NATION
OF NATIONS

Here is not merely a nation but a teeming nation of nations.
—WALT WHITMAN

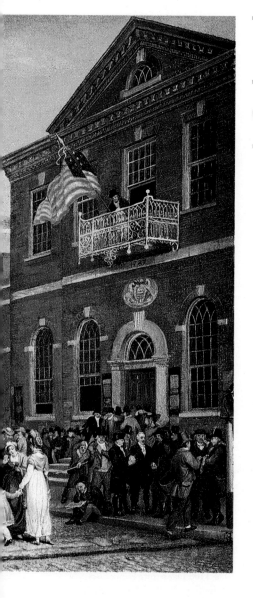

NATION
OF NATIONS

JAMES WEST DAVIDSON

WILLIAM E. GIENAPP
The University of Wyoming

CHRISTINE LEIGH HEYRMAN
Brandeis University

MARK H. LYTLE
Bard College

MICHAEL B. STOFF
The University of Texas, Austin

ALFRED A. KNOPF   *New York*   1991

Permissions Acknowledgement

315 From Charles A. Johnson, *Frontier Camp Meeting*, copyright 1955, 1985, SMU Press. Reprinted with permission; 921 Reprinted by permission of Smithsonian Institution Press from *Smithsonian Collection of Classic Jazz*. © Smithsonian Institution, Washington, D.C., pp. 4–5; 923 Excerpt from Claude McKay, "If We Must Die" from *White Shadows*. Copyright © 1981 Twayne Publishers, a division of G. K. Hall & Co., Boston. Reprinted with permission; 942 From Gordon Thomas and Max Morgan-Witts, *The Day the Bubble Burst: The Social History of the Wall Street Crash of 1929*, Doubleday & Co., 1979; 1106 Taken from Frank Levy, *Dollars and Dreams: The Changing American Income Distribution*. © 1987 Russell Sage Foundation. Used with permission of the Russell Sage Foundation; 1143 Adapted from Richard Day, "The Economics of Technological Change and the Demise of the Sharecropper," *American Economic Review* 57 (1967) [Figure 3], with additional data from the U.S. Department of Agriculture, Economic Research; 1206 Excerpt from Nikki Giovanni, "The True Import of Present Dialogue: Black vs. Negro" from *Black Feeling, Black Talk, Black Judgment*, William Morrow & Co., © 1968, 1970 by Nikki Giovanni; 1259 Taken from Frank Levy, *Dollars and Dreams: The Changing American Income Distribution*. © 1987 Russell Sage Foundation. Used with permission of the Russell Sage Foundation; 1260 From "I Am Changing My Name to Chrysler" by Tom Paxton. © Copyright 1980 Accabonac Music. All Rights Reserved. Used by permission.

CONTENTS

LIST OF MAPS AND CHARTS   xxiii
PREFACE   xxvii

PART 1

THE CREATION OF A NEW AMERICA   2

CHAPTER 1   Old World, New Worlds   8

The Meeting of Europe and America   11
  The Portuguese Wave   *14*   The Spanish and Columbus   *16*

Early North American Cultures   17
  The First Inhabitants   *17*   Societies of Increasing Complexity   *18*

The European Background of American Colonization   21
  Life and Death in Early Modern Europe   *21*   The Conditions of
  Colonization   *23*

Spain's Empire in the New World   25
  Spanish Conquest   *25*   Spanish Colonization   *27*

The Prelude to England's American Colonization   29
  Backdrop to the Reformation   *30*   The Teaching of Martin
  Luther   *31*   The Contribution of John Calvin   *32*   The English
  Reformation   *33*   The English Colonization of Ireland   *34*

England's Entry into the New World   35
  The Failures of Frobisher and Gilbert   *36*   Raleigh's Roanoke
  Venture   *38*

  DAILY LIVES: "Barbaric" Dress—Indian and European   40

CHAPTER 2   The First Century of Settlement in the Colonial
  South   44

English Society Takes Shape on the Chesapeake   47
  The Virginia Company   *48*   Reform and a Boom in Tobacco   *49*
  Settling Down on the Chesapeake   *52*   The Founding of Maryland
  and the Renewal of Indian Wars   *54*   Changes in English Policy in
  the Chesapeake   *55*

Chesapeake Society in Crisis   56
  The Conditions of Unrest   *56*   Bacon's Rebellion and Coode's

Rebellion *57*   From Servitude to Slavery *59*   The Chesapeake
Gentry *62*

From the Caribbean to the Carolinas 65
Paradise Lost Beyond the Line *65*   The Founding of the
Carolinas *67*   Early Instability *70*   White, Red, and Black: The
Search for Order *72*   The Founding of Georgia *74*

The Spanish Borderlands 76

DAILY LIVES: A Taste for Sugar 68

CHAPTER 3 **The First Century of Settlement in the Colonial
North 80**

The Founding of New England 83
The Puritan Movement *84*   The Pilgrim Settlement at Plymouth
Colony *85*   The Puritan Settlement in Massachusetts Bay *87*

New England Communities 89
New England Families *89*   Local Life in Early New England *92*
Deviance and Dissent *94*   Heresy *96*   Goodwives *98*   White
and Indians in Early New England *99*

The Middle Colonies 100
The Founding of New Netherlands *101*   English Rule in New
York *102*   The League of the Iroquois *103*   The Founding of
New Jersey *105*   Quaker Odysseys *105*

Adjustment to Empire 108
The Dominion of New England *109*   The Aftershocks of a
Glorious Revolution *110*   Leisler's Rebellion *111*   Royal
Authority in America in 1700 *112*

DAILY LIVES: The Rituals of Mourning 90

Generations of the Republic: The First Anglo-Americans (1640–1700) 114

CHAPTER 4 **The Mosaic of Eighteenth-Century America 118**

Forces of Division 121
Immigration and Natural Increase *121*   Older Rural
Communities *123*   The Settlement of the Backcountry *126*
Social Conflict on the Frontier *129*   Boundary Disputes and
Tenant Wars *130*   Eighteenth-Century Seaports *131*   Social
Conflict in Seaports *135*

Slave Societies in the Eighteenth-Century South 136
The Slave Family and Community *137*   Slave Resistance in the
Eighteenth Century *138*

Enlightenment and Awakening in America 140
The Enlightenment in America *140*   The First Great
Awakening *141*   The Aftermath of the Great Awakening *143*

The Anglo-American Worlds of the Eighteenth Century 144
Urban Life in England and America *145*   Economic Development

and Inequality *145*   Politics in England and America *148*   The English Opposition and American Political Thought *149*   The Imperial System Before 1760 *151*

Toward the Seven Years' War   153

DAILY LIVES: Transatlantic Trials   124

PART 2
THE CREATION OF A NEW REPUBLIC   156

CHAPTER 5   Toward the War for American Independence   160

The Seven Years' War   162
The Years of Defeat *162*   The Years of Victory *163*   Postwar Expectations *167*

The Imperial Crisis   168
New Troubles on the Frontier *169*   George Grenville's New Measures *169*   The Beginning of American Resistance *172*   The Townshend Acts *178*   Resistance Revived *181*   The Empire Strikes Back *182*   Toward the Revolution *184*   The First Continental Congress *185*   The Last Days of the British Empire in America *187*   The Fighting Begins *189*   *Common Sense* *190*

DAILY LIVES: The Rituals of Revolutionary Protest   176

CHAPTER 6   The American People and the American Revolution   192

The Decision for Independence   194
The Second Continental Congress *195*   American Loyalists *197*

The Fighting in the North   202
The Two Armies at Bay *202*   Laying Strategies *204*   The Campaigns in New York and New Jersey *205*   Capturing Philadelphia *206*   Disaster at Saratoga *208*

The Turning Point   209
An Alliance Formed *209*   Winding Down the War in the North *211*   The Home Front in the North *214*

The Struggle in the South   215
The Siege of Charleston *215*   The Partisan Struggle in the South *216*   Greene Takes Command *218*   African-Americans in the Age of Revolution *220*

The World Turned Upside Down   222

DAILY LIVES: Radical Chic and the Revolutionary Generation   198

CHAPTER 7   Crisis and Constitution   226

Republican Experiments   229
The State Constitutions *229*   From Congress to Confederation *231*

The Temptations of Peace   232
The Temptations of the West   *233*   Slavery and Sectionalism   *239*
Wartime Economic Disruption   *241*

Republican Society   243
The New Men of the Revolution   *243*   Urban Artisans   *246*   The
New Women of the Revolution   *246*   The Attack on
Aristocracy   *248*

From Confederation to Constitution   250
The Jay–Gardoqui Treaty   *250*   Shays' Rebellion   *251*   The
Framing of the Federal Constitution   *252*   Ratification   *255*

DAILY LIVES: The Spirits of Independence   244

Generations of the Republic: The First African-Americans (1740–1800)   258

CHAPTER 8   The Republic Launched   262

1789: A Social Portrait   264
The Subsistence Economy of Crèvecoeur's America   *265*   The
Commercial Economy of Franklin's America   *269*   The Constitution
and Commerce   *271*

The New Government   272
Washington's Character   *272*   Organizing the Government   *273*
The Bill of Rights   *274*   Hamilton's Financial Program   *275*
Opposition to Hamilton's Program   *276*   The Specter of
Aristocracy   *279*

Expansion and Turmoil in the West   279
The Resistance of the Miamis   *280*   The Whiskey Rebellion   *280*
Pinckney's Treaty   *282*

The Emergence of Political Parties   282
The French Revolution   *283*   Washington's Neutral Course   *284*
The Federalists and Republicans Organize   *285*   The 1796
Election   *287*   Federalist and Republican Ideologies   *288*

The Presidency of John Adams   289
The Quasi-War with France   *290*   Suppression at Home   *290*
The Election of 1800   *292*   Political Violence in the Early
Republic   *292*

DAILY LIVES: The Rise of "Vile Electioneering"   294

CHAPTER 9   The Jeffersonian Republic   298

Jefferson in Power   300
The New Capital City   *301*   Jefferson's Character   *302*
Jefferson's Political Philosophy   *302*   Republican Principles   *304*
Jefferson's Economic Policies   *304*   John Marshall and Judicial
Review   *305*   The Jeffersonian Attack on the Judiciary   *307*

Jefferson and Western Expansion   307
The Louisiana Purchase   *308*   Lewis and Clark   *309*

Whites and Indians on the Frontier   311
The Course of White Penetration   *311*   The Second Great
Awakening   *312*   Black Hoof and the Choice of Assimilation   *316*
The Prophet, Tecumseh, and the Pan-Indian Movement   *318*

The Second War for American Independence   320
Neutral Rights   *321*   The Embargo   *322*   Madison and the Young
Republicans   *323*   The Decision for War   *324*   National
Unpreparedness   *325*   "A Chance Such as Never Will Occur
Again"   *327*   The British Invasion   *327*   The Hartford
Convention   *329*

America Turns Inward   329
Monroe's Presidency   *330*   The Monroe Doctrine   *330*   The End
of an Era   *332*

DAILY LIVES: The Frontier Camp Meeting   314

PART 3

THE REPUBLIC TRANSFORMED AND TESTED   334

CHAPTER 10   The Opening of America   338

The Market Revolution   340
The New Nationalism   *341*   The Cotton Trade   *342*   The
Transportation Revolution   *342*   The Canal Age   *343*
Steamboats   *344*   Railroads   *346*   Agriculture in the Market
Economy   *347*   John Marshall and the Promotion of
Enterprise   *350*   General Incorporation Laws   *351*

A Restless Temper   352
Population Growth   *353*   The Federal Land Rush   *354*
Geographic Mobility   *356*   Urbanization   *356*

The Rise of Factories   357
Technological Advances   *358*   Textile Factories   *359*   Industrial
Work   *362*   The Shoe Industry   *362*   The Labor Movement   *363*

Social Structures of the Market Society   364
The Distribution of Wealth   *365*   Social Mobility   *366*
Materialism   *366*   The Redefinition of Time   *367*   The Market at
Work: Three Examples   *367*

Prosperity and Anxiety   369
The Panic of 1819   *370*   The Missouri Crisis   *371*

DAILY LIVES: Floating Palaces of the West   348

CHAPTER 11   The Rise of Democracy   374

Equality and Opportunity   377
The Tension between Equality and Opportunity   *378*

The New Political Culture of Democracy   379
The Election of 1824   *380*   Anti-Masonry and the Defense of

Equality   *380*   Social Sources of the New Politics   *382*   The
Acceptance of Parties   *383*   The Politics of the Common Man   *384*

Jackson's Rise to Power   385
John Quincy Adams' Presidency   *385*   President of the
People   *386*   The Political Agenda in the Market Economy   *387*

Democracy and Race   388
Accommodate or Resist?   *388*   Trail of Tears   *390*   Free Blacks in
the North   *392*   The African-American Community   *394*   The
Minstrel Show   *395*

The Nullification Crisis   396
The Growing Crisis in South Carolina   *396*   Calhoun's Theory of
Nullification   *397*   The Nullifiers Nullified   *398*

The Bank War   399
The National Bank and the Panic of 1819   *399*   Biddle's Bank   *400*
The Clash between Jackson and Biddle   *401*   The Bank
Destroyed   *402*   Jackson's Impact on the Presidency   *402*

Van Buren and Depression   403
"Van Ruin's" Depression   *403*   The Whigs' Triumph   *405*

The Jacksonian Party System   408
Democrats, Whigs, and the Market   *408*   The Social Bases of the
Two Parties   *410*   The Triumph of the Market   *410*

DAILY LIVES: The Log Cabin Campaign   406

CHAPTER 12   The Quest for Perfection   412

Revivalism and the Social Order   415
Finney's New Measures   *416*   The Philosophy of the New
Revivals   *416*   Religion and the Market Economy   *417*   The
Significance of the Second Great Awakening   *418*

Women's Sphere   419
Women and Revivalism   *419*   The Idea of Domesticity   *420*   The
Middle-Class Family in Transition   *424*

American Romanticism   425
Emerson and Transcendentalism   *425*   The Clash Between Nature
and Civilization   *426*   Songs of the Self-Reliant and Darker
Loomings   *427*

The Age of Reform   429
Utopian Communities   *429*   Robert Owen and New Harmony   *431*
The Temperance Movement   *432*   Educational Reform   *433*   The
Asylum Movement   *434*

Abolitionism   435
The Beginnings of the Abolitionist Movement   *435*   The Spread of
Abolitionism   *437*   Opponents and Discontents   *439*   The
Women's Rights Movement   *440*   The Schism of 1840 and the
Decline of Abolitionism   *441*

Reform Shakes the Party System   442
Women and the Right to Vote   *442*   The Maine Law   *443*
Abolitionism and the Party System   *444*

DAILY LIVES: Early Bloomers   422

Generations of the Republic: Families of the New Democracy (1815–1875)   446

CHAPTER 13   The Old South   450

The Social Structure of the Cotton Kingdom   453
The Boom Country Economy   *453*   The Upper South's New
Orientation   *455*   The Rural South   *457*   Distribution of
Slavery   *458*   Slavery as a Labor System   *459*

Class Structure of the White South   460
The Slaveowners   *460*   Tidewater and Frontier   *462*   The Master
at Home   *463*   The Plantation Mistress   *464*   Yeoman
Farmers   *466*   Urban Society   *468*   Poor Whites   *468*

The Peculiar Institution   469
Work and Discipline   *470*   Slave Maintenance   *471*
Resistance   *472*

Slave Culture   474
The Black Family   *474*   Slave Songs and Stories   *475*   The Lord
Calls Us Home   *478*   The Slave Community   *479*   Free Blacks
in the South   *480*

Southern Society and the Defense of Slavery   481
The Virginia Debate of 1832   *481*   The Proslavery Argument   *482*
Closing Ranks   *483*   Sections and the Nation   *484*

DAILY LIVES: A Slave's Daily Bread   476

CHAPTER 14   Western Expansion and the Rise of the Slavery
Issue   486

Destinies: Manifest and Otherwise   489
The Roots of the Doctrine   *490*   The Mexican Borderlands   *491*
The Texas Revolution   *492*   The Texas Republic   *494*

The Trek West   495
The Overland Trail   *498*   Women on the Overland Trail   *498*
Indians and the Trail Experience   *499*

The Political Origins of Expansion   501
Tyler's Texas Ploy   *501*   Van Overboard   *502*   To the
Pacific   *503*   The Mexican War   *503*   Opposition to the
War   *505*   The Price of Victory   *505*   The Rise of the Slavery
Issue   *507*

New Societies in the West   508
Farming in the West   *508*   The Gold Rush   *509*   Instant City:
San Francisco   *511*   The Mormon Experience   *512*   Temple City:
Salt Lake City   *513*   Shadows on the Moving Frontier   *514*

Escape from Crisis   515
  A Two-Faced Campaign   *516*   The Compromise of 1850   *517*
  Away from the Brink   *519*

  DAILY LIVES: Seeing the Elephant on the Overland Trail   496

CHAPTER 15   The Union Broken   522

Sectional Changes in American Society   525
  The Growth of a Railroad Economy   *526*   The New Commercial
  Agriculture   *527*   Rising Industrialization   *530*   Immigration   *530*
  Southern Complaints   *533*

The Political Realignment of the 1850s   534
  The Kansas–Nebraska Act   *536*   The Collapse of the Second
  American Party System   *537*   The Know-Nothings   *538*   The
  Republicans and Bleeding Kansas   *539*   The Caning of Charles
  Sumner   *540*   The Election of 1856   *541*

The Worsening Crisis   543
  The *Dred Scott* Decision   *543*   The Panic of 1857   *544*   The
  Lecompton Constitution   *545*   The Lincoln–Douglas Debates   *546*
  The Beleaguered South   *551*

The Road to War   552
  Harpers Ferry   *552*   A Sectional Election   *553*   Secession   *554*
  The Outbreak of War   *555*   The Roots of a Divided Society   *556*

  DAILY LIVES: Uncle Tom by Footlights   548

CHAPTER 16   Total War and the Republic   560

The Demands of Total War   562
  Political Leadership   *563*   The Border States   *564*

Opening Moves   565
  Blockade and Isolate   *566*   Grant in the West   *567*   Eastern
  Stalemate   *569*

Emancipation   571
  The Logic of Events   *572*   The Emancipation Proclamation   *573*
  Black Americans' Civil War   *573*

The Confederate Home Front   575
  The New Economy   *575*   Southern Women   *576*   Confederate
  Finance and Government   *577*   Hardship and Suffering   *578*

The Union Home Front   579
  Government Finances and the Economy   *579*   A Rich Man's
  War   *580*   Women and the Work Force   *581*   Civil Liberties and
  Dissent   *583*

Gone for a Soldier   584
  Camp Life   *584*   Southern Individualism   *588*   The Changing
  Face of Battle   *589*

The Union's Triumph   591
  Lincoln Finds His General   *593*   War in the Balance   *594*   The
  Twilight of the Confederacy   *596*

The Impact of War 598

DAILY LIVES: Hardtack, Salt Horse, and Coffee   586

CHAPTER 17   Reconstructing the Union   602

Presidential Reconstruction   604
Lincoln's Plan   *605*   The Mood of the South   *606*   Johnson's
Program of Reconstruction   *606*   The Failure of Johnson's
Program   *608*   Johnson's Break with Congress   *609*   The
Fourteenth Amendment   *611*   The Election of 1866   *612*

Congressional Reconstruction   613
The Land Issue   *614*   Impeachment   *615*   Reconstruction and
the Constitution   *616*

Reconstruction in the South   617
Black Officeholding   *617*   Southern White Republicans   *618*   The
New State Governments   *619*   Economic Issues and
Corruption   *620*

Black Aspirations   621
Experiencing Freedom   *621*   The Black Family   *624*   The
Gospel and the Primer   *625*   New Working Conditions   *626*   The
Freedmen's Bureau   *627*   Planters and a New Way of Life   *628*

The Abandonment of Reconstruction   630
The Election of Grant   *630*   The Grant Administration   *632*
Growing Northern Disillusionment   *633*   The Triumph of White
Supremacy   *634*   The Disputed Election of 1876   *636*   Racism
and the Failure of Reconstruction   *638*

DAILY LIVES: The Black Sharecropper's Cabin   622

PART 4

THE UNITED STATES IN AN INDUSTRIAL AGE   642

CHAPTER 18   The Rise of a New Industrial Order   646

The Development of Industrial Systems   649
Natural Resources and Industrial Technology   *650*   Systematic
Invention   *651*   Transportation and Communication   *653*
Finance Capital   *656*   The Corporation   *656*   A Pool of
Labor   *657*

Railroads: America's First Big Business   659
A Managerial Revolution   *660*   Competition and
Consolidation   *661*   The Role of Finance   *662*

The Growth of Big Business   664
Growth in Consumer Goods   *664*   Carnegie Integrates Steel   *665*
Rockefeller and the Great Standard Oil Trust   *666*   The Mergers of
J. Pierpont Morgan   *668*   Corporate Critics   *669*

Workers Respond to an Industrial Culture   671
The Workers' World   *671*   The Systems of Labor: Early
Unions   *675*   The Knights of Labor   *675*   The American
Federation of Labor   *676*   The Limits of Industrial Systems   *677*

DAILY LIVES: The Rise of Information Systems   654

CHAPTER 19   The Rise of an Urban Order   682

The Rise of Cities   684
The Urban Explosion   *685*   The Great Global Migration   *686*
The Immigrant in the City   *688*   The Shape of Cities   *690*
Urban Transport   *690*   Bridges and Skyscrapers   *692*   Slum and
Tenement   *693*

Running and Reforming the City   695
Boss Rule   *695*   The Social Conscience of the City   *697*

City Life and Culture   699
The Urban Middle Class at Home   *699*   Victorian Mores   *703*
School Days   *704*   College Years   *706*   Palaces of
Consumption   *707*   Arts and Entertainment   *709*

DAILY LIVES: Gender Roles and Fashions in the 1890s   700

Generations of the Republic: The Family in an Urbanizing Culture (1860–1920)   714

CHAPTER 20   Agrarian Domains: The South and the West   718

The Southern Burden   721
Cotton in the New South   *722*   Sharecropping   *723*   Southern
Industry   *727*   The Colonial South   *728*

The Rise of Jim Crow   730
Segregation   *730*   Disfranchisement   *732*

The Transformed West   733
Native Americans and the Western Environment   *734*   Whites and
the Western Environment   *736*

The War for the West   738
War   *739*   Last Stands   *740*

The Western Boom   744
Rail Towns and Cattle Drives   *744*   Cattle Kingdom   *748*

The Final Frontier   750
The Land Rush   *751*   A Plains Existence   *752*

DAILY LIVES: The Frontier Kitchen of the Plains   754

CHAPTER 21   The Failure of Traditional Politics   758

The Politics of Paralysis   761
The Party Stalemate   *761*   Congressional Politics   *766*   The
White House from Hayes to Harrison   *769*   Ferment in the States
and Cities   *771*

The Revolt of the Farmers   772
The Harvest of Discontent   *772*   The Alliance Movement   *773*
The People's Party   *776*

The Depression of 1893   777
The Depths of Depression   *778*   The Rumblings of Unrest   *779*
Democrats Under Fire   *780*

The New Realignment   781
The Battle of the Standards   *782*   Campaign and Election   *784*
Jim Crow Politics   *784*   The African-American Response   *786*
McKinley in the White House   *788*

DAILY LIVES: The Bosses Throw a Party   762

CHAPTER 22   The New Empire   790

Visions of Empire   792
Imperialism, European-Style and American   *794*   The Shapers of
Foreign Policy   *794*   The Ideology of Imperialism   *799*

Stirrings of Empire   800
Canada   *800*   Mexico   *801*   William Henry Seward   *802*   The
United States and Latin America   *804*   Prelude in the Pacific   *805*
Crisis in Venezuela   *807*

The Imperial Moment   808
Mounting Tensions   *809*   The Imperial War   *810*   The Cuban
War   *812*   Peace and Empire   *814*   America's First Asian
War   *816*   An Open Door in China   *817*

The Roots of Russian–American Conflict   818
Conflicting Ideology   *818*   Diverging Interests   *819*

DAILY LIVES: The New Navy   796

CHAPTER 23   The Progressive Era   822

The Roots of Progressive Reform   825
The Progressive System of Beliefs   *826*   The Progressive
Method   *828*

The Search for the Good Society   829
The Rediscovery of Poverty   *830*   Expanding the "Woman's
Sphere"   *831*   Social Welfare and Social Justice   *832*   Woman
Suffrage   *833*

Controlling the Masses   835
Stemming the Immigrant Tide   *835*   The Curse of Demon
Rum   *838*   Prostitution   *839*   Vaudeville Cleans House   *839*

The Politics of Municipal and State Reform   840
The Reformation of the Cities   *841*   Progressivism in the
States   *842*

Progressivism Goes to Washington   843
TR in Action   *844*   The Square Deal   *846*   Bad Food and
Pristine Wilds   *848*   The Troubled Taft   *849*   The Election of

1912 *851*   Woodrow Wilson and the Politics of Morality *854*
The Mixed Legacy of Progressivism *857*

DAILY LIVES: "Amusing the Million" 836

CHAPTER 24   The United States and the Old World Order   860

Progressive Diplomacy 863
The Big Stick in the Caribbean *864*   A "Diplomatist of the
Highest Rank" *865*   Taft and Dollar Diplomacy *866*

Woodrow Wilson and Moral Diplomacy 868
Missionary Diplomacy *869*   Intervention in Mexico *870*

The Road to War 871
The Guns of August *872*   American Neutrality *872*   The
Diplomacy of Neutrality *874*   Preparedness *876*   The Election
of 1916 *877*   The Final Peace Offensive *878*

War and Society 879
The Slaughter of Stalemate *879*   "You're in the Army Now" *880*
Mobilizing the Economy *882*   War Work *883*   Propaganda and
Civil Liberties *886*   Over There *887*

The Lost Peace 889
The Treaty of Versailles *889*   The Battle for the Treaty *894*
Red Scare *895*

DAILY LIVES: The Doughboys Abroad 890

PART 5

THE PERILS OF DEMOCRACY 898

CHAPTER 25   The New Era   902

The Roaring Economy 906
The Boom Industries *906*   The Automobile *907*   The Business
of America *909*   The Consumer Culture *911*

A Mass Society 913
The New Woman *913*   Mass Media *918*   "Ain't We Got
Fun?" *920*   The Art of Alienation *921*   A "New Negro" *922*

Defenders of the Faith 923
Nativism and Restriction of Immigration *924*   The "Noble
Experiment" *925*   KKK *926*   Fundamentalism versus
Darwinism *928*

Republicans Ascendant 929
The Politics of Normalcy *930*   The Policies of Mellon and
Hoover *930*   The Election of 1928 *933*

DAILY LIVES: The Beauty Contest 914

Generations of the Republic: The Modern Family (1900–1960) 936

CHAPTER 26   Crash and Depression   940

The Great Bull Market   943
The Rampaging Bull   *943*   Chinks in the System   *944*   The Great Crash   *945*

The American People in the Great Depression   947
Hard Times   *948*   The Depression Family   *951*   A Depression Culture   *954*   "Dirty Thirties": An Ecological Disaster   *959*   The Fate of Outsiders   *962*

The Tragedy of Herbert Hoover   964
The Failure of Relief   *965*   The Hoover Depression Program   *966* Stirrings of Discontent   *969*   The Election of 1932   *971*

DAILY LIVES: The Control of Narcotics   956

CHAPTER 27   The New Deal   974

The Early New Deal (1933–1935)   976
The Democratic Roosevelts   *977*   The First Hundred Days   *979* The Riddle of Recovery   *982*

A Second New Deal (1935–1936)   985
Voices of Protest   *985*   The Second Hundred Days   *988*   The Election of 1936   *991*

The New Deal and the American People   992
Outsiders Under the New Deal   *993*   A New Deal for Women   *995*   The Rise of Organized Labor   *996*   "Art for the Millions"   *998*

The End of the New Deal (1937–1940)   1002
"Packing" the Courts   *1002*   More Troubles   *1004*   The Legacy of the New Deal   *1005*

DAILY LIVES: Post Office Murals   1000

CHAPTER 28   America's Rise to Globalism   1008

The United States and the Collapse of the Versailles System   1010
Economic Diplomacy   *1011*   Avoiding War   *1011*   Becoming a Good Neighbor   *1013*

The Diplomacy of Isolationism   1014
Neutrality and Appeasement   *1014*   War in Europe   *1018* Disaster in the Pacific   *1021*

Misfortunes of War   1025
Strategies for War   *1025*   Gloomy Prospects   *1026*   A Grand Alliance   *1027*   The Naval War in the Pacific   *1028*   Turning Points in Europe   *1028*

Those Who Fought   1030
The Wartime Military Branches   *1030*   Women at War   *1033* Over There   *1033*   Science Goes to War   *1034*   Total War   *1035* D-Day and the Fall of the Third Reich   *1036*   Two Roads to Tokyo   *1037*

War and Diplomacy **1040**
War Aims *1040*   The Road to Yalta *1041*   The Fallen
Leader *1043*

DAILY LIVES: Air Power Shrinks the Globe   1038

CHAPTER 29   War on the Home Front   1046

The Sinews of War **1049**
War Production *1049*   The Story of Rubber *1050*   The Miracle
of Production *1052*

War Work **1053**

War and Consumption **1053**
Willow Run *1057*   Women Workers *1057*

A Question of Rights **1059**
Little Italy *1060*   Concentration Camps *1060*   Minorities on the
Job *1063*   At War with Jim Crow *1065*

Politics as Usual **1066**
Paying the Piper *1066*   1942: A Farewell to Reform *1068*
Organized Labor *1068*   1944: A Fourth Term *1070*

Victory **1071**
The Holocaust *1071*   The United Nations *1073*   Ending the
War *1074*   Atomic Diplomacy *1075*

DAILY LIVES: Dress on the Home Front   1054

PART 6

THE UNITED STATES IN A NUCLEAR AGE   1078

CHAPTER 30   Cold War America   1082

Conversion: "The American People Want a Rest" **1085**
Postwar Work *1085*   The New Deal at Bay *1086*

The Rise of the Cold War **1087**
The View from West and East *1089*   Toward Containment *1091*
The Truman Doctrine *1091*   The Marshall Plan *1092*   The Fall
of Eastern Europe *1093*   The Atomic Shield versus the Iron
Curtain *1095*   Atomic Deterrence *1096*

The Cold War at Home **1097**
HUAC, Hollywood, and Hiss *1097*   The Ambitions of Senator
McCarthy *1101*

The Culture of Prosperity **1102**
Soldiers as Civilians *1102*   The Baby Boom *1103*   Hail,
Suburbia *1104*   The Flickering Gray Screen *1107*

The Politics of Frustration **1108**
The Fair Deal *1110*   Beyond Containment *1110*   Korea *1112*
K1C2: The Election of 1952 *1115*

DAILY LIVES: Film Noir in an Uncertain Cold War   1098

CHAPTER 31   The Suburban Era   1118

Transforming Wheels   1120

The Shape of the Suburbs   1122
American Civil Religion   *1123*   "Homemaking" Women in the
Workaday World   *1124*   The "Organization Man" in a
Conglomerate World   *1125*

The Politics of Calm   1129
Modern Republicanism   *1130*   The Fall of Joseph McCarthy   *1131*
The Politics of the Middle   *1133*

Nationalism in an Age of Superpowers   1133
To the Brink?   *1134*   The Covert Side of the "New Look"   *1136*
The Superpowers   *1137*   Thaws and Freezes   *1140*

Civil Rights and the New South   1142
The New South's Effect on Blacks   *1142*   The Movement for Civil
Rights   *1143*

The Culture Wars   1147
Juvenile Delinquency   *1148*   Rock and Roll: Idiom of a Youth
Culture   *1148*   The Unblinking Eye   *1149*   Abstract Art and
Architecture   *1150*

DAILY LIVES: The New Suburbia   1126

CHAPTER 32   Liberalism and Beyond   1152

A Liberal Agenda for Reform   1155
The Social Structures of Change   *1155*   The Election of
1960   *1156*   The Hard-Nosed Idealists of Camelot   *1157*

New Frontiers   1159
The Missiles of October   *1160*   The (Somewhat) New Frontier at
Home   *1164*   The Reforms of the Warren Court   *1165*

The Civil Rights Crusade   1166
Riding to Freedom   *1166*   Liberalism at High Tide   *1168*   The
Fire Next Time   *1170*   Black Power at the Ballot Box and on the
Street   *1172*

Lyndon Johnson and the Great Society   1174
The Origins of the Great Society   *1175*   The Election of
1964   *1176*   The Great Society   *1177*

The Counterculture   1179
Activists on the New Left   *1179*   The Rise of the
Counterculture   *1182*   The Rock Revolution   *1183*   The West
Coast Scene   *1185*

DAILY LIVES: The Politics of Dress   1180

Generations of the Republic: The Baby Boomers (1940–)   1188

CHAPTER 33   The Vietnam Era   1192

The Road to Vietnam   1195
Escalation at Tonkin Gulf   *1199*   Rolling Thunder   *1200*

Social Consequences of the War   1202
The Soldiers' War   *1202*   Technology and Its Limits   *1203*   The War Comes Home   *1206*

The Unraveling   1208
Tet Offensive   *1208*   The Shocks of 1968   *1210*   Whose Silent Majority?   *1212*

The Nixon Era   1214
Vietnamization—And Cambodia   *1215*   Morale in a No-Win War   *1216*   The Move Toward Détente   *1217*   The New Federalist   *1219*

"Silent" Majorities and Vocal Minorities   1221
Hispanic Activism   *1221*   The Choices of Native Americans   *1223*   Social Politics and the Court   *1224*   Us versus Them   *1225*   Triumph   *1226*   The End of an Era   *1227*

DAILY LIVES: The Race to the Moon   1204

CHAPTER 34   The Age of Limits   1230

The Limits of Reform   1232
Environmentalism   *1233*   Consumerism   *1235*   Feminism   *1238*   The Activist Legacy   *1242*

Political Limits: Watergate   1242
The Perils of Power   *1243*   Break-In   *1244*   To the Oval Office   *1245*

A Ford, Not a Lincoln   1248
Kissinger Regnant   *1248*   The Decline of American Hegemony   *1249*   Détente   *1252*   An Embattled Presidency   *1253*   The Election of 1976   *1255*

Jimmy Carter: Restoring the Faith   1256
The Carter Style   *1256*   The Moral Equivalent of War   *1257*   A Sick Economy   *1259*   Leadership, Not Hegemony   *1260*   The Middle East: Hope and Hostages   *1262*

DAILY LIVES: Fast-Food America   1236

CHAPTER 35   A Nation Still Divisible   1266

The Conservative Rebellion   1269
Born Again   *1270*   The Liberal Media   *1273*   The Election of 1980   *1275*

Prime Time with Ronald Reagan   1276
The Great Communicator   *1276*   The Reagan Agenda   *1277*   The Reagan Revolution in Practice   *1279*   The Surge in Military Spending   *1281*   The Election of 1984   *1283*

Second-Term Blues   1284
Triumph before the Storm   *1285*   Standing Tall   *1285*   Clean Hearts and Dirty Hands in Central America   *1287*   The Iran–Contra Connection   *1288*   Cover Blown   *1291*   From Cold War to Glasnost   *1292*

The Reagan Legacy and an Unfinished Social Agenda   1293
The Uncertain Legacy   *1293*   Unsolved Problems   *1294*   A
Question of Civil Rights   *1298*   The New Immigration   *1298*
The Election of 1988   *1302*

DAILY LIVES: Life in the Underclass   1296

Appendix   A.1

Declaration of Independence   A.1

The Constitution of the United States of America   A.5

Presidential Elections   A.17

Presidential Administrations   A.21

Justices of the Supreme Court   A.32

A Social Profile of the American Republic   A.34
Population   *A.34*   Vital Statistics   *A.34*   Life Expectancy   *A.35*
The Changing Age Structure   *A.36*   Regional Origin of
Immigrants   *A.37*   Recent Trends in Immigration   *A.37*
American Workers and Farmers   *A.38*   The Economy and Federal
Spending   *A.39*

Maps   A.40

Bibliography   A.45

Photo Credits   A.77

Index   A.83

LIST OF MAPS AND CHARTS

The Geography of Exploration 12
  European Exploration in the Sixteenth Century 12
  Atlantic Ports in Europe and Newfoundland 13
  Volta do mar 13
Indians of North America, Circa 1500 19
Spanish America, Circa 1600 28
Colonies of the Chesapeake 53
The American Transatlantic Slave Trade, 1450–1760 59
The Carolinas and the Caribbean 71
Early New England 86
Patterns of Settlement in the Eighteenth Century 122
Estimated Population by Region, 1720–1760 132
Estimated Population of Colonial Cities, 1720–1770 132
The Distribution of American Population, 1775 137
Overseas Trade Networks 152
The Seven Years' War in America 162
European Claims in North America, 1750 and 1763 166
The Appalachian Frontier, 1750–1775 171
Patterns of Allegiance 200
The Fighting in the North, 1775–1777 207
The Fighting in the South, 1780–1781 217
Western Land Claims, 1782–1802 235
The Ordinance of 1785 238
Ratification of the Constitution 256
The Geography of Subsistence and Commercial America 266
  Subsistence and Commercial America 266
  Population Density, 1790 267
  Male/Female Population, 1790 267
Hamilton's Financial System 275
The Election of 1800 293
Exploration and Expansion: The Louisiana Purchase 310
The Frontier Camp Meeting 315
The Indian Response to White Encroachment 317
American Imports and Exports, 1790–1820 322
The War of 1812 326

The Transportation Network of a Market Economy, 1840   345
Time of Travel, 1800 and 1830   346
Prices of Corn, Wheat, and Western Land, 1815–1860   355
Land Sales, 1815–1860   355
The Missouri Compromise and the Union's Boundaries in 1820   371
The Election of 1824   381
Indian Removal   389
The Spread of White Manhood Suffrage   393
The Election of 1840   409
Annual Consumption of Distilled Spirits, 1710–1920   433
Cotton and the Other Crops of the South   456
The Spread of Slavery, 1820–1860   458
Southern Population, 1860   460
A Plantation Layout   461
Sioux Expansion and the Horse and Gun Frontier   489
The Mexican Borderlands   493
The Overland Trail   500
The Mexican War   504
Territorial Growth and the Compromise of 1850   517
The Geography of Railroads   528
   Railroads in 1850 and 1860   528
   Rail Connections in Philadelphia, 1860   529
   Rail Connections in the Midwest, 1860   529
Prices of Cotton and Slaves, 1815–1850   533
The Kansas–Nebraska Act   535
The Emergence of the Republican Party   542
The Election of 1860   553
The Pattern of Secession   555
The War in the West, 1861–1862   568
The War in the East, 1861–1862   570
The Changing Magnitude of Battle   590
The War in the East, 1863–1865   592
The War in the West, 1863–1865   595
The Southern States During Reconstruction   614
A Georgia Plantation After the War   627
The Election of 1876   637
Steel Production, 1880 and 1914   649
Occupational Distribution, 1880 and 1920   658
Railroads, 1870 and 1890   663
Boom and Bust Business Cycle, 1865–1900   670
Population and Immigration, 1800–1920   687
Streetcar Suburbs in Nineteenth-Century New Orleans   691
The Geography of the Postwar South   724
   Cotton Production, 1859 and 1899   724
   Plantation Labor and Tenantry   725
   Farm Tenantry, 1900   725
Spending on Education in the South   731
Natural Environment of the West   735
The Indian Frontier   741
The Mining and Cattle Frontiers   745

The Election of 1896   **785**
Imperialist Expansion, 1900   **793**
U.S. Trade, 1870–1910   **798**
The Spanish-American War   **812**
The United States in the Pacific   **815**
Woman Suffrage   **834**
The Voting Public, 1860–1912   **852**
Republican and Democratic Parties' Share of Popular Vote, 1860–1912   **853**
The Election of 1912   **855**
Panama Canal—Old and New Transoceanic Routes   **862**
American Interventions in the Caribbean, 1898–1930   **867**
The Course of War in Europe, 1914–1917   **872**
The Election of 1916   **877**
The Final German Offensive and Allied Counterattack, 1918   **888**
Areas of Population Growth   **905**
The Election of 1928   **933**
Unemployment, 1925–1945   **949**
Federal Budget and Surplus/Deficit, 1920–1940   **968**
The Election of 1932   **971**
The Tennessee Valley Authority   **983**
The Election of 1936   **991**
What the New Deal Did . . .   **1006**
World War II in Europe and North Africa   **1018**
The Geography of Global War   **1022**
   Supply Routes to U.S.S.R.   **1022**
   The Spaces of the Pacific   **1022**
   Pacific Campaigns of World War II   **1023**
The Impact of World War II on Government Spending   **1067**
Cold War Europe   **1094**
The United States Birth Rate, 1900–1984   **1103**
Internal Population Movement After World War II   **1106**
The Election of 1948   **1109**
The Korean War   **1113**
Asian Trouble Spots   **1135**
Mechanically Harvested Cotton, 1949–1960   **1143**
The Election of 1960   **1157**
The World of the Superpowers   **1160–1161**
Civil Rights: Patterns of Protest and Unrest   **1168**
Growth of Government, 1955–1985   **1177**
The Geography of Vietnam   **1196**
Levels of U.S. Troops in Vietnam   **1201**
The Election of 1968   **1213**
Oil and Conflict in the Middle East   **1251**
OPEC Oil Prices, 1973–1987   **1254**
Income Projections of Two-Income Families, 1967–1984   **1259**
The Election of 1980   **1275**
Central American Conflicts, 1974–1988   **1289**
Hispanic and Asian Populations   **1299**
The Election of 1988   **1303**

PREFACE

History is both a discipline of rigor, bound by rules and scholarly methods, and something more: the unique, compelling, even strange way in which we humans define ourselves. We are all the sum of the tales of thousands of people, great and small, whose actions have etched their lines upon us. History supplies our very identity—a sense of the social groups to which we belong, whether family, ethnic group, race, class, or gender. It reveals to us the foundations of our deepest religious beliefs and traces the roots of our economic and political systems. It explores how we celebrate and grieve, sing the songs we sing, weather the illnesses to which time and chance subject us. It commands our attention for all these good reasons and for no good reason at all, other than a fascination with the way the myriad tales play out. Strange that we should come to care about a host of men and women so many centuries gone, some with names eminent and familiar, others unknown but for a chance scrap of information left behind in an obscure letter.

Yet we do care. We care about Sir Humphrey Gilbert, "devoured and swallowed up of the Sea" one black Atlantic night in 1583, about George Washington at Kips Bay, red with fury as he takes a riding crop to his retreating soldiers. We care about Octave Johnson, a slave fleeing through Louisiana swamps trying to decide whether to stand and fight the approaching hounds or take his chances with the bayou alligators, about Clara Barton, her nurse's skirts so heavy with blood from the wounded, she must wring them out before tending to the next soldier. We are drawn to the fate of Chinese laborers, chipping away at the Sierras' looming granite; a Georgian named Tom Watson seeking to forge a colorblind political alliance; and desperate immigrant mothers, kerosene in hand, storming Brooklyn butcher shops that had again raised prices. We follow, with a mix of awe and amusement, the fortunes of the quirky Henry Ford ("Everybody wants to be somewhere he ain't"), turning out identical automobiles, insisting his factory workers wear identical expressions ("Fordization of the Face"). We trace the career of young Thurgood Marshall, crisscrossing the South in his own "little old beat-up '29 Ford," typing legal briefs in the back seat, trying to get black teachers to sue for equal pay, hoping to get his people somewhere they weren't. The list could go on and on, spilling out as it did in Walt Whitman's *Leaves of Grass:* "A southerner soon as a northerner, a planter nonchalant and hospitable, / A Yankee bound my own way. . . . a Hoosier, a Badger, a Buckeye, a Louisianian or Georgian. . . ." Whitman embraced and celebrated them all, inseparable strands of what made him an American and what made him human:

> In all people I see myself, none more and not one a barleycorn less,
> And the good or bad I say of myself I say of them.

To encompass so expansive an America Whitman turned to poetry; historians have traditionally chosen *narrative* as their means of giving life to the past. That mode of explanation permits them to interweave the strands of economic, political, and social history in a coherent chronological framework. By choosing narrative, they affirm the multicausal nature of historical explanation—the insistence that events be portrayed in context. By choosing narrative, they are also acknowledging that, while long-term economic and social trends shape societies in deep and significant ways, events often take on a logic (or illogic) of their own, jostling one another, being deflected and redirected by unpredictable successions of personal decisions, sudden deaths, natural catastrophes, and chance. There are literary reasons, too, for preferring a narrative approach, since it supplies a dramatic force usually missing from more structural analyses of the past.

In some ways, surveys like this one are the natural antithesis of narrative history. They strive, by definition, to be comprehensive: to furnish a broad, orderly exposition of their chosen field. Yet to cover so much ground in so limited a space necessarily deprives readers of the pacing and context of more detailed accounts. Then, too, the resurgence of social history—with its concern for class and race, patterns of rural and urban life, the spread of market and industrial economies—lends itself to more analytic, less chronological treatments. The challenge facing historians is to incorporate these areas of research without losing the narrative drive that propels the story or sacrificing the chronological flow that orients readers to the more familiar events of our past.

Lately there has been increased attention to the worldwide breakdown of so many nonmarket economies, and by inference, to the greater success of the market societies of the United States and other capitalist nations. As our own narrative makes clear, American society and politics have indeed come together centrally in the marketplace. What Americans produce, how and where they produce it, and the desire to buy cheap and sell dear have been defining elements in every era. That market orientation has created unparalleled abundance and reinforced striking inequalities, not the least a society in which, for two centuries, human beings themselves were bought and sold. It has made Americans powerfully provincial in protecting local interests and internationally adventurous in seeking to expand wealth and opportunity.

It goes without saying that Americans have not always produced wisely or well. The insistent drive toward material plenty has levied a heavy tax on the global environment. Too often quantity has substituted for quality, whether we talk of cars, education, or culture. When markets flourish, the nation abounds with confidence that any problem, no matter how intractable, can be solved.

When markets fail, however, the fault lines of our political and social systems become all too evident.

In the end, then, it is impossible to separate the marketplace of boom and bust and the world of ordinary Americans from the corridors of political maneuvering or the ceremonial pomp of an inauguration. To treat political and social history as distinct spheres or hostile camps is counterproductive. The primary question of this narrative—how the fledgling, often tumultuous confederation of "these United States" managed to transform itself into an enduring republic—is not only political, but necessarily social. In order to survive, a republic must resolve conflicts between citizens of different geographic regions and economic classes, of diverse racial and ethnic origins, of competing religions and ideologies. The resolution of these conflicts has produced tragic consequences, perhaps, as often as noble ones. But tragic or noble, the destiny of these states cannot be understood without comprehending the social dimension of the story.

A word about organization and strategies. The narrative is divided into six parts, each beginning with a brief essay setting American events of the period in a global context. We believe it important to make clear that the United States did not develop in a geographic or cultural vacuum and that the broad forces shaping it also influenced other nations. Thus we compare the extraordinary demographic growth of colonial America with the worldwide eighteenth-century rise in population; the effects of democratic and industrial revolutions here with those abroad; the massive voluntary migrations of the nineteenth century to many parts of the globe. We examine the rise of industrial societies of the twentieth century and the environmental constraints to growth as we approach the twenty-first. Each essay ends with a time line comparing political and social events in the United States with developments elsewhere.

Throughout the book we have sought to sustain a narrative approach, starting with introductory episodes for each chapter. Complementing the narrative for each chapter is a two-page essay, "Daily Lives," focusing on one of five topics that give insight into the lives of ordinary Americans: clothing and fashion; time and travel; food, drink, and drugs; political culture; public and private spaces. These topics recur regularly throughout the book, providing additional thematic continuity. Each chapter concludes with a summary of significant events; full and up-to-date bibliographies can be found at the back of the book.

For each of the book's six parts, we have included an essay, "Generations of the Republic," which takes one generation of Americans and charts its progress from birth, childhood, and adolescence through courtship, marriage, adulthood, and old age. In moving from the first Anglo-Americans (Part 1) to the baby boomers born in the 1940s and 50s (Part 6), we have sought to integrate recent research on family structure and demographics with a sense of how national events affected the lives of ordinary citizens. In effect, we are applying a narrative approach to illuminating the intersection of biography and history.

Any account of a republic with a global reach must be geographically grounded. We have taken particular care in developing the maps for this book, working closely with the cartographers to create geographically detailed yet clear renderings. Full captions are provided whenever necessary; a number of maps are unique to this book, while many others include unusual information. In addition, six geographic essays explore such topics as the commercial and subsistence regions of the young republic, the economics of cotton in the post–Civil War South, and the geographic aspects of the war in Vietnam.

In addition to characterizing the American experience through a complement of paintings, photographs and drawings, we have tried to convey a sense of change over time by incorporating into the book's design contemporary printers' ornaments. The initial blocks opening each chapter have been taken from type specimen books of different eras; similarly, the decorative drawings have come from contemporary engravings.

We are grateful to a host of readers whose comments and suggestions helped improve an earlier draft of this manuscript. They include Carol Berkin, Baruch College and the Graduate Center of the City University of New York; Roger W. Biles, Oklahoma State University; Carol Brown, Houston Community College; Victor Chen, Chabot College; Mario S. DePillis, University of Massachusetts, Amherst; Lynn Dumenil, Claremont McKenna College; Robert Elam, Modesto Junior College; Robert G. Fricke, West Valley College; James L. Gormly, Washington and Jefferson College; Peter Iverson, Arizona State University; George Juergens, Indiana University; Mark H. Leff, University of Illinois at Urbana-Champaign; John McCardell, Middlebury College; Gerald W. McFarland, University of Massachusetts, Amherst; Dennis C. Rousey, Arkansas State University; James C. Schneider, University of Texas, San Antonio; Lewright B. Sikes, Middle Tennessee State University; Gregory Holmes Singleton, Northeastern Illinois University; David Sloan, University of Arkansas, Fayetteville; Donna J. Spindel, Marshall University; Thomas E. Terrill, University of South Carolina; Stephen G. Weisner, Springfield Technical Community College; Frank J. Wetta, Galveston College; and William Bruce Wheeler, University of Tennessee, Knoxville. In addition, many friends and colleagues contributed their advice and constructive criticism in ways both small and large. These included Michael Bellesiles, Lawrence A. Cardoso, Dinah Chenven, James E. Crisp, R. David Edmunds, Drew McCoy, James McPherson, Stephen E. Maizlish, Harold Silesky, David J. Weber, and Virginia Joyner.

The division of labor for this book was determined by our respective fields of scholarship: Christine Heyrman, the colonial era, in which Europeans, Africans, and Indians participated in the making of both a new America and a new republic; William Gienapp, the ninety years in which the young nation first flourished, then foundered on the issues of section and slavery; Michael Stoff, the post–Civil War era, in which industrialization and urbanization brought the nation more centrally into an international system constantly disrupted by depression and war; and Mark Lytle, the modern era, in which Americans finally faced the reality that even the boldest dreams of national greatness are bounded by the finite nature of power and resources both natural and human. Finally, because the need to specialize inevitably imposes limits on any project as broad as this one, our fifth author, James Davidson, served as a general editor and writer, with the intent of fitting individual parts to the whole, as well as providing a measure of continuity, style, and overarching purpose. In producing this collaborative effort, all of us have shared the conviction that the best history speaks to a larger audience.

We began the writing of this book as friends; what is perhaps more unusual, given the strains of such undertakings, is that over the years our friendship deepened. The responsibility for such a happy outcome no doubt rests squarely on the shoulders of our editor, Christopher Rogers. He conceived the project, brought the authors together, consistently pushed us to make this the best book it could be, and marshalled the unstinting support of our publisher for its completion and production. Authors could ask for no more from an editor.

JAMES WEST DAVIDSON
WILLIAM E. GIENAPP
CHRISTINE LEIGH HEYRMAN
MARK H. LYTLE
MICHAEL B. STOFF

PART 1

THE CREATION OF A NEW AMERICA

It is now nearly half a millennium—a full 500 years—since the civilizations of Europe and Africa first made sustained contact with those of North America. The transformations arising out of that event have been astonishing. To gain a rough sense of the scale involved, both in time and space, we start not at the beginning of our story but somewhere nearer its midpoint: retracing the route taken by Meriwether Lewis, First Infantry, USA, as he embarked from Washington, D.C., July 4, 1803.

Lewis, on orders from President Thomas Jefferson, planned to cross the continent with his friend William Clark and a party of assistants; they would be the first Americans to do this. Leaving the cluster of buildings and muddy avenues then known as Washington, Lewis followed the rutted wagon road up the Potomac to Harpers Ferry and made his way across the Alleghenies, that range of mountains which had kept the English colonists hemmed in along the Atlantic coastal plain for 200 years. From Pittsburgh he proceeded by boat down the Ohio, where the wild squirrels were so numerous they could be seen crossing the river in herds. (Lewis' dog, Scannon, finding himself in canine heaven, jumped overboard and retrieved more than a few, which Lewis skinned, fried, and pronounced "a pleasant food.") Clark came aboard at Louisville and the two men continued down to the junction of the Mississippi, then beating upstream to the village of St. Louis.

The true journey began the following spring: up the broad Missouri, which,  together with the Mississippi, constituted one of the longest river systems in the world. The party passed first through lush, tall prairie grass ("from 5 to 8 feet high") and then into the short-grass plains. To Lewis, these resembled nothing so much as a "beautiful bowling-green in fine order," dotted by "immence herds of Buffaloe, deer Elk and Antelopes which we saw in every direction feeding on the hills and plains." The party pressed on through the Dakotas and Montana into the Rockies, seeking the ultimate headwaters of the Missouri. Finally, in August 1805, Lewis reached his watershed—a "handsome bold running Creek of cold Clear water," whose westward flow would eventually take him to the Pacific.

But stop for a moment with Lewis: midway between two oceans, straddling a continental divide and half a millennium of American history. From his vantage point, what can we see?

At first glance, we see pretty much what we expect to see at the beginning of American history: a magnificent and empty "virgin wilderness," rolling on and on across the continent. Even more to the point, because we live in the twentieth century, we tend to take for granted that this vast territory, stretching from ocean to ocean, will become united as a continental republic under a single national government; but only hindsight makes this proposition seem natural. In 1800 the sheer size of the land made the idea of unifying such a territory difficult to grasp. After all, Lewis had traveled a full 1200 miles merely to reach St. Louis, then another 2700 to the headwaters of the Missouri. In 1805 the nation amounted to over 1.5 million square miles. Vast as that was, nearly 2 million more square miles remained to be annexed before the United States would attain its present size.

But it was more than size that made the new "Louisiana Territory" which Lewis and Clark traversed hardly the stuff of continental republics. It was a diverse array of cultures, which for many years had been claimed by the Spanish but in fact was controlled primarily by scores of independent Indian nations. Some of these were hunter-gatherer societies, dispersed in bands across the land; others, especially to the south, had developed highly sophisticated urban cultures or the means of growing crops carefully cultivated through irrigation. Just how diverse the landscape was can be seen by the methods Lewis and Clark used to communicate. With no common language spanning the territory, speechmaking became a series of translations that reflected the route over which the party had traveled. In Idaho, for example, Clark addressed the Tushepaw tribe in English; his speech was translated into French by a trapper in the party; then a second  trapper translated into Minataree, a language which the trapper's Indian wife, Sacajawea, understood. Sacajawea, later renowned as the sole female member of the party, had grown up farther west with the Shoshone, so she in turn translated the Minataree into Shoshone, which a boy from the Tushepaw nation understood. He translated the Shoshone into his own people's tongue.

If the Louisiana Territory seemed a patchwork of governments and cultures, the rest of America was almost as heterogeneous. Spain, Britain, and Russia all continued to claim parts of it, with France too keeping an eye out for possible conquests. During the 1790s Clark had acted as an American intelligence agent, floating up and down the Ohio and Mississippi rivers keeping track of the foreign powers still active on what were then U.S. borders. The "U. States" themselves remained a group of colonies only recently unified. Jefferson, who possessed the vision to send Lewis and Clark on their continental mission, had nonetheless long been in the habit of referring to Virginia as "my country." Indeed, the various states contained a patchwork of languages and cultures nearly as diverse as those farther west. Dutch-speaking patroons could be found along New York's Hudson River, Welsh and German farmers along Pennsylvania's Lancaster Pike, Swedes in

3

Delaware, Gaelic-speaking Scots scattered up and down the Appalachian back-country, blacks using the African-English Gullah dialect along the Carolina coast. Many of these settlers knew more about their homelands in Europe or Africa than they did about other regions of North America.

In fact, many colonists gained a sense of what other regions were like only during the American Revolution. "Law! Is he a Yankee?" asked one Philadelphia lady of a soldier in the Continental Army. "I thought he was a Pennsylvanian. I don't see any difference between him and other people." Even in the nineteenth century, Americans might understandably be confused about the geography beyond their neighborhoods. Frederick Law Olmsted reported this conversation with a farmer riding on a train near Charleston, South Carolina, during the 1850s:

> "How do you go," the man asked, "w'en you get to Charleston?"
> "I am going on to New Orleans."
> "Is New York beyond New Orleans?"
> "Beyond New Orleans? Oh, no."
> "In New Orleans, is't?"
> "What?"
> "New York is somewhere in New Orleans, ain't it?"
> "No; it's the other way—beyond Wilmington."
> "Oh! Been pretty cold thar?"
> "Yes; there was a foot and a half of snow there, last week, I hear."
> "Lord o'massy! why! have to feed all the cattle!—whew!—ha!—whew! don't won-ner ye com' away."

Evidently this farmer had only vague ideas of the nation existing beyond his neighborhood. But even informed Americans of the 1850s doubted whether the United States could survive the bitter differences then growing between North and South. To resolve them took four years and the bloodiest war in the nation's history. It was by no means clear in the 1850s that a continental republic would survive.

Thus our first task in studying the American past becomes one of translation. We must view events not with the jaded eyes of the late twentieth century but with the innocent eyes of an earlier era. Then the foregone conclusions vanish. How does the American nation manage to unite millions of square miles of territory into one governable republic? How do New Orleans and New York come to be linked in a complex economy as well as in a single political system? Such questions take on even more significance when we recall that Europe—roughly the same size as the United States—is today still divided into 32 independent nations speaking some 33 languages, not to mention another 100 or so spoken within the Soviet Union. A united Europe has not emerged there, despite noble intentions and a Common Market economic system.

How, then, did this American republic—this "teeming nation of nations," to use Walt Whitman's phrase—come to be? In barest outline, that is the question which drives our narrative across half a millennium.

To Europeans in the mid-fifteenth century, of course, the idea of a republic across the sea was even more fantastic than the "Islands of the Blessed"—those mythical lands in the far mists of the Atlantic dreamed of by monks. Scandinavian seafarers had sailed as far west as Greenland by the end of the tenth century; in 1001 a party of men and women under Leif Ericsson established an encampment known as Vinland that endured several seasons, but news of his discoveries never reached the rest of Europe. In 1450, about the time Christopher Columbus was born, only the first stirrings of Western expansion had begun. Localism held sway even more than it did in Lewis and Clark's America.

Europe, in fact, was not a particularly formidable area of the globe. The fastest growing power in the region was the Turkish Ottoman Empire, which in 1453 had captured Constantinople as a beachhead for further expansion into Europe. True, the Italian city-states of Genoa and Venice controlled flourishing trading outposts in Asia Minor. But the Turks were also cutting into these. Within Europe, political organization remained fragmented. Italy was divided into five major states and an equal number of smaller territories. The Germanic peoples were united loosely in the Holy Roman Empire (which, as historians have long delighted in pointing out, was neither holy, Roman, nor an empire). French kings ruled over only about half of what is now France. Spain was divided into several kingdoms, with some areas held by Christians, others by Islamic Moors, whose forebears came from Africa. England, a contentious little nation, was beginning a series of bitter civil conflicts among the nobility, known eventually as the Wars of the Roses. The only country pushing beyond the boundaries of the known European world was Portugal, whose sailors were slowly advancing down the coast of Africa in search of gold and slaves.

Localism was evident in other ways. Europe in 1450 was far from being the urban commercial society it is today. London, which today has a population of 6 million or 7 million, held only about 50,000 people; Paris, something more than 100,000. Most people lived in rural or village settings. Moving goods from one region to another was extremely difficult. Land routes were by and large only rutted paths, except for the ancient Roman roads. Wheeled carts were sometimes used to haul loads, but more often it was simply pack animals or human porters bearing goods over the mountain passes of the Alps. Rivers and canals provided another option, but lords repeatedly taxed boats that crossed their territories. (On the Seine River, greedy tollkeepers lay in wait every six or seven miles.) Travel across the Mediterranean Sea and along Europe's northern coastlines was possible, but storms and pirates made the going dangerous and slow. Under good conditions, a ship might reach London from Venice in only 9 days; under bad, it might take 50. In addition, since 1347 western Europe had been repeatedly decimated by bubonic plague. A population once totaling more than 50 million had dropped to about 37 million by 1450.

European peoples at this time had some dealings—though not extensive—with Africa. What contact there was arose primarily from sharing the Mediterranean Sea. North African culture had been shaped since the seventh century by the religion of Islam, whose influence spread even up through Spain. Farther south in Africa, the kingdom of Songhai prospered along the Niger River. But Africans from these interior regions were linked with Europeans primarily through trading caravans, which made their way across the Sahara with African gold—essential to Europe's economy. The west African coast, which faced the Atlantic, was only beginning to receive the attention of the Portuguese. Their coming would drastically alter the patterns of African–European trade. Ultimately these changes would transform the Americas as well.

If Europe in 1450 was less unified and dynamic than we might have imagined, the civilizations of North and South America were more complex than they have sometimes been painted. We have already noted the popular image of America before 1492 as a "virgin wilderness." Yet this stereotype is profoundly misleading. Research over the past several decades indicates that North and South America were much more populous than historians once thought. Earlier estimates suggested that when Europeans arrived about 10 million people were living in Central and South America, with another million living north of Mexico. More recently these figures have been raised tenfold, to perhaps as many as 100 million people in Central and South America and 10 million north of Mexico.

Such numbers—which remain conjectural and imprecise—nevertheless lead to startling conclusions. In 1492, when Columbus landed on Hispaniola, that island alone may have held some 7 million to 8 million people—a number roughly equal to the entire population of Spain. (England at the time had only 4 million to 5 million people.) Tenochtitlán, capital of the Aztec empire, held an estimated 250,000 inhabitants, probably double the size of the largest European cities of the day. Such dense urban populations were supported by sophisticated agricultural techniques, including canals, irrigation, and drainage systems.

North America was far from being as heavily populated as the lands to the south, but neither was it sparsely settled. From one end of the continent to the other, native cultures actively shaped their environments, regularly burning the forests and plains to promote the growth of vegetation as well as animal populations, which they harvested. As we shall see, their agricultural achievements were so remarkable that they eventually revolutionized eating habits across the rest of the globe.

Here then are three worlds—Europe, Africa, the Americas—poised on the brink of contact. What social and economic forces led so many Europeans—desperate and opportunistic, high-minded and idealistic—to turn westward in pursuit of their dreams? How did the civilizations of North and South America react and adjust to the European invaders? And not least, how did the mix of cultures from Africa, Europe, and North America come together to create what was truly a new America, in which some of the most independent-minded individuals prospered in provinces that exhibited some of the harshest examples of human slavery? These are among the questions we seek to answer as our narrative unfolds.

CHRONOLOGY

AMERICAN EVENT	YEAR	GLOBAL EVENT
Leif Ericsson establishes Vinland in Newfoundland	1001	
	1215	Mongols begin 60-year conquest of China
	1271–1295	Marco Polo travels to China from Venice
Rise of the Aztec empire	ca. 1300	
	1347	Bubonic plague reaches Europe; population of 50 million drops 30–40 percent by 1400
Formation of the Iroquois League	late 1400s	
Columbus reaches America	1492	Reconquista drives Muslim Arabs from Spain
	1498	Vasco da Gama reaches India
	1517	Luther launches Protestant Reformation
European diseases waste central Mexico; population falls from ca. 25 million to 1 million in 1600, a 95% mortality	1520s	
Cortés conquers Aztec empire	1521	
Silver boom in Mexico, Bolivia	1550s	
	1602	Dutch East India Company founded
Jamestown established	1607	
Santa Fe founded	1610	
Pilgrims land at Plymouth	1620	
Sugar boom in Caribbean	1640s	
	1642	Outbreak of English Civil War
	1660	Restoration of English monarchy: Charles II ascends throne
Carolinas founded	1663	
Chesapeake labor system depends increasingly on black slavery	1680s	
La Salle follows the Mississippi	1682	
	1687	Isaac Newton's Principia Mathematica, on gravitation, published
	1688	Glorious Revolution in England; constitutional monarchy of William III and Mary
Glorious Revolution in America	1688–1691	
King William's War	1689–1697	War of the League of Augsburg
Rice boom in South Carolina	1700s	
Queen Anne's War	1702–1713	War of the Spanish Succession
French found New Orleans	1718	
The Great Awakening	1730s–1750s	
	1738	John and Charles Wesley begin preaching Methodism in England
King George's War	1740–1748	War of the Austrian Succession
Benjamin Franklin founds the American Philosophical Society	1743	

1

Old World, New Worlds

ll the world lay before them. Or so it seemed to mariners from England's seafaring coasts, pushing westward toward unknown lands in the far Atlantic.

The scent of the new land came first—not the sight of it, but the sounds and smells, wafted from beyond the horizon, delicious to mariners who had felt nothing but the rolling sea for weeks on end. In northerly latitudes around June, it would be the scent of fir trees or the sight of shore birds wheeling about the masts—signs of favor worthy of an Our Father or a Hail Mary from the grateful sailors. Straightaway the captain would call for a lead to be thrown overboard to sound the depths; at its end was a hollowed-out socket with a bit of tallow in it, so some of the sea bottom would stick when hauled up. Even out of sight of land, a good sailing master could tell where he was by what came up—"oosy sand," indicating a location north of the Scilly Isles, or perhaps "soft worms" or "popple-stones as big as beans." But if the ship was approaching unknown shores, the captain's hope would be to sight land early in the day, allowing time to work cautiously toward an untried harbor on uncharted tides.

Since the time of King Arthur, the English living along the rugged southwestern coasts of Devon and Cornwall had followed the sea. From the wharves of England's West Country seaports, like Bristol, Exeter, and Plymouth, ships headed west and north to Ireland, bringing back timber for houses, barrels and casks, and animal hides. Or they turned south, crossing the English Channel to trade with other Atlantic ports, bringing back wines from French Bordeaux and olive oil or luxurious figs and raisins from the Spanish and Portuguese coasts. In return, West Country ports offered woven woolen cloth and codfish, caught wherever the likeliest prospects beckoned.

In the early fifteenth century, prospects had taken West Country sailors north and west, toward Iceland. The amount of dried cod brought back had been not only essential for trade but also a crucial staple in the diet, especially over the barren winter months. By the 1480s, however, the West Country fisherfolk were taking a beating from the Icelanders, whose mariners preferred to keep the catch for themselves and trade with the Germans and the Danes. The brawling and killing that plagued the fishing grounds persuaded some of the more enterprising English to sail farther west. Old maps, after all, claimed that the bountiful *Hy-Brasil*—Gaelic for "Isle of the Blessed"—lay vaguely to the west of Ireland.

Over the next dozen years, a few ships ventured every other year or so

With sails bellying in a gale, the Dutch ship in this Verbeek painting has furled the rest of its canvas. When Humphrey Gilbert's ship went down in a similar storm, the last a nearby vessel saw was the stern lantern (visible on this ship too) wink out.

West Country fisherfolk from England weighed anchor and sailed from harbors like this one, painted during the 1480s. The ship at left is being towed by a longboat to a position where it can hoist sail and set off. In the foreground is a primitive lighthouse: an iron cresset on a pole, holding a smoky warning fire.

beyond the known routes, but with little luck. Into this eddy of interest stepped an Italian, a citizen of Venice named Giovanni Caboto, whom the English called John Cabot. Cabot had obtained the blessing of King Henry VII to hunt for unknown lands, and he wisely took to Bristol to outfit himself. In the spring of 1497 his lone ship set out to the west, and this time the return voyage brought news of a "new-found" island where the trees were tall enough to make fine masts and the codfish were plentiful. After returning to Bristol, Cabot marched off to London to inform His Majesty, received 10 pounds as his reward, and with the proceeds dressed himself in dashing silks. The multitudes of London flocked after him, wondering over "the Admiral"; then Cabot returned triumphantly to Bristol to undertake a more ambitious voyage—the search for a northwest passage to Asia. He set sail with five ships in 1498 and was never heard from again, presumably a victim of the North Atlantic.

Still, Bristol folk were not about to let a gale or two distract them from reports of cod. In the 1500s they began to fish regularly the relatively shallow Grand Banks off the island of Newfoundland, as it came to be called. The teeming waters attracted a swarm of Europeans, not only from England but also from Portuguese harbors like Aveiro and Viana, French ports scattered along Brittany and Normandy, and Spanish villages facing the Bay of Biscay. By 1550, perhaps 400 vessels and 1200 men arrived in Newfoundland for the annual fishing season.

The trip was not easy. Individual merchants or a few partners outfitted small ships with provisions, fishing boats, and a complement of guns to ward off both sea-roving pirates and "privateers"—pirates who looted with royal approval. As early in the season as they dared, crews of 10 or 20 would catch the spring easterlies, leaving astern the horizon of familiar roofs and the primitive lighthouse burning its smoky coal. Aboard ship, only the officers were given bunks; seamen slept in odd spaces below decks. Rats were such a constant plague that the law of the sea required carrying at least one cat aboard every ship. In Newfoundland waters, sailors had to look sharp for icebergs and even more dangerous "growlers"— chunks of ice the size of houses, which floated barely concealed just below the water, ready to do a ship in.

Weeks after setting sail the sailors sighted land—fog-shrouded beaches fringing thick pine forests, seals and walruses along the rocks offshore, and the encircling sea filled with cod and flounder, salmon and herring. Throughout the summer men launched little ketches from rickety, hastily constructed stages in each harbor and fished offshore all day and into the night. With lines and nets, and baskets weighted with stones, they scooped fish from the sea and then dried and salted the catch on the beach. Some of the Spanish went after whales, which they hauled ashore, cut up, and boiled into oil. And crews from every European country traded with the native Beothuks and Micmacs, who shared their summer fishing grounds and the skins of fox and deer.

For those who tired of the long weeks at sea, Newfoundland offered St. John's, which by the 1550s had become the hub of the North Atlantic fishery. Portuguese, English, and French fishing vessels all dropped anchor there, either to take on supplies in the spring or to prepare for the homeward voyage in autumn. Only the Spanish kept their distance. In St. John's, masters haggled over the price of fish and bartered for items they could not get at home. Here the port admiral, usually the master of the first vessel to arrive each season, struggled to settle disputes over stolen boats, contested beaches, and personal insults. And here, amid the swilling and scuffling and squabbling, there was always a great deal of talk, for these seafarers knew as much as anyone about the new world of wonders that was opening to Europeans. They were acquainted with names like Cristoforo Colombo, the Italian from Genoa whom Cabot might have known as a boy. They listened to Portuguese tales of sailing around the Horn of Africa in pursuit of spices and to stories of empires to the south, rich in gold and silver, which Spanish treasure ships were bringing home.

Indeed, Newfoundland was one of the few places in the world where so many ordinary folk of different nations could gather and talk, crammed aboard dank ships moored in St. John's harbor, huddled before blazing fires on its beaches, or crowded into smoky, makeshift taverns. And when the ships sailed home in autumn the tales went with them, repeated in the tiniest coastal villages by those pleased to have cheated death and the sea one more time. Eager to fish, talk, trade, and take profits, West Country mariners were almost giddy at the prospect of Europe's expanding horizons.

THE MEETING OF EUROPE AND AMERICA

Most of the captains, pilots, and seafarers who fished the waters of Newfoundland's Grand Banks remain anonymous today. Their lives are lost to the historical

The Geography of Exploration

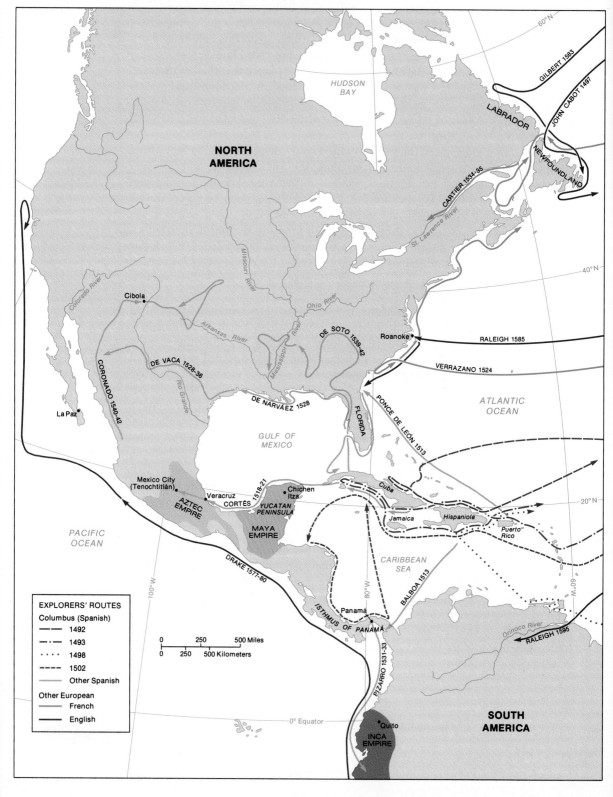

HUDSON
BAY

**NORTH
AMERICA**

GILBERT 1583

JOHN CABOT 1497

LABRADOR

NEWFOUNDLAND

CARTIER 1534-35

St. Lawrence River

Missouri River

Ohio River

Cibola

Colorado River

Arkansas River

Mississippi River

DE SOTO 1539-42

Roanoke

RALEIGH 1585

DE VACA 1528-36

CORONADO 1540-42

Rio Grande

DE NARVÁEZ 1528

VERRAZANO 1524

ATLANTIC
OCEAN

40° N

60° N

La Paz

FLORIDA

PONCE DE LEÓN 1513

GULF OF
MEXICO

Mexico City
(Tenochtitlán)

Veracruz
CORTÉS

1518-21

Chichen
Itza

Cuba

AZTEC
EMPIRE

YUCATAN
PENINSULA

Jamaica

Hispaniola

Puerto
Rico

20° N

MAYA
EMPIRE

PACIFIC
OCEAN

DRAKE 1577-80

CARIBBEAN
SEA

BALBOA 1513

80° W

60° W

100° W

Orinoco River

ISTHMUS OF PANAMA

Panama

RALEIGH 1595

PIZARRO 1531-33

**SOUTH
AMERICA**

0° Equator

Quito

INCA
EMPIRE

EXPLORERS' ROUTES

Columbus (Spanish)

——— 1492
—·—·— 1493
········· 1498
– – – – 1502
——— Other Spanish

Other European
——— French
——— English

| 0 | | 250 | | 500 Miles |
| 0 | 250 | | 500 Kilometers | |

Spain dominated the first hundred years of exploration and settlement in the Americas. Columbus and his successors first established a base of operations at Hispaniola and then subjugated Puerto Rico (1509), Jamaica (1510), and Cuba (1511). Ponce de León pressed north to Florida, Balboa traversed the Panamanian isthmus to discover the Pacific, and in 1519 Cortés began his conquest of the mainland.

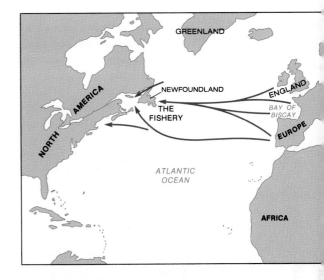

But Spain was only one of several countries whose Atlantic coast encouraged them to press westward in search of profitable trade (top right). Spanish and French fisherfolk, whose ports lay on the Atlantic's Bay of Biscay, joined other French sailors from Brittany and Normandy as well as English "West Country boys" at the Grand Banks off Newfoundland, where the shallows of the continental shelf yielded abundant stores of cod and other fish.

Farther south, the Portuguese and Spanish had developed different strategies for sailing west (bottom right). During the fifteenth century, they used the prevailing breezes of the northeast trades to head south and west to the Madeira Islands, colonized by Portugal, and the Canaries, settled by Spain. But how to sail home, against the winds? The technique sailors hit upon was to travel farther *west*, but north as well, until they reached a latitude where the prevailing westerlies carried them back to Europe. The Portuguese called this maneuver the *volta do mar*—returning by sea.

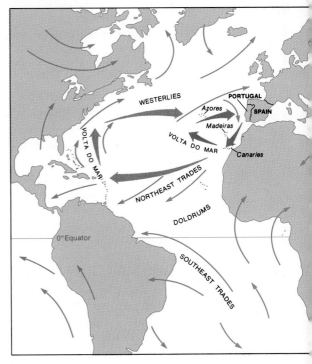

Columbus and the Spanish who followed him applied the same technique on a grander scale: dropping south to the Canaries to catch the northeast trades to the Caribbean, then heading north on the return trip to pick up the westerlies. The technique was refined even further when the pilot of Ponce de León's expedition discovered the currents of the Gulf Stream that surged eastward between Florida and Cuba. Soon all Spanish fleets were returning home by sailing not south of Cuba but north, harnessing both ocean currents and the winds.

record except for a few recollections or a line or two in royal archives about voyagers who presented to the Crown exotic "hauwkes," wildcats, or "popinjays" (a bright bird of any unusual sort) "brought from the Newfounde Island." Yet it is well to begin with these anonymous fisherfolk, for the European discovery of the Americas cannot be looked upon simply as the voyages of a few bold explorers. The expansion of European peoples and culture that began in the 1450s could not have occurred without a series of gradual but telling changes in the fabric of European society.

Some of these changes were technological, arising out of advances in navigational skills, the art of shipbuilding, and the use of gunpowder. Some were social, involving the development of trade networks of the sort that linked Bristol with ports as far afield as those of Iceland and Spain. Some were demographic, bringing about a rise in Europe's population after a devastating century of plague. Some changes were religious, adding a dimension of devout belief to the political rivalries that fueled discoveries in the Americas. And some changes were political, making it possible for feudal kingdoms to centralize and extend their bureaucratic influence across the ocean. Portugal, Spain, France, and England—all possessing coasts along the Atlantic—led the way in exploration, spurred on by acclaimed Italian "admirals" like Caboto and Colombo, Spanish *conquistadores* like Cortés and Pizarro, and English sea dogs like Humphrey Gilbert and Walter Raleigh. Ordinary folk rode these currents too. The great and the small alike were propelled by forces that were remolding the face of Europe.

The Portuguese Wave

In 1450 all of the world known to western Europeans was Asia and Africa. Most mariners of the day confined their voyages to the coast of western Europe, inching gingerly along the shores between Norway and the southern tip of Spain, seldom daring to lose sight of land, and putting into port often. Since the beginning of the fifteenth century, the boldest seafarers had groped down the coast of western Africa—half-expecting to be boiled alive in the Atlantic as they approached the equator. Europeans had traded with Asia through the Muslims of the eastern Mediterranean and across an overland route called the "Silk Road," but they had only vague notions about the contours of "the Indies"—China and Japan, the Spice Islands, and the lands lying between Thailand and India. What little they knew, they had learned mainly from Marco Polo, whose account of his travels in the East was not published until 1477, more than 150 years after his death. Even then, many learned men in Europe doubted his reports of the Great Khan's Cathay (China) and dismissed his Cipango (Japan) as a mythical island.

But a revolution in the European knowledge of geography began in the middle decades of the fifteenth century. As the picture of the known world changed, so did the world itself. Ever-widening networks of travel and trade connected Europeans to new peoples, economies, and civilizations beyond western Europe. The Portuguese took the lead in pushing beyond the traditional bounds, encouraged by Prince Henry, known as the Navigator. The devout Henry, a member of Portugal's royal family in the middle of the fifteenth century, was not as much consumed by dynastic ambitions as he was curious about finding out "things which were hidden from other men, and secret." Like others of his day, he had heard tales of Prester John, a Catholic priest reputed to rule a Christian kingdom somewhere in Africa or Asia, on the eastern flank of the Muslim world. Henry dreamed of joining forces with Prester John and trapping the Muslims in a vise. To that end, he subsidized a series of expeditions down the coast of west Africa. And at Cape St. Vincent, the westernmost point of all Europe on the Portuguese coast, he founded an informal school of navigation, dispensing to shipmasters information about wind and currents, as well as navigational charts.

Portuguese merchants, who may or may not have credited the existence of Prester John, never doubted that there was money to be made in Africa. Unlike Spain, Portugal possessed no coast bordering the Mediterranean with easy access to its trade. As an alternative, its merchants invested in Prince Henry's voyages and in return gained trading monopolies of ivory and slaves, grain and gold. A few may have hoped that the voyages down the coast of west Africa would lead to a direct sea route to the Orient. By discovering such a route, Portugal would be able to lower the cost of importing Asia's silks, dyes, drugs, perfumes, and spices by cutting out the Muslim middlemen who controlled all of Europe's Asian trade through Mediterranean ports.

At the same time that Portugal's merchants were establishing trading posts or "factories" along the west coast of Africa, its mariners were discovering islands in the Atlantic. Before 1400, the Portuguese had found the Canary Islands, and in the 1420s they colonized both Madeira and the Azores; settlers planted sugar cane and grape vines and imported slaves from Africa to work their fields.

Portuguese mariners might have pressed farther west, but for the daring of Bartolomeu Dias. In 1488 Dias distracted the Portuguese from the Atlantic by rounding the Cape of Good Hope on the southern tip of Africa and sailing far enough up that continent's eastern coast to claim discovery of a sea route to India. Ten years later Vasco da Gama reached India itself, and Portuguese interests ultimately extended to Indochina and China. The Portuguese did not settle large numbers of their own people in Asia, but they scattered factories, garrisons, and missions throughout the Indies. And although Portugal's explorers never encountered the like of Prester John, its merchants replaced the Muslims as masters of trade to the Orient.

By the turn of the century, all of seafaring Europe eagerly sought the services of Portuguese pilots, prizing their superior maps and skills with the quadrant. That instrument made for a fairly accurate determination of latitude, allowing ships to plot their position after months out of the sight of land. The Portuguese had also pioneered the caravel, a light ship that afforded greater power against contrary winds and more maneuverability in rough seas than did heavier vessels. More seaworthy than the lumbering galleys of the Middle Ages, caravels combined longer, narrower hulls, a shape built for speed, with triangular lateen sails, which allowed for more flexible steering. Advances in firearms over the previous century led the Portuguese as well as other Europeans to mount cannons on their ships. The superior firepower made it possible to defeat Asian navies, even when the Europeans were outnumbered.

Following the discovery of a route to India, Portuguese attention turned largely to building an empire in the East Indies, although Portugal continued to

This stately ivory mask made by an African artist in the early sixteenth century for the Court of Benin (present-day Nigeria) is adorned with several small heads of white men, representing Portuguese explorers and traders who had first arrived in Benin in 1472.

dominate trade along Africa's west coast. When yellow fever, malaria, and other African diseases kept the Portuguese from colonizing the mainland, they set up way stations on islands off the African coast, such as the Cape Verdes and, farther south, São Tomé. There, Africans converted to Christianity by missionaries intermarried with European traders to form a culturally mixed society that became a linchpin of the Atlantic trade in African slaves. In the centuries to come, hundreds of thousands of slaves would be shipped to the Portuguese colony of Brazil, whose shores were discovered when a storm blew Pedro Álvares Cabral off course in 1500. But the Atlantic slave trade did not blossom in earnest until after Spain had made a much greater mark on the Americas.

The Spanish and Columbus

From among the international community of seafarers and pilots, it was a sailor from Genoa, Cristoforo Colombo, who led the Spanish to the Americas. Columbus (the Latinized version of his name survives) had knocked about in a number of harbors. In 1472 the red-haired, ruddy-faced young man of 25 traveled to Lisbon, picking up valuable navigation skills sailing Portugal's merchant ships to Madeira, west Africa, and the North Atlantic. His North Atlantic travels took him to Iceland and western Ireland, possibly even to England's West Country. In the Irish port of Galway, Columbus saw two boats drift into the harbor, bearing the dead bodies of "a man and a woman of extraordinary appearance." Most likely they were Lapps or Finns, the victims of a shipwreck. But everyone in Galway, including Columbus, assumed that they were Chinese, "blown across" the Atlantic.

That evidence only confirmed Columbus in his conviction that the quickest route to the Indies lay westward, across the Atlantic—and that his destiny was to prove it. Perhaps a mere 4500 miles, he reckoned, separated Europe from Japan. His wishful estimate raised eyebrows whenever Columbus asked European monarchs for the money to meet his destiny. Most educated Europeans agreed that the world was round, but they also believed that the Atlantic barrier between themselves and Asia was far wider than Columbus allowed and that it was impossible to navigate. The kings of England, France, and Portugal dismissed him as a crackpot.

Almost a decade of ridicule and rejection had grayed Columbus' red hair when Spain's monarchs, Ferdinand and Isabella, finally consented to subsidize his expedition in 1492. Even then, it was not so much confidence in Columbus as spite against Portugal that dictated Spanish support. For the past 20 years the two monarchs had worked to unite Spain and drive the Muslims out of their last stronghold on the peninsula, the Moorish kingdom of Granada. In 1492 they completed this *reconquista*, or battle of reconquest, expelling many Jews as well. Yet the Portuguese, by breaking the Muslim stranglehold on trade to Asia, had usurped the role of scourge of Islam that Spain coveted for itself. Ferdinand and Isabella were so desperate to even the score with their neighboring kingdom that jealousy overcame common sense: they agreed to take a risk on Columbus.

Columbus' first voyage across the Atlantic could only have confirmed his conviction that he was destiny's darling. His three ships, no bigger than fishing vessels that sailed to Newfoundland, plied their course over placid seas, south from Seville to the Canary Islands and then due west. On October 11, branches, leaves, and flowers floated by their hulls, signals that land lay near. And just after midnight, a sailor spied cliffs shining white in the moonlight. On the morning of

October 12, the *Niña*, the *Pinta*, and the *Santa Maria* made for a shallow, sapphire bay, and their crews disembarked and knelt on the white coral beach. Then Christopher Columbus, by the authority of Spain Admiral of the Ocean Sea and Governor and Viceroy of all he surveyed, christened the place San Salvador (Holy Savior).

Like so many men of destiny, Columbus did not recognize his true destination. Certain that God intended him to find the Indies, he resisted recognizing the novelty of his discovery. He was off by about 8000 miles. At first Columbus confused his actual location, the Bahamas, with an island off the coast of Japan. He coasted Cuba and Hispaniola (Haiti), expecting at any moment to catch sight of gold-roofed Japanese temples or to happen upon a fleet of Chinese junks. He encountered instead a gentle, generous people who knew nothing of the Great Khan, but who showed him around their islands. Columbus' journals note that they wore little clothing, but they did wear jewelry—tiny pendants of gold suspended from the nose. These trinkets they exchanged gladly for glass beads and hawks' bells, and they directed Columbus to the source of their finery, Hispaniola. He dubbed the Arawak people "Indians," as befitting inhabitants of the Indies.

Columbus crossed the Atlantic three more times between 1493 and 1504. On his second voyage he established a permanent colony at Hispaniola and explored other Caribbean islands; on his third voyage he reached "the Spanish Main" (or mainland)—Venezuela on the continent of South America; and on his last voyage he made landfalls throughout Central America—Honduras, Nicaragua, Costa Rica, and Panama. Everywhere he looked for proof that these lands formed part of Asia—probably, he came to believe, the Malay Peninsula.

Columbus died rich in titles, treasure, and tales—everything but recognition. During the last decade of his life, most Spaniards no longer believed that Columbus had discovered the Indies or anyplace else of significance. And shortly after his death in 1506, another Italian stamped his own name on the New World. Amerigo Vespucci, a Florentine banker with a flair for self-promotion, cruised the coast of Brazil in 1501 and again in 1503. His sensational report of his travels misled Martin Waldseemüller, a young German mapmaker, into giving Vespucci credit for discovering the barrier between Europe and Asia, and so naming it "America."

EARLY NORTH AMERICAN CULTURES

The Americas were a new world only to European latecomers. To the Asian peoples and their native American descendants who had settled the continents tens of thousands of years earlier, Columbus' new world was their own old world. But it is doubtful that the first nomadic hunters who crossed from Siberia over the Bering Strait to Alaska considered themselves discoverers or recognized what they had found—a truly new world, one wholly uninhabited by humans.

The First Inhabitants

The first passage of people from Asia to America probably took place during a prehistoric glacial period—either before 35,000 B.C. or about 10,000 years later—when huge amounts of the world's water froze into sheets of ice. Sea levels dropped so drastically that the Bering Strait became a broad, grassy plain. Across that land bridge between the two continents both humans and animals escaped icebound Siberia for ice-free Alaska. Whenever the first migration took place, the movement of Asians to America continued, even after 8000 B.C. when world temperatures rose again, and the water from melting glaciers flooded back into the ocean, submerging the Bering Strait. The 56-mile stretch of water froze in winter, paving an icy path to America; even in summer, small boats could hop from one continent to another across the Diomedes Islands. Over a span of 25,000 years settlement spread down the Alaskan coast, then up river valleys and along mountain passes deeper into the North American mainland, and finally throughout Central and South America.

Native Americans remained nomadic hunters and gatherers for thousands of years, as did many Europeans, Africans, and Asians of those millennia. Increasingly, however, American cultures diversified, especially after about 5500 B.C., when the peoples of central Mexico discovered how to cultivate food crops; this skill slowly spread north to other tribes. This "agricultural revolution" allowed native American societies to grow much larger, and each developed distinctive forms of economic, social, and political organization. By the end of the fifteenth century, the inhabitants of North America, perhaps 10 million people, spoke as many as 1000 languages, some as different from each other as English is from Chinese. Columbus erred doubly by calling the native Americans "Indians," not only mistaking continents but also attributing to peoples a cultural unity that had vanished long before 1492.

The simplest Indian societies were those that still relied on hunting and gathering—like the Shoshone of the Great Basin (parts of present-day Nevada, Oregon, and Idaho); the Eskimos of the Arctic; and the Serrano, Cahuilla, Luiseño, and Diegueño of southern California, Arizona, and the Baja peninsula of Mexico. Stark deserts and frozen tundra defied cultivation and yielded food supplies that could sustain nomadic bands numbering no more than about 50 people. Families occasionally joined together for a collective hunt or wintered in common quarters, but for most of the year they dispersed across the landscape, the women gathering plants and seeds, making baskets, and cooking meals while the men hunted for meat and hides. Political authority was invested in either the male family head or the "headman" of a small band; "shamans"—any tribesmen claiming spiritual powers—enlisted the supernatural to assist individuals.

Societies of Increasing Complexity

In the densely forested belt that stretched from Newfoundland to the Bering Strait, resources more generous than those of the tundra to the north made for larger populations and more closely knit societies. Northeastern bands like the Montagnais, the Micmac, and the Penobscot and northwestern tribes like the Yellowknife and the Beaver traveled forests of evergreen in moccasins and snowshoes, stalking deer, elk, moose, bear, and caribou; they speared fish in icy lakes and swift streams from birch-bark canoes. Their environment encouraged cooperative economic pursuits: leading men assigned several families to specific territories that they hunted together, dividing the returns among the whole band. Religious beliefs enhanced the solidarity of kin groups: each family had a "totem," a particular animal from which they claimed descent.

While men dominated Indian bands based on hunting by virtue of their skill

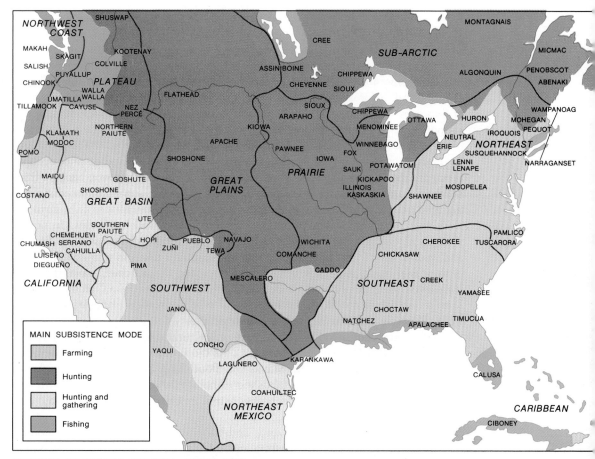

INDIANS OF NORTH AMERICA, CIRCA 1500

and knowledge of the terrain, women assumed more influence in societies that relied for part of their food on settled agriculture. Among the Pueblo peoples of Arizona and New Mexico, the Hopi and Zuñi tribes, men hunted bison and cultivated corn and beans, but women owned the fields, the crops, and even the tools. They also owned the sun-baked dwellings of adobe and stone, some of which rose to several stories, that housed the families of their daughters. By 1540 some 70 Pueblo villages flourished, harboring populations much larger than those of nomadic tribes. More reliable food supplies swelled the size and number of lineages or clans, families sharing a common ancestry, who together formed the Hopi and Zuñi tribes.

Despite the scale of Pueblo society, it remained egalitarian: a council of religious elders drawn from the different clans governed each village. But Pueblo religious ceremonies, in contrast to those of simpler Indian societies, involved the whole tribe, not just families or individuals. Elaborate rituals celebrated tribal unity and sought the gods' blessing for hunts and harvests that secured the common welfare. Thousands of miles to the northeast and in a natural setting far different from the semiarid Southwest, the Iroquois created a remarkably similar culture. There, too, property and inheritance passed through the mother's side of the family, and tribal councils united family kinship networks in a larger alliance.

More complex Indian civilizations arose in the bountiful environments of the Pacific Northwest and the coastal region reaching from Virginia to Texas. The seas and rivers from eastern Alaska to northern California teemed with salmon, cod, and halibut and hosted humpback whales, seals, and otters; the Southeast's fertile soil and temperate climate encouraged the cultivation of maize, rice, and a variety of fruits, and its forests were filled with deer, bear, and bison. Diligent harvesting of these resources and the development of techniques to preserve food supplies supported large, settled tribes.

Far less egalitarian than nomadic hunting bands or even the Pueblo and Iroquois, these tribes developed elaborate systems of status and distinct occupational groups, including a special caste of priests. Chiefs, if they won backing from powerful families, could exercise considerable authority: storing and redistributing food among the tribe's members, assigning certain families to fish, farm, or work at handicrafts, and conducting wars to expand tribal territories. In northwestern chiefdoms, each individual had a place in hierarchies based on lineage and wealth; the richest families kept slaves—captives taken in war—as emblems of their high rank. Among southeastern tribes like the Natchez, social divisions were even more firmly etched. Below the chief, or "Great Sun," stood his advisers, a hereditary nobility of lesser "Suns," who demanded elaborate deference from the lowly "Stinkards," the common people.

Even more advanced were the vast agricultural empires of Mesoamerica—south and central Mexico and Guatemala. As the Roman empire was declining in Europe, the civilization of the Mayas was flourishing in the lowland jungles of Central America. The Mayas established elaborate urban centers, filled with palaces, bridges, aqueducts, vapor baths, astronomical observatories, plazas, and temples topped by pyramids. Their priests developed a written language, their mathematicians discovered the zero, and their astronomers devised a calendar more accurate than any then existing and calculated the revolution of the moon and the recurrence of solar eclipses.

The Aztecs, who invaded central Mexico from the north in the fourteenth century, built on the achievements of the Mayas and later civilizations like the Toltecs. Within a century, conquest and diplomacy had created an empire of several million people that extended west from the Gulf coast to the Pacific and south to Guatemala. The Aztec capital, Tenochtitlán, transformed a once-marshy island on a lake into a glittering metropolis with a population in 1400 of perhaps a quarter of a million—several times the size of London. The Great Temple of the Sun dominated the center of the city, and through the causeways and canals leading to Tenochtitlán flowed gold, silver, exotic feathers, cotton cloaks, cocoa, and millions of pounds of maize, trade goods and tribute from other Mexican city-states conquered by the Aztecs.

Warfare enlarged and enriched the empire, but its primary purpose was to maintain a steady supply of human captives for sacrifice. Aztecs believed that they were the chosen people—chosen to nourish the earth by sustaining the life of the sun. Each year priests wielding razor-sharp obsidian knives sliced open the chests of thousands of captives and offered up to the sun hearts still beating, the essence of life.

Although early modern Europeans were shocked at the extent of the sacrifices and the accompanying cannibalism, crusading Christians should not have found unfamiliar the sense of mission and destiny underlying the Aztec ritual of human sacrifice. In other ways, too, the world of the Aztecs was not dissimilar to the societies of early modern Europe. Like Europe's peasants, Aztec farmers lived in permanent villages; their merchants and specialized craftworkers clustered in large cities, organized themselves into guilds, and clamored for protection from the government. And, as in Europe, noble and priestly classes commanding land and followers took the lead in politics and religion and exacted tribute from the common people. Although these Indian empires did not know the use of the wheel or iron, they had sophisticated methods of irrigation, architecture, and the manufacture of pottery, jewelry, and textiles.

Yet, for all their similarities, there was at least one crucial difference between Aztec civilization and that of Europe in 1500: Aztec territorial expansionism did not take the form of colonization or overseas settlement that spanned the oceans—indeed, the globe. That difference reflected a host of distinctive changes in European social, economic, and political development during the fourteenth and fifteenth centuries. It was these transformations that made it possible for bold sailors like Columbus and Cabot or anonymous fisherfolk and traders to dream of profit, glory, and empire.

THE EUROPEAN BACKGROUND OF AMERICAN COLONIZATION

Long before Europeans discovered America, they had invented it. Centuries before Columbus, stories abounded of an island across the Atlantic, a garden paradise of riches and plenty. Plato told of Atlantis, a kingdom lying beyond the Pillars of Hercules (Strait of Gibraltar), reputed for its wise men and valiant warriors. Medieval bards embellished the tale of St. Brendan, a fifth-century Irish abbot whose crew of monks, they claimed, sailed to islands in the Atlantic and encountered a whale that talked and birds that sang in Latin. Throughout the Middle Ages, wishful cartographers crowded the Atlantic with other enchanted islands like Hy-Brasil along with sea monsters and griffins.

Of course, the invention of America did not bring about its discovery. Not mere dreams but a complex constellation of historical circumstances impelled explorers of the fifteenth and sixteenth centuries to explode the boundaries of their old world. Europe in 1450 was slowly emerging from centuries of economic and political localism. It was recovering, too, from the onslaught of a continent-wide epidemic that had reduced its population by a third. As stronger, more centralized nation-states put advances in technology and trade at the service of their ruling monarchs, the temper of these vibrant, often chaotic times mixed a sense of crisis with a sense of possibility. It was this special blend of desperation and idealism that made the New World more than a dream of metaphysical philosophers and medieval monks.

Life and Death in Early Modern Europe

In the fourteenth and the fifteenth centuries, at the beginning of the Renaissance, Europe's interest in island paradises became especially keen. The Europe graced by the genius of Michelangelo and Leonardo da Vinci, Machiavelli and Petrarch, was also a world riddled with war, disease, and uncertainty. The conditions of life and death whetted the taste for fantasy and escapism. Ninety percent of Europe's people, widely dispersed in small villages, made their living from the land. But perhaps as few as one-fifth of all peasants owned enough land to feed themselves, and all faced the constant prospect of food shortages and outright famine. Warfare, bad weather, poor transportation, and low grain yields conspired to create a fragile food supply, and undernourishment produced a population prone to disease.

Under these circumstances, life was nasty, brutish, and usually short. One-quarter of all children died in the first year of life, and people who reached the ripe age of 40 counted themselves fortunate. Men and women usually married in their mid-twenties, and as a result, most children came to maturity having lost one or both parents. Parents deliberately tried to instill in their children the toughness needed to survive in a harsh world. Boys and girls of all classes commonly lived away from home between the ages of 7 and 10, receiving schooling or military training or serving apprenticeships as craftsworkers or domestic servants.

It was a world of sharp inequalities, where nobles and aristocrats enjoyed several hundred times the income of peasants or craftsworkers. It was a world with no strong, centralized political authority, where kings were weak and warrior lords held sway over small towns and tiny principalities. It was a world of hierarchy, dependence, and deference, where the upper classes provided land and protection for the lower orders. It was a world of violence and sudden death, where public executions commanded enormous crowds and where homicide, robbery, and rape occurred with brutal frequency. It was a world where security and order of any kind seemed so fragile that people clung to tradition and feared innovation and change.

Into that world in 1347 came the Black Death, which by 1351 had swept away one-third of Europe's population. The crisis of epidemic disease disrupted both agriculture and commerce, triggering a depression that lasted until the end of the fourteenth century. Recovery came slowly, over the course of a century. As Europe's population began to grow again after 1500, its cities sprang back to life; merchants revitalized old trading networks, and peasants reclaimed land for cultivation. Fewer people meant larger shares of wealth for all: the relative scarcity of workers and consumers made for better wages, lower prices, and more land.

But by the time of Columbus' arrival in America, nearly 150 years after the outbreak of the Black Death, Europe again confronted its old problem: too many people were competing for a limited supply of food and land. Throughout the sixteenth century most Europeans suffered a steady decline in the quality of their lives. Diets became poorer, land and work less available, wages lower, the peasantry more impoverished, and crime and begging more widespread. As Europe's population growth strained the limits of its resources, inflation compounded the recurrence of food and land shortages. Prices doubled at the end of the fifteenth century and then quadrupled between 1520 and 1590. To keep pace with the "Price Revolution," landlords raised rents, adding to the burden of Europe's peasantry.

The climate of scarcity, disorder, and uncertainty prevailing in Europe during the first century of exploration and colonization fostered among the hopeful and the desperate alike a belief that the New World offered an opportunity to renew the Old. That mixture of hope and desperation led Europeans to idealize America as a source of riches and plenty. Columbus wrote of Hispaniola: "This island and all others are very fertile to a limitless degree. . . . There are very large

St. Sebastian Interceding for the Plague-stricken City captures the desperation of Europeans during an outbreak of the Black Death. While a priest reads prayers over the bodies being buried in a common grave, a man suddenly taken by the plague writhes in agony. In the background, a cart moves through the street to collect more corpses. At the upper left St. Sebastian, a Christian martyr, intercedes with God to end the suffering.

tracts of cultivated land. . . . There are birds of many kinds, and fruits in great diversity. In the interior there are mines and metals, and the population is without number." Columbus and many of his contemporaries expected that the American cornucopia would provide land for the landless, work for the unemployed, and wealth beyond the wildest dreams of the daring.

The Conditions of Colonization

While the scale of scarcity and disruption in sixteenth-century Europe made colonizing the Americas attractive, other changes made settling the New World practical. The improvements in maritime technology that made travel at sea more precise—and made the Portuguese such respected pilots—led also to a general expansion of trade. By the late fifteenth century Europe had broken free from the limited, localized commercial exchange of the Middle Ages. Transcontinental trading networks now linked merchants in Lisbon, Seville, Amsterdam, and London to Africa and Asia. Europe's merchants and bankers created more efficient techniques of exchange and finance to support commerce across the longer distances. And if rising prices and rents pinched Europe's peasantry, inflation enriched those who had goods to sell, money to loan, and acreage to let. Wealth flowed into the coffers of sixteenth-century traders, financiers, and landlords, creating a pool of surplus capital that investors could plow into colonial development. Both the commercial networks and the private fortunes essential to sustaining overseas trade and settlement were in place by the time of Columbus' discovery.

The direction of Europe's political development during the fifteenth and sixteenth centuries also paved the path for American colonization. After 1450 strong monarchs enlarged the sphere of royal power in many European countries. Henry VII, the founder of England's Tudor dynasty, Francis I of France, and Ferdinand and Isabella of Spain initiated the trend, forging nation-states from the autonomous towns and tiny principalities of the Middle Ages and increasing royal authority at the expense of warrior lords who had earlier held sway over smaller areas. As European political organization became more coherent and as kings and queens tightened their control over territory, people, and resources, the prospects for overseas expansion flourished. The larger, more centrally organized states were able to marshal the resources necessary to support colonial outposts and to sustain the professional armies and navies capable of protecting empires abroad.

Successful colonization depended on more than dreams and daring. It was the growing power of monarchs as well as commercial and technological development in early modern Europe that allowed the Spaniards and the Portuguese, the Dutch, the French, and the English to establish permanent settlements—even empires—in another world lying an ocean away. That accomplishment had earlier eluded Scandinavians like Leif Ericsson because they lacked the political power that could be continuously and forcefully projected. They also lacked a network of trade dense enough to sustain colonies and the capital to back them in their formative years.

Similarly, the character of Aztec society limited its potential for expansion. For all of their sophistication in other technologies, the Aztecs lacked knowledge of ocean navigation, which not only limited the scope of their movement but also restricted commercial development and merchant wealth. Although their trading networks reached far into Central America and the North American Southwest, Aztec merchants relied entirely on overland routes and trafficked mainly in luxury goods for a limited market—precious stones and metals, jaguar skins, and rare feathers—a trade resembling medieval Europe's commerce with Asia. And while Europe's traders were enhancing their power and status, often in a partnership with aristocrats, Aztec merchants were losing out in a struggle with the nobility. By the end of the fifteenth century, Aztec nobles had succeeded in curbing the influence of commercial families, had even executed some merchants and seized their estates.

Equally important, Aztec political organization by 1500 had not become as centralized as that of western European states. Aztec rulers had not established their sovereign authority over powerful nobles and clans. These groups still raided neighboring city-states and evened scores with their enemies—with or without chiefly approval. The absence of centralized power made it impossible for the Aztecs to coordinate a more ambitious expansion and impeded the consolidation of their empire. While their armies put down disturbances in conquered territories, protected trade routes, and plundered subjugated peoples, the Aztecs never actively colonized, never exported their people or their way of life to other places. Nor did they integrate diverse subject tribes into their own culture. Instead, conquered city-states retained their distinctive languages and customs—and harbored a lingering hostility toward Aztec rule. The result was an empire vulnerable to division from within and to attack from abroad.

SPAIN'S EMPIRE IN THE NEW WORLD

By the reckoning of the Aztecs it was the year 12-House, a time, they believed, when the fate of the whole world hung by a thread. According to their calendar, a 52-year cycle had come to an end, a transition always pregnant with peril. Now the gods might extinguish the sun with a flood or a great wind, might even send the sky crashing down on the earth. The end of this particular cycle had been marked with chilling omens. Aztec scribes reported that a comet flared across the heavens, seeming "to bleed fire, drop by drop, like a wound in the sky"; mysteriously, a fire broke out in the Great Temple. And in one of the canals, fishermen caught a bird "the color of ashes" with a strange mirror in the crown of its head. They brought the creature to their ruler, Moctezuma II, who looked in the mirror and saw ranks of men mounted on animals resembling deer and moving across a plain. Everyone was terrified by the portents.

Two years later, the Aztecs' worst fears were fulfilled. Dust rose in whirlwinds on the roads from the hooves of horses and the boots of men in battle array, some glittering in iron from head to foot. Coats of mail and weapons crashed and rattled; flags flapped like bats above metal helmets; dogs raced ahead of the column, muzzles uplifted, ropes of saliva running from their jaws. "It was as if the earth trembled beneath them, or as if the world were spinning . . . as it spins during a fit of vertigo," one Aztec scribe recorded. This was no image in a magic mirror: Hernando Cortés and his army of Spaniards were marching on Tenochtitlán. By Cortés' calculations, it was A.D. 1519.

Spanish Conquest

To Cortés and the other Spanish explorers who had followed Columbus across the Atlantic over the previous quarter century, a new and remarkable world was opening. By 1513 the Spanish had explored and mastered the Caribbean basin. In that year too, Vasco Nuñez de Balboa crossed the Isthmus of Panama and glimpsed the Pacific Ocean. North and South America were revealed as continents of vast size, separated from Asia by another ocean. And Ferdinand Magellan finally did reach the Orient by sailing west across the vast Pacific; after his death in the Philippines in 1521, his shipmates completed the first circumnavigation of the globe.

From their bases in the islands of the Caribbean, the Spanish pressed outward, mounting expeditions in search of profits and treasure whenever an ambitious military commander could scrape together the necessary soldiers and supplies. To the north they met mostly with disappointment. Juan Ponce de León vainly scoured the shores of the Florida peninsula for the fabled "Fountain of Youth," while Pánfilo de Narváez trekked along the west side of Florida and over the Gulf Plains, a route that Hernando de Soto subsequently followed as far as the Mississippi River. Between 1540 and 1542 Francisco Vásquez de Coronado moved through Arizona, New Mexico, Texas, Oklahoma, and Kansas. But reports of fantastic cities of gold proved to be merely the stuff of dreams.

During these same decades, however, the Spanish found golden opportunities elsewhere. Those who had first rushed to Hispaniola immediately started scouring the island for gold—and enslaving Indians to work the mines. As for Cortés, when the envoys of Moctezuma met him on the road to Tenochtitlán in

1519 and attempted to appease him with gold ornaments and other gifts, an Indian witness recorded that "the Spaniards burst into smiles. . . . They picked up the gold and fingered it like monkeys. . . . Their bodies swelled with greed. . . . They hungered like pigs for that gold." For nearly half a year Cortés dominated the vacillating Moctezuma by imprisoning him in his own capital. The Aztecs drove the Spanish out after Moctezuma's death, but Cortés returned with reinforcements, set siege to Tenochtitlán, and in 1521 conquered it. The Aztec empire lay in ruins.

To the conquistadors—a motley lot of minor nobles, landless gentlemen, and professional soldiers—the Americas seemed not only a golden but also a most timely opportunity. Resentment of the Spanish monarchy's growing strength at home inspired in such men dreams of conquest abroad. Cortés and other conquistadors aimed to recreate in the New World a much older world. They dreamed of eluding the reach of expanding royal authority by establishing themselves as a powerful feudal nobility in America, one that would enjoy virtual independence from the Spanish Crown, buffered by the Atlantic.

For a time the conquistadors succeeded beyond their wildest expectations. By the 1540s Cortés and just 1500 men had taken all of Mexico and the southwestern portion of North America; by the 1550s the ruthless Pizarro brothers and an even smaller band of conquistadors had sailed along South America's Pacific coast and overthrown the Incas in Peru, an Andean civilization as impressive as that of the Aztecs. They also laid claim to Ecuador, Chile, Argentina, and Bolivia.

How did the conquistadors—a handful of Spanish gentlemen heading a rabble of soldiers, seamen, rustics, and criminals—bring down Indian empires in the span of a generation? To begin with, the Spanish enjoyed the edge of surprise and technological superiority. The sight of ships and the explosion of guns terrified the Indians. Just as strange and daunting were enormous mastiffs and mounted invaders, men on horseback whom the Indians took at first to be single creatures. The only domesticated animals known to the Aztecs were small dogs; the Spanish provided them with their first glimpse of horses and, later, cattle, sheep, oxen, pigs, goats, donkeys, mules, and chickens.

What delivered a more lasting shock to Indian civilizations was exposure to European infections. Smallpox, influenza, typhus, and measles, disease strains against which they had no defense, ravaged the people of entire villages and tribes. Tenochtitlán surrendered to Cortés after a siege of 85 days, during which many died from starvation but many more died of smallpox contracted from the Spanish. Everywhere that the conquistadors invaded, disease was their ally against Indian resistance.

An equally important factor in the rapidity of the conquest was the political disunity within Indian empires. The Aztecs and Incas had subjugated the native Indian populations of Mexico and Peru just 100 years before the Spanish invasion. They established themselves in cities as a noble and priestly aristocracy and collected tribute from Indian peasants, but they took no steps to conciliate the conquered. Disaffection with Aztec and Inca rule afforded the conquistadors eager

The dignity and grace of this Mexican woman drawn in the 1550s, possibly by a Spanish priest, may reflect the sympathetic influence of the missionary Bartolemé de Las Casas—sentiments most Spaniards did not share.

allies among the subject Indian tribes. But by aiding the Spanish overthrow of the Aztecs and the Incas, the native Indians only substituted one set of overlords for another.

Spanish Colonization

The conquistadors did not long enjoy their mastery over the New World. The Spanish monarchs who had just subdued a feudal aristocracy at home were not about to allow a new colonial nobility to arise across the Atlantic. The Crown bribed the conquistadors into retirement—or was saved the expense when blood-thirsty men like the Pizarro brothers were assassinated by their own followers. The task of governing Spain's new colonies passed from the conquistadors to a small army of officials, soldiers, lawyers, and Catholic bishops, all appointed by the Crown, reporting to the Crown, and loyal to the Crown. Headquartered in urban centers like Lima and Mexico City (the city that arose from the ashes of Tenochtitlán), an elaborate, centralized bureaucracy administered the Spanish empire, closely regulating every aspect of economic and social life.

Few Spaniards besides imperial officials settled in the New World. By the end of the sixteenth century only about 5 percent of the colonial population was of Spanish descent, the other 95 percent being either Indian or African. Even by 1800 only 300,000 Spanish immigrants had come to Central and South America. Indians remained on the lands that they had farmed under the Aztecs and the Incas, now paying Spanish overlords their taxes and producing valuable commodities for export, principally cochineal (a red dye) and livestock. The Indians were not enslaved outright by the Spanish, but they were compelled to work for their new masters for specified periods of time, a system of forced labor known as *encomienda*. The Spanish also established sugar plantations in the West Indies; these were worked by black slaves who were being imported from Africa in large numbers by 1520.

Spain's colonies returned even more spectacular profits to the mother country after 1540, when silver deposits were discovered in both Mexico and Peru. Silver mining developed into a large-scale capitalist enterprise requiring substantial investment and efficient production techniques. European investors and Spanish immigrants who had profited from cattle raising and sugar planting poured their capital into the necessary equipment—stamp mills, water-powered crushing equipment, and pumping machinery. To supply the mines' labor requirements, the Spanish government introduced another form of forced labor known as *repartimiento*. Whole villages of Indians were pressed into service in the mines, joining black slaves and free white workers employed there.

In the last decades of the sixteenth century the economies of Mexico and Peru revolved solely around the mines. By 1570 the town of Potosí, the site of a veritable mountain of silver, had become larger than any city either in Spain or its American empire, with a population of 120,000. Local farmers who supplied mining centers with food and Spanish merchants in Seville who exported European goods to Potosí profited handsomely. So, too, did the Spanish Crown, which claimed one-fifth of all the silver extracted from the mines. All told, between 1500 and 1600 some 16,000 tons of silver was exported from Spanish America to Europe.

The growth of Spain's New World empire strengthened the political and economic developments in Europe that had made colonization possible. The crea-

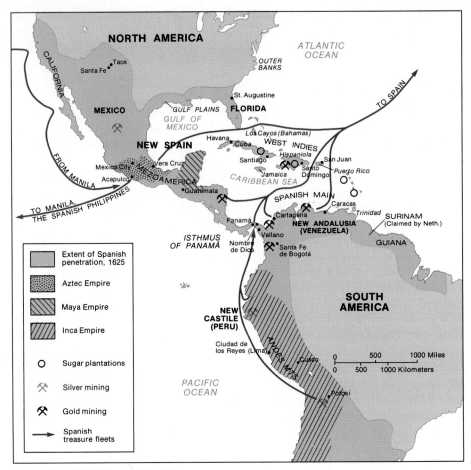

SPANISH AMERICA, CIRCA 1600

By 1600 Spain was extracting large amounts of gold and silver from Central and South America, as well as profits from sugar plantations in the Caribbean. Each year Spanish treasure ships ferried bullion from mines like Potosí to the Isthmus of Panamá, where it was transported by land to the Caribbean coast, and from there to Spain. An expedition from Acapulco sailed annually to the Philippines as well, returning with Asian spices and other trade goods.

tion of an imperial bureaucracy in Spanish America reinforced royal power by extending the Crown's dominion and enlarging the number of men in the monarch's service. Similarly, the growth of colonial economies returned large rewards to Europe's investors, concentrating more and more wealth in the hands of landlords, merchants, and bankers. In addition, the influx of American silver increased Europe's money supply, fueling inflation as well as increasing trade to eastern Europe and Asia, regions that demanded hard cash in return for their exports. Finally, the boom in Spanish America encouraged capitalist forms of economic organization, since the silver mines of Mexico and Peru were models of mass production. Brought into existence by the capital of private investors, they were more advanced than any enterprise existing in sixteenth-century Europe.

The Spanish colonization of America quickened the pace at which the Old

World developed more modern forms of economic and political organization. But that "progress" was purchased at a fearful human cost. The native population of the Americas in 1500 may have equaled that of Europe, but by 1600 it was not one-tenth of Europe's. Indian tribes were devastated not only by warfare and hard labor, but also by disease. The Indians of the Caribbean were virtually wiped out within a century; in Mesoamerica, a native population of 20 million was reduced to 2 million.

Well before European contact took its full toll among Indian tribes, the Spanish conquest came under attack. In the 1530s Bartolomé de Las Casas, a Spanish Dominican priest who became a bishop in southern Mexico, spoke out against the exploitation of the natives and called for the Spanish monarchy to return American lands to their rightful Indian owners. Las Casas' writings, reprinted in many translations and illustrated with gruesome drawings, circulated throughout Europe, becoming the basis of the "Black Legend" of Spanish tyranny and oppression in the New World.

Few of Las Casas' countrymen shared his scruples. They justified their conquest by claiming that they had "delivered" the Indians from Aztec and Inca tyranny. Enlightened emissaries of a superior culture, they were replacing native "barbarism" and "paganism" with European civilization and Christianity. The extent of the Spanish conquest itself fostered a heady sense of superiority. By the beginning of the seventeenth century Spain's dominions in the New World spanned 8000 miles, stretching from Baja California to the Straits of Magellan. It was the greatest empire known to Europe since ancient Rome. The prevailing mood was captured by the portrait of a Spanish soldier that adorns the frontispiece of his book about the West Indies. He stands with one hand on his sword and the other holding a pair of compasses on top of a globe. Beneath is inscribed the motto "By compasses and the sword/More and more and more and more."

THE PRELUDE TO ENGLAND'S AMERICAN COLONIZATION

While the Spanish reached for more in the Americas, England remained a small island nation. For the first several decades of the sixteenth century, the English Crown refused to entertain any schemes for poaching on Spain's colonial preserves. Caution was dictated by the strategic importance of Spain as an ally against a common rival, France, and the commercial value of England's cloth trade to the Netherlands, which was then controlled by Spain. To be sure, privateers like the senior Walter Raleigh looted Spanish silver ships, and buccaneers like John Hawkins tried to muscle in on the Caribbean slave trade. But these pirates—to use the less diplomatic term—only caused trouble for an England eager to conciliate imperial Spain. As the Spanish inched up the Atlantic coast in the 1560s, fortifying a base at St. Augustine, Florida, and claiming territory as far north as the Outer Banks of North Carolina, the English quietly abandoned a project to colonize the coast of present-day South Carolina.

Still, there were those English who remained restless. Sir Walter Raleigh senior was an expression of the same West Country culture that had sent enterprising fishermen across to Newfoundland. And his own swashbuckling career stamped a lasting impression on his impetuous brood of boys, especially his step-son, Humphrey Gilbert, and his namesake, the young Walter Raleigh. With Spain's empire looming before them, they envisioned more than plunder: they wanted to conquer the empire itself—or at least carve out for England an empire that would rival it. As they came of age during the 1560s and early 1570s they might have seriously disrupted English plans to remain on good terms with Spain, except that they were distracted by other alternatives to adventuring in America. One alternative lay in the upheavals arising out of the Protestant Reformation, which had turned all of sixteenth-century Europe into a battleground.

Backdrop to the Reformation

During the Middle Ages, the Roman Catholic church defined what it meant to be a Christian in western Europe. Like the other institutions of medieval society the Catholic church was a hierarchy. At the top was the pope in Rome, and under him were the descending ranks of other spiritual lords—cardinals, archbishops, bish-ops. At the bottom of the Catholic hierarchy were parish priests, each serving his own village, as well as monks and nuns living in monasteries and convents. But medieval popes were weak, their power felt little in the lives of most Europeans. Like political units of the era, religious institutions of the Middle Ages were local and decentralized.

Between about 1100 and 1500, the Roman Catholic church and the Papacy gradually increased their control over the lives of Europeans. Just as the kings of Europe were growing more powerful during those centuries, so too was the pope. Just as the nations of Europe were consolidating, so too was the Catholic church. As the church grew in wealth and power, a large bureaucracy of ecclesiastical officials emerged, and the Papacy exerted greater influence over Europe's politics. The Catholic church acquired land throughout Europe and added to its income with tithes (church taxes) and the sale of church offices. In the thirteenth century, church officials also began to sell "indulgences." For ordinary believers, who ex-pected to spend time after death purging their sins in purgatory, the purchase of an indulgence promised to shorten that punishment, by supposedly drawing on the "treasury of merit" amassed by the good works of Christ and the saints.

By the fifteenth century the Catholic church and the Papacy were enor-mously powerful, but both were weakened by their very success. Church officials had become caught up in bureaucratic concerns and secular politics. The more their affairs isolated them from the laity—the mass of ordinary believers—the less responsive they became to popular religious needs. Secular preoccupations all too often corrupted the church with a crass materialism. Popes and bishops flaunted their wealth. Poorly educated parish priests neglected their pastoral duties. Ca-tholicism in 1500 was no more corrupt than it had been a century earlier; but as the church gained power, its abuses became more visible.

Most lay people were not hostile to the church. They were indifferent. But although they found the institutional church irrelevant, a sharp anxiety over salva-tion and an intense need for religious assurance gripped Europeans in the fif-teenth and sixteenth centuries. Popular piety swelled in response to the sweeping and disorienting changes overtaking Europe—sporadic recurrences of the plague, the widening gulf between rich and poor, the new importance of commerce, the rise in prices, and the discovery of America. And with the invention of printing

St. Anthony Tormented by Demons evokes the sense of social and spiritual crisis pervading early modern Europe. The engraver, Martin Schongauer, was a contemporary of Luther.

with movable type in the mid-fifteenth century, more people had access to religious books and imagery.

The Teachings of Martin Luther

Into this climate of heightened spirituality stepped Martin Luther, a would-be lawyer who, thrown to the ground by a bolt of lightning from a passing thunderstorm in 1505, forsook his career and entered a monastery. Like many of his contemporaries, Luther was consumed by fears over his eternal fate. He was convinced that he was damned, and he could not find any consolation in the Catholic church. Catholic doctrine taught that men were saved by faith in God and by their own good works—by leading virtuous lives, partaking of the sacraments, making pilgrimages to holy places, and praying to Christ and the saints. Since he believed that human nature was innately evil, Luther despaired of being able to lead a life that "merited" salvation. If men and women are so bad, he reasoned, how could they ever win their way to heaven with good works?

Luther finally broke through his despair by reading the Bible, which convinced him that God did not require fallen mankind to earn salvation or to achieve grace. Salvation, he concluded, came by faith alone, the "free gift" of God to undeserving sinners. The ability to live a good life could not and must not be the *cause* of salvation, but its *consequence:* once men and women believed that they had saving faith, moral behavior was possible. That idea, known as "justification by faith alone," Luther elaborated between 1513 and 1517.

Luther's own experience put him in touch with the universal spiritual problem of his age, the need for assurance of salvation. At the same time, as Luther was ordained a priest and then assigned to teach at a university in Wittenberg, Germany, he was becoming more critical of the Catholic church as an institution. In 1517 he posted on the door of a local church 95 theses attacking the Catholic hierarchy for selling salvation in the form of indulgences.

What was new about Luther was not that he broke openly with Catholic teachings. Nor was it that he criticized the church as an institution. Challenges to Catholicism had cropped up throughout the Middle Ages, and some of the heretical groups of the fifteenth century—the Hussites of Bohemia, the Waldensians of Italy, and the Lollards of England—had anticipated some of Luther's theological ideas and his objections to the church. What was new about Luther was the passion and force that infused his attacks, his ability to write—in the blunt, earthy Germanic tongue—what many of this contemporaries thought and felt. The "gross, ignorant asses and knaves at Rome," he warned, should keep their distance from Germany, or else "jump into the Rhine or the nearest river, and take . . . a cold bath."

The pope and his representatives in Germany tried to silence Luther, as they had successfully suppressed earlier heretics. Their opposition only pushed the reformer toward more radical positions. He asserted that the church and its hierarchy were not infallible; only the Scriptures were without error. He argued that every person should read and interpret the Bible for himself or herself. The Catholic church, on the other hand, claimed that only certain theologians approved by the church had the necessary training to interpret Scripture—and that Martin Luther was not among them.

For defying the authority of the pope, Luther was excommunicated. He responded with an even more fundamental attack on the Catholic church in which he propounded an idea known as "the priesthood of all believers." Catholic doctrine held that salvation came only through the church and its clergy, a uniquely privileged group that was holier than the laity and possessed special access to God. Luther asserted that the whole hierarchy of popes, cardinals, and bishops was unnecessary and contrary to the Bible, that every person had the power claimed by priests. It followed for Luther that if the clergy had no special power to mediate between man and God, neither did the rituals and ceremonies that they performed. He believed that only two of the church's seven sacraments, baptism and communion, could be shown to exist in the Bible and that inner devotion and religious feeling were much more important than outward display and ceremony.

Although Luther had not intended to start a schism within Catholicism, independent Lutheran churches were forming in Germany by the 1520s. And during the 1530s, Luther's ideas spread throughout Europe, where they were eagerly taken up by other reformers.

The Contribution of John Calvin

The most influential of Luther's successors was John Calvin, a Frenchman who also had abandoned law for theology. Calvin agreed with Luther that men could not merit their salvation. But while Luther's God was a loving deity who extended his mercy to fallen, corrupt men, Calvin conceived of God as a majestic and terrible sovereign, all-knowing and all-powerful, the controlling force in human history who would ultimately triumph over Satan. To bring about that final vic-

Martin Luther.

tory, Calvin believed, God had designated certain people as his chosen agents for ushering in his heavenly kingdom. These people—"the saints," or "the elect"—had been chosen by a God who could foresee and shape the flight of the smallest sparrow. The elect alone were "predestined" for eternal bliss in heaven.

Calvin's emphasis on predestination led him to another distinctively Protestant notion—the doctrine of calling. How could a person learn whether he or she belonged to the elect who were saved? Calvin answered: strive to behave like a saint. God expected his elect to serve the good of society by unrelenting work in a "calling," or occupation, in the world. In place of the Catholic belief in the importance of good works, Calvin emphasized the goodness of work itself. Success in attaining discipline and self-control, in bringing order into one's own life and the entire society, revealed that a person was among the elect.

Calvin fashioned a religion to reshape the world. Out of his ideas flowed a militant, uncompromising, reformist impulse. Whereas Luther believed that Christians should accept the existing social order and established political authority, Calvin called on Christians to become activists, tailoring both society and government to conform with God's laws laid down in the Bible. He wanted all of Europe to become like Geneva, the Swiss city that he had converted into a holy commonwealth where the elect regimented the behavior and morals of everyone else.

Unlike Luther, Calvin was not a charismatic religious genius. But he had the French flair for systemizing doctrine in a way that could be applied to the work of reformation everywhere in Europe and, later, in America. And unlike Luther, who had aimed his writings primarily at a German audience, Calvin addressed his most important book, *The Institutes of the Christian Religion* (1536), to Christians throughout Europe who were dissatisfied with the Catholic church. Reformers from every country flocked to Geneva to learn more about Calvin's ideas.

The English Reformation

While the Reformation went forward, King Henry VIII of England was striving for a goal more modest than those of Martin Luther and John Calvin. He wanted only to sire a male heir to carry on the Tudor dynasty. When his wife, Catherine of Aragon, the daughter of the king of Spain, gave birth to a daughter, Mary, Henry decided to do something less modest: to prove that his marriage to Catherine had been unlawful and to get it annulled by the pope. Pope Clement VII, under pressure from Spain, refused, and so Henry divorced Catherine without papal consent in 1527 and married his mistress, Anne Boleyn.

Henry then widened this breach with Rome by dissolving England's monasteries, seizing all church lands, and making himself the head of the Church of England. In 1534 Parliament formalized the relationship with the Act of Supremacy. To ensure that the break with the pope would be permanent, Henry sold church lands at bargain prices to powerful members of the English gentry. But Henry, who fancied himself a theologian, had no fondness for Protestant doctrine. Under his leadership the Church of England remained essentially Catholic in teachings and rituals.

That changed in 1547 with the accession of Edward VI, the male heir that Henry had finally sired with his third wife, Jane Seymour. Anne Boleyn, who had produced another mere daughter, Elizabeth, had lost her head for that offense among others. During the brief reign of the boy king Edward, England's militant

Protestants began to press for a more radical reformation of the English church. They enjoyed considerable influence until Edward's early death in 1553 brought his elder half-sister, Mary, a Catholic and the wife of Philip II of Spain, to the English throne. Determined to reverse the English Reformation, "Bloody Mary" martyred many Protestants and drove others into exile on the Continent, some taking refuge in Geneva, Calvin's holy commonwealth. But Mary died before she could return England to the Catholic fold, and Anne Boleyn's "mere" daughter, Elizabeth I, took the crown in 1558, proclaiming herself "the Palladium of Protestantism."

With the accession of Elizabeth, the Protestants exiled by Mary rushed back to England, their enthusiasm to reform the church there burning hotter than before because of their stay in Geneva. But the new queen had other ideas. While she was willing to commit the Church of England to the Protestant cause, Elizabeth stopped short of embracing radical Calvinism. Her more zealous subjects remained a vocal minority, calling for the English church to purge itself of bishops, elaborate ceremonies, and other vestiges of Catholicism. Because of the austerity and zeal of such Calvinist reformers, their opponents proclaimed them "Puritans."

The Protestant Reformation shattered the unity of Christendom. Spain, Ireland, and Italy remained firmly Catholic, but England, France, Scotland, the Netherlands, and Switzerland developed either dominant or substantial Calvinist constituencies. Much of Germany and Scandinavia opted for Lutheranism. As competing religious loyalties coalesced, brutal wars and internal uprisings racked sixteenth-century Europe. Protestant and Catholic antagonists slaughtered each other in the name of Christianity.

In the long run, the Reformation's legacy of religious strife intensified European interest in colonization, as religious rivalries were played out in America. But in the 1560s France's bloody half-century of religious wars supplied some of England's young West Country gentlemen with a substitute for adventuring in America. In 1562 Humphrey Gilbert, followed by Walter Raleigh a few years later, crossed the English Channel to fight on the side of the Huguenots, French Calvinists locked in a struggle with French Catholics. And when the opportunities for winning Protestant supremacy and personal glory waned in France, Gilbert and the younger Raleigh looked elsewhere. By the late 1560s they had departed for Ireland.

The English Colonization of Ireland

The colonization of Ireland would serve as a rough model for later efforts in America. In 1565 the English began a concerted effort to bring Ireland under their control by military conquest and colonization. Fearing that Catholic Ireland would be used by the French or the Spanish as a base for invading England, Queen Elizabeth encouraged a number of her subjects, mainly gentlemen and aristocrats from the West Country, to sponsor private ventures for subduing the native Irish and settling English families on Irish land. The English enterprise in Ireland, like the Reformation in Europe, influenced the future course of American settlement.

Elizabethans saw Ireland as a place far outside the English periphery, a "famous island in the Virginia sea," peopled by a strange and savage race. Although all of Ireland professed Catholicism, the Irish church had never conformed completely to the worship prescribed by Rome, and many pre-Christian customs and traditions survived. The English invaders of Ireland, almost all ardent Protestants, regarded the native inhabitants as barbarians sunk in paganism and superstition. As one Englishman reported, "They blaspheme, they murder, commit whoredome, hold no wedlocke, ravish, steal and commit all abomination without scruple."

Thus did the English justify their conquest of Ireland by proclaiming their duty to teach the Irish the discipline of hard work, the rule of law, the refinement of manners, and the truth of Christianity. But before the Irish could be "delivered" from the darkness of superstition and their "thralldom" to Irish landlords, they had to be "civilized"—preferably as the servants and tenants of English landlords. And while they were learning civilized ways, the Irish would not be allowed to buy land or hold office or serve on juries or give testimony in courts or learn a trade or bear arms.

When the Irish rejected that program for their "liberation" and rebelled, the English savagely repressed native resistance, indiscriminately slaughtering men, women, and children, combatants and civilians. Most English in Ireland, like most Spaniards in America, believed that pagans and barbarians who resisted civilization and Christianity should be subdued at any human cost. No scruples stopped Humphrey Gilbert from planting the path to his camp in an insurgent county with the severed heads of Irish rebels.

The logic of England's conquistadors in Ireland was chilling: it sanctioned the savage repression of any "inferior race." More ominous still, not only Gilbert but also Raleigh and many other West Country gentry who colonized Ireland during the last half of the sixteenth century later turned their attention toward North America. After their apprenticeship in Ireland, where, Gilbert concluded, "neither reputation, or profytt is to be wonne," they wanted more.

ENGLAND'S ENTRY INTO THE NEW WORLD

After hard service in France and Ireland, Gilbert and Raleigh returned to England in the 1570s, assumed places at Elizabeth's glittering court, and flaunted their reputations as bold knights. Their more moderate and perhaps more modern contemporaries at court considered the two swaggering gentlemen insufferable if not downright dangerous, much as the Spanish officials distrusted their unbridled conquistadors. Cautious administrators who had been enlarging the royal bureaucracy ever since the reign of Henry VIII feared that the likes of Gilbert and Raleigh would never subordinate their pursuit of individual fame and family fortune to the larger aims of the Crown and the state. The court buzzed with gossip of Gilbert's vain boasting and Raleigh's epic pride, "which exceedeth [that] of all men alive."

Still, England in the 1570s was receptive to the schemes of such hotheaded warrior lords for challenging Spain overseas. English Protestantism, English nationalism, and English economic interests had fused to swell support for English exploration and colonization.

The turning point for the English came when the Calvinist Dutch rebelled during the 1570s against their rule by Catholic Spain. The Spanish retaliated savagely against the Netherlands' resistance, sacking the city of Antwerp and killing 8000 people. The destruction of Antwerp cost the English their major market for cloth on the continent of Europe, a loss that compounded the problems of Elizabethan merchants. Even before the troubles in the Netherlands, the market for English textiles was becoming saturated, the glut producing periodic depressions in the cloth industry and trade. Both difficulties prompted English merchants to look elsewhere for markets and investment opportunities. They combined in joint stock companies to develop a trade with Africa, Russia, the East Indies, and the Mediterranean. These private corporations, in which many shareholders pooled small amounts of capital, allowed investors to finance large ventures at minimal risk. These corporations also began to plow money into Atlantic privateering voyages and pressed Elizabeth to unleash England's sea rovers on Spain's silver ships.

Joining English merchants in the new interest in overseas exploration were gentry families, many of whom shared with traders a desire for new ventures in which to invest their capital. The gentry had a second concern as well. The high birth rate among England's upper classes throughout the sixteenth century had produced a surplus of younger sons, who stood to inherit no share of family estates. The shortage of land for their offspring at home stirred up support within gentry ranks for England to lay claim to land across the Atlantic.

With the support of England's landed and commercial elites, Elizabeth now needed little encouragement to adopt a more belligerent stance toward Spain. But she got more encouragement from Spain itself. The Spanish made no secret of wanting to restore England to the true faith of Catholicism, by armed invasion if necessary. In 1570 the pope excommunicated Elizabeth, and the Spanish ambassador plotted her assassination. By 1572 the queen was permitting her subjects to assist the Dutch rebels.

As Humphrey Gilbert stepped forward to aid the Dutch, he hoped that Elizabeth might be ready to challenge Spain in the New World as well. In 1577 he presented the queen with "A Discourse on How Her Majesty May Annoy the King of Spain," a proposal to conquer Spanish Cuba and Santo Domingo and then use the two islands as bases for destroying Spanish power on the mainland. Although Elizabeth probably agreed with Gilbert's view that Spanish Catholics were "at open and professed war with God himselfe," she was not prepared to annoy the king of Spain to the point of provoking open warfare. Even so, she winked at the freebooting of English pirates on the Spanish Main and closely watched with interest the exploits of a new generation of English explorers in North America.

The Failures of Frobisher and Gilbert

The adventurer who first caught the queen's eye was Martin Frobisher, a formidable professional sailor from Yorkshire, the veteran of slaving voyages to west Africa, privateering raids in the Atlantic, the fighting in Ireland, and other unsavory enterprises. A full-length contemporary portrait of Frobisher—face frozen in a glare, a horse-pistol fixed in his fist—conveys his character. In 1576 he set his sights on another search for the Northwest Passage to Asia.

After sailing as far as the bay north of Labrador that now bears his name, Frobisher returned to England with an Eskimo (plucked, kayak and all, from the Atlantic) and a shiny black stone. The unfortunate Eskimo died soon after, but experts attested that Frobisher's rock was gold ore. The sensational news prompted the queen and several of her courtiers to take the unusual step of forming a joint stock company to establish a military outpost and mining camp at this "new Peru." It was the closest that the English state had come to underwriting a colonial expedition.

Frobisher made two more voyages in 1577 and 1578, kidnaping three more Eskimos and hauling back nearly 2000 tons of black rock. These Eskimos also died shortly after arriving in England, and the rest of Frobisher's cargo, upon closer inspection, turned out to be "fool's gold." Frobisher's reputation fell under a cloud.

Because Gilbert had refused to invest in this fiasco, Frobisher's disgrace became Gilbert's opportunity. In 1578 Elizabeth granted Gilbert a vague patent— the first English colonial charter—to explore, occupy, and govern any territory in the New World "not actually possessed of any Christian prince or people." That charter, ignoring Indian claims to North America, made Gilbert the lord and proprietor of all the land lying between Florida and Labrador. His power was limited only by provisions that his colonists were to enjoy all the liberties and privileges of Englishmen and that his laws had to be "agreeable" to those of England.

In planning his American colony, Gilbert continued to dream of a mineral-rich empire that would rival Spain's holdings. But he hoped for more. For some years he had tried to interest Elizabeth in settling the New World with "such needie people of our Countrie which now trouble the common wealth, and through want here at home, are inforced to commit outragious offences, whereby they are dayly consumed with the Gallows." In the 1580s, his detailed plans for a settlement included encouraging the immigration of the English poor to his colony by providing them with free land and farm implements. Gilbert also provided his projected settlement with a civil government, consisting of a governor and 13 councilors "to be chosen by consent of the people," a legal code, and a system of Anglican parishes, schools, and clergymen.

It was the blueprint for building a better society, one that would guarantee land, employment, and liberty to England's poor. It was also a formula for recreating an older, nearly feudal world in America. Gilbert pictured himself and his heirs as manorial lords of an agricultural colony of grateful and loyal tenants, collecting rents, providing for defense, and, like Spain's conquistadors, enjoying considerable independence from the Crown.

In June 1583 Gilbert finally set sail. Ever the knight-errant, he took along a poet to set down in Latin verse "the gests and things worthy of remembrance happening in this discovery." By August, Gilbert had sailed into St. John's harbor to find the usual international crew of fishermen. Gilbert formally claimed the land for England (John Cabot's voyage of a century earlier having been forgotten by nearly everyone) and then set out to probe the coast of Nova Scotia when storms forced him to head for home. North of the Azores, the *Golden Hind* and the *Squirrel* met foul weather and high waves. Gilbert, commanding the smaller *Squirrel*, sat on deck with characteristic bravado, reading a book. "We are as neere to Heaven by sea as by land," he shouted across the heaving swells. The men aboard the *Golden Hind* recognized the words of Thomas More, whose *Utopia*—a description of an ideal society in the New World—Gilbert held in his hand. Gilbert was nearer to heaven than he knew: around midnight, the crew of

Martin Frobisher, 1588.

the *Golden Hind* saw the lights of the *Squirrel* extinguished and the ship "devoured and swallowed up by the sea."

Raleigh's Roanoke Venture

Raleigh had been eager to accompany his stepbrother's ill-fated expedition, but Elizabeth showered so many favors on him, it had been hard to leave. He was dining on food from palace kitchens, living in "a bravely furnished lodging," complete with a bed covered in green velvet and silver lace and adorned with spangled plumes of white feathers; he was supporting a retinue of 30 gallants, all sporting gold chains.

Still, Raleigh was restless. Even if Gilbert had perished at sea, others were succeeding spectacularly. Another West Country adventurer, Sir Francis Drake, had circumnavigated the globe by 1580. Drake had sailed around the southern tip of South America and surprised the Spanish treasure ships in the Pacific—which Spain looked on as its own sea in almost proprietary fashion. Drake then sailed north, claimed northern California for England, hunted for the Northwest Passage, crossed the Pacific and opened trade with the Portuguese Spice Islands in the East Indies, and then repeated the feat of Magellan's crew by sailing home. Elizabeth was impressed enough to knight him on the deck of his own ship.

And if Drake's daring voyage was not enough, two other men who never left England were calling attention to the possibilities of colonies abroad. Richard Hakluyt was a lawyer who neglected the law in favor of mastering the new geography of the world and corresponding with merchants in Spanish and Portuguese colonial possessions. He imparted to his nephew, a clergyman of the same name, a similar passion for spreading knowledge of overseas discoveries. From that time forward, the younger Hakluyt neglected his pastoral duties in favor of publicizing North America. The younger Hakluyt wrote for Elizabeth, at the behest of Raleigh, an eloquent plea for the English settlement of America, titled *A Discourse Concerning Westerne Planting*.

The temperate and fertile lands of North America, argued Hakluyt, would provide a perfect base from which to harry the Spanish, search for a Northwest Passage, and extend the influence of Protestantism. But he also stressed the commercial advantages of colonies—as sources of commodities that England could not produce, as markets for woolens that England could not sell nearer to home, and as havens for people whom England could not employ. Like Humphrey Gilbert, he believed that settling America would solve the problem of overpopulation.

Still wary of the king of Spain, Elizabeth stopped short of lending state support to any such venture. But in 1584 she granted Raleigh a patent to settle American lands nearly identical to the patent that she had given Gilbert. By the summer Raleigh had sent two able gentlemen of his retinue, Philip Amadas and Arthur Barlowe, across the Atlantic, their two small ships coasting the Outer Banks of present-day North Carolina. Amadas and Barlowe established cordial relations with the Roanoke tribe, exchanging gifts and hospitality with these "very handsome, goodly people" ruled by a "werowance," or chief, named Wingina. The expedition returned home, painting an idyllic picture of natives "most gentle, loving, and faithfull, void of all guile and treason," much as Columbus had to the

Sir Walter Raleigh, 1577.

Spanish almost a century before. The enthusiastic Hakluyt promptly envisioned a colony that would become the Mexico of England, full of tidewater plantations producing bananas, pineapples, and sugar cane, mulberry trees supporting a silk industry, and mountains yielding gold. Elizabeth immediately knighted Raleigh and allowed him to name the new land "Virginia," after his virgin queen. The following summer a full-scale expedition returned to Roanoke Island.

Raleigh apparently aimed to establish on Roanoke a mining camp and a military garrison modeled on Frobisher's venture of the 1570s. To lead the company of 108 men, he tapped a West Country relative, Sir Richard Grenville, and as governor of the new colony he named Ralph Lane: both were veterans of the Irish campaigns. He also recruited a scientist, Thomas Hariot, to study the country's natural resources and native cultures, and an artist, John White, to make drawings of the Virginia Indians. Their inclusion was a stroke of genius. *A Briefe and True Reporte of the New Found Land of Virginia* (1588), written by Hariot, illustrated by White, and translated into Latin, French, and German, served as one of the principal sources about North America and its Indian inhabitants for more than a century. But Raleigh's choice of Grenville and Lane to lead the expedition was a fatal error of judgment. Even his fellow conquistadors in Ireland considered Lane intolerably proud and greedy. As for Grenville, even Lane considered him intolerably proud, greedy, and violent: he was given to breaking wineglasses between his teeth and then swallowing the shards to show that he could stand the sight of blood, even his own.

Both men alienated the natives of Roanoke almost as soon as they set foot on American soil. After Grenville missed one of his silver cups, he accused the Indians of theft and burned one of their villages. Wingina overlooked the incident, invited the Englishmen to settle on Roanoke Island, supplied them with corn and built them weirs to trap fish. But after a year, with the English still apparently content to sponge indefinitely off the Indians—and indifferent when their cattle trampled Indian cornfields—Wingina's hospitality ran out. Rumors that the chief planned to weaken the English by starvation before finishing them off with bows and arrows prodded Lane to mount a preemptive strike. On the night of July 1, 1586, at the watchword "Christ our victory," Lane and his men attacked Wingina's main village, killing and beheading the chief. All that averted an overwhelming counterattack was the timely arrival of Drake and Frobisher, who had promised Raleigh that they would look in on his colony after freebooting up and down the Caribbean. They ended up evacuating the settlement's 102 survivors, who piled onto the pirate fleet and put an ocean between themselves and the avenging Roanokes.

Raleigh was not daunted, however. He decided to organize a second expedition to plant a settlement on a site farther north, in the Chesapeake Bay. And rather than colonizing with miners and military men, Raleigh projected an agricultural community modeled on Humphrey Gilbert's manorial dreams. He recruited 119 men, women, and children, members of the English middle class, granting each person an estate of 500 acres. He also appointed the artist John White as governor; the delighted White bought a suit of armor for ceremonial occasions.

From the moment of first landfall in July 1587, everything went wrong. Their expedition's pilot, Simon Ferdinando, insisted on putting off the colonists at Roanoke Island rather than the Chesapeake, so he could head off to raid Spain's annual convoy of silver ships. But even before Ferdinando weighed anchor, the settlers were skirmishing with the local Indians: one colonist killed, an Indian

Daily Lives

CLOTHING AND FASHION

"Barbaric" Dress—Indian and European

It was remarkable to sixteenth-century Europeans how many things seemed to be missing from Indian culture. Even more remarkable, the Indians themselves did not seem to notice. Michel de Montaigne, a French philosopher who had never been to America but liked to talk with explorers and read their accounts, managed to compile quite a list. According to Montaigne, Indians had "no kind of traffic [trade], no knowledge of letters, no intelligence of numbers, no name of magistrate, nor of politics, no use of service [servants], of riches, or of poverty, no contracts, no successions, no partitions, no occupation but idle, no apparel but natural. . . ." When other Europeans, with and without experience in America, made similar lists, they never failed to mention that last crucial item missing in Indian culture—clothing. Even European men and women who could not read and who never traveled beyond their villages associated America's inhabitants with nakedness, for woodcuts, engravings, and paintings showed native peoples either entirely nude or clad in the skimpiest of loincloths or grass skirts.

Europeans interpreted the simplicity of Indian dress in two different ways. Some saw the lack of clothing—like their supposed lack of commerce, law, government, and religion—as evidence of "barbarism." Andre Thevet, a shocked French visitor to Brazil in 1557, voiced this point of view when he attributed nakedness to native lasciviousness. If the Indians could weave hammocks, he sniffed, why not shirts? But other Europeans esteemed unashamed nakedness as the Indians'

badge of innocence. As remnants of a bygone "golden age," they believed, Indians needed clothing no more than government, laws, regular employment, or other corruptions of civilization. Jean de Lery, another French traveler to Brazil, remarked that the elaborate clothes and jewels worn by Parisian women were "without comparison a source of greater evils than the ordinary nudity of the savage women who in their natural state are not a whit less beautiful."

In fact, Indians were no more "naked" than they were without trade, politics, employment, or religion. While the simplest tribes of the Caribbean and Brazil wore little, the members of more advanced Indian cultures in Central and North America covered themselves with animal pelts sewn into mantles and robes, breechclouts, leggings, and moccasins. They wrought bird feathers into headdresses and ear decorations and fashioned reptile skins into belts and pouches. Even more formidably clad were the Eskimos of the far North, who dressed head to foot in sealskin suits with waterproofed seams, turning the furry side inward for warmth in the winter and outward in the summer.

By the late sixteenth century, Europeans, and especially the English, were paying more heed to what the Indians wore, hoping to assure prospective colonists that the natives would not affront European standards of modesty. Captain John Smith, for example, left detailed descriptions of the attire of Virginia's tribes, noting in a telling comparison that "the better sort use large mantels of deare skins not much differing in fashion from the Irish mantels." Even more reassuringly, Smith added, "The women are alwaies covered about their midles with a skin and very shamefast [modest] to be seen bare."

Daily Lives

Later accounts of Indian dress also advertised the riches of America. In a narrative of his voyage to Roanoke in 1584, Arthur Barlowe remarked that the wife of a local Indian leader sported a fur-lined cloak, a band of white coral about her forehead, and long pendant pearl earrings "of the bigness of good pease."

If natives struck whites as starkly underdressed, Europeans seemed, by the Indians' standards, grotesquely over-dressed. Indeed, European fashion was ill-suited to the environment between the Chesapeake and the Caribbean. Elizabethan gentlemen strutted in silk stockings attached with garters to padded, puffed knee breeches, topped by long-sleeved shirts and tight quilted jackets called "doublets." Men of lesser status wore coarse woolen hose, canvas breeches, shirts, and fitted vests known as "jerkins"; when at work, they donned aprons of dressed leather. Women wore gowns with long, full skirts, low-cut bodices, aprons, and hosiery held up by garters. Ladies went in silk and wore hoods and mantles to ward off the sun, while the rest dressed in flannels or canvas and covered their heads with linen caps or coifs. Both sexes favored long hair, and men sported mustaches and beards. Such fashions complicated life in the American environment, especially since heavy clothing and even shoes rotted rapidly from sweat and humidity. The pungent aroma of Europeans also compounded the discomfort of natives who came in contact with them. For despite sweltering heat, the whites who swaddled themselves in woolens and brocades also disdained regular bathing and regarded Indian devotion to daily washing as another uncivilized oddity.

It would have been natural for Indians to wonder why the barbaric newcomers did not adapt their dress to a new setting. The answer may be that for Europeans—entering an alien environment inhabited by peoples whom they identified as "naked savages"—the psychological risk of shedding familiar apparel was simply too great. However inappropriate or even unhealthy, heavy, elaborate dress afforded the comfort of familiarity and distinguished "civilized" newcomer from "savage" native in America.

Columbus meeting the natives on Hispaniola.

village razed in retaliation, and an Indian executed. Sensing that the situation on Roanoke could rapidly become desperate, White sailed back with Ferdinando, hoping to bring reinforcements.

Unfortunately for White, he returned home just when King Philip of Spain had reached the end of his patience with England. It was 1588, and the massive Spanish navy, the Armada, was marshalling for an assault on England. Elizabeth was enlisting every seaworthy ship and able-bodied sailor in her realm to stave off invasion. Blocked by the war with Spain and distracted by another scheme to colonize a large plantation in Ireland, Raleigh left the Roanoke colonists to shift for themselves. White could not return to Roanoke Island until 1590, three years later. To herald his arrival, White's party sounded a trumpet, "and afterwards many familiar English tunes of songs, and called to them friendly." There was no answer. The empty fort, no more than a few cottages in a clearing, gave no clue of the colony's fate, save for a few letters carved on a post: CROATOAN. It was the name of a nearby island off Cape Hatteras.

Had the Roanoke colonists fled to Croatoan for safety? Had they moved to the mainland and joined Indian tribes in the interior? Had they been killed by Wingina's people? The historical record remains silent on the fate of the "lost colony." When a storm blew up, damaging his ship and spoiling his supplies, White was forced to sail back to England, leaving behind the little cluster of cottages that would soon be overgrown with vines and his suit of armor that was already "almost eaten through with rust."

All of the world lay before them. Or so it had seemed to the young men from England's West Country who dreamed of gold and glory, conquest and colonization. But the sixteenth-century world had defied the expectations and defeated the dreams of England's would-be conquistadors. In 1600, over a century after Columbus' first crossing, not a single English settlement existed anywhere in the Americas. The Atlantic had swallowed up Gilbert and his hopes for a manorial utopia; Raleigh's ventures foundered on the rock of royal ambition.

Raleigh had left behind his Virginia schemes to sail to South America in quest of El Dorado, a rich city somewhere near Guiana, rumored to be ruled by descendants of the Aztecs. But in 1603, Elizabeth's death brought to the English throne her cousin James I, the founder of the Stuart dynasty. The new king arrested the old queen's favorite for treason, and Raleigh languished for 15 years in the Tower of London. Set free in 1618 at the age of 64, he returned to Guiana, his lust for El Dorado undiminished. Along the way, he plundered some Spanish silver ships, defying James' orders. It was a fatal mistake, for England had made peace with Spain. By annoying the king of Spain, he had also annoyed the king of England: Raleigh lost his head.

James I did not want to annoy the king of Spain; he wanted to imitate him. The Stuarts were even more determined than the Tudors to enlarge the sphere of royal power. Royal ambition meant, among other things, that there would be no recreation of the old feudal world in America. It meant that there would be no role in America for a warrior nobility of conquistadors, no room for a kingdom ruled by the likes of Sir Walter Raleigh. Instead, there would be English colonies in America like the new outpost of Jamestown, planted on the Chesapeake Bay in Virginia in 1607. There would be English colonies in America named for English kings and queens and ruled by English royalty and their loyal, efficient bureaucrats. And there would be English colonies yielding commodities and revenues that enriched the English monarchy and the English state. Settling America would strengthen English monarchs, paving their path to greater power, just as the dominions of Mexico and Peru had augmented the authority of the Spanish crown. America would be the making of kings and queens.

Or would it? For some in the Old World, weary of the tyranny of conquistadors and sea rovers, the order and security that Crown rule and centralized states promoted in western Europe would be enough. But others, the desperate and idealistic men and women who sailed to the world that lay before them, would want more.

SIGNIFICANT EVENTS

ca. 50,000–25,000 B.P. (before the present)	First Asian penetration of the Americas
ca. 1300 A.D.	Rise of the Aztec empire
1271–1295	Marco Polo travels to China from Italy
1347	First outbreak of the Black Death
1420s	Portuguese settlements in the Atlantic islands
1488	Dias rounds the tip of Africa
1492	Columbus discovers America
1497	John Cabot discovers Newfoundland
1498	Da Gama reaches India
1517	Luther posts his 95 theses
1519–1522	Magellan circumnavigates the globe
1521	Tenochtitlán surrenders to Cortés
1540	Discovery of silver in Mexico and Peru
1558	Elizabeth I becomes queen of England
1565	England begins its conquest of Ireland
1576–1578	Frobisher searches for Northwest Passage
1583	Gilbert's quest for a North American colony
1584–1590	Roanoke voyages

2

The First Century of Settlement in the Colonial South

n the year 1617, as Europeans counted time, on a bay they called the Chesapeake, in a land they named Virginia, an old Indian chief surveyed his domain. It had all worked according to plan, and Powhatan, werowance of the Pamunkeys, had laid his plans carefully. While in his prime, the tall, robust man had drawn some 30 smaller tribes along the Virginia coast into a powerful confederacy. He had pressed southward, subjugating and exacting tribute from the other Algonkian-speaking tribes of the Tidewater. He had installed his relatives as their new leaders and as his new vassals. By 1607 Powhatan's confederacy numbered nearly 9000. In imposing political unity on the Virginia tribes, Powhatan conquered formidable obstacles. The natives of Virginia, like the tribes who inhabited the length of eastern North America, were a seminomadic people. They lived for most of the year in small villages and ranged seasonally with the game over tribal hunting and fishing grounds. Rivalries over trade, territorial boundaries, and leadership had often erupted into armed conflict. Some tribes in the Tidewater had fiercely resisted incorporation into the confederacy. To the west, another challenge had confronted Powhatan. From the gentle, rolling hill country lying between the falls of great rivers and the Appalachian Mountains the Monacans and Manahoacs had threatened the security of the infant confederacy. These interior tribes of the Piedmont had also controlled the trade in copper, a metal that the coastal tribes fashioned into decorative objects.

After 1607 Powhatan had been compelled to take into account yet another tribe as he consolidated his empire. They came by sea, crammed into three ships, 100 men and 4 boys, all clad in heavy, outlandish clothing, many dressed in gaudy colors. The English, as the tribe called themselves, followed a river deep into his territory and built a fort on a swampy, mosquito-infested site that they called Jamestown—a dubious way to honor their werowance, whom they called King James I.

Powhatan had not been surprised. His people had heard about, perhaps even encountered, other overdressed whites—the English settlers of the ill-fated Roanoke colony and the Spanish and French explorers, missionaries, and slavers who had scouted, preached, and plundered along the southeastern coast of North America during the late sixteenth century. The English had larger boats and louder, more lethal weapons than his own people possessed. But the Indians

The early southern gentry idealized their life as one of grace, plenty, and independence—qualities evoked by this painting, The Plantation. *Typically, this plantation fronts a river, ensuring good access to the markets for tobacco and rice across the Atlantic.*

quickly learned how to use guns, and they vastly outnumbered the English, who seemed, like those late of Roanoke, unlikely to live long and prosper in Powhatan's land.

Powhatan had not been frightened: he saw that the English were an inferior race of people. The feckless English could not manage to feed themselves, even in the rich Chesapeake region encompassing most of present-day Virginia and Maryland. Along the coast, where whites first settled, the forests abounded with deer, elk, and buffalo; the streams teemed with sturgeon and the shoals with shellfish. With bows and arrows, spears and nets, Indian men brought in an abundance of meat and fish. The fields tended by Indian women yielded generous crops of corns, beans, squash, and melon, and edible nuts and fruits—hickory and black walnuts, mulberries, grapes, and strawberries, plums and persimmons—grew wild. Still the English starved, and not just during the first few months of their settlement, but for several years thereafter.

Powhatan could understand why the English refused to grow food. Cultivating crops, like building houses, or making clothing, pottery, and baskets, or caring for children, was women's work, beneath manly dignity. And the English settlement included no women until two arrived in the fall of 1608. Yet even after more women came, the English still starved, and they expected—no, they demanded—that the Indians supply them with food.

Most incredible to Powhatan was that the inferior English considered themselves a superior people. They boasted incessantly about the power of their god— they had only one—and spoke contemptuously of the Indians' "devil-worship" of "false gods." The English also boasted incessantly about the power of their king, who expected Powhatan to become his vassal. The English had even planned a "coronation" at Jamestown to crown Powhatan as a "subject king." Powhatan had not been impressed. "If your king has sent me presents," he responded, "I also am a king, and this is my land. . . . Your father is to come to me, not I to him, nor yet to your fort, neither will I bite at such a bait." In the end, the English did come to Powhatan, only to find what "a fowle trouble there was to make him kneele to receave his crowne . . . [he] indured so many perswasions, examples and instructions as tired them all. At last by leaning hard on his shoulders, he a little stooped, and . . . put the Crowne on his head." In return for the English king's presents, Powhatan sent James I his mantle and a pair of old shoes.

It was inconceivable to Powhatan—his kneeling before the English werowance, the ruler of so savage a race. When his own subjects withheld food or defended their land from these invaders, the English retaliated, not only by burning Indian villages, fields, and canoes, but also by murdering Indian women and children. When the Indians made war, they killed the male warriors of rival tribes, but adopted their women and children. And the English could not tell one tribe from another. If an Indian tribe from outside the confederacy attacked a white settlement, the English, in their confusion, were likely to retaliate by pillaging and murdering Indians allied to Powhatan. To make matters worse, the English could not even keep order within their own tribe. Too many of them wanted to be chiefs, and they squabbled constantly among themselves.

Only one man among the English, a brash fellow called Captain John Smith, had been able, briefly, in 1608, to impose discipline on the rest. Powhatan had granted him a grudging respect, despite Smith's capacity for such extravagant boasting that even other English seemed modest by comparison. Smith bragged endlessly of his earlier exploits across the seas, where he had fought as a soldier of fortune, and of his irresistible appeal to beautiful women, who had rescued him from harrowing perils. A rough man, he had bullied the Indians for food and would have enslaved them, had it been in his power. Even so, Smith had taken a genuine interest in Indian ways and he, alone among the English, learned to tell one tribe from another. Unfortunately, Smith returned to England in 1609 after being injured when some of the whites' gunpowder blew up by mistake. Thereafter the English returned to squabbling and starving.

Small wonder that shortly after Smith's departure, the whole miserable tribe of English had prepared to leave Jamestown for good. Only the arrival of another ship carrying supplies and more settlers had turned them back. And small wonder that some English had deserted their settlement to live among Powhatan's people. Anyone could see the superiority of Indian culture to English ways.

The temptation to wipe out the helpless, troublesome, arrogant tribe of Eng-

No stranger to self-promotion, Captain John Smith included this portrait of himself and verses celebrating his ennobling exploits at the beginning of his *Description of New England* (1616). After his brief stay in Jamestown, Smith explored the New England coast, but he always hoped for an opportunity to return to Virginia.

lish—or simply to let them starve to death—had been almost overwhelming. But if Powhatan often wore a "sour look," as John Smith noticed, he had never launched a major offensive against the invaders. On the contrary, the food provided by his people was all that had kept Jamestown going for several years. Powhatan had allowed the source of his aggravation to survive because he had decided that even the English had their uses—as an addition to his empire. English manpower, English trading goods, and, most important, English guns would provide him with the support to quell resistance within his confederacy and to subdue his Indian rivals in the Piedmont. In 1614, Powhatan had cemented his claim on the English and their weapons with the marriage between his favorite child, Pocohontas, and a white settler, John Rolfe.

By 1617 events had vindicated Powhatan's strategy of suffering the English presence. His empire flourished, ready to be passed on to his brother, Opechancanough. Internal dissension within the confederacy had diminished, and the power of his Piedmont rivals had been broken. Powhatan's people still outnumbered the English, who seldom starved outright now but continued to quarrel and sicken and die. Only one thing had changed in the Chesapeake by 1617: the English were clearing woodland along the rivers and planting tobacco.

That was the doing of Powhatan's son-in-law, Rolfe, a man as strange as any of his tribe, all of them eager to accumulate wealth and worldly goods. Rolfe had been obsessed with finding a crop that could be grown in Virginia and then sold for gain across the sea. By the incomprehensible standards of the English, he had succeeded: his experiments with planting and selling a South American strain of tobacco were leading many other English to imitate the practice. Odder still, not women but men tended the tobacco fields. Here was more evidence of English inferiority. Men wasted long hours laboring when they might supply their needs with far less effort and enjoy the rest of the time allotted them by the gods.

In 1617 Powhatan, werowance of the Pamunkeys, surveyed his empire, and sometime in that year, he looked no longer. He had lived long enough to see the tobacco fields lining the riverbanks, straddling the charred stumps of felled trees. Knowing the English as he did, Powhatan had not been surprised by the sight of such plantations, and he had not been frightened. For he had overcome the greatest danger to his empire: he had prevailed over the other Indian tribes. He died believing that he had bent the English to his purposes—died, perhaps blessedly, before those stinking weeds spread over the length of his land and sent his hard-won empire up in smoke.

ENGLISH SOCIETY ON THE CHESAPEAKE

While the chief of the Chesapeake was expanding his dominions and consolidating his power, the king of England was doing the same. James I's ambition to enhance the wealth and power of his people and, not incidentally, himself, entangled the fate of England's infant empire with that of Powhatan.

The English and other European powers had an idea about how to attain national wealth and influence. That idea, which had been the guiding principle of Europe's commercial development and expansion for 200 years, was named "mercantilism" by the eighteenth-century economist Adam Smith. Mercantilists called for the state to supervise, regulate, and protect industry and commerce. Their primary objective was to enrich the nation by fostering a favorable balance of trade. Once the value of exports exceeded the cost of imports, they theorized, gold and silver would flow into home ports. If a nation could dispense entirely with imports from other countries, so much the better—and it was here that the idea of colonies entered the mercantilist scheme. Colonial planters and farmers, miners and loggers would supply raw materials that the mother country could not produce, while colonial consumers swelled demand for the finished goods and financial services that the mother country could provide. Convinced that colonies would enhance national self-sufficiency, mercantilists urged states to sponsor overseas settlements.

Mercantilist notions appealed to Europe's ambitious monarchs. A thriving trade meant that larger revenues from taxes and customs duties would fill royal coffers, increasing royal power. That logic led James I to lend his approval to the private venture that brought the first white settlers to the Chesapeake.

The Virginia Company

In 1606 the king granted a charter to Richard Hakluyt and a number of English merchants, gentlemen, and aristocrats, incorporating them as the Virginia Company of London. The members of the new joint stock company promptly sold stock in their venture to English investors, as well as awarding a share to those willing to settle in Virginia at their own expense. With the proceeds from the sale of stock, the company planned to send to Virginia hundreds of poor and unemployed people as well as scores of skilled craftsworkers. These laborers were to serve the company for seven years in return for their passage, pooling their efforts to produce any commodities that would return a profit to stockholders. Like Gilbert and Raleigh before them, the investors hoped to make money by discovering gold in the New World, as the Spanish had in the sixteenth century. If that failed, they hoped that North America might yield other valuable commodities—furs, pitch, tar, lumber, or sassafras, which Spanish merchants were hawking throughout Europe as a cure for a less popular American import, syphilis. In the spring of 1607, the Virginia Company's first expedition—104 men and boys aboard the *Godspeed*, the *Discovery*, and the *Susan Constant*—sailed into the Chesapeake Bay and up the Powhatan River, renaming it the James. Some 30 miles upstream, they founded Jamestown.

That was the first of many mistakes. Jamestown's first settlers had pitched their fort on an inland site ideally suited to prevent a surprise attack from the Spanish. Unfortunately, the marshy, thickly forested peninsula was also ideally conducive to malaria, especially during the steamy summer settling over the Chesapeake. Even for healthy men willing to work hard, cultivating such land would have been a daunting task. But Jamestown's settlers, weakened by bouts of malaria and then beset by dysentery, typhoid, and yellow fever, died by the scores, and those who survived were left listless and debilitated.

Many of Jamestown's first settlers—gentlemen who expected to lead rather than to work—had little taste for labor even before ill health claimed whatever inclination to work they might have had. Most other members of the early colonizing parties were gentlemen's servants and craftsmen—goldsmiths, jewelers, refiners, even a perfumer—men who were accustomed to labor but who did not regard growing crops as their line of work. The settlers resorted to bullying and begging

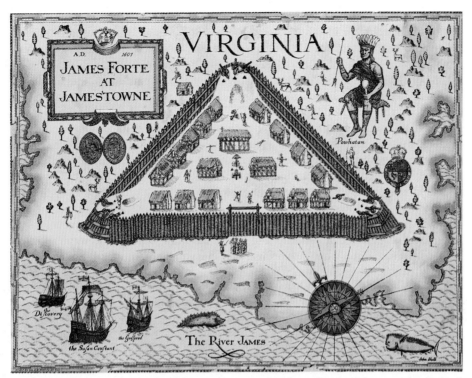

In Jamestown's early years its military orientation was clear. The fort's heavy palisades and its strategic location upriver and some distance inland underscore the colonists' concern for defense—as does the imposing figure of Powhatan seated at the right.

food from Powhatan's people, but the Indians' liberality was less than reliable, especially after the departure of John Smith. Food shortages produced chronic malnutrition, which heightened the colonists' susceptibility to disease, and even more drastic consequences. Only 60 of Jamestown's 500 inhabitants lived through the winter of 1609–1610, known as the "starving time." Some desperate colonists unearthed and ate corpses; one settler even butchered his wife.

Reports of starvation and staggering death rates stiffened the Virginia Company's resolve: in 1611 it imposed on the colonists what amounted to martial law. Company officials in Virginia organized the settlers into work gangs and inflicted draconian punishments on the lazy and the disorderly. Still the company failed to turn a profit. And after 1617, skirmishes with the Indians became more brutal and frequent, as rows of tobacco plants encroached on tribal lands farther and farther inland. The "noxious weeds" were equally an embarrassment to advocates of colonization at home in England. After a decade of settlement, Virginia's sole contribution to the empire was the smoke filling England's taverns and brothels. Even James I, whose standards of hygiene and morality often caused his own courtiers to wince, condemned the use of tobacco as a filthy and dissipated habit.

Reform and a Boom in Tobacco

Desperate to salvage their investment and their respectability, the company managers instituted in 1618 the sweeping reform program advocated by a principal stockholder, Sir Edwin Sandys. To attract more capital and colonists to Virginia, the company established a "headright" system for granting land to individuals. Those already settled in the colony received 100 acres apiece, new settlers each received 50 acres, and anyone who paid the passage of other immigrants to Virginia—either family members or servants—received 50 acres per "head." The company also dispensed with martial law, allowing the planters to elect a representative assembly, which, along with a governor and an advisory council appointed by the company, had the authority to make laws for the colony. The House of Burgesses met for the first time in 1619, commencing what would become a strong tradition of representative government in the English colonies. Finally, the company attempted to encourage a more diverse economy by ordering that no colonist could grow more than 100 pounds of tobacco annually and by dispatching to Virginia an assortment of skilled workers—vintners, ironworkers, brickmakers, and glassblowers.

The new measures to encourage migration met with immediate success. For several years both free immigrants and bound laborers surged into Virginia. Of the bound laborers, some were indentured servants who agreed to work a set number of years, usually four to seven, for the planters paying the cost of their passage. Others were sharecropping tenants who were to cultivate company land under the direction of its agents in the colony; for seven years they were to turn half of their earnings over to the Virginia Company, and at the end of their terms of service, they were to receive 50 acres.

Free immigrants poured into Virginia, too, for during the 1620s the tobacco economy took off. As demand soared and prices peaked in European markets, those with an eye for profits took their chances in Virginia, planted every inch of their farms in tobacco, and reaped windfalls. Because of the gains that free settlers stood to make by growing tobacco, the effort to diversify Virginia's economy failed. That was just one casualty of the tobacco boom; another was the lives of most English men and women who came to Virginia during the 1620s.

Those who crossed the Atlantic to Virginia during that decade were in the vanguard of an English migration to the Chesapeake that numbered between 130,000 and 150,000 over the seventeenth century. Drawn from the ranks of ordinary English working people, the immigrants were predominantly men, outnumbering women by six to one; typically young, ranging in age between 15 and 24; and generally, because of their youth, without skills or wealth. Three-quarters of all the newcomers arrived in the Chesapeake as indentured servants.

For most of the new servants, the crossing to Virginia was simply the last of many moves, each undertaken in the hope of finding work. While England's population had been expanding since the middle of the fifteenth century, changes in agriculture, chiefly the conversion of arable land for crops to pasturage for sheep, had steadily reduced the need for farm laborers. A severe recession in the English textile industry early in the seventeenth century augmented the problem of employing a growing number of people. The search for work pushed young men and women out of their villages, sending them through the countryside and then into the cities. Down and out in London, Bristol, or Liverpool, some decided to make their next move across the Atlantic and signed indentures. Pamphlets promoting immigration promised a bounteous natural environment, a balmy climate, and, once servants finished their terms, abundant land and quick riches. If the recruits to the Chesapeake did not credit completely these rosy promises, the lack of work, the low wages, and the high prices in old England made them desperate enough to try their luck in the New World anyway.

Even the most skeptical immigrants must have been shocked at what they found. The death rate in Virginia during the 1620s was higher than that of England during times of epidemic disease. The life expectancy for Chesapeake men who reached the age of 20 was a mere 48 years; for women it was lower still. Servants fared worst of all, since malnutrition, overwork, and abuse made them vulnerable to disease. And as masters scrambled to make quick profits, they extracted the maximum amount of work before death carried off their laborers. An estimated 40 percent of servants never regained their freedom because they did not survive to the end of their indentured terms.

The expanding cultivation of tobacco also claimed many lives by putting unbearable pressure on Indian land. Following Powhatan's death in 1617, leadership of the confederacy passed to Opechancanough, who watched, year after year, the tobacco mania grow. In March 1622 he coordinated a full-scale attack on white settlements that killed about one-fifth of the white population of Virginia. Swift English reprisals wiped out whole tribes and cut down an entire generation of young Indian men. As tragic as the casualties on both sides was the view of Indians that the events of 1622 fixed in the minds of the English—the belief that all Indians were treacherous and cunning, incapable of being civilized and incorporated into English colonial society. Back in England, John Smith predicted the consequence: the Virginians now saw "just cause to destroy them [the Indians] by all meanes possible."

The aftermath of the Indian war revealed to English investors the true state of their Virginia venture. It came to light that unscrupulous company officials in the

---

The Smokers, painted by Adriaen Brouwer, a seventeenth-century Dutch artist, suggests that the use of tobacco was both popular and disreputable. Native American peoples like the Costa Rican man shown at the right had been cultivating and smoking tobacco long before the arrival of Europeans.

colony had commandeered tenants to work their private plantations instead of company lands. The Virginia Company, despite the tobacco boom, was plunging toward bankruptcy. Nor was that the worst news. Stockholders discovered that their colony numbered just 1240 inhabitants after the upheaval in 1622. More than 3500 people had immigrated to Virginia after 1619, joining several hundred settlers who had arrived earlier. The Indian war had claimed 345 colonists. What accounted for the deaths of so many others? An investigation by the king brought out the whole truth: shiploads of servants and tenants, more dead than alive from scurvy, had been disgorged on Virginia shores without adequate supplies of food and clothing. Labor-hungry planters had snatched up the survivors, buying and selling their contracts like any other commodity, starving and driving human beings out of sheer greed. As one servant observed, Virginia masters used English men, women, and children "like damned slaves." James I dissolved the Virginia Company and took control of the colony himself in 1624.

Settling Down in the Chesapeake

The 1630s and 1640s brought beleaguered colonists some respite from the chaos of the first decades of Virginia's settlement. Although servants still streamed into the colony, the price of tobacco leveled off, which meant that planters were less likely to drive their servants to death in search of overnight fortunes. As the fever of the tobacco boom broke, a more settled social and political life emerged in Virginia. The same shrewd, ruthless tobacco planters who had become wealthy by monopolizing land now began to consolidate their gains through political power. They established local bases of influence in Virginia's counties, serving as justices of the peace and sheriffs, maintaining roads and bridges, collecting taxes, and supervising local elections. There they organized all able-bodied adult males into militias for local defense. There they established and served in vestries, the governing bodies of local Anglican parishes, hiring the handful of clergy who came to Virginia and providing for the neighborhood poor.

The biggest tobacco planters of each county also dominated colony politics. Even though King James had replaced the Virginia Company's government by charter with his own royal administration, the colony's elected assembly continued making laws for the colony. Along with the council (the upper house of the legislature), the assembly stoutly resisted interference in Virginia's affairs from the royal governor, the king's representative.

While the structure of colony and local government took shape, Virginia's population grew. As tobacco became less lucrative, planters raised more corn and cattle, and mortality rates declined as food supplies rose. The growing number of men who survived servitude found greater opportunity in the Chesapeake during the 1630s and 1640s than would have been theirs in England. The majority of freed servants, after a few years of working as hired hands or tenant farmers, managed to save enough money to buy their own land and become independent planters. That status was attained by few farmers in England, most of whom remained the tenants of gentlemen and aristocrats.

For the women who survived servitude in the Chesapeake, prospects were even better. With wives at a premium, single women stood a good chance of improving their status by marriage—far better than women back in England. Some impatient planters even bought women servants out of their indentures. If they outlived their husbands, widows inherited handsomely and often contracted even more advantageous second—and third—marriages.

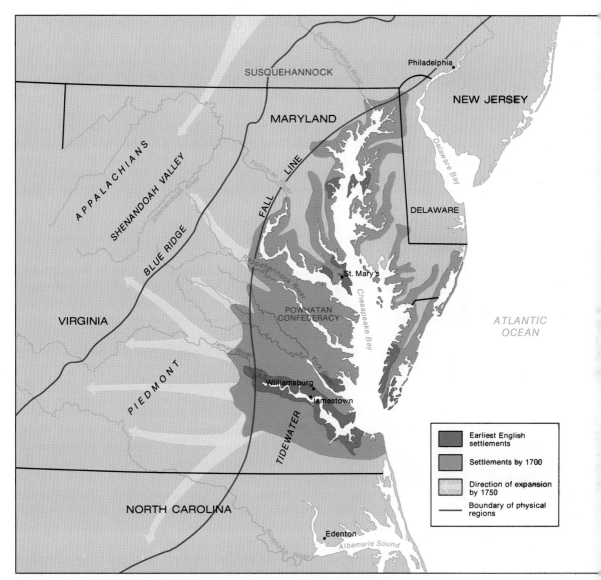

COLONIES OF THE CHESAPEAKE
Settlements in Virginia and Maryland spread out along the many bays of the Chesapeake, where tobacco could easily be loaded from plantation wharves. The "fall line" on rivers, dividing Tidewater and Piedmont regions, determined the extent of commercial agriculture, since ships could not pick up exports beyond that point.

By the middle of the seventeenth century, Virginia numbered about 15,000, with more servants and free immigrants coming to the colony every year. The increase of inhabitants and the rapid depletion of the soil by tobacco fed an eagerness for fresh land. But two impediments stood between the Virginians and the new territory that they coveted. The first problem was the creation of a second colony in the Chesapeake.

The Founding of Maryland and the Renewal of Indian Wars

In 1632 Cecilius Calvert, Lord Baltimore, received a charter from Charles I making him the absolute owner of 10 million acres on the Chesapeake Bay. Although Elizabeth I and her royal successors were suspicious of lordly gentlemen with designs on the New World, James I wanted to reward the loyalty of Cecilius' father, George. The king also wanted to please his queen, who, like the Calvert family, was Catholic. Lord Baltimore named the new colony Maryland in her majesty's honor and immediately set about fashioning in the New World a safe haven for what he valued in the Old World. To protect his cherished religion, Calvert established Maryland as a refuge for Catholics and extended complete religious freedom to all Christians. And to protect his cherished aristocratic order, Calvert attempted to recreate in Maryland a nearly feudal domain.

Unlike Virginia, which was first settled by a private corporation and later converted into a royal colony, Maryland was founded by a single aristocratic family. The first of several such "proprietary" colonies, Maryland was the private preserve of the Calverts, who held absolute authority to grant land, administer justice, and establish a civil government. All of these powers they exercised, granting estates, or "manors," to their friends, carving Calvert holdings into smaller farms for ordinary immigrants, and collecting annual "quitrents," fees for use of the land, from Calvert "tenants"—every settler in the colony. While the largest landowners dispensed local justice in manorial courts and made laws for the entire colony in a representative assembly, the Calverts appointed a governor and a council to oversee their own interests. Humphrey Gilbert and Walter Raleigh would have admired everything about the Calverts' lordly domain—except the toleration of Catholics.

Virginians, on the other hand, liked nothing at all about Maryland. Worse than the annoyance of Catholic neighbors was the problem of economic competition. By 1640 Maryland had 2000 inhabitants, virtually all of them pursuing the profitable business of planting tobacco on land desired by the Virginians. And the Marylanders were only one impediment to Virginia's expansion. The other was the remnant of the Powhatan confederacy, which had lost none of its determination to repel the white invaders. The solution was obvious: Virginians tried to incite the Indians to attack Calvert's colony.

But Opechancanough and his people had some old scores to settle, as well as some new resentments. They had not forgotten the reprisals of 1622, and by the 1640s Virginia's white settlers, blocked by Maryland from moving north and east along the Chesapeake Bay, were pressing west again onto Indian land. Opechancanough also had some new ideas about how to settle the score: he hoped that white Marylanders hated white Virginians enough to cast their lot with the Indians. Old and feeble but still formidable, Opechancanough rallied a new generation of Indians and in 1644 launched full-scale hostilities against the encroaching Virginia planters. The Indians again sustained the more severe losses, and the support they had hoped for from white Marylanders never materialized. Yet the Chesapeake tribes still mounted a determined resistance, one that in absolute numbers inflicted as many casualties on the Virginia planters as the attacks in 1622.

Virginians gradually resigned themselves to the existence of Maryland, and the two colonies came to resemble each other closely. Counties modeled on Virginia's system of local government replaced Calvert's manorial courts. The Maryland assembly became as obstreperous in resisting the power of the proprietor as

Virginia's legislature was in challenging the influence of the royal governor. But Maryland's imitation of Virginia was too faithful to be flattering. Maryland continued to develop an economy devoted to the cultivation of tobacco, and the competition continued to make Virginians miserable.

Changes in English Policy in the Chesapeake

In the 1630s and 1640s the king did not intervene, even belatedly, to ease tensions in the Chesapeake. Engulfed in a political crisis and then a civil war, England made no effort to protect the Indians by curbing white expansion or to reconcile Virginia and Maryland by diversifying the tobacco economy.

A storm gathered over England as the Stuarts, ever ambitious to enlarge the authority of the monarchy, found that they lacked the financial ability to pay for that authority. Throughout the first four decades of the seventeenth century James I and his son and successor, Charles I, sought to dispense with the nuisance of ruling with Parliament. James I made a great point of defending the right of kings to generally do whatever they pleased, and, in particular, to raise money through taxes and customs duties levied without the consent of Parliament. Even more eager than his father to dispense with Parliament, Charles dissolved that body in 1629 when its members condemned him for usurping the power of the purse. The landed gentlemen and merchants who sat in Parliament regarded representative government as indispensable, especially when it came to consenting to taxes, and they resisted royal bullying.

Unlike the successful absolutist monarchs of France and Spain, Charles had no way of getting money without Parliament's approval, no large royal bureaucracy, and no standing army. That left Charles no choice but to reconvene Parliament in 1640 when the Scots invaded England. By that time, many members of Parliament had decided that the Stuart kings themselves might be dispensable. In 1642 Parliament and its Puritan allies squared off against Charles I and his royalist supporters, defeated them in battle, and, in 1649, beheaded the king as a public criminal. For 11 years thereafter, from 1649 to 1660, England was a republic ruled, for most of that time, by Oliver Cromwell, first as head of Parliament's New Model Army, and later as the Lord Protector.

Cromwell took advantage of the end of civil war to turn England's attention to its American colonies. Under his regime Parliament passed legislation that prohibited England's principal commercial rival, the Dutch, from trading with English possessions overseas. Taking a more aggressive tack, he sent English forces to attack the shipping and colonial settlements of Spain and France and in 1652, inaugurated a series of wars with the Dutch, conflicts that would flare up in 1664 and again in 1672.

Cromwell's death in 1658 virtually ended the republican experiment in ruling without a king. Hatred of his repressive regime, which was more a military dictatorship than a true republic, restored to the throne of England a member of the Stuart family who promised never to dispense with Parliament. This was Charles II, the politically adroit son of the beheaded Charles I. Yet the determination of Cromwell and Parliament to make English colonies contribute to the parent country's prosperity outlived both the Lord Protector and the republic.

Indeed, almost immediately Charles II set out to implement a consistent colonial policy in a series of regulations known as the Navigation Acts. The first, passed in 1660, gave England and English colonial merchants a monopoly on the shipping and marketing of all colonial goods. It also specified certain "enumerated commodities" that the colonies could send only to England or other British ports, a list that included sugar, tobacco, cotton, ginger, and indigo (a blue dye). In 1663 Parliament added another regulation: the Staple Act gave Britain a virtual monopoly on the sale of European manufactured goods to Americans by stipulating that most imports going to the colonies had to pass through England. In 1673 a third Navigation Act levied duties on the coastal trade of the American colonies and provided for customs officials to collect imposts and enforce commercial regulations. Parliament later made minor modifications in the Navigation Acts, adding rice and naval stores (masts, pitch, tar, and turpentine) to the category of enumerated commodities in 1704 and 1705, prohibiting the colonies from exporting certain textiles by the Wool Act of 1699 and exporting hats by the Hat Act of 1732, and offering bounties and eliminating duties to encourage the colonial production of indigo and pig and bar iron. All of these regulations were designed to ensure that England—and no foreign nations or their merchants—would profit from all colonial production and trade.

CHESAPEAKE SOCIETY IN CRISIS

The turmoil of England's revolution had little lasting effect on Virginia and Maryland. The long decades of neglect only confirmed Chesapeake inhabitants in their inclination to act with considerable independence from their homeland. It was the measures instituted by Restoration kings Charles II and James II and their Parliaments that had a more dramatic impact on colonials. Accustomed to conducting their affairs as they pleased— and they were often pleased to trade with the Dutch—Chesapeake planters chafed under the new restrictions that limited their commerce to England. What was worse, the curtailing of colonial freedom after 1660 coincided with a downturn in colonial fortunes. In the effort to consolidate its empire, England inadvertently deepened the economic and social difficulties of Chesapeake society.

The Conditions of Unrest

Even before the passage of the Navigation Acts, the Chesapeake colonies had been headed for trouble. The problem began when inhabitants had started to live longer. More servants survived their terms of service, set up as independent tobacco planters, and competed with established growers for land and a share of the profits. More planters meant more production, and overproduction sent the price of tobacco plummeting, especially between 1660 and 1680. With the cost of land rising and the price of tobacco falling, opportunities for newly freed servants diminished sharply after the middle decades of the seventeenth century, especially in Virginia. To maintain their advantage, the biggest planters bought up all of the prime property along the coast. The scarcity of land forced freed servants to become tenants or to settle on unclaimed land in the interior. Either way, these poorer men lost. Depending on bigger planters for land and credit made the small farmers vulnerable to debt; moving to the frontier made them vulnerable to Indian attack.

Freed servants who managed to become small planters or tenants did not enjoy a comfortable livelihood or a secure existence. And after the passage of the Navigation Acts, demands on their slim resources included not only taxes levied by the county government and fees charged by local officials, but also export duties on tobacco collected by England. During the hard times after 1660, many small planters fell deeply into debt to those who had rented them land or advanced them credit, and some were forced back into servitude. By 1676 one-quarter of Virginia's free white men were landless.

An alarming number of former servants were unable to gain a foothold even as tenants. They became the vagabonds of Virginia, young bachelors who owned only the clothes on their backs—and their guns. They roamed from place to place, sometimes squatting on someone else's land, sometimes working as hired hands, sometimes living off whatever game they could shoot or livestock they could steal.

Diminishing opportunity in the 1660s and 1670s provided the tinder for social and political unrest. As the discontent of small planters mounted and the number of young, armed vagabonds multiplied, so did the apprehensions of Virginia's big planters. The assembly of the colony lengthened terms of servitude, hoping to limit the number of servants entering the free population, and curtailed the political rights of landless men, hoping to stifle opposition by depriving them of the vote.

Efforts to repress popular resentment only generated a spate of mutinies among servants and protests over rising taxes among small planters. By the early 1670s the situation had become so explosive that Virginia's royal governor, Sir William Berkeley, feared what might happen if the colony required defense from a European power or the Indians. If he mobilized the militia and marched them off to defend the coastline or the frontier, would Virginia's servants find in the absence of their masters a chance to rebel? Or would the militia—comprised mainly of small planters—turn their guns against the colony's government instead of the enemy? Berkeley's alarm deepened in 1673 when the Dutch, displeased at being excluded from the Chesapeake trade by the Navigation Acts, dispatched four armed vessels to Virginia and set fire to the tobacco fleet.

Bacon's Rebellion and Coode's Rebellion

Virginia survived the Dutch assault, but Berkeley's apprehensions were realized just three years later: civil war erupted in 1676. What set off the conflict among white Virginians was a renewal of hostilities with red Virginians. After Opechancanough's offensive of the 1640s, the Susquehannocks and several smaller Indian tribes living along the Potomac River had retreated to the northwest. By the 1670s white expansion again threatened these tribes, and they resisted with raids on frontier plantations. Berkeley favored a policy of building forts to contain the Indian threat, but frontier farmers opposed his plan as an expensive and ineffective way to defend their scattered plantations. As they clamored for a punitive expedition against the Indians, Nathaniel Bacon stepped forward to spearhead the bloody reprisals.

Wealthy and well connected, Bacon had arrived recently from England, expecting every consideration—including official permission to trade with the Indians from his frontier plantation. Berkeley, along with a few select friends, already held a monopoly on the Indian trade, and the governor declined to include Bacon. Stung by Berkeley's rebuff, Bacon switched his interests from Indian trading to

Indian fighting: he took up the cause of his poorer neighbors on the frontier against their common enemy, the governor. Bacon also received support from other monied, ambitious immigrants who resented being excluded from Berkeley's circle of power and patronage.

In the summer of 1676 Bacon appeared in Jamestown with a body of armed men and extracted from the assembly an authorization to kill Indians. While Bacon carried out that grisly business, indiscriminately slaughtering friendly as well as hostile tribes, Berkeley rallied his supporters and declared him a rebel. Bacon retaliated by turning his forces against those led by the governor. Both sides sought allies by offering freedom to servants and slaves willing to join their ranks. Many were willing: for months the partisans of Bacon and Berkeley plundered one another's plantations. In September 1676 Bacon reduced Jamestown itself to a mound of ashes. It was only his death from dysentery a month later that snuffed out the rebellion. Berkeley, with the belated assistance of 1000 soldiers from England, finally reimposed order.

On the heels of the civil war in Virginia, political upheaval engulfed Maryland. The extraordinary powers of that colony's proprietors, the Calvert family, had from the first created consternation among settlers. And after 1660, against a background of deepening economic depression, antagonisms intensified. A growing number of substantial Maryland planters, like some of Bacon's followers, resented their exclusion from political power and privilege. The Calvert family and their favorites, like Berkeley's circle in Virginia, monopolized political offices. Maryland's small farmers, like Virginia's, suffered from taxes and customs duties that siphoned off their profits and from new laws that whittled away their political privileges. They too wanted a less expensive and more representative government. Compounding the tensions in Maryland were religious enmities: the Calverts and their friends were Catholic, but many of the colony's inhabitants, including its most successful planters, were Protestants.

The unrest among Maryland planters, both humble and powerful, came to a head in July 1689. John Coode, a former member of the assembly, gathered an army, captured the proprietary governor, seized the Calvert family's plantation, and took the grievances of his Protestant Association to authorities in England. There Coode received a sympathetic hearing; the Calverts' charter was revoked and not restored until 1715, by which time the family had embraced Protestantism.

After 1690 the warring factions within the Chesapeake colonies' elite gradually worked out an accommodation that eased competition among them. The leading planters, newer as well as earlier settlers in Virginia, Protestants as well as Catholics in Maryland, parceled out among themselves the spoils of political office. That more inclusive distribution of power and privilege ensured that no future Nathaniel Bacon or John Coode could mobilize disgruntled elites against the government. The great planter families dominated the assembly and the council of both colonies, and by acting in concert, they managed to curb the power of royal and proprietary governors for decades thereafter.

The greater unity among the Chesapeake's leading families did not redress that region's most fundamental problem. The sharp inequality of white society, a gulf between rich and poor planters etched ever more deeply by the troubled tobacco economy, persisted long after Bacon's Rebellion in Virginia and Coode's Rebellion in Maryland. All that saved white society in the Chesapeake from a renewal of internal crisis was the growth of black slavery.

From Servitude to Slavery

Like the tobacco plants that came to command the length of Powhatan's land, a labor system based on slavery had not figured in the first plans for the Chesapeake. Both early promoters and planters had preferred importing English servants to importing alien African slaves. Black slaves, because they served for life, were more expensive than white workers, who served for several years. Since neither whites nor blacks lived long, cheaper servant labor was the logical choice. The number of blacks in the Chesapeake remained small for most of the seventeenth century, comprising just 5 percent of all inhabitants in 1675.

The first blacks landed in Virginia in 1619, brought by the Dutch, who dominated the slave trade until the middle of the eighteenth century. The lives of those blacks, and the lives of those who followed during the next few decades, resembled those of white servants, with whom they shared harsh work routines and living conditions. White and black bound laborers socialized with each other and formed sexual liaisons; they conspired to steal from their masters and ran away together—and if caught, they endured similar punishments. There was more common ground: many of the first blacks did not arrive directly from Africa, but

---

THE AFRICAN TRANSATLANTIC TRADE: 1450–1760

Of all the American colonies, Brazil received the largest proportion of slaves (about 32 percent), although the total numbers shipped to the Caribbean sugar islands during this period were greater. Only 4 percent of the trade went to North America. As the map indicates, the Islamic slave trade also continued to flourish, carrying roughly as many slaves along its routes across the Sahara, the Red Sea, and the Indian Ocean.

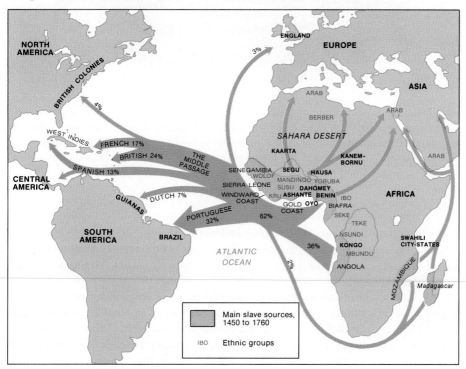

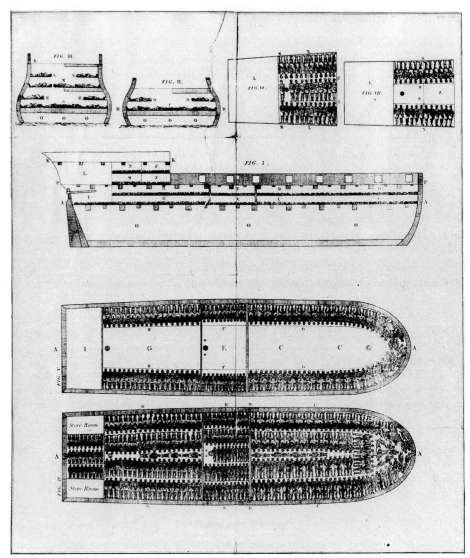

Eighteenth-century slave ships were actually more crowded than this architect's diagram suggests, because traders expected that many slaves would die during the Atlantic crossing. Congestion only contributed to the spread of disease and high rate of shipboard mortality.

came from the Caribbean, where some had learned English and adopted Christian beliefs. And not all blacks in the early Chesapeake were slaves: a few were indentured servants and a handful were free. At least one free black Virginian owned a slave himself.

A number of changes after 1680 caused planters to invest more heavily in slaves than in servants. First, declining mortality rates in the Chesapeake made slaves the more profitable investment. Although slaves were still more expensive than servants, planters could now expect to get many years of work from their bondspeople—and title as well to the children that they would now live long enough to have. At the same time, the flow of white servant migrants was falling off, in response to rumors of brutal conditions in the colonies and a new interest in keeping English workers at home to labor in new English factories and textile mills. Finally, while the supply of white servants was dwindling, the pool of available black labor was widening. When the Royal African Company lost its monopoly on the English slave trade in 1698, other merchants entered the market and swelled the number of Africans sold by British dealers to 20,000 annually.

More than 80 percent of the blacks caught up in the forced migration to America during the decades after 1680 came directly from Africa. They came mainly from agrarian tribes in Angola on the southwest coast of Africa and from the hinterlands of Senegambia, the Windward Coast, and the Gold Coast, an area lying between the Senegal and Niger rivers and the Gulf of Benin. Seized by other Africans, the captive blacks were yoked together at the neck and marched hundreds of miles through the interior to the coast. Some attempted suicide by eating clay; others died of hunger, exhaustion, and exposure. When slaves arrived at coastal trading posts, they were held in pens until their numbers constituted a full cargo for sale and shipment by European dealers.

For those who survived the trauma of capture and the long trek to the ocean, there remained the deadly hurdle of the Middle Passage, a journey of 5000 miles across the Atlantic to America. Perhaps 100 to 200 black men, women, and children were crowded onto each slave ship, but an estimated one out of every six did not live through the crossing. Shipmasters crammed their human cargo onto platforms built between the decks of their vessels, tiers spaced so low that even sitting upright was impossible. Among white sailors and slaves alike, the death toll from disease, especially dysentery, was staggering. Some of the captives tried to starve themselves to death; others fomented mutinies. Both forms of resistance were met with brutal repression.

Those captives who survived the Middle Passage reached their destinations in American ports numb and exhausted; now they faced more challenges to staying alive. The first year in the colonies was the most lethal for new, unseasoned slaves. The sickle cell genetic trait gave blacks a greater immunity than whites had to malaria, but slaves were highly susceptible to respiratory infections. One-quarter of all blacks died during their first year in the Chesapeake, and among Carolina and Caribbean slaves, mortality rates were even higher. In addition to the new disease environment, Africans were forced to adapt to lives without freedom in a wholly unfamiliar country and culture.

The Chesapeake's conversion from a labor system based on servitude to one based on slavery transformed the size, composition, and character of its black population. By 1740 forty percent of all Virginians were black, and most were African-born. Unlike blacks who had arrived earlier, they had no familiarity with English language and culture. Not only larger and more distinctively African, the black community was also locked into a more debased status by the late decades of the seventeenth century. Laws limiting manumission, the freeing of slaves by masters, inhibited the growth of a free black population. Other legislation systematically separated the races: free blacks were forbidden to own white servants; interracial marriages and sexual relationships were punished by stiff penalties. The legal code also fostered white contempt for blacks: while masters were prohibited from whipping their white servants on the bare back, slaves had no such protection. And "any Negro that shall presume to strike any white" was to receive 30 lashes for the rash act.

By consigning blacks to a servile status and defining them as property, the new laws both reflected and encouraged racism among whites of all classes. The spread of racism greatly reduced the likelihood that antagonism between rich and poor would erupt into armed conflict. White servants and small planters came to perceive slaves as inferiors; racial hatred alienated exploited whites from exploited blacks. Instead of identifying with the plight of the slaves, the Chesapeake's poor whites prided themselves on being free, the formal equals of the great planters.

The leaders of the Chesapeake colonies cultivated white supremacy and white solidarity by improving economic prospects for freed servants and lesser planters. The Virginia assembly made provisions for servants to get a better start once they became free, ensuring that fewer would falter as small farmers and slip back into servitude. Legislators also lowered taxes, allowing lesser planters to keep more of their earnings, and widened the franchise, affording most white male Virginians a channel to express their grievances through voting. Economic trends also contributed to the greater security and prosperity of poorer whites after the last decades of the seventeenth century. In response to a moderate but steady swell of demand in Europe, tobacco prices rose slightly and then stabilized. As a result of Bacon's genocidal campaign against the Virginia Indians in 1676, new land became available. Even the domestic lives of lesser men improved as the numbers of men and women in the white population evened out around the turn of the century.

After 1700 the Chesapeake evolved into a more stable society. Gone were the bands of wild, landless, young bachelors one step ahead of the law, the small body of struggling lesser planters one step ahead of their creditors, and the great mass of exploited servants one step away from rebellion. Virginia and Maryland became colonies of farming families, most of them small planters who owned between 50 and 200 acres, who held no slaves—or at most two or three—and who accepted, usually without question, the social and political leadership of their acknowledged "superiors." The ruthless tobacco barons and swaggering conquistadors of the seventeenth century were supplanted at the top of society by great planters who styled themselves the "gentry."

The Chesapeake Gentry

The new Chesapeake gentry were the sons of well-to-do London merchant families, powerful commercial clans whose capital and connections had allied them, by interest and intermarriage, with England's landed gentlemen. Entrepreneurial fathers, some of them investors in the old Virginia Company, sent their sons to the Chesapeake between 1640 and 1670 to create prosperous plantations and to establish family interests in the New World. Their coolly calculating sons and their descendants achieved those objectives, not by the feckless gambling and heedless exploitation practiced by the Chesapeake's former profiteers, but by shrewd use of family land, capital, and influence, careful planning, and skillful estate management.

Their fortunes rested in part on the cultivation of tobacco on thousands of acres by hundreds of slaves. But the gentry made their real money from even more lucrative commercial sidelines: they collected and marketed the tobacco crops of their lesser neighbors; they sold these smaller families English manufactured goods from stores maintained on their home plantations; they provided legal

George Booth, the son of a
wealthy planter family in Glouces-
ter County, Virginia, was being
raised for mastery. The young
man's self-assured stance, the bow
and arrows, the dog at his feet
clutching the kill, the classical
busts of women flanking his figure,
and his family estate in the distance all suggest the gentry's concern for controlling the natural
and social worlds.

advice, lent money, speculated in land, dispensed medical services, and hired out
slaves to the whole county. Unlike the rough-hewn barons of the tobacco boom,
the gentry's profit did not depend on wringing work from poor whites. It hinged
instead on wringing work from black slaves while converting their white "inferiors" into modestly prosperous small planters and paying clients.

But the gentry wanted more than money: they wanted respect. The earliest
leaders of the Chesapeake, men of no breeding or learning, had been satisfied
with making their fortunes and then heading home for England. The merchants'
sons who succeeded them at the top of society, men with better educations and
higher social ambitions, planned to stay in the Chesapeake and to acquire not only
wealth, but also the dignity and status of gentlemen.

The gentry sought—and received—the deference of the colony's lesser inhabitants in a host of ways. In the realm of politics, they looked forward to election
days, when most men in the county came to cast their ballots, each in turn approaching the gentleman candidate of his choice. Some yeomen offered a brief,
flattering speech before awarding their vote, and the winning candidate afterward
treated his supporters to "bumbo," a potent rum punch. On militia days, when
every able-bodied man in the county over the age of 16 mobilized to perform
military drills, gentlemen officers led the exercises and then invited everyone to
their plantations for refreshments. On court days, defendants and plaintiffs testified respectfully before gentlemen justices of the peace, bedecked in wigs and
robes and seated on raised benches, and during recesses all participants repaired
to the neighboring tavern. And each Sabbath morning, when many in the county
came to worship at the Anglican chapel, families filed soberly into the church in
order of their social rank, with the gentlemen vestry heading the procession. The

little enclaves for public assembly that sprang up at the central crossroads of each county—courthouse and church, tavern and training field—served as theaters in which the new Chesapeake gentry dramatized their superiority and lesser men displayed their deference.

The plantation societies of Virginia and Maryland remained as unequal after 1700 as they had been a century earlier—indeed, even more so, for the conversion to slavery steadily deepened economic and social distinctions within the white population. Those who owned slaves enjoyed a decided edge over those who did not. And leading men still had little but disdain for poorer whites: the gentry regarded small planters and white servants alike as a lazy, stupid, and dissipated lot. But while extreme economic inequality persisted, social tension among whites eased. The naked domination of white servants and poorer planters by unscrupulous scoundrels was replaced with the exploitation of slaves by great planters who fancied themselves the equals of English gentlemen and the patriarchs of Chesapeake society.

As "fathers" to county and colony, the gentry cultivated reputations for responsibility. They served in political office not only to pursue private interest but also to advance the public good. And as "fathers" of their plantations and neighborhoods, the gentry kept a close watch over the public and private affairs of everyone, both black and white, bound and free. They decided whether to advance more credit or sue a lesser planter struggling with debt; whether to beat or administer medicine to a slave complaining of sickness; whether to indulge or discipline a white overseer or servant drinking to excess.

While maintaining strong ties to local society, the Chesapeake gentry also enjoyed a more cosmopolitan culture. Unlike their lesser neighbors, the great planter families were connected to a world wider than the county. As major marketers of tobacco, they hosted the visiting captains of English commercial vessels that sailed upriver from Chesapeake Bay to dock at their plantations. As representatives to the assembly or members of the governor's council, they convened to hear the latest news from England and to conduct public business in the tiny capitals of Williamsburg, Virginia, and Annapolis, Maryland. And as proud fathers, they sent their sons to England for a university education, rather than entrusting them to the Chesapeake's only institution of higher learning, the College of William and Mary, which was chartered in 1693.

The gentry prized such contacts with the greater Anglo-American world. They prized them so much that they were slow to recognize that their dependence on England might someday expose them to a dangerous contradiction. Their dilemma was that in addition to wealth and respect, the new Chesapeake gentry also wanted independence. "I am dependent upon no one but Providence," boasted William Byrd, one of Virginia's biggest planters.

He was wrong. True, Byrd and other members of the gentry dominated Chesapeake society and politics with little interference from England for decades after 1700. But planter power remained subject to check by authorities in the parent country—the monarchy and Parliament. Equally crucial, control over the tobacco trade, the basis of gentry prosperity and prestige, rested elsewhere. English and Scottish merchants supplied credit, banking, and marketing services, while Parliament determined imperial economic policy.

Gentlemen planters like Byrd were dependent in other ways as well. While the great gentry families created in their counties nearly self-sufficient home plantations, it was slave skill and slave labor that supported their operation. Black men and women grew the food, planted the tobacco, erected the buildings, tended the livestock, sewed the clothing, cobbled the shoes, and performed the host of other tasks that sustained gentry "self-sufficiency." And it was the clientage and acknowledgment of small planters that contributed to gentry profit and prestige.

The Chesapeake gentry, who so prized independence, also wanted wealth and respect, for which they had to depend on England, on lesser planters, and on their own slaves. That contradiction—of being independent-minded and dependent at the same time—would eventually undermine the stable social world over which the Chesapeake gentry held sway.

FROM THE CARIBBEAN TO THE CAROLINAS

During the same decade that the English invaded Powhatan's land, they began to colonize the Caribbean. A century earlier, Columbus had charted the route: ships picked up the trade winds off Madeira and the Canary Islands and headed west across the Atlantic. Dolphins and flying fish trailed in their wake, and paradise awaited at journey's end. There the surf broke over shores rimmed with white sand and jagged rocks; beaches rose sharply to coral terraces, then to broad plateaus or mountain peaks shrouded in rain forests and lush jungles. Wild hogs and cattle, turtles, fish of every sort, and figs and oranges, pomegranates, pineapples, papayas, guavas, melons, and yams promised a life of ease and plenty to all comers.

Paradise was lost to the Indians of the Caribbean, or at least to those few remaining alive. European diseases, combined with Spanish exploitation, had eliminated virtually all the natives of Hispaniola by the 1520s; over the next century those living in Cuba, Puerto Rico, and Jamaica would follow. Disease, spread by Spanish slaving expeditions, guaranteed the same fate for the Bahamas and the Lesser Antilles Islands. And the "paradise" that remained was filled with plants and animals that would have been strange to natives only a century earlier. The hogs and cattle, now wild, had been imported by Europeans, as had the figs, oranges, pomegranates and African yams. This ecological migration of flora and fauna would continue to transform the Caribbean, as well as the Americas, in the century to come.

Paradise was lost to the English as well. At first they came to the Caribbean intending not to colonize but to steal from the Spanish. Even after 1604 when some English settled on the islands, few intended to stay. Yet the English ended up not only establishing permanent plantation colonies in the West Indies, but also extending themselves from the Caribbean to a new colony on the North American mainland. Because of the strong West Indian influence, South Carolina developed a social order in some ways distinct from that of the Chesapeake or, indeed, any place in America north of paradise. But white society in early South Carolina moved toward stability and consolidation in a manner similar to that of Virginia and Maryland.

Paradise Lost Beyond the Line

The English had traded and battled with the Spanish in the Caribbean since the 1560s. During the decades of war with Spain after 1588 the islands served as bases for English privateers, staging grounds from which they conducted an illicit trade with Spanish settlements, sacked the coastal towns, and plundered silver ships bound for Seville. Until the 1630s English investors plowed more money into commerce and piracy in the Caribbean than any other overseas venture.

Even after the war with Spain ended in 1604, fighting in the Caribbean continued, for the West Indies lay "beyond the line," outside of the territorial claims ratified by European treaties. That left any nation with the courage to face the Spanish free to settle and trade in the Caribbean. And that left the Spanish free to wipe out any interlopers, if they had the strength. But they did not. Weakened by decades of warfare, Spain could not hold the West Indies; the Dutch drove a wedge into Caribbean trade routes, and the French and the English began to colonize the islands.

In the 40 years after 1604, some 30,000 immigrants from the British Isles planted crude frontier outposts on St. Kitts, Barbados, Nevis, Montserrat, and Antigua. The settlers—some free, many others indentured servants, and almost all young men—devoted themselves to working as little as possible, drinking as much as possible, and returning to England as soon as possible. They cultivated for export a poor quality of tobacco, which returned just enough to maintain straggling settlements of small farms.

Then, nearly overnight, sugar cultivation transformed the Caribbean. In the 1640s Barbados planters learned from the Dutch how to process sugar cane. The Dutch also supplied African slaves to work the cane fields and marketed the sugar for high prices in the Netherlands. Sugar plantations and slave labor rapidly spread to other English and French islands as Europeans developed an insatiable sweet tooth for the once scarce commodity. In meeting the demand, West Indian planters outstripped all of their competitors in the Mediterranean and Portuguese Brazil. Caribbean sugar made more money for England than the total volume of commodities exported by all of the mainland American colonies. Barbados, the largest and most prosperous island, became the jewel of the Caribbean, and the Caribbean, the diadem of England's overseas empire.

The biggest planters of Barbados and the other islands battened on the sugar boom. In the 50 years after 1640 a few hundred families claimed the best growing land and imported thousands of slaves; they amassed fabulous fortunes and dominated island politics. They housed and fed themselves with unbridled extravagance; they dressed with opulent vulgarity; they entertained with frantic gaiety. By 1680 Caribbean nabobs were the richest people in English America.

But even its great planters could not have confused the West Indies with paradise. Throughout the seventeenth century, yellow fever and other tropical diseases took a fearful toll, and island populations grew only because of immigration. A precarious food supply compounded the problem of disease: with every acre of land planted in sugar, West Indians had to import all that they consumed from Britain and North America. The scramble for land shunted small farmers, still the majority of the white population, onto tiny plots that supported bare subsistence.

The desperation of bound laborers posed another threat. After the conversion to sugar, black slaves gradually replaced white indentured servants in the cane fields. By the end of the seventeenth century a quarter of a million Africans had been transported to the English West Indies; a few decades later, blacks outnumbered whites by a ratio of four to one. Fear of servant mutinies and slave rebellions frayed the nerves of island masters. They tried to contain the danger by imposing harsh slave codes and inflicting brutal punishments on white and black laborers alike. But planters paid a high price for their security: they lived under a constant state of siege. One visitor to Barbados observed that whites fortified their homes with parapets from which they could pour scalding water on attacking servants and slaves. During the first century of settlement, seven major slave uprisings shook the English islands.

As more people, both white and black, squeezed onto the islands, some settlers looked for a way out. With all of the land in use, the Caribbean no longer offered opportunity to freed servants or even planters' sons. It was then that the West Indies started to shape the history of the American South.

The Founding of the Carolinas

At the end of England's civil war, Sir John Colleton, a royalist friend of Charles I, had gone into exile beyond the line in the Caribbean. After the restoration of the Stuarts in 1660 Colleton returned to England, hoping to obtain a charter for a mainland colony to be settled by the overflow from the Caribbean. In England Colleton met Sir William Berkeley, the newly appointed royal governor of Virginia, who knew that the inhabitants of his colony needed room to expand as well. Together the two men set their sights on the area south of Virginia and enlisted in their venture a number of other aristocratic, influential favorites of Charles II. By 1663 they had become joint proprietors of a place they called, in honor of the king, the Carolinas.

The northernmost part of that proprietary grant already harbored a few hardy souls from Virginia who had squatted around Albemarle Sound. The proprietors duly dispatched a governor and granted a representative assembly to that desolate region, and about 40 years later, in 1701, they set it off as a separate colony, North Carolina. The place quickly proved a disappointment. Lacking good harbors and navigable rivers to the interior, the colony had no convenient way of marketing its produce. Settlement aroused little enthusiasm among either the proprietors or any prospective inhabitants. North Carolina remained a small, poor colony, its sparse population engaged in general farming and the production of naval stores.

The southern portion of the Carolina grant held far more promise, especially in the eyes of one of its proprietors, Sir Anthony Ashley Cooper, earl of Shaftesbury. In 1669 he sponsored an expedition of a few hundred English and Barbadian immigrants, who planted the first permanent settlement in South Carolina. By 1680 the colonists, now numbering about 1000, established the center of economic, social, and political life at the confluence of two rivers called the Ashley and the Cooper after Sir Anthony and named the site itself Charleston after the king.

Cooper had big plans for his Carolina colony. Charleston's location at the hub of a network of river routes leading into the interior would permit full exploitation of the region's commercial potential. The favorable prospects for trade, coupled with the proprietors' provisions for liberal land grants and promises of complete religious toleration and representative government, would lure settlers in droves. These droves of settlers would enrich the proprietors by paying quitrents, a halfpenny per acre annually.

Such plans were big enough to satisfy most of the Carolina proprietors, who regarded their venture simply as land speculation. But Cooper, like Gilbert and Raleigh before him, and like the Calverts of Maryland, hoped to create an ideal

Daily Lives

FOOD/DRINK/DRUGS

A Taste for Sugar

It is said that shortly before his death in A.D. 735, the Venerable Bede, an English abbot, bequeathed a precious treasure to his brother monks. His legacy consisted of a cache of spices, including a little stock of sugar. What separated Bede's world, where sugar was counted a costly luxury, from twentieth-century Americans' world of ever-present sweetness was the discovery of America and the establishment of plantation economies in the Caribbean and Brazil.

Europeans acquired their first knowledge of sugar from the cultural exchange produced by an earlier surge of expansion—the Arab conquests in the Mediterranean, North Africa, and Spain during the seventh and eighth centuries. From then until the fourteenth century, Europe's merchants imported small quantities of sugar at great expense from Arab plantations, as well as from distant Persia and India, countries that had produced sugar since A.D. 500.

Throughout the Middle Ages and the early modern era, only the royal and the rich of Europe could indulge their desire for sugar, and even those privileged classes partook sparingly. Europeans classified sugar as a spice, like the equally scarce and exotic pepper, nutmeg, ginger, and saffron. Apothecaries doled out small doses as medicine for sore throats, stomach disorders, and infertility; it was also used as a remedy for the Black Death and tooth decay. The cooks of castle kitchens seasoned food and sauces with a pinch of sugar or sprinkled it on meat, fish, fowl, and fruit to preserve freshness—or to conceal rot. Only on great occasions did the confectioners of noble families dare to splurge, fashioning for courtly feasts and rituals great baked sugar sculptures of knights and kings, horses and apes, called "subtleties." Until the eighteenth century, those who consumed sugar as a medicine, spice, preservative, or decorative dessert were distinguished from the ranks of commoners as persons of consequence.

For the rest of Europe, life was not as sweet. While the rich and royal savored sugary treats, the diets of ordinary people

Once harvested, sugar cane in the West Indies was crushed, as in this sugar mill. The juice was collected and channeled to the sugar works, where it was concentrated through boiling and evaporation. This neat diagrammatic picture belies the harsh conditions of labor and high mortality slaves experienced: sweetness came at a steep price.

The Sugar Mill.

Daily Lives

ran to monotonous, meager starches. The staff of everyday life consisted of bread, peas, beans, and, in good years, a little milk, butter, and cheese. The occasional pig slaughtered, rabbit trapped, or fish caught supplied stray protein for the poor. Sugar, like the other trappings of power and status, only lordly families possessed.

That pattern of consumption started to change as Europeans turned to African slave labor to grow sugar for them. The sugar plantations established by Spain and Portugal in the fourteenth century on Madeira and the Canary Islands became steppingstones across the Atlantic to the creation of veritable sugar factories in the Caribbean colonies of England and France.

The impact of American sugar production on European diets manifested itself slowly but dramatically over a long span of time. By the sixteenth and seventeenth centuries, Europe's merchant classes could imitate elite patterns of eating by pouring sugar into pastries and puddings. And by the middle of the eighteenth century, an increasingly large and inexpensive supply from the Caribbean was making sugar essential to the poorest Europeans. Among England's laboring classes, another colonial import—Indian tea, laced heavily with sugar—emerged as the preferred complement to an otherwise cold supper of bread. Sweet tea and bread comprised the entire diet of those at the bottom of English society. Cheaper, warmer, and more stimulating than milk or beer (its principal competitors), sugared tea won the loyalty of England's mass market and ranked as the nonalcoholic beverage of national choice. By the nineteenth century, English working families were also combining sugar and starch by pouring treacle (molasses) over porridge and spreading jams or marmalades on their bread.

Europe and America affected each other in many ways, but diet figures among the more fundamental conditions of life altered by colonization. More than coffee, chocolate, rum, or tobacco—indeed, more than any of the other "drug foods" produced by the colonies except tea—sugar provided a major addition to the diet of the English and other Europeans. In Britain alone, consumption per capita rose about 400 percent over the eighteenth century as more and more people used more and more sugar.

Even though sugar changed gradually from a coveted luxury belonging only to the lordly to a basic foodstuff commanding a mass market, its association with power persisted. But by the eighteenth century, it was no longer the *consumption* of sugar that bestowed status. On the contrary, as sweeteners found their way into the barest cupboards, the rich and royal probably used less sugar than the poor and powerless. Instead, after 1700 it was the *production* of sugar that conferred power. Planters who grew it, merchants who shipped and sold it, industrialists who refined it, and statesmen who taxed it discovered in sugar sources of profit and distinction less perishable than the "subtleties" of noble banquets or the legacy of the Venerable Bede.

society in America. Cooper's utopia was one in which a few landed aristocrats and gentlemen would rule with the consent of many smaller propertyholders. With his personal secretary and physician, John Locke, Cooper drew up an intricate scheme of government, the Fundamental Constitutions. The design provided Carolina with a proprietary governor and a three-tiered order of hereditary nobility—proprietors, landgraves, and caciques. These nobles would constitute a Council of Lords and recommend all laws to a Parliament elected by lesser landowners.

The Fundamental Constitutions met the same fate as other grand manorial dreams for America. Frontier conditions defied all efforts to establish elaborate feudal domains. Instead, both of the Carolinas plunged into the political contention typical of other proprietary regimes like Maryland: assemblies resisted the great powers granted to the proprietary governors; ordinary settlers protested against paying quitrents claimed by the proprietors. Political unrest in North Carolina triggered three separate rebellions against proprietary rule between 1677 and 1711, with near-anarchy prevailing in intervening years. In South Carolina opposition to the proprietors gathered strength more slowly, but in the end it exploded with equal force.

Early Instability

Immigrants from Barbados, the most numerous among the early settlers, quickly assumed a dominant role in South Carolina politics, and, just as quickly, they voiced objections to proprietary power. To offset the influence of the Barbadians, most of whom were Anglican, the proprietors encouraged the migration of other groups—principally French Huguenots and English Presbyterians and Baptists—and awarded them political office. Their arrival in the colony only compounded tensions, cleaving South Carolinians into two camps with competing political and religious loyalties.

While both factions battled over proprietary rule, settlers dispersed along the coastal plain north and south of Charleston, establishing scattered plantations and searching for a profitable export. The first colonists raised grains and grazed cattle, foodstuffs that they regularly exported to the West Indies. South Carolinians also developed a large trade in deerskins and other animal pelts with coastal tribes like the Yamasee and the Creeks of the interior. More numerous than the Indians of the Chesapeake and even more deeply divided by old antagonisms, the Carolina tribes competed to become the favored clients of white traders. Southeastern Indian economies quickly became dependent on English guns, rum, and clothing.

Out of all these circumstances there developed another profitable sector of the early Carolina economy—Indian slavery. To satisfy their debts to white traders, Indians enslaved and sold to white buyers large numbers of men, women, and

---

THE CAROLINAS AND THE CARIBBEAN
The map underscores the geographic link between West Indian and Carolina settlements. Emigrants from Barbados dominated politics in early South Carolina, while Carolinians provided foodstuffs, grain, and cattle to the West Indies. As South Carolinians began growing rice, Caribbean slave ships found it an easy sail north and west to unload their cargoes in Charleston.

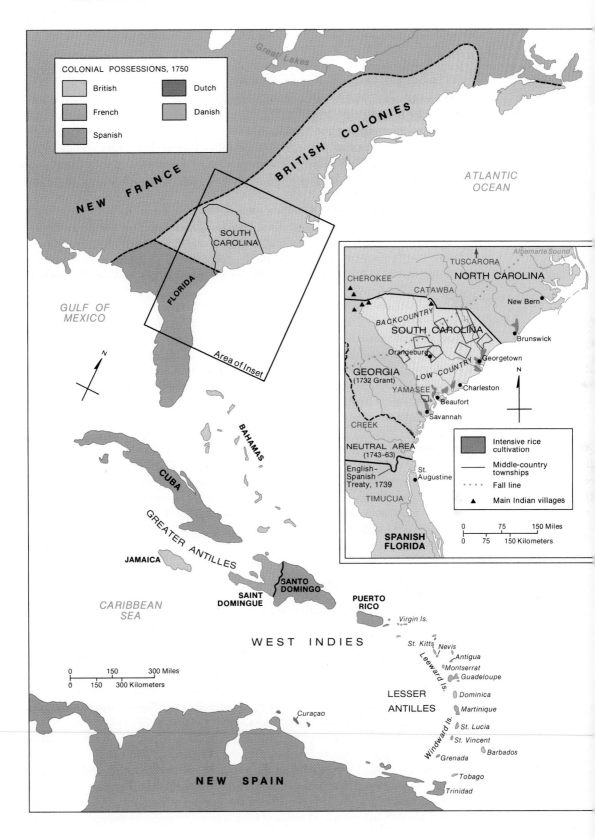

children from rival tribes taken in war. Although Carolinians exported many of the captives to New England and the West Indies, Indian slavery existed in the colony for a century.

Provisions, deerskins, and Indian slaves proved less lucrative for South Carolinians than rice. Paddy fields sprouted from the marshy lowlands around Charleston as rice became the colony's cash crop by the opening decades of the eighteenth century. Commanding good prices and being in constant demand in Europe, rice yielded less spectacular rewards than Caribbean sugar, but larger and more reliable returns than Chesapeake tobacco. It made South Carolina the richest colony and South Carolina rice planters the richest people on the mainland of North America.

Unfortunately, South Carolina's natural environment, so well suited for rice production, was less well suited for human habitation. For a century after the colony's initial settlement, appalling mortality rates prevented many planters from living long enough to appreciate their prosperity. The miasmic swamps of the lowland coast, perfect breeding grounds for mosquitoes and deadly microbes, defied survival and reproduction among men and women. Weakened by chronic malaria, settlers succumbed in epic numbers to yellow fever, smallpox, and respiratory infections. The white population grew slowly, through immigration rather than natural increase, and numbered a mere 10,000 by 1730.

The first generations of South Carolinians had little in common but the harsh conditions of frontier existence. Most colonists lived on isolated plantations, making only occasional trips to Charleston. Early deaths fragmented families and inhibited the development of native-born communities. Immigration after 1700 only intensified the colony's ethnic and religious diversity, adding Swiss and German Lutherans, Scots-Irish Presbyterians, Welsh Baptists, and Spanish Jews. Local institutions that might have enhanced order and a sense of solidarity remained extremely weak for more than a century after the first settlement. The colony's only courts were in Charleston; churches and clergymen of any denomination were scarce. On those rare occasions when early Carolinians came together, they gathered at Charleston to escape the pestilent air of their plantations, to sue each other for debt and to haggle over prices, or to fight over religious differences and proprietary politics.

White, Red, and Black: The Search for Order

By the opening decades of the eighteenth century, South Carolina, like the early Chesapeake, seemed slated for a future of strife. While internal weaknesses impaired social stability, external dangers threatened English settlement with extinction. The Spanish rattling their sabers in Florida, the French filtering into the Gulf region, and the pirates lurking along the North Carolina coast imperiled the security of settlement. But most menacing were the Indians, and in 1715 they struck. The Yamasee launched a series of carefully coordinated assaults that nearly pushed white Carolinians into the sea.

Once the allies and trading partners of white settlers, the Yamasee had subdued and enslaved smaller tribes like the Tuscarora. Then their own debt to Carolina merchants mounted, and the Yamasee realized that they might share the fate of the shattered Tuscarora. Allied with the Creeks, the Yamasee executed the most successful pan-Indian offensive in the eighteenth-century South. As Indians raided plantations within 30 miles of Charleston, refugees streamed into the city, and rumors flew throughout North America that Yamasee success would inspire assaults all along the coast. All that saved South Carolinians was their timely alliance with the Cherokee, another strong interior tribe. The Cherokee had also become dependent on English trading goods, and to meet their own needs, they were willing to make common cause with white Carolinians and to mount a counterattack against the Yamasee and the Creeks.

Although white settlement in South Carolina survived the Yamasee uprising, proprietary rule did not. As colonists reeled from the devastation of the Indian war, opposition mounted against the proprietors, who had done nothing to protect their vulnerable colony from the Spanish, the French, and the Indians. The proprietors were equally indifferent to the economic difficulties arising from the cost of defense. Military expenditures had saddled Carolinians with a depreciating currency, rising taxes, and growing indebtedness, but the proprietors had been unable to brake the colony's descent into economic crisis. Even Presbyterians, Baptists, and Huguenots, once the mainstay of proprietary support, had shifted their sympathies because they disapproved the proprietors' attempts to establish the Church of England as South Carolina's officially sanctioned religion.

Unified in their hatred of the proprietors yet divided over the route to economic recovery, planters and merchants waged a bitter struggle that nearly tore the colony apart during the 1720s. Mass meetings and mob actions so disrupted government that it all but ground to a halt during the latter years of that decade. Finally, in 1729, the Crown formally established royal government; the following year economic recovery did much to ease local tensions. Even more important in bringing greater political stability to South Carolina, whites in the colony recognized that unity within their ranks was essential, if they were to counter the Spanish in Florida and the French and their Indian allies to the southwest. Still more crucial for white Carolinians was maintaining a unified front against black Carolinians.

Black slaves brought by their Barbadian masters had been among the earliest inhabitants of South Carolina. During the first decades of settlement, frontier conditions and the scarcity of labor had forced masters to temper their treatment of slaves and to allow them greater freedom within bondage. Whites and blacks shared chores on small farms, and on isolated stockraising plantations, called "cowpens," black cowboys ranged freely over the countryside, chasing the cattle being fattened for market. The pioneer economy accorded blacks considerable autonomy and a variety of employments, and their familiarity with subtropical environments gave them an advantage over all whites except the Barbadian emigrants. White settlers could not have confused lowland South Carolina with the English countryside, but blacks found southern topography and climate remarkably similar to those of West Africa. Masters had much to learn from slaves who could identify useful plants and animals and suggest methods of cultivation and stockraising best suited to the environment. Black contributions to the defense of the colony also reinforced racial interdependence and muted white domination. From the first years of settlement to the Yamasee War, whenever the Spanish, the French, or the Indians threatened, blacks were enlisted in the militia.

After white Carolinians turned to rice as their cash crop, they depended on blacks no less—in fact, planters began to import slaves in larger numbers because of West African skill in rice cultivation. But whites now feared their dependence on blacks a great deal more. As early as 1708 blacks had become a majority in the colony, and by 1730 they outnumbered whites by two to one. Like Caribbean planters, white Carolinians instituted repressive slave codes that converted their colony into an armed camp and snuffed out the freedoms that blacks had enjoyed earlier.

The ever-present threat of revolt on the part of the black majority gave all white South Carolinians, whatever their religion, politics, or ethnic background, an incentive to cooperate among themselves. Despite the persistence of high death rates and cultural differences, despite the continuing isolation of planter families and the lack of strong local civil and religious institutions—against all odds, white South Carolinians prospered and political peace prevailed after 1730. Any course except harmony would have extracted too high a price.

In South Carolina there emerged a society both more opulent and more embattled than that of the Chesapeake. In its extremes of planter prosperity and black degradation, the surface splendor of Charleston and the actual vulnerability of the entire colony, South Carolina resembled the English Caribbean more closely than it did Virginia or Maryland. On the other hand, white Carolinians, like Chesapeake planters, tied their fortunes to a single staple crop, found themselves in debt to British merchants and financiers, prided themselves on being white and free, and held in contempt the enslaved black and Indian population. Even more than the Chesapeake's biggest planters, low country Carolina's leading men depended for their wealth on the very people whom they deeply feared—the black slaves who tended their rice fields and the Indians who supplied them with pelts and slaves.

The Founding of Georgia

After 1730 South Carolinians could take comfort not only from their new prosperity and new political harmony, but also from the founding of a new colony on their southern border. South Carolinians liked Georgia a great deal more than the Virginians had liked Maryland, for the colony formed a defensive buffer between British North America and Spanish Florida.

Enhancing the military security of South Carolina was only one reason for the founding of Georgia. More important to General James Oglethorpe and other idealistic English gentry was the aim of aiding the "worthy poor" by providing them with land, employment, and a new start in a better society. They projected a colony of hardworking small farmers who would produce silk and wine, sparing England the need to import both commodities from other countries. That dream seemed within reach when George II made Oglethorpe and his friends the trustees of the new colony in 1732, granting them a charter for 21 years, after which time Georgia would revert to royal control.

Unlike the Virginia Company's inadequate and haphazard provisions for Jamestown, Georgia's trustees exercised strict oversight in their colony. They selected with meticulous care those poor families who were to be transported "on charity," a group including not only English but Germans, Swiss, Austrians, Scots, and even a few Italians. The trustees did not, as legend has it, empty England's debtors' prisons to populate Georgia: they freed few debtors but recruited from every country in Europe paupers who seemed willing to work hard—and who professed Protestantism. They sponsored their resettlement and provided each with 50 acres of land, tools, and a year's worth of supplies. They also encouraged settlers who could pay their own way to immigrate, by allotting them larger tracts of land. Much to the trustees' consternation, that generous offer was

The Yuchi were neighbors of one of Georgia's early settlements, and one of the newly emigrated German colonists painted this watercolor of a Yuchi celebration. Judging from the guns hanging at the back of the shelter, these Indians were already trading with whites.

taken up not only by many hoped-for Protestants, but also by several hundred Ashkenazim (German Jews) and Sephardim (Spanish and Portuguese Jews), who established a thriving community in early Savannah.

The trustees enforced several regulations to ensure that Georgia became a small farmers' utopia. Rather than selling land the trustees simply gave it away, but none of the colony's settlers could receive more than 500 acres. The trustees also prohibited Georgians themselves from selling land or from willing their farms to female heirs, thus preventing daughters from combining their inheritances with their husbands' land to form large estates. As a further precaution against great plantations, the trustees outlawed slavery, not out of any concern for blacks but to cultivate habits of industry and to sustain equality among whites. The same considerations led the trustees to ban the importation and consumption of all hard liquor.

This design for a virtuous and egalitarian utopia for poor families was greeted with little enthusiasm by Georgians. They lobbied for the opening of a free market in land, claiming that many of the individual grants made by the trustees consisted only of sandy soil and pine trees, acreage not suited to farming. They also argued that the colony could never prosper until the trustees revoked their ban on slavery and followed the example of booming South Carolina. Since the trustees had provided for no elective assembly, settlers could express their discontent only by moving across the border—which many did during the early decades.

Careful planning and good intentions had not been enough to realize the trustees' utopian dreams. As mounting opposition to their policies threatened to depopulate the whole colony, the trustees caved in. They revoked their restrictions on land, slavery, and liquor a few years before the king assumed control of the colony in 1752. The death of the trustees' vision made Georgia a magnet for immigrants from Europe, the West Indies, and the other mainland North American colonies. Under royal control, Georgia continued to develop an ethnically and religiously diverse society, similar to that of South Carolina, and a comparable economy based on rice cultivation and the Indian trade.

THE SPANISH BORDERLANDS

When the English founded Jamestown, Spanish claims in North America extended from a feeble fort at St. Augustine, Florida, in the east to a western flank of garrison towns (*presidios*) and Catholic missions in New Mexico. During the seventeenth century, as Chesapeake planters developed a tobacco economy and Carolinians cleared their frontier, the Spanish sustained their initial colonizing efforts in the Southwest. Juan de Oñate founded Santa Fe in 1610; the Jesuit Eusebio Francisco Kino established missions in Arizona and Baja California later in the seventeenth century. As English colonial societies matured in the Southeast over the first half of the eighteenth century, the Spanish were establishing more missions and *presidios* at San Antonio and elsewhere in Texas. The spread of Spanish influence to California took place later, possibly because of a persistent misconception among Europeans that California was an island. It was not until the last half of the eighteenth century that Spanish soldiers and missionaries led by the Franciscan friar Junípero Serra established 20 communities along California's coastal plain.

Since the borderlands of the Southwest lacked the mineral wealth and the large native populations of Mexico and Peru, Spain took relatively little interest in that part of its empire and the region developed slowly. Cattle-raising became the basis of the borderlands' economy: mounted cowboys, *vaqueros*, rounded up the herds that roamed over the vast open ranges of scattered ranches, or *haciendas*. After the roundup, or *rodeo*, the cattle were slaughtered for sale to the south and to supply the soldiers of the *presidios*. The garrisons, in turn, protected Spanish settlements in the Southwest from the French, who infiltrated the region in the eighteenth century, and they protected Spanish claims in northern California from English and Russian traders.

The Spanish also attempted to strengthen their hold on the borderlands by incorporating native tribes into colonial society. The principal instrument for attaining that objective was the mission community. Each mission consisted of a quadrangle, dominated at the center by a large church. Homes, workshops, granaries, and stables clustered around the church. Spanish missionaries, chiefly members of the Franciscan and Dominican orders, gathered the Indians into the missions and taught them European agricultural techniques and crafts, as well as the Spanish language and Catholic doctrine. Native Indian men sometimes served mission villages as civil officials and judges, but always under the close scrutiny of the Catholic clergy.

Unlike the English, the Spanish projected a place in their colonies for the Indians, and they made sustained efforts to "civilize" and Christianize them. The role that the Spanish envisioned for the Indians in their settlements was a subservient one—docile servants for Spanish officers, pious agricultural laborers and artisans for Spanish missionaries and *hacendados* (ranchers), willing laborers for Spanish mine owners. The Indians might not have accepted such a fate without a determined struggle, but the deadly contagion of European diseases had devastated the small southwestern and Pacific coastal tribes.

The Indians still managed to mete out defiance. The Apache adopted the horses introduced by the Spanish and became expert cattle rustlers. Indians forced into the missions regularly ran away and occasionally organized major insurrections. The Yaqui uprising of 1740 in northwest Mexico left over 1000 Spanish dead. The Tepehuanes and the Tarahumaras of northern Mexico and the Hopi of the American Southwest also held out against Spanish rule for long periods.

The most sustained and successful Indian resistance was the Great Pueblo Revolt in 1680, which drove the Spanish out of New Mexico for more than a decade. Popé, an Indian spiritual leader in Taos, coordinated an uprising of several Pueblo tribes that vented the full force of their hatred of Spanish rule. They murdered priests, piled their bodies on altars, and set the churches on fire. They killed families in outlying *haciendas* and burned their Spanish-style houses to the ground. They even exterminated the livestock introduced by the Spanish. The attack wiped out one-fifth of the Spanish population of 2500 and sent survivors scurrying for refuge down Dead Man's Road to El Paso, Texas. After the Pueblo victory, one candid colonial official observed that "they are very happy without religious [Catholic missionaries] or Spaniards." Only after four attempts at reconquest and the outbreak of a plague among the Pueblos did the Spanish reassert their control over New Mexico.

The Spanish in the Southwest attempted to regulate every aspect of native life by drawing local tribes into missions. Here, Catholic priests have marshalled the Indian inhabitants of a mission in Carmel, California, to welcome a visiting European dignitary.

Empire . . . utopia . . . independence. . . . For more than a century after the founding of Jamestown, those dreams inspired the inhabitants of the Chesapeake, the Carolinas, and Georgia, the Caribbean, and the American Southwest. The regions served as staging grounds where kings and commoners, free and unfree, men and women, red, white, and black played out their hopes. Most met only disappointment and many, disaster.

The dream of an expanding empire faltered for the Spanish, who found no new El Dorado to the north. It failed the expectations of England's early Stuart monarchs, who found themselves embroiled in revolution at home. And the dream foundered fatally for Powhatan's successors, who were unable to resist both white diseases and land-hungry tobacco planters. So, too, the dream of a feudal utopia carried by the Calvert family into Maryland and by Cooper into the Carolinas sank like Gilbert's ship, buffeted by the frontier and finally engulfed by swells of opposition to lordly rule. The Georgian trustees could not transplant across the Atlantic their dream of a utopia for the poor, and the dream of a Spanish Catholic utopia brought by missionaries to the American Southwest dimmed with Indian resistance.

The dream of independence proved the most deceptive of all, especially for the inhabitants of England's colonies. Just a bare majority of the white servant immigrants to the Chesapeake survived to enjoy freedom, and not all of those earned freedom from hardship and insecurity. Not only in the Chesapeake but also in the Caribbean and the Carolinas, real independence eluded the English planters. Poorer people relied on richer people for land and leadership; the richest looked to England as the ultimate source of economic and political power. And everywhere in the American South and Southwest, white people's lingering dreams could be realized only through the labor of the least free members of colonial societies—Indians and blacks, whose own dreams of empire or independence had met an even more cruel defeat.

SIGNIFICANT EVENTS

late 1500s	Formation of Powhatan's confederacy
1603	James I becomes king of England; beginning of Stuart dynasty
1604	First English settlements in the Caribbean
1607	English settle Jamestown
1610	Founding of Santa Fe
1619	First blacks arrive in Virginia
1620s	Tobacco boom in Virginia
1622	White–Indian warfare in Virginia
1624	Virginia becomes a royal colony
1625	Charles I becomes king of England
1632	Calvert founds Maryland
1640s	The sugar boom begins in the Caribbean
1660	Parliament passes the first of the Navigation Acts
1669	First permanent settlement in South Carolina
1676	Bacon's Rebellion in Virginia
1680	Pueblo Revolt in New Mexico
1689	Coode's Rebellion in Maryland
ca. 1700	Rice boom begins in South Carolina
1715	Yamasee uprising in South Carolina
1732	Chartering of Georgia

3

The First Century of Settlement in the Colonial North

hey came to her one night while she slept. Into her dreams drifted a small island, and on the island were tall trees and living creatures, one of them wearing the fur of a white rabbit. When she told of her vision, no one took her seriously, not even the wise men among her people, shamans and conjurers whose business it was to interpret dreams. No one, that is, until two days later, when the island appeared to all, floating toward shore. On the island, as she had seen, were tall trees, and on their branches—bears. Or creatures that looked so much like bears that the men grabbed their weapons and raced to the beach, eager for a good hunt and hungry for a great feast sent by the gods. They were disappointed. The island was not an island at all, but a strange wooden ship planted with trees. And the bears were not bears at all but a strange sort of men whose bodies were covered with hair. Strangest among them, as she had somehow known, was a man dressed all in white. He commanded great respect among the bearlike men as their shaman, or "priest."

In that way, foretold in the dreams of a young woman, the Micmac Indians living along the north Atlantic coast in 1869 recounted their tribe's first meeting with whites more than two centuries earlier. Uncannily, the traditions of other northern tribes record similar dream portents of the European arrival: "large canoes with great white wings like those of a giant bird," filled with pale, bearded men bearing "long, sharp knives" and "long black tubes." Perhaps the dreamers gave shape in their sleep to stories heard from other tribes who had actually seen white strangers and ships. Or perhaps the Indians of the north Atlantic coast and Canada, long before they ever encountered Europeans, imagined them, just as medieval monks fantasized the Isles of the Blessed. The first whites seen by those tribes might have been English or Dutch, but probably, like the party met by the Micmacs, they were French, the most avid early adventurers in the northern reaches of the New World.

While Indians dreamed of ships and strangers, the dreams of some French explorers were more fabulous and far-fetched. At first, in the sixteenth century, the French dreamed of finding a northwest passage to Asia, a discovery that would bring their nation riches rivaling those of the Spanish and the Portuguese. That quest captivated Giovanni de Verrazzano, a Florentine navigator in the service of Francis I, who coasted the continent from North Carolina to Nova Scotia in 1524.

Mrs. Elizabeth Freake and Baby Mary, *by an anonymous New England artist (1670–1674). Unlike the South, where family life developed slowly, northern colonial society was based from the beginning on the family.*

The same prospect shimmered before the hopeful eyes of Jacques Cartier, whose quarry also included "Saguenay," a kingdom of fabulous riches reputed to exist in northern reaches just as surely as Prester John's principality thrived somewhere in the Muslim world. Instead of Saguenay, Cartier discovered the St. Lawrence River in 1535. The French attempted to settle at the present site of Quebec several years later, but, failing to find precious minerals, they confined their efforts to fishing and fur trading for the next 50 years. The French did not plant a permanent colony in North America until 1605, when a company of merchants established Port Royal in Acadia (Nova Scotia).

The French quickly realized the limits of Port Royal's location: the Appalachian highlands cut off Acadia from the rest of Canada. Eager for access to the vast North American hinterland, the French shifted the center of their settlement back to the St. Lawrence valley, where Samuel de Champlain founded Quebec in 1608. He planned to follow from Quebec the elaborate network of rivers and lakes leading into the interior, exploring the continent for the furs that it would yield and for the passage to the Pacific that it might hold. With the returns of the fur trade, he hoped to finance the immigration of settlers, who would build a strong colony for France in America.

A quarter of a century after the founding of Quebec, Canada had neither attracted a large contingent of colonists nor revealed a northwest passage. But the handful of settlers in New France—about 100 soldiers, traders, and missionaries—had established amicable relations with the local Indian tribes. There were the Algonquin and Montagnais of the St. Lawrence valley, skilled nomadic hunters and eager traders who rubbed the arms and torsos of the French in gleeful greeting. In the broad, fertile meadows and rich forests around Georgian Bay there was Huronia, a nation of expert fishermen, woodsmen, and hunters, 25,000 strong. More settled than the St. Lawrence tribes, the Huron lived in a score of semipermanent villages, longhouses enclosed by a palisade and surrounded by the corn fields that women tended.

The French formed profitable partnerships with these native peoples. Tribesmen hunted beaver, otter, and raccoon and then wore the pelts until they turned soft and supple enough to be converted into felt for fashionable European hats. Indians also supplied the skins of mink and marten, finery favored by European government officials and churchmen to display their rank. The French had a name for what New France had become by 1630—a *comptoir*, a storehouse for the skins of dead animals, not a proper colony.

That began to change when other Frenchmen with their own dreams took responsibility for Canada. Louis XIII and his chief minister, Cardinal Richelieu, hoped that American wealth might be the making of France and its monarchs. In the 1630s, they granted large tracts of land and a trading monopoly to a group of private investors, the Company of the Hundred Associates. The Associates brought a few thousand French farmers across the Atlantic, dispersed them over 200 miles of company lands along the St. Lawrence, and established upstream from Quebec the towns of Montreal and Trois-Rivières.

Religious zeal, as much as the hope of profit, spurred France to renew its commitment to colonization. The Catholic Church throughout Europe was basking in a revival of religious piety and confidence as a result of the Counterreformation, an effort to correct those abuses that had prompted the Protestant Reformation. Catholic reformers called for ending the sale of indulgences and church offices, improving the education of parish priests, enforcing celibacy among the clergy, and making the church more responsive to popular spiritual needs. To reclaim members lost to Protestantism and to arrest the spread of Lutheran and Calvinist "heresies," the Counterreformation launched an aggressive campaign of repression in Europe and missionary work abroad. In France, the Catholic majority persecuted Protestant Huguenots and targeted Canada as a field ripe for religious imperialism. The shock troops of the Counterreformation, not only in the Americas but also in India and Japan, were the Jesuits. One of several new religious orders founded during the Counterreformation, the Jesuits, whose order is the Society of Jesus, specialized in educating the sons of upper-class families and in spreading Catholic teachings to foreign lands. With Richelieu's encouragement, Jesuit missionaries streamed into Canada to assist other French settlers in bringing the Indians the "right" kind of Christianity.

In the Jesuits' dreams began France's formidable "responsibility" in America. The Indians of the north Atlantic coast shared with the southern tribes a supreme confidence in the superiority of their own cultures. The Jesuits, at least at first, seemed unlikely to shake that conviction. In Indian eyes, the Jesuits were a joke— men encumbered by their effeminate robes, deformed by their "very ugly" beards, and disqualified from physical pleasure by their vow of celibacy. The Jesuits were also a nuisance. Not content with establishing missions in French settlements and Indian villages, they undertook "flying" missions to the nomadic tribes, tagging along with Indian trappers. Once in the wilderness, the Jesuits were a disaster—tangling their legs as they tried to master snowshoes, trying for a first and last time to stand in a bark canoe, refusing to carry any weapons, and sponging off the Indians for food and shelter.

Some Indians gradually formed a better opinion of the French and their priests. The French were brave. Their traders, known as *coureurs du bois*, and their soldiers often adopted the Indian way of life and married Indian women. Even better, the French were still relatively few. Interested primarily in trade, they had no designs on Indian land. The Jesuits, too, won acceptance among some tribes. Their sincere lack of interest in Indian land, Indian furs, and Indian women made them a novelty among white men, while their relative immunity to the diseases that killed many Indians confirmed their claims to superior power. And once the Jesuits got the hang of native tongues, they exhibited a talent for smooth talk that the Indians, who prized able oratory, greatly admired. The Jesuits returned the admiration: unlike many of their countrymen, they saw the Indians not as savage brutes, but as innately civil and good.

Jesuit persistence slowly paid off. Missionaries reached every tribe within a radius of several hundred miles from Quebec. Christian factions formed in many tribes, especially those in which shamans or important families embraced the new religion. Part of the Jesuits' appeal was that they accepted and even appreciated much of Indian culture. The Jesuits never wavered in their determination to supplant Indian religions with Catholicism, but they did not try to convert the Indians into French men and women. If the natives chose to become Catholics in their religion, while retaining the rest of their culture, it was all to the good—a good deal better than their becoming English and Protestant.

THE FOUNDING OF NEW ENGLAND

The English regarded the northern part of North America as a place that only the mad French could endow with possibility. English fishermen who strayed from

Newfoundland to the coast of Acadia and New England carried home descriptions of the long, lonely stretch of coast, rockbound and rugged, washed by the waves of the slate gray Atlantic. Long winters of numbing cold and heavy snowfalls alternated with short summers of steamy heat. There were no minerals worthy of mining, no crops worthy of export, no large population of natives suitable for enslaving. To prospective investors and settlers the Chesapeake, with its temperate climate and long growing season, appeared a more likely spot.

In truth, of course, Indian tribes had successfully inhabited the territory that came to be called New England for at least 10,000 years. Each spring they set fires while the forests were still wet, to burn away the underbrush and make traveling and hunting easier. Such burnings encouraged the growth of deer and other game populations and gave early New England forests an almost parklike appearance. Elsewhere, Algonkian women tended fields of corn, beans, and pumpkins—not one crop per field as Europeans did, but mixed together in single patches, to help keep down weeds. By the beginning of the seventeenth century, perhaps 100,000 Algonkian-speaking men and women hunted, fished, and farmed in the area reaching from the Kennebec River in Maine to Cape Cod.

Until 1620, the English remained unimpressed with the region's potential. Increasingly, however, deteriorating conditions in the Old World began to produce the peculiarly intense blend of desperation and idealism that was required to settle an uninviting, unknown world. Just as the crusading militancy of the Catholic Counterreformation shaped the French colonization of Canada, the uncompromising zeal of John Calvin's followers inspired the first English settlements on the north Atlantic coast. Because of the Protestant Reformation, religious faith became more and more a matter of controversy during the seventeenth century. Compounding the religious crisis were mounting political tensions and continuing problems of unemployment and recession. Times were bad—so bad that the anticipation of worse times to come swept men and women to the shores of New England. The drama that unfolded there differed in almost every way from the ordeal taking place at the same time in the Chesapeake colonies and the Carolinas.

The Puritan Movement

The settlement of New England started with a king who chose his enemies unwisely. James I, shortly after succeeding Elizabeth I in 1603, vowed to "harry out" of his realm radical Protestant reformers. That angered the Puritans, the radicals whom James had in mind, and it angered some members of Parliament with Puritan sympathies. Next the king attempted to levy taxes without the consent of Parliament. That angered every member of Parliament and many other English besides. The anger of these two groups did not bode well for James' reign. In Parliament, he faced politically ambitious landowners and merchants, who were convinced that law was on their side. And in the Puritans he faced a determined band of zealots who were convinced that God was on their side.

The Puritans were less remarkable for what they believed than for the intensity with which they believed it. Like all Christians, Protestant and Catholic, the Puritans believed that God was all-knowing and all-powerful. And like all Calvinists, the Puritans emphasized that idea of divine sovereignty known as predestination. At the center of their thinking was the belief that God had determined the outcome of history, including the eternal fate of every human being, before the beginning of time. Logically, believing in predestination should have made men and women despairing or passive, resigned to their preordained fates. But psychologically, the effect on the Puritans was just the opposite: predestination was the engine driving their social and political activism.

Far from sinking into pessimism, the Puritans called predestination "a comfortable doctrine," because it provided their lives with meaning, order, and a clear sense of purpose. They had the assurance that a sovereign God was firmly directing the fate of individuals, nations, and all of creation. Far from lapsing into passivity, the Puritans strove to play their parts in the divine drama of history and to discover in their performances some evidence of personal salvation.

The divine plan, as the Puritans understood it, called for them to reform evils in both church and society along the lines laid down by John Calvin. What stood between them and the reformation of England was the state. Instead of promoting purity in the churches and order in society, the English government, it seemed to the Puritans, impeded the progress of reform. It tolerated drunkenness, theatergoing, gambling, extravagance, public swearing, and Sabbath-breaking. It condoned popular pastimes rooted in pagan custom and superstition—sports like bear-baiting and maypole-dancing and festivals like the celebration of Christmas and saints' days. What was worse, the state had not gone far enough in purifying the English church. The Puritans deplored the "corruptions" of Roman Catholicism that still infected the Church of England: the hierarchical offices of bishops and archbishops, ecclesiastical courts, elaborate ceremonies in which priests wore ornate vestments, making communion a kind of literal sacrifice, in which wine was turned into blood before an altar. Too many Anglican clergy were "dumb dogges" in Puritan eyes, too poorly educated to instruct the laity in the truths of Scripture or to deliver a decent sermon. Finally, the Church of England included everyone in the nation, saint and sinner alike. To the Puritans, belonging to a church was no birthright. They wished to limit church membership and the privileges of baptism and communion to the visibly godly.

The refusal of English monarchs to take stronger measures to reform church and society turned the Puritans into their outspoken critics. Elizabeth I had tolerated this opposition, but James I would not endure it and intended to rid England of these malcontents. With some of the Puritans, known as the Separatists, he seemed to succeed.

The Pilgrim Settlement at Plymouth Colony

The Separatists were Puritans who concluded that the Church of England was too corrupt to be reformed from within. They abandoned Anglican worship and met secretly in small congregations of like-minded men and women. From their first appearance in England during the 1570s, the Separatists suffered persecution from the government—fines, imprisonment, and in a few cases, execution. Always a tiny minority within the Puritan movement, the Separatists were pious people from humble backgrounds, craftworkers and farmers without the resources or the numbers or the inclination to challenge the state. By 1608 one Separatist congregation, a group at Scrooby, had become so dismayed by the depravity of Stuart England that they migrated to Holland.

The move to Holland proved to be just the first of their trials. Although the Dutch government permitted complete freedom of religion, the Separatists were disappointed by low-paying jobs, alarmed when their children adopted Dutch customs, and distressed by desertions from their own ranks to other religions.

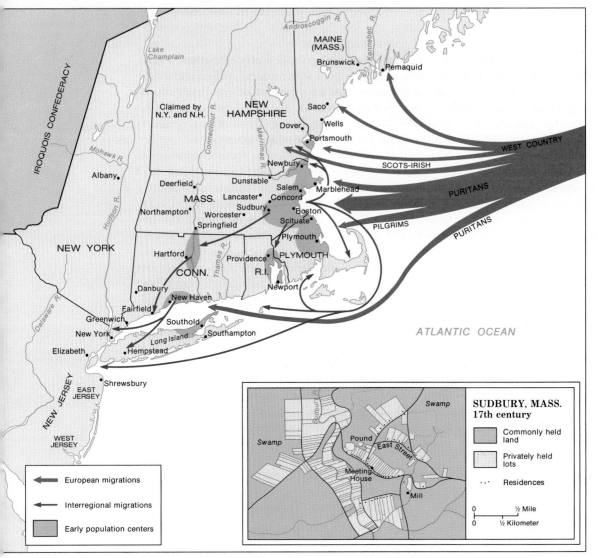

EARLY NEW ENGLAND
Despite some variety among emigrants to New England, the region remained relatively
homogenous and stable, with everyday life centered in small towns like Sudbury (located to
the west of Boston). Most families lived close to one another in houses clustered around the
meetinghouse, in contrast to the decentralized plantations of the South. The privately held
farm lots were mixed together as well, so that neighbors worked and lived in close contact
with each other.

They wanted a place where their pure churches and communities could flourish,
free of hardship, corruption, distraction, and competition. Some decided to move
to Virginia.

What fate would have greeted the gentle, unworldly Separatists of Holland if
they had actually settled in the Chesapeake during the decade of the tobacco
boom can only be imagined. But a series of mistakes—including an error in chart-

ing the course of their ship, the *Mayflower*—landed the little band in New England instead. In November 1620, some 88 Separatist "Pilgrims," sick with scurvy, weakened by malnutrition, and shaken by a shipboard mutiny, disembarked at a place that they called Plymouth on the coast of present-day southeastern Massachusetts. Neither the site nor the season seemed auspicious, as one of their leaders, William Bradford, later remembered:

> For summer being done, all things stand upon them with a weatherbeaten face, and the whole country, full of woods and thickets represented a savage hue. If they looked behind them, there was the mighty ocean which they had passed and was now as a main bar and gulf to separate them from all the civil parts of the world.

For some, the shock was too great. Dorothy Bradford, William's wife, is said to have fallen overboard from the *Mayflower* as it lay anchored off Plymouth. It is more likely that she jumped to her death.

Few Pilgrims could have foreseen founding the first permanent white settlement in New England, and many did not live long enough to enjoy the distinction. The season was far too late to plant crops, and the colonists had failed to bring an adequate supply of food with them. By the spring of 1621, half of the immigrants had died. Plans for attaining self-sufficiency through hunting and fishing proved impractical too, for the Separatists knew little of firearms and even less about fish. Their efforts to establish a summer fishery on Cape Ann ended in an inglorious retreat after a company of English fishermen laid claim to the same spot with muskets leveled. English merchants who had financed the *Mayflower* voyage failed to send supplies to the struggling colony.

Plymouth might have become another doomed colony if the Pilgrims had not received better treatment from native inhabitants than they did from their English backers. Samoset and Squanto, two Indians who had learned to speak English from visiting fishermen, introduced the settlers to native strains of corn and arranged a treaty between the Pilgrims and the region's main tribe, the Wampanoags, who sought the English as allies against their enemies, the Narragansetts. Peace with them prevailed for 50 years, enabling the white settlers of Plymouth to survive.

The Pilgrims also set up a government for their colony, the basis of which was the Mayflower Compact. That agreement provided for a governor and several assistants to advise him, all to be elected annually by Plymouth's adult males. The Plymouth settlers had no clear legal sanction for their claim to land or their government, for they had neither a royal charter nor approval from the Crown. But English authorities, distracted by more pressing problems, left the tiny colony of farmers alone.

The Puritan Settlement at Massachusetts Bay

Among the Crown's distractions were other Puritans—the Presbyterians and the Congregationalists—who were still striving to reform church and society in England. But the 1620s brought them only fresh discouragements. In 1625 Charles I inherited his father's throne and all of his enemies in Parliament and among the Puritans. Charles dealt with political dissent by dissolving Parliament in 1629. He dealt with religious dissent by supporting a group of archconservative Anglicans led by Archbishop William Laud, proponents of stringent measures for suppressing Puritanism. Laud purged England's parishes of ministers with Puritan leanings and reintroduced Roman Catholic rituals and practices into the Church of England.

Increased persecution appeared to the Puritans a fearful portent that England was slipping toward the edge of apocalypse. Many believed that great catastrophes were at hand which would usher in the second coming of Jesus Christ. As their disillusionment deepened into desperation, some concluded that it might be more prudent to cross the Atlantic—then press for reform and await Christ's return.

The Puritans who became interested in American colonization came from the ranks of the Congregationalists. They shared with the Separatists in Old and New England a commitment to Calvinism and a common view of church government. Both groups believed that each congregation should be self-governing and independent of any higher authority. But the Congregationalists differed from the Separatists in their desire to remain within the Church of England, as well as in their social background and temperament.

It was a group of energetic, experienced, and established Congregationalist merchants, landed gentlemen, and lawyers who organized the Massachusetts Bay Company in 1629. Alienated from their own society, these able Puritan leaders aimed to build a better society in America, an example to the rest of the world. Unlike the Separatists, they were imbued with a strong sense of mission and destiny; they claimed that they were not abandoning the English church but regrouping for another assault on corruption from across the Atlantic. They began by organizing a mass exodus to Massachusetts Bay that had the precision and efficiency of a military maneuver and the aggressive, martial spirit of a crusade. One of the immigrants, Edward Johnson, described his fellows as "Soldiers of Jesus Christ," who "for England's sake . . . are going from England to pray without ceasing for England."

The Massachusetts Bay Company first dispatched advance parties of several hundred settlers, who established the town of Salem as a Puritan foothold on the coast well north of Plymouth. Then the company procured a royal charter confirming its title to most of present-day Massachusetts and New Hampshire and securing its rights to govern the region. That accomplished, the stockholders promptly voted to transfer the company to Massachusetts Bay and elected as their first governor John Winthrop, a pious, tough-minded Puritan lawyer and landed gentleman. Winthrop sailed from England in 1630, taking with him a dozen other company stockholders and a fleet of men and women committed to the Puritan cause. "We shall be as a city on a hill," Winthrop declared during the crossing to his fellow passengers on the ship *Arbella*. The Winthrop fleet steered a straight course for Salem, landing on the spot as spring planting season began.

To guarantee that the settlers would govern themselves without interference from London, Winthrop carried across the Atlantic the royal charter of the Massachusetts Bay Company. Leaders of the migration believed that the charter supplied them with an unimpeachable title to settle and to rule, and they made the most of their opportunity. Once established in the Bay Colony, Winthrop and the other stockholders transformed the charter for a mere trading company into the framework of government for a colony. The company's governor became the

John Winthrop, the first governor of the Massachusetts Bay Colony.

colony's chief executive and the company's other officers, the governor's assistants. The charter provided for annual elections of the governor and his assistants by company stockholders, the freemen. But to create a broad base of support for the new government, Winthrop and his assistants expanded the freemanship in 1631 to include every adult male church member. Being committed to Puritanism rather than owning company stock became the requirement for political participation. "The way of God hath alwayes beene to gather his churches out of the world," Winthrop remarked; "Now the world, or civill state, must be raised out of the churches."

The governor, his assistants, and the freemen together comprised the General Court of the colony, which passed all laws, levied taxes, established courts, and made war and peace. In 1634 the whole body of the freemen stopped meeting and instead each town elected representatives or deputies to the General Court. Ten years later, the deputies constituted themselves as the lower house of the Bay Colony legislature, and the assistants formed the upper house. By refashioning a company charter into a civil constitution, Massachusetts Bay Puritans gained full control of the government under which they would live. In the New World they fulfilled their dream of shaping society, church, and state to their liking.

NEW ENGLAND COMMUNITIES

Contrary to all expectations, New England proved more hospitable to the English than did the Chesapeake. The character of the initial migration itself gave New England settlers an advantage, for most arrived not as young, single, indentured servants, but in family groups. The heads of New England's first households were typically free men—farmers, artisans, and merchants, most of whom were skilled and literate. Since husbands usually migrated with their wives and children, the ratio of three men to two women within the population was fairly evenly balanced at the outset. There was never in New England a large number of young, single men like those who contributed to the volatility of Virginia society.

Most immigrants, some 21,000, came in a cluster between 1630 and 1642. Thereafter the flow of new arrivals tapered off because of the outbreak of the English Civil War. The concentrated settlement of New England within the short span of 12 years meant that these colonies, unlike the Chesapeake, escaped the strain of absorbing a steady stream of newcomers throughout the seventeenth century. Rapid settlement also made for social solidarity, because immigrants shared a common set of experiences and ideals. The "Great Migration" of 1630 to 1642 was a movement of Puritans unified by persecution and a strong sense of religious mission—the desire to create a purer church and to establish an ordered society modeled on Scripture.

New England Families

Like-minded Puritan emigrants and their progeny lived long and prospered in New England, and their very longevity fostered a sense of continuity. New Englanders lived nearly twice as long as Virginians and about 10 years longer than English men and women. The first generation of colonists lived to an average age

Daily Lives

PUBLIC SPACE/PRIVATE SPACE

The Rituals of Mourning

Two hours past midnight on a Boston Sabbath, Samuel Sewall awoke to the cries of his eldest daughter, Hannah, and rushed downstairs to her bedside. The 44-year-old woman was in a "restless" state and, from the looks of the sober-faced attending relatives, near death. Sewall roused his wife, Hannah's stepmother, and sent for his son, the Reverend Joseph Sewall, and other neighborhood clergy, who joined the family, watching and reading psalms at the deathbed. Later that morning he pinned a note to the door of the Old South meetinghouse: "Prayers are desired for Hannah Sewall as drawing Near her end." Then he attended Sabbath services, where the minister led the prayers for the dying woman. When he returned from public worship, Sewall found his daughter dead.

Like most New Englanders, Hannah Sewall died at home, and there her body remained for a period of private mourning. In her case, this period of necessity would be short, for both the sweltering mid-August heat and the nature of her illness dictated that burial take place quickly, within two days. By Monday Hannah lay in a coffin in the "best room" of her father's house; near the windows "opened for coolness," Sewall's slave, a man named "Boston," kept vigil over the corpse through the night. "Her pleasant Countenance was very Refreshing to me," Sewall noted in his diary. "I hope God had delivered her from her fears."

Samuel Sewall was practiced at pious resignation to divine will, for death had stopped often at his household, more frequently than at most New Englanders'. By the time of Hannah's death, he had buried

On the elaborate headstone of John Foster (d. 1681) Father Time attempts to stay the hand of a skeletal Death from extinguishing the candle of earthly life; the sun of redemption rises above both figures, promising eternal life to the godly. The Foster headstone contains more biographical allusions than most other early markers. The Latin inscription below, composed by Increase Mather, a Boston minister, celebrates Foster's career as an astronomer and publisher of almanacs. It reads: "Living thou studiest the stars; dying, mayest thou, Foster, I pray, mount the skies and learn to measure the highest heaven."

two wives; of his 16 children, 7 had died in infancy and another was stillborn. Hannah's death might also have come as a relief: she had "languished" for a long time and possibly suffered from ill health all her life, for she died, at age 44, unmarried. But however familiar death was to his family or however welcome Hannah's release from suffering, Sewall deeply felt his loss. Grief and distraction intruded as he listed in his diary his last efforts to comfort his

Daily Lives

daughter and to ready her corpse for burial: "I do not remember the exact order of these things," he admitted.

To master his sorrow, Sewall threw himself into preparations for Hannah's funeral, the ritual of public mourning. By 1724, the year of her death, New England funerals had become elaborate and costly affairs, especially those for members of leading families like the Sewalls. They began the public ritual of death by sending a pair of gloves, a symbol of fellowship, to each person invited to the funeral. They also presented relatives, friends, and local clergy with mourning rings, bands wrought of gold and engraved or enameled with death's heads (winged skulls), coffins, and skeletons. On Tuesday, August 18, the Sewall family, outfitted in elegant black mourning clothes, were joined by other relatives and friends in a solemn procession behind Hannah's coffin, to which were pinned elegies composed by Boston clergy. Although New England funerals were civil ceremonies, one of the ministers would offer a prayer before the burial, once the pallbearers and the horse-drawn hearse had led the assembly to a nearby graveyard.

To those attending Hannah Sewall's burial, cemeteries, although public property, were steeped in spiritual significance. Puritans regarded the graveyard not as a final resting place but rather as a way station between this world and the next. Like other Christians, they viewed death as both destructive and regenerative: the dissolution of the body but, for the elect, the final stage of the spiritual resurrection that had begun in the conversion experience. The shape of the gravestones suggested a doorway, a passage from earthly life to eternal afterlife; the most popular motifs of gravestone art—the winged skull of death's head and the winged head of a cherub—represented the ascent of the soul to heaven. Less common images of peacocks, flowering vines, and hearts also bespoke immortality, as did more elaborate allegorical designs: skeletons grasping scythes and seated on winged hourglasses, representing death's reign over time. Above them might stand a giant sun, signifying Christ's ultimate victory over the natural process of decay.

Such gravestones, carved by local stonecutters and often erected weeks and sometimes years after burial had taken place, served many purposes. Epitaphs recorded the age, date of death, and, occasionally, more detailed biographical information, philosophical reflection, or moral exhortation. Although most epitaphs expressed solemn sentiments ("READER/ REMEMBER DEATH"), a few adopted a lighter tone. Consider, for example, the punning inscription for one Captain Hezekiah Stone:

Beneath this Stone Death's Prisoner Lies
The Stone Shall move the Prisoner Rise.

Like the other rituals surrounding the Puritan way of death, both private and public, gravestones helped console friends and relatives to the loss of loved ones and remind the living of their own mortality. At the same time, these memorials served as reminders for future generations, inscribing on New England's landscape the lives and deaths of individuals and, indeed, whole families, who had sustained the Puritan mission in the New World.

of 70, and nearly one-fifth survived into their eighties. Rates of mortality among infants and children in New England were also significantly lower than those in the Chesapeake and England. Ninety percent of all children reached adulthood, and most young people grew up knowing both of their parents and even their grandparents. While the premature deaths of parents splintered Chesapeake families, two adult generations were often on hand to encourage order within New England households.

The probable cause of New Englanders' longer lives was their less temperate but more healthful northern climate. They also managed to escape infection from the epidemics that devastated both the Chesapeake and seventeenth-century Europe. Whatever the cause of longevity, the consequence for New England was a dynamic rate of population growth. While the populations of Europe and the Chesapeake barely reproduced themselves, the number of New Englanders doubled about every 27 years. Families were large, the typical household consisting of seven or eight children who survived to maturity. Along with low mortality rates, a more balanced sex ratio contributed to the brisk rate of reproduction. Because there were roughly equal numbers of men and women in the population, most New Englanders could and did marry. By 1700, New England and the Chesapeake each had populations of approximately 100,000. But whereas the southern population grew because of continuing immigration, New England's expanded through natural increase.

Local Life in Early New England

As immigrants arrived in the Bay Colony after 1630, they spread out rapidly from the first centers of settlement at Salem, Charlestown, and Boston, establishing an arc of small villages around the Massachusetts Bay. Within a decade settlers pressed into Connecticut, Rhode Island, and New Hampshire. Connecticut and Rhode Island received separate charters from Charles II in the 1660s, securing to their inhabitants title to land and power to govern. But as early as the 1640s, Massachusetts successfully staked its claim to New Hampshire, which did not become a separate colony until 1679; by 1658 the handful of families settled along the coast of present-day Maine had also accepted the Massachusetts Bay Colony's authority.

The families who spread throughout the New England landscape proceeded in an orderly way that laid the groundwork for a coherent organization of local life. Unlike the Virginians, who scattered across the Chesapeake to isolated plantations, most New Englanders distributed themselves into tightly knit communities that resembled the places that they had left behind in England. Often families who had left the same village or congregation back in England formed a community together in the New World. They petitioned the colony government for a tract of land in order to establish a town. All prospective adult townsmen initially owned in common this free grant of land, along with the right to set up a local government.

Townsmen gradually parceled out among themselves the land granted by the colony, with each family receiving a lot for a house, lying at the center of the village, along with farmland in adjacent fields. The distribution of land was remarkably even, the typical family holding about 150 acres. But farmers left much of their acreage uncultivated, a legacy for future generations, for most had only the labor of their own families to develop their farms. While the early Chesapeake abounded with discontented servants, tenant farmers, and landless men, almost every adult male in rural New England owned property.

The economy that supported most of New England's families and towns offered few chances for anyone to get rich. By diligent cultivation, farmers could coax enough yield from the land to feed their families, but the climate and soil would not support the production of a cash crop like tobacco, rice, or sugar. Lacking the resources to sustain a profitable commercial agriculture, New England farmers also lacked the Chesapeake planters' incentive to import shiploads of servants and slaves or to create large plantations.

The farmers who labored for subsistence in the New England countryside established strong institutions that contributed to the coherence of social life. First and foremost was the family, described by the Puritans as a "little commonwealth," a government in miniature that was the basis of social and civil order. The strong patriarchal fathers who governed the "little commonwealth" of the Puritan family exacted strict obedience from all of their children, even after they had reached maturity.

To foster local order New Englanders created, quite deliberately, another important institution—the village leadership. Few members of the English upper class migrated to New England, but the Puritan colonists, like most other seventeenth-century English, believed firmly in the importance of hierarchy. They thought that a measure of social inequality was natural, inevitable, and essential to a stable society. Because early New Englanders desired to be less equal than they were, each town favored certain families in its land distribution, awarding them a little more than the average allotment. The heads of these favored families were often ministers or other men who had received university degrees. Or they were millers or other artisans who possessed some skill of unusual service to the community. Or they were men who had enjoyed some wealth and standing back in England. They became the "town fathers" and took the lead in directing local affairs. The rest of the community generally accepted their authority, for all agreed that some men were more suited to rule than others. The trust that most New Englanders accorded their leaders had no counterpart in the Chesapeake experience, where the credibility of the early elite was constantly challenged.

Equally important in preserving local order was the church. Unlike Chesapeake immigrants, New Englanders arrived in the colonies with a full supply of ministers. Settlers formed churches as quickly as they founded towns. In the churches, the Puritans realized their ideal form of ecclesiastical organization—the independent, self-governing congregation. Each village church conducted its own affairs, hiring and dismissing ministers, admitting and disciplining members. The autonomy of each congregation guaranteed that local churches never clashed with higher religious authorities, for none existed. Bishops and synods had been left behind in the Old World. And membership in the churches was voluntary: men and women joined Congregational churches by consent, not compulsion.

But membership in New England churches was not available to anyone for the asking. Candidates for membership had to submit to a rigorous scrutiny to satisfy the church that they had experienced "conversion." The Puritans understood conversion to mean a turning of the heart and soul toward God, an inward transformation that was reflected by an outwardly godly and disciplined life. Believers who had some hope that they had experienced this inner spiritual rebirth and gained admission to church membership on that basis were called "visible saints."

Most early New Englanders sought and received church membership, a status that entitled them to receive communion and to have their children baptized. Widespread membership enabled the churches to oversee public morality and to discipline backsliders for a variety of offenses ranging from drunkenness to adultery. Although the churches of New England could not inflict corporal punishment on their members or fine them, as church courts did in England, Puritan churches could and did censure and excommunicate wayward members for misbehavior. And everywhere in New England except Rhode Island, civil laws obliged every settler to attend worship services on the Sabbath and every taxpayer to contribute to the support of the Puritan clergy.

Another feature of New England's religious life spared its clergy from becoming the targets of criticism and controversy. Although the Congregational churches exerted enormous informal influence over public and private life alike, they held no formal, legal power. Puritan ministers did not serve as officers in the civil government, and the Congregational churches owned no property. Even the meetinghouse was the property of the town, not the congregation. The separation between church and state in New England was not complete, but it had progressed further there than in most nations of the Old World. Catholic and Anglican church officials wielded real temporal power in European states, and the churches held extensive tracts of land.

Finally, there was the town meeting, the basis of local self-government. In every New England village, all white adult male inhabitants gathered regularly at the meetinghouse to decide matters of local importance, and virtually all of them could vote for town officials. The town fathers generally took the lead at these meetings, presenting an agenda of public business and making recommendations. But decisions were reached by the unanimous agreement of the entire body of townsmen. Consensus was a practical necessity, because the town fathers had no way to enforce unpopular decisions, no means to bring into line a reluctant majority or even a recalcitrant minority.

Colony governments in early New England also evolved into representative and responsive political institutions. Typically the central government of each colony, like the General Court of Massachusetts Bay, consisted of a governor and a bicameral legislature, including an upper house, or council, and a lower house, or assembly. These officials were elected annually by the freemen—white adult males entitled to vote in colony elections. Voting qualifications for colony elections varied in New England but the number of men entitled to vote comprised a much broader segment of society than in seventeenth-century England. Many qualified voters, however, did not bother to exercise their right to elect colony officials. For most ordinary farmers, town elections and local affairs loomed much larger than colony politics. And New England's small, inexpensive colony governments intruded little into the daily lives of most settlers. The Bay Colony's General Court, like its counterparts in other New England colonies, concerned itself mainly with parceling out land to new towns, making war and peace with native peoples, and mediating relations with England.

Deviance and Dissent

Although most aspects of life in early New England fostered order, its inhabitants had not fashioned wholly harmonious communities. The Puritans sometimes disagreed among themselves, and there were some people in New England who found the Puritans themselves most disagreeable.

Along the edges of New England settlement, several communities departed dramatically from typical patterns of Puritan life—and their inhabitants had no desire to conform. One such outpost was Marblehead, a fishing port north of Boston on the Massachusetts coast. Marbleheaders were a volatile mixture of immigrant fisherfolk from England's West Country, Wales, Ireland, and the French-speaking Isle of Jersey in the English Channel. Most eked out a spare subsistence as suppliers and employees of Boston merchants, who managed Marblehead's fishery and pocketed most of its profits. Fishermen and mariners competed fiercely for credit and customers in Boston—and for the company of the few women in Marblehead. They sought solace for the shortage of both at the town's many taverns, which inspired frequent street brawls and drunken cavorting. Since most Marbleheaders had come to New England mainly to catch fish, they had little commitment to creating a community life of any kind, let alone the Puritan variety. Local government remained weak for most of the seventeenth century, and inhabitants managed to avoid founding a local church for 50 years.

Similar problems blighted Springfield in western Massachusetts, a frontier settlement in the fertile Connecticut River valley. A single powerful family, the Pynchons, founded Springfield as a center of the fur trade and later developed a thriving commercial agriculture. The Pynchon family recruited most of Springfield's inhabitants—a motley assortment of Scottish convicts and English indentured servants—for their labor rather than their lives of piety and restraint.

Raucous, chaotic "company towns" like Marblehead and Springfield had more in common with the settlements of the early Chesapeake than with the rest of New England. Financed by profit-minded merchants, these places suffered from severe social disarray because of the great gulf between rich and poor and the exploitation of labor. Puritan Massachusetts tolerated these towns because their inhabitants produced what few commodities New England could trade to the rest of the world. Outside of the Connecticut River valley, New England's stony soil yielded just enough to feed farming families. But Marblehead's abundant supplies of fish found a ready market in Catholic Spain and Portugal and among the slaves of English sugar planters in the West Indies. Similarly, the surplus of Springfield's grain and livestock commanded a good price among Caribbean planters, and English consumers coveted furs. In exchange, New Englanders acquired wine, sugar, molasses, textiles, and iron goods—commodities that they needed but could not produce.

Still, less-than-Puritan places like Marblehead and Springfield were few and far between. A more common cause of conflict in early New England than ethnic diversity and economic inequality was the tension that resulted when immigrants of different English backgrounds tried to live together. Variations in English local customs produced disagreement among townsmen about the proper way of distributing land or farming it, regulating livestock, or allocating rights to marshes and woodlands.

As the first generation passed from the scene, disagreements of this sort died and other quarrels arose to take their place. The typical town conflict of the late seventeenth century was triggered by the movement of households. As local population expanded and the centers of towns became overcrowded, many young families relocated in outlying districts, village "suburbs." Since moving made churches and schools at the center of towns too distant, the "outlivers" petitioned the town meeting to create convenient institutions of their own or to split off as a separate town. Reluctant to lose taxpayers, the town meeting often resisted, and a running battle between the two factions resulted.

These conflicts within New England towns were little more than tempests in a teapot. Most discord amounted to little more than petty quarrels among members of a community who agreed on fundamentals. A far more serious source of conflict in early New England was religion.

Heresy

While most of the men and women who settled in New England called themselves Puritans, that name did not imply a single, uniform code of belief and practice. Instead, Puritanism encompassed a spectrum of religious persuasions, all aimed at carrying out the impulse of the Protestant Reformation and the ideas of John Calvin. The Puritan Separatists in Plymouth Colony, for example, believed that religious purity required renouncing the Church of England, while the Bay Colony's Puritans clung to the hope of reforming the Anglican Church from within. The Puritans of the Bay Colony even differed among themselves about how to organize church life. Because individual Congregational churches were free to go their own way, each had its own distinctive way of admitting members, conducting divine worship, or hiring a minister. Over time, the diversity among Congregational churches inevitably increased. Many adopted more liberal standards for determining who might be admitted, be baptized, or take communion.

During the earliest years of settlement, religious diversity led to the founding of new colonies in New England. In 1636 Thomas Hooker, the minister of Cambridge, Massachusetts, led part of his congregation to Connecticut, where they established the first English settlement. Somewhat more liberal than other Bay Puritans, Hooker favored less stringent standards for church membership. He also opposed the Bay's policy of restricting its civil franchise to church members. By contrast, New Haven, a separate colony until its incorporation by Connecticut in 1662, started in 1638 as the preserve of strict Puritans who found Massachusetts a little too liberal. Massachusetts recognized its southern neighbors, including Separatist Plymouth, as colonies within the Puritan fold, respectable suburbs of Winthrop's city on a hill.

The same could not be said about Rhode Island, for that little colony on Narragansett Bay began as a ghetto for heretics. While voluntary migration formed Connecticut and New Haven, enforced exile filled Rhode Island with Puritans whose radical ideas unsettled the rest of Massachusetts.

Roger Williams, Rhode Island's founder, had come to New England in 1631, serving as a popular and respected minister of Salem. But soon Williams announced that he was a Separatist, like the Pilgrims of Plymouth. He encouraged his congregation and the entire Bay Colony to break all connections to the corrupt Church of England. He also urged a more complete separation of church and state than most Puritans were prepared to accept, and later in his career he endorsed full religious toleration. Finally, Williams denounced the Bay's charter—the legal document that justified Massachusetts' existence—on the grounds that the king had no right to grant land that he had not purchased from the Indians. Even more provocatively, he urged Massachusetts to inform the king of his mistake immediately. With Charles so hostile to Puritans, Massachusetts leaders hardly wished to call attention to themselves and so ordered that Williams be deported to England. Instead he chose to flee the colony in the dead of winter to live with the Indians. In 1636, Williams became the founder and first citizen of Providence, later to be part of Rhode Island.

The artist who sketched this Quaker meeting called attention to one of that sect's most controversial practices by placing a woman at the center of his composition. Women were allowed to speak in Quaker worship services and to preach and proselytize at public gatherings of non-Quakers. The Puritans roundly condemned this liberty as contrary to the teachings of St. Paul.

Another brilliant and charismatic heretic from Massachusetts arrived soon after. Anne Hutchinson, a skilled midwife and the spouse of a wealthy merchant, emigrated to Boston in 1634 for the pleasure of hearing John Cotton, formerly her minister in England. Enthusiasm for Cotton's eloquence started her on a course of explaining his sermons to gatherings of her neighbors—and then to elaborating ideas of her own in which many of the Bay's leaders detected the dangerous heresy of "Antinomianism," meaning "against the law."

The Bay Puritans, like all Calvinists, denied that men and women could "earn" salvation by conforming their lives to God's laws. That stark denial of human ability—the insistence that divine grace alone could save fallen mankind— offered individuals little incentive for good behavior. But most Puritans tempered that conviction with another belief that did more to encourage orderly and disciplined conduct: they held that individuals might be able to discern in their capacity to lead a godly life the *sign* that they had been saved by divine grace. A minority in the Puritan movement, including Anne Hutchinson, rejected the notion that upright living could constitute evidence of salvation; she contended that outward obedience to God's commandments indicated nothing whatsoever about the inward state of the soul. She was certain that those predestined for salvation knew it intuitively and could recognize the same grace in others.

When most of the Bay Colony's ministers denounced her, Anne Hutchinson denounced them. Her attack on the clergy, along with the popularity of her preaching among many important merchant families, prompted the Bay Colony government to expel Hutchinson and her followers for sedition in 1638. Despite a spirited and intelligent defense of her position during her trial, she made a fatal slip by claiming that she had received divine revelation directly from the Holy Spirit. That assertion sealed her fate, for the Puritans held that revelation had ended in biblical times and that those who believed otherwise belonged in Rhode Island. Anne Hutchinson stopped there briefly before moving on to Long Island, where she died in an Indian attack—to the satisfaction of many in Massachusetts Bay.

The devil of religious controversy assumed the shape of a woman in later cases of dissent as well. The Quakers, one of the most radical religious groups spawned by the Protestant Reformation in England, sent Ann Austin and Mary Fisher as their first missionaries to the Bay, and women were among the most active and determined early converts. Mary Dyer was hanged for her persistence along with three Quaker men in 1656. Like the Antinomians, the Quakers attached great significance to an inward state of grace, called the "Light Within." Through that inner light, the Quakers claimed, God revealed his will directly to believers, enabling men and women to attain spiritual perfection. Because they held that everyone had immediate access to God, the Quakers also dispensed with a clergy and the sacraments.

Goodwives

If Anne Hutchinson and Mary Dyer had been men, their ideas would still have been deemed heretical. On the other hand, if these women had been men, they might not have become heretics. As men, they might have found other ways to assert their extraordinary intelligence and magnetism, other avenues to power and approval. But life in colonial New England offered women, especially married women, little scope to exercise their ability and authority.

Most adult women were hardworking farm wives who cared for large households of children, to which a new baby was added every two years. Between marriage and middle age, most New England wives were pregnant except when breast-feeding. When they were not nursing or minding children, mothers were producing and preparing much of what was consumed and worn by their families. They planted vegetable gardens and pruned fruit trees, salted beef and pork and pressed cider, milked cows and churned butter, kept bees and tended poultry, cooked and baked, washed and ironed, spun, wove, and sewed. Most women had only their daughters to assist in this exhausting round of chores. Their contributions to feeding, clothing, and raising their families left farm wives little time for tidy housekeeping—as more leisured and affluent female visitors from larger towns like Boston churlishly observed.

What farm women themselves minded more than the drudgery and dirt— conditions that they shared with men—was the tedium of their repetitive household duties. While husbands and sons engaged in jobs on the farm that changed with the seasons, conducted business in town, took trips to the village mills, and went off to hunt or fish, housebound wives and daughters were locked into a humdrum daily routine with little time for themselves. "A continual sameness reigns throughout the year," complained one New England matron.

Most women suffered legal disadvantages as well, because English common law and colonial legal codes accorded married women no control over property.

Wives could not sue or be sued; they could not make contracts; and they surrendered to their husbands any property that they possessed before marriage. Divorce was almost impossible to obtain until the late eighteenth century. Only widows and a few single women had the same legal rights as men, and even these women could not vote in colony elections.

The one arena in which women could attain something approaching equal standing with men was the churches. Although Puritan women could not become ministers, after the 1660s they comprised the majority of church members. In some congregations, membership enabled them to vote for ministerial candidates and to voice opinions in cases of admission and discipline. For many New England women, religion was a source of social identity.

Whites and Indians in Early New England

New England Puritans were far more concerned to define and perfect the principles of the Protestant Reformation among themselves than to impart their faith to other peoples. While French missionaries carried Catholicism to tribes in every place reached by traders, the Puritans made only a few halfhearted efforts to bring Protestantism to the natives of New England.

Although most white settlers in New England, like those in the Chesapeake, insisted on the "savagery" of the Indians, the Puritans had much in common with native peoples. Both groups relied on the same resources and the same combination of seasonal activities—fishing in spring and summer, hunting in winter, cultivating and harvesting food crops in spring and fall. And, to an even greater degree than among the Puritans, Indian political authority was local. No central government like Powhatan's confederacy or the English colonial governments consolidated New England's tribes. Within each village, a single leader known as the "sachem" or "sagamore" directed economic life, administered justice, and negotiated with other tribes and English settlers. And like the officials of New England towns, a sachem's power depended on keeping the trust and consent of his people. Like the town fathers, the sachems cultivated reputations for spirituality to enhance their claims to leadership.

The Indians of New England shared one other characteristic with the English: no love was lost among neighboring nations. The antagonism among the English, Spanish, Dutch, and French was equaled in intensity by the animosities among the Abenaki, Pawtucket, Massachusett, Narragansett, and Wampanoag tribes of the north Atlantic coast. The rivalries kept different tribes from forging an effective defense against white colonials. New England settlers, like those in the Chesapeake, exploited Indian disunity, playing one tribe off against another. What made the white strategy of "divide and conquer" easier still was that the competition for trade magnified rivalries among the tribes, just as it heightened conflict among European nations.

If the New England tribes had been able to unify, they might have resisted the English longer. Still, they would have confronted a deadly enemy against which they had no defense—disease. Even before the Pilgrims landed, an epidemic introduced in 1618 by visiting fishermen ravaged the Massachusett and Pawtucket tribes, leaving the coast of New England "a widowed land." As contact with Europeans increased, epidemics recurred with deadly frequency, drastically reducing tribal populations.

With only the shattered remnants of the coastal tribes inhabiting the areas where New England colonials first settled, conflicts between the two groups occurred infrequently at first. But when white settlers began to push into Connecticut, they encountered the Pequots, a tribe still numerous and strong enough to marshal a staunch resistance. Had the Pequots allied with their neighbors, the Narragansetts, they could have retarded English expansion southward. But the Narragansetts, bitter enemies of the Pequots, cast their lot with the English instead. Together they prosecuted a brutal campaign that virtually destroyed the Pequots in 1637. A few years later, in 1643, the English, eyeing Narragansett lands, turned against their former allies, joined forces with the Narragansetts' rivals, the Mohegans, and mobilized for an assault. To avoid following the Pequots into oblivion, the Narragansetts ceded a large tract of their territory to white settlers. As the Puritans established themselves as "the dread and sovereign lords" of the Connecticut River valley, only a few objected to their aims and methods, among them Roger Williams. "God Land," he warned one of Connecticut's leaders, "will be (as it now is) as great a God with us English as God Gold was with the Spanish."

The destruction of the Pequots and the submission of the Narragansetts left the Wampanoags of Plymouth as the only coastal tribe capable of resisting Puritan encroachment. For nearly 50 years they had been allied with Plymouth settlers, but in the 1660s their sachem Metacomet, whom the English called King Philip, decided that Indian clients of the English inevitably lost their lands, their lives, and their dignity. In 1675 he organized a pan-Indian uprising: the Narragansetts, Mohegans, and Nipmucs joined the Wampanoags in an offensive that devastated white settlements throughout the New England frontier. By the spring of 1676, Metacomet's forces were pressing toward the coast, raiding towns that lay within 20 miles of Boston.

What finally halted the Indian advance was not a successful colonial counterattack, but shortages of food and ammunition and the outbreak of disease. Metacomet called for assistance from the Abenaki, a powerful Maine tribe, and from the Iroquois of New York. His efforts were in vain; these tribes withheld their support, not wishing to jeopardize their trade with the English. By the summer of 1676 the Indian offensive had collapsed. Some of the tribes surrendered, while others fled for refuge farther west. Metacomet met his death in battle, and his wife and son along with many other Indians were sold as slaves to Caribbean planters. The remnants of the surviving tribes submitted to resettlement in villages supervised by the white victors.

In seventeenth-century New England, as in the Chesapeake, the clash between the tribes and white settlers culminated in violence that threatened the very survival of both groups. Ultimately, the Puritans broke the back of Indian resistance, but at a fearful cost to both sides. Perhaps 20,000 English and Indians lost their lives in Metacomet's War; scores of colonial towns and tribal villages lay in ruins.

THE MIDDLE COLONIES

The settlements planted between Connecticut and Maryland are aptly called the Middle Colonies, for while the inhabitants of New York and New Jersey, Pennsylvania and Delaware enjoyed more secure lives than most southerners, they lacked the basis for consensus that lent New England its remarkable stability. Instead, in each of the Middle Colonies an assortment of ethnic and religious groups vied for wealth from farming and the fur trade and chafed under the rule of political institutions less responsive and representative than those to the north and south.

The Founding of New Netherlands

By the beginning of the seventeenth century the Calvinist Dutch had finally freed their homeland from Spanish domination. Having won independence, they were equally determined to compete with Spanish merchants and to contain the spread of Spanish Catholicism. Along the Amazon River and the African coast, forts and trading posts of the Dutch West India Company protected and promoted Dutch commerce while harrying Spanish competitors. Least important to the company was its sole outpost in North America, New Netherlands, founded in 1624. The company had some interest in tapping the furs of the interior, scattering a few trading posts along the Hudson, Connecticut, and Delaware rivers. But the Dutch did not intend to plant permanent communities in America; enjoying both prosperity and religious freedom at home, they were far less inclined than the English to emigrate.

Thus New Netherlands' population was as small and scattered as New England's was large and concentrated. Most of the few settlers were clustered in the village of New Amsterdam on the tip of Manhattan Island at the mouth of the Hudson. One-hundred and fifty miles upriver lay Fort Orange (Albany). By the

---

New Amsterdam (later New York City) in about 1626. Despite having this outpost in New Netherlands, the Dutch had far more interest in vying with the Portuguese for control of commerce with the Far East than in competing with the English for the fur trade in North America.

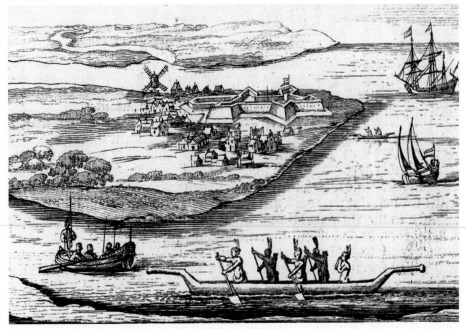

1660s a few other farming villages dotted the west end of Long Island, upper Manhattan Island, Staten Island, and the lower Hudson valley. In all, there were fewer than 9000 New Netherlanders—a diverse array of Dutch, Belgians, French, English, Portuguese, Swedes, Finns, and Africans. The first blacks had arrived in 1626, imported as slaves; some later became free, intermarried with whites, and even owned white indentured servants.

This ethnic diversity ensured a variety of religions. Although the Dutch Reformed Church predominated, other early New Netherlanders professed Lutheranism, Congregationalism, Quakerism, and Catholicism. There were Jews as well, refugees from Portuguese Brazil, who were required by law to live in a ghetto in New Amsterdam. To New Englanders, accustomed as they were to more homogeneous communities, New Netherlands must have seemed a veritable Babel, a bustling confusion of languages, customs, and beliefs. Nevertheless, as early as the 1640s, a substantial number of New Englanders, drawn by promises of cheap land and local self-government, planted farming communities on eastern Long Island.

New Netherlanders recognized that their differences complicated the creation of a stable civic order, and the Dutch West India Company did little to ease the strain. Most of the colony's governors were inefficient, corrupt, and dictatorial, and no elective assembly was established. New Netherlanders felt little loyalty to either the company or its representatives. To make matters worse, the company provided scant protection for its outlying settlers; when it did attack neighboring Indian nations it did so savagely, leading to an increased level of violence. By the time the company went bankrupt, in 1654, it had virtually abandoned its American colony.

New Englanders on Long Island, who had insisted on a free hand in regulating their own villages, began to demand a voice in running the colony as well. Their example prompted Dutch towns to advance claims to self-government. By the 1660s, the New Englanders had gone further still, openly challenging Dutch rule and calling for English conquest of the colony.

English Rule in New York

The English were, of course, already in the midst of an ongoing rivalry with Holland for maritime and commercial supremacy. In 1652 antagonism flared into a conflict that lasted for two years, the first Anglo-Dutch War. Four years later the English were spoiling for a renewal of hostilities. More than 100 English ship captains complained to Oliver Cromwell in 1658 that "the Dutch eat us out of our trade at home and abroad . . . and call us 'English Dogs,' which doth much grieve our English spirits. They will not sail with us, but shoot at us and by indirect courses bring their goods into our ports, which wrongs not only us but you in your customs."

Charles II took up the challenge, tempted by the disarray of New Netherlands. Brushing aside Dutch claims, he granted his brother James, the duke of York, a proprietary charter that included all of New Netherlands to Delaware Bay, as well as Maine, Martha's Vineyard, and Nantucket Island. In 1664 James sent an invading fleet, whose mere presence caused the Dutch to surrender without even a show of resistance. Governing the new colony, however, proved more of a problem.

The establishment of English rule in New York, as it was renamed, improved the efficiency of colonial administration but did little to ease ethnic tensions, encourage settlement, or promote political stability. James made a determined effort to appease the Dutch. He allowed them to remain in the colony, confirmed their land titles, permitted their merchants direct trade to Holland, and tolerated the Dutch Reformed Church. But the Dutch remained restive under English rule. When Holland briefly reconquered the colony during the third Anglo-Dutch War in 1673, they rejoiced. When New York was returned to England by treaty a year later, they reluctantly submitted again to foreign rule. Only a generation of intermarriage and acculturation would finally ease these frictions.

James also failed to win the goodwill of Long Island's Puritans. He instituted a legal code based on English practice, the Duke's Laws; but he refused to establish an elective assembly. The settlers, in turn, refused to pay taxes to what they termed his "arbitrary" government. James, whose aversion to assemblies dated from the beheading of his royal father at the direction of Parliament, grudgingly gave in to the demand for such a body in 1683. But he repudiated the first act of the new assembly, the Charter of Liberties, which would have guaranteed New Yorkers basic civil and political rights. On top of everything else, James' Catholicism aroused suspicion and antagonism among both Long Island Puritans and Dutch Calvinists.

Political upheaval and discontent discouraged settlers from coming to New York. By 1698 the whole colony numbered only 18,000 inhabitants. New York City, the former New Amsterdam, was an overgrown village of a few thousand, still dependent on Boston for shipping and trade. James enjoyed little in the way of revenues from his proprietary colony.

The League of the Iroquois

The Indian tribes around New York City and the lower Hudson valley fell prey to the same forces that shattered the natives of New England and the Chesapeake. They resisted English land hunger for decades, but recognized too late the importance of united action. Farther into the interior, however, contact with European fur traders strengthened the Iroquois nation, which had already united in a remarkable league.

The dynamics of the situation resembled those at work in early South Carolina. Like the tribes of South Carolina, the Indians of northern New York became important suppliers of fur pelts to white traders. As in the Carolinas, powerful tribes dominated the upper Hudson, far outnumbering whites. The handful of Dutch and, later, English traders had every reason to cultivate goodwill among the Indians. But while mutual economic interests promoted peace between white New Yorkers and Indians, the fur trade heightened tensions among the northern interior tribes. At first the Mahicans had supplied furs to the Dutch, but by 1625 the game in their territory had been exhausted and the Dutch had taken their business to the Iroquois. When the Iroquois faced the same depletion of fur-bearing animals in the 1640s, they found a solution. With Dutch encouragement and Dutch guns, the Iroquois hunted the neighboring Huron nation virtually to extinction and seized the rich Canadian forests where the Huron had trapped for the French. In every respect except the conduct of a slave trade in Indian captives, the brutal warfare in the north resembled the conflicts that competition for English trade had also brought upon Carolina's tribes.

The extermination of the Huron left the Iroquois undisputed Indian lords of the northern frontier. More successfully than Powhatan's confederacy in the Ches-

Converts of the French Jesuits, these women of the Caughnawaga tribe are kneeling before a statue of the Virgin Mary taking vows of celibacy. One cuts her hair, in imitation of the practice of Catholic nuns. Both French Catholic and English Protestant missionaries condemned the long hair favored by Indian women and men alike as a symbol of native pride.

apeake or Canada's Huronia, the Iroquois managed to consolidate disparate tribes into a coherent political unit, 12,000 strong. This union of the Five Nations (to become six after the Tuscaroras joined them in 1712) included the Mohawk, Oneida, Cayuga, and Seneca tribes, stretching from the lands around the upper Hudson in the east to the Genesee River in the west.

Iroquois legend attributes the consolidation to the work of Hiawatha, a Mohawk sachem, who was inspired by a vision to unify the northern tribes. By the late sixteenth century a council of 49 chiefs presided over the League of the Iroquois, making decisions for all villages and prohibiting feuding and blood revenge among them. Political strength enabled the Iroquois to deal effectively with their Algonkian rivals in New England as well as European newcomers. As the favored clients of the Dutch and, later, the English, they became opponents of the French, who had allied with the Hurons.

The League's remarkable achievement rested on an even more remarkable form of political and social organization, one in which both sexes shared authority. The most powerful women anywhere in colonial North America were the matriarchs of the Iroquois. Matrilineal kinship formed the basis of Iroquois society, as it did among the Pueblos of the Southwest: when men married, they joined their wives' families, households over which the eldest female member presided. But unlike Pueblo women, Iroquois matriarchs wielded political influence as well. The most senior Iroquois women selected the confederation's council of chiefs, advised them, and "dehorned"—removed from office—those deemed unfit. Throughout the eighteenth century, the League of the Iroquois would continue to figure as a major force in North America.

The Founding of New Jersey

The colony of New Jersey took shape in the shadow of its more notable neighbors to the north. Its inhabitants were less united and powerful than the Iroquois, less wealthy and influential than New Yorkers, and less like-minded and self-governing than New Englanders.

New Jersey's beginnings had promised greater distinction. In 1664 James, duke of York, bestowed on two of his favorites, Lord Berkeley and Sir George Carteret, 5 million fertile acres lying west of the Hudson and east of the Delaware River. To attract settlers, New Jersey's new proprietors adopted the same strategy that they were using in their other colonies, the Carolinas. They guaranteed religious freedom, generous land grants, and self-government in a representative assembly to all inhabitants in exchange for a small quitrent, an annual fee for the use of the land. The proprietors' terms and the lure of rich land appealed to a group of Puritans, who moved there from New Haven. There they encountered another group of Puritans from eastern Long Island.

The Long Islanders, however, had settled in New Jersey not at the invitation of Berkeley and Carteret, but under a conflicting grant from Governor Richard Nicolls of New York, whose colony claimed title to New Jersey. Unaware that James had already given New Jersey to his friends, Nicolls granted the Long Islanders land there, as well as the right to government by their own assembly. The Long Islanders announced that they had not come to New Jersey to pay quitrents or to submit to autocratic rule.

To complicate matters even more, Berkeley and Carteret decided to divide New Jersey into east and west and sell both halves to Quaker investors. New Jersey's Puritan inhabitants, unhappy with any proprietorship, became apoplectic at the prospect of heretical Quakers running their colony. But New Jersey was not destined to develop as the center of Quaker settlement in the New World. Although some English Friends migrated to West Jersey, the Quakers quickly decided that neither of the Jerseys compared favorably with Pennsylvania and sold both to speculators. In the end, the Jerseys were dominated neither by Puritans nor by Quakers, but became patchwork colonies of English, Scots, Irish, Dutch, French Huguenots, Germans, and West Indians. These settlers established small family farms and clustered in neighborhoods where inhabitants shared a common religion or national origin. When the Crown reunited east and west and converted New Jersey into a royal colony in 1702, it was still overshadowed by more notable settlements to the north and, now, to the south.

Quaker Odysseys

A spirit of religious and political idealism similar to that of New England infused the settlement of Pennsylvania, making it an oddity among northern proprietary colonies. The oddity began with an improbable founder, William Penn. Young Penn devoted his early years to disappointing his distinguished father, Sir William Penn, an admiral in the royal navy. After being expelled from college, he traveled in Europe, dabbled in law, and seemed generally at loose ends, until at last he settled upon a career that may have made his eminent father yearn for mere disappointment. For the son had been captivated by the doctrines of the Quakers; this youthful interest in the Society of Friends quickly deepened into a lifelong commitment to put into practice its teachings. By the 1670s William Penn had emerged as one of the movement's acknowledged leaders.

English Quakerism had by the 1660s shed some of its more extreme practices, taken up during the previous heady decade of revolt and religious enthusiasm. But the Friends still adhered to ideas that most people regarded as odd. They affected a deliberately plain and severe manner of dress. They withheld from their social superiors the customary marks of respect, such as bowing, kneeling, and removing their hats. They refused to swear oaths or to make war. They allowed women to speak in their meetings and to travel about preaching as "Public Friends." That pattern of behavior bespoke their disdain of pride and worldliness and their embrace of egalitarian ideals. It was the logical conclusion of the Quaker belief that all men and women shared equally in the "Light Within." Some 40,000 English merchants, artisans, and farmers embraced Quakerism by 1660, and many suffered for their convictions, paying fines and enduring imprisonment and corporal punishment.

Since the English upper class has always welcomed eccentricity among its members, it is perhaps less surprising that young William Penn's Quakerism did nothing to diminish his standing at the Stuart court or his friendship with Charles II. More surprising is that royal favor took the extravagant form of presenting Penn with all the land between New Jersey and Maryland. A royal charter of 1681 made the 37-year-old Penn the absolute proprietor of the only ungranted land left along the North American coast, a territory nearly as large as England. Perhaps the king was repaying Penn for the large sum that his father had lent the Stuarts. Or perhaps the king was hoping to export England's troublesome Quakers to a preserve presided over by his trusted personal friend.

Whatever the reason for Charles' generosity, the energetic Penn lost no time in making the most of his New World windfall. He envisioned planting a prosperous settlement that would provide a refuge for persecuted Quakers and produce revenue for its proprietor in the form of quitrents. Recruiting settlers required planning, because the pace of English migration to America had slowed by the 1680s, and Quaker meetings, the most likely source of colonists, were scattered throughout the British Isles and the continent of Europe. To publicize his colony, Penn printed pamphlets in several languages extolling its attractions.

The response was overwhelming. In 1682, just a year after being chartered, Pennsylvania received 4000 settlers. Within five years its population had tripled, and by 1700 it stood at 21,000. The only early migration of equal magnitude was the Puritan colonization of New England.

Perhaps half of Pennsylvania's settlers arrived as indentured servants: the families of free farmers and artisans made up the rest of the immigrants. The majority were English, Irish, and Welsh Quakers, but newcomers also included

William Penn, the founder of Pennsylvania.

Catholics, Lutherans, Baptists, Anglicans, and Calvinists. Not all new Pennsylvanians came from the British Isles; Quakers from Germany and Holland joined the exodus. And in 1682 when Penn purchased and annexed the Three Lower Counties (later the colony of Delaware), his settlement included the Dutch, Swedes, and Finns living there, about 1000 people. Finally, Quakers from other American colonies—West Jersey, Maryland, and New England—flocked to the new homeland.

These experienced American farmers and established merchants brought with them agricultural skills and trading connections that contributed to Pennsylvania's spectacular economic growth. Industrious Quaker landowners speedily sowed their rich lands into a sea of wheat, which was exported along with pork, beef, and lumber to the Caribbean by enterprising Quaker merchants. The center of the colony's trade was the seaport of Philadelphia, a superb natural harbor situated at the confluence of the Delaware and Schuylkill rivers. Boasting a population of 5000 by 1700, Philadelphia equaled New York City in size and soon outstripped its northern competitor.

Rural settlement radiated rapidly from Philadelphia, first stretching along the Delaware River. After 1700 settlers moved west along the Schuylkill and later across the Susquehanna River. In contrast to New England's landscape of villages, the Pennsylvania countryside was dotted with dispersed farmsteads. Commercial agriculture required larger farms, which kept settlers at some distance from one another. As a result, the county rather than the town became the basic unit of local government in Pennsylvania.

Another reason that farmers did not need to cluster their homes within a central village was that the local Indian tribe, the Lenni Lenapes (also called Delawares by the English), posed no threat. Thanks to two of the odder Quaker beliefs—their commitment to pacifism and their conviction that the Indians rightfully owned their land—peace prevailed between native Pennsylvanians and newcomers. Before he sold any land to white settlers, Penn purchased it from the Indians. He also prohibited the sale of alcohol to the tribe, strictly regulated the fur trade, and learned the language of the Lenni Lenapes. "Not a language spoken in Europe," he remarked, "hath words of more sweetness in Accent and Emphasis than theirs."

"Our Wildernesse flourishes as a Garden," Penn declared late in 1683, and in fact, his colony lived up to all of its advance promises. New arrivals readily acquired good land on liberal terms; Penn's Frame of Government instituted a representative assembly and guaranteed all inhabitants the basic English liberties of habeas corpus (the right to bail) and trial by jury. In addition, all faiths enjoyed complete freedom of worship.

Like the Puritans, Penn yearned to reform the political and religious errors of Europe by creating a model society across the seas. And like the Puritans, he believed that government should be based on contract and consent. Penn even shared with the Puritans the view that the state should by law promote morality, virtue, and Christian values. But he parted company with most New England Puritans on the point of religious toleration. While the Puritans believed that the government should support "true religion" and persecute dissenters, Penn vehemently opposed religious establishments. Undeviating in his devotion to liberty of conscience, he endorsed a nearly complete separation of church and state.

Despite Pennsylvania's prosperity and religious peace, political harmony did not follow. Because Penn believed that the colony would survive and prosper only with the backing of the wealthy, he sold rich investors large tracts of land to persuade them to settle. As an added inducement, he conferred on them trade monopolies and political power. Penn's Frame of Government gave the sole right to initiate legislation to the council, a body comprised of those large landowners. The colony's representative assembly could only accept or reject bills sent down by the council. The citizens of Pennsylvania, having been given much, wanted more. Members of the assembly battled relentlessly for the right to initiate legislation. Farmers opposed Penn's efforts to make orderly allotments of land and to collect quitrents. The Dutch, Swedish, and Finnish inhabitants of the Three Lower Counties, non-Quakers who felt no loyalty to Penn, chafed at being annexed to the colony and agitated for separation.

Adding insult to injury, even the Quaker merchants and landowners who owed their privileges to Penn tried to increase their influence by challenging proprietary rule. Their attacks found a receptive audience among settlers, fully half of whom could vote. Penn's carefully laid plans ran afoul of his prickly fellow Quakers who, accustomed to defying civil and religious authority in the Old World, bristled against proprietors in America.

Penn finally bought peace in the place that he now called "this licentious wilderness"—but at the price of approving a complete revision of his original Frame of Government. In 1701 the Charter of Privileges, Pennsylvania's new constitution, stripped the council of its legislative power, leaving it only the role of advising the governor. The charter also limited Penn's privileges to the ownership of ungranted land and the power to veto legislation. A unicameral assembly, the only single-house legislature in the colonies, dominated Pennsylvania's government.

Pennsylvania continued to prosper, and Philadelphia became the commercial and cultural center of England's North American empire. The colony's Quaker inhabitants continued to squabble over politics, both among themselves and with their Anglican and Presbyterian neighbors. And as the interior of the colony became peopled with groups with no "odd" ideas about Indian rights—mainly Germans and Scots-Irish—the Lenni Lenapes and other tribes were intimidated into moving farther west. As for William Penn, he returned to England and spent some time in a debtors' prison after being defrauded by his unscrupulous colonial agents. He died in 1718, an ocean away from his American utopia.

ADJUSTMENT TO EMPIRE

In the year 1685, from the city of London, a new English king surveyed his American domains. The former duke of York, now James II, had hoped that America might contribute to the making of England and, incidentally, to the making of kings and queens. Like earlier Stuart monarchs, James hoped to ride to power on a wave of imperial wealth, just as Spain's monarchs had during the sixteenth century. The Stuarts had chartered the private trading companies of Virginia, Plymouth, and Massachusetts Bay, and they had handed out to their aristocratic favorites huge tracts of land—Maryland, the Carolinas, New York, New Jersey, and Pennsylvania—all in the name of encouraging colonial settlement. But Stuart expectations had exceeded Stuart commitments. Their governments had resisted supplying military or financial assistance to the new outposts, leaving those details to private investors. Until Parliament passed the first Navigation Acts in 1660, England had lacked even a coherent policy for regulating colonial trade.

As a result, when James II came to the throne in 1685, there were a great many places in North America named for English monarchs, but only three colonies, New Hampshire, New York, and Virginia, over which England exercised direct rule through royally appointed governors and councils. What was worse, ungrateful colonists were resisting their obligations to enrich the English state and its rulers. While Chesapeake planters grumbled over the customs duties levied on tobacco, New Englanders flouted the Navigation Acts altogether and traded openly with the Dutch. The Puritans could have paid the tariffs and prospered still, but they delighted in defying the dictates of Stuart monarchs and Restoration Parliaments. The New Yorkers were shaping up as an equally intractable lot, as James, the former duke of York, remembered all too well. Elsewhere—in New Jersey, the Carolinas, and Pennsylvania—settlement was still too raw and recent to seem anything but anarchic. Yet even in the new colonies, the stirrings of resistance to proprietary authority did not bode well.

What was needed, in James' view, was first to bring Massachusetts to heel. Because of their charter, the inhabitants of the Bay Colony were, as one English statesman observed, "a people almost upon the brink of renouncing any dependance of the Crowne." James' brother, Charles II, had laid the groundwork for dealing with truculent Massachusetts. In 1664 he had authorized the same commission charged with seizing New Netherlands to look in on Massachusetts Bay. Their reports of flagrant violations of the Navigation Acts prompted Parliament in 1673 to authorize the placement of customs agents in colonial ports to suppress illicit trade.

The commission also inspired Charles II to form the Lords of Trade and Plantations, a committee charged with overseeing colonial affairs. In 1679 the Lords of Trade further tightened the reins of command by rejecting the Bay's longstanding claim to New Hampshire, making it a separate royal colony instead. When reports of Puritan defiance continued to surface, Charles II delivered the decisive blow: an English court annulled the charter of Massachusetts in 1684, leaving the Bay Colony without a legal basis for its claim to the privilege of self-government. The presiding judge declared that Massachusetts was "a Company of Rebells the King should send a fleet to subdue."

The Dominion of New England

Charles died the following year, leaving James II to complete the reorganization of Massachusetts' affairs. In 1686, at the king's urging, the Lords of Trade consolidated the colonies of Connecticut, Plymouth, Massachusetts Bay, Rhode Island, and New Hampshire into a single entity to be ruled by a royal governor and a royally appointed council. By 1688 he had added New York and New Jersey to his royal domain, now called the Dominion of New England. Indulging the Stuart distaste for representative government, James also abolished all northern colonial assemblies. The king's aim to centralize authority over such a large territory made the Dominion not only a royal dream but a radical experiment in English colonial administration.

The transition to royal rule proceeded without opposition; even Massachusetts submitted without armed intervention from England. Yet the Dominion government assumed from the outset a military cast. Sir Edmund Andros, a tough professional soldier sent to Boston as the Dominion's royal governor, quickly came to vie with his king for the title of most unpopular man north of Pennsylvania. Andros imposed autocratic rule and implemented policies guaranteed to alienate every segment of New England society, even those few colonial leaders who had at first urged accommodation to royal government. He strictly enforced the Navigation Acts, thus stagnating trade and infuriating not only merchants, but sailors, fishermen, dockworkers, and artisans in the maritime trades. He appropriated a Congregationalist meetinghouse for Anglican worship and immediately angered devout Puritans. He invalidated all title to land granted under the old charter, incensing farmers and speculators. He imposed arbitrary taxes, censored the press, and prohibited town meetings, thereby outraging virtually everyone.

The Aftershocks of a Glorious Revolution

While northern colonials endured Andros with a great deal of ill humor, the English were deciding that they had taken enough from his royal master. James II had revealed himself as the wrong sort of Stuart—one who tried to dispense with Parliament and who embraced Catholicism. As they had before with Charles I, Parliament dispensed with the king. In a quick, bloodless coup d'état known as the Glorious Revolution, Parliament forced James into exile in 1688 and placed on the throne of England his daughter, Mary, and her Dutch husband, William of Orange. Mary was the right sort of Stuart, a staunch Protestant who would abide by her agreement to rule with Parliament as a monarch limited by the unwritten English constitution of customs and law. The accession of William and Mary halted the drift toward royal power in England and America and established the supremacy of Parliament.

The deposing of James II was so popular among New Englanders that they rose in revolt against his Dominion governor even before Parliament officially proclaimed the succession of William and Mary. On April 18, 1689, as soon as news reached Boston that William had landed in England, the town's militia seized Andros and sent him home to England. Bay leaders restored the old charter government, while Increase Mather, an eminent minister from Boston, negotiated in London with the new monarchs.

William and Mary officially dismembered the Dominion and reinstated representative assemblies everywhere in the northern colonies. Connecticut and Rhode Island retained their old corporate charters, but Massachusetts received a new charter in 1691. The terms of that charter incorporated Massachusetts, Plymouth, and present-day Maine into a single royal colony headed by a governor appointed by the Crown rather than elected by the people. It also made property ownership rather than church membership the basis of the franchise and imposed religious toleration. Henceforth the Bay Colony's civil goverment had no power to persecute religious dissidents like Anglicans and Quakers, and these groups were also exempted from paying taxes to support the Congregationalist clergy.

The new charter did not satisfy all New Englanders, accustomed as they were to virtual independence from the Crown and from official suppression of religious dissent. And many were badly shaken by the years of uncertainty and upheaval after the old charter had been revoked in 1684. Those anxieties and the search for scapegoats may have found an outlet in the mass accusations of witchcraft that began at Salem Village, Massachusetts (now Danvers), in 1692. Like most early modern Europeans, New Englanders believed in wizards and witches, men and women who acquired supernatural powers by signing a compact with Satan. Before 1692 courts in both Massachusetts and Connecticut had tried scores of people accused of practicing witchcraft, usually women of middle age or older, and some of those convicted had been executed. What was unique about the Salem Village outbreak was its scale and intensity: hundreds of people were accused of witchcraft, more than 100 were imprisoned, and 20 were executed.

No single cause seems to have triggered the Salem episode. Bitter rivalries among families lay behind some of the accusations; others grew out of disputes between near neighbors over boundaries and livestock. These antagonisms may have festered into charges of witchcraft because the revocation of the old charter in 1684 dismantled the judicial system, which usually had settled such petty grievances, and new courts were not established until 1692. The first court created under the new charter was empowered to investigate only the witchcraft charges that had started to crop up in Salem Village, a restriction that probably encouraged many people with old grudges to accuse their adversaries of witchcraft. Religious hatreds could have fueled the hysteria, too, for many of the accused witches were kin, spouses, or close friends of Baptists, Quakers, or Anglicans—heretical groups feared and despised by a Puritan majority now bound by law to tolerate dissent.

If the tragedy at Salem Village vented tensions that had built up over a period of drastic change, it was the last aftershock of the political earthquake that had shaken New England. Its inhabitants adjusted to the political realities of royal rule and quickly came to regard their new charter as a decided improvement on the Dominion. That rapid adaptation both reflected and reinforced the basic stability of New England society. By contrast, the violence and vicious political infighting that plagued New York after 1691 at once reflected and reinforced that colony's essential instability.

Leisler's Rebellion

Word of revolution in England and rebellion in Massachusetts galvanized New Yorkers into armed opposition in May 1689. Declaring their loyalty to William and Mary, the New York City militia forced from office Francis Nicholson, the young, arrogant military officer who served as the Dominion's lieutenant governor. In his place they appointed one of their own leaders, Jacob Leisler, a German immigrant who had attained modest prosperity as a merchant.

Since James II had won few friends in New York, there was no opposition to the rebellion. But Leisler could not consolidate the support for his authority, strongest among Protestant Dutch farmers, artisans, and small shopkeepers. At the same time, the leaders of the colony—an intermarried elite of English and Dutch merchants—considered Leisler a dangerous upstart and a threat to their own influence. After royal rule was restored to New York in 1691, Colonel Henry Sloughter, the new governor, adopted the merchants' suspicions of Leisler. In May 1691 a jury comprised entirely of Englishmen convicted Leisler and his son-in-law, Jacob Milburne, of treason. Their executions lent a long life to the bitter political rivalries that the rebellion had intensified in New York. When Leisler and Milburne were reburied in a Dutch cemetery in 1698, some 1200 people, a quarter of New York City's population, marched in the funeral procession. For decades thereafter, political factions fought each other for advantage.

Royal Authority in America in 1700

In the wake of political upheaval at home and abroad, England confined its colonial efforts to reaping maximum profit from the American trade. A series of measures passed in 1696 put more muscle into monitoring colonial commerce. Parliament enlarged the number of customs officials stationed in each colony to oversee the Navigation Acts. Colonial governors took oaths to uphold the regulations, and customs officers received broader legal powers to search warehouses for contraband goods. To help prosecute smugglers, Parliament established colonial vice-admiralty courts, tribunals without juries presided over by royally appointed justices. And to keep current on all colonial matters, the king appointed a new Board of Trade to replace the old Lords of Trade. The new enforcement procedures generally succeeded in curtailing the contraband traffic, channeling colonial trade through England, and quelling American resistance to the Navigation Acts.

That was enough for England and its monarchs for half a century thereafter. With the Glorious Revolution, the steam went out of the Stuart drive to consolidate their empire. English kings and queens forswore any aspirations to impose on North America the strict, centralized administration of colonial life that the Dominion had attempted. Political readjustment at home and the distractions of wars with Spain and France dictated a policy toward the colonies that Edmund Burke, an English political philosopher, later termed "salutary neglect."

True, there were at the end of the seventeenth century more American colonies directly ruled by the Crown. By 1700 royal governments had been established in Virginia, New York, Massachusetts, and New Hampshire; New Jersey, the Carolinas, and Georgia would shortly be added to the list. Proprietary rule persisted only in Pennsylvania and Maryland; Connecticut and Rhode Island alone retained their old corporate charters granting full powers of self-government. Royal rule meant that the monarch appointed governors and (everywhere except Massachusetts) also appointed their councils. Royally appointed councils could veto any law passed by the representative assembly, royally appointed governors could veto any law passed by both houses; and the Crown could disallow any law passed by both houses and approved by the governor.

Still, the sway of royal power remained more apparent than real after 1700. The Glorious Revolution had established once and for all that Parliament's authority would be supreme in the governing of England, putting distinct limits on royal power. In the colonies, members of representative assemblies grew more adept at dealing with royal governors and more entrenched in power. They protected most jealously their strongest lever of power—the right of the lower houses to levy taxes.

The political reality of the assemblies' power reflected a social reality as well. The colonies of 1700 were no longer mere beachheads along the Atlantic, run from 2000 miles away by English joint stock companies. They were no longer the blueprints of absentee proprietors with dreams of establishing lucrative feudal domains or benevolent utopian kingdoms. The close-knit Puritan towns of New England, the heterogeneous farmlands of the Middle Colonies—even the plantation economies of the Chesapeake and the Carolinas—were becoming more firmly rooted societies with social dynamics of their own. Their laws and traditions were based not only on what they had brought from England, but on the conditions of life in America. The Stuarts had hoped that America might be the making of English kings and queens, and the Glorious Revolution swept away that hope. But social realities had already ensured that Stuart hopes of controlling American development would prove no more practical than proprietary dreams or joint stock ventures.

Still, the dream of empire would revive among England's rulers in the middle of the eighteenth century—in part because the same dream had never died among the rulers of France. By 1663, Louis XIV had decided that kings could succeed where the enterprise of private French traders had failed: he placed New France under royal rule. Thereafter France's fortunes in America steadily improved. Soldiers strengthened Canada's defenses; colonists and traders expanded the scope of French influence; the Jesuits made more converts among the tribes of the interior—and even among the Iroquois, who had previously been raiding French farms and trading posts. Under the Sun King, as Louis was known to admiring courtiers, royal rule became absolute and the hopes for empire grew absolutely. Louis and his heirs would continue their plans for the making of France by contending for empire with the English, both in the Old World and in the New.

SIGNIFICANT EVENTS

late 1500s	Formation of the League of the Iroquois
1535	Cartier discovers the St. Lawrence
1608	Champlain founds Quebec on the St. Lawrence; Separatists flee to Holland
1620	Pilgrims land at Plymouth
1624	Dutch found New Netherlands
1630	Winthrop fleet arrives at Massachusetts Bay
1637	Pequot War
1642–1648	English Civil War
1649	Charles I executed
1660	English monarchy restored: Charles II becomes king
1664	New Netherlands becomes English New York; founding of New Jersey
1675–1676	Metacomet's War
1681	Founding of Pennsylvania
1685	James II becomes king of England
1686	Dominion of New England established
1688	Glorious Revolution; William and Mary become monarchs of England
1689	Massachusetts Bay overthrows Andros; Leisler's Rebellion in New York
1692	Witchcraft trials in Salem
1696	Creation of the Board of Trade and Plantations

Generations of the Republic

The First Anglo-Americans (1640–1700)

Thirteen-year-old Rachel lay awake in the dark loft, listening to the regular breathing of her two stepbrothers and the servant girl who lay beside her. In the darkness of the small, half-story room squeezed under the steep roof of her stepfather's Maryland house, she drifted toward sleep. Waking with a sudden start, she whispered the word that now described her: *orphan*. Not only was she an orphan, but her mother, dead three days, had named no guardian for her. At the sound of footsteps in the hall room beneath her, Rachel sat upright and crept quietly from her straw mattress to the ladder leading below and listened intently to the exchange that might determine her fate.

She could identify each person in the hall. She recognized the commanding voice of a local gentleman, a wealthy planter and member of the county court, the body charged with appointing guardians for orphans. She heard the respectful responses of her few remaining kinfolk and friends. There was her 21-year-old brother, Thomas, who worked the small farm he had inherited from their parents. There were her godparents, who had attended her baptism into the Anglican church at the crossroads 10 miles distant.

And there was her stepfather, the man who had become her mother's second husband.

Rachel's natural father had died five years earlier. Like most men in the Chesapeake, he had come out of England as a young indentured servant. Unlike many, he had survived the rigors of servitude, then worked for a few years as a hired hand, and finally, in his late twenties, scraped together enough money to buy his own land. A year later he married Rachel's mother, a former servant herself, in her mid-twenties. Like many immigrant brides, she was pregnant with her husband's son at the time of their marriage. Rachel's father considered himself luckier than most men along the Chesapeake, where males outnumbered females by six to one and a quarter remained bachelors all their lives. And he had lived to the ripe old age of 48, the average life expectancy for men, before succumbing to typhoid fever.

Rachel's mother had fared well after her husband's death. His will granted her full responsibility for the farm and the children. Like most people in the early Chesapeake, he had no other kin who could have assumed those obligations. But the estate had not amounted to much: it included no servants or slaves. The new widow might have been forced to bind out

her children as servants, simply to provide for their support, if a neighboring planter had not promptly proposed marriage.

Rachel and Thomas had not resented their mother remarrying. Most widows in the Chesapeake took a second and even a third husband, and most marriages were broken within 10 years by the death of one partner. And when Rachel and Thomas moved into their new stepfather's household, which included two young sons from his previous marriage, they took it in stride. Many other children up and down the Bay lived in complicated households that included stepparents, stepsiblings, and half-siblings.

But then her mother had become pregnant. Rachel had watched the matrons from neighboring plantations gather in the hall of her stepfather's home to help her mother from the bed to the birthing stool. Her mother, by then in her early forties, delivered what might have been her last baby even if she had been healthy. But only hours later the infant died, and a few days later Rachel's mother succumbed to complications of childbirth compounded by malaria—the chronic condition that dogged so many settlers, month in and out, and which pregnancy made worse. Many other women in the Chesapeake met the same fate. And many of their children found themselves orphaned, as had Rachel: one-fifth of all youngsters lost both parents before their thirteenth birthday and one-third by their eighteenth birthday.

Even so, Rachel knew that she was lucky just to be alive, since so many of the other children she had seen at church over the years had died of one malady or another. Indeed, one out of every four children born in the Chesapeake did not survive into their teens. And in a society dominated by immigrants with few ties to one another, she was lucky to still have a small circle of adults who might look after her. The county court usually bound out orphans without kin or friends as servants to any planter looking for another laborer. She was lucky, too, because her mother, before her remarriage, had deeded the major part of her first husband's land to Thomas, securing his future as a small planter, and reserved two cows as her daughter's inheritance and modest dowry.

What would the future hold? If Rachel became the ward of her stepfather, or her godparents, or even her brother, they might mismanage her inheritance or mistreat her. Even if they did not, she would be obliged to work for part of her keep, since her inheritance would not yield enough income for her support. If she remained with her stepfather, he would surely favor his own boys over Rachel—or he might marry yet again, perhaps to a woman who would resent the young girl. On the other hand, Rachel could expect to marry out of any unpleasant situation in a few years. Most native-born girls who were not indentured to a master married between 16 and 19, much earlier than their servant-mothers had. And since men

still outnumbered women—by a ratio of three to one in Rachel's generation—even the orphaned daughter of a small planter could choose among suitors. Choose she would, too, and freely, for Rachel no longer had parents alive to influence her selection of a husband.

Still, the world of the Chesapeake did not present a particularly wide array of choices. Rachel and her brother Thomas expected to replicate their parents' lives, he as a small planter, she as a small planter's wife, both of them marrying into nearby farm families. They did not look for futures of greater wealth, higher social rank, education exceeding bare literacy, or travel to distant places. The possibility of real change, of not repeating their parents' lives, never occurred to them.

Far to the north of the tiny, weather-beaten frame house where Rachel listened from the loft, hundreds of miles up the coast, a slightly larger home of similar design nestled amid some 60 others in a small New England village. This house offered even less privacy than that of Rachel's stepfather, for its occupants included a family of eight, and their neighbors lived moments rather than miles away. But Edward, a boy of about Rachel's age, found nothing exceptional in his crowded life.

While Edward's family—his father, mother, and several brothers and sisters—constituted an average New England household, only folk far wealthier than ordinary farmers enjoyed more commodi-ous living quarters. But what most families lacked in space within their homes, they more than made up for in the acres that they owned outdoors: long strips of land for crops, radiating out from the village center, and fat plots of meadow, marsh, and woodland for grazing, hay, and fuel—scattered where nature saw fit. Although the typical New England farm was half the size of a Chesapeake plantation, Edward's father was still rich in land beyond the wildest dreams of any English yeoman.

That land, coupled with a healthy northern climate, allowed early New Englanders to become rich in children—and rich in relatives of every kind. Rachel counted herself fortunate that her parents had lived into their forties and left her among a few familiar faces; Edward's family formed a phalanx of interminable and seemingly indestructible kin. Both sets of his grandparents, who had emigrated from England as young married couples with small children and settled in this very village, were still alive in their sixties. And they might live 10 or even 20 years longer. Most of their now-grown children—Edward's mother and father and his legion of aunts and uncles—had reached maturity and married in the same village. There they bore their own children, wives becoming pregnant every two years, as soon as they weaned their most recent baby. While Edward's parents, grandparents, aunts, and uncles each maintained separate households, the intimate scale of village society ensured that he encoun-

tered his near and distant kin every day of his life.

The land, too, gave New England's long-lived fathers great authority over their children. Land commanded power, respect, and submission to parental standards, for sons and daughters relied on legacies of farms in order to marry and establish their own families. The subordination to patriarch rule extended for some sons even into middle age, for most fathers waited until the end of their long lives before deeding land to their heirs.

Long before he realized that his future livelihood depended on his father's pleasure, Edward had learned to submit to authority. After his second birthday, his parents started to discipline him whenever he stubbornly misbehaved, making plain by a severe look, a scolding, or a switching their expectation that Edward conform his will to their wishes. At the age of 10 he was sent by his parents to serve his uncle's household, where he lived for two years. It was a common practice among New England parents, an antidote to their fears of coddling and indulging beloved children. During his several winters of study at the village school, Edward learned that his willful ways were the legacy of Adam and Eve to the whole human race. "In Adam's Fall, We Sinned All," read his primer. Twice each week in the meeting house the minister taught the same lesson, urging upon his congregation that conversion alone could make "a new creature," a Christian who preferred

God's will to his or her own. Throughout the long sermons, which seemed even longer on winter Sabbaths so cold that the bread froze and rattled on the communion plate, Edward and the other village boys wriggled and dozed in the drafty back pews under the watchful eye of the sexton, who rang the steeple bell, buried the dead, and kept order among the young.

The lessons took. Edward and most members of his generation accepted the authority of their elders and came to understand parental discipline as a sign of affection and concern. They adopted and celebrated their values, admired and even lionized their parents and grandparents. As adults they sought to imitate and replicate patriarchal culture. And since New England parents lived long enough to be more than memories to their offspring, they exerted considerable influence over the choices of mates and careers made by the next generation. Matters in the Chesapeake were very different. Even if parents there attempted to discipline their children, early death made that authority impossible to sustain. By their teens, many southern youngsters were already independent, making their own way without assistance from kin or friends. The broken, discontinuous families that afforded a full measure of freedom but little certainty stood in sharp contrast to the secure but insulated existences of young people in New England.

4

The Mosaic of Eighteenth-Century America

y the time the hundred and fifty or so Iroquois sat facing the colonial commissioners the morning of June 29, 1754, the rain had passed and the sky had cleared—a good thing, considering the downpours of the past few days. The Hudson River had risen nearly 14 feet, overflowing its banks, tearing sloops from their moorings, drowning the corn in nearby fields, and even pushing up against the palisade fence surrounding the frontier settlement of Albany, New York. The rains, though, had not stopped the meeting. In front of the governor's house, servants had set up about 10 long wooden planks, upon which the delegates from the Six Nations of the Iroquois now sat. The commissioners themselves, 25 in all, were not about to make do with planks; each had his own chair. They represented seven colonies, from Massachusetts Bay on the north to Maryland on the south.

Governor James DeLancey of New York stood and read a proclamation of welcome, pledging to "brighten the Chain of Friendship" between the Iroquois and the English and to keep that "antient Covenant Chain . . . Inviolable and Free from Rust." As each paragraph of the governor's speech was translated, the Iroquois were presented with a decorative belt, to which they responded with a ceremonial "*Yo-heigh-eigh*," shouted in unison. The noise sounded little more than "a kind of universal Huzzah" to one of the New Hampshire commissioners, who was new to such meetings. But sharper ears were more attuned to Iroquois diplomacy. Normally, each nation voiced its agreement individually: six *Yo-heigh-eighs* coming one after another. By mixing them together, noted one observer, the delegates "had a mind to disguise that all the Nations did not universally give their hearty assent to the Covenant." The Iroquois League was not as united in its friendship as first appearances indicated.

Unity—and not merely the unity of the Iroquois—was very much on the mind of one commissioner from Philadelphia. Several chairs to the left of Governor DeLancey sat the most influential member of the Pennsylvania delegation, Benjamin Franklin. Forty-eight years old and in the prime of life, Franklin recognized that the question of whether the Iroquois would unite in an alliance was only half the issue for this congress at Albany. Equally important was whether the British colonies could unite, to deal in an effective way with France's threat throughout North America. Franklin had a plan for bringing the colonies together, but whether they would pay any heed remained an open question.

By the mid-eighteenth century, Philadelphia was the largest city in the colonies and the second largest in all the British empire. Its busy harbor served not only as a commercial hub but also as the disembarkation point for thousands of immigrants.

In a sense, the plan grew out of a lifetime of experience, for the imperial rivalry between England and France had begun well before Franklin's birth and had flared, on and off, throughout his adult years. In 1689, in the wake of the Glorious Revolution, England had joined the Netherlands and the League of Augsburg (several German-speaking states) in a war against Louis XIV, France's ambitious Sun King. While the main struggle raged on the continent of Europe, French and English colonials, joined by their Indian allies, skirmished across the Atlantic in what was known as King William's War. The Treaty of Ryswick in 1697 signaled a brief interlude in the fighting, but the Anglo-French struggle resumed in 1702, four years before Franklin was born, and continued throughout his early childhood, until the treaty of Utrecht brought peace in 1713.

At stake between the two imperial powers was not so much control over people or even territory but control over trade. In North America France and England vied for access to the rich sugar islands of the Caribbean, a monopoly on the supply of manufactured goods to New Spain, and title to the fur trade. For a quarter of a century following the peace of Utrecht, France and England waged a kind of cold war, vying for position and influence. The British had the advantage of numbers: nearly 400,000 subjects in the colonies in 1720, compared to only about 25,000 French spread along a thin line of fishing stations and fur trading posts. The French, however, had strengthened their chain of forts, stretching from the mouth of the Mississippi north through the Illinois country and into Canada. The forts helped channel the flow of furs from the Great Lakes and the Mississippi River valley into Canada, thus keeping them out of the clutches of English traders.

And strategically, the forts neatly encircled England's colonies, confining their settlement to the eastern seaboard. By midcentury, about 50,000 farmers, traders, and missionaries lived in French America, and wheat had joined furs as a profitable export.

When fighting again engulfed Europe and the colonies in 1744, the results were inconclusive. King George's War, as the colonials dubbed it, was ended by the peace of Aix-la-Chappelle (1748), which essentially restored the status quo. The French, seeing English traders and settlers filter steadily into the Ohio River valley, moved in 1752 to protect their interests in the region, building a new line of forts south of Lake Erie to the Ohio River. Two years later they erected Fort Duquesne at the strategic forks of the Ohio, flush against the border of Franklin's Pennsylvania. The news of Fort Duquesne startled Pennsylvania and other colonies into sending commissioners to Albany in 1754 to coordinate efforts to deal with the worsening crisis. Franklin put the message plainly in his newspaper, the *Pennsylvania Gazette*, in a cartoon of a snake cut into segments. It was inscribed "Join, or Die."

Throughout this imperial maneuvering, the Iroquois League maintained a cool neutrality toward its white rivals. Where once the League had been willing to attack New France in order to maintain control of the fur trade, by the eighteenth century it had become equally suspicious that the English were perhaps using the Iroquois merely as "a Pack of Hounds" to hunt the French. On July 2, three days after Governor DeLancey's welcoming speech, the Albany commissioners heard the frank reply of Hendrik, a Mohawk chief. The English and the French "are both Quarrelling about lands which belong to us," Hendrik complained. "And such a Quarrel as this may end in our destruction." Furthermore, while English farmers from Pennsylvania and Virginia continued to settle on Indian lands, English soldiers seemed incapable of resisting the French. "Look about your Country and see," Hendrik concluded contemptuously,

> you have no Fortifications about you no not even to this City, tis but one step from Canada hither and the French may easily come and turn you out of your Doors. . . . Look at the French, they are Men, they are fortifying every where—but we are ashamed to say it, you are all like Women, bare and Open without any Fortifications.

For the time being, the commissioners could do little to satisfy Iroquois doubts, except lavish as much hospitality as their straitened budgets would allow. In the end, Hendrik and the other delegates made evasive promises of loyalty, and then hauled away 30 wagons full of presents.

But would the colonies themselves unite? That was Franklin's worry. On the way to the Albany Congress he had sketched out a tentative political framework for colonial cooperation. Working with several others at the meeting, he proposed establishing a federal council composed of representatives from each colony, presided over by a president-general appointed by the Crown. The council would assume all responsibility for colonial defense and Indian policy, defraying the cost of building forts and patrolling harbors by taxes levied on all Americans. The commissioners were bold enough to accept the plan, having experienced face to face the reluctance of the Iroquois and the reality of the French threat. Franklin sailed back down the Hudson with his plan endorsed and a call from the commissioners to establish "one general government" for British North America.

But the union born at Albany was smothered by the jealous colonies, who were unwilling to sing *yo-heigh-eigh* either in unison or separately. Not a single assembly approved the Albany Plan of Union. New Englanders and Pennsylvanians did not want to help secure the claims of Virginians to the upper Ohio valley. Virginians, along with New Jerseyans, had refused even to attend the congress. And no American legislature was ready to surrender its cherished and exclusive right to tax inhabitants of its own colony—not to a federal council or any other body. "Everyone cries, a union is necessary," Franklin wrote Governor Shirley of Massachusetts in disgust; "but when they come to the manner and form of the union, their weak noodles are perfectly distracted." If the Albany Congress proved one thing, it was that American colonials were emphatically and hopelessly divided.

FORCES OF DIVISION

Franklin, of course, should have known better. He was a practical man, not given to idle dreams, and he certainly recognized the many forces of disunion at work in America. He knew that the colonies were divided by ethnic, racial, and religious differences and prejudices. Year after year small wooden ships sailed into American seaports to disgorge a bewildering variety of immigrants—especially in Philadelphia, where Franklin had lived since 1723. From his efforts to reorganize the post office Franklin knew, too, that Americans were separated by vast distances, poor transportation, and slow communications. And he knew how much frontier districts distrusted seaboard communities and how the eastern seaboard disdained the backcountry. Taken all in all, the British settlements in America were, in the eighteenth century, a diverse and divided lot.

Immigration and Natural Increase

One of the largest immigrant groups—250,000 black men, women, and children—had come to the colonies from Africa not by choice but in chains. White arrivals included a substantial number of English immigrants, but also a quarter of a million Scots-Irish, the descendants of seventeenth-century Scots who had regret-

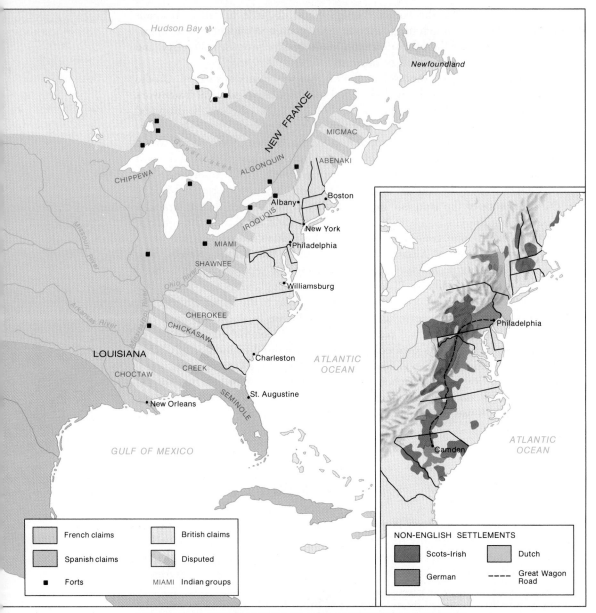

PATTERNS OF SETTLEMENT IN THE EIGHTEENTH CENTURY

The French, English, and Indian nations all jockeyed for power and position across North America during the eighteenth century. The French expanded their fur trade through the interior, while English settlement at midcentury began to press the barrier of the Appalachians. Many non-English settlers spilled into the backcountry: the Scots-Irish and Germans followed the Great Wagon Road through the western parts of the Middle and southern colonies while the Dutch and Germans moved up the Hudson River valley. Albany, where Franklin journeyed in 1754 for the Albany Congress, was one natural pivot point in the rivalry—a place where Iroquois, French, and Indian interests converged.

ted settling in northern Ireland; perhaps 135,000 Germans; and a sprinkling of Swiss, Swedes, Highland Scots, and Spanish Jews. Most non-English white immigrants were fleeing lives rent by famine, warfare, and religious persecution. All of the voyagers, English and non-English, risked the hazardous Atlantic crossing. And many mortgaged their freedom to redeem the price of passage by signing indentures to work as servants in the New World.

The immigrants and slaves who arrived in the colonies between 1700 and 1775 swelled an American population that was already growing dramatically from natural increase. The birth rate in eighteenth-century America was triple what it is today. Most women bore between five and eight children, and most children survived to maturity. Even larger families of 10 or more children were not uncommon—Franklin was the youngest son in a family of 17 children. After about 1700, low rates of infant mortality and long life expectancy, the rule in the northern colonies since the seventeenth century, also became more typical in the South.

Franklin knew, better than most colonials, the dimensions of American growth, both from immigration and through reproduction. In a 1751 essay on the subject, he recognized the social and political consequences of the population explosion. People of different races speaking different languages, believing in different religions, and cherishing different customs created distinctive environments that ranged over a wide expanse of territory. This diversity, coupled with the hectic pace and sheer scale of expansion after 1700, made it hard for Americans to share any common identity. Far from fostering political union, almost every aspect of social development set Americans at odds with one another.

Older Rural Communities

Once they disembarked at American ports, the free immigrants needed places to live and ways of earning a livelihood. So, too, did the burgeoning ranks of native-born Americans coming of age every year: about half of the colonial population in 1775 was under 16. The places that probably appealed to many immigrants and younger Americans were the scores of older rural communities lining the coast or lying a few miles inland.

Even after a century of colonization, most northern settlements remained isolated villages of several hundred inhabitants living in simple family farmsteads built of logs, stone, or brick. In the older parts of New England, family farms of about 100 acres radiated along dirt roads from country towns, the centers of social life. Here farmers bartered small stocks of produce at village stores for what their families could not make at home—sugar, molasses, rum, spices, salt, chocolate, tea, iron ploughs and scythes, and English textiles. Here men and women gathered at village taverns to tipple, smoke, and gossip. Here families flocked on the Sabbath to worship at white steepled meetinghouses and to listen to long sermons delivered by the best educated man in the community, the village minister. Here, several times during the year, men convened at the same meetinghouse to discuss village business.

The stony soil of New England's coast, now worn with a century of use, afforded most families just enough to feed themselves. Outside of the rich Connecticut River valley, it was almost impossible to turn a profit by farming. But most farmers owned the land they worked, and there were no marked extremes of wealth or poverty.

Daily Lives

TIME AND TRAVEL

Transatlantic Trials

A mountain of water swelled from the slate gray Atlantic, towering over the *Jamaica Packet*, then toppled onto the small wooden passenger ship. The impact hurled Janet Schaw and her maid about their cabin like rag dolls. As seawater surged in, the two women struggled to grasp something, anything, to keep from drowning. Outside, it was panic and pandemonium as the ship pitched wildly, "one moment mounted to the clouds and whirled on the pointed wave," the next plunging prow first into the heaving ocean. Four men lashed to the helm fought for control, while the rest of the crew worked with hands "torn to pieces by the wet ropes." The ship's provisions— hogsheads of water, coops of chickens, and barrels of salted meat—snapped from their fastenings and careened across the deck before bouncing overboard.

For more than two days the *Jamaica Packet* hurtled in the grip of the gale. Then its foremast splintered, and the ship flipped onto its side. Passengers, crew, and furniture crashed "heels over head to the side the vessel had laid down on." Schaw found herself "swimming amongst joint-stools, chests, [and] tables" in her cabin and listening to the sound of "our sails fluttering into rags." It would have been the end of the *Jamaica Packet* if, at that moment, its masts had not washed overboard. With the weight of the masts gone, the ship righted itself, reeling all aboard "with equal violence to the other side," as "a second deluge of sea water" swept the vessel.

Schaw, "a lady of quality," as she described herself, was traveling by the finest accommodations from Great Britain to America in the age of sail. For those passengers who could not pay full fare for a private cabin on the *Jamaica Packet*, the storm was worse. Twenty-two or more indentured servants from Scotland in that year of 1774 were bound aboard ship for the West Indies. Unlike ladies and gentlemen "of quality," these desperate, impoverished families of farmers and fishermen had agreed with British merchants to work for labor-hungry American masters in return for the costs of passage. And, like the thousands of others who came to America in the eighteenth century, they were consigned to steerage, the between-decks area or "upper hold."

Perhaps four to five feet high, that space was a congested, foul-smelling dormitory, crowded with narrow wooden bunks arranged in tiers about two feet apart. It was impossible for most people to stand in steerage or to sit up in a bunk, where as many as four people huddled together at night. Sanitary facilities consisted of a few wooden buckets filled with seawater; candles and fish-oil lanterns

Daily Lives

supplied the only light; the sole source of air was the hatch opening onto the deck.

When the storm struck, the hatch had been closed and fastened tightly to keep the holds from filling with water. But as waves dashed over the decks, water seeped and then streamed into steerage, forcing its occupants to stand, clutching their children to keep them from being crushed or suffocated as the storm tumbled everyone from one side of their dark, watery prison to the other. For nine days they stood in water, soaked to the skin, without a fire or any food except raw potatoes and moldy biscuit. And they were without light or fresh air, except for one young man and his pregnant wife. During the storm the woman miscarried, and her "absolutely distracted" husband, Schaw reported, somehow forced open the hatch and carried her up to the deck, reviving the unconscious woman and saving her life. When at last the servants were allowed to come up on deck, they discovered that all of their belongings had been swept overboard.

What followed the servants up to the deck, to the horror of all, was a stench "sufficient to raise a plague aboard." But the luck of the *Jamaica Packet* held, for it escaped not only shipwreck but epidemic disease. Passengers on other transatlantic voyages were not so fortunate. Throughout the eighteenth century notices of ships "lost at sea" or of passengers who slipped overboard in storms filled colonial newspapers. Even on voyages graced with good weather, all aboard suffered from a week of seasickness. Outbreaks of epidemic disease—smallpox, influenza, typhus, and diphtheria—were common. Contributing to the problem of pestilence were the cramped, airless quarters of most travelers bound for America: indentured servants and some convict laborers. Although even cabin passengers complained of wet and cold, they could stroll the deck at will. But servants and convicts were confined to the hold for most of the voyage—anywhere from two to three months.

Along with poor ventilation and primitive sanitation, meager diets left steerage occupants prey to infection. Full-paying passengers received the same rations as ships' officers and often brought a private stock of provisions, but those in steerage subsisted on a stingy allotment of oatmeal, molasses, bread, and meat, much of it wet, moldy, or spoiled. Often their water was brackish. Aside from a few peas, they had no vegetables or fruit. Debilitated by malnutrition, dysentery, and fever, they became vulnerable to deadlier microbes. Although there are no reliable statistics for shipboard mortality during the eighteenth century, estimates range from 3 percent of all passengers to as high as 10 to 15 percent, a rate comparable to that for slave ships during the Middle Passage across the Atlantic.

For all who ventured abroad, transatlantic travel was tedious and dirty at best, fraught with hazard and horror at worst. Those who risked the crossing routinely made out wills and sought the prayers of friends and relatives. But disease and danger at sea discriminated against the poor, indentured servants, and convict laborers who comprised the majority of eighteenth-century emigrants.

In the Middle Colonies, farms of slightly larger size lay at a greater distance from smaller central places, often only a crossroads where all of the county occasionally gathered at a tavern, a country store, a courthouse, or a church. The fertile soil south of Connecticut afforded farm families there not only subsistence but often a surplus of livestock and grain, which they sent to Philadelphia or New York City for export. Because of such commercial opportunities, wider disparities in wealth existed in some settled communities of the Middle Colonies. But since most farmers owned land, inequality was not pronounced.

In established northern rural communities, there had emerged a local "squirearchy" comprised of the wealthier farmers. These families, at the pinnacle of the village pecking order, owned more land than their neighbors and supplemented their farm income by keeping stores, milling wheat or logs, or practicing law. Year after year, they provided leadership for their localities, directing civic life and church affairs.

In the oldest counties of the Virginia and Maryland Tidewater and in the Carolina low country, stability and prosperity also prevailed. Like the rural areas of the Middle Colonies, coastal southern counties specialized in commercial agriculture. Chesapeake planters cultivated tobacco for export; low-country farmers grew rice and indigo. But southern farms were even larger than those in the Middle Colonies, and even greater distances isolated planters from each other. Not only longer physical distances, but also greater social distances separated inhabitants of settled plantation districts. Through a combination of farming, shopkeeping, land speculation, and professional practice, the gentry amassed estates that far exceeded those of ordinary planters. And after 1700, gentry property included a growing number of black slaves. Wealth won the deference of lesser planters: social authority and political office passed from one generation of southern gentlemen to the next. Like their northern counterparts, these local leaders administered justice, supervised civic life, and oversaw public order and morality.

To white immigrants from Europe, weary of war or worn by want, America's settled towns and counties must have seemed safe havens. But by the beginning of the eighteenth century, many coastal communities could no longer accommodate even the children of long-time settlers, let alone newcomers from Europe. In older New England towns, three and four generations were putting pressure on a limited supply of land, while wasteful farming practices had depleted the soil of its fertility. Farther south, earlier settlers had already snatched up the choice farmland of Philadelphia's outlying counties, the prime tidewater tobacco property, and the best low-country rice swamps.

With older rural communities offering few opportunities to either native-born or newly arrived white families, both groups were forced to create new communities in new places. Blacks alone among eighteenth-century immigrants were settled in established rural districts, the plantations of the tidewater and the low country. The uprooting and resettlement of Europeans, Africans, and native sons and daughters created three distinctive kinds of societies in eighteenth-century America: the raw frontier county, the urban seaport, and the plantation slave community.

The Settlement of the Backcountry

The obvious outlet for hard-pressed settlers was the frontier. A few hardy Scots-Irish established enclaves in Maine and in the territory that was to become Vermont. But for the most part, the peopling of New England's interior was left to the descendants of old Yankee families. Throughout the eighteenth century, young men, often brothers or cousins who had grown up in the same coastal village, brought their brides to Maine, New Hampshire, or Vermont. There they felled trees, planted farmsteads, and named tiny hamlets after their hometowns back in southern New England.

Better opportunities to acquire plentiful land at cheaper prices lay south of New York, especially in the backcountry of Pennsylvania, Virginia, and the Carolinas. There, Germans, Scots-Irish, and other settlers formed farming communities that were distinct from both the plantation districts of the southern coast and the rural villages of the North. Backcountry families dispersed across the landscape, enduring greater isolation than any other Americans. In one new Virginia Piedmont county, about 3000 settlers were scattered over 5000 square miles. Farm families spread over this distance seldom had contact with anyone outside of the members of their own households. The nearest courthouse could lie as far as a day's ride from many farmsteads; taverns and churches were often just as distant.

If the isolation of the frontier inhibited the development of strong social bonds, so did the rapid rate at which people came to and left western communities. Many Americans migrated west only to roam restlessly within the backcountry: some families pulled up stakes three and four times before settling down permanently. It was not uncommon for as many as one-third of the members of a frontier county to move on after a few years—to be replaced by an even larger number of newcomers. Houses reflected the transiency of frontier settlements. Framed structures were the exception; most families crowded into filthy, fragile, one-room shacks, earth-fast structures built on posts sunk in the ground and walled with mud, turf, or crude logs.

Backcountry economies afforded most families a bare existence. Large portions of the interior were cut off from access to water transport, lying on unnavigable rivers above the fall line. Unable to float their crops downriver to seaport markets or to drive cattle or cart crops overland on primitive dirt paths, farmers grew only enough to feed their households, selling to new settlers whatever small surplus remained. Not only poor transportation but also the lack of labor kept frontier farmers from tapping the commercial potential of their lands. Most backcountry inhabitants could not afford to invest in a slave or even a servant. They had at their disposal only the labor of family members.

The lack of opportunity to engage in trade or to buy bound labor made the frontier, more than anywhere else in America, a society of equals. Most backcountry families lived on their own farms of about 200 to 400 acres. They had sons enough to cultivate a small fraction of that total acreage, and daughters enough to help with the never-ending household chores of cooking, weaving, spinning, sewing, making candles and soap. Together, their efforts yielded just enough to sustain their families. All of the worldly goods of a typical family consisted of livestock, farm implements, a few pots, knives, and blankets.

What the frontier gained in equality it may have lost in stability. In the backcountry there were no southern gentlemen or northern squires to supply continuous, experienced local leadership. There was only a handful of farmers in each county set above their neighbors by a few extra acres or a single slave. To these relatively inexperienced and uneducated men fell the thankless tasks of overseeing public order as justices of the peace or officers in the local militia or representatives to colonial assemblies. It was hard for men who had so little authority over

This log cabin, built in the North Carolina backcountry in 1782, would have been dark inside, given the lack of windows. The spaces between the logs in such cabins were usually chinked with thin stones or wedges of wood, then daubed with mortar.

their fellows to police sprawling backcountry communities; not surprisingly, coarse and aggressive behavior dominated frontier life. Backcountry men and women mated out of wedlock, swore in public, drank to excess, and brawled at any provocation.

Nor were the churches much help in promoting law and order. Most western-ers could not at first afford to build churches, and their widely dispersed home-steads deterred them from attending public worship. The few clergy willing to endure the rigors of preaching from one backcountry neighborhood to another were either exceptional zealots or, as frontier folk described them, "notorious evil-livers"—drunkards, womanizers, and other scoundrels. While churches loomed large in the lives of Americans on the coast, most western families, al-though often deeply pious, had only haphazard or occasional contact with orga-nized religion.

Among the least enviable lives in eighteenth-century America were those of frontier women. Besides doing the usual chores of farm women, western wives and daughters joined male family members in the fields. One traveler from the East expressed his astonishment at seeing German women in western Pennsylva-nia "at work abroad on the Farm mowing, Hoeing, Loading Dung into a Cart." Perhaps even more difficult to endure than the greater demands on their labor was the loneliness of their lives. Most women had little enthusiasm for moving far away from family and old friends, and they often had trouble adjusting to the primitive conditions of the backcountry. Equally distressing was the distance separating their homesteads from those of female neighbors. The reactions of women to being uprooted and resettled in a wilderness cabin can be guessed at from the assurance that one Scottish husband offered his wife: "We would get all these trees cut down . . . [so] that we would see from house to house."

Social Conflict on the Frontier

Benjamin Franklin knew about the lure of the frontier. He had observed the hordes of Scots-Irish and German immigrants disembarking at Philadelphia and lingering there just long enough to scrape together the purchase price of western land. He had seen workers in his own printshop grow restless with city life and light out for the frontier. From his point of view, the backcountry performed a valuable service by siphoning off surplus people from congested eastern settlements and endowing them with enough land to make a living. But he knew, too, that the frontier was an American Pandora's box: once opened, the West unleashed discord and conflict. Backcountry communities were themselves volatile and violent places. And the settlement of the frontier fostered deep political divisions between the eastern seaboard and the backcountry.

These fissures fueled struggles in almost every colony, and in some, they widened into violent conflict. In Pennsylvania, Franklin himself mediated one contest between East and West. In 1763 a band of Scots-Irish farmers known as "the Paxton Boys" protested the government's inadequate protection of frontier settlers by killing a number of Indians. Then they took their protests and their guns to Philadelphia, marching as far as Lancaster before Franklin intervened and promised redress of their grievances.

North and South Carolina did not get off as easily. In both colonies, legislatures dominated by coastal planters refused to grant equitable political representation and extend basic legal institutions to inland settlers. In response to eastern intransigence, two protest movements emerged in the Carolina interior, each known as the Regulation.

Beginning in the 1760s, backcountry South Carolinians sought to "regulate" into extinction gangs of horse thieves and cattle rustlers who preyed on farm families. The outlaws stormed into lonely plantations, burned farm buildings, stole livestock, kidnaped and raped women, tortured and murdered men. Disgusted by the inaction of South Carolina's assembly, which refused to set up courts in the backcountry, westerners formed vigilante groups and administered grisly frontier justice to the marauders, as well as to any hapless drifters and trappers caught in their dragnets. Threats to march on Charleston itself finally panicked eastern political leaders into extending the court system, but bitter memories of eastern indifference lingered among the Regulators.

If local government in western South Carolina was nonexistent, in North Carolina it was corrupt. Here frontier disaffection ran even deeper. Wealthy lawyers and merchants, backed by big eastern planters, moved into the western parts of the colony, shouldered aside local farmers, and seized control of politics. The new leaders used the machinery of government to exploit frontier settlers, charging exorbitant fees for legal services, imposing high taxes, and manipulating debt laws. Led by the largest local planters, frontier settlers petitioned the governor and the assembly for redress in 1766 and tried to vote the corrupt out of office. When that failed, a virtual civil war erupted in the backcountry. Dubbing themselves the "Regulation," western farmers seized county courts, liberated their jailed leaders, and at last squared off 2000 strong against an eastern militia led by the governor. The militia won at the Battle of Alamance in 1771, but the brutal repression of frontier discontent left westerners in North Carolina with an enduring hostility to the seaboard.

Ethnic differences exacerbated the political tensions between East and West. While people of English extraction predominated along the Atlantic coast, Germans, Scots-Irish, and other white minorities were concentrated in the interior. Many English colonials eyed the new immigrants with disdain and mistrust, regarding them as culturally inferior and even politically subversive. In 1729 Bostonians greeted the arrival of a boatload of Irish immigrants with a riot; a few years later, a mob in Worcester, Massachusetts, set fire to a Scots-Irish Presbyterian church. Farther south, the Scots-Irish also stirred strong animosities. Charles Woodmason, an Anglican missionary in the South Carolina backcountry, deplored the influx of "5 or 6000 Ignorant, mean, worthless, beggarly Irish Presbyterians, the Scum of the Earth, the Refuse of Mankind," who "delighted in a low, lazy, sluttish, heathenish, hellish life."

German immigrants were generally credited with greater industry as well as higher standards of sexual morality and personal hygiene. But like the clannish Scots-Irish, the Germans preferred to live, trade, and worship among themselves. They exhibited little admiration for English political institutions, even less interest in citizenship, and a decided aversion to military service. By 1751 Franklin was warning that the Germans would always retain their separate language and customs: instead of Anglicizing the Germans, the Pennsylvania English would be overrun by "the Palatine Boors." Even in South Carolina, a colony desperate for white settlers because of its black majority, the assembly considered restricting German immigration.

Boundary Disputes and Tenant Wars

The settlement of the frontier also triggered disputes between colonies over their boundaries. At the root of the confusion were the old colonial charters, whose vague definitions of western borders allowed groups of settlers and land speculators from different colonies to lay claim to the same tract of land. Thus was New York drawn into frays with Connecticut and Massachusetts, and Pennsylvania with Connecticut and Virginia.

The most serious of these border wars pitted New York against some farmers from New England who had settled in present-day Vermont: Ethan Allen and the Green Mountain Boys. In the 1760s, New York, backed by the Crown, claimed land that Allen and his friends had already purchased from New Hampshire. When New York tried to invalidate New England land titles and to extend its political jurisdiction over Vermont, it reaped a whirlwind of opposition. For more than a decade Allen spearheaded a successful guerrilla resistance, harassing Yorker settlers and officials, occupying Yorker courthouses, and setting up a competing judicial system in the Green Mountains.

The spread of settlement also set the stage for mass revolts by farm tenants in areas where proprietors controlled vast amounts of land. While outright ownership of land was the exception among rural folk in Europe, it was the rule in America. Throughout the eighteenth century, colonial governments regularly granted or sold land to any interested buyers; for those willing to settle in remote western districts, allotments were liberal and prices affordable. Even those who started out renting farms managed to end up as independent landowners. Still, in a few areas of the Middle Colonies, tenancy struck a deeper root. In eastern New Jersey, prominent proprietors pressed squatters for quitrents on land that had become increasingly populated and therefore more valuable. When the squatters, many of them strong-willed migrants from New England, refused to pay rents, buy the land, or move, the proprietors began evictions, touching off riots in the 1740s.

In New York's Hudson River valley several prominent merchant families had received large manorial estates in the 1680s from the royal governor. They established themselves on these tracts as resident landlords and recruited poor Dutch and German immigrants as tenants. By the middle of the eighteenth century, there were about 30 manors around New York City and Albany, totaling some 2 million acres and worked by several thousand tenants. Their labor produced a large surplus of wheat and livestock and a handsome profit for the great Yorker landlords.

The terms of tenancy in the Hudson valley were fairly generous, because Yorker landlords had to compete with other colonies to attract laborers. But tenancy under any terms was unacceptable to the New Englanders who had moved there. They squatted on Yorker manors, fended off all attempts at eviction, and preached their ideas about owning land to Dutch and German tenants. Armed insurrection exploded in 1757 and again, more violently, in 1766. Tenants refused to pay rents, formed mobs, stormed the homes of landlords, and prepared to march on New York City. The rebels dispersed only when a regiment of British soldiers arrived armed with a cannon.

Eighteenth-Century Seaports

Most Americans on the move found homes, if not havens, in frontier communities. Others, drawn by opportunity or desperation, made places for themselves in a different environment—colonial seaports. Cities like Boston, New York, Philadelphia, and Charleston, founded as coastal villages in the seventeenth century, became magnets for migrants and mushroomed into major commercial centers by the opening decades of the eighteenth century.

Benjamin Franklin's Philadelphia offered a waterfront fringed with wharves and dotted with warehouses, streets crowded with a jumble of shops, taverns, and homes, and a skyline punctuated by the spires of churches and the towers of public buildings. It was the second largest city of all the British empire, but by modern standards Philadelphia was small, with just 35,000 inhabitants in 1770. New York, Boston, Charleston, and Newport were its closest competitors in the colonies. The scale of city life was small in another way too. All of New York City was clustered at the southern tip of Manhattan Island; all of Boston could be traversed in a walk of less than an hour. Only Philadelphia's population had sprawled into suburbs. And it was a rare building that rose more than two stories high.

Because of their tiny total area, colonial seaports were teeming, congested places. Human occupants competed for places on crude sidewalks and narrow streets of gravel or rough cobblestone with cattle and sheep being driven to the butcher and with carts, carriages, and horses conveying produce and passengers, often at breakneck pace. Pedestrians, vehicles, and livestock alike vied for right of way with roaming herds of swine and packs of dogs. Despite the density of settle-

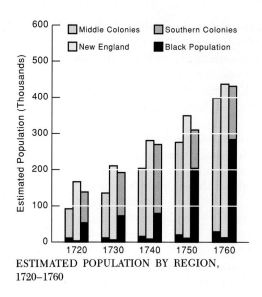

ESTIMATED POPULATION BY REGION, 1720–1760

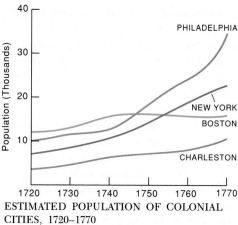

ESTIMATED POPULATION OF COLONIAL CITIES, 1720–1770

While Boston's population remained stable after 1740, it was surpassed by the sharp growth of New York and, especially, Philadelphia.

ment and traffic, colonial cities were relatively clean compared to European towns of equal size. While public sanitation still left much to be desired, most city governments improved the state of sewers, drains, and streets during the eighteenth century. Only New York remained so filthy that it defied human habitation.

The size of cities fostered intimacy among inhabitants. Most faces seen on the streets were familiar, and nearly everyone could recognize one group—the merchants. They managed commerce, the lifeblood of urban economies. Traders in New York and Philadelphia dealt in the produce of their towns' rich hinterland, dispatching corn, wheat, cattle, and horses to feed West Indian planters and to power island sugar mills. New England merchants trafficked in fish, a staple in the diet of Caribbean slaves and Iberian Catholics; masts and timber, items in demand by the British navy; and rum, a popular export to almost any place. Charleston's dealers sent indigo and rice to Britain, the indigo for English dyemakers, the rice for shipment to Europe. With the returns of the export trade, merchants in every colonial city imported the coveted luxuries produced in England—fine cloth, pottery, and tea—along with large lots of cheaper textiles and farming implements.

Their wealth made merchants a dominant force in political as well as economic life. They monopolized city governments and shared power in colonial assemblies with lawyers and the largest farmers and planters. By the middle of the eighteenth century, an increasing amount of wealth and political influence was concentrated in the hands of urban trading families. But the merchant class was not a closed oligarchy: new entrepreneurs with ready skills or fortunate marital connections were always entering the ranks of the city elite.

Most of those mobile citizens rose from the ranks of skilled craftworkers, the artisans who comprised the middling classes of colonial cities. No large-scale domestic industry produced goods for a mass market. Instead, the households of master craftworkers, usually including a few younger and less skilled journeymen artisans and very young, unskilled apprentices, filled orders for specific items placed by individual purchasers. Some artisans specialized in the maritime trades, the greater rewards going to master mariners, shipbuilders, and blacksmiths who forged anchors and iron fittings, the lesser returns to ropemakers and sailmakers who fashioned rigging. Master craftworkers who processed and packed raw materials for export—butchers, millers, and rum distillers—might also realize a substantial profit, as could those artisans in the luxury trades—gold- and silversmiths, jewelers, cabinet and carriage makers. Ranking below the master craftworkers in the most lucrative trades were those who served the basic needs of city dwellers— the men and, occasionally, women who baked bread, mended shoes, combed and powdered wigs, sewed simple clothing, cut hair and beards, and tended shops and taverns.

On the lowest rung of the city's social hierarchy were free and bound workers. The free labor force included journeymen artisans who were still perfecting their skill in a particular craft and young, able-bodied men who shipped out as sailors and fishermen or who loaded cargo onto ships docked in harbors. At the very bottom of the social order were unfree laborers—young boys serving apprenticeships to local master craftworkers and indentured servants doing menial labor for merchants or artisans.

Black men and women also made up a substantial part of the bound labor force of colonial seaports, not only in southern Charleston but in northern cities as well. While the vast majority of slaves imported from Africa were destined for a lifetime in tobacco fields and rice swamps, a smaller number were sold to urban merchants and craftsmen. Working as porters at the docks, assistants in craft shops, or as servants in wealthy households, blacks made up almost 20 percent of New York City's population and accounted for 10 percent of the inhabitants of Boston and Philadelphia.

The character of northern slavery changed decisively during the middle of the eighteenth century, when wars raging in Europe strangled the supply of white indentured servants to the colonies. Northern whites turned to slaves as substitutes for servants and started importing large numbers of blacks directly from Africa. In the two decades after 1730, one-third of all immigrants arriving in New York harbor were black; by 1760, blacks comprised over three-quarters of all bound laborers in Philadelphia. The preference of white merchants for importing African men upset what had been an equal balance of black men and women in colonial seaports, making it difficult for the newcomers to enjoy a normal family life. The recently arrived Africans also lacked immunity to American diseases, and many did not survive their first northern winter: the death rate among urban blacks was double that for whites.

But those who did survive infused into urban black culture a new awareness of a common West African past. The resurgence of African traditions appeared most vividly in an annual event known as "Negro election day." The festival, similar to one conducted throughout West Africa, was celebrated by blacks in seaports throughout New England and the Middle Colonies. The day's revels began with black men and women—some dressed in their masters' clothes or mounted on their horses—parading to the music of fiddles, banjos, drums, and tambourines. They proceeded to select black "kings," "governors," and "judges," who duly "held court" and settled minor disputes among white and black members of the community. "Negro election day" did not challenge the established racial order with its temporary and ritualized reversal of roles. But it did allow the black community to honor their own leaders.

The availability of black maids and cooks as well as the pool of free domestic

The Old Plantation affords a rare glimpse of life in the slave quarters. At this festive gathering, both men and women dance to the music of a molo (a stringed instrument similar to a banjo) and drums. The insets show a gudugudu drum and a stringed kora, instruments common throughout Africa and similar to those depicted in the painting.

servants made for leisured lives among women from well-to-do white families in colonial seaports. Even those women who could not afford the luxury of household help spent less time and energy doing domestic work than farming wives and daughters. Although some housewives grew vegetables in backyard gardens or kept a few chickens, large markets stocked by outlying farmers supplied most of the food for urban families. Most women were also relieved of the laborious chore of spinning and weaving: they bought their cloth at dry goods stores instead. Because they purchased what farm women had to produce, urban wives could devote more time to keeping up houses and appearances. The daughters of the well-to-do, in particular, had greater leisure for visiting friends and reading. Unlike girls in rural areas, whose labor was vital to family welfare, these young urban women learned "the mysteries of housewifery" only to prepare themselves for their future domestic roles.

All colonial women were expected to devote themselves to caring for households, husbands, and children and to find fulfillment in the domestic sphere. But cities offered to women who had to support themselves a number of employments.

Young single women from poorer families commonly spent a few years before marriage working in more affluent households as maids, cooks, laundresses, seamstresses, or nurses for infants and the infirm. Prostitution was another possible line of work, but less secure because of public opposition. More respected and lucrative occupations for women, all requiring long apprenticeships and expert skill, included midwifery, millinery, and "mantua making"—the "Genteel way of Making up" fashionable dresses and cloaks. Although wives of artisans and retailers sometimes assisted in their husbands' businesses, and, as widows, often continued to manage groceries, taverns, and printshops, most women worked in jobs that more closely resembled traditional female roles. And even in cities, less than one out of every ten women worked outside their own homes.

The people who lived in cities, perhaps one out of every twenty Americans, enjoyed a more stimulating and diverse environment than most colonials. The wealthiest could attend an occasional ball or concert; those living in liberal New York or Charleston might even see a play performed by touring English actors. The middling classes could choose among weekly newspapers and a varied stock at local bookshops and could converse with other tradespeople at private social clubs and fraternal societies. The lower classes, along with their betters, found diversion in drink, horse racing, cockfighting, and bull and bear baiting. Occasionally members of all social classes converged at taverns to see traveling exhibitions of trained dogs and horses, exotic displays of "Great White Bears" and "Arabian camels," or the spectacular waxworks of one John Dyer, featuring "a lively Representation of Margaret, Countess of Herrinburg, who had 365 Children at one Birth."

But city dwellers, then as now, paid a price for the variety of their lives. Commerce was fraught with risk: ships sank, small markets abroad glutted, and wars disrupted trading patterns. Natural and human disasters could send shock waves through the delicate economies of colonial seaports, bankrupting merchants and leaving craftworkers and laborers out of work. When trade slowed down, the lowest classes were the first to feel the pinch. The ups and downs of seaport economies, combined with the steady influx of immigrants, swelled the ranks of the poor in all cities by the mid-eighteenth century. While the major seaports established workhouses to employ the able-bodied poor, these institutions were a place of last resort for their intended occupants. Cities continued to aid most of the dependent by doling out small subsidies of money, food, and firewood.

Not only economic life but often life itself was more precarious for city dwellers, who endured epidemic disease more frequently than country folk. The deadly microbes of smallpox and yellow fever, introduced to American ports by sailors and immigrants, spread rapidly among closely packed populations. And because of urban congestion, fire was an ever-present danger as well. Although buildings of brick were slowly supplanting the wooden frame structures of an earlier era, a spark from a single clogged chimney flue could quickly set afire surrounding dwellings, engulfing overcrowded neighborhoods in a catastrophic blaze.

Social Conflict in Seaports

Cities were social tinderboxes too. Just as rapid westward movement churned up trouble on the frontier, the swelling of urban populations sparked discord in seaports. The jumbled assortment of English, Scots-Irish, Germans, Swiss, Dutch, French, and Spanish jostled uneasily against one another in the compact quarters of Philadelphia and New York. To make matters worse, religious differences contributed to ethnic animosities. Jewish funerals in New York, for example, drew crowds of the hostile and the curious to cemeteries, where they heckled the mourners. Even when hostility did not turn to violence, ethnic and religious differences often split city residents in urban political contests.

Antagonism between rich and poor also stirred up unrest. Some merchant families flaunted their wealth, building imposing mansions in town and maintaining country estates. Merchants clad in scarlet coats clambered out of elegant carriages and strutted to their counting houses in gaudily striped shoes. Their wives shivered in fashionably low-cut gowns of French design, encumbered by hoop petticoats and weighed down with lavish jewelry. During hard times, symbols of merchant opulence like expensive coaches and full warehouses became favorite targets of mob vandalism. Crowds also congregated to intimidate and punish other groups who provoked popular hostility—unresponsive politicians, prostitutes, and "press gangs." Impressment, attempts on the part of the British navy to dragoon colonial service, triggered some of the most violent urban riots.

SLAVE SOCIETIES IN THE EIGHTEENTH-CENTURY SOUTH

The divisions and social diversity of seaports paled, however, when set beside those of another society in eighteenth-century America. There was no colonial environment so deeply unequal, varied, and violent as the plantation district of the southern coast.

When Thomas Jefferson wrote the Declaration of Independence in 1776, nearly half of the people in his own colony of Virginia were slaves. Even by the first decade of the eighteenth century, a majority of South Carolinians were black, and by 1720 slaves made up two-thirds of that colony's population. By 1775 one out of every five Americans was of African ancestry, and over 90 percent of all American blacks lived in the South, most along the seaboard. Here, on tobacco and rice plantations, slaves fashioned an African-American society and culture as distinctive as the other provincial settings of the eighteenth century. But blacks began to build stable families and communities only late in the eighteenth century, and against formidable odds.

Whether a slave was auctioned off to the Chesapeake or to the Lower South shaped his or her future in important ways. Slaves in the low country of South Carolina and Georgia lived on plantations with as many as 50 other blacks, about half of whom were African-born. Slaves residing in large lowland quarters, virtually black villages, had infrequent contact with either their masters or the rest of the sparse white population. In some districts of South Carolina there were seven or eight blacks for every white. Planters who could afford the luxury of absentee ownership escaped the lowland malarial climate for the healthier air of Charleston. Other masters owned several plantations and traveled from one to another. In their absence, white overseers and black "drivers," the most experienced slaves, supervised work routines.

That work was arduous, for rice required constant cultivation. Blacks tended young plants and hoed fields in the sweltering summer heat of the mosquito-infested lowlands. After midcentury when some planters adopted "tidal cultivation," irrigating their fields by regulating the flow of rivers, slaves spent the winter

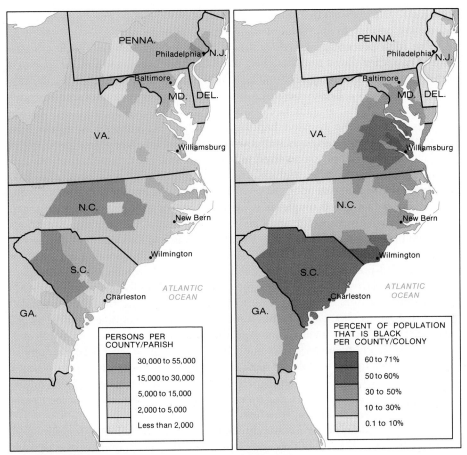

THE DISTRIBUTION OF THE AMERICAN POPULATION, 1775
The African-American population expanded dramatically during the eighteenth century, especially in the southern colonies. While the high volume of slave imports accounts for most of the growth in the first half of the century, natural increase was responsible for the rising black population during later decades.

and early spring building dams and canals and the summer overseeing sluices and floodgates.

Many Chesapeake slaves, like those in Carolina, were African-born, but most lived on smaller plantations with fewer fellow blacks. Throughout the eighteenth century, more than half lived on plantations of less than 20 slaves. Less densely concentrated than in Carolina, Chesapeake slaves also had more contact with whites. Unlike Carolina's absentee owners, gentlemen in the Upper South actively managed their estates and subjected their slaves' performance to closer scrutiny.

The Slave Family and Community

By contrast, in the Carolina low country, the density of black settlement afforded slaves the opportunity to cultivate a separate sphere in the quarters. The widespread use of the "task system" rather than gang labor on Carolina plantations also widened the window of freedom within slavery. When a slave had completed his assigned task for the day, one planter explained, "his master feels no right to call upon him." During such free time blacks tended garden plots, growing vegetables and raising poultry to supplement their own diets or to sell.

The high percentage of African-born blacks everywhere in the South also made it easier for slaves to retain their tribal cultures. African influence appeared in the slaves' distinctive agricultural skills and practices, folktales, music, dances, superstitions, and religious beliefs. Christianity won few converts among eighteenth-century slaves, in part because most blacks preferred traditional African religions. Whites also resisted baptizing their slaves, fearing that blacks who shared their masters' religious status would become less tractable.

Whenever possible, slaves lived in family groups, the typical household consisting of a husband, wife, and children. Some gradually developed elaborate kinship networks that extended over several plantations in a single neighborhood, maintaining family ties through visits, with or without their masters' permission. But not all slaves were so fortunate. The smaller size of Chesapeake plantations narrowed opportunities for slaves in the Upper South to find partners, and in the Lower South, two out of every three slaves were male. The South Carolina slave population did not contain equal numbers of men and women until 1790.

Even for slaves fortunate enough to find mates, family life was fragile. Although some planters encouraged permanent unions among their bondspeople, hoping that family ties would foster reproduction and discourage running away, slave marriages had no legal status. And the slave family was only as stable as a master's health and finances were sound. If a planter fell on hard times, members of black families might be sold off to different buyers to meet his debts. When a master died, black families might be divided among surviving heirs. Even under the best circumstances, fathers might be hired out to other planters for long periods or sent to work in distant quarters.

After the middle of the eighteenth century, a number of changes enhanced the strength and solidarity of the black family and the slave community. As slave importation began to taper off, the rate of natural increase among blacks started to climb. In the Tidewater and the Virginia Piedmont, the black population grew more rapidly than the white, and even in the Lower South, slave communities began to increase because of reproduction rather than importation. As the proportion of new Africans dropped and the number of native-born blacks grew, the ratio of men to women in the slave community became more equal. Those changes and the appearance of more large plantations, even in the Chesapeake, created more opportunities for blacks to form families.

As the number of native-born blacks increased, so did a distinctive African-American culture in the slave quarters. Glimpses of it begin to appear in planters' diaries and travelers' accounts toward the end of the eighteenth century. In 1774, one young English visitor to the Maryland Tidewater described "a Negro Ball" held on one spring Sabbath day, "the only days that these poor creatures have to themselves." To the music of a banjo, a gourd fitted out with four strings, the assembled slaves danced. They also sang together, "very droll music indeed," which related "the usage they have received from their Masters or Mistresses in a very satirical stile and manner."

Slave Resistance in the Eighteenth Century

What the young Englishman had witnessed at the "Negro Ball" was not only an African-American entertainment, but also a subtle expression of resistance and a strategy for survival. While the influx of white immigrants to the backcountry contributed to upheaval on the frontier, the concentration of slaves on the southern coast generated conflict in plantation districts.

Slave resistance took several forms. Among newly arrived Africans, collective attempts at escape were most common. Groups of "saltwater" slaves, often made up of newcomers from the same tribe, fled inland and formed "Maroon" communities of runaways. These efforts were usually unsuccessful because the Maroon settlements were large enough to be easily detected; Carolinians even enlisted the Cherokee to return runaways for a reward.

More acculturated blacks adopted subtler ways of subverting slavery. William Byrd, a Virginia planter, unwittingly recorded in his diary a catalogue of the range of resistance tactics deployed by slaves on his plantation. He complained about house servants challenging his orders, damaging his furniture, stealing his liquor, and engaging him and his wife in elaborate contests of will; he fretted over field hands who broke his tools and dragged out their tasks. Domestics and field hands alike faked illness, feigned stupidity and laziness, pilfered from the storehouse, hid in the woods for weeks at a time, or simply took off to visit other plantations. It never dawned on Byrd that there was a pattern to slave behavior and that every recalcitrant act was another grain of sand scattered in the gears of his plantation.

The more that slaves became accustomed to English ways, the more likely they were to resist their condition and to escape—successfully. The largest group of blacks who made good on a flight to freedom were slave artisans. Because of their work, these craftworkers were accustomed to moving about the countryside from one job to another on different plantations. Because they spoke fluent English and possessed valuable skills, they could survive once they slipped away from their masters. And because they ran away individually, the slave artisans were more difficult to track down. Most disappeared into colonial seaports, where they practiced their craft or became sailors.

Rebellion against bondage also involved violence. Whites in communities with substantial numbers of blacks lived in gnawing dread of arson, poisoning, and insurrection. Four slave conspiracies were reported in Virginia during the first half of the eighteenth century. In South Carolina, more than two decades of abortive uprisings and insurrection scares culminated in the Stono Rebellion of 1739, the largest slave revolt of the colonial period. Nearly 100 blacks, led by a slave named Jemmy, seized arms from a store in the low-country district of Stono and killed several whites before they were caught and killed by the white militia.

The Stono Rebellion triggered other unsuccessful slave uprisings and reports of slave conspiracies throughout the colonies in 1740 and 1741. But throughout the eighteenth century, slave rebellions occurred far less frequently on the mainland of North America than in the Caribbean or Brazil. Whites outnumbered blacks in all of the colonies except South Carolina, and only there did rebels have a haven for a quick escape—Spanish Florida. Faced with these odds, most slaves reasoned that the risks of rebellion outweighed the prospects for success—and most sought opportunities for greater personal freedom within the slave system instead.

Despite the growing rebelliousness of blacks, southern planters continued to import African slaves in large numbers during the eighteenth century. The practice mystified Franklin, revealing at least one gap in his knowledge—the crucial importance of slavery in the southern economy. But unlike some of his Quaker neighbors in Pennsylvania, who were beginning to object to slavery on moral and humanitarian grounds, Franklin's reservations—like his opposition to German immigration—were overtly racist. "Why increase the sons of Africa by planting them in America," he asked, "where we have so fair an opportunity, by excluding all blacks and tawnys, of increasing the lovely white and red?"

ENLIGHTENMENT AND AWAKENING IN AMERICA

All of the differences among eighteenth-century Americans resulted in more than clashes of economic interests and conflicts between regions, races, and ethnic groups. Diversity also made for fundamental differences in the ways that Americans thought and believed. City dwellers were more attuned to European culture than were people living in small inland farming villages, and both were more cosmopolitan than settlers scattered across the frontier. White males from well-to-do families of English ancestry were far more likely to receive college educations than those from poorer or immigrant households, white women of every class and background were excluded from higher education, and slaves received no education at all. Where they lived, how well they lived, whether they were male or female, native-born or immigrant, slave or free—all these variables fostered among Americans distinctive world views, differing attitudes and assumptions about the individual's relationship to nature, society, and God.

The Enlightenment in America

The diversity of Americans' inner lives became even more pronounced during the eighteenth century because of the Enlightenment, an intellectual movement that started in Europe during the seventeenth century. The leading figures of the Enlightenment, the "philosophes," stressed the power of human reason to promote progress by revealing the laws governing both nature and society. By acquiring a clear understanding of these laws, they believed, people could control their lives and improve the quality of society and government. The philosophy of the Enlightenment struck a shallow root in the American colonies. Its influence was confined mainly to the most skilled seaport artisans and some elite colonial families of city merchants, northern country squires, and southern planters. Only well-to-do families had the resources, the leisure, and the education to read the latest books from Europe. The new outlook that they adopted contrasted sharply with that of less privileged and well-educated colonials.

Franklin's career epitomized the Enlightenment's impact on the colonies. Like other Americans who imbibed the "new learning," he was most impressed by its emphasis on useful knowledge and experimentation. He pondered air currents and then invented a stove that heated houses more efficiently. He toyed with electricity and then invented lightning rods to protect buildings in thunderstorms. Other amateur American scientists also hoped to understand and master the natural world: they constructed simple telescopes to observe the transits of Venus and Mercury; they filled botanical gardens with plants and identified and classified animal species native to North America; they sought to explain epidemics in terms of natural causes and supported inoculation, a new medical procedure for immunizing people against smallpox. They experimented with new farming techniques and wrote treatises on increasing the productivity of agriculture.

Clubs were organized to discuss the latest European ideas about science, philosophy, literature, and social betterment. Typical of these groups was the American Philosophical Society, founded by Franklin in 1743 and dedicated to "Experiments that let Light into the Nature of Things, tend to increase the Power of Man over Matter, and multiply the Conveniencies or Pleasures of Life."

Enlightenment ideas were also disseminated among young men of affluent families through American colleges. While many scions of colonial families were still educated in England, six colleges had been established in America by 1763: Harvard (1636); William and Mary (1693); Yale (1701); the College of New Jersey (later Princeton, 1746); King's College (later Columbia, 1754); and the Academy and College of Philadelphia (later the University of Pennsylvania, 1755). The founders of some of these institutions had intended them primarily to train ministers, but by the eighteenth century their graduates included lawyers and merchants, doctors and scientists. Most colleges offered courses in mathematics and the natural sciences that taught students algebra and such advanced theories as Copernican astronomy and Newtonian physics.

Even some clergy educated at American colleges were touched by the Enlightenment, the new spirit being reflected in the more liberal theology that they developed and preached to their congregations. By 1740, this "rational Christianity" commanded a small following among Americans, usually Anglicans or liberal Congregationalists. In place of the Calvinist religion of mystery and miracle, rationalists asserted the essential reasonableness of Christianity. Their God was not the Calvinists' inscrutable Jehovah, but a benevolent, nearly genial deity who opened salvation to all, not just a small, predestined elite. According to the rationalists, religious life consisted in doing good works: they muted the Calvinist emphasis on human sinfulness and dispensed altogether with the Calvinist insistence on a heart-wrenching conversion. Some reduced religion to a moral science— Franklin drew up lists of virtues in a ledger and then kept an account of his progress toward perfection.

Enlightenment philosophy and rational Christianity did not affect the outlook of most Americans. Even among members of the elite the appeal of these newer currents was far from universal. The great majority of colonials still looked for ultimate truth in God's revelation in the Bible rather than human reason, and explained the workings of the world in terms of divine providence rather than natural law. By the mid-eighteenth century, over half of all white men (and a smaller percentage of white women) were literate, and most children of every class except slaves received some training in reading, writing, and basic arithmetic at home, in village "dame schools" run by widows or unmarried women, or in schools set up for apprentices by their masters. Even so, such rudimentary educations could not have carried most American readers through such learned treatises of the philosophes as John Locke's essay on human psychology, Newton's explanation of the law of gravity, or Voltaire's attacks on traditional Christianity.

The inroads of rationalism in America, although slight, still convinced some clergy that they needed to promote among colonials not only religion but "true religion"—Calvinism. Out of their concerns came the revival that swept the colonies during the middle decades of the eighteenth century.

The First Great Awakening

The westward flow of immigrants, the concentration of more people in seaports, and the forced settlement of many slaves in the coastal South—all three movements of people over the eighteenth century—set the stage for mounting social

To Nathan Cole, a Connecticut farmer who witnessed one of George Whitefield's sermons, the preacher appeared "almost angelical; a young, slim, slender youth before thousands of people with a bold, undaunted countenance. . . . He looked as if he was clothed with authority from the Great God . . . and my hearing him preach gave me a heart wound."

tensions. And in the 1740s, a single dramatic episode supplied Americans with yet another source of division. Ironically, that event was a religious revival. Even more ironically, participation in the revival, known as the first Great Awakening, was the only experience that a large number of people everywhere in the colonies had in common. And the man who sparked the Great Awakening, George Whitefield, an English evangelist and one of the founders of the Methodist Church, was the only public figure whose name was known to all eighteenth-century Americans.

Of course, Americans had been fighting over religion well before the Great Awakening. In most New England colonies, minorities of Anglicans, Baptists, and Quakers had battled the established Congregational Church for more than a century, first seeking relief from outright persecution and political discrimination and later exemptions from paying taxes to support the Puritan clergy. In the southern colonies, even smaller congregations of Presbyterians, Baptists, and Quakers had waged a similar struggle against the established Anglican Church. And in the Middle Colonies, where religious toleration prevailed, a patchwork of denominations and smaller sects—Quakers, Presbyterians, Lutherans, Mennonites, Dunkards, and others—competed ferociously for members.

The spread of population westward heightened the competition and fostered a sense of crisis in American church life. The clergy recognized that many inhabitants of the backcountry were deprived of religious consolation and the ordered social life offered by churches. And many ministers, especially the strict Calvinists among the Congregationalists, Presbyterians, and Reformed, feared that large numbers of lay people might abandon the faith of their ancestors and embrace rational Christianity—or lose all faith.

The first stirrings of religious excitement began among the congregations of a handful of evangelical Calvinists who urged the necessity of conversion. There was William Tennent, a Scots-Irish immigrant who settled with his four sons, all ministers, in Bucks County, Pennsylvania. The Tennents aroused religious enthusiasm among their fellow Presbyterians throughout the Middle Colonies and in the 1730s founded the "Log College"—the institution that came to be called Princeton—to train other preachers. Among New England Congregationalists, clergy awakened "backsliders" to a proper anxiety over salvation by preaching about local epidemics or earthquakes or the premature deaths of young people. Among them was Jonathan Edwards, a tall, thin, intensely intellectual Yale graduate who served as the pastor at Northampton, Massachusetts. By the mid-1730s, Edwards' preaching, which combined lyrical descriptions of God's saving grace with sheer psychological terrorism, had promoted "frontier revivals" throughout the Connecticut River valley. "The God that holds you over the pit of hell, much as one holds a spider or some loathsome insect over the fire, abhors you and is dreadfully provoked," Edwards declaimed to one congregation, ". . . there is no other reason to be given, why you have not dropped into hell since you arise in the morning, but that God's hand has held you up."

These local revivals were mere tremors compared to the earthquake of enthusiasm that shook the colonies with the arrival in the fall of 1739 of George Whitefield, the handsome, cross-eyed "boy preacher." What Whitefield preached in the churches and open fields of America was nothing more than what other Calvinists had been saying for centuries: sinful men and women were totally dependent for salvation on the mercy of a pure, all-powerful God. But Whitefield presented the message in novel ways. He and his many eager imitators among colonial ministers turned the church into a theater. With dramatic gestures and sometimes copious tears, in low, ominous monotones or in ringing cadences, divines preached sermons laden with vivid, terrifying images of the torments of hellfire. The pathos, simplicity, and stark violence of such performances appealed to people of all classes, ethnic groups, and races. Whitefield toured America from New England to Georgia; by the time he sailed back to England in January 1741, thousands of awakened souls were joining churches, many of them newly formed.

The Aftermath of the Great Awakening

Whitefield also left in his wake a gathering storm of controversy. Throughout the colonies, conservative and moderate clergy questioned the unrestrained emotionalism of the evangelicals and the disorder and discord that attended the revivals. "Our presses are forever teeming with books, and our women with bastards," one antirevivalist sighed. Many members of the awakened laity now openly criticized their old ministers as cold, unconverted, and uninspiring. To supply the missing fire, some laymen—"and even Women and Common Negroes"—took to "exhorting" any audience willing to listen. The most popular prorevival ministers turned "itinerants," traveling like Whitefield from one town to another. Battles raged within congregations and whole denominations over the challenge to clerical authority by lay exhorters and itinerants, as well as the evangelical approach to conversion from "the heart" rather than "the head."

The Awakening left Americans sharply polarized along religious lines. Quakers (who by now had become much soberer than their seventeenth-century forebears) gained new members among conservatives who disapproved of the revivals' excesses. So did the Anglicans. On the other hand, Baptists and "Separate" Congregationalists gained a host of evangelical radicals, who demanded pure churches of converted believers. The largest single group of churchgoing Americans remained within the Congregational and Presbyterian denominations, but they divided internally between advocates and opponents of revivals.

While congregations splintered and denominations bickered, the fires of revivalism spread to the frontier. As the enthusiasm on the seaboard burned down to embers, the Presbyterians of the Middle Colonies and the Baptists of New England spread the gospel in the backcountry of Pennsylvania, Virginia, the Carolinas, and Georgia. From the mid-1740s until the 1770s, scores of new churches were formed. As in the East, the "awakenings" caused contention. Ardent Presbyterian converts in the Carolina backcountry harassed Anglican priests and disrupted their services by loosing packs of dogs in local chapels. In parts of Virginia, Anglicans took the offensive against the somber Baptists. Their severe, ascetic, and egalitarian morality sounded a silent reproach to the hard-drinking, high-stepping, horse-racing, slaveholding Chesapeake gentry. County officials, prodded into action by resentful Anglican parsons, fined Baptist ministers, intimidated and imprisoned them, and occasionally even whipped them.

While the West was turning toward evangelical Calvinism, the most powerful people on the southeastern coast remained Anglican, and, in the Middle Colonies, Quaker. As a result, the seaboard and the backcountry residents found themselves quarreling over religious as well as political and ethnic issues. Inevitably, civil governments were drawn into the fray. In colonies where one denomination received state support, other churches lobbied legislatures for disestablishment, an end to the favored status of Congregationalism in Connecticut and Massachusetts and of Anglicanism in the southern colonies.

And so a divided and diverse lot of Americans found themselves at odds with one another—whether over religion, ethnic origins, or backcountry versus seaboard disputes. And Benjamin Franklin, who made it his business to know, knew well the extent of the divisions as he made his way toward Albany in the spring of 1754, dreaming improbably of American political union. He had himself counted his fellow citizens, despairing over the influx of Germans, Scots-Irish, Africans, and other non-English newcomers. He had lived in two booming seaports, and he had felt the explosive force of the frontier. He personified the Enlightenment— and he knew all about the Great Awakening. The day that George Whitefield preached on the steps of the Philadelphia courthouse, there stood Franklin, an unrepentant rationalist, ignoring the sermon and working his way through the crowd to compute the distance traveled by the evangelist's voice.

Why, then, could Franklin, who knew how little held the colonials together, sustain his hopes for political unity? The answer may be that even in 1754, the majority of colonial men and women were of English descent. And these free, white Americans liked being English. That much they had in common.

THE ANGLO-AMERICAN WORLDS OF THE EIGHTEENTH CENTURY

Most Americans prided themselves in being English. When colonials named their towns and counties, they named them after places in their parent country. When colonials established governments, they turned to England for their political models. They frequently claimed "the liberties of freeborn Englishmen" as their birthright. Even in diet, dress, furniture, architecture, and literature colonists adopted English standards of taste.

Yet the physical separation of the colonies across the wide Atlantic meant that American society had developed in ways significantly different from Great Britain.* Americans who visited their parent country quickly discovered the differences, which set them to thinking what it really meant to be English. Some differences made Americans feel inferior, ashamed of their rustic manners when compared with London's sophistication. But Americans also came to appreciate the comparative simplicity of their culture and the greater equality of their society. In particular, they judged colonial political arrangements to be more representative and responsive than those in England. Most Americans still liked being English, but they especially liked being English in America.

Urban Life in England and America

England was a more urban society than America. Although three-quarters of England's people lived in the countryside, a considerable number passed some part of their lives in cities. While most Americans on the move struck out for the frontier, the English gravitated toward urban settings. Perhaps one out of every six English men and women lived for a time in London, a teeming colossus by eighteenth-century standards with a population of 675,000 in 1750.

Nothing in their experience at home could have prepared colonials for their first exposure to London. Ninety percent of all Americans lived in towns of less than 2000, and the complexity of life even in major colonial seaports was dwarfed by that of London. Those who could afford to gloried in London's luxury and elegant diversions. They roamed the British Museum. They gawked at cathedrals and lounged in coffeehouses. They strolled through fashionable shops, fingering fine textiles, trying on spectacles, and inspecting handsome carriages. They had their portraits painted by celebrated artists like Joshua Reynolds. They savored concerts and operas, and they could even be found in Drury Lane, enjoying, perhaps with a twinge of Puritan guilt, English stage plays.

But the underside to this splendor left colonials with grave misgivings. London seethed with filth, crime, and desperate poverty. The poor and the unemployed, beggars and thieves, pickpockets and prostitutes crowded into its gin-soaked slums, taverns, and brothels. The city's death rate was double the birth rate, in large part because of heavy consumption of alcohol by the poor. The contrast between the polite refinements enjoyed by a wealthy few Londoners and the abject misery of the many disquieted colonial observers. Ebenezer Hazard, an American Quaker, knew for certain that he was not in Philadelphia, but instead in "a Sink of Sin."

Economic Development and Inequality

What sustained the growth of London and the urbanization of all England was a higher level of commercial and industrial development than existed in any of the

---

*When England and Scotland were unified in 1707, the nation as a whole became known officially as Great Britain, its citizens as British.

colonies. Most English men and women worked at agriculture, but it had become a big business, aimed at producing surplus food for city dwellers or for export abroad. By the mid-eighteenth century, the average English farm was a large-scale capitalist enterprise. Members of the gentry rented their estates to tenants, members of the rural middle class, or entrusted the management of their lands to stewards. Tenants and stewards then hired men and women from the swollen ranks of England's landless to perform the actual farm labor. At most, a mere quarter of the English actually owned the land that they farmed.

Bigness was the byword in other sectors of the economy as well. Mines and textile factories had become familiar sights, backed by large financial institutions and corporations like the Bank of England, Lloyd's of London, and the East India Company. By contrast, the average American family farm was small—a few hundred acres of land owned by the people who worked it. Production on most farms outside of the coastal South and the Delaware and Hudson valleys was geared to subsistence rather than trade. Manufacturing remained limited both by British mercantilist restrictions and the inclinations of colonials to farm instead.

The opportunities for great wealth provided by England's more developed economy created deep class distinctions, as did the inherited privileges of the aristocracy. The gulf between the rich and the poor yawned widest in London, but inequality of every kind was woven into the fabric of society. The members of the English upper class, the landed aristocracy and gentry, made up less than 2 percent of England's population but owned 70 percent of its land. By right of birth, English aristocrats claimed membership in the House of Lords; by custom, certain powerful gentry families dominated the other branch of Parliament, the House of Commons. England's titled gentlemen shared power and wealth and often family ties with the rich men of the city—major import and export merchants, successful lawyers, and lucky financiers. They too exerted political influence through the House of Commons.

The colonies had their own elites, but no true aristocracy or formally titled ruling class, no group gaining political privilege by hereditary right. On the contrary, the biggest American merchants and planters could trace their ancestries no higher than to England's merchants and minor gentlemen, and most derived from humbler backgrounds. Even the wealthiest colonial families lived in markedly less magnificence than their English counterparts. Probably the finest mansion in eighteenth-century America, William Byrd's Westover plantation, was scarcely a tenth the size of the marquis of Rockingham's country house, which was longer than two football fields.

If the English upper classes were more splendid, its lower classes were larger and worse off than their American counterparts. Less than a third of England's inhabitants belonged to the "middling sort" of traders, professionals, artisans, and tenant farmers. More than two-thirds eked out marginal existences at the bottom of society. By contrast, the colonial middle class took in nearly three-quarters of the white population, who prospered thanks to the availability of relatively cheap land. With labor scarce and wages for both urban and rural workers 100 percent higher in America than in England, it was much easier for Americans to accumulate savings and then buy a farm of their own. Most whites who began life on the bottom of society did not remain there throughout their lives.

Americans were divided in their opinion of England's social and economic development. On the one hand, gentlemen planters from the colonies envied the techniques English estate managers had introduced to make their fields more

Coffeehouses like this establishment in London were favorite gathering places for eighteenth-century Americans visiting Britain. Here merchants and mariners, ministers and students, lobbyists and tourists warmed themselves, read newspapers, and exchanged gossip about commerce, politics, and social life.

productive. Colonial entrepreneurs admired the ingenuity of English mills, mines, and canals. And they saw nothing amiss in women and children working long hours in factories. On the other hand, Americans disdained some members of the English upper class, whose incomes from land sustained extravagant, slothful, and dissolute habits. Just as alarming was the eagerness among London's big bankers and brokers to speculate in stocks or engage in shady financial maneuvering.

Americans were equally fascinated and uneasy about the habits of royalty and aristocracy. Benjamin Rush, a Philadelphia physician, felt in the House of Lords as if he "walked on sacred ground," begged his guide for permission to sit on the throne therein, and, once ensconced, sat "for a considerable time." Other colonials gushed over the grandeur of aristocratic estates and imported suits of livery for their servants, tea services for their wives, and wallpaper for their drawing rooms. They exported their sons to Britain for college educations at Oxford and Cambridge, medical school at Edinburgh, and legal training at London's Inns of Court.

But the aping of English ways was accompanied by a tinge of apprehension. One Philadelphia Quaker ordered an elegant English coach complete with coat-of-arms—but then reconsidered and removed the crest. When sons educated in England came home wearing dandified silks and affecting foppish manners, planter and merchant fathers complained that higher education had left their boys not only incompetent but impertinent. Fashionable English slang such as "Split me, Madam!" "By Gad!" and "Dam me!" fell hard on parental ears.

Americans harbored even greater doubts about English inequality. They recognized that England's ruling classes purchased their luxury and leisure at the cost of the rest of the nation. In his *Autobiography*, Benjamin Franklin painted a devastating portrait of the idle, dissipated, and degraded lives of his fellow workers in a London printshop. With no hope of bettering themselves, the printers drowned their disappointments by drinking throughout the workday, even more excessively on the Sabbath, and then faithfully observing the holiday of "St. Monday's" to nurse their hangovers. Franklin wondered about a society that suffered the many to live "below the Savage State so that a few may be raised above it." While accepting hierarchy as natural and desirable, many Americans felt that gross inequality of wealth would endanger liberty. They regarded the idle parasites among England's rich and poor alike as ominous signs of a degenerate nation.

Politics in England and America

American sentiments about English government were simpler. They venerated the British constitution of government but abhorred the actual workings of English politics. That judgment was ungenerous at best, for British political life had become remarkably stable over the eighteenth century. In large part it had done so because those who governed England ignored theories of what was supposed to be in favor of what worked.

In theory, England's "balanced constitution" was designed to give every order of English society some place in the workings of government. While the Crown represented the monarchy and the House of Lords the aristocracy, the House of Commons represented the democracy, the people of England. An ideal equilibrium was supposed to exist among the three elements of monarchy, aristocracy, and democracy, and that balance produced political harmony. In fact, the monarch's executive ministers had become dominant by adroit "managing" of the legislative branch, Parliament. The executive created support for their policies through a system of "influence" or patronage—or, put more bluntly, bribery.

Over the course of the eighteenth century, a large executive bureaucracy had evolved, in order to enforce laws, collect taxes, and prosecute the nearly constant wars in Europe and America. The power to appoint all military and treasury officials, customs and excise collectors, judges and justices of the peace lay with the monarch and his or her ministers. They used the spoils of office to win support among members of Parliament. By the middle of the eighteenth century, almost half of all members of Parliament also held Crown offices or government contracts.

Royal patronage was also deployed to manipulate parliamentary elections. In some of England's smaller districts, the majority of the electorate were royal officeholders. In other cases, the executive branch used money or liquor to bribe local voters into selecting their candidates. The small size of England's electorate fostered executive influence. Perhaps just one-fifth of all adult males were enfranchised. And many electoral districts were not adjusted to keep pace with population growth and resettlement. The notorious "rotten boroughs" each elected a member of Parliament to represent fewer than 500 easily bribable voters, while some large cities like Manchester and Leeds, newly populous because of industrial growth, had no representation in Parliament at all.

Americans liked to think that their colonial governments replicated the ideal structure of the English constitution. In terms of formal organization, there were similarities. Every colony except Connecticut and Rhode Island had a royal governor who represented the monarch in America. Every colony also had a bicameral (two-house) legislature: the democratically elected lower house or assembly, like the House of Commons, stood for popular interests, while the upper house or council, some elected and others appointed, more roughly approximated the House of Lords. Like members of Parliament, most colonial legislators came from among the elite.

But these formal similarities masked real differences between English and colonial governments. On the face of it, royal governors had much more power than the English Crown. Unlike kings and queens, royal governors could veto laws passed by assemblies; they could dissolve those bodies at will; they could create courts and dismiss judges. However, governors who asserted their full powers quickly ran afoul of their assemblies, who objected that such overwhelming authority endangered popular liberty. And in any showdown with their assemblies, most royal governors had to give way, for they lacked the lubricant of English politics—the lucrative government offices and contracts that bought loyalty. The colonial legislatures possessed additional leverage, since all of them retained the sole authority to levy taxes.

But even if the governors had enjoyed greater patronage powers, their efforts to "manage" colonial legislatures would have been stymied by the sheer size of the American electorate. There were too many voters in America to bribe. Over half and possibly as many as 70 percent of all white adult colonial men were enfranchised. Property requirements were the same in America as in England, but widespread ownership of land in the colonies allowed most men to meet the qualifications easily.

The American electorate was not only too big to bribe, but it was also more watchful. Representatives were required to reside in the districts that they served, and a few even received binding instructions from their constituents about how to vote. Representation was also apportioned according to population far more equitably than in England. Eighteenth-century Americans endorsed the notion of "actual representation": they believed that officials should serve the local interests and needs of those who directly elected them. Since they were so closely tied to their constituents' wishes, American legislators were far less susceptible than members of Parliament to executive pressure and influence.

All these peculiarities of American political life fostered a phenomenon historians have called "the rise of the assemblies." The royal governors' lack of patronage steadily diminished executive influence over colonial legislatures, allowing assemblies a decided edge in any political contest. Increasingly confident of their power and importance, the assemblies styled themselves miniature Parliaments, entitled to all of the privileges of the original body in England.

The English Opposition and American Political Thought

The desire of colonial legislatures to emulate Parliament was part of the wider reverence in which Americans held the English constitution. But while Americans agreed that the English constitution was nothing short of "the most happy and excellent form of government" ever devised, many were appalled by the reality of English politics. John Dickinson, a young Pennsylvanian training as a lawyer in London, recoiled in horror from the conduct of a parliamentary election in 1754. The king and his ministers had spent over 100,000 pounds to sway support for their candidates, he wrote to his father, and "If a man cannot be brought to vote as he is desired, he is made dead drunk and kept in that state, never heard of by his family and friends, till all is over and he can do no harm."

The English artist William Hogarth's satirical rendition of an English election mirrored the reservations of many Americans about the political culture of the mother country.

Americans like John Dickinson found their own dark conclusions reinforced by the writings of a group of English known as the "Country Party," also called "the Opposition." The Opposition drew their inspiration from the English Civil War a century earlier, when thinkers like John Milton, Algernon Sydney, and James Harrington had consistently upheld the rights of the individual against the power of the state. Even now, the Opposition argued, the danger to liberty still loomed. The Glorious Revolution of 1688 had not gone far enough in reforming English politics. The ever-expanding executive branch of government was steadily corrupting Parliament and depriving the electorate of its liberty.

Underlying the Opposition's conception of politics was a nearly Calvinist view of sinful human nature. In their eyes humankind was not ruled by principle but driven by passion and insatiable ambition. Politicians, the most selfish and depraved of all people, would always conspire against liberty to enhance their own power. They had to be watched at all times: the price of liberty was eternal vigilance. In pressing their case for reform, the Opposition advocated adult manhood suffrage and proportional representation. They also favored binding representatives to their constituencies by residential requirements and instructions. Only the reform of politics and the restoration of virtue to public and private life, the Opposition believed, could save England from certain disaster.

Such sentiments were strongly put, but in fact, Opposition thinkers occupied only the fringes of English political life. They drew from radicals and religious dissenters on the extreme left and conservative landed gentlemen on the extreme right of the political spectrum. An odd lot, they included the gifted historian Catherine Macaulay; Henry St. John Bolingbroke and Robert Viscount Molesworth, two aristocratic politicians out of power; Benjamin Hoadley, an Anglican priest; and Joseph Priestley, a clergyman and chemist. Best known to Americans were John Trenchard, a lawyer, and Thomas Gordon, a schoolteacher, who collaborated on *Cato's Letters*, a series of scathing essays against the political establishment. But whether intellectuals, teachers, or clergy, they had drifted far from England's political mainstream.

American colonists, however, revered the English Opposition. Their assessment of English society confirmed American anxieties about England, while their program for political reform bore a flattering resemblance to how colonial politics operated. The Opposition also shared with Americans a lurking suspicion of people at the center of power—for both groups were far enough on the fringes of imperial politics to imagine the worst.

The Imperial System Before 1760

In England most citizens remained complacent and unconcerned about the condition of government. In their view, the Glorious Revolution of 1688 had worked: peace prevailed in public life, except for the mutterings of the Opposition. As for the Americans, the English thought about them little, understood them less, and wished neither to think more about them nor to understand them better.

It would be hard to overstate just how insignificant North America was in the English scheme of things. Those few Britons who thought about America at all saw colonials as seedy rustics who resembled the "savage" Indians more than the "civilized" English. As a London acquaintance remarked to Thomas Hancock, it was a pity Mrs. Hancock had to remain in Boston when he could "take her to England and make her happy with Christians." Americans on the receiving end of British scorn bristled, like the Marblehead fish merchant Robert Hooper, who complained to his London agent about being cheated by an English trader. "Do tell him," Hooper fumed, "that we are not quite Indians, although living in an Indian country."

The same indifference contributed to England's haphazard administration of its colonies. The Board of Trade and Plantations, created from the Lords of Trade in 1696, remained for the rest of the colonial period the major agency monitoring American affairs. The Board gathered information about Atlantic trading and fishing, reviewed laws and petitions drawn up by colonial assemblies, and exchanged letters and instructions with royal governors. But the Board of Trade was only an advisory body, reporting to the king's ministers and passing on information to other government agencies but unable to act. The English bureaucrats who knew the most about America were not the same bureaucrats who decided on colonial policies.

Real authority over the colonies was scattered among an array of other agencies—the secretary of state for the Southern Department, the Treasury, the Admiralty Board, and the War Office. Each agency staked out its own tiny administrative area: the Treasury oversaw customs and gathered other royal revenues; the Admiralty Board enforced regulations of trade; the War Office orchestrated colonial defense. But these departments were distracted by domestic and international responsibilities; colonial affairs stood at the bottom of their agendas. Furthermore, most British officials in America seemed equally indifferent to America. While some governors, customs collectors, and other officials were honest and competent, the king and his ministers commonly passed out the plums of colonial jobs in payment for political support, not in recognition of administrative ability. That standard saddled the colonies with some choice royal officials, eager to profit

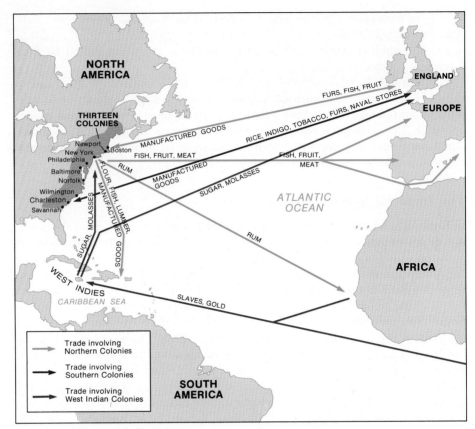

OVERSEAS TRADE NETWORKS
Commercial ties to Spain and Portugal, Africa, and the Caribbean sustained the growth of
both seaports and commercial farming regions on the British North American mainland and
enabled colonials to purchase an increasing volume of finished goods from England. The
proceeds from exports in foodstuffs and lumber to the West Indies and trade in fish to Spain
and Portugal enabled northern merchants and farmers to buy hardware and clothing from
the mother country. Southern planters financed their consumption of English imports and
their investment in African slaves with the profits from the sale of tobacco, rice, and indigo
abroad.

from their office and then retire. Some royal appointees never even set foot in
America, selling their offices to the highest bidder.

But no group in England's government was more indifferent to America than
Parliament. Members were content to consign colonial affairs to the king's ministers and the executive bureaucracy. Aside from passing an occasional law to regulate trade, restrict manufacturing, or direct monetary policy, Parliament made no
effort to assert its authority in America. The Lords and Commoners assumed that
their sovereignty extended over the entire empire, and nothing had occurred to
make them think otherwise.

In sum, England's decentralized colonial administration was chaotic, inefficient, and corrupt. And for the colonies, it worked quite well. The very weakness
of imperial oversight minimized the chances for conflict and left Americans with a
great deal of freedom.

Even England's regulation of trade rested lightly on the shoulders of Americans, for most colonial commerce flowed naturally into the channels prescribed by mercantilist restrictions. Southern planters were obliged to send their rice, indigo, and tobacco to Britain only, but they enjoyed favorable credit terms and experienced wholesaling from English merchants. Colonials were prohibited from finishing iron products and exporting hats and textiles, but they had no strong interest in developing domestic industries. Americans were required to import all manufactured goods through England, but by doing so, they acquired high-quality goods at low prices. At little sacrifice, Americans abided by imperial regulations: illicit trade was minimal in volume, sugar, molasses, and tea being the only commodities routinely smuggled.

Basking in benign neglect, the colonies prospered. During the eighteenth century America steadily produced more, earned more, and consumed more imported goods. American exports commanded high prices and met with steady demand. And by doing almost nothing about the colonies, England benefited as well, reaping a harvest of raw materials and a burgeoning market of ready colonial consumers. By 1770 one-third of England's total trade went to the colonies.

In this manner, the British empire muddled on to the mutual satisfaction of most people on both sides of the Atlantic. Prosperity and political autonomy allowed most Americans to like being English, despite their misgivings about the mother country. The beauty of it was that Americans could be English in America, enjoying higher birth rates, less squalid cities, more economic opportunity, greater political equality, and superior virtue. If imperial arrangements had remained as they were in 1754, the empire might have muddled on indefinitely. But because of the French and the Indians on the American frontier, the British empire began to change. And those changes made it increasingly hard for Americans to be English in America.

TOWARD THE SEVEN YEARS' WAR

In the late spring of 1754, while Benjamin Franklin dreamed of unifying Americans, a young man from Virginia dreamed of military glory. As Franklin rode toward Albany, the young man, an inexperienced, impulsive officer, led his company of Virginia militia toward Fort Duquesne, the French stronghold on the Forks of the Ohio.

Less than a year earlier, the king's ministers had advised royal governors in America to retard—by force if necessary—the French advance into the Ohio country. Virginians welcomed the order, for many leading politicians there held stock in the Ohio Company, a group of speculators who claimed hundreds of thousands of acres in the disputed territory. The Virginia government organized an expedition against Fort Duquesne, placing at its head the tall, strapping, red-haired young planter. He combined an imposing presence with the aloof self-possession of an English gentleman, and he wanted, more than anything, to become an officer in the regular British army.

But events in the Ohio country during that spring and summer did not go George Washington's way. French soldiers easily captured Fort Necessity, the crude outpost near Fort Duquesne that Washington's troops had hastily constructed. In early July, as the Albany Congress was debating, Washington was surrendering to a French force in the Pennsylvania backcountry and beating a retreat back to Virginia. By the end of 1754, Washington had resigned his militia command and retired to his plantation at Mount Vernon. His humiliation at Fort Necessity had dashed his dreams of martial glory and a regular army commission: he had no future as a soldier.

With the rout of Washington and his troops, the French grew bolder and the Indians, more restless. The renewal of war between England and France was imminent by the beginning of 1755. This time the contest between the two powers would be conclusive, the question of sovereignty over North America decided once and for all. That, at least, was the dream of William Pitt, who was about to become the most powerful man in England.

Even by the standards of English politicians, William Pitt was an odd character. Egotistical and devious, he inspired the loathing of his king, George II, and many of his colleagues. He also suffered devastating bouts of gout and depression that disabled him for months, even years, at a stretch. Yet despite his opportunism, his cold, disdainful manner, and his fragile health, Pitt always managed to recoup his political losses and return to power.

What kept Pitt alive was a strong sense of destiny—his own and that of England. His dream for England, imparted by his grandfather, "Diamond Pitt," a bloody-minded India merchant, was commercial supremacy. England must seize the world's trade, for trade meant wealth and wealth meant power. As early as the 1730s, Pitt knew that the only power in Europe that stood between England and its destiny was France—and that the balance of power in Europe would be decided in America. Deprived of Canadian timber, French planters in the West Indies would lack fuel, driving up the price of their sugar, and the French navy would lack masts, driving down their strength at sea. The entire market for manufactured goods in the New World would be lost to France. And, incidentally from Pitt's point of view, the British colonies would enjoy complete security.

During King George's War, Pitt had repeatedly mesmerized the House of Commons and the nation with his spellbinding oratory about England's imperial destiny. But troubled by the mounting cost of fighting, the government opted to accept peace with France in 1748, dismissing Pitt's proposal to mount an attack on Quebec, the key to all of Canada. In dejection and frustration Pitt retired from public life.

But while Pitt sulked in his library and nursed his gout, the rivalry for the American frontier moved toward a showdown. The French pressed their front lines eastward; the English pushed for land westward; chiefs like Hendrik maneuvered for position. Sustained by every dispatch from America, Pitt clung to his dream of English commercial dominion and French defeat. And by the late spring of 1754, as Benjamin Franklin and George Washington rode toward their defeats, William Pitt knew that he would have his war and his way.

Other dreams would wait longer for fulfillment. The Albany Congress had demonstrated that a few enlightened Americans like Franklin had seen beyond the diversity of a divided colonial world—beyond backcountry Presbyterians who quarreled with Philadelphia's Quaker pacifists, parochial Yankee Congregationalists who confined their charity to New England, and prickly Anglican gentry who projected the borders of the southern colonies to the Pacific Ocean. But it would take another war, one that restructured an empire, before some Americans saw in themselves a likeness that was not English.

SIGNIFICANT EVENTS

1636	Harvard College founded
1689–1697	King William's War (War of the League of Augsburg)
1701	Yale College founded
1702	Anne becomes queen of England
1702–1713	Queen Anne's War (War of the Spanish Succession)
1714	George I becomes king of England, beginning Hanover dynasty
1727	George II becomes king of England
1730s	Tennents' "Log College" founded (becomes College of New Jersey at Princeton in 1746)
1730s–1740s	Rise in importation of black slaves in northern colonies
1739	George Whitefield's first preaching tour in America; Stono Rebellion in South Carolina
1743	Franklin founds the American Philosophical Society
1744–1748	King George's War (War of the Austrian Succession)
1751	Franklin's essay on population
1754	The Albany Congress; Washington surrenders at Fort Necessity
1760–1769	South Carolina Regulation
1763	Paxton Boys march in Pennsylvania
1766	Tenant rebellion in New York
1766–1771	North Carolina Regulation (Battle of Alamance, 1771)

PART 2

THE CREATION OF A NEW REPUBLIC

As the shrewd Benjamin Franklin had observed in the course of his wide involvement in colonial affairs, the population of British North America was doubling approximately every 25 years. This astonishing rate was quite possibly the fastest in the world at the time. Even so, the North American surge in population was merely the most striking example of a more general global trend at work in the second half of the eighteenth century. In terms of sheer numbers, China led the way. Its population of 150 million in 1700 had doubled to over 313 million by the end of the century. African and Indian populations seem to have risen too, although historians have analyzed trends there less closely. Europe's total rose from about 118 million in 1700 to about 187 million a century later, the greatest growth coming on its eastern and western flanks, in Great Britain and Russia.

This worldwide rise, unprecedented in previous history, occurred for a variety of reasons. Climate may have been one: in Europe, at least, warmer and drier seasons produced generally better harvests.* Furthermore, health and nutrition improved globally with the spread of native American crops. Irish farmers discovered that a single acre planted with the lowly American potato could support an entire family. The tomato added crucial vitamins to the Mediterranean diet, while maize provided more calories per acre than any European or African grain. In China, the American sweet potato made great headway, being planted in hilly regions where rice would not grow.

Not only plants but diseases also were carried back and forth by European ships, and these too affected world population. As we have seen, contact between previously isolated peoples produced extreme mortality from epidemics, enabling European invaders like Hernando Cortés to conquer populous civilizations. Simi-

larly, the Pilgrims unwittingly blessed Divine Providence for allowing them to take over deserted fields that had been cleared and farmed by Indians only recently struck down by disease. By 1800 the more globally isolated peoples—those living in Australia or on the North American plains, for instance—still remained at risk, but increased biological resistance to European and African diseases allowed the Indian and mestizo populations in Peru and Mexico to grow rapidly. The frequent circulation of diseases worldwide led to a more stable environment, in which populations began to swell.

During the same years that Europeans were explor-

*The already dry Middle East seems to have been one area whose population was not expanding, and it may have been hurt by the climate changes.

ing the Atlantic frontiers of North and South America, Slavic and Romanian pioneers were pushing eastward into the Eurasian steppes, turning sparsely settled pastoral lands into feudal manors and farms. Farther north in forested lands unsuitable for farming, Russian fur traders had crossed the Urals by 1580 and were advancing steadily eastward across the river systems of Siberia, until they reached Okhotsk on the Pacific in the 1630s. By the 1780s the advance guard of Russian pioneers (*zemleprokhodtsy*, the "crossers of land") had reached Alaska and the Pacific American coast, encountering western Europeans who had been trapping their way across the forests and streams of Canada.

Both flanks of this European thrust often depended on forced labor, especially in agricultural settings. As we have seen, the institution of slavery in North America became increasingly restrictive over the course of the seventeenth century. And the number of slaves imported to North America paled when compared with the thousands shipped by the Portuguese to the slave markets of Rio de Janeiro. Similarly, along the frontiers of eastern Europe, the plight of serfs worsened from 1500 to 1650, as empty lands were being taken up and the demand for labor increased. In 1574 Polish nobles received the right to do entirely as they pleased with their serfs—including execution, if they chose. By 1603, Russian peasants were forbidden to move from one estate to another, being routinely sold along with the land they worked; in 1649 the czar issued even more restrictive laws.

As the currents of European Enlightenment swirled along the frontier peripheries of North America during the eighteenth century, so too they penetrated eastern Europe. Russia's Peter the Great absorbed many ideas when he traveled, sometimes incognito, to England and western Europe, and he attempted to Westernize Russia during his reign (1689–1725). Even more artistically enlightened was Catherine the Great (1762–1796), who imported Western architects, sculptors, and musicians to her court at St. Petersburg. But her limits to toleration were made brutally clear in 1773. The same year that a group of rowdy Americans were dumping tea into Boston harbor, a Cossack soldier named Emelian Pugachev launched a peasant rebellion, grandly proclaiming himself emperor and issuing decrees abolishing serfdom and taxes. Serfs in the Ural and Volga river valleys flocked to his ragtag army. Catherine ruthlessly executed Pugachev and scattered his followers; in 1775 she granted Russian nobles even more absolute control over their serfs.

To make the obvious comparison—between a failed Russian revolution for liberty and the triumph of American colonials—would be somewhat smug. Liberty-loving American merchants like John Hancock and genteel tobacco planters like George Washington were hardly in the position of serfs. A more appropriate link might be made between Russian serfs and American slaves, since both groups supplied the forced labor along the frontiers of European expansion. But the slaves, whose African homelands lay thousands of miles away, found the long odds of rebellion equally as formidable as did Russian serfs. Ironically, white Americans may have been able to fight so vigorously for their liberties precisely because they had made revolt by a class of forced laborers so difficult.

Americans rebelled in 1775 not out of a serf's desperation; quite the opposite. The Seven Years' War ended in 1763 with the French being driven out of North America, the British colonists thriving thanks to a wartime boom, and American hopes high. Thomas Mayhew, a respected Boston minister, voiced the opinion of many colonials when he envisioned a glorious empire spreading across the continent in the century to come. "I do not mean an independent one," he added carefully, but in 1763 the qualification was hardly necessary. Most white Americans were quite pleased with the prospect of being English. With the significant exception of the slave class, the distance between the poorest and richest Americans was smaller than anywhere in Europe. And the British tradition of representative government ensured a broader involvement of citizens in colonial government. Thus the American Revolution was hardly inevitable in 1776—and most certainly it did not appear so in 1763. The timing of the break with Great Britain was the result of specific decisions made on both sides of the Atlantic.

America's isolated position on the periphery of European expansion certainly created conditions that made separation likely at some point. Most colonials, used to relative social equality among white Americans, blanched at what they saw as English luxury and corruption—as we have seen. English governing elites, when they bothered to notice Americans, usually found them provincial and naive. Under different circumstances, the move for independence might have come in 1800, or even 1867, as it did for Canada. But the break came earlier, and surprisingly—given the experience of the Albany Congress of 1754—ended in the creation of a new American Republic.

CHRONOLOGY

AMERICAN EVENT	YEAR		GLOBAL EVENT
	1630s		Russian fur traders reach the Pacific Coast
English found Hudson's Bay Company, rival for French fur trade	1670		
English and French increase penetration of Ohio valley	1740s–1750s		
	ca. 1750		Global population rise
Franklin publishes essay on population	1751		
	1751–1772		Denis Diderot's *Encyclopedia* published, popularizing the ideas of the Enlightenment
Albany Congress meets	1754		
French and Indian War	1754–1763		Seven Years' War
	1762		Catherine the Great becomes empress of Russia
	1763		Proclamation of 1763 issued, to contain British colonials east of the Alleghenies
	1764		Sugar Act passed, beginning British attempt to increase colonial revenues
Stamp Act protests and riots	1765		
Boston Tea Party	1773		Pugachev leads revolt of Russian peasants
American Revolution	1775–1783		
Paine's *Common Sense* published	1776		
Noah Webster publishes American spelling book	1783		
Constitutional Convention meets	1787		Wolfgang Amadeus Mozart composes *Don Giovanni*
First presidential inauguration	1789	WASHINGTON	French Revolution begins
	1797	ADAMS	
	1799		Napoleon comes to power in France
First peaceful transfer of power between rival parties	1801	JEFFERSON	
	1803		Britain and France resume war
Tecumseh organizes Pan-Indian confederacy	1809	MADISON	
Treaty of Ghent ends War of 1812	1814		Congress of Vienna meets to bring political stability to Europe
Jackson defeats British at New Orleans	1815		Napoleon defeated at Waterloo
	1817	MONROE	
	1820		King George III dies
Monroe Doctrine proclaimed	1823		
	1825	ADAMS	

5

Toward the War for American Independence

mericans liked being English. They had liked being English from the beginning of colonial settlement, and they liked it even more as time went on. But Americans most liked being English for a few golden years after 1759. One wonderful day during those golden years—September 16, 1762—Bostonians turned out to hear a sermon preached by a local minister, the Reverend Jonathan Sewall. Later that day they began to imbibe inspiration from another source, just as Puritan and almost as potent: they drank "many loyal healths" and consumed "a vast quantity of liquor." Doubly inspirited, the inhabitants of Boston savored the pageantry of a public celebration. Soldiers mustered on the Common in stirring martial display; bells pealed from the steeples of local churches; the charge of guns fired from the battery resounded through towns; strains of orchestra music from a concert floated over the city's crowded streets and narrow alleys. As daylight drifted into darkness, bonfires illuminated the city's neighborhoods. Many loyal healths later that evening, General John Winslow of Marshfield leapt onto a table and danced to the tinkle of glassware shattering on the tavern floor. But no matter. It was a day to make merry. And Winslow was a local hero, an officer who had served in the Seven Years' War.

The occasion of Boston's celebration was the Spanish surrender to British forces at Havana, Cuba. Spain's capitulation in August 1762 marked the end of the Seven Years' War, sometimes called the French and Indian War. When the great news reached the North American mainland in early fall, celebrations like the one in Boston broke out all over the colonies. But the party in America had begun long before, with a string of stellar British triumphs in French Canada in the glorious year of 1759, and it continued through 1760 when all of Canada fell to Anglo-American forces and the youthful King George III acceded to the throne of England. The revels resumed in 1762, when the British conquered all comers, and climaxed in February of 1763 with the Treaty of Paris, which formally ended the war. Britain had become the new Rome, the largest and most powerful empire in the Western world. Americans were among His Majesty's proudest subjects.

Thirteen years after the celebration of 1762, Boston was a different place. In less than a generation, deep affection for Britain had been supplanted by deadly enmity. Pride in belonging to the empire had shriveled to a shrill conviction that England conspired to enslave its colonies. Boston led the way, drawing the other colonies deep into the logic of resistance and, by 1775, into outright rebellion. Bostonians had initiated many of the colonial petitions and resolves against British authority. They had ignited the rioting, when words did not work. They had

160

"To have a standing army!" wrote one Bostonian in 1768. "Good God! What can be worse to a people who have tasted the sweets of liberty! Things are come to an unhappy crisis!" Paul Revere engraved this print of British redcoats arriving in Boston.

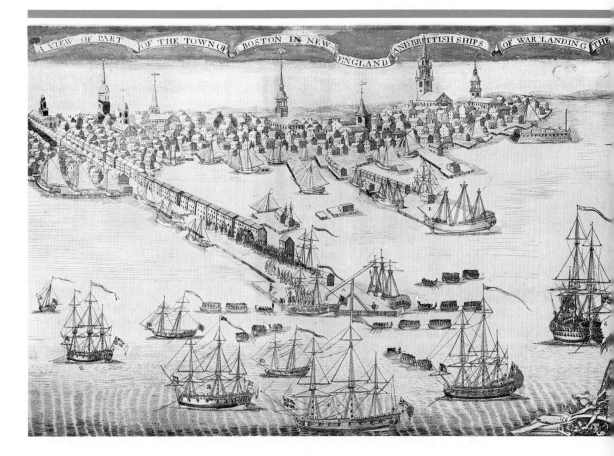

harassed British officials, baited British troops, and destroyed British property. In 1775, they were laying plans for war against the British empire.

Oddly enough, Americans, even Bostonians, still liked being English, even as they readied for war in 1775. It was only the inhabitants of England that they couldn't stand. History plays tricks of all sorts on the dead. But few twists in history are more ironic than the fate dealt that generation of Americans who loved being English. In the light of historical hindsight, they were members of a revolutionary generation, the men and women who made the war for independence. But by their own lights, they were members of a postwar generation, jealous of their rights as Britons and elated at belonging to the all-conquering empire. It was that intense pride in being British that drove Americans into rebellion. After 1763, both a long process of evolution and the individual men who ran the empire would not allow Americans to be English.

Even before the Seven Years' War, some Americans recognized that divergent courses of social and political development made them different from the English. After the Seven Years' War, events demonstrated to more Americans that they were not considered the political equals of the English who lived in England. Colonials did not accept easily the defeat of their dreams of being English. But as their disillusionment with the British empire deepened, they began to discover a new identity as Americans. As that discovery unfolded, they declared their independence from being English.

THE SEVEN YEARS' WAR

The Seven Years' War actually lasted nine years. It was a global conflict fought on four continents by the two reigning imperial powers of the eighteenth century. The struggle pitted Britain and its ally, Prussia, against France, in league with Austria and Spain. The battle raged from 1754 until 1763, and it ranged over the continent of Europe, the coast of west Africa, India, the Philippines, the Caribbean, and North America.

The Years of Defeat

The war started in the Pennsylvania backcountry after the longstanding contest over the Ohio River valley among the English, the French, and the Indians led to George Washington's surrender at Fort Necessity in 1754. The episode stiffened

THE SEVEN YEARS' WAR IN AMERICA
After Washington's surrender and Braddock's defeat in the Pennsylvania backcountry, the British and French waged their final contest for supremacy in North America in the backcountry of New York and Canada.

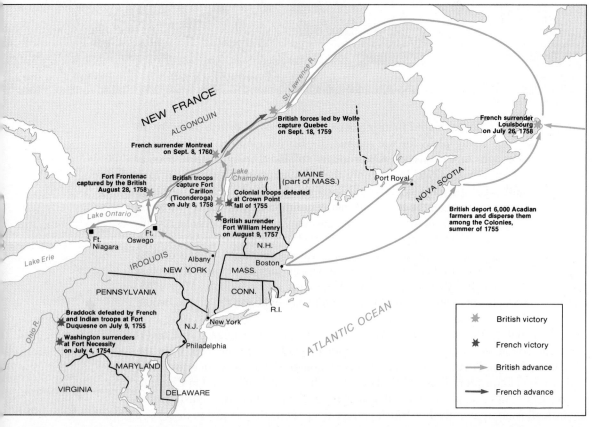

Britain's resolve to remove French encroachments along the American frontier and to assert its claims to the Ohio country. In the summer of 1755, two under-strength British regiments led by an underskilled commander, Major General Edward Braddock, slowly advanced through the densely forested backcountry toward the French outpost at Fort Duquesne on the Forks of the Ohio. On July 9, as the British approached Duquesne, they were ambushed and cut to pieces by a party of French and Indians. Washington led the mortally wounded Braddock and the remnants of his army in a retreat.

During the summer of Braddock's defeat, New Englanders fared somewhat better against the French. New England forces expelled French defenders from two small garrisons along the Nova Scotia frontier and then deported 6000 Acadian farmers. Most Acadians professed to be neutral, but their ancestors had been French; the English suspected they might be susceptible to intrigue from nearby Quebec. Their lands were confiscated, and they were dispersed throughout the colonies. Farther to the west in the fall of 1755, troops from New York and New England tried and failed to capture the French stronghold at Crown Point on Lake Champlain. The Americans got only as far as the head of Lake George when they were beset by a party of French and Indians. Colonials billed the costly but indecisive encounter as a victory and on the site of the battle built Fort William Henry.

But no amount of doubletalk could put a better face on the failures that followed for two disastrous years. When England and France formally declared war in May 1756, John Campbell, the fourth earl of Loudoun, took command of the North American theater. Loudoun insisted on personal command over provincial troops in all of the colonies, as well as sufficient money and men on demand from colonial assemblies. Provincial soldiers and civilian leaders alike hated Lord Loudoun. They balked at his efforts to centralize control over the military and dragged their heels at his demands for troops and supplies.

Meanwhile, the French moved to strengthen their position in Canada, appointing a new commanding general, Louis Joseph, the marquis de Montcalm. Montcalm immediately smashed British defenses at Fort Oswego on the southern shore of Lake Ontario, plunging New Yorkers into a panic. Then he snuffed out American hopes to advance up Lake Champlain, by fortifying French strength on its southern end with Fort Carillon. From Carillon Montcalm pressed south toward Lake George and laid siege to Fort William Henry. Its British defenders surrendered in August 1757, after just six days, alarming New Englanders. While Montcalm prospered in North America, the British and their Prussian allies were taking a beating from the French in Europe and in India as well. The lethal combination of Loudoun's ineptitude and Montcalm's daring brought the American war effort almost to a standstill by the end of 1757.

During the years when the French juggernaut seemed unstoppable, Americans looked for help from the strongest tribes of the interior—the Iroquois in the North, the Creek, Choctaw, and Cherokee in the South. Instead, Benjamin Franklin's worst fears were realized: most tribes adopted neutrality or joined the French. After Braddock's defeat in 1755, Indian raiders set ablaze English frontier settlements from New England to Georgia. Over the next three years, as France seemed certain to carry the continent, the attacks mounted in intensity.

The Years of Victory

As the news of the war worsened throughout 1756 and 1757, in England the political fortunes of William Pitt improved. By 1758 Pitt had ended his retirement, maneuvered himself into the head of the ministry, and assumed personal control over the war, "I know that I can save this country and that no one else can," he declared. Whatever his weaknesses may have been, Pitt was a great war minister. He knew exactly how to handle the French. Leaving the fighting in Europe to the Prussians, Pitt lobbed the mortar of British muscle at North America, mobilizing the British army and navy as well as American troops for an amphibious assault against the French fortress at Louisbourg. He dispatched other naval squadrons to blockade France itself, cutting off the lifeline to Canada.

Pitt also knew just how to handle the Americans. He recalled Lord Loudoun, replaced him with James Abercromby, a new commander who had far more limited authority over colonial troops, and sent new requests for men and money directly to each colonial assembly—accompanied by promises of reimbursement in gold and silver. Americans, who found the combination of political and military autonomy and real money irresistible, renewed their enthusiasm for the war effort.

France enjoyed its last victory on North American soil in July 1758, when Montcalm beat back a British assault on Fort Carillon. Less than three weeks later, the British seized control of the St. Lawrence when Louisbourg fell before the combined force of the Royal Navy, the British regular army, and provincial troops led by Lord Jeffrey Amherst. In August of 1758, Lieutenant Colonel John Bradstreet and a force of New England volunteers strangled France's frontier defenses by capturing Fort Frontenac on the northeast shore of Lake Ontario at the western end of the St. Lawrence. The fall of Frontenac left isolated and indefensible Forts Niagara and Detroit on the Great Lakes and the chain of posts lining the Ohio valley. By the end of 1758, the French had been routed in the interior and abandoned by their Iroquois allies. The Indians, seeing the turning tide of the battle, switched their allegiance back to the English. Anglo-American troops, George Washington among them, even claimed Fort Duquesne, the site of Braddock's defeat, renaming it Pittsburgh.

The British succeeded even more brilliantly in 1759. During July of that year, forces under Amherst pushed the French first from Fort Carillon, renamed Ticonderoga, and then from Crown Point. Meanwhile, more than 200 miles to the north, Brigadier General James Wolfe was proceeding more impulsively. As soon as the spring ice had melted, Wolfe sailed up the St. Lawrence with 9000 men and waited outside the walls of Quebec. Within lay Montcalm and his army. Months passed, and Quebec towered still secure atop a well-fortified palisade. On September 13, Wolfe gambled and won, decoying and splitting French defenses with a daring and dangerous stratagem. Naval squadrons landed Wolfe's men beneath a steep path leading up the bluff to Quebec. They scaled the heights to a plateau known as the Plains of Abraham. Montcalm might have won by holding out behind the walls of his fortress and awaiting reinforcements, but he matched Wolfe's recklessness and offered battle instead. Five days later both Wolfe and Montcalm lay dead, along with 1400 French soldiers and 600 British and American troops. Quebec had fallen.

The tide of war turned toward Britain in other theaters as well during 1759. John Clive routed the French in India; English offensives captured French sugar islands in the Caribbean and French trading posts in Africa; the British navy destroyed its rival's fleet when the French attempted to break the blockade; the Prussians, subsidized by Pitt, held their own in Europe.

The campaigns of 1760 ended the fighting in North America. Three branches

Executing General Wolfe's daring strategy, British soldiers climb the cliffs to the Plains of Abraham, laying siege to the city. The fall of Quebec in 1759 presaged the end of France's empire in North America.

of the Anglo-American army closed in on Montreal. The city and its surrounding territory were defenseless, with enemy forces in control of Louisbourg, the major strategic points on the St. Lawrence, Frontenac and Quebec, and Crown Point and Lake Champlain. On September 8, the governor general of New France surrendered, and New France was no more.

Elsewhere in the world, the war was also winding down—much to the dismay of William Pitt. He wanted to press the British advantage by attacking Spain's colonial possessions. But the new king of England, George III, liked Pitt even less than had his grandfather, George II. The king also worried over the expense of the war—the mounting national debt and high taxes. When George III refused to carry the struggle to Spain, Pitt resigned in protest. Spain vindicated Pitt by entering the war on the side of France in 1762, and intermittent conflict continued until the British subdued Manila in the Philippines and Havana a few months later, bringing the Spanish to the bargaining table.

The Treaty of Paris, signed in February 1763, ended the French presence on the continent of North America. The terms confirmed British title to all French territory east of the Mississippi as well as to Spanish Florida. France ceded to its ally Spain all of its land lying west of the Mississippi and the port of New Orleans. Despite Britain's overwhelming victory, France retained and regained some valuable colonial possessions and commercial rights—its sugar islands in the West Indies, its trading posts and slave stations in west Africa, and its factories and warehouses in India. Britain's generosity to its defeated rival was the doing of Pitt's replacement as first minister, Lord Bute, who believed that England's future security lay in balancing power among European nations.

The peace made at Paris was welcomed by most war-weary Britons, but it did not please everyone. "Like the peace of God," jeered the English radical John

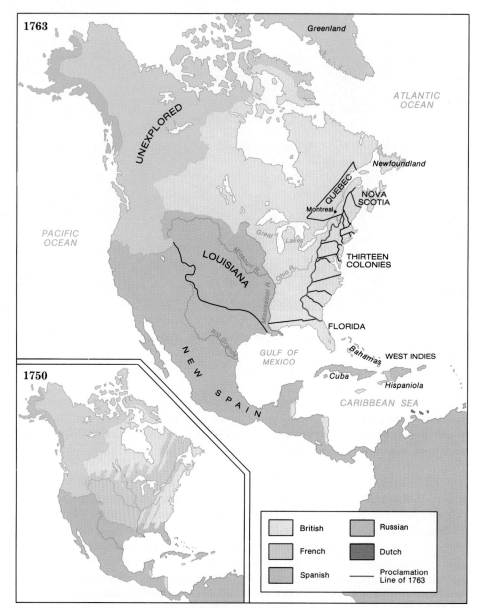

EUROPEAN CLAIMS IN NORTH AMERICA, 1750 AND 1763
The British victory in the Seven Years' War secured their title to a large portion of the present-day United States and Canada. While colonials hoped to settle the newly won territory, statesmen in London intended to restrict westward movment with the Proclamation of 1763.

Wilkes, "it passeth all understanding." And the concessions to French commerce disgusted Pitt, dashing his dreams of undisputed dominion for British trade. Crippled by gout, exhausted, and almost incapable of speech, he roused himself to denounce the treaty before the House of Commons: "We retain nothing although we have conquered everything."

Postwar Expectations

While Pitt fumed, the colonies overflowed with great expectations. The end of the war, they were sure, meant the end of high taxes. The terms of the peace, they were confident, meant the opening of the Ohio valley's limitless tracts of fertile land. It was certainly the start of an era of security and prosperity—and to some Americans, nothing less than the dawning of the millennium. In a sermon much like the one Jonathan Sewall gave during the bonfires and celebrations of 1762, the Reverend Thomas Barnard told his congregation in Salem, Massachusetts,

> Now commences the Aera of our quiet Enjoyment of those Liberties. . . . Safe from the Enemy of the wilderness. . . . Here shall be the late founded Seat of Peace and Freedom. Here shall our indulgent Mother, who has most generously rescued and protected us, be served and honoured with Growing Numbers, with all Duty, Love, and Gratitude till Time shall be no more.

The prosperity of the war years alone made for a mood of optimism. British military spending and Pitt's subsidies had created a boomlet for farmers, merchants, artisans, and anyone else who had anything to do with supplying the army or navy. Provincials also took pride in their contributions to the winning of the war. Only a few colonies had withheld appropriations altogether. The rest, led by Virginia and Massachusetts, raised an average of 20,000 troops every year until 1762 and despite Pitt's subsidies, paid about half of the cost themselves. And although the British regular army had shouldered much of the actual fighting, the provincial irregular troops had participated in most major engagements.

Even more impressive to Americans than their own contributions to the struggle were the blood and treasure expended by England in defense of the colonies. In global terms, William Pitt cared relatively little about securing the American frontier, but that did not stop colonials from flattering themselves on their importance to the empire. William Smith, Jr., a New York lawyer, was confident that Britain's wealth and power had been "vastly enhanced since the Discovery of the New World." A fellow colonial waxed even more self-congratulatory, contending that without America's trade, "the people in Britain would make but a poor figure, if they could even subsist as an independent nation." Postwar Americans fully expected to be accorded more consideration within the British empire, a larger and more equal status. Now, as one anonymous pamphleteer put it, Americans would "not be thought presumptuous, if they consider[ed] themselves upon an equal footing" with English in the parent country.

If Americans took pride in being British, most English officials in America thought that they had done a poor job, during the war, of showing it. Many complained that local assemblies had been downright niggardly in supporting the fighting. Although the American contribution was actually substantial, the version of their role put forward, predictably, by Lord Loudoun was the one that stuck in the minds of Britons back home. Colonial legislators, he charged, "assumed to themselves what they call Rights and Privileges . . . to screen them, from giving any Aid." British commanders also heaped abuse on provincial troops. Wolfe, considered by Americans a demigod of martial valor, had not returned the compliment. Before meeting his end at Quebec he had remarked that "the Americans are in general the dirtiest, most contemptible, most cowardly dogs that you can conceive."

What enraged British officials more than Americans' lack of generosity or bravery was their determination to turn a profit from the war. Customs officials and royal governors reported a sharp rise in violations of the Navigation Acts, alleging that there was "scarce a man in all that country who was not concerned in the smuggling trade." The worst of it was the insouciance of American merchants and mariners. Caught redhanded with contraband tea from the neutral Dutch and even illegal molasses from the enemy French, the smugglers coolly explained that their illicit trade helped to pay for the fighting!

The British on the scene concluded that the Americans were selfish and self-interested, unconcerned with the welfare of the empire as a whole. In the defense of the colonies, Britain had accumulated a huge national debt that would saddle the nation with high taxes for years to come. And they were repaid with American ingratitude—or perhaps even worse. With the French finally removed from North America, some Britons suspected that colonials would make a bid for independence. As early as 1755, Josiah Tucker, a respected English political economist, had warned that "to drive the French out of all North America would be the most fatal step we could take." Ironically, independence entered the calculations of some people in England long before it was ever considered by Americans.

What might prevent or at least forestall independence, the British recognized, was the depth of intercolonial division. In fact, the few leaders who gave any thought at all to America counted on continuing disunity to diffuse any sentiment for independence. Yet the rivalries over western land and local quarrels also promoted an instability that threatened the British presence in North America. The more observant English worried about what Americans, especially those on the frontier, might do to each other and to the Indians.

Americans in 1763 were not revolutionaries-in-the-making. They were patriotic British subjects of the postwar generation. Americans in 1763, deeply divided among themselves, were not even "Americans." But most postwar English colonials expected to enjoy a greater and more equal status in the empire. And most Britons had no inclination to accord them that influence. The differing expectations of the colonies' place in the empire poised the postwar generation for crisis. A conflict was not inevitable, but it came in the course of human events.

THE IMPERIAL CRISIS

It was common sense. Great Britain had waged a long and costly war to secure its empire in America; it needed now to consolidate its gains. Whatever the deficiencies of Americans in English eyes, the value of their land, labor, and trade contributed greatly to the wealth of England. The empire's North American territory required adequate protection, its administration needed centralization and tightening, and its colonies had to be made as profitable as possible to the parent nation. The decision to centralize the empire dictated the British decision to leave several thousand troops in America after the Seven Years' War. The British army would prevent France from trying to regain its lost territory. Maintaining a military presence would also ensure the submission of the non-English inhabitants in the newly conquered provinces—the French in Canada, the Spanish in Florida.

New Troubles on the Frontier

Keeping troops in North America made sense because of the Indians, too. The fall of New France made native Americans restless. They knew that with the removal of the French from the West, English traders, speculators, and settlers would swarm into the region. The Indians also knew that without the French as trading partners, the tribes were in a weaker position to resist white incursions. No longer could they play the French off against the British to gain favorable trading terms. No longer could they count on a steady supply of arms and ammunition from European rivals competing for their furs. Many tribes had hoped to preserve the balance of power among Europeans by throwing their support to the French during the Seven Years' War—until English victory became imminent. Now, with the French gone, the Indians were edgy, expecting the worst, and the British were worried.

Even as Anglo-American forces, joined by the Iroquois, fought to victory in Canada, the Cherokees had started terrorizing backcountry settlements in South Carolina. The Cherokee War raged until 1761, when troops under Amherst crushed the Indian insurgents. Deprived of French guns, shot, and powder, the Cherokee cause was doomed to defeat. Only an alliance with the other Indian power of the southern interior, the Creeks, could have turned the tide of battle toward the Cherokees. But the Creeks had long memories: the Cherokees had refused to come to their assistance earlier, during the Yamasee War of 1715. Now it was the Creeks who stayed on the sidelines, forcing the Cherokees to submit to a peace treaty in 1761. Despite the Cherokee surrender, the British believed that it was only a matter of time before colonials blundered into another Indian war.

Events bore out British fears. In the early 1760s, a Lenni Lenape prophet, Neolin, began advising the tribes to return to their ancient ways and resist the spread of white settlement. Pontiac, an Ottawa chief, embraced Neolin's message of renaissance and rebellion. In May 1763 he organized an attack on Fort Detroit, a British outpost on the Great Lakes. Other tribes joined Pontiac's offensive—the Shawnee, Chippewa, Huron, Lenni Lenape, Miami, Potawatomi, and Seneca. Throughout the summer of 1763, as the defenders of Detroit held out, the Indians captured all of the other British outposts west of Pittsburgh. British troops and American militia finally smothered Pontiac's Rebellion, as shortages of supplies again forced the tribes to terms. But deadly skirmishing bled backcountry settlements in Pennsylvania, Maryland, and Virginia until the end of 1764.

After the outbreak of Pontiac's Rebellion, British policymakers found another use for troops in America—to enforce the newly issued Proclamation of 1763. This order, issued by the administration's Board of Trade, prohibited white settlement past the crest of the Appalachian Mountains. Restricting westward movement might mollify Indian fears, the British hoped, and so preclude future conflicts. It might also keep the combustible colonials confined to the seaboard, where they were more easily subject to the control of colonial administrators. It might even encourage Americans to settle in the new territories of Nova Scotia and Florida, diluting the strength of potentially disloyal French and Spanish inhabitants.

George Grenville's New Measures

A final reason for keeping troops in the colonies occurred to the British by 1764: an armed presence could encourage American compliance with other new and equally sensible measures for tightening the empire. Those new measures were the solutions of George Grenville, the First Lord of the Treasury, to the fiscal problems confronting England after the Seven Years' War.

Britain's national debt had doubled in the decade after 1754, and adding to that burden was the drain of supporting troops in the colonies. Grenville recognized that English taxpayers alone could not shoulder the costs of winning and maintaining an empire: heavy taxes and a postwar trade recession were already triggering sporadic protests among hard-pressed Britons. Americans, by contrast, paid comparatively low taxes to their colonial governments and little in trade duties. Indeed, Grenville discovered that the colonial customs service paid out four times more in salaries to its collectors than it gathered in duties, operating at a net loss of 6000 pounds sterling every year. The returns from customs were negligible, because Americans systematically evaded the Molasses Act of 1733.

The Molasses Act imposed a hefty duty of six pence on every gallon of molasses imported from the French and Dutch sugar islands. Parliament had designed that tariff to encourage colonists to consume more British molasses, which carried a higher price but came duty-free. But New England merchants, who distilled molasses into rum and then traded it to the southern colonies and to west Africa, claimed that the British sugar islands could not keep pace with the demands of their distilleries. Regrettably, the merchants were compelled to import more molasses from the French and Dutch. More regrettably, to keep their costs low and the price of their rum competitive, they were compelled to bribe customs officials. With the going rate for bribes ranging from a halfpenny to a penny and a half per gallon, the entire arrangement offered a substantial break to merchants and a tidy sum for customs inspectors. Highly regrettable; highly profitable.

George Grenville reasoned that if Americans could pay out a little under the table to protect an illicit trade, they would willingly pay a little more to go legitimate. Parliament agreed and in April 1764 passed the Revenue Act, commonly called the Sugar Act. On the face of it, Americans benefited because the act lowered the duty on foreign molasses to three pence a gallon. But this time Grenville intended to enforce the duty and to crack down on American smugglers. The Sugar Act required shipmasters to submit elaborate papers enumerating every item in their cargoes when entering or clearing colonial ports. Even common sailors had to declare the contents of their sea chests. Those caught on the wrong side of the law were to be tried in admiralty courts, where verdicts were handed down by royally appointed judges—not juries of Americans more likely to sympathize with their fellow citizens than to convict.

By tightening customs enforcement, Grenville hoped to realize a more substantial revenue from the American trade. His were modest aims: he did not expect Americans to help reduce England's national debt or even to defray the entire cost of their defense. To meet his objectives, Grenville made other modest proposals, all approved by Parliament. In the same month as the Sugar Act was passed, Parliament also approved the Currency Act, which prohibited the colonies from making their paper money legal tender. That prevented Americans from paying their debts to British traders in currency that had fallen to less than its face value. Then there was the Quartering Act, passed in May 1765, which obliged any colony in which troops were stationed to provide them with suitable accommodations. That contributed to the cost of keeping British forces in America. And a few months earlier, in March 1765, Parliament had passed the Stamp Act.

The Stamp Act placed taxes on legal documents, customs papers, newspa-

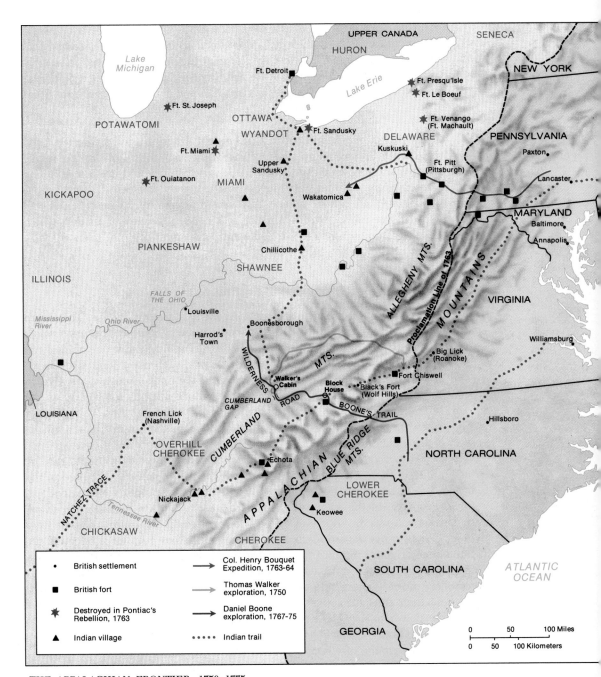

THE APPALACHIAN FRONTIER, 1750–1775

Made bold by the presence of British forts and soldiers, land-hungry colonials spilled into the west through the Cumberland Gap, a notch in the chain of mountains stretching the length of the North American interior. Only Indians and some white hunters knew of the Cumberland Gap before it was scouted in 1750 by Dr. Thomas Walker and a party of Virginians on behalf of a company of land speculators. In 1763, Indians led by Pontiac seized eight British forts before troops under Colonel Henry Bouquet stopped the offensive at Bushy Run, Pennsylvania. In 1775 Daniel Boone took the first large party of pioneers through the Cumberland Gap and established a fort at Boonesborough in present-day Kentucky.

pers, almanacs, college diplomas, playing cards, and dice. After November 1, 1765, all these items had to bear a stamp signifying that their possessor had paid the tax. Violators of the Stamp Act, like those infringing the Sugar Act, were to be tried without juries in admiralty courts. The English had been paying a similar tax for nearly a century, so it seemed to Grenville and Parliament that Americans could have no objections, especially since the revenues raised would help to pay for American defense.

Every packet boat from London that brought Americans news of another one of Grenville's measures dampened postwar optimism. For all of the real differences between the colonies and England, Americans still held much in common with the English, including definite ideas about why the British constitution, British customs, and British history all served to protect liberty and the rights of the empire's free-born citizens. And for that reason, the new measures, which seemed like common sense to Grenville and Parliament, did not make sense to Americans.

The Beginning of American Resistance

Like the English, Americans feared and mistrusted standing armies. They were familiar with a classic pamphlet, *An Argument, Shewing, that a Standing Army Is Inconsistent with a Free Government* (1697), by John Trenchard, one of the English Opposition politicians to whom Americans paid such close heed. Trenchard, and others like him, had pointed out that an army unchecked by firm civilian control could all too easily use its power to reduce citizens to slavery, as the Turkish empire and other "despotic kingdoms" demonstrated. And while English redcoats were hardly Turkish mercenaries, Americans did not take kindly to any sort of army standing between them and the coveted lands to the west.

Like the English, Americans believed that they should be taxed only by assemblies of their representatives. Like the English, Americans adhered to the axiom laid down by the liberal philosopher John Locke: property guaranteed liberty. Property, in this view, was not merely real estate, or wealth, or material possessions; it was the source of strength for every individual, providing the freedom to act, to live according to one's own lights, as one pleased. Protecting the individual's right or property was the principal responsibility of government, for if personal property was not sacred, then neither was personal liberty. The obvious corollary in this equation of power and liberty was that no people should be taxed without their consent or that of their elected representatives. The power to tax was the power to deprive a person of property; therefore, it was the power to destroy. Yet both the Sugar Act and the Stamp Act were taxes passed by members of Parliament, none of whom had been elected by colonials.

Finally, Americans, like the English, prized the right of trial by jury as one of their basic constitutional liberties. Yet both the Sugar Act and the Stamp Act would prosecute offenders in the admiralty courts, not through the duly constituted local courts. The acts thus deprived colonials of the freedom claimed by all other English men and women.

In sum, Grenville's new measures implied that Americans were not the political equals of the English living in England. They were not entitled to protection from standing armies, to taxation by consent, or to trial by jury. The psychological impact on Americans was devastating. The sting of British social snobbery, always a sore point among provincial visitors to London, now assumed a more ominous political cast. To be treated like second-class citizens wounded Americans' pride and mocked their postwar expectations. George Grenville had reduced colonials to political nonentities. The great dreams of the role that the colonies would play in the British empire evaporated, leaving behind the bitter dregs of disappointment. And after the passage of the Stamp Act, dismay mushroomed into militant protest.

Britain's determination to centralize its empire after 1763 was a disaster of timing, not just psychologically but also economically. By then, Americans were in the throes of a recession. The boom produced in the colonies by government spending during the war had collapsed once subsidies were withdrawn. American merchants were left with full stocks of imported goods gathering dust on their shelves; farmers lost the brisk and lucrative market of the army.

American response to the Sugar Act reflected a preoccupation with painful postwar readjustments. New England merchants led the opposition, objecting to the Sugar Act principally on economic grounds. They contended that enforcing a lower duty on foreign molasses would ruin the rum trade, a cornerstone of the suddenly shaky colonial economy. But with the passage of the Stamp Act, the terms of the imperial debate widened, and resistance within all of the colonies intensified.

The Stamp Act hit all Americans, not just New England merchants. It laid a levy on anyone who made a will, filed a deed, traded out of a colonial port, bought a newspaper, consulted an almanac, graduated from college, took a chance at dice, or played cards. More important, the Stamp Act represented the first outright attempt by Parliament to tax the colonies directly. In the past, Parliament had passed legislation affecting the colonies and had regulated their trade. These regulations often amounted to a kind of indirect tax: the Sugar Act raised revenues at the same time that its tariff regulated trade, and the Quartering Act also required an outlay of public funds. But the Stamp Act served notice that Parliament possessed the rightful authority to raise a revenue by directly taxing the colonials.

That assertion provoked an unprecedented development: the first display of American unity. A nearly unanimous chorus of outrage greeted Parliament's claim that it could tax the colonies. During the spring and summer of 1765, American assemblies passed resolves denying Parliament that authority. The right to tax Americans belonged to colonial assemblies alone, they argued, by the law of nature and the liberties guaranteed in charters and in the British constitution.

Virginia's assembly, the House of Burgesses, took the lead in protesting the Stamp Act, prodded by Patrick Henry. Just 29 years old in 1765, Henry had tried his hand at planting in western Virginia before recognizing his real talent—demagoguery. Blessed with the eloquence of an evangelical preacher, the dashing charm of a southern cavalier, and a mind uncluttered by much learning, Henry parlayed his popularity as a fast-talking lawyer into a place among the Burgesses. He took his seat just 10 days before introducing the Virginia Resolves against the Stamp Act. Although Henry's heated attack on Parliament's authority alienated some of the older Burgesses, his defiant rhetoric stirred the blood of younger members. It also aroused the admiration of another westerner, a gangly young law student with political ambitions who watched the debate over the Stamp Act from the back of the chamber. His name was Thomas Jefferson.

The Burgesses passed Henry's resolutions upholding their exclusive right to tax Virginians. But they stopped short of adopting those that called for outright resistance to the Stamp Act. When news of Virginia's stand spread to the rest of

Visual imagery brought home the urgency of resistance to Americans who could not read political pamphlets or radical newspapers. This detail from an engraving by Paul Revere includes a liberty tree, from which is hung an effigy of the Boston stamp distributor, and a beast busily destroying the Magna Carta while trampling American colonials. The date on the tree, August 14, 1765, marked the first Stamp Act riot in Boston.

the colonies, other assemblies followed suit, affirming that the sole right to tax Americans resided in their elected representatives. In October 1765, delegates from nine colonies convened in New York, where they prepared a joint statement of the American position and petitioned the king and Parliament to repeal both the Sugar Act and the Stamp Act.

Meanwhile, American political leaders turned to the press to arouse popular opposition to the Stamp Act. Disposed by the writings of the English Opposition to think of politics in conspiratorial terms, they warned that Grenville and the king's other ministers schemed to deprive the colonies of their liberties by unlawfully taxing their property. The Stamp Act was only the first step in a sinister design to impoverish and then to enslave Americans. Whether or not dark fears of a ministerial conspiracy haunted most Americans in 1765, many resisted the Stamp Act. The merchants of Boston, New York, and Philadelphia agreed to stop the importation of English goods to pressure British traders to lobby for repeal. In every colony, organizations emerged to ensure that the Stamp Act, if not repealed, would never be enforced.

The new extralegal resistance groups, which styled themselves the "Sons of Liberty," consisted of traders, lawyers, and prosperous artisans. With great success, they mobilized the middling and lower ranks of seaport society in opposition to the Stamp Act. In every colonial city, crowds of sailors, dockworkers, poor artisans, apprentices, and servants burnt the stamp distributors in effigy, insulted them on the streets, demolished their offices, and attacked their homes. One hot night in August 1765, a mob went further than the Sons of Liberty had planned. They set on the stately mansion of Thomas Hutchinson, the unpopular lieutenant governor of Massachusetts and the brother-in-law of the colony's stamp distributor, looting and all but leveling the place by morning. Committed to a resistance in the name of protecting private property, the Sons of Liberty afterward took care to keep crowds under tighter control. In most cases, the mere show of popular force sufficed: by the first of November, the day that the Stamp Act took effect, all of the stamp distributors had resigned.

As American port dwellers rioted and colonial assemblies resolved, a reprieve from the Stamp Act was already in the works back in England. The man who came—inadvertently—to America's relief was none other than George III. The young king was a good man, industrious and devoted to the empire, but he was also immature and not overendowed with intellect. Unfortunately, George knew his limitations, and the anxiety that he was unequal to his great responsibilities compounded his emotional instability. These insecurities made the young king an irksome master, and he ran through ministers as rapidly as his father Frederick had run through mistresses. By the end of 1765, George had dismissed Grenville for reasons unrelated to the uproar in America and appointed a new first minister, the marquis of Rockingham. Rockingham had opposed the Stamp Act from the outset, and he had no desire to enforce it. He received support from London merchants, who were beginning to feel the pinch of the colonists' nonimportation campaign and so pushed for repeal. Although Parliament was prepared to stand by the Stamp Act, especially after hearing reports of rioting and insolent colonial resolves from across the Atlantic, Rockingham and his merchant allies secured repeal in March 1766.

When news of the Stamp Act's demise reached America in May, jubilant celebrations erupted throughout the colonies. As fireworks and rockets soared over seaports, repeal restored to some Americans their earlier optimism. In truth, celebrations were not in order: the Stamp Act crisis did not augur well for the future of imperial relations. It had decided nothing about the extent of Parliament's authority in America, and it had demonstrated dramatically to Americans just how similar in political outlook they were to one another and just how different they were from the British.

Americans had found that they shared the same assumptions about the meaning of representation. To counter colonial objections to the Stamp Act, Grenville and his supporters had claimed that Americans *were* represented in Parliament, even though they had elected none of its members. Americans were virtually represented, Grenville insisted, for each member of Parliament stood for the interests of the whole empire, not just those of the particular constituency that had elected him.

Americans could see no virtue in virtual representation, and they rejected the British view that divorced representation from direct election. The newly recognized American consensus was that colonials could be truly represented only by those whom they had actually elected. Their view, known as actual representation, emphasized that elected officials were directly responsible for their constituents.

Americans also had discovered that they agreed about the extent of Parliament's authority over the colonies: it stopped at the right to tax. Colonials did not contend that Parliament had no authority over them; they readily conceded its right to legislate and to regulate trade for the good of the whole empire. But taxation, in the American view, was no part of the power to pass laws or to regulate trade: taxation was the free gift of the people through their representatives.

Members of Parliament were not amused by the American assessment of their rightful power. They brushed aside colonial petitions and resolves, all but ignoring their constitutional argument. To make its authority perfectly clear, Parliament accompanied the repeal of the Stamp Act with a Declaratory Act, asserting that it had the power to make laws for the colonies "in all cases whatsoever." But the Declaratory Act clarified nothing: did Parliament understand the power of legislation to include the power of taxation?

Daily Lives

POLITICAL CULTURE

The Rituals of Revolutionary Protest

On the first night of November 1765, the city of New York glowed with unaccustomed light. The Stamp Act was to have taken effect on that date, but the colony's stampmaster had long since resigned his office. What had frightened him into resignation could be seen in the ominous moving shadows of men, women, and children, hundreds of them. The flaring torches and flickering candles that they carried aloft through the city's crooked streets cast on storefronts and doorways dark images of a crowd protesting the "death of Liberty."

Bringing up the rear of the procession was a seaman, bearing atop his head an old chair in which was seated a paper effigy. It represented Cadwallader Colden, "the most hated man in the province" and—as New York's temporary governor—the local representative of British authority. The crowd marched to the center of town, shouting insults at Colden's figure and peppering it with pistol shots. When some of the marchers decided that their effigy should evoke the Roman Catholic pope, the chief symbol of arbitrary power to colonial Americans, they broke into Colden's stable and appropriated his fine coach for a proper papal throne. A second group joined the crowd, bearing their own carefully designed piece of portable political theater—a gallows illuminated with two lanterns. Hanging from the gallows were effigies of Colden and the devil, the "grand Deceiver of Mankind." The entire assembly climaxed the evening by burning the effigies in a bonfire and then vandalizing homes of several Stamp Act supporters.

Similar protests had been staged throughout the colonies, in major seaports and small hamlets, following Boston's rioting against the Stamp Act. Some crowds held mock trials of local stampmasters or unpopular British officials and then tarred and feathered, beat, hung, or burned their effigies. Other crowds enacted mock funerals, parading effigies in carts or coffins to the accompaniment of tolling church bells. Despite local variations, certain symbols appeared repeatedly: devils and gallows, lanterns and the paraphernalia of papal authority. And virtually every town that protested the Stamp Act acquired in the process another political symbol, the "liberty tree." Whether a living tree or a rough-hewn pole, the liberty tree became the center of protests and celebrations, bedecked with lanterns or adorned with flagstaffs used to signal meetings of the local Sons of Liberty. Townsfolk gathered under liberty trees to protest measures like the Townshend duties and the Tea Act, to intimidate loyalists and customs informers with mock trials, and to mark the anniversaries of events like the Boston Massacre.

The frequency and the political focus of this rioting were new to the decade preceding the Revolution. Still, the actions taken resembled those of earlier colonial crowds in their direction and restraint. Previous protests against merchants who hoarded goods, houses of prostitution, or supporters of smallpox inoculation had not been spontaneous, uncontrolled outbursts of popular passion. Crowds chose their targets and their tactics carefully and then carried out the communal will with a minimum of violence and destruction.

Equally striking, the resistance after 1765 drew on rituals and symbols surrounding traditional forms of protest, pun-

Daily Lives

A Pope's Day parade in mid-eighteenth-century Boston. Boys dressed as the devil's imps accompany a cart bearing an effigy of the pope.

ishment, and celebration. For centuries before the Revolution, for example, crowds on both sides of the Atlantic had meted out to prostitutes, adulterers, or henpecked husbands punishments known in England as "rough music." That ritualized round of humiliation and abuse included tarring and feathering or placing around the neck of the malefactor a halter with a placard naming his or her crime. The targets of rough music were also ridden "skimmington": placed on the back of a donkey, pelted with mud and dung, and driven out of town to the accompaniment of hooting laughter and beating drums.

An even more important inspiration for resistance rituals came from Pope's Day, an elaborate annual celebration of anti-Catholic sentiment which started in Boston early in the eighteenth century. Craftworkers and apprentices from both the North End and South End of town fashioned a cart bearing a lantern, effigies of the pope and the devil, and signs reading "The devil take the pope" and "North [or South] End Forever." Local boys with blackened faces and jester's caps played the part of the "devil's imps," taunting the

pope's effigy as laboring people from both ends of town paraded their carts through the streets. Each group tried to destroy the other's creation before the final bonfire at the end of the evening.

As Americans appropriated the symbols of the past for their rituals of political resistance, their borrowing took an odd twist. Pope's Day, the ritual prototype for later protests, was in fact a colonial adaptation of an English celebration of monarchy, Guy Fawkes Day. In 1605 Fawkes, a Catholic, had been foiled in his attempt to assassinate James I, a failure that the English annually commemorated with a parade ending with burning the conspirator in effigy. In colonial America an effigy of the pope took the place of the Catholic Fawkes; in resistance rituals after 1765 hated British officials took the place of the pope. Beginning in 1776 Americans celebrated public readings of the Declaration of Independence by parading, burning, and burying effigies of George III. Strangely enough, Americans had converted symbols and ceremonies designed to honor monarchy to represent the ritualized killing of a king.

The Townshend Acts

In the summer of 1766, George III—again inadvertently—gave Americans what should have been an advantage by changing ministers again. The king replaced Rockingham with William Pitt. Suddenly popular with his king, Pitt was doubly the darling of the Americans for his prosecution of the Seven Years' War and his opposition to the Stamp Act. Almost alone among British politicians, Pitt had grasped and agreed with the colonists' constitutional objections to taxation.

During the debate over repeal of the Stamp Act, Pitt rose in the House of Commons to affirm that Parliament's sovereignty over the colonies notwithstanding, Americans possessed all the rights of English citizens. Those rights included being taxed only by their representatives. Grenville's application of virtual representation to the colonies Pitt dismissed as "the most contemptible idea that ever entered into the head of man." America's spirited opposition to the Stamp Act drew Pitt's admiration, and he warned Parliament of the perils of threatening colonial liberties: "America, if she fell, would fall like a strong man. She would embrace the pillars of the state and pull down the constitution along with her." Grenville rose to defend his modest proposals: "Tell me when the colonies were emancipated?" he asked. "I desire to know when they were made slaves!" Pitt shot back.

If the man who believed that Americans were "the sons not the bastards of England" had been well enough to govern, matters between Great Britain and the colonies might have turned out differently. But almost immediately after Pitt took office, his health collapsed, and he went into seclusion. Power passed into the hands of Charles Townshend, the brilliant but erratic Chancellor of the Exchequer.

Unlike Pitt, Townshend had little understanding of the colonies and even less comprehension of their constitutional objections to taxation. His twin concerns were to strengthen the authority of Parliament and the power of royal officials in the colonies at the expense of American assemblies and to raise more revenue at the expense of American taxpayers. In 1767, he persuaded Parliament to tax the lead, paint, paper, glass, and tea that Americans imported from Britain.

To clip the wings of colonial assemblies, Townshend advanced several strategies. First, he instructed the royal governors to take a firmer hand with their recalcitrant legislatures. To set the example, he singled out for punishment the New York legislature, which was refusing to comply with provisions of the Quartering Act of 1765. The troops that were left on the western frontier after the Seven Years' War had been pulled back into colonial seaports in 1766, in part to economize on costs, but also to quiet agitation over the Stamp Act. The largest contingent came to New York. That colony's assembly protested, claiming that the cost of quartering the troops constituted a form of indirect taxation. But Townshend was determined to enforce the Quartering Act, and Parliament backed him, suspending the New York assembly in 1767 until it agreed to toe the mark.

In an even more ominous encroachment on colonial autonomy, Townshend dipped into the revenue from his new tariffs to free royal officials from their financial dependence on the assemblies. Governors and other officers like customs

This 1766 porcelain of *Lord Chatham and America* attests to the popularity of William Pitt, Earl of Chatham, among Americans who resisted the Stamp Act. The artist's representation of "America" as a black kneeling in gratitude echoes the colonists' association of taxation with slavery.

collectors and judges had heretofore received their salaries from colonial legislatures. The assemblies lost that crucial leverage when Townshend found a different way to pay colonial bureaucrats.

Townshend's policies not only liberated royal officials from colonial control but also enlarged their numbers. To ensure more effective enforcement of all the duties on imports, he created an American Board of Customs Commissioners, who appointed in turn a small army of new customs collectors. Townshend also established three new vice-admiralty courts in Boston, New York, and Charleston to bring smugglers to justice. At the same time, he instituted a new cabinet office for handling American affairs, the secretary of state for the colonies.

In Townshend's efforts to centralize the British empire, Americans saw new evidence that they were not being treated like the English. In newspapers and pamphlets colonial leaders reiterated their earlier protests against taxation. The most widely read publication, "A Letter from a Farmer in Pennsylvania," was the work of John Dickinson. If not quite a Pennsylvania farmer, Dickinson had developed from a young law student disgusted by the corruption of British politics into a Philadelphia lawyer disgusted by the policies of Parliament. He urged Americans to protest the Townshend duties with a show of superior virtue. Through hard work, thrift, simplicity, and home manufacturing, Americans could reduce their consumption of imported English luxuries. American self-reliance, Dickinson argued, would advance the cause of repeal.

As John Dickinson's star rose over Philadelphia, the Townshend Acts also dealt the destiny of another man farther north. He was 46 years old in 1768, and had failed at almost everything. His aspirations of becoming a minister he had surrendered while still a student at Harvard; his ventures as a merchant ended in bankruptcy; his improbable stint as a tax collector left all of Boston in the red. These credentials disqualified Samuel Adams for any career except politics. By the 1760s, he was a leader in the Massachusetts assembly. The Townshend Acts made him the consummate political organizer and agitator in America. First his enemies and later his friends claimed that Adams had decided on independence for America as early as 1768.

Adams started small. In February 1768, he persuaded the Massachusetts assembly to send other colonial legislatures a circular letter condemning the Townshend Acts and calling for a united American resistance. He got more than he had expected. From Virginia, the House of Burgesses responded in May with hopes for "a hearty union" against any British measures that "have an immediate tendency to enslave them [the colonies]."

While John Dickinson and Samuel Adams whipped up public indignation against the Townshend Acts, the Sons of Liberty surfaced again in every colonial seaport, orchestrating the opposition in the streets. Customs officials, like the stamp distributors before them, became targets of popular hatred. But the customs collectors gave as good as they got, using the flimsiest pretexts to justify seizing American vessels for violating royal regulations and shaking down American merchants for what amounted to protection money. The racketeering in the customs service brought tensions in Boston to a flashpoint in June 1768 after officials seized and condemned the *Liberty*, a sloop belonging to one of the city's biggest merchants, John Hancock. Bostonians vented their anger in a night of

John Dickinson, a moderate who defended American rights but hoped for reconciliation.

rioting. A crowd of several thousand swept through the streets, searching out and roughing up customs officials.

The new secretary of state for the colonies, Lord Hillsborough, raised the ante. He dispatched two regiments of troops to Boston to protect the customs collectors and to wrest control of the city from the Sons of Liberty. The presence of British soldiers in Boston affronted its inhabitants in every way. The redcoats disembarked in the fall of 1768 and paraded into town under the cover of warships lying off the harbor. In the days and months that followed, citizens accustomed to coming and going as they pleased bristled when challenged on the streets by armed sentries. Even more disturbing to Bostonians was the execution of British military justice on the Common: British soldiers were whipped savagely for breaking military discipline, and desertion was punished by execution.

Despite the risk, desertion was fairly common because of the disadvantages of being a British soldier in Boston. They were regularly reviled by the citizenry and occasionally pelted with stones, snowballs, dirt, and human excrement. The British regulars were particularly unpopular among Boston's laboring classes because they competed with them for jobs. Off-duty soldiers were permitted to moonlight as maritime laborers, and they sold their services at much cheaper rates than the wages paid to locals. By 1769, brawls between British regulars and waterfront workers broke out with disturbing frequency.

With some 4000 redcoats coming into contact daily with some 15,000 Bostonians under the sway of Samuel Adams, what happened on the night of March 5, 1770 was almost inevitable. A crowd gathered around the customshouse for the sport of heckling its guard of 10 soldiers. When the confrontation turned ugly, the redcoats panicked: they fended off the volley of insults, snowballs, and chunks of ice hurled by the mob with live fire, hitting 11 rioters and killing 5. Adams and other propagandists seized upon the incident: labeling the bloodshed "the Boston Massacre," they publicized the "atrocity" throughout the colonies. The radical *Boston Gazette* framed its account in an eye-catching black-bordered edition complete with a drawing of five coffins.

Even before the Boston Massacre, intercolonial resistance had been gathering momentum. The *Liberty* riot of 1768 and the arrival of British troops in Boston a few months later galvanized colonial assemblies into action. Most legislatures joined Virginia's Burgesses in endorsing the Massachusetts circular letter and in protesting the Townshend Acts. The colonies also adopted agreements not to import or to consume British goods. The reluctance among some merchants to revive nonimportation in 1767 gave way to greater enthusiasm by 1768, and by early 1769, such agreements were in effect throughout the colonies.

The Stamp Act crisis had also called forth intercolonial cooperation and tactics like nonimportation. But the protests against the Townshend Acts raised the stakes by creating new institutions to carry forward the resistance. Subscribers to the nonimportation agreements established "committees of inspection" to enforce the ban on trade with Britain. Merchants who refused to stop importing opened themselves to retribution meted out by the committees, who claimed authority from "the people." The committees denounced recalcitrant traders in the newspapers, vandalized their warehouses, forced them to stand under the gallows, and sometimes resorted to tar and feathers. In effect, the committees of inspection, although they had no formal, legal sanction, operated like shadow governments.

After 1768, the resistance also brought a broader range of Americans into the politics of protest. Artisans, who recognized that nonimportation would spur domestic manufacturing, began to organize as independent political groups. In many towns, women took an active part in opposing the Townshend duties. The "Daughters of Liberty" took to heart John Dickinson's recommendations: they forswore English finery in favor of homespun clothing, served coffee instead of tea, and boycotted shops that persisted in selling British goods.

While Townshend's policies intensified the insurgency in America, at least part of his program was meeting with opposition in England as well. Finally the obvious had dawned on members of Parliament: by taxing British exports of paint, lead, paper, and glass, they were losing more in trade than they gained in colonial revenues. Duties only discouraged sales to Americans and encouraged them to manufacture at home. The argument for repeal was overwhelming, and the way had been cleared by the unexpected death of Townshend shortly after Parliament adopted his proposals.

But American defiance of the Townshend Acts stiffened the spine of Parliament. The stalemate was broken only by the king's appointment of Lord North as his new first minister at the beginning of 1770. North convinced Parliament to repeal all of the Townshend duties except the one on tea, allowing that tax to stand as a source of revenue and as a symbol of Parliament's authority.

Resistance Revived

For more than two years, colonial protest subsided. Repeal of the Townshend duties took the wind from the sails of American resistance, restoring to imperial relations some of their former harmony. And internal problems preoccupied Americans after 1770—the Regulator movements in the Carolinas and the contest over western land waged by Connecticut, Pennsylvania, and Virginia. But the quiet was deceptive, for the controversy between England and the colonies had not been resolved. Americans still paid the Sugar Act's duty on molasses and Townshend's tariff on tea, taxes to which they had not consented. Americans were still subject to trial in admiralty courts, tribunals that operated without juries. Americans still lived with a standing army in their midst, a threat to basic freedoms. Beneath the banked fires of protest burned the live embers of Americans' political inequality. Any shift in the wind could fan those embers into flames.

The wind shifted on Narragansett Bay in 1772, running aground the *Gaspee*, a British naval schooner. Since the ship had been in hot pursuit of Rhode Island smugglers, eight boatloads of Providence residents, led by a prominent merchant, celebrated its misfortune in the middle of the night with a bonfire built on the deck of the *Gaspee* after the ship had been boarded and its crew beaten up and put ashore. British officials sent a special commission to look into the burning of the ship, intending once again to bypass the established colonial court system. That violation of common law procedure reignited the imperial crisis, and American resistance flared again.

It did so through an ingenious mechanism, the committees of correspondence. Established all across the colonies by the legislative assemblies, the committees took it upon themselves to draw up statements of American rights and grievances, to distribute these documents within and among the colonies, and to solicit responses from towns and counties. The brainchild of Samuel Adams, the committee structure constituted a new communications network, one designed to

Samuel Adams, a radical who masterminded colonial resistance tactics.

foster an intercolonial consensus on resistance to British measures. Adams had worked too long as a politician not to recognize the need to develop allies, to coordinate plans of action, to embolden wavering supporters to act through the example of others. The arguing and cajoling, the evening meetings at taverns—such techniques might work in lining up local support for a Boston town meeting, but the committees of correspondence provided the badly needed means to rally support on an intercolonial basis. The strategy succeeded admirably, and not only between colonies. The committees spread the scope of the resistance from colonial seaports into rural areas, engaging farmers and other country folk in the opposition to Britain.

The committees had much to talk about when Parliament passed the Tea Act in 1773. The law was an effort to bail out the bankrupt East India Company by granting that corporation a monopoly on the tea trade to Americans. Since the company could use agents to sell its product directly, cutting out the middlemen, the new low price undercut that charged by colonial merchants—even when the duty of three pence per pound was added, and even when smugglers tried to compete using illegal Dutch tea. Thus although the Tea Act would hurt American merchants, it promised to make tea cheaper for ordinary Americans. Still, many colonials saw the act as Parliament's ploy to lull them into accepting its authority to tax the colonies. They set out to deny that power, once and for all.

By the fall of 1773, the Sons of Liberty had resumed their agitation in American seaports. Colonial newspapers denounced the merchants to whom the East India Company had consigned shipments of tea; mobs collected around their warehouses; mass meetings gathered to decry the latest step in the plot to enslave the colonies. In early winter of 1773, the tempest over the Tea Act peaked in Boston, with popular leaders calling for the cargoes to be returned forthwith to England. Thomas Hutchinson, now the governor of Massachusetts, was determined that the tea would be landed and stored.

On the evening of December 16, thousands of Bostonians, as well as farmers from the surrounding countryside, packed into the Old South Meetinghouse to hear Samuel Adams announce that Hutchinson had denied clearance to vessels attempting to carry the detested tea back to England. Some members of the audience knew that Adams had more on the evening's agenda than denouncing the governor, and they awaited their cue. It came when Adams told the meeting that they could do nothing more to save their country. War whoops rang through the meetinghouse, the crowd spilled onto the streets and out to the waterfront, and the Boston Tea Party commenced. From the throng emerged 50 "Indians" clad in blankets, their faces smeared with paint to disguise their identities. The party boarded three vessels docked off Griffin's Wharf, broke open casks containing 90,000 pounds of tea, and brewed a beverage worth 10,000 pounds sterling in Boston harbor.

The Empire Strikes Back

George III, his ministers, and Parliament responded to the destruction of the tea first with shock, then with disgust, and finally with grim determination. The Tea Party proved to British satisfaction that Americans aimed at independence. Lord North concluded that "we are now to dispute whether we have, or have not, any authority in that country."

To show that they did, Parliament speedily assented to the Coercive Acts,

While the new political activism of some American women often amused male leaders of the resistance, it inspired the scorn of some partisans of British authority. When the women of Edenton, North Carolina, renounced imported tea, this British cartoon mocked them.

dubbed in the colonies the "Intolerable Acts." In March 1774, two months after hearing of the Tea Party, Parliament passed the Boston Port Bill, closing that harbor to all oceangoing traffic until such time as the king saw fit to reopen it. He would not see fit until America recompensed the East India Company for their tea. During the next three months, Parliament approved three other "intolerable" laws designed to isolate and punish Massachusetts. The Massachusetts Government Act handed over the colony government to royal officials: henceforth, the Crown would nominate that colony's council and the royal governor would appoint and remove most officials. Sheriffs would become royal appointees rather than freemen, and it was given to them to select juries. Town meetings henceforth would require royal permission. The Impartial Administration of Justice Act permitted any royal official accused of a crime in Massachusetts to be tried in England or in another colony. The Quartering Act allowed the billeting of British troops in private households—not only in recalcitrant Massachusetts, but in all the colonies.

Many Americans saw the Coercive Acts as proof of a deliberate plot to enslave the colonies. The taxes and duties, laws and regulations of the last decade— measures that the king's ministers and Parliament regarded as commonsensical steps to centralize British authority in America—many colonials perceived as a sinister conspiracy against their liberties.

The source of this conspiratorial interpretation of the recent past lay in the writings of the English Opposition, which held that human history recorded the same story, time and time again. It was a tale of power overwhelming liberty. Those who had power would always seek more; those who had more power would inevitably become corrupt, unless checked by a virtuous and vigilant people. An especially popular treatment of this theme appeared in a series of essays by Trenchard and Gordon, *Cato's Letters* (1720–1723), which was reprinted repeatedly in America. Trenchard, Gordon, and others of the Opposition asserted that ambitious politicians always pursued the same strategies to supplant representative government and popular freedom with tyranny and despotism. They pointed to the sad lessons of the ancient republics of Greece and Rome, whose citizens had fallen prey to the powers of tyrants and dictators. They held up more recent examples of Venice, Sweden, and Denmark, whose republican traditions had all degenerated within the past century. Power overwhelming liberty: colonials discerned that same dark scenario unfolding in America.

First, English theorists warned, the people of a republic were impoverished by costly wars—something the colonists could well appreciate after the Seven Years' War. Then the government loaded the people with taxes to pay for those wars—as in the case of the Sugar Act or the Stamp Act or the Townshend duties. Next the government stationed a standing army in the country, ostensibly to protect the people, but actually to consolidate the strength of those in power. And of course, troops had been unloaded in Boston harbor, were quartered in New York, and were making trouble wherever they appeared. Then, the Opposition warned, worthless and wicked men were favored with public offices and patronage to secure their loyalty and support for the foes of liberty. And how else could one describe the royal governors, customs collectors, and judges whose salaries derived from the revenues of the Townshend duties? Then those in power would deliberately promote luxury, idleness, and extravagance to weaken the moral fiber of the people—like the consumption encouraged by the low prices ensured by the Tea Act. Finally, those in power would try to provoke the people to violence in order to justify new oppression. And week after week in the spring of 1774, reports of the Coercive Acts and other legislative outrages came across the waters.

With the passage of the Coercive Acts, many more Americans came to believe not only that distant powers plotted to enslave the colonies but also that the conspirators included a large number of British political leaders. At the time of the Stamp Act and again during the agitation against the Townshend Acts, most Americans had confined their suspicions to the king's ministers. By 1774, those implicated in that conspiracy included more than a handful of ministers—Parliament itself had fallen under suspicion. Americans everywhere were thoroughly alarmed. The Coercive Acts prompted an outpouring of support for "suffering Boston," and the committees of correspondence worked unceasingly to rally support. From one colony after another came calls for an intercolonial congress—like the one that had met during the Stamp Act crisis—to determine the best way to defend their freedom.

In 1754 the Albany Congress had found the colonies too divided to agree on any course of action in the common defense. In 1765 the Stamp Act Congress had shown greater resolve, but the occasion for action passed. In 1774 Americans were united in opposition, convinced that the threat to their liberties was real. But many remained unsettled about where the logic of their actions might be taking them: toward a denial that they were any longer English.

TOWARD THE REVOLUTION

By the beginning of September 1774, when the First Continental Congress met, the news from Massachusetts was bad. The colony verged on anarchy, it was reported, as its inhabitants resisted the enforcement of the Massachusetts Government Act. When British soldiers had raided an arsenal at Charlestown where radical leaders were stockpiling arms and ammunition, thousands of militia throughout the colony had mobilized and marched to defend Boston. On that occasion, known as "the Powder Alarm," the volunteers had finally dispersed, and the episode ended without bloodshed. But the 55 delegates meeting at Carpenter's Hall in Philadelphia feared that there would be more confrontations and more violence.

In the midst of this atmosphere of crisis, they also had to take one another's measure. Many of the delegates had not traveled outside their native provinces; even those who had were hardly familiar with all the customs and circumstances of the other colonies. (All but Georgia sent representatives.) Lawyers compared notes on how their respective colonial governments justified their rights as British subjects, how their laws were encoded. Delegates learned more about their distant neighbors' economies, customs, and temperaments. Although the representatives encountered a great deal of diversity, they quickly discovered that they held in common an esteem of certain "republican" virtues: simplicity and self-reliance, industry and thrift, and, above all, disinterested commitment to the public good. Individual delegates were delighted to discern among men from other colonies those virtues that they had once attributed only to themselves. Most members of the Congress also shared a common mistrust of England, associating the mother country with vice, extravagance, and corruption.

Still, as delegates took one another's measure, they found that their perceptions were not entirely in accord. Massachusetts in particular brought with it a reputation—well deserved, considering Samuel Adams was along—for radical action and a willingness to use force to accomplish its ends. John Adams, another delegate (and a cousin of Samuel Adams), reported that other colonies were suspicious of the Massachusetts representatives. "We have been obliged to keep ourselves out of sight, and to feel pulses, and to sound the depths; to insinuate our sentiments, designs, and desires by means of other persons, sometimes of one province, and sometimes of another."

The First Continental Congress

In an atmosphere charged with apprehension and excitement, the delegates settled down to business. Their agenda was to reach a consensus on the basis of American rights, the limits of Parliament's power, and the proper tactics for resisting the Coercive Acts. Congress quickly agreed on the first point. They affirmed what most Americans had argued since 1765: the law of nature, the colonial charters, and the British constitution were the foundations of American liberties. On the two other issues, Congress plied a middle course between the demands of the more radical delegates and the reservations of conservatives.

In a Declaration of Rights and Grievances, adopted on October 14, 1774, the delegates asserted the right of the colonies to tax and legislate for themselves. Since the time of the Stamp Act, most Americans had insisted that Parliament had no authority to tax the colonies. Subsequent events—including the suspension of the New York legislature, the Gaspee Commission, and, most recently, the Coercive Acts—had demonstrated that Parliament could undermine colonial liberties by legislation as well as by taxation. The Declaration of Rights reflected that recognition, defining the limits of Parliament's power over Americans more narrowly than colonials had a decade earlier.

The repudiation of Parliament's power to legislate for the colonies doomed to defeat a strategy for accommodation with England favored by the most conservative members of the Congress. Their leading advocate, Joseph Galloway of Pennsylvania, proposed a plan of union with Britain similar to the one set forth by the Albany Congress in 1754: a grand council of the colonies would handle all common concerns, its enactments subject to review and veto by Parliament, and all acts of Parliament affecting America would require the approval of the grand council. A majority of delegates judged that Galloway's proposal left Parliament too much leeway in legislating for Americans, and they rejected his plan. Galloway, who knew a good politician when he saw one, blamed Samuel Adams' maneuverings for his defeat. Adams, he commented, "eats little, sleeps little, thinks much, and is most decisive and indefatigable in the pursuit of his objects."

Although the Congress denied Parliament the right to impose taxes or to make laws, delegates stopped short of declaring that it had no authority at all in the colonies. They grudgingly approved Parliament's regulation of trade, but "only from the necessity of the case," that is, because of the interdependent economy of the empire. And although some American pamphleteers were attacking the king for plotting against American liberties, Congress acknowledged the continuing allegiance of the colonies to George III. In other words, the delegates called for a return to the situation that had existed in the empire before 1763, with Parliament regulating trade and the colonies exercising all powers of taxation and legislation.

On the question of resistance, Congress acceded to the desires of its most radical delegates by drawing up the Continental Association, an agreement to cease all trade with Britain until the Coercive Acts were repealed. They agreed that their fellow citizens would immediately stop drinking East India Company tea, and that by December 1, 1774, merchants would no longer import goods of any sort from Britain. A ban on the export of American produce to Britain and the West Indies would go into effect a year later, during September 1775—the lag being a concession to southern rice and tobacco planters, who wanted to market their crops.

Although the Association provided for the total cessation of trade favored by radical delegates, Congress did not approve another part of their agenda—making preparations for war. From the outset of the convention, Samuel Adams and some of the other Massachusetts delegates had quietly worked to commit the Congress to mobilizing colonial defenses. Adams' designs were not farfetched. A story had been spreading among the delegates that George Washington, when he heard of the Boston Port Bill, had "offered to raise and arm and lead one thousand men at his own expense, for the defense of his country."

On September 16, a Boston silversmith named Paul Revere rode breathlessly into Philadelphia with news. Revere had worked with Adams before, providing the press with more than a few inflammatory engravings to strengthen the radicals' causes, including one of the Boston Massacre. Now he had a copy of the Suffolk Resolves, drawn up by Bostonians and other inhabitants of Suffolk County a month earlier. The resolutions set forth the sufferings of Massachusetts in inflammatory language and called for civil disobedience to protest the Coercive Acts. Congress endorsed the Suffolk Resolves to underscore American solidarity.

But when Revere rode into town again on October 16, this time to announce that the British were fortifying Boston, he received a cooler response from Congress. A few of the southern delegates joined in the spirit of the Boston radicals: Patrick Henry thundered that "Arms are a Resource to which We shall be forced";

Christopher Gadsden of South Carolina proposed an immediate attack on British troops in Boston; Richard Henry Lee of Virginia wanted Congress to call for the evacuation of the city. Among the majority of delegates, however, restraint prevailed. They refused to be stampeded by the manipulation of Adams, the saber-rattling of southern hotspurs, or the histrionics of Revere. Congress approved a defensive strategy of civil disobedience but drew the line at authorizing proposals to strengthen and arm colonial militias.

The First Continental Congress, although determined to bring about repeal of the Coercive Acts, held firm in its resistance to a revolutionary course of action. If British officials had responded to its recommendations and restored the status quo of 1763, the war for independence might have been postponed—perhaps indefinitely. On the other hand, even though the Congress did not go to the extremes urged by the radicals, its decisions drew Americans further down the road to independence.

The successful conduct of a continental congress itself fostered the cause of American unity. Despite the differing backgrounds of delegates and the separate interests of individual colonies, the Congress forged compromises and attained remarkable unanimity on the key issues of colonial rights and the tactics of resistance. More important, the delegates discovered that they shared a common set of values—a commitment to the republican virtues of simplicity and industry—embodied in the Association. To their mutual satisfaction, members of Congress came away concluding, with Caesar Rodney of Delaware, that "more sensible, fine fellows you would never wish to see."

The Last Days of the British Empire in America

Most Americans shared the delegates' enthusiasm for the achievements of the First Continental Congress. They expected that the Association would bring about a speedy repeal of the Coercive Acts. But most of the delegates, although proud of their unity, were less sanguine about the future. They anticipated war with England, even if they were unwilling to commit Congress itself to preparing for it.

The same apprehension that America was slipping toward a showdown with Britain led other men to denounce the doings of Congress. Joseph Galloway warned his countrymen that he had detected within Congress "the ill-shapen diminutive brat, Independency." Conservatives dreaded that outcome. If the authority of Parliament was denied, they predicted, the colonies would be in "a perfect state of nature," destitute of any supreme director to settle differences among themselves. Americans would quarrel over land claims and other contended issues, and the result would be civil war. Conservatives also warned that a break with Britain would mean the triumph of democracy in America. They believed that the colonies had more to fear from the certain anarchy and mob rule that would follow independence than from the British Parliament.

The man in America with the least enthusiasm for the actions of the Continental Congress was the one who sat in the hottest seat in the colonies, that of the governor of Massachusetts. He was General Thomas Gage, who had replaced Thomas Hutchinson in 1774 and now watched as royal authority crumbled in Massachusetts and the disintegration spread to other colonies.

In October 1774, a desperate Gage dissolved the Massachusetts legislature, which then reconstituted itself as a Provincial Congress and assumed the government of the colony. The new Provincial Congress promptly took over tax collection, appropriating 20,000 pounds for arms and ammunition and creating a committee to supply and direct the militia. Gage then started to fortify the Boston Neck with cannon and pleaded with the ministry for more troops—only to find his fortifications damaged by saboteurs and his requests for reinforcements ignored by Britain. Gage at last dispatched scouts to map the roads leading out of Boston, but his scouts were detected and sent packing by farmers. And when he made a show of drilling his troops, the Provincial Congress announced it would muster the militia if more than 500 British regulators moved out of Boston.

Outside Boston, the friends of royal authority fared no better. Farmers in western Massachusetts forcibly closed the county courts, turning out royally appointed justices and establishing their own tribunals. Popularly elected committees of inspection charged with enforcing the Association took over towns everywhere in Massachusetts, not only restricting trade, but also regulating every aspect of local life. The committees converted their communities into "Christian Spartas," societies of virtuous republicans who condemned "effeminate" English luxuries like tea and fine clothing and "corrupt" leisure activities like dancing, gambling, and racing. The committees also dispatched spies to report on any citizen unfriendly to the resistance. "Enemies of American liberty," who engaged in illegal trade, illicit consumption, or "disloyal" behavior, faced public censure, and in some places, intimidation and punishment at the hands of angry mobs.

Throughout the colonies a similar process was under way. During the winter and early spring of 1775, provincial congresses, county conventions, and local committees of inspection were emerging as de facto governments, supplanting royal authority at every level. As the spectacle unfolded before General Gage, he concluded that only force could subdue the colonies. But it would take more than he had at his command.

With Massachusetts on the verge of armed revolt, most Britons received reports from the colonies with utter indifference. The chaos in America merited hardly a mention during the parliamentary elections held in November 1774. In most English circles, Edmund Burke observed, "any remarkable highway robbery on Hounslow Heath would make more conversation than all of the disturbances in America."

By the end of 1774, Gage had persuaded the king and Parliament that the colonies were in rebellion, but most politicians still regarded the American resistance as the work of "a rude rabble" in Boston fired by a few radical agitators like Samuel Adams. Few British policymakers understood the seriousness of the situation, but one who did was William Pitt. No longer a minister but now a member of Parliament, Pitt put before that body a radical program for reconciliation in January 1775. He urged the withdrawal of all troops from Boston, the repeal of the Coercive Acts and all other measures objectionable to Americans, and the passage of legislation promising that the colonies could not be taxed without their consent. In return for these concessions, the colonies would grant the Crown a perpetual revenue.

Would the adoption of Pitt's proposals have undermined the momentum of the resistance and restored the colonies to the empire? There is no way to know: Parliament spurned Pitt's program and instead, in February, approved an address to the king declaring that the colonies were in rebellion. A few weeks later, it approved a carrot-and-stick policy proposed by Lord North as a final means to settle the dispute. For the stick, Parliament closed the Atlantic fishery to New

England ships and restricted their trade to Britain and the West Indies. Balancing this punishment with a conciliatory offer, Parliament agreed to suspend its taxation of any colony that made adequate provision on its own for the support of civil and military government. But no mention was made of how much revenue would be required or what each colony's proportion might be. It hardly mattered, for no one in America took Lord North's offer seriously.

The Fighting Begins

As spring came to Boston, the city waited. A band of artisans in the North End, organized as spies and express riders by Paul Revere, watched General Thomas Gage, waiting for him to act. Gage waited for word from Lord North and watched the hostile town. On April 14, word from North finally arrived: the general was to seize the leaders of the Provincial Congress. That would behead the rebellion, North said. If the arrest of resistance leaders triggered violence, Gage was to suppress the insurrection with force. That would nip revolution in the bud. General Gage knew better—the situation required more than a quick police action— but he also knew that he had to do something.

On the night of April 18, the sexton of Christ Church in Boston's North End hung two lamps in the steeple. It was a signal that British troops were moving out of Boston by water. They had crossed the Back Bay in boats around midnight, beginning a march toward the arms and ammunition stored by the Provincial Congress in Concord. As the lamps flashed the signal to Charlestown, Revere and a comrade, William Dawes, set out on a hard ride to arouse the rest of the countryside.

When the news of a British march reached Lexington, the local militia of about 70 farmers, chilled and sleepy, mustered on the Green at the center of the little rural town. Lexington Green lay directly on the road to Concord. At about four in the morning, 700 British troops appeared on the Green, and their commander, Major John Pitcairn, ordered the Lexington militia to disperse. The Americans, badly outnumbered and probably overawed, began to comply. A shot rang out—whether the British or the Americans fired first is unknown—then two volleys burst from the ranks of the redcoats. With a cheer, the British set off for Concord, five miles distant, leaving eight Americans dead on Lexington Green.

By dawn, hundreds of volunteers from nearby towns were surging into Concord. From as far west as Worcester other companies were on the march, heading for the same site. The British entered Concord at about seven in the morning and encountered no opposition as they moved on their target, a house lying across the North Bridge that spanned the Concord River. While three companies of British soldiers conducted a futile search for American arms, three others, posted on the bridge itself, had the misfortune to find American arms—borne by the rebels and fired at the badly deployed redcoats with deadly effect. By noon, the British were retreating to Boston.

The narrow road from Concord to Boston's outskirts became a corridor of carnage, Americans in pursuit firing on the column of fleeing redcoats from the cover of fences and forests. By the end of April 19, the British had sustained 273 casualties; the Americans, 95. It was only the beginning. By evening of the next day, perhaps 20,000 militia had converged on Boston and were digging in for a long siege.

Common Sense

The bloodshed at Lexington Green and Concord's North Bridge irrevocably committed Americans to a course of rebellion—and that course of rebellion, to independence. That was the conclusion drawn by Thomas Paine, who urged other Americans to do the same.

In point of fact, Paine was hardly an American at all. He was born in England, apprenticed first as a corsetmaker, appointed later a tax collector, and fated finally to become midwife to the age of republican revolutions. Paine came to Philadelphia late in 1774, set up as a journalist, and made the American cause his own. "Where liberty is, there is my country," he declared. In January 1776, he wrote a pamphlet to inform Americans of their identity as a distinct people and their destiny as a nation. *Common Sense* enjoyed tremendous popularity and wide circulation, selling 120,000 copies within three months of its publication.

After Lexington and Concord, Paine wrote, as the imperial crisis passed "from argument to arms, a new era for politics is struck—a new method of thinking has arisen." That new era of politics for Paine was the age of republicanism. He derided monarchy as a foolish and dangerous form of government, one that ran counter to the dictates of reason as well as the word of the Bible. King George himself Paine rechristened as "the Royal Brute of Britain," a "sullen Pharaoh" who had enslaved the chosen people of the new age—the Americans.

By ridicule and remorseless argument, Paine severed the ties of America's allegiance to the king. George III was no well-meaning but misinformed monarch in the thrall of evil ministers and a corrupt Parliament. In Paine's view, George III was the principal villain of the piece, nothing more than "a crowned ruffian," like all other kings before him. Nor did Paine stop there. He rejected the idea that Americans were or should want to be English. Britain, he told his readers, had nurtured the colonies out of self-interest rather than attachment. Far from being a tender parent, the so-called mother country was a parasite on colonial wealth and a predator on colonial liberties. That the colonies occupied a huge continent an ocean away from the tiny British Isles proved that nature itself had fashioned America for independence. There was more: "By the common order of nature, it is evident that they belong to different systems. England to Europe, America to itself." England lay locked in Europe, doomed to the corruption of an Old World. The New World liberated America to become an "asylum of liberty."

Americans liked being English, but being English hadn't worked. Perhaps that is another way of saying that over the course of nearly two centuries colonial society and politics had evolved in such a way that the identity between Americans and English no longer fit. By the end of the Seven Years' War, the colonies had established political institutions—institutions that made the rights of "freeborn Britons" more evident and available to ordinary citizens in America than in the nation that had created those liberties. Perhaps, then, most Americans had succeeded *too* well at becoming English, regarding themselves as political equals entitled to basic constitutional freedoms. No matter. In the space of less than a generation, the logic of events made clear that for all the English and Americans

Thomas Paine, author of *Common Sense.*

shared, in the distribution of political power they were fundamentally at odds. And the call to arms at Lexington and Concord made retreat impossible.

On that point Paine was clear. It was the destiny of Americans to be republicans, not monarchists. It was the destiny of Americans to be independent, not subject to British dominion. It was the destiny of Americans to be American, not to be English. That, according to Thomas Paine, was common sense.

SIGNIFICANT EVENTS

1755	Braddock defeated by French and Indians
1756	England and France declare war
1759	Decisive English victory at Quebec
1760	George III becomes king of England
1763	Treaty of Paris ends the Seven Years' War; Pontiac's Rebellion; royal proclamation prohibits settlement west of the Appalachians
1764	Sugar Act; Currency Act
1765	Stamp Act; Quartering Act
1766	Repeal of the Stamp Act; Declaratory Act
1767	Townshend duties; Parliament suspends New York assembly
1770	Boston Massacre; repeal of most Townshend duties
1772	Gaspee Commission
1773	Boston Tea Party
1774	Coercive Acts; First Continental Congress meets at Philadelphia
1775	Battles of Lexington and Concord
1776	Thomas Paine's *Common Sense* published

6

The American People and the American Revolution

 t was a perfect morning in the middle of June. From a high place in the city—Beacon Hill, perhaps, or Copse Hill—General Thomas Gage looked down on the peninsula of Boston. His gaze traveled over the church belfries and steeples, the roofs of brick and white frame houses basking serenely in the warm air of early summer. Then he shifted his spyglass, focusing on a figure far in the distance across the Charles River. The man was perched on the parapet of a crude fortification on Breed's Hill, an elevation lying a little below Bunker Hill on the Charlestown peninsula. Gage took the measure of his enemy: an older man, past middle age, clad all in homespun, a sword swinging beneath his coat, a broad-brimmed hat shading his eyes. As he passed the spyglass to his ally, a king's man, an American loyalist, Gage asked Abijah Willard if he knew the man on the parapet. Willard peered across the Charles and identified his own brother-in-law, Colonel William Prescott. The member of an eminent Massachusetts family and a veteran of Amherst's assault on Louisbourg during the Seven Years' War, Prescott was now a leader in the rebel army laying siege to Boston. Atop the parapet, Prescott deliberately exposed himself to British fire from Boston harbor, a gesture to hearten his men.

"Will he fight?" Gage wondered aloud. The loyalist studied his kinsman. "I cannot answer for his men," Willard replied, "but Prescott will fight you to the gates of hell."

Fight they did on June 17, 1775, both William Prescott and his men. The evening before, three regiments drawn from the thousands of New England militia who had converged on British-occupied Boston after the bloodshed at Lexington and Concord followed Prescott from Cambridge to the Charlestown peninsula. There, all through the hot, dusty night, they built on Breed's Hill a redoubt of deep trenches and high earthen walls. At the first light of day, General Gage awakened to the boom of a cannonade from Boston harbor: his warship, the *Lively*, had spotted the new rebel outpost on Breed's Hill and opened fire. By noon barges were ferrying British troops under Major General William Howe across the half-mile of river that separated Boston from Charlestown. The 1600 raw rebel troops tensed at the sight of scarlet-coated soldiers streaming ashore, glittering bayonets grasped at the ready. Their eyes stung from the acrid smoke of bombardments fired from British warships and the battery on Copse Hill. Their ears re-

Eleven years after the event, the American artist John Trumbull painted Battle of Bunker's Hill *(1786), a canvas executed in the currently fashionable mode of grand historical painting, designed to commemorate (and elevate) an occasion of note.*

sounded with the din of guns roaring and an enemy massing. The rebels were farmers and craftworkers, not professional soldiers, and they were frightened out of their wits.

But Prescott and his men held their ground. The British charged Breed's Hill twice, and both times the defenders allowed them to close before raining lead into their lines. Howe watched in horror the stream of fire felling his troops. Finally, during the third British frontal assault, the rebels ran out of ammunition and were forced to withdraw; redcoats swarmed over the redoubt, savagely bayoneting its handful of remaining defenders. By nightfall the British had taken Breed's Hill and the rest of the Charlestown peninsula. They had bought a dark triumph at the cost of 228 dead and 800 wounded. The British could not afford to win another such victory, one officer remarked, and Howe agreed.

The cost came high in loyalties as well. The fighting on Breed's Hill fed hatred of Britain, the sense of betrayal that had been building since April. Throughout America, preparations for war intensified: militia in every colony mustered; communities stockpiled arms and ammunition. From as far south as Virginia came reports that "a phrenzy of revenge" had "seized all ranks of people." Back in New England, civilians fled Charlestown, which had been ravaged in a fire lit by the British shelling of Breed's Hill. Fearful of another British strike, the inhabitants of neighboring communities also sought refuge farther inland with friends and kinfolk. "The roads filled with frightened women and children, some in carts with their tattered furniture, others on foot fleeing into the woods," recalled Hannah Winthrop, one of their number. Militia companies from every town and hamlet in the colony started to converge on the hills around Boston, cordoning off the capital. From nearby Watertown the rebel leader James Warren reported that "it is Impossible to describe the Confusion in this place, Women and Children flying into the Country, armed Men Going to the field, and wounded Men returning from there fill the Streets."

The bloody and indecisive fight on the Charlestown peninsula known as the Battle of Bunker Hill actually took place on Breed's Hill. And the exchange between Thomas Gage and Abijah Willard that is said to have preceded the battle may not have taken place at all. But the story has persisted in the folklore of that war for colonial liberation called the American Revolution. Whether it really happened or not, the conversation between Gage and Willard raised the question that both sides wanted answered: were Americans willing to fight for independence from British rule? It was one thing, after all, to oppose the British ministry's policy of taxation; it was another to support a rebellion for which the ultimate price of failure was hanging for treason. It was fine enough to be stirred by the rhetoric of Thomas Paine's *Common Sense;* it was another matter for farmers and their wives to find soldiers marching through newly sown fields, stealing their chickens. And it was another matter entirely for men to wait nervously atop a hill as the seasoned troops of one's own "mother country" marched toward them with the firm intent to kill.

Indeed, the question "will they fight?" was revolutionary shorthand for a host of other, deeper queries concerning how ordinary men and women would react to the tug of loyalties between long-established colonial governments and a long-revered parent nation and monarch. For recent immigrants, the question of loyalties concerned their feelings about their neighbors and their new-found land. For slaves, the question revolved around their allegiance to masters who spoke of liberty, or to their masters' enemies, who promised liberation. For those who led the rebels, it was a question of strengthening the resolve of the undecided, coordinating resistance, instilling discipline—translating the *will* to fight into the ability to do so. And for those who believed the rebellion was a madness whipped up by artful politicians, it was a question of whether to remain silent or risk speaking out; whether to take up arms for the king or flee. All these questions were raised, of necessity, by the act of revolution. But the barrel of a rifle shortened them to a single, pointed question: will you fight?

THE DECISION FOR INDEPENDENCE

The delegates to the Second Continental Congress gathered on May 10, 1775, just one month after the battles at Lexington and Concord. As the armies of Britain and America faced each other across the siege lines surrounding Boston, the delegates meeting together again at Philadelphia considered whether independence or reconciliation offered the best way to protect the liberties of their colonies.

For a brash, ambitious lawyer from Braintree, Massachusetts, British depravity dictated only one course. "The Cancer [of official corruption] is too deeply rooted," wrote John Adams, "and too far spread to be cured by anything short of cutting it out entire." Yet during the spring and summer of 1775, even ardent advocates of independence like Adams and his kindred spirit, Virginia's Richard Henry Lee, did not openly seek a separation from Britain. Even the impulsive Adams recognized that reconciliation still appealed to many both in Congress and in the colonies. If the radicals' objective of independence was ever to be achieved, greater agreement among Americans had to be attained. Moderates and conservatives clung to the hope of reconciliation and harbored deep misgivings about independence: they had to be brought along slowly.

The Second Continental Congress

To bring them along, Congress adopted the "Olive Branch Petition" in July 1775. Drawn up by Pennsylvania's John Dickinson, the document affirmed American loyalty to George III and asked the king to disavow the policies of his principal ministers. At the same time, Congress issued a declaration denying that the colonies aimed at independence. Yet, less than a month earlier, Congress had authorized the creation of a rebel military force, the Continental Army, and had issued paper money to pay for the troops. Americans had taken up arms only to protect their rights, the delegates insisted, and would lay them down once Britain had redressed their grievances.

Congress not only mobilized for war but also cast about for allies among Britain's other colonies. The planters of the British West Indies, too remote and too dependent on England, were dismissed as potential supporters, but the "oppressed Inhabitants of Canada" were invited to send delegates to the Second Continental Congress. Some Americans had regarded Canadians as "fellow sufferers" for a "common liberty" ever since Parliament passed the Quebec Act in 1774. That legislation provided for the rule of Canada by a royal governor and a council, but no representative assembly; it also officially recognized the Roman Catholic church and extended the bounds of the province to include all land between the Mississippi and Ohio rivers. While the Quebec Act outraged the partisans of American liberty, Protestantism, and land speculation, the 80,000 inhabitants of Canada, most of whom were Catholic, applauded Parliament's toleration of their religion and the expansion of their territory. Since most Canadians were also French, they had little sympathy for a struggle for "British liberties." When Canadians declared either loyalty to the king or indifference to the American cause, Congress sponsored several unsuccessful invasions of Canada, approving the first almost immediately after it created the Continental Army.

A Congress that sued for peace while preparing for war was a contradiction that British politicians did not even try to fathom, least of all Lord George Germain, the new, tough-minded American secretary. Germain would hear nothing of negotiating: he was determined to bring Americans to heel by force. George III proved just as stubborn. He refused to receive the Olive Branch Petition, and in the fall of 1775 he informed Parliament of "a desperate conspiracy" for independence in America. By the end of that year Parliament had shut down all trade with the rebellious colonies and had ordered the Royal Navy to seize colonial merchant ships on the high seas. The remaining royal governors also lent their influence to snuffing out any chance of reconciliation. In November 1775, Virginia's Lord Dunmore offered freedom to any slaves who would rebel against their masters and join

In John Trumbull's painting the Committee of Five, including Adams (left), Jefferson (second from right), and Franklin (right) submit the Declaration of Independence to the Continental Congress. John Hancock, the president of the Congress, is reported to have remarked, "We must be unanimous; there must be no pulling different ways; we must all hang together." Franklin is said to have rejoined, "Yes, we must indeed all hang together, or most assuredly, we shall all hang separately."

the British. During January of the next year, Dunmore ordered the shelling of Norfolk, Virginia, reducing that town to a smoldering rubble.

The blast of British belligerence withered the cause of reconciliation within Congress and the colonies. Support for independence gained momentum from the overwhelming public reception of Thomas Paine's *Common Sense* in January 1776. The radicals in Congress realized that the future was theirs and were ready to act. In April 1776 the delegates opened American trade to every nation in the world except Great Britain; a month later Congress advised the colonies to establish new state governments. And on June 7, Richard Henry Lee offered the motion "That these United Colonies are, and of right ought to be, free and independent States, that they are absolved from all allegiance to the British Crown, and that all political connection between them and the State of Great Britain is, and ought to be, totally dissolved."

Congress debated Lee's motion but then postponed a final vote until July. There was still some lingering opposition among delegates from the Middle Colonies, and a committee appointed to write a declaration of independence needed time to complete its work. That committee included some of the premier political leaders in Congress: John Adams, Benjamin Franklin, Connecticut's Roger Sherman, and New York's Robert Livingston. But the man who did most of the drafting was a young planter and lawyer from western Virginia, a learned and imaginative devotee of the Enlightenment.

Thomas Jefferson was just 33 years old in the summer of 1776 when he sequestered himself in his second-floor lodgings on the outskirts of Philadelphia, pulled a portable writing desk onto his lap, and wrote the statement that would explain American independence to a "candid world." In the document's brief opening section, Jefferson set forth a general justification of revolution that invoked the "self-evident truths" of human equality and "unalienable rights" to "life, liberty, and the pursuit of happiness." To underscore the finality of America's break with Britain, the Declaration's case for revolution rested squarely on the doctrine of natural rights. These rights had been "endowed" to all persons "by their Creator," the Declaration pointed out; thus there was no need to appeal to the narrower claim of the "rights of Englishmen."

While the first part of the Declaration served notice that Americans no longer considered themselves English, its second and longer section implicitly denied Parliament any authority in the colonies. In its detailed history of American grievances against the British empire, the Declaration alluded only once to Parliament. Instead, for every infringement of American liberty, the Declaration blamed the last acknowledged link between Britain and the colonies—George III. This second section specifically justified an American revolution by showing the "long train of abuses and usurpations," the design for "absolute despotism" authored by the king. Unlike Paine's *Common Sense*, the Declaration indicted only the reigning king of England; it did not attack the institution of monarchy itself. But like *Common Sense*, the Declaration affirmed that government originated in the consent of the governed and upheld the right of the people to overthrow oppressive rule. And it referred hopefully to Americans as "one people."

Later generations have debated what Jefferson meant by "the pursuit of happiness" and whether he had either women or black Americans in mind when he wrote the famous phrase "all men are created equal." His own contemporaries in Congress did not pause to consider these questions: they adopted the Declaration of Independence on July 4, 1776.

American Loyalists

Colonial political leaders edged toward independence, drawn by their own interests, their commitment to preserving constitutional liberty, and events that extinguished any prospect of reconciliation. In the end, they embraced independence because they believed that a majority of Americans would support a revolution to bring it about.

But the sentiment for independence was not universal. Those who would not back the rebellion, partisans of the king and Parliament, who numbered perhaps one-fifth of the population in 1775, proclaimed themselves "loyalists." Their rebel opponents dubbed them "tories"—"a thing whose head is in England, whose body is in America, and whose neck ought to be stretched." That division made the Revolution a conflict that pitted Americans against one another as well as the British. In truth, the war for independence was the first American civil war.

Many who took up the king's cause had not lacked sympathy for the resistance. Loyalist leaders like Joseph Galloway, Daniel Dulany, and Daniel Leonard actually opposed the Stamp Act in 1765 and disapproved of imperial policy thereafter. It was not until the crisis reached a fever pitch in 1774, after the Boston Tea Party, that a large number of colonials cast their lot with the king. Even then many

Daily Lives

CLOTHING AND FASHION

Radical Chic and the Revolutionary Generation

Women and men of revolutionary America sought to invest themselves with virtue as they escaped British "corruption." The most zealous partisans of colonial rights took that "investiture" to a literal extreme: they made and wore particular clothing as an emblem of political commitment and aspiration. What workshirts, faded denim jeans, and "love beads" were to student radicals of the 1960s, gowns, shirts, and breeches made of "homespun" were to members of the revolutionary generation. In the 1760s homespun, any coarse cloth made in America, became a badge of imperiled innocence and cultural alienation.

Donning homespun bespoke the wearer's virtue: he or she had forsworn fine fabrics along with all the other "effeminate" and "enslaving" English luxuries. Clothes sewn from domestic textiles identified the men and women who wore them as friends of liberty, freed from the vanity and foppishness of British fashion and the humiliating dependence on British imports. As early as 1766 the radical press called for increased domestic industry to offset American reliance on English cloth and beamed its pleas particularly at the women who managed colonial households. A Rhode Islander writing in the *Providence Gazette* remarked in 1767, "We must after all our efforts depend greatly upon the female sex for the introduction of œconomy among us."

By 1769 radical propaganda had produced a new ritual of American resistance, the patriotic spinning competition. Wives and daughters from some of the wealthiest and most prominent families, women who had heretofore vied to outdo each other in acquiring the latest English finery, were the featured players in this novel form of political theater. Its setting was usually the home of a local minister where, early in the morning, "respectable" young ladies, all dressed in homespun, assembled with their spinning wheels. They spent the day spinning furiously, stopping only to sustain themselves with "American produce . . . which was more agreeable to them than any foreign Dainties and Delicacies" and to drink herbal tea. At the end of the day the minister accepted their homespun cloth and delivered an edifying sermon to all present. That was a large group, often including from 20 to 100 "respectable" female spinners as well as hundreds of other townsfolk who had come to watch the competition or to provide food and entertainment. The Reverend Ezra Stiles of Newport, Rhode Island, hosted a spinning bee that drew, by his estimate, 600 spectators.

Women reveled in the new attention and value that the male resistance movement and the radical press now attached to a common and humdrum domestic task. By the beginning of 1769 New England newspapers were giving extensive coverage to spinning bees and their female participants, sometimes termed the "Daughters of Liberty." Front pages overflowed with praise of female patriotism: "The industry and frugality of American ladies must exalt their character in the Eyes of the World and serve to show how greatly they are contributing to bring about the political salvation of a whole Continent."

Spinning competitions and the vogue of wearing homespun served two political purposes. First, the bees actively enlisted American women in the struggle against Britain. The wives and daughters from families of every rank were made to feel

Daily Lives

Hunting shirts like the one worn by this rifleman (second figure from the right) captured the imagination of the French army officer in America who made these watercolor sketches of uniforms of revolutionary soldiers. The enlistment of blacks (infantryman at the far left) drew the artist's attention as well.

that they could play an important role in the resistance by imitating the elite women showcased in public spinning spectacles. Every woman could display her devotion to liberty by encouraging industry and frugality in her own household. Many women took pride in the new political importance that radical propaganda attributed to domestic pursuits. Writing to her English cousin, Charity Clarke of New York City cast herself as one of America's "fighting army of amazones . . . armed with spinning wheels." Although "heroines may not distinguish themselves at the head of an Army," the young woman assured her cousin, American women could still defend their "new arcadia" from "arbitrary power" by clothing its inhabitants "with the work of our hands."

Spinning bees and "dressing down" in homespun also contributed to the solidarity of the resistance by narrowing the visible distance between rich and poor Americans. In accounts of spinning competitions, the radical press emphasized that the spinners came from "as good families as any in town," demonstrating that even daughters of the elite sacrificed for the cause of resistance by embracing domestic economy and simplicity. And what genteel women wove, leading men wore. On public occasions throughout the revolutionary crisis, radical leaders appeared in homespun, an ostentatious display of both their patriotic virtue and their identification with poorer Americans who could not afford British finery. When they returned to their home counties to muster local militia companies, many southern gentlemen—indeed, most members of the Virginia House of Burgesses—adopted homespun "hunting shirts," long, loose, full-sleeved frocks that reached past the thigh. This staple of the attire of ordinary frontiersmen since the beginning of the eighteenth century at once united the gentry with ordinary men of the backcountry while declaring their superiority to the corrupt mother country.

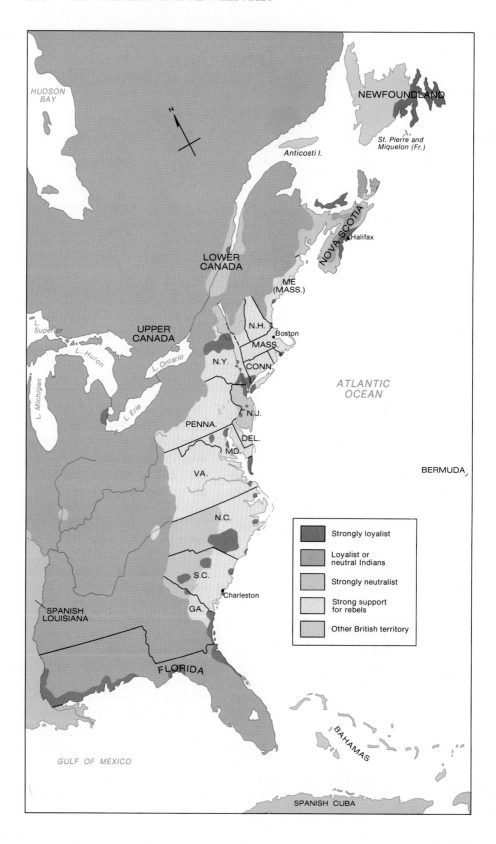

HUDSON
BAY

NEWFOUNDLAND

St. Pierre and
Miquelon (Fr.)

Anticosti I.

NOVA SCOTIA

Halifax

LOWER
CANADA

ME
(MASS.)

L. Superior

UPPER
CANADA

N.H.

Boston

MASS.

L. Huron

L. Ontario

N.Y.

CONN

L. Michigan

L. Erie

ATLANTIC
OCEAN

N.J.

PENNA.

DEL.

MD.

VA.

BERMUDA

N.C.

Strongly loyalist

Loyalist or
neutral Indians

Strongly neutralist

S.C.

Charleston

Strong support
for rebels

Other British territory

SPANISH
LOUISIANA

GA.

FLORIDA

BAHAMAS

GULF OF MEXICO

SPANISH CUBA

who did so voiced objections to the Tea Act. But worse than British taxation, in their view, was the radicalism of American resistance—the dumping of tea into Boston harbor, the forming of the Association, and the flouting of royal authority.

If any single characteristic distinguished the loyalists' thinking, it was their deep conviction of the divisiveness and instability of colonial society. If Americans won independence, they feared, the chaos of civil war would envelop the continent. Without the British around to maintain order, controversies among Americans would mushroom into armed conflicts. On the eve of the Revolution, Jonathan Boucher, a New York loyalist of uncanny prescience, warned:

> See ye not that after some few years of civil broils all the fair settlements in the middle and southern colonies will be seized on by our more enterprising and restless fellow-colonists of the North. . . ? O 'tis a monstrous and unnatural coalition; and we should as soon expect to see . . . the wolf and the lamb feed together, as Virginians to form a cordial union with the saints of New England.

Predictably, the king and Parliament commanded the strongest support in New York, New Jersey, Pennsylvania, and the Carolinas, colonies that had been wracked by severe internal strife earlier in the eighteenth century. In these colonies a history of struggle not only sharpened worries of future upheaval, but old adversaries also took different sides in the Revolution. The Carolina backcountry emerged early as a stronghold of loyalist sentiment, principally because some former frontier Regulators refused to make common cause with their old enemies, the coastal planters, most of whom advocated independence. The same reasoning held among the former land rioters of New York and New Jersey. If their old landlord opponents opted for the rebel cause, the tenants took up loyalism. Everywhere that controversies over land tenure and political representation had raged before the Revolution, the losers in those contests gravitated toward loyalism during the Revolution.

Other influences also fostered allegiance to the king. About 10 percent of the loyalists were government officials who owed their jobs to the empire or major city merchants who depended on British trade. Those Anglicans living outside the South retained strong ties to the parent country because of their membership in the Church of England. Loyalists were also disproportionately represented among recent emigrants from the British Isles. The inhabitants of Georgia, the newest colony, inclined toward the king, as did the Highland Scots, many of whom had arrived in the colonies as soldiers during the Seven Years' War or had worked for a short time in the southern backcountry as tobacco merchants and Indian traders.

Although a substantial minority, loyalists were the least of the problems facing republican leaders. While there were supporters of the king in all the colonies, they never became numerous enough anywhere to pose a serious threat to the Revolution. A more serious problem was posed by the British army, the most formidable in Europe. An even more serious problem was posed by those very Americans who claimed that they wanted independence. For the question remained: would they fight?

PATTERNS OF ALLEGIANCE
While most New Englanders rallied behind the rebel cause, support for the Revolution was not as widespread in the Middle and southern colonies.

THE FIGHTING IN THE NORTH

Perhaps more numerous than either diehard loyalists or dedicated rebels, at least in the summer of 1775, were Americans who wished to remain neutral. Strictly from a military standpoint, staying neutral made a lot more sense than fighting for independence. Even the most ardent advocates of American rights had reason to harbor second thoughts, given the odds against the rebel colonists defeating the armed forces of the British empire. And no friend of the American cause sized up the dismal chances of a rebel victory more accurately than George Washington.

June of 1775 found Washington, 43 years old, in Philadelphia, a delegate to the Second Continental Congress. He attended its deliberations dressed—a bit conspicuously—in his officer's uniform. The other delegates listened closely to his opinions on military matters, for Washington was the most celebrated American veteran of the Seven Years' War still young enough to lead a campaign. Better still, he was a southerner, who, if chosen to command Congress' forces, could bring his region into what thus far had remained mostly New England's fight. John Adams proposed that Congress accept the volunteer forces surrounding British-held Boston as a Continental Army and appoint a commander-in-chief. He made no secret of his preference for Washington, and the Congress followed his lead.

The Two Armies at Bay

So Washington found himself, only a month later, outside Boston in the once-quiet college town of Cambridge, the commander-in-chief of the Continental Army. Maturity had muted some of the impulsiveness and ambition that marred his performance at Fort Necessity in 1754. But the grave, dignified Virginia planter who took charge of the rebels massing around boston had lost none of his admiration for the British army.

There was much to admire. Highly trained, ably commanded, and efficiently equipped, the king's troops were seasoned professionals. Rigorous drills and often savage discipline administered by an aristocratic officer corps welded rank-and-file soldiers, men drawn mainly from the bottom of British society, into a formidable fighting machine. They marched in precise formations, loaded and discharged their muskets on orders, held ranks under fire, and fought with the courage instilled by stringent military regimen. At the height of the campaign in America, reinforcements brought the number of British troops to 50,000, their strength augmented by some 30,000 Hessian mercenaries from Germany and the support of half the ships in the British navy, the largest in the world.

Washington was more modest about the army under his command, and he had a great deal to be modest about. At first Congress recruited his fighting force of 16,600 rebel "regulars," the Continental Army, from the ranks of local militia bands, armed civilians from everywhere in New England who converged on Boston in 1775. Although a flurry of patriotic enthusiasm swelled enlistments briefly during 1775, for the rest of the war Washington's Continentals suffered chronic shortages of men and supplies. Even strong supporters of the Revolution did not want to join the regular army. They disdained the low pay and strict discipline and feared the disease and danger that were the lot of a professional soldier. Most men preferred to fight instead as members of local militia units, the "irregular" troops who turned out as adjuncts to the regular army whenever British forces came close to their neighborhoods.

The general reluctance to join the Continental Army created a host of difficulties for its commander and for Congress. Washington wanted and needed an army whose size and military capability could be counted on in long campaigns. He could not create an effective fighting force out of civilians who mustered out occasionally with the militia or enlisted for short stints in the Continental Army. Washington's insistence on a professional military establishment clashed with the inclinations of most republican leaders. They feared standing armies and idealized "citizen-soldiers," volunteers who took up arms whenever needed, as the backbone of the common defense. "Oh, that I was a soldier," John Adams rhapsodized in 1775, "I will be.—I am reading military books. Everyone must and will and shall be a soldier."

But not everyone became a soldier. The dwindling number of volunteers gradually overcame republican scruples about standing armies. In September 1776 Congress set terms in the Continental Army at a minimum of three years or for the duration of the war and assigned each state to raise a certain number of troops. They offered every man who enlisted in the army a cash bounty and a yearly clothing issue; enlistees for the duration were offered 100 acres of land as well. Still the problem of recruitment persisted. Less than a year later, Congress recommended that the states adopt a draft. Some passed conscription laws, but Congress had no authority to compel the states to meet their troop quotas.

Even in the summer of 1775, before enlistments fell off, Washington was worried. As his Continentals laid siege to British-occupied Boston, he measured them against the adversary and found them wanting. Not only were his Continentals complete strangers to military drill and discipline, they regularly shirked the most basic responsibilities of soldiers. The rank and file slipped away from camp at night; they left sentry duty before being relieved; they took potshots at the British; they tolerated filthy conditions in their camps. Inexperienced officers provided no real leadership. And the several thousand militia lending occasional support around Boston were even more stubbornly independent, undisciplined, and dirty.

Then there were "the Women of the Army." When American men went off to fight, their wives usually stayed at home. To women then fell the sole responsibility for running farms and businesses, raising children, and keeping households together. They helped to supply the troops by sewing clothing, making blankets, and saving rags and lead weights for bandages and bullets. Other women on the home front organized relief for the widows and orphans of soldiers and protests against merchants who hoarded scarce commodities. But the wives of poor men who joined the army were often left with no means to support their families. Thousands of such women—one for every 15 soldiers—drifted after the troops. In return for half-rations, they cooked and washed for the soldiers, and, after battles, nursed the wounded, buried the dead, and scavenged the field for clothing and equipment. An even larger number of women accompanied the redcoats: their presence was the only thing that Washington did not admire about the British army and could barely tolerate in his own. From the beginning to the end of the Revolution, Washington fumed that women were "a clog upon every movement" of the Continentals.

It was fortunate that Washington no longer lusted for fame and military glory, because his army seemed likely to bring him humiliation and defeat. He could only set aside his doubts about the prospects for military victory and set about imposing discipline on officers and men alike. As soon as Washington assumed command, he issued orders that covered everything from the proper procedure for standing guard to restrictions on "profane cursing, swearing, and drunkenness." He tried repeatedly to get rid of the "Women of the Army" as well—without success. The services that they performed were indispensable, and women followed the troops throughout the war.

Laying Strategies

At the same time that he tried to bring order to the ranks, Washington designed a defensive strategy to compensate for the weakness of his army. To avoid exposing raw rebel troops on "open ground against their Superiors in number and Discipline," he planned to fight the British from strong fortifications. In March 1776, Washington barricaded his Continentals on Dorchester Heights, an elevation commanding Boston harbor from the south.

Even before the besieging rebels encroached on Dorchester Heights, General William Howe, who had replaced Gage as the head of the British land forces in North America, had decided to back out of Boston. Now the certain peril that rebel artillery on the Heights would pose to British warships in Boston harbor prodded Howe into an immediate evacuation. By March 27, 1776, the occupying army of 5000 British regulars had departed for Halifax, Nova Scotia.

The evacuation of Boston marked Britain's abandonment of their first strategy for reclaiming colonies—strangling the insurgency in Massachusetts—in favor of another approach. By now the British had discerned that they were up against more than a Yankee rabble aroused by a few agitators. More than a quick, directed strike against New England would be required to arrest the cancer of resistance. Instead, the situation called for Britain to wage a conventional war in America, capturing major cities and crushing the Continental forces in a decisive battle. Military victory, the British believed, would enable them to restore political control and reestablish imperial authority.

The first target was New York City. General Howe and Lord George Germain, the new American secretary charged with overseeing the war, chose that seaport for its central location, its excellent harbor, and—they hoped—its large loyalist population. They planned for Howe's army to move from New York City up the Hudson River, meeting ultimately with a smaller complement of British troops under General Sir Guy Carleton coming south from Canada. Either the British drive would lure Washington into a major engagement, drubbing the Continentals, or, if unopposed, the British offensive would cut America in two, smothering resistance to the south by isolating New England.

The strategy seemed sound enough, but the two men charged with its execution hobbled British efforts from the outset. General Howe took to extremes the conventional wisdom of eighteenth-century European warfare, which aimed as much at avoiding heavy casualties as winning victories against the enemy. The difficulty and expense of recruiting, training, and maintaining professional soldiers dictated conservative strategies of battle. Concern for preserving manpower dominated Howe's approach throughout his American campaigns, addicting him to caution when greater daring would have carried the day. Howe's brother, Admiral Lord Richard Howe, the head of naval operations in America, also refrained from pressing the British advantage. A true eccentric among the English of his day, Richard Howe actually liked Americans. Torn between the ministry's orders to subdue the colonies by military force and his personal desire for reconciliation, Admiral Howe prosecuted the war halfheartedly. The reluctance of both of the

Howe brothers to fight became the formula for British frustration in the two years that followed.

The Campaigns in New York and New Jersey

However cautiously, General William Howe and his army sailed from Halifax and landed on Staten Island in New York harbor during July 1776. Admiral Richard Howe followed with reinforcements by sea. The Continentals marched from Boston and fortified Brooklyn Heights on Long Island, the key to the defenses of New York City on Manhattan Island. By mid-August, 32,000 British troops, including 8000 Hessians, the largest expeditionary force of the eighteenth century, faced Washington's army of 23,000.

At dawn on August 22, the Howe brothers moved on Long Island. Although the British easily pushed the rebel army from Brooklyn Heights back across the East River to Manhattan, the Howe brothers lingered on Long Island for almost a month. While the rebel militia deserted in droves and his supplies dwindled, Washington waited in Manhattan, wondering whether to defend New York City or withdraw. Just as he prepared to pull out, marching his army north through Harlem, the Howe brothers at last lurched into action, ferrying their forces to Kip's Bay, just a few miles south of Harlem. When the British landed, the handful of rebel defenders at Kip's Bay fled—straight into the towering wrath of Washington, who happened on the scene of their humiliation. Enraged by the rout, the general lost his habitual self-restraint, flogged both officers and men with his riding crop, and came close to being captured himself.

On the next day, September 16, the rebels managed to hold back the wave of British advance at Harlem Heights. The Howe brothers, still reluctant to hit hard with everything they had, let Washington's army escape from Manhattan to Westchester County on the mainland. Throughout the fall of 1776, General Howe's forces followed as Washington's fell back, first northward into New York and then southward into New Jersey. By mid-November the British advance picked up speed, and the rebels stepped up their retreat across New Jersey into a desperate race for the Delaware River. With the pursuing British army at his heels, Washington reached Trenton and ferried his forces across the river to Pennsylvania on December 7. There Howe suspended his pursuit, pulling back most of his army to winter in New York City and leaving the Hessians to hold the British line of advance along the New Jersey side of the Delaware River.

In spite of everything, Washington decided that the campaign of 1776 was not over. Although the British had harried the Continentals from their positions throughout New York and New Jersey, although the retreat had shriveled rebel strength to only 3000 men, half of whose enlistments would end with the year, and although the winter cold had settled over the Northeast, Washington wanted to play one last card.

His gamble paid off. On a frosty Christmas night, as it rained, sleeted, and snowed, Washington floated his forces back across the Delaware, their boats dodging chunks of ice. As dawn broke, the Continentals picked their way across roads sheeted with ice and blanketed with snow and finally slid into Hessian-held Trenton at eight in the morning. One thousand German soldiers, disabled by their spirited Christmas celebration and caught completely by surprise, quickly surrendered.

When word of Washington's daring exploit reached Howe in New York City,

he ordered to Trenton forces under his subordinate officer, Charles, Lord Cornwallis. But Washington's luck held. On January 3, 1777, the Continentals slipped
past Cornwallis' main force and struck at a smaller British detachment on the
outskirts of Princeton, New Jersey. The rebel victories at Trenton and Princeton
whittled away the British hold on New Jersey. Cornwallis withdrew to New
Brunswick, while Washington's army watched the enemy from their winter camp
at Morristown, just 25 miles from New York City.

The rebels enjoyed the view from Morristown. During that winter of 1776–
1777, the British alienated the very civilians whose loyalties they had hoped to
cultivate. In New York City the presence of the main body of the British army
brought shortages of food and housing and fostered constant friction between
soldiers and city dwellers. In the New Jersey countryside still held by the Hessians, the situation was even worse. Forced to live off the land, the Germans
aroused resentment among local farmers by seizing "hay, oats, Indian corn, cattle,
and horses, which were never or but very seldom paid for," as one loyalist admitted; ". . . in many instances their families were insulted, stripped of their beds
with other furniture—nay, even of their very wearing apparel." The Hessians
ransacked and destroyed homes and churches; they kidnaped and raped young
women.

Instead of protecting civilians and nurturing loyalist sentiment, the British
army menaced local peace and prosperity. Americans who had had enough of the
king's men could take their allegiance elsewhere, for Washington had demonstrated at Trenton and Princeton the credibility of the Continental Army as a
fighting force. The result was a surge of popular support for the revolutionary
cause throughout the region: bands of militia irregulars on Long Island, along the
Hudson River, and all over New Jersey rallied and raided British patrols and
foraging parties.

Capturing Philadelphia

Spring came and passed into summer in 1777 before word filtered down to the
anxious Continentals in Morristown that the British were on the move again—
boarding ships in New York harbor. General Howe had not changed his strategy:
he still hoped to entice the Continentals into a decisive engagement or to seize a
major American seaport, control the surrounding countryside, and solicit loyalist
support. But Howe had now decided to goad the Americans into battle by capturing Philadelphia. Rather than risk his army on a march through hostile New Jersey, he intended to approach the rebel capital by sea. In July Howe's army of
15,000 set sail, leaving behind a force of 7300 to hold New York.

In early August rebel spies sighted on the Chesapeake Bay the British convoy
carrying Howe's army. As the redcoats disembarked on the Maryland shore and
headed for Philadelphia, 50 miles away, Washington's army, swelled to 11,000,
hurried south from New Jersey. Washington had hoped to stay on the strategic
defensive, holding his smaller army together, harassing the enemy, but avoiding
full-scale engagements. Howe's march on Philadelphia made that impossible: he
could not allow the British to seize the fledgling nation's capital.

On September 11 the two armies joined battle at Brandywine Creek, where
the British scored a major victory and the Continentals beat a disorganized retreat. The rebels managed to stay between the advancing British and the city until
September 26, when Howe decoyed the Continentals up the Schuylkill River and

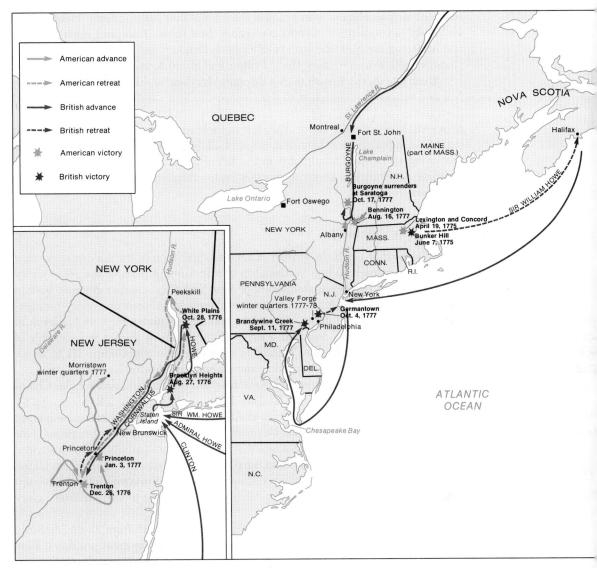

Legend:
- American advance
- American retreat
- British advance
- British retreat
- ★ American victory
- ★ British victory

QUEBEC

St. Lawrence R.

Montreal
Fort St. John

NOVA SCOTIA

Halifax

MAINE
(part of MASS.)

BURGOYNE

Lake
Champlain

N.H.

Burgoyne surrenders
at Saratoga
Oct. 17, 1777

SIR WILLIAM HOWE

Lake Ontario   Fort Oswego

Bennington
Aug. 16, 1777

Lexington and Concord
April 19, 1775

NEW YORK   Albany

MASS.

Bunker Hill
June 7, 1775

Hudson R.

CONN.

R.I.

PENNSYLVANIA

Valley Forge
winter quarters 1777-78

N.J.   New York

Germantown
Oct. 4, 1777

NEW YORK

Peekskill

White Plains
Oct. 28, 1776

Brandywine Creek
Sept. 11, 1777

Philadelphia

Hudson R.

HOWE

MD.

Delaware R.

NEW JERSEY

Morristown
winter quarters 1777

DEL.

Brooklyn Heights
Aug. 27, 1776

VA.

ATLANTIC
OCEAN

WASHINGTON

CORNWALLIS

Staten
Island

SIR. WM. HOWE

New Brunswick

ADMIRAL HOWE

Chesapeake Bay

Princeton

CLINTON

Princeton
Jan. 3, 1777

Trenton   Trenton
Dec. 26, 1776

N.C.

THE FIGHTING IN THE NORTH, 1775–1777

claimed Philadelphia. He quartered his main force of some 9000 men in German-town, a village five miles northwest of the city. Washington struck back quickly, surprising the British at Germantown in the dawn of October 4, but Howe's troops recovered and forced another rebel retreat.

Germantown was a miss for Washington—but it was a near miss, too close for Howe's comfort. The Americans could take satisfaction not only from a new pride that sustained the army even in defeat, but also from the difficulties that blighted the British even in victory. Although the British held Philadelphia, rebel-held forts along the Delaware blocked the flow of supplies and reinforcements into the capital until mid-November. The natives of the conquered city were restless, too. In Philadelphia, as in New York, British occupation jacked up demand and prices for food, fuel, and housing. While inflation hit hardest at the poor, the wealthy resented British officers who became their uninvited house guests. Everyone in Philadelphia complained of redcoats looting their shops, trampling their gardens, and harassing them on the streets. Elizabeth Drinker, the wife of a Quaker merchant, confided in her diary that "I often feel afraid to go to bed."

Even worse, the British march through Maryland and Pennsylvania had terrified and outraged civilians, who fled before the army and then returned to find their homes and barns bare, their crops and livestock gone. Everywhere Howe's men went in the middle states, they left in their wake Americans with compelling reasons to support the rebels. But worst of all, just days after Howe marched his occupying army into Philadelphia in the fall of 1777, another British commander in North America was surrendering his entire army to rebel forces at Saratoga, New York.

Disaster at Saratoga

The calamity that befell the British at Saratoga had been in the making ever since the previous winter. While Washington was reclaiming parts of the New Jersey countryside and Howe was simmering in New York City, another general, back in London, was jockeying for an independent command. Glamorous, glory-mongering John "Gentleman Johnny" Burgoyne had served under Sir Guy Carleton in Canada. After Carleton bungled a drive into New York during the summer of 1776, Burgoyne went back to Britain to urge Germain and George III to attack from Canada again, this time under more aggressive leadership—his own.

Burgoyne proposed to cut off New England by pressing down Lake Champlain and then south along the Hudson River to Albany. He left vague exactly what he would do once he got as far as Albany and exactly how his maneuvering would isolate New England, but Germain and the king asked no questions. Nor did they try to coordinate Burgoyne's drive with the movements of Howe's army, who might have assisted by heading north up the Hudson. Howe, bent on taking Philadelphia and unwilling to share military glory with Burgoyne, offered no support; and Burgoyne, bent on taking Albany and unwilling to share military glory with anyone, requested none.

Burgoyne began his campaign by calling for support from those "friendly civilians" whom the British consistently expected to find in great numbers. Few stepped forward, especially after Burgoyne's bullying threat to unleash the Iroquois against frontier settlements. Nevertheless, at the end of June 1777 Burgoyne set out from Quebec with a force of 9500 redcoats, 2000 women and children, and an elaborate baggage train that included the commander's silver dining service, his dress uniforms, and numerous cases of his favorite champagne. As the British marched into New York, a handful of Continentals and a horde of New England militia assembled at Bemis Heights, an elevation 200 feet above the Hudson River and several miles below Saratoga, under the command of General Horatio Gates. An elderly, rough-hewn man, "Granny" Gates enjoyed great popularity with his troops, but he exercised little discipline and shared with the Howe brothers a lack of daring.

If the rebels in New York lacked an effective commander, the British under Burgoyne faced an even more formidable disadvantage—the treacherous terrain from Quebec to Albany. The route before them led over a winding road, broken by boulders and felled trees and knit together with long, ramshackle bridges that swayed over yawning ravines. Burgoyne's huge entourage lumbered southward like a stately royal caravan gone astray, the rigors of the journey exhausting men, horses, and supplies. To replenish his stocks, Burgoyne dispatched a foraging party of 600 Hessians to the Connecticut River, only to have them stopped at Bennington, Vermont, and mauled by a much larger rebel force under Brigadier General John Stark.

As the dispirited Burgoyne continued his halting advance toward Albany, Gates and several thousand rebels were fortifying Bemis Heights. On September 19, scouts nested high in the trees spied the glitter of bayonets and alerted Gates to the British approach. Benedict Arnold, a dashing young officer who had organized several heroic but futile rebel forays into Canada, persuaded a reluctant Gates that British fire would pry open the rebel fortifications. Arnold led the forces that descended from Bemis Heights and swarmed into the surrounding woods, meeting Burgoyne's men in a clearing at Freeman's Farm. Arnold spearheaded repeated charges across the clearing, and the British rallied and returned the assaults. At the end of the day, British reinforcements finally pushed the rebels back from a battlefield piled high with the bodies of soldiers from both sides. Burgoyne's army, bleeding after its mangling at Freeman's Farm, hemorrhaged as it started back toward Canada with the rebels in deadly pursuit. On October 17, Burgoyne stopped his flight at Saratoga and surrendered his entire army to Gates.

Saratoga changed everything. With Burgoyne's surrender, the British did not lose their military superiority in America, but they lost something just as important: the conviction that the war was theirs to win. And with Burgoyne's surrender, the rebels did not gain irresistible momentum on the battlefield, but they did succeed in convincing France that, with a little help, the Americans might well reap the fruits of victory. The new British uncertainty and the new French alliance soon transformed the American Revolution into a global war.

THE TURNING POINT

France had been waiting since 1763 for revenge against Britain. Humiliated by defeat in the Seven Years' War, the French yearned for an opportunity to reclaim their fisheries in the North Atlantic, to secure their colonies in the Caribbean, and to reassert their supremacy in Europe. Since the mid-1760s, as France's agents in America sent home reports of a rebellion brewing, a scheme for evening the score with Britain had been taking shape in the mind of the French foreign minister, Charles Gravier de Vergennes. In the disaffected Americans he reckoned that France might find willing allies against Britain.

An Alliance Formed

Vergennes approached his prospective allies cautiously. He wanted to make certain that the rift between Britain and its colonies would not be reconciled. He also wanted to make certain that the rebels in America stood a fighting chance. Although France had been secretly supplying the Continental Army with guns and ammunition since the spring of 1776, Vergennes would go no further than covert assistance—until Saratoga.

Congress approached their former French enemies with equal caution. In November 1775 they deputized a secret committee to solicit foreign aid, and after declaring independence they aimed at open recognition and assistance from France. But would France, the leading Catholic monarchy in Europe, make common cause with the republican rebels? A few years earlier American colonials had fought against the French in Canada; only recently they had renounced a king; and for centuries they had overwhelmingly adhered to Protestantism. And if Congress contracted an alliance with France, what would the French want in return?

The string of defeats dealt the Continental Army during 1776 convinced Congress that they needed the French enough to accept both the contradictions and the costs of such an alliance. In November Congress appointed a commission to negotiate not only aid from France but also a formal alliance. That commission included Silas Deane of Connecticut, Arthur Lee of Virginia, and a past master at achieving the improbable, Benjamin Franklin, whose arrival in Paris created a sensation.

Because of their sophistication, the French prized innocence, which they associated with America. In spite of their sophistication, they mistook Benjamin Franklin for an American innocent. From the moment Franklin stepped onto French soil, sporting a simple fur cap and a pair of spectacles (something no fashionable Frenchman wore in public), he was hailed as a homespun sage, sprung from the unspoiled wilderness of Philadelphia. While Franklin basked in his popularity among the Parisians, who stamped his face on everything from the top of snuffboxes to the bottom of porcelain chamber pots, he knew that public adulation would not produce the alliance sought by Congress. Franklin could do nothing more to advance the rebel cause—until Saratoga.

British officials played nicely into his hands, for at the beginning of 1778, just weeks after news of Burgoyne's surrender crossed the Atlantic, they authorized a commission headed by Lord Carlisle to negotiate a peace settlement. The Carlisle Commission made an offer that Congress could not have refused two years earlier. They invited Americans to return to the empire as it had existed before 1763—no parliamentary taxes, no oppressive legislation, but also, of course, no independence. Franklin knew that Congress would dismiss the peace overtures, but the anxious Vergennes did not. So the simple, straightforward American turned the screws, playing on French fears that the Carlisle Commission might reconcile Britain with its former colonies.

Determined to weaken England and convinced by Saratoga that the Continental Army could win, Vergennes willingly succumbed to Franklin's pressure. In February 1778, France signed a treaty of commerce and friendship and a treaty of alliance, which Congress approved in May. Under the terms of the treaties, both parties agreed to accept nothing short of independence for America, and France pledged to renounce all future claims in continental North America and to relinquish any territory captured in the war. The alliance left the British no option other than to declare war on France. Less than a year later Spain joined France, hoping to recover territory lost to England in earlier wars.

As the Revolution widened into a European war after 1778, the British could take some comfort from being able, once again, to think about Americans as little as possible. Hostilities with France and Spain posed a grave peril, but at least the British understood how to wage and win a war against European powers. The same could not be said about the struggle in America. There the British had fought bravely, captured major cities, and gained important victories—but their con-

The French public's infatuation with Franklin knew no bounds, as this painting, entitled *The Genius of Franklin*, illustrates.

quests failed to restore political control. They knew how to win battles, but they could not figure out how to extinguish the rebellion. After 1778, few British officials even tried to figure it out. The struggle with France and Spain absorbed their attention; the war in America became a sideshow.

Winding Down the War in the North

Preparing to fight France dictated a reorganization of British strategy and command in America. No longer could the British concentrate on crushing the Continental Army; instead they would disperse their forces to fend off challenges all over the world. George III and his ministers also decided to deploy some of the troops in America to attack France's possessions in the West Indies, the rich sugar islands. In May, Sir Henry Clinton replaced William Howe as commander-in-chief and received orders to cut his commitments in Philadelphia and withdraw to New York City. There, and in Newport, Rhode Island, Clinton was to maintain defensive bases for harrying northern coastal towns. But the strategic future lay southward. Clinton planned to dispatch some 5000 men to the Caribbean and another 3000 to Florida. In addition, the British laid plans for a new offensive drive in the American South.

Before dawn on June 18, 1778, the British army of 10,000 men started out of Philadelphia and overland toward New York. That same morning, word of the British march reached rebel headquarters. Clinton's cumbersome column of men and supply trains snaking slowly northward was a target too tempting to be resisted by Washington and his Continentals at Valley Forge.

Some 11,000 rebel soldiers had passed a harrowing winter in that isolated spot, starving for want of food, freezing for lack of clothing, huddling in miserable huts, and hating the British who lay 18 miles away in Philadelphia. The army also cursed their own countrymen, for the misery of the soldiers resulted from congressional weakness and disorganization and civilian corruption and indifference. Congress lacked both money to pay and maintain the army and an efficient system for dispensing provisions to the troops. And most farmers and merchants preferred contracting to supply the British, who could pay handsomely, to doing business with financially strapped Congress and the Continentals. What little did reach the army often was food too rancid to eat or clothing too rotten to wear. Perhaps 2500 perished at Valley Forge, the victims of cold, hunger, and disease.

Why did civilians who considered themselves patriotic allow the army to suffer? Probably because by the winter of 1777, the Continentals came mainly from social classes that received little consideration at any time. The middle-class farmers and artisans who had laid siege to Boston in 1775 had stopped enlisting. Respectable, propertied rebels wanted nothing to do with the Continental Army. As for the virtuous "citizen-soldier" rising to the defense of the Republic, "I knew it to be impossible," John Adams snapped, in an abrupt change of mind. Serving in their stead were single men in their teens and early twenties, some who joined the army out of desperation, others who were drafted, still others who were hired as substitutes for the more affluent. The landless sons of farmers, unemployed laborers, drifters, petty criminals, vagrants, indentured servants, slaves, even captured British and Hessian soldiers—all men with no other means and no other choice—were swept into the Continental Army. "The most undisciplined, profligate Crew that were ever collected," was how James Warren of Massachusetts described the army. The social composition of the rebel rank and file had come to resemble that of the British army.

It is the great irony of the Revolution: a war to protect liberty and property

The soldiers depicted in this 1777 illustration condemn civilian neglect and the profiteering of private contractors who supplied the Continental Army. Such grievances would provoke mutinies within the army before the end of the fighting.

First Soldier: "Keep up courage, my boys, we will soon bring those villains to terms."

Second Soldier: "These d__d Extortioners are the worst enemies to the country."

Third Soldier: "I serve my country for sixteen pence a day, pinched with cold."

was waged by those Americans who were poorest and least free. The army did not forget the misery that they endured not only at Valley Forge, but also for the two winters that followed.

The beginning of spring in 1778 brought a reprieve. Supplies arrived at Valley Forge, and so did a fellow calling himself the Baron von Steuben. A penniless Prussian soldier of fortune, the Baron came to the Continental Army recommended by Franklin. Although Washington's men had shown spirit and resilience ever since Trenton, they still lacked discipline and training. Those defects and more von Steuben began to remedy. Barking orders and spewing curses in German and French, the Baron (and his translators) drilled the rebel regiments to march in formation and to handle their bayonets like proper Prussian soldiers. By the summer of 1778, morale had rebounded as professional skill and pride fused solidarity among Continental ranks in the crucible of Valley Forge.

Spoiling for action after their long winter, Washington's army, now numbering nearly 13,500, set out to harass Clinton's army as it headed for New York. The Continentals caught up with the British force on June 28 at Monmouth Courthouse and got more than they bargained for. The long, confused battle ended in a draw; after both armies retired for the night, exhausted by combat and summer heat, Clinton's forces slipped away. A week later the British reached safety in New York City.

With the Battle of Monmouth Courthouse, the Continental Army had come of age, holding its own against the best army in Europe. Washington longed to launch an all-out assault on New York City, but he lacked the necessary numbers. And with the defenses of New York secured, Clinton had fulfilled his objectives: he would not offer battle. The main force of the Continental Army camped at White Plains outside of occupied New York City and waited. The war in the north had stalemated.

Now the fighting between the Continental Army and civilian rebel leaders began. While Washington waited outside New York City, his army started to come apart. During two hard winters, resentments mounted among the rank and file over spoiled food, inadequate clothing, and arrears in pay. Petitions to Congress and the state legislatures produced pensions for the officers but no improvements for their men. The army responded with mutinies. Between 1779 and 1780 officers managed to quell uprisings in three New England regiments. But in January 1781 both the Pennsylvania and New Jersey lines mutinied outright and marched on Philadelphia, where Congress had reconvened. Order returned only after Congress promised back pay and provisions and Washington put two ringleaders in front of a firing squad.

Trouble also loomed on the western frontier. From a fortress at Detroit, a British official named Henry Hamilton, known, for good reason, as the "Hair Buyer," stirred up the Great Lakes tribes to attack settlers in Kentucky and West Virginia. In October 1778 Hamilton himself led some Indians south into the Illinois–Indiana country and took Vincennes from a handful of rebel Virginians. A few months later, the rebels, led by a burly young Virginian named George Rogers Clark, known—since scalping was hardly restricted to the Indians—as "Long Knife," drove the "Hair Buyer" from Vincennes.

After the disastrous winter at Valley Forge, Baron Friedrich Wilhelm von Steuben helped to restore the morale and to improve the military skills of Continental soldiers.

While Clark and his few hundred troops helped to contain Indian raids in the Old Northwest, General John Sullivan led an expedition against the Iroquois in upstate New York. From Fort Niagara loyalists under Major John Butler and Iroquois fighters under a Mohawk chief, Thayendanegea (called Joseph Brant by the English), had conducted a series of bloody raids along the New York and Pennsylvania frontiers. Sullivan and his expedition routed the marauders and retaliated, burning over 40 Indian villages.

Both the British and the rebels sought support from the Indians, because the most powerful tribes determined the balance of power on the frontier. Most of the tribes maintained their neutrality, but those who took sides usually joined the British, who had tried to stem the tide of Americans taking Indian lands.

The Home Front in the North

While fighting continued on the frontier and English and Hessian troops made occasional attacks on Connecticut coastal towns in 1779, the stalemate in the North afforded most civilians a welcome respite from the war. Since the outbreak of the fighting at Lexington and Concord, every movement of troops—or rumor of movement—had pitched the inhabitants of threatened neighborhoods into a panic. Refugees on foot and in carts hastily packed with their belongings filled the roads, fleeing the advancing armies. "By this time the Cannon began to roar," wrote Mary Silliman, a Connecticut mother who escaped a British coastal raid with her two-year-old son Selleck, "which pleased Selleck, and he would mimic them by saying *bang, bang.* But they were doleful sounds in our ears." Those who remained to protect their homes and property ran multiple risks. They might be caught in the crossfire of contending forces, endangered by the fighting itself, or cut off from supplies of food and firewood. Loyalists who remained in areas occupied by rebel troops faced harassment, imprisonment, or the confiscation of their property; rebel sympathizers endured similar fates in regions held by the British. Disease, however, was no respecter of political allegiances: military camps and occupied towns spawned epidemics of dysentery and smallpox that devastated civilians as well as soldiers, rebels and loyalists alike.

When the war moved on, the families who had remained and the refugees who returned confronted their losses—crops and livestock stolen, fences and barns demolished, churches and meetinghouses converted into barracks and stables. While plundering armies destroyed and damaged civilian property wherever they marched, military demands disrupted family economies throughout the northern countryside. The seasons of intense fighting drew men off into military service just when their labor was most needed on family farms. Wives and daughters were left to assume the "outside duties" of husbands and sons while coping with loneliness, anxiety, and grief. Often enough, the disruptions, flight, and loss of family members left lasting scars. Two years after she fled before Burgoyne's advance into upstate New York, Ann Eliza Bleecker confessed to a friend, "Alas! the wilderness is within: I muse so long on the dead until I am unfit for the company of the living."

Although such wounds could be searing, many women vigorously supported the revolutionary cause in a variety of ways. The Daughters of Liberty continued to join their brethren in harassing loyalists who refused to commit themselves to the rebel cause; one outspoken dissident found himself surrounded by Daughters who stripped off his shirt, covered him with molasses, and plastered him with flower petals. In Massachusetts a crowd of some 400 women marched on a local merchant who was hoarding coffee, newly popular in the wake of the tea boycotts. In more genteel fashion, a group of well-to-do women founded the Ladies Association of Philadelphia, an organization that divided the city into districts and went door-to-door, collecting contributions. The idea spread to four other states, with women collecting not only money but medicines, food, and pewter to melt for bullets.

THE STRUGGLE IN THE SOUTH

Between the fall of 1778 and the summer of 1781, while Washington waited outside New York City and tried to control his mutinous army, the British stormed the American South. The few English politicians and generals who were still thinking about America after 1778 believed that the war could be won in that region. Loyalists, they believed, lay thick on southern ground, especially in the backcountry. Festering resentment of the seaboard, a rebel stronghold, bred among frontier folk a readiness to take up arms for the king at the first show of British force. On the other hand, southern rebels—especially the vulnerable planters along the coast—could never afford to turn their guns away from their slaves. So, at least, the British theorized. All that was needed, they concluded, was for the British army to establish a beachhead in the South and then, in league with loyalists, drive northward, pacifying the population while pressing up the coast. The idea had been already tried in the summer of 1776, when Clinton and Admiral Peter Parker had attempted an invasion of Charleston. Although some in the backcountry stood ready to support the British, the rebels held the coast, and their fire from Sullivan's Island in Charleston harbor drove the British back to sea. By 1778 the British were ready to try again.

The Siege of Charleston

The southern strategy worked well for a short time in a small place. In November 1778, Clinton detached 3500 troops to Savannah, Georgia. The resistance in the tiny colony quickly collapsed, and a gratifyingly large number of loyalists turned out to help the British invaders subdue the remnants of rebel forces and to reimpose royal control over Georgia. Everything was proceeding according to plan until the British reached South Carolina.

During the last days of 1779, an expedition under Clinton himself set sail out of New York City; for nearly a month, rain, snow, and high waves buffeted the British fleet. After drying out on Tybee Island off the Georgia coast, the troops mucked through the malarial swamps of Johns and James islands to the mainland of South Carolina. By then, April had arrived in the low country. Unseasonably warm weather made the area a heaven for sandflies and mosquitoes and a hell for human beings. Sweltering and swatting, redcoats weighted down in their woolen uniforms inched their siegeworks down the peninsula lying between the Ashley and Cooper rivers. At the tip of that neck of land stood the city of Charleston, and every night of burrowing in the soggy sand brought the British closer.

But they advanced at great cost. From "the Citadel," a fortification constructed across the northern end of the neck, more than 5000 Continental soldiers and South Carolina militia commanded by Major General Benjamin Lincoln threw everything that they had at the British. All day long the rebels fired rifles and muskets: by night they bombarded the enemy with a deadly assortment of projectiles—shards of glass, broken shovels, pickaxes, hatchets, and flatirons. The redcoats battered back with mortar shells and canisters filled with bullets. As the British pushed onward, each side could see by day the carnage in the other's camp; by night more men were maimed and killed in the murky, humid darkness. By the beginning of May, Clinton's siege lines lay within yards of the rebel Citadel, and his shelling was setting fire to houses within the city. On May 12 Charleston surrendered.

Much to Clinton's relief, he had not been obliged to destroy Charleston in order to save it for the British. His aim was not to devastate the city, but to pacify its defenders. To woo support, he paroled and pardoned many of his prisoners of war. Then he erred fatally by insisting that both military and civilian leaders take an oath of loyalty to the British cause. That demand rankled the rebels, forcing many back into active opposition. Even worse, Clinton's tender of pardons and paroles provoked the resentment of South Carolina's loyalists.

But Clinton did not stay in his conquered city long enough to experience the opposition aroused by his policies. By the end of June 1780 he was sailing back to New York, leaving behind 8300 men to reclaim the rest of South Carolina for the king and to carry the British offensive northward to Virginia. The man that Clinton left in command was his jealous and ambitious, but able subordinate, Charles, Lord Cornwallis.

The Partisan Struggle in the South

Even before Congress declared independence, civil war had erupted between local bands of rebels and loyalists in the South. Although loyalists were scarce in Charleston and along the coast, the king's supporters were more numerous in the Carolina backcountry. The rebel slogan "no taxation without representation" rang hollow to western farmers denied an equitable voice in eastern-dominated Carolina legislatures. The legacy of the Regulator movements had convinced many on the frontier that the Crown would be their best defense in any future contest with the coast. In fact, some frontier loyalists regarded the seaboard's strong support for independence as nothing more than a strategy for gaining a free hand in dealing with the backcountry.

In the summer and fall of 1775 the supporters of Congress and the new South Carolina revolutionary government denounced, mobbed, tortured, and imprisoned men who refused to sign the newly adopted Association. But these attacks only hardened loyalist resolve, as roving bands seized ammunition, mobilized to break their leaders out of jail, and besieged rebel outposts. Still, South Carolina's revolutionary government kept the upper hand. Reinforcements from the coast joined rebel militia on the frontier in defeating and disbanding loyalist forces in the backcountry.

But the fall of Charleston in 1780 aroused the dormant loyalists on the frontier, while the loss of the entire Continental line at Charleston made southern revolutionaries more willing to adopt new and unconventional modes of warfare. Out of loyalist vengefulness and rebel desperation issued the brutal partisan strug-

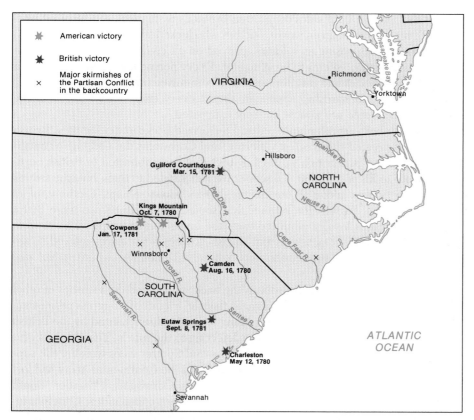

THE FIGHTING IN THE SOUTH, 1780–1781

gle that seared the southern backcountry after 1780. A bloody guerrilla war of
ambush, arson, and atrocity, reprisal and counterreprisal raged in the Carolinas
for the duration of the Revolution. Neighbors and even families fought and killed
each other as members of roaming rebel and tory militias.

By the fall of 1780, the resistance had gathered real momentum, as rebel
irregulars picked up victories and popular support. Francis Marion, the "Swamp
Fox," and his band of white and black raiders cut British lines of communication
between Charleston and the interior. Another rebel leader, the "Gamecock,"
Thomas Sumter, bloodied loyalist forces throughout the central part of South
Carolina. Farther west, rebel over-the-mountain men capped the successes of
Marion and Sumter at the Battle of King's Mountain in October 1780. The revolu-
tionaries surrounded loyalist forces on a ridge running across the border between
North and South Carolina and then, from the cover of pine trees, picked off enemy
soldiers with long rifles.

Most families on the Carolina frontier wished only for a restoration of order.
Like civilians in the middle states, those in the South lost property to pillaging
soldiers: crops and livestock were snatched, slaves were stolen, and fences, fruit
trees, and farm buildings were pulled down for firewood. But the intensity of
partisan warfare in the backcountry produced unprecedented desolation and destruction. British troops and their loyalist allies plundered plantations and assaulted local women; rebel militias whipped suspected British supporters and

burned their farms; both sides committed brutal assassinations and tortured prisoners. To make matters even worse, outlaws who lurked around the fringes of both armies, sometimes posing as soldiers, preyed on all civilians. All of society, observed one minister, "seems to be at an end. Every person keeps close on his own plantation. Robberies and murders are often committed on the public roads. . . . Poverty, want, and hardship appear in almost every countenance . . . and the morals of the people are almost entirely extirpated."

Although both armies plundered and terrorized backcountry families, British depradations created the greatest suffering, and Cornwallis did nothing to conciliate civilians. One farmer in a western district that had submitted to British occupation wrote to his cousin that "no sooner we had yielded to them but [the British army] set to Rob us taking all our livings, horses, Cows, Sheep, Clothing, of all sorts, money . . . in fine Everything that sooted them. Untill we were Stript Naked." A Carolina loyalist admitted that "the lower sort of People, who were in many parts originally attached to the British Government, have suffered so severely . . . that Great Britain has now a hundred enemies, where it had one before."

By the end of 1780, the disorder in the backcountry and the victories of rebel irregulars had persuaded most Carolinians that the friends of Congress rather than the king's men could ensure stability. Many loyalists, disenchanted by the British army's lack of support and respect, were defecting to the rebels. That was lucky for the rebels, for while the forces under Marion and Sumter were winning the support of backcountry civilians, American regulars in the Continental Army had lost a major engagement to the main British force under Cornwallis at Camden, South Carolina. The Continentals, led by their new southern commander, General Horatio Gates, had been pushed into a conventional battle that they were unprepared to fight. On a brutally hot August day, redcoats scattered the rebels in all directions, with their general himself leading a headlong scramble back to safety in Hillsboro, North Carolina. Gates' rapid retreat, in the irreverent view of Washington's young aide, Alexander Hamilton, "did admirable credit to the activity of a man at his time of life." In the fall of 1780, Congress replaced Gates with Washington's candidate for the southern command, Nathanael Greene, an able, energetic, 38-year-old Rhode Islander and a veteran of the northern campaigns.

Greene Takes Command

Greene vindicated Washington's confidence by intuitively grasping the military situation in the South. He understood the needs of his men—1400 hungry, ragged, and demoralized troops—and instructed von Steuben to lobby Virginia for food and clothing. He understood the importance of the rebel irregulars, and sent Lieutenant Colonel Henry "Lighthorse Harry" Lee to assist Marion's raids. He understood the weariness of southern civilians, and insisted that his men refrain from plundering the countryside for provisions. He understood the problems of the backcountry terrain, and directed Thaddeus Kosciuszko, a Polish officer and engineer who had lent his services to the rebels, to scout the fords of rivers and to build flatboats for quick crossings.

Above all, Greene understood that his forces could never hold the field

General Nathanael Greene.

against the whole British army. That led him to break the first rule of conventional warfare: he divided his army. In December 1780, he dispatched to western South Carolina a detachment of 600 men under the command of his comrade from the northern campaigns, Brigadier General Daniel Morgan of Virginia.

Back at the British camp, Cornwallis and Lieutenant Colonel Banastre Tarleton could hardly believe their intelligence reports. Tarleton urged a quick assault on Greene, but Cornwallis worried that Morgan and his rebels, if left unchecked, might mobilize the entire Carolina backcountry. On the other hand, Cornwallis reckoned that he could not commit his entire army to the pursuit of Morgan's men, for then Greene and his troops might try to retake Charleston. The only solution, unconventional to be sure, was for Cornwallis to divide *his* army. That he did, sending Tarleton and 1100 men west after Morgan. Cornwallis had played right into Greene's hands: the rebel troops might be able to defeat a British army split into two pieces. And if some of the redcoats could be tired out even before the battle by weeks of running after Morgan, so much the better.

For two weeks Morgan's men led Tarleton's troops on a breakneck chase across the Carolina countryside, until mid-January 1781, when the British finally cornered the rebels at an open meadow called Cowpens. With the Broad River at their backs, Morgan's troops had nowhere to run, so they stood and fought. For once it was the British who panicked and lost the fight, prodded into a premature and disorganized attack by the impetuous Tarleton.

When Cornwallis took up the chase, Morgan and Greene reconnoitered and agreed to keep going until the British army wore out. After another month of running, Cornwallis called a temporary respite at Hillsboro, North Carolina, and issued invitations to all local loyalists to join his forces. Few recruits appeared. By now Cornwallis was beginning to suspect that there were not many loyalists left in the Lower South. To ensure that loyalist ranks remained thin, Greene decided to make a show of rebel force. He chose as his battleground Guilford Courthouse, a tiny village set on a hill overlooking a forested valley. On a brisk day in March, the two sides joined battle, each sustaining severe casualties. Cornwallis finally forced Greene to retreat rather than risk the loss of his army. But the high cost of victory at Guilford Courthouse convinced Cornwallis to end his pursuit. "I am quite tired of marching about the country in quest of adventures," he informed Clinton.

Cornwallis now conceded that he could not put down the rebellion in the Carolinas. He realized that the British had wildly exaggerated the strength of southern loyalism. But unlike Washington, Cornwallis had not put behind him the hunger for military glory. Outfoxed in the Carolinas, he still believed he could win the war with a decisive victory against the Continental Army. The theater that he chose for the showdown was the Chesapeake Bay.

While Cornwallis turned north, the rebel militia routed loyalist defenders from most of their forts in the South Carolina interior. By the end of May, as the entire backcountry arrayed against them, the British were planning to evacuate Camden. Even the redcoats' ability to beat back Greene's army in a final encounter at Eutaw Springs in September gained them no advantage. The remaining British garrisons at Charleston and Savannah simply waited out the end of the war.

The southern campaign could have gone differently. If the British had swept into the Carolinas with a stronger force in 1776, if they had seized Charleston then, and if they had nursed loyalist support in the backcountry, they could have crushed the Revolution. But when the British were repulsed at Charleston in 1776, they neglected the South for nearly four years and abandoned the king's

Rebel Americans were able to hold the southern backcountry because of the courage and determination of militias like the one depicted in this nineteenth-century painting. Francis Marion's company was unusual among southern militias because it included blacks.

supporters to the Carolina rebels. During those four years, the rebels smothered loyalism and proved that the revolutionary governments could maintain order. Even after Charleston finally fell to the British in 1780 and loyalists renewed their opposition, the rebels, working through their militia, still commanded the support of most civilians. In 1780, as in 1775, the rebels held the edge in the struggle for the hearts and minds of southern civilians. The resilience of their militia sowed the seeds of British frustration and, finally, British defeat.

Most American officers had few kind words for the militia. They complained constantly about the militia's lack of discipline, its habit of melting away when homesickness set in or harvest approached, and its record of cowardice under fire in conventional engagements. But if the militia faltered and fled from set-piece battles, they shone in guerrilla fights. When set the task of ambushing supply trains and dispatch riders, harrying bands of local loyalists, or making forays against isolated British outposts, the militia came through. The majority of southerners refused to join the British or to provide the redcoats with food and information, because they knew that once the British army left their neighborhoods, the rebels would always be back. The Continental Army in the South lost many conventional engagements, but the irregulars kept the British from restoring political control over the backcountry.

African Americans in the Age of Revolution

The British lost the South not only because they overestimated loyalist sentiment and underestimated the rebel militia, but also because they did not enlist widespread support among those Americans who would have fought for liberty *with* the British—the slaves.

Black Americans, virtually all in bondage, made up one-third of the population between Delaware and Georgia. White revolutionaries fully expected the British to turn slave rebelliousness to their strategic advantage. As early as 1775, rumors spread throughout the colonies that the British were planning to instigate slave revolts and that the slaves were waiting to assist the British in return for freedom. Janet Schaw, an English woman visiting her brother's North Carolina plantation in July of 1775, reported that his neighbors had heard that the loyalists were "promising every Negro that would murder his master and family he should have his Master's plantation. . . . The Negroes have got it amongst them and believe it to be true."

Wracked by the fear of slave conspiracies, southern revolutionaries began to take precautions. Marylanders disarmed blacks and issued extra guns to the white militia. Charlestonians hanged and then burned the body of Thomas Jeremiah, a free black and a highly skilled harbor pilot, who was convicted of urging others that the British "were come to help the poor Negroes." Throughout the South, white loyalists accused of stirring up the slaves were mobbed, tarred and feathered, and, in one instance, packed off to Britain. When he invaded the South in 1779, Clinton repeated Lord Dunmore's offer to free all slaves who joined the British.

But in London there was considerable opposition to the policy of encouraging slave runaways and recruiting blacks into the army. British leaders dismissed Dunmore's ambitious scheme to raise a black army of 10,000 and another plan to create a southeastern sanctuary for black loyalists. Turning slaves against masters, they recognized, was not the way to conciliate southern whites.

Southern fears of insurrection made the rebels even more reluctant to enlist blacks as soldiers. Since the beginning of the resistance to Britain, white southerners had worried that the watchwords of liberty and equality would spread to the slave quarters. As Charlestonians protested the Stamp Act in 1765, Henry Laurens, a local merchant and political leader, reported that local blacks "in thoughtless imitation" took up the cry of "Liberty." The spectacle of slaves shouting "Liberty!" in the streets so unsettled white Charlestonians that the city "was thrown under arms for a week" and the countryside was alerted. By 1775 southerners were even more concerned that blacks would seize on the disruption to make a revolution of their own.

That fear prompted Congress to bar blacks from the Continental Army. But as the rebels became more desperate for manpower, policy changed. Northern states actively encouraged black enlistments, and in the Upper South, some states allowed free blacks to join the army or permitted slaves to substitute for their masters. Even in South Carolina, where resistance to arming blacks remained intense, a few fought in racially mixed militias like Marion's raiders.

Blacks themselves sought freedom from whichever side seemed most likely to grant it. Even before Dunmore invited Virginia slaves to desert their masters in 1775, a group of blacks offered him their services, and at least 800 reached his floating headquarters off Norfolk harbor. Thousands more flocked to Clinton's forces after the fall of Charleston. For many the hope of liberation proved an illusion: they died of disease in army camps or were sold back into slavery in the West Indies. But some served the British army as laborers, spies, and soldiers. An estimated 5000 blacks served in the revolutionary army in the hope of gaining freedom. In addition, the number of runaways soared during the Revolution, especially in the Upper South, where there was a more acculturated black population, familiar with the countryside and fluent in English. All told, some 55,000 slaves fled to freedom, some escaping behind British lines, others into the North.

While several thousand solitary fugitives fought on either side and thousands of other individuals and families ran for freedom, the slave revolts so dreaded by southern whites never materialized. Possibly the boldest slaves were drawn off into the armies; possibly greater white precautions discouraged would-be insurrectionists. In South Carolina, where the potential for revolt was greatest, slaves preferred staying on plantations to risking a collective resistance and escape in the midst of the fierce partisan warfare.

THE WORLD TURNED UPSIDE DOWN

It was a perfect summer on the Chesapeake. A glove of warm, moist air gathered over the fingers of deep green peninsulas and smaller spits and necks of land

The world turned upside down: The British lay down their arms at Yorktown.

reaching into the bay. The scent of salt wafted from the creeks and coves, rivers and swamps cleaving the mainland. That soothing June of 1781 was all the sweeter to Charles, Lord Cornwallis, because waiting for him on the Chesapeake was an ally—a king's man—the newly turned loyalist, Benedict Arnold.

Arnold was a disillusioned man. Distressed by his personal finances and disgusted by Congress' shabby treatment of the Continental Army, he had started exchanging rebel secrets for British money in 1779 before defecting outright in the fall of 1780. But disappointment and disgrace had not lessened his ambition. A few months later, Arnold and 1500 redcoats were marauding along the Virginia coast, striking as far inland as Richmond. And in that perfect summer of 1781 he joined forces on the Chesapeake with another disillusioned man whose ambition had also survived disappointment and disgrace. Together Cornwallis and Arnold set about fortifying a site on the tip of the peninsula formed by the York and James rivers, a place called Yorktown.

Meanwhile, Washington and his French ally, the Comte de Rochambeau, met in Connecticut to plan a major attack. An able strategist, Rochambeau urged a coordinated land–sea assault on the Virginia coast: he had learned that a large French fleet from the West Indies might be in the Chesapeake Bay to blockade

Cornwallis. Washington insisted instead on a full-scale offensive against New York City. Just when the rebel commander was about to have his way, Clinton received a daunting number of Hessian reinforcements, and word arrived that a French fleet under the Comte de Grasse was headed for the Chesapeake.

By the end of September, 7800 Frenchmen, 5700 Continentals, and 3200 militia had sandwiched Yorktown between the devil of an allied army and the deep blue sea of French warships. "If you cannot relieve me very soon," Cornwallis wrote to Clinton, "you must expect to hear the worst." At last the British navy did arrive—seven days after Cornwallis surrendered to the rebels on October 19, 1781. When Germain carried the news from Yorktown to the king's first minister, Lord North replied, "Oh, God, it is over." Then North resigned, Germain resigned, and even George III murmured something about abdicating.

It need not have ended at Yorktown. But Cornwallis' defeat drained away what little was left of British resolve to smash the American rebellion. The timing of Yorktown made all the difference. At the end of 1781 and early in 1782, the British army received setbacks in the other theaters of the war: India, the West Indies, and Florida. The French and the Spanish were everywhere in Europe as well, gathering in the English Channel, planning a major offensive against Gibraltar. The cost of the fighting was already enormous. British leaders recognized that the rest of the empire was at stake and set about cutting their losses in America.

The Treaty of Paris, signed on September 3, 1783, was a diplomatic triumph for the American negotiators, Benjamin Franklin, John Adams, and John Jay. They dangled before Britain the possibility that a magnanimous settlement might weaken American ties to France. The British jumped at the bait. They recognized the independence of the United States and agreed to generous boundaries for the new nation: the Mississippi River on the west, the 31st parallel on the south, and the present boundary of Canada on the north. American negotiators then persuaded a skeptical France to approve the treaty by arguing that, as allies, they had to present a united front to the British. When the French finally persuaded Spain, the third member of the alliance, to reduce its demands on Britain for territorial concessions, the treaty was an accomplished fact. The Spanish settled for Florida and Minorca, an island in the Mediterranean.

Those present at Yorktown on that clear autumn afternoon in 1781 watched as the second-in-command to an "indisposed" Lord Cornwallis surrendered his superior's sword—first, in a face-saving gesture, to the French commander Rochambeau, who politely demurred and pointed to the American general, Washington, who proudly demurred and pointed to *his* second-in-command, Benjamin Lincoln. Some witnesses recalled that British musicians arrayed on the green played "The World Turned Upside Down." Their recollections may have been faulty, but the story has persisted as part of the folklore of the American Revolution—and with some justification. The world *had*, it seemed, turned upside down with the coming of American independence. The colonial rebels shocked the British with their answer to the question: would they fight?

The answer had been yes—but on their own terms. By 1777 most propertied Americans avoided fighting in the Continental Army. Yet whenever the war reached their homes, farms, and businesses, sufficient numbers of Americans gave their allegiance to the new confederation by turning out with rifles or supplying homespun clothing, food, or ammunition. The men fought in the militia, rallying around Washington in New Jersey, Gates in upstate New York, Clark on the frontier, Greene and Lincoln, Marion and Sumter in the Carolinas. Middle-class

Americans fought, some from idealism, others out of self-interest, but always on their own terms, as members of the militia. At Saratoga and in the Carolina back-country, these "citizen-soldiers" turned the world upside down by defeating professional armies.

Of course, the militia did not bear the brunt of the fighting. That responsibility fell to the Continental Army, which by 1777 drew its strength from the poorest ranks of American society. Yet even the Continentals, despite their desperation, managed to fight on their own terms. Some asserted their rights by raising mutinies, until Congress redressed their grievances. All of them, as the Baron von Steuben observed, behaved differently from European soldiers. Americans followed orders only if the logic of commands was explained to them. The Continentals, held in contempt by most Americans, turned the world upside down by sensing their power and asserting their measure of personal independence.

Thus did a revolutionary generation turn the world upside down. Descended from desperate, idealistic, and self-interested men and women who settled colonies named for kings and queens, ruled by kings and queens whose absolutist and mercantilist ideals sought to enrich the power of their bureaucratic states—these Americans rebelled against a king. They wanted more than a monarch. But what more did they want? What awaited in a world turned upside down by republican revolutionaries?

SIGNIFICANT EVENTS

1775 — Second Continental Congress convenes at Philadelphia; Congress creates the Continental Army; Battle of Bunker Hill

1776 — Publication of *Common Sense;* British troops evacuate Boston; Declaration of Independence; British occupy New York City, forcing Washington to retreat through New Jersey into Pennsylvania; Washington counterattacks at Battle of Trenton

1777 — British summer drive to occupy Philadelphia: battles of Brandywine Creek, Germantown; Burgoyne surrenders at Saratoga; Continental Army encamps for winter at Valley Forge

1778 — Carlisle Commission sues for peace; France allies with rebel Americans; France and Britain declare war; British shift focus to the South: Savannah falls

1780 — British occupy Charleston; partisan warfare of Marion, Sumter; rebel victory at King's Mountain, South Carolina; Nathanael Greene takes southern command

1781 — Engagements at Cowpens, Guilford Courthouse; Cornwallis surrenders at Yorktown

1783 — Treaty of Paris

7

Crisis and Constitution

 am not a Virginian, but an American," Patrick Henry declaimed to the Virginia House of Burgesses. Most likely he was lying. Certainly no one listening took him seriously, for the newly independent patriots did not identify themselves as members of a nation. They would have said, as Thomas Jefferson did, "Virginia, Sir, is my country." Or as John Adams wrote to another native son, "Massachusetts is our country." Jefferson and Adams were men of wide political vision and experience: both were leaders in the Continental Congress and more inclined than most to think nationally. But like other members of the revolutionary generation, they harbored strong local loyalties. "Americans" identified deeply with their home states and even more deeply with their home counties and towns.

When did the inhabitants of 13 separate states begin to think of themselves as Americans? The war for independence itself fostered a new sense of national identity among some participants. Marching together from one state to another in ragged uniforms, enduring enemy fire from British cannon—not to mention soggy "firecake," a flatbread from their own army commissary—Washington's Continentals were the first group whose experience awakened a camaraderie and an allegiance to a truly national institution, the army. These men may have been the first "Americans."

But if military men came to think in terms of loyalty to a national cause, most political leaders did not. Allegiance to the states, not the Union, determined the shape of the first republican political experiments. For a decade after independence, the revolutionaries were less committed to creating an American nation than to organizing 13 separate state republics. The Declaration of Independence referred explicitly not to *the* United States, but *these* United States. It envisioned not one republic so much as a federation of 13, like the independent but linked city-state republics of Switzerland.

Only when peace was restored during the decade of the 1780s were Americans forced to think through the consequences of their revolution. The Declaration proclaimed that these "free and independent states" had "full power to levy war, conclude peace, contract alliances, establish commerce." Did that mean that New Jersey, as a free and independent state, could sign a trade agreement with France, excluding the other states? If the United States was to be more than a loose federation, how could it assert power on a national scale? Similarly, American borderlands to the west presented problems. If these territories were settled

226

During the summer of 1787 the Constitutional Convention met at the old State House in Philadelphia (pictured here in 1799). Because passersby strolled by the windows, the delegates kept them closed to maintain privacy—and sweltered in the summer heat.

The portraits of Captain and Mrs. Samuel Chandler, a New England couple, project the virtuous rectitude of the new republican era. Husband and wife share the same direct, disarming gaze, a mixture of wariness and resolution. To the portrait of Captain Chandler, a proud veteran of the Revolution, the artist added a battlefield scene in the background.

by Americans, would they eventually join the United States? Go their own ways as independent nations? Become new colonies of Spain or England? None of these political questions had been fully answered.

Such problems were more than political; they were rooted in social realities. For a political union to succeed, Americans needed some sense of national identity. There had to be social bonds linking one citizen with another. When it came right down to it, what united a Vermont farmer working his stubborn, rocky fields and a South Carolina nabob, presiding over a vast rice plantation? What bonds existed between a leather-shirted Kentuckian rafting the Ohio River and a Salem merchant sailing all the way to China for porcelain? Could a republic be strong enough to unite these "Americans" politically yet still reflect their widely different identities? Could it be strong enough to raise money and regulate trade without unfairly promoting one economic class or geographic region at the expense of another?

And in a society where all citizens were said to be "created equal," the inevitable social inequalities had to be confronted. How could women participate in the Revolution's bid for freedom if they were not free to vote or to hold property? How could blacks feel a bond with white Americans when so often the only existing bonds had been forged with chains? To these questions there were no answers in 1781, none, at least, with the ring of finality. And as the decade progressed, the sense of crisis deepened. Americans worried that the center could not hold, that factions and selfish interest groups would pull "these" United States irrevocably apart. The republican union that had been formed, spread out as it was over so many miles, constituted a truly unprecedented venture. A good deal of experimenting would be needed if it was to succeed.

REPUBLICAN EXPERIMENTS

The enduring hold of local loyalties accounts in part for the enormous enthusiasm among revolutionary leaders for creating new state governments, but it also accounts for the lack of concern about designing national institutions. After independence was declared in July 1776, many of America's best political minds were engaged in drawing up constitutions for their individual states. Thomas Jefferson deserted the Continental Congress, leaving the conduct of the war and national affairs to other men. He wanted to address the more important business of creating Virginia's new government.

In truth, the state constitutions were crucial political experiments, the first efforts at applying republican principles to American actualities. The states faced the task of designing institutions that would carry out the republican commitment to a government of and by the people. All of the revolutionaries agreed that the people—not a king or a few privileged aristocrats—should rule. Giving effective form to that ideal might require some trial and error, but of one thing Americans were absolutely certain: republican governments were not suited to large territories. That axiom appeared in the writings of every major republican thinker read by Americans, the most influential being Montesquieu.

Americans took the axiom to heart. Inevitably, they believed, national legislatures grew indifferent to popular concerns, being distant from their far-flung constituents. Without being under the watchful eye of the people, they escaped popular control and soon degenerated into despotism. Thus revolutionary leaders thought of republican government in terms of the states. Efforts to form a single national republic would be doomed to failure, they reasoned. A federation of small state republics would stand a far better chance of enduring.

The State Constitutions

Colonial experience as well as republican theory shaped the framing of the first state constitutions. The states retained the basic form of their old colonial governments, most providing for a governor and a bicameral legislature. Only Georgia and Pennsylvania dispensed with both the governor and the upper house of the legislature. But while the structure of most new constitutions resembled those of the old colonial regimes, the balance of power among the branches of government shifted dramatically.

From the republican perspective in 1776, the greatest problem of any government lay in curbing executive power. What had driven Americans into rebellion was the abuse of authority by the king, his ministers, and their agents in the colonies, the royal governors. To ensure that the executive could never again threaten popular liberty, the new states either accorded almost no power to their governors or abolished that office entirely. The governors had no authority to convene or dissolve the legislature. They could not veto the legislatures' laws. They could not grant land or erect courts. Most important from the republican point of view, governors had few powers to appoint other state officials. All these limits were designed with one aim in mind: to deprive the executive of any patronage or other form of influence over the legislature. By reducing the governor to a cipher, Americans hoped to preserve their states from the corruption that they deplored in British political life.

What the state governors lost, the legislatures gained. In the decade after

1776 most American republicans believed that liberty would be best served by making legislatures the dominant force in the government. The colonial assemblies, after all, had led the staunch opposition to Britain, defended American freedom, and embodied the will of the people. The course for state constitution makers was clear: grant legislatures a lion's share of power and take steps to make assemblies truly representative.

To realize the ideal of actual representation, the new constitutions called for annual elections and stipulated that candidates for the legislature had to live in the district they represented. Some states also reapportioned representation on the basis of population, and many asserted the right of constituents to instruct the men elected to office. Although no state granted universal manhood suffrage, most reduced the amount of property required of qualified voters. American republicans believed that the major purpose of government was to protect property and that only men who owned property possessed the independence necessary to participate in political life. But the new property qualifications were low enough to allow most white men the vote, and Georgia and Pennsylvania went as far as opening the franchise to all taxpayers.

While the legislatures reigned supreme over state executives, the judiciary was also rendered dependent on popular favor. State supreme courts were either elected by the legislatures or appointed by an elected governor. In one sense, the sum of these constitutional changes was fairly democratic. A majority of voters within a state could do whatever they wanted, unchecked by governors or courts. On the other hand, the arrangement opened the door for legislatures to turn as tyrannical as governors. The revolutionaries brushed that prospect aside: republican theory assured them that the people would never oppress themselves.

By investing all power in popular assemblies, Americans abandoned the British system of mixed government. In an equally momentous departure from British

Americans responded to independence with rituals of "killing the king," like this New York crowd in 1776, which is pulling down a statue of George III. Americans also expressed their mistrust of monarchs and their ministers by establishing new state governments with weak executive branches.

practice, the revolutionaries insisted on written state constitutions. They were determined to set down the fundamental law in an actual document that defined the extent of government's power and the full scope of popular liberty. Whenever government appeared to exceed the limits of its authority, Americans wanted to have at hand the contract between rules and ruled. Americans had discovered the necessity for written constitutions in their experience with the British constitution. That much-admired system of government was an unwritten constitution— not an actual document but a collection of parliamentary laws, customs, and precedents. When eighteenth-century Englishmen used the word "constitution," they meant the existing arrangement of government. But Americans believed that a constitution should be a written code that stood apart from and above government, a law superior to government, a yardstick against which the people measured the performance of their rulers. If Britain's constitution had been written down, available for all to consult, would American rights have been violated? No, the republican rebels reasoned, and so they came to write their own state constitutions. These documents circulated widely on both sides of the Atlantic, were translated and published in France and other European countries, and were touted as models of enlightened political organization.

From Congress to Confederation

While Americans were lavishing attention on their state constitutions, the national government nearly languished, a neglected stepchild during the decade after 1776. With the coming of independence, the Second Continental Congress assumed responsibility for conducting the common business of the federated colonies. It created and maintained the Continental Army, issued currency, and negotiated with foreign powers. But while Congress functioned as a central government by common consent, it lacked any legal basis for its authority. To redress that need, in July 1776 Congress appointed a committee to draft a constitution for a national government. The more urgent business of waging and paying for the war made for delay, as did the consuming interest in framing state constitutions. Congress finally approved the first national constitution in November 1777, but it took four more years for all of the states to ratify these Articles of Confederation.

The Articles of Confederation provided for a government by a national legislature—essentially a continuation of the Second Continental Congress. This body had the authority to declare war and make peace, conduct diplomacy, regulate Indian affairs, appoint military and naval officers, and requisition men from the states. In affairs of finance it could coin money and issue paper currency. Extensive as these responsibilities were, Congress lacked important powers. It could not levy taxes or even regulate trade. The crucial power of the purse rested entirely with the states, which were to contribute funds to the common expense at congressional request. Nor could Congress do more than recommend particular policies to the states; it had no authority to enforce its resolutions. All final power to make and execute laws lay with the states. In addition, the states retained control over a potential source of large revenues, the undistributed tracts of western land granted to them under their old colonial charters.

Beyond these limitations, the very organization of the new government fostered a weak, discontinuous leadership. Delegates to Congress were appointed annually by state legislatures, and no delegate could serve more than three out of every six years. Often the states dispatched men of little ability to sit as their representatives in Congress, and even after the fighting had ended, its meetings shifted from Philadelphia to Princeton to Annapolis to New York City. Even worse, the national government had no distinct executive branch. Congressional committees, constantly changing in their membership, not only had to make laws but had to administer and enforce them as well. With no executive to carry out the policies of finance, war, and foreign policy, the federal government's influence was extremely limited.

These weaknesses appear more evident in hindsight than Congress perceived in 1777. It was no easy task to frame a new government in the midst of a war. Day in, day out, delegates were harried enough keeping up with news of battles, demands from the army for more arms and men, squabbles over which general should command which troops, complaints from individual states—even the threat of their own capture by the British, which caused them to pack their bags hastily on several occasions.

Beyond such distractions, most American statesmen of the 1770s had given little thought to federalism, the organization of a United States. Political leaders simply had not yet perceived the need for a defined distribution of power between the states and the central government. With the new nation in the midst of a military crisis, Congress assumed—correctly in most cases—that the states did not have to be forced to contribute men and money to the common defense. To have given significant powers to the national government would only have aroused opposition among the states, each jealous of its independence. Sam Adams, the Boston rebel leader, expressed the consensus of political opinion when he declared that "every legislature of every colony ought to be the sovereign and uncontrollable Power within its own limits of territory." Creating a strong national government would also have antagonized many Americans, who after all had just rebelled against the distant, centralized authority of Britain's king and Parliament. As Edward Rutledge of South Carolina observed, "The inhabitants of every Colony consider themselves at liberty to do as they please on almost every occasion."

Primed by republican political theory and guided by their experience as colonials, the revolutionaries set about creating a loose confederation of 13 independent state republics under a nearly powerless national government. They succeeded so well that the United States almost failed to outlast the first decade of its independence. The problem was that republican theory and lessons from the colonial past were not always apt guides to postwar realities. Only when events forced Americans to think nationally did they begin to consider the possibility of reinventing "these United States"—this time under the yoke of a truly federal republic.

THE TEMPTATIONS OF PEACE

The surrender of Lord Cornwallis to George Washington's forces at Yorktown in 1781 marked the end of military crisis in America. But as the threat from Britain receded, so did the source of American unity. No longer endangered by a common enemy, the 13 independent states fell to bickering among themselves. The many differences among Americans, most of which lay submerged during the struggle for independence, surfaced in full force. And neither the states nor the national government proved equal to the conflicts arising from the intrigues of foreign powers or the domestic dislocations of the postwar period.

The Temptations of the West

The greatest opportunities and the greatest problems for postwar Americans awaited in the West. The frontier, of course, had long provided land for an expanding population. Even before the Revolution, settlers had pushed into the backcountry, especially of Pennsylvania, Virginia, and the Carolinas. Some hardy frontiersmen had even defied British authority by crossing the Proclamation Line of 1763 and had risked Indian retaliation by venturing into tribal lands over the Appalachians. After the Revolution, the movement to the western portions of the new states assumed such massive scale that the population of the backcountry outstripped that of the seaboard in some places. And with the boundary of the United States now set at the Mississippi River, more migrating families spilled across the Appalachians, planting farmsteads and raw frontier towns throughout Ohio, Kentucky, and Tennessee.

Frontier growth was explosive. By 1790 places that had been almost uninhabited by whites in 1760 held over 2.25 million people, one-third of the nation's population. By 1800 that proportion approached one-half. The scope of movement attained momentous dimensions; except for the first colonization of the early seventeenth century, never before or since has such a large percentage of white Americans lived in newly settled communities.

The frontier was explosive in another sense too. After the Revolution, as before, the West was a source of sharp conflict. American claims to sovereignty all the way to the Mississippi were by no means taken for granted by covetous European powers. And even if Americans could ignore the intrigues of Europeans or the claims of Indians, they faced a question of their own national identity. How would the nation incorporate the newly settled territories? Would they come in as states on an equal footing with the original 13 states? Would they be ruled as dependent colonies? Could the federal government reconcile conflicting interests, cultures, and traditions over so great an area? The fate of the West, in other words, constituted a crucial test of whether "these" United States could grow and still remain united.

With independence won, the Confederation still faced the problem of enforcing American claims to its northwestern and southwestern frontiers. Both the British from their base in Canada and the Spanish in Florida and Louisiana hoped to chisel away at American boundaries. Their considerable success in the 1780s exposed the weakness of Confederation diplomacy. Before the ink was dry on the Treaty of Paris, Britain's ministers were secretly instructing Canadians to maintain their forts and trading posts inside the United States' northwestern frontier. They reckoned—correctly—that with the Continental Army disbanded, the Confederation had no troops to force the British to withdraw. When Congress protested this treaty violation, the British pointed out that Americans were in violation too. The treaty required that neither side hinder the collection of private debts contracted before the war and that Congress recommend that the states restore confiscated loyalist property. But several states had passed laws prohibiting British subjects from suing to recover debts and property in America. Congress could do nothing to compel the states to abide by the terms of the treaty and repeal the offending legislation. With Congress unable to bring the states into line or to raise troops for defense, the British stayed on in their northwestern garrisons and savored the humiliation of the Confederation.

The British also attempted mischief along the Confederation's northern borders, principally with Vermont. For decades, Ethan Allen and his Green Mountain Boys had waged a war of nerves with neighboring New York, which claimed Vermont as part of its territory. The Vermonters kept the controversy going after the Revolution, petitioning Congress for statehood and demanding independence of both New York and New Hampshire. When Congress dragged its feet, the British tried to woo Vermont into their empire as a province of Canada. That flirtation with the British pressured Congress into granting Vermont statehood in 1791.

The loyalty of the southwestern frontier was far less certain. By 1790 more than 100,000 settlers had poured through the Cumberland Gap to reach Kentucky and Tennessee. Along with the farmers came speculators, who bought up large tracts of land from the Indians. But the commercial possibilities of the region depended entirely on access to the Mississippi and the port of New Orleans, since it was far too costly to ship southwestern produce over the rough trails east across the Appalachians. And the Mississippi route was still dominated by the Spanish, who controlled Louisiana as well as forts along western Mississippi shores as far north as St. Louis. The Spanish, seeing their opportunity, closed the Mississippi to American navigation in 1784, hoping to sway the Southwest into their empire. Without free access to an ocean port, the inhabitants of western Virginia, Kentucky, and Tennessee seriously considered secession from the United States. Already dissatisfied by the neglect of the states and Congress, they were clamoring as well for protection from local Indians, who had occasionally reacted to white settlements on their land with retaliatory raids. While the Confederation temporized, unable to do anything to guarantee frontier military or economic objectives, western loyalties hung in the balance.

The West posed not only international difficulties but also internal problems. Throughout the colonial era, frontier settlers had protested their lack of influence in legislative affairs. Although most northern states moved quickly to extend representation to frontier districts, the southern states proceeded more slowly. North Carolina, whose western Regulators had nearly launched a civil war before the Revolution, once again saw protests and riots erupt when its constitution did not extend full representation to the western counties. A new state of Franklin was actually formed and its legislature met for several years in the mid-1780s. Virginia experienced similar problems.

Even more demoralizing were the continuing arguments among states over conflicting land claims. The old royal charters for some colonies—Georgia, the Carolinas, Virginia, Connecticut, Massachusetts, and New York—had extended their boundaries all the way to the Mississippi and beyond. But the charters were as vague as they were generous, granting both Massachusetts and Virginia, for example, undisputed possession of present-day Wisconsin. An even knottier problem arose because the charters of other states—Maryland, Delaware, Pennsylvania, Rhode Island, and New Jersey—limited their territories to within a few hundred miles of the Atlantic coast. "Landed" states like Virginia wanted to secure control over their chartered territory. "Landless" states like Maryland called on Congress to restrict the boundaries of landed states and to convert western lands into a domain administered by the Confederation.

The landless states had good reasons for favoring control over the West by

WESTERN LAND CLAIMS, 1782–1802
The Confederation's settlement of conflicting western land claims was an achievement essential to the consolidation of political union. Some states asserted that their original charters extended their western borders to the Mississippi River. A few states, like Virginia, claimed western borders on the Pacific Ocean.

Congress. The landed states, they argued, enjoyed an unfair advantage from the large revenue that could be gained from selling their western claims. That revenue would allow landed states to reduce taxes, and lower taxes would lure settlers from the landless states. Meanwhile, landless states would have to raise taxes to make up for the departed citizens, forcing a continuing downward cycle.

The landless states had a few less high-minded reasons for opposing the landed states. Before the Revolution, speculators, who numbered among the most prominent citizens of landless Pennsylvania, Maryland, and New Jersey, had purchased tracts in the West from Indians, and some had nearly received royal approval of their purchases before independence inconveniently intervened. These speculators now joined forces with the political leaders of the landless states to lobby for congressional ownership of all western lands except those tracts that they had already purchased from the Indians.

The landless states, however, had lost the opening round of the contest over

ownership of the West. The Articles of Confederation acknowledged the old charter claims of the landed states. But Maryland, one of the smallest landless states,
refused to ratify the Articles. Since every state had to approve the Articles before
they were formally accepted, the fate of the United States hung in the balance.
One by one the landed states relented. The last holdout, Virginia, in January 1781
ceded its charter rights to land north of the Ohio River. In a moment of uncharac-
teristic modesty, the Virginians conceded that they might have trouble extending
republican government over the entire territory allotted them in their charter—a
substantial portion of the North American continent. Once Virginia ceded, Maryland stepped into line, ratifying the Articles in February 1781, four long years
after Congress had first approved them.

The West triggered controversy in yet another way: by the sort of people
being elected to political office. The state legislatures of the 1780s were both
larger and less aristocratic than the old colonial assemblies. A newer, more democratic spirit leavened legislative proceedings. The new representatives were often
less wealthy, less socially prominent, and less educated. Before the Revolution no
more than a fifth of the men serving in the assemblies were middle-class farmers
or artisans; government was almost exclusively the domain of the wealthiest merchants and planters. After the Revolution twice as many state legislators were men
of moderate wealth. The shift was more marked in the North, where middle-class
men predominated among representatives; but in every state, some men of the
middling sort attained political power.

This spread of democracy resulted chiefly from the surge of westward settlement. As backcountry districts grew, the number of their representatives increased, swelling both the size of state legislatures and western influence within
them. One telling sign of the change was that many states moved their capitals
from the coast farther inland to sites more accessible for frontier delegates. The
new western influence also guaranteed that more men who were not rich or cultivated would sit in legislatures, since backcountry districts tended to be less developed economically and culturally. Voters did not repudiate the wealthy leaders
who had led the movement for independence, but because of greater western
representation, older elites became a much smaller and less powerful group
within the legislatures.

Some republican gentlemen accepted the new situation. One eminent Virginian observed that the House of Burgesses in 1776 was "composed of men not
quite so well dressed, nor so politely educated, nor so highly born as some I have
formerly seen, but they are the people's men (and the People in general are
right)." Not all patriots were as pleased, however. Some gentlemen—no doubt a
minority—condemned all notions of "the equality of mankind," preferring the
more cynical doctrine that "the many were made for the few." Others, while
endorsing government by popular consent, still doubted whether the people
themselves were fit to rule.

The problem, conservative republicans argued, was that the new legislators
lacked a "larger view" of politics. Rougher, blunter, more single-minded, the new
western delegates concerned themselves only with the narrow interests of their
particular constituents, not with the good of the whole. They were too wedded to
their localities and too easily swayed by the demands of a short-sighted and often
selfish electorate. They seemed, to conservatives at least, to lack the cardinal
republican virtue of "disinterestedness." And if state legislatures could not rise
above petty bickering and narrow self-interest, how long would it be before civic
virtue and a concern for the general welfare simply withered away?

By the early 1780s movements were already afoot in many states to amend the new constitutions by reducing the powers of democratic legislatures. Furthermore, fears of democratic excess influenced policy at the national level when Congress finally came to decide what to do with the Northwest Territory.

Carved out of the land ceded by the states to the national government, the Northwest Territory comprised the present-day states of Ohio, Indiana, Illinois, Michigan, and Wisconsin. With so many white settlers moving into these lands, Congress was faced with a crucial test of its federal system. As the national government, how could it expand the confederation of states beyond the original 13 colonies? If a peaceful and orderly way could not be devised, the new territories might well break off and become independent countries or even colonies of Spain or Britain. Congress dealt with the issue of expansion by adopting three ordinances.

The first, drafted by Thomas Jefferson in 1784, proposed a division of the Northwest Territory into 10 states, each to be admitted to the Union on equal terms as soon as its population equaled that in any of the existing states. In the interim, Jefferson provided for democratic self-government of the territory by all free adult males according to any state constitution. A second ordinance of 1785 set up an efficient mechanism for dividing and selling public lands. The Northwest Territory was surveyed into townships of six square miles along lines running east–west and north–south. Each township was then divided into 36 lots of one square mile, or 640 acres. Congress also established land offices in all of the states to organize public auctions, stipulating that a lot was the smallest unit that could be purchased and setting the price per acre at not less than one dollar in specie.

Eager for anticipated revenue, Congress waited—in vain—for buyers to flock to the land offices. The cost of even a single lot—$640—was too steep for most farmers, especially since Congress required payment in specie, not paper money. Disappointed by the dearth of buyers and desperate for funds, Congress finally succumbed to a proposition submitted by a private company of land speculators who offered to buy some 6 million acres in present-day southeastern Ohio, using badly depreciated paper money. That several members of Congress numbered among the company's stockholders no doubt added to enthusiasm for the deal.

The transaction concluded, Congress sweetened the bargain by calming the speculators' worries that incoming settlers might enjoy too much self-government. For decades, eastern entrepreneurs had been warning that backcountry folk were "uncivilized, and little better than barbarians.—They are lazy, licentious, and lawless—and, instead of being useful members of society, are become seditious and dangerous to the community." In short, these were not the sort of people the speculators wanted to trust with self-government. Congress accordingly scrapped Jefferson's democratic design and substituted the Northwest Ordinance of 1787.

That ordinance swept aside self-government and provided for a period in which Congress held sway in the territory through its appointees—a governor, a secretary, and three judges. When the population reached 5000 free adult males, a legislature was to be established, although its laws required the governor's approval. A representative could sit in Congress but had no vote. When the population reached 60,000, the inhabitants might apply for statehood, and the whole Northwest Territory was to be divided into not less than three or more than five states. The ordinance also guaranteed basic rights—freedom of religion and trial by jury—and provided for the support of public education.

Congress' settlement ignored just one important consideration: the Indian nations who were settled on the land had never relinquished their claim to it. That

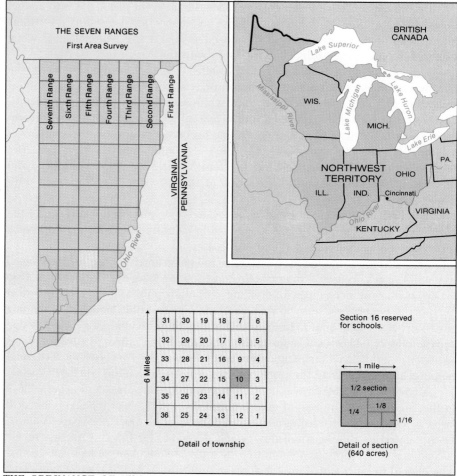

THE ORDINANCE OF 1785
Surveyors entered the Northwest Territory in September of 1785, imposing on the land regular grids of six square miles to define new townships, as shown on this range map of a portion of Ohio. Farmers purchased blocks of land within townships, each one mile square, from the federal government or from land speculators. This pattern was followed in mapping and settling public lands all the way to the Pacific Coast.

the British had ceded the territory to the states and the states to the Confederation made no difference to the Shawnee, the Chippewa, the Ottawa, and the Potawatomi, who had never ceased to regard the land as theirs. After the Revolution, these nations formed a league to enforce their right of ownership and to stop white settlement at the Ohio River. Confrontation could not be avoided indefinitely, but in 1790, only about 4300 whites had settled in the Northwest, the largest number around Cincinnati.

In the final analysis, the Northwest Ordinance slighted tribal land rights, discriminated economically against small farmers, and retreated politically from Jefferson's ideal of self-governing democracy for the frontier. On the other hand, Congress had succeeded in extending republican government to the West and incorporating the frontier into the federal system. It did not make the mistake of keeping its new territories as dependent colonies of the older, more powerful states. In that sense, the Northwest Ordinance became the most enduring legacy of government under the Articles of Confederation.

Congress left the Northwest another legacy: it outlawed slavery throughout the territory. And this had an unlooked-for, almost ironic consequence. The Northwest Ordinance went a long way toward establishing a federal system that minimized tensions between the East and the West, which had been a major source of postwar conflict. The Republic now had a peaceful, orderly way to expand its federation of states. Yet by limiting the spread of slavery in the northern states, Congress deepened the critical social and economic differences between North and South, evident already in the 1780s. For the time being, conflict between the two sections remained muted. But the tensions that erupted into civil war in 1860 were mounting in the wake of the Revolution.

Slavery and Sectionalism

When white Americans declared their independence, they owned nearly half a million black Americans. African-Americans of the revolutionary generation, most of them enslaved, comprised 20 percent of the total population of the colonies in 1775, and nearly 90 percent of them lived in the South. But few political leaders, either in Congress or in the state legislatures, directly confronted the issue of whether slavery should be permitted to exist in a truly republican society.

On the rare occasions when political discussion strayed toward the subject of slavery, southerners bristled defensively. Theirs was a difficult position, fraught with contradictions, especially for ardent republicans. On the one hand, they had condemned parliamentary taxation as tantamount to political "slavery" and had rebelled, declaring that all men were "created equal." On the other hand, enslaved blacks formed the basis of the South's plantation economy. To surrender slavery, southerners believed, would be to usher in economic ruin. And in much of the South, slavery was an entrenched part of the social system.

Some planters in the Upper South resolved the dilemma they felt by freeing their slaves. In any case, the economies of Maryland and Virginia were shifting away from tobacco toward wheat, a crop demanding a good deal less labor. With less need to maintain a large slave work force, Virginia and Maryland liberalized their manumission statutes, laws providing for freeing slaves. Between 1776 and 1789, most southern states also joined the North in prohibiting the importation of slaves, and a few antislavery societies appeared in the Upper South. But no southern state legally abolished slavery. Most planters continued to hold human property and defended their right to do so in the name of republicanism.

To modern eyes, the irony in that position is obvious. Yet it is important to remember that equality was not the only ideal held by eighteenth-century republicans. For them the concept of property was equally crucial. Property provided a man and his family with security, status, and wealth. More important, it provided a measure of independence: to be able to act firmly and rationally, without fear or favor of other men. People without property were dangerous, republicans believed, because the poor could never be politically independent. When English republicans discussed people without property, they were concerned chiefly with their country's large number of white poor and unemployed. Some political theorists there even recommended that the state enslave propertyless people or incarcerate them in workhouses.

Negro Methodists Holding a Meeting in a Philadelphia Alley evokes the vibrancy of African-American religious life in the city that became a haven for free blacks. The artist, Pavel Petrovich Svinin, was a Russian diplomat who traveled throughout America, praised its religious freedom, and predicted the end of slavery.

Republicans in the American South followed a similar line of reasoning. Slavery was necessary, they argued, because free, propertyless black people would constitute a political threat to the liberty of propertied whites. Ending slavery would undermine the stability of the new nation. And, of course, to the white masters who held them, slaves were property, assets that provided wealth, status, independence. Subordinating human rights to property rights, southern republicans reached the paradoxical conclusion that freedom—for whites—depended on keeping one-fifth of the population in bondage.

The North followed a different course. Because its economy was far less dependent on slave labor, emancipation did not run counter to entrenched economic interests. Antislavery societies, the first founded by the Quakers in 1775, spread throughout the northern states during the next quarter century. Over the same period, the legislatures of most northern states provided for the immediate or gradual abolition of slavery. Freedom for most northern blacks came slowly, but by 1830 there were fewer than 3000 slaves out of a total northern black population of 125,000.

The Revolution, which had been fought for liberty and equality, did little to change the status of most black Americans. All the same, a larger number of blacks than ever before became free during the war and in the decades following. Some had escaped slavery by serving in the military. Both the British and the Americans emancipated slaves who joined their ranks. The British evacuation at the end of the war also liberated tens of thousands of slaves, who were resettled in England, Canada, the West Indies, and Sierra Leone. Furthermore, an unprecedented number of blacks took advantage of the chaos created by the war in the South, fleeing from the plantations in an escape to freedom. And after the war, while the northern states took steps to abolish slavery, manumissions rose sharply in the Upper South.

All these developments fostered the growth of free black communities, especially in the Upper South and in northern cities. By 1810 free blacks comprised 10 percent of the total population of Maryland and Virginia. The composition of the postwar free community changed as well. Before independence, most free blacks had been either mulattoes—the offspring of interracial unions—or former slaves too sick or aged to have value as laborers. By contrast, the free population of the 1780s became darker skinned, younger, and healthier. This group injected new vitality into black communal life, organizing independent schools and churches for the growing number of "free people of color."

Yet for all those changes, there were more blacks enslaved in 1800 than in 1776. Slavery had continued to grow in the Lower South as the rice culture of the Carolinas and Georgia expanded and as the new cotton culture spread to the backcountry districts and beyond, into the Alabama and Mississippi frontiers. Because of the high demand for slaves in the Lower South, most Virginia and Maryland planters who had turned to growing wheat did not release their slaves, but sold them to ready buyers among rice and cotton growers. And in the Lower South, the commitment to slave labor meant that virtually no free black communities or white-sponsored antislavery societies could prosper.

After the Revolution, slavery ceased to be a national institution. It became the "peculiar institution" of a single region, the American South. Because the overwhelming majority of black Americans lived in the South, the end of slavery as a national institution affected few blacks. But it determined the political future for white Americans. The isolation of slavery in one section set North and South on radically different courses of social development, sharpening economic and political divisions. As early as 1778, South Carolina's William Henry Drayton predicted that northern and southern interests would naturally diverge "from the nature of the climate, soil, and produce of the several states." That phrase was Drayton's delicate device to avoid even mentioning the word slavery.

Wartime Economic Disruption

With the outbreak of the Revolution, Americans had suffered an immediate and costly loss of the manufactured goods, markets, and credit that Britain had formerly supplied. Hardest hit were southern planters, who had to seek new customers for their tobacco, cotton, and rice as well as finding new sources of capital to finance production. British bounties had for years encouraged the indigo plantations of South Carolina. Without that subsidy, the industry was dealt a crippling blow from which it never recovered. And the liberation of tens of thousands of slaves deprived many masters of their investment in a labor force.

Northerners faced hard times as well. Most northern cities were occupied for a time by British troops, whose presence disrupted commercial activity. Even after the army had departed, British naval vessels and privateers patrolled northern harbors, crippling the fishing industry and menacing the carrying trade. Thrown out of work, maritime craftsmen, dockside laborers, and sailors migrated to rural areas or joined the army.

Matters did not improve with the coming of peace. Desperate for markets,

Americans now found that both the British and the French colonies in the Caribbean were closed to their trade. But both France and Britain flooded the new states with their manufactures, and postwar Americans, eager for luxuries, indulged in a most unrepublican spending spree. The flurry of buying left some American merchants and consumers as deeply in debt as their governments. When loans from private citizens and foreign creditors like France and Holland had proved insufficient to finance the fighting, both Congress and the states printed paper money—a whopping total of $400 million. The paper currency was backed only by the government's promise to redeem the bills with money from future tax receipts, since politicians balked at the unpopular alternative of levying taxes during the war. For the bills to be redeemed, the government had to survive. Consequently, each rebel military reversal was followed by a decline in the value of American currency.

By the end of 1776, when Continental forces sustained a series of defeats, paper money started to depreciate dramatically. By 1781 it was virtually without value, and Americans coined the expression "not worth a Continental." The printing of paper money combined with a wartime shortage of goods set off an inflationary spiral of scarcer and scarcer goods costing more and more worthless dollars. In this spiral, creditors were gouged by debtors, who paid them back with depreciated currency. At the same time, soaring prices for food and manufactured goods eroded the buying power of wage earners and small farmers. And the end of the war brought on demands for prompt repayment from the new nation's foreign creditors as well as from soldiers seeking back pay and pensions.

Under the Articles of Confederation, Congress was hamstrung by the crisis. With no power to regulate trade, it could neither dam the stream of imported goods rushing into the states nor stanch the flow of gold and silver to Europe to pay for these items. With no power to prohibit the states from issuing paper money, it could not halt depreciation. With no power to regulate wages or prices, it could not curb inflation. And with no power to tax, it could not make any headway in reducing the public debt. Efforts to grant Congress greater powers met with determined resistance from the states. In 1781 and again in 1783, a group that included Alexander Hamilton, John Jay, and Robert Morris proposed that Congress be allowed to levy a 5 percent duty on all imports. The income generated by the impost would have given the Confederation a source of independent revenue to help repay the national debt. But the states still jealously guarded their power to tax. They refused Congress any revenue of its own, fearing the first steps toward "arbitrary" and "aristocratic" government.

Within states, too, economic problems fomented disaffection and discord. War always offers the chance for large profits, especially for those with an eye to the main chance. Some major merchants, creditors, and large commercial farmers had profited handsomely by selling supplies to the army at high prices or by preying on enemy vessels as privateers. Eager to protect their windfall, they lobbied state legislatures for an end to inflationary monetary policy. That meant passing high taxes to pay wartime debts, a paper currency that was backed up with gold and silver, and an active policy to encourage foreign trade.

Small farmers and urban artisans retaliated, pressing legislatures for programs that met their needs. Rural subsistence farmers, often in debt, pitted themselves against merchant and creditor interests, urging low taxes, a moratorium on debt payments, and a policy of cheap money and easy credit. Artisans opposed merchants by calling for protection from low-priced foreign imports that competed with the goods they produced. They set themselves against farmers as well by demanding price regulation of the farm products they consumed. In the continuing struggle, the state legislatures became the battleground of competing economic factions, each bent on gaining its own particular advantage.

As the 1780s wore on, conflict mounted toward crisis. The original political structures created by American revolutionaries proved poorly equipped to cope with postwar social and economic divisions. So long as the individual states remained sovereign, jealously guarding their prerogatives and the power of the purse, the Confederation was crippled—unable to conduct foreign affairs effectively, unable to set coherent economic policy, unable to deal with discontent in the West—in short, "frittered down to the impotent condition in which it now stands," as one observer noted in 1787. And political leaders who had counted on the civic virtue of their countrymen found that private interest proved more powerful than republican disinterestedness. With the body politic slowly rending itself to pieces, leaders like George Washington and James Madison of Virginia, James Wilson and Robert Morris of Pennsylvania, and Alexander Hamilton and John Jay of New York became convinced that the only way to quell the clashes among Americans was to strengthen the central government. Whether the states could be convinced to surrender power remained to be seen.

REPUBLICAN SOCIETY

While leaders with power and influence tried to decide how America should define itself politically, ordinary men and women were finding their own ways to reshape American society and culture. Inspired by the Declaration's ideal of equality, some Americans chafed at the subordinate position assigned to them under the old colonial order. Westerners, newly wealthy entrepreneurs, urban artisans, and women all claimed greater liberty, power, and recognition. These groups differed in their aspirations and goals, but all of them were, in some sense, challenging "patriarchy." The authority of the traditional "fathers" of government, society, and the family came under a new scrutiny; the impulse to defer to social superiors became less automatic. The new assertiveness demonstrated how deeply egalitarian assumptions were taking root in American culture.

The New Men of the Revolution

The Revolution gave rise to a new sense of social identity and a new set of ambitions among several groups of men who had once accepted obscurity. Westerners, especially, had rising expectations that sprang from the rapidly changing conditions of frontier communities. As one Kentuckian explained to James Madison, the western migrants "must make a very different mass from one which is composed of men born and raised on the same spot. . . . They see none about them to whom or to whose families they have been accustomed to think themselves inferior." Contemporaries saw clearly that frontier mobility weakened deference to eastern elites.

The war also offered opportunities to clever entrepreneurs, and these men too had their aspirations. Often these entrepreneurs were not the same men who

Daily Lives

FOOD/DRINK/DRUGS

The Spirits of Independence

If God had intended man to drink water, Ben Franklin remarked, He would not have made him with an elbow capable of raising a wine glass. Colonials from all across America, regardless of their theology, agreed with Franklin on the virtues of drink. The ruddy glow of colonial cheeks (still visible in the portraits hung in museums) reflected not only good health and ardent republican virtues, but also substantial daily doses of alcohol. Colonials consumed about twice as much alcohol as Americans today, though in different forms. Beer was not popular, the only sort consumed being a weak, homemade "small beer" containing about one percent alcohol. Only the wealthy, like Franklin, could afford imported Madeira and port wines. On the other hand, the produce of apple orchards allowed Americans northward from Virginia to drink their fill of hard cider. Far and away the most popular distilled liquor was rum, a potent 90 proof beverage (45 percent alcohol) that they sipped straight or mixed with water and sugar to make "toddies."

Special occasions were especially convivial. The liquor flowed freely at ministerial ordinations in New England towns, at court days in the tidewater South, at house-raisings, corn-huskings, and quilting bees on the frontier, and at weddings, elections, and militia musters everywhere in the colonies. But Americans did not confine their drinking to occasional celebrations. Some, like John Adams, started the day with a tankard of hard cider. Others, merchants and craftworkers, broke the tedium of late mornings and early afternoons by sending the youngest apprentice in the shop out for

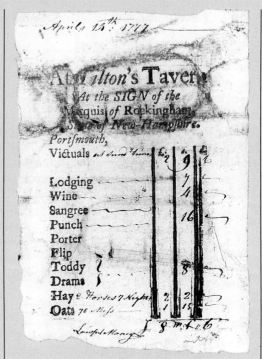

This tavern bill from New Hampshire indicates that in 1777 whiskey was still too rare to be listed.

spirits. Laborers in seaport docks and shipyards, fishermen and sailors at sea, and farm workers in the countryside commonly received a daily allotment of liquor as part of their wages. And at night, men of every class enjoyed a solitary glass at home or a sociable one at a local tavern.

Socialization into the drinking culture started in childhood. Parents permitted youngsters to sip the sweet dregs of a glass of rum, and when young men entered their teens, they joined their fathers at the tavern. Women drank too, although more often at home, and they sometimes explained their use of distilled liquor as serving some "medicinal" purpose. Even slaves got their share, despite laws restricting their consumption of alcohol.

Daily Lives

Thomas Jefferson, whose presidential administration invented the Washington cocktail party, complained that for every glass of wine drunk by his guests, his resourceful slaves stole three.

Early Americans did not drink because they regarded alcohol as healthful, but their faith that it provided an added comfort. Until the middle of the eighteenth century, most colonials (and Europeans) considered spirits a source of physical strength and an essential supplement to their diet, as well as a remedy for colds, fevers, snakebite, and, ironically, depression. They did not condone public drunkenness, but they saw nothing amiss in the regular use of alcohol or even in occasional intoxication.

The easy acceptance of drinking prevailed for most of the colonial period for two reasons. First, until about 1760s, frequent access to the strongest spirits, rum, lay beyond the means of most Americans. Second, the leaders of local communities were able to oversee most public drinking and to keep disorder to a minimum. But by the middle of the eighteenth century some Americans developed misgivings about the drinking culture. Increased production and importation led the price of rum to drop anywhere from 30 to nearly 50 percent. With a gallon of rum selling so cheaply, an ordinary laborer could earn enough in a day to stay "drunk as a lord" for the rest of the week. And as distilled liquor became cheaper, taverns proliferated, making it impossible for community leaders to monitor the popular consumption of alcohol.

The new concern that the drinking of rum fostered crime and social disruption prompted the first steps toward temperance reform. By the 1770s, Quakers like Anthony Benezet were urging that alcohol, like slavery, was an "unrepublican vice," for both forms of bondage deprived their victims of liberty and the capacity for rationality and self-control. Some members of the medical profession also joined early temperance ranks, most notably Benjamin Rush, who publicized new theories about the detrimental effects of drink upon health which he had learned in Edinburgh.

While the advocates of more moderate consumption won support among some educated elites, most Americans altered their drinking habits by consuming *more* hard liquor. Rum, the liquor of choice, received a setback during the Revolution when the British blockade cut drastically the import of both rum and the molasses from which it was made. It became so scarce that Patrick Henry, while governor of Virginia, was embarrassed into serving his guests home-brewed beer. After the war distillers tried to recover their trade, but consumption dropped from 8 million gallons in 1770 to only 7 million in 1789, even though the American population had nearly doubled during that time. Rum lost much of its ground to a new rival, whiskey. Before the 1780s few Americans drank whiskey or were even familiar with it. But significant numbers of immigrants, arriving from Scotland and Ireland in the last quarter of the eighteenth century, brought with them the techniques of efficient, small-still grain distilling.

Whiskey was democratic and cheap, for it could be made in the lowliest backcountry farmhouse. It was patriotic, since it did not depend on imports from the Caribbean. Gradually these "spirits of independence" supplanted rum, not only in the frontier West but also in the urban East. Consumption of alcohol was on a steady rise that would finally result, half a century after the Revolution, in calls for temperance reform.

had prospered before the war, for the fair fortunes and high social position of some families did not survive the Revolution. The biggest losers were loyalists, whose ranks included a disproportionate number of government officials, large landowners, and major merchants. At a stroke independence swept away their political prominence while revolutionary governments confiscated their properties. Whig politicians, some men of humble social backgrounds, assumed loyalist power and government offices. Land speculators, gambling on an American victory, bought up loyalist property, selling off tracts to smaller buyers at a handsome profit.

The loyalists were not alone in suffering reversals. Wartime disruptions ruined some major merchants and planters who had supported independence. But others with a quick eye for profit stepped in. Some northern merchants turned to privateering; others profited from military contracts; many large commercial farmers in the Middle Colonies made a killing from the high prices for food caused by wartime scarcity and army demand.

The Revolution effected no dramatic redistribution of wealth; in fact, the gap between rich and poor increased during the 1780s. Many elite families weathered the war years well, retaining their property and prestige into the nineteenth century. But those families newly enriched by the Revolution came to demand and receive status and power during the postwar period. Their wealth allowed them to compete with established elites, the former "fathers" of colonial society, for social recognition and political influence. The republican ideal of "an aristocracy of merit" justified their claims to social leadership.

Urban Artisans

The dominance of society's traditional "fathers" met with resistance from city craftsmen as well. Before the imperial crisis, manufactured items had been produced in houses and small shops. Presiding was the master craftsman, who imparted the "mystery" of his art to younger, less experienced journeymen and even younger, unskilled apprentices. Journeymen and apprentices not only worked under their master's roof but usually lived under it also. The master supervised their private lives as well as their initiation into his trade. After the Revolution the "patriarchal" organization of the crafts began to give way to a more impersonal, contractual system of production. As domestic manufacturing expanded, the distinction between home and shop grew. Journeymen and even apprentices moved out of their masters' households and away from paternalistic supervision. They took their pay in cash rather than in room and board. Recognizing that their interests were often distinct from those of masters, journeymen formed new organizations to secure higher wages. Between 1786 and 1816, skilled urban laborers organized the first major strikes in American history. A new sense of solidarity among urban laborers translated into political activism, and workers expressed their objectives in republican rhetoric.

The New Women of the Revolution

Not long after the fighting with Britain had broken out, Margaret Livingston of New York wrote to her sister Catherine, "You know that our Sex are doomed to be obedient in every stage of life so that we shant be great gainers by this contest." By war's end, however, Eliza Wilkinson from rural South Carolina was complaining boldly to a woman friend: "The men say we have no business with political matters

. . . it's not our sphere. . . . [But] I won't have it thought that because we are the weaker Sex (as to bodily strength my dear) we are Capable of nothing more, than minding the Dairy . . . surely we may have enough sense to give our Opinions."

What separated Margaret Livingston's resignation from Eliza Wilkinson's assertion of personal worth and independence was the Revolution. For many American women, the war was a politicizing experience. Eliza Wilkinson, for one, had managed her parents' plantation during the war and defended it from British marauders. Other women discovered similar reserves of skill and resourcefulness. When soldiers returned home, some were surprised to find their wives and daughters, who had been running family farms and businesses, less submissive and more self-confident.

Beyond savoring their newfound independence, some women took republican promises of equality to heart, claiming greater political and domestic liberty. Like westerners, self-made capitalists, and city artisans, these women challenged traditional authority. They objected to men monopolizing political life and husbands ruling the family like patriarchs of old. Their protests were seldom heeded.

American men had not fought a revolution for the equality of American women. In fact, male revolutionaries gave no thought whatsoever to the role of women in the new nation, assuming that those of the "weaker sex" were incapable of making informed and independent political decisions. The English Opposition tradition, the main influence on American republican thought, contributed to the widespread conviction that women were politically irrelevant. These radical thinkers—among them, ironically, the gifted historian Catherine Macaulay— wrote virtually nothing about the relationship of women to the state. Most women of the revolutionary generation agreed that the proper female domain was the home, not the public arena of politics. Those with political interests and opinions usually apologized for expressing their views on public matters. When the widow of the head of Georgia's revolutionary government, Ann Gwinnet, wrote to warn the Continental Congress that the officer corps in her state was rife with loyalists, she added, "These things (tho from a Woman, and it is not our sphere, yet I cannot help it) are all true."

But occasionally women of the revolutionary generation openly displayed their keen political interests and advanced their claims to political consideration. When a loosely worded provision regarding voting requirements in the New Jersey state constitution enfranchised "all free inhabitants" owning a specified amount of property, white widows and single women went to the polls. Until 1807, when the state legislature amended the law, unmarried women qualified as legal voters and exercised that right.

Even though women's primary sphere remained the home, the Revolution brought about changes. Reformers like Benjamin Rush and Judith Sargent Murray argued that only educated and independent-minded women could raise the informed and self-reliant citizens that a republican government required. The notion of "republican motherhood" contributed to the most dramatic change in the lives of women after the war—the spread of female literacy.

Mercy Otis Warren, the sister of James Otis and the wife of James Warren, another Massachusetts political leader, lent her talent as a writer to the causes of American independence and education for women.

Between 1780 and 1830, the number of American colleges and secondary academies rose dramatically, and some of these new institutions were devoted to educating women. Not only did the number of schools for women increase, but these schools also instituted a solid academic curriculum. At the Young Ladies Academy of Philadelphia, which Rush helped to establish in 1787, students learned reading, arithmetic, English grammar and composition, rhetoric, and geography. Missing from the female curriculum were natural philosophy (science), advanced mathematics, and classics, subjects still restricted to male scholars. On the other hand, needlework no longer dominated the course of instruction for women.

The reform of women's education that began after the war resulted in a closing of the literacy gap between the two sexes. By 1850—for the first time in American history—there were as many literate women as there were men. That change came slowly, hampered by the view shared by members of both sexes that academic study for women was self-indulgent, useless, or even dangerous—a luxury that made women "masculine," ridiculous, and, above all, unfit for domestic life. To counter popular prejudices, the defenders of female education contended, schooling for women would produce the ideal republican mother. An educated woman, as one graduate of a female academy claimed, would "inspire her brothers, her husband, or her sons with such a love of virtue, such just ideas of the true value of civil liberty . . . that future heroes and statesmen shall exaltingly declare, it is to my mother that I owe this elevation."

The Revolution also prompted a number of states to reform their marriage laws, making divorce somewhat easier. In New England divorce rates rose, reflecting less willingness on the part of wives to tolerate domestic tyranny and more sensitivity on the part of judges to the rights of women within marriage. Divorce was still extremely unusual in the North and almost impossible in the South, yet the Revolution at least raised the possibility that equality should affect private as well as public lives.

While women won better schooling and greater freedom to divorce, they actually lost ground in the realm of property rights. After the Revolution courts became more lax about preserving dower rights, the widow's legal claim to one-third of her spouse's real estate. Married women still could not sue or be sued, make wills or contracts, or buy and sell property; any wages that they earned went to their husbands. All personal property that wives brought into a marriage became the possession of their spouses, as did the rents and profits of any real estate.

Even the new notion of "republican motherhood," while enhancing the significance of what women did within the home, relegated them to the domestic sphere. In the end, women as independent actors in the political world remained as invisible to the framers of the federal constitution in 1787 as they had been to John Adams when Abigail petitioned him in 1776 to act on behalf of "the ladies." The only reference to women in *The Federalist Papers* warns that the intrigues of mistresses and courtesans often threatened the stability of governments.

The Attack on Aristocracy

Why wasn't the American Revolution more revolutionary? Independence secured the full political equality of white men who owned property, but most had enjoyed such equality before the war. The Revolution fostered greater personal freedom for women and prompted some states and individuals to emancipate slaves, but by and large it left the major legal barriers to equality unchanged. Women were still deprived of political rights, blacks of human rights. Why did the revolutionaries stop short of extending equality to the most unequal groups in American society—and with so little sense that they were being inconsistent?

In part, the lack of concern was rooted in republican ideas themselves: lacking property, women and blacks were easily read out of the political nation, consigned to the custody of husbands and masters. In part, the oversight was the product of prejudice: the perception of women and blacks as naturally inferior beings. But it was also the product of a deep conservatism among the revolutionaries. Political innovators though they were, American republicans in their social vision looked backward. Their obsession with traditional inequities kept them from conceiving of social justice in more progressive terms.

The revolutionaries thought of themselves as engaged in a great struggle for equality, and so they were. Yet most defined that battle in traditional and limited terms. During the Middle Ages, the feudal system had created a class of princes, dukes, knights, and other aristocrats, who had become bloated with the power of inherited privileges. Bishops, archbishops, and other "spiritual lords" had also come to rule over the thoughts and beliefs of free citizens. In the eyes of republicans, the real threat to liberty lay in the privileges of those "lords spiritual and temporal"—privileges that had to be eliminated from the political system, root and branch. Republicans were interested in leveling off the top of society, not in raising up the bottom. When they looked for legal abuses, they saw the unfair legal practices inherited from medieval Europe, but they remained blind to the legal inequalities that kept blacks enslaved and women dependent.

No matter that America was devoid of aristocrats and bishops and that no individuals or groups enjoyed formal privileges. Republicans sought out and exposed any traces of aristocracy they could find. If elaborate powdered wigs smacked of lordly privilege, then city crowds might find themselves treated to a Fourth of July parade like the one in Philadelphia witnessed by a local resident: a dirty woman wearing a "very high Head dress" was "exhibited thro the Streets" with an eager mob swirling around her, symbolically beating "Drums etc. by way of ridiculing that very foolish fashion." In similar spirit, reformers attacked the Society of Cincinnati, a group organized by former officers of the Continental Army in 1783. The society, which was nothing more sinister than a social club for veterans, was harried for its policy of passing on its membership rights to eldest sons. In this way, critics charged, the Cincinnati was creating artificial distinctions and perpetuating a hereditary warrior nobility. Bowing to public pressure, the society eventually disbanded.

More significant was the dismantling of state-supported churches. Every state except Delaware, New Jersey, Pennsylvania, and Rhode Island had a religious establishment—the Anglican church in New York and the South, the Congregational church in New England. Since the 1740s, dissenters who did not worship at state churches had protested laws that taxed all citizens to support the clergy of established denominations. They also objected to the licenses that colonial governments required their own ministers to have. After the Revolution, dissenters argued that if all citizens were to be treated as equals, the privileges of religion had to be ended. Pointing to their contributions to winning the war for independence, dissenters urged that they were entitled to a full share of liberty in the new republic. As more and more dissenters became voters, state legislators paid heed and finally abolished the special legal privileges of the Anglican and Congregational churches. But the trend toward disestablishment had been under way well before the Revolution, and the new laws were mainly the capstone of the process.

Many of the republican efforts at reform seem in retrospect misdirected and occasionally ridiculous. While only a handful of revolutionaries worked for the education of women and the emancipation of slaves, enormous zeal went into fighting threats from a feudal past that had never existed in America. Yet if most revolutionaries struck at shadows, the darkness of aristocrats and bishops seemed real to them—and indeed remained real in many parts of Europe. Their determination to sweep away every residue of formal privilege ensured that these forms of inequality never took root in America. And if eighteenth-century Americans did not extend equality to women and racial minorities, it was a failure that they shared with later revolutionary movements that promised more. The political institutions that American republicans created did not by any stretch of the imagination bring total equality. But over the years the strength of those institutions has allowed the extent of equality to grow.

FROM CONFEDERATION TO CONSTITUTION

While Americans sought to realize the republican commitment to equality in many walks of life, leaders in Congress wrestled with the problem of preserving the nation itself. By the mid-1780s the survival of the United States was in doubt. Two events—one foreign, one domestic—brought American republicans to the disturbing conclusion that neither the Confederation nor the state legislatures were able to remedy the fundamental difficulties facing the nation.

The Jay–Gardoqui Treaty

The international episode that pushed the United States to the brink of dissolution was a debate over a proposed treaty with Spain. In 1785 settlers along the southwestern frontier remained restive over their trade route to New Orleans. Accordingly, Congress instructed its secretary of foreign affairs, John Jay, to negotiate an agreement with Spain preserving American navigational rights on the Mississippi River. The Spanish emissary, Don Diego de Gardoqui, proved the more formidable diplomat. He inveigled Jay into an arrangement by which the United States would actually relinquish all rights to the Mississippi for 25 years. In return, Spain would acknowledge American territorial claims in the Southwest and grant trading privileges to American merchants.

Jay, a New Yorker, leapt to the bait. He knew northern merchants took a keen interest in finding new markets, and he chose to overlook the expense to the South at which this northern opportunity was gained. Southwestern settlers in the Ohio valley, most of them migrants from Virginia and the Carolinas, regarded the proposed treaty as nothing short of betrayal, and they told Congress so. The treaty was never ratified, but the hostility stirred up during the debate revealed how strong sectional feelings were. Gardoqui's clever bid to deepen southwestern mistrust of the Confederation worked. Southwestern leaders like James Wilkinson, a former Revolutionary War general, and Daniel Boone began accepting bribes from the governor of New Orleans with the understanding that they would en-courage pro-Spanish sympathies among their neighbors.

Shays' Rebellion

On the heels of the Confederation's foreign humiliation came an internal ruckus that challenged the notion that individual states could maintain order in their own territories. The problem surfaced in western Massachusetts, where many small farmers were close to ruin. By 1786 farm wages and prices had fallen sharply and farmers were selling little produce. Yet they still had to pay mortgages on their farms, still had other debts, and were perpetually short of money. The time-honored tactics that legislatures used to help debtors were to lower taxes and fees and simply to print more money. Stay laws could be passed, too, temporarily forbidding creditors from foreclosing on farmers' property. (Foreclosures could include more than land: sometimes creditors took away farmers' personal tools, household goods, and even clothing.) In 1786 the lower house of the Massachu-setts legislature obliged the farmers with a package of relief measures.

But creditors in eastern Massachusetts, determined to safeguard their own investments, persuaded the upper house to defeat the measures. The farmers then took matters into their own hands. In the summer of 1786 they met in extralegal conventions, demanding that the upper house of the legislature be abol-ished and that the relief measures go into effect. By autumn the farmers had turned from words to deeds, rising 2000 strong in armed rebellion. Led by Cap-tain Daniel Shays, a veteran of the Revolution, mobs closed the county courts to halt creditors from foreclosing on their farms and marched on the federal arsenal at Springfield. The state militia quelled the uprising by February 1787, but the insurrection left many in Massachusetts and the rest of the country thoroughly shaken.

Alarmed conservatives saw Shays' Rebellion as the consequence of democ-racy carried to radical extremes. "The natural effects of pure democracy are al-ready produced among us," lamented one republican gentleman; "it is a war against virtue, talents, and property carried on by the dregs and scum of man-kind." But the farmers who took up arms under Daniel Shays were no impover-ished rabble. They were reputable members of western communities who wanted their property protected and believed that government existed to provide that protection. The Massachusetts state legislature had been unable to safeguard the property of farmers from the inroads of recession or to protect the property of creditors from the armed debtors who closed the courts. It had failed, in other words, to fulfill the most fundamental aim of republican government.

What if such violent tactics spread? Other states with discontented debtors feared what the example of western Massachusetts might mean for their own future—not to mention the future of the Confederation itself. But by 1786 Shays' Rebellion supplied only the sharpest jolt to the movement toward creating a stronger national government already under way. Even before Shays rose in arms, a group of Virginians had urged Congress to authorize a meeting of the states that would consider setting up a uniform system of commercial regulations. Once as-sembled at Annapolis in September 1786 the delegates from five states agreed to a more ambitious undertaking. They called for a second, broader meeting in Phila-delphia, which Congress approved, for the "express purpose of revising the Arti-cles of Confederation." The die was now cast; but the outcome was by no means certain.

The Framing of the Federal Constitution

It was the wettest spring anyone could remember. The 55 men who traveled to Philadelphia in May 1787 came over muddy roads and through unceasing rainstorms, arriving drenched and bespattered. They wondered if the honor of being chosen a delegate to the convention made up for the discomfort. Fortunately, most of the travelers were men in their thirties and forties, young enough to survive a good soaking. And since most were gentlemen of some means—planters, merchants, and lawyers with powdered wigs and prosperous paunches—they could recover from the rigors of their journey in the best accommodations offered by America's largest city.

The delegates came from all of the states except one. Rhode Island, ever the maverick, refused to send a representative. The rest of New England supplied shrewd backroom politicians—Roger Sherman and Oliver Ellsworth from Connecticut, and Rufus King and Elbridge Gerry, Massachusetts men who had learned a trick or two from Sam Adams. The middle states marshaled much of the intellectual might: two Philadelphia lawyers, John Dickinson and James Wilson, and one Philadelphia financier, Robert Morris. There was Alexander Hamilton, the mercurial and ambitious young protégé of Washington, and his fellow New Yorker, the aristocratic Gouverneur Morris. South Carolina provided fiery orators, Charles Pinckney and John Rutledge.

It was "an assembly of the demi-gods," gushed Thomas Jefferson, who was not there. Along with John Adams, Jefferson was serving as a diplomat in Europe when the convention met. In fact, the only delegate who looked even remotely divine was the convention's presiding deity. Towering a full half foot taller than most of his colleagues, George Washington exuded his ineffable self-possession from a chair elevated on the speaker's platform where the delegates met, in the Pennsylvania State House.

It would have been hard to find a less likely candidate for patriotic icon than Washington's fellow Virginia delegate, James Madison. Short and slightly built, bookish and retiring, the 36-year-old Madison had no profession except hypochondria; he read a great deal and dressed in black. He was not a commanding presence like Washington or as celebrated as other Virginia delegates like George Mason, the author of that state's bill of rights, or Edmund Randolph, its eccentric governor. Nonetheless, Madison was an astute politician. He possessed limitless patience and was brilliant without being dogmatic. The convention belonged to him: more than anyone else, James Madison shaped the framing of the federal Constitution.

The delegates from 12 different states had two things in common. First, they were men of considerable political talent and experience. Most had served in Congress; others had drafted state constitutions or served as state governors. One-third were veterans of the Continental Army and 34 were lawyers. Second, the delegates all recognized the need for a stronger national government. So when the Virginia delegation introduced Madison's outline for a new central government, the convention was ready to listen.

James Madison, the scholar and statesman whose ideas and political skill shaped the Constitution.

What Madison had in mind was a truly national republic, not a confederation of independent states. His "Virginia Plan" proposed a central government with three branches—legislative, executive, and judicial—with Congress having the power to veto all state legislation. In place of the Confederation's single assembly, Madison substituted a bicameral legislature, with a lower house elected directly by the people and an upper house chosen by the lower from nominations made by state legislatures. Representatives to both houses would be apportioned according to population—a change from practice under the Articles, in which each state had a single vote in Congress. Madison also revised the structure of government that had existed under the articles by adding an executive, who would be elected by Congress, and an independent federal judiciary.

After two weeks of debate over the Virginia Plan, William Paterson, a lawyer from New Jersey, presented a less radical counterproposal. While his "New Jersey Plan" increased Congress' power to tax and to regulate trade, it kept the national government as a unicameral assembly, with each state receiving one vote in Congress under the policy of equal representation. Smaller states like New Jersey opposed proportional representation because it would give larger, more populous states greater influence in Congress. The delegates summarily dispatched Paterson's plan, rejecting it within four days. Most recognized the need for stronger measures and supported Madison's design for changing the structure of the central government. But the delegates were seriously divided over the apportionment of representation. While smaller states pressed for each state having an equal vote in Congress, larger states backed Madison's provision for basing representation on population.

Underlying the dispute over representation was an even deeper rivalry between southern and northern states. While northern and southern populations were nearly equal in the 1780s, and the South's population was growing at the more rapid rate, the northern states were more numerous. Giving the states equal votes would put the South at a disadvantage. Southerners feared being outflanked in Congress by the northern states and felt that only proportional representation would protect the interests of their section.

As the wettest spring that anyone could remember burned off into the hottest summer, the division over representation deepened into a deadlock. Temperatures soared, tempers shortened, and the delegates suffered the daily torture of staring at a large sun emblazoned across the speaker's chair occupied by Washington. The stifling heat was made even worse because the windows remained shut all day, to keep any news of the proceedings from drifting out onto the Philadelphia streets and upsetting the delicate negotiations.

Finally, as the heat wave broke, so did the political impasse. On July 2 a committee headed by Benjamin Franklin, who at 81 had been trying to form a national union before some of the delegates were born, weighed in with a compromise. States would be equally represented in the upper house of Congress, each state legislature appointing two senators to six-year terms. That appeased the smaller states. But in the lower house of Congress, which alone could initiate money bills, representation was to be apportioned according to population: every 30,000 inhabitants would elect one representative for a two-year term. A slave was to count as three-fifths of a free person in the calculation of population, and the slave trade was to continue until 1808. That appeased the larger states and the South.

The Constitution was drawn up and debated, and by the end of August the

As the Constitution is signed, Benjamin Franklin, second from left, looks on; Washington presides. "The business being closed," Washington wrote, "the members adjourned to the City Tavern, dined together and took cordial leave of each other."

convention was prepared to approve the final draft. The delegates agreed that the executive, now called the president, would be chosen every four years. Direct election, however, seemed out of the question—after all, how could citizens in South Carolina know anything about a presidential candidate who happened to live in distant Massachusetts, or vice versa? But if voters instead chose presidential electors, those eminent men likely would have been involved in national politics, would have known the candidates personally, and would be prepared to vote wisely. Thus the Electoral College was established, with each state's total number of senators and representatives determining its share of electoral votes. It was a cumbersome device, but one that guaranteed that the president would not owe his office to Congress.

An array of other powers assured that the executive would remain independent and strong: he would have command over the armed forces, authority to conduct diplomatic relations, responsibility to nominate judges and officials in the executive branch, and the power to veto congressional legislation. Just as the executive branch was made independent, so too the federal judiciary was separated from the other two branches of government. Madison believed that this clear separation of powers was essential to a balanced republican government.

Madison's only real defeat came when the convention refused to give Congress veto power over state legislation. Still, the new bicameral national legislature enjoyed much broader authority than Congress had under the Confederation, including the power to tax and to regulate commerce. The Constitution also clipped the wings of state legislatures, prohibiting them from levying import and export duties, coining money or issuing paper currency, relieving debtors of their contractual obligations, and conducting foreign relations. The Constitution and the acts passed by Congress were declared the supreme law of the land, taking precedence over any legislation passed by the states. And changing the Constitution would not be easy—amendments could be proposed only by a two-thirds vote of both houses of Congress or in a convention requested by two-thirds of the state legislatures. Ratification of amendments required approval by three-quarters of the states.

On September 17, 1787, thirty-nine of the forty-two delegates remaining in Philadelphia signed the Constitution. It was fortunate that the signatories included so many lawyers, for the summer's proceedings had been of such dubious legality that a battery of skilled attorneys would be needed to make them seem otherwise. Charged only to revise the Articles, the delegates had instead written a new frame of government. Not only had they written a new constitution, but one with no bill of rights—the majority of delegates had deemed that unnecessary. In addition, to speed up ratification, the convention decided that the Constitution would go into effect after only nine states had approved it, overlooking the fact that even a revision of the Articles would have required the assent of all state legislatures. As for the state legislatures, the delegates determined to bypass them altogether, declaring that the people themselves would pass judgment on the Constitution in special ratifying conventions. To serve final notice that the new central government was a republic of the people and not merely another confederation of states, Gouverneur Morris of New York hit on a happy turn of phrase to introduce the Constitution. "We the People," the document begins, "in order to form a more perfect union. . . ."

Ratification

With grave misgivings on the part of many, the states called for conventions to decide whether to ratify the new Constitution. Those with the gravest misgivings—the anti-Federalists as they came to be called—voiced familiar republican fears. Expanding the power of the central government at the expense of the states, they warned, would lead to corrupt and arbitrary rule by new aristocrats. Extending a republic over a large territory, they cautioned, would separate national legislators from the interests and close oversight of their constituents. With so many different regions and interests and classes of people, factions would soon tear the government apart.

Madison responded to these objections in *The Federalist Papers*, a series of 85 essays written with Alexander Hamilton and John Jay and published in a New York City newspaper during the winter of 1787–1788. He countered anti-Federalist concerns over the centralization of power by pointing to the ingenious system of checks and balances built into the Constitution. Each separate branch of the national government would, Madison explained, keep the others within the limits of their legal authority. The mechanism would prevent the executive from oppressing the people while preventing the people from oppressing themselves.

To answer anti-Federalist objections to a national republic, Madison drew on the iconoclastic ideas of an English philosopher, David Hume. According to Hume, the conventional wisdom of Montesquieu and other liberal thinkers was all wrong: large size was not a liability but an asset for a republic. The larger a territory, the more likely were multiple political interests and parties—so many that no single faction could dominate. Instead, each would cancel out the others.

Ratification of the Constitution

STATE	DATE	VOTE FOR	VOTE AGAINST
Delaware	December 8, 1787	30	0
Pennsylvania	December 12, 1787	46	23
New Jersey	December 18, 1787	38	0
Georgia	January 2, 1788	26	0
Connecticut	January 9, 1788	128	40
Massachusetts	February 16, 1788	187	168
Maryland	April 26, 1788	63	11
South Carolina	May 23, 1788	149	73
New Hampshire	June 21, 1788	57	47
Virginia	June 25, 1788	89	79
New York	July 26, 1788	30	27
North Carolina	November 21, 1789	194	77
Rhode Island	May 29, 1790	34	32

Madison reformulated Hume's argument in his famous tenth essay in *The Federalist Papers*, arguing that in a great republic, "the Society becomes broken into a greater variety of interests, of pursuits, of passions, which check each other, whilst those who may feel a common sentiment have less opportunity of communication and contact."

The one criticism Madison could not get around—and the issue that became the core of anti-Federalist opposition to the Constitution—was the absence of a bill of rights. The convention delegates had not drawn up a specific national bill of rights because they believed that provisions in the Constitution as well as the state constitutions themselves provided sufficient protection for personal freedoms. But the anti-Federalists were not assured, and they called for an explicit statement of rights to secure the freedoms of individuals and minorities from being violated by the federal government. Madison finally promised to place a bill of rights before Congress immediately after the Constitution was ratified.

Throughout the early months of 1788, anti-Federalists continued their opposition. Although their followers were widespread, they lacked the articulate and influential leadership that rallied behind the Constitution and commanded greater access to the public press. In the end, too, anti-Federalist fears of a tyrannical centralized power proved less compelling than federalist prophecies of the chaos that would follow if the Constitution was not adopted. Many agreed with Hamilton that the alternative to ratification was "anarchy and Convulsion."

By June 1788 all of the states except three had voted in favor of ratification—New York, North Carolina. The last holdout—to no one's surprise Rhode Island—finally accepted the Constitution in May 1790. Madison's pledge to provide a bill

The American artist Thomas Sully's idealized likeness of Patrick Henry conveys his subject's intensity. Henry's eloquence and passion as on orator made a vivid impression on his contemporaries.

of rights took the form of the first 10 amendments to the Constitution, adopted by three-quarters of the states by the end of 1791. The amendments protected the freedoms of speech, religion, press, and assembly, as well as the right to bear arms and to trial by jury. In a real sense, they were the anti-Federalists' most impressive legacy.

Within the life span of a single generation, Americans had declared their independence twice. In many ways the liberation claimed from Britain in 1776 was less remarkable than the intellectual freedom that Americans achieved by assenting to the Constitution. The Constitution represented a triumph of political imagination and pragmatism and a repudiation of some ancient and cherished republican axioms. It was a recognition that experience could be the only reliable guide to politics.

Americans were afraid to change their minds, but many did. Committed at first to limiting executive power and asserting legislative supremacy, Americans at last ratified a constitution that provided for an independent executive and a balanced government. Committed at first to preserving the sovereignty of the states, Americans at last established a national government with authority independent of the states. Committed at first to the proposition that a national republic was impossible, Americans at last created an impossibility that still endures. Such thinking was hardly consistent, but "a foolish consistency," wrote philosopher Ralph Waldo Emerson half a century after 1787, "is the hobgoblin of small minds." It would have been a fitting epitaph for the revolutionary generation.

Not all of the old revolutionaries agreed. The narrow majorities by which the Constitution was ratified reflect the continuing influence of localistic sentiments. Among the loyal supporters of undiluted state sovereignty was Patrick Henry. He refused to attend the Constitutional Convention in 1787 because he "smelt a rat." He became an ardent anti-Federalist, lending his impassioned oratory to the cause of defeating ratification. "I am not a Virginian, but an American," Henry had once declared. Most likely he was lying. Or perhaps Patrick Henry, a southerner and a slaveholder, could see his way clear to being an "American" only so long as sovereignty remained firmly in the hands of the individual states. That was a position which, 70 years later, would rise again to haunt the Union.

SIGNIFICANT EVENTS

1777	+	Continental Congress approves the Articles of Confederation
1781	+	Articles of Confederation ratified
1784	+	Spain closes the Mississippi River to American navigation
1785	+	Jay–Gardoqui Treaty negotiated but not ratified
	+	Shays' Rebellion; Annapolis convention calls for revising the Articles
1787	+	Congress adopts the Northwest Ordinance; Constitutional Convention
1787–1788	+	Publication of *The Federalist Papers*
1788	+	New Hampshire becomes ninth state to ratify Constitution
1791	+	Bill of Rights adopted

Generations of the Republic

The First African-Americans (1740–1800)

What were their memories of the world as first they found it? Perhaps some remembered the snug darkness or the dank, dirt floor of home, a spare one-room hut. Perhaps some remembered its familiar objects—straw bedding, coarse woolen blankets, wooden barrels that served as seats, a grindstone for making corn into meal. Perhaps they remembered their mother or father, sitting before the fireplace, smiling, calling the familiar name they had been given by someone else: Molly or Betty, Jack or Jemmy.

Or did the world outdoors leave more of an impression? Some may have remembered the yard fronted by identical huts, an enclosed space filled during the day with chickens and small children—their brothers and sisters, cousins and playmates—and presided over by an ancient woman, wrinkled by the sun, worn by work—their grandmother, or even great-grandmother. Perhaps they remembered glimpsing in the distance the dark figures of mothers and fathers, aunts and uncles, older brothers and sisters, as they weeded, hoed, or harvested from daybreak to sundown in tobacco fields and

rice swamps. Perhaps they remembered watching their mothers breaking from work long enough to suckle the infants left lying in the shade.

Evenings in the quarters no doubt etched themselves vividly. The whole village of kin, in-laws, and friends came together, often cooking a communal meal of cornbread and bits of pork. Perhaps they remembered the men after supper sharing liquor and stories of how they had contrived to get the contraband spirits. Perhaps they remembered the runaways who sometimes came after dark to take shelter in the quarters.

Many must have remembered fondly Sundays and holidays, when family members not seen every day came to visit—fathers, grown brothers and sisters, and more distant kin and friends from neighboring plantations. Exuberant singing and dancing to the beating of drums and the strumming of banjos marked these reunions. Cross-plantation networks of families and friends also convened more solemn gatherings—meetings for religious worship and commemorations of the dead. Funerals, usually held a month after bur-

ial, often included a ritual of drinking the dead to a new home, as some said, in west Africa.

The African-American children born into slavery on southern plantations could not count west Africa among their memories. It was only through their immigrant parents that these native-born children came to know of the world their elders had lost. The older generation told of the initiation ceremonies and puberty rites, the marriage customs and religious beliefs, the hunting and farming practices, the legends and tales of conjuring and sorcery of tribes to which they had once belonged: the Ibos and Ibidios, the Efkins and Mokos. They told of African relatives they would never see again and African names they no longer heard.

Equally foreign to the black children growing up after 1750 was the earlier America of their parents, the Africans brought to the Chesapeake and the Carolinas in the four decades after 1700, the time of heaviest importation. This older generation had survived the trauma of captivity, the Middle Passage, and sale at slave auctions. They had been thrust into a bewildering new world: a sea of unfamiliar faces, a clamor of different languages, a host of demands from men and women who called themselves masters. Theirs was a world of ceaseless, monotonous labor, performing the plantation's most menial tasks. Theirs was a world of count-

less efforts to escape. Theirs was a world in which death stalked life, especially during the first grim year of "seasoning," when one-quarter of all black immigrants succumbed to disease or despair.

The earliest generations of enslaved Africans confronted a world of constant struggle and conflict, not only with deadly diseases against which they had no immunity and with masters against whom they had few defenses, but also with their fellow slaves. Coming from a number of diverse west African tribes, each with a separate language or dialect and distinctive cultures and kinship systems, the "new Negroes" often had little in common with one another, and even less in common with the American-born black minority. Native-born blacks enjoyed better health, command of English, and experience in dealing with whites. They were also more likely to enjoy a family life, for their advantages probably made them the preferred partners of black women, who were outnumbered two to one by black men. And since immigrant women waited two or three years before marrying, some immigrant men died before they could find a wife, and many never married. Africans resented native-born men as rivals in the competition for wives, and some immigrants held in particular contempt native converts to Christianity.

But by the 1730s in the Chesapeake, and a few decades later in the Carolinas,

births began to outnumber deaths in the slave quarters. As the black population began to grow by natural increase, slave importations tapered off. As native-born blacks predominated, the balance between men and women started to even out, reinforcing the growth of population by reproduction. As the black population expanded, the size of plantations also grew apace. In the Chesapeake as well as in the Carolinas, slave quarters on larger plantations came to resemble black villages of interrelated kin. And as the immigrant generations were replaced by native-born blacks, earlier sources of tension and division within the slave community disappeared.

Forming a family had also become somewhat easier by the 1750s. Because men still outnumbered women, most black males married later than whites, around age 30; black women married in their late teens, at about the age of southern white brides. Although some newly married black couples set up their own households after the birth of their first child, most black wives, even on larger plantations, did not share that home with their husbands. For unlike southern whites, blacks refused to marry their cousins, a taboo that forced many young men to choose mates from neighboring plantations. These husbands and fathers resided in barracks with other men on separate plantations, visiting their wives and children as often as they could.

Because of these changes, black children of the mid-eighteenth century came of age in a plantation society more stable than that known by earlier generations. These members of a new African-American majority generally lived in households with their mothers and some of their brothers and sisters, and more than half of all youngsters on larger plantations lived with both parents. In addition, many members of a child's extended family—grandparents, uncles, aunts, and cousins—often lived on the same plantation or close enough to allow frequent visits.

African-Americans coming of age later in the eighteenth century not only had fuller domestic and social lives, but some also engaged in work more varied than heavy labor in the fields. White masters, especially the owners of large plantations, trained some native blacks in skilled trades that did not require literacy, apprenticing them as blacksmiths, coopers, masons, potters, carpenters, miners, shoemakers, millers, and boatmen. Slave women acquired skills as cooks, laundresses, dairymaids, and nurses. In the 1770s, a large number who learned the crafts of weaving and spinning supplied much of the cloth previously imported from England. The determination of white masters to make their plantations as self-

sufficient as possible fostered a class of skilled black workers, both male and female.

To be sure, the harsh realities of slavery still intruded into the lives of African-American children. Masters, not slave parents, named the infants born on their plantations, and their preferences ran to diminutives and nicknames. Between the ages of 7 and 10, youngsters were sent to work alongside adult slaves in the fields, and between the ages of 10 and 14, many either left their parental home to live with relatives or were sold to neighboring planters.

The most basic conditions of life remained fraught with uncertainty. Virtually every southern slave experienced a forced separation from the family at some time in his or her life. Although some planters encouraged permanent unions among their bondspeople, hoping that family ties would increase reproduction and discourage runaways, slave marriages had no legal status. And the slave family was only as stable as a master's health and finances were sound. If a master fell on hard times, members of black families might be sold off to different buyers to meet his debts. When a master died, slave families were divided among the heirs. Even in the best circumstances, fathers might be separated from their families for long periods, hired out to other planters or sent to work on distant quarters.

Two other developments disrupted black efforts to fashion domestic and communal bonds. Most important was the migration of many white slaveholding families from the coast to the interior. Between 1755 and 1782, masters on the move resettled fully one-third of all adult blacks living in Tidewater Virginia, mostly men and women in their teens and early twenties, in the valleys of the Piedmont, hundreds of miles from their families and friends. There these young people had to begin again the long process of establishing families and elaborating kinship networks. Another unsettling event was the American Revolution, when southern blacks were confronted with a choice between remaining on their plantations or risking a trek across the embattled countryside to escape behind British lines. Perhaps 2 to 3 percent of the Chesapeake's slave population—3000 to 5000 people— cast their lot with the British, nearly half of them women with children.

By the end of the seventeenth century, a drop in mortality rates and the decline of indentured servitude allowed many southern whites to create a more stable web of family, kin, and friends. Blacks faced more daunting odds. But the sustaining ties of family and friendship became part of most African-American lives in the decades before the Revolution.

8

The Republic Launched

he news spread outward from the centers of ratification like ripples from pebbles dropped in a pond. Normally news traveled slowly in the eighteenth century, but express riders spurred their horses through the night. New Hampshire, the ninth state to ratify, sent messengers south on June 21 and in three days New York City had received the news. The next day Philadelphia learned and the ripple kept spreading: through Delaware, on to Maryland, and then farther south. Meanwhile in Richmond, the Virginia convention ratified on June 25, and its news began traveling north, the two ripples crossing at about two hours before dawn on June 28, in the village of Alexandria. New Hampshire to Virginia—500 miles in one week.

West of the Alleghenies in Pittsburgh, rumors were spreading so fast that eager Federalists persuaded themselves that Virginia had ratified five days before it actually did. Some 1500 citizens assembled on Grant's Hill to hear an orator proudly announce that the Anti-Federalist "frogs of the marsh" would no longer threaten the Republic because their pond was "about to be dried up." In Albany, New York, opponents of the Constitution accepted the news less calmly. Filling their pockets with stones, they bombarded the local Federalist parade. Out in the Southwestern Territory, word of the new union didn't reach the Creek nation until April 1789, when American officials announced, somewhat pompously, that the United States was "now governed by a President who is like the old King over the great water. He commands all the warriors of the thirteen great fires . . . and when peace shall be established he will be your father, and you will be his children." The Creeks were neither impressed nor notably inclined to become anyone's children.

As always, the celebrations were symbolic. The crowd at Pittsburgh lit nine bonfires—each representing a state that had ratified—and then let the flames spread to four other brush piles, those states yet to join. When Pennsylvania ratified, a few seamen managed to load a boat onto a wagon and haul it through Philadelphia's streets. One of the sailors stood in the bow, throwing out a sounding line and calling, "Three and twenty fathoms, foul bottom," or sometimes, "Six-and-forty fathoms, sound bottom, safe anchorage." Onlookers were puzzled about the meaning until someone realized that the number of fathoms referred to the vote: the Federalists had won by a margin of 46 to 23. Up in Boston, citizens

The corner of Wall and Water Streets in New York City was the location of the Stock Exchange and the Tontine Coffee House, both meeting places for the merchants and brokers of commercial America.

sang an epic poem about ratification to the tune of "Yankee Doodle." Its final stanza concluded:

> So here I end my Fed'ral song,
> Composed of thirteen verses;
> May agriculture flourish long
> And commerce fill our purses!

The symbols were important, illustrating as they did Americans' hopes for the Republic and what it might become. Yet the bonfires, parades, and solemn pronouncements could not mask large uncertainties. Joining together under the "new federal roof" involved more than wrangling over political philosophy. Could the new government succeed in uniting so many diverse factions and regions? The visions Americans had for the nation were formed largely by the social backgrounds from which they came. A Yankee merchant from Salem whose "purse," as the song put it, was being filled by commerce from the new China trade had economic interests and cultural traditions quite different from a farmer in the Virginia backcountry whose agriculture was "flourishing long" by the raising of hogs and tending of a few acres of corn. What were the social contours of the American Republic as its new federal government was launched?

1789: A SOCIAL PORTRAIT

When the Constitution went into effect, the United States stretched from the Atlantic Ocean to the Mississippi River. The first federal census, compiled in 1790, put the population at approximately 4 million people, divided about evenly between the northern and southern states. Virginia, the largest and most populous state, contained over half again as many residents as Pennsylvania, its nearest rival. New York, whose settlers lived primarily in the Hudson River valley, ranked only fifth, behind not only Virginia and Pennsylvania, but also Massachusetts and North Carolina. Formal boundaries could be deceptive, however, since the Republic's population was overwhelmingly concentrated along the eastern seaboard within 50 miles of the Tidewater. Only about 100,000 settlers lived beyond the Appalachians in the Tennessee and Kentucky territories, which were soon to become states. The area north of the Ohio River was virtually unsettled by whites. The great westward surge of population, which would be a major phenomenon of the nineteenth century, was just beginning.

Within the Republic's boundaries were two major social groups that lacked effective political influence: African-Americans and Indians. In 1790 blacks numbered 750,000, almost one-fifth of the total population. Over 90 percent lived in the southern states from Maryland to Georgia, most of them slaves who worked on tobacco and rice plantations. But there were free blacks as well, their numbers increased by the ideals of liberty that the Revolution had fostered. In 1790 the free black population was larger, relative to the total African-American population, than at any time before the Civil War. The census did not count the numbers of Indians living east of the Mississippi. North of the Ohio, the powerful Miami Confederacy discouraged settlement, although during the 1780s a smallpox epidemic had decimated their numbers. To the south, five strong, well-organized tribes with a total population somewhere between 50,000 and 100,000—the Creeks, Cherokees, Chickasaws, Choctaws, and Seminoles—dominated the region below the Ohio from the Appalachians to the Mississippi River. In 1790 in other words, Indian nations wielded effective control of more territory within the United States than the United States itself did.

That situation would soon change, however, as the white population continued to double approximately once every 22 years. Immigration contributed only a small part to this astonishing increase, for on average, fewer than 10,000 incoming Europeans arrived annually between 1790 and 1820. The primary cause was natural increase, making the United States preeminently a nation of youth. In 1790 almost half of all white Americans were under 16 years old and the average American woman gave birth to nearly eight children. Because of the extremely high birth rate (no nation in the world today can match it), women did not live as long, and thus males made up slightly more than half the population, at least among whites.* The age at first marriage was about 25 for men, 24 for women; because of the preponderance of males on the frontier, it was significantly lower in newly settled areas (on average perhaps 21 for males and less for females), which contributed to the high birth rate.

---

*Because the 1790 census did not include significant data on the black population, many of the statistical figures quoted for this era apply only to whites.

This youthful, burgeoning population remained overwhelmingly rural. Only 24 towns or cities boasted a population of 2500 or more, and 19 out of 20 Americans lived outside them. In fact, in 1800 over 80 percent of American families engaged in agriculture, a figure more than double that for England, the most industrialized country of the day. Throughout rural America, the movement of people, goods, and information was slow. The news of the Constitution's ratification traveled much faster than most newspapers, letters, or cargoes. Most roads were still little more than dirt paths hacked through the forest, with stumps cut off at 16 inches (so axles would just clear them) and large trees sometimes left in the roadway. They choked with dust in dry periods and became a sea of mud after rains. When the new government took office, there was not a soundly paved road anywhere in the country. South of Richmond and westward over the Appalachians, travel conditions were even worse.

The primary means of written communication were the mails and newspapers. The United States had a regular postal system, but it was so expensive that it was used principally by businesses rather than individuals. In 1790 the country had 92 newspapers, published weekly or semiweekly, mostly in towns and cities along major avenues of transportation. There were few post offices—only 75 in 1790 to serve a population of almost 4 million. Americans off the beaten path led isolated lives, with only an occasional traveler offering a window to the larger world.

Life in such isolated regions contrasted markedly with the bustling environment of urban centers like New York and Philadelphia. But perhaps the most basic division in American society lay not so much between the cities and the countryside, important as that was. What would divide Americans most broadly over the coming decades was whether they were primarily subsistence farmers, living on the produce of their own land and labor, or whether they were tied more closely to the larger commercial markets of a far-flung world. As the United States began its life under the new federal union, the distinction between a subsistence economy and a commercial economy was a crucial one.

The Subsistence Economy of Crèvecoeur's America

Most rural Americans lived off the produce of their own land in a barter economy. It was this world of small American farms and farm families that a French naturalist and author, Hector St. John de Crèvecoeur, described so well.

Crèvecoeur arrived in the British colonies in 1759 and almost immediately began wandering: riding over the rutted roads that led to the farms of New England and New York, fording the streams between the scattered settlements of Ohio and Kentucky, knocking the dust of Virginia off his clothes, stopping to talk at taverns along the roads to Philadelphia, and finally settling for a number of years as a farmer in the Hudson River valley. A surveyor and a salesman, he visited not only the older settled areas along the Atlantic coast but also the interior, crossing the Appalachians and traveling down the Ohio River and through the region of the Great Lakes. Crèvecoeur was not only curious but literate as well, and his *Letters from an American Farmer*, published in 1783, asked the question that had so often recurred to him: "What then is the American, this new man?"

For Crèvecoeur, what distinguished American society was the widespread equality of its people, especially the rural farmers. Americans were hostile to social pretensions and anything that smacked of aristocratic privilege. Further-

Subsistence and Commercial America

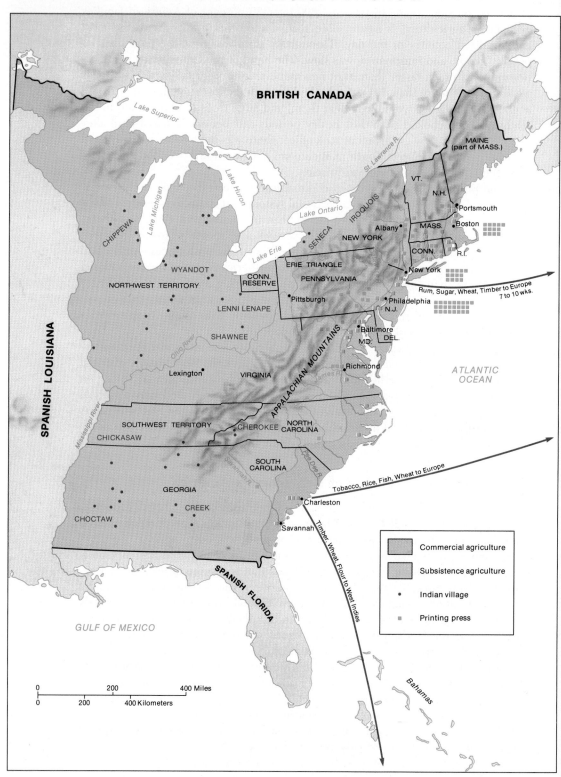

BRITISH CANADA

Lake Superior

Lake Michigan

Lake Huron

St. Lawrence R.

MAINE
(part of MASS.)

VT.

N.H.

Portsmouth

Lake Ontario

IROQUOIS

MASS.

Boston

CHIPPEWA

SENECA

NEW YORK

Albany

Lake Erie

ERIE TRIANGLE

CONN.

R.I.

WYANDOT

New York

NORTHWEST TERRITORY

CONN.
RESERVE

PENNSYLVANIA

Rum, Sugar, Wheat, Timber to Europe
7 to 10 wks.

LENNI LENAPE

Pittsburgh

Philadelphia

N.J.

SPANISH LOUISIANA

SHAWNEE

Ohio River

Baltimore

MD.

DEL.

Lexington

VIRGINIA

Richmond

ATLANTIC
OCEAN

James R.

Mississippi River

APPALACHIAN MOUNTAINS

SOUTHWEST TERRITORY

CHEROKEE

NORTH
CAROLINA

CHICKASAW

SOUTH
CAROLINA

Pee Dee R.

GEORGIA

Savannah R.

Tobacco, Rice, Fish, Wheat to Europe

CREEK

Charleston

CHOCTAW

Savannah

Timber, Wheat, Flour to West Indies

SPANISH FLORIDA

GULF OF MEXICO

Bahamas

	Commercial agriculture
	Subsistence agriculture
•	Indian village
▪	Printing press

0   200   400 Miles

0   200   400 Kilometers

The geography of the young Republic played a large part in determining which areas would become commercial and which would remain semisubsistent. To prosper, commerce demanded relatively cheap transportation to move goods; hence the commercial economy was largely confined to settled areas along the coast and to navigable rivers below the fall line. Since commerce depended on an efficient flow of information and goods, newspapers flourished in these areas. As we have already seen in Chapter 4 (see map on page 137), the highest proportions of blacks were concentrated along the commercial southern coasts and rivers. In limited areas of Kentucky and Tennessee, commercial agriculture based on slavery had begun to take root, but full-scale operations could not develop in the trans-Applachian West so long as Spain controlled the mouth of the Mississippi River.

Population density was greater in commercial areas (left), not only because of the presence of cities, but also because domestic markets flourished as labor became more specialized. (Workers who did not raise their own food needed to buy it, along with other necessities.) Population density decreased in some older settled regions, as in New England, where the shortage of good land drove young men westward in search of opportunity. In southeastern Pennsylvania, an area of intensive commercial agriculture, the high birth rate and declining farm size were beginning to exert similar pressure on the younger generation.

The linkage of western migration and economic opportunity produced distinctive sex ratios in different areas of the country (bottom right). In New England, the migration of young men westward created a surplus of females in older areas, a sign of declining economic prospects stemming from poor soil, excess population, and exhausted fields. By the same token, males predominated in frontier regions. Many pioneers were unmarried men, and only after they established farms and achieved a measure of economic security did they marry and begin to raise a family.

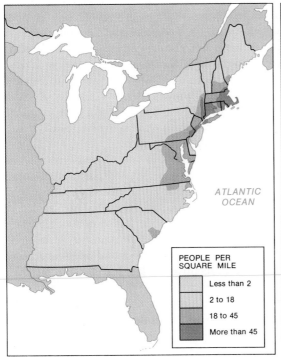

PEOPLE PER SQUARE MILE

Less than 2

2 to 18

18 to 45

More than 45

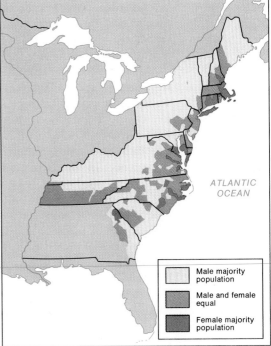

Male majority population

Male and female equal

Female majority population

more, the conditions of the country promoted equality. The abundance of land provided citizens with the freedom and opportunity to live decently, rather than go hungry or idle, as in Europe. In effect, Crèvecoeur was describing a freehold utopia—a society of small farms, where property was widely distributed, where people supported themselves by growing what they needed, and where the population was not divided into the wealthy few and the desperate many. (Like most of his contemporaries, Crèvecoeur glided rather quickly over the plight of black slaves.) "We are the most perfect society now existing in the world," he boasted.

Although Crèvecoeur waxed romantic about the conditions of American life, he painted a reasonably accurate portrait of most of the interior of the northern states and the backcountry of the South. Wealth in those areas was hardly distributed equally, but it was spread fairly broadly. And subsistence remained the goal of most families. "The great effort was for every farmer to produce anything he required within his own family," one European visitor noted. In such an economy, women played a key role. In addition to helping care for the children and maintaining the home, a wife had to be skilled in making articles such as clothes, hats, candles, and soap, since the cost of buying such items was prohibitive. In his report on manufacturing in the 1790s, Alexander Hamilton estimated that household manufacturing produced two-thirds to three-fourths of the clothing in this country. The prevalence of homemade articles, with their awkward shapes and ill-fitting cut, was responsible for the rustic appearance that set off the rural inhabitant from the city dweller.

With labor scarce and expensive, farmers also depended on the cooperation of their neighbors, who helped one another in clearing fields, building homes, and harvesting crops. What small surplus farmers produced was used in local exchange rather than sold for cash in a distant market. In this barter economy, money was seldom seen and was used primarily to pay taxes, settle accounts, and purchase imported goods. "Instead of money going incessantly backwards and forwards into the same hands," a French traveler wrote, residents in the countryside "supply their needs . . . by direct reciprocal exchanges. The tailor and the bootmaker go and do the work of their calling at the home of the farmer who requires it and who, most frequently, provides the raw material for it and pays for the work in goods. . . . They write down what they give and receive on both sides and at the end of the year they settle a large variety of exchanges with a very small quantity of coin." Even ministers were often paid in kind. In 1798 John Shackleford's Baptist parishioners in South Elkhorn, Kentucky, paid him by donating wheat, pork, flour, beef, sugar, tallow, and whiskey; only a handful gave cash.

Indian economies throughout the backcountry were also based primarily on subsistence. In the division of labor, women were responsible for raising crops, while men fished or hunted—not only for meat, but also for skins to make clothing. Indians did not domesticate cattle, sheep, or pigs, but they managed and "harvested" deer more than was evident at first glance. Once or twice a year, villagers would burn the surrounding forests, resulting in an almost parklike environment free of underbrush, full of large, well-spaced trees and open meadows. The Indians fired the forests, noted one perceptive Yankee traveler, "to produce fresh and sweet pasture for the purpose of alluring the deer to the spots on which they had been kindled." Because Indians followed game more seasonally than white settlers, their villages were moved to several different locations over the course of a year. But both whites and Indians in a subsistence economy moved periodically to new fields after the old ones were exhausted. Indians consumed

Work in semisubsistence rural families was done by both sexes and often involved cooperation among neighbors. While a woman milks the cow, a group of men assist in the difficult labor of burning felled trees and plowing a new field with an eight-oxen team.

firewood more prodigiously than whites and were forced to relocate villages closer to new supplies of timber, but they exhausted agricultural lands less quickly than most whites, because they planted beans, corn, and squash in the same field, a technique that better conserved soil nutrients.

Despite the popular image of both the independent "noble savage" and the self-reliant yeoman farmer, virtually no one in the rural backcountry operated within a truly subsistence economy. While farmers tried to grow most of the food their families ate, they normally bought salt, sugar, coffee, and molasses. Often they depended on trade with their neighbors for extra food and agricultural produce. In addition, necessities such as iron, glass, lead, and powder had to be purchased, usually at a country store, and many farmers hired artisans to make items such as shoes and to weave cloth. Similarly, even before white contact, Indians had wide trade networks of their own (obsidian, mined in the Rockies and used for arrowheads, made its way by trade as far east as the Mississippi valley). And Indians quickly became enmeshed in the wider realm of European commerce, exchanging furs for iron implements or items of ornamentation and dress.

The Commercial Economy of Franklin's America

Outside the backcountry, other regions of the United States were tied much more closely to a commercial economy, where specialized merchants, artisans, and even farmers did not subsist on what they produced, but instead sold goods or services in a wider market and lived on their earnings and profits. Cities and towns, of course, played a key part in the commercial economy, but so did the agricultural regions near the seaboard and along navigable rivers. Farmers in these areas, such as Virginia planters who exported tobacco to London and Pennsylvania farmers who shipped grain to Barbados, were part of a much wider commercial network.

For commerce to flourish, goods had to move from producers to market cheaply enough to reap profits. Cost-effective transportation was available to the planters of the Tidewater South, and city merchants used their access to the sea to establish trading ties to the West Indies and Europe. But urban artisans and workers were also linked to this market economy, as were many farm families in the Hudson valley, southeastern Pennsylvania, and southern New England. Where transportation was limited or prohibitively expensive, an economy of barter and semisubsistence persisted, since it cost as much to ship goods a mere 30 miles over primitive roads as to ship by boat 3000 miles across the Atlantic to London. And because backcountry farmers could sell produce only locally, they had no reason to increase production. "It was of no importance to the farmer, that his fields, with careful cultivation, would yield from 50 to 100 bushels of corn per acre," an Ohio pioneer recalled, "when a fourth part of the quantity would answer his purpose, there being no market for a surplus."

Good transportation and the opportunity to profit from wider markets set commercial society apart from Crèvecoeur's world in another way: its wealth was less equally distributed. In the Tidewater South, a small number of planter families monopolized wealth and status. Most backcountry southerners, although not poor, were clearly inferior socially to the planter class. Similarly, American cities were becoming more stratified as the number of propertyless citizens increased and the wealthiest families controlled a greater percentage of a city's total wealth. By 1790, the richest 10 percent of those living in cities and plantation districts owned about 50 percent of the wealth. In the backcountry, the top 10 percent was likely to own 25 to 35 percent.

Crèvecoeur argued that the American tradition of equality had sustained a society of small farm families, bound together in a community of relative equals. But he failed to see how much that equality rested on isolation. Without access to market, one could aspire only so high. Where the market economy operated more fully, however, Americans were more acquisitive and materialistic. Europeans were struck by this desire for wealth and emphasis on money. Material well-being was increasingly the means to status in American society, and the Revolution and its aftermath stimulated the competitive spirit. "Man here weighs everything, calculates everything, and sacrifices everything to his interest," one foreign visitor reported. Although semisubsistence farm families were eager to rise in life and acquire material goods, only those in the commercial economy could realistically pursue these dreams.

The man who gained international renown as a self-made citizen of commercial America was Benjamin Franklin. In his writings and in the example of his own life, Franklin offered a vision of the new nation that contrasted with Crèvecoeur's ideal of a subsistence America. Franklin symbolized the urban and commercial order that was emerging from colonial society, a process that extended from the Revolution into the early nineteenth century. He had arrived in Philadelphia as a runaway apprentice, but by hard work and natural talent rose to be one of the leading citizens of his adopted city.

The preface to Franklin's popular *Poor Richard's Almanack*, as well as his countless essays, spelled out simple maxims for Americans seeking the upward path. "The way to wealth is as plain as the way to market," he advised. "It depends chiefly on two words, industry and frugality." The aphorisms flowed effortlessly from his pen. "Remember that time is money." "Keep thy shop, and thy shop will keep thee." "God gives all things to industry." To Franklin, success and wealth were moral obligations, and success was a reflection of one's virtue. Though he did not say so explicitly, the kind of success he preached depended on taking advantage of commerce and a wider market. As a printer, Franklin's hard work paid off because he could distribute his almanacs and newspapers to ever-greater audiences. As an inventor, he trafficked in a marketplace of ideas that could flourish only in an urban culture, where libraries and social interchange spread ideas freely. As a land speculator hoping to make money in the Ohio backcountry, he anticipated the market price of land being driven up by the spread of settlement and markets westward. Franklin lived what he preached: the commercial life of acquisition and wealth, of social mobility and the potential of the free individual.

By the time he died in 1790, the commercial economy had reached a plateau. The markets for American agriculture were so limited that most farmers had no incentive to increase their yields by adopting the newer techniques of crop rotation and fertilizing with manure. Without profits made from shipping surplus produce to market, American agriculture suffered from a scarcity of capital. Thus farmers lacked the means to boost farm efficiency by increasing the size of their farms, by specializing in the production of a single grain, or by buying better tools. The high birth rate created population pressures that compounded this problem, as farms were further divided from one generation to the next. Even in prosperous commercial regions such as southeastern Pennsylvania, the declining size of farms reduced their profitability; a growing number of farmers were tenants rather than independent operators. Although the West acted as a magnet to draw off surplus population, since Indians still held much of the prime agricultural land and the Spanish controlled the mouth of the Mississippi River, opportunity was severely constricted. Even when western farmers were allowed to ship their surplus to market through New Orleans, their livelihood remained subject to foreign control.

The ethics of Franklin's marketplace, which looked forward to the opening up of opportunity in American society, threatened to destroy Crèvecoeur's egalitarian America. In 1790, the ideal that Crèvecoeur had so eloquently described still held sway across much of America. But the political debate of the 1790s showed clearly that Franklin's world of commerce and markets was slowly transforming the nation.

The Constitution and Commerce

In many ways, the fight over ratification of the Constitution represented a struggle between the commercial and the subsistence-oriented elements of American society. Urban merchants and workers as well as commercial farmers generally rallied behind the Constitution. They participated in a larger market and took a broader, more cosmopolitan view of the nation's future. As a result, they were much more willing to see the government play a role in the economy and especially in promoting foreign trade. Franklin, predictably, supported the Constitution. So did Madison and Washington, both planters whose wealth depended on trade and commerce. Robert Morris, another framer at the convention, was a leading merchant whose expertise in finance helped the young Republic during the Revolution.

Americans who remained a part of the subsistence barter economy tended to oppose the Constitution. More provincial in outlook, they feared concentrated power and harbored deep suspicions of cities and commercial institutions, were outspoken foes of aristocracy and special privilege, and in general just wanted to be left alone. They were a majority of the population, but they were not easily mobilized, lacked prestigious leaders, and did not have the access to communication that their opponents enjoyed. In defeat they remained suspicious that a powerful government would tax them to benefit the commercial sectors of the economy. They clung, like Crèvecoeur, to a vision of a rural, freehold utopia.

And so in 1789 the United States embarked on its new national course, with two rival visions—both somewhat hazy and not clearly expressed—of the direction that the fledgling Republic should take. Whose vision of America would prevail? This question—as much social as it was political—increasingly divided the generation of revolutionary leaders during the 1790s.

THE NEW GOVERNMENT

Whatever the Republic was to become, Americans were agreed on one thing: George Washington personified it. The certainty that Washington would be the nation's first president induced the delegates at the Constitutional Convention to invest more power in the executive than they might otherwise have done. His prestige aided the Federalists immensely in rallying support for ratification. When the first Electoral College cast its votes, Washington was unanimously elected, the only president in history so honored. John Adams became vice president.

Washington knew full well the challenges that faced him. "My movements to the chair of government will be accompanied by feelings not unlike those of a culprit who is going to the place of his execution," he confessed, for he was loath to leave his plantation at Mount Vernon. But his strong sense of duty obliged him to bow to the inevitable, and in April 1789 he journeyed to New York, the temporary federal capital. Along the route crowds gathered for a glimpse of him and to cheer. Almost every town organized an official welcome and celebration, culminating in a gigantic reception in New York City, complete with arches over the streets, booming guns in the harbor, and girls strewing flowers ahead of him as he made his way to his living quarters.

The Federalists—supporters of the Constitution—called the new government "the great experiment," for they were intensely aware that throughout history democratic republics had ultimately degenerated into quarreling factions, as with the city-states of ancient Greece, or ended in dictatorships, as had happened in Cromwell's England and Caesar's Rome. No republic—not England, or Rome, or the Swiss city-states—had stretched over a territory as large as the United States' 890,000 square miles. Loyalty to the new Republic, with its new and untried form of government and diversity of peoples and interests, rested to a great degree on the trust and respect Americans accorded Washington.

Washington's Character

Time has transformed Washington from a man into a monument: remote and unknowable, stiff, unbowing, impenetrable. Even during his own lifetime, Washington had no close friends in public life and discouraged familiarity, even among his closest acquaintances. "I could never be on familiar terms with the General—a man so cold, so cautious," one foreigner testified after visiting Mount Vernon. In a famous story, perhaps apocryphal but widely circulated because it captured the essence of Washington's character, Gouverneur Morris on a dare put his arm on the general's shoulder and greeted him casually; Washington stepped back, icily removed Morris' hand, and glared at him until the poor man fled in mortification. Washington cultivated his aloofness deliberately, believing it would enhance his power and sense of command.

As much as he craved honor and military fame, Washington did not hunger for power. Although he had a temper described as "volcanic" when it exploded, he learned with age to control it. He tried to endure criticism patiently, yet he bitterly resented it, a feeling that deepened during his presidency because he had accepted the office reluctantly. In an age of brilliant political theorists, Washington was not an original thinker, although he was far from dull. At a loss to give an instant opinion, he fell into the habit of asking for advice and then making his decision only after he had weighed the options carefully. But once he adopted a policy, he always assumed responsibility for it.

The president also provoked criticism by the pomp with which he conducted the government. Washington, who was one of the richest men in America, enjoyed the luxuries that wealth brought. Critics complained about his formal public receptions, the large number of servants, and the coach emblazoned with his coat of arms—all aristocratic habits. James Madison remarked that "the satellites and sycophants which surround him [Washington] had wound up the ceremonials of the government to such a pitch of stateliness which nothing but his personal character could have supported, and which no character but his could ever maintain."

Organizing the Government

Washington realized that as the first occupant of the executive office, everything he did was fraught with significance. "I walk on untrodden ground," he commented. "There is scarcely any part of my conduct which may not hereafter be drawn into precedent."

The Constitution made no mention of a cabinet. Yet the drafters of the Constitution, aware of the experience of the Continental Congress under the Articles of Confederation, clearly assumed that the president would have some system of advisers. Congress authorized the creation of four departments—War, Treasury, State, and Attorney General—whose heads were to be appointed with the consent of the Senate. Under Madison's guidance, Congress rejected the proposal that these department heads could be removed only with the Senate's approval, thereby reaffirming the independence of the executive.

Washington chose Alexander Hamilton to be secretary of the treasury and Thomas Jefferson to head the State Department. For the other two positions, Washington selected men of lesser note: Henry Knox, an old colleague from the Revolution, for secretary of war, and Edmund Randolph of Virginia as attorney general. Initially the president did not meet regularly with his advisers as a group, but gradually the idea of a cabinet that met to discuss policy matters evolved. Any meaningful role for the vice president, whose duties were largely undefined by the Constitution, soon disappeared. Washington gradually excluded Adams from cabinet discussions, and before the end of the first term, the vice presidency had sunk into the political backwaters from which it has never emerged.

Congress faced several crucial decisions, including the establishment of a system of federal courts. The Constitution created a federal Supreme Court, but beyond that was silent about the court system. The Judiciary Act of 1789 set the size of the Supreme Court at six members; it also established 13 federal district courts and three circuit courts of appeal. Supreme Court justices spent much of their time serving on these circuit courts, a distasteful duty whose long hours "riding the circuit" caused one justice to grumble that Congress had made him a "traveling postboy." The Judiciary Act made it clear that federal courts had the right to review decisions of the state courts and specified cases over which the Supreme Court would have original jurisdiction. Washington appointed John Jay of New York, a staunch Federalist, as the first chief justice.

The Bill of Rights

Congress also confronted the demand for a bill of rights, which had become an issue during the debate over ratification. Among the 200 some amendments suggested during the ratification debates, there were about 80 proposed changes to the Constitution. They included a prohibition of standing armies (the bane of Republicans) and, most ominous to proponents of the Constitution, a restriction of the federal power to tax. Already critics in some states had called for a new convention to revise the Constitution. Madison sought to forestall any large-scale tinkering by submitting a bill of rights more to his liking in the House of Representatives, where he led the Federalist forces. By focusing on civil liberties, he hoped to win over well-meaning opponents of the Constitution without weakening federal power.

Ultimately Congress sent 12 amendments to the states. The 10 that were ratified—known as the Bill of Rights—became part of the Constitution in December 1791. Their passage by Congress helped persuade North Carolina (1789) and Rhode Island (1790), the two holdouts, to join the Union. So Madison's shrewd tactic succeeded. The advocates of strong federal power, like Hamilton, were relieved that "the structure of the government, and the mass and distribution of its powers" remained unchanged. At the same time, the Bill of Rights fixed firmly the 10 amendments that were destined to be of such importance in defining personal liberty in the United States.

Among the rights guaranteed were freedom of religion, the press, and speech, as well as the right to assemble and petition and the right to bear arms. The amendments also established clear procedural safeguards, including the right to a trial by jury and protection against illegal searches and seizures. They prohibited excessive bail, cruel and unusual punishment, and the quartering of troops in private homes. The last two amendments were intended to calm fears about the federal government having unlimited power and to silence the objection that by enumerating certain basic rights, other, unlisted rights would be denied the people. Madison was careful, however, to phrase these amendments in the most general terms. The Tenth Amendment, for example, declared that "the powers not delegated to the United States by the Constitution, nor prohibited by it to the States, are reserved to the States respectively, or to the people." At the same time, an attempt in Congress to apply these same guarantees to state governments failed, and almost a century would pass before Congress moved, during Reconstruction, to prevent states from interfering with certain basic rights.

Hamilton's Financial Program

Before adjourning, Congress called on Alexander Hamilton, as secretary of the treasury, to prepare a report on the nation's finances. Hamilton undertook the assignment eagerly, for he did not intend to be a minor figure in the new administration.

Hamilton never forgot that he was a self-made man. His father was a Scottish merchant of noble birth, his mother the talented, headstrong daughter of a West Indies physician. But Hamilton's parents never married, and his father eventually deserted the family. Raised largely by his mother, who became a storekeeper, Hamilton grew up on the islands of the West Indies, scarred by the stigmas of poverty and illegitimacy. To compensate, he became a driven personality, who craved respectability and money and remained extremely sensitive about his reputation. "My blood is as good as that of those who plume themselves upon their ancestry," he once asserted. Marriage to the daughter of a wealthy New York politician gave him influential connections he could draw on in his political career. As a military aide to Washington during the Revolution, his devotion was so great as to suggest that the general had become the father figure he lacked as a child.

Ever restless, searching always for the bold or masterful stroke, Hamilton was unable to curb his penchant for intrigue, his feelings, and his tongue, characteristics that made him many enemies. Moreover, he was haughty and overbearing, and, for all his ability, he was jealous and could not tolerate any rival. He was a brilliant thinker and, at times, a shrewd leader, yet he was a turbulent and explosive personality who felt out of place in the new, increasingly democratic society that was emerging around him. Hamilton's political principles were unique among the leaders of the Revolution. He deeply admired British culture and the British

HAMILTON'S FINANCIAL SYSTEM
Under Hamilton's financial system, over 80 percent of federal revenues went to pay the interest on the national debt.

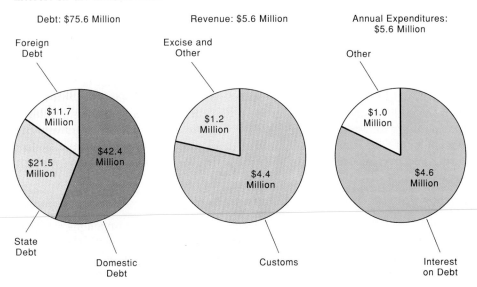

Debt: $75.6 Million   Revenue: $5.6 Million   Annual Expenditures: $5.6 Million

Foreign Debt   Excise and Other   Other

$11.7 Million $1.2 Million $1.0 Million

$42.4 Million $4.4 Million $4.6 Million

$21.5 Million

State Debt   Customs   Interest on Debt

Domestic Debt

constitution, and he abhorred democracy. "All communities divide themselves into the few and the many," he declared. "The first are rich and wellborn, the other the mass of the people. . . . The people are turbulent and changing; they seldom judge or determine right."

Still, despite the accusations of his enemies, he was not a monarchist. At the Constitutional Convention he had proposed that the president serve for life, but had not wanted the office to be hereditary. His experience in the army impressed on him the necessity of a vigorous government, so that he was more inclined to use force than most of his colleagues. Convinced that human nature was fundamentally selfish, Hamilton believed that the government needed to appeal to the self-interest of the rich and wellborn in order to succeed. "Men," he observed succinctly, "will naturally go to those who pay them best." He took as his model Great Britain, whose greatness he attributed to its system of public finance and its preeminence in commerce and manufacturing. Thus Hamilton set out to achieve two goals: to use federal power to encourage manufacturing and commerce, to make the United States economically strong and independent of Europe; and to link the interests of the wealthy with those of the new government.

Neither of these goals could be achieved until the federal government solved its two most pressing financial problems: revenue and credit. Without revenue, it could not be effective. Without the faith of merchants and other governments that it would repay its debts, it would lack the ability to borrow money. Hamilton proposed not only that all $52 million of the federal debt be paid in full (or funded), but that the government also assume responsibility for the remaining $25 million in debts that individual states owed. He hoped that these twin policies of funding and assumption would put the new federal government on a sound financial footing and enhance its power. Convinced that the critical power of government was the power to tax, Hamilton also proposed a series of excise taxes to help pay off the debt, including a controversial 25 percent levy on whiskey.

After heated debate, Congress deadlocked over funding and assumption. Several southern states, especially Virginia, were unhappy about assumption, because they had already paid off part of their debts and did not relish the prospect of being taxed to assist heavily indebted states like Massachusetts. Finally, over dinner with Hamilton, Jefferson and Madison of Virginia agreed to support his proposal if, after 10 years in Philadelphia, the permanent seat of government was located in the South, on the Potomac River between Virginia and Maryland. Aided by this understanding, funding and assumption finally passed Congress. In 1791 Congress also approved a 20-year charter for the first Bank of the United States. The bank would hold government deposits and issue bank notes that would be received in payment of all debts owed the federal government, thus providing the country with a sound paper currency. Congress proved less receptive to the remainder of Hamilton's program, although a limited tariff to encourage manufacturing and several excise taxes, including the one on whiskey, won approval.

Opposition to Hamilton's Program

The passage of Hamilton's program caused a permanent rupture among supporters of the Constitution. Madison, who had collaborated closely with Hamilton in the 1780s, broke with his former ally over funding and assumption. Jefferson, who disliked personal confrontation, finally went over to the opposition when Hamilton announced plans for a national bank. Eventually the two warring factions

A study in contrasts, Jefferson and Hamilton increasingly came into conflict in Washington's administration. Despite his aristocratic upbringing, Jefferson (left) was awkward, loose-jointed, reserved, and ill-at-ease in public. Testifying before a congressional committee, he casually lounged in a chair and spoke in a rambling, nonstop manner. "Yet he scattered information wherever he went," conceded Senator Maclay of Pennsylvania, "and some even brilliant sentiments sparkled from him." Hamilton, though short of stature, cut a dashing figure with his erect bearing, strutting manner, meticulous dress, and carefully powdered hair. Declared the wife of the British ambassador: "I have scarcely ever been more charmed with the vivacity and conversation of any man."

organized themselves into political parties: the Republicans, led by Jefferson and Madison, and the Federalists, led by Hamilton and Adams.* But the divisions emerged slowly over several years.

Hamilton's program rekindled many of the concerns that had surfaced during the struggle over ratification of the Constitution, for it promoted the commercial sector at the expense of subsistence-agrarian groups. The ideology of the Revolution had long stressed that republics were extremely fragile, and that they always contained groups who sought power in order to destroy popular liberties and overthrow the republic. Having escaped an alleged British conspiracy to enslave them, some Americans saw in Hamilton's program an internal threat to establish a privileged and powerful financial aristocracy—perhaps even a monarchy, given the high-handed and intriguing methods of the secretary of the treasury. Even worse, there was considerable doubt that Hamilton ever intended to retire the national debt, which he planned to convert into a source of credit in society.

Who, after all, would benefit from the funding proposal? As the value of notes issued by the Continental Congress diminished during and after the Revolution, speculators had bought them up for a fraction of their face value from small farm-

*The Republican party of the 1790s, sometimes referred to as the Jeffersonian Republicans, is not to be confused with the modern-day Republican party, which originated in the 1850s.

ers and workers. If the government ultimately redeemed the debt, speculators would profit accordingly. By 1790 an estimated four-fifths of this paper was in the hands of speculators. Equally disturbing, some members of Congress had been buying up the notes prior to the adoption of Hamilton's program. Nearly half of the members of the House owned U.S. securities. Madison urged that only the original holders of the debt be reimbursed in full, and that subsequent purchasers be paid the market value before funding (about 50 percent of the face value), but Hamilton rejected this idea. Merchants and commercial speculators were precisely that class of people he hoped to bind to the new government.

Similarly, when stock in the Bank of the United States went on sale, speculators snapped up all the shares in an hour. The price of a share skyrocketed from $25 to $300 in two months. Jefferson was appalled by the mania Hamilton's program encouraged. "The spirit of gambling, once it has seized a subject, is incurable," he asserted. "The taylor who has made thousands in one day, tho he has lost them the next, can never again be content with the slow and moderate earnings of his needle."

The national bank struck its critics as a dangerous mimicking of English corruption. After all, the Bank of England played a powerful role not only in fueling the English economy but in controlling Parliament by making loans to members, electing directors and stockholders, and attaching the new moneyed men to the government. Hamilton's program, Benjamin Rush warned, would inexorably "introduce among us all the corruptions of the British funding system." Jefferson railed that bank directors and members of Congress with loans from the bank would take their marching orders from the Treasury Department rather than represent their constituents. English-style corruption seemed to be taking root as "paper men" became rich not by producing anything substantial with their own hard work, but by shuffling paper, trading notes, and benefiting from the financial legislation they themselves passed. These fears were heightened by the fact that Americans had little experience with banks—only three existed in the country when the Bank of the United States was chartered. One congressman expressed a common attitude when he said that he would no more be caught entering a bank than a house of prostitution.

Then, too, banks and commerce were a part of the urban environment that rural Americans so distrusted. To them, cities seemed sores of corruption, teeming with propertyless and dependent citizens under the control of the rich. Although most granted that a certain amount of commerce was necessary, they believed that it should remain subordinate. Hamilton's program, in contrast, would encourage manufacturing and urbanization, developments that history showed to be incompatible with liberty and equality. Moreover, the tariff favored one group in society—the manufacturers—at the expense of other groups. Such favoritism would enrich the few, concentrate wealth, and destroy the values and social fabric necessary to preserve republicanism.

As wealth became concentrated, so would power in the hands of the federal government. Republicans had long been suspicious of concentrated power, and after Congress approved the bank bill, Washington hesitated to sign it, uncertain of its legality. When he consulted his cabinet, Jefferson and Randolph argued that the Constitution did not specifically authorize Congress to charter a bank. (Madison, who supported them, recalled that the Constitutional Convention had rejected a proposal that Congress be authorized to charter corporations.) All three men upheld the idea of strict construction—that the Constitution should be interpreted narrowly and the federal government restricted to powers expressly delegated to it. To allow Congress to decide that a bank charter was constitutional would make the federal government the judge of its own powers. There would be no safeguard against the abuse of power.

Hamilton countered that the Constitution contained implied as well as enumerated powers. He particularly emphasized the clause that permitted Congress to make all laws "necessary and proper" to carry out its duties. A bank would be useful in carrying out the enumerated powers of regulating commerce and maintaining the public credit; therefore Congress had a right to decide whether the specific means proposed should be employed. The Constitution, after all, could not possibly anticipate all emergencies and future developments. To be effective, the government needed flexibility to meet its responsibilities. In the end, Washington was persuaded by Hamilton's forceful arguments and signed the bill.

The Specter of Aristocracy

The alarm over what a "standing army" might do, the threat posed by a powerful bank, the secretary of the treasury's outspoken efforts to woo the rich—all these concerns made Hamilton's opponents fear the rise of an aristocracy in the United States. While Americans did not insist on an equal division of property and wealth, they did cherish the Revolutionary ideal that all individuals were of equal moral worth. They were hostile to arrogance and haughtiness among the upper classes, and to anything that harked back to the aristocratic traditions of Europe. Because Hamilton's program deliberately aided the rich and created a class of citizens whose wealth derived from the federal government, it strengthened these traditional fears. "Money will be put under the direction of government," charged Philip Freneau, a leading Republican editor, "and the government will be put under the direction of money."

Many who opposed Hamilton's financial program had also been against the Constitution, but leadership of the opposition fell to Jefferson and Madison, who had staunchly worked for ratification. The political divisions of 1788 did not survive intact into the 1790s, but Anti-Federalism generally carried over into the emerging Republican party. Although Jefferson and Madison were planters, and well accustomed to the workings of the marketplace, they still distrusted cities and commerce and Hamilton's aristocratic ways.

Economically Hamilton's program was a success. With the government's credit restored, it was able to borrow at home and abroad. The national bank checked the inflation of the previous two decades and created a sound currency. And the government's policies stimulated investment and capitalistic enterprise. At the same time, the administration demonstrated that the federal government would not be paralyzed as it had been under the Articles. Hamilton's theory of implied powers and broad construction gave the nation the flexibility necessary to respond to unanticipated crises.

EXPANSION AND TURMOIL IN THE WEST

Under terms of the peace treaty of 1783, Britain ceded to the United States the territory between the Appalachian Mountains and the Mississippi River. Nevertheless, when the new government began functioning, British troops continued to hold the forts in the Northwest and Indian tribes controlled most of this region. To demonstrate the government's effectiveness, the Washington administration moved to extend control over the West.

The Resistance of the Miamis

In the Treaties of Fort Harmar, made in 1789 with the Iroquois and the Miami Confederacy (composed of eight western tribes headed by the Miami), the United States recognized the rights of Indians to their lands and their right to negotiate as sovereign powers. The government promised that land would be transferred through treaties rather than by separate negotiations of land companies and individual settlers with tribes. Nevertheless, the government was determined to clear Indian titles in order to promote white settlement and to prevent costly wars on the frontier. Recognition of Indian sovereignty was only a tactic to hasten Indian removal.

Although Indian titles to most of Kentucky and about one-quarter of Tennessee had been cleared by 1790, north of the Ohio the Miami Confederacy still blocked white settlement. Standing together, the Miami, Shawnee, and Lenni Lenape refused to make any cessions. The Washington administration decided to resort to force, but the Indians defeated American military expeditions under General Josiah Harmar in 1790 and General Arthur St. Clair in 1791. St. Clair's defeat, in which over 600 soldiers were killed, was particularly devastating. Encouraged by their victory, the Miami Confederacy insisted that peace would be possible only if the United States accepted the Ohio River as the boundary dividing white from Indian lands.

Washington responded by mounting yet another military expedition, this one led by General Anthony Wayne, a hero of the Revolution. Although British officials in the area encouraged Indians to resist American settlement, they refused to come to their allies' aid. Wayne marched an army of 2000 into the Ohio wilderness and at the Battle of Fallen Timbers in August 1794 won a decisive victory, breaking the Indians' hold on the Northwest. In the Treaty of Greenville, negotiated in 1795, Wayne forced the tribes to cede the southern two-thirds of the area between Lake Erie and the Ohio River. No previous Indian cession had been larger, and it opened up the Northwest to white settlement.

The Whiskey Rebellion

Westerners approved of the administration's military policy against the Indians, but they were far less pleased with the enactment in 1791 of a new excise tax on distilled liquors. No other action brought the question of federal power more directly to the attention of the ordinary citizen. Indeed, since Hamilton pushed the whiskey tax precisely to demonstrate the power of the new government, he was almost eager for an outbreak of popular resistance. Farmers in the western districts of several states, especially Pennsylvania, defied federal officials and refused to pay. In the barter economy west of the Appalachians, where barrels of whiskey were sometimes used as currency, about the only way farmers could profitably export surplus grain was to distill it and bring the liquor to market. But Hamilton saw the matter as a question of authority. "Shall there be government, or no government?" he asked.

The West during the 1790s was a society in turmoil. Most property owners

Frontier farmers in Pennsylvania tar and feather a federal tax collector during the Whiskey Rebellion. In response to such acts of violence and defiance, Washington called out the army in 1794. Marching to western Pennsylvania, the troops restored order but found few rebels.

along the frontier found it hard to make ends meet, and a number were forced to sell their land and become tenants on what had been their own property. Thus wealth became more concentrated in the hands of fewer individuals. The whiskey tax was unpopular in many rural areas, but opposition was strongest on the frontier, where residents fiercely resisted any outside control and where the sale of whiskey made the greatest difference in providing poor families with a bit of extra income. Resistance was most pronounced in areas with the greatest number of tenants, who resented the more commercially minded larger landowners of their region. Many of these miserably poor farmers turned out at mass meetings to condemn the tax and protest against having to support government officials and the burdensome national debt. Beset by economic dislocation, they directed their resentment not just at the authorities, but also at wealthy landowners, merchants, and other symbols of an alien urban cosmopolitan culture.

When the protests flared into the Whiskey Rebellion, an alarmed Washington led an army of 13,000 men—larger than he had commanded at Yorktown—into the Pennsylvania countryside to awe the populace and subdue the rebels. He soon returned to Philadelphia, but the zealous Hamilton accompanied the army the entire way to Pittsburgh. To his disappointment the army met no organized resistance; it had to be satisfied with taking 20 prisoners, all obscure men who posed no threat to the government. Two were convicted of treason, but Washington pardoned both since they were mentally incompetent. As Jefferson scoffed, "An insurrection was announced and proclaimed and armed against, but could never be found." Even some of Hamilton's allies conceded that he had overreacted. "Elective rulers can scarcely ever employ the physical force of a democracy," one remarked, "without turning the moral force, or the power of public opinion, against the government."

Pinckney's Treaty

Less controversial was Washington's effort to strengthen the hold on the West by negotiating a treaty with Spain. That nation still controlled Florida and the mouth of the Mississippi and had never agreed to a northern boundary between its possessions and the United States. Increasingly afraid that the United States might form an open alliance with Great Britain, the Spanish government readily agreed to all concessions sought by Washington's emissary, Thomas Pinckney of South Carolina. Pinckney's Treaty set the 31st parallel as the southern boundary of the United States and granted Americans free navigation of the Mississippi, with the right to deposit goods at New Orleans for reshipment to ports in the East and abroad. Not surprisingly, the Senate approved the treaty unanimously in 1796. No longer could Spain try to detach the western settlements from American control by promising to open the Mississippi to their trade.

THE EMERGENCE OF POLITICAL PARTIES

It is ironic that political parties developed in the 1790s, because members of the revolutionary generation fervently hoped that they would not take root in the United States. "If I could not go to heaven but with a party, I would not go at all," remarked Jefferson. Yet the United States was the first nation to establish truly popular parties.

The fear of parties was a heritage of the Revolution and English political thought. Radical English theorists like John Trenchard and Thomas Gordon condemned parties because they divided society, were dominated by narrow special interests, and placed selfishness and party loyalty above a concern for the public welfare. This was a rather accurate portrait of parties in Britain, where personal and factional advantage often outweighed other considerations and many members of Parliament routinely exchanged their votes for offices, pensions, and lucrative contracts. American thinkers differed over whether it was possible to keep parties down permanently, but no influential leader embraced the idea that they were necessary or good.

In an aristocratic society like that of Great Britain, where most common people could not vote, political factions were much freer to pursue their own private interests. But in the United States, if party members hoped to hold office, they had to offer a broad program attractive to a wider constituency. Thus the material contours of American society actually aided the rise of parties. Because property ownership was widely diffused, the nation had a broad suffrage, and the Revolution, by lowering property requirements in many states, had increased the number of voters still further. As representatives of economic and social interest groups, parties were one way a large electorate could make its feelings known. In addition, the United States had the highest literacy rate in the world and the largest number of newspapers, further encouraging political interest and participation. Finally, the fact that well-known patriots of the Revolution ended up in both the Federalist and the Republican camps helped defuse the charge that either party represented continued hostility to the Revolution or the Constitution.

The French Revolution

While domestic issues initially split the supporters of the Constitution, divisions over foreign affairs crystallized the new parties. Since the creation of the Republic, Americans had argued that their mission was to serve as an example to other nations. The American Revolution would be a beacon for the oppressed in other societies. Thus when the French Revolution began in 1789, Americans hailed it as the first stirring of liberty on the European continent. Each new ship from overseas brought exciting news: the Bastille prison had been stormed in July; the new National Assembly had abolished feudal privileges and adopted the Declaration of the Rights of Man. France seemed on the way to establishing its own just society.

By 1793, however, enthusiasm for the French Revolution began to cool, as word came that the king and queen had been executed and that the radical Jacobin party had inaugurated a reign of terror. Some 20,000 French men and women, including many of the nobility and other "enemies" of the Revolution, met their end on the guillotine. The French republic even outlawed Christianity and substituted the worship of Reason. Finally in 1793 republican France and monarchical England went to war. Whether America should continue its old alliance with France or support Great Britain fundamentally divided American politics.

Hamilton and his allies viewed the French Revolution as sheer anarchy. Its mad leaders seemed to be destroying the very institutions that held civilization together: the church, social classes, property, law and order. The United States, Hamilton argued, should renounce the treaty of alliance with France signed in 1778 and side with Britain. Fisher Ames, a congressman from Massachusetts, spoke for the Federalists when he declared: "Behold France, an open hell, still ringing with agonies and blasphemies, still smoking with suffering and crimes, in which we see perhaps our future state." For Jefferson and his followers, the issue was republicanism versus monarchy. France was a sister republic, and despite deplorable excesses, its revolution was spreading the doctrine of liberty. Britain remained repressive and corrupt, presided over by the same tyrannical king who had made war on the colonies. As secretary of state, Jefferson argued that the United States should maintain its treaty of alliance with France and insist that as neutrals, Americans had every right to trade with France as much as with England.

As tempers flared between the two factions, each side suspected the worst of the other. To the Jeffersonians, Hamilton and his friends seemed part of a monarchist conspiracy—"monocrats," they dubbed them. "The ultimate object of all this," Jefferson said of Hamilton's policies, "is to prepare the way for a change, from the present republican forms of Government, to that of a monarchy." As for the Hamiltonians, they viewed Jefferson and his faction as "mobocrats"— domestic agents of an international conspiracy designed to import the subversive doctrines of the French Jacobins. Foreign affairs became a distorting lens through which each party perceived an alternate destiny that threatened the Republic. Years later, when calm reflection was possible, John Adams conceded that both parties had "excited artificial terrors."

Washington's Neutral Course

Although Washington did not actively involve himself in the economic affairs of the government, from the beginning he took a keen interest in foreign affairs. Furthermore, he entered office convinced that the United States must remain independent of Europe and its incessant quarrels and wars. Thus Washington repeatedly tempered Jefferson's efforts to support France.

Under international law, neutrals could trade with belligerents as long as the trade had existed prior to the outbreak of hostilities and did not involve war supplies. Neither France nor Great Britain, however, was willing to respect neutral rights in the midst of their desperate struggle. They began intercepting American ships and confiscating cargoes. In addition, Britain, which badly needed manpower to maintain its powerful navy, impressed into service American sailors it suspected of being British subjects. Despite these abuses, Hamilton still supported a friendly policy toward Britain. Beyond his horror of the French Revolution, he realistically recognized, as did Washington, that the United States was not strong enough to challenge Britain militarily. It therefore needed to maintain commercial ties between the two nations, avoid an open alliance, and gain time for the nation to grow and develop.

In addition, the secretary of the treasury's domestic program depended critically on trade with Britain, which purchased 75 percent of America's exports (mostly foodstuffs and naval supplies), as well as providing 90 percent of imports. The war in Europe stimulated the demand for American grains, drove the price up on the world market, and created unprecedented prosperity in America. During

Typifying the rising party spirit of the 1790s, this anti-Republican cartoon portrays Washington with American troops repulsing an invasion of bloodthirsty French radicals. Jefferson and Citizen Genêt attempt to hold his chariot back, while a dog (presumably an ardent Federalist) sprays a Republican newspaper.

the decade, the total value of American exports increased nearly fourfold. At the same time, American ships almost completely took over the carrying trade between the United States and Europe. All parts of the commercial economy shared in this new prosperity, not only merchants, but also workers and businessmen in the cities, sailors, the shipbuilding industry, and farmers who sold their surplus at high prices in the domestic or European market.

While Hamilton and Jefferson struggled within the cabinet for Washington's support, the arrival in April 1793 of "Citizen" Edmond Genêt, the French minister to America, further muddied the diplomatic waters. As the minister traveled from Charleston to Philadelphia, he was greeted by enthusiastic crowds sympathetic to the French cause. Genêt, a hot-blooded zealot without much of a head on his shoulders, became giddy from the reception. "I live in a round of parties," he boasted to the French government. "Old man Washington can't forgive my success." He embarrassed even Jefferson when he began commissioning American privateers to attack British shipping in the Caribbean and set up courts in American ports, run by French consuls, who officially condemned the seized cargo. Washington, who had already issued a proclamation of American neutrality, angrily demanded the French minister's recall. Genêt's American popularity collapsed, and when a new French government at home called for his arrest, he decided rather hastily to settle in New York rather than return to France and lose his head permanently.

For its part, Great Britain continued to run roughshod over American rights on the high seas and to maintain the garrisons in U.S. western territories that it had promised to evacuate in 1783. In addition, it closed the West Indies, a traditional source of trade, to American ships. In March 1794 Washington appointed John Jay as a special minister to negotiate the differences between the two countries. Unfortunately, Jay had little leverage with which to bargain, and Hamilton undercut his position further by secretly informing the British minister that the United States would take no action regardless of the outcome of Jay's mission. In the end, Jay persuaded the British only to withdraw their troops from the western territories, but the West Indies remained closed to American shipping except under the most restrictive conditions (which the Senate subsequently refused to accept). Britain continued to impress sailors and violate neutral rights. Jay's Treaty, in essence, reinforced the United States' position as an economic satellite of Britain; only reluctantly did Washington submit it to the Senate.

The treaty debate was bitter. Republicans denounced Jay and hung him in effigy, a mob stoned Hamilton in the streets, and Washington testified that the public was agitated "in a higher degree than it has been at any period since the Revolution." At the center were the old Revolutionary fears of an external threat to American independence (whether France or Great Britain) and of an internal threat (either from secret monarchists or subversive democrats). In June 1795, the Senate approved Jay's Treaty by exactly the two-thirds vote required, 20–10.

The Federalists and Republicans Organize

The war in Europe, Jefferson commented, "kindled and brought forward the two parties with an ardour which our own interests merely, could never excite." Like-minded members of Congress had worked together planning strategies and votes almost from the beginning, but by the mid-1790s they were organizing on a national basis. At first, Hamilton had given no thought to forming a party; he intended merely to rally support for the government and his policies. Yet the Federalist party grew naturally out of the voting bloc in Congress that enacted Hamilton's legislative program and, once formally organized, represented an important break with the past. Increasingly, Washington drew closer to Federalist advisers and policies. In effect, he became the symbol of the party, although he clung to the vision of a nonpartisan administration and never recognized the extent to which he had become a party leader.

The guiding genius of the opposition movement was Hamilton's one-time colleague James Madison. Jefferson, who resigned as secretary of state at the end of 1793, became the symbolic head of the party, much as Washington headed the Federalists. But, unconvinced of the wisdom and necessity of such a party, he was reluctant to lead it. Madison acted much more vigorously, conferring over strategy and lining up the Republican voting bloc in the House. The disputes of 1794 and 1795—Jay's Treaty, the whiskey tax—gave the Republicans issues with which to take the offensive, and they began organizing on the state and local levels. Unlike the Federalists, who cloaked themselves in Washington's mantle and claimed to be the upholders of the government and the Constitution, the opposition had to overcome the ingrained idea that an opposition party was seditious and therefore illegitimate. Because of broad support for the Constitution, Republican leaders had to be careful to distinguish between opposing the administration and opposing the Constitution. For in an atmosphere where French revolutionary tribunals routinely overthrew one another and British factions constantly intrigued, it was by no means clear that an opposition party could arise without threatening the very government itself.

As the two parties took shape, voting in Congress became increasingly partisan, with more and more members allying with one faction or the other. In the first two Congresses, party votes occurred mostly on Hamilton's economic program and the organization of the government. In the third and fourth Congresses, party questions included foreign affairs and domestic issues such as western problems and the Whiskey Rebellion. By 1796 even minor matters were debated in party caucuses and decided by partisan votes.

Gradually, party organization filtered downward to local communities. John Beckley, the clerk of the House of Representatives, was a key Republican partisan who took the lead in setting up effective party machinery. In 1796 Beckley managed the Republican campaign in Pennsylvania. In an age when deference remained a central feature of American politics, Beckley recruited prominent residents to endorse the Republican cause, relying on them to distribute political pamphlets and handbills. A shrewd tactician, he secretly sent copies of one Anti-Federalist broadside over primitive mountain trails to circulate in the western part of the state, and only later work its way east, so that the Federalists in Philadelphia would have no time to issue a counterattack. Once party leaders had agreed on a list of presidential electors, Beckley hired express riders to distribute tickets throughout the state. Since voters at the polls had to write out the name of the electors and could not use printed lists, Beckley also instructed local leaders to use friends and family members to write out as many tickets as possible beforehand, to be given to unprepared voters. In a state where only 12,000 votes were cast in the election, he distributed 30,000 electoral tickets and thousands of handbills and addresses. It was an unprecedented effort.

The 1796 Election

As long as Washington remained head of the Federalists, they enjoyed an insurmountable advantage over their opponents. But in 1796 the weary president, stung by the vituperation heaped on him by the opposition press, announced that he would not accept a third term in office. Just as he had refused during the Revolution to assume dictatorial powers, so in 1796 he voluntarily relinquished power, setting a two-term precedent that other presidents would follow until Franklin Roosevelt. In his Farewell Address to his fellow citizens, he warned against the dangers of parties and urged a return to the earlier nonpartisan system. Since the "nonpartisan" system envisioned the Federalists guiding the government, the manifesto amounted to an electioneering tract; still, it voiced Washington's genuine fear of party strife. But that vision had become obsolete: parties were an effective way of expressing the interests of different social and economic groups within the nation. When the Republicans chose Thomas Jefferson to oppose John Adams, the possibility of a nonparty constitutional system disappeared.

The framers of the Constitution did not anticipate that political parties would run competing candidates for both the presidency and the vice presidency. They assumed that, of those running for president, the candidate with the most electoral votes would win and the second highest would become vice president. Hamilton, ever the intriguer, disliked both Adams and Jefferson and tried to manipulate the electoral vote so that the Federalist vice presidential candidate, Thomas Pinckney of South Carolina, would be elected president. Hamilton attempted to persuade several Federalist electors to vote for Pinckney but not Adams; the scheme backfired when some of Adams' supporters learned of the plan and refused to vote for Pinckney. In the ensuing confusion, Adams won with 71 electoral votes, and his rival, Jefferson, gained the vice presidency with 68 votes.

In their constituencies, the two parties reflected basic divisions in American life. Geographically, the Federalists were strongest in New England, with its extensive commercial ties to Great Britain and its powerful tradition of hierarchy and order. Moving farther south, the party became progressively weaker. Of the southernmost states, the Federalists enjoyed significant strength only in aristocratic South Carolina. The Republicans won solid support in subsistence areas like the West, where Crèvecoeur's farmers were only weakly linked to the market. The middle states, with more complicated economic and social divisions, were closely contested, although the most cosmopolitan and commercially oriented elements remained the core of Federalist strength.

The Republicans won over most of the old Anti-Federalist opponents of the Constitution, and their coalition contained some who had firmly backed the new union. These supporters included some commercial farmers in the North and planters in the South and, increasingly, urban workers and small shopkeepers who were repelled by the aristocratic tone of the Federalists. In many communities, especially towns that were rising economically, the Republicans were led by ambitious men of new wealth who felt excluded by the entrenched Federalist elite. For similar reasons, Jefferson attracted the support of immigrants from France and Ireland, who felt culturally excluded, as well as members of religious sects such as the Baptists and Methodists, who resented the power and privileges of New England's established Congregational Church.

Federalist and Republican Ideologies

In different ways, each party was drawn toward certain traditions of the past as well as toward newer social currents that would shape America in the nineteenth century.

Most Federalists viewed themselves as a kind of natural aristocracy making a last desperate stand against the excesses of democracy. They clung to the notion that a nation's political and social leaders should be identical, that the upper class should rule over their social and economic inferiors. In supporting the established social order, most Federalists opposed unbridled individualism. They believed that society's needs took precedence over the individual's and that each class fulfilled a particular role in society. Government should regulate individual behavior for the good of society and protect property from the violent and unruly. Pessimistic in their view of human nature, Federalists were almost obsessed by fear of the "mob." Unthinking and easily manipulated, the masses were dangerous when led by a demagogue who sought power by setting the poor against the rich. In a republic, they argued, popular power had to be restrained, and the role of the people was to choose leaders from society's best men.

Although the Federalists resolutely opposed the rising tide of democracy and individualism, they were remarkably forward-looking in their economic ideas. (Hamilton and his allies here took the lead.) They sensed that the United States would become the major economic and military power of their vision only by prospering through commerce and economic development. To that end, the government ought to use its power not only to protect property, but to actively encourage growth of commerce and manufacturing.

The Republicans, in contrast, viewed Federalist attitudes and policies as evidence of corruption that was eating away at American morals, just as had occurred in England prior to 1776, when Americans finally declared their independence. Thus Republican ideology harked back to the traditional Revolutionary fear that government power threatened liberty, that agriculture had to be dominant over commerce, that wealth and luxury threatened to corrupt the ideals of American society. Over and over Republicans emphasized the threat of corruption: the Treasury was too powerful and was corrupting Congress; the anti–Whiskey Rebellion army would be used to enslave the people; broad construction of the Constitution would make the federal government all-powerful.

Despite their emphasis on agriculture, Republican leaders like Jefferson and Madison recognized that commerce was essential. Yet they were not forward-looking in their economic ideals. The only real need they saw for commerce was to sell America's agricultural surplus abroad; hence they insisted that commercial interests remain secondary to agriculture. When Jefferson considered the merits of developing industry, he instinctively felt republican values would be preserved by limiting it to household manufacturing. And Republicans failed to appreciate the role financiers played in accumulating capital and promoting economic development. Instead, Republicans focused on the abuses of "paper wealth"— speculators, bank directors, stockjobbers, and holders of the public debt.

Whereas the Jeffersonians looked backward in their economic values, rejecting the ideals of urbanization and industrialization that would dominate American society in the nineteenth century, they were more farsighted in matters of equality and personal liberty. Their faith in the people put them much more in tune with the emerging egalitarian temper of society. Eagerly they embraced the virtues of individualism, hoping to reduce government to the bare essentials in order to free individuals to develop to their full potential without interference. And they looked to the West as the means to preserve opportunity and American values.

THE PRESIDENCY OF JOHN ADAMS

As president, John Adams became the nominal head of the Federalists, but in many ways he was out of step with his party. Unlike Hamilton, he felt no pressing need for the government to aid the wealthy, nor was he fully committed to the commercial–industrial vision that Hamilton held. As a crusty revolutionary leader who in the 1780s had served in England as American minister, Adams also opposed any alliance with Britain. Increasingly he and Hamilton clashed, not only over policies but also over party leadership. Part of the problem stemmed from personalities. Adams was so abrasive and thin-skinned, it was difficult for anyone to get along with him, and Hamilton's secret intrigues in the 1796 election had not improved relations between the two men. Although Hamilton had resigned from the Treasury Department in 1795 to practice law in New York City, key members of Adams' cabinet remained loyal to him and turned to him on a regular basis for advice. Indeed, they opposed Adams so often that the frustrated president sometimes dealt with them, according to Jefferson, "by dashing and trampling his wig on the floor." The feud between the two rivals did not bode well for the Federalist party.

John Adams, who believed that pageantry and pomp were essential to government, proposed in 1789 that the president's title be "His Highness the President of the United States and Protector of the Rights of the Same." He wore this sword at his own inauguration in the vain hope that it would lend dignity. Sarcastic Republicans, noting his paunchy figure, gleefully bestowed a title of their own: "His Rotundity."

The Quasi-War with France

Adams began his term trying to balance relations with both Great Britain and France. Since the terms of Jay's Treaty had been so favorable to the British, the French in retaliation set their navy and privateers to raiding U.S. shipping. To resolve the conflict, in 1797 Adams sent three envoys, John Marshall, Charles Cotesworth Pinckney, and Elbridge Gerry, to France. In what became known as the XYZ Affair (because in the official documents the administration substituted the letters X, Y, and Z for the names of the French officials involved), the French minister Talleyrand demanded a personal bribe of $250,000 and a "loan" of $12 million to the French treasury before negotiations could even begin. The American representatives refused and Marshall and Pinckney returned home. When the affair became known, a tremendous public outcry against France ensued.

Confronted with such deeply felt anger, Federalist leaders saw a chance to retain power by exploiting the national emergency and going to war with France. With war fever running high, Congress in 1798 repudiated the French treaty of 1778, authorized 40 ships for a newly created Department of the Navy, and created a new army of 12,500 men. Republicans suspected that the purpose of the army was not to fight the French army—none existed in North America—but to crush the opposition party and establish a military despotism. All that remained was for Adams to whip up popular feeling and lead the nation into war.

But Adams hesitated, afraid he would become a scapegoat if his policies failed. He preferred to have France declare war in order to unite the country solidly behind his leadership. Furthermore, he distrusted standing armies and preferred the navy as the nation's primary defense. So an unofficial naval war broke out—the so-called Quasi-War—as ships in each navy openly and freely raided the fleets of the other, while Britain continued to impress American sailors and seize ships suspected of trading with France.

Believing that war with France offered a solution to all his party's problems, Hamilton took the lead in getting Congress to enlarge the army without Adams' support. Then, when Adams summoned Washington out of retirement to head the American forces, the aged general insisted that Hamilton be his second in command. Since Washington was only a figurehead, Hamilton wielded effective control of the army. He dreamed of seizing Louisiana and Florida, which were held by France's ally Spain, as a way to make the army acceptable to the American people, and even toyed with the idea of marching the army through Virginia in order to provoke resistance and justify suppression of the Republican party. Urging that Virginia be put "to the test of resistance," he disclosed that he was ready to use the army "to subdue a *refractory and powerful State.*"

But Hamilton's hot-headed behavior helped cool Adams' martial ardor. The president delayed accepting enlistments and commissioning officers, and the new army never reached more than a third its authorized size. Moreover, the British defeat of the French fleet in 1798 ended any threat of French invasion. Adams recognized that only in times of crisis could a standing army gain widespread support, and as he caustically observed in 1799, "At present there is no more chance of seeing a French army here than there is in Heaven."

Suppression at Home

Before the threat of war had diminished, however, Federalist leaders attempted to suppress disloyalty at home. In the summer of 1798 Congress passed several measures known together as the Alien and Sedition Acts. The Alien Act authorized the president to arrest and deport aliens suspected of having "treasonable or secret" leanings. Although never used, the act directly threatened nonnaturalized immigrants, many of whom were prominent Jeffersonians. Immigrant voters—again, most of them Republican—were also penalized by the Naturalization Act, which increased from 5 to 14 years the length of residency before a newcomer could become a naturalized citizen. Most controversially, the Sedition Act established heavy fines and even imprisonment for writing, speaking, or publishing anything of "a false, scandalous and malicious" nature against the government or any officer of the government. To cries that such censorship violated the First Amendment's guarantees of freedom of speech and the press, Federalists replied that sedition and libel were not protected by the Constitution.

Because of the heavy-handed way it was enforced, the Sedition Act quickly became a symbol of tyranny. Federalists directed it with single-minded zeal against a number of prominent Republican editors, convicting and imprisoning them. Several Republican papers ceased publication, and the act even brought to justice one unfortunate tippler who had proclaimed his fervent hope that a cannonball might hit the president in his rear. In all, 25 were arrested under the law and 10 convicted and imprisoned, including Matthew Lyon, a Republican member of Congress from Vermont. What would have been an unpopular law in any event became doubly obnoxious because of the partisan fashion in which Federalists used it.

The crisis over the Sedition Act forced Republicans to develop a broader concept of freedom of the press. The prevailing view had been that newspapers ought not to be restrained before publication, but that they could be punished afterward for libel. Jefferson and others now argued that the American government was uniquely based on the free expression of public opinion—not just in elections every two years, but in continuous discussion and debate. Thus criticism of the government was not a sign of criminal intent. Only overtly seditious acts, not opinions, should be subject to prosecution. The courts eventually adopted this view, although once in power the Republicans did not hesitate to prosecute Federalist editors for libel, especially in the state courts. Finally, the Supreme Court settled the issue in *United States v. Hudson and Goodwin* (1812), ruling that there was no such crime as seditious libel under the Constitution. The decision heralded a new and more absolute view of freedom of speech guaranteed by the First Amendment.

Meanwhile, however, the Republican-controlled legislatures of Virginia and Kentucky responded to the crisis of 1798 by each passing a set of resolutions. Written secretly by Madison for Virginia and Jefferson for Kentucky, they formulated the doctrine of state interposition. The Constitution, they claimed, was a compact between sovereign states, which delegated strictly limited powers to the federal government. When the government exceeded those limits and threatened the liberties of citizens, states had the right to interpose their authority. The logical conclusion of this reasoning was that the states, and not the federal courts, had the authority to decide whether the federal government had exceeded its power.

But Jefferson and Madison were not ready to rend a union that had so recently been forged. They hoped the Virginia and Kentucky resolutions would rally public opinion to the Republican cause, but they did not encourage Virginia or Kentucky to resist federal authority by force. And other states openly rejected the doctrine. As the Adams administration came to a close, the Alien Act quietly expired in June 1800 and the Sedition Act in March 1801. Once in power, the Republicans repealed the Naturalization Act.

The Election of 1800

With a naval war raging on the high seas and the Alien and Sedition Acts precipitating a storm at home, Adams suddenly shocked his party by appointing three new commissioners to reopen negotiations with France. It was a courageous act, for Adams not only split his party in two, but also ruined his own chances for reelection by forcing Hamilton's pro-British wing of the party into open opposition. Yet the nation as a whole benefited, for France signed a peace treaty ending its undeclared war. Adams, who bristled with pride and independence, termed this act "the most disinterested, the most determined and the most successful of my whole life."

With the Federalist party split, Republican prospects for 1800 brightened. Again the party chose Jefferson to run against Adams, along with Aaron Burr for vice president. Their efficient party organization coordinated the campaign, subsidizing Republican newspapers, circulating the Virginia and Kentucky resolutions as propaganda, and mobilizing supporters. In contrast, the Federalists' high-handed policies, disdain for the masses, and insensitivity to public opinion doomed them in a republic where the suffrage was so broad. The political journalist Noah Webster put his finger on his fellow Federalists' problem when he said: "They have attempted to resist the force of public opinion, instead of falling into the current with a view to direct it."

Sweeping to victory, the Republicans won control of both houses of Congress for the first time, gaining 40 seats from the Federalists in the House alone. Jefferson outdistanced Adams, 73 electoral votes to 65, although Adams ran ahead of his party and proved more popular with the rank-and-file Federalists and the southern wing of the party. But once again, the election demonstrated the fragility of the fledgling political system. Jefferson and Burr received an equal number of votes, but the Constitution, with no provision for political parties, did not distinguish between the votes for president and vice president. With the election tied, the decision lay with the House of Representatives, where each state was allotted one vote. Since Burr refused to step aside for Jefferson, the election remained deadlocked for almost a week, until the Federalists, who eventually decided that Jefferson represented the lesser of two evils, allowed his election on the thirty-sixth ballot. In 1804 the Twelfth Amendment corrected the problem, specifying that electors were to vote separately for president and vice president.

Political Violence in the Early Republic

It had been a tense moment: the leadership of the Republic hanging on bitter party votes in the House, Federalists willing to chance the unscrupulous Burr to escape "the fangs of Jefferson." Some even swore they would "go without a constitution and take the risk of civil war." Indeed, the hindsight of a later day makes it easy to forget how violent and unpredictable the politics of the 1790s had been.

Some of the violence was physical. Irate crowds roughed up federal marshals who tried to enforce the whiskey tax; Benjamin Bache, the leading Republican newspaper editor in Philadelphia, plunged into a street brawl with his Federalist

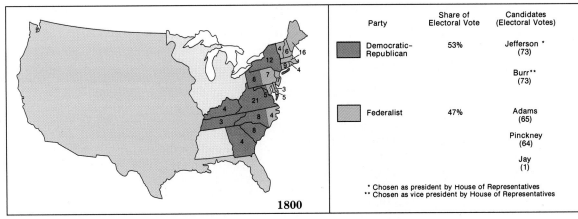

Party	Share of Electoral Vote	Candidates (Electoral Votes)
Democratic-Republican	53%	Jefferson * (73)
		Burr** (64)
Federalist	47%	Adams (65)
		Pinckney (64)
		Jay (1)

* Chosen as president by House of Representatives
** Chosen as vice president by House of Representatives

1800

THE ELECTION OF 1800

rival, John Fenno; Representative Matthew Lyon of Vermont spit in the eye of Representative Roger Griswold of Connecticut, the two of them wrestling on the floor of Congress, going at each other with cane and fire tongs. Mobs threatened the leaders of both parties, and at the height of the crisis of 1798–1799, President John Adams actually smuggled guns into his home for protection. But most of the violence was emotional and rhetorical, as reflected in the era's abusive political language. Republicans accused patriots like Washington and Hamilton of being British agents, tyrants, and monarchists; Federalists portrayed Jefferson as an irreligious Jacobin, and the Republicans as "blood-drinking cannibals." Washington complained that he was abused "in such exaggerated and indecent terms as could scarcely be applied . . . to a common pickpocket." In 1797 Jefferson noted that normally political differences did not extend to social relations, but "it is not so now. Men who have been intimate all their lives, cross the streets to avoid meeting, and turn their heads another way, lest they should be obliged to touch their hats."

What accounts for this remarkable estrangement of the leaders of the Revolution and the amount of violence—both real and rhetorical—in the first decade of the Republic? For one, Federalists and Republicans alike knew how fragile a form of government republicanism had proved over the long course of history. Its repeated failure created grave uncertainty about the American experiment. Then too, the ideology of the American Revolution stressed the need to be on constant guard against conspiracies to subvert liberty. Domestic suspicions were all too quickly magnified by turbulent foreign events, as Federalists perceived threats to the country from the subversive and violent French Revolution, and Republicans detected the age-old corruptions of power and aristocracy in an alliance with the British.

In such overheated circumstances, both Republicans and Federalists readily assumed the worst of one another. In 1798, for example, Washington contended that the Republican party aimed at nothing less than to "change the nature" of the government and "subvert the Constitution." American leaders lacked a satisfactory intellectual framework with which to interpret events of the 1790s. Neither side grasped that in a democracy, political parties were essential institutions, needed to express the differences between social and competing interests and to

Daily Lives

POLITICAL CULTURE

The Rise of "Vile Electioneering"

When George Washington launched the new federal government in 1789, American politics remained a relatively hierarchical affair. Most ordinary citizens deferred to their social "betters," accepting the notion that political leadership belonged to the rich, the educated, and the articulate. Politics was not a full-time profession, and politicians devoted only part of their energies to public life. Nominations, which were the result of deliberations among a handful of leaders, were simply announced in the local press, and elections were decided on a personal rather than a party basis. As a result, most voters did not bother to participate in the political process. In Newburyport, Massachusetts, for example, only 12 percent of the town's eligible voters cast ballots in the 1792 congressional election.

The rise of political parties in the 1790s transformed America's political culture, involving ordinary citizens more than ever before. Previously, competition for voters' support had been limited to the South, where candidates were expected to treat voters to drinks on election day and, in some communities, to stand at the polls soliciting support. But extensive campaigning for weeks before the election was unusual and often condemned.

By 1800, however, "the vile practice of electioneering," as one contemporary termed it, had spread throughout the nation. Since the Jeffersonian Republicans were at first excluded from most avenues of power, they took the lead in electioneering, holding mass meetings at which they dispensed free food and drinks while party leaders addressed the crowd. They arranged so many political barbecues that

Federalist leader Fisher Ames, looking down his aristocratic nose, dismissed Republicans as "ox-eating fools." They also organized campaign committees, furnished written or published ballots in states where these were required, and distributed party propaganda far and wide. On election day, volunteers manning a fleet of vehicles transported supporters to the polls, where party leaders addressed those waiting to vote and had an ample supply of tickets and often liquor on hand.

Believing themselves the natural leaders of society and equating electioneering with corruption, Federalists at first spurned the new techniques as "too degrading." Instead, they tried to stymie Republican electioneering through intimi-

In this detail of an early nineteenth-century painting by Rudolf Krimmel, party workers bring electors to the Philadelphia polls in carriages, while voters argue about candidates and celebrate.

dation. In the 1799 election in New York City, for example, wealthy Federalist merchants warned cartmen that they would be fired if they voted the Republican ticket; and then they stood watch in laboring wards on election day to observe how individuals voted. (Voting by secret ballot did not appear in American politics until after the Civil War.) By 1800, however, a number of Federalists began to electioneer in a frantic effort to keep the despised Jefferson out of the presidency.

The new partisan attitudes spilled over into virtually all areas of daily life. Federalists in Salem, Massachusetts, expelled Republicans from the local dancing club, even though the Republicans came from respected and wealthy families. In commercial centers, Federalists and Republicans established rival banks, rival insurance companies, and even rival wharfs. Party members began attending different churches, hoping in part to hear partisan sermons blasting the opposition. As a result of these agitations, election-day proceedings became much more tumultuous. Even in normally staid Boston, "confusion, wrangling, and even uproar" prevailed as rival organizations distributed their ballots outside the polls.

Both parties developed ingenious methods to swell their vote: they paid the taxes of poorer voters, transferred workers to doubtful districts, and delayed ships' scheduled departures to herd the crews to the polls. In the sharply contested 1800 election, resourceful New Jersey Federalists took advantage of the state's ambiguous election law and beat back the Republican challenge with the votes of wives, daughters, and other women. In Charleston, Federalists handed out specially colored tickets, so that merchants, bankers, and other influential men could be sure of how their employees voted.

The hardest-fought contest in 1800 occurred in New York City. Both parties mounted all-out efforts in the April legislative election, since the legislature would select the presidential electors. For the Republicans, the wily Aaron Burr kept a record on virtually every voter in the city, assigned party members to collect contributions from well-heeled sympathizers, presided over countless strategy sessions, and had party workers plaster the city with handbills. One merchant wrote in his diary: "Col. Burr kept open house for nearly two months, and Committees were in session day and night. . . . Refreshments were always on the table and mattresses for temporary repose in the rooms." The Federalists, led by Alexander Hamilton, overcame their scruples at mixing with the masses and pitched in. "I have not eaten dinner for three days and have been constantly upon my legs from 7 in the morning till 7 in the afternoon," reported one Federalist at the climax of the campaign. Burr's hard work paid off when the Republicans carried New York City by only 250 votes, assuring them of the state's electoral vote. The election of Jefferson in 1800 was truly a party triumph, in which efficient organization paved the way to success.

The American party system had not yet become entirely modern. Politics continued to be a sideline rather than a career for party leaders, and party coalitions depended on networks of friends, relatives, and business associates. A good deal of political activity remained secret, while parties were still looked on with suspicion. Nevertheless, in the decade since the adoption of the Constitution, political culture had been fundamentally transformed.

help resolve them peacefully. Instead, each party considered the other a faction, and therefore illegitimate; and each hoped fervently to reestablish a one-party system. Not until after 1815 did there develop an American political ideology that recognized the necessity of parties and the government's role in promoting economic development.

As John Adams prepared to leave office, he looked back on the 12 years that his Federalist party had held power with mixed feelings. Under Washington's firm leadership and his own, the Federalists had made the Constitution a workable instrument of government. They had proved that republicanism was compatible with stability and order, and they had established economic policies and principles of foreign affairs that even their opponents would continue. The Union had been strengthened, the Constitution accepted, and prosperity had returned. Perhaps those achievements, along with the Revolution's glorious heritage, would be a monument that history would long remember.

But most Federalists took no solace in such reflections. For the forces of history seemed to be running against them. With the world they knew and sought to preserve rapidly disintegrating, they had waged one last desperate battle to save it—and had lost. The champions of order and hierarchy, of government by the well-born, of a society in which social betters guided their respectful inferiors, had been vanquished by the ignorant and unwashed rabble, led by that archdemagogue Thomas Jefferson. Federalists shared fully the view of the British minister, who concluded in 1800 that the entire American political system was "tottering to its foundations."

The great American experiment in republicanism had failed. Of this most Federalists were certain. And surely, if history was any judge, the destruction of liberty and order would soon follow.

SIGNIFICANT EVENTS

1789	First session of Congress; Washington inaugurated president; French Revolution begins; Judiciary Act passed
1790	Funding and assumption approved; Harmar's defeat
1791	Bank of the United States chartered; St. Clair's defeat; first ten amendments (Bill of Rights) ratified
1792	Washington reelected
1793	Execution of Louis XVI; war breaks out between France and England; Washington's Neutrality Proclamation; Genêt Affair
1794	Battle of Fallen Timbers; Whiskey Rebellion
1795	Jay's Treaty ratified; Treaty of Greenville signed
1796	Pinckney's Treaty ratified; first contested presidential election— Adams defeats Jefferson
1798	XYZ Affair; Alien and Sedition Acts passed; Virginia and Kentucky resolutions
1798–1799	Quasi-War with France
1800	Adams sends new mission to France; Jefferson defeats Adams
1801	The House elects Jefferson president

9

The Jeffersonian Republic

 n September 29, 1800, after a long and rocky courtship, Margaret Bayard quietly married Samuel H. Smith. In many ways, there was nothing unusual in their union. Despite religious differences (she was a Presbyterian, he belonged to no church), they had much in common: they were from prominent families, well educated, accustomed to life's comforts, and at ease in society. Still, even though they were second cousins, Margaret's father consented to the marriage only reluctantly, for the Bayards were staunch Federalists, and Smith was an ardent Republican. Indeed, Thomas Jefferson had asked Smith, a Republican editor in Philadelphia, to follow the government to Washington, D.C., and establish a party newspaper in the new capital. After the wedding ceremony, the couple traveled to the new seat of government on the banks of the Potomac River.

The Smiths arrived in the capital in early October. Renting two adjacent buildings, Samuel established a printing office in one, while Margaret set up housekeeping in the other. On the last day of the month, he began publishing the *National Intelligencer*, the first national newspaper in the United States. Servants were scarce and unreliable, so Margaret had to prepare meals for her husband's employees as well as her family. Moreover, Washington was little more than a raw village of 3200 souls, offering few social outlets. Yet thanks to her husband's connections, Margaret soon became acquainted with the nation's political leaders. Her social charm and keen intelligence made her home a center of Washington society.

Predisposed by her upbringing to view Federalists as models of refinement and intelligence, Margaret Smith expected the head of the Republican party to be coarse and vulgar. Instead, when she met Jefferson about a month after her arrival, she found herself captivated by his gracious manners, sparkling conversation, and gentlemanly bearing. Whatever remained of her Federalist sympathies vanished, and she became (perhaps as her father feared) a devoted supporter of the new president.

On March 4, 1801, in eager anticipation, she went to the Senate chamber to witness Jefferson's inauguration. The chamber was packed, but the members of Congress nonetheless reserved one side for the ladies present. To emphasize the change in attitude that the new administration represented, Jefferson walked to the capitol, accompanied by a few government officials and well-wishers, along with a small body of Maryland militia carrying flags and beating drums. Absent

"We have met the enemy and they are ours," reported Captain Oliver Perry after defeating the British on Lake Erie in 1813. His triumph, revealed in this contemporary painting (detail), was celebrated by an increasingly nationalistic citizenry.

were the elaborate ceremonies and flourishes of the Federalists; absent too were the silver-buckled shoes, knee breeches, and wigs that had been the hallmarks of a Revolutionary gentleman. As cannon roared in the background, Jefferson ascended the capitol steps at noon. Since the new president delivered his inaugural address in almost a whisper, few of the assembled crowd heard much of what he said. Then Chief Justice John Marshall, a Virginian but a Federalist whom Jefferson deeply distrusted, administered the oath of office. When the ceremony was over, the new president returned to his lodgings at Conrad and McMunn's boardinghouse, where he declined a place of honor and instead took his accustomed seat at the foot of the table. Only several weeks later did he finally move to his official residence.

As Margaret Smith proudly watched the proceedings, she could not help thinking of the most striking feature of this transfer of power: it was peaceful. "The changes of administration, which in every government and in every age have most generally been epochs of confusion, villainy and bloodshed, in our happy country take place without any species of distraction, or disorder." After the violence of the Revolution, the fierce controversies of the previous decade, and the harsh rhetoric of the election of 1800, the peaceful assumption of power by the opposing party—the first such occurrence in the nation's history—was indeed remarkable.

After the inauguration, Mrs. Smith returned home. A steady stream of visitors called during the day to offer congratulations and celebrate the party's triumph. With a mixture of surprise and pride, she reported that even three Federalists (one her cousin) called and stayed for two hours, drinking tea with members of the other party. With memories still fresh of the heated campaign and the struggle in the House before Jefferson was finally elected, this display of civility was noteworthy. The Republic had weathered a serious trial.

Like Margaret Bayard Smith, the country had shifted its allegiance to the Republican party. The new president's inauguration represented a break with the Federalist past, and once in power, Jefferson ambitiously set out to reshape the government and society in accord with Republican principles. Jefferson later referred to his election as "the Revolution of 1800," asserting that it "was as real a revolution in the principles of our government as that of 1776 was in its form." That statement is an exaggeration, perhaps. But the rule of the Republican party during the following two decades set the nation on a distinctly more democratic tack. And in working out its relationship with Britain and France, as well as with the Indian nations of the West, America achieved a sense of its own nationhood that came only with time and the passing of the Revolutionary generation.

JEFFERSON IN POWER

Thomas Jefferson was the first president to be inaugurated in the new capital of Washington, D.C. In 1791 George Washington had commissioned Pierre Charles L'Enfant, a French architect and engineer who had served in the American Revolution, to draw up plans for the new seat of government. L'Enfant designed a city with broad avenues, statues and fountains, parks and plazas, and a central mall. The capitol building and the president's home dominated L'Enfant's design, with streets radiating out from these and other major buildings and crossing the rectangular pattern of streets at various angles. In keeping with their belief that government was the paramount power in a nation, the Federalists intended that the city would be a new Rome—a cultural, intellectual, and commercial center of the Republic.

The New Capital City

The reality of the new city, however, fell far short of this grandiose dream. The site selected by Washington was located in a swampy river bottom near the head of navigation on the Potomac. The surrounding low-lying hills rendered the spot oppressively hot and muggy during the summer. Removed as it was from the thriving commercial centers of the country, the capital had no business or society independent of the government. Nondescript boardinghouses, where members of Congress and government officials lived when in town, represented the main commercial activity. Cattle roamed the Mall, as they would throughout much of the century. The streets were filled with tree stumps and became impenetrable seas of mud after a rain. Much of the District was covered with woods and virtually all of it remained unoccupied. Residents and visitors boasted of the excellent hunting along the streets and even around the capitol's walls. So undeveloped was the town that in 1801 a group of congressmen returning from a party wandered lost in the woods all night.

When the government moved to its new residence in 1800, the capitol, built on a small hill to emphasize the dominance of the legislative branch in a republic, was not yet finished. The Senate chamber, where Jefferson took the oath of office,

Washington in 1800 barely resembled L'Enfant's grand design. When Jefferson was inaugurated, only one wing of the capitol was completed, and a primitive Pennsylvania Avenue ran more than a mile through the woods to connect it with the unfinished executive mansion.

was the only part of the capitol that had been completed. The executive mansion was unfinished as well, although it had been occupied since November when the Adamses had moved in for the last few months of John Adams' presidency. Except for its classical architecture, the city gave no indication of emulating the great centers of antiquity. A British diplomat grumbled over leaving Philadelphia, the previous capital, with its large population, bustling commerce, regular communication with the outside world, and lively society, to conduct business in "what was . . . scarce any better than a mere swamp."

Yet the isolated and unimpressive capital reflected the new president's attitude toward government. Distrustful of centralized power of any kind, Jefferson deliberately set out to remake the national government into one of limited scope. He took as his ideal precisely what the Federalists had striven to avoid—a government, in Hamilton's words, "at a distance and out of sight," which commanded little popular attention and touched few people's daily lives.

Jefferson's Character

Jefferson himself reflected that vision of modesty. Even standing nearly 6 feet, 3 inches, with red hair now mostly gray, the 57-year-old president lacked an impressive presence. He dressed so carelessly in frequently ill-fitting clothes that William Plumer, a New Hampshire Federalist, mistook him for a servant when he called at the executive mansion. Despite his wealth and genteel birth into Virginia society, Jefferson disliked pomp and maintained an image of republican simplicity. His habit of conducting business in a frayed coat and slippers dismayed dignitaries who called on him decked out in ribbons and lace.

Contemporaries noted his genial disposition. While he wrestled with occasional bouts of despair, he was on the whole an unshakable optimist. "I steer my bark with Hope in the head," he once declared, "leaving fear astern." Although he was a writer of literary elegance, his "soft and gentle" voice made him a poor public speaker, prompting him to send written messages to Congress rather than deliver them in person, as Washington and Adams had done. And he preferred to accomplish his political business in private conversations or at his renowned dinner parties, where he charmed his guests with his easy conversation and informal manners. The normally critical John Qunicy Adams, who eventually abandoned the Federalist party for the Republicans, declared, "You never can be an hour in this man's company without something of the marvelous."

Jefferson's Political Philosophy

Jefferson spelled out his political principles in the Declaration of Independence and his first inaugural address. For him, every person possessed certain inherent natural rights, which he defined as "life, liberty, and the pursuit of happiness." As John Locke had argued, government existed to secure these rights and derived its authority from the consent of the governed. Defending the wisdom of the people, Jefferson considered "the will of the majority" to be "the Natural law of every society" and "the only sure guardian of the rights of man." Although he conceded that the masses might err, he was confident they would soon return to correct principles. His faith in human virtue exceeded that of most of the founding generation, yet in good republican fashion, he feared those in power. Government seemed to Jefferson a necessary evil. Unlike the Federalists, he wanted to free individuals from its economic regulations and incentives and let the market control the distribution of goods and rewards in society.

In Jefferson's vision of the ideal society, agriculture was a morally superior way of life. "Those who labour in the earth are the chosen people of God, if ever he had a chosen people," he wrote in *Notes on the State of Virginia* (1787). Like Crèvecoeur, Jefferson praised rural life for nourishing the values of honesty, independence, and virtue that were essential in a republic. Government would "remain virtuous . . . as long as [the American people] are chiefly agricultural," he assured his associate James Madison. "When they get piled upon one another in large cities, as in Europe, they will become corrupt as in Europe." Rather than encouraging the development of large-scale factories, Jefferson wanted to preserve small household manufacturing, which was an integral part of the rural economy. Commerce should exist primarily to sell America's agricultural surplus. He was never able to overcome his earlier conviction, rooted in the classical republican ideology of the Revolution, that cities and commerce promoted speculation, greed, and useless luxury and self-indulgence.

Jefferson was a product of the Enlightenment, with its faith in the power of human reason to perfect society and decipher the universe. A self-taught architect of considerable merit, he designed the first buildings at the University of Virginia, in which he took a special interest because of his belief in the importance of education. He also submitted a plan for the president's home in the new capital. As an amateur scientist, he kept meticulous records of his observations and farming activities and invented many practical gadgets, including a more efficient plow and a machine that made a copy of his letters to help him carry on his voluminous correspondence. His estate at Monticello reflected his multifaceted interests. The house, which he designed, was built from bricks manufactured on the premises. Its rooms were filled with his inventions, scientific equipment, including a telescope and a set of meteorological instruments (he recorded data for years in hopes of being able to predict the weather), and specimens and artifacts collected from all over the world. His library of 6500 volumes, reputedly the finest in the country, was ultimately purchased by the government and became the nucleus of the Library of Congress.

Although Jefferson asserted that "the tree of liberty must be refreshed from time to time by the blood of patriots and tyrants," his reputation as a radical was undeserved. He did not support universal suffrage, he did not speak out for women's rights, and he did not advocate allowing women to vote. He clung to the traditional republican idea that voters should own property and thus have a stake in society. He proposed to broaden the suffrage, not by abolishing property requirements, which he believed would allow men dependent on others to control elections, but by giving propertyless men 50 acres from the public domain. Such a policy would maintain his cherished agrarian community. After 1790 his once-bold condemnation of slavery grew increasingly mute, and in the last years of his life he rebuked critics of the institution who sought to prevent its expansion westward. One of the largest slaveholders in the country, he treated his slaves indulgently yet took steps to protect his investment by tracking down runaways and, on occasion, selling slaves. Nor did his belief in free speech mean that he rejected the traditional idea that seditious libel was an offense government could prosecute. Although he did not seek to renew the Sedition Act, which had expired with Adams' presidency, Jefferson had no qualms about state governments punishing seditious behavior.

Slaveholding aristocrat and apostle of democracy, lofty theorist and pragmatic politician, Jefferson was an exceedingly complex, and at times contradictory, personality. But like most politicians, he was flexible in his approach to problems and tried to balance ends and means. And like most leaders, he quickly discovered that he confronted very different problems in power than he had in opposition.

Republican Principles

Once Jefferson settled into the executive mansion, he took steps to return the government to the republican ideals of simplicity and frugality. In place of the elaborate presidential receptions held by Washington and Adams, he opened his office to all callers and received them in order of arrival. At social affairs he paid no attention to rank or seniority, much to the discomfort of foreign dignitaries and upper-crust guests left to scramble for places at the table.

When the inaugural address was printed and circulated, it proved to be a carefully crafted work laying out what Jefferson termed "the essential principles of republican government." The states rather than the federal government, he asserted, were "the most competent administrators for our domestic concerns and the surest bulwarks against antirepublican tendencies." He stressed too that the civil authorities must always retain control of the military, long a firm republican conviction. He also affirmed his belief in individualism and a government that would leave people "free to regulate their own pursuits of industry and improvement." Jefferson particularly went out of his way to conciliate the vanquished Federalists. "Though the will of the majority is in all cases to prevail," he concluded, " . . . the minority possess their equal rights, which equal law must protect, and to violate would be oppression." In acknowledgment of Hamilton's fiscal policies, he promised to uphold the government's credit and protect commerce as the "handmaiden" of agriculture. Agreeing with Washington, he proposed friendship with all nations and "entangling alliances" with none. Urging Americans to unite for the common good, he declared, "We have called by different names brethren of the same principles. We are all republicans—we are all federalists."

The election of 1800 established the legitimacy of an opposition party in American politics, and Jefferson, in his inaugural address, seemed to endorse the validity of a party system. In reality, he hoped to restore one-party rule to the country by winning over moderate and honest Federalists and isolating the party's extremists, whom he still attacked as monarchists. "Nothing shall be spared on my part to obliterate the traces of party and consolidate the nation," he pledged, "if it can be done without the abandonment of principle."

Jefferson's Economic Policies

But what would Jefferson do about Hamilton's economic program? As he promised in his inaugural address, Jefferson proceeded to cut spending, reduce the size of the government, and begin paying off the national debt. Unless the debt was paid, he warned Albert Gallatin, his talented secretary of the treasury, "we shall be committed to the English career of debt, corruption and rottenness, closing with revolution." Even though the government was absurdly small by modern standards, with almost no employees other than those in the post office and army and navy, Jefferson considered it much larger than necessary. He abolished the internal taxes enacted by the Federalists, including the notorious tax on whiskey, and thus was able to get rid of all tax collectors and inspectors. "What farmer, what mechanic, what laborer, ever sees a tax gatherer in the United States?" boasted Jefferson in 1805. Land sales and the tariff duties would supply the funds needed to run the government.

The most serious spending cuts were made in the military branches, upon which the Federalists had placed such emphasis. Jefferson slashed the army budget in half, reducing the army to 3000 men stationed in the West. In a national emergency, Jefferson reasoned, the militia would be adequate to defend the country. He reduced the navy to an even greater extent. During the Quasi-War with France, the Federalists had launched a program to strengthen and expand the navy; Jefferson brought this work to a halt and replaced the navy's frigates with a fleet of small gunboats designed to guard the coast. The gunboats captured Jefferson's fancy because they were cheap, but in the long term they proved totally inadequate to defend the nation in war.

By such steps, Jefferson made significant progress toward paying off Hamilton's hated national debt. He lowered it from $83 million to only $57 million by the end of his two terms in office, despite the added financial burden of the Louisiana Purchase. Still, Jefferson did not dismantle entirely the Federalists' economic program. Funding and assumption could not be reversed—the nation's honor was pledged to paying these debts, and Jefferson fully understood the importance of maintaining the nation's credit. The tariff had to be retained as a source of revenue to meet the government's expenses. But more surprising, Jefferson argued that the national bank should be left to run its course until 1811, when its charter would expire. In fact, he actually expanded the bank's operations and began to contend, in words reminiscent of Hamilton, that he favored "making all the banks Republican, by sharing deposits among them in proportion to the [political] dispositions they show." His goal, he confessed to Gallatin, was "to detach the mercantile interest from its enemies and incorporate them into the body of its friends."

In effect, practical politics had triumphed over agrarian economics. "We can never get rid of his [Hamilton's] financial system," Jefferson confessed. "It mortifies me to be strengthening principles which I deem radically vicious, but this vice is entailed on us by the first error." Throughout his presidency, Jefferson frequently put pragmatic considerations above unyielding principles. As he himself expressed it, "What is practicable must often control what is pure theory." Other Republicans were less happy with such compromises. A small, intransigent wing of the party, led by John Randolph and John Taylor, both of Virginia, accused Jefferson of abandoning the principles of strict construction and agrarian virtue that had called the party into being.

John Marshall and Judicial Review

Having lost both the presidency and control of Congress in 1800, the Federalists moved before Jefferson took office to shore up their control of the remaining branch of government by expanding the size of the federal court system. The Judiciary Act of 1801 created 6 circuit courts and 16 new judgeships, along with a number of marshals, attorneys, and clerks. Federalists justified these "midnight appointments" executed by Adams in the last hours of his term on the grounds that the expanding nation required a larger judiciary. Jefferson, however, understandably saw matters differently. "The Federalists, defeated at the polls, have retired into the Judiciary," he fumed, "and from that barricade . . . hope to batter down all the bulwarks of Republicanism." In 1802, by a strict party vote, Congress repealed the 1801 law. Elimination of the new courts left their judges without jobs, prompting Federalists to protest that the action was illegal because the Constitution provided that judges were appointed for life and could be removed from office only for misconduct. The Republicans, determined to bring the judiciary under party control, forged ahead.

Under newly appointed Chief Justice John Marshall, the Supreme Court declined to challenge Congress' action on the courts. But before leaving office Adams had made a number of last-minute appointments, among them William Marbury as justice of the peace for the District of Columbia. When James Madison assumed the office of secretary of state under the new administration, he found a batch of undelivered commissions, including Marbury's. Wishing to appoint a loyal Republican, Jefferson instructed Madison not to hand over these commissions, whereupon Marbury sued under the Judiciary Act of 1789. Since that act gave the Supreme Court original jurisdiction in cases against federal officials, the case of *Marbury v. Madison* went directly to the Court in 1803.

Chief Justice Marshall, himself a Federalist, faced a dilemma. If he persuaded his colleagues to rule in favor of Marbury, Jefferson and Madison would almost certainly defy the Court and badly damage its prestige. On the other hand, a ruling in favor of Madison would amount to conceding that the Court had no legitimate check on the executive branch—a responsibility that Marshall believed the Constitution had clearly given the Court. In writing the majority opinion, the chief justice showed himself to be politically adroit and judicially farsighted. He avoided both pitfalls by ruling against Marbury on technical grounds, while at the same time affirming the Court's greatest power, the right to review statutes and interpret the meaning of the Constitution.

"It is emphatically the province of and duty of the judicial department to say what the law is," he wrote in upholding the doctrine of judicial review. This idea meant that the Court "must of necessity expound and interpret" the Constitution and the laws when one statute conflicted with another or when a law deviated from the Constitution. Marshall found that the section of the Judiciary Act of 1789 that granted the Supreme Court original jurisdiction in the case was unconstitutional. Since the Constitution specified those cases the Court had such jurisdiction over, they could not be enlarged by statute. Thus Marshall was able both to deny Marbury's petition and to assert that the executive branch was not above the law. Jefferson could hardly defy the ruling, since it required no action on his part. *Marbury v. Madison* was so critical to the development of the American constitutional system that it has been called the keystone of the constitutional arch.

Marshall and his colleagues subsequently asserted the power of the Court to review the constitutionality of state laws in *Fletcher v. Peck* (1810) when it struck down a Georgia law. It also brought state courts under the scrutiny of the Supreme Court in *Martin v. Hunter's Lessee* (1816), denying the claim of the Virginia Supreme Court that it was not subject to the authority of the federal judiciary, and in *Cohens v. Virginia* (1821), in which it asserted its right to review decisions of state courts on issues arising under the Constitution. During his tenure on the bench, Marshall extended judicial review to all acts of government. It

John Marshall.

took time for the doctrine to be accepted, but since Marshall's time the Supreme Court has successfully defended its position as the final arbiter of the meaning of the Constitution.

The Jeffersonian Attack on the Judiciary

Having disposed of Adams' last-minute appointments, the Republicans proceeded to attack Federalist judges who had been particularly obnoxious during the party battles of the 1790s. Jefferson argued that impeachment was not limited to criminal acts but was an appropriate political device to remove any judge who was unacceptable to two-thirds of the Senate. That, he claimed, would make the judiciary responsive to the public will. The administration began by seeking to remove John Pickering of New Hampshire, a federal district judge. Pickering, who was both insane and an alcoholic, had delivered rambling tirades against the Republican party from the bench. In 1803, after the House had impeached him, he was convicted and removed by the Senate.

Encouraged by this success, the administration turned its attention to Associate Justice Samuel Chase of the Supreme Court. An ultra-Federalist, Chase had interpreted the Sedition Act in a blatantly partisan fashion to ensure convictions against Republicans. In continuing their attack, Jefferson and his advisers ignored the uneasiness of some Republicans over using the impeachment process to remove judges who had committed no crime but merely held opinions opposed to those of the party in power. The House impeached Chase on political charges, but in the Senate trial his lawyers argued that impeachment was limited to indictable offenses. While acknowledging that Chase had perhaps been indiscreet, they claimed he had committed no crime. A majority of senators voted to convict, but since a two-thirds vote was necessary for removal, Chase was acquitted. A number of Republican senators refused to expand the meaning of impeachment to include political transgressions.

In the end, even Jefferson, who believed the trial had been mismanaged, accepted Chase's acquittal without protest. Republicans decided to wait for death and retirement to give them eventual control of the remaining branch of the government through presidential appointments.

JEFFERSON AND WESTERN EXPANSION

The Federalists feared the West as a threat to social order and stability. Thus when they passed an act in 1796 authorizing the sale of federal land, they regarded it as a revenue measure rather than the means to develop the country and kept the price of land high. It sold for a minimum of $2 an acre, with a required purchase of at least 640 acres, over four times the size of the typical American farm. Jefferson and the Republicans, on the other hand, viewed the West as the means to preserve the values of an agrarian republic. In 1801, the Republican Congress reduced the minimum purchase to 320 acres and established a four-year credit system to pay. The intention was to encourage rapid settlement of the interior, and in fact land sales boomed under the new law. Most of the sales, however, were to speculators and land companies rather than individual settlers.

Jefferson realized that as settled regions of the country became crowded, the excess population would seek opportunity elsewhere. Without fresh, cheap land to the west, many rural residents would migrate to the cities in search of work. Such a development, he believed, would be a calamity for the security of an agrarian republic, since western society evidenced a greater degree of equality in day-to-day affairs. Wealth and property were more widely distributed than in the East, where urbanization and commercial development led to a growing concentration of wealth. America's vast spaces provided land that would last for a thousand generations, Jefferson predicted in his inaugural, enough to transform the United States into "an empire of liberty." Moreover, the West was overwhelmingly Republican, and thus the admission of each new state would also strengthen his party and hasten the demise of the Federalists. From the Jeffersonian perspective, western expansion was a blessing economically, socially, and politically.

The Louisiana Purchase

Jefferson recognized the importance of the Mississippi River to western interests. Because Spain's New World empire was disintegrating, Americans were confident that before long they would gain control of Florida and of the rest of the Mississippi, either through purchase or military occupation.

This comforting prospect was shattered, however, when Spain secretly ceded Louisiana, which encompassed the territory between the Mississippi River and the Rocky Mountains, to France. That nation had emerged from the convulsions of revolution led by a bold young military commander, Napoleon Bonaparte. Under his rule, France had become the most powerful nation on the European continent, with the military might to protect its new colony and block American expansion. American anxiety intensified when Spain, while still in control of Louisiana, suddenly revoked Americans' right to navigate the lower Mississippi guaranteed by Pinckney's Treaty (page 282). Americans believed (incorrectly, it turned out) that Spain had acted at the behest of France. Western farmers, who were thus denied access to the sea, angrily protested Spain's high-handed action. If this were not enough, word came that Spanish officials, dangling the bait of access to the Mississippi, were intriguing again with American settlers in the West to detach the region from the United States.

Jefferson saw that if he could buy New Orleans and West Florida from the French, the United States would gain control of the entire Mississippi. He dispatched James Monroe to Paris to join Robert Livingston, the American minister, in negotiations. "There is on the globe one single spot, the possession [i.e., possessor] of which is our natural and habitual enemy," Jefferson reminded them. "It is New Orleans." Should they fail to acquire the city, he instructed them to seek an alliance with Great Britain, whose navy offered the only possible protection. "The day that France takes New Orleans, we must marry ourselves to the British fleet and nation," he observed with a notable lack of enthusiasm.

In the meantime, however, Napoleon lost interest in Louisiana. He had intended to use the region to feed the slaves on the sugar-rich island of Santo Domingo (Haiti), but a military expedition to reestablish French control ended in disaster. Furthermore, with war looming again in Europe, he desperately needed money, so in April 1803 he offered to sell not just New Orleans, but all of Louisiana to the United States. This proposal flabbergasted Livingston and Monroe. Their instructions said nothing about acquiring all of Louisiana; and they certainly had not been authorized to spend what the French demanded. On the other hand, here was an unprecedented opportunity to dramatically expand the boundaries of the United States. Pressed for an immediate answer, Livingston and Monroe wanted to consult Jefferson but worried that the French might withdraw the offer as suddenly as they had made it. So the American ministers haggled over a few details, took a deep breath, and agreed to purchase Louisiana for approximately $15 million. Striking one of the most extraordinary bargains in the history of the United States, they had doubled its size by adding some 830,000 square miles.

Such was Talleyrand's haste to conclude the agreement that the boundaries of Louisiana were not even specified. When Livingston pointed out this omission, the opportunistic French foreign minister characteristically replied, "You have made a noble bargain for yourselves, and I suppose you will make the most of it." The millions of acres of fertile farmland, untold natural resources, and control of the vital Mississippi River and its tributaries were indeed a noble bargain, and Livingston recognized it. "From this day," he asserted, "the United States take their place among the powers of the first rank."

Jefferson, naturally, was immensely pleased at the prospect of acquiring so much territory, which seemed to guarantee the survival of his agrarian republic. At the same time, he found the legality of the act deeply troubling. He himself had set forth the doctrine of strict construction in the Kentucky resolutions of 1798, and clearly, the Constitution did not specifically authorize the acquisition of territory by treaty. Jefferson went so far as to draw up a constitutional amendment authorizing the acquisition of Louisiana, but ratification would take time, and Livingston and Monroe urged haste. In the end, Jefferson sent the treaty to the Senate for ratification, noting privately, "The less we say about constitutional difficulties the better." Once again pragmatism had triumphed over theory in Jefferson's presidency. His desire for an agrarian empire of liberty took precedence over his states' rights principles.

The Louisiana Purchase was generally popular, even in Federalist New England. The Senate ratified the treaty 24–7 and Congress appropriated the necessary funds. West Florida, which bordered part of the lower Mississippi, remained in Spanish hands, and Jefferson's efforts to acquire this region, either by threats or by purchase, were unsuccessful. Nevertheless, western commerce could flow down the Mississippi unimpeded to the sea. The Louisiana Purchase would rank as the greatest achievement of Jefferson's presidency.

Lewis and Clark

As early as the 1780s Jefferson's interest in the West had led him to propose an expedition to California. The project had never gotten off the ground, but early in 1803, even before the Louisiana Purchase was completed, Congress secretly appropriated $2500 to send an exploring party up the Missouri River to the Pacific. To head this expedition, Jefferson selected his private secretary, Meriwether Lewis, a Virginian who had served in the army in the West and who was an acute and knowledgeable observer. Lewis selected William Clark, a younger brother of Revolutionary War hero George Rogers Clark, as co-commander.

Jefferson instructed Lewis and Clark to map the region and make detailed observations concerning the soil, climate, rivers, minerals, and plant and animal life. They were also to investigate the feasibility of an overland route to the Pacific, particularly whether the Missouri River "may offer the most direct and practicable water communication across this continent for the purposes of commerce." When the Spanish minister inquired about the purposes of the expedition (once across the Rockies, it would be in Spanish territory), Jefferson blandly informed him they were solely geographic. But in truth, he hoped also to engage in diplomacy with the Indians in the West and assure them of the United States' friendship (and weaken their ties to Spain). Equally important, by pushing onward to the Pacific, Lewis and Clark would strengthen the American title to Oregon, which several nations claimed but none effectively occupied.

In the spring of 1804, Lewis and Clark, accompanied by 48 men, embarked from near St. Louis. They laboriously pushed their boats up the Missouri River to present-day North Dakota, where they spent the winter with the Mandans. The next spring, they headed west again. In their difficult trek over the Rockies, they were aided by a French-Canadian trader and his wife Sacajawea, a member of the Shoshone tribe who served as guide and interpreter in dealing with various Indian peoples. Only with great difficulty did the expedition get through the rugged mountains ahead of the winter snows. Having crossed the Continental Divide, the party floated down first the Snake and then the Columbia River to the Pacific.

EXPLORATION AND EXPANSION: THE LOUISIANA PURCHASE
The vast, largely uncharted Louisiana Purchase lay well beyond the most densely populated areas of the United States. The Lewis and Clark expedition along with Lieutenant Zebulon Pike's exploration of the upper Mississippi River and the Southwest opened the way for westward expansion.

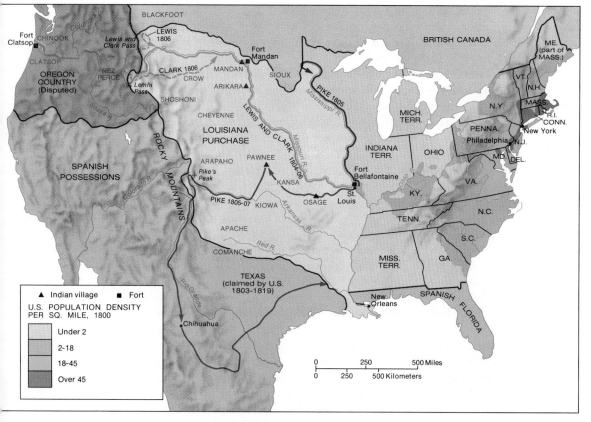

After spending a bleak winter in Oregon, vainly waiting for a ship that would take them back, the company returned in 1806 over the Rockies. Having traveled across half the continent in both directions, navigated countless rapids, and conducted negotiations with numerous tribes, Lewis and Clark arrived in St. Louis in September, two and a half years after they had departed. The expedition fired the imagination of Americans about the exotic lands of the newly acquired Louisiana Purchase, as well as the Pacific Northwest. Lewis and Clark had collected thousands of useful plant and animal specimens (for a time, two grizzly bear cubs they had captured were kept on the grounds of the White House). They discovered several passes through the Rockies and produced a remarkably accurate map, their most valuable contribution to western exploration.

WHITES AND INDIANS ON THE FRONTIER

In their trek across the continent, Lewis and Clark fought only one skirmish with Indians. The expedition's dealings remained peaceful partly through vigilance and caution, but also because a small party of whites hardly threatened the Indians living west of the Mississippi. The situation was different farther east, where for some years settlers had been streaming through the passes and into the fertile lands of the Ohio River valley. Whereas in 1790 only about 100,000 whites lived in the West, by 1800 that number had jumped to almost 400,000, and a decade later, to over a million. By 1820 more than 2 million whites lived in a region they had first entered only 50 years earlier.

In this backcountry, where white and Indian cultures mixed and often clashed, both peoples experienced the breakdown of their own traditional cultural systems. White immigrants pushing into Indian territory often lacked the structures of community such as churches, schools, and legal institutions. Indians, for their part, were attracted to some elements of white culture, such as the benefits of trade goods. But whites, with their unceasing hunger for Indian land, their more settled agricultural ways, domesticated animals, and fenced-in fields, placed severe stress on Indian cultures.

The Course of White Penetration

Following the Treaty of Greenville (page 280), white settlers poured into the Ohio Territory. Travelers were amazed at the number of people heading west by wagon and flatboat. "From what I have seen and heard," one girl wrote while crossing Pennsylvania bound for the West, "I think the State of Ohio will be well fill'd before winter,—Waggons without number, every day go on." The pattern of settlement remained the same: in the first wave came backwoods families who laboriously cleared a few acres of forest by girding the trees, removing the brush, and planting corn between the dead trunks. Their isolated one-room log cabins were crude, dark, and windowless, with mud stuffed between the chinks, the furniture and utensils sparse and homemade. Such settlers were mostly squatters, without legal title to their land, depending largely on their own resources. As a region began to fill up these incurably restless pioneers usually sold their improvements and headed west again.

The waves of settlement that followed were more permanent. These men and women completed the work of clearing the land and improving a farm. Many were young unmarried men who left crowded regions in the East seeking new opportunities. Their migration, which relieved population pressures back home, contributed to the imbalance of males and females on the frontier. Once established, they quickly married and started families. Like the pioneers before them, most engaged in semisubsistence agriculture; as their numbers increased and a local market developed, they switched to surplus agriculture, growing and making much of what the family needed while selling or exchanging the surplus to obtain essential items. "The woman told me that they spun and wove all the cotton and woollen garments of the family, and knit all the stockings," a visitor to an Ohio farm wrote. "Her husband, though not a shoemaker by trade, made all the shoes. She manufactured all the soap and candles they used." The wife sold butter and chickens to get money to buy coffee, tea, and whiskey.

The Second Great Awakening

It was the most sparsely settled regions that became famous for a second wave of revivals that swept across the nation beginning in the 1790s. Like the first national outpouring of religious concern 50 years earlier, the Second Great Awakening was not limited to the frontier. Revivals flourished among Congregationalists in New England and Presbyterians in central New York and Pennsylvania. They roused young students at college campuses like Hampden-Sydney and Washington College in Virginia (1787) and at Yale in Connecticut (1802). But even in the East, there was widespread concern that the newer, less developed areas of the country needed religion most. Beginning in 1798 the Congregationalists set up a missionary society to send ministers westward, and the Baptists and Presbyterians quickly followed suit.

The Methodists, however, had the most effective organization for spreading the gospel in remote areas. As soon as a district could be organized, a devout "circuit rider"—not necessarily a minister—would be appointed to travel the countryside, stopping at isolated cabins, handing out tracts, and preaching to small groups anywhere he could. One competing Presbyterian missionary ruefully noted that "into every hovel I entered I learned that the Methodist missionary had been there before me." It became common wisdom among country folk that when blizzards or thunderstorms were especially severe, "nobody was out but crows and Methodist preachers."

In June 1800 three Presbyterian ministers and a Methodist held an especially successful four-day meeting along the Red River in Kentucky. The audience, moved to tears by their sins and the prospect of eternal life, began to fall to the ground and shriek for mercy as John McGee, the Methodist preacher, begged them to "let the Lord Omnipotent reign in their hearts." News of the meeting spread quickly; several more meetings were held in the area during the summer, and people came from 50 and 100 miles around, camping in makeshift tents and holding services out of doors. This new form of worship, the camp meeting, reached its climax at Cane Ridge, Kentucky, in August 1801. At a time when the largest city in the state had only 2000 people, over 10,000 gathered for a week to hear dozens of ministers.

Men and women earnestly examined their hearts; scoffers came, half-mocking, half-fearful of what they might see. For rural folk accustomed to going to bed

Although the clergy at camp meetings were male, women played prominent roles, often pressing husbands to convert. The audience here is predominantly female, including those sitting on the "anxious bench" below the preacher.

soon after dark, the sight of hundreds of campfires flickering throughout the woods far into the night, reinforced by the endless singing, praying, and crying, was a powerful tonic indeed. "The vast sea of human beings seemed to be agitated as if by storm," recalled one skeptic, who himself was converted at Cane Ridge. "I counted seven ministers all preaching at once. . . . Some of the people were singing, others praying, some crying for mercy in the most piteous accents. . . . At one time I saw at least 500 swept down in a moment as if a battery of a thousand guns had been opened upon them, and then immediately followed shrieks and shouts that rent the very heavens." In the overwhelming emotion of the moment, converts might dance, bark, laugh hysterically, or jerk uncontrollably, hair flying, the whole body shaking, as they sought to gain assurance of their salvation.

In the South, blacks, including slaves, attended camp meetings and enthusiastically participated in the tumultuous services. Indeed, revivals were a major force in spreading Christianity to African-Americans and producing slave conversions. Revivalists' clear and vivid speech, their acceptance of the moral worth of every individual regardless of race, and their emphasis on the conversion experience rather than the forms of religion and abstract theology had the same appeal to blacks, who had little formal schooling, as it did to poorly educated whites. Blacks worshiped separately from and sometimes together with whites. The revivals also produced black preachers, who exhorted whites as well as blacks. Some slaveholders, especially in eastern plantation districts, worried that camp meetings might foster racial egalitarianism, but revivalists concentrated on bringing slaves to Christ rather than questioning society's institutions. As with whites, the Baptist and Methodist churches received the bulk of African-American converts.

The revivals quickly found critics, who decried the emotionalism and hysteria they produced. For a time Presbyterians and Baptists withdrew from camp meetings, leaving the field to the more enthusiastic Methodists. But as the country became more settled, even the Methodists took pains to set well-defined limits on camp meeting revivals. They restricted admittance, patrolled the grounds, and attempted to maintain a sober atmosphere.

Daily Lives

PUBLIC SPACE/PRIVATE SPACE

The Frontier Camp Meeting

The Cane Ridge revival, one of the earliest along the frontier, was a chaotic and disorganized affair. But as western clergy became more experienced with outdoor camp meetings, they standardized the format. About a week in advance, organizers chose a forest clearing, removed nearby underbrush, erected pulpits, and constructed benches for the worshipers. Usually the camp went up near an established church, which provided lodging for the ministers. Since an adequate water supply was essential, camps were located near springs, creeks, or rivers. Being near a navigable river also improved access to the meeting. A good site needed dry ground, shade so worshipers could escape the blazing sun, pasturage for the horses, and wood for tent poles and fuel.

The meeting site might be laid out in a horseshoe, a rectangle, or, most popularly, a broad circle. But in each case the tents of the worshipers formed a ring around the outdoor auditorium where services were held. As participants began to arrive, a supervisor directed drivers where to park carriages or wagons, tether animals, and pitch tents. At a large meeting, where as many as 200 tents covered the site, they were set up in several rows with streets in between to allow easy access. To help people find their lodgings, the streets were sometimes even named. This outer perimeter constituted the meeting's private spaces. Here, beneath tents of sailcloth or even shelters patched together from old blankets and sheets, individuals could withdraw from the larger group to find relative solitude, cook meals in front of campfires, and sleep on rude beds of straw or simply on the ground. Often several families shared a tent.

Worshipers were naturally drawn toward the central public space, where they filled bench after bench at the periodic call of a bugle. Few would have been inclined to fall asleep at such meetings, but the benches made it difficult to do so, for unlike most church pews they had no backs. Rising above the listeners, at one or both ends of the clearing, stood the preachers' pulpit. Sometimes it was merely a 10-foot-square platform on stilts, other times it was more elaborate, with several levels and a roof. Services were held in the open, where neither rain nor thunderstorms would interrupt them. At night time, the dancing light and shadows produced by the candles, torches, campfires, and fire altars (earthen covered platforms) at each corner created a spectacular effect and heightened the feeling of awe.

The democracy of the frontier did not automatically break down customary social constraints. For reasons of authority as well as practicality, the ministers' pulpit rose above the congregation. And the audience itself was segregated: women were seated on one side of the clearing, men on the other. In the South, blacks who attended camp meetings were relegated to an area behind the pulpit, where they set up their own camp and conducted their own services.

Since the avowed purpose of camp meetings was to "revive" religion and produce an alteration in listeners' hearts, the meeting site provided what was known as an "anxious bench" for those whose souls struggled in the agony of conversion. Several rows of planks were set aside for such "mourners," directly in front of the pulpit. Thus the design of the space focused the attention of both the congregation and the

Daily Lives

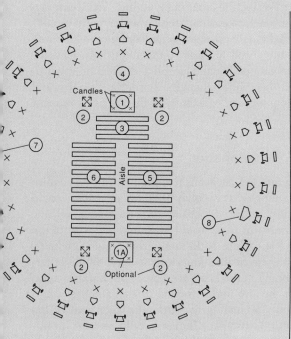

CODE

× Cooking fires–illumination also from candles in trees
△ Tents
🛏 Wagons
▱ Horses
1. Speakers' stand–candles for illumination
2. Earthen covered fire platforms
3. Mourners' bench
4. Blacks' worship area
5. Seats–women's side
6. Seats–men's side
7. Preachers' tent
8. Boarding tent

Source: Adapted from Charles A. Johnson, *The Frontier Camp Meeting: Religion's Harvest Time* (Dallas: SMU Press, 1955), pp. 43 and 47.

near the anxious benches. (Again, curtains separated the male and female sections, and blacks had their own mourning tents.)

But the demarcations between public and private, male and female, and even black and white could be broken down. As excitement grew, several services might be held simultaneously, some people praying, others singing, shouting, or listening to ministers who stood on wagons or makeshift platforms of felled trees. And when formal services ended, men and women often continued singing and exhorting in small groups, going into the woods to pray, and searching one another's souls by campfires late into the night. Indeed, the social mixing and spontaneous excitement were great enough that meeting sponsors quickly learned that supervision was necessary to prevent unseemly activities. The nearby forest, the many tents, and nightfall all offered temptations for drinking, carousing, or lovemaking. Official patrols regularly investigated suspicious activities and monitored sleeping arrangements.

On the final day whites and blacks would join together in a singing and marching festival before disbanding to their more humdrum daily routines. Successful camp meetings depended on more than the talents of the clergy and the enthusiasm of participants. In their layout they were carefully planned and regulated communities in the forest, designed to reduce the distance between public and private space and thereby instill a sense of religion in all of the activities that took place in the meeting, as well as those that would be resumed in the regular world.

ministers on the mourners, who were exhorted and prayed over in hopes that they would receive a new birth in Christ. Sometimes the anxious bench became so crowded with the stricken that they could hardly move. As camp meetings became increasingly organized, separate mourning tents were set up on the edge of the arena

Revivals like Cane Ridge provided an emotional release from the hard and isolated life on the frontier. For a moment, pioneers could forget the drabness and squalor of their lives, the pains and sorrows they endured as they struggled to carve an existence out of the forest. For families that enjoyed little social interaction with others, revivals offered a chance to participate in a wider social gathering, to renew old friendships and make new ones, while relieving pent-up emotions. For those at the bottom of the social hierarchy, the revivalists' message emphasized an individual's ability to gain personal triumph and salvation, regardless of his or her station in life. In the swiftly changing borderlands north and south of the Ohio River, where society seemed constantly in flux, revivals brought a sense of uplift and comfort.

Black Hoof and the Choice of Assimilation

As white settlers continued to pour into the backcountry, the pressure to acquire Indian lands increased. Jefferson endorsed the policy that Indian tribes would either have to assimilate into American culture by abandoning their seminomadic hunting practices and becoming farmers or they would have to move west of the Mississippi River. There, isolated from white settlement, they could gradually develop the skills and values necessary to fit into American society. While Jefferson defended these alternatives as being in the best interests of the Indians, since otherwise they faced extermination, he also understood that such a policy would conveniently enable the government to clear Indian titles to lands east of the Mississippi. By adopting an agricultural existence, Indians would be able "to live on smaller portions of land," he noted, adding, "While they are learning to do better on less land, our increasing numbers will be calling for more land." And call they did. Between 1800 and 1810 whites pressed Indians into ceding more than 100 million acres in the Ohio River valley.

The hard truth about white policies toward the Indians was that however enlightened individuals might be, the demographic pressure of high birth rates and aggressive expansion ensured conflict between the two cultures. Anglo-Americans—whether Crèvecoeur's yeoman farmers or Franklin's commercial traders or devout Methodist circuit riders—never doubted the superiority of their ways. As William Henry Harrison, governor of the new Indiana Territory, confessed in 1801, "A great many of the Inhabitants of the Fronteers consider the murdering of the Indians in the highest degree meritorious." And even a student of the Enlightenment like Jefferson could become cynical. Corresponding with Harrison, he encouraged the policy of selling goods on credit, in order to lure Indians into debt. "When these debts get beyond what the individuals can pay," the president observed, "they become willing to lop them off by a cession of

---

THE INDIAN RESPONSE TO WHITE ENCROACHMENT
With land cessions and white western migration placing increased pressure on Indian cultures after 1790, news of the Prophet's revival fell on eager ears. It spread especially quickly northward along the shores of Lake Michigan and westward along Lake Superior and the interior of Wisconsin. Following the Battle of Tippecanoe, Tecumseh eclipsed the Prophet as the major leader of Indian resistance, but his trips South to forge political alliances met with less success.

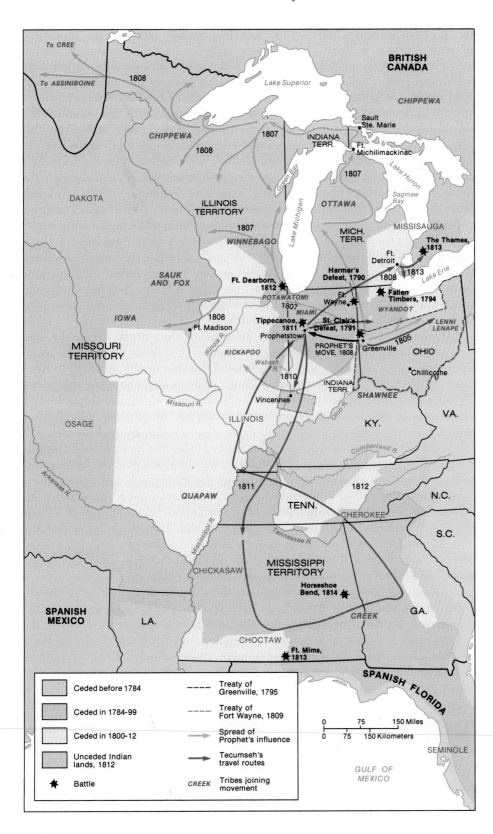

To CREE

To ASSINIBOINE

BRITISH
CANADA

1808

Lake Superior

CHIPPEWA

Sault
Ste. Marie

1807   INDIANA
TERR.

Ft.
Michilimackinac

CHIPPEWA

1808

Green Bay

1807

DAKOTA

ILLINOIS
TERRITORY

Lake Huron

Saginaw
Bay

OTTAWA

MISSISAUGA

1807

WINNEBAGO

Lake Michigan

MICH.
TERR.

Ft.
Detroit

The Thames,
1813

SAUK
AND FOX

Ft. Dearborn,
1812

Harmar's
Defeat, 1790

1808

1813

Lake Erie

POTAWATOMI

Ft.
Wayne

Fallen
Timbers, 1794

IOWA

1808

1807

MIAMI

WYANDOT

MISSOURI
TERRITORY

Ft. Madison

Tippecanoe,
1811

Prophetstown

St. Clair's
Defeat, 1791

LENNI
LENAPE

Illinois R.

KICKAPOO

PROPHET'S
MOVE, 1808

Greenville

1805

OHIO

Wabash R.

1810

INDIANA
TERR.

Chillicothe

Missouri R.

Vincennes

SHAWNEE

VA.

OSAGE

ILLINOIS

Ohio R.

KY.

Cumberland R.

Arkansas R.

1811

1812

N.C.

QUAPAW

TENN.

CHEROKEE

S.C.

Mississippi R.

Tennessee R.

SPANISH
MEXICO

LA.

MISSISSIPPI
TERRITORY

Horseshoe
Bend, 1814

CREEK

GA.

CHICKASAW

CHOCTAW

Ft. Mims,
1813

SPANISH FLORIDA

	Ceded before 1784	- - -	Treaty of Greenville, 1795
	Ceded in 1784-99	- - -	Treaty of Fort Wayne, 1809
	Ceded in 1800-12	→	Spread of Prophet's influence
	Unceded Indian lands, 1812	→	Tecumseh's travel routes
★	Battle	CREEK	Tribes joining movement

0   75   150 Miles
0   75   150 Kilometers

SEMINOLE

GULF OF
MEXICO

lands." Such were the rationalizations of the man who hoped to spread a white agrarian "empire of liberty" westward.

The loss of so much land to white settlement had a devastating effect on traditional Indian cultures by reducing hunting grounds and making game and food scarce. "Stop your people from killing our game," the Shawnees complained in 1802 to federal Indian agents. "At present they kill more than we do. They would be angry if we were to kill a cow or hog of theirs, the little game that remains is very dear to us." Tribes also became dependent on white trade to obtain blankets, guns, metal utensils, alcohol, and decorative beads. To pay for these goods with furs, Indians often overtrapped, which forced them to invade the lands of neighboring tribes, provoking wars. The debilitating effects of alcohol were especially marked during these years. Indians turned to alcohol as a means of coping with cultural stress, and increased production in white backcountry settlements during the 1790s and early 1800s made whiskey readily available. Technological advances in the design of small stills made distilling corn much easier and by far the most profitable way to market surplus grain.* Indeed, during these years, white consumption of alcohol was also rising, a symptom of the adjustment of white society to urban and industrial stresses which the temperance movement of the 1820s and 1830s attempted to deal with.

Among the Shawnees in the Ohio River valley, the cultural stresses brought about by white expansion led to alcoholism, growing violence among tribe members, family disintegration, and the collapse of the clan system designed to regulate relations among different villages. These problems might have been alleviated by separating from white culture, but the Shawnees had become dependent on trade for articles they could not produce themselves. The question of how to deal with the encroaching white culture became a matter of anguished debate.

Chief Black Hoof, one signer of the Treaty of Greenville, embraced assimilation, hoping to help his people adapt to white ways. He accepted the treaty provisions ceding some Shawnee lands in exchange for trade goods and a government annuity and traveled to Washington in 1801 to request a deed guaranteeing his people the remaining Shawnee lands in western Ohio, where they would "raise good Grain and cut Hay for our Cattle" as whites did. The astonished secretary of war, Henry Dearborn, refused to provide any deed (Jefferson, after all, wanted *Indians* to cede land, not whites); but he promised "ploughs and other useful tools." So a group of Shawnees settled in permanent villages in the Auglaize River valley, built log houses, wore garments like those of whites, and, aided by government officials and Quaker missionaries, took up agriculture. For several years the experiment appeared promising, but after the government refused to pay the federal agent who had been providing technical support, Black Hoof's followers became discouraged. As their independence steadily eroded and they became more dependent on their government annuities, even Black Hoof admitted, "The white people has spoiled us. They have been our ruin."

The Prophet, Tecumseh, and the Pan-Indian Movement

Other Shawnees decided not to adopt white ways, but to revitalize their culture by severing all ties with the white world. In such efforts, Indian religion often

*From 1802 to 1815 the federal government issued more than 100 patents for distilling devices, more than 5 percent of all patents granted during these years.

played a central role. During the 1790s a revival of religious fervor led by Handsome Lake took hold among the Iroquois, following the loss of most of the Iroquois lands and the collapse of their military power in western New York. Among the Shawnees, Lalawethika, also known as the Prophet, sparked a religious revival. The Prophet's early life was undistinguished: he was a poor hunter and as a child accidentally blinded himself in the right eye with an arrow. His portly build and homely looks reinforced his unsightly appearance, and the ridicule of his fellow tribe members drove him to alcoholism. Then suddenly in April 1805 he lapsed into a trance so deep that he was given up for dead. When he revived, he spoke of having died and been reborn. In this vision and others he later received, he outlined a new creed for the Shawnee. Renouncing alcohol, he took a new name, Tenskwatawa (The Open Door), to express his mission to "reclaim the Indians from bad habits and to cause them to live in peace with all mankind."

He urged the Shawnee to renounce whiskey and white goods and return to their old ways of hunting with bows and arrows and eating traditional foods like corn and beans. "You must not dress like the White Man or wear hats like them," he exhorted, ". . . and when the weather is not severe, you must go naked Excepting the Breach cloth, and when you are clothed, it must be in skins or leather of your own Dressing." Seeking to revitalize Shawnee culture, the Prophet condemned intertribal violence, promoted monogamous marriage, and denounced the idea of private instead of communal property. Except for guns, which could be used in self-defense, his followers were to discard all items made by whites.

Not only trade but also fraternizing with Americans was forbidden. Indian wives of white men were to leave their husbands and return to the tribe, and children of mixed parentage were to be barred from the village. Setting up his headquarters first in Greenville, Ohio, and then at his own village of Prophetstown in Indiana in 1808, Tenskwatawa led a religious revival among the tribes of the Northwest, who were increasingly concerned about the loss of their lands. Just as thousands of white settlers traveled to Methodist or Baptist camp

Tenskwatawa, "the Open Door," shown in traditional dress, led a religious movement to revitalize Shawnee culture. After the Battle of Tippecanoe, he was supplanted as leader of the movement by his brother Tecumseh, who advocated political unity to preserve Indian lands and cultures.

meetings deep in the woods, where preachers denounced the evils of liquor and called for a return to a purer way of life, so thousands from northern tribes as far away as Wisconsin and Minnesota traveled to the Prophet's village for inspiration.

While Tenskwatawa's strategy of revitalization was primarily religious, his older brother Tecumseh turned to political and military solutions. William Henry Harrison described Tecumseh as "one of those uncommon geniuses which spring up occasionally to produce revolutions and overturn the established order of things." Tall and athletic, an accomplished hunter and a renowned warrior, Tecumseh at first played only a secondary role in his brother's religious movement. But in 1809 when the Lenni Lenape and Miami tribes ceded yet another 3 million acres in Indiana and Illinois under the Treaty of Fort Wayne, Tecumseh concluded that spiritual revival was inadequate to safeguard Indian lands. Repudiating this treaty, he urged tribes to forget their ancient animosities and unite under his leadership to protect their lands from white incursions. As he traveled throughout the Northwest, preaching his message of unity and resistance, hundreds of young braves rallied to his movement. Tecumseh's confederacy brought together the Wyandot, Chippewa, Sauk and Fox, Winnebago, Potawatomi, and other tribes. As Tecumseh began to overshadow the Prophet, Harrison aptly termed him "really the efficient man—the Moses of the family."

Tecumseh's message of pan-Indian unity and centralized authority ran counter to many facets of traditional Indian cultures. He asked villages to pay less attention to their local leaders and join his larger movement; he also called on tribes to unite with their traditional enemies in a common cause. While the amount of support he received was impressive, his following never matched that of the Prophet's earlier revivals. After proselytizing among the northwestern tribes, Tecumseh in 1811 toured through the South, where he encountered greater resistance. In general, the southern tribes were more prosperous, more acculturated, and felt less immediate pressure on their land base than did northern tribes. In addition, the Choctaws and Chickasaws refused to forget longstanding feuds with northern tribes.

So Tecumseh's southern mission ended largely in failure. To compound his problems, while he was away, a force of Americans under Governor Harrison fought off an attack launched by the Prophet at the Battle of Tippecanoe in November and then destroyed Prophetstown. As a result, Tecumseh had to continue his uphill battle for unity under discouraging circumstances. He became convinced that the best way to contain white expansion was to play off the Americans against the British, who maintained their interest in the Great Lakes region. Indeed, by 1811 the two nations were on the brink of war.

THE SECOND WAR FOR AMERICAN INDEPENDENCE

As Tecumseh pushed his campaign for a pan-Indian alliance, Jefferson, paying much more attention to partisan politics, looked to restore American political unity by wooing all but the most extreme Federalists into the Republican camp. Jefferson easily won reelection in 1804 over Charles Cotesworth Pinckney, the Federalist candidate, carrying 15 of 17 states. With the Federalists discredited by their vocal reactionary wing, and with the Republicans controlling three-quarters of the seats in Congress, Jefferson's goal of one-party rule seemed near at hand.

That unity was threatened, however, by growing Republican factionalism and, more important, by renewed fighting in Europe. Only two weeks after Napoleon agreed to sell Louisiana to the United States, war broke out between France and Great Britain. As in the 1790s, the United States found itself caught between the world's two greatest powers. In his struggle to maintain American neutrality, Jefferson's controversial policies momentarily revived the two-party system.

Neutral Rights

Initially, the war's disruption of European agriculture stimulated the American economy, since raw materials, especially foodstuffs, were in great demand overseas. As the fighting drove most nonneutral ships from the seas, American shipping dominated the carrying trade. The nation's foreign trade doubled between 1803 and 1805. Moreover, because the British navy prevented any direct trade with the French colonies, the reexport trade flourished. American ships transported sugar, coffee, and other goods from colonies in the West Indies and Latin America to an American port, unloaded the cargo and paid a duty, then reloaded the cargo and carried it to Europe. Britain initially ignored these broken voyages, but in 1805 its Admiralty courts ruled that such voyages violated the British blockade, and therefore the ships and cargo could be seized.

Adding to American anger, the British navy again resorted to impressment of sailors and even passengers from American ships. British authorities refused to recognize the right of its citizens to emigrate and become Americans, insisting that even if naturalized by the United States, they remained subjects of the Crown. Anywhere from 4000 to 10,000 sailors were impressed by British naval officers, who were not always terribly concerned about distinguishing between naturalized and native-born Americans. Isaac Clark, for example, was a native of Randolph, Massachusetts, yet he was taken from the American ship *Jane* in June 1809 after it was stopped by the British. When he presented papers attesting to his American citizenship, the English captain tore them up and threw them overboard. Refusing to work, he was put in irons, given a daily allowance of a biscuit and a pint of water, and once a week received two dozen lashes. Finally, half-starved and physically broken, Clark gave in. He served in the British navy for over two and a half years until wounded in action against a French frigate. While in a hospital he was freed through the intervention of the American consul. Voicing American indignation over such cases, John Quincy Adams characterized impressment as an "authorized system of kidnapping upon the ocean."

By 1805, the war had demonstrated the British navy's clear superiority on the sea, while Napoleon's army enjoyed a similar decisive edge on land. Adopting a strategy of attrition, each country began to raid America's ocean commerce with the other side. Between 1803 and 1807, Britain seized over 500 American ships, France over 300. Insurance rates soared, yet trading with the belligerents was so profitable that American merchants willingly ran the risks. Knowledgeable observers claimed that even if only one ship in three reached its destination, the owner reaped a handsome profit.

But in 1806 the British government tightened the screws further by proclaiming a blockade of France and northern Europe. Napoleon in turn issued the Berlin Decree of 1806, which established his own "Continental System" prohibiting British merchants and shipping from European markets. The following year the British adopted a set of regulations over neutral shipping known as the Orders in Council, which stipulated that any ship trading with France or its satellites had to

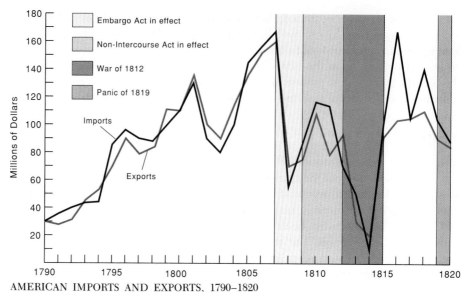

AMERICAN IMPORTS AND EXPORTS, 1790–1820
The prosperity of the 1790s is reflected in steadily rising foreign trade. Note the sharp drop after the Embargo Act and during the war.

stop first at a British port, pay a duty, and get a license. Napoleon retaliated with the Milan Decree of 1807, which announced that any ship that stopped in Britain in conformity with the Orders in Council would be treated as a British ship, subject to seizure. American merchants, caught in the middle, saw the number of seized ships again increase. An irate Jefferson said of France and England, "The one is a den of robbers, the other of pirates."

The war of nerves came to a head in June 1807, when the British frigate *Leopard* stopped the U.S. warship *Chesapeake* while still in American territorial waters just outside Norfolk, Virginia. When the British demanded the right to search the ship and seize British deserters, the American commander indignantly refused, since no nation claimed the right to impress sailors from a warship. The *Leopard* then fired three salvoes point blank into the *Chesapeake*, killing 3 and wounding 18. When the American ship struck its colors, a British boarding party seized four sailors who had deserted from the Royal Navy, three of them Americans (including two blacks). News of the high-handed British behavior inflamed public opinion, as politicians and editors called for the country to redress the humiliations it had suffered. Jefferson testified that "never, since the battle of Lexington, have I seen the country in such a state of exasperation as at present."

The Embargo

Yet Jefferson shrank from declaring war. He announced instead a program of "peaceable coercion," designed to protect neutral rights without war. The plan not only prohibited American ships from trading with foreign ports, it stopped the export of all American goods. Staying at home would keep American ships out of trouble on the high seas. In addition, Jefferson was confident that American exports were so essential to the two belligerents, they would quickly agree to respect American neutral rights. In December 1807 Congress passed the Embargo Act.

The president had seriously miscalculated. France did not depend on American trade and so managed well enough, while British ships quickly took over the carrying trade as American vessels lay idle. Under the embargo, American exports plunged from $108 million in 1807 to a mere $22 million a year later; simultaneously, imports fell from almost $145 million to barely $58 million. As the center of American shipping, New England port cities were hurt the most and protested the loudest.

More disturbing, American merchants and shippers resorted to smuggling and open defiance of the law, outdoing one another in devising ways to circumvent the regulations. Congress passed a series of supplementary laws to close loopholes, and the administration resorted to increasingly harsh enforcement procedures that could be justified only by a loose reading of the Constitution. Jefferson stubbornly refused to admit his mistake, but during his last months in office he simply gave up trying to enforce the act.

Madison and the Young Republicans

Following the example set by Washington, Jefferson did not seek a third term. A caucus of Republican members of Congress selected James Madison, Jefferson's secretary of state and close political collaborator, to run against Federalist Charles Cotesworth Pinckney. Influenced by younger members, who recognized the necessity of party organization and appeals for popular support, the Federalists mounted an energetic campaign, yet in the end Madison triumphed easily. Still, Pinckney swept all of New England, where feeling against the embargo was highest, and his party gained 24 seats in Congress. To younger Federalists, who advocated accommodation to the prevailing political attitudes and techniques, the party seemed on the verge of a revival.

Few men have assumed the presidency with more experience than James Madison. A leading nationalist in the 1780s, the father of the Constitution, a key floor leader in Congress, the founder of the Republican party, Jefferson's secretary of state and closest adviser, Madison had spent over a quarter of a century in public life. Yet his tenure as president proved disappointing, in large degree because of his character. Few had maneuvered more adeptly in the House or performed more loyally in the cabinet. But Madison lacked the force of leadership and the inner strength to impose his will on less capable men. Slight and frail-looking, he suffered from periodic seizures and was terrified that he was an epileptic. (It is not clear from what disease, if any, the seizures stemmed.) His weak voice, lack of personal charm, and failure to appeal to women scarred him further. He married his vivacious wife, Dolley, late in life, only to have his inadequacy heightened when the union produced no children. Madison compensated by pursuing intellectual achievement with a furious intensity, but his brilliant accomplishments never overcame his sense of inferiority.

With a president reluctant to fight for what he wanted, leadership passed from the executive branch to Congress. In the process, the Republican party, which had begun to fragment under Jefferson, became more factionalized. In 1810, of the 142 members of the House of Representatives 63 were swept out of office. They were replaced by a new generation of Republicans, led by the adroit and magnetic 34-year-old Henry Clay of Kentucky, who gained the rare distinction of being elected Speaker in his first term. These younger Republicans were much more nationalistic than the generation led by Jefferson and Madison. They sought an ambitious program of economic development and were aggressive expansionists, especially those from frontier districts. Their feisty willingness to go to war earned them the name of War Hawks. Though they numbered fewer than 30 in Congress, they quickly became the driving force in the Republican party.

The Decision for War

During Jefferson's final week in office in early 1809, Congress had repealed the Embargo Act, replacing it with the more moderate Non-Intercourse Act. Hoping to induce the two great powers to respect neutral rights, the new act reopened trade with all nations except Britain and France; it authorized the president to resume trade with either nation that lifted its trade restrictions. In 1810, Congress passed an even more poorly thought-out piece of legislation, Macon's Bill Number 2, introduced by Nathaniel Macon of North Carolina. It authorized trade with France and England, but decreed that if one of the two belligerents agreed to stop interfering with American shipping, trade with the other would be prohibited.

In this situation, Napoleon cleverly outmaneuvered the British by announcing that he would not enforce his Continental System. Madison eagerly took the French emperor at his word and reimposed a ban on trade with England. It soon became clear that Napoleon had no intention of lifting restrictions, and French raiders continued to seize American ships. But Madison, who had boxed himself into a corner, refused to rescind his order unless the British revoked the Orders in Council. In the disputes that followed, American anger focused on the British, who seized many more ships than the French and continued to impress American sailors. Westerners also accused the British of stirring up hostility among the Indian tribes.

Jefferson's and Madison's policies had a cumulative effect. With the Continent closed to British goods and with exports to the United States cut by some 80 percent, hard times fell on British merchants. As the depression in England deepened, pressure mounted for the government to modify its policy. Finally, on June 16, 1812, the British ministry suspended the Orders in Council. But it was too late. Two days earlier, unaware of the impending British decision, the United States had declared war on Britain.

Angered by the continued British violations of American neutrality and pressed by the War Hawks to defend American honor, Madison on June 1 asked for a declaration of war. The vote for war was 79 to 49 in the House and 19 to 13 in the Senate; to a large extent, the division followed party lines, with every Federalist voting against war. As the representatives of commercial interests, particularly in New England, Federalists were convinced that war would ruin American commerce; they also still identified with Britain as the champion of order and conservatism. The handful of Republicans who joined the Federalists represented coastal districts, which were most vulnerable to the Royal Navy.

Clearly, the vote for war could not be explained as a matter of outraged Americans protecting neutral rights. The coastal areas, which were most affected,

Jefferson in rags because of the Embargo Act.

preferred trade over high principle, while members of Congress from the South and the West, regions that had a less direct interest in the issue, clamored most strongly for war. The War Hawks were led by Henry Clay of Kentucky, John C. Calhoun of South Carolina, Felix Grundy of Tennessee, and Peter Porter of western New York. Their constituents were consumed with a desire to seize additional territory in Canada or in Florida (which was owned by Britain's ally Spain) and were outraged by British intrigues with the Indians along the frontier.

Overriding all these considerations was the conviction that Britain had never accepted the verdict of the American Revolution. American independence, the War Hawks were convinced, hung in the balance. A war against Great Britain would destroy both the internal and external enemies of republicanism by forcing the British to respect American rights and by strengthening the Republican party at home against its domestic foes. For insecure Americans, hungering for acceptance in the community of nations, nothing rankled more than being treated by the British as colonials. John Quincy Adams expressed this point of view when he declared: "In this question something besides dollars and cents is concerned and no alternative [is] left but war or the abandonment of our rights as an independent nation."

National Unpreparedness

With Britain preoccupied by Napoleon, the War Hawks expected that the United States would win an easy victory. The British fleet certainly posed no threat to the interior of the country. The conquest of Canada, Jefferson asserted, was simply a matter of marching.

In truth, the United States was totally unprepared for war. While a handful of frigates like the U.S.S. *Constitution* (known affectionately as *Old Ironsides*) fought commendably in individual actions, collectively they were woefully outnumbered. Against the world's most powerful navy, Jefferson's vaunted gunboats could do nothing to lift the British blockade of the American coast, which bottled up the country's merchant marine and most of its navy. But the Great Lakes, which were inaccessible to the Royal Navy, held the key to the naval war, and when hostilities began neither side had an advantage on these waters. The American army included only a few thousand men, led largely by inexperienced junior officers or Revolutionary War veterans well past their prime. The militia numbered an additional 690,000, but the best units were in disaffected New England. When Congress moved to increase the size of the army to 75,000, even the most hawkish states failed to meet their quotas. Congress was also reluctant to levy taxes to finance the war.

Full of hope, the American army launched a three-pronged invasion of Canada from Detroit in the West, Niagara in western New York, and Lake Champlain along the New York–Canada border. In the West, the timid General William Hull marched only a few miles into Canada before suddenly returning to Detroit, where he surrendered to the British without firing a shot. The invasions from New York also proved a fiasco when militia units refused to leave the state and cross into Canada. American forces were defeated at Niagara, and the march on Montreal from Plattsburgh also had to be abandoned.

American forces fared better in 1813, as both sides raced to build a navy on the strategically located Lake Erie. Led by Commander Oliver Hazard Perry, the Americans prevailed in the decisive battle at Put-in-Bay. Fighting between the

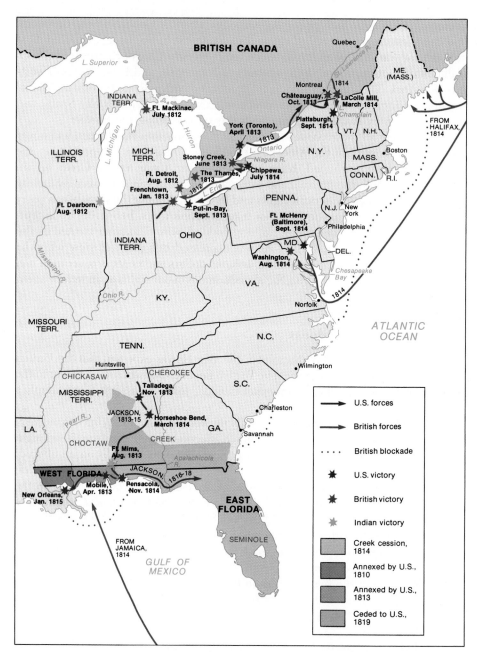

THE WAR OF 1812

After the American victory on Lake Erie and the defeat of the western Indians at the Battle of the Thames, the British adopted a three-pronged strategy to invade the United States, culminating with an attempt on New Orleans. But they met their match in Andrew Jackson, whose troops marched to New Orleans after fighting a series of battles against the Creeks and forcing them to cede a massive tract of land.

two squadrons was fierce, and at one point Perry transferred to another ship to continue the battle after his flagship was knocked out of commission. This victory gave the United States control of Lake Erie and greatly strengthened the American position in the Northwest.

"A Chance Such as Will Never Occur Again"

While the United States struggled to rally its forces, Tecumseh saw the need for the Indians to drive Americans out of the western territories. When a number of chiefs spoke in favor of siding with the Americans against the British, Tecumseh retorted, "Here is a chance . . . such as will never occur again—for us Indians of North America to form ourselves into one great combination." Joining up with the British, Tecumseh traveled south in the fall to talk again with his Creek allies. To coordinate a concerted Indian offensive for the following summer, he left a bundle of red sticks with eager Creek soldiers. They were to remove one stick each day from the bundle and attack when the sticks had run out.

A number of the older Creeks were more acculturated and preferred an American alliance. But about 2000 younger "Red Stick" Creeks launched a series of attacks, culminating with the destruction of Fort Mims along the Alabama River in August 1813. Andrew Jackson, the major general of the Tennessee militia, summoned 2000 volunteers and set out after the Creeks. Once again, the Indians' lack of unity was a serious handicap. Warriors from the Cherokee, Choctaw, and Chickasaw tribes, who were the Creeks' traditional enemies, joined Jackson's army. At the Battle of Horseshoe Bend in March 1814, these allied forces soundly defeated the Red Sticks. Jackson promptly dictated a peace treaty under which the Creeks ceded 22 million acres of land in the Mississippi Territory. They and the other southern tribes still retained significant landholdings, but Indian military power had been broken in the Southwest.

Farther north, Perry's victory on Lake Erie meant trouble for Tecumseh. With his supply lines cut, British General Henry Proctor abandoned the area around Detroit and retreated north. American forces under General William Henry Harrison pursued, and in October they defeated the British and their Indian allies at the Battle of the Thames. In the midst of heavy fighting Tecumseh was slain—and with him died any hope of a pan-Indian movement. In the short time of his power, he could not overcome the divisions and suspicions among tribes, especially in the South, where the forces of acculturation had taken stronger hold.

The British Invasion

As long as the war against Napoleon continued, the British were unwilling to divert army units to North America. But in 1814 Napoleon was at last defeated. Free to concentrate on the war in America, the British devised a coordinated strategy to invade the United States in the northern, central, and southern parts of the country. The main army headed south from Montreal but was checked when Captain Thomas Macdonough destroyed the British fleet on Lake Champlain.

In the meantime, a smaller British force landed in Maryland, marched on Washington, burned a number of public buildings, including the capitol and the president's home, and withdrew. To cover the scars of this destruction, the executive mansion was painted with whitewash and became known as the White House. The burning of the capital was a humiliating event (President Madison and his wife

During the Battle of New Orleans, American troops under Jackson entrenched behind breastworks, while their artillery raked the advancing British forces with deadly fire. The ladders needed to scale the American works quickly became entangled in the disorganized British assault. The portrait of Jackson (right) was done shortly after the battle.

Dolley were abruptly forced to flee, leaving their dinner to be eaten by the British), but the defeat had little military significance. The main objective of the British forces was Baltimore, where for 25 hours their fleet bombarded Fort McHenry in the city's harbor. Francis Scott Key, an American detained aboard a British ship, saw "the rockets' red glare, the bombs bursting in air"—and, at dawn, the American flag still flying above Fort McHenry. He hurriedly penned the verses of "The Star Spangled Banner," which was eventually adopted as the national anthem. The British abandoned their attempt to capture Baltimore.

The third British target was New Orleans, where a formidable force of 7500 British troops, mostly veterans fresh from the European theater, faced a motley collection of American regulars, western frontiersmen from Kentucky and Tennessee, citizens of the city, including several companies of free African-Americans, Choctaws, and—for an added dash of color—a group of pirates. The Americans were commanded by Major General Andrew Jackson, who had crushed the Red Stick Creeks. Not satisfied with defeating the Creeks, Jackson had invaded Spanish Florida contrary to his orders and occupied Pensacola and Mobile, solidifying American control of all of West Florida, over which the United States now assumed jurisdiction.

Taking charge of the defense of New Orleans, Jackson deployed his forces on a carefully chosen site five miles below the city. Protecting his flanks were the Mississippi and a swamp; in front lay an open field over which the enemy would have to advance. The Americans constructed a set of breastworks behind a dry canal bed and dug in. When the British attacked on January 8, 1815, the ladders needed to scale the American earthworks were at the rear rather than in front of the attacking column. When this mix-up was discovered, the attacking troops halted within range of the American guns while those to the back attempted to bring the ladders forward. In the prevailing confusion, Jackson's artillery raked the enemy with deadly fire, and the British finally broke and ran. In the two-hour battle, British losses exceeded 2000 men, of whom 291 were killed and over 1200 wounded (another 500 were missing); Jackson lost only 21: 8 killed and 13 wounded. It was a stunning victory, which made the general an overnight hero. As the victor over hardened British veterans who themselves had vanquished Napoleon, Jackson enabled Americans to forget the war's many failures and to boast that once again the United States had humbled the world's greatest military power.

The Hartford Convention

In December 1814, while Jackson was organizing the defense of New Orleans, New England Federalists met in Hartford to map strategy against the war. Yankee merchants, contemptuous of "Mr. Madison's War," had continued to trade with the enemy during the war, while New England governors declined to make available the state militias. Finally the Massachusetts legislature called for a convention to discuss New England's grievances. Connecticut and Rhode Island sent delegates, but only three counties in New Hampshire and one in Vermont were represented.

The delegates endorsed a series of proposed amendments to the Constitution which showed their displeasure with the government's economic policies. Embargoes could be enforced for no more than 60 days; Congress would not be permitted to restrict foreign trade or declare war without a two-thirds vote. The delegates indicated their resentment of southern power by proposing the abolition of the three-fifths clause of the Constitution, which provided that five slaves would count as three free persons in determining congressional representation, a measure that boosted southern representation in Congress. To limit the power of the West, they proposed that Congress require a two-thirds vote to admit new states. Although a few extremists thought secession from the Union might be necessary, the moderates in control at Hartford merely sent a committee to Washington to present the convention's demands. To their dismay, it arrived in the capital just as news of Andrew Jackson's victory was being trumpeted on the streets. The burst of national pride badly undercut the Hartford Convention's position, as did a second piece of news from across the Atlantic: American negotiators in Ghent, Belgium, had signed a treaty ending the war. Hostilities had ceased, technically, on Christmas Eve 1814, two weeks before the Battle of New Orleans.

Like the war itself, the Treaty of Ghent accomplished little of significance. Impressment, neutral rights, the boundary between the United States and Canada, American trade and fishing rights—all these issues were either ignored or referred to future commissions for settlement. As John Quincy Adams succinctly commented, "Nothing was adjusted, nothing was settled—nothing in substance but an indefinite suspension of hostilities was agreed to." Both sides were simply relieved to end the conflict.

AMERICA TURNS INWARD

In the wake of the war's end came an outburst of American nationalism—one that could not have flowered in 1776, when "these United States" had first fought Britain for independence. Those states had united before their citizens could develop a strong sense of national identity. But the War of 1812, capped by Jackson's victory, strengthened Americans' confidence in their country's destiny.

The upsurge in nationalism sounded the death knell of the Federalist party. The resistance of New England Federalists to the embargo and their disloyalty during the war had already weakened the party elsewhere, and the Hartford Convention tainted it with disunion and treason. Although it had made its best showing in years at the outbreak of the war (Madison had been reelected in 1812 by a margin of only 128 electoral votes to 89), the party's support collapsed in the 1816 election. Madison's secretary of state, James Monroe, handily defeated Federalist Rufus King of New York. In 1820 Monroe ran for reelection unopposed. The Federalists' strength in the House likewise collapsed; by 1818 they could count only 27 members of the House, compared to 156 Republicans.

Monroe's Presidency

The spirit of postwar harmony produced the so-called Era of Good Feelings, presided over by James Monroe, the last president of the Virginia dynasty and of the revolutionary generation. Monroe, like Jefferson before him, hoped to eliminate political parties, which he considered unnecessary in a free government. Like Washington, he thought of himself as the head of the nation rather than of a party.

Monroe's greatest achievements were diplomatic, accomplished largely by his astute secretary of state, John Quincy Adams. Adams, the son of President John Adams, already had compiled a distinguished diplomatic record, for while often harsh and overbearing, he was nevertheless a skillful negotiator. Adams thought of the Republic in continental terms; he was intent on promoting expansion to the Pacific, which he considered the avenue of trade with the Orient. Such a vision required dealing with Spain, which had never recognized the legality of the Louisiana Purchase. In addition, between 1810 and 1813 the United States had occupied and unilaterally annexed Spanish West Florida.

Spain, however, was preoccupied with events farther south in the Americas. In the first quarter of the nineteenth century, its colonies one after another had revolted and established themselves as independent nations. These revolutions increased the pressure on the Spanish minister to America, Luis de Onís, to come to terms with the United States. Furthermore, in 1818 Jackson marched into East Florida and captured several Spanish forts. Jackson had exceeded his instructions, but Adams understood well enough the additional pressure this aggression put on Onís and refused to disavow it.

Fearful that the United States might next invade Texas or other Spanish territory, Spain agreed to the Transcontinental, or Adams–Onís Treaty in February 1819. Its terms set the boundary between American and Spanish territory all the way to the Pacific. Spain not only relinquished its claims to the Pacific Northwest, but also ceded Florida in exchange for the U.S. government assuming $5 million in claims against Spain by American citizens. In exchange for the line to the Pacific, the United States abandoned its contention that Texas was part of the Louisiana Purchase. Adams had wanted Texas, but he wanted the line to the Pacific even more, understanding the strategic commitment to expanding across the continent. "The acknowledgement of a definite line of boundary to the South Sea [Pacific] forms a great epoch in our history," he confided to his diary.

The Monroe Doctrine

The United States came to terms not only with Spain, but, even more important, with Great Britain as well. Following the War of 1812, the British abandoned their

Thomas Sully's portrait of John Quincy Adams (1825) includes an open map symbolizing his significant contribution to national expansion during his eight years as secretary of state.

connections with the western Indian tribes and no longer attempted to block American expansion to the Rocky Mountains. In a growing spirit of cooperation, the two countries signed a commercial treaty that ended British discrimination against American trade, a sore point ever since the Revolution. The Rush–Bagot Agreement in 1817 limited naval forces on the Great Lakes and on Lake Champlain. In 1818 the countries agreed to the 49th parallel as the northern boundary of the Louisiana Purchase and also to joint control of the Oregon Territory for 10 years, subject to renewal.

In this atmosphere of goodwill, George Canning, the British foreign secretary, proposed in August 1823 that the United States and Britain issue a joint statement that would keep European powers from meddling in Latin America. Spain was clearly too weak to reestablish control of its former colonies, but Britain feared that Russia, Austria, and Prussia, which had joined together in the Holy Alliance, or France might intervene on Spain's behalf. Canning proposed that the United States and Britain declare that neither sought to expand in Latin America and that they opposed the transfer of Spain's colonies to any foreign power.

Monroe was inclined to accept the British offer, and both Jefferson and Madison urged him to do so. But John Quincy Adams forcefully argued that the United States should not make any pledge against acquiring territory in the future, particularly in Texas, Mexico, and the Caribbean, where Americans thought Cuba might come under its sway. Adams also worried that in any joint statement the United States would appear to be merely a junior partner, coming along "as a cock-boat in the wake of a British man-of-war." In addition, Adams was concerned over Russia's steady advance down the west coast of North America. Monroe finally agreed to make an independent statement.

He included it in his annual message to Congress, on December 2, 1823. Monroe reaffirmed that the United States would not intervene in European affairs, a principle of American foreign policy since Washington's Farewell Address. And he also announced that the United States would not interfere with already established European colonies in the Western Hemisphere. But any intervention, he warned, in the new republics of Latin America would be considered a hostile act: "The American continents . . . are henceforth not to be considered as subjects for future colonization by any European powers." The essence of this policy, which was Adams' handiwork, was the concept of two worlds, one old and one new, each refraining from interfering in the other's affairs.

Canning, upon hearing of Monroe's message, was irked: it was the British fleet, not any presidential declaration, that blocked European intervention in Latin America. American public opinion hailed Monroe's statement and then promptly forgot it. Only years later would it be referred to as the Monroe Doctrine. Still, it represented the culmination of the American quest since 1776 for independence and sovereignty. The very fact that Britain had proposed a joint declaration demonstrated that, at last, the parent nation recognized its offspring as a legitimate and sovereign nation. Monroe's declaration underlined that the United States would not act in world affairs as a satellite of Britain. Ever since the adoption of the Constitution, the issue of independence had been at the center of American politics: in Hamilton's quarrel with Jefferson over whether to favor Britain or France, in the response to the French Revolution, in the debate over the embargo, and finally in 1812 with the second war for American independence.

The End of an Era

The growing reconciliation with Great Britain ended the external threat to the Republic. Isolated from Europe and protected by the British fleet, the United States was free to turn its attention inward, to concentrate on expanding across the vast continent and on developing its resources. Yet how would the nation be developed? Jefferson had dreamed of an "empire of liberty," delighting in western expansion because it would preserve a nation of small farmers, like those Crèvecoeur had written about during the 1780s. Indeed, Jefferson seemed to have achieved his political goal of a one-party system, for by 1820 the Federalist party had dwindled to insignificance. "Our government is now so firmly on it's republican tack, that it will not be easily monarchized by forms," he assured Lafayette.

Yet the younger, more nationalistic Republicans were speaking of internal improvements, protective tariffs to help foster American industries, better roads and canals to link farmers with towns, cities, and wider markets. The tone of these new Republicans was not aristocratic, like the Federalists of old, but their dream of a national, commercial republic resembled Franklin's and Hamilton's more than Jefferson's. The new young westerners were aggressive: they looked to profit from speculation in land, from the increasing market for cotton, from the new methods of industrial manufacturing. If these people represented the rising wave across America, what would be the fate of Crèvecoeur's semisubsistence farm communities? The answer was not yet clear.

In one of those remarkable coincidences that Americans hailed as a sign of Providence's favor, Thomas Jefferson and John Adams died within hours of each other on July 4, 1826, the fiftieth anniversary of the adoption of the Declaration of Independence. The lives of these two giants of the Revolution—Jefferson, the ever-hopeful, self-styled revolutionary Virginia gentleman, and Adams, the prickly, independent Federalist of Braintree—intertwined with one another in the fabric of the nation's development. Partners in the struggle to secure American independence, they had become bitterly estranged in the heated party battles of the 1790s and resumed a warm friendship only after their public careers had drawn to a close. Their reconciliation was in tune with the rise of American nationalism, but their time was past. Leadership belonged now to a new generation of Americans who confronted different problems and challenges. Revolutionary America had passed from the scene. The dawn of a new nation was at hand.

SIGNIFICANT EVENTS

1790s	Second Great Awakening begins
1801	Adams' "midnight" appointments; Marshall becomes chief justice; Jefferson inaugurated in Washington; Cane Ridge revival
1802	Judiciary Act of 1801 repealed
1803	*Marbury v. Madison*; Louisiana Purchase; war resumes between Great Britain and France
1804–1806	Lewis and Clark expedition
1805	Prophet's revivals begin
1806	Non-Importation Act
1807	*Chesapeake* affair; Embargo Act passed
1808	Madison elected president
1809	Non-Intercourse Act passed; Tecumseh's confederacy organized
1810	Macon's Bill Number 2; *Fletcher v. Peck*
1810–1813	West Florida annexed
1811	Battle of Tippecanoe
1812	War declared against Great Britain
1813	Battle of Lake Erie; Tecumseh killed
1813–1814	Creek War
1814	Washington burned; Hartford Convention; Treaty of Ghent
1815	Battle of New Orleans
1816	*Martin v. Hunter's Lessee*; Monroe elected president
1817	Rush–Bagot Agreement
1818	United States–Canada boundary fixed to the Rockies; Joint occupation of Oregon
1819	Transcontinental Treaty; United States acquires Florida
1819–1823	Panic and depression
1820	Monroe reelected
1823	Monroe Doctrine

PART 3
THE REPUBLIC TRANSFORMED AND TESTED

Two remarkable transformations began sweeping the world in the late eighteenth century; so wrenching and far-reaching were these changes that both have been called revolutions. The first was a cascade of political revolts that led to increased democratic participation in the governing of many nation-states. The other was the application of machine labor and technological innovation to agricultural and commercial economies known as the industrial revolution.

Proclaiming the values of liberty and equality, Americans in 1776 led the way in what would become a succession of democratic revolutions. As we have seen, the bold act of revolution did not in itself solve the question of how regional and economic antagonisms could be adjusted peacefully in the new nation-state. Not until the Republicans succeeded the Federalists was a tradition of peaceful political change established within the framework of the Constitution. And not until a new generation of leaders arrived on the scene during the second war for independence did a national consciousness fully bloom.

These were notable milestones, but internationally, the center of revolutionary attention had shifted in 1789 to France. There, as in America, the ideals of the Enlightenment played a part in justifying democratic revolution; and French liberals like the Marquis de Lafayette were also inspired by the example of the United States. Still, the crowds marching through the streets of Paris adopted a more radical and violent stance, reflecting the onerous burdens that the feudal system exacted from peasants and workers as well as other pressures affecting

France. The worldwide rise in population of the previous half-century had left the French capital overcrowded, underfed, and thoroughly unruly—and the French citizenry that much more willing to arm themselves and march on the Bastille, on the palace at Versailles, against any perceived enemies of the Revolution. The countryside, too, suffering from a series of bad harvests, rose up in protest, sometimes brutally. Paradoxically, the population pressure that had pushed matters to a crisis was relieved as the Revolution gave way to the emperor Napoleon, whose wars of conquest killed almost as many French soldiers as the nation's natural in-

334

crease was producing. When Napoleon was at last defeated at the Battle of Waterloo (1815), Louis XVIII reestablished the French monarchy.

In Latin America, however, movements of democracy and nationalism spread. Just as England had attempted to pay for its colonial defenses with additional revenue from its colonies, so the Spanish Crown raised taxes in the Americas, with predictable results. The Creole class—Spanish who had been born in America—resented the preferential treatment given the *peninsulares*—colonial residents born in Spain—who often held a monopoly on administrative positions. Although the Spanish colonies lacked the tradition of representative assemblies found in North America, the writings of Jefferson and Thomas Paine circulated, as did translations of the French *Declaration of the Rights of Man*. From 1808 to 1821 Spain's American provinces declared their independence one by one. Democracy did not always root itself in the aftermath of these revolutions, but democratic ideology remained a powerful social catalyst.

The industrial revolution was less violent but no less dramatic in its effects. It began in Great Britain, where an increasing proportion of that nation's burgeoning population had begun to develop a more diversified commercial economy. A string of canal-building projects improved its transportation network toward the end of the eighteenth century, just as a similar movement would develop in the 1820s and 1830s in the United States. In Britain, too, James Watt in 1769 invented an engine that harnessed the power of steam, and innovations in textile production led to the use of water and later steam power to drive mechanical looms. As steam power was applied to transportation, both in ships and rail locomotives, the reach of commercial markets widened. Regular shipping made it possible to bring Egyptian cotton from Alexandria to factories in British Manchester and American cotton from the Arkansas Red River country to New England. Just as  skilled workers like Samuel Slater smuggled the new technology out of England to the United States, others like William Cockerill set up factories in Europe, as the capabilities of steam and industrial manufacturing spread to the continent.

In many ways the narrative of the young American republic is the story of how one nation worked out the implications of these twin revolutions, industrial and democratic. It was only after the War of 1812 that a market economy began rapidly to transform the agricultural practices of Crèvecoeur's subsistence America. Urban areas of the North became more diversified and industrial, as young women took jobs in textile mills and young men labored at flour mills processing grain to be shipped east. The impact of industry on the North is probably clear enough in the popular imagination; what is sometimes less appreciated is how the industrial revolution transformed the rural South. Cotton would never have become king there without the demand for it created by textile factories or without the ability to "gin" the seeds out of cotton by Eli Whitney's invention. (The "gin" in *cotton gin*, after all, is a clipped southern pronunciation of the word "engine.") Nor could cotton production have flourished without industrial advances in transportation, which allowed raw materials and factory goods to be shipped worldwide.

As the industrial and democratic revolutions developed side by side, the United States had to resolve the conflicts that the two presented each other. On the one hand, the advances in industry and commerce made it possible for resourceful entrepreneurs to reap profits on a scale that Americans of Crèvecoeur's day could never have imagined. They also created a labor force more impoverished than most Americans had been. The industrial revolution, in other words, made possible a society in which Americans could become both richer and poorer than they had ever been before—a society more stratified and more unequal. At the same time, the democratic revolution spreading across America was calling for greater equality among all citizens. This potential contradiction was one Americans wrestled with throughout the era.

Furthermore, although the industrial revolution transformed both the North and the South, it transformed them in conflicting ways. Although the economies of the two regions depended on each other, slavery came increasingly to be the focus of disputes between them. The industrial revolution's demand for cotton increased both southern profits and a demand for slave labor. Yet the spread of democratic ideology worldwide was creating increased pressure to abolish slavery everywhere. In France, the revolutionary government struck it down in 1794; the British empire outlawed it in 1833, about the time that American abolitionists, influenced by their British friends, became more active in opposing it. In eastern Europe, the near-slavery of feudal serfdom was being eliminated as well: in 1848 within the Hapsburg empire; in 1861 in Russia; in 1864 in Romania.

If the purpose of a democratic republic is to resolve conflicts among its members in a nonviolent manner, then in 1860 the American republic failed. It took four years of bitter fighting to reconcile the twin paths of democracy and industrial development. Given the massive size of the territory involved in the dispute and the different ways in which industry affected the North and South, it is perhaps not surprising that a union so diverse did not hold without the force of arms. That the separation was not final—that in the end, reunion emerged out of conflict—is perhaps one reason why the tale is so gripping.

CHRONOLOGY

AMERICAN EVENT	YEAR		GLOBAL EVENT
Stamp Act Congress	1765		Spinning jenny invented
	1769		Steam engine invented
American Revolution begins	1775		
	1789	WASHINGTON	French Revolution begins
First American textile mill	1790		
Whitney invents cotton gin	1793		
Slave revolt in Haiti	1794		France abolishes slavery
	1797	ADAMS	
	1801	JEFFERSON	
Wars for independence in Latin America	1804–1824		
	1809	MADISON	
Cotton trade is the major expansive force in the American economy	1815–1839		
	1817	MONROE	
Erie Canal completed	1825	ADAMS	First rail line in England
Mexico abolishes slavery	1829	JACKSON	
Total U.S. rail mileage, 13 miles	1830		Revolutionary movements in Europe
Indians removed from Southwest	1830–1838		
American Anti-Slavery Society founded	1833		Slavery abolished within British empire
McCormick patents mechanical reaper	1834		
	1837	VAN BUREN	
Total U.S. rail and canal mileage, 3300 miles each	1840		
	1841	HARRISON TYLER	
	1845	POLK	Irish potato famine begins
Outbreak of Mexican War	1846		Repeal of British Corn Laws
Immigration from Europe rises			
Seneca Falls convention for women's rights	1848		Serfdom abolished within Hapsburg empire
			Revolutions in Europe
	1849	TAYLOR	
Total U.S. rail mileage, 8900 miles	1850	FILLMORE	Total rail mileage: Britain, 15,900; Germany, 9500; France, 4700
	1853	PIERCE	
Kansas–Nebraska Act; Thoreau's *Walden* published	1854		Crimean War begins
	1857	BUCHANAN	
	1860		Italy unified
Civil War begins	1861	LINCOLN	Serfdom abolished in Russia
Emancipation Proclamation	1863		
Reconstruction begins	1865	JOHNSON	
	1868		Meiji Restoration in Japan
	1869	GRANT	
	1871		Germany unified
End of Reconstruction	1877	HAYES	

10

The Opening of America

In the years before the Civil War, the name of Chauncey Jerome could be found traced in neat, sharp letters in a thousand different places across the globe: everywhere from the fireplace mantels of plantation nabobs to the log huts of Illinois prairie farmers, the residences of English greengrocers, and even in Chinese hongs, the trading houses along the banks of the Pearl River at Canton. For Chauncey Jerome was a New England clockmaker, whose clever, inexpensive, and addictive machines had conquered the markets of the world.

Truly a self-made man, Jerome was born in 1793 in Canaan, Connecticut. His father was a blacksmith and wrought-iron maker. After just three winters of schooling he went to work at the age of nine, first in his father's smithy and then as an apprentice to a house carpenter. When the carpentry business turned slack during the winter months, he worked making dials and cases for clocks. Duty called during the War of 1812, but when peace came, Jerome tried several jobs before buying some clock movements and wood veneers and setting up a clock-making business. For several years he eked out a living peddling his products from farmhouse to farmhouse.

Then in 1824 Jerome's career took off. The epitome of the Yankee mechanic, he designed a "very showy" bronze looking-glass clock, whose models sold as fast as he could manufacture them. Between 1827 and 1837 his factory produced more clocks than any other in the country. But when the Panic of 1837 struck, Jerome's business dropped off so sharply that he had to scramble to avoid ruin.

Looking for a new opportunity, he set out to produce an inexpensive brass "one-day" clock—so called because its winding mechanism kept it running that long. Traditionally, only the movements of expensive eight-day clocks had been fashioned from brass. The wood in one-day clocks was cheaper, but it had to be seasoned for an entire year and the clock's wheels and teeth had to be painstakingly cut by hand. Furthermore, wooden clocks could not be exported overseas because the humidity on board ship swelled the wood and ruined them. Jerome's new brass version proved more accurate than earlier types and cheaper to boot. Costs came down further when he began to use interchangeable parts and combined his operations for making cases and movements within a single factory in New Haven, Connecticut. By systematically organizing the production process, Jerome brought the price of a good clock within the reach of ordinary people. So popular were the new models that his hapless competitors began attaching Jerome labels to their own inferior imitations.

"There are very many young ladies at work in the factories that have given up milinary dressmaking and school-keeping for to work in the mill," wrote Malenda Edwards in 1839. This young woman was one of them.

Disaster struck again in 1855, when Jerome went into partnership with several unreliable associates. Within a few years, his business faltered, then failed. At the age of 62, the once-prominent Chauncey Jerome found himself working again in a clock factory as an ordinary mechanic. He lived his last years in poverty.

Jerome rose higher than most Americans of his generation, and he fell further. Yet his fellow citizens shared his dreams of wealth and success and at the same time were haunted by the fear—so vividly illustrated in his own life—of losing everything. Not only material comforts vanished; so did respect. "One of the most trying things to me now," he confessed in his autobiography, "is to see how I am looked upon by the community since I lost my property. I never was any better when I owned it than I am now, and never behaved any better. But how different is the feeling towards you, when your neighbors can make nothing more out of you. . . . You are passed by without notice."

Chauncey Jerome's life spanned the transition from the old master–apprentice system of production to the beginnings of mechanization and the rise of the factory system. By 1850 the notion of independent American farmers subsisting primarily on what they themselves produced (Crèvecoeur's vision of the 1780s) had become a dream of the past. In its place stood a commercial republic, in which a full-blown national market encompassed most settled areas of the country.

The notion of the market is crucial here. Americans tied themselves to one another eagerly, even aggressively, through the mechanism of the free market. They sold cotton or wheat and bought manufactured cloth or brass one-day clocks. They sold pork, beef, or tobacco and purchased shoes or the new ladies' magazines. They mortgaged land and houses not merely to establish a family estate, but to speculate and profit. They relied, even in many rural villages, on cash and paper money instead of bartering for goods and services. In short, a market economy bound Americans to one another in increasingly complex ways. American life moved from less to more specialized forms of labor; from subsistence-oriented to more commercially oriented outlooks; from face-to-face local dealings to impersonal, distant transactions; from the mechanically simple to the technologically complex; and from less dense patterns of settlement to more complex arrangements in cities and towns. Such were the changes Chauncey Jerome witnessed—indeed, changes he helped to bring about himself, with his clocks that divided the working days of Americans into more disciplined, orderly segments.

As these changes swirled around him, Jerome sensed that somehow society had taken on a different tone—that the marketplace and its ethos had become dominant. "It is all money and business, business and money which make the man now-a-days," he complained. "Success is every thing, and it makes very little difference how, or what means he uses to obtain it." The United States, according to the foreign visitor Francis J. Grund, had become "one gigantic workshop, over the entrance of which there is the blazing inscription *'No admission here except on business.'*"

THE MARKET REVOLUTION

A truly national system of markets began to grow following the War of 1812 and was in full swing by the 1820s, when the United States entered a period of unprecedented economic expansion. As it grew, the economy became varied enough to sustain and even accelerate its growth. Before the war, it had been tied largely to international trade. The United States exported staples like cotton, wheat, tobacco, and timber; if the nations that bought these commodities suddenly stopped doing so, as happened during the European wars of the 1790s and again after 1803, the domestic economy suffered. Since so many Americans remained rural and primarily self-sufficient—as in the America idealized by Crèvecoeur—they could not absorb any increase in producer goods.

But the War of 1812 marked the turning point in the creation and expansion of a domestic market. First the embargo and then the war itself stimulated the growth of manufacturing, particularly in textiles. In 1808 the United States had 8000 spindles spinning cotton thread; by 1811 the number had risen to 80,000 and at the end of the war there were around 130,000—a greater than 15-fold increase in less than a decade. War had also bottled up capital in Europe, and when peace was restored this capital flowed into the United States, further stimulating growth. Finally, the war experience led the federal government to adopt policies designed to spur economic growth, particularly a protective tariff, the national bank, and aid for internal improvements.

The New Nationalism

In the aftermath of the war with Britain, leadership passed to a new generation of the Republic—younger men such as Henry Clay, John C. Calhoun, and John Quincy Adams, who were ardent nationalists eager to use the power of the federal government to promote the rapid development of the nation. Increasingly dominant within the Republican party, they were impatient with the old-fashioned ideas of Jefferson and Madison and advocated the "New Nationalism," a set of economic policies designed to foster the prosperity of all regions of the country and bind the nation more tightly together.

Even Madison saw the need for increased federal activity, especially given the problems the government experienced during the war. The national bank closed its doors in 1811, when its charter expired, and in its absence state bank notes had multiplied, and their variety and uncertain value had produced financial chaos. In his message to Congress in December 1815, Madison, who had led the fight against Hamilton's national bank in 1791, noted that the country had changed a great deal since the adoption of the Constitution, and that a national bank had become essential for the American economy. Congress responded by chartering the Second Bank of the United States for a period of 20 years. It had a capital of $35 million (compared to $10 million for Hamilton's first bank), which made it easily the largest and most powerful bank in the country.

The war had also highlighted the need for greater economic independence. Madison thus endorsed a mildly protective tariff to aid the fledgling American industries that had sprung up during the embargo and the war. The tariff of 1816 set an average duty of 20 percent on imports of woolen and cotton cloth, iron, sugar, and other items. Because duties raised the prices of imported goods, competing American products gained an advantage in the domestic market. The Middle Atlantic states and the West voted for the tariff by a large margin, while even Federalist New England, whose prosperity was closely tied to imports, lent the Republican measure moderate support. But in a portent of sectional tensions, many southern representatives opposed the tariff.

Madison also recommended that the government provide aid for internal improvements such as roads, canals, and bridges. The war had demonstrated how cumbersome it was to move troops or supplies overland. Madison, however, believed that a constitutional amendment was needed to permit federal funds to be used for local projects. To nationalists such as Clay and Calhoun, this proposal was one more example of Madison's outmoded ideas. Calhoun brushed aside Madison's constitutional scruples and championed the so-called Bonus Bill, under which the $1.5 million bonus the national bank paid the government for its charter was to be distributed to the states for internal improvements. The president vetoed the bill, but this represented only a temporary setback for the nationalists. Even Madison was willing to support projects broader in scope, and his successor, James Monroe, approved additional ones.

The Cotton Trade

The most important cause of American economic development after 1815 was the growth of the cotton trade. By the end of the eighteenth century, southern planters had discovered that cotton would grow in the lower part of the South. At first, however, the only profitable type of cotton was the long-fibered, silky variety that flourished in a narrow band along the South Carolina and Georgia coast and on the islands offshore. A short-fibered variety grew upland, but it contained sticky green seeds that could not be easily separated from the lint by hand. The necessary technological breakthrough occurred in 1793, when Eli Whitney, a Connecticut Yankee working as a tutor on a Georgia plantation, invented a simple but ingenious device that removed seeds from the cotton.

The impact of the cotton gin was dramatic. Whereas before, a slave could clean only a pound of cotton a day by hand, with a gin one person could clean 50 pounds. The heavy demand for cotton by British textile mills sent prices on the world market soaring. By 1840 the South produced over 60 percent of the world supply, which accounted for almost two-thirds of all American exports.

The cotton trade was the major expansive force in the economy until 1839—and not only in the South. Northern factories increasingly made money by turning raw cotton into cloth, while northern merchants reaped profits from shipping the cotton and then reshipping the textiles. Planters used the income they earned to purchase foodstuffs from the West and goods and services from the Northeast. After 1839 the cotton trade became less of an economic stimulus, but its explosive expansion in the critical earlier period enabled the country to sustain internal economic growth.

The Transportation Revolution

For a market economy to become truly national, a transportation network linking various parts of the nation was essential. The network was crucial not so much for moving people as it was for moving goods. (A market economy, after all, did not require a farmer to travel regularly to St. Louis or New York, but his grain had to get there efficiently and cheaply.) The economy had not become self-sustaining earlier partly because the only means of transporting goods cheaply was by water. Thus trade was limited largely to coastal and international markets, for even on rivers, bulky goods moved easily in only one direction—downstream.

Whitney's cotton gin.

All that changed, however, with the revolution in transportation. New areas were drawn quickly into the market, while the speed and cost required to move goods across land dropped dramatically. From 1825 to 1855—the span of a single generation—the cost of transportation on land fell 95 percent, while its speed increased fivefold.

The Canal Age

Canals attracted considerable investment capital, especially after the success of the wondrous Erie Canal. Built between 1818 and 1825, the Erie Canal stretched 364 miles from Albany on the Hudson River to Buffalo on Lake Erie. Its construction, the dream of Governor De Witt Clinton of New York, was an act of faith, for in 1816 the United States had only 100 miles of canals, none longer than 28 miles. Jefferson, hardly a man of limited vision, called the idea of such a canal "little short of madness."

For much of its distance the Erie Canal ran through forest, disease-ridden swamps, and unsettled wilderness. The canal's engineers, headed by Benjamin Wright, were largely self-taught, but they made up in ingenuity what they lacked in training. Improving on European tools, they devised a special scraper for excavating, a cable and screw that allowed one man to pull down even the largest trees, and a stump-puller that could remove up to 40 stumps a day. Along the route they discovered limestone, which made a superior cement that hardened under water. Still, no ingenuity could get around the grueling work of clearing trees when the route led straight through a swamp.

The Erie Canal promoted urban growth, economic development, and bustle along its route. Here boatmen guiding their craft past busy laborers on shore provide an indication of the commerce that quickly flourished on the waterway.

When finished in 1825, the canal was 40 feet wide and 4 feet deep; it had 83 locks with a combined ascent and descent of 675 feet and 18 aqueducts across various rivers. The one at Little Falls was 1184 feet long with a massive central arch 70 feet across. The project, which cost New York $7.5 million, paid for itself within a few years. Indeed, traffic was so heavy that it soon strained the Erie's capacity. Before its completion, shipping a ton of goods from Buffalo to New York City had cost over 19 cents a mile; with the canal in operation the cost dropped to less than 3 cents, and by 1860 it had fallen to less than a penny. Where its busy traffic passed, settlers flocked, and with them came commerce and new markets. Haphazardly constructed towns like Syracuse, Rochester, and Lockport sprang up and thrived by moving goods, serving markets, and creating new demand. Between 1820 and 1840 the number of people employed in manufacturing in the region rose 262 percent, while those engaged in commerce and navigation swelled by 1000 percent. "Everything in this bustling place appears to be in motion," wrote one English traveler about Rochester in 1827. "Here and there we saw great warehouses, without window sashes, but half-filled with goods, and furnished with hoisting cranes, ready to fish up the huge pyramids of flour barrels, bales, and boxes lying in the streets." And the steady flow of goods eastward gave New York City a dominant position in the scramble for control of western trade.

Indeed, New York's rivals such as Philadelphia and Baltimore were soon frantically trying to build their own canals to the West. Western states like Ohio and Indiana constructed canals to link interior regions with the Great Lakes. Wasted money and a number of foolish schemes brought several overextended state governments to the verge of bankruptcy, but the general attitude among citizens was that without cheap transportation and access to markets, farmers in the state could never prosper. The public's enthusiasm for canals increased support for government involvement in the economy. By 1840 the nation had completed over 3300 miles of canals—a length greater than the distance from New York City to Seattle—at a cost of about $125 million. Almost half of that amount came from state governments.

By 1850 the canal era was over. The depression of 1839 caused several states to halt or slow their construction, especially since many poorly planned canals lost money. Still, whether profitable or not, canals sharply reduced transportation costs and stimulated economic development in a broad belt along their routes.

Steamboats

Because of its vast expanse, the United States was particularly dependent on river transportation. But shipping goods downstream from Pittsburgh to New Orleans took 6 weeks, while the return trip required 17 weeks or more in keelboats pushed laboriously by hand against the current. Consequently, only the lightest and most valuable goods could be profitably shipped upstream. Steamboats, however, substantially reduced both the cost and time of river travel. A trip from New Orleans to Louisville dropped from 90 to 8 days, while upstream costs were cut by 90 percent.

John Fitch, an ingenious mechanic, had exhibited a working prototype of a steamship to the members of the Constitutional Convention in Philadelphia in 1787, but his work was ignored. Twenty years later Robert Fulton demonstrated the commercial possibilities of propelling a boat with steam when his ship, the *Clermont,* traveled from New York City to Albany on the Hudson River. But the

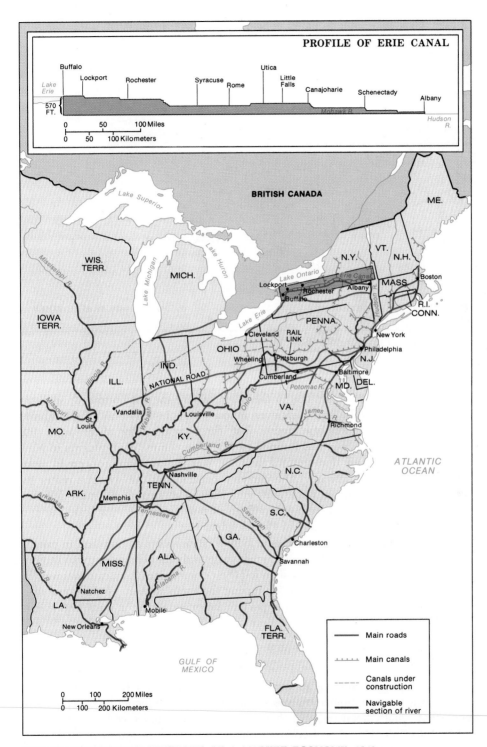

PROFILE OF ERIE CANAL

THE TRANSPORTATION NETWORK OF A MARKET ECONOMY, 1840
Canals played their most important role in the Northeast, where they linked eastern cities
to western rivers and the Great Lakes. On the Erie Canal, a set of locks raised and lowered
boats in a series of steps along the route. Steamboats were most crucial in the extensive
river systems of the South and the West.

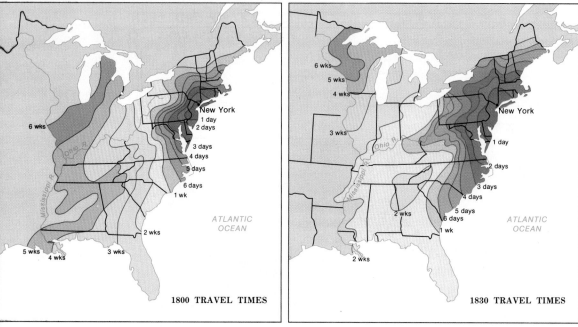

TIME OF TRAVEL, 1800 AND 1830

steamboats greatest impact was in the West, where the flat-bottomed, shallow-draft boats could haul heavy loads even in low water. In 1817 only 17 steamboats were operating on western rivers; just three years later there were 69, and by 1855, the number had jumped to 727. The volume of shipments to New Orleans doubled every decade until the Civil War. Since steamboats could make many more voyages annually, the carrying capacity on the western rivers increased a hundredfold between 1820 and 1860. The steamboat, marveled one westerner, "brings to the remotest village of our streams . . . a little Paris, a section of Broadway, or a slice of Philadelphia."

Governments did not invest as heavily in steamboats as they had in canals, except for providing funds to remove river snags and other obstacles to navigation. Although by 1860 the railroads had ended their dominance, the steamboat was the major form of western transportation during the establishment of a national market economy, and it was the most important factor in the rise of manufacturing in the Ohio and upper Mississippi valleys.

Railroads

The first significant railroads appeared in the 1830s. By and large, they were seen not as a way to revolutionize transportation, but merely as feeder lines to the more important canals. Soon enough, though, communities perceived that their economic future depended on having adequate rail links. Chicago's eventual dominance among western cities grew out of its early commitment to railroads, and Boston, Baltimore, and Charleston, which all lacked important inland waterways, led the way in the construction of regional rail networks.

The country had only 13 miles of track in 1830, but 10 years later railroad and canal mileage were almost exactly equal (3325 miles). During the next decade, the railroad network rapidly expanded, reaching a total of 8879 miles by 1850. Railroads did not always cut the cost of transporting goods over land; canals and steamboats were usually cheaper. But railroads were approximately twice as fast as steamboats, offered more direct routes, and could operate year-round. After 1850, railroads would increasingly become the dominant form of transportation in the country, but initially canals and steamboats were the key to creating a national market.

Agriculture in the Market Economy

The new forms of transportation had a remarkable impact on Crèvecoeur's yeoman farmer. Before the canal era, a farmer could not ship corn profitably outside his immediate neighborhood—unless, of course, he transformed it into a more transportable commodity such as whiskey. Wheat, for example, could be shipped at a profit no farther than 50 miles. But once cheap transportation became available, farmers eagerly sought to increase their yields and ship the surplus to distant markets for sale. Output per worker surged upward as farmers began cultivating more acres and working longer hours. They also began adopting scientific farming methods, including crop rotation and the use of manures as fertilizer. State governments encouraged the circulation of agricultural information through fairs and state agricultural departments, while farm journals advised interested subscribers on the latest advances in fertilizers, plows, and plant varieties.

The transportation revolution also encouraged regional agricultural specialization. Marginal lands in New England and the Northeast could no longer compete with wheat yields of western farms. Eastern farmers, if they did not pull up and move west, shifted to other crops and particularly engaged in dairying and truck farming, for they could now sell milk, vegetables, and fruit to the rapidly growing urban areas. Other farmers began raising sheep. The center of wheat production moved steadily westward, so that by 1850, Wisconsin and Illinois were developing into major wheat-producing states.

All these changes linked farmers more tightly to a national market system. They were now more likely to deal in cash and credit, forsaking the barter system previously used between neighbors. Instead of marketing crops themselves, as they had in the past, farmers dealt with regional merchants, middlemen in a far-flung distribution system. Like southern planters, western wheat farmers increasingly sold in a world market. Poor harvests in Europe, as well as the repeal of Britain's protectionist Corn Laws in the 1840s, created a great demand for American wheat. Banks and distributors advanced farmers credit, and those who anticipated the ups and downs of prices in markets hundreds of miles away were most likely to profit from this system. More and more, farmers competed in a market controlled by impersonal forces centered in distant locations.

As transportation and market networks spread, they fed on themselves, growing larger, connecting more areas of the nation, and allowing further specialization. The South increasingly concentrated on staple crops for export and the West grew foodstuffs, particularly grain, while the Northeast became the center of manufacturing. Although foreign commerce expanded too, it was overshadowed by the dramatic growth in domestic markets, which absorbed more and more of the goods and services being produced. Even though Americans were producing

Daily Lives

TIME AND TRAVEL

Floating Palaces of the West

Plying the Mississippi River and its many tributaries, the western steamboat carried both freight and passengers, but it won its greatest fame as a mode of travel. The most luxurious boats, dubbed "floating palaces," offered accommodations far beyond the experience of the average American. Steamboats also provided the cheapest form of inland transportation before the Civil War: by midcentury, cabin passage for the 1400-mile trip from Louisville to New Orleans was only $12 to $15.

On the earliest steamboats, passengers were housed on the main deck along with the cargo. As the boats became larger, designers added a second or boiler deck (which, despite its name, was not where the boilers were located). Eventually a third level was added, the hurricane or texas, which contained additional accommodations for the officers and passengers. The boiler deck's saloon was the center of steamboat society, with the ladies' parlor at one end and the barroom at the other. Besides serving as a dining room and lounge, it provided the sleeping quarters. Berths were arranged in two tiers on both sides of the saloon and, at least on the better boats, each contained bedding and a mattress. Gentlemen were not allowed in the ladies' cabin except by invitation or if they were traveling with their wives. Women entered the saloon only for meals.

Steamboats also offered passage on the main deck for about one-fifth the price of a regular ticket. Primarily the poor, immigrants, and blacks, these passengers had no living quarters or toilet facilities and had to provide their own food. Then too, boiler explosions, collisions, and sinkings from snags caused a much higher loss of life among lower deck passengers, who were closer to the water and had less warning. Between 1811 and 1851, some 44 steamboats collided, 166 burned, 209 exploded, and 576 hit obstructions and sank. And in the four years before 1852, when Congress passed a law governing steamboat safety, more than 1500 people lost their lives in steamboat accidents.

The steamboat was, as many travelers remarked, a "world in miniature," carrying slaves and planters, farmers and manufacturers, merchants and frontier families, soldiers and Indians, ministers and professional gamblers. Regular passengers generally had little contact with those on the lower deck, but as fares steadily dropped, people of widely different wealth and position were thrown together in the main cabin and mingled with a democratic familiarity. Women spent their time talking, sewing, caring for children, and strolling the deck. Men passed the time in conversation, drinking, and gambling. The bar was the center of the male social world, where as one minister remarked, "whiskey is used just as freely as water." Gambling was rife on steamboats, as many men, temporarily freed from the moral restraints of home, eagerly dealt themselves into card games.

The most famous vessels on the rivers boasted intricately carved gingerbread facings, painted a glistening white and trimmed in gold leaf—an architectural style known as Steamboat Gothic. Sophisticated Europeans found the effect garish and vulgar: "an indefinable sham splendor all around, half disgusting and wholly comical." To rustic westerners and southerners, however, the decor represented elegance beyond anything they had seen. Some, unaccustomed to the finery, gave the furnishings rather hard usage. Owners

The luxurious saloon furnishings on the Mississippi steamboat, the *Princess*.

had to post rules against whittling the furniture and sleeping with boots on.

For all their luxurious veneer, steamboats lacked amenities that later travelers would take for granted. Most six-by-six staterooms had two narrow shelves to sleep on and no lighting or heat. The washrooms in the main cabin contained tin basins and pitchers of cold water, a comb and brush, and a communal toothbrush. One traveler complained that there were only two towels for 70 men on one boat. Water, both for drinking and washing, came directly from the river and was laden with silt. Furthermore, the average riverboat hardly lived up to the standards of the most famous packets. In 1843 John James Audubon journeyed from Louisville to St. Louis on what he described as "the very filthiest of all filthy old rat-traps I ever traveled in." He grumbled particularly about a leaky roof, threadbare sheets, and pillows filled with corn husks.

Steamboat food was ample but often poorly prepared and saturated with grease. In the main cabin 30 or more dishes were placed on the table and diners grabbed whatever they wanted. Unused to such variety, some passengers simply gorged themselves on the dishes near at hand rather than selecting what they wanted. It was a common saying that "steamboat living was entirely too rich for any one to stand it long without ruining the stomach."

In maintaining law and order, the captain was aided by the passengers, who, in the tradition of the frontier, sometimes formed their own courts to deal with those charged with minor offenses. Travelers accused of theft, illicit sexual relations, or gambling disputes might find themselves flogged or put ashore at some desolate spot. In one case, when a young man and woman traveling together as "cousins" aroused suspicion, the passengers insisted on an investigation by the boat's officers, who discovered the pair sharing a berth. At the next stop, while the boat waited, indignant passengers marched the couple ashore, rounded up a minister, and compelled them to get married.

Despite the discomforts of swarming mosquitoes, heat from the boilers, and noisy engines at all hours of the night, observers agreed that journeying by steamboat was far more pleasant than taking a stagecoach, the principal alternative in the West before 1850. With their churning paddlewheels, gingerbread decks, and belching smokestacks, these gaudy vessels were the grandest showpieces of life on the Mississippi.

more goods than ever before, only in 1835 did American exports exceed those of 1807, the last year before the embargo.

Thus the cities of the East no longer looked primarily to the sea; they looked to southern and western markets. That, indeed, was a revolution in markets.

John Marshall and the Promotion of Enterprise

For a national market system to flourish, a climate favorable to investment had to exist. As it happened, the Supreme Court became the branch of the federal government most aggressive in protecting the new forms of business central to the growing market economy.

As chief justice, John Marshall presided over the Court from 1801 to 1835. Despite his informal, almost sloppy personal manners, he was a commanding figure: tall and slender, with twinkling eyes and a hearty laugh that was as contagious as it was disarming. His forceful intellect was reinforced by his genial ability to persuade. A strong nationalist, he convinced his colleagues time after time to uphold the supremacy of the federal government over the states, its power to promote economic growth, and the sanctity of private property.

In the case of *McCulloch v. Maryland* (1819), the Court had to decide whether the Second Bank of the United States, chartered by Congress in 1816, was constitutional. Maryland had levied a tax on the Baltimore branch of the national bank, which John McCulloch, the cashier, refused to pay, and the case went to the Supreme Court. Asserting that "the power to tax involves the power to destroy," Marshall, speaking for the Court, upheld the constitutionality of the national bank and struck down the tax. Just as Alexander Hamilton had argued during the 1790s in the debate over the first national bank, Marshall pointed out that the Constitution gave Congress the power to make all "necessary and proper" laws to carry out its delegated powers. If Congress believed that a bank would help it meet its responsibilities, such as maintaining the public credit and regulating the currency, then it was constitutional. The bank only had to be useful, not essential. "Let the end be legitimate," Marshall wrote, "let it be within the scope of the Constitution, and all means which are appropriate, which are plainly adapted to that end, which are not prohibited . . . are constitutional." By upholding Hamilton's doctrine of implied powers, Marshall enlarged federal power to an extraordinary degree.

He also encouraged a more freewheeling commerce in *Gibbons v. Ogden* (1824). Under a New York law, Aaron Ogden held a monopoly on steamboat traffic on the Hudson River between New Jersey and New York City. Gibbons, who had a federal license to operate a steamboat, set up a competing line and Ogden sued. The case gave Marshall a chance to define the greatest power of the federal government in peacetime, the right to regulate interstate commerce. In striking down the New York monopoly, the chief justice gave the term *commerce* the broadest possible definition, declaring that it covered all commercial intercourse, and that Congress' power over interstate commerce could be "exercised to its utmost extent." The result was increased business competition, not just on the Hudson but throughout society.

At the heart of most commercial agreements were private contracts, made between individuals or companies. Marshall took an active role in defining the meaning of contract law, which was then in its infancy. The case of *Fletcher v. Peck* (1810) showed how far he was willing to go to protect private property. The case grew out of a grant of land the Georgia legislature made in 1795 to a group of speculators. When it was discovered that the speculators had bribed some of the representatives, the next legislature rescinded the grant. Because some individuals had already purchased property from the original grantees, thinking their title was valid, the case eventually made its way to the Supreme Court. The justices unanimously struck down the law rescinding the land grant. A grant was a contract, Marshall declared, and since the Constitution forbade states from impairing "the obligation of contracts," the legislature could not interfere with the grant once it had been made. Although the framers of the Constitution probably meant contracts to refer only to agreements between private parties, Marshall made no distinction between public and private agreements, thereby greatly expanding the meaning of the contract clause.

In another decision (*Sturges v. Crowninshield*, 1819), the Court also defined a debt as a binding contract and limited the power of state legislatures, through bankruptcy laws, to interfere with the collection of debts. But the most celebrated decision Marshall wrote on the contract clause was in *Dartmouth College v. Woodward*, also decided in 1819. This case arose out of the attempt of the state of New Hampshire to alter the charter that George III had granted in 1769 to the college's trustees. The Court overturned the state law on the grounds that state charters were also contracts and could not be altered by later legislatures. By this ruling, Marshall intended to protect corporations, which conducted business under charters granted by individual states. Yet his arguments could be used to preserve monopolies from competition and to defend corporations from regulation in the public interest. So extreme was Marshall's position that courts eventually had to modify some of his decisions.

Thus the Marshall Court sought to encourage economic risk taking by protecting property and contracts, by limiting state interference, and by creating a climate of business confidence. Like other Federalists, Marshall distrusted the masses and believed that state laws were the major obstacle to economic development. During his years on the bench, he upheld the view that commerce and economic enterprise were the agents of progress.

General Incorporation Laws

Corporations were not new in American business, but as the economy expanded they grew in numbers. From the beginning, banks had been established by acts of incorporation, and their success encouraged other businesses to adopt this mode of organization. Corporations continued beyond the lives of the individuals who created them, and by pooling investors' resources, they provided a means to raise capital for large-scale undertakings. Corporations also offered the advantage of limited liability: an investor was liable for the corporation's debts only to the extent of the amount he or she had invested. A recent innovation, this legal concept put limits on a person's financial risk. Small and medium-sized businesses continued to be run as partnerships and individual ventures, but banks, insurance companies, railroads, and manufacturing firms, which required greater capital, increasingly were incorporated.

Originally, state legislatures were required to approve a special charter for each new corporation. But with the number of applications steadily increasing, this procedure became too cumbersome. Beginning in the 1830s, states adopted general incorporation laws. Any applicant who met certain minimum qualifications would automatically be granted a corporation charter. This reform made it much easier and faster to secure a charter and stimulated organization and manipulation of the national market.

A RESTLESS TEMPER

"An American . . . wants to perform within a year what others do within a much longer period," observed Francis Lieber, a German who emigrated and became a noted American political scientist. Between 1815 and 1850, as new markets were opened up, fresh fields plowed, canals dug, and faster steamboats built, the nation reverberated with almost explosive energy. The famous French commentator Alexis de Tocqueville was astonished, like most Europeans, at the restless mobility of the average American. "Born often under another sky, placed in the middle of an always moving scene, himself driven by the irresistible torrent which draws all about him, the American has no time to tie himself to anything, he grows accustomed only to change, and ends by regarding it as the natural state of man."

This emphasis on speed—seen in the mobility of Americans, the expansiveness of the new market, the sense of boundless possibilities—affected nearly every aspect of American life. Steamboat captains vied with one another for the honor of having the fastest boat on the river, their sweaty stokers in the boiler rooms piling log after log into the fires until—all too often—the pressurized engines exploded, ripping the vessel apart. To the visiting English novelist Charles Dickens, traveling under these conditions seemed like taking up "lodgings on the first floor of a powder mill." In railroad cars, Americans could not sit still long enough to abide the European system of providing individual passenger compartments; instead, American cars had a center aisle, allowing their ever-restless passengers to wander the length of the train. American transportation technology emphasized speed over longevity: unlike European railroads, which were sturdy and heavy, American railroads were lightweight, hastily constructed, with little heed paid to the safety or comfort of passengers. Americans even ate quickly, looking neither right nor left, only at their plates, bolting the food down in complete silence. In America, insisted one disgruntled European, food was "pitchforked down."

The new American way of building manifested a similar emphasis on speed. Before the 1830s, American houses were held together with mortises and joints. This method of construction was sturdy, but it required master craftsmen to hew the joints by hand. The pressure to build many houses quickly in areas with few skilled carpenters led to the use of new light frames, made of two-by-fours nailed together, to which the walls, roof, and floor were also attached with nails. Derisively called "balloon frame" houses, they cost less than half the price of a traditional house, and they could be built in a week by workers with only minimal training. Ironically, balloon frame houses proved stronger and lasted longer than traditional houses. Moreover, they were perfectly adapted to the American penchant for moving: the owner simply removed the nails, hauled the lumber to a new site, and reassembled the building.

Horatio Greenough, an American sculptor who returned to the United States in 1836 after an extended stay abroad, was amazed and a bit frightened by the pace

Europeans were shocked that Americans bolted their food or gorged themselves on any-thing within reach, as this English drawing indicates. Such habits reflected both the indif-ferent preparation of food and the frenetic tempo of American life.

that confronted him. "Go ahead! is the order of the day," he observed. "The whole continent presents a scene of scrambling and roars with greedy hurry." If the economic hallmark of this new order was the growth of a national market, there were social factors that also contributed to the new, restless America.

Population Growth

The American population continued to double about every 22 years—more than twice the birth rate of Great Britain. The census, which stood at fewer than 4 million in 1790, surpassed 9 million in 1820. By 1850, there were 23 million people living in the United States. Although the birth rate peaked in 1800, it evidenced only a slow decline before 1840. In the 1840s, which was a period of rapid urbanization, it dropped about 10 percent, the first significant decrease in American history. In cities, couples tended to be older at marriage and families were smaller, in part because the labor of children was not as critical to the family's welfare. At the same time, many basic population characteristics changed little throughout the first half of the nineteenth century: life expectancy did not improve significantly, the population was very young, and early marriage and family formation remained the norm, especially in rural areas.

From 1790 to 1820, natural increase accounted for virtually all of the country's population growth. But immigration, which had been disrupted by the Napoleonic Wars in Europe, revived after 1815. In the 1830s, some 600,000 immi-grants arrived, more than double the number in the quarter century after 1790, and this increase was just a foretaste of the flood of newcomers that reached America beginning in the late 1840s.

The vast areas of land available for settlement absorbed much of the burgeon-ing population. "Old America seems to be breaking up, and moving westward," Morris Birkbeck, an Englishman, declared in 1817. By 1850 almost half of the

American population lived outside the original 13 states, and well over 2 million lived beyond the Mississippi River. The population west of the Appalachian Mountains doubled in the decade 1810–1820, and it doubled again the following decade. By 1840, more than one American in three lived in the trans-Appalachian West.

The Federal Land Rush

As the tide of settlers pushed west, the federal government avidly encouraged them. In the great prosperity after 1815, speculation in western lands reached frenzied proportions as the government sold land on credit. Whereas in 1800 only 68,000 acres of the public domain had been sold, 1.3 million acres were sold in 1815, mostly to speculators, and in 1818 sales peaked at a staggering 3.5 million acres, an area larger than the state of Connecticut. In the ensuing depression that began in 1819, numerous speculators were ruined, and many farmers lost their farms. Congress reacted by abolishing credit sales and demanding full payment in cash, but it tempered this policy by lowering the price of the cheapest lands from $2.00 an acre to $1.25 (the best lands, sold at auction, fetched considerably higher prices, however). It also reduced the minimum tract to 80 acres, which meant that an ordinary farm could be purchased for a hundred dollars.

Squatters on public land, however, clamored for the right of preemption: the right to buy at the minimum price the land they had cleared and put into production before it was offered for sale at auction. Under federal law, squatters who had moved onto land before it had been surveyed and legally opened could be evicted without compensation by the rightful owner, although the owner, to avoid trouble, often paid something for the improvements. The issue of preemption divided those who favored rapid settlement of the West from those who wanted to increase federal revenue. In the 1830s, Congress moved toward the right of preemption by passing a series of special acts, which allowed the preemption of certain lands in the public domain. Finally, in 1841, it approved a general preemption law.

Even with these new laws, speculators purchased most of the public lands sold, since there was no limit on the amount of acreage an individual or land company could buy. These land speculators, who intended to hold property until it rose in value and then sell it, played a leading role in settlement of the West. Naturally, they could not afford to allow land to remain unsettled indefinitely, so to hasten sales, they usually sold land partially on credit—a vital aid to poorer farmers. They also provided loans to purchase needed tools and supplies. To repay these loans, farmers had to grow a commercial crop, and hence they needed access to markets. Many farmers became speculators themselves, buying up property in the neighborhood, keeping it until the population increased, and then selling their surplus to latecomers at a tidy profit. "Speculation in real estate has been the ruling idea and occupation of the western mind," one Englishman reported in the 1830s. "Clerks, laborers, farmers, storekeepers merely followed their callings for a living while they were speculating for their fortunes."

With the westward surge of the population came the admission of new states. In the 20 years before 1810, only four states entered the Union, whereas during the next decade no fewer than five were added. Four more came in by 1840, including Missouri and Arkansas, both west of the Mississippi. By 1860 seven additional states had joined the Union, including California and Oregon on the Pacific Coast.

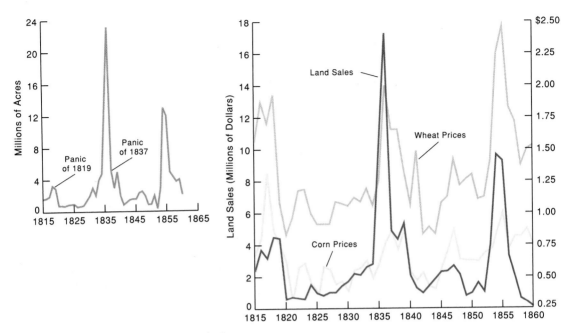

WESTERN LAND SALES AND THE PRICE OF CORN AND WHEAT

Western farmers' expectations of future income were tied to the price of corn and wheat. As commodity prices rose, farmers eagerly bought land on credit, anticipating that future profits would enable them to pay off their mortgages. As the chart illustrates, when wheat and corn prices fell sharply in the Panic of 1819, land sales plummeted and many farmers who had purchased on credit found themselves unable to pay their debts; a similar pattern is apparent in the 1830s. In the South there was a comparable relationship between land sales and the price of cotton.

Purchases of Public Land

YEAR	PRICE PER ACRE	MINIMUM ACREAGE	TERMS OF SALE
1785	$1.00	640	Cash
1796	2.00	640	One-half cash; 1 year to pay balance
1800	2.00	320	Payment over 4 years
1804	2.00	160	Payment over 4 years
1820	1.25	80	Cash
1832	1.25	40	Cash
1841	Preemption (squatter could buy up to 160 acres at minimum price of $1.25 per acre)		
1854	Graduation (price of unsold lands reduced over time to a minimum of 12.5 cents per acre)		

Geographic Mobility

Given such rapid settlement, geographic mobility became one of the most striking characteristics of the American people. The 1850 census revealed that nearly half of all native-born free Americans lived outside the state where they had been born. In Boston from 1830 to 1860 perhaps one-third of the inhabitants changed their place of residence each year. Unlike European peasants, who had a strong attachment to the village where their families had lived for generations, the typical American "has no root in the soil," visiting Frenchman Michel Chevalier observed, but "is always in the mood to move on, always ready to start in the first steamer that comes along from the place where he had just now landed." Americans had become much more mobile than they were during the colonial or Revolutionary era, and Chevalier thought the national emblem should be a steamboat or locomotive.

It was the search for opportunity, more than anything else, that accounted for such restlessness. An American moved, noted one British observer, "if by so doing he can make $10 where before he made $8." Alexis de Tocqueville commented that "in the United States a man builds a house to spend his latter years in it, and he sells it before the roof is on; he plants a garden, and lets it just as the trees are coming into bearing; he brings a field into tillage, and leaves other men to gather the crops; he embraces a profession, and gives it up; he settles in a place, which he soon afterwards leaves to carry his changeable longing elsewhere."

Urbanization

Even with the growth of national markets, the United States remained a rural nation. Nevertheless, a significant rise in urbanization occurred during the period. In 1820 there were only 12 cities with a population of more than 5000; by 1850, there were nearly 150. In 1820 the census classified only about 9 percent of the American people as urban (living in towns with a population of 2500 or more). Forty years later, the number had risen to 20 percent. Indeed, the four decades after 1820 witnessed the fastest rate of urbanization in American history. As a result, the ratio of farmers to urban dwellers steadily dropped from 15 to 1 in 1800 to 10.5 to 1 in 1830, and 5.5 to 1 in 1850. The most heavily urbanized area of the country was the Northeast, where in 1860 more than a third of the population was urban.* The South, with only 10 percent of its population living in cities, was the least urbanized. Improved transportation, the declining productivity of many eastern farms, the beginnings of industrialization, and the influx of immigrants all stimulated the growth of cities.

In 1850 six cities had populations exceeding 100,000. The largest, New York (which then did not include the city of Brooklyn), contained over half a million people, and older cities like Philadelphia, Boston, Baltimore, and New Orleans continued to be major urban centers. Equally significant was the rise of cities in the West. By 1850 Cincinnati and St. Louis each had over 100,000 people, and Chicago, which in 1830 had only about 8000 inhabitants, topped 50,000. Indeed, at the century's midpoint, 40 percent of the nation's total urban population lived in interior cities.

---

*The Northeast includes New England and the Middle Atlantic states (New York, Pennsylvania, and New Jersey). The South comprised the slave states plus the District of Columbia (page 455n).

St. Louis, a major urban center that developed in the West, depended on the steamboat to sustain its commerce, as this 1859 illustration makes clear.

All of these changes—the amazing growth of the population, the quickening movement westward, and the rising migration to the cities—pointed to a fundamental reorientation of American development. Expansion was the keynote of the new America, and the prospects it offered thrilled Americans. "Our population is destined to roll its resistless waves to the icy barriers of the north, and to encounter Oriental civilization on the shores of the Pacific," proclaimed former New York governor William H. Seward in 1846.

THE RISE OF FACTORIES

Another crucial element in the country's accelerating economic growth was the beginning of industrial manufacturing. This development required not only technological innovation but also a reorganization of the labor used to manufacture goods.

Before 1815 manufacturing had been done in homes or shops by skilled artisans, who turned out a small number of finished goods, often made to order for local customers. As master craftworkers, they imparted the secrets of their trades to apprentices and journeymen. In addition, women often worked in their homes part-time under the putting-out system, in which merchant capitalists supplied raw material from which these women made finished or partially finished articles. Weaving was traditionally done at home by both men and women, and many farm families manufactured items such as brooms and fans during the winter months.

After 1815, however, this older form of manufacturing began to give way to large-scale factories with machinery tended by unskilled or semiskilled laborers. The creation of a domestic market, the development of cheap transportation, the rise of cities, and the availability of capital and credit all stimulated the shift to factory production.

Technological Advances

Many of the earliest technological innovations were developed in England, including James Watt's steam engine (1769), spinning machinery, and the power loom. But Americans often improved on these inventions or adapted them to more extensive uses. In contrast to the more traditional societies of Europe, "everything new is quickly introduced here," one visitor commented in 1820. "There is no clinging to old ways; the moment an American hears the word 'invention' he pricks up his ears." To encourage experimentation, the United States established the Patent Office in 1790 and provided that inventors would enjoy exclusive use of a registered patent for 17 years. The number of patents averaged 77 a year during the first decade of the nineteenth century; by 1850 it had risen to nearly 1000 a year. Indeed, from 1790 to 1860 the United States granted more patents than England and France combined.

To protect their economic advantage, the British forbade the export of any textile machinery or drawings of such machines as well as the emigration of any craftworker trained in their design and construction. American legislatures countered by offering rewards to those who could provide plans, and in 1790, a 21-year-old English mill worker named Samuel Slater emigrated, pretending to be a farmer and carrying the necessary plans in his head. Backed by Moses Brown, a Providence merchant, Slater designed and built the first textile mill in America. Two decades later, the Boston merchant Francis Cabot Lowell imitated British designs for a power loom and then improved on them. In fact, American tinkering and innovation soon made the home-built models more efficient than the English originals.

The first machines were often complex and required highly skilled workers to build and repair the individual gears, cogs, and other parts. Eli Whitney had a better idea. Having won a contract to produce 10,000 rifles for the government, he developed machinery that would mass produce parts that were interchangeable from rifle to rifle. Such parts had to be manufactured to very rigid specifications, and it took Whitney a number of years to achieve the precision needed. But once the process was perfected, these parts allowed a worker to assemble a rifle quickly with only a few tools. As an experiment, a British commission studying Whitney's techniques disassembled a set of guns Whitney had produced over a 10-year period and mixed the parts together. Then one of Whitney's workers astonished the commission by selecting parts at random and assembling a gun without difficulty. Simeon North applied the same principle to the production of clocks and made the famous Connecticut clock affordable for the first time to most families; Chauncey Jerome followed North's example and soon surpassed him.

What rail and steam engines did for transportation, Samuel F. B. Morse's telegraph did for communications. Morse patented his device in 1837, but it was not until 1844 that he used a government subsidy to construct an experimental line from Washington to Baltimore. Soon telegraph lines fanned out in all directions, linking various parts of the country in instantaneous communication. By 1852 there were 23,000 miles of lines laid, and by 1860, over 50,000 miles. The telegraph to California was completed the following year. The new form of communication sped business information, helped link the transportation network, and allowed newspapers to provide their readers with up-to-date news.

Indeed, the invention of the telegraph and the perfection of a power press (1847) by Robert Hoe and his son Richard revolutionized journalism. The mechanical press sharply increased the speed with which sheets could be printed over the old hand method. Mass-produced newspapers, crammed with the latest news, became readily available. The penny press—newspapers costing only a penny, which was within reach of ordinary families—gained huge circulations through a skillful combination of news, gossip, and sensationalism. "These papers are to be found in every street, lane, and alley; in every hotel, tavern, counting-house, [and] shop," one editor noted. "Almost every porter and dray-man, while not engaged in his occupation, may be seen with a paper in his hands." Hoe's press had a similar impact on book publishing, as thousands of copies could now be printed at a price that mass audiences could afford.

Lacking a large pool of highly skilled workers, the United States took the lead in inventing machine tools that did not require great skill to operate. Whenever possible, American manufacturing relied on mechanization over human labor. The use of light machine tools and interchangeable parts constituted the American system of manufacturing.

Textile Factories

The factory system originated in the Northeast, where through lucrative foreign trade investors had accumulated the capital needed for expensive equipment, water power was abundant, good transportation facilities were available, and banks and other commercial institutions already existed. As in England, the production of cloth was the first manufacturing process to make use of the new technology on a large scale. Initially, factories like Samuel Slater's merely spun thread, which was then put out to be handwoven. But ultimately all of the processes of manufacturing cloth were brought together in a single location, from opening the cotton bales to weaving the cloth, and machines did virtually all the work.

In 1813 a group of wealthy Boston merchants, the most important of whom were Francis Cabot Lowell and Nathan Appleton, chartered the Boston Manufacturing Company and established the first fully integrated textile factory at Waltham, Massachusetts. Expanding their highly profitable operations, these investors, known as the Boston Associates, then organized the Merrimack Manufacturing Company and set up operations at Chelmsford—which was renamed Lowell, Massachusetts. Intended as a model community, Lowell soon became the most famous center of textile manufacturing in the country.

Its founders sought to avoid the misery and wretchedness that characterized the factory system in England. Instead of relying primarily on child labor or a permanent working class, Lowell employed daughters of New England farm families, and thus women were the first factory workers in the United States. Male supervisors lived in company houses; female workers stayed in company boarding-houses under the watchful eye of a matron. To its many visitors, Lowell presented an impressive scene, the town "new and fresh," with "a pile of huge factories, each five, six or seven stories high," wrote one visitor. "By the side of these larger structures rise numerous little wooden houses, painted white, with green blinds, very neat, very snug, very nicely carpeted, and with a few small trees around them. . . . [There are also] fancy-goods shops . . . vast hotels in the American style . . . canals, water wheels, water falls, bridges, banks, schools, and libraries." Female workers were encouraged to attend lectures and use the library; they even published their own magazine, the *Lowell Offering*. In this seemingly utopian setting, the Boston Associates intended to combine paternalism with high profits.

In reality, factory life involved a regimen of punctuality, strict work rules, and long hours of tedious, repetitive work. At Lowell, for example, workers could be fined for lateness or misconduct, such as talking on the job. The company forbade alcohol as well as cards and gambling in the shop or mill yard. Employees who did not go to church on the Sabbath were to remain inside, improving themselves by reading, writing, or other uplifting activities. The women's morals in the boardinghouses were strictly guarded; male visitors were allowed only in the presence of a chaperone, and there was a 10 p.m. curfew. Work typically began at 7 a.m. (earlier in the summer) and continued until 7 at night, six days a week. With only 30 minutes for the noon meal, many workers had to run to the boardinghouse and back to avoid being late. Winter was the "lighting up" season, when work began before daylight and ended after dark. The only light after sunset came from whale oil lamps that filled the long rooms with smoke. Even in summer the factories were poorly lit and badly ventilated. Although the labor was hard, the female operators received wages that were considered good by the standards of the time. They earned from $2.40 to $3.20 a week, depending on their skill and position, compared to less than a dollar a week for domestic servants and seamstresses, two of the most common jobs women held.

The average "mill girl," as they were called, was between 16 and 30 years of age. Contrary to a widely held assumption, most were not working to support their families back home on the farm. Their departure reduced the financial burden on the family, but most of the women kept their earnings in order to accumulate some money for perhaps the first time in their lives, to sample some of life's pleasures, and to save for a marriage dowry. "I must . . . have something of my own before many more years have passed," Sally Rice wrote when her parents asked her to return home to Somerset, Vermont. "And where is that something coming from if I go home and earn nothing? . . . I have but one life to live and I want to enjoy myself as well as I can." Like Rice, few women in the mills intended to work permanently, and most stayed no more than five years before marrying, taking up housekeeping, and raising a family. Mill workers often quit periodically to return home, then came back and, if they had left in good standing, resumed work. These interruptions from the tedious routine, the sense of sisterhood that united women in the boardinghouses, and their view of the situation as temporary rather than permanent, all made it easier for farm daughters to adjust to the stress and regimen the factory imposed on them.

Mary Paul went to work in the Lowell mills in November 1845 at the age of 15. The daughter of a rural New England family, she was working as a domestic servant when she asked her father for permission to go to Lowell. "I am in need of clothes which I cannot get about here," she explained, "and for that reason I want to go to Lowell or some other place." Two friends from her hometown of Barnard, Vermont, helped her find her first job, from which she earned $128 in 11 months; apparently she did not send any of it back to her father. After four years she returned home, but now found the "countryfied" style too confining and eventually left again. During the next seven years, she moved about and supported herself in several occupations, until at age 27 she married the son of a former Lowell boardinghouse keeper. Mary Paul's urban experiences had altered her outlook, and like the majority of mill workers traced in one study, she did not return to farm life, settling down instead in nearby Lynn, where her husband got a job in the marble works.

As competition in the textile industry intensified, factory managers undertook

Long hours and punctuality: that is the message of this Lowell timetable. Often accustomed to a less regimented life on a farm, laborers complained of the pace of the machines and the tyranny of the factory bell that summoned and dismissed them each day.

TIME TABLE OF THE LOWELL MILLS,

To take effect on and after Oct. 21st, 1851.

The Standard time being that of the meridian of Lowell, as shown by the regulator clock of JOSEPH RAYNES, 43 Central Street

	From 1st to 10th inclusive.				From 11th to 20th inclusive.				From 21st to last day of month.			
	1st Bell	2d Bell	3d Bell	Eve.Bell	1st Bell	2d Bell	3d Bell	Eve.Bell	1st Bell	2d Bell	3d Bell	Eve.Bell
January,	5.00	6.00	6.50	•7.30	5.00	6 00	6.50	•7.30	5.00	6.00	6.50	•7.30
February,	4.30	5.30	6.40	•7.30	4.30	5.30	6.25	•7.30	4.30	5.30	6.15	•7.30
March,	5.40	6.00		•7.30	5.20	5.40		•7.30	5.05	5.25		6.35
April,	4.45	5.05		6.45	4.30	4.50		6.55	4.30	4.50		7.00
May,	4 30	4.50		7·00	4.30	4.50		7.00	4.30	4.50		7 00
June,	"	"		"	"	"		"	"	"		"
July,	"	"		"	"	"		"	"	"		"
August,	"	"		"	"	"		"	"	"		"
September,	4.40	5.00		6.45	4.50	5.10		6.30	5.00	5.20		•7.30
October,	5.10	5.30		•7.30	5.20	5.40		•7.30	5.35	5.55		•7.30
November,	4.30	5.30	6.10	•7.30	4.30	5.30	6.20	•7.30	5.00	6.00	6.35	•7.30
December,	5.00	6.00	6.45	•7.30	5.00	6.00	6.50	•7.30	5.00	6·00	6.50	•7.30

* Excepting on Saturdays from Sept. 21st to March 20th inclusive, when it is rung at 20 minutes after sunset.

YARD GATES,

Will be opened at ringing of last morning bell, of meal bells, and of evening bells; and kept open Ten minutes.

MILL GATES.

Commence hoisting Mill Gates, Two minutes before commencing work.

WORK COMMENCES,

At Ten minutes after last morning bell, and at Ten minutes after bell which "rings in" from Meals.

BREAKFAST BELLS.

During March "Ring out"........at....7.30 a. m........."Ring in" at 8.05 a. m.
April 1st to Sept. 20th inclusive.....at....7 00 " " .... " " at 7.35 " "
Sept. 21st to Oct. 31st inclusive.....at....7.30 " " .... " " at 8.05 " "
Remainder of year work commences after Breakfast.

DINNER BELLS.

"Ring out"..... ....12.30 p. m........."Ring in".... 1.05 p. m.

In all cases, the *first* stroke of the bell is considered as marking the time.

to raise productivity. In the mid-1830s the mills began to increase the workloads. The most commonly used methods were the speed-up (increasing the speed of the machines), the stretch-out (increasing the number of machines each operator tended), and the premium system (paying bonuses for high productivity). Skilled women could make more money under the new system, but they had to work much harder to do so. The average worker's productivity rose by 71 percent, but her wages went up only 16 percent. Even these changes in work rules failed to maintain previous profits, and on several occasions factories cut wages.

The decline of paternalism and the ever-quickening pace of work finally provoked resistance among the women in the mills. Several times in the 1830s wage cuts precipitated strikes in which a minority of workers walked out. Management retaliated by firing strike leaders, hiring new workers, and blacklisting women who refused to return. In the 1840s, workers' protests focused on the demand for a 10-hour day. Perhaps a third of the female workers signed petitions calling for the shorter workday, but the legislature, siding with the owners, concluded that working conditions were not the state's responsibility.

As the mills expanded, a smaller proportion of the workers lived in company boardinghouses and moral regulations were relaxed. But the greatest change was a shift in the work force from native-born females to Irish immigrants. The Irish, who had comprised only 8 percent of the Lowell work force in 1845, made up almost half by 1860. In addition, 30 percent of the workers were men, and the number of children in the mills (many of whom also were Irish) doubled. The arrival of the Irish, who were desperately poor and did not view their situation as temporary, signaled the creation of a permanent working class. It also eventually led to a lowering of wages and a narrowing of the gap between the highest and lowest paying jobs in the factory.

Industrial Work

The transition to an industrial labor force with values and behavior patterns that were attuned to factory work was not a smooth one. Before the rise of the factory, artisans had worked within the home. Apprentices were considered part of the family and subject to the discipline and control of the master. Masters were responsible not only for teaching their apprentices a trade, but also for providing them some education and for supervising their moral behavior. Journeymen took pride in their work, knowing that if they developed their skills and were frugal, they could eventually set themselves up in a shop and become respected master artisans. Nor did skilled craftsmen work by the clock, at a steady pace, but rather in bursts of intense labor alternating with slow seasons, their work frequently interrupted for a pint of ale, a bit of gossip, or even a prank or two.

The factory, however, changed that. Pride in craftsmanship gave way to rates of productivity. Goods produced by factories were not as finished or elegant as those done by hand. Instead, the emphasis was on mass producing articles of lower quality that could be sold cheaply. At the same time that workers lost pride in their work, they were required to discard old habits. Industrialism demanded a worker who was sober, dependable, and self-disciplined. The machines, whirring and clacking away, set a strict schedule that had to be followed. Absenteeism, lateness, and drunkenness hurt productivity and, since work was specialized, disrupted the regular factory routine. Thus industrialization not only produced a fundamental change in the way work was organized, but also transformed the very nature of work.

The first generation to experience these changes did not adopt the new attitudes easily, and many workers persisted in the old ways. The factory clock became the symbol of the new work rules. One mill worker who finally quit complained revealingly about "obedience to the ding-dong of the bell—just as though we are so many living machines." With the loss of personal freedom also came the loss of pride in one's work and a sense of place in the community. Unlike the master–apprentice relationship, factories sharply separated workers from management, and few workers rose through the ranks to supervisory positions. In areas of the economy where factory production became dominant, even fewer could achieve the artisan's dream of setting up one's own business, since handcrafted goods were too expensive to be sold to any but the wealthy. Even well-paid workers sensed their decline in status.

The Shoe Industry

Shoemaking illustrates one way the artisan tradition came to be undermined. If Lowell was the symbol of the textile industry, nearby Lynn was the center of shoe manufacturing. Traditionally, a skilled cobbler possessed a good knowledge of leather, had the ability to cut out the various parts of a shoe, and could stitch and glue those parts together. He then sold the shoes in the same shop where he and his apprentices made them. Unlike the textile industry, shoemaking was not rapidly transformed by a shift to heavy machinery. That came only later, in the 1860s. But expanding transportation networks and national markets nevertheless fundamentally altered this business.

Micajah Pratt began selling shoes in 1812, a business in which his father John had prospered by selling to customers in New England. However, the younger Pratt found that if he could meet the demand for cheaply made shoes, there were ready markets in the South and West that he could ship to, beyond his father's traditional customers. Responding to these new opportunities, he hired workers to produce shoes in larger and larger central shops. He cut costs further by using new production techniques, such as standardized patterns and sole-cutting machines. Pratt eventually employed as many as 500 men and women and produced about a quarter-million pairs of shoes annually. Other shoe manufacturers adopted similar strategies.

With the shoe industry serving as a magnet, Lynn's population doubled every 20 years, yet so great was the national market that manufacturers could not keep pace with demand. More and more they hired farmers, fishermen, and their families, many of whom lived in other towns, putting out part-time work at home. Women and girls sewed the upper parts of a shoe, and men and boys attached the bottoms. While slow, this mode of production allowed wages to be reduced still further. A few highly paid workers performed critical tasks like cutting the leather, but most of the work was done either in large central shops or in homes. No longer able to make an entire shoe, workers lost their sense of craftsmanship and with it their status. In little more than a generation, shoemaking ceased to be a craft. Though not organized in a factory setting, it had become essentially an assembly-line process.

The Labor Movement

In this newly emerging economic order, workers sometimes organized to protect their rights and traditional ways of life. In the 1820s, workers formed political parties in several eastern cities. Such craftsmen as carpenters, printers, and tailors organized, and in 1834 individual unions came together in the National Trades' Union.

The leaders of these groups argued that labor was degraded in American society: workers endured long hours, low pay, and low status. Instead of a society where individuals were rewarded according to the value of their labor, the idle rich enslaved the industrious poor. Thus labor leaders, unlike most American social thinkers of the day, accepted the idea of conflict between different classes. They did not believe that the interests of workers and employers could be reconciled, and they blamed the plight of labor on monopolies, especially banking and paper money, and on machines and the factory system.

If the unions' rhetoric sounded radical, the solutions they proposed were moderate. Reformers agitated for public education, abolition of imprisonment for debt, political action by workers, and effective unions as the means to guarantee social equality and restore labor to its former honored position. In that sense, labor reformers looked to the ideology of the Revolution rather than to the notion of a working-class movement. Proclaiming the republican virtues of freedom and equality, they attacked special privilege, denounced the lack of equal opportunity, and decried workers' loss of independence. "As our fathers resisted unto blood the lordly avarice of the British ministry," affirmed the Lowell strikers in 1836, "so we, their daughters, never will wear the yoke which has been prepared for us."

The labor movement gathered some momentum in the decade before the Panic of 1837, but in the depression that followed, labor's strength collapsed. During hard times, few workers were willing to strike or engage in collective action. Nor did skilled craftsmen, who instituted the union movement, feel a particularly strong community of interest with semiskilled factory workers and unskilled laborers. More than a decade of agitation did finally bring the 10-hour day to most industries by the 1850s; and unions also campaigned hard for the right to strike, something that the authorities had long looked upon as an illegal conspiracy to restrain trade. Unions also confronted hostile public opinion, which held them guilty of price fixing contrary to the public good. In 1842, however, Chief Justice Lemuel Shaw of the Massachusetts Supreme Court upheld the basic right to strike in the case of *Commonwealth v. Hunt*. Gaining this right was a milestone in the history of the labor movement, but in the years before the Civil War the ruling had little impact.

Workers were united in their resentment of the industrial system and their loss of status, but they were divided by ethnic and racial antagonisms, gender, conflicting religious perspectives, occupational differences, party loyalties, and disagreements over tactics. And despite their longing for Revolutionary equality, most workers were unable to do much to ease the changes brought by the technologies of the factory system. For them, the factory and industrialism were not agents of opportunity but reminders of their loss of independence and a measure of control over their lives.

SOCIAL STRUCTURES OF THE MARKET SOCIETY

Laborers, farmers, and merchants were among the social groups affected by the rapidly developing economy. The revolution in markets, however, also restructured American society as a whole.

Historian William McNeill observes that "civilized societies were created and are sustained by dint of occupational differentiation and specialization." Clearly, the opening up of America to the market allowed society to become much more specialized. Transportation networks made it possible for farmers to concentrate on producing certain crops, while factories could focus on making a single item such as cloth or shoes. The growth of cities with their dense patterns of settlement made possible the development of more complex social relationships among buyers, sellers, and distributors. The rise of the factory system made the process of manufacturing more specialized through a division of labor. No longer did cobblers produce a pair of shoes from start to finish; the operation was broken down into more specialized (and less skilled) tasks. There was, as McNeill puts it, more "occupational differentiation."

This process evolved at different rates. Textiles and milling were completely mechanized, whereas other sectors of the economy, such as shoes and men's clothing, depended little on machinery. Slow to use steam engines, American manufacturing relied largely on water power. Moreover, large factories were the exception rather than the rule; except in fully mechanized industries, much of the manufacturing was done in smaller shops with few employees. Nevertheless, the tendency was toward more technology, greater efficiency, and increasing specialization. Textile factories illustrated this latter development. Initially textile companies built their own machinery and marketed their products, but eventually they began to purchase machines from firms that specialized in machinery construction and they sold their cloth to wholesalers who in turn marketed it.

These more complex structures had consequences for the home as well as the workplace. For the average eighteenth-century American woman, the home was a workplace where she produced items like thread, cloth, clothing, and candles. With the growth of factories, household manufacturing all but disappeared. As a result, women lost many of the economic functions they had previously performed in the family unit. Again, textiles are a striking example. Between 1815 and 1860, the price of a yard of cotton cloth fell from 18 to 2 cents. Because it was cheaper, smoother, and more brightly colored than homespun, most women purchased cloth rather than make it themselves. Similarly, the development of ready-made men's clothing reduced the amount of sewing women did. In urban centers, more men purchased clothing from retail stores. As Chapter 12 will make clearer, the growth of industry led to an economic reorganization of the family and a new definition of women's role in society.

The Distribution of Wealth

As American society became increasingly specialized and differentiated, greater extremes of wealth began to appear. Chauncey Jerome and Micajah Pratt demonstrated that if one's market were the nation—or even the world—greater riches could be amassed than by selling door to door, or even town to town. And as the new markets created fortunes for the few, the factory system lowered the wages of many ordinary workers by dividing labor into smaller and less skilled tasks.

Indeed, recent studies of local tax records have documented a growing concentration of wealth at the top of the social pyramid after 1815. Wealth was most highly concentrated in large eastern cities and in the cotton kingdom of the South, but everywhere the tendency was for the rich to get richer and own a larger share of the community's total wealth. In New York, Brooklyn, Boston, and Philadelphia, the top 1 percent of the wealthholders owned a quarter of the total wealth in 1825; by 1850, they owned half. Similar trends appeared in western cities, such as Cincinnati and St. Louis.

In contrast, those at the base of the social pyramid held a smaller percentage of a community's wealth. In Connecticut towns during the years 1831 to 1851 the number of inhabitants listed as having no property increased by 33 percent. In Cincinnati the bottom half of the city's taxpayers held 10 percent of the wealth in 1817; in 1860 their share had dropped to less than 3 percent. By 1860, in fact, 5 percent of American families owned more than 50 percent of the nation's wealth. Significantly, in villages where the market revolution had not penetrated, wealth tended to be less concentrated. Among rural towns in Massachusetts, wealth was most evenly distributed in precisely those towns that were the most economically stagnant.

In a market society, the rich were able to build up their assets because those with capital were in a position to increase it dramatically by taking advantage of new investment opportunities. As a result, family fortunes generally persisted from one generation to the next. Although a few men, such as Cornelius Vanderbilt and John Jacob Astor, vaulted from the bottom ranks of society to the top, most of the nation's richest individuals came from wealthy families. In one study of four major eastern cities, over 90 percent of the rich had wealthy parents, whereas only 2 percent had been born poor.

Social Mobility

The existence of great fortunes is not necessarily inconsistent with the idea of social mobility or property accumulation. Although the gap between the rich and the poor widened after 1820, even the incomes of most poor Americans rose, because the total amount of wealth produced in America had become much larger. From about 1825 to 1860, the average per capita income almost doubled to $300, a figure that exceeded that of western Europe. Europeans were impressed by how hard Americans worked, and also by their high standard of living. A Scottish immigrant testified that "the generality of working people in the United States live more sumptuously than most middle class people in England." Voicing the popular belief, a New York judge proclaimed, "In this favored land of liberty, the road to advancement is open to all."

Recent research indicates that such social mobility existed, but not to the degree claimed by contemporaries. In Philadelphia, during each decade between 1820 and 1860, perhaps 15 percent of the population who remained in the city improved their income or place of residence. At the same time, the proportion of those who lost wealth or status increased sharply until it roughly equaled the rate of upward mobility. Movement up and down was highest among those who worked in the lowest paying jobs. In the end, most laborers—or more often their sons—did manage to move up the social ladder, but only a rung or two. Few unskilled workers rose higher than to a semiskilled occupation. Even the children of skilled workers normally did not escape the laboring classes and enter the middle-class ranks of clerks, managers, or lawyers. For most workers, improved status came in the form of a savings account or home ownership, which gave them some security during economic downswings and in old age.

Materialism

Europeans who visited the United States during these years were struck by the degree to which Americans were preoccupied with material goods and achievements. The new generation did not invent materialism, but the spread of the market after 1815 made it much more evident. "I know of no country, indeed," Tocqueville commented, "where the love of money has taken stronger hold on the affections of men." And in 1836 the American writer Washington Irving coined the classic phrase that captured the spirit of the age when he spoke, in one of his stories, of "the almighty dollar, that great object of universal devotion throughout the land."

In a nation that had no legally established aristocracy, no established church, and class lines that were only informally drawn, wealth became the most obvious symbol of status. As one magazine explained, "Wealth is something substantial. Everybody knows that and feels it. Birth is a mere idea, which grows everyday more and more intangible." Materialism reflected more than a desire for physical comfort and luxury. It also represented a quest for respect and recognition. "Americans boast of their skill in money making," one contemporary observed, "and as it is the only standard of dignity and nobility and worth, they endeavor to obtain it by every possible means."

The emphasis on money and material goods left its mark on the American character. Often enough, it encouraged sharp business practices and promoted a greater tolerance of wealth acquired by questionable means. Families were rated by the size, not the source, of their fortunes. Americans also emphasized practicality over theory. "In no country in the civilized world," remarked Tocqueville, "is less attention paid to philosophy than in the United States." The esteem of the founding generation for intellectual achievement was often lost in the scramble for wealth that seemed to consume those who were developing new markets.

The Redefinition of Time

It was no accident that Chauncey Jerome's clocks spread across the land along with the market economy. The new methods of doing business required that society be structured more precisely. Actually, rural Americans who paced themselves according to the natural rhythms of a day were, in their own way, quite sophisticated about time. An Illinois farmer, for example, divided the last hours before sunrise into no less than eight different stages: long before day, just before day, just coming day, just about daylight, good light, before sunup, about sunup, and finally sunup. Factory life, however, required a more regimented time, where work commenced at the sound of a bell, workers kept machines going at a constant pace, and the day was divided into hours and even minutes.

Clocks began to invade private as well as public space. Before Chauncey Jerome and his competitors began using standardized parts, only the wealthy could afford clocks. But beginning in the 1830s, even farmers became more sensitive to time as they became integrated into the marketplace. As one frontier traveler reported in 1844, "In Kentucky, in Indiana, in Illinois, in Missouri, and here in every dale in Arkansas, and in cabins where there was not a chair to sit on, there was sure to be a Connecticut clock."

The Market at Work: Three Examples

To sense how much America was leaving behind Crèvecoeur's vision of a land of subsistence farmers, consider three examples of the new market economy, from a small city on the East Coast to the distant frontier of the Rocky Mountains.

In 1820, Kingston, New York, was a small, rural-oriented community of 1000 people, located along the Hudson River halfway between New York City and Albany. But in 1828 the Delaware and Hudson Canal linked Kingston with the Pennsylvania coal fields, jolting the town out of its economic lethargy. The rise of the coal trade stimulated local commerce, marked the shift to a cash economy, and greatly increased the number of banks and the variety of businesses. While still seasonal, the rhythm of life in Kingston changed. With the spring thaw still came a quickening of activity, but it now focused on the docks, stores, and canal boats rather than on planting and harvest. By 1850 Kingston had a population of 10,000, ten times that of 1820.

Its landscape changed too. Whereas in 1820 most storekeepers and craftsmen conducted business from their homes, by 1850 a commercial district had developed. As had already happened in the largest cities, Kingston's stores became specialized, some handling china and glassware, others dry goods, clothing, or jewelry and watches. Some blocks of the downtown area were devoted almost entirely to one type of trade or business. In addition, most of the manufacturing facilities were confined to two sections on the city's outskirts. Residential areas were separate from the commercial center and had become segregated along class lines, with the elite of the community, skilled workers, and unskilled laborers each living in their own neighborhoods. By midcentury, street signs and gas lamps were going up, and numbers were being assigned to buildings. Kingston had passed the urban threshold.

A thousand miles west, the small settlement of Sugar Creek, Illinois, presented an even more rural setting. The first white settlers had moved to Sugar Creek in 1817, just as the market revolution was getting under way. At that point, the village's pioneers were less worried about the market than about simply surviving. The land they plowed was not on the prairie (the available plows could not cut prairie grass roots), but in forests, where girdled trees often remained standing among the crops until they could be cleared. The roads to larger towns like Springfield were mere cart paths, winding hither and yon among the trees.

By the 1840s and 1850s, the market economy had made inroads at Sugar Creek. True, a farmer like Eddin Lewis might still keep an account book noting that James Wilson came by for "six days work planting corn [$]3.00." That was the traditional barter system in action, for no cash actually changed hands—Lewis was simply keeping tabs, noting also when he helped Wilson, so that eventually the account could be balanced. But Lewis had also begun to drive pigs down the road to St. Louis, where he received cash in return. By 1848 he was shipping south 6000 pounds of barreled pork, as well as lard and 350 bushels of corn. Wealth had become more concentrated in Sugar Creek, too: the richest farmers owned more land, which they rented to poorer tenants. Well-to-do farmers grew a few lucrative crops, which freed their wives from having to produce large amounts of butter for the market to make ends meet. Sugar Creek, in other words, was becoming more specialized, more stratified in terms of wealth, and more tied into regional and national markets.

Another thousand miles west a different sort of American roamed, who might at first seem the least connected to the bustle of urban markets. These were the legendary mountain men. Traveling across the Great Plains, along upland streams, and over the passes of the Rockies, hard-bitten outdoorsmen like Jim Bridger, Jedediah Smith, and James Walker wore buckskin hunting shirts, let their unkempt hair grow to their shoulders, and stuck pistols and tomahawks in their belts. In good times they feasted on buffalo blood, raw liver, and roasted hump; when game was scarce, some were not above holding their hands "in an ant-hill until they were covered with ants, then greedily [licking] them off," as one veteran trapper recalled. Wild and exotic, the mountain men quickly became romantic symbols of the American quest for individual freedom.

Yet these wanderers too were inextricably tied to the market. During their heyday, from the mid-1820s to the early 1840s, they hunted beaver, whose pelts were shipped east and turned into fancy hats for gentlemen. The fur trade was not a sporting event but a business, dominated by organizations like John Jacob Astor's American Fur Company, and the trapper was the agent of a vast economic structure that stretched from the mountains to the eastern cities and even to Europe. The majority of these men went into the wilderness not to flee civiliza-

Alfred Jacob Miller's *Caravan en Route* shows the annual procession of trade goods being shipped west during the fur trappers' heyday. Despite their colorful lifestyle, trappers were employees in a large-scale business enterprise organized along corporate lines and dominated by large fur companies.

tion, but to make money, and their ultimate goal was to accumulate capital in order to set themselves up in society. Of those who survived the fur trade, almost none remained permanently outside the bounds of civilization. In one sample of 446 trappers whose careers could be traced, only 5 stayed in the wilderness; 36 became ranchers or farmers, 22 transformed themselves into shopkeepers and traders, 10 became skilled workers, and 2 became bankers. Seven, capitalizing on their fame, entered politics. Far from repudiating society's values, the mountain men sought respectability and success as defined by the society they had temporarily left. They, like farmers, were expectant capitalists for whom the West was a land of opportunity.

PROSPERITY AND ANXIETY

The mountain men, the farmers of Sugar Creek, and the workers of Kingston were all alert to the possibilities of the market. Indeed, many citizens, buoyed by the expansion of their nation's frontiers and its economy, began to view history in terms of an inevitable and continuous improvement. "The irresistible tendency of the human race is therefore to advancement," historian George Bancroft argued in 1835. "The movement of the species is upward, irresistibly upward."

In fact, however, the path of commerce was not steadily upward. Rather it advanced in a series of wrenching boom–bust cycles: accelerating growth, followed by a crash and then a depression. The country remained extraordinarily prosperous from 1815 until 1819, only to sink into a depression that lasted from 1819 to 1823. The next cycle extended from 1823 to 1843, the economy expanding slowly during the 1820s, followed by almost frenzied speculation and investment in the 1830s. Then came the inevitable contraction in 1837, and the country suffered an even more severe depression from 1839 to 1843. The third cycle stretched from 1843 to 1861, again following the familiar pattern: gradual economic growth during the 1840s, followed by frantic expansion in the 1850s, and a third depression that began in 1857 and lasted until the Civil War began in 1861. In each of these depressions, thousands of workers were thrown out of work, overextended farmers lost their farms, and many businesses closed their doors.

In such an environment, prosperity, like personal success, seemed all too fleeting. Because Americans believed the good times would not, could not last— that the bubble would burst and another "panic" set in—their buoyant optimism was often tinged with a sense of insecurity and anxiety. They knew too many individuals like Chauncey Jerome, who had been rich and then lost all their wealth in a downturn. With the economy subject to such extreme fluctuations and seemingly impersonal forces, a person could be dragged down through no fault of his or her own.

The Panic of 1819

The initial shock of this boom-and-bust psychology came with the Panic of 1819, the first major depression in the nation's history. And like most American economic disasters, it was tied to events in Europe. From 1815 to 1818 cotton had commanded truly fabulous prices on the Liverpool market, reaching 32.5 cents a pound in 1818. The high prices meant high profits, and as eager investors looked for new opportunities, the federal government extended liberal credit to those who bought land. Similarly, the new national bank encouraged merchants and farmers to expand and buy more land and catch the rising tide. In the heady prosperity of the new economic order, few Americans preached the old republican values of simplicity and frugality.

But in 1819 world demand for American staples suddenly dropped. The price of cotton collapsed and took the rest of the economy with it. As the inflationary bubble burst, land values, which had been driven to unprecedented heights by the speculative fever, plummeted 50 to 75 percent almost overnight. As the economy went slack, so did the demand for western foodstuffs and eastern manufactured goods and services, sending the nation into a severe depression.

Because the market economy had spread to new areas, this economic downturn affected many Americans. The impact of the panic was not confined to cities and commercial centers, but it was felt in the countryside as well. Many farmers, especially in newly settled regions, had bought their land on credit, and farmers in established areas had expanded their operations in anticipation of future returns. When prices fell, both groups were hard-pressed to pay their debts. Moreover, because so many new cotton plantations had sprung up in the Southwest, many more southerners were now deeply enmeshed in the market. And because they sold most of their staples abroad, their income was especially vulnerable to fluctuations in the world market.

The Missouri Crisis

The Panic of 1819 brought an end to the optimism that had followed the War of 1812. The New Nationalism's spirit of cooperation gave way to jealousy and conflict between competing interests and social groups. Scrambling to weather the economic storm, southern planters, Yankee merchants, and western farmers looked first to their own welfare. So it was probably not surprising that smoldering sectional animosities flared again in 1819, when the Missouri Territory applied for admission as a slave state.

Before the crisis over Missouri, slavery had not been a major issue in American politics. Congress had debated the institution when Jefferson called for the prohibition of the African slave trade in 1808, the earliest year this could be done under the Constitution. Antislavery forces prevailed then, and Congress had outlawed the trade. Louisiana entered the Union in 1812 as a slave state—the first from the Louisiana Purchase—and in 1818 Missouri asked permission to come in too. It did not have a climate suitable for growing cotton and was thus unlikely to be a substantial slaveholding state. In the absence of any specific federal legislation, however, slavery had crossed the Mississippi River into the Louisiana Purchase. By 1820 there were 10,000 slaves in the Missouri Territory out of a total population of 66,000.

Since the adoption of the Constitution, four free states (Vermont, Ohio, Indiana, and Illinois), and five slave states (Kentucky, Tennessee, Alabama, Mississippi, and Louisiana) had been admitted to the Union. That made the tally in Congress 11 free and 11 slave states. As the federal government became stronger and more active, both the North and the South became increasingly anxious about maintaining their political power. The North's greater population gave it a majority in the House of Representatives, 105 to 81. The Senate, of course, was evenly balanced, since each state had two senators regardless of population. But Maine, which up to now had been part of Massachusetts, requested admission as the

THE MISSOURI COMPROMISE AND THE UNION'S BOUNDARIES IN 1820

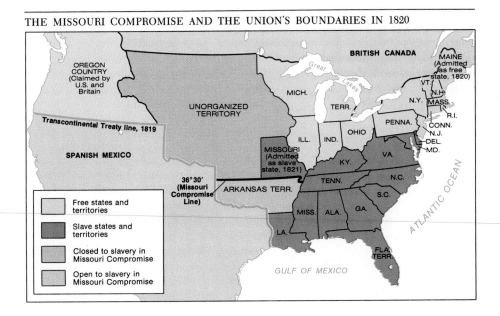

twelfth free state, which would upset the balance unless Missouri came in as a slave state. This was the delicate state of affairs in 1819 when Representative James Tallmadge of New York suddenly introduced an amendment designed to establish a program of gradual emancipation in Missouri.

The debate that followed was bitter. One New York paper argued that the issue "involves not only the future character of our nation, but the future weight and influence of the free states. If now lost—it is lost forever." The Richmond *Enquirer* made the same point from the southern perspective when it declared that if the North prevailed, "Virginia influence will be heard of no more." In addition, for the first time Congress directly debated the morality of slavery. The House approved the Tallmadge amendment, but the Senate refused to accept it, and the two houses deadlocked.

When Congress reconvened in 1820, Henry Clay of Kentucky, the Speaker of the House and a leading spokesman for the New Nationalism, proposed what came to be known as the Missouri Compromise. Under its terms, Missouri was admitted as a slave state and Maine as a free state. In addition, slavery was forever prohibited in the remainder of the Louisiana Purchase north of 36°30' (the southern boundary of Missouri). This division gave the North most of the Louisiana Purchase. The only remaining portion where slavery could exist was Arkansas, which was organized as a slave territory and eventually admitted as a slave state (1836). Clay's proposal, the first of several sectional compromises he would engineer in his long career, won congressional approval, ending the crisis. But southern fears for the security of slavery and northern fears about its spread remained. As Thomas Jefferson had gloomily predicted, "A geographical line, coinciding with a marked principle, moral and political, once conceived and held up to angry passions of men, will never be obliterated; and every new irritation will mark it deeper and deeper."

Yet sectional tensions, while ominous, tended to ebb and flow with events. The Panic of 1819 affected the political life of the nation in even more direct ways, for as the depression deepened and hardship spread, Americans saw government policies as at least partly to blame. The postwar nationalism, after all, had been based on a growing acceptance of the idea that government should stimulate economic development through a national bank and protective tariff, by improving transportation, and by opening up new lands. As Americans struggled to make sense out of their new economic order and their own personal situation, they began to take more direct control of the government that was so actively shaping their lives. During the 1820s, the popular response to the market and the Panic of 1819 produced a strikingly new kind of politics in the Republic.

SIGNIFICANT EVENTS

1790	Slater's textile mill opens
1793	Eli Whitney invents the cotton gin
1798	Whitney develops system of interchangeable parts
1807	Fulton's *Clermont* initiates regular steamboat service on the Hudson River
1810	*Fletcher v. Peck*
1810–1820	Cotton boom begins in the South
1811	First steamboat trip from Pittsburgh to New Orleans
1813	Waltham system initiated
1816	Second Bank of the United States chartered; protective tariff enacted
1818–1825	Erie Canal constructed
1819	*Dartmouth College v. Woodward*; *McCulloch v. Maryland*; *Sturges v. Crowninshield*
1819–1823	Panic and depression
1820	Missouri Compromise; Lowell mills established
1824	*Gibbons v. Ogden*
1825–1850	Canal era
1830	Baltimore and Ohio Railroad begins passenger service
1834	National Trades' Union founded
1837	Panic
1839–1843	Depression
1841	Preemption Act
1842	*Commonwealth v. Hunt*
1844	Samuel F. B. Morse sends first telegraphic message
1847	Rotary printing press invented

11

The Rise of Democracy

The notice, printed in the small but estimable newspaper of Monticello, Mississippi, made the rounds along the Pearl River. The readers peered at the advertisement by candlelight, in rough log cabins tucked along the piney woods trails; or perhaps together, among a knot of idlers lounging comfortably outside the county courthouse; or perhaps even over in Natchez, shooting billiards barefoot in the late afternoon light while trying to keep the mosquitoes at bay. Someone who knew how to read might happen on the notice and then, grinning, share it with the rest of the crowd. A traveler, the advertisement proclaimed, had lost a suitcase while fording the Tallahala River; the contents included "6 ruffled shirts, 6 cambric handkerchiefs, 1 hair-brush, 1 tooth-brush, 1 nail-brush. . . ."

And as the list went on, the reaction of the listeners would inevitably shift from amusement to disdain and beyond. ". . . 1 pair curling tongs, 2 sticks pomatum . . . 1 box pearl-powder, 1 bottle Cologne, 1 [bottle] rose-water, 4 pairs silk stockings, and 2 pairs kid gloves." The howls of derision that filled the air could only have increased upon learning that anyone finding said trunk was requested to contact the owner—Mr. Powhatan Ellis of Natchez.

Powhatan Ellis was no ordinary backcountry traveler. Born into a genteel Virginia family that claimed descent from Pocahontas, Ellis had moved in 1816 to the raw Southwest to seek his fortune. With his cultivated tastes, careful dress, and stately dignity, he upheld the tradition of the gentleman politician. In Virginia he would have commanded respect—indeed, in Mississippi he had been appointed district judge and United States senator. But for the voters along the Pearl River, the advertisement for his trunk of ruffled shirts, hair oils, and fancy "skunkwater" proved to be the political kiss of death. His opponents branded him an aristocrat and a dandy, and his support among the piney woods farmers evaporated faster than a morning mist along Old Muddy on a sweltering summer's day.

No one was more satisfied with this outcome than the resourceful Franklin E. Plummer, one of Ellis' political enemies. In truth, while the unfortunate Powhatan Ellis had lost a trunk fording a stream, he had never placed the advertisement trying to locate it. That was the handiwork of Plummer, who well understood the new playing field of American politics in the 1820s. If Powhatan Ellis typified the passing political world of the revolutionary era, Plummer was a product of the raucous democratic system emerging in its place. Leaving his home in New England during the hard times following the Panic of 1819, he had worked

A Whig parade in Philadelphia, 1840, painted by Francis Schell. "It seems as though every man, woman, and child preferred politics to anything else," wrote one politician at the end of the campaign.

his way downriver to New Orleans, then headed inland to Mississippi. Settling in a new community, he set himself up as an attorney, complete with a law library of three books. Plummer's ambition, shrewdness, and oratorical talent compensated for his lack of legal training, and he became the first member of the legislature elected from his county.

Plummer's ambition soon flowed beyond the state capital. In 1830 he announced his candidacy for Congress against Colonel James C. Wilkins, a wealthy Natchez merchant, military hero, and member of the state's ruling political clique. The uncouth Plummer seemed overmatched against such a distinguished opponent, and at first few observers took his candidacy seriously. In his campaign, however, he boldly portrayed himself as the champion of the people battling against the aristocrats of Natchez. Contrasting his humble background with that of his opponent, Plummer proclaimed: "We are taught that the highway to office, distinction and honor, is as free to the *meritorious poor* man, as to the *rich;* to the man who has risen from obscurity by his own individual exertions, as to him who has inherited a high and elevated standing in society, founded on the patrimony of his ancestors." Taking as his slogan "Plummer for the People, and the People for Plummer," he was easily elected.

Plummer was a campaigner who knew how to affect the common touch. Once, while canvassing the district with his opponent, the pair stopped at a farmhouse. When his opponent, seeking the farmer's vote, kissed the daughter, Plummer picked up a toddling boy and began picking red bugs off him, telling the enchanted mother, "They are powerful bad, and mighty hard on babies." On another occasion, while his opponent slept, Plummer rose at dawn to help milk the family's cow—and won another vote. He was a master at secretly planting false stories attacking himself in the press, and then bringing forth personal testimonials of well-known men defending his character and denouncing the charges against him.

As long as Plummer maintained his image as one of the people, fighting their battles against aristocrats, he remained invincible. But in 1835 when he became a candidate for the U.S. Senate, his touch deserted him. Borrowing money from a Natchez bank, he purchased a stylish coach, put his servant in a uniform, and campaigned across the state. Having become beholden to the wealthy, he abruptly dropped his attacks on banks and aristocrats. His followers abandoned him and he was soundly defeated. He died in 1852 in obscurity and poverty. Ah, Plummer! Even the staunchest of nature's noblemen may stumble, prey to the temptations of power and commerce!

Indeed, Franklin Plummer was being pulled two ways by the forces transforming American society. As the previous chapter explained, the growth of commerce and new markets opened up opportunities for more and more Americans during these years. "Opportunity" was one of the bywords of the age. Through his connections with bankers and the well-to-do, Plummer saw the opportunity to accumulate wealth, to hire a servant and a coach, to gain status and respect. It was the growth of a market economy that made these opportunities possible, not only for Plummer, but also for farmers speculating in western lands and shoe merchants in Lynn seeking profits by selling throughout the country.

Yet at the same time that new markets were producing a more stratified, unequal society, the nation's politics were becoming more democratic. The new political system that developed after 1820 was strikingly different from the system of the early Republic. Just as national markets linked the regions of America

As this nattily dressed oyster seller suggests, clothes were not much help in sorting out social status in America. Although the clothing of the upper class was often made of finer material and was more skillfully tailored, by the 1820s the less wealthy were wearing similar styles. One visitor expressed amazement at seeing common workers in sleek coats, glossy hats, and doeskin gloves.

economically, the new system of national politics involved more voters than ever before, adopted more democratic electioneering techniques, and created a new class of politicians. Plummer's world reflected that new political culture. And its central feature—another byword on everyone's lips—was "equality." What was the relation between the new equalities of politics and the new opportunities of the market?

EQUALITY AND OPPORTUNITY

Middle- and upper-class Europeans who visited the United States during these decades were especially sensitive to how much of an egalitarian society America had become. Coming from the more traditional and stratified society of Europe, they were immediately struck—often unfavorably—by the "democratic spirit" that had become "infused into all the national habits and all the customs of society." Europeans spent only a few days traveling American roads before the blunt contours of Franklin Plummer's world were brought home to them.

To begin with, they discovered that only one class of seats was available on stagecoaches and rail cars. And these were filled according to the rough-and-ready rule of first come, first served. In steamboat dining rooms or at country taverns, everyone ate at a common table—sitting alongside their fellow "democrats," sharing food from the same serving plates, and ordering from a common menu. As one upper-class gentleman complained, "The rich and the poor, the educated and the ignorant, the polite and the vulgar, all herd on the cabin floor, feed at the same table, sit in each others laps, as it were." Being ushered to bed at an inn, visitors found themselves lodged 10 to 12 people a room, often with several bodies occupying a single bed. Fastidious Europeans were horrified at the thought of sleeping with unwashed representatives of American democracy.

Indeed, the democratic "manners" of Americans seemed positively shocking. Europeans were used to social inferiors speaking only if spoken to. But Americans felt free to strike up a conversation "on terms of perfect equality," with no sense that they were intruding. Frances Trollope, the mother of the English novelist Anthony Trollope, was offended by the "coarse familiarity of address" between classes, while another visitor complained that in a nation where every citizen felt free to shake the hand of another, it was impossible to know anyone's social station. This informality—a forward, even *rude* attitude—was not limited to shaking hands. At theaters, it was hard to get patrons to remove their hats so those behind them could see. And American men seemed always to be slouching when they sat, their feet propped up on a nearby stool, legs dangling this way or that, bodies lying full length on a bench; "perfectly indescribable," sniffed Mrs. Trollope. Not only that, they chewed tobacco and spit constantly—in the national Capitol, in courts and hospitals, even on the floor in homes (although one visitor at least claimed that no gentleman would spit in the living room). Fanny Kemble, an English actress who toured the United States and eventually married an upper-class southerner, reported that on an American steamboat "it was a perfect shower of saliva all the time."

When Plummer took on airs, he made the mistake of dressing his servant in a formal uniform. Few servants in America stood for such unrepublican treatment. An American "will not wear a livery," one visitor explained, "any more than he will wear a halter around his neck." Those who did hire themselves out refused to be called "servants," insisting on the term "help" and on being treated as part of the family. They took their meals at the same table and refused to be summoned by bells. Indeed, except in the South, where black slaves served their owners through the legally enforced system of slavery, no permanent class of domestic servants existed in America. Before the first large wave of immigration began in the mid-1840s, wealthy families often could not hire "help" at any price.

Americans were self-consciously proud of such democratic behavior, which they viewed as a valued heritage of the Revolution. One European reported that a tailor refused to come to his room to fit him for a suit, since to do so would be "unrepublican." And the keelboaters who carried the duke of Orléans—the future King Louis-Philippe of France—on a trip down the Mississippi made their republican feelings plain when the keelboat ran aground. "You kings down there!" called the captain. "Show yourselves and do a man's work, and help us three-spots pull off this bar!" The ideology of the Revolution made it clear that, in the American deck of cards at least, "three-spots" counted as much as jacks, kings, and queens. Kings were not allowed to forget that—and neither was Franklin Plummer.

The Tension Between Equality and Opportunity

While Americans extolled opportunity and equality, a fundamental tension existed between these values, because widespread opportunity would inevitably produce inequality of wealth. In Crèvecoeur's America, a rough equality of wealth and status had prevailed because of the lack of opportunity. In 1800, shoemakers in Lynn, with no way to ship large quantities of shoes across the country, could not become wealthy. Without steamboats or canals, farmers in Jefferson's day could not market surplus grain for profit. But by the 1820s and 1830s, as the opportunities of the market expanded, wealth became much more unevenly distributed. Thus the new generation had to confront contradictions in the American creed that their parents had been able to conveniently ignore.

By equality, Americans did not mean equality of wealth or property. Calls for the redistribution of property were doomed to failure. "I know of no country where profounder contempt is expressed for the theory of permanent equality of property," Alexis de Tocqueville wrote. Thomas Skidmore, a New York City labor leader, did argue that inherited property should be confiscated and redistributed. But even the workers' movement spurned him as too radical. Nor did equality mean that all citizens had equal talent or capacity. Americans realized that individuals possessed widely differing abilities, which inevitably produced differences in wealth. "Distinctions in society will always exist under every just government," Andrew Jackson declared. "Equality of talents, or education, or of wealth cannot be produced by human institutions."

What Americans upheld, in the final analysis, was the equality of opportunity, not equality of condition. Self-made men such as John Jacob Astor, whose fortune came from the western fur trade, were celebrated as the fulfillment of the American dream—examples to be emulated. "True republicanism requires that every man shall have an equal chance—that every man shall be free to become as unequal as he can," one American commented. In a world of expanding markets, increasing national wealth, and an economy that could go bust as well as boom, Americans agreed that one of the primary objectives of government was to safeguard opportunity. Thus the new politics of democracy walked hand in hand with the new opportunities of the market.

THE NEW POLITICAL CULTURE OF DEMOCRACY

The stately James Monroe, with buckled shoes and breeches, his hair powdered and tied in a queue, was not part of the new politics. The last president of the Revolutionary generation, he was suspicious of political parties and rejoiced in the Era of Good Feelings, when party competition seemed to be dying. But as he neared the end of his second term in 1824, a host of new leaders in the Republican party looked to succeed him. Traditionally, a congressional caucus selected the party's presidential nominee; in 1824, the Republican caucus settled on William H. Crawford of Georgia. But Crawford's rivals condemned "King Caucus" as undemocratic. Rejecting the party's official nominee, three other Republicans continued to seek the presidency, all of them ardent nationalists. John Quincy Adams, son of the second president, had once been a Federalist, but as Monroe's secretary of state he strongly pushed for American expansion. John C. Calhoun, Monroe's secretary of war, and Henry Clay, the Speaker of the House, both supported the national bank, a protective tariff, and federal aid for internal improvements.

None of these men bargained on the sudden emergence of another Republican candidate, Andrew Jackson, the hero of the Battle of New Orleans. Jackson was an unexpected choice, for among all previous presidents, only Washington had been a military leader; the others had each spent a long apprenticeship in public office. Jackson had served in the House and the Senate for only three years, and he had briefly been governor of the Florida Territory. At first no one took his candidacy seriously, including Jackson himself. But soon the general's supporters and rivals began receiving reports of his popularity. One of Calhoun's lieutenants in Pennsylvania sent word that Jackson sentiment was strong among "the grog shop politicians of the villages and rabble of Philadelphia and Pittsburgh." From Cincinnati an observer wrote, "Strange! Wild! Infatuated! All for Jackson!" Savvy politicians soon flocked to his standard, but it was the people who first made Jackson a serious candidate.

The Election of 1824

Calhoun eventually dropped out of the race, but that still left four candidates, none of whom received a majority of the popular vote. Jackson led the field, however, and finished first in the Electoral College with 99 votes. Adams had 84, Crawford 41, and Clay 37. Under the Twelfth Amendment, the House was to select a president from the top three candidates. Clay, though himself eliminated, held enough influence as Speaker of the House to name the winner. After a private meeting between the two, he threw his support to Adams, who was elected.

Two days later, Adams announced that Clay would be his new secretary of state; in each of the previous three administrations, the secretary of state had succeeded to the presidency. Jackson and his supporters promptly took up the charge of a "corrupt bargain" between Adams and Clay. Before Adams had even assumed office, the 1828 race was under way.

Even more significant, the election of 1824 had shattered the old party system. The Federalists were long gone, the Republicans hopelessly divided. Political competition would not wither away in a permanent era of good feelings, for the simple reason that differing economic, social, and regional elements in society would continue to advance conflicting interests. But as the old system was breaking up, what would replace it? Henry Clay and John Quincy Adams began to organize a new party, known as the National Republicans to distinguish it from Jefferson's old party, while Jackson's disgruntled supporters were beginning to call themselves Democrats. To muddy the waters even further, a third party arose out of a controversy that erupted in 1826.

Anti-Masonry and the Defense of Equality

The controversy centered on a secret organization known as the Freemasons (or simply Masons), a fraternal group whose chapters had spread through Europe and America during the eighteenth century. Members like George Washington and Benjamin Franklin shared the Enlightenment's belief in the power of reason and the idea of progress, while embracing the Masons' moral commitment to temperance, charity, and hard work. Members were taught this code through secret initiation rituals as they gradually rose through various "degrees" of membership. By 1826, the 150,000 American Masons were predominantly business leaders, manufacturers, and professionals, and the order especially attracted ambitious young men eager to take advantage of the contacts it provided. While Masons were often above average in wealth, their power and prestige stemmed more from the number of public offices they held. In Genesee County, New York, for example, where the Erie Canal was spawning new markets and new fortunes, half of the county's officeholders and an even larger proportion of town officers were Masons.

It was along the canal that William Morgan, a disgruntled Mason, announced

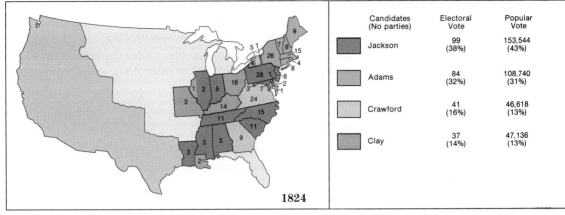

Candidates (No parties)	Electoral Vote	Popular Vote
Jackson	99 (38%)	153,544 (43%)
Adams	84 (32%)	108,740 (31%)
Crawford	41 (16%)	46,618 (13%)
Clay	37 (14%)	47,136 (13%)

1824

ELECTION OF 1824

in 1826 that he intended to publish a book exposing the secrets of the order. Not long after, he was seized by a group of Masons and, crying "Murder," forced into a closed carriage and spirited off into the night. Morgan was never seen again, but little doubt exists that he was murdered, allegedly near Niagara Falls. Indignant citizens in western New York demanded an investigation, and when prominent Masons used their power to thwart it, the Anti-Masonic movement, which demanded eradication of the order, mushroomed. By 1830 the Anti-Masons had organized in 10 states as a political party. William Wirt, Monroe's former attorney general, ran for president on its ticket in 1832.

In national terms, Morgan's disappearance was a relatively minor incident, but it touched raw nerves in an egalitarian society. The Masons, with their secret rituals and shadowy influence, seemed a sinister threat to equality and opportunity. One of the secret oaths its members swore was to advance a "brother's" best interest "by always supporting his military fame and political preferment in opposition to another." Confronted with the power of such an "aristocratic" order, how could ordinary citizens compete? "The direct object of freemasonry," one Anti-Masonry writer charged, "is to benefit the few at the expense of the many, by creating a privileged class, in the midst of a community entitled to enjoy equal rights and privileges." The Anti-Masons argued that in a society of equals, the rule of law should settle disputes—not aristocratic power or secret connections. They looked for new ways to organize politically, to involve more citizens in politics, and to reform society through public opinion and voting.

As a rule, Anti-Masonry was strongest in the most populous, rapidly developing, market-oriented towns. Poor farmers who lacked access to markets but wanted it, as well as farmers in newly opened areas who had become dependent on city banks and merchants for credit or who wanted new roads or canal lines to come their way, were often suspicious of Masonic officeholders. Anti-Masonry also represented a fervent desire to Christianize society and root out organizations like the Masons that exalted reason over traditional religion. The movement was especially powerful in communities with many churches, and it attracted strong support from evangelical Protestants, particularly Baptists, Methodists, Presbyterians, and Congregationalists. In attacking Masonry as an infidel society, the Anti-Mason movement represented a protest against the increasingly secular aspects of American life, which the spread of the market had strengthened.

The new parties were one indication of how much the political system was in flux. By the mid-1830s, what historians now call the second American party system would be in place. The National Republicans gave way to the Whigs, a new party whose organization absorbed many members of the fading Anti-Masons. The Democrats, as the other major party, came together under the leadership of Andrew Jackson. Once established, the second American party system dominated the nation's politics until the 1850s.

Social Sources of the New Politics

Why was it that a new style and new system of politics emerged in the 1820s? We have already seen that a revolution in markets was under way: stimulated by new transportation networks, a more diversified economy, and a more stratified and urbanized society, was emerging. We have seen, too, the immense westward migration, the scramble to bring new land into the market, and the speculative land boom that collapsed in the Panic of 1819. The rise of the new political culture was rooted in these social conditions. During the sharp depression that followed, many Americans became convinced that government policy had aggravated, if not actually produced, hard times. Consequently, they decided that the government had a responsibility to relieve distress and promote prosperity.

The connection made between government policy and economic well-being was the fundamental cause of a rising popular interest in politics during the 1820s. For the first time, large numbers of Americans saw politics as relevant to their daily lives. As agitation mounted for government, especially at the state level, to provide assistance, voters demanded leaders who would respond to the popular will. In several states, notably Kentucky, a movement arose for the legislature to provide debtor relief by enacting a moratorium on the collection of debts. Elections soon became the means through which the majority expressed its policy preferences, by voting for candidates pledged to specific programs. The older style of politics, where a representative took the lead in shaping opinion rather than following it, gave way to the notion that representatives were to carry out the will of the people, as expressed in the results of elections.

As more citizens championed the "will of the people," pressures mounted to open up the political process. Most states had traditionally required voters to own a certain amount of property, to guarantee that they had a "stake in society" if they were to vote on matters concerning the common good. By 1824, only four states (Virginia, North Carolina, Rhode Island, and Louisiana) maintained significant property qualifications for voting. In the others, something approximating white manhood suffrage, under which all free white males were allowed to vote, prevailed. Similarly, property requirements for officeholders were reduced or dropped.

Presidential elections became more democratic as well. In 1800, when Jefferson was elected, only two states allowed the voters rather than the legislature to choose presidential electors. By 1832 South Carolina was the only state that had not reformed its system. States also began casting their electoral votes for president in a single bloc, rather than by districts. This winner-take-all principle increased the power of the most populous states and made it all but impossible for minor parties to wield power or control the election of president. And because a candidate had to carry a number of states in different sections of the country, the backing of a national party, with effective state and local organizations, became essential.

As Jefferson's old Republican party splintered, reformers objected to the legislative caucus as a way of choosing party candidates. Other techniques were tried,
such as Jackson's nomination by the Tennessee legislature and Calhoun's endorsement in a public letter signed by a small number of congressmen. But it was the
Anti-Masons who pioneered what they argued was a more democratic approach: a
party convention to nominate candidates and approve a platform on the crucial
issues of the election. By 1832 the other parties were also bringing delegates
together at conventions to select state and local tickets, write party platforms, and
celebrate partisan fellowship.

As the new reforms went into effect, voter turnout soared. In the 1824 presidential election, only 27 percent of eligible voters bothered to go to the polls.
Four years later, the proportion had more than doubled to 56 percent, and in
1840, the apex of the second party system, 78 percent of eligible voters cast ballots, probably the highest turnout in American history. In some states over 90
percent voted in national elections. As the Democrats and the Whigs became truly
national parties fielding competitive slates, voter interest intensified.

The Acceptance of Parties

All these developments worked to favor the rise of a new type of politician: one
whose life was devoted to party service and who often depended for his living on
public office. As the number of state-sponsored internal improvement projects
increased during the 1820s, so did the number of government jobs that could
support party workers. No longer was politics primarily the province of the
wealthy, who often served out of a sense of duty and spent only part of their time
on public affairs. Instead, the profession became an important avenue of social
mobility. Political leaders were much more likely to come from the middle ranks
of society, especially outside the South. Many became economically established
after entering politics, but as Franklin Plummer demonstrated, large sums of
money were not required to conduct a campaign. Indeed, given the new state of
affairs, a successful politician had to mingle with the masses, voice their feelings,
and identify with them—requirements that put the wealthy elite at a disadvantage.

In many ways, Martin Van Buren epitomized the new political leader. The
son of a New York tavernkeeper, Van Buren was a self-made man who used his
success as a lawyer to launch his political career. A master organizer and tactician,
he built alliances and gained power even though he lacked a charismatic style.
Like Van Buren, whose career took him to the U.S. Senate and eventually the
White House, the new breed of politician was beholden to the party system and
highly adept at manipulation and party management.

Indeed, it was Van Buren who played a decisive role in promoting a dramatic
new attitude toward political parties. The older Revolutionary generation, like
Washington, Jefferson, and Monroe, regarded political parties as dangerous and
destructive—necessary evils at best. Van Buren took a more positive attitude.
Parties were not only "inseparable from free governments," he argued, but "in
many and material respects . . . highly useful to the country." He conceded that
they were subject to abuse, like any organization, but insisted that they were
essential for dealing with the inevitable conflicts that arose in any free political
system. Competing parties would scrutinize each other and check abuses, at the
same time that they kept the masses informed and politically involved.

"The Will of the People the Supreme Law" reads the banner at this county election. One of the few occasions when most of the men would assemble at the village, election day remained an all-male event, as well as a time of excitement, heated debate, and boisterous celebration. As citizens give their oath to an election judge, diligent party workers dispense free drinks, solicit support, offer party tickets, and keep a careful tally of who has voted. Liquor and drinking are prominently featured: one voter enjoys another round, a prospective voter who is too drunk to stand is held up by a faithful party member, and on the right one groggy partisan is obviously the worse for wear.

Parties also subjected private individuals to discipline and control. If leaders were to be politically successful, they had to consider more than their own personal ambitions. In addition, patronage became a crucial means of holding parties together by rewarding members for faithful service. Finally, parties, by uniting the different sections in a single political organization, helped dampen sectional rivalries. For Van Buren, who had been badly shaken by the Missouri crisis of 1820, parties and the discipline they wielded provided the means to keep the slavery issue out of national politics—which virtually all politicians agreed was essential if the Union was to be preserved.

The Politics of the Common Man

The Jacksonian era has been called the Age of the Common Man. Certainly in politics the ordinary citizen was celebrated as never before. Andrew Jackson, one of the first political leaders to grasp this change, invoked the often-expressed refrain of American politics when he insisted, "Never for a moment believe that the great body of the citizens . . . can deliberately intend to do wrong." To be born in a log cabin became a great advantage, and party leaders everywhere avoided aristocratic airs when on the stump. "I have always dressed chiefly in *Home spun* when among the people," one North Carolina congressman explained. "If a Candidate be dressed Farmerlike he is well received and kindly remembered by the inmates of the Log Cabin, and there is no sensation among the children or the *chickens.*"

Politics became mass entertainment, with campaign hoopla frequently over-shadowing issues. Parades complete with floats and marching bands, massive rallies sometimes involving thousands of people, glee clubs, torchlight processions, barbecues, picnics, and free whiskey were used to rouse voters. Treating to drinks became an almost universal campaign tactic. One Kentucky politician admitted that electoral success depended on understanding that "the way to men's hearts is down their throats." Although politicians talked often about principles, political parties were pragmatic organizations, intent on gaining and holding power, and no party could long survive if it did not have a realistic chance of electing a president.

The new politics created an enthusiastic electorate with strong loyalties. By the time the second party system reached maturity, most voters identified with one of the two major parties and supported its candidates through thick and thin. Given such strong loyalties, elections became deeply felt battles between two competing armies, led by men who claimed that the very survival of the Republic hinged on the outcome.

Certainly the politics of the "common man" had distinct limits. Women and slaves were not allowed to vote, nor could free African-Americans (except in a few states) and Indians. Nor did the parties always deal effectively with (or even address) basic problems in society. Still, the importance of Van Buren's insight was fundamental. If the United States was to expand and prosper, the political system had to resolve peacefully differences among competing interest groups, regions, and social classes.

JACKSON'S RISE TO POWER

The new democratic style of politics first appeared on the state and local levels: Van Buren deftly working behind the scenes in New York; Amos Kendall of Kentucky campaigning in favor of debtor relief; Davy Crockett of Tennessee carefully dressed in frontier garb and offering voters a drink from a jug of whiskey and a chew from a large plug of tobacco. But the national implications of these changes were not clear until Andrew Jackson came to power in 1829 as the head of a new, well-organized party. John Quincy Adams might have created a mass-based party when he assumed the presidency in 1825, but while Adams could think nationally— even continentally—about America's future, he was temperamentally unsuited to the task.

John Quincy Adams' Presidency

Adams had been a talented diplomat and a great secretary of state. Intelligent and far-seeing, he was eminently fit to be president—except that he had hardly a political bone in his body. The cold and tactless Adams could build no popular following, and his first message to Congress even urged members not to be "palsied by the will of our constituents." As a committed nationalist, he proposed a series of far-reaching programs to promote internal improvements, manufacturing and agriculture, and exploration of the interior, as well as to support the arts, literature, and the sciences. But such sweeping recommendations left his opponents aghast, and since Adams would not deign to seek support for them, his proposals languished.

Nor would Adams take any steps to gain reelection, though he earnestly desired it. Despite urgent pleas from Henry Clay and other advisers, he declined to remove from federal office men who actively opposed him. Since Adams refused to be a party leader, Clay undertook to organize the National Republicans. But with a reluctant candidate at the top of the ticket, Clay labored under serious handicaps.

Meanwhile, Jackson and his advisers were putting together a new party, the Democrats, to promote his candidacy. Because the party was made up of conflicting interests, its leaders decided against adopting any specific platform, and Jackson remained vague about his own position on many issues. Under these conditions, the 1828 campaign quickly degenerated into a series of scurrilous attacks on the candidates' personal characters, splattering mud on all involved. Meanwhile, party lieutenants (like Van Buren and Calhoun for Jackson and Clay for the National Republicans) organized meetings and barbecues, mobilized the party apparatus, and got out the vote.

Aided by enormous majorities in the South, Jackson won the election handily. Adams carried New England and ran well in the mid-Atlantic states, but he showed little strength in the South and West. In one sense, the significance of the election was clear. It marked the beginning of politics as Americans have practiced it ever since, with two disciplined national parties actively competing for votes, an emphasis on pageantry over issues, and the resort to mass electioneering techniques. Yet in terms of public policy, the meaning of the election was anything but clear. The people had voted for Jackson as a national hero without any real sense of what he would do with his newly won power.

President of the People

Certainly the people looked for change. "I never saw such a crowd here before," Daniel Webster wrote as inauguration day approached. "Persons have come 500 miles to see General Jackson, and they really seem to think that the country is rescued from some dreadful danger!" Some 15,000 supporters cheered wildly after Jackson was sworn in, and only with difficulty did he make his way through the crowd that rushed up the capitol steps to congratulate him.

At the White House, pandemonium reigned. Elbowing aside the invited dignitaries, thousands of ordinary citizens pushed inside to catch a glimpse of their idol. The new president had to flee after being nearly crushed to death by wellwishers. The crowd trampled on the furniture, broke glass, smashed mirrors, and ruined carpets and draperies. Finally the refreshments were moved to the lawn to disperse the mob and keep the executive mansion intact. "It was a proud day for the people," boasted Amos Kendall, one of the new president's advisers. "General Jackson is their own president." Supreme Court Justice Joseph Story was less enraptured: "I never saw such a mixture. The reign of King Mob seemed triumphant."

Whether loved as a man of the people or hated as a demagogue leading the mob, Jackson was the representative of the new democracy. The first president from west of the Appalachians, he was a product of the frontier, where so many Scotch-Irish families like his own had settled. As a young lawyer, he moved to the Tennessee frontier and became the new state's attorney general. He had a quick mind but limited schooling and little use for learning; after his death a family intimate acknowledged that the general had never believed that the Earth was round. A man of action rather than thought, his decisiveness served him well as a soldier and also in the booming economy around Nashville, where he established himself as a large landowner and slaveholder.

Tall and wiry, with flowing white hair, Jackson carried himself with a soldier's bearing. He had mellowed with age, yet he was never a man to provoke. His troops had nicknamed him Old Hickory out of respect for his toughness, but that strength sometimes became arrogance, and he could be a bully and a tyrant. Toward his enemies he was vindictive, taking opposition as a personal slight. So sensitive was he about his and his wife's reputations that he engaged in several duels and carried a bullet from one near his heart for the rest of his life. Upon leaving the presidency he remarked that his only regret was that he had never had the opportunity to shoot Henry Clay or hang John C. Calhoun.

For all these flaws, Jackson was a shrewd politician. He knew how to manipulate men and could be affable or abusive as the occasion demanded. He would sometimes burst into a rage to get his way with a hostile delegation, only to chuckle afterward, "They thought I was mad." He also displayed a keen sense of public opinion, reading the shifting national mood better than any of his contemporaries.

As the nation's chief executive, he defended the spoils system, under which public offices were awarded to political supporters, as a democratic reform. Rotation in office, he declared, would guard against insensitive bureaucrats who believed that they held their positions by right. During eight years he replaced about 20 percent of the 10,000 federal employees—more than his predecessors, but hardly a wholesale housecleaning. The cabinet, he believed, existed more to carry out his will than to offer counsel, and he had no qualms about removing members who disagreed with him. For advice, Jackson turned more regularly to an informal group of friends, who soon came to be known as the "Kitchen Cabinet." Throughout his term he remained a strong executive who insisted on his way—and usually got it.

The Political Agenda in the Market Economy

Jackson took office at a time when the market economy was spreading through America and the nation's borders were expanding geographically. The three major problems his administration faced were directly caused by the growing pains of this expansion. First, the demand for new lands put continuing pressure on Indians, whose valuable cornfields and hunting grounds could produce marketable commodities like cotton and wheat. Second, as the economies of the North, South, and West became more specialized, their rival interests forced a confrontation over the tariff. Jackson was faced with the difficult question of how the national government might resolve the disputes among different regions. And finally, the booming economy focused attention on the role of credit and banking in society, and on the new commercial attitudes that had become a central part of the developing market economy. The president attacked all three issues in his characteristically combative style.

DEMOCRACY AND RACE

As a planter, Jackson well understood the international demand for cotton that was drawing new lands into the market. He had gone off to the Tennessee frontier in 1788, a rowdy, ambitious young man who could afford to purchase only one slave. Swept up in 1795 in the speculative mania, he bought 50,000 acres on the future site of Memphis. By 1820 44 slaves worked his plantation, the Hermitage; that number grew to nearly 100 by the time he became president. In other words, Jackson pursued the opportunities of the market like so many other Americans on the frontier, and his popularity derived not only from defeating the British, but also from subduing Indians and opening their lands to white settlement. Through military fighting and treaty negotiating, he was personally responsible for obtaining about a third of Tennessee for the United States, three-quarters of Florida and Alabama, a fifth of Georgia and Mississippi, and a tenth of Kentucky and North Carolina.

Even so, in 1820 an estimated 125,000 Indians remained east of the Mississippi River. In the Southwest, the Choctaws, Creeks, Cherokees, Chickasaws, and Seminoles—known as the five "civilized" tribes because their activities and institutions most closely approximated those of whites—retained millions of acres of prime land in the heart of the cotton kingdom. Led by Georgia, southern states demanded that the federal government clear these titles. In response to this mounting pressure, Monroe in 1824 proposed to Congress that the remaining eastern tribes be relocated west of the Mississippi River.

As white pressure for removal intensified during the Jacksonian era, a shift in the attitude toward Indians and race became increasingly apparent. Earlier leaders like Jefferson had argued that although Indian and white cultures could not long coexist side by side, Indians might gradually adopt white ways. By the 1820s, however, more and more Americans began to argue that the Indian could never be "civilized" but was a permanently inferior savage who would always block progress. Before 1815, whites had generally attributed cultural differences among whites, blacks, and Indians to the environment; after 1815 the dominant white culture stressed "innate" racial differences that could never be eradicated.

Accommodate or Resist?

The clamor among southern whites for removal placed the southwestern tribes in a difficult situation. Understandably, they all strongly rejected the idea of removal from their lands. They diverged, however, over how to respond. Among the Seminoles, mixed-bloods (those with white as well as Indian ancestry) took the lead in urging military resistance to any attempt to expel them. Among the Cherokees, on the other hand, mixed-bloods led by John Ross argued that resistance was hopeless and advocated a program of accommodation. They would adopt white ways and live in a manner that would make removal legally impossible. After a bitter struggle, the mixed-blood accommodationists carried the day and in 1827 the Cherokees adopted a written constitution modeled after that of the United States. They also declared themselves an independent nation, enacting the death penalty for any member who sold tribal lands to whites without consent of the governing general council. Developing their own alphabet, they published a bilingual newspaper, *The Cherokee Phoenix*. Similarly, the neighboring Creeks moved to centralize authority by strengthening the power of the governing council at the ex-

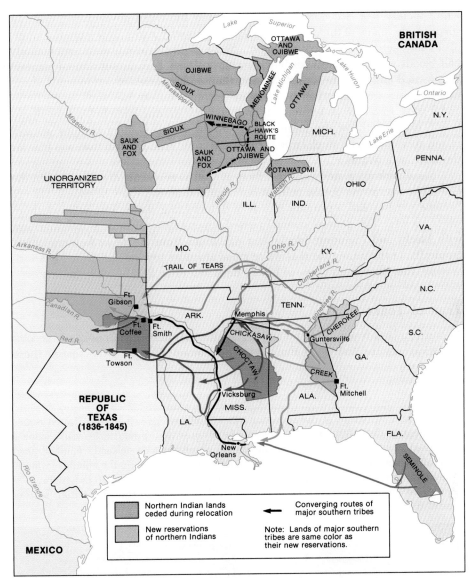

INDIAN REMOVAL

During Jackson's presidency, the federal government concluded nearly 70 treaties with Indian tribes, in the Old Northwest as well as in the South. Under their terms, the United States acquired approximately 100 million acres of Indian land.

pense of local towns. They too made it illegal for individual chiefs to sell any more land to whites.

The division between traditionalists and those favoring accommodation reflected the fact that Indians had been drawn into a web of market relationships too. Indeed, their production of commercial crops such as cotton reinforced the perception among whites that these tribes were more "civilized." While the Cherokee tribe as a whole had prospered, more and more families began clearing their own land and selling the surplus rather than sharing property communally, as they had in the past. Cherokee society became more stratified and unequal, just as white society had. Economic elites dominated the tribal government, and not surprisingly, many of the new laws dealt with property rights. Nor were the Cherokees untouched by the cotton boom. Some of the tribe's leaders, particularly half-bloods who could deal easily with white culture, became substantial planters who owned large numbers of slaves and thousands of acres of cotton land. Slaveholders were wealthier, had investments in other enterprises such as gristmills and ferries, raised crops for market, and were the driving force behind acculturation. Three-fourths of the members of Cherokee slaveholding families were of mixed ancestry, and a much larger proportion could read English than was true for the tribe as a whole.

Slaveholding created value conflicts as well as economic divisions within the Cherokee nation. As cotton cultivation expanded among the Cherokees, slavery became harsher and a primary means of determining status, just as in southern white society. The general council passed several laws forbidding intermarriage with blacks and excluding blacks and mulattoes from voting or holding office. Ironically, at the same time that white racial attitudes toward Indians were deteriorating, the Cherokees' view of blacks drew closer to that of white society.

Trail of Tears

As western land fever increased and racial attitudes hardened, a policy of accommodation was the last thing that whites welcomed. Jackson, who shared these

The Choctaws were one of the southern tribes forcibly removed by the United States government in the 1830s. Here, a Choctaw family, led by a proud male, walks along a Louisiana bayou. Tocqueville watched one group, which included sick and wounded, newborn babies, and elderly members near death, cross the Mississippi in the middle of winter. "They possessed neither tents nor wagons, but only their arms and some provisions. . . . No cry, no sob, was heard among the assembled crowd. . . . Their calamities were of ancient date, and they knew them to be irremediable."

feelings, was determined as president to bring the matter of Indian removal to a head. During his first year in office, he watched sympathetically as the Georgia legislature overturned the Cherokee constitution and declared Cherokee laws null and void. It also decreed that Indians would be tried in state courts, although it excluded them from sitting on juries or testifying against whites. Pointing to these developments, the president prodded Congress to allocate funds for Indian removal. In 1830 Congress finally passed a removal bill.

But the Cherokees brought suit in federal court against Georgia's actions, as did sympathetic white missionaries. In 1832 in the case of *Worcester v. Georgia*, the Supreme Court, in an opinion written by Chief Justice John Marshall, sided with the Cherokees. Indian tribes had full authority over their lands, Marshall ruled, and thus Georgia had no right to extend its laws over Cherokee territory. Pronouncing Marshall's decision "stillborn," Jackson ignored the Court's edict and went ahead with plans for removal.

Although Jackson assured Indians that they could be removed only voluntarily, he paid no heed when state governments harassed tribes into surrendering lands. Under the threat of coercion, the Choctaws, Chickasaws, and Creeks reluctantly agreed to move to tracts in present-day Oklahoma. In the process, Indians unaccustomed to white law and notions of property fell victim to shameful frauds. Land-hungry schemers forged sales contracts, enticed intoxicated Indians to sign papers they did not understand, and conspired with the state courts to cheat tribal members. As much as 90 percent of the western land allotments may have fallen into the hands of speculators. Then too, the lure of easy money influenced some tribal leaders to push for emigration. Chief Greenwood LeFlore, a prosperous and powerful Choctaw slaveowner, urged his tribe to relocate, even though he remained behind on his plantation in Mississippi.

The Cherokees held out longest, but to no avail. In order to deal with more pliant leaders of the tribe, Georgia authorities kidnapped Chief John Ross, who had led the tribe in resisting relocation, and threw him into jail. Ross was finally released but not allowed to negotiate the settlement, which stipulated that the Cherokees leave their lands no later than 1838. When that time came, most refused to go. In response, President Martin Van Buren had the U.S. Army round up resistant members and put them in detention camps. Many, leaving the lands they knew so intimately, touched the trunks of trees one last time before they were forced, at bayonet point, to join the westward march. Of the 15,000 who traveled this Trail of Tears, approximately one-quarter died along the way of exposure, disease, and exhaustion. John Ross' wife was one, succumbing to pneumonia after she had given her blanket to a sick child during a snowstorm. As for the western tracts awaiting the survivors, they were smaller and generally inferior to the rich lands that had been taken from the Cherokees.

Some Indians chose resistance. In the Old Northwest, a group of the Sauk and Fox led by Black Hawk recrossed the Mississippi into Illinois in 1832 and were crushed by federal troops and the militia. More successful was the resistance of a minority of Seminoles under the leadership of Osceola. Despite his death, they held out until 1842 in the Everglades of Florida before being subdued at a cost of some $50 million and more than 1500 soldiers' lives. Seminole casualties were

The leader of the antiremoval faction, Cherokee chief John Ross was the son of a mixed-blood mother and a Scottish trader.

equally high by the time most had been removed to Oklahoma. In the end, only a small number of southern tribe members were able to escape removal. Most were relegated to worthless lands that whites did not want.

Except for a few missionaries and eastern reformers, Americans expressed little regret over the treatment of the eastern tribes. In his Farewell Address in 1837, Jackson defended his policy by piously asserting that the eastern tribes had been finally "placed beyond the reach of injury or oppression, and that [the] paternal care of the General Government will hereafter watch over them and protect them." Indians knew the bitter truth of the matter. Without effective political power, they found themselves at the mercy of the pressures of the marketplace and the hardening racial attitudes of white Americans.

Free Blacks in the North

Unlike Indian removal, discrimination against free blacks and the lessening of black opportunity in this period did not depend directly on presidential action. Still, it was Jackson's Democratic party, which so vigorously trumpeted its belief in democracy, that was also the most strongly proslavery and the most hostile to black rights. The intensifying racism that paradoxically accompanied the emergence of democracy in American life bore down with particular force on free African-Americans. "The policy and power of the national and state governments are against them," commented one northerner. "The popular feeling is against them—the interests of our citizens are against them. Their prospects . . . are dreary, and comfortless."

In the years before the Civil War, the free states never had a significant free black population.* In 1860, about 226,000 free blacks, one-quarter of whom were mulattoes, lived in the North. Although they constituted less than 2 percent of the North's population, most states enacted a series of laws to keep African-Americans in an inferior position.

Most northern blacks lacked any meaningful political rights. Black males could vote on equal terms with whites in only five New England states. In New York, the only other state where any African-Americans could vote, they were required to have property worth at least $250, which effectively disfranchised all but a handful of black males. (White males, in contrast, did not have to meet any property requirement.) In 1840, some 93 percent of the northern black population lived in states that completely or practically excluded them from the franchise. Moreover, in New Jersey, Pennsylvania, and Connecticut, blacks lost the right to vote after having previously enjoyed that privilege.

Blacks were also denied basic civil rights that whites enjoyed. Five states prohibited blacks from testifying against whites, and either law or custom excluded African-Americans from juries everywhere except Massachusetts. In addition, Ohio, Indiana, and Illinois passed black exclusion laws prohibiting free blacks from immigrating into the state. These laws were seldom enforced, but they were available to harass the African-American population, as were laws requiring free blacks to post bonds of $500 to $1000 (a sum beyond the means of most whites as well as blacks) for "good behavior." When officials in Cincinnati, following an anti-black riot, enforced such a law in 1829, fully half the city's African-American residents departed.

*For a discussion of free blacks in the South, see Chapter 13, pages 430–431.

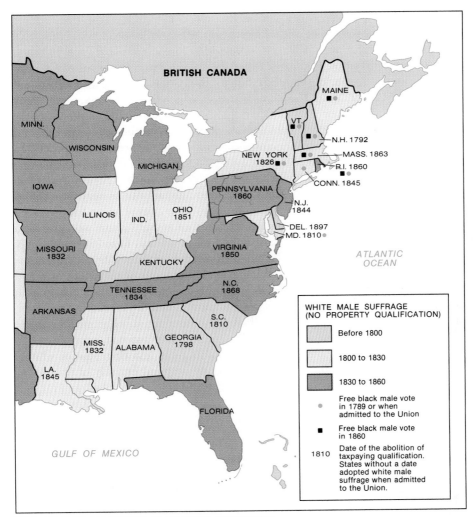

THE SPREAD OF WHITE MANHOOD SUFFRAGE
Although white manhood suffrage became the norm during the Jacksonian era, in a number of states free black males who had been voting by law or by custom (until 1834 in Tennessee) actually lost the right to vote. After 1821 a $250 property requirement disfranchised about 90 percent of adult black males in New York.

Segregation, or the physical separation of the races, was widely practiced in the free states. African-Americans were excluded from or assigned to special, separate sections on railroads, steamboats, stagecoaches, and omnibuses. Throughout the North, they could not go into most hotels and restaurants, except as servants of wealthy whites, and if permitted to enter at all, they sat in the corners and balconies of theaters and lecture halls. If they worshiped in white churches, they were relegated to separate pews and took communion after white members. In virtually every community, black children were excluded from the public schools or forced to attend overcrowded and poorly funded separate schools. Commented one English visitor: "We see, in effect, two nations—one white and another black—growing up together . . . but never mingling on a principle of equality."

During these years, whites took to the streets to vent their hostility against blacks in a number of cities with a significant African-American population. No fewer than five major anti-black riots occurred in Philadelphia between 1832 and 1849. After the 1849 riot, Frederick Douglass, the most prominent African-American leader in the North, observed: "No man is safe—his life—his property—and all that he holds dear, are in the hands of a mob, which may come upon him at any moment—at midnight or mid-day, and deprive him of his all."

Discrimination relegated African-American males to the lowest paying and most unskilled jobs in society: servants, sailors, waiters, and common laborers. In Philadelphia in 1838, 80 percent of employed black males were unskilled laborers, and three of five black families had less than $60 total wealth. African-American women normally continued working after marriage, mostly as servants, cooks, laundresses, and seamstresses, since their wages were critical to the family's well-being. Fearing economic competition and loss of status, white workers were overtly hostile to black workers, and skilled black artisans found it increasingly difficult to practice their craft. Excluded from trade unions, African-Americans willingly became strikebreakers. "Whenever the interests of the white man and the black come into collision," one foreign observer noted, "the black man goes to the wall. It is certain that, wherever labor is scarce, there he is readily employed; when it becomes plentiful, he is the first to be discharged." Forced into abject poverty, free blacks suffered from inadequate diet, were more susceptible to disease, and in 1850 had a life expectancy 8 to 10 years less than that of whites.

"At times I feel it almost impossible not to despond entirely of there ever being a better day for us," despaired Charlotte Forten, a free black in Philadelphia. "None but those who experience it can know what it is—this constant, galling sense of cruel injustice and wrong."

The African-American Community

African-Americans responded to this oppression by founding self-help societies, and the black community centered on institutions such as black churches, schools, and mutual aid societies. African-American leaders often emphasized the importance of thrift, industry, and morality as the means to rise in society, but these qualities could not negate white prejudice. A black convention movement began in the early 1830s, bringing together representatives of these various state and local societies. These conventions agitated against slavery in the South and for equal rights in the North. After 1840 black frustration generated a nationalist movement that emphasized racial unity, self-help, and for some, renewal of ties with Africa.

Because of limited economic opportunity, the African-American community was not as diversified as white society in terms of occupation and wealth. But there were distinctions, made not only in terms of wealth but of skin color. In general, lighter skinned blacks, called mulattoes, had greater opportunity to become more literate and skilled than their darker neighbors, had a better chance of finding employment and thus were better off economically, and were more likely to be community leaders. Mulattoes' feelings of superiority were reflected in marriage choices. In Philadelphia, for example, only 8 percent of black marriages in 1850 were between mulattoes and darker-skinned blacks. "They have as much caste among themselves as we have," lamented the abolitionist Sarah Grimké, "and despise the poor as much I fear as their pale brethren."

Minstrel sheet music (left) illustrates the racist attitudes that pervaded Jacksonian democracy. Blacks, played by whites, were made to appear ridiculous through grotesque physical features, exaggerated poses, and pretentious airs. In contrast, the black sawyer (right) working in New York City evidences the dignity free blacks maintained in the face of hostility and discrimination.

The Minstrel Show

During the first half of the nineteenth century, a popular culture directed toward the masses developed in response to rising urbanization. Originating in the 1830s and 1840s and playing to packed houses in cities and towns throughout the nation and even in the gold fields of California, the minstrel show became the most popular form of entertainment in Jacksonian America. Featuring white actors performing in blackface, these shows revealed the deep racism embedded in American society. They dealt in the broadest of racial stereotypes; their advertisements ridiculed blacks, with bulging eyeballs, flat noses, large lips, and gaping mouths, as physically different. The skits themselves portrayed blacks as buffoons, speaking in heavy dialect, performing outlandish dances, and singing almost compulsively.

Although popular throughout the country, minstrelsy's primary audience was in northern cities, and its basic message was that African-Americans could not cope with freedom and therefore did not belong in the North. Blacks in slavery were portrayed as happy and contented, whereas free blacks were invariably caricatured either as strutting dandies who aped white ways or as helpless ignoramuses. Longing to return to the South, one character declared, "Dis being free is worser den being a slave." Drawing its patrons from workers, Irish immigrants, and the poorer elements in society, minstrelsy assured these white champions of democracy that no matter what their situation, they were superior to blacks.

The unsettling economic, social, and political changes of the Jacksonian era heightened white anxiety. Under intense pressure to succeed, whites were haunted by the fear of failure, and this fear was magnified because of the popular yet unrealistic expectation that anyone could become rich. In truth, 20 to 40 percent of white adult males during this period never accumulated any property. Their lack of success stimulated racism, which served as an effective outlet to relieve personal tensions. Subjecting blacks to legal disabilities ensured that even the poorest whites would enjoy an advantage in the race for wealth and status. "The prejudice of race appears to be stronger in the states that have abolished slavery than in those where it still exists," Tocqueville noted, "and nowhere is it so intolerant as in those states where servitude has never been known."

Racism, whether directed against African-Americans or Indians, offered whites a refuge from the frustrations of uncertain status in a supposedly egalitarian society. The power of racism in Jacksonian America stemmed in part at least from the fact that equality remained part of the nation's creed, while it steadily receded as a social reality.

THE NULLIFICATION CRISIS

Indian removal and black discrimination provided one answer to the question of who would be given equality of opportunity in the new democracy of the 1820s and 1830s. Indians and African-Americans would not. The issue of nullification raised a different, but equally pressing question. In a republic as large as the United States, how would various regions or interest groups accommodate their differences? The market revolution, we have seen, led the North, South, and West to specialize economically. Each region had its own particular interests, and when economic conditions became especially severe, the conflicts became more evident.

The Growing Crisis in South Carolina

South Carolina had been particularly hard hit by the depression of 1819. When prosperity returned to the rest of the nation, many of the state's cotton planters remained economically depressed. With lands exhausted from years of cultivation, they could not compete with the fabulous yields of frontier planters in Tennessee, Alabama, and Mississippi. To make matters worse, the policy of Indian removal opened up millions of acres of rich new land that competed with their own.

Under these difficult conditions, South Carolinians increasingly viewed federal tariffs as the cause of their miseries. Congress raised the duty rates in 1816 and again in 1824. The tariff of 1824 included high duties on imported agricultural goods such as wool, hemp, wheat, and liquor, which protected western farmers. Duties on imported textiles encouraged manufacturing in New England, and iron duties were particularly important to Pennsylvania's mining and forging industries. Southerners bitterly assailed the tariff as an unfair tax that raised the prices of goods they imported by as much as 50 percent, while benefiting other regions of the nation.

South Carolina, the one southern state in which blacks outnumbered whites, had been growing progressively more sensitive about the institution of slavery. Moreover, in 1822 a slave conspiracy led by Denmark Vesey, a free black carpenter in Charleston, had been thwarted only at the last moment. A brilliant leader, highly intelligent, literate, and well traveled, Vesey argued that slavery was a violation of republicanism and Christianity. He devised a careful plan to seize control of the city in a series of coordinated attacks and raise the standard of black liberty, but several slaves betrayed the conspiracy shortly before it was scheduled to go into operation. Alerted to the impending danger, Charleston authorities arrested Vesey and his lieutenants, who were speedily tried, convicted, and either executed or banished. Nevertheless, whites remained panic-stricken, since they were convinced that many conspirators had escaped detection and were still in their midst.

With popular fears aroused, South Carolinians felt strongly that additional constitutional protection was needed for slavery. They feared that the constitutional doctrine of broad construction and implied powers, which was used to justify enactment of protective tariffs, might also be used to end slavery. "In contending against the tariff, I have always felt that we were combatting against the symptom instead of the disease," argued Chancellor William Harper of South Carolina. "Tomorrow may witness [an attempt] to relieve . . . your slaves."

Other southern states opposed the 1824 tariff as well, though none so vehemently as South Carolina. When Congress, over the protests of the state's representatives, raised the duty rates still higher in 1828 with the so-called Tariff of Abominations, South Carolina's legislature defiantly published a response, the *South Carolina Exposition and Protest*. This document outlined for the first time the theory of nullification. Only later was it revealed that the author was the second highest official of the federal government itself: Vice President John C. Calhoun.

Calhoun's Theory of Nullification

Educated at Yale and at the most distinguished law school in the country, Calhoun was the most impressive intellect of his political generation. A humorless, driven man, he displayed a fondness for theoretical abstractions that set him apart from his more practical-minded colleagues. During the 1820s, as the crisis in South Carolina deepened, Calhoun made his slow but steady journey away from nationalism toward an extreme states' rights position. When he was elected Jackson's vice president, South Carolinians assumed that tariff reform would be quickly forthcoming. But not long after Jackson took office, he and Calhoun quarreled over a number of matters, and Calhoun lost all influence in the administration.

In his theory of nullification, Calhoun grappled with the problem of how to protect the rights of a minority in a political system based on the rule of the majority. Madison and Jefferson had addressed this question in the Virginia and Kentucky resolutions (page 291), but Calhoun was the first to work out a fully coherent theory. The Union, he argued, was a compact between sovereign states. Thus the people of each state, acting in special conventions, had the right to nullify any federal law that exceeded the powers which the Constitution had granted Congress. If a popular convention declared a law unconstitutional, it would become null and void in that state. Congress then could either yield and repeal the law or propose a constitutional amendment expressly giving it the power in question. If the amendment was ratified and added to the Constitution, the nullifying state could then either accept the decision or exercise its ultimate right as a sovereign state and secede from the Union.

When Senator Robert Hayne of South Carolina explained Calhoun's theory

As Daniel Webster outlines his nationalist theory of the Constitution and the Union, Senator Robert Hayne of South Carolina sits (front, center) with his hands together. Leaning forward on his desk at the extreme left, Vice President Calhoun listens intently. The Senate gallery is filled, with most of the seats occupied by women, evidence of widespread interest in politics.

on the floor of the Senate, Senator Daniel Webster of Massachusetts replied sharply that the Union was not a compact of sovereign states. The Constitution began with the words "We the people," and it was the people, and not the states, who had created it. "It is the people's constitution, the people's government, made for the people, made by the people, and answerable to the people." Webster also argued that the federal government did not merely act as the agent of the states, but that it had sovereign powers in those areas where it had been delegated responsibility. Finally, Webster pointed out that the doctrine of judicial review gave the Supreme Court, and not the states, the final authority to determine the meaning of the Constitution. Expressing the hope that he would never see the Union rent by "fraternal blood," Webster closed with the affirmation, "Liberty and Union, now and forever, one and inseparable."

The Nullifiers Nullified

When Congress passed another tariff in 1832 that failed to give the state any relief, South Carolina's legislature called for the election of delegates to a popular convention, which overwhelmingly adopted an ordinance in November that declared the tariffs of 1828 and 1832 "null, void, and no law, nor binding upon this state, its officers or citizens" after February 1, 1833. The convention established legal penalties for any state or federal officer who attempted to collect the tariff duties and prohibited any appeals to the federal courts.

Jackson, who had spent much of his life defending the nation and expanding its borders, was not about to tolerate any defiance of his authority or the federal government's. In his Proclamation on Nullification, issued in December 1832, he reiterated Webster's nationalist arguments and added a last one of his own—the idea that the Union was perpetual. Under the Constitution, he insisted, there was no right of secession. The United States was a nation, not a league, and secession would destroy the nation. Surprisingly, it had taken 40 years since the adoption of the Constitution to develop this point. Warning the citizens of South Carolina that nullification was treason, Jackson vowed that he would unflinchingly enforce the tariff laws. To reinforce his threat, in March Congress passed the Force Bill, a largely symbolic law that reaffirmed the president's powers to use the army and navy to quell any insurrection.

Yet Jackson was also a skillful politician. At the same time he threatened South Carolina, he urged Congress to reduce the tariff rates. By holding out the hope of tariff reform, he managed to isolate South Carolina from the rest of the southern states. With no other state willing to follow South Carolina's lead, Calhoun reluctantly joined forces with Henry Clay to work out a compromise tariff, which Jackson signed on March 1, the same day he signed the Force Bill. The nullifiers eagerly accepted the compromise, reassembled their popular convention, and repealed the nullifying ordinance. Then, in a move of symbolic defiance, the delegates nullified the Force Bill! Jackson, however, chose to ignore this meaningless gesture, and the crisis came to an end.

The nullification crisis was a triumph of nationalism, and Jackson quickly became a nationalist hero and a symbol of the Union. Whatever its virtues as a theory, Calhoun's doctrine had proven too radical in practice for the rest of the South. No doubt the fact that Jackson was a southerner had also helped. And the resulting compromise had managed to balance the economic interests of the North, South, and West.

But the controversy did strengthen the sense among many southerners that they were becoming a permanent minority. "It is useless and impracticable to disguise the fact," concluded nullifier William Harper, "that we are divided into slave-holding and non-slaveholding states, and this is the broad and marked distinction that must separate us at last." As that feeling grew, it was not nullification, but the threat of secession that ultimately became the South's primary weapon. Although few Americans recognized it then, by 1832 the time had passed when a state might secede peacefully.

THE BANK WAR

Jackson comprehended the political ties that bound the nation, but he understood less well the economic and financial connections that linked different regions of the country through banks and national markets. In particular, the president was suspicious of the national bank and the power it possessed. His clash with the Second Bank of the United States brought on the greatest crisis of his presidency.

The National Bank and the Panic of 1819

Chartered by Congress in 1816 for a 20-year period, the Second Bank of the United States suffered in its early years from woeful mismanagement. During the frenzied speculation between 1816 and 1818, it recklessly overexpanded its operations. When the depression hit in 1819, the Bank, under new management, rigorously contracted credit by calling in loans. The West and the cities were especially hard hit. Senator Thomas Hart Benton of Missouri charged that the national bank foreclosed on so much property that it owned entire towns. Cautious policies put the Bank on a sound financial footing again, but William Gouge, a Philadelphia journalist and economist, charged, "The Bank was saved and the people were ruined." Critics viewed the Bank's policies not as a consequence, but as the cause of the financial downswing. To many Americans, the Bank had already become a monster.

The psychological effects of the Panic were almost as momentous as the economic. The American people had been rapidly pulled from the old agrarian order into a national market economy. From the midst of dizzying prosperity and unbounded optimism, they were suddenly plunged into privation and despair. The shock made the 1820s a time of soul searching, during which many uneasy farmers and workers came to view the hard times as punishment for having lost sight of the revolutionary virtues of simplicity, frugality, and hard work. The call to restore the old Republic and its values found a ready audience. For such Americans, unsettled by the changes that were sweeping the land, banks became a symbol of the commercialization of American society and the rapid passing of a simpler way of life.

Biddle's Bank

In 1823 Nicholas Biddle, a rich, 37-year-old Philadelphia businessman, became president of the national bank. Biddle was intelligent, well educated, and thoroughly familiar with the banking system, but he was also impossibly arrogant. Setting out boldly to restore the Bank's damaged reputation and provide the nation with a sound credit system, he made the Bank of the United States something like a central bank that regulated the amount of credit available in the economy. Government revenues, which came primarily from tariff duties and land sales, were paid largely in state bank notes—paper money issued by state-chartered banks. Because the Treasury Department deposited United States funds in the national bank, the notes of state banks from all across the Union came into its possession. If Biddle believed that a state bank was overextended and had issued more notes than was safe, he presented them to that bank and demanded they be redeemed in specie (gold or silver). Because banks rarely had enough specie reserves to back all the paper money they issued, the only way a state bank could continue to redeem its notes was to call in its loans and reduce the amount of its notes in circulation. This action had the effect of lessening the amount of credit in the economy.

On the other hand, if Biddle felt that a bank's credit policies were reasonable, he simply returned the state bank notes to circulation without presenting them for redemption. Being the government's official depository gave Biddle's Bank enormous power over state banks and over the economy. As Biddle tactlessly commented under questioning by a congressional committee, "There are very few [state banks] which might not have been destroyed by an exertion of the powers of the bank."

Yet Biddle did not use this power irresponsibly. By skillfully regulating the credit supply, he gave the United States a sound paper currency, which the expanding economy needed. Many appreciative bankers supported the national bank, although in the West, where the need for credit was particularly acute, some resented its restraints. Critics also noted that whatever public services it performed, the Bank was a private institution that put stockholders' profits first. Under Biddle's direction, it had opened 29 branches by 1830 and was a financial colossus. The Bank made 20 percent of the country's loans, issued one-fifth of the total bank notes, and held fully a third of all deposits and specie.

Although the Bank had strong support in the business community, workers were often critical of the paper money system. They were frequently paid in depreciated state bank notes that could be redeemed for only a portion of their face value, a practice that deprived them of part of their wages. To avoid being cheated, they called for a "hard money" system—using only gold and silver for currency. Hard money advocates viewed bankers and financiers as profiteers who manipulated the paper money system to enrich themselves at the expense of honest, hardworking farmers and laborers.

The Clash Between Jackson and Biddle

Jackson's own experiences left him with a deep distrust of banks and paper money. In 1804 his Tennessee land speculations had brought him to the brink of bankruptcy, from which it took years of painful struggle to free himself. Reflecting on his personal situation, he became convinced that banks and paper money threatened to corrupt the Republic. He also concluded that the Constitution prohibited banks and that gold and silver were the only constitutional currency. Lacking an understanding of how a credit system and paper money contributed to economic expansion, Jackson had no appreciation of the vital services performed by the national bank.

As president, Jackson periodically called for reform of the banking system, but Biddle refused even to consider curbing the Bank's powers. Already distracted by the nullification controversy, Jackson warned Biddle not to inject the bank issue into the 1832 campaign. Wishing to generate an issue for the upcoming election, Clay and Webster prodded Biddle into applying for a renewal of the Bank's charter in 1832, four years before it was to expire. When Biddle did so, Jackson was furious. "The Bank is trying to kill me," he stormed to Van Buren, *"but I will kill it."*

Despite the president's opposition, Congress passed a recharter bill in the summer of 1832. Immediately Jackson vetoed it as unconstitutional (rejecting Marshall's earlier ruling in *McCulloch v. Maryland*). He went on to condemn the Bank as an agent of special privilege and as inconsistent with the republican principle of equality, because it made "the rich richer and the potent more powerful." Holding up the Bank as a symbol of aristocracy, the president pledged to protect "the humble members of society—the farmer, mechanics, and laborers" against "the advancement of the few at the expense of the many."

As Jackson's veto message revealed, to a large extent the struggle over the national bank pitted traditional farmers and workers against the world of commerce and national markets. Jackson's strongest supporters were workers and farmers outside the commercial economy and those who were ill at ease over or hurt by the changes that the market produced in their lives. Speculators who desired an inflationary credit system also hailed Jackson's opposition to the Bank—not because they distrusted banks and wanted a "hard money" policy, but because they wanted all restraints lifted from state banks. Individuals who were more comfortable with the new commercial ethos rallied to the Bank's defense. Ultimately, most of them would end up as members of the opposing Whig party.

The Bank Destroyed

When Congress failed to override Jackson's veto, the recharter of the Bank became a central issue of the 1832 campaign. Jackson's opponent was Henry Clay, a National Republican who eagerly accepted the support of Biddle and his national bank. Indeed, Biddle may have spent as much as $100,000 of the Bank's funds in the futile campaign to defeat Jackson. Once reelected, the president was determined to destroy the Bank. He believed that as a private corporation the Bank wielded a dangerous influence over government policy and the economy, and he was justly incensed over its intervention in the election.

His strategy was simple. Since the government had nearly $10 million in Biddle's vaults, the president would cripple the Bank by ordering the deposits withdrawn. When his secretary of the treasury pointed out that such a policy was against the law, Jackson transferred him to another office. When the new secretary also refused, Jackson fired him. Finally, he found in Roger Taney a secretary of the treasury willing to carry out his edict. Taney (pronounced "Taw-ney") did not withdraw the deposits en masse; he merely began drawing against them to pay the government's debts, while depositing new revenues in state banks. The Senate censured Jackson for his action, but Old Hickory remained defiant.

Biddle fought back by deliberately precipitating a brief financial panic in 1833. As the Bank contracted credit, businessmen flocked to Washington seeking relief. Jackson was unmoved. "Go to Biddle," he snapped. "I never will restore the deposits. I never will recharter the United States Bank, or sign a charter for any other bank." Again, Biddle had blundered in this naked display of the Bank's power, for he alienated many supporters in the business community and eventually had to relent. Jackson's victory was complete. When the Bank's charter expired in 1836, no national banking system replaced it. Instead, Jackson continued depositing federal revenues in selected state banks, soon nicknamed "Pet Banks" by his opponents. While some were responsibly managed, political considerations carried more weight in their selection, as a large majority were controlled by Democrats.

Jackson's Impact on the Presidency

Jackson approached the end of his administration in triumph. Indian removal was well on its way to completion, the nullifiers had been confounded, and the "Monster Bank" had been destroyed. A strong-willed general who had never been shy about acting forcefully, Jackson immeasurably enlarged the power of the presidency. "The President is the direct representative of the American people," he lectured the Senate when it opposed him. "He was elected by the people, and is responsible to them." With this declaration, Jackson redefined the character of the presidential office and its relationship to the people.

Jackson also converted the veto into an effective presidential power. During his two terms in office, he vetoed 12 bills, compared with only 9 for all previous presidents combined. Moreover, where previous presidents had vetoed bills only on strict constitutional grounds, Jackson felt free to block laws simply because he thought them bad policy. The threat of such action became an effective way to shape pending legislation to his liking, which fundamentally strengthened the power of the president over Congress. The development of the modern presidency began with Andrew Jackson.

VAN BUREN AND DEPRESSION

With the controls of the national bank removed, state banks rapidly expanded their loans and the amount of paper money in circulation. The total value of bank notes jumped from $82 million in January 1835 to $120 million in December 1836. As the currency expanded, so did the number of banks: from 329 in 1829 to 788 in 1837. A spiraling inflation set in, as prices rose 50 percent after 1830 and interest rates by half as much. Anti-bank Democrats were aghast. Fumed Senator Thomas Hart Benton: "I did not join in putting down the Bank of the United States to put up a wilderness of local banks."

As prices rose sharply, so did speculative fever. By 1836 land sales, which had been only $2.6 million four years earlier, approached $25 million. Almost all of these lands were bought entirely on credit with bank notes, many of which had little value. The opening of extensive Indian tracts for sale fueled the fever. Men seeking land poured into the Old Southwest, and as one observer wryly commented, "under this stimulating process prices rose like smoke." In July 1836, Jackson, seeking to apply the brakes to the economy, issued the Specie Circular, which decreed that the government would accept only specie for the purchase of public land. Land sales drastically declined, but the speculative pressures in the economy were by now too great to be reversed. The Specie Circular remained in effect until May 1838, when Congress repealed it.

"Van Ruin's" Depression

During Jackson's second term, his opponents had gradually coalesced into a new party, the Whigs. Taking their name from the English party that had resisted monarchical tyranny, they charged that "King Andrew I" was a tyrant who abused his veto power, trampled on the Constitution, and dangerously concentrated power in the presidency. Henry Clay led the new party, and his American System, designed to spur national economic development through a protective tariff, a national bank, and federal aid for internal improvements, formed the core of its program. In 1836 the Democrats' presidential nominee was Martin Van Buren, who had replaced Calhoun as Jackson's vice president during his second term. The Whigs ran not one candidate but three: Daniel Webster in New England, Hugh Lawson White in the South, and William Henry Harrison in the West. In so doing, the party hoped to prevent Van Buren from getting a majority of the electoral votes and thus send the election to the House. But while Van Buren was a lackluster candidate, he carried the election and assumed office in March 1837.

Van Buren had less than two months in office to savor his triumph before the speculative mania of the previous few years collapsed. An oversupply drove down the price of cotton on the international markets, and nervous investors began a rush on banks to redeem paper notes for hard cash. In May, as the New York banks ran out of gold and silver reserves, they suspended specie payments. The

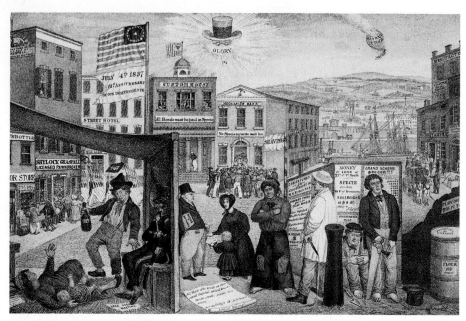

This Whig cartoon blames the Democratic party for the depression that began during Van Buren's administration. Barefoot workers go unemployed and women and children beg and sleep in the streets. Depositors clamor for their money from a bank that has suspended specie payments, while the pawnbroker and liquor store do a thriving business and the sheriff rounds up debtors.

news spread as fast as stagecoaches and steamboats could travel, and everywhere banks faced the same crisis. The economy recovered partially, but in 1839, following a record crop and declining British demand, the bottom fell out of the cotton market and the country entered a serious depression. Arising from causes that were worldwide, the depression demonstrated how deeply the market economy had penetrated American society. It was not until 1843 that the economy revived.

But public opinion identified hard times with the policies of the Democratic party. As federal revenues declined, Van Buren cut government spending, further constricting the economy. He also steadfastly opposed a new national bank and instead sought to divorce government from banking. In 1840 Congress approved his proposal for an Independent Treasury to keep the government's funds. Its offices were forbidden to accept paper currency, issue any bank notes, or make any loans. The government's money would be safe, as Van Buren intended, but it would also remain unavailable to banks to make loans and stimulate the economy. In addition, the system produced a perpetual shortage of specie as it accumulated in Independent Treasury vaults, thus further curtailing economic investment.

Whigs countered by demanding a protective tariff, continuation of state internal improvement projects, protection of corporations, and expansion of the banking and credit system. In states where the Whigs gained power, they increased the number of banks, expanded the supply of paper money, and called for positive government programs to promote economic recovery.

As the depression deepened, thousands of workers were unemployed and countless businesses failed. Cotton prices, which had stood at 17 cents a pound before the depression, fell to a low of 6 cents. Suffering was particularly acute among urban workers and their families. An estimated 50,000 were unemployed in New York City, 2000 shoemakers representing 40 percent of the work force were thrown out of work in Lynn, and the mills in Lowell were idle; nationally wages fell 30 to 50 percent. "Business of all kinds is completely at a stand," wrote New York businessman and civic leader Philip Hone in 1840, "and the whole body politic sick and infirm, and calling aloud for a remedy."

The Whigs' Triumph

For the 1840 presidential campaign the Whigs turned to William Henry Harrison, a military hero who had defeated the Shawnee at Tippecanoe and the British at the Battle of the Thames during the War of 1812. By 1840 the Whigs had done much to perfect their party's national organization, and they entered the campaign in high spirits, especially since the Democrats had rather glumly renominated Van Buren. The Whigs' strategy was simple. In the midst of the worst depression of the century, they employed the democratic electioneering techniques that Jackson's supporters had perfected to portray Harrison as a man of the people. Van Buren, of course, was painted in the opposite colors. Whig broadsides claimed that he wore a corset, ate off gold plates with silver spoons—even that "Sweet Sandy Whiskers" indulged in the effeminate custom of using cologne. Shades of Franklin Plummer!

In contrast, when one Democratic newspaper editor (allegedly quoting a disgruntled Whig) sneered that Harrison would be content to spend his days drinking hard cider in a log cabin, Whig rallies began featuring hard cider and log cabins to reinforce Harrison's image as a man of the people. Ironically, Harrison had been born into one of Virginia's most aristocratic families and was living in a 16-room mansion in Ohio. But the Whig campaign, by portraying the election as a contest between aristocracy and democracy, was perfectly attuned to the prevailing national spirit.

Both parties used the new campaign techniques—parades, barbecues, liberty pole raisings, and mass meetings—to stir up enthusiasm among the voters. And just as the Panic of 1819 had roused the voters to action, the depression and the two parties' response to it kindled voters' interest. The result was a record turnout, as nearly four-fifths of the eligible voters went to the polls. Some 900,000 new voters were mobilized between 1836 and 1840, and the Whigs won over three-fifths of them. Voters who were hurt most severely by falling prices blamed the Democrats for hard times and strongly backed the Whigs. Democrats, on the other hand, recruited thousands of new voters who feared the probanking legislation passed by Whigs in various states in 1838 and 1839. Although the popular vote was fairly close (Harrison led by about 150,000 votes out of 2.4 million cast), in the Electoral College he won an easy victory, 234 to 60.

The "log cabin" campaign marked the final transition from the deferential politics of the Federalist era to the stridently egalitarian politics that had emerged in the wake of the Panic of 1819. The Whig and Democratic parties, now closely competitive and national in their organization, attracted great popular support. As the *Democratic Review* conceded after the Whigs' victory in 1840, "We have taught them how to conquer us."

Daily Lives

POLITICAL CULTURE

The Log Cabin Campaign

"Political life to an American citizen, has all the fanaticism of religion and all the fascination of gambling." So concluded one knowledgeable American during the Jacksonian era, and he spoke accurately enough. The Whigs' legendary "log cabin" campaign of 1840 was in many respects the first modern presidential campaign, with both parties involving ordinary Americans in a multitude of ways.

The sheer number of participants in 1840 was unprecedented. Whigs, who led the way in innovation, organized a rally on the battlefield at Fort Meigs, in Ohio, which reputedly attracted more than 25,000 men, women, and children. Thousands marched in parades in New Jersey and Ohio, but the largest political demonstration the country had ever seen occurred in Baltimore at the Young Men's Whig Convention. Spectators jammed rooftops, balconies, and sidewalks to witness the three-mile-long parade of delegates accompanied by artillery, bands, carriages with dignitaries, at least eight log cabin floats, and over a thousand banners and transparencies. The festivities, which continued for two full days, included hour after hour of speeches, a balloon ascension, and a fancy-dress ball.

Although women lacked the right to vote, by 1840 they were cheering party processions, riding on floats, and attending political meetings. This was a sharp break with tradition, and at first women caught up in the excitement felt uneasy. In 1840 Mary Todd, the future wife of Abraham Lincoln, confessed that her support of Harrison had led her into the rather "unladylike profession" of politics. "Yet at such a crisis," she countered, "whose heart could remain untouched?" Once again the Whigs were innovators, specifically inviting women to attend party rallies. As Thomas Corwin, the Whig candidate for governor in Ohio, declared, "Ladies should become interested in subjects affecting the welfare and very existence of our common country."

Most women remained in the background of the campaign, but some became more active, delivering political speeches and conducting meetings. On Harrison's behalf, Lucy Kenney published *The Strongest of All Governments Is That Which is Most Free*, one of the first political pamphlets written by an American woman. "This way of making politicians of their women is something new under the sun," acknowledged one Georgia Democrat. Democrats initially resisted the trend, but of necessity soon plunged in.

In an era when social diversions were relatively limited, the new political techniques aimed to entertain as they forged bonds of party commitment. The variety of activities was limited only by the imagination of party organizers: political clubs, pole raisings, bonfires, fireworks, barbecues and picnics, debates and stump speaking. Before a mammoth 1840 Whig meeting in Ohio, party volunteers baked 20,000 pounds of bread and prepared 200 bushels of potatoes, 600 pounds of butter, 70 sheep, 80 slabs of bacon, 21 steers, and "numerous other provisions" for the expected throng. (Small wonder that Whigs saluted the contribution of women in their songs and speeches.) One member of Congress acknowledged that it was a hardship for many voters to attend rallies, but added that "the fun, the joy, the excitement . . . repaid them for the loss of time and the necessary expenditures of money and energy it required."

Daily Lives

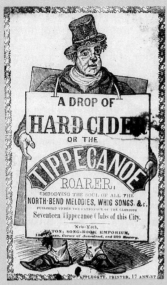

Whig song book, 1840.

The Whigs' 1840 campaign for the first time popularized party songs. Male and female glee clubs sang partisan tunes, publishers brought out campaign song books, and newspapers printed the most popular lyrics. "Nobody cared how sorry the doggerel might be," one western politician recalled, "if it contained a hit at the opposite party . . . or a rattling chorus." In the best democratic tradition of Franklin Plummer, Whigs crooned:

Old Tip he wears a homespun coat
He has no ruffled shirt-wirt-wirt.
But Mat he has the golden plate
And he's a little squirt-wirt-wirt.

Democrats countered with a serenade mocking General Harrison's tactful silence during the campaign:

Another gourd for General *Mum*,
Whose fame is like his fav'rite drum;
Which when most empty makes
  most noise,
Huzza for General Mum, my boys!

Even if the lyrics were mostly nonsense, commented Whig editor Horace Greeley, "people like the swing of the music," and "after a song or two they are more ready to listen to the orators."

Drinking went hand in hand with the new democratic politics: rural taverns and urban saloons were frequently centers of party activity, and liquid refreshment was mandatory at rallies. Whig gatherings featured barrels of hard cider (and sweet cider for the temperate). Capitalizing on the fervor of 1840, Edmund C. Booz, an enterprising distiller, hit on the brilliant strategy of marketing his liquor in bottles shaped like log cabins. Soon known as booze bottles, they added a new word for liquor to American speech.

Party souvenirs, too, were widely marketed for the first time. Arising in the morning, a loyal Whig could shave with Tippecanoe Shaving Soap, don a Harrison suit complete with log cabin buttons, knot his Harrison necktie, fold his Harrison handkerchief, and pin on a Tippecanoe badge. He could check the weather forecast in the *Harrison Almanac*, write his friends on Harrison stationery, and smoke Tippecanoe Tobacco. In the evening, with his wife outfitted in a dress made from calico printed with Harrison's picture and log cabins and carrying a Harrison fan, he might saunter down to Whig headquarters to sing selections from *The Tippecanoe Roarer*.

Witnessing the popular fervor of the 1840 campaign, former president John Quincy Adams wrote in his diary, "Here is a revolution in the habits and manners of the people. Where will it end?" Adams' terminology was apt: nothing less than a revolution in the structure and behavior of American politics had occurred. Enthusiastic popular involvement would remain the hallmark of the party system for the remainder of the nineteenth century.

THE JACKSONIAN PARTY SYSTEM

It is easy, given the hoopla of hard-cider campaigning, to be distracted from the central fact that the new political system was directly shaped by the social and economic strains of an expanding nation. Despite the efforts of both parties to avoid campaigning on the issues, Whigs and Democrats held different attitudes toward the changes brought about by the market, banks, and commerce.

Democrats, Whigs, and the Market

The Democrats had supported Jackson in his war against a national bank and stuck with Van Buren through the depression, as he tried to check the harm of speculating banks. Through it all, they tended to view society as a continuing conflict between "the people"—farmers, planters, and workers—and a set of greedy aristocrats—bankers, stock jobbers, and investors—who manipulated the banking system for their own profit. Idle social parasites, this paper money aristocracy was the enemy of the nation's traditional Revolutionary virtues, for it encouraged speculation and the desire for sudden, unearned wealth. For Democrats, the Bank War became a battle to restore the old Jeffersonian Republic, to preserve the values of simplicity, frugality, hard work, and independence. The Bank was a monster, a symbol of the corporate power that menaced the Republic. This is what Jackson meant when he said that removal of the deposits from Biddle's Bank would "preserve the morals of the people."

Jackson shrewdly understood the power private banks could wield and the dangers they posed to a democratic society. Yet Democrats, in effect, wanted the rewards of the market without sacrificing the virtues of a simple agrarian republic. They wanted the wealth that the market offered, without the competitive, changing society, the complex dealings, the dominance of urban centers, and the loss of independence that came with it. Whigs, on the other hand, were more comfortable with the market. For them, commerce and economic development were agents of civilization. "Our course is onward, straight onward, and forward," Daniel Webster proclaimed. ". . . we shall elevate [our country] to a pitch of prosperity and happiness, of honor and power, never yet reached by any nation beneath the sun."

Nor did the Whigs envision any conflict in society between farmers and mechanics on the one hand and businessmen and bankers on the other. Economic growth would benefit everyone by creating jobs, stimulating demand for agricultural products, raising national income, and expanding opportunity. The government's responsibility was to provide a well-regulated economy that guaranteed opportunity for citizens of ability. In such an economy, banks and corporations were not only useful but necessary, as was a sound currency that was at least partly paper. A North Carolina Whig well expressed the party's vision of society: "We are all one family. . . . All should be mutual friends and helpers to each other, and who ever aids and assists his fellow men from good motives, by lending money, by affording employment by precept or example, is a benefactor to his fellow men."

Whigs and Democrats differed not only in their attitudes toward the market, but also about how active government should be. Despite Andrew Jackson's inclination to be a strong president, Democrats as a rule believed in limited government, particularly at the federal level. They feared power as a threat to individual-

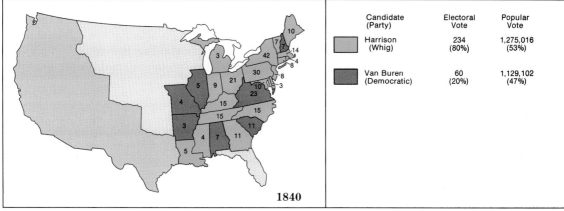

Candidate (Party)	Electoral Vote	Popular Vote
Harrison (Whig)	234 (80%)	1,275,016 (53%)
Van Buren (Democratic)	60 (20%)	1,129,102 (47%)

1840

ELECTION OF 1840

ism and freedom. To restrain excessive power, they believed that government had a responsibility to destroy monopolies and special privileges and open the market to equal access and free competition. As one New Jersey Democratic newspaper declared, "All Bank charters, all laws conferring special privileges, with all acts of incorporation, for purposes of private gain, are monopolies, in as much as they are calculated to enhance the power of wealth, produce inequalities among the people and to subvert liberty."

In *Charles River Bridge v. Warren Bridge* (1837), the Supreme Court strengthened the vision of an expanding capitalistic society undergirded by free competition. The opinion was written by Chief Justice Roger B. Taney, whom Jackson had appointed in 1835 to succeed John Marshall. At issue was whether the state of Massachusetts, which had given a charter to the Charles River Bridge Company to build a toll bridge, could give another company a charter to construct an adjacent free bridge. The toll bridge company sued, claiming that construction of the competing bridge would make its property worthless. In his opinion, Taney held that the public interest was an overriding concern, and that any ambiguity in the charter should be resolved in favor of the people. By striking down the idea of implied monopolies, the Court sought to promote equality of opportunity and economic progress.

In keeping with this philosophy of limited government, Democrats also rejected the idea that moral beliefs were the proper sphere of government action. Religion and politics, they believed, should be kept clearly separate. More fearful of concentrated power, Democrats believed that limited government would best preserve individual liberty, and they viewed humanitarian legislation as an interference with personal freedom. On the other hand, they supported debtor relief, which in their view curbed the wealthy aristocrats who tyrannized the common worker.

The Whigs, in contrast, viewed government power positively. They believed that it should be used to protect individual rights and public liberty, and that it had a special role where individual effort was futile. By regulating the economy and competition, the government could assure equal opportunity. In the absence of government control, the rich would monopolize power and wealth.

But for Whigs the concept of government promoting the general welfare went beyond the economy. Northern Whigs in particular also believed that government power should be used to foster the moral welfare of the country. They were much more likely to favor temperance or antislavery legislation, aid to education, and the reform of prisons or asylums. Whigs portrayed themselves not only as the party of prosperity, but also as the party of respectability and proper behavior.

The Social Bases of the Two Parties

In some ways, the social makeup of the two parties was similar. To be competitive, Whigs and Democrats both had to have significant support among farmers, the largest group in society, and workers. Since most Americans were in the middle ranks of society, neither party could carry an election by appealing exclusively to the rich or the poor.

The Whigs, however, enjoyed disproportionate strength among the business and commercial classes, especially after the Bank War drove a number of businessmen out of the Democratic party. They appealed to planters who needed credit to finance their cotton and rice trade in the world market, to farmers who were eager to ship their surpluses at a profit, and to workers who were eager to improve themselves. Democrats attracted farmers isolated from the market or uncomfortable with it, workers alienated from the emerging industrial system, and rising entrepreneurs who felt excluded and were eager to break monopolies and open the economy to newcomers like themselves. The Whigs were strongest in the towns, cities, and rural areas that were fully integrated into the market economy, whereas Democrats dominated areas of semisubsistence farming that were more isolated and were economically languishing or declining. Attitude toward the market, rather than economic position, was more important in determining party affiliation.

The Triumph of the Market

Clearly, then, Jacksonian politics evolved out of the social and economic dislocation produced by rapidly expanding economic opportunity. Yet efforts to reverse some of the effects of the market while preserving its benefits were doomed to failure. Some Democrats followed up the destruction of the national bank by mounting a drive to eliminate all state banks as well. But in the states where they succeeded, so much hardship and financial chaos ensued that some system of banking was soon restored. The expansion of the economy after 1815 had caught farmers as well as urban residents in an international network of trade and finance, tying them with a tightening grip to the price of cotton in Liverpool or the interest rates of the Bank of England. There was no rolling back the market in a return to the ideals of Crèvecoeur.

Still, Americans had evolved a system of democratic politics to deal with the conflicts that the new order produced. The new national politics—like the new markets spreading across the nation—had become essential structures uniting the American nation. They provided an ideology of equality and opportunity, which stood as a goal for the nation even if crucial elements of society, like women, blacks, and Indians, were excluded. The new politics developed a system of truly national parties, competing with one another, involving large numbers of ordinary Americans, resolving differences through compromise and negotiation. Along with the market, democracy had become an integral part of American life.

SIGNIFICANT EVENTS

1819–1823	Panic and depression
1822	Denmark Vesey conspiracy
1823	Biddle becomes president of the Bank of the United States
1824	Tariff duties raised; Jackson finishes first in presidential race
1825	House elects John Quincy Adams president
1826	William Morgan kidnapped
1827	Cherokees adopt written constitution
1828	Tariff of Abominations; *South Carolina Exposition and Protest*; Jackson elected president
1829	Cherokee blood law
1830	Webster–Hayne debate; Indian Removal Act
1830–1838	Indians removed from Southwest
1831	Anti-Masonic party holds first nominating convention
1832	*Worcester v. Georgia*; Jackson vetoes recharter of the national bank; Black Hawk War; Jackson reelected; South Carolina nullifies tariff; Jackson's Proclamation on Nullification
1833	Force Bill; Tariff duties reduced; Jackson removes deposits from the Bank of the United States
1833–1834	Biddle's panic
1834	Whig party organized
1835–1842	Second Seminole war
1836	Specie Circular; Van Buren elected president
1837	*Charles River Bridge* case; Panic
1838	Trail of Tears
1839–1843	Depression
1840	Independent Treasury Act; Harrison elected president
1842	First professional minstrel troupe.

12

The Quest for Perfection

nyone unfamiliar with Boston would have mistaken the short, plain, rustic fellow for a stranger. His speech, with talk of God's "creeturs" or "nat'ral" occurrences, was that of a rural Yankee, a pious farmer, perhaps, come to gaze reverently upon the imposing Hanover Street Church. Spanking new in 1826, the church boasted a facade of rough-hewn granite and a main floor that sloped toward the pulpit, allowing every member of its thriving congregation to see as well as hear anyone who spoke from it. All the more curious, then, was the purposeful, almost proprietary way that this unkempt man bustled about the church. Come Sunday morning, however, visitors understood the unusual behavior of this rough-hewn man. For then he would mount the stairs to the pulpit, fasten his wide-set, burning eyes on his audience, and blaze forth denunciations of dancing, drinking, dueling, or "infidelity," all the while punctuating his sermon with pump-handle strokes of the right hand. In 1826 the Reverend Lyman Beecher was probably the most celebrated minister of the Republic, and the pulpit of Hanover Street was his to command.

Nor were Beecher's ambitions small. His goal was nothing less than to bring the kingdom of Christ not only to Boston but to the nation and the entire world as well. Like most respectable clergy of the day, Beecher had studied the intriguing final book of the New Testament, the Revelation to John. The Revelation set forth visions of what would come to pass in the latter days of the Earth. It foretold a thousand years of peace and triumph, when the saints would rule and evil would be banished from the world. These obscure prophecies of a glorious millennium had been analyzed for years, not only by noted ministers like Jonathan Edwards but also by scientists like Isaac Newton and Joseph Priestley, the discoverer of oxygen. Beecher was convinced that the long-awaited millennium might well begin in the United States.

Personal experience had long reinforced this unfailing optimism. Born to a shrewd, sturdy lineage of New England blacksmiths in the year before the colonies declared their independence, Beecher entered Yale College during the high tide of postwar nationalism—and, some said, the lowest ebb of religion among young people. Many of his fellow Yale students boasted of reading deist books like Thomas Paine's *Age of Reason*, which ridiculed the "superstitions" of the Bible. Yale's devout president, Timothy Dwight, did not silence Yale's young infidels; instead, he challenged them to open and frank debate. His energetic arguments, vigorous eloquence, and sheer endurance swept students up in the revivals of the

The Way of Good and Evil *extolls the importance of family, religion, education, and hard work, all virtues in the millennial quest for perfection.*

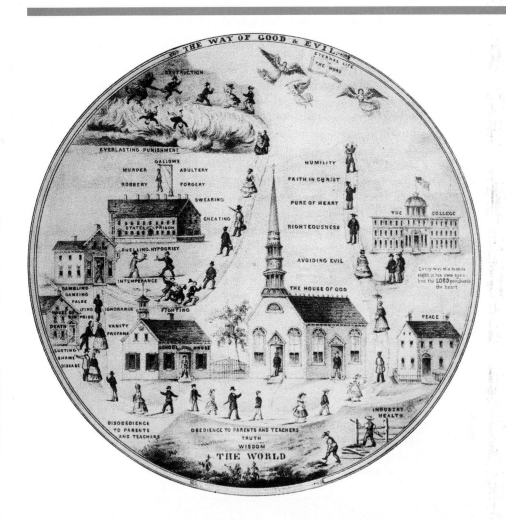

Second Great Awakening that came to many colleges in 1802. Among those converted was Beecher.

As a minister, Beecher first did the Lord's work in a small Long Island fishing town, then moved in 1810 to Litchfield, Connecticut, a prosperous community noted for its fine law school and excellent female academy. But his boundless energy also went into raising a family of 11 children, every one of whom he prayed would take leading roles in bringing the kingdom of God to America. Beecher was no stodgy Puritan. He loved to wrestle on the floor with his sons or climb the highest trees, scrambling energetically for nuts. With his daughters he went "berrying," and young Harriet Beecher delighted in such expeditions, coming back "with a six quart pail full of berries and her dress wet up to her knees." But the religious dimension of their lives was constant: two services on Sunday, a weekly prayer meeting, and a monthly "concert of prayer," where the devout met to pray for the conversion of the world. Beecher's son Thomas remembered the daily prayers and the commanding, deep voice of his father: "Overturn and overturn till He whose right it is shall come and reign, King of nations and King of saints."

If the kingdom were to come, there would clearly have to be a sweeping transformation of the world, not only of individual souls but also of families, communities, and entire nations. Beecher joined other Protestant ministers in supporting a host of religious reforms and missionary efforts. In 1810 the American Board of Commissioners for Foreign Missions was established, followed by the American Bible Society (1816) and the American Tract Society (1825), whose Bibles and religious pamphlets blanketed every sleepy hamlet in the country. Societies sprang up to promote Sunday schools and minister to sailors and the poor. By 1830 the most important of these organizations made up the loosely united "Benevolent Empire." To Beecher these were signs of the coming kingdom.

In 1826, as the new pastor at Hanover Street, Beecher was determined to combat Unitarianism, which seemed to him Boston's most threatening perversion of Christianity. Upper-class and cultured, Unitarian churches counted among their members many of Boston's merchant and banking elite, as well as lawyers, judges, and Harvard professors. They were the sort of people who borrowed many books from the Boston Atheneum, who attended concerts of the Haydn and Handel Choral Society, who employed exotic Asian servants and stocked their private gardens with peacocks. To Beecher their liberal, rational theology was little more than a "halfway house on the road to infidelity," for Unitarians rejected the divinity of Jesus, referring to him only as Teacher and Redeemer, not as the Son of God. They disdained revivals as entirely too emotional and distrusted the notion that a conversion experience was essential to leading a Christian life. Beecher's aim as "the great gun of Calvinism" was to destroy these pernicious beliefs, "roots and all."

But he had artillery enough left over for other targets. Constantly Beecher denounced the sins of playing cards and gambling with dice. He agitated to outlaw

Lyman Beecher (center) with his family in 1855. Five of his six sons, all of whom were ministers, stand in back. In front, daughters Catharine (holding his arm to steady it for the long exposure) and Isabella are on the left; Harriet, the author of *Uncle Tom's Cabin*, is at the far right.

lotteries that were so popular among the lower classes. He outspokenly condemned those who drank to excess, and he sought to close the booths that sold grog on the Boston Common. And he denounced Roman Catholic priests and nuns as superstitious, devious agents of "Antichrist"—that seven-headed, ten-horned beast described so vividly in the book of Revelation. By the late 1820s a new wave of immigrants had begun to arrive in the United States, many of them Catholics from Ireland and Germany. Such newcomers, as well as other working people who enjoyed rum, whiskey, or lotteries, did not appreciate Beecher's efforts at "moral reform." When a blaze broke out in the basement of his church in 1830, local firefighters rushed to Hanover Street—for the pleasure of watching while that splendid structure burned to the ground. The fires of spiritual reform had been checked, temporarily, by a blaze of a literal sort.

Any fire, real or spiritual, is a bit unpredictable as it spreads from one scrap of tinder to the next. So it proved with reform movements of the 1820s and 1830s: they moved in diverging, sometimes contradictory ways. What did it mean, after all, to bring in Christ's kingdom? The goals of the early reform societies were moral rather than social. Leaders like Beecher sought to convert individuals and to church the unchurched, with the help of religious revivals and benevolent associations. Their conservative aim, as he expressed it, was to restore America to "the moral government of God." Other Christians, however, began to focus on social abuses and to demand more radical solutions. The degradation of slavery, the inequality of women in society, the abuses of prisons and asylums—these social evils needed to be attacked directly, they argued. Ironically, while Lyman Beecher remained in the conservative mainstream, many of his children went well beyond his own strategies for hastening the millennium. They spoke out for abolition, women's rights, and education in ways that left their father distinctly uncomfortable. In their activities, Beecher family members reflected the diversity of the reform impulse itself.

REVIVALISM AND THE SOCIAL ORDER

Society during the Jacksonian era was undergoing deep and rapid changes. It was expanding economically through the revolution in markets, as its citizens competed for status and wealth through the gospel of democratic individualism. In a nation where fortunes could be won and lost almost overnight, some reformers sought stability and moral order in religious community. The bonds of unity created by a revival brought a sense of peace in the midst of a society in change. Revivals could provide a sense of strength and discipline, too, in an emerging industrial culture that demanded sobriety and regular working habits. Other reformers, however, sought to check the excesses of Jacksonian America by radically remaking institutions or devising utopian, experimental ways of living and working together. The drive for renewal, in other words, led reformers sometimes to preserve social institutions, other times to overturn them. It led them sometimes to liberate, other times to control. And the conflicting ways in which these dynamics operated could be seen as the revivals of the Second Great Awakening were transformed by the electric career of Charles Grandison Finney.

Finney's New Measures

In 1821, before Lyman Beecher had even moved his family to Boston, a young lawyer in western New York experienced a soul-shattering religious conversion. Immediately he abandoned his legal career and announced that he was now on retainer to God. He began preaching throughout New York as an itinerant free-lance revivalist, joining with settled ministers who invited him to address their congregations. Eventually he was ordained in the Presbyterian church, although he lacked any formal theological training. Then he conducted a series of spectacular revivals in the booming port cities along the new Erie Canal between the mid-1820s and the early 1830s—the final, climactic phase of the Second Great Awakening. As a result of these revivals in upstate New York, Charles Finney, lawyer-turned-evangelist, gained national attention.

There were many reasons for his extraordinary appeal. Tall and spare, a handsome man with a penetrating gaze, Finney, like George Whitefield before him, had a marvelous voice that he could project a great distance and modulate at will. His power over an audience was such that when he described the descent of a sinner into hell, those in the back of the hall rose to witness the final plunge. The secret of his success lay less in his presence than in his use of special revivalistic techniques—"the new measures"—and his casual attitude toward religious doctrine.

The new measures that Finney popularized in upstate New York had been developed on the frontier in places like Cane Ridge. They included using blunt, direct speech; holding "protracted meetings" night after night to build up excitement and emotion; praying for sinners by name; encouraging women to testify in public gatherings; and placing sinners on the "anxious bench" at the front of the church, where the entire congregation could witness their struggle for conversion. "A revival is not a miracle," Finney coolly declared, "it is a purely scientific result of the right use of constituted means." He even wrote a manual for ministers explaining how to "work up" a revival with the new measures.

The Philosophy of the New Revivals

Finney walked in the footsteps of a long tradition of Protestant evangelicals.* But by his day, many optimistic, individualistic Americans found the traditional doctrines of John Calvin and Jonathan Edwards difficult to endorse. A mysterious, inscrutable God who predetermined the fate of every human being seemed unreasonable and undemocratic to citizens of a republic founded on common sense and natural rights. And Calvin's insistence that men and women had inherited Adam's original sin and could do nothing to attain salvation hardly appealed to a generation that condemned hereditary distinctions, celebrated human dignity, and praised ability and activity.

These strict Calvinist doctrines had already been modified by a fast friend of Lyman Beecher, Professor Nathaniel Taylor of the Yale Divinity School. His "New

---

*The word *evangelical* derives from a Greek word meaning the bringing of good news—in this case, the Gospel. Protestant evangelicals consistently stressed the need for individuals to undergo an emotionally wrenching conversion experience and subsequent rebirth stemming from an awareness of sinful guilt, and Christ's act of atoning, through his death, for their sins.

Charles Finney, about 1834.

Haven theology" rejected the doctrine of original sin, in which Adam and Eve's sin had been passed on in human nature as a hereditary taint. Although men and women would inevitably sin, Taylor acknowledged, as rational beings they had sufficient free will to resist their natural inclination toward evil. Taylor thus denied that salvation was exclusively the doing of God; instead it was the duty of ministers to induce sinners to accept of their own free will God's gift of salvation.

Finney popularized these notions, couching liberal Calvinism in a language that his audience could easily understand. But that process pushed him further than Taylor dared go toward minimizing human sinfulness and emphasizing human free will. Leaving the Lord little role in the drama of human deliverance, Finney insisted that men and women were free moral agents and that all who wanted to could be saved. To those anxious about their salvation, he thundered, "Do it!" Finney's approach also made emotion paramount. While his revivals were not as tumultuous as those on the southern frontier, shrieks and groans, the cries of agonized prayers, and uncontrolled crying resounded throughout the hall. Like the camp meetings, Finney's methods were designed to precipitate outbursts of emotion and to prepare sinners to accept conversion. He justified their use on the grounds of success, pointing to the large numbers who had been saved.

With such changes within reach of every individual, what might be in store for the society at large? "If the church would do her duty," Finney confidently predicted, "the millennium may come in this country in three years." He advised his young converts that they should take as their goal "the complete reformation of the whole world." And by the 1830s Finney had taken to preaching not merely faith in human progress, but something more—human perfectibility. This new theology of "perfectionism" maintained that a benevolent God was progressively revealing his will to a reasonable mankind—so plainly that in time even the common people would understand these ultimate truths and successfully live up to them. Finney boldly asserted that all Christians should "aim at being holy and not rest satisfied until they are as perfect as God."

By bringing more aggressive techniques to the practice of revivalism, by preaching an optimistic message of free will and salvation to all, Finney and his many eager imitators among western ministers transformed Protestantism. But not all clergy applauded his achievement. For Beecher, as well as many supporters of the Second Great Awakening, Finney's new measures went too far, the emotionalism of his revivals ran to excess, and his theology of perfectionism verged on heresy. When the two men met at New Lebanon, Connecticut, in 1827 to discuss their differences, Beecher warned that if Finney tried to bring his brand of revivalism to Massachusetts, "I'll meet you at the State Line, and call out all the artillery-men, and fight you every inch of the way to Boston." Undeterred, Finney promoted his new measures in New York, western Pennsylvania, and even New England. As for Beecher, by 1832 he had decided to outflank all of his adversaries— Finney in upstate New York, the Unitarians in Boston, even the pope in Rome— by moving west to take over the presidency of Lane Seminary in Cincinnati. There he planned to train the right sort of revivalists to save the frontier for true religion and to bring about the kingdom of God in America.

Religion and the Market Economy

The controversies over revivalism and perfectionism were not remote theological disputes. Revival audiences responded to the call for reform partly because they were disquieted by the rapid social changes Americans were experiencing. In the

North, evangelical religion proved strongest not in isolated backwaters, but in areas emerging from the frontier stage and entering the market economy. Rochester, New York, a burgeoning flour-milling center on the Erie Canal, epitomized the social environment that spawned revivals. When Charles Finney came to town in the winter of 1830–1831, Rochester was a community in crisis. It had grown in a decade and a half from a village of 300 souls to a commercial city of more than 20,000. That wrenching expansion produced sharp divisions among the town's leaders, a large working class that increasingly lived apart from employers and beyond their moral control, and a rowdy saloon culture catering to canal boatmen and other transients. Many members of the business community were indifferent to religion and the spiritual state of their employees.

Finney preached almost daily in Rochester for six months. One resident remembered that "you could not go upon the streets and hear any conversation, except upon religion." In cooperation with the local ministers, Finney brought thousands to accept his message of voluntary salvation. Church membership doubled during the revival, and by the time he left, members were actively at work in the community, spreading the gospel. Religion helped bring order to what had been a chaotic and fragmented city.

Although revivals like Finney's Rochester triumph drew converts from all segments of American society, they appealed especially to the middle class: lawyers, merchants, retailers, and manufacturers—men who played central roles in the larger market economy and invested in factories and railroads. The market put intense pressure on these upwardly mobile citizens, who regarded success as a moral obligation and a reflection of individual character. At the same time, the oscillations of the economy—boom, then bust—intensified their fear that success would be fleeting. Religion provided a way in which to cope with the tensions and uncertainties of their own lives.

In addition to businessmen and professionals, workingmen were among the converted. Joining a church symbolized their desire to get ahead in the new economy by accepting moral self-discipline. To a striking degree, social mobility walked hand in hand with church membership. In Rochester two-thirds of the workers who were church members improved their occupational status in a decade: they were far more likely than unchurched workers to own their own shop or business or to become skilled employees. By contrast, workingmen who did not join a church rarely stayed in town more than a few years, and those who stayed were likely to decline in status.

Although revivalists like Finney cared more about saving souls than about savings accounts, evangelical Protestantism reinforced values that were necessary to succeed in the new competitive economy. The market and the factory required a disciplined, reliable, responsible work force. Churchgoers accepted the values of hard work, sobriety, and punctuality; they internalized the demand for restraint and self-control. Religion was also a means of social control in a disordered society. Again, that aim was far from the purpose of the revivalists, who had their gaze fixed firmly on the millennium. But the revivals promoted social order through the mechanism of self-restraint. And many employers put pressure on workers to give up their drinking habits, on and off the job, and to embrace religion.

The Significance of the Second Great Awakening

Tocqueville claimed that he knew of "no country in the world where the Christian religion retains a greater influence over the souls of men than in America." He did not exaggerate. And as a result of the Second Great Awakening, the dominant form of Christianity in America became evangelical Protestantism. Membership in the major Protestant churches of pre–Civil War America—Congregational, Presbyterian, Baptist, and Methodist—soared during the first half of the nineteenth century. By 1840 an estimated half of the adult population was nominally connected to some church, with the Methodists emerging as the largest Protestant denomination in both the North and the South. Numbering just 58,000 members in 1790, Methodists claimed over a million members in 1844. Unlike the more Calvinistic Congregationalists, Presbyterians, and Baptists, the Methodists from the beginning embraced the doctrine of free will and honed their revival skills.

Evangelicalism was in harmony with the basic values of early nineteenth-century Americans. Its emphasis on the ability of the individual to bring about his or her salvation endorsed the American belief in individualism. The revivals appealed to ordinary people and catered to a mass audience without social distinctions, which reinforced the American belief in democracy and equality. Anti-intellectual in their thrust, revivalists emphasized the individual's feelings and conscience as the source of truth and scorned carefully reasoned theological discourses. Success oriented, the revivals varied tactics to gain the most converts and were invincibly optimistic. Finney's doctrine of perfectionism was perfectly attuned to the spirit of the age.

WOMEN'S SPHERE

But not all—or even a majority—of Americans who flocked to revivals or joined reform societies were men. On the contrary, female converts outnumbered males by about three to two. Usually the initial convert in a family was a woman, and many men who converted were related to women who had come forward earlier. In Utica, New York, for example, the majority of men who joined the churches were relatives of women who had preceded them in membership.

Women and Revivalism

Women played such a prominent role in the Second Great Awakening in part because of changes in their own social universe. During the early nineteenth century, Americans placed increasing emphasis on romantic love as a factor in marriage. In the new conjugal marriage, couples married less often to enhance property and status, and more often because they shared a mutual affection. With sons and daughters demanding the right to choose their own partners, parents played a smaller part in arranging marriages. Marriage was still deemed important for a woman's happiness, and it remained essential for her economic security. But a woman's prospects for marriage became less certain with the decline of the parental role in matchmaking. And in older areas such as New England, this uncertainty was compounded by the migration of so many young men to the West, creating a shortage of eligible bachelors.

The new unpredictability of their lives drew young women toward religion. Although everywhere in America women made up the backbone of the churches, those between the ages of 12 and 25 were especially susceptible to conversion. Joining a church heightened a young woman's sense of initiative and gave her a sense of purpose. Church membership also provided friendships and support and, by establishing respectability and widening her social circle, enhanced her chances of marriage.

Furthermore, the changing economic order of the Jacksonian era brought unfamiliar pressures to bear on wives and mothers. Most men now worked outside the home, while the rise of factories led to a decline in part-time work such as spinning, which women had once performed to supplement family income. Moreover, except on the frontier, home manufacturing was no longer essential, for the family purchased articles that women previously had made, such as clothing, shoes, soap, and candles. A number of occupations that had been open to women earlier, including medicine and shopkeeping, were now closed to them.

The Ideal of Domesticity

This increasing separation of the household from the workplace converted the home into a female domain. As such, it took on a new social identity. Idealized as a repository of virtue and a barrier against the disorder of the outside world, the home became a sanctuary and the mother its patron saint. This new view of women's role—almost a "cult of domesticity"—was elaborated largely by clergy and female authors in countless sermons, advice manuals, and pieces of sentimental fiction for an urban middle-class audience. But the ideal's significance and acceptance had far-reaching consequences.

The cult of domesticity was based on the notion of separate sexual spheres. Each sex, it was said, had a part of life in which it reigned supreme. Whereas men were breadwinners responsible for the family's financial security, women were care-givers, concerned with and finding fulfillment in others. If men's sphere was the outside world, women's sphere was the home, where they were to dispense love and comfort and teach moral values to husbands and children. "Love is our life our reality, business yours," Mollie Clark told one suitor. Women were also held to a higher standard of sexual purity. Although regarded as physically weaker and therefore reliant on male protection, women were believed to be stronger morally. A man's sexual infidelity, while hardly condoned, brought no lasting shame. But for a woman to "fall" before marriage or to stray afterward was to court everlasting disgrace and social isolation. Under this double standard, men were expected to be aggressive, while women were to be passive, to submerge their identities in those of their husbands. Tocqueville commented that "in no country has such constant care been taken, as in America, to trace two clearly distinct lines of action for the two sexes, and to make them keep pace with the other, but in two pathways which are always different."

Most Jacksonian women did not see this ideology as a rationale for male dominance. On the contrary, women played an important role in creating the cult of domesticity, none more than Lyman Beecher's daughter Catharine. Like the earlier advocates of "republican motherhood," she argued that making the home a female domain gave women real power as moral custodians of the nation's future. To raise children in Christian virtue and to provide solace for family members were crucial responsibilities. So too was the proper care of a middle-class household, and she wrote several books on the "science" of domestic management, detailing the most efficient, economical, and sanitary methods of preparing food and keeping house. Catharine Beecher was also a leading advocate of training women to become schoolteachers. Conceiving of the school as an extension of the

As business affairs grew increasingly separate from the family in the nineteenth century, the middle-class home became a female domain. As a wife and mother, a woman was to dispense love and moral guidance to her husband and her children.

home, she maintained that teachers, like mothers, should instill sound moral values in children. Because of their naturally pious character and their affection for children, women were ideally suited to be teachers and should receive greater educational opportunities.

Most women hardly had the time to make the ideal of domesticity the center of their lives. Farm women had to work hard and constantly, while lower-class families could not get by without the wages of female members. Still, most middle-class women accepted and tried to live up to the ideal, and many found the effort confining. "The great trial is that I have nothing to do," one complained. "Here I am with abundant leisure and capable, I believe, of accomplishing some good, and yet with no object on which to expend my energies." For such women, religion and reform offered two socially accepted outlets for their talents.

Their socially defined role as the guardians of religion and morality helps explain the prominence of women among revival converts, but religious activities offered other rewards as well. It was the one way that women could exert influence over society and the one area where wives were freed from subordination to their husbands. Finney allowed men and women to pray together, and he permitted women to lead the congregation in prayer. For some male critics, this was the most dangerous of his new measures, for it implied a certain equality between the sexes. One unhappy man in Rochester complained about the effect of Finney's visit to his home: "He *stuffed* my wife with tracts, and alarmed her fears, and nothing short of meetings, night and day, could atone for the many fold sins my poor, simple spouse had committed." Then, getting to the heart of the matter, he added, "She made the miraculous discovery, that she had been 'unevenly yoked.' From this unhappy period, peace, quiet, and happiness have fled from my dwelling, never, I fear, to return."

Daily Lives

CLOTHING AND FASHION

Early Bloomers

As Elizabeth Smith Miller cultivated her garden in the spring of 1851, her thoughts wandered from the flowers and vegetables to her muddy, bedraggled skirt. Those long, trailing flounces seemed to catch on every stalk and branch; layers of stiff petticoats made stooping to weed and plant almost impossible; her snug corset kept her short of breath. Irritated and uncomfortable, Miller resolved then and there to free herself from bondage to those "fettering folds" by designing a simpler outfit. The result was a loose-fitting dress that reached a few inches below her knees and a pair of trousers that tapered at the ankle, resembling "harem pants." "It would be suitable dress for a journey to California," one dubious but diplomatic family member remarked. Miller remained undaunted. "What is Life," she rejoined, "but a journey to California—to that Eldorado of higher development in pursuit of which one should cast off every impediment."

In her eagerness to "cast off every impediment," Elizabeth Miller epitomized the perfectionist spirit of early Victorian America, and her chosen object of reform became women's dress. The daughter of Gerrit Smith, a wealthy landowner and merchant from upstate New York who endorsed abolition, temperance, and women's rights, Miller enlisted in the cause of dress reform feminists like her cousin, Elizabeth Cady Stanton, and Amelia Bloomer, the editor of a temperance newspaper, *The Lily*. After Bloomer's newspaper publicized Miller's design, other journalists dubbed the outfit "bloomers," and Cady Stanton, along with many other women prominent in the suf-

frage movement, adopted the costume.

Dress reform attracted adherents with a variety of social agendas. Some feminists, like Elizabeth Miller, simply sought greater freedom of movement. Cady Stanton, for example, commended bloomers to all busy wives and mothers "who wash and iron, bake and brew, carry water and fat babies upstairs and down, bring potatoes, apples, and pans of milk from the cellar, run our own errands, through mud or snow, shovel paths, and work in the garden." "'The drapery,'" she concluded, "is quite too much—one might as well work with a ball and chain." Other feminists went further, seeing dress reform as essential to establishing the equality of the sexes. Sarah Grimké contended that "so long as we submit to being dressed like dolls, we can never rise to the stations of duty and usefulness from which they [men] desire to exclude us." Many women members of utopian socialist communities like Oneida, Brook Farm, and New Harmony adopted the bloomer costume for similar reasons, applauding dress reform as a leveling, democratic influence.

A consensus concerning the need to simplify women's dress reached well beyond the ranks of feminists and utopian thinkers. Health reformers like the followers of Sylvester Graham joined with more orthodox members of the medical community in condemning the vogue of "tight-lacing" corsets. Some physicians warned that tight lacing impaired the ability of women to bear healthy children by narrowing the pelvis, while others charged that the practice could result in broken ribs, collapsed lungs, weakened abdominal walls, and uterine disorders. Catharine Beecher, who instituted a regimen of health-promoting calisthenics at her female seminaries, agreed with feminists that confining corsets and "seas" of crino-

Daily Lives

line petticoats restricted ease of movement. The members of female moral reform societies also took up the cause, contending that addiction to fashion and finery encouraged prostitution. A similar suspicion of high style pervaded sentimental novels of the period, literature written largely by and for women.

But not all Victorians agreed on the need for dress reform. *Harper's Bazaar*, a popular women's magazine, stood with tradition by declaring that "we believe in the petticoat as an institution older and more sacred than the Magna Carta." Critics associated bloomers with the radicalism of upstate New York's "Burned-Over District," where it had been created, and with the free love theories of the Oneida Community, where it reigned as the prevailing fashion. Others charged that bloomers resembled the garments worn by prostitutes in big city brothels, while pious skeptics pointed to the biblical prohibition against women wearing trousers. Most middle-class Americans, steeped in both Scripture and the doctrine of "separate spheres," strongly identified wearing pants with masculinity and believed that bloomers would make women men's "rivals" rather than their "counterparts." Even Cady Stanton's father lamented that she had made "a guy" of herself by appearing in the new costume.

By the 1860s, bloomers had fallen from favor even among feminists. The outfit proved difficult to make, and even Elizabeth Miller admitted that her creation did not "sit" gracefully. More to the point, the flurry over fashion distracted attention from the cause of women's rights. Susan B. Anthony abandoned bloomers when she noticed that men stared at her ankles instead of listening to her talk. Perhaps most important, many suffragists became convinced that women's degradation was rooted in laws and institutions, not in dress. "We have no reason to hope that pantaloons would do more for us than they have done for man himself," Cady Stanton wrote. "The negro slave enjoys the most unlimited freedom in his attire . . . yet in spite of his dress and his manhood, too, he is a slave still."

Despite the new importance of affection in marriage, women gave emotionally much more to other family members than they received in exchange, and they turned to other women for comfort and support. Thus benevolent organizations supplemented religious revivals, weekly services, and prayer in consoling women and providing an outlet for expression. These societies fostered close friendships among women eager for companionship. This "sisterhood"—the common sense of identity and shared experiences—helped sustain not only home missionary societies and maternal associations, but also other reform movements launched by women to aid females of the lower classes, including movements to reclaim prostitutes.

The Middle-Class Family in Transition

As the middle-class family adapted to the increased pressures of a competitive market society by becoming a domestic haven of moral virtue, it developed a new structure and new set of attitudes closer in spirit to the modern family. One basic change was the rise of privacy. The family was increasingly seen as a sheltered retreat from the outside world. It became the center of emotional comfort, reassurance, and support. In addition, the pressures to achieve success led middle-class young adults to delay marriage. A man was expected to be sufficiently established to support a wife before he married. Owning a house and having a wife who did not work became important symbols of success.

Smaller family size was a result of the delay in marriage as well, since wives began bearing children later. But especially among the urban middle class, women began to use birth control to space children further apart and minimize the risks of pregnancy. The methods were primitive by modern standards: abstinence from intercourse, extended breastfeeding, condoms, and crude vaginal diaphragms and sponges. In addition, it has been estimated that before 1860 one abortion was performed for every five or six live births. These practices contributed to a decline in the birth rate, from slightly more than 7 children per family in 1800 to 5.4 in 1850—a 25 percent drop. Although the birth rate had been falling gradually since the turn of the century, it dropped more abruptly beginning in the 1830s. Family size was directly related to the success ethic. A smaller family indicated an effort at self-restraint, but, more important, it showed that the family recognized the necessity of living within its means. In the cities, large families were increasingly identified with low-status immigrants and were viewed as evidence of economic irresponsibility. An economic asset on the farm, children were a financial burden in the new society, where extended education and special training were needed to succeed.

Indeed, more parents showed greater concern about providing their children with advantages in the race for success. Middle-class families were increasingly willing to bear the additional expense of educating their sons to prepare them for a career in business. Sons remained in the family longer and entered the work force later; often they were in their early twenties by the time they left home. In general the parents' sacrifice accomplished its purpose: sons who went to school longer and left home later tended to be more successful and achieve a higher status. Middle-class families also frequently equalized inheritances rather than giving priority to the eldest son or favoring sons over daughters.

AMERICAN ROMANTICISM

American Protestantism, with its drive for millennial perfection, played a central role in the reform movements of the Jacksonian era—whether it was Charles Finney "praying up" a revival or Catharine Beecher reordering the habits of American women. Yet the temper of those movements would have been strikingly different without another influential current of thought, that of Romanticism.

As an intellectual movement, Romanticism began in Europe as a reaction to the Enlightenment. The Enlightenment had placed reason at the center of human endeavor; Romanticism emphasized instead the importance of intuition and emotion as sources of truth. It gloried in the unlimited potential of the individual, who might soar if freed from the artificial restraints of oppressive institutions. Romanticism extolled humanitarianism; it sought to experience and identify with the suffering of the oppressed, in the way that Lord Byron, the tempestuous English poet who died in 1824 working for Greek independence, did.

All of these attitudes, values, and thought helped separate the world of Jacksonian America from the Enlightenment temperament of the Revolutionary generation. In exalting inner feelings and heartfelt convictions, Romanticism reinforced the emotionalism of religious revivals. Philosophically, its influence was strongest among intellectuals who took part in the Transcendental movement and in the dramatic flowering of American literature. And like millennial revivalism, Romanticism offered its own paths toward perfection.

Emerson and Transcendentalism

Above all, Romanticism produced individualists. Thus Transcendentalism is difficult to define, for its members resisted being lumped together. It blossomed in the mid-1830s, when a number of Unitarian clergy like George Ripley and Ralph Waldo Emerson resigned their pulpits, loudly protesting the church's smug, lifeless teachings. To Lyman Beecher, Unitarians were threatening because their rationalism took them too far toward infidelity. To Ripley and Emerson, Unitarian rationalism did not go far enough. "In how many churches, by how many prophets, tell me," demanded Emerson, "is man made sensible that he is an Infinite Soul; that the heavens and the earth are passing into his mind; that he is drinking forever the soul of God?" The new "Transcendentalist Club" attracted a small following among other young Boston intellectuals who were likewise unhappy, including Margaret Fuller, Bronson Alcott, and Orestes Brownson.

Like European Romantics, American Transcendentalists emphasized feeling over reason, seeking a spiritual communion with nature. By *transcend* they meant to go beyond or to rise above—specifically above reason and beyond the material world. Every human being contained a spark of divinity, Emerson avowed, by participating in what he called the "Over-Soul," the divine force flowing through all of creation. Transcendentalists also shared in the Romantic's glorification of the individual. "Trust thyself. Every heart vibrates to that iron string," Emerson ad-

Ralph Waldo Emerson.

vised. "The root and seed of democracy is the doctrine, judge for yourself." If freed from the artificial constraints of traditional authority, the individual had infinite potential. So optimistic was Transcendentalism in its view of human nature, it essentially denied the existence of evil.

Transcendentalism had much in common with Jacksonian America—optimism, individualism, and an egalitarian spirit. "I am *Defeated* all the time," Emerson declared, "yet to Victory I am born." The psychology of boom-and-bust left no place for the finality of defeat. Although the details of Emerson's philosophy lay beyond the grasp of all but a handful of intellectuals, thousands flocked to hear him lecture. Like the devout at Finney's revivals, who sought to perfect themselves and bring about the millennium, those who heard Emerson were infused with the spirit of optimistic reform.

As the currents of Romanticism percolated through American society, the country's literary tradition came of age. In 1820 educated Americans still tended to ape the fashions of England and Europe: American readers bought seven English books for every three written in the United States. But as the population grew and education expanded, American writers developed their own distinctive styles and examined the customs, opinions, and character of American society. Improved printing presses allowed for cheaper, mass-produced American books, and better transportation made possible a wider distribution of printed material across the nation. By 1850 for every British book, two American books were sold in the United States.

Emerson's address "The American Scholar" (1837) constituted a declaration of literary independence. "Our long dependence, our long apprenticeship to the learning of other lands draws to a close," he proclaimed. "Events, actions arise, that must be sung, that will sing themselves." His call inspired a generation of writers.

The Clash Between Nature and Civilization

At the time Emerson spoke, James Fenimore Cooper was already making his mark as the first distinctive American novelist. In the Leatherstocking Tales, a series of five novels written between 1823 and 1841, Cooper chronicled the life of the frontiersman Natty Bumppo. Leatherstocking, as Bumppo was also known, was hardly drawn with realism; decades later, Mark Twain would hoot at Cooper's crude dialogue, and the poet James Russell Lowell gleefully said of Cooper that "the women he draws from one model don't vary/ All sappy as maples and flat as a prairie."

But the tales did examine two basic yet contradictory impulses within American culture. On the one hand, Natty Bumppo represented the nobility and innocence of the wilderness. At the same time, the novels portrayed the culture of the frontier as a threat to the civilization Cooper prized so highly. In one scene in *The Pioneers* (1823), as villagers along the New York frontier slaughter thousands of pigeons, Leatherstocking laments the wanton destruction, only to hear a townsman express surprise that anyone would "grumble at the loss of a few pigeons. . . . If you had to sow your wheat twice, and three times, as I have done," he continues, "you wouldn't be so massyfully feeling'd toward the devils. Hurrah, boys! scatter the feathers." As the market expanded and the hinterlands began to develop and exploit their resources, American thought betrayed an inward dread that the advance of civilization would destroy the natural simplicity of the land.

Natty Bumppo, the self-reliant solitary individual, stood halfway between the savage and civilized worlds, not comfortable embracing either.

Henry David Thoreau, too, used nature as a backdrop for his literary explorations; he also was concerned with the conflict between the unfettered individual and the constraints of society. A disciple of Emerson, Thoreau grew up in Concord, Massachusetts, where he became part of Emerson's circle. Eventually he undertook to live by himself to demonstrate the advantages of self-reliance. Building a cabin on the edge of Walden Pond on land owned by Emerson, Thoreau lived in relative solitude for 16 months, recording his observations in his journal, which became the basis for one of the classics in American literature, *Walden* (1854).

Thoreau argued that only in nature could one find true independence, liberty, equality, and happiness. By living simply, it was possible to master oneself and the world. Thoreau's own isolation from society, however, was less than total. When lonely or hungry, he walked to Emerson's home nearby for conversation and a slice of Lidian Emerson's apple pie, and most of the materials he used to build his "wilderness" cabin were store-bought. Still, *Walden* eloquently denounced the frantic competition in an industrial society for material goods and wealth. "Money is not required to buy one necessity of the soul," Thoreau maintained. "I see my townsmen, whose misfortune it is to have inherited farms, houses, barns, cattle, and farming tools. . . . Who made them serfs of the soil?" It seemed only too clear that "the mass of men lead lives of quiet desperation."

Thoreau's individualism was so extreme that he rejected any institution of society that contradicted his personal sense of right. "The only obligation which I have a right to assume, is to do at any time what I think right," he wrote in his essay "On Civil Disobedience." He extolled the individual over the democratic will of the majority. "Any man more right than his neighbors constitutes a majority of one already," he claimed. Thoreau's anarchism finally led him to refuse to pay his poll tax as a protest against the Mexican War. After spending a night in jail, he was released when his aunt paid the tax. Voicing the anti-institutional impulse of Romanticism, he took individualism to its antisocial extreme.

Songs of the Self-Reliant and Darker Loomings

In contrast to Thoreau's exclusiveness, Walt Whitman was all-inclusive, embracing American society in its infinite variety. A journalist and laborer in the New York City area, Whitman proclaimed that "the genius of the United States is . . . always most in the common people. Their manners, speech, dress, friendships . . . are unrhymed poetry." In taking their measure in *Leaves of Grass* (1855), he pioneered a new, modern form of poetry, unconcerned with meter and rhyme and using the line as the basic unit. Baffled by his innovative free verse, put off by his informal use of slang, most critics were offended by his frank imagery and sexual references.

"Simmering, simmering," as he later said, when Emerson "brought me to a boil," Whitman accepted fervently the idea that America was the hope of the future. Conceiving himself the representative of all Americans, he exuberantly

Walt Whitman, poet of democracy.

titled his first major poem "Song of Myself."

> I am your voice—It was tied in you—In me it began to talk.
> I celebrate myself to celebrate every man and woman alive.

Like the Transcendentalists, Whitman exalted the emotions, nature, and the individual, while endowing these ideas with a more joyous, democratic spirit.

More brooding in spirit was Nathaniel Hawthorne, who lived for a time in Concord and also participated in the Transcendental commune at Brook Farm. After his father's death, Hawthorne's mother withdrew into herself, leaving Nathaniel to make his way emotionally on his own. He became gloomy and introspective, unable to partake of Emerson's sunny optimism and repelled by the self-centered outlook of Thoreau. Convinced of the power of the past to shape future generations, Hawthorne wrote of the reality of evil and its place in the human heart. In *The Scarlet Letter* (1850), set in New England's Puritan era, Hawthorne spun the tale of Hester Prynne, condemned to wear the scarlet A (adulteress) for bearing an illegitimate child. His sympathies obviously lay with Prynne, even though she was guilty of the sin of pride, while his greatest condemnation fell on her neighbors, who judged her without compassion. Like the Puritans, who both attracted and repelled him, Hawthorne had no illusions about creating a world without evil, and he rejected the American belief that a person or society could free itself from the past.

Hawthorne found a soul mate in Herman Melville, who became a close friend. But unlike Hawthorne, who was recognized by his contemporaries and supported himself by his writing, Melville died in poverty and obscurity. Not until the twentieth century did literary scholars elevate him to the first rank of American authors. His masterpiece, *Moby-Dick* (1851), drew on his youthful experiences aboard a whaling ship. The novel's Captain Ahab relentlessly drives his ship and crew in pursuit of the great white whale Moby-Dick, to whom he had lost a leg. In his unbridled quest for success the fierce captain becomes, in Melville's telling, a powerful symbol of American character and values: the prototype of the ruthless businessman despoiling nature's resources. "Swerve me?" he asks at one point. "The path to my fixed purpose is laid with iron rails, whereon my soul is grooved to run. Over unsound gorges, through the rifled hearts of mountains, under torrents' beds, unerringly I rush!" In *Moby-Dick* Melville repudiated the materialistic emphasis of American individualism.

Even more adamantly than Hawthorne, Melville rejected the spark of divinity that Emerson saw within each individual. Ahab is Emerson's self-reliant man, but in him, self-reliance is transformed into a dangerous monomania. A law unto himself, Ahab chases the whale with such relentless ferocity that he destroys his ship, its crew, and himself. *Moby-Dick*'s universe is morally ambiguous, rejecting the view that goodness must always triumph. Instead, individuals find themselves isolated and in spiritual anguish, doomed to a lifelong pilgrimage in search of the meaning of life and one's proper place in the infinite cosmos.

More clearly than any other writer, Melville recognized the dilemma created by Romanticism's emphasis on emotion and the individual. On the one hand,

Herman Melville.

Americans celebrated the unlimited power of the free individual. Liberated from institutional restraints, human possibilities seemed unlimited to Romantic philosophers. Yet as older traditions and institutions dropped away, the new individualism also led to a competitive materialism devoid of the older sense of community. How, Melville seemed to be asking, could American society be made perfect, if it was based on self-interested materialism and individualism?

But awash in the unbounded opportunities opening before them, most Americans preferred to celebrate, with Emerson, the glories of democracy and the individual's quest for perfection.

THE AGE OF REFORM

Both Romanticism and perfectionism held the potential for inspiring radical democratic change. While the earlier benevolent societies had aimed at a more conservative reformation of individual sinners, the more radical offshoots of Romanticism and perfectionism sought to remake society at large. The new ideas invited ordinary people to determine what good needed doing independent of the clergy and to equate their decision with the Lord's will.

Some schemers and dreamers for a better world harbored decidedly eccentric notions. The reformer Sylvester Graham, who argued that diet determined character, won lasting fame by having a cracker named after him. Graham also advocated frequent bathing, exercise, wearing loose-fitting clothing, and avoiding sex except for purposes of procreation. While he gained a small following, most Americans ignored him—except for commercial bakers, who, knowing a threat when they saw one, mobbed this champion of homemade bread.

Even stranger than Graham's theory of diet was the vogue of phrenology. Based on an alleged science of the mind, phrenology purported to chart aspects of human character by studying the form and shape of the head. Eager urban audiences paid for lectures explaining the system, rural families subscribed to mail order courses, and thousands visited salons to have bumps on their heads examined and their character analyzed, including young men uncertain about a career, for phrenology promised to discover the occupation that would best match a person's talents. In all, the fad suited the needs of a people anxious to succeed.

Utopian Communities

Other reformers proposed more radical changes in society by establishing utopian communities. These experiments aimed at reforming the world through example, and all sought to restore a spirit of unity and cooperation in place of competitive individualism. Some were directly linked to religion, but even the secular communities shared the optimism of perfectionism and millennialism.

One of the most long-lived utopian experiments had its sources in an eighteenth-century millennial movement: the Shakers, led by Ann Lee. The illiterate daughter of an English blacksmith, Lee believed that God had a dual nature, part male and part female. In a series of ecstatic visions, she became convinced that, just as Christ had come to earth exemplifying the male side of God, through her own person a spiritual Second Coming would be achieved. Persecuted in England, she left for America in 1774 with eight followers.

Mother Ann, as she was known, died in 1784, after making a number of converts in New England and New York. But the Shakers' greatest growth came during the years of the Second Great Awakening, when Lee's successors traveled to revivals (including the great camp meeting at Cane Ridge, Kentucky) to make their own converts. The new disciples founded about 20 communal settlements to put into effect Mother Ann's teachings. Influenced by the Quakers, Lee had preached a life of spiritual simplicity. Like the early Quakers, she and her followers sometimes shook in the fervent public demonstration of their faith—hence the name Shakers. Convinced that the end of the world was at hand and that there was no need to perpetuate the human race, Shaker communities practiced celibacy, separating the sexes as far as practical. Men and women normally worked apart, ate at separate tables in silence, entered separate doorways, and had separate living quarters. The Shakers' religious services provided an emotional release in their otherwise carefully regimented lives. Central to these services was dancing, which was sometimes carefully regulated, other times wild and spontaneous. At its peak after 1820, the sect had an estimated 6000 members.

Shaker communities accorded women unusual authority and equality. Community tasks were generally assigned along sexual lines, with women performing household chores and men laboring in the fields. But leadership of the church was split equally between men and women. Since marriage and families had been abolished, women were freed from many traditional burdens. By the mid-nineteenth century, a majority of members were female.

Property in Shaker settlements was owned communally and controlled by the church hierarchy. The sect's members worked hard, lived simply, and impressed outsiders with their cleanliness and order. They prospered through a combination of agriculture and crafts, and they became famous for the clean, simple lines of their architecture and furniture. Lacking any natural increase, membership began to decline after 1850, and by the end of the century the Shakers had been reduced to a small remnant.

The Oneida Community, founded by John Humphrey Noyes, also set out to alter the relationship between the sexes, though in a rather different way. Noyes, a convert of Charles Finney, was expelled from his ministry in the Congregational church for his heretical ideas on perfectionism. While Finney argued that men and women should strive to achieve perfection, Noyes announced that he had reached this blessed state. Unlike Finney, he contended that once a person was saved, he or she became incapable of sinning. Settling in Putney, Vermont, with a band of like-minded followers, Noyes relieved women of what he termed "kitchen slavery." Under his system, they cooked only at breakfast and thereafter were free from household duties until the next morning.

Noyes' ideas of liberation, however, went beyond the kitchen. After he had been spurned by the woman he wished to marry, he evolved the doctrine of "complex marriage." Exclusive love for one person was antisocial and dangerous to a community, he argued, since all members should be bound to one another. Rejecting traditional marriage, Noyes concluded that it was not sinful for the members of his commune to have sexual relations with one another. Confronted with the hostility of his Vermont neighbors, who emphatically did not share these views, Noyes in 1848 moved his unorthodox community to Oneida, New York.

The practice of complex marriage did not lead to unrestrained self-indulgence. Oneida couples were allowed to have intercourse only with the approval of the community and after a searching examination of their motives. Eventually Noyes even undertook experiments in planned reproduction. Acting on his conviction that good character was inherited, a committee of Oneidans selected "scientific" combinations of parents to produce morally superior children. Despite his radical ideas about marriage and women's work, Noyes was hardly a feminist. He unambiguously believed that men were superior to women and that this superiority was part of the order of the universe. In his eyes, the ultimate ideal for a woman was to become "what she ought to be, a female man."

Noyes' real concern was not to liberate women but to overcome social and intellectual disorder and in so doing, achieve a new synthesis between religion and society. Under his charismatic leadership, the Oneida Community grew to over 200 members in 1851. But in 1879 an internal dispute drove him from power, and without his guiding hand the community soon fell apart. In 1881 its members reorganized as a joint stock company and prospered by manufacturing silver, an enterprise still in existence.

Robert Owen and New Harmony

The hardship and poverty that accompanied the growth of industrial factories sparked another attempt at utopian reform by Robert Owen, himself a Scottish industrialist. Determined to create a society that balanced both agriculture and manufacturing, Owen believed that the character of individuals was shaped by their surroundings, and that by changing those surroundings, one could change human character. In this sense he was an environmentalist. His utopianism was based on science and reason, not religion, yet he shared the belief in the perfectibility of human nature and society.

Owen came to the United States in 1824 and purchased property in Indiana to found his community of New Harmony. Confident that he could reform anyone, he accepted all who wanted to join. Unfortunately, most of the 900 or so volunteers who flocked to New Harmony lacked the skills, commitment, and discipline needed to make the community a success. Bitter factions that split the settlement were made worse when Owen tried to ease frictions through open discussion and debate. Owen also rashly surrendered control of the textile mill, the economic basis of the community, to its members; this socialist scheme soon failed. Having lost most of his own fortune, Owen dissolved the community in 1827. Over 20 other American communities were founded on Owen's theories, none particularly successful.

By 1840 Owen had been eclipsed in socialist circles by a French theorist and reformer, Charles Fourier. Fourier also envisioned communities of cooperative labor, but his system was not true communism, for investors shared profits produced by the community, as in a business corporation. Instead of adopting environmentalism, Fourier based his theories on his own science of human nature. An individual's personality was determined by the mixture of 12 passions, Fourier argued; laborers who took jobs suited to their personalities would find work a pleasure, not drudgery. Because Fourierism attracted support from some intellectuals and received lavish publicity in Horace Greeley's New York *Tribune*, it gained much attention in the United States. At least 28 cooperative communities were established, but none lasted long.

The experience of New Harmony and other communities demonstrated that the United States was poor soil for socialistic experiments. Wages were too high and land too cheap to interest most Americans in collectivist ventures. And individualism was too strong to create a commitment to cooperative action.

The Temperance Movement

The most significant reform movements of the period sought not to withdraw from society, but to change it directly. One of the most determined of these was the temperance movement.

The origins of the campaign lay in the heavy drinking of the early nineteenth century. Liquor had been part of American life since the founding of the colonies, but after the Revolution, alcohol consumption reached unprecedented levels. From 1800 to 1830 the annual per capita consumption of distilled spirits rose from three gallons to more than five, the highest level in American history and nearly triple present-day levels. The per capita figure, of course, included women and children, who did much less imbibing than men; on average in the late 1820s, an adult male drank nearly half a pint daily of whiskey, gin, brandy, or rum. Whiskey was cheap and plentiful, and anxiety-ridden Americans sought relief in the bottle, as well as drinking routinely at house raisings, quilting parties, weddings, and funerals. Anne Royale, whose travels often took her cross country by stage, reported, "When I was in Virginia, it was too much whiskey—in Ohio, too much whiskey—in Tennessee, it is too, too much whiskey!" The social costs for such habits were high: broken families, abused and neglected wives and children, sickness and disability, poverty and crime. The temperance movement undertook to eliminate these problems by curbing drinking.

Led largely by clergy, the movement initially focused on drunkenness and did not oppose moderate drinking. But in 1826 the American Temperance Society was founded, taking voluntary abstinence as its goal; during the next decade approximately 5000 local temperance societies were founded. Three important changes occurred in the antidrinking movement between 1820 and 1850, reflecting this shift toward total abstinence. First, ardent spirits were redefined to include beer and wine, whose consumption was no longer acceptable. Second, temperance advocates increasingly concentrated their attack on the liquor traffic rather than the consumer. And finally, the movement entered the political arena and lobbied for state laws to prohibit the manufacture and sale of liquor. Despite legal setbacks and the unwillingness of many politicians to lend support, the temperance movement produced a sharp decline in the annual per capita consumption of alcohol after 1830. By the middle of the next decade it had fallen below two gallons.

The temperance movement lasted longer and attracted many more supporters than other reforms: it appealed to young and old, to men and women, to urban and rural residents, to workers and businessmen. And it was the only reform movement with significant support in the South. One reason for its wide appeal was the campaign's use of revival techniques. The Washington Temperance Society, founded by reformed alcoholics, aimed to save drunkards through personal testimony, using the language of the common people and deliberately emphasizing emotion. At the climax of these meetings, members of the audience were invited to step forward, like converts in a revival, and take the pledge.

Other factors strengthened the movement's appeal. The rise of democracy

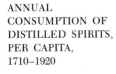

ANNUAL
CONSUMPTION OF
DISTILLED SPIRITS,
PER CAPITA,
1710–1920

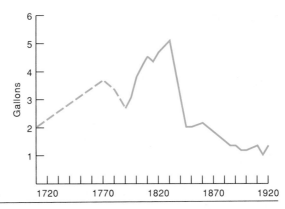

necessitated sober voters; the rise of industry required sober workers. Temperance also appealed to the upwardly mobile—professionals, small businessmen, and skilled artisans anxious to improve their social standing by acquiring reputations for self-discipline. Finally, the temperance movement strongly appealed to women. To a striking degree, its literature stressed the suffering that men inflicted on women and children. As defenders of the home, women saw drinking as a threat to family security; participation in the temperance campaign provided an important avenue of self-assertion and a way for women to uphold their domestic mission.

Educational Reform

In 1800 Massachusetts was the only state requiring free public schools supported by community funds. The well-to-do generally were educated in private academies or by tutors, and some of the poor attended church or charity schools. Even where public schools existed, the one-room buildings crowded in as many as 80 students of various ages and ability levels, to be taught by a single harassed, overworked, and underpaid teacher.

The call for tax-supported education arose first among workers, as a means to restore their deteriorating position in society. But middle-class reformers quickly took control of the movement, with an intent to uplift common citizens, educate boys to vote wisely when they came of age, and make equal opportunity a reality. Horace Mann, the leading proponent of common schools, hailed education as "the great equalizer of the conditions of men" and contended that it would eliminate poverty. Reformers appealed to business leaders by arguing that the new economic order needed educated workers.

Mann convinced Massachusetts to create a state board of education, which he oversaw from 1837 to 1848. Under his leadership, the state adopted a minimum-length school year, provided for training of teachers, increased their pay, and improved the curriculum by including subjects such as history, geography, and various applied skills. Massachusetts also took the lead in requiring every town with a population of 500 or more to establish a high school. This innovation was slow to catch on elsewhere; by 1860 the nation could count only about 300 high schools, fully a third of which were in Massachusetts. Moreover, compulsory attendance was rarely required, and out of necessity many poor parents sent their children to work instead of school, particularly at the secondary level. Still, by the 1850s the number of schools, attendance figures, and school budgets had all increased sharply. Educational reformers enjoyed their greatest success in the Northeast and the least in the South, where planters opposed paying taxes to educate poorer white children.

Educational opportunities for women also expanded. Teachers like Catharine Beecher and Emma Hunt Willard established a number of private girls' schools, putting to rest the objection of many male educators that fragile female minds would not be able to absorb large doses of mathematics, physics, or geography. In 1833 Oberlin became the nation's first coeducational college; four years later Mary Lyon founded Mount Holyoke, the first American college for women. Students at Holyoke led a rigorous life, not only studying hard but helping out with the housekeeping. On Thanksgiving Day one relieved student recorded that "we all had the privilege of sleeping as long as we wished in the morning, provided we were ready for breakfast by 8 o'clock. I rose at five, an hour later than usual and worked two hours and a half before breakfast."

The Asylum Movement

After 1820 there was also a dramatic increase in the number of asylums of every sort—orphanages, jails, and hospitals. The proponents of asylums called for isolating and separating the criminal, the insane, the ill, and the dependent from outside society, and the goal of care shifted from confinement to reform.

The prison reform movement tried to separate youthful offenders from older, hardened criminals, to end imprisonment for debt, and to abolish public executions. But it was American efforts to rehabilitate prisoners that attracted international attention. Tocqueville originally came to the United States to examine and report on prisons. Pennsylvania and New York developed systems to isolate prisoners, introducing the measures of solitary confinement and absolute silence to give inmates time to reflect on their past errors. The reformers assumed that environment produced criminal behavior and that the new prison regimen would rehabilitate criminals. The new measures were not very effective, however: under the strain of isolation, some inmates went insane or committed suicide.

Other reformers lobbied to improve care for the mentally ill. Dorothea Dix, a Boston schoolteacher, took the lead in advocating state-supported asylums for the insane. She attracted much attention to the movement by her report detailing the horrors to which the mentally ill were subjected, including being chained, kept in cages and closets, and beaten with rods. In response to her efforts, 28 states maintained mental institutions by 1860.

Like other reform movements, the push for new asylums and better educational facilities reflected overtones of both liberation and control. Asylums freed prisoners and the mentally ill from the harsh punishments and abuses of the past, but the new techniques of rehabilitation forced prisoners to march in lockstep. Education brought with it freedom, but some enthusiastic reformers seemed to hope that schools would become as orderly as prisons.

ABOLITIONISM

Late in the fall of 1834, Lyman Beecher was in the midst of his own continuing efforts to "overturn and overturn" on behalf of the kingdom of God. As planned, he had left Boston in 1832 to assume leadership of Lane Seminary, which boasted a distinguished faculty, handsome new buildings, an ample library, and a hilltop setting commanding a panoramic view of Cincinnati and the Ohio River. The school made an admirable beachhead for converting and evangelizing the West, for it had everything that an institution for training ministers needed— everything, that is, except students. In October 1834, all but 8 of Lane's 100 students had deserted after months of bitter fighting with Beecher and the trustees over the issue of abolition.

Beecher knew the source of his troubles: a disheveled, charismatic student named Theodore Dwight Weld, who had been firing up his classmates at Lane, filling their heads with the necessity for immediately freeing the slaves of America. Beecher was not surprised, for Weld had been converted by that firebrand Finney. He knew, too, that Theodore Weld had been influenced by the arguments of William Lloyd Garrison, whose abolitionist newspaper had, in 1831, sent shock waves across the entire nation. Indeed, Beecher's troubles at Lane Seminary provided only one example of how reform, when loosed, could move in paths unexpected by those who began it.

The Beginnings of the Abolitionist Movement

William Lloyd Garrison symbolized the transition from a moderate antislavery movement to the more militant abolitionism of the 1830s. A sober, religious youngster deeply influenced by his Baptist mother, Garrison apprenticed as a printer and in the 1820s edited a newspaper sympathetic to many of the new reforms. In 1829 he was enlisted in the antislavery cause by the Quaker Benjamin Lundy. The Quakers had long opposed slavery, and Lundy had founded antislavery societies in several southern states and edited a Baltimore newspaper, *The Genius of Universal Emancipation*. Calling for a gradual end to slavery, he supported colonization, a strategy for overcoming southern fears of emancipation by transporting free blacks to Africa. Under the auspices of the colonizationists, the first group of former slaves was sent to Liberia in West Africa in 1822.

Once engaged in the antislavery cause, Garrison developed views far more radical than Lundy's. Within a year of moving to Baltimore to help edit Lundy's paper, he was convicted of libel and imprisoned. Upon his release, he hurried back to Boston, determined to publish a new kind of antislavery journal. On January 1, 1831, the first issue of *The Liberator* appeared, and abolitionism was born. In appearance, the bespectacled Garrison seemed frail, almost mousy, but in print he was abrasive, vituperative, and uncompromising. "On this subject, I do not wish to think, or speak, or write with moderation," he proclaimed. "I am in earnest—I will not equivocate—I will not excuse—I will not retreat a single inch—AND I WILL BE HEARD." Repudiating gradual emancipation and embracing "immediatism," he declared that freedom had to come at once. He denounced colonization as a racist movement and upheld the principle of racial

William Lloyd Garrison (shown left at age 30) and Theodore Dwight Weld represented different wings of the abolitionist movement. Garrison's growing radicalism led him to repudiate organized religion in the struggle against slavery. Weld, on the other hand, preferred to work through the evangelical churches and cooperated with the clergy.

equality. He insisted on no compensation to slaveowners and urged the use of "moral suasion" to convince southerners voluntarily to renounce slavery as a sin.

Garrison attracted the most attention, but other abolitionists spoke with equal conviction. Wendell Phillips, from a socially prominent Boston family, could hold listeners spellbound with his speeches; Lewis Tappan and his brother Arthur, two New York City silk merchants, boldly placed their wealth behind the causes they believed in; James G. Birney, a southern slaveholder, converted to abolitionism after wrestling with his conscience; and Angelina and Sarah Grimké, the daughters of a South Carolina planter, left their native state to speak against the institution. And there was Angelina's future husband, Theodore Weld, the restless student at Lane Seminary who had fallen so dramatically under Garrison's influence.

To abolitionists, slavery seemed a contradiction of the principle that all human beings had been created with natural rights. Then too, it went against the Romantic spirit of the age, which celebrated the individual's freedom and self-reliance. Already involved with other humanitarian campaigns, reformers condemned slavery as the most inhumane of institutions, because of the breakup of marriages and families by sale, the harsh punishment of the lash, the lack of access to education, and the sexual abuse of black women. But most of all, abolitionists condemned slavery as outrageously contrary to Christian teaching. So persistent and firmly made were their religious objections that the churches were forced to face the question of slavery head-on. In the 1840s the Methodist and Baptist churches split into northern and southern organizations over the issue. In making their indictment of slavery, abolitionists did not debate how abolition might affect the economy of the South or southern whites. To them, slavery was a moral, not an economic question. As one Ohio antislavery paper declared, "We believe slavery to be a sin, always, everywhere, and only, sin—sin, in itself."

The Spread of Abolitionism

Garrison and others organized the New England Anti-Slavery Society in 1832 with about 75 members. In 1833 he joined with merchant Lewis Tappan and with Theodore Weld to establish a national organization, the American Anti-Slavery Society, which served as an umbrella for a loosely affiliated network of state and local societies. During the years before the Civil War, perhaps 200,000 northerners belonged to an abolitionist society.

Abolitionists were concentrated in the East, especially New England, and areas that had been settled by New Englanders, such as western New York and northern Ohio. The movement was not strong in cities or among businessmen and workers. Most abolitionists were young, generally in their twenties and thirties when the movement began, and had grown up in rural areas and small towns in middle-class families. Intensely religious, many had been profoundly affected by the revivals of the Second Great Awakening. Whatever their background, they shared a deep alienation from American society—its materialism, its crass politics. More and more they came to feel that slavery was the fundamental cause of the Republic's degraded condition.

Certainly Theodore Weld felt that way when in 1833 he enrolled in Lane Seminary. Immediately he began to implement a plan endorsed by Tappan and Garrison for making Lane Seminary a strategic western center of abolitionist activity. He culled a nucleus of abolitionist sympathizers from the ranks of his fellow students and assigned each an uncommitted classmate, a man who needed to be convinced that slavery was not simply *a* problem, but *the* problem facing the nation. "Thus we carried one after another," Weld recalled. By the time Beecher arrived to assume the Lane presidency a year later, he confronted a student body dominated by committed abolitionists, impatient of any position that stopped short of Garrison's immediatism.

The radicalism of Lane students was also made clear in their commitment to racial equality. Unlike some abolitionists, who opposed slavery but disdained blacks as inferior, Lane students mingled freely with Cincinnati's large free black community. Rumors that the town's residents, alarmed by the "amalgamation" of free blacks and students, intended to demolish the school panicked Beecher and Lane's trustees into taking drastic measures in the summer of 1834. They prohibited any discussion of slavery on campus, dissolved Lane's antislavery society, restricted contact with the black community, and ordered students to return to their academic work. The response of the Lane rebels was decisive. "Who that has an opinion and a soul will enter L. Sem now?" one asked, "Who can do it without degrading himself?" All except a few left the school and enrolled at Oberlin College. That desperate, debt-ridden institution agreed to their demands for guaranteeing freedom of speech, admitting black students, and hiring Charles Finney as professor of theology.

But Finney fared no better than Beecher with the Lane rebels. In the end, he too concluded that reform generated discord, distracting Christians from the greater good of promoting revivals. Both men conceived of sin in terms of individual immorality, not unjust social institutions and prejudices. To the abolitionists, most of them younger men and women, America could never become a godly nation until slavery was abolished. "Revivals, moral Reform, etc. will remain stationary until the temple is cleansed," concluded Weld bluntly.

As such sentiments spread, free blacks, who always constituted the majority of subscribers to Garrison's *Liberator*, became a mainstay of the movement. Their unwavering support provided them with an opportunity to strike a blow against the discrimination and hostility that pervaded northern society. Many abolitionists challenged discrimination as a denial of the American principle of equality, and free African-Americans provided important support and leadership for the movement.

Frederick Douglass assumed the greatest prominence. Having escaped from slavery in Maryland, he became an eloquent critic of its evils. Initially a follower of Garrison, Douglass eventually broke with him and started his own newspaper in Rochester. Other important black abolitionists included Martin Delany, William Wells Brown, William Still, and Sojourner Truth. Most blacks endorsed peaceful means to end slavery, but David Walker in his *Appeal to the Colored Citizens of the World* (1829) urged slaves to use violence to end bondage. Aided by many others of their race, these men and women battled against racial discrimination in the North as well as slavery in the South.

A network of antislavery sympathizers developed in the North to convey runaway slaves to Canada and freedom. While not as extensive or as tightly organized as contemporaries claimed, the Underground Railroad hid fugitives and transported them northward from one station to the next. Free blacks, who were more readily trusted by wary slaves, played a leading role in the Underground Railroad. One of its most famous conductors was Harriet Tubman, an escaped slave of great daring and resourcefulness. Returning to the South at least 19 times, she escorted more than 200 slaves, including several members of her own family, to freedom.

An escaped slave, Harriet Tubman (far left) made several forays into the South as a "conductor" on the Underground Railroad. Shown here with one group that she led to freedom, she was noted for her stealth and firm determination, qualities that helped her repeatedly to outwit her pursuers.

Opponents and Discontents

The drive for immediate abolition faced massive obstacles, no matter how fervent its advocates. With slavery increasingly pivotal to the economic life of the South (Chapter 13), the abolitionist cause was received there with extreme hostility. And in the North racism was equally entrenched, as the case of Prudence Crandall demonstrated. A Quaker schoolteacher, Crandall opened a boarding school for black girls in 1833 in Canterbury, Connecticut, with the backing of several well-known abolitionists. Town residents harassed her by breaking her windows, poisoning her well with manure, and attempting to destroy the school building. When all else failed, town officials induced the legislature to pass a law closing the school, and Crandall was arrested and imprisoned. Racism was so deeply ingrained that even abolitionists like Garrison, whose attitudes were far in advance of the general public's, treated blacks paternalistically, contending that they should occupy a subordinate place in the antislavery movement.

As support for abolition spread, opponents reacted harshly. Southerners, immune to "moral suasion," forced opponents of slavery to flee the region. In the North anti-abolitionist mobs attacked antislavery speakers. A Boston mob seized Garrison in 1835 and paraded him with a noose around his neck; another mob burned to the ground the headquarters of the American Anti-Slavery Society in Philadelphia. And in 1837 in Alton, Illinois—across the river from the slave state of Missouri—Elijah Lovejoy was murdered when he tried to protect his printing press from an angry crowd. The leaders of these anti-abolitionist mobs were not the rabble of the streets but, as one of their victims noted, "gentlemen of property and standing." Prominent leaders in the community, they reacted vigorously to the threat that abolitionists posed to their power and prosperity, and to the established order.

The progress of the abolitionists was further limited by divisions among the reformers themselves. Given the Romantic individualism of the era, it became all too easy for groups of reformers to splinter and diverge. Finney, maintaining that revivals provided the road to perfection, watched in dismay as his convert Theodore Weld became a rabid abolitionist. Lyman Beecher, more conservative than Finney, saw his son Edward put aside his preaching to stand guard over Elijah Lovejoy's printing press the evening before the editor's murder. Within another decade, Beecher would see his daughter Harriet Beecher Stowe write the most successful piece of antislavery literature in the nation's history, *Uncle Tom's Cabin*. And finally the abolitionists themselves splintered, shaken by the harsh opposition they encountered and unable to agree on the most effective response. The more conservative reformers argued that abolitionism needed to broaden its appeal to northerners. Confident that American society, although in need of reform, was basically sound, they counted on political action to end slavery. But for Garrison and his followers, the mob violence demonstrated that slavery was only part of a deeper national disease. All American institutions must be overthrown, all values changed.

By the end of the decade, Garrison had formulated a program for the total reform of society—root-and-branch abolitionism. He embraced perfectionism and pacifism, denounced the clergy, urged members to leave the churches, and called for an end to all government. Adopting the slogan "No Union with Slaveholders," he condemned the Constitution as proslavery—"a covenant with death and an agreement with hell"—and publicly burned a copy one July 4th. Finally, he argued that politics was inherently corrupting and that no person of conscience could vote or otherwise participate in the political system. This platform was radical enough on all counts; but the final straw for Garrison's opponents was his endorsement of women's rights as an inseparable part of abolitionism.

The Women's Rights Movement

Women faced many disadvantages in American society. They were kept out of most jobs, denied political rights, and given only limited access to education beyond the elementary grades. And they had no legal control over their property. When a woman married, her husband became the legal will of the marriage and gained complete control of her assets. If a marriage ended in divorce, the husband was awarded custody of the children. Any unmarried woman was made the ward of a male relative.

When abolitionists divided over the issue of female participation, women found it easy to identify with the situation of slaves, since both were victims of male tyranny. The attacks on female abolitionists and attempts to keep them from exerting influence in the movement produced the first major documents of American feminism. Sarah and Angelina Grimké took up the cause of women's rights after they were criticized for speaking to audiences that included men as well as women. Sarah responded with *Letters on the Condition of Women and the Equality of the Sexes* (1838), arguing that women deserved the same rights as men. Abby Kelly, another abolitionist, remarked that women "have good cause to be grateful to the slave," for in "striving to strike his irons off, we found most surely, that we were manacled *ourselves.*"

Two abolitionists, Elizabeth Cady Stanton and Lucretia Mott, launched the women's rights movement after they were forced to sit behind a curtain, screened from other delegates, at a world antislavery convention held at London in 1840. In 1848 Stanton and Mott organized a conference in Seneca Falls, New York, that attracted an attendance of about a hundred. The meeting issued a Declaration of Sentiments (modeled after the Declaration of Independence) that began, "All men and women are created equal." There followed a catalog of the wrongs that men had inflicted on women, a device paralleling the first Declaration's indictment of George III.

The Seneca Falls convention approved resolutions calling for educational and professional opportunities for women, passage of laws giving them control over their property, recognition of legal equality, and repeal of laws awarding the father custody of the children in divorce. The most controversial proposal, and the only resolution that did not pass unanimously, was one demanding the right to vote. Thus the Seneca Falls convention established the arguments and the program for the women's rights movement for the remainder of the century.

The women's rights movement won few victories before 1860. Several states gave women greater control over their property, and a few made divorce easier or granted women the right to sue in courts. But disappointments and defeats far outweighed these early victories. Still, many of the important leaders in the crusade for women's rights that emerged after the Civil War had already taken their places at the forefront of the movement. They included Stanton, Susan B. Anthony, Lucy Stone, and—as Lyman Beecher by now must have expected—one of his daughters, Isabella Beecher Hooker.

Elizabeth Cady Stanton, one of the instigators and guiding spirits at the Seneca Falls convention, photographed with two of her children about that time.

The Schism of 1840 and the Decline of Abolitionism

It was Garrison's position on women's rights that finally split antislavery ranks already divided over other aspects of his growing radicalism. The showdown came in 1840 at the national meeting of the American Anti-Slavery Society, where the key battle was waged over allowing women to hold office in the organization. Some of Garrison's opponents favored women's rights but opposed linking this question to the slavery issue, insisting that it would drive off potential supporters. By packing the convention, Garrison carried the day, and his opponents, led by Lewis Tappan, resigned to found the rival American and Foreign Anti-Slavery Society.

The schism of 1840 marked the end of abolitionism as an important movement in American society. Crippled by the division of resources and supporters, neither national organization was of much significance thereafter. Although abolitionism heightened moral concern about slavery, it failed to convert the North to its program, and throughout its existence its supporters remained an infinitesimal minority. For all the courage they showed—and that was considerable, given the scorn of so many of their neighbors—their movement suffered from an excess of individualism and a repeated tendency toward extremism. Furthermore, the abolitionists had no realistic, long-range plan for eliminating so deeply entrenched an institution. When attempts at moral persuasion failed, they fell back on harsh rhetoric. Garrison even boasted that "the genius of the abolitionist movement is to have *no* plan." Abolitionism demonstrated the severe limits of Emersonian self-reliance as a solution to deeply rooted social problems.

REFORM SHAKES THE PARTY SYSTEM

The crusading idealism of revivalists and reformers inevitably collided with the hard reality that society could not be perfected by converting individuals. Despite the arguments of the temperance movement, some Americans continued to drink. For all the zeal of the abolitionists, slavery showed no signs of disappearing. Even the revivalist tide had lost its force by the end of the 1830s. Several campaigns, including those to establish public schools and erect asylums, had operated within the political system from the beginning. But a growing number of other frustrated reformers abandoned the principle of voluntary persuasion and looked to governmental coercion to achieve their goals. In America's democratic society, politics promised a more effective means to impose a new moral vision on the nation. Declared a writer in the *American Temperance Magazine*, "The speculative has yielded to the practical. . . . In this sense, moral suasion is moral balderdash."

Old-line politicians did not particularly welcome the new interest. Moral questions such as temperance and antislavery, which cut across party lines, threatened to detach regular party members and disrupt each party's unity and voting base. Because the Whig and Democratic parties had formed around economic questions rather than moral ones, both drew on evangelical and nonevangelical voters. Yet it was precisely for this reason that moral reform, by mobilizing evangelical voters, threatened the Jacksonian party system.

Both religion and reform helped shape that system, through ethnic and religious loyalties. Whigs attracted immigrant groups that most easily merged into the dominant culture, such as the English, Welsh, and Scots. Democrats, on the other hand, recruited more Germans and Irish, whose drinking habits, more lenient observance of the Sabbath, and (among Catholics) use of parochial schools made native-born citizens suspicious. As the self-proclaimed party of respectability, Whigs especially attracted the support of high-status native-born church groups, including the Congregationalists and Unitarians in New England and Presbyterians elsewhere. Democrats appealed to the lower-status Baptists and Methodists. For all their evangelical ways, these groups usually lacked the prestige and social acceptance of the Presbyterians and Congregationalists, with whom they often clashed. Both parties also attracted freethinkers and the unchurched, but the Democrats had the advantage because they resisted demands for temperance and sabbatarian laws, such as the prohibition of Sunday travel.

Women and the Right to Vote

As the focus of change and reform shifted toward the political arena, women in particular lost influence. As major participants in the benevolent organizations of the 1820s and 1830s, they had circulated petitions, sought new members, and used their efforts on behalf of "moral suasion." But since women could not vote, they felt excluded when reformers turned to electoral action to accomplish their goals. By the 1840s, female reformers increasingly demanded the right to vote as the means to reform society. Nor were men blind to what was at stake: one reason they so strongly resisted female suffrage was because it would give women real power.

The temperance and abolitionist movements, both of which turned to political action in the 1840s, helped convince women of the importance of gaining the ballot. Previously, many female reformers had accepted the right of petition as their most appropriate political activity. But *The Lily*, a women's rights paper, soon changed its tack. "Why shall [women] be left only the poor resource of petition?" it asked. "For even petitions, when they are from women, without the elective franchise to give them backbone, are of but little consequence." The right to vote would remain the key demand of the women's rights movement until 1920, when the Nineteenth Amendment was ratified.

The Maine Law

The political parties could resist the women's suffrage movement, since most of its advocates lacked the right to vote. Less easily put off were temperance advocates. As early as 1825 Lyman Beecher had called for banning the sale of distilled spirits, and the antiliquor crusade turned to political action in the 1840s. Although drinking had significantly declined in American society, it had not been eradicated, and the arrival after 1845 of large numbers of German and Irish immigrants, who were accustomed to drinking, made voluntary prohibition even more remote. In response, temperance advocates decided to attack the supply of liquor by enacting state laws outlawing the manufacture and sale of alcoholic beverages; they demanded stiff penalties, including jail sentences, for individuals guilty of selling liquor. Antiliquor reformers reasoned that if liquor was unavailable, the attitude of drinkers was unimportant—they would be forced to reform whether they wanted to or not.

In taking up the cause of prohibition, the antidrinking movement gained the support of the evangelical churches, which condemned drinking even in moderation. Consequently, the issue of prohibition cut across party lines, with large numbers of Whigs and Democrats on both sides of the question. When party leaders tried to dodge the issue, the temperance movement adopted the strategy of endorsing for the legislature only candidates who pledged to support a prohibitory law. As a result, a growing number of legislators committed themselves to the antiliquor cause. To win additional recruits, temperance leaders emulated techniques used in political campaigns, including house-to-house canvasses, parades and processions, bands and singing, banners, picnics, and mass rallies.

The major triumph came in 1851 in Maine's legislature. The Maine Law, as it was known, provided stiff penalties for selling liquor in the state; it also provided for search and seizure of private property, thereby strengthening the powers of enforcement. In the next few years a number of states enacted similar laws, although most were struck down by the courts or subsequently repealed. Nevertheless, prohibition remained a divisive political issue throughout the century.

While prohibition was temporarily defeated, the issue badly disrupted the unity of the two parties. It detached a number of voters from both coalitions, greatly increased the extent of party switching, and brought to the polls a large number of new voters, including many "wets" who wanted to preserve their right to drink. By dissolving the ties between many voters and their party, the temperance issue played a major role in the eventual collapse of the Jacksonian party system in the 1850s.

Abolitionism and the Party System

Abolition remained the most divisive issue to come out of the benevolent movement. Even during the 1830s, when abolitionists were not focusing on the political arena, a dispute arose over the use of the federal mails. In 1835 abolitionists distributed over a million pamphlets through the post office. Since these were sent to southerners as well as northerners, a wave of excitement swept over the South when the first batches arrived. Former senator Robert Hayne led a Charleston mob that burned sacks of United States mail containing abolitionist literature, and postmasters in other southern cities refused to deliver the material. The Jackson administration allowed southern states to censor the mail and close the post office to abolitionists, who protested that their civil rights had been violated. In reaction, the number of antislavery societies in the North nearly tripled.

With access to the mails impaired, abolitionists began flooding Congress with petitions against slavery. Most called for its abolition within the District of Columbia, which was under the jurisdiction of Congress. Asserting that Congress had no power over slavery, angry southern representatives demanded action, and the House adopted the so-called gag law in 1836. The provision automatically tabled without consideration petitions dealing with slavery. Claiming that the right of petition was also under attack by slavery's champions, abolitionists gained new supporters. In 1844 the House finally repealed the controversial rule.

The censorship of the mails and the attack on the right of petition were serious tactical mistakes by southern leaders. These acts allowed abolitionists to speak out as defenders of white civil liberties and to broaden significantly the appeal of the antislavery movement. Abolitionists outside William Lloyd Garrison's circle were convinced that by forming a third party they could force the slavery issue into the political arena. In 1840 these political abolitionists founded the Liberty party and nominated for president James Birney, a former slaveholder who had converted to abolitionism. Birney received only 7000 votes, but the Liberty party was the seed from which a stronger antislavery political movement would grow.

Since they were not tied to either major party, political abolitionists were freed from the restraints that national parties imposed on their members in order to maintain unity. Always seeking to enlarge their popular support, abolitionists did not hesitate to push controversial questions. In doing so, they functioned like a pressure group on the major parties, goading them to commit themselves, to take more radical positions. In closely divided northern states their votes continued to be critical.

After two decades of fiery revivals, benevolent crusades, utopian experiments, and Transcendental philosophizing, the ferment of reform had spread through urban streets, canal town churches, frontier clearings, and congressional halls. Part and parcel of the era, it shared the nation's individualistic, optimistic temperament. But the sheer diversity of reform—its conservative impulse to control as well as its more radical, liberating tendencies—meant that its effects varied. The quest for perfection could impel Henry Thoreau to secede temporarily from society altogether or convince Sarah Grimké to engage in activities formerly restricted to men. It could reinforce the new order of industrial labor by preaching the virtues of sobriety or scandalize the God-fearing with tales of communal marriage. Fires, once burning, spread in unpredictable ways.

Abolition, potentially the most divisive issue, seemed still under control in 1840. Birney's small vote, along with the disputes between the two national anti-slavery societies, encouraged party leaders in the belief that the slavery issue had run its course—that the party system had successfully turned back this latest threat of sectionalism. But the growing northern concern about slavery highlighted differences between the two sections. Despite the strength of evangelicalism in the South, the reform impulse spawned by the revivals was largely confined to the North. Discredited by their association with abolitionism, reform movements generally found little support below the Mason–Dixon line, a situation that heightened southern distinctiveness. The party system confronted the difficult challenge of holding together sections that, although sharing much, were also diverging in important ways. To the residents of both sections, the South increasingly seemed to be a unique society with its own distinctive way of life.

SIGNIFICANT EVENTS

1787	First Shaker commune established
1821	New York constructs first penitentiary
1824	New Harmony established
1824–1837	Peak of revivals
1826	James Fenimore Cooper's *The Last of the Mohicans* published; American Temperance Society founded
1829	David Walker's *Appeal to the Colored Citizens of the World*
1830–1831	Charles Finney's revival at Rochester
1831	*The Liberator* established
1833	American Anti-Slavery Society founded; Oberlin College admits women
1834	Lane Seminary rebellion
1835	Abolitionists' postal campaign
1836	Transcendental Club established
1836	Gag law passed
1837	Massachusetts establishes state board of education; Ralph Waldo Emerson delivers "The American Scholar" address; Mount Holyoke Seminary commences classes; Elijah Lovejoy killed
1838	Sarah Grimké's *Letters on the Condition of Women and the Equality of the Sexes* published
1840	Schism of American Anti-Slavery Society; Liberty party founded
1841	Fourierist phalanx established
1843	Dorothea Dix's report on treatment of the insane
1844	Gag law repealed
1848	Oneida Community established; Seneca Falls convention
1850	Nathaniel Hawthorne's *The Scarlet Letter* published
1851	Maine adopts prohibition law; Herman Melville's *Moby-Dick* published
1854	Henry David Thoreau's *Walden* published
1855	Walt Whitman's *Leaves of Grass* published

Generations of the Republic

Families of the New Democracy (1815–1875)

An Englishman, Frederick Marryat, was visiting the United States in the 1830s when he witnessed a scene—all too common, for his taste—of youthful disobedience. The youngster in question was only three years old, scampering about in the rain. "Johnny my dear, come here," his mother called.

"I won't," cried Johnny.

"You must, my love, you are all wet, and you'll catch cold."

"I won't," repeated the lad.

"Come, my sweet, and I've something for you."

"I won't."

At this point the exasperated mother begged her husband, "Do, pray, make Johnny come in."

"Come in, Johnny," called the father.

"I won't."

"I tell you, come in directly, sir—do you hear?"

"I won't," replied the child, as he ran off. The father smiled at Marryat and remarked, "A sturdy republican, sir." To Marryat the conclusion was obvious: "Anyone who has been in the United States must have perceived that there is little or no parental control."

Whether or not the American family was consistently different from its European counterpart, its character was evolving steadily away from that of earlier generations of Americans. As the young Republic expanded, families adapted to the changes that were transforming society: unprecedented mobility, heightened commercialization, accelerating industrialization and urbanization. In conjunction, a new concept of the family emerged, more democratic in structure and modern in orientation.

To begin with, American families were getting smaller. After a century of extraordinary population growth, the birth rate began to decline. Between Jefferson's election in 1800 and the Civil War, the fertility rate dropped almost 25 percent. By twentieth-century standards American families remained large, averaging 5.4 children in 1850, but the average before 1800 had been close to 8 children. Family size was diminished by infant mortality, which remained at about 20 percent among whites and was even higher on the frontier and among African-Americans.

The smaller size of families reflected economic choices, a new conception of

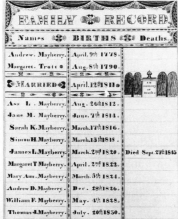

marriage and the family, and a desire among women for greater personal freedom. Such considerations surfaced first among the urban middle class created by the market economy. Separating themselves from the working class, these families consciously reduced the number of children in order to increase their own standard of living and improve their children's prospects for success. The birth rate was higher among immigrants and working-class families, who spent less money on education and sent children to work at an earlier age, but it also gradually declined. The birth rate of African-Americans, on the other hand, showed no significant falling off, and would not until after emancipation. Blacks had a strong sense of family, but the economic incentives that motivated whites to reduce family size affected them less, since slaves were denied control over their own lives. Because free blacks were allowed to work only in the lowest paying jobs, they depended, as did poor immigrant families, on the income of children to make ends meet.

The ideal of the democratic family that developed after 1800 was based on greater personal affection, not only between husband and wife, but also between parents and children. The new family was child-centered: relations with children were emotionally less distant and—as Marryat observed—discipline was less severe. Children were seen as individuals with special needs, and companies began producing books, toys, and furniture designed specifically for children. By mid-century the concept of the family vacation had developed, along with new family-oriented celebrations such as Christmas, Thanksgiving, and birthday parties.

With fewer children, mothers could lavish more attention on each child. Anxious about raising their sons and daughters properly, women read a host of books on child nurture directed specifically at them. Whereas the Puritan tradition had stressed the "breaking and beating down" of a child's "natural pride," nineteenth-century parents emphasized the importance of affection rather than strict control.

The new generation of children also tended to remain at home longer. Eighteenth-century parents had put out older children as apprentices and servants in order to reduce their financial burden, but families now delayed their children's departure in order to extend their education and increase their chances of success. A growing number of children, especially among the urban middle class, lived at home until their late teens and even early twenties. Adolescence (a term that now came into common use) was recognized as a separate stage of life, distinct from childhood, with its own needs and problems.

In the new world of the market, aspiring parents hoped to raise children who were independent, responsible, orderly,

and self-disciplined. Too strict control of children would stifle self-reliance, an essential quality in an intensely competitive society. Yet these attitudes were a source of tension, too. Because sons remained at home longer, they were more dependent economically and emotionally on their parents; at the same time, they spent a larger part of their days at school away from home and were expected to be independent, "sturdy" republicans. Daughters felt new pressures as well. Since they had no crucial economic role at home, more of them received a better education and supported themselves by working in factories and teaching. Yet upon marriage they were expected to sacrifice their interests to being a wife and mother.

The independence of youth extended to choosing a marriage partner. The colonial custom of parents arranging suitable marriages was no longer observed. Financial considerations, although still important, took second place to physical attraction and emotional compatibility. Earlier generations had identified romantic love with immaturity, but the new generation, taking its cue from novels and popular literature, elevated love to the central force in marriage. Still, falling in love could be risky—how could one know if such feelings were deceptive? "Of all the foolish things under the sun, the most foolish and saddest is for very young and ignorant people to rush into marriage under the impression that they are 'in love,'" reflected Lydia Sigourney. "'In love' they are crazy, and they make themselves miserable for life, for want of a little sense."

Most parents did not interfere with courtship and couples were allowed considerable time alone. But young women especially were responsible for seeing that passionate exchanges did not lead to premarital intercourse. Emma Hadley, a clever young Quaker, said of youthful courting:

The boys they go courting they dress very
    fine
To keep the girls up 'tis all their design
They will hug them and kiss them
    and flatter and lie
And keep the girls up till they are ready to
    die.

As etiquette books formulated a new set of rituals designed to solemnize marriage, weddings among the urban upper and middle class became more elaborate. Church services supplanted civil ceremonies, and instead of only a few close family members in attendance, weddings became gala social events. Earlier, American brides had often worn gray or brown, but now social convention dictated a white dress, veil, and a wreath of flowers in the hair. Most couples had one or two bridesmaids and groomsmen, but elaborate weddings involved as many as a dozen.

Because of the cost, wedding ceremonies for most working-class and rural families remained simple and were held at home. And slaves were often denied any formal ceremony, allowed only to observe the tradition of "jumping the broomstick" before the slave community.

After the wedding, new responsibilities greeted husband and wife. "An entirely new life opened," Priscilla Page recalled; "duties, interests, associations hitherto unknown forcibly presented themselves; new cares and anxieties replaced the old ones, and life together assumed a more serious aspect." The transition to married life was often more difficult for women, since marriage now represented a sharp break in women's lives, with new work and responsibilities.

On a much greater scale than with any previous American generation, war disrupted families and lives. In 1861 in both the North and the South, lovers, sons, brothers, and fathers marched off to war. Many never came back; many others returned maimed and disabled, unable to resume their former roles in society. For slaves, emancipation brought control over their families, and in freedom African-Americans quickly sought to model their family life after that of whites. Among whites, the war left countless women widows and children without fathers. Few white families on either side were not touched by personal loss. With so many shattered lives, the Civil War was a wrenching experience for this generation.

In old age and retirement, parents depended on their own resources, and if necessary their children, for care and support. With no pension plans (except for Union veterans), and with most couples able to save only limited amounts for later years, perhaps 70 percent of men over 65 continued to work. Some fathers sought to provide for the couple's final years by giving a son the family farm or business in exchange for being taken care of in old age. Care for elderly parents put pressures on both generations. Having worked hard all their lives, parents worried about falling into poverty in their final years, while their children's independence was limited by continuing obligations and parental supervision. Couples might be able to spend a few years in retirement together after their children were grown, but these years tended to be few. Indeed, at mid-century in half of the families one of the parents died before the youngest child was married.

Thus the family too was touched by the nineteenth-century revolution in markets, urban development, and industry. The new democratic family developed gradually, flourishing at different rates and in different places. But the changes were revolutionary nonetheless. Frederick Marryat had good reason to be surprised at these "sturdy republicans."

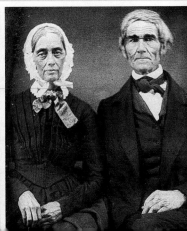

13

The Old South

The myth of the Old South has long engaged the popular imagination. It was, in legend, a land of chivalrous gentlemen and ladies fair, of moonlight and magnolias, of elegant aristocrats and dutiful slaves. But the reality of the Old South was far more complex. Where, then, is the real Old South to be found?

The impeccably dressed Colonel Daniel Jordan, master of 261 slaves at Laurel Hill, strolls down his oak-lined lawn to the dock along the Waccamaw River, a day's journey north of Charleston in All Saints Parish. Here he boards the steamship *Nina*, which on its regular run passes other rice plantations with names like True Blue, Weehawka, Forlorn Hope, and Oryzantia, whose vast irrigated fields front the river on either side. On Fridays, it is Colonel Jordan's custom to visit the exclusive Hot and Hot Fish Club, founded by his fellow low-country planters, to play a game of lawn bowling or billiards, and be waited on by black servants in livery as he sips a mint julep—or even more remarkable, a shivering-cold glass of ice water—in the refined and genteel atmosphere that for him is the South.

Several hundred miles to the west another steamboat, the *Fashion*, makes its way along the Alabama River, tying up to take on cotton at landings so crude that trees offer the only available moorings. Near the village of Claiborne, one of the passengers is upset by the steamboat's slow pace. Tall and thin, he is wearing a ready-made suit, which unfortunately seems to have been tailored with a short, fat figure in mind. The hilt of a large knife protrudes from his waistcoat. He has been away from his plantation in the Red River country of Texas and is eager to get back. "Time's money, time's money!" he mutters to anyone who will listen. "Time's worth more'n money to me now; a hundred percent more, 'cause I left my niggers all alone; not a damn white man within four mile on 'em." When asked what they are doing, since the cotton crop has already been picked, he says, "I set 'em to clairin', but they ain't doin' a damn thing—not a damn thing, they ain't. . . . I know that as well as you do. That's the reason time's an object. I told the capting so, when I came aboard: says I, 'Capting,' says I, 'time is in the objective case with me.' No sir, they ain't doin' a damn solitary thing; that's what they are up to. . . . But I'll make it up, I'll make it up when I get thar, now you'd better believe." For this Red River planter, time is money and cotton is his world—indeed, cotton is what the South is all about. "I am a cotton man, I am, and I don't car who knows it," he proclaims. "I know cotton, I do. I'm dam' if I know anythin' but cotton."

Plantation Burial, *painted about 1860 by John Antrobus, portrays a black slave community from a Louisiana plantation burying a loved one. Religion played a central role in the life of slaves.*

In the bayous of the Deep South, only a few miles from where the Mississippi Delta meets the Gulf, the South is a far different place. There, Octave Johnson hears the dogs coming: as many as 20, he judges, from the strength of their baying. Johnson is a runaway slave and has been for over a year. He fled from a Louisiana plantation in St. James Parish when the work bell rang so early it was too dark to see, and his overseer threatened to whip him for staying in bed. To survive, he hides in the swamps four miles behind the plantation—stealing turkeys, chickens, and pigs when he gets the chance. Some days he meets slaves at work in the field and swaps his meat for their cornmeal or some matches. The example his freedom sets, uncertain a life as it is, seems alluring to his fellow slaves. Over the year, nearly 30 others have joined him. The band sleeps on logs and burns cypress leaves to keep away the mosquitoes.

The sound of the dogs warns Johnson and his companions that the hound master Eugene Jardeau is out again. This time when the pack bursts upon them, the slaves do not flee, but set about killing as many dogs as possible. Then they throw themselves into the bayou, the hounds following, and alligators make short work of another six. Johnson isn't pleased by the notion of mixing with alligators, but he isn't terrified either. "The alligators [prefer] dog flesh to personal flesh," he explains later. For Octave Johnson, the real Old South is a matter of weighing one's prospects between the uncertainties of alligators and the overseer's whip— and deciding when to say no.

Ferdinand Steel and his family were not forced, by the flick of the lash, to rise

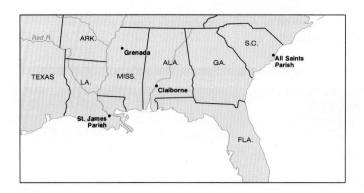

at five in the morning. They rose because the land demanded it; and it was their duty to do the work of the Lord. Steel, in his twenties, owned 170 acres of land in Carroll County, Mississippi, not many miles from the Yalobusha River. Not yet married, he had moved there from Tennessee with his widowed mother, sister, and brother in 1836, only a few years after the Choctaws had been compelled to give up the region and march west. His life was one of continuous hard work. After family prayers each morning, he would milk the cows, feed the horses, and then come to breakfast. Except for a midday respite, he was out in the fields until sundown, tending corn, a little wheat, and some watermelons. His mother Eliza and sister Julia had plenty to keep them busy: making lye soap by the long, messy process of boiling ashes with animal fat, or fashioning dippers out of gourds, or sewing dresses, shirts, and "pantiloons" for the men. Always there was work to do, droughts to worry about, or accidents and misfortune. Steel had castrated a calf and it had died—probably, he felt, because he had performed the operation when the moon was in the wrong phase.

The Steel family grew cotton, too, but not with the single-minded devotion of the planter aboard the *Fashion*. Self-sufficiency and family security always came first, and Steel's total crop amounted to only five or six bales. His profit was never sufficient to consider buying even one slave. In fact, he would have preferred not to raise any cotton. "We are to[o] weak handed," he wrote in his diary. "We had better raise small grain and corn and let cotton alone, raise corn and keep out of debt and we will have no necessity of raising cotton." But the five bales meant cash, and cash meant that when he went to market at nearby Grenada on Saturday afternoons, he could buy sugar and coffee for the family, gunpowder and lead, a bit of calico for the women, and quinine to treat the malaria that was so common in those parts. Sunday was the Lord's day, and often Steel's family found their hearts melted to tenderness by the sermon of an itinerant Methodist preacher. Though fiercely independent, Steel and his scattered neighbors came together often enough, to help each other raise houses, clear fields, shuck corn, or quilt. Worshiping or playing, working or eating, they depended on one another and were bound together by blood, religion, obligation, and honor. For rural farmers like Ferdinand Steel, these ties were the real South.

The portraits could go on: different people, different Souths, all of them real. Such contrasts underscore the futility of trying to isolate one "true" South, or even of trying to define a regional identity. The label itself—the *South*—suggests a definition based on geography; yet the South was a land of great geographic diversity. Encompassing in 1860 the fifteen slave states plus the District of Columbia, it extended from the Tidewater coastal plain along the Atlantic seaboard to the prairies of Texas; from the Shenandoah and Tennessee valleys to the Gulf coast, from the hill regions and mountains of western Virginia and North Carolina to the swampy Mississippi Delta with its semitropical climate. Nor did geographic boundaries set the South apart from the rest of the country. Only the Ohio River separated the North and South, and it was an avenue of trade rather than a source of division.

Yet despite its many differences of people and geography, the South was bonded by ties so strong, they eventually outpulled those of the nation itself. Sectional loyalty led in the end to civil war. To understand what made the South a region, we cannot merely take one particular portrait and elevate it: we cannot decide, for example, that Octave Johnson rather than Colonel Jordan was the "real" South. Instead, we must see how so many different people and races and classes formed a single southern society.

At the heart of this unity was an agricultural system that took advantage of the region's warm climate and long growing season. Cotton required 200 frost-free days, and rice and sugar even more, which meant that in the United States these crops could be grown only in the South. These staples tied the South to the international economy. Furthermore, the emphasis on staple crops and the prestige accorded agriculture discouraged the growth of cities and made it more difficult for a diversified economy to develop. And most important, this rural agricultural economy was based on the institution of slavery, which had far-reaching effects on all aspects of southern society. It shaped not only the culture of the slaves themselves, but the lives of their masters, and even of farmers and herdsmen in the hills and backwoods, who saw few slaves during their day-to-day existence. To understand the Old South, then, we must understand how the southern agricultural economy and the institution of slavery affected the social class structure of both whites and blacks.

THE SOCIAL STRUCTURE OF THE COTTON KINGDOM

We have already seen (Chapter 10) that the spread of cotton stimulated the nation's remarkable economic growth after the War of 1812, both in the North, with its textile factories, and the South, with the expansion of the plantation system. Demand sent the price of cotton soaring on the international market and southerners scrambled westward to reap the profits to be made in the cotton sweepstakes. Just as tobacco had turned the Chesapeake Bay region into a boom country during the seventeenth century, cotton produced new fortunes in the 1820s, 1830s, and 1840s from the fresh lands of the Southwest.

The Boom Country Economy

Letters, newspapers, and word of mouth all brought tales of the "black belt" region of Alabama, where the dark, loamy soil was particularly suited to growing cotton. Tremendous yields also came from the alluvial soils deposited along the Mississippi River's broad reaches. As southern agricultural practices rapidly exhausted the soil in older fields, the policies of Indian removal soon opened up new tracts in Alabama, Mississippi, Louisiana, and then Arkansas. "The *Alabama Fever* rages here with great violence and has *carried off* vast numbers of our Citizens," a North Carolinian wrote in 1817. "I am apprehensive if it continues to spread as it has done, it will almost depopulate the country." A generation later, in the 1830s, immigrants were still "pouring in with a ceaseless tide," an Alabama observer reported, including "'Land Sharks' ready to swallow up the home of the redmen, or the white, as opportunity might offer."

By the 1840s, planters even began to leave Mississippi and Alabama—virgin territory at the turn of the century—to head for the new cotton frontier along the Red River and up into Texas. A traveler in 1845 saw many abandoned and desolate farms in Mississippi, which a decade later the northern visitor Frederick Law Olmsted called "Gone to Texas" farms. Texas cotton production jumped from 58,000 bales in 1850 to 432,000 in 1860. Indeed, by the eve of the Civil War the Gulf states produced three-fourths of all the cotton grown in the United States. Equally amazing, nearly a third of the total crop came from *west* of the Mississippi River.

As Senator James Henry Hammond of South Carolina boasted in 1858, cotton was king in the Old South. True, the region devoted more acreage to corn, which was the major crop of nonslaveholders, but cotton was the primary export and the major source of southern wealth. It accounted for over half of America's exports from 1815 to 1860, and by 1860 the United States produced three-fourths of the world's supply of cotton.

In this romanticized Currier and Ives print of a cotton plantation, field hands are waist-deep in the fields while other slaves haul the picked cotton to be ginned and then pressed into bales. Looking on are the owner and his wife. Picking began as early as August and continued in some areas until late January. Because the bolls ripened at different times, a field had to be picked several times.

This boom fueled the southern economy so strongly that, following the depression of 1839–1843, it grew faster than the northern economy. Southern per capita income (with slaves included) was 20 percent lower than the national average in 1860, but it was higher than that of the Northwest, which had been settled at the same time as the cotton belt. Moreover, among whites, per capita income in the South actually exceeded that of the free states, though wealth was not as evenly distributed in the plantation South as in northern agricultural areas. Yet the gap between the richest and the poorest southern whites was not significantly different from the gap in northern cities.

The surface of prosperity, however, masked basic problems in the economy—problems that would become more apparent after the Civil War. Much of the South's new wealth resulted from migration of its population to more productive western lands. The amount of unsettled prime land was not unlimited, and once it was settled, the South could not sustain forever its rate of expansion. Nor did the shift in population alter the structure of the southern economy, stimulate technological change, or improve the way goods were produced and marketed. Fundamentally dependent on its exports, the South failed to develop internal markets, which would have generated economic growth and increased specialization among its citizens.

The Upper South's New Orientation

As cotton transformed the boom country of the Deep South, agriculture in the Upper South also adjusted.* Improved varieties and more scientific agricultural

*The Upper South included the border states (Delaware, Maryland, Kentucky, and Missouri) and Virginia, North Carolina, Tennessee, and Arkansas. The states of the Deep South were South Carolina, Georgia, Florida, Alabama, Mississippi, Louisiana, and Texas.

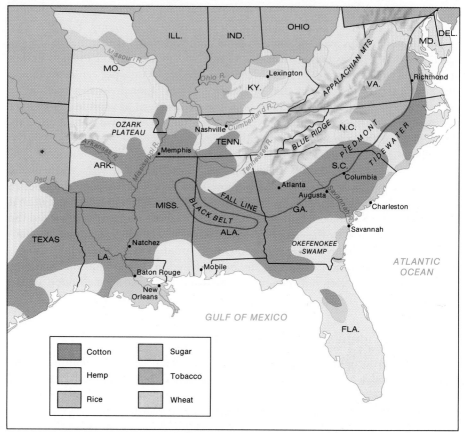

COTTON AND OTHER CROPS OF THE SOUTH

By 1860, the cotton kingdom extended across the Lower South into the Texas prairie and up the Mississippi River valley. Tobacco and hemp were the staple crops of the Upper South, where they competed with corn and wheat. Rice production was concentrated in the swampy coastal region of South Carolina and Georgia as well as the lower tip of Louisiana. The sugar district was in southern Louisiana.

practices reversed the decline in tobacco, which had begun in the 1790s. More important, however, farmers in the Upper South made wheat and corn their major crops. As early as 1840 the value of wheat grown in Virginia was twice that of tobacco.

Because the new crops required less labor, planters in the Upper South found themselves with a surplus of slaves, whom they regularly sold to cotton and sugar planters in the Deep South. This flow of slaves strongly shaped the southern economy—indeed, some planters in the Upper South maintained a profit margin only by selling surplus slaves. The demand in the Deep South for field hands drove their price steadily up from 1820 to 1860. By the late 1850s a prime field hand, who would have sold for $600 in the early 1840s, commanded as much as $1500. Even with increased labor costs, southern agriculture flourished. In 1800 a slave's labor produced less than $15 worth of crops on average, but by 1860, the figure had risen to about $125.

The Rural South

The Old South, then, was expanding, dynamic, and booming economically. But the primary focus on agriculture meant that its social structure would remain overwhelmingly rural. In 1860 in the South, 84 percent of the labor force was engaged in agriculture, compared to 40 percent in the North. Although the South on the eve of the Civil War had slightly less than 40 percent of the population, it raised 50 percent of the nation's cattle, 60 percent of the hogs, 90 percent of the mules, and 50 percent of the corn. And of course it had no competition in the production of tobacco, cotton, sugar, rice, and hemp.

Conversely, the South lagged badly in manufacturing. A few towns like Columbus, Alabama, had small textile factories where "cracker girls" from the countryside earned from $8 to $12 a month running the spindles, but less than 15 percent of the capital invested in manufacturing went to southern factories. Because these were built on a smaller scale than those in the North, they produced only 9 percent of the nation's manufactured goods. The South even trailed the new states of the Northwest like Indiana and Illinois, where the manufacturing capital invested was greater than that of the seven states of the Deep South combined. During the 1850s, some southern propagandists urged greater investment in industry to diversify the South's economy, but so long as the high profits from cotton continued, the movement made little headway. Most slaveholders did not encourage the development of an industrial, urban economy, which would have undermined their power.

With so little industry, few cities developed in the South. New Orleans, with a population of 169,000 in 1860, was the only city of significant size. (Baltimore and St. Louis, both located in slave states, were not really southern in their value systems or economic orientation.) Whereas in 1860 Indiana and Illinois had 40 cities with a population over 2500, the entire Deep South combined had only 33. North Carolina, Alabama, Mississippi, Arkansas, and Texas did not contain a single city with a population of 10,000. Only 1 in 10 southerners lived in cities and towns in 1860, compared to 1 out of 3 persons in the North.

Innovation and education often accompany an urban culture, and the South evidenced far less interest in education. The nation's best colleges were in the North, and many wealthy southerners sent their sons to these schools, much to the dismay of some southern leaders. At the secondary level, southern facilities were virtually nonexistent, except for private academies serving the children of the rich. Southern politicians, who spoke for the planter class, argued that education was the responsibility of the family, not the state. Thus free public schools were rare, especially in the rural districts that comprised most of the South. Georgia in 1860 had only one county with a free school system, and Mississippi had no public schools outside its few cities.

The net effect of fewer schools, lower attendance, and shorter school terms was that white children on average spent only one-fifth as much time in school as did their northern counterparts. Since laws forbade the education of black slaves, and whites were seldom in school, illiteracy rates were much higher in the South. Among native-born whites, the 1850 census showed that 20 percent were unable to read and write. The comparable figure was 3 percent in the Middle states and 0.4 percent in New England. In some areas of the South, over a third of all whites were illiterate.

Distribution of Slavery

Even more than agrarian ways, slavery set the South apart. In 1776, slavery had been a national institution. Legally enslaved African-Americans could be found rolling barrels on the wharves of Boston, serving meals in the mansions of Rhode Island merchants, tending stock on New Jersey farms, and stoking iron forges in Pennsylvania. One by one, however, the northern states freed their slaves, so that by the 1820s, slavery was virtually confined to the states south of Pennsylvania and the Ohio River. It became the South's "peculiar institution." Thus slavery must be

THE SPREAD OF SLAVERY, 1820–1860

Between 1820 and 1860, the slave population of the South shifted south and westward, concentrating especially heavily in coastal South Carolina and Georgia, in the black belt of central Alabama and Mississippi (so named because of its rich soil), and in the Mississippi valley. Small farms with few slaves predominated in cotton-growing areas that lacked good transportation, such as northern Georgia, and in regions with poor soil, such as the piney woods of southern Mississippi.

understood not only in the searing personal terms of human bondage, but also as a social and economic system that bound southern whites and blacks together in a multitude of ways.

Slaves were not evenly distributed throughout the region. More than half lived in the Deep South, where blacks outnumbered whites in both South Carolina and Mississippi by the 1850s. Elsewhere in the Deep South, the black population exceeded 40 percent in all states except Texas. In the Upper South, on the other hand, whites greatly outnumbered blacks. Only in Virginia and North Carolina did the slave population exceed 30 percent. In Delaware, it was a minuscule 1.5 percent.

The distribution of slaves showed striking geographic variations within individual states as well. Virginia's Tidewater and Piedmont regions, for example, had significant slave populations, whereas the hilly and mountainous western part of the state had relatively few slaves. A similar pattern prevailed in most other states. In areas of fertile soil, flat or rolling countryside, and good transportation, slavery and the plantation system dominated; in the pine barrens, areas isolated by lack of transportation, and hilly and mountainous regions, small family farms and few slaves were the rule.

Almost all slaves, male and female, were used in agriculture, with only about 10 percent living in cities and towns. On large plantations, a few slaves were domestic servants, and others were skilled artisans—blacksmiths, carpenters, or bricklayers—but most toiled in the fields. Some slaves found work in extractive industries such as turpentine production and lumbering, others along the docks, or in industry. But by and large, the demand for slaves as agricultural workers drove their purchase price so high that they were seldom used elsewhere in the southern economy. Only about 5 percent of the South's manufacturing employees in the 1850s were slaves.

Slavery as a Labor System

Slavery was, first and foremost, a system to manage and control labor. Other than the work performed by farm families, slaves supplied virtually all southern agricultural labor. Southern whites, like northern farmers, refused to hire out as farm laborers, except to save enough money to buy a farm of their own. The plantation system, with its extensive estates and large labor forces, could never have developed without slavery, nor could it have met the world demand for cotton and other staples. Slavery, in other words, made the mass production of agricultural staples possible.

And it remained a highly profitable investment. The average slaveowner spent perhaps $30 to $35 a year to support an adult slave; some expended as little as half that. Allowing for the cost of land, equipment, and other expenses, a planter could expect one of his slaves to produce more than $78 worth of cotton—which meant that even at the higher cost of support, the planter expropriated about 60 percent of the wealth produced by a slave's labor. For those who pinched pennies and drove slaves harder, the profits were even greater. In terms of investment, planters generally received about as high a return on human property as they would have by putting their money into land, factories, or railroads. As a result, slaves represented an enormous capital investment, worth more than all the land in the Old South.

By concentrating wealth and power in the hands of the planter class, slavery shaped and influenced the tone of southern society. Planters were not aristocrats in the European sense of having special legal privileges or formal titles of rank. Still, the system encouraged southern planters to think of themselves as a landed gentry upholding the aristocratic values of pride, honor, family, and hospitality. The planters gained wealth and prestige from their ownership of other human beings, and the law gave masters wide discretion in controlling plantation slaves— just as medieval lords had exercised nearly absolute power over their serfs.

Whereas slavery had existed throughout most of the New World at the beginning of the century, by the 1850s the United States, Cuba, and Brazil were the only slaveholding nations left in the Americas. Public opinion in Europe and in the North had grown more and more hostile to the institution, causing southern whites to feel increasingly like an isolated minority defending an embattled position. Yet white southerners tenaciously clung to slavery, for it was the base on which the South's economic growth and way of life rested. As one Georgian observed on the eve of the Civil War, slavery was "so intimately mingled with our social conditions that it would be impossible to eradicate it."

CLASS STRUCTURE OF THE WHITE SOUTH

Tradition divided southern society into three classes: planters, slaves, and poor whites. In reality, the class structure of the Old South was considerably more complex. Because of the institution of slavery, the social structure of the antebellum South differed in important ways from that of the North. Even so, southern society was remarkably fluid and as a result class lines were not rigid.

The Slaveowners

In 1860 the region's 15 states had a population of 12 million, of which roughly two-thirds were white, one-third were black slaves, and about 2 percent were free

SOUTHERN POPULATION, 1860

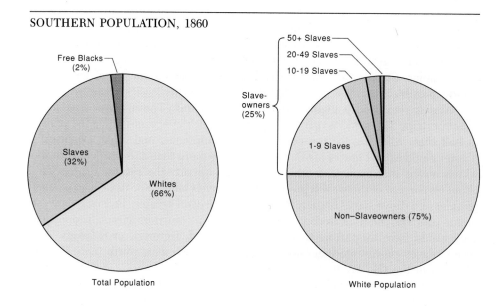

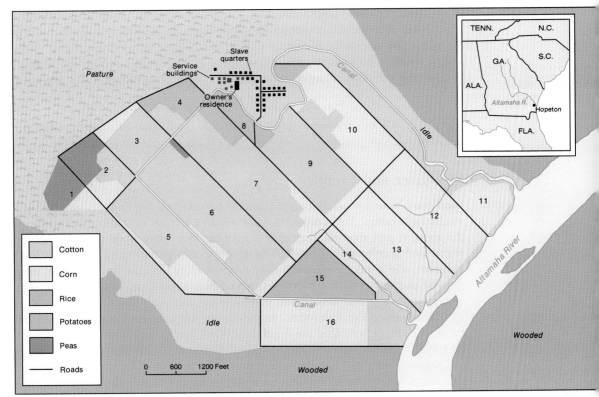

A PLANTATION LAYOUT

Often covering a thousand acres or more, a plantation contained several fields and usually extensive uncleared woods. Service buildings might include a smoke house, stables, a gin house (for cotton) or a rice mill, and an overseer's dwelling. Like most large plantations, Hopeton produced a considerable amount of foodstuffs, but it grew both rice and cotton as staples. Most plantations concentrated on a single cash crop.

blacks. Of the 8 million whites, only about 2 million, or one-quarter, either owned slaves or were members of slaveowning families. Thus the typical white southerner was not a slaveowner at all, but belonged to a yeoman farmer family whose members worked the land themselves. Moreover, most slaveowners owned only a few slaves, usually at most one slave family. If one uses the census definition of a planter as a person who owned 20 or more slaves, only about 1 out of every 30 southern whites belonged to families of the planter class.

A planter of consequence, however, needed to own at least 50 slaves, and there were only about 10,000 such families—less than 1 percent of the white population. This privileged group made up the aristocracy at the top of the southern class structure. Owners of large numbers of slaves were very rare. Out of 8 million southern whites, only about 2000 like Colonel Daniel Jordan owned 100 or more slaves. Although limited in size, the planter class nevertheless owned over half of all slaves and controlled over 90 percent of the region's total wealth. The average slaveholder was 14 times as rich as the average nonslaveholder.

The typical plantation had 20 to 50 slaves and 800 to 1000 acres of land. On a larger estate, slaves would have to walk more than an hour to reach the farthest fields, losing valuable work time. Thus larger slaveowners usually owned several plantations. An overseer managed the slaves on each, while the owner attended to administrative and business matters. The slaves were divided into field hands, skilled workers, and house servants, with one or more slaves serving as "drivers" to assist the overseer. Planters pioneered the application of capitalistic methods, including specialization and division of labor, to agriculture, and the best-run plantations resembled "factories in the fields." Yet they remained labor-intensive operations. Of the southern staples, only the production of sugar was heavily mechanized.

Tidewater and Frontier

Southern planters shared a commitment to preserve slavery as the source of their wealth and stature. Yet in other ways they were a diverse group. On the one hand, the tobacco and rice planters of the Atlantic Tidewater were part of a settled region and a culture that reached back 150 to 200 years. Alabama, Mississippi, Arkansas, and Texas, by contrast, were just emerging from the frontier stage, since the vast majority of their settlers had arrived after 1815. Consequently, the society of the Southwest was newer, rawer, and more volatile.

It was along the Tidewater, especially the bays of the Chesapeake and the South Carolina coast, that the legendary "Old South" was born. Here, masters erected substantial homes, some—especially between Charleston and Columbia—the classic white-pillared mansions in the Greek revival style. For Virginia planters, social life centered on their plantations, in contrast to the South Carolina nabobs, who often gravitated to the city of Charleston, especially during the gay winter social season. While these planters were practical men rather than philosophers, more than a few were urbane and polished. Upriver from the Tidewater, most country gentry were more rustic. They enjoyed a leisurely life, fought duels to defend their reputations, and were bound to one another by strong ties of kinship.

The ideal of the Tidewater South was the country gentleman of the old English tradition. An Irish visitor observed that in Maryland and Virginia the great plantation residences were "exactly similar to the old manor houses of England" and that their occupants lived in "a style which approaches nearer to that of the English country gentleman than what is to be met with anywhere else on the continent." As in England, the Episcopal Church remained the socially accepted road to heaven; also as in England, the local gentry often served as justices of the peace, administering the local courts and dispensing justice. Here, too, family connections continued to be important in politics: there were fewer upstart Franklin Plummers to challenge aristocrats like Powhatan Ellis.

While the newer regions of the South boasted planters with cultivated manners (Jefferson Davis of Mississippi was one), as a group the cotton lords were a different breed. They were basically entrepreneurs who had moved west for the same reason so many other Americans had: to make their fortunes. Some were planters fleeing the exhausted soils of the Tidewater; others were the sons of planters seeking to improve their lot. Not a few were northerners with an eye for opportunity, such as Henry Watson, who went south as a young tutor, settled in Greensboro, Alabama, and became a leading planter. Overseers sometimes rose into the ranks of slaveowners, as Ephraim Beanland of Mississippi did. Merchants and businessmen like Maunsel White of New Orleans invested their profits in a plantation; land speculators rode the land grabs of the 1830s into the ranks of the elite. But by and large, the wealthy planters of the cotton gentry were self-made men, who through hard work, aggressive business tactics, and good luck had risen from ordinary backgrounds. For them, the cotton boom offered the opportunity to move up in a new society that lacked an entrenched elite.

"Time's money, time's money." For men like the impatient Texan, time was indeed money, slaves were capital, and cotton by the bale signified cash in hand. This business orientation was especially apparent in the cotton kingdom, where planters sought to maximize profits and constantly reinvested their returns in land and slaves. As one visitor remarked of Mississippi slaveholders: "To sell cotton in order to buy negroes—to make more cotton to buy more negroes, 'ad infinitum,' is the aim and direct tendency of all the operations of the thorough-going cotton planter: his whole soul is wrapped in the pursuit." One shocked Virginian who visited Vicksburg claimed that its citizens ran "mad with speculation" and did business "in a kind of phrenzy." And indeed there was money to be made. The combined annual income of the richest thousand families of the cotton kingdom approached $50 million, while the wealth of the remaining 666,000 families amounted to only about $60 million.

Stately mansions could be found in a few areas, especially along the Mississippi between Natchez and Vicksburg and below Baton Rouge. In general, though, elegant homes were uncommon in the cotton South, coming into their own only during the 1850s and later. Most planters lived more humbly. Although they ranked among the richest citizens in America, their homes were often simple one- or two-story, unpainted wooden frame houses. A visitor to one Georgia plantation reported that the house did not have a pane of glass in the windows, a door between the rooms, or a ceiling other than the roof. A traveler in central Mississippi in 1839 spent the night in "the *Mansion House* of the plantation, a cabin with two rooms and a passage between, the one room was occupied by barrels of pork, flour, and plough and its appendages, a few old saddles, some peas spread on the floor, etc. The other served as a parlour, dining room, chamber, etc." "If you wish to see people worth millions living as [if] they were not worth hundreds," advised one southwestern planter in 1839, ". . . come to the land of cotton and negroes."

Few of the new cotton lords had a strong commitment to education; fewer still absorbed the culture and learning of the traditional country gentleman. During his extensive journeys in the South, the noted New Yorker Frederick Law Olmsted declared that he "did not see, except perhaps in one or two towns, a thermometer, nor a book of Shakespeare, nor a piano or sheet of music, nor a good reading lamp, nor an engraving or copy of any kind, or a work of art of the slightest merit. A large majority of all these houses were residences of slaveholders, a considerable proportion cotton planters."

The Master at Home

Whether tending a Tidewater plantation or carving out a cotton estate on the Texas frontier, the master had to coordinate a complex agricultural operation. He gave daily instructions concerning the work to be done, settled disputes between slaves and the overseer who supervised the slaves, and generally handed out the rewards and penalties. In addition, the owner made the critical decisions concerning which fields to use, what crops to plant, and when to send crops to market. Planters had to watch expenses and income carefully, and they often sought to expand their production by clearing additional fields, buying more land or slaves, or investing in machinery such as cotton gins. As in any business, these decisions required a sound understanding of the domestic and international market as well as anticipation of future swings.

In performing his duties, the plantation owner was supposed to be the "master" of his crops, his family, and his slaves. Defenders of slavery often held up this paternalistic ideal—the care and guidance of dependent children—as the keystone of southern society. With slaves, as with children, the relationship included instilling proper behavior by any discipline necessary. White southerners expected that the duties and responsibilities each had for the other would promote a genuine bond of affection between the caring master and his loyal slaves.

In real life, the forces of the market and a desire for success made this paternalistic ideal less evident among masters. Some conservatives, located in the more traditional, long-settled areas of the South, did condemn the increasingly material scramble for wealth on the cotton frontier, a pursuit that led to an excessive exploitation of slaves and land. Still, Tidewater planters were concerned with money and profits as much as the self-made cotton lords were. Indeed, some of the most brutal forms of slavery existed on the rice plantations, where the absenteeism of many Tidewater planters, combined with the sheer numbers of slaves, made close personal ties impossible. Except for a few domestic servants, owners of large plantations generally had little contact with their slaves. Nor could paternalism mask the reality that slavery everywhere rested on violence, racism, and exploitation.

The Plantation Mistress

Upper-class southern white women, like those in the North, grew up with the ideal of domesticity, reinforced by the notion of a paternalistic master who was lord of the plantation. The proper southern woman was religious, pure, and submissive, and she focused attention on family and home. As the guardian of moral standards, she dispensed love and comfort along with moral guidance in her role as wife and mother. But the plantation mistress soon discovered that, given the demands placed on her, the ideal was hard to fulfill.

A genteel lady, after all, enjoyed a certain amount of leisure. Once a young southern woman married and became a plantation mistress, she was often shocked by the magnitude of her responsibilities. Nursing the sick, making clothing, tending the garden, caring for the poultry, and overseeing every aspect of food preparation were all her domain. She also had to supervise and plan the work of the domestic servants and distribute clothing. "This morning I got up late having been disturbed in the night," wrote one harried Carolina mistress, "hurried down to have something arranged for breakfast, . . . had prayers, got the boys off to town. Had the [sewing] work cut out, gave orders about dinner, had the horse feed fixed in hot water, had the box filled with cork: went to see the carpenters working on the negro houses . . . now I have to cut out the flannel jackets." Small wonder that Sarah Williams, the New York bride of a North Carolina planter, admitted that her mother-in-law "works harder than any Northern farmer's wife I know."

Unlike female reformers in the North, upper-class southern women did not openly challenge their role, but there is evidence that they found their sphere confining. The greatest unhappiness stemmed from the never-ending task of managing the slaves. "These women have less chance to live their own lives than if

Sarah Pierce Vick, the mistress of a plantation near Vicksburg, Mississippi, pauses to speak to one of her slaves, who may be holding feed for her horse. A plantation mistress had many duties and, while enjoying the comforts brought by wealth and status, often found her life more difficult than she had anticipated before marriage.

they were African missionaries," Mary Chesnut, the wife of a prominent South Carolina planter, observed. "They have a swarm of blacks about them like children under their care." Another southern woman, voicing her dislike for her position, confessed, "I do not see how I can live my life amid these people! To be always among people whom I do not understand and whom I must guide, and teach and lead on like children. It frightens me." Yet without the labor of slaves, the lifestyle of these women was an impossibility.

Some women drew a parallel between their situation and that of the black slaves. Both were subject to male dominance, and independent-minded women found the subordination of marriage difficult. Commented Mary Chesnut, "There is no slave, after all, like a wife." And Susan Dabney Smedes, in her recollection of growing up on an Alabama plantation, recalled that "it was a saying that the mistress of a plantation was the most complete slave on it." Some women particularly bristled at their lack of independence and at the necessity of obeying men. "How men can be blustering around, making everybody uncomfortable, simply to show that they are masters and we are only women and children at their mercy!" exclaimed Mary Chesnut. Her father-in-law, she observed, was amiable so long as those beneath him did as he expected, "but he is as absolute a tyrant as the Czar of Russia . . . or the Sultan of Turkey."

Many women were deeply discontented, too, with the widespread double standard for sexual behavior and with the daily reminders of miscegenation some had to face. A man who fathered illegitimate children by slave women suffered no social or legal penalties, even in the case of rape (southern law did not recognize such a crime against slave women), whereas a white woman guilty of adultery lost all social respectability. Miscegenation placed a particular strain on the ideals of plantation mistresses. Like all wives, their duties required them to preserve the sanctity of marriage and the wholesomeness of family life. But they were also required to oversee the welfare of their slaves as additional "family"—at the same time that they knew their husbands might be siring children out of wedlock and violating the lines of racial caste so crucial to maintaining the peculiar institution.

Mary Chesnut, who knew the reality of miscegenation firsthand from her father-in-law's liaisons with slave women and discussed it more frankly than most, sneered in her diary at the assumptions of male superiority. "All the time they seem to think themselves patterns—models of husbands and fathers," she fumed, bitter at the enforced silence among wives. "Like the patriarchs of old, our men live all in one house with their wives and concubines; and the mulattoes one sees in every family partly resemble the white children. Any lady is ready to tell you who is the father of all the mulattoes one sees in everybody's household but her own. Those, she seems to think, drop from the clouds. My disgust sometimes is boiling over." She discovered that her views were shared by other planters' wives. One spoke of "violations of the moral law that made mulattoes as common as blackberries," and another recalled, "I saw slavery in its bearing on my sex. I saw that it teemed with injustice and shame to all womankind and I hated it."

Even women whose husbands or sons had not engaged in such behavior often felt constrained and chafed at the legal restraints marriage imposed. Some preferred to work for themselves, often running their own businesses, and thus maintain control of their own property. Married women found such lack of control a particular grievance. The ups and downs of cotton prices and the boom–bust cycles of the economy finally led some southern states to protect the property women brought with them when they married by establishing a separate estate over which women had greater control.

Still, only a small minority of women questioned either their place in southern society or the corrosive influence of slavery. Even fewer were willing to forgo the physical and material comforts that slavery made possible, despite the burdens it imposed on them. Racism was so pervasive within American society that the few white southern women who privately criticized the institution displayed little empathy for the plight of slaves themselves, including black women. Whatever the burdens of the plantation mistress, the experiences that made her a "slave" to her duties as an upper-class woman were hardly akin to the bondage of slavery itself.

Yeoman Farmers

In terms of numbers, yeoman farmers and their families were the backbone of southern society, accounting for well over half the southern white population. They owned no slaves and farmed the traditional 80 to 160 acres, like northern farmers. About 80 percent of the males owned their own land and the rest rented or hired themselves out to other farmers, hoping one day to acquire their own homestead. They settled almost everywhere in the South, except in the rice and sugar districts and valuable river bottomlands of the Deep South, which were monopolized by large slaveowners. Like Ferdinand Steel, most were semisubsistence farmers who raised primarily corn and hogs, along with perhaps a few bales of cotton or some tobacco, which they sold to obtain the cash needed to buy items like sugar, coffee, and salt. The more enterprising sought to produce a surplus of food to sell locally or in a more distant market, and in areas like Virginia's Shenandoah Valley, wheat production thoroughly tied yeoman farmers and small slaveowners to the commercial economy. Some were not so much farmers as herdsmen, who set large herds of scrawny cattle or pigs to forage in the woods until it was time for the annual drive to market. Yeoman farmers lacked the wealth of planters, but they had a pride and dignity that earned them the respect of their richer neighbors.

Southern farmers led more isolated lives than their northern counterparts. The population density was thinner, towns were less numerous, and there were

A majority of white southerners were members of nonslaveholding yeoman farm families. Respected and relatively prosperous, these families nevertheless often lacked many comforts. A number, such as this German farm family in Texas, lived in log cabins.

fewer roads, canals, or railroads to ease travel. Yet the social activities of these people were not much different from those of northern farmers. Religion played an important role, and the church was the center of the community. Camp meetings, held in late summer after the crops were laid by but before harvest time, were both a soul-wrenching experience and a valued time for socializing. As in the North, neighbors also met to exchange labor and tools, always managing to combine work with play. Men raised a house for a new family or for a bride and groom, the women prepared a feast, then everyone had a square dance in the evening. The men rolled logs to clear fields of dead trees, turning the activity into a contest of strength. Women met for quilting bees, where they pieced such traditional patterns as log cabin, flying geese, and oak leaf cluster. Adults and children alike would gather at a barn to shuck corn; in the evening glow of lanterns, the jug would be passed around, rival teams would compete, or a couple of the stoutest voices would lead a chorus of "Round up the corn, boys, round up the corn . . . pull off the shucks, boys, pull off the shucks" and "Give me a dram, sir, give me a dram." County fairs, court sessions, militia musters, political rallies—these too were occasions that brought rural folk together.

Hard work helped improve the lot of these farm families, but the southern economic system put limits on how far ordinary farmers could progress. Planters monopolized the best farmlands, particularly those tracts along riverways with ready access to market. Since yeoman farmers lacked cheap slave labor, adequate transportation, and access to credit, they could not compete with planters in the production of staples. And when it came to selling their corn and wheat, small farmers conducted only limited business with planters, who usually grew as much of their own foodstuffs as possible. In the North, cities became a market for small farmers, but in the South, where the staple economy did not stimulate the growth of towns and cities, this internal market was much smaller.

Thus while southern yeoman farmers were not poor, they suffered from a chronic lack of money and the absence of conveniences that northern farm families enjoyed, such as cast iron stoves, sewing machines, ready-made clothing, and good furniture. And the lack of public schooling hurt ordinary farmers more than wealthy planters, who could afford private tutors. A few chafed at the absence of greater opportunities. Josiah Hinds, who hacked a farm out of the isolated woods of northern Mississippi, worried that his children were growing up "wild" and complained, "Education is but little prized by my neighbours, although honest and industrious . . . and if the corn and cotton grows to perfection . . . it is enough, provided it brings a fare price, and hog meat is at hand to boil with the greens."

In some ways, then, the worlds of the yeoman farmers and the upper-class planters were not only different, but also in conflict. Still, a hostility between the two classes did not emerge. Yeoman farmers admired planters and looked up to them. Realistically or not, they aspired to join the gentry themselves. And even whites who owned no slaves accepted slavery as a means of controlling blacks. If slaves were freed, they would compete directly with white farmers; as slaves, they remained members of an inferior social caste based on race. "Now suppose they was free," one poor farmer told Frederick Law Olmsted. "You see they'd all think themselves as good as we." Racism and fear of blacks were sufficient to keep nonslaveholders loyal to southern institutions. In 1849 in Kentucky, where nearly 90 percent of the voters were nonslaveholders, support for a program of gradual emancipation won only 10,000 votes—showing how firmly whites of all classes supported slavery.

Urban Society

In many ways urban society paralleled rural society in the South. At the top were the merchants, businessmen, and professionals, who generally allied themselves with the planters. Down a notch were the mechanics and tradesmen, part of the southern middle class. They ranked higher than farm laborers or factory workers, and a few even owned slaves. At the bottom were the unskilled white laborers, who did work such as building the canals and railroads of the South. To avoid losing valuable slaves, planters often hired Irish workers to perform such dangerous jobs as draining malarial swamps. The most notable feature of all these groups was their small size—less than 8 percent of the population in 1860 lived in towns with a population over 4000—which reflected the minor role urban life played in the South.

Poor Whites

The poorest white southerners lived on land that no one else wanted: the wiregrass region of southeastern Georgia, the sand hills of central South Carolina, the pine barrens of the coastal plains from Virginia to southeastern Mississippi. In their backgrounds, they were similar to other southerners, but they were the least efficient, the least enterprising, and the least lucky of the rural white population. Shiftless and lazy, extremely superstitious, and largely illiterate, they lived in squalor in rude, unchinked, windowless log cabins. They resided in the remotest areas, inaccessible to market, and were often squatters without title to the land they were on. Many of the men were not really farmers, but spent their time hunting and fishing while women did the domestic work, including what farming they could manage. Other southern whites scorned them as crackers, white trash, sandhillers, and clay eaters.

Circumstances made their poverty difficult to escape. Consuming a monotonous diet of corn, pork, and whiskey, they suffered from malnutrition. And the poor lands they inhabited were prime country for malaria and the hookworm parasite, afflictions which sapped their energy, made them listless, and gave them yellow, sallow complexions. Olmsted described one woman whom he found sitting before the fire in her piney woods cabin: "apparently young," but her face "dry and impassive as a dead man's. . . . Once in about a minute, [she] would suddenly throw up her chin, and spit with perfect precision into the hottest embers of the fire."

The number of poor whites in the Old South has been difficult to estimate. They were found more often in the eastern coastal plain than in the new regions of the Southwest. Their numbers were probably magnified by visitors to the South, who tended to classify most natives they encountered either as wealthy planters or poverty-stricken squatters, ignoring the vast majority of "plain folk." There may have been as few as 100,000 poor whites or as many as a million; probably they numbered about 500,000, or a little more than 5 percent of the white population.

Because poor whites often traded with slaves, exchanging whiskey for stolen goods, planters considered them a nuisance as well as contemptible, and often bought them out, simply to rid the neighborhood of them. For their part, poor whites resented planters much more than did most yeoman farmers. Still, their hostility toward blacks grew stronger. Poor whites refused to work alongside slaves, to perform any work commonly done by them, and vehemently opposed ending slavery. Emancipation would remove one of the few symbols of their status—that they were, at least, free.

THE PECULIAR INSTITUTION

Slaves were not free. That overwhelming fact must be understood before anything is said about the kindness or the cruelty individual slaves experienced; before any consideration of healthy or unhealthy living conditions; before any discussion of how slave families coped with hardship, rejoiced in shared pleasures, or worshiped in prayer. The lives of slaves were affected day in and day out, in big ways and small, by the basic reality that slaves were not their own masters. If a slave's workload was reasonable, it remained so only at the master's discretion, not because the slave determined it to be. If slaves married or visited family or friends on a nearby plantation, they could do so only with the master's permission. If they raised a family, they could remain together only so long as the master did not separate them by sale. Whatever slaves wanted to do, they had always to consider the response of their masters.

When power is distributed as unequally as it was between masters and slaves, every action on the part of the enslaved involved a certain calculation, conscious or unconscious. The consequences of every act, of every expression or gesture, had to be considered. In that sense, the line between freedom and slavery penetrated every corner of a slave's life, and it was an absolute and overwhelming distinction. Not even the most miserable, poverty-stricken white, wearing rags or going hungry or living in the draftiest log hovel, ever asked to be a slave.

One other stark fact reinforced the sharp line between freedom and slavery: slaves were distinguished on the basis of color. While the peculiar institution was an economic system of labor, it was also a caste system based on race. The color line of slavery made it much easier to brand blacks as somehow different. It made it easier to rationalize the institution of slavery and to win the support of yeoman farmers and poor whites, even though in many ways the system held them back. And when emancipation finally arrived, the practice of racism remained, in both the North and the South. All this is to say that slavery must be understood on many levels: not only as an economic system, but as a racial and cultural one; not only in terms of its outward conditions of life and labor, but also through the inner demands it made on the soul.

Work and Discipline

The vast majority of African-Americans in the South were slaves, but the conditions they encountered varied widely, depending on the size of the farm or plantation, the crop being grown, the personality of the master, and whether he was an absentee owner. On small farms, slaves worked in the fields with the owners and had much closer contact with whites. The Upper South, where such holdings were common, had a reputation for treating slaves less harshly. On large plantations, on the other hand, most slaves rarely saw the master. Instead, they dealt with the overseer, who had not invested in them personally, was being paid for the size of the harvest he brought in, and was therefore often harsh in his approach. The largest plantations, which raised rice and sugar, also required the longest hours and the most grueling labor.

On large plantations, the house servants and the drivers were accorded the highest status. Skilled artisans such as carpenters and blacksmiths were also given special recognition and, like house servants, worked in the fields only in emergencies. The hardest work was done by the field hands, both men and women. Sometimes field hands were separated into specialties. In the summer of 1854, Olmsted watched a group of Mississippi slaves return to work in the fields after a thunderstorm. "First came, led by an old driver carrying a whip, forty of the largest and strongest women I ever saw together; . . . they carried themselves loftily, each having a hoe over the shoulder, and walking with a free, powerful swing like [soldiers] on the march." Behind them were the plowhands on the mules, "the cavalry, thirty strong, mostly men, but a few of them women." Bringing up the rear was "a lean and vigilant white overseer, on a brisk pony."

Toil began just before sunrise and continued until dusk. Tasks varied according to the crop, but plantations required a year-round routine, and masters were always able to find work for slaves. One Alabama planter informed his father in Connecticut, "There is no leisure, no long sleeping season such as you have in New England." In addition, most planters tried to grow a substantial portion of their food supply, which meant that slaves also had charge of corn and livestock (mostly hogs). Corn and cotton required attention in alternating sequences, and therefore many planters preferred to plant both crops to keep the slaves constantly busy.

Some planters used a gang system for working their slaves, in which an overseer or a driver supervised gangs of 20 to 25 adults. Although this approach ex-

Black slave driver.

tracted long hours of reasonably hard labor, the gangs had to be constantly supervised and shirkers were difficult to detect. Other planters preferred the task system, under which each slave was given a specific daily assignment. An able-bodied man, for example, would be required to break up 1200 square feet of rice field with a spade, or a woman to sow half an acre with rice seed. Slaves could work at their own pace, and when the assigned tasks were completed, they were finished for the day. This system gave slaves an incentive to do rapid but careful work and freed overseers from having to closely supervise the work. On the other hand, slaves resisted vigorously if masters tried to increase the workload. The task system was most common in the rice fields, whereas the gang system predominated in the cotton districts. Many planters used a combination of the two.

During cultivation and harvest, slaves were in the field 15 to 16 hours a day, eating a noonday meal there and resting before resuming labor. Work was uncommon on Sundays, and frequently only a half day was required on Saturdays. Even so, the routine was taxing by the standards of the day. "We get up before day every morning and eat breakfast before day and have everybody at work before day dawns," an Arkansas cotton planter reported. "I am never caught in bed after day light nor is any body else on the place, and we continue in the cotton fields when we can have fair weather till it is so dark we can't see to work."

Often masters gave rewards to slaves who worked diligently. A field hand whose tools passed inspection at the end of the year might receive a week's extra ration of rice, peas, molasses, meat, and tobacco. But the threat of punishment was always present. Slaves could be denied passes to visit other plantations on Sunday; their food allowance could be reduced or their workload increased; and if all else failed, they could be sold. The most common instrument of punishment was the whip, emblem of the master's authority. The frequency of its use varied from plantation to plantation, but few slaves escaped the lash entirely. "We have to rely more and more on the power of fear," planter James Henry Hammond acknowledged. "We are determined to continue masters, and to do so we have to draw the reign tighter and tighter day by day to be assured that we hold them in complete check."

Slave Maintenance

Planters generally bought cheap cloth for slave clothing and each year gave adults at most only a couple of outfits and a pair of shoes. By the end of the year, field hands were usually in tatters. Few had enough clothing or blankets to keep warm when the weather dipped below freezing. Some planters provided well-built housing, but more commonly slaves lived in cramped, poorly built cabins that were leaky in wet weather, drafty in cold, and furnished with a few crude chairs, benches and a table, perhaps a mattress filled with corn husks or straw, and a few pots and dishes. The floor was dirt, and cooking was done in the fireplace, which also supplied the heat for the cabin.

Sickness among the hands was a persistent problem for slaveowners. In order to keep medical expenses down, they treated sick slaves themselves and called in a doctor only for desperate cases. One overseer included among the skills necessary for the job "a tolerable knowledge" of medicines and sufficient skill in surgery "that he may be able with *safety* to open a vein, extract a tooth, or bandage a broken limb." Even conscientious masters often employed harmful treatments and dispensed quack patent medicines that promised to cure a wide variety of ailments. Conditions varied widely, but on average, a slaveowner spent less than a dollar a year on medical care for each slave.

Some plantations had hospitals to care for the sick; other slaveowners expected slaves who were sick to be cared for by family members. When she took up residence on her husband's plantation in Georgia, Fanny Kemble was shocked that the hospital had only a dirt floor, the rooms were filthy, and the patients did not have a bed or mattress but simply lay on the floor.

Defenders of slavery exaggerated when they claimed that the standard of living for American slaves exceeded that of free workers in the North. On the other hand, slaves fared much worse in Latin America, where the heavy imbalance of males over females prevented anything like a normal family life, and harsher treatment, harder labor, and greater incidence of disease resulted in a much higher mortality rate. Only by continually importing new slaves from Africa could Latin American societies maintain their labor force. The United States, by contrast, was the only slave society in the Americas where the slave population increased naturally—indeed, at about the same rate as the white population.

Still, a deficient diet, inadequate clothing and shelter, long hours of hard toil, and poor medical care resulted in a lower life expectancy among slaves compared to whites in the United States. Infant mortality among slaves was more than double that of the white population; for every 1000 live births among southern slaves, more than 200 died before the age of five. For those who survived infancy, slaves had a life expectancy about 8 years less than whites. As late as 1860, fewer than two-thirds of slave children survived to the age of 10.

Resistance

Given the wide gulf between freedom and slavery, it was only natural that slaves resisted the bondage imposed on them. The most radical form of resistance was rebellion. In Latin America, slave revolts were relatively frequent, involving hundreds and even thousands of slaves and pitched battles in which large numbers were killed. Such struggles were rare in the United States. Unlike slave societies such as Brazil and Jamaica, in the Old South whites outnumbered blacks almost everywhere, and the influence and power of the civil government was much stronger. Then too, the South offered less suitable terrain to establish the fugitive slave colonies that developed in Latin American jungles and mountains. Furthermore, African-born slaves, most of whom had grown up free, were most likely to revolt in Latin America, whereas the African slave trade had been closed off much earlier in the United States. By 1820, a majority of U.S. slaves were native-born. Finally, in the United States slave family life was stronger and more important, which mitigated against desperate rebellion. Slaves recognized the odds against them, and many potential leaders became fugitives instead. What is remarkable is that American slaves revolted at all.

Early in the nineteenth century several well-organized uprisings were barely thwarted. In 1800 Gabriel Prosser, a slave blacksmith, carefully recruited perhaps a couple hundred slaves in hopes of marching on Richmond, setting fire to the city, and capturing the governor. But a heavy thunderstorm postponed the attack and a few slaves then betrayed the plot. Prosser and other leaders were eventually captured and executed. Denmark Vesey's conspiracy in Charleston in 1822 met a similar fate (page 396). Both of these rebellions were elaborately planned, and both were hurt by their sheer size. The larger any group of conspirators, the greater chance that the plot would be betrayed.

The most famous slave revolt, led by a Virginia slave preacher named Nat Turner, was smaller and more spontaneous. Turner, who lived on a farm in the southeastern part of the state, enjoyed unusual privileges. His master, whom he described as a kind and trusting man, allowed him to read and write, encouraged him to study the Bible and preach to other slaves on Sundays, and gave him great personal freedom. Spurred on by an almost fanatic mysticism, Turner became convinced from visions of white and black angels fighting that God intended to punish whites, and that he had been selected "to carry terror and devastation" throughout the countryside. One night in 1831 following an eclipse of the sun, he and six confederates stole out and murdered Turner's master and family. Gaining some 70 recruits as they went, Turner's band eventually killed 57 white men, women, and children. Along the way, the members voiced their grievances against slavery and announced that they intended to confiscate their masters' wealth.

The revolt lasted only 48 hours before being crushed. In the aftermath as many as 200 slaves, most of whom were innocent, were killed by unnerved whites. Turner himself eluded pursuers for over two months but finally was captured, tried, and executed. This uprising was quickly put down, but it left whites throughout the South with a haunting uneasiness. Turner's master had been kind; Turner himself seemed a model slave. Yet in a world where masters held such power over human property, who could read the true emotions behind the mask of obedience?

Few slaves followed Turner's violent example. But there were other, more subtle ways of resisting a master's authority. Whatever the theory, in practice slavery was an institution in which the master was not all-powerful and the slave helpless; slaves found countless ways to disrupt the daily routine. Most dramatically, they could do as Octave Johnson did: say no, put down their tools, and run away. With the odds stacked heavily against them, few runaways escaped safely to freedom except from the border states. More frequently, slaves fled to nearby woods or swamps to avoid punishment or protest their treatment. Often they remained away for weeks while other slaves served as intermediaries in negotiations with the owner or overseer. Some runaways stayed out only a few days; others, like Johnson, held out for months.

Many slaves resisted by abusing their masters' property. They mishandled animals, broke tools and machinery, misplaced items, and worked carelessly in the fields. Many of these misdeeds arose simply from the lack of incentive to perform well; others, however, were conscious obstruction. Olmsted observed one field gang that stopped hoeing every time the overseer turned his back. Slaves also sought to trick the master by feigning illness or injury and by hiding rocks in the cotton they picked. Slaves complained directly to the owner about an overseer's mistreatment, thereby attempting to drive a wedge between the two. The most common form of resistance, and a persistent annoyance to slaveowners, was theft. Slaves became adept at stealing produce from the master's garden, watermelon, chickens (telltale feathers had to be buried, not burned, for masters recognized the smell), hogs (clubbed quickly, to keep them from squealing), and even cattle. Slaves often distinguished between "stealing" from each other and merely "taking" from white masters. "Dey allus done tell us it am wrong to lie and steal," recalled Josephine Howard, a former slave in Texas, "but why did de white folks steal my mammy and her mammy? Dey lives clost to some water, somewhere over in Africy. . . . Dat de sinfulles' stealin' dey is."

In the end, the typical slave was neither a rebel nor a childlike adult, but an individual who lived his or her life with as much dignity as possible. To do so often required the slave to wear an "impenetrable mask," one bondsman recalled. "How much of joy, of sorrow, of misery and anguish have they hidden from their tormentors." Slaves learned to outwit their masters. Frederick Douglass, the most famous fugitive slave, explained that "as the master studies to keep the slave ignorant, the slave is cunning enough to make the master think he succeeds." When emancipation came, former slaves dropped their masks, and white masters were amazed at the transformation. "We planters could never get at the truth," one slaveowner wrote after the Civil War. "So deceitful is the Negro that as far as my own experience extends I could never in a single instance decipher his character."

SLAVE CULTURE

Trapped in bondage, facing the futility of revolt, slaves could at least forge a culture of their own. By the nineteenth century, American slaves had been separated from much of their traditional African heritage, but that did not mean they had fully accepted the dominant white culture. Instead, slaves combined strands from their African past with customs that evolved from their life in America. This slave culture was most distinct on big plantations, where the slave population was large and slaves had more opportunity to live apart from white scrutiny.

The Black Family

Maintaining a sense of family was one of the most remarkable achievements of African-Americans in bondage, especially given the odds against it. Southern law did not recognize slave marriages as legally binding, slave parents did not have complete authority over themselves or their children, black women faced the possibility of rape by the master or overseer without legal recourse, and husbands, wives, and children had to live with the fear of being sold and separated. From 1820 to 1860 more than 2 million slaves were sold in the interstate slave trade, one of the greatest forced migrations in world history, and perhaps 600,000 husbands and wives were separated by such sales. The chance that a slave family would be broken up—children taken from parents, brothers separated from sisters—was even greater.

Still, family ties remained strong, as slave culture demonstrated. The marriage ceremony among slaves varied from plantation to plantation: sometimes it consisted of the tradition of jumping over a broomstick in the presence of the slave community; sometimes it was no more than the master giving verbal approval; sometimes there was a formal religious ceremony in the planter's Big House. Whatever the ceremony, slaves viewed the ritual as a public affirmation of commitment to the couple's new duties and responsibilities. Although young men and women often engaged in premarital sex, they were expected to settle down, choose a partner, and become part of a stable family. It has been estimated that at least one in five slave women had one or more children before marriage, but most of these mothers eventually married. "The negroes had their own ideas of morality, and they held them very strictly," the daughter of a Georgia planter recalled.

None of the slaves for sale at this Richmond auction betrays outwardly the pain and anguish of being physically inspected by prospective owners, bid upon, and sold. Mary Chesnut, an upper-class South Carolinian, was once walking with a European visitor past a sidewalk slave sale. "If you can stand that," she remarked, "no other Southern thing need choke you."

"They did not consider it wrong for a girl to have a child before she married, but afterwards were very strict upon anything like infidelity on her part."

The traditional nuclear family of father, mother, and children was the rule, not the exception, among slaves. Families headed by the mother and with an absent father (unless sold by the master) were not typical. Within the marriage, the father was viewed as the traditional head of the family; wives were to be submissive and obey their husbands. Labor in the quarters was divided according to sex: women did the indoor work such as cooking, washing, and sewing, and men did outdoor chores, such as gathering firewood, hauling water, and tending the animals and garden plots. The men also hunted and fished to supplement the spare weekly rations. "My old daddy . . . caught rabbits, coons an' possums" recalled Louisa Adams of North Carolina. "He would work all day and hunt at night."

Beyond the nuclear family, slaves developed strong kinship networks. Normally the master allowed a slave couple to name their children, and most were named after a relative. The ties of kin also promoted a sense of community. Aunts and uncles were expected to look after children who lost their parents through death or sale. When children were sold to a new plantation, a family in the slave quarters took them in. Thus all members of the slave society drew together in an extended network of mutual obligation.

Slave Songs and Stories

In the songs they sang, slaves expressed some of their deepest feelings about love and work and the joys and sorrows of life. "The songs of the slave represent the sorrows of his heart," commented Frederick Douglass. Surely there was bitterness as well as sorrow when slaves sang:

Daily Lives

FOOD/DRINK/DRUGS

A Slave's Daily Bread

Once a week on most plantations, slaves lined up to receive their rations from the master. Though the allotments varied from one plantation to the next, they were predictable enough: for each adult slave about a peck of cornmeal, three or four pounds of bacon or salt pork, and some molasses for sweetener. Some masters added vegetables, fruits, or sweet potatoes in season, but only on rare occasions did slaves receive wheat flour, beef, lean meat, poultry, eggs, or milk (which was reserved for children when it was available at all, and was usually in soured form).

In terms of simple calories, this ration was ample enough to sustain life. Frederick Law Olmsted, who traveled extensively in the South in the 1850s, reported that slaves had enough to eat but that their fare was generally "coarse, crude, and wanting in variety." A careful modern study of slave diet concludes that on the eve of the Civil War, the standard daily ration was over 3000 calories, and that adult slaves received almost 5400 calories, which exceeds today's recommended levels of consumption. But over 80 percent of the daily calories came from corn and pork, and this monotonous fare of hog-and-hominy, while sufficient in bulk, lacked several essential nutrients as well as enough protein. Diet-related diseases such as pellagra and beriberi were often noted among the slave population. This malnutrition was due more to ignorance than miserliness or willful neglect on the part of masters. Although slaveowners and their families enjoyed more variety in their food and better cuts of meat, they too lacked a balanced diet.

On some plantations, masters left all cooking to the slaves, who would make breakfast and their noon meal before going to work in the morning, taking dinner with them to eat in the fields. After the day's labor was done, they came home to fix a light supper. Other masters established a plantation kitchen where regular cooks prepared breakfast and dinner, though supper remained the responsibility of the individual slave or family. On these plantations, a noon meal was brought to the fields. In general, the quality of food preparation was better under this system because slaves were often too exhausted after work to put much time or care into cooking. Naturally enough, however, slaves preferred to fix meals according to their own taste and eat as a family in some privacy, even if their quarters were hardly luxurious. Fanny Kemble reported that on her husband's Georgia plantation the slaves sat "on the earth or doorsteps, and ate out of their little cedar tubs or an iron pot, some few with broken iron spoons, more with pieces of wood, and all the children with their fingers." The cooking itself was done in front of a large fireplace, perhaps four feet wide, using long-handled frying pans, dutch ovens that nestled in the coals, or pots that were hung from poles swung over the fire.

Slaves resorted to various means to enliven their drab diet. Wherever their masters permitted it, they tended their own vegetable gardens after work or raised chickens and other animals. Not only did this practice provide eggs and other items not included in the weekly rations, but it also enabled slaves to sell their surplus to the master or in town and use their earnings to buy small quantities of luxuries such as coffee, sugar, and tobacco. Slaves also raided the master's smokehouse, secretly slaughtered his

Daily Lives

When slaves working in the fields became dizzy from the heat, they sometimes called out, "I see a monkey." "Monkey pots" like this one brought water and relief.

stock and killed his poultry, and stole from neighboring plantations. Richard Carruthers, a former slave, recalled, "If they didn't provision you 'nough, you just had to slip round and get a chicken." Even slaves who received relatively large rations resorted to midnight forays to obtain higher-quality food and to trade stolen goods for tobacco and whiskey.

Hunting and fishing provided fresh meat as well as variety. Slaves who worked all day still had plenty of incentive to stir out at night to hunt raccoon or opossum. "The flesh of the coon is palatable," admitted Solomon Northup, a black who had tasted both southern and northern cooking, "but verily there is nothing in all butcherdom so delicious as a roasted 'possum." Possum was parboiled to soften it up and then roasted with lard over the fire, along with sweet potatoes. As one slave song put it:

De way ter cook de 'possum nice,
Carve 'im to de heart,
First parbile 'im, stir 'im twice,
Carve 'im to de heart.

Den lay sweet taters in de pan,
Carve 'im to de heart;
Nuthin' beats dat in de lan'.
Carve 'im to de heart.

Squirrel meat, though tougher, could be boiled long enough to soften it up for squirrel pie served with dumplings. Rabbits, especially young ones, were tender enough to fry.

Along with such meat might come "hoecakes," a popular dish made by slapping a bit of cornmeal dough on the blade of a hoe and holding it over the coals. Vegetables were boiled in a pot with a bit of hog jowl, each new vegetable thrown in at the appropriate cooking time: beans first, then cabbage when the beans were half done, then squash, and finally okra. Whenever they could get them, slave cooks used spices to flavor their dishes. Some spices, such as sesame seeds, had come from Africa with the slaves. Red pepper, native to the Americas, added zing to innumerable dishes.

Holidays on the plantation, when the master would provide a banquet for the hands, provided a welcome break from the usual daily fare. On these occasions, slaves could fill up on beef, mutton, roast pig, coffee, wheat bread, pies, and other dishes only rarely tasted. Although masters generally tried to keep whiskey away from their slaves, some slaveowners made an exception at Christmas. Feasting was one of the slaves' "principle sources of comfort," one ex-slave testified. "Only the slave who has lived all the year on his scanty allowance of meal and bacon, can appreciate such suppers."

> We raise the wheat
> They give us the corn
> We bake the bread
> They give us the crust
> We sift the meal
> They give us the husk
> We peel the meat
> They give us the skin
> And that's the way
> They take us in

Yet songs were also central to the celebrations held in the slave quarters: for marriages, Christmas revels, and after harvest time. And a slave on the way to the fields might sing,

> Saturday night and Sunday too
> Young gals on my mind.
> Monday morning 'way 'fore day.
> Old master's got me gwine.
> Peggy does you love me now?

Slaves expressed themselves through stories as well as song. Most often these folk tales used animals as symbolic models for the predicaments slaves found themselves in. The best known of these, the cunning Brer Rabbit, was a weak fellow who defeated larger animals like Brer Fox and Brer Bear by using his wits. Such stories passed from generation to generation in the slave quarters. Some undoubtedly had their origins in traditional African "trickster" folk tales; others grew out of the slaves' own experiences. Sometimes the identity of the trickster was no longer symbolic, but the slave. Because these latter stories contained more overt hostility to whites, slaves usually told them only among themselves. But the message, whether direct or symbolic, was much the same: to laugh at the master's foibles and teach the young how to survive in a hostile world.

The Lord Calls Us Home

At the center of slave culture was religion. Slaveowners encouraged a carefully controlled form of religion among slaves, based on their own version of the gospel, as an effective means of social control. Masters provided slaves with a minister (often white), set the time and place of services, and usually insisted that a white person be present. "Church was what they called it," one former slave protested, "but all that preacher talked about was for us slaves to obey our masters and not to lie and steal. Nothing about Jesus was ever said and the overseer stood there to see that the preacher talked as he wanted him to talk." Disenchanted, some slaves repudiated all religion. Henry Bibb, a fugitive slave, maintained that "this kind of preaching has driven thousands into infidelity." Others continued to believe in conjuring, voodoo, and various practices derived from African religion.

Most slaves, however, sought a Christianity firmly their own, beyond the control of the master. On many plantations, they met secretly at night, in the quarters or at "hush harbors" in the safety of the woods, where a rhythmic singing and dancing, modeled on the ring shout of African religion, would begin: some "clapping their hands and beating time with their feet," one witness reported;

others "walking around in a ring . . . [striking] into the shout step, observing most accurate time with the music." As one slave preacher recalled, "The way in which we worshiped is almost indescribable. The singing was accompanied by a certain ecstasy of motion, clapping of hands, tossing of heads, which would continue without cessation about half an hour. The old house partook of the ecstasy; it rang with their jubilant shouts, and shook in all its joints." In an environment where slaves, for most of the day, were prevented from expressing their deepest feelings, such meetings served as a satisfying emotional release.

Religion also provided slaves with values to guide them through their daily experiences and give them a sense of self-worth. From their gospel's Christian roots, slaves learned that God, through the love of Jesus, would redeem the poor and downtrodden and raise them one day to honor and glory. Rejecting the teaching of some whites that slavery was punishment, slave preachers told their congregations that they were the chosen people of God, and that on the final Day of Judgment, masters would be punished for their sins. "This is one reason why I believe in hell," a former slave declared. "I don't believe a just God is going to take no such man as my former master into His Kingdom."

Again, song played a central role. Slaves sang religious "spirituals" at work and at play as well as in religious services. Seemingly meek and otherworldly, the songs often contained a hidden element of protest. Frederick Douglass disclosed that when slaves sang longingly of "Canaan, sweet Canaan" they were thinking not only of the Bible's Promised Land, but of the North and freedom. When slaves heard "Steal Away to Jesus" sung in the fields, they knew that a secret devotional meeting was scheduled that evening. Songs became one of the few ways slaves could openly express their yearning for freedom, in the approved language of Christianity. While a song's lyrics might speak of an otherworldly freedom from sin in heaven, their hearts were considering a this-worldly escape from physical bondage. Even so, slaves sometimes ran afoul of white authority. At the beginning of the Civil War one group of slaves was jailed in South Carolina for singing "We'll soon be free/When the Lord calls us home."

Religion, then, served not only to comfort slaves after days of toil and sorrow. It also strengthened the sense of togetherness and common purpose and held out the promise of eventual freedom in this world and the next. The faith that "some ob dese days my time will come" was one of the most important ways that slaves coped with bondage and resisted its pressure to rob them of their self-esteem.

The Slave Community

While slaves managed with remarkable success to preserve a sense of self-worth in a culture of their own, the hard reality of slavery made it impossible to escape fully from white control. Whites constantly intruded in slaves' daily lives and in a wide variety of ways tried to make them dependent. Even the social hierarchy within the slave quarters could never remain entirely free from the white world. Slave preachers, conjurers, and herb doctors held status that no white conferred, but the prestige of a slave driver rested on the authority of the white master. Similarly, skilled slaves and house servants often felt superior to other slaves, an attitude masters consciously promoted. "I considered my station a very high one," one master's body servant confessed. Light-skinned slaves sometimes deemed their color a badge of superiority. Fanny Kemble recorded that one woman begged to be relieved of field labor, which she considered degrading, "on 'account of her color.'"

But the realities of slavery and white racism inevitably drove blacks closer together in a common bond and forced them to depend on each other to survive. Slaves who helped masters capture runaways or curried favor by reporting other slaves' misbehavior were unusual. And new slaves on a plantation were immediately instructed in the mysteries of the quarters, including such vital matters as the best strategies for avoiding punishment. The slave community was their only sanctuary in an otherwise hostile environment. Walled in from the individualistic white society beyond, slaves out of necessity created their own community.

Free Blacks in the South

Of the 4 million blacks living in the South in 1860, only 260,000—about 7 percent—were free. Over 85 percent of them lived in the Upper South, with almost 200,000 in Maryland, Virginia, and North Carolina alone. Mississippi, by contrast, had only 773 free blacks in the entire state, and of all African-Americans living in the Deep South, only 1.5 percent were free. Free blacks were also much more urban than either the southern white or slave populations. In 1860 almost a third of the free African-Americans in the Upper South, and over half in the Lower South, lived in towns and cities. As a rule free African-Americans were more literate than slaves, and they were disproportionately female. They were also much more likely to have mixed ancestry, especially in the Lower South. Only 10 percent of all slaves were classified as mulattoes, compared to four times as many free blacks. Compared to free African-Americans in the North, a greater proportion in the South were skilled artisans and were materially better off.

Still, most free blacks lived in rural areas, although usually not near plantations. Planters adamantly refused to hire them or sell them land, fearing their presence would corrupt slaves. Most eked out a living in low-paying unskilled jobs, but some did well enough to own slaves themselves. In 1830 about 3600 did, although commonly their "property" was their own wives or children, purchased because they could not be emancipated under state laws. A few, like William Tiler Johnson of Natchez, were full-blown slaveowners, however. Johnson invested his earnings from barbering in a farm and eventually hired a white overseer to supervise his 15 slaves. As one of the free African-American elite, he went to the theater, attended horse races, gave his daughters music lessons, and subscribed to six newspapers. In 1852, however, he came to a tragic end when he sued a white neighbor in a boundary dispute. Johnson won in court, but his white adversary murdered him in revenge, and since the witnesses were black, and state law forbade blacks from testifying against whites, the murderer was acquitted.

While highly unusual, Johnson's life illustrated the limits placed on even extraordinarily talented free blacks. And after Nat Turner's rebellion of 1831, southern legislatures moved to restrict free blacks even further. Most states in the Deep South prohibited whites from freeing slaves in their wills, and some required any emancipated slaves to leave the state. All states forbade the entry of free African-Americans, and those already living there were subject to ever greater restrictions. They had to carry their free papers, could not assemble when they wished, were subject to a curfew, often had to register or be licensed to work, and could not vote, hold office, or testify in court against whites. In the final analysis, free African-Americans were hedged in so tightly because they were a glaring contradiction of the idea that bondage was the natural condition of blacks.

As Johnson's life also illustrated, lighter-skinned free blacks in the South, as in the North, tended to set themselves apart from darker-skinned blacks, free or slave. In such cities as Charleston and New Orleans, they established separate social and cultural organizations and maintained their own exclusive social network. Economically dependent on white customers, they developed close connections with whites, yet were never accepted in the white world. Free African-Americans occupied an anomalous position in southern society, well above black slaves but distinctly beneath even poorer whites. They were victims of a society that had no place for them.

SOUTHERN SOCIETY AND THE DEFENSE OF SLAVERY

From wealthy planters to yeoman farmers, from free black slaveholders to poor white mountain families, from cotton field hands to urban craftworkers, the South was a remarkably diverse region. But as we have seen, it was united by its dependence on staple crops and above all by the peculair institution of slavery, the labor system that supported those crops. As the South's economy became more and more dependent on slave-produced staples, and even poor farmers shared the dream of becoming "cotton gentry," slavery became more central to the life of the South, to its culture and its identity.

The Virginia Debate of 1832

At the time of the Revolution, the leading critics of slavery had been southerners— Jefferson, Washington, Madison, and Patrick Henry among them. But beginning in the 1820s, in the wake of the controversy over admitting Missouri as a slave state, southern leaders became less apologetic about slavery and more aggressive in defending it. The turning point occurred in the early 1830s, when the South found itself increasingly under attack. It was in 1831 that William Lloyd Garrison began publishing his abolitionist newspaper, *The Liberator*, and in that year too, Nat Turner launched his revolt, which frightened so many white southerners.

In response to the Turner insurrection, a number of Virginia's western counties, where there were few slaves, petitioned the legislature to adopt a program for gradual emancipation. Between January 16 and 25, 1832, the House of Delegates engaged in a remarkable debate over the merits of slavery. Some antislavery advocates advanced the traditional religious and moral arguments; others pointed to the American belief in natural rights. But most often they focused on how much slavery hurt whites, by retarding southern economic development and draining Virginia of its white population by driving nonslaveholders to free states in the West. These arguments did not sway the more powerful slaveowning classes, even in the Upper South. In the end, the legislature refused, 73–58, to consider legislation to end slavery. The majority was unwilling even to label slavery an evil.

The Virginia debate represented the last significant attempt of southerners to take action against slavery. Most felt that the subject was no longer open to debate. Only in Tennessee, when a constitutional convention in 1834 rejected by a lopsided vote any consideration of gradual emancipation, and in Kentucky, when candidates pledged to gradual emancipation failed to win a single seat in the 1849 state constitutional convention, was the issue raised again. Instead, during the

1830s and 1840s, southern spokesmen defended slavery as a positive good, not just for whites but for blacks. As John C. Calhoun proclaimed in 1837, "I hold that in the present state of civilization, where two races of different origin, and distinguished by color and other physical differences, as well as intellectual, are brought together, the relation now existing in the slaveholding states between the two is, instead of an evil, a good—a positive good."

The Proslavery Argument

Politicians like Calhoun were not alone. Southern leaders, whether slaveholders or not, justified slavery in a variety of ways. Those favoring religious sanction argued that under the law of Moses, Jews were authorized to enslave heathens; and throughout the Bible, no Old Testament prophet, no Apostle, not even Christ himself had ever condemned slavery. Some proslavery writers suggested that God had brought blacks and whites into existence through two separate (and unequal) creations, but for orthodox southern Christians this was heresy. Instead, most white southerners accepted the idea of a single creation and traced slavery's origins instead to the curse of Canaan, in which Canaan (the allegedly black grandson of Noah) was made a servant in punishment for his father's sin. Jefferson Davis summarized the biblical defense of slavery when he declared that slavery "was established by the decree of Almighty God."

Defenders of the institution also pointed out that classical Greece and Rome depended on slavery. The Greek philosopher Aristotle had argued that individuals of superior talent properly became masters over those of inferior ability. They even cited John Locke, that giant of the Enlightenment, who had recognized slavery in the constitution he drafted for the colony of Carolina. Slavery, however, benefited not only "civilization" and its masters, but also slaves themselves. Blacks belonged to an intellectually and emotionally inferior race, apologists argued, and therefore lacked the ability to care for themselves and were sexually licentious. "Providence has placed [the black man] in our hands for his good, and has paid us from his labor for our guardianship," contended James Henry Hammond, an eminent planter and senator from South Carolina, whose "guardianship" of several hundred slaves had netted him a tidy fortune.

Apologists sometimes argued that slaves in the South lived better than factory workers in the North. Masters cared for slaves for life, whereas northern workers had no claim on their employer when they were unemployed, old, or no longer able to work. In making this argument, southerners exaggerated the material comforts of slavery and minimized the average worker's standard of living—to say nothing, of course, about the value of freedom. Still, to many southerners, slavery seemed a more humane system of labor relations, one that kept southern society free from the social turmoil and disorder that plagued the North. George Fitzhugh, the most original of the proslavery writers, placed heavy emphasis on these ideas in his book *Cannibals All!* and other writings. Fitzhugh advanced a class-based theory of society in which superior individuals by right dominated those who were inferior.

Defenders of slavery did not really expect to influence opinion in the North. Their target was more often slaveowners themselves. As Duff Green, a southern editor and one of Calhoun's advisers, explained, "We must satisfy the consciences, we must allay the fears of our own people. We must satisfy them that slavery is of itself right—that it is not a sin against God—that it is not an evil, moral or politi-

This 1841 proslavery cartoon contrasts the treatment of American slaves, who are allegedly well fed, clothed, and cared for, with the plight of unemployed, sick, and starving English factory workers. Defenders of slavery made the same comparisons with northern laborers.

cal. In this way only," he went on, "can we prepare our own people to defend their institutions."

Closing Ranks

Of course, not all southerners could quell their doubts. To take only one example, Robert Scott, an antislavery advocate in the Virginia debate of 1832, was publicly calling slavery "an institution reprobated by the world" as late as 1849. Still, a remarkable change in southern opinion seems to have occurred in the three decades before the Civil War. Outside the border states, few southern whites after 1840 would admit even in private that slavery was wrong. And those who opposed slavery found themselves harassed and sometimes assaulted. Southern newspapers refused to print articles criticizing slavery, and southern mobs destroyed the presses of antislavery papers and threatened the editors into either keeping silent or leaving the state for their personal safety. Southern mails were closed to abolitionist propaganda, and by the 1850s there were even attempts to prevent the circulation of northern magazines or newspapers. Academic freedom also came under attack, as defenders of the South's institutions scrutinized textbooks, administrators, and faculty members. By suppressing even minor dissent on slavery, southern leaders helped to effect greater unity by intimidating critics or driving them into exile. Southerners like James Birney and Sarah and Angelina Grimké left their native region to carry on the fight against slavery from the free states.

Increasingly, too, the debate over slavery spread to the national political arena. Before 1836, Andrew Jackson's enormous popularity in the South blocked the formation of a competitive two-party system. His strong stand against South Carolina and nullification and his destruction of the national bank alienated some groups in the South, who became the nucleus of the Whig party, but Jackson remained overwhelmingly popular with the masses. The emergence of the abolitionist movement in the 1830s left many southerners uneasy, and when the Democrats nominated the northerner Martin Van Buren in 1836, southern Whigs seized the opportunity to build up their party. Emphasizing the need to safeguard southern institutions, they charged that Van Buren could not be counted on to meet the abolitionist threat. The Whigs made impressive gains in the South in 1836, carrying several states and narrowing the margin between the two parties significantly. The election marked the beginning of party rivalry in the South.

In later presidential elections, both parties in the South exploited the politics of slavery by attacking the opposing party through its northern supporters. This tactic was less successful in state elections, however, since both parties were led by slaveholders and were committed to protecting slavery. In addition, the depression that began in 1837 focused the attention of southern voters on economic matters. Southern Whigs appealed to the commercially oriented members of society: planters, business leaders and merchants, bankers, professionals, residents of cities and the plantation black belts. Democrats won their share of slaveowners, but the party's strongholds were the more isolated regions of small independent farmers. As in the North, class and occupation were less important than one's economic and moral outlook. Southern voters most comfortable with the market and the changes it brought gravitated toward the Whig party. And since Whigs supported tariffs to stimulate local industries, hemp growers in Kentucky and sugar planters in Louisiana supported the Whigs, for their crops needed protection from cheaper imports. On the other hand, those farmers who feared the loss of personal independence that banks and commercial development brought with them tended to support the Democratic party.

During the Jacksonian era, most southern political battles did not revolve around the slavery issue. Still, Whigs and Democrats had to be careful to avoid the stigma of antislavery. And politicians who hoped to suppress or ignore the slavery issue came under mounting pressure from John C. Calhoun and his followers. Frustrated in his presidential hopes by the nullification crisis in 1832–1833, Calhoun's sincere wish to preserve the South's way of life merged imperceptibly with his national ambitions. Insistently, even recklessly, he agitated the slavery issue, introducing inflammatory resolutions in Congress upholding slavery, seizing on the abolitionist mailing campaign to demand censorship of the mails, leaping to his feet to insist on a gag law to block antislavery petitions. During the 1830s and early 1840s, few southern politicians followed his lead, but they did become extremely careful about being the least critical of slavery or southern institutions. They knew quite well that, even if their constituents were not as fanatical as Calhoun, southern voters overwhelmingly supported slavery. And such agitation, along with the continued debate between proslavery and abolitionist forces, contributed to the eventual emergence of slavery as a national issue.

Sections and the Nation

Viewing the events of the 1830s and 1840s with the benefit of hindsight, one cannot help but concentrate on the Civil War looming on the horizon, a sharp reminder of the major differences dividing the North and the South. Yet both northerners and southerners had much in common as Americans.

The largest group in both sections was composed of independent farmers who cultivated their own land with their own labor and were devoted to the principles of personal independence and social egalitarianism. Although southern society was more aristocratic in tone, both sections were driven forcefully by the quest for material wealth and prosperity. The Texas Red River planter for whom "time was in the objective case" did not take a back seat to the Yankee clockmaker Chauncey Jerome in the scramble for success and status. White Americans in both sections aspired to rise in society, and they looked to the expanding opportunities of the market to help them do so. Moreover, both northerners and southerners linked geographic mobility to opportunity, and both pushed westward with astonishing frequency in search of better land and a new start.

Many Americans, North and South, also adhered to the teachings of evangelical Protestantism, viewing emotion as central to the religious experience and accepting the need for atonement and rebirth. Southern churches were less open to social reform, primarily because of its association with abolitionism; and southern churches, unlike most in the North, defended slavery as a Christian institution. Eventually both the Methodist and the Baptist churches split into separate northern and southern organizations over this issue, but their attitudes on other matters often coincided.

Finally, northerners and southerners shared a belief in democracy and white equality. Southern as well as northern states embraced the democratic reforms of the 1820s and 1830s, and the electorate in both sections favored giving all white males the vote and making public officeholders responsible to the people. The existence of the planter class created greater tensions in southern society between democracy and the aristocratic side of southern life. But in both sections running for public office required celebrating the "voice of the people." Southerners insisted that the equality proclaimed in the Declaration of Independence applied only to whites (and really only to white males), but the vast majority of northerners in practice took no exception to this attitude. Both sections agreed on the necessity of safeguarding equality of opportunity rather than equality of wealth.

With so much in common, it was not inevitable that the two sections should come to blows. Indeed, economically they complemented one another, since to a large extent they did not compete in the crops they grew or the articles they manufactured. Certainly, before 1840 few politicians believed that the differences between the two sections were decisive. It was only in the mid-1840s, when the United States embarked on a new program of westward expansion, that the slavery issue began to loom ominously in American life, and Americans began to question whether the Union could permanently endure, half slave and half free.

SIGNIFICANT EVENTS

1800	Gabriel's revolt
1815–1860	Spread of the cotton kingdom
1822	Denmark Vesey conspiracy
1830–1840	Proslavery argument developed
1830–1860	Agricultural reform movement in Upper South
1831	Nat Turner Rebellion
1832	Virginia debate on slavery
1844	Methodist church divides into northern and southern organizations
1845	Baptist church divides

14

Western Expansion and the Rise of the Slavery Issue

At first the Crows, Arapahos, and other Indians of the Great Plains paid little attention to the new people moving out from the forests far to the east. After all, nations like the Crow had hunted buffalo for as long as they could remember and had called the plains their own. But the new arrivals were not to be taken lightly. Relentlessly they pushed westward: up the Missouri River, along the Platte, toward the Rocky Mountains. Armed with superior weapons and bringing a great many women and children, their appetite for land seemed unlimited. They attacked the villages of the Plains Indians, ruthlessly massacred women and children, and forced defeated tribes to live on reservations and serve their economic interests. In conflict after conflict, they drove the Mandans off their homelands, made the Arikara scatter up the Missouri, and looked to take over the hunting grounds of the Cheyenne and the Crow. In little more than a century and a half—from the first days when only a handful of their hunters and trappers had come into the land—they had become the masters of the plains.

The invaders who established this political and military dominance were *not* the strange "white men," who also came from the forest. During the 1830s and early 1840s, whites were still few in number. The more dangerous people—the ones who truly worried the Plains tribes—were the Sioux.

Although westward expansion is a firmly entrenched part of the American myth, it is usually told as a one-dimensional tale, centering on the wagon trains pressing on toward the Pacific. But frontiers, after all, are the boundary lines between contrasting cultures or environments; and during the nineteenth century, those in the West were shifting, skirmishing with one another, and adapting. Frontier lines moved not only east to west, as with the white and Sioux migrations, but also from south to north, as Spanish culture diffused; and west to east, as Asian immigrants came to California. Furthermore, frontiers marked not only human but animal boundaries as well. Horses, cattle, and pigs, all of which had been imported from Europe, moved across the continent, usually in advance of European settlers, and often transformed the way Indian peoples lived. Frontiers

The Spirit of Progress dominates John Gast's painting of Manifest Destiny. *In reality, the movement of the frontier was hardly one-dimensional, as Hispanic, Indian, Asian, and white cultures clashed.*

could also be technological, as in the case of trade goods and firearms. Moreover, as we have already seen, disease moved across the continent, with disastrous consequences for natives who had not acquired immunity to European micro-organisms.

Three frontiers altered the lives of the Sioux: those of the horse, the gun, and disease. The horse frontier spread originally from the southwest, where the Spanish first taught Indians to ride. As horses began to run wild or were stolen by neighboring tribes, their habitat spread north and east, well ahead of white settlement. On the other hand, the Spanish, unlike English and French traders, refused to sell firearms to Indians, so the gun frontier moved in the opposite direction, from northeast to southwest. The two waves met and crossed along the upper Missouri during the first half of the eighteenth century—at a time when Ben Franklin rode to Albany, New York, along his western frontier, the Spanish remained a thousand miles to the south, and only a few French traders had penetrated the Mississippi valley. For the tribes that possessed them, horses provided greater mobility, both for hunting bison and for fighting. Guns, too, conferred obvious advantages, and the arrival of these new elements inaugurated an extremely unsettled era for Plains Indian cultures.

The Sioux were first lured from the forest onto the Minnesota prairie during the early 1700s to hunt beaver, whose pelts could be exchanged with white traders for manufactured goods, and buffalo, whose meat offered a reliable food supply. Having obtained guns in exchange for furs, the Sioux could drive the Omahas, Otos, Cheyennes, and Missouris (who had not yet acquired guns) south and west. Much like the Iroquois in New York a century earlier, the Sioux used their strategic position to dominate the western fur trade. But by the 1770s their previous advantage in guns had disappeared, and any further advance up the Missouri was blocked by powerful tribes such as the Mandans and Arikaras. These peoples were primarily horticultural, raising corn, beans, and squash and living in well-fortified towns. They also owned more horses than the Sioux, which made it easier for them to resist attacks.

But the third frontier, disease, threw the balance of power toward the Sioux after 1779. European traders inadvertently brought smallpox with them onto the prairie. The horticultural tribes were hit especially hard because they lived in densely populated villages, where the epidemic spread more easily. Observing this decimation, the Sioux abandoned their tentative experiments with agriculture and instead developed a nomadic culture centered on the buffalo hunt. They began a second wave of westward expansion in the late eighteenth century, so that by the time Lewis and Clark came through in 1804, they firmly controlled the upper Missouri as far as the Yellowstone River.

The Sioux's nomadic life enabled them to avoid the worst ravages of disease, especially the smallpox epidemic of 1837, which reduced the plains population by as much as half. They also benefited from government vaccination programs in the 1830s and 1840s, after several U.S. forts were established on the Missouri. Indeed, the Sioux became the largest tribe on the plains and was the only one whose high birth rate approximated that of whites, their population doubling perhaps every 20 years. From an estimated 5000 in 1804, they grew to 25,000 by the 1850s. Their numbers increased Sioux military power as well as the need for new hunting grounds. During the first half of the nineteenth century, they pushed farther up the Missouri, conquered the plains west of the Black Hills, and won control of the hunting grounds on the Platte River. By the 1840s, when whites began to traverse the region in large numbers, the Sioux had become the most powerful tribe on the plains.

So the "Sioux frontier" was multidimensional, involving shifting boundaries of trade, animals, guns, and disease. Each of these factors disrupted the political and cultural life of the Great Plains. And as white Americans moved westward, their own frontier lines produced similar disruptions, not only between white settlers and Indians, but also between Anglo-American and Hispanic cultures. To Americans in the East, hearing tales of covered wagons along the Platte, the frontier saga seemed a stirring tale of "progress" moving west. To ranchers in New Mexico or California, this migration threatened their status as the predominant upper class. For the Chinese who had come to the gold fields of California, it meant creating a civilized enclave among the *fon kwei* (foreign devils), who mocked long pigtails and wore incredibly coarse clothes.

Ironically, perhaps the greatest instability created by the moving frontiers occurred in established American society. As the political system of the United States struggled to incorporate territories, the North and South engaged in a fierce debate over whether the new lands should become slave or free. What, after all, was the destiny of "these" United States? (Americans, remember, still used the plural.) Just as the Sioux's cultural identity was brought into question by the moving frontier, so too was the identity of the American Republic.

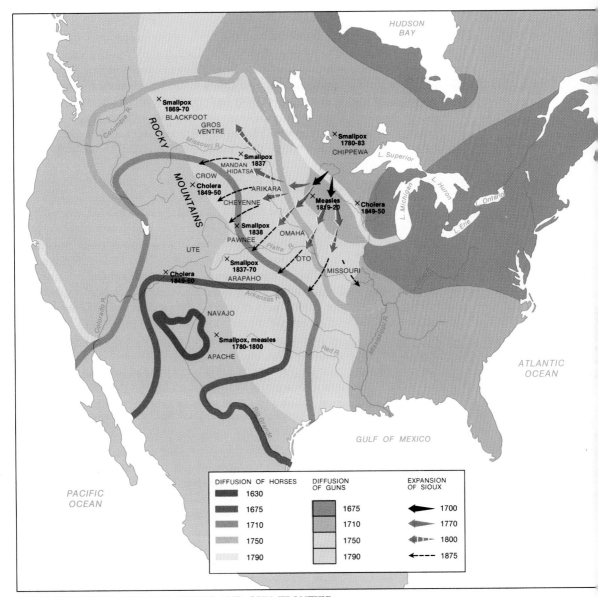

SIOUX EXPANSION AND THE HORSE AND GUN FRONTIER
In 1710 the horse and gun frontiers had not yet crossed, but by 1750 the two waves began to overlap. The Sioux pushed west during the early eighteenth century thanks to firearms; they were checked from further expansion until the 1770s, when smallpox epidemics again turned the balance in their favor.

DESTINIES: MANIFEST AND OTHERWISE

"Make way . . . for the young American Buffalo—he has not yet got land enough," bellowed one American politician in 1844. "We will give him Oregon for his summer shade," Texas "as his winter pasture," and "the use of two oceans— the mighty Pacific and the turbulent Atlantic" to quench his thirst.

In the space of a few years, the United States acquired Texas, California, the lower part of the Oregon Territory, and the lands between the Rockies and California: nearly 1.5 million square miles in all. To many a "young Buffalo," such acquisitions seemed only proper. John L. O'Sullivan, a prominent Democratic editor in New York, struck a responsive chord when he declared that it had become the United States' "manifest destiny to overspread the continent allotted by Providence for the free development of our yearly multiplying millions." The cry of "Manifest Destiny" soon echoed in other editorial pages and in the halls of Congress.

The Roots of the Doctrine

Many Americans had long believed that their country had a special, even divine mission. The Protestant version of this conviction could be traced back to John Winthrop, who assured his fellow Puritans that God intended them to build a model "city upon a hill" for the rest of the world to emulate. During the Revolution, many Americans, including the Reverend Ebenezer Baldwin of Danbury, Connecticut, expected that the colonies would one day become "a great and mighty Empire; the largest the World ever saw." Revivalists of the Second Great Awakening like Charles Finney (pages 416–417) spoke similarly of a coming Christian "millennium": a thousand years of peace and prosperity toward which America, by its example, would lead the way.

Manifest Destiny also contained a political component, inherited from the ideology of the Revolution. Baldwin, for example, had argued that the holy American empire would be founded on the "principles of Liberty and Freedom, both civil and religious." In the mid-nineteenth century, future president James Buchanan echoed this dream of a nation "extending the blessings of Christianity and of civil and religious liberty over the whole North American continent." By "civil liberty," he meant a democracy with widespread suffrage, no king or aristocracy, and no established church. In that sense, Manifest Destiny reflected the democratic reforms of the Jacksonian era. But it was a social and economic system, too, that Americans believed should spread around the globe. That system, they argued, encouraged a broad ownership of land, individualism, and the free play of economic opportunity. This doctrine had its self-interested side, of course, for American business interests recognized the value of the fine harbors along the Pacific Coast and hoped to make them American. As Senator Thomas Hart Benton proclaimed, the West was the road to India. By traveling it, a lucrative trade with the Orient would grow and flourish.

Finally, underlying other assumptions about Manifest Destiny was a persistent and widespread racism. The same belief in racial superiority that was used to justify Indian removal under Jackson, to uphold slavery in the South, and to excuse segregation in the North also proved handy to defend expansion westward. The United States had a duty to regenerate the backward peoples of America, declared politicians and propagandists. Their reference was not so much to Indians—who stubbornly refused to assimilate into American society—but to Mexicans, whose Christian nation had its roots in European culture. The Mexican race "must amalgamate and be lost, in the superior vigor of the Anglo-Saxon race," proclaimed O'Sullivan's *Democratic Review*, "or they must utterly perish."

Before 1845 most Americans assumed that expansion would be achieved peacefully. American settlement would spread westward and, when the time was

ripe, neighboring provinces, like ripe fruit, would fall into American hands naturally. Neither mountains nor deserts nor (in their eyes) backward cultures could
stand in the way. Nor did Americans doubt in which direction their country's
destiny pointed. Texas, New Mexico, Oregon, and California—areas that were
sparsely populated and weakly defended—dominated the American imagination.
As this destiny became more manifest (to them, at least), Americans became less
willing to wait patiently for the fruit to fall.

The Mexican Borderlands

The heart of Spain's American empire was Mexico City, where spacious boulevards spread out through the center of the city and the University of Mexico, the
oldest university in North America, had been accepting students since 1553, a full
85 years longer than Harvard. From the Mexican point of view, the frontier was
1000 miles to the north, reached over rutted trails by burro caravan, a four-week
journey to Texas, another two weeks to New Mexico, and three months by land
and sea to the missions of California. Spain had established these provinces as
buffers to protect its flanks from the Russians, whose traders had been wandering
down the California coast, and from French settlements in Louisiana. But being so
isolated, the provinces of California, New Mexico, and Texas developed largely
free from supervision.

California's settlements were anchored by four coastal *presidios*, or forts,
built by the Spanish at San Diego, Santa Barbara, Monterey, and San Francisco.
Between them lay 21 Catholic missions, each 14 leagues, or one day's journey,
from the next. Run by a handful of Franciscans (there were only 36 at the time of
Mexican independence), the missions controlled enormous tracts of land and were
the center of California's economic activity. Gigantic herds of cattle and irrigated
fields were tended by about 20,000 Indians, nominally converted to the Christian
faith, who worked for all practical purposes as slaves. In 1834 the missions' holdings included 400,000 cattle, 300,000 sheep and swine, and 60,000 horses.

Following Mexican independence, the demand for cattle hides
and government redistribution of
church lands created a flamboyant
new society in Mexican California
centered on the *rancho*. Forming
a rural aristocracy, the *rancheros*
controlled gigantic estates and vast
herds of cattle, supervised by
workers who were virtual slaves.

When Mexico won its independence from Spain in 1821, California at first was little affected. But as the Mexican Congress began carrying out reforms, it freed the Indians of California in 1833 and stripped the Catholic Church of its lands. These were turned over to Mexican cattle ranchers, usually in massive grants of 50,000 acres or more. The new *rancheros* ruled their estates much like great planters of the antebellum South. Labor was provided by Indians, who once again were forced to work for little more than room and board. Indeed, the mortality rate of Indian workers was twice that of southern slaves and four times that of the Mexican Californians. The *rancheros* lived in as much ease and comfort as their isolated existence allowed. They became famous for their lavish hospitality, horsemanship, broad-brimmed hats, and brightly decorated clothes. At this time the Mexican population of California was approximately 4000.

By the 1820s and 1830s, Yankee traders were sailing around South America and up the Pacific to California, bringing everything from cloth and axes to brass buttons adorned with eagles. Ships moved up and down the coast trading for dried hides and tallow; when their holds were full they set sail for home. As ranchers began to play off rival merchants, the Yankees established their own agents in California to buy hides year-round and store them in warehouses until a company ship arrived. These agents were the first Americans to settle permanently in California, and their glowing letters home lured others west. Still, in 1845 the American population amounted to only 700.

Spanish settlement of New Mexico was more dense: the province had about 44,000 inhabitants in 1827. But like California, its society was dominated by *ranchero* families who grazed large herds of sheep along the upper Rio Grande valley between El Paso and Taos. A few individuals controlled most of the wealth, while their workers eked out a meager living. Mining of copper and gold was also important, and here too, the profits enriched a small upper class. Spain had long outlawed any commerce with Americans, but in 1821 several traders from Missouri ventured forth, returning with the news (as one ingenious speller phrased it) that "the mackeson [Mexican] province Has de Clared Independence of the mother Cuntry and is desirous of a traid With the people of the united States." Soon yearly caravans were making the long journey along the Santa Fe Trail, banding together for safety in a single wagon train. Approaching their destination, the traders would wash, don bright handkerchiefs, and parade into town shooting pistols, cracking whips, and wending their wagons through the plaza to the cheers of Santa Fe's 3000 inhabitants. While this trade flourished over the next two decades, developments in the third Mexican borderland, neighboring Texas, eroded relations between Mexico and the United States.

The Texas Revolution

Just as the new government in Mexico had opened New Mexico to trade, it hoped to encourage emigrants to Texas, where only about 3000 Mexicans, mostly ranchers, lived. In 1821 Moses Austin, an American, received a grant from the Spanish government to establish a colony of 300 families. When Austin died, his son Stephen took over the project, laying out the little town of San Felipe de Austin along the Brazos River. By 1824 over 300 families had received large grants of land at almost no cost and the colony's population exceeded 2000. Stephen Austin was only the first of a new wave of American land agents, or *empresarios*, who obtained permission from Mexican authorities to settle families in Texas. Ninety

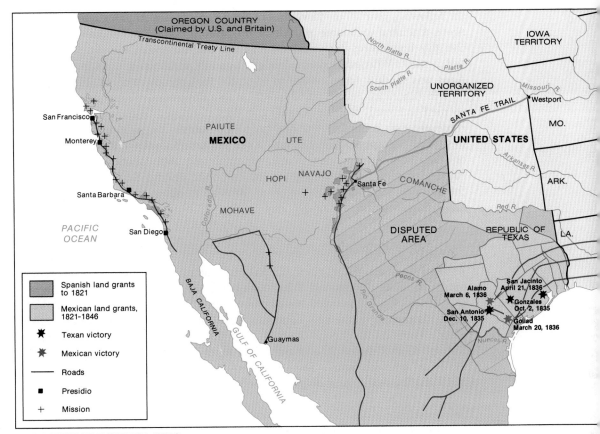

THE MEXICAN BORDERLANDS

percent of the new arrivals came from the South, and some, intending to grow cotton, brought slaves with them.

Tensions between Mexicans and Americans grew with the Texas economy. Most settlers from the States were Protestant, and although the government did not enforce its law that all citizens become Catholic, it barred Protestant churches. In 1829 Mexico abolished slavery, then looked the other way when Texas slaveholders evaded the law by forcing workers to sign lifetime indenture contracts. In the 1830s the Mexican government began to have second thoughts about American settlement and passed laws prohibiting any new immigration and levying stiff duties on goods imported from the United States. But Texans were most disturbed because they had little say in their government. Their province was allotted only 2 of 12 representatives in the more densely populated state of Coahuila, whose capital lay 700 miles away.

For a time, the Mexicans enforced these policies only erratically and in 1833 allowed American immigration to resume. But the flood of new settlers only made the situation worse, for by 1835 the American white population of 30,000 was nearly 10 times the number of Mexicans in the territory. The government also seemed determined to enforce the abolition of slavery. Hoping to work out a compromise, Stephen Austin journeyed to Mexico City in 1833, only to be thrown in jail because he advocated a Texan government independent of Coahuila. Events the following year seemed even more threatening when Antonio Lopez de Santa Anna, a general with large ambitions, dissolved the Mexican Congress, abolished the state legislatures (including the one in Texas–Coahuila), and proclaimed himself dictator. Worried Texans intercepted an official dispatch reporting that Santa Anna was sending troops north to reinforce the corrupt customs officials.

To Americans reared on tales of their own Revolution, the sequence of events seemed ominously familiar. Hadn't the English refused to grant the colonists full representation in Parliament? And hadn't a tyrannical king sent troops to America to support corrupt customs officials? As in the American Revolution, "committees of safety and correspondence" spread among the settlements, and when Santa Anna led a disciplinary military expedition north, a ragtag Texas army drove back the advance party and then captured Mexican troops in nearby San Antonio. A full-scale revolution was under way.

The Texas Republic

As Santa Anna massed his troops for a decisive attack, a provisional government on March 2, 1836, proclaimed Texas' independence. The constitution of the new republic of Texas borrowed heavily from the U.S. Constitution, except that it explicitly prohibited the new Texas Congress from interfering with slavery. Meanwhile, Santa Anna's troops overran a Texan garrison at an old mission in San Antonio known as the Alamo and killed all of its 187 defenders, including the legendary western figures Davy Crockett, Jim Bowie, and William Travis. The Mexicans, however, paid dearly for the victory, losing over 1500 men. The massacre of another force at Goliad after it had surrendered further inflamed American resistance.

But anger was one thing; organized resistance was another. It fell to the commander of the Texas forces, Sam Houston, to discipline his troops. Of striking physique and something of an eccentric, Houston had a flair for wearing gaudy clothing to attract attention (he once set tongues wagging by appearing at a ball in a suit of black velvet lined with white satin and sporting a large hat trailing plumes of feathers). His successful political career in his home state of Tennessee might have continued, except that the failure of his marriage led him to resign abruptly as governor and go live with the Indians. Eventually he made his way to Texas, where his intellectual ability, courtly manner, and unexcelled talent as a stump speaker propelled him to the forefront of the independence movement. His sturdy six-foot frame enabled him to endure great physical hardship, a quality that served him well as commander of the small Texas army. Steadily retreating eastward, Houston adeptly forged his ragged army into a disciplined fighting force.

By late April Houston was ready to fight. Reinforced by eager volunteers from the United States, Houston's army advanced along the San Jacinto River, taking advantage of the Mexican army's habit of enjoying an afternoon siesta. "Hold your fire! God damn you, hold your fire!" Houston commanded as his troops fell upon Santa Anna's startled men. With the first Mexican volley rattling overhead, the Texans fired and charged, shouting "Remember the Alamo!" Fif-

Sam Houston, the first president of the Texas Republic, often sported gaudy clothing. A staunch nationalist, he worked for the annexation of Texas to the United States. This detail from a portrait painted between 1846 and 1859 shows the aging lion's firm determination.

teen minutes of spirited combat ended in total victory and the capture of Santa Anna.

Threatened with execution, the Mexican commander signed treaties recognizing Texas' independence and establishing the Rio Grande as the southern boundary of the Texas Republic. The Mexican Congress (which had been reestablished in 1835) later repudiated the agreements as having been signed under duress and launched several invasions into Texas, none of which was successful. In the meantime, Houston assumed office in October 1836 as the first president of the new republic, determined to bring Texas into the Union as quickly as possible. (In a referendum, only 61 of the 6000 who cast ballots opposed annexation.)

As an old Tennessee crony of Andrew Jackson, Houston assumed that the United States would find the acquisition of such a rich and inviting territory irresistible. But Jackson worried that such a step would revive the debates over slavery and sectionalism. Since that might hurt Martin Van Buren's chances in the 1836 presidential election, Jackson temporized. Only on his last day in office did he extend formal diplomatic recognition to the Texas Republic. Van Buren, distracted by the economic panic that erupted shortly after he took office and fearful of stirring up sectional tensions, took no action during his term.

Rebuffed, Texans decided to go their own way and strengthen their economy. In the 10 years following independence, the Lone Star Republic attracted over 100,000 immigrants by offering free land grants of 1280 acres to families and 640 acres to single men. As Texas sought diplomatic recognition and economic aid from Europe, some of its citizens talked grandly of expanding their republic to the Pacific. But Mexico refused to recognize Tex ´ independence, and the vast majority of its citizens still wished to join the United States, where most of them, after all, had been born. There matters stood when the Whigs and William Henry Harrison won the presidency in 1840.

THE TREK WEST

As thousands of Americans were moving into Texas, a much smaller trickle headed toward the Oregon country. Since 1818 the United States and Great Britain had occupied that territory jointly, as far north as latitude 54°40', but the only white settlement of any size was the trading headquarters of the Hudson's Bay Company, along the Columbia River. Then in 1833, in response to a fanciful report that Indians in Oregon wanted to be instructed in the white man's "Book of Heaven," several denominations eagerly sent missionaries west. The first, Methodist Jason Lee, erected a settlement in the Willamette valley in 1834, only to discover that the Indians there had been largely wiped out by an epidemic. But what Lee lacked in converts he made up for by publicizing Oregon's virtues back East. By 1836 American settlers outnumbered the British in the Willamette valley.

Pushed by the Panic of 1837 and six years of depression and pulled by tales of Oregon's lush, fertile valleys and the frost-free climate along California's Sacramento River, many American farmers struck out for the West Coast. Missouri was "cleaned" out of money, worried farmer Daniel Waldo, and his wife was even more adamant about heading west: "Well, Dan Waldo, if you want to stay here another summer and shake your liver out with the fever and ague, you can do it;

Daily Lives

TIME AND TRAVEL

Seeing the Elephant on the Overland Trail

In an era when traveling circuses proved a welcome though rare attraction, Americans used the expression "I have seen the elephant" to indicate they had gotten all—or considerably more—than they had bargained for. To the quarter of a million men and women who migrated overland to the Pacific coast, "seeing the elephant" meant ceasing to be a greenhorn by overcoming hardship and succeeding. The greeting, "Have you seen the elephant?" became the unofficial password of the Overland Trail.

Some walked, rode horseback, or accompanied mule pack trains, but the overwhelming majority of emigrants traveled in wagons. There were faults aplenty with these: they were cumbersome, liable to break, and difficult to maneuver. But they could haul more pounds per animal, did not have to be packed each day, could carry the sick and injured, and could be arranged in a defensive circle at night. Most often, emigrants modified a common farm wagon, about 10 feet long, for their purposes. The wooden bed, which had to be of seasoned hardwood to withstand the extremes in temperature and moisture, was arched over by cloth or waterproofed canvas that could be closed at each end. Many owners adorned their wagon covers with personal information and slogans or decorated them with paintings and pictures of animals (the elephant was a popular choice), so they would stand out in the crowd. Because of the many streams and rivers to be crossed, the bottom was caulked or covered with canvas so it would float.

Pulled usually by four to six oxen, one wagon provided sufficient space to carry provisions and gear for a family of four. Most farm families were larger, however, and took at least one additional wagon. Packed within was a supply of bacon, breadstuffs (mostly flour), and coffee. Because fuel was scarce on the treeless prairie and water boiled at lower temperatures at high altitudes, rice and beans were not taken in large quantities. For sleeping, families brought blankets and frequently a tent; a well-equipped wagon might have a feather bed laid over the packed possessions in the wagon. Parents normally slept there for privacy while children used the tent.

Before starting, the adult male members of a company elected their leaders. In the first years, when trains often ran to 30 wagons or more, a complex set of rules and procedures was adopted. With experience, these were simplified. Often decisions were openly discussed and then made by majority vote. Disputes inevitably arose, and leaders were sometimes deposed midjourney. Samuel Tetherow recalled that his father, the captain of an 1845 train, "was capable as well as popular. . . . But if you think it's any snap to run a wagon train of 66 wagons with every man in the train having a different idea of what is the best thing to do, all I can say is that some day you ought to try it."

At first, overlanders were gripped by a spirit of adventure; this feeling soon passed, as the monotonous daily routine set in. Women rose before daybreak to cook breakfast and food for lunch; the men followed at around 5 to care for the animals; the train was off at 7 with the call of a bugle. Men and older sons walked alongside the team or herded stock in the rear. Women and children could ride in the wagon as it jolted along, but before long

Daily Lives

Leaving home   Arrival in California

Joseph Goldsborough Bruff's sketches of "Seeing the Elephant" on the way west included a confident overlander leaving home—and arriving in California.

they walked as much as possible to conserve the animals' strength. After a noonday stop for a cold lunch, the journey resumed; by midafternoon the men seemed almost asleep as they plodded under the baking sun beside their teams. At evening camp the men attended to the animals, which, in addition to the oxen, usually included at least one horse used for hunting, rounding up stray livestock, and scouting. Many emigrants drove cattle too, and families with small children often took a milk cow. Meanwhile, the women and children collected buffalo dung for fuel and hauled water. Women cooked the evening meal and afterward washed the dishes, took care of the bedding, cleaned the wagons, aired provisions, and mended clothes. After a guard was posted, the exhausted emigrants turned in for the night.

For most of the trip, travelers relied on the family as the basic unit of labor. Yet mutual assistance was critical, especially once the Great Plains were crossed and the Rockies loomed ahead. The final third of the route lay across deserts, along twisting rivers with numerous and difficult crossings, on narrow paths barely wide enough for a wagon, and over the Sierra Nevadas. Wagons had to be double- and triple-teamed up steep grades, and hoisted over canyon walls with ropes, chains, and winches. Since most wagons lacked brakes, drivers locked the wheels when going down steep slopes, dragged a weight behind, or lowered the wagon by a rope attached to a tree. Company members also worked cooperatively by selling or trading food, taking in individuals abandoned along the trail, and helping when members were too sick to work. At some desert crossings, a tradition developed: travelers used supplies left by earlier groups, then hauled water and grass back after they had safely crossed, to replenish the supplies for the next party.

Improvements in the 1850s shortened the trip and reduced the hardships. Still, it required considerable courage to embark on the journey and resilience and fortitude to complete it. "To enjoy such a trip," an anonymous overlander testified, "a man must be able to endure heat like a Salamander, . . . dust like a toad, and labor like a jackass. He must learn to eat with his unwashed fingers, drink out of the same vessel with his mules, sleep on the ground when it rains, and share his blanket with vermin. . . . It is a hardship without glory." When they reached their new homes, those who traveled the Overland Trail could boast that they had, indeed, seen the elephant.

but in the spring I am going to take the children and go to Oregon, Indians or no Indians. They can't be any worse than the chills and fever!" The wagon trains began rolling west.

The Overland Trail

Only a few hundred emigrants reached the West in 1840 and 1841, but in 1843 over 800 crossed the mountains to Oregon, and from then on, they came by the thousands. Every spring brought a new rush of families to Independence or later St. Joseph, Missouri, or to Council Bluffs, Iowa, where they waited for the spring rains to end and the trails to become passable. Meantime, they traded horses or mules, bought blankets and frying pans at street auctions, compared trail guide-books, and practiced snapping the whip over oxen to get the wagons moving. "Whoo ha! Go it boys! We're in a perfect *Oregon fever.*" The migration was pri-marily a family enterprise, and many couples had only recently married. Most adults were between 20 and 50, since the hard journey discouraged the elderly. Furthermore, the price of emigration was high enough to exclude most poor. A family of four needed about $600 to outfit their journey, although they could recoup two-thirds of the cost at the end of the trip by selling the wagon and oxen.

The Oregon Trail followed the Platte River to South Pass, where it made a relatively easy crossing of the Rockies, and then turned north and followed the Snake and the Columbia rivers to the Willamette valley. Several forks angled southwest to northern and central California. Caravans of 20 to 30 wagons were not uncommon the first few years, but after 1845, parties traveled in smaller trains of 8 to 10 wagons. Large companies used up the grass quickly, discipline was more difficult to maintain, and breakdowns (and hence halts) were more frequent. The trip itself lasted about 6 months, since the wagons normally covered only 15 miles a day, and the weather, repairs, deaths, and other eventualities necessitated occa-sional halts.

Women on the Overland Trail

The journey west placed a special strain on many wives and mothers, for the rugged life along the trail disrupted the sense of the home as a moral center and nursery for the family. What lay ahead, in an unsettled country far from older family ties? Not all wives were as eager as Dan Waldo's to find the answer. "Poor Ma said only this morning, 'Oh I wish we never had started,'" one daughter reported, "and she looks so sorrowful and dejected." Another disgruntled woman wondered "what had possessed my husband, anyway, that he should have thought of bringing us away out through this God forsaken country."

Sheer necessity put new demands on women and eventually altered their roles. At first, parties divided work by sex, as had always been done back home. Women cooked, washed, sewed, and took care of the children, while men drove the wagons, cared for the stock, stood guard, and did other heavy labor. Within a few weeks, however, women found themselves engaged in the distinctly unlady-like task of gathering buffalo dung for fuel on the treeless plains, or pitching in to help repair wagons or construct a river bridge. When men became exhausted, sick, or injured, women stood guard and drove the oxen. The change in work assignments proceeded only in one direction: few men undertook "women's work." And no matter how late the previous night's chores had continued, women had to be up before daybreak, ahead of the men, fixing a fire and the next morning's meal.

The extra labor did not bring women new authority or power within the family, nor, by and large, did they seek it. Women resisted efforts to blur the division between male and female labor and struggled to preserve their traditional role and image. Quarrels over work assignments often brought into the open long-simmering family tensions. One woman reported that there was "not a little fighting" in their company, "invariably the outcome of disputes over divisions of labor." The conflicting pressures a woman might feel were well illustrated by Mary Ellen Todd, a teenaged daughter who spent hours practicing how to crack the bullwhip. "How my heart bounded," she recalled, "when I chanced to hear father say to mother, 'Do you know that Mary Ellen is beginning to crack the whip.' Then how it fell again when mother replied, 'I am afraid it isn't a very lady-like thing for a girl to do.' After this, while I felt a secret joy in being able to have a power that set things going, there was also a sense of shame over this new accomplishment."

As women strove to maintain a semblance of home on the trail, they often experienced a profound sense of loss. The Sabbath, which had been ladies' day back home and an emblem of women's moral authority, was often spent working or traveling, especially once the going got rough. "Oh dear me I did not think we would have abused the sabbath in such a manner," wrote one guilt-stricken female emigrant. Women also felt the lack of close companions, to whom they could turn for comfort. One woman, whose husband separated their wagon from the train after a dispute, sadly watched the other wagons pull away: "I felt that indeed I had left all my friends to journey over the dreaded plains without one female acquaintance even for a companion—of course I wept and grieved about it but to no purpose."

Often fatigued, their sense of moral authority eroded, their ultimate home uncertain, women complained, as one put it, that "we had left all civilization behind us." Civilization to women meant more than law, government, and schools; it also meant their homes and domestic mission. Once settled in the West, they strove to reestablish that order.

Indians and the Trail Experience

The nations whose lands were crossed by white wagon trains reacted in a number of ways to the westward tide. The Sioux, who had long been trading with whites, were among the tribes who regularly visited overlanders to trade for blankets, clothes, cows, rifles, and knives. The Sioux were sharp negotiators, who "in every case get the best of the bargain," remarked one overlander, while another, Catherine Haun, asserted that the Indian was "a financier of no mean ability and invariably comes out A1 in a bargain." As white migrants flooded the overland routes, they took a heavy toll on the Plains Indians' way of life: the emigrant parties scared off game and reduced buffalo herds, overgrazed the grass, and depleted the supply of wood. Having petitioned unsuccessfully in 1846 for government compensation, the Sioux decided to demand payment from the wagon trains crossing their lands. Whether parties paid or not depended on the relative strength of the two groups, but whites complained bitterly of what seemed to them naked robbery.

Their fears aroused by sensational stories, overland parties were wary of Indi-

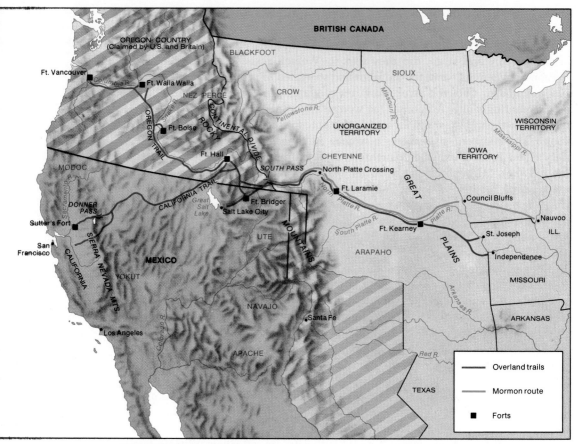

THE OVERLAND TRAIL
Beginning at several different points, the Overland Trail followed the Platte and Sweetwater rivers across the plains to South Pass, where it crossed the Continental Divide. The trail split again near Fort Hall. Between 1840 and 1860 over a quarter of a million emigrants made the trek. With news of the gold strikes in 1849, the flow of westward emigrants increased and shifted toward California.

ans, but this menace was greatly exaggerated, especially on the plains. Few wagon trains were attacked by Indians, and less than 4 percent of deaths on the trail were caused by Indians; in actuality, emigrants killed more Indians than were killed by Indians. Most attacks occurred during the last third of the trip, which was the most dangerous segment. Violence flared occasionally between whites and Indians, mostly after the number of travelers rose sharply during the 1850s, but for overlanders the most aggravating problem posed by Indians always was theft of stock. Many companies completed the journey without encountering a single hostile Indian, and others received valuable assistance from Indians, who acted as guides, directed them to grass and water, transported stock and wagons across rivers, and traded various goods.

As trail congestion and conflict increased, the government constructed a string of forts to protect emigrants and in 1851 summoned the Plains Indians to a conference at Fort Laramie. Although some tribes refused to attend, about 10,000

Indians assembled. The United States government agreed to make an annual payment as compensation for the damages caused by the wagon trains but also required tribes to confine themselves to areas north or south of a corridor through which the Overland Trail ran. This first treaty with the Plains Indians foreshadowed the reservation approach already in use east of the Mississippi. Some tribes were unwilling to surrender their freedom of movement and refused to agree; the Sioux, the most powerful tribe on the plains, signed and then ignored the terms.

THE POLITICAL ORIGINS OF EXPANSION

President William Henry Harrison made the gravest mistake of his brief presidential career when he ventured out one raw spring day, bareheaded and without an overcoat, to buy groceries at the Washington fish and meat markets. Shortly after, the 68-year-old president caught pneumonia and died, only a month into his administration.

For the first time in the nation's history, a vice president succeeded to the nation's highest office upon the death of the president. The prospect pleased virtually no one. John Tyler of Virginia had been a Democrat who supported states' rights so strongly that, during the nullification crisis, he was the only senator to vote against the Force Bill. After that, Jackson and the Democrats would have nothing to do with him, so Tyler joined the Whigs. The Whigs were hardly overjoyed, since Tyler was a strict constructionist and often suspicious of Whig plans to use federal power to develop the economy. But in 1840 they put him on the ticket with Old Tip anyway, in order to balance the ticket sectionally. In the rollicking 1840 campaign, the Whigs sang all too accurately: "And we'll vote for Tyler, therefore,/Without a why or wherefore."

Tyler's Texas Ploy

A proud Virginia planter, Tyler was extremely vain, a quality his marriage to a glamorous heiress 30 years his junior had only puffed up further. His courteous manner and personal warmth masked a rigid, doctrinaire mind. Repeatedly, when Henry Clay and the Whigs in Congress passed a major bill, Tyler opposed it. After Tyler twice vetoed bills to charter a new national bank, disgusted congressional Whigs held a caucus and expelled their president from the party, sarcastically referring to him as "His Accidency." Most Democrats, too, avoided the man they viewed as an untrustworthy "renegade."

Tyler, in short, was a man without a party. Surrounded by a small group of flatterers whom critics sneered at as "the corporal's guard," the president had almost no support in the country except among federal officeholders, who could be fired if they did not endorse him. Still, Tyler's intense ambition led him to covet a term of his own. His advisers, nursing their own personal and political dreams, convinced him that the right popular issue could win him another four years in the White House, either as a Democrat or as an independent candidate. These political operators began to whisper in Tyler's ear that the issue he needed to carry the 1844 election was the annexation of Texas.

That advice came mostly from Democrats disgruntled with Martin Van Buren and his followers. Van Buren was, in their eyes, an ineffective leader who had stumbled through a depression and in 1840 gone ignominiously down to defeat. They "mean to throw Van overboard," reported one delighted Whig, who caught wind of the plans. "There is music ahead." Van Buren's principal opponent was Robert Walker, a Pennsylvania Democrat who had moved to Mississippi. Walker and his allies set out in 1842–1843 to propagandize on behalf of annexing Texas. The campaign included rumors (inaccurate, as it proved) that Britain was ready to offer economic aid if Texas would abolish slavery. An independent Texas would block American expansion westward, and a free Texas would, in southern eyes, threaten slavery in the United States. Under his advisers' prompting, Tyler secretly opened negotiations to bring Texas into the Union. Convinced the nation would rally behind him, he sent the resulting treaty to the Senate for ratification in April 1844.

Van Overboard

As the politicians watched this drama unfold, they looked to see what position Clay and Van Buren, the two presidential front runners, would take on Texas. Although rivals, Clay and Van Buren were both moderates who wanted to avoid dividing their parties over slavery. The previous fall, Van Buren had paid a two-day social call on Clay in Kentucky, and they apparently agreed to keep Texas out of the campaign. In late April, both men issued letters opposing annexation on the grounds that it threatened the Union and would provoke war with Mexico.

As expected, the Whigs unanimously nominated Clay on a platform that ignored the expansion issue entirely. The Democrats, however, had a more difficult time. Under Walker's lead, the Democratic convention adopted a rule (used in 1836 and then dropped in 1840) requiring a two-thirds vote to nominate a candidate. When Van Buren won a majority but not two-thirds, the convention deadlocked. Finally, on the ninth ballot, the delegates turned to James K. Polk of Tennessee. Polk had been a supporter of both Jackson and Van Buren, but he was also pro-Texas. Having served in Congress for 14 years, four of them as Speaker, he was hardly unknown, but no one had expected him to be selected. The 1844 Democratic platform called for the "reannexation" of Texas (under the claim it had been part of the Louisiana Purchase) and the "reoccupation" of Oregon, all the way to its northernmost boundary at 54°40'.

Angered by their defeat, Van Buren's supporters in the Senate joined the Whigs in decisively defeating Tyler's treaty of annexation, 35–16. But during the presidential campaign, the issue would not go away. Tyler, who had been nominated as an independent candidate by an assembly of federal officeholders, was finally flattered into bowing out, leaving the pro-Texas voters to Polk. Henry Clay, on the other hand, found many southerners slipping out of his camp because he opposed annexation; backtracking, he announced that he would be glad to see Texas annexed if it could be done without war or dishonor and without threatening the Union. And in the North, a few antislavery Whigs turned to James G. Birney, running on the Liberty party ticket.

In the end, Polk squeaked through by 38,000 votes out of nearly 3 million cast. A 5000-vote margin in New York decided the election in his favor. If just half of Birney's 15,000 ballots there had gone to Clay, Clay would have carried the state and been narrowly elected president. Whigs poured out their wrath on the political abolitionists, charging that by refusing to support Clay, they had made the annexation of Texas, and hence the addition of slave territory to the Union, inevitable. And indeed, with only a few months remaining in his term, Tyler again asked Congress to annex Texas—this time by a joint resolution, which required only a majority in both houses rather than a two-thirds vote for a treaty in the Senate. In the new atmosphere following Polk's victory, the resolution passed (just barely in the Senate) and on March 3, 1845, his last day in office, Tyler invited Texas to enter the Union.

To the Pacific

Hardworking and intense, the humorless Polk pursued his objectives as president with a dogged determination. He lacked personal charm, was calculating and often deceitful, and was not particularly brilliant in his maneuvering. But the life of politics consumed him, he knew his mind, and he could take the pounding when the political brawling got rough. Embracing a continental vision of the United States, Polk not only endorsed Tyler's offer of annexation but looked beyond, hoping to gain the three best harbors on the Pacific: San Diego, San Francisco, and Puget Sound. That meant wresting Oregon from Britain and California from Mexico.

The new president brushed aside any notion of continuing joint occupation of Oregon with Britain. The American title was "clear and unquestionable," he claimed. To pressure the British, he convinced Congress to give the required one-year notice terminating the joint occupation of the territory. "Great Britain was never known to do justice to any country . . . on her knees before her," Polk insisted. His blustering was reinforced by the knowledge that American settlers in Oregon outnumbered the British 5000 to 750. On the other hand, Polk hardly wanted war with a nation as powerful as Great Britain. So when the British offered, in June 1846, to divide the Oregon Territory along the 49th parallel, he readily agreed.* The arrangement gave the United States Puget Sound, which had been the president's objective all along. Even more important, the settlement left Polk free to deal with Mexico, for by June the two nations were already at war.

The Mexican War

Texas, of course, had been the issue. In 1845 Congress admitted it to the Union as a slave state, but Mexico had never formally recognized Texas' independence and insisted, moreover, that its southern boundary was the Nueces River. Texans countered that Santa Anna had accepted the Rio Grande, 130 miles to the south, as the boundary. In fact, Texas had never controlled the disputed region, and if its claim had been taken literally, the Rio Grande border would have encompassed New Mexican territory all the way to Santa Fe—lands still controlled by Mexico. Polk, already looking toward the Pacific, supported the Rio Grande boundary.

When Mexico broke off diplomatic relations after Texas came into the Union, Polk countered by sending American troops under General Zachary Taylor across

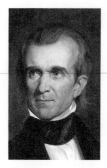

---

*Britain retained Vancouver Island, however, where the Hudson's Bay Company headquarters was located.

James K. Polk, continentalist (detail from an 1846 portrait by George Healy).

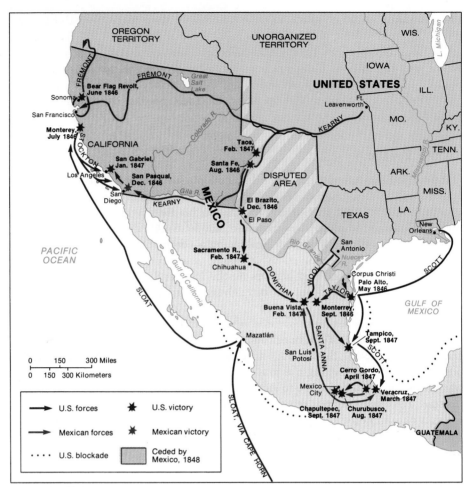

THE MEXICAN WAR

the Nueces. At the same time, knowing that the unstable Mexican government desperately needed money, he attempted to buy territory to the Pacific. Sending John Slidell of Louisiana to Mexico as his special minister, Polk was prepared to offer $2 million in return for clear title to the Rio Grande boundary, $5 million for the remaining part of New Mexico, and up to $25 million for California. But Mexican public opinion was so hostile to the idea of ceding more territory that the Mexican government collapsed for even permitting Slidell to set foot in the country. "Depend upon it," reported Slidell, as he departed in March 1846, "we can never get along well with them, until we have given them a good drubbing."

On orders from Washington, General Taylor had cautiously crossed the Nueces with 4000 troops in July 1845. For almost six months he camped on the south bank, hoping to prevent any clash between his forces and the Mexican army. Once the Slidell mission had failed, Polk ordered Taylor to proceed south to the Rio Grande. From the Mexican standpoint, the Americans had invaded their country and occupied their territory. For his part, Polk wanted to be in position to defend the disputed region if the two countries went to war. He also hoped that the Mexican army might attack Taylor's force and make war inevitable.

On May 9, the president resolved to send Congress a war message that cited Mexico's refusal to negotiate with Slidell as the reason to begin hostilities. As he began work on it, word arrived that on April 25 Mexican forces had crossed the Rio Grande and attacked some of Taylor's troops, killing 11 Americans. Polk quickly revised his war message, placing the entire blame for the war on Mexico. "Now," he told Congress on May 11, "after reiterated menaces, Mexico has passed the boundary of the United States, has invaded our territory, and shed American blood upon American soil. War exists, and notwithstanding all our efforts to avoid it, exists by the act of Mexico herself." The administration sent a bill to Congress calling for volunteers and requesting money to supply American troops.

Opposition to the War

The war with Mexico posed a dilemma for Whigs. They were convinced (correctly) that Polk had provoked it in order to acquire more territory from Mexico, and many northern Whigs accused the president of seeking to extend slavery. But they remembered, too, that the Federalist party had doomed itself to extinction by opposing the War of 1812. If Mexico had attacked American soldiers, it seemed political suicide to vote against Polk's request for supplies. Throughout the conflict, they voted for supply bills, but at the same time they strenuously attacked the conduct of "Mr. Polk's War." One young member of the House, Abraham Lincoln of Illinois, submitted a set of resolutions asking Polk to inform Congress whether the Mexicans living in the area where Taylor was attacked "have ever submitted themselves to the government or laws of Texas or of the United States, by consent or by compulsion, either by accepting office, or voting at elections, or paying tax, or serving on juries, or having process served on them, or in any other way." Lincoln, of course, knew the answer was no. Crossing the Nueces was invasion, pure and simple.

Sentiment for the war was strongest in the Old Southwest and most of the Old Northwest. It was much weaker in the East, where antislavery "Conscience Whigs" were prominent. "If I were a Mexican," Senator Thomas Corwin of Ohio affirmed in the Senate, "I would tell you, . . . 'we will greet you with bloody hands and welcome you to hospitable graves.'" In 1847 the Massachusetts legislature resolved that the war was unconstitutionally begun by the president, and that it was being fought to extend slavery and strengthen the South. With their party deeply divided over the issue of the expansion of slavery, Whigs opposed the acquisition of any territory from Mexico.

The Price of Victory

When the war began, a military exploring party under the command of Colonel John C. Frémont was already in California, and the Pacific squadron was off the coast of Monterey, waiting for official word that war had started. (In 1842, the previous American commander, under the mistaken notion that war had broken out with Mexico, had stormed into Monterey Bay and captured the town, only to return it with great embarrassment to Mexican authorities when he discovered his error.) In addition, Polk immediately ordered Colonel Stephen W. Kearny to march from Fort Leavenworth, capture Santa Fe, and then proceed to California.

Before word of hostilities arrived in California, a group of impetuous American settlers around Sacramento launched the "Bear Flag Revolt" in June and

The fortified heights of Chapultepec fell in 1847 to Winfield Scott's invading forces, but not without fierce resistance by young Mexican cadets. Like the partisans of the Alamo, who gained fame in Texas lore, the defenders of Chapultepec won an honored place in Mexican history.

proclaimed California an independent republic. Aiding the rebels, Frémont attacked the Mexican forces at Monterey and assumed command of the rebellion. The American navy squadron quickly captured Monterey and San Francisco and then transported Frémont's troops to the southern part of the state, where resistance continued. Kearny and his force soon arrived to aid in mopping up. By January 1847 California was safely in American hands.

Meanwhile, Taylor moved south from the Rio Grande, and in a hard-fought battle took possession of the major Mexican city of Monterrey. His popularity soared when a Mexican army under Santa Anna, who was back in power, attacked him at the Battle of Buena Vista. Although outnumbered four to one, Taylor's forces had the advantage of highly mobile artillery, which throughout the campaign helped him beat back Mexican assaults. Once Santa Anna retreated, the war in the northern provinces was essentially over.

Military victory gave Polk the territory he sought from the beginning; now he wanted only peace. But the Mexican people, inspired by nationalist fervor, refused to support any government that sued for peace, and so Polk decided to invade the heart of the country. An American army commanded by General Winfield Scott sailed to Veracruz in March 1847 and captured that key port. Scott then moved inland, brilliantly fighting a series of engagements, beginning with a decisive victory in the Battle of Cerro Gordo and culminating with the storming of the stone palace of Chapultepec, overlooking Mexico City. On September 14, Scott entered the capital and Mexico surrendered.

The war had cost $97 million and 13,000 American lives, mostly as a result of disease. Yet the real cost was even higher. By bringing vast new territories into the Union, the war forced the explosive slavery issue to the center of national politics and threatened to upset the balance of power between North and South. When the Mexican War began, Ralph Waldo Emerson had been prophetic: "The United States will conquer Mexico," he wrote, "but it will be as the man who swallows the arsenic which brings him down in turn. Mexico will poison us."

The Rise of the Slavery Issue

When the second party system emerged during the 1820s, Martin Van Buren had championed political parties as one way to forge links between North and South that would strengthen the Union. But the widening gulf between northern and southern interests so stretched the bonds of union that politicians from the two sections found it increasingly hard to work with one another. On the Democratic side, President Polk did nothing to ease this problem.

Polk was a politician to his bones: constantly maneuvering, promising one thing, doing another, making a pledge, taking it back—using any means to accomplish his ends. As his term wore on, the pro-southern bent of this Tennessee slaveholder embittered Democrats from the North and West. Western Democrats, for example, had struck a deal for southern votes to pass a bill to improve harbors and river navigation, voting in return with southern Democrats to lower the tariff. But then Polk vetoed the river and harbors bill. Northerners also complained that Polk had compromised with the British on Oregon at the same time that he had used military force to defend Texas' absurd boundary claims.

This festering discontent finally erupted in August 1846 when Polk requested $2 million from Congress, as he vaguely explained, to "facilitate negotiations" with Mexico. Everyone in Washington knew that the purpose of the money was to bribe the Mexican government to cede territory to the United States.

A group of northern Democrats had come to the end of the line. On August 8, David Wilmot, an obscure Pennsylvania congressman, startled Democratic leaders by introducing an amendment to the $2 million bill. The Wilmot Proviso, as the amendment became known, barred slavery from any territory acquired from Mexico. The measure passed the House of Representatives several times, only to be rejected in the Senate. Still, it revealed mounting sectional tensions. When first introduced, every northern congressman except two (both Democrats) voted in favor of the proviso, while every southern representative except two (both Whigs) voted against it.

Wilmot himself was hardly an abolitionist. Indeed, he hoped to keep not only slaves but all blacks out of the territories. Denying any "morbid sympathy for the slave," he rose to "plead the cause of the rights of white freemen. I would preserve for white free labor a fair country . . . where the sons of toil, of my own race and color, can live without the disgrace which association with negro slavery brings upon free labor." The Wilmot Proviso aimed not to destroy slavery in the South, but to confine the institution to those states where it already existed. Northerners who opposed slavery on moral grounds rallied behind the proviso, but the issue also attracted a much larger group of people—who felt that both slavery and blacks were a curse.

Abolitionists had long contended that slaveholders were an oligarchy—a "Slave Power"—that dominated the South and were consciously plotting to extend their sway over the rest of the country. The political maneuverings of slave-holders like Tyler, and especially Polk, convinced growing numbers of northerners that the Slave Power existed. To them, slavery seemed an aristocratic institution, which threatened the republican society established by the Revolution. Northern fears of a Slave Power, like southern fears of abolitionist conspiracies, disclosed the growing sensitivity to regional differences.

The issue of slavery in the territories became more than an abstract debate once Polk's representative in Mexico, Nicholas Trist, negotiated the Treaty of Guadalupe Hidalgo. Under the treaty, ratified in 1848, the United States acquired New Mexico and Upper California in return for approximately $18 million. That translated into a half million square miles of territory along with about 75,000 Spanish-speaking inhabitants. After the Louisiana Purchase, it was the largest territorial acquisition in American history. And with the United States in control of the Pacific Coast from San Diego to Puget Sound, Polk's continental vision had become a reality.

NEW SOCIETIES IN THE WEST

As Hispanic, Indian, Asian, and Anglo-American cultures mixed, the patterns of settlement along the frontier varied widely. Some recreated the farm economies and small towns of the Anglo-American East; others continued the cattle-ranching life of the Hispanic West. In California the new settlements were overwhelmingly shaped by the rush for gold after 1848. And in the Great Basin around Salt Lake, the Mormons established a society whose sense of religious mission was as strong as that of the Puritans.

Farming in the West

The overlanders expected to replicate the societies they had left behind. Once a wagon train arrived at its destination, members scattered in search of employment, a good farm site, or a town in which to practice a profession. Most families who completed the marathon trip were so low on supplies, they could hardly afford to waste time. "Friday, October 27.—Arrived at Oregon City at the falls of the Willamette," read one pioneer diary. "Saturday, October 28.—Went to work." For farmers, that meant clearing land and building a home. The high cost of transport made supplies and equipment expensive; furthermore, credit was not readily available, and markets were small and inaccessible. The Overland Trail took its toll on family possessions too, so that many of the cabins lacked the amenities that farm families had become accustomed to back East. "I baked 18 loaves of bread," recorded Mary Walker in Oregon. "A hard job for our old baker. What a handy thing an oven would be."

In the Willamette valley, the first large group of emigrants adopted a constitution setting up the machinery of government. Elsewhere, the process was repeated over and over again. Although violence was frequent on the frontier, farming communities, which contained many families, tended to resolve problems by traditional means. Churches took longer to establish, for ministers were hard to recruit, congregations were often not large enough to support a church, and many frontier settlers had grown indifferent if not hostile to religion. As the population grew, however, a more conventional society evolved: towns and a middle class developed, the proportion of women increased, and the population became more stable. The presence of women, both as teachers and as strong advocates of education, made possible the establishment of schools.

As towns expanded to serve the neighboring countryside, they provided stores, newspapers, cultural institutions, and better transportation. While opportunity was greater on the frontier than in the East and early arrivals had a special advantage, the development of the market and a transportation network meant that success and wealth would not be equally distributed throughout the community. More and more, the agricultural frontier of the West resembled the older society of the East. Wealth became concentrated, some families fell to the lower rungs of society, and those who were less successful left, seeking yet another fresh start.

The Gold Rush

In January 1848, while constructing a sawmill along the American River, a carpenter and engineer named James Marshall noticed gold flecks in the millrace. More discoveries followed, and by May eager prospectors were stampeding to the Sierra foothills. Word took a season to trickle east, then spread like wildfire, and the following spring the Overland Trail was jammed with eager "forty-niners." Some 80,000 emigrants journeyed to California that year, about 55,000 of whom took the overland route. The popular song that had once serenaded travelers to the boom country of Louisiana was quickly updated: "Oh, Susannah, don't you cry for me,/ I'm gone to California with my wash-bowl on my knee." In only two years, from 1848 to the end of 1849, California's population jumped from 14,000 to 100,000. By 1852 it stood at twice that figure, and in 1860 it was 380,000. California's glittering promise would always have a special allure for restless Americans.

For those intent on making a fortune and returning home, there was no question of putting down roots. Camps literally appeared and died overnight, as word of a new strike sent miners racing off to yet another canyon, valley, or streambed. Most settlements were hardly more than a single street, littered with debris and lined with stores, buildings, and miners' shacks—dirty, uncomfortable, and often no more than blankets or cloth tacked to a wooden frame in order to hold down costs. Almost always a saloon and gambling hall, which might double as a hotel and sometimes a brothel, was the most prominent building in town. Over 80 percent of the prospectors who poured into these settlements were Americans; most hailed from the Mississippi valley, but Yankees and free African-Americans were there as well. Mexicans, Australians, Hawaiians, Chinese, French, English, and Irish also came. Whatever their nationality, the new arrivals were overwhelmingly unmarried men in their twenties and thirties.

The constant movement, the hard labor of mining, the ready cash, and the rootlessness all contributed to the instability of camp society. "There is an excitement connected with the pursuit of gold which renders one restless and uneasy— ever hoping to do something better," explained one forty-niner. Removed from the traditional forms of social control, miners felt and behaved as if they had left civilization behind. Gambling, swearing, drinking, and fighting were commonplace. As a Denver paper complained during that territory's gold rush a few years later, as soon as "men of decent appearance" reached a mining camp, they "sang low songs, walked openly with the painted courtesans with whom the town teems, and generally gave themselves up to what they term 'a time!'" Secure in the knowledge that "their women folks were safe and snug in their distant homes . . . these [former] gentlemen announced that they were going 'the whole hog or none.'"

Only about 5 percent of gold rush emigrants were women or children; given this relative scarcity, men were willing to pay top dollar for women's domestic skills. Women supported themselves by cooking, sewing, and washing, as well as running hotels and boarding houses. "A smart woman can do very well in this country," one woman informed a friend in the East. "It is the only country I ever was in where a woman received anything like a just compensation for work." Yet women's earnings depended on those of the miners, and as the mines played out, their wages declined accordingly. Regardless, they suffered no shortage of suitors. "Even I had men come forty miles over the mountains, just to look at me," Eliza Wilson recalled, "and I never was called a handsome woman, in my best days, even by my most ardent admirers."

Women went to the mining frontier to be with their husbands, to make money, or to find adventure. By far the class most frequently seen in the diggings were prostitutes, who numbered perhaps 20 percent of female Californians in 1850. Many had practiced their trade elsewhere before coming to the mining districts. Those handsome enough to set themselves up in "high-class" houses made tidy fortunes. But for those who had aged or were less attractive, "cribs" were rented: tiny, foul, windowless rooms with a cot, a chair, and a blur of faces at 50 cents apiece. In such circumstances, life was grim, violent, and uncertain.

Predictably, mining the miners offered one of the more reliable roads to prosperity. Perhaps half the inhabitants of a mining town were shopkeepers, businessmen, and professionals who serviced prospectors; also conspicuous were gamblers, card sharks, and other shady characters, all bent on separating the miner from his riches. In such an atmosphere, violence was prevalent, so when a new camp opened, miners adopted a set of rules and regulations to govern it, including a mining code and local government. Justice was dispensed promptly, either by a vote of all the miners or by an elected jury. After witnessing one such trial, a European visitor commented, "I never saw a court of justice with so little humbug about it." While effective when administered fairly, the system at times degenerated into lynch law.

Observers spoke of the democratic spirit in the diggings. "The only capital required is muscle and an honest purpose," boasted one. Yet such assertions overlooked strongly held nativist prejudices: when frustrated by a lack of success, American miners directed their hostility toward foreigners, whom they scorned with such derogatory names as "greasers" (Mexicans) and "chinks" (Chinese). The miners ruthlessly exterminated the Indians in the area, mob violence drove Mexicans out of nearly every camp, and the Chinese were confined to claims abandoned by Americans as unprofitable. Efforts to exclude all foreigners from mining failed, but the state eventually enacted a foreign miners' tax, which fell largely on the Chinese. Free African-Americans felt the sting of discrimination as well, both in the camps and in state law. White American miners proclaimed that "colored men were not privileged to work in a country intended only for American citizens."

Before long, the most easily worked claims had been played out. Moreover, with 100,000 miners in the state by 1852, competition steadily drove down the average daily earnings from $20 in 1848 to $6 in 1852. That was still higher than eastern wages, but goods and services cost significantly more too. As gold became increasingly difficult to extract, highly capitalized companies using heavy equipment dominated the industry. Shafts were dug deep into the ground, high-pressure water jets tore away ore-bearing gravel, and veins of quartz rock were blasted out and crushed in large stamping mills. Virtually all of this was done by miners working for wages rather than prospecting for themselves. Thus control of the mining industry passed into the hands of capitalists and corporate executives. Men who had come to California filled with visions of wealth usually found only shovels of mud. And as the era of the individual miner passed, so too did most mining camps and the unique society they spawned.

Instant City: San Francisco

When the United States assumed control of California, San Francisco had a population of perhaps 200. But thousands of emigrants took the water route west, passing through San Francisco's harbor on their way to the diggings. Some stayed, others returned from the mines to settle down, and by 1856 the city's population had jumped to an astonishing 50,000. In a mere eight years the city had attained the size New York had taken 190 years to reach.

The product of economic self-interest, San Francisco developed in a helter-skelter fashion. Land prices soared, speculation was rampant, and commercial forces became paramount. The business streets presented a bedlam of noise and commotion, one visitor reporting that "the throng of men of all classes, characters, and nations, with carts and animals, equaled Wall Street before three o'clock." The city plan was a neat gridiron, but it paid no heed to the hilly terrain, and streets along the waterfront were projected precariously into the bay on piles driven into the water, until dirt from the hills being leveled could be carted down to fill in the cove. To complicate matters, south of Market Street the streets were laid out at a 45° angle to the original survey, which clogged the flow of traffic.

Commercial sentiment was so strong that almost no land was reserved for public use, and the city government took virtually no role in directing development. The town appeared insubstantial, with people living in tents or poorly constructed, half-finished buildings. Junk and rubbish littered the streets and goods were piled everywhere because of the lack of warehouse space. Property owners defeated a proposal to widen the streets, prompting the city's leading newspaper to complain, "To sell a few more feet of lots, the streets were compressed like a cheese, into half their width." The city's population was strikingly heterogeneous, and visitors reported that an amazing assortment of languages could be heard. Ethnic neighborhoods included Little Chile for South Americans, a French quarter, Sydneytown, where Australians dominated, Chinatown, and a Jewish section. In 1860, the city was 50 percent foreign-born.

The most distinctive of the ethnic groups was the Chinese. They had come to *Gum San*, the land of the golden mountain, because China in the 1840s had experienced considerable economic distress. Between 1849 and 1854, some 45,000 Chinese went to California. Like the other gold seekers, they were overwhelmingly young and male, and they wanted only to accumulate savings and return home to their families. (Indeed, only 16 Chinese women were recorded as arriving before 1854.)

When the Chinese were harassed in the mines, many found work in San Francisco as launderers. The going rate at the time for washing, ironing, and starching shirts was an exorbitant $8 per dozen; many early San Franciscans actually found it cheaper to send their dirty laundry to Canton or Honolulu, to be returned several months later. The Chinese quickly stepped in, for it took little capital to start a laundry—soap, scrub board, iron, and ironing board. Soon the price for washing shirts dropped to $2 a dozen. Other Chinese around San Francisco set up restaurants or worked in the fishing industry. In these early years, they found Americans less hostile, so long as they stayed away from the gold fields. In 1850 a San Francisco newspaper, the *Alta California*, predicted optimistically that "the China Boys will yet vote at the same polls, study at the same schools and bow at the same altar as our countrymen." As immigration and the competition for jobs increased, however, anti-Chinese sentiment intensified.

Gradually, San Francisco took on the trappings of a more orderly community. The city government established a public school system, erected street lights, created a municipal water system, and halted further filling in of the bay. Fashionable neighborhoods sprouted on several hills, as high rents drove many residents from the developing commercial center of the city. Industry was relegated to the area south of the city; several new working-class neighborhoods grew up near the downtown section. Churches and families became more common. By 1856, when the city and county were consolidated, the city of the gold rush had been replaced by a new city whose stone and brick buildings gave it a sense of permanence.

The Mormon Experience

The society spawned by the gold rush—in the makeshift mining towns and the chaotic progress of San Francisco—was a product of largely uncontrolled economic pressures. The society that evolved in the Great Basin of Utah exhibited an entirely different but equally remarkable growth. Salt Lake City became the center of a religious kingdom established by the Church of Jesus Christ of Latter-day Saints. Church members, known generally as Mormons, streamed west by the thousands during the 1840s. But unlike most families on the Overland Trail, they were united by a common faith and closely bound by persecution. Salt Lake City reflected the discipline and unity of their movement, whose roots reached back to the "Burned-Over District" of western New York, an area where the religious fires of revivalism flared up regularly.

The church had been founded in Palmyra, New York, by a young man named Joseph Smith. In 1827, at the age of only 22, Smith announced that he had discovered a set of golden tablets on which was written the *Book of Mormon*. The tablets, translated by Smith, told the story of some lost tribes of Israel, who came to America and established a Christian civilization, only to be exterminated by the Indians. Proclaiming that he had a commission from God to reestablish the true church, Smith gathered a group of devoted followers. Although he was a robust, cheerful, and magnetic person, Smith's unorthodox teachings provoked bitter persecution wherever he went: first in Ohio and then Missouri, where mob violence hounded his settlement out of the state. Finally he obtained a charter from the Illinois legislature to establish a Mormon community at Nauvoo. Thousands of followers settled there, but hostility again mounted after rumors circulated around the state that Smith had announced to his inner circle a new revelation sanctioning plural marriage, or polygamy. In 1844, following a dispute with dissident Mormons, the state threw him in jail in Carthage, Illinois, where an anti-Mormon mob murdered him.

Leadership of the church fell to Brigham Young, who lacked Smith's religious mysticism but was a brilliant organizer. Studying the reports of various explorers, Young decided to move his followers to the Great Basin. In 1844, the region was still part of Mexico, which had not authorized any settlement, but it could be farmed with irrigation and was a thousand miles from settled areas of the United States, promising the freedom to live and worship without interference. In 1847 the first thousand settlers began building at Salt Lake, the vanguard of thousands more who extended Mormon settlement throughout the valley of the Great Salt Lake. Thanks to energetic mission work in Great Britain and Scandinavia as well as the East, over 30,000 emigrants had moved to Utah by 1860, and the Mormons had established over 96 separate communities. In 1849 they erected the state of Deseret with Brigham Young as governor and applied for admission to the Union.

The Mormon success rested on a community-oriented effort firmly controlled by the church elders and Brigham Young. Families were given only as much farmland as they could use. Water for irrigation was owned by the community and the bishops assigned each user an appropriate share. And since church officials also held the government positions, church and state were not separated. Young had supreme power in legislative, executive, and judicial matters as well as religious affairs.

The most controversial church teaching was the doctrine of polygamy, which Young finally sanctioned publicly in 1852. Although the arrangement might have been expected to place special pressures on Mormon wives, visitors reported with surprise that few seemed to rebel against the practice. Some plural wives developed close friendships; indeed, in one sample almost a third of plural marriages included at least two sisters. If the wives lived together, the system allowed them to share domestic work. When the husband established separate households, some wives enjoyed greater freedom, since the husband was not constantly present. Many women testified that plural marriage was difficult to accept, yet because polygamy distinguished Mormonism from other religions, plural wives saw it as a badge of pride and as an expression of their religious faith. "I want to be assured of *my position in God's estimation,*" one plural wife explained. "If polygamy is the Lord's order, we must carry it out."

Temple City: Salt Lake City

Brigham Young and his advance party had laid out the "temple city" of Salt Lake in 1847, determined to avoid the commercial worldliness, speculation in property, and competitive individualism that had plagued the earlier Mormon settlement at Nauvoo. City lots were not sold but distributed by lottery; they could not be subdivided for sale, and real estate speculation was forbidden. Water and timberlands were held in common and their use was governed by church leaders. As one church apostle recalled, these rules "created a community of interest which could not have been felt under other circumstances."

The city itself was conceived on a grand scale, in a checkerboard grid well suited to the level terrain. Streets were all 132 feet wide (compared with 60 feet in early San Francisco), and each square block contained eight home lots of 1.25 acres each. Unlike early San Francisco, the family was the basic social unit in Salt Lake City, and almost from the beginning the city had an equal balance of men and women. Families were to use part of their lot to grow food in order to increase the community's self-sufficiency. Regulations specified that sidewalks were to be a standard width, and homes were to be set 20 feet back from the sidewalks and constructed of adobe. The planners also provided for four public squares in various parts of the city. As with the kingdom of Deseret itself, Salt Lake City lacked any traditional secular authority. The city was divided into 18 wards, each under the supervision of a bishop. Holding civil as well as religious power, the bishops were responsible for fencing, constructing irrigation ditches, and building and maintaining the bridges across the ditches in their wards.

By 1853 the city already covered four square miles. As the city expanded, the original plan had to be modified to accommodate the developing commercial district by dividing lots into sizes more suitable for stores. Experience and growth also eventually dictated smaller blocks and narrower streets, but the city still retained its spacious appearance and regular design. Through religious and economic discipline church leaders succeeded in preserving a sense of unity and common purpose in an urban setting, while making a "desert bloom."

Shadows on the Moving Frontier

Transformations like Salt Lake City and San Francisco were truly remarkable. But it is important to remember that Americans were not coming into a trackless, unsettled wilderness. As frontier lines crossed, 75,000 Mexicans had to adapt to the new American rule.

In theory, the Treaty of Guadalupe Hidalgo guaranteed that Mexicans would be "maintained and protected in the free enjoyment of their liberty and property." So long as Mexicans continued to be a sizable majority in a given area, their influence was strong. But as Anglo emigrants became more numerous, they scorned Mexicans and demanded conformity to American customs. When Mexicans remained faithful to their heritage, language, and religion, these cultural differences worked to reinforce Hispanic powerlessness, social isolation, and economic exploitation.

New Mexico had the largest Hispanic population as well as the fewest Anglos in the former Mexican territory. As a result, the upper-class Mexicans who owned the land and employed large numbers of mixed-blood workers on their ranches managed to maintain their position. This class had established American allies during the Santa Fe trade, and their connections grew stronger as American businessmen slowly entered the territory in the 1850s. Neither group had much interest in the lower-class Hispanics, whom both exploited.

In contrast, the rush of American emigrants quickly overwhelmed Hispanic settlers in California and Texas. Even in 1848, before the discovery of gold, Americans in California outnumbered Mexicans two to one, and by 1860 Hispanics amounted to only 2 percent of the population. Ironically, the descendants of the Spanish, who had opened their own American frontier three centuries earlier by exploiting Indians in the silver mines, now found themselves subject to the California "foreign" miners' tax and driven out of the gold fields by Anglo mobs who had equally firm notions about their own superiority.

During the gold rush, the 200 or so *ranchero* families (who together owned about 14 million acres) prospered because of the demand for beef to feed the miners. But changes in California land law required verification of the *rancheros'* original land grants by a federal commission. Since the average claim took 17 years to complete and imposed complex procedures and hefty legal fees, many *ranche-*

ros lost large areas of land to Americans. Lower-class Mexicans scratched out a bare existence on ranches and farms, or in the growing cities and towns. Despised by the dominant Anglo majority and without skills and resources, they were often reduced to extreme poverty.

Mexicans in Texas were also greatly outnumbered: they totaled only 10 percent of the population in 1840 and 6 percent in 1860. Stigmatized as inferior, they were the poorest group in free society. One response to this dislocation, an option commonly taken by persecuted minorities, was social banditry. Just as the Shawnee prophet Tenskwatawa a half century earlier sought to drive out American intruders and restore the purity of Indian cultures, a number of Mexican bandits gained fame by attacking and robbing Anglos. The most famous was Joaquín Murieta of California, a semifictional character whose legend actually drew on the exploits of several men. Another folk hero, less shrouded in legend, was Juan Cortina. A member of a displaced landed family in southern Texas, Cortina was driven into resistance in the 1850s by American harassment. He began stealing from wealthy Anglos to aid poor Mexicans, proclaiming, "To me is entrusted the breaking of the chains of your slavery." His sizable band of followers staged a daring attack on Brownsville in 1859, then eluded the U.S. Army by retreating into Mexico. Cortina continued to raid Texas border settlements until the Mexican army, under intense American pressure, finally imprisoned him. While failing to produce any lasting change, Murieta and Cortina demonstrated the depth of frustration and resentment among Hispanics over their abuse at the hands of the new Anglo majority.

ESCAPE FROM CRISIS

With the return of peace, Congress continued to debate what to do with its newly won territories, especially whether to allow slavery within them. David Wilmot had already thrown down the gauntlet of the northern opposition with his proviso to outlaw slavery in any new territory. John C. Calhoun, representing the extreme southern position, countered that slavery ought to be legal in all territories. The federal government had acted as the agent of all the states in acquiring the land, he argued, and southerners had a right to move there and take their property with them, including slaves. Only when the residents of a territory drafted a state constitution could they decide the question of slavery.

Between these extremes were two moderate positions. One proposed extending the Missouri Compromise line of 36°30′ to the Pacific. That approach would have continued the policy, dating back to the 1780s, of dividing the national domain between the North and the South. The other proposal, championed by Senators Lewis Cass of Michigan and Stephen A. Douglas of Illinois, was to allow the people of the territory rather than Congress to decide the status of slavery. This solution, which became known as popular sovereignty, was left deliberately ambiguous. Could settlers of a new territory prohibit slavery any time they wished or only at the time it was admitted as a state, as Calhoun argued? Hoping to avoid further polarization, Cass, Douglas, and other supporters of popular sovereignty left northerners and southerners to draw their own conclusions.

In 1848 the two moderate approaches would probably have appealed to most

Americans. Over the next decade, however, they became increasingly unacceptable to both the North and the South. When Congress organized the Oregon Territory in 1848, under pressure from the northern-controlled House, it prohibited slavery there, since even southerners admitted that the region could not support slave-labor crops like cotton, rice, and tobacco. But this seemingly straightforward decision made it impossible to apply the Missouri Compromise to the other territories. Without Oregon as a part of the package, the greater share of the remaining land would be open to slavery, something the North balked at. Almost inadvertently, one of the two moderate solutions by the summer of 1848 had been discarded.

A Two-Faced Campaign

In the election of 1848, both major parties tried to avoid disrupting national politics with the slavery issue. The Democrats nominated Lewis Cass, a supporter of popular sovereignty. The Whigs bypassed all their prominent leaders and nominated General Zachary Taylor, still basking in the fame of his victories in the Mexican War. Taylor was a southerner and a slaveholder, but he had not previously identified with the Whig party and had taken no position on any public issue. In fact, he had never even voted. The Whigs adopted no platform and planned instead to emphasize the general's war record.

But the slavery issue would not quietly go away. A number of dissatisfied factions came together to form the new antislavery Free Soil party. Alienated by Polk's policies and still angry over the 1844 convention, northern Democrats loyal to Van Buren spearheaded its creation, and they were joined by "Conscience Whigs," who repudiated Taylor's nomination because he was a slaveholder. Furthermore, political abolitionists like Salmon P. Chase left the Liberty party in favor of this broader coalition. To widen its appeal, the Free Soil platform focused on the dangers of extending slavery rather than on the evil of slavery itself. Allow it to exist in the present slave states, party members agreed, but any new states entering the Union must be free. "Free soil" as much as antislavery was the key. Ironically, the party's convention named as its candidate Martin Van Buren—the man who for years had struggled to keep the slavery issue out of politics. William Lloyd Garrison and other strong abolitionists saw the choice of Van Buren as an example of the compromises reformers would be forced to make in the political arena.

With the Free Soilers strongly supporting the Wilmot Proviso, the Whigs and Democrats could not ignore the slavery question. Since Taylor had taken no position on the subject, the Whigs ran a deliberately sectional campaign. Northern party leaders promised audiences that Taylor would not veto the Wilmot Proviso if it passed Congress, while southern Whigs insisted he would protect the interests of his native South. Similarly, northern Democrats claimed that popular sovereignty would allow the new territories to vote themselves free, while southern Democrats assured slaveholders that they would have equal access to territories won with the nation's common blood and treasure.

In this two-faced, sectional campaign, the Whigs won their second national victory. Taylor kept the core of Whig voters in both sections (Van Buren as well as Cass, after all, had long been Democrats). But especially in the South, where the contest pitted a southern slaveholder against two northerners, Taylor won many more votes than Clay had in 1844. As one southern Democrat complained, "We have lost hundreds of votes, solely on the ground that General Cass was a North-

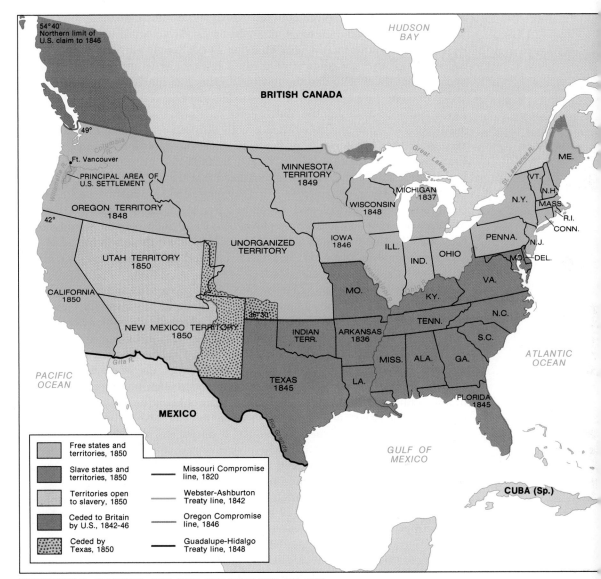

TERRITORIAL GROWTH AND THE COMPROMISE OF 1850

erner and General Taylor a Southern man." Furthermore, Van Buren polled five times as many votes as the Liberty party had four years earlier, further splitting the nation along sectional lines. It seemed that the national system of political parties was being gradually pulled apart.

The Compromise of 1850

Once he became president, Taylor could no longer remain silent. The territories gained from Mexico had to be organized; California, crowded with would-be miners, even in 1849 had gained enough population to be admitted as a state. In the

Senate the balance of power between North and South stood at 15 states each. Whichever way California went, it would break the sectional balance.

Taylor was a forthright man of action ("Old Rough and Ready," his troops called him), but he was an utter political novice. As an ardent nationalist, he decided that the way to end the territorial crisis was simple. Even Calhoun conceded that entering states had the right to ban slavery. The solution, Taylor therefore reasoned, was to skip the controversial territorial stage. So the president sent agents to California and New Mexico with instructions to set the machinery in motion for both territories to draft constitutions and apply for statehood directly. Even more shocking to southern Whigs, he indicated his support for admitting both as free states because he was convinced that slavery would never flourish in them. When Congress convened in December 1849, California had drafted a constitution and applied for admission as a free state. Taylor indicated that New Mexico (which then included most of Arizona, Utah, and Colorado) would soon do the same. All that remained was for Congress to admit these two free states and the crisis would be over. Instead, Taylor touched off the most serious sectional crisis the Union had yet confronted.

Into this turmoil stepped Henry Clay, now 73 years old and nearing the end of his career. Clay had been a savvy cardplayer all his life; he loved the bargaining, the wheeling and dealing, the late-night trade-offs eased along by a pint of bourbon. Thirty years earlier he had engineered the Missouri Compromise, and in 1833 he had helped defuse the nullification crisis. Clay decided that a grand compromise was now needed to end all disputes between the North and South and save the Union. Already, Mississippi had summoned other southern states to meet in a convention at Nashville to discuss the crisis, and extremists were pushing for secession. The issues rankling both sides went beyond the question of the western territories. Many northerners considered it disgraceful that slaves were bought and sold in the nation's capital, where slavery was still permitted. Southerners complained bitterly that northern states ignored the 1793 fugitive slave law and prevented them from reclaiming runaway slaves.

Clay's compromise, submitted in January 1850, addressed all of these issues. California, he proposed, should be admitted as a free state, which represented the clear wishes of most settlers there. The rest of the Mexican cession would be organized as two territories, New Mexico and Utah, under the doctrine of popular sovereignty. Thus slavery would not be prohibited from these regions. Clay also proposed that Congress abolish the slave trade but not slavery itself in the District of Columbia, and that a new, more rigorous fugitive slave law be passed. To reinforce the idea that both North and South were yielding ground, Clay combined most of these provisions (and several others adjusting the Texas–New Mexico border) in a larger package known as the Omnibus Bill.

With the stakes so high, the Senate debated Clay's proposal for six months. Daniel Webster of Massachusetts, always solemn and deep-voiced, seemed more somber than usual when he delivered a pro-compromise speech on the seventh of March. "I wish to speak today not as a Massachusetts man, not as a Northern man, but as an American. . . . I speak today for the preservation of the Union. Hear me for my cause." Calhoun, whose aged, crevassed face mirrored the lines that had been drawn so deeply between the two sections, was near death and too ill to deliver his final speech to the Senate. But he listened, a silent specter, as a colleague read it for him. The "cords of Union," he warned—those ties of interest and affection that held the nation together—were snapping one by one. Only

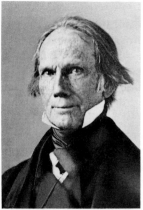  

The Great Triumvirate, Clay, Webster, and Calhoun, served the public together for almost four decades. Clay (left) and Webster (center) supported the Compromise of 1850, whereas the dying Calhoun's last speech opposed it. By midcentury, power was passing to a new generation of politicians more accustomed to sectional conflict and less amenable to compromise. (All pictures are details from portraits.)

equal treatment of the South and an end to the agitation against slavery could preserve the Union. William Henry Seward of New York, a younger voice speaking for the antislavery forces, proclaimed that "all legislative compromises . . . [are] radically wrong and essentially vicious." In the matter of human bondage, "a higher law" than the Constitution had to be obeyed.

Clay, wracked by a hacking cough, spent long hours trying to line up the needed votes. But for once, the great whist enthusiast had misplayed his hand. The Omnibus Bill required that the components of the compromise be approved as a package. But extremists in Congress from both regions combined against the moderates and rejected the bill. With Clay exhausted and his strategy in shambles, Democrat Stephen A. Douglas assumed leadership of the pro-compromise forces. One by one, he submitted the individual measures for a vote. By September 17, all the separate bills had passed and become law. Northern representatives provided the necessary votes to admit California and abolish the slave trade in the District of Columbia, while southern representatives supplied the edge needed to organize the Utah and New Mexico territories and pass the new fugitive slave law. On the face of it, everyone had compromised. But in truth, only 61 members of Congress, or 21 percent of the membership, had supported all of the Compromise or had abstained on one vote and supported the remaining measures. Nearly 80 percent had voted against some part of it.

Away from the Brink

President Taylor had threatened a veto, but he died suddenly on July 9, and the new president, Millard Fillmore, threw his support behind Clay and Douglas. The Compromise of 1850 became law and the Union, it seemed, was safe.

The general public, both North and South, rallied to the Compromise. At the convention of southern states in Nashville, the fire-eaters—the radical proponents of states' rights and secession—found themselves voted down by more moderate voices. Even in the Deep South, coalitions of pro-Compromise Whigs and Democrats soundly defeated secessionists in subsequent state elections. Nevertheless, most southerners felt that a firm line had been drawn. With California's admission, they were now outnumbered in the Senate, so it was even more crucial that slaveholders be granted equal legal access to the territories. They announced that any breach of the Compromise of 1850 would justify secession. During the 1830s and 1840s, few southerners had asserted the right of secession; but by 1850 a majority accepted it in the abstract as the South's ultimate recourse, although they refrained from exercising it.

The North, for its part, found the new fugitive slave law the hardest measure of the Compromise of 1850 to swallow. Denying an accused runaway a trial by jury, it provided that the case was to be decided by a special commissioner. The commissioner would receive a $5 fee if he freed the accused fugitive but $10 if he returned him or her to slavery. In addition, the law required that all citizens assist federal marshals in its enforcement. Harriet Beecher Stowe's popular novel *Uncle Tom's Cabin* (1852) presented a powerful moral indictment of the law—and of slavery as an institution. Despite sentimental characters, a contrived plot, and clumsy dialect, Stowe's story profoundly moved its readers. It described the plight of the slave without resorting to the harsh rhetoric of the abolitionists. Emphasizing the duty of Christians toward the downtrodden in this crisis, the book reached a greater audience than any previous abolitionist work, heightening moral opposition to the institution.

In reality, however, fewer than 1000 slaves a year ran away to the North, and many of those never reached freedom. Despite some cases of well-publicized resistance, the 1850 fugitive slave law was generally enforced in the free states. From 1850 to 1856, an estimated 200 blacks were arrested under its provisions, and only 12 of them were forcibly rescued. Many northerners did not like the law, but they were unwilling to tamper with the Compromise. Stephen Douglas spoke accurately when he boasted in 1851, "The whole country is acquiescing in the compromise measures—everywhere, North and South. Nobody proposes to repeal or disturb them."

And so calm returned. In the lackluster 1852 presidential campaign, both the Whigs and the Democrats endorsed the Compromise, and Franklin Pierce, a little-known New Hampshire Democratic politician, soundly defeated the Whig candidate Winfield Scott. Even more significant, the antislavery Free Soil candidate received only about half as many votes as Van Buren had four years before. The slavery issue was losing political force. To maintain party unity, both parties had abandoned sectional issues, and public opinion seemed willing to stand by the Compromise of 1850. It appeared that the Republic had weathered the storm unleashed by the Wilmot Proviso and could direct its attention once more to the economic development of the continent.

But the moving frontier still had changes to work. It had leaped from the Mississippi valley all the way to the Pacific, but in between remained territory still unorganized. And as the North became increasingly industrialized and the South more firmly committed to an economy based on cotton and the peculiar institution, the conflict between the two sections would shatter the Jacksonian party system, reinvigorate the slavery issue, and shake the Union to its foundation.

SIGNIFICANT EVENTS

1725–1850	Sioux expansion on the Great Plains
1821	Mexico wins independence; Santa Fe trade opens
1823	First American settlers in Texas
1829	Mexico tries to abolish slavery in Texas
1830	Mexico attempts to halt American migration to Texas; Joseph Smith founds Mormon church
1835	Texas Revolution
1836	Texas Republic established; Battle of the Alamo; Santa Anna defeated at San Jacinto
1841	Tyler becomes president
1842	Webster–Ashburton Treaty
1843	Large-scale migration to Oregon begins
1843–1844	Tyler's secret negotiations with Texas
1844	Tyler's Texas treaty rejected by the Senate; Joseph Smith murdered; Polk elected president
1845	United States annexes Texas; phrase "Manifest Destiny" coined
1845–1846	Slidell's unsuccessful mission
1846	War declared against Mexico; Bear Flag Revolt in California; Oregon Treaty ratified; Wilmot Proviso introduced
1847	Mormon migration to Utah; U.S. troops occupy Mexico City
1848	Gold discovered in California; Treaty of Guadalupe Hidalgo; Free Soil party founded; Taylor elected president
1849	Gold rush; California drafts free state constitution
1850	Nashville convention; Taylor dies and Fillmore becomes president; Compromise of 1850 enacted
1850–1851	South rejects secession
1851	Fort Laramie Treaty
1852	Harriet Beecher Stowe's *Uncle Tom's Cabin* published; Pierce elected president

15

The Union Broken

Into town they rode, several hundred strong, their faces flushed with excitement. They were unshaven, big, rough-talking men, "wearing the most savage looks" and "armed . . . to the teeth with rifles and revolvers, cutlasses and bowie-knives." Out in front of the procession, an American flag flapped softly in the warm May breeze. Alongside it was another flag, a crouching tiger emblazoned on black and white stripes, followed by banners proclaiming "Southern Rights," "South Carolina," and "The Superiority of the White Race." At the rear rolled five artillery pieces, which were quickly dragged into range of the town's main street. Josiah Miller, the editor of the Lawrence *Kansas Free State*, watched intently from a window in his office. "Well, boys," he predicted, "we're in for it."

For the residents of Lawrence, Kansas, a community of less than 1000 people along the banks of the Kansas River, the worst seemed at hand. Founded by the New England Emigrant Aid Company, a Yankee association that recruited settlers in an effort to preserve Kansas for freedom, Lawrence was the headquarters of the free state movement in the territory. Accepting Stephen Douglas' idea that the people should decide the status of slavery, the town's residents intended to see to it that under popular sovereignty Kansas entered the Union as a free state. Emigrants from the neighboring slave state of Missouri were equally determined that no "abolition tyrants," "negro thieves," or "philanthropic knaves" control the future of the territory. There had been conflict in Kansas almost immediately: land disputes, horse thievery, shootings on both sides—even two tar-and-featherings. (Actually, lacking feathers, the proslavery vigilantes had settled for tar and cotton.)

In the ensuing turmoil, the federal government seemed to back the proslavery forces, much to the anger of the free-staters. Finally, in the spring of 1856, a U.S. District Court indicted several of Lawrence's leading citizens for treason and federal marshal Israel Donaldson called for a posse to help make the arrests and to put down any resistance. That was all the encouragement proslavery forces needed. "War to the knife, and knife to the hilt," raged one proslavery newspaper, the *Squatter Sovereign*. Donaldson's posse, swelled to an army by eager volunteers from across the Missouri border, arrived outside Lawrence on the night of May 20.

Meanwhile, Lawrence's "committee of safety" had agreed on a policy of nonresistance. The next morning it instructed residents to give no provocation, not even to congregate in groups on the streets. Most of those indicted had prudently fled, but Donaldson arrested two men without incident; then, hoping to cement the uneasy peace, the proprietors of the newly completed Free State Hotel in-

A torchlight parade staged by the Republican Wide-Awakes, New York City, 1860. In remarkably few years, the new sectional party sensed victory within its reach in the presidential election.

vited several of the group to dinner, including Donaldson and former U.S. senator David Rice Atchison of Missouri. After the meal, Donaldson returned and dismissed his posse, announcing that his purpose had been accomplished. But Sheriff Samuel Jones, one of its members, had a score to settle. During his previous visit to Lawrence, someone had taken a potshot that wounded him in the back; now the irate sheriff, falsely claiming that he had a court order, took over the band and led its cheering members into the hated free state town at three o'clock in the afternoon.

The thoroughly liquored "army" quickly degenerated into a mob and, ignoring the pleas of some leaders, went on a drunken spree. The mob burst into the offices of two newspapers, the *Herald of Freedom* and the *Kansas Free State*, smashed the presses, broke up type, and threw assorted printing material into the Kansas River. Then the crowd unleashed its wrath on the now-deserted Free State Hotel, which, with its 18-inch-thick walls, concealed portholes, and parapet, resembled a fort. Sheriff Jones and his followers unsuccessfully attempted to batter it down with cannon fire; they then set off two kegs of gunpowder in the basement to no avail. Finally, after carefully confiscating the hotel's liquor supply, they put a torch to the building. After destroying additional private property, the mob, with a few final whoops and hurrahs, rode off, leaving the residents of Lawrence unharmed but thoroughly terrified. As they departed, a worried Atchison exclaimed, "And the eyes of the nation are on Kansas!"

Retaliation by free state partisans was not long in coming. Hurrying north along a different road to Lawrence, an older man with a grim visage and steely eyes that would not be shaded by his dirty straw hat heard the news the next morning that the town had been sacked. Old Man Brown, as everyone called him, was on his way with several of his sons to provide reinforcements. A severe, God-fearing Calvinist (some of his neighbors would have called him a fanatic), John Brown was also a staunch abolitionist who had once remarked to a friend that he believed "God had raised him up on purpose to break the jaws of the wicked." News that the free-staters had not resisted the "slave hounds" from Missouri made him livid. Brooding over these events, Brown decided not to push on to Lawrence; instead, he ordered his followers to sharpen their heavy cutlasses. When one of the other volunteers warned Brown to behave with caution, he exploded. "Caution, caution, sir. I am eternally tired of hearing the word caution. It is nothing but the word of Cowardice."

On the night of May 24, 1856, three days after the Lawrence raid, Brown headed toward Pottawatomie Creek with a half dozen others, including four of his sons. As a damp wind beat against their coats, the party silently approached a dark cabin, cutlasses drawn. When James Doyle, a proslavery man from Tennessee, opened the door, Brown and his men charged in, declaring that they were "the Northern Army" come to serve justice. Terrified, Doyle's wife Mahala stood in the shadows with her young daughter, crying. As Brown marched Doyle and his three sons off, she begged him to spare her youngest, and the old man relented. The others were led no more than 100 yards down the road before Owen and Salmon Brown set upon them, broadswords slashing and hacking, until the three men lay in a bloodied heap along the trail. Old Man Brown then walked up to James Doyle's body and put a bullet through his forehead. Before the night was done, two more cabins had been visited and two more proslavery settlers brutally executed. Not one of the five murdered men owned a single slave or had any connection with the attack on Lawrence.

In the days that followed, as guerrilla bands prowled the plains, prudent

The Free State Hotel was destroyed and burned by the proslavery band that attacked Lawrence, Kansas, on May 21, 1856. News of the so-called "Sack of Lawrence" greatly agitated northern public opinion and strengthened the struggling Republican party.

Kansans armed themselves when traveling. Families refused to open their doors at night; and the news of the tumult, as Senator Atchison had predicted, soon reached outraged audiences in both the North and the South. "Everybody here feels as if we are upon a volcano," remarked one congressman in Washington.

The country was indeed atop a smoldering volcano that would finally erupt in the spring of 1861, showering death and destruction across the land. Popular sovereignty, the last remaining moderate solution to the controversy over the expansion of slavery, had failed dismally in Kansas. The violence and disorder in the territory provided a stark reply to Stephen Douglas' proposition: What could be more peaceable, more fair than the notion of popular sovereignty?

SECTIONAL CHANGES IN AMERICAN SOCIETY

The road to war was not a straight or short one. Six years elapsed between the Compromise of 1850 and the crisis in "Bleeding Kansas"; another four would pass before the first blows between North and South were struck. And the process of separation involved more than hot tempers, bumbling politicians, and an unwillingness to negotiate. As we have seen, Americans were bound together by a growing transportation network, by national markets, and by a national political system. These social and political ties—the "cords of Union," Calhoun called them—could not be severed all at once. Increasingly, however, the changes occurring in American society heightened sectional tensions. As the North continued to industrialize, its society came increasingly into conflict with that of the South, while the Old Northwest, which had long been an ally of the South, became more closely linked to the East. The coming of Civil War, in other words, involved changes in the social and economic systems as well as the political.

The Growth of a Railroad Economy

By the time the Compromise of 1850 produced a lull in the tensions between North and South, the American economy had left behind the depression of the early 1840s and was roaring again with speculative optimism. The basic structure of the economy, however, was changing. Cotton remained the nation's major export, but it was no longer the driving force for American economic growth. After 1839, this role was taken over by the construction of a vast railroad network covering the eastern half of the continent.

By the 1840s most states recognized that railroads were essential to a thriving commerce, and construction of a national rail network was under way. By 1850, the United States possessed more than 9000 miles of track; 10 years later, it had over 30,000 miles, more than the rest of the world combined. During the 1850s, much of the new construction occurred west of the Appalachian Mountains—over 2000 miles in Ohio and Illinois alone. The South lagged behind the North, yet in 1860 almost a third of the nation's total mileage was located in the southern states. As rail networks expanded, they were also combined into integrated systems, or trunk lines, that brought long sections of track under a single management. The New York Erie, for example, ran all the way from the Hudson River north of New York City to Lake Erie. Soon after, Erastus Corning, an Albany banker and financier, created a rival line, the New York Central, by merging a number of small lines running from Albany to Buffalo.

To help secure adequate transportation, businessmen and farmers subscribed to railroad company stock. In heavily populated areas, where the freight and passenger traffic was heavy, investors usually profited quickly. Western railroads, however, ran through less settled areas and were especially dependent on public aid. State and local governments made loans to rail companies, invested in their stocks and bonds, backed them with government credit, and sometimes exempted them temporarily from taxes. About a quarter of the cost of railroad construction came from state and local governments, but federal land grants were crucial too. In 1850 the Illinois Central, which was charted to run south from Chicago to Mobile on the Gulf of Mexico, received almost 2.6 million acres of land from the public domain along its tracks. By mortgaging or selling the land to farmers, the railroad raised most of the needed construction capital and also stimulated settlement, which increased its business and profits. By 1860 Congress had allotted about 28 million acres of federal land to 40 different companies.

The effect of the new lines rippled outward through the economy. Farmers along the tracks began to specialize in cash crops and market them in distant locations. With their profits they purchased manufactured goods that earlier they might have made at home. A newspaper in Athens, Tennessee, noted that before the railroad reached its region, the surrounding counties produced about 25,000 bushels of wheat, which sold for less than 50 cents a bushel. Once the railroad came, farmers in these same counties grew 400,000 bushels and sold their crop at a dollar a bushel. Railroads also stimulated other areas of the economy, notably the mining and iron industries. By 1860 half of the domestic output of bar and sheet iron was used by railroads, and pig iron production stood at 920,000 tons, almost triple what it had been only 20 years earlier.

On a national map, the rail network in place by 1860 looked impressive, but appearances were deceiving. Roadbeds had not yet been standardized, so that no fewer than 12 different gauges, or track widths, were in use. Furthermore, cities at the end of rail lines jealously strove to maintain their commercial advantages, not wanting to connect with competing port cities, for fear freight would pass through to the next city down the line. Philadelphia, for example, was linked to the west through the Pennsylvania Railroad, to the north with two lines running toward New York, and to the south with a line toward Baltimore. But the two lines from New York stopped well short of Philadelphia, and the lines from the south and west did not connect with each other, even though they used the same gauge.

Still, the new rail networks shifted the direction of western trade. Traditionally, the mighty Mississippi, the Ohio, and the Missouri rivers linked the Old Northwest with the South. In 1840 most grain produced upstream was shipped by water to the bustling port of New Orleans. But there were disadvantages to water travel, even by steamboat. Low water made travel risky in summer; and by the time farmers in Missouri, Illinois, and the country of the upper Mississippi were finished harvesting crops, ice began shutting down river travel. Products such as lard, tallow, and cheese quickly spoiled if stored in New Orleans' sweltering warehouses. And transferring freight at the crowded harbor of St. Louis or New Orleans was woefully inefficient.

With the new rail lines, traffic from the Midwest increasingly flowed west to east. Chicago, which had no rail connections at the beginning of 1848, was served by over 2000 miles of track by 1855. It became the region's hub, connecting the farms of the upper Midwest to New York and other eastern cities. Loading and unloading freight was a lot easier beside rail warehouses and grain elevators than at river ports, where water levels rose and fell unpredictably. Whereas eastern merchants had enough capital to extend credit to western shippers, in New Orleans, as elsewhere in the South, capital was largely tied up in slaves. Thus while the value of goods shipped by river to New Orleans continued to increase, the South's overall share of western trade dropped dramatically. The old political alliance between the South and West, based on shared economic interests, was weakened by the new patterns of commerce.

The New Commercial Agriculture

The growing rail network was not the only factor that led farmers in the Northeast and Midwest to become more commercially oriented. Another was the sharp rise in international demand for grain. After 1846, the repeal of the protective English corn laws opened up English markets. European crop failures and the Crimean War (1853–1856) also increased demand. Wheat, which in 1845 commanded $1.08 a bushel in New York City, fetched $2.46 in 1855; the price of corn nearly doubled during the same period. Farmers responded by specializing in cash crops, borrowing to purchase more land, and investing in equipment to increase productivity.

Improved technology made it possible to meet the increased demand. John Deere's steel plow allowed midwestern farmers to cut through the thick roots of prairie grass without the soil sticking to the blade. Cyrus McCormick refined a

The Geography of Railroads

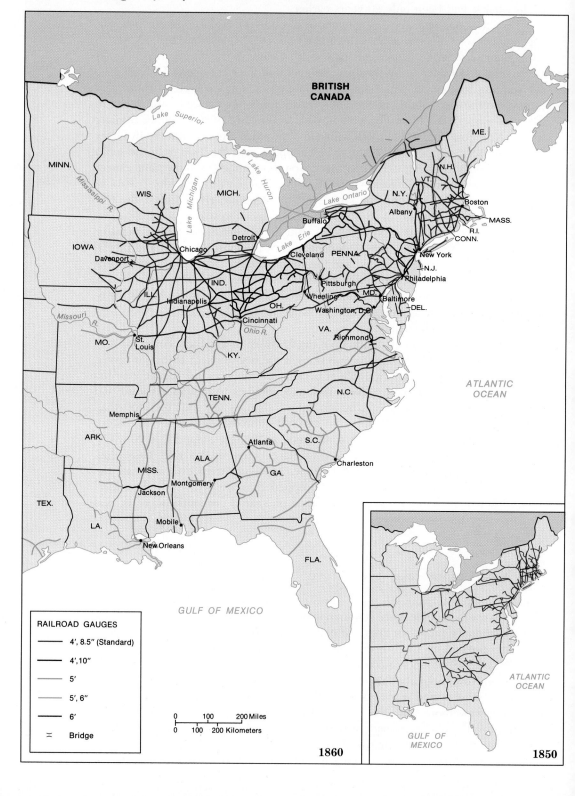

BRITISH CANADA

ME.

N.H.

VT.

MINN.

Lake Superior

Lake Huron

Lake Michigan

WIS.

MICH.

Lake Ontario

N.Y.

Albany

Boston

MASS.

R.I.

CONN.

Buffalo

Lake Erie

IOWA

Davenport

Chicago

Detroit

Cleveland

PENNA.

New York

N.J.

Philadelphia

IND.

Pittsburgh

Wheeling

MD.

Baltimore

DEL.

Indianapolis

OH.

Washington, D.C.

Missouri R.

Mississippi R.

MO.

St. Louis

Cincinnati

Ohio R.

VA.

Richmond

ATLANTIC OCEAN

KY.

TENN.

N.C.

Memphis

ARK.

Atlanta

S.C.

ALA.

Charleston

MISS.

GA.

Montgomery

Jackson

TEX.

Mobile

LA.

New Orleans

FLA.

GULF OF MEXICO

RAILROAD GAUGES

— 4', 8.5" (Standard)

— 4', 10"

— 5'

— 5', 6"

— 6'

≍ Bridge

0   100   200 Miles

0   100   200 Kilometers

1860

ATLANTIC OCEAN

GULF OF MEXICO

1850

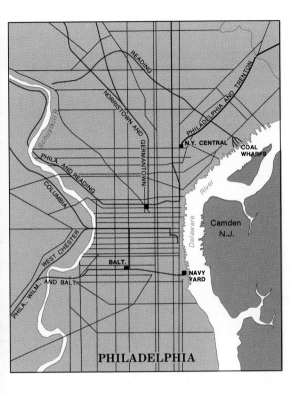

PHILADELPHIA

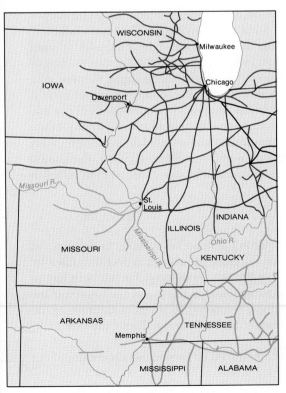

During the 1850s, a significant amount of railroad track was laid in the United States. Total track mileage is misleading, however. Despite the cobweb of lines crisscrossing the nation, the United States still lacked a fully integrated rail network in 1860. A few trunk-line roads had combined a number of smaller lines into a single system to facilitate shipment; the Baltimore and Ohio, for example, extended to Wheeling on the Ohio River, and the Pennsylvania connected Philadelphia and Pittsburgh. But the existence of five major track gauges, as well as additional minor ones, meant that passengers and freight often had to be transferred from one line to the next. North-south traffic was disrupted not only by gauge differentials, but also by the lack of bridges over the Ohio.

Even in a city like Philadelphia, where most of the railroads were the same gauge, traffic was hindered by the failure to connect the different lines. Passengers and freight had to be transported in wagons, carts, and coaches through the city's crowded streets to another line. Teamsters, cartmen, stagecoach drivers, and others whose livelihood depended on the need for local transportation bitterly fought efforts to link rail lines.

In the decade before the Civil War, railroad construction produced a dramatic shift in the economic orientation of the West. Before 1850, western trade had flowed primarily down the Ohio and Mississippi rivers on steamboats to St. Louis and New Orleans. In the 1850s, however, railroads transported an increasing proportion of western grains and foodstuffs eastward to New York, Philadelphia, and other major cities. Recognizing this threat to the steamboat industry, the St. Louis Chamber of Commerce tried to prevent construction of a crucial railroad bridge over the Mississippi near Davenport, Iowa; indeed the Chamber's attorney was even jailed on suspicion of attempted arson. But by the end of the decade, Illinois rail lines reached into Iowa and Missouri, and Chicago had emerged as the major rail hub of the Midwest.

mechanical reaper. Problems in harvesting had long limited the amount of grain farmers could grow, for they had only a short time to cut it before it spoiled. The reaper allowed as much as 14 times more wheat to be harvested with the same amount of labor. John Deere established a factory in Moline, Illinois, in 1847, the same year that McCormick set up headquarters in Chicago. McCormick was soon selling 1000 reapers a year and could not keep up with demand, while Deere turned out 10,000 plows annually.

By 1860 midwestern states produced for market more wheat, corn, beef, and pork than any other region. Again the shift in commercial agriculture had an effect on the political balance. "The power of cotton over the financial affairs of the Union has in the last few years rapidly diminished," the *Democratic Review* remarked in 1849, "and bread stuffs will now become the governing power."

Rising Industrialization

On the eve of the Civil War, 60 percent of the American labor force was still employed in agriculture. But in 1860 for the first time, less than half the workers in the North were engaged in agriculture. The expansion of commercial agriculture spurred the growth of industrial labor, for out of the 10 leading American industries, 8 processed raw materials produced by agriculture; these included flour milling and the manufacture of textiles, shoes, and woolens. The only exceptions were iron and machinery. Industrial growth also spurted during the 1850s as water power was increasingly replaced by steam. Only a fixed number of rivers and falls were available for water-power sites, and in the Northeast, these had largely been occupied. For industry to spread, another source of power was essential.

Most important, the factory system of organizing labor and the technology of interchangeable parts spread to other areas of the economy. The textile industry, we have seen, first brought workers together in factories. Many industries during the 1850s adopted interchangeable parts, which required that a product's components be machined to very fine tolerances. Isaac Singer began using them in 1851 to mass produce sewing machines, an invention patented only five years earlier. In turn, sewing machines made possible the ready-made clothing industry, while shoe manufacturers adapted the machines to concentrate all steps of their production under a single roof. Similarly, the workers who assembled farm implements performed a single step in the process over and over again. By 1860, the United States had nearly a billion dollars invested in manufacturing, almost twice as much as in 1849.

Immigration

The surge of industry depended on having a large labor force to support the factory system. Natural increase helped swell the population to over 30 million by 1860, but this accounted for only part of the new labor force, for the birth rate in the United States had actually begun to decline. On the eve of the Civil War the average white mother bore five children, compared to seven at the turn of the century. But the beginning of mass immigration to America during the mid-1840s kept population growth soaring.

In the 20 years from 1820 to 1840, about 700,000 newcomers had entered the United States. That figure jumped to 1.7 million in the 1840s, then to 2.6 million in the 1850s. Though even greater numbers arrived after the Civil War, as a percentage of the nation's total population, the wave from 1845 to 1854 was the largest influx of immigrants in American history. From the British Isles alone, a fleet of 1000 ships transported immigrants back and forth; in 1854, one of the heaviest years, 51 ships left Liverpool in June, carrying nearly 22,000 passengers. Whether traveling as individuals or as families, most of the newcomers were young people in the prime of life: in 1856 out of 224,000 arrivals, only 31,000 were under 10 and 20,000 were over 40.

Although fares were low, the journey, which lasted from six weeks to three months depending on the weather, was anything but comfortable. The cheapest passage was the cramped, crowded quarters of steerage, where the food was bad, the air noxious, and sanitation inadequate. Sickness weakened the passengers, and sometimes epidemics decimated them. "Dyin' like rotten sheep thrown into a pit," one Irish immigrant recalled, "and the minit the breath is out of our bodies, flung into the sea to be eaten up by them horrid sharks." Once disembarked in the United States, newcomers were set upon by runners for various boardinghouses and railroad companies, as well as swindlers who tried to take advantage of them. Tickets, printed with enticing pictures of a train, steamboat, or canal packet, were hawked at exorbitant rates, after which hopeful immigrants might find themselves herded, for example, onto a "night boat" from New York to Albany, with no shelter from the rain or cold, and only a hard deck to sleep on. Deaths from exposure on the lines to Albany alone were estimated in the thousands.

Certainly the booming economy and the lure of freedom drew immigrants to America, but they were also pushed by deteriorating conditions in Europe. In Ireland, a potato blight which struck in 1846 produced widespread famine. Already desperately poor and oppressed by English landlords, the Irish faced hunger, starvation, and the ravages of epidemics that swept across the Emerald Isle. Out of an Irish population of 9 million, as many as a million perished, while a million and a half more emigrated, two-thirds to the United States. The tide continued, though at a lesser rate, even after the potato crop recovered in 1849.

The Irish tended to be poorer than other immigrant groups of the day, generally younger sons and daughters of farm families, who had become a burden to their families because Irish landholdings and farms were so small. Mostly unmarried, they often arrived as individuals rather than as part of a family, and they sent money home to support their relatives. Although the Protestant Scotch-Irish con-

New York was the major port of entry for immigrants in the 1840s and 1850s. Here a group of Irish immigrants debark at New York in 1847.

tinued to emigrate, as they had in large numbers during the eighteenth century, the decided majority of the Irish who came after 1845 were Catholic. Because they were poor and unskilled, the Irish congregated in the cities, where the women performed domestic service and took factory jobs and men did manual labor.

Germans and Scandinavians also had economic reasons for leaving Europe. They might be small farmers whose lands had become marginal or who had been displaced by landlords, or skilled workers thrown out of work by industrialization. Others fled religious persecution. Some, particularly among the Germans, left after the liberal revolutions of 1848 failed. Many celebrated the free institutions of the United States and advertised them in letters home. "I am living in God's noble and free soil, neither am I a slave under others," wrote a Swede who settled in Iowa in 1850. Since coming to America, he added, "I have not been compelled to pay a penny for the privilege of living. Neither is my cap worn out from lifting it in the presence of gentlemen." An approving Dutch woman reported that schools were free, taxes low, and while "the finery is great, one cannot discern any difference between the cobbler's wife and the wife of a prominent gentleman."

Immigration reached its highest levels during periods of prosperity, then declined significantly after 1857, when the country entered another depression. Newcomers testified that the pace of work was faster and more regular in the United States, but wages were high and the food abundant and cheap. "Nearly all people eat meat three times a day," marveled a woman from Holland.

Although many Germans and Scandinavians arrived in modest straits, few were truly impoverished, and many could afford to buy a farm or start a business. Scandinavians and the Dutch were most often farmers; Germans included workers and shopkeepers and thus settled in cities and towns as well as the countryside. Unlike the Irish, Germans tended to emigrate as families, and wherever they settled they formed social, religious, and cultural organizations to maintain their language and customs. Whereas the Scandinavians, Dutch, and English immigrants were Protestant, half or more of the Germans were Catholics.

As a result of the immigrant tide, many American cities by 1860 contained a sizable foreign-born population. The Irish were especially numerous in eastern cities, particularly Boston, New York, and Philadelphia. Germans had established enclaves there too, but they were more dominant in western cities like Cincinnati, Chicago, Milwaukee, and St. Louis. By 1860 a majority of the population in Chicago, St. Louis, and San Francisco was foreign-born.

Factories came more and more to depend on immigrant labor, since newcomers would work for lower wages and were less willing to protest harsh working conditions. The meager pay seldom supported a family, so both parents and all but the youngest children often had to work. The shift to an immigrant work force could be seen most clearly in the textile industry, where over half the workers in New England mills were foreign-born by 1860. Mostly Irish, they found that American employers gave them only the lower paying jobs and excluded them from company housing. Rising ethnic tensions between native- and foreign-born workers, as well as among immigrants of various nationalities, made it difficult for workers to unite.

The massive influx of immigrants also strained city resources. Immigrants who could barely make ends meet were forced to live in overcrowded, unheated tenement houses, damp cellars, and even shacks. A building might appear as "a high, respectable-looking brick house on the outside," one New York journalist reported, but "within, the hall was dark and reeking with the worst filth. . . . The upper part of the house was filled with little narrow rooms, each one having five or six occupants; all very filthy. The people seemed very poor, honest Irish, not long here, and without work, usually." Such urban slums became notorious for crime and drinking, which took a heavy toll on families and the poor. In the eyes of many native-born Americans, immigrants were to blame for driving down factory wages and pushing American workers out of jobs. Overarching these complaints was a fear that America might not be able to assimilate the new groups, with their unfamiliar social customs, strange languages, national pride, and foreign traditions. Such fears precipitated an outburst of political nativism in the mid-1850s.

Southern Complaints

Industrialization affected the South, too, though in different ways. With British and northern factories buying cotton in unprecedented quantities, southern planters prospered in the 1850s. Like those of northern commercial farmers, their operations became more highly capitalized to keep up with the demand. But northern capital went into machinery like McCormick's harvester; white south-

---

SLAVE PRICES VERSUS COTTON PRICES
From 1815 to 1850, cotton and slave prices generally moved together, as southerners plowed their profits from growing cotton into buying more land and slaves. During the 1850s, however, the booming southern economy and bumper cotton crops drove the price of slaves steeply upward compared to cotton prices, squeezing slaveowners' profit margins and heightening southern anxieties about the future.

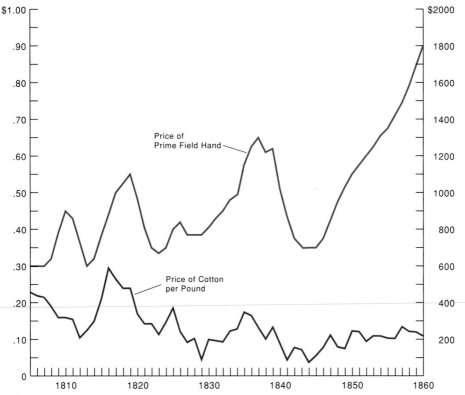

erners invested in slaves. During the 1850s, the price of prime field hands reached record levels at New Orleans and other southern markets.

Still, a number of southern nationalists, who advocated that the South should be a separate nation, pressed for greater industrialization to make the region more independent. "At present, the North fattens and grows rich upon the South," one Alabama newspaper complained in 1851.

> We purchase all our luxuries and necessities from the North. . . . Our slaves are clothed with Northern manufactured goods, have Northern hats and shoes, work with Northern hoes, ploughs, and other implements. . . . The slaveholder dresses in Northern goods, rides in a Northern saddle . . . sports his Northern carriage . . . reads Northern books. . . . In Northern vessels his products are carried to market, his cotton is ginned with Northern gins, his sugar is crushed and preserved by Northern machinery; his rivers are navigated by Northern steamboats.

So long as investments in cotton and slaves absorbed most of the South's capital, efforts to promote southern industry were doomed. Even with northern rail networks siphoning away the trade of western farmers, southern planters found railroads a less attractive investment, since these roads' profits were limited by the region's dispersed population, lack of cities, and restricted domestic market.

Despite southern prosperity, the section's leaders repeatedly complained that the North had used its power over banking and commerce to convert the South into a colony. In the absence of any significant southern shipping, northern middlemen controlled the South's commodities through a complex series of transfers from planter to manufacturer. Storage and shipping charges, insurance, port fees, and commissions, which added an estimated 20 percent to the cost of cotton and other commodities, went into the pockets of northern merchants, shippers, and bankers. Rather than viewing this as part of the process necessary for international trade, southerners complained that northern middlemen were nonproducing parasites. The idea that the South was a colony of the North was inaccurate, but southerners found it a convincing explanation of the North's growing wealth. More important, it reinforced their resistance to federal aid for economic development, which they were convinced would inevitably enrich the North at southern expense. This attitude further weakened the South's political alliance with the West, which needed federal aid for transportation.

White southerners also feared that the new tide of immigration would shift the sectional balance of power. Immigrants did settle in the South's few cities (in 1860 New Orleans' white population was 44 percent foreign-born) and some German farmers settled in Texas. But for the most part immigrants shunned the South because they did not want to compete with cheap slave labor. The lack of industry and the limited demand for skilled labor also shunted immigrants northward. As a result, the North surged even further ahead of the South in population, thereby strengthening its control of the House of Representatives and heightening southern concern that the North would rapidly settle the western territories.

THE POLITICAL REALIGNMENT OF THE 1850s

When Franklin Pierce (he pronounced it "Purse") assumed the presidency in 1853, he was only 48 years old, the youngest man yet to be elected president. He

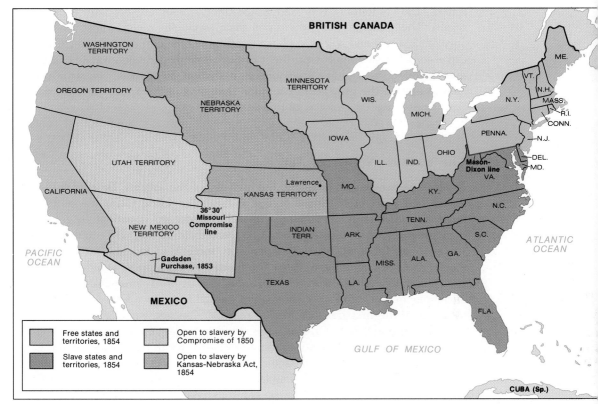

THE KANSAS-NEBRASKA ACT
When the Kansas-Nebraska Act of 1854 opened the remaining portion of the Louisiana Purchase to slavery under the doctrine of popular sovereignty, conflict between the two sections focused on control of Kansas, directly west of the slave state of Missouri.

was also a supporter of the "Young America" movement of the Democratic party, which enthusiastically anticipated extending democracy across the globe, securing new markets to promote American prosperity, and annexing additional territory to the United States. Its boastful spirit was epitomized in 1853 by a Philadelphia newspaper that spoke of the United States as bound on the "East by sunrise, West by sunset, North by the Arctic Expedition, and South as far as we darn please."

The believers in Young America considered themselves a dynamic, can-do lot, who felt it idle to argue about slavery and sectionalism when the nation could be developing. But they failed to comprehend how deeply American society was divided, and how each new plan for annexation would stir up renewed opposition. In 1853 Pierce did manage to conclude the Gadsden Purchase, thereby gaining control of about 45,000 square miles of Mexican desert and the most feasible southern route for a transcontinental railroad.

Pierce's major goal, Cuba, generated even fiercer debate. For years many Americans had assumed the United States would eventually acquire Cuba, and in 1848 Polk had authorized offering Spain up to $100 million for the island. Pierce was ready to raise the price, but Spain showed no interest. Then in 1854, three American ministers meeting at Ostend in Belgium sent the president a confidential recommendation. If Cuba could not be purchased, they argued, it should be seized. The contents of this "Ostend Manifesto" soon leaked, with predictable results. The acquisition of Cuba, a rich sugar-producing region where slavery had once been strong and still existed, was inexorably linked to the question of slavery expansion. The notion of acquiring it through naked aggression was so unpopular that Pierce was forced to repudiate the suggestion. In any case, he soon had his hands full with the proposals of another Democrat of the Young America stamp, Senator Stephen A. Douglas of Illinois.

The Kansas–Nebraska Act

Douglas too was eager to revive the fortunes of the sagging Democratic party. Stocky and short of stature (5 feet, 4 inches), the Little Giant was ambitious, bursting with energy, brimming with self-confidence, impatient to get things done, pugnacious in debate—always, it seemed, in motion. He could improvise strategies on the spot, but his impetuosity sometimes led him into rash judgments. As chairman of the Senate's Committee on Territories, Douglas was eager to organize federal lands west of Missouri as part of his program for economic development. As a citizen of Illinois, he wanted Chicago selected as the eastern terminus of the first transcontinental railroad. Chicago would never be chosen over St. Louis and New Orleans unless the remainder of the Louisiana Purchase was organized, for any northern rail route would have to run through that region.

Under the terms of the Missouri Compromise of 1820, slavery was prohibited in this portion of the Louisiana Purchase. But Douglas had already tried in 1853 to organize the area while keeping the ban on slavery intact, and his bill had been defeated by southern votes in the Senate. Douglas reintroduced his bill organizing this territory in January 1854. Bowing to a good deal of southern pressure, the Illinois leader agreed to remove the prohibition on slavery that had been in effect for 34 years, although he acknowledged that this action would "raise a hell of a storm."

As finally written, the bill created two territories: Kansas, directly west of Missouri, and a much larger Nebraska Territory, located west of Iowa and the Minnesota Territory. The Missouri Compromise was explicitly repealed. Instead, popular sovereignty was to determine the status of slavery in both territories, though it was left unclear whether residents of Kansas and Nebraska could prohibit slavery at any time, or only at the time of statehood, as southerners insisted. Still, most members of Congress assumed that Douglas had split the region into two territories so that each section could claim another state: Kansas would be slave and Nebraska free.

The Kansas–Nebraska Act outraged northern Democrats, Whigs, and Free Soilers alike. The Missouri Compromise was not just another statute, they argued, but an inviolable compact between the two sections. Critics rejected Douglas' contention that popular sovereignty would keep the territories free; the bill, they charged, was meant to give the Slave Power new territory. As always, most northerners spoke little of the moral evils of slavery; it was the expansion of slavery and the Slave Power that concerned them. So great was the northern outcry that Douglas joked he could "travel from Boston to Chicago by the light of my own [burning] effigy."

Once President Pierce endorsed the bill, Senate passage was assured. The real fight came in the House, where the North held a large majority. The president put intense pressure on his fellow northern Democrats, and finally the bill passed by a narrow margin, 113–100. Pierce signed it on May 30, 1854, and the Missouri Compromise was repealed.

The Collapse of the Second American Party System

In a sense, the furor over the Kansas–Nebraska Act was like the fault line of an earthquake zone. The jagged scar across the political landscape was visible evidence of the underlying social and economic tensions that had developed between the North and South. Since the 1820s and 1830s, the Jacksonian party system had bound the Union together. Both the Whig and the Democratic parties were national in scope, bringing together like-minded leaders from the North and the South. But as the moving frontier brought in new territories, the balance of political power tipped and the second American party system collapsed. Voters who had been loyal to one party for years, even decades, began switching allegiances, while new voters were mobilized. By the time the process of realignment was completed, a new party system had emerged, divided this time along clearly sectional lines.

In part, the old party system decayed because new problems had replaced the traditional issues of both Whigs and Democrats. Jacksonian Democrats had achieved many of their political reforms, and the latest round of prosperity undermined their campaign against banks as the agents of economic "privilege." The Whigs, whose strength lay within the Protestant mainstream, tried to expand their base by appealing to Catholics and recent immigrants, a tactic that backfired by alienating many of the party's traditional supporters. Then too, after 1850 Protestant reformers began agitating for the prohibition of alcohol, a question that deeply divided Whigs. In several key states the party was in complete disarray by the end of 1853. Finally, both the Whigs and Democrats were targets of a popular feeling that the existing parties were little more than corrupt engines of plunder designed "to keep a lot of 'Old Fogies' in office." Some citizens called for reform; others simply stopped voting. "There is prevailing generally a sort of 'don't care a damn' spirit," admitted one Ohio Whig in 1853.

Thus the party system was already weakened when the Kansas–Nebraska Act divided the two major parties along sectional lines. The northern Whigs, who unanimously opposed the bill, found themselves deserted by all of their southern colleagues, except for a few border-state Whigs. Indeed, many southern Whigs soon left the party for the Democrats. Although Franklin Pierce had convinced half the northern Democratic representatives to vote for Douglas' bill, the party paid the price in the elections that fall, losing 66 of the 91 northern Democratic seats and control of the House of Representatives.

In such an unstable atmosphere, with party loyalties badly weakened, independent parties flourished. The antislavery forces, which had earlier sparked the Liberty and Free Soil parties, united with Whigs and anti-Nebraska Democrats in the new antislavery Republican party. Their hopes were jolted, however, when another new party capitalized upon widespread fears aroused by the recent flood of immigrants and surged to the political forefront.

The Know-Nothings

New York City was the primary gateway for immigrants, and it was here in 1850 that a secret society, the Order of the Star-Spangled Banner, was formed. The society, which entered the political arena as the American party, proclaimed its unbridled hostility to the growing political power of Catholics and immigrants. Its members were sworn to secrecy and instructed to answer inquiries by replying "I know nothing." In 1853, the Know-Nothings (as they were quickly dubbed) began organizing in several other states; after only a year they had become the fastest growing party in the nation. Not coincidentally, 1854 also marked the peak of the new wave of immigration.

Taking as its slogan "Americans should rule America," the American party advocated that immigrants be forced to wait not 5 but 21 years before becoming naturalized citizens, and it called on voters to oust from office corrupt politicians who openly bid for foreign and Catholic votes. Know-Nothings denounced illegal voting by immigrants, the rising crime and disorder in urban areas, and immigrants' more easygoing observance of the Sabbath. (Germans, for example, enjoyed congregating on Sunday in beer gardens rather than engaging in solemn contemplation at home.) Indeed, because the Irish as well as the Germans often drank more heavily than native-born Americans, the prohibition movement had strong nativist overtones and gained the support of many Know-Nothings. Behind a great many of their specific complaints lay a virulent anti-Catholicism. Know-Nothings were convinced that the "undemocratic" hierarchy of priests, bishops, and archbishops, controlled by the pope in Rome, was conspiring to undermine American democracy.

The party especially attracted the support of young native-born American workers, who bore the brunt of the economic dislocations caused by industrialization and had to compete with immigrants for jobs. To workers, their jobs threatened and their status declining, immigrants and Catholics seemed obvious symbols of the unwanted transformation. And in the election of 1854, joined by sympathetic farmers and some members of the middle class, they voted in remarkable numbers for nativist candidates in key northern states like New York, Pennsylvania, Ohio, and Massachusetts.

The Know-Nothing triumph spelled doom for the Whigs, as the rank and file deserted in droves to the Know-Nothings. Fueled by its success, the American party turned its attention south, and in a few months it had organized in every state of the Union. By 1855, perhaps a million voters had enrolled in its lodges, as Know-Nothing candidates triumphed for the first time in Maryland, Kentucky, and Texas. Know-Nothing leaders confidently predicted that they would elect the next president.

Yet only a year later—by the end of 1856—the party had collapsed as quickly as it had risen. Lack of experience was one reason. Many Know-Nothing officeholders proved woefully incompetent, while in some states ambitious politicians quickly took over the movement and used it for their own purposes. Worse, party members often fell to bickering among themselves and failed to enact their program: voting reforms, a longer period of naturalization, and laws meant to check the power of the Catholic church. When firm deeds failed to follow strong words, supporters became disillusioned. The party's secrecy, too, seemed out of tune with a free republican spirit and in some cities, Know-Nothing gangs stole ballot boxes or attacked immigrants to prevent them from voting. Such actions made a mockery of the American party's claim to be a patriotic reform organization.

But the death knell of the party was rising sectional tensions. In 1855 a majority of northern delegates walked out of the American party's national convention when it adopted a proslavery platform. The 1856 convention brought a repeat of the same scene. This time, however, the bulk of the northern Know-Nothings left for good and joined the other new party, the Republicans. This party, unlike the Know-Nothings, had no base in the South. It intended to elect a president by sweeping the free states, which controlled a majority of the electoral votes. With Democratic strength concentrated more and more in the South, and the Republicans gaining in the North, the party system was realigning along sectional rather than national lines.

The Republicans and Bleeding Kansas

Initially, the Republicans looked no more like a viable party than any of the other short-lived antislavery parties of the period. In the summer of 1854, following passage of the Kansas–Nebraska Act, party organizers tried to capitalize on antislavery sentiment to attract Whigs, anti-Nebraska Democrats, and Free Soilers, but voters seemed more concerned about other issues: immigration in some states, temperance in others, and longstanding partisan antipathies in still others. To many moderate Whigs and Democrats, the Republican party seemed too radical. In 1855 Republican candidates met defeat almost everywhere they ran. A Democratic newspaper expressed the prevailing view when it declared, "Nobody believes that this Republican movement can prove the basis of a permanent party."

Such predictions, however, did not take into account the Kansas issue, and the emotions that it stirred. Most early settlers migrated to Kansas for the same reasons other Americans headed west—the chance to prosper in a new land. But Douglas' idea of popular sovereignty transformed the settlement of Kansas into a referendum on slavery in the territories: people voted with their feet. Thus a group of Massachusetts free-staters organized the New England Emigrant Aid Company, a joint stock venture designed to make a profit by investing in Kansas land and improvements while peopling the territory with antislavery advocates. This was one Yankee venture that failed on both counts; it sent few settlers to Kansas, and it was soon bankrupt.* But to the proslavery residents of Missouri's western counties, free state communities like Lawrence appeared as ominous threats. "We are playing for a mighty stake," former senator David Rice Atchison insisted. "If we win, we carry slavery to the Pacific Ocean; if we fail we lose Missouri, Arkansas and Texas and all the territories; the game must be played boldly."

In 1854 and 1855, during the first Kansas elections to select a delegate to Congress and a territorial legislature, Missourians took Atchison's advice to heart. In these elections they poured over the Kansas border, seized the polls, overawed the election judges, and voted en masse. Later congressional investigations concluded that over 60 percent of the votes were cast illegally. This massive fraud tarnished popular sovereignty at the outset and greatly aroused public opinion in the North. It also provided proslavery forces with a commanding majority in the Kansas legislature, where they promptly expelled the legally elected free state members and enacted a stringent legal code designed to intimidate antislavery

*It sent no more than 750 settlers in 1854 and fewer than 900 the following year; of these, perhaps a third left.

settlers. This Kansas Code, which attacked such time-honored rights as freedom of speech, impartial juries, and fair elections, became for northerners a symbol of tyranny. Mobilized into action, the free-staters in the fall of 1855 organized a separate government in Topeka, drafted a state constitution prohibiting slavery, and asked Congress to admit Kansas as the seventeenth free state in the Union.

Such a polarized situation triggered increased violence between the two factions in 1855 and again in the spring of 1856. Some of the bloodshed was typical of the anarchy common to most frontiers and had little to do with the slavery question. But since Kansas was distant from the more settled areas of the country, each report became fodder for propagandists on either side. For southerners, the free state Kansans were abolitionists preaching moral righteousness as an excuse to cheat southerners out of their property and rights. For their part, northern Republicans made little distinction between whiskey-soaked "border ruffians" and more peaceable southern settlers.

The Caning of Charles Sumner

In the ensuing congressional debate over the situation in Kansas, few were more heated in condemning the proslavery electoral frauds and violence than Senator Charles Sumner, a Republican from Massachusetts. A strong antislavery man, Sumner made no secret of his contempt for those who defended what he saw as an evil institution. In May, only a few days before the proslavery attack on Lawrence, he delivered a scathing speech entitled "The Crime Against Kansas," which included several deliberately insulting remarks about the state of South Carolina and one of its senators, 60-year-old Andrew P. Butler, a courtly, well-liked gentleman.

Butler was not in Washington at the time, but his cousin Preston Brooks was. A congressman from South Carolina, Brooks was especially outraged because Sumner had insulted an elderly blood relation, mocking his state and section. Several days later, on May 22, Brooks strode into the Senate after it had adjourned and approached Sumner, who was seated at his desk addressing mail. Announcing that he considered the speech "a libel on South Carolina and Mr. Butler," Brooks took his gutta-percha cane and struck the senator sharply on the head. Sumner, surprised and stunned by the blow, struggled to rise but his desk, bolted to the floor, restrained him. The emotion of the moment swept Brooks up and, furiously, he delivered blow after blow to Sumner's bleeding head, his cane shattering into three pieces from the vehemence of the attack. Sumner finally wrenched the desk from the floor with his legs and staggered forward, blinded by blood and vainly trying to ward off the blows. Brooks continued hitting him until another member of Congress finally restrained him. Sumner collapsed unconscious.

Northerners were electrified to learn that a senator of the United States had been beaten senseless in the Senate chamber. The next day, news of the "sack of Lawrence," which had occurred one day earlier, arrived. But what caused even greater consternation in the North was southern reaction to Sumner's caning, for in his own region, Preston Brooks was promptly lionized as a hero. Resolutions endorsed his action, souvenir canes descended on him, and supporters feted him with dinners and receptions. Influential papers like the Richmond *Enquirer* urged that other notable Republican members of Congress "be lashed into submission." Instantly, the Sumner caning breathed life into the fledgling Republican party. Its claims about "Bleeding Kansas" and the Slave Power now seemed credible. Sumner, whose injuries proved severe enough to keep him away from the Senate until

The caning of Senator Charles Sumner by Representative Preston Brooks of South Carolina inflamed public opinion. In this northern cartoon, the fallen Sumner, a martyr to free speech, raises his pen against Brooks' club. In the background several prominent Democrats look on in amusement. Rushing to capitalize on the furor, printmakers did not know what the obscure Brooks looked like and thus had to devise ingenious ways of portraying the incident. In this print, Brooks' face is hidden by his raised arm.

SOUTHERN CHIVALRY — ARGUMENT versus CLUB'S.

1860, was reelected anyway in 1857 by the Massachusetts legislature, his chair left vacant as a symbol of southern brutality.

The Election of 1856

Given the storm that had arisen over Kansas, Democrats concluded that no candidate associated with the repeal of the Missouri Compromise had a chance to win. That eliminated President Pierce and the ever-ambitious Senator Douglas. Instead, the Democrats turned to James Buchanan of Pennsylvania, an old party warhorse whose supreme qualification was that he had been out of the country when the Kansas–Nebraska Act was passed.

The American party, which had been badly split by the Kansas issue, nominated former president Millard Fillmore. The Republicans chose John C. Frémont, the western explorer and adventurer who had helped liberate California during the Mexican War. Considerably younger than Fillmore and Buchanan, the dashing Frémont seemed to many a fresh face. His only known opinions were on the subject of slavery, which he opposed in the territories. That suited the Republicans, whose platform denounced slavery as a "relic of barbarism" and who demanded that Kansas be admitted as a free state. Throughout the summer the party hammered away on Bleeding Sumner and Bleeding Kansas. "A constantly increasing excitement is kept up by the intelligence coming every day from Kansas," wrote one knowledgeable observer. "I have never known political excitement—I ought rather to say exasperation—approach that which now rages."

A number of basic principles guided the Republican party, especially the ideal of free labor. Slavery degraded labor, Republicans argued, and would inevitably drive free labor out of the territories. Condemning the South as a stagnant, hierarchical, and economically backward region, Republicans extolled the North as a fluid society of widespread opportunity, where enterprising individuals could improve their lot through hard work and self-discipline. Stopping the expansion of slavery, in Republican eyes, would preserve this heritage of opportunity and economic independence for white Americans. This notion of free labor, which drew a great deal from the traditional Protestant ethic, was of course an idealized vision. Republicans by and large remained blind to the growing concentration of wealth in the North and the extent to which industrialization closed off avenues of social mobility for poor laborers.

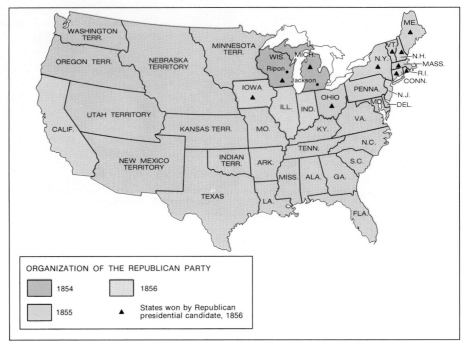

THE EMERGENCE OF THE REPUBLICAN PARTY
In the first two years after its founding in 1854, the Republican party enjoyed only limited
success in the North. The turning point came in 1856, when Frémont won a plurality of the
popular vote in the North, carried all but five of the free states, and finished second in the
presidential contest.

Also important was the moral opposition to slavery, which works like Harriet
Beecher Stowe's *Uncle Tom's Cabin* had strengthened. Republican speakers and
editors stressed that slavery was a moral wrong, that it was incompatible with the
ideals of the Republic and Christianity. Emerging as a prominent Republican
leader, Abraham Lincoln spoke out eloquently in the decade against the evil of
slavery. "Never forget," he declared on one occasion, "that we have before us this
whole matter of the right and wrong of slavery in this Union, though the immediate question is as to its spreading out into new Territories and States."

More negatively, Republicans gained support by shifting their attacks from
slavery itself to the Slave Power, or the political influence of the planter class.
Since the party's founding, the New York *Times* explained, its "specific aim was to
dislodge the slaveholding interest from the ascendency it had acquired over the
Federal government, and to render it forever impossible for it to regain that
supremacy." Pointing to the Sumner assault and the incidents in Kansas, Republicans contended that the Slave Power had set out to destroy the liberties of northern whites. Since concern for the welfare of blacks was weak in the North, the
focus on the rights of whites gave Republicans a more potent appeal. "The issues
now before the people," one Republican insisted in the 1856 campaign, "are those
of Despotism or Freedom. The question has passed on from that of slavery for
negro servants, to that of tyranny over free white men."

All these fears played on a strong northern attachment to the heritage of the

American Revolution. Republicans argued that just as the nation's founders had battled against slavery, tyranny, aristocracy, and minority rule, so the North faced the unrepublican Slave Power. "If our government, for the sake of Slavery, is to be perpetually the representative of a minority, it may continue republican in form, but the substance of its republicanism has departed," argued the Cincinnati *Commercial*. And a New Hampshire Republican paper warned in 1856 that "the liberties of our country are in tenfold the danger that they were at the commencement of the American Revolution. We then had a distant foe to contend with. Now the enemy is within our borders."

News of the violence in Kansas and Sumner's caning nearly won Frémont the presidency, despite his inexperience. He ran ahead of both Buchanan and Fillmore in the North, and won 11 free states out of 16. Had he carried Pennsylvania plus one more, he would have been elected. Still, Buchanan all but swept the South (losing only Maryland to Fillmore) and won enough free states to push him over the top, with 174 electoral votes to Frémont's 114 and Fillmore's 8. Clearly, the Republican party had supplanted the Whigs in the two-party system. For the first time in American history, an antislavery party based entirely in the North threatened to elect a president and snap the bonds of union.

THE WORSENING CRISIS

President James Buchanan had spent much of his life in public service: over 20 years in the House and the Senate, secretary of state under Polk, as well as minister to Russia and to Great Britain. A tall and heavy-set man with flowing white hair, Buchanan struck White House visitors as exceptionally courteous; an eye defect caused him to tilt his head slightly forward and to one side, which reinforced the impression of deference and attentiveness. Yet underneath this facade, he was cold, humorless, and calculating. At bottom a timid man, he had a strong stubborn streak, deeply resented opposition, and overrated his ability to enforce party discipline on those who disagreed with his policies. Throughout his career, Buchanan had taken the southern position on sectional matters. His closest associates remained southerners, and he proved remarkably insensitive to the concerns of northern Democrats.

Moderates in both the North and the South hoped that the new president's diplomatic skills would steer the country clear of Republican radicals and secessionists of the Deep South, popularly known as "fire-eaters." But on March 6, 1857, only two days after Buchanan's inauguration, the Supreme Court gave the new administration a jolt with one of the most controversial decisions in its history.

The *Dred Scott* Decision

The owner of a Missouri slave named Dred Scott had taken him to live for several years in Illinois, a free state, and in the Wisconsin Territory, where slavery had been banned by the Missouri Compromise. Scott had returned to Missouri as a slave, but aided by some antislavery people eventually sued for his freedom. Residence in a free state and a free territory had made him free, he argued. His case ultimately went to the Supreme Court, which had to decide two questions. First, was Scott, a black person, a citizen of Missouri who had the legal right to sue in federal court? And second, if he could sue, was he free by virtue of his having resided in free territory? The Court's decision was so complex that every justice wrote his own opinion, but all five southern members of the Court, plus two northerners, ruled 7–2 that Scott remained a slave. In the majority opinion Chief Justice Roger Taney argued that Scott had voluntarily returned to Missouri and that under Missouri law, which took precedence, he was a slave.

Had the Court stopped there, the public outcry would have been minimal. But the Court majority believed that they had a judicial responsibility to deal with the larger controversy between the two sections, and Chief Justice Taney, in particular, wanted to strengthen the judicial protection of slavery. Taney, a former Maryland slaveowner who had emancipated his slaves, ruled that blacks could not be and never had been citizens of the United States. Instead, he insisted that at the time the Constitution was adopted, blacks were "regarded as beings of an inferior order, so far inferior that they had no rights which the white man was bound to respect." In addition, since Scott had based part of his appeal on the fact that the Missouri Compromise outlawed slavery in the western part of the Wisconsin Territory, the Court ruled that the Compromise was unconstitutional. Congress, it declared, had no power to ban slavery from *any* territory of the United States.

While southerners rejoiced at this unexpected outcome, Republicans were flabbergasted. Their platform declared, after all, that Congress ought to prohibit slavery in all territories. In effect, the Court had ruled their central goal unconstitutional and upheld the extreme southern position. Horace Greeley, the Republican editor of the New York *Tribune*, fumed that the decision was "entitled to just so much moral weight as would be the judgment of a majority of those congregated in any Washington bar-room." Abraham Lincoln was more restrained. "We know the court . . . has often over-ruled its own decisions," he observed, "and we shall do what we can to have it over-rule this." But the decision was sobering. If all territories were now open to slavery, how long would it be before a move was made to reintroduce slavery in the free states? That was precisely what southern Democrats conspired to do, Republican leaders argued.

But the decision also was a blow to Douglas' moderate solution of popular sovereignty. If Congress had no power to prohibit slavery in a territory, how could it authorize a territorial legislature to do so? While the Court did not rule on this point, the clear implication of the *Dred Scott* decision was that popular sovereignty was also unconstitutional. The Court, in effect, had adopted the extreme Calhounite view that slavery was legal in all the territories. In so doing, the Court, which had intended to settle the question of slavery in the territories once and for all, succeeded only in heightening the sense of crisis and strengthening the forces of extremism in American politics.

The Panic of 1857

As the nation grappled with the *Dred Scott* decision, an economic depression aggravated sectional conflict. Once again, boom gave way to bust as falling wheat

Chief Justice Roger Taney.

prices and contracted credit hurt commercial farmers and overextended railroad investors. The Panic of 1857 was nowhere near as severe as the depression of 1837–1843, but the psychological results were far-reaching, for the South remained relatively untouched. With the price of cotton and other southern commodities still high, southern secessionists hailed the panic as proof that an independent southern nation was economically feasible. *DeBow's Review,* the leading commercial journal in the South, argued that southern wealth was real and permanent, whereas northern wealth rested on paper and was fictitious. And James Henry Hammond, a senator from South Carolina, boasted: "What would happen if no cotton was furnished for three years? England would topple headlong and carry the whole civilized world with her save the South. No, you dare not make war on cotton. No power on earth dares to make war on it. Cotton is king."

For their part, northerners sought decisive federal action to bolster the economy—the sort which so many southerners had long opposed. When the North proposed a moderate increase in the tariff duties, which were at their lowest level since 1815, southerners opposed even this moderate measure. Under southern pressure, Buchanan also vetoed bills to improve navigation on the Great Lakes and to give free farms to western settlers. Many businessmen and conservative ex-Whigs concluded that the United States would never be able to develop in the face of southern obstructionism. And the Republicans, hoping to broaden their party's base, began to add economic planks to their platform. Economic issues, in other words, were becoming sectional ones.

The Lecompton Constitution

While the *Dred Scott* decision and economic depression further weakened the bonds of Union, Kansas remained at the center of the political stage. By June 1857, when the territory elected delegates to a convention to draft a state constitution, the worst of the marauding had ended. But free-staters boycotted the election because the voting districts had been unfairly drawn up. As a result, the proslavery majority at the convention meeting in Lecompton promptly drew up a constitution that made slavery legal. Even more boldly, they decided not to allow Kansas voters the chance to reject the constitution. In the referendum that followed, voters could choose only whether to admit additional slaves into the territory; they could not vote against either the constitution or slavery. Once again, free-staters boycotted the election and the Lecompton constitution was approved. In the meantime, however, the free state forces gained control of the territorial legislature and submitted the whole constitution in another referendum, when it was overwhelmingly rejected. In debating the admission of Kansas as a state, Congress had to decide which of the two results to accept.

As an adherent of popular sovereignty, President Buchanan had pledged to support a free and fair vote on the Lecompton constitution. But the outcome offered him the unexpected opportunity to satisfy his southern supporters by pushing the Lecompton constitution through Congress. This was too much for Douglas, who had staked so much on the idea of popular sovereignty. Breaking party ranks, he denounced the Lecompton constitution as a fraud. Nevertheless, the administration prevailed in the Senate. Buchanan now pulled out all the stops

Dred Scott.

to gain the necessary votes in the House, where northern representation was much stronger, to admit Kansas as a slave state. But after one of the fiercest political struggles in American history, the House rejected the Lecompton constitution. In a compromise, Congress, using indirect language, returned the constitution to Kansas for another vote. This time it was decisively defeated, 11,300 to 1788. No doubt remained that as soon as it had sufficient population, Kansas would come into the Union as a free state.

The attempt to force slavery on the people of Kansas drove many conservative northerners to join the Republicans, making that party the most likely victor in 1860. And Douglas, once the Democrats' strongest candidate, now found himself at odds with the Buchanan administration and assailed by the southern wing of his party. On top of that, in the summer of 1858 Douglas faced a desperate fight in his race for reelection to the Senate against Republican Abraham Lincoln.

The Lincoln–Douglas Debates

"He is the strong man of his party . . . and the best stump speaker, with his droll ways and dry jokes, in the West," Douglas commented when he learned of Lincoln's nomination to oppose him. "He is as honest as he is shrewd, and if I beat him my victory will be hardly won." As a Whig, Lincoln had served several terms in the state legislature during the 1830s and 1840s; he had been in Congress two years but had been out of public office for almost a decade. He was a gangly man, with gaunt face, high cheekbones, deep-socketed gray eyes, and a shock of unruly hair. He appeared awkward as he spoke, never knowing quite what to do with his large, muscular hands, and his voice, though strong and clear, sometimes seemed shrill. But his finely honed logic, his simple, eloquent language, and his sincerity carried the audience with him. His sentences, as spare as the man himself, had none of the oratorical flourishes common in that day; they merely laid out propositions to be examined and pondered. "If we could first know *where* we are, and *whither* we are tending, we could then better judge *what* to do, and *how* to do it," Lincoln began, in accepting his party's nomination for senator from Illinois in 1858. And then he went on to dissect Douglas' notion that popular sovereignty could somehow settle the crisis over slavery.

We are now far into the *fifth* year, since a policy was initiated, with the *avowed* object, and *confident* promise, of putting an end to slavery agitation.

Under the operation of that policy, that agitation has not only, *not ceased*, but has *constantly augmented*.

In my opinion, it *will* not cease, until a *crisis* shall have been reached, and passed.

"A house divided against itself cannot stand."

I believe this government cannot endure, permanently half *slave* and half *free*.

I do not expect the Union to be *dissolved*—I do not expect the house to *fall*—but I *do* expect it will cease to be divided.

It will become *all* one thing, or *all* the other.

Either the *opponents* of slavery, will arrest the further spread of it, and place it where the public mind shall rest in the belief that it is in course of ultimate extinction; or its *advocates* will push it forward, till it shall become alike lawful in all the States, *old* as well as new—*North* as well as *South*.

The message echoed through the hall and across the pages of the national press.

Superb debaters, Douglas (left) and Lincoln nevertheless had very different speaking styles. The deep-voiced Douglas was constantly on the attack, drawing on his remarkable memory and showering points like buckshot in all directions. Employing sarcasm and ridicule rather than humor, he never tried to crack a joke. Lincoln, who had a high-pitched voice and a rather awkward platform manner, developed arguments more methodically, and relied on his sense of humor and unmatched ability as a storyteller to drive his points home to the audience.

Born in the slave state of Kentucky, he had grown up mostly in southern Indiana and central Illinois. He could split rails with the best frontiersman, loved telling stories, and was at home mixing with ordinary folk: lifting weights at a county fair or "standing backs" with a tall man in the crowd to see who had the advantage of height (Lincoln was 6 feet, 4 inches). Yet his intense ambition had lifted him above the rural backwoods from which he came. He compensated for a lack of formal schooling through disciplined self-education, and moving to the capital in Springfield, he became a shrewd courtroom lawyer of respectable social standing. For all that, he stood apart from his society in many ways. He did not drink, and so hated the sight of blood that he did not hunt. He was unswayed by frontier revivalism and, although profoundly sensitive to the power of religion, did not belong to any organized church. Known for his sense of humor, he was nonetheless subject to fits of acute depression, and his eyes often mirrored a deep melancholy.

Lincoln's first love was always politics. At only 25, he entered the state legis-

Daily Lives

PUBLIC SPACE/PRIVATE SPACE

Uncle Tom by Footlights

By 1850 American theaters were a popular, though controversial focal point for public entertainment. The Puritans had roundly condemned plays of any sort, and even in the mid-nineteenth century many ministers and religious critics frowned on theatergoing as an idle diversion. Still, the rise of cities made possible the large audiences needed to support long-run productions. The stage became a medium for mass entertainment, which attracted not only the working classes but, increasingly, the urban middle class.

In 1852 George C. Howard, the head of the Museum Theater in Troy, New York, was casting about for new material. He decided to take up the issue of slavery, which had recently engaged the nation's attention through a controversial new novel, *Uncle Tom's Cabin*. Written by Harriet Beecher Stowe, one of the Reverend Lyman Beecher's energetic daughters, the book's first 5000 copies sold out in two days. Soon four power presses were running night and day (except Sundays) trying to keep up with the demand. Over 300,000 copies were printed in the first year. In the South, although many communities banned the novel, it was read by a remarkable number of the curious.

In trying to turn the novel into a play, Howard faced substantial problems. While full of vivid and dramatic incidents, the plot of *Uncle Tom's Cabin* followed a host of characters to a multitude of locales. When a debt-ridden Kentucky family is forced to sell some of its slaves, George and Eliza Harris, a mulatto slave couple, learn that their young son is to be one of them. Eliza flees north to freedom across the ice-choked Ohio River, her child

clinging to her breast. At the same time, Tom, an older slave and a devout Christian, submits to his sale and is taken south. There he meets Evangeline St. Clare, an innocent, golden-haired child, who convinces her father to buy Tom and take him to their home in New Orleans. For a time Tom is treated kindly, but after both Evangeline and her father die, Tom is sold to Simon Legree, a hard-drinking, blasphemous Yankee, who owns a plantation on the Red River in Louisiana. When Tom steadfastly refuses to whip other slaves, Legree beats him to death; Tom is a martyr to his faith in God and his love for his fellow man.

Compressing this complex story was not easy. Then, too, no American play on the subject of slavery had been produced. Many theater managers believed that the public would not accept a black hero. Indeed, black characters were rare on stage except in minstrel shows. But Howard liked the idea of casting his four-year-old daughter Cordelia (already an experienced trouper) as young Eva, and he decided to proceed. A member of the repertory company, George Aiken, wrote an adaptation that focused on Tom's experiences in the St. Clare household.

The play ran successfully for four weeks prompting Aiken to write a sequel, *The Death of Uncle Tom*, based on the Legree section of the novel; finally he combined the two plays into a 6-act, 30-scene epic that took an entire evening to perform. To make the plot coherent would have required almost twice as many scenes, so Aiken actually sacrificed coherence for playability. Aiken's adaptation became the classic stage version of *Uncle Tom's Cabin*. From Troy the production moved to New York City, where it ran for an unprecedented 325 performances and then achieved similar triumphs in other

Daily Lives

In this playbill advertising a production of *Uncle Tom's Cabin*, vicious bloodhounds pursue Eliza clutching her child as she frantically leaps to safety across the ice-choked Ohio River.

northern cities. No play had ever attracted such large audiences.

Aiken had a good eye for the dramatic: a slave auction, Eva's death after a long illness, and Tom's defiance of Legree when threatened with a whipping. ("My soul a'nt yours, mas'r; you haven't bought it—ye can't buy it.") Eliza's flight across the icy Ohio River—described in two paragraphs in the book—became one of the major scenes, with a pack of bloodhounds added for good measure. Furthermore, since audiences of melodrama were accustomed to comic interludes between dramatic scenes, Aiken expanded the humorous potential of certain characters and added a new one, Gumption Cute, a swindling slavecatcher. As in minstrel shows, blacks were played by whites wearing lampblack.

Despite these additions, the play remained essentially faithful to the book's antislavery message. And Howard worked hard to attract a new middle-class audi-

ence. He banned the prostitutes who so often frequented theaters, and in the lobby displayed the endorsements of prominent religious leaders and reformers on posters. A further innovation, matinee performances, attracted women and children. As one reporter for the New York *Atlas* commented, instead of newsboys and apprentices, he saw "many people who have been taught to look on the stage with horror and contempt." Even Harriet Beecher Stowe, who disapproved of having her book turned into a play, at last discreetly attended a performance, her head carefully covered with a shawl. And in a departure from the normal policy of New York theaters, blacks were allowed to attend, seated in a segregated section accessible through a separate entrance.

The play moved audiences of all backgrounds. After wrestling with his religious scruples, John Kirk, a traveling salesman from Chicago, finally went to see a production. He laughed uproariously at the humor, but confessed, "My laughing soon turned to weeping. The appeals of the dying little Eva to her father, for Uncle Tom's freedom, were overwhelmingly affecting. . . . I must confess that I never saw so many white pocket handkerchiefs in use at the same time, and, for the same purpose before. I was not the only one in that large audience to shed tears I assure you." Equally striking, the play affected the workers and apprentices who made up the theater's normal clientele. Traditionally hostile to abolitionism, these groups cheered wildly over Eliza's escape and shouted approval of her antislavery speeches. By providing vivid images of the cruelties and suffering under slavery, theatrical presentations of *Uncle Tom's Cabin*, even more than the book, heightened the sectional tensions that increasingly divided the nation in the 1850s.

lature and went on to become one of the leaders of the Whig party in Illinois. He fervently admired Henry Clay and his economic program. But after 1848, with Illinois staunchly Democratic, his political activities waned until the repeal of the Missouri Compromise rekindled his zeal. He eventually joined the Republican party and became one of its key leaders in the state. In a series of seven joint debates, Lincoln challenged Douglas to discuss the issues of slavery and the sectional controversy. Crowds of 5000, 10,000, and even 15,000 men, women, and children gathered all across Illinois by torchlight, or in drizzling rain, or under a blazing sun, to support their candidate and weigh the issues.

In a state that was antislavery but also strongly racist, Douglas sought to portray Lincoln as a radical whose "House Divided" speech preached sectional warfare. The nation *could* endure half slave and half free, Douglas declared, so long as states and territories were left alone to regulate their own affairs. Accusing Lincoln of believing that the black man was his equal, Douglas suggested sarcastically that his opponent could now accept the black man as "his brother," whereas Douglas was already on record that the American government had been "made by the white man, for the white man, to be administered by the white man."

Lincoln countered by insisting that the spread of slavery was a blight on the Republic. Even though Douglas had voted against the Lecompton constitution, he could not be counted on to oppose slavery's expansion, for he had already admitted that he didn't care whether slavery was voted "down or up." That, after all, was what popular sovereignty was all about. For his part, Lincoln denied any "perfect equality between the negroes and white people" and opposed allowing blacks to vote, hold office, or intermarry with whites. But, he concluded,

> Notwithstanding all this, there is no reason in the world why the negro is not entitled to all the natural rights enumerated in the Declaration of Independence, the right to life, liberty and the pursuit of happiness. . . . I agree with Judge Douglas [that the negro] is not my equal in many respects—certainly not in color, perhaps not in moral or intellectual endowment. But in the right to eat the bread, without leave of anybody else, which his own hand earns, *he is my equal and the equal of Judge Douglas, and the equal of every living man.*

In the debate held at Freeport, Illinois, Lincoln asked Douglas how the people of a territory could lawfully exclude slavery before statehood, since the *Dred Scott* decision seemed to make that impossible. Douglas answered, with what became known as the Freeport Doctrine, that slavery could exist only with the protection of positive law, and that whatever abstract rights slaveowners possessed, they would not bring their slaves into an area that did not have a slave code. Therefore, Douglas explained, if the people of a territory refused to pass a slave code, slavery would never be established there.

In a close race, the legislature elected Douglas to another term in the Senate.* But on the national scene, southern Democrats angrily repudiated him and condemned the Freeport Doctrine. And although Lincoln lost, Republicans thought his impressive performance marked him as a possible presidential contender for 1860.

---

*State legislatures elected senators until 1913, when the Seventeenth Amendment was adopted. While Lincoln and Douglas both campaigned for the office, Illinois voters actually voted for candidates for the legislature who were pledged to one of the senatorial candidates.

The Beleaguered South

While northerners increasingly feared that the Slave Power was conspiring to extend slavery into the free states, southerners worried that the "Black Republicans" would hem them in and undermine their political power.

The very factors that brought prosperity during the 1850s stimulated the South's sense of crisis. As the price of land and slaves rose sharply, fewer small farmers could hope to become slaveowners. The proportion of southerners who owned slaves had dropped almost a third since 1830. Land also was being consolidated into larger holdings. Between 1850 and 1860, the average farm size rose in the South by 20 percent: in Alabama from 289 to 346 acres, and in Mississippi from 309 to 370 acres. Planters were increasing their wealth at the expense of the bottom half of society. In earlier decades, small farm families might have pushed westward, as many continued to do during the 1850s by moving to Texas. But California and Kansas had been closed to southern slaveholders—unfairly, in their eyes—and the *Dred Scott* decision had been negated.

Several possible solutions to the South's internal crisis had failed. Agricultural reform to restore worn-out lands had made significant headway in Virginia and Maryland, but elsewhere the rewards of a single-crop economy were just too great. Like most Americans, southerners preferred to exploit the soil and then move west. In some counties, over half the slaveholders left in a decade. Another alternative—industrialization—had also failed. Indeed, the gap between the North and the South steadily widened in the 1850s. More controversial was the movement to reopen the African slave trade, which became the cry of many fire-eaters after 1850, but which never attracted wide support in the South. A few militant southerners launched their own private military expeditions in the Caribbean during the 1850s, hoping to add Cuba, Mexico, or Nicaragua to the United States as slave territories. But all of these "filibustering" expeditions came to naught. They demonstrated, however, how much the sense of internal crisis made southerners more willing to consider aggressive and extremist solutions.

The South's growing sense of moral and political isolation made this crisis more acute. By the 1850s, slavery had been abolished throughout most of the Americas, and in the United States the South's political power was steadily shrinking. The House had been lost decades ago, the Senate in 1850, and only the expansion of slavery held out any promise of new slave states needed to preserve the South's political power and protect its way of life. For a growing number of southerners, geographic expansion had become a panacea for the section's problems. "The truth is," fumed one Alabama politician, " . . . the South is excluded from the common territories of the Union. The right of expansion claimed to be a necessity of her continued existence, is practically and effectively denied the South."

To defend their embattled way of life, southern whites appealed to the heritage of the Revolution. For them, republicanism consisted of individual liberty, self-government, and equality of opportunity for all whites. Slavery was the linchpin of this system, for it preserved equality among whites and guaranteed all whites, regardless of wealth, a certain pride and status. "Break down slavery," Governor Henry Wise of Virginia maintained, "and you would with the same blow destroy the democratic principle of equality among men." A Georgia newspaper echoed those sentiments: "Slavery," it insisted, "is the best foundation for a *permanent* republican government."

THE ROAD TO WAR

After 1854 a series of blows weakened the forces of compromise and moderation at the nation's political center. But none struck with the force of the news from the quiet town of Harpers Ferry, Virginia. Behind it was none other than John Brown of Pottawatomie.

Harpers Ferry

In 1857 Brown had returned to the East from Kansas, consumed with the idea of attacking slavery in the South itself. Financed by a number of prominent northern reformers (who were unaware of his role in the Pottawatomie killings), Brown gathered a small force of 21 followers, including five free blacks, with the design of fomenting a slave insurrection. On the night of October 16, 1859, they attacked the unguarded federal armory at Harpers Ferry. It fell easily enough, but no slaves rallied to his standard, for the area had few to begin with. Before long the alarm went out and Brown found himself holed up in the armory's engine house with hostile townspeople taking potshots at his army of liberation. Charging with bayonets fixed, federal troops commanded by Colonel Robert E. Lee soon captured Brown and his band.

The "invasion" itself was an ill-planned, dismal failure, as were most of the enterprises Brown undertook in his troubled life. But the old man knew well how to bear himself with a martyr's dignity. At his trial he made an impassioned case against slavery. "Had I so interfered in behalf of the rich, the powerful, the intelligent, the so-called great," he declared, ". . . it would have been all right. Every man in this court would have deemed it an act worthy of reward rather than punishment. . . . I believe that to have interfered as I have done in behalf of [God's] despised poor, is no wrong, but a right." On December 2, 1859, Virginia hanged Brown for treason.

John Brown's enduring legacy sprang not from his ill-conceived raid but from the popular reaction to his cause. With the election of 1860 looming and victory seemingly within their grasp, Republicans sought to distance themselves from abolitionist radicals. Hurriedly they denounced Brown's raid as "the gravest of crimes." But other northerners were less cautious. Ralph Waldo Emerson described Brown as a "saint, whose martyrdom will make the gallows as glorious as the cross," and on the day of his execution, church bells tolled in many northern cities. Only a minority of northerners endorsed Brown, but southerners were shocked by such public displays of sympathy. And they were firmly convinced that the Republican party was secretly connected to the raid. The legislatures of Alabama, Mississippi, and Florida all passed resolutions declaring that the election of a Republican president would justify secession, while countless southerners for the first time seriously considered the prospect. "I have always been a fervid Union man," one North Carolina resident wrote, "but I confess the endorsement of the Harpers Ferry outrage has shaken my fidelity and I am willing to take the chances of every probable evil that may arise from disunion, sooner than submit any longer to Northern insolence and Northern outrage."

John Brown.

A Sectional Election

When Congress convened in December, only three days after John Brown was executed, there were ominous signs everywhere of the growing sectional rift. Intent on destroying Douglas' Freeport Doctrine, southern radicals in Congress issued a platform for the 1860 election which demanded a federal slave code to protect slavery in the territories. Northern Democrats denounced this demand as provocative, since no settlers in any territory had requested such protection. Moreover, for them to support such a platform spelled political death. As one Indiana Democrat put it, "We cannot carry a single congressional district on that doctrine in the state."

The Democratic convention met in April in Charleston, South Carolina, the hotbed of southern extremism. The packed galleries cheered on the fire-eaters, who boldly pressed their demand for a federal slave code as a way to force Douglas out of the race. An angry Senator George Pugh of Ohio spoke for the Douglas forces: "Gentlemen of the South, you mistake us,—you mistake us. We will not do it." After six days of heated debate, the convention adopted the Douglas platform upholding popular sovereignty, whereupon the delegations from the entire Deep South, plus Arkansas, walked out. Unable to agree on a candidate, the convention adjourned to reassemble two months later in Baltimore. There, Douglas was nominated, but most of the remaining southern Democrats left in disgust. Joining with the Charleston seceders, they nominated their own candidate, Vice President John C. Breckinridge of Kentucky, on a platform supporting a federal slave code. With a northern and a southern Democratic candidate in the field, the last major national party had shattered.

In May the Republicans convened in Chicago. In the end, the delegates turned to Abraham Lincoln, who could help carry his doubtful home state of Illinois, was a moderate on slavery, and was acceptable to all factions of the party, including the Germans and the former Know-Nothings. Republicans also sought to

THE ELECTION OF 1860
Although Lincoln did not win a majority of the popular vote, he still would have been elected even if the votes for all three of his opponents had been combined, since he won a clear majority in every state he carried except California, Oregon, and New Jersey (whose electoral votes he split with Douglas).

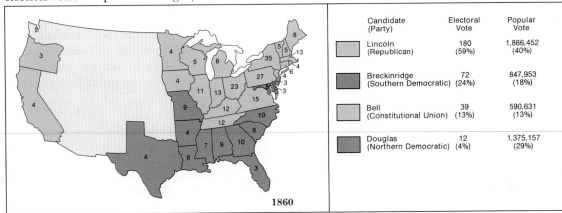

Candidate (Party)	Electoral Vote	Popular Vote
Lincoln (Republican)	180 (59%)	1,866,452 (40%)
Breckinridge (Southern Democratic)	72 (24%)	847,953 (18%)
Bell (Constitutional Union)	39 (13%)	590,631 (13%)
Douglas (Northern Democratic)	12 (4%)	1,375,157 (29%)

1860

broaden their appeal by adding to their platform several economic planks that endorsed a moderately protective tariff, a homestead bill, and a northern transcontinental railroad.

The election that followed was really two contests in one. In the North, which had a majority of the electoral votes, only Lincoln and Douglas had any chance to carry a state. In the South, the race pitted Breckinridge against John Bell of Tennessee, the candidate of the Constitutional Union party, which represented yet another attempt to create a national conservative party. When the votes were counted, Lincoln had less than 40 percent of the popular vote and virtually no support in the South. But he won 180 electoral votes, 27 more than needed for election. Breckinridge ran first in the South and swept the Deep South. The two sectional parties (Lincoln and Breckinridge) had overwhelmed the two Unionist parties (Douglas and Bell). Douglas, the only candidate with support in all areas of the country, finished second in the popular vote but won only 12 electoral votes. For the first time, the nation had elected a president who headed a completely sectional party and who was committed to stopping the expansion of slavery.

Secession

Although the Republicans had not won control of either house of Congress, Lincoln's election struck many southerners as a blow of terrible finality. Lincoln had been lifted into office on the strength of the free states alone. With Republicans opposing slavery in the territories, the South's power base could only diminish. Although the Supreme Court had traditionally checked the abuses of majority rule, Republicans refused to accept the *Dred Scott* decision and had spent the last four years bitterly assailing the Court.

What would Lincoln do, once in office? It was not unrealistic, southern radicals argued, to believe that he would use federal aid to induce the border states to voluntarily emancipate their slaves. Once slavery disappeared there, and new states were added, the necessary three-fourths majority would exist to approve a constitutional amendment abolishing slavery. Or perhaps Lincoln might send other John Browns into the South, to stir up more slave insurrections. The Montgomery (Alabama) *Mail* accused Republicans of intending "to free the negroes and force amalgamation between them and the children of the poor men of the South." Reinforcing these arguments was the comforting opinion held by many white southerners that secession was not only constitutional, but it would also be peaceful.

Secession now seemed the only alternative left to protect southern equality, liberty, and the Constitution itself. South Carolina, which had first challenged federal authority in the nullification crisis, was determined to force the other southern states to act. On December 20, 1860, a popular convention unanimously passed a resolution seceding from the Union and declaring the state once again independent. The rest of the Deep South quickly followed, and on February 7, 1861, the states stretching from South Carolina to Texas organized the Confederate States of America and elected Jefferson Davis president.

The voting for delegates to the secessionist conventions in the Deep South was not a rerun of the recent presidential contest. As the regular Democratic candidate, Breckinridge had been strong in the traditionally Democratic hill counties and other areas of small farms and few slaves. In the secession elections, however, these Democratic yeoman farmers backed Unionist candidates, whereas

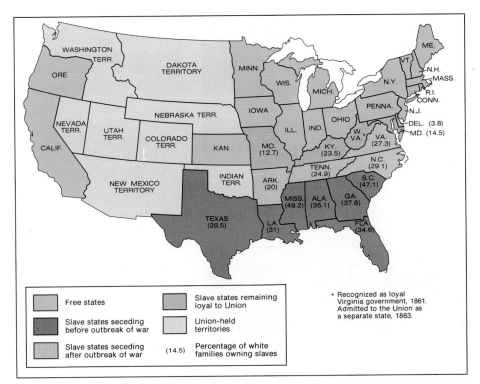

THE PATTERN OF SECESSION
Led by South Carolina, the Deep South seceded between Lincoln's election in November and his inauguration in March. The Upper South did not secede until after the firing on Fort Sumter. The four border slave states never seceded and remained in the Union throughout the war. As the map indicates, secession sentiment was strongest in states where the highest percentage of white families owned slaves.

slaveowners, many of whom had voted for Bell in the presidential election, endorsed secession by decided margins. As a general rule, the higher the concentration of slaves in a county, the greater was its support for secession. When the issue shifted to protecting slavery, slaveholders chose secession. Certainly large numbers of nonslaveholders backed secession also, but in its driving force, secession was a slaveholders' revolution.

But the Upper South and the border states declined to follow, hoping that once again Congress could patch together a settlement. Senator John Crittenden of Kentucky, who now held the seat of the Great Compromiser himself, Henry Clay, proposed extending to the Pacific the old Missouri Compromise line of 36° 30′. Slavery would be prohibited north of this line and given federal protection south of it in all territories, including any acquired in the future. Furthermore, Crittenden proposed an "unamendable amendment" to the Constitution, forever preserving slavery in states where it already existed. To reassure jittery southerners, Crittenden introduced these and several other provisions designed to protect slaveowners as constitutional amendments rather than ordinary statutes.

But the Crittenden Compromise was doomed, for the simple reason that the two groups who were required to make concessions—Republicans and secessionists—had no interest in doing so. "The argument is exhausted," representatives from the Deep South announced, even before Crittenden had introduced his

When Confederate batteries opened fire on Fort Sumter, Charleston civilians climbed to their roofs to witness the bombardment. "The women were wild, there on the housetop," one Charleston woman reported. "Prayers from the women and imprecations from the men, and then a shell would light up the scene." The Civil War had begun.

package. Although President-elect Lincoln maintained a public silence, he privately threw all his influence against any compromise that permitted slavery in new territories. "We have just carried an election on principles fairly stated to the people," he commented. "Now we are told in advance, the government shall be broken up, unless we surrender to those we have beaten, before we take the offices. If we surrender, it is the end of us, and of the government."

The Outbreak of War

As his inauguration approached, Lincoln pondered what to do about secession and the seizure of federal property, including forts, arsenals, and customshouses, by the seceded states. In his inaugural address on March 4, he sought to reassure southerners that he had no intention, "directly or indirectly, to interfere with the institution of slavery in the States where it exists." He pledged to enforce the fugitive slave law. But he maintained that the Union of the states was a solemn compact that no state "upon its own mere motion" could break unilaterally. "The Union of these states is perpetual," he declared, echoing Andrew Jackson's Proclamation on Nullification. He also announced that he intended to "hold, occupy and possess" federal property and collect customs duties under the tariff. Appealing to the "bonds of affection" that united all Americans, he told southerners in closing that the choice between peace and war rested with them.

Lincoln hoped for time to work out a solution, but on his first day in office he learned that Major Robert Anderson, commander of the federal garrison at Fort Sumter, one of the few remaining federal outposts in the South, had just informed the government that he was almost out of food. Located on an artificial island in the middle of Charleston harbor, the fort had been isolated since January by southern forces hoping to starve the occupants into submission. Anderson's dispatch indicated that without additional supplies, he would have to capitulate within six weeks. For a month Lincoln looked for a way out, but he finally sent a relief expedition. As a conciliatory gesture, he notified the governor of South Carolina that supplies were being sent, and that if the fleet were allowed to pass, only food, and not men, arms, or ammunition, would be landed.

The burden of decision now shifted to Jefferson Davis. From his point of view, secession was a constitutional right, and the Confederacy was not a spurious but a real government. To allow the United States to hold property and maintain military forces within the Confederacy would destroy its claim of independence. Lincoln's decision to resupply Fort Sumter, Davis argued, was an act of aggression. After two days of debate with his cabinet, he ordered the commander at Charleston, General Pierre Beauregard, to demand the immediate surrender of Fort Sumter and, if refused, to open fire. When Anderson declined the ultimatum, Confederate batteries began shelling on April 12 at 4:30 a.m. Some 33 hours and 5000 rounds of artillery later, Anderson surrendered. When in response Lincoln called for 75,000 volunteers to put down the rebellion, four states in the Upper South, led by Virginia, also seceded. Matters had passed beyond compromise.

The Roots of a Divided Society

And so the Union was sundered. After 70 years, the forces of sectionalism and separatism had finally outpulled the ties binding "these United States." Why did affairs come to such a pass?

In some ways, we have seen, the revolution in markets, the improving technologies of transportation, the increasingly sophisticated systems of credit and finance, all served to tie the nation together. The cotton planter who rode the steamship *Fashion* along the Alabama River ("Time's money! Time's money!") was wearing ready-made clothes manufactured in New York from southern cotton. Chauncey Jerome's clocks from Connecticut were keeping time not only for commercial planters, to whom time was money, but for Lowell mill workers like Mary Paul, who learned to measure her lunch break in minutes. Wheat farmers in Athens, Tennessee, and Ottumwa, Iowa, were interested in the Crimean War, because the war affected the price of wheat, and the price of wheat affected the profits that could be made shipping their grain by the new railroad lines. American society had become far more specialized, and therefore far more interdependent, since the days of Crèvecoeur's self-sufficient farmer of the 1780s.

But a specialized economy had not brought unity. For the North, specialization meant more factories, a higher percentage of urban workers, and a greater number of cities and towns—themselves signs of specialization. Industry affected midwestern farmers as well, for their steel plows and McCormick reapers allowed them to farm larger holdings and required greater capital investment in the new machines. For its part, the South was transformed by the industrial revolution too, as textile factories made cotton the booming mainstay of its economy. But for all its growth, the region remained largely a rural society. Its prosperity stemmed from expansion westward into new areas of cotton production, and the dominant planter class reinforced the concepts of honor, hierarchy, and deference.

Above all, the intensive labor required to produce cotton, rice, and sugar made slavery an inseparable part of the southern way of life—"so intimately mingled with our social conditions," as one Georgian admitted, "that it would be impossible to eradicate it." An increasing number of northerners viewed slavery as evil, not so much out of high-minded sympathy toward slaves, but as a labor system that threatened the republican ideals of white American society.

If the United States had not grown so dynamically—if its frontier had not swept so quickly toward the Pacific—the nation might have been able to postpone the day of reckoning on slavery. It might have found ways to compromise or to rationalize its creed that "all men are created equal," until some form of gradual emancipation could have been adopted. But the luxury of time was not available. The new territories became the battlegrounds for two contrasting ways of life, with slavery at the center of the debate. Nor did those Americans, North and South, black and white, who saw the issue in moral terms think the question should be postponed.

It fell to the political system to try to adjudicate sectional conflict, through debate within the framework of a democratic republic and through a system of national parties that represented various interest groups. But the political system had critical weaknesses. The American system of electing a president gave the winning candidate a state's entire electoral vote, regardless of the margin of victory. (Lincoln, with a total of 1.9 million ballots cast for him, received 180 electoral votes; Douglas, with 1.3 million, received only 12.) That procedure made a northern sectional party possible, since the Republicans could never have carried an election on the basis of popular vote alone. In addition, the four-year fixed presidential term allowed Pierce and Buchanan to remain in office, pursuing disruptive policies on Kansas, even after the voters had rejected those policies in 1854 and 1858. Finally, since 1844 the Democratic party had required a two-thirds vote to nominate its presidential candidate. Unintentionally, this requirement made it difficult to pick any truly forceful leader and gave the South a veto over the party's candidate. Yet the South, by itself, could not elect a president.

The nation's republican heritage also contributed to the political system's vulnerability. Ever since the Revolution, when Americans accused the king and Parliament of deliberately conspiring to deprive them of their liberties, Americans had been accustomed to suspecting the motives of political opponents. Such an outlook often stimulated exaggerated fears, unreasonable conclusions, and excessive reactions. For their part, Republicans emphasized the existence of the Slave Power bent on eradicating northern rights, while southerners accused the Black Republicans of conspiring to destroy southern equality. Each side viewed itself as defending the country's republican tradition from an internal threat; each side came to feel that defeat would mean the end of republicanism.

In 1850, southerners might have been satisfied if their section had been left alone and the agitation against slavery had ended. But a decade later, many Americans both North and South had come to accept the idea of an irrepressible conflict between two societies, one based on freedom, the other on slavery, in which only one side could ultimately prevail. At stake, it seemed, was control of the nation's future. As a weary Abraham Lincoln looked back to the beginning of the conflict four years later, he noted, "Both parties deprecated war, but one of them would *make* war rather than let the nation survive, and the other would *accept* war rather than let it perish, and the war came."

SIGNIFICANT EVENTS

1834	McCormick patents mechanical reaper
1837	John Deere patents steel plow
1840–1860	Expansion of railroad network
1846–1854	Mass immigration to United States
1849–1860	Cotton boom
1850	Illinois Central is first land grant railroad
1852	Pierce elected president
1853	Gadsden Purchase; Know-Nothings begin expanding
1854	Kansas–Nebraska Act; Republican party organized; Ostend Manifesto; peak of immigration
1854–1855	Height of Know-Nothings' popularity
1855	Fighting begins in Kansas; Republican party organizes in key northern states
1856	Free state "government" established in Kansas; "Sack of Lawrence"; caning of Charles Sumner; Pottawatomie massacre; first railroad bridge built across the Mississippi; Buchanan elected president
1857–1861	Panic and depression
1857	*Dred Scott* decision; Lecompton constitution drafted
1858	Congress rejects Lecompton constitution; Lincoln–Douglas debates
1859	John Brown's raid on Harpers Ferry
1860	Democratic party ruptures at Charleston; Lincoln elected president; South Carolina secedes
1861	Rest of Deep South secedes; Confederate States of America established; Crittenden Compromise defeated; war begins at Fort Sumter; Upper South secedes

16

Total War and the Republic

"**O**ff they went, one and all," a congressman reported, "off down the highway, over across fields towards the woods, anywhere, everywhere, to escape." Panic-stricken, their faces streaked and blackened by the powder of their cartridges, they threw away their knapsacks, their canteens, their cartridge boxes, even their rifles—everything—as they fled. In their headlong rush, they shoved aside officers who tried to stop them, ignored congressmen waving revolvers, and raced frantically by the wagons, caissons, and civilians' carriages that clogged the roads. They didn't stop until they reached Washington.

July 21, 1861, had begun as a festive outing. For weeks the drumbeat in Horace Greeley's influential New York *Tribune* had been "Forward to Richmond! The Rebel Congress must not be allowed to meet there on the 20th of July!" As the Union army under the command of General Irvin McDowell moved toward the Confederates concentrated at Manassas Junction, members of Congress, joined by jaunty male and female sightseers, their picnic baskets filled with provisions and fine wines, drove buggies and other conveyances the 25 miles from Washington to see the battle that would crush the rebellion.*

In truth, both armies were composed of raw, undisciplined troops. Few had ever marched together, or fired their rifles in coordinated fashion; indeed, they were more likely to mill about and shoot their own comrades by mistake. Worse yet, neither side had ever deployed such massive bodies of men before: McDowell commanded 30,000 troops against General Pierre Beauregard's 22,000. (During the Mexican War, American armies had usually numbered from 5000 to 10,000.) The fighting surged back and forth near a stream called Bull Run, until Confederate reinforcements under General Thomas "Stonewall" Jackson turned the tide. Railroads had allowed Jackson to transfer his forces in timely fashion; and it was here that he won his nickname, for holding his line so staunchly.

After McDowell ordered a retreat, his green Union soldiers panicked when fired upon while on the road, and the retreat became a rout. Discipline dissolved, the army degenerated into a mob, and a stampede began. All the next day in a drizzling rain, the mud-spattered troops straggled into the capital. The remnants

*The Union and Confederacy often gave different names to a battle. The Confederates called the first battle Manassas; the Union, Bull Run.

Winslow Homer's Rainy Day in Camp, *realistically portrays the tedium and discomfort of camp life. In the world's first total war, victory depended on massing and bringing to bear the North's superior resources.*

of various regiments mingled pell-mell. William Russell, an English reporter, asked one pale officer where they were coming from. "Well, sir, I guess we're all coming out of Virginny as far as we can, and pretty well whipped too," he replied. "I know I'm going home. I've had enough of fighting to last my lifetime."

The rout at Bull Run sobered the North. Gone were dreams of ending the war with one glorious battle. Gone was the illusion that 75,000 volunteers serving three months could crush the rebellion. As one perceptive observer noted, "We have undertaken to make war without in the least knowing how."

Still, it was not surprising that both sides underestimated the magnitude of the conflict. As the conduct of war had evolved in Europe, fighting between armies consisted largely of maneuverings that took relatively few lives, did little damage, respected private property, and left civilians largely unharmed. In that respect, the Mexican War was like the War of 1812 or the American Revolution. The Civil War, on the other hand, was the first war anywhere whose major battles routinely involved over 100,000 troops. So many combatants could be equipped only through the use of factory-produced weaponry; they could be mobilized and moved only with the help of railroad networks; and they could be sustained only through the concerted efforts of civilian society as a whole. The morale of the population, the quality of political leadership, and the utilization of industrial and economic might were all critical to the outcome. By the time the fighting ended, few Americans had not been personally touched by the bloody conflict, and society had been fundamentally transformed. Quite simply, the Civil War was the first total war in history.

THE DEMANDS OF TOTAL WAR

When the war began, the North had an enormous advantage in manpower and industrial capacity. The Union's population was 2.5 times larger, and its advantage in white men of military age even greater. The North had a stronger navy and merchant marine, it produced more iron, firearms, and textiles, and it had in place more railroad track and rolling stock. Creating goods worth $1.5 billion, its 110,000 establishments dwarfed in capacity the 18,000 Confederate manufacturing concerns, whose products were worth $155 million.

From a modern perspective, the South's attempt to defend its independence against such odds would seem a hopeless cause. Yet this view indicates how much the conception of war has changed since then. European observers, who knew the strength and resources of the two sides, believed that the Confederacy, with its large area, poor roads, and rugged terrain, could never be conquered. Indeed, the South enjoyed definite strategic advantages. To be victorious, it did not need to invade the North or capture a single mile of territory—only to defend its own land, prevent the North from destroying its armies, and break the Union's will to fight. Southern soldiers knew the topography of their home country better, and a friendly population regularly supplied them with intelligence about Union troop movements.

The North, in contrast, had to invade and conquer the Confederacy and destroy the southern will to resist. To do so, its armies would be forced to use

Resources of the Union and the Confederacy, 1861

	UNION	CONFEDERACY	UNION ADVANTAGE
Total population	22,300,000	9,100,000*	2.5 to 1
White male population (18–45 years)	4,600,000	1,100,000	4.2 to 1
Bank deposits	$207,000,000	$47,000,000	4.4 to 1
Value of manufactured goods	$1,730,000,000	$156,000,000	11 to 1
Railroad mileage	22,000	9,000	2.4 to 1
Shipping tonnage	4,600,000	290,000	16 to 1
Value of textiles produced	$181,000,000	$10,000,000	18 to 1
Value of firearms produced	$2,290,000	$73,000	31 to 1
Pig iron production (tons)	951,000	37,000	26 to 1
Coal production (tons)	13,680,000	650,000	21 to 1
Corn and wheat production (bushels)	698,000,000	314,000,000	2.2 to 1
Draft animals	5,800,000	2,900,000	2 to 1
Cotton production (bales)	43,000	5,344,000	1 to 124

*Slaves accounted for 3,500,000, or 40 percent.

Sources: U.S. Census 1860; E. B. Long, *The Civil War Day by Day* (New York: Doubleday, 1971), p. 723.

thousands of soldiers to defend long supply lines into enemy territory, a situation that significantly reduced the northern advantage in manpower. Only half the Union troops, compared to three-fourths of the Confederates, were available for combat duty. Yet in the end, the Union's resources and population proved so superior that the Confederacy was not only invaded and conquered but also utterly destroyed. By 1865 the Union forces had penetrated virtually every part of the 500,000 square miles of the Confederacy and were able to move almost at will. The Civil War demonstrated the capacity of a modern society to overcome distance and terrain with technology.

Political Leadership

To sustain a commitment to total war required effective political leadership, especially in a democracy, where coercion of the populace has limits. The task of leadership fell on Abraham Lincoln and Jefferson Davis, who ironically had been born within a hundred miles of each other in Kentucky, before both their families moved west.

The Davises chose Mississippi, where they became part of planter society on the cotton frontier. Assisted in his early life by his wealthy older brother, Jefferson Davis was accustomed to life's advantages. He had been educated at Transylvania University and then West Point. After fighting in the Mexican War, he became one of the South's leading advocates in the Senate, as well as serving as Franklin Pierce's secretary of war. Tall and stately, sensitive about his reputation, the new Confederate president looked and acted like an aristocrat. Although he was extremely hardworking and committed to the cause he led, he quarreled tactlessly with generals and politicians, nursed grudges, and refused to work with those he personally disliked. "He cannot brook opposition or criticism," one member of the Confederate Congress testified, "and those who do not bow down before him have no chance of success with him."

Not surprisingly, a man of such temperament was not well suited to rousing the southern people. His cabinet, with whom he was often at odds, changed constantly; 14 men held its six posts in four years. Yet for all Davis' personal handicaps, he faced an institutional one even more daunting. To meet the demands of total war, he would need to centralize and increase the authority of the government beyond anything the South had ever experienced. And yet the Confederate States of America had seceded in opposition to control by the federal majority. With the doctrine of states' rights so crucial to southern ideology, even a popular leader would have faced serious obstacles in coordinating resistance.

When Lincoln took the oath of office, his national experience consisted of one term in the House of Representatives. He had never held an administrative office, and even his friends worried that his new task was beyond him. But Lincoln was a shrewd judge of character and a superb politician. To achieve a common goal, he willingly overlooked withering criticism and personal slights. (The commander of the Union army, General George McClellan, for one, continually snubbed the president and referred to him as "the original Gorilla.") He was not easily humbugged, overawed, or flattered, and never allowed personal feelings to blind him to his larger objectives. "No man knew better how to summon and dispose of political ability to attain great political ends," one contemporary commented.

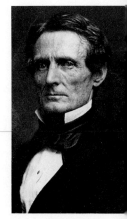

Jefferson Davis.

"This is essentially a People's contest," Lincoln asserted at the start of the war, and few presidents have been better able to communicate with the average citizen. Several times a week, the president opened the White House doors to the general public to hear their praise, complaints, or requests—his "public opinion baths," he called them. He regularly visited Union troops in army hospitals, at field encampments, and on the parade ground, more often than not astride some horse too small to accommodate his lanky frame. "The boys liked him," wrote Joseph Twichell, from a Connecticut regiment, "in fact his popularity with the army is and has been universal." Always Lincoln reminded the public that the war was being fought for the ideals of the Revolution and the Republic. It was a test, he remarked in his famous address at Gettysburg, of whether a nation "conceived in Liberty, and dedicated to the proposition that all men are created equal" could "long endure." The politician in him recognized that without popular support, he could not wage a successful, full-scale war. But his eloquence also sprang from a deep personal anguish, as he witnessed the death and suffering the war produced. Uncorrupted by power, Lincoln remained to the end a man of compassion and humility.

He also proved the more effective military leader. Jefferson Davis took his title of commander-in-chief literally, priding himself on his West Point training and interfering with his generals even on the smallest matters. But he failed to formulate an effective overarching strategy. In contrast, Lincoln read quite clearly the lessons of the disaster at Bull Run. He accepted General Winfield Scott's suggestion that the army and navy surround the Confederacy, cut off its supplies, and slowly strangle it into submission, just as the anaconda snake squeezes its prey. But unlike Scott, he realized that an "anaconda plan" was not enough. As the blockade tightened, the South would have to be invaded and defeated, not only on an eastern front in Virginia, but in the West, where Union control of the Mississippi would divide the Confederacy fatally. Lincoln understood that the Union's superior manpower and matériel would become decisive only when the Confederacy's resources were stretched along a broad front. The Union forces could then break through at the weak points. This novel idea of a simultaneous advance languished several years before the president found generals willing or able to execute it.

Lincoln was not the North's only advantage in leadership. The existence of political parties also contributed to the Union's successful conduct of the war. When southerners seceded, they deliberately suppressed parties, believing that their absence would promote national unity. The result was precisely the opposite. Without parties, Davis lacked the means to mobilize support. Confederate politics deteriorated into a paralyzing system of personal loyalties, while local politicians tended to focus on their own state's narrow interests. In the North, party organizations linked state and local loyalties with a national cause. In addition, elections served as referenda on policy, and every election was a step toward nationalizing the war effort.

The Border States

When the war began, the balance of forces between North and South remained uncertain because four border slave states—Delaware, Maryland, Kentucky, and Missouri—remained in the Union. Only Delaware was certain to stay, and Lincoln's immediate political challenge was to retain the loyalty of the others. Maryland especially was crucial, for if it was lost, Washington itself would have to be abandoned.

The danger became immediately apparent when pro-Confederate forces destroyed the railroad bridges near Baltimore and isolated Washington. Only with difficulty was the administration able to move troops to the city. Once the capital was safe, Lincoln moved vigorously—even ruthlessly—to secure Maryland. He suspended the writ of habeas corpus, the right under the Constitution of an arrested person either to be charged with a specific crime or to be released, and then held without trial prominent Confederate sympathizers (including the mayor and chief of police of Baltimore), suppressed pro-Confederate newspapers, and mounted a massive show of force in Baltimore. As the fall state election approached, Union troops arrested 27 members of the legislature as well as outspoken secessionists who tried to vote on election day. This intimidation ensured that Unionists won a complete victory. The election ended any possibility that Maryland would join the Confederacy.

At the beginning of the conflict, Kentucky officially declared its neutrality. Lincoln was quoted as saying that he hoped to have God on his side, but that he had to have Kentucky. "I think to lose Kentucky is nearly to lose the whole game," he wrote. "Kentucky gone, we can not hold Missouri, nor, as I think, Maryland. These all against us, and the job on our hands is too large for us." Union generals requested permission to occupy the state, but the president refused, preferring to act cautiously and wait for Unionist sentiment to assert itself. After Unionists won control of the legislature in the summer election, a Confederate army entered the state, giving Lincoln the opening he needed. He quickly sent in troops, and Kentucky stayed in the Union.

In Missouri, where controversy over slavery stretched back to the statehood debates of 1820, skirmishing broke out between Union and Confederate sympathizers. Eventually the pro-Confederate governor was deposed by an extralegal Unionist government. Not until March 1862, when the Union scored a victory at Pea Ridge in northern Arkansas, was Missouri secure from any Confederate threat. Even so, guerrilla warfare continued in the state throughout the remainder of the war. In Virginia, internal divisions led to the creation of a new border state, as the hilly western counties where slavery was not strong refused to support the Confederacy. After adopting a congressionally mandated program of gradual emancipation, West Virginia was formally admitted to the Union in June 1863.

The Union scored an important triumph in holding the border states. The population of all five equaled that of the four states of the Upper South that had joined the Confederacy, and their production of military supplies—food, animals, and minerals—was greater. Furthermore, Maryland and West Virginia contained key railroad lines and were critical to the defense of Washington, while Kentucky and Missouri gave the Union army access to the major river systems of the western theater, down which it launched the first successful invasion of the Confederacy.

OPENING MOVES

As with so many Civil War battles, the Confederate victory at Bull Run achieved no decisive military results. But a sobered Congress authorized the enlistment of half a million volunteers, to serve for three years. As public clamor forced Lincoln to replace General Scott, he named a new commander of the Union army, 34-year-old George McClellan, a West Point graduate who had been working as a railroad executive when the war began. Energetic and ambitious, McClellan was a model of businesslike efficiency, and he set to work on the much-needed task of organizing and drilling the Army of the Potomac. Indeed, for the rest of 1861 both sides devoted their energies to assembling and training armies that dwarfed any previously assembled on the continent.

Blockade and Isolate

Assigned the formidable task of blockading some 3550 miles of Confederate coastline, the U.S. Navy had only 42 ships in commission at the beginning of the war. Unlike their army counterparts, however, few naval officers resigned to accept Confederate commissions. By the spring of 1862, the Union fleet had secured several key bases, including Roanoke Island off North Carolina, the sea islands off South Carolina and Georgia, and Fort Pulaski guarding the entrance to Savannah. The navy also began building fleets of powerful gunboats to operate on the rivers. In April 1862, Flag Officer David G. Farragut ran a gauntlet of Confederate fire rafts, armor rams, and shore batteries to capture New Orleans, the Confederacy's largest port. Memphis, another important river city, fell to Union forces in June.

The blockade was hardly leakproof, and Confederates slipped through it using fast, low ships. Still, southern trade suffered badly. Only 800 vessels evaded Union patrols in the first year of war, compared with the 6000 ships that had docked in 1860. Unable to match the Union navy ship for ship, the Confederacy resorted to technological innovation, by converting the wooden U.S.S. *Merrimack* into an ironclad gunboat. Rechristened the *Virginia*, it steamed out in March 1862 to meet the Union fleet at Hampton Roads and damaged a third of the ships before engine trouble forced it to retire. But the next day a new Union ironclad, the *Monitor*, battled it to a standoff; the Confederates were forced to scuttle the *Virginia* when they evacuated Norfolk in May. After that, the Union's naval supremacy was secure.

The South looked to diplomacy as another means to lift the blockade. With cotton so vital to European economies, especially Great Britain's, southerners believed Europe would formally recognize the Confederacy and come to its aid. To increase economic pressure, the Davis administration deliberately withheld cotton that was waiting shipment, rather than rush it overseas before the Union blockade became effective. The North, for its part, claimed that it was merely putting down a domestic insurrection, and Secretary of State William Seward warned European nations against intervening in America's internal affairs. Yet Lincoln's proclamation of a blockade had the effect of giving the Confederacy belligerent status, since a country legally could not blockade itself. European countries extended belligerent status to the government at Richmond, which allowed the Confederacy to purchase supplies abroad and outfit privateers in foreign ports.

A diplomatic crisis erupted in November 1861 when a Union navy ship, acting without orders, stopped a British mail packet, the *Trent*, on the high seas and removed James Mason and John Slidell, two Confederate diplomats who were traveling to Europe. The British government vigorously protested this action, since international law did not authorize the seizure of individuals as contraband.

Amid war talk on both sides of the Atlantic, Lincoln defused the crisis by ordering Mason's and Slidell's release, while refusing to make a formal apology, as the British demanded.

The bumper cotton crop of 1860 initially undermined king cotton diplomacy, for European manufacturers had a large surplus on hand. By 1862, however, supplies were dwindling and the Confederacy mounted a new campaign to win recognition. France was ready to agree, but not unless Britain followed suit. The British prime minister, Lord Palmerston, favored the South, but he hesitated to act until Confederate armies proved themselves strong enough to fend off the North. Meanwhile, new supplies of cotton from Egypt and India enabled the British textile industry to recover. In the end Britain and the rest of Europe refused to recognize the Confederacy. As the blockade continued to tighten, the South was left to stand or fall on its own resources.

Grant in the West

In the western war theater, the first decisive Union victory was won by a short, shabbily dressed, cigar-chomping general named Ulysses S. Grant. An undistinguished student at West Point (he graduated twenty-first in a class of 39), Grant had become lonely and depressed in the army and, drinking heavily, eventually resigned his commission. In civilian life he failed at everything he tried, and when the war broke out he was a store clerk in Galena, Illinois. Almost 39, he enlisted as a colonel in the Illinois militia, and two months later became a brigadier general.

Grant's self-effacing demeanor gave little indication of his military potential. He was a quiet, ordinary-looking man, who disliked ceremony and bore himself in distinctly unmilitary fashion. The gaze of his blue eyes, however, disclosed iron determination. Alert to seize any opening, he remained extraordinarily calm and clear-headed in battle. He absorbed details on a map almost photographically, and in battles that spread out over miles, he was superb at coordinating an attack on horseback. He would "try all sorts of cross-cuts," recalled one staff officer, "ford streams and jump any number of fences to reach another road rather than go back and take a fresh start." Grant also took full advantage of the telegraph to track troop movements, stringing new lines as he advanced and keeping his communications open. (Some of his Union telegraphers were so adept that they could receive messages before a station was set up, by touching the end of the wire to their tongues to pick up Morse code.) Hard-headed and unromantic, Grant grasped that attention to detail and hard fighting, not fancy maneuvering, would bring victory. "The art of war is simple," he once explained. "Find out where your enemy is, get at him as soon as you can and strike him as hard as you can, and keep moving on."

Grant realized that rivers were avenues into the interior of the Confederacy, and in February 1862, supported by Union gunboats, he captured Fort Henry on the Tennessee River and shortly after, Fort Donelson on the Cumberland. These victories forced the Confederates to withdraw from Kentucky and middle Tennessee. Grant continued south with 40,000 men, but he was surprised on April 6 by General Albert Johnston, who had marched his army through dense woodland to Shiloh, just north of the Tennessee–Mississippi border. Johnston was killed in the day's fierce fighting, but by nightfall his army had driven the Union troops back to the Tennessee River, while others huddled disconsolately in the forest as a cold rain fell. William Tecumseh Sherman, one of Grant's subordinates, found the general standing under a dripping tree, his coat collar drawn up against the damp,

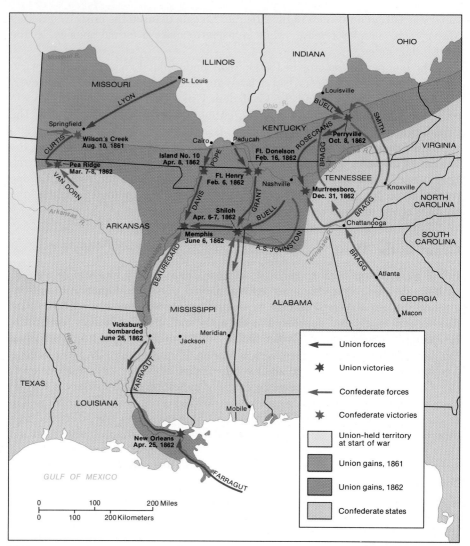

THE WAR IN THE WEST, 1861–1862
Grant's push southward stalled after his costly victory at Shiloh; nevertheless, by the end of 1862 the Union had secured Kentucky and Missouri, as well as most of Confederate Tennessee and the upper and lower stretches of the Mississippi River.

puffing on a cigar. Sherman was about to suggest retreat, but something in Grant's eyes, lighted by the glow of his stogey, made Sherman hesitate. So he said only, "Well, Grant, we've had the devil's own day, haven't we." "Yes," replied Grant. "Lick 'em tomorrow, though." With the aid of reinforcements which he methodically ferried across the river all night, Grant counterattacked the next morning and drove the Confederates from the field.

But victory came at a high price. Shiloh inflicted over 23,000 casualties: virtually as many Americans were killed or wounded in two days as in the Revolution, the War of 1812, and the Mexican War combined. "The scenes on this field would have cured anyone of war," Sherman testified. Grant, who had previously doubted the commitment of Confederate troops, came away deeply impressed by their determined fighting. "At Shiloh," he wrote afterwards, "I gave up all idea of saving the Union except by complete conquest."

Eastern Stalemate

Grant's victories did not impress a number of his envious colleagues, who argued that he drank too much and should be relieved of command. But Lincoln was unmoved. "I can't spare this man. He fights." That was a quality in short supply farther east, where General McClellan directed operations.

The short, handsome McClellan was nicknamed "Little Napoleon" by his admirers, and he did little to discourage the comparison. But beneath his arrogance and bravado lay a self-doubt that rendered him excessively cautious. As the months dragged on and McClellan did nothing but train and plan, Lincoln's frustration grew. "If General McClellan does not want to use the army I would like to *borrow* it," he remarked acidly. In the spring of 1862 the general finally moved against Richmond, the Confederate capital. Transporting 130,000 troops by ship to the mouth of the James River, he began inching his way up the peninsula between the James and York rivers. Habitually overestimating his opponent's strength, he was incapable of seizing the initiative. He threw up siegeworks instead of launching a direct assault, or maneuvered and called for reinforcements instead of striking directly for Richmond. After two and a half months, when he had finally advanced to within five miles of the capital, General Joseph Johnston attacked him near Fair Oaks, from which he barely escaped.* Worse for him, when Johnston was badly wounded, the formidable Robert E. Lee took command of the Army of Northern Virginia.

Lee, an impeccably dressed, gentlemanly commander, had entered the war somewhat reluctantly. ("I must say that I am one of those dull creatures that cannot see the good of secession," he confessed at the beginning of the conflict.) But he could not bring himself to raise his sword against his native Virginia. From his army days, Lee knew McClellan personally and understood how to fight him. Where McClellan was cautious and defensive, Lee was daring and ever alert to assume the offensive. His first name, one of his colleagues commented, should have been Audacity: "He will take more chances, and take them quicker than any other general in this country." Lee was aided by Stonewall Jackson, a deeply religious Calvinist whose rigorous discipline honed his troops to a hard edge. At the Battle of Seven Days McClellan parried the attacks of Lee and Jackson with his own brilliant maneuvering, but he stayed on the defensive. As McClellan retreated to the protection of the Union gunboats, Lincoln ordered the Peninsula campaign abandoned and placed John Pope in command. Lee won another victory, this time over Pope, at the second Battle of Bull Run. As the badly whipped Pope retreated back to Washington, Lincoln restored McClellan to command.

Realizing that the Confederacy needed a decisive victory, Lee convinced Davis to allow him to invade the North, hoping to detach Maryland and isolate Washington. But as his army crossed into Maryland, a copy of Lee's orders, wrapped around three cigars and accidentally left at a campsite by a Confederate officer, fell into Union hands. From this paper McClellan learned that his own forces vastly outnumbered Lee's—yet still he hesitated before launching a series of badly coordinated assaults near Antietam Creek on September 17. Scrambling

*Not to be confused with Albert Johnston, the Confederate general in the western theater killed at Shiloh.

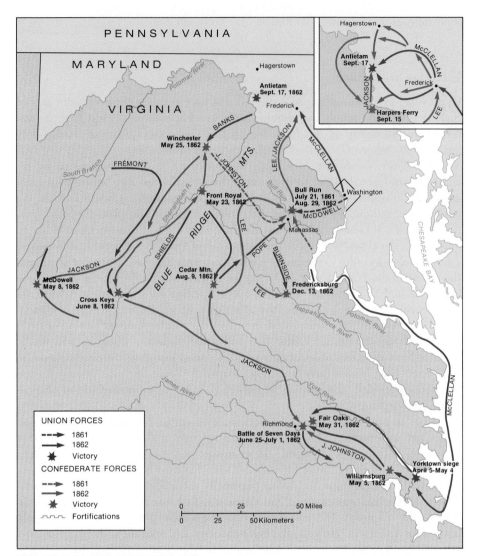

THE WAR IN THE EAST, 1861–1862
McClellan's campaign against Richmond failed when Joseph Johnston surprised him at Fair Oaks. Taking command of the Army of Northern Virginia, Lee drove back McClellan in the Seven Days battles, then won a resounding victory in the second Battle of Bull Run. He followed up by invading Maryland, dividing his forces to take advantage of McClellan's caution, and captured Harpers Ferry. McClellan checked his advance at Antietam. The Army of the Potomac's devastating defeat at Fredericksburg ended a year of frustration and failure for the Union in the eastern theater.

desperately, Lee barely beat back these attacks; the bloody exchanges horrified both sides for their sheer carnage. "Where the line stood the ground was covered in blue," recounted a Georgia soldier. "I could have walked on them without putting my feet on the ground." Within the space of seven hours, nearly 5000 soldiers were killed and another 18,000 wounded, making it the bloodiest single day in American history. When Lee, worried about his overextended supply lines, decided to withdraw, McClellan allowed the Army of Northern Virginia to escape.

With almost 23,000 casualties, Antietam was the bloodiest single day of the war. A group of Confederate soldiers were photographed where they fell along the Hagerstown Pike, the scene of some of the heaviest fighting. Said one Union officer of the fighting there: "Men, I cannot say fell; they were knocked out of the ranks by dozens."

Exasperated beyond measure with McClellan's habitual problem of "the slows," as Lincoln put it, the president relieved him from his command in November.

The winter of 1862 was the North's Valley Forge, as morale sank to an all-time low. It took General Ambrose Burnside, who assumed McClellan's place, little more than a month to demonstrate his utter incompetence. In December at the Battle of Fredericksburg, he ordered a direct assault on an impregnable Confederate position. The disastrous encounter inflicted 12,600 casualties on the North, compared to fewer than 5000 for the Confederates. Lincoln replaced Burnside with "Fighting Joe" Hooker. In the West, Grant had emerged as the dominant figure, but the Army of the Potomac still lacked a capable commander, the deaths on both sides kept mounting, and no end to the war was in sight.

EMANCIPATION

In 1858, Lincoln had proclaimed that an American "house divided" could not stand and that the United States would eventually become either all slave or all free. At the time, he had worried that the movement was toward slavery.

When the house did divide, Lincoln hesitated to move against slavery. He perceived, accurately, that most northern whites were not deeply committed to emancipation. He feared the social upheaval that such a revolutionary step would cause, and he hoped not to alarm the wavering border states. Thus when Congress met in special session in July 1861, Lincoln fully supported a resolution offered by Senator John J. Crittenden of Kentucky, which declared that "this war is not waged for any purpose of overthrowing or interfering with the rights or established institutions of these States, but to defend and maintain the supremacy of the Constitution and to preserve the Union." Even with most of the southern members of Congress gone, the Crittenden Resolution passed the House 117 to 2 and the Senate by 30 to 5.

Still, a minority of Republican radicals like Senator Charles Sumner and Horace Greeley pressed Lincoln to adopt a policy of emancipation. Slavery had caused the war, they argued; its destruction would hasten the war's end. Lincoln, however, placed first priority on saving the Union, not ending slavery. "My paramount object in this struggle *is* to save the Union, and is *not* either to save or to destroy slavery," he affirmed in 1862 in a public letter to Greeley. "If I could save the Union without freeing *any* slave I would do it, and if I could save it by freeing *all* the slaves I would do it, and if I could save it by freeing some and leaving others alone, I would also do that." This statement outlined Lincoln's policy during the first year of the war.

The Logic of Events

As the Union army began to occupy Confederate territory, slaves flocked to the Union camps. Octave Johnson, the runaway who hid in the Louisiana bayous for over a year (page 451), was only one of many slaves who presented themselves to occupying forces. In May 1861, the army adopted the policy of declaring runaway slaves contraband of war, and refused to return them to their rebel owners. In the Confiscation Act of August 1861, Congress provided that slaves used for military purposes by the Confederacy would become free if they fell into Union hands. Lincoln adhered to this position for a year but went no further. When two of his generals, acting on their own authority, abolished slavery in their districts, the president countermanded their orders.

By the time Congress reconvened in December 1861, opinion was beginning to shift. Introduced a second time, the Crittenden Resolution was soundly defeated, with Republicans voting against it almost three to one. Congress also prohibited federal troops from capturing or returning fugitive slaves, banned slavery from all the territories (thus ignoring the *Dred Scott* decision), and freed the 2000 slaves living in the District of Columbia with compensation of their owners. In July 1862 it took even more radical action by passing the Second Confiscation Act, which declared that the slaves of anyone who supported the rebellion would be freed if they came into federal custody. Unlike the first act, it did not matter whether the slaves had been used for military purposes. If vigorously enforced, the law would have led to virtual emancipation throughout the Confederacy.

Lincoln signed this bill, then proceeded to ignore it. Instead, he emphasized state action, since slavery was a domestic institution. In his first annual message to Congress, he proposed that the federal government provide grants to compensate slaveowners in any state-sponsored program of emancipation, to be completed by the year 1900. He also urged delegations of free blacks who visited him to organize colonization programs to Africa. Having lived all their lives in America, the delegates failed to see the virtues of moving to a land they had never seen. Twice the president summoned representatives from the border states and urged them to act before the war destroyed slavery of its own momentum. Both times they rejected his plea.

These failed attempts led Lincoln to suggest a new policy when he met with his cabinet on July 22—to issue a proclamation freeing at least some slaves. He was increasingly confident that the border states would remain in the Union, and he wanted to strike a blow that would weaken the Confederacy militarily. By making the struggle one of freedom versus slavery, such a proclamation would also undermine Confederate efforts to obtain diplomatic recognition. Accepting Seward's advice, Lincoln decided to wait for a Union military victory so that the act would not appear one of desperation.

The Emancipation Proclamation

Two months later, the victory at Antietam provided the opportunity. On September 22, Lincoln announced that all slaves within rebel lines would be freed unless the seceded states returned to their allegiance by January 1, 1863. When that day came, the Emancipation Proclamation went formally into effect. Excluded from its terms were the Union slave states, all of Tennessee, and the areas of Virginia and Louisiana that were under Union control. In all, about 830,000 of the nation's 4 million slaves were not covered by its provisions. Since Lincoln justified his actions on strictly military grounds, he believed that there was no legal right to apply it to areas not in rebellion.

Southerners denounced the proclamation as an attempt to incite their slaves to rebellion. Nor did Europeans immediately praise the move. Its principle, sneered a London paper, was "not that a human being cannot justly own another, but that he cannot own him unless he is loyal to the United States." Yet in the long run, European public opinion swung toward the Union. In the North, Republicans generally favored Lincoln's decision, while the Democrats made it a major issue in the 1862 elections. "Every white man in the North, who does not want to be swapped off for a free Nigger, should vote the Democratic ticket," urged one party orator. While the Democrats improved their showing in the elections that year, the results offered no clear verdict on the proclamation, since the Republicans increased their vote in some areas of the North.

Despite the mixed reaction, the Emancipation Proclamation had immense symbolic importance, for it redefined the nature of the war. The North was fighting, not to save the old Union, but to create a new nation. The war had become remorseless revolution.

Black Americans' Civil War

Contrary to southern whites' fear that a race war would erupt behind the lines, slavery did not explode during the war: it simply disintegrated. Well before federal troops entered an area, slaves took the lead in undermining the institution by openly challenging white authority and claiming greater personal freedom for themselves. For the first time, whites lost control of the slave labor force. One experienced overseer reported in frustration that now the "slaves will do only what pleases them, go out in the morning when it suits them, come in when they please, etc." In addition, the number of instances of slaves refusing to submit to punishment rose. The wife of a Texas planter wrote that she had discontinued whipping, for it only made matters worse. Throughout the Confederacy the vital psychological relationship between master and slave was strained, and sometimes it snapped.

Early in the conflict slaves concluded that emancipation would be one consequence of a Union victory. Perhaps as many as half a million—one-seventh of the total slave population of the Confederacy—fled to Union lines. Even in areas where escape was impractical, a remarkable number of slaves learned the news of the proclamation and rejoiced. One, who found out just before she was to serve her master's dinner, asked to be excused to get water from a nearby spring. Once safely out of earshot of the house, she gave free rein to her feelings. "I jump up and scream, 'Glory, glory hallelujah to Jesus! I'se free! I'se free! Glory to God, you come down an' free us; no big man could do it.' An' I got sort of scared, afeared somebody hear me, an' I takes another good look, an' fall on de groun' an' roll over, an' kiss de groun' fo' de Lord's sake, I's so full o' praise to Masser Jesus."

Slaves who entered the Union lines faced an uncertain reception. Manifesting a deep-seated racism, northern troops were often hostile. The ex-slaves, called freedmen, ended up living in refugee or contraband camps that were overcrowded, disease-ridden, and provided only rudimentary shelter and food. "The poor Negroes die as fast as ever," one northern missionary reported. "The children are all emaciated to the last degree and have such violent coughs and dysenteries that few survive."

Convinced that blacks would not work on their own initiative, the U.S. government put some contrabands to work as cooks, teamsters, woodchoppers, and other unskilled laborers. But their wages fell well below those paid whites for the same work. In the Mississippi valley, where two-thirds of the freedmen under Union control were located, most were forced to work on plantations leased or owned by loyal planters. This policy was officially adopted in the summer of 1863 as a way to free the army from the cost of supporting former slaves and strengthen Unionism in the South. Freedmen had no say in the contracts negotiated between military authorities and planters, found themselves strictly disciplined, and had so many deductions taken from their wages that in the end most received only room and board. In short, the conditions often approximated slavery. The abolitionist Lydia Maria Child was prophetic when she predicted that if the slaves were freed "merely as a war necessity, everything must go wrong, if there is no heart or conscience on the subject."

The Emancipation Proclamation also announced that blacks would be accepted in the navy and, more controversially, the army. Throughout its history, the navy had been hard-pressed to get enough recruits, and as a result that service had always included some black sailors. African-American troops had also fought during the Revolution and the War of 1812, but they had been quickly discharged at the end of the war and had never served in the regular army. Resistance to accepting blacks in the army remained especially strong in the Midwest. Northern blacks themselves were divided over whether to serve, given the hostility of so many whites. But Frederick Douglass spoke for the vast majority of African-American people when he argued that once a black man had served in the army, there was "no power on earth which can deny that he has earned the right of citizenship in the United States."

Black men, including runaway slaves, joined the Union army and navy beginning in 1863. This photograph shows Hubbard Pryor after enlistment. As soldiers, former slaves developed a new sense of pride and confidence.

In the end, over 200,000 black men served in the Union forces, about 10 percent of the Union's total military manpower. Some, including two of Douglass' sons, were free, but most were former slaves who enlisted after escaping to the Union lines. As a concession to the racism of white troops, blacks served in segregated units under white officers. Initially they were relegated to undesirable duties such as heavy labor and burial details. They were paid only $10 a month, with $3 deducted for clothing. Whites, by contrast, received $13 a month plus a $3.50 clothing allowance. After an 18-month struggle, Congress in June 1864 granted equal pay retroactively to African-American soldiers.

After successfully agitating for the chance to fight, black soldiers impressed whites with their courage under fire. It "completely revolutionized the sentiment of the army with regard to the employment of Negro troops," a War Department official reported, after viewing the fierce battle at Millikin's Bend, Louisiana, in June 1863. Ultimately 37,000 African-American servicemen gave their lives, a rate of loss about 40 percent higher than among whites. Blacks had good reason to fight fiercely: they knew that the freedom of their race hung in the balance, they hoped to win civil rights at home by their performance on the battlefield, they resented racist sneers about their loyalty and ability, and they knew that capture might mean death. The effect on African-American pride was also apparent. Slaves admired the confidence of the new black recruits, while for their part, African-American soldiers relished being liberators. One soldier, who discovered his former master among the prisoners he was guarding, summed up the situation succinctly. "Hello, massa!" he called cheerfully, "bottom rail on top dis time!"

THE CONFEDERATE HOME FRONT

Nowhere was the effect of war more complete than within the Confederacy. These changes were especially ironic, since the southern states had seceded in order to preserve their traditional ways. Not only did the war send hundreds of thousands of "Johnny Rebs" off to the front, but it also put extreme burdens on the women and families at home. It fundamentally transformed the southern economy and forced the Confederate government to become more centralized. And of course it ended by destroying the institution of slavery, which the South had gone to war to preserve.

The New Economy

With the Union blockade tightening, the production of foodstuffs became crucial to the South's economy. Many men who normally worked in the fields had gone to fight, and with the lessening of discipline slaves became increasingly assertive, stole livestock, refused to work, or ran off. More and more plantations switched from cotton to raising grain and livestock, and some state and local organizations tried to limit the amount of cotton grown, to encourage the transition. As a result, cotton production dropped from 4.5 million bales in 1861 to 300,000 in 1864, but even so, food production declined. By the last two years of the war, the shortage had become serious.

Southern planters had resisted industrialization before the war, but the Union blockade made it impossible to rely on European manufactured goods. So the Confederate War Department began building and running factories, as well as taking over the region's mines. It also regulated private manufacturers by offering contracts and draft exemptions for their workers if they switched to the production of war goods. Though the Confederacy never became self-sufficient, its accomplishments were impressive. As Josiah Gorgas, head of the Confederate Ordnance Department, noted,

> We began in April, 1861, without an arsenal, laboratory or powder mill of any capacity, and with no foundry or rolling mill except at Richmond, and before the close of 1863, . . . we had built up foundries and rolling mills, smelting works, chemical works, a powder mill far superior to any in the United States, and a chain of arsenals, armories and laboratories equal in their capacity and their improved appointments to the best of those in the United States.

In fact, the Confederacy sustained itself far better in industrial goods than it did in agricultural produce. It was symbolic that when Lee surrendered, his troops had sufficient guns and ammunition to continue, but they had not eaten in two days.

While the Confederacy remained a rural society, its urban areas expanded and became more influential. Richmond more than tripled in population, while Atlanta, a minor upcountry Georgia town, grew into a major urban center because it was located at a critical rail junction. For the first time, urban residents in the South developed a separate identity and a consciousness of their importance.

Southern Women

Southern white women took an active, even an intense role in the war. Some gained notoriety as spies; others smuggled medicine, guns, clothing, and shoes into the South, often taking advantage of the large hoop skirts then in fashion. Women also spent a good deal of time knitting and sewing clothes for soldiers. "We never went out to pay a visit without taking our knitting along," recalled a South Carolina woman. Perhaps most important, with so many men fighting, women took charge of agricultural production. As one Georgia soldier told his wife, "You must be man and woman both while the war lasts." On plantations, the mistress often supervised the slaves, as well as the wrenching shift from cotton to foodstuffs. "All this attention to farming is uphill work with me," one South Carolina woman confessed to her army husband.

The war also opened up new jobs off the farm. Given the manpower shortage, "government girls" became essential to fill the burgeoning Confederate bureaucracy, and with economic conditions so desperate, the secretary of the treasury found he had 100 applications for every vacancy. Initially women were paid half the wages of male co-workers, but by the end of the war they had won equal pay. Women also staffed the new factories springing up on the southern landscape, undertaking even dangerous work that normally would have been considered off limits. A majority of the workers in the South's munitions factories were women, some of whom lost their lives in accidental explosions.

Thus the war brought the harsh realities of hardship and risk to southern women. But when the fighting was over, they had become more assertive, more realistic, and more confident. "Of all the principles developed by the late war," wrote one Alabama planter, "I think the capability of our Southern women to take care of themselves was by no means the least important."

Confederate Finance and Government

The most serious domestic problem the Confederate government faced was finance, for which officials at Richmond never developed a satisfactory program. The South had few banks and only $27 million in specie when the war began. European governments refused to float major loans, which left taxation as the unappealing alternative. Only in 1863 did the government begin levying a graduated income tax (from 1 to 15 percent), a series of excise taxes, and, most controversial, a tax-in-kind on farmers which, after exempting a certain portion, took one-tenth of their agricultural crops. Even more unpopular was the policy of impressment, which allowed the army to seize private property for its own use, often with little or no compensation.

Above all, the Confederacy financed the war effort simply by printing paper money not backed by specie, some $1.5 billion, which amounted to three times more than the federal government issued. The result was runaway inflation, so that by 1865 a Confederate dollar was worth only 1.7 cents in gold and prices soared to 92 times their prewar base. Prices were highest in Richmond, where flour sold for $275 a barrel by early 1864, coats for $350, shoes $125, potatoes $25 per bushel, and butter $15 a pound. By the end of the war, flour had reached an astronomical $1000 a barrel. Inflation that ate away at their standard of living was one of the great wartime hardships borne by the southern people.

In politics even more than finance, the Confederacy exercised far greater powers than those of the federal government before 1861. Indeed, Jefferson Davis strove to meet the demands of total war by transforming the South into a centralized, national state. Backed by the Confederate Congress, he sought to limit state authority over military units and create a truly national army. To do this required a draft, for enlistments had fallen off dramatically after the early rush of enthusiasm. In April 1862 the Confederacy passed the first national conscription law in American history, drafting all white males between 18 and 35 unless exempted. As conditions worsened, those age limits widened to 17 and 50, mobilizing virtually the entire military-age white population. Civilians, too, felt the effects of government control, for in 1862 the Congress authorized Davis to invoke martial law and suspend the writ of habeas corpus. For the duration of the conflict Richmond fell under martial law.

Critics protested that Davis was destroying states' rights, the cardinal principle of the Confederacy. Concerned foremost about their states' safety, governors wanted to be able to recall troops if their own territory was threatened. Governor Joseph Brown of Georgia refused to provide state troops for the defense of Atlanta, since he was afraid they would be placed under Confederate control, while Zebulon Vance of North Carolina insisted that all blankets and uniforms produced by the state's textile mills be reserved for North Carolina troops. When President Davis suspended the writ of habeas corpus, his own vice president, Alexander H. Stephens, accused him of aiming at a dictatorship. Davis, however, used those powers for a limited time, only with the permission of Congress, and only where northern invasion threatened.

But the Confederate draft, more than any other measure, produced an outcry. The original law exempted a number of unimportant occupations, including postmen and editors, and it allowed the rich to provide substitutes, at a cost that eventually rose, on the open market, to as much as $6000. The Confederacy abolished this privilege in the last year of the war, but as one Georgia leader complained, "It's a notorious fact if a man has influential friends—or a little money to spare he will never be enrolled." Most controversially, the draft exempted from service one white man on every plantation with 20 or more slaves (later reduced to 15). This law was designed to preserve control of the slave population, but more and more nonslaveholders complained that it was a rich man's war and a poor man's fight. Denouncing the war as a slaveholders' plot, one Alabama yeoman claimed that "all they want is to git you pumped up and go to fight for their infernal negroes and after you do their fighting you may kiss their hind parts for all they care." In some counties where the draft was unenforceable, conscription officers ventured only at risk to their own safety.

Hardship and Suffering

By the last year of the conflict, food shortages had become so severe that ingenious southerners were brewing parched rye, corn, or acorns instead of coffee, cooking with blackberries and molasses oil instead of vinegar, and using sorghum in place of sugar. One scarce item for which there was no substitute was salt, essential for curing meat. Scarcity bred speculation and hoarding: merchants bought up large quantities of food and supplies to resell at high prices and thus profit from the inflationary spiral. Some states tried to regulate prices and punish extortion, but the laws were unenforceable. The high prices and food shortages led to riots in several southern cities, most seriously in Richmond early in April 1863. About 300 women and children chanting "Bread!" and armed with knives, hatchets, and pistols, marched into the business section, wrecked a number of stores, and helped themselves to bread, food, and other items. Nor were rural areas immune

Precipitated by the high price of food and growing shortages, a series of food riots shook the Confederacy in 1863. In the capital of Richmond, a group of desperate women, some of them armed, ransacked bakeries and other stores until troops rushed to the scene.

from these outbreaks. Country women attacked wagon trains carrying supplies and on several occasions even invaded towns and looted stores.

As always, war corroded the discipline and order of society. With prices rising, the value of paper money dropping, and the future uncertain, many Southerners frantically pursued money and spent it in frenzied haste. The governor of Florida criticized "a wide spread desire for speculation and wealth, which have overcome obligations of patriotism and endangered the very existence of the Confederate States." Gambling halls were crowded with revelers seeking relief, while soldiers on furlough drank heavily, aware of their increasingly poor chances of survival at the front. Even in the army, theft became more common, and during the last two years of the war soldiers could not leave their property unattended. In Richmond, the House of Representatives was robbed and Jefferson Davis' favorite horse stolen.

The search for escape from the grim reality of the war led to a forced gaiety for those who could afford it. "The cities are gayer than before the war," one refugee reported, "—parties every night in Richmond, suppers costing ten and twenty thousand dollars." Walking home at night after spending several hours at the bedside of a dying soldier, Judith McGuire passed a house gay with laughter, music, and dancing. "The revulsion was sickening," she wrote in her diary. "I thought of the gayety of Paris during the French Revolution, and the hall at Brussels the night before the battle of Waterloo, and felt shocked that our own Virginians, at such a time, should remind me of scenes which we were wont to think belong only to a foreign society." The war was a cancer that ate away, not only at southern society, but at the southern soul itself.

THE UNION HOME FRONT

Since the war was fought mostly on southern soil, northern civilians rarely felt its effects directly. Yet to be effective, the North's economic resources had to be organized and mobilized. Stimulated by government purchases, the northern economy boomed and the war accelerated the process of industrialization.

Government Finances and the Economy

To begin with, the North required a comprehensive system to finance its massive campaign. Taxing the populace was an obvious means, and taxes paid for 21 percent of Union war expenses, compared to only 1 percent of the Confederacy's. In August 1861 Congress passed the first federal income tax, 3 percent on all incomes over $800 a year. When that, along with increased tariff duties, proved insufficient, Congress enacted a comprehensive tax law in 1862 that for the first time brought the tax collector into every northern household. Excise fees taxed virtually every occupation, commodity, or service; income and inheritances were taxed, as were corporations and consumers. A new bureaucracy, the Internal Revenue Bureau, oversaw the collection process.

The government also borrowed heavily, through the sale of some $2.2 billion in bonds, and financed the rest of the war by issuing paper money. In 1862 Congress authorized notes known as greenbacks because of their distinctive color on one side. In all, $431 million was printed. Although legal for the payment of debts, they could not be redeemed in specie and therefore their value fluctuated. Congress also established a national banking system, allowing nationally chartered banks to issue notes backed by U.S. bonds. By taxing state bank notes at a steep 10 percent, Congress drove competing paper money out of circulation and for the first time gave the United States a uniform national currency. This arrangement remained the country's banking system until the Federal Reserve System was established in 1913.

During the 1850s, the Republicans appealed to Whigs and commercially minded citizens with measures to develop the national economy. During the war, Lincoln and the Republican-controlled Congress similarly encouraged industry and trade. Tariffs to protect industry from foreign competition rose so sharply that by the end of the war, some duties were 100 percent, and the average rate was 47 percent, compared to 19 percent under the 1857 tariff. To encourage development of the West, the Homestead Act of 1862 granted 160 acres of public land—the size of the traditional American family farm—to those who settled and improved the land for five years. Over a million acres were distributed during the war years alone. And the Land Grant College Act of 1862 donated the proceeds from certain land sales to finance public colleges and universities. Eventually 69 institutions of higher learning were created under its provisions, many in the West.

A Rich Man's War

Over the course of the war, the government purchased more than $1 billion worth of goods and services. The army in particular was a voracious consumer. Shoes wore out every three months and uniforms every six. Goods lost or destroyed on the march and in battle had to be replaced. In response to this heavy demand, many sectors of the economy boomed, fortunes were made, and business prospered. Wages rose 42 percent between 1860 and 1864, but workers did not fully share in the prosperity because inflation and higher tariffs sent the price of consumer goods up 76 percent. Adjusted for inflation, workers' average real income dropped from $363 in 1860 to $261 in 1865, which meant that the working class paid a disproportionate share of the burden of financing the war.

The Republican belief that government should play a major role in the economy also fostered a cozy relationship between business and politics. In the rush to profit from government contracts, some suppliers succumbed to the temptation to sell inferior goods at inflated prices. Uniforms made of "shoddy"—bits of unused thread and recycled cloth—were fobbed off in such numbers that the word became an adjective describing inferior quality. Unscrupulous dealers sold clothing that dissolved in the rain, shoes that fell apart, spoiled meat, broken-down horses, and guns that would not fire. A War Department investigation later revealed that at least 20 percent of government expenditures involved fraud.

Stocks and dividends rose with the economy, as investors scrambled after profitable new opportunities. Cotton especially excited the avarice of speculators, since the Union blockade had driven its price up to $1.90 a pound in Boston. With cotton going begging for 20 cents a pound on southern wharves, smuggled shipments multiplied. Treasury agents and military authorities were either bribed to provide passes to go through the lines or were active participants in the trade. The Confederate government quietly traded cotton for contraband such as food, medicine, and enough arms and equipment to maintain an army of 50,000 men, according to Union investigators. One of them, Charles Dana, reported in 1863 that in the Mississippi valley, "The mania for sudden fortunes made in cotton has to an alarming extent corrupted and demoralized the army. Every colonel, captain or quartermaster is in secret partnership with some operator in cotton."

Speculation during the last two years of the war became particularly feverish and the fortunes made went toward the purchase of ostentatious luxuries. New York City had never seen so much imported foreign finery, while the Chicago *Tribune* admitted: "We are clothed in purple and fine linen, wear the richest laces and jewels and fare sumptuously every day." Like Richmond in the Confederacy, Washington became the symbol of this moral decay. Prostitution, drinking, and corruption reached epidemic proportions in the capital, and for the wealthy, festivities and social gatherings became the means to shut out the numbing horror of the casualty lists.

Women and the Work Force

Even more than in the South, the war opened new opportunities for northern women. Countless wives ran farms while their husbands were away at war. One traveler in Iowa reported, "I met more women driving teams on the road and saw more at work in the fields than men." But the trend toward mechanization and commercial farming made the northern labor shortage less severe. By 1865 three times as many reapers and harvesters were in use as in 1861, while production per agricultural worker increased by a greater percentage from 1860 to 1870 than in any decade before 1890. With the price of grain driven up by government purchases and increased demand in Europe, northern agriculture prospered.

Beyond the farm, women increasingly found work in industry, filling approximately 100,000 new jobs during the war. As in the South, they worked as clerks in the expanding government bureaucracy. The work was tedious, the pace frenzied, the workload heavy: copying reports and correspondence in large volumes, keeping accounts in ledgers often too heavy to lift, counting stacks of currency. Some supervisors would not even allow women to work in the office, instead assigning them papers to take home as "piecework." But the new jobs offered satisfactions as well, including good wages, a sense of economic independence, and a pride in having aided the war effort.

The war also allowed women to enter and eventually dominate the profession of nursing. After the Revolution they had been excluded from medical careers, and army doctors opposed their presence in military hospitals during the Civil War. "Our women appear to have become almost wild on the subject of hospital nursing," protested one physician. He conceded that female volunteers might provide "delicate, soothing attentions . . . which . . . none know so well how to give as do noble, sensible, tenderhearted women"; but he shuddered to "imagine a delicate refined woman assisting a rough soldier to the close-stool, or supplying him with a bedpan." Women lobbied vigorously to overcome such objections, and their service in the wards of the maimed and dying reduced the hostility to women in medicine.

Led by Drs. Emily and Elizabeth Blackwell, Dorothea Dix, who became head of army nurses, and Clara Barton, the founder of the American Red Cross, women fought the bureaucratic inefficiency of the army medical corps. One of the most famous army nurses was Mary Ann "Mother" Bickerdyke, who attacked the

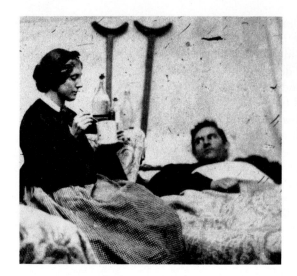

A nurse tends a wounded Union soldier in a military hospital in Nashville, Tennessee. Despite the opposition of army doctors, hundreds of female volunteers worked in army hospitals for each side. Nursing became a female profession after the war.

problem of health care in the western armies head on. Ignoring the established lines of military authority, she ordered hospitals cleaned, kitchens established, bathing facilities constructed, and incompetent employees removed. She became famous for ordering army officers around, prompting Grant to joke that she "outranks everybody, even Lincoln." With her heavyset figure and simple attire, she became a familiar sight at battlefields, aiding those in need.

Clara Barton, like so many other nurses, often found herself in battlefield hospitals, where death and suffering were massive. During the battle of Fredericksburg, she wiped the brows of the wounded and dying, bandaged wounds, and applied tourniquets to stop the flow of blood. She later recalled that as she rose from the side of one soldier, "I wrung the blood from the bottom of my clothing, before I could step, for the weight about my feet." She steeled herself at the sight of amputated arms and legs casually tossed in piles outside the front door as the surgeons cut away, yet she found the extent of suffering overwhelming. She was jolted by the occasional familiar faces among the tangled mass of bodies: the sexton of the church in her hometown, his face drenched in blood; a wayward boy she had befriended years ago; an officer who had kindly assisted her on the way to the front, already dead when she discovered him. Sleeping in a tent nearby, she drove herself to the brink of exhaustion until the last patients were transferred to permanent hospitals. She then returned to her home in Washington where she broke down and wept.

Before 1861 teaching too had been dominated by males, but the war accelerated the profession's transition into a largely female preserve. In both North and South, the shortage of men forced school boards to turn to women, who could be paid half to two-thirds of what men received. As wages were driven down, men increasingly left the educational profession for other occupations, whereas teaching often became not a temporary occupation but a career for women. Women also contributed to the war effort through volunteer work. The United States Sanitary Commission was established in 1861 to coordinate relief efforts and raise money to provide medical supplies and care. Women performed much of the fund-raising at the local level, organizing fairs, collecting supplies, wrapping bandages, and working in hospitals alongside paid nurses. Such activity extended female involvement in humanitarian reform movements.

Civil Liberties and Dissent

With the government attempting to mobilize northern society, Lincoln did not hesitate to curb dissenters. Shortly after the firing on Fort Sumter, he suspended the writ of habeas corpus in specified areas, clearing the way for the detention of anyone suspected of disloyalty or activity against the war. Although the Constitution permitted such suspension in time of rebellion or invasion, Lincoln did so without consulting Congress (unlike President Davis), and he used his power far more broadly, expanding it in 1862 to cover the entire North for cases involving antiwar activities. The president also decreed that those arrested under its provisions could be tried under the stricter rules of martial law by a military court. Eventually at least 14,000 individuals were arrested, most of whom were never charged with a specific crime or brought to trial, and were released as arbitrarily as they had been apprehended.

Democrats attacked Lincoln as a tyrant bent on destroying the Constitution. When Clement Vallandigham, a prominent Ohio Democratic congressman, called for an armistice in May 1863, he was arrested by the local military commander and tried and convicted by a military commission. In the ensuing uproar, Lincoln adroitly sidestepped controversy by commuting the prison sentence to banishment to the Confederacy. Vallandigham eventually made his way to Canada, returning to the United States in 1864 to actively campaign for the Democratic party. Lincoln ignored him, convinced he was doing the Democrats more harm than good. The Supreme Court refused to review the case, which in effect upheld his conviction. Once the war was over, however, the Court changed its position. In *Ex parte Milligan* (1866) it struck down the military conviction of a civilian accused of plotting to free Confederate prisoners of war. The Court ruled that as long as the regular courts were open, civilians could not be tried by military tribunals. The decision became one of the landmarks of constitutional law in defense of civil liberties.

Republicans labeled those who opposed the war Copperheads, conjuring up the image of a venomous snake waiting to strike the Union. Constituting the extreme peace wing of the Democratic party, Copperheads were most often either

In this 1862 painting, Lincoln battles the Copperhead dragon to preserve the Union. He is held back by an Irish Tammany Hall Democrat, who invokes the Constitution and democracy to oppose the war effort. The heavy-handed caricature of the Irish was common in Republican propaganda during the war.

transplanted southerners, who had settled the lower portion of the Ohio valley, or urban Irish Catholics. Both groups hated the Republicans and both had been hurt by the economic changes produced by the war. In protesting the administration's probusiness policies, including the tariff, the national banking acts, and aid to railroads, Copperheads were the forerunners of the Grangers and other agrarian reform movements that developed after 1865.

More than anything else, Copperheads reviled the draft as an attack on individual freedom and an instrument of special privilege. According to the provisions enacted in 1863, a person would be exempt from the present (but not the future) draft by paying a commutation fee of $300, about a year's wages for a worker or ordinary farmer. Or those drafted could hire a substitute, the cost of which was beyond the reach of all but the wealthy. Approximately 118,000 men did so, and another 87,000 paid the commutation fee. In areas of notable Copperhead sentiment, draft officials were shot at and the drawing of names precipitated riots, but the most common form of resistance was draft evasion. Perhaps 160,000 northerners illegally evaded the draft.

In July 1863, when the first draftees' names were drawn in New York, workers in the Irish quarter rose in anger. They hated the rich, who could avoid service, and they resented even more being asked to risk their lives to free black people, who competed with them for the lowest paying jobs. Rampaging through the streets, the mob attacked draft officials and the police, then turned their wrath on a number of prominent Republicans and wealthy individuals. Soon after, they proceeded to African-American neighborhoods, burning the Colored Orphan Asylum and lynching blacks who fell into their hands. The rioting continued for four days until troops rushed from the battle of Gettysburg finally restored order. At least 74 people were killed, the worst loss of life from any riot in American history.

GONE FOR A SOLDIER

By war's end, approximately 2 million men had served the Union cause and another million the Confederate. The common wisdom of the day was that a disproportionate number were poor, but modern research indicates otherwise. In both the North and South, farmers and farm laborers accounted for the largest group of soldiers, whereas unskilled workers, who were poorer than other groups, were actually underrepresented. A study of enlistments for Concord, Massachusetts, reveals that for those under 30, men without property were twice as likely to serve as those with property. But fighting was a job for the young (almost 40 percent of entering soldiers were 21 or younger), and the large majority of males that age, no matter what social class they came from, did not own property.

Camp Life

Soldiers spent most of their time in camp, perhaps as many as 50 days, on average, for every day spent in battle. The near-holiday atmosphere of the early months, when army life seemed like a gigantic campout, soon gave way to dull routine. Men from rural areas, accustomed to the freedom of the farm, complained about the endless recurrence of reveille, roll call, and drill. "When this war is over," one

Soldiers leaving for war often had their picture taken with their loved ones. The Confederate soldier on the left posed with his two sisters. On the right a member of the Union forces sits with his family for a farewell portrait. Such photographs are reminders of how much the war and its mounting death toll touched civilians on both sides as well as soldiers.

Rebel promised, "I will whip the man that says 'fall in' to me." Troops in neither army cared for the spit and polish of regular army men. "They keep us very strict here," noted one Illinois soldier; "it is the most like a prison of any place I ever saw."

Camp life was often unhealthy as well as unpleasant. Poor sanitation, miserable food, exposure, and primitive medical care contributed to widespread sickness and disease. Officers and men alike regarded army doctors as nothing more than quacks and tried to avoid them. It was a common belief that if a fellow went to the hospital, "you might as well say good bye." Twice as many soldiers died from dysentery, typhoid, and other diseases as from wounds.

Treatment at field hospitals was a chilling experience. A Union colonel, wounded at Port Hudson, recounted that as he was taken into a poorly lit cotton press building filled with wounded men. "I could not help comparing the surgeons to fiends. . . . In the middle of the room was some 10 or 12 tables just large enough to lay a man on; these were used as dissecting tables and they were covered with blood; near and around the tables stood the surgeons with blood all over them and by the side of the tables was a heap of feet, legs and arms."

More than anything else, ignorance was responsible for these conditions and practices. Many army doctors were capable by the standards of the time, but nothing was known about germs or how wounds became infected. Having lived through the revolution in medical science, a federal surgeon was appalled as he looked back on his Civil War experience:

> We operated in old blood-stained and often pus-stained coats. . . . We used undisinfected instruments from undisinfected plush-lined cases, and still worse, used marine sponges which had been used in prior pus cases and had been only washed in tap water. If a sponge or an instrument fell on the floor it was washed and squeezed in a basin of tap water and used as if it were clean. Our silk to tie blood vessels was undisinfected. . . . We dressed the wounds with clean but undisinfected sheets, shirts, tablecloths, or other old soft linen rescued from the family ragbag. . . . We knew nothing about antiseptics and therefore used none.

Daily Lives

FOOD/DRINK/DRUGS:

Hardtack, Salt Horse, and Coffee

"If a person wants to know how to appreciate the value of good vi[c]tuals he had better enlist," a Vermont soldier declared. "I have seen the time when I would have been glad to [have] picked the crusts of bread that mother gives to the hogs." Whether in the field or in quarters, food was generally Johnny Reb's and Billy Yank's first concern.

At the beginning of the war, the prescribed daily allowance for each soldier included 12 ounces of pork or 20 ounces of beef, a pound or more of bread or flour, and ample quantities of rice, beans, sugar, and coffee. That allotment was more generous than any received by a European soldier, and for nearly three years, the Union army raised its allowance beyond even that. While both armies experienced serious shortages from time to time, in general northern soldiers had more food and in greater variety than their opponents. By April 1862 the Confederacy was forced to reduce the daily ration, because of shortages, bureaucratic inefficiency, and the lack of adequate transportation. Eventually the allowance for Confederate soldiers dropped to a third of a pound of bacon and a pound of flour or meal—and even this was seldom provided, leaving the average Rebel to complain more about the quartermaster corps than about Yankees.

Meat, bread, and coffee: these were the soldier's mainstays. The meat was either pork or beef and was usually salted to preserve it. Soldiers, who called salt pork "sowbelly" and pickled beef "salt horse," preferred the former, since the beef was so briny it was inedible unless thoroughly soaked in water. Many soldiers left salted beef in a creek overnight before they tried to eat it.

Union soldiers normally were given wheat bread or flour, but for Confederates cornbread was the standby. This monotonous fare prompted a Louisiana soldier near the end of the war to grumble, "If any person offers me cornbread after this war comes to a close I shall *probably* tell him to—go to hell." Both armies often replaced bread with hardtack, crackers half an inch thick that were so hard soldiers dubbed them "teethdullers." Cynics claimed that they were more suitable for building breastworks, and some Yanks insisted that the "B.C." (for Brigade Commissary) stamped on the boxes they came in referred to their date of manufacture. They became moldy and worm-infested

An infantry private from New York eats a meal in camp.

Daily Lives

with age, and hence veterans preferred to eat them in the dark.

Coffee was the other main staple, eagerly and amply consumed. Because of the Union blockade, the Confederacy could not get enough, and Rebel troops resorted to various substitutes, none of which produced a very appealing brew. Despite official opposition, troops often fraternized during lulls in the fighting, swapping tobacco, which was in short supply on the Union side, for coffee and sugar, which Confederates desired most. When the two armies spent the winter of 1862 camped on opposite sides of the Rappahannock River, enlisted men ferried cargoes of sugar and coffee to one bank and tobacco to the other, using makeshift toy boats.

In an effort to create portable rations, the Union War Department produced an experimental "essence of coffee," a forerunner of the instant variety. But the beverage was so vile the men would not drink it, and it was eventually abandoned. More long-lasting was the use of dehydrated potatoes, which few men ever developed a taste for, and desiccated mixed vegetables, which were issued in hard, dry cakes that troops dubbed "baled hay." The only practical way of serving this concentrate was in soup, but the resulting product reminded one officer of "a dirty brook with all the dead leaves floating around promiscuously." The shortage of fruits and vegetables was one of the main deficiencies of the Civil War soldiers' diet.

Troops in both armies supplemented their diet by foraging (the army's polite term for stealing), although Union soldiers, being most often in enemy territory, relied more heavily on this tactic. Hungry troops regularly raided pigpens, poultry houses, orchards, gardens, cornfields, and smokehouses. Attempts to limit this activity to regularly appointed groups were largely ineffective. A Massachusetts soldier serving in North Carolina told his parents in 1862, "When we first started the colonel tried to prevent our foraging but he quickly found out that all that was nonsense and before we got back we were as expert at it as any of the old hands."

During training and in winter quarters, cooks normally prepared food for an entire company. Neither army, however, established a cooks' or bakers' school, and soldiers contended that officers regularly selected the poorest soldiers to be cooks. "A company cook is a most peculiar being," one soldier recalled after the war. "He generally knows less about cooking than any other man in the company. Not being able to learn the drill, and too dirty to appear on inspection, he is sent to the cook house to get him out of the ranks." Once the army went on the march, men usually cooked for themselves or formed a mess of four to eight soldiers, taking turns cooking. Either way, food was rarely prepared with any skill and was laden with grease. In addition, troops often lacked adequate utensils and learned to bake bread on a board, fry food in half a canteen, and roast meat and dough at the end of a stick.

By war's end, soldiers on both sides had developed a new appreciation for food. One hungry Texan promised that when he got home he was going "to take a hundred biscuit and two large hams, call it three days rations, then . . . eat it all at *one* meal." A poetic Yankee summed up the situation succinctly:

The soldiers' fare is very rough,
The bread is hard, the beef is
  tough;
If they can stand it, it will be,
Through love of God, a mystery.

Conditions were even worse in the Confederate hospitals, for the Union blockade produced a shortage of medical supplies, and Confederate doctors often had to resort to native-grown substitutes.

The boredom of camp life, the horrors of battle, and the influence of an all-male society all corrupted morals. Profanity and heavy drinking were widespread, while one Mississippian reported that after payday games of chance were "running night and day, with eager and excited crowds standing around with their hands full of money." As in the gold fields of California, the absence of women stimulated behavior that would have been checked back home by the frowns of family and society. Prostitutes flooded the camps of both armies. An Illinois private stationed in Pulaski, Tennessee, wrote home that there were four brothels in town and added that the price schedule in each was reasonable. "You may think I am a hard case," he conceded, "but I am as pious as you can find in the army."

With death so near, some soldiers sought solace in religion. Devotional activities intensified when troops settled into winter quarters and the fighting let up. Among Confederate troops, a wave of revivals swept the ranks during the last two years of the war, producing between 100,000 and 200,000 conversions. "In all my life, I never witnessed more displays of God's power in the awakening and conversion of sinners," testified a southern Methodist chaplain. These revivals deepened the sense of duty and visibly improved morale. No doubt southern leaders' heavier emphasis on religion contributed to the greater religious fervor in the Confederate camps, but significantly the first major revivals occurred after the South's twin defeats at Vicksburg and Gettysburg. Then too, as battle after battle thinned Confederate ranks, the prospect of death became increasingly real.

Southern Individualism

Despite obvious similarities, Confederate soldiers differed from their northern counterparts in ways that reflected fundamental qualities of southern society. Observers commented on the lack of discipline among Confederate troops—they had "a sort of devil-may-care, reckless, self-confident look." While Union soldiers came grudgingly to accept discipline as a necessity of war, many southerners were "not used to control of any sort and were not disposed to obey anyone except for good and sufficient reason given," one Rebel noted. "There never has been discipline in the armies of the Confederacy," commented one Richmond paper, "but instead thereof a kind of universal suffrage, which fights when it chooses and straggles when it feels like it." Many Confederates discarded equipment on the march and lagged behind, while others left without permission to take care of affairs back home, then returned to the ranks.

This disrespect for authority affected the ordinary soldier's relations with his officers. Like Union soldiers, Confederates complained about officers' special privileges, but they were far more likely to threaten or even physically assault their superiors when dissatisfied. Contributing to the lack of discipline, Confederates insisted on electing all officers through the rank of colonel. The Union army had discarded this democratic tradition soon after the war began, but electioneering constantly disrupted Confederate units. Officers were obliged to court the favor of their troops, and most of those known as strict disciplinarians were eventually defeated. Professional military men unanimously opposed the practice, but the Confederate Congress maintained it out of political considerations. A Confederate general fumed that the law should have been entitled "An act to disorganize and dissolve the army."

Moreover, upper-class southerners often felt that social class should override military rank. "It is galling for a gentleman to be absolutely and entirely subject to the orders of men who in private life were so far his inferiors," declared one socially prominent soldier. Another who was ordered to the guardhouse shouted to his captain, "I will not do it. I was a gentleman before I joined your company and by God you want to make a damned slave of me."

At the beginning of the war, when both armies were little more than disorganized mobs, the rural individualism of southerners was not a severe handicap. But as the Union army became increasingly organized, Confederate indifference to discipline took its toll. Northern soldiers who came from a more economically complex society were more familiar with impersonal organizations and accustomed to greater order and social control, and urban factory workers especially were used to a strict regimen. In a total war, which would be won by superior organization and the mobilization of resources, this difference between the two armies became more significant with each year of the fighting.

The Changing Face of Battle

As in all modern wars, technology revolutionized the conditions under which Civil War soldiers fought. Smoothbore muskets gave way to the rifle, so named because of the grooves etched into the barrel to give a bullet spin, as the basic infantry weapon. A new bullet, the minié ball, allowed the rifle to be easily loaded, and the invention of the percussion cap rendered it serviceable in wet weather. Under these improved circumstances, the number of misfires in 1000 rounds dropped from 411 to fewer than 5. Most significant, however, was the rifle's improved range of 1000 yards—four times greater than that of the old musket.* As a result, soldiers fought each other from greater distances and battles took much longer to fight and produced many more casualties—yet paradoxically they were much less decisive in outcome since modern armies, unless enveloped, are often battered but rarely annihilated in battle.

Under such conditions, the defense became a good deal stronger than the offense. The larger artillery pieces also adopted rifled barrels, but they still lacked good fuses and accurate sighting devices and could not effectively support attacking troops. Loaded with canister or grapeshot, however, they were a deadly defensive weapon, functioning like huge sawed-off shotguns that decimated advancing infantry at close range. Confederate General D. H. Hill described the devastating barrage as his men charged the Union line at Malvern Hill: "As each brigade emerged from the woods, from 50 to 100 guns opened upon it, tearing great gaps in its ranks. Most of them had an open field half a mile wide to cross, under the fire of field artillery and heavy ordnance. It was not war—it was murder."

The rising casualty lists bore down most heavily on the ordinary soldier. During the Crimean War, the charge of the English Light Brigade became notorious as an example of excessive sacrifice. Its casualty rate was a dismaying 37 percent, but that paled beside the experience of the 1st Minnesota or the 26th North Carolina at Gettysburg, which each lost 85 percent of its members, the highest loss sustained by any regiment in a Civil War battle. Over 100 regiments on both sides suffered more than 50 percent casualties in a single battle.

Every battle produced its skulkers and heroes, its miraculous escapes and

---

*The spin of a bullet leaving a rifle increased not only accuracy, but also velocity, which provided the extra range.

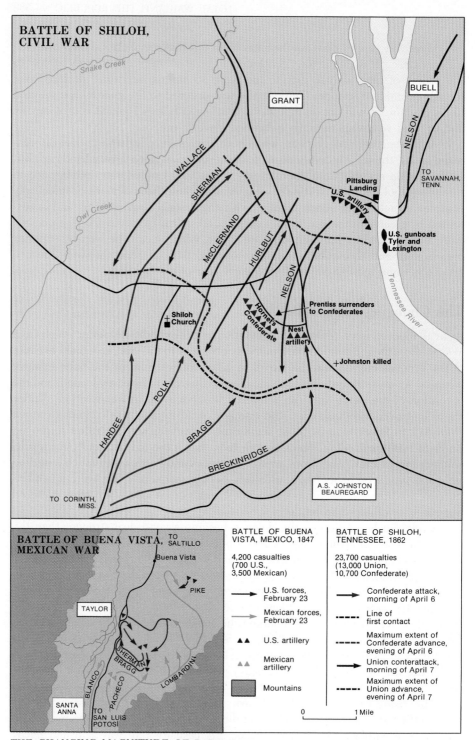

BATTLE OF SHILOH, CIVIL WAR

Snake Creek

GRANT

BUELL

NELSON

WALLACE

SHERMAN

Owl Creek

McCLERNAND

HURLBUT

NELSON

Pittsburg Landing

TO SAVANNAH, TENN.

U.S. artillery

U.S. gunboats Tyler and Lexington

Prentiss surrenders to Confederates

Shiloh Church

Hornet's Confederate Nest artillery

Tennessee River

Johnston killed

HARDEE

POLK

BRAGG

BRECKINRIDGE

A.S. JOHNSTON BEAUREGARD

TO CORINTH, MISS.

BATTLE OF BUENA VISTA, MEXICAN WAR

TO SALTILLO

Buena Vista

PIKE

TAYLOR

SHERMAN BRAGG

BLANCO

PACHECO

LOMBARDINI

SANTA ANNA

TO SAN LUIS POTOSÍ

BATTLE OF BUENA VISTA, MEXICO, 1847

4,200 casualties
(700 U.S.,
3,500 Mexican)

→ U.S. forces,
February 23

→ Mexican forces,
February 23

▲▲ U.S. artillery

▲▲ Mexican
artillery

■ Mountains

BATTLE OF SHILOH, TENNESSEE, 1862

23,700 casualties
(13,000 Union,
10,700 Confederate)

→ Confederate attack,
morning of April 6

----- Line of
first contact

----- Maximum extent of
Confederate advance,
evening of April 6

→ Union conterattack,
morning of April 7

----- Maximum extent of
Union advance,
evening of April 7

0   1 Mile

THE CHANGING MAGNITUDE OF BATTLE

During the Mexican War at Buena Vista, the American army of 4800 men was overextended trying to defend a two-mile line against 15,000 Mexicans. At Shiloh, by contrast, battle lines stretched almost six miles. (The maps are drawn to the same scale.) Against 40,000 Confederates, Grant galloped back and forth, rallying some 35,000 troops organized under five subordinates and coordinating the overnight reinforcement of 25,000 troops. The size of the armies, the complexity of their organization, the length of battle lines, and the number of casualties all demonstrate the extent to which the magnitude of battle had changed.

590

daring deeds, its gallows humor and wrenching tragedy. But as the haze of gunfire covered the land (smokeless powder had not yet been invented) and the constant spray of bullets mimicked rain pattering through the treetops, soldiers discovered that their romantic notions about war had no place on the battlefield. Men witnessed horrors they had never envisioned as civilians and choked from the acrid stench of decaying flesh and mortal slaughter. They realized that their efforts to convey to those back home the gruesome truth of combat were inadequate. "No tongue can tell, no mind can conceive, no pen portray the horrible sights I witnessed this morning," a Union soldier wrote after Antietam. And yet they tried.

An Indiana soldier at Perryville (7600 casualties): "It was an awful sight to see there men torn all to pieces with cannon balls and bom shells[.] the dead and wounded lay thick in all directions." A Confederate soldier at Shiloh (23,000 casualties): "O it was too shocking too horrible. God Grant that I may never be the partaker of such scenes again. . . . when released from this I shall ever be an advocate of peace." An Ohio soldier at Antietam (23,000 casualties), two days after the fighting: "The smell was offul . . . there was about 5 or 6,000 dead bodes decaying over the field . . . their lines of battle Could be run for miles by the dead[.] they lay long the lines like sheavs of Wheat[.] I could have walked on the boddees all most from one end too the other." A Georgian, the day after Chancellorsville (30,000 casualties): "It looked more like a slaughter pen than anything else. . . . The shrieks and groans of the wounded . . . was heart rending beyond all description." A Maine soldier who fought at Gettysburg (50,000 casualties): "I have Seen . . . men rolling in their own blood, Some Shot in one place, Some another. . . . our dead lay in the road and the Rebels in their hast to leave dragged both their baggage wagons and artillery over them and they lay mangled and torn to pieces so that Even friends could not tell them. You can form no idea of a battle field. . . . I hope none of my brothers will Ever have to go into a fight."

In the face of what Charles Francis Adams, Jr., termed "the carnival of death," soldiers braced themselves with a grim determination to see the war through to the end. Not glorious exploits, but endurance and tenacity became the true measure of heroism.

THE UNION'S TRIUMPH

In the spring of 1863, matters still looked promising for Lee. At the battle of Chancellorsville, he and Stonewall Jackson had brilliantly defeated Lincoln's latest commander, Joseph Hooker. But when Jackson returned from scouting the battle zone, he was accidentally shot by one of his own sentries. He died a few days later—a severe setback for Lee, who mourned that he had lost his "right arm." Determined to take the offensive and perhaps even capture a major northern city, Lee invaded Pennsylvania in June with an army of 75,000. Lincoln's newest general, George Gordon Meade, warily shadowed the Confederates, carefully keeping his forces between them and Washington. On the first of July, advance parties from the two armies accidentally collided at the town of Gettysburg. Both sides rushed up reinforcements, and the war's greatest battle ensued.

For once, it was Lee who had the extended supply lines and was forced to fight on ground chosen by his opponent. After two days of assaults failed to break the Union left or right, Lee made the greatest mistake of his career, sending 15,000 men under General George Pickett in a charge up the center of the Union

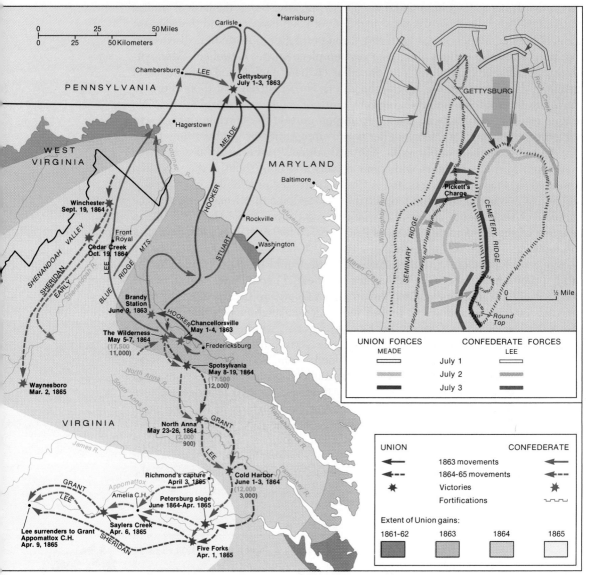

THE WAR IN THE EAST, 1863–1865

Lee won his most brilliant victory at Chancellorsville, then launched a second invasion of
the North, hoping to score a decisive victory. When the two armies accidentally collided at
Gettysburg on July 1, 1863, the Union's Army of the Potomac was driven back through the
town until it took up a strong defensive position, shaped like a fish hook and anchored by a
hill at each end. On July 2 the Confederate attack drove back the Union's left flank, but
failed to dislodge the right. Lee's assault on the center of the Union line July 3 (including
Pickett's charge) ended in a decisive defeat, and the Army of Northern Virginia retreated to
the Confederacy. In 1864 Grant delivered a series of heavy blows against Lee's outnumbered forces in Virginia. Despite staggering losses, Grant relentlessly pressed on in a ruthless demonstration of total war. (Note the casualties listed for the spring and summer of
1864; from mid-May to mid-June Grant lost nearly 60,000 men, equal to Lee's total
strength.) Sheridan's devastating raids that fall against the civilian farms of the Shenandoah
helped deprive Lee of desperately needed supplies. Too weak to defend Richmond any
longer, Lee surrendered at Appomattox Courthouse in April 1865.

line on Cemetery Ridge. "Pickett's division just seemed to melt away in the blue musketry smoke which now covered the hill," one Confederate officer wrote. "Nothing but stragglers came back." The Union casualties of more than 23,000 represented a quarter of Meade's effective strength, but Lee lost between 25,000 and 28,000—more than a third of his troops. Never again was he able to assume the offensive.

Lincoln Finds His General

To the west, Grant had been trying for months to capture Vicksburg, one of the two remaining Rebel strongholds on the Mississippi. In a daring maneuver, he left behind his supply lines and marched inland, calculating that he could feed his army largely from the produce of Confederate farms, weakening southern resistance in the process. These were the tactics of total war, and seldom had they been tried before Grant used them. His troops defeated two Confederate armies, then drove the defenders of Vicksburg back into the city and starved them into submission. On July 4, as news of Gettysburg was telegraphed to Lincoln, Vicksburg surrendered to Grant. With the fall of Port Hudson, Louisiana, four days later, the Mississippi was completely in Union hands. Grant had divided the Confederacy and isolated Arkansas, Texas, and part of Louisiana from the rest of the South.

He followed this victory by opening up a supply line over the Tennessee mountains around Chattanooga, relieving Union forces that had been surrounded there. With Chattanooga safe by November, the Union army was poised for a thrust into Georgia. Grant's performance confirmed Lincoln's earlier judgment that "Grant is my man, and I am his the rest of the war," while an enthusiastic Congress now bestowed on him the rank of lieutenant general, held before only by George Washington. In March 1864 Lincoln brought Grant east and put him in command of all the Union armies.

Grant recognized that the Union had always possessed the resources to wear down the Confederacy, but that its larger armies had "acted independently and without concert, like a balky team, no two ever pulling together." He intended to change that. While he launched a major offensive against Lee in Virginia, William Tecumseh Sherman, who replaced Grant as commander of the western army, would drive a diagonal wedge through the Confederacy from Tennessee across Georgia. Grant's orders to Sherman were as blunt as his response had been that rainy night when the two had conferred at Shiloh: "Get into the interior of the enemy's country so far as you can, inflicting all the damage you can against their war resources."

In May and June 1864, Grant fought a series of fierce battles with Lee. Recognizing the importance a breakthrough in Virginia would have on northern morale, Grant tried to maneuver Lee out of the trenches and into an open battle. But Lee was too weak to win head-on, so he opted for a strategy of attrition: entrenching, holding lines dearly, hoping to inflict such heavy losses that the northern will to continue would waver and Lincoln would be defeated at the polls. It was a strategy that nearly worked, for Union casualties were staggering: in a month of heavy fighting, the Army of the Potomac lost 60,000 men—the size of Lee's entire army at the beginning of the campaign. Grant lost two soldiers for every Confederate who fell, yet at the end of the campaign his reinforced army was larger than when it started, whereas Lee's was significantly weaker.

After especially bloody losses at the battle of Cold Harbor, Grant changed tactics. Unable to flank the Confederates any farther to the east, he marched his army south toward Petersburg, which guarded the last remaining rail link between Richmond and the rest of the Confederacy. When the city managed to hold out until Lee arrived, Grant settled into a protracted siege, counting on his numerical superiority to stretch Lee's line to the breaking point. A siege would be agonizingly slow, but he saw no other option. In the west, meanwhile, the gaunt and grizzled Sherman, who was famous for his blunt, unceasing talk and passionate nature, fought his way to the outskirts of Atlanta by July. He had great confidence in his rough-hewn army, which by now had been seasoned by several years of hard campaigning. But Atlanta was heavily defended and gave no sign of capitulating. "Our all depends on that army at Atlanta," wrote Mary Chesnut, based on her conversations with Confederate leaders. "If that fails us, the game is up."

War in the Balance

The game was nearly up for Lincoln as the 1864 election approached. In 1863, the victories at Gettysburg and Vicksburg sparked Republican victories, including the defeat in Ohio of Clement Vallandigham, whom the Democrats had nominated for governor despite his Copperhead record. Public opinion seemed to be swinging toward emancipation. But as the Union draft swept more and more northerners south to death, and Grant and Sherman bogged down on the Virginia and Georgia fronts, even leaders in Lincoln's own party began to mutter out loud that he was not equal to the task.

Perhaps the most remarkable thing about the 1864 election is that it was held at all. Indeed, before World War I, the United States was the only democratic government in history to carry out a general election in wartime. But Lincoln firmly believed that to postpone it would be to lose the priceless heritage of republicanism itself: "We cannot have free government without elections, and if the rebellion could force us to forego or postpone a national election, it might fairly claim to have already conquered and ruined us." Exploiting his control of the party machinery, Lincoln easily won the Republican nomination. Endorsing Lincoln's wartime leadership, the Republican platform stipulated that the Confederacy's unconditional surrender was the only acceptable peace term and, at the president's insistence, called for adoption of a constitutional amendment abolishing slavery. To balance the ticket, Lincoln selected Andrew Johnson, the military governor of Tennessee and a prowar Democrat, as his running mate. The two men ran under the label of the "Union" party.

The Democrats nominated George McClellan, the former Union commander. Their platform, written largely by Vallandigham, pronounced the war a failure and called for an armistice and a peace conference. Warned that a cessation of fighting would lead to disunion, McClellan partially repudiated this position, insisting that "the Union is the one condition of peace—we ask no more." In private he made it clear that if elected he intended to restore slavery. Lincoln was gloomy about his prospects, as well as those of the Union itself. On August 23 he had his cabinet members sign a sealed envelope without revealing its contents. Inside was a statement which declared: "This morning, as for some days past, it seems exceedingly probable that this Administration will not be reelected. Then it will be my duty to so cooperate with the President-elect as to save the Union between the election and the inauguration; as he will have secured his election on such ground that he cannot possibly save it afterwards." But then Admiral Farragut won a dramatic victory at Mobile Bay, and a few weeks later, in early Septem-

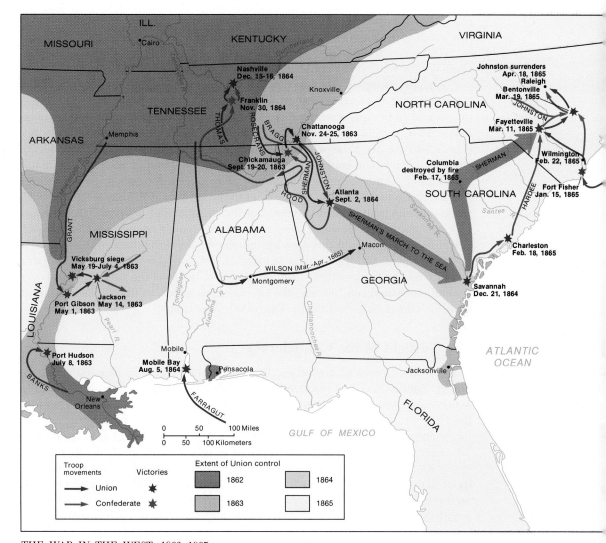

THE WAR IN THE WEST, 1863–1865
The Union continued its war of mobility in the western theater, bringing more Confederate territory under its control. After Grant captured Vicksburg the entire Mississippi lay in Union hands. His victories at Lookout Mountain and Missionary Ridge, near Chattanooga, ended the Confederate threat to Tennessee. In 1864 Sherman divided the Confederacy by seizing Atlanta and marching across Georgia; then he turned north. When Joseph Johnston surrendered, several weeks after Lee's capitulation at Appomattox, the war was effectively over.

ber, Sherman finally captured Atlanta. As Secretary of State Seward gleefully noted, "Sherman and Farragut have knocked the bottom out of the Chicago [Democratic] nominations."

Polling an impressive 55 percent of the popular vote, Lincoln won 212 electoral votes to McClellan's 21. Eighteen states allowed soldiers to vote in the fields, and Lincoln received nearly 80 percent of their ballots. One lifelong Democrat described the sentiment in the army: "We all want peace, but none any but an honorable one. I had rather stay out here a lifetime (much as I dislike it) than consent to a division of our country." As Grant recognized, the victory at the ballot box was "worth more than a victory in the field both in its effect on the Rebels and in its influence abroad." Jefferson Davis remained defiant, but the last hope of a Confederate victory was gone.

Equally important, the election of 1864 ended any doubt that slavery would be abolished in the reconstructed Union. The Emancipation Proclamation had not put an end to the question, for its legal status remained unclear. Lincoln argued that as a war measure, it would have no standing once peace returned; and in any case, it had not freed slaves in the border states or those parts of the Confederacy already under Union control. Thus Lincoln and the Republicans believed that a constitutional amendment was necessary to secure emancipation.

Congress had passed an amendment in the spring of 1864 that freed all slaves without compensating their owners, but the measure did not pass by the necessary two-thirds vote in the House. Following Lincoln's triumph, it came before Congress again. Lincoln threw all his influence behind the drive to round up the necessary votes, and it passed on January 31, 1865. By December, enough states had ratified the Thirteenth Amendment to make it part of the Constitution. Later generations would call Lincoln "the Great Emancipator," a title he merited most from his efforts on behalf of the Thirteenth Amendment.

The Twilight of the Confederacy

In the wake of Lincoln's reelection, the Confederate will to resist rapidly disintegrated. Southerners had never fully united behind the war effort, but the large majority had endured great suffering to uphold it. As Sherman pushed deeper into the Confederacy, and General Philip Sheridan mounted his devastating raid on the Shenandoah Valley, the war came home to southern civilians as never before. "We haven't got nothing in the house to eat but a little bit o meal," wrote the wife of one Alabama soldier in December 1864. ". . . Try to get off and come home and fix us all up some and then you can go back. . . . If you put off a-coming, 'twont be no use to come, for we'll all . . . [be] in the grave yard." He deserted. In the last months of the fighting, over half the Confederacy's soldiers were absent without leave.

After the fall of Atlanta, Sherman gave a frightening demonstration of the meaning of total war. General John Hood moved his Confederate army into Tennessee, in the rash hope of luring Sherman out of Georgia. Instead, Sherman sent only a portion of his forces to keep Hood occupied, and then imitated Grant's strategy by abandoning his supply lines for an audacious 300-mile march to the sea. His 57,000 men proceeded virtually unopposed, not in search of battle, but on an intimidating campaign of total war. Sherman intended to deprive Lee's army of the supplies it desperately needed to continue and to break the southern will to resist. Or as he bluntly put it, "to whip the Rebels, to humble their pride, to follow them to their recesses, and make them fear and dread us."

In four columns the army covered about 10 miles a day, cutting a path of destruction 50 miles wide. "We had a gay old campaign," one of his soldiers wrote. "Destroyed all we could not eat, stole their niggers, burned their cotton and gins, spilled their sorghum, burned and twisted their railroads and raised Hell generally." Sherman paid particular attention to the railroads, so that by the time he had finished tearing up scarce track and burning key bridges, Confederate armies were effectively separated from the resources of their population. Sherman esti-

The war's greatest generals, Ulysses S. Grant (left) and Robert E. Lee (right), confronted each other in the eastern theater during the last year of the war. A member of a distinguished Virginia family, the impeccably dressed Lee was every inch the aristocratic gentleman. Grant, a short, slouched figure with a stubby beard, dressed indifferently, often wearing a private's uniform with only the stars on his shoulders to indicate his rank. But his determination is readily apparent in this picture, taken at his field headquarters in 1864.

mated that his army did $100 million in damage, of which $20 million was necessary to supply his army and the rest was wanton destruction. On December 22 he captured Savannah and turned north. His troops wreaked havoc in South Carolina, which they considered the seedbed of the rebellion.

Meanwhile, General George H. Thomas defeated Hood's forces in December at Nashville, leaving the interior of the Confederacy essentially conquered. Only Lee's army remained, entrenched around Petersburg, Virginia, as Grant relentlessly extended his lines, stretching the Confederates thinner and thinner. In desperation, Lee attacked, hoping to break through the Union defenses, but in vain. The only remaining option was to abandon Richmond, which fell soon after, on April 3.

Westward Grant doggedly pursued the Army of Northern Virginia for another hundred miles. After Union forces captured supplies waiting for Lee at Appomattox Courthouse and also blocked his retreat south, the weary gentleman from Virginia asked to see Grant. As the victorious northern commander rode to where Lee was waiting, a Union band along the road struck up "Auld Lang Syne." His baggage somewhere back in the rear, Grant arrived in a mud-splattered private's shirt with only three stars pinned to the shoulder to signify his rank. Accepting Grant's terms, Lee surrendered on April 9, 1865. As he waited for his horse, Lee looked sadly across the fields and woods in the direction where his army waited—now prisoners. As one of Grant's aides recalled, "He thrice smote the palm of his left hand slowly with his right fist in an absent sort of way," then mounted. Grant saluted by raising his hat; Lee raised his respectfully and rode off at a slow trot. "On our part," one federal officer wrote, there was "not a sound of trumpet . . . nor roll of drum; not a cheer . . . but an awed stillness rather."

With Lee's army gone, remaining resistance throughout the Confederacy collapsed within a matter of weeks. Visiting the captured city of Richmond on April 4, Lincoln was enthusiastically greeted by the black population. He looked "pale, haggard, utterly worn out," noted one observer. The lines in his face showed how much the war had aged him in only four years. Often his friends had counseled rest, but Lincoln had observed that "the tired part of me is *inside* and out of reach." Day after day, the grim telegrams had arrived—so many wounded, so many dead—or the mothers had come to see him in his "public opinion baths," begging him to spare their youngest son because the other two had died in battle. Congressman Isaac Arnold was once shocked to find Lincoln telling one of his innumerable jokes after particularly severe Union losses, and rebuked him for such levity in a time of war. The president broke down, his whole body shaking. If he did not joke or tell stories, he explained as tears flowed down his cheeks, the burden became too much to bear.

Back in Washington, the president received news of Lee's surrender with relief. But massive problems remained. How exactly would the seceded states be brought back into the Union? Could the wounds of a house divided fully heal? The night of April 14, Lincoln, seeking a welcome escape, went to see a comedy at Ford's Theater. In the midst of the performance John Wilkes Booth, an unstable actor and Confederate sympathizer, slipped into Lincoln's balcony box and shot him with a derringer; then he jumped to the stage shouting the state motto of Virginia, "*Sic semper tyrannis*"—Thus be it ever to tyrants—and fled. Lincoln died the next morning without regaining consciousness. As he had called upon others to do in his Gettysburg Address, the sixteenth president had given his "last full measure of devotion" to the Republic.

THE IMPACT OF WAR

The assassination, which capped four years of bloody war, left a tiredness in the nation's bones—a tiredness "*inside*" and not easily within reach. In every way the conflict had produced fundamental, often devastating changes. There was, of course, the carnage. Approximately 620,000 men on both sides lost their lives, almost as many as in all the other wars the nation has fought from the Revolution through Vietnam combined. In material terms, the war cost an estimated $20 billion, or about 10 times the value of all slaves in the country in 1860, and more than 11 times the total amount spent by the federal government from 1789 to 1861. Although northern expenditures slightly exceeded those of the South, white southerners bore a much higher cost per capita. The war's ravages destroyed perhaps $1.5 billion in property, most of it within the Confederacy. Even without adding the market value of freed slaves, southern wealth declined 43 percent, transforming what had been the richest section in the nation (on a white per capita basis) into the poorest.

The staggering demands of total war also stimulated industrialization, especially in the heavy industries of iron and coal, machinery, and agricultural implements, while the probusiness finance and tax policies of the Republican party encouraged the formation of larger corporations and industries in the years ahead. The war also forced manufacturers to supply and equip the army on an unprecedented scale over distances of up to a thousand miles. One consequence was that businesses of necessity became larger, and truly national industries, producing for a national rather than local market, emerged in flour milling, meat packing, clothing and shoe manufacture, and machinery making.

Politically, the war dramatically changed the balance of power. The South lost its substantial influence, as did the Democratic party, while the Republicans emerged in a commanding position. And above the divisions of party, the Union's military victory signaled the triumph of nationalism. No longer could theorists like John C. Calhoun argue that the Union was a voluntary confederacy of sovereign states. It was perpetual, as Andrew Jackson had first suggested—truly an indivisible nation. In an important symbolic change, Americans now spoke of the United States in the singular rather than the plural. Julia Ward Howe's "Battle Hymn of the Republic" had referred to the divine vengeance that would be wreaked by the war's "terrible swift sword"; yet out of this fiery trial, the Republic was reborn stronger and more durable than before.

In the short run, the price was disillusion, ashes, and bitterness. The South faced a painful period of reconstruction in the shadow of its military defeat, while blacks anxiously waited to see whether they would be incorporated into the political and economic life of the nation. The war's corrosive effect on morals left American life and politics more corrupt and made the idealism of antebellum humanitarian reform seem almost innocent by comparison. Millennialism and perfectionism were victims of the war's appalling slaughter, forsaken for a new emphasis on practicality and power, order and discipline, materialism and science. As the war unfolded, the New York *Herald* recognized the deep changes: "All sorts of old fogy ideas, manners, and customs have gone under, and all sorts of new ideas, modes, and practices have risen to the surface and become popular."

George Ticknor, a prominent author and critic who was sensitive to shifting intellectual and social currents, reflected on the changes that had shaken the nation in only a few short years. The war, it seemed to him, had left "a great gulf between what happened before it in our century and what has happened since, or what is likely to happen hereafter. It does not seem to me as if I were living in the country in which I was born."

SIGNIFICANT EVENTS

1861 — Border states remain in the Union; Union blockade proclaimed; Lincoln suspends writ of habeas corpus in selected areas; Battle of Bull Run; Crittenden Resolution; First Confiscation Act; *Trent* affair

1862 — Forts Henry and Donelson captured; *Monitor vs. Virginia (Merrimack);* Battle of Shiloh; slavery abolished in the District of Columbia; Confederacy institutes draft; New Orleans captured; Homestead Act; Union Pacific Railroad chartered; Land Grant College Act; Second Confiscation Act; Union income tax enacted; McClellan's Peninsula campaign fails; second Battle of Bull Run; Battle of Antietam; preliminary Emancipation Proclamation; Lincoln suspends writ of habeas corpus throughout the Union; Battle of Fredericksburg

1863 — Emancipation Proclamation; National Banking Act; Union institutes draft; Confederacy enacts general tax laws, initiates impressment; bread riots in the Confederacy; Battle of Chancellorsville; West Virginia admitted to the Union; Battle of Gettysburg; Vicksburg captured; New York City draft riots

1864 — Grant becomes Union general in chief; Wilderness campaign; Battle of Mobile Bay; fall of Atlanta; Lincoln reelected; Sherman's march to the sea

1865 — Congress passes Thirteenth Amendment; Sherman's march through the Carolinas; Lee surrenders; Lincoln assassinated; Thirteenth Amendment ratified

1866 — *Ex parte Milligan*

17

Reconstructing the Union

On November 19, 1866, Joseph Davis sold his plantations Hurricane and Brierfield, located on a large bend of the Mississippi River south of Vicksburg. In one sense, there was nothing unusual in this transaction. Like other southern planters financially ruined by the war, Davis had decided to quit agricultural operations. Yet the sale was bound to attract attention, since Joseph Davis was the elder brother of Jefferson Davis. In fact, before the war the Confederate president had operated Brierfield as his own plantation, even though his brother retained legal title to it. In truth, however, this sale was so unusual that the two parties agreed to keep it secret, and with good reason. The purchasers, Benjamin Montgomery and his sons, were black, and Mississippi law prohibited blacks from owning land.

Though a slave, Montgomery had been the business manager of the two Davis plantations before the war. Displaying unusual talent and ambition, he had also obtained Joseph Davis' permission to open a store on Hurricane Plantation and had developed considerable business expertise, operating on his own line of credit in New Orleans and dealing with white as well as black customers. In 1863, when the fighting reached the area around Vicksburg, Montgomery fled to Cincinnati, where his mechanical ingenuity landed him a job in a boatyard. With the coming of peace, however, he returned to Davis Bend, where the federal government had established a settlement of independent black farmers to whom it leased plots of land on confiscated plantations—Joseph Davis' among them. Reopening his plantation store, as well as beginning planting operations, Montgomery emerged as the leader of the African-American community at the Bend.

Then, in 1866, President Andrew Johnson pardoned Joseph Davis and restored his lands. Black hopes of creating a permanent settlement of independent farmers at Davis Bend were thrown into doubt. But when Joseph Davis took possession of Brierfield and Hurricane, he was over 80 years old. He lacked the will and stamina to rebuild and start over again. Unlike many one-time slaveholders, however, Davis still felt bound by obligations to his former slaves, and he remained deeply interested in their welfare. Convinced that with proper encouragement African-Americans could succeed economically in freedom, he sold his land secretly to Benjamin Montgomery in order to promote black self-help. Only when the law prohibiting blacks from owning land was overturned in 1867 did Davis publicly confirm the sale to his ex-slave.

A Visit from the Old Mistress, *by Winslow Homer, captures the conflicting, often awkward emotions felt by both races after the war.*

For his part, Montgomery undertook to fulfill the dream of his former master to create a model society at Davis Bend where African-Americans could prosper through mutual cooperation. Moving with his family into what had once been the home of Jefferson Davis, Montgomery guided the settlement with a paternalistic hand, much like Joseph Davis had earlier. He rented land to black farmers, hired others to work his own fields, sold supplies on credit, and ginned and marketed the crops. To the growing African-American community, he constantly preached the gospel of hard work, self-reliance, and education.

Severe difficulties, including the destruction caused by the war, several disastrous floods, insects, droughts, and declining cotton prices, dogged these farmers. Yet before long, cotton production exceeded that of the antebellum years. In 1870 the black families at Davis Bend produced 2500 bales, more than twice the amount produced by whites on a neighboring plantation with the same acreage. In fact, in that year the Montgomerys accounted for over half of all the cotton bales produced by African-Americans in the state's 20 richest cotton counties. The following year they bought Ursino Plantation, which adjoined their holdings. The addition of 1500 acres to the 4000 they had purchased from Joseph Davis made them reputedly the third largest planters in the state, and they won national and international awards for the high quality of their cotton. Their success was an inspiration and example of what African-Americans, given a fair chance, might accomplish.

The experiences of Benjamin Montgomery during the years after 1865 were not those of most southern blacks, who did not own land or have a powerful white benefactor. Yet Montgomery's dream of economic independence was shared by all African-Americans. As one black veteran noted, "Every colored man will be a slave, and feel himself a slave until he can raise him own *bale of cotton* and put him own mark upon it and say dis is mine!" Blacks could not gain effective freedom simply through a proclamation of emancipation, no matter how well intentioned. They also needed to live in a society where they had economic power of their own—to become the largest cotton planter in the district, like Montgomery, or simply a farmer with a plot of land no one could unfairly take away.

For nearly two centuries, the laws had prevented slaves from possessing such economic power. Inevitably, if such conditions were to be overturned, blacks needed political power too. The whole theory that underlies a democratic republic is that social conflict—between different classes, economic groups, or regions—may be peacefully resolved if all groups share power in the political arena. For 200 years, African-Americans lacked that power, and the conflict and inequality that had built up in American society had led to civil war. In political terms, the Republic would have to be reconstructed in order to share power with a major group of Americans who had been previously denied it.

To achieve that goal in a land where racism had distorted society for so long in both the North and the South would be a major task. War, in its blunt way, had roughed out the contours of a solution, but only in broad terms. Clearly, African-Americans would no longer be slaves. The North, with its industrial might, would be the driving force in the nation's economy and retain the dominant political voice. It had the power to set the terms for admitting the defeated Confederate states back into the Union. But beyond that, the outlines of a reconstructed Republic remained vague. How much effective power would blacks receive? How would the North and South readjust their economic and social relations? These questions lay at the heart of the problem of Reconstruction.

PRESIDENTIAL RECONSTRUCTION

Even in the early months of the war, Abraham Lincoln had considered Reconstruction his responsibility. In devising a program, Lincoln never lost sight of its political consequences. Elected with less than 40 percent of the popular vote in 1860, he was acutely aware that the Republican party had no real strength in the South. Once the states of the Confederacy were restored to the Union, they would again have 22 senators and 63 representatives, as well as 85 votes in the Electoral College. The Republicans inevitably would be weakened unless they evolved into more than a sectional party. Lincoln looked to the old Whigs, who supported many of the Republicans' economic programs, to build up a southern wing of the party. By a generous peace, he hoped to attract white southerners and assure his party's continuing national supremacy.

Lincoln's Plan

As the Union army conquered parts of the Confederacy, Lincoln set up a flexible program of Reconstruction in a Proclamation of Amnesty and Reconstruction, issued in December 1863. A minimum of 10 percent of the qualified voters from 1860, having taken a loyalty oath to the Union, could organize a state government. The new state constitution had to be republican in form, abolish slavery, and provide for black education. High-ranking Confederate leaders were not eligible to take the loyalty oath, although Lincoln did not require that the new state government bar them from public life. Once these requirements had been met, the president would recognize the new civilian state government.

Lincoln also assured southerners that there would be no mass arrests, trials, and executions, for he had no desire to create any Confederate martyrs. He indicated that he would be generous in granting pardons and did not rule out compensation for slave property. Moreover, while he suggested to the Unionist governor of Louisiana that it would be wise to permit a few black men to vote, "as for instance, the very intelligent and especially those who have fought gallantly in our ranks," Lincoln did not demand social or political equality for blacks. Nor did he envision any long-term federal assistance to former slaves. Although he seemed to be moving toward requiring limited black suffrage in the disloyal southern states, he recognized pro-Union governments in Louisiana, Arkansas, and Tennessee that allowed only white men to vote.

The Radical Republicans, who constituted the most militant antislavery wing of the party, found Lincoln's approach much too lenient. Radical members of Congress like Charles Sumner and George W. Julian had been openly condemning slavery and the Slave Power for over a decade. They had led the struggle to make emancipation a war aim and now were in the forefront in advocating rights and privileges for the freedmen. They were also disturbed that Lincoln had not enlisted Congress in devising Reconstruction policy. Lincoln argued that the rebellious states had never left the Union because secession was illegal. Therefore, the executive branch should bear the responsibility for restoring proper relations with the former Confederate states. The Radicals, on the other hand, believed that in seceding, these states had ceased to exist; consequently, it was Congress' duty to set the terms under which they would regain their rights in the Union. Though the Radicals often disagreed with each other on matters of detail, they were united in a determination to readmit southern states only after slavery had been ended, black rights protected, and the power of the planter class destroyed.

Led by Senator Benjamin Wade of Ohio and Representative Henry Winter Davis of Maryland, Congress proposed that Confederate states would be ruled temporarily by a military governor. Under the Wade–Davis bill, state conventions could meet to draft a new state constitution only when fully half the white adult males took an oath of allegiance. The constitution had to renounce secession as illegal, abolish slavery, and repudiate all debts incurred by the Confederate government, ensuring that those who bought Confederate bonds and loaned money to finance the rebellion would not be repaid. To qualify as a voter or to serve as a delegate to the constitutional convention required a second oath, the so-called ironclad oath, attesting that a person had never voluntarily aided or supported the Confederacy. Since only a small minority of white southerners could take this oath in good conscience, this bill would have given political power to the hard-core Unionists in each state.

When the Wade–Davis bill passed on the final day of the 1864 congressional session, Lincoln exercised his right of a pocket veto and the bill died.* The Radicals bitterly assailed the president, but if anything, their strident objections won him wider popular support. Still, his own program could not succeed without the assistance of Congress, which refused to count the electoral votes of the reconstructed states in the 1864 election or seat Unionist representatives who had been elected to Congress from Louisiana or Arkansas. By April 1865, with the war in its last days, Lincoln appeared willing to make concessions to the Radicals. He suggested that he might favor different—and conceivably more rigorous—Reconstruction plans for different states. At his final cabinet meeting, he acknowledged that perhaps he had gone too fast on Reconstruction and approved in principle a proposal by Secretary of War Edwin Stanton to place the defeated South temporarily under military rule.

But only a few days later Booth's bullet found its mark, and Lincoln's final approach to Reconstruction would never be known. Would he have continued to push for moderation? Or being a practical politician, would he have made peace with the Radicals and pushed ahead with a firmer hand? How would the South respond to any plan of "Reconstruction"?

The Mood of the South

Northerners worried about the attitude of ex-Confederates at war's end. During Lincoln's visit to Richmond, he had ridden along deserted, rubble-strewn streets past charred buildings, to be greeted by a dusty silence. Hundreds of white southerners peered out windows, "but it was a silent crowd," recalled one of his guards. "There was something oppressive in those thousands of watchers without a sound, either of welcome or hatred." In the wake of defeat, the immediate reaction among whites was one of shock, despair, and hopelessness. Some southerners, of course, were openly antagonistic. A North Carolina innkeeper remarked bitterly that Yankees had stolen his slaves, burned his house, and killed his sons, leaving him only one privilege: "to hate 'em. I git up at half-past four in the morning, and sit up till twelve at night, to hate 'em." Most Confederate soldiers were less defiant, having had their fill of war; and even among hostile civilians there was a pervasive feeling that the South must accept northern terms. A South Carolina paper admitted that "the conqueror has the right to make the terms, and we must submit."

This psychological moment was critical. To prevent a resurgence of resistance, the president needed to lay out in unmistakable terms what white southerners had to do to regain their old status in the Union. A confusion in policy, or a wavering on the terms of how political power was to be shared in the reconstructed Union, could only increase the likelihood that southerners would resist the logic of the war's victory. Perhaps even a clear and firm policy would not have been enough. But Lincoln was no longer president, and as events would prove, the executive power now rested in less capable hands.

Johnson's Program of Reconstruction

Andrew Johnson, the new president, had been born in North Carolina and eventually moved to Tennessee, where he supported himself as a tailor. His wife taught

*If a president does not sign a bill after Congress has adjourned, it has the same effect as a veto.

him to read and write. Something of a demagogue, he rose to political power in eastern Tennessee, where there were few slaves, by portraying himself as the champion of the people against the wealthy planter class. "Some day I will show the stuck-up aristocrats who is running the country," he vowed as he began his political career. "A cheap purse-proud set they are, not half as good as the man who earns his bread by the sweat of his brow." In Tennessee, he campaigned for a free, tax-supported public school system, and when he went to Congress, he led the fight for a homestead act to grant free land from the public domain to small farmers. He had not opposed slavery before the war—in fact, he hoped to disperse slave ownership more widely in southern society. Although he accepted emancipation as one of the consequences of the war, Johnson remained an inveterate racist with no concern for the welfare of blacks. "Damn the negroes," he said during the war, "I am fighting these traitorous aristocrats, their masters."

Johnson had been the only southerner to remain in the Senate when his state seceded in 1861. In Congress, he had joined with the Radicals in calling for stern treatment of southern rebels. "Treason must be made odious and traitors must be punished and impoverished," he proclaimed in 1864. After serving as military governor of Tennessee following its occupation by Union forces, Johnson, a Democrat, was tapped by Lincoln in 1864 as his running mate on the rechristened "Union" ticket.

The Radicals expected Johnson to uphold their views on Reconstruction, and upon assuming the presidency he spoke of trying Confederate leaders and breaking up planters' estates. In reality, the grounds of agreement between Johnson and the Radicals were quite narrow. Unlike most Republicans, Johnson strongly supported states' rights and decentralization. He opposed government aid to business and romanticized the self-sufficient yeoman farmer he had championed in Tennessee politics. Given such differences, conflict between the president and the majority in Congress was inevitable. But Johnson's abrasive personality and politi-

Andrew Johnson was a staunch Unionist, but his contentious personality and inflexibility masked a deep-seated insecurity, which was rooted in his humble background. As a young man, he worked and lived in this rude tailor shop in Greenville, Tennessee.

cal shortcomings made the situation worse. Scarred by his humble origins, he remained throughout his life an outsider. When challenged or criticized, he became tactless and inflexible, alienating even those who sought to work with him.

At first, Johnson seemed to be following Lincoln's policy of quickly restoring the southern states to their rightful place in the Union. Like Lincoln, he prescribed a loyalty oath southern whites would have to take to receive pardon and amnesty. Those who took the oath would have their property, except for slaves, restored and would regain their civil and political rights. Like Lincoln, Johnson excluded high Confederate officials from this group, but he added those with property worth over $20,000, which included his old foes in the planter class. These groups had to apply to the president for individual pardons.

Loyal state governments could be formed after a provisional governor, appointed by the president, called a state convention and supervised the election of delegates. Voters and delegates had to qualify under the 1860 state election laws and take the new loyalty oath. Once elections were held to choose a governor, legislature, and members of Congress, Johnson announced he would recognize the new state government, revoke martial law, and withdraw Union troops. Again, the plan was similar to Lincoln's, though more lenient. Johnson did not require southern states to repeal their ordinances of secession, repudiate the Confederate debt, or ratify the proposed Thirteenth Amendment abolishing slavery. He only recommended that they do so.

The Failure of Johnson's Program

The southern delegates who met to construct new governments soon demonstrated that they were in no frame of mind to follow mere recommendations. Several states, instead of repudiating their ordinances of secession, merely repealed them, refusing to yield in principle the right to secede. Mississippi and Texas rejected the Thirteenth Amendment, while Georgia ratified it with the provision that slaveholders be compensated. South Carolina and Mississippi refused to repudiate the Confederate debt.

Most damaging, however, was that none of the new governments allowed blacks any political rights, and none made any effective provision for black education. Mississippi was the first to act in August 1865, but Johnson, instead of pressing harder for change, telegraphed the provisional governor with suggestions on how to appear to comply with his terms without provoking northern public opinion. Give the vote only to the tiny minority of literate black males and those who owned property worth more than $250, he advised. "This you can do with perfect safety and, ... as a consequence, the radicals, who are wild upon negro franchise, will be completely foiled." But the new southern governments refused to make even that gesture. In addition to denying black political rights, each state passed a series of laws, often modeled on the earlier slave code, that applied only to African-Americans.

The black codes did grant African-Americans some rights they had been denied as slaves. They legalized marriages from slavery and allowed blacks to hold and sell property and to sue and be sued in state courts. Yet their primary intent was to keep African-Americans as propertyless agricultural laborers without political rights and with inferior legal rights. The new freedmen could not serve on juries, could not testify against whites, and could not marry whites. And their freedom to work as they pleased was severely limited. South Carolina forbade blacks from engaging without a special license in anything other than agricultural labor; Mississippi prohibited them from buying or renting farmland; Louisiana required that agricultural laborers make contracts within the first 10 days of January that bound them for the entire year. Most states ominously provided that blacks who were vagrants could be arrested and hired out to landowners.

Although several northern states had narrowly defeated their own proposals to give black men the vote, most northerners were incensed by the restrictive black codes. "We tell the white men of Mississippi that the men of the North will convert the State of Mississippi into a frog pond before they will allow such laws to disgrace one foot of the soil . . . over which the flag of freedom waves," proclaimed the Chicago *Tribune*. Carl Schurz, a Radical Republican orator and politician who toured the South at Johnson's request, wrote that the black codes were "a striking embodiment of the idea that although the former owner has lost his individual right of property in the former slaves, the blacks at large belong to the whites at large."

Southern voters under Johnson's plan defiantly elected governors and members of Congress who were by and large prominent Confederate military and political leaders, headed by Alexander Stephens, the vice president of the Confederacy, who was elected senator from Georgia. At this point, Johnson faced a critical decision. He could have called for new elections or admitted that a different program of Reconstruction was needed. Yet for all his rabble rousing, he recoiled from the prospect of social and economic upheaval in the South. Although he had smarted for years at "the taunts, the jeers, the scowls" of upper-class planters, at the same time, he craved their respect. When they began flocking to the White House, begging for pardons and praising his conduct, he found it enormously gratifying. He began to issue special pardons almost as fast as they could be printed; in the next two years he pardoned some 13,500 Confederates. Confronted with southern defiance, Johnson capitulated and failed to follow through on his original goals.

In private, Johnson warned southerners against a reckless course. Publicly he put on a bold face, announcing that Reconstruction had been successfully completed. But many in the new Congress thought it a failure, and the stage was set for a serious confrontation.

Johnson's Break with Congress

The new Congress was by no means of one mind. The most conservative element, a small number of Democrats and conservative Republicans, backed the president's program of immediate and unconditional restoration. At the other end of the spectrum, a larger group of Radical Republicans, led by Thaddeus Stevens, Charles Sumner, Benjamin Wade, and others, was bent on fundamentally restructuring southern society and making it over on a northern model. Reconstruction must "revolutionize Southern institutions, habits, and manners," thundered Representative Stevens. "The foundations of their institutions must be broken and relaid, or all our blood and treasure have been spent in vain."

As a minority, the Radicals could accomplish nothing without the aid of the Moderate Republicans, the largest bloc in Congress. Led by William Pitt Fessenden, Lyman Trumbull, and John Sherman, the Moderates hoped to avoid conflict

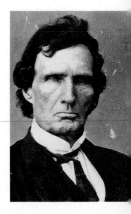

Thaddeus Stevens, Radical leader in the House.

This drawing by Thomas Nast expresses northern condemnation of the black codes enacted in the South after the war. On the left, a black man accused of crime is sold as punishment, while on the right another freedman is whipped in front of a blindfolded justice.

with the president, and they had no desire to foster social revolution in the South. But they wanted to keep Confederate leaders from reassuming power and readmit southern states only after they had fulfilled certain conditions. Finally, while they had no sympathy for the idea of racial equality promoted by many Radicals, the Moderates saw the need to extend federal protection to the freedman, who, Trumbull declared, would "be tyrannized over, abused, and virtually reenslaved without some legislation by the nation for his protection."

The central issue dividing Johnson and the Radicals was the place of African-Americans in American society. Johnson, along with other racists, accused his opponents of seeking "to Africanize the southern half of our country." The Radicals, on the other hand, championed civil and political rights for blacks, particularly the right to vote. Convinced that southern white Unionists were too small a nucleus to build a party around, Radicals believed that the only way to maintain loyal governments and develop a Republican party in the South was to give black men the ballot. Moderates, however, feared too much of an emphasis on black rights would alienate northern voters. But they agreed with Radicals that the new southern governments were too harsh toward blacks and too defiant toward the victorious North. In December 1865, when southern representatives to Congress appeared in Washington, a majority in Congress voted to exclude them. They also appointed a joint committee, chaired by Moderate William Fessenden, to look into Reconstruction.

The growing split with the president became clearer when Congress passed a bill extending the life of the Freedmen's Bureau. Created in March 1865 during the last days of the war, the Bureau provided emergency food, clothing, and medical care to war refugees (including whites) and took charge of settling freedmen on abandoned lands. The new bill not only continued these duties, but also called for the Bureau to supervise special courts to resolve disputes involving freedmen and to set up and support schools for southern blacks. This bill passed with virtually unanimous Republican support, but to the surprise of Moderates, Johnson vetoed the measure, charging that the Bureau's military courts lacked the fundamental guarantees of juries and rules of evidence. (African-Americans, of course, could neither sit on the juries nor testify against whites under the state laws approved by Johnson.) Even more alarming, the president claimed the bill was unconstitutional because southern representatives had been excluded from Congress, which if accepted would mean that any legislation passed by Congress was unconstitutional. Still, Congress failed to override the veto.

Johnson also vetoed a civil rights bill designed to overturn the more flagrant provisions of the black codes. The law made African-Americans citizens of the United States and granted them the right to own property, make contracts, and have access to courts as parties and witnesses. It also provided that federal courts could take jurisdiction if state courts discriminated against blacks. Johnson vetoed the bill on the grounds that it granted greater safeguards to blacks than whites. For most Republicans, Johnson's action was the last straw. In April 1866 Congress overrode his veto, the first major legislation to be enacted into law over a presidential veto in American history. Congress then approved a slightly revised Freedmen's Bureau bill in July and promptly overrode the president's veto. Only three Republicans in the Senate supported the president. "He has broken the faith, betrayed his trust, and must sink from detestation to contempt," observed Senator Fessenden. Johnson's refusal to compromise drove the Moderates into the arms of the Radicals.

The Fourteenth Amendment

To prevent unrepentant Confederates from taking over the reconstructed state governments and denying blacks basic freedoms, the Joint Committee on Reconstruction proposed an amendment to the Constitution, which passed both houses of Congress with the necessary two-thirds vote in June 1866. In effect, the amendment, coupled with the Freedmen's Bureau and civil rights bills, represented the Moderates' terms for Reconstruction.

The amendment put a number of matters beyond the control or discretion of the president. It guaranteed repayment of the national war debt and prohibited repayment of the Confederate debt, which Johnson had not insisted on. To counteract the president's wholesale pardons, the amendment disqualified prominent Confederates from holding office and provided that only Congress by a two-thirds vote could remove this penalty. Radicals had pushed for a provision giving the franchise to blacks, but Moderates balked, convinced that many white northerners would oppose such a provision. Instead, the amendment merely gave Congress the right to reduce the representation of any state that did not have impartial (male) suffrage. The practical effect of this provision, which Radicals labeled a "swindle," was to allow northern states to continue a policy of white suffrage if they wished, for they had few blacks and would not be penalized. Southern states, on the other hand, had significant African-American populations and risked losing part of their representation in Congress by adhering to white suffrage.

The most important provision of the amendment, Section 1, defined an American citizen as anyone who had been born in the United States or naturalized. Blacks thereby automatically became citizens, effectively repealing the Supreme Court's ruling in the *Dred Scott* case. Section 1 also prohibited states from abridging "the privileges or immunities" of citizens, depriving "any person of life, liberty, or property, without due process of law," or denying "any person . . . equal protection of the laws." The framers of the amendment probably intended to prohibit laws that applied to one race only, such as the black codes; or that made certain acts felonies when committed by blacks but not whites; or that decreed different penalties for the same crime when committed by whites and blacks. The framers probably did not intend to prevent African-Americans from being excluded from juries or segregated in schools and public places.

Still, Section 1 used general phrases for the rights it enumerated: "privileges and immunities," "due process of law," and "equal protection of the laws." The authors deliberately made those guarantees broad, to cover unanticipated abuses. And indeed, the first section of the Fourteenth Amendment has been the basis for more litigation than the rest of the Constitution combined, and one of the greatest safeguards of individual liberty and equal rights.

Ratification of a constitutional amendment does not require the president's approval; still, Johnson denounced the proposed amendment and urged southern states not to ratify it. Ironically, the president's own state ignored his advice, and one gleeful foe sent Congress a telegram announcing Tennessee's approval, which concluded, "Give my respects to the dead dog in the White House." Congress readmitted the state with no further restrictions. All the other seceded states rejected the amendment.

The Election of 1866

With Congress and the president at loggerheads, Johnson took his case to the people. In the election of 1866, he hoped to build a new National Union party, rallying Democrats, southern whites, and conservative Republicans on the platform of immediate readmission of the southern states. When a national convention in Philadelphia in August attracted few Republicans, Johnson became a man virtually without a party.

News that summer of major race riots in Memphis and New Orleans heightened northern concern. Forty-six blacks died when white mobs invaded the black section of Memphis, burning homes, churches, and schoolhouses; about the same number were killed in New Orleans when whites attacked both black and white delegates to a convention supporting black suffrage. "The negroes now know, to their sorrow, that it is best not to arouse the fury of the white man," boasted one Memphis newspaper. In the face of such attitudes, Johnson, who launched a tour of the East and Midwest to drum up support for his cause, found it difficult to convince audiences that white southerners were fully repentant. To make things worse, he conducted his campaign "swing around the circle" as if he were stumping the backwoods of Tennessee, trading insults with hostile crowds, responding in kind when they heckled him, and ranting that the Radicals were traitors. Even his supporters found the performance humiliating.

Not to be outdone, the Radicals vilified Johnson as a traitor aiming to turn the country over to rebels and Copperheads. Resorting to the tactic of "waving the bloody shirt," they appealed to voters by reviving bitter memories of the war and sectional distrust. In a classic example of such rhetoric, Governor Oliver Morton of Indiana proclaimed that "every bounty jumper, every deserter, every sneak who ran away from the draft" was a Democrat; everyone "who murdered Union prisoners," every

> New York rioter in 1863 who burned up little children in colored asylums, who robbed, ravished and murdered indiscriminately . . . called himself a Democrat. In short, the Democratic party may be described as a common sewer and loathsome receptacle, into which is emptied every element of treason North and South.

Such rhetoric became a Republican campaign staple for many years.

The voters soundly repudiated Johnson, as the Republicans won over a two-thirds majority in both houses of Congress, every northern gubernatorial contest, and control of every northern legislature. The Radicals had reached the height of their power, propelled by genuine alarm among northerners that Johnson's policies would lose the fruits of the Union's victory and leave the ruling class of the South undisturbed.

CONGRESSIONAL RECONSTRUCTION

With a clear mandate in hand, Republicans devised their own program of Reconstruction. The first Reconstruction Act was passed in March 1867 and, like all other subsequent pieces of Reconstruction legislation, was promptly repassed over Johnson's veto. The 10 unreconstructed states were divided into five military districts, each under a military commander with authority over the provisional state governments. In enrolling voters, officials were to include black adult males but not those former Confederates who were barred from holding office under the Fourteenth Amendment. Delegates to the state conventions would frame constitutions that provided for black suffrage and disqualified prominent ex-Confederates from office; the first state legislatures to meet under the new system were required to ratify the Fourteenth Amendment. Once these steps were completed and Congress approved the new state constitution, a state could send representatives to Congress.

Southern whites found these requirements so obnoxious, they preferred to remain under military rule; thus officials took no steps to register voters. Congress then enacted a second Reconstruction Act, also in March, ordering the local military commanders to enroll voters and put the machinery of Reconstruction into motion. Johnson's efforts to limit the power of military commanders produced a third act, passed in July, which upheld their superiority in all matters and confirmed their power to remove officials and reject voters' loyalty oaths. Southerners then adopted a strategy of delay, hoping that a Democratic victory in the 1868 presidential election would lead to repeal of all the Reconstruction acts. When elections were held to ratify the new state constitutions, southern whites boycotted them in large numbers. In Alabama, the first state to vote on a new constitution, only 43 percent of registered voters participated, less than the required majority. Congress was not to be daunted. It passed the fourth Reconstruction Act

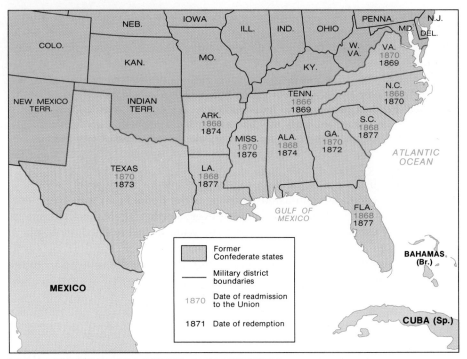

THE SOUTHERN STATES DURING RECONSTRUCTION

(March 1868), which required ratification of the constitution by only a majority of those voting rather than those who were registered. (Congress applied this act retroactively to Alabama and readmitted the state under its new constitution.)

By June 1868, Congress had readmitted the representatives of seven states. Georgia's state legislature expelled its black members once it had been readmitted, granting seats to those barred by Congress from holding office. Congress ordered the military commander to reverse these actions and Georgia was then admitted a second time in July 1870. Texas, Virginia, and Mississippi did not complete the process until 1869.

The Land Issue

While the political process of Reconstruction proceeded, Congress confronted the question of whether it was sufficient to give former slaves political and civil rights alone. Radical Republicans argued that without economic independence, blacks would enjoy only nominal freedom. Certainly many blacks felt that way. At a meeting with Secretary of War Edwin Stanton near the end of the war, African-American leaders declared, "The way we can best take care of ourselves is to have land, and till it by our own labor." Since slaves had been deprived of the right to own property before the war, Congress debated whether they should now be compensated.

During the war, the Second Confiscation Act had authorized the government to seize and sell the property including land of supporters of the rebellion. General Sherman had also issued his Special Order No. 15 in January 1865, granting blacks 40-acre homesteads on abandoned lands along the South Carolina and

Georgia coasts inland for 30 miles. In June 1866 President Johnson ruled that the Second Confiscation Act of 1862 applied only to wartime, and he also overturned Sherman's order. But Congress continued to debate the matter of confiscation from December 1865 until early 1867.

Thaddeus Stevens, the leader of the Radical Republicans in the House, advocated confiscating 394 million acres of land from about 70,000 of what he termed the "chief rebels" in the South, who comprised less than 5 percent of the South's white families. He proposed to give 40 acres to every adult male freedman and then sell the remaining land, which would amount to nine-tenths of the total, to pay off the public debt, compensate loyal southerners for losses they suffered during the war, and fund veterans' pensions. "How can republican institutions, free schools, free churches, free social intercourse exist in a mingled community of nabobs and serfs?" Stevens asked. "If the South is ever to be made a safe Republic, let her lands be cultivated by the toil of the owners or the free labor of intelligent citizens." Land, he insisted, would be far more valuable to blacks than the right to vote.

But even some Radicals believed it sufficient to give black men the ballot and pass laws protecting black rights. With Americans' strong belief in self-reliance, little sympathy existed for the idea that government should support any group or that blacks deserved special consideration. In addition, land redistribution represented an attack on property rights, another cherished American value. "A division of rich men's lands amongst the landless," argued the *Nation*, a Radical journal, "would give a shock to our whole social and political system from which it would hardly recover without the loss of liberty."

By 1867 land reform was dead. Except for property that had already been sold during the war under the Confiscation acts, seized land was returned to its former owners. Few freedmen acquired land after the war, a development that severely limited African-Americans' economic independence and left them vulnerable to white coercion. Certainly the failure to provide an economic foundation for black freedom helped undermine Reconstruction. That this decision was the basic cause of the failure of Reconstruction, however, is doubtful. In the face of white hostility and institutionalized racism, African-Americans probably would have been no more successful in protecting their property than they were in maintaining the right to vote, especially once the federal government refused to use its power to protect them. Southern whites no doubt would have devised ways to dispossess most black landowners.

Impeachment

Throughout 1867 the battle between the executive and legislative branches settled into a predictable rhythm: Congress would pass a bill, the president would veto it, Congress would override. But Johnson had other ways of undercutting congressional Reconstruction. He interpreted the new laws as narrowly as possible. He removed military commanders who vigorously enforced the laws, and his belligerence alarmed even Moderates. "Is the President crazy . . . ?" asked one. "I am afraid his doings will make us all favor impeachment." Congress fought back, directing the president to issue orders to the five military commanders in the southern states only through the general of the army, Ulysses S. Grant. Congress even limited Johnson's control of his cabinet through the Tenure of Office Act, which forbade him from removing any member without the Senate's consent. The

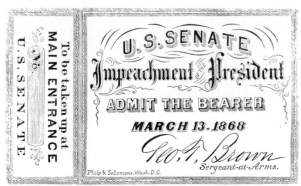

Facsimile of a ticket of admission to the impeachment trial of President Andrew Johnson.

intention of this law was to prevent him from firing Secretary of War Edwin Stanton, the only remaining Radical in the cabinet.

When Johnson tried to dismiss Stanton in February 1868, the determined secretary of war barricaded himself in his office (where he remained night and day for about two months). On February 24, the House of Representatives angrily approved articles of impeachment. The articles focused on the violation of the Tenure of Office Act, but the charge with the most substance was that Johnson had conspired to systematically obstruct Reconstruction legislation. In the trial before the Senate, his lawyers argued that a president could be impeached only for an indictable crime, which Johnson clearly had not committed. They also claimed that the president had fired Stanton merely to test the constitutionality of the Tenure of Office Act, while simultaneously they argued inconsistently that the Tenure of Office Act did not apply to Stanton, since he had been appointed by Lincoln and not Johnson. The Radicals countered that impeachment applied to political offenses and not merely criminal acts, a position James Madison had supported during the drafting of the Constitution.

In May 1868, after a three-month trial at which Johnson did not appear, the Senate voted 36–19 to convict, one vote short of the two-thirds majority needed. The seven Republicans who had joined the Democrats in voting for acquittal were uneasy about using impeachment as a political weapon. In addition, the president pro tempore of the Senate, Benjamin Wade of Ohio, was in line to succeed Johnson, and his radical views on Reconstruction as well as women's rights and the currency frightened Moderates. Their vote against conviction established the precedent that a president could be removed from office only for indictable offenses, which greatly lessened the effectiveness of the threat of impeachment.

Reconstruction and the Constitution

Impeachment represented an attempt by Congress to establish its supremacy in the federal government. The Supreme Court also became a target of congressional pressure and control. Democrats, who were a hopeless minority in Congress, increasingly looked to the Court to overthrow the Reconstruction acts. For their part, Republicans worried that the *Milligan* decision (page 583), which struck down military trials for civilians during wartime, was a sign that the Court might declare the Reconstruction acts unconstitutional, since they provided for military rule and trials in the southern states. Republicans' fears crystallized when the

Court agreed to hear the appeal of an editor from Mississippi named William McCardle, who had been arrested under the Reconstruction acts and tried by a military commission. The first Reconstruction Act had given federal courts jurisdiction over certain cases, to protect freedmen from state courts. Congress responded by retroactively denying federal courts jurisdiction in such appeals and the Court, unwilling to challenge Congress, ruled in *Ex parte McCardle* (1868) that it had no jurisdiction.

Indeed, throughout this era the Court decided several relevant cases on very narrow grounds and declined to rule on the constitutionality of the Reconstruction acts. In *Texas v. White* (1869) it ruled that secession was illegal and the Union perpetual, and asserted that it was up to Congress to guarantee a republican government in each state. But it perceived, properly, that Reconstruction was an extraordinary situation, one the Constitution had never anticipated. Had the Court challenged Congress on such a highly political matter, it would have precipitated a constitutional crisis that would have led to a concerted effort to restrict the Court, if not destroy its power. Restraint on the Court's part proved wise.

RECONSTRUCTION IN THE SOUTH

The waning power of the Radicals in Congress, evident in the failure to remove Johnson, meant that the success or failure of Reconstruction increasingly hinged on developments in the southern states themselves. Power in these states rested with the new Republican parties, representing a coalition of southern blacks, southern whites, and transplanted northerners.

Black Officeholding

Black men formed the bulk of the Republican voters in the South—perhaps as much as 80 percent. Almost from the beginning, they insisted that they were the only sizable loyal population in the South and lobbied for the right to vote. When they finally received the franchise, they were not about to support the Democratic party and its appeal to white supremacy. As one Tennessee Republican explained, "The blacks know that many conservatives [Democrats] hope to reduce them again to some form of peonage. Under the impulse of this fear they will roll up their whole strength and will go entirely for the Republican candidate whoever he may be."

Yet, even though African-American males eagerly accepted the ballot, they never held office during Reconstruction in proportion to their voting strength. They lacked a majority in any southern legislature; only in South Carolina, where they constituted over 60 percent of the population, did they control even one house of the legislature. No African-American was ever nominated or elected governor. Only in South Carolina did a black judge serve on a state supreme court. Between 15 and 20 percent of the state officers and 6 percent of the congressmen in Reconstruction were black. Two blacks from Mississippi served in the U.S. Senate, and 15 blacks served in the House. In reality, only in South Carolina, where they held 52 percent of all state and federal elective offices, did black officeholding approach their proportion of the population.

This engraving shows a black politician addressing former slaves at a political meeting in the South during the 1868 presidential campaign. Although only men could vote, black women are also in the audience. Commented *Harper's Weekly* when this picture appeared, "Does any man seriously doubt whether it is better for this vast population to be sinking deeper and deeper in ignorance and servility, or rising into general intelligence and self-respect?"

Those who held office came from the top levels of African-American society. Among state and federal officeholders, perhaps four-fifths were literate, and over a quarter had been free before the war, both marks of distinction in the black community. Their occupations also set them apart: two-fifths were professionals (mostly clergy), and of the third who were farmers, nearly all owned their own land. Others were skilled workers or ran small businesses. Among blacks in Congress, all but three had a secondary school education, and four had gone to college. Jonathan Gibbs, the Florida secretary of state, was a graduate of Dartmouth and the Princeton Theological Seminary, and Francis Cardozo, who served as secretary of state and treasurer in South Carolina, had attended several colleges in England. Senator Blanche Bruce of Mississippi was the son of a white planter and had been educated on his father's plantation. In their political and social values, African-American leaders were more conservative than the rural black population, and they showed little interest in land reform. Like whites, they ranged from the talented to the incompetent.

Southern White Republicans

The failure of Congress to disfranchise Confederates meant that the Republican party had to secure white votes to stay in power. Blacks were a majority of the voters only in South Carolina, Mississippi, and Louisiana. Opponents labeled southern whites who allied with the Republican party scalawags, a pejorative term referring to scrubby cattle. An estimated quarter of southern whites at one time voted Republican, including prominent southerners like General James Long-

618

street, one of Robert E. Lee's key commanders, and James Lusk Alcorn, a wealthy Mississippi planter. Although the party appealed to some wealthy southern Whigs, they were outnumbered by Unionists from the upland counties and hill areas who were largely yeoman farmers. Such voters were attracted to Republican promises to rebuild the South, restore prosperity, create public schools, and open isolated areas to the market with railroads.

The other group of white Republicans in the South hailed originally from the North: carpetbaggers, they were derisively called, allegedly poor and ignorant men who arrived with all their worldly possessions stuffed in a carpetbag, ready to loot and plunder the defeated South. Some did, certainly, but northerners who moved south came for a variety of reasons. Those in political office were especially well educated and, although they constituted only a small percentage of Republican voters, they controlled almost a third of the offices, especially the higher ones. More than half of all southern Republican governors and nearly half of Republican congressmen and senators were originally northerners.

The Republican party in the South had difficulty agreeing on a program or maintaining unity. Scalawags were especially susceptible to the race issue and social pressure. "Even my own kinspeople have turned the cold shoulder to me because I hold office under a Republican administration," testified a Mississippi Republican. As blacks pressed for more recognition and a greater share of the offices, southern whites increasingly defected to the Democrats. Carpetbaggers, by contrast, were less sensitive to race and more strongly committed to the party. A number had previously worked for black rights and education, although most felt that blacks needed guidance and should be content with minor offices. The friction between carpetbaggers and blacks was minor compared to scalawags' resentment of carpetbaggers, intruders who in their eyes had seized offices that rightfully belonged to native southerners. As a result, southern Republicanism was riven by growing factionalism.

The New State Governments

The new state constitutions in the South included a number of significant reforms. In older states the earlier inequitable legislative apportionment, which discriminated against the interior counties, was replaced by a fairer system. Many previously appointive offices were made elective, and property requirements for office-holding were abolished. In South Carolina, for the first time, voters were allowed to vote for the president, governor, and other state officers.* The Radical state governments also assumed some responsibility for social welfare and established the first statewide systems of public schools in the South. The new governments also substantially increased state aid to the insane, the handicapped, and the poor. Women's rights were also enlarged, and divorce was finally legalized in South Carolina.

Although the Fourteenth Amendment prevented high Confederate officials from holding office, virtually all the new state constitutions refused to place any additional penalties on them. Only Alabama and Arkansas temporarily forbade some ex-Confederates from voting. Understandably, the strongest advocates of harsh penalties were southern Unionists, who often had suffered at the hands of

*Previously, presidential electors as well as the governor had been chosen by the South Carolina legislature.

their Confederate neighbors and who believed that political power in the reconstructed South rightfully belonged to them. African-American delegates, on the other hand, generally opposed any penalties. They argued that blacks and whites had to live together in the South, and such penalties could lead only to growing bitterness between the races.

All of the new constitutions proclaimed the principle of equality and granted black adult males the right to vote, but on social relations they were much more circumspect. No state outlawed social segregation, and South Carolina and Louisiana were the only states requiring integration in public schools. Even so, that requirement was ignored except in New Orleans and at the University of South Carolina. Sensitive to status, mulattoes were more insistent on eliminating social discrimination, but white Republicans refused to adopt such a radical policy.

Economic Issues and Corruption

The problems of economic reconstruction were as difficult as those of politics. Major sections of the South lay in ruins; its people, white and black, faced dire poverty. Charred and gutted buildings scarred cities like Columbia, Atlanta, and Richmond; rail networks were broken up; central South Carolina, where Sherman's army had struck, was described as "a broad black streak of ruin and desolation."

The Republican governments in the South sought to encourage industry by providing subsidies, loans, and even exemption from taxes for a certain number of years. These governments also largely rebuilt the southern railroad system, often offering lavish aid and privileges to railroad corporations. In the two decades after 1860, the region doubled its manufacturing establishments, and centers like the Birmingham iron and steel industry became symbols of a new industrial South. Yet the harsh reality was that the South steadily slipped further behind the economy of the North, which had boomed throughout the war. Between 1854 and 1879, 7000 miles of railroad track were laid in the South, but in the same period 45,000 miles were constructed in the rest of the nation. Social disorder also discouraged outside investment, and southern energy and capital initially were devoted simply to rebuilding what the war had destroyed. The Radical governments could not create the prosperity that they unrealistically promised in hopes of gaining the support of upper-class southerners.

The expansion of government services and the cozy relationship with business leaders offered sometimes irresistible temptations for corruption. In many southern states, officials regularly resorted to fraud and received bribes and kickbacks for their award of railroad charters, franchises, and other contracts. The tax rate grew as expenditures went up, so that by the 1870s it was four times the rate of 1860. By 1872, the debts of the 11 states of the Confederacy had increased $132 million. In Florida between 1868 and 1874 the state debt grew tenfold; in South Carolina in only three years it increased to almost six times its previous size.

Corruption, however, was not only a southern problem. The decline in morality was nationwide, as scandals in the federal administration and in northern state governments revealed. During these years, the Democratic Tweed Ring in New York City stole more money than all the Radical Republican governments in the South combined. Moreover, corruption in the South was hardly limited to Republicans. Many Democrats and white businessmen participated in and profited from the corrupt practices, both before and after the Radical governments were in power. In Louisiana, where corruption had flourished long before Reconstruction, Governor Henry Warmoth, a carpetbagger, told a congressional committee the legislature was as good as the people it represented. "Why, damn it," he testified, "everybody is demoralizing down here. Corruption is the fashion."

While fraud contributed to the public debt in the South, most of the increase came from the cost of rebuilding. In fact, most of the debt represented grants to railroads. In addition, freeing millions of slaves greatly increased the number of citizens eligible for government services. The new public school systems, even if inadequately funded, meant that state taxes were bound to increase.

Corruption in Radical governments undeniably existed, but southern whites exaggerated its extent for partisan purposes. Conservatives as bitterly opposed the Radical regime in Mississippi, which was untainted by any significant financial scandal, as they did the notoriously corrupt Republican governments in Louisiana and South Carolina. In the eyes of most southern whites, the real crime of the Radical governments was that they recognized blacks in the distribution of offices and tried to protect the civil rights of black Americans. Race was the conservatives' greatest weapon and would prove the most effective means to undermine Republican power in the South.

BLACK ASPIRATIONS

Emancipation came to slaves in different ways. For some it arrived during the war when Union soldiers entered an area; for others it came some time after the Confederacy's collapse when Union troops or officials announced that they were free. On some plantations the news set off a wild celebration—a "Day of Jubilee" and thanksgiving—while other slaves received the news with no outward reaction. But after the initial celebration, what did freedom mean to people who had been in bondage all their lives?

Experiencing Freedom

The first impulse was to think of freedom as a contrast to slavery, to understand the new state of affairs in terms of limitations on white behavior and a release from the most oppressive aspects of bondage—the whippings, the work routine, the breakup of families. Above all, freedom meant that African-Americans were now their own masters and that their labor would be for their own benefit. One Arkansas freedman, who earned his first dollar working on a railroad, recalled that when he was paid, "I felt like the richest man in the world."

Freedom also meant movement, the right to travel without a pass or white permission. In the first months after the war, former slaves clogged the roads of the South. For some, this was a way to experience the thrill of moving about freely. For others, it was an attempt to find lost family members, to visit relatives, or to return to the place where they had grown up either to resettle or just to visit. Some never found the kin they sought, while others wept when reunited at last with husbands, wives, and children.

Freedom also included finding a new place to work. Changing jobs was a concrete way to break the psychological ties of slavery. Blacks especially deserted masters who had been harsh and cruel, but even planters with reputations for kindness and fairness sometimes found most of their former hands had departed. The cook who left a South Carolina family, even though they offered her higher

Daily Lives

PUBLIC SPACE/PRIVATE SPACE

The Black Sharecropper's Cabin

On the plantations of the Old South, slaves had lived in cabins along a central path in the shadow of the white master's "big house" or the overseer's dwelling. These quarters were the center of their community, where marriages and other festivals were celebrated, family life went on, and slaves shared a sense of kinship. With the coming of emancipation, however, freedmen looked to rid themselves of the old quarters, which stood as a symbol of bondage and of close white supervision. Hence when white landowners switched to a system of sharecropping or tenant farming, African-Americans either dismantled their old cabins and hauled them to the plots of land they rented or simply built new housing. This enabled them to live on the land they farmed, just as white farmers and tenants did. It also provided a greater measure of privacy.

In selecting a cabin site, freedmen tried to locate within a convenient distance of their fields, but close to the woods as well, since cutting wood was a year-round task for boys. To improve drainage, cabins were often built on a knoll or had a floor raised above the ground; in low-lying areas, stone or log piers were used. A nearby stream, spring, or well provided not only water but a place to cool butter and other perishable dairy products.

Like slave cabins, sharecroppers' dwellings were one story high with a gable roof, about 16 feet square, and built usually of logs chinked with mud. The few windows had shutters to protect against the weather; glass was rare. Though the inside walls normally lacked plaster or sheeting, they were given a coat of whitewash annually to brighten the dark interior and make the room seem larger. To provide a bit of cheer, the womenfolk often covered the walls with pictures from seed catalogues and magazines. The floor, packed dirt that was as smooth and hard as concrete, was covered with braided rugs made from scraps of cloth and worn-out clothing.

The main room served as kitchen and dining room, parlor, bathing area, and the parents' bedroom. To one side might be a homemade drop-leaf table (essential because of cramped space), which served as a kitchen work counter and a dining table. The other side of the room had a few plain beds, their slats or rope bottoms supporting corn shuck or straw mattresses. (Featherbeds were considered a remarkable luxury.) The social center of the room was the fireplace, the only source of heat and the main source of light after dark. Pots and pans were hung on the wall near the fireplace, and the mother and daughters did the cooking stooped over an open fire. Since the family usually could not afford to buy matches, the fire was rarely extinguished. Some earthen or tin dishes, steel eating utensils, assorted containers, a rifle or shotgun, and a few prized possessions (usually displayed on the mantlepiece over the fireplace) rounded out the family's furnishings. Clothing was hung on pegs in the wall. If the family owned a trunk, the parents' Sunday clothes and valuables would be stored in it.

The fireplace was constructed of smooth stone; the chimney was made of small logs notched together and covered with several layers of clay to protect it from the heat. It often narrowed toward the top, and sometimes its height was extended by empty flour barrels, for a taller chimney drew better. That made for a hot-

Daily Lives

Chimneys on share-croppers' cabins were often tilted deliber-ately, so they could be pushed away from the house quickly if they caught fire.

ter fire and kept smoke from blowing back down into the house and sparks away from the roof. After the evening meal, the family gathered around the fireplace, the children to play with homemade dolls and toys, the mother to sew, and the father perhaps to play the fiddle. At bedtime, a trapdoor in the ceiling offered access up a ladder to the loft beneath the gabled roof. Being cold and dark, it was used only for sleeping. Normally the parents and infants slept downstairs, older children upstairs until the girls reached puberty, after which they slept downstairs too. The children often slept on pallets on the floor, as had been the case in slavery.

In the summer, cooking was done outdoors over an open fire. Women preferred to cook under a tree, which offered some protection from rain as well as relief from the sun and the high humidity. Sharecropper families rarely had separate cooking rooms attached to or next to the cabin. Separate kitchens, which were a sign of prosperity, were more common among black landowners and white tenant farmers.

Gradually, as black sharecroppers were able to scrape together some savings, the quality of their homes improved. By the end of the century, frame dwellings were more common, and many older log cabins had been covered with wood siding. The newer homes were generally larger, with wood floors, and often had attached rooms such as a porch or kitchen. In addition, glass panes covered the windows, roofs were covered with shingles instead of planking, and stone and brick chimneys were less unusual. A narrow stairwell, often with a door to shut out cold drafts, provided access to the loft; underneath it was a closet for additional storage. Ceramic dishes were more frequently seen, and wood-burning stoves made cooking easier for women and provided a more efficient source of heat.

Without question, the cabins of black sharecroppers provided more space than the slave quarters had, and certainly more freedom and privacy. Still, they lacked many of the comforts that most white Americans took for granted. Such housing reflected the continuing status of black sharecroppers as poverty-stricken laborers in a caste system based on race.

wages than her new job, explained, "I must go. If I stays here I'll never know I'm free." And a black preacher told a group of freedmen in Florida: "So long as the shadow of the great house fall across you, you ain't going to feel like no free man and no free woman. You must all move to new places that you don't know, where you can raise up your head without no fear of Master This and Master The Other."

Symbolically, freedom meant, too, having a full name. As slaves, African-Americans often had no surname, but with the coming of freedom, more than a few took the name of some prominent individual, such as Washington or Jefferson, or else some leading figure in the community. More common, however, was to take the name of the first master in the family's oral history as far back as it could be recalled. Most freedmen, on the other hand, retained their first name in slavery, especially if they had been named by their parents (as most slaves were). It had been their form of identity in bondage, and for those separated from their family it was the only link with their parents. But whatever name they took, it was important to blacks that they made the decision themselves without white interference.

The Black Family

African-Americans also sought to strengthen the family in freedom. Since slave marriages had not been recognized as legal, thousands of former slaves insisted on being married again by proper authorities. Although not required by law, these wedding ceremonies represented a reaffirmation of commitments made earlier. This new right created a dilemma for those who had been forcibly separated from a spouse in slavery and subsequently remarried. Should they return to their first spouse or remain with the current one? The Freedmen's Bureau urged blacks in this predicament to take the spouse with whom they had the greatest number of dependent children, but the final decision rested with the individuals. Laura Spicer, who had been separated from her slave husband, received a series of wrenching letters from him after the war. He had thought her dead, had remarried, and had a new family. "I would come and see you but I know you could not bear it," he wrote.

> You know it never was our wishes to be separated from each other, and it never was our fault . . . I had rather anything to had happened to me most than ever have been parted from you and the children. As I am, I do not know which I love best, you or Anna . . . I do not think I would die satisfied till you tell me you will try and marry some good, smart man that will take good care of you and the children; and do it because you love me; and not because I think more of the wife I have got than I do of you. The woman is not born that feels as near to me as you do.

A family decision that had major economic repercussions for agricultural labor was the insistence of black men that their wives would not work in the fields as they had in slavery. As in white families, black fathers deemed themselves the head of the family and the breadwinner and acted legally for their wives. "The [black] women say they never mean to do any more outdoor work," one planter reported, "that white men support their wives and they mean that their husbands shall support them." African-American families also often withdrew their children from labor. In negotiating contracts, a father demanded the right to discipline his children. All these changes were designed to insulate the black family from white control.

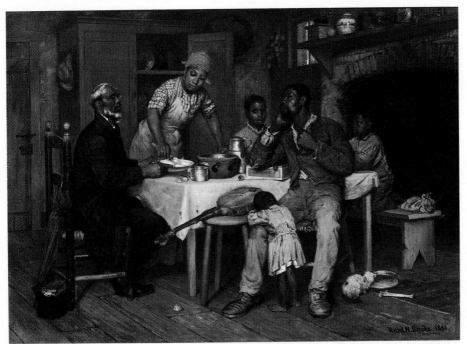

Making the rounds of the parish, a black minister shares a meal with some of his parishioners. Such meals were a welcome supplement to a clergyman's scanty salary. Black ministers were important leaders of the African-American community in freedom.

The Gospel and the Primer

In freedom, the schoolhouse and the black church became essential institutions in the black community. Next to ownership of land, African-Americans saw education as the best hope for advancement. "My Lord, Ma'am, what a great thing learning is!" a South Carolina freedman told a northern teacher. "White folks can do what they likes, for they know so much more than we." Initially, northern churches and missionaries, working with the Freedmen's Bureau, set up black schools in the South. The Bureau also spent over $400,000 to support black colleges, including Howard University in Washington, which were founded to train future African-American leaders and teachers to staff black schools.

The freedmen's schools were not free and required a substantial commitment on the part of the family of those who enrolled. Tuition represented 10 percent or more of a laborer's monthly wages, yet these schools were full. Blacks eagerly came; one school official reported they were simply "crazy to learn." Many parents sent their children to school by day and attended classes themselves at night. Eventually, the freedmen's schools were replaced by the new public school systems, which by 1876 had enrolled 40 percent of African-American children.

Black adults had good reasons for seeking literacy. They wanted to be able to read the Bible, to defend their newly gained civil and political rights, and to protect themselves from being cheated. Slavery had bred a deeply ingrained suspicion of whites, and as one elderly Louisiana freedman explained, giving children an education was better than giving them a fortune, "because if you left them even

$500, some man having more education than they had would come along and cheat them out of it all." White resistance stimulated this desire for education. Black schools were often destroyed, and white teachers threatened and even murdered. Both races saw in the postwar South that education would undermine the old servility that slavery had fostered. More than other Americans, blacks knew that education would overthrow the legacy of slavery.

For the first time in the South, blacks were allowed to establish their own churches. Most slaves had attended white churches or services supervised by whites, and northern organizations like the African Methodist Episcopal Church had been banned. Once free, African-Americans quickly established their own congregations led by black preachers. In the first year of freedom, the Methodist Church South lost fully half of its black members. By 1870, the Negro Baptist Church had increased its membership threefold compared to 1850, and the African Methodist Episcopal Church expanded at an even greater rate.

Indeed, black churches were so important because they were the only social organization in the African-American community actually controlled by blacks. Black ministers were respected leaders. An officer of the American Missionary Association reported that "the Ebony preacher who promises perfect independence from White control and direction carried the colored heart at once." Many of the black men elected to office during Reconstruction were preachers. Just as in slavery, religion offered African-Americans a place of refuge in a hostile white world and provided them with hope, comfort, and a means of self-identification.

New Working Conditions

For blacks, freedom involved more than just receiving pay for labor performed; they sought to remove all the emblems and habits of servitude. Owning land would have best provided them with economic independence, but the few feeble attempts at land reform failed. Blacks remained a largely propertyless class, forced to work for former masters and landowners. Whites insisted, as they had before the war, that blacks would not work without compulsion. Except for paying wages, they tried to retain the old system of labor, including close supervision, gang labor, and discipline by the whip or other physical punishment. African-Americans, however, not only refused to work under this system; they demanded time off to devote to their own work and leisure interests. Convinced that working at one's own pace was part of freedom, they simply would not work as long or as hard as they had in slavery. Because of shorter hours and the withdrawal of children and women from the fields, work output declined by an estimated 35 percent. Blacks also refused to live in the old slave quarters located near the master's house. Instead, they erected cabins on distant parts of the plantation. Wages initially were $5 or $6 a month plus provisions and a cabin; by 1867, they had risen to an average of $10 a month.

Such changes in the labor system eventually led to the rise of the sharecropping system. Under this arrangement, African-American families farmed separate plots of land and then at the end of the year divided the crop with the owner. The farmer's share depended on whether he supplied the seeds, animals, and implements, but the normal arrangement was an equal division of the crop between the sharecropper and the landowner. Although sharecropping was not the same as owning a farm, blacks believed it offered higher status and greater personal freedom than being a wage laborer. One black defended his right to leave the planta-

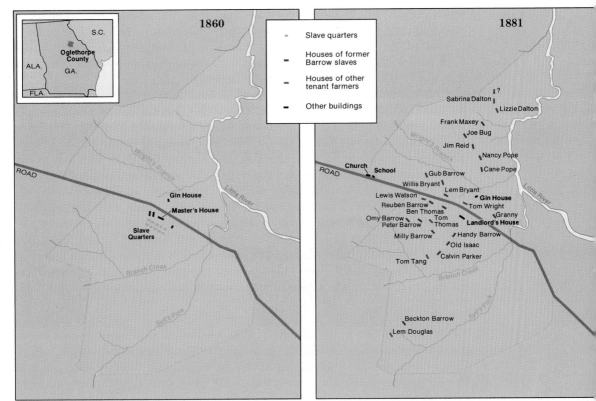

A GEORGIA PLANTATION AFTER THE WAR
After emancipation, sharecropping became the dominant form of agricultural labor in the South. Black families no longer lived in the old slave quarters, but dispersed themselves to separate plots of land that they farmed themselves. At the end of the year each sharecropper turned over part of the crop to the white landowner.

tion at will without permission of the owner. "I am not working for wages," he declared, "but am part owner of the crop and as I have all the rights that you or any other man has I shall not suffer them abridged." Actually, black per capita agricultural income increased 40 percent between 1857 and 1879, since white landlords were unable to expropriate as large a share of black earnings as they had in slavery.

The Freedmen's Bureau

The task of supervising the transition from slavery to freedom on southern plantations fell to the Freedmen's Bureau, a unique experiment in social policy supported briefly by the federal government. Created as an agency of the War Department, the Bureau provided relief for refugees, helped settle freedmen on abandoned lands, and put them back to work. During the summer of 1865 the Bureau provided 150,000 daily rations, a third of which went to whites; from 1865 to 1870 it issued 2 million rations, built 40 hospitals, and treated 450,000 patients. But the Bureau's major task was to protect the freedmen's economic rights. Approximately 550 local agents supervised and regulated working conditions in an attempt to bring order to southern agriculture after the war. The racial attitudes of Bureau agents varied widely, as did their commitment and competence. Since their guidelines were vague, they used their own judgment to settle cases, and they depended on the army to enforce their decisions.

Most agents encouraged or required written contracts between white planters and black laborers, specifying not only wages, but the conditions of employment. Agents adjudicated disputes, sometimes intervening to protect freedmen from unfair treatment. But agents also used their power to get African-Americans who had migrated to the cities back on the plantations. They preached to the freedmen the gospel of work and the need to be orderly and respectful. Given such attitudes, blacks increasingly complained that Bureau agents were mere tools of the planter class. "They are, in fact, the planters' guards, and nothing else," claimed the New Orleans *Tribune*, a black newspaper. Agents did provide important help to planters. They insisted that blacks not desert at harvest time; they arrested as vagrants those who violated their contracts or refused to sign new ones at the beginning of the year. One observer reported, "Doing justice seems to mean seeing that the blacks don't break contracts and compelling them to submit cheerfully."

The primary means of enforcing working conditions were the Freedmen's Courts, which Congress created in 1866 because of persistent discrimination against African-Americans in the state courts. These new courts functioned as military tribunals and often the agent was the entire court, hearing testimony and then rendering a verdict. These courts were more sympathetic to freedmen in some states than others. In 1867 one agent summarized the Bureau's experience with the labor contract system: "It has succeeded in making the freedman work and in rendering labor secure and stable—but it has failed to secure to the Freedman his just dues or compensation."

In 1869, with the Bureau's work scarcely under way, Congress ordered it to prepare to shut down. Even the Radical Republicans did not want to create a permanent welfare agency. By 1872 the Bureau had gone out of business, leaving behind a mixed record. Its major accomplishment was freedmen's schools, but the absence of any program for significant land redistribution ensured that its contributions would be limited. The disbanding of the Bureau, the most effective and efficient agency that protected blacks' civil and political rights, signaled the beginning of the northern retreat from Reconstruction.

Planters and a New Way of Life

Planters and other southern whites faced emancipation with dread. Unwilling to live with free blacks, some planters fled to the North, the West, or even to foreign countries like Mexico and Brazil. Most, however, stayed, searching for a system to replace slavery. "All the traditions and habits of both races had been suddenly overthrown," a Tennessee planter recalled, "and neither knew just what to do, or how to accommodate themselves to the new situation."

The old ideal of a paternalistic planter, which required a facade of black subservience and affection, gave way to an emphasis on strictly economic relationships. Mary Jones, a Georgia slaveholder before the war who did more for her workers than the law required, complained of their disrespectful language, imper-

Black education was one of the significant changes freedom brought during the era of Reconstruction. Here a group of black students pose with their books outside their crude schoolhouse.

tinent gestures, and poor work. But her patience snapped when two workers accused her of trickery and hauled her before a Freedmen's Bureau agent, with whom she won her case. Upon returning home, she announced to the assembled freedmen that "in doubting my word they offered me the greatest insult I ever received in my life; that I have considered them friends and treated them as such but now they were only laborers under contract, and only the law would rule between us." The subservience that planters had demanded and taken for granted—touching one's hat, the obsequious, smiling demeanor, the fawning guise of gratitude—now melted away in freedom. Only with time did planters develop new norms and standards to judge black behavior. What in 1865 had seemed insolence was viewed by the 1870s as the normal attitude of freedom.

Slavery had been a complex institution that welded blacks and whites together in intimate relationships, but under the new system planters increasingly embraced the ideology of segregation. Planters kept dealings with African-Americans to a minimum. Since emancipation significantly reduced the social distance between the races, whites sought psychological separation. Segregation—the legal separation of the races—became an institution to buttress white status. By the time Reconstruction ended, white planters had developed a new set of values to replace those of slavery. Their new way of life was reflected in the institutions of sharecropping and segregation and undergirded by a militant white supremacy. Planters endured, but with emancipation, they lost their pride, confidence, and some of their identity.

Nor did planters regain the economic prosperity of the antebellum years.

Rice plantations, which were not suitable to tenant farming, largely disappeared after the war. The cotton crops in 1865 and 1866 failed, and it was not until 1877 that cotton production consistently exceeded the prewar level. Furthermore, cotton from new areas such as India, Egypt, and Brazil now competed with American cotton, while the world demand grew at a much slower rate after 1865 than it had earlier. Cotton prices began a long decline, and southern per capita income suffered as a result. Cotton plantations continued to dominate southern agriculture, but many planters' income declined sharply. Most escaped total collapse, but by 1880 the value of southern farms had slid 33 percent below the level of 1860.

THE ABANDONMENT OF RECONSTRUCTION

The Radical Republicans had failed to impeach Johnson by one vote—a narrow margin, but effective nevertheless. The Radicals' influence was waning and the Republican party was being drained of the crusading idealism that had stamped its early years. Ulysses S. Grant was hardly the cause of this change, but he certainly came to symbolize it.

The Election of Grant

Grant had not identified with the Radical wing of the party until Johnson used the general as a pawn in his struggle with Congress. In relieving Stanton, Johnson had tried to maneuver Grant to take his place, and in the process drove the general into an alliance with the Radicals. Afraid of sinking into obscurity, Grant yearned to be president, the only office that would be a promotion for him. Immensely popular, he was the natural choice of Republicans in 1868. Since the Republican platform called for repayment of the national war debt in gold, which pleased businessmen but hurt workers and farmers, the Democrats proposed a more inflationary monetary policy. That appealed to many debtor farmers (who were helped by inflation), and the Democrats also hoped to pick up votes of whites who disapproved of Republican policies on behalf of the freedmen.

Grant easily defeated his opponent, former governor Horatio Seymour of New York, in the Electoral College, but his popular margin was only 300,000 votes. With a ticket headed by a great military hero, the close vote shocked Republican leaders. Although Grant would have won in the Electoral College even without the estimated 450,000 votes he received from southern blacks, a majority of whites had voted for Seymour. The 1868 election helped convince Republicans that an amendment securing black suffrage throughout the nation was necessary.

In February 1869 Congress sent the Fifteenth Amendment to the states for ratification. It forbade any state from denying the right to vote on grounds of race, color, or previous condition of servitude. Some Radicals had hoped to forbid literacy or property requirements, to protect blacks further; others wanted a simple declaration that all adult male citizens had the right to vote. But the Moderates feared that only a conservative version could be ratified, since many northerners were increasingly worried about the number of immigrants who were again enter-

Declining to adopt her husband's name, Lucy Stone (right) was a major figure in the women's rights movement after the Civil War. Northern women who had worked for emancipation during the war protested the failure to grant them the right to vote along with male freedmen during Reconstruction.

ing the country. As a result, the final amendment left loopholes that eventually allowed southern states to disfranchise African-Americans.

Radicals saw the Fifteenth Amendment as an antidote to the hypocrisy of the Fourteenth Amendment, which fastened black suffrage only upon the South (and even there, only by indirection). "We have no moral right to impose an obligation on one part of the land which the rest will not accept," one Radical leader declared. Party leaders also felt that the small black vote might be critical to the Republicans in closely contested northern states. The amendment was ratified in March 1870, in part with the votes of the four southern states that had not completed the process of Reconstruction and thus were also required to endorse this amendment before being readmitted to Congress.

Proponents of women's suffrage were gravely disappointed at the refusal of Congress to prohibit voting discrimination on the basis of sex as well as race. Many of the women's suffrage supporters had been associated with the abolitionist movement earlier and had worked hard to get the Thirteenth Amendment ratified. The Women's Loyal League, led by Elizabeth Cady Stanton and Susan B. Anthony, had pressed for first the Fourteenth and then the Fifteenth Amendment to recognize women's public role, but even most Radicals, contending that black rights had to be assured first, were unwilling to back women's suffrage. The Fifteenth Amendment ruptured the feminist movement. While disappointed that women were not included in its provisions, Lucy Stone and the American Woman

Suffrage Association urged ratification of the amendment. Anthony and Stanton, on the other hand, broke with their former allies among the Radicals, denounced the amendment, and organized the National Woman Suffrage Association to work for passage of a new amendment giving women the ballot. This division continued to hamper the women's rights movement in the future.

The Grant Administration

Grant lacked the moral commitment to make Reconstruction succeed. Unsure of himself socially, he gravitated toward the wealthy elements in American society, the businessmen and financiers that the party increasingly aided. He was ill at ease with the political process, lacked trustworthy advisers, and, haunted by his undistinguished career before 1861, had an abiding fear of failure. Grant's simple and taciturn style, while superb for commanding armies, did not serve him as well in politics, and his well-known resolution withered when he was uncertain of his purpose or goal. His bewilderment over the complex political problems he confronted made him appear pathetic, a handicap that even his good intentions could not overcome.

A series of scandals wracked Grant's presidency, so much so that "Grantism" soon became a code word in American politics for corruption, cronyism, and venality. Although Grant did not profit personally, those close to him dipped freely into the public till. Loyal to his friends, he displayed little zeal to root out corruption or bring the guilty to justice. His relatives were implicated in a scheme to corner the gold market, his private secretary escaped conviction for stealing federal whiskey revenues only because Grant interceded on his behalf, and his secretary of war, who was selling Indian trading post contracts, resigned to avoid impeachment. James W. Grimes, one of the party's founders, denounced the Republican party under Grant as "the most corrupt and debauched political party that has ever existed."

Nor was Congress immune from the lowered tone of public life. The Crédit Mobilier, a corporation established to build the Union Pacific Railroad, siphoned huge profits from the coffers into its directors' hands, but a number of bribed congressmen successfully headed off an investigation. In such a climate ruthless state machines, led by men who favored maintaining the status quo, came to dominate the Republican party. Office and power became ends in themselves, and party leaders worked in close cooperation with northern industrial interests.

At the same time, the Radicals who had spearheaded the movement for a rigorous program of Reconstruction were passing from the scene. Thaddeus Stevens died in August 1868, shortly after Johnson's impeachment trial. Benjamin F. Wade and George Julian were defeated, and Charles Sumner, who got into a tug of war with the Grant administration over an attempt to annex the island of Santo Domingo, was stripped of his chairmanship of the foreign relations committee by the Senate. The few Radicals still active in public life increasingly repudiated Grant and the Republican governments in the South. Congress in 1872 passed an amnesty act, removing the restrictions of the Fourteenth Amendment on office holding, except for about 200 to 300 ex-Confederate leaders.

As corruption in both the North and South worsened, reformers in the party became more interested in cleaning up government than in protecting black rights. These liberal Republicans, who considered themselves "the best men," opposed the continued presence of the army in the South, denounced the corrup-

Grant swings from a trapeze while supporting a number of associates accused of corruption. Among those holding on are Secretary of the Navy George M. Robeson (top center), who was accused of accepting bribes in the awarding of navy contracts; Secretary of War William W. Belknap (top right), who was forced to resign for selling Indian post traderships; and the president's private secretary Orville Babcock (bottom right), who was implicated in the Whiskey Ring scandal. Though not personally involved in the scandals during his administration, Grant was reluctant to dismiss supporters accused of wrongdoing from office.

tion of southern governments as well as the national government, and advocated free trade and civil service reform. In 1872 they broke with the Republican party and nominated for president Horace Greeley. The editor of the New York *Tribune* and a one-time Radical, Greeley was disillusioned with Reconstruction and urged a restoration of home rule in the South. Democrats decided to back the Liberal Republican ticket. The Republicans renominated Grant, who, despite the defection of Radicals such as Sumner, Carl Schurz, and E. L. Godkin of the *Nation*, won an easy victory with 56 percent of the popular vote.

Growing Northern Disillusionment

During Grant's second term, Congress passed the Civil Rights Act of 1875, the last major piece of Reconstruction legislation. Up until this time, Congress had refused to challenge segregation and racial discrimination practiced by individuals and corporations. The 1875 law prohibited racial discrimination in all public accommodations, transportation, places of amusement, and juries. Congress, however, rejected a ban on segregation in public schools, which was almost universally practiced in the North as well as the South. While some railroads, streetcars, and public accommodations in both sections were desegregated after the law passed, the federal government made little attempt to enforce the law, and it was ignored throughout most of the South. In 1883 the Supreme Court struck down its provisions except that relating to juries.

Despite passage of this law, northern public opinion was, in fact, growing increasingly disillusioned with Reconstruction. Northerners were bothered by the corruption and dishonesty of the southern governments and tired of the violence and disorder in the South. Even at the height of Reconstruction, the support for black rights owed more to antisouthern than problack motives. "People are becoming tired of abstract questions," one Republican paper commented. "The negro question, with all its complications, and the reconstruction of the Southern states, with all its interminable embroilments, have lost much of the power they once wielded."

At the same time, a number of Republicans were attracted to Lincoln's old strategy of forging an alliance with southern whites. Influential northern business leaders were particularly eager to establish conditions favorable to investment in the South. They began to look to southern conservatives, many of whom were proponents of the idea of a New South based on urbanization and industry, to restore order and political stability. William Dodge, a wealthy New York capitalist, wrote in 1875: "What the South now needs is capital to develop her resources, but this she cannot obtain till confidence in her state governments can be restored, and this will never be done by federal bayonets." It had been a mistake, he went on, to make southern blacks feel "that the United States government was their special friend, rather than those with whom their lot is cast, among whom they must live and for whom they must work. We have tried this long enough," he concluded. "Now let the South alone."

As the agony of the war became more distant and Republicans got less mileage out of waving the bloody shirt, economic matters drew public attention away from Reconstruction. The Panic of 1873 marked the beginning of a severe depression that lasted for four years. Some 3 million people were thrown out of work, and much of the wrangling in Congress about how to revive the economy centered on the question of the currency. In 1874 Grant vetoed a bill to increase the supply of greenbacks, and the next year Congress adopted the policy of requiring greenbacks to be convertible to gold by 1878. The question of inflation and the gold standard would remain a central political issue for the remainder of the century (page 782).

But in its immediate political consequences, the depression led to a surge in Democratic strength. Battered by the panic and the corruption issue, the Republicans lost a shocking 77 seats in Congress in the 1874 elections, and along with them control of the House of Representatives for the first time since 1861. The Democrats scored striking gains in every region of the country, even winning the Massachusetts governorship for the first time in 40 years. "The truth is our people are tired out with the worn out cry of 'Southern outrages'!!" one Republican concluded. "Hard times and heavy taxes make them wish the 'ever lasting nigger' were in hell or Africa." Republicans spoke more and more about cutting loose the southern governments to enhance the party's strength in the North.

The Triumph of White Supremacy

As northern commitment to Reconstruction declined, southern Democrats set out to overthrow the remaining Radical governments. Already white southerners were deserting the Republican party by the thousands. A white Republican in Mississippi justified his decision to leave the party on the grounds that otherwise, his children had no future. "No white man can live in the South in the future and act with any other than the Democratic party unless he is willing and prepared to live a life of social isolation and remain in political oblivion."

To poor whites who lacked social standing, the Democratic appeal to racial solidarity offered great comfort. As one explained, "I may be poor and my manners may be crude, but I am a white man. And because I am a white man, I have a right to be treated with respect by Negroes. That I am poor is not as important as that I am a white man; and no Negro is ever going to forget that he is not a white man." The large landowners and other wealthy groups that led southern Democrats objected less to blacks voting, in part because they did not face social and economic competition from them, but also because they were confident that if outside influences were removed, they could control the black vote. When Wade Hampton, a wealthy planter, ran for governor in South Carolina in 1876, he pledged that if elected he would "observe, protect, and defend the rights of the colored man as quickly as any man in South Carolina."

Democrats also resorted to economic pressure to undermine Republican power. The lack of a secret ballot strengthened the hand of white conservatives. White landlords refused to hire or take on as sharecroppers African-Americans who voted Republican. In heavily black counties, white observers at the polls took down the names of blacks who cast Republican ballots and published them in local newspapers. A Mississippi paper urged planters to "discharge . . . every laborer who persists in the diabolical war that has been waged against the white man and his interest ever since the negro has been a voter."

But terror and violence proved the most important means used to overthrow the radical regimes in the South. A number of paramilitary organizations, of which the Ku Klux Klan was the most famous, broke up Republican meetings, terrorized white and black Republicans, assassinated Republican leaders and candidates, and prevented blacks from voting. Founded in 1866 in Tennessee, the Klan represented all social classes, although the leaders were often locally prominent planters. Most of the members were young men in their twenties and thirties, and many were Confederate veterans. The Klan and similar organizations functioned as an unofficial arm of the Democratic party.

Congress finally moved to break the power of the Klan with the Force Act of 1870 and the Ku Klux Klan Act of 1871. These laws made it a felony to interfere with the right to vote; they also authorized use of the army, suspension of the writ of habeas corpus, and removal of Klan supporters from juries. The Grant administration eventually suspended the writ of habeas corpus in nine South Carolina counties and arrested hundreds of suspected Klan members throughout the South. Although these actions weakened the Klan, terrorist organizations continued to operate underground.

What became known as the Mississippi Plan was inaugurated in 1875, when Democrats decided to use as much violence as necessary to carry the state election. Several local papers trumpeted, "Carry the election peaceably if we can, forcibly if we must." Democratic clubs, organized into irregular military companies, paraded in black areas to intimidate voters, dispersed Republican meetings, and assassinated Republican leaders. When Republican Governor Adelbert Ames requested federal troops to stop the violence, Grant's advisers warned that sending troops to Mississippi would cost the party the Ohio election. In the end, the administration told Ames to depend on his own forces. As the attorney general

Two Ku Klux Klan members pose in full regalia. Violence played a major role in overthrowing the Radical governments in the South. One South Carolina paper openly praised Klan attacks on blacks and the Republican Union Leagues:

> Born of the night, and vanish by day;
> Leaguers and niggers, get out of the way!

explained, "The whole public are tired out with these annual autumnal outbreaks in the South, and the great majority are now ready to condemn any interference on the part of the government."

Bolstered by this terrorism, the Democrats swept the election. Violence and intimidation prevented as many as 60,000 black and white Republicans from voting, converting the normal Republican majority into a Democratic majority of 30,000. The victors boasted that Mississippi had been "redeemed."

The Disputed Election of 1876

With the Republican party on the defensive across the nation, the 1876 presidential election was crucial to the final overthrow of Reconstruction. Only three states—Louisiana, South Carolina, and Florida—still remained in Republican hands, and Democrats were prepared to use the Mississippi Plan to carry them in 1876.

The Republicans nominated Ohio governor Rutherford B. Hayes to oppose Samuel Tilden, a Democrat who had won fame by prosecuting the corrupt Tweed Ring in New York City. Once again, violence prevented an estimated quarter of a million Republican votes from being cast in the South, and the outcome was in doubt. Tilden had reported majorities in South Carolina, Florida, and Louisiana, but Hayes' supporters also claimed them. Hayes needed all three states to be elected, for even without them, Tilden had amassed 184 electoral votes, one short of a majority. Tilden also had a clear majority of 250,000 in the popular vote. Although the Democrats also claimed to have carried the governorships and legislatures in South Carolina, Louisiana, and Florida, the Republican canvassing boards in power disqualified enough Democratic votes to give each state to Hayes.

To arbitrate the disputed returns, Congress established a 15-member electoral commission: 5 members each from the Senate, the House, and the Supreme Court. As originally constituted, the commission divided evenly between 7 Republicans and 7 Democrats, with Supreme Court Justice David Davis, who had been a Republican and was now a political independent, as the swing vote. But when Davis was elected to the Senate from Illinois, he declined to serve on the commission and was replaced by a Republican member of the Court. By a straight party vote of 8–7, the commission awarded the disputed electoral votes—and the presidency—to Hayes.

When angry Democrats threatened a filibuster to prevent the electoral votes from being counted, Republicans scrambled to head off a stalemate. On February 26, key Republicans met with southern Democrats at the Wormley Hotel in Washington and reached an informal understanding, later known as the Compromise of 1877. Hayes' supporters agreed to withdraw the troops and not oppose the new white state governments if Democrats would drop their opposition to Hayes' election. Southerners, for their part, pledged to treat blacks fairly and respect their rights. Hayes was quite happy with this deal, for he hoped to rebuild his party in the South by appealing primarily to whites who were former Whigs. Assurances that Republicans would help pass federal aid for a number of southern internal improvement projects also helped in a minor way to ease Democratic objections.

Once in office, Hayes withdrew military support for the Republican governors in South Carolina and Louisiana, who had claimed victory. Those administrations promptly collapsed, and Democrats took control of the remaining two states of the Confederacy. By 1877, the entire South was in the hands of the Redeemers, as they called themselves, and Reconstruction and Republican rule had come to an end.

THE ELECTION OF 1876

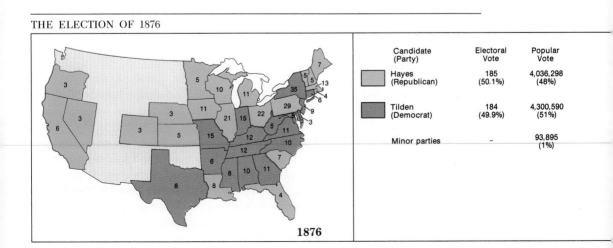

Candidate (Party)	Electoral Vote	Popular Vote
Hayes (Republican)	185 (50.1%)	4,036,298 (48%)
Tilden (Democrat)	184 (49.9%)	4,300,590 (51%)
Minor parties	–	93,895 (1%)

1876

In a crowded Supreme Court chamber, lawyers for both Hayes and Tilden present evidence to the electoral commission (seated on the rostrum at left) created to decide the outcome of the 1876 election. Members of all branches of government listen to the testimony, along with a number of socially prominent women, including Cornelia Adele Fassett, the artist who painted the scene from which this detail is taken.

Racism and the Failure of Reconstruction

Reconstruction failed for a multitude of reasons. The reforming impulse that had created the Republican party in the 1850s had been battered and worn down by the war. The new materialism of industrial America inspired in many a jaded cynicism about the corruption of the age and a desire to forget the uncomfortable issues of the past. In the South, African-American voters and leaders inevitably lacked a certain amount of education and experience; elsewhere, Republicans were divided over policies and options. Yet beyond all these obstacles, the sad fact remains that the ideals of the war and Reconstruction were most clearly defeated by a deep-seated racism that permeated American life. Racism was why the white South so unrelentingly resisted Reconstruction; racism was why most northern whites had little interest in black rights except as a means to an end, to preserve the Union or to safeguard the Republic; racism was why northerners were willing to write off Reconstruction, and with it the welfare of black Americans. Ever since the mid-seventeenth century, the system of slavery had been based on race. While Congress might pass a constitutional amendment abolishing the peculiar institution, it could not overturn at a stroke the social habits of two centuries.

Certainly the political equations of power, in the long term, had been changed. The North had fought tenaciously during the war to preserve the Union, and in doing so, had retained the power to dominate the economic and political destiny of the nation. With the overthrow of Reconstruction, the white South had won back in time of peace some of the power it had lost through war. But even with white supremacy triumphant across the land, African-Americans did not remain on the same social footing as before the war. They were no longer slaves, and blacks who walked dusty roads in search of family members, sent their children to school, or worshiped in churches they controlled, knew what a momentous change this was. Even under the exploitive sharecropping system, black income rose 40 percent in freedom. Then too, the principles of "equal protection" and "due process of law" had been written into the Constitution and would be available for later generations to use in resurrecting the Radicals' goal of racial equality.

But this was a struggle left to future generations. For the time being, the clear trend was away from change, reform, or hope—especially for blacks like Benjamin Montgomery and his sons, the owners of the old Davis plantation in Mississippi. In the 1870s bad crops, falling cotton prices and land values, and other misfortunes undermined the Montgomerys' financial position. At the same time, white violence against blacks made them more dependent than before on white goodwill, and in 1875 Jefferson Davis, who was now in dire economic circumstances himself, sued to have the sale of Brierfield invalidated. Davis acknowledged that he had never received legal title to the land, but he contended that his brother Joseph, who had died in 1870, had given him the plantation years ago to operate as his own.

In 1876, a lower court ruled against Davis, since he had executed his brother's will for four years without challenging its validity. But with the overthrow of Mississippi's Radical government, the political winds in the state shifted, and Davis appealed to the state supreme court, which now had a white conservative majority. The court, in a politically motivated decision, awarded Brierfield to Davis in 1878, and the Montgomerys lost Hurricane as well. The final outcome was not without bitter irony. In applying for restoration of his property after the war, Joseph Davis had convinced skeptical federal officials that he, and not his younger brother, held legal title to Brierfield. Had they decided instead that the plantation belonged to Jefferson Davis, it would have been confiscated.

But the waning days of Reconstruction were times filled with such ironies: of governments "redeemed" by violence, of Fourteenth Amendment rights designed to protect black people being used by conservative courts to protect giant corporations, of reformers searching elsewhere for other causes. Repudiated by its northern supporters and unmourned by public opinion, Reconstruction was over.

Benjamin Montgomery, together with his sons, purchased Jefferson Davis' plantation along the Mississippi River after the war. A former slave, Montgomery pursued the dream of black economic independence by renting land to black farmers at Davis Bend.

SIGNIFICANT EVENTS

1863	Lincoln outlines Reconstruction program
1864	Lincoln vetoes Wade–Davis bill; Louisiana, Arkansas, and Tennessee establish governments under Lincoln's plan
1865	Freedmen's Bureau established; Johnson becomes president; Presidential Reconstruction; Congress excludes representatives of Johnson's governments; Thirteenth Amendment ratified; Joint Committee on Reconstruction established
1865–1866	Black codes enacted
1866	Civil Rights bill passed over Johnson's veto; Memphis and New Orleans riots; Fourteenth Amendment passes Congress; Freedmen's Bureau extended; Ku Klux Klan organized; Tennessee readmitted to Congress; Republicans win decisive victory in congressional elections
1867	Congressional Reconstruction; Tenure of Office Act; Control of the Army Act
1867–1868	Constitutional conventions in the South; blacks vote in southern elections
1868	Johnson impeached but acquitted; Fourteenth Amendment ratified; Grant elected president
1869	Fifteenth Amendment passes Congress; *Ex parte McCardle*
1870	Last southern states readmitted to Congress; Fifteenth Amendment ratified; Enforcement acts
1871	Ku Klux Klan Act
1872	General Amnesty Act; Freedmen's Bureau dismantled; Liberal Republican revolt
1873–1877	Panic and depression
1874	Democrats win control of the House
1875	Civil Rights Act; Mississippi Plan
1876	Disputed Hayes–Tilden election
1877	Compromise of 1877; Hayes declared winner of electoral vote; last Republican governments in South fall

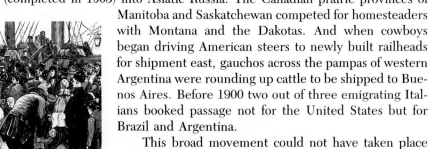

PART 4

THE UNITED STATES
IN AN
INDUSTRIAL AGE

The Statue of Liberty has now stood watch over New York harbor for more than a hundred years. In that time the tired, poor, huddled masses of immigrants who passed beneath her torch have become, to late-twentieth-century Americans, anonymous parts of a continuing stream, stretching back in the mind's eye to the English Pilgrims, the French fur traders along the St. Lawrence, and the Spanish friars of Old California. But the nineteenth-century stream of immigrants arriving at Ellis Island was different from the large majority of those who had traveled to America in an earlier age. Innovations in transportation, communications, and industry created an international network that made possible for the first time voluntary migration on a massive scale.

Before 1820 substantial numbers of people had moved to North and South America, but for the great majority the choice had hardly been voluntary. Perhaps 7.8 million Africans were brought to the Americas during those years, virtually all as slaves. That number was four to five times the number of Europeans who came during the same period. In contrast, between 1820 and 1920 nearly 30 million free immigrants arrived from Europe.

Nor was this flood directed only toward America. At least as many Europeans left their homelands for other regions of Europe or the world. While millions of immigrants were taking trains across the American plains in search of jobs and homesteads, millions more from eastern Europe followed the Trans-Siberian Railway (completed in 1905) into Asiatic Russia. The Canadian prairie provinces of Manitoba and Saskatchewan competed for homesteaders with Montana and the Dakotas. And when cowboys began driving American steers to newly built railheads for shipment east, gauchos across the pampas of western Argentina were rounding up cattle to be shipped to Buenos Aires. Before 1900 two out of three emigrating Italians booked passage not for the United States but for Brazil and Argentina.

This broad movement could not have taken place without a widening global network of communication, markets, and transportation. Some of the effects of the industrial transformation had been felt well before the end of the nineteenth century. Indeed, the Civil War was a consequence, in part, of the conflicting ways in which the North and the South had evolved. Though still relatively rural, the northern economy had begun to urbanize by 1860, with textile mills clustered in factory towns along New England rivers, and railroads from the Midwest opening up commercial markets for grain and dairy products. The South remained overwhelmingly rural, but industry shaped it nonetheless, as New England and European factories clamored for southern cotton to spin into fabric and "ready-made" clothing. The demand for cotton ensured that the slave labor system firmly entrenched itself in the South, until at last the issue of whether the nation could endure half-slave and half-free was decided by force of arms.

By the end of Reconstruction, urbanization and industrialization were well under way, not only in America but also in Europe. The British, whose innovations had sparked the revolution in industry, also discovered its devastating side effects. Population swelled in urban areas of Great Britain, as rural workers flocked after factory jobs. Without efficient transportation, the workers were forced to live within walking distance of the factories. The resulting overcrowding and filth were almost stupefying: families jammed into dark, pungent row houses built with few windows along narrow alleyways and streets where open sewers flowed with garbage. In London one construction engineer reported that the overflow from privies had collected to the depth of three feet in the cellars of nearby houses.

Spurred on by a deadly cholera epidemic in 1848, British social reformer Edwin Chadwick completed a long and hard-fought campaign to install a system of cheap iron pipes and tile drains to provide running water and sewers throughout major cities. In addition, French and German research during the 1860s and 1870s established the germ theory of disease, which confirmed the need for better sanitation. Other urban planners took note of the radical renovation of Paris begun by Baron Georges Haussmann. Under Haussmann's direction, workers tore down the city's medieval fortress walls, widened its major streets into boulevards, and set aside land for green and pleasant parks. American cities had no ancient walls and fewer narrow roads, and since Americans were less tradition-bound, they were often more willing to rebuild and enlarge. Their innovations led Europeans to adopt horse-drawn streetcars and, later, electric trolleys. By establishing an intracity transportation network, the old "walking cities" were able to add suburbs, partially easing the crush of earlier industrial crowding.

As hubs of the new industrial networks, where immigrants and newcomers from the countryside flocked, cities needed efficient links to raw materials, as well as markets for their finished products. Much of the late nineteenth century can be seen as a scramble of Western nations for raw materials and markets. Miners combed the hills of California for gold in 1849, as they did two years later in Victoria, Australia. In South Africa, the rush was for diamonds discovered along the Vaal and Orange rivers and gold near present-day Johannesburg. In Canada, Australia, Argentina, and New Zealand, agriculture and stock-raising moved steadily toward larger, more commercialized operations. All of these enterprises extracted value from previously untapped natural resources, funneling commodities into the growing global network.

The end result of the scramble was the age of imperialism, as the European powers sought to dominate their newly acquired territories. The United States joined the rush somewhat late, in part because the nation had consumed so much of its energies extracting raw materials from its own "colonial" regions, the burgeoning West and the conquered South. Incorporating these two regions into a national industrial dominion raised unpleasant questions of power, just as imperialism itself did. European imperialists justified their rule over nonwhite races in Darwinian fashion, as the survival of the fittest. "The path of progress is strewn with the wreck . . . of inferior races," one English professor proclaimed in 1900. The British poet Rudyard Kipling even suggested that Europeans see themselves as making a noble sacrifice on behalf of their subject peoples. "Take up the White Man's Burden—," he exhorted them:

> Send forth the best ye breed—
> Go bind your sons to exile
> To serve your captives' need.

All too clearly, however, the needs being served were usually not those of the "captives." Imperialism certainly did not serve the needs of coolie laborers of Kipling's India, who died by the thousands clearing virgin jungles for tea plantations; or black miners in South Africa laboring for nearly slave wages; or Chinese workers in Australia and the United States, excluded and segregated after both gold rushes; or southern black sharecroppers, oppressed by a system of racism; or American Indians, driven off their lands by successive waves of prospectors, cowhands, and sodbusters.

The racist undercurrent of both European imperialism and American expansion was something most whites of the era ignored. But farmers in both the South and the West did lash out at industrial "robber barons" and railroad "monopolists," who seemed to epitomize the abuses of the new industrial order. The social strains arising out of these wrenching changes were reflected in the American political system, first in the Populist movement of the 1890s and then in the tide of progressivism that became prominent at the turn of the century. In Europe, too, industrializing nations responded to pressures for political reform, passing social legislation that included the first social security systems and health insurance.

Through imperialism, then, the modern industrial states spread their political dominion across the world, as migrants traveled in search of jobs and land, merchants sought new markets, industries explored and extracted raw materials, and nations established colonial regimes. The United States, too, joined this global order of commerce, political alliances, and rivalries—an order that finally collapsed with the coming of World War I.

CHRONOLOGY

AMERICAN EVENT	YEAR		GLOBAL EVENT
Commodore Perry visits Japan	1853		
	1859		Darwin's *On the Origin of Species* published
Transcontinental railroad completed	1869	GRANT	Suez Canal completed
Rockefeller founds Standard Oil	1870		Franco-Prussian War
			Britain produces half the world's pig iron
Bell invents telephone	1876		Refrigerated ships permit export of beef from Argentina
Battle of Little Bighorn			
Reconstruction ends	1877	HAYES	
	1880s		Pogroms against Russian Jews spur emigration
American Federation of Labor founded	1881	GARFIELD	
	1881	ARTHUR	
Twain's *Huckleberry Finn* published	1885	CLEVELAND	Berlin Conference concluded; European powers partition Africa
			Indian National Congress formed
	1888		Slavery abolished in Brazil
	1889	HARRISON	Germany enacts a social security system
			Japan establishes the Meiji Constitution
Sherman Antitrust Act	1890		
Three-year depression begins	1893	CLEVELAND	
Plessy v. Ferguson upholds segregation	1896		
First U.S. subway opens (Boston)	1897	MCKINLEY	
Spanish-American War	1898		Germany modernizes navy
Carnegie Steel produces more steel than all Great Britain	1900		Boxer Rebellion in China
			Freud's *Interpretation of Dreams* published
J. P. Morgan creates U.S. Steel	1901	ROOSEVELT	
	1904		Outbreak of Russo-Japanese War
			Social welfare legislation in France
	1905		Trans-Siberian railroad completed; revolution in Russia
			Einstein begins work on relativity
Sinclair's *The Jungle* published	1906		
U.S. troops intervene in Nicaragua	1909	TAFT	
	1910		Mexican Revolution begins
Armory Show, New York City, introduces modern art	1913	WILSON	
Panama Canal opened	1914		World War I begins
United States enters World War I	1917		Russian Revolution
Senate rejects Versailles Treaty	1919		Treaty of Versailles signed
Women's suffrage ratified (Nineteenth Amendment)	1920		
	1921	HARDING	

18

The Rise of a
New Industrial Order

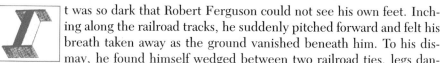 t was so dark that Robert Ferguson could not see his own feet. Inching along the railroad tracks, he suddenly pitched forward and felt his breath taken away as the ground vanished beneath him. To his dismay, he found himself wedged between two railroad ties, legs dangling in the air. That was enough. Scrambling back to solid ground, he retreated along the tracks to the railroad car, where he sat meekly until dawn.

Ferguson, a Scotsman visiting America in 1866, had been in Memphis only two days earlier, ready to take the "Great Southern Mail Route" from the Mississippi River east some 850 miles to Washington. Things had gone badly from the start. About 50 miles down the track, a broken bridge at the Hatchie River forced him from the train and onto a ferry across the river. Bumping along another 10 miles in a mule-drawn truck, he arrived at Brownsville, Tennessee, where he was told the rail line did not resume for at least 40 miles, a distance impossible to travel in less than two days. Disheartened, he decided to return to Memphis and try another rail route.

The "excursion" to Memphis, due to leave the town of Big Hatchie at 10 a.m., arrived at four in the afternoon, six hours late. By seven Ferguson had traveled half of the 50-mile journey when the train suddenly stopped. It was dinnertime, not for the passengers but for the conductor, engineer, and stoker. The crew left the engine idling while they ate. Barely three hours later came another wrenching stop as the train derailed several miles outside of Memphis.

A few passengers decided to hike the remaining distance to Memphis, banding together for mutual protection against any toughs who might be lurking beyond the city's gaslights. Ferguson followed but lagged farther and farther behind in the darkness. It was then that he fell between the tracks and retreated to the safety of the railcar. At dawn he discovered how narrow his escape had been: just ahead, the tracks led out onto a high river bridge, consisting of nothing more than cross rails supported on trestles. Ferguson had trouble managing them even in daylight.

Before he finally reached Washington, Robert Ferguson traveled six days more, with connections between lines that took anywhere from a few hours to an entire evening. Meals were not served "on board," nor were there any sleeping

In a fiery display giant egg-shaped Bessemer converters remove carbon from molten iron ore to make steel at Andrew Carnegie's steelworks in Pittsburgh.

cars. Railside inns were primitive and usually crowded. "It was certainly what the Americans would call 'hard travelling,'" he snorted; "—they do not make use of the word 'rough,' because roughness may be expected as a natural condition in a new country."

Southern rail lines had been hit hard by the Civil War, but northern travelers encountered similar difficulties. Bridges across major rivers were scarce. One line would end, and passengers and freight would be forced to transfer to another because rail gauges—the width of the track—differed from line to line. Accommodations were still fairly primitive. The Reverend Newman Hall, visiting from England in 1867, rode his first "sleeping car" from Niagara to Chicago and was roused at six in the morning for a "wash-up" of "towels, soap, &c." To eat, he had to purchase apples from a boy roaming the aisles, who cheekily stopped to finger Newman's diamond stickpin.

A mere 20 years later, rail passengers traveled in relative luxury. T. S. Hudson, another British tourist, launched a self-proclaimed "Scamper Through America" in 1882. It took him just 60 days to go from England to San Francisco and back. He traveled across the entire continent on a ticket booked by a single agent in Boston. Such centralization would have been unthinkable in 1866 when, in any case, the transcontinental railroad was still three years from completion. Hudson's trains had Pullman Palace cars with luxurious sleeping accommodations and a breakfast menu offering coffee, tea, and iced milk; broiled meats (including "game in their season"); hot breads and rolls; eggs prepared in every imaginable style; fried bacon, sausage, oysters, and trout; relishes, vegetables, fruits, even chocolate—all for 75 cents. Newly installed air brakes made the trains he rode safer and their stops less jarring. Bridges appeared where none had been before, including a "magnificent" span over the Mississippi at St. Louis, with three arches of "five hundred feet each, approached by viaducts, and, on the western shore, also by a tunnel."

Hudson also found himself in the midst of a communications revolution. Traveling west across the plains, he was struck by the number of telephone poles along the route. Salt Lake City, to his surprise, had launched its own phone exchange. The problem remained of adjusting to local times, for each town still set its clocks by the sun. (New York and Boston, for example, were 11 minutes and 45 seconds apart.) By 1882, there were some 50 rail systems of time, no two identical. To aid passengers, stations often had several clocks showing the time on different lines along with one showing "local mean time." Had Hudson waited another year for his "scamper," the railroads would have reinvented time for him. In 1883, independently of any government or court, the railroad companies divided the country into four standard time zones, called "railroad time," to which cities and towns soon adjusted. Congress did not get around to making the four zones official until 1916.

What made America in the 1880s so different from the 1860s was a new industrial order. The process of industrialization had begun much earlier, at least three decades before the Civil War. Small factories had produced light consumer goods like clothing, boots and shoes, and furniture. They catered largely to local markets in what was predominantly an economy of farmers and merchants. After the 1850s the industrial economy matured and a new industrial order flowered. The transformation, remarkable as it was, brought not only progress but pain. In 1882, the year T. S. Hudson scampered comfortably across America, an average of 675 workers were killed on the job every week.

THE DEVELOPMENT OF INDUSTRIAL SYSTEMS

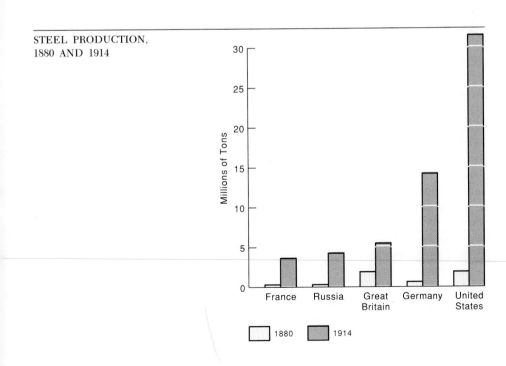

The new industrial order can be best understood as the emergence of a host of complex industrial systems that became woven into the fabric of everyday life. Look, for example, at the industrial systems required to build the bridge across the Mississippi that Hudson so admired. When James B. Eads constructed his soaring 515-foot arches in 1874, he needed steel, which was refined from iron ore most likely from the Mesabi range in Minnesota. At Mesabi, giant mechanized shovels scraped up the ore and in a few swings loaded an entire freight car. A transportation revolution, in the form of heavy-duty railroads, ore boats, and ore carriers, then moved the ore and other materials to a manufacturing center, perhaps near Pittsburgh, Pennsylvania. High-quality anthracite coal, probably from the mines of western Pennsylvania, fired the blast furnaces. The factory system—in this instance, a steel mill—provided the machinery and manpower to finish the steel. The costs of creating such a system—buying giant shovels, financing transportation, underwriting steel plants, hiring labor—ran into the millions of dollars. Investment banks and stock markets in New York and Chicago furnished the money. Not just laborers but a national network of industrial systems built the Eads bridge.

The industrializing of America after the Civil War is not the story of one but of many processes, all linked, all acting together to forge an industrial nation. Americans tied the country's natural resources into an interlocking system. They used technological innovations to streamline communication and transportation networks. They organized complex bureaucracies and coordinated workers through new techniques of management. They generated capital and dispersed ever

STEEL PRODUCTION, 1880 AND 1914

Millions of Tons

France   Russia   Great Britain   Germany   United States

1880   1914

greater amounts of it. Without the entwining of such facilities there would have been no Eads bridge—and no industrial America.

Natural Resources and Industrial Technology

The earliest European settlers had waxed eloquent about the "merchantable commodities" of America, whether the glittering silver mines of the Spanish empire or the hardwood forests that stretched from New England halfway across the continent. What set the new industrial economy apart from that older America was the scale, range, and efficiency of exploiting resources. New industrial technologies, most of them developed initially in Europe, made possible the use of natural riches in ways undreamed of only decades earlier.

Iron, for example, had been made into steel for use in the blades of fine swords as far back as the Middle Ages. In the 1850s, however, Henry Bessemer in England and William Kelly in Kentucky independently discovered a way to convert iron into steel in large quantities. To heat iron ore the new "Bessemer process" required egg-shaped converters, some the size of small houses and capable of holding five tons of molten metal. At precisely the right moment and in exactly the right places, the converters blew drafts of hot air through the mixture to burn out the carbon that made iron brittle.

By the late 1870s, the Bessemer process had reduced the price of steel from $100 to $40 a ton. Steel quickly became the construction material of the age. For railroads, steel rails were lighter than iron, could support 20 times as much weight, and lasted 20 years instead of 3. Steel girders replaced the old cast iron frames of buildings, and steel cables supported new suspension bridges. By the 1870s, steel shovels, saws, and nails were common at construction sites.

Under the impact of industrial technology some worthless natural resources became valuable. Petroleum had once been little more than an annoyance—a smelly, thick liquid that bubbled to the surface of springs and was used occasionally as patent medicine. By the middle of the nineteenth century, distillation processes changed it into paraffin for making candles and sealing jars, oil for lubricating machinery, and kerosene for lighting lamps. Within a few years, chemists added to the list of petroleum products varnish, grease, polish, and paint.

Such innovation made oil into an even bigger business. Two subsequent events turned it into a major industry. In 1859, near Titusville, Pennsylvania, Edwin M. Drake drilled an oil well that tapped pools of petroleum below the surface. Then, in 1859, the Frenchman Etienne Lenoir constructed the first practical internal combustion engine. By the late 1870s, George Selden, a lawyer from Rochester, New York, had begun experimenting with gasoline-driven engines that powered road vehicles. In the twentieth century these "automobiles" would transform social and economic life in America and would help, along with vast natural reserves of petroleum, to make the American oil industry preeminent in the world.

The environmental price of industrial technology soon became all too evident. Loggers cut down the forests of the Pacific Northwest with a ruthless efficiency that threatened to destroy them. Mining scarred the land, and industrial wastes befouled lakes and rivers. At the turn of the century the Monongahela River, site of the huge Homestead steel mill, was so polluted local residents doubted that even microbes could survive in it. After a cloudburst trees around the mill were gray with soot.

Systematic Invention

The United States had always lagged behind Europe in basic scientific research, but for sheer inventiveness, the 40 years following the Civil War have rarely been matched in American history. Between 1790 and 1860, 36,000 patents had been registered with the government. Over the next three decades, the U.S. Patent Office granted more than 500,000; and in one year, 1897, the office issued over 21,000 patents, more than the total number recorded during the 1850s.

Even the process of invention became systematized. In the first half of the nineteenth century new inventions usually had come from practical tinkerers, operating by trial and error. While such lone operators continued to make important contributions, the process of industrialization required more orderly innovation. Small-scale inventors experimenting in machine shops were replaced by "invention factories"—highly capitalized research labs. Inventing became not only a system but also a business.

No one did more to bring system and order to invention than Thomas Alva Edison. Born in 1847, Edison spent his adolescence tinkering with electricity and telegraphs. At the age of 21, he went to work for a New York brokerage house and promptly improved the design of the company's stock tickers. With the $40,000 bonus he received, he set himself up as an independent inventor. For the next five years, Edison patented a new invention almost every five months. Before he was 30 he had come up with a "quadraplex" (he also invented the word) capable of sending four messages over a single telegraph wire, an electric voting machine, an "electric pen," a mimeograph, and a host of other marketable items.

Thomas Edison's unkempt hair, often matted with oil and dust, his wrinkled suit, and acid-stained hands belied his meticulous intellect and devotion to the dollar. "Anything that won't sell," he said, "I don't want to invent."

Edison was not content with unstructured tinkering. In 1876 he moved 15 of his workers to Menlo Park, New Jersey, where he created the first "scientific" factory, determined to turn out "minor" inventions every 10 days and "a big thing every six months or so." Like a manufacturer, he subdivided the work among gifted inventors, engineers, toolmakers, and others, including a mathematical physicist. An orderly bureaucracy evolved, and in 1878 it became a full-blown business—the Edison Electric Light Company.

Edison aimed at nothing less than bringing electricity into the homes of America. Before Edison's innovations, the only electric alternatives for lighting streets were arc lamps, which tended to short-circuit and were far too bright for use indoors. For Edison, the solution was not merely technical but social, which meant solving the problem of marketing and distribution as well. What was needed, he realized, was a unified electric system: a central power station to send out electric current; a network of wires to every home; thousands of small lights to illuminate households.

To launch his enterprise, Edison enlisted the backing of several major banking houses. When his system became practical in 1882, Edison shrewdly chose to illuminate the Wall Street financial district first. It looked, said a reporter, "like writing by daylight." Potential investors were impressed, and soon Edison power plants, organized by his private secretary Samuel Insull, sprang up everywhere. Correcting a critical mistake Edison had made, inventor George Westinghouse relied on high-voltage alternating current instead of Edison's low-voltage direct current, which could travel only a mile or two. He then installed transformers to reduce voltage back to low levels for household use. Despite initial skepticism over safety (for years "to Westinghouse" meant to electrocute), the improvements worked. By 1898 there were nearly 3000 power stations in America, lighting some 2 million bulbs.

Electricity was more flexible than earlier sources of energy. Factories no longer had to be built near rivers and falls to make use of their power. Before the end of the century, electricity was running automatic looms, trolley cars, subways, and factory machinery. Electricity not only revolutionized industry; it also worked in the homes of ordinary citizens. The electric motor, developed commercially by Westinghouse and Nikola Tesla in 1886, ran everything from sewing machines to phonographs.

George Eastman revolutionized photography by developing a system that substituted the ordinary consumer for the skilled professional. In 1879 he patented the "dry plate," which replaced the hundred pounds of chemicals photographers had to carry to take pictures. He spent the next several years trying to find a way to get his product to consumers. In 1888 he marketed the "Kodak" camera, a black box containing a strip of celluloid film. It weighed just over two pounds and cost $25. After 100 snaps of the shutter, the owner simply sent the camera back to the store or factory and waited for the developed photos, along with a reloaded camera, to return by mail. "You press the button—we do the rest" was Eastman Kodak's apt slogan. By the mid-1890s the company had done the rest so often that it was worth $8 million.

What united these innovations was the notion of rationalizing inventions—of making a systematic business out of them. The Westinghouse Electric Company

Thomas Edison's gramophone, patented in 1877.

and the General Electric Company both set up their own research labs, as did E. I. Du Pont de Nemours & Company (1911), the U.S. Rubber Company (1913), the Standard Oil Company of New Jersey (1919), and the Bell Telephone Company (1925). Researchers themselves formed professional organizations like the American Chemical Society. By the middle of the twentieth century, the research laboratory had spread beyond business to the federal government, universities, trade associations, even labor unions.

Transportation and Communication

Abundant resources and new inventions such as electric motors remained worthless to industry until they could be moved to processing plants, factories, and offices. But with over three and a half million square miles of land, the distance from resources to factories to markets, negligible in Europe, was huge in the United States. Where 100 miles of railroad track would suffice for hauling raw or finished materials in Germany and England, 1000 miles was necessary in America. Furthermore, railroads in Europe usually appropriated existing roads and horse tracks for their rail lines; in America the routes more often broke new ground, opening areas to settlement and exploitation.

An efficient internal transportation network tied the country into an emerging international system. Steam-powered ships, introduced before the Civil War, assumed greater importance in the 1870s, pushing barge traffic on American rivers and carrying passengers and goods across the oceans. Ever-larger ships with more powerful engines cut the time of transatlantic travel in half, to about 10 days. Between 1870 and 1900, the value of American exports tripled. Eventually the rail and water transportation systems became entwined. By 1900 railroad companies owned nearly all of the country's domestic steamship lines.

Goods could be transported efficiently across large distances only with an effective communications network in place. First put into service in 1844, by the end of the Civil War the telegraph had 76,000 miles of line in the United States as well as a transatlantic cable. By the 1870s cables stretched underwater to Japan and China, and before the turn of the century they reached Africa and South America. In the United States the telegraph developed side by side with railroads, which allowed poles and wires to be set up along their rights of way in exchange for free telegraphic service. By the turn of the century a million miles of wire crisscrossed the continent, handling some 63 million messages a year.

A second innovation in communication, the telephone, vastly improved on the telegraph. Alexander Graham Bell, a Scot who emigrated to Boston in 1871, was teaching the deaf when he began experimenting with the electrical transmission of speech. Using pairs of telegraph instruments with receiving and transmitting reeds to get the right pitch, he and his young assistant, Thomas Watson, succeeded in sending a "twang" across the wires in 1875. Nine months later, on March 10, 1876, Bell's "telephone" finally transmitted the first intelligible words at their true pitch.

The telephone transformed communications. In 1878, when President Rutherford B. Hayes installed one in the White House, the instrument was still a curiosity. The same year, New Haven, Connecticut, opened the first telephone exchange in America. By 1895 there were 310,000 telephones in America; five years later there were 1.5 million. The telephone patent, issued in 1876, proved to be the most valuable ever granted. In the scramble for profits, the Bell Telephone

Daily Lives

TIME AND TRAVEL
The Rise of Information Systems

"Mr. Watson, come here. I want you." With those seven words, transmitted to his assistant on March 10, 1876, Alexander Graham Bell ended years of frustrating experimentation and ushered in the age of the telephone. At first Bell's electrical toys were purchased by individuals who wanted to connect two places, perhaps their home and business or their factory and office. Within a year, however, the advantages of such direct communication led to the first intercity hookup, between New York and Boston. Before the turn of the century, the Bell-organized American Telephone and Telegraph Company had combined over 100 local telephone companies to furnish business and government with long-distance service. When rates began to drop after 1900, telephones found their way into more and more American homes. The number of telephones installed jumped from 1,355,000 in 1900 to 10,535,000 in 1915 to 20,200,000 in 1930.

During the first half of the nineteenth century, information had traveled largely through the mails, which meant that it moved slowly. It took as many as 10 days for newspapers from New York to reach Indiana in 1841. In 1844 Samuel F. B. Morse succeeded in sending the first message across electrical wires, thereby achieving instantaneous communication. By 1860 telegraph wires stretched across the nation and replaced the fastest existing means of communication—the pony express.

The telegraph had obvious drawbacks. Instantaneous communication was by no means direct. Messages had to be taken to a telegraph office, where trained

Systems of finance and communication intersected at Wall Street, New York City, where the nation's most important investment banks and markets were located. In 1888 a snowstorm blanketed the district.

clerks could translate them into "Morse code," an unwieldy language of dots and dashes developed by the inventor for transmission by electrical impulse. When they arrived at the receiving station, messages were recast into comprehensible language, then carried by hand to their precise destination. This was a far cry from the telephone, which was both instantaneous *and* direct. Callers could speak to each other immediately and without the aid of intermediaries.

Daily Lives

The "speaking telegraph," as Bell called his invention, revolutionized communication, cutting time and obliterating distances. The telephone and a host of other innovations were the basis of the information system required of any thriving industrial nation. Information was a precious commodity, every bit as essential to the functioning of the economy as natural resources, finance capital, factories, and labor. The increased specialization at all stages of production, with raw materials from one area being processed in an urban industrial center and then distributed widely to other regions, required information about markets, prices, and supply sources—and required it quickly. Just as the rail system came to overshadow the earlier nineteenth-century steamboats and canal packets as efficient means of moving commodities, the telephone gradually superseded the telegraph as an efficient means of moving information.

Another such device that helped businesses to grow and prosper was the typewriter. C. Latham Sholes, a Milwaukee printer and editor, had been tinkering with an automatic numbering machine when a friend suggested he develop a mechanical letter-writing device. In 1868 he patented the "Type-Writer," and by the 1870s the Remington Arms Company was mass-producing them. Decorated with floral designs, these early machines rested on a sewing machine stand with a treadle that operated the carriage return. By the early twentieth century the typewriter had taken its modern shape—a keyboard with upper- and lower-case letters and a carriage that allowed typists to see the output.

At first typewriters were used mainly by writers, editors, ministers, and others from the world of letters. (Legend has it that Mark Twain's *The Adventures of Tom Sawyer* was the first book manuscript to be typed.) Impressed by the speed, uniformity, and legibility of typewriting, business executives began using the machines. Early critics charged that "machine-made" letters were too impersonal, and when farmers complained about receiving them, Sears, Roebuck hired secretaries to write their business letters by hand. Nevertheless, machine writing soon became standard business practice. As it did, the value of elegant and distinctive handwriting declined. Colleges of penmanship began to disappear, replaced by new vocational schools that taught shorthand and typing.

The need for speed and efficiency in the office led to other innovations. Carbon paper, designed for making a typewritten copy along with the original, was patented in 1872. In 1890 Alfred Dick invented the mimeograph to reproduce many copies of a single document cheaply, a communications boon not only to businesses but also to churches, reform organizations, and political groups. By the mid-twentieth century, as the processes of photography were applied to the problem of reproducing documents, xerography, or photocopying, would advance the communications revolution still further. And when photocopying was combined with telephonic and satellite technology in the late twentieth century, fax machines would enable senders to transmit over the phone facsimiles of documents instantaneously across the globe from business to business or home to home. Communications, like the rest of the new industrial order, were steadily becoming more rationalized and efficient, permitting the rapid distribution of information to those who needed or desired it.

Company fought off challenges from competitors and suits from rivals who claimed that their contributions were worth a share of the rights.

Along with typewriters (1867), ticker tape machines (1867), and adding machines (1888), telephones modernized offices and eased business transactions. In 1915, when the American Telephone and Telegraph Company opened the first transcontinental line, a business executive in New York could speak instantaneously to someone in San Francisco. The telephone was also part of a social revolution in America. Like the railroad and the telegraph, it compressed distances and homogenized the country. In time, remote households on farms and in villages would be connected to distant neighbors and to vital services offered by hospitals and fire departments.

Finance Capital

As industry grew, so did the demand for investment capital—the money spent on land, buildings, and machinery. The sheer scale of enterprise required more funds than ever before. In the 1870s an average iron and steel firm employed fewer than 100 workers to produce just under 4000 tons of material a year. The capital invested amounted to about $150,000. In 1900 the same firm employed four times as many workers, produced over ten times as much steel, and required almost $1 million. Not surprisingly, the amount of invested capital increased twelvefold over those years.

The need for capital was great especially because so many new industrial systems were being put into place at the same time. In the old days, a steamboat could be set afloat for the price of the boat itself. A railroad, on the other hand, had enormous start-up costs before it could even begin to run. Miles of track had to be laid, engines and cars bought, depots constructed, and so on. Similarly, electric utilities had to string wires, make light fixtures available, and build generating plants before they could function. In other words, an industrial process involving so many expensive systems could not take shape until someone raised money to build the systems.

Where did the money come from? For the first three-quarters of the nineteenth century investment capital came primarily out of the savings of the firms that used it. In the last half of the century "capital deepening"—a process essential for industrialization—took place. Simply put, as national wealth increased people began to save and invest more of their money. This meant that greater amounts of capital were available to companies seeking to start up or expand.

Savings and investment grew increasingly attractive with the development of a sophisticated network of financial institutions. Commercial and savings banks, investment houses, and insurance companies all gave savers increased opportunities to channel money to industry. The New York Stock Exchange, in existence since 1792, became the major conduit for connecting eager investors with money-hungry firms. By the end of the century it had established itself as the primary instrument for exchanging securities and making capital available to industry.

The Corporation

Finance, like natural resources, technology, transportation, and communication, was just one piece of the industrial mosaic. For those business leaders with the skill to put all the pieces together, large profits awaited. This was the era of the notorious "robber baron," and to be sure, sheer ruthlessness and a disregard of legal niceties went far in the fortune-building game. "Law? Who cares about law!" railroad magnate Cornelius Vanderbilt once bellowed. "Hain't I got the power?"

To survive in the long term, however, business leaders could not depend on ruthlessness alone. The growing scale of enterprise and the money required to run it led them to adapt an old device, the corporation, to new needs. Corporations had existed since colonial times, when governments granted charters of incorporation to organizations that ran such public facilities as turnpikes, canals, and banks. After the Civil War the modern corporation came into being as an instrument for mobilizing capital and protecting business holdings.

The corporation had several advantages over more traditional forms of ownership, such as the single proprietorship and the partnership. A corporation could raise large sums quickly by selling "stock certificates," or shares in the enterprise, to the public. It could also outlive its owners because it required no legal reorganization if one of them died. It limited liability because owners were not personally responsible for corporate debts. And it separated owners or stockholders from the actual running of the company, which permitted professional managers to operate complex businesses with unprecedented efficiency. So overwhelming were these advantages that even before the turn of the century, two-thirds of all manufactured products in the United States were made by corporations.

A Pool of Labor

Last, but hardly least important for the success of the new industrial order, was a pool of labor. All industrializing nations required workers, but in the United States demand was so great that the native population alone could not fill it. In 1860 it took about 4.3 million workers to run all the factories, mills, and shops in the United States. By 1900 there were approximately 20 million industrial workers in America.

Gas company employee in Chicago, 1891.

Europe was a primary recruiting ground. In the late nineteenth century poverty, oppression, and mechanization conspired to push Europeans from farms into cities and finally off the continent entirely. Meanwhile, economic opportunity pulled them to America. The Labor Contract Law, repealed in 1885, allowed prospective employers to recruit laborers abroad, pay their passage, then deduct the cost from their wages. Industrialists were among the most aggressive recruiters, advertising in newspapers, distributing pamphlets, and sending agents to Europe. When iron workers arrived in the United States from Sweden in the 1880s, they often knew only three words of English: "Charlie—Deere—Moline" (Charlie being the president of the John Deere Plow Company in Moline, Illinois).

An unprecedented wave of immigration flooded American shores. Over 8 million people arrived between 1870 and 1890, another 14 million by 1914. Eastern and southern Europe, where mechanized agriculture and religious persecution simultaneously took hold, replaced northern and western Europe as the chief sources of immigration. Most of the new arrivals settled in industrial cities. Often unskilled, many of them peasants, they went to work in factories and mines or on construction and road gangs. In at least 21 major manufacturing or mining industries two out of every three employees were new immigrants from eastern and southern Europe or African-Americans from the South.

To get those jobs they relied on well-defined networks of friends and relatives, together with a new breed of labor brokers. Tough and savvy immigrants themselves, these contractors met newcomers at the dock, promising work and serving as a funnel to the new world. For their trouble they took a healthy cut of the immigrants' wages and overcharged them for goods. Among Italians they were known as "*padrones*," and by the end of the nineteenth century they controlled two-thirds of the labor in New York.

Following such prescribed paths tended to concentrate one group or another within certain industries or at specific jobs. Poles, Slavs, and Italians began to fill the mines of Pennsylvania; Greeks worked in the textile mills of New England. In

OCCUPATIONAL DISTRIBUTION, 1880 AND 1920

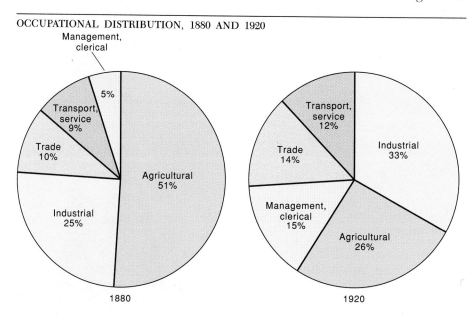

1880

1920

one Pittsburgh steel mill, Serbians clustered in the blooming mill, Poles in the hammer shop. Russian and Polish Jews, skilled tailors and seamstresses in the old country, went into needle trades of New York. But whatever they did, hard-pressed immigrants were willing to accept less pay and put in more hours than those they replaced. "Immigrants work for almost nothing," complained one native-born laborer, "and seem to be able to live on wind—something which I cannot do."

At the same time a massive migration of rural Americans—some 11 million between 1865 and 1920—provided a source of home-grown labor for industrial cities. Driven from the farm by machines and bad times or just following dreams of a new life, they moved first to small and then perhaps to larger cities. Unlike the vast majority of immigrants, they could often read and write English. At the very least they could speak the language and understand American ways. In iron and steel cities as well as coal-mining towns, they sometimes commanded better industrial jobs or served as supervisors and foreman. More often they lacked the skills for higher paying work. If they could get them, they found jobs instead in retail stores or offices and slowly entered the new urban middle class of white-collar workers.

Unless, of course, they were black. Most African-Americans continued to work the cotton fields of the South, but a small number, nearly 300,000, moved to northern cities between 1870 and 1910. Like the new immigrants, they sought to escape discrimination and find jobs. Unlike many of those immigrants, few blacks returned home. More often they stayed in the industrial cities and brought their families, one by one. They failed to escape discrimination but did find work—usually in low-paying jobs as day laborers and janitors or laundresses and domestic servants. By 1890 only 7 percent of all black men worked in industry.

The development of an industrial labor force extracted high human costs. The daily work rhythms of a European peasant, a black field hand, and a midwestern farmer were quite different from the 12-hour shifts of a Pittsburgh steelworker or a woman plucking tobacco from cigarette-rolling machines in North Carolina. Monotonous, alienating, and difficult, such work was as dangerous as it was dehumanizing. In the last third of the nineteenth century the United States had the highest rate of industrial accidents in the world, another component in the emerging industrial order. Labor would pay dearly for economic progress.

RAILROADS: AMERICA'S FIRST BIG BUSINESS

At the center of the new industrial systems were the railroads, helping to spread communications networks, efficiently moving freight, reinventing time. Steel rails even redefined the geography of America. Unlike canals, which ran only between bodies of water, railroads could move goods and raw materials wherever track was laid. Under their impact the commercial axis of the nation shifted from New York and New Orleans, with its heavy reliance on river and coastal shipping, to New York and Chicago. Railroads also stimulated economic growth, simply because they required so many resources to get things built. By the 1850s they furnished the largest single market in the country for iron and devoured large quantities of coal, wood, felt, glass, rubber, and brass. In the 1880s, three-fourths of all the steel made in the United States went into rails. By lowering transportation costs railroads allowed manufacturers to reduce prices and thereby attract more buyers. To control their far-flung operations, they pioneered new techniques of management, soon adapted to the needs of other business.

In time the railroad became a cultural symbol of American might, energy, and foresight. The poet Walt Whitman called the locomotive the "emblem of motion and power—pulse of the continent." Those who drove them, like the 6-foot, 4-inch John Luther "Casey" Jones (who really did drive the Cannonball Express between Memphis and Canton, Illinois), became folk heroes. Everyone along the New York-to-Chicago route knew that the New York Central and the Pennsylvania were making the run in 27 hours. Whole towns turned out to greet an incoming train, and the most impressive building in any hamlet was likely to be not a church or the city hall or the municipal court, but the railroad depot.

A Managerial Revolution

To the men who ran them, railroads were primarily businesses, and the railroad business was growing so fast that new ways of organizing and financing it were essential. With operations extending over hundreds of miles, railroad lines had to construct and maintain an immense inventory of engines, cars, tracks, shops, terminals, stations, warehouses, office buildings, bridges, and even telegraph lines. In the 1850s, one of the largest industrial enterprises in America, the Pepperell textile mills of Maine, employed no more than 800 workers. By the early 1880s the Pennsylvania Railroad had nearly 50,000 people on its payroll. Railroads serviced untold numbers of customers, and the facilities of any one line would take literally weeks to see. Each day managers had to make countless decisions involving the delivery of freight and the safety of passengers. From setting rates to determining costs and profits, everything required a level of coordination unknown in earlier businesses.

To achieve it, railroads found themselves forced to develop new systems of management. Here the so-called "trunk lines" were innovators. Scores of early companies had serviced local networks of cities and communities, often with less than 50 miles of track. During the 1850s four great trunk lines emerged east of the Mississippi to connect the shorter branch, or "feeder," lines. By the outbreak of the Civil War, the Erie, the Baltimore and Ohio, the Pennsylvania, and the New York Central all furnished roads under a single management that linked the eastern seaboard with the Great Lakes and western rivers. After the war, the South and West organized their own trunk lines, largely with capital from Europe and the North.

Simply keeping track of the money was a major task, since conductors, station agents, freight agents, and scores of other employees were involved in paying out or collecting cash. To supervise and account for the funds, the Baltimore and Ohio separated the management of finances from all activities involving the movement of trains. Accounting was handled by a special section called the controller's office, working directly with another new financial section, the treasurer's office. The treasurer watched over and helped allocate revenue raised by the sale of securities and from profits. Both offices came under the jurisdiction of a new vice president, whose sole duty was to oversee finances.

The operations of large lines spawned a business bureaucracy staffed by a new style of business executive. Typically these bureaucrats were not entrepreneurs who started or owned businesses but a class of managers, subordinate to owners but having wide authority over daily operations. By the first two decades of the twentieth century nearly a third of the prominent business executives born between 1861 and 1880 had climbed the bureaucratic ladder. A hundred years earlier, only 5 percent had reached the top by working through their organizations. Cautious by nature, this managerial elite preferred to negotiate and administer rather than compete.

Daniel McCallum, a talented engineer and inventor, was the prototype. As general superintendent of the New York and Erie in the 1850s, he drew up the first table of organization for an American company—a tree with roots representing the president and board of directors, five branches comprising the main operating divisions, and leaves standing for the local agents, train crews, and others. Information moved up and down the chain of command so that managers could get daily reports to and from the separate parts. Even within small units like the machine shop, hierarchy prevailed. The duties of each grade were carefully prescribed, and every employee wore an insignia on his uniform for easy identification of both grade and job.

Soon railroads were dividing their operations, giving local superintendents the power to move passengers and freight, while the "central office" concentrated on the broader problems of cost, competition, and expansion, based on information from the field. By the turn of the century, the railroads had led a managerial revolution in American industry. Central offices operated as corporate nerve centers, housing functional divisions responsible for purchases, production, transportation, sales, and accounting. A new class of "middle managers" ran them and imposed new order. What was going on, in other words, was a process of economic rationalization of business practices. Executives, managers, and laborers were being taught to work in increasingly precise and coordinated ways.

Competition and Consolidation

While managers made operations more systematic, the struggle among entrepreneurs to achieve dominance in the railroad industry was at times anything but precise and rational. In the 1870s and 1880s, competition to attract profitable business reached fierce proportions.

More than any other contemporary enterprise, railroads were saddled with enormous "fixed costs"—expensive equipment, huge payrolls, high debts. These remained constant regardless of the volume of traffic. To generate more revenue, railroads constructed more lines in hopes of increasing their traffic. Soon the railroads had overbuilt. (Recall that Robert Ferguson could choose from more than one line running from Memphis to Nashville.) With so much excess capacity, railroad owners schemed desperately to win new accounts. They gave free passes to favored shippers, promised them free sidings constructed at their plants, offered free land to bring businesses and traffic to their territory.

Nothing worked better than manipulating prices. Managers lowered rates for freight that was shipped in bulk, on long hauls, or on return routes (since the empty cars were coming back anyway). When those tactics failed, they used "rebates," secret kickbacks to preferred customers, which dropped prices below the posted rates of competitors. Losses were recouped by overcharging small shippers like farmers. Such competition could prove fatal to some railroads. When the economy plunged, or if a weak line sought to improve its position, savage rate wars broke out. In the shakeout caused by the depression of 1873, some 40 percent of all railroad bonds went into default; 65 lines declared bankruptcy by 1879.

One way to prevent the ravages of competition was to consolidate: buy up competing lines. But that could lead to even fiercer war. From 1866 to 1868 Cornelius Vanderbilt of the New York Central waged a futile battle to gain control of the Erie, headed by a trio of railroad sharks: the corporate buccaneer Daniel Drew, the flamboyant speculator James Fisk, Jr., and the subtle, calculating, and utterly unscrupulous Jay Gould (a "perfect eel," according to one railroad president). They fought Vanderbilt in the courts, where each side brought its own attorneys and bought its own judges. They fought him in the legislature, where both sides bribed legislators to vote their way. (The going rate, it was said, was $15,000 apiece.) They fought on the streets with gangs of hired toughs. They even patrolled the seas with Fisk serving as admiral of a Hudson River flotilla armed with riflemen.

Eventually the "Erie Wars" ended in a standoff. The Erie paid Vanderbilt a huge ransom; Gould and Drew retained effective control of the company until they turned against each other. By 1877, the Erie was bankrupt, mismanaged and drowned in a sea of "watered stock" (stock issued in excess of the company's true assets). Gould emerged unscathed. When he died of tuberculosis at the age of 56 in 1892, his estate totaled $74 million.

The strategies of consolidation developed by railroad managers were more productive. During the 1870s a number of regional railroad federations were created to pool traffic among their members and divide the profits equitably. Pooling was designed to remove the incentive for cutting rates. Without the force of law, however, these associations failed to control competition. In the end the rail wars subsided only when the strongest lines bought up their competitors.

In the East purchases, leases, and mergers accomplished the task. In the West new construction produced self-contained systems like the Atchison, Topeka and Santa Fe. By 1890 that rail line stretched from Chicago to the Pacific coast and operated over 9000 miles of track. But in the depression of 1893, it too went bankrupt, the victim of management's overambitious vision. Railroad executives learned a lesson: although they had gained some control through consolidation, they had also overexpanded. By the mid-1890s, a third of the mileage of American railroads was tied up in foreclosure or bankruptcy proceedings.

The Role of Finance

In the early days many railroads had relied on state governments for financial aid. When the depression of the late 1830s and early 1840s turned states stingy, promoters looked to counties, cities, and towns for bonds and other commitments. In the 1850s and 1860s western promoters went to Washington seeking federal assistance. Congress responded with loans of $65 million to six western railroads and lavish grants of land that totaled more than 131 million acres. Even so, federal support helped to build only about 8 percent of the nation's railroads.

So executives developed new ways of raising capital from private investors. At first people living near the ends of the rail lines, who stood to gain more from construction, received stock in exchange for their land or their labor. Investors in Europe or in eastern cities had more money, and promoters soon tapped them by offering bonds, the preferred instrument of nearly all American railroads for rais-

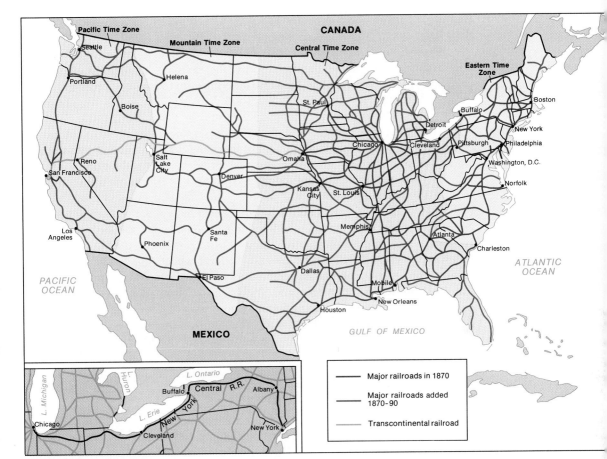

RAILROADS, 1870–1890

On the eve of the Civil War there were 31,000 miles of track in America, most of it east of the Mississippi. By the end of the century, the railroad network stretched from one end of the country to the other, with more miles of track than in all of Europe combined, including Russia. New York and Chicago, linked by the New York Central trunk line, became the new axis of commerce in America.

ing capital. These interest-bearing certificates promised regular payments to investors and involved no ownership of the line.

Beginning around 1850, the financial needs of railroads outreached the capacities of local banks and stock exchanges. The New York Stock Exchange, already growing, expanded even more rapidly as the securities of railroad corporations began to be listed and traded there. Over the same period, investment banking houses developed financial networks through which they found and distributed capital. The banks were soon marketing railroad and other industrial securities abroad as well as in the United States. As late as 1898 Europeans owned nearly a third of all American railroad securities. At home, life insurance companies became a prominent source of capital. Organized in the 1840s, when reliable mortality tables were first drawn up, the companies blossomed during the 1870s by introducing innovative group and industrial insurance contracts. By the turn of the century life insurance companies had over $1.5 billion to invest, and a third of their assets went into railroad bonds.

Because investment bankers played such prominent roles in controlling the flow of funds, they found themselves advising railroads about their affairs. If a company fell into bankruptcy, bankers sometimes served as the "receivers," who oversaw the property until the firm returned to financial health. By absorbing smaller lines into larger ones, eliminating rebates, and stabilizing rates, the bankers helped to reduce competition. In the process, they often came to control the companies they advised. Their system of financing not only underwrote the network of transportation; it also imposed new order and centralization.

By 1900, the application of industrial systems had transformed the railroads. With a capital investment of $11 billion, some 200,000 miles of track were in operation, with six groups of railroads owning over 80 percent of those miles. Time zones allowed for coordinated schedules on a national level; standard track gauges permitted easy cross-country freighting. Passengers were traveling 16 billion miles every year. To that total could be added wheat, corn, and hogs, which moved from the Great Plains, cotton and tobacco from Mississippi and North Carolina, lumber from Oregon and Wisconsin, oil from Pennsylvania, and coal from West Virginia to the great factories and mills of Chicago, Pittsburgh, and Birmingham. Finished products made the return trips, and everything moved with a predictable regularity that allowed businesses to plan and prosper.

THE GROWTH OF BIG BUSINESS

The process of system building continued to spread through other industries. Although most entrepreneurs still functioned on a small scale, many businesses grew big. Like the railroads, they adopted several operating strategies. Combination—a loose alliance of enterprises under a large national organization—helped to coordinate operations over vast distances. And consolidation—blending separate companies into one corporation—actually integrated operations under a single corporate headquarters and permitted unprecedented control.

These giant industrial organizations were put together in a number of ways. Some firms grew horizontally by absorbing several competitors engaged in the same activity. For other companies the issue was assuring access to raw materials and markets. These firms grew vertically, acquiring the successive stages needed to make and sell a product. Some combined the two strategies, spreading vertically up toward consumers and down toward raw materials as well as horizontally outward over competitors. By the end of the century, innovative instruments of control—the trust and the holding company—pumped big business to remarkable proportions. The overall aim was to create an environment that provided managers with greater predictability and more influence over materials and markets. In the process business leaders reorganized the economy, concentrated power, and laid the foundations of a modern business system.

Growth in Consumer Goods

By the 1860s salt producers in Michigan were locked in deadly competition. Salt processing and other industries that specialized in consumer products for ordinary home use had low start-up costs, so they often were beset by stiff competition. In Michigan the presence of too many salt makers had sent prices plummeting. Seeing salvation in combination, they drew together (like the railroads) in an informal pool, the Michigan Salt Association, in 1869. They voluntarily agreed to allocate production, divide markets, and set prices—at double the previous rate. Horizontal combination saved them. By the 1880s there was a whiskey pool, a cordage pool, and countless rail and other pools. Informal pools ultimately proved to be unenforceable and unsatisfactory (and after 1890 they were considered illegal restraints on trade), but other forms of horizontal growth, such as formal mergers, spread in the wake of an economic panic in the 1890s.

Some entrepreneurs, like Gustavus Swift, adopted a vertical growth strategy and ended up integrating several different activities under one company. Swift, a New England butcher, moved to Chicago in the mid-1870s. Aware of the demand for fresh beef in the East, he acquired new refrigerated railcars to ship meat from western slaughterhouses and a network of ice-cooled warehouses in eastern cities to hold the meat. By 1885 he had created the first national meat-packing company. Swift moved forward, even closer to consumers, by putting together a fleet of wagons to distribute his beef to retail butchers. He moved back toward his own raw materials, extending and coordinating the purchase of cattle at the Chicago stockyards. He built plants to make chemicals, fertilizers, and other by-products. By the 1890s the Swift Company was a fully integrated, vertically organized corporation operating on a nationwide scale. Other meat packers followed, and soon Swift, Armour and Company, and 3 other giants—together called the "Big Five"— controlled 90 percent of the beef shipped across state lines.

Carnegie Integrates Steel

Industrialization encouraged integration in heavy industry as well. Here Andrew Carnegie led the way. More than any of his contemporaries, Carnegie's life was entwined with the industrial revolution. His father, a hand weaver in Scotland, had been thrown out of work by machines. When the family emigrated to Allegheny, Pennsylvania, in 1848, 12-year-old Andrew found his first jobs in industry— as a bobbin boy in a textile mill and later as a machine wiper deep in the cellar of a factory. For the rest of his days, the scent of machine oil made him ill.

When the telegraph came to Pittsburgh, Carnegie became a messenger boy, then a skilled operator whose talent and hard work drew the attention of Thomas Scott, a local superintendent of the Pennsylvania Railroad. Scott needed a personal telegrapher and secretary; Carnegie got the job. Over the next 12 years, as Scott rose (ultimately to become president of the railroad), Carnegie followed along. In 1859, at the age of 24, he was appointed superintendent of the Pennsylvania's western division.

Under Scott's shrewd tutelage, Carnegie learned how to manage a railroad and how to make money from money. Through attention to detail, resourcefulness, initiative, and quick action, he made things work. When wrecked freight cars blocked service, Carnegie coolly ordered them burned. His colleagues swallowed hard, but the procedure soon became standard practice for the Pennsylvania Railroad. With a tip and a loan from Scott, Carnegie profited from investments in the first sleeping car, the first iron railroad bridge, a locomotive factory, and finally a local iron factory that became the nucleus of his steel empire.

In 1872, on a trip to sell railroad bonds in England, Carnegie chanced to see the Bessemer process in action. Awe-struck by the fiery display, he jumped aboard the first steamer home and announced his intention to build the biggest steel mill in the world. In 1875 he did, in the midst of a severe depression. Over the next 25 years, he added mills at Homestead and Keystone, Pennsylvania, moved from railroad building to city building, and won a contract for supplying steel for the Brooklyn Bridge in 1876. His structural steel went into New York City's elevated railway, the frames of early skyscrapers, and the Washington Monument.

Carnegie succeeded, in part, by taking advantage of the boom-and-bust business cycle of the late nineteenth century. He jumped in during hard times, building and buying when equipment and businesses came cheap. He also had a knack for finding skilled managers, like Henry Clay Frick and Charles M. Schwab, who employed the administrative techniques pioneered on the railroads. Carnegie set managers against each other in races to quicken the pace of production. The winners received handsome bonuses, the losers embarrassing telegrams: "Puppy dog Number Two has beaten puppy dog Number One on fuel." Competition was also Carnegie's way of dealing with rival steelmakers. To undercut contenders, he would scrap new machinery, a new mill, even his own workers for the sake of efficiency and low costs. A beneficent federal government helped too. The federal decision to build an all-steel navy in the mid-1880s furnished added demand for his product, while protective tariffs helped to keep British steel from the American market.

The final key to Carnegie's success was expansion and still more expansion: horizontally, by purchasing and constructing more and larger steel mills; and vertically, by buying up sources of supply, transportation, and sales. Beneath the Thomson, Homestead, and Keystone mills lay a supporting network of industries: giant furnaces for making pig iron and giant ovens for making coke; 40,000 acres of coal land; fleets of railway cars and ore-carrying steamers; a shipping company; a docking company; and nearly two-thirds of the Mesabi iron ore range. Controlling such an integrated system, Carnegie could assure a steady flow of materials from mine to mill and market as well as profitable investments at every stage along the way. In 1900 his company turned out more steel than Great Britain and made $40 million dollars in profits.

Integration of the kind Carnegie employed expressed the logic of the new industrial age. More and more, the industrial activities of society were being linked in one giant, interconnected process.

Rockefeller and the Great Standard Oil Trust

John D. Rockefeller accomplished in oil what Carnegie achieved in steel. And he went further, developing an innovative business structure—the trust—that promised even greater power. Rockefeller was as taciturn and cold as Carnegie was warm and charming. While Carnegie looked on religion with skepticism, Rockefeller was a devout believer who taught Bible classes at Cleveland's Erie Street Church. "God gave me my money," he once remarked. More earthly powers shaped his approach to business. In the rough-and-tumble commercial world of the late nineteenth century, his father had been an able tutor. "I cheat my boys

John D. Rockefeller.

every time I get a chance," the elder Rockefeller once explained. "I want to make them sharp."

In John's case, he succeeded beyond his wildest imaginings. After a stint of bookkeeping in commission houses, the young Rockefeller entered the refining business in 1862. Cleveland was just emerging as a commercial center on the shores of Lake Erie, owing to its location near one of the early oil fields and to the competition of railroads for its trade. By 1870 Rockefeller and his partners controlled nearly a fifth of all the city's refining facilities.

In 1870 Rockefeller and his associates incorporated their business as the Standard Oil Company (Ohio), looking for even greater gains. Unlike the competitive Carnegie, Rockefeller put his faith in combination, achieved through alliances, "voluntary" associations, and cooperation. But oil refining, like steelmaking, was a jungle of competitive firms, so Rockefeller proceeded to twist arms. In the name of higher cooperation, he used bribery, spying, railroad rebates, phony companies, and price-slashing to eliminate rivals or persuade them to join him. When necessary he undersold them with high-quality products. He moved horizontally to gain control of refining, succeeding so well that by 1880, a decade after Standard Oil had incorporated, he headed an alliance of companies that together commanded 90 percent of the nation's oil refining capacity. Rockefeller also grew vertically all the way back to drilling for oil and forward into selling its products.

How could he maintain and control such an empire? Through the 1870s Rockefeller relied on informal pools and other business combinations. Because they had no legal standing, they proved too weak. Corporations, though legal entities, were restricted by state law. In Ohio, where Rockefeller operated, corporations were forbidden from owning plants in other states or stock in out-of-state companies. Another device was called for, and Samuel C. T. Dodd, an ingenious lawyer who became chief counsel of Standard Oil, came up with one in 1879. The "trust," as Dodd conceived it, was a quasi-legal arrangement under which a corporation's stockholders surrendered their shares "in trust" to a central board of nine directors. The directors could "hold, control, and manage" all property. In exchange, stockholders received certificates of trust that paid dividends (a handsome 30 to 48 percent in the case of Standard Oil).

In 1882 the Standard Oil Company of Ohio formed the country's first great trust. For six years, until a New York state investigation unmasked it, the arrangement was kept secret. Since no one was any the wiser, Rockefeller and his associates could testify with straight faces that they had "harmonized" the industry rather than conspired to restrain it. Secret or not, the trust brought Rockefeller what he had so relentlessly sought—centralized management of the oil industry. The Standard Oil Trust, worked out over the next several years, included 14 companies and controlled 26 more.

Trusts surmounted the legal barriers states had erected to regulate corporations, and immediately the form was copied by businesses that dealt in copper, sugar, cottonseed oil, rubber, leather, and farm machinery. Just as quickly, trusts developed unsavory reputations for extortion and monopoly. In time most people came to regard any large combination of capital as a trust, whether it was a formal voting trust (like Standard Oil) or a looser affiliation of giant companies (like the "Big Five" Beef Trust). The average citizen, one observer noted sarcastically, was born to profit the milk trust and died to profit the coffin trust. In practice, no trust was a true monopoly that completely controlled an entire industry. Trusts generally were "oligopolies" in which a few large firms dominated an industry.

The Mergers of J. Pierpont Morgan

The voting trust was only a steppingstone to an even more effective means of avoiding competition, managing people, and controlling business: the corporate merger. The idea of two companies merging—one company buying out another—remained impractical until 1889, when New Jersey became the first of several states to permit corporations to own other companies. The following year, the need to find a substitute for the trust increased when that arrangement was outlawed by Congress under the Sherman Antitrust Act of 1890. So the ever-inventive Samuel Dodd came up with the "holding company," a corporation of corporations that had the power to hold shares of other companies. Many industries converted their trust arrangements into holding companies, and in 1899 Dodd created the Standard Oil Company of New Jersey, an immense holding company for Rockefeller's oil empire.

Two years later came the biggest corporate merger of the era, the creation not of a lawyer but of a financial wizard named J. Pierpont Morgan. After the Civil War Morgan had become head of the powerful investment house that bore his father's name. Born rich, he made the House of Morgan richer still by buying, holding, and merging companies. For 50 years after the Civil War Morgan had a hand in reorganizing almost every important American enterprise: railroads, coal, steel, steamships, electricity. His orderly mind abhorred chaotic competition, especially when it threatened the profitability of his investments. "I like a little competition," he was quoted as saying, "but I like combination more." Between 1892 and 1902 he was instrumental in creating such massive consolidations as General Electric, American Telephone and Telegraph, and International Harvester.

Morgan's greatest triumph was in steel, where for years Carnegie had refused to combine with his rivals. In January 1901, with the threat of a colossal steel war looming, Morgan convinced Carnegie to put a price tag on his company. When a messenger brought the scrawled reply back—over $400 million—Morgan merely nodded and said, "I accept this price." Within three months he had bought Carnegie's eight largest competitors and announced the formation of the United States Steel Corporation.

A mammoth holding company, U.S. Steel embraced every aspect of steelmaking from ore beds to finishing plants. It gobbled up over 200 manufacturing and transportation companies, 1000 miles of railways, and the whole Mesabi iron range. It employed over 170,000 workers and controlled 60 percent of America's steel capacity. U.S. Steel was the largest industrial combine the world had ever seen and America's first billion-dollar corporation. Capitalized at $1.4 billion, its value was greater than the national debt. All the same, it was a bloated giant with far too many costs ever to realize Morgan's dream of high profits.

What Morgan helped to create in steel was rapidly coming to pass in other industries. A wave of mergers swept through American business in the wake of the depression of 1893. As the economy plunged, cutthroat competition bled businesses until they were eager to sell out. Over 1200 companies "disappeared" in mergers in 1899 alone. Within industries, giants grew almost overnight. By 1904 a single firm came to account for 60 percent or more of the total output in each of 50 different industries. The economic results were mixed. Bigness helped to bring down prices. Economies of scale—the reduced cost of each item that resulted from the production of many—lowered prices and increased profits. Consolidation also eliminated the perils of cutthroat competition, which demoralized business leaders and threatened the benefits of industrialization. Yet the merger movement never succeeded in wholly ending competition. The market shares of the giants steadily declined as smaller and more aggressive firms stole business and as new companies entered the industry. Still, the big firms were there to stay.

Corporate Critics

Many Americans were not pleased about the development of corporate giants. Industrialization and the growth of big business might have helped to rationalize the economy, increase national wealth, and tie the country together, but they also exploited workers, concentrated power, corrupted politics, and widened the gap between rich and poor. According to the census of 1890, the richest 9 percent of the people held nearly three-quarters of all wealth in America. By the turn of the century, one American in eight (nearly 10 million people) lived below the poverty line.

In truth, the concentration of wealth was not much different from what it had been in 1850. What had changed was the rise of a visible new class of millionaires. They lived ostentatiously, and much of the country hated them for it. Two Vanderbilt mansions on New York's Fifth Avenue alone cost a total of $14 million. The family owned seven altogether, in addition to several country estates. The anger of ordinary people sometimes boiled over. When the kidnapper of Eddie Cudahy, the son of a prominent member of the beef trust, confessed to the crime, the jury acquitted him all the same.

New York's wealthy called their elaborate summer homes "cottages," but they were mansions by any standard. The Breakers, designed by Richard Morris Hunt for Cornelius Vanderbilt II, looks like an Italian palace and has this grand music room among its 70 rooms. Now open to the public, the mansion cost $5 million to build.

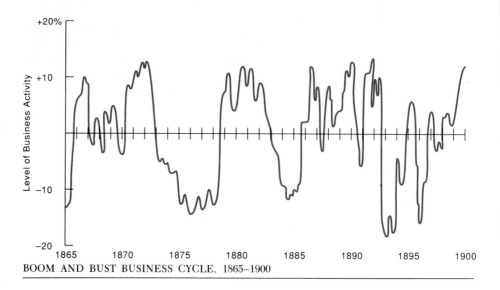

BOOM AND BUST BUSINESS CYCLE, 1865–1900

Industrialization also subjected the national economy to enormous disruptions. The banking system could not always keep pace with the demand for capital, and businesses failed to distribute enough of their profits to workers to sustain purchasing power. Supply often outstripped demand. A vicious cycle of boom and bust developed. Three severe depressions—1873–1879, 1882–1885, and 1893–1897—ravaged the country in the last third of the nineteenth century. With hard times came fierce competition as companies struggled to survive, collapsed, or were bought at bargain prices. Faced with shrinking markets, managers worked harder to cut costs, and the industrial barons earned their reputations for ruthlessness.

Corporate apologists justified the system by applying Charles Darwin's new theories of evolution to society at large. Distorting Darwin, British philosopher Herbert Spencer maintained that in society, as in biology, only the "fittest" survived. How prosperously they survived reflected how fit they truly were. His American apostle, William Graham Sumner, defended property and privilege by arguing that competition was natural and had to proceed without any restraints, including government regulation. Millionaires, in his view, were simply the "product of natural selection." Such "Social Darwinism" found ready adherents among businessmen, who applauded their own survival in the business jungle even as they worked to reduce the very competition they extolled.

For all the contemporary celebrations of wealth and big business, many Americans longed for a more promising future. A group of radical social prophets offered one by mounting a powerful attack on corporate capitalism. Henry George, a journalist and self-taught economist, advanced an arresting scheme to redistribute wealth in *Progress and Poverty* (1879). It became one of the best-selling books ever published in America. Trying to explain how poverty could continue when industrial progress had created great wealth, George pointed to greedy landowners who held their property until labor, technology, and speculation on nearby sites raised the price. He called the profit thereby reaped an "unearned increment." He proposed a "single tax" on all such property to bring an end to monopoly landholding and eliminate all other taxes. "Single-tax" clubs sprang up throughout the country, and with the support of labor, George nearly won the race for mayor of New York in 1886.

Edward Bellamy, a journalist turned novelist, tapped the same vein of popular resentment with his utopian novel *Looking Backward* (1888). The hero, a Boston millionaire, falls asleep in 1887 and awakens Rip Van Winkle–like in the year 2000. His competitive, caste-ridden society is gone. In its place he finds an orderly utopia, managed in military fashion by a vast, government-controlled trust. Cruel exploitation, class divisions, political corruption, and disparities in wealth have vanished. Instead abundance is shared equally, and "fraternal cooperation" has replaced competition. Bellamy called it "nationalism," and the idea soon spawned more than 160 clubs in 27 states. His followers called for redistribution of wealth, civil service reform, and nationalization of railroads and utilities.

Less popular but equally hostile to competitive capitalism was the Socialist Labor party, formed in 1877. Dominated for many years by Daniel De Leon, a West Indian immigrant, it advocated revolution through class conflict and worker control over the means of production. De Leon's unyielding emphasis on purity of theory attracted more intellectuals than workers. The Socialist Labor party found some adherents in the ethnic communities of the great industrial cities but never polled more than 82,000 votes. Party members, bent on gaining popular and trade union support, revolted and in 1901 founded the more successful Socialist Party of America. Here and elsewhere workers were beginning to organize their own responses to industrialism.

WORKERS RESPOND TO AN INDUSTRIAL CULTURE

The new systems of industrialization, far-reaching as they were, could hardly fail to shape the lives of ordinary workers. It was they who struggled most to adjust to the new industrial order and they who sought to bring the large processes within their control.

The vast steel mills, the cramped tenement sweatshops, the dank tunnels of the coal fields—all demanded workers, whether "greenhorns" from abroad, "hayseeds" from the countryside, children, adults, blacks, whites, Mexicans, or Asians. Furthermore, the new industrial systems required people to work in new and foreign ways. Farmers or peasants, accustomed to timing themselves by the daily position of the sun, now learned to live by the clock and work in the twilight of gaslit factories. Instead of being self-employed or paid by a boss whom they knew and could bargain with, industrial workers had to deal with foremen, were paid by the hour or the piece, and had the pace of their work set by relentless cycles of machines. Increasingly they bore the brunt of depressions, faced periodic unemployment, worked under dangerous conditions, and lived in substandard housing.

The Workers' World

By 1880 the number of nonagricultural laborers had risen above the number of farm workers for the first time in American history. Five million Americans toiled in manufacturing, construction, and transportation—more than three times the number employed a generation earlier. Though small shops could still be found at the end of the century, industrial work had grown big and harsh.

In 1881, for example, when the Pittsburgh Bessemer Steel Company opened its new mill in Homestead, Pennsylvania, nearly 400 men and boys went to work on its 60 acres of sheds. To keep the mill going 24 hours a day, they worked every day but Christmas and the Fourth of July, 12 hours a day one week, 12 hours a night the next, except for the weekly "swing shift." Then the Saturday night crew took Sunday off, and the Sunday swing worked 24 hours straight. In the furnace room, ovens and huge pits ("gaping like the mouth of hell," wrote novelist Hamlin Garland) emitted terrible heat that quickly exhausted men who tended them. The incessant vibration of machinery and the screeching of cold saws rang in the ears of workers, making some of them deaf. Shiny grains of steel covered their clothing and coated their lungs. There were no breaks of any kind, not even for lunch, and no shower rooms. "Home is just the place where I eat and sleep," one steelworker said. "I live in the mills."

Few industrial laborers had it quite so bad. Less than 1 percent of all jobs were in iron and steel mills in 1880. Still, Homestead reflected a common pattern of industrial work: mechanization and mass production, the dictatorship of the clock, subdivision of labor, intricate organization, and brutal conditions. By the turn of the century, most of those earning wages in industry worked 6 days a week, 10 hours a day. They held jobs that increasingly required more machines and fewer skills. Repetition of small tasks replaced fine craftsmanship. In the 1880s, for example, almost all the 40 different jobs that went into making a pair of shoes could be performed by a "green hand" with a few days of instruction at a simple machine.

New high-speed machines also brought danger to the workplace. If a worker succumbed to boredom, fatigue, or simple miscalculation, disaster could strike. Each year of the late nineteenth century some 35,000 wage earners were killed by industrial accidents. In Pittsburgh iron and steel mills alone, in one year 195 men died from hot metal explosions, asphyxiation, and falls, some into pits of molten metal. Men and women working in textile mills were poisoned by the thick dust and fibers in the air; similar toxic atmospheres injured those working in anything from twine-making plants to embroidery factories. Railways, with their heavy equipment and unaccustomed speed, were especially dangerous. In Philadelphia over half the railroad workers who died between 1886 and 1890 were killed by accidents. For injury or death, workers and their families could expect no payment from employers, since the idea of worker's compensation was unknown.

Industrial workers almost never saw an owner. The foreman exercised complete authority over the unskilled in his section, hiring and firing them and even setting their wages. A worker with a complaint, an industrialist observed, "stood just about as much chance to get in to see any one . . . as he would to get into the Kingdom of Heaven." Skilled workers had much greater freedom; yet in time even they yielded to technology and organization. Carpenters found that machine-made doors were replacing the ones they had before constructed at the site, while painters no longer mixed their own paints. More and more, labor became a commodity and workers cogs in a vast industrial machine. "I regard my people," one manager stated, "as I regard my machinery. So long as they can do my work for what I choose to pay them, I keep them, getting out of them all I can."

Higher productivity was the aim. It received a powerful boost from Frederick

W. Taylor, who revolutionized working conditions in the steel industry. Taylor was obsessed with efficiency. As a boy, he had invented the overhand pitch to deliver a baseball with new speed and precision. In steel plants during the 1870s and 1880s, he undertook careful time-and-motion studies of workers' movements, set up standard procedures, and offered pay incentives to those who surpassed his production quotas. In a famous application of his theories, he designed 15 ore shovels, each for a separate task to be performed in a specific way, so that 140 men were able to do what had previously required a crew of 600. The company cut its costs in half, and the remaining shovelers got a raise. By the early twentieth century "Taylorism" had become a full-blown philosophy, complete with its own professional society. "Management engineers" prescribed routines from which workers could not vary. Work itself was thus separated from the planning of work, and labor was managed as yet another part of an integrated system.

For all the high ideals of Taylorism, ordinary workers refused to perform as simple cogs. Many European immigrants, accustomed to celebrating numerous saints' holidays, continued to take those days off, regardless of factory work rules. (The Greek Orthodox church had more than 80 festivals a year, while Polish weddings lasted as long as five days.) When the pressure of six-day weeks became too stifling, workers took an unauthorized "blue Monday" off. Often they simply walked off the job, took another "greenhorn" opening in another industry, or packed up and moved to a new city. Come spring and warm weather, the turnover in factories rose significantly, just as it decreased in the fall. At the turn of the century, factories reported turnover rates of more than 100 percent in the course of a year. That meant that the Armour meat-packing plant in Chicago, for example, had to hire 8000 new workers in 1914 just to stay fully staffed.

Workers who stayed on the job earned low wages. Before 1900, an unskilled laborer could expect between $1.25 and $1.50 for 10 hours of work, a skilled one perhaps twice that amount. It took about $600 to make ends meet, but most manufacturing workers made just under $500 a year. Native white Americans tended to earn more than immigrants, those who spoke English more than those who did not, men more than women, and all others more than African-Americans and Asians. By 1900, some 1.7 million children worked in factories and fields, more than double the number 30 years earlier. On average, their paychecks were three times smaller than those of adult males. Parents often had no choice but to send their children to work. As one union leader observed of coal miners, "Absolute necessity compels the father in many instances to take the child into the mine to assist him in winning bread for the family."

Women worked outside the home too. Farm women had always labored on the family homestead, but by 1870 one out of every four nonagricultural workers was female. In general they earned one-quarter of what men did. Nearly all were single and young, anywhere from their mid-teens to their mid-twenties. Most lived in boarding houses or at home with their parents, where they usually contributed their wages to the family kitty. Once married, they took on a life of full-time housework and child rearing.

Only 5 percent of married women held paying jobs in 1900. That figure can be misleading, since home-bound women who needed money earned it by increasing their housework with extra laundry or sewing or by taking in boarders. And industrialization inevitably pushed women out of the traditional domestic women's sphere and into new jobs. The census of 1890 listed 369 occupations in America. Women worked in all but nine. Mainly they had jobs considered exten-

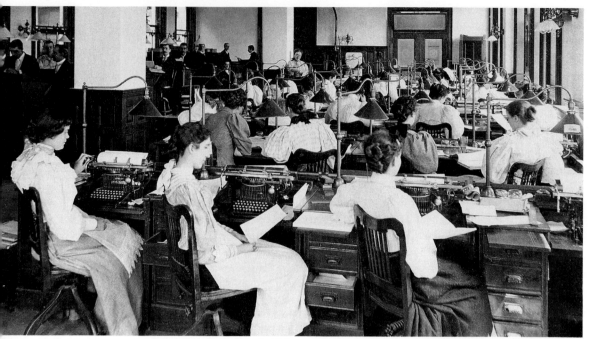

Clerks' jobs, traditionally held by men, increasingly came to be filled by women as inventions like the typewriter and telephone created new opportunities for office work.

sions of housework: food processing, textiles and millinery, and cigar making. By far the largest number of jobs available to women were in clothes manufacturing and domestic service. New methods of management and marketing opened new avenues of employment for some women as "typewriters," "telephone girls," bookkeepers, and secretaries. On rare occasions they entered the professions, though law and medical school administrators continued to see them as unworthy invaders. Instead, ambitious, educated women became nurses, librarians, and teachers. Their presence effectively "feminized" these pursuits, making them women's work and driving men upward into managerial slots or out of these occupations entirely.

African-Americans, even more than women, faced discrimination in the workplace. Paid less than whites and relegated to the most menial employment, blacks found their greatest opportunities in industry as "scabs" to replace striking white workers. Once a strike ended, they were themselves replaced—and hated by whites all the more. The service trades furnished the largest single source of jobs, though black craftsmen and a sprinkling of professionals could usually be found in cities. The pattern of black employment in Washington, D.C., was typical. In 1870 the population of the nation's capital included 410 black waiters, 133 black carpenters, and one black lawyer. Most single black women in the South worked for wages as laundresses and domestic servants. If married, they were five times more likely than married white women to work outside their homes.

Whatever their separate experiences, American workers did improve their lot, at least in the aggregate. Though the gap between rich and poor widened, ordinary laborers, with the exception of African-Americans, made measurable gains. Wages rose, prices fell, and the number of hours on the job declined. Not that workers rose from "rags to riches." Few could expect to repeat the experience of an Andrew Carnegie. But for most there was a chance to rise. About one-quarter of the manual laborers in one study entered the middle class in their own lifetimes. And most workers believed in the American dream of success, even if they did not fully share in it.

The Systems of Labor: Early Unions

Working longer to save a few pennies, walking off the job in exhaustion or disgust, taking in boarders—these were the ways most workers coped with the new systems of industrial America. Yet such responses were the actions of individuals against the complex structures being set in place around them. For ordinary workers to have any effect on the process of industrialization they had to combine, just as businesses had. They needed to integrate horizontally—which for workers meant organizing not just locally but on a national scale. And they needed to integrate vertically: to coordinate their actions along a wide range of jobs and skills, just as Andrew Carnegie coordinated the production of steel, all the way from the iron ranges of Minnesota to the delivery of finished steel girders. For workers, labor unions were their systematic response to industrialization.

In the United States the earliest unions had been formed before the Civil War among such craftsmen as iron molders, machinists, printers, and cigar makers. Railroad "brotherhoods" had also appeared, more in an effort to furnish insurance for those hurt or killed on the job than to exert economic leverage on bosses. Such organizations remained local, exclusively male, and weakened by small membership and divided power. Once in a while a nationwide craft organization such as the National Typographic Union emerged, but on the eve of the Civil War only six national unions existed in the whole country.

After the war, a group of craft unions, brotherhoods, and reformers banded together as the National Labor Union (NLU). Although national in scope, the goals of the organization looked backward. Using the language of abolitionism, the NLU called for an end to "wage-slavery" and spoke longingly of a mythic, simpler past when workers employed themselves. It vigorously opposed anything, including strikes, that encouraged members to think of themselves as a working class. By the early 1870s, the NLU claimed over half a million members, but it faded quickly once the depression of 1873 set in.

The Knights of Labor

Similarly nostalgic and visionary but much more successful was a national union born in secrecy, amid elaborate ritual. This was the Noble and Holy Order of the Knights of Labor. Founded by Uriah Stephens and a group of Philadelphia garment workers in 1869, the Knights remained small and fraternal for a decade. Their strongly Protestant tone repelled Catholics, who made up almost half the work force in many industries. Then in 1879, as the 1873 depression waned, the Knights elected Terence V. Powderly their Grand Master Workman. Handsome, dynamic, Irish, and Catholic, Powderly threw off the Knights' secrecy, dropped their religious rituals, and opened their ranks. He called for "one big union" that would embrace the "toiling millions"—skilled and unskilled, men and women, natives and immigrants, all religions and all races. Within half a dozen years, membership rose from 10,000 to 100,000; by 1886, it reached nearly 730,000.

Like the NLU, the Knights saw workers as producers, denied by monopoly and special privilege "the full enjoyment of the wealth they create." Nothing short of a radical reordering of society would do. "The aim of the Knights of Labor—properly understood—is to make each man his own employer," said Powderly. He hated the word "class," shunned labor violence, and urged harmony. His would be a cooperative economy of mines, factories, and railroads, owned and operated by workers. They would pool their resources and share their profits.

The Knights knew that such a radical vision might take years to realize. In the interim they set up over 140 cooperative workshops, sponsored political candidates in 200 cities and towns, and pressed for short-term reform. Their platform advocated the eight-hour workday, regulation of trusts, the prohibition of child and convict labor, and the abolition of liquor. They were, in fact, prescribing not only an economic system but also a social plan, guided by Christian moralism. Only when citizens put aside greed, sloth, and dishonesty, they argued, would class divisions and corruption fade away.

It was one thing to proclaim a united national organization but another to coordinate the activities of so many members. Powderly disapproved of strikes, but soon found his local members engaged in quite a few of them. During the mid-1880s, when such stoppages wrung concessions from the western railroads, the Knights attracted thousands of new recruits. But the organization soon became associated with unsuccessful strikes and violent extremists. And the gains against the railroads were wiped out when Jay Gould and his Texas and Pacific Railroad broke the locals striking against it. By 1890, the Knights of Labor teetered on the edge of extinction.

The American Federation of Labor

The Knights' position as the premier union in the nation was usurped by the rival American Federation of Labor (AFL). The AFL reflected the practicality of its leader, Samuel Gompers. Born in a London tenement, the son of a Jewish cigar maker, he had emigrated in 1863 with his family to New York's Lower East Side. Gompers had little use for Terence Powderly's radical vision of a cooperative commonwealth. Pragmatic and conservative, he accepted capitalism and the wage system. In his view, workers were "a distinct and practically permanent class." So he sought to organize those with the most leverage—craftsmen. Above all, Gompers wanted results: higher wages, fewer hours, improved safety, increased benefits. By bargaining with employers and using strikes or boycotts when necessary, his "pure and simple unionism" was designed to win better conditions for those with skills.

Using the Cigar Makers' Union as his base, Gompers helped found the first national federation of craft unions in 1881. In December 1886, when it was reorganized as the American Federation of Labor, 25 labor groups joined, representing some 150,000 mostly skilled laborers. It was labor's answer to the corporation and trust: a consolidated organization for controlling resources (in this case labor) and competition (for jobs). From 1886 until his death in 1924, Gompers fought off socialists, allied himself with whichever major party supported labor, stressed gradual, concrete gains, and transformed the AFL into the most powerful amalgamation of trade unions in the country. By 1901 it had over a million members, almost a third of all skilled workers in America.

Gompers was less interested in vertical integration: combining skilled and unskilled workers. For most of his career, he preserved the prerogatives of crafts-men and acceded to their prejudices against women, blacks, and immigrants. Only two locals—the Cigar Makers' Union and the Typographers' Union—accepted women, and most affiliates restricted black membership through high entrance fees, technical examinations, and other discriminatory practices.

Despite the success of the AFL, the laboring classes did not organize them-selves as systematically as the barons of industrial America. Union membership never included more than 2 percent of the whole labor force and less than 10 percent of all industrial workers. Skewed by different languages and nationalities, deeply divided over race and gender, raised to value self-reliance, working men and women resisted unionization during the nineteenth century. In fact, workers often regarded such collective activities as alien, subversive, and un-American.

The Limits of Industrial Systems

As managers sought to increase their control over the workplace, workers often found themselves at the mercy of the new industrial order. Few could count on full-time employment, even when the economy was booming. One out of every three workers could expect to be out of work for at least three or four months a year. Changes in markets and weather brought seasonal unemployment, New machines that replaced old human skills led to structural or technological unem-ployment. And regular tailspins in the economy—on average one every five or six years—brought cyclical unemployment. In such hard times the industrial system was driven to its limits, and workers bore the brunt of it. Managers sped up work to increase labor productivity, insisted on longer hours, laid off hundreds, and cut wages.

When a man's pay dropped and his anger and frustration rose, when his wife began working all night to make ends meet and fell asleep during the day while taking care of her children, when food prices suddenly jumped—violence might well erupt. "A mob of 1,000 people, with women in the lead, marched through the Jewish quarter of Williamsburg last evening," wrote the New York *Times* in 1902, "and wrecked half a dozen butcher shops. Men and women who were seen coming out of the shops with meat and chickens in their hands were attacked. In the throng of women leaders of the mob there were many who carried bottles of kerosene oil."

Workers' strikes served more often than mobs as an outlet for protest. Most strikes broke out spontaneously, organized by informal leaders in a factory. "Mal-vina Fourtune and her brother Henry Fourtune it was them who started the strike," confessed a company informer in Chicopee, Massachusetts. "They go from house to house and tells the people to keep up the strike." Nor were strikes limited to the years of depression. Thousands of rallies and strikes were staged on behalf of the eight-hour workday, in good times as well as bad, by union and nonunion workers alike.

In 1877 Americans received an early view of labor troubles to come. When the Baltimore and Ohio Railroad cut wages by 20 percent, a crew in Martinsburg, West Virginia, seized the local depot and refused to let the trains move. The spontaneous strike spread to other eastern lines and then west to California until two-thirds of the nation's tracks were shut down. As strikebreakers came in, railyard after railyard went up in flames. Local police, state militia, and federal troops, sometimes fighting pitched battles with mobs supporting strikers, finally

Labor strikes, some of them bloody, plagued the late nineteenth century. Most involved working conditions rather than wages. Here labor and management confront each other directly. One striker reaches for a stone while an anxious mother looks on.

restored order after 12 days. The first nationwide strike in American history left 100 people dead and $10 million worth of railroad property in rubble. "This may be the beginning of a great civil war in this country, between labor and capital," read one newspaper editorial. In the face of violence, middle- and upper-class Americans came to fear the "Sampson-like strength" of labor.

Strikes became epidemic in the late nineteenth century. Between 1880 and 1900, some 6.6 million workers staged over 23,000 strikes. In 1886 alone, a record 610,000 workers were out of jobs as a result of strikes, lockouts, and shutdowns. The most violent episode of that year started innocently enough, at a rally at Haymarket Square in Chicago. Anarchists were protesting the brutality of police who had earlier killed two workers during a lockout at the McCormick Harvester Company. The turnout—around 3000—was disappointingly low, the speeches long-winded, the crowd placid and bored. As rain drenched the gathering, police moved into the square and ordered everyone to disperse. Moments later a bomb exploded, instantly killing one officer and mortally wounding six others. The police opened fire, and the crowd fired back. In addition to the 7 policemen who died, 70 more were injured. At least four civilians were killed and uncounted numbers hurt.

Conservatives charged that organized labor had encouraged the violence and anarchy of the "Haymarket Massacre." Even though the identity of the bomb thrower was never established, the courts found eight anarchists guilty of conspiracy to murder. Four were hanged, one committed suicide, and three later were pardoned by Governor John P. Altgeld. Even ordinary citizens called for action against radicals in laborers' clothing. Cities enlarged their police forces and states built more National Guard armories on the borders of working-class neighborhoods.

During the troubled 1890s federal and state governments firmly sided with business. In 1892, in the remote Coeur d'Alene district of Idaho, striking silver miners and company guards fought a guerrilla war until federal troops quashed the strike. In July of that year the Amalgamated Iron and Steel Workers, a powerful AFL affiliate, struck the Homestead steel mill after Carnegie's managing partner, Henry Clay Frick, cut wages by 20 percent and refused to improve working conditions. Determined to destroy the union, Frick imported 300 Pinkerton detectives to drive off picketing workers. The hired thugs arriving by barge under cover of darkness were suddenly engaged in a furious gun battle and beaten savagely as they marched to the main gate. When the melee ended, 10 strikers and 3 Pinkertons lay dead. Within days the governor had called out 8000 state militia; on July 15 the mill reopened under military guard. "I will never recognize the Union, never, never!" Frick insisted. By mid-November he had replaced most of the workers, broken the strike, and crippled the union for decades.

A broader confrontation between labor and capital took place just two years later. George Pullman, inventor of the plush Palace Car and owner of the company that built it, was a benevolent despot. He was determined to ensure efficiency on the job by controlling the lives of his workers. In the 1880s he built for his 5000 workers a model town south of Chicago on the shores of Lake Calumet. Pullman was a clean and pretty town, free of alcohol but never free from discontent. In addition to difficult working conditions, residents resented Pullman's relentless control over this compulsory heaven. "We are born in a Pullman house," one of them complained, "fed from the Pullman shop, taught in the Pullman school, catechized in the Pullman church, and when we die, we shall be buried in the Pullman cemetery and go to the Pullman hell."

As the depression of 1893 deepened, Pullman laid off workers, cut wages five times in one year, and refused to reduce the high rents charged for company houses. In 1894 frustrated workers struck. They managed to convince Eugene V. Debs' American Railway Union to support them by boycotting all trains that used Pullman cars. The General Managers Association, an organization of 24 midwestern railroads, appealed to President Grover Cleveland for federal help. On the slim pretext that the strike obstructed delivery of the United States mail (strikers had actually been willing to handle mail trains so long as they contained no Pullman cars), Cleveland secured an injunction halting the strike and ordered several thousand special deputies into Chicago to enforce it. In the rioting and looting that followed, 12 people died and scores were arrested. Debs and other union leaders were eventually sent to jail for defying the injunction. After his release, a bitter Debs became the foremost socialist leader in America.

At Pullman and in other labor disputes the central question, whatever the public issues, was power. Employers always enjoyed the advantage. They hired and fired workers, set the terms of employment, and controlled the workplace. To most of them, unions were a curse they fought to destroy with a formidable arsenal. "Yellow dog" contracts forced workers to forswear union membership. "Blacklists" circulated the names of labor agitators. Lockouts kept protesting workers from plants, and labor spies infiltrated their organizations. Workers were paid with "scrip," company money redeemable only at company stores charging inflated prices. With abundant migrant and immigrant labor, employers could replace strikers and so break their strikes. "I can hire one half the working class to kill the other half," Jay Gould once remarked.

When strikes spread, the government aided management not only with troops but also with powerful new legal weapons. The injunction had been used with devastating effect in the Pullman strike to stop workers from interfering with their employer's business. When the Supreme Court upheld Debs' sentence in *In re Debs* (1895), it legalized the federal injunction against the railway strikers. As the Court saw it, the strike hindered interstate commerce, an action deemed illegal under the Sherman Antitrust Act. The Sherman Act, intended to control monopolies, was thereby turned against labor. By the end of the century employers had weathered the protests of workers and emerged as masters of the mightiest industrial economy on earth.

The new industrial order was hard won, and its benefits were unevenly apportioned. The exploitative power of business grew as the number of those in control shrank. The gulf between the rich and the poor, always present, became more apparent. Laborers found themselves with fatter pay checks but less independence and satisfaction from their jobs. Yet the overall gain for the American economy was undeniable. On average, real wages rose for laborers, and Samuel Gompers agreed that "the social conditions of the working people have improved very materially within the past 35 years." At the end of the Civil War the United States had been fourth in the world in industrial production. By the mid-1890s the value of American manufactured goods nearly totaled those of France, Britain, and Germany combined, and by 1900 America ranked first among all industrial nations.

Whether rich or poor, worker, entrepreneur, or industrial baron, Americans were linked by new industrial systems, drawn closer to one another than ever before. Ore scooped from Mesabi might end up in a steel girder on James Eads' Mississippi bridge or in a steel pin bought by a California housewife or in a McCormick reaper slicing across the Nebraska plains. When a textile worker in Massachusetts struck, a family in Alabama might well pay more for clothes. A man in Cleveland now set his watch to agree with the time of a man in New York and vice versa, regardless of the sun. Such changes might seem effortless to someone like T. S. Hudson, scampering across the rails of America in 1882. But as the nineteenth century drew to a close, material progress seemed to go hand in hand with social upheaval. Americans had not yet adjusted to either.

SIGNIFICANT EVENTS

1859 — First oil well drilled near Titusville, Pennsylvania

1866 — Transatlantic cable links United States and Great Britain; National Labor Union founded

1868 — Philip Armour opens meat-packing factory in Chicago

1869 — Knights of Labor created

1870 — John D. Rockefeller incorporates Standard Oil Company of Ohio

1872 — George Westinghouse perfects air brakes; Crédit Mobilier scandal

1873 — Cable cars first used (in San Francisco); E. Remington and Sons begins making typewriters; Carnegie Steel Company founded; Panic of 1873

1874 — Massachusetts enacts first ten-hour workday law for women

1876 — Alexander Graham Bell invents telephone

1877 — Railroad wage cuts lead to violent strikes; Thomas Edison invents phonograph

1879 — Edison develops the incandescent light bulb; Henry George's *Progress and Poverty* published

1882 — Rockefeller's Standard Oil Company becomes the nation's first trust; Thomas Edison's electric company begins lighting New York City

1883 — Railroads establish standard time zones

1886 — American Federation of Labor organized; Haymarket Square bombing

1891 — Edison's motion picture camera patented

1892 — Homestead Steel strike

1893 — Panic of 1893

1894 — Pullman strike

1901 — U.S. Steel Corporation becomes the nation's first billion-dollar company

19

The Rise of an
Urban Order

raziano's bootblack stand in the old County Court House off Foley Square was jammed with people. Almost everybody needed a shine, but practically nobody had come to get one. They were there to see George Washington Plunkitt, ward boss of Manhattan's Fifteenth Assembly district. Plunkitt sat above the din like an Irish king, dispensing favors and philosophy to loyal constituents. His crown was a top hat, his throne a chair perched atop the unassuming stand. On the wall behind him hung his coat of arms—crossed American flags cradling photographs of other party leaders. Doing whatever he could to help his people, he asked nothing in return except their votes on election day.

As one of the powers of Tammany Hall, the Democratic party organization that dominated New York City politics from 1850 to 1930, Plunkitt knew how to get those votes. On one typical day a bartender from his district woke him at two in the morning to bail a fellow saloonkeeper out of jail. Plunkitt didn't get back to sleep until after three, only to be roused by fire engines at six. He rushed to the fire to help burned-out tenants find food, clothing, and shelter at a nearby hotel.

After squeezing in breakfast, he visited the police court and secured the release of four drunken constituents "by a timely word with the judge." Half an hour later, at the Municipal Court, he directed one of his district captains to act as counsel for a widow in an eviction case and paid the rent of a poor family about to be dispossessed. As he left he handed the father a dollar for food. By eleven he was home again, where four men awaited him in search of jobs. It took him three hours, but he found work for all of them.

With barely enough time to eat lunch, he rushed to two funerals—one Italian over by the ferry, and one Jewish and closer to home. At both rites he stood conspicuously in front of the houses of worship to make certain he was seen. Then he dashed to a "Hebrew confirmation" at a local synagogue. By seven in the evening he was at district headquarters presiding over a meeting of his election captains. Each reported on the voters in his district: their attitudes toward Tammany, their needs and troubles, and the "best way to reach them."

The business of "the organization" thus cared for, Plunkitt went to a church fair at eight. He bought chances on everything, treated the children to ice cream,

Theodore Groll captures Washington Street, Indianapolis, at dusk in this detail from a painting done in the 1890s. The trolley cars are still horse-drawn (not electrified), but the telephone pole gives proof of the new urban era at hand.

kissed the little ones, flattered the mothers, and took the fathers around the corner for a quick drink. Then it was back to the clubhouse, where he promised some constituents a subscription for a new church bell. He bought tickets for an excursion of parishioners and a baseball game between two teams in his district. Before leaving, he told two dozen pushcart peddlers he would visit the precinct station in the morning to register their complaints of police harassment. He arrived at a Jewish wedding reception at half past ten (having already sent the bride "a handsome wedding present") and finally got to bed at midnight.

Such relentless exertion helped to make Plunkitt a fortune. Born to Irish immigrant parents in a shantytown called "Nanny Goat Hill" on Manhattan's Upper West Side, he died a millionaire in 1924 at the age of 82. His pluck and practicality would have made him the envy of the most successful industrialists. Like the Carnegies and Rockefellers, his rise from butcher boy to political boss was fueled by fierce ambition. City politics was his way out of the slums in a world that otherwise favored the rich, the educated, and the well established.

In the late nineteenth century the needs of rapidly growing cities and the people who lived in them gave political bosses like George Washington Plunkitt their chance. "I seen my opportunities and I took 'em," Plunkitt used to say. Every city building contract, every tax assessment, municipal bond issue, and rental on city property, every franchise and charter for a new business offered Plunkitt and his cronies an opportunity for lining their pockets with kickbacks, payoffs, and profits made from inside knowledge of city projects. This was "boodle," or honest graft (not to be confused with "black" graft, which came from vice and extortion). In Plunkitt's world boodle was the just reward for public service that normally paid so little.

How much boodle bosses collected depended on how successfully their organization controlled municipal politics. Control, in turn, hinged on electing the right officials, or as Plunkitt would have said, "turning out the vote." In the end, this whole system hung on the personal loyalty of bosses to immigrants and immigrants to bosses. That explains why Plunkitt spent so much time catering to his constituents. "When a poor man comes . . . for help," said one city boss, "we don't make one of those damned fool investigations like these city charities. No, by God, we fill his belly and warm his back and vote him our way."

Plunkitt's New York was the first great city in history to be ruled by men of the people in an organized and continuing fashion. Bosses and their henchmen came from the streets and saloons, the slums and tenements, the firehouses and funeral homes. More remarkable still, their families had only recently arrived in America. Usually bosses were immigrants or their children. Most remarkable of all, other great cities were ruled by them too. While the Irish of Tammany Hall ran New York, Germans governed in St. Louis, Scandinavians in Minneapolis, and Jews in San Francisco. In the late nineteenth century, the golden door of opportunity opened onto the city.

THE RISE OF CITIES

The modern city was the product of industrialization. The vast systems of communication and transportation, of manufacturing, marketing, and finance, of labor and management converged in the industrial city. Cities contained the great investment banks, the smoky mills and dingy sweatshops, the spreading railroad yards, the tenements and mansions, the new department stores and skyscrapers. They drew people like magnets from places as far away as Lincoln, Nebraska, and Minsk in Russia. By the end of the nineteenth century industrial cities had come of age. America—once an agrarian republic—was becoming urban, with tens of millions of "urbanites," an urban landscape, and a growing urban culture.

The Urban Explosion

"We cannot all live in cities," reformer Horace Greeley lamented just after the Civil War, "yet nearly all seemed determined to do so. . . . 'Hot and cold water,' baker's bread, gas, the theater, and the streetcars . . . indicate the tendency of modern taste." The city had all the household conveniences, temples of entertainment, and newfangled transports imaginable—and more: the best stores, the best restaurants, the best schools, the best newspapers, and virtually every museum, library, art gallery, bookshop, and orchestra. The city housed the delights of the age and most of the opportunity. Promising wages high enough to buy this good life, cities beckoned native-born Americans and a generation of immigrants to realize their dreams of success.

During the 50 years after the Civil War, world population rose by about 50 percent. The population of the United States quadrupled—from 23 million to 92

Realist painters like George Bellows, scorned by their critics as the "Ashcan School," captured the grittiness and vibrancy of teeming cities. Here Bellows evokes the cliff-dwelling ancestors of the Pueblo Indians with a turn-of-the-century scene of urban life. Like all his work, *Cliff Dwellers* makes dramatic use of light and dark, relying heavily on line, mass, and color to achieve naturalism.

million. Yet the number of people living in American cities increased nearly sevenfold. The census of 1870 defined a city as containing 8000 people or more. Ten years earlier, only one American in six qualified as a city dweller; in 1870 one in four did; in 1900, one in three. By 1910 nearly half the nation was urban.

Densely populated Europe and Asia boasted only a few cities of a million or more. In America giants sprouted overnight. Chicago (which rose from a swamp) had only 30,000 people in 1850, but it approached the million mark by 1890, making it the fastest growing metropolis in the world. So confident were city fathers of continued expansion that they laid new streetcar lines far into open cornfields. Just two American cities contained populations of over 500,000 at the outbreak of the Civil War. There were six when the century turned. Three—New York, Chicago, and Philadelphia—had more than a million each.

Cities grew in every region of the country, some faster than others. The Northeast and upper Midwest, where industrialization took hold earliest, were far more urban than the West and the South, although big cities could be found in those regions as well. Atlanta and Nashville (later Louisville, Memphis, Dallas, and Houston) boomed under the influence of railroads. In Birmingham, a steel town founded in Alabama in 1871, one early resident recalled that "property changed hands four or five times a day" during the real estate craze of the 1880s. Los Angeles had barely 6000 people in 1870. By 1900 it was the second largest city on the Pacific coast with a population of 100,000 and a set of nearby "satellite" towns, including Azusa (named, said its founders, "from A to Z in the USA!").

Size alone does not make a modern city. Without efficient ways of moving people and tying diverse functions together, without the means to control resources and capital, no settlement, however large, can perform as an organic, integrated unit, the mark of a modern metropolis. In the United States, the dynamic instruments of industry and commerce, along with striking advances in urban technology, helped to transform swelling towns into modern metropolises. Some cities became famous for their main product: Milwaukee for beer, Tulsa for oil, Houston for railroad cars, and Hershey, Pennsylvania, for chocolate. The giants continued to diversify. New York, the nation's banker, printer, and commercial center, also produced clothing and cigars. Chicago became the leading butcher, packer, and granary and by 1870 began to move into steelmaking.

The Great Global Migration

In the nineteenth century the world was moving to town. By some estimates 60 million people left farms and villages for cities between 1820 and 1920. Everywhere in Europe the forces of change pushed people off the land. After the mid-1820s and the end of the destructive Napoleonic Wars a cycle of baby booms continued at 20-year intervals for the rest of the century. Improved diet and sanitation, abetted by Louis Pasteur's pathbreaking discovery that bacteria cause infection and disease, reduced deaths. The population of Europe doubled between 1750 and 1850. Meanwhile the use of machinery enhanced productivity but cut the need for agricultural labor. In 1896 it took one man in a wheat field to do the work 18 had done just 60 years earlier.

Surplus farm workers became a ragtag army of rural migrants. Pushed from the land by machines, they were pulled by machines into the great industrial cities of Europe. The prospect of good pay and shorter hours drew them to urban factories. The young especially saw their fortunes in the city. In America those who stayed behind agonized as they watched their towns being robbed of the future.

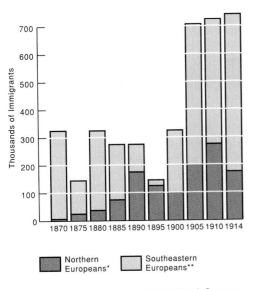

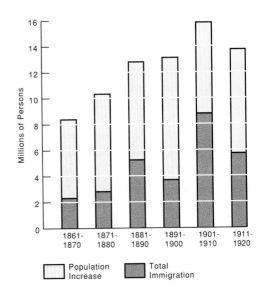

Northern Europeans*   Southeastern Europeans**

Population Increase   Total Immigration

*Includes immigrants from Great Britain, Ireland, Germany, and the Scandinavian countries.
**Includes immigrants from Poland, Russia, Italy, and other Baltic and East European countries.

IMMIGRATION AND POPULATION, 1860–1920

Frightened and envious, they shared Thomas Jefferson's view of cities as "ulcers on the body politic." The result was a voluminous literature of urban fear with sensational titles like *The Spider and the Fly; or, Tricks, Traps, and Pitfalls of City Life by One Who Knows* (1873) and *Metropolitan Life Unveiled; or the Mysteries and Miseries of America's Great Cities* (1882). No doubt their vivid pictures and splashy accounts seduced as many breathless readers as they repelled. By 1910 a third of all city dwellers had come from the American countryside.

Another quarter came from overseas, the crest of a tidal wave of immigration that began to hit American shores in the mid-1880s. Until then most immigrants had come from northern and western Europe—first the English, Scotch, Dutch, and French in the eighteenth century, then Germans, Scandinavians, and Irish in the mid-nineteenth century. Beginning in the 1880s "new" immigrants with swarthier faces appeared from southern and eastern Europe. Some were fleeing political and religious persecution. The assassination of Czar Alexander II in 1881 brought a resurgence of anti-Semitic pogroms in Russia. Polish and Russian Jews escaped by the tens of thousands from their "shtetls," or villages, into crowded European cities and then on to the new "Promised Land" across the Atlantic. Others left to evade diseases like cholera, which swept across southern Italy in 1887. But most came for the same reasons as migrants from the American countryside—a job, more money, a fresh start.

Ambitious, hardy, and resourceful, immigrants found themselves tested at every step of their journey. They were uprooted from old ways and old friends. Most left mothers and fathers, brothers and sisters, wives and children behind. In many cases it was too expensive to bring relatives along, at least on the first trip (the price one-way was about $50 in 1904). Wayfarers often stole across heavily guarded borders, sometimes on foot, sometimes by train. They traveled for weeks to reach a port like Le Havre in France or Bremen in Germany. If they could find no lodgings, they slept in the streets. At dockside, shipping lines vaccinated, disinfected, and examined them to ensure against their being returned at company expense (by 1907, some 40,000 emigrants had been rejected at Liverpool alone).

It took from one to two weeks to cross the Atlantic. Immigrants spent most of that time below decks in "steerage" compartments one passenger described as "a kind of hell that cleanses a man of his sins before coming to the land of Columbus." When they finally reached America (the main receiving station opened in 1892 on Ellis Island in New York's harbor), they still had to pass a dreaded medical examination that weeded out the physically and mentally unfit. No wonder the immigrant's arrival was, in the words of the hero of an immigrant novel, *The Rise of David Levinsky* (1917), "like a second birth to him. Imagine a new-born babe in possession of a fully developed intellect. Would it ever forget its entry into the world? Neither does the immigrant forget his entry into a country which is, to him, a new world in the profoundest sense."

Immigrants arrived in staggering numbers—over 6.3 million between 1877 and 1890, some 30 million by 1920. In 1907 alone, 1.2 million landed. By the turn of the century immigrants made up nearly 15 percent of the population. Most newcomers were young, between the ages of 15 and 40. They usually came from farms and tiny hamlets. Few spoke English, had skills, or had much education. They worshiped mainly in Catholic, Greek, or Russian Orthodox churches and Jewish synagogues. Almost two-thirds were men, a large number of whom came solely to make money for buying land or starting businesses back home. Some changed their minds and sent for relatives to join them, but returnees were common enough to have a name—"birds of passage." For every 100 eastern and southern Europeans who arrived between 1908 and 1910, 44 went back.

Jews were the singular exception. Over half came from cities and had been tailors, merchants, and artisans in Europe. Almost all stayed and brought their families with them. There was little else they could do. As one Jewish immigrant wrote of his Russian homeland, "Am I not despised? Am I not urged to leave? . . . Do I not rise daily with the fear lest the hungry mob attack me?"

The Immigrant in the City

When they put into port, the first thing newcomers were likely to see was a city—perhaps Boston, New York, or later Galveston, Texas. Enough of them traveled inland so that by the turn of the century three-quarters of the residents of Minnesota and Wisconsin and nearly two-thirds of Utah had at least one foreign-born parent.* Most immigrants, worn by physical and financial exhaustion, settled in cities, no matter where they came from. Even Italians, Slavs, and Greeks whose families had farmed for generations looked to cities for quick money.

Friends or labor contractors or just the drift of people speaking familiar tongues drew them to specific neighborhoods. Immigrants usually clustered together on the basis of their villages or provinces, reflecting old world habits and prejudices. In America Greeks from Athens still considered Spartans ignorant and belligerent, while Spartans found Athenians effete and decadent. Sometimes it seemed that only mutual mistrust of Sicilians united northern Italians with those from the central provinces. New York contained no "Little Italy" but distinct groups of Italians—Neapolitans and Calabrians in the Mulberry Bend district,

---

*Mormons serving as missionaries in Europe and Great Britain especially swelled Utah's population with converts.

Genoese on Baxter Street, northerners west of Broadway and on Sixty-ninth Street. Wherever they ended up, Jews tended to settle according to the regions in which they had lived in Europe.

Cities developed a well-defined mosaic of ethnic communities, but these neighborhoods were constantly in flux. As many as half the residents moved every 10 years, often to better quarters. More recent arrivals from Italy, Russia, and the Balkans replaced earlier ones from Ireland and Germany. Despite popular perceptions, no other group of immigrants lived like the Chinese in urban ghettos composed exclusively of one nationality. Racial prejudice forced the Chinese together, and local ordinances kept them from buying their way out. Though one nationality usually dominated a neighborhood, there was always a sprinkling of Poles, Slavs, or Greeks in Italian and Jewish areas and vice versa.

Ethnic communities served both as refuges from the strangeness of American society and springboards to a new life. In their neighborhoods immigrants could find comrades who spoke their native tongue and theaters that performed national plays and music, even as they were assaulted everywhere by a new language and culture. Familiar foods, sometimes prepared at ethnic restaurants like the German Luchow's or the Italian Mamma Leone's, competed with expensive American fare whose consumption was a sign of status and acceptance. The *Jewish Daily Forward* and scores of other foreign-language newspapers reported events from the homeland but also gave eager readers profiles of local leaders, advice on voting, and tips on adjusting to life in America. Organizations such as the Hebrew Immigrant Aid Society, the Polish National Alliance, and the Society for the Protection of Italian Immigrants furnished fellowship and assistance, usually in the newcomers' native languages. They also fostered assimilation by sponsoring baseball teams, insurance programs, libraries, and English classes.

Houses of worship were always at the center of immigrant life. They often catered to the practices of individual towns or provinces; yet occasionally they cast off orthodoxy under the cultural pressure of American experience. With Irish priests dominating the American Catholic church many immigrants formed new churches with priests from their homelands. Eastern European Jews began to break the old proscription against sitting next to their wives and daughters in synagogues, and the Orthodox churches of Armenians, Syrians, Rumanians, and Serbians gradually lost their national identifications.

Immigrants worked in factories, in the construction and needle trades, or as common laborers on the street. Their backgrounds and cultural values influenced the kinds of jobs they took. Italians, for example, were committed to family above individual success and were wary of children who did better than their parents. All but one of the nearly 500 bootblacks in New York in 1894 were Italian. Because Chinese men did not feel washing or ironing was women's work, more than 7500 of them could be found in San Francisco laundries by 1880. Sewing ladies' garments seemed unmanly to many native-born Americans but not to Russian and Italian tailors. Slavs tended to be the most physically robust of the new immigrants and valued steady income over education. They pulled their children out of school, sent them to work, and worked themselves in the mines for better pay than in factories.

On the whole, immigrants married later and had more children than the native-born. Greeks and eastern European Jews prearranged marriages according to tradition. They imported "picture brides," betrothed by mail and often from the same village as their prospective husbands. After marriage men ruled the household, but women managed it. Although child-rearing practices varied, immigrants resisted the relative permissiveness of American parents. Youngsters were expected to contribute, like little adults, to the welfare of the family. Caught between the past and the present, immigrants clung to tradition and assimilated slowly. Children adjusted more quickly, despite heart-rending clashes with their elders. They soon spoke English like natives, married whomever they pleased, and worked their way out of old neighborhoods.

The Shape of Cities

Cities of the late nineteenth century still exhibited the ringed residential pattern that had emerged in the old "walking cities" earlier in the century. In those days the professional and upper classes had lived within walking distance of their offices and shops in the city center. As the middle and upper classes moved outward from an increasingly industrial core, the poor, some immigrants, blacks, and lower-class laborers filled the inner void. They took over old factories and brownstones, shanties and cellars; they crammed themselves into dank tenements; and by sheer weight of numbers they transformed these areas into the slums of the central city.

Curled around the slums was the "zone of emergence," an income-graded band of those on their way up—second-generation city dwellers, factory workers, skilled laborers, and professional mechanics—living in progressively better tenements and neater row houses. Their residents had escaped poverty but could still slip back in hard times. Farther out was the suburban fringe, home to the white-collar managers and executives, who lived in larger houses on individual lots. With income determining residence, cities developed a concentric and fragmented look. Yet for all their differences, the circles of settlement held together as a part of a massive and interdependent whole.

Urban Transport

One reason cities remained whole was urban transportation. In the middle of the nineteenth century the horse-drawn railway had begun conveying people, some 35 million people a year in New York and 6.5 million in Boston. The railways' problems were legendary: so slow, a person could walk faster; so crowded (according to Mark Twain), you "had to hang on by your eyelashes and your toenails"; so dirty, thousands of tons of smelly horse manure were left in their wake every day.

Civic leaders came to understand that the modern city could not grow, much less survive, without improved transportation. One far-fetched scheme—trolley cars pulled by steam-driven cables up the steep hills of San Francisco—worked well enough so that Chicago, Seattle, and several other cities installed similar systems in the 1880s. Cable lines and steam locomotives were elevated on trestles high above crowded streets in New York and Chicago. New York completed the first elevated line in 1870. By the early 1880s its lines were hauling 175,000 passengers a day. The system spread to Kansas City, Chicago, and other large cities that could afford it. None of the breakthroughs quite did the trick. Cables remained slow and unreliable; "els" were dirty, ugly, and noisy.

It took electricity to rescue city travelers. In 1888 Frank Julian Sprague, a naval engineer who had once worked for Edison, installed the first electric trolley line, a 12-mile stretch of track in Richmond, Virginia, with overhead wires to power 40 cars. The ingenious Sprague also designed a multiple-unit system of control that permitted individual cars to be powered, lighted, and braked inde-

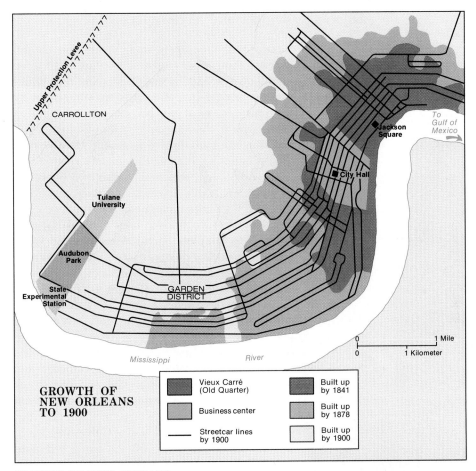

GROWTH OF
NEW ORLEANS
TO 1900

▧	Vieux Carré (Old Quarter)		▧	Built up by 1841
▨	Business center		▨	Built up by 1878
—	Streetcar lines by 1900		☐	Built up by 1900

GROWTH OF NEW ORLEANS
Streetcars helped cities to spread beyond business districts while still functioning as organic wholes. By 1900, lines in New Orleans reached all the way to Audubon Park and Tulane University, bringing these once distant points within the reach of city dwellers and creating "streetcar suburbs."

pendently or together by a master switch located in any one of them. Streetcars moved along at the daunting speed of 12 miles an hour, twice as fast as horses traveled. By 1902 electricity drove nearly all city railways.

Sprague's innovations prompted the electrification of els and made possible the most dramatic advance in urban transport, "subways." The smoke and soot of the steam locomotives made the air of tunnels barely breathable in the first underground lines in London. Between 1895 and 1897 Boston built the first underground electric line, a mile and a half long, under Tremont Avenue. New York followed quickly in 1904 with a subway that ran from City Hall on the southern end of Manhattan north to 145th Street.

The rich had long been able to keep homes outside city limits, traveling to and fro in private carriages. New systems of mass transit freed the middle class and even the poor to live miles from work. Now for a nickel or two (the fare included a free transfer), anybody could ride from central shopping and business districts to the suburban fringes and back again. The segmented and sprawling city, held together by a network of moving vehicles, widened its reach out into suburbs.

Bridges and Skyscrapers

Since cities often grew along rivers and natural harbors, their separate parts sometimes had to be joined over water. The principles and techniques of river bridges had already been worked out by the railroads, most notably in Octave Chanute's bridge across the Missouri by Kansas City (1869) and James B. Eads' bridge across the Mississippi at St. Louis (1874). It remained for a German immigrant and his son, John and Washington Roebling, to make the bridge a symbol of urban growth.

The Roeblings built one of the wonders of the day: the Brooklyn Bridge. Begun in 1870, it took 13 years to complete, cost $15 million, and killed 20 men (including designer John Roebling). President Chester A. Arthur, his cabinet, and several governors attended the opening in 1883. Before them stood the longest suspension bridge in the world—over a mile across the East River with a passageway wide enough for a footpath, two double carriage lanes, and two railroad lines. Its arches were cut like the windows of a giant cathedral and its supporting cables hung, said one awe-struck observer, "like divine messages from above." Soon other suspension bridges spanned the railroad yards in St. Louis and the bay at Galveston, Texas. By 1909 there were over 350 new bridges of more than 500 feet in length.

Even as late as 1880 church steeples still dominated the urban landscape, towering over squat factories and office buildings. The increasing value of urban land put a premium on using available space to its limits. Congestion, which forced railways up on trestles over streets or underground, pushed buildings ever higher. Most large structures were built of masonry, with huge load-bearing walls that restricted floor space and supported no more than a dozen or so stories. The use of cast iron columns in factories and warehouses left more room to house large machines and stores of merchandise. Strong, durable, and fire-resistant "cloudscrapers" made of all cast iron were soon serving as office buildings and department stores too.

Steel, tougher in tension and compression, turned cloudscrapers into skyscrapers. First used in Chicago in William LeBaron Jenney's 10-story Home Insurance Building (1885), steel frames and girders raised buildings to heights of 30 stories by the end of the century. "Instead of the building's being a shell," wrote architectural historian Lewis Mumford, "it became essentially a skeleton . . . with a tough external skin." Studded with plate glass windows, Daniel Burnham's Reliance Building (1894) in Chicago looked to contemporaries like "a glass tower fifteen stories high."

It was no accident that many of the most stunning new skyscrapers arose in Chicago, for the city had burned nearly to the ground in 1871. The "Chicago School" of architects helped to rebuild it. A young maverick of the crowd, Louis H. Sullivan, promised a new urban profile in which the skyscraper would be "every inch a proud and soaring thing, rising in sheer exaltation that from top to bottom is a unit without a single dissenting line." In the Wainwright Building (1890) in St. Louis, the Prudential Building (1895) in Buffalo, and the Carson, Pirie, and Scott department store (1889–1904) in Chicago, Sullivan produced towering structures that symbolized the modern industrial city.

For a building to be a "soaring thing" and still habitable required solutions for some practical problems. Heating with a fireplace in each of hundreds of rooms would have been too costly. A more efficient system of steam or hot water circulating through pipes came into use in the 1870s. When William Baldwin finally perfected the "radiator" in 1874, high-rise buildings became year-round dwellings. To move people from the bottom to the top of tall buildings quickly and safely, Elisha Graves Otis developed a trustworthy, fast elevator in 1861. By the 1890s faster electric elevators made "the passenger seem to feel his stomach pass into his shoes," reported one visitor to Chicago.

Slum and Tenement

Far below the skyscrapers, jammed into block after block, lay the slums and tenements of the inner city. In cramped rooms and sunless hallways, along narrow alleys and in basements (some flooded every day by tidewaters) lived the city poor. Some worked there, too, in "sweaters' shops" where as many as a dozen and a half people labored and slept in dingy two-room flats. Writing in vivid detail in *How the Other Half Lives* (1890), reporter and photographer Jacob Riis brought his readers into the teeming tenement:

> Come over here. Step over this baby—it is a baby, spite of its rags and dirt— under these iron bridges called fire-escapes, but loaded down, despite the innocent watchfulness of the firemen, with broken household goods, with washtubs and barrels, over which no man could climb from a fire. This gap between dingy brick walls is the yard. That strip of smoke-colored sky up there is the heaven of these people.

By the late nineteenth century all cities had such slums and tenements. The worst ones were in New York, where land rentals were highest and the pressure of incoming immigrants was greatest. Crime flourished in places called "Bandit's Roost," "Bottle Alley," "Hell's Kitchen," and "Kerosene Row." Bands of young toughs (with names like the "Alley Gang," the "Sewer Rats," and the "Rock Gang") stalked the streets in search of thrills and easy money. The darker forms of vice—gambling, prostitution, and alcoholism—claimed their victims most readily in the slums. The poor usually turned to crime when all else had failed. "Let God Almighty judge who's to blame most," said a 20-year-old prostitute supporting a sickly mother and four younger brothers and sisters, "I that was driven, or them that drove me to the pass I'm in."

Disease was a constant and killing companion. Practices that had been safe in the open air of small villages helped turned crowded cities into hellholes. Until the late 1860s pigs and other animals roamed freely in the streets of New York. Visitors to one slum in the Midwest were shocked to discover a group of Greeks slaughtering sheep in a filthy basement and Italian ragpickers sorting their latest finds from the city dump in a courtyard filled with children. Tightly packed tenements and streets piled high with refuse were breeding grounds for deadly microbes. On the Lower East Side of New York nearly 1000 people dwelled on every acre of land in 1894, each of them a powerful transmitter of disease to family and neighbors.

Slum dwellers, often living on subsistence diets, were especially susceptible to epidemics. Cholera, typhoid, and a nasty outbreak of yellow fever in Memphis at the end of the 1870s killed tens of thousands. Tuberculosis was even deadlier. As late as 1900, among infectious diseases it ranked behind only influenza and pneumonia *combined* as a killer. Slum children—in fact all city children—as well as migrants from American farms who had little previous exposure to diseases were the most vulnerable. Infant mortality in cities was twice that of rural areas. In 1882 only half of the children born in Chicago could expect to reach the age of five, and almost a quarter of all children born in American cities in 1890 died before their first birthday.

The installation of new sewage and water purification systems helped. The modern flush toilet came into common use after the turn of the century. Until then water closets and communal privies, some catering to as many as 800 people, served the purpose. All too often cities dumped waste into old private vaults or, worse, into local rivers used for drinking water. In 1881 an exasperated mayor of Cleveland called the Cuyahoga River "an open sewer through the center of the city." The stench rising from open privies, from alleys filled with garbage, and from stagnant water, said a resident of one city, was "enough to knock you down."

Slum housing was often as dangerous as the water. An early tenement like New York's Gotham Court, built in 1850, was little more than a five-story barracks, 234 feet long and 34 feet wide, wedged between two alleys. Half the rooms of this "unventilated and fever breeding structure," as one observer called it, had no windows at all. The tubercle bacillus flourished. In 1879 New York enacted a new housing law, which required a window in all bedrooms of new tenements. Architect James E. Ware won a competition with an innovative design that contained an indentation at the middle of each side of the building. When the indentations of two tenements abutted each other, a shaft about five feet wide was formed. It furnished a small measure of air and light for interior rooms and made each building look like a giant dumbbell from above.

Originally hailed by reformers as a major improvement, Ware's dumbbell tenement spread over such cities as Cleveland, Cincinnati, and Boston "like a scab," said one disgruntled city dweller. Squeezed onto lots barely 25 by 100 feet, the dumbbell had as many as eight stories. Each contained 14 rooms divided into four apartments. Up to 16 families lived on a floor, which had but two toilets in the hall. With 10 tenements to a block, ordinary streets housed as many as 4000 people.

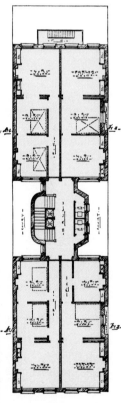

SECOND STORY.

"Dumbbell" tenements were designed to use every inch of available space in the standard 25 by 200 foot city lot while providing ventilation and reducing the spread of disease.

Overcrowding soon turned the reform into a dangerous blight. The much-vaunted airshafts became giant silos for trash, which blocked what little light had formerly entered, and carried fires from one story to the next. In 1890 Jacob Riis estimated that three-fourths of his poverty-stricken "Other Half" lived in tenements. When the New York housing commission met in 1900, after 33 years of tenement legislation, it concluded conditions were worse than when reformers started.

RUNNING AND REFORMING THE CITY

Those running the new industrial cities struggled to develop a more efficient way to govern their diverse populations. Many city charters dating from the eighteenth century included a cumbersome system of checks and balances. Mayors, city councils, and state legislatures checked each other so often that it was difficult to get anything done. The mayor vetoed the council; the council ignored the mayor. Jealous state legislatures allowed cities only the most limited and unpopular taxes, such as those on property. But to the cities more than the states fell the responsibility for providing services. Municipal government grew into a tangle of little governments—fragmented, dispersed, often at odds with one another. By 1890, Chicago had 11 branches of government, each a powerful fiefdom with its own hierarchy, regulations, and taxing authority. By the early twentieth century New York City had 1400 separate agencies.

At the very moment when such decentralization increasingly paralyzed cities, schools had to built, streets paved, garbage collected, sewers dug, fires fought, utility lines laid. The middle and upper classes, sources of political leadership for generations, were being drawn into business and moving to the suburban fringes, where they lost interest in governing the city (though not in how the city was governed). Meanwhile the dizzying pace of change left residents little time for planning. "Even the present," wrote Theodore S. Case in his 1888 history of Kansas City, "is more than they can keep up with."

Boss Rule

"Why must there be a boss," journalist Lincoln Steffens asked Boss Richard Croker of New York, "when we've got a mayor—and a city council?" "That's why," Croker broke in. "It's because we've got a mayor and a council and judges—*and*— a hundred other men to deal with." In other words, the boss and his system furnished cities with the centralization, authority, and services they so sorely needed.

Bosses ruled through the political machine. Often, like New York's Tammany Hall, the machines dated back to the late eighteenth and early nineteenth centuries as fraternal and charitable organizations. Over the years they became centers of political power, shifting their concern from the voting rights of the propertyless to the voting habits of immigrants. In New York the machine was Democratic; in Philadelphia, Republican. Some were less centralized, as in Chicago; some less ethnically mixed, as in Detroit. But wherever they appeared they both served and exploited the community.

The political machine bore a striking resemblance to the corporation. Like a corporate executive, the boss looked on politics as a profession and treated it as a business. His office might be a saloon, a funeral home, or, as in the case of George Washington Plunkitt, a shoeshine stand. His managers were party activists, arranged in a hierarchy with local committeemen reporting to district captains, captains to district leaders, and district leaders to the boss or bosses who ran the machine. Like a businessman, the boss sought to harmonize the competition or destroy it. His machinery was power and money; his workers, the party hacks; his consumers, the voting public.

The stock and trade of the machine was simple: a Christmas turkey, a load of coal for the winter, flowers for the sick, legal assistance and help with the authorities. "I think that there's got to be in every ward somebody that any bloke can come to—no matter what he's done—and get help," said Boston ward leader Martin Lomasney. *"Help, you understand; none of your law and justice, but help."* Bosses sponsored fun too—ball teams, glee clubs, torchlight parades, ward balls, and joy rides up the river with bands playing and drink flowing, even nursing bottles for the tiny ones. "You can't do nothin' with the people," said William Devery after organizing a joyride up the Hudson River for 10,000 of his New York constituents, "unless you do somethin' for 'em."

This crude welfare system not only won votes for machine-sponsored candidates; it also served as a form of public philanthropy. Private charities proved unable to cope with the crush of urban despair. By helping people, bosses also offered a path for advancement to the least privileged and a method of Americanization for the most foreign. To the unskilled, the boss doled out jobs in public construction. For bright, ambitious young men, he had places in city offices or in the party itself. These represented the first steps into the middle class. Help came in more basic forms too—English-language classes, guidance at the polls, speedy naturalization—which began to turn foreigners into grateful citizens.

It was votes that bosses really wanted. They went to almost any lengths to get them. William Tweed, whose ring ruled New York briefly in the 1860s and 1870s, streamlined the process of naturalization. His ward leaders filled out applications for citizenship, then had judges running for reelection sign them—up to 1000 a day. Every day 1000 new Americans became 1000 new supporters of Boss Tweed. "Little Bob" Davies of Jersey City was adept at mobilizing the "graveyard vote." He drew names from tombstones to pad lists of registered voters and hired "repeaters" to vote under the phony names. Democratic boss "Hinky Dink" Kenna of Chicago's First Ward liked to get his fraudulent names from the Hospital for the Insane at Dunning. Dunning inmates, he said, were more astute than Republican voters.

When reformers introduced the Australian (secret) ballot in the late 1880s to prevent fraud, bosses pulled the "Tasmanian dodge," premarking the election ticket to assure the vote went their way. Failing that, they dumped whole ballot boxes into the river or drove unpersuaded voters from the polls with gangs of barroom thugs. In an age when men alone had the right to vote, the most fearsome election day terrorists were women hired to intimidate opponents' voters: Euchre Kate Burns, the champion female heavyweight brick hurler of New York; Battle Annie, the ferocious leader of the Battle Row Ladies Social and Athletic Club; and Hell-Cat Maggie, who filed her front teeth to points and wore long artificial nails of brass. When she went tearing through the polls, nails clawing and teeth flashing, even the bravest citizen fled.

Why did bosses go to such lengths? Some, like "Honest" Ed Flynn of the Bronx, simply loved the game of politics. More often bosses loved money. Their ability to get it was limited only by their ingenuity or the occasional success of an outraged reformer. The record for brassiness must go to Boss Tweed. During a reign of barely a dozen years, Tweed bilked New York City out of millions of dollars. His masterpiece of graft was a chunky three-story courthouse in lower Manhattan originally budgeted at $250,000. When Tweed was through, the city had spent over $13 million—and the building was still not finished. Each window, consisting of a wooden frame, glass, and a small awning, was worth $12.50; each cost the city $8000. For carpeting valued at $13,000, the bill came to $350,000. The New York *Times* estimated that 65 percent of the total went back to the Tweed Ring. Tweed died in prison, but with such profits to be made, it is no wonder that bosses rivaled the pharaohs of ancient Egypt as builders.

In their fashion bosses played a vital role in the industrial city. Rising from the ranks of those they governed, they guided immigrants into American life and helped some of the underprivileged escape poverty. They forged a massive construction program that changed the urban landscape. Most of all they modernized city government by uniting it and making it perform. Choosing the aldermen, municipal judges, mayors, and administrative officials, bosses exerted new control that allowed them to provide the contracts and franchises needed to run cities.

The price was often outrageous. Inflated taxes, extorted revenue, unpunished vice and crime were only the obvious costs. A woman whose family enjoyed Plunkitt's Christmas turkey might be widowed by an accident to her husband in a sweatshop kept open by timely bribes. Filthy buildings might claim her children, as corrupt inspectors ignored flagrant violations. Buying votes and selling favors, bosses turned democracy into a petty business—as much a "business," said Plunkitt, "as the grocery or dry-goods or the drug business."

The Social Conscience of the City

Urban blight and the condition of the poor, particularly the immigrant poor, inspired social as well as political activism, especially within the churches. Some ministers told their middle-class flocks that poverty resulted from weak character and a lack of morality. Others, like the popular Congregationalist minister Josiah Strong, simply concluded the city was "a menace to society." Along with a host of anxious economists and social workers, these church leaders blamed the trouble on new immigrants and urged restrictions on their entry. In the 1880s and 1890s nativist organizations like the American Protective Association and the Immigration Restriction League attacked Catholics and other non-Protestant newcomers. In 1897 the first bill requiring literacy tests to reduce immigration passed Congress, but President Grover Cleveland vetoed it.

Other clergymen took their missions to the slums, bridging the distance between the middle class and the poor. They became the social conscience of the city. Beginning in 1870 Dwight Lyman Moody, 300-pound former shoe salesman, joined gospel singer and organist Ira David Sankey to win armies of lowly converts with revivals in Boston, Chicago, and other cities. Evangelists helped to found American branches of the British Young Men's Christian Association and the Salvation Army. By the end of the century the Salvation Army had grown to 700 corps staffed by some 3000 officers. They ministered to the needy with food, music, shelter, and simple camaraderie.

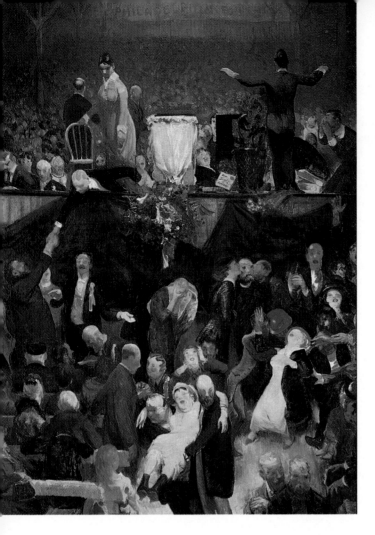

A small group of ministers rejected the old ethos that personal guilt explained sin and turned to a new "Social Gospel." They believed individual salvation would come through the betterment of society, not the other way around. The influential Congregationalist minister Washington Gladden in *Applied Christianity* (1886) and other books spread the word that the church was responsible for performing good social works. Souls could be saved only if the bodies that contained them were first well fed, housed, and clothed. Charles L. Sheldon, a minister from Topeka, Kansas, asked readers of his best seller *In His Steps* (1896) to follow the lead of the charitable citizens of the fictitious town of Raymond. When confronted with the social ills of poverty, drunkenness, and slum life they asked themselves, "What would Jesus do?" Houses of worship, such as William Rainford's St. George's Episcopal Church in New York, became centers of social activity with boys' clubs and gymnasiums, libraries, glee clubs, and industrial training programs.

Church-sponsored programs often repelled the immigrant poor, who saw them as thinly disguised missionary efforts. Immigrants and other slum dwellers were more receptive to a bold new experiment called the settlement house. An agency of social reform imported from Great Britain (which had begun to grapple with the problems of the industrial city earlier in the century), the American settlement house first appeared on the Lower East Side of New York in 1886. Situated in the worst slums, these early community centers were run by middle-class women and men to help the poor and foreign-born. At the turn of the century there were over 100 of them, the most famous being Jane Addams' Hull House in Chicago (1889). In 1898 the Catholic church sponsored its first settlement house in New York, and in 1900 Bronson House opened in Los Angeles to aid the Hispanic community.

High purposes moved settlement workers. Leaving comfortable middle-class homes, they moved into the settlement houses. They dedicated themselves (like the "early Christians," said one) to service and sacrifice. They sought to teach new immigrants American ways and to create a community spirit that would foster "right living through social relations." Like political bosses, they helped, providing everything from day nurseries to playgrounds and libraries. Armed with statistics and personal experiences, they also entered the world of politics, lobbying for social legislation to regulate tenement housing, the working conditions of women, and the improvement of schools.

As they set about their work, settlement workers never lost sight of practicality or the humanity of their clients. Immigrants were to be made American, but they were also to be encouraged to preserve their heritages through festivals, parades, and museums. If the blight of the cities could be ended, decency, creativity, and wholesomeness would go a long way. "The delicious sensation to be found in a swimming pool," Jane Addams wrote, would doubtless outweigh the temptation "to play craps in a foul and stuffy alley."

CITY LIFE AND CULTURE

Settlement workers and other middle-class reformers offered Americans a startling look at the underside of the city, but a grand view of life at the top was available to anybody who strolled along Nob Hill in San Francisco, the North Shore of Lake Michigan near Chicago, or the Main Line outside Philadelphia. In New York, architect Richard Morris Hunt and the firm of McKim, Mead & White transformed Fifth Avenue into the most spectacular residential showplace in the country. William H. Vanderbilt's $11 million mansion on the corner of Fifty-First Street was actually three palaces under one roof. Just down Fifth Avenue was his grandfather's mansion, a limestone replica of a French château.

Few saw the insides with their gold walls, carvings, and Renaissance tapestries, their staircases and ceilings (in some cases ripped from medieval castles and shipped across the Atlantic). No matter—new, mass circulation newspapers gave anybody who wanted it a peek at the socially prominent. Before the Civil War, James Gordon Bennett, publisher of the New York *Herald*, pioneered journalistic voyeurism with lurid tales of what went on behind the potted palms at fancy dress balls. By the 1880s most newspapers had society pages. The upper crust of New York was a prime topic even in small cities like Mobile, Alabama. In 1889 its local paper devoted almost an entire issue to the 282 marriageable ladies of the Social Register, complete with their personal and financial assets. Under the guise of "news," high-toned city life invaded even the provinces of America.

The Urban Middle Class at Home

Between the top and the bottom stretched the vast and ill-defined middle of urban society—educated professionals, white-collar clerks and salesmen, shopkeepers,

Daily Lives

CLOTHING AND FASHION

Gender Roles and Fashions in the 1890s

At Chicago's vast Columbian Exposition of 1893, the Women's Building displayed the latest fashions of an industrial nation. A stunning new simplicity ruled, and the audience liked it. Dresses had less bulk. Skirts were shorter, waists wider and less confining. Shoes tipped at gentler angles on shrunken heels. As the models glided through the hall, women expressed "their great desire to be free from the bondage of skirts," one surprised journalist reported; "—women, too, who would, one would suppose, rather die in long skirts than let the world know they had legs." That same year the *Ladies Home Journal*, a respected women's magazine, proclaimed the female right to choose clothing for comfort. This was not quite a revolution in fashion, but it did signal a significant change, not only in what women were wearing but also in the roles they were playing in American society.

Through most of the nineteenth century Victorian convention dictated middle-class standards in women's dress. Strenuously laced steel-and-bone corsets pushed breasts up, stomachs in, and derrières out. The "Good Sense" corset waist even came in sizes to fit children. The resulting wasplike figure accentuated the image of women as procreators. So did outward apparel. Ankle-length skirts were draped over bustles, hoops, and petticoats—all of which made hips look larger, to suggest fertility. Wide-brimmed hats and high-heeled shoes stressed a delicate femininity. This complicated style bespoke wealth, status, and proper modesty, setting off middle- and upper-class women from those below, whose often shapeless

figures and plain clothes signaled drudgery and poverty.

Such elegance was cumbersome and sometimes debilitating. Corsets ("an instrument of human torture," one woman called them) constricted movement, circulation, and breathing. Internal organs pressed unnaturally against each other. Ribs occasionally cracked; uteruses sagged. Fainting spells and headaches were all too common. High collars, whether of satin or linen, chafed and choked. Yards of pleats could cake with ice in winter or overheat the wearer in summer. The sheer size of a full skirt, observed one women, meant "the wearer had to bunch it in great folds and devote

Daily Lives

one hand to nothing else but the carrying of it." With petticoats the costume weighed as much as 30 pounds. These clothes were designed for little except restricting the women who wore them.

Victorian morality gave men greater leeway in fashion as in conduct. At home they were figures of authority; outside they were free to make their way with few social encumbrances. Clothes, with the exception of stiff paper collars on shirts, expressed male independence. The dark suit coats and full, cuffless trousers afforded ample comfort. A paunchy waist, prominently displayed, signified success. For "dandies," there were checkered pants, floral waistcoats, and heavy gold watch chains.

In the 1840s health reformers and liberal educators had begun to attack women's dress. Feminists like Susan B. Anthony and Elizabeth Cady Stanton abandoned their corsets and donned "bloomers"—long-sleeved, high-necked, loose tunics worn over baggy trousers. Few women followed their lead, but by the 1890s new social and economic forces made simpler styles more acceptable. Health reformers continued to press their case, adding a new emphasis on the need for women to exercise more. New sports that included women became popular: ice-skating in the 1850s; croquet in the 1860s; and bicycling, the most vigorous of all, in the 1880s. Tennis and golf caught the fancy first of the wealthy and, after the turn of the century, of the middle class. All demanded greater movement and the clothes to make it possible.

As more women entered college and went to work, they grew impatient with convention. Women began to associate plainer dress not with the poor or with radical feminists but with new and appealing role models like college students, office clerks, and sports enthusiasts. Fashion became more sensible, reflecting the needs of these new women. Looser and lighter undergarments replaced corsets and bustles. "Shirtwaist" blouses (styled after men's shirts), skirts to the ankle, tailored suits, and lower heeled oxfords made getting to and from the office easier and work once there more efficient.

Meanwhile a revolution in the manufacture of clothing was quietly taking place. Before the Civil War, most garments were made at home. A ready-made–clothing industry had already begun to develop, but it specialized in refinishing castoffs and making only the cheapest grades of new clothes for sailors, slaves, and miners. Steady improvements on the sewing machine, along with the army's demand for uniforms during the Civil War, boosted sales and led to a new science of sizing. The development of cutting machines, pressers, and buttonholers allowed "ready-made" clothes to increase the range of styles offered in volume. In 1890 the value of factory-made clothing for women was under a third that of men's wear. But by 1914 it had soared to half a billion dollars, $20 million more than men's.

Ready to wear or not, newer styles failed to catch on immediately. Novelist Edna Ferber remembered that neighbors in her hometown of Appleton, Wisconsin, disapproved of her mother wearing shirtwaists and shorter skirts in the 1890s. Skirts generally remained long until World War I, and most women put on some kind of corset until the 1920s. Yet greater comfort was here to stay, and so were new roles for women.

corporate managers and executives, public employees, and their families. The earnings of the middle class had risen nearly 30 percent between the Civil War and the 1890s. By the turn of the century just over a third owned their homes. Often two or three stories in height, made of brick or brownstone, these suburban row houses stood within easy reach of new streetcars that could whisk residents to downtown business and shopping districts.

Houses of the nineteenth century served a variety of functions. The top floor of bigger homes contained a modest ballroom that doubled as a family room; in smaller homes it became a sewing room or a guest room for boarders. On the story below were the bedrooms and on the bottom floor, the living room, dining room, pantry, and kitchen. The most notable innovation of the household was the bathroom. Usually there was only one, so bedrooms still contained old-fashioned washstands. But new central heat gave urban bathers the luxury of no longer having to break through the ice that once covered washbowls on wintery mornings.

Technology had its greatest impact on the kitchen. More than any other room, it was a blend of tradition and progress. A "combination" stove (which could be fired by wood or coal if the gas failed) dominated the room. The "refrigerator," a newer and larger version of the old icebox, stood in the pantry, a telltale drip pan betraying its continued reliance on ice. Despite the likely presence of gas jets or electric lighting by the end of the century, a row of candles and kerosene lamps stood ready for use. Many middle-class homes had servants to do the cooking, laundry, and cleaning. According to one estimate about 25 percent of urban households had live-in servants. On call about 100 hours a week, off but one evening and part of Sunday, the average maid received room, board, and $2 to $5 a week in salary.

A woman was measured by the state of her home, which experts said shaped her family. "A clean, fresh, and well-ordered house," stipulated domestic adviser Shirley Murphy in 1883, "exercises over its inmates a moral, no less than physical influence, and has a direct tendency to make members of the family sober, peaceable, and considerate of the feelings and happiness of each other." The woman of the house was expected to prepare elaborate meals, clean, launder, and sew. Each took considerable time. Baking bread, for example, required nearly 24 hours from start to finish. In 1890, when bread was widely available at bakeries and grocery stores, four of five loaves were still made at home.

By the 1890s a cornucopia of commercially prepared foods eased some of the burdens of housework. Brand names began to appear, trumpeting a new age of convenience through consumerism—Campbell's soup, Quaker oats, Pillsbury flour, Jell-O, Canada Dry ginger ale, and Cracker Jacks, just to name a few. New appliances such as "self-working" washers and hand-pumped "vacuum" cleaners offered mechanical assistance, but shredded shirts and aching arms testified that mechanization was sometimes more trouble than it was worth.

The day had already begun to assume its modern form. Families rose early, and to the sound of a mechanical alarm rather than the crow of a rooster. City breakfasts were less hearty but more varied than country fare. Oatmeal and farina supplemented eggs, chops, and other meats. After breakfast the household dispersed. Children walked to grammar school or rode trolleys to high school. Fathers

Processed food labels for tin cans, ca. 1880.

commuted on streetcars to their places of business downtown. Mothers oversaw the domestic routine. The greatest boon to their mornings was the demise of the big noonday dinner. Husbands took their lunches at restaurants or saloons, and children ate at school. A quick cold meal of sandwiches, chicken, or leftovers sufficed for mother, maid, and any preschoolers at home.

Married women of the middle class were supposed to use their free time "to keep up intellectually, to look young and well and be fresh and bright." Lollie Osborn, a homemaker who lived near New York City, spent the winter of 1895 improving her mind "at Literature class," "at reading class at Lizzie Simonds," and "at Astronomy." Outside of literary clubs some women read uplifting religious novels like Lew Wallace's *Ben Hur* (1880) or popular "romances," frowned upon because of their titillating themes. Mrs. E. D. E. N. Southworth, the best-selling woman novelist of the nineteenth century, had heroines who were invariably strong, manipulative, and sensual. They defied contemporary mores through affairs of the heart and an occasional murder of passion.

A middle-class homemaker could also "go downtown" to shop or lunch with a friend. She might spend her afternoons doing needlepoint, an acceptable diversion because it combined the old virtues of housewifery with the new interest in arts and crafts. Or she could curl up with one of the new women's magazines such as the *Ladies Home Journal* for hints on dress, cooking, and home decorating and advice on health and manners.

The family reassembled at the end of the day for supper, a full meal of fish or roast meats, potatoes, canned and fresh vegetables, and breads, followed by a new treat from the refrigerator for dessert—ice cream. Nobody stayed long at the table to chat. Young girls raced to the porch steps to visit friends; boys went off for a game of baseball or "leap-frog"; fathers hurried to lodge meetings or sat smoking cigars and reading newspapers in the den or living room (either of which they could have completely to themselves); mothers cleaned up, then perhaps played the piano or looked at new three-dimensional slides through "magic lanterns." Increasingly, family members found themselves separated from each other and in the company of people their own age. Only on weekends did the routine vary. Toward the end of the nineteenth century, Saturday became less of a workday and more of a family day. Sunday mornings remained a time for dressing up and going to church, still an important center of family life. Afternoons had a more secular flavor with shopping trips (city stores often stayed open) and visits to lakes, zoos, and amusement parks (usually built at the end of trolley lines to attract more riders). In towns and villages, where the pace was slower and living less diversified, Sunday afternoons might offer only dinner and naps or reading, followed by another church service in the evening. In one form or another, outside institutions—fraternal organizations, uplift groups, athletic teams, and church groups— began to intrude on middle-class urban family life.

Victorian Mores

Taking its name from from the long-reigning British queen, Victorianism—a disciplined and prudish code of personal conduct—dictated middle-class behavior. It stressed sobriety, industriousness, self-control, and modesty, all designed to tame a turbulent urban-industrial society. When working-class Americans failed to follow middle-class cues, cultural reformers preached directly to them. In 1874

Frances Willard, fearing the corrosive effects of alcohol on the family, founded the Women's Christian Temperance Union. Under her leadership the WCTU worked relentlessly against the consumption of alcohol and for sexual purity and other middle-class virtues. At the turn of the century it had enlisted 500,000 members and was the largest women's organization in the country.

Anthony Comstock crusaded with equal vigor. A self-appointed custodian of public virtue, Comstock began in 1871 a 41-year campaign against obscenity that led to some 3600 arrests. His targets varied from the despicable to the harmless. In one two-year period he reported seizing 130,000 pounds of vice-ridden books, 194,000 pictures and photos, and precisely 60,300 "articles made of rubber for immoral purposes and used by both sexes." In 1873 President Ulysses S. Grant signed the so-called Comstock Law, a statute suppressing trade and circulation of "obscene literature and articles of immoral use." Two days later Comstock went to work as a special agent for the Post Office.

Crusaders like Comstock were not simply missionaries of a stuffy morality. They were apostles of a middle-class creed of social control and discipline. Inspired by their fear of disorder in an interdependent urban society they believed that the road to ruin lay behind the door of every saloon, dance hall, gambling parlor, or bedroom. And given the increasing incidence of alcoholism, venereal disease, gambling debts, unwanted pregnancies, divorce, industrial accidents, and other ills, moralists had cause for alarm. If taken to extremes either by individuals or society at large, such social pathologies could easily produce chaos and violence in the teeming cities of the late nineteenth century.

The insistence with which moralists warned against impropriety suggests that many people did not take their message to heart. Three-quarters of women surveyed toward the turn of the century reported that they desired and enjoyed sex. If some women did not, said physician Elizabeth Blackwell, they probably feared pain, injury from childbirth, or awkward sexual encounters.

Bold women challenged convention openly. Victoria Woodhull, publisher of *Woodhull & Claflin's Weekly*, divorced her husband, ran for president in 1872 on the Equal Rights party ticket, and pressed the case for sexual freedom. "I am a free lover!" she shouted to a riotous audience in New York's Steinway Hall. "I have the inalienable, constitutional, and natural right to love whom I may, to love as long or as short a period as I can, to change that love every day if I please!" While she made a public case for freedom of sexual choice, in private she followed convention. Like other social radicals, Woodhull believed in strict monogamy and romantic love for herself, just as middle-class readers of romance novels did.

Feminist writer Charlotte Perkins Gilman, author of *Women and Economics* (1898), disputed the ideals of womanly purity, domesticity, and idleness. After suffering a crippling depression in 1885 she wrote *The Yellow Wall Paper*, a fictionalized account of her illness that compared the confinement of a mental patient with the lot of a wife. For Susan B. Anthony sexual politics boiled down to female disfranchisement. She rallied women to demand the vote through the National American Woman Suffrage Association (1890). Despite such telling attacks on conventional behavior, most Americans heeded the message of the traditional moralists in spirit, if not in deed.

School Days

Public education was another powerful tool for imposing order and control on the city. The campaign for public education begun in the Jacksonian era did not have a serious impact until after the Civil War. As late as 1870 half the children in the country received no formal education at all. The average citizen had taken only four years of classes, and one in five Americans could not read. Then a great educational awakening occurred, as business required better educated workers and the number of compulsory state-supported school systems grew.

Attendance in public schools more than doubled between 1870 and 1900. The length of the school term rose from 132 to 144 days. Illiteracy fell by half. At the turn of the century, nearly all the states outside the South had enacted compulsory education laws. Almost three out of every four school-age children were enrolled. Yet an ordinary adult still had attended for only about five years, and less than 10 percent of those eligible ever went to high school.

The average school day started early, but by noon most girls were released (the assumption being they required less formal education than boys). Curricula stressed fundamentals—reading, writing, and arithmetic—but courses in manual training, science, and physical education were added as the demand for technical knowledge grew and opportunities to exercise shrank. In the classroom teachers had absolute control. Students learned by rote, sitting in silent study with hands clasped or standing erect while they recited phrases and sums. "Don't stop to think," barked a Chicago teacher to a class of terrified youngsters in the 1890s, "tell me what you know!"

A rigid social philosophy underlay the harsh discipline. In an age of industrialization, massive immigration, and rapid change, school curricula taught conformity and values as much as simple facts and figures. Teachers were supposed to be drillmasters, hammering their charges into shape for the sake of society. "Teachers and books," wrote New Jersey College Professor John L. Hart in 1879, "are better security than handcuffs and policemen." In *McGuffey's Reader*, a standard textbook used in grammar schools throughout the nineteenth century, students learned not only how to read but also how to behave. Hard work, Christian ethics, and obedience to authority would lead boys to heroic command, girls to blissful motherhood, and society to harmonious progress.

African-American students had to deal with the special problems of discrimination and segregation. As the federal commitment to Reconstruction faded, so did the impressive start made in public education for blacks. Yet they were so eager for education that by the end of the century nearly half of black America could read. It was a remarkable achievement, for most of the first generation of former slaves had been illiterate. Worse still, for nearly 100 years after the Civil War, the doctrine of "separate but equal," finally upheld by the Supreme Court in *Plessy v. Ferguson* (1896), kept black and white students apart but scarcely equal. By 1882 public schools in a half dozen southern states were segregated by law, the rest by practice. Underfunded and ill-equipped, serving dirt-poor families whose every member had to work, all-black schools drew only about a third of the South's black children.

Like African-Americans, many immigrants saw education as a way of getting ahead, while some educators saw it as a means of Americanizing immigrants. "Education," declared a New York principal, "will solve every problem of our national life, including that of assimilating our foreign element." Few public schools paid special attention to immigrants. Educators assumed that immigrant and native-born children would learn the same lessons and turn out the same way. But toward the end of the century, as immigration mounted, eastern cities began to offer night classes in English and civics for foreigners. When public education proved inadequate or failed to address their needs, immigrants established their

own schools. Catholics, for example, started an elaborate expansion of their parochial schools in 1884. Public or private, the education of immigrants served the
same purpose: teaching fundamentals while promoting citizenship through wholesome values. "The first step in civilization," wrote Father Paul Tymkevich of the
Greek Catholic church, "is to acquire good habits, and where can they acquire
them? On the streets? In the saloons?"

School was obviously the place, and by the 1880s educational reforms were
already promoting "good habits" and marketable skills. A number of reforms came
from Germany, already a center of innovation. Opened first in St. Louis in 1873,
American versions of "kindergartens" put four- to six-year-olds in orderly classrooms while parents went off to work. "Normal" or teacher-training schools multiplied, so that in 1900 almost one teacher in five had a professional degree. Science
and manual training supplemented more conventional curricula. Such vocational
studies supplied industry with better educated workers and also helped to control
them by reducing union influence over apprenticeship. By 1890, 36 cities had
vocational high schools.

College Years

Increasingly colleges served the urban industrial society, not by controlling mass
habits but by providing a corps of leaders and managers. Early in the nineteenth
century, most Americans had regarded higher learning as effete and irrelevant. Of
the few who sought higher education, many preferred the superior universities of
Europe to those in the United States. As American society became more organized, mechanized, and complex, the need for professional, technical, and literary
skills brought greater respect for what colleges could teach. The Morrill Act of
1862 generated a dozen new state colleges and universities, eight mechanical and
agricultural colleges, and six black colleges.

Private philanthropy added more. In 1873 Johns Hopkins, who had acquired
part of his fortune from ownership of the Baltimore and Ohio Railroad, bequeathed $7 million to found the university that bore his name. John D. Rockefel-
ler reestablished the University of Chicago (1890), while railroad baron Leland
Stanford endowed Stanford University (1891) with $24 million. The number of
colleges and universities nearly doubled between 1870 and 1910. Their enrollments swelled to a third of a million. At that time the 16 universities of France had
40,000 students, a figure that roughly equaled the number of faculty of American
institutions.

The "college man" enjoyed new respect as universities flourished. Small-
town boys and girls admired him and children's novels like *Frank Merriwell at
Yale* celebrated his exploits. No longer depicted as a wastrel or bookworm, he was
now informed and virile. The upper middle class had a new ideal—the educated
rogue in a ribbed turtleneck sweater. At his side, the envy of all to see, was a new
phenomenon—the "co-ed." Before the Civil War women could attend only three
private colleges. After the war they had new ones for themselves, among them
Smith (1871), Wellesley (1875), and Bryn Mawr (1885). Many land-grant colleges,
chartered to serve all people, admitted women from the start. By 1910 some 40
percent of college students were women, almost double the 1870 figure. Only one
college in five refused to accept them.

Potent myths continued to make college life hard for women. As Dr. Edward
Clarke of the Harvard Medical School told thousands of students in *Sex in Educa-*

tion (1873), the rigors of a college education could lead the "weaker sex" to physical or mental collapse, infertility, and early death. Women's colleges therefore included a stringent program of physical activity to keep students healthy. In addition to an academic curriculum similar to that of the best men's schools, women found an array of conventional courses in "domestic science" available to them. Pioneered in the 1870s by coeducational schools, they were developed to counter the claim that higher education would be of no value to most women. The first of these "Ladies Courses" had been a series of lectures on cooking offered by the wife of the president of Iowa State College. Eventually they included sewing and the application of chemistry to foods. Some women's colleges such as Bryn Mawr resisted, but 18 land-grant colleges, mostly in the West, had organized departments of home economics by 1905.

The practical impulse in higher education inspired several new black colleges. In the late nineteenth century, few institutions mixed races and most refused the rare African-American applicant who sought admission. Church groups and private foundations, such as the Peabody and Slater funds (supported by white philanthropists from the North), underwrote black schools after Reconstruction. By 1900, when a total of 700 black students were enrolled, about 2000 had graduated from college. Some, through hard work and persistence, had even graduated from institutions generally considered reserved for whites.

By the turn of the century, higher learning, though pursued by less than 5 percent of college-age Americans, extended more and more beyond college. In keeping with the new emphasis on practical training, professional schools multiplied. American universities adopted the German model requiring young faculty members to perform scholarly research as part of their training. The number of medical schools more than doubled between 1870 and 1900; the number of medical students almost tripled. Ten percent of medical students were women (a peak enrollment that soon shrank as the medical profession became more organized and exclusive). The number of law schools (a uniquely American development) jumped from 51 in 1880 to 102 in 1900, while schools of nursing grew by 300 percent. New professionals swelled the ranks of the middle class. Slowly the professional was becoming a new force in the society of urban America, replacing the ministers and gentlemen freeholders of an earlier day as community leaders.

Palaces of Consumption

In the city, middle- and working-class urbanites had access to a new material culture that was leveling and homogenizing American society. In the eighteenth century clothes signaled status. As sewing machines became household items in the nineteenth century, common people began wearing garments that fit them and made them look more like the well-to-do. The demand for hundreds of thousands of uniforms during the Civil War encouraged mass manufacturing, and new immigrants skilled at the needle trades supplied the labor. A revolution in clothing substituted store-bought "ready-made" garments for those manufactured at home or consigned to high-priced tailors. By 1890 millions of boys and men dressed in "ready-to-wear." Similar shifts affected the food people ate and the furnishings in their homes.

Young girl selling newspapers in New York, ca. 1895.

Well-made, inexpensive merchandise in standard sizes and shapes found outlets in new palaces of consumption called "department stores" (so named because they displayed their goods in separate sections or departments). The idea was imported from France, where shopping arcades had been built as early as the 1860s. Unlike the small exclusive shops of Europe, department stores were palatial, public, and inviting. Rising several stories, like the Cast Iron Palace of A. T. Stewart in New York, they were usually found in central business districts, where they were easily accessible by streetcars and other public conveyances.

A trip to the department store offered a day's entertainment. In addition to shopping, patrons found restaurants, dance floors, and beauty salons. Most of the new stores had intricate facades that sometimes duplicated Venetian palazzos. There were large plate glass windows filled with enticing merchandise that invited strollers to participate in the new pastime of "window shopping." The wide, unbroken interiors, painted in soft colors, imparted a dreamlike quality to rooms with appealing displays of furniture, housewares, and clothing.

Retailers did not rely on their stores alone to woo customers. From the start they publicized their wares in daily newspapers. Under the impact of new printing techniques and aggressive publishers such as Joseph Pulitzer, newspapers broadened their coverage, sought out sensational "news" stories, and increased their circulation. The advertisements of department stores contributed to their success and also helped to keep them free of the political subsidies that prejudiced newspapers in France and Italy. Between 1870 and 1900 the amount of money spent on advertising quadrupled.

Emile Zola, the French novelist and crusading journalist, observed that department stores "democratized luxury." Anyone could enter free of charge, handle the most elegant and expensive goods, and buy whatever was affordable. When consumers found goods too pricey, department stores pioneered "lay-away" plans, which allowed for deferred payments. Free delivery and free return or exchange of purchases helped to make buying and selling a public affair built on policies offered to all, not just the favored customers of exclusive fashion makers. The department store also educated people. It showed them models of what proper families owned and taught them the correct names for things like "women's wear" and "parlor furniture." Mass production, along with massive advertising campaigns, was beginning to produce a mass culture.

Slowly popping up in city after city, "chain stores" (a term coined in America) served a similar function but without frills. They catered to the working class, who could not afford department stores, and operated on a "cash-and-carry" basis. Owners kept their costs down by buying large quantities to fill the small stores in their long neighborhood chains. The Great Atlantic and Pacific Tea Company, founded in 1859, was the first. It gradually added other groceries to its list of teas. By 1876 there were 76 A & P branches, all featuring the distinctive red-and-gold facade. F. W. Woolworth opened his first "5-and-10-cent" store in 1879. In the twentieth century such centrally operated chains would drive local merchants out of business.

Rural Americans, far from department and chain stores, joined the community of consumers by mail. From a loft over a livery stable in Chicago, Aaron Montgomery Ward started sending a price sheet to farmers in 1872. By cutting out the middleman Ward promised savings of 40 percent on fans, parasols, needles, trunks, harnesses, cutlery, and scores of other goods. In 1884 his catalogues boasted 10,000 items, each illustrated by a lavish woodcut. Country folk came to rely on Ward for almost all their needs, even things he could not possibly supply. "As you advertise everything for sale that a person wants," one faithful customer reasoned, "I thought I would write you, as I am in need of a wife, and see what you could do for me."

Similarly, Richard W. Sears and Alvah C. Roebuck built a $500 million mail order business by 1907. In the early 1900s Sears, Roebuck was distributing 6 million catalogues every year. Schoolrooms that had no encyclopedia used a Ward's or Sears' catalogue instead. Children were drilled in reading and spelling from it. They learned arithmetic by adding up orders and geography by studying the postal zone maps. When asked where the Ten Commandments came from, one farm boy replied without hesitation that they came from Sears, Roebuck.

Americans were already beginning to think of themselves as consumers, even as machines and factories weakened the old work ethic of individual productivity. Reaching out from city to countryside, a vast community of consumption was growing. Rural free delivery of mail, standardized by the Post Office in 1898, and the inauguration of parcel post in 1913 made everyone's home a potential marketplace. Increasingly city businesses sold the same goods to farmer and clerk, rich and poor, native-born and immigrant. Common patterns and articles of consumption bound up the nation as never before.

Arts and Entertainment

People in cities turned leisure into a consumer item, spending time and money in new ways. While churchgoing remained a primary leisure activity, hundreds of new fraternal, business, civic, and patriotic organizations sprang up. Members paid annual dues to a special fellowship that reduced the anonymity and isolation of urban life and furnished important contacts in the community. Sports, traditionally the province of the rich, slowly broadened their appeal. The recently imported English game of tennis attracted new players at country clubs but few in public parks. Most people regarded it as a game for women and frail men. Polo and golf, which required expensive equipment, considerable space, and some training, were also limited to the country-club set.

Croquet had wider appeal, since it required less skill and special equipment. Perhaps as important, it could be enjoyed in mixed company, like the new national craze of bicycling. Bicycles evolved from the unstable "ordinary" with its large front wheel to the "safety" bike, which had equal-sized wheels, a dropped middle bar, pneumatic tires, and coaster brakes. By the early 1890s, Americans owned more than a million bicycles (a good one cost about $100, far beyond the reach of a factory worker). On Sunday afternoons city parks became crowded with cyclers, and cycling clubs such as the League of American Wheelmen began lobbying for better roads.

More and more women rode the new safety bikes along with the earlier tricycles. Their participation was governed by elaborate rules, including a strict proscription against riding alone. But cycling broke down conventions too. Inevitably it required looser garments, freeing women from corsets. Lady cyclists demonstrated that they were hardly too fragile for physical exertion. Tandem bikes encouraged couples to ride together. In 1896, at the height of the fad, one enterprising manufacturer even brought out an unadorned black bicycle for widows in mourning.

Mannered sports of the wealthy and middle class had their counterparts in organized spectator sports that attracted crowds from every walk of life. Baseball overshadowed all others. For city dwellers with dull work, cramped quarters, and isolated lives, baseball offered the chance to join thousands of people for an exciting outdoor spectacle. In the 1890s it was attracting crowds of 60,000. Like roller skating, baseball began as a fashionable exercise played in natty blue trousers and straw hats, attended by ladies and gentlemen in stylish coaches, and followed by a formal dinner. Boston teamsters soon confirmed its status as a "democratic" sport of amateurs by scheduling games on the Common before work.

Slowly the game took its modern form: in 1869 the first professional team, the Cincinnati Red Stockings, appeared; umpires called balls and strikes; the overhand replaced the underhand pitch; fielders put on gloves and catchers, protective gear; lively experimental balls that produced scores of 201 to 11 were abandoned. Newspapers began covering baseball in specialized sports sections with detailed statistics for fans. Teams from eight cities formed the National League of Professional Baseball Clubs in 1876, followed by the American League in 1901. In 1903 the Boston Red Sox beat the Pittsburgh Pirates in the first World Series. League players were distinctly working class, with few of the high salaries of today's professionals. When the players tried to unionize and form their own league, owners beat them back.

Horse racing, bicycle tournaments, and other sports of speed and violence helped to break the dullness, frustration, and routine of the industrial city. In 1869, without pads or helmets, Rutgers beat Princeton in the first intercollegiate football match. By the 1890s the service academies and state universities fielded teams. But not everyone cheered. Cornell University forbade its team from playing the University of Michigan. "I will not permit 30 men to travel 400 miles," said President White in 1873, "to agitate a bag of wind." Despite protests against rising death tolls (18 players died in 1905), football soon attracted crowds of 50,000 or more. Then, beginning in 1891 when Dr. James Naismith nailed a peach basket to the gymnasium wall at the Y.M.C.A. Training School in Springfield, Massachusetts, "basketball" became the indoor interlude between the outdoor sports of spring and fall.

Variety also marked social life in the city. Workingmen took their dates to dance halls and boxing exhibitions, staged in small rings used for variety acts between fights. Wealthier couples went to theaters and symphonies. A "star system," developed long in advance of Hollywood, promised audiences their favorite actors. Popular melodramas gave theatergoers a chance to escape the ambiguities of modern life. The audience booed villains, cheered heroes, shuddered for heroines, and marveled at tricky stage mechanics that made ice floes move and players float upward to heaven. Whatever was happening on the street, virtue and honor triumphed at every performance of Harriet Beecher Stowe's *Uncle Tom's Cabin* and Augustin Daley's *Under the Gaslight*, the two biggest attractions at the end of the century. Even "serious" theater, such as the tragedies of Shakespeare, furnished excitement—swordplay, gasping deaths, and gloriously anguished monologues.

Cities put together symphony orchestras, expert ones in New York and Chicago, half-professional and half-amateur ones in smaller cities. To appeal to broad audience tastes, the orchestras played a mixture of popular tunes, John Philip Sousa marches, and the music of classical European composers. Theatergoers with lighter tastes relished weak American imitations of operettas by Gilbert and Sullivan and home-grown vaudeville revues. Touring companies bringing city culture

The catcher wears no mitt in this 1875 painting of two baseball players, by Thomas Eakins. Eakins, a master of realism, shocked his staid faculty colleagues at Philadelphia's Pennsylvania Academy of Fine Arts by working from live nude models and by painting scenes and portraits that, while insightful and penetrating, did not always flatter their subjects.

to small towns caused such excitement that crowds gathered at the train station to greet them.

In towns and cities a stunning assortment of music filled the air. Organ grinders churned out Italian airs on street corners; steam-powered calliopes tooted spirited waltzes from amusement parks and riverboat decks; in bandstands brass ensembles played German-style concerts of the latest compositions of Patrick Gilmore. By 1900 the sale of phonograph records had reached 3 million, helping to make popular music a big business. Ballads like "My Mother Was a Lady" ran to nostalgia, moralism, and sentimentality. Topical songs celebrated the discovery of oil, the launching of baseball's National League, and the changing styles of women's clothing. In Scott Joplin's "Maple Leaf Rag" (1899) the lively syncopation of ragtime heralded the coming of jazz.

As the nineteenth century drew to a close the city was reshaping the country, just as the industrial system was creating a more specialized, diversified, and interlocking national and even international economy. Most Americans were ambivalent about this process. The old Jeffersonian bias against cities warred with the gospel of material progress and wealth that cities so dramatically embodied. Cities beckoned migrants and immigrants with unparalleled opportunities for work and pleasure. The playwright Israel Zangwill celebrated the city's transforming power in his 1908 Broadway hit *The Melting Pot*. "The real American," one of his characters explained, "is only in the Crucible, I tell you—he will be the fusion of all the races, the coming superman."

Where Zangwill saw a melting pot with all its promise for a new super race, champions of traditional American values like the widely read Protestant minister Josiah Strong saw "a commingled mass of venomous filth and seething sin, of lust, of drunkenness, of pauperism, and crime of every sort." Economist David A. Wells, alarmed at rising rates of heart disease and mental illness, bemoaned what he called these "diseases of civilization." "Never was there, perhaps, more hollowness of heart than at present, and here in the United States," wrote poet Walt Whitman. The gap between rich and poor yawned most widely in cities. Progress and poverty, as Henry George observed, seemed to go hand in hand.

Both the champions and critics of the late nineteenth century had a point. Corruption, crudeness, and immorality were no more or less a part of the cities than the vibrancy, energy, and opportunities that drew people to them. In the end moral judgments, whether pro or con, missed the point. Forces much deeper than individual vices and virtues gave cities their new form. Integrated systems of transportation, manufacturing, communications, capital accumulation, and the mass distribution of goods and culture had cities as their indispensable nodes. Those cities grew so rapidly, and in such an unplanned, helter-skelter fashion, that their disorderliness threatened the operation of the very systems that helped to bring them into being.

Somehow the political system had to find within the traditions of a democratic republic a way to bring order out of this seeming chaos. More would be needed than Jacob Riis' moralistic warnings to the privileged few to observe the desperate plight of "the Other Half." People divided by wealth, race, ethnicity, religion, region, social class, age, cultural habits, and gender had somehow to be shaped into a coherent whole. The arbitrary rule of the bosses would have to give way to government that met the industrial order's need for efficiency, the public's need for services, and the need of the poor for compassion, all at a price society could afford. Since Americans could not agree that modern urban life was desirable in the first place, they would have great difficulty finding any way to make their cities work.

SIGNIFICANT EVENTS

1869 — Cincinnati Red Stockings become first professional baseball team; Rutgers beats Princeton in first intercollegiate football game

1870 — Elevated railroad begins operation in New York City

1871 — Fire destroys most of Chicago

1872 — William "Boss" Tweed convicted of defrauding city of New York

1873 — Comstock Law enacted

1874 — Women's Christian Temperance Union founded

1875 — Dwight Moody begins urban evangelical revivals

1876 — First National League baseball game; Central Park completed in New York City; Johns Hopkins University opens nation's first graduate school

1879 — F. W. Woolworth opens first "5-and-10-cents" store

1882 — Chinese Exclusion Act

1883 — Brooklyn Bridge opens

1885 — Home Life Insurance Building, world's first skyscraper, built in Chicago

1886 — Statue of Liberty dedicated

1887 — Edward Bellamy's *Looking Backward, 2000–1887* published; free mail delivery in all communities with 10,000 or more people

1888 — Nation's first electric trolley line begins operation in Richmond, Virginia

1889 — Hull House opens in Chicago

1890 — Jacob Riis' *How the Other Half Lives* published

1891 — Basketball invented

1892 — Ellis Island opens as receiving station for immigrants

1893 — World's Columbian Exposition in Chicago

1894 — Immigration Restriction League organized

1896 — *Plessy v. Ferguson*

1897 — Boston opens nation's first subway station

Generations of the Republic

The Family in an Urbanizing Culture (1860–1920)

The generation born after 1860 lived in an America suspended between two worlds, one urban and the other rural. By the end of the nineteenth century, nearly half of all Americans dwelled in cities, contrasted with only 20 percent in 1860. The urban middle class became firmly established, and for the first time in American history agricultural workers made up less than half of the labor force.

Following a pattern set earlier in the century, the rate of population growth continued to decline. Traditionally birth rates had been highest along the frontier, where abundant land represented opportunity for succeeding generations and so encouraged fertility. As the frontier slowly receded, birth rates fell: the average number of children born to a white woman was 5.2 in 1860; by 1890 it was 3.9. High infant mortality kept most families even smaller, usually to about 3 children.

This decline was widespread: it not only affected virtually all classes, races, and ethnic groups but touched other Western nations as well. Historians speculate that the change reflected the impact of a rising urban middle class, maturing industrial economies, and changing ideals of the family. For middle-class families, reducing family size made sense, given the premium on urban dwelling space and the opportunity to improve their own material lives by raising fewer children. Higher birth rates among immigrants and working-class urbanites remained common, but in time even these families began to shrink as they improved their status, spent more money on educating their children, and sent fewer of them to work at a young age. Despite declining birth rates, the nation as a whole remained young. The population pyramid retained its classic shape—wide at the youthful base and narrower toward the elderly top.

The experiences of those growing up in the new urban environment differed widely, in large measure depending on class and economic status. The parents of the new urban middle class viewed families as havens, away from the bustle of the city's business district, its sooty factories, and the threat of strikes and labor violence. Chaos might reign in the industrial city, but orderliness, tranquillity, and hierarchy ruled the Victorian home. Seventeenth-century notions of children as inherently sinful had given way to greater optimism about their capacity to be shaped. By the late nineteenth century

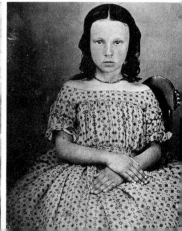

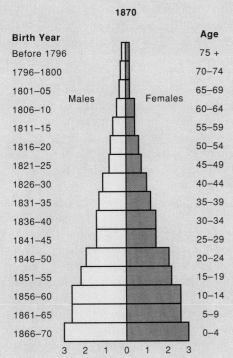

1870

Birth Year		Age
Before 1796		75 +
1796–1800		70–74
1801–05	Males Females	65–69
1806–10		60–64
1811–15		55–59
1816–20		50–54
1821–25		45–49
1826–30		40–44
1831–35		35–39
1836–40		30–34
1841–45		25–29
1846–50		20–24
1851–55		15–19
1856–60		10–14
1861–65		5–9
1866–70		0–4

3 2 1 0 1 2 3

As middle- and upper-class youngsters reached the age of courtship, they faced increasingly elaborate rituals. Sixteen was the recommended age for young women to start "keeping company" with men, though they could begin as early as fourteen. Flirting was an accepted means for women to seize the romantic initiative normally reserved for men. New leisure activities such as roller skating and bicycle riding gave couples acceptable ways to hold hands in public or be alone together. The new urban culture also offered women greater opportunity to be self-supporting than their mothers and grandmothers had. As a result, more than one woman in ten never married, the highest proportion in American history. (Among college-educated women the percentage was even higher.) "I don't want to be married," a young schoolteacher told her beau. "I can take care of myself."

Men had responsibility for proposing marriage and, once accepted, an obligation to seek the approval of their fiancées' father. Since the prospective husband was expected to support his wife and children, he had to outline his financial prospects. Women remained subordinate, and once engaged they were expected to obey their betrothed as they had their father. They also were to remain pure and innocent until marriage, whereupon they were advised to control the "lower natures" of their husbands by cultivating their own supposed indifference to sex. Despite this

clergy and child experts were advising parents that "bad habits" resulted from improper training, not innate depravity.

Thus children required gentle nurturing, usually at the hands of the mother. It began in infancy with a new emphasis on breast-feeding. As children grew, "reason and affection" were the favored tools for training. Parental advisers now condemned the practice of wrapping babies tightly, viewing swaddling clothes as "so many bonds by which [the baby] is restrained of the natural freedom of its body."

advice, so often tendered by marriage manuals of the day, middle-class Americans became more conscious of sexuality as an emotional dimension of a satisfying union, not merely a function to be performed for the purposes of procreation. The stereotype of the frigid, repressed Victorian marriage is at best overdrawn.

Middle-class weddings were often lavish affairs, with printed invitations for the larger ones. Gifts were often displayed on the day of the marriage and enviously inspected by the guests. Around 1870, when the cost of photography dropped, wedding portraits became popular. Taken well after the ceremony, they usually commemorated the bride alone. Also by the 1870s, a growing railroad network helped spawn a new institution—the honeymoon resort. Hotels at Saratoga and Niagara Falls, New York, greeted new couples with band music and offered special honeymoon suites to make memorable the interlude between courtship and married life.

The gritty realities that confronted urban working classes made any talk of family "havens" or elaborate weddings somewhat fanciful. Most families moved frequently, in search of work, and lived in cramped quarters. To supplement family incomes as many as 30 percent took in boarders, usually unmarried men and women between the ages of 20 and 35. (In some cities, nearly half the immigrants who arrived toward the end of the century had boarders in their homes.) In such households mothers took responsibility for child rearing, often working outside the home as well to help support the family. The consequence of such pressures could be grim. Gertrude Moselle, a black journalist in New York writing a column of advice to women, warned working mothers against the practice of drugging their children or locking them in closets to keep them out of mischief while the mothers were absent.

In the "family economies" of the working classes, key decisions—over whether and whom to marry, over work and education, over when to leave home—tended to be made on the basis of collective rather than individual needs. Though boys were more likely to work than girls, daughters in immigrant families often went to work at an early age so sons could continue their education. It was customary for one daughter to remain unmarried so she could care for younger siblings or aged parents. Young men and women generally worked for seven years before marrying and often did not establish their own households until their early thirties.

The rise of urban centers even affected family lives in rural areas, as a larger proportion of young farm men were drawn to the opportunities in the city. By the second or third generation of settlement many farming communities consisted of close networks of female kin, since daughters often married neighbors

and set up house near their parents. The bonds of family and kinship were equally strong among African-Americans, the vast majority of whom lived in the southern countryside. Black families had existed in slavery, though with restrictions on visitation for slave couples belonging to different masters and with constant threats of separation by sale. The strength of such attachments became clear after the Civil War when thousands of former slaves wandered the South in search of spouses, siblings, and children separated by sale or war. As late as 1900, so many ex-slaves were seeking relatives that one Virginia newspaper created a special section—"Do You Know Them?"—to satisfy the demand for information.

Beginning in the 1880s, in both rural and urban settings, American mortality rates began gradually declining. (There were notable exceptions among African-Americans; see page 938.) In cities, the decline resulted from a host of factors: the coming of purer water, better access to medical care, pasteurized milk, and—by the early twentieth century—improvements in sewage systems. As a result of the drop in mortality, the population grew steadily older. By 1900 about 6.5 percent of all Americans were 60 or older, compared to 4 percent in 1860. Still, with so few members of society reaching old age, no fixed policy toward retirement existed in most businesses. Voluntary retirement did increase. In 1920 some 60 percent of

men 65 and older continued to work, down from the 75 percent who had worked in 1870. The growth of the factory system helped to account for the decline by accelerating retirement among workers who could not keep pace. Those who continued to work often found themselves moved from assembly lines to lower-paying janitorial jobs.

Poverty among the aged increased. As late as 1922 no state had enacted a workable old-age pension system, despite recognition (dating from around 1910) that old age was becoming a social problem. By 1930 one elderly American in four was dependent on some form of assistance. Most relied on savings or help from families, but many found themselves in asylums and state poorhouses, the majority of whose populations were 65 or older. Not until 1935 did Congress enact a national pension program in the Social Security Act, at least 50 years later than most European countries. Even then its provisions and support were limited. Society still held that individuals were responsible for themselves, whatever their age.

In their declining years this generation saw America assuming its characteristic twentieth-century shape, in which the urban middle classes achieved a dominant social position. Births were becoming less frequent, and the population was steadily growing older and more diverse. Modern America was coming of age with the passing of this generation.

20

Agrarian Domains:
The South and the West

he news spread across the South during the late 1870s in a variety of ways: sometimes merely as rumors, passed by word of mouth in the cotton fields. Perhaps a man came around with a handbill, telling about cheap land to be had. Or it might be in a letter from friends or relatives, read aloud to the congregation at church. The news spread in different ways, but in the end, the talk always spelled *Kansas*.

Few black farmers had been to Kansas themselves, of course. But more than a few knew that Old John Brown had lived there before coming east to launch his famous raid on Harpers Ferry. Kansas was a state where it seemed black folk might be able to live more freely. "You can buy land at from a dollar and a half to two dollars an acre," wrote one settler to his friend in Louisiana, also noting another distinct advantage. "They do not kill Negroes here for voting." *The Colored Citizen*, a newspaper in Topeka, received so many inquiries that it printed advice on how to travel and where to settle, concluding, "COME WEST. COME TO KANSAS." Even more enticing were the chromoliths—colored promotional handbills showing "freedman's homes" with floor-length French windows, living rooms with young children playing the piano, black mothers directing a host of servants in the kitchen and fathers hauling home turkeys and deer from the verdant prairies.

In 1878 such prospects excited hundreds of black families already stretched to their limits by economic hardship and political violence. With Rutherford Hayes president and Reconstruction officially superseded by white "redemption," the future in the South seemed uncertain indeed. Henry Adams, founder of the Negro Union Co-operative Aid Association in Louisiana, sent 150 members of his organization across the South to study the plight of ordinary blacks. By 1877 he had concluded that migration out of the South was the best solution available. But there were individuals aplenty who needed no committee to come to that conclusion. "Colored people are looked upon by the white people with disdain and scum," one black farmer from Texas complained. "I have suffered the bukes and scums long enough down South here."

St. Louis first learned of these rumblings in the first raw days of March 1879, as steamers from downriver began unloading unusual numbers of freedmen. Some came with belongings and money; others had little more than the clothes on their

Blasting away with pressurized water jets, miners loosen gold-bearing gravel. Such techniques damaged the environment in the rush to exploit western resources. The artist, Mrs. Jonas Brown, lived in Idaho City during the height of its gold rush.

backs. While the weather was still cold, they sought shelter beneath tarpaulins along the river levee, built fires by the shore and got out frying pans to cook their meals while their children jumped rope nearby. By the end of April over 6,000 had arrived; by the end of 1879, over 20,000. When the crowds became too much for the wharves and temporary shelters, the city's black churches banded together to shelter the "refugees," feed them, and help them continue toward Kansas. The news that rail passage would not be free, as many rumors had it, did not shake their almost millennial faith in their mission. "We's like de chilun ob Israel when dey was led from out o' bondage by Moses," one explained, referring to the exodus from Egypt across the Red Sea. "Dis is our Red Sea, right hyah in St. Louis, atween home an' Kansas, an' if we sticks togeder an' keeps up our faith we'll git to Kansas and be out o' bondage for shuah." So the "Exodusters," as they became known, pressed onward.

Adjusting to the new land was often not easy, any more for black emigrants than for whites. Both northerners and southerners were accustomed to forested country, where lumber was plentiful for building houses and for cooking. The Exodusters were not prepared for the harsh Kansas winters either. "Kansas has the roughest wind you ever run across in *your* life," commented one; another was dismayed to find that cotton did not flourish in prairie soil. "If I were back home I might get in a crop of cotton; but I cannot make enough here." Those who did manage to settle on farms met with the hatred of cattlemen whose herds grazed the prairies. One settler from Nicodemus, an early black colony, wrote the governor of Kansas, begging him to "please get rede of the Catel we are so rounded with the hured [herders] do not care for us."

In the end, more black emigrants settled in the growing towns like Topeka, Lincoln, or Kansas City. Men might get jobs as hired hands, while the women worked as washerwomen. With luck, couples made $350 a year, saved a bit of it for a home, and put down roots. Bill Sims, an emigrant who settled in Ottawa, Kansas, put down roots literally—working at tree husbandry for a living. When his wife died, he promised her on her deathbed that he would educate their two daughters. By the 1930s, when he was in his nineties, he could boast that his oldest had been the "first colored girl to ever graduate" from Ottawa University; his other daughter had become a schoolteacher. And on the courthouse grounds at the center of town, the trees he had planted years before were still standing.

Sims and the host of Exodusters who poured into Kansas were part of a more general flood westward. In 1879, as blacks traveled up the Mississippi to St. Louis, a thousand white emigrants arrived in Kansas every week. Special trains brought settlers to the plains, all eager to start anew, whether they were farmers from Pennsylvania or Russian Mennonites newly emigrated. During the 1870s, Nebraska's population increased from 123,000 to over 450,000; during the 1880s the number of Kansans jumped from a million to a million and a half. "We have plenty of room for all creation," boasted a newspaper in Olathe, Kansas.

Yet the spirit of boosterism and hope could not mask serious strains in the rapidly expanding nation, especially in the South and West. The boom economies of cotton, cattle, and grain all depended on urban markets. The market for cotton lay with the textile mills of New England (and, increasingly, the "New South"), while the demand for beef and western grains came from metropolitan centers. Especially during hard times, westerners and southerners saw themselves as the victims of a colonial economic system, in which their fortunes were controlled by the industries of the Northeast. Like colonial subjects of European imperialists, the West and South exported inexpensive raw materials and imported more expensive manufactured goods. And as rural people, they found themselves alienated from a culture that was increasingly urban.

The more rural South and West were also marked by the conflicts of race and ethnicity, just as the centers of industry had been. The racism of these regions provided the rationale for creating a society based on caste; violence offered one means to establish and sustain it. The Exodusters of 1879 had left the South in large part because of the increasing violence of white "Redeemers." On the western ranges racism took the form of open warfare between whites and Indians, whose cultures clashed directly. (The cowboys, after all, could not have expanded their rangeland farther west so long as the Indians' wild cattle—the buffalo—dominated the grazing lands of the Plains.) Against Hispanics, Asians, and African-Americans, whites adopted a mixture of physical intimidation, segregation, and other legal mechanisms that denied minorities the rights of citizens.

As the two regions became tied more closely to the industrial Northeast, the tensions and imbalances between the regions subjected the national political system to stresses even in boom times. Drought, exhausted mines, overcut timberlands, and overproduction in cattle and grain demonstrated the limits of the regions' economies. The inevitable adjustments were often wrenching.

THE SOUTHERN BURDEN

In the era following Reconstruction a faith in economic progress flourished in the South. Propagandists for this ideal, led by Henry Grady of the Atlanta *Constitution*, envisioned a "New South" based on bustling industry, cities, and commerce. The business class and its values would displace the old planter class as southerners raced "to out-Yankee the Yankee." Yet while Grady spread the gospel of laissez-faire capitalism and economic diversity, no amount of hopeful rhetoric could change the economic structure of the South as an agrarian society. As late as 1890 the census counted less than 10 percent of all southerners as urban dwellers, compared to more than 50 percent in the North Atlantic states. The South had not only fewer large cities but also fewer small towns, which had become an important source of economic diversification in the Midwest.

Even more relevant to the South's problems, its antebellum economy had depended largely on slave labor. In 1860 the value of slaves in the five cotton states—Alabama, Louisiana, South Carolina, Georgia, and Mississippi—had amounted to 60 percent of all agricultural wealth, whereas the value of farmlands and buildings amounted to less than a third. In Harrison County, Texas, for example, a typical slaveholding family owned $10,000 worth of property in slaves, three times the value of their land and buildings. This fundamental fact ensured that slaveholders tried to concentrate their wealth in slaves, not land, which often seemed almost disposable. Planters would clear new fields, plow them, exhaust them in a few years, and move on in search of new profits rather than settling down, as prosperous northern farmers did. Not only the larger "cotton lords" but smaller operators too carried their wealth in slaves. A farmer who owned only three slaves had a greater investment in his human property than the average nonslaveholding farmer had in all his assets combined.

Thus while northern society in the 1840s and 1850s was building canals and rail links, developing towns that would serve surrounding farms and drive up land values, southerners were accumulating comparatively little wealth in land, factories, buildings, or transportation facilities. The railroads and canals that did exist tied staple crop areas to ports rather than opening the back country to economic development. The southern economy that emerged from the Civil War was therefore decentralized, isolated, and agricultural.

Certainly publicists like Henry Grady were right about the South's potential. The region extending from Delaware south to Florida and west to Texas and Oklahoma took in a third of the nation's total area, a third of its arable farm lands, two-thirds of the land with over 40 inches of rainfall each year, vast tracts of lumber, and rich deposits of coal, iron, oil, and fertilizers. But to overcome the devastation inflicted by the war and the loss of wealth based on slaveholding, southern entrepreneurs needed to wage a major campaign to catch up with the rest of the nation. Indeed, they did better than popular myth would suggest. In rates of growth for urban areas, as well as for mining, textiles, lumber, and railroad building, the postwar South equaled or surpassed other regions of the country.

Still, the South lagged far behind. The war had abolished slavery, but it had not wiped out the inferior status of blacks, who continued to receive distinctly lower wages for their labor than did northern or western workers. This economic hardship not only worked a disservice to blacks, but it depressed the wage scale for the region as a whole. Despite all its natural and human resources, the South remained the poorest section of the United States well into the twentieth century. It was the low-wage market that unified the experience of blacks and whites who were otherwise separated by caste and culture.

Cotton in the New South

One barrier to economic development arose from continued reliance on agricultural staples like tobacco, rice, sugar, and especially cotton. Although southerners had boasted that cotton was king in the region and nation during the 1850s, between 1870 and 1900 the number of acres planted in cotton more than doubled. In a turnabout, as the use of fertilizers increased, the crop spread eastward into areas that had once been considered marginal for cotton.

In good years, southern farms were more profitable than those in other regions. But from 1880 to 1900 the world demand for cotton grew at only about 2.7 percent per year, so prices fell. Even as cotton farmers worked to increase their productivity, they lost ground. While farms in other parts of the country were becoming larger, more efficient, and tended by fewer workers per acre, the average size of a southern farm fell. This partly reflected the breakup of large plantations before the war, but it also was caused by a continued high birth rate in the South. In other regions of the country, the number of children born per mother was dropping, but in the South, the continuing large family size meant that fewer acres of land were available for each person to cultivate. Thus even though the southern economy kept pace with national growth, per capita income fell behind. Before 1900, the South prospered in only a few pockets, such as South Carolina's fertilizer regions, Birmingham's steel industry, and areas of Kentucky, North Carolina, and Virginia that benefited from a rise in tobacco prices.

Some southern farmers sought roads to prosperity other than cotton. George Washington Carver, of Alabama's Tuskegee Institute for blacks (page 786), persuaded many poor farmers to plant peanuts. But most southern soils were too acidic and the rains too heavy in the spring for grains and legumes to flourish. Corn and other food crops offered a hedge against poor cotton prices, but they brought in no cash. Parasites and diseases plagued cattle herds, reducing weight and milk yields. Work animals like mules were raised more cheaply in other regions. As much as southerners might seek alternative sources of income, cotton still dominated the region's economic life. "When southern cotton prices drop, every man feels the blow," one observer commented; "when cotton prices advance, every industry thrives with vigor."

Sharecropping

Emancipation during the Civil War had brought to John Solomon Lewis and other former slaves not only freedom from servitude, but hopes of economic independence. In the era after the war Lewis rented land to grow cotton in Tensas Parish, Louisiana. The devastations of war followed by the severe depression of the 1870s dashed his hopes. "I was in debt," Lewis explained, "and the man I rented land from said every year I must rent again to pay the other year, and so I rents and rents and each year I gets deeper and deeper in debt."

Lewis' lament expressed the plight of small farmers both black and white in the cotton South. The South's best lands remained in the hands of large plantation

---

"Forty acres and a mule" had been the dream of newly freed slave families at the end of the Civil War; sharecropping or tenant farming was more often their lot. At least 'croppers had the advantage of living in cabins much closer to the fields they worked. This scene was sketched in 1901 by H. T. West.

The Geography of the Postwar South

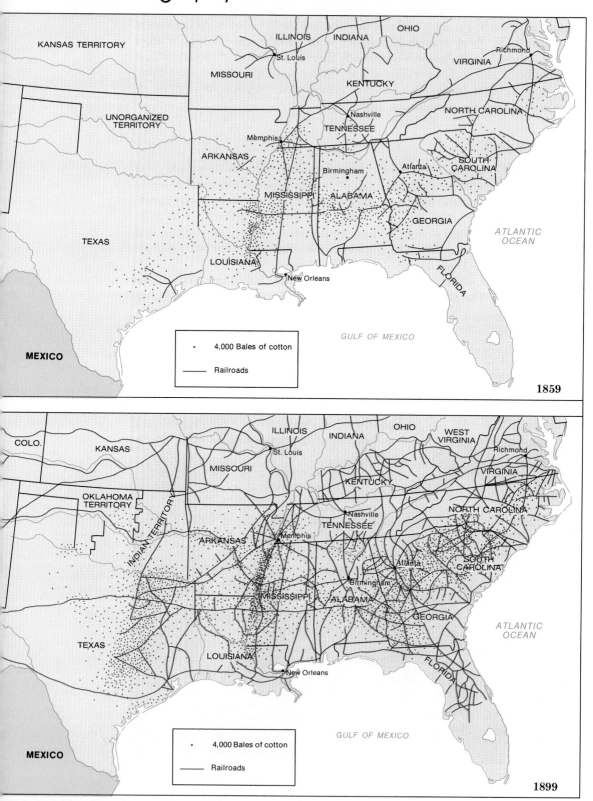

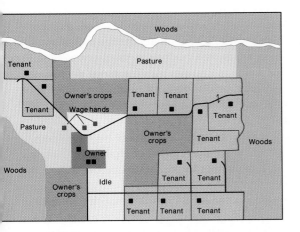

In 1860 slaves accounted for nearly 60 percent of the agricultural wealth in the cotton states stretching from South Carolina to Louisiana. The value of farm lands and buildings amounted to less than a third. Emancipation changed all that. With slaves no longer "property" that could be controlled or moved at will, land itself became an important measure of worth. Southern planters and farmers who had once been "labor lords" became landlords to whom property now meant land. This shift was reflected in the geography of the postwar South.

Railroads increased the value of land by opening up interior markets; after the Civil War, southerners eagerly participated in the nationwide railroad boom, in marked contrast with the pre-war years. By 1890 (see maps at left) an enlarged rail network was well established. Cotton production also rose sharply. In southeastern regions, where soils had been thought "exhausted," fertilizers increased output. Farther west, more intensive use of labor increased per acre yields. In both cases, greater crop volume enhanced the value of land, to the advantage of farmers and planters alike.

As the new agricultural system stabilized after 1880, large landowners divided their holdings into plots that they worked for themselves, bringing in wage laborers who lived in quarters the owners provided (see map at left) and land that they rented to tenants or sharecroppers. On the one hand, wage laborers allowed landowners the flexibility of bringing in workers for peak harvesting seasons, then laying them off later; on the other hand, sharecroppers and tenants, having signed a yearly contract, provided the security of knowing someone would be there to work the land. Because wage laborers had to travel from farm to farm in order to continue working, they tended to be young, single males. Sharecroppers and tenants were usually families who preferred to stay in one place.

Shortages of capital needed to establish independent farms made tenantry the dominant pattern in southern agriculture after the war (see map below). But notice that by 1900 tenantry accounted for much of the farm labor in areas of the trans-Mississippi West settled under the generous terms of the Homestead Act of 1862. There, too, low crop prices, the heavy cost of land and equipment, and severe environmental conditions forced independent farmers into tenantry.

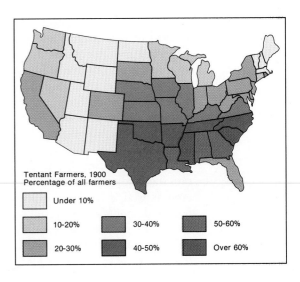

Tentant Farmers, 1900
Percentage of all farmers

Under 10%
10-20%
20-30%
30-40%
40-50%
50-60%
Over 60%

owners. Those owners had little cash to pay wages for farm labor. And only a few among the land-hungry freedmen or poor whites had the wherewithal to acquire land of their own. So, like Lewis they rented, and like Lewis they saw their debts pile up. The average tenant in the Deep South from Alabama to Texas seldom had more than 15 to 20 acres. Since cotton was king and money scarce, rents were generally set in pounds of cotton rather than in dollars. Usually the amount added up to about one-quarter to one-half the value of a farmer's annual crop. If a tenant was lucky enough to find a generous planter, or if an area had a shortage of tenant farmers, or if the tenant had tools and farm animals of his own, then the terms of the rent might be less burdensome.

This system of farming on shares, or sharecropping, would not have proven so ruinous if the South had possessed a more equitable system of credit. But before they could sell their crop in the fall, farmers without cash had to borrow money in the spring to buy their seeds, tools, and other necessities. The only source for those supplies in most areas of the South was the local store. When John Solomon Lewis and other tenants entered the store they saw two prices, one for cash and one for credit. The credit price might be as much as 60 percent higher, in effect a 60 percent interest charge. By contrast, merchants in New York City seldom charged their customers more than 6 percent to buy on credit. The only asset most sharecroppers could offer as security was a mortgage or lien on their crops. This meant in turn that the shopkeeper rather than the sharecropper had first claim on the crop until the debt was paid off, a practice that was known as the crop–lien system.

Many planters recognized that running a store was a way to increase profits. They would rent the land and then sell the goods needed to farm. At the same time storeowners without land often held mortgages on nearby farms. As farms failed, the merchants took them through foreclosure, thereby becoming large landholders themselves. Most tenants found they were twice indebted: they owed part of the crop to the landlord and the remainder to the shopkeeper—more often than not the same person.

The combination of sharecropping and crop liens led to debt peonage. Economic dependence robbed the small farmers of their freedom. The landlord–shopkeeper could insist that sharecroppers devote their efforts solely to producing profitable crops rather than foodstuffs. In the post–Civil War South that almost always meant cotton, which yielded more value per acre than any other crop. Instead of raising corn and hogs, sharecroppers had to use credit to buy food imported from the Midwest. One observer noted that Louisiana farmers "had not as much as twenty-five to fifty dollars cash money (about the value of one 400- to 450-pound bale) at the end of any one year. That they always, at the owner's mode of settling, was in his debt. Yet, they did not even have half enough to eat or scarcely anything to wear."

The problems of ginning and marketing made matters worse. Few areas had more than a single cotton gin, so that no price competition existed. Most landlords insisted that tenants bring raw cotton to their mills to be ginned and baled, at a rate the landlord set himself. And most landlords claimed the right to market the crop as well, which was especially onerous to black sharecroppers. "The white people do not allow us to sell our own crops," blacks regularly remarked. "When we do, we do it at risk of our lives, getting whipped, shot at, and often some get killed." Or as one disgruntled farmer complained, "We had to carry the cotton to the gin of the man who owned the land we rented, and he would take it all from us." Though statistics show that blacks were economically better off in freedom than in slavery, sharecropping, crop liens, and monopolies on ginning and marketing added up to inequality and crushing poverty for the South's small farmers.

Southern Industry

By the 1880s many southerners came to believe that industrialization was the only way the South could shed its yoke of poverty. The gospel of the New South swept some localities with the fervor of a religious camp meeting. By soaking up unemployed agricultural labor, new industries would become as much social as business enterprises. "People were urged to take stock . . . for the town's sake, for the poor people's sake, literally for God's sake," one writer explained.

In many ways the crusade for a New South was crowned with success. Southern industrial production from 1869 to 1909 grew faster than the national rate. So did productivity for southern workers. A boom in railroad building after 1879 furnished the region with a good transportation network. The number of industrial workers tripled (209,000 to 600,000), as did the value of manufactures.

In two areas, cotton textiles and tobacco, southern advances were especially striking. Aided by easy access to cotton fiber and abundant cheap labor, 161 cotton mills were in operation by 1880. That number jumped to 400 by 1900, with the mills employing almost 100,000 workers. Local custom dictated that most textile workers be whites, drawn from the ranks of poorly paid agricultural wage earners escaping the competition of blacks, or mountain folk escaping the poverty of poor soils. Many mills employed entire families, though it soon became clear that older men used to working outdoors in a rhythm dictated by the sun and seasons lacked the temperament demanded to tend spindles and looms. But over time, as southern farm folk were socialized to the monotonous rhythms of indoor factory work for wages, they became competitive with workers from other regions of the United States and western Europe.

The tobacco industry also thrived in the New South. Before the Civil War American taste in tobacco had run to cigars, snuff, and chewing tobacco. By the 1880s popular taste in the North shifted to a new product, cigarettes. (Southern men tended to consider them effeminate.) James Bonsack had coincidentally in-

Textile production was critical to the industrial expansion of the New South. Most mill towns attracted entire families, almost all of them white. Conditions were generally cramped, noisy, and unsafe. These women at the White Oaks Mills in Greensboro, North Carolina, are measuring and sewing denim.

vented in 1880 a machine that made it possible to roll vast numbers of cigarettes at low cost. The growing popularity of smoking was reflected in the rate of annual tobacco consumption, which soared from 1.5 pounds per person in 1860 to 5.5 pounds in 1900. Americans spent more money on tobacco than on clothes or shoes. The health consequences of the new fad would not become evident until nearly a hundred years later.

The sudden taste for smoking offered southerners a rare opportunity to control a major national market. But the factories were so hot, the smells so strong, and the work so unskilled that whites generally refused the jobs. James Buchanan Duke solved the labor problem by hiring Russian Jewish immigrants to train local blacks in the techniques of tobacco work. Then he adopted the Bonsack machine to mechanize cigarette rolling. A vigorous national advertising campaign and ruthless use of promotional gimmicks allowed Duke to destroy or buy out his competitors. By 1890 he had built his American Tobacco Company into a major trust that dominated the industry.

The Colonial South

Jobs in textiles and tobacco paid better wages than agricultural labor and thus formed the basis of industrial growth. These industries also encouraged urbanization and investment of capital for regional development, but they could not by themselves lift the region from poverty. Both reflected the prevailing low-wage pattern of southern agriculture rather than the higher wage patterns of the industrial Northeast and upper Midwest. During the same period when the heavy flood of immigrants was expanding both work forces and markets in other sections of the nation, low wages discouraged immigrants from settling in the South. Isolated from the international labor pool, the southern labor force grew almost exclusively from natural increase.

The realities of southern economic life were more accurately reflected in lumber and steel than in tobacco and textiles. In the postwar era, the South possessed over 60 percent of the nation's timber resources. With soaring demand to meet the needs of the nation's rapidly growing towns and cities, lumber became the South's leading industry and number one employer. If anything, however, aggressive lumbering left the South far poorer. Corrupt state governments and relaxed federal timber policy allowed northerners and foreigners to acquire huge forest tracts at prices far below their actual value. Most of the timber was sold as raw lumber rather than finished products such as cedar shingles or newsprint, though the manufacture of furniture did flourish in North Carolina.

Logging camps were set up as isolated and temporary settlements. Visitors described the predominantly black work force as "single, homeless, and possessionless." The ruthless overcutting and other bad lumbering practices typical in all regions during this exploitative era destroyed the southern forests' capacity for self-renewal and led to severe problems of soil erosion and flooding. Having devastated the forests around their camps, the loggers quickly moved on to repeat their acts of destruction elsewhere. The sawmills to which they sent the cut timber were scarcely more permanent. The workers, mostly single, young black men, had little time to forge bonds of common interest among themselves or roots in the local community. Most mills operated for only a few years in any one place before the owners followed the loggers to a new area. They generally left without having contributed significantly to local development.

The fact that most mill workers were black added to the industry's relative isolation from nearby towns. Logging and lumbering provided young southern blacks the single greatest source of employment. The work was unskilled, dirty, dangerous, and temporary. High turnover and low morale often led southerners to blame the workers, not the operators, for the industry's low standards. As one critic complained, "The sawmill negro is rather shiftless and is not inclined to stay in any one location and consequently there is little incentive on the part of the owner or operator to carry on welfare work in any extensive manner." In fact, most blacks left the mills in search of higher wages or to settle down to sharecropping in order to marry and support families.

Even more symptomatic of the South's economic woes was the failure of the iron and steel industry to meet the expectations of the New South's promoters. By burning coke as a fuel to produce pig iron, Chattanooga, Tennessee, and Birmingham, Alabama, became major centers for foundries. Birmingham had the special advantage of being located closer than any other industrial center to *both* iron and coal deposits. By the 1890s the Tennessee Coal, Iron, and Railway Company (TCI) had turned its Birmingham facilities into the major producer of iron pipe for use in the gas, water, and sewer lines vital to urban growth. Unfortunately for Birmingham, its iron deposits were ill suited to produce the kinds of steel in high demand. By 1907 TCI had become so financially strapped that it had to sell out to the giant U.S. Steel Corporation, controlled by northern interests.

The disappointing contribution of the lumber and iron industries to southern economic growth was paralleled by other leading industries such as mining, chemical fertilizers, cottonseed oil, and railroads. Though all these industries grew dramatically in employment and the value of their products, they failed to meet the rosy predictions of the apostles of the New South. The region remained largely rural, agricultural, and poor.

Southerners of the day as well as modern historians have argued that the South suffered from the exploitation of outside financial interests. The region was in short a colonial economy, they claimed, relying for its wealth on extractive products such as minerals and timber or staple crops whose value had not increased through processing into finished goods. Profits that might have been used to foster development in the South were siphoned off to other regions, as decisions affecting the region's economic health were made in New York or Pittsburgh, not in Atlanta or New Orleans.

More recent analysis. however, suggests that economic growth lagged due to three factors peculiar to the South, rather than any conspiracy of outside capitalists. First, the South began to industrialize later than the Northeast, so northern entrepreneurs and workers had a head start on learning the new manufacturing techniques. Northern workers could be more productive, not because they were more energetic or disciplined, but because they were more experienced. Once Southern workers overcame that differential, they competed equally. Second, the South commanded only a small technologically skilled community to guide its industrial development. Since northern engineers and mechanics seldom followed northern capital into the region, few people were available to adapt modern technology to southern conditions. Southerners who did want to remain in the region found it difficult. For example, George Gordon Crawford, a Georgian who eventually became director of Tennessee Coal and Iron's Alabama operations, had to travel to Germany to receive his graduate education and then spent 15 years mastering steel operations at the Carnegie plant in Pennsylvania before returning to his homeland. Thus the South found itself importing advanced technologies and machinery even when they were ill adapted to southern conditions. The Bessemer process, for instance, did not work well with the type of iron ore found near Birmingham.

Southerners might have overcome this problem by upgrading the region's work force through better education. But no region in the nation spent as little on schooling as the South. Even before the war southern leaders were hostile to government services in general, largely to keep taxes low. The elite cared little about educating ordinary whites and openly resisted educating blacks. Education, they contended, "spoiled" otherwise contented workers and led them to demand higher wages and improved conditions. More important, better educated workers often left the region in search of higher paying jobs. Nor did the region invest heavily in technical colleges and engineering schools like the ones northern capitalists funded at Cornell University (1865) and the Massachusetts Institute of Technology (1859).

The lack of education was a critical factor behind the third and most central source of southern poverty, the isolation of the southern labor market. In 1900 agriculture still dominated the southern economy, and it required an unskilled, low-paid work force of sharecroppers and wage laborers. Ever fearful of outside influences that might spread discontent among the industrial and agricultural poor, southerners perpetuated conditions that also discouraged much needed outside human and capital resources. The South remained poor because it received too little, not too much, outside investment.

THE RISE OF JIM CROW

When Reconstruction and Radical Republican rule ended in the South after 1876, northerners gave up any pretense of protecting black freedmen. To achieve sectional reconciliation, whites both North and South were willing to sacrifice the rights of blacks. Southerners were relieved that in the matter of race relations they would be "left alone" by the federal government. That laissez-faire approach suited northern former champions of black rights like *The Nation* magazine, which had come to doubt whether former slaves could participate in "a system of government for which you [northern readers] and I have much respect." The Compromise of 1877 (page 637) guaranteed that blacks would remain free but did not guarantee political equality.

Segregation

Whatever their politics before the war, the Redeemer politicians who came to power in southern states afterward adopted a probusiness posture. Mostly Democrats, they were eager to develop the New South and reap benefits from its economic expansion. To attract the business-oriented elements—bankers, railroad promoters, industrial leaders—the ruling Democrats sometimes referred to themselves as Conservatives or conservative Democrats. As their part of the bargain, the Redeemers assured anxious northerners that home rule would not mean the wholesale political disfranchisement of the freedmen. So long as freed blacks identified their interests with those of conservative whites, leading southerners like

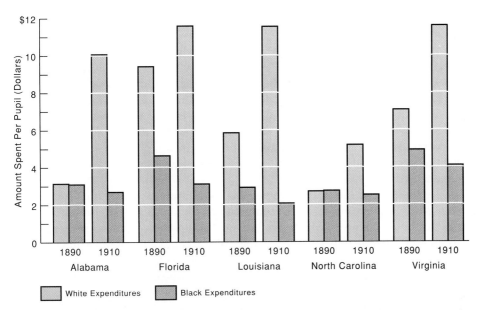

Source: Data from Robert A. Margo, *Disfranchisement, School Finance, and the Economics of Segregated Schools in the U.S. South, 1890-1910* (New York: Garland Press, 1985), table I-1.

SPENDING ON EDUCATION IN THE SOUTH
BEFORE AND AFTER DISFRANCHISEMENT
With disfranchisement and segregation, education was separate, but hardly equal for blacks and whites.

Alexander Stephens of Georgia, Wade Hampton of South Carolina, and L. Q. C. Lamar of Mississippi saw no reason to "take [blacks] out of politics as a factor or leading issue." And blacks did continue to entertain clear ideas about their political interests, to vote, and to hold some minor public offices, especially in states like South Carolina, where black majorities held the balance between rival political factions.

Whatever tolerance had existed began to disappear in the 1880s, as the new Redeemer governments moved to formalize a "Jim Crow" system of segregation.* As more blacks moved into southern towns and cities to compete for jobs with whites, and as their status as free laborers (and often voters) blurred the social line between them and poor whites, pressures increased to separate blacks as social inferiors. That was made somewhat difficult by the Civil Rights Act of 1875, in which Congress had guaranteed persons of every race the right to use public facilities such as hotels, theaters, and railroads. But when a number of blacks sued after being denied those rights, the Supreme Court ruled (in the *Civil Rights Cases*, 1883) that the 1875 law was invalid. Hotels and railroads were not "public" institutions, the Court argued narrowly; they were owned by private individuals. The Fourteenth Amendment was thus said to protect citizens from violations of their civil rights only by states, not by private individuals. The national policy of laissez faire in race relations could not have been made any clearer, and southern legislatures got the message.

*The term "Jim Crow," to denote a policy of segregation, originated in a song of the same name sung in minstrel shows of the day.

Within 20 years every southern state had enacted a legal system of racial separation. The earliest laws limited segregation largely to schools and trains, but soon a complex web of Jim Crow statutes had drawn a color line indelibly in prisons, parks, hotels, restaurants, hospitals, and virtually all public places except streets and stores. And again the Supreme Court accepted the new state of affairs in *Plessy v. Ferguson* (1896). That decision upheld a Louisiana law requiring segregated railroad facilities by arguing that segregation did not constitute discrimination under the equal protection clause of the Fourteenth Amendment, so long as accommodations for both races were equal. In reality, of course, the segregated facilities stigmatized blacks. Such facilities were always separate but seldom met the standard of equality.

By the turn of the century segregation was firmly in place. Jim Crow effectively stifled significant economic competition. Jobs such as those in textile mills were restricted largely to whites, while skilled and professional blacks were generally allowed to serve only a black clientele. Blacks could enter some white residential areas only as servants and hired help. They were barred from juries and generally received far stiffer penalties than whites who committed similar crimes. And as the law became entrenched, so did social custom. Blacks always called whites, even those of lower status, Mister, Miss, and Ma'am, but to whites, no matter what age or profession blacks might be, they were called by first name or more simply Sister or Boy. If any black crossed the lines drawn by whites, the consequences were often violent. A rapid increase in lynchings accompanied the rise of Jim Crow. Of the 187 lynchings averaged in each year of the 1890s, some 80 percent occurred in the South, where the large majority of victims were black.

Disfranchisement

"The best friends of the colored men are the old slaveholders," politician Wade Hampton told a group of black voters in 1878. " . . . They will defend your right to vote because it gives to the South infinitely more power than we ever had before." Hampton and other conservative Democrats espoused this policy so long as black voters marched to the polls to vote their way. But if wooing failed, whites resorted to various forms of coercion. Implicit on many occasions was the threat of violence if blacks did not vote according to instruction. One Mississippi newspaper observed in 1883 that should freedmen "not vote with the Democrats, it would be better for them and the county that they refuse to participate in the election. The weather might be warm that day and they might get sun-struck." Whether by persuasive appeal, bribery, fraud, or intimidation, the conservative Democrats did regularly manage to remain in power with the help of blacks.

Those who sought to reform either the political or economic system courted black votes too. The issues varied from state to state—"greenback" currency reforms, public school legislation, complaints about the laws that allowed convict labor (poor whites as well as blacks) to be hired out—but in each case, the threat of an alliance between poor whites and poor blacks was always there. Conservatives began to argue that it might be better if blacks were disfranchised, eliminating even their minimal influence in politics.

Mississippi, which during Reconstruction had led the move to "redeem" its state from Radical Republicans, in 1890 again took the lead in disfranchising black voters. In a constitutional convention, delegates required that voters henceforth would be required to pay a poll tax and pass a literacy test. Such tests made it possible to eliminate the great majority of black voters, especially if election officials interpreted the requirements strictly. Poll taxes were first adopted in the North and South to fund schools. Since many blacks were too poor to pay even a small amount, the new poll tax would keep them from voting. Then, too, Mississippi required that the tax be paid in advance and the receipt presented on the day of voting, a cumbersome and discouraging procedure. Conservative Democrats favored the plan because it reduced not only black voting but also that of poor whites, who were most likely to join opposition parties. Before Mississippi's new constitution went into effect, there were 257,305 eligible voters in the state; in 1892, after its adoption, that number plummeted to 76,742.[*]

Conservatives in other southern states were envious. "We would do well to imitate the wise politicians of Mississippi," noted one Alabama journal. "The poll tax gets rid of most of the negro votes there," wrote an enthusiastic Louisiana observer, "but it gets rid of a great many whites at the same time—in fact a majority of them." But for just that reason, the issue of voter disfranchisement remained explosive in many southern states. As more and more small farmers angrily challenged the corruption of conservative Democratic rule in the early 1890s, some held out for an alliance with black voters to change the system. Once that challenge failed, the move for disfranchisement swept the rest of the South by the end of the century, with devastating results for blacks.

THE TRANSFORMED WEST

The West, like the South, has been defined not so much as a particular place but as a distinctive culture shaped by an unusual set of conditions. For historian Frederick Jackson Turner, writing in the 1890s, the West was shaped by the frontier, an area of "free land" to be found beyond the point of white settlement. In the ethnocentric fashion of his age, Turner ignored the presence of rich and varied tribal cultures beyond the frontier, where Indians hardly considered their lands "free" for use by whites. By the time the Civil War broke out, the frontier of white settlement had moved beyond the Mississippi, but it had "jumped" across the Great Plains to the Pacific, as "Overlanders" settled the farmlands of California and Oregon. The frontier then pushed east from the Pacific coast, following miners into the Sierra Nevadas. At the same time, farmers and ranchers pushed west from the Mississippi into what had been popularly known as "the Great American desert."

Most areas of this Great Plains region, west of the 98th meridian, receive less than 20 inches of rainfall a year. In the Great Basin area of Utah, Nevada, and eastern California the climate is even drier. In extreme cases, the air becomes so dry that rain evaporates before hitting the ground. The infrequent stands of timber cluster along river bottoms, making wood for housing and fences scarce. To eastern farmers accustomed to ready access to water, timber, and tillable land, the region between the 98th meridian and the fertile valleys of the West Coast at first seemed suitable for neither man nor beast. Many Overlanders of the 1840s and 1850s compared its vast windy spaces to the oceans, a "sea of grass" stretching to the horizon crossed by "prairie schooners."

---

[*]It was perhaps doubly ironic that the convention, convinced that lower-class whites as well as blacks would oppose the changes, simply declared the new constitution adopted. They never allowed it to be ratified in a popular vote.

Native Americans and the Western Environment

Easterners who watched the wagons head west liked to conjure up the image of a "trackless wilderness," but in truth, even in the 1840s the Great Plains and mountain frontier comprised a region in which Spanish, Anglo-American, and Native American cultures were interacting with one another in unstable, swiftly changing ways. The horse, introduced into North America by the colonial Spanish, had spread by the eighteenth century across the plains. By the nineteenth century the Comanche, Cheyenne, Sioux, Kiowa, Blackfoot, Apache, and other tribes were among the great equestrians of the world. The mobility they attained on horseback significantly increased the area in which they could hunt the buffalo, and it transformed many of their cultures from a relatively settled, village-centered, horticultural way of life to a more aggressively nomadic existence.

Under the Indian Removal Act of 1830 the forced relocation of eastern tribes to lands west of the Mississippi also disturbed intertribal patterns. The dry climate of the western plains was an environment for which the woodland cultures of eastern tribes were ill-suited. Western tribes such as the Comanche, Pawnee, and Osage resented the intrusion of the newcomers, who raided their camps and drove off livestock. The Sioux, perhaps the most feared warriors of the Plains in the mid-nineteenth century, had emerged from the forests of the Great Lakes only a century earlier. They were able to expand partly because they began using firearms before other tribes and partly because they escaped the worst ravages of white diseases, which decimated many plains tribes.

Some whites—usually those who had the least contact with native Americans—viewed Indians as "noble savages," whose "natural" way of life remained in harmony with the elements, a myth still perpetuated by far too many scholars. To be sure, the population density of Indian settlement remained low enough so that their impact on the western environment was relatively small compared with later white settlement. And Indians could be remarkably inventive about making the most of the resources around them. The bark of the cottonwood proved good food for horses during the winter, while the buffalo supplied not only meat but also bones for tools, fat for cosmetics, and sinews for thread. But Indians had traditionally hunted bison by stampeding them over cliffs, which resulted in tremendous waste of food. They irrigated crops, set fires on the plains to improve the game and vegetation, and in other ways actively altered their environment.

By the mid-nineteenth century they had also become enmeshed in a web of white trade, supplying furs in return for firearms, cloth, metal tools, and jewelry. Since the environment could sustain only a finite amount of use, Indians suffered, just as white trappers did, when the fur trade led to overtrapping. And the Sioux nation expanded so aggressively because its increasing population forced the tribe to enlarge its base of resources. It would be misleading, then, to view native societies in the Great Plains as isolated from white cultures, living as they had from time out of mind. For more than a century, the West had been in dramatic flux, as white and Indian cultures borrowed and adapted from one another, often clashing in competition for the region's limited resources.

Whites and Indians found themselves in conflict because their values were so much at odds. Generalizations about Indians in the West are hard to sustain because their cultures were as varied as the western environment. Although big-game hunting was common among western Indians, the nomadic buffalo culture of the Great Plains was hardly representative. Along the Pacific Northwest coast the

The cultures of western Indians were remarkably varied, ranging from the nomadic Plains tribes to the more settled peoples of the northwest coast who lived off the sea. This Sioux woman gathers firewood; the photograph was taken by Edward Curtis, who spent many years recording the faces and lives of western tribes.

Yuroks, Coos, Umpqua, Chinook, and other tribes hunted the woods and mountains for bear, moose, elk, and deer. They also took from the ocean whales, seals, and a variety of fish. The Klamaths, Yakimas, and Walla Wallas moved into the river valleys for the great salmon runs. Where the land was less bountiful, Indian tribes lived close to starvation. Utes, Shoshones, Paiutes, and Pavistos scoured the hot, arid Great Basin deserts to eke out a diet of rabbits, snakes, insects, roots, berries, seeds, and nuts. The early Hohokams and later the Havasupais, Pima, and other tribes in New Mexico and Arizona developed irrigation to allow farming of beans, squash, and corn in the arid climate.

Despite such diversity, Indian tribes did share certain values. Most were small, extended kinship groups in which the well-being of the community outweighed the needs of the individual. While some tribes were materially better off than others, the gap between rich and poor within tribes was seldom large. Egalitarian material culture tended to promote egalitarian decision making. The Cheyenne, for example, employed a council of 44 to advise the chief.

What most separated white and Indian cultures were attitudes toward the land and all that was on it. Man, for the Indians, was not a transcendent being, but a single part of a complex web of animals, plants, and other natural elements—all with souls of their own. Whereas Europeans viewed nature as a resource to be exploited, the Indians saw it as sacred. The Taos of New Mexico, for example, believed that each spring the pregnant earth issued new life. To avoid disturbing "mother" earth, they removed the hard shoes from their horses and themselves walked in bare feet or soft moccasins. Whites were mystified by the attitude of Chief Somohalla of the Wanapaun tribe who explained why his people refused to farm: "You ask me to plow the ground! Shall I take a knife and tear my mother's bosom? . . . You ask me to cut grass and make hay and sell it, and be rich like white men! But how dare I cut off my mother's hair?"

Such reverence for the land gave Indians a religious loyalty to special places. The Taos centered their spiritual and economic life on Blue Lake in northwest New Mexico, the source of life and the revelations of the great spirit of the universe. The Shoshone in eastern California came to Coso Hot Springs for healing and worship. To white migrants from the East or from Europe, these places had no special meaning. Where the Sioux saw in the Black Hills the sacred home of Wakan Tanka, the burial place of the dead and the site of their "vision quests," whites saw the possibility of gold and grass for grazing their herds. From such misunderstandings came conflict. To some white Americans, the Indians seemed a hopelessly savage people whose just fate was extermination. To other whites, moved by Christian zeal or "enlightened" sympathy, the Indian was a child, an inferior being, who needed to be first protected and then assimilated into American society. To survive either killing or kindness, Indians had to find ways to resist both forms of attack.

Whites and the Western Environment

The balance of power between white and Indian cultures changed dramatically in the years following the Civil War. For Indians it was a time of transition and rebuilding as well as military defeat and despair. For white Americans the new industrial order created both the means and the motive to close the final western frontiers. Transcontinental rail lines, standardized rail gauges and freight systems, telegraph lines to coordinate communications, systems of large-scale finance and military power, and rapidly growing urban markets all made it easier to accelerate white settlement in the West, especially in the least settled areas of the Great Plains.

Even among whites, however, attitudes varied as to how Americans should take advantage of the frontier region. As repeated discoveries of gold and silver brought whites into Indian territory, many adopted the confident, booster outlook of Missouri politician William Gilpin. To Gilpin, the Indians seemed just one more impediment that would be pushed aside by the expansive force of the American people. Only the lack of vision among those in the East prevented the nation from opening the West for exploitation, he told an Independence, Missouri, audience in 1849. What was most needed were cheap lands and a railroad linking the two coasts "like ears on a human head."

By 1868 the dreams of western expansionists were becoming reality. A generous Congress had granted the West its two greatest wishes: free land, under the Homestead Act of 1862, and a transcontinental railroad. As the new governor of Colorado, Gilpin told a July Fourth audience that the resources of the region were so limitless that the land would one day support over a billion people. The limited rainfall and water resources did not daunt him, for in his eyes the West was a garden, not "the Great American desert" it had been called for so many years. If the rains did not come, farmers would find all the water they needed in artesian wells deep underground. Once the land had been planted, the rains would develop naturally, Gilpin assured his listeners, for he subscribed to the popular myth that "rain follows the plow."

Unlike the visionary Gilpinites, John Wesley Powell actually knew something about water and farming. After service in the Civil War that cost him his right arm, Major Powell, a geologist, had come west in 1869 to lead a scientific expedition down the Green and Colorado rivers through the Grand Canyon. No whites had

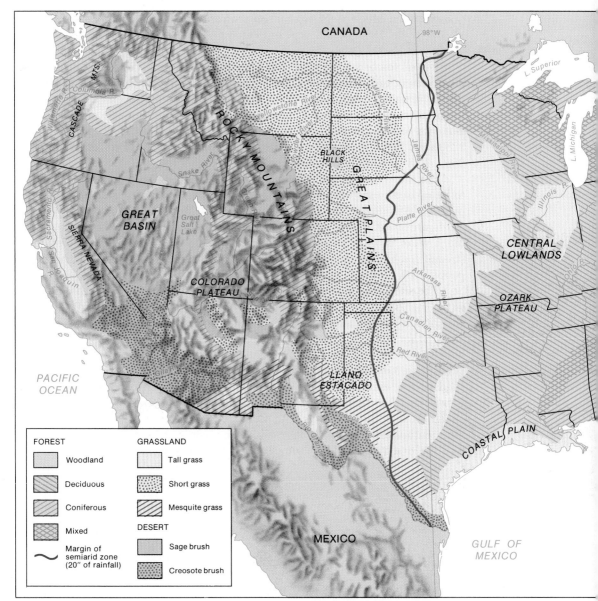

NATURAL ENVIRONMENT OF THE WEST
With the exception of the Pacific Northwest in Oregon and Washington, few areas west of the 20-inch rainfall line receive enough annual precipitation to support agriculture without irrigation. Consequently water has been the key to growth and development in the area west of the 98th meridian, encompassing over half the land area of the continental United States. The dominance of short grasses and coniferous (evergreen) trees reflects the rainfall patterns.

ever made that trip; indeed most people doubted it could be done. Powell not only survived, but he also repeated the feat in 1871, impelled as much by his fascination with Indian customs as with the remarkable terrain. Capitalizing on his success, he told Congress that the development of the West required more scientific planning. Much of the region had not yet even been mapped or its resources identified. In 1880 Powell was appointed director of the recently formed U.S. Geological Survey.

Powell too had a vision of the West, in his case based on the realities of the environment rather than the power of myth. In the East, where rainfall was adequate, a family could make a decent living farming a plot even half of the maximum 160 acres allotted settlers under the current policy for sale of federal land. But eastern land law had little relevance in a region whose arid climate rendered 1280 acres barely enough for farming, while grazing a small herd required at least 2560. And with no water at all, most land was useless.

For the West to grow in an orderly fashion, Powell believed that the laws had to be revised to suit the environment. The key was to treat water, not land, as a precious commodity. In the water-rich East, the English tradition of riparian rights prevailed. Those who owned the banks of a river or stream controlled as much water as they might take regardless of the consequence for others downstream. Such a practice in the West, Powell recognized, would enrich the few people with access to water while spelling ruin for the rest.

The alternative was to allow the community to distribute water to the benefit of the many rather than the powerful or privileged few. To that end the federal government would have to establish political boundaries defined by watershed areas rather than the grid pattern of settlement, which dated back to the Northwest Ordinances of the 1780s. Scientifically based planning would replace the laissez-faire custom under which the unregulated individual or corporation pursued narrow ends of profit with little regard for its environmental costs or the greater social good. But Powell's scientific realism could not overcome the vision of the West as the new American Eden. Development would proceed with the same enthusiasm for laissez faire and immediate results as captivated the East. And the first victims of this unrestrained expansion were Indians.

THE WAR FOR THE WEST

Since Andrew Jackson began moving eastern tribes beyond the Mississippi River, federal officials considered the Great Plains marginal land that could safely be given to the Indians. White estimates of the land began to change with a series of gold and silver discoveries beginning in 1848. By 1851 federal officials introduced a policy of "concentration," trying to get various tribes to sign treaties limiting the boundaries of their hunting grounds. Such treaties were often claimed to be settlements that would last "forever," but time after time, land-hungry pioneers squatted on Indian lands, then demanded protection from the government. The government, in turn, forced new, more restrictive agreements on the western tribes. In the Pacific Northwest, for example, many Indians had welcomed the first farmers, but by the 1850s the pressures on their land had become disruptive. Territorial governor Isaac Stevens, by often devious means, induced representatives of the Cayuse, Yakima, Walla Walla, and Nez Percé to cede millions of acres of land on which they had once freely hunted.

By 1862 the lands of the Santee Sioux had been similarly whittled down to a strip 10 miles wide and 150 miles long along the Minnesota River. Lashing out in frustration, the tribe attacked several undefended white settlements along the Minnesota frontier. The alarmed governor informed Washington that a full-scale war had broken out. In response, General John Pope came to St. Paul declaring his intention to wage a war of extermination. "They are to be treated as maniacs or wild beasts and by no means as people with whom treaties and compromises can be made," he instructed his officers. When Pope's forces under Colonel Henry Sibley captured 1800 Sioux braves, vindictive Minnesotans were outraged that President Lincoln would authorize the hanging of only 38.

War

The campaign under General Pope was the opening phase of a guerrilla war that raged intermittently between the U.S. Army and western Indians for some 30 years. The conflict gained momentum in November 1864, when a force of Colorado volunteers under Colonel John Chivington fell upon a band of friendly Cheyenne gathered at Sand Creek under the protection of the army. Black Kettle, the Cheyenne chief, raised an American flag to indicate friendship, but Chivington was having none of it. "Kill and scalp all, big and little," he told his men. When the massacre ended, all 80 Cheyenne, including women and children, lay dead. Settlers and soldiers alike felt the consequences of Chivington's unprovoked brutality, as virtually all the plains Indians joined the Sioux efforts to drive the whites from their lands.

The Sand Creek massacre was severely criticized by many eastern reformers, who understood the sources of Indian violence. The commission appointed to negotiate peace terms in 1867 observed that "when the progress of settlement reaches the Indian's home, the only question is, 'How best to get his land.' When they are obtained, the Indian is lost sight of." Fair-minded generals like George Crook and O. O. Howard honored treaty obligations and tried to inform insensitive politicians about the injustices that provoked Indian hostility. But the gap between the two cultures was so great that even reformers were largely unwilling to consider the possibility of allowing Indians to continue their traditional lives, protected from white encroachment. Instead they campaigned to turn nomadic Indians into farmers with 160-acre plots of land. General Pope, who went on to become commander of the Department of the Missouri, recognized the folly of this notion but proposed the equally unlikely solution of making Indians into stock raisers and cattlemen.

In the end, war was only one of several determining factors in the defeat of tribal cultures. Over the course of centuries only an estimated 4000 Indians (and about 7000 whites) were killed in direct warfare—a paltry few compared to the casualty lists of the Civil War. Far more devastating were white diseases, which continued to take their toll, and the debilitating influence of liquor. On the Great Plains the railroad disrupted the migratory patterns of the buffalo and in turn the patterns of the hunt. Tourist parties came west on the trains to bag the buffalo from railside; and when hides became popular back east, commercial companies hired hunters who could mow down over 100 bison an hour. In three short years, from 1872 to 1874, approximately 9 million of the herd were killed. By 1883 bison were nearly extinct on the plains. In other areas mining, farming, grazing herds, and fencing disrupted the Indians' traditional hunting and farming lands.

Last Stands

Among those who joined in Cheyenne raids on white settlements after Sand Creek was a young Sioux named Crazy Horse. His western band had always worried that too much contact with whites would destroy the Indian way of life. As the Civil War ended, veteran troops swelled the ranks of the western army assigned to protect the Northern Pacific Railroad and to open a trail from the gold fields of western Montana through Sioux country along the South Platte River. Crazy Horse led regular raiding parties that made that trail unsafe for soldiers and civilians. In December 1866 Captain William Fetterman, a brash commander who believed his 80 men could make short work of any Sioux war party, rode straight into an ambush Crazy Horse had helped set. There were no survivors.

This campaign was effective enough to cause federal negotiators to sign a treaty in 1868 promising to abandon the trail to the gold fields, as well as three military posts. It agreed also to the establishment of two large Indian reservations, one in Oklahoma and the other in the western Dakotas. But many of the Sioux did not understand that the terms restricted them to hunting in the area of the Powder River and Bighorn country and to living in a reservation area of South Dakota west of the Missouri. To protect the transcontinental route and the trail to Montana, the treaty banned all trade between whites and Indians along the Platte. Thus the tribes could not replenish their supplies of guns, ammunition, and blankets. Much to the Indians' dismay, the army began to harass bands that traveled outside the reservation area.

Only Chief Sitting Bull's northern Tetons and their Cheyenne allies had refused to sign the treaty, and Crazy Horse joined them, determined to draw a firm line. But in the summer of 1874 Colonel George Armstrong Custer flagrantly disregarded the 1868 treaty by leading an expedition into *Pa Sapa*, the sacred Black Hills of the Sioux. Custer, a Civil War veteran, had gained fame among the plains tribes as a "squaw killer" for his cruel warfare against the Indians of western Kansas. Among white critics he was known for his monumental vanity and publicity-seeking ways. When his expedition returned, its members spread rumors that the Black Hills were rich with gold "from the grass roots down." As prospectors poured into Indian country, the army made little effort to keep them out. Once again, federal negotiators tried to force another treaty to gain control of the Black Hills, but when that failed, President Grant ordered all "hostiles" in the area rounded up and driven onto the reservations.

The stage was set for a showdown, as the Cheyenne allied with the Sioux for the first time under the leadership of Crazy Horse. Against them marched several army columns, including Custer's 7th Cavalry, a force of over 600 troops. Custer, ever eager to win fame, arrived at the Little Big Horn River a day earlier than the other columns. Hearing a rumor of a native village nearby, he impulsively attacked, only to discover that he had stumbled onto an encampment of over 12,000 Sioux and Cheyenne, extending for almost three miles. From a deep ravine Crazy Horse charged Custer, killing him and some 250 soldiers.

"It is a good day to die!" Crazy Horse cried—the traditional war cry. Even in the midst of victory he spoke truly. For while Custer had been conquered, the railroads still stood ready to continue their work, the prospectors remained eager to make fortunes, and soldiers continued to come from the East. By late summer the Sioux were forced to split into small bands to evade the army sent to punish

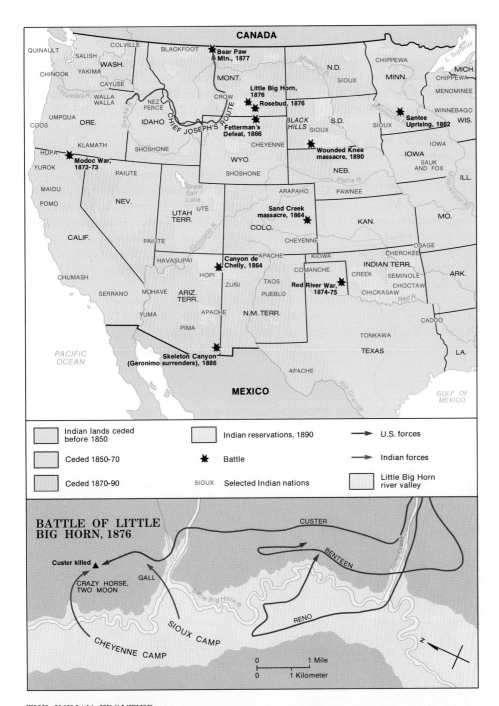

THE INDIAN FRONTIER

As conflict erupted between Indian and white cultures in the West, the government sought increasingly to concentrate tribes on reservations. Resistance to the reservation concept helped unite the Sioux and Cheyenne, traditionally enemies, in the Dakotas during the 1870s. Along the Little Big Horn River, the impetuous Custer underestimated the strength of his Indian opponents and attacked before the supporting troops of Reno and Benteen were in a position to aid him.

them. While Sitting Bull barely escaped to Canada, Crazy Horse and 800 with him surrendered after a winter of suffering and starvation.

The battles along the Platte and upper Missouri rivers did not end the war between whites and Indians, but never again would such a substantial threat be mounted. Even peaceful tribes like the Nez Percé of Idaho found no security once whites began to hunger for their land. The Nez Percé had become effective breeders of livestock, rich in horses and cattle that they grazed in the meadows of grass west of the Snake River canyon. That did not prevent the government from trying to force them onto a small reservation. Rather than see his people humiliated, Chief Joseph led a band of almost 600 toward Canada, pursued by the U.S. Army. In just 75 days the Nez Percé traveled over 1300 miles. Every time the army closed to attack, Chief Joseph and his warriors drove them off. But before they could reach the border they were trapped, and the chief's words of surrender were eloquent: "Hear me, my chiefs, I am tired; my heart is sick and sad. From where the sun now stands I will fight no more forever." The government then shipped the defeated tribe to Oklahoma, where disease and starvation finished the destruction the army had begun.

Almost as mythic as the name of Crazy Horse was Geronimo, whose band of Apaches was the last to succumb to white conquest. In 1872 Cochise, the great battle chief of the Apache, had accepted peace terms and moved his people onto a reservation in the Arizona territory. Geronimo decided to keep up the fight, re-

---

More than warfare, acculturation threatened the survival of traditional Indian ways. By 1905, some 20 years after his surrender, Geronimo had adopted Christianity and other white ways (including this top hat). He rode as a celebrity that year in Theodore Roosevelt's inaugural parade.

treating across the Mexican border into a mountain camp and from there leading sporadic raids on settlements and ranches across the territories. Terrified whites begged Washington for protection, but not until 1886 did the army finally capture Geronimo and send him to an exile in Florida.

By 1887 reformers recognized that the policy of concentrating Indians on reservations was a failure. Deprived of their traditional lands and culture, the reservation tribes became dependent on the government. And whites who coveted the resources of reservation lands were quick to violate treaty terms. Railroad barons like Collis P. Huntington and Jay Gould had ignored Apache rights as they ran tracks across the reservation. In a spirit that mingled good intentions and unbridled greed, Congress adopted the Dawes Severalty Act of 1887 to end reservation policy and bring once-nomadic Indians into white society as farmers and small landowners.

In practice, the Dawes Act was more destructive than any blow struck by the army, because it attacked the communal tribal structure upon which Indian life was based. Lands held in common would now be allotted to individuals: 160 acres to the head of a family and 80 acres to single adults or orphans. But as John Wesley Powell had warned, small homestead farms in the West would not support a family—white or Indian—unless they were irrigated. And most Indians of the region had no experience with farming, managing money, or other white ways. The sponsors of the Dawes Act, knowing that whites might swindle Indians out of their private holdings, arranged for the government to hold title to the land for 25 years, but that did not stop unscrupulous speculators from "leasing" lands. Furthermore, all reservation lands not allocated to Indians were opened to non-Indian homesteaders. Few Indians were able to assimilate into white society as the Dawes Act intended.

Against such a bleak future, many Indians sought solace in dreams of the past. In 1890 a religious revival spread when word came from the Nevada desert that a humble Paiute named Wovoka had received revelations from the Great Spirit. Wovoka told the pilgrims that God wanted them "to be good and love one another, and not fight, or steal, or lie." With that message God also sent a dance. Wovoka preached that if they adopted his message and mystical rituals, the dead Indians would come back, whites would be driven out of the land, and game would be thick again. As the rituals spread from tribe to tribe, alarmed settlers called the strange shuffling and chanting the "Ghost Dance." The army moved to stop the proceedings among the Sioux, for fear of another uprising. The great Sitting Bull himself was killed in one scuffle, while the 7th Cavalry, Custer's old unit, set out to track down other members of the tribe. At Wounded Knee the cavalry fell upon one band and with devastating machine-gun fire killed at least 200 men, women, and children.

Wounded Knee was a last symbolic act of violence against an independent Indian way of life. After 1890 the real battle was over assimilation, not extinction. The system of markets, rail and freight networks, and extractive industries was linking the Far West with the rest of the nation, replacing free-roaming bison with herded cattle and sheep, nomadic tribes with prairie sodbusters, and sacred hunting grounds like the Sioux's *Pa Sapa* with gold fields. Armed with the Dawes Act and often pressed by those with designs on Indian lands, reformers sought to use a combination of education, citizenship, and allotments to draw Indians from their communal lives into white society. Most Indians were equally determined to preserve their tribal ways and a sense of themselves as a separate people.

THE WESTERN BOOM

Though opportunity in the West lay in the land and its resources, wealth also accumulated in the towns. Each time a speculative fever hit the region, new communities sprouted to serve those who rushed in to strike it rich. The boom began with the "forty-niners" of 1849 and San Francisco; in the next few decades new hordes threw up towns in Park City, Utah; Tombstone, Arizona; Deadwood in the Dakota Territories; and other promising sites. Then in the 1860s came the railroads, which created cities like Denver and would awaken sleepy communities like Los Angeles. Railroads opened the Great Plains to the cattle drives that in the 1870s brought the great herds to "cowtowns" like Sedalia, Missouri; Dodge City, Wichita; and Abilene, Kansas; and Cheyenne, Wyoming. Fast behind the cattle boom came the sodbusters by the late 1870s to turn the thick prairie soils left open by the destruction of the buffalo herds. By the 1890s the once unsettled Great Plains were dotted with towns, crisscrossed by rails, and divided into farms, ranches, and Indian reservations. Historian Frederick Jackson Turner could announce by 1893 that the frontier had closed.

The gold and silver strikes established a pattern the other booms would follow. Stories of easy riches would attract small entrepreneurs. The populations of boom towns were largely male (as much as 90 percent) and almost half foreign-born. Someone entering the local saloon could expect to hear English, the Irish brogue, German, French, Spanish, Chinese, Italian, Hawaiian, and various Indian dialects. Once the quick profits were gone, a period of consolidation brought more order to towns and larger scale to enterprise. In the mine fields, that meant corporations with the capital to invest in high-pressure hydraulic water jets to blast ore loose and other heavy equipment to crush rock and extract silver and gold from deeper veins. In their concern to secure quick profits, such operations often led to environmental disaster as floods, mud slides, and dirty streams threatened the livelihood of farmers in the valleys below. In state and territorial governments bitter disputes erupted between agricultural and mining interests.

Conflict erupted, too, between the corporations and the paid labor force that replaced the prospectors. Struggles between the companies and miners seeking union recognition, better wages and hours, and improved working conditions sometimes turned into pitched battles. In Coeur d'Alene, Idaho, in 1892, troops seeking to break a strike killed seven miners. The miners, refusing to knuckle under, created the Western Federation of Miners, which in the decade after 1893 attracted some 50,000 members and a reputation as one of the nation's most militant unions. In short, the mining frontier, which had begun as a rowdy and individualistic collection of small-scale prospectors, had been integrated into the industrial system of wage labor, large-scale resource extraction, and high-finance capital.

Rail Towns and Cattle Drives

As William Gilpin had predicted in 1849, the development of the West awaited the coming of the railroads. Before the gold spike joined the Central and Union Pacific at Promontory Point, Utah, in 1869, travel across the West was slow and dusty. Mail, cargo, and people moved on stagecoaches, wagons, horseback, and

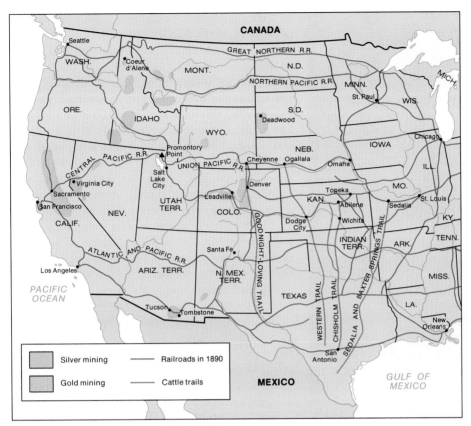

THE MINING AND CATTLE FRONTIERS

In the vast spaces of the West, railroads, cattle trails, and gold mining usually preceded the arrival of settlers in large enough numbers to establish towns and cities. The railroads forged a crucial link between the region's natural resources and urban markets in the East and in Europe, but by transsecting the plains they also disrupted the migratory patterns of the buffalo herds, undermining Plains Indian cultures while opening the land to cattle grazing and farming.

foot. Given the vast distances and sparse population, entrepreneurs had little opportunity to follow the eastern practice of building local railroads from city to city.

But such difficulties put no end to dreaming, especially for the likes of Collis P. Huntington. A transplanted New Yorker, Huntington soon discovered that the way to make a fortune was not in the hunt for gold but by supplying the boom society that came with the rush for mineral wealth. Setting up a hardware business in Sacramento, he often strapped bags of gold to his waist and rowed out into San Francisco harbor to meet incoming supply ships. Before they could land, he had bought up the entire cargo, which he then sold at highly inflated prices. Huntington understood all too well the credo of the West in those early days: "It pays to be shifty in a new land." He and three other Sacramento business leaders, Mark Hopkins, Leland Stanford, and Charles Crocker—the "Big Four" (all happened to be ample in girth as well as in wealth)—incorporated the Central Pacific Railroad.

In 1862 the Central Pacific won from Congress the opportunity to build the western link of the transcontinental railroad eastward from San Francisco. To the Union Pacific Corporation fell the right to construct the section from Omaha westward. But the real money in this and other ventures lay not so much in the revenues from passengers and freight, but from generous loans and gifts of federal and state lands. For every mile of track completed, the rail companies received twenty sections of land in the states along the route and forty sections per mile in the territories. (One section equaled 6,400 acres or ten square miles.) By the time the Central and Union Pacific railroads were completed, they had received some 45 million acres. Fraudulent stock practices, corrupt accounting, and wholesale bribery (with the complicity of the vice-president and at least two members of Congress) enabled the promoters to earn large profits.

General Grenville Dodge, an army engineer on leave to the Union Pacific, recognized that the immense labor force needed to build the railroad might be recruited cheaply from the mass of Irish and other European immigrants. He drove his workers with ruthless army discipline, completing as much as ten miles of track in a single day. Charles Crocker had no similar source of cheap labor in California for the Central Pacific, since the gold rush era had passed. Worse yet, he faced the formidable task of forging a route through the Sierra Nevadas. When his partner Leland Stanford suggested imported Chinese labor, Crocker dismissed him with a laugh—at first. But it was some 10,000 Chinese laborers ("the Asiatic Contingent of the the Grand Army of Civilization," one observer dubbed them) who accomplished the daunting task. With wheelbarrows, picks, shovels, and baskets they advanced eastward, building trestles like the one at Secrettown (left) and chipping away at the steep Sierras' looming granite walls. On the worst stretches they averaged only eight inches a day.

Once the Chinese crews had broken into the flat country of the desert basin, the two railroads raced to claim as much federal land as possible. Labor bosses pushed their men with blatant appeals to racism. In the resulting scramble, the two sides passed each other, laying over two hundred miles of parallel track before the government ordered them to join at Promontory Point, Utah, in the spring of 1869. The headlong rush had involved waste and the cutting of corners: many sections of the first track had been thrown up on narrow embankments and over flimsy bridges. Still, East and West were finally linked across the American continent. Writer Bret Harte described the Central and Union Pacific engines as

> Facing on a single track
> Half a world behind each back.

Over 75 western railroads benefited from similar government generosity. The Northern Pacific line, from Minnesota to Seattle, received almost twice as much land as the Central Pacific and the Union Pacific. The Atchison, Topeka, and Santa Fe, which followed the old Santa Fe Trail, acquired some 3 million acres. Only the Great Northern, the last of the major transcontinental lines, built its track without federal aid.

The rail companies recognized the strategic value of their enterprise. If the key to getting rich off the gold rush was supplying miners, the key to prospering in the developing West was control of the means of transport. Just by threatening to bypass a town, a powerful railroad could extract important concessions on rights of way, taxes, and loans. No one topped Collis Huntington for ruthlessness and audacity. "If the Great Wall of China were put in his path, he would attack it with his nails," an acquaintance remarked. To Huntington the Big Four assigned the task of managing Congress, judges, and local officials. "If a man has the power to do great evil and won't do right unless he is bribed to do it, I think . . . it is a man's duty to go up and bribe the judge," he admitted with characteristic bluntness.

When Los Angeles resisted Charles Crocker's demands for major concessions, the Big Four threatened to ruin the town by leaving it off their route. As an example to Angelenos they bypassed nearby San Bernardino and simply built another town, Colton. After acquiring waterfront land in Oakland, the Central Pacific eventually gained control of all the railroad, ferry, and dock land around the rim of San Francisco Bay. And as huge landowners with control of transportation, the railroads had an enormous influence on the development of farming and cattle grazing.

Westerners developed a peculiar ambivalence toward government and the railroads. Both were necessary for growth and development of the region. Yet, in the words of the Sacramento *Union*, miners, small ranchers, farmers, and the newly settled towns found their lives hinging on decisions made by "coldhearted, selfish, sordid" robber barons and officials in Washington, over whom they had little direct control. Such antagonism helps explain the legends that abounded concerning the exploits of train robbers like the James brothers, Jesse and Frank, and the Hole-in-the-Wall Gang, led by Butch Cassidy and the Sundance Kid. If the railroads could, with government support, rob the people, then the train robbers were latter-day "Robin Hoods," giving the railroads a little of their own medicine.

So the railroads sparked urban growth in coastal cities like Seattle, San Francisco, and Los Angeles, where sea and land transportation routes met. Los Angeles, a sleepy town of 6000 people in the 1870s, jumped to over 50,000 with the coming of the Southern Pacific and the Santa Fe. San Francisco and Oakland prospered as major transportation centers after the gold rush ended. For western cities of the interior like Denver, Cheyenne, Abilene, and Wichita, growth came with the joining of the railroads to the great cattle trails.

In many ways Wichita, Kansas, typified the scattered towns and cities that sprouted as the West opened to speculative fever. Wichita, on the Arkansas River, first served as a campsite for Indians and fur traders. After the Civil War, land speculators recognized that the proximity to the Chisholm Trail would bring the cattle herds and the hungry and thirsty cowpokes who drove them to Abilene. When the railroad came through in 1872 the boom began in earnest. Area farmers now had far wider access to distant markets. And towns like Wichita offered farmers and cowhands alike an escape from the isolation that was their common lot. In the five years after 1869 the town's population grew from 300 to 2500 people.

Cattle Kingdom

The towns thrived, of course, on the business of ranchers, whose longhorn steers were driven to market beginning in 1866. Mexican ranchers had introduced not only the cattle but the basic techniques for their management with a minimum of cost and labor. The ranchers allowed their herds to roam the range freely, identified only by a distinctive mark or brand. Each spring the cowboys rounded up the herds, branded the calves, and selected the steers to send to market. Anglo-Americans who came to Texas readily adopted the Mexican equipment: the tough mustangs and broncos (horses suited to managing the mean longhorns), the branding iron for marking the herds, the corral for holding cattle, and the lariat for roping. So too the cowboys donned the distinctive Mexican outfits—chaps, spurs, and a broad-brimmed hat.

Clara Williamson painted this herd on the long drive north from Texas. Cowboys normally worked in pairs, opposite each other, as shown here; the chuck wagon can be seen at the rear of the train. So strenuous was the work that each cowboy brought with him about eight horses, so fresh mounts would always be available.

When the early routes to Sedalia, Missouri, proved unfriendly, a more direct route through easier country along the Chisholm Trail, running from San Antonio to Abilene and Ellsworth, made the cattle drive practical. But the railroads that carried cattle east also brought farmers determined to close the open ranges of western Kansas. The resourceful Texans had soon blazed new trails, the Western to Dodge City and the Goodnight-Loving to Pueblo, Denver, and Cheyenne.

Since cattle grazed on the open range, early ranches were relatively small. Most had a house for the rancher and his family, a bunk house for the cowboys and other hired hands, and some grazing lands. Ranchers either owned the lands and herds or managed them for corporations and investors. Women were rare in the masculine world of cattle and cowboys. Most were ranchers' wives, who cooked, nursed the sick, and helped run the ranch. By necessity these women were strong and resourceful. When Helen Wiser Stewart of Nevada learned in July 1884 that her husband had been murdered, she took over operation of the ranch. Her life was an endless round of buying and selling cattle, managing the hands, and tending to her family. She did heavy physical labor as well, gathering crops, racking wine, grubbing mesquite, slaughtering hogs, and tending her garden.

After the Civil War veterans of the Confederate army made up the majority of the cowhands who tended the herds in Texas. But at least a third of all cowboys were black freedmen and Mexicans. Some cowhands dreamed of setting aside enough wages to start a herd of their own. A few took the easier route of cattle rustling. But in the end, most became wage laborers employed by the large corporate enterprises that came to dominate the industry. When Richard King, founder of the huge King Ranch of Texas, made $50,000 on the drive of 1875, he paid his 43 hands (over half of them Hispanic) anywhere from $43.20 a month for the most experienced to $25 for ordinary horse wranglers. Once again, the eastern pattern of economic concentration and labor specialization was being applied in the West.

Life in the saddle was far from romantic. For his labors, a cowboy was fed, housed, and paid a wage of about a dollar a day. No more than 12 hands tended from 2000 to 5000 head along the trail. During the drives of some 800 miles, lasting several months, the hands spent long hours chasing strays, guarding against human and animal predators, and heading off stampedes. Heavy dust clung to the skin and a cough brought up black phlegm from the lungs. There were days when the sun shone and the spectacle of the herd elevated spirits. More often, though, the cowboy reached the end of the day gloomy and heartsick, his stomach hurting from hunger, his body aching with fatigue. His only relief came in the raucous cattle towns where saloonkeepers, card sharps, and dance hall madams waited to separate him from his hard-earned wages.

The cattle boom that began with the first long drive of 1866 reached its peak from 1880 to 1885. Ranchers came to expect profits of 25 to 40 percent a year. Millions of dollars poured into the west from eastern and foreign interests eager to cash in on soaring cattle prices. Ranching corporations extended the open range from Texas into Wyoming and Montana. But as in all booms, forces were at work bringing the inevitable bust. High profits swelled the size of the herds and led to overproduction, increased foreign competition, and sagging beef prices. The big ranchers sometimes banded together to squeeze out the cowhands and farmers who sought to start herds of their own. In 1892 a range war broke out between the hired guns of the Wyoming Stockgrowers' Association and the small independent ranchers. The same forces that led to consolidation of industrial firms began to drive the small operators out of the cattle business.

Cattle ranchers were not the only entrepreneurs with an eye on the public domain. Rising food prices and cheap lands brought farmers into the Great Plains too. The "nesters," as ranchers disdainfully called them, fenced off their lands, resulting in a continually shrinking open range. Vast grants to the railroads limited the area of free land, while ranchers intent on breeding heavier cattle with more tender beef began to fence in their stock to prevent them from mixing with inferior strays. Even after Congress declared it illegal to fence the public domain, nesters and cattlemen fought an intermittent guerrilla war to establish their conflicting claims.

And cows were not the only grazing animals the Mexicans had introduced to the West. Cattlemen had particular contempt for the sheep raiser and his "woolies." Sheep tended to crop grasses so short that they ruined land for cattle grazing. To protect the range they saw as their own from the "hooved locust," cattlemen attacked shepherds and their flocks. On one occasion raiders along the Green River in Wyoming clubbed 8000 sheep to death. The sheep raiser–cattle rancher feuds produced violence often more severe than that between the farmers and ranchers.

In the end it was nature that imposed its own limits on the boom. There was simply not enough grass along the trails to support the millions of head on their way to market. The need to buy feed and land to raise hay drove costs up. Diseases like "Texas fever" sometimes wiped out entire herds. Then in 1886 and 1887 came two of the coldest winters in recorded history. The winds brought blizzards that drove wandering herds up against fences, where they either froze or starved to death. Exhaled breath congealed into sheets of ice so heavy a cow could not raise its head. Summer brought no relief, as severe heat and drought dried up waterholes and scorched the grasslands. In the Dakotas, Montana, Colorado, and Wyoming, losses ran as high as 90 percent. Future president Theodore Roosevelt was among the easterners who lost investments.

By the 1890s the open range and the long drives had disappeared. What prevailed were the cattle corporations like the King Ranch of Texas, with sufficient capital to acquire and fence vast grazing lands, hire ranchers to manage the herds, and pay for feed during winter months. The free and independent cowboy sitting tall in the saddle lived on mostly in the mythology of western writers and Hollywood movies.

THE FINAL FRONTIER

In the 1860s they had come in a trickle; in the 1870s they became a torrent. They were farmers from the East and Midwest, black freedmen from the South, and immigrants from Europe. What bound them together was a hunger for land based on their rural and peasant backgrounds. They had read railroad and steamship advertisements and heard stories from friends about millions of acres of fertile lands in the plains west of the 98th meridian. New, hardier strands of wheat like the "Turkey Red" imported from Russia, improved farm machinery, and techniques like dry farming made it possible to raise crops under harsh climatic conditions. The number of farms in the United States increased from around 2 million on the eve of the Civil War to almost 6 million in 1900.

The Land Rush

So intense was the craving for land that in March and April of 1889 some 100,000 people traveled by wagon, horseback, carriage, buckboard, mule, and on foot to a line across the Oklahoma panhandle. These were "Boomers," gathered for the greatest land rush in history. On April 22, 1889, with a signal from the U.S. cavalry, the Boomers raced across the line to claim some 2 million acres of Indian territory opened for settlement. And beyond the line lay the "Sooners"—those who had jumped the gun and hidden in gullies and thickets, ready to leap out one minute after noon to claim a stake in prosperity.

Even though more land would be settled after 1900 than before, the Oklahoma land rush marked the end of the opening of the West. No longer would geographers be able to mark a line on a map demarcating the point where settlement ended. Even before then the myth of the garden had foundered on the realities of weather and uncertain markets. Overproduction, combined with competition from newly opened lands in Canada, Argentina, Russia, and Australia, steadily drove down prices from the 1870s to the early twentieth century. Wheat, which sold for as much as $1.60 a bushel during the Civil War, fell as low as 49 cents during the 1890s and would not rise over a dollar until the demands of World War I drove prices up. Periods of above-average rain inevitably gave way to dry cycles. Farmers, like cattle ranchers, suffered through the drought and fierce winter cold of 1886 and 1887. They, especially, had to confront the harsh realities of a dry, treeless land that left families isolated in the vast loneliness of its boundless horizons. So even as the hopeful crowds lined up in Oklahoma, thousands of others abandoned their farms to escape mounting debts. Some returned east while others headed farther west, pursuing what one historian described as "the mirage of an infinity of second chances."

The West never conformed to the myth popular in the East that a poor farmer, with fortitude, self-reliance, and luck, could prosper on free and fertile land. For one thing, most of the desirable land in the West was not free. For every acre the government granted under the Homestead Act (80 million by 1900) farmers bought six. Land that the government had granted to Indians, the states, or the railroads had to be purchased. And the best lands were those near the railroad tracks that gave access to eastern markets. By the 1890s railroad land sold for around $25 an acre, compared to $1.25 if bought under the Homestead Act.

Speculators managed to control much of the choicest land, purchasing large blocks from states eager to raise revenues. Or they employed shills willing to establish a "dummy entry" on a quarter section and then turn it over to the speculator for a modest fee. Some even built cabins on wheels, which they could move from section to section to comply with the law's requirement for a building on the land. Others dropped a cup of water on the ground to meet the terms of the Desert Land Act of 1877, which entitled a farmer to 640 acres if the land was irrigated within three years.

Land was not the only expense for newly settled farmers. Farming the plains required substantial investment in equipment. Only a steel plow could cut the dense root systems of prairie grasses. The threat of cattle trampling the fields forced farmers to erect fences. Lacking wood, they found the answer in barbed wire, first marketed by an Illinois farmer, Joseph Glidden, in 1874. Between 1880 and 1900 the sale of barbed wire imported from the East grew from 80 million to 297 million pounds per year. And with little rain, many farmers had to install windmills and pumping equipment to draw water from deep underground.

On the vast open prairies, successful farming in export staples, especially wheat and oats, demanded heavy investment in machinery: special plows and harrows (which turned the heavy sod before spring rains and harrowed quickly to capture moisture once it fell) to permit dry farming; threshers, combines, and harvesters to bring in the crop; and powerful steam tractors to pull the heavy equipment. The average farmer spent what was for the poor a small fortune, about $785 on machinery alone and another $500 for land. The bigger operators often invested 10 or 20 times as much. Farms of over 1000 acres, known as bonanza farms, were most common in the wheatlands of the northern plains. The resulting efficiencies made a great difference. A steam tractor working one of the huge bonanza farms could simultaneously plow, harrow, and seed up to 50 acres a day—about 20 times more than a single person could do without machinery. Against such competition, small-scale farmers could scarcely compete. Like small farmers in the South, many westerners became tenants on land owned by others. Bonanza farmers hired as many as 250 laborers to work each 10,000 acres in return for room, board, and as little as 50 cents a day in wages.

A Plains Existence

For poor farm families, life on the plains meant a sod house or a dugout carved out of the hillside for protection from the winds. Tough, root-bound sod was cut into bricks about a foot wide and three feet long and laid edgewise to create walls three feet thick; sod bricks were laid over rafters for a roof. The average house was seldom more than 18 by 24 feet, and in severe weather it had to accommodate animals as well as people. One door and usually no more than a single window provided light and air. A sod house had the advantage of being cheap, too heavy to blow away in the wind, and too wet to catch fire. The thick walls kept the house warm in winter and cool in summer. In the spring, wildflowers and grass turned the roof into a small garden.

But bad weather made the disadvantages all too apparent. A heavy, soaking rain or snow could bring the roof down, or at the least allow mud and water to seep into the living area, where wooden floors were an uncommon luxury. Katherine Gibson of the Dakota territories recalled that no sooner had she lighted the stove one cold fall morning than she was beset by a rattlesnake and its offspring. She escaped through the window. As soon as a home was established, armies of flies, gnats, mosquitoes, and fleas moved in. Privacy was nearly impossible for families of six or more. Whenever they could afford to do so, farm families erected a wood frame house and turned the sod hut over to the livestock.

The heaviest burdens of farm life fell on the women, who faced a seemingly infinite variety of chores and deprivations. Stores were scarce and money for supplies even scarcer. Matches, window glass, kerosene for light and heat, and soap for laundry were generally unavailable. That meant long days over hot tubs preparing tallow wax for candles or soaking ashes and boiling lye with grease and pork rinds to make soap. Equally time-consuming was the sewing of clothing. Some families brought carding brushes and spinning wheels, but wool in the first years of settlement was often in such short supply that resourceful women used hair from wolves and other wild animals. Wagon covers and tents were often the only other cloth available. Buttons had to be fashioned from old spoons.

Even worse than disease and the shortage of basic necessities were the hard-

Sod houses built on the treeless plains were limited in size by a shortage of wood needed to support the roof, which often was over a foot thick. Having to haul possessions over long distances obviously restricted what a family could carry.

ships imposed by the natural elements. Women in the Southwest lived in dread of the stinging centipedes and scorpions that inhabited wall cracks. For the farmers from Missouri to Oregon, nothing spelled disaster like the locusts that periodically descended without warning. Swarms were sometimes more than 100 miles long, beating against the houses like hailstones. Though they seldom bothered people, they stripped all vegetation in their paths, including the bark of trees. They even devoured the laundry on the line and curtains in the windows. Many a farm family survived the harsh weather only to see an entire year's labor destroyed in a day. "I saw heaps of grasshoppers as large as a washtub," Elizabeth Roe recalled. "They commenced on a forty acre field of corn at 10 o'clock and before night there was not an ear of corn or green leaf to be seen."

The hot summers, disease, Indian wars, isolation, and material deprivation all taxed the courage of pioneer farm families, but winter had its special horrors. Blizzards could sweep the plains for days, piling snow to the rooftops and halting

Daily Lives

FOOD/DRINK/DRUGS

The Frontier Kitchen of the Plains

Out on the treeless plains the Indians had adjusted to scarcity of food, water, and other necessities by adopting a nomadic way of life. Their small kinship groups moved each season to wherever nature supplied the food they needed. Such mobility discouraged families from acquiring extensive material possessions. Tools and housing had to be light and portable. Even tribes that raised crops as part of their subsistence cycle often moved with the seasons.

White settlement was different. Farmers, ranchers, and townspeople rooted themselves to a single place. What the surrounding countryside could not supply had to be brought from afar, generally at great effort and expense. In areas distant from the railroad or other transportation links, families generally had to learn either to do without or to improvise from materials at hand. Keeping food on the table was nearly impossible some seasons of the year. Coffee and sugar were staples in such short supply that resourceful women invented a variety of substitutes. "Take a gallon of bran, two tablespoonsful of molasses, scald and parch in an oven until it is somewhat browned and charred," one women suggested. Something as simple as finding water suitable for drinking or cooking became a problem in many western areas, where the choice might be between "the strong alkaline water of the Rio Grande or the purchase of melted manufactured ice (shipped by rail) at its great cost." To prepare for the lean winter months, women stocked their cellars and made wild fruits into leathery

A box mill was essential for grinding the coffee beans and "stretchers"—rye, barley, and other grains used to extend coffee, which was often in short supply on pioneer farms.

cakes, eaten to ward off the scurvy that resulted from vitamin deficiency.

Gardening, generally a woman's responsibility, brought variety to the diet and color to the yard. The legume family of peas and beans, in particular, provided needed protein. Superstition had it that plants which grew above ground, like peas, beans, and squash, should be planted in the new moon, whereas root plants such as carrots, potatoes, radishes, and turnips went in as the moon waned. As the moon rose, the theory went, plants rose; as it dropped, so did the root plants. Flowers were much prized but seldom survived the winds, heat, and dry periods. Dishwater and laundry water helped keep them alive. One woman was so excited by the discovery of a hardy dandelion that she cultivated it with care and planted its seeds each spring.

Daily Lives

Until rail lines made shipment of goods cheap and Sears, Roebuck "wishbooks" brought mail order to the frontier, a woman's kitchen was fairly modest. A cast iron stove, which sold for $25 in the East, was in such demand and so expensive to ship that it fetched $200 in some areas of the West. One miner's wife in Montana during the 1870s considered her kitchen "well-furnished" with two kettles, a cast iron skillet, and a coffeepot. A kitchen cupboard might be little more than a box nailed to a log. In sod houses cooking could be difficult after a cloudburst. One "soddie" recalled that her kitchen remained snug and dry during a rainstorm, but she discovered that the downpour had taken its toll as the water seeped slowly through the thick roof. After the sun came out, the still-waterlogged roof began to leak. She ended up frying pancakes on her stove under the protection of an umbrella while the sun shone brightly outside.

Without doctors, circumstances forced women to learn the rudiments of caring for the hurt and sick. Most folk remedies did little more than ease pain. Whiskey and patent medicines, often more dangerous than the disease, were used to treat a range of ills from frostbite to snake bite and from sore throats to burns and rheumatism. Settlers believed that onions and gunpowder had valuable medicinal properties. Cobwebs could bandage small wounds; turpentine served as a disinfectant. Mosquitoes were repelled with a paste of vinegar and salt. One woman in Wyoming prevented winter snow blindness by burning pitch pine until it was black and smudging the skin below the eyes with it to cut glare. Most parents thought the laxative castor oil could cure any childhood malady. And if a family member had a fever, one treatment was to bind the head with a cold rag, wrap the feet in cabbage leaves, and then force down large doses of sage tea, rhubarb, and soda. Some women adapted remedies used on their farm animals. Sarah Olds, a Nevada homesteader whose family was plagued by fleas and lice, recalled that "we all took baths with plenty of sheep dip in the water. . . . I had no disinfectant . . . so I boiled all our clothing in sheep dip and kerosene."

Gradually, as the market system penetrated the West, families had less need to improvise in matters of diet and medicine. Through catalogs one might order spices like white pepper or poultry seasoning and appliances such as grinders for real coffee. If a local stagecoach passed by the house, a woman might send her eggs and butter to town to be exchanged for needed store-bought goods like threads and needles. It took a complex commercial network to bring all that the good life required to a land that produced few foods and necessities in abundance.

all forms of travel. Stockade fences built to keep the blizzards out and the animals safe made many a farm house seem like a prison. After living through several severe Dakota winters, Mary Woodward was amused by an eastern poet's romantic view of a winter snowfall. "I doubt if there is a poet living who possesses enough vim to write a poem about a Dakota blizzard. I guess a blizzard would knock all the poetry out of a man."

In the face of such hardships many westerners found comfort in religion. Though Catholics and Jews came West, evangelical Protestants dominated along the frontier, in the mining towns, and in other western communities. Worship offered an emotional outlet, some intellectual stimulation, a means of preserving older values, and a source of hope. Circuit riders compensated for the shortage of preachers, while camp meetings offered an opportunity for socializing; both brought contact with a wider world. In many communities it was the churches that first instilled order on public life. Through church committees westerners could deal with local problems like the need for schools or charity for the poor.

The sense among westerners and southerners that they were outside the American mainstream came not so much from their isolation from the industrial Northeast or Midwest, but from their links to it. The struggle by promoters of a New South to out-Yankee the Yankee could not overcome the region's low wage structure and high fertility rates. And so by 1900 southerners earned half as much as the national average—$509 versus $1165. The promoters of a fertile West had greater success in adopting the techniques of large-scale industry and investment to mining, cattle ranching, and farming. But they too discovered limits to an arid land, whose mineral and timber resources were not endless and where rain, contrary to William Gilpin's hopes, did not follow the plow. Like easterners, ordinary citizens in the West found that large corporations with near-monopoly control over markets and transportation bred inequality, unfair business practices, and widespread resentment.

These regional upheavals could not help but affect the political system as conflicts of class and race and region spilled over into the national arena. By the late 1880s and early 1890s, an agrarian revolt had begun to sweep the South and West. In both sections disillusionment and despair turned to bitterness as more small farmers, both black and white, found themselves enslaved to debt and driven toward bankruptcy, tenancy, or wage labor. It was small wonder that the South and West gave rise to a "People's party," determined to end the "business as usual" approach of the Democratic and Republican parties.

SIGNIFICANT EVENTS

1849–1859	Gold and silver strikes open western mining frontier
1862	Homestead Act; Minnesota Sioux uprising begins Plains Indian wars
1864	Chivington massacre
1866	Drive to Sedalia, Missouri, launches cattle boom
1869	Completion of first transcontinental railroad; Powell explores the Grand Canyon
1872–1874	The great buffalo slaughter
1874	Black Hills gold rush; barbed wire patented
1876	Battle of Little Big Horn; Nez Percé resist relocation
1877	Compromise of 1877 ends Reconstruction; Crazy Horse surrenders; Desert Land Act
1879	Height of Exoduster migration to Kansas
1880	Bonsack cigarette-rolling machine invented
1883	*Civil Rights Cases*
1885–1887	Severe winter and drought cycle in the West
1887	Dawes Severalty Act
1889	Oklahoma opened to settlement
1890s	Tennessee Coal, Iron, and Railway Company makes Birmingham, Alabama, a major steel center
1890	Ghost Dance Indian religious revival; Wounded Knee
1892	Union violence at Coeur d'Alene, Idaho; Wyoming range wars
1893	Frederick Jackson Turner's "Frontier Thesis" presented
1896	*Plessy v. Ferguson* upholds separate but equal doctrine

21

The Failure of Traditional Politics

he Democratic brass band gathered on a hot September day in Sparta, Georgia, to play a few patriotic numbers. Set up at one end of the grove, it launched tune after tune, each louder than the last. At the other end of the crowd, from a platform in the semiwooded countryside, Tom Watson addressed the assembled folks. On the surface, it was a scene reenacted all across America in that election season: brass bands, barbecues, and ballyhoo. But this was 1892—not an ordinary election year—and the assembly at Sparta was profoundly unsettling to many observers.

To begin with, the Democratic band that played so loudly at the far end of the grove did not belong to Tom Watson, the campaigner. Watson, a Congressman from northeast Georgia, had left the Democratic ticket in disgust and was running on behalf of a new third party, the Populists. His opponent's gathering was down the grove less than a mile away, and the band had come over to whoop it up and distract Watson's followers. What seemed especially unsettling to the rival Democrats was that the Watson crowd was largely black. Blacks still went to the polls in Georgia in 1892; and most of them knew, from the habits of the past decades, the way they were supposed to vote if they wanted to stay healthy. On Election Day the white owner they sharecropped for or some other local worthy would gather 25 or 50 blacks and march them off single file, down a dusty road to the polls. Blacks remembered well enough the nights in the 1870s when the Ku Klux Klan galloped through the countryside, and southern whites "redeemed" their states. Redeemer politicians treated blacks courteously enough during election season, so long as they voted the way they were meant to.

As the band continued playing, a Democrat on horseback pushed his way into Watson's Populist crowd shouting, "A free dinner for everybody; you are all invited down to the barbecue—white and colored!" Watson had no dinner plans but he had his lungs. "You may have the trees," he shouted to the rider, "but we have got the men; and these men are not going to be enticed away from free, fair discussion of these great public questions by any amount of barbecued beef!" Nor did the crowd move. They wanted to hear Watson out.

Thomas E. Watson was no ordinary farmer and no typical southern politician. He was, in fact, the single largest landowner in Georgia, with more tenants on his land than his grandfather had owned slaves. Yet like some other members of the

New York City's Democratic party machine grew out of the Tammany Society, an eighteenth-century fraternal order named for a Lenni Lenape chief who welcomed William Penn. Here, Tammany Hall is decorated for the Democratic Convention of 1868.

landed class, Watson identified with the poor farmers, tenants, small landholders, and impoverished industrial workers who rallied to the Populist party. During the past two decades, the price of cotton had fallen steadily at the same time that deflation had increased the value of money. For farmers in debt, these conditions meant that paying back loans had become even more expensive. Land in the South was so cheap that farmers could not mortgage it; merchants and banks would allow them only to take out "liens"—obligations to pay back their debts from the sale of future crops. If the crops fell short or prices dropped, they lost their land. Each year fewer farmers owned the land they tilled; a third had become tenants by the time the 1892 election rolled around. "Hundreds of farmers will be turned adrift, and thousands of acres of our best lands be allowed to grow up in weeds. . . . The roads are full of Negroes beggings homes," one newspaper editor warned. Urban workers were equally desperate. The mills that belched the smoke of Henry Grady's New South left their workers in "rooms wherein eight and ten members of one family are stricken down, where pneumonia and fever and measles are attacking their emaciated bodies; where there is no sanitation, no help or protection from the city, no medicine, no food, no fire, no nurses—nothing but torturing hunger and death."

Such folk acted "like victims of some horrid nightmare . . . powerless—oppressed—shackled," Watson observed. To him the agents of ruin were all too evident. They included the huge railroad companies, which charged exorbitant fees to ship cotton, and the industrialists and finance capitalists, who held a "monopoly of power, of place, of privilege, of wealth, of progress." Nor was Watson alone in his views, for many western as well as southern farmers were experiencing hard times. Watson and eight members of Congress from the West had organized a splinter party, called the Populists, or People's party. It ran its first major candidates in the 1892 elections.

Throughout the campaign Watson received continual threats against his life and later regarded it as something of a "miracle" that he hadn't been killed. The hatred resulted not so much from his social program (though proposals like nationalizing the railroads upset many conservatives) as from his decision to build a political alliance between poor whites and poor blacks, against the Republican industrialists of the Northeast and the conservative Democratic ruling class of the South. Watson told his racially mixed audiences that both Democrats and Republicans wanted to keep them divided from each other:

> You are kept apart that you may be separately fleeced of your earnings. You are made to hate each other because upon that hatred is rested the keystone of the arch of financial despotism which enslaves you both. You are deceived and blinded that you may not see how this race antagonism perpetuates a monetary system which beggars both.

As the campaign of 1892 heated up, white Populists found themselves barred from their churches by hostile fellow citizens, denied credit at local stores, even driven from their homes. Citizens of both races nevertheless worked eagerly for Watson. One young black preacher, the Reverend H. S. Doyle, made over 60 speeches in the candidate's behalf; when Doyle was threatened with a lynch mob, Watson gave him haven on his own lands and mobilized some 2000 Populists to protect him. They arrived on "buggies and horses foaming and tired with travel." "We are determined," said Watson, "in this free country that the humblest white or black man that wants to talk our doctrine shall do it, and the man doesn't live who shall touch a hair of his head, without fighting every man in the people's party."

Still, upright intentions could not outweigh fraud and outright violence. As many as 15 blacks died in the Democratic campaign of intimidation. Whiskey was

Georgia firebrand Tom Watson in 1904.

dispensed liberally to persuade citizens to vote Democratic; blacks were trucked in from across the South Carolina line to vote; many Democrats voted repeatedly as ballot boxes were stuffed. Even cash bribes routinely changed hands. After winning through such a convincing show of force, Watson's opponents expected that their adversary had learned his lesson—was so badly beaten that he would have to be laid out in state, like a corpse at a funeral. Watson was having none of it. "We decided not to die," he announced, on behalf of his party. "We unanimously decided to postpone the funeral."

The conditions breeding rebellion and resistance in the South and West would not go away. By the early 1890s the national system of politics as usual was not working. An economic and social revolution had been reshaping America, creating industrial and financial systems of remarkable size, cities whose social diversity and stratification had become much greater than the cities of prewar America, regional economies in the South and West whose raw materials had been drawn into national and international markets over which farmers and ordinary workers had little control.

The political system changed much more slowly. Real social and economic problems were allowed to simmer unattended. Pressures built in the 1890s as the business cycle plunged and a great depression worked its stringent discipline, throwing millions out of work and driving many to violent protest. Politicians were forced to change and adjust. Men and women like Watson ensured that politics could not go on as usual.

THE POLITICS OF PARALYSIS

As he traveled through the United States in the 1880s and 1890s, Moisei Ostrogorski, a Russian political scientist, observed that "the constituted authorities are unequal to their duty." Ostrogorski was part of an invasion of foreign visitors who had come to see the American democratic experiment in action. By the end of the century they were in agreement: the experiment was imperiled, the victim of private greed, middle-class indifference, and political mediocrity. In fact, there were deeper problems—the widening gulf between rich and poor, the growing power of corporate industry, the wretched poverty of city and farm, the endless cycle of boom and bust, the needs of blacks, women, Indians, and other Americans. They had scarcely been addressed, let alone resolved. Politics, the traditional medium of resolution, was grinding into paralysis as Republicans and Democrats fought to a dangerous stalemate.

The Party Stalemate

Another foreign visitor to America in the 1880s, the British historian and diplomat Lord James Bryce, concluded that "neither party has any clean-cut principles, any distinctive tenets. . . . All has been lost, except office or the hope of it." Bryce's judgment, echoed by generations of historians, is too harsh. That the two parties seemed so similar and produced so little were marks of the delicate balance of power on which partisan politics rested in the Gilded Age. From 1877 to 1897 Republicans inhabited the White House for 12 years, Democrats for 8. Margins of victory were paper thin. In 1880, for example, the Republicans won the presiden-

Daily Lives

POLITICAL CULTURE

The Bosses Throw a Party

Chicago's First Ward Ball was a lavish if chaotic affair held in the city's spacious Coliseum. Mounted by ward bosses "Bathhouse" John Coughlin and Michael "Hinky Dink" Kenna, the annual bash had something for everyone. With wine merchants pledged to spend $1500 each, waiters paying $5 just to work the floor, and ordinary tickets running $3 apiece, Hinky Dink and the Bath turned a $20,000 profit in 1907. That was enough to replenish their war chest for the 1908 elections. The 20,000 revelers had thoroughly enjoyed themselves, downing 10,000 quarts of champagne and 30,000 quarts of beer. "Enjoy" was perhaps too tame a judgment. Riotous, drunken carousers stripped unguarded young women naked, overran a lurid "circus act," and smashed a 35-foot bar. "If a great disaster had befallen the Coliseum last night," reported the unamused *Tribune*, "there would not have been a second story worker, a dip or plug ugly, porch climber, dope fiend or scarlet woman remaining in Chicago."

Reformers railed against the "vile orgy," but Hinky Dink and the Bath paid no heed. For 1908 the Coliseum was again rented and the liquor license—all neat and legal—renewed. When the *Tribune* threatened to publish the names of any "better grade" politicians or business leaders (the ball's biggest supporters) who attended, Hinky Dink himself took charge of promoting ticket sales. Any house of ill repute employing two more prostitutes than the year before received an additional 50 tickets to sell. A barber who had been allowed the privilege of placing his pole on the city sidewalk free of charge was encouraged to show his gratitude by purchasing tickets and giving them away. Every saloonkeeper and theater owner in the ward received an extra block to dispose of, and those who refused could be found cooling their heels in jail or suddenly deprived of their mortgages. A few could not be found at all.

When a bomb mysteriously shattered the back windows of the Coliseum two days before the party, Bathhouse John blamed reformers. Asked to compromise with them, the Bath winked: "All right. . . . We won't let parents bring their children." Still, he made a few concessions. Pickpockets were told they were no longer welcome at this year's event and warned that they would be driven from the city if anyone reported a theft. Two hundred burly ward heelers, collectors, and party thugs, each wearing a bright blue ribbon, were detailed as bouncers. (Trusted precinct captains and ward jobholders got red ribbons to identify them as clerks in the cloakroom.) A hundred extra policemen were put on duty to control the crowd.

As night fell on the appointed date, Bathhouse John hurried to the Coliseum from a meeting of the city council. As an alderman, he had just voted against a low bid from an unfriendly contractor to construct a new city hall. He arrived at the celebrations to find 15,000 people jammed along Wabash Avenue waiting to enter. Rushing inside, he spoke briefly to Hinky Dink, checked the preparations one last time, and cried, "O.K.! Let 'em in."

The crowd flooded the hall, knocking over tables and potted palms, crashing like a giant wave onto the bars, and spilling finally into the annex and basement. Some were already in their cups; others demanded beer so ferociously that bartenders had no time to ask for payment. Soon the empty champagne bottles were piled

Daily Lives

Michael "Hinky Dink" Kenna and "Bathhouse" John Coughlin, bosses of Chicago's notorious First Ward and "Lords of the Levee."

high atop tables, the better for Hinky Dink and the Bath to see how the party and the "take" were coming along. The hall became a madhouse, so tightly packed that "even those already drunk were forced to stand erect." High above the throng, in the royal boxes, sat a more dignified group of fun-lovers—the important lawyers, politicians, railroad executives, and businessmen, all wearing masks to avoid detection by reporters.

Then the ladies arrived—painted, daringly dressed, and ready for an evening of sport (despite already having put in half-shifts at the local brothels). At midnight sharp, a huge procession gathered at one end of the Coliseum and strutted, 25 abreast, across the floor. At the head of the Grand March stood Hinky Dink and the Bath, trailed by an army of card sharps and gamblers, prostitutes, pimps and madams, female impersonators, tramps, dive owners, and other assorted characters of unsavory reputation. Then Bathhouse John gave the nod, and the band struck up the evening's theme: "Hail! Hail! The Gang's All Here!"

Loyal voters continued dancing, brawling, and drinking until near dawn, when the Bath called for a final chorus or two of "Home, Sweet Home." A sleepy-eyed Coughlin tarried a bit longer to count receipts. With all the gate crashers and cheapskates, the take was less than $20,000, but no matter—there was always next year!

Chicago's First Ward Ball was not the only such party, only the most notorious. All across turn-of-the-century America similar scenes were enacted. Whether in Boss Cox's Cincinnati, Boss Behrman's New Orleans, or Boss Reuf's San Francisco, political machines were mounting barbecues, boatrides, and balls to raise funds and reward their followers. Reformers might fulminate, but bosses like Hinky Dink and the Bath continued to levy tribute and rule the wards for years to come.

tial race by only 7000 votes out of more than 9 million cast. No president had a majority of his party in both houses of Congress for his entire term. Democrats won control of the House in 1874, lost it in 1880, regained it in 1882, only to lose it in 1888 and win it again in 1890. Republicans held the Senate throughout the period (except for 1879–1881), but between 1876 and 1890 they enjoyed a margin of more than three for only two years.

With elections so tight, the parties orchestrated mass spectacles to bring out the vote. "For three months," reported a British observer, "processions, usually with brass bands, flags, badges, crowds of cheering spectators, are the order of the day and night from end to end of the country." In cities political machines turned out loyal followers on cue. Party workers distributed leaflets and pinned campaign buttons on passers-by, while local postmasters (party appointees) delivered campaign pamphlets with the mail. Picnics and rallies, highlighted by spellbinding speakers, drew people from miles away. Campaigns stressed entertainment and symbols, lest either party risk losing precious votes. "Political oratory," remarked still another foreign traveler, was "not directed towards instruction, but towards stimulation." When election day finally arrived, stores closed and businesses shut down. At political clubs and corner saloons men lined up to get voting orders (along with free drinks) from ward bosses. In the countryside, fields went untended as farmers took their families to town, cast their ballots, and bet on the outcome.

It is no wonder that an average of nearly 80 percent of those eligible cast their ballots in presidential elections between 1876 and 1900, a figure higher than any time since. Even so, the electorate was only a small percentage of the population. Between 1876 and 1892, less than one American in five voted in presidential elections. Other than white males, few citizens even met voting qualifications. Only in Wyoming, Utah, Idaho, and Colorado could women vote in national elections. In 1875 the Supreme Court ruled in *Minor v. Happersett* that states could deny women their franchise. The efforts of the National Woman Suffrage Association to enact a constitutional amendment granting women the right to vote failed miserably, and between 1870 and 1910 almost a dozen states defeated similar referenda.

Party loyalty was unwavering. In every election, 16 states could be counted on to vote Republican, 14 Democratic. Only in Connecticut, New Jersey, Illinois, New York, Indiana, and Ohio were the results ever in doubt. National victories often hung on their returns. Both parties courted them with money, time, and—most flattering of all—presidential candidacies. Between 1868 and 1900 these states produced five of six Republican and four of six Democratic candidates for president. Ohio alone supplied four Republican presidents, New York four Democratic candidates for president.

Republicans and Democrats did have similarities but also clear differences. Both parties supported business and condemned radicalism; neither offered embattled farmers and workers much help. Democrats believed in states' rights and a decentralized, limited government. They were often naysayers, especially to spending. Their regional center of power was the South, which embraced the party not only because Democrats had led the Old Confederacy and "redeemed" it from Reconstruction but also out of fear that federal authorities might try again to protect the rights of African-Americans.

Urban political machines and their immigrant constituents composed a second wing of the Democratic party. The cultural politics of religion and ethnicity

Even as a teenaged printer's apprentice around 1850, Samuel Clemens seemed a cocky "man of letters," displaying his name on a printer's stick. By 1873 his humorous essays and books, published under the pen name of Mark Twain, had made him famous. When he and Charles Dudley Warner published a satirical novel, its title, *The Gilded Age*, became synonymous with an era rife with political spoils and corruption. Twain's masterpiece, *The Adventures of Huckleberry Finn* (1884), combined a realistic ear for dialect with humor that, at bottom, reflected a somber view of human nature.

guided them. Often members of ritualistic religions such as Roman Catholicism, German Lutheranism, and Judaism, they saw salvation in following the rituals of their faith, not in dictating codes of conduct for all society. For an Italian Catholic or a Russian Jew, morality was an individual and family matter. They regarded the Democratic party as a protector of liberty because it opposed such moral and ethnic controls as prohibition of alcohol, Sunday-closing laws, and English-only public schools.

Whereas the Democrats were the party of localism and restraint, the Republicans had begun to develop a national vision and invoke modest federal activism. Drawing on their Whig heritage, they promoted economic growth through the Homestead Act (1862), subsidies to railroads, and protective tariffs. Business interests therefore formed the solid core of their support, around which a substantial portion of the middle class rallied. With memories of emancipation and Reconstruction, African-Americans too voted for the party of Lincoln. (Black voting power, of course, had dwindled as white Democrats "redeemed" the South.) By 1890 well over a million surviving veterans remained loyal to the Grand Old Party. Regionally Republicans could count on the Northeast and Midwest to offset Democratic control of the South. And ethnically they drew on Anglo-Saxon Protestant sects that put their faith in the value of good works to encourage pious behavior throughout society. In the Republican party, which had risen to power with moral condemnations of slavery, these pietistic groups found eager supporters of social controls such as prohibition.

Both parties suffered from deep divisions and personal feuds. The Republicans were split among various factions with colorful labels like "Stalwarts," "Half-Breeds," and "Mugwumps" (an Algonkian word meaning "chief"). Stalwarts looked for leadership to "Lord" Roscoe Conkling, the haughty and vain senator from New York. Tall, graceful, a former boxer, Conkling summed up his philosophy in one line: "I do not know how to belong to a party a little." He and his followers hewed to the old tenets of Republicanism, especially its commitments to Reconstruction and establishing the Republican party in the South. Most of all they believed in the time-honored political traditions of acquiring power and dispersing the "spoils" (federal, state, and local offices) to supporters and party workers.

No less a master of spoils was the charming, sharp-tongued senator from Maine, James G. Blaine, who led the Half-Breeds. These forward-looking party members embraced the new Republicanism of economic nationalism, tariff protection, and the development of an urban industrial society. Opposed to both factions were the Mugwumps. Elitist and socially prominent, out of touch with the mass of voters, they wanted to end corruption and replace the spoils system with a rational civil service that employed men of wealth, education, and standing. Essentially conservative, they favored a limited supply of money and laissez-faire government. For their part the Democrats, as ardent a collection of spoils-seekers as the Stalwarts and Half-Breeds, were split among southern white supremacists and family farmers, urban machine politicians, and business interests bent on lowering tariffs.

Impassioned reformers usually created their own political instruments. Some formed nonpartisan groups that aligned themselves behind issues rather than parties. Opponents of alcohol formed the Women's Christian Temperance Union (1874) and the Anti-Saloon League (1893). Champions of the rights of women joined the National Woman Suffrage Association (1890), a reunion of two branches of the women's suffrage movement that had split in 1869. Formal political parties sometimes crystallized around a single concern or a particular group. Advocates of prohibition rallied to the Prohibition party (1869). Those who sought inflation of the currency formed the Greenback party (1874). Disgruntled farmers in the West and South created the Populist, or People's, party (1892). All drew scores of supporters from both conventional parties, but as single-interest groups, they mobilized minorities, not majorities.

Congressional Politics

Congressional politics focused on the well-worn issues of regional conflict, patronage, tariffs, and money. With the presidency weakened by the impeachment of Andrew Johnson, the scandals of Ulysses S. Grant, and the contested victory of Rutherford B. Hayes in 1876, Congress enjoyed the initiative in making policy. Time after time, legislators squandered it amid electioneering and party infighting.

Some divisive issues were the bitter legacy of the Civil War. Well into the 1880s Republicans symbolically waved the "bloody shirt" by labeling Democrats the "party of treason," responsible for the war between the states and unworthy of governing. "Not every Democrat was a Rebel," they reminded voters, "but every rebel was a Democrat." South of the Mason–Dixon line, Democrats waved the bloody shirt too, only it was the Republicans who were called traitors.

The war's politics also surfaced in the lobbying efforts of veterans. The Grand Army of the Republic, an organization of over 400,000 former Union soldiers, petitioned the government for pensions to make up for poor wartime pay and to support the widows and orphans of their fallen comrades. By the turn of the century Union army veterans and their families were receiving $157 million annually, one of the largest programs of public assistance in American history. Veterans of the Confederacy, on the other hand, got nothing except small pensions from several southern states.

Less divisive but more relevant was the campaign for a new method of staffing federal offices. Since the early nineteenth century, government jobs had been awarded by political victors, who simply gave them away to loyal followers regardless of their qualifications. After elections, winners faced an army of office seekers, "lying in wait . . . like vultures for a wounded bison." President Hayes found that even his wife was hounded by applicants, and Benjamin Harrison despaired that he spent as many as six hours a day dealing with them during the first 18 months of his presidency.

The increasing size of the federal bureaucracy made the situation almost intolerable by the late 1880s. From barely 53,000 people on the payroll at the end of the Civil War, the federal government had grown to 166,000 by the early 1890s. In addition, far more government jobs required special skills. For example, the use of typewriters (20 of them were hammering away at the Justice Department by the mid-1880s) meant that literacy and intelligence alone no longer qualified someone for a clerkship. As government expanded, the need for scientists, engineers, and other well-trained professionals grew accordingly.

Dismantling the spoils system, whatever the need, stirred great controversy. American politics rested on patronage. Without it, politicians—from presidents to lowly ward captains—feared that they could attract neither the workers nor the money required to run their parties. Reacting to the scandals of the Grant administration, a group of young independents, generally well educated and well-to-do, banded together in 1881 to form the National Civil Service Reform League. The league promoted the British model of civil service based on examination and merit. Defenders of the spoils system called the reform "snivel service," with neither party in Congress willing to take action when it held power (and thus controlled patronage). Presidents, not nearly so dependent on appointees for influence, could more easily afford to advocate reform.

The assassination of President James A. Garfield in 1881 by Charles Guiteau, a demented and frustrated office seeker, finally produced a clamor for reform. In 1883 the Civil Service Act, or Pendleton Act, created a bipartisan civil service commission to administer competitive examinations for a select number of federal jobs. It also outlawed the assessments political leaders charged their appointees and established an orderly, nonpartisan method of promotion. While the new system applied to only 10 percent of all federal jobs, presidents could expand the list. By 1896 almost one federal worker in two came under civil service (though whether the new system actually improved the quality of bureaucrats was hotly debated).

As much as any issue, the protective tariff ignited popular emotions while baffling politicians. The tax on imports of manufactured goods and some agricultural products had been created early in the century to protect developing "infant industries." Since then the debate on whether to increase or lower tariffs had set regions and interest groups against one another. Northern and eastern industrialists supported high schedules to keep up the prices of their foreign competitors. So did laboring men and women, who wanted to protect their wages and jobs. Southerners saw the tariff as more unfair protection for the industrial Northeast and opposed it on all but the products made within their region. Farmers, while favoring protection for agriculture, wanted rates on manufactured goods reduced. Consumers maintained that high tariffs gouged them by keeping prices up, regardless of the jobs they preserved.

As promoters of economic growth, Republicans usually favored high tariffs.

Democrats generally sought reduction to encourage foreign trade and cut the federal surplus. In 1890, when Republicans controlled the House, Congress enacted the McKinley Tariff (1890), which raised schedules to an all-time high. The McKinley Tariff also contained a novel twist, a reciprocity clause to promote foreign trade. The president was given authority to lower rates if other countries did the same. In 1894 Democrats in the House, supported strongly by President Grover Cleveland, succeeded in reducing rates, only to be thwarted by some 600 Senate amendments restoring most cuts. In 1897 the Dingley Tariff raised rates still higher but soothed reductionists by broadening reciprocity.

Just as murky and emotional was the currency controversy. Until about the mid-1800s American money, like that of other nations, was coined from both gold and silver. In this policy of "bimetallism," the Treasury periodically adjusted the number of grains of each metal in the dollar according to the price of gold and silver bullion on the open market. The need for more money during the Civil War led Congress to issue "greenbacks"—currency printed on green paper that was not redeemable in gold or silver. For the next decade and a half Americans argued over whether to print more unsupported paper money or take it out of circulation entirely. In 1878 the "Greenback" party polled over a million votes and elected 14 representatives to Congress. Yet fear of inflation led Congress first to reduce the number of greenbacks in circulation, then in 1879 to make what remained convertible into gold on demand. The currency and the question faded from the scene.

Meanwhile a more heated battle was developing over silver-backed money. In a sense it pitted "have-nots" against "haves." The have-nots of business— aggressive entrepreneurs interested in starting new ventures—were hungry for capital to build factories, warehouses, or railroads. They wanted more silver coined to expand the money supply. Prices would rise and interest rates would fall, an ideal situation for eager new businessmen.

Farmers also looked to silver for salvation. Some had bought cheap land from railroads or from the government on credit. Others borrowed every year to purchase seed and equipment for planting and harvesting. As the prices of wheat, corn, and other agricultural products steadily slipped, these farmers found themselves unable to pay their debts. They blamed "the money power"—gold-oriented northeastern bankers and financiers—for keeping the supply of money low and interest rates high. Inflation, they believed, would increase farm prices and fatten farmers' profits. It would even cheapen their debts by permitting them to repay loans with dollars worth less than those originally borrowed. Western miners, who had just hit a mother lode of silver, also supported bimetallism.

Bankers, other creditors, and established businessmen—the haves—stood firmly for "sound money," a limited supply of currency that rested on the time-honored standard of gold. It was an article of their faith that dollars exchangeable for gold induced the business confidence required for prosperity by keeping the monetary system tight and stable. "Atheism is not worse in religion," declared the New York *Christian Advocate* in 1878, "than an unstable or irredeemable currency in political economy."

By the early 1870s the United States and Europe used so little silver that Congress stopped coining it. A silver mining boom in Nevada soon revived demands for coining the metal. In 1878 the Bland–Allison Act inaugurated a limited form of silver coinage. The Treasury was required to purchase between $2 million and $4 million worth of silver each month. Pressure for unlimited coinage of silver—coining of all silver presented at United States mints—mounted as silver production quadrupled between 1870 and 1890. Under the Bland–Allison Act, moreover, the money supply was growing too slowly for inflationists. Each year the government was able to buy all the silver it needed with fewer and fewer dollars because new discoveries reduced silver prices. The money supply grew too slowly. By 1890 the pressure to coin silver had reached such a level that President Harrison and Republican leaders in Congress adopted the Sherman Silver Purchase Act. The government was obligated to buy 4.5 million ounces of silver every month regardless of the price. Paper tender called "treasury notes," redeemable in either gold or silver, would pay for it. The compromise satisfied both sides only temporarily, and by the mid-1890s silver was again a hot issue.

The White House from Hayes to Harrison

From the 1870s through the 1890s a run of nearly anonymous presidents presided over the country. Not all were mere caretakers; some tried to revive the office, but Congress continued to reign supreme in Washington. Despite the criticism of modern historians, such legislative supremacy more closely reflected the intentions of the Founding Fathers. The dynamic presidency is more a product of twentieth-century circumstances and political values.

The first of the "Ohio dynasty" (three presidents from 1876 to 1900), Republican Rutherford B. Hayes was, in the opinion of one Democratic leader, "far better than four years of unrest which we should undoubtedly have had if Tilden had occupied the office of President." ("Rutherfraud" Hayes, as the angry losers called him, had reversed the popular election victory of Samuel Tilden in 1876 with secret deals for contested electoral votes.) A Harvard-trained lawyer, wounded veteran of the Civil War, and reform governor of Ohio, Hayes was moderate in his personal habits. When Rutherford and "Lemonade Lucy" Hayes threw a dinner party, said one guest, "the water flowed like champagne." As president, Hayes moved quickly to end Reconstruction and tried unsuccessfully to woo southern Democrats with promises of economic support. He pursued civil service reform so staunchly that one angry spoilsman called him "George Washington." Making few inroads against the spoils system, he left office after a single term, happy to be "out of a scrape."

Republican James Garfield succeeded Hayes, but not for long. Another former soldier from Ohio, Garfield won by a handful of votes and spent his first hundred days in the White House besieged by office hunters and indecisively trying to placate the rival Half-Breed and Stalwart sections of his party. On July 2, 1881, Garfield was shot while standing in a Washington railroad station, on route to a vacation in New England. "I am a Stalwart and Arthur is President now!" shouted Charles Guiteau, the crazed assassin who had failed to receive an appointment in the administration. Garfield lingered for 11 weeks before succumbing to his wounds. Chester A. Arthur, a "spoilsman's spoilsman" and protégé of party boss Roscoe Conkling, was president. "Chet Arthur, President of the United States," exclaimed a dismayed Republican. "Good God!"

"He isn't 'Chet' Arthur any more," concluded one former associate soon after the inauguration. To almost everyone's surprise, the fastidious Arthur turned out to be an honest president. He transformed the gloomy and dilapidated White House into an elegant social center. He broke with machine politicians, including his mentor Roscoe Conkling. He worked to lower the tariff, warmly endorsed the

Handsome and urbane, Chester A. Arthur was the era's most fashionable and least distinguished president.

new Civil Service Act, and reduced the federal surplus by beginning construction of a modern navy. Such even-handed administration left him little chance for renomination from party leaders. Half-Breeds regarded him as a Stalwart, Stalwarts as a renegade. Arthur could never have accepted anyway; he was dying and knew it.

The election of 1884 was, in the words of a contemporary, the "vilest" ever waged. It pitted Half-Breed Senator James Blaine, the beloved "Plumed Knight" from Maine, against Democrat Grover Cleveland, the former mayor of Buffalo and governor of New York. Despite superb talents as a leader and vote-getter, Blaine was haunted by renewed charges that he helped to secure illegal favors for the Little Rock and Fort Smith Railroad. "Grover the Good," on the other hand, had won a well-deserved reputation for honesty by fighting corruption and the spoils system in New York. The diligent and portly Cleveland, sighed a reporter, "remains within doors constantly, eats and works, eats and works, and works and eats." Unfortunately Cleveland, a bachelor, spent enough time away from work to father an illegitimate child. "Above all, tell the truth," he instructed his campaign managers, when the scandal broke, whereupon Republicans throughout the country broke into a chant of "Ma, ma, where's my pa?" In the last week of the tight race, Democrats circulated among the numerous Irish-Catholic voters of New York the statement of a local Protestant minister that labeled Democrats the party of "Rum, Romanism, and Rebellion" (alcohol, Catholicism, and the Civil War). Most of the Irish who had been tempted to support Blaine returned to the Democratic fold and New York swung to Cleveland. When Cleveland won the election (by a mere 25,000 out of 10 million votes), Democrats told Republicans where to find the bachelor father: "Gone to the White House, ha, ha, ha!"

A Chinese laborer, queue in hand, proudly displays patches in support of the 1888 Democratic presidential candidate Grover Cleveland and his running mate, Allen B. Thurman. Cleveland and Thurman lost to Benjamin Harrison and Levi P. Morton.

Cleveland was the first Democrat elected to the White House since James Buchanan in 1856. He pleased reformers, especially Mugwumps who had deserted the Republican party to support him, by expanding the civil service. Businessmen praised his conservative devotion to gold, economy, and efficiency. He endorsed the growth of federal power by supporting the Interstate Commerce Act (1887), new agricultural research, and federal arbitration of labor disputes.

Cleveland's presidential activism remained limited. He vetoed two of every three bills brought to him, more than twice the number of all his predecessors combined. Toward the end of his term, embarrassed by the large federal surplus, Cleveland finally exerted leadership by attacking the tariff as "the vicious, inequitable, illogical source of taxation" and pledging to lower it. The Republican-controlled Senate blocked this move, and in 1888 Republicans nominated a sturdy defender of protectionism, Benjamin Harrison, the grandson of President William Henry Harrison. Cleveland won a plurality of the popular vote but lost in the Electoral College. Since the Republicans also won both houses of Congress, 1888 marked the most sweeping victory for either party in nearly 20 years.

Benjamin Harrison (called by his colleagues the "human iceberg") worked hard, rarely delegated management, and turned the White House into a well-regulated office. Cautiously active, he began to bring the presidency back to life. As a former senator, he understood the value of executive advice and pressure; he offered both at informal dinners at the White House with leaders of the House and Senate, in trial balloons released to reporters, and in well-timed messages to Congress. He helped to shape the Sherman Silver Purchase Act (1890), kept up with the McKinley Tariff (1890), and accepted the Sherman Antitrust Act (1890), which limited the control exerted by business combinations over markets. At his urging the House passed a Federal Elections Bill to protect the rights of black voters. Democrats denounced it as a "force bill" and filibustered it to death in the Senate. Yet by the end of Harrison's term in 1892, Congress had completed its most productive term of the era, including the first billion-dollar peacetime budget. To Democratic taunts of an extravagant "Billion Dollar Congress," Republican House Speaker Thomas Reed shot back, "This is a billion-dollar country!"

Ferment in the States and Cities

It would be misleading to focus only on Washington. Most people expected little from the federal government. It was closer to home that public pressure mounted. Ambivalence about the growth of big business, discontent over discriminatory shipping rates, and widespread anxiety about political corruption and urban decay produced a ferment in the states and cities. Experimental and often effective, state programs set important precedents for later action and represented some of the era's boldest initiatives in public policy.

Starting in 1869 with Massachusetts, states established commissions to investigate and regulate industry. By the turn of the century, almost two-thirds of the states had them. The first commissions gathered and publicized information on shipping rates and business practices and furnished advice on public policy. In the Midwest, on the Great Plains, and in the Far West, merchants and farmers upset over unfair railroad rates and rebates to large shippers pressed state governments for action. In Sacramento, California, one newspaper published a schedule of freight rates to various places in Nevada, showing that lower rates had been charged by wagon teams before the railroads were built. On the West Coast and in the Midwest, state legislatures empowered commissions to end rebates and monitor rates. In 1870 Illinois became the first of several states to define railroads as public highways subject to regulation, including setting maximum rates.

Concern over the condition of cities and their politics led to state municipal conventions, the first in Iowa in 1877. Philadelphia sponsored a national conference on good city government in 1894, and a year later reformers founded the National Municipal League. Within two years it had over 200 branches. Its model city charter advanced such far-sighted reforms as separate city and state elections, limited franchises for utilities, and more authority for mayors. Meanwhile cities and states in the Midwest enacted pietistic laws closing stores on Sundays, prohibiting the sale of alcohol, and making English the language of public schools—all in an effort to control the habits of newcomers from abroad.

THE REVOLT OF THE FARMERS

In 1890 the politics of complacency cracked. Lavish expenditures of the "Billion-Dollar Congress" on pensions and public works, together with the overall expansion of federal authority, angered many voters. Beginning in the late 1880s, a severe agricultural depression hit. In 1887 and again in 1889 droughts withered crops. Yet overproduction caused prices to fall, and a wave of foreclosures drove thousands of desperate farmers from the western plains.

Farmers had no trouble explaining why. "We went to work and plowed and planted," said one woman. "The rains fell, the sun shone, nature smiled, and we raised the big crop they told us to; and what came of it? Eight cent corn, ten cent oats, two cent beef and no price at all for butter and eggs—that's what came of it. Then the politicians said we suffered from over-production." Overproduction there had been, but as the previous chapter made clear, farmers suffered from a great deal more—declining prices, discriminatory railroad rates, heavy mortgages, and widespread poverty. It was only in 1890 that the political resentment building up for a decade or more boiled over on a national scale. "The farmer fed all other men," an angry speaker concluded, "and lived himself upon scraps."

The Harvest of Discontent

The revolt of the farmers, which came eventually to be known as Populism, first stirred on the southern frontier, swept eastward from Texas to the other states of the Old Confederacy, and then spread through the western plains. The exasperation from which it sprang was global. Farmers found the labor-saving machines that plowed their fields, harvested their crops, and hauled the crops to market were also producing price-deflating surpluses. Between 1860 and 1890, wheat output in the United States leaped from 173 million to 449 million bushels, cotton from 5.3 million to 8.5 million bales. By the late 1880s the price of wheat had dropped by 50 percent; that of cotton, 80 percent. In Kansas prices fell so low that families burned corn for heat.

Farmers blamed their troubles on obvious inequalities: manufacturers were protected by the tariff; railroads charged high rates; bankers held their mounting debts; and expensive middlemen stored and processed their goods. All seemed to profit at the expense of farmers. The true picture was fuzzier. The tariff protected industrial goods but supported many agricultural commodities. Railroads rates, however high, actually fell from 1865 to 1890. And it was true that mortgages were heavy, yet most were short, no more than four years. Farmers often refinanced them, using the money to buy additional land and machinery that increased their output and their incomes as well as their debts. Middlemen did make handsome profits, but increasingly millers and grain elevator operators were coming under state regulation.

In hard times, of course, none of this mattered. And in the South many poor farmers seemed condemned to hard times forever. Credit lay at the root of their problem. To plant and harvest their crops, southern farmers had to borrow money. When prices fell, they borrowed still more, stretching the financial resources of the South beyond their meager limits. Within a few years after the Civil War, Massachusetts' banks had five times as much money as all the banks of the Old Confederacy. The South became a giant debtors' pen.

The burden of debt fell most heavily on poor farmers. Increasingly they labored under the vicious crop–lien system, which operated throughout the South (page 726). From start to finish this debasing system shackled poor southern farmers to a single crop and a single merchant, in the process depriving them of land and liberty. Beginning in the 1870s, nearly 100,000 farmers a year picked up stakes throughout the Deep South, scrawled the initials "GTT" (Gone to Texas) on their doors, and fled west to escape the system—only to find it waiting for them. Others stood and fought, as one pamphlet exhorted in 1889, "not with glittering musket, flaming sword and deadly cannon, but with the silent potent and all-powerful ballot, the only vestige of liberty left."

The Alliance Movement

Before farmers could vote together, they had to get together. Life on the farm was harsh, drab, and most of all isolated. As late as 1900 an average farmer worked 68 hours a week (the average industrial worker put in 56 hours). Their clothes were mostly homespun, meals mainly potatoes, bread, and salt pork. On the Great Plains, weeks might pass before someone happened by. The Sears, Roebuck catalog was the only link many farmers had to the world outside their communities.

The earliest impulses to organize grew out of such social conditions. In 1867, Oliver Hudson Kelley, a government clerk stunned by the dullness of rural southern life, founded the Patrons of Husbandry. It was designed to brighten the lives of farmers and broaden their intellectual horizons. Local "granges"—neighborhood chapters of a few dozen members—brought farmers and their families together to pray, sing, and learn new farming techniques. The Grangers sponsored fairs, picnics, dances, lectures—anything to break down the loneliness of farm life. After a slow start the Grange grew quickly as the depression of 1873 sent farmers in search of solace. By 1875 there were 800,000 members in 20,000 locals, mostly in the Midwest, South, and Southwest.

Generally the Grangers swore off politics, but in a pattern repeated again and again among farmers, socializing soon led to economic and political action. Grangers began to pool their money to create cooperatively owned enterprises for buying and selling, for milling and storing, and for banking and manufacturing. In the early 1870s they lobbied midwestern legislatures to adopt "Granger laws" regulating rates charged by railroads, grain elevator operators, and other middlemen.

Eight "Granger cases" came before the Supreme Court in the 1870s. In *Munn v. Illinois* (1877), the most important, the justices upheld the right of Illinois to regulate private property (in this case, giant elevators used for storing grain) so long as it was "devoted to a public use." Later decisions limited regulation of railroads, ruling that states could not determine rates of carriers that crossed state lines. Congress responded in 1887 by creating the Interstate Commerce Commission, a federal agency that could regulate commerce among the states. It was supposed to investigate railroad rates and practices and stop rebates and pooling arrangements. It had little real power of enforcement, but it was a key step toward establishing the public right to control private corporations.

As the depression of 1873 waned, the Patrons of Husbandry lost members. By the end of the 1880s, stimulated by another slump in prices, a host of new organizations had blended into what the press called the Alliance Movement. The Southern Alliance, formed in Texas in 1875, spread rapidly after Dr. Charles W. Macune took command in 1886. A doctor and lawyer as well as a farmer, Macune was a tireless organizer and innovative thinker. What he had in mind was expanding Texas' network of local chapters, or suballiances, into a national network of state Alliance Exchanges. Together they would avoid the high charges of middlemen by pooling their resources to buy supplies and equipment and to store and market their crops. Hostile business leaders called the idea socialism, but Macune was no socialist. Like other farmers, he merely wanted to increase his profits, protection, and freedom to maneuver.

Soon the Southern Alliance was publicizing its activities in local newspapers, publishing a journal, and sending lecturers to 43 states and territories. By 1890 it claimed more than a million members. Hoping at first to stay within the framework of the traditional party system, the Southern Alliance tried to win over the Democratic party. "Pitchfork" Ben Tillman in South Carolina and Tom Watson in Georgia—still a loyal Democrat—successfully challenged regular Democrats.

Across the South, Alliance cooperatives sprang up, and at first the results seemed marvelous. Macune claimed that his new Texas Exchange saved farmers 40 percent on plows and 30 percent on wagons. When the jute trust—the manufacturers who made the bags used in the cottonfields—raised prices in 1888, Alliance leaders organized a boycott that brought prices back down. But most Alliance cooperatives were managed by farmers without the time or experience to succeed. Usually opposed by irate local merchants, the ventures were bound to fail. For a brief period, however, between 1886 and 1892, the cooperatives multiplied throughout the South, challenging accepted ways of doing business.

Although the Southern Alliance admitted no blacks, it did encourage African-American farmers to organize. Founded by a small group of white and black Texans in 1886, the Colored Farmers' National Alliance and Cooperative Union maintained branches in every southern state. By 1891 there were about a quarter of a million members. Activities were largely secret, since public action often brought swift, sometimes deadly, retribution from white supremacists. When Ben Patterson organized a strike of black cotton pickers near Memphis in 1891, white mobs hunted down and lynched 15 strikers, including Patterson. The murders went unpunished and the Colored Farmers' Alliance began to founder.

The idea of farm cooperation swept northward to the states of the Midwest and Great Plains in the form of the National Farmers' Alliance, or Northwestern Alliance, created in 1880. In June 1890 Kansas organizers formed the first People's party, a local political alternative that would respond to grassroots needs. Meanwhile the Southern Alliance changed its name to the National Farmers' Alliance and Industrial Union, incorporated the strong Northern Alliances in the Dakotas and Kansas, and made the movement truly national in scope.

The key to Alliance success was not organization but leadership, not simply from a few at the top but from hundreds in the middle. Specially trained Alliance lecturers traveled across states, organized suballiances, and taught members about complex national issues such as money and finance and local issues like building and expanding cooperatives. Rugged, red-haired William Lamb in Texas, Georgia firebrand Tom Watson, Ignatius Donnelly, the utopian novelist and orator from Minnesota, and "Sockless" Jerry Simpson in Kansas founded new branches throughout the South and Great Plains, reminding farmers who stood for them, who against them.

In a movement remarkably free of gender prejudice, women were as important as men. "Wimmin is everywhere," noted one observer of the "wonderful picnicking, speech-making Alliance summer of 1890." The observation seemed literally true of Mary Elizabeth Lease. In the summer of 1890 alone she gave some 160 speeches, several over two hours long. An indomitable supporter of temperance, woman's suffrage, union labor, and the Alliance, she hurled sentences, said one woman, "like Jove hurled thunderbolts." Seeing wasted corn burned for heat or piled along railroad tracks, she told farmers to "raise less corn and more hell." And she attacked northeastern financiers: "It is no longer a government of the people, by the people, and for the people," she told farmers eager for easy answers, "but a government of Wall Street, by Wall Street, and for Wall Street."

In 1890 members of the Alliance meeting in Ocala, Florida, produced the "Ocala Demands," a platform that urged reduced tariff rates, an end to national banks, rigid regulation of railroads, free coinage of silver, a federal income tax, and popular election of senators—this last designed to make government more responsive to public opinion. Its most innovative feature came again from the inventive Charles Macune. His "subtreasury system" called on the federal government to build warehouses where farmers could store their crops until prices rose, instead of having to sell them on a glutted market, as they did under the crop–lien system. To tide them over, farmers would receive greenbacks covering 80 percent of the market value of the crop, a government loan to be repaid when the crops were sold.

In the elections of 1890 the old parties faced the challenge of hostile farmers across the nation. Working within the Democratic party, southern Alliancemen measured candidates by the "Alliance yardstick" (their willingness to support Alliance demands) and nearly gained control. They elected four governors, gained control of eight legislatures, and sent 44 congressmen and three senators to Washington. In the Great Plains, the Alliance drew farmers from the Republican party. Newly created farmer parties elected five congressmen and two senators in Kansas and South Dakota and took over both houses of the Nebraska legislature. Where they did not elect their own candidates, their presence helped to account for Democratic victories over Republican incumbents.

Mary Elizabeth Lease, the "Kansas Pythoness," was admitted to the bar as a young woman but soon turned to radical activism. A charismatic speaker, she campaigned for Populist candidates in the 1890s, on one occasion warning the industrial Northeast that "the people are at bay, let the bloodhounds of money beware."

The People's Party

The successes of 1890 raised the ambitions as well as the political consciousness of farmers. In the West especially, Alliance organizers began to dream of a national third party, free from the corporate influence, sectionalism, and racial tensions that split both Republicans and Democrats. It would be a party not just of farmers but of the downtrodden, including industrial workers.

As the presidential election approached, a convention of 900 labor, feminist, farm, and other reform delegates (100 of them black) met in St. Louis in February 1892. "The fruits of the toil of millions," Ignatius Donnelly told the audience,

> are boldly stolen to build up colossal fortunes, unprecedented in the history of the world, while their possessors despise the republic and endanger liberty. From the same prolific womb of governmental injustice we breed two great classes—paupers and millionaires.

Moved to wild enthusiasm, delegates rushed the podium to grasp Donnelly's hand. They founded the People's, or Populist, party and called for a convention to nominate a ticket for the presidential election. At first southerners held back from such independence, clinging to their strategy of boring from within the Democratic party. When newly elected southern congressmen failed to support Alliance programs, southern leaders like Tom Watson abandoned the Democrats and began recruiting black and white farmers for the Populists.

The national Populist convention met in Omaha, Nebraska, on July 4, 1892. "It was a religious revival," exclaimed one observer, "a crusade, a pentecost of politics in which a tongue of flame sat upon every man." The Populists adopted a platform that harkened back to Ocala two years earlier. Its preamble, the impassioned work of Ignatius Donnelly, promised to restore government "to the hands of the people." Planks advocated the subtreasury plan, unlimited coinage of silver and an increase in the money supply, direct election of senators, an income tax, and government ownership of railroads, telegraph, and telephone. To attract wage earners the party endorsed the eight-hour workday, restriction of "undesirable" immigration, and a ban on the use of Pinkerton detectives in labor disputes—for the Pinkertons had engaged in a savage gun battle with strikers that year at Andrew Carnegie's Homestead steel plant. The interests of "rural and civic labor," the platform declared, were the same, "their enemies . . . identical." The only somber note was struck before the convention opened when Leonidas Polk, president of the Farmers' Alliance and the leading candidate for the presidential nomination, died. Delegates turned to the old greenbacker and Union general, James B. Weaver, carefully balancing the ticket with a one-legged Confederate veteran as his running mate.

The Populists enlivened the otherwise dull campaign, as Democrat Grover Cleveland and Republican incumbent Benjamin Harrison refought the election of 1888. Mary Elizabeth Lease joined Weaver on trips through the South and West, where they drew crowds that "could only be counted by the acre." In the Northwest, Ignatius Donnelly, running for governor of Minnesota, made 150 speeches to nearly 10,000 voters in a campaign he described as the "liveliest ever seen" in the state. Meanwhile Tom Watson campaigned in Georgia, bringing white and black supporters together.

The results were mixed. Weaver polled over a million votes, the first third-party candidate to do so. He carried Kansas and four western states with 22 electoral votes. Populists ran strongest among western farmers and silver miners, who found the party's stand on currency particularly appealing. When local votes were tallied, Populists elected 3 governors, 5 senators, 10 congressmen, and nearly 1500 members of state legislatures.

For all the Populists' successes, the election revealed dangerous weaknesses in the party. Ignatius Donnelly ran a disappointing third in the Minnesota gubernatorial race. In the Northeast and most of the Midwest Weaver lost badly. In southern states Weaver won more than a quarter of the vote only in Alabama. Worst of all for the southern Populists, Tom Watson lost his seat in Congress through the traditional tactics of fraud and intimidation. (In Augusta alone, his Democratic opponent received twice as many votes as there were legal voters.) For all of Watson's determination to fight on, southern conservatives were appalled by his open courtship of blacks.

Across the nation thousands of voters changed political affiliations in the election of 1892, but most often they switched from the Republican to the Democratic party, and not to the Populists. No doubt the campaign of intimidation and repression hurt the People's party in the South. In the North, the Populists also failed to win over labor and most city dwellers. Both were more concerned with family budgets than low farm prices, high farm debt, and limited supplies of money. Inflation, after all, was bound to hurt consumers, especially those workers whose wages could not keep pace with rising prices. And the darker side of Populism put off many Americans. Its rhetoric was often violent; it spoke ominously of conspiracies and stridently in favor of immigration restriction. Ignatius Donnelly might expound on the ills of farmers one moment, but the next he might be publishing an anti-Semitic novel like *Caesar's Column*, prophesying a depraved world ruled by an international Jewish oligarchy. Most fatal for the Populists, they failed to attract a majority of farmers. Even the Alliance lost members.

In 1896 and 1900 Populists nominated candidates for the presidency; neither won. The party's moment had passed. It left an exhilarating momentum and a legacy of unfinished business, including proposals for a subtreasury system, popular election of senators, and an income tax. In one form or another all would be enacted into legislation in the future. For the present, the People's party demonstrated two conflicting truths: how far from the needs of many ordinary Americans traditional parties had drifted and how difficult it would be to break their hold on the political system.

THE DEPRESSION OF 1893

In 1892 Grover Cleveland won an impressive victory in his third race for the White House, carrying seven northern states as well as the Solid South. For the first time since the Civil War Democrats also controlled both houses of Congress. Helped by working-class voters who had been revolted by the pitched battles, gunfire, and deaths in the Homestead Steel Strike, the Democrats increased their strength in industrial cities and among wage earners. Business executives remained calm. "I am very sorry for President Harrison," wrote Henry Clay Frick, manager of the Homestead plant and normally a Republican, "but I cannot see that our interests are going to be affected one way or the other by the change of administration."

The economy, not the new administration, soon shattered business confidence. In the recovery from the depression of 1873, the economy had gradually but relentlessly overexpanded: railroads overbuilt, businesses borrowed to finance expansive new projects, farmers increased their production by purchasing farm machinery on credit. The capability to borrow was essential for economic expansion, of course; but under the new industrial order, the fortunes of industry, labor, and farmers became tied so closely to one another and to international developments that a major downturn in one area affected other sectors of the economy. Even before Cleveland's inauguration ominous signs appeared that credit was crumbling. The Philadelphia and Reading Railroad, deeply in debt to finance the building of new stations, bridges, and tracks, declared bankruptcy. A major British banking firm had already failed spectacularly in 1890, causing British investors to retrench by selling their American investments for gold. This in turn contributed to a drain in U.S. gold reserves as the depression in Europe steadily worsened. In mid-February a flurry of panic selling hit the New York Stock Exchange. Stockholders sensed that uncertain currency values, glutted markets, depressed agricultural prices, and declining exports had sapped economic strength. By April the gold reserves of the U.S. Treasury had dropped below the critical $100 million mark.

On May 5, 1893, after a wave of bankruptcies had destroyed major firms across the country, stock prices sank to all-time lows. By the end of the year, 600 banks and 15,000 businesses had failed, among them such symbols of stability as the Northern Pacific, Union Pacific, and Santa Fe railroads. Officials considered closing the Stock Exchange. The new industrial order had brought prosperity to some farmers by opening larger markets to them and tied Americans closer together with better communications and transportation networks, but the price of interdependence now became obvious. Without some way to control the excesses of the boom-and-bust business cycle, depression would be visited upon the nation on as large a scale as the booming prosperity had been. The economic costs were all too quickly paid in human currency.

The Depths of Depression

The depression of 1893, the deepest to that date in the nation's history, lasted until 1897. Charles Francis Adams, Jr., railroad baron and descendant of two presidents, called it a "convulsion." The depression revived doubts about the price of industrialization, sparked labor violence and near class warfare, and produced a new awareness of how intertwined American society had become.

The most obvious problem was the sheer lack of jobs, the effect of a failing industrial economy. In August 1893 unemployment stood at 1 million; by January 1894, 2 million; by the middle of 1894, 3 million. At the end of the year nearly one worker in five was out of a job. Washington, D.C., newspapers reported "a vast army of unemployed, and men pleading for food who have never before been compelled to seek aid." Every night at every police station in Chicago, from 60 to 100 people sought shelter. In Detroit the needy transformed vacant lots into "Pingree Potato Patches" (named for the mayor of the city). In Pasadena, California, they dined at soup kitchens bitterly nicknamed "Cleveland Cafes." In the South and Great Plains states, farm prices fell below the cost of production. Western cattle went to market for a few dollars; repossessed machinery sat in sheriffs' lots. As one desperate Kansas farmer bluntly put it, "The problem is how to live."

The federal government had no program at all. "While the people should

The Massachusetts-born illustrator Charles Dana Gibson, famous for his portraits of well-bred young women in the 1890s, tackles a different subject in this ink drawing, a bread line of mixed classes during the terrible depression of 1893.

patriotically and cheerfully support their Government," President Cleveland had said at his inauguration, "its functions do not include the support of the people." The states offered little more. Relief, like poverty, was considered a private matter. The burden fell on local charities, benevolent societies, churches, labor unions, and ward bosses. In city after city, citizens organized relief committees to cope with distress. They distributed bread and clothing until their meager resources gave out under the weight of want. At one point Chicago saloons were giving free lunches to an estimated 60,000 people a day. Others were less generous. As the popular preacher Henry Ward Beecher told his congregation, "No man in this land suffers from poverty unless it be more than his fault—unless it be his sin."

The scale of hardship began a slow change in thinking about poverty. "The individual crawled as best he could, through the wreck," wrote historian Henry Adams, "and found many values of life upset." People saw that anyone could be thrown out of work—an industrious neighbor, a factory foreman with 20 years on the job, a bank president. One survey of the working class revealed that as late as 1901 half the heads of households had no jobs. Working- and middle-class families took in boarders, laundry, and sewing to make ends meet. With so many fathers and husbands unemployed, more and more wives and children left home to work. In the 1890s the number of laboring women jumped from 4 million to 5.3 million, mainly in exploitative fields such as domestic and clerical work.

In the South, where half the nation's working children were employed, child labor rose by 160 percent in textile mills during the decade. Concern over the young became so acute that middle-class women created the League for the Protection of the Family in 1896. Among other things it advocated compulsory education to keep children out of factories and mines. Older attitudes were gradually giving way to new ideas about the social causes of poverty and the responsibilities of public and private agencies.

The Rumblings of Unrest

Even before the depression, rumblings of unrest rolled across the land. The Great Railway Strike of 1877 touched off nearly two decades of labor unrest. In the late

1880s and early 1890s violence erupted at the Haymarket Square in Chicago, at the Carnegie steel plant in Homestead, Pennsylvania, and in the silver mines of Coeur d'Alene, Idaho, where federal troops finally crushed the strike. After 1893 discontent mounted as wages were cut, employers laid off employees, and factories closed. During the first year of the depression, 1400 strikes sent more than half a million workers from their jobs. The worst one idled 170,000 coal miners in Pennsylvania and the Midwest, where strikers bombed mine shafts, dynamited coal trains, and fought state militias.

Uneasy business executives and political leaders saw the hand of radicals in these uprisings. Harking back to a popular revolt in Paris in 1871 that had toppled the government and instituted a "Commune," or worker-controlled regime, American businessmen became convinced that only force could keep peace and preserve the republic. When a strike at George Pullman's Palace Car factory in 1894 led thousands of western rail workers to walk out in sympathy, a young Theodore Roosevelt, then serving as a Civil Service commissioner, advised his fellow citizens, "The sentiment now animating a large portion of our people can only be suppressed as the Paris Commune was suppressed, by taking ten or a dozen of their leaders out, standing . . . them against a wall and shooting them dead. These leaders are plotting a social revolution and the subversion of the American Republic." Roosevelt, however, was hyperventilating. Although radicals had been involved in many of the strikes, they were a tiny minority. Anarchism, which sought to abolish government entirely, had never attracted more than a handful of Americans, and socialism suffered from internal dissension and lack of strong leadership in the United States.

The depression of 1893 had unleashed another force: simple discontent with government inaction. By the spring of 1894 masses of unemployed—perhaps 10,000 in all—were wandering the roads, some slowly forming into small armies. On Easter Sunday, "General" Jacob Coxey, a 39-year-old Populist and factory owner, launched the "Tramps' March on Washington" from Massillon, Ohio. His "Commonweal Army of Christ" of some 500 men, women, and children descended on Washington at the end of April to offer "a petition with boots on," in Coxey's words, for a public works program of road-building. The government jobs would be financed through the issuance of $500 million in paper money.

The press covered the march as if it were a foreign invasion. "For every two sloggers in Coxey's ranks there was at least one reporter," recalled an amused journalist. Along the way Secret Service men mingled with the army's privates to report on their progress. In Washington President Cleveland's staff tightened security around the White House. Other "armies" mobilized across the country: an 800-person contingent left from Los Angeles; a San Francisco battalion of 600 swelled to 1500 by the time it reached Iowa.

On May 1 Coxey's troops, armed with "clubs of peace," massed at the foot of the Capitol. When Coxey entered the Capitol grounds, 100 mounted police routed the demonstrators and arrested him for trespassing on the grass. Nothing came of the protest, save unmistakable evidence of growing demand for federal action. Faced with a sputtering industrial economy, ordinary citizens had sought in Washington, rather than their state capitals, the court of last resort.

Democrats Under Fire

Grover Cleveland had barely entered office when the depression struck. The country blamed him; he blamed silver. In his view the Sherman Silver Purchase

Act of 1890 had cut business confidence by forcing the government to buy silver. The new silver reserve, in turn, had pushed the gold reserves out of the Treasury and brought on panic. Repeal of the act, Cleveland believed, was the only way to recovery. When India dropped silver as a basis for its currency late in June 1893, Cleveland called Congress into special session to roll back the Sherman Act. Congress did, after considerable debate, in November. But this bit of economic tinkering only strengthened the resolve of the "silverites" in the Democratic party to overwhelm Cleveland's conservative "gold" wing.

Even worse for the president, who had staked his reputation on it, repeal of silver purchases brought no economic revival. In the short run abandoning silver hurt the economy by contracting the money supply just when some inflation might have helped stimulate it. Worst of all, the battle over repeal had siphoned off the support Cleveland needed for his principal goal, reducing the tariff. The best Democrats in Congress could do was the Wilson–Gorman Tariff Act (1894), which reduced some schedules, raised others, and enacted a modest income tax to make up for lost revenues. A year later even the tax provision fell when the Supreme Court invalidated it.

As panic and unemployment spread across the country, Democrats were buried in state after state in the congressional elections of 1894. They lost both the House and Senate. "The truth is," said one senator, "there was hardly an oasis left in the Democratic desert." The Democrats' disaster did not favor the Populists, who elected only four senators and four representatives. Everywhere disgruntled voters had turned to the Republicans. Dropping moralistic reforms and stressing national activism, Republican candidates cut deeply into traditional sources of Democratic support. With the Democrats confined to the solid South, the politics of stalemate was over and the Republicans reigned. All that remained for them was to capture the White House in 1896.

THE NEW REALIGNMENT

Despite occasional praise for handling crises like the Pullman strike and mediating a dispute over Venezuela's boundary, Cleveland's popularity wilted. He enjoyed no practical relations with Congress; he seldom spoke or traveled; his mail shrank to that of an average citizen. Cancer of the jawbone (for which he had undergone a secret operation) also took its toll on his health and energy. By the end of 1895 the president was spending his remaining days in the White House on family matters, routine paperwork, and plans for retirement. His would-be successors, however, were lining up for the campaign of 1896, which proved to be one of the five or six most critical elections in the republic's history.[*] Its results, coming in the midst of a deep depression, ended by reordering the political landscape and leaving behind the "Gilded Age" of bloody shirt politics, slim party margins, and low-profile presidents.

---

[*]Political scientists consider five elections, in addition to the contest of 1896, as critical shifts in voter allegiance and party alignments: the Federalist defeat of 1800, Andrew Jackson's rise in 1828, Lincoln's Republican triumph of 1860, Al Smith's Democratic loss in 1928; and—perhaps—Ronald Reagan's conservative tide of 1980.

The Battle of the Standards

From the start, the campaign of 1896 was a "battle of the standards," with both major parties absorbed in the question of whether gold or silver should become the nation's monetary standard. As the self-proclaimed promoters of business interests, most Republican leaders saw gold as the stable base upon which to build confidence and prosperity. At their nominating convention in St. Louis, the party enthusiastically adopted a platform calling for "sound money" supported by gold. Senator Henry M. Teller of Colorado, a lonely dissenter, rose with tears in his eyes to offer a silver substitute, then led 23 followers from the convention hall when it was voted down almost 8 to 1.

Marcus Alonzo Hanna, a shrewd Ohio industrialist and party leader, had carried the gold plank to the convention and had been maneuvering for almost a year to win the nomination for William McKinley, former congressman and now governor from Ohio. Patient, principled, and tolerant, McKinley was no pawn of Hanna's but a power in his own right. He had championed every aspect of Republican nationalism, mastered the arts of political management, and stood firmly for the high protective tariff that bore his name. Cautiously he endorsed gold. Thanks to Hanna's organizational skills, McKinley was nominated on the first ballot. As a result, the convention spent far less time in contentious wrangling among regional party chieftains. Increasingly, the issues being raised at political conventions encompassed the whole nation, rather than sectional concerns.

As for the Democrats, four years of agitation, depression, and party fragmentation had left them in disarray. Throughout Cleveland's term, disappointed silverites wanted nothing to do with his conservative policies, pressing instead for "free and independent" coinage of silver. They argued that if the Treasury freely minted all the silver presented to it, independent of other nations, the supply of money would increase, prices would rise, and the economy would revive. "The blood of commerce," wrote one silverite, "will again flow through the arteries of business; industry will again revive; millions of men will find employment; (and) the hand of greed will be stricken from the throat of prosperity."

As much as anything, free silver was a social protest of the South and West against the financial aristocracy of the gold-bound Northeast. Associated with rural, debt-ridden farm folk (whose debts would be diminished by currency inflation), silver implied the superiority of country life over city life. Most of all, in the words of young Nebraska congressman William Jennings Bryan, it stood for the "work-worn," "dust-begrimed" people against arrogant wealth. In speech after speech, article after article, silverites pressed their case, nowhere more effectively than in William Harvey's best-selling pamphlet, *Coin's Financial School* (1894). It reached tens of thousands of readers with the common sense of Coin, its young hero. Fighting for silver, he "was like a little monitor in the midst of a fleet of wooden ships."

As Democrats assembled in Chicago for their convention, William Jennings Bryan was ready to seize the hour. Just 36 years old, Bryan was steeped in the rural virtues of grassroots democracy. He looked, reformer Robert La Follette remembered, "like a young divine"—"tall, slender, handsome," with a rich melodic voice that could reach the back rows of the largest halls (no small asset in the

"Gold Bug" pin worn by supporters of McKinley's gold standard in the election campaign of 1896.

days before electric amplification). He had served two terms in Congress and worked as a journalist. He favored a low tariff, opposed Cleveland, and came out somewhat belatedly for free silver. Confessing total ignorance of the issue in 1892, he explained, "The people of Nebraska are for free silver and I am for free silver. I will look up the arguments later." Slowly, systematically, he organized a quiet boom for his nomination in 1896.

Silverites controlled the convention from start to finish. They paraded with silver banners, wore silver buttons, and won a plank in the anti-Cleveland platform calling for the free and unlimited coinage of silver. The high point came when Bryan stepped to the lectern, threw back his head, and offered himself to "a cause as holy as the cause of liberty—the cause of humanity." The audience rose as one, cheered wildly, then listened as Bryan spoke for "the plain people of this country," for "our farms" and against "your cities," for silver and against gold. The crowd was in a near-frenzy as he reached the dramatic climax and spread his arms in mock crucifixion:

> Having behind us the producing masses of this nation and the world, supported by the . . . toilers everywhere, we will answer their demand for a gold standard by saying to them: You shall not press down upon the brow of labor this crown of thorns, you shall not crucify mankind upon a cross of gold.

The next day the convention nominated him for the presidency.

Populists were in a quandary. They had expected the Democrats to stick with Cleveland and gold, sending dissident silverites headlong into their camp. Instead, as they saw it, the Democrats had plagiarized their platform and stolen their

---

William Jennings Bryan made the first of his three presidential bids in 1896, when he ran on both the Democratic and Populist tickets. Passionate in his convictions and devoted to the plain people, the "Great Commoner" is depicted in this hostile cartoon as a Populist snake devouring the Democratic party.

thunder. "If we fuse [with the Democrats] we are sunk," complained one Populist. "If we don't fuse, all the silver men we have will leave us for the more powerful Democrats." At a convention racked with bitter debate, the fusionists nominated Bryan for president. The best antifusionists could do was drop the Democrats' vice presidential candidate, Maine shipbuilder Arthur Sewall, in favor of that agrarian rebel who had set Georgia aflame, Tom Watson.

Campaign and Election

Bryan waged an extraordinary campaign on limited financial resources. He traveled 18,000 miles by train, gave as many as 30 speeches a day, and reached perhaps 3 million people in 27 states. The nomination of the People's party actually did more harm than good by labeling Bryan a Populist (which he was not) and a radical (which he definitely was not). Devoted to the "plain people," Bryan spoke for rural America and Jeffersonian values: small farmers, small towns, and small government. Anticipating a new, more active campaign style, he tried to "educate" voters, but in the end he preached largely to the converted.

McKinley knew he could not compete with Bryan's barnstorming, so he stumped sedately from his front porch in Canton, Ohio. This gave his campaign a folksy appearance, which belied the reality. Marcus Hanna, a politician of the industrial age, relied on modern techniques of organization and marketing to put his candidate across. He advertised McKinley, in Theodore Roosevelt's words, "as if he were patent medicine." Hanna constructed a well-oiled campaign machine that brought tens of thousands of delegations by train into Canton and paraded them to McKinley's doorstep. On one day alone, McKinley addressed some 80,000 people with promises of a "full dinner pail." Hanna saturated the country with millions of leaflets, along with 1400 speakers attacking free trade and free silver. Conservatives, frightened by what they viewed as Bryan's dangerous radicalism, poured at least $4 million into McKinley's campaign.

Bryan's silver-tongued oratory proved no match for Republican money and organization. On election night, Bryan sat at home in Lincoln, Nebraska, as three telegraph operators brought him bulletin after bulletin spelling defeat. Both candidates tallied more votes than any of their predecessors. Bryan had 6.5 million, McKinley 7.1 million, making him the first candidate since Grant to receive a clear majority. More important than numbers was where the votes came from. McKinley carried the Northeast and the Midwest, four border states, and California and Oregon in the Far West. In the industrial cities he routed Bryan. The Republicans combined old support from businessmen, farmers and veterans with broader backing from wage earners to create a national coalition that dominated politics for the next 30 years. As in 1892, blacks continued to vote mainly for Republicans, when they were permitted to vote at all.

Jim Crow Politics

The violence that threatened Tom Watson's biracial campaign was the crest of a wave of racism that engulfed America in the late 1800s. "New" immigrants from eastern and southern Europe and new overseas colonies of Hispanics, Filipinos, and Hawaiians helped breed a powerful race hatred to justify control. In the South longstanding racism deepened and was enlisted into a political purpose— preventing a biracial alliance that might topple white conservative Democrats from power. But the white supremacy campaign, ostensibly directed at African-

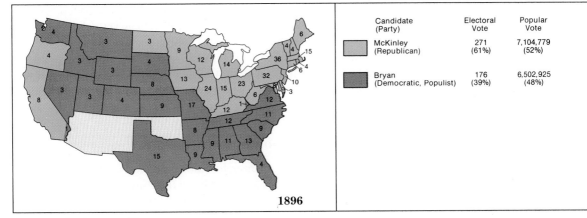

Candidate (Party)	Electoral Vote	Popular Vote
McKinley (Republican)	271 (61%)	7,104,779 (52%)
Bryan (Democratic, Populist)	176 (39%)	6,502,925 (48%)

1896

THE ELECTION OF 1896

Americans, had a broader target, political insurgents from below, as much white as black. When Mississippi designed a new constitution in 1890 to disfranchise blacks and many poor whites as well (page 732), some southern states hesitated to follow suit, because conservatives feared losing the fraudulent black votes that often gave them victory in elections. Conservatives, badly shaken by the Populist uprising of poor whites in the 1890s, demanded that if African-Americans were disfranchised (which would hurt conservatives, who controlled the votes of their black tenants and sharecroppers), the vote of potentially radical poor whites had to be reduced too.

After the defeat of Populism in the mid-1890s, the only question was which whites would be supreme, insurgents like the poor farmers who joined the People's party or conservative landholders. Eventually an all-white combination of conservatives and "reformers"—those disgusted by the frequent spectacle of election-stealing by using blocks of black votes—passed disfranchisement laws throughout the South. Between 1895 and 1908, the disfranchisement campaigns won out in every southern state. Sometimes the disfranchisement laws relied on the complicated procedure of charging poll taxes and demanding that receipts be shown at the polls, as in Mississippi. Sometimes literacy tests were used as a barrier. Where African-American voters were concentrated in large numbers, some states gerrymandered, or remapped the boundaries of election districts, to render black votes ineffective. "Grandfather clauses" allowed citizens to vote only if their grandfathers had cast ballots in elections held before 1860 (or 1866 in some cases)—a provision that excluded all blacks. By charging blacks with petty crimes, the states could often make them ineligible to vote. If these devices did not remove enough voters, politicians sometimes arranged for circuses and other entertainments to tour black districts before elections and collect poll tax receipts as the price of admission. Without these receipts, black voters would not be permitted to cast their ballots.

Populists and other reformers who agreed to the disfranchisement movement hoped that loopholes would permit poor whites to vote despite poll taxes and literacy tests. In practice, however, many whites were barred from the polls. In Louisiana, for example, under the new provisions the number of citizens voting was cut from 294,000 to 93,000, excluding virtually all the black voters and almost half the whites. The disfranchisement campaign also succeeded in splitting insurgent whites from blacks, as the tragic fate of Tom Watson demonstrated. Only a dozen years after his biracial campaign of 1892, Watson was actively promoting black disfranchisement in Georgia. "What does Civilization owe to the negro?" he asked bitterly. "Nothing! *Nothing!!* NOTHING!!!" In 1920, after more than a decade of baiting blacks (as well as Jews and Catholics), the Georgia firebrand was finally elected to the Senate. Watson, who began with such high ideals, gained power only by abandoning them.

The African-American Response

White reformers who supported disfranchisement claimed that race relations would actually improve, because blacks would learn their proper "place" in southern society. But to mount a successful campaign for disfranchisement, its supporters constantly inflamed racial passions. They staged "White Supremacy Jubilees" and complained, as the Atlanta *Journal* did, that the black man grew "more bumptious in the street. More impudent in his dealings with white men." The number of lynchings peaked during the 1890s, almost tripling in the first three years and averaging over a hundred a year for the whole decade. Most took place in the South. In Atlanta and New Orleans, white mobs terrorized blacks for several days in the new, heightened atmosphere of tension.

Under such circumstances, African-Americans were forced to work out a response to the climate of intolerance. It came in 1895 from Booker T. Washington. Born a slave, Washington struggled after the war to survive as a laborer and coal miner while attending school. In 1872 he learned of the Hampton Institute, founded by a former Union general to teach blacks skilled trades. After working his way through Hampton, Washington vowed to extend a similar opportunity to blacks in the lower South. In 1881 he accepted an offer from Alabama to establish an industrial and agricultural school at Tuskegee, Alabama. Its debut was far from auspicious, for the Tuskegee Institute opened in a log shack with 30 students and a single instructor.

Washington persevered, achieving almost overnight fame when he spoke to an audience of whites and blacks about race relations in Atlanta in 1895. "I love the South," he reassured white listeners. He conceded that white prejudice existed throughout the region but suggested that blacks should not try to fight it. "The agitation of questions of social equality is the extremist folly," he concluded. Instead, African-Americans should work for economic betterment. Every laborer who learned a trade and increased his savings through hard work would earn respect from whites. And those earnings would amount to "a little green ballot" that "no one will throw out or refuse to count." Thus Tuskegee's curriculum was designed to provide blacks with vocational skills for farming, manual trades, and industrial work.

Whites in both the North and the South hailed Washington's "Atlanta Compromise" as a solution to racial harmony. For blacks, it made the best of an increasingly difficult situation; for whites, it struck the note of patient humility they were so eager to hear. Washington, himself an astute politician, discovered that philanthropists across the nation hoped to make Tuskeegee an example of their generosity. He was the honored guest of Andrew Carnegie at his imposing Skibo Castle; Collis Huntington, one of the California "Big Four" rail magnates, became his friend; aboard the yacht of a Standard Oil executive he discussed "public and social questions." Throughout, Washington preached accommodation. He accepted segregation (so long as separate facilities were equal) and qualifications on voting (if they applied to whites as well). Above all Washington preached economic self-improvement designed to reach common black folk in fields and factories. In 1900 he organized the National Negro Business League to help establish black businessmen as the leaders of their people. The rapid growth of local chapters (320 by 1907) helped him extend his influence over the affairs of African-American communities across the country.

Not all black leaders accepted Washington's call for racial self-effacement. The most outspoken critic was W. E. B. Du Bois, a scholar with a far different vision. Born in western Massachusetts, Du Bois received training in history and economics at Fisk, Harvard, and the University of Berlin. In 1903, as a professor at Atlanta University, he leveled a broad attack on Washington's philosophy in *The Souls of Black Folk*. Du Bois saw no benefit for African-Americans in sacrificing intellectual growth for narrow vocational training. Nor was he willing to abide the permanent stigma that came from the South's discriminatory caste system. A better future would come only if blacks struggled politically to achieve suffrage and equal rights.

Instead of exhorting black folks to pull themselves slowly from the bottom up, Du Bois called on the "talented tenth," a cultured black vanguard, to blaze a trail of protest. In 1905 he founded what became known as the Niagara movement, to press for immediate political and economic equality. By 1909 a coalition of blacks and sympathetic whites had transformed the Niagara movement into the National Association for the Advancement of Colored People (NAACP). Middle class and elitist, it mounted legal challenges to the Jim Crow system of segregation. For sharecroppers in southern cotton fields and laborers in northern factories—the mass of African-Americans—the strategy offered little relief.

In keeping with Booker T. Washington's emphasis on manual training, Tuskegee Institute, opened in Alabama in 1881, was training 1400 students in 30 trades by 1900. Academic subjects received attention, too, as evidenced by this photograph of a history class (segregated by gender) learning about Captain John Smith and Pocahontas.

Neither accommodation nor legal agitation would suffice, but in the "Solid South" (as well as an openly racist North) it was Washington's patient approach that articulated an agenda for most African-Americans. The ferment of the early 1890s, among black Populists and white, was replaced by a lily-white Democratic party that dominated the region but remained largely a minority party on the national level.

McKinley in the White House

The Republican party came out of the election of 1896 not only as the grand new party but also as a dynamic instrument of government in Washington. The Republicans built an organization that could command votes, raise money, and mobilize public opinion. It combined traditional conservatives with forward-thinking leaders from the professions, education, business, and journalism. In William McKinley Republicans had a skillful chief with a national agenda. Unlike his Gilded Age predecessors, he began to reorganize the executive branch and make it more vigorous. McKinley cultivated news reporters, openly walked the streets of Washington, and charmed the public with warm handshakes and flowers from his own lapel. With a firm but delicate touch, he curbed the power of old-time state bosses like Thomas Platt of New York and Matthew Quay of Pennsylvania. When need be, he prodded Congress to action. In all these ways, he foreshadowed "modern" presidents, who would lead their party rather than act as executive caretakers.

Fortune at first smiled on McKinley. When he entered the White House the economy had already begun its recovery, as the cycle of economic retrenchment hit bottom. Factory orders were slowly increasing, causing a drop in unemployment; farm prices climbed. New discoveries of gold in Alaska and South Africa expanded the supply of money without causing the "gold bugs" to panic that it was being destabilized by silver. Freed from the burdens of the economic crisis, McKinley called a special session of Congress to make good on a campaign promise— tariff revision. In July 1897 the Dingley Tariff raised protective rates still higher but allowed the tariffs to come down if other nations lowered theirs.

McKinley also sought a solution for resolving violent railroad strikes, like the Pullman conflict, through government mediation. The Erdman Act of 1898 set up the machinery for doing so. Reformers had been complaining that the large industrial monopolies and trusts needed regulation as well, and McKinley laid plans for moving in that direction. But the same expansiveness that had pushed an industrial nation across the continent and shipped grain and cotton to international markets also drew the country into conflict and war. McKinley soon found himself facing a crisis with Spain that monopolized the attention of his fellow citizens. Regulation—and a true age of reform—would have to await the next century.

On New Year's Eve at the State House in Boston a midnight ceremony ushered in the twentieth century. The crowd celebrated with psalms and hymns. There was a flourish of trumpets, and everyone sang "America." The Reverend Edward Everett Hale, too deaf to hear anything but the brass, nonetheless recorded his sober impression: "The whole service was very satisfactory and I am writing under the influence of its solemnity."

Solemn and patriotic, the American people had weathered a decade of partisan jockeying, disorder, and violence. The conflicts arrayed a discontented South and West against the industrial Northeast and Midwest; whites against blacks, striking miners and workers against Pinkerton guards and hard-nosed industrialists. The political system, which through a policy of laissez faire had mostly ignored the social forces of urbanization and industrialization that were changing America, took the first steps of adjustment. In the race between Bryan and McKinley, it seemed that an older agrarian America was facing off against the new industrial order. The soul of the nation, divided just 30 years earlier by a civil war, had again been at stake.

The dawn of the new century brought an end to an era of political uncertainty and a decade of social upheaval. Prosperity returned at home; empire beckoned abroad. Still, deep divisions—between rich and poor, farmers and factory workers, men and women, native-born and immigrant—split America. A younger generation of leaders stood in the wings, fearful of the schisms but confident it could forge ties to bridge them. As Theodore Roosevelt looked eagerly toward war with Spain and the chance to expand American horizons, he did not mince words with one of his older opponents. "You and your generation have had your chance. . . . Now let us of this generation have ours!"

SIGNIFICANT EVENTS

1867	Patrons of Husbandry ("Grange") founded
1869	Prohibition party founded; Massachusetts establishes first state regulatory commission
1874	Greenback party organized
1874	Women's Christian Temperance Union formed
1875	First Farmers' Alliance organized
1877	*Munn v. Illinois*
1878	Bland–Allison Silver Purchase Act
1881	President James Garfield assassinated; Chester Arthur sworn in as president; Booker T. Washington founds Tuskegee Normal and Industrial Institute in Alabama
1887	Interstate Commerce Commission created
1890	National Woman Suffrage Association created; Sherman Antitrust Act; Wyoming enters the Union as the first state to give women the vote; Sherman Silver Purchase Act; McKinley Tariff; Southern and Northwestern Alliances adopt "Ocala Demands"
1892	Populist party formed; Grover Cleveland elected president
1893	Panic of 1893; Sherman Silver Purchase Act repealed
1894	"Coxey's Army" marches on Washington to demand public works for the unemployed
1895	National Municipal League founded
1896	League for the Protection of the Family organized, William McKinley elected president
1903	W. E. B. Du Bois' *The Souls of Black Folk* published
1909	National Association for the Advancement of Colored People founded

22

The New Empire

mericans found the British wherever they looked abroad, or so it seemed. Through their navy, through missionaries from the Church of England, through manufacturers, merchants, and bankers, the British had footholds in India, Africa, the Middle East, China, the Pacific. But Americans after the Civil War were particularly galled by the influence Great Britain wielded in their own backyard. The Monroe Doctrine might assert that the United States was supreme in the Western Hemisphere, but around the Caribbean the British Navy piped the tune.

If the United States hoped to build a canal across Central America—and many Americans did—they had to share it with the British under the terms of the Clayton–Bulwer Treaty of 1850. Year after year British pounds flowed into Nicaragua, El Salvador, Guatemala, Honduras, and Costa Rica to pay for railroads and to finance their governments. When Honduras refused to pay its debts in 1872, the British navy shelled a Honduran port. Even after the government in Tegucigalpa caved in, the British decided to take over nearby Belize and turn it into British Honduras. In so doing they simply ignored the claim of Nicaragua to the same territory. In fact, the British even assumed control over the Miskito Coast of Nicaragua, which, very conveniently, offered one of the most promising sites for the eastern end of an isthmian canal. By 1900 British investors had placed all five Central American governments in the thrall of debt.

Perceptive and ambitious Americans recognized that if the British could use their navy and bankers to muscle into Central America, the United States could too. The profits from American factories and farms could open doors of trade and influence and a modern navy could help keep them open. Although English investors might buy up government securities and public utilities, Americans could gain control over the productive facilities and transportation upon which the economies of developing nations increasingly depended. For an American with the proper enterprise and bold enough plans—someone like Minor Keith, for instance—the reward might prove immense.

In 1871 this "apple-headed little man with the eyes of a fanatic," as he would later be described by the writer John Dos Passos, had arrived in Costa Rica to build railroads for which the British supplied the financing. Costa Rica had a classic one-crop colonial economy based on coffee beans. As Keith supervised construction of the railroads, he also began to tap a new market by buying bananas to ship to the United States for sale at a hefty profit. He used some of his earnings

In 1858 the United States signed its first commercial treaty with Japan. The Japanese were not especially impressed with people they viewed as barbarians; only after forceful intervention in 1867 by Western powers did Japan permit substantial commerce.

in 1884 to refinance the Costa Rican debt of $12 million to the British. The grateful government in return granted him a 99-year lease on the railroad, 800,000 acres of fertile land, and freedom from import duties on the equipment he needed for railroad and plantation construction projects.

As soon as he received the land, Keith began to create banana plantations under the control of his Tropical Fruit Company. The railroads he built, like those of southern planters in the United States, linked the plantations to the coast rather than connecting key towns and cities. Despite its huge debt for construction, Costa Rica was left without a viable internal transportation network. At the same time, Keith complemented his economic influence by cultivating political connections. Marriage to the daughter of a former president increased his sway over a government already receptive to his financial inducements. In 1899 he extended his private empire even further by merging Tropical Fruit with Boston Fruit to create the United Fruit Company.

By the early twentieth century Keith had almost single-handedly turned Costa Rica into the prototypical "banana republic" and the United States into the dominant foreign power. The country imported five times more from the Americans than from the British. United Fruit had almost equal influence in Guatemala, and Honduras would fall under the influence of Keith's company by the 1920s. Central Americans came to call the company, with its vast landholdings, railroads, and steamship lines, "the octopus."

Keith's direct involvement in the affairs of Central American states was not the only way to use economic resources to expand American influence. Numerous Americans had products they wanted to sell in foreign markets. Southern farmers exported half their cotton crop, western wheat farmers earned some 30 to 40 percent of their income from overseas markets, John D. Rockefeller's Standard Oil Company shipped about two-thirds of its refined products abroad, Cyrus McCormick supplied Russian farmers with the reaper, and Thomas Edison and Alexander Graham Bell established England's telephone service in the 1880s. But no American product sold more widely than the sewing machines of the Singer Company. All over the globe Singer found markets for a machine that was practical, profitable, and labor saving for its users.

The lure of overseas profits took Singer to Europe in the 1850s. The depressions of the 1870s, 1880s, and 1890s convinced the company that foreign sales were essential to smooth out domestic ups and downs. "We never get tired of ding-donging this matter of exports . . . for we hope we will wake [the sewing machine trade] up and make them go to work as eagerly abroad as they ever did at home," one industry journal stated. By 1900 Singer had 60,000 sales agents spread out over every inhabited part of the globe and its name had entered some foreign languages as the word for sewing machine. For many of the world's people, that little machine was their sole contact with the United States, its economy, and its culture.

Singer's most coveted market lay in China, but it was a difficult one to penetrate because the culture was so strange to most Americans. From John MacIntyre, a sympathetic Scotch Presbyterian missionary stationed there, Singer representatives learned that every business deal would involve a complex web of "compradors," or middlemen. If strangers bargained, a mutual friend or relative was needed to settle differences and guarantee the contract. Tailors, the most promising customers, had a deep aversion to innovation. Accustomed to loosely stitched seams, they disdained the tight stitching the Singer machine produced. But spurred on by the depression of 1893, the company made a concerted effort to sell Chinese officials on the virtues of the "iron tailor." Machines were introduced into the Dowager Empress Tzu Hsi's industrial training schools, free schools were established to teach machine sewing, and new machines were developed to produce a loose chain stitch. Singer had learned that in China one had to become Chinese to succeed. Although the vast market of Americans' dreams never materialized, Singer established the presence of the United States and the missionaries of its cultural, economic, and religious gospel in Asia.

VISIONS OF EMPIRE

By the grand plans of Minor Keith and the small stitches of Singer; by sales of Iowa grain and the salvation of Indochinese souls; even, finally, by navy gunboats and political strong-arming, the United States entered the new imperial race. Since the 1840s expansionists had spoken of a divine and Manifest Destiny to overspread the North American continent from the Atlantic to the Pacific. Even after the Civil

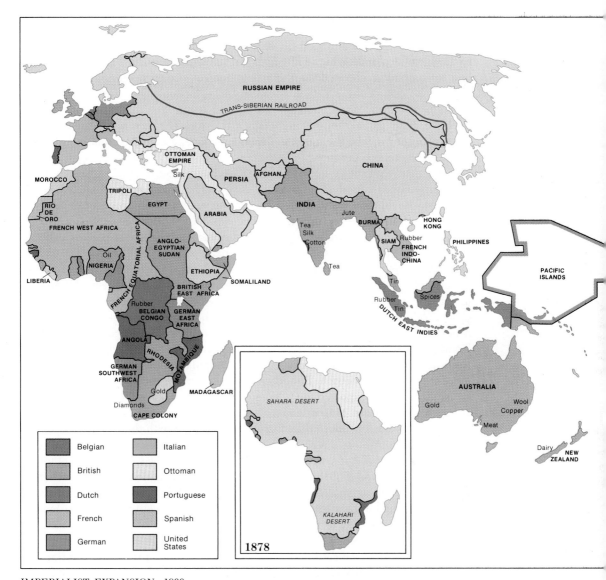

IMPERIALIST EXPANSION, 1900
A comparison of Africa in 1878 (inset) and 1900 shows how quickly Europeans extended their colonial empires. Often resource-poor countries like Japan and England saw colonies as a way to acquire raw materials, such as South African diamonds and tin from Southeast Asia. Closer scrutiny shows that four of the most rapidly industrializing countries—Germany, Japan, Russia, and the United States—had few if any overseas possessions, even in 1900. And while China appears to be undivided, all the major powers were eagerly establishing spheres of influence there.

War, some Americans still cast covetous glances at Canada to the north and Mexico and Cuba to the south. More often, however, their interest came to center on distant lands, which, unlike the Louisiana and Gadsden purchases or the territories acquired after the Mexican War of 1846, did not border on the United States.

Imperialism, European-Style and American

Spain and Portugal maintained the shrinking remnants of colonial empires dating to the age of exploration in the fifteenth and sixteenth centuries. England, France, and Russia had accelerated their efforts to control foreign peoples and lands. But toward the end of the nineteenth century, the technology of arms and the networks of communication, transportation, and commerce made the prospect of effective, truly global empires especially attractive. The race for overseas empire was well under way by the time the Americans, Japanese, and Germans entered in the late nineteenth century.

For many Americans accustomed to a heritage of continental expansion, overseas imperialism raised some difficult issues. The tradition growing out of the American Revolution painted the nation as an exceptionally free and democratic one, untainted by the corrupting influences of Old World monarchies, aristocracies, or hierarchical churches. Whereas Americans tended to see narrow and selfish interests directing the expansion of European powers, they were more likely to imagine themselves the bearers of a selfless Protestant Christianity, the economic benefits of free enterprise capitalism, and the blessings of democracy. No doubt a majority of Americans felt the world's far reaches would benefit from an expansion of such values. Even so, differences arose over how aggressive and self-interested American imperialism ought to be. The naked way in which Great Britain, France, and Germany scrambled for possessions in the Niger and Congo basins of tropical Africa in the 1880s certainly stirred popular opinion in America toward a more competitive approach. But other Americans preferred a more indirect imperialism that simply exported ideas, commerce, and influence. To them the paths of Minor Keith or Isaac Merritt Singer seemed more practical.

While Americans more than Europeans wrestled with the problem of justifying imperial control in the name of the ideals of democracy, similar social, economic, and political forces drew them into the imperial race. The growth of industrial networks linked more and more Americans to international markets, whether they were Arkansas sharecroppers depending on the price of cotton in world markets or Pittsburgh steelworkers whose jobs might continue only so long as orders for railroad steel from entrepreneurs like Minor Keith kept their factories in business. The development of efficient transoceanic steamship lines greatly facilitated international commerce. Singer was only one of many corporations, in Europe as well as America, looking to world markets. As economic systems became more tightly knit and integrated and political systems became more responsive to the interests of industrialists and finance capital, a scramble for domination of markets and distant lands was perhaps inevitable. Nations looked to project their interests, economically, militarily, and culturally.

The Shapers of Foreign Policy

Although the climate for expansion and imperialism was present at the end of the nineteenth century, the small farmer or steelworker had little if any concern about how the United States might advance its ends abroad. A small minority of informed interest groups shaped the debate over foreign policy and imperialism. They were Christian missionary groups, the navy lobby, business interests, commercial farm interests, and a small intellectual and political elite who followed American affairs in the wider world.

American overseas missionary work began in earnest in the 1840s with Protestant missions in China, which set out to convert the "heathens" to Christianity. By the late nineteenth century American missionaries had spread out to other parts of the western Pacific region and the Middle East, where they encountered people with profound cultural differences that often made them unreceptive to the Christian message. The missionaries came to believe that the natives first had to become Western in culture before becoming Christian in belief. To that end they sought to introduce Western goods, education, and systems of governmental administration—any "civilizing medium," as the Reverend McIntyre had remarked when he helped Singer gain a foothold in China. Yet most American missionaries, especially those to China, were not territorial imperialists. They assumed instead "the white man's burden" of introducing civilization to the "colored" races of the world. To that end they set up vocational training schools and Western-style universities, stores, and hospitals, but they opposed direct military or political intervention. At home their representatives lobbied in Congress and from the pulpit for expanded commercial activities to support their evangelical efforts.

In the 1870s a young American woman complained to English wit Oscar Wilde that her country, unlike Europe, had no classical ruins, no curiosities. "No ruins! No curiosities!" Wilde countered. "You have your Navy and your manners." Certainly, American naval officers could agree with Wilde's scathing sarcasm. By 1880 the once-proud Civil War fleet of over 600 warships was rotting and rusted with neglect. Only 48 could actually fire a gun. In effect, the United States had no functional navy to protect overseas interests.

Budgetary deprivation also spelled disaster for the graduates of the Naval Academy bent on a military career. Without ships, they could not find commands or avenues for promotion. Such dead-end prospects did not suit the temperament of young men drawn from the nation's elite. The average navy officer came from an upper-middle class business or professional family, belonged to an establishment Protestant denomination like the Episcopalians or Presbyterians, and married a woman from a respected eastern family. Many of these young and discontented officers joined with similarly inclined business leaders to lobby Congress to establish a modern navy with steam-powered, steel-hulled ships. Half a century later, this growing combination of business, military, and political lobbyists would become known as the military-industrial complex, and it would influence the nation significantly.

In the 1880s it was Captain Alfred Thayer Mahan who formulated the ideas of these officers and business leaders into a theory of navalism that exerted a powerful influence over the thinking of his generation. The United States, Mahan argued, required a navy prepared to do more than protect coastal waters. Great nations had always relied on foreign trade to enhance their wealth and power, especially in times of chronic industrial overproduction and sharp depressions, as had occurred repeatedly after the Civil War. The United States thus needed to make a concerted effort to expand foreign trade. And the only way to protect access to foreign markets was with large cruisers and battleships. These ships, operating far from American shores, would need coaling stations and other resupply facilities throughout the world.

Mahan's logic and the benefits that a shipbuilding program would bring American factories persuaded Congress in the 1880s to begin rebuilding the navy. Steel ships replaced those with wooden hulls. Between 1882 and 1893 the United States went from the world's twelfth to its seventh naval power and ten years later

Daily Lives

TIME AND TRAVEL

The New Navy

Early on February 3, 1874, a fleet of chunky monitors and steam frigates and sloops lumbered out of Key West at a tortoiselike 4.5 knots. It was the largest assembly of American naval power since the Civil War, but to the officers watching from shore, the overage armada was a lamentable sign of weakness. "It became painfully apparent to us that the vessels before us were in no respect worthy of a great nation like our own," declared one commodore. "Two modern vessels of war," a future admiral later observed, "would have done us up in thirty minutes."

During the Civil War the United States Navy had reached its pinnacle with over 600 ships, 65 of them ironclads. But almost immediately after the war the country began dismantling the fleet. War debts, Reconstruction, and industrial development dominated national interest. With 3000 miles of ocean as protection and no colonies to defend, a large blue-water fleet seemed unnecessary. Even steamships, though superior to vessels under sail, seemed unwarranted since the United States had no coaling stations in foreign waters to fuel them. All naval vessels were therefore required to have full sail power. The number of propeller blades on steamships was reduced from four to two to improve sailing ability. Boilers and engines were replaced by smaller ones or removed entirely. By 1878 the number of sailors had shrunk to 6000, the smallest force since the presidency of Andrew Jackson, and the United States Navy ranked twelfth in the world—behind Denmark and Chile.

Meanwhile technology was transforming the navies of Europe. Compound engines, improved armor plating, self-propelled torpedoes, and large rifled guns revolutionized naval warfare. In 1873, as the United States Navy fell into disrepair, the British launched the *Devastation*, a single-masted, steam-driven vessel with heavy armor and powerful twin turrets. A forerunner of the modern battleship, it could steam across the Atlantic and back without stopping for coal. Less than a decade later, a British fleet smashed Alexandria, Egypt, whose fortifications were sturdier than those of American ports.

Anxieties about foreign navies and dreams of empire led Congress in 1883 to appropriate $1.3 million for four modern vessels—the cruisers *Atlanta, Boston,* and *Chicago,* 3000 to 4500 tons; and the 1500-ton dispatch boat *Dolphin.* The "ABCD" ships were the first of a new steel fleet designed to raise the United States Navy to world-class status. These early "protected" cruisers (so named for the armored deck built over boilers, engines, and other machinery) were an odd mix of old and new. All three had full sail rigs yet were completely electrified and contained watertight compartments and double bottoms. The *Chicago* had twin propellers but engines and boilers so antiquated that one observer compared them to a saw mill. The steel breechloading guns were vast improvements over the iron muzzle-loaders; yet gunners still aimed them the old-fashioned way, by looking down the barrels through open sights.

Before the turn of the century, the navy had commissioned additional protected cruisers, larger armored cruisers, and its first full-sized battleships—the *Indiana, Massachusetts,* and *Oregon,* each over 10,000 tons. (Soon after 1900 giant battleships were displacing 20,000 tons; on the eve of World War I they reached

Daily Lives

Passengers on riverboats and yachts saluted the new steel-hulled, steam-powered American fleet as it steamed triumphantly up the Hudson River after naval victories in the Spanish–American War. Within a few years, these modern ships would be obsolete, as rapid innovations in naval warfare fed an international arms race.

over 30,000 tons.) With five more first-class battleships commissioned by 1896, the United States Navy rose to fifth place in the world. The prestige of naval service had risen, too, and with it the number of sailors: nearly 10,000 in uniform. A Naval War College had been created in 1884 to train officers in the science of naval war, and in 1891 states established naval militia units, which became the nucleus of the Naval Reserve.

Service aboard the new navy, as always, reflected the privileges of rank. Commanders lived in wood-paneled luxury and dined on specially prepared cuisine, capped by coffee, brandy, and cigars. The crew ate salted meats, beans, and potatoes. Officers had private quarters, while enlisted men, so the saying went, lived under the place where they slept and slept under the place where they ate. At night the tables and benches used for dining in the common quarters were stowed between overhead beams from which hammocks were hung. Battery drill was held twice a day, but under fire American

marksmanship proved poor. During one battle in the Spanish–American War, Americans fired more than 8000 shells at four fleeing Spanish crusiers. An examination of their hulks later revealed only 120 hits.

By 1907 the new navy had come of age, and in that year President Theodore Roosevelt sent 16 of its newest battleships on a 46,000-mile, 14-month world tour. Ironically the Great White Fleet (named for the gleaming white hulls of its ships) was already out of date. In 1906 Great Britain had commissioned the *Dreadnought*, a warship whose gunnery rendered all of its competitors obsolete. Unlike conventional battleships with guns of varying sizes, the *Dreadnought* carried mostly big guns that gave it more than twice the firepower of anything afloat. In a single stroke the new American navy, the product of a quarter-century of effort, was outclassed—but not for long. By the end of World War II, another quarter-century away, the United States Navy would outclass the world.

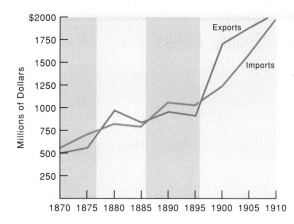

BALANCE OF U.S. IMPORTS
AND EXPORTS, 1870–1910
The green areas indicate an unfavorable balance of trade.

to third. Navy officers had already taken the initiative to establish a greater American presence in Korea, Haiti, Samoa, and Hawaii. With a modern navy, the United States had both the motive and means to become an imperial power. Only the question of method remained to be solved.

The majority of the business class had little concern with foreign trade in the late nineteenth century. They had, after all, ample opportunity to find new markets and cheap raw materials in burgeoning urban areas with the opening of the West and the rise of the New South. The expansion of the railroads offered seemingly endless opportunities for profitable investment of surplus capital. All the same, at least three groups from the business community did pursue overseas interests. Most obviously, shipbuilders, import–export businesses, and steamship lines looked abroad, since all of them had a direct stake in foreign commerce. Any steps that promoted foreign trade served their interests. Second, adventurers like Minor Keith recognized that, although the risks of investment in underdeveloped economies were greater, the potential profits were spectacular. Most investments went into developing raw materials from mining and foodstuffs. Railroads and shipping lines to move those goods were also popular. Finally, as in the case of Singer, there were manufacturers who saw hundreds of millions of Chinese and other native people as potential customers for their products. Foreign sales were especially alluring to manufacturers in industries suffering from chronic overproduction.

Perhaps even more vocal in generating pressure to expand American overseas markets was a fourth group: the large commercial farmers and the industries that processed farm produce. The rapid growth of urban markets had encouraged an even more rapid increase in farm production. When farmers began producing more than urban markets could absorb, they began to look abroad for relief from depressed prices.

In addition to missionaries, navy careerists, and certain members of the business class, a small, generally well-educated, influential group of individuals also promoted the cause of imperialism. This elite group—widely traveled, politically well connected—communicated with one another through books, journal articles, lectures, and informal social contacts. It included such lights as Henry and Brooks Adams, sons of diplomat Charles Francis Adams, grandsons of former President and Secretary of State John Quincy Adams, and great-grandsons of John Adams. Brooks and Henry were almost born to assume a role in guiding the destiny of the United States, but neither had any taste for active political life. They exercised their influence through their writing and political friends like Henry Cabot Lodge, the Massachusetts senator and one of America's first holders of a doctorate (in political science from Harvard); young Theodore Roosevelt, the patrician son of one of New York City's most distinguished merchant families; and John Hay, an Illinois lawyer who had the good fortune to befriend Abraham Lincoln and inherit a large fortune through his wife's father. By the 1890s Alfred Mahan, too, was a respected member of this circle.

All these men were expansionists. They accepted and in one way or another helped define and popularize most of the era's theories on culture, race, and economics that justified the American drive toward empire. By a curious irony of history, many of these same ideas were used by anti-imperialists, who often favored expansion but felt it was a tactical mistake to acquire colonies.

The Ideology of Imperialism

It is an unusual culture indeed that does not fancy its own ways superior to those of foreign peoples. To take one example among many, the Cheyenne of the Great Plains called themselves "the people," or simply "the human beings," implying that no one else had fully achieved that rank. So, too, the civilizations arising out of western Europe at the end of the Middle Ages generally assumed the superiority of their cultures. But because of their remarkable expansion across the globe, the confidence and aggressiveness of Western beliefs became especially marked in the late nineteenth century. Not surprisingly, Americans and Europeans who sought to explain their successes over nonwhite or aboriginal populations gave themselves credit for superior government, the spread of a system of international markets, dynamically expanding industrial capacity, and technological advances in weapons and communications. All these seemed material symbols confirming the favor of divine providence.

Yet as we have also seen, the success of western European expansion into colonial North America also benefited from ecological factors (page 157). European diseases, animals, and plants often devastated and disrupted the new worlds they entered. The coming of smallpox and measles; of pigs, cattle, and horses; and of sugar and wheat played equally important roles in opening the Western Hemisphere and the Pacific basin to European domination. In areas like the Middle East, Asia, and Africa, where populations already possessed hardy domesticated animals and plants (as well as their own devastating disease pools), European penetration was far less complete. Still, journalist Finley Peter Dunne's Irish characters Mr. Hennessy and Mr. Dooley best expressed the confidence with which Americans and Europeans viewed their self-proclaimed superiority. "'We're a gr-reat people,' said Mr. Hennessy earnestly. 'We ar-re,' said Mr. Dooley. 'We ar-re that. An' the best iv it is, we know we ar-re.'"

With a confidence so sublime, scholars, academics, and scientists soon developed a number of theories justifying European and American expansion in terms of race. Charles Darwin's *On the Origin of Species* (1859) had popularized the notion that among animal species, the fittest survived through a process of natural selection, and Social Darwinists like Herbert Spencer in England and William

Graham Sumner in the United States argued that the same laws of survival governed the social order. By natural as well as divine law, the fittest people—those descended from Anglo-Saxon and Teutonic stock—would assert their dominion over the lesser peoples of the world. When applied aggressively, the theory of white supremacy could rationalize the wholesale slaughter and enslavement of native populations who resisted. When combined with the somewhat more humane notions of the "white man's burden," conquest included not only the "burden," or obligation to impose order, but also the opportunity to uplift the "lower" races by teaching them Western ideas, converting them to Christianity, and introducing law and government. Patricians like Theodore Roosevelt and Henry Cabot Lodge eagerly accepted such notions.

Perhaps more compelling than either cultural or racial motives for American expansion was the commercial imperative. The recurrent depressions of the late nineteenth century reminded Americans of the unpredictable disorder in the nation's economy. The Populists had proposed a monetary solution to depression: inflate the currency with free silver. The business community generally attempted to limit the swings of the free market through consolidation into monopolies and trusts, which would then avoid overproduction and destructive competition. High protective tariffs to keep out foreign goods was yet another solution. But as the National Association of Manufacturers explained, "Our manufacturers have outgrown or are outgrowing the home market" and "expansion of our foreign trade is [the] only promise of relief." In and out of government, leading public figures called for a campaign to "find markets in every part of the habitable globe" and to "open trade wherever we can." Imperialist policies, whether defined as an expansion of United States boundaries, the acquisition of colonies, or merely the achievement of a controlling influence, offered the opportunity to increase foreign trade, enhance American prestige, and guarantee future security.

STIRRINGS OF EMPIRE

Even when the inhabited United States encompassed little more than a baker's dozen of former colonies clustered along the Atlantic seaboard, Thomas Jefferson had dreamed of an American "empire of liberty" that one day would stretch from sea to sea. Jefferson supposed it might take a thousand generations before American pioneers had vaulted the continent, but it took a mere 40 years, and the wines of such expansionist fruits proved sometimes heady. The dream of a truly continental American republic—one that absorbed Canada and Mexico to boot—had not died out after the Civil War.

Canada

To the north lay Canada, still a British colony and still a target for American expansionists like Lincoln's secretary of state, William Henry Seward. Canadian territory took in a landmass second in size only to Russia, though its population was largely clustered in the areas of Ontario and Quebec, bordering the United States. Political unrest in 1837 had led the British by 1841 to merge French-speaking Lower Canada (Quebec) with English-speaking Upper Canada (Ontario) to form a united Canada Province. At the time of the American Civil War the Canadians were prepared for a peaceful separation from England and the creation of an independent Canada.

The continuing interest of American expansionists in the territory to the north also spurred the British to redefine Canada's status. In 1866 Congress had put financial pressure on Canada by cutting back on the amount of free trade and fishing privileges that had been negotiated between the two countries. With enough pressure, the expansionists in Congress speculated, Canadians hurt by the loss of American markets might favor annexation. In addition, neither President Andrew Johnson nor Ulysses S. Grant made any attempt to stop raids into Canada conducted periodically by the Irish Fenian Brotherhood. Canadians correctly suspected that annexation was the price the United States would extract for calling off the Irish. At the same time, the United States made extraordinary demands on Britain to pay indemnities for damages caused by Confederate raiding vessels built in England. The only way Britain could repay those damages, proponents in Congress recognized, was to cede Canada to the United States.

But in 1867 Britain eased the discontent in Canada over its colonial status by adopting the British North America Act, which organized Ontario, Quebec, New Brunswick, and Nova Scotia into a single confederation possessing greater power for self-government and an independent foreign policy. Under the Anglo-American Treaty signed in 1871 the United States settled its claims for compensation. Canada, like the United States, experienced increasing immigration from Europe and expansion into its western plains. By 1871 Manitoba and British Columbia had both achieved provincial status, comparable to American statehood. Even though disputes erupted between the United States and the new Canadian government over questions of boundaries, fishing rights, seal hunting, and tariffs, most Americans decided that it was more profitable to trade with Canada than to annex it.

Mexico

Mexico posed possibilities and problems of a different sort. During the Civil War, France's new emperor, Napoleon III, had occupied Mexico City with a French army and soon after established a puppet monarchy under Austria-Hungary's Archduke Maximilian, now Emperor Maximilian of Mexico. Only French bayonets kept the ineffectual Maximilian in power. Once the distractions of the Civil War eased, the United States made increasingly menacing noises about the new regime. Napoleon III quickly realized that social unrest in Mexico, coupled with the threat of invasion by the battle-hardened Union army, rendered his North American ambitions chancy at best. As soon as he withdrew his troops, the puppet government fell and Maximilian was executed by Mexican partisans.

Freedom from the French did not bring stability to Mexico or free it from the designs of diehard American continentalists. These included a group of veteran army officers who had suddenly found themselves without any wars to fight, Texas Rangers who coveted Mexican cattle and grazing lands, and a number of political opportunists. If a border war could be provoked, these schemers reasoned, the officers would have new commands, the Rangers could legally steal Mexican stock, and Texas would gain new lands to govern. Commercial and business interests, however, opposed such schemes. They preferred friendly economic ties with the new regime of Porfirio Díaz to the uncertainties of war and the conquest of a potentially hostile people. In 1881 Secretary of State James G. Blaine laid con-

tinentalism to rest forever. The United States had no territorial designs whatsoever in Mexico, he announced. It sought only the opportunity to invest its "large
accumulation of capital."

William Henry Seward

No one did more to initiate the idea of a "New Empire" for the United States than
William Henry Seward. Possessed of "a slouching, slender figure," as Henry
Adams once described him, Seward had "a head like a macaw; a beaked nose;
shaggy eyebrows; unorderly hair and clothes; hoarse voice; offhand manner; free
talk and perpetual cigar." As secretary of state under Lincoln and Andrew Johnson, his skillful diplomacy averted direct European interference in the Civil War,
and the breadth of his intellect and vision led him to dream dreams beyond those
of most politicians. Though his own efforts to shape a new American empire ran
into opposition in Congress, he glimpsed the course American expansion would
take over the next 40 years.

Seward rested his expansionist policies on what he perceived as two central
political laws. The first, based on his reading of history, was that "empire has, for
the last three thousand years . . . made its way constantly westward . . . until
the tides of the renewed and decaying civilizations of the world meet on the shores
of the Pacific Ocean." In his view, the surge of industrialization had only accelerated that pace of westward movement. Seward thus concluded that the United
States needed to be prepared to win the great battles among the commercial
nations for supremacy in the Far East. His second maxim underscored how that
battle should be won: the great empires of the future, he believed, would be
commercial, not military. "The nation that draws the most materials and provisions from the earth, and fabricates the most, and sells the most of productions and
fabrics to foreign nations, must be, and will be, the great power of the earth."
Thus the American empire would not require colonies. Rather the United States
asked only for unrestricted access to Asian markets on nondiscriminating terms.
That idea formed the basis of the "open-door" concept, which guided both British
and American Far Eastern policy.

Seward assiduously pursued American links to Japan, Korea, and China. For
him, a transcontinental railroad served to tie eastern factories to western ports
and, from there, to the western Pacific. His diplomatic efforts led to the Burlingame Treaty of 1868, which made it possible for the railroads to recruit Chinese
labor to build the western half of the first transcontinental line. For similar reasons
Seward pressed for the construction of a canal across the Central American isthmus. And though he opposed direct colonialism in Asia, he advocated that the
United States acquire a string of Pacific island colonies, protectorates, or naval
stations, through which the United States could defend a canal and the sea lanes to
China.

Seward's dreams of opening the Far East to American commerce bore little
fruit in his lifetime. Chinese society and Chinese markets remained for the most
part tightly closed to American penetration, as the Singer Sewing Company's
difficulties demonstrated. Moreover, the shabby treatment of the Chinese in California, compounded by the insulting restrictions placed on Asian immigrants in
1882, aggravated Sino-American relations. The efforts of American missionaries
often aroused antiforeign resentment among Chinese nationalists. What access
Americans had to the China market was largely the result of British determination
to prevent other powers from further carving China into exclusive spheres.

Commodore Matthew Perry, seen by a Japanese artist and by the Western eye of the camera.

Japan proved an even more elusive prize. Earlier in the century, novelist Herman Melville referred to Japan as the "double-bolted land." Except for a single port at Nagasaki open to Dutch traders, Japan's ruling feudal lords kept their isolated, agricultural land closed to foreigners. That lasted until 1853, when an American naval unit under Commodore Matthew Perry arrived to "open" Japan to the West. Perry specifically sought ports for trade and refueling ships as well as protection for American sailors off wrecked whaling ships. The Japanese had never seen steam-powered ships before. To them Perry's flotilla was an invasion by "barbarians in floating volcanoes."

Despite the terror he had inspired, Perry had opened the door to Japanese trade no more than a crack. Thus in 1867 the American warship *Wyoming* joined British and French naval units determined to break Japanese resistance to foreign trade, by force if necessary. Unwilling to suffer the fate of China by becoming a dependent colonial economy, the Japanese launched an internal revolution under the Meiji restoration (1868–1912), which in little more than a decade transformed Japan into a modern power and a rival to Western hegemony in the Pacific. In its subsequent diplomatic efforts with Japan, the United States concentrated not on dominating the Japanese home market, but in securing Japanese support for an open door in China.

Korea at first seemed a more promising Asian market for American penetration. Some commercial opportunities opened in the 1860s, and in 1882 Navy Commodore Robert Shufeldt made the United States the first Western country to have formal trade and diplomatic ties with a country so isolated that Westerners called it the "hermit kingdom." Though technically a dependency of China, Korea became more vulnerable to other nations as Chinese control weakened. A remarkable American diplomat, business promoter, and missionary, Horace Allen, worked diligently to protect Korean autonomy from foreign predators while maintaining an open door to trade. Other nations had little incentive to see Allen's efforts succeed. The Russians wanted to dominate Korea to protect the eastern terminus of the Trans-Siberian Railroad in Vladivostok (see map, p. 793). The Japanese viewed an independent Korea as a knife pointed at their home islands. As the fruit of victory in successive wars with China (1894–1895) and Russia (1904–1906), Japan established exclusionary dominion over Korea.

The meager success of American initiatives in the Far East demonstrated that Seward's vision was far ahead of both opportunity and domestic political support. Even close to home he had difficulty transforming vision into policy. The transcontinental railroad, Atlantic cable, and high tariffs he supported did become realities. But when he tried in 1865 to buy the Virgin Islands with their fine harbors, Denmark insisted on more than the $5 million Seward offered. Congress balked at paying a higher price. President Grant finally killed the proposed treaty. Seward's hopes to buy Iceland, Greenland, and Samana Bay on Santo Domingo and to annex revolution-riddled Cuba, European-controlled Caribbean islands, Tiger Island off Honduras, and Hawaii all ran into domestic and foreign opposition.

Seward did make two notable territorial acquisitions. An American naval officer raised the Stars and Stripes over Midway Island in 1867. Though of no great importance by itself, Midway was a way station to Asia and close to Hawaii, where missionary planters were already establishing an American presence. More notably, Seward engineered the purchase of Alaska, a territory of some 591,000 square miles, twice the size of Texas. By the 1850s the Russian government had lost enthusiasm for its beachhead in North America. Besides, St. Petersburg sensed that if it did not sell Alaska, the Americans might seize it.

Following the Civil War, Seward opened negotiations with the Russians without informing either President Johnson or Congress; then, in March 1867 he simply presented Congress with a treaty and a bill of sale for $7.2 million. Critics derided the acquisition of the "Polar Bear Garden," or "Frigidia," when the United States had not even settled the vast western lands it owned. But key senators and congressmen, like Charles Sumner of Massachusetts, recognized that Alaska, with its vast potential natural resources, was cheap at many times that price. And other members of Congress, unpersuaded by high-minded arguments of imperial strategy, accepted the logic of bribes liberally dispensed by the Russian ambassador. Within 10 days the Senate approved the Alaskan purchase, though the House stalled for over a year.

The United States and Latin America

Many Americans did not accept Seward's conviction that history's future lay in the Far East. They thought Latin America offered the best opportunity for new markets—if obstacles to American penetration could be overcome. One impediment, as we have seen, was the British presence in Central America. James G. Blaine, "the plumed knight" from Maine, who became secretary of state under James Garfield and again under Benjamin Harrison, believed the time had come to establish American supremacy under the Monroe Doctrine in fact as well as in principle. Blaine tried to persuade Great Britain to cancel the Clayton–Bulwer Treaty and give the United States exclusive control over any canal built in the region. More important, he looked for some means to shift the region's import market from British to American goods.

At the same time Blaine sought some way to end the political disruptions and constant warfare that threatened to undermine hemispheric markets. Mexico against Guatemala, Chile against Argentina, Nicaragua against Honduras, Chile against Peru and Bolivia, and even a threat of war between Chile and the United States in 1891 demonstrated the quarrelsome nature of hemispheric relations. Internal factional rivalries, unstable governments, and British and American meddling all contributed to unrest.

The best way to ease tensions, Blaine believed, as well as promote regional trade, was a conference among the nations of the hemisphere. For nearly a decade his idea went unheeded, but in 1889 the secretary of state presided over the first Pan-American Congress, with delegates from 17 nations. Blaine suggested a "customs union," designed to reduce trade barriers in the Americas and, conveniently, allow the United States to exploit its less developed neighbors. He also urged arbitration as a way to prevent the escalation of tensions into armed conflict. Hindered by the Argentinian and Chilean delegates, who were deeply suspicious of American motives, the meeting ended only with an agreement to establish a Pan-American Union to foster peaceful understanding. Blaine thus found himself forced to pursue separate talks and use less subtle arm-twisting in order to gain the tariff reductions he sought. If a nation balked, he threatened to invoke provisions of the 1890 McKinley Tariff to ban the products of their single-crop economies. Only three nations—Colombia, Haiti, and Venezuela—had the will to resist.

Prelude in the Pacific

Preoccupation with Latin America did not quiet all interest in the Pacific, where the United States vied with Great Britain and Germany for the islands of Samoa. In 1878 a treaty gave America the rights to the harbor at Pago Pago. When the Germans sent marines to secure their interests in 1889, the British and Americans reinforced their naval presence. Only a fortuitous typhoon, which destroyed the rival ships, staved off an escalating conflict. The three powers then peacefully carved up the islands, with the United States retaining Pago Pago.

The primary target for American expansionists was not Samoa but Hawaii, earlier known as the Sandwich Islands. If the United States wanted to fashion a bracelet of trade across the Pacific to China, Hawaii was the jewel in the middle. It would afford a fine naval base and a way station along the route to Asia. As early as the 1780s an American merchant ship had stopped at the Sandwich Islands on its journey to China. By the 1840s missionaries and merchants so dominated the port at Honolulu that one historian described it as "Yankee as New Bedford." Though Polynesian culture and local rule survived for several more decades, the process of political, economic, and cultural absorption was under way. The missionaries were godly, but their descendants were a remarkably practical lot: they saw the possibilities for a harvest not only of Polynesian souls but of sugar as well. Thus they undermined local culture by converting the islanders to Christianity while they acquired large tracts of property on which they produced sugar for export to the United States.

European imperialists, eager for their own way stations in the Pacific, would have been happy to possess Hawaii. But the United States, while not yet ready to annex the islands, had by the 1880s asserted virtual control over them. Although an 1875 treaty admitted Hawaiian sugar duty-free into the states, Hawaiians paid a high price for that advantage, for their prosperity now depended on the American

Sugar was the key to Hawaii's English- and American-dominated plantations. Polynesians were culturally ill-suited to the backbreaking labor sugar cultivation demanded. Planters filled their labor needs by recruiting Japanese workers like this one.

market. In 1886 they granted the United States naval rights to Pearl Harbor. Finding themselves hopelessly outmaneuvered, the British could only ask the Americans to keep the islands neutral and trade open to all nations.

The McKinley Tariff of 1890 changed matters dramatically, however, by removing sugar from the list of exempt items. Hawaiian planters recognized that if the islands were annexed, the tariffs would no longer apply to them. Unfortunately for their cause, in 1891 Queen Liliuokalani brought to the throne a nationalist rule much less sympathetic to American ways. As a nationalist, she firmly believed that Hawaii should remain in the hands of its native peoples. And as a monarchist, she firmly believed those hands should be hers, and not those of planter interests dominating a constitutional legislature. So the sugar planters began plotting and in January 1893 staged a revolt. Their success was conveniently assured when the American minister to Hawaii, John Stevens, ordered ashore sailors of the U.S.S. *Boston* on the pretense of protecting Americans. Faced with heavily armed opposition, the queen capitulated, leaving a commission of planters, four American and one British, in control.

While Stevens had acted without direct orders from Washington, President Harrison supported his efforts. On his own initiative Stevens also recognized the new government, placed it under the protection of the United States, and urged President Harrison to annex the islands, though the native Hawaiians had given no indication they desired to become Americans. Eager to preempt any British designs, Harrison signed an annexation treaty with the American-dominated commission from Hawaii.

Before the Senate could act to ratify, Grover Cleveland took office and immediately put the treaty on hold. Cleveland was hardly a foe of expansion, but as his secretary of state, Walter Gresham, expressed it, the administration was "unalterably opposed to stealing territory, or of annexing people against their consent, and the people of Hawaii do not favor annexation." The idea of incorporating the nonwhite population also troubled Cleveland. So matters stood, for a time, at a stalemate. But given the strength of expansionist sentiments in the rising generation of Americans, the stalemate could not last indefinitely.

Crisis in Venezuela

Gold, with its universal capacity to muddy the waters out of which it was panned, stirred trouble again in the jungles of Venezuela. In the 1880s prospectors unearthed a 32-pound nugget in the region between Venezuela and British Guiana. Almost 10 years earlier the Venezuelans had begun to complain about British incursions on their borderlands. Not coincidentally, those lands included the mouth of the Orinoco River, a potential gateway to trade in the interior of South America's northern coastal region.

Determined to preserve the sanctity of the Monroe Doctrine but lacking the navy to oppose British actions, the United States unsuccessfully recommended that the disputed claims be arbitrated. In 1895, with the British still threatening to adjust the border unilaterally, the United States sent a stiffly worded protest that Britain's expansive claims against Venezuela impinged on the "safety," "honor," and "welfare" of the United States. The mood in Washington had become much more truculent now that a naval building program was under way, and, in the midst of economic depression, Congress was hardly in the mood to see Great Britain close off a promising market. Arbitration, the Cleveland administration insisted, was the only way for Britain to avoid more forceful American intervention in an area where the United States was "practically sovereign" and "practically invulnerable as against any or all other powers." What form that intervention might take Secretary of State Richard Olney was careful not to say.

Secretary of State Olney's cable arrived when much of the Foreign Office was away on summer vacation. Not until November did Britain's prime minister issue another tepid rejection of arbitration. The outraged Cleveland, unwilling to back down but unwilling to risk war, issued what amounted to an ultimatum. The United States would send a commission to set the boundary, and if the British did not arbitrate, more forceful American action would follow. The British ambassador warned London that "in Congress and among the public [exists] a condition of mind which can only be described as hysterical." Theodore Roosevelt, the pugnacious police commissioner of New York City and usually a foe of Cleveland, applauded the president's menacing posture: "Let the fight come if it must; I don't care whether our sea coast cities are bombarded or not; we would take Canada."

But cooler heads found the prospect of war with Great Britain unacceptable. The scare had disrupted American financial markets as British investors withdrew funds. Believers in the superiority of the Anglo-Saxon race saw no reason why people of the same background should fight one another. Nor, in fact, did Cleveland. He wanted only to force the British to accept peace on terms acceptable to the United States. In that he succeeded. Eager to avoid conflict with the United States, the British agreed to arbitrate and in the end a compromise settlement left Venezuela with what it most wanted, control of access to the Orinoco.

In reality few Americans, including Cleveland, had ever cared much about Venezuela's interests. What the administration most wanted was an opportunity to assert American power and influence in world affairs. Venezuela offered an outlet for the jingoistic spirit of the age: many nations, including the United States, adopted a belligerent posture on foreign policy issues both large and small. That aggressive tone in newspapers and political speeches reflected the expansionary nationalism of most Americans in the late nineteenth century. The Venezuelan crisis thus put new teeth into the Monroe Doctrine, as the United States moved to assume hegemony in the Western Hemisphere.

Ironically, the dispute marked the end, rather than the increase of tensions between Great Britain and the United States. Once dominant among European powers, Great Britain increasingly found itself facing a formidable rival, Germany, which had been unified under Otto von Bismarck's iron hand and was now rapidly industrializing. In Asia, both Russia and Japan threatened to close off markets Britain sought, while the 1899 Boer War with white Afrikaaners in South Africa drained British energy and resources. The Foreign Office recognized that allowing Americans a free hand in the Western Hemisphere was a small price to pay for friendly assistance in keeping trade doors open around the world. The treaty Secretary of State John Hay concluded with British Ambassador Sir Julian Pauncefote in 1901 symbolized the new era of Anglo-American friendship. Under the Hay–Pauncefote Treaty, Britain ceded its interest in building a canal across the Latin American isthmus, while the United States pledged to leave such a canal open to ships of all nations.

THE IMPERIAL MOMENT

The year 1895 signaled a major shift in relations among the imperial powers. The United States had confronted Britain over Venezuela, Japan humiliated China in the Sino-Japanese War, and revolution in Cuba threatened the last bastion of Spain's shrunken New World empire. Americans had long cast a covetous eye on that sugar-rich island some 90 miles southwest of the tip of Florida. Outside the small white Spanish minority, few Cubans benefited from the island's plantation economy. In the wake of an unsuccessful revolutionary struggle from 1868 to 1878 the majority of the island's black and mulatto population suffered from dire poverty and severe political repression from their Spanish overlords.

After almost 15 years of planning and plotting from exile in the United States, Cuban revolutionary leader José Martí returned to Cuba in 1895 to renew the struggle for independence. With cries of *Cuba libre*, the rebels on February 24 began their fight by cutting railroad lines, destroying sugar mills, and burning the cane fields. The Cuban economy was already staggering from a drop in sugar exports resulting from duties imposed by the United States in 1894, in the midst of a severe national depression. That crisis made the local populace sympathetic to Martí's cause. By 1896 the rebels controlled more than half the island. All that time Martí and his followers worried about what the United States might do. They knew their island had long been a target of American expansionists and economic interests. "I have lived in the bowels of the monster," Martí said in reference to the United States, "and I know it."

The Spanish struck back with brutal violence. Governor-General Valeriano Weyler instituted a reconcentration program, under which his soldiers herded a half million Cubans from their homes into fortified camps. Filth, disease, and starvation killed as many as 200,000 of these prisoners. Outside the camps, Weyler's forces made war on the countryside, polluting the drinking water, killing farm animals, and burning crops.

Mounting Tensions

Americans had toyed with the notion of annexing Cuba since before the Civil War, when the island's slave-driven sugar plantations offered southerners a way to add slave territory to the United States to balance the increasing number of free states. During the 1890s the Cleveland administration had little sympathy for Martí's revolution. Cleveland doubted that the predominantly black Cuban population was capable of self-government and feared that any move for independence from Spain might lead to chaos. Already the revolution had caused widespread destruction of American-owned property. Cleveland settled on a policy that would throw American support to neither Spain nor the rebels: opposing the rebellion, but pressuring Spain to grant Cuba a measure of autonomy.

That halfway approach did not satisfy Republicans in Congress, who pressed Cleveland to recognize the Cuban belligerents. As a result, when Spain refused to lighten its oppressive hand in Cuba, Cleveland found himself trapped. He wanted to end Spanish brutality, but he did not want war. He wanted to continue the commercial penetration of Cuba, but he did not want to annex the island. So Cleveland and Secretary of State Olney continued to warn Spain of American interest in Cuba, doing little more than rattling teacups.

Ardent expansionists like Theodore Roosevelt, Henry Cabot Lodge, and John Hay had already convinced Republicans in their 1896 platform to call for American annexation of Hawaii, the construction of a Nicaraguan canal, purchase of the Virgin Islands, and further naval expansion. For Cuba they called for recognition of independence, a step that, if taken, would likely lead to war with Spain. The new president, however, was only a moderate expansionist. Like Blaine, William McKinley believed that the United States had dominant interests in Latin America. Like Mahan, he favored a large navy, insular bases, and a vigorous foreign trade. At first McKinley acted privately to press Spain to cease its repression of the rebels and to avoid actions that sent American citizens to Cuban jails and destroyed American property.

In October 1897 Spain did promise to remove the much-despised Weyler, to end the reconcentration policy, and to offer Cuba far greater autonomy. That shift in Spanish policy encouraged McKinley to reject calls for a more belligerent course. But events soon proved that dominant elements of the Spanish army in Cuba were renewing their efforts to crush the rebels and uphold Spain's honor. Conservative and pro-army elements opposed to reform rioted in the streets of Havana. McKinley dispatched the battleship *Maine* to show that the United States might take stiffer measures.

Then in February 1898 the State Department received a stolen copy of a letter to Cuba sent by the Spanish minister in Washington, Enrique Dupuy de Lôme. So did William Randolph Hearst, a pioneer of sensationalist, or "yellow," journalism. "WORST INSULT TO THE UNITED STATES IN ITS HISTORY," screamed the headline of Hearst's New York *Journal*. What had de Lôme actually said? It was insulting enough that he had dismissed McKinley as "a would-be politician," but, more tellingly, he admitted that Spain had no intention of reforming its Cuban policies. It intended to fight until the rebels were beaten. Spain immediately recalled de Lôme, but the damage had been done. Most Americans believed Spain had purposely deceived the United States. McKinley recognized that he had few options short of war.

It was at this point, on February 15, 1898, that a series of explosions ripped through the hull of the *Maine* as it lay at anchor in Havana harbor. Some 260 American sailors died. The cause of the blasts to this day remains unclear, but most Americans of the day irrationally concluded that Spanish agents had sabotaged the ship. The reality that Spain had little reason to provoke a war it could ill afford to fight did not penetrate the popular emotional outcry. The cautious McKinley sought a diplomatic solution, but he also asked Congress to appropriate $50 million "to get ready for war."

Meanwhile Theodore Roosevelt, the bumptious assistant secretary of the navy, sought to overcome the caution of the president and John Long, his boss in the Navy Department. With Long away, Roosevelt ordered Commodore George Dewey to prepare his Asiatic naval squadron to attack the Spanish fleet in the Philippines should war break out. That has led to the myth that Roosevelt secretly promoted war in the Pacific. In fact, the navy in 1896 had developed plans for a Philippine attack, so though Roosevelt acted a bit precipitately, his order was consistent with administration policy. McKinley was not as bellicose as ardent imperialists like Roosevelt, but, like most of the leaders of his party, he did consider overseas expansion a way to revive the economy in the aftermath of the 1890s depression.

The pressures for war simply proved too strong for McKinley to resist for long. On April 11 he asked Congress to authorize "forceful intervention" by the United States to establish peace in Cuba. Congress responded nine days later with a resolution that recognized the independence of Cuba, insisted on the withdrawal of Spanish forces, and gave the president authority to use the army and navy to enforce American demands. In the midst of this war rhetoric Congress adopted another measure, the Teller Amendment, with almost no fanfare. The amendment renounced any aim to annex Cuba, a gesture that seemed to cast the decision for war in a humanitarian rather than an imperialist light. "We cannot look idly on while hundreds of thousands of innocent human beings . . . die of hunger close to our doors," argued Senator George Hoar of Massachusetts. In truth, many supporters of the amendment feared the burden the United States would be forced to assume for Cuba's debts and its deeply impoverished black population. Certainly idealism and moral outrage had led many Americans down the path to war. But in this instance, less lofty ambitions for empire, expanded trade, and military glory offer a better explanation for what John Hay would call a "splendid little war."

The Imperial War

Many Europeans expected war between Spain and the United States to be an even fight. Most Americans thought otherwise. They welcomed the Spanish–American War as if it were a sporting event like a heavyweight prizefight. The army was swamped with volunteers, including an unlikely cavalry troop of cowboys and eastern college dudes put together by Theodore Roosevelt. Ohio alone had almost 100,000 volunteers. Beating a decrepit Spain would be no harder than "robbing an old gypsy woman in a vacant lot after a night fair," jested the young writer Sherwood Anderson.

For the 5462 men who died in the Spanish–American War there was little splendid about the event. Only 379 of the dead actually gave their lives in battle. The rest suffered from accident, disease, and the mismanagement of an unprepared army. Its total force numbered only 30,000, none of whom had been trained for fighting in tropical conditions or dealing with tropical disease. The sudden expansion to 60,000 troops and 200,000 volunteers overtaxed the supply system, which operated largely through graft and inefficiency. Troops often fought with weapons left over from the Civil War, sweltered in winter wool uniforms, and were given tinned rations that were diseased, rotted, or poisoned. Thus American soldiers went to war facing more dangerous conditions on their own bases than under enemy fire.

Fortunately for the United States, naval battles largely determined the outcome of the Spanish–American War. The decision to modernize the fleet during the 1890s paid almost immediate dividends. Prepared by orders from Theodore Roosevelt (which had been blessed, after the fact, by the approval of President McKinley), Admiral George Dewey ordered his battle squadron from China toward the Philippines as soon as war was declared. Few Americans had heard of the islands; fewer still could easily have located them on a globe. McKinley himself actually followed the news from the southwest Pacific on an old textbook map. The navy, however, had marked the Philippines as a key target, and on April 30, under cover of darkness, Dewey's squadron slipped by the shore guns of Corregidor in Manila Bay (see map on p. 812).

The battle that followed was one of the most one-sided and decisive in American military history. It began on May 1, 1898, with Dewey's laconic command at 5:40 a.m., "You may fire when ready, Gridley." And fire they did, until 8 a.m., when the Americans stopped briefly for breakfast. Five hours later the entire Spanish squadron of 10 ships lay at the bottom of Manila Bay. Three hundred eighty-one Spaniards had died; only eight Americans were wounded, and one sailor died of a heart attack. Dewey had no plans to follow up his victory with an invasion. In fact, his fleet carried no troops with which to take Manila. Only after he learned of Dewey's success did President McKinley order American troops to the Philippines.

News did not reach the American people until May 7, but then the entire nation went wild. Victory seemed to confirm American military prowess. In Dewey people found the hero for whom they thirsted. As one bit of newspaper doggerel exulted:

> Oh, dewy was the morning
> Upon the first of May,
> And Dewey was the admiral,
> Down in Manila Bay.
> And dewy were the Spaniards' eyes,
> Them orbs of black and blue,
> And dew we feel discouraged?
> I dew not think we dew!

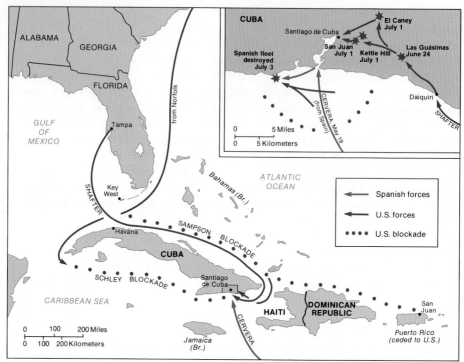

THE SPANISH-AMERICAN WAR
Had the Spanish-American War depended largely on ground forces, the ill-prepared U.S. Army might have fared poorly. But the key to success, in both Cuba and the Philippines, was naval warfare, in which the recently modernized American fleet had a critical edge. Proximity to Cuba also gave the United States an advantage in delivering troops and supplies and in maintaining a naval blockade that isolated Spanish forces.

Meanwhile, another Spanish fleet had slipped into Santiago harbor in Cuba before the U.S. Navy reached the area. American forces under Admiral William Sampson soon set up a blockade, assuming that the Spanish would try to sneak out at night. After being bottled up for five weeks, the Spanish instead made a desperate daylight dash for the open seas on July 3. So startled were the Americans that several of their ships nearly collided in an effort to sink their hopelessly exposed foes. All seven Spanish ships were sunk with 474 casualties, compared with only one dead and one wounded among the Americans. Cuba was now effectively cut off from Spain and the war virtually over.

The Cuban War

Before the outbreak of hostilities, Tampa was a sleepy coastal Florida town with a single railroad line. As the port of embarkation for the Cuban expeditionary force it became a hive of activity. Its overtaxed facilities soon broke down, with the inevitable unhealthy food and unsafe sanitation, as well as an ineffable miasma of plain human stench.

Into this scene of disease and chaos came yet another source of tension. President McKinley had authorized the army to raise five volunteer regiments of black soldiers. Despite the resistance of most state governors, the army finally accepted about 10,000 soldiers the Spanish came to call "smoked Yankees." But as Sergeant Frank Pullen of the black 24th Infantry Regiment remarked, to most white Americans, "we were 'niggers.'" Like most southern towns, Tampa and Lakeland were largely segregated, so that the 4000 blacks stationed there could sail off to die freeing the peasants of Cuba, but they could not buy a soda at the local drugstore. "Is America any better than Spain?" one dismayed black chaplain wondered. As the expeditionary force prepared to leave in early June, anger turned to violence. After drunken white troops shot at a black child, black troops in Tampa struck back. The ensuing riot left 3 whites and 27 blacks wounded.

Matters were scarcely less chaotic as the disorganized troops and hundreds of reporters finally scrambled aboard ships. There they sat for a week; on June 14 they sailed toward Santiago and battle. By June 30 the 17,000 regulars and volunteers had landed, to challenge some 24,000 Spanish troops, many equipped with more modern rifles. The following day 7000 Americans stormed up heavily fortified San Juan Hill and nearby Kettle Hill. Their objective was the high ground to

By the time of the Spanish-American War, blacks had been largely disfranchised and segregated; one of the few rights they preserved was the right to die for their country. Black veterans of the western Indian wars along with volunteers, segregated and commanded by white officers, made up almost a quarter of the American force that invaded Cuba. The Spanish soldiers dubbed them "smoked Yankees." Here, the all-black Tenth Cavalry supports a charge by Colonel Teddy Roosevelt's Rough Riders at the battle of San Juan Hill.

the north and east of Santiago. Among them Lieutenant Colonel Theodore Roosevelt thrilled at the experience of battle as he yelled to his Rough Riders (most of whom could not hear his rather high, squeaky voice), "Gentlemen, the Almighty God and the just cause are with you. Gentlemen, *Charge!*" After Roosevelt had repeated the call a second time, charge they did, though the battle cost the Americans over 1500 casualties. Without a fleet to cover them or any way to escape, the Spanish garrison surrendered on July 17. In the Philippines, a similar brief skirmish preceded the American taking of Manila on August 13. John Hay's "splendid little war" had ended in less than four months.

Peace and Empire

Conquering Cuba and the Philippines proved easier than deciding what the United States should do with them. The Teller Amendment renounced any American intention to exercise sovereignty over Cuba. But clearly the United States had not freed the island to see chaos reign or American business and military interests excluded. And what of the Philippines—and Puerto Rico, which American forces had taken without a struggle? Powerful public and congressional sentiment pushed McKinley to claim empire as the fruits of victory.

The president himself favored such a course. The battle in the Pacific highlighted the need for naval bases and coaling stations. "To maintain our flag in the Philippines, we must raise our flag in Hawaii," the New York *Sun* insisted. And on July 7 McKinley did just that as he signed a joint congressional resolution annexing Hawaii.

The Philippines presented a far more difficult problem. Filipinos had greeted the American forces as liberators, not colonial successors to the Spanish. The popular leader of the rebel forces fighting against Spain, Emilio Aguinaldo, had returned to the islands on an American ship. But to the rebels' dismay, McKinley insisted that the islands were under American authority until the peace treaty settled matters. Such a settlement no doubt would include permanent American control. McKinley had no intention of leaving Spain in charge and no desire to see the islands fall to such imperial rivals as Britain, Germany, and Japan. Without control of the entire island of Luzon, American military advisors warned, its capital, Manila, was indefensible as a naval base. Nor, McKinley felt certain, were the Filipinos in any way capable of self-government. Aguinaldo and his rebels understandably thought otherwise. In June Aguinaldo declared himself president of a new Philippine republic.

Many influential Americans took a strong stand against annexation. This was not, however, simply an argument for or against empire. Most members of the anti-imperialist movement, which included such prominent figures as former president Grover Cleveland, steel baron Andrew Carnegie, and novelist Mark Twain, did favor expansion in some form. Rather, business leaders among the anti-imperialists believed the United States could enjoy the economic fruits of the Philippines without the cost and consequences of incorporating the islands into the American system. Annexation would involve the United States far more deeply and undesirably in the politics of Asia. More important, a large fleet would be necessary to defend the islands. To the imperialists that was precisely the point. The United States should seek markets in Asia; and a large fleet was crucial to the interests of a powerful commercial nation.

Racist ideas shaped both sides of this argument. Imperialists believed that the

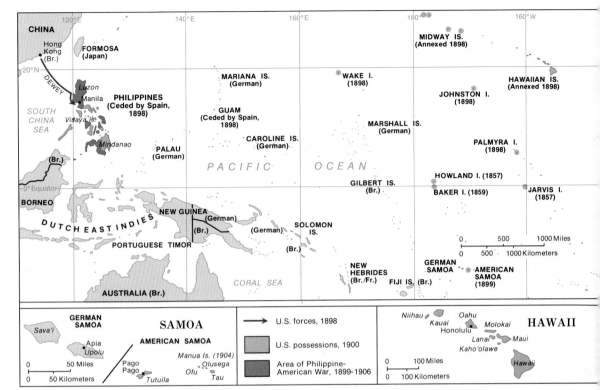

THE UNITED STATES IN THE PACIFIC

In the late nineteenth century both Germany and the United States emerged as major naval powers and as contestants for influence and commerce in China. The island groups of the Central and Southwest Pacific, though of little economic value, had potential strategic significance as bases and coaling stations along the routes to Asia. Rivalry (as in the case of Samoa) sometimes threatened to erupt into open conflict. Control of Hawaii, Midway, Samoa, Guam, and the Philippines gave the United States a string of strategic stepping-stones to the Orient.

racial inferiority of nonwhite peoples made the Philippine occupation necessary. But where the imperialists were willing to assume the "white man's burden" by annexing the Philippines, the anti-imperialists feared racial intermixing and the possibility that Asian workers would flood the American labor market.

Moreover, they believed that dark-skinned people could never develop the capacity for self-government. The Constitution made no provision for governing people without representation or equal rights. Rule in the Philippines would be successful only at the point of bayonets wielded by permanent troops of occupation. The precedent of government by force might imperil American liberties at home. Imperialists envisioned a benevolent government under which the United States would teach the virtues of democracy, Western civilization, and Christianity,[*] thus preparing the Philippines for self-rule.

---

[*]In point of fact, most Filipinos were already Catholic after many years under Spanish rule.

Still, in the Senate debate over the Treaty of Paris, the imperialists had the overwhelming support of the president, Congress, and public opinion. Even an anti-imperialist like William Jennings Bryan, defeated by McKinley in 1896, supported the treaty, in which Spain surrendered title to Cuba, ceded Puerto Rico and Guam to the United States, and for $20 million ceded the Philippines as well. Eager to see war ended, Bryan believed that once the United States possessed the Philippines it could free them.

The imperialists had other notions. Having acquired an empire and a modern navy to protect it, the United States could rightfully assert its claim as one of the great powers of the world. But managing a new empire proved far more difficult than acquiring it.

America's First Asian War

Conflict between the American occupation forces and the Philippine rebels erupted even before the capture of Manila. The Americans might hold the city, but the rebels controlled the countryside. As the Senate debated annexation, a rebel and an American patrol clashed outside the city. The guerrilla war that followed lasted more than three years, claiming 5000 American lives, 25,000 rebel soldiers, and 200,000 Filipino civilians.

The savagery of the fighting was spurred on by the deep racial antagonism on the part of most American soldiers toward people they described as "cross-eyed kakiak Ladrones." Successful resistance by such a supposedly inferior people too often turned frustration to brutality and torture. To avenge a rebel attack on unarmed troops, one American officer swore he would turn the surrounding country-

The American decision to occupy the Philippines rather than give it independence forced Filipino nationalists to fight U.S. troops, as they had already been fighting the Spanish since 1896. Forces like the ones pictured at the right were tenacious enough to require more than 70,000 Americans (left) to put down the rebellion. Sporadic, bloody guerrilla fighting continued until 1902 and other incidents persisted until 1906.

side into a "howling wilderness." Before long the 70,000 American troops had resorted to a garrison strategy that was embarrassingly reminiscent of the reconcentration policy of "Butcher" Weyler in Cuba. The war came to an unresolved end in 1902 only after the Americans managed to capture Aguinaldo, and his Filipino supporters finally lost hope.

In contrast to the bitter guerrilla war, the United States did practice a relatively benevolent colonial rule. Directed by Governor William Howard Taft, a program of modernization brought new schools, improved roads, cleaner cities, more productive agriculture, and factories, which won the support of the Filipino elite. The United States played a similar role in Puerto Rico, where, as in the Philippines, executive authority resided in a governor appointed by the president. Under the Foraker Act of 1900 Puerto Ricans were given a voice in their government, a nonvoting representative in the U.S. House of Representatives, and tariff advantages. All the same, many Puerto Ricans chafed at the idea of permanent second-class status. Some favored eventual admission to the United States as a state, while others advocated independence, a division of opinion that persists to the present day.

An Open Door in China

Interest in Asia had spurred the United States to annex the Philippines; annexation of the Philippines further whetted American interest in Asia. As always, the possibility of markets in China—whether for Christian souls or consumers— proved the greatest attraction. But both the British, who had garnered most of China's export trade, and Americans were worried about China being carved up by other imperial powers. Japan had gone to war with China in 1895 and defeated it, encouraging Russia, Germany, Japan, and France to demand additional trading concessions. Each nation sought to establish a "sphere of influence" in which its commercial and military interests were supreme. Often this meant discrimination against the interests of rival powers. Since Britain and the United States hoped only for the benefits of trade rather than new colonies, they sought some means to limit further foreign demands while leaving China open to the trade of all nations.

At the urging of a British customs official from China, Secretary of State John Hay in 1899 circulated the first of several "open-door" notes to the imperial powers. Hay asked only that the powers keep their spheres of influence in China open; he did not ask them to relinquish those spheres or to refrain from extending them. All of the powers accepted Hay's proposal with qualifications, but he announced that the open door was now an international policy.

Americans less familiar with imperial ambitions believed that Hay's note might actually protect China. In reality, it reflected the gap between American ambitions and power in Asia. The United States lacked the military, economic, or diplomatic means to create the fabled China market or to prevent other powers from partitioning China. Only the fear that the United States might tip the delicate balance by siding with a rival power led the Japanese and European powers to respond to Hay's note.

Events soon threatened the balance Hay sought to maintain. Disgruntled Chinese nationalists, known to Westerners as Boxers (their symbol was a fist), formed secret societies to drive the the *fon kwei*, or foreign devils, from their country. The Manchu empress secretly supplied them with arms and political support. Egged on by the empress, the Boxers murdered hundreds of Christian missionaries and their followers and besieged foreign diplomats and citizens in Beijing. All of the European nations sent troops to quell the uprising. Hay and McKinley sent 2500 Americans to join the march to the capital city. Along the way the angry armies did not restrain themselves against those they viewed as "slanty-eyed Celestials," confiscating valuables and committing atrocities against the civilian population.

Fearful that once in control of Beijing the conquerors might never leave, Hay dispatched a second open-door note. This time he asked the foreign powers to respect China's territorial and administrative integrity as well as access to its markets. At the same time he encouraged local Chinese authorities to suppress the Boxers and withdrew American troops once the rebellion had ended. No other foreign power endorsed this proposal, but many Americans assumed it now had the same status as the Monroe Doctrine: a principle recognized in theory and practice by other imperial powers.

Yet Hay never committed the United States to upholding the open door with anything more than words; he even briefly explored the possibility of America carving out a naval coaling station in China. It took a note from the imperial Japanese to remind him that such a step contradicted the principle he himself had enunciated. The open-door notes amounted to no more than an expression of American interests and an announcement that the United States was now committed to the preservation of stability in Asia.

THE ROOTS OF RUSSIAN–AMERICAN CONFLICT

"There are two great nations in the world which, starting from different points, seem to be advancing toward the same goal: the Russians and the Anglo-Americans. . . . Each seems called by some secret design of Providence one day to hold in its hands the destinies of half the world." To people living after World War II, such an observation seems self-evident, but when Alexis de Tocqueville made it in 1835, both Russia and the United States stood on the periphery of world affairs.

For much of the nineteenth century, in fact, Europe's most reactionary monarchy and the revolutionary New World republic maintained cordial relations. They did so by stressing their mutual interests rather than their profound ideological and cultural differences. As peripheral powers separated by great distances, they had few points of potential geographical conflict. Russian–American commerce benefited both nations and each nation viewed the other as a potential counterweight to a common enemy—Great Britain. Thus the United States maintained a sympathetic attitude toward Russia in 1854 as it battled England and France during the Crimean War. The Russians returned the favor by frustrating French and British proposals to interfere in the American Civil War. The sale of Alaska to the United States in 1867 marked the high point of Russian–American cooperation. From then on, however, their interests began to diverge and conflicting ideologies soured their once cordial ties.

Conflicting Ideology

As American power increased and British–American rivalry eased, many Americans began to see Russia as a rival power. Where Britain supported the open door in China, the Russians clearly had imperial designs on Manchuria. And the more they learned about the czar's government, the more Americans objected to its repressive policies and its secret police. They were shocked to learn about the horrors of exile in the Siberian labor camps. But no issue did more to arouse American popular opposition to the czarist government than anti-Semitism. Official Russian policy restricted Russian Jews to an area of settlement in eastern Poland and western Russia called the Pale. Other laws limited Jewish educational and economic opportunities. Young Jewish men at the age of 12 faced over 30 years of forced military service. When revolutionaries assassinated Czar Alexander II in 1881, a bad situation became worse. The government condoned pogroms that for the next 30 years led to the beating and killing of Jews, the looting of shops, and illegal confiscation of property.

In the 1880s the population of the United States included only 250,000 Jews, mostly of German extraction. Their vocal protests, however, aroused the sympathies of other Americans as well as the State Department, which interceded when the pogroms affected American Jews traveling or living in Russia. On other occasions the State Department reminded the Russian government of the American commitment to religious freedom. The Russians replied that since the United States did not see fit to treat its minorities equally, the principle should not be binding on Russia either.

By the 1890s the pogroms had turned Jewish immigration to the United States from a trickle to a torrent. American Jewish leaders and humanitarians became more insistent that the government take some action to curtail Russian anti-Semitism. At first John Hay and President Theodore Roosevelt (who succeeded McKinley in 1901) refused. "What possible advantage would it be . . . to the Jews of Russia, if we should make a protest against these fiendish cruelties and be told it's none of our business?" Hay asked Jewish financier Jacob Schiff.

Insistent public protest led the politically shrewd Roosevelt in this case to let domestic concerns reverse his support for nonintervention. He agreed to forward a petition to the Russian government, which the Russians refused to accept. All the same, the United States had taken an important step. An ideological principle rather than a material interest had influenced American relations with Russia. If anything, American protests worsened the treatment of Russian Jews and certainly aggravated Russian–American relations. Roosevelt, however, reaped political benefits from a grateful American Jewish community. Jewish leaders, in turn, had demonstrated that influential pressure groups could affect the course of American foreign policy.

Diverging Interests

By the 1890s Russian and American economic interests had begun to diverge as well. As the United States came to work more closely with Britain, both powers began to regard Russia as a threat to the open door in China. Manchuria, a Chi-

This Russian-Jewish immigrant was one of millions who fled anti-Semitic violence in the region of Russia and Poland known as the Pale. Immigration officials placed the "K" on his coat to indicate a suspected hernia condition. Some diseases and disabilities were grounds for refusing immigrants' admission to the United States.

nese province southeast of Siberia, became an area in which American and Russian geographic interests clashed. Part of the Trans-Siberian Railroad, built in the 1890s, passed through Manchuria, and the new transportation link gave the Russians a commercial advantage in Asia over its European rivals. In the wake of the Boxer Rebellion, the Russians had occupied the entire province and then refused to withdraw. In 1902 Britain responded by forming an alliance with Japan.

The United States did not formally associate itself with this anti-Russian pact, but Americans supported it as a barrier to Russian ambitions. The American consul in Manchuria had recently warned that Russia "will annihilate American trade here . . . become a serious obstacle to the extension of our trade in all the Orient, and eventually a menace to our higher civilization." Thus when the Russians extended their occupation in 1903, Secretary of State Hay called the action "injurious to our legitimate interests" and characteristic of "a government with whom mendacity is a science." Rumors quickly spread in Washington of a possible Russian–American war, encouraged by traveler, writer, and lecturer George Kennan among others. Kennan (a distant relative of the well-known Soviet expert George F. Kennan) was one of the few Americans familiar with Russia and an archfoe of the czarist regime. Kennan knew that war was unlikely, but he recognized that the new course of American empire had forever ended "the sentimental friendship that has long been supposed to exist between the governments of Russia and the United States."

That was more the choice of American than Russian leaders. The goals of Russian foreign policy remained what they had long been: secure frontiers, access to the open seas (beyond merely the Baltic and Black seas), ethnic and religious solidarity at home, and a stable balance of power in Europe. In the late nineteenth century it was the United States whose goals had changed. A nation once content with continental expansion had set its sights across the seas. Foreign markets beckoned to its merchants and manufacturers. It had transformed its feeble navy into a force capable of projecting power into distant lands. Traditionally tied by culture and history to western Europe, its people now included those who had called eastern and southern Europe home. This gave the United States more reason to involve itself in the internal affairs of foreign nations, as it did increasingly with Russia in the twentieth century. Here lay the distant roots of the Russian–American conflict that has dominated international affairs since World War II.

To men like Alfred Thayer Mahan, Brooks and Henry Adams, Theodore Roosevelt, and John Hay, American interests would be secure only when they had been established worldwide. These expansionists were confident that as a world power the United States had embarked on the course destined for it by divine providence. It could maintain its high principles of democracy and equality without descending to the cynical power politics of imperialism. But to one French diplomat, perhaps more accustomed to the corrosive effects of wheeling and dealing in the corridors of international power, it seemed that the Americans had tempted fate rather than destiny. With a whiff of Old World cynicism he remarked, "The United States is seated at the table where the great game is played, and it cannot leave it."

SIGNIFICANT EVENTS

1850	Clayton–Bulwer Treaty
1853	Commodore Perry visits Japan
1867	Alaska acquired; British North America Act creates Canadian confederation; fall of Maximilian in Mexico
1871	Minor Keith arrives in Costa Rica
1878	Samoan Treaty
1881	Revolutionaries assassinate Czar Alexander II; anti-Jewish pogroms begin in Russia
1882	Chinese Exclusion Act; Commodore Shufeldt negotiates treaty with Korea
1889	First Pan-American Congress
1890	Mahan's *The Influence of Sea Power Upon History, 1660–1783* published; Naval Appropriations Bill launches modern navy
1891	Chile–United States war threat
1893	Controversy over annexation of Hawaii
1893–1896	Depression encourages expansionist policies
1894–1895	Sino-Japanese War
1895	Venezuelan boundary dispute; Martí revives Cuban revolution
1898	Sinking of the U.S.S. *Maine;* war with Spain; Teller Amendment; Dewey captures the Philippines; Tampa riots; Treaty of Paris; Hawaii formally annexed; Anti-Imperialist League established
1898–1902	Philippine insurrection
1899	First open-door notes
1900	Boxer Rebellion; second open-door notes; Foraker Act establishes civil government in Puerto Rico
1901	Hay–Pauncefote Treaty
1902	British–Japanese anti-Russian pact

23

The Progressive Era

 uitting time, March 25, 1911. The streets of lower Manhattan were just beginning to swell with people. Glancing upward, a passer-by noticed "a great swirling, billowing cloud of smoke," sweeping "like a giant streamer out of Washington Square and down upon the beautiful homes in lower Fifth Avenue." The Asch Building, home of the Triangle Shirtwaist Company, was on fire.

Five hundred people, largely Jewish and Italian immigrants, had been working at the Triangle factory for nearly 12 hours as smoke began to fill the evening sky. Since half past seven in the morning they had been making "shirtwaists," the tailored blouses worn by young women working in offices. Most of the factory workers were young women, too, many under 25. Some were children as young as 8. In fact, so many youngsters could be found laboring in the city's garment factories, recalled one seamstress, that "the corner of the shop would resemble a kindergarten."

Throughout the industry wages and working conditions were horrid. Adults earned from $3 to $15 a week, children as little as $1.50, without overtime pay no matter how heavy the schedule. Workers sat on chairs without backs and bought their needles and thread—even the electric power—from their bosses. If employees arrived late or made a mistake on the job, they were fined or sent home with no pay.

Two years earlier Triangle workers had struck the company because it routinely fired union members. Some 18,000 dressmakers and waistmakers from the city's 600 manufacturers joined them. In mid-February 1910, while New Yorkers were buying sheet music for "Heaven Will Protect the Working Girl," the companies finally settled. The largest firms made concessions on wages and hours but refused to recognize the union. At Triangle dangerous working conditions remained: fire escapes stayed broken; no sprinkler system was installed; and doors were locked each morning to keep union organizers out and workers in.

The Triangle blaze broke out in the lofts and spread quickly from floor to floor. Terrified seamstresses groped through fire and smoke toward exits, only to find them shut tight. All the fire escapes but one collapsed in the heat. Children with hair on fire jumped from top-floor windows. "Spectators saw again and again pitiable companionships formed in the instant of death—girls who placed their arms around each other as they leaped," one news story read. They fell 10 stories before their bodies hit the sidewalk or were impaled on the building's iron guard rails.

Personal magnetism, expansive vision, and shrewd use of the press enabled Theodore Roosevelt to transform the presidency into a vital center of public action. This cartoon detail depicts him as an American Caesar, triumphantly parading through Washington.

One hundred forty-six people, mainly young women, died. A few days later 80,000 New Yorkers joined the silent funeral procession as it moved slowly up Fifth Avenue in the rain. A quarter of a million watched. "This is not the first time that girls have been burned alive in the city," union leader Rose Schneiderman told a mass meeting at the Metropolitan Opera House. "Every year thousands of us are maimed." New York's governor appointed a commission to investigate the tragedy. Over the next four years its recommendations produced 56 state laws—the most far-reaching labor code in the country—regulating fire safety, hours, machinery, and home work.

The Triangle fire horrified the nation and underscored what many Americans already knew: modern industrial society had created profound strains, widespread misery, and deep class divisions. Corporations and trusts grew to sizes previously unimagined, bought and sold legislators, dictated the terms of their own profit. Men and women worked around the clock in unsafe factories for wages that barely supported them. Eight- and nine-year-olds went into coal mines and came out missing fingers or limbs. Some never came out at all. If they survived to adulthood, they faced an early death from lungs blackened by coal dust.

Americans everywhere felt the pinch of the new industrial order. In cities tenement-bred tuberculosis took the lives of the disadvantaged. Violent criminals threatened people and property; saloons tied the poor and working class to dishonest political machines. In the countryside even successful farmers could not control the high rates of shippers. Sharecroppers and tenants helplessly suffered the poverty and ignorance that stripped them of dignity and opportunity. Across prosperous America, a mild but relentless inflation, averaging about 3 percent a year, shrank the wallets of the middle class. "It was a world of greed," concluded one disillusioned garment worker; "the human being didn't mean anything."

But human beings did mean something to adherents of the great reform movement that had already begun to reshape America. Progressivism had emerged in the mid-1890s and would last through World War I. It sprang from many impulses: desires to curb the advancing power of corporations and end widespread corruption; efforts to bring order and efficiency to economic and political life; attempts by new interest groups to make business and government more

In 1911 the fiery deaths of 146 people at the Triangle Shirtwaist Company shocked the nation. Firefighters arrived within minutes, but their ladders could not reach the top stories. Trapped by locked doors, those who failed to escape perished within or leaped to their deaths on the streets below. Following the horrifying episode New York enacted the most ambitious labor code in the country.

responsive to their needs; moralistic urges to rid society of such perceived evils as drink and prostitution. The ideology of progressivism mixed elements of liberal concern for the poor and working class with conservative efforts to stabilize business and avoid social chaos. At times progressivism embraced such diversity that historians have despaired of finding any coherence in it.

If progressivism did anything, it tried to reduce the dangerous effects of industrialization, immigration, and urbanization by softening their impact on people. The aftermath of the Triangle fire offers a case study of progressivism in action. Tragedy led to publicity and investigation, which generated the outrage and evidence necessary for change. Amid the clamor for reform, legislators adopted laws to set things right. To keep things right, progressives looked to an aroused public opinion and to government, often in the form of strong executive agencies staffed by impartial experts.

Progressivism began in the cities, where the wellspring of misery was fullest, political corruption deepest, and social division clearest. Organized mostly by angry, idealistic members of the middle class, it percolated up from neighborhoods to city halls and state legislatures. Though usually pursued through the medium of politics, the goals of progressives were broadly social. Progressives wanted nothing less than to create a "good society" (shaped largely in a middle-class mold) where people could live decently, harmoniously, and prosperously.

Progressives understood that only government had the resources for such a broad-based reformation. Under their leadership the modern activist state was born. It emerged at the national level in the presidencies of Theodore Roosevelt and Woodrow Wilson. No one political party monopolized progressivism; no single group controlled it. In 1912 it gave birth to the Progressive, or "Bull Moose," party, but by then it extended well beyond politics into every realm of American life.

THE ROOTS OF PROGRESSIVE REFORM

The wrenching depression of 1893 forced reformers to focus on the need to humanize the industrial system. They came to realize that despite differences in their social backgrounds and political concerns, they shared a common goal: the improvement of society. Ordinary people found common causes that cut across lines of class, religion, and ethnicity. If streetcar companies raised fares while service deteriorated, if processors doctored food with harmful additives, all consumers suffered.

The result was not a coherent progressive "movement" but a set of loosely affiliated movements. Some progressives struggled to provide efficient government and honest politics. Others attempted to widen the regulation of business. Some fought for social justice for the urban poor, others for social welfare to protect children, women, factory workers, or consumers. Still others wanted to purify society by prohibiting alcohol and drugs, restricting immigration, stamping out slums, and ending prostitution. Although independent forces, these groups often combined when their causes overlapped.

Progressivism had its nostalgic streak, for some progressives aimed at redeeming such traditional American values as democracy, opportunity for the individual, and a spirit of public service. In this quest progressives were often paternalistic, seeking to impose their ideals no matter what the less "enlightened" poor or oppressed might view as their own best interests. Yet if the ends of progressives were traditional, their means were modern. They made use of the latest techniques of organization, management, and science—fighting the excesses of the new industrial and urban order with its own systems and methods.

The Progressive System of Beliefs

Moderate modernizers, progressives accepted the American system as sound, in need only of adjustment. In adopting this gradual approach, many drew on the increasingly popular Darwinian theories of evolution. With its notion of slowly changing species, evolution undermined the acceptance of fixed principles that had guided social thought in the Victorian era. Progressives saw an evolving landscape and ever-shifting values; thus they placed less emphasis on absolute truths and more on the relativity of ideas. With an eye to results, their prime concern was not so much "Is it true?" but "Does it work?" Philosopher Charles Peirce called this way of thinking "pragmatism," and William James, the Harvard psychologist, became its most famous popularizer. For James, the new philosophy meant "looking away from first things, principles, 'categories,' supposed necessities; and of looking towards last things, fruits, consequences, facts."

Progressives also denied the traditional Calvinist doctrine of innate sinfulness or depravity—sheer "human cussedness." They viewed human potential as more good than evil and spoke of "the essential nobility of man." But human advancement and social improvement were only possible, never automatic. One skeptical wit remarked that Theodore Dreiser, an eminent novelist of the era, possessed an abiding faith in humanity—then saw Pittsburgh and lost all hope. The barb was in jest, but it had its hook. Progressives, having seen the mean side of the industrial city, somehow had to deal with the existence of crime and vice. Some progressives agreed that evil and ugliness were "largely, if not wholly, products of environment." People went wrong, as Fremont Older of the San Francisco *Bulletin* explained it, because of "what happens to them."

Progressives thought they could change people by changing "what happens to them." Social reformer Jane Addams liked to tell the story of Marcella, a poor but decent girl who stole some silk to make a dress for a fancy ball. Neither the authorities nor the girl's mother could understand, but Addams felt she did. Marcella had been driven to crime by circumstances—poverty and temptation. Improve her environment, and she would flower. "Life in the Settlement," Addams wrote, "discovers above all what has been called 'the extraordinary pliability of human nature,' and it seems impossible to set any bounds to the moral capabilities which might unfold under ideal civic and educational conditions."

Pragmatism led educators, social scientists, and lawyers to adopt new approaches to reform. John Dewey, the preeminent educator of the progressive era, along with his wife, Alice, founded a new School of Pedagogy at the University of Chicago in 1896; it was based on the notion that human thought evolved in relation to the environment in which it was developed. Instead of forcing students to memorize abstract and unconnected facts at a teacher's command, Dewey wanted to "make each one of our schools an embryonic community life, active with the types of occupations that reflect the life of the larger society." By letting students unbolt their desks from the floor, move their chairs around, and learn by doing, schools could teach real life. Education would be a fountainhead of reform—in Dewey's words, "the deepest and best guarantee of a larger society which is worthy, lovely, and harmonious."

The blending of environmentalism and expertise led John B. Watson to "behavioral" psychology and the belief that human beings could be shaped at will. "Give me a dozen healthy infants," Watson later wrote, ". . . and my own specified world to bring them up in, and I'll guarantee to take any one at random and train him to become any specialist I might select, doctor, lawyer, artist, merchant, chief, and yes, even beggarman and thief, regardless of his talents, tendencies, abilities, vocations and race of his ancestors."

Most environmentalists were less extreme than Watson. Sociologist Edward A. Ross in *Social Control* (1901) looked at industrialized life—"its wolfish struggle for personal success, its crimes, frauds, exploitation and parasitism"—and stressed the need for restraints. In *The Theory of the Leisure Class* (1899) Thorstein Veblen, an economist, outraged genteel Americans by describing them with the detachment that an anthropologist might have reserved for some exotic tribe in Borneo. Reclusive and defiant, Veblen irreverently rejected the notion that the rich and respectable labored primarily to produce valued goods and services. Rather, he claimed, they strove to outdo each other in showing off their wealth ("pecuniary emulation") and expending labor to buy, maintain, and display their many-roomed mansions, multicourse banquets, and multilayered evening dresses ("conspicuous consumption"). Indeed, he concluded, the business class promoted an economy of waste and scarcity as they scrambled for profits. In *The Engineers and the Price System* (1921) Veblen argued that only expert planning could create an efficient and orderly industrial system.

Lawyers and legal theorists applied their own brand of pragmatism and environmentalism. Justice Oliver Wendell Holmes, Jr., appointed to the Supreme Court in 1902, rejected the idea that the traditions of American law ought to be regarded as universal and unalterable, interpreted in an august manner from the bench. "Long ago," Holmes remarked, "I decided I was not God." To him law was a living organism to be interpreted according to the needs of a changing society. The "life of the law," he wrote in *The Common Law* (1881), "has not been logic; it has been experience."

Experience was where Denver Judge Ben Lindsey looked when he handed down a verdict. Presiding over one of the first juvenile courts in the country, the "Kids' Judge" examined the home life of youthful offenders before he ruled. All too often he discovered poverty, illness, and joblessness. Environment, not heredity, produced juvenile delinquents, Lindsey believed, so he used the new authority of his court to take them from dysfunctional homes and make them wards of the state. In several states, supervised probation replaced suspended sentences to ensure that bad habits stayed broken. Yet in this urge to do good, progressives revealed an uncomfortable inclination to intrude into private lives and to limit individual choice.

"Sociological jurisprudence," as this environmental view of the law came to be known, found its most creative practitioner in Louis D. Brandeis. Brandeis believed that law must "guide by the light of reason," which meant bringing the conditions of everyday life to bear in any court case. Shaken by the Homestead steel strike, Brandeis turned away from his corporate practice to become the self-proclaimed "people's lawyer." When laundry-owner Curt Muller challenged an Oregon law limiting the working day of women to 10 hours, the National

Consumers' League retained Brandeis to defend the law before the Supreme Court in 1908. Surrounded by boxes of reports from social workers, doctors, factory inspectors, and other experts, Brandeis documented the damaging effects of long hours of work on the health and morals of women. His brief in *Muller v. Oregon* (prepared by his sister-in-law Josephine Goldmark) contained only 2 pages of legal precedents; the remaining 102 pages detailed the sociology of working women. The Supreme Court upheld the Oregon law and in so doing gave legal sanction to the "Brandeis Brief."

The Progressive Method

Seeing the nation riven by diverse ethnic and interest groups, progressives tried to restore a sense of community and common purpose through the ideal of a single public interest. Christian ethics were the guide, applied expertise and planning the instruments. "There are two gospels I always want to preach to reformers," Theodore Roosevelt told a conference on city improvement. "The first is the gospel of morality; the next is the gospel of efficiency." From the physical and social sciences progressives borrowed the latest methods for systematically gathering and analyzing data, making diagnoses, and prescribing solutions. In the modern corporation they found an appealing model for organization. Like corporate executives, progressives relied on careful management, coordinated systems, and specialized bureaucracies to carry out reforms.

Between 1902 and 1912 a new breed of investigative reporters publicized wrongdoers by name and described their deeds in vivid detail. Most exposés began as articles in mass circulation magazines. Samuel McClure, publisher since 1893 of a magazine bearing his name, sent Lincoln Steffens out to discover the unsavory ties between business and politics. Steffens' startling exposé, "Tweed Days in St. Louis," appeared in the October 1902 issue of *McClure's*. The first installment of Ida M. Tarbell's *History of the Standard Oil Company*, another stinging, well-researched indictment, followed in November. As *McClure's* annual circulation jumped to 370,000, competitors quickly adopted the new style. *The Ladies Home Journal* exposed the evils of patent medicines; *Everybody's* featured Thomas W. Lawson on crooked finance and Charles Edward Russell on the beef trust. Soon a full-blown literature of exposure was covering everything from prostitution and health care to insurance companies, urban poverty, and child labor.

Theodore Roosevelt called the new breed of journalists "muckrakers," after the man who raked up filth and ignored beauty in John Bunyan's seventeenth-century classic, *Pilgrim's Progress*. Journalist Ray Stannard Baker chose to differ: muckraking flourished, and deserved to, he argued, "because the country for years had been swept by the agitation of soap-box orators, prophets crying in the wilderness, and political campaigns based upon charges of corruption and privilege which everyone believed or suspected had some basis of truth, but which were largely unsubstantiated." By documenting dishonesty and blight, muckrakers helped to arouse public indignation. Most likely, no broad reform movement of American institutions would have taken place without them.

To move beyond exposure to solutions, progressives stressed volunteerism and collective action. They drew on the organizational impulse that seemed everywhere to be bringing people together. Between 1890 and 1920 nearly 400 new organizations appeared. Some, like the National Consumers' League, grew out of

John D. Rockefeller, oil baron and multimillionaire, was a favorite target of the investigative journalists Theodore Roosevelt dubbed "muckrakers." A sympathetic cartoon in the
magazine *Judge* beseeches them to relent. "Boys," reads the caption, "don't you think you
have bothered the old man just about enough?"

efforts to promote general causes, in this instance protecting consumers and workers from exploitation. Others, such as the National Tuberculosis Association,
aimed at solving a specific problem. Reflecting the new emphasis on expertise, the
professions also organized. Groups like the American Medical Association and the
American Society of Mechanical Engineers standardized their procedures, licensed their members to keep out charlatans, and informed the public about their
professional goals.

When voluntary action failed to produce results, progressives looked to government as the agent for protecting the public welfare. Disdainful of legislators
controlled by special interests and political bosses, they tried to strengthen the
executive branch by enhancing the power of mayors, governors, and presidents.
At all levels—local, state, federal—new agencies and commissions staffed by impartial experts began to investigate and regulate society—from the activities of
lobbyists and railroad companies to the state of public health.

THE SEARCH FOR THE GOOD SOCIETY

If progressivism ended in politics, it started with social reform: the shock of excesses in slums, the need to reach out, to do something to bring the "good society"
a step closer. In 1890, a year after Jane Addams founded her famous settlement
house in Chicago, the New England Kitchen opened in downtown Boston. Ellen
Richards, a chemist-turned-home economist, designed the Kitchen to sell cheap,

wholesome food to the working poor. For a few pennies, customers could choose from a menu that included beef broth, boiled hominy, cracked wheat, and spiced beef. To ensure the highest nutrition, Richards had every dish tested in her laboratory at the Massachusetts Institute of Technology.

The New England Kitchen was an exercise as much in social as in nutritional reform. Women freed from the drudgery of cooking could seek gainful employment. As a "household experiment station" and gathering place for information on "the food supply of the masses," the Kitchen tried to educate the poor about how best to prepare wholesome meals. It also sought to Americanize immigrants with standard foods and, according to philanthropist Pauline Shaw, to produce a "rival to the saloon." As she saw it, poor diets fostered drinking, especially among the lower classes.

For all these good intentions, the New England Kitchen usually served as an inexpensive eatery for middle-class working women and students rather than a resource for the poor or an instrument of Americanization. ("Oh!" one Irish mother reported her son saying when she served an Indian pudding. "You can't make a Yankee of me that way!") Still, the New England Kitchen reflected the pattern of reform that characterized so many progressive ventures: the mix of middle-class professionalism with lower-class uplift, the hope of creating the outlines of a new and better world.

The Rediscovery of Poverty

Social reformers often chose to live in slums, among the poor. There they saw poverty in a new light. During the 1890s urban reformer and pioneer photographer Jacob Riis (page 693) used lantern slide shows to introduce middle-class urbanites to the look of poverty. The slides appeared artless—merely recording the desperate poverty before the camera—but Riis' moralistic narrative used them much the way the earlier English novelist Charles Dickens had used his melodramatic tales to attack the abuses of industrialism. Riis' photographic essays were followed by an even greater naturalism in fiction and painting. Novelists such as Theodore Dreiser and Frank Norris spun tales of city dwellers struggling to survive with body and soul intact. The "Ashcan School" painted city life in all its gritty realism. Several artists of this group had been illustrators on metropolitan dailies and many—photographer Alfred Stieglitz and painters like John Sloan, George Luks, and George Bellows—chose slums, tenements, and dirty streets as subjects. Poverty began to look less ominous and more heart-rending.

Between 1908 and 1914 the Russell Sage Foundation produced six large volumes of facts and figures documenting how wretchedly urban workers lived, how dangerously they labored in factories, how poorly they were paid, how relentlessly disease struck them down. The gathering weight of evidence indicated a vicious social cycle that trapped its victims for generations. The children of paupers would likely be paupers themselves, not because of heredity but because of deprivation. No one did more to publicize this view than Robert Hunter. In researching his book *Poverty*, Hunter discovered no fewer than 10 million Americans (out of a population of about 80 million) living in poverty. As a cure he recommended a hodgepodge of progressive social legislation: prohibition of child labor; public day nurseries; pensions for the sick, the unemployed, and the elderly; sanitary legislation for tenements and factories; maximum hour and minimum wage laws; and limitations on immigration.

A new profession—social work—developed out of the settlement house movement. Like doctors (from whom they drew inspiration), social workers studied hard data to diagnose the problems of their "clients." Unlike nineteenth-century philanthropists, the new social workers refused to do things to or for people. Instead they worked with their clients, enlisting their help to solve their own problems. A social worker's "differential casework" attempted to treat individuals case by case, each according to the way the client had been shaped by environment.

No amount of middle-class goodwill and scientific endeavor could entirely eradicate poverty. Most progressives continued to see the problem as a by-product of political and corporate greed, of the evil environment of urban slums, and of "institutions of vice" like the saloon. They saw less clearly how deeply rooted poverty had become in rural areas made marginal by large-scale, mechanized agriculture, in urban areas where the unskilled congregated, and in individuals suffering from a range of pathologies—alcoholism, drug addiction, mental illness—that defied cure by even the most enlightened policies. Poverty was in reality a single symptom of a host of personal and social ills.

Expanding the "Woman's Sphere"

Progressive social reform attracted a disproportionate number of women, seeking what Jane Addams called "the larger life." Like most Americans, women were living longer and becoming better educated. Between 1870 and 1910, the proportion of women among college students had doubled to 40 percent of all American students. Meanwhile more women remained unwed and the divorce rate skyrocketed—from 1 in 21 marriages in 1880 to 1 in 9 by 1916. (Two-thirds were instigated by wives, most of them unhappy with the quality of married life.)

Single, well-educated women turned most often to professions that involved the traditional role of nurturer—nursing, library work, and teaching. Custom and prejudice barred them from other choices. The faculty at the Massachusetts Institute of Technology refused to allow Ellen Richards, the first woman in America to earn a degree in science, to pursue a doctorate, even though they hired her to run the gender-segregated "Woman's Laboratory" for training public school teachers. Only about 1500 women lawyers practiced in the whole country. In 1910 women comprised barely 6 percent of licensed physicians. That figure rapidly declined as male-dominated medical associations grew in power and discouraged the entry of women. Professions dominated by women began to define themselves in modern terms just as those largely consisting of men did. In a manner characteristic of other women's activities, teaching (still the occupation of 9 of 10 professional women) increasingly set standards of admission and monitored its members. In 1905 teachers created the National Education Association, which lobbied for government certification of teachers.

Educated women frequently discovered that their families stood in their way. "All my plans for a 'career' have been knocked to atoms," wrote one Wellesley College graduate, forced to stay home to care for her mother. "You can put me down as still alive, though." Some educated and professional women tried not simply to widen the boundaries of their sphere but to destroy them. In *Women and Economics* (1898) feminist Charlotte Perkins Gilman condemned the conventions of womanhood—femininity, marriage, maternity, and domesticity—as enslaving and obsolete. She argued for a radically restructured society with large apartment houses, communal arrangements for child rearing and housekeeping, and cooperative kitchens to free women from economic dependence on men.

Margaret Sanger, a visiting nurse on the Lower East Side of New York, sought to free women from the bonds of chronic pregnancy. "Women," she believed, "cannot be on equal footing with men until they have complete control over their reproductive functions." The insight came as a revelation one summer evening in 1912, when she was called to the home of an immigrant family on Grand Street. Sadie Sachs, a mother of three who had nearly died after an earlier self-induced abortion, had succeeded this time in killing her unborn child—and herself. Sanger vowed that night to "seek out the root of the evil, to do something to change the destiny of mothers whose miseries were as vast as the sky." She became a crusader for what she called "birth control." By distributing information on contraception, she hoped to prevent unwanted pregnancies among poor women. Some middle-class women joined the movement, largely to control the size of their own families and those of new immigrants.

For many middle- and upper-class women, it was often women's clubs that extended their sphere into the world at large. Founded in the 1880s and 1890s, over 500 women's clubs totaled some 160,000 members by the turn of the century. Banding together in the General Federation of Women's Clubs, they began to turn their attention from cultural self-improvement to social improvement— funding libraries and hospitals, supporting schools and settlement houses, eventually endorsing such controversial causes as woman suffrage and unionization.

Single or married, militant or moderate, professional or lay, more and more middle-class urban women thus became "social housekeepers." From their own homes they turned their attention to the homes of their neighbors and from there to all of society.

Social Welfare and Social Justice

In this "bigger family of the city," as one reformer called it, settlement workers bridged traditional charity and progressive reform. Like old-style philanthropists, they volunteered to staff the settlement houses, where the urban poor and foreign-born were exposed to middle-class virtues: thrift; cleanliness; orderliness; refinement; manners; culture; responsibility; and citizenship. They also offered language and cooking classes, day nurseries, and clubs for men and women. All were designed to teach immigrants American ways, lift the destitute from the slums, and help those who failed to make it out. In 1891 there were 6 settlement houses in the country; by 1910 there were over 400, most located in the worst slums and united by a national organization. Increasingly, however, settlement reformers turned to government to supplement individual charity by passing laws and establishing public agencies to promote improved housing, safer factories, parks, and playgrounds, and the abolition of child labor.

As settlement workers became more organized and professional, they helped to shape government policy. Lawrence Veiller worked at the University Settlement in New York before Governor Theodore Roosevelt named him as secretary of the newly created Tenement House Commission. In 1901 New York enacted a new tenement code based on a bill Veiller had drafted. Other states soon copied the law, which required fire escapes, a window in each room, and a water closet for each apartment. Julia Lathrop, a Vassar College graduate, spent 20 years at Hull-House in Chicago before becoming the first head of the new federal Children's Bureau in 1912. By then two-thirds of the states had adopted some child labor legislation, although loopholes exempted newsboys and countless other

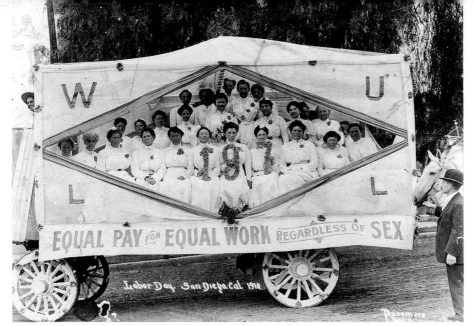

By 1900 one-fourth of the nonfarm labor force was female. On average, women industrial workers made three dollars a week less than unskilled men. Here at a Labor Day parade in San Diego in 1910 women demand equal pay for equal work.

youngsters from coverage. Under Lathrop's leadership, Congress was persuaded to pass the Keating–Owen Act (1916), forbidding goods manufactured by children to cross state lines.*

Florence Kelley, who, like Addams and Lathrop, had worked at Hull-House, spearheaded the campaign that led the Illinois legislature to pass an eight-hour workday law for women in 1893. The state supreme court invalidated it, so Kelley began a nationwise crusade to mobilize public opinion and local consumers' groups. As general secretary of the National Consumers' League, she organized boycotts of companies that treated employees inhumanely. In the wake of the *Muller* decision in 1908, most states enacted laws restricting the number of hours women could work.

Woman Suffrage

Ever since the conference for women's rights held at Seneca Falls in 1848, women reformers had been pressing for the right to vote on the grounds of simple justice and equal opportunity. The suffrage campaign continued sporadically for another half century, but it was firmly opposed by a host of antisuffrage organizations that included many men and women, the Catholic church, and assorted liquor interests (which feared that giving women the vote would strengthen the drive for prohibition).

Progressives embraced women's suffrage as one means to clean up government. Many reformers believed the "purer sensibilities" of women would help cleanse the political process of selfishness and corruption. Such an argument accommodated traditional views of gender differences, not gender equality. The suffrage movement benefited, too, from new leadership. In 1900 Carrie Chapman Catt, a woman of great personal charm, political finesse, and organizational skill,

---

*The Supreme Court struck down the law in 1918 as an improper regulation of local labor; nonetheless, it focused greater attention on the abuses of child labor.

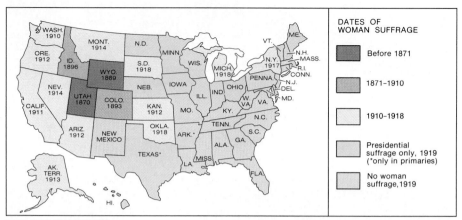

WOMAN SUFFRAGE

Western states were the first to grant women the right to vote. Sparsely populated and more egalitarian than the rest of the nation, the West was used to women participating fully in settlement and work. Other sections of the country, notably the Midwest, granted them partial suffrage that included voting for school boards and taxes. Suffragists encountered the most intractable resistance in the South, where rigid codes of social conduct elevated women symbolically but shackled them practically.

became president of the National American Woman Suffrage Association. Along with Anna Howard Shaw (a Boston social worker who succeeded her in 1904), Catt mapped a strategy of education and persuasion at the state level. Less traditional and more accustomed to having women work side by side with men, western states came around first, with victory in Washington in 1910. By 1914 California, Oregon, Arizona, Kansas, Nevada, and Montana had granted women the vote in state elections, as Illinois had in presidential elections.

The slow pace of progress drove some suffragists to more militant tactics. In 1903 women in England chained themselves to lampposts, engaged in hunger strikes while in prison, and physically attacked politicians. In 1913 Alice Paul, a young Quaker activist who had worked with English suffragists, organized 5000 women to parade in protest at President Woodrow Wilson's inauguration. Half a million people watched as a near-riot ensued. The suffragists were hauled to jail, stripped naked, and thrown into cells with prostitutes. A year later Paul formed the Congressional Union, dedicated to passing a constitutional amendment through disruptive pressure if need be. The Suffrage Association came to support the amendment, too, but Paul would not settle for their more sedate lobbying techniques. Allying her Congressional Union with western women voters in the militant National Woman's party, her forces picketed the White House in 1917. When jailed, the protesters refused to eat. The resulting attention and sympathy, plus the need for support from women once the United States entered World War I, led the House of Representatives to pass a woman suffrage amendment in 1918, and in 1920 the Nineteenth Amendment granting women the right to vote became law.

CONTROLLING THE MASSES

The drive for social justice reflected the optimistic, tolerant impulses of progressivism; the pursuit of social "welfare" for the masses, its paternalistic instincts. But more than a few progressives feared they were losing their country to aliens, ethnics, and city low-lifes. To maintain control they sometimes went beyond their basic strategy of education and sought restrictive laws to uplift and refashion the behavior of the masses. In doing so, the progressive custodians of culture sometimes allied themselves with more traditional evangelical Protestants.

To such uneasy reformers, cities seemed the place where sin flourished: races jostling uneasily, strange Old World cultures clashing with "all-American" customs, long Chinese pigtails or Hasidic Jewish sidelocks lending a discordant air to city crowds; saloons and dance halls luring youngsters and impoverishing laborers; prostitutes walking the streets; vulgar vaudeville shows and motion pictures pandering to uneducated audiences. The city challenged reformers possessed of Protestant, middle-class values to convert this riot of diverse customs and ways into a homogeneous society conceived in their own image.

Stemming the Immigrant Tide

During the late nineteenth century, racism in the form of Jim Crow laws restricted the social and economic opportunities of blacks in the South, but that region was hardly the only area where discrimination flourished. Asians, Hispanics, and Indians faced similar restrictions in the West, as did "new" immigrants from southern and eastern Europe in the North. By 1900 more than 10 million Americans out of a total population of nearly 80 million had been born in Europe. Another 26 million had foreign-born parents, largely from Mediterranean and Slavic countries. Under these conditions a new science called "eugenics" quickly lent respectability to ideas popular among "older stock" middle-class Americans that the newcomers were biologically inferior. By 1914 more magazine articles discussed eugenics than slums, tenements, and living standards combined. Eugenicists, who advocated selective breeding for human improvement, believed that heredity determined everything. "Observe immigrants," wrote sociologist Edward A. Ross in 1912; "you are struck by the fact that from ten to twenty percent are hirsute, low-browed, big-faced persons of obviously low mentality. . . . They clearly belong in skins, in wattled huts at the close of the Ice Age."

For some old-line Americans, assimilation was not only undesirable—it was impossible. "What can you expect of the Americanism of a man whose breath always reeks of garlic?" sneered a member of the Daughters of the American Revolution. Middle-class urban reformers, despairing over the link between immigrants and political machines, reduced immigrant voting power by increasing residency requirements. In many states only native-born and fully naturalized citizens could vote. Madison Grant, a Park Avenue patrician and amateur zoologist, helped to popularize the notion that the "lesser breeds" threatened to "mongrelize" America. In *The Passing of the Great Race* (1916) Grant warned that "race suicide" threatened the United States. Mixing with inferior immigrants, he argued, "gives us a race reverting to the more ancient, generalized and lower type."

More enlightened reformers such as Jane Addams stressed the "gifts" immi-

Daily Lives

PUBLIC SPACE/PRIVATE SPACE

"Amusing the Million"

In May 1903 an opening-night crowd of 45,000 patrons poured through the massive gates of Luna Park at Coney Island, just south of Brooklyn. Before them, one journalist reported, was "an enchanted, storybook land of trellises, columns, domes, minarets, lagoons, and lofty aerial flights . . . a world removed—shut away from the sordid clatter and turmoil of the streets." Those who spent their days in crowded tenements rolling cigars or sleeping nights in stuffy apartments might well blink in awe at the scene. A quarter of a million electric lights, strung like shimmering pearls, studded the buildings. At the flick of a switch, night turned into day: "Tall towers that had grown dim suddenly broke forth in electric outline and gay rosettes of color, as the living spark of light traveled hither and thither, until the place was transformed into an enchanted garden, of such a sort as Aladdin never dreamed."

Everywhere spectacle greeted the crowds. Fantastic winged griffins adorned "The Dragon's Gorge"; a huge dolphin fountain gushed water from the base of the main tower. Barkers with megaphones extolled a Venetian city with actual gondoliers, Irish and Eskimo villages, a Japanese garden, and a bustling Asian Indian celebration complete with gilded chariots, exotic dancers, soldiers, and "real Eastern people." There were sideshows and rides galore: the "Switchback" Railroad, a forerunner of the roller coaster; and the immensely popular "Shoot-the-Chutes," which sent flat-bottom boats careening down a steep incline into a lagoon. As if that were not enough, visitors could witness a genuine disaster. In "Fire and Flames," a four-story building burst into flames on cue, as mock firefighters doused the blaze and mock residents jumped from top floors to safety nets below.

Luna Park was the second of three new amusement parks that together formed Coney Island. And Coney Island was but one (albeit the largest and most famous) of a host of similar parks that popped up across the country at the turn of the century. Soaring urban populations, increases in leisure time and spending money, and new trolley systems that made for cheap excursions from the city led to the opening of Boston's Paragon Park and Revere Beach, Philadelphia's Willow Grove, Cleveland's Euclid Beach, Atlanta's Ponce de Leon Park, Denver's Manhattan Beach, and Los Angeles' Venice Beach.

All traded in entertainment, but of a sort different from earlier forms of urban recreation. In the second half of the nineteenth century Victorian reformers had promoted two influential models of public entertainment, the spacious city park and the grand public exposition. Both were intended to instruct as well as amuse, reducing the potential for urban disorder by raising public taste and reforming public conduct. When it opened in 1858, New York City's Central Park became a model pastoral retreat in the midst of the city. Its rustic paths, tranquil lakes, and woodsy views were designed as respites from the chaos of urban life. Becalmed by such natural beauty, even the rudest fellows would feel, said designer Frederick Law Olmsted, "a distinctly harmonizing and refining influence."

The World's Columbian Exposition of 1893 in Chicago also reflected an elevated

Daily Lives

The Venice Amusement Park in California was dubbed by its founders "the Coney Island of the Pacific."

vision of society. The most impressive of a host of "world's fairs," it was a fully planned neoclassical "White City" (named for the fake marble used to construct it) built on the shores of Lake Michigan, a symbol of order, unity, and civic virtue. Exhibits were housed in buildings that looked as if they had been transplanted from Renaissance Italy. They encircled an enormous basin whose shimmering waters highlighted "The Republic," a 100-foot statue draped in a toga and holding an eagle perched on a globe. Here was the Victorian ideal of a city—modern yet classic, planned and unified, inspiring to all who gazed on it.

Some amusement parks, like Venice Beach in California, self-consciously mimicked the Chicago Exposition, though on a much smaller scale. Others, like Coney Island, built dream worlds all their own. But wherever they operated, amusement park owners knew what the planners of Chicago's fair only reluctantly learned: people wanted to have fun. Adjacent to the White City had stood the Midway Plaisance, a mile-long recreational area bustling with theaters, restaurants, exotic Indian tepees, German castles, and the Persian palace of Eros where "Little Egypt" danced the "hootchy-kootchy." A gigantic steel wheel, designed especially for the Exposition by George Ferris, carried visitors 250 feet into the air for only 50 cents. The Midway's privately sponsored attractions easily lured more people than the free public exhibits of the White City.

Amusement parks expressed not the civic values of the White City but the commercial values of the Midway. Parks were in the business, said one owner, of "amusing the million." Coney Island's Luna Park claimed 5 million paying customers in a single season, drawing patrons from all social classes and ethnic groups. Jostling with crowds, eating ice cream and hot dogs, riding "Shoot-the-Chutes," even the new immigrant could feel gloriously American. A sense of solidarity drew visitors together, and the zaniness of the setting loosened social restraints. Instead of the genteel values of sober industry, thrift, and orderly conduct, amusement parks encouraged abandon, extravagance, and gaiety. They heralded the rise of mass culture, invading public space with the private dreams of multitudes.

grants brought to their adopted culture: folk dances, music, handicrafts, and of course exotic foods. With characteristic paternalism, reformers hoped to "Americanize" the foreign-born (the term was newly coined), especially through education. Peter Roberts, a progressive educator, developed a lesson plan for the Young Men's Christian Association that taught immigrants to dress, tip, buy groceries, and vote. In Milwaukee factories English was taught so immigrant workers could read safety signs. But some lessons were far from practical. In 1916 burly men who labored by day could be found nightly in Cleveland schools copying "I am a yellow bird. I can sing. I can fly."

Progressive reformers revealed their intolerant side as they sought an end to unrestricted entry for immigrants. Here, too, they employed organization, investigation, education, and legislation. Active since the 1890s, the Immigration Restriction League pressed Congress in 1907 to require a literacy test for admission into the United States. Instead the Senate appointed the Dillingham Commission to study the matter. Despite evidence that no correlation existed between the new immigrants and feeble-mindedness, crime, epilepsy, or tuberculosis, the commission's 42-volume report concluded that unlimited immigration created unmanageable social problems. The commission endorsed a literacy test to stem the tide. To the delight of many ethnic groups, Presidents Taft and Wilson vetoed it in 1913 and 1915. Congress nonetheless overrode Wilson's second veto in 1917.

The Curse of Demon Rum

Tied closely to concern over immigrants was an attack on saloons. Part of a broader effort to clean up cities, the antisaloon campaign also drew strength from the century-old crusade to ban alcohol. By 1900 the danger seemed greater than ever. Consumption had increased to over two gallons a year per person. By 1909 there was one saloon for every 300 city dwellers. Over half the population of Boston and Chicago visited a bar at least once a day. In inner cities, immigrants and the working-class poor made up most of the clientele.

Whether drinkers or teetotalers, progressives or conservatives, reformers agreed that saloons were the societal equivalent of "a nest of rats." Taverns and social clubs seemed to be at the center of a host of social problems—gambling and prostitution, political corruption, drug trafficking, unemployment, and poverty. Few temperance reformers recognized the complex cycle of social decay that produced such problems, fewer still the important social role played by saloons as "workingmen's clubs." The saloon was often the only place to cash a check, borrow money, find out about jobs, eat a cheap meal, take a bath, or sit with a group of friends.

Led by the Anti-Saloon League, reformers concentrated efforts to prohibit the sale of alcohol at local and state levels. A massive publicity campaign bombarded citizens with pamphlets and advertisements. Doctors cited scientific evidence linking alcohol to cirrhosis, heart disease, insanity, and other serious illnesses. Social workers connected drink to the deterioration of the family; employers, with accidents on the job and lost efficiency. By 1917 three out of four Americans lived in dry counties, and nearly two-thirds of the states had adopted laws that outlawed the manufacture and sale of alcohol, to stop profiteering from human pain and corruption (most reformers considered a ban on drinking unrealistic and intrusive).

Prostitution

No urban vice worried reformers more than prostitution, the "social evil" that threatened a generation of young city women with a fate reformers thought much worse than death. The Chicago Vice Commission of 1910 estimated the city had 5,000 "full-time" and 10,000 occasional prostitutes. Even Muncie, Indiana, a city of just 11,000 people, had 20 to 25 brothels, each with four to eight women. Along the urban frontier the low wage scale of women workers encouraged the increase in prostitution. "I don't propose to get up at 6:30," wrote Maimie Pinzer, a Philadelphia prostitute, "to . . . work in a stuffy room . . . until dark, for $6 or $7 a week, when I could . . . spend an afternoon with a congenial person and in the end have more than a week's work could pay me." On average, prostitutes earned five times the income of a factory worker. Most needed only to walk the streets to find willing customers. For many the risks of being exploited by pimps or "uncongenial" clients seemed worth taking.

An unlikely group of reformers united to fight the vice: feminists who wanted husbands to be as chaste as their wives; social hygienists worried about the spread of venereal disease; and immigration restrictionists who regarded the growth of prostitution as yet another sign of inferiority in the new arrivals. Progressives naturally saw the problem in economic and environmental terms. Most agreed with the conclusion of the Illinois Vice Commission of 1916 that "poverty causes prostitution."

Other Americans—and some progressives—considered prostitutes the victims of city life and male predators. Rumors of a vast and lucrative "white slave trade" spread across the country. Men armed with hypodermic needles, so the story went, traveled crowded streetcars and stalked amusement parks, dance halls, and vaudeville shows seeking likely targets to drug and abduct. While the average female rider of the streetcar was hardly in danger of villainous abduction, every city had cribs with locked doors where a substantial fraction of women (at least 10 percent of all prostitutes by conservative estimates) were held in bondage and forced into prostitution. As real abuses blended with sensationalism, Congress passed the Mann Act (1910), prohibiting the interstate transport of women for immoral purposes. By 1918 reformers succeeded in getting states to close previously tolerated "red light" districts in most cities. As with prohibition, progressives went after those who made money from misery.

Vaudeville Cleans House

Some targets of reform chose to police themselves, as in the case of vaudeville show proprietors. Vaudeville enjoyed its heyday from 1890 to the mid-1920s. The mix of rowdy performers—singers, jugglers, acrobats, magicians, animal acts, and comics—reflected urban vitality and tastes. Skits often drew on the experience of immigrants, and early comedy teams had names like "The Sport and the Jew," "Irish by Name but Coons by Birth," and "Two Funny Sauerkrauts."

Seeing housewives with children as a source of new profits, resourceful theater managers began to specialize in "straight, clean variety shows" to attract the middle-class family trade. Tony Pastor, a former choir boy and circus performer, opened the first vaudeville theater on Fourteenth Street in New York in 1881. Within a few years he was producing the kind of show, as comedian Fred Stone later said, "to which any child could bring his parents." By 1910 other owners

Balconies at vaudeville shows, like this one depicted by Charles Dana Gibson, attracted a wide variety of customers. Most seats cost $1, and theater owners scheduled performances from morning until night. "After breakfast go to Proctor's," read one advertisement, "after Proctor's go to bed."

went even further to attract families. The Keith–Albee Circuit, the most powerful and far-flung of the vaudeville chains, tacked notices backstage that warned performers not to say "slob" or 'son-of-a-gun' or 'hully-gee' . . . unless you want to be canceled peremptorily." In the interest of good taste, all of its chorus girls wore stockings.

Not all owners were so puritanical. The bare midriffs of "Ziegfeld girls" and the ethnic jokes of Webber and Fields packed houses through the 1920s. Nevertheless, vaudeville had become middle-class, mass entertainment. It was also big business. Nearly one in five city dwellers went to a show once every seven days. The self-imposed purity policies allowed theater owners to broaden appeal, avoid outside censorship, and attract citizens as solid as Woodrow Wilson, a regular customer during his tenure as governor of New Jersey.

THE POLITICS OF MUNICIPAL AND STATE REFORM

The reform of character, the cure for poverty, the movement to liberate women and care for slum children, the need to take the profit out of human misery—all these problems seemed soluble with reform in government. Jane Addams learned as much literally outside the doors of her beloved Hull-House. For months during the early 1890s, garbage piled up all along Halstead Street, until the filth and stench finally drove Addams and her fellow workers to city hall in protest—700 times in one summer—but to no avail. Like most cities, Chicago was ruled by a corrupt band of city fathers for whom garbage collection was a plum, awarded to the company that paid the most for the job. City garbage inspectors won their posts by serving the machine, and garbage collection remained erratic, especially in poor neighborhoods, where boxes overflowed with stinking refuse.

Having normally avoided politics, Addams submitted a bid for garbage removal in the ward. It was thrown out on a technicality. She then got herself appointed as a garbage inspector and dogged collection carts for almost a year, but boss politics kept things dirty. So Addams ran candidates against local ward boss Johnny Powers in 1896 and 1898. The flamboyant Powers, tossing cigars to the men and nickels to the children, won both times. Undaunted, Addams continued her campaigns for honest government and social reform, not only at city hall but in the Illinois legislature and in Washington as well. Politics turned out to be the only way to clean things up.

The Reformation of the Cities

"Sometimes, I think they'se poisonin' the life in the big city," said Mr. Dooley, the philosophical barkeep who was the creation of political satirist Finley Peter Dunne. "The flowers won't grow there." On the other hand, corruption blossomed: mayors and city councils controlled by boss-dominated machines; city contracts for sale to the highest corporate bidders; city offices filled with political hacks and cronies. Party rule seemed always at the heart of the trouble, and for middle-class reformers, the urban battleground furnished the first test of political reform.

A series of colorful mayors demonstrated that cities could be run humanely, even without changing the structure of government. In Detroit, shoe factory magnate Hazen Pingree squeaked to victory in the mayor's race of 1889 on the immigrant votes of Germans and Poles. Moral but never self-righteous, he opposed child labor, tolerated Sunday drinking, and attacked Bible reading in public schools. He cut costs and fought city bosses, a utility overcharging for street lighting, and a monopolistic street railway company. By the end of his fourth term, Pingree had built parks and public baths, modernized transit and taxes, created a city-owned light plant, and started a work-relief program to combat the depression of 1893. Similarly, Tom Johnson, mayor of Cleveland from 1901 to 1909, launched an educational campaign from a portable tent that held 4000 people. Among other things, he limited municipal franchises to a fraction of their previous 99-year terms. Like Pingree and Johnson, Mayor Samuel Jones of Toledo also put his city in the utility business. By 1915 nearly two out of three cities across the nation had copied some form of this "gas and water socialism."

Tragedy sometimes dramatized the need for effective government and led to change. On a hot summer night in 1900 a tidal wave rolled in from the Gulf of Mexico and smashed the port city of Galveston, Texas. Flood waters killed one out of every six residents. The municipal government sank into confusion and partisan wrangling. In reaction business leaders won approval of a new city charter under which a special commission replaced the mayor and city council. Each of its five commissioners controlled a municipal department, and together they enacted ordinances to run the city. By 1920 nearly 400 cities had adopted the commission plan to enhance efficiency and check party rule in municipal government.

In some cities also concerned about raising efficiency and reducing partisanship, elected officials appointed an outside expert or "city manager" to run things. At lower levels experts took charge of services: engineers oversaw utilities; accountants, finances; doctors and nurses, public health; specially trained fire fighters and policemen, the safety of citizens. Broad civic reforms attempted to break the corrupt alliance between companies doing business with the city and the bosses who controlled poor and immigrant voters. City-wide elections replaced the old ward system, while civil service laws helped to create a nonpartisan bureaucracy. Most urban reforms resulted in stronger middle-class rule. Ethnic voters lost power, but city government gained efficiency.

Progressivism in the States

"Whenever we try to do anything, we run up against the charter," complained the reform mayor of Schenectady, New York. Charters granted by the state governments defined the powers of cities. The rural interests that generally dominated state legislatures rarely gave cities adequate authority to levy taxes, set voting requirements, draw up budgets, control penal and mental institutions, or legislate moral reforms. State legislatures under the influence of business interests, party machines, and county courthouse rings were often as corrupt as city halls. Reformers therefore tried to place their candidates where they could do some good—in the governors' mansions.

State progressivism found its fullest scope in the Midwest, largely under the charismatic leadership of Robert La Follette. A graduate of the University of Wisconsin, La Follette early in his career won election to Congress by toeing the party line of high tariffs and the gold standard. But after being buried in 1890 by a Democratic landslide, the "regular" Republican was soon transformed. Practicing law in Wisconsin, La Follette was outraged when a Republican boss offered him a bribe to sway a judge in a railroad case. "The power of this corrupt influence . . . should be broken," he recalled deciding. In 1900 he won the governorship as an uncommonly independent Republican.

Over the next six years "Battle Bob" La Follette made Wisconsin, in the words of Theodore Roosevelt, "the laboratory of democracy." A magnetic stump speaker, La Follette could reach the public more easily than party insiders. So he rooted out the old Republican machine and pressed for the "Wisconsin idea," the most comprehensive program of state reform in American history. His legislation calling for a direct primary, a mechanism designed to break the hold of state machines and party bosses, transferred party nominations from back rooms at conventions and caucuses to the voters at large. Under his relentless urging, Wisconsin established a railroad rate commission, forced railways to lower charges, and raised railroad taxes. The legislature passed laws to control lobbyists, conserve the environment, and expand the civil service. Among his most notable "firsts" were a state income tax, a state commission to oversee factory safety and sanitation, and a Legislative Reference Bureau at the University of Wisconsin. La Follette transformed the university into a superb educational institution as well as an employment service and advisory board for state government.

Other states copied the Wisconsin idea or hatched reform schemes of their own. By 1916 all but three had direct primary laws. To break the power of party organizations and make officeholders directly responsible to the public, progressives worked for three additional reforms: the initiative (which allowed voters themselves to introduce legislation), the referendum (which allowed them to enact or repeal it), and the recall (which allowed them to remove elected officials). By 1912 a dozen states had adopted initiative and referendum, seven recall. That same year the Seventeenth Amendment to the Constitution permitted the direct election of senators, previously selected by state legislatures. Somewhat ironically, many city bosses supported the amendment, since it gave their voters a larger role while limiting the power of their rival state bosses and legislative cronies to hand pick the members of the United States Senate.

Almost every state established regulatory commissions, especially for railroads and utilities. Through them reformers curtailed favoritism shown to certain businesses and mediated conflicts among interest groups. Commissions had the power to hold public hearings, subpoena executives, and examine company books. Some could set maximum prices and rates. Yet it was not always easy to define, let alone serve the "public good." All too often commissioners found themselves refereeing battles within industries—between carriers and shippers, for example—rather than between "the interests" and "the people." In such cases, especially if the commission staff itself came from the business community, the "regulators" found themselves doing the bidding of the industries they were supposed to regulate.

Social welfare received special attention from the states. The lack of workers' compensation for injury, illness, or death on the job had long drawn fire from reformers and labor leaders. In Germany and England, accident insurance had guaranteed payment since the nineteenth century. American courts, however, still operated on the common-law assumption that employees assumed the risks of work. When hurt, maimed, or killed, workers and widows collected damages only if they proved employer negligence. Most victims received nothing. In 1902 Maryland finally adopted the first workers' compensation act. By 1916 most states had laws requiring insurance for factory accidents. Following the lead of New York in 1910, more than half the states passed employer liability laws by 1914. Thirteen states also provided pensions for widows with dependent children.

More and more it was machine politicians who pressed for such welfare reforms. Progressives had attacked the power of parties to control elections (and in the process reduced party loyalty and hence voter turnout). Boss politics, however, survived, in part because it adapted to the climate of reform. In New York City, where Tammany Hall dominated politics, the infamous Democratic machine promoted statewide legislation to safeguard working children and end industrial hazards. After the Triangle fire of 1911, it was Senator Robert F. Wagner and Assemblyman Alfred E. Smith, both Tammany Democrats, who led the fight for a new labor code. Working-class "urban liberalism" thus became a powerful instrument of reform.

PROGRESSIVISM GOES TO WASHINGTON

On September 6, 1901, Leon Czolgosz stood nervously in line, among a crowd of well-wishers waiting to shake hands with President William McKinley at the Pan-American Exposition in Buffalo, New York. Unemployed and bent on murder, Czolgosz shuffled toward McKinley, eyes downcast, a bandage concealing the pistol in his hand. As the president reached out, Czolgosz fired two bullets into his chest. "Don't let them hurt him," cried McKinley as he slumped into a chair. Doctors searched in vain for the bullets, one of which was lodged near his spine. No one thought to use the new X-ray machine on display at the exposition. Eight days later the president was dead.

The mantle of power passed to Theodore Roosevelt, at 42 the youngest president ever to hold the office. His succession was an accident, for party leaders had seen the vice presidency as a way of removing him from political power. Accident or not, Roosevelt made the most of it. "It is a dreadful thing to come into the presidency this way," he remarked, "but it would be a far worse thing to be morbid about it." When Roosevelt entered the White House in 1901, the presidency was weak and rudderless, despite McKinley's best efforts. Both houses of Congress lay in conservative hands. National reform was a distant dream. When Roosevelt left the office in 1909, the president had become the center of attention and his powers had grown broader than at any time since Lincoln. Surely progressivism would have come to Washington without Roosevelt, and while there he was never its most daring advocate. In many respects, he was quite conservative. Yet without Roosevelt progressivism would have had neither the broad popular appeal nor the buoyancy with which he infused it.

TR in Action

"TR," as so many Americans called him, was the scion of seven generations of wealthy New Yorkers. A small and sickly boy, he suffered from fits of asthma that sent him running into the cold night air for relief. His eyes were so bad that he saw the world as a blur until he got his first pair of glasses at age 14. Through rigorous exercise and boxing lessons he built his body. He learned to ride and shoot, roped cattle in the Dakota Badlands, mastered judo, and later in life climbed the Matterhorn, hunted African game, and explored the Amazon. While vigor ruled his life, a

---

Bull-necked and barrel-chested, Theodore Roosevelt was "pure act," said Henry Adams. T.R. may have had the attention span of a golden retriever, as one critic charged, but he also embodied the great virtues of his day—honesty, hard work, constancy, courage, and, while in power, self-control.

hard moralism guided his conscience. He disciplined his emotions with obsessive denial. When his wife died in childbirth (ironically on the same day his mother died), he banished her from memory by destroying their love letters and ripping her photographs from their frames.

In choosing politics, Roosevelt defied the traditions of the American gentry. Well-bred families like the Roosevelts saw politics as a dirty business for more ordinary folk. But at the age of 23, barely out of Harvard, Roosevelt won election to the New York State Assembly. At 28 he ran unsuccessfully for mayor of New York, then in rapid succession became a civil service commissioner in Washington, New York City police commissioner, assistant secretary of the navy, and the Rough Rider hero of the Spanish–American War. At the age of 40 he won election as reform governor of New York and two years later as vice president. Arms flailing, fists pounding, his mouth locked in a toothy grin, TR remained a solid Republican, personally flamboyant but committed to mild change only.

To the Executive Mansion (which he officially renamed the "White House"), Roosevelt brought a passion for order, a commitment to the public, and a sense of presidential possibilities. Most presidents believed the Constitution set specific limits on their power. As Roosevelt saw it, the president could do anything not expressly forbidden by the Constitution. Recognizing the value of popular support, he gave reporters the first press room in the White House and fed a favored few all the stories they could write. He was the first president to play tennis, ride in an automobile, fly an airplane, and dive in a submarine—and everyone knew it.

To dramatize racial injustice, Roosevelt invited black educator Booker T. Washington to lunch at the White House in 1901. Southern journalists called it "treason," but for Roosevelt the gesture served both principle and politics. His lunch with Washington was part of a "black and tan" strategy to build a biracial coalition among southern Republicans. He denounced lynching and appointed blacks to important federal offices in Mississippi and South Carolina. Understanding the limits of political feasibility, Roosevelt went no further. In 1906, when

Atlanta exploded in a race riot that left 12 people dead, he said nothing. Later that year he discharged "without honor" three entire companies of black troops because a few unidentified soldiers had shot up Brownsville, Texas. All lost their pensions.

The Square Deal

"My business," said Roosevelt, surveying his presidency as he left the White House in 1908, "was to take hold of the conservative party and turn it into what it had been under Lincoln, that is, a party of progressive conservatism." Underneath it all, Roosevelt feared extremes and was bent on heading off radical change. In his hands government would use mild reform to save conservatism from its sometimes hidebound resistance to change.

That course was not easy in Washington, where an archconservative "Old Guard" dominated the Republican party and Congress in 1901. In the Senate the "Big Four"—Nelson W. Aldrich of Rhode Island, John Spooner of Wisconsin, Orville H. Platt of Connecticut, and William B. Allison of Iowa—protected business, resisted reform, and looked suspiciously at the young presidential upstart. In the House, power revolved around Speaker Joseph G. Cannon of Illinois, a politician dedicated to protecting the status quo.

Roosevelt could not long follow the cautious course McKinley had charted. He had more energetic plans for government. He accepted growth—whether of business, labor, or capital—as natural. In his pluralistic system, big labor would counterbalance big capital, big farm organizations would offset big food processors, and so on. Big government would mediate among them all. That way, he believed, everyone could count on a fair result. Later, as he campaigned for a second term in 1904, Roosevelt named this program the "Square Deal."

In a startling display of presidential initiative, Roosevelt in 1902 intervened in a strike that idled 140,000 miners in the hard coal industry. Operators, led by coal magnate George Baer, refused workers' demands for higher wages and fewer hours and would not even recognize their union, the United Mine Workers. As Americans faced a winter without heat, public anger at the operators' inflexibility mounted. When Roosevelt summoned both sides to the White House, John A. Mitchell, the young president of the United Mine Workers, agreed to arbitration, but owners balked. In desperation Roosevelt leaked word to Wall Street that the army would take over the mines if the owners did not come to terms. Never before had the government intervened on behalf of labor; seldom had a president acted so boldly. In late October 1902 the owners settled, granting miners a 10 percent wage hike and a nine-hour day in return for increases in coal prices and no recognition of the union. Roosevelt was equally prepared to intervene on behalf of management, as he did when he sent federal troops to end strikes in Arizona in 1903 and Colorado in 1904. His aim was to establish a vigorous presidency prepared to deal squarely with both sides.

Roosevelt especially needed to face the issue of economic concentration, since financial power had become increasingly consolidated in large trusts following a wave of mergers at the end of the century. As large firms swallowed smaller ones, many Americans feared that monopoly would destroy individual enterprise and free competition. A series of government investigations revealed a rash of corporate abuses—rebates, collusion, "watered" stock, and payoffs to government officials. The courts, with judges sympathetic to business interests, showed little inclination to dismember the giants or blunt their power. In *United States v. E. C. Knight* (1895), the Supreme Court crippled the Sherman Antitrust Act by ruling that the law applied only to commerce and not manufacturing. The decision left the American Sugar Refining Company in control of 98 percent of the nation's sugar factories.

In his first State of the Union message, Roosevelt told Congress that he did not oppose business concentration per se. As he saw it, large corporations were both inevitable and beneficial. He wanted to regulate, not destroy them, to make them fairer and more efficient. Only then would the economic order be humanized, its victims protected, and class violence forestalled. "Trusts are creatures of the State, and the State not only has the right to control them, but it is in duty bound to control them wherever the need of such control is shown," he said in 1902. Trusts, like individuals, had to be held to strict standards of morality. Conduct, not size, was the yardstick TR used to measure "good" and "bad" trusts.

Because he shared progressive faith in the power of publicity to marshal public opinion and keep business in line, Roosevelt moved immediately to strengthen the federal power of investigation. He called for the creation of a Department of Commerce with a Bureau of Corporations that could compel companies to hand over their records. Congressional conservatives shuddered at the prospect of putting corporate books on display. Finally, after Roosevelt charged that John D. Rockefeller was orchestrating the opposition, Congress enacted the legislation and added two assistant attorneys general to the Justice Department to prosecute more antitrust cases. In 1902, without prior warning, Attorney General Philander Knox filed suit under the Sherman Act against the Northern Securities Company, a mammoth holding company with a virtual monopoly over railroads in the Northwest. Not only was the holding company unpopular with farmers and travelers, but its founders, Morgan, Rockefeller, James J. Hill, and E. H. Harriman—all notorious business barons—also had bloated the company stock with worthless certificates. Here, clearly, was a symbol of the "bad trust."

Stunned by the suit, Morgan himself hurried to the White House. "If we have done something wrong," he told Roosevelt and Attorney General Knox, "send your man [the attorney general] to my man [Morgan's lawyer] and they can fix it up." "We don't want to fix it up," said Knox. "We want to stop it." A trust-conscious country cheered as the Supreme Court ordered the company to dissolve in 1904. "Even Morgan no longer rules the earth," declared one journal, "and other men may still do business without asking his permission." Ultimately, the Roosevelt administration brought antitrust suits against some 44 behemoths, including the Standard Oil Company, the American Tobacco Company, and the Du Pont Corporation.

Roosevelt always preferred regulation to antitrust action. The old problems of the railroads, for example, were newly underscored by a recent round of consolidation that had contributed to higher freight rates and higher prices. Roosevelt pressed Congress to revive the ineffective Interstate Commerce Commission (ICC). In 1903 Congress enacted the Elkins Act, which gave the ICC power to end rebates. On this occasion, as on others, business supported reform because it served its interests. At last railroads were saved from the costly practice of granting special reductions to large shippers.

By the election of 1904 bold initiatives had won the president broad popular support. He trounced two rival candidates, conservative Democrat Alton B. Parker, a lackluster jurist from New York, and Eugene V. Debs of the Socialist party.

It was the most lopsided victory since the election of James Monroe in 1820. No longer, Roosevelt boasted, was he a "political accident." Having strengthened his hold on the Republican party, he returned to reforming the railroads. Within weeks of the election, he launched new suits against roads and corporations that still granted rebates. Standard Oil alone, he declared, had profited "enormously" from secret rail rates. Meanwhile he put steady pressure on Congress to grant the ICC power to set maximum rates.

Conservatives in his own party opposed such federal meddling in the private sector; staunch progressives, goaded by Robert La Follette, demanded the addition of a controversial provision for disclosing the value of all rail property. In 1906, after two years of struggle, the president negotiated a compromise, typical of his cautious approach to reform. The Hepburn Railway Act enlarged the ICC, empowered it to set a ceiling on rates, and broadened its jurisdiction to include sleeping car companies, ferries, bridges, and terminals. Nestled among the fine print was a provision for ICC control of interstate pipelines—aimed, no doubt, at Rockefeller's Standard Oil Company. No provision for valuation appeared. La Follette and other progressives were furious, but with the Hepburn Act Roosevelt drew nearer to his goal of continuous federal supervision of business.

Bad Food and Pristine Wilds

Extending the umbrella of government regulation to consumers, Roosevelt belatedly threw the weight of the presidency behind two campaigns for healthy foods and drugs. In 1905 Samuel Hopkins Adams, a reporter for *Collier's Weekly*, wrote that in its patent medicines "Gullible America" would get "huge quantities of alcohol, an appalling amount of opiates and narcotics," and even worse additives—axle grease, acid, and glue. The concoctions, claimed advertisers, could cure everything from abscesses and cancer to tumors and ulcers. In 1905 industry lobbyists had succeeded in blocking several pure food and drug bills in Congress, despite a presidential endorsement.

Adams sent the samples he had collected to Harvey Wiley, chief chemist at the Agriculture Department. Wiley's "Poison Squad" produced scientific evidence supporting Hopkins' charges. Then the appearance of Upton Sinclair's *The Jungle* early in 1906 drove Congress to act. Intended to recruit people to socialism with an indictment of the exploitative labor system in the meat packing industry, the novel contained vivid descriptions of the slaughter of cattle infected with tuberculosis, of meat covered with rat dung, and of men falling into cooking vats and going out to consumers as "Durham's Pure Leaf Lard." Readers paid scant attention to the plight of the workers, but their stomachs turned at the thought of what they might be consuming at the breakfast table. The Pure Food and Drug Act of 1906 sailed through Congress in the wake of the book. The Meat Inspection Act soon followed. Even industry leaders realized that more effective government regulation was one way to restore public confidence in their products and enlarge their market abroad.

Roosevelt came late to the consumer cause, but on conservation he led the nation. An outdoors enthusiast, he galvanized growing public concern over the reckless exploitation of natural resources. His chief forester, Gifford Pinchot, persuaded him that rational, planned management under federal regulation was needed to protect the natural domain.

In the western states water was the problem. Economic growth, even survival, depended on access to it. Inequitable local and state water policy repeatedly provoked controversy and violence, and many progressives campaigned for a federal program of water distribution to replace the chaotic web of rules. Senator Frederick Newlands, a Democrat from Nevada, introduced the Reclamation Act of 1902 to set aside proceeds from the sale of public lands in the South and West for irrigation projects. Though the self-financing provisions of the bill cost western politicians some political leverage, the Reclamation Act applied progressive means to the conservationist end of putting federal resources behind western development.

The conservationist concept of efficient water use often conflicted with the more radical vision of preservationists, led by naturalist and wilderness philosopher John Muir. Muir, the founder of the Sierra Club (1892), hoped to maintain such natural wonders as Yosemite and its neighboring Hetch-Hetchy valley in a state "forever wild" to benefit future generations. Many conservationists saw such valleys only as sites for dams and reservoirs. Controversy exploded after 1900 when San Francisco announced plans to establish a reservoir in the Hetch-Hetchy valley. For 13 years Muir waged a publicity campaign against the "temple destroyers" and "devotees of ravaging commercialism." Pinchot enthusiastically backed San Francisco's claim; Roosevelt, torn by his friendship with Muir, did so more tepidly. Not until 1913 did President Woodrow Wilson finally decide the issue in favor of San Francisco. Conservation had won over preservation.

Still, Roosevelt advanced many of Muir's goals. Over the protests of cattle and timber interests, the president added nearly 200 million acres to government forest reserves, placed coal and mineral lands, oil reserves, and water-power sites in the public domain, and enlarged the national park system. When Congress tried to block Roosevelt, he relied on his own ample view of executive authority to get the job done, appropriating another 17 million acres of forest before Congress could pass a bill limiting him. He also set in motion national congresses and commissions on conservation, mobilizing governors from across the country and, like a good progressive, setting hundreds of experts to work applying science, education, and technology to the problems.

As Roosevelt grew bolder in his assertion of public interests, conservatives, many from his own party, lashed back. Roosevelt's record, so far, had been modest, but his chief accomplishment—invigorating the presidency—had the potential for promoting deeper reform. When a financial panic hit Wall Street in 1907, business leaders and conservatives blamed the president. Roosevelt, in turn, pointed to the "speculative folly and the flagrant dishonesty of a few men of great wealth." But having declared he would not run again in 1908, Roosevelt (just 50 years old) prepared to hand the reins of his party and office to William Howard Taft.

The Troubled Taft

Early on the morning of March 4, 1909, while snow swirled outside the White House, Taft readied himself for his inauguration. Over breakfast with Roosevelt, he warmed in the glow of recent Republican victories. Taft had decisively beaten William Jennings Bryan in the "Great Commoner's" third and last run for the presidency. Republicans had retained control of Congress as well as a host of legislatures in northern states. Reform was at high tide, and Taft was ready to continue in the Roosevelt tradition.

William Howard Taft (left), a full-bodied 300 pounds, enjoyed golf more than politics.

"Will," as Roosevelt liked to call him, was his hand-picked successor. A distinguished jurist, the first governor-general of the Philippines under American rule, and Roosevelt's secretary of war, Taft had demonstrated great administrative skill. He could be charming, was often funny, and was always honest. His size—nearly 300 pounds—reflected his tastes and temperament. He ate too much, slept too long, and disliked strife and political maneuvering. He preferred conciliation to confrontation. Even Roosevelt had doubts. "He's all right," TR had told a reporter on inauguration day. "But he's weak. They'll get around him. They'll"—and here Roosevelt pushed the reporter with his shoulder—"lean against him."

The standard-bearer of conservative Republicans was Joseph G. Cannon, the Speaker of the House. Every committee assignment, every patronage appointment, every bill required "Uncle Joe's" approval. Thirty progressive House members were hoping to curb these dictatorial powers—and they had Taft's blessing. But Cannon had no intention of backing down without a fight. He threatened to block any reduction of the tariff if the congressional revolt continued. Taft, who wanted tariffs lowered, caved in so that the tariff bill would pass. When progressives later broke Cannon's power without the president's help, they scorned Taft's lack of backbone. And Taft's compromise went for naught, since Senate protectionists led by Nelson W. Aldrich peppered the tariff bill with some 800 amendments, which raised rates nearly to their old levels. With both wings of the party disenchanted with his waffling, Taft lost control of Republicans in Congress.

The ties between Taft and the progressives were stressed even further in a dispute over conservation. Taft had appointed Richard Ballinger as secretary of the interior over the opposition of Chief Forester Pinchot. Ballinger and Taft, like Pinchot, were genuine conservationists. Through their efforts more land was protected than Roosevelt had saved during all his years in office. But Taft and Ballinger sought to weaken the centralized federal power that Roosevelt and Pinchot used to pursue their goals. When Ballinger opened a million acres of Pinchot-protected public lands for sale, Pinchot rebelled. He unearthed a report that claimed shady dealings had led to the transfer of Alaskan public coal lands to a syndicate that included J. P. Morgan. Taft stood by Ballinger. Out of frustration Pinchot took his case to the press and to Congress early in 1910, whereupon Taft fired him for insubordination. The Ballinger–Pinchot controversy, as it became known, led some progressives to label Taft the "friend of thieves and the enemy of honest men." They began to look longingly across the Atlantic, where TR was stalking lions in Africa.

In the off-year elections of 1910, Republicans—conservative and progressive alike—were swept from office. Democrats won the industrial Northeast and Midwest. The new state lawmakers, largely from the ranks of immigrants, advanced social welfare in the form of worker's compensation, utilities regulation, and pro-labor laws. For the first time in 16 years Democrats controlled the House of Representatives. Republicans clung to a nominal majority in the Senate. There a small band of independent-minded progressives held the balance of power.

Despite the failures of his leadership, Taft was no conservative apologist. For the next two years he pushed Congress to enact a progressive program regulating safety standards for mines and railroads, creating a federal children's bureau, and setting an eight-hour workday for federal employees. Taft's support of a constitutional amendment permitting graduated income taxes was sometimes ardent, sometimes tepid, but in the end proved decisive. Early in 1913 the Sixteenth Amendment was added to the Constitution. Many historians have viewed it as the most important reform of the century, for it eventually gave the federal government the financial resources to increase the scope of its responsibilities. Yet no matter what he achieved, Taft somehow managed to alienate conservatives and progressives without retaining the support of either. That spelled trouble for the Republicans as the presidential election approached.

The Election of 1912

In June 1910 Roosevelt had come home, exuberant as ever and laden with hunting trophies. He was confronted with an unhappy Taft and a fractious party. Angry progressives were threatening to bolt. Party loyalty kept Roosevelt quiet through most of 1911, though in private he described Taft as a "flubdub with a streak of the second-rate." Roosevelt could not contain himself any longer when, in October 1911, Taft pricked him on the particularly sensitive matter of busting trusts. Taft, like TR, accepted trusts as natural, but he failed to make Roosevelt's distinction between "good" and "bad" ones. He demanded, more impartially, that all trusts be prevented from restraining trade. In his four years as president, Taft initiated nearly twice as many antitrust suits as Roosevelt had in seven years.

In October 1911 the Justice Department filed suit against U.S. Steel, charging the company with having violated the antimonopoly clause of the Sherman Act by acquiring the Tennessee Coal and Iron Company. Roosevelt, while president, had personally accepted the acquisition to stave off a financial collapse. To see the Taft administration now prosecuting U.S. Steel irked him immensely, for the suit not only blurred his distinction between "good" and "bad" trusts but also seemed to censure his behavior as president. Taft, complained Roosevelt confidentially, "was playing small, mean, and foolish politics."

TR decided to play big, high-minded, and presidential. Already, in a speech at Osawatomie, Kansas, in 1910, he had called for a "New Nationalism," a sweeping program that stressed planning and efficiency at the hands of a powerful national executive. The New Nationalism recognized the value of collectivism—big business, big government, big labor—but insisted on protecting the interests of

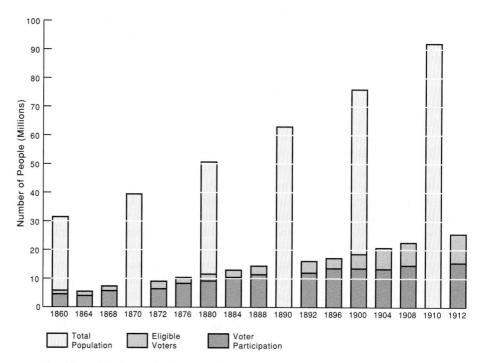

Note: The census years 1870, 1890, and 1910 were not election years.

THE VOTING PUBLIC, 1860–1912

Between 1860 and 1910 the population and the number of eligible voters increased nearly threefold. As reforms of the early twentieth century reduced the power of political machines and parties, the percentage of voter participation actually declined.

individuals. The community, Roosevelt declared, had the right to regulate property "to whatever degree the public welfare may require."

Based partly on the ideas of progressive theorist Herbert Croly, the New Nationalism harked back to Alexander Hamilton's brand of federalism, with its reliance on a strong central government. But it hoped to combine that brand of federal leadership with a respect for the rights of individuals at the core of Thomas Jefferson's republicanism. As Roosevelt elaborated his New Nationalism, he defended economic concentration so long as government could control it by national incorporation and regulation. His program would support labor through compulsory investigation of labor disputes and limits on court injunctions against unions. It would control wealth by taxing income and inheritances. It embraced social justice in the eight-hour workday, workers' compensation, child labor laws, minimum wages for women, and "equal suffrage"—a nod to women and loyal black Republicans. Occasionally Roosevelt even suggested that conservative judges might be curbed by putting in place a "recall" system for judicial decisions.

All that remained was to find some stalwart, energetic president to put the New Nationalism into effect. "My hat is in the ring!" Roosevelt announced in February 1912, to the surprise of few. "The fight is on and I am stripped to the buff!" Taft responded by claiming that the New Nationalism had won support only from "destructive radicals," "political emotionalists," and "neurotics." In fact, the enormously popular Roosevelt won most of the primaries; but by the time Repub-

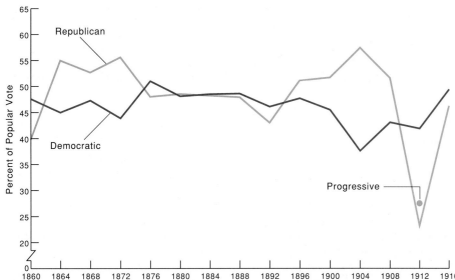

REPUBLICAN AND DEMOCRATIC PARTIES' SHARE OF POPULAR VOTE, 1860–1912
In the last quarter of the nineteenth century the Republican and Democratic parties were
deadlocked until the Republicans became the majority party in 1896. In 1912 the parties
splintered, TR ran as a Progressive, and Republican fortunes plummeted.

licans met in Chicago in June 1912, Taft's use of patronage and promises had won
him the nomination.

A frustrated Roosevelt bolted and took progressive Republicans with him.
Two months later, amid choruses of "Onward Christian Soldiers," delegates to the
newly formed Progressive party nominated Roosevelt for the presidency. "We
stand at Armageddon," he told a crowd of nearly 10,000, "and we battle for the
Lord." At one point Roosevelt bellowed at reporters, "I'm feeling like a bull
moose!"—and Progressives had a symbol for their party. The Democrats met in
Baltimore, jubilant over the prospect of facing a divided Republican party. On the
verge of regaining the White House after a 16-year absence, delegates chose as
their candidate Woodrow Wilson, the reformist governor of New Jersey.

Wilson saw Roosevelt, not Taft, as his major opponent. He immediately countered the New Nationalism with his "New Freedom," a reiteration of Louis Brandeis' program to free the American people from the control of large concentrations
of wealth and power. Wilson rejected the managed economy of the New Nationalism. He wanted to free the marketplace. Instead of Roosevelt's "regulated monopoly," Wilson proposed a "regulated competition." Only by enforcing strict limits
on size and removing artificial barriers to commerce could concentration be controlled and free enterprise preserved. Nothing less than liberty was at stake. "If
America is not to have free enterprise," he said in October 1912, "then she can
have freedom of no sort whatever." Though he accepted social justice as an admirable goal, Wilson feared that government-sponsored social welfare programs
would threaten constitutional freedoms. "Liberty," he warned, "has never come
from government," only from the "limitation of governmental power"—
sentiments Jefferson no doubt would have endorsed.

Increasingly voters found Taft's conservatism beside the point. And in an age of reform, even the socialists looked good. Better led, financed, and organized than ever before, the Socialist party had increased its membership to nearly 135,000 by 1912. Socialist mayors ran 32 cities, from Schenectady, New York, to Berkeley, California. The party also had an appealing candidate in Eugene V. Debs, a home-grown Indiana radical. Crisscrossing the country on a train dubbed the "Red Special," Debs had won 400,000 votes for president in 1904. Now, in 1912, he summoned voters to make "the working class the ruling class of the nation and the world." As for trusts, he proposed simply to nationalize them.

On election day voters gave progressivism a resounding endorsement. Wilson won 6.3 million votes, Roosevelt 4.1 million. Debs received almost a million votes, whereas the conservative Taft attracted just 3.6 million. Thus the progressive candidates combined had a 3 to 1 margin, and the Democrats won control of both houses of Congress. Though shaken by his defeat, Roosevelt remained optimistic about reform: "The Progressive movement must and will go forward even though its progress is fitful."

Woodrow Wilson and the Politics of Morality

Soon after the election Woodrow Wilson told William McCombs, chairman of the Democratic National Committee, "I wish it clearly understood that I owe you nothing." Taken aback, McCombs reminded Wilson of his sturdy service during the presidential campaign. Wilson replied: "God ordained that I should be the next President of the United States. Neither you nor any mortal could have prevented that!"

Born in Virginia in 1856, Woodrow Wilson grew up believing, as he put it, "in predestination and election." A minister's son and a devout Presbyterian, he dismissed those who disagreed with him as plain "wrong." Gyrating between Christian love and Calvinist severity, he could be warm and generous one moment, cold and petty the next.

To compensate for a learning disability (probably dyslexia), Wilson developed a near-photographic memory. He studied the words and cadences of great speakers, then wandered the woods reciting their speeches. Like most southerners, he loved the Democratic party, hated the tariff, and accepted the necessity of racial separation. Under his presidency, segregation would return to Washington for the first time since Reconstruction.

Bored and disheartened by a career in law, Wilson turned to political science, earned a doctorate from Johns Hopkins, and taught at Bryn Mawr, Wesleyan, and Princeton. Political science persuaded him that a president must act as a "prime minister," directing and uniting the party, shaping legislation and opinion, exerting continuous leadership. In 1902 he became president of Princeton and helped to transform it into one of the nation's finest schools. His tenure was often controversial, however, and as in later crises in Washington, if pushed, Wilson retreated into a sanctimonious moralism that made compromise difficult. He escaped academic politics in 1910, when Democratic party bosses helped elect him governor of New Jersey, and after a successful term of reform, president in 1912.

The New Freedom in Action

In power Wilson was a model of executive leadership. He went to Congress, the first president since John Adams to appear in person. He kept party discipline

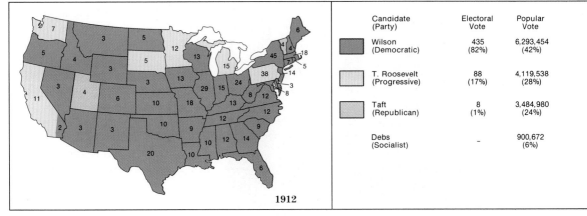

Candidate (Party)	Electoral Vote	Popular Vote
Wilson (Democratic)	435 (82%)	6,293,454 (42%)
T. Roosevelt (Progressive)	88 (17%)	4,119,538 (28%)
Taft (Republican)	8 (1%)	3,484,980 (24%)
Debs (Socialist)	–	900,672 (6%)

1912

THE ELECTION OF 1912

tight, threatened to veto bills he did not like, and mobilized public opinion when confronted with congressional obstruction. During his presidency progressivism peaked.

Lowering the high tariff was Wilson's first order of business. Progressives regarded the tariff as yet another example of the unrestrained power of trusts, and in Wilson's view it weakened competition by protecting American manufacturers. Roosevelt had avoided the tariff; Taft had bungled its revision; Wilson moved quickly and forcefully to reduce it. Addressing Congress directly he declared, "We must abolish everything that bears even the semblance of privilege or of any kind of artificial advantage." When protectionists in the Senate threatened to raise rates, Wilson appealed directly to the public. "Industrious" and "insidious" lobbyists had descended on Washington to block reform, he told the press. A "brick couldn't be thrown without hitting one of them."

The Underwood–Simmons Tariff of 1913 marked the first downward revision in 19 years and the biggest since before the Civil War. It lowered most rates from 40 percent to 25 percent and placed many new items on the free list. To compensate for lost revenue, Congress enacted a graduated income tax, permitted under the newly adopted Sixteenth Amendment. It applied solely to corporations and the tiny fraction of Americans who earned more than $4000 a year. It nonetheless began a momentous shift in government revenue from its nineteenth-century base—public lands, alcohol taxes, and customs duties—to its twentieth-century base—personal and corporate incomes.

Wilson turned next to the knotty problem of money and banking. Early in 1913 the Pujo Committee, created by Congress to investigate the "money trust," revealed "a spider web of interlocking Wall Street directorates" that concentrated control of the nation's credit system in a few powerful investment firms. Without a stable but flexible currency, Wilson's free market would be enslaved to the great investment banks, which could choke industry and commerce with high interest rates or tight money. As a banking reform bill moved through Congress in 1913, opinion split sharply over its design. Wall Street wanted a privately controlled, centralized banking system that could issue currency and set interest rates. Rural Democrats, led by Senator Carter Glass of Virginia, favored a decentralized sys-

Woodrow Wilson, 28th president of the United States, was the first Ph.D. in the White House and the first president to hold open press conferences.

tem of regional banks run by local bankers. Populists and progressives, including Bryan, La Follette, and Brandeis, wanted public control.

Wilson reconciled their differences in the Federal Reserve Act of 1913. The new Federal Reserve System contained not one central bank, but 12 regional banks (scattered deliberately around the country) that held reserves for commercial banks. A central Federal Reserve Board in Washington, appointed by the president, supervised the whole system. It could regulate credit and the money supply by setting the interest rate it charged member banks, by buying or selling government bonds, and by issuing paper currency (called Federal Reserve notes) backed by a combination of gold and government credit. Each Federal Reserve Bank was owned and directed by local member banks. Thus the Federal Reserve Act sought to stabilize the existing order by making currency more elastic and credit easier to obtain. As it turned out, the conservatives Wilson appointed to the Federal Reserve Board failed to understand how their power to expand and contract the nation's money supply influenced the health of the economy. Later financial upheavals would show that mistakes made by the Federal Reserve System could be as devastating as those made by private bankers on Wall Street.

When Wilson took on the trusts, he moved a bit closer toward the New Nationalism of Theodore Roosevelt. The Federal Trade Commission Act of 1914 created a bipartisan executive agency to oversee business activity. The end—to enforce orderly competition—was distinctly Wilsonian, but the means—an executive commission to regulate commerce—were pure Roosevelt. The Federal Trade Commission (FTC) had wide investigatory powers, could order corporate compliance, and had the power to prosecute against "unfair trade practices." The FTC proved to be more of a guide than a sheriff. It gave advance warning of government disapproval and, through consent decrees, persuaded companies to make changes without having to convict them of anything. Wilson, like Roosevelt, was no extremist. He chose commissioners sympathetic to the business community and accepted a revision in the law that gave the conservative courts power to review all FTC decisions.

Roosevelt would have stopped there, but Wilson complemented regulation with the Clayton Antitrust Act of 1914. The Clayton Act outlawed some of the worst corporate malpractices—price discrimination, holding companies, and interlocking directorates—but only when they "tend to create a monopoly." Action on these practices was at the government's discretion. More and more, the Wilson administration chose to regulate rather than break up bigness. The Justice Department filed fewer antitrust suits than the Taft administration had and negotiated more "gentlemen's agreements" (voluntary agreements by companies to change practices) than had Roosevelt.

By November 1914, tariff and banking reform, regulatory legislation, a graduated income tax, and a new antitrust law—all impressive and important accomplishments—adorned Wilson's two-year-old presidency. Yet voters seemed lukewarm toward the New Freedom. In the elections of 1914 Republicans cut Democratic majorities in the House and won important industrial and farm states. To strengthen his hand in the presidential election of 1916, Wilson began edging slowly toward the social programs of the New Nationalism he had earlier criticized as paternalistic and unconstitutional. He signaled the change in 1915 when he nominated his close adviser Louis D. Brandeis to the Supreme Court. The "people's lawyer," Brandeis had fought for the very social reforms lacking from Wilson's agenda. With Wilson's staunch support, Brandeis broke the tradition of conservatism and anti-Semitism that had previously kept Jews off the Court.

Wilson had been cool to labor and social reform and was unwilling to exempt strikes and boycotts from antitrust prosecution. But in 1916 he effectively dropped his opposition to such "class legislation" by signing the Seamen's Act, to provide federal protection for the rights and working conditions of merchant seamen. Wilson maneuvered for passage of the Keating–Owen Child Labor Act (declared unconstitutional in 1918) and workers' compensation for federal employees. Just before the election he intervened to avert a nationwide strike of rail workers. Despite his reservations about federal intrusion in the economy, he later signed the Adamson Act, mandating an eight-hour day for workers on all interstate railroads.

Farmers and women also gained his support. The Federal Farm Loan Act and the Warehouse Act furnished farmers with long-term, federally supported, low-interest loans based on the value of their crops and land. The Federal Highway Act of 1916 helped farmers on their way to market by granting aid to states that improved their roads. In 1915 Wilson even endorsed state action to grant women the right to vote.

"The future," Woodrow Wilson had written in 1914, "is clear and bright with promise of the best things." As the presidential campaign of 1916 approached, the future looked brighter still. Under Wilson's administration, progressivism had reached high tide. He himself had come reluctantly to accept big government and big business. He had also learned the value of protective social legislation. Like Theodore Roosevelt, Wilson harnessed the chief executive to change. Together they made the presidency newsworthy and the president noteworthy. For good or ill, Americans thereafter looked to the White House for leadership and direction.

The Mixed Legacy of Progressivism

Reform, then, had taken the country far during the first heady decade and a half of the twentieth century. Seeing chaos in the modern industrial city, progressives worked to reduce the damage of poverty, eliminate the dangers of industrial work, control the rising immigrant tide, and spread a middle-class ideal of morality. In city halls and state legislatures, they looked to break the power of special corporate interests and entrenched political machines. In Washington, they enlarged government and broadened its mission from simple caretaker to promoter of public welfare. Progressivism did not always succeed, in part because powerful forces opposed it, in part because the progressive vision was limited and fuzzy. Progressives sometimes betrayed their own reformist ideals by denying blacks, Asians, and other minorities racial equality and by attempting to Americanize foreigners rather than accept the rich contributions of their cultures. And efforts to regulate business fell short of the protection intended. Too often regulatory agencies were captured by the very interests they were supposed to oversee.

For all its sweeping claim to reform, progressivism left the system of market capitalism largely intact. But the Gilded Age's philosophy of laissez faire—of giving private enterprise a free hand—had been clearly rejected. Both state and federal governments had established their right to regulate the actions of private corporations for the public good. That public good, progressives believed, could be exposed through vigorous publicity brought about by commissions, investigative hearings, activist presidents. The reforms achieved through these means— the eight-hour day, woman suffrage, direct election of senators, graduated income taxes, public ownership of utilities—began to address the problems of an urban industrial society. Under progressive leadership, the modern state—active and interventionist—was born. A sense of mastery, so characteristic of twentieth-century reform, replaced the awful feeling of drift that had dominated the 1890s.

Such accomplishments invigorated American faith in progress as the new century unfolded. A higher civilization of enlightened culture, peace, and prosperity seemed within reach. But in 1914, as progressivism crested in America, the guns of a hot August shattered an uneasy calm in Europe and plunged the world into war. Few people anywhere were prepared for the carnage that followed.

SIGNIFICANT EVENTS

1890 — New England Kitchen opens; General Federation of Women's Clubs organized

1892 — Sierra Club founded

1893 — Illinois legislature enacts eight-hour workday law for women; Anti-Saloon League created

1895 — *United States v. E. C. Knight*

1899 — National Consumers League founded

1900 — Galveston, Texas, creates first commission form of government

1901 — Leon Czolgosz assassinates President William McKinley; Theodore Roosevelt becomes president; Robert La Follette elected reform governor of Wisconsin; Socialist Party of America founded

1902 — Bureau of the Census created; Northern Securities Company dissolved under Sherman Antitrust Act; anthracite coal miners strike in Pennsylvania; Maryland adopts first workers' compensation law

1903 — Department of Labor and Commerce created; Elkins Act passed; Wisconsin is first state to enact direct primary; Wright brothers' flight

1904 — Lincoln Steffens' *The Shame of the Cities* published; Robert Hunter's *Poverty* published; Theodore Roosevelt elected president

1906 — Hepburn Act strengthens Interstate Commerce Commission; Upton Sinclair's *The Jungle* published; Meat Inspection and Pure Food and Drug acts passed

1907 — William James' *Pragmatism* published

1908 — Henry Ford introduces the Model T; *Muller v. Oregon*; William Howard Taft elected president

1909 — Payne–Aldrich Tariff; Ballinger–Pinchot controversy

1910 — Mann Act passed

1911 — Triangle Shirtwaist fire

1912 — Progressive ("Bull Moose") party nominates Theodore Roosevelt for presidency; Woodrow Wilson elected president

1913 — Sixteenth Amendment and Seventeenth Amendment passed; Underwood–Simmons Tariff enacted; Federal Reserve Act passed; Keith–Albee Circuit opens Palace Theater in New York

1914 — Clayton Antitrust Act passed; Federal Trade Commission created

1916 — Margaret Sanger organizes New York Birth Control League; Keating–Owen Child Labor Act passed; Woodrow Wilson reelected president

1917 — Congress enacts literacy test for new immigrants

1920 — Nineteenth Amendment passed

24

The United States
and the Old World Order

n 1898, when the battleship *Oregon* steamed from San Francisco Bay to its battle station in the Caribbean during the Spanish–American War, it had to travel around the tip of South America, a journey of over two months. The delay was more than embarrassing; it was dangerous. As an emerging naval power, the United States needed a canal farther north to link the Atlantic and Pacific. A path between the seas, most likely across Central America, would also speed American trade; between 1890 and 1900 the value of American exports had jumped from $845 million to nearly $1.4 billion.

From the days of the sixteenth-century conquistador Francisco Pizarro, travelers had crossed through the jungles of the Panamanian isthmus (later acquired by Colombia) on foot, horseback, or mule train, taking their chances with muddy trails and tropical diseases. Only in the 1850s, when the first true transcontinental railroad cut through Panama, did the trip cease to be a nightmare.

The commercial and strategic possibilities of a canal had long inspired dreamers. A French diplomat who had been involved in building the Suez Canal, Ferdinand de Lesseps, planned to cut across the isthmus in the 1880s. The venture was brought low by yellow fever and problems insuperable without more advanced engineering. Teddy Roosevelt was equally visionary about the possibility of a canal and even more energetic at mustering the resources and confidence to complete the task. "With Roosevelt," said one engineer, "anything is possible."

"I took the isthmus," Roosevelt later told a crowd of cheering students at Berkeley. In a way he did. In 1901 Roosevelt persuaded Britain to give up its rights to a joint canal enterprise, then authorized Secretary of State John Hay to negotiate with Colombian chargé d'affaires Tomas Herran. The Hay–Herran Convention (1903) leased to the United States a strip across the Panamanian region of Colombia, the site of the earlier French attempt to link the Atlantic with the Pacific. Meanwhile Roosevelt agreed to pay the old de Lesseps Company $40 million for its equipment and other assets.

Suddenly the Colombians drew back. Hoping for more money and a firmer guarantee of sovereignty, their senate refused to accept the treaty. The Colombi-

On November 11, 1918, six hours after the armistice was signed in a railroad car in the forest of Compiègne, France, the guns of World War I fell silent. At 3 a.m. news reached the United States, which burst into wild celebrations.

ans, fumed TR, were "highwaymen," "blackmailers," and "inefficient bandits," barring "one of the future highways of civilization." He convinced himself that the order and stability of the region required action. Privately, Roosevelt talked of seizing Panama; instead he settled on fomenting a revolution.

Phillipe Bunau-Varilla, a French engineer with the de Lesseps Company, told Roosevelt of a budding independence movement in Panama. Roosevelt let it be known that he would welcome a revolt. On November 3, 1903, on schedule and without bloodshed, the Panamanians took over. The next day the cruiser *Nashville* dropped anchor offshore to prevent Colombia from landing troops on the isthmus. Two days later, far quicker than diplomatic convention dictated, the United States recognized the new Republic of Panama; and within two weeks, Bunau-Varilla, acting for the Panamanian government, signed a treaty with the United States for a renewable lease on a canal zone 10-miles in width. Panama received $10 million plus an annual rent of $250,000 (the same terms earlier offered to Colombia). The Chicago *American*, one of the few critics of this affair, called it "a rough-riding assault upon another republic over the shattered wreckage of international law and diplomatic usage." Roosevelt never apologized, but in 1921, when oil had been discovered there, Congress voted $25 million to Colombia. One historian later dubbed it "canalimony."

To underscore the importance of the canal, Roosevelt himself traveled to Panama, the first president ever to leave the country while in office. Arriving early in November 1906 on the new 16,000-ton *Louisiana*, the largest battleship in the

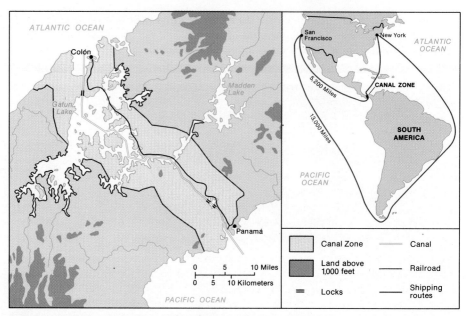

PANAMA CANAL—OLD AND NEW TRANSOCEANIC ROUTES
Tropical forests cover three-fourths of Panama, including the Canal Zone. Vegetation is denser at high elevations, but tightly packed even below 1000 feet. The terrain is rugged, but the distance saved by the canal (nearly 8000 miles) made the ordeal of construction worthwhile.

fleet, he timed his visit with the rainy season in order to see the canal site at its foulest. "If we shrink from the hard contests," he once said, "then the bolder and stronger people will pass us by."

Soaked from head to toe, his huge panama hat and white suit sagging about his body, Roosevelt made the canal tour a public event. He had Dr. William Gorgas, exterminator of the deadly yellow fever–bearing mosquito, take him in person through the hospital at Ancon. At the cuts, he asked black workers about their complaints, walked railroad ties, splashed through labor camps, and made speeches in the pouring rain. "This is one of the great works of the world," he boasted to an assembly of diggers.

As Roosevelt clambered aboard a giant 95-ton Bucyrus steam shovel, he saw proof of his boast—the largest trench yet cut in the earth's surface. When completed in 1914 it stretched some 40 miles across the Isthmus of Panama. Three years of planning and seven years of construction went into it, and its final cost, $352 million, was four times what had been spent on the Suez Canal when it opened in 1869. Crews working on the Panama Canal dug the equivalent of a Suez Canal every three years. "Everything," reported one journalist who visited the site in 1911, "is on a colossal scale." The locks of the canal, used to raise and lower water levels, were 1000 feet long and rose higher than a six-story building. Three Statues of Liberty could be laid end to end in any one of them with room to spare. The volume of concrete poured to make just one of the three main locks was enough to build a wall 8 feet high, 12 feet thick, and 133 miles long.

Nearly 6000 men lost their lives from disease and accidents. About 4500 were blacks, among 30,000 black laborers imported from the West Indies for the back-breaking job of digging the canal. They worked 10 hours a day, 6 days a week, for 10 cents an hour (considered good wages at the time). To emphasize the difference between black and white workers, blacks were paid in silver, whites in gold.

The Panama Canal embodied Roosevelt's muscular policy of respect through strength. "I do not believe," he told Taft after leaving office, "in our taking any position anywhere unless you mean to shoot." He tripled the size of the army and doubled the navy's strength. He modernized the armed forces, created a general staff for military planning and mobilization, and established the Army War College. As a pivot point between the two hemispheres, his canal would allow the United States to flex its strength across the globe. These widening horizons came about largely as an outgrowth of its commercial and industrial expansion in the world, just as the imperialist drives of England, France, Germany, Russia, and Japan reflected the spread of their own industrial and commercial might.

In the ensuing rivalry, the industrialized powers often contested with one another for spheres of influence. The United States, steeped in democratic ideals, frequently seemed uncomfortable with the dirty business of "spheres of influence" or baldly stated dreams of empire. Roosevelt's embrace of the canal showed how far some progressives had come, however, in being willing to intervene, influence, and actively shape the world order. In domestic affairs TR did not oppose big trusts, only "bad" ones. Abroad, he saw no problem with the United States exercising power globally, so long as power was wielded in a "good" way. As in the matter of judging trusts, the distinction between good and bad was not always easy to make, and control was not easy to maintain. The expansionist diplomats, whether idealistic or cynical, had convinced themselves they could maintain global order by a series of political alliances. In the end, that system of alliances and spheres of influence did not suffice, and the old order collapsed in a terrible world war.

PROGRESSIVE DIPLOMACY

The progressive era was the busiest period in American diplomacy since the eve of the Civil War. In the aftermath of the war with Spain, the United States intervened in China and Latin America, dominated the Caribbean and Central America, and fought a world war. American diplomacy became assertive and nationalistic. Diplomatic and defense budgets climbed steadily, from less than $200 million in 1900 to $1 billion in the war year of 1917.

Progressive diplomacy, like progressive politics, stressed moralism and order. Progressives pursued these aims abroad as they had at home—by stretching executive power and shaping the environment. In their hands manifest destiny, once confined to the continent, assumed global proportions. "Of all our race," Albert Beveridge told his fellow senators in 1900, "[God] has marked the American people as His chosen nation to finally lead in the redemption of the world." A widely held belief in the superiority of Anglo-American institutions lay at the core of Beveridge's faith. Implicit in his remark was the growing notion—shared by all leaders—that northern Europeans were superior in other ways as well. The darker peoples of the tropical zones, observed educator and anti-imperialist David Starr Jordan, dwelled in "nature's asylum for degenerates."

Aggressive economic expansion underlay the commitment to a "civilizing" mission. Shocked by the depression of 1893, American manufacturing and agricultural interests looked to markets abroad to ease the burdens of overproduction at home. By 1900 the United States stood first in the world among industrial nations. Five years later tractors, sewing machines, and other manufactured goods replaced agricultural commodities as America's chief exports. When World War I ended in 1918, the United States found it had become the largest creditor in the world. American-based corporations like Singer Sewing Machine and Standard Oil of New Jersey operated all over the globe. Every administration in the twentieth century committed itself to opening the doors of trade to American interests and keeping them unobstructed.

The Big Stick in the Caribbean

"Walk softly and carry a big stick," Roosevelt once remarked, but in the Caribbean he and his successors moved both loudly and mightily. The Panama Canal gave the United States a commanding strategic and commercial position in the Western Hemisphere. Its existence required the country to "police the surrounding premises," explained Secretary of State Elihu Root. Roosevelt moved promptly to make the Caribbean an American lake. Before granting Cuba independence in 1902, the United States reorganized its finances and included in the Cuban constitution the so-called Platt Amendment. According to its terms, the United States could intervene if Cuban independence were threatened or internal disorder broke out. Under its provisions, American troops occupied the island from 1906 to 1909 and again from 1917 to 1923.

Apart from his higher aim of encouraging stable governments that would be fiscally responsible and open to investment, Roosevelt worried quite practically that instability would open the Caribbean to deeper European penetration. Ever since the Monroe Doctrine of 1823 asserted American opposition to further European colonization of the Western Hemisphere, the United States had sought to keep foreign powers out of the region. In the early twentieth century the rising

Theodore Roosevelt visited the site of the Panama Canal in 1906. Relentlessly curious, he had to know everything, from the salary of engineers to the proper techniques for operating this giant Bucyrus steam shovel. "It is greater work than you, yourselves, at the moment realize," he told workers.

scale of Latin American debts to European powers invited their intervention. "If we intend to say hands off to the power of Europe," Roosevelt told Elihu Root, "then sooner or later we must keep order ourselves." Roosevelt did not shrink from the challenge. The great powers could minimize dangers by counterbalancing each other, much as big government offset big business at home, and each of them, including the United States, had an obligation to keep order in its own sphere of influence while avoiding encroachment on another's. Going well beyond Monroe's concept of resisting foreign intrusions, Roosevelt asserted an American hegemony over the Caribbean.

An early test of resolve came when British and German gunboats blockaded Venezuela for refusing to pay debts in 1902. Roosevelt successfully urged arbitration on both sides. When the Dominican Republic defaulted on its debts in 1904, Roosevelt stretched the Monroe Doctrine from a warning to keep Europe out into an American pledge to move in. Decrying "chronic wrongdoing or impotence," the president appointed the United States "policeman of the West." If Latin American nations failed to keep their affairs in order, the United States would do it for them. Under this "Roosevelt Corollary," the United States assumed responsibility for the internal affairs of several Caribbean states. In 1905, with the navy just off the coast, American agents took control of Dominican customs and tax services to ensure payment of debts. Within two years the United States established protectorates over Cuba and Panama.

A "Diplomatist of the Highest Rank"

Roosevelt exercised ingenuity rather than force in Asia. He did not consider it within the American sphere, and in any event few of his countrymen would have supported armed intervention half a world away. Roosevelt, therefore, committed himself only to maintaining an "open door" of equal commercial access to China and to protecting the Philippines, "our heel of Achilles." The key lay in offsetting Russian and Japanese ambitions to dominate the region. When Japan launched an attack on Russian holdings in the Chinese province of Manchuria in 1904, Roosevelt privately cheered the audacious Japanese, "a great civilized nation." To his way of thinking, the Russians were little more than "a menace to the higher life of the world." Still, he worried that an unchecked Japan might threaten American interests in China and the Philippines. He looked for an end to the war that would balance power in the region.

In 1905 both sides accepted Roosevelt's offer to mediate. At the U.S. Naval Base in Kittery, Maine, just across the river from Portsmouth, New Hampshire, he tried to keep angry diplomats from each other's throats. "I am having my hair turned gray by dealing with the Russian and Japanese peace negotiators," the president complained to his son. Roosevelt's skillful intercession finally produced the Treaty of Portsmouth in August 1905, leaving Japan as the dominant naval power in the Far East. Further negotiations secured a Japanese promise not to invade the Philippines in return for recognition of Japan's control over Korea. Roosevelt thus agreed to shut the open door in a portion of Asia in order to secure American interests throughout the Far East. For his efforts in ending the Russo–Japanese War he received the Nobel Peace Prize in 1906.

The Japanese government signed the peace treaty, but not without resentment among Japanese nationalists. Anger surfaced in a protest lodged not against Roosevelt, but against the San Francisco school board. In 1906 San Francisco school authorities, succumbing to racial prejudice, segregated the city's 200 Asian students. In Japan citizens talked of war over the insult to national honor. Roosevelt, fuming at those "infernal fools in California," summoned the mayor of San Francisco and seven school board members to the White House. In exchange for an end to the segregation order Roosevelt offered to arrange a mutual restriction of immigration between Japan and the United States. In 1907 all sides accepted his "gentlemen's agreement."

Relations between the two nations reached a new peak of harmony in 1908 when the Root–Takahira Agreement affirmed the status quo in the Pacific, the independence of China, and the open door in the Far East. In case Japan or other nations thought of upsetting the Pacific balance, Roosevelt conceived of a grand gesture of American might. He sent 16 sleek white battleships, many of them launched during his administration, on a global tour in the summer of 1907. The "Great White Fleet," as Roosevelt cheerfully called it, made its most conspicuous stop in Japan in 1908. Some Europeans predicted armed disaster. Instead, cheering crowds turned out in Tokyo and Yokohama. The show of force heralded a new age of American naval might but had an unintended consequence: it spurred Japanese navalists to expand their fleet, thus threatening the balance of Pacific power Roosevelt had sought to secure.

Roosevelt's policies toward Japan reflected two of his central beliefs: American interests were global and armed conflict between great powers should be avoided. When Germany and France seemed on the verge of war over control of the North African colony of Morocco in 1905, Roosevelt arranged for an international conference in Algeciras, on the coast of Spain. Breaking a century of isolation from European affairs, he sent American delegates. The peaceful outcome, favorable to France and the stability of Europe, pleased him. In the summer of 1908 the United States and 43 other nations again met at the Hague in the Netherlands to set limited rules for war. Horrified at the destructiveness of new weaponry, they outlawed poison gas but held back from banning aerial balloons, battleships, airplanes, and submarines.

Watching Roosevelt in his second term, an amazed London *Morning Post* dubbed him a "diplomatist of the highest rank." Abroad and at home his brand of progressivism was grounded in an enthusiastic nationalism, mixed force with finesse, and sought always to achieve balance and order. For all his strenuous efforts, however, disorder still threatened. Imperial rivalries, empires both rising and falling, an unchecked naval arms race, and domestic unrest in Europe threatened to plunge the world into war.

Taft and Dollar Diplomacy

Roosevelt's hand-picked successor, William Howard Taft, was TR's opposite—prudent, legalistic, and cooperative. Rather than wielding force or finesse, Taft preferred to promote American interests by encouraging private corporations to invest abroad, particularly in the Caribbean and China. American capital, managed wherever possible by American financiers, would help to achieve prosperity, keep peace, and tie debt-ridden nations to the United States instead of Europe. "Dollar diplomacy," Taft explained, simply amounted to "substituting dollars for bullets." As it turned out, he and his prickly secretary of state, Philander Knox, relied on both.

South of the Rio Grande Taft and Knox (himself a corporation lawyer) treated the restless nations of Latin America like ailing corporations, injecting capital and

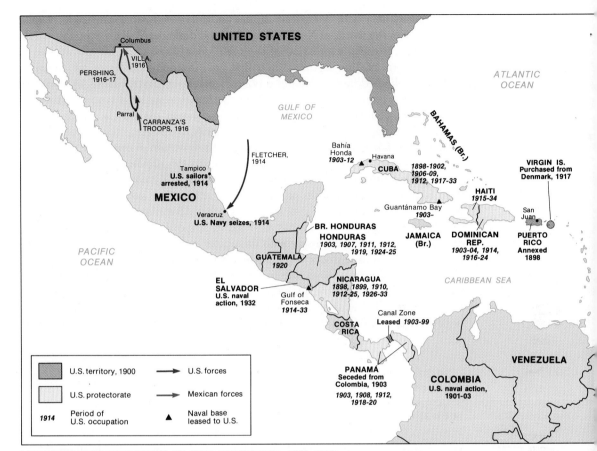

AMERICAN INTERVENTIONS IN THE CARIBBEAN, 1898–1930
In the first three decades of the twentieth century, U.S. diplomacy transformed the Caribbean into an American lake as armed and unarmed intervention became part of the country's diplomatic arsenal.

reorganizing management. Aided by the State Department, American money flowed across the border. One-half of all American investments abroad were in Latin America by the time Taft left office in 1912. Taft and Knox convinced American investors to supply credit to Honduras to pay off European bondholders in 1909. A year later Taft got American bankers to take over the national bank of chronically unstable Haiti.

In Nicaragua dollar diplomacy was not enough. An American-supported revolt against the unfriendly dictator José Zelaya had brought Adolfo Díaz to power in 1909. When the Nicaraguan legislature balked at American demands to take over its customs house and national bank, a U.S. warship dropped anchor off the coast. The lawmakers changed their minds, but in 1912 a revolution reinstated Zelaya. Taft sent 2000 marines to protect American lives and property, an assignment that lasted on and off for more than a dozen years.

Taft found he could assure American influence in the Caribbean far more easily than in Asia. Where Roosevelt had tried to conciliate Japan, Taft tried to strengthen China with American capital and increased American trade. Dollar diplomacy, in the words of New York banker and diplomat Willard Straight, would become the financial expression of the open door. Knox and Taft saw an end to foreign control of Manchuria as their first goal. So dominant were the Japanese that they collected taxes, appointed police, and supervised Chinese all along the railroads they operated. Knox tried to organize an international syndicate through which China could buy back the railroads from Japan and Russia. When Russia, England, and Japan refused to cooperate in 1910, the scheme fell apart. Encouraged by the Chinese, Knox then elbowed his way into a British, French, and German venture to finance a new rail line across the province of Hukuang. The Japanese and Russians also demanded entry, then paralyzed the resulting consortium to protect their spheres of influence. The best Taft and Knox could do was dragoon American bankers into lending a paltry $2 million to China.

Failure dogged Taft overseas as it did at home. In the Caribbean his dollar diplomacy was linked so closely with unpopular regimes, corporations, and banks that Woodrow Wilson dissociated himself from it as soon as he took office. In the Far East Taft's initiatives only intensified rivalry with Japan and made China more suspicious of all foreigners, including Americans. In 1911 the southern Chinese provinces rebelled against foreign intrusion and overthrew the monarchy. Only persistent pressure from the White House kept "dollar diplomacy" in Asia alive at all.

WOODROW WILSON AND MORAL DIPLOMACY

Before running for public office Woodrow Wilson had devoted his academic life to studying politics, Congress, and the presidency. His political touch was therefore surest at home. Abroad he felt his way through unknown territory. Just before his inauguration in 1913 he confessed to a friend, "It would be the irony of fate if my administration had to deal chiefly with foreign affairs." Wilson, it turned out, lacked the sense of irony to deal with what fate had in store.

To the diplomacy of order, force, and finances he brought a commitment to justice, democracy, and Christian values. He revived Jefferson's notion of the United States as a beacon of freedom for the world and then went a step beyond: he wanted the country, with its newfound power, to become an active promoter of peace, human rights, and social progress. "We are chosen, and prominently chosen," Wilson asserted in 1910, "to show the way to the nations of the world how they shall walk in the paths of liberty." Such paternalism only thinly masked the assumption of Anglo-American superiority that Wilson shared with his predecessors and other Western leaders.

Wilson's evangelical democracy had a practical side. In the twentieth century foreign markets would serve as America's new frontier. "Our industries have expanded to such a point," he warned in the campaign of 1912, "that they will burst their jackets if they cannot find free outlets in the markets of the world." Wilson's genius lay in reconciling this commercial self-interest with global interests. As he saw it, exporting American democracy and capitalism would promote stability and progress throughout the world.

Missionary Diplomacy

Solitary and self-assured, Wilson served as his own vicar of foreign policy. Circumventing the State Department, he sent personal emissaries to foreign leaders and often typed his own dispatches. Sometimes he even left his secretary of state uninformed about important initiatives. When in doubt, Wilson usually turned to his trusted personal friend, Edward M. House. A private citizen and presidential kingmaker, the honorary "Colonel" House had seen in Wilson's ascent his own road to power and influence behind the scenes. Those who sought to reach the president learned first to go to New York to see the man who had become his alter ego.

In his secretary of state, William Jennings Bryan, Wilson found an ardent public preacher for spreading the blessings of democracy and Christianity. As an evangelical and a pacifist, this thrice-frustrated presidential candidate served mineral water and grape juice at State Department receptions. Like Wilson, Bryan had no experience in foreign affairs. He distrusted the elite corps of foreign affairs experts and appointed politically "deserving Democrats" to key posts around the world. All too often they were as ill equipped and unsophisticated as Bryan himself.

In 1913, many progressives harbored a utopian hope that nations could settle their differences peaceably, if given the chance. Bryan offered that chance through treaties of conciliation with some 30 nations, including Great Britain, France, and Italy. (Ominously, Germany refused to sign one.) Completed in 1914, on the eve of World War I, these "cooling-off" agreements placed disputes before international commissions of investigation, usually for a year. Commissions of "experts," after all, had been at the heart of so many progressive domestic reforms. According to these agreements, neither disputant could further arm itself or declare war until the commission rendered an opinion.

In Asia and the Pacific Wilson gave early signals of his desire to put "moral and public considerations" ahead of the "material interests of individuals." Soon after entering the White House he pulled American bankers out of the Chinese railroad consortium. Observing that the terms of its loan required foreign control of tax collection and expenditures, he pledged to aid China without undermining its sovereignty. The United States became the first major power to recognize the new Republic of China after a revolution in 1911 toppled the last Manchu emperor, and in 1915 strongly opposed Japan's "Twenty-one Demands" for control of the country. At the end of Wilson's first administration the Philippines gained limited self-government, the first step toward the eventual independence granted in 1946.

In the Caribbean and Latin America, despite promises of change, Wilson found himself resorting to armed intervention. Like Taft and Roosevelt, he failed to appreciate the near impossibility of trying to graft American-style democracy and capitalism onto countries with indigenous traditions and aspirations. In August 1914 he convinced Nicaragua, already occupied by American troops, to yield control of a naval base and grant to the United States an alternative canal route. By the end of his administration U.S. troops were still stationed there and also in the Dominican Republic, Haiti, and Cuba. All of them were economically dependent on the United States and all were virtual American protectorates. Missionary diplomacy, like its predecessors, spread its gospel with steel and cash.

Intervention in Mexico

A lingering crisis in Mexico made a final mockery of Wilson's moral diplomacy in Latin America. In 1911 President Francisco Madero, an aristocratic reformer, overthrew the aging dictator, Porfirio Díaz. Despite efforts to modernize his country, Díaz had succeeded mainly in enriching himself and a few powerful families. Most Mexicans remained poor and uneducated in a population deeply divided among whites, Indians, and mestizos. Díaz kept Mexico financially afloat by encouraging foreign investment in oil, railroads, land, and mines. United States corporations owned nearly half the investment property.

Backed by the middle class, Madero set about raising taxes on foreign holdings, canceling concessions, and nationalizing properties. His reforms plunged the country into political turmoil for two years. The climax came on February 22, 1913, when General Victoriano Huerta surrounded the presidential palace, arrested Madero, and had him killed. Foreign investors endorsed Huerta, a conservative militarist likely to protect their holdings. Most European nations recognized the new regime immediately, but Wilson refused to accept the "government of butchers." He wanted to extend into Mexico the same principles progressivism fostered at home: orderly government and a democratic rule of law. So he threw his support to rebel leader Venustiano Carranza, on the condition that Carranza participate in American-sponsored elections. No Mexican, least of all Carranza and his "constitutionalists," was ready to lose face by tolerating such heavy-handed interference. They rejected the offer. Having few options, Wilson supplied the rebels with arms anyway.

Wilson's distaste for the Huerta regime was so great that he used a minor incident as a pretext for armed intervention. In April 1914 the paymaster and crew of the U.S.S. *Dolphin* landed without permission in the Mexican port city of Tampico. Local police promptly arrested them, only to release the sailors with equal speed. Unappeased, their squadron commander demanded a 21-gun salute to the American flag to salve the honor of the United States. Huerta refused to salute a nation that did not recognize his regime unless the Americans returned the salute to Mexico. Learning of a German shipload of weapons about to land at Veracruz, Wilson broke the impasse by ordering American troops to take the port city, expecting a bloodless occupation. Instead, marines encountered stiff resistance as they stormed ashore; 126 Mexicans and 19 Americans were killed before the city fell. The intervention accomplished the unlikely feat of uniting the rival Mexican factions in a moment of shared rage.

With Mexico and the United States edging toward war, Wilson accepted an offer from Argentina, Brazil, and Chile (the "ABC powers") to mediate. As talks convened, a bankrupted Huerta resigned and Carranza formed a new constitutionalist government. Under the guidance of the ABC powers the United States evacuated Veracruz in November 1914. Wilson, still irked by Carranza's hostility over American intervention, threw his support to Francisco "Pancho" Villa. The wily, peasant-born general had broken from the government, and with Emiliano Zapata, another peasant leader, he kept a rebellion flickering.

A year later, when Wilson finally accepted reality and recognized the Carranza regime, Villa turned against the United States. In January 1916 he abducted 17 Americans from a train in Mexico and executed them. In March, after months of shooting up border towns, he galloped into Columbus, New Mexico, killed 19 people, and left the town in flames. While Senator Henry Cabot Lodge denounced Villa as a murderous peon, Wilson sent 6,000 troops into Mexico to capture him.

Led by General John "Black Jack" Pershing (who would later command the American Expeditionary Force in Europe), the army chased Villa across northern Mexico on horseback, in automobiles, and with airplanes. There were bloody skirmishes with Mexican troops, but not Villa; he and his rebels eluded the Americans for several months. As the goose chase turned wilder and wilder, Carranza withdrew his consent for U.S. troops to invade Mexican soil. Early in 1917 Wilson ordered Pershing home. The "punitive expedition," as the president called it, poisoned Mexican–American relations for the next 30 years.

Like a good progressive, Wilson had wanted "to teach the South American republics to elect good men." Condescending and impatient, he failed to realize the irrelevance of his bright vision and the presumptuousness of his methods. Imposing progressive ideals of law, democracy, and gradual reform on an impoverished country like Mexico, riven with class, racial, and ethnic strife and torn by revolution, virtually guaranteed a hostile reception.

THE ROAD TO WAR

In the century before the world order shattered in 1914, Europe's population had more than tripled. As the ranks of its middle and working classes swelled, discontent with industrial society deepened. Antagonisms among rival empires grew; nationalism rose and militarism flourished alongside it. These profound social strains led Europe down the road to war.

In theory—the theory of hard-nosed, "realistic" diplomats—war should not have come. A system of interlocking alliances, fashioned by Europe's great powers

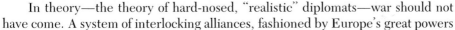

General John J. "Black Jack" Pershing led U.S. forces into Mexico on a "punitive action" to catch rebel leader Pancho Villa "dead or alive." Villa (pictured below) eluded the Americans for several months before they abandoned the expedition. Audacious and ruthless, he was worshiped by Mexican peasants, who extolled his exploits in folktales and ballads after his assassination in 1923.

at the turn of the century, was designed to maintain a reasonable balance of power. But what was reasonable? Led by the stiff-necked Kaiser Wilhelm II, Germany dreamed of a glorious empire and allied itself with Turkey and Austria–Hungary. The established imperialist powers—England and France—had committed themselves to Germany's foe, Russia, promising one another guns and troops in case of war. By the summer of 1914 Europe was a powder keg ready to explode.

The Guns of August

The unlikely spark was Archduke Franz Ferdinand, benign heir to the Austro–Hungarian throne. On June 28, 1914, the archduke and his wife were gunned down by a Slavic nationalist. Austria–Hungary mobilized to punish Serbia, which was rumored to be responsible for the assassination. Mobilization prompted a protective response from Russia (with 6 million men, the largest army in Europe) on behalf of the Serbs and led Germany and France to call out their troops. On July 28, after a month of insincere demands for apologies, Austria attacked Serbia. Early in August German siege cannons with barrels the size of freight cars and shells a yard long hammered the forts of neutral Belgium. The Germans were marching on France, and these guns of August heralded the first global war.

Germany's plan for a quick knockout blow against France not only failed but also set in motion a chain of events that ultimately brought most of the world's major powers into the war. By early August, five German columns were slicing west through Belgium toward Paris. "The smell of half a million unbathed men," wrote a news reporter, hung about Belgian towns for days, nauseating evidence of an invading army again on the move. Meanwhile 11,000 trains carrying nearly 2 million soldiers sped across eastern Europe to Russia. Great Britain, responding to the violation of Belgium's neutrality and rallying to aid the French, declared war on Germany on August 4, 1914.

Like dominoes, the other industrial nations fell into line: Japan, Italy, Romania, and Greece to the side of "Allies" Britain, France, and Russia; Bulgaria to "Central Powers" Germany, Austria–Hungary, and Turkey. Armies fought from the deserts of North Africa and the Near East to the plains of Flanders; fleets battled off the coasts of Chile and Sumatra. Soldiers came from as far away as Australia and India. Nearly 8 million never went home.

American Neutrality

The outbreak of war in Europe shocked most Americans. Few were prepared to do anything about it. Among them was President Wilson, who called an emergency cabinet meeting to issue a declaration of neutrality and to approve a plan for evacuating Americans stranded in Belgium. Then he hurried to the bedside of his wife, whose failing health absorbed him throughout the crisis. Early in August, as Germany marched on France and Russia, Ellen Wilson died. For an instant the president seemed near collapse. Personal grief mixed with contempt as he watched Europe disembowel itself. "The more I read about the conflict across the seas," Wilson wrote a friend, "the more open it seems to me to utter condemnation."

Wilson slowly came to see in the calamity an opportunity for a new world order. Neutral America would lead warring nations to "a peace without victory."

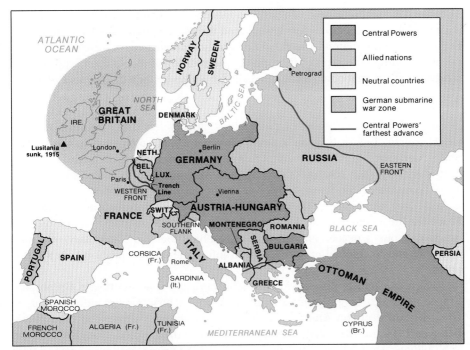

THE COURSE OF WAR IN EUROPE, 1914–1917
When World War I erupted between the Central and Allied Powers in 1914, few countries in Europe remained neutral. The armies of the Central Powers penetrated as far west as France and as far east as Russia, but by 1917 the European war had settled into a hideous standoff along a deadly line of trenches on the western front.

Selfish nationalism would give way to cooperative internationalism, Christian charity and fellowship would replace power politics, progressive faith in reason and gradual change would triumph over irrational conflict. Everything hinged on American neutrality. Only if the country stood above the fray could America achieve a higher peace. Americans, Wilson declared in 1914, must remain "neutral in fact as well as in name, impartial in thought as well as action."

Neutrality would be difficult, but impartiality was impossible. Nearly 9 million Americans of German and Austrian descent naturally had sympathy for the Central Powers, while Irish-Americans, almost 5 million in number, shared those sympathies on the grounds of England's centuries-old domination of Ireland. On the other hand, the bonds of language, culture, and history tied the majority of Americans to Great Britain. Wilson himself, who had long venerated British institutions of government and law, could not escape feeling tugged toward the Allies. Meanwhile gratitude for French aid during the American Revolution still lived. When the first American division marched through Paris years later, its commander stopped to salute Lafayette's tomb with the cry, "Nous voilà, Lafayette!"— Lafayette, we are here!

Germany aroused different sentiments. Although some progressives admired German social reforms, most Americans saw Germany as an iron military power bent on world conquest. For years newspapers had featured photographs of the uniformed Kaiser, strutting arrogantly, a monocle clutched in his eye, looking like an imperial robber baron. Americans read British propaganda—some based on real events, some manufactured, some merely embellished—of the pillage of innocent Belgium, the rape of its women, the murder of its children, and the destruction of its national treasures, all by spike-helmeted, bayonet-wielding "Huns."

Even though hundreds of young Americans slipped across the border to enlist in the Canadian army, most of their fellow citizens felt that neutrality was the wisest course. Before the war a peace movement had taken seed in the United States, nourished in 1910 by a gift of $10 million from Andrew Carnegie. In 1914 a host of social justice reformers, led by Jane Addams, Charlotte Perkins Gilman, and Lillian Wald, condemned the war as the offspring of militarists, munitions makers, and imperialists. They founded the Women's International League for Peace and Freedom and the American Union Against Militarism. Calling on Wilson to convene a peace conference, they lobbied for open diplomacy, disarmament, an end to colonial empires, and an international organization to settle disputes.

Even as pacifists pressed for peace, American economic ties to Britain and France created a tangible investment in Allied victory. Commanding the seas, Great Britain drew on American resources—munitions, arms, food, and fibers. Between 1914 and 1916 trade with the Allies more than tripled, from $800 million to $3 billion. After faltering briefly in 1914, the American economy boomed with the flood of war orders. The Allies eventually borrowed over $2 billion from American banks to finance their purchases. By contrast, a British blockade reduced American "contraband" commerce with the Central Powers to a trickle.

The Diplomacy of Neutrality

The blockade sorely tested Wilson's patience with Great Britain. British warships forced American vessels into port and seized cargoes. The British navy mined the North Sea. British censors opened American mail to Europe. British authorities refused to allow the United States to trade with Germany's neutral neighbors. They even barred British companies from dealing with "blacklisted" American firms that did business with Germany. Wilson insisted that the Allies respect the trading rights of neutral nations, but he never forced the issues of freedom of the seas and commercial rights to the point of rupture. He feared that strong retaliation, such as embargoing arms to the Allies, would deprive Britain of its most powerful weapon—the navy—and tip the balance toward Germany, a land power.

Dependent on American supplies, the British pursued a policy of reducing German–American trade without souring British–American relations. When Britain forbade cotton from being sold to the Central Powers in 1915, it arranged to buy American surpluses. It also agreed to compensate American firms for their losses when the war was over. By the end of 1915 the United States had all but accepted the British blockade of Germany, while American supplies continued to flow to England. True neutrality was dead as America became the quartermaster of the Allied war effort.

While Wilson looked for diplomatic leverage to bring the belligerents to the peace table, Secretary of State Bryan called for "real neutrality," evenhanded treatment of all combatants. On those grounds he opposed loans to the Allies. "Money," Bryan said in 1914, "is the worst of all contrabands because it commands everything else." Later that year he gave in, only to become embroiled in a hot debate over a dreadful new weapon—the submarine.

Early in 1915 Germany mounted a counterblockade of Great Britain with two dozen submarines, or *Unterseeboote*, called U-boats. Before submarines, sea raiders generally were required to stop their targets, examine their cargoes, and allow crews and passengers to escape. If the U-boats surfaced to obey these conventions, they risked being rammed or blown from the water. So submarines attacked without warning and spared no lives. In February 1915 Berlin announced that U-boats would torpedo enemy vessels within a war zone around the British Isles. Even neutral ships were at risk, since British vessels often flew neutral flags as cover. Invoking international law and national honor, President Wilson threatened to hold Germany to "strict accountability" for any American losses. Germany promised not to sink any American ships, but within a month a new issue—the safety of American passengers on belligerent vessels—claimed the headlines.

On the morning of May 7, 1915, the British passenger liner *Lusitania* appeared out of a fog bank off the coast of Ireland on its way from New York to Southampton. The commander of the German U-20 could hardly believe his eyes as the giant ship, displacing some 30,000 tons, filled the viewfinder of his periscope. He fired a single torpedo. A tremendous roar followed as one of the *Lusitania*'s main boilers exploded. The ship stopped dead in the water and soon listed so badly that lifeboats could barely be launched. Within 18 minutes it slid beneath the waves with a sound, recalled one survivor, "like a terrible moan." Nearly 1200 men, women, and children perished, including 128 Americans.

Former President Theodore Roosevelt charged that such an "act of piracy" demanded war against Germany. Wilson, horrified at this "murder on the high seas," still urged restraint. "There is such a thing as a man being too proud to fight," he said a few days later. "There is such a thing as a nation being so right that it does not need to convince others by force." Instead he sent three notes of protest demanding that Germany disavow submarine warfare, compensate the victims, and agree to stop sinking passenger liners. Secretary Bryan wanted equal protests lodged against both German submarines and the British blockaders. He suspected that the *Lusitania* carried munitions and was thus a legitimate target. To "rely on passengers to protect her from attack," Bryan argued, was "like putting women and children in front of an army." In Wilson's mind the two were scarcely equivalent. The blockade killed only trade; submarines killed people. Rather than endorse the policy, Bryan resigned and was replaced as secretary of state by Robert Lansing, a pro-Allied lawyer in the State Department.

Germany, battling on two fronts in Europe, wanted to keep the United States out of the war. When two Americans died in August 1915 after the torpedoing of the British steamer *Arabic*, Germany apologized, offered an indemnity, and pledged not to sink passenger liners without warning. But in February 1916 a desperate Germany declared submarine warfare on all *armed* vessels, belligerent or neutral. A month later a U-boat commander mistook the French steamer *Sussex* for a mine layer and torpedoed the unarmed vessel as it ferried passengers and freight across the English Channel. Several Americans were injured. The *Arabic* pledge seemed suddenly empty.

Pressed to the breaking point, Wilson issued an ultimatum on April 18. If Germany failed to stop sinking nonmilitary vessels, the United States would cut diplomatic relations. War would surely follow. Without enough U-boats to control the seas, the Kaiser accepted. According to the *Sussex* pledge of May 4, 1916,

The ideal of neat, sharply defined spaces for living and fighting is exemplified by these model trenches in northern France (left). Trench warfare, wrote one general, was "marked by uniform formations, the regulation of space and time by higher commands down to the smallest details . . . fixed distances between units and individuals." The reality (below) was something else again.

Germany agreed to Wilson's terms, all but abandoning the submarine campaign. For a time tensions between the two countries eased. The *Sussex* pledge gave Wilson a major victory, but with a grave risk. His ultimatum was so tough that if Germany resumed unrestricted submarine attacks, the honor and prestige of the United States would require war. "Any little German [U-boat] commander," Wilson told his cabinet, "can put us into the war at any time by some calculated outrage."

Preparedness

While pacifist groups condemned the war and any hint of involvement in it, corporate leaders and Republican party spokesmen claimed the nation was woefully unprepared to fight or even to keep peace. The army numbered only 80,000 men in 1914, the navy just 37 battleships and a handful of new "dreadnoughts," or supercruisers. Advocates of "preparedness" called for a navy larger than Great Britain's, an army of millions of reservists, and universal military training.

Wilson at first resisted efforts to "turn America into a military camp," even when Theodore Roosevelt criticized him for "milk and water" diplomacy. As his frustration with German submarines rose, Wilson ordered the War Department to plan for military expansion. In November 1915 he proposed a volunteer army of 400,000, and in January 1916 he toured the country promoting preparedness and promising "a navy second to none."

By the middle of 1916 Wilson's steady pressure persuaded Congress to double the army, increase the National Guard, and begin construction of the largest navy in the world. To foot the bill progressives pushed through new graduated taxes on incomes and estates as well as additional levies on corporate profits. Higher rates on the wealthy would largely underwrite the preparedness program. Whoever paid for it, most Americans in 1916 were thinking of preparedness for peace, not war.

The Election of 1916

As the Democratic National Convention opened in St. Louis in June 1916, former New York Governor Martin Glynn was determined to talk of Americanism and preparedness, just as President Wilson had instructed. Glynn began what he expected to be a dull recitation of the precedents for American neutrality. Warming to his audience, he cited case after case of Wilson's diplomatic maneuvers, each one punctuated with screams of "What did we do? What did we do?" from the crowd. "We didn't go to war! We didn't go to war!" Glynn shouted back. The next day Wilson was renominated by acclamation. Within weeks his campaign had taken up "He Kept Us Out of War" as its slogan. The Democrats had discovered the political power of peace.

The Republicans had already nominated Charles Evans Hughes, a moderate progressive, the former governor of New York, and later a Supreme Court justice. With his endorsement of "straight and honest" neutrality, Hughes too endorsed

THE ELECTION OF 1916

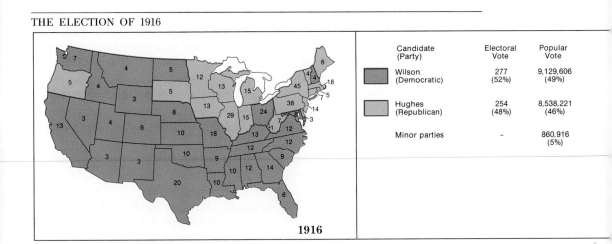

Candidate (Party)	Electoral Vote	Popular Vote
Wilson (Democratic)	277 (52%)	9,129,606 (49%)
Hughes (Republican)	254 (48%)	8,538,221 (46%)
Minor parties	–	860,916 (5%)

1916

peace. It won the loyalty of German-American voters, whether he liked it or not. Hughes also turned away from the saber rattling of Theodore Roosevelt, whose presidential overtures were spurned by party leaders. "The country wasn't in a heroic mood," Roosevelt wrote soon after the Republican convention. As the election approached, Democrats took full-page advertisements in newspapers across the country: "If You Want WAR, Vote for HUGHES! If You Want Peace with Honor VOTE FOR WILSON!" Voters liked the pledge enough to give Wilson a slender majority. He carried the South and key states in the Midwest and West on the tide of prosperity, progressive reform, and promises of peace. As the British ambassador reported, "Americans desire nothing so much as to keep out of war."

The Final Peace Offensive

Twice since 1915 Wilson had sent Colonel House to European capitals in behind-the-scenes attempts to negotiate a peace settlement. With the election over, Wilson opened his final peace offensive. But when he asked the belligerents to state their terms for a cease-fire, neither the Allies nor the Central Powers accepted. Total war had committed both sides totally to victory. Frustrated, fearful, and genuinely agonized, Wilson in a dramatic speech to the Senate on January 22, 1917, called for "a peace without victory." There could be no victor or vanquished, only "a peace among equals."

As Wilson spoke a fleet of U-boats cruised north toward the British Isles. Weeks earlier German military leaders had persuaded the Kaiser to take one last gamble to starve the Allies into submission in six months. On January 31, 1917, the German ambassador in Washington informed Secretary of State Lansing that unrestricted submarine warfare would be resumed the next day.

The collapse of his dream to keep the country from war shook Wilson, but still he clung to it. As he told Secretary of State Lansing, the future of "'white civilization' and its domination over the world rested largely on our ability to keep this country intact." On February 4 Wilson severed relations with Germany, though later that month Congress refused his bill to arm merchant ships. Then British authorities handed him an intercepted telegram from the German foreign secretary, Arthur Zimmermann, to the Kaiser's ambassador in Mexico. In the event of war, the ambassador was instructed to offer Mexico guns and money to attack the United States. After victory, Mexico would receive its "lost territory in Texas, New Mexico, and Arizona." Wilson released the Zimmermann telegram to the press on March 1. Stunned and outraged, the House of Representatives passed Wilson's bill immediately, but La Follette and other opposition senators stalled until the session ran out. On March 9, acting on his own, Wilson ordered gun crews aboard merchant ships and thereafter told them to shoot U-boats on sight.

The logic of events now propelled a reluctant nation toward war. On March 12 U-boats torpedoed the American merchant vessel *Algonquin*. On March 15, with Russia in the midst of a shattering revolution, the abdication of Czar Nicholas II threw a major ally into chaos. By the end of the month U-boats had sunk nearly 600,000 tons of Allied and neutral shipping. For the first time reports came to Washington of the desperate condition of Allied armies and of their cracking morale. The president could wait no longer.

On April 2, accompanied by armed cavalry, Wilson rode down Pennsylvania Avenue, trudged up the steps of the Capitol, and delivered a stirring message of war to a joint session of Congress. He summoned Americans not to their flag but to a higher purpose: "the ultimate peace of the world and for the liberation of its people, the German people included: for the rights of nations great and small . . . to choose their way of life." "The world," he said, "must be made safe for democracy." The United States had to enter "the most terrible and disastrous of wars." "God helping her, she can do no other."

Despite opposition (6 votes in the Senate; 50 in the House), the war resolution passed quickly. American entry into the war boosted Allied confidence at a critical moment. Wilson had not wanted war, but now it seemed the only way to realize his vision of a higher peace.

WAR AND SOCIETY

The first "world war" enlisted whole societies in the pursuit of victory. Governments not only fielded armies, but they mobilized industry, controlled labor, and rationed food as well. For the first time civilians died in air attacks. In 1915 the German Zeppelin L-13, hovering at 8000 feet, dropped a load of bombs that killed 17 Londoners. In the United States, despite substantial opposition to the war, traditions of cooperation and volunteerism led people to pull together. Even though its citizens never came under direct attack, war still shaped American society in peculiarly progressive ways.

The Slaughter of Stalemate

While the United States prepared to win the Great War, the Allies were coming perilously close to losing it. They had halted the initial German assault at the River Marne, north of Paris, in September 1914. The war then settled into a grisly stalemate. A continuous, immovable front stretched from Flanders to the border of Switzerland. Troops dug ditches, six to eight feet deep and four to five feet wide, to escape bullets, grenades, and artillery. Twenty-five thousand miles of these "trenches"—enough to circle the globe—cut a muddy scar across Europe. Men lived in them for years, prey to disease, lice, and a plague of rats. One British sergeant left a tomcat in the mess hall overnight to dispose of the rodents. He returned the next morning to find the cat disposed of, fur and all.

The military fruits of industrial technology turned all assaults into bloodbaths. Soldiers bravely charged "over the top," only to be shredded by machine guns that fired 600 rounds a minute. Poison gas choked them in their tracks. Barbed wire strung them out and made them easy targets. Giant howitzers lobbed shells on them from positions too distant to see. "The advantage is all with the shell," wrote one veteran, "and you have no comeback." The German siege of Verdun in 1916 cost 680,000 lives; later that year a million men died in the valley of the Somme River during four months of fighting. Even in quiet times 7000 British soldiers were killed or wounded every day. Only late in the war did new armored "landships"—code-named "tanks"—return the advantage to the offense by surmounting the trench barriers with their caterpillar treads.

By then Vladimir Lenin, a revolutionary Marxist exiled to Switzerland during the early stages of the Russian Revolution, was speeding home to Petrograd aboard a special train provided by the Germans. In November 1917 he led the

Bolshevik party to power in Russia, and in December his lieutenant, Leon Trotsky, opened peace negotiations with Germany in the Polish city of Brest-Litovsk. While Russia lapsed into civil war, Germany transferred a million soldiers to the western front in preparation for the spring offensive. A dispirited Allied army settled in for another cold winter. "We will wait," said a French commander, "for the tanks and the Americans."

"You're in the Army Now"

Many Americans went to war assuming their role would be limited to economic and military aid. "Congress," a prominent senator had declared in mid-April 1917, "will not permit American soldiers to be sent to Europe." The Allies' desperate plight forced the General Staff of the Army into a crash program for sending a million men to Europe by the spring of 1918. To raise such a fighting force, Congress passed the Selective Service Act in May 1917. Feelings about the draft ran from strong opposition to enthusiastic support. "There is precious little difference," protested Democratic House Speaker "Champ" Clark in 1917, "between a conscript and a convict." Progressives were more inclined to see military service as an opportunity to overcome class antagonisms in America: "Universal [military] training will jumble the boys of America all together, . . . smashing all the petty class distinctions that now divide, and prompting a brand of real democracy."

After local draft boards opened their doors, 24 million men registered. Almost 3 million Americans were drafted; another 2 million volunteered. Most were white, and all were young, between the ages of 21 and 31. Several thousand women served as clerks, telephone operators, and nurses. But there were people who opposed the war and military service. A handful of tenant farmers, blacks, and Indians in two Oklahoma counties protested in the "Green Corn Rebellion." Official reports put the number of draft evaders at 300,000, though many more went unreported. Others, including some 4000 conscientious objectors, simply requested exemptions.

Most of the 2 million American troops who landed in Europe looked forward to service. "Here was our one great chance for excitement and risk," wrote a volunteer later. "We could not afford to pass it up." In a nation of immigrants, nearly one draftee in five had been born in another country. Training often aimed at educating and Americanizing ethnic recruits. In special "development battalions" drill sergents barked out orders while volunteers from the YMCA taught American history and English. Not all camps sought assimilation. "We are not in this war to make American citizens," read a staff report, "we are in to win the war." At Camp Gordon in Georgia, Italians and Slavs drilled full-time in two distinct units. Commanders spoke their languages; chefs cooked them Italian and Slavic dishes; and no one bothered with Americanization.

African-Americans volunteered in disproportionately high numbers and quickly filled the four rigidly segregated Regular Army and eight National Guard units that already existed for them. White officers commanded almost every one. A training program at Fort Des Moines graduated a single class of 639 black officers, all below field rank and all assigned to one experimental division—controlled by whites. Historically barred from skilled trades and often too poor to support their families, blacks failed to get exemptions at the same rate as whites. They made up about 10 percent of the population but 13 percent of the draftees. Only one in five sent to France actually saw combat (compared to two of every three whites). Southern Democrats had opposed training African-Americans to arms, fearful of the prospect of putting "arrogant, strutting representatives of black soldiery in every community." Most were trained for menial tasks, serving as stevedores aboard navy ships in the Atlantic and common laborers in support units in Europe.

Racial violence sometimes exploded among the troops. The worst episode occurred in Houston in the summer of 1917. Seasoned black regulars, harassed by white soldiers and the city's Jim Crow laws, rioted and killed 17 white civilians. Their whole battalion was disarmed and sent under arrest to New Mexico. Thirteen troopers were condemned to death and hanged within days, too quickly for appeals even to be filed.

The progressive impulse did not ignore an army often in need of reforming. Testing intelligence became a standard procedure for all recruits, most of whom had fewer than seven years of education (for immigrants, fewer than five; for southern blacks, fewer than three). One in four could not read at all. "Mental meddlers," as one general called the psychologists, administered new intelligence tests to inductees. The impersonal tests were an improvement over impression, prejudice, and personal influence. Yet what at the time seemed such a scientific advance in organizational management often measured little more than class origins. Questions such as "Who wrote 'The Raven'?" and "Where was the Overland car manufactured?" exposed background rather than intelligence. More than half the Russian, Italian, and Polish draftees and almost 80 percent of blacks showed up as "inferior." The army stopped the testing program in January 1919, but schools across the country adopted it after the war, reinforcing prevailing ethnic and racial prejudices.

New recruits, including these black ones at Camp Meade in Maryland, were each issued a clothing slip, which was then stamped with a number.

While war raged in Europe, moral crusaders waged a war against sin at home. Temperance leaders pressured the War Department to prohibit the sale of liquor to anyone in uniform in the vicinity of training camps. The army also declared war on venereal disease. "A Soldier who gets a dose is a Traitor!" warned one poster. The Commission on Training Camp Activities produced thousands of pamphlets, films, and lectures on dangers of sexual misconduct. The drive constituted the first serious sex education many young Americans had ever received. When Premier Clemenceau generously offered to establish licensed houses of prostitution, customary for French troops, Secretary of War Newton Baker exclaimed, "My God . . . don't show this to the President or he'll stop the war."

Mobilizing the Economy

To arm, clothe, feed, and transport an army of nearly 5 million required a coordinated national effort. The production of a single ammunition shell brought more than a dozen components from every section of the country (plus vital nitrates shipped from Chile through the Panama Canal) to assembly plants in New Jersey, Virginia, and Pennsylvania and from there to military installations or Atlantic ports. At the Treasury Department Secretary William Gibbs McAdoo fretted over how to finance the war, which cost, finally, $32 billion, at a time when the entire national debt ran to only $2 billion. New taxes paid about a third of the war costs. The rest came from loans financed through "Liberty" and "Victory" bonds and war savings certificates.

Bond drives served a dual purpose. They raised national fervor as well as money. "We capitalized the profound impulse called patriotism," McAdoo explained. At huge rallies, celebrities exhorted Americans to buy bonds. Boy Scouts sold them under the slogan "Every Scout to Save a Soldier." All five bond issues were oversubscribed—and no wonder. "Every person who refuses to subscribe," McAdoo told a crowd in California, ". . . is a friend of Germany." The Federal Reserve System expanded the money supply to make borrowing easier. By 1920 the national debt climbed to $20 billion, and, through inflation, the consumer price index nearly doubled from 1916.

With sweeping grants of authority under the Overman Act (1918) and other new statutes, President Wilson constructed a massive bureaucracy to run the home front. What actually emerged was a managed economy, similar to the New Nationalism envisioned by Theodore Roosevelt. Nearly 5000 new executive agencies employed thousands of business leaders, the readiest source of expert managers. For a nominal "dollar-a-year," they served their country and built a partnership between business and government. Industrial and trade associations such as the Chamber of Commerce tied industry to a network of federal agencies. It was never clear who gained most. Antitrust suits, as the attorney general later recalled, were simply put "to sleep until the war was over." Business influence grew, and corporate profits tripled.

With rapid conversion on such a grand scale, bottlenecks inevitably occurred. In March 1918 mounting criticism led Wilson to name Wall Street wizard Bernard Baruch to the War Industries Board (WIB) with orders to sort out the mess. Under Baruch's leadership, the WIB had the authority to set production schedules, allocate resources, standardize procedures, and coordinate government purchases. Aware that such broad powers might be deemed unconstitutional, Baruch worked indirectly. Lucrative contracts helped him persuade manufacturers to shift to war goods. The WIB covered all costs and guaranteed a profit. When a businessman refused WIB requests, Baruch threatened to marshal public opinion to make him "such an object of contempt and scorn in your home town that you will not dare to show your face there."

As war made battlefields out of wheat fields in Europe, the government encouraged American farmers to make up the loss. The Lever Act (1917) authorized Wilson to create the Food Administration. Herbert Hoover, who had saved starving refugees as chairman of the Commission for Relief in Belgium in 1914, was appointed administrator. Like Baruch, Hoover mobilized what he called "the spirit of self-sacrifice." Huge publicity campaigns promoted "wheatless" and "meatless" days each week and encouraged families to plant "victory" gardens. Half a million people went door to door to enlist housewives in the cause of food conservation. "Do not permit your child to take a bite or two from an apple and throw the rest away; nowadays even children must be taught to be patriotic to the core," joked *Life*. Spurred by high prices, farmers brought ever more marginal lands into cultivation, as their real income increased 25 percent. When in later years prices fell and rain did not, both farmers and their land would suffer from the rush to maximize profits and production.

A Fuel Administration met the army's energy needs by increasing production and limiting domestic consumption. Transportation snarls required more drastic action. In December 1917 the U.S. Railroad Administration simply took over rail lines for the duration of the war. Government coordination, together with a new system of permits, got freight moving. Federally imposed "daylight savings time" stretched the workday and saved fuel as well. Railroad workers turned out to be among the chief beneficiaries of nationalization. Their wages grew by $300 million. Treasury Secretary McAdoo, a master organizer who also served as railroad administrator, ordered equal pay for women and fought discrimination against blacks. Railroad unions won government recognition, an eight-hour day, and a grievance procedure. For the first time in decades labor unrest subsided and trains finally ran on schedule.

The size and scope of government increased enormously during the 18 months of American participation in the war. The number of federal employees soared from just under 400,000 in 1916 to over 850,000 by 1918. The modern bureaucratic state received a powerful boost. Speeding trends already under way, a host of federal agencies and committees centralized authority and cooperated with business and labor to meet the demands of war. The wartime bureaucracy was quickly dismantled at the end of the war, but it set a powerful precedent for the future.

War Work

The war benefited working men and women, though not as much as their employers. Government contracts guaranteed high wages, an eight-hour day, and equal pay for comparable work. To keep people on the job, federal contracting agencies encouraged employers to "manage" personnel. Arsenal officers and munitions contractors attended special classes at Dartmouth College to learn the young science of personnel management. American industry moved one step closer to the

War posters exhorted Americans to pull together for victory.

"welfare capitalism" of the 1920s, in which employers used profit-sharing, company unions, and personnel departments to forestall worker discontent.

During the war, personnel management was not enough to guarantee industrial peace. In 1917 American workers called 4450 strikes, the most in American history. To keep factories running smoothly, President Wilson created the National War Labor Board (NWLB) early in 1918. The NWLB arbitrated over 1000 labor disputes, helped to increase wages and decrease hours, and established overtime pay. In return for pledges not to strike, it guaranteed the rights of unions to organize and bargain collectively. NWLB examiners oversaw elections for shop committees in the steel industry, long impervious to unionization. When the Smith and Wesson arms plant in Springfield, Massachusetts, and the Western Union telegraph company discriminated against union employees, the government commandeered both firms.

Given such sympathetic federal support, organized labor grew. President Samuel Gompers of the American Federation of Labor (AFL), the nation's largest union, represented labor on Wilson's National Defense Council and later on the War Labor Board. Membership in the AFL increased from 2.7 million members in 1916 to nearly 4 million in 1919. On Armistice Day Gompers complained that labor had yet to achieve all the gains it needed. What rights had been won, Gompers justifiably feared, would end with peace.

War work sparked massive internal migrations of labor to meet shortages as the war choked off immigration from abroad and the draft depleted manpower at home. Factory owners scoured the country for a fresh labor supply. Industrial cities, no matter how small, soon swelled with newcomers. Between 1917 and 1920, some 100,000 Mexicans crossed the border into Texas, California, New Mexico, and Arizona. Some Mexican-Americans left segregated barrios in the West for northern war plants. Most worked on farms and ranches, freed from military service by the deferment of all agricultural labor.

Northern labor agents fanned out across the South to recruit young blacks. African-American newspapers like the Chicago *Defender* summoned them north to the "Land of Hope." "I beg you, my brother, to leave the benighted land," urged one editor. "Get out of the South." Over the war years more than 400,000 migrated to the booming industrial centers of the North. The number of African-Americans in Chicago more than doubled. In Cleveland it quadrupled; in Detroit it jumped sixfold. Towns like Hattiesburg, Mississippi, were decimated by the drain. Finally, under pressure from southern politicians, the U.S. Employment Service suspended its program to assist blacks moving north.

Largely unskilled and semiskilled, blacks took factory jobs in the steel mills of Pennsylvania, the war plants of Massachusetts, and the brickyards of New Jersey. Mostly rural backgrounds left them unprepared for life in the city. The new arrivals, noted one magazine, were often "crowded into dark rooms, . . . shivering with the cold from which they do not know how to protect themselves." The Urban League and other voluntary organizations tried to meet the housing shortage, but the basic problems—high rents and low wages—remained unresolved.

W. E. B. Du Bois and other African-American leaders urged their followers to "forget our special grievances and close our ranks shoulder to shoulder with our own white fellow citizens." So they did, deferring dreams of equality and material gain until the war was over. In France, where 200,000 blacks served, only 42,000 saw combat. Four regiments of the all-black 93rd Division, brigaded with the French army, were among the first Americans in the trenches and among the most decorated units in the U.S. Army. Three of the regiments later received the Croix de Guerre for heroism.

At home the war aggravated racial tensions. Southern lynching parties murdered 38 blacks in 1917 and 58 in 1918. In 1919, after the war ended, more than 70 were hung, some still in uniform. Housing shortages and job competition helped to spark race riots across the North. In almost every city blacks, stirred by war rhetoric of freedom and democracy, showed new militancy by fighting back. In mid-1917 some 40 blacks and 9 whites died when East St. Louis erupted in racial violence. During the bloody "red summer" of 1919 race wars broke out in Washington, D.C., Omaha, Nebraska, and New York City. In July a two-week reign of racial terror began in Chicago after whites stoned a black who had drifted into their section of a segregated beach. Thousands were burned out of their homes, hundreds injured, and 38 killed—15 whites and 23 blacks.

Just as the war lured African-Americans to northern factories, it brought as many as a million more women into the labor force. Most were young and single. Sometimes they took over jobs once held by men as railroad engineers, drill press operators, and electric lift truck drivers. The prewar trend toward higher paying jobs temporarily intensified. More and more women worked in offices, schools, hospitals, and telephone exchanges. Some of the most spectacular gains in defense and government work evaporated after the war. When the country demobilized, tens of thousands of women lost jobs as army nurses, defense workers, and wartime administrators. Agencies such as the Women's Service Section of the Railroad Administration, which fought sexual harassment and discrimination, simply went out of business, while organized labor remained hostile.

The constraints of war brought more women than ever into the job market. These women work on a production line manufacturing bullets. The novelty of the situation seems evident from the fashionable high-heeled high-button shoes that they wear—ill-suited to the conditions in an armaments plant.

Propaganda and Civil Liberties

"Once lead this people into war," President Wilson said before American entry into the conflict, "and they'll forget there ever was such a thing as tolerance." Americans did succumb to a ruthless hysteria during World War I, but they had help. Intense prewar opposition to American participation coupled with pressing fears over public apathy led the president to create the Committee on Public Information (CPI), headed by George Creel, a California newspaperman. Surrounding himself with old muckrakers such as Ida Tarbell and Ray Stannard Baker, Creel launched what he called "a fight for the *minds* of men, for the 'conquest of their convictions.'" The CPI mobilized artists to design colorful war posters, including James Flagg's famous "I Want *You* for the U.S. Army." It distributed 75 million pamphlets, issued 6000 press releases, and sponsored war expositions attended by 10 million people in two dozen cities.

Initially committed to a simple "faith in the fact," the CPI soon developed into the most powerful propaganda mill the nation had ever known. An army of "Four-Minute Men," 75,000 fast-talking orators, invaded movie theaters, lodge halls, schools, and churches to keep patriotism at "white heat" with four minutes of war tirades. The CPI organized "Loyalty Leagues" in ethnic communities and sponsored parades and rallies, including a much-publicized immigrant "pilgrimage" to the birthplace of George Washington. Such propaganda often worked. People whose anthem had been the pacifist song "I Didn't Raise My Boy to Be a Soldier" were singing George M. Cohan's patriotic "Over There" six months later.

The line between patriotic appeal and intolerance proved impossible to maintain. Overly enthusiastic parents enlisted their five-year-olds in paramilitary clubs like the "Khaki Babes." As war hysteria mounted, volunteerism blossomed into an orgy of "100-percent Americanism." Immigrants, aliens, radicals, and pacifists came under suspicion as a coercive urge to conformity took hold. German-Americans naturally became special targets. Local influenza epidemics were blamed on German spies contaminating water supplies. In Iowa the governor made it a crime to speak German in public. Hamburgers were renamed "Salisbury steak"; German measles, "liberty measles." In April 1918 a mob outside of St. Louis seized Robert Praeger, a naturalized German-American who had tried to enlist in the navy, bound him in an American flag, and lynched him. After deliberating for 25 minutes a jury found the leaders not guilty.

In 1917 Congress gave hysteria more legal bite. The Espionage Act provided $10,000 fines and 20-year sentences for anyone convicted of obstructing military operations (including recruitment), aiding the enemy, or mailing treasonous material. In 1918 the Sedition Act outlawed in one broad stroke "any disloyal, profane, scurrilous, or abusive language about the form of government of the United States, or the Constitution of the United States, or the flag of the United States, or the uniform of the Army or Navy." Under these acts, 1500 citizens were arrested for offenses including denouncing the draft, criticizing the Red Cross, and complaining about taxes. Opponents of the war, especially radical groups, suffered most. The Industrial Workers of the World (IWW), a militant labor union centered in western states, saw the war as a battle among capitalists and threatened to strike mining and lumber companies in an anti-war protest. In September 1917 federal agents raided the Chicago headquarters of the IWW—familiarly known as the "Wobblies"—seized membership lists and office equipment, and arrested 113 of its leaders in the name of patriotism. The crusade succeeded in destroying the union.

Similarly, when the Socialist party stridently opposed the "capitalist" war, the postmaster general banned a dozen Socialist publications from the mail, though the party was a legal organization that had elected mayors, municipal officials, and congressmen. In June 1918 government agents arrested Eugene V. Debs, the Socialist candidate in the presidential election of 1912, for an antiwar speech to the Socialist convention in Canton, Ohio. Promptly found guilty of sedition, Debs received a 10-year sentence. Running for the presidency from his jail cell in 1920, he received nearly 1 million votes.

The Supreme Court endorsed the aggressive wartime assaults on civil liberties and dissent. In *Schenck v. United States* (1919), the Court unanimously affirmed the conviction of a Socialist party officer who had mailed pamphlets urging potential army inductees to resist the draft. "When a nation is at war," wrote Justice Oliver Wendell Holmes, Jr., "many things that might be said in time of peace are such a hindrance to its effort that their utterance will not be endured." Schenck's pamphlets, Holmes concluded, created "a clear and present danger" for the safety of the nation. Holmes and his associate Louis Brandeis later sought to narrow the scope of the *Schenck* decision, but in *Abrams v. United States* (1919) the majority upheld, by 7–2, the verdict against Russian immigrant Jacob Abrams, whose pamphlets had denounced an American intervention in Russia to fight the Bolsheviks. Although Holmes saw no "clear and present danger," the Court ruled that the pamphlets tended to discourage the American war effort.

Over There

American forces began to reach France in the fall of 1917, but it was not until March 1918 and the German spring offensive that they helped to turn the tide. General John Pershing, commander of the American Expeditionary Force (AEF), wisely held his raw troops out of battle for several months of additional training. Pershing had kept his force separate, in part because American politicians wanted the AEF to preserve its identity, in part because Allied generals disagreed over strategy. Pershing understood, too, that "when the war ends, our position will be stronger if our army acting as such shall have played a distinct and definite part." But as the German army advanced within 50 miles of Paris, Pershing rushed 70,000 American troops to the front.

Early in May American units helped to block the Germans at the town of Château-Thierry. Four weeks later they met the German spearhead at Belleau Wood. When the French sounded retreat, one marine captain snorted, "Retreat, hell!" and the Americans attacked instead, even though it cost half their force to drive the Germans out of the woods. Two more German attacks, one at Amiens, the other just east of the Marne River, ended in costly German retreats. On September 12, 1918, half a million American soldiers and a smaller number of French troops overran the German stronghold at Saint-Mihiel in four days. Even as the strategic initiative shifted to the Allies, the slaughter continued. As nearly 900,000 Americans moved north along a 24-mile front between the Meuse River and the Argonne Forest, five undermanned and dispirited German divisions, just over 100,000 men, held them off for almost two months. According to one estimate 10 Americans died for every dead German in the Meuse-Argonne campaign.

As the German army retreated and war weariness drained morale at home, Germany's civilian leaders sought an armistice. They hoped in particular to negotiate terms along the lines laid out by Woodrow Wilson in a speech to Congress in

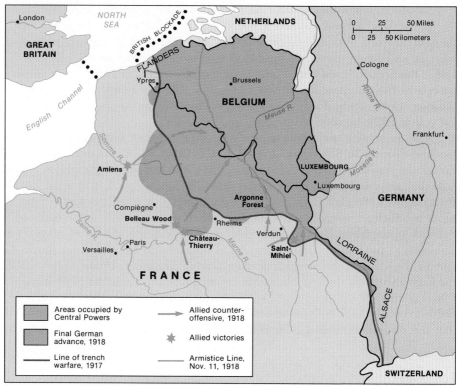

THE FINAL GERMAN OFFENSIVE AND ALLIED COUNTERATTACK, 1918
On the morning of March 21, 1918, the Germans launched a spring offensive designed to cripple the Allies. Sixty-three German divisions sliced through Allied lines for the first time since 1914 and plunged to within 50 miles of Paris. The tide turned in July, when the Germans were stopped at the Marne. The Allied counterattack, with notable American successes at Château-Thierry, Belleau Wood, Saint-Mihiel, and Meuse-Argonne, broke the German war effort.

January 1918. In it, Wilson presented his vision for a postwar peace that encompassed "Fourteen Points." The key provisions called for open diplomacy, free seas and free trade, disarmament, national self-rule, and an "association of nations" acting together to keep peace—nothing less than a new world order with an end to selfish nationalism, unilateral action, and war. Wilson the progressive was applying the tactics and goals of domestic reform to the taming of world-class rivalries.

Allied leaders were not all impressed. "President Wilson and his Fourteen Points bore me," French Premier Georges Clemenceau said. "Even God Almighty has only ten!" But Wilson's idealistic platform had also been designed to save the Allies deeper embarrassment. Almost as soon as it came to power in 1917, the new Bolshevik government in Moscow had begun publishing secret treaties from the czar's archives. Those treaties revealed that the Allies had gone to war for selfish ends such as the acquisition of territories and colonies, not the high principles they claimed. Wilson had given their cause a nobler purpose. His ideals stirred deep yearnings among German liberals. On October 6 Wilson received a telegram from Berlin requesting an immediate armistice. Within a month Turkey and Austria surrendered. Early in November the Kaiser was overthrown and fled to neutral Holland. On November 11, 1918, just before dawn, German officers filed into Allied headquarters in a converted railroad car near Compiègne, France, and signed the surrender.

The guns of August fell silent for the first time in four years. Of the 2 million Americans who had served in France, 50,000 had died in combat and 230,000 had been wounded. By comparison, the war claimed 1.8 million Germans, 1.7 million Russians, 1.4 million French, 1.2 million Austro-Hungarians, and nearly a million Britons. The American contribution had nonetheless been crucial to victory, providing vital convoys at sea and fresh, confident troops on land. The United States emerged from the war stronger than ever. Europe, on the other hand, looked forward—as one newspaper put it—to "Disaster . . . Exhaustion . . . Revolution."

THE LOST PEACE

As the S.S. *George Washington* approached the coast of France in mid-December 1918 the mist suddenly lifted, an omen of good hope. On board were the president of the United States, a group of advisers called the "Inquiry," and an entourage that included Committee on Public Information chief George Creel, there to make a movie of the historic mission. Woodrow Wilson was going to represent the United States at the peace conference at Versailles, outside Paris, where a world of problems awaited settlement. Large portions of European cities and farmlands had been shelled into ruin, scarred with trenches, barbed wire, and the debris of war. Fifty million people lay dead or maimed from the fighting. Starvation and typhus spread across the continent, eventually killing another 6 million people in the first year of peace. In eastern Europe especially, the social order had broken down and revolution unsettled the land. Poles fought with Czechs, Slavs with Italians, Turks with Greeks, Bolshevik "Reds" with czarist "Whites," Jews with Arabs. With the old world order so evidently in shambles, it seemed clear to Wilson that vigorous, immediate action was imperative.

Thus the president hand-picked the Peace Commission that accompanied him, including only loyal supporters like Secretary of State Lansing and Colonel House. Not a single member of the Republican-controlled Senate was included. What promised to make negotiations easier at Versailles, however, created a crippling liability in Washington, where Republicans cast a hostile eye on the impending Democratic peace treaty.

The Treaty of Versailles

Woodrow Wilson was the first president in office to meet with a foreign head of state; in fact, he met leaders of 27 nations from five continents. The most important were David Lloyd George, the prime minister of England, who had promised to squeeze Germany "until the pips squeak"; French premier Georges Clemenceau, nicknamed "Le Tigre" and obsessively dedicated to French security; and Vittorio Orlando, prime minister of Italy, who kept a covetous eye on neighboring

Daily Lives

TIME AND TRAVEL

The Doughboys Abroad

At ten in the morning on July 20, 1917, Secretary of War Newton Baker tied a blindfold over his eyes, reached into a huge glass bowl at the Senate Office Building, and drew the first number in a new draft lottery. The United States, with barely 180,000 men in the service, had begun to raise an army. During the first weeks after American entry into World War I, only 32,000 more volunteered. Yet by the time the conflict ended 16 months later, nearly 2 million men had donned uniforms, learned the manual of arms and close order drill, and gone off to fight in Europe. For the first time the New World was invading the Old, and for most of those who went, it was their first trip from home.

Armed against the enemy, scrubbed and clothed, drilled until they dropped, the "doughboys" marched out of their training camps and up the gangplanks of the "Atlantic Ferry"—the ships that conveyed them to Europe. The infantrymen were called "doughboys" for the "dough" of clay that soldiers had used to clean their white belts in the 1850s. Each man was outfitted with a pack, a weapon, a set of uniforms, and a "safety" razor, a new device that quickly altered American shaving habits.

Almost half the soldiers sailed on British vessels. Some were fortunate enough to ship out on refitted luxury liners, but most made the voyage in converted freighters. "Assigned quarters below decks," one private reported, "the blackest, foulest, most congested hole that I ever set foot into." A few who never made it across died from anthrax in the horsehair of their new shaving brushes. It was a poignant taste of things to come. Disease killed more Americans than enemy fire. Nearly 50,000 troops died in the influenza pandemic of 1918.

The first American troops, a division of army regulars and a battalion of marines, arrived in France at the end of June 1917. Two months later the first volunteers landed, wearing spring parade uniforms and carrying just 10 rounds of ammunition apiece. They were squeezed into "40-and-8's"—French freight cars designed to hold 40 men and 8 horses—and carried inland to training areas. In the end the American Expeditionary Force purchased more of its supplies in Europe than it shipped from the "arsenal of democracy" in the United States. The American doughboy typically wore a steel helmet modeled on the British "Tommy" and fought with French artillery. More often than not American fliers went aloft in European-made planes.

With the United States at war for only 18 months (from April 1917 to November 1918), most American soldiers spent more time in training and on leave than in the trenches. To keep the men from becoming restless, company commanders marched their troops against imaginary enemies in never-ending exercises. "Every hill in this vicinity has been captured or lost at least ten times," wrote one weary infantryman who had to keep training even after the armistice. Soldiers complained about "cooties" (lice) and food (so bad that many reported a 10 percent weight loss within weeks of arriving). Most of all they hated military discipline. Used to freewheeling individualism and equality, Americans of all ranks abhorred hierarchy and subordination.

Enlisted men groused about army life, but touring France, whether on leave

Daily Lives

After months of training state-side, the American Expeditionary Force sailed to Europe on the troop ships of the "Atlantic Ferry." Most soldiers departed from Hoboken, New Jersey, and almost half made the journey aboard British vessels.

or in troop transports, awed them. Paris was both exhilarating and titillating, with women who danced the "Can-Can" and cried "oo-la-la." In fact, warned an army journal, too many soldiers expected France to be an "international Coney Island, a universal pleasure resort." As it turned out, the sheer beauty of the place impressed them more than the entertainment. Most of the doughboys arrived in the spring and summer of 1918, when France was awash in color. "The country is green and covered with flowers," observed a young infantryman. "It is a continuous garden."

The antiquity of Europe struck the doughboys even more. "The church here," one wrote, "is very, very old, probably built sometime in the 12th or 13th century. Saint Louis the Crusader, King of France, attended a service there on three occasions and Jeanne d'Arc was there several times." The Europeans seemed old too. Elderly women in black shawls of mourning often were the only ones left in shattered villages, deprived by war of their men. "My but the people are old fashioned," remarked a soldier. "They still

harvest with cradles and sickles." Everything endorsed the American myth of the Old World as hidebound and worn and the New as modern and vital.

It was as if they had become crusaders, off on what one doughboy called "a glorious adventure" to save beleaguered Europe. They witnessed "thrilling air fights" from the ground and spectacular artillery fire—often from a distance. Up close, the shellfire could maim and kill, sometimes leave men frozen with "shell shock." Disillusion and discontent overcame British and French troops after years in the trenches, but most doughboys never fought long enough to lose their sense of wonder and delight. A year after the war ended a veteran wrote: "I know how we all cried to get back to the States. But now that we are here, I must admit for myself at least that I am lost and somehow strangely lonesome. These our own United States are truly artificial and bare. There is no romance or color here, nothing to suffer for and laugh at." Their tours of duty were short, but the doughboys traveled far.

territory. Together with Wilson they comprised the "Big Four." War had united them; now peacemaking threatened to divide them.

In December Wilson traveled to Europe to prevent, in his words, "a peace of loot or spoliation." Everywhere he went, cheering throngs greeted him. In Paris 2 million people threw flowers in his path as he made his way down the Champs-Elysées; in Italy the most enthusiastic crowds of all hailed him as the "peacemaker from America." And Wilson believed them, unaware of how determined the victors were to punish the vanquished Germans.

The sweeping reforms he proposed had taken Allied diplomats by surprise. Hungry for colonies that had been German and eager to see Germany crushed and disarmed, their secret treaties already divided the territories of the Central Powers. Germany offered to surrender on the basis of Wilson's Fourteen Points, but the Allies refused to accept them. When Wilson threatened to negotiate peace on his own, Allied leaders finally agreed—but only for the moment.

Noticeably absent when the peace conference convened on January 18, 1919, were the Russians. Fearful of the spread of revolutionary communism, none of the Western democracies had recognized the Bolshevik regime in Moscow. Instead, France and Britain were helping to finance Bolshevik adversaries in a civil war. They had blockaded Russian ports, landed troops on Russian soil, and persuaded President Wilson to send a small expeditionary force to Siberia in 1918, then another to Vladivostok on the Sea of Japan in 1919. The Soviets would neither forgive nor forget this instrusion.

During the grueling negotiations, Wilson was forced to yield several of his Fourteen Points. The European Allies resisted even putting free trade and freedom of the seas on the agenda. His "open diplomacy" was conducted behind closed doors by the Big Four themselves. Peace without victory gave way to a

On June 28, 1919, representatives of the new German republic were herded into the Hall of Mirrors in the old world palace of Louis XIV at Versailles, just outside Paris. Glumly they signed the peace treaty, which they had never seen before. The Germans, observed one reporter, suffered a "horrible humiliation." Here, Woodrow Wilson (in the red chair) sits with the other Allied leaders.

"guilt clause" that placed responsibility for the war on Germany. Worse still, the Allies saddled their enemies with reparations that eventually reached the impoverishing sum of $33 billion. The only mention of disarmament involved Germany, which was permanently barred from rearming.

Wilson did achieve a number of successes. He convinced Clemenceau to scale down demands for $200 billion in German payments in exchange for promises of aid if Germany attacked France. His pleas for national self-determination led to the creation of a dozen new states in Europe, including Yugoslavia, Hungary, and Austria. (Poland and Czechoslovakia, also carved from the empires of the Central Powers, contained millions of Germans whose national affiliation was thus violated.) Although former colonies were not granted the sovereignty Wilson desired, they gained new status as "mandates" of the victors, who were obligated to prepare them for eventual independence. The old German and Turkish empires in the Middle East and Africa became the responsibility of France and England, while Japan took over German possessions in the Far East.

Wilson never lost sight of his main concern—a League of Nations. He had given so much ground precisely because he believed such a body could correct any mistakes in the peace settlement. As constituted, the League was composed of a general Body of Delegates, a select Executive Council, and a Court of International Justice. Members promised to submit all war-provoking disagreements to arbitration and to isolate aggressors by cutting off commercial and military trade. Article X (which Wilson called "the heart of the convenant") bound members to respect one another's independence and territory and to join together against attack. "A living thing is born," the president told a general session of the conference in mid-February 1919. "It is definitely a guarantee of peace."

Wilson left immediately for home to calm congressional opposition. The previous October he had called on Americans to endorse his liberal peace plan by returning Democratic majorities to Congress. Instead, disaffected by wartime controls, attacks on civil liberties, and new taxes, voters gave both houses to the Republicans. A slim majority of two in the Senate put Wilson's archrival, Henry Cabot Lodge of Massachusetts, in the chairman's seat of the all-important Foreign Relations Committee. A Harvard-educated disciple of T.R., Lodge bristled at the notion of Wilson as the foremost intellectual in Washington. "I never expected to hate anyone in politics with the hatred I feel toward Wilson," he confessed.

While most of the country favored the League, Lodge was set against it. Lodge loved the Republican party more than world peace and certainly did not want the Democrats to win votes by taking credit for the treaty. Yet less partisan motives also moved him. For decades he had fought to preserve American freedom of action in foreign affairs. Now he believed Americans were being asked to "subject our own will to the will of other nations." Securing the signatures of 37 senators, enough to block passage of any treaty, Lodge rose in the Senate just before midnight on March 3 to read a "round robin" resolution against the League. "Woodrow Wilson's League of Nations died in the Senate tonight," concluded the New York *Sun*. Wilson began to suffer again from the mind-numbing headaches that always afflicted him under pressure.

Early in March the president returned to Paris for a final round of horse-trading with the Europeans. He withdrew often to nurse a stubborn case of influenza and bang out new amendments on his battered old typewriter. A twitch that had developed at his left eye now convulsed the whole left side of his face. Mindful of Senate critics, he engineered three changes he thought would satisfy them: keeping domestic affairs free from League interference; preserving the Monroe Doctrine; and permitting members to quit with two years' warning. The Allies exacted a price, including Japanese control of Shantung and additional reparations for the British. Forced to sign a treaty they had no role in writing, the Germans suffered a terrible national humiliation of crushing debt, impounded colonies, and war guilt.

The Battle for the Treaty

Wilson was about to suffer his own humiliation. On July 10, 1919, just one day after returning home, he drove to Capitol Hill to present the treaty to the Senate. "Dare we reject it and break the heart of the world?" he asked the senators. Fourteen Republicans and four Democrats were happy to do just that. "Irreconcilable" opponents of internationalism, they vowed to kill what one of them called "the unholy thing with the holy name." Twenty-three "strong reservationists," led by Lodge, sought to amend the treaty with major changes requiring Allied approval. Twelve "mild reservationists" wanted minimal alterations, mainly interpretive in nature.

Wilson's only hope of winning the necessary two-thirds majority lay in combining loyal Democrats with Republican "mild reservationists." But temperamentally the president could not abide compromise. Worn out by the concessions already wrung from him in Paris, he resisted more change at home and, despite his doctor's warnings, took his case to the people in a month-long railroad stump across the nation.

In Pueblo, Colorado, before a crowd of 10,000, he gave perhaps the greatest oration of his career, speaking movingly of American soldiers killed in France and American boys whom the League one day would spare from death. Listeners wept openly. That evening, utterly exhausted, the president collapsed in a spasm of pain. On October 2, four days after returning to the White House, he fell to the bathroom floor, knocked unconscious by a stroke. For six weeks Wilson could do no work at all, and for months after he worked only an hour or so a day. His second wife, Edith Bolling Wilson, his secretary, and his doctor handled the routine business of government, concealing the seriousness of his condition from the country. Wilson recovered slowly but never fully. He walked only with the aid of a cane, became more irritable, and at times broke into tears. More and more the battle for the treaty consumed his fading energies.

On November 19 Lodge finally reported the treaty out of committee, appending exactly 14 amendments (to match Wilson's Fourteen Points). The most important asserted that the United States assumed no obligation under Article X of the treaty to come to the aid of League members if their territory or political independence were violated, unless Congress consented. Whatever ill will Lodge bore Wilson, his objections did not destroy the treaty but only weakened it by protecting the congressional prerogative to declare war. Wilson believed Lodge had delivered a "knife thrust at the heart of the treaty" and refused to accept any changes. "The Senate must take its medicine," he told the French ambassador.

Under orders from the president, Democrats joined Republicans and "irreconcilables" to defeat the treaty with Lodge's reservations. An attempt to pass the unamended treaty failed. Although four-fifths of the senators favored it in some form, Wilson and Lodge stubbornly refused to compromise. When the modified treaty came before the Senate for final consideration in March 1920, 21 Democrats disobeyed the president by voting for it, enough to produce a 49–35 majority but seven votes short of the necessary two-thirds. The Treaty of Versailles was dead, and loyal Democrats had been forced to deliver the killing blow. Not until July 1921 did Congress enact a joint resolution ending the war. The United States, which had fought separately from the Allies, made a separate peace as well.

Red Scare

Peace abroad did not bring peace at home. On May Day 1919, six months after the war ended, mobs in a dozen cities broke up Socialist parades, injured hundreds, and killed three people. Later that month, when a spectator at a Victory Loan rally in Washington refused to stand for the national anthem, a sailor shot him in the back. The stadium crowd applauded. On the floor of the Senate Kenneth McKellar of Tennessee advocated sending citizens with radical beliefs to a penal colony on Guam.

The spontaneous violence and extremism occurred because Americans believed they were under attack. Rapid and unplanned demobilization had brought inflation, unemployment, and a chilling wave of strikes—3600 in 1919 alone. Over 350,000 steel workers and 450,000 coal miners struck for higher wages as the nation plunged into postwar turmoil. In Boston even the police walked off their jobs. When a strike by conservative trade unionists paralyzed Seattle for five days in January, Mayor Ole Hanson draped his car in an American flag and led troops through the streets in a show of force. Hanson blamed radicals, while Congress ascribed the national ills to Bolshevist agents, inspired by the revolution in Russia.

In truth, the menace of communist subversion was entirely overblown. With Socialist Eugene V. Debs in prison, his dwindling party numbered only about 30,000. Radicals at first hoped that the success of the Russian Revolution would help reverse their fortunes. But they discovered that most Americans found the prospect of "Bolshevik" revolution threatening, especially after March 1919, when the new Russian government formed the Comintern to foment revolution in other countries. Furthermore, in 1919 John Reed and Benjamin Gitlow deserted the Socialists to form the more radical Communist Labor party. About the same time, a separate Communist party was created, mostly by Slavic radicals (fewer than 7 percent of whom could speak English). In all, both parties could count no more than 40,000 members.

On April 28, Mayor Hanson received a small brown parcel at his office, evidently another present from an admirer of his tough patriotism. It was a homemade bomb. Within days, 20 such packages were discovered, including ones sent to John D. Rockefeller, Supreme Court Justice Oliver Wendell Holmes, and Postmaster General Albert Burleson. On June 2 bombs exploded simultaneously in eight different cities. One of them demolished the front porch of A. Mitchell Palmer, attorney general of the United States. The bomb thrower was blown to bits in the explosion, but enough remained to identify him as an Italian anarchist from Philadelphia. Americans, already edgy over Bolshevism and labor militancy, assumed they were under attack by an organized conspiracy to overthrow the government.

Palmer, a Quaker and a staunch progressive, hardened in the wake of the bombings. With an emergency appropriation of $500,000 he launched an antiradical campaign on November 7, 1919. The Palmer raids in a dozen cities rounded up hundreds of suspects, who were held in violation of their legal rights. On December 21, 1919, a total of 249 aliens, most of whom had no criminal records, were marched aboard the army transport *Buford* (nicknamed the "Soviet Ark") and deported to the Soviet Union. Among them were radicals Emma Goldman and Alexander Berkman, several philosophical anarchists pledged against violence, and a few communists.

A new round of raids began in January 1920. In a single night, government agents invaded private homes, meeting halls, and pool parlors in 33 cities. They took nearly 2000 alleged communists into custody without warrants. Beatings often accompanied the arrests. Prisoners were marched through streets in chains, crammed into dilapidated jails, and held incommunicado without hearings. Arrests continued at the rate of 200 a week through March. State after state passed new statutes outlawing radical unions, and local vigilance committees even screened the loyalty of schoolteachers. In Centralia, Washington, vigilantes spirited radical labor organizer Wesley Everest from jail, castrated him, and hanged him from the Chehalis River bridge as they riddled his body with bullets. The county coroner ruled it a suicide.

Such wholesale abuses of civil liberties provoked a backlash. After the New York legislature expelled five duly elected Socialists in 1919, responsible politicians—from former presidential candidate Charles Evans Hughes to Ohio Senator Warren Harding—denounced the action. A revolt against Palmer by the Labor Department, where assistant secretary Louis Post refused to issue more deportation orders, ended the "deportation delirium" early in 1920. Then Palmer overreached himself by predicting a revolutionary uprising for May 1, 1920. Buildings were put under guard and state militia called to readiness. Nothing happened. Four months later, when a wagonload of bombs exploded on Wall Street, Palmer conjured up a Bolshevik conspiracy. Despite 33 deaths and over 200 injuries,

On September 16, 1920, as lunch-hour crowds filled the heart of New York's financial district, a wagonload of bombs exploded at the corner of Broad and Wall streets. Thirty-three people were killed and over 200 injured in the blast, probably the work of deranged anarchists. All of the dead were workers—runners, stenographers, and clerks. The nation, though horrified, saw no communist plot, as Attorney General A. Mitchell Palmer charged. The Red Scare at last was over.

Americans assumed it was the work of a few demented anarchists (which it probably was) and went about business as usual.

Not for another 20 years would the United States assume a leading position in international affairs. And the spirit of reform at home waned as well. When war came, progressivism had furnished the bureaucratic weapons to organize the fight, but the push for social justice and toleration had been overshadowed by a patriotic frenzy.

War changed Americans in important ways. They experienced a centralized and planned economy for the first time. Propaganda shaped diverse ethnic, racial, social class, and gender differences into a uniform set of national issues. Such singlemindedness would not quickly disappear. War work drew millions from country to city, from farm to factory. The army mixed millions of recruits from thousands of hometowns. They did not simply learn to fight. Some learned to read, to sleep in a bed, to eat regular meals, and to take regular baths. After seeing Europe, they returned like tourists in uniform to tell of its wonders. Provincial America became more cosmopolitan, urban, and homogenized. With the war over, the nation turned from idealistic crusades to the practical business of getting and spending.

SIGNIFICANT EVENTS

1901	Hay–Pauncefote Treaty authorizes U.S. to build canal across the Central American isthmus
1902	Platt Amendment ratified
1904	Roosevelt Corollary to Monroe Doctrine
1905	Treaty of Portsmouth ends Russo–Japanese War
1907	"Gentlemen's agreement" with Japan; "Great White Fleet" embarks on world tour
1911	Mexican Revolution erupts
1913	Secretary of State William Jennings Bryan begins negotiating "cooling-off" treaties
1914	U.S. Navy invades Veracruz; Archduke Franz Ferdinand assassinated; World War I begins; Panama Canal opens
1915	Japan issues Twenty-one Demands; Germany proclaims war zone around British Isles; *Lusitania* torpedoed; Secretary of State Bryan resigns; *Arabic* pledge; Wilson endorses preparedness
1916	*Sussex* pledge; General John Pershing invades Mexico in pursuit of Pancho Villa; Wilson reelected president
1917	Wilson calls for "peace without victory"; Germany resumes unrestricted submarine warfare; Zimmermann telegram released; Russian Revolution breaks out; U.S. enters World War I; Selective Service Act passed; War Industries Board created
1918	Wilson's Fourteen Points for peace; Eugene Debs jailed under Sedition Act; influenza epidemic; Germany sues for peace; armistice declared
1919	Paris Peace Conference; *Schenck v. United States* affirms Espionage Act; Red Summer; Chicago race riot; Senate rejects Treaty of Versailles
1920	Palmer raids; Red Scare

PART FIVE
THE PERILS
OF DEMOCRACY

In the wake of World War I, the editors of the American progressive journal *The New Republic* despaired that "the war did no good to anybody. Those of its generation whom it did not kill, it crippled, wasted, or used up." With the specter of Russian Bolshevism looming, parliamentary governments across Europe struggled to establish what President Warren Harding in the United States called "normalcy": a mixture of material prosperity and political stability.

By the mid-1920s despair had given way to hope. The postwar recession lifted. Woodrow Wilson's vision of a world made safe for democracy no longer seemed a naive hope. In both political and material terms democracy seemed to be advancing almost everywhere. Great Britain eliminated restrictions on suffrage for men; and between 1920 and 1928 women gained the vote in both Britain and the United States. Hapsburg Germany transformed itself into the Weimar Republic, whose constitution provided universal suffrage and a bill of rights. Across central and eastern Europe, the new nations carved out of the old Russian and Austro-Hungarian empires, along with the previously independent Romania, Bulgaria, Greece, and Albania, attempted to create governments along similarly democratic lines.

The winds of political reform blew from Europe across the Middle East through Asia. No longer were the nationalists of these areas willing to see their people and resources exploited for the benefit of foreigners. Nor were they willing to see their cultures erased by Westerners. Some Asians, like Mao Tse-tung in China and Ho Chi Minh in Indochina, saw in communism the means of liberation for their oppressed peoples. But even Asian Marxists aligned themselves with the

powerful force of nationalism. In India, the Congress party formed by Mohandas K. Gandhi (1869–1948) brought together socialists and powerful industrial capitalists. Through tactics of nonviolence and boycotts of British goods, Indian nationalists wrested concessions from the British on political representation, economic autonomy, and eventual self-government. In Turkey, Kemal Atatürk in 1923 abolished the sultanate and established the Turkish Republic with all the trappings of a Western democratic state.

The spread of democracy had a material side as well. The credibility of parliamentary governments depended heavily on their ability to restore and maintain prosperity. In the second half of the 1920s the world economy expanded. Scientific and technological discoveries created new products, while improving and lowering the costs of old ones. Some optimists suggested that innovations in manufacturing, like Henry Ford's moving assembly line, augured an era where plenty would replace want. Increased earnings encouraged a democratic culture of consumption, whether it was buying radios in France or Western-style fashions in Tokyo (below, left). Products like the automobile, once available only to the rich, were increasingly accessible to people of all classes. Ford himself became an international hero and German and Russian engineers used the term *Fordismus* to characterize modern industrial techniques.

Along with the automobile the mass media introduced a revolution in world culture. The impact of movies, radio, and mass circulation magazines, while greatest in the United States, was felt around the globe. Some social critics saw in the pervasive reach of the media a way to overcome the divisions among people and the disintegrative force of modern society. The movie camera, observed social critic Lewis Mumford, brought ordinary people into the public world. Once-remote people and places became accessible and famil-iar. Stories, names, phrases, images, and ideas could become the common property of all. "In short, it seems to be the nature of radio to encourage people to think and feel alike," two prominent psychologists concluded. Consumption of culture as well as manufactured goods seemed to walk hand in hand with the democracy of the masses.

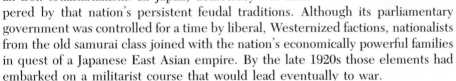

But often the foundations upon which democracy rested were fragile. The Bolsheviks, led by Lenin and the young Joseph Stalin, demonstrated how readily talk of "the masses" and "democratic socialism" could mask an iron totalitarianism. In Japan, democracy was hampered by that nation's persistent feudal traditions. Although its parliamentary government was controlled for a time by liberal, Westernized factions, nationalists from the old samurai class joined with the nation's economically powerful families in quest of a Japanese East Asian empire. By the late 1920s those elements had embarked on a militarist course that would lead eventually to war.

While conservative nationalists tolerated democratic forms, they worried that communism would spread its infection beyond the Soviet Union's boundaries. Nowhere were those fears deeper than in Italy. With the parliamentary government seemingly paralyzed by postwar unrest, Benito Mussolini and his *Fasci di Combattimento*, or fascists, under the cover of parliamentary means, used terrorism, murder, and intimidation to defeat their enemies. Through the mass media they spread antidemocratic propaganda and promoted an "all-embracing" single-party state, outside which "no human or spiritual values can exist, let alone be desireable." They rejected both the liberals' belief in political parties and the Marxist concept of class solidarity in favor of the glorified nation-state dominated by the middle class, small business people, modest property owners, and small farmers.

Fascism thus gave a sinister twist to the liberal ideal of national solidarity, but one that others embraced as a no-nonsense means of blunting Marxism. Adolf Hitler, like many Germans, resented the stinging defeat that war brought in 1919. Like Mussolini, Hitler too used the politics of discontent to rise to power. And having achieved it in 1933, his Nazi party destroyed democracy. Under one-party rule, the Gestapo secret political police ensured that Germans expressed only those ideas that conformed to the views of their national leader, the *Führer*.

Hitler succeeded partly because the prosperity of the 1920s was shattered worldwide by the corrosive hardships of the Great Depression. Farmers were particularly hard-hit: during the 1920s the opening of new lands to cultivation had already led to overproduction. In Java, for example, the use of scientific agricultural techniques created a glut in the sugar market. By 1930 the price of wheat, measured in gold, reached its lowest point in four hundred years. And those urban unemployed who walked the street in search of a job ("I seek work of any sort," reads the German's sign on the preceding page.) were often ready to believe that only the forceful leadership of one could unite the many. Even in the United States, the business newspaper *Barron's* voiced the thoughts of more than a few when it mused that "a mild species of dictatorship" might "help us over the roughest spots in the road ahead."

Still, the rise of Hitler and Mussolini shook those who had faith in the possibilities of mass politics. While Franklin Roosevelt had used his radio "fireside chats" to bring government closer to the people, Hitler's fiery speeches and mass rallies seemed bent on encouraging racist fears and controlling public opinion. While Hollywood produced films that overwhelmingly affirmed popular faith in democratic government, a capitalist economy, and the success ethic, the German director Leni Riefensthal used her cinematic gifts to combine myth, symbolism, and documentary into an evocation of the *Führer* as a pagan god of strength and a Christian savior. The "mass" aspects of the media were a two-edged sword. Perceptive critics recognized that even in democracies, mass culture was devoted primarily to the entertainment and escapism of light comedy and melodrama rather than serious social criticism.

Thus the Depression shook both the political and material pillars of democratic culture. On the eve of World War II the number of European democracies had been reduced from twenty-seven to ten. Latin America was ruled by a variety of dictators and military juntas that differed little from the dictatorships of Europe. China suffered not only from invasion by Japan's militarists and civil war but also from the corrupt and ineffectual one-party dictatorship of Chiang Kai-shek. Almost alone, the New Deal attempted to combat the Depression through the methods of parliamentary democracy. The totalitarian states that had promised stability, national glory, and an end to the communist menace instead led the world to chaos and war from which both communism and democracy emerged triumphant.

CHRONOLOGY

AMERICAN EVENT	YEAR		GLOBAL EVENT
	1920s		Inflation plagues defeated Germany
First commercial radio station on the air (KDKA, Pittsburgh) Prohibition takes effect	1920		
	1921	HARDING	Washington Conference on naval armaments
Sinclair Lewis' *Babbitt* published	1922		Mussolini marches on Rome James Joyce's *Ulysses* published
Teapot Dome scandal exposed	1923	COOLIDGE	Atatürk establishes Turkish Republic
F. Scott Fitzgerald's *The Great Gatsby* published Scopes trial debates evolution	1925		
Stock market boom underway	1928		Kellogg–Briand Pact outlaws war
Stock market crash	1929	HOOVER	Stalin's power consolidated
	1931		Depression spreads to Europe Japan invades Manchuria
Bonus Army arrives in Washington	1932		
"Hundred days" of the New Deal	1933	ROOSEVELT	Hitler becomes chancellor of Germany
Prohibition ends Good Neighbor Policy announced "Second New Deal" program Isolationists pass Neutrality Act	1935		Italy invades Ethiopia
	1936		Civil war breaks out in Spain
FDR fails to enlarge the Supreme Court	1937		Japan attacks China
	1938		Germany annexes Austria Munich Conference placates Hitler
John Steinbeck's *The Grapes of Wrath* published	1939		Nazi–Soviet nonaggression pact Germany invades Poland; World War II
America First Committee formed	1940		U.S.S.R. invades Baltic nations, Finland German blitzkrieg sweeps Europe
Roosevelt supports preparedness Black unions press for integration of government-contract jobs Pearl Harbor attacked; U.S. enters war	1941		Germany attacks U.S.S.R. Nazis begin systematic extermination of Jews and other subject peoples
U.S. wins Battle of Midway Japanese-Americans interned	1942		Japan occupies the Philippines North Africa campaign
Race riots in Detroit and Los Angeles	1943		Allies invade Italy Jean-Paul Sartre's *Being and Nothingness* published
American war production peaks	1944		D-Day invasion of Normandy U.S. recaptures the Philippines
Roosevelt dies	1945	TRUMAN	Allies capture Berlin Atomic bomb dropped on Japan World War II ends

25

The New Era

On Armistice Day 1918 the "Gospel Car" pulled into Tulsa, Oklahoma. Bold letters on one side announced "Jesus Is Coming—Get Ready"; those on the other side asked "Where Will You Spend Eternity?" Aimee Semple McPherson, the vivacious red-headed driver, was on her way to conquer the West. Just before Christmas she arrived in Los Angeles "with ten dollars and a tambourine." For the next three years she wandered in and out of the state before landing in San Diego. With the highest rates of illness and suicide in California, it was the perfect place for Sister Aimee to preach the healing message of her "Foursquare Gospel." Her first revival attracted 30,000 people, who witnessed her first "miracle": a paralytic walked.

Billed as the "world's most pulchritudinous evangelist," Sister Aimee had a Pentecostal message for her flock. "I am not a healer," she readily confessed. "Jesus is the healer. I am only the little office girl who opens the door and says, 'Come in.'" After the miracle in San Diego, her fame quickly spread. She returned triumphantly to Los Angeles, at the time more of an enormous village than a real metropolis. In the decade of the 1920s almost three-quarters of a million people, many of them from the nation's rural heartland, had migrated there in search of opportunity, sun, and perhaps salvation. In heading west, most had lost touch with the traditional Protestant denominations at home. Sister Aimee put her traveling gospel tent away and attended that lost flock at her doorstep.

And what a doorstep she created. The Angelus Temple was pure Hollywood. To the blare of trumpets on New Year's Day in 1923 she unveiled a $1.5 million dollar structure graced by a 75-foot, rotating electronic cross, visible at night from 50 miles away. Inside was a 5000-seat auditorium, radio station KFSG (Kall Four Square Gospel), a wardrobe room that rivaled those of the movie studios, a "Cradle Roll Chapel" for babies, and a "Miracle Room" filled with the crutches, trusses, wheelchairs, and other aids Sister Aimee's cured faithful had discarded. Services were not simply a matter of hymn, sermon, and prayer. Aimee staged pageants, Holy Land slide shows, dramatized sermons, circuses, and healing sessions to ease the pain and boredom of the folks who flocked to see her.

Sister Aimee succeeded because she was able to blend the old with the new. Her lively sermons had a simple message, easy to remember. They carried the spirit of what people were calling the "New Era." Casting aside hellfire evangelism, wrote one observer, Sister Aimee "substituted the cheerfulness of the playroom for the gloom of the morgue." Where country preachers menaced their

The pulsating rhythms of the Jazz Age are captured in this vibrant painting by Archibald Motley. The New Orleans–born artist was one of a group of black genre painters in the 1920s who became part of the Harlem Renaissance.

congregations with visions of eternal damnation, she gave her faithful, "flowers, music, golden trumpets, red robes, angels, incense, nonsense, and sex appeal." To that she also added the sophistication of the booming media industries of the 1920s. She had a nose for publicity, a great capacity for self-dramatization, and a gift for improvising new activities to entertain her followers. Here was one brand of evangelism eminently suited to a new consumer age.

Aimee Semple McPherson was hardly the only evangelist to use technology. In Fort Worth, Texas, the Reverend J. Frank Norris of the First Baptist Church built a 6000-seat amphitheater, set aglow by spotlights. If the lights failed to bring the faithful to Christ, advertising would. Bruce Barton, founder of a major advertising agency, became concerned that Christ no longer had the proper "image." In *The Man Nobody Knows* (1925), he portrayed Jesus as the thoroughly modern businessman, a bibulous socializer who had, after all, changed water into wine at the wedding feast at Cana and whose parables of wisdom were the "most powerful advertisements of all times." Barton explained how Christ had "picked up twelve men from the bottom ranks of business and forged them into an organization that conquered the world." With the Savior himself said to be blessing mass marketing, it was small wonder that so many Americans embraced a consumer culture. Half a million of them bought Barton's book.

Modernizing the way the gospel was spread was just one symptom of the

"New Era." Writing in 1931, journalist Frederick Lewis Allen found the changes of the preceding decade so overwhelming that he could not believe that 1919 was *Only Yesterday*, as he titled his book. To give some sense of the transformation, Allen introduced his readers to "Mr. and Mrs. Smith," a moderately well-to-do couple living in a city apartment. Among the images that struck Allen (as well as disapproving conservatives) was the revolution in Mrs. Smith's fashions. No longer was she wrapped in a heavy, formless dress hanging to the floor. Her hemline exposed her ankles as it raced toward her knees. Her petticoats and corsets had vanished. Her dress was straight and long-waisted. She wore flesh-colored stockings of silk or rayon (which "flappers," the more adventurous women of her day, rolled at the top). She had "bobbed," or cut, her hair to the popular, near-boyish length, and flattened her breasts, all in an effort to gain greater freedom of movement. In 1919 Mrs. Smith had used face powder but never other cosmetics, the surest sign of "a scarlet career." By the end of the decade she was applying rouge every day, visiting a "beauty parlor" regularly, and using one of the 2500 brands of perfume and 1500 face creams on the market.

With Prohibition in full force, Mrs. Smith and other women of her day were walking into illegal "speakeasy" saloons and ordering drinks as readily as did men. In the trendy hotels she and her husband danced to "jazz" (so popular by the mid-twenties that the "Jazz Age" became another name for the decade). Modern couples like the Smiths sprinkled their conversations with references to "repressed sexual drives" and the best methods of contraception. But the most striking fact about Allen's description of these "average" Americans was that they lived in the city. The census of 1920 showed that for the first time just over half of the population were urbanites. Here, in urban America, the New Era worked its changes and sent them rippling outward.

Yet the Smiths of Frederick Allen's imagination were in many ways hardly average. According to the census tables, nearly as many Americans still lived on isolated farms, in villages, and in small towns. In fact, many "city" dwellers lived out there too. By defining a city as any place with 2500 people, the Census Bureau had created hundreds of statistical illusions. Boston with its millions of inhabitants ranked in the census tables alongside Muncie, Indiana, just under 37,000 people, and Sac Prairie, Wisconsin, whose population hovered barely above the mystical mark of 2500, and tiny Hyden, Kentucky, along the Cumberland plateau of eastern Kentucky. As late as 1927 nearly all American farms lacked electricity; two-thirds of American homes had no washing machines or vacuum cleaners and half had no telephones; 95 percent were without refrigerators; and despite the amazing growth of the medium, 70 percent had no radio. Most citizens, the Smiths aside, still clung to the values of an earlier America and still lived there too.

The poet August Derleth grew up in Sac Prairie, and as a 10-year-old in 1919 he could hear the "howl of wolves" at night. The town observed changing seasons not with new fashions but by the appearance and disappearance of plants and animals. Sac Prairie was a world of farming and gossip and fishing, of men swapping stories over potbellied stoves, of barn-raisings, and of harvest moon dances—all within a few hours' drive of the state capital at Madison. In Hyden, Kentucky, Main Street was still unpaved, livestock roamed at will, and the lots on either side

Sister Aimee Semple McPherson in her evangelical robe.

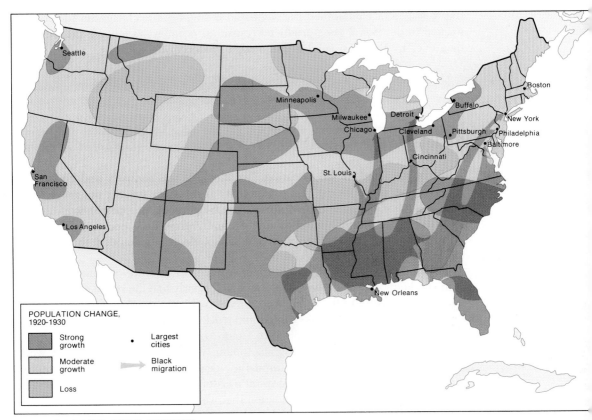

AREAS OF POPULATION GROWTH

In the 1920s the population of urban America grew by some 15 million, at the time the greatest ten-year jump in American history. Spurred first by the industrial demands of World War I and then by declining farm income, cities grew largely by depopulating rural areas. The biggest gains were in the South and West, where farmers followed opportunity to cities in climates similar to their own. In the most dramatic manifestation of the overall trend, more than a million African-Americans migrated from the rural South to the urban North in hopes of escaping poverty and discrimination.

had fences to keep front yards and gardens free of animals. By 1930 there were still only 10 automobiles in the county, and god-fearing Baptists not only worshiped together as their parents had before them but also repaired to the Middle Fork of the Kentucky for an open-air baptism when they declared their new birth in Christ. They would have nothing to do with flapper girls and "paint" or the showy miracles of Aimee McPherson.

As much as some Americans resisted the transforming forces of modern life—technology, corporatism, bureaucratization, and consumerism—the New Era could not be ignored or walled out. Modernism mixed uneasily with traditionalism in the 1920s. Automobiles had come to Hyden, no matter how few in number, and in Tennessee, a few hundred miles down the road, the mass media had flocked to a spectacular trial involving Darwinian evolution. Whether Americans embraced the New Era or condemned it, they could not ignore the changes in society that worked to develop a mass-produced consumer economy, a culture shaped more than ever by the mass media, and a more materialistic society.

THE ROARING ECONOMY

If anything roared in the "Roaring Twenties," it was industry and commerce. America was in the midst of a productivity revolution, turning out more goods with less labor. Manufacturing output rose 64 percent, output per workhour 40 percent. Between 1922 and 1927 the economy grew by 7 percent a year—the largest peacetime growth rate ever. The sale of electricity doubled; the consumption of fuel oil more than doubled.

Technology was partly responsible. All over the country old machines were being junked for new. Between 1919 and 1927 nearly half the steam engines in the United States went to the scrap heap. Steam turbines and steam shovels, electric motors, belt and bucket conveyors, dump trucks, and countless other mechanized innovations became commonplace in factories and at work sites—all improving productivity. As automatic and semiautomatic machinery replaced 200,000 workers each year, a new phrase entered the vocabulary: "technological unemployment." Even so, the labor force grew at a faster rate than the population. And for the larger percentage of the population that worked, wages improved too, climbing nearly $150 for industrial workers between 1919 and 1927.

As the industrial economy matured, more and more consumer items appeared on store shelves—cigarette lighters, wristwatches, radios, antifreeze fluids, Pyrex glass cooking utensils, panchromatic film. Given the improvement in productivity, prices were stable, and some even fell. The cost of a tire and an inner tube tumbled from $30 in 1914 to nearly half that amount by 1929. Americans enjoyed the highest standard of living any people had ever known. Yet for all the prosperity, the average American depositor increased savings by only $11 in 1928. Most people saved nothing. Personal debt was rising two and a half times faster than personal income. Sooner or later buying power would be exhausted and the roaring economy would grind to a chilling stop.

The Boom Industries

Along with technology, new "boom industries" promoted economic growth. A short recession in 1921 gave way to a massive construction boom to make up for the wartime backlog in demand for offices, homes, factories, and warehouses. During the twenties New York got a new skyline, topped in 1931 when the Empire State Building rose to the world record height of 86 stories. Soon cities the size of Beaumont, Texas, Memphis, Tennessee, and Syracuse, New York, boasted buildings of at least 21 stories. Residential construction doubled as people fanned out from cities to suburbs. Near Detroit, suburban Grosse Point grew by 700 percent; Shaker Heights, outside of Cleveland, by 1000 percent; Beverly Hills by 2500 percent. The construction of roads made settling in the suburbs possible and poured millions of dollars into the economy. In 1919 Oregon, New Mexico, and

Colorado hit on a new idea for financing road building—a tax on gasoline. Within a decade every state had one. At the end of the war only 7000 miles of hard-surfaced roads existed; by 1927 there were 50,000; and by 1928 a tourist could drive from New York as far west as St. Mary's, Kansas, and never leave a paved highway.

Construction stimulated other businesses and industries: steel, concrete, glass, lumber, wiring, home mortgages, and insurance. The demands of war already had spurred the chemical and synthetics industries. In the 1920s rayon transformed the textile business; cellophane, used to wrap everything from leftovers to cigarettes, doubled in sales each year from 1924 until the end of the decade. Meanwhile the urban diet became more varied as interest in nutrition climbed. Shipments of fresh fruits and vegetables soared, and vitamins, publicized with new zeal, appeared on breakfast tables. "Kitchenettes" in small city apartments boosted the canning industry. Between 1914 and 1929 purchases of canned milk nearly tripled. City families could dine at home on canned soup, canned meat and vegetables, and canned fruit for dessert.

The Automobile

The most important boom industry involved the automobile. The first cars had appeared on streets at the turn of the century but for many years remained expensive toys for the rich. By 1920 there were 10 million in America, a sizable number; by 1929 that had jumped to 26 million, one for every five people (compared to one for every 43 in Britain and one for every 7000 in Russia). During the decade automakers bought one-seventh of the nation's steel. They were the leading purchasers of rubber, plate glass, nickel, and lead. By 1929 it was estimated that one American in four derived employment directly or indirectly from automobiles.

Henry Ford made this revolution possible by pushing the principles of standardization and mass production to such ruthless extremes that the automobile became available to the masses at a price most could afford. At the age of 16, Ford walked away from the family farm in Dearborn, Michigan. In 1902, after a decade of tinkering and building autos, he saw his flame-shooting "999" race car roar to a world speed record of 70 miles per hour. Trading on his fame he founded the Ford Motor Company in 1903 and in 1907 announced his dream: to build a "motor car for the multitude." "Everybody wants to be somewhere he ain't," Ford said. The way to succeed was to make all the cars alike, "just like one pin is like another pin when it comes from a pin factory." In 1908 Ford perfected the Model T. It had a 20-horsepower engine and a body of steel. It was high enough to ride the worst roads, and it came in one color: black.

Priced at $845, the Model T was cheap by industry standards, but still too costly, and it took too long to build—12 hours for the chassis alone—to fulfill its designer's dream. Two Ford engineers suggested copying a practice of Chicago meat-packing houses, where beef carcasses were carried on moving chains past a line of meat dressers. In 1914 Ford introduced the moving assembly line. A conveyor belt, positioned waist high (to eliminate bending or walking), propelled the chassis at six feet per minute as stationary workers put the cars together. The process cut assembly time in half. By 1925 the process had been so well streamlined that new Model T's were rolling off the assembly line every 10 seconds. At $290, almost anybody could buy one. By 1927 Ford had sold a total of 15 million "tin lizzies," making him the giant of the automobile industry, not only in America but throughout the world.

Ford, the greatest industrialist of the twentieth century, was also a social prophet. Unlike most of his contemporaries, he praised the benefits of a "doctrine of high wages," pointing out that workers with extra money in their pockets would stimulate enough consumption—of autos, clothing, all the new products—to sustain a booming prosperity. In 1915 his plants in Dearborn established the "Five-Dollar Day," twice the going wage rate in Detroit. He reduced working hours from 48 to 40 a week and cut the work week to five days. By 1926 he employed 10,000 blacks, many of whom had advanced far enough to hire and fire whites. His methods simplified each operation so much that he could employ even the disabled.

Yet Ford workers were not happy. Ford himself admitted that the routinized operations on his assembly line were "so monotonous that it scarcely seems possible that any man would care to continue long at the same job." By 1915 labor turnover at Ford plants had reached over 300 percent a year. The Five-Dollar Day was designed partly to keep workers at Ford, and it did: within two years turnover dropped to 40 percent. Ford recouped his profits by speeding up the assembly line. Anything that reduced efficiency was barred. Ford workers could not talk, sing, whistle, smoke, or sit on the job. They wore frozen expressions called "Fordization of the Face" and communicated in the "Ford Whisper" without moving their lips. A "Sociological Department" sent company inspectors to workers' homes to encourage "thrift, honesty, sobriety, better housing, and better living generally." In Ford factories an "Education Department" ran "Americanization" classes where immigrant workers learned English, proper dress, and even etiquette, as well as plant procedures.

Sometimes Ford's paternalism led to tyranny. The company fired nearly a thousand Greek and Russian workers, who as Orthodox Christians celebrated Christmas 13 days later than other Christian sects. "If these men are to make their home in America," said a Ford official, "they should observe American holidays." Unions were barred, and when advertisements for 3000 jobs brought 25,000 men to the Rouge Assembly Plant on January 2, 1929, company guards drove them off with fire hoses. In 14-degree temperature the water froze almost as soon as it hit the men. Only 600 found employment that day. Ford didn't mind a bit of social revolution, so long as it was on his own terms.

General Motors copied Ford's production techniques but not his business strategies. Where Ford, the inventive mechanic with an eighth-grade education, operated on instinct, college-educated Alfred Sloan, manager of GM, combed statistics for market trends. Where Ford centralized operations, GM decentralized them. "Policy," Sloan liked to say, "may originate from anywhere." While Ford tried to sell everyone the same car, GM created "a car for every purse and purpose." There were Cadillacs and Buicks for the well-to-do, Chevrolets for the modest. GM cars had flashy designs, plush upholstery, self-starters, and hydraulic brakes. They came in a rainbow of colors, and every year the look changed. In an increasingly standardized society, these details allowed people to view their automobiles as symbols of distinction and social prestige. Only in 1927 did Ford realize that efficiency and economy were not enough. He dropped the Model T, retooled his factories, and introduced the upscale Model A in 1928 in an array of colors.

By making automobiles available to the masses, the growing industry

Henry Ford at the turn of the century.

changed the face of America. The spreading web of paved roads fueled urban sprawl, real estate booms in California and Florida, and a new roadside culture. Thousands of "auto camps" opened to provide tourists with tents and crude toilets. "Auto clubs" like the Tin Can Tourists Association (named for the tin can tied to the radiator cap of a member's car) sprang up to aid travelers. Automobile travel broke down provincialism and advanced standardized dialects and manners. By 1930 almost two farm families in three had cars. When asked why her family had bought a Model T when they had no indoor plumbing, a farm woman replied, "You can't go to town in a bathtub." Across the country the automobile gave the young unprecedented freedom from parental authority. After hearing 30 cases of "sex crimes" (19 of which had occurred in cars), an exasperated juvenile court judge in Indiana declared that the automobile was "a house of prostitution on wheels." It was, of course, much more. The automobile was to the 1920s what the railroad had been to the nineteenth century: the catalyst for economic growth, a transportation revolution, and a cultural symbol.

The Business of America

A generation earlier, progressives had criticized business for its social irresponsibility (even as reformers adopted business techniques and helped businesses to stabilize whole industries). Patriotic and productive service in the war enhanced the reputation of businessmen, and after a brief postwar recession, the return of prosperity in 1922 deepened respect for them. When Harvard established a graduate school of business administration in 1924, it was a sign that business had become a "profession," whose mastery required special training.

In the 1920s business also became a form of public service. A new middle class of civil servants, sales representatives, and salaried managers thrived on pep, boosterism, and good cheer. Immortalized in Sinclair Lewis' *Babbitt* (1922), they joined the Kiwanis or the Rotary Club, worshiped Henry Ford, and shared his belief that in business the "fundamentals are all summed up in the single word, 'service.'" President Calvin Coolidge echoed the theme in 1925: "The business of America is business. The man who builds a factory builds a temple. The man who works there worships there."

Encouraged by federal permissiveness, a wave of mergers swept the country. Between 1919 and 1930, some 8000 firms disappeared as large ones swallowed small. Oligopoly, where a few firms dominated whole industries, grew increasingly common. At the end of the decade, four companies packed nearly three-quarters of all American meat; another four rolled nine-tenths of all cigarettes. National chains began to replace local "mom and pop" stores. One bag of groceries in ten came from the Great Atlantic and Pacific Tea Company. A & P's chain of 15,000 red-and-gold stores did more business than the Ford Motor Company. One mammoth holding company, Drug, Incorporated, owned 10,000 Rexall drugstores, 706 Liggett stores, the Owl chain on the West Coast, and huge drug companies like Vick Chemical, Bayer Aspirin, and Bristol-Myers. Almost every pill that Americans bought over the counter came from Drug, Incorporated or a business owned by the company.

This expansion and consolidation meant that the capital of the nation was controlled not by a host of individuals, or even by a concentration of rich "captains of industry," but by large, bureaucratic organizations in which management was divorced from ownership. The economy became "corporatized." By 1929 half the total industrial income was concentrated in 100 corporations. Nearly one-fifth of all national wealth had shifted from private to corporate hands. Stocks and bonds were becoming so widely dispersed that few individuals held more than 1 or 2 percent of the shares in any company. The 20 largest shareholders in U.S. Steel owned only 5.7 percent of the stock among them.

Modern bureaucratic management made it possible for huge corporations to run their empires ever more efficiently. Control of business policy was passing from entrepreneurs to a salaried bureaucracy of executives and plant managers. They formed a new elite, which no longer aimed to own a business; instead they wanted to work their way up a corporate ladder. They were less interested in risk than productivity and stability. Mergers left them with more resources, and increasingly managers shoveled earnings back into their companies to expand physical plants and to carry on research for future development. By the end of the decade more than a thousand firms had research laboratories.

At Harvard and other new schools of business, through new journals, professional societies, and consultants, corporate leaders learned the techniques of "scientific management," an innovative system for standardizing business procedures. In the nineteenth century a Carnegie or a Rockefeller applied his quick mind and indomitable will to business. In the 1920s management was the key—to selling, budgeting, financing, even personnel. Like Alfred Sloan at General Motors, managers divided and subdivided their enterprises. Central headquarters planned for the future, while semi-independent divisions took care of daily operations. It was still experimental. Most businesses, for example, began to use budgets to plan their expenditures and capital outlays only after 1922.

Scientific management stressed good relations between managers and workers. Businesses preferred to retain laborers and avoid the expense of training new ones. A new form of labor relations emerged, designed to keep workers in factories and trouble-making unions out. In 1921, after a rash of postwar strikes, the National Association of Manufacturers, the Chamber of Commerce, and other employer groups launched the "American Plan." Backed by a million dollars in business pledges, it aimed at opening "closed shops," where only union members were allowed to work. Employers made workers sign agreements (dubbed "yellow dog contracts" by unions) disavowing union membership, infiltrated their organizations with company spies, locked them out of factories if they protested, and boycotted firms that hired union labor.

The benevolent side of the American Plan involved a social innovation called "welfare capitalism." Leading exponents such as General Electric and Bethlehem Steel built clean, safe factories, installed cafeterias and hired trained dietitians, formed baseball teams and glee clubs. Millions of workers enrolled in company unions (called by critics "Kiss-Me Clubs," for their lack of power). They nonetheless offered what few traditional unions could match: health and safety insurance, a grievance procedure, and representation for African-Americans, women, and immigrants. Several hundred firms encouraged perhaps a million workers to buy company stock. The Western Electric Company introduced rest breaks, provided free refreshments, and shortened the workday. Productivity increased immediately.

Still, such welfare capitalism embraced only about 5 percent of the work force and often gave benefits only to skilled laborers, the hardest to replace. Most companies cared more for productivity than contented workers. At a steel mill where tired workers lost their hands in steel sheet cutters, foremen handcuffed

A shop steward.

them to a lever that pulled their arms away from descending blades in the interest of safety. "There they work, chained to their machines, as galley slaves were chained to their oars," wrote one visitor. In the interest of increasing productivity, other machines displaced laborers. Throughout the decade unemployment never dropped below 5 percent, and in ailing industries like coal mining it averaged 30 percent. According to one estimate, almost one American family in six was "chronically destitute." In the 1920s a family of four could live in "minimum health and decency" on $2000 a year. The average industrial wage was $1304 a year, so many families needed more than one wage earner to just get by.

Over a million children, ages 10 to 15, still worked full-time in 1920, some for as little as 20 cents an hour. In Passaic, New Jersey, a textile town, the sons and daughters of Hungarian and Polish immigrants went into the mills at 13 so their families could survive. Some of the worst conditions existed in the textile town of Gastonia, North Carolina. Parents and children worked 10- to 12-hour shifts around the clock in 90-degree heat. To wring more production from the mill, managers imposed "stretch-outs," the textile equivalent of assembly-line speed-ups. In 1927, in the most famous strike of the decade, 2500 mill hands left their jobs, and even strikebreakers walked out. Eventually unsympathetic local authorities ended the strike, presaging a national trend. A year later there were only 629 strikes in the whole country, a record low. Union membership plummeted from almost 5 million in 1921 to less than 3.5 million in 1929. "The AF of L machinery," observed a despondent union official, "has practically collapsed."

The Consumer Culture

By the time of World War I, the network of industrial and manufacturing systems—in communications, sales, and distribution—had penetrated enough of the country to create mass markets. As the industrial base matured with the production of more consumer goods, prosperity in the 1920s hinged increasingly on consumption. Business leaders began to look at workers (in fact at all their fellow citizens) as "consumers." Henry Ford's doctrine of high wages was based on the assumption that more take-home pay would raise mass purchasing power, increase demand and production, and bring down costs. The flip side of his doctrine was low prices, which would lift mass sales still higher. If this continued, prosperity would reign without end.

Everything rested on consumers: they now had to be courted. Wives ceased to be homemakers and became purchasers of processed food and manufactured goods. Husbands were no longer just workers but bill-payers—consumers of mortgages and other forms of credit. As more employees got two-week (unpaid) vacations, even leisure became consumable. So, as one government report observed, "it is preeminently the problem of marketing, and especially the creation of demand, which has held the attention of business executives." Consumption (as reflected in sales) was the final key to prosperity, and consumption hinged on two modern innovations: advertising to increase demand and credit to help consumers buy.

Before World War I advertising had been a grubby business. Most top advertising executives were former copywriters for patent medicines. Around the turn of the century, however, advertising began a critical shift from emphasizing the virtues of products to stressing the wants of consumers. During the war the Committee on Public Information demonstrated the power of advertising as an instrument of mass persuasion, and soon businesses were shaping the tastes of consumers, convincing them that almost any want could be bought. Behavioral psychologists like John B. Watson, who left Johns Hopkins University for an advertising agency in the 1920s, showed advertisers how to develop more sophisticated techniques. Like the war propaganda, advertising copy aimed increasingly at emotions and cynically regarded the "average normal American," in the words of one executive, as having the "literate capacity of a 12- or 14-year-old."

More than anyone else, Albert Lasker developed modern advertising in America. Lasker, the owner of Chicago's largest advertising firm, Lord and Thomas, created copy that was hard-hitting, forthright, positive—and often fantastical. To boost the sales of Lucky Strike cigarettes Lord and Thomas advertisements suggested that smoking made people slimmer and more courageous. "Lucky's" became one of the most popular brands in America. Other advertisers were even less scrupulous. Bogus doctors and dentists endorsed all kinds of products, some downright dangerous. Millions were told to brush their teeth with toothpaste containing potassium chloride—eight grams of which could kill a human being. (At least one person committed suicide by eating a tube.) "Halitosis," plucked from the pages of an obscure medical dictionary, was used to sell Listerine mouthwash, and Lifebuoy soap thrived on fears of "B.O." ("body odor"). The bottom line was to sell not products, but desires: health, popularity, social prestige.

Advertisers declared war on the traditional virtues of thrift and prudence. A generation earlier debt had been considered unrespectable, the result of wantonness or disaster. When sociologists Helen and Robert Lynd completed an exhaustive study of Muncie, Indiana (*Middletown*, 1929), they found almost no family without debts. Installment buying, once confined largely to sewing machines and pianos, grew into the tenth biggest business in the United States. The automobile industry led the way. In 1919 Alfred Sloan created millions of new customers by establishing the General Motors Acceptance Corporation, the first consumer credit organization in the country. Ten years later it was the largest sales financing company in the world, and more than two-thirds of all automobile sales were on time payments. By 1929 consumer debt had jumped 250 percent, to $7 billion, almost twice the amount of the federal budget. The consumer culture encouraged Americans to borrow today so they could buy what advertising convinced them they wanted for tomorrow. At the end of the decade Americans were buying over 60 percent of their cars, radios, and furniture on the installment plan. By persuading them that what was new was also desirable, advertising also helped to propagate modernism.

A MASS SOCIETY

The increasingly consumer-oriented structure of the American economy played a central role in shaping a modern culture of consumption. During the late nineteenth century the economy had boomed, too, but a larger part of its energies went into the development of heavy industry and non–consumer goods: greater steel capacity and the growth of national rail, communications, and energy networks. As the economy shifted to consumer goods and the modern ethic of high spending and high consumption worked its way into American society, life changed. The new systems of distribution and mass marketing led not simply to a higher standard of living but also to a mass culture, with tastes less regional and diverse. More and more Americans read the same weekly magazines, saw the same films, heard the same radio programs, and had the same idols.

Other aspects of the new mass culture weakened many of the traditional ties that bound Americans together. Local communities and churches, which had often been the arbiters of what was moral and proper, sometimes found their authority undercut by the tastes of moviemakers in Hollywood or magazine writers in New York. The automobile gave families, and individuals within families, the independence to travel at their convenience. Families saw their role in educating their children decrease as the bureaucratic institution of the school steadily expanded its influence. The New Era was witness to "a vast dissolution of ancient habits," remarked columnist Walter Lippmann. In the place of those habits came many of the forces of modern life: independent women, free and easy love, standardized culture, the energy and impersonality of cities, the alienation of intellectuals.

The New Woman

The "New Woman," charged critics, was at the bottom of what Frederick Lewis Allen called the "revolution in manners and morals" that characterized the twenties. Before the war women were arrested for smoking cigarettes in public, using profanity, appearing on public beaches without stockings, driving automobiles without men beside them, and wearing slacks or shorts. Judges heard such cases not just in small towns but in cities like New York and Chicago as well. Wartime America ended many of these restrictions. With so many women bagging explo-

Daily Lives

CLOTHING AND FASHION

The Beauty Contest

On a sunlit day early in September 1921 eight young women stood nervously on the boardwalk at Atlantic City, New Jersey. For a week the seaside resort had presented a succession of swimming exhibitions, dance contests, and automobile races. A giant parade featured clowns, bands, a float carrying King Neptune escorted by mermaids, and the boardwalk's famous rolling chairs draped with flowers. With the exception of the clowns all the marchers wore bathing suits, even the mayor and the members of the city council and chamber of commerce. They had been instrumental in organizing the week's central event—a national beauty contest to select the first "Miss America."

The American beauty contest drew on a heritage that dated back to medieval festivals, which often included a competition for the most attractive woman. In colonial times the traditional May Day celebration crowned a Queen of the May as a symbol of fertility. By the middle of the nineteenth century many cities began holding festivals to publicize their virtues and attract settlers. Queens played a vital role, embodying fruitfulness and community. Though physical beauty mattered in the selection, qualities such as civic leadership and popularity also counted.

The flamboyant huckster P. T. Barnum created the modern beauty contest. In 1854 Barnum conceived of a competition among women to judge their appearance at his high-class American Museum in New York. As first prize he offered a diamond tiara (or a dowry if the winner were unmarried), but Victorian codes of conduct prohibited such public displays, and Barnum attracted only contestants

of "questionable reputation." To lure middle-class women, he announced that "daguerrotypes," or photographs, could be submitted. Participants did not even have to send their names. Barnum sold his museum before he received the photographs, but the idea quickly spread to newspapers and later to the new mass-circulation dailies. When the promoters of the St. Louis Exposition advertised a beauty contest in 1905, some 40,000 women applied.

Carnivals, fairs, and "dime museums" (where for 10 cents one could see midway curiosities and stage entertainment) had begun holding beauty contests with entrants actually present. Catering to

Margaret Gorman of Washington, D.C., crowned in 1921 as the first Miss America.

Daily Lives

working-class customers whose social conventions were not rigid, the shows produced few complaints. Around the turn of the century, as mass advertising and mass entertainment spread across the country, chorus girls and models gained acceptance. "Bathing beauties" began cropping up at summer resorts and on the silver screen. The legitimate beauty contest, with middle-class audiences and participants, was simply the next step.

Despite public pronouncements, the contestants at the Miss America pageant came not from the nation at large but from eight nearby cities, each of which had conducted local competitions. Promoters had conceived of the pageant as a way of extending the summer season past September 1, but Victorian prudishness threatened the venture. The contest measured physical beauty alone, with the high point being a bathing suit competition. (Only later did the pageant add a talent show.) After the turn of the century, bathing suits had grown alarmingly scant, exposing arms and discarding billowy bloomers in favor of revealing tights. Straight-laced visitors might balk at the sight of middle-class women strutting seminude before a panel of judges.

Aware of such perils, organizers depicted entrants as wholesome, conventional, and unsophisticated. None of the contestants were permitted to wear short "bobbed" hair or makeup—both symbols of the racy modern woman. Models, theatrical performers, and other "professional beauties" competed separately. Famous women's illustrators lent legitimacy by serving as judges. Howard Chandler Christie alone judged the first contest, but the following year Norman Rockwell and two other artists joined the panel. To underscore the lightheartedness of the pageant, local police dressed like Keystone Kops, the bumbling heroes of Mack Sennett's comedy films.

As the contestants waited anxiously, officials announced the winner—Margaret Gorman of Washington, D.C. She looked like Mary Pickford, the screen star dubbed "America's Sweetheart" by the press. Like Pickford, Gorman radiated innocence and athletic vigor. "She represents the type of womanhood America needs," observed Samuel Gompers of the American Federation of Labor, "—strong, red-blooded, able to shoulder the responsibilities of home-making and motherhood."

The Miss America pageant was an immediate success. Newspapers across the country reported the results. In 1922 representatives of 58 cities competed, and a crowd of 200,000 watched the opening parade. Five years later the number of contestants had jumped to 75, including some from distant California and Alaska. The much-feared protests nonetheless materialized. In 1928 organizers were forced to cancel the pageant when hotel owners objected that their middle-class clientele found the display offensive. The pageant was revived again in 1935, and a Miss America has reigned ever since.

Miss America and other beauty contests evolved as Victorianism declined in the early twentieth century, but the lengths to which pageant organizers went to gain respect demonstrated the strength of the older social codes. The Miss America pageant in particular came to symbolize the middle-class ideal of womanhood. Physical beauty remained the chief component, marriage and motherhood the chief ends. The message was graphic: men competed in sports gear, business attire, and professional garb; women in bathing suits. That fashion would be slow to change.

sives, running locomotives, and drilling with rifles, the old taboos often seemed antiquated or plain silly.

Before the war disseminating birth control information by mail had also been a crime. By the armistice there was a birth control clinic in Brooklyn, a National Birth Control League, and later an American Birth Control League led by Margaret Sanger. Sanger's crusade had begun as an attempt to save poor women from the burdens of unwanted pregnancies. Hostile authorities confiscated the literature she mailed discussing sex education, venereal disease, and contraception, and in 1914 she fled the country to evade arrest. By the 1920s she had become less a radical crusader for the poor than a feminist advocate of "new ideals of sex," which she hoped would transform the sex act from "biological necessity" to "a psychic and spiritual avenue of expression." Her message found a receptive middle-class audience. Surveys showed that by the 1930s nearly 90 percent of college-educated couples practiced contraception.

Being able to a degree to control the matter of pregnancy, women felt less guilt about enjoying sex. In 1909 Sigmund Freud had come to America to lecture on his theories of coping with the unconscious and overcoming harmful repressions. Freud's complex ideas sailed blissfully over the heads of most Americans, but as popularized in the 1920s by crusaders like Sanger, they gave the clear impression that sexuality was a key to health. In a consumer culture preoccupied with self-gratification, sexual fulfillment became an important ingredient. Anybody could learn to free suppressed desires and consequently enjoy a richer life. To help them, Sears, Roebuck began listing books such as *Ten Thousand Dreams Interpreted* and *Sex Problems Solved*.

"Street selling was torture for me," Margaret Sanger recalled of her efforts to promote the *Birth Control Review*. Hecklers often taunted Sanger and her colleagues. "Have you never heard God's word to 'be fruitful and multiply and replenish the earth'?" one asked. The reply came back, "They've done that already."

Cocktail in hand, cigarette in mouth, the New Woman became a symbol of liberated womanhood. If she was up to the latest wrinkle, she wore a close-fitting felt hat and lots of makeup, had a long-waisted dress and two strings of beads, unbuckled her galoshes, and called herself a "flapper." She was, wrote F. Scott Fitzgerald, the chronicler of the decade, "lovely and expensive and about nineteen." The flapper, though, was hardly an accurate symbol of the age. Certainly women in the 1920s gained a measure of power and independence. With passage of the Nineteenth Amendment in 1920 the United States became the twenty-second nation to grant women the vote, and in 1924 two women—Nellie Ross in Wyoming and Miriam ("Ma") Ferguson in Texas—were elected governors, the first female chief executives. But the deserved fame of a few women was one thing, the daily working patterns of American life another. Over the decade, the female labor force had grown by more than 2 million, making one worker in every five female. That represented an increase of barely 1 percent. As late as 1930 nearly 60 percent of all working women were African-American or foreign-born, generally holding low-paying jobs in domestic service or the garment industry.

The new age did offer some new career choices for women. The consumer culture spawned a preoccupation with appearance that led to the opening of some 40,000 beauty parlors staffed by hairdressers, manicurists, and cosmeticians. "Women's fields" carved out by progressive reformers expanded opportunities in education, libraries, and social welfare. In many ways extensions of women's domestic sphere, these fields nevertheless became more professionalized in the 1920s. Specialized training and licensing required more education. Women earned a higher percentage of doctoral degrees (from 10 percent in 1910 to 15.4 percent in 1930) and held more college teaching posts than ever (32 percent). In most areas, professional men resisted the "feminization" of the work force. The number of women doctors dropped by almost 3000, a 50 percent decline, as medical schools imposed restrictive quotas and some 90 percent of all hospitals rejected female interns.

Having won the vote, most women did not use it, and when they did, they voted with their husbands or families along lines of class, region, and ethnicity, not gender. A few activists succeeded in winning passage of the Sheppard–Towner Federal Maternity and Infancy Act in 1921 to fight high rates of infant mortality. But by the end of the decade it had lapsed. Even the most obstreperous flapper, if she wed, ended up in a conventional marriage that tied her to home and family.

In the wake of its greatest success, the hard-won vote for women, the feminist movement splintered. The National Woman Suffrage Association disbanded in 1920, at the prompting of its most distinguished member, 65-year-old Carrie Chapman Catt. In its place the League of Women Voters was begun to encourage informed voting. For the more militant Alice Paul and her allies, that was not enough. Their National Woman's Party, founded in 1916, began to press for a constitutional Equal Rights Amendment (ERA).

Strongest support for the ERA came from middle-class women. Social workers and others familiar with the conditions under which women labored opposed it. Death and injury rates for women were nearly double those for men in the same industries. Barred from most unions, working-class women had won some protection only because they were women. To them the ERA meant losing the protection as well as the benefits they derived from mothers' pensions and maternity insurance. Joined by most men and a majority of Congress they fought the amendment to a standstill.

Mass Media

In balmy California, where movies could be made year-round, Hollywood helped to give the New Woman notoriety as a temptress and trend-setter. When Theda Bara (the "vamp") appeared in *The Blue Flame* in 1920, crowds mobbed theaters all along the East Coast. Clara Bow, the "It" girl, became a featured player. "It" was sex appeal, and the only others who had "It," explained novelist Elinor Glyn, were "Rex, the wild stallion, actor Tony Moreno, [and] the Ambassador Hotel doorman." And just as Hollywood came to dictate the standards of physical attraction, it became the arbiter of taste and fashion in countless other ways because motion pictures were a virtually universal medium: there was no need for literacy or fluency, no need even for hearing, given the simple stories parading across the silent screen.

Motion pictures, invented in 1889, had first been shown in tiny neighborhood theaters called "nickelodeons." For a nickel, almost anyone, children included, could afford to walk into the dark, overheated theater. The screen flickered with moving images as an accompanist played music on a tinny piano. The audience was anything but silent. The theater reverberated with the cracking of Indian nuts, the day's equivalent of popcorn, while young cowboys shot off their Kilgore repeating cap pistols during dramatic scenes. Often children read the subtitles aloud to their immigrant parents, translating into Italian, Yiddish, or German. After the first feature-length film, *The Great Train Robbery* (1903), productions became rich in spectacle, attracted middle-class audiences, and turned into America's favorite form of entertainment.

By 1926 more than 20,000 theaters offered customers overstuffed seats, live music, and a celluloid dream world—all for 50 cents or less. At the end of the decade, they were drawing over 100 million people a week, roughly the equivalent of the national population. In Muncie, Indiana—the "Middletown" of America—nine theaters opened their doors at 1 p.m. and closed at 11 at night, 7 days a week, 12 months a year. Every theater had two films, and each changed programs two or three times a week. Westerns were the staple of five theaters, and a comedy star named Harold Lloyd was the town favorite. Next to Lloyd comedies, movies with "sex appeal" drew the biggest audiences. *Flaming Youth* packed houses in 1924 with promotions that promised "neckers, petters, white kisses, red kisses, pleasure-mad daughters, sensation-craving mothers, by an author who didn't dare sign his name." Rudolph Valentino, whose dark good looks seduced a generation of moviegoers, traded on raw sexuality to become the era's premier matinee idol. When he died of peritonitis at the age of 31, the line of mourners stretched over a mile through the streets of New York.

Radio came into its own as a mass medium. In the spring of 1920 Frank Conrad of the Westinghouse Company in East Pittsburgh rigged up a research station in his barn and began sending out phonograph music and baseball scores to local wireless operators. An ingenious Pittsburgh newspaper began advertising radio equipment to "be used by those who listen to Dr. Conrad's programs." In October 1920 Westinghouse officials opened the first licensed broadcasting station in history, KDKA, to stimulate sales of their supplies. By 1921 the number of licensed stations had jumped to 28; half a year later there were 430. Radios—"furniture that talks," comedian Fred Allen called it—were soon being purchased by millions of Americans.

At first radio was seen as a civilizing force, an agent of cultural uplift that

The Roxy, the largest theater in the world when it opened in 1926, in all its palatial glory. Such lavish movie houses sought to attract more prosperous middle-class audiences with splendor reminiscent of European cathedrals. On the night the Roxy opened, pealing chimes marked the beginning of the show, whereupon a man dressed as a monk strode onto center stage, pointed to the balcony, and declared, "Let there be light!" Blazing spotlights then set the orchestra aglow. "Does God live here?" asked a little girl in a *New Yorker* cartoon.

could beam high-toned programs to an audience of individuals and small groups. "The air is your theater, your college, your newspaper, your library," trumpeted one ad in 1924. After a rocky start, commercial broadcasting slowly took hold as the ownership of sets spread to less affluent listeners. By 1931 advertisers were paying $10,000 an hour for a national hook-up, and the gross income of the the the National Broadcasting Company, launched only five years earlier, was $150 million. Nearly one home in three had a radio. Almost the entire nation listened to "Amos 'n' Andy," a comedy about blacks created by two white vaudevillians in 1929. People refused to answer their telephones during the program, and in smaller cities movie theaters stopped their shows to tune it in so patrons would not leave.

Radio changed national habits. At night families gathered around the radio instead of the hearth. Rather than going out to hear music people listened to it on the radio. Together with movies, radio cut deeply into the traditional audiences of vaudeville. After all, noted *Broadcasting* magazine, "You can get Eddie Cantor on the air for nothing." The aged, the sick, and the isolated could be, as one advertisement declared, "at home but never alone." Across the country, linked by nothing but airwaves, Americans were finding themselves part of a vast new community.

Print journalism also developed broader systems of distribution during the 1920s. In 1921 DeWitt Wallace, a veteran with a knack for condensing magazine stories, borrowed $5000 from friends and relatives, set up business in the basement of a Greenwich Village speakeasy, and mailed out the first issue of *Reader's Digest* to 1500 subscribers. Within a decade circulation stood at half a million. In 1923 Henry R. Luce and Briton Hadden, classmates at Yale, rewrote news stories in a snappy style, mixed them with photographs, and created the country's first national newspaper, *Time* magazine. By 1927, 55 giant chains distributed 230 newspapers with a combined circulation of 13 million. Though they controlled under 10 percent of all papers, the chains pioneered modern mass news techniques. Editors relied on central offices or newspaper syndicates to prepare editorials, sports, gossip, and Sunday features for a national audience.

"Ain't We Got Fun?"

"Ev'ry morning, ev'ry evening, ain't we got fun?" ran the 1921 hit song. As the average hours on the job decreased from 47.2 in 1920 to 42 by 1930, spending on amusement and recreation shot up 300 percent. Some of the spare time went into fads of the new mass culture. To mark their individuality and win notoriety people sat on flagpoles, swallowed goldfish, and entered dance marathons. In 1922 no home was considered complete without a mah-jongg set, a Chinese board game that had its own national association. As leisure time expanded, upper-class sports like tennis and golf spread to the middle class and created heroes—Bill Tilden in tennis, Bobby Jones in golf.

Spectator sports came of age. In 1921, some 60,000 fans paid $1.8 million to see Jack Dempsey, the "Manassas Mauler," knock out French champion Georges Carpentier. Millions more listened as radio took them ringside for the first time in sports history. Universities constructed huge stadiums for football—a 60,000-seater at Berkeley; a 64,000-seater at Ohio State. By the end of the decade college football games outdrew major league baseball, and Harold "Red" Grange, the "Galloping Ghost" of the University of Illinois, became the first athlete to make the cover of *Time*.

Baseball still remained the national pastime. An ugly World Series scandal in 1919 led owners to appoint Judge Kenesaw Mountain Landis "czar" of the sport early in the decade. His iron rule reformed the game. In 1920 the son of immigrants revolutionized it. George Herman "Babe" Ruth hit 54 homers (more than any other whole team hit that year), batted .376, and made the New York Yankees the first baseball club to attract a million fans in one season. A heroic producer in an era of consumption, Ruth was also baseball's bad boy, "our national exaggeration," said one writer. He smoked, drank, cursed, and chased every skirt in sight. Under the guidance of his personal manager, Christy Walsh (the first modern sports agent), Ruth became the highest paid player in the game and made a fortune endorsing everything from automobiles to clothing.

At parties old diversions—charades, card tricks, recitations—vanished as dancing took over. The ungainly camel-walk, the sultry tango, and in 1924 the frantic Charleston were the urban standards. Country barns featured a revival of square dancing with music provided by Detroit's WBZ, courtesy of Henry Ford. And from the turn-of-the century brothels and gaming houses of New Orleans,

Memphis, and St. Louis came a rhythmic, compelling music that swept into night-clubs and over the airwaves: jazz.

The term "jazz" had illicit sexual overtones when bestowed by whites, who found its bolder style of playing and its origins in the community to be little more than immoral "race music." But jazz was a remarkably complex blend of several older African-American musical traditions. It grew most directly out of "the blues," whose haunting melodies were often sung or played with a quavering, passionate pitch:

> The moon looks lonesome when it's shining through the trees.
> Yes, the moon looks lonesome, shining through the trees.
> And a man looks lonesome when his woman packs up to leave . . .

The new jazz bands combined the soulfulness of the blues with the brighter synco-pated rhythms of ragtime music. Jazz bands usually used five to eight instruments—a few trumpets, trombones, a rhythm section of drums and a plucked string bass, a piano or perhaps a banjo. Their distinct style came from a marvellous improvising. Most music compositions, whether the symphonies of Brahms or the marches of John Phillip Sousa, were written out in advance and played note by note. A jazz piece provided only a backdrop, a kind of rough musical framework. Within these limits, musicians would embellish the melody, playing off one another, encourag-ing their partners to go them one better.

The jazz style spread when the "Original Dixieland Jazz Band" (hardly origi-nal but possessed of the advantage of being white) recorded a few numbers for the phonograph. The music became a sensation in New York in 1917 and soon spread to other parts of the country. Black New Orleans stalwarts like Joe "King" Oliver's Creole Jazz Band began touring; in Chicago Oliver introduced audiences to a young cornet player named Louis Armstrong, who became a leading jazz musician and arranger in his own right. In 1924 Paul Whiteman inaugurated respectable "white" jazz in a concert at Carnegie Hall, and George Gershwin was soon adapt-ing its rhythms to musicals and symphonic compositions like "Rhapsody in Blue." Guardians of good taste and propriety denounced such music as "intellectual and spiritual debauchery." Whiteman disagreed: "Jazz is the folk music of the machine age."

The Art of Alienation

Painters of the Ashcan School continued to find subjects, in the words of teacher Robert Henri, "anywhere, everywhere," but mostly where they always had—in the strident life of the industrial city. George Bellows painted violent prizefights, the most famous of which depicted Argentina's Luis Firpo knocking Jack Dempsey from the ring. Charles Sheeler broke with the gauzy, artistic photography of the past. He snapped the machine age, shot by raw shot, most notably in a study of Henry Ford's Rouge Assembly Plant. Georgia O'Keeffe moved in the opposite direction. As warm as Sheeler's work was cool, her paintings represented passion and sexuality in near-abstract shapes and bold colors.

Before the war a generation of young writers had begun rebelling against Victorian purity. During the war years many lost faith in reason and progress, seeking relief from a comforting "nihilism" that denied all meaning in life. When the conflict ended they launched a brilliant assault on small towns, big business, conformity, technology, and material culture. Some fled to the urban bohemia of Greenwich Village in New York City. Others, called expatriates, simply left the country for the artistic freedom of London and Paris (where the rising value of the dollar also made living cheaper). Their alienation helped to produce a literary outpouring unmatched in American history.

On the eve of World War I the poet Ezra Pound had predicted an "American Risorgimento" that would "make the Italian Renaissance look like a tempest in a teapot." From Europe the expatriate Pound began to make it happen. Abandoning rhyme and meter, he decried the "botched civilization" that had produced the war. Another voluntary exile, T. S. Eliot, bemoaned the emptiness of modern life in his epic poem *The Waste Land* (1922). Ernest Hemingway captured the disillusionment of the age in his novels *The Sun Also Rises* (1926) and *A Farewell to Arms* (1929), where resolution came as it had in war—by death.

At home Sherwood Anderson led a revolt against small-town life. In 1912, at the age of 36, Anderson walked out of his paint factory in Elyria, Ohio. After a nervous breakdown, in 1919 he published his masterpiece, *Winesburg, Ohio*, a series of short stories connected by place and mood. Compassionate but pessimistic, Anderson examined the underside of the small town. He wrote about frustrated spinsters, repressed businessmen, pimply teenagers. Some were near suicide; all had sex on their minds. No American novel of the period had greater influence on those that followed.

A year later Minnesota-born Sinclair Lewis, the first American to win a Nobel Prize in literature, wrote *Main Street*. A scathing vision of small-town life in the Midwest, the book described "savorless people, gulping tasteless food, . . . saying mechanical things about the excellence of Ford automobiles, and viewing themselves as the greatest race in the world." It sold 3 million copies. His next novel, *Babbitt* (1922), dissected small-town businessman George Follansbee Babbitt, a peppy realtor from fictional Zenith. Faintly absurd and supremely dull, Babbitt was the epitome of the average.

The novels of another Minnesotan, F. Scott Fitzgerald, glorified youth and romantic individualism but found redemption nowhere. His heroes, like Amory Blaine in *This Side of Paradise* (1920), spoke for a generation "grown up to find all Gods dead, all wars fought, all faiths in man shaken." Like most writers of the decade, Fitzgerald saw life largely as a personal affair—opulent, always self-absorbing, and ultimately tragic. It was "characteristic of the Jazz Age," he wrote, "that it had no interests in politics at all."

John Dos Passos, whose novels pulsed with the energy and edginess of the machine age, was a notable exception. The child of Portuguese immigrants, Dos Passos embraced individualism and communism equally, fought entrenched power, and saw the country as divided along class, ethnic, and racial lines. "All right," he said in *The Big Money* (1931), the last volume of his searing *U.S.A.* trilogy, "we are two nations."

A "New Negro"

As World War I seared white intellectuals, so too did it galvanize blacks. Postwar unemployment and racial violence dashed blacks' hopes for equality with white

Born in Jamaica in 1887, Marcus Garvey founded his "Back to Africa" movement in 1914. He went to prison for mail fraud in 1925, but it was like "jailing a rainbow," said one observer. President Coolidge pardoned Garvey in 1927, then deported him to Jamaica.

America. Common folk in urban slums found an outlet for their alienation in a charismatic nationalist from Jamaica named Marcus Garvey.

Garvey had come to America in 1916, bringing with him an organization and a dream. The Universal Negro Improvement Association (UNIA) was Garvey's vehicle for returning Africans to Africa and Africa to Africans. He decried racial prejudice and stressed black superiority, pride, education, and industry. "Up you mighty race," he told his followers, "you can accomplish what you will." By 1920 Garvey claimed 4 million followers. Even his harshest critics admitted there were at least half a million members in more than 30 branches of his organization. It was the first mass movement of African-Americans in history. When Garvey spoke at the first national convention of the UNIA in 1920, more than 25,000 supporters jammed Madison Square Garden in New York to hear him preach black nationalism and separatism.

In 1925 Garvey's dream shattered. He was convicted of mail fraud for having oversold stock in his Black Star Line, the steamship company founded to take Africans back to Africa. The movement fell apart, but its audacious spirit infected other African-Americans. As Garvey rose to prominence a renaissance of black literature, painting, and sculpture was brewing in Harlem. The first inklings came in 1922 when Claude McKay, another Jamaican immigrant, published a book of poems entitled *White Shadows*. McKay mixed defiance with racial pride in his most famous poem, "If We Must Die."

> If we must die, let it not be like hogs
> Hunted and penned in an inglorious spot, . . .
> Like men we'll face the murderous, cowardly pack,
> Pressed to the wall, dying but fighting back!

Often supported by white patrons, or "angels," young black writers and artists found their subjects in the street life of cities, the folkways of the rural South, or further back in the primitivism of preindustrial cultures. Though generally not promoters of racial protest, the young artists of the Harlem Renaissance drew on the new assertiveness of African-Americans as well as on the alienation of white intellectuals. In 1925 Alain Locke, a black professor from Howard University, collected a sampling of their works in *The New Negro*. The title reflected not only a new artistic movement but a new racial consciousness as well.

DEFENDERS OF THE FAITH

Like the races, America itself was divided. One part of the nation looked ahead, the other back. Modernists rushed toward a glorious future of machines, organization, middle-class urban living, and cosmopolitan tolerance. Traditionalists followed a cherished older faith, associated with rural life and valuing neighborliness, small communities, and comfortable sameness.

The two had stood side by uneasy side for decades. In the 1920s the emergence of a mass society sharpened awareness of the differences—and the dangers—each saw in the other. As modernism transformed the country, traditional culture hardened, looking on change with suspicion and diversity with dismay. If urban cosmopolitans could be patronizing about the "rubes" and "hayseeds" from the country, country folk could be mean-spirited and intolerant in return. They could draw support from their allies—rural migrants to cities and an embattled Protestant elite. All were determined to defend the older order against the modern age.

Nativism and Restriction of Immigration

In May 1920 Nicola Sacco and Bartolomeo Vanzetti, two Italian aliens and admitted anarchists, were indicted for a shoe company robbery and murder in South Braintree, Massachusetts. Most of the evidence linking them to the crime was circumstantial. In July 1921, after a jury found them guilty, Judge Webster Thayer sentenced them to death. For the next six years they appealed the decision. Each time Thayer denied their motions, even when a Rhode Island gang member confessed to the crime.

The case, seemingly a straightforward robbery and murder, became one of the most celebrated of the decade. Critics charged that Sacco and Vanzetti were innocent, convicted only for being foreign-born radicals. Whatever the merits of their case, the two never received a fair hearing. Testimony at their trial often focused on their anarchist beliefs, draft evasion, and foreign birth. Thayer himself had called them "anarchist bastards" in private. When a special commission including the presidents of Harvard and the Massachusetts Institute of Technology denied clemency, the forces of upper-class respectability seemed aligned against them. For protesters around the world, Sacco and Vanzetti were symbols of bigotry and prejudice. In August 1927, when they were executed, 50,000 marchers wearing red armbands followed the funeral procession for eight miles to bid a final farewell.

By then, nativism—a rabid hostility to foreigners—had produced the most restrictive immigration laws in American history. In the aftermath of World War I immigration was running close to 1 million a year, almost as high as prewar levels. Most immigrants came from eastern and southern Europe; the majority were Catholics and Jews. With just over half the American population white and of native-born parents, alarmists like novelist Kenneth Roberts worried that unrestricted immigration would produce "a hybrid race of people as worthless and futile as the good-for-nothing mongrels of Central America and Southeastern Europe." Appreciating the benefits of a shrunken labor pool, the American Federation of Labor supported restriction too.

Led by Henry Cabot Lodge of Massachusetts and Hiram Johnson of California, in 1921 Congress enacted emergency legislation that established an annual limit on immigration. A quota set the number of entrants at 350,000 a year and parceled them out on the basis of 3 percent of each nationality living in the United States as of 1910. Asian immigration was banned entirely. Three years later the National Origins Act cut the quota to 150,000, pushed the base year back to 1890 (before the bulk of southern and eastern Europeans arrived), and made the restrictions permanent.

The National Origins Act fixed the pattern of immigration for the next four decades. Immigration from southern and eastern Europe was reduced to a trickle, while the steady flow of northern and western Europeans continued. In Congress support for restriction was especially strong among rural members who saw limiting immigration as a matter not only of race and religion but also of beliefs and loyalties. "On the one side," declared a representative from Kansas during the debate, "is beer, bolshevism, unassimilating settlements and perhaps many flags—

on the other is constitutional government; one flag, stars and stripes." The great movement of Europeans to America, a migration of classes and nationalities that had been unimpeded for 300 years, came largely to an end.

The "Noble Experiment"

In the same years that Sacco and Vanzetti were appealing their case, the "noble experiment" of Prohibition was under way. The Eighteenth Amendment, banning the sale, manufacture, importation, and transportation of liquor, took effect in January 1920. For nearly a hundred years reformers had tried to reduce the consumption of alcohol. Progressive temperance arguments stressed efficiency, public health, and the corrupting influence of the saloon. In World War I the need to feed starving war victims prompted the conservation of grains for food. Meanwhile hysterical patriots questioned the loyalties of breweries with German names and fellow citizens who drank beer and ale.

Where in force, Prohibition was not total: as private citizens, Americans could still keep liquor in their homes and serve drinks to their friends. They simply could not make, sell, or import any "intoxicating beverage." The Volstead Act, an enforcement statute passed in September 1919, defined an "intoxicating beverage" as one containing 0.5 percent alcohol. The act permitted the use of existing stocks of liquor for religious and medicinal purposes and allowed the manufacture of industrial alcohol—but only if rendered poisonous.

Prohibition never stamped out liquor, but it did reduce consumption (as much as half by some accounts). Despite the availability of "moonshine" and hard cider, drinking declined in rural areas. Cities recorded fewer deaths from alcohol and fewer arrests for drunkenness. From the start, however, enforcement was underfunded and understaffed. The Justice Department's Prohibition Bureau consisted of 1500 agents. The entire Pacific Northwest never had more than 20 agents to cover it. Not one was given an airplane, a boat, or an automobile. Their salary of $2000 a year amounted to a license to steal. One New York agent banked over $1.6 million in four months on the job. Other agents, like Izzy Einstein and his partner Moe Smith, were honest and dedicated. Disguised as everything from rabbis to college deans, they made nearly 3000 arrests. Still others, frustrated and poorly trained, relied on quick triggers, pistol whippings, or their fists.

Prohibition had always been unpopular with a sizable minority of Americans. In southern Florida people drilled holes in coconuts, added brown sugar, waited three weeks, and enjoyed a pungent "cocowhiskey." Some citizens, like Alice Roosevelt Longworth, wife of the Speaker of the House of Representatives, made their own home brew in copper stills purchased at hardware stores. A few states never ratified the Eighteenth Amendment; others refused to enact local enforcement statutes.

The consequences of so vast a social experiment as Prohibition were often unexpected. Prohibition reversed the prewar trend toward beer and wine, since hard liquor brought greater profits to bootleggers. Ironically, it advanced the cause of women's rights: saloons had discriminated against "ladies," having them enter by a separate door; speakeasies welcomed them. A democratic air prevailed inside, where everybody broke the law together. Prohibition also helped to line the pockets—and boost the fame—of gangsters. "Scarface" Al Capone moved from New York to Chicago in 1920. Seven years later he was the best known mobster in America, with a $60 million empire of alcohol, gambling, extortion, prostitution, and drugs. Thousands of poor immigrants looked to bootlegging to move them out of the slums, and cities erupted in a mayhem of violence among rival gangs.

Prohibition worked best as cultural and class legislation. Support for Prohibition had always been strongest among Protestant evangelical churches, including Baptists and Methodists. And there had always been a strong antiurban and anti-immigrant bias among reformers. As it turned out, cities recorded the steepest decline in drinking, especially among working-class ethnics, just as reformers had hoped. Only the rich had enough money to drink regularly without risking death or blindness, the common effects of cheap, tainted liquor. Working-class Americans, concentrated like the wealthy in cities, had a strong incentive to avoid the only liquor they could afford. Not only did they find themselves deprived of alcohol, but they lost the saloon as well. The saloon had functioned as their labor exchange, union hall, and social club as well as a source of corruption, but Prohibition turned it into a speakeasy for the middle and upper classes. Workers went to the movies or enjoyed radio instead. Traditionalists might celebrate the triumph of the "noble experiment," but most urbanites either ignored or resented it.

KKK

On Thanksgiving Day 1915, just outside Atlanta, 16 men trudged up a rocky trail to the crest of Stone Mountain. Leading them was William Simmons, 35 years old, tall and thin, formerly a circuit-riding Methodist minister and fraternal organizer. As night fell the assembly gathered around a burning wooden cross and by its light swore allegiance to the Invisible Empire, Knights of the Ku Klux Klan. A week later they received a preliminary charter from the state of Georgia. The KKK was reborn.

The modern Klan, a modified throwback to the hooded order of Reconstruction days (p. 635), reflected the particular insecurities of the New Era. Any white man could join the old Klan, but the new one admitted only "native born, white, gentile Americans." No Catholics could enter the order. Members believed in 100 percent Americanism and feared "foreigners" as much as African-Americans. In Texas Klansmen fed off hatred for Mexicans; in California, for Japanese; in New York, for Jews and other immigrants. Unlike the hooded night riders of old, the reborn Klan was not confined to the rural South. By the 1920s the capital of the Klan was Indianapolis, Indiana, and it had chapters in towns and cities as well. More than half of its leadership and over a third of its members came from metropolises of more than 100,000 people. Even the urban Northeast succumbed. In May 1923, Klansmen gathered, 10,000 strong, in New Brunswick, New Jersey, barely out of sight of New York City, and set a 62-foot cross ablaze.

The new Klan drew on the culture of small-town America. It was philanthropic, patriotic, and avowedly fraternal. Its elaborate regalia and rituals included white-hooded sheets and satin robes; titles of "Imperial Wizard," "Exalted Cyclops," and "Klaliff"; songs called "klodes"; and a secret handshake. A typical Klan gathering involved whole families, drawn together by fireworks, a barbecue, hymn-singing, oaths of loyalty to flag and country—all capped by the burning of a giant cross. Often working-class Americans of old Protestant stock, Klan members usually found themselves at the bottom of an industrialized, urbanized society. With few skills, they lived on the edge of unemployment and poverty, threatened by blacks and immigrants, anxious about changing codes of conduct, "moral

A raw and brutal form of racial violence, lynching continued to be a national scourge well into the 1920s and 1930s, when Paul Cadmus drew this searing study entitled *To the Lynching!* In 1919 alone more than seventy African-Americans were lynched, some of them returning soldiers still in uniform. In 1921, at the prompting of the National Association for the Advancement of Colored People, Representative L. C. Dyer of Missouri introduced the first antilynching bill in Congress. Despite passage in the House, the bill was filibustered to death by southerners in the Senate. Later antilynching bills met similar fates.

decay," and the rise of cities. Klan membership gave them reassurance and undreamed-of status. They could "klasp" each other's hands, converse in secret language, and feel as secure as any small-town lodge member.

Klansmen lived with the hope of restoring an older America. They fought for laissez-faire capitalism and fundamental Protestantism; white supremacy; chastity, fidelity, and parental authority; Prohibition; law and order; and an America free of foreigners. When benign methods failed they resorted to brutality—floggings, kidnapings, acid mutilations, and murder. In Houston a woman accused of bigamy, a doctor suspected of performing abortions, and a lawyer who accepted blacks as clients were whipped, tarred, and feathered. A naturalized citizen in Alabama was lashed for marrying a native-born woman. The Klan played so heavily on a fear of Catholics that when a train rumored to be carrying the pope pulled into Kokomo, Indiana, a mob stoned it.

Klan members may have distrusted the New Era's new values, but like so many other schemes of the decade, the Klan itself was dedicated to making money. Using modern promotional techniques, two professional fund-raisers, and an army of 1000 salesmen (called "kleagles"), the Klan enrolled a million new members by the end of 1921. By 1922 some 5000 applications were pouring in every day, and soon there were perhaps 5 million members. Moving into politics, the Klan won control of legislatures in Indiana, Texas, Oklahoma, and Oregon. It was instrumental in electing six governors, three senators, and thousands of local officials. In 1924 the KKK became so powerful that it blocked the Democratic National Convention from adopting a plank condemning it.

At the height of its strength, the Ku Klux Klan began to unravel. In an attempt to prove their power, 50,000 Klansmen marched down Pennsylvania Avenue in August 1925, but a violent thunderstorm burst over the rally like an omen of doom and sent Klansmen scurrying for shelter. Across the country in elections for mayor, governor, or senator, Klan-backed candidates lost as conventional politicians fought back. Sex scandals and financial corruption rocked its leadership and embarrassed members who saw themselves as guardians of morality. In November 1925, David Stephenson, grand dragon of the Indiana Klan and the most powerful leader in the Midwest, was sentenced to life imprisonment for rape and second-degree murder. The Klan never recovered.

Fundamentalism versus Darwinism

Although Aimee Semple McPherson and Bruce Barton adapted their religions to the cultural changes of the New Era, many Protestants, especially in rural areas, felt as though they had been under steady assault over the past half century. They felt threatened by the tide of Catholic and Jewish immigrants who poured into the country demanding a place in America. Equally troubling was the secular culture of modern life and its fluid morality, as well as scientific theories about geology, the age of the earth, and a skepticism about the possibility of miracles. The number of churches steadily declined during the decade. Despite an increase of nearly 13 million in church membership, many pastors reported fewer and fewer of their flock actually in attendance. Some pastors abandoned Sunday evening services altogether. Others attempted to reconcile the Bible with the modern world by stressing Jesus' ethical teachings rather than dealing with the miracle-oriented questions of bodily resurrection and the Day of Judgment, heaven, and hell.

Troubled conservatives had combined, as early as the late 1870s, to combat modernist influences. Between 1909 and 1912 two wealthy Los Angeles laymen, Lyman and Milton Stewart, subsidized a series of booklets known as *The Fundamentals*, which were sent to "every pastor, evangelist, minister, theological professor, theological student, Sunday school superintendent, YMCA and YWCA secretary in the English speaking world." The 3 million copies distributed stressed the "verbal inerrancy" of scripture: every word of the Bible was literally true. Proponents of this view, who after 1920 were increasingly known as "fundamentalists," saw themselves as defenders of traditional religion. Yet their literal reading of scripture was hardly traditional, for many Christian theologians in the past had interpreted various passages of scripture allegorically.

Fundamentalists maintained effective ministries nationwide, and they could be found among Presbyterians, Methodists, and other denominations. They were strongest in the South, however, especially among Baptists. Nothing disturbed them more than Darwinian theories of evolution, which by definition denied the divine origin of humankind and made the creation story of Adam and Eve either fanciful mythmaking or at best a parable. In 1925 George Washington Butler, a part-time schoolteacher and clerk of the Round Lick Association of Primitive Baptists, succeeded in convincing his fellow Tennessee legislators to make it illegal to teach that "man has descended from a lower order of animals."

Tennessee was neither the first nor the last state to seek legal means to restrain the onslaught of modern scientific ideas. Oklahoma, Florida, Mississippi, and Arkansas all passed similar statutes. What made Tennessee exceptional was the decision of some skeptics in the town of Dayton to test the legality of Butler's law. In the spring of 1925 a slender, bespectacled biology teacher named John T. Scopes was charged with violating the statute by teaching evolution. Behind the scenes, Scopes' sponsors were as much preoccupied with boosting their town's commercial fortunes as with the defense of free speech. When the Scopes trial opened in July it took on the flavor of a championship boxing match. Hot dog, lemonade, and sandwich stands lined the streets; vendors sold everything from Bibles to stuffed monkeys; loudspeakers relayed court proceedings to the thousands of people who stood outside, cooling themselves with toothpaste company fans that read "Do Your Gums Bleed?" Millions more listened over the radio to the first trial ever broadcast. Inside the courtroom, trial judge John Raulston sat beneath a banner advising "Read Your Bible Daily."

On one side of the bench stood Clarence Darrow, the most famous defense lawyer in the country and a professed agnostic, who had journeyed from Chicago to act as co-counsel for Scopes. Opposing him was William Jennings Bryan, the three-time presidential candidate who had recently joined the antievolution crusade. It was urban Darrow against rural Bryan in what Bryan described as a "duel to the death" between Christianity and evolution.

When Judge Raulston ruled that scientists imported by the defense could not be called on behalf of evolution (their testimony was considered "hearsay" because they had not been present at the Creation), the defense virtually collapsed. To keep the trial going (and to save his skin from angry vendors and town boosters) Judge Raulston agreed to let Darrow put Bryan on the stand. Darrow made him admit, to the horror of many of his followers, that the Earth was not made "in six days of 24-hours." In the end, the Dayton jury took eight minutes to find Scopes guilty and fine him $100. But by then the trial had become more of a national joke than a confrontation between darkness and light. The New Era would continue to be condemned in many quarters, but it could not be repealed. The larger issue of how much religious beliefs could influence public education in a nation where church and state were constitutionally separated would remain relevant as scientific, religious, and cultural standards clashed.

REPUBLICANS ASCENDANT

On March 4, 1921, Woodrow Wilson limped from the White House to a waiting automobile, took a seat beside President-elect Warren G. Harding, and rode down Pennsylvania Avenue to the Capitol. After the inauguration Wilson returned to his S Street house and lived the remaining three years of his life in bitter seclusion. Harding, the former Republican senator from Ohio, had won a smashing victory over Ohio governor James Cox and his young running mate, Franklin D. Roosevelt. "It wasn't a landslide," said Wilson's personal secretary after the election, "it was an earthquake." The Republicans were again ascendant.

"The change is amazing," wrote a Washington reporter shortly after the inauguration. "The populace is on a broad grin." The contrast in presidents could not have been more striking. Wilson had been ill, reclusive, and austere. Harding was handsome, warm, and lovable. Wilson had kept his own counsel; Harding promised to bring the "best minds" into the cabinet and let them run things. For the first time in four years, sentries disappeared from the gates of the White House, tourists walked the halls, and reporters freely questioned the president. The reign of "normalcy," as Harding called it, began. "By 'normalcy' I don't mean the older order," he had said during the campaign, "but a regular steady order of things. I mean normal procedure, the natural way, without excess." That Christmas, in a typical gesture of goodwill, Harding released socialist Eugene Debs from jail and invited him to dinner at the White House.

The Politics of Normalcy

"Normalcy" turned out to be anything but normal. After eight years of Democratic rule, Republicans controlled the White House from 1921 to 1933 and both houses of Congress from 1919 to 1931. For only the second time since Reconstruction one party ruled Washington for a decade. Fifteen years of reform gave way to eight years of consolidation and cautious uses of government. A strong executive fell into weak hands. The cabinet and the Congress set the course of the nation.

Harding and his successor, Calvin Coolidge, were content with delegating power. To the cabinet Harding appointed some men of true quality: Charles Evans Hughes as secretary of state; Henry C. Wallace as secretary of agriculture; and Herbert Hoover as secretary of commerce. He also made, as *The New Republic* put it, some "unspeakably bad appointments": his old crony Harry Daugherty as attorney general and New Mexico Senator Albert Fall as interior secretary. In the end they undermined his administration. Daugherty sold influence for cash and resigned in 1923. Three years later only a divided jury saved him from jail. In 1929 Fall became the first cabinet member to be convicted of a felony. In 1922 he had accepted bribes of over $400,000 for secretly leasing naval oil reserves at Elk Hill, California, and Teapot Dome, Wyoming, to private oil companies.

Harding died suddenly in August 1923, before the scandals came to light, leaving Vice President Coolidge to clean up the mess. Though Harding would be remembered for a lackluster reign of normalcy, his tolerance and moderation had a calming influence on the strife-ridden nation. Slowly he had even begun to lead. In 1921 he created a new Bureau of the Budget that brought modern accounting techniques to the management of federal revenues. Toward the end of his administration he averted a scandal from the Veterans' Bureau and set an agenda for Congress that included expanding the merchant marine.

To his credit Calvin Coolidge handled Harding's sordid legacy with skill and dispatch. He created a special investigatory commission, prosecuted the wrongdoers, and restored the confidence of the nation. Decisiveness, when he chose to exercise it, was one of Coolidge's hallmarks. As governor of Massachusetts, he had ended the Boston police strike in 1919 with a firm declaration: "There can be no right to strike against the public safety by anybody, anywhere, anytime." He was honest and ascetic, privately talkative but notoriously tight-lipped in public. He believed in small-town democracy and minimalist government. Practicing what he preached, he slept 11 hours a day while president, more than any of his predecessors. "One of the most important accomplishments of my administration," he observed later, "has been minding my own business." Above all Coolidge worshiped wealth. "Civilization and profits," he once said, "go hand in hand."

As president his popularity rivaled Harding's. In an age of consumption and ballyhoo, his Yankee frugality and taciturn manner reassured Americans, off on an orgy of spending. Barely half the qualified voters cast ballots in the election in 1924, but they returned Coolidge to the White House by a margin of nearly two to one. Coolidge gave the credit to "Divine Providence." In fact the victory was yet another sign that Americans had wearied of reform, delighted in surging prosperity, and approved of the business-dominated Republican government. Whether the policies served the economy or the nation well in the long term, however, was open to question.

The Policies of Mellon and Hoover

Coolidge retained most of Harding's cabinet, including two of its most powerful members, treasury secretary Andrew Mellon and commerce secretary Herbert

Hoover. Mellon, a favorite of Old Guard Republicans, revived traditional Republican conservatism; Hoover developed innovative policies that reflected the new mass-production economy. Both placed themselves in service of business; as a result, the role of government in the economy grew. After a brief postwar decline, moreover, the number of federal employees increased by over 40,000 between 1921 and 1930.

Mellon, president of aluminum giant Alcoa, was the third richest man in the country (behind Ford and Rockefeller). He believed that prosperity "trickled down" from rich to poor through investment, which in turn raised production, employment, and wages. For more than a decade he devoted himself to cutting government spending and reducing taxes on high incomes. The rich would benefit from the lower taxes, invest more, and invigorate the economy. In 1921 Mellon got Congress to repeal the excess-profits tax on corporations, but progressives blunted his efforts to slash income taxes, 75 percent of which were paid by the wealthiest 2 percent of Americans. Bolstered by the Coolidge landslide, in 1926 he persuaded Congress to end all gift taxes and halve the estate tax and to cut the maximum income tax from 40 to 20 percent. In 1928 he reduced corporation and consumption taxes still further.

Business leaders applauded the Mellon tax program, which almost completely reversed the progressive tax policies of the Wilson era. They had contributed $8 million to Harding's campaign in 1920, and they profited most from the tax cuts. They also benefited from the narrow economic nationalism pushed by conservatives—tariff revision. In 1921 Congress, worried about rising imports from Europe, passed an emergency tariff act to increase the moderate rates of the 1913 Underwood–Simmons Tariff. In 1922 the Fordney–McCumber Tariff lifted schedules even higher. Farmers, who supported the increase, won protection too—but at a price. For each dollar they gained by keeping out agricultural products, costs on manufactured goods they needed rose by $3.50.

Herbert Hoover, a mining engineer who had made himself a millionaire, transformed the lowly Commerce Department into one of the most active agencies in Washington. Among insiders he was known as "Secretary of Commerce and Under Secretary of Everything Else." Unlike Mellon, Hoover was no narrow conservative. Dedicated to efficiency, distribution, cooperation, and service, he espoused a progressive capitalism that tried to navigate between centralization

Andrew Mellon, secretary of the treasury and the millionaire head of an aluminum monopoly, is flanked by Grace and Calvin Coolidge on the lawn of the White House. A disciple of business, President Coolidge believed that what was of "real importance to wage-earners was not how they might conduct a quarrel with their employers but how the business of the country might be so organized as to insure steady employment at a fair rate of pay. If that were done there would be no occasion for a quarrel, and if it were not done a quarrel would do no good."

and laissez faire to serve public needs. Called "associationalism," it sought to bring stability and order to industry by relying on trade associations, industry-wide organizations of business firms. By 1929 there were nearly 2000 of them. Government provided advice, statistical information, and forums for business leaders to exchange ideas, set standards for industries, and cooperate in developing markets. At the same time Hoover promoted welfare capitalism, encouraging firms to sponsor company unions, pay employees decent wages, and develop responsible social programs that protected workers from factory hazards and unemployment.

In government and industry Hoover declared war on waste. To "Hooverize" meant to economize, save, and share. The newly created Division of Simplified Practices of the Commerce Department held more than 1200 conferences and helped industries standardize everything from accounting procedures to toilet paper. The real efficiencies thereby gained saved businesses millions. Meanwhile the Overseas Market Division worked to expand foreign markets and fought international cartels in raw materials such as rubber, silk, and nitrates. Government and business, building on the ties developed during World War I, dropped all pretense of a laissez-faire economy and forged a corporate commonwealth. "Never before, here or elsewhere," boasted the *Wall Street Journal*, "has a government been so completely fused with business."

Postwar trends pushed farmers outside the magic circle of Republican prosperity. By far the biggest business in America, farming had an investment value greater than manufacturing, all utilities, and all railroads combined. A third of the population relied on farming for their livelihood. Yet the farmers' portion of the national income had shrunk from 16 percent in 1919 to 9 percent by 1929. The government withdrew price supports for wheat and ended its practice of feeding refugees with American surpluses. The postwar impoverishment of Europe reduced the export market. Wartime speculation in farmland and heavy equipment purchases doubled farmers' prewar mortgage debt. New dietary habits meant that average Americans of 1920 ate 75 fewer pounds of food than they had 10 years earlier. The development of synthetic fibers like rayon drove down demand for natural wool and cotton fibers. And the 1920 harvest brought what farmers wanted least—bumper crops to drive prices down further. In one year American farmers suffered a net loss estimated at $6 billion.

In 1921 a group of southern and western senators organized the "farm bloc" to unite farm-district congressmen behind agricultural legislation. Over the next two years they brought stockyards, packers, and grain exchanges under federal supervision. The Capper–Volstead Act (1922) exempted farm cooperatives from antitrust actions, and the Intermediate Credit Act (1923) created 12 banks for low-interest farm loans. Regulation and cheap credit were not enough, so in 1924 Senator Charles McNary and Representative Gilbert Haugen proposed a radical plan to raise American farm prices by selling staple crop surpluses abroad. Since it did not address the central problem of overproduction and would have sent agricultural prices plummeting overseas, McNary–Haugenism was doomed to fail. When Congress passed the bill in 1927 and again in 1928, President Coolidge vetoed it.

For four years President Coolidge continued to run a "businessman's government." His administration balanced the budget, scaled down the federal debt, reduced corporate, estate, and income taxes, and decreased antitrust suits. Serious economic imbalances were ignored. Insulated from government regulation, corporations grew and corporate profits soared. But workers reaped far fewer gains in wages, purchasing power, and bargaining power. Although welfare capitalism promised compensating benefits, only a handful of companies put the philosophy into practice. Those that did often used it simply to weaken independent unions. Most farmers languished throughout the decade. When President Coolidge vetoed the price supports of McNary–Haugenism, he offered nothing in their place. High tariffs protected American manufacturers but left desperate Europeans with no place to send their exports. And on Wall Street shaky methods of finance and investment were leaving a dangerous legacy. "Nero fiddled while Rome burned," observed H. L. Mencken. "Coolidge only snores."

The Election of 1928

On August 2, 1927, the fourth anniversary of Calvin Coolidge's elevation to the presidency, 30 reporters assigned to cover his vacation entered a mathematics classroom at the Rapid City High School in South Dakota for a presidential press conference. As they filed past Coolidge, he handed each a slip of paper on which was typed a terse message: "I do not choose to run for President in nineteen twenty-eight."

Republicans, bowing to the will of "Silent Cal," nominated Herbert Hoover as his successor. Hoover was not a politician but an administrator who had never run for public office. His entire campaign consisted of seven speeches, delivered in typical Hoover fashion—head bent, eyes riveted to the page, left hand nervously jiggling the keys in his pocket. However flat the midwestern tones of his delivery, his message was bland: "We in America today are nearer to the final triumph over poverty than ever before in the history of any land." Republican prosperity would be difficult for any Democrat to beat. Hoover—Iowa-born Quaker, self-made millionaire, dry (he drank no alcohol), perhaps the most admired official in America—would make the task impossible.

The Democratic party, on the other hand, continued to be dangerously polarized between its rural supporters in the South and West and urban laborers in the

THE ELECTION OF 1928
Historians still debate whether the election of 1928 was a pivotal one that produced a significant political realignment. Hoover cracked the solidly Democratic South, which returned to the Democratic fold in 1932. On the other hand, Democrat Al Smith won the twelve largest cities in the country, all of which had voted Republican in 1924 but stayed in the Democratic fold in 1932.

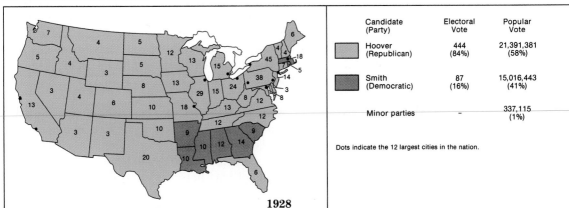

Candidate (Party)	Electoral Vote	Popular Vote
Hoover (Republican)	444 (84%)	21,391,381 (58%)
Smith (Democratic)	87 (16%)	15,016,443 (41%)
Minor parties	–	337,115 (1%)

Dots indicate the 12 largest cities in the nation.

1928

Northeast. The two factions had clashed during the 1924 convention, where rural delegates had rallied behind William Gibbs McAdoo. McAdoo, a former secretary of the Treasury and wartime head of the Railroad Administration, was as dry as a desert on the subject of Prohibition, openly criticized city life, and enjoyed the endorsement of William Jennings Bryan and the Ku Klux Klan. To boot, he was Woodrow Wilson's son-in-law, the heir apparent to the presidency. But the urban wing of the party was set on New York governor Alfred E. Smith, a Tammany Hall politician, the grandchild of Irish immigrants. As governor he combined support for social legislation with fiscal orthodoxy, administrative economy, and honest politics. The 1924 convention had deadlocked at 102 ballots before finally settling on an entirely different compromise ticket: conservative Wall Street lawyer John W. Davis and Charles W. Bryan, the radical governor of Nebraska and brother of William Jennings Bryan. The ticket was less balanced than "schizoid." It won fewer votes than any Democratic presidential team in the twentieth century. Robert La Follette, running for president in 1924 as an independent Progressive, fell only 3.5 million votes short of the Davis–Bryan total.

By 1928 the shift in population toward cities had given the urban wing control of the party. Al Smith won the nomination on the first ballot, even though his liabilities were evident. He had a jarring New York accent. When he spoke "poisonally" on the "rha-dio" to voters across America, they winced collectively. He claimed jokingly not even to know what states were west of the Mississippi River. Though he pledged to enforce Prohibition, he campaigned against it. He even took an occasional drink, which produced the spurious rumor that Smith was not only wet but a hopeless alcoholic. Most damaging of all, he was Catholic, at a time when anti-Catholicism remained virulent in many areas of the country. Baptist ministers in the South and Methodists in the North advised their flocks to "Vote as You Pray," and they did. Nearly 60 percent of the eligible voters turned out to give all but eight states to Hoover. The solidly Democratic South cracked for the first time, as the Republicans carried Texas, Florida, Kentucky, Virginia, and North Carolina. No Democrat could have beaten the Republicans, but Smith's urban roots, wetness, and Catholicism deepened defeat.

Buried in the returns were the stirrings of a major political realignment. Rhode Island and Massachusetts, industrial states that had voted Republican in 1924, voted Democratic, moved by a formidable Catholic vote. The 12 largest cities in the country had gone to the Republicans in 1924, but in 1928 the Democrats won them by slight margins. Western farmers, ignored by Republicans for a decade, also voted for Smith. The Democrats were becoming the party of the cities and of immigrants, a tangible nucleus around which to build a powerful vote-getting machine. Meanwhile a new kind of electorate was emerging. No longer were voters part of a vast partisan army. Instead they were embedded in a culture of consumption. Parties courted them with newspaper advertisements and, recognizing the value of publicity, persuaded them with radio "spots." In 1929 the Democrats created the first public relations department in American politics.

Modern times came to America in the 1920s. Changes building for half a century accelerated during World War I and converged with unprecedented force. Despite Harding's pledge of a return to normalcy, Americans faced growing economic concentration as fewer corporations controlled more business and a strong state became involved in monitoring personal habits like drinking. As the culture of mass society triumphed, traditional religious and parental authority declined, to the dismay of many Americans who clung to older ways of thought and action even as they experimented with new ones. This ambivalence between the old and the new produced paradoxes. Conventional small-town matrons coexisted with nonconformist flappers, Henry Ford's nostalgia for square dancing with his innovations in mass production. Traditional values continued to assert themselves in a modern culture. A business economy produced greater government intervention. A mass society looked to heroic individuals like Babe Ruth and Rudolph Valentino.

No greater hero existed than Charles Lindbergh. After his solo flight across the Atlantic in 1927 he and his plane, the *Spirit of St. Louis*, returned home aboard the warship *Memphis*. Eight other flyers had died trying to cross the ocean; Lindbergh alone succeeded. As he sailed up the Potomac, he received an honor previously reserved only for heads of state, a 21-gun salute. President Coolidge brought him to the White House. Four million screaming fans buried him with ticker tape as he rode through the streets of New York. Lindbergh, wrote one reporter, "fired the imagination of mankind." Never had one person mastered a machine so completely or conquered nature so gallantly. To Americans ambivalent about mass productivity and mass consumption here was a sign. Perhaps they could control the New Era without losing their cherished individualism. For a brief moment it seemed possible.

SIGNIFICANT EVENTS

1903 — First feature-length film, *The Great Train Robbery*, released

1909 — Sigmund Freud comes to America

1914 — Henry Ford introduces moving assembly line

1915 — Modern Ku Klux Klan founded

1916 — Marcus Garvey brings Universal Negro Improvement Association to America

1919 — Eighteenth Amendment outlaws alcohol use

1920 — First commercial radio broadcast; Nineteenth Amendment grants women right to vote; Warren Harding elected president

1921 — Congress enacts quotas on immigration; Budget and Accounting Act; Sheppard–Towner Federal Maternity and Infancy Act; American Birth Control League organized; first Miss America crowned

1922 — Capper–Volstead Act; Fordney–McCumber Tariff raises rates; Sinclair Lewis' *Babbitt* published; T. S. Eliot's *The Waste Land* published

1923 — *Time* magazine founded; Harding dies; Calvin Coolidge becomes president; Harding scandals break

1924 — Coolidge elected president

1925 — Bruce Barton's *The Man Nobody Knows* published; John T. Scopes convicted of teaching evolution in Tennessee; Alain Locke's *The New Negro* published

1927 — Charles Lindbergh's solo flight across the Atlantic; McNary–Haugen farm bill vetoed; Sacco and Vanzetti executed; first "talking" film, *The Jazz Singer*, released

1928 — Herbert Hoover elected president

1929 — Robert and Helen Lynd's *Middletown* published

Generations of the Republic

The Modern Family (1900–1960)

In the first half of the twentieth century the forces of modern life overwhelmed traditionalism. Urbanism, ethnicity, the progressive drive to use expertise to mold society—all these forces shaped Americans born at the turn of the century. This generation saw the demographic balance tip from farm to city, lived through unprecedented prosperity and depression, and fought two world wars. It was indeed the first modern generation.

As industrial cities grew, American families continued their century-long contraction. By 1900 the average mother was giving birth to three or four children, compared with seven or eight a century earlier. Fertility still remained higher on the farm than in the city, while birth rates among immigrants inched above those of the urban middle class.

Historians still do not know why fertility declined, but it seems likely that the growth of cities, a desire among women for greater personal freedom, and new medical advances were responsible. City living inhibited family size. On farms children could soon be put to work at home or in the fields, but in crowded urban apartments they meant more mouths to feed and less room for other family members or rent-paying boarders. Limiting the number of newborns thus became a way to improve standards of living for the whole family.

At the same time, cosmopolitan, middle-class women believed they could gain greater personal freedom by controlling their sexual lives. After the turn of the century, they relied increasingly on contraception. In 1906, almost a decade before Margaret Sanger began her crusade for birth control, a physician reported that "hardly a single middle class family" did not expect him to help "prevent conception." By 1922 nearly three-quarters of the women questioned in one study used contraceptives. Among working-class and ethnic wives, however, knowledge of modern contraceptive techniques or access to them remained rare.

Declines in infant mortality also seem to have contributed to falling birth rates. Though still high, deaths of those under a year old dropped to one in ten, half the number a century earlier. With more children likely to survive into adulthood, there was less incentive to continue having them. Medical advances reduced in-

fectious diseases, particularly among infants and toddlers. And after the turn of the century cities began requiring that milk be pasteurized to kill bacteria and apartments ventilated to combat tuberculosis.

Childhood diseases were by no means wiped out. A mother probably spent most of her time nursing sick children. A knife cut could easily become infected and leave a child fever-ridden for days. Measles required a month of bed rest, pneumonia six months. The global influenza pandemic of 1918 killed 550,000 people in the United States alone, 10 times the number of Americans who died in World War I.

Under the impact of progressive reforms, childbirth—like other aspects of American life—became the province of trained experts. In 1900 a woman was likely to give birth at home, without an anesthetic or even a physician; after the turn of the century, male doctors trained in obstetrics began to replace midwives. Anesthetics came into use, and the use of forceps, which in the hands of untrained attendants had mangled many newborns, was curbed. By the mid-1930s almost 4 women in 10 delivered in a hospital. (By 1945 the number was nearly 8 in 10.)

Child rearing, once left entirely to the family, became community business, as middle-class mothers found themselves bombarded with expert advice. Seeing children as active creatures with special needs, progressive professionals advanced a new ideal of "scientific mothering." They recommended imposing regularity, detachment, and control, not only to produce healthy toddlers but eventually to produce an orderly, efficient society as well. Children were to be subject to rigid eating and sleeping schedules. Thumbsucking was discouraged and so was caressing, lest early sexual drives be overstimulated.

At school, "Little Mothers' Leagues" sent young girls home with special injunctions for their working-class and immigrant parents: "Don't give the baby herring; Don't give the baby beer to drink; Don't let the baby eat dirty things from the floor that she threw down at first; also pickle." The government's newly created Children's Bureau collected the prevailing wisdom in a pamphlet, *Infant Care* (1914), designed for the "average mother." "The care of the baby," it read, "is readily reduced to a system." Among immigrant families children sometimes became interpreters of the new regimen for parents who could neither speak nor understand English. "Please," one child wrote to the Children's Bureau, "can you send me your book 'Infant Care' in Greek. We can read American, but mother cannot."

Not all parents were inclined to follow the "experts'" often unrealistic advice. Complained one Wisconsin woman, "Most of the advice I have read says—

Fruite in plenty a bath every morning—gentle exercise . . . music—pleasant surrounding now I have a perfectuly fine husband and a loveing home but here is my day—get up at 5 a.m. hustle breakfast for 5, wash dishes help milk feed pigs clean up bakeing-scrubbing washing . . . where could I have the time for a bath every morn?"

As blacks increasingly moved to the city, limited opportunities placed sharp pressures on their families. Blocked from holding even factory jobs by discrimination in hiring, many black males remained chronically unemployed or were forced to work at the most menial labor. Poor housing and diet (especially a deficiency in protein) left both children and parents prey to disease. A study in 1917 in one New York City district showed that 90 percent of black infants had rickets. For pregnant mothers, rickets meant a much higher likelihood of dying during or after birth, due to puerperal fever or toxemia. Life expectancy rates among blacks, especially the women, appear to have *worsened* significantly in the half-century after the Civil War, at a time when white rates were improving. With families forced to endure such conditions, black churches attempted to provide support. By the 1920s they had established day-care services for working parents, scout troops for their children, and couples clubs for young marrieds. But urban conditions continued to be corro-

sive for those at the bottom of the social ladder.

In an industrial society that stressed technical skill, more children attended school and stayed longer. By the 1920s, for the first time in American history, a majority of teenagers went to high school instead of work. College enrollment, though still low, reached 10 percent of the eligible population by 1928; in 1890 it had been less than 3 percent. The intrusion of outside institutions like schools also meant that children spent more of their time outside the family among people their own age. By the 1920s a full-blown "peer culture" emerged. Revolving around school and friends, its components were remarkably modern—athletics, clubs, sororities and fraternities, dating, proms, "bull sessions," and moviegoing.

Tolerance for premarital sex seems to have grown in the 1920s ("necking" and "petting" parties replaced sedate tea parties), but the new subculture of youth still tied sexual relations to love. Casual sex remained rare; what changed was the point in the courtship at which sexual intimacy occurred. A growing minority of young women reported having premarital intercourse, for example, but only with their future husbands. A rigidly supervised courtship was replaced by unsupervised dating and "going together." A boy picked up his "date" usually just by honking the horn of his car. Once on the road

they were truly on their own, free from parental control.

For all the frivolity and rebelliousness it promoted, the new peer culture of the 1920s, as historian Paula Fass observed, "also subscribed to specific work values: aggressive and directed competition, merit through association, and a carefully calibrated system of prestige." These tended to fuse young adults to the larger social culture. Conformity remained the norm. Even the notorious "flappers," who wore short skirts and short hair and rouged their cheeks, usually ended up in conventional marriages that emphasized the roles of wife and mother. Modern marriage did, however, place a new premium on "companionate" values. Compatibility, emotional fulfillment, and sexual satisfaction were lauded above financial security, status, and procreation. In the words of one survey, couples envisioned "a perfect consummation of both personalities that would involve all phases of mutual living."

As this generation approached middle age in the 1930s prosperity gave way to the greatest depression in modern history. Reflecting a sense of caution about the future, marriage and birth rates fell sharply. The rate of population increase dropped from 16.1 percent in the 1920s to 7.2 in the 1930s. More women sought employment outside their homes to supplement family incomes. For those who remained at home, household chores consumed even more of their time. "Labor-saving" devices, introduced over the previous half-century, ended up making more work for women by upgrading standards of cleanliness. Automobiles added to their burdens by transforming mothers into part-time chauffeurs for their children. And the deepening depression often led to more hours canning vegetables, making clothes, and stretching family budgets with homebound businesses like laundering and baking.

Continuing the trend of the previous hundred years, old age and dying shifted from a family to a community experience, presided over by professionals. The New Deal set in place Social Security, which would be expanded gradually to cover more older citizens. And Americans of this generation were far more likely than their parents to die in a hospital or to have their bodies prepared at a funeral home. They were also likely to pay much more for the services. In 1900 a typical undertaker recommended minimum charges of $5 for washing and dressing the body, $10 for embalming, and $8 to $10 for a hearse; in the early 1960s Americans paid an average of nearly $1500 for an elaborate funeral that included body preparation, casket, burial vault or plot, flowers, clergy, and cemetery charges. Shaped by experts and oriented toward consumers, modern life governed this generation even in death.

26

Crash and Depression

igh above Columbus Circle in New York City a gigantic electric sign blinked out the happy injunction: "You should have $10,000 at the age of 30; $25,000 at the age of 40; $50,000 at the age of 50." And in the pages of the *Ladies Home Journal* John J. Raskob, who had run the Finance Committee at General Motors and who listed his profession as "capitalist," told people how. "Everyone ought to be rich," he declared: $15 a month, "wisely invested," would be worth $80,000 in 20 years. In the 1920s, when 4 families in 10 earned less than $1500 a year, that was rich.

As the decade wore on, some people did grow rich. In 1914 there were 7000 millionaires; in 1928 there were 35,000. Between 1919 and 1928 the number of six-figure incomes doubled. Easy money obsessed the nation. The volume of sales on the New York Stock Exchange jumped 400 percent from 1923 to 1928. Other exchanges in Chicago, St. Louis, San Francisco, and Los Angeles registered similar gains. Buyers were less concerned about the assets of a company than about the prospects for a rise in the price of its stock. A simple dictum governed the market: buy low, sell high; buy high, sell higher.

Possibilities for profit were everywhere, including far-off Florida. In 1929 the Marx Brothers broke into films with *The Cocoanuts,* a zany farce about real estate scams in the Sunshine State. "You can get stucco," says Groucho as he pitches a land deal. "Oh, can you get stucco!" Thousands of investors had gotten "stucco" when "land fever" hit southern Florida in the mid-1920s. Before World War I Miami was largely mangrove jungle and bug-infested swamp. Attracted by 80-degree temperatures in winter, developer Carl G. Fisher cleared the jungle, drained the swamp, put up a sea wall, and built a three-mile causeway from the beach to the mainland. Miami became the fastest growing city in America. The Miami *Herald* carried more advertising than any other newspaper in the world. Miami, residents boasted, was "the Magic City." By 1925 city lots were going for $20,000 apiece, sight unseen.

In Palm Beach, 75 miles up the coast from Miami, oceanfront property sold for $3300 a foot, up from $4.65 just three decades earlier. "Buy anywhere," said locals. "You can't lose." Gertrude Shelby, a journalist who went to Florida to write about the boom, put down a binder of $2500 on 34.5 acres, sold it before paying the first installment, and made $13,000 in one month. The Florida boom was on. So many people arrived in the summer of 1925 that famine threatened the state, and ice could be obtained only by doctor's prescription.

In the 1930s, Dorothea Lange pioneered a new realism in photography—grim, unvarnished, and poignant. Nowhere did she better capture the shattering effects of the Great Depression than in these pictures of a heavily mortgaged Georgia cotton farmer.

One mid-September night in 1926, Miami barometers dropped to 27.75—the lowest reading to date in North America. Wind howled through the city at 130 miles per hour as 20-foot waves pounded sea walls and washed away beaches. The swamp reclaimed landfills. Speculators discovered an awful truth: southern Florida lay in the middle of the hurricane belt. In one night 100 Miamians drowned; 40,000 lost their homes. Property damage in the state ran to $300 million. Reality punctured the vast speculative bubble. The value of oceanfront lots dropped from $2000 to $700 a foot. Hundreds went bankrupt; thousands lost their land to foreclosures.

Though Florida land values plummeted, the boom laid the foundation for later development, but stock market scams and speculation did nothing except turn the financial center of the nation into a gambling den. Outright swindles in phony stocks (oil wells and mines were the most popular) netted con artists more than $600 million a year. Some stock maneuvering was legal but deceptive. Favored "insiders"—from wealthy speculators like Bernard Baruch to the president of the United States—were placed on "preferred lists" at brokerage houses and tipped off about impending issues. They bought discounted stocks in advance, then sold them on the market for a tidy profit. Insiders formed "stock pools" to drive up prices so they could make a quick killing. In 1928 a group that included John Raskob pushed Radio Corporation of America stock from $90 to $109 a share. They made $5 million by selling the stock one week later.

More middle-class people were trading too, boosting the level of ignorance almost as much as the volume of sales. Once the province of the wealthy, Wall Street buzzed with tales of the dumb luck of simple folk. An actor was said to be $40,000 richer for having bought stock in just four companies. A waiter at the Exchange's Luncheon Club was supposed to have made $90,000 by investing on the basis of customers' shop talk. A group of pages from the floor of the New York Stock Exchange captured the national mood in a song they wrote for their bosses:

> O hush thee, my babe, granny's bought some more shares.
> Daddy's gone to play with the bulls and the bears,
> Mother's buying on tips and she simply can't lose,
> And baby shall have some expensive new shoes.

The stock market dominated the news. Millions watched it as closely as they watched their favorite baseball team. Even those with no money followed sales and prices just like they counted home runs and figured batting averages. In Saginaw, Michigan, and Amarillo, Texas, people shook open their morning papers to the financial pages. In Steubenville, Ohio, and Storm Lake, Iowa, they gathered at brokerage houses to watch the daily fluctuations in stocks. Some bought and sold; a few got rich quick; most shoveled their profits into the market again. Even if they lost money it did not matter. "Everybody ought to be rich"—and anyone could be. Another Florida bubble might develop at any moment; each business day brought fresh quotations on the ticker tape; untold riches were just around the corner.

So it seemed in the late 1920s, as the New Era careened toward disaster. Behind electric signs directing the pursuit of wealth and slogans exhorting it, beneath stock deals and land booms, the economy was honeycombed with weaknesses, and in 1929 it began to collapse.

THE GREAT BULL MARKET

As the last business day of the year drew to a close in 1928, the floor of the New York Stock Exchange radiated optimism. In Wall Street parlance the "bulls"—those who buy stock—had routed the "bears"—those who sell. In fact it was the greatest bull market in history as eager buyers drove prices higher and higher. Nineteen twenty-eight had been a record year with over 90,500,000 shares traded. General Electric jumped from $124 a share to $221; American Can from $70 to $117; and the Radio Corporation of America from $85 to a breathtaking $420. More remarkable still, RCA never paid a dividend. Its skyrocketing price alone was enough to keep buyers clamoring for more.

Strolling across the quarter-acre, felt-padded floor of the New York Stock Exchange, Superintendent William Crawford welcomed the New Year with a confident assertion: "The millennium's arrived"; but Alexander Noyes, a veteran financial analyst, was worried. Despite the opulence of the New York Exchange and the swelling volume of trade, there was trouble in this financial paradise. It was built on economic quicksand. Noyes knew it could not last. "Something has to give," he told reporters in the fall of 1929. Less than a month later, the Great Bull Market fell in a heap.

The Rampaging Bull

The Great Bull Market had been building for most of the decade. In the early twenties a day when 2 million shares were traded was noteworthy; by mid-decade 3 million–share days still created a stir; by 1928 4 million–share days left smug brokers convinced the stock market bubble might never burst.

No one knows exactly what caused the orgy of speculation on the market. Speculation had infected the culture, and the market was not immune. In fact a new breed of aggressive outsiders had helped to spread the speculative fever. In search of quick profits, these traders had invaded the exchanges at the start of the decade. The "Establishment," which consisted of the leading investment bankers and their clients, had ruled Wall Street since the late nineteenth century. Its members, including such leaders as J. P. Morgan, Paul Warburg, and Otto Kahn, shared both background and outlook. They came from wealthy eastern families, went to Ivy League schools, and supported the Republican party. They stood for moral rectitude, financial stability, and sound investment practices. But in the 1920s their control of the market weakened. Rich outsiders from the Midwest—William Durant of General Motors, the seven Fisher brothers from Detroit, the flamboyant Jesse Livermore—plunged in, bought millions of shares, and helped to send prices soaring.

Rambunctious individuals may have ignited the boom, but new personnel and innovative financial devices allowed it to grow. Hundreds of young "customer men"—largely untrained "go-getters"—flooded investment houses to handle the booming business. Like automobile salesmen, they had quotas to meet and were awarded bonuses for high volume. Before long, as one student of the market put it, "uninitiated brokers were selling stocks to an uninformed public." New investment trusts allowed buyers with only a few hundred dollars to participate in a portfolio of "glamour stocks." The first such trust, International Securities Trust of

America, had been formed in 1921. By 1929 a new investment trust was opening every other day. Several were created by people who simply wanted to sell their own securities. Some owned shares in other investment trusts. In this financial house of cards if one trust failed, it could bring down others, since their only assets might be stock in other investment trusts. Profits were so great, however, that by 1927 even the Establishment had become involved in such risky ventures.

Money to fuel the market became plentiful. From 1922 to 1929, some $900 million dollars worth of gold flowed into the country, a sign of international faith in the American economy. Bankers could lend up to $13 for every $1 of gold they held, so the money supply expanded by $6 billion. Over the decade corporate profits grew by 80 percent. At interest rates as high as 25 percent, more could be made from lending money to brokers (who then made "brokers' loans" to clients buying stock) than from constructing new factories or taking on sound investments. Borrowed over the phone, lent with the purchased stock as collateral, this "call money" could be collected, or called in, at any time and was usually renewable. It provided the sort of loan speculators crave—one that did not tie up their cash. By 1929 Bethlehem Steel had over $157 million in the "call money market," and brokers' loans had almost tripled from two years earlier.

"Margin requirements," the cash actually put down to purchase stock, had dropped as low as 10 percent but hovered around 50 percent for most of the decade. Thus buyers had to come up with only half the price of a share; the rest was financed by borrowing from brokers. As trading reached record heights in August 1929, the Federal Reserve Board finally tried to dampen speculation by raising the interest, or "rediscount," rate charged by the Federal Reserve System for loans to member banks. Higher interest rates would make borrowing more expensive and, authorities hoped, gently reduce inflated stock prices. They were wrong, for it was already too late.

Chinks in the System

If the economy had been sound, nothing could have shattered it. But the economy was not sound. With national attention riveted on the stock market, hardly anyone noticed the warning signs. The construction and automobile industries, key spurs to the prosperity of the New Era, began to lose vitality by 1928 as consumer demand sagged. Residential construction slackened throughout the year, and in the last 10 months of 1929 building permits dropped by 65 percent. Construction fell to the levels of 1921, when the country had been in a deep recession. Meanwhile mortgaged indebtedness had more than doubled, from $13 billion in 1922 to $27.1 billion in 1929. Americans increasingly were gambling their futures on the soundness of the economy.

Automobile sales continued to rise, but at a much slower rate after 1925. By 1929 the automobile industry and ancillary industries like tires and oil were badly overbuilt. Automakers cut back on orders for steel, glass, and other components; industrial production declined; commodity prices dropped. An alarming growth in business inventories, from $500 million in 1928 to $1.8 billion in 1929, further dampened productivity. A deflationary cycle of sinking prices and wages took hold. Increases in consumer spending slowed to a lethargic 1.5 percent for 1928–1929.

The danger signs reflected genuine trouble. For 10 years business had increased profits at twice the rate of productivity. Without strong labor unions or government support, real wages increased only about 11 percent, far below rises in production. Mass purchasing power never kept pace with productivity and consumer demand, so people made up the difference between what they earned and what they bought by borrowing. Increasingly consumers bought "on time," paying off purchases a little each month. During the decade consumer debt rose by 250 percent. Few could afford to keep spending at that level. Nor could the distribution of wealth sustain prosperity. By 1929, 1 percent of the population owned 36 percent of all personal wealth. The savings of the top 60,000 families equaled those of the bottom 25 million families. The wealthy had more money than they could possibly spend; the working and middle classes did not have enough to keep the economy growing.

Unemployment began to increase as early as 1927, revealing growing softness in the economy. By early 1928 the director of the Charity Organization Society in New York reported that unemployment was worse than at any time since the end of World War I. In the fall of 1929 there were 3 million people out of work, many of them in textiles, coal mining, lumbering, and railroads—all "sick" industries suffering from overexpansion, reduced demand, and weak management. Most farmers had been in a recession since the end of World War I. They had 16 percent of the national income in 1919 but only 9 percent in 1929. As more of them went bust, so did many rural banks.

During the twenties nearly 6000 banks failed, mostly in rural areas. Mismanagement, greed, and the emergence of a new type of executive—half banker, half broker—led banks to divert more funds from investment to speculation. "The banks," observed one writer, "provided everything for their customers but a roulette wheel." The uniquely decentralized American banking system left no way to set things right. At the end of the decade half of the 25,000 banks in America lay outside of the Federal Reserve System. Its controls even over member banks were weak. And no government agency monitored the stock exchanges at all. Soon even elite banks were caught up in shady deals. In 1928 Charles Mitchell, president of National City Bank, sold $90 million worth of Peruvian bonds. His own auditors had reported the Peruvian government was likely to default, but Mitchell floated the bonds anyway. That year he earned over $1 million in bonuses from his bank's security-selling subsidiary. When the Peruvian government refused to pay bondholders, their holdings were as worthless as used ticker tape.

Corporations operated unchecked by any countervailing power. The federal government encouraged consolidation. Big business gained so much control over the marketplace that changes in demand had little effect on prices. Managers had so much influence over the workplace that workers received much less pay than their productivity warranted. High profits and the Mellon tax program helped to make many corporations wealthy enough to avoid borrowing, so even changes in interest rates could not control them. Free from government regulation, fluctuating prices, and the need for loans, businessmen ruled the economy. And they ruled badly.

The Great Crash

On Thursday morning, October 24, 1929, the gallery of the New York Stock Exchange was packed with visitors, including the former British Chancellor of the Exchequer Winston Churchill. Trouble was in the air. The day before, a sharp break downward had capped a week of falling prices. Speculators had begun to

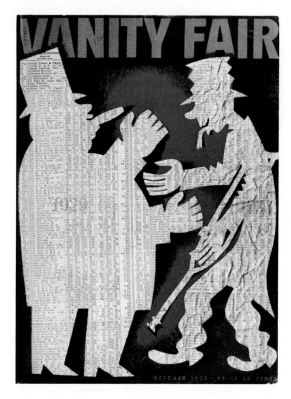

On "Black Tuesday"—October 29, 1929—the stock market collapsed in the greatest single day of losses Wall Street had ever experienced. The long slide actually began in September and did not end until mid-November. In those ten weeks, the value of stocks on the New York *Times* industrial index dropped by half.

take their profits. Other traders exhausted their margins and had no more money to spend. After only an hour, millions of shares went up for sale. There were no buyers.

As a torrent of orders to sell flooded the New York Stock Exchange, prices plunged. Panic set in. By the end of "Black Thursday" the ticker tape was running more than four hours late. Nearly 13 million shares had been traded—a record. Losses stood at $3 billion, another record. Representatives of 35 of the largest brokerage houses on Wall Street issued a joint statement of reassurance to their customers across the country: "The worst has passed."

The worst had just begun. Prices rallied for the rest of the week, buoyed by a bankers' buying pool organized at the House of Morgan. The following Tuesday, October 29, 1929, the bubble burst. Over 16 million shares changed hands. Stockholders lost $10 billion. In a single day almost as much money in capital value vanished as the United States had spent on World War I. The biggest gainer of the decade, RCA, which had peaked earlier at $450 a share, eventually dropped to $32. Within a month industrial stocks lost half of what they had been worth in September. It was the greatest crash so far in history—and it continued for almost four years. At their peak in 1929 stocks had been worth $87 billion. In 1933 they bottomed out at $18 billion. The exchanges were littered with casualties, including boxer Jack Dempsey, the first millionaire athlete. He lost $3 million and went broke.

The Great Crash did not cause the Great Depression, but it did damage the economy in several ways. Although only about 500,000 people were actually trading stocks by the end of the decade, many of them were the people whose investments helped to sustain prosperity. Thousands of middle-class investors lost their savings and their futures. They had bought cars, houses, clothing, and other consumer items on the promise to pay when stock profits came in, and profits never came. The credit structure of the nation was suddenly in jeopardy. Commercial banks, some heavily loaded with corporate stocks, others sunk deeply into the call money market, reeled in the wake of the crash. Business confidence sank, and American optimism withered.

The Great Crash signaled the start of the greatest depression in the history of the nation. The gains of the twenties were wiped out in a few years. By 1933 the gross national product had fallen by almost half. Manufacturing was less than it had been in 1913. The automobile industry was operating at under 20 percent of its 1929 capacity, the steel industry at 12 percent. By some estimates 85,000 businesses failed, and major railroad systems like the Missouri Pacific went into receivership. American foreign trade fell by more than two-thirds.

The shock waves helped to topple already fragile economies in Europe. American loans, investments, and purchases had propped up a shaky Europe since the end of World War I. When they stopped, European governments defaulted on war debts. More European banks failed; more businesses collapsed. Unemployment surged. Europeans scrambled to protect themselves. Led by Great Britain in 1931, 41 nations abandoned the gold standard. With currency no longer redeemable in gold, foreign governments hoped to expand their supplies of money. Such devaluation, they hoped, would make exports cheaper and increase foreign trade. Each simultaneously raised tariffs to protect its industries from inexpensive foreign goods. So devaluation failed, and the resulting trade barriers only deepened the crisis.

Declining sales at home and abroad sent crop prices in the United States to new lows. Wheat fell from $1.05 a bushel in 1929 to 39 cents in 1932, corn from 81 cents to 39 cents a bushel, cotton from 17 cents to 6 cents a pound. In 1932 a wagonload of oats could not buy a $4 pair of Thom McCann shoes. Farm income dropped by more than half—to a paltry $5 billion. The contagion of rural bank failures spread to the cities. Nervous depositors rushed by the thousands to withdraw their cash. Even healthy banks could not bear the strain. In August 1930 every bank in Toledo but one failed. Between 1929 and 1933 collapsing banks took over $20 billion in assets with them.

Fearing that the United States would soon abandon the gold standard, foreign investors traded their dollars for gold. As gold vanished from the country, the money supply contracted. Gold reserves began to grow again only after the Federal Reserve Board raised short-term interest rates in October 1931. By then money was so scarce that the banks could not meet domestic needs. Stores in the state of Washington accepted wooden money; Iowa towns issued scrip; the city of Knoxville printed its own currency. In the first three years after the crash total productivity dropped from $103 billion to $56 billion. National income fell by half, factory wages by almost half. The economy spiraled downward, and no one could stop it. Overexpansion of major industries, uneven distribution of wealth and income, the relative decline in mass purchasing power, a weak banking and corporate structure, and plain economic ignorance were the underlying causes.

THE AMERICAN PEOPLE IN THE GREAT DEPRESSION

"When a great many people are unable to find work," said Calvin Coolidge in 1930, "unemployment results." Between 1929 and 1932 U.S. Steel laid off all of its

225,000 full-time employees. An average of 100,000 people lost their jobs every week in the first three years after the crash. By 1932 more than 13 million were jobless. At least one worker in four could find no work at all. In the industrial cities the toll was staggering. A million unemployed walked the streets of New York; over half a million roamed the streets of Chicago. In Cleveland half the working force had no jobs; in Toledo, more than three-quarters were without work. By 1931 even white-collar workers, usually safe in past depressions, were unemployed. "Time was when a white collar case was an event," wrote one social worker. "Not so today."

The Great Depression was a great leveler, reducing differences in the face of common deprivation. The New York seamstress without enough piecework to pay her rent felt the same frustration and anger as the Berkeley student whose college education was cut short when the bank let her father go. Most husbands had some job; most wives continued as homemakers; and most Americans got by as best they could, often cooperating with one another, practicing a ruthless underconsumption to make ends meet. "We lived lean," recalled one Depression victim. So did most of the American people—black and white, northern and southern, urban and rural.

Hard Times

When asked in 1932 whether there had ever been anything like the Great Depression, the economist John Maynard Keynes replied, "Yes, it was called the Dark Ages, and it lasted four hundred years." In the 1930s hard times lasted 10 years, the longest depression in American history. In 1940, some 7.5 million Americans (roughly 14 percent of the labor force) were still without jobs. Five future presidents—John Kennedy, Richard Nixon, Gerald Ford, Ronald Reagan, and George Bush—grew up during the Great Depression, and no one who lived through the ordeal forgot it. In one way or another, it changed everybody, even those who did not suffer directly. "I had been a conformist, a Southern snob," recalled Virginia Durr, who became a pioneer in the battle for civil rights. "What I learned during the Depression changed all that. I saw a blinding light like Saul on the road to Damascus."

Three years after the Great Crash nearly one American in three had no income. Half the labor force was either unemployed or underemployed. People set forest fires in Washington State so they could be hired to put them out. An Arkansas man walked 900 miles in search of work. New York City department stores required college degrees for elevator operators; professors drove taxicabs. Armtorg, the Russian trading company, received an average of 350 applications a day from Americans who wanted to settle in the Soviet Union. Throughout the decade emigration from the United States exceeded immigration into the country. Most left because they could find no work in America.

Even before the Great Crash a great many Americans were having trouble making a living. The Depression publicized their plight. In the golden year of 1929, economists at the Brookings Institution calculated that for the barest necessities a family of four required $2000 a year—more money than 60 percent of American families earned. By 1932 the average family had an annual income of $1348, barely enough to survive. Only one family in five had as much as $3000 a year to spend.

Even members of the middle class suffered a sickening descent. One defendant in Brooklyn, charged with vagrancy for sleeping in a vacant lot for 46 days,

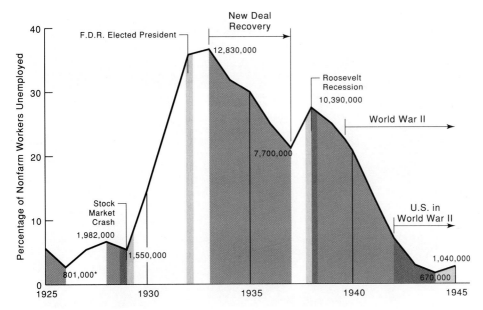

New Deal
Recovery

F.D.R. Elected President

12,830,000

Roosevelt
Recession
10,390,000

World War II

7,700,000

Stock
Market
Crash

1,982,000

U.S. in
World War II

1,550,000

1,040,000

801,000*

670,000

*Unemployed totals for entire labor force.
UNEMPLOYMENT, 1925–1945
The dark bands mark significant events during the era.

had served as a civil engineer for the governments of Panama, China, and Vene-zuela. The man who knocked at the door for a handout at night, noted a New York *Times* reporter, "might be the same fellow who a few months or a year ago had cheerfully O.K.'d your loan at the bank or had written editorials in your news-paper or had been the vice president of a leading real estate company."

National morale sank. "The energy of the country has suffered a strange paralysis," said one observer. "We are in the doldrums, waiting not even hopefully for the wind which never comes." The nation's capital looked grim. "I come home from the Hill every night filled with gloom," wrote a Washington correspondent in 1932. "I see on the streets filthy, ragged, desperate-looking men, such as I have never seen before." In New York and Boston, soup kitchens opened and bread lines formed. Midwestern schoolteachers donated their salaries to feed their stu-dents at lunch. A teacher told one haggard girl to go home and get some food. "I can't," she replied. "This is my sister's day to eat."

Millions stayed alive by foraging like animals. In Chicago people stood at local dumps, waiting for the next garbage truck. When one pulled away from the pile, read a 1932 report, a crowd of 35 "started digging with sticks, some with their hands, grabbing bits of food and vegetables." One widow always removed her glasses before eating so she would not see the maggots. In Kentucky people ate violet tops, wild onions, and weeds previously thought fit only for cattle.

Big-city hospitals began receiving new patients ill primarily from starvation. The New York City health department reported that more than one schoolchild in five suffered from malnutrition. In the coal-mining regions of West Virginia and Illinois almost every child fed by the American Friends Service Committee was underweight. Diseases associated with malnutrition, like pellagra, increased, es-pecially in the South. Despite reassurances from public officials and chambers of commerce that "no one has starved," the New York City Welfare Council reported

Shantytowns (called "Hoovervilles" after President Herbert Hoover) sprang up around most cities as the Depression deepened. Sometimes the down-and-out turned to desperate action. In 1931 a hunger riot broke out when the unemployed stormed a grocery store in Oklahoma City. Meanwhile thousands occupied the Seattle County–City Building to protest conditions there. Two years later in Chicago, 55 citizens were arrested when they were found tearing down a four-story building and taking it away brick by brick.

29 victims of starvation and 110 dead of malnutrition in 1932. Most were children.

Unable to pay mortgages or rent, many families lived off the generosity of forgiving landlords. Some traded down to smaller quarters; others lost their homes. In 1932 some 273,000 families were evicted. In a single day in April, an estimated one-fourth of Mississippi went to auction. People sought shelter anywhere. In Oakland, California, they lived in unsold sewer pipes. Near the Salt River in Arizona miners camped under bridges. In every large city women could be found sleeping on subways. Men huddled in abandoned factories. In winter the homeless begged to be sent to a warm jail cell. A New York couple set up house in a Central Park cave and lived there for an entire year. By 1932 between 1 million and 2 million Americans were homeless wanderers, among them an estimated 25,000 nomadic families. The Missouri Pacific caught 13,745 migrants hitching illegal rides in 1929 and 186,028 in 1931. They were part of what one federal report later called a "migration of despair."

Victims of the Depression overthrew the governments of seven Latin American countries, but in the United States most citizens turned their anger inward. "People blamed themselves, not the system," said one woman. "They felt they had been at fault: . . . 'if we hadn't bought that old radio' . . . 'if we hadn't bought that second-hand car.'" Shame, self-doubt, and pessimism became epidemic. "I'm just no good, I guess," a Houston woman told a caseworker in 1934. "I've given up ever amounting to anything." Most tried to keep up appearances. Men resharpened old razor blades, rolled their own cigarettes, and used 25-watt bulbs to save electricity. Women retailored their dresses for their daughters and sewed together lengths of sheets to equalize wear. Families went through old Christmas cards so they could be sent to different friends next year.

It was often a losing battle. "The unemployed have been so long without food—clothes—shoes—medical care—dental care etc—we look pretty bad," wrote an Oklahoma woman. "And we look and feel a little worse each day." There was no escaping anxiety. "What will become of us?" wondered an Arizona man. "I've lost twelve and a half pounds this last month, just thinking." Rates of mental illness and suicide rose. "No home, no work, no money," despaired a Pennsylvania man as he pled for a "human" method to dispose of his family in 1934. "We cannot go along this way."

A few people profited from the Depression. Albert Fuller sent a corps of salesmen from home to home to sell his brushes. Business grew by $1 million a year. With crude oil selling for 10 cents a barrel in west Texas, J. Paul Getty began acquiring oil wells cheaply. In 1932 he gained control of the Pacific Oil Corporation. Each year of the Depression cigarette sales increased as smokers switched from cigars to less expensive cigarettes. The Mason family was able to keep its factory in Muncie operating at full capacity until 1935 as Americans again were canning their food in Mason jars, reversing the trend toward commercially canned goods. Fear of pregnancy and extra mouths to feed boosted sales of contraceptives to $250,000 a year. In some families sex became a form of therapy. "Life is terrible," said a California woman worried about her unemployed husband. "You must try all the time to keep him from going crazy. And many times—that's the only way."

The Depression Family

"I have watched fear grip the people in our neighborhood around Hull House," wrote Jane Addams in 1931, "men and women who have seen their margin of savings disappear; heads of families who see and anticipate hunger for their children before it occurs. That clutch of cold fear is one of the most hideous aspects." The "clutch of cold fear" led many young couples to put off having children: births per 1000 women of childbearing age dropped from 97.4 in 1929 to 75.7 in 1933, part of a long-term decrease aggravated in the early years of the Depression. For the first time in three centuries the curve of population growth was leveling off. Unable to foresee World War II and the "baby boom" to follow, experts predicted a "baby crop shortage."

After 1929 the marriage rate plunged; it did not begin to recover until 1934. An estimated 800,000 marriages were postponed—some forever. "Do you realize how many people of my generation are not married?" a Chicago educator later told an interviewer. By 1930 the number of women between the ages of 25 and 30 who never married had increased 30 percent over the previous five years. Throughout the decade divorce declined (largely because of expense) but desertion, the "poor man's divorce," increased.

Studies found that the Depression did not break up families so much as it magnified tendencies already present. Weak families languished or fell apart; strong ones hung together and grew closer. The Burtons of Saginaw, Michigan, had a steady marriage before Mr. Burton lost his business in the early 1930s. He moved his family to Ann Arbor, where he took a job as a salesman. His income dropped from $10,000 to $3000 a year. His wife took in boarders, remained cheerful and ambitious, and pulled together with her husband. Everyone regarded her as the "family heroine." The Rileys, another Michigan family—but one already on shaky ground—sank into a morass of anxiety, resentment, and debt. After his unsuccessful law practice failed, Mr. Riley turned to gambling, his wife became callous, and their 24-year old daughter took on the roles of chief breadwinner and family leader. She resented both of her parents.

When unemployment struck, such role reversals were not uncommon. Men without work grew listless and discouraged after a few weeks at home. Work had defined them as productive members of society. Suddenly they had nothing to do. "One of the worst things was occupying your time, sensibly," recalled Ward James, fired from his publishing job in 1935. "You'd go to the library. You took a magazine to the room and sat and read. I didn't have a radio. I tried to do some writing and found I couldn't concentrate. The day was long. There was nothing to do evenings. I was going around in circles, it was terrifying." Mr. Riley spent his days at the local pool hall. Other husbands put on ties and jackets each morning, but instead of going to the office they went to distant neighborhoods to sell Two-in-One shoe polish or cheap neckties door-to-door. In a culture that stressed self-reliance and self-help, such men felt like failures and blamed themselves.

Most of the country's 28 million homemakers stayed at home. During the Depression their routines were less disrupted than their husbands', but demands on them grew. Poor rural women, the wives of tenants and sharecroppers, experienced the fewest changes. They had long since adjusted to poverty. As always they did field and farm work, cared for their families, and still deferred to their husbands. In middle-class families strong women like Mrs. Burton often rose to fill roles vacated by defeated husbands. "I did what I had to do," said one woman. "I seemed to always find a way to make things work."

The role of homemaker took on added importance. The typical middle-class family in the Depression had one or two children and lived in a rented house or apartment (few Americans owned their homes in the 1930s). Between 1929 and 1933 living costs dropped almost 25 percent, but family incomes tumbled by 40 percent. Homemakers watched family budgets with a close eye. They substituted less expensive fish for red meat or dropped meat from their menus altogether. Jell-O, the cheapest all-purpose dessert, enjoyed new popularity. Corn, tomatoes, and pole beans sprang up in backyards and vacant city lots. Families took in relatives and boarders. Some wives started home businesses selling baked goods, making dresses, or operating kitchen beauty parlors. Returning to "Middletown" for a follow-up study in 1935, sociologists Helen and Robert Lynd discovered an increase in prostitution. Working-class wives were selling themselves to keep their families going.

More and more women worked outside their homes, largely to supplement meager family incomes. Some critics claimed they took jobs from men. "There are approximately 10,000,000 people out of work in the United States today," wrote Norman Cousins in 1939, "there are also 10,000,000 or more women, married and single, who are jobholders. Simply fire the women, who shouldn't be working anyway, and hire the men. Presto! No unemployment. No relief rolls. No depression." Such thinking was sheer nonsense. Past discrimination in employment had relegated most women to "women's work," traditionally secretaries, schoolteachers, and social workers. Over half the female labor force worked in domestic service or the garment trades. Most unemployed men would have been reluctant to take such jobs, even if they were available.

An evicted sharecropper stands with his child. In 1930 such children faced a grimmer future than their parents. Throughout the South, where most African-Americans lived, the difference in the quality of education accorded whites and what was available to blacks widened between 1900 and 1940. By the first year of the Great Depression more money was being spent on school buses for whites than on new schools for blacks.

In the 1930s discrimination still dogged working women. Their jobs paid little. Live-in maids, the elite of domestic servants, got $8 a week; pieceworkers in the textile mills of Lawrence, Massachusetts, got $4. It was worse for married women. Opinion polls showed more than three in four Americans believed that wives belonged at home. Frances Perkins, later secretary of labor, denounced "the pin money worker" as a "menace to society." Few school districts would hire married women, and half had a policy of firing them. Between 1932 and 1937 federal authorities prohibited more than one member of a family from working for the civil service. Three-quarters of those forced to resign were women. The proportion of women in the work force rose anyway, approaching 25 percent by 1940, and most new women workers were married. Wages for women rose, too, until they were 63 percent of men's.

The nation's 21 million children could not escape feeling some anxieties. "The children all seem to be so excitable and high-strung these days," reported a New York City kindergarten teacher. "I can't help thinking it's due to the distress at home." Enrollment in public schools and colleges grew as prospects for employment sank. By 1940 three of four high school–aged children were attending school, compared to less than half in 1930. Extended schooling now kept children out of the labor force. Universities, still reserved for a privileged few, drew 1.2 million students, or 7.5 percent of the college-age population. The long-term trend toward a highly educated public continued.

A *Literary Digest* survey in 1931 showed that eight-year-olds still wanted to be cowboys, aviators, and army officers if they were boys, movie stars if they were girls. But by age 18 they had developed a new practicality. Boys looked forward to being lawyers, engineers, and architects, girls to making careers as stenographers and secretaries. Gone were the swashbuckling, goldfish-swallowing college students of the 1920s. "The present day college generation is fatalistic," observed the editors of *Fortune* magazine. "It keeps its shirt on, its pants buttoned, its chin up, and its mouth shut."

953

As many as 250,000 children took to the road, some to relieve families of their support, others just to wander. Most youngsters stayed at home; indeed, for a child of unemployed parents life barely extended beyond the front door. "The unemployed man and his wife have no social life," wrote one observer in 1934. "The only visitors they have are their married children with their families." The picture was not so bleak for everyone, but after a decade of being drawn apart by automobiles and mass entertainment, the middle-class family turned inward. Church attendance declined; the spending of recreational groups dropped by half; a third of the Grange and rural women's clubs vanished; millions of telephones were taken out; even the mails lightened.

The home and family emerged as the center of recreation and companionship. People dreamed of exuberant activity—playing tennis, swimming, or boating—but surveys showed that they actually spent their free time reading newspapers and magazines, listening to the radio, and going to the movies, in that order. "There was a lot of visiting back and forth in the evenings," recalled one man, "games of penny ante poker, monopoly, and bridge, sampling the newly legal beer and whiskey, going to picnics, discovering golf at a nearby country club which had opened its course to all-comers at one dollar greens fee."

The Great Depression forever marked the generation that lived through it. Countless women came to associate working outside the home with crisis and financial distress. The middle-class dream of a wife freed from working for wages, weakened in the 1920s, reasserted itself. "Some day, Dear Sister," a union officer told one spouse unhappy about married women with jobs, "I hope we will reach that economic ideal where the married woman will find her place in the home caring for children, which is God's greatest gift to women and her natural birthright." Whether in the renewed importance of homemaking and family life or the reemergence of home industries, Americans retreated into traditionalism.

Some never forgot the humiliation of life in the Depression. "Shame? You tellin' me?" recalled a businessman. "I would go stand on that relief line. I would look this way and that and see if there's nobody around that knows me: I would bend my head low so nobody would recognize me. The only scar that is left on me is my pride, my pride." The lasting legacy of humiliation and fear—that the bottom would fall out again; that life would be leveled once more; that the next depression might not end—this was what one writer called an "invisible scar." "Security to me is not what we have," said a woman who grew up in the 1930s, "but what we can do without."

A Depression Culture

In a decade when uncertainty and fear dominated their feelings, middle-class Americans threw themselves into games that depended on rationality as well as chance. Contract bridge, with its system of bidding and play, Parker Brothers' board game Monopoly, which rewarded orderly investing in real estate, and pinball, the ultimate machine-age game that carried the injunction "Do Not Tilt," were Depression favorites. All relied on rules and skill as well as luck. In more physical games, sheer endurance became a virtue. Six-day bicycle races staged a comeback, and dance marathons, another contest for survival, kept partners on the floor 45 minutes out of every hour, 24 hours a day, sometimes for weeks on end.

The Depression produced more sober fashions: longer skirts and hair, fewer long waists, more curves. A desire to escape the here-and-now helped to make best sellers of *The Good Earth* (1931), Pearl Buck's saga of China, and Margaret Mitchell's Civil War epic, *Gone with the Wind* (1936). New skepticism about business led Fred Schlink to write *100,000,000 Guinea Pigs*, a sequel to *Your Money's Worth* (1927), his earlier exposé of false advertising. By 1935 the two books had sold half a million copies. Reflecting the new tight-fistedness, consumer cooperatives multiplied more than tenfold during the decade.

Hungry for diversions, people still flocked to spectacles, just as they had in the 1920s. A World's Fair in Chicago in 1933 and a second in New York in 1939 both attracted large crowds. Families living a limited life found cheaper pursuits than they had a decade earlier. Stamp collecting quadrupled during the 1930s. There were fads for knitting and jigsaw puzzles. Boxtop contests and other games of chance held out hope of turning bad luck good. Inaugurated in 1930, the Irish Sweepstakes became the most successful lottery in the world within five years. Nearly every adult in Colorado was involved in the chain-letter craze of 1935.

With a wider audience than ever, record sales increased a hundredfold between 1934 and 1937. Classical music enjoyed new popularity as tastes turned to a more controlled, full-bodied sound. By 1939 there were over 270 symphony orchestras in the country; only 17 had existed in 1915. More than 10 million families listened to symphonic music and opera each weekend on radio. Popular music became more melodic and cheerful. Pop hits were usually romantic ("Stardust"), often sentimental ("Red Sails in the Sunset"), and occasionally poignant ("Brother, Can You Spare a Dime?"). "Swing," a commercialized jazz, dominated the charts, and "big bands," orchestras that played popular favorites at nightclubs and theaters, capitalized on the continuing dance craze. In 1937 Benny Goodman, the "King of Swing," drew an audience of nearly 4000 when he opened at the Paramount Theater in New York City. Couples added the acrobatic "jitterbug" and exotic Latin imports like the rumba to such durable favorites as the fox trot.

By the end of the decade almost 9 families in 10 owned radios. People depended on the radio for almost everything—news, sports, and weather; music and entertainment; advice on how to bake a cake or find God. Radio entered a golden age of commercialism. At an average price of $50 (down from $100 in 1929), a radio brought variety programs like "Major Bowes' Amateur Hour," comedy shows with George Burns and Gracie Allen, and soap operas such as "One Man's Family" and "Against the Storm" to some 27 million listeners. A hair-raising adventure like "The Lone Ranger" (first broadcast in 1933) became so popular that by 1939 it was being heard three times a week on 140 stations.

Radio continued to bind the country culturally. A teenager in Splendora, Texas, could listen to the same wisecracks from Jack Benny, the same music from Guy Lombardo as kids in New York and Los Angeles. In 1938, when Orson Welles broadcast H. G. Wells' classic science fiction tale, *The War of the Worlds*, Americans everywhere listened to "Invasion from Mars," and many believed it. In Newark, New Jersey, cars jammed roads as families rushed to evacuate the city; church services in Indianapolis came to a hurried end so parishioners could scurry to safety; in a small town in Washington State the power suddenly failed and women fainted in the streets, convinced the end was at hand. The nation, used to responding to radio advertising and bombarded with continual reports of impending war in Europe, was prepared to believe almost anything, even invaders from Mars.

In Hollywood an efficient but autocratic "studio system" churned out a record number of feature films. Eight motion picture companies produced more than two-thirds of them. Color, first introduced in features in *Becky Sharp* (1935), soon

Daily Lives

FOOD/DRINK/DRUGS

The Control of Narcotics

The problem was old, and the new president intended to attack it firmly. Early in his first administration he sent his personal adviser to the federal commissioner of narcotics with an unmistakable message: no clemency for drug pushers. If the commissioner ever forwarded such a recommendation to the White House, he was to attach his own resignation. The public would stand for nothing less than strict enforcement of the law, and neither would Franklin Roosevelt.

As Roosevelt entered the White House in 1933, narcotics had been under federal control for two decades. But it had taken a half century before that to recognize the social costs of addiction. In the nineteenth century, a host of drugs offered Americans increasing control over tension and pain. Laudanum, or tincture of opium, had been used since the Renaissance to calm nerves, induce sleep, and relieve gastrointestinal illnesses such as cholera, food poisoning, and parasites. Chloroform and ether had served as anesthetics since the 1850s, and chloral hydrate (the famed "knockout drops" of sensational novels) was developed in 1868. Morphine, derived from opium in 1803, was a potent painkiller, while heroin, isolated in 1898, promised "heroic" therapy as an analgesic and sedative. Cocaine was made not from opium but from the South American coca leaf in the late 1850s. By the 1880s testimonials from authorities as diverse as Sigmund Freud and former surgeon general of the army William Hammond praised it as an anesthetic and stimulant, even as a cure for opiate addiction.

These addictive drugs became commonly available in a host of products. The exhilarating qualities of cocaine made it a favorite ingredient in medicines, wines, tonics, and, until 1903, in the soft drink Coca-Cola. Morphine and other opiates had worked their way into popular over-the-counter medicines like "Mrs. Winslow's Soothing Syrup" and "Hooper's Anodyne, the Infant's Friend." In the 1880s many doctors continued to believe that narcotics administered hypodermically were nonaddictive, and by the 1890s anyone could order a hypodermic kit from Sears, Roebuck for $1.50. Still, with drug use on the rise, the detrimental effects soon became obvious. By the turn of the century, conservative estimates placed the total number of abusers in the country at about 1 million.

As early as 1860 some states had begun regulating the use of pure narcotics, but strong traditions of individualism and privacy made control difficult and uneven. The emergence of the United States as a world power at the end of the nineteenth century gave domestic reformers a powerful boost. They had long argued that addiction was a foreign contagion, and in the early years of the twentieth century they pressed for the United States to mount an international war on drugs. Naturally such moral leadership abroad required moral rectitude at home.

As concern for public health and individual morality peaked during the progressive era, new laws brought narcotics slowly under federal control. The federal government had regulated opium through import taxes since the late nineteenth century. The Pure Food and Drug Act of 1906 required labeling of ingredients, including narcotics. In 1909 Congress excluded the

Daily Lives

The fruits of a drug raid in the 1920s. Until 1930, when the Federal Bureau of Narcotics was created, drug agents operated under the Treasury Department's Narcotics Division.

importation of opium for other than medical uses. Finally, in 1914 it enacted the more comprehensive Harrison Anti-Narcotic Act, which permitted only federally registered dealers to dispense morphine, cocaine, opium, and heroin. Physicians were allowed to issue the substances for medicinal purposes but had to file records of their prescriptions with federal authorities.

Once the prohibition of alcohol went into effect in 1920, the Treasury Department (given authority over enforcement) created a special Narcotics Division. As alcohol prohibition declined in popularity, supporters of the Harrison Act succeeded in establishing a separate Federal Bureau of Narcotics in 1930. It was this bureau's commissioner to whom Roosevelt wrote his stern memorandum.

A disturbing pattern ran through the history of narcotics control. The most ardent campaigners often believed that certain drugs would make feared minorities unmanageable. In the late nineteenth century opium had been linked to the Chinese, raising alarm that its use would promote sexual contact with white women. At the turn of the century, cocaine was believed to endow blacks with cunning, hostility, and superhuman strength. (The fear that "cocainized" blacks could not be stopped by .32-caliber bullets is said to have led many southern police departments to arm themselves with .38-caliber pistols.) Heroin was used to explain the violence and promiscuity of adolescents in urban gangs in the 1920s. And in the 1930s, as pressure mounted for federal control of cannabis, or marijuana, local officials in southwestern states said smoking it increased crime among Mexican immigrants.

In each instance anxieties peaked amid social crisis: a glut of low-paid Chinese workers in the depression-filled 1890s; a battle for political control of blacks at the turn of the century; the rise of an unruly youth culture in the 1920s; and high unemployment among Mexican immigrants in the Great Depression of the 1930s. In 1937, despite resistance from an understaffed and underfunded Narcotics Bureau, Congress enacted the Marijuana Tax Act, which resulted in total prohibition. "America is a nation of drug-takers," wrote one authority in 1881. By the 1930s the nation had taken steps to change its habits.

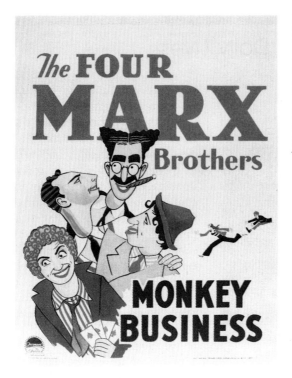

Lunatic social jesters, the Marx brothers turned convention topsy-turvy in the 1930s. Their antics made the Depression-spawned prospect of social disorder fun. *Monkey Business* (1931), their first Hollywood film, unleashed Groucho, Chico, Harpo, and Zeppo on a gang of crooks.

complemented sound, which had debuted in the 1927 version of *The Jazz Singer*. Neither alone could keep movie theaters full. As attendance waned early in the Depression, big studios like Metro-Goldwyn-Mayer, Columbia, Warner Brothers, and Universal sought to lure audiences back with films designed to shock, titillate, and just plain entertain in the midst of crisis.

Popular movies often played on deep national emotions. Horror movies such as *Frankenstein* (1931) and *Dracula* (1931) drew on anxieties about the dangers of tampering with the natural order of things. Early Depression gangster movies like *Little Caesar* (1931), *The Public Enemy* (1931), and *Scarface* (1932) allowed Americans ambivalent about the ethic of success to root for misfits who challenged it and still applaud their just demise. The Marx Brothers made fun of social disorder in *Monkey Business* (1931) and *Duck Soup* (1933), while Walt Disney's *Three Little Pigs* (1933) scoffed at it in the cartoon's hit song, "Who's Afraid of the Big Bad Wolf?" *She Done Him Wrong* (1933) catapulted Mae West to the top of box-office favorites by mixing sex with West's bawdy humor. ("Haven't you ever met a man who could make you happy?" Cary Grant asks her. "Sure, lots of times," she replies.) Busby Berkeley's choreography for *42nd Street* (1933) and *Gold Diggers of 1933* (1933) and Fred Astaire and Ginger Rogers, first paired in *Flying Down to Rio* (1933), leavened spirits in musicals that stressed teamwork and cooperation. Only toward the end of the decade did Hollywood develop a social conscience in such films as *Dead End* (1937), *Angels with Dirty Faces* (1938), and *The Grapes of Wrath* (1941).

By the mid-1930s more than 6 Americans in 10 were going to the movies at least once a week. They saw tamer films as the industry regulated movie content in the face of growing criticism. To avoid censorship and boycotts from such groups as the Legion of Decency (a watchdog group created in 1933 by the Catholic church), studios agreed to stiffen already existing regulations. "Evil and good are never to be confused," stated the Motion Picture Production Code of 1934. Producers could not depict homosexuality, abortion, drug use, or sex. Actors could utter no profanities. Even the word "sex" was banned. If they were featured in bed, couples had to be clothed and one foot of each partner had to touch the floor. Traditional middle-class morality reigned on the "silver screen." As a result most Depression movies, like most of popular culture, tended to preserve the basic social and economic tenets of American culture.

"Dirty Thirties": An Ecological Disaster

On the morning of Armistice Day 1933, the wind began to blow through Beadle County, South Dakota. Soon it was blowing at 60 miles an hour. It carried away almost everything that was not nailed down. "By noon," reported R. D. Lusk from the Karnstrum farm, "it was darker than night." When Lusk stepped outside, he ran smack into "a wall of dirt one's eyes could not penetrate, but it could penetrate the eyes and ears and nose. It could penetrate the lungs until one coughed up black." When the wind finally died down, the Karnstrum farm, like the rest of Beadle County, was changed. Lusk no longer saw any fields, "only sand drifting into mounds. . . . There was no longer a section-line road fifty feet from the front door. It was obliterated. In the farmyard, fences, machinery, and trees were gone, buried. The roofs of sheds stuck out through drifts deeper than a man is tall."

On and off the winds blew for 10 years. Between 1932 and 1939 an average of nearly 50 storms a year howled across the Great Plains. The "black blizzards" lasted anywhere from an hour to three and a half days. In 1935 one storm carried twice as much earth from the plains as had been dug out to make the Panama Canal. Visibility was so limited, said an observer, "Lady Godiva could ride thru streets without even the horse seeing her." Some cities burned their street lights 24 hours a day. In one small town a seven-year-old lost his way in the gloom. Days later he was found suffocated under a drift. "This is the ultimate darkness," despaired one Kansan in the midst of a dust storm. "So must come the end of the world."

One of the worst ecological disasters in modern history, the dust storms transformed 1500 square miles from the Oklahoma panhandle to western Kansas into a gigantic "Dust Bowl." From 1932 to 1936 drought parched fields and pastures and made sand dunes of plowed land. Record temperatures scorched the earth. The thermometer topped 100 degrees in Vinita, Oklahoma, every day for over a month in 1934. By 1936, reported *Newsweek*, the nation was "a vast simmering cauldron." That year the heat killed 4500 people. Nature alone was not to blame. "The dirty thirties," wrote one historian, "were primarily the work of man." The semiarid lands west of the 98th meridian were not suitable for intensive agriculture or livestock grazing. Sixty years of use and abuse had stripped the Great Plains of its natural vegetation. Without sod, the land lay defenseless against the elements. When the dry winds came, one-third of the Great Plains just blew away.

For protection people wore gauze masks, swabbed their nostrils with Vaseline, and covered their windows with paraffin-soaked rags, all to no avail. Tiny

"Black blizzards" dwarfed all man-made structures. The drought that gave rise to the huge dust storms lasted from 1932 until 1936, and few who lived through one ever forgot. "Noon was like night," reported a conductor on the Santa Fe railroad. "There was no sun, and, at times, it was impossible to see a yard. The engineer could not see the signal lights." In a single day in 1934, 12 million tons of western dirt fell on Chicago.

particles of dust covered everything—bedspreads, dinner plates, bread dough. Food crunched to the bite. An epidemic of respiratory infections and a new disease, "dust pneumonia," broke out among farm families in the plains states. Autopsies of dead cattle showed their lungs caked with mud; fish died from lack of oxygen in dust-coated rivers. As far east as Memphis people covered their faces with handkerchiefs to filter the air they breathed. Yellow grit from Nebraska collected on the window sills of the White House, and ships 300 miles off the East Coast found bits of Montana and Wyoming on their decks.

All told, some 3.5 million plains people abandoned their farms. As many as nature forced off their land were pushed out by landowners or corporations. Large-scale commercial farming was slowly spreading into the heartland of America. Huge "factories in the field," commercial farms were advancing east across the Great Plains from California, where 10 percent of the farms grew more than 50 percent of the crops. As in industrial America, the strategy was to consolidate and mechanize, increase production, cut labor costs, and raise profits. As farms grew in size, so did the number of tenants. In most Dust Bowl counties less than half the land was owned by the people who lived on it. American agriculture was turning from a way of life into an industry, American farmers from independent yeomen into common laborers. "We are not husbandmen," sighed an agricultural spokesman. "We are not farmers. We are producing a product to sell."

In the 1920s there had been a net migration of 6 million Americans, most of them young or black, from farms to towns and cities. During the Depression the trend reversed itself. By 1935 the largest number of people in American history—

33 million—were living on farms. The Great Plains, by contrast, were the only states that suffered a net loss of residents during the decade; 10,000 houses were left vacant on the high plains alone; 9 million acres of farmland went untended. The "exodusters" joined a growing migration of rural refugees. No one knows how many became migrants, but relief offices around the country did report a change in the typical migrant family. No longer black or brown, it was white and native-born, typically a young married couple with one child, leaving a farm or town on the Great Plains or in the South and traveling west.

Most did not travel far, perhaps to the next county. Long-distance migrants—many from Oklahoma, Arizona, and Texas—usually set their sights on California. Handbills and advertisements promised jobs picking fruit and harvesting vegetables. If they were like the Joad family in John Steinbeck's classic *The Grapes of Wrath* (1939), they drove west along Route 66 through Arizona and New Mexico, their belongings piled high atop rickety jalopies, heading for their Promised Land. Over 350,000 Oklahomans arrived in California during the decade. So many came that "Okie" came to mean any Dust Bowler, even though most of Oklahoma lay outside the Dust Bowl.

During the decade nearly two of every five migrants ended up in California, increasing its population by 1.1 million, the largest jump of any state. The poor were only a small minority of new arrivals, but enough came to make local citizens edgy. In 15 months, 86,546 destitute migrants crossed the California border, more than the total number of migrants for the first two years of the gold rush. By the middle of the decade the Los Angeles police had begun forming "bum blockades" to keep them out. "Negroes and Okies upstairs," read one sign in a San Joaquin Valley theater. Native-born whites had never encountered such discrimination before.

Only one in two or three migrants actually found work. At peak season California needed no more than 175,000 pickers. The labor surplus allowed growers to set their own terms. A migrant family could expect to earn about $450 a year, less

"Arkies" from Arkansas and "Okies" from Oklahoma fled west from the ravages of dust storms and farm tenancy.

than half the subsistence level. Those that did not work formed wretched enclaves called "little Oklahomas." The worst were located in the fertile Imperial Valley. There at the end of the decade relief officials discovered a family of 10 living in a 1921 Ford. When the mother, suffering from tuberculosis and pellagra, was told to go, she responded vacantly, "I wonder where."

The Fate of Outsiders

The Chavez family lost their farm in the North Gila River valley of Arizona in 1934. They had owned the small homestead near Yuma for two generations, but the Depression pushed them out. Cesar, barely six years old at the time, remembered only images of his family's departure: a "giant tractor" leveling the corral; the loss of his room and bed; the family piling into a Chevy for the journey west; his father promising earnestly to buy another Arizona plot someday.

The elder Chavez could never keep his promise. Instead he and his family lived on the road, "following the crops" in California. Like the Joads, the Chavez family roamed the West Coast in search of work. In eight years Cesar went to 37 schools. The whole family was forced to sell their labor to unscrupulous contractors for less than $10 a week. The father joined the strikes that hit the Imperial Valley in the mid-1930s, but they were crushed. "We were trapped," recalled Cesar. "Some people put this out of their minds and forget it. I don't." Thirty years later he founded the United Farm Workers of America, the first union of migratory workers in the country.

The Chavezes resembled the Joads in every way but one: they were Mexican-Americans. The Joads had found a few sympathetic store owners on their way west. When the Chavezes entered a roadside restaurant, a young waitress greeted them coldly: "We don't serve Mexicans here. Get out." In an America still strictly segregated, she never thought twice about refusing service to outsiders, whether they were brown or black. "White trade only" read the sign out front. "Every time we thought of it," said Cesar, "it hurt us."

The Spanish had inhabited the Southwest for nearly 400 years, producing a rich culture that mixed Old World and Indian civilizations. By the turn of the twentieth century there were nearly 300,000 Mexican-Americans in the United States, largely in the Southwest. In the following decade Mexicans fleeing poverty and revolution nearly doubled the Latino population of Texas and New Mexico. In Arizona this group more than doubled; in California it quadrupled. During the war labor shortages led Washington to sponsor a bracero (day laborer) program, and in the 1920s American farmers opened a campaign to attract Mexican farm workers, who would accept low wáges. By 1930 the census listed nearly 1.5 million Mexicans living in the United States.

A deep ambivalence had always characterized American attitudes toward Mexicans, but the onset of the Great Depression turned most communities against them. Fearful of being burdened with their relief, cities like Los Angeles found it cheaper to ship them back to Mexico. Some migrants left voluntarily, but others were forced out. Beginning in 1931 the federal government launched a series of deportations, or "repatriations," of Mexicans, including their American-born children (who by law were citizens of the United States).

During the decade the Latino population of the country declined by 500,000. Most of those who remained lived in poverty. The average income of Mexican-American families in Crystal City, Texas, in the Rio Grande valley was $506 a year, a sum that represented the combined income of parents and children. Fewer than two Mexican-American children in ten completed five years of school.

Hard times were nothing new for African-Americans. "The Negro was born in depression," one black man said. "It only became official when it hit the white man." Depressed agricultural prices and rampant discrimination had spurred a great African-American migration from the Deep South on the eve of World War I. It continued through the 1920s, when over 800,000 moved to northern cities. Like their rural counterparts, these new urbanites found prosperity elusive, and as the Depression deepened black unemployment skyrocketed. By 1932 it reached 50 percent, twice the national level. Unemployed whites demanded that blacks be fired from their jobs as garbage collectors, street cleaners, elevator operators, and bellhops. A white clerk in Marianna, Florida, no different from millions of Americans, reasoned that "a nigger hasn't got no right to have a job when there are white men who can do the work and are out of work." By 1933 several cities reported between 25 and 40 percent of their black residents with no support but relief payments. Even skilled blacks who retained their jobs had their wages cut by half, according to one study of Harlem in 1935.

African-Americans made do as they had for years. "We had one big advantage," attested one black man. "Our wives could go to the store and get a bag of beans or a sack of flour and a piece of fat meat, and they could cook this. And we could eat it. . . . Now you take the white fella, he couldn't do this. His wife would tell him: Look, if you can't do any better than this, I'm gonna leave you." Migration from the rural South dropped to half of what it had been a decade earlier. As late as 1940 three of four African-Americans lived in rural areas; yet conditions there were just as bad as in cities. Forty percent of all black workers in the United States were farm laborers or tenants. In 1934 one study estimated the average income for black cotton farmers at under $200 a year.

The Depression aggravated racial prejudice. "Dust has been blown from the shotgun, the whip, and the noose," reported *The New Republic* in 1931, "and Ku Klux Klan practices were being resumed in the certainty that dead men not only tell no tales but create vacancies." Lynchings tripled between 1932 and 1933. In 1932 the Supreme Court ordered a retrial in the most celebrated racial case of the decade. In 1931 nine black teenagers had been accused of raping two white women on a train bound for Scottsboro, Alabama. Within weeks all-white juries had found the boys guilty and sentenced eight of them to death. The convictions rested on the testimony of the women, one of whom later admitted the boys had been framed. Appeals kept the case alive for most of the decade. In the end charges against four of the "Scottsboro boys" were dropped, while the other five received substantial prison sentences. One fled to Michigan, where the governor rejected demands to extradite him to Alabama.

Like many African-Americans, George Baker refused to be victimized by the Depression. In 1915 he had moved from Georgia to Harlem, changed his name to M. J. Divine, and founded a religious cult that promised followers an afterlife of full equality. In the 1930s "Father Divine" stressed economic cooperation and opened shelters, or "heavens," for regenerate "angels," black and white alike. His soup kitchens and missions fed 3000 hungry souls a day in Harlem, and soon the cult spread to other American cities and even abroad. Urban blacks had found a new messiah.

Some rural blacks joined the Southern Tenant Farmers Union, organized in 1934 by black and white tenants in Arkansas. "The landlord is always betwixt us, beatin' us and starvin' us and makin' us fight each other," an old black man advised the founders. "There ain't but one way for us to get him where he can't help himself and that's for us to get together and stay together." The union published its own newspaper, the *Sharecropper's Voice,* and attracted national support from Socialists and other radicals. Landlords became uneasy with union demands for a greater share of federal subsidies and an end to arbitrary evictions. Planters and riding bosses broke up union meetings and horsewhipped organizers. Although they won few concessions, union members hung together. Elsewhere the Depression divided black and white Americans, but in the Arkansas delta hard times drew them closer.

THE TRAGEDY OF HERBERT HOOVER

A cold, gray morning sent shivers through the crowd huddled in front of the Capitol on March 4, 1929. Herbert Hoover had just been sworn in as the thirty-first president of the United States. His voice, always a monotone, came booming over the loudspeakers: "I have no fears for the future of our country. It is bright with hope." Engineer, businessman, secretary of commerce for eight years, Herbert Hoover embodied executive competence and efficiency. No one seemed better suited to anticipate trouble or resolve it. "We were in a mood for magic," recalled journalist Anne McCormick of the inauguration. "We had summoned a great engineer to solve our problems for us; now we sat back comfortably and confidently to watch the problems being solved."

Within seven months a "depression" (a term coined by Hoover to minimize the crisis) had struck. Try as he might, he could not beat it. The magic failed, and the nation turned against him. "People were starving because of Herbert Hoover," one angry mother told her son in 1932. "Men were killing themselves because of Herbert Hoover, and their fatherless children were being packed away to orphanages . . . because of Herbert Hoover." The charge was unfair, but it stuck. Hoover's presidency, begun with such promise, became the worst ordeal of his life. Near the end of his term in 1932 he moaned that "all the money in the world could not induce me to live over the last nine months. The conditions we have experienced make this office a compound hell." He nonetheless felt duty-bound to accept his party's renomination for the presidency. His ordeal soon turned into a tragic and humiliating rejection.

The Failure of Relief

By the winter of 1931–1932 the story was the same everywhere: too little money, too many destitute. Private charities, the traditional sources of aid, had long since dried up. In 1932 Hull House, once a model of progressive benevolence, stood in "proud irrelevance." It was flooded, continued the critic Edmund Wilson, with a "sea of misery." In New York, city employees had been donating 1 percent of their salaries to feed the needy since 1930; yet New Yorkers were starving to death. The Red Cross furnished free vegetable seeds when the city council of Midland, Texas, gave land to the unemployed. There was not enough money to supply free food. "Compared to the size of the problem," wrote one historian, "it was like using a peashooter to stop a rhinoceros." By 1932 private charity had dwindled to 6 percent of all relief funds.

City resources were quickly depleted by an estimated 30 million destitute people. In 1930 the Emergency Work Bureau of New York City provided temporary jobs, or "work relief," for 37,000 people a week. The city had at least 300,000 unemployed. In Philadelphia relief payments to a family of four totaled $5.50 a week, the highest in the country. In New York the total was $2.39. The dimensions of the crisis sharpened the problems of discrimination as well. Houston and Dallas refused to grant any relief to African-Americans and Mexicans, and some cities gave nothing to unmarried people or childless couples, no matter how needy they were.

As property values fell and businesses failed, nearly 30 percent of taxes owed went unpaid. Deprived of revenue, cities stopped paving roads, repairing sidewalks, and plowing snow. Relief was expendable too. In 1931 New Orleans refused all new applications for aid. Oklahoma City began arresting unemployed men, charging them with vagrancy, and ordering them out of town. By the end of 1931, Detroit, Boston, Buffalo, and scores of other cities were bankrupt. When mayors sought loans, banks required them to cut relief rolls. The mayor of Detroit, which provided welfare for 50,000 families, dropped one-third of them so he could borrow money from automakers to keep the city running. By 1932 more than 100 cities had no relief appropriations at all.

Cities clamored for help from state capitals, but after a decade of extravagant spending and sloppy bookkeeping, many of the states were already running in the red. As businesses folded and property values tumbled, tax bases shrank and with them state revenues. Michigan, one of the few states to provide any relief, sliced funds from over $2 million in 1931 to $860,000 in 1932. Until New York established its Temporary Emergency Relief Administration in 1931, no state even had an agency to handle the problem.

Some people refused to accept help. By 1932 only one eligible family in four was receiving public assistance in cities. Contrary to popular stereotypes, recipients were reluctant to take aid. The "right people," said the wife of an unemployed railroad worker, never took "something for nothing." Like most Americans she regarded accepting cash or food as a sign of personal failure. When her husband told her they would have to go on relief, she gasped. To go on relief, said one man, was to endure a "crucifixion." Before applications could even be considered, all property had to be sold, all credit exhausted, all relatives declared flat broke. After a half-hour grilling about his family, home, and friends, one applicant left, "feeling I didn't have any business living any more." Hostile to the idea of public assistance, officials attached every possible stigma to aid. In 1932 residents of Lewiston, Maine, voted to bar all welfare recipients from the polls. Ten states had already written property requirements for voting into their constitutions. The destitute were being disfranchised.

The Hoover Depression Program

Every night he stayed at the White House during the Great Depression President Hoover dined in regal splendor. He had thought about economizing but decided it would be bad for the morale of the country. If he changed his habits one bit, it might be taken as a sign of lost confidence. So each evening Hoover entered the dining room in black tie, ready to consume seven full courses. Uniformed buglers heralded his arrival and departure with glittering trumpets, even when the only guest was his wife.

It was not that Herbert Hoover was insensitive—far from it. He never visited a bread line or a relief shelter because he could not bear to see suffering. When the press criticized him he withdrew, wounded and hurt. The cruel rumors that circulated about him—that dogs instinctively disliked him; that he had master-minded the kidnaping and murder of Charles Lindbergh's infant son in 1932; that roses wilted in his hands—were as painful as they were ridiculous. Hoover was doing all he could to promote recovery, more than any of his predecessors, and still he was scorned. His natural sullenness turned to self-pity. "You can't expect to see calves running in the field the day after you put the bull to the cows," Calvin Coolidge reassured him. "No," said an exasperated Hoover, "but I would expect to see contented cows."

Hoover's frustration was understandable. He had never failed before. Or-phaned into poverty at nine, he became one of the first graduates of Stanford University in 1895, an expert engineer, and the owner of one of the most success-ful mining firms in the world. Before he turned 40, he was a millionaire. As a good Quaker he balanced private gain with public service. Saving starving refugees in war-torn Europe and flood victims at home, he became known as the greatest humanitarian of his generation. Finns added a new word to their vocabulary: to "hoover" meant to help.

From the fall of 1930 onward, Hoover assumed full responsibility for ending the crisis—and as humanely as possible. Treasury Secretary Andrew Mellon urged him to "liquidate labor, liquidate stocks, liquidate the farmers, liquidate real estate." Hoover ignored the advice and eased Mellon out of the administra-tion. When Democratic leaders in Congress demanded all federal employment and salaries be cut by 10 percent, Hoover called the idea "heartless and medie-val." Instead he worked 18 hours a day, cut his own salary, and developed a program to actively fight the Depression. His unprecedented strategy was grounded in Hoover's longstanding commitment to voluntarism, his faith in the power of capitalism to revive itself, and his conviction that too much government action would create an intrusive federal bureaucracy that threatened public free-doms and private initiative. Unfortunately the strategy was based on two widely held but faulty assumptions: the Depression was temporary and it had originated in the faltering economies of Europe.

Herbert Hoover.

Hoover understood the vicious cycle of rising unemployment and falling demand and knew the necessity for investment. So he invited business leaders to the White House and secured their pledges to maintain employment, wages, and prices. To further bolster public confidence, he not only decided to maintain his dining habits but also varied the rest of his routine as little as possible and minimized the seriousness of the collapse. Again and again he reassured Americans that "conditions are fundamentally sound" and that the "depression is over." When recovery proved elusive, Hoover's credibility vanished (so thoroughly that journalist Edward Angley published all of the president's sunny forecasts in 1931 and called the book *Oh Yeah!*).

Hoover tried to stimulate the economy indirectly to encourage private and local initiative. Right after the crash he demanded a tax cut to put more money into people's hands. In 1930 Congress happily complied. Toward the end of the year, he created the President's Emergency Committee on Employment (PECE) under Colonel Arthur Woods to encourage local relief programs. The Federal Farm Board, created in 1929 to stabilize agriculture, promoted the sale of farm commodities through cooperatives. In 1931 Hoover prompted Congress to expand the lending powers of the Federal Land Banks by $125 million and later urged the establishment of home-loan banks to discount mortgages. He endorsed and signed the Hawley–Smoot Tariff (1930), raising tariff walls to new heights to protect the United States from cheap foreign goods. He declared a one-year moratorium on payments of reparations and war debts in 1931 to give Europeans economic breathing space. At home he increased spending on public works to prime the economic pump. Before he was done, his public building program overshadowed those of all of his predecessors.

The program was in keeping with Hoover's associational philosophy, developed during his years as Commerce secretary (see pp. 931–932), of using government to promote private and local action. But nothing worked. Employers tried to keep their pledges; yet within months they were forced to reduce wages and lay off workers. Tax cuts were followed by tax increases when government spending and reduced revenues threw the federal budget out of balance. In 1932 Congress passed the largest peacetime tax increase in American history in order to make up the difference. The Revenue Act of 1932, supported by the president, brought added funds into the Treasury but stymied recovery by undermining investment and consumption. More trouble followed. In April 1931 Colonel Woods resigned as head of PECE after the president had rejected his recommendation for greater federal involvement in relief. Late in 1931 Hoover appointed the Organization on Unemployment Relief under Walter Gifford, president of the American Telephone and Telegraph Company. Less than a year later Gifford, who counseled against federal participation, confessed that he did not know how many people were unemployed.

The Hawley–Smoot Tariff was the greatest disaster of all. Over a thousand of the nation's leading economists had petitioned Hoover not to sign it. It left American loans as the only prop for European exports, brought on a wave of retaliation, and choked world trade. The Federal Farm Board was innovative in 1929 but never designed to handle the collapse of agriculture that took place after the crash. Woefully undercapitalized, it also failed to attack the principal farm problem, overproduction. Even public works did not induce recovery. Spending, which ran to more than $1 billion by the end of Hoover's administration, scarcely approached what was needed. To give even half the estimated unemployed jobs on

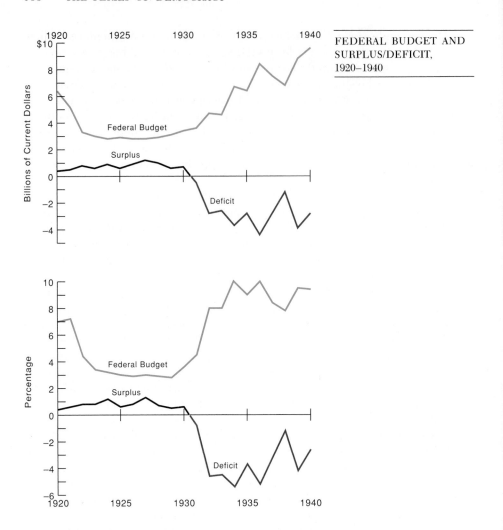

FEDERAL BUDGET AND
SURPLUS/DEFICIT,
1920–1940

public works would have cost $10 billion in 1932, when the entire federal budget amounted to only $3.2 billion.

Between 1930 and 1932 some 5100 banks failed in America as panicky depositors withdrew their funds. Losses amounted to over $3.2 billion. Yielding to pressure from congressmen and enlightened bankers, Hoover called for a revival of the War Finance Corporation of 1918. Early in 1932, the Reconstruction Finance Corporation (RFC) was mustered into service to fight the Depression. With a capital stock of $500 million (and the power to borrow four times that amount), the RFC could lend money to banks and their chief corporate debtors—insurance companies and railroads. Within three months bank failures dropped from 70 a week to 1 every two weeks. The Glass–Steagall Banking Act (1932) eased credit by allowing the Federal Reserve to use government bonds as a basis for $2 billion in new issues of currency.

From the start Hoover rejected the idea of direct federal relief for the unemployed. Critics pointed out that he had no compunctions about furnishing relief for banks, but Hoover did not budge. He feared that a dole or giveaway program (of the kind being used in Britain) would damage the character of recipients. "We are dealing with the intangibles of life and ideals," he reminded Americans. In particular, federal experiments with relief could have unhealthy results for the whole nation, perhaps even creating a permanently dependent underclass. Administration would be expensive and a bureaucracy would be needed to police the program. Not only would the state be meddling in the lives of its citizens, but also "direct relief from the Federal government would bring an inevitable train of corruption and waste." Hoover assumed neighborliness and cooperation would be enough. When Congress appropriated $45 million to save the livestock of drought-stricken Arkansas farmers in 1930, he vetoed an additional $25 million to feed farm families. Congress restored most of the cuts.

In 1930, as unemployment topped 4 million, Americans sent a new Congress to Washington. The off-year elections reduced the Republican majority to one in the Senate and gave Democrats a slim lead in the House. After rejecting Democratic proposals for federal public works and a federal employment service, Hoover slowly softened his stand on federal relief. In 1932 he dictated the terms of his own surrender in the Emergency Relief and Construction Act. It authorized the RFC to lend up to $1.5 billion for "reproductive" public works like toll bridges and slum clearance. The Treasury could lend an additional $350 million for public buildings such as post offices. Another $300 million was made available to states for direct relief of the unemployed. Neither Hoover nor Congress expected these loans to be repaid. Even so, they were woefully inadequate: when the governor of Pennsylvania requested funds to furnish the destitute with 13 cents a day for a year, the RFC sent him only enough for 3 cents a day.

Stirrings of Discontent

Hoover had given ground on relief, but like the rest of his Depression program it was too little and came too late. "The word revolution is heard at every hand," one writer noted in 1932. Three years into the Great Depression some observers wondered if capitalism had given out. Here and there bands of desperate people took matters into their own hands. In Wisconsin the Farm Holiday Association, under the leadership of Milo Reno, dumped thousands of gallons of milk on highways in a vain attempt to raise prices. Ten thousand striking miners formed a 48-mile motor car "Coal Caravan" that worked its way in protest across southern Illinois. In March a demonstration turned ugly when communist sympathizers led a hunger march on Henry Ford's Rouge Assembly Plant in Dearborn, Michigan. As 3000 protesters surged toward the gates, Ford police drenched them with hoses, then opened fire at point-blank range. Four marchers were killed and more than twenty wounded.

For all the stirrings of discontent, revolution was never a real danger. By 1932 the Communist party of the United States had 20,000 members, up from 6500 in 1929, but it was hardly a potent political force. Under the slogan "Starve or Fight!" the communists staged dozens of food, unemployment, and eviction protests. They led unionizing drives and courted intellectuals and the oppressed with their commitment to labor and civil rights. Deeply suspicious of Marxist doctrine, most Americans were unsympathetic. Fewer than 1000 African-Americans joined the party in the early 1930s, and in the election of 1932 the communist presidential candidate, William Z. Foster, polled just over 100,000 votes. At first belligerent and hostile to established politics, the communists adopted a more cooperative strategy to contain Adolf Hitler, whose Nazi party had won control of Germany in 1933. The Soviet Union ordered Communist parties in Europe and the United

States to join with liberal politicians in a "popular front" against Nazism. Thereafter party membership peaked in the mid-1930s at about 80,000.

Hoover was compassionate but only to a point. When 1600 communist-led hunger marchers came to Washington in December 1931, he was determined to protect their right to protest. The president ordered blankets, tents, a field kitchen, and medical aid for them. Washington police stood guard over their parade, and Hoover himself received their petitions at the White House. In January 1932 James Cox, a Catholic priest from Pittsburgh, led 10,000 unemployed men through Washington in a motorcade eight miles long. Hoover listened sympathetically as the priest pleaded for public works and a tax on the rich.

The veterans who descended on the capital half a year later received a different reception. In the summer of 1932 a ragtag army of World War I veterans came to Washington to cash in their Adjusted Compensation Certificates. In 1924 Congress had sent out about 3.5 million certificates for wartime service. Called "bonuses," they were due to mature at an average of $1000 each in 1945. Penniless and hungry, the veterans marched on Washington to press for immediate payment. Walter Waters, one of the leaders, was typical. He had served overseas with the 146th Field Artillery and had been discharged in June 1919. By 1930 he was married, assistant superintendent of a cannery in Portland, and happy. A year later he was destitute, his job and savings gone, possessions pawned, and his prospects bleak. The only thing of value he owned was his Adjusted Compensation Certificate.

In May 1932 Congressman Wright Patman from Texas introduced a bill for immediate payment of bonuses. Waters and 300 other veterans set out from Portland on a march to press their case in Washington. By the time they reached the capital in June, the "Bonus Expeditionary Force" had swelled to 15,000, the largest protest in the city's history. Bonus Army leaders met with congressional representatives, but the president refused to see them. For the first time since the armistice the gates of the Executive Mansion were chained shut.

Hoover dismissed the veterans as a special-interest lobby eager to feather an already soft nest. Veterans' benefits accounted for 25 percent of the federal budget, the largest single item. The cost of their bonuses—$2.3 billion—would have nearly doubled the deficit. Hoover was prepared to veto any bonus bill. When the House enacted one, the Senate spared him the trouble by blocking it. Some of the veterans went home, but about 10,000 stayed to dramatize their plight. Besides, they had nowhere else to go.

The Bonus Army conducted itself peaceably, drilling, parading, and policing its own. The few radicals in its ranks were quickly isolated. When two men were killed late in July as Washington police tried to evict some of the veterans from federal buildings, Hoover called in the army. He wanted nothing more than unarmed military support for the police; what he got was a bloody rout. Dressed in jodhpurs and all his medals, Army Chief of Staff General Douglas MacArthur personally led four troops of cavalry brandishing sabers, followed by six tanks and a column of infantry.

The operation commenced at dusk on July 28, 1932. First the soldiers cleared the Federal Triangle with bayonets and tear gas. A horrified Dwight Eisenhower, one of MacArthur's aides, watched helplessly as Major George S. Patton, Jr., rode down a crowd of Bonus marchers in the last mounted charge of the United States Cavalry. MacArthur then turned to the Bonus Expeditionary Force encampment on the Anacostia Flats across the Potomac River. Despite President Hoover's orders to halt, the general razed the camp that night. As the smoke drifted over the Capitol the next morning, the Bonus marchers had vanished. Among the routed veterans, who included some 300 casualties, was Joseph T. Agelino. In 1918 he had received the Distinguished Service Cross for saving the life of a young officer named George S. Patton, Jr.

Hoover took responsibility for everything but offered the lame excuse that Bonus marchers were "not veterans" but "Communists and persons with criminal records" bent on insurrection. An exhaustive survey of the Bonus Army conducted by the Veterans Administration belied the claim. More than 9 of 10 marchers had been veterans, nearly 7 of 10 had served overseas, and 1 in 5 was disabled. What they really wanted was food and jobs. Sadly, Hoover could provide neither. In Albany, New York, Governor Franklin Roosevelt, outraged by the bloodshed, exploded: "There is nothing inside the man but jelly." Like the hero of a classical tragedy, Herbert Hoover, prophet of the New Era, came tumbling down.

The tragedy was made all the more poignant by Hoover's considerable accomplishments. However cautiously he responded to the Depression, he had taken unprecedented federal action. Through the Reconstruction Finance Corporation the federal government intervened directly into the peacetime economy for the first time. With the Emergency Relief and Construction Act it assumed responsibility for relief, again for the first time. It underwrote the incomes of farmers through the Federal Farm Board and tried to save the homes of the middle class with mortgage loans. But nothing had been enough. Trapped by fears of big government and committed to the associational formula of private initiative and voluntary cooperation, Hoover could go no further.

The Election of 1932

Sensing the opportunity to recapture the White House for the first time since 1920, buoyant Democrats gathered in Chicago in June 1932 for their national convention. The platform blamed the Depression on the Republicans, called for a 25 percent cut in federal spending, and promised a balanced budget. It also vowed somehow to provide federal public works and unemployment relief. When the

THE ELECTION OF 1932

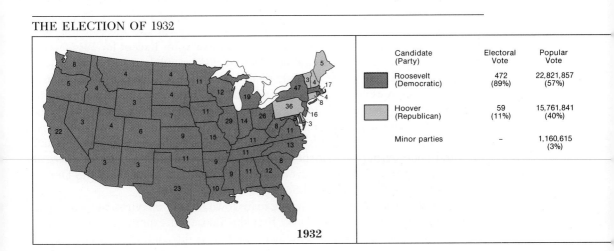

Candidate (Party)	Electoral Vote	Popular Vote
Roosevelt (Democratic)	472 (89%)	22,821,857 (57%)
Hoover (Republican)	59 (11%)	15,761,841 (40%)
Minor parties	–	1,160,615 (3%)

1932

convention heard the plank calling for repeal of Prohibition, pandemonium broke loose for 25 minutes. Uniting traditional supporters from the South and West with city dwellers from the Northeast, New York Governor Franklin D. Roosevelt swept all challengers aside on the fourth ballot. Effervescent and inspiriting, Roosevelt broke tradition by flying to Chicago to accept the nomination himself. "I pledge you," he told delegates, "I pledge myself, to a new deal for the American people." In that instant, Roosevelt found his campaign slogan—"the New Deal." Moments later, when an organ bellowed "Happy Days Are Here Again," he had a campaign song.

The Republicans refused to abandon the somber Hoover. In June 1932 their national convention opened in Chicago and endorsed his Depression program to the last detail. The party platform opposed government spending and direct federal relief and favored an extension of the tariff. On Prohibition, delegates waffled with a plank so ambiguous that neither side was pleased. Hoover was renominated by acclamation in a hall one-third empty. Thoughtlessly the band struck up "California, here I come/Right back where I started from." "I have seen many conventions," reported H. L. Mencken from the press gallery, "but this is the worst."

The campaign was over before it began. "I had little hope of re-election," Hoover later explained, "but it was incumbent on me to fight it out to the end." He believed the future was at stake. As he saw it, the contest was between more than two men or two parties. It was between two philosophies of government: the dangerous federal activism of Democrats against the voluntarism and prudent leadership of Republicans. Roosevelt, Hoover warned, would increase federal spending, inflate the currency, reduce the tariff, and "build a bureaucracy such as we have never seen in our history." Hoover called instead for balanced budgets, confident press releases, a cautious program of public works and government loans, and the mobilization of private resources.

Lacking a national following, Roosevelt tailored his appeal to as broad a constituency as possible. In Iowa he called himself a "farmer"; to the Commonwealth Club of San Francisco he prescribed a stiff dose of economic planning to ensure recovery. He demanded both a balanced budget and more federal relief for the unemployed. He attacked Hoover as a "profligate spender," then went on to describe his own costly program for expanding federal public works. Columnist Walter Lippmann called him a "balanced antithesis." "The country yearned for a Messiah," wrote one disappointed reporter. "Mr. Roosevelt did not look or sound like a Messiah," only "the one sure means of rebuking the party in power."

Election day brought a thundering rebuke of Hoover and the Republicans. Roosevelt received nearly 58 percent of the popular vote. Except for 1912, when the party was divided, no Republican presidential candidate had ever lost so badly. Norman Thomas, one of the few radicals in the race, won for the Socialists proportionately fewer votes than in 1912 or 1920. Democrats held majorities in both houses of Congress. As telling as their magnitude were the returns themselves. Roosevelt carried the South and West and almost all the industrial states. Immigrants, Catholics and Jews, farmers and industrial laborers, city dwellers and the rural poor—groups dissatisfied with Republican rule even before the Great Depression—were being galvanized into a vast coalition. With them the Democratic party would dominate politics for decades to come.

Early the next morning, returning to his town house from victory celebrations at the Biltmore Hotel in New York, Franklin Roosevelt experienced a rare moment of doubt. As his son James helped him to bed, he confessed, "I am afraid I may not have the strength to do this job. After you leave me tonight, Jimmy, I am going to pray. . . . I hope you will pray for me, too."

The challenge was daunting: over 12 million unemployed, an average of 30 banks failing every week, factories idle, farms on the auction block, prices plummeting. Hoover had recognized the need for action but failed to stop the terrible slide. People who had scorned government, including businessmen, were baffled and now looked to Washington. The nation awaited Roosevelt, but no one knew whether he would be equal to the job, not even the president-elect himself. All Roosevelt knew was that he would try anything to help. In one of his first acts as president, he ordered that no one telephoning the White House for aid be shut off. Someone in the administration would be found to answer every call.

SIGNIFICANT EVENTS

1926 — Miami real estate bust

1928 — Great Bull Market begins to peak

1929 — Herbert Hoover inaugurated; stock market crash; Federal Farm Board created

1930 — Hawley–Smoot Tariff raises rates; President's Emergency Committee on Employment created

1931 — Repatriation of Mexicans; Scottsboro boys arrested; New York establishes Temporary Emergency Relief Administration; President's Organization on Unemployment Relief created

1932 — Glass–Steagall Banking Act; Reconstruction Finance Corporation established; Emergency Relief and Construction Act; Farm Holiday Association formed; Bonus Army marches on Washington, D.C.; Franklin Roosevelt elected president

1933 — Walt Disney's *Three Little Pigs;* Legion of Decency formed; Motion Picture Production Code; "black blizzards" begin to create Dust Bowl

1934 — Southern Tenant Farmers Union organized

1935 — *Becky Sharp,* first color film; Communist party announces popular front

1936 — Margaret Mitchell's *Gone with the Wind* published

1937 — Marijuana Tax Act

1938 — Orson Welles' radio broadcast of *Invasion from Mars*

1939 — John Steinbeck's *The Grapes of Wrath* published

27

The New Deal

inner, South Dakota, November 10, 1933. "Dammit, I don't WANT to write to you again tonight. It's been a long, long day, and I'm tired." All the days had been long since Lorena Hickok began her odyssey four months earlier. She often felt tired and sometimes out of sorts, especially when *Time* magazine had run that "damned article" about her. "I suppose I am 'a rotund lady with a husky voice' and 'baggy clothes,'" she admitted. But to call her "peremptory," to say that she had gotten her job as special investigator for the Roosevelt administration merely because she was a friend of the president's wife—that was too much!

True enough, when the new federal relief administrator had first come looking for an agent, Eleanor did recommend "Hick." Friendship had gone no further. Talent and experience put Hickok on the federal payroll. A hard-nosed reporter, she had been the first woman hired by the Associated Press. In the days when women were routinely handed delicate assignments, she covered politics, kidnapings, and worse. "One time I slept with a murderess," she recalled proudly of an interview. "There was only one bed, so she and I slept together."

Whatever *Time* wrote, Hickok knew she was doing an important job. Riding trains and airplanes, driving along roads so full of ruts you couldn't tell them from ploughed fields, traveling through "every man's land—and no man's land," she was reporting on Depression America. In three years she covered 7000 miles across 32 states—from the capital's notorious slums to a New England potato harvest to the Imperial Valley of California, where the thermometer in her car registered 126 degrees Fahrenheit.

Before she began her journey, she regarded the unemployed as most Americans did—a faceless legion of "muffled figures, backs curved against the wind, selling apples on the street corners." They were "chiselers" and "shovel-leaners" who lived on government handouts and make-work projects because they did not want regular jobs. The cross-country trek changed her. A national crisis became a series of personal crises, each with its own face and story, together adding up to a portrait of deprivation, anguish, and often courage.

Hickok found that the federal government's relief program, barely a year old, was making a difference. Half a billion dollars was being funneled into states, localities, and private charities. By the end of 1933 a million farm families were on relief. And more was needed. "Seems like we just keep goin' lower and lower," the 16-year-old daughter of a North Carolina sharecropper told Hickok. For two

Franklin Roosevelt was inaugurated on March 4, 1933. Skies were overcast, but the previous day's rain had stopped. Washington, wrote a reporter, "welcomes the 'new deal,' even though it is not sure what the new deal is going to be."

weeks, she, her sister, and their father had been living in a tobacco barn outside of Raleigh. Somehow hope still flickered in her determined blue eyes. Hickok couldn't explain it until she noticed that pinned to the girl's bosom, "as one wears a brooch," was a campaign button from the 1932 election—"a profile of the President." Hope sprang from the man in the White House.

Before Franklin D. Roosevelt and the New Deal, few Americans had any contact with the federal government. In 1932 the vast majority of them paid no federal income taxes. Federal welfare payments and public works projects had yet to be initiated. There were no government guarantees of minimum wages and maximum hours. Social Security did not exist, and federal deposit insurance, the sole protection for the funds of depositors, would not be enacted for another year. The old order was widely perceived to have failed, and nothing, least of all government, seemed capable of reviving it. The only federal institution people knew at all was the local post office, and these days it usually delivered bad news.

A change was perceptible, Hickok reported. In Pennsylvania, "The Federal government is hugely important." She found people all over America talking about federal programs. Perhaps it was Washington's long-awaited contributions to relief or maybe the new farm subsidies; just as likely it was Roosevelt. Wherever she went, Hickok seldom heard voters describe themselves as "Republicans"

Lorena Hickok (left) met Eleanor Roosevelt (right) in 1928 and thereafter served as her unofficial press adviser. She traveled with Eleanor during Franklin's campaign for the presidency in 1932, arranged her women-only press conferences, and became her closest friend. (In the center of this photograph is Paul Person, governor of the Virgin Islands.)

or "Democrats" any more. Instead they said they were "for the President." "This fellow Roosevelt is really trying to help us," one South Dakota farmer told her.

The mails carried other signs that plain people were looking to the president and the federal government as never before. During the first weekend after the inauguration nearly half a million letters and telegrams poured into the White House. For years the average remained between 5000 and 8000 a day, a new presidential record. It took a staff of 50 just to handle Roosevelt's public correspondence. In four years President Hoover had required only one.

Over half the letters came from those at the bottom of the economic heap. Most sought help, offered simple words of praise, or just expressed heartfelt gratitude. It seemed, wrote a Kansas man in 1932, "as though some Moses had come to alleviate us of our sufferings." Whatever the individual messages, their collective meaning was clear: Franklin D. Roosevelt and the New Deal had begun to restore hope and confidence. For the first time, Americans believed the federal government would help them through a great crisis. Here, if anywhere, is the true essence of what historians would call the "Roosevelt Revolution."

THE EARLY NEW DEAL (1933–1935)

On March 4, 1933, as the clocks struck noon, Eleanor Roosevelt wondered if it was possible to "do anything to save America now." One-fourth of the work force was unemployed; 30 million families had no means of support; there wasn't enough money in the Treasury to meet the federal payroll. Eleanor looked at her husband, who had just been sworn in as thirty-second president of the United States. Franklin Roosevelt removed his hand from the 300-year-old family Bible, turned to the podium, and solemnly addressed the crowd, now over 100,000: "Let me assert my firm belief that the only thing we have to fear is fear itself—nameless, unreasoning, unjustified terror." Heeding the nation's call for action, he promised to convene Congress into special session and exercise "broad Executive power to wage a war against the emergency." The crowd broke into thunderous applause. Eleanor was terrified. "One has the feeling of going it blindly," she explained a few hours later, "because we're in a tremendous stream, and none of us know where we're going to land."

The New Deal unfolded in two legislative bursts, one in the hundred days after the inauguration, another in the hundred days at the end of 1935. Often chaotic and sometimes contradictory, the program pursued three broad goals: recovery, relief, and reform. Though recovery remained elusive, there were notable achievements in relief and reform. Above all the New Deal created a limited "welfare state." It never reached all Americans, but for the first time government was committed to maintaining minimum standards of well-being for those in need. Despite his dominating presence Franklin Roosevelt was not the New Deal. It was also the product of Congress, the Supreme Court, and ordinary Americans. Sometimes they pushed the New Deal further than Roosevelt wanted to take it; sometimes they set limits he disliked. Regardless, the New Deal reshaped America.

The Democratic Roosevelts

Franklin Delano Roosevelt understood the gravity of the crisis better than anyone. A friend told him that if he succeeded, he would go down as the greatest president in history. "If I fail," he replied, "I shall be the last one." Roosevelt had no intention of failing, but he was not quite sure how he was going to succeed. "Take a method and try it," he instructed his staff. "If it fails, try another. But above all try something." He had no master blueprint, no "economic panaceas or fancy plans." He was a pragmatist who improvised, he told reporters, like a football quarterback calling a play only when he had seen how the last one turned out.

One thing he did know beforehand: Americans were ready for change. Together he and Eleanor gave it to them, beginning with the White House itself. No more footmen; no more buglers; and above all, no more seven-course meals as Hoover had served. Instead visitors got fare fit for a boardinghouse, capped by a desert of a pineapple slice with two cherries and a walnut swimming in watery whipped cream. Roosevelt's lunches—hash and one poached egg—cost 19 cents. With millions of Americans on the edge of starvation, anything more would have been unseemly.

Almost nothing Roosevelt did was unseemly. Born of an old Dutch patrician family in New York, he had been pampered as a boy by an overbearing mother and an elderly, indulgent father. He grew up idolizing his cousin Theodore Roosevelt and mimicked his path to the presidency, except that Franklin was a Democrat. Like Theodore, he was graduated from Harvard University (in 1904), won a seat in the New York State legislature (in 1910), secured an appointment as assistant secretary of the navy (in 1913), and ran for the vice presidency (in 1920). Along the way he even married Theodore's niece Eleanor, a shy girl with a toothy grin, fantastic energy, and an unshakable commitment to social justice.

Though the Democrats lost the election of 1920, party bosses agreed that Franklin Roosevelt, barely 38 years old, had a bright future. Then disaster struck. On vacation at the family retreat in Nova Scotia in the summer of 1921, he returned from sailing only to succumb to a numbing fatigue. Normally vigorous, he could barely move. Doctors diagnosed the illness as poliomyelitis, a dreaded crippler when it did not kill. It paralyzed Roosevelt from the waist down. Confined to a wheelchair for the rest of his life, he could walk only with the aid of crutches and heavy steel braces.

Roosevelt seemed to emerge from the ordeal with greater patience, deeper conviction, and more empathy for the unfortunates of the world. The disease probably enhanced his appeal to Depression America. When they saw Roosevelt, voters imagined not a spoon-fed aristocrat but a man who had triumphed over personal adversity. In 1928, the year of Al Smith's disastrous presidential race, Roosevelt won the governorship of New York. A progressive like cousin Theodore, he stressed conservation of human as well as physical resources. As governor he pressed for old-age pensions and endorsed unemployment insurance in New York. In the wake of the stock market crash, he was the first governor to provide unemployment relief. Aid to the jobless, said Roosevelt, "must be extended by Government, not as a matter of charity, but as a matter of social duty." In 1931 New York's Temporary Emergency Relief Administration became the first state relief agency.

In the governor's mansion or the White House, Roosevelt was a natural leader. He loved power. "Wouldn't you be President, if you could?" he asked a visitor. "Wouldn't anybody?" He bubbled with enthusiasm. Meeting Franklin Roosevelt, said Winston Churchill, was like "uncorking a bottle of champagne!" His mind was "quick," observed editor William Allen White, but "superficial." Common sense ruled him, and he made no decisions that could be put off. Everything was on a "24-hour basis" so that all his options could be preserved until the last instant. A conventional budget balancer, he could be bold when it came to social reform. He adopted no single ideology. He cared little about political principles. What he wanted were results.

Two traits made Roosevelt a peerless politician—an unshakable faith in himself and the ability to persuade others. Radiating charm, he delighted in manipu-

Most photographers acceded to White House wishes that President Roosevelt never be shot from the waist down. After coming down with polio, Roosevelt helped to transform the ramshackle resort at Warm Springs, Georgia (where this picture was taken), into a treatment center for victims of the disease.

lating those around him. His deep voice and infectious smile were irresistible. And for all his high breeding he never lost the common touch. Roosevelt could take a difficult subject like banking, said humorist Will Rogers, and explain it so that anyone understood it, even bankers. Roosevelt could be ruthless and deceitful (for years he carried on a secret affair with Lucy Mercer Rutherford, his wife's former social secretary); yet he found it nearly impossible to fire anybody. It did not matter, for Roosevelt retained power by scattering it among competing agencies. Only the president had the authority to resolve their differences. "Bring it to Poppa," he told his staff, and time after time they did.

Regularly he reached out to the American people. Almost single-handedly he shifted the locus of newsmaking from New York to Washington. He held an unequaled number of press conferences (998) and became the first president to hire a press secretary. During Roosevelt's administration the United Press wire service tripled its Washington staff. His famous "fireside chats" brought Roosevelt into the homes of his countrymen. "My friends," he said in the first of 16 radio broadcasts, "I want to tell you what has been done in the last few days, why it was done, and what the next steps are going to be." During the campaign he had promised to remember the "forgotten man," and when he spoke Americans felt as if he had each of them in mind. "It was a sacred time," recalled one women of the fireside chats, "as if a father was talking to his children who were afraid."

Roosevelt relied on his wife, more than any president before him had, and Eleanor redefined what it meant to be First Lady. After the inauguration he sent her to visit the second encampment of the Bonus marchers. She ended up leading them in a sing-along. "Hoover sent the army, but Roosevelt sent his wife!" said one of them. Never had a president's wife been so visible. She was the first one to hold weekly press conferences. Her column, "My Day," appeared in 135 newspapers, and her twice-weekly broadcasts made her a radio personality second only to her husband. She became his eyes, ears, and legs, traveling 40,000 miles a year on behalf of the downtrodden. Secret Service men gave her the code name "Rover."

Eleanor claimed modestly that she was nothing more than a "spur" to action. Her husband used her, she said, as he did everyone because she "served his purposes." He served hers as well. She pressed him to hire more women and blacks, supported antilynching and anti–poll tax measures when he would not, and transformed the First Lady's office into a lobby for the underdog. By 1939 public opinion polls showed that more Americans approved of her than of her husband. Her modesty aside, the Democratic Roosevelts formed the most potent political team in American history.

The First Hundred Days

In his first hundred days in office Roosevelt orchestrated the enactment of 15 major pieces of legislation—a record that stood until Lyndon Johnson's Great Society of the 1960s. Congress shaped the programs, but with a sense of urgency and speed rarely seen on Capitol Hill. So rapidly were bills sent from the White House to Congress and back again that even the president confessed to being "a bit shell-shocked." Government began to dominate American economic life so much that conservatives feared the end of capitalism. But Roosevelt's aim was to save capitalism, though that did mean modifying it.

Before the election Roosevelt had gathered a group of economic advisers called the "Brains Trust." Headed by Columbia University professors Raymond

Moley, Rexford G. Tugwell, and Adolf Berle, the Brains Trust disagreed with Hoover's conclusion that the Depression was spawned overseas. Like Roosevelt they saw the Depression as the home-grown product of corporate greed, Republican mismanagement, and a massive failure of consumer purchasing power. Blending progressive New Nationalism with the more recent associationism of the 1920s, the Brains Trusters prescribed a multifaceted program under federal direction: experimentation to achieve recovery, reforms to end abuses and restore confidence, limits on production to boost prices, and centralized economic planning.

The first step toward recovery was saving the banks. When Roosevelt arrived in Washington he already had a draft of new banking legislation in hand. Since the crash 5500 banks had failed. The country's 18,569 banks had only about $6 billion on hand in cash to cover $41 billion in deposits. Even the soundest banks held most of their deposits in mortgages, securities, and other investments, all of which had fallen to a fraction of their former value. More currency was needed. Yet at the very time the Treasury was being called on to expand the money supply investors were squirreling away the gold on which it was based. By the eve of the inauguration governors in 38 states had temporarily closed their banks to stem the tide. Reflecting popular resentment, *Time* magazine coined a new word, "bankster," by combining "banker" with "gangster."

On March 5, the day after the inauguration, Roosevelt issued a decree halting all transactions in gold and proclaiming a four-day bank "holiday." The euphemism snapped the tension of the previous winter. Instead of panicking, Americans responded as if it were a holiday. They devised ingenious ways of conducting business—from using local currencies called "scrip" to bartering services for goods. (One Wisconsin wrestler signed a contract for a can of tomatoes and a peck of potatoes.) Roosevelt called Congress into special session on March 9 and introduced emergency banking legislation to shore up the system. By unanimous shout, the House passed the measure, sight unseen. The Senate, with a handful of dissents, followed later in the day. A haggard Roosevelt signed it that night.

The Emergency Banking Act was scarcely a radical measure. Instead of nationalizing banks it simply extended federal assistance to them. Sound banks would be reopened immediately with government support; troubled banks would be handed over to federal "conservators," who would help reorganize their assets. Federal loans would be available to keep them afloat. On Sunday, March 12, Roosevelt explained what was happening in the first of his fireside chats. Half the people in America had radios; nearly one in three tuned in. In calm, uncluttered language the president reassured the public that the banks were safe again. The next day deposits exceeded withdrawals, and two days later the stock market had its largest one-day increase in history. "Capitalism was saved in eight days," said one Roosevelt adviser.

Other financial measures buoyed public confidence in government and the economy. On March 10 Roosevelt requested sweeping powers to cut the federal budget by $400 million in veterans' payments and $100 million in salaries. Congress passed the Economy Act after only two days' debate. Later that spring a second Glass–Steagall Banking Act separated investment from commercial banking to limit speculation by bankers. Tucked into the statute was one of the most important achievements of the New Deal: federal insurance of bank deposits. Roosevelt opposed it on the grounds that it would underwrite weak banks, but Congress enacted it anyway. Soon the Federal Deposit Insurance Corporation was guaranteeing bank deposits up to $2500. Fewer banks failed during the rest of the decade than in the best year of the twenties. To clean up Wall Street, the Securities Act of 1933 reduced the advantage of insiders by requiring advance disclosure of information about new stocks. In 1934 the Securities Exchange Act established a new federal agency, the Securities and Exchange Commission, to police the stock market. Stricter regulation of banking and investment laid the groundwork for recovery.

The relief of human suffering was a second goal of the first hundred days. Middle-class Americans were a primary target. In 1932 a quarter of a million families lost their homes. During the first half of 1933 more than 1000 homes were foreclosed every day. The Home Owners' Loan Act helped one out of every five homeowners refinance their mortgages. To keep people from starving until recovery took hold, Congress created the Federal Emergency Relief Administration (FERA) in May 1933. Sitting amid unpacked boxes, gulping coffee and chain-smoking, former social worker Harry Hopkins began disbursing its $500 million appropriation as if, said a colleague, he were "turning on a fireplug." Hopkins spent $5 million in his first two hours on the job. To avoid charges of "federal dictatorship," the money came in matching grants to states, which then administered them as a dole, or giveaway program. In its two-year existence, FERA furnished over $1 billion in direct assistance to states, localities, and private charities. The system had its flaws. It left critical decisions over eligibility and dispersal in local hands, where local prejudices sometimes ruled. Poorer states, able to put up less, received less.

Like Hoover, Roosevelt feared that any public assistance might become a "narcotic," but he recognized the need for temporary aid in the depths of the Depression. Of the two possibilities he preferred work relief to cash allotments. Giving a person a job in exchange for a paycheck "preserves a man's morale," Hopkins explained. "It saves his skill. It gives him a chance to do something socially useful." As the winter of 1933–1934 approached, Hopkins persuaded Roosevelt to expand relief with a program to tide the unemployed over the chilly season. The Civil Works Administration (CWA) gave jobs, some of them useful, others makeshift and shoddy, to some 4 million Americans. Wages averaged $15 a week, hardly adequate but more than twice FERA payments. The work itself was as important as the money. "When I got that [CWA identification] card it was the biggest day of my whole life," an unemployed insurance man told Lorena Hickok. "At last I could say, 'I've got a job.'" Alarmed at the high cost of the program, Roosevelt disbanded the CWA in the spring of 1934. For the next year and a half, the FERA remained the principal source of public aid.

Another work relief program established during the hundred days proved to be more creative. The Civilian Conservation Corps (CCC) was Roosevelt's pet project, combining his concern for conservation with a compassion for youth. The CCC took unmarried 18- to 25-year-olds from relief rolls and sent them into the woods and fields of America. They protected and restored forests, beaches, rivers, and parks at wages of $1 a day. During its 10-year lifetime, the CCC provided 2.5 million jobs, all of them for men (which prompted some critics to chant, "Where's the she, she, she?").

The cause of conservation received a more powerful boost in May 1933, when Roosevelt signed an act creating the Tennessee Valley Authority (TVA). Long a dream of Nebraska senator George Norris, this experiment in regional development and social engineering aimed at transforming one of the poorest regions of the country. The TVA, still functioning today, began with the construction of a series of dams in seven states on the Tennessee River to control flooding, improve navigation, and generate cheap electric power. Soon, for the first time, thousands of rural families could flip a switch to get light or turn a knob to hear the latest news on the radio. TVA-generated electricity also served as a "yardstick" for measuring the prices of private utilities. In an effort to encourage "grassroots democracy," the TVA cooperated with state and local officials in social programs, from controlling malaria to furnishing library bookmobiles and constructing recreational lakes. Like many New Deal programs, the TVA has a mixed legacy. It saved 3 million acres from erosion, multiplied the average income in the valley tenfold, and repaid its original investment in federal taxes. It also pushed thousands of families from their land and became one of the worst polluters in the country.

The Riddle of Recovery

After years of Hoover paralysis, Roosevelt's first hundred days finally broke national despair. The economic depression proved more resistant. Though Roosevelt regarded recovery as his primary goal, the New Deal never reached it. Conditions did improve, but the Depression persisted. As late as 1939 industrial production had yet to reach 1929 levels. Nearly 10 million Americans walked the streets in search of work, and displaced farm families still huddled around campfires on western highways. Perhaps no one could have solved the riddle of recovery, but Roosevelt tried.

At first the president experimented with quick monetary fixes. In 1933 he took the nation off the gold standard by prohibiting banks from redeeming currency in gold coin and outlawing the export of gold. Then he reduced the value of the dollar by buying gold on the open market. Devaluation, he hoped, would make American goods cheaper for foreign buyers and raise commodity prices at home. By November 1934 the program had failed. Yielding to pressure from western farmers and miners, he began buying silver to inflate the currency and raise prices. This scheme also ended in failure. Investment, not artificially inflated prices, was the key to recovery.

In June 1933 Roosevelt launched a two-pronged attack on the many ills of industry: sagging prices and purchasing power, overproduction, "cut-throat" competition, unemployment, and declining wages. The National Industrial Recovery Act created two new agencies, the Public Works Administration (PWA) and the National Recovery Administration (NRA). Originally designed to work in tandem, they soon went separate ways. Harold Ickes, the irascible secretary of the interior, took over the PWA. Its purpose was to prime the economic pump by stimulating heavy industry and providing jobs with $3.3 billion in public works. Fearing waste and corruption, "Honest Harold" oversaw each project personally. He spent money so slowly that the PWA never achieved its goal. But it did make spectacular additions to the national inventory of public structures, including the Triborough Bridge and Lincoln Tunnel in New York, the port city of Brownsville in Texas, and the aircraft carriers *Yorktown* and *Enterprise*.

The National Recovery Administration took on the gargantuan tasks of maintaining prices, wages, and employment while controlling production and competi-

An NRA blue eagle decal.

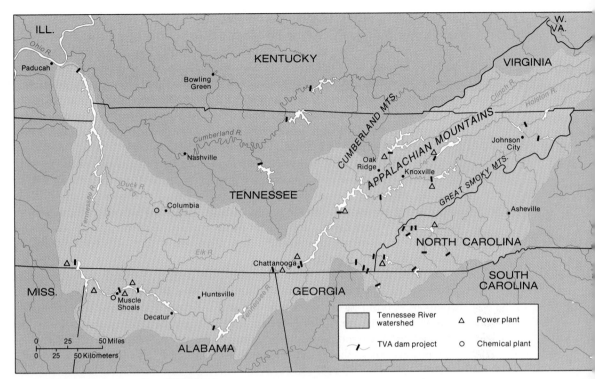

THE TENNESSEE VALLEY AUTHORITY
The Tennessee River basin encompassed parts of seven states. Rivers honeycombed the area, which received some of the heaviest rainfall in the nation. A long-time dream of Senator George Norris, the Tennessee Valley Authority, created in 1933, constructed some twenty dams and improved five others over the next twenty years to control chronic flooding and erosion and to produce cheap hydroelectric power and fertilizers.

tion. Building on Hoover initiatives in the associational movement, Roosevelt cast the NRA as "a partnership in planning" between government and industry. NRA administrator Hugh Johnson had his doubts about chances for success: "This is just like mounting the guillotine on the infinitesimal gamble that the ax won't work." Johnson, a rough-hewn veteran of the cavalry, had served with the War Industries Board during World War I. He hoped to rekindle the wartime spirit of unity by calling on businessmen, laborers, and consumers to cooperate again.

Under the watchful eye of government, industries developed "codes of fair practices" to limit production, divide it among the various companies, and stabilize prices. In return government suspended antitrust laws to allow for business cooperation. Each code also promised labor improved working conditions, outlawing such practices as child labor and sweatshops. Section 7a of the original legislation, modeled on the War Labor Board, further protected workers by guaranteeing union rights to bargain with management and requiring codes to set minimum wages and maximum hours. To guard their interests consumers were promised a voice in making and administering codes.

Eventually more than 600 codes governed industries ranging from major ones like steel, oil, and construction to minor ones such as horse hair dressing and the manufacture of shoulder pads. No business was forced to comply. Instead Johnson, a superb showman, relied on voluntary participation, promoted through patriotic campaigns. Casting about for a symbol of compliance, he hit on a blue eagle with the legend "We Do Our Part." Soon Blue Eagle decals appeared all over the country—in storefronts, in factories, even on the backs of chorus girls' costumes. On the Boston Common Mayor James Curley led 100,000 children in a pledge to "buy only where the Blue Eagle flies." For 10 hours New Yorkers watched a quarter of a million people march down Fifth Avenue for the Blue Eagle. More than 2 million employers pledged to abide by the codes.

The NRA leavened national spirits but failed to bring about recovery. Big businesses dominated code-making. To guarantee profits they restricted production and raised prices, usually enough to cover forced increases in wages. "This was scarcity economics," wrote one historian, "and it meant reduced purchasing power." Businesses could survive, but without increasing production there would be no incentive for expansion and new investment. Under such conditions hard times could last indefinitely.

Disillusioned, owners of smaller businesses refused to comply with the codes. Even participating firms found ways to avoid labor reforms and wage increases. Company-sponsored unions competed with independent unions; collective bargaining often became a sham. Labor leaders began to refer to the NRA as the "National Run Around." Consumers, promised representation in the NRA, had no real power. Soon they started complaining about "NRA prices and Hoover wages." On May 27, 1935, in *Schecter Poultry Corp. v. United States*, the Supreme Court struck down the NRA. The justices unanimously ruled that the NRA exceeded federal power over interstate commerce and that its codes represented "an unconstitutional delegation of legislative power" to an executive agency. Publicly distressed over the grounds of the decision, Roosevelt was privately relieved to be rid of this "awful headache."

New Deal efforts to revive agriculture turned out better. Agriculture secretary Henry A. Wallace planned to increase farm prices by attacking the age-old problem of overproduction. Under the Agricultural Adjustment Act of 1933 farmers would be paid for *not* planting crops. A tax on processors—millers, cotton ginners, and the like—would finance the government subsidies under this program of "domestic allotments." In theory surpluses would be reduced, commodity prices would rise, and agriculture would recover. In practice the Agricultural Adjustment Administration (AAA) did help to increase prices of the seven major commodities it covered: cotton, corn, tobacco, rice, wheat, hogs, and dairy products. For the first time in more than a decade farm income grew (from $5.5 billion in 1932 to $8.7 billion in 1935). The Commodity Credit Corporation extended loans on crops kept in storage, a revival of the Populists' old subtreasury plan (see page 775). Loans were pegged slightly higher than market value as an additional spur to prices.

Not all of the gains were attributable to government. In 1934 and 1935 dust storms, droughts, and floods, particularly in the Great Plains and in the South, helped to reduce harvests and boost prices. The AAA, moreover, failed to distribute its benefits equally. Like the NRA, the AAA favored big producers. To preserve democratic procedure, Roosevelt insisted that the program be voluntary and that local farmers themselves choose the plots to be left fallow. Large farmers controlled decision-making. In the South this frequently meant cutting the acreage of tenants and sharecroppers or forcing them from the land. Even when they reduced their own acreage, large farmers often increased yields since they had the money and equipment to cultivate more intensively. The New Deal stabilized the farm economy and set the pattern of future farm programs, but it also accelerated the trend toward large-scale, corporate "agribusiness."

In 1936 the Supreme Court declared the processing tax of the AAA unconstitutional in *Butler v. U.S.* A hastily drawn replacement, the Soil Conservation and Domestic Allotment Act of 1936, subsidized farmers for practicing "conservation" but paid them from general revenues instead of a special tax on processors. Farmers received benefit payments for taking soil-depleting staples off the land, thereby achieving reduction indirectly. Agents from the new Soil Conservation Service were so successful in educating farmers about scientific land use that production still increased. A second Agricultural Adjustment Act in 1938 returned production quotas.

Other agencies tried to help impoverished farmers. The Farm Credit Administration refinanced about a fifth of all farm mortgages. In 1935 the Resettlement Administration gave marginal farmers a fresh start by moving them to better land, and beginning in 1937 the Farm Security Administration furnished low-interest, long-term loans to help tenants buy family-size farms. In neither case did the rural poor have much political clout, and appropriations from Congress were never enough. In the end fewer than 5000 families (of a projected 500,000) were resettled, and less than 2 percent of tenant farmers got loans.

A SECOND NEW DEAL (1935–1936)

The early New Deal had tried to satisfy as many people as possible. Without a clear following, Roosevelt had catered to a variety of interests, acting as a broker who responded first to one group, then to another. The result was a makeshift concoction of "alphabet agencies." Organized groups—bankers, large farmers, big businesses—benefited most; unorganized groups—sharecroppers, tenants, the downtrodden—scarcely at all. Yet the focus remained broad, and all the activity, even when it was contradictory, had rekindled hope. In 1934 voters gave the Democrats an unprecedented endorsement by strengthening their majorities in Congress and handing them all but seven governorships. Never before had a party in power increased its popular vote in an off-year election. The "broker state," as it came to be called, made for good politics, whatever its economic shortcomings.

In 1935 politics helped to shift the course of the New Deal. Pressed by the persistence of unemployment and depression, worried about the 1936 presidential election, and stung by the hostility of many businesses, Roosevelt began to respond to calls for deeper change. Neither a radical nor a conservative, he moved in the direction he always wanted to go, "slightly to the left of center." A "second New Deal" emerged. It abandoned the partnership with business, addressed more directly the needs of the dispossessed, and stressed liberal reform. Even more than the early New Deal, this second New Deal brought the federal government into the lives of ordinary Americans.

Voices of Protest

"The revolutionary spirit burgeons," wrote historian William Leuchtenburg, "not when conditions are at their worst but as they begin to improve." The early successes of the New Deal invigorated its critics as well as its friends. One April day in 1934 a mob of 6000 stormed the Minneapolis city hall, tossing sticks, stones, and lumps of coal through the windows during a meeting of the city council. The rioters demanded government work at a living wage and greater relief. That summer in San Francisco longshoremen walked off the job and ignited a general strike that paralyzed the city. In the fall 1000 relief workers in Denver struck, infuriated by a cut in relief payments. All told, 1.5 million workers took part in some 1800 strikes in 1934. Conditions were improving but not quickly enough. Across the country voices of protest gathered strength.

A few angry voices came from the right, as businessmen accused Roosevelt of favoring labor and farmers. Some charged him with amassing enough power to become an American Hitler. The embattled rich were most nervous of all. "Five Negroes on my place in South Carolina refused work this Spring . . . saying they had easy jobs with the government," reported a retired Du Pont executive. Moved by his predicament, a group of corporate leaders and conservative Democrats founded the American Liberty League in August 1934 to protect the rights of property and the people who held most of it. Despite spending over $1 million in publicity, the League inflicted no serious wounds on Roosevelt or the New Deal. Few considered the plight of the wealthy a problem.

Louder voices came from the left. In Minnesota, Governor Floyd B. Olson of the Farmer–Labor party demanded more aid for farmers and workers. "I hope," he said in 1932, "that the present system of government goes right down to Hell." By 1934 he was calling himself a "radical" and soon toying with a third-party presidential campaign for 1936. In California discontented voters took over the Democratic party and nominated novelist Upton Sinclair, a Socialist, for the governorship. Running under the slogan "End Poverty in California" (EPIC), Sinclair proposed the distribution of surpluses through a production-for-use plan. Under his administration the state would confiscate idle factories and land and permit the unemployed to work for their own benefit. Republicans, anxious about the threat to private property, mounted a devastating counterattack. Hollywood tycoons contributed fake newsreels depicting Sinclair as a Bolshevik, atheist, and freelover. Sinclair lost the election but won nearly 1 million votes.

Huey P. Long represented a greater threat. The flamboyant senator from Louisiana had ridden to power on a wave of rural discontent. Born on a family farm in the Louisiana hill country, Long was reared on the rhetoric of radical Populism. "There wants to be a revolution," his father once told him. Huey decided to make one happen by redistributing wealth in America. Comical and ruthless, he called himself the "Kingfish" (after a character in the popular "Amos 'n' Andy" radio show) and promised to make "every man a king" by "sharing our wealth." His plan was simple: the government would limit the size of all fortunes and incomes so that every family could be given an estate of $5000, enough to buy a house, an automobile, and a radio. There would be a guaranteed annual income of $2500. The young would get scholarships, the old pensions. By 1935, one year after its founding, the Share Our Wealth organization boasted 27,000 clubs and files containing nearly 8 million names.

Louisiana Governor and Senator Huey Long promised to make "every man a king," but critics predicted that only Long would wear the crown. Power-hungry and charismatic, the "Kingfish" made no secret of his presidential aspirations.

In the early years of the Depression, demonstrations of the unemployed, some organized by Communists and other radicals, broke out all over the country. On March 6, 1930, a Communist-led protest at Union Square in New York turned into an ugly riot. In 1935 Communist parties, under orders from Moscow, adopted the more cooperative strategy of allying with democratic and socialist groups against facism, proclaiming in the United States that "Communism is twentieth century Americanism."

Despite his gross underestimates of what it would take to subsidize the have-nots, Long was addressing a real problem, the uneven distribution of wealth in America. As governor of Louisiana (some called him "dictator"), he had attacked wealthy corporations, built bridges and roads in the poorest sections of the state, and given free schoolbooks to children, black and white alike. So when Long told the Louisiana legislature which bills to enact, when his private police force kidnaped political opponents, when he feathered his own financial nest, the downtrodden of Louisiana looked the other way. Democratic National Committee members shuddered at polls showing that the Kingfish might capture 3 million to 4 million votes in 1936, enough to put a Republican in the White House. The Kingfish himself might even make it there in 1940. But late in 1935, as he strode through the corridors of the Louisiana capitol, Long was shot to death by a disgruntled constituent whose father-in-law had been wronged by the Long political machine.

Father Charles Coughlin was Long's urban counterpart. As urban middle- and working-class people slipped into poverty, the Detroit "Radio Priest" grew in popularity. In weekly broadcasts from the Shrine of the Little Flower he offered bewildered followers—mainly ethnic Catholics from the lower middle class of the urban North—a simple explanation for their plight. A conspiracy of international bankers had toppled the world economy by manipulating currencies based on gold.

Like Long, Coughlin also touched on a real problem, the inadequate supply of money. And like the Kingfish, Coughlin exploited rather than solved it. He promised to end the Depression by such simple strokes as nationalizing banks, spreading work, and using silver to inflate the currency. (None would have

987

worked, since they would have dampened investment, one key to recovery.) Drawing on old Populist suspicions of eastern bankers and later spewing an ugly anti-Semitism, his radio sermons were soon drawing 30 million to 40 million listeners, the largest audiences in the world. At first Coughlin supported the New Deal, but when the president refused to adopt his schemes, he broke with the administration and Franklin "Double-Crossing" Roosevelt. In 1934 he created the National Union for Social Justice to rally his supporters. As the election of 1936 approached, it loomed as an ominous specter on the political horizon.

A more kindly challenge came from Dr. Francis Townsend, a 67-year-old physician who had retired from the public health service. One morning he looked out of his bathroom window to see three old women scavenging for food in an alley. Across the country aged Americans on shrinking incomes faced unemployment and illness without pension plans or medical insurance. Townsend vowed to bring their humiliation and suffering to an end. In 1934 he set up Old Age Revolving Pensions, Limited, to promote his plan for furnishing aid to the elderly and at the same time promoting recovery. Townsend proposed to pay citizens 60 years or older $200 a month provided they quit their jobs, surrender all other income, and spend the money within 30 days. The program would be financed by a 2 percent tax on commercial transactions.

As much as the elderly needed assistance, the Townsend plan was economic hokum. Townsendites expected to spend over half the national income to compensate less than one-tenth of the population. The plan would create no new jobs, and its 2 percent sales tax would fall on everyone, including impoverished American consumers. Yet the allure of the Townsend movement was undeniable. In 1935 almost 9 in 10 Americans believed that some form of government old-age pensions was necessary. By 1936 Townsend clubs counted 3.5 million members, most of them small businessmen and farmers at or beyond retirement age. The clubs gave them more than hope for added income: they provided a place where the elderly could socialize with people their own age, who saw things as they did, who believed they could save the economy and return the nation to old truths. Members brought Bibles to Townsend club meetings, sang hymns, and harrangued against alcohol, necking, wild youth, and big-city ways. Most of all they believed in Townsend and his plan. Under his leadership, the elderly became a new force in politics.

The Second Hundred Days

Reporting on the state of the Union to the new Congress in January 1935, the president struck a moderate tone as he looked to the coming year, "a genuine period of good feeling, sustained by a sense of purposeful progress." Even as he spoke, the forces of discontent—from businessmen on the right to demagogues on the left—were pushing him to bolder action, and so was Congress. Democrats, who controlled more than two-thirds of both houses, were prepared to outspend Roosevelt in extending the New Deal to more of their constituents. His advisers were pushing too. "Boys—this is our hour," crowed Harry Hopkins. "We've got to get everything we want—a works program, social security, wages and hours, everything—now or never." The result was a new flurry of legislation in 1935—"the second hundred days"—stressing longer term relief and more sweeping reform.

To ease the plight of the jobless Roosevelt first proposed a massive program of work relief. Despite a decline of 2 million from the ranks of the unemployed, millions more remained jobless at the end of 1934. "The forgotten man is still forgotten," a Pennsylvania worker wrote to Eleanor Roosevelt in 1935. In April 1935 Congress enacted the Emergency Relief Appropriation Act. Its $4.8 billion allocation (the largest to date in peacetime) was designed to put people to work. Some of the money went to the new National Youth Administration (NYA). It gave part-time employment to more than 4.5 million young people, almost half of them students. The Public Works Administration and the Civilian Conservation Corps also received funds, but the largest share went to the new Works Progress Administration (WPA) with super-relief administrator Hopkins at the helm.

Since the WPA aimed at disbursing most of its money in wages, its projects were usually of the pick-and-shovel variety. Constrained by rules against competing with private industry, WPA workers were sometimes forced into "boondoggles" like raking leaves or digging and filling holes. Critics called the program "We Piddle Around," yet Hopkins showed remarkable ingenuity in finding useful work. The WPA built or improved 20,000 hospitals, schools, airports, and playgrounds. WPA workers taught art classes to the mentally disturbed in a Cincinnati hospital; drafted a Braille map for the blind in Watertown, Massachusetts; and rode a packhorse pulling a library through the hills of Kentucky. Though pay averaged only $55 a month (barely half the annual subsistence level), 80 percent of the WPA budget went to wages. In 1935 alone, the agency employed over 3 million people, and before it was ended in 1943, it gave work to over 8.5 million. The WPA was a bold experiment, but it never reached Roosevelt's goal of giving jobs to all who could work.

The Social Security Act (1935) was intended to help the aged, infirm, and other "forgotten" men and women. Roosevelt favored what he called a "cradle-to-grave" system, an all-embracing social insurance program. Reflecting the limits of political feasibility, the Social Security Act was something less. It created a national system of old-age insurance funded by payroll taxes on employers and workers; state and federal funds for the care of the destitute over the age of 65; a federal–state system of unemployment insurance; and national aid to the states, on a matching basis, for care of dependent mothers and children, the crippled, and the blind, and for public health services.

For all its coverage, Social Security had defects. Compared to social insurance in Europe, the program was conservative and skimpy. Pension payments were not scheduled to begin until 1942 and would be no more than $10 to $85 a month, with subsidies to dependent children and the handicapped usually averaging less—and all inadequate even by Depression standards. Contrary to Roosevelt's wishes, Social Security also failed to cover everyone. To win the votes of southerners worried about its effect on race relations, the legislation excluded farmers and domestic servants, doubtless the neediest but often black. The payroll tax was another problem. It took money from workers and thereby reduced demand for goods at a time when mass purchasing power was already too low. Roosevelt had nonetheless insisted on the tax. Bad economics again made good politics, since retiring citizens would have a right to pensions because they had paid for them. "With those taxes in there," Roosevelt slyly observed, "no damn politician can ever scrap my social security program."

Social Security marked a historic reversal. The gospel of self-help was counterbalanced by a new social contract, however narrow. For the first time the federal government acknowledged the social rights of citizens and its responsibility to protect them. The welfare state, foreshadowed in the temporary relief measures of the early New Deal, was made permanent.

Congress may not have gone as far as Roosevelt wished on Social Security, but its labor legislation pushed him beyond his natural limits. A symbolic father to so many of his countrymen, Roosevelt regarded labor with similar paternalism. He wanted things done for workers, not by them. He had chosen a social worker, Frances Perkins, rather than a labor leader as secretary of labor. She agreed that enactment of Social Security, along with provisions for maximum hours and minimum wages, was what the New Deal needed to do for working men and women.

Robert F. Wagner, the liberal senator from New York, believed such government paternalism was not enough. The son of a janitor, Wagner was the strongest friend of labor in Congress. He wanted workers to be able to fight their own battles. In 1933 he pressed for the inclusion of Section 7a in the NRA to protect the rights of labor to organize and bargain collectively. When the agency was invalidated by the Supreme Court, Wagner sought to protect organized labor directly. Enacted in the summer of 1935 (with only the belated blessings of the president), the National Labor Relations Act, known as the "Wagner Act," created a National Labor Relations Board to supervise elections in plants and factories where workers wanted to organize. Once workers decided to join a union and selected their representatives by secret ballot, management had to negotiate with them. No company could engage in "unfair labor practices" such as firing employees for union activity or fostering company-controlled unions. The Wagner Act forced unions on no one but did guarantee the right of workers to band together and bargain collectively. It was, said admirers, "labor's Magna Carta." By 1941 the number of unionized workers had doubled.

Roosevelt responded to growing business hostility by turning openly against the wealthy and powerful. The Banking Act of 1935 centralized control of the money market in the Federal Reserve Board. By coordinated manipulation of interest rates and money supply government could influence the economy more than ever. The nation's financial capital moved from Wall Street to Washington. The Public Utilities Holding Company Act (1935) ordered the breakup of utility empires, long the target of progressive reformers. The giant holding companies produced nothing but inflated profits for speculators and high prices for consumers. Roosevelt wanted to dissolve them. The legislation, weakened by the powerful utilities lobby, ended up limiting their size. The Revenue Act of 1935 (called the "Wealth Tax Act") threatened to "soak the rich" but in the end brought only moderate taxes on high incomes and inheritances. Diluted like the holding company act, it was still a political victory for New Dealers, though mostly a symbolic one. "I am now on your bandwagon again, having slipped off," a Philadelphian told the president.

The second hundred days, like the first, wrought no fundamental changes in American life. The country was still capitalist, still democratic, still opposed to extremism. But there had been important shifts. Orthodox but practical, Roosevelt moved slowly to the left, in part to ward off the challenges of Long, Coughlin, and Townsend, in part to catch up with his own constituents. The price was business hostility, which surely inhibited recovery. As his partnership with business ended, he directed innovations more toward reform than the constant goal of recovery. No longer seeking to please everyone, Roosevelt turned to his natural allies, the down-and-out, the working and middle classes, liberal reformers, and rank-and-file Democrats. In 1935 his motives had been a mixture of instinctive decency and cold-blooded politics. His success would be measured in the election of 1936.

The Election of 1936

A June rain drenched the crowd of over 100,000 packed into the Franklin Field stadium in Philadelphia. No one minded. Loyal Democrats, they were there to see the president accept his nomination for a second term. As Roosevelt moved stiff-legged up the ramp, he reached down to shake the hand of a friend and suddenly pitched forward, falling to the ground. "Clean me up!" he snapped, his famous composure momentarily broken. Seconds later the curtain hiding the stage parted, and the president, now calm and unsoiled, flashed a smile at the cheering throng. "This generation of Americans," he told them, "has a rendezvous with destiny." It was a virtuoso performance because Roosevelt expected the coming election to turn on a single issue. "It's myself," he told one staffer, "and people must be either for me or against me."

The Republicans nominated Alfred M. "Alf" Landon of Kansas, the only Republican governor elected in 1932 who still survived in office. A former Bull Moose Progressive, Landon favored the regulation of business, the preservation of civil liberties, and several New Deal measures. Republicans outspent Democrats $14 million to $9 million in one of the first big-money advertising campaigns that would mark later presidential races. Yet despite his bulging war chest, Landon lacked luster as well as issues. Even his theme song (the old Oregon Trail ballad "Oh, Susanna") was out of tune with an electorate uninterested in reviving a bygone era. Landon and his running mate, Chicago publisher Frank Knox, were reduced to rebutting the New Deal with promises of retrenchment, a balanced budget, and a return to the gold standard.

Roosevelt ignored his opponents. He even ignored his own party. Instead he depicted himself as the leader of a great liberal crusade that knew no partisan lines. He turned the election into a contest between haves and have-nots. His most blistering attacks were launched at big business, already lost to him. The forces of "organized money are unanimous in their hate for me," he told a roaring crowd at New York's Madison Square Garden, "and I welcome their hatred." When the wealthy returned fire at Liberty League confabs and Chamber of Com-

THE ELECTION OF 1936

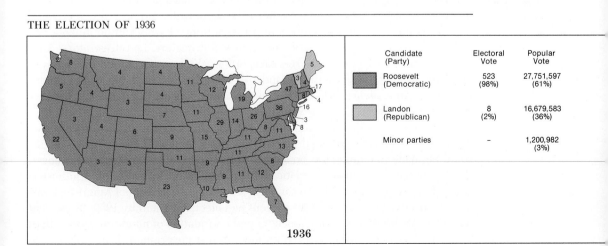

Candidate (Party)	Electoral Vote	Popular Vote
Roosevelt (Democratic)	523 (98%)	27,751,597 (61%)
Landon (Republican)	8 (2%)	16,679,583 (36%)
Minor parties	–	1,200,982 (3%)

1936

merce dinners, they only strengthened Roosevelt's hand. "At last we have a Man in the White House," wrote an Oregon woman,"and not a puppet of organized Wealth."

The strategy deflated the Republicans, discredited the right, and coopted the newly formed Union Party of Townsendites, Coughlinites, and the remnants of Huey Long's movement. The returns shocked even experienced political observers. Roosevelt won the largest electoral victory ever recorded—523 to 8. He received a whopping 60.8 percent of the popular vote and beat Landon by over 11 million votes. The Republican challenger won only two states, Maine and Vermont. "If Landon had given one more speech," quipped veteran reporter Dorothy Thompson, "Roosevelt would have carried Canada, too." Union party candidate William "Liberty Bill" Lemke of North Dakota polled only 882,000 votes; Socialist Norman Thomas recorded just 187,000. After the election, Father Coughlin, recalling the persecution of Christ, announced his retirement from politics.

Roosevelt's margin of victory came from those near the bottom of the economic ladder. Approximately 6 million more people cast ballots in 1936 than in 1932; 5 million of them voted for Roosevelt. Most were members of the poor and working classes expressing their support for the New Deal. More than 8 out of 10 trade union members, unskilled workers, and relief recipients voted for Roosevelt. Class replaced region as the dominant element in American politics.

A dramatic realignment took place, as important as the Republican rise to power in 1896. The Democrats reigned as the new majority party for the next 30 years. The "Roosevelt coalition" rested on three main pillars: traditional Democratic support in the South; the big cities, particularly ethnics and African-Americans; and labor, both organized and unorganized. The minority Republicans became the party of big business and small towns.

THE NEW DEAL AND THE AMERICAN PEOPLE

The lights did not go on in the Hill Country of Texas until 1939. Before then, local farmers read books after dusk and milked cows before dawn by the light of 25-watt kerosene lamps. Hill Country wives washed eight loads of laundry a week, all by hand. They hauled 200 gallons of water a day from wells and heated seven-pound "sadirons" on wood-burning stoves to press clothing. Farms had no milking machines, no washers, no automatic pumps or water heaters, no refrigerators. After sundown people could barely see each other. While other Americans enjoyed evenings listening to Jack Benny and the Lone Ranger on radio, Hill Country farmers sat in a silence broken only by their own voices. "Living—just living— was a problem," recalled one woman.

The reason for this limited life was simple: the Hill Country had no electricity. Utility companies resisted electrifying rural America because more money could be made in cities. Thus no agency of the Roosevelt administration changed the way people lived more dramatically than the Rural Electrification Administration (REA), created in 1935, at a time when less than 10 percent of American farms had electricity. Six years later 40 percent had electricity, and by 1950, 90 percent did. In 1935 the REA began to encourage the formation of nonprofit cooperatives to bring electricity to the farm. With low-interest government loans, the co-ops strung thousands of miles of power lines into the countryside. In the Smoky Mountains, along the Upper Peninsula of Michigan, on the slopes of the Continental Divide, and in the Hill Country of central Texas, communities saw their churches, stores, schools, and homes set aglow with a dazzling new light. Electric machines eased the drudgery of rural people; radios cut their isolation; light bulbs reduced the strain on their eyes and even improved the school grades of their children, who could now study at night. The New Deal did not always have such a marked impact; its overall record was mixed. But time and again it changed the lives of ordinary people as government never had before.

Outsiders Under the New Deal

In 1932 most African-Americans voted as they had since Reconstruction—for Republicans, the party of Abraham Lincoln and emancipation. But disenchantment with decades of broken promises of equality was spreading. "Go turn Lincoln's picture to the wall," publisher Robert Vann of the Pittsburgh *Courier* told black readers. "That debt has been paid in full." Not only did African-Americans turn Lincoln's picture to the wall; they replaced it with Roosevelt's. By 1934 they were voting for Democrats, and in 1936 they mounted a full-blown revolution in politics. "Let Jesus lead you and Roosevelt feed you," a black preacher told his congregation on the eve of the election. Three of four black voters cast their ballots for Roosevelt in 1936. By 1938 nearly 85 percent of black respondents in one poll counted themselves as Roosevelt Democrats.

The New Deal accounted for the dramatic change. Roosevelt's indifferent record on civil rights as governor of New York gave way to greater concern once he entered the White House. Never an open advocate of complete equality, he regarded African-Americans as one of many groups whose interests he brokered. Even that was an improvement over his predecessors. The federal government had been racially segregated since the days of Woodrow Wilson, and in the late 1920s black leaders referred to Hoover as "the man in the lily-White House."

Under Roosevelt government began once again to be racially integrated. Passionate partisans of civil rights like Eleanor Roosevelt and Secretary of the Interior Harold Ickes brought blacks into the administration. Political scientist Clark Foreman and economist Robert C. Weaver became advisers on racial affairs and later on black economic problems. Mary McLeod Bethune, who had risen from a sharecropper's shack to found Bethune–Cookman College, ran a division of the National Youth Administration. In May 1935, as the second New Deal began, Roosevelt issued Executive Order 7046 banning discrimination in the new Works Progress Administration.

African-Americans also pressed for such changes. Important as both symbols and contributers, black administrators formed the "Black Cabinet" to help shape federal policy. Outside of government the Urban League continued to lobby for economic advancement, and the NAACP drafted legislation to make lynching a federal crime. (Though publicly against lynching and privately in favor of the bill, Roosevelt refused to make the outlawing of lynching "must" legislation. He feared losing the support of southern congressmen he needed "to save America.") When NRA wage differentials ended up reducing the salaries of black workers in the

Mary McLeod Bethune.

South or NRA codes resulted the loss of their jobs to whites, black newspapers were quick to rename the agency "Negroes Ruined Again." In New York's Harlem the Reverend John H. Johnson organized the Citizens' League for Fair Play in 1933 to persuade white merchants to hire black clerks. After picketers blocked storefronts, hundreds of African-Americans got jobs with Harlem retailers and utility companies. Racial tension over employment and housing continued to run high, and in 1935 Harlem exploded in the only race riot of the decade.

Discrimination persisted under the New Deal. Government efforts to promote "grassroots democracy" often gave control of federal programs to localities, where prejudice produced inequalities. Relief payments to black clients in Atlanta, Georgia, averaged $19.29 a month; whites received $32.66. When local farm committees decided to retire acreage under the AAA, black sharecroppers and tenants were often the ones put out of production. New Deal showplaces like the TVA's model town of Norris, Tennessee, and the subsistence homestead village of Arthurdale, West Virginia, were closed entirely to blacks. Officials feared integration would promote trouble in these communal paradises.

African-Americans did benefit from the New Deal, but more as dispossessed citizens than as a disadvantaged race. The federally run WPA, whose employment practices were based on need, hired blacks for almost 20 percent of its jobs, even though they comprised less than 10 percent of the population. The minimum WPA wage of $12 a week was twice what many of them had earned before. Public Works Administrator Ickes established the first quota system for hiring blacks (based on their percentage of the local work force). By 1941 the number of African-Americans working for the government exceeded their percentage of the population.

Training programs, including Mary McLeod Bethune's enormously successful Office of Minority Affairs, helped to reduce black illiteracy from 16.4 percent to 11.5 percent by the end of the decade. Life expectancy jumped from 49 to 55 years for black women and from 47 to 52 years for black men in the 1930s. (Among whites it rose from 63 to 67 for women and from 60 to 62 for men.) Countless blacks shared the sentiments of a Washington cab driver who explained that he had voted for Roosevelt and the Democrats because they "favor the little man, and I've been a little man all my life."

The nearly 1 million Mexican-Americans in the United States received little assistance from the New Deal. Hispanic culture sometimes impeded relief efforts. The Mexican folk tradition of self-help inhibited some from seeking aid, while others remained unfamiliar with claim procedures. Still others failed to meet residency requirements. Low voter turnout and a high proportion of aliens among Mexican-Americans reduced their political power and the attention paid to their interests. Uneducated and unskilled, they often toiled as migrant farm workers outside the reach of many New Deal programs, including Social Security.

Throughout the Southwest and California, the Civilian Conservation Corps and the Works Progress Administration did help with jobs on the land and in construction. On Capitol Hill Dennis Chavez of New Mexico, the only United States senator of Hispanic descent, succeeded in channeling relief and other federal funds into Spanish-speaking communities. During the decade Hispanics, like blacks, were mired in poverty but developed enough faith in Roosevelt to switch from the Republican to the Democratic party.

After decades of neglect Indians found themselves the subjects of new federal interest. Indian families on reservations rarely earned more than $100 a year.

Their infant mortality rate was the highest in the country; their life expectancy the shortest; their education—usually no more than five years—the lowest. Their rate of unemployment was three times the national average. The Dawes Severalty Act of 1887 had sought to make Indians independent landowners, but poverty forced many to sell their federal allotments to white farmers and ranchers. By the 1930s Indian landholding had shrunk from 138 million to 48 million acres, most of it desert.

Commissioner of Indian Affairs John Collier, a social worker who had long fought for Indian rights, reversed the trend by acquiring land for Indians through federal and state grants. Indian Bureau agents tried to improve soil conservation by discouraging overgrazing and encouraging economic independence. Federal credit unions were organized on reservations, and federal funds underwrote Indian business ventures. Collier began to end years of assimilationist policies by promoting cultural pluralism and racial pride among the tribes. The Indian Bureau hired so many Indians that they made up more than a fourth of its employees by the end of the decade.

The Indian Reorganization Act of 1934 tried to revive traditional life and resurrect the tribal system. A special Court of Indian Affairs removed Indians from the jurisdiction of states. Tribes gained control of Indian lands. Elders were urged to celebrate festivals, artists to work in native styles, children to learn the old languages. Indians themselves were divided over Collier's policies. The Pueblos, with a strong communal spirit and already functioning communal societies, favored them. The tribes of Oklahoma and the Great Plains tended to oppose them. Individualism, the profit motive, and an unwillingness to share property with other tribe members fed resistance. So did age-old suspicion of all government programs, along with the genuine Indian desire for assimilation. The Navajos, under the leadership of J. C. Morgan, rejected the Indian Reorganization Act in 1935. Morgan saw tribal government as a step backward, and his people bitterly opposed Collier's efforts to discourage overgrazing by reducing the number of sheep. To the Navajos sheep had deep cultural meaning.

A New Deal for Women

The broker government of the New Deal was sensitive to a wide range of interests, and women quickly took advantage of the situation. Led by Eleanor Roosevelt and Secretary of Labor Frances Perkins, women invaded government. They headed the Women's and Children's bureaus of the Labor Department, directed the Mint, and served as assistant secretary in the Treasury Department. They found their greatest opportunities in the newly created agencies of the New Deal, where their appointments encroached less on the traditional preserves of men. Women worked on the consumers' advisory board of the NRA, helped to administer the relief program, and won appointments to the Social Security Board. Florence Jaffrey Harriman and Ruth Bryan Owen became the first women diplomats and Ohio judge Florence Allen the first woman on the Federal Court of Appeals. Many of them were friends, often with professional ties, and they formed a network of activists who informally promoted women's interests and liberal reform.

The New Deal achieved a mixed record in helping women. Three-fourths of the NRA codes included provisions for equal pay to women workers. The remaining quarter, covering industries like cloakmaking, electronics, and commercial laundries, which employed a high percentage of women, set lower minimum wages for them. The Works Progress Administration hired nearly half a million women in 1936, roughly 15 percent of all WPA workers. At the time, almost a quarter of the work force was composed of women. Men on WPA projects were paid $5 a day, women only $3. Social Security aided women with dependent children but excluded domestic servants, most of them women. The Federal Emergency Relief Administration built 17 camps for women in 11 states, while the National Youth Administration and the WPA created projects to train women and put them to work. On the other hand, the Civilian Conservation Corps employed no women at all.

Women became part of the Democratic party machinery as never before. At the 1936 Democratic National Convention in Philadelphia 219 women served as delegates, and over 300 stood by as alternates. (Only 60 were delegates at the Republican convention.) Eight women made seconding speeches. Under the leadership of social worker Mary W. "Molly" Dewson, the Women's Division of the Democratic National Committee played a critical role in the election. Thousands of women mounted a "mouth-to-mouth" campaign, literally traveling from door to door to drum up support for Roosevelt and other Democrats. When the ballots were finally tallied, women formed an important part of the new Roosevelt coalition.

The Rise of Organized Labor

The New Deal boosted the fortunes of organized labor by creating a hospitable environment for unionization. At the outset of the Depression under 3 million of the 48 million workers in America belonged to labor organizations. The nation's premier union, the American Federation of Labor (AFL), paid little attention to industrial workers. Historically bound to skilled labor, notoriously uncomfortable with the ethnics and African-Americans who worked in mass-production factories, and downright hostile to women, the AFL ignored major industries like rubber, automobiles, and steel. Under the protection of Section 7a of the National Recovery Administration the AFL increased its membership, but its cautious president, William Green, sought cooperation with management.

The thundering, barrel-chested John L. Lewis, head of the United Mine Workers (UMW) since 1919, led the drive to unionize the mass of unskilled laborers. Tough, charismatic, egotistical, and ambitious, Lewis voted for Hoover in 1932, then promptly called on Roosevelt at the White House in 1933. When the new president offered nothing but consolation for the sagging UMW, Lewis returned to the coal fields with a message he had somehow divined: "The President wants you to join a union." Within a year the UMW had 400,000 members. Raising his sights, Lewis called for the creation of a Steel Workers' Organizing Committee (SWOC) and for the admission of the United Auto Workers into the AFL. AFL leaders accepted the proposals, only to ignore them.

At the annual AFL convention in Atlantic City in 1935, Lewis demanded a commitment to the "industrial organization of mass production workers." The delegates, mostly from craft unions, voted down the proposal. "I was seduced," Lewis growled, "I am enraged, and I am ready to rend my seducers limb from limb." Near the end of the convention he made good on his threat. As he passed "Big Bill" Hutcheson of the carpenters union, angry words passed between the two. Lewis spun and with a single punch sent Hutcheson sprawling in a bloody heap. The blow signaled the determination of industrial unions to break the AFL's domination of organized labor. Three weeks later, on November 10, 1935, Lewis and the heads of seven other AFL unions announced the formation of the Committee for Industrial Organization (CIO). Charging the CIO with "dual organization" and "fomenting insurrection," the AFL suspended the rogue unions in 1936. The CIO, later rechristened the Congress of Industrial Organizations, turned to the unskilled.

CIO representatives concentrated on the mighty steel industry, which had clung tenaciously to the "open" or nonunion shop since the great strike of 1919. In other industries, the rank and file did not wait. Emboldened by the recent passage of the Wagner Act, a group of rubber workers at three companies in Akron, Ohio, spontaneously sat down on the job in early 1936. The new strategy worked at two of the companies. Since the strikers occupied the plants, managers could not replace them with strikebreakers. Nor could the rubber companies call in the military or police without the possibility of destroying their own property. The leaders of the United Rubber Workers Union opposed the "sit-downs," but when the Goodyear Tire & Rubber Company laid off 70 workers, 1400 workers struck on their own. A picket line, running some 11 miles around the facility, sprang up outside. Eventually Goodyear settled by recognizing the union and accepting its demands on wages and hours.

The biggest strikes erupted in the automobile industry. Automobile production had developed the assembly line to a fine art. "Where you used to be a man," complained one Chevrolet worker, "now you are less than their cheapest tool." Periodic speed-ups left laborers without a moment's rest. "When I get home I'm so tired I can't even sleep with my wife," said one of them. The new United Auto Workers (UAW) wanted to move cautiously, so workers took things into their own hands. The General Motors Company had exploited employees for years. Its 20 top executives earned $200,000 a year; its line workers barely $1000. A series of spontaneous strikes at General Motors plants in Atlanta, Kansas City, and Cleveland spread to Fisher Body No. 2 in Flint, Michigan, late in December 1936. Singing the unionists' anthem, "Solidarity Forever," workers took over the plant while wives, friends, and fellow union members handed food and clothing through the windows. When local police tried to break up supply lines, they were driven off in a hail of nuts, bolts, coffee mugs, and bottles.

In the wake of this "Battle of Running Bulls" (a reference to the retreating police), Governor Frank Murphy called out the National Guard, this time not to arrest but to protect strikers. Faced with the prospect of class warfare and little support from authorities, General Motors surrendered in February 1937. Less than a month later U.S. Steel capitulated without a strike, granting recognition to SWOC, a wage boost, and a 40-hour work week. By the end of the year every automobile manufacturer except Henry Ford had negotiated with the UAW. Bloody violence accompanied some drives, most notably in the effort to unionize the Republic Steel Company in Chicago. Police killed 10 strikers there on Memorial Day, 1937. Yet sooner or later much of industrial America was unionized. Rubber, electronics, and heavy metals all succumbed. In 1941, under the pressure of an impending war, even Henry Ford gave in.

Middle-class Americans, generally sympathetic to the union drives of the thirties, were horrified by sit-down strikes. The lack of respect for private property smacked of radicalism. In 1939 the Supreme Court outlawed the tactic. A momentous transfer of power had nonetheless taken place, and with relatively little bloodshed. By 1940 nearly one worker in three belonged to a union. The unskilled developed a powerful voice in the CIO (though the craft unions of the AFL still outnumbered them by more than a million). Women's membership in unions tripled between 1930 and 1940, and blacks made impressive gains. Millions of workers in the domestic and service trades, not to mention millions more on the farm, remained unorganized, but independent unions were at last a permanent feature of industrial America.

Through it all government played an important but secondary role. Roosevelt stood aside, favoring neither labor nor management. "A plague o' both your houses," he declared when the CIO tried to unionize the steel industry. The Wagner Act afforded laborers nothing more than the opportunity to organize and protection if they chose to. The workers themselves, galvanized by leaders like John L. Lewis, Walter Reuther of the United Auto Workers, and Philip Murray of the Steel Workers' Organizing Committee, won their own victories.

"Art for the Millions"

Under the influence of the New Deal the fine arts—from writing to painting, music, theater, and the new "art" form of photography—became a government project for the first time. Like everyone else, artists needed help. It made no sense, believed Harry Hopkins, to give a concert pianist or a Shakespearean actor a job digging ditches. Here was an opportunity to blend decency, culture, and democracy. Paid by the federal government, trained professionals would get financial assistance and preserve their talents. At the same time the government could bring art to the masses by employing skilled artists on public programs. Americans would taste high culture, some for the first time. "Art for the millions," as one administrator called it, was the dream of the New Deal.

"Federal One" was the bureaucratic umbrella of the Works Progress Administration that covered the arts programs. The Federal Writers Project (FWP) was perhaps the least controversial program. Under the direction of journalist Henry Alsberg, the FWP produced about a thousand publications. Its 81 state, territorial, and city guides were so popular that commercial publishers happily printed them. Reflecting the renewed interest in Americana, the FWP collected folklore, studied ethnic groups, and recorded the reminiscences of 200 former slaves.

The FWP employed established writers like Conrad Aiken, new ones including John Cheever, Jack Conroy, and Saul Bellow (later to win the Nobel Prize for literature), and black writers Richard Wright, Arna Bontemps, Zora Neale Hurston, Ralph Ellison, and others. "Actually to be paid for writing," Ellison exulted, "why that was a wonderful thing!" Little time was reserved for creative writing on the job, but work weeks averaged only about 30 hours. Richard Wright completed his acclaimed *Native Son*, a stinging novel of racial discrimination, in his spare time.

Nicolai Sokoloff, conductor of the Cleveland Symphony Orchestra, headed the Federal Music Project (FMP). At its peak it employed some 15,000 out-of-work musicians. For a token charge, Americans could hear the music of Bach and Beethoven. Touring orchestras brought FMP-commissioned compositions like those of Aaron Copland to people across the country, and professional musicians gave lessons for free. Musicologist Charles Seeger collected American folk songs, while the Composers Forum Laboratory gave creative talents like William Schuman their first serious hearings.

Holger Cahill, an authority on folk art, ran the Federal Art Project (FAP).

Watercolorists and draftsmen painstakingly prepared the *Index of American Design*, which offered elaborate illustrations of American material culture—andirons, skillets, figureheads from ships, even cigar-store Indians. At night hundreds of artists taught sculpture, painting, clay modeling, and carving in country churches, settlement houses, and schools. Jackson Pollock, Willem de Kooning, Anton Refregier—all destined to become important artists—made it through the Depression by painting for the government.

The most notable contribution of the FAP came in the form of murals. Under the influence of Mexican muralists Diego Rivera and José Clemente Orozco, American artists covered the walls of post offices and airports with huge murals glorifying American life and work. Frank treatments of class conflict often alienated conservatives and opened the FAP to charges of "communist infiltration" at the end of the decade. By then Americans (most of whom Roosevelt believed never had seen a "fine picture") could walk into San Francisco's Coit Tower and gaze at Victor Arnautoff's magnificent *City Life*. When the FAP held an exhibition at the New York World's Fair in 1940, over 2 million people filed through. Despite variations in quality Roosevelt was pleased. "Some of it good," he said, "some of it not so good, but all of it native, human, eager, and alive."

The Federal Theater Project (FTP) aroused the most controversy and probably reached the greatest number of people. As head of the FTP, Hallie Flanagan made government-supported theater vital, daring, and relevant. *Living Newspapers* dramatized headlines of the day; under the direction of Orson Welles and John Houseman an all-black company (one of 16 "Negro Units") set Shakespeare's *Macbeth* in Haiti, complete with voodoo priestesses and a corps of African drummers. Touring companies took classics to small towns, and on summer nights city children watched *Punch and Judy* and *Jack and the Beanstalk* from park benches. All told some 30 million people saw Federal Theater productions in its four-year history. Most of them had never seen stage actors before.

Some productions raised the eyebrows of congressional conservatives. *The Revolt of the Beavers*, a thinly veiled attack on capitalism, depicted a revolution of exploited, working-class beavers. *Triple-A Plowed Under*, a success with critics and ticket-buyers alike, exhorted farmers and consumers to band together against greedy middlemen. In 1938 and 1939 the House Committee to Investigate Un-American Activities under Martin Dies of Texas examined the FTP as "a branch of the Communistic organization." When Hallie Flanagan quoted sixteenth-century playwright Christopher Marlowe during her testimony, committee members asked whether he was a Communist. The WPA budget of 1939 cut the FTP, bringing government-sponsored theater to a quick end.

The documentary impulse to record life permeated the arts in the 1930s. Novels such as Erskine Caldwell's *Tobacco Road*, feature films like John Ford's *The Grapes of Wrath* and *How Green Was My Valley*, and government-sponsored documentaries by Pare Lorentz, *The River* and *The Plow That Broke the Plains*, stirred the social conscience of the country. Word and image were masterfully wed in the collaborative work of writer James Agee and photographer Walker Evans. *Let Us Now Praise Famous Men*, the chronicle of three tenant farm families, sold only 600 copies when it was published in 1941 but remains an unforgettable portrait of the 1930s.

New Dealers had more practical motives for promoting documentary realism. They wanted to undercut criticism of New Deal relief measures. In 1937 Rexford Tugwell established an Information Division in his Resettlement Administration.

Daily Lives

PUBLIC SPACE / PRIVATE SPACE
Post Office Murals

"How can a finished citizen be made in an artless town?" asked the postmaster of Pleasant Hill, Missouri, in 1939. Such weighty matters as citizenship and art might have seemed beyond an ordinary postmaster, but he did not think so—and neither did the New Dealers in Washington. They had just made his post office the recipient of a new painting entitled *Back Home: April 1865*, and in the eyes of the postmaster, they had performed a commendable service. His town, like so many others scattered across America, had been "wholly without objects of art." Now it had one that showed common people at an epic moment in history, the end of the Civil War. Townsfolk saw it every day, and every day it made them a bit more aware of their history, more comfortable with art, and more appreciative of the heritage of democracy.

The Fine Arts Section (FAS) of the Treasury Department, which sponsored the artwork for Pleasant Hill, was but one of the programs for artists underwritten by the New Deal. The largest and most famous, the Works Progress Administration's Federal Art Project (1935–1943), produced 18,000 easel paintings, 17,000 sculptures, and 2500 murals. It employed thousands of needy artists, mostly in the large cities where they lived, and placed their work in state and municipal institutions.

The Treasury Department had a similar mission but a different focus. Beginning in 1934, it commissioned artwork for federal buildings, over which it enjoyed jurisdiction. During its nine-year existence, the FAS hired 850 artists (one-sixth of whom were women) and commissioned nearly 1400 works. Unlike relief agencies, which handed out work on the basis of financial need, FAS artists competed for contracts on particular jobs. Most were for the 1100 new post offices built during the New Deal.

Post offices were an ideal medium for democratizing art. Often at the center of town, the rectangular brick buildings bespoke solidity, permanence, and service. They linked the community with a wider world and served as the junction of local and national interests. They were tangible symbols of the federal government, perhaps the only contact many citizens had with Washington. Yet rather than emphasizing government might with portraits of national heroes or friezes of eagles and flags, post office murals depicted the daily routines of common citizens, usually from the community or the region. Local committees helped to select both the artists and the subjects, and whenever possible local artists did the work. Here, as elsewhere in the New Deal, regard for community participation was meant to temper the sense that people were surrendering control to an intrusive central government.

From the artists' point of view the post office was hardly an ideal setting. Muralists required space and light, but most post office buildings were small and dark. The available walls, often no more than 6 by 12 feet, were usually above the postmaster's door at the end of a long, cramped lobby with hanging light fixtures and vestibules that obstructed vision. The giant murals of Diego Rivera, whose work had glorified the Mexican Revolution in the 1920s, were inspirational but also controversial. Post office muralists painted on a smaller scale and avoided controversy. They drew fewer figures and arranged them in the foreground to draw the atten-

Daily Lives

Back Home: April 1865, presented to the Pleasant Hill, Missouri, post office in 1939, was commissioned by the Fine Arts Section of the Treasury Department as part of its program to democratize American art by adorning public buildings with it.

tion of viewers. Sometimes they used geometric designs that carried the eye across the disruptive door or vertical lines that broke the painting into three parts.

In a decade of fear and insecurity, the murals stressed the continuity of past and present, suggesting old virtues that had made the country great would help it to overcome the current crisis. Grand themes were distilled to simple essences and timeless symbols embodied in plain experiences: a family enjoying a Sunday picnic; friends picking fruit; skaters gliding across a frozen pond; workers stringing electric wire; children waiting for the postman. Family, work, community—the enduring qualities of American life, at once ordinary and ideal, local and national—bound the country together in good times and bad.

More often than not, regionalism influenced subject matter: colonial and urban scenes in New England and the Mid-Atlantic states; agriculture and country life in the South; the frontier and Indian and Spanish culture in the West.

Rarely were artists permitted to deal with inflammatory subjects like war, radicalism, or poverty. And when locals did not like the results, they made their displeasure known. In Watonga, Oklahoma, Cheyennes gathered at the post office to protest as unfair and inaccurate a mural depicting Indians. Asked by a reporter if he were going to scalp the artist, Chief Red Bird replied that was "bow-and-arrow, horse-and-buggy-day business." The Cheyenne were "streamlined," he said. "We picket post office."

The quality of the murals varied greatly, but in the end they achieved their aim of reaching common folks by combining the ordinary and the aesthetic. Almost always they communicated a harmonious vision of America, inspiring viewers with faith in progress and faith in themselves. "How important it is," said Supreme Court Justice Harlan Stone, after seeing a mural in Big Spring, Texas, "that the humble people of this country should be impressed with the fact that the artist finds beauty and dignity in their life."

He placed Roy Stryker, his former Columbia University teaching assistant, in charge of its Historical Section. Stryker hired a cadre of talented photographers, not so much to furnish them with relief but to have an unvarnished record of the Great Depression to blunt anti–New Deal journalists and politicians. Later transferred to the Farm Securities Administration, the group included Russell Lee, Dorothea Lange, Ben Shahn, Walker Evans, and Marion Post Wolcott. Raw and haunting, their photographs turned history into art.

THE END OF THE NEW DEAL (1937–1940)

Signs of recovery were visible everywhere by the end of 1936. Apple vendors vanished from street corners, breadlines from cities. In Detroit more automobiles came rolling off assembly lines than at any time since 1929. Utility companies were billing more kilowatt-hours of electricity than ever. Industrial output had doubled since 1932. From the winter of 1932 to the fall of 1936 farm income had almost quadrupled.

Roosevelt and the New Deal had made a difference. The Farm Credit Administration prevented an average of 300 farm foreclosures a day. A loan from the Federal Housing Authority helped Pueblo chief Albert Looking Elk Martinez replace his adobe hearth with a gas stove and put linoleum over his dirt floor. "Your work saved our humble little home from the Deed Trust sharks," wrote a California real estate broker. "Life is 1000% better since you took Charge of our United States."

Still, full recovery remained elusive. National income was only half again as large as it had been in 1933. "I see one-third of a nation ill-housed, ill-clad, ill-nourished," Roosevelt told the crowd at his second inauguration on January 20, 1937 (the first January inauguration under new federal legislation). One dark cloud drifted toward the White House from the Supreme Court, whose recent rulings threatened to nullify the New Deal. Sensing the full depth of his power, with unprecedented popularity and bulging majorities in Congress, Roosevelt vowed to reform the federal judiciary. It was the biggest mistake of his presidential career. The move stunned the nation and marked the beginning of the end of the New Deal.

"Packing" the Courts

In its first 76 years the Supreme Court had invalidated only two acts of Congress; between 1920 and 1933 it struck down portions of 22 laws. This new judicial activism, spearheaded by a conservative majority, rested on a narrow view of the constitutional powers of Congress and the president. As the New Deal broadened those powers it came under judicial attack.

In 1935 the Court wiped out the NRA on the grounds that manufacturing was not interstate commerce and thus lay beyond federal regulation. In 1936 it canceled the AAA, reducing federal authority under the taxing power and the general welfare clause of the Constitution. In *Moorehead v. Tipaldo* (1936) the Court ruled that a New York minimum-wage law was invalid because it interfered with the right of workers to negotiate a contract. A frustrated Roosevelt complained that the Court had thereby created a "'no-man's land,' where no government—

Roosevelt's plan to "pack" the courts came under furious attack as a naked power grab and vindictive assault on the Supreme Court itself. Here cartoonist John Berryman lampoons the president as Roosevelt asks Interior Secretary and Public Works Administrator Harold Ickes if he would construct a new, bigger Supreme Court building flying FDR's flag.

State or Federal" could act. It seemed that no law would be safe, not the Wagner Act, not wages and hours legislation, not even Social Security.

Roosevelt knew he was the first president since James Monroe to serve four years without making a Supreme Court appointment. He had little more luck with federal judgeships, where Republicans outnumbered Democrats by more than two to one in 1933. By adding new judges to the federal benches Roosevelt planned to redress the balance. Masking his true intentions, he announced early in February 1937 that the federal courts were overburdened. Sitting judges were often too "aged or infirm" to keep up. In the interests of efficiency Roosevelt proposed to "vitalize" the judiciary with new members. When a 70-year-old judge who had served at least 10 years failed to retire, the president would add another. He wanted to appoint as many as six new justices to the Supreme Court and 44 new judges to the lower federal courts.

Roosevelt took such electrifying action because he regarded courts as political, not sacred, institutions. He had ample precedent for altering even the Supreme Court. Only in 1869 did Congress set its size at 9 (there had been as few as 5 and as many as 10 justices). Most Americans, however, still clung to such cherished symbols of stability. Few accepted Roosevelt's efficiency argument, and no one on Capitol Hill (which abounded with 70-year-olds) believed that seven decades of life necessarily made one incompetent. Worse still, Roosevelt unveiled the proposal without warning. Conservative–liberal antagonisms within Congress, even within his own party, fed the fight. "Boys," said the angry Democratic chairman of the House Judiciary Committee, "here's where I cash in my chips."

Suddenly, as if by judicial magic, the Court began reversing itself. By a vote of five to four in *N.L.R.B. v. Jones and Laughlin Steel Corporation*, the justices upheld the Wagner Act in April 1937. A month later they sustained the Social Security Act as a legitimate exercise of the commerce power. And when Justice Willis Van Devanter, a staunch conservative born before the Civil War, retired in 1937, Roosevelt at last could make a Supreme Court appointment. He nonetheless pressed ahead with court reform. When Democrat after Democrat abandoned him, Roosevelt finally accepted a substitute measure that ignored his proposal to appoint new judges. He later claimed to have won the war over the Court (eventually he named five justices), but victory came at a high price. The momentum of

1003

the 1936 election was squandered; the unity of the Democratic party was de-stroyed; and opponents learned that Roosevelt could be beaten. A conservative coalition of Republicans and rural Democrats had found the first of several com-mon causes.

More Troubles

As early as 1936 Secretary of the Treasury Henry Morgenthau, Roosevelt's closest friend in the cabinet, began to plead for fiscal restraint. The economic omens were good, he argued, so the administration should reduce spending, balance the bud-get, and let business lead the way to full recovery. "The patient might scream a bit when he was taken off narcotics," Morgenthau reasoned, but the time had come "to strip off the bandages, throw away the crutches," and allow the economy to "stand on its own feet."

In the case of Roosevelt, Morgenthau was preaching to the converted. The president had never been comfortable with the alarming deficits prescribed by theorists like John Maynard Keynes. The British economist had developed a star-tling new theory that called on government to spend its way out of depression. When good times returned, government could pay off its debts through taxes. Such "countercyclical" activity (spending in bad times, taxing in good) should take place only in the absence of private investment, Keynes cautioned. Many Ameri-cans, including Federal Reserve Board chairman Marriner Eccles, had come inde-pendently to similar conclusions, but not Roosevelt. Even after meeting with Keynes in 1934, the president dismissed his "rigmarole of figures," later confess-ing that he had not understood a word of the economist's most important work, *The General Theory of Employment, Interest, and Money.*

As stock prices crept up and unemployment dipped, Roosevelt ordered cuts in federal spending. Early in 1937 he slashed WPA relief rolls by half and virtually halted PWA operations; the Federal Reserve Board tightened credit; the govern-ment began to collect $2 billion in new social security taxes. In the fall of 1937 the economy collapsed. Industrial activity plummeted, eliminating all the gains made since 1935. In three months the Dow Jones stock averages fell by 75 points. At the end of the year unemployment stood at 10.5 million. The president, sounding strangely like Hoover, told his cabinet to "sit tight and keep quiet," but the "Roo-sevelt recession" only deepened. Finally the spenders in this administration con-vinced him to propose a $3.75 billion omnibus measure in April 1938. Facing an election, Congress happily restored WPA cuts, quadrupled farm subsidies, and embarked on a new shipbuilding program. The economy revived but never recov-ered. Keynesian economics was vindicated, though for years after not generally accepted.

With Roosevelt vulnerable, the conservative coalition in Congress began to block the New Deal. Conservatives gutted a public housing law, wrote regional differentials into the minimum wage provision of the Fair Labor Standards Act (which also established maximum hours), and limited a presidential bill to reorga-nize the executive branch. Roosevelt's principal success came in a renewed attack on business. The Anti-Trust Division of the Justice Department under Thurman Arnold launched a campaign against big business, while Congress created the Temporary National Economic Committee to investigate corporate abuses. These were small consolations. The president, wrote Harold Ickes in August, "is punch drunk from the punishment that he has suffered recently."

Roosevelt struck back in the off-year elections of 1938. Across the West and

South he tried to purge Democrats who had deserted him, but every one of the five senators he targeted for defeat won reelection. Only in his home state of New York did he succeed, unseating Representative John J. O'Connor, the unfriendly chairman of the House Rules Committee. Republicans gained 13 governorships, 8 Senate seats, and 81 House seats. Democrats still held majorities in both houses, but the impetus was gone. For all intents and purposes the New Deal had passed into history.

The Legacy of the New Deal

As an active reform movement, the New Deal lasted only five years, from 1933 to 1938. It failed in its primary mission to end the Depression. Although the federal budget grew from $3.2 billion in 1932 to $9 billion in 1939, New Dealers never spent enough to make up for lost private investment. It was World War II that proved to be the agent of recovery. By 1945, after four years of war, federal expenditures stood at an astounding $100 billion, and only in 1943 did unemployment finally dip below its 1929 level.

Furthermore, New Dealers never achieved any fundamental change in the distribution of wealth and income. They never intended to, but in the end the wealthy received such a large proportion of all income that not enough mass purchasing power existed to sustain consumption and employment. Without consumption and employment, there was little incentive for businesses to mount further investment. The equation was simple, said Brains Truster Adolf Berle. "Unless the national income was pretty widely diffused there were not enough customers to keep the plants going."

Though it was a response to an immediate crisis, the New Deal fell within the progressive tradition. Like progressivism it sought to conserve capitalism by ending its abuses, regulating its excesses, and softening its impact. In doing so the New Deal relied, again like progressivism, on government activism, moderate reform, expertise, and new executive agencies. Despite its ultimate failure to bring about recovery, it left a lasting legacy. It placed responsibility for prosperity squarely with government, as a shaper and regulator of the economy. No administration would ever be able to escape this responsibility. In its securities and banking regulations, unemployment compensation, and maximum hours and minimum wage requirements the New Deal created stabilizers to forestall another breakdown. Strengthening the Federal Reserve system and enhancing control over credit made Washington, not Wall Street, the financial center of the nation.

Roosevelt modernized the presidency. He turned the White House into the heart of government, setting the public agenda, spreading new ideas, initiating legislation, and assuming responsibility for the whole nation. It became the place where decisions were made. A clerk calculated that Roosevelt made 35 decisions for every decision made by Calvin Coolidge. The power of Congress and of local and state governments diminished as a result, while the federal bureaucracy grew. In 1932 there were 605,000 federal employees; by 1939 there were nearly a million. Though later critics would charge the New Deal with creating an unwieldy, expensive, and dangerous bureaucracy, conversion to a war economy would have been perilously slowed without it. It is also important to remember that the size of government exploded during World War II, not the New Deal. By 1945 the number of federal employees had soared to 3.5 million.

The manifest failures of the private economy and private charity and of local and state governments promoted the expansion of federal authority. When mayors

What the New Deal Did . . .

	RELIEF	RECOVERY	REFORM
FOR THE FARMER:	Rural Electrification Administration (1936) Farm Security Administration (1937)	Agriculture Adjustment Act (1933)	
FOR THE WORKER:		National Industrial Recovery Act (1933)	National Labor Relations Act (1935) Fair Labor Standards Act (1938)
FOR THE MIDDLE CLASS:	Home Owners' Loan Act (1934)		Revenue ("Wealth Tax") Act (1935) Public Utilities Holding Company Act (1935)
FOR THE NEEDY:	Federal Emergency Relief Act (1933) Civilian Conservation Corps (1933) Civil Works Administration (1933) National Public Housing Act (1937) Emergency Relief Appropriation Act (1935)		
FOR PROTECTION AGAINST FUTURE DEPRESSIONS:			Federal Deposit Insurance Corporation (1933) Securities Exchange Act (1934) Social Security Act (1935)

and governors could not feed the people of their cities and states, Americans looked to Washington as the court of last resort. People came to feel that the federal government was concerned with their welfare. Roosevelt embodied the state as protector. "My mother looks upon the President as someone so immediately concerned with her problems and difficulties," wrote an insurance man, "that she would not be greatly surprised were he to come to her house some evening and stay to dinner." Home loans, farm subsidies, bank deposit insurance, relief payments and jobs, pension programs, unemployment insurance, aid to mothers with dependent children, guarantees of minimum wages and maximum hours—all touched the lives of ordinary Americans and made them more secure.

Never enough to furnish complete security, these programs were never intended to. The welfare state had limits. Most of its relief measures were designed to last no longer than the crisis itself. Millions of sharecroppers, migrants, domestic servants, and minorities fell through even its more nearly permanent safety nets. The commitment of the New Deal to furnishing minimum standards of subsistence for every American, not its failure to do so, won Roosevelt their support. He was, after all, almost the first to try.

At a time when dictators and militarists had taken hold in Germany, Italy, Japan, and Russia, the New Deal strengthened democracy in America. Roosevelt's "broker state" invigorated interest groups that had previously been unrepresented. It broadened access to government for unions, farm organizations, ethnic minorities, and some women. Under the AAA and the Wagner Act, for example, staple farmers and industrial workers actually voted to determine which crops to cut and whether to join a union. Like the welfare state, Roosevelt's broker state had its limits. The administration never developed ways to protect people who belonged to no organizations. The unorganized, like slum dwellers and most blacks, often found themselves ignored.

Under Roosevelt's leadership the Democratic party, divided and crippled for decades, became a mighty force in American politics. In a quiet but profound revolution, African-Americans were brought rapidly into the party's fold and its constituencies were further widened to include labor and farmers. Political attention shifted from the cultural divisions of the 1920s to bread-and-butter issues. In 1932 people had argued about Prohibition and European war debts. By 1935 they were debating Social Security, labor relations, tax reform, public housing, and the TVA. With remarkable speed, the New Deal had become part of American life.

During the 1930s the United States found a middle way between the extremes of communism and fascism. Blending public and private controls, the New Deal attempted to humanize industrial society and generate prosperity without sacrificing capitalism and democracy. Government—particularly the executive branch—took the lead. Yet New Dealers from the president down recognized that they could not do everything. "I never believed that the Federal government could solve the whole problem," Eleanor Roosevelt told the National Youth Congress in February 1939. "It bought us time to think. . . . Is it going to be worth while?" Only future generations could say.

SIGNIFICANT EVENTS

1933 — Franklin Roosevelt inaugurated as president; bank "holiday"; "hundred days" legislation passed; repeal of Eighteenth Amendment (Prohibition); Townsend movement begins

1934 — Securities and Exchange Commission; American Liberty League; Indian Reorganization Act

1935 — Emergency Relief Appropriation Act; Rural Electrification Administration authorized; *Schecter Poultry Corp. v. United States* invalidates National Recovery Administration; Huey Long organizes Share Our Wealth Society; "second hundred days" legislation passed; Father Charles Coughlin creates National Union for Social Justice; Huey Long assassinated

1936 — *Butler v. U.S.* invalidates Agricultural Adjustment Administration; Soil Conservation and Domestic Allotment Act; Congress of Industrial Organizations formed; Roosevelt reelected; United Auto Workers union begins sit-down strikes; John Maynard Keynes' *The General Theory of Employment, Interest, and Money* published

1937 — Roosevelt announces court "packing" plan; Roosevelt recession

1938 — Fair Labor Standards Act sets minimum wages/maximum hours; Congress establishes Temporary National Economic Committee

1939 — Marian Anderson gives a concert at the Lincoln Memorial; Executive Reorganization Act

28

America's Rise to Globalism

J ohn Garcia, a native Hawaiian, worked as a pipe-fitter's apprentice at the Pearl Harbor Navy Yard in Hawaii. On Sunday, December 7, 1941, he was enjoying a lazy day off. By the time his grandmother came rushing in to wake him at eight that morning, it was already too late. "The Japanese were bombing Pearl Harbor," he recalled her yelling to him. John listened in disbelief. "I said, 'They're just practicing.'" "No," his grandmother replied. It was real. He catapulted his huge frame from bed, ran to the front porch, and caught sight of the antiaircraft fire in the sky. "Oh boy" were his only words.

Hopping on his motorcycle, he sped the four miles to the harbor in 10 minutes. "It was a mess," he remembered. The U.S.S. *Shaw* was in flames. The battleship *Pennsylvania*, a bomb nesting one deck above the powder and ammunition, was about to blow. When ordered to put out its fires, he refused. "There ain't no way I'm gonna go down there," he told the navy officer. Instead, he spent the rest of the day pulling bodies from the water. There were so many he lost count. He couldn't tell "how many were alive and how many were dead."

Surveying the wreckage the following morning, he noted that the battleship *Arizona* "was a total washout." So was the *West Virginia*. The *Oklahoma* had "turned turtle, totally upside down." It took two weeks to get all the fires out. John and his fellow workers spent the next month cutting through the *West Virginia*'s superstructure, trying to save the men trapped inside. "About three hundred men we cut out of there were still alive by the eighteenth day." John's girlfriend was not. She had been killed by an errant American shell as she prepared for church on Sunday morning.

The world had been at war since 1939, but Americans had largely been spared. Two vast oceans had seemed to protect the United States—until now. The surprise attack at Pearl Harbor suddenly transformed the Pacific into an avenue of potential assault. All along the West Coast panic spread as radio reports carried the news that America was on the verge of war. Dennis Keegan, a young college student at the University of San Francisco, could not believe it, even though his younger brother Bill was training in Canada to fly with the Royal Air Force. "These places were so far away from us," Dennis said after hearing about Pearl Harbor. "It just didn't seem possible that we were at war."

1008

Images of its battleships in flames sent the United States into global war, although the losses at Pearl Harbor were more shocking than disabling. The West Virginia, *shown here, settled to the shallow bottom with guns still firing and was later repaired.*

That night Keegan drove into downtown San Francisco. Market Street was "bedlam." "The United Artists Theater had a huge marquee with those dancing lights, going on and off," he recalled. "People were throwing everything they could to put those lights out, screaming Blackout! Blackout!" The next day a false army report of 30 Japanese planes flying toward the coast triggered air-raid sirens throughout the city. Unsubstantiated rumors put Japanese aircraft carriers off the mouth of the Columbia River. Blackouts were declared as far inland as Boise, Idaho.

Los Angeles turned trigger-happy. A young policeman named Tom Bradley (who later served as mayor of the city) heard "sirens going off, aircraft guns firing." "Here we are in the middle of the night," he said, "there was no enemy in sight, but somebody thought they saw the enemy." In January 1942 the Rose Bowl was moved from Pasadena, California, to Durham, North Carolina. Early that same year submarines shelled Santa Barbara. The Japanese also floated balloons carrying incendiary devices from ships off the coast. One reached Iowa without doing any damage.

The Japanese attack on Pearl Harbor created a sense of panic along the West Coast of the United States. Hasty defenses like these sandbags stacked in front of the telephone company in San Francisco were thrown up to ward off an attack that never came.

Although the Japanese never came any closer, in a world with long-range bombers and submarines, no place seemed safe: this was global war, the first of its kind. Arrayed against the Axis powers of Germany, Italy, and Japan were the Allies—Great Britain, the Soviet Union, the United States, China, and the Free French. Their armies fought from the Arctic to the southwestern Pacific, in the great cities of Europe and Asia and the small villages of North Africa and Indochina, in malarial jungles and scorching deserts, on six continents and across four oceans. Perhaps as many as 100 million people took up arms; some 40 million to 50 million lost their lives.

Tragedy on such a scale taught the generation of Americans who fought the war that they could no longer isolate themselves from any part of the world, no matter how remote it might seem. Manchuria, Ethiopia, and Poland had once seemed far away, yet the road to war had led from those distant places to the United States. Retreat into isolation had not cured the worldwide depression or preserved the peace. Most Americans now came to believe that to avoid other such disasters once this war was ended, the United States must assume far wider responsibility for managing the world's geopolitical and economic systems.

THE UNITED STATES AND THE COLLAPSE OF THE VERSAILLES SYSTEM

The outbreak of World War II had its roots in the devastation of World War I, when almost an entire generation of young men had been killed or maimed in five years of carnage. War debts eroded economic health. The political disorganization of central Europe and Asia produced vacuums of power soon filled by the forces of fascism. The nations dissatisfied with the terms of the peace—Germany, the Soviet Union, Italy, Poland, Japan—sought to achieve unilaterally what the victors had denied them at Versailles. Faced with an unstable world economy, the United States turned away from collective action. In one of his final speeches Warren Harding declared that American participation in the League of Nations was an issue as "dead as slavery." That did not mean the United States would simply isolate itself from world affairs. Bankers and businessmen eagerly pursued markets abroad. Sometimes they worked under government auspices, sometimes independently. In general, though, little consensus existed about how the United States could work with other nations to ensure peace and prosperity.

Economic Diplomacy

The World War I victors saddled Germany with $33 billion in war costs, partly to repay their own war debts to the United States. When Germany defaulted on reparations in 1923, French forces occupied the Ruhr valley, the industrial heartland of Germany. Germany struck back by inflating its currency, a move that dramatized the crushing burden of debt. In 1923 Germans carried bushels of money to pay for food. Runaway inflation wiped out the savings of the middle class, shook confidence in the new German Weimar Republic, and soon threatened the economic structure of all Europe.

Emerging from the war as the leading creditor nation of the world, the United States, more than any nation, had some capacity to bring order to the world's economic systems. Congress instead acted first to protect American prosperity by adopting the highly restrictive Fordney–McCumber Tariff in 1922. Only then did the Harding administration respond to the growing crisis in Europe. To temper German inflation American business leaders Charles G. Dawes and Owen D. Young persuaded the victorious Europeans to adopt a plan to scale down reparations. In return the United States promised to help stabilize the German economy. Encouraged by the State Department, American bankers made large loans to Germany, which the Germans used to pay their reparations. The European victors then used the money to repay their war debts to the United States, which amounted to taking money out of one American vault and depositing it in another. In 1926 the United States also reduced European war debts. Canceling them altogether would have made more sense, but few Americans were that forgiving. As President Coolidge remarked, "They hired the money, didn't they?"

The United States sought to maintain world trade by promoting American business overseas. Multinational corporations eager to develop markets and facilities abroad made use of a new consular service that provided them with business information, while the Departments of State and Commerce pressed to keep open markets Europeans and Japanese threatened to close. In the Middle East, the United States pressured the British to allow American oil companies to participate in major oil operations in Iraq, Kuwait, and Bahrain Island. American capital constructed branch factories in Scandinavia, mined tin in Bolivia, developed rubber plantations in the Dutch East Indies. With high tariffs restricting the American market, the nations of Europe had difficulty expanding economies burdened by reparations and war debts. The Dawes Plan helped to stabilize Germany but did nothing to calm European fears that German militarism might revive.

Avoiding War

The end of World War I failed to halt an arms race among the great powers. The United States vied with Britain, France with Italy, and Japan with nearly everyone for naval supremacy. Within the United States two factions sought to end military escalation, but for different reasons. A variety of pacifists and peace activists blamed the arms race between Germany and England for having brought the world to war in 1914. They believed disarmament would secure peace forever.

Republicans in the tradition of Theodore Roosevelt had few qualms about military rivalry but worried about spiraling costs. With a small single-ocean fleet, for example, Japan could threaten British and American interests in the Pacific basin. Yet both Great Britain and the United States chose to maintain navies in two oceans.

In an effort to cut the budget and still protect China and the Philippines, Secretary of State Charles Evans Hughes invited eight nations to a naval disarmament conference in Washington, D.C., in November 1921. Barely had the delegates taken their seats when Hughes offered an electrifying proposal. Scrap 2 million tons of capital ships (battleships and battle cruisers), he said, and cancel those under construction. The plan would sink more tonnage than had been destroyed in the history of naval warfare. A "tornado of cheering" welled up, as delegates whooped, waved their hats, and embraced each other. Hughes proposed to save their treasuries from bankruptcy.

Three major treaties emerged from the Washington Naval Conference. A Five-Power Agreement froze capital ship construction for 10 years and limited maximum capital tonnage to 500,000 tons for the United States and Great Britain, 300,000 for Japan, and 167,000 each for France and Italy. It was the first disarmament treaty in modern history. Britain, the United States, France, and Japan also signed a Four-Power Agreement to respect one another's holdings in the Pacific. Finally, a Nine-Power Pact guaranteed the independence and territorial integrity of China. Political restraint would substitute for naval strength.

What seemed so bold on paper proved ineffective in practice. French resentment over low ratios tied to Italy rather than Japan led France to refuse limits on land armaments and smaller warships such as submarines, cruisers, and destroyers. Soon the arms race concentrated on these areas. The Soviet Union and Germany had been completely excluded. In 1922 the two outcast nations met at Rapallo, Italy, where they agreed on a secret plan for German remilitarization, in violation of the Treaty of Versailles.

Peace advocates continued to seek some way to prevent war. At the same time the French sought some means to prevent any revival of German military strength. French Foreign Minister Aristide Briand in 1928 proposed a bilateral Franco-American treaty outlawing war. Under pressure from both pacifists and isolationists at home, American Secretary of State Frank Kellogg transformed Briand's proposal into an international treaty against war. Every major nation except the Soviet Union joined the Kellogg–Briand Pact of 1928. "Peace is proclaimed," said Kellogg as he signed the document with a foot-long pen made of gold. In fact most people recognized the pact as a harmless gesture, at best a sign of hope. Whatever hope it did represent proved forlorn.

Neither the Kellogg–Briand Pact nor the Washington Conference treaties directly addressed the upheavals in China. For years rival factions had warred ruthlessly among themselves, agreeing only that foreign powers should leave. In 1927 the Nationalists, led by Chiang Kai-shek, consolidated power by massacring thousands of their Communist party allies. Civil war flared intermittently for the next 20 years. Meanwhile Japanese nationalists, eager to secure raw materials and markets for their resource-poor island nation, moved to control the Shantung peninsula and Manchuria, two regions they believed vital to Japan's future as a world power. In 1931 the Japanese Military Command in Manchuria used an explosion on the rail lines near Mukden as a pretext to justify military occupation of the whole province. A year later the Japanese converted Manchuria into a puppet state and named it Manchukuo.

The Western powers faced a quandary. Japanese moderates wanted to restrain their military adventurists in China, but the military factions in Japan would probably be strengthened if the United States and Europe imposed sanctions. President Herbert Hoover had cautiously supported investigation by the League of Nations; then, when the Japanese took over Manchuria in 1932, he instructed Secretary of State Henry Stimson to announce that the United States refused to recognize any violation of open-door principles, infringement of American rights, dismembering of China, or breaches of the Kellogg–Briand Pact. Even though Stimson had wanted to do more, this policy of nonrecognition became known as the Stimson Doctrine. The principle, no matter how sound, failed to restrain Japan. Within a month Japanese cruisers were shelling Shanghai, a port city in China. When the League of Nations condemned Japan in 1933, the Japanese simply withdrew from the League. The seeds of war in Asia had been sown.

Becoming a Good Neighbor

The history of American restraint in Europe and Asia had no counterpart in Latin America. By 1924 the United States was running the financial affairs of 10 nations south of the border. Harding had landed troops in Honduras, and in 1927 the Coolidge administration used marines in Nicaragua to keep Mexican-supported rebels from gaining power. When rebel leader César Augusto Sandino (who would later inspire the "Sandinista" rebels of the 1970s) refused to participate in American-supervised elections, Coolidge ordered the marines to stay.

By the late 1920s interventionism under the Roosevelt Corollary (page 865) had become both an embarrassment and a potential liability. No European state was likely to violate the Monroe Doctrine. A few Latin American states, moreover, had grown strong enough to resist direct interference by the United States in defense of North American interests. Even Coolidge relented and in 1927, rather than confront Mexico over the confiscation of American-owned properties, he sent Ambassador Dwight Morrow to ease tensions. The Depression gave the United States added incentive to improve hemispheric relations. In 1933, when critics compared the American position in Nicaragua to Japan's in Manchuria, Secretary Stimson ordered the marines to withdraw. In those gestures and President Hoover's efforts to cultivate goodwill south of the border lay the roots of a "Good Neighbor" policy.

Under Franklin Roosevelt being a good neighbor meant correcting the political (but not the economic) inequities between the United States and Latin America. At the seventh Pan-American Conference in 1933, his administration accepted a resolution denying any country "the right to intervene in the internal or external affairs of another." Roosevelt completed the withdrawal of marines from Nicaragua and Haiti. In 1934 he negotiated a treaty with Cuba that renounced the American right to intervene under the Platt Amendment (page 864). Henceforth the United States would replace direct military influence with indirect economic influence. Secretary of State Cordell Hull embarked on a crusade to lower tariffs under the new Trade Agreements Act (1934), which led to agreements with six Latin American (and seven European) nations. In 1936 Roosevelt crowned the Good Neighbor policy by opening the Pan-American Conference in Buenos Aires with a speech declaring that outside aggressors "will find a Hemisphere wholly prepared to consult together for our mutual safety and our mutual good."

The greatest test of the Good Neighbor policy came in 1937 and 1938, when

Bolivia and Mexico expropriated the properties of American oil companies. Roosevelt's desire to protect American interests was compromised by his fear that intervention would drive Mexico into arrangements with Japan, Germany, or Italy. When an arbitration committee awarded the oil companies $24 million rather than the $450 million they demanded, Roosevelt accepted the decision.

With the threat of war approaching in Europe, the Roosevelt administration found a new Latin willingness to cooperate over hemispheric protection. At the Havana Conference in 1940 all the ministers agreed to treat an attack on one nation as an attack on all. By the end of the year Roosevelt had worked out defense agreements with every Latin American country but one. The United States could now face war with the American hemisphere largely secured.

THE DIPLOMACY OF ISOLATIONISM

During the 1920s Benito Mussolini had capitalized on appeals to Italian nationalism and fears of communism to assume power in Italy. Having destroyed all political opposition, he declared himself the leader, *Il Duce*, and adopted a program of national solidarity and state management of the economy while spinning dreams of a new Roman empire. Mussolini embodied the rising force of fascism. Then on March 5, 1933, one day after the inauguration of Franklin Roosevelt, the German Reichstag (Parliament) gave Adolf Hitler control of Germany. Magnetic and mystical, Hitler headed the National Socialist, or "Nazi," party. Riding a wave of anti-communism and anti-Semitism, the Nazis promised to unite all Germans in a Greater Third Reich that would last a thousand years. Just over a week earlier, Yosuke Matsuoka had led the Japanese withdrawal from the League of Nations. Under the lead of militarists, Japan began to carve out its own Greater East Asia Co-Prosperity Sphere. By the end of the decade the rise of fascism and militarism in Europe and Asia brought the world to war.

Neutrality and Appeasement

"It's a terrible thing," Franklin Roosevelt said in the mid-1930s, "to look over your shoulder when you are trying to lead—and to find no one there." As much as he wanted the United States to play a leading role in bringing order to world affairs, Roosevelt often found the nation reluctant to follow. Though the Depression was international in scope, most politicians clamored for national solutions. Only when a potential economic interest was involved could Roosevelt command wide support for foreign initiatives. For example, businessmen welcomed his decision in 1933 to recognize the communist regime in Russia. Not only did Roosevelt hope recognition would increase Russian–American trade, but he also thought the Soviet Union would help contain Japanese expansion in Asia and fascism in Europe.

For every step Roosevelt took toward internationalism abroad, the Great Depression forced him home again. In 1933 he sent a delegation under Secretary of State Cordell Hull to participate in the London Economic Conference. Europeans were seeking to reduce war debts, lower American tariff barriers, and stabilize the value of currency. Roosevelt refused to allow Hull even to discuss war debts or tariff reduction. After dramatically dispatching White House adviser Raymond Moley with a message for the Conference, he rejected a proposal on currency stabilization. With the United States mired in the Depression he wanted no foreign entanglements to inhibit his attempts to revive the economy.

Roosevelt's rejection of an international policy was politically shrewd. Programs to combat the Depression at home gained broad support; efforts to resolve crises abroad provoked controversy. In 1935 Senate hearings conducted by Gerald P. Nye of North Dakota revealed that bankers and munitions makers, so-called "merchants of death," had made enormous profits during World War I. The committee report implied, but could not prove, that business interests had even steered the United States into war. "When Americans went into the fray," declared Senator Nye, "they little thought that they were there and fighting to save the skins of American bankers who had bet too boldly on the outcome of the war and had two billions of dollars of loans to the Allies in jeopardy."

Nye's charges fed the debate over the growing threat to peace. By 1935 leading public figures agreed war was imminent; they agreed, too, that the United States should stay out. But on the question of what policy to follow the divisions were profound. Internationalists like the League of Women Voters and former secretary of state Henry Stimson favored collective security. "The only certain way to keep out of a great war is to prevent war," Stimson declared; "the only hope of preventing war . . . is by the earnest, intelligent, and unselfish cooperation of the nations of the world towards that end."

Isolationists opposed the collective security formula. Yet the simple isolationist or internationalist tag does not adequately describe the range of people and opinions in this debate. The isolationists themselves were deeply divided. Their camp included liberal reformers like George W. Norris and conservatives like Robert A. Taft of Ohio, a concentration of midwesterners as well as major leaders from both coasts like Senator Hiram W. Johnson of California and Representative Hamilton Fish of New York, and a number of Democrats as well as leading

A flag company of Hitler youth parade past their *Führer*, Adolf Hitler (centered in the balcony doorway). Hitler's shrewd use of patriotic and party symbols, massed rallies, and marches exploited the possibilities for mass politics and propaganda.

Republicans. What united the isolationists was not party, ideology, or region, but a shared opposition to war and a belief that the United States should avoid alliances or political commitments to other nations. Pacifists added yet another element to the debate. Powerful groups like the Women's International League for Peace and Freedom insisted that disarmament, not the League of Nations or other collective security schemes, was the only road to peace.

It was internationalist Charles Warren who gave the isolationists a strategy to avoid war. If bankers' loans, arms shipments, and American travel on belligerent ships had pulled the United States into World War I, Warren proposed laws to prohibit these activities when another conflict broke out. Debate in Congress centered on a proposal to prohibit the sale of arms to all belligerents in time of war. Internationalists opposed the idea, arguing that the embargo should apply only to aggressor nations to prevent the aggressors from striking when they were ready, leaving their unprepared victims without access to arms. The president, internationalists suggested, should use the embargo selectively. Isolationists, however, did not want to give Roosevelt that power and they had the votes they needed. The Neutrality Act of 1935 required an impartial embargo of arms to all belligerents. The president had authority only to determine when a state of war existed.

Roosevelt had wavered throughout this debate, seeming at times to favor legislation and at times to oppose it. He had threatened to veto the bill but accepted it when it was limited to six months. Even so, he warned, it might "drag us into war rather than keeping us out." The isolationists were reluctant to grant what Roosevelt wanted: discretionary power to respond flexibly to crises.

The limitations of congressional neutrality became immediately apparent. In October 1935 Benito Mussolini ordered Italian forces into the North African country of Ethiopia. Against tanks and planes, the troops of Emperor Haile Selassie fought with spears and flintlock rifles. Roosevelt immediately invoked the Neutrality Act in hopes of depriving Italy of war goods. Italy needed not arms, but oil, steel, and copper, none of which fell under the Neutrality Act. When Secretary Hull called for a "moral embargo" on such goods, hard-pressed American businesses shipped them anyway. With no effective opposition from the League of Nations or the United States, Mussolini quickly completed his conquest. Congress then extended neutrality into 1936, adding a prohibition on loans or credits to belligerents.

Neutrality legislation also benefited Nazi dictator Adolf Hitler. On March 7, 1936, two weeks after Congress renewed the Neutrality Act, German troops thrust into the demilitarized area west of the Rhine. In the face of this flagrant violation of the Treaty of Versailles, Britain and France did nothing, while the League of Nations sputtered out a worthless condemnation. Roosevelt remained aloof. The Soviet Union's lonely call for collective action fell on deaf ears.

In 1931 the Spanish monarchy had been replaced by a democratic republic. In July 1936 Generalissimo Francisco Franco, emboldened by Hitler's success, led a rebellion against the newly elected Popular Front government. When civil war erupted, Spain became a staging ground for World War II. Hitler and Mussolini sent supplies, weapons, and troops to Franco's fascists, while the Soviet Union and Mexico aided the left-leaning government. The war divided opinion in Europe and America. Catholics supported the anticommunist Franco forces. Leftists embraced the Loyalists, who backed the democratic government. Some 3200 American citizens, the "Abraham Lincoln Brigade," joined the Spanish Loyalists' fight against fascism. Over half this rag-tag force of soldiers, nurses, and ambulance drivers died in the struggle. In the face of domestic political divisions Roosevelt stood by, even though until 1937 the neutrality laws did not apply to civil wars. By 1939 the Spanish republic had fallen to Franco.

As the world edged toward war, Congress struggled to keep America safe. Immediately after the outbreak of the Spanish Civil War, financier Bernard Baruch suggested a way to permit American trade (and thus to promote recovery at home) without risking war. Belligerents could buy supplies other than munitions but would have to pay beforehand and carry the supplies on their own ships. "Cash-and-carry" was adopted in the Neutrality Act of 1937. If war spread, the British navy would ensure that supplies reached England.

Cash-and-carry worked well in Europe but not in Asia. Japan, after provoking a clash with Chinese forces at the Marco Polo Bridge south of Beijing, invaded southern China in 1937. In a thinly veiled effort to give China continued access to American goods, Roosevelt refused to invoke neutrality. This policy benefited Japan, which had conducted a greater volume of trade with the United States. Without the discretion to impose embargoes selectively, Roosevelt could do little else.

By 1937 war seemed inevitable in both Europe and Asia, especially after Germany, Japan, and Italy signed the Anti-Comintern Pact. Ostensibly a pledge of mutual support against the Soviet Union, the agreement created a Rome–Berlin–Tokyo axis that paralyzed Europe with fear. Roosevelt groped for some way to contain these "bandit nations." In 1937 he joined with the French and British to condemn Japan's war against China. That October he gave his first foreign policy speech in 14 months. Seeming to favor collective action, he called for an international "quarantine" of aggressor nations. The isolationist press was quick to condemn the president. The large majority of editorial opinion, however, applauded the president's remarks. For reasons that are unclear, Roosevelt retreated from the position he had boldly staked out. When Japanese planes sank the American gunboat *Panay* on China's Yangtze River that December, he meekly accepted an apology for the unprovoked attack.

The president was simply too beleaguered on the domestic front to risk confrontation with powerful isolationists over foreign policy. His "court-packing" plan in 1937 (page 1002) had emboldened his opposition among both conservative Democrats and Republicans. When Roosevelt again asked Congress to give him discretionary authority over the arms embargo in 1939, he suffered a discouraging defeat. "Well, Captain," Vice President John Nance Garner told him, "we may as well face the facts. You haven't got the votes, and that's all there is to it."

What made Roosevelt's impotence so frustrating was the growing menace of Nazism in Europe. In 1938 German troops entered Austria in yet another violation of the Treaty of Versailles. Hitler then insisted that the 3.5 million ethnic Germans in the Sudetenland of Czechoslovakia be brought into the Reich. With Germany threatening to invade Czechoslovakia, in September 1938 Britain's prime minister Neville Chamberlain and French premier Edouard Daladier flew to Munich, where they struck a deal to appease Hitler. Czechoslovakia would give up the Sudetenland in return for German pledges to seek no more territory in Europe. The Munich Pact, Chamberlain announced to cheering English crowds, would bring "peace in our time." Six months later, in open contempt for the European democracies, Hitler took over the remainder of Czechoslovakia. "Appeasement" became synonymous with betrayal, weakness, and surrender.

War in Europe

By 1939 Hitler made little secret of his intentions to recapture territory lost to Poland after World War I. Russia was the key to his success. If Soviet leader Joseph Stalin joined the Western powers, Hitler might be blunted. But Stalin, who coveted eastern Poland, suspected the West of seeking to turn Hitler against him. On August 24, 1939, the foreign ministers of Russia and Germany signed a

WORLD WAR II IN EUROPE AND NORTH AFRICA
Coordination of Allied strategy was crucial to victory. As Soviet forces engaged the bulk of the Axis armies across a huge front, the defense of Stalingrad prevented Hitler from reinforcing Rommel against the British in North Africa. After winning North Africa, the Allies turned north to knock Italy out of the war. The final key to defeating the Nazis was the invasion of Western Europe at Normandy. D-Day would not have been possible had the Allies been unable to use England as a base to gather their forces. (1939 boundaries are shown.)

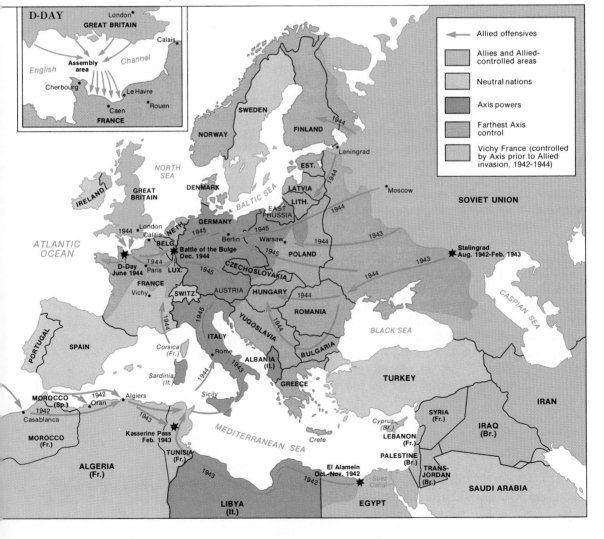

nonaggression pact, shocking the rest of the world. The secret protocols (revealed after World War II) of the Molotov–Ribbentrop Agreement freed Hitler to invade Poland without having to fight a two-front war. Stalin could extend his western borders by bringing the Baltic states (Latvia, Estonia, and Lithuania), eastern Poland, and parts of Romania and Finland into the Soviet sphere.

On the hot Saturday of September 1, 1939, German tanks and troops lunged into Poland. "It's come at last," Roosevelt sighed. "God help us all." Within days France and England declared war on Germany. Stalin quickly moved into eastern Poland, where German and Russian armor took just three weeks to crush the Polish cavalry. As Hitler consolidated his hold on eastern Europe, Stalin turned to Finland. Many Americans were eager to support the Finnish cause, especially since the Finns alone had paid their war debts. But isolationists in Congress gutted a Finnish aid bill.

As spring arrived in 1940, Hitler moved to protect his sea lanes by capturing Denmark and Norway. The French retreated behind their Maginot Line, a steel and concrete fortification at the German border, while German panzer divisions supported by airpower knifed through Belgium and Holland in a *blitzkrieg*—a "lightning war." The Low Countries fell in 23 days, giving the Germans a route into France. By May 1940 a third of a million British and French troops lay pinned on the beaches of Dunkirk. Only a strenuous rescue effort, staged by the Royal Navy and a flotilla of English pleasure craft, saved them—clearing the way for the German march to Paris. On June 22, less than six weeks after the German invasion, France capitulated—in the very railway car where Germany had surrendered in 1918.

Suddenly, only Britain stood between Hitler and the United States. If the Nazis got control of the British fleet, the Atlantic Ocean could easily become a gateway to America. Isolationists mobilized in the America First Committee to keep the country out of war. Ohio Senator Robert Taft, aviator Charles Lindbergh, and Socialist party presidential candidate Norman Thomas endorsed the idea of a "Fortress America." They believed that hemispheric defenses alone could protect the nation from any onslaught. At the other end of the spectrum, in 1940 internationalists formed the Committee to Defend America by Aiding the Allies. Headed by editor William Allen White, it boasted some 600 chapters and supported aid to England short of war. Anyone who thought the Nazis would wait until the United States was ready, claimed one of its advertisements, was "either an imbecile or a traitor."

By the spring of 1940 Roosevelt had abandoned impartiality in favor of outright aid to the Allies. In May he requested funds to motorize the army (it had only 350 tanks) and build 50,000 airplanes a year (fewer than 3000 planes existed, most of them outmoded). Despite isolationist opposition he had persuaded Congress to adopt a bill for the first peacetime draft in history. Congress, earlier planning to slash the military budget, voted over $17 billion for defense.

Then came summer and the onslaught of thousands of German fighter planes and heavy bombers to soften Great Britain for a German invasion from occupied France. In addition, German submarines were sinking British convoys at an alarming rate. As radio reporters relayed graphic descriptions of London in flames and Royal Air Force pilots putting up a heroic defense, a majority of Americans became convinced that the United States should help Britain win the war, though few favored military involvement. So Roosevelt adopted policies designed to help the British help themselves. In September 1940 he agreed to give Britain 50 old destroyers in return for leases on British bases in the Western Hemisphere and a pledge not to let the Germans capture their navy. The destroyers-for-bases deal, Roosevelt told the nation, was the most important "reinforcement of our national defenses that has been taken since the Louisiana Purchase."

In the 1940 election campaign isolation was no longer the issue. Both Roosevelt and his Republican opponent, Wendell Willkie, favored an internationalist course short of war. In defeating Willkie, Roosevelt promised voters that "your boys are not going to be sent into any foreign wars." He portrayed the United States, instead, as "the great arsenal of democracy." Since the British no longer could pay for arms under the provisions of cash-and-carry, Roosevelt proposed a scheme to "lease, lend, or otherwise dispose of" arms and supplies to countries whose defense was vital to the United States. That meant sending supplies to England on the dubious premise that they would be returned when the war ended. Roosevelt likened "lend-lease" to loaning a garden hose to a neighbor whose house was on fire. Isolationists saw that lend-lease was a way to tie the United States more closely to the Allied cause. Senator Robert Taft thought "chewing gum" made a better comparison than a garden hose. After a neighbor used it, "you don't want it back." In March 1941, over the angry cries of isolationists, a large majority in Congress voted to pass the Lend-Lease Act.

By the summer of 1941 the United States and Germany were on the verge of war. For two months American destroyers had been escorting British ships as far as Iceland (though Roosevelt insisted it was a "patrol," not a convoy). The United States extended its defensive sphere to include Greenland and Iceland. Then Hitler, as audacious as ever, broke his alliance with the Soviet Union and in June 1941 launched a surprise invasion. The Allies expected a swift Russian collapse. Soviet armies had fought poorly in the Finnish War, and Stalin's purges three years earlier had decimated the officer corps. But the Russians threw up a heroic resistance, and Roosevelt extended lend-lease to the Soviet Union in August 1941.

That month Roosevelt also held secret meetings with the new British prime minister, Winston Churchill, on warships on Argentia Bay, off the coast of Newfoundland. Both leaders recognized the value of cooperation. Almost every day since England and Germany had gone to war, the two men had exchanged phone calls, letters, or cables. Churchill wanted Roosevelt to save Britain from bankruptcy and defeat. Roosevelt believed that if England collapsed, the United States would confront Germany and Japan alone. The Argentia meetings cemented the friendship between Roosevelt and Churchill—one key to Allied victory. The two leaders also issued the Atlantic Charter to define Allied war aims. The Charter condemned aggression and embraced the "Four Freedoms"—freedom of speech and expression, freedom of worship, freedom from want, and freedom from fear—which Roosevelt had proposed in a January speech. When talk turned to a postwar international organization, Roosevelt hedged. He wanted to avoid any commitment that might mire him, like Woodrow Wilson, in domestic controversy.

By the time Churchill and Roosevelt met at Argentia Bay, American destroyers in the North Atlantic were already stalking German U-boats and reporting their whereabouts to British commanders. Despite Hitler's orders to avoid engaging American patrols, several incidents occurred, including the sinking in October of the destroyer *Reuben James* with the loss of over 100 American sailors. Although public support for efforts to assist the Allied cause was growing, Roosevelt's policies still provoked angry debate. Interventionists criticized Roosevelt for being too cautious; isolationists attacked him for being too provocative and for

During World War II Franklin Roosevelt and British Prime Minister Winston Churchill developed the closest relationship ever between an American president and the head of another government. The two distant cousins shared a sense of the continuities of Anglo-American culture and of the global strategy of the war.

deceiving the American people. As late as September 1941 eight of ten Americans were against going to war. Roosevelt believed only an unprovoked attack would unite public opinion behind a declaration of war. He did not suspect that Japan, not Germany, would solve the problem for him.

Disaster in the Pacific

Preoccupied by the fear of German victory in Europe, Roosevelt sought to avoid a showdown with Japan. Hitler seemed the more dangerous enemy, who needed to be dealt with first. The navy, Roosevelt told his cabinet, had "not got enough ships to go round, and every little episode in the Pacific means fewer ships in the Atlantic." But precisely because American as well as European attention was centered on the conflict in Europe, Japan was emboldened to expand militarily into Southeast Asia.

Living on a string of crowded islands, possessing few resources, the Japanese nationalists envisioned a new order in the western Pacific. Through the "Greater East Asia Co-Prosperity Sphere," Japan would replace the European powers in Asian markets and promote just enough development to nurture local support for Japanese domination. To Japanese leaders, the Co-Prosperity Sphere was simply an Asian Monroe Doctrine. To American leaders, it threatened the principles of the open door and the survival of Chinese independence. Japan had been waging

The Geography of Global War

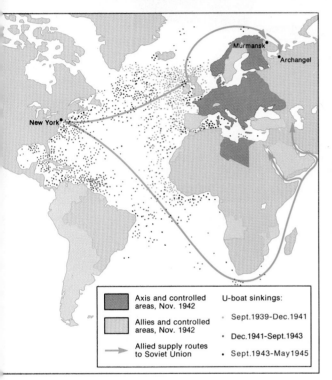

Axis and controlled areas, Nov. 1942

Allies and controlled areas, Nov. 1942

Allied supply routes to Soviet Union

U-boat sinkings:

· Sept.1939-Dec.1941

· Dec.1941-Sept.1943

· Sept.1943-May1945

the region with the outline of the United States overlaid, in scale. The war had to be fought over an area which, in terms of the Western Hemisphere, was like placing the U.S. Army's Australian center of operations somewhere in South America. On the same scale, Tokyo would lie far up in northern Canada, Iwo Jima somewhere in Hudson Bay, Guam in Quebec, Tarawa and Guadalcanal in the mid-Atlantic, Singapore in Utah, Manila in North Dakota, central Java in Texas, Midway Island near Iceland, and Hawaii off the coast of Scotland.

Such extraordinary distances spurred the United States to devise a two-front strategy to defeat Japan (map, right). MacArthur's army forces used Australia as a base of operations in the southwest Pacific, aiming for the Philippines and the southeast coast of China. Once those areas were secured, forces could then launch air attacks and finally, if necessary, a full-scale invasion of Japan. The navy, under command of Admiral Nimitz, set out to destroy the Japanese fleet and to conduct a series of amphibious landings on island chains in the central Pacific. Once Japan's

In the world's first truly global war, the need to coordinate and supply troops and materiel became paramount. During World War II U.S. factories produced more goods than the three Axis powers combined. But as German U-boats took a heavy toll on Allied shipping in the North Atlantic, the problem became delivering those goods where they were needed. The solution was a logistical nightmare: send supplies to Russia on a 12,000-mile odyssey around Africa to the Persian Gulf and then across Iran by land. The elimination of German submarines and the recapture of the Mediterranean area greatly eased the shipping problem and, as much as any single battle, ensured victory.

In the Pacific the problem was one of sheer distance. To impress upon newly arrived officers the vastness of the war theater, General MacArthur showed them a map of

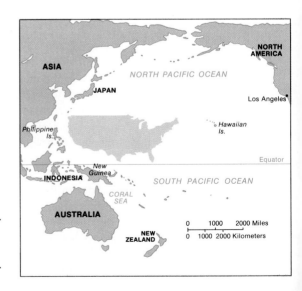

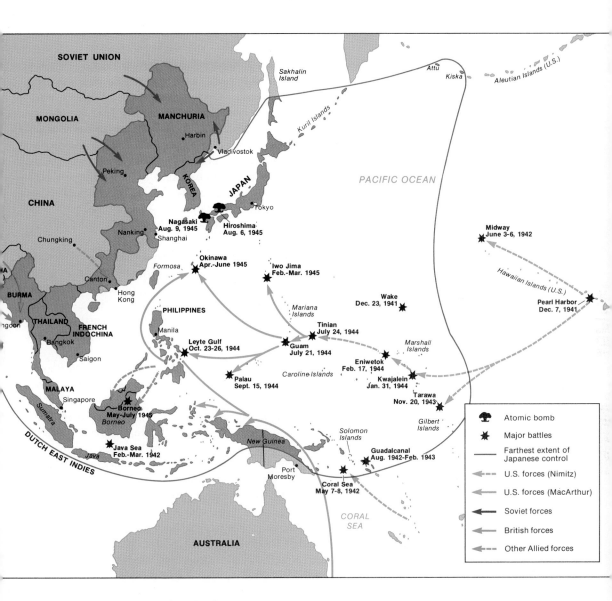

SOVIET UNION

MONGOLIA

MANCHURIA

• Harbin

• Vladivostok

Sakhalin
Island

Attu

Kiska

Aleutian Islands (U.S.)

Kuril Islands

PACIFIC OCEAN

Peking •

CHINA

KOREA

JAPAN

• Tokyo

Nanking •

Chungking •

Nagasaki
Aug. 9, 1945
Shanghai

Hiroshima
Aug. 6, 1945

Midway
June 3-6, 1942

Formosa

Okinawa
Apr.-June 1945

Iwo Jima
Feb.-Mar. 1945

Canton •

BURMA

Hong
Kong

PHILIPPINES

Mariana
Islands

Wake
Dec. 23, 1941

Hawaiian Islands (U.S.)

ngoon

THAILAND

FRENCH
INDOCHINA

Bangkok •

Manila •

Tinian
July 24, 1944

Pearl Harbor
Dec. 7, 1941

Leyte Gulf
Oct. 23-26, 1944

Guam
July 21, 1944

Marshall
Islands

• Saigon

Palau
Sept. 15, 1944

Eniwetok
Feb. 17, 1944

MALAYA

Caroline Islands

Kwajalein
Jan. 31, 1944

Singapore •

Borneo
May-July 1945
Borneo

Tarawa
Nov. 20, 1943

Sumatra

DUTCH EAST INDIES

Java Sea
Feb.-Mar. 1942
Java

New Guinea

Solomon
Islands

Gilbert
Islands

Guadalcanal
Aug. 1942-Feb. 1943

Port
Moresby

Coral Sea
May 7-8, 1942

CORAL
SEA

AUSTRALIA

Legend:

🌳 Atomic bomb

✳ Major battles

— Farthest extent of
Japanese control

‹--- U.S. forces (Nimitz)

‹— U.S. forces (MacArthur)

◀— Soviet forces

◀— British forces

‹--- Other Allied forces

navy had been destroyed and Okinawa captured, U.S. bombers devastated Japanese cities from the air. British forces launched separate operations in Burma, forces under Chiang Kai-shek occasionally engaged Japanese forces on China's mainland, and in August 1945, Soviet troops attacked northern China.

war on China since 1937 and by the summer of 1941 its forces controlled the China coast and all major cities. By occupying French Indochina (now Vietnam) in July, Japan stood ready to conquer all of the Southeast Asian peninsula and the oil-rich Dutch East Indies.

Japan's thrust into Indochina forced Roosevelt into action. He embargoed trade, froze Japanese assets in American banks, and barred shipments of vital scrap iron and petroleum. His actions divided the Japanese cabinet. Military leaders were willing to risk war to achieve security, but Prime Minister Fumimaro Konoye proposed instead a summit meeting with Roosevelt to iron out major differences. In fact, the two nations' goals were so at odds that no diplomatic resolution was possible. The Japanese military demanded that Konoye win recognition of recent conquests and Japanese dominance of Asia. At a meeting in Washington, Secretary of State Cordell Hull told Ambassador Kichisaburo Nomura that Japan must renounce the Tripartite Pact with Italy and Germany and withdraw from China before summit talks could begin. Even as Hull and Nomura talked, the Japanese military were planning to capture the East Indies. In October General Hideki Tojo, leader of the militants, replaced the more moderate Konoye; the war party had complete control of the government. Secretly the Japanese began preparing to attack American positions in Guam, the Philippines, and Hawaii. They planned one final round of diplomacy before striking. When Japanese Ambassador Nomura learned from Secretary Hull in late November that the United States still insisted on complete withdrawal from China, Japanese militarists decided on war.

As the Hull–Nomura talks collapsed, American military leaders urged Roosevelt to avoid direct conflict until the United States had built up its national defenses. Massive Japanese troop movements southward indicated an assault on British and Dutch holdings. If the Japanese attacked American possessions, most expected the blow to fall on Guam or the Philippines. In late November a Japanese armada slipped from Hitokappu Bay in the remote Kuril Islands, then part of Japan. Observing strict radio silence, the six carriers and their escorts steamed across the North Pacific toward the American base at Pearl Harbor in Hawaii. On Sunday morning, December 7, 1941, as a Western Union messenger pedaled to deliver an alert to the base commander, the first sortie of Japanese planes roared down on the Pacific Fleet lying at anchor. For over an hour the Japanese pounded the harbor and adjacent airfields. Altogether 19 ships—the heart of the Pacific Fleet—were sunk or battered. Practically all of the 200 American aircraft were damaged or destroyed. More than 2400 men died. Only the aircraft carriers, by chance on maneuvers, escaped the worst naval defeat in American history.

In Washington, Secretary of War Henry Stimson could not believe the news as it was relayed to his office. "My God! This can't be true, this must mean the Philippines." Later that day the Japanese did attack the Philippines, along with Guam, Midway, and British forces in Hong Kong and the Malay peninsula. On December 8, Franklin Roosevelt told a stunned and grieving nation that "yesterday, December 7, 1941" was "a date which will live in infamy." America, the "reluctant belligerent," was in the war at last.

The Japanese had given Adolf Hitler no warning about the attack, but on December 11, 1941, Germany and Italy honored their treaty with Japan by declaring war on the United States. Hitler apparently thought he had little to lose, since Germany and America were already fighting an undeclared war in the Atlantic. He certainly miscalculated the willingness and capacity of Americans to fight. Such errors in judgment ultimately doomed his dream of a thousand-year Reich.

Had Roosevelt known the attack on Pearl Harbor was coming, as some of his critics and enemies have charged? After all, American intelligence had cracked Japan's diplomatic codes. Much information indicated that Pearl Harbor was at risk. Yet Roosevelt not only refused diplomatic compromise but also left the fleet exposed, seeming almost to provoke an attack to bring the United States into the war. Was it mere coincidence that the vital aircraft carriers were at sea, leaving obsolete battleships to bear the brunt of the attack. Since the attack on Pearl Harbor so neatly served Roosevelt's purposes, many critics argue that he must have contrived to bring it about. This argument is circumstantial, not factual. Roosevelt, wanting to fight Germany more than Japan, would have preferred an incident in the Atlantic rather than the Pacific. More important, the intelligence signals were confusing and analysts lost track of the Japanese fleet as it moved toward Hawaii. Evidence pointed more to an attack on Guam or the Philippines.

No one in Japan believed a surprise attack would bring victory against the United States—only time to consolidate a defensive perimeter that would prove impenetrable to the weak-willed Westerners. And no one in America thought the Japanese audacious or sophisticated enough to raid Pearl Harbor, some 4000 miles from Japan. Such cultural misperceptions had deadly consequences for both sides. They explain the coming of war better than any conspiracy theory.

MISFORTUNES OF WAR

On December 8, 1941, few Americans could have found much cause for hope in the smoking wreckage of ships and planes that had once been the heart of the United States' forces in the Pacific. Over the next four years one of history's great ironies unfolded. Uniting the American people as nothing else, the stunning defeat at Pearl Harbor doomed the Axis. To the Allies' resolve to defeat militarism and fascism were now added the enormous material and human resources of the United States. Victory would not come easily, nor would the alliance of the British-American democracies with the Soviet communist dictatorship be easy to sustain. The Allies needed to forge a strategy that would win both the war and the peace to follow.

Strategies for War

Two world leaders sensed better than most what Pearl Harbor meant. One was Admiral Yamamoto Isoruku, head of the Japanese navy and the man who planned the attack. The other was Winston Churchill, prime minister of England. Yamamoto had mixed feelings about the United States, where he had served several tours of duty as a young officer. He dismissed its navy as a "social organization of golfers and bridge players," yet he admired its capacity for industrial organization and production. He had warned of the folly of making war on the United States, but if Japan insisted on war, Yamamoto urged a paralyzing opening blow. He promised victory at Pearl Harbor and a free hand in the Pacific for six months, no more. As it turned out six months was not quite enough.

Winston Churchill greeted the news of Pearl Harbor with elation and shock. "We have won the war," he thought and that night slept "the sleep of the saved and thankful." Great Britain would no longer stand alone in the North Atlantic and the Pacific wars. Two weeks later Churchill headed to Washington to coordinate strategy with Franklin Roosevelt. At the meeting (code-named ARCADIA) the two leaders announced production schedules for ships, planes, and armaments that were so large some critics openly laughed—at first. A year later combined British, Canadian, and American production boards not only met but exceeded the schedules.

Roosevelt and Churchill also planned grand strategy. Outraged by the attack on Pearl Harbor, many Americans thought the United States should concentrate on Japan. The two leaders reaffirmed an earlier decision to defeat Germany first. The Pacific war would be fought as a holding action. To assure effective cooperation the two established the Combined Chiefs of Staff, a unified British-American military command based in Washington. The Arcadia Conference also led to a definition of war aims—sufficiently idealistic to rally support for the war and broad enough to avoid specific commitments. The Declaration of the United Nations (the countries at war with the Axis), made on January 1, 1942, called for easing restrictions on trade among nations, demanded disarmament of aggressors, and hinted at participation in some future security system—ultimately the United Nations.

Gloomy Prospects

In 1942 the Allies could plan for victory only on faith. German armies controlled almost all of Europe. Having narrowly survived the Battle of Britain, the British had forestalled a German invasion from France, but no counterattack to liberate France or the Low Countries seemed remotely possible. By the end of the summer the Nazis stood before the Soviet Union's three major cities—Leningrad, Moscow, and Stalingrad. British and American leaders doubted the Russians could long survive the Nazi onslaught. In North Africa General Erwin Rommel's Afrika Korps swept into Egypt and stood within striking distance of the Suez Canal—a crucial link to the resources of the British Empire.

The critical battle for the North Atlantic appeared equally precarious. As soon as prowling German U-boats spotted a convoy, they would attack in groups called "Wolfpacks." So deadly were they that merchant sailors developed a grim humor about sleeping. Those on freighters carrying iron ore slept above decks, since the heavily laden ships could sink in less than a minute. On a ship with general cargo seamen slept with clothes on and doors open to ease their escape. On oil tankers, however, sailors closed their doors, undressed, and slept soundly. If a torpedo hit, no one would survive. U-boat sailors called the first six months of 1942 "the American hunting season," as they sank 400 Allied ships in United States' territorial waters. All of America's productive capacity would mean nothing if supplies never reached Europe.

In the Far East the situation was desperate. After Pearl Harbor Japanese forces invaded the Philippines, British Malaya, and the Dutch East Indies. The British bastion of Singapore fell in just one week, and in March, at the Battle of Java Sea, the Japanese navy destroyed almost the entire remaining Allied naval force in the western Pacific. In April 1942 General Douglas MacArthur, commander of American forces in the Philippines, fled to Australia with his family in a small patrol boat. In what appeared to be an empty pledge, he vowed, "I shall return." The closest thing to success was the heroic but doomed fight of American and Philippine troops on Bataan and Corregidor. Unprepared for a mass surrender, the victorious Japanese led some 76,000 survivors on a "death march" that cost 10,000 lives. By the summer no significant Allied forces stood between the Japanese and India or Australia. The Japanese even captured two undefended islands in the Aleutian chain off the coast of Alaska. Americans feared that the West Coast of the United States might be next.

The chain of spectacular victories disguised fatal weaknesses within the Axis alliance. Japan and Germany were fighting separate wars on two fronts. They never coordinated strategies. Vast armies in China and Russia drained them of both manpower and supplies. Fearful of alienating domestic support, Hitler had not placed German industry on a full war footing before 1942. Japanese industry depended on a steady flow of materials from conquered territories. Disrupted shipping could cripple the war economy. Most important, the Axis had conquered too much territory too quickly. Brutal occupation policies alienated subject populations and forced Axis armies to leave large occupying forces to maintain control and move supplies. The Nazis diverted precious resources into the extermination of Europe's Jews, Slavs, and Gypsies. Resistance movements grew as the victims of Axis aggression fought back.

A Grand Alliance

Defeat at first obscured the Allies' strengths. Chief among these were the manpower of the Soviet Union and the productive capacity of the United States. Relatively safe from the fighting, Americans could concentrate their efforts on producing enough food and war materials to supply two separate wars at once. By the end of the war American factories had turned out 300,000 airplanes, 87,000 warships, 400,000 artillery pieces, 102,000 tanks and self-propelled guns, and 47 million tons of ammunition.

The Allies benefited too from exceptional leadership. The "Big Three"— Joseph Stalin, Winston Churchill, and Franklin Roosevelt—all had shortcomings but were able to maintain a unity of purpose that eluded Axis leaders. All three understood the global nature of the war. To a remarkable degree they managed to set aside their differences in pursuit of a common goal—the defeat of Nazi Germany. The arch-anticommunist Churchill pledged Britain's resources to assist the defense of the world's largest communist state. The anti-imperialist Roosevelt poured American resources into the war effort of two of Europe's major imperial powers.

Whenever differences of ideology, national interest, or military objectives threatened to split the alliance, the Big Three managed a compromise. In 1942 Stalin made three demands on his allies: recognition of his territorial ambitions in eastern Europe, including the former Baltic states and parts of Poland, Finland, and Romania; huge shipments of war materiel; and the opening of a second front in western Europe. The last demand was the most vital. By the end of the year the Soviets were facing 3.5 million Axis troops along a 1600-mile front in eastern Europe. One diplomat remarked that Stalin's foreign minister knew only four words in English: "yes," "no," and "second front."

Churchill and Roosevelt refused all three of Stalin's demands. In 1942 the Western Allies did not have enough supplies for their own forces, much less for Stalin's. Even if they could assemble the materiel, they did not have enough ships to carry it. Nor were Churchill and Roosevelt willing to jeopardize Allied harmony by discussing postwar Russian territorial ambitions. And in 1942 the Allies simply lacked sufficient trained soldiers, landing craft, and air support for a successful invasion of Europe.

Churchill himself flew to Moscow in August 1942 to give Stalin the bad news: no second front in Europe until 1943. Postponed again until mid-1944, the second front became a source of festering Russian suspicion. But after an initial surge of anger over the postponement, Stalin accepted Churchill's rationale for a substitute action, a British–American invasion of North Africa set for the end of 1942. Code-named Operation Torch, the North African campaign could be mounted quickly, would bring British and American troops into direct combat with the Germans, and stood an excellent chance of succeeding. Here was an example of the personal contact that assured Allied cooperation. The alliance sometimes bent but never broke.

The Naval War in the Pacific

Despite the Allied decision to concentrate on defeating Germany first, the earliest signs of success came in the Pacific. At the Battle of Coral Sea in May 1942 planes from the aircraft carriers *Yorktown* and *Lexington* stopped a large Japanese invading force headed for Port Moresby in New Guinea. For the first time in history two fleets fought without seeing each other. The age of naval aviation had arrived. The Japanese fleet actually inflicted greater damage but decided to turn back to nurse its wounds. Had they captured Port Moresby, the Japanese could have severed Allied shipping routes to Australia.

A daring bit of Allied showmanship led the Japanese High Command into the decisive battle of the Pacific war. Desperate for some good war news, President Roosevelt had urged the Joint Chiefs to bomb the Japanese home islands as soon as possible. On April 18, 1942, sixteen Army B-25 bombers rolled off the deck of the navy aircraft carrier *Hornet*. All of them bombed Tokyo before crash landing along the China coast. The "Doolittle raid," named for its commander, Colonel James Doolittle, inflicted only slight physical damage but humiliated the Japanese army and navy. To extend Japan's defenses, Admiral Yamamoto ordered the capture of Midway, a small island guarding the approach to Hawaii.

The Americans, in possession of decoded Japanese transmissions, were ready. On June 3, as the Japanese main fleet bore down on Midway, a patrol plane from the American carrier task force spotted smoke from the ships. Caught between attacks on Midway, the Japanese were not fully prepared to defend themselves. Planes from the carriers *Hornet, Enterprise,* and *Yorktown* sank four enemy carriers, a cruiser, and three destroyers. The United States lost only the *Yorktown.* More important, the Japanese lost many of their best carrier pilots, who were more difficult to replace than planes. The Battle of Midway broke Japanese naval supremacy in the Pacific and stalled Japan's offensive. In August 1942 American forces launched their first offensive—on the Solomon Islands, east of New Guinea. With the landing of American marines on the key island of Guadalcanal, the Allies started on the bloody road to Japan and victory.

Turning Points in Europe

By the fall of 1942 the Allies were seeing successes in the European war. Erwin Rommel's Afrika Korps had pushed as far east as El Alamein, 75 miles from the port of Alexandria, by July 1, 1942, but the Germans were too exhausted to move

U.S. marines stage an amphibious landing at Tarawa. On this 300-acre island in the Gilberts, west of Hawaii, 4700 Japanese troops had built a complex chain of fortifications. Just reaching the beach and crossing it, the marines suffered 1500 deaths or injuries. By the time the Japanese surrendered, all but 17 Japanese and almost 1000 Americans had died, with over 2000 wounded.

farther. Rather than follow up Rommel's successes, Hitler sent reinforcements to the Russian front to buoy a collapsing situation. On October 24 British forces under General Bernard Montgomery counterattacked. With bagpipes skirling in the night, Montgomery's forces broke through Rommel's lines. Weeks later, the Allies' Operation Torch, Churchill's second-front invasion of North Africa, began, under the command of General Dwight D. Eisenhower, with attacks at Oran and Algiers in Algeria and Casablanca in Morocco. An American defeat in February 1943 at the Kasserine Pass in Tunisia was followed by a string of victories under General George S. Patton. By May 1943 Rommel had fled from North Africa, abandoning 300,000 German troops.

Success in North Africa provided a stirring complement to the dogged Russian stand at Stalingrad. From August 1942 until February 1943 Axis and Soviet armies, each with over a million troops, fought one of the bloodiest engagements in history. Each side suffered more casualties than the Americans did during the entire war. When it was over, the Russian lines had held. The Germans lost an army and their momentum; Stalin's forces went on the offensive, moving south and west through the Ukraine toward Poland and Romania. By the fall of 1942 the Allies had also gained the edge in the war for the Atlantic. Boatyards launched record tonnages of new ships. Improved air patrols, new convoy systems, and better antisubmarine weapons—such as improved depth charges and sonar, which located submerged vessels by bouncing sound waves off them—helped sink 785 out of the nearly 1200 U-boats the Germans built. Success in the North Atlantic allowed troops and supplies to reach Europe and Stalin's beleaguered forces.

THOSE WHO FOUGHT

World War II opened a new world to its combatants. Nineteen-year-olds who had never left home found themselves swept off to Europe or the South Pacific. Many of them looked forward to combat. "I was going to gain my manhood," recalled one soldier. But combat soon hardened such troops. The same soldier, after taking part in an assault on the French coast, concluded that war was "a nightmare." Looking at newly arrived troops, he now had but one thought: "You poor innocents." Only a feeling of camaraderie sustained him, a "special sense of kinship," he called it. "The reason you storm the beaches," he said, "is not patriotism or bravery. It's that sense of not wanting to fail your buddies."

War brought together Americans from all regions, social classes, and ethnic backgrounds. It afforded women and minorities a chance to dispel many stereotypes. Soldiers were subjected to regimentation, hierarchy, and obedience—all unnatural to civilians living in a democracy. The regimentation was necessary because a successful global war required coordination from the platoon on the battlefield to the high commands in Washington, from the farms and shop floors to the executive offices of large corporations and government bureaucracies. Mobilization for war had its benefits. For one, rapid expansion of the economy finally brought an end to the Depression.

The Wartime Military Branches

The military services had been out of favor during the interwar years. Congress denied the military enough funds even to maintain adequate supplies and modern equipment. Generals and admirals spent most of their time in bitter interservice rivalry for greater shares of restricted budgets. With low pay and little chance for advancement, many able officers left. Leadership became stagnant. Success often resulted from skill at bridge or golf rather than military command.

With the outbreak of war in Europe, military spending in the United States rose rapidly. The president mobilized the National Guard and won approval of a peacetime draft. When Pearl Harbor came, the army had 1.6 million men in uniform. By 1945 it had over 7 million, the navy 3.9 million, the army air corps 2.3 million, and the marines 600,000. Increases in size and equipment transformed the services into huge organizations. The navy, for example, opened the war with 4500 vessels, including 17 battleships, 7 large carriers, and 18 heavy cruisers. By the time peace came, there were 91,000 vessels of various sizes. The army air corps had 9000 planes in 1941 but only 1100 fit for combat. By 1945 its pilots flew over 72,000 planes.

A revised draft law enabled the military to take men between the ages of 20 and 44 for a term that lasted until the war ended. A later amendment limited the

As the United States prepared for war the military found itself desperately short of equipment. Here a plank laid over a wooden tripod served trainees as a substitute field gun. Such shortages lasted until the nation converted its industry to full-time war production.

upper age to 38 and reduced the lower to 18. By 1945 some 31 million American males had registered for the draft. Out of that pool nearly 10 million were inducted. Another 5.3 million men and women volunteered. Over 200,000 women joined the auxiliary branches of the services. Minorities enlisted in unusually large numbers because the military offered training and opportunities unavailable in civilian life.

Once drafted or enlisted, many Americans traveled far from home for the first time. One young soldier who had never been outside of the Midwest wrote, "I was absolutely bowled over by Europe, the castles, the cathedrals, the Alps. It was wonderment." By 1943 the army provided temporary housing for 5 million people in all parts of the country. The average soldier had about a year's worth of training: 13 weeks of "basic," 26 weeks of advanced training with an assigned division, and a final 13 weeks under simulated combat conditions. Even if they had worked in factories, young Americans were unprepared for the regimentation, limits on their personal freedom, and loss of individual identity imposed by military life. They had to adopt new habits: regular hours, three meals a day, and personal hygiene, including the army haircut.

Griping about shared indignities and incompetent leaders became a reflex. Many boys grew homesick, yet for most young men the military opened new regional, social, and ethnic horizons. "The first time I ever heard a New England accent," said a midwesterner, "was at Fort Benning. The southerner was an exotic creature to me. The people from the farms. The New York street smarts." More than any other social institution the military acted as a melting pot. It also offered educational opportunities and job skills or suggested the need for them. "I could be a technical sergeant only I haven't had enough school," reported one Navaho soldier in a letter home to New Mexico. "Make my little brother go to school even if you have to lasso him." Not all that soldiers and sailors learned was of redeeming

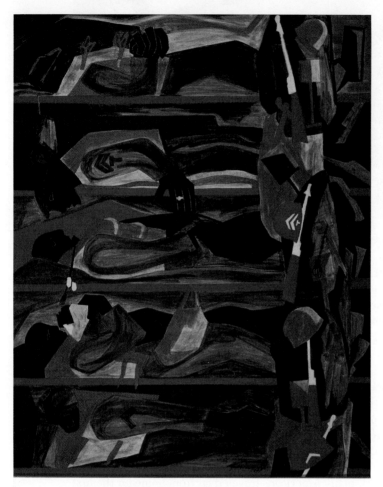

In *Shipping Out* black artist Jacob Lawrence, a veteran of the New Deal's Federal Arts Project, commemorated black troops heading overseas in the crowded confines of a troop ship. African-Americans served in segregated units more often in service roles than in combat. It was ironic that, in a war against Nazi racism, race remained a central issue among Americans.

value. Gambling, prostitution, drinking, and thievery were as much a part of military life as spit and polish and close-order drill.

Prejudice against blacks and other minorities carried over from civilian life. The army was strictly segregated and generally assigned blacks to noncombatant roles as cargo handlers, laborers, or mess personnel. The navy accepted them only as cooks and servants. At first the air corps and marines would not take them at all. In time leaders of the black community pressured the military to ease segregation and allow black soldiers to play a more active role. The army did form some black combat units, usually with white officers, and a black air corps unit. It even promoted Colonel Benjamin O. Davis to brigadier general. The marines enlisted some blacks and found that given adequate training, effective leadership, and an opportunity, black units fought with heroism. Segregation still remained the rule. The American Red Cross even kept "black" and "white" blood plasma separated, as if there were a difference.

Sometimes racial tensions led to open fighting between black and white troops. More common was the anguish suffered by a group of blacks stationed in Salina, Kansas. One day the owner of a restaurant blocked their entrance: "You boys know we don't serve colored here." They knew, of course; no place in town served blacks. But from the doorway, they stared in disbelief as lunch was served to German prisoners of war. "If we were *Untermenschen* in Nazi Germany," said one of the black soldiers, "they would break our bones. As 'colored' men in Salina, they only break our hearts." Despite the persistence of such prejudices, over a million black men and women served during the war.

Women at War

World War II brought an end to the military as an exclusive male enclave that women entered only as nurses. During the prewar mobilization, Eleanor Roosevelt and other women leaders had campaigned for a regular military organization for women. The War Department came up with a compromise that allowed women to be "in the army but not of it," as one observer noted. The Women's Army Auxiliary Corps (WAAC) brought women into the army but with inferior status and lower pay. By 1943 the "Auxiliary" had dropped out of the title: WAACs became WACs, with full army status, equal ranks, and equal pay. (The navy had a similar force called the WAVEs.)

Women could look with a mixture of pride and resentment on their wartime military service. Thousands served close to the battlefields, where they labored as technicians, mechanics, radio operators, postal clerks, and secretaries. While filling a vital need, these were largely traditional female jobs that implied a separate and inferior status. Until 1944 women were prevented by law from serving in war zones, even as noncombatants. There were women flyers, but they were restricted to shuttling planes behind the lines. WAVEs and WACs had limited social opportunities. While on duty their lives were heavily regulated. At many posts they lived behind barbed wire and could move about only in groups under armed escort.

Over There

Service in the military did not necessarily mean fighting in the war. The army used almost 2 million soldiers just to move supplies. In the Pacific theater only one enlisted man in three and two of five officers actually saw combat. Most battles were reasonably short, followed by long periods of waiting and preparation. One army division was in action for only one month in a year and a half. Soldiers in the European theater stayed longer on the front lines, often several months in a row. On the other hand, they usually spent less time overseas and had safer rear-area bases and healthier recreational facilities than those elsewhere.

In the Pacific conditions barely improved when soldiers left the front lines. Enemies stalked them everywhere. Dysentery, typhus, and even plague were as dangerous as the Japanese. On many days the thermometer rose over 110 degrees Fahrenheit. Most personnel lived in dirt-floored tents without screens, and disease-bearing insects took a heavy toll. Over 40 percent of all infantry soldiers in the Pacific were treated at least once for malaria. Showers were rare; fresh food was rarer still. The average soldier ate canned foods, called "K-rations," which were long on calories and short on flavor. One marine claimed that during his two years in the Pacific he had seen fresh eggs less than five times.

Wherever they fought, American soldiers usually lived in foxholes dug by hand with small shovels. Whenever possible they turned a hole in the ground into a home. "The American soldier is a born housewife," observed war correspondent Ernie Pyle. No sooner did a soldier settle in than he tried to tidy his makeshift home for visitors. Between battles, movies were about the only entertainment many troops had. Each film was a tenuous link to a more comfortable world at home, a place American soldiers yearned for with special intensity. It was not a country or an idea for which they fought so much as a set of memories—a house with a green lawn, a car, Mom and Pop, and a slice of pie.

As with most wars, the infantry bore the brunt of the fighting and dying. They suffered 90 percent of the battlefield casualties. World War II at least brought great advances in the treatment of wounds. Innovations such as the Mobile Auxiliary Surgical Hospital (MASH) and air evacuation saved countless lives. The use of antibiotics and improved treatment of the wounded saved many who would have died. Yet war is ultimately a bloody business. Almost 400,000 Americans died and over 600,000 were wounded before the war ended.

Science Goes to War

Before American entry into the war, British and American cryptographers, using advanced communications technologies, had cracked both the German and Japanese secret codes, gaining access to war plans and enabling the Allies to anticipate Axis troop movements. That was just one way in which scientists demonstrated their importance to the war effort. Some American scientists warned that failure to keep pace with enemy advances could prove fatal. In June 1941 Roosevelt appointed Vannevar Bush head of the Office of Scientific Research and Development (OSRD). Its mission was to organize the scientific community for war. Bush brought together scientists and engineers from private industry, universities, and the military as well as émigré scientists who had fled to the United States to escape fascism. For the first time America became an international center of scientific research.

Early reversals in the war revealed defects in the equipment and strategic thinking of Allied forces. The success of aircraft against battleships spelled the end of an era in naval warfare. The aircraft carrier and the submarine would become the keys to naval supremacy. The Battle of Britain and the European air war spurred the development of a new generation of fighter planes and long-range bombers. To combat enemy bombers and submarines, English and American scientists rushed to perfect electronic detection devices such as radar and sonar.

While sonar was helping to win the submarine war in the North Atlantic, American submarines were wreaking their own devastation on Japanese shipping in the Pacific. By 1944 the home islands faced serious shortages of vital raw materials. Of the 8 million tons of shipping with which Japan entered the war, American submarines sent 5 million to the bottom of the sea by late 1944. Above the water, the newly developed techniques of radar-controlled naval and antiaircraft gunnery gave American ships a decided edge in crucial sea battles. It was possible to hit targets obscured by darkness, fog, or smoke. One of the most crucial technical advances was also one of the best kept secrets of the war, the proximity fuse. By placing a small radio device in a warhead, scientists created a shell that did not need to hit a target to destroy it. Use of the proximity fuse accounted for the success of American antiaircraft guns against Japanese planes and German V-1 bombs.

Scientific advances saved lives as well as destroying them. New techniques for using blood plasma and whole blood meant that more wounded soldiers could survive. Insecticides, pesticides, and drugs limited the spread of infectious diseases like malaria and syphilis, which are often more deadly than bullets. Penicillin had its first widespread use in World War II. The health of the nation actually improved during the war. Life expectancy rose by three years overall (five years for blacks). Infant mortality was cut by more than a third, and in 1942 the nation recorded its lowest death rate in history.

Science sometimes proved a two-edged sword. The pesticide DDT helped to control malaria and other diseases that are spread by insects. Only later did DDT's dangerous ecological consequences become apparent. Some advances had long-term benefits not fully clear until after the war. In figuring out how to break codes, find submarines, or hit targets from high altitudes, mathematicians often had to deal with complex calculations. To speed their work, engineers designed new machines to manipulate numbers at great speed. Thus the war ushered in the Computer Age.

So, too, did it bring on the Atomic Age. In 1938 German scientists discovered the process of atomic fission: when bombarded by atomic particles, atoms of uranium-235 split, releasing an enormous amount of energy. If properly harnessed, fission could furnish the power to run great cities or the bombs to destroy them. Emigré scientists like Enrico Fermi, Albert Einstein, and Leo Szilard understood all too well the military potential of the German discovery. In 1939 they had alerted President Roosevelt to the possibility that the Nazis were developing atomic weapons. He ordered OSRD to make atomic fission research a top priority. Within a few years over 100,000 scientists, engineers, technicians, and support workers from the United States, Canada, and England at 37 installations across the country were engaged in the largest research and development effort in history, code-named the Manhattan Project.

Atomic bomb development was one of the most tightly guarded secrets of the war. Security was designed to keep the Russians as much as the Germans or Japanese in the dark. Roosevelt and Churchill did not intend to share their atomic monopoly with friend or foe, despite the urging of the respected Danish physicist Niels Bohr, who feared that a lack of international agreement would lead to an arms race. The key to success was not so much secret discoveries, but money (the project cost $2 billion) and industrial, scientific, and technical resources to produce nuclear fuels and a bomb design.

Total War

Under the new conditions of war, air power became crucial to many battles. Control of the air was necessary for amphibious operations as well as for traditional land warfare. Planes could disrupt troop movements, break supply lines, spot enemy formations, and attack defensive fortifications. Air-power strategists had a more aggressive vision for heavy bombers. Large waves of planes could attack industrial and military targets deep in enemy territory, devastate the home front, and cripple the enemy war effort. The first test of such "strategic bombing" came in 1942, when 1134 planes of the British Royal Air Force (RAF) destroyed some

20,000 homes, 1500 stores and offices, and about 60 factories around Cologne, Germany. Horrific as that sounds, the attack did not level the city, as RAF planners had predicted. Indeed, later studies indicated that for all the damage done, strategic bombing did not substantially reduce Axis productivity, which actually increased until the last months of the war. Still, it disrupted Japanese and German industry, brought the war home to the civilian population, and diverted enemy forces from the front to home defense.

Raids on Dresden and on Tokyo symbolized the horrors of the new technology. Dresden, a charming German city almost untouched by the twentieth century, had been largely ignored until February 1945. The RAF hit it first; then, with fires still raging, the American bombing wave struck. A huge inferno drew all the oxygen out of the center city, so that victims who did not burn suffocated. The city and its 60,000 people died. In March 340 American bombers hit Tokyo with incendiary bombs. The resulting "firestorms," whipped by strong winds, leveled 16 square miles, destroyed 267,000 homes, left 83,000 dead, and injured 41,000. The heat was so intense that the water in canals boiled. With long-range air power the traditional "front line" vanished. Everyone became a potential combatant, every village a potential target in a total war.

D-Day and the Fall of the Third Reich

After driving the Germans from North Africa in May 1943, Allied strategists yielded to Churchill's plan to slice into the "soft underbelly of the Axis" by invading Italy through Sicily. Late in July, two weeks after a quarter of a million British and American troops had landed on Sicily, Mussolini fled to German-held northern Italy. Although Italy surrendered early in September, Germany continued to pour in reinforcements. It took the Allies almost a year of bloody fighting to get to Rome, and at the end of the war they had yet to break German lines. Along the eastern front, Soviet armies steadily pushed the Germans out of Russia and back toward Berlin.

In January 1944 General Dwight D. Eisenhower, fresh from battle in North Africa and the Mediterranean, took command of the massive Allied preparations for Operation Overlord, the cross-Channel invasion of the continent. By June all attention focused on the coast of France, for Hitler, of course, knew the Allies were approaching. He suspected they would hit Calais, the French port city closest to the British Isles. Allied planners did their best to convince the Germans that was their plan, even placing fake armaments across the English Channel. On the morning of June 6, 1944, the invasion began—not at Calais but on the less well-fortified beaches of Normandy. Almost 3 million men, 11,000 aircraft, and over 2000 vessels took part in the D-Day operation.

As Allied forces hit the beaches, luck and Eisenhower's meticulous planning favored their cause. German attempts to defeat airborne troops, dropped by parachute behind coastal defenses, left Utah beach lightly defended. Persuaded the Allies still wanted Calais, Hitler delayed the movement of two reserve divisions. His indecision allowed the Allied forces to secure a foothold. Over the next few days more than 1.5 million soldiers landed on the beaches—but they still had to move inland. The hedgerows that separated the fields of frugal Norman farmers provided the Germans with effective barriers against troops and tanks. The Allied advance from Normandy took almost two months, not several weeks as expected.

The complicated logistics of maintaining supply lines were as important as the heroics of troops during the D-Day invasion. Like Ulysses Grant during the Civil War, Dwight Eisenhower was a master of such details.

Once Allied tanks broke through German lines their progress was spectacular. In August Paris was liberated, and by mid-September the Allies had driven the Germans from France and Belgium.

All went well until December 1944, when Allied forces under General Omar N. Bradley stalled in the Ardennes Forest because of fuel shortages. Hitler, risking one last, desperate gamble, threw in his reserves on December 16, 1944. The Germans succeeded in pushing back the Allied lines along a 50-mile bulge toward Bastogne. There the Germans trapped the 101st Airborne Division. When asked to surrender, General Tony MacAuliffe sent back a one-word reply: "Nuts!" His troops held, General George Patton raced to the rescue, and the last German offensive collapsed. The Battle of the Bulge, as it was called, delayed the Allied invasion of Germany by six weeks, but Hitler lost 200,000 men and 600 tanks he could not replace. Little stood between the Allies and Berlin.

Two Roads to Tokyo

In the Pacific, American forces defied the conventional military wisdom. Instead of concentrating military force against a weak point in enemy lines, the American forces were split into two campaigns. The navy favored the tactic of leapfrogging from island to enemy-held island, using amphibious warfare conducted by naval forces and marines. Army General Douglas MacArthur argued for recapturing the Philippines as a staging area for the liberation of China and the invasion of Japan. In the bleak days of 1942 MacArthur—flamboyant and jaunty with his dark sunglasses and corncob pipe—had emerged (with the help of his public relations

Daily Lives

TIME AND TRAVEL

Air Power Shrinks the Globe

War has always been a great accelerator of social change, often in unanticipated ways. So World War II advances in air power and strategic bombing eventually changed the international order. In the short term, both the Allied and Axis powers hoped to use aircraft to damage enemy resources and morale in order to bring about surrender. But the new tactics for accomplishing this goal led to the development of missiles and long-range bombers, whose ultimate consequences included shrinking the effective distances between nations and even realigning international relations.

During World War I, airplanes had played only a secondary role in military strategy. While the popular imagination thrilled to the stories of dogfights and "flying aces," relatively primitive airplanes were hampered by short flying ranges and an inability to carry heavy loads. Between the two wars, airframes grew stronger, engines more powerful, and payloads greater. Air-power strategists began to suggest that concerted waves of planes could attack industrial and military targets deep in enemy territory, which before had remained safe unless ground troops had fought their way overland to reach them. Hitler grasped the strategic possibilities and insisted that Germany's air force as well as its army rearm and modernize.

Once Hitler's bold offensive had subdued France in the opening moves of the war, Air Marshal Herman Goering predicted that bombers from the German *Luftwaffe* would soon bring England to its knees. The Battle of Britain, fought during the winter of 1940–1941, signaled the start of the age of modern air warfare. For the first time in history, one nation tried to conquer another from the skies. Goering's boast failed; England continued doggedly to resist, demonstrating that air-power theorists had exaggerated the potentials of strategic bombing. And while Allied bombing contributed to victory, it succeeded largely through the sustained pattern of destructiveness, not from any startling technological innovation. In the last year of the war heavy bombers dropped almost 2 million tons of bombs on Germany alone, three times as much as in the previous four years.

To ensure the success of aerial warfare, aircraft designers on both sides had to make their planes bigger and faster. On the first major raid the English launched, they used the Wellington bomber, a plane 65 feet long with a wing span of 86 feet and a bomb load of 1500 pounds. By contrast, the B-29s that bombed Hiroshima and Nagasaki only three years later were some 99 feet long, with a wing span of 141 feet and a capacity of up to 10 tons. The Wellington flew 255 miles an hour and cruised as high as 12,000 feet, with a range of 2200 miles, whereas the new B-29s could travel over 350 miles an hour, at altitudes up to 30,000 feet, with a range of up to 5000 miles—more than double the Wellington's. During these same years, German scientists looked to increase the speed and range of their weaponry with a new V-1 pilotless "buzz bomb" (named for the sound of its jet engine) and the V-2 rocket, the first true missile used as a weapon. Launched from bases in Europe, V-1's and V-2's easily reached targets in England. For all the terror they inspired, however, they were not accurate and the Germans could not launch them in sufficient quantities to mount a decisive threat.

Germany and Britain also rushed to produce the first fighter planes with jet

Daily Lives

The Boeing Stratocruiser was a modified version of the B-29 that carried atomic bombs to Hiroshima and Nagasaki. As a commercial airliner, it made transatlantic travel a practical reality by virtue of its range and carrying capacity.

engines. Hitler foolishly insisted on using Germany's jets as bombers—where sheer speed was not essential—rather than as fast interceptors, which would have given German pilots an edge in air combat. Too few were produced to make a real difference, and technical problems made the new "rocket" planes as dangerous to their pilots as the enemy. Similarly, the Japanese had designed a piloted "rocket bomb" that could race on its suicidal mission at over 500 miles an hour. None ever hit an Allied ship.

Although these technologies proved indecisive in the war, the competition to create longer range aircraft capable of carrying heavier payloads led to far-reaching changes in the postwar world. With some modifications the B-29 bomber was reborn as the Boeing Stratocruiser, capable of carrying over 80 passengers from the United States to Europe without stopping to refuel. The British, having pioneered jet propulsion, introduced by 1952 the first commercial jet airliner, the De Havilland Comet. By 1955, when Boeing introduced its 707 jet, 200 passengers could be carried up to 4000 miles at 550 miles an hour. It was now possible to work in both New York and Los Angeles on the same day. Cheap flights from Puerto Rico to New York encouraged hundreds of thousands of Hispanic immigrants to come to the continental United States. Travel to Europe, Hawaii, or the Orient was no longer restricted to the very rich.

Equally significant, the technology of air power encouraged a fundamental change in most Americans' perception of the world. In 1919, at the end of World War I, Americans were determined not to become involved again in the affairs of Europe. Between the wars Arthur Vandenberg, a Republican senator from Michigan, was one of the nation's leading isolationists. That was before Pearl Harbor and before Vandenberg visited London during the war. As German V-1 and V-2 missiles brought terror from the skies, the senator came to believe that an isolationist policy no longer made sense. Physical distance would never again be a safeguard from attack, because air power had reshaped the strategic map of the world. The United States was now a matter of hours, not days, away from both friends and potential enemies.

officers) as America's only military hero. To refuse him command would erode public faith in the war effort. For that reason the Combined Chiefs of Staff had given him control of the southwestern Pacific. MacArthur believed the future of America lay in the Far East and that the Pacific theater, not the European, should have top priority. He warred constantly with his superiors in Washington, complaining that they were scheming to deny him troops and supplies. In March 1943 the military chiefs agreed to his plan for a westward advance along the northern coast of New Guinea toward the Philippines and Tokyo.

By July 1944 the navy's leapfrogging campaign had reached the Marianas, east of the Philippines. From there B-29 bombers could reach the Japanese home islands. As a result, Admiral Chester W. Nimitz, commander of the Pacific Fleet, proposed bypassing the Philippines in favor of a direct attack on Formosa (now Taiwan). MacArthur, outraged, accused the U.S. Joint Chiefs of Staff and the president of breaking a promise he had made "to eighteen million Christian Filipinos that the Americans would return." President Roosevelt himself came to Hawaii to resolve the impasse between Nimitz and MacArthur, giving MacArthur the green light. Backed by over 100 ships of the Pacific Fleet, MacArthur splashed ashore on the island of Leyte in October 1944 to announce his return.

The decision to invade the Philippines led to savage fighting until the war ended. As the retreating Japanese armies left Manila, they tortured and slaughtered tens of thousands of Filipino civilians. The United States suffered 62,000 casualties redeeming MacArthur's pledge to return. A spectacular U.S. Navy victory at the Battle of Leyte Gulf spelled the end of the Japanese Imperial Navy as a fighting force.

WAR AND DIPLOMACY

The coordination of Russian, British, and American efforts in far-flung theaters of war went beyond military strategy. The Allies had to negotiate constantly in order to set supply priorities, choose commanders in combined operations, and divide and administer conquered territories. Inevitably, the questions of war slid into questions about the peace that would follow. What would happen to occupied territories? How would the Axis powers be punished? After World War I the powers of Europe met at Versailles to mete out justice, peace, and a stable world order. Those dreams had collapsed in a mere 20 years; now millions more were dead. The peace had to be won as well as the war. If not, the cycle of violence might never end.

War Aims

Although Roosevelt and Churchill had spelled out their war aims in the Atlantic Charter of 1941, the Allies did not necessarily accept all its provisions. Churchill himself had reservations about the principle of self-determination. It was all very well for restive colonials to be given a greater voice in their own affairs, he argued, but he had "not become the King's First Minister to preside over the liquidation of the British Empire." Churchill also believed that only a stable European balance of power, not an international agency, could preserve peace. In his view the

Soviet Union was the greatest threat to postwar peace, and so he courted the United States as a counterweight.

Suspicious of the capitalist powers, Premier Joseph Stalin seemed unwilling to trust Russian security to their goodwill or to an international body. He left no doubt that the Soviet Union would ignore the Atlantic Charter whenever it conflicted with Soviet interests. An expansive notion of Russian security defined his war aims. Twice in the last 20 years Germany had marched through eastern Europe to invade Russia, and expelling them during this latest drive cost the Soviet Union some 20 million people—nearly 8 percent of its population. (By contrast the United States lost less than 0.5 percent of its population.) For future protection Stalin expected to annex the Baltic states, once Russian provinces, along with bits of Finland and Romania and about half of prewar Poland. In eastern Europe and other border areas such as Iran, Korea, and Turkey, he wanted "friendly" neighbors. It soon became apparent that "friendly" meant regimes subservient to Moscow. As for Asia, Stalin hoped to drive Japan off the mainland and return Russia to the position it had held under the czars.

The kind of peace Franklin Roosevelt sought was unclear. He opposed Churchill's balance of power plan and did not share his almost obsessive distrust of Russia. At the same time, he wished to allay Stalin's suspicions and bring the Soviet Union into an international peacekeeping system. Early on, Roosevelt promoted his own balance of power, which he called the "Four Policemen." The Soviet Union, Great Britain, the United States, and China would guarantee peace through military cooperation. The concept was badly flawed. China was hardly a great power and could not keep peace in Asia; Roosevelt had included it only because he wanted an international order, not an exclusively Western one. Furthermore, the Four Policemen did not involve a major continental power aside from the Soviet Union. The security of Europe would rest on Stalin's cooperation. Finally, smaller countries, largely pawns in this system, might not take kindly to the four cops patrolling the beat.

By 1944 Roosevelt had discarded the Four Policemen in favor of an international organization based on a new League of Nations. Having served under Woodrow Wilson in World War I, Roosevelt shared his internationalism and particularly his faith in collective security. Equally important, a broad spectrum of influential Americans wanted to resurrect the League. This time, however, all the great powers would participate, including the United States. Whether Churchill and Stalin—or the American people as a whole—would accept the idea was not yet clear.

The Road to Yalta

The outlines of a postwar settlement—and the sticking points where a settlement was most unlikely—were worked out in a series of summit conferences of the Allied leaders. In January 1943, with Rommel on the defensive in North Africa and Morocco newly liberated, President Roosevelt met Winston Churchill at Casablanca. Stalin had not come; he never left Soviet-occupied territory. He was angry about the delay of a second front in the west and worried that the Americans and British might make a separate peace with Germany, leaving the Soviet Union alone to continue the war. To reassure him, Roosevelt announced with Churchill's blessings that the war would end only with the "unconditional surrender" of all enemies. Just what that meant was not always clear, even to Roosevelt.

By November Italy's surrender was in hand, the war against Germany was going well, and Churchill and Roosevelt agreed to make the hazardous trip to Teheran, Iran, so the Big Three could meet for the first time. Here each leader had a chance to take the personal measure of the other. ("Seems very confident," Roosevelt said of Stalin, "very sure of himself, moves slowly—altogether quite impressive.") The president used the occasion to work his considerable charm on Stalin, teasing Churchill for Stalin's benefit, keeping it up "until Stalin was laughing with me, and it was then that I called him 'Uncle Joe.'" Stalin finally won the commitment to the D-Day operation he had so long been seeking; in return he promised to launch a spring offensive to prevent the transfer of German troops to the west. He also reaffirmed the earlier Russian pledge to join the war against Japan once Germany was beaten. In the matter of winning the war, the Allies hammered together a united front. Teheran was the high point of cooperation among the Big Three.

There had been differences, however, most significantly over the postwar peace rather than the conduct of the war. How large these differences were became clearer in February 1945, at the final meeting of the Big Three, at the Russian resort city of Yalta, located on the Black Sea. By then, Russian, British, and American troops were all closing in on Germany. Roosevelt arrived tired, ashen. The trip to Yalta would have taxed the resources of a robust young man, and Roosevelt was neither youthful nor healthy. At 62, limited by his paralysis, he also suffered from heart disease, hypertension, and hardening of the arteries. His doctors had urged him to follow a less demanding schedule and he listened patiently, then ignored their advice, keeping to his busy schedule without reducing his consumption of cigarettes and cocktails. And he was mindful that although Germany was all but beaten, Japan still held out in the Pacific. Under no circumstances did he want Stalin to withdraw his promises to enter the fight against Japan or to join a postwar international organization.

Churchill, for his part, arrived at Yalta profoundly mistrustful of Soviet intentions. As Germany and Japan disintegrated, he saw vacuums of power opening up in Europe and Asia, which the Russians appeared only too eager and able to fill. Most diplomats in the American State Department and a growing number of military officers and politicians agreed. It seemed to them that Britain and the United States needed to work together to rein in Soviet ambitions. The problem was particularly evident in the disagreements over Poland, raised at first during the Teheran Conference. Hitler's invasion of Poland had touched off the war, and Britain fought in part to ensure the survival of an independent Polish state.

Stalin, on the other hand, saw Poland as the historic corridor of invasion for Russia's enemies. As Soviet troops reentered Poland, he insisted he would recognize only the Communist-controlled government at Lublin, whereas Britain and the United States backed an exile government in London. Stalin also demanded that Russia receive territory in eastern Poland, for which the Poles would be compensated with German lands. That was hardly the "self-determination" called for in the Atlantic Charter. Roosevelt saw that he could not force Stalin's hand, since Soviet troops occupied all of Poland. So he proposed a compromise. Poland would have a coalition government, including representatives from both Lublin and London. Free elections held after the war would settle the question of who should rule. The Soviets would also receive the territory they demanded in eastern Poland, and the western boundary would be established later.

Similarly, the Allies remained at odds about Germany's position in the postwar era. Stalin was determined that Germany would never invade Russia again. Many Americans shared his desire to have Germany punished and its war-making capacity eliminated. At the Teheran Conference, Roosevelt and Stalin proposed that the Third Reich be drastically dismembered, split into five powerless parts. In the following months Secretary of the Treasury Henry Morgenthau had even come up with a plan to dismantle German industry and limit Germany to an agrarian economy. Churchill briefly accepted the idea but then reconsidered, fearful of repeating the economic disaster that followed World War I. A healthy European economy required an industrialized Germany. And Churchill was much less eager to bring low the nation that was the most natural barrier to Russian expansion.

As with Poland, the Big Three avoided a clear definition of terms for Germany. It would be divided into separate occupation zones (France would receive a zone carved from British and American territory). Four powers would jointly occupy Berlin, while an Allied Control Council supervised the national government. Reparations became the final sticking point. Stalin insisted on $20 billion to compensate Russia for its wartime losses. He needed German resources to rebuild his own shattered economy. Churchill and Roosevelt accepted that figure only as a "basis for discussion" at a later date.

When the Big Three turned their attention to the Far East, Stalin held a trump card. Fierce Japanese resistance on Okinawa and Iwo Jima, where American casualties exceeded 70,000, plus the horror of kamikaze attacks, persuaded Roosevelt that only a bloody invasion of the home islands could force Japan to surrender. He came to Yalta determined to win Stalin's agreement to enter the Pacific war at the earliest date. Many British and Americans feared Stalin would wait until the invasion of Japan before sending his troops into Manchuria to reap the fruits of victory. Instead Stalin agreed to declare war within three months of Germany's defeat, but his price was high. Stalin wanted to reclaim Russia's losses in the Russo-Japanese War of 1904–1906: renewed control of the Kuril Islands and the island of Sakhalin, the port of Darien, and control over the Chinese Eastern and South Manchurian railroads. Although Stalin had been supporting the Communist forces under Mao Tse-tung, in return for the Allied concessions in Asia he was willing to sign a friendship pact with Chiang Kai-shek's nationalist government.

The agreement on China, like all the agreements reached at Yalta, depended on Stalin's willingness to cooperate, in this case with Chiang. In public Roosevelt put the best possible face on what Allied leaders had achieved. A new world organization would "provide the greatest opportunity in all history" to secure the peace. And as if to lay to rest the specter of isolation that had destroyed Wilson's dream, Roosevelt told Congress, "We shall take responsibility for world collaboration, or we shall have to bear the responsibility for another world conflict." Privately Roosevelt was less sanguine. He told his friend Sam Rosenman as they worked on his speech to Congress that he doubted, "when the chips were down, Stalin would be able to carry out and deliver what he had agreed to."

The Fallen Leader

The Yalta Conference marked one of the last and most controversial chapters of Franklin Roosevelt's presidency. Critics charged that the concessions to Stalin had been too generous—a violation of Atlantic Charter principles and a threat to

American national interests. Poland had been betrayed; China sold out; the United Nations crippled at birth. Those critics offered various explanations for the president's failures: his ill health, his naiveté, his hubris, even communist infiltration of his entourage.

Yalta was no "sellout"; it was a diplomatic success for Russia based on its military role in Europe. Roosevelt conceded little that Stalin could not have taken for himself. By 1945, after four years of bloody sacrifice, Soviet troops controlled most of eastern Europe. The president had come to Yalta with two goals. Above all he wanted to guarantee Soviet entry into the Pacific war. That he achieved (though the successful development of the atom bomb would change the significance of Stalin's declaration of war). Second, Roosevelt hoped that Stalin would honor the spirit of the Yalta pledges by holding free elections and promoting self-determination in areas liberated by Russian armies. Even Winston Churchill, an outspoken critic of Soviet ambitions, concluded that although "our hopeful assumptions were soon to be falsified . . . they were the only ones possible at the time."

Roosevelt himself sensed the hollowness of Stalin's vows. On March 23, 1945, he told a friend, "We can't do business with Stalin. He has broken every one of the promises he made at Yalta." That did not mean that Roosevelt had lost his faith in postwar cooperation. Rather, he seemed to have decided that future deals with the Russians must involve a quid pro quo, or trade-off. In that spirit, the president had already refused to share atomic secrets or to commit the United States to financing postwar reconstruction without political concessions.

What peace Roosevelt would have achieved we can never know. He returned from Yalta visibly ill. On April 12, 1945, while sitting for his portrait at his vacation home in Warm Springs, Georgia, he complained of a "terrific headache," then suddenly fell unconscious. Two hours later Roosevelt was dead, the victim of a cerebral hemorrhage that deprived many Americans of the only president they had ever known. Not since the assassination of Lincoln had the nation been so grieved by a loss. Under Roosevelt's leadership government had become a protector, the president a father and friend, and the United States the leader in the struggle against Axis tyranny. Eleanor recalled how many Americans later told her that "they missed the way the President used to talk to them. . . . There was a real dialogue between Franklin and the people."

Franklin Roosevelt guided the nation through the deepest depression in its history and then to the verge of global greatness. The man who replaced him was Harry S. Truman. "Who the hell is Harry Truman?" the chief of staff had asked when Truman was nominated for the vice presidency in 1944. Into his untested hands now fell the awesome responsibility for victory in war and peace.

SIGNIFICANT EVENTS

1921–1922	Washington Naval Disarmament Conference
1922	Fordney–McCumber Tariff
1923	German inflation
1924	Dawes Plan
1926–1933	United States involvement in Nicaragua's internal affairs
1928	Kellogg–Briand Pact
1929	Crash signals onset of worldwide economic crisis
1930	Hawley–Smoot Tariff
1931–1932	Japan invades Manchuria; Stimson Doctrine
1933	London Economic Conference; Roosevelt recognizes the Soviet Union
1935	Nye Committee hearings; first Neutrality Act
1936	Second Neutrality Act; Buenos Aires Conference
1937	Third Neutrality Act (cash-and-carry); Roosevelt's quarantine speech; *Panay* incident
1938	Munich meeting; settlement of Mexican appropriation crisis
1939	Fall of Czechoslovakia; Molotov–Ribbentrop Pact; World War II begins in Europe
1940	Germany launches blitzkrieg against Low Countries and France; America-First Committee and Committee to Defend America by Aiding the Allies formed; Roosevelt supports preparedness and peacetime draft; destroyers-for-bases deal; Roosevelt wins third term
1941	Congress adopts Lend-Lease Act; Germany invades Soviet Union; Roosevelt and Churchill sign Atlantic Charter; Japan occupies Indochina; Roosevelt imposes embargo against Japan; Pearl Harbor attacked; Hitler and Mussolini declare war on the United States
1942	Declaration of the United Nations; submarine war in the Atlantic; Bataan and Corregidor fall; battles of Guadalcanal, Coral Sea, and Midway fought; American and British troops invade North Africa; WACs receive full status; Manhattan Project begins
1943	Churchill and Roosevelt announce unconditional surrender at Casablanca; British-American forces invade Italy; Big Three meet at Teheran
1944	D-Day invasion of France; Battle of the Bulge; U.S. forces return to Philippines; island-hopping campaign reaches Guam and Saipan; Allies invade Germany
1945	Yalta Conference; Roosevelt dies; Truman becomes president

29

War on the Home Front

I n 1940 Washington was still a sleepy provincial southern city with but one function, the operation of a national government. Unlike Paris, London, or Rome, it had no cosmopolitan glitter. It had just one legitimate theater and a hopelessly inept professional baseball team. Haute cuisine ran to the deep-fat fried. Washington's summers were so hot and steamy the British ambassadors were entitled to wear the same outfits, including pith helmets, that diplomats wore in Southeast Asia and tropical Africa. A third of the city was black, rigidly and completely segregated and except for a small middle class forced to live in slum shacks without plumbing or electricity. Young Americans eager to make their mark in the world avoided Washington. The 200,000 people with government jobs were clerks, secretaries, and bureaucrats paid to move paper, not to worry about politics and public policy.

Ten years of the New Deal had done little to shake the city out of its provincial ways. The city's small southern social elite largely ignored the army of social workers, economists, labor specialists, and lawyers who had come to town eager to heal the nation's sick economy. By 1940 New Deal efforts had shown mixed results. Some 10 million workers and about a third of all blacks were still unemployed. New Deal agencies by 1940 took little initiative beyond doling out public monies to their various constituents of poor farmers, unemployed workers, and special interest groups. Many New Dealers had left Washington once it was clear that the conservatives had frustrated the spirit of reform.

Leon Henderson was not among them. He believed that the war engulfing Europe and Asia offered an opportunity to bring new vitality to New Deal programs. As foreign war orders heated up the economy, critical raw materials needed for planes, ships, and guns went to make automobiles, radios, and toasters. Shortages, black marketeering, and inflation threatened to disrupt the recovery from 10 years of depression. Henderson had a plan to turn a motley collection of bureaucracies into an efficient government capable of managing a vast wartime economy. Even a year before Pearl Harbor, he understood that the capacity of the United States to produce war goods could spell the difference between victory and defeat. The economy needed more central direction, more planning, if it was to produce on the scale required for a global effort to defeat fascism.

Henderson's friends were not surprised that he thought in such broad terms. They considered him a brilliant, if decidedly eccentric economist. He had a volcanic temper, a midriff that overflowed his waistline, and a way of stepping on

With war industries depending so heavily on the labor of women and minorities, patriotic posters exhorted them to support the troops overseas. "WOW," ordinarily a slang term for an attractive woman, here stands for Women Ordnance Workers.

political toes that ought to have been avoided. When angered he had been known to punch taxi drivers and slam his fist through a table. Now his anger was directed at government inefficiency. To lead his attack he needed Roosevelt's full support. So he did what New Dealers had long done when they had a big headache; he took it to "Poppa." The president's secretary gave him an hour to make his case.

Henderson arrived at the Oval Office with thick stacks of papers, a swirl of graphs and charts, and a young lawyer, David Ginsburg, to help explain it all. Roosevelt took one look at the armada of paper and must have sensed the magnitude of what Henderson had in mind. So he did what he always did when confronting issues he hoped to avoid; he launched a diversionary counterattack. From his desk he produced papers of his own. These were blueprints for temporary office buildings that the president had agreed must be built along the Mall that stretched between Capitol Hill and the Washington Monument. The various defense agencies had grown so fast that the government had run out of space to house them.

Long years in government had taught Roosevelt that temporary structures, whether buildings or agencies, had a way of becoming permanent. Some of the hideous buildings thrown up during World War I were still in use. That would not happen this time, the president insisted. The "tempos" would be so ugly that nobody could want to keep them and so flimsy they would collapse in less than 10 years. What did Henderson and Ginsburg think of them, he wanted to know. For an hour the three discussed the blueprints—where the doors would go, how many floors the buildings should have, and just how ugly they might be. Henderson fidgeted as his precious hour frittered away. By the time he left, nothing had been decided, none of his questions heard or answered, and nothing done to prepare the government or the nation for war.

Roosevelt, like the nation, was simply not yet prepared to face the complex task of coordinating so vast an undertaking. He knew little and cared less about the details of copper shortages that disrupted munitions manufacturing, of railroad bottlenecks that slowed the shipment of Allied war goods, or a thousand and one other components of the emerging war economy. Only when matters became critical would he find some way to deal with them. Thus when war came, the nation had yet to transform itself into the arsenal of democracy.

The war condensed into four years social, economic, and political changes that might ordinarily take decades to achieve. With 12 million men and women in uniform, labor-hungry war factories gobbled up the jobless. Women, blacks, and Hispanics found unprecedented opportunity. Unemployment virtually disappeared. After years of depression-spawned penny-pinching, people had money again. Where war industries located, boom towns sprang up overnight. The West Coast, for example, had less than 10 percent of the population in 1940 yet it produced 20 percent of all war goods. Experts estimated that 25 to 50 years of economic growth had been squeezed into 3 years. Prefabricated houses, much like Roosevelt's tempos, appeared all over the country to contain the workers as small towns turned into cities overnight. Federal authorities ordered 42,000 units at the start of 1942 alone. Within a year they had ordered tens of thousands more. Most communities expected to tear them down once the war ended and the workers moved on.

Like other cities throughout the nation, Washington too became a boom town with prefabricated offices and housing. In the year after Pearl Harbor 70,000 people arrived; government employment grew by over 5000 people each month.

The population of the metropolitan area soared to over a million. Traffic congested the city streets at all hours of the day. New government war agencies proliferated. To the TVA and SEC were added the WPB, OPA, WMC, BEW, NWLB, FEA, and worst of all an agency that issued regulations for plumbers—the PWPGSJSISIACWPB. No one in Washington could have identified what all those initials stood for.

These agencies would not all simply disappear when the war ended. Some were reborn as postwar agencies; thus the OSS (Office of Strategic Services) became the CIA (Central Intelligence Agency). Others shifted their functions and many of their war workers to permanent agencies like the War and Navy departments. Power became more centralized in the federal government. Like government, big business, big labor, and big agriculture grew bigger still and sent their representatives to Washington to lobby for government support.

None of this happened with the kind of planning that Henderson had hoped to achieve. His own efforts to impose rationing and fight inflation as director of the Office of Price Administration mired him in endless controversy. Roosevelt dumped him in 1943. Henderson had his measure of vindication because the tempos, like so much of the largely unplanned expansion of government and big business, survived the end of the war. No matter how ugly, no matter how flimsy, they defied Roosevelt's careful attempt at planned obsolescence. Most remained in use until the 1960s, housing all those offices necessary in a government that had assumed responsibilities on a global scale. World War II had transformed Washington from a provincial southern city into the capital of the free world.

THE SINEWS OF WAR

In December 1941, within weeks of Pearl Harbor, Franklin Roosevelt announced production schedules so ambitious that few Americans believed they were possible. The president's goals staggered the imagination: 60,000 airplanes, 45,000 tanks, 20,000 antiaircraft guns, and 8 million tons of merchant shipping by the end of 1942. The figures were so astonishing partly because the shortages facing the United States were so severe. At some training bases, recruits drilled with broomsticks rather than rifles. Pilots flew training planes made of plywood. Unless the American economy expanded quickly and efficiently, the war might be lost in the factories before it could be won on the battlefields.

War Production

The process of gearing up was far from smooth. Scarred by the Depression, manufacturers resisted expanding plant capacity. Revived consumer spending encouraged production of civilian rather than military goods. Roosevelt was reluctant to make enemies of business leaders whose support he needed for war conversion. Thus he initially gave federal war agencies few of the powers Henderson envisioned. Severe bottlenecks had resulted. Electric power, steel, aluminum, railroad equipment, and skilled workers were all in short supply. The military agencies allocated scarce resources to favored producers so generously that parts, raw materials, and labor were in short supply. The key to successful conversion lay with the automobile industry, which consumed some 80 percent of the nation's rubber, 18 percent of its steel, and 14 percent of its copper. Domestic automobile sales had grown in 1941, so automakers were reluctant to convert to war production. Until they began to make badly needed tanks and planes, industrial output would lag far behind growing war demand.

In early 1942 President Roosevelt recognized the need for more direct control. He established the War Production Board (WPB) under the direction of former Sears, Roebuck president Donald M. Nelson. On paper, Nelson's powers were impressive. He was charged with responsibility for nothing less than administering the war economy. Under the Second War Powers Act of 1942 Congress gave the WPB authority to allocate resources and organize factories in whatever way promoted national defense. In one of its first acts, the WPB ordered an end to all car and truck production. Once accustomed to new models every year, the American people would now drive their present cars until the end of the war.

In practice, Nelson was scarcely the dictator the economy needed. Other federal agencies with their own czars controlled petroleum, rubber, and labor resources. Nelson also allowed the military agencies to continue their own procurement. They placed most of their orders with the largest industrial firms, with whom they had long done business. Not only did small businesses suffer, but the concentration of economic power in the hands of large corporations increased significantly. Rather than exercise controversial authority over industry, Nelson offered lucrative inducements to encourage voluntary compliance. Even then, it was not until the late spring of 1942 that the auto industry actually ceased producing cars.

By 1943 President Roosevelt realized that Nelson could not bring order out of chaos. Bottlenecks still hampered production. The president created the new Office of War Mobilization (OWM) and installed Supreme Court Justice James F. Byrnes as director. Widely respected as a political facilitator, Byrnes became the dictator the economy needed. His authority was so great and his access to Roosevelt so direct that he became known as the "assistant president." By assuming control over vital materials such as steel, aluminum, and copper, OWM allocated them on a more systematic basis. The logjams disappeared.

The Story of Rubber

The history of industrial mobilization is too complicated to tell in a short space. Every industry from transportation to petroleum to metals to agriculture had its special problems meeting the needs of war. The story of rubber is representative.

Rubber may not seem as vital as steel or gasoline, but jeeps, trucks, tanks, planes, and a host of other machines cannot function without it. Each tank required about a ton of rubber; each battleship as many as 75 tons. By 1942 war planners realized that the United States faced a crippling shortage. Before Pearl Harbor, 90 percent of raw rubber was imported from Southeast Asia. War with Japan cut off the source of supply. Prewar imports from South America amounted to only a trickle. Synthetic rubber was a possible substitute, but the United States produced only 40,000 tons in 1941, when almost a million were needed.

What had caused this shortfall, and, more important, what could be done to remedy it? Assistant Attorney General Thurman Arnold offered a shocking answer to the first question. The Standard Oil Company of New Jersey (later Exxon) had developed methods for producing a synthetic rubber called Buna-S. Standard had then entered a cartel agreement with a German chemical company, I. G. Farben, which gave Farben control over the patents. Worse yet, Standard had maintained the cartel even after Germany declared war! Once Arnold began an antitrust suit in 1942 Standard agreed to turn over the patents to the government. The delay cost crucial months in launching the synthetic rubber industry in America.

Standard Oil was not the only company exposed. Senator Harry S. Truman, head of the watchdog committee for defense industries, opened hearings on corporate collusion, while Arnold prepared antitrust cases against General Electric, Du Pont, and other major corporations with similar patent-pooling agreements. The War and Navy departments overruled him. They feared that businesses would concentrate on fighting the suits rather than producing war goods. After 1943 antitrust enforcement took a holiday.

Whatever the antitrust policies of the government, synthetic rubber would take time to produce. To supplement supplies, Roosevelt launched a drive to collect scrap rubber. He urged Americans to turn in their "old tires, old rubber raincoats, old garden hose, rubber shoes, bathing caps, [and] gloves." The president was after more than rubber. His appeal stoked the volunteer spirit that kept the nation behind the war. Whenever possible, the president preferred voluntarism to the compulsion of law. It worked. Americans surrendered over 450,000 tons of scrap in just four weeks. Even though most of it was never actually used, the drive allowed people to contribute to the war effort.

Conservation turned out to be more productive. If people drove less, they could keep their tires longer. Gasoline rationing was one way to limit auto use. But like so many good ideas, rationing offended special interests. Oil companies resisted any limit to consumption and state governors worried about the loss of revenues with reduced gasoline taxes. Unhappier still were the motorists for whom unlimited driving was linked to freedom. One party leader eager to avoid retribution from angry drivers in the 1942 congressional elections suggested that "an appeal by the President for voluntary cooperation will get patriotic support and will be politically safer." So Roosevelt created a nonpartisan committee that proposed mandatory gasoline rationing and a crash program for manufacturing synthetic rubber, which Roosevelt imposed only after the elections.

When war cut off the United States from its rubber supply in Malaysia, old tires were recycled to help meet the shortage. Most Americans were unable to replace their car tires during the four years the United States was at war. The manufacturers of synthetic rubber eventually eased the crisis.

Synthetic rubber rather than rationing finally resolved the crisis. To create this new industry, the administration made several decisions that illustrate how the war accelerated industrial consolidation. Roosevelt appointed William M. Jeffers, a business executive, as rubber director in late 1942. Jeffers, in turn, staffed his agency with executives from the rubber industry. The government then spent over $700 million to build new plants around the country. For a token fee it leased the plants to established companies, which ran them for a guaranteed profit. In addition, the industry chose to use a petroleum process for Buna-S rather than one based on grain alcohol, which American farmers supported.

By 1944 Jeffers' agency had ended the rubber shortage. The synthetic process produced some 800,000 tons of rubber, roughly 87 percent of annual need. One plant in West Virginia produced as much rubber as 20 million trees. There would be a price to pay. Synthetic production caused far more pollution than conventional methods. And after the war, the large rubber companies bought the war factories for about one-tenth of the actual cost. Companies like Goodyear and Firestone became even larger and more entrenched. The story of rubber, with both its successes and hidden costs, could be repeated for most industries.

The Miracle of Production

During World War II America worked a miracle of production as important to victory as any battle. Two years after Pearl Harbor American factories doubled the output of Germany, Italy, and Japan combined. From 1939 to 1945 the gross national product grew from $91 billion to $166 billion. (In World War I it had not changed significantly.) Manufacturing rose by 96 percent and transportation volume by 109 percent. Shipbuilding increased by almost 2000 percent. What made this possible was not only centralized planning but also massive conversion of industries, large and small. While the "Big Three"—Ford, General Motors, and Chrysler—generated some 20 percent of all war goods, small business also played a vital role. A manufacturer of model trains, for example, made bomb fuses.

Henry J. Kaiser, a California industrialist, symbolized the creative financing and management that made such an accomplishment possible. His lobbyists in Washington found him generous government loans for building factories. He also circumvented restrictions to find the steel he needed. By offering extravagant wages and benefits, including day care for the children of working mothers, he lured workers to his new shipyards, most of which were located on the West Coast. By applying assembly line techniques he reduced the time required to build cargo vessels (known as Liberty ships) from almost a year to 56 days. His yards finished one in a record 14 days. Speed had its price: Liberty ships were slow and barely seaworthy. (One of them actually split in half at its launching.) Despite an occasional misstep, Kaiser built ships in the quantity the war effort demanded.

The aircraft industry also transformed the industrial landscape of the West Coast. In 1939 aircraft factories employed about 46,000 workers and built almost 6000 planes. When production peaked in 1944, the industry had 2.1 million workers producing almost 100,000 planes. Most of the new factories were located around Los Angeles, San Diego, and Seattle, where large labor pools, temperate climates, and available land made the locations attractive.

The military relied on large, established firms in part because they had more experience producing in large volume. At the same time lucrative war contracts helped large corporations increase their dominance over the economy. In 1939 firms with over 500 employees produced just under half the nation's goods. This total had risen to 62 percent in 1944. Workers in companies with over 10,000 employees amounted to just 13 percent of the work force in 1939; by 1944 they comprised over 30 percent.

In agriculture a similar phenomenon occurred. The number of sharecroppers and tenants dropped by a third, the farm population in general by almost a fifth. Yet farm productivity increased by 30 percent. This was achieved by consolidating small farms into large ones, using more tractors, and spreading more artificial fertilizers. Large commercial farming by corporations rather than individuals (later called "agribusiness") came to dominate the agricultural sector. Its political agents in the Farm Bureau Federation guaranteed high commodity prices and a powerful voice in Washington after the war.

Almost as important as the benefits of rising wages, increased savings, and higher status were less tangible gains that came from new pride in work done for a common cause. Civilians volunteered for civil defense, hospitals, or the many scrap drives. Tiny "victory" gardens added 8 million tons of food to the harvest in 1943; car pooling conserved millions of tires; deferred consumption limited inflation. Children became "Uncle Sam's Scrappers" and "Tin-Can Colonels" as they scoured vacant lots for valuable trash. One 13-year-old in Maywood, Illinois, collected over 100 tons of paper between Pearl Harbor and D-Day. Movie stars donated their talents to sell war bonds. Morale ran high because people believed that every contribution, no matter how small, helped defeat the Axis.

WAR WORK

War production brought back prosperity, but not without stresses. Unemployment, which stood at almost 7 million in 1940, virtually disappeared by 1944. Jeff Davies, president of Hoboes of America, reported in 1942 that 2 million of his members were "off the road." In retirement communities like San Diego nearly 4 retirees in 10 returned to work. Employers, eager to overcome the labor shortage, welcomed handicapped workers. The hearing impaired found jobs in deafening factories; dwarfs became aircraft inspectors because they were able to crawl inside wings and other cramped quarters. By the summer of 1943 nearly 3 million children aged 12 to 17 were working. Mail deliverers were in such short supply that the Post Office began to zone and number the nation's cities.

By 1945 average income had jumped to nearly $3000 a year, twice what it had been in 1939. Farm income rose by 250 percent. The distribution of wealth shifted in favor of those with lower incomes. The top 5 percent, who had received about a quarter of all income in 1940, dropped to 16 percent in 1944 (though their real income actually rose). Personal savings tripled. Demands for loans dropped so dramatically that banks were charging interest rates of only 2.5 percent.

War and Consumption

Newly affluent Americans often discovered that store shelves were empty of the goods they wanted most. Whether essentials such as food and clothing or luxuries

Daily Lives

CLOTHING AND FASHION

Dress on the Home Front

World War II dislocated American lives in endless ways. Millions went into the armed services; tens of millions moved to new areas to work in war industries. For most of those who left home, high war wages and the exposure to new opportunities compensated for the disruption of leaving familiar ways behind. Frankie Cooper, for one, decided the time had come to leave the family chicken farm in rural Kentucky, where she had lived for all her 21 years. Together with her husband and two small children she headed to East St. Louis, an industrial city on the Illinois bank of the Mississippi River.

In Kentucky Cooper had lived without indoor plumbing, electricity, a telephone, or department stores. She had never driven a car and made most of her dresses from chicken-feed sacks. In East St. Louis Cooper discovered a new world. War work brought her and her husband a prosperity they had never known. Now she could afford to buy clothes off the rack, ready made. Having never worn stockings, Cooper did not mind that silks and nylons were in short supply. A woman could always resort to painted-on stockings, or leg makeup, so long as she was careful to paint the seam straight.

Newfound prosperity made it much easier to live with wartime restrictions. The War Production Board designed rules to save on scarce materials and promote efficiency in the workplace. By 1942 it had banned full skirts, pleats, patch pockets (rule L-85, "no fabric over fabric"), and zippers. Order M-217 sought to conserve leather by limiting shoes to six colors. In an effort to save wool, the government forbade the manufacture of suits with two pairs of pants (which wore out faster than coats), vests, double-breasted lapels, and cuffs. Most of the changes were intended to be so subtle that old suits would not seem out of style. A new look might stimulate "a buying rush for 'victory suits,' which would defeat the conservation aim of the order."

Shortages forced the WPB to order a reduction in the fabric for women's bathing suits as well. Gone were the single-piece suits with billowing skirts. In came the two-piece look featuring a bare midriff. The *Wall Street Journal* concluded that "the two-piece bathing suit now is tied in with the war as closely as the zipperless dress and the pleatless skirt." After surveying women to find out which cosmetics were essential to morale, the War Production Board ruled that bath oil was in, bath salts out, and that face powder, lipstick, rouge, and deodorant were crucial.

Many changes came without any government coercion. The military cut of women's coats, low-cut shoes for comfort on the job, shorter hair less likely to catch in machinery, and simple jumpers or pinafores made to look like uniforms were all practical adjustments to wartime necessity. Freed from the domination of Parisian styles, American designers developed their own look. Wide, padded shoulders in both men's and women's suits gave way to a more natural shoulder and, for women, bare arms. Ballerina-length gowns replaced floor-length evening dresses. Smaller hats that complemented the natural styles displaced the large, frilly ones popular during the 1930s. Interchangeable skirts and blouses, coupled with hats, gloves, purses, and other accessories, allowed women to create a large wardrobe with fewer clothes.

Daily Lives

Having waited so long in line, this woman decided she could not wait to return home before putting on her strictly rationed nylon stockings.

And the shortage of rubber encouraged the redefinition of women's ideal body shape. Girdles were no longer available to rein in unsightly bulges. *McCall's*, a popular women's magazine, advised its readers to "stay slim for healthy beauty and morale. . . . Go slow on fats and sweets. And take exercise." In fact, *McCall's* was defining not simply new fashion, but a new lifestyle. Both women and men would now lead more active lives. To accommodate this new pattern, clothing became more casual. Women and men were far more likely to wear slacks, light blouses, and open-collared shirts in public.

The war had left the United States on the verge of a sexual revolution that was reflected in the new fashions but went far beyond clothing. Sleeveless blouses and dresses, two-piece bathing suits, and shorts exposed far more of the female body than had ever before been acceptable. That look was not only more revealing, but also softer and more feminine. Feminists would later charge that it reflected a male preoccupation with women as sex objects. As the nation turned from war work to postwar domesticity, advice columns urged women to assume more feminine roles, especially since returning veterans yearned for "admiration, or at least submissiveness." While a career might yield social prestige, only through marriage and child rearing, roles that were "protective or nurturing, passive and receptive," could women realize their biological destiny. Such warnings were far from the last word. Over the course of the next 40 years Americans would choose clothing styles that reflected a continual redefinition of gender roles, sexual practices, marital relationships, and the image of how the human body ideally should look.

like liquor and cigarettes, consumers found their desires restricted by shortages and rationing. Problems were most severe in cities like Los Angeles, Detroit, New Orleans, and Washington, D.C., which boomed with new war workers. Schools, public transportation, and other municipal services could not keep pace. Even people with the money had difficulty finding a house or an apartment at any price.

The public reaction hardly suggested a nation tightening its belt for war. "Americans are finding fun," noted one report, "—and lots of it." Liquor consumption increased by 30 percent. The city of Minneapolis ran out of whiskey. Attendance at movie theaters and night clubs reached new peaks. In 1944 wagering at race tracks was two and a half times greater than it had been in 1940. The average sale in department stores was $2 before the war; by 1944 it had soared to $10. Scarcity of cloth inspired new fashions like the women's two-piece bathing suit and men's pants without cuffs. Pocket book sales skyrocketed from several hundred thousand to 40 million by the end of the war. The demand for Bibles was so great that they had to be rationed.

Rationing and price controls were imposed by the Office of Price Administration (OPA) to restrain consumers with bulging wallets. Under Leon Henderson OPA established a system to allot such goods as sugar, gasoline, meats, butter, and shoes. Consumers received coupons that allowed them to buy set amounts at fixed prices. To restock their shelves, merchants had to return the coupons to the government. Local boards determined the coupon quota for each family. Abuses were unavoidable. People with connections could receive additional allotments by pleading special hardships. Meanwhile merchants complained that OPA had set prices too low.

Henderson lacked the weapons to halt inflation. The OPA had no way to limit wages or farm prices. Increased income left consumers with billions to spend. He did try to impose a maximum price ceiling ("General Max"), but wholesalers and retailers found ways to avoid its restrictions. They substituted inferior goods or sold on the black market instead. Public hostility to OPA reached such a crescendo in 1943 that Henderson resigned. Eager consumers snapped up goods in quantities that often defeated the purpose of government restrictions. Though most Americans abided by the rationing program, those willing to pay the price could find almost anything on the illegal "black market." On the black market in Philadelphia a $5 pair of shoes could be purchased for $7, while in Washington, D.C., boneless ham sold for $1.25 a pound, almost twice the legal price.

Resourceful entrepreneurs discovered a gold mine in the war. Robert Woodruff of Coca-Cola demonstrated shrewdness that made patriotism pay dividends. He avoided the restrictions of sugar rationing by persuading the military that Coke was vital to the morale of soldiers and sailors. Everywhere American forces went, Coke went with them. One dismayed doctor on a malaria-infested South Pacific island opened a shipment of quinine only to discover he had been sent Coke instead. Woodruff did not make unusual profits from his wartime operations. Rather, he managed to make the American thirst for Coke a global phenomenon. Coca-Cola's reward came after the war when it sold its product worldwide. Similarly, Philip Wrigley convinced the army that soldiers would fight better if each K ration package contained a stick of Wrigley Spearmint gum. War workers could ward off boredom and fatigue with timely chewing. The combined appeal to patriotism and wartime necessity made gum, like Coke, an essential product.

Slower speeds conserved gas and rubber.

Willow Run

In every city swollen with new workers the war boom created similar strains. Old residents resented the disruption of their communities. Pressures on housing aggravated already simmering racial tensions. Families suffered as they moved into new communities where living space and schools were crowded; parents were away at work or at war; and local government could not meet the demand for services.

Perhaps more than any other town or city, Willow Run, Michigan, came to symbolize wartime dislocations. In 1941 Henry Ford picked this site 27 miles west of Detroit for his new bomber factory. At its height in 1944 the main plant covered 67 acres and employed 42,000 workers, about 40 percent of whom were women. Willow Run also attracted many poor southerners unaccustomed to life in an industrial community. The population of the county around Willow Run grew by almost 50 percent within two years.

Available housing did not increase to accommodate the newcomers. Federal plans to build the community ran afoul of a variety of interests. Realtors and property owners feared a glut of housing after the war when the factory shut down. Republican politicians assumed they would lose control, as new residents swelled the ranks of the Democratic party. If taxes rose and property values fell, the old residents would suffer. Faced with stiff local opposition, the government reduced the scale of its proposed housing project. Voters rejected a plan to build new schools.

Willow Run nearly buckled under the weight of the war boom. In one two-story house, five men slept in the basement, a family of five lived on the first floor, four people rented the second floor, nine men had cots in the garage, and four families parked trailers in the yard. Sewage polluted water supplies and led to periodic outbreaks of dysentery. Medical facilities could not provide most people with basic care. The schools had to run double sessions to meet demand. Many workers quit rather than abide the indignities of such a life. For others, particularly newcomers from the South, conditions were little worse and often better than those they had left behind.

Women Workers

World War II improved the economic status of women, but it did not alter conventional views about gender roles. Women's work was acceptable so long as it was seen as temporary and not as the beginning of a sexual revolution. World War I had had little long-term impact on women. By 1920 women faced layoffs, renewed job discrimination, and segregation into traditionally female jobs. Until World War II employment for women rose only in domestic service and clerical work, significantly the lowest paying jobs.

Real gains for women came after 1941 as the military and war industries absorbed the reserve pool of male workers. With as many as 12 million men in uniform, women (especially married women) became the largest untapped source of labor. Suddenly the popular media, which had discouraged them from competing with men for jobs, now urged them to enlist in the work force. Labor shortages forced traditionalists to stifle complaints that working at jobs considered masculine would create a nation of "Amazon women." What faithful wife or sister could sit at home when the media warned that shortages of war goods threatened the lives of American soldiers? A former schoolteacher recalled listening to a conversation at a

Between 1940 and 1945 the female labor force increased over 50 percent. Many women performed jobs that once were considered exclusively male. Lionized with nicknames such as "Rosie the Riveter," women like this airplane factory worker proved that many gender stereotypes had no basis in reality.

friend's house: "She and her sister at the dinner table were talking about the best way to keep their drill sharp in the factory. I never heard anything like this in my life. It was just marvelous." "Rosie the Riveter" and "Commando Mary" symbolized the flood of women workers who heeded their country's call.

These women were not mostly young and single, as women workers of the past had been. From 1940 to 1945, some 6.5 million women entered the work force, over half for the first time. A majority were either married or between 55 and 64 years old. Having accounted for just one worker in four in 1940, women amounted to more than one in three by 1945. Patriotism alone could not explain their willingness to leave families and homes for the factories. Rising war wages were a powerful inducement. Indeed, with husbands who earned low military pay many families could not get by without additional income. Other families discovered that dual incomes allowed a rapid improvement in standards of living.

Many women preferred the relative freedom of work and wages to the confines of home. With husbands off at war, millions of women had more free time as the demand for household services declined. Wartime restrictions limited leisure activities. Work provided a satisfying outlet for the unutilized energy of women. In part this satisfaction reflected an improvement in the quality as well as quantity of jobs. Black women in particular realized dramatic gains. Once concentrated in low-paying domestic and farm jobs with erratic hours and tedious labor, some 300,000 rushed into factories that offered higher pay and more regular hours. Given the chance to learn such skills as welding, aircraft assembly, and electronics, women shattered many stereotypes about their capabilities.

Most Americans assumed that when the war ended veterans would pick up their old jobs and women would return home. "We were sold a bill of goods," remembered one woman. "They were hammering away that the woman who went to work did it to help her man, and when he came back, she cheerfully leaped back to the home." Surveys showed that the vast majority of Americans, whether male or female, continued to believe that child rearing was a woman's primary responsibility. The birth rate, which had fallen during the Depression, began to rise in 1943 as prosperity returned.

The war thus led to few structural changes to accommodate the new circumstances of women as both mothers and workers. Women with young children needed day care. The government was slow to provide even minimal facilities. And where they did exist, many mothers were reluctant to use them. They or other family members continued to care for children. Working mothers thus tended to have higher absentee rates and work shorter hours. For them, the demands of the job remained secondary to those of the home.

Other traditional barriers blocked women from altering economic structures. Most professions restricted the entry of women into graduate programs or other career paths. As women flooded into government bureaucracies, factory production lines, and corporate offices few received managerial status. Supervision remained man's work. Many employers found ways to circumvent government regulations ordering equal pay for men and women. General Motors, for one, simply changed its old job classification from overtly discriminatory male–female designations to equally restrictive "heavy–light" categories. Women, of course, were left in "light," lower paying jobs. Even when the government discovered such practices, it was reluctant to enforce its own rules. Economists feared that raising wages for women would spur inflation.

Social trends acted as another brake on advances for women. Wartime statistics revealed stresses undermining the family and threatening public morality. Alcohol abuse, teenage prostitution, divorce, and juvenile delinquency all were on the rise. Some observers blamed such trends on working mothers, who were said to neglect their families. In fact, there was no clear evidence that the families of mothers who stayed home fared any better than those where mothers held outside jobs. The real problem lay with extraordinary mobility during the war. Crowded into new communities with inadequate schools and recreational facilities, young people had few outlets for their energies. Some towns tried to occupy them with roller skating, dancing, and bowling. When trouble came, the children of newcomers were more likely to be arrested than were children familiar to local police. Rather than build new recreational facilities, concerned public agencies were just as likely to recommend compulsory rules restricting mothers from work. Only labor shortages prevented the acceptance of such rules. The war inspired a change in economic roles for women without fomenting a revolution in attitudes about gender. That would come later.

A QUESTION OF RIGHTS

Franklin Roosevelt and his administrators saw national unity as vital to victory. That meant minimizing tensions across lines of race, ethnicity, and social class. Roosevelt condemned the assaults on civil liberties committed during the frenzy of World War I. There would be no repetition of the raids on dissident groups, of mobs menacing immigrants, or of appeals to spy on one's neighbors. Americans in general were horrified by Japanese and Nazi atrocities, especially toward the "lesser breeds" of Asia and Europe. It was difficult to practice racism at home while fighting it abroad, but it was not impossible. The war sometimes aggravated intolerance, raising serious questions of minority rights.

Little Italy

Aliens from enemy countries fared far better in World War II than in World War I. Immigration restriction had greatly reduced the numbers of foreigners who had not yet become citizens. When war came there were about 600,000 Italian aliens and 5 million Italian-Americans in the United States. Whether aliens or citizens, all had struggled during the Depression. Most still lived in Italian neighborhoods centered around churches, fraternal organizations, and clubs. Some had been proud of Mussolini and supported *Fascismo*. "Mussolini was a hero," recalled one Italian-American, "a superhero. He made us feel special," especially with anti-Italian prejudices so strong. All that stopped after Pearl Harbor. During the war, Italian-Americans unquestioningly pledged their loyalties to the United States.

At first the government treated Italians without citizenship (along with Japanese and Germans) as "aliens of enemy nationality." They could not travel without permission, enter strategic areas, or possess shortwave radios, guns, or maps. By 1942 few Americans believed that German- or Italian-Americans posed any kind of danger. Eager to keep the support of Italian voters in the 1942 congressional elections, Roosevelt chose Columbus Day, 1942, to lift restrictions on Italian aliens. The segregation of Italian-Americans ended. Henceforth they would maintain their ethnic unity as a matter of choice, not necessity.

Concentration Camps

Japanese-Americans, whether aliens or citizens, did not find similar tolerance. Far more than the Italians, the 127,000 Japanese in the United States had remained separated, often because state laws and local custom created complex barriers to assimilation. In the western states where they were concentrated around urban areas, most Japanese could not vote, own land, or live in decent neighborhoods. Approximately 47,000 Japanese aliens, known as "Issei," were ineligible for citizenship under American law. Only their children could become citizens.

This near-apartheid system forced most Japanese-Americans to remain isolated from the mainstream of American life. Despite such restrictions, some Japanese achieved success in farming and small businesses like landscaping. Their accomplishments sometimes added to the hostility of white neighbors. Pearl Harbor intensified ugly racial prejudice. One California undertaker captured popular sentiment when he announced, "I'd rather do business with a Jap than with an American."

By February 1942 West Coast politicians began to press the Roosevelt administration to evacuate the Japanese from their communities. It did not seem to matter that about 80,000 were American citizens, called "Nisei," and that no evidence indicated they posed any threat whatsoever. To some politicians, lack of evidence seemed proof in itself. California Attorney General Earl Warren thought it significant that no sabotage had been reported. "It looks very much to me," he stated, "as though it is a studied effort not to have any until the zero hour arrives.

American propaganda during World War II was not as hysterical as it had been during World War I. Still, hostile images of the enemy stirred popular fears. While Germans were sometimes shown as brutal, it was more common to associate the Japanese with racism, brutality, and savagery.

This is the Enemy

. . . That was the history of Pearl Harbor. I can't believe the same thing isn't planned for California." General John De Witt, commander of West Coast defenses, was more blunt: "A Jap's a Jap. . . . It makes no difference whether he is an American citizen or not." In response, the War Department in February 1942 drew up Executive Order 9066, which allowed the exclusion of any person from designated military areas. Under De Witt's authority, the order was applied only on the West Coast against Japanese-Americans.

Even that violation of Nisei rights did not satisfy more racist elements. Forty percent of the people on the West Coast believed that all Japanese were loyal to another government. To the north, Canada had already ordered all Japanese males between 18 and 65 to work camps away from the Pacific coast. In the United States vigilante violence soon broke out against the Japanese and their property. Pressure for removal mounted. "Put them all into concentration camps," one man was quoted as saying, "and work it out after the war's over!" By late February Roosevelt had agreed that both Issei and Nisei would be evacuated from the West Coast. But where would they go? When some 9000 moved on their own initiative, politicians from other states complained loudly. The army thus began in March to ship the entire Japanese community to "assembly centers."

Sudden removal imposed numerous hardships, many of them unnecessary. Few Japanese had time to arrange for the care or sale of property left behind. Most incurred heavy financial losses as they sold out far below market value. Their distress became a windfall for people who had long resented their economic competition. Once the Japanese reached the assembly centers at race tracks, fair grounds, and other temporary sites they encountered other indignities. The army had not prepared the sites to offer basic sanitation, comfort, or privacy. "We lived in a horse stable," remembered one young girl. "We filled our cheesecloth with straw—for our mattress." The authorities at least had the decency to keep families together.

The question of where to send the detainees was not resolved until September 1942. Milton Eisenhower, who headed the War Relocation Authority (WRA), had hoped to distribute people in small numbers to CCC-style work camps. That plan ran into opposition from state officials. Instead, most of the Japanese were interned in 10 camps in remote areas of seven western states. Notions that the camps might become self-sufficient communities proved wishful thinking. Even resourceful farmers could not raise food in arid desert soil.

No claim of humane intent could change the reality—these were concentration camps. Internees were held in wire-enclosed compounds by armed guards. Temporary tar-papered barracks housed families or small groups in single rooms. Each room had a few cots, some blankets, and a single light bulb. That was home. Bathing, meals, laundry, and recreation all took place in communal facilities. Attempts to introduce community self-government failed. Relocation had undermined the prestige of traditional elder leaders. The younger Nisei, who usually spoke English, were better able to deal with the authorities but were often more hostile.

Some Japanese within the camps protested, and rioting occasionally erupted. That only hardened opposition to a WRA plan that had permitted some 17,000 Nisei to leave the camps during 1943. In response, over 18,000 Japanese designated as disloyal were sent to a special camp at Tule Lake in California. About 8000 of these asked to go to Japan rather than suffer further indignities. Yet when given the chance to enlist, thousands of Nisei distinguished themselves in combat. Despite all they had suffered they accepted the one right left them—to die for their country.

Having created the camps, the government eventually found them hard to close. As late as 1944 the War Department warned that the West Coast would not tolerate rapid release of the Japanese. Many of the internees were now afraid to leave the relative safety of camps for life in hostile communities, but there was no reason to keep the camps open. Roosevelt finally decided after his reelection in 1944 that the time had come to let the Japanese go. As of January 1945 all Japanese had permission to leave at will. In late 1945 the WRA closed the last of the camps and one of the sorriest chapters in American history.

Even the Supreme Court lent its authority to the policy. In the case of *Hirabayashi v. United States* (1943) the Court upheld the discriminatory military curfew aimed at Japanese citizens. The majority opinion stated baldly that "residents having ethnic affiliations with an invading enemy may be a greater source of danger than those of different ancestry," even though the army had never demonstrated that any danger existed. The unanimous decision masked a divided Court. Justice Frank Murphy, who had wanted to dissent, got his chance in *Korematsu v. United States* (1944). The Court this time ruled that exclusion of Japanese-American citizens in wartime was legal. With the support of Justices Owen Roberts and Robert Jackson, Murphy criticized his colleagues for their automatic deference to a military decision and the "legalization of racism." Such an opinion had influence. On the same day in *Ex parte Endo* the Court declared it illegal to detain loyal citizens more than temporarily. That did little to help Mitsue Endo. She had spent over two years in a relocation camp waiting for the Court to decide her case.

Concentration camps in America did not perpetuate the horror of Nazi death camps, but they were built on racism and fear. Worse, they violated the traditions of civil rights and liberties for which Americans believed they were fighting.

Minorities on the Job

The war gave minority leaders an opportunity to press for broader civil rights. "A jim crow army cannot fight for a free world," the NAACP declared. The Pittsburgh *Courier*, a major black newspaper, advocated the "Double V"—"victory over our enemies at home and victory over our enemies on the battlefields abroad." Such ideas of racial justice had been the driving force in the life of A. Philip Randolph, long an advocate of greater black militancy. Randolph had demonstrated his gifts as an organizer and leader of the Brotherhood of Sleeping Car Porters, the most powerful black labor organization. He was determined to secure for blacks their rights in defense industries and the armed forces. "The Administration leaders in Washington will never give the Negro justice," Randolph argued, "until they see masses—ten, twenty, fifty thousand Negroes on the White House lawn." In 1941 he began to organize a march on Washington.

By using executive orders, President Roosevelt could have granted almost all of Randolph's demands aimed to end segregation in the government, defense industries, unions, and the armed forces. Only Randolph's insistence that the government refuse collective bargaining rights to unions closed to blacks required congressional action. The president, however, had never been a stalwart opponent of racial discrimination. He would have preferred to placate Randolph with a few kind words and gestures, but Randolph refused to be charmed. He predicted that 100,000 blacks would march on Washington in mid-1941 if Roosevelt did not act.

Under pressure from Randolph, the president in June 1941 finally issued Executive Order 8802. Federal policy now banned racial discrimination in the employment of workers in government or defense industries. To carry out that policy, the order established the Fair Employment Practices Commission (FEPC). In some ways that was the boldest step toward racial justice since the Civil War era. But the FEPC had only marginal success in breaking down barriers against blacks and Hispanics. It was one thing to ban discrimination, quite another to enforce that ban in a society still deeply divided by racial prejudice.

Mexican farm workers offer a case in point. During the Depression western farmers paid them below-subsistence wages, offered squalid housing, and sometimes left them stranded in the countryside between picking seasons. As unemployed white workers sought farm jobs, pressure mounted to reverse the flow of Mexican immigration. Traditional discrimination in education, housing, and jobs grew more severe. Local authorities discovered that it was cheaper to deport Mexicans, even some who were citizens or in the United States legally, than to provide relief to which they were entitled.

The war reversed that pattern. Efforts by the FEPC opened industrial jobs in California's shipyards and aircraft factories, which had previously refused to hire Hispanics. Thousands migrated from Texas, where job discrimination was most severe, to California, where war work created new opportunities. Labor shortages led the southwestern states to join with the Mexican government under the bracero (contract labor) program to recruit Mexican labor.

In Texas, by contrast, antagonism to braceros ran so deep that the Mexican government tried to prevent workers from going there. In 1942 the FEPC began to investigate systematic discrimination in the oil and mining industries. With support from labor unions company officials blocked Hispanics from training programs and job advancement. In this case, the State Department stymied the inquiry because Assistant Secretary Sumner Welles claimed that hemispheric relations might suffer. Disclosures would also afford Axis agents a wealth of propaganda with which to embarrass the United States. Not until late 1943 was the FEPC able to proceed.

Black Americans experienced similar frustrations. Early wartime prosperity bypassed them almost entirely. In 1941 half a million blacks were still unemployed while another two million worked at marginal, low-paying jobs. Over half of all defense jobs were closed to minorities. For example, with 100,000 skilled and high-paying jobs in the aircraft industry, blacks held about 200 janitorial positions. The federal agency charged with placing workers honored local employment practices. Generally that meant "whites only." The Office of Production Management refused to introduce antidiscrimination clauses into defense contracts. Unions segregated black workers or excluded them entirely. One person wrote to the president with a telling complaint: "Hitler has not done anything to the colored people— it's people right here in the United States who are keeping us out of work and keeping us down." Discrimination in housing, restaurants, transportation, and hotels added to the sense of grievance.

Eventually the combination of labor shortages, pressures from black leaders, and initiative from government agencies opened the door to more skilled jobs and higher pay. The federal government increased its employment of blacks from 60,000 to over 200,000. Beginning in 1943 the United States Employment Service rejected requests with racial stipulations. The National Labor Relations Board announced it would no longer certify unions that barred minorities. Faced with a dwindling labor pool, many employers finally opened their doors. By 1944 blacks, who accounted for almost 10 percent of the population, held 8 percent of the jobs. The wage gap narrowed so that black men (and white women) earned about 65 percent as much as white males. The lure of industrial jobs drew some 400,000 blacks from southern farms where they had eked out livings in sharecropping and tenant farming. About half went to the West Coast, half to the Northeast and Upper Midwest.

White hostility to blacks was never far from the surface. In Philadelphia in 1943 the local streetcar company claimed its union contract prevented the hiring of blacks as motormen (drivers) or conductors. Nonetheless, the FEPC ordered the company to upgrade some blacks. After considerable foot-dragging eight blacks received promotions by July 1944. On August 1 several hundred white workers struck to protest the upgrading of blacks. The city's 1600 streetcars, 600 buses, and 500 railway cars stopped. Since Philadelphia was one of the nation's most vital industrial centers, the government moved quickly to crush the strike. Eight thousand army troops manned the streetcars and kept the peace. FBI agents arrested strike leaders. Two days after it began, the strike was ended.

The victory in Philadelphia was an exceptional case. When the government confronted a more powerful union, like the Brotherhood of Locomotive Firemen and Engineers, it was not as forceful. A railroad strike could have brought the entire economy to a halt. In the large majority of cases, employers and unions defied FEPC orders for equal treatment of minorities. As the war ended, the old practice of "last-hired, first-fired" resumed. Even in postwar boom industries like car making, minorities were quickly downgraded to lower paying jobs.

At War with Jim Crow

At the beginning of World War II three-fourths of the 12 million black Americans lived in the South. Hispanic Americans, whose population exceeded a million, were concentrated in a belt along the United States–Mexican border. When jobs for minorities opened in war centers, blacks and Hispanics became increasingly urban. Whether rural or urban, both groups suffered from deeply entrenched systems of segregation that denied them basic rights to decent housing, jobs, and political participation. The explosiveness of that prejudice became clear in 1942. Competition for housing and the use of public facilities like parks, beaches, and transportation between whites and rapidly expanding minority populations became fierce.

In some cities government funds created new housing. One such project built in Detroit was named to honor the black poet and abolitionist Sojourner Truth. It included 200 units for black families. Federal authorities had picked a site for the houses along the edge of a Polish neighborhood. When the first black families tried to move in, they faced an angry mob of whites. Finally, local officials had to send several hundred National Guardsmen to protect the newcomers, as Ku Klux Klan members looked on menacingly.

The incident only provoked Detroit blacks and whites into greater confrontations. On a hot evening in June 1943, the simmering hatreds boiled over. At first scattered fighting broke out among blacks and whites returning from a local park. Suddenly, widespread gunfire, looting, and mob violence broke out. Angry blacks assaulted white workers leaving night shifts. White mobs dragged blacks off streetcars and buses. Police and snipers exchanged rifle fire. Six thousand soldiers from nearby bases finally imposed a troubled calm, but not before the riot had claimed 34 lives and property damage was widespread. Refusing to take black grievances seriously, local officials accused the NAACP and the "militant" Negro press for stirring up trouble. The black community charged that the police, shooting indiscriminately at blacks, did nothing to stop white rioters.

Detroit was not the only racially divided city, and blacks were not the only victims. Hispanics in southern California suffered the same indignities as black Americans. By 1943 overt Anglo hostility had come to focus on the *pachucos*, or "zoot suiters." These were young Hispanic men and boys who had adopted the outrageous style of Harlem hipsters: greased hair, swept back into a ducktail; broad-shouldered, long-waisted suit coats; baggy pants, pegged at the ankles, polished off with a swashbuckling keychain. The Los Angeles city council passed an ordinance making it a crime even to wear a zoot suit. For most "zooters" this style was a modest form of rebellion; for a few it was a badge of criminal behavior; for white servicemen it was a target for racism.

In June 1943 taunting turned to violence. Sailors from the local navy base invaded Hispanic neighborhoods in search of zooters who had allegedly attacked

The loose fit and pegged ankles of the zoot suit made it ideal for the jitterbug, a dance craze that swept the country in the era of big jazz bands. When the fashion became especially popular with urban Hispanic and black minorities, "zoot suiters" found themselves the targets of local officials and angry servicemen who resented the outrageous look of this teen subculture.

servicemen. The self-appointed vigilantes grabbed innocent victims, tore their clothes, cut their hair, and beat them bloody. When Hispanics retaliated, the police arrested them, all the while ignoring the actions of white servicemen. Irresponsible newspaper coverage made matters worse. "ZOOTERS THREATEN L.A. POLICE," charged one Hearst paper.

Accusations against zooters could not long mask the cause of the violence. Los Angeles in 1943 had limited recreational facilities for servicemen. Living outside American society, Hispanics offered convenient targets for servicemen's unfocused energies and irrepressible prejudices. Soon after the "zoot-suit riots," a citizens committee created at the urging of California Governor Earl Warren placed the blame where it belonged—on both sides. Underlying Hispanic anger were the grim realities of filthy housing, unemployment, disease, and white racism. All that added up to a level of poverty that wartime prosperity eased but in no way resolved.

Minority leaders realized some legal gains during the war. The Congress of Racial Equality (CORE), a nonviolent civil rights group inspired by the Indian leader Mohandas K. Gandhi, used sit-ins and other peaceful tactics to desegregate some restaurants and movie theaters. In 1944 the Supreme Court outlawed the "all-white primary," an infamous device used by southerners to exclude blacks from voting in primary elections within the Democratic party. Because Democratic candidates in the South often ran unopposed in the general elections, the primary elections were usually the only true political contests. In *Smith v. Allwright* the Court ruled that since political parties were integral parts of public elections, they could not deny minorities the right to vote in primaries. In so ruling the Court opened a legal door to further assaults on the Jim Crow system. "I see World War II as having been a step on the first rung of the ladder," concluded one black soldier. "But I wouldn't want to wish it on anybody else." With race as with gender, the war sowed the seeds of future upheaval. Hispanic, black, and Indian veterans would play leading roles in the postwar struggle for equality.

POLITICS AS USUAL

Politics did not go into eclipse after Pearl Harbor. As Roosevelt told reporters, "Dr. New Deal" had retired so that "Dr. Win-the-War" could go about his business. Politics nonetheless proceeded as usual. The increasingly powerful anti–New Deal coalition of Republicans and rural Democrats saw in the war an opportunity to attack liberal programs they had long resented. The president, for his part, was a politician who never lost sight of election returns. Without an electoral mandate (whether a Democratic Congress in 1942 or a fourth presidential term in 1944) Roosevelt could not achieve the victory he sought in war and peace.

Paying the Piper

One of the most difficult questions Roosevelt faced was how to pay the enormous cost of fighting the war. The federal budget, only about $9 billion in 1939, jumped to $100 billion by 1945. The national debt soared from $49 billion in 1941 to $259 billion by the end of the war. The money came from three major sources: taxes,

THE IMPACT OF WORLD WAR II ON GOVERNMENT SPENDING
Note that after both world wars nonmilitary government spending was greater than in the prewar eras.

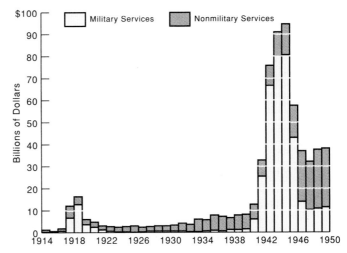

borrowing, and inflation (which amounts to a hidden tax). Tax receipts accounted for about 41 percent; borrowing provided the remainder. As personal income rose, inflation threatened to eat away higher earnings.

Americans agreed on little beyond controlling the war profits of individuals and corporations. Liberal New Dealers urged Roosevelt to pursue the tax and fiscal policies recommended by British economist John Maynard Keynes. Steeply graduated individual and corporate taxes would restrict inflation while falling on those best able to pay. Compulsory war bond purchases could further check prices through forced savings. The progressive tax structure would also lead to a more equitable distribution of wealth. Conservatives viewed such proposals as socialistic schemes to "soak the rich." They believed, quite correctly, that the liberal revenue program was designed to achieve social reform. They proposed voluntary war bond drives and sales taxes that would ease inflation by limiting consumption. In this case low- and middle-income taxpayers would shoulder most of the burden.

The Roosevelt approach mixed conservative and liberal elements: it was voluntary and compulsory, regressive and progressive. The Treasury Department sold war bonds through advertising campaigns rather than enforced savings. A volunteer group, the War Advertising Council, organized publicity for bond drives. Manufacturers without products to sell paid instead for war bond advertisements. Their motives were not entirely patriotic. The advertisements kept the names of companies like General Electric and General Motors in the public eye, while much of their cost could be written off company taxes.

The Treasury Department had concluded that higher taxes were the best way to limit inflation and generate needed revenue. Vote-conscious politicians winced, but the Treasury recommended a highly progressive tax bill anyway. Secretary Morgenthau proposed surtaxes on personal and corporate incomes and higher taxes on excess profits (to limit war profiteering), estates and gifts, luxury items, and scarce war goods. The most innovative feature of Morgenthau's bill was the new payroll deductions. No longer would taxpayers have to set aside money to pay the Internal Revenue Service (IRS) at the end of the year.

Conservatives in Congress balked at such sweeping reforms. They continued to press for sales taxes. After six months of wrangling, in which Roosevelt gave no support to Morgenthau's bill, the Revenue Act of 1942 emerged, in the president's words, as "the greatest tax bill in American history." It was something less. Gone were most of the progressive features. To placate supporters of the sales tax, the administration agreed to a 5 percent tax on incomes over $624 a year. That provision struck hardest at low-income workers, most of whom would pay federal taxes for the first time. Some 13 million people paid in 1941; under the Revenue Act almost 50 million would fall into the IRS net. A 1943 bill required employers to collect taxes through payroll deductions.

Future tax bills ran into similar opposition. In 1944 Congress passed a bill so laced with favors to business and empty of new revenue provisions that Roosevelt vetoed it. He charged Congress had provided "relief not for the needy but for the greedy." House Majority Leader Alben Barkley of Kentucky, a staunch New Dealer, resigned in outrage at the presidential slight of Congress. Both houses overrode Roosevelt's veto. Even though the president and Barkley patched up their quarrel, equitable taxation had suffered an irreversible defeat.

1942: A Farewell to Reform

The fight over taxes reflected deeper political currents running against the New Deal. New Deal foes moved quickly to eliminate the Civilian Conservation Corps, the National Youth Administration, and the largely ineffectual National Resources Planning Board. They gutted the Farm Security Administration and blocked moves to extend Social Security and unemployment benefits. They also thwarted Thurman Arnold's antitrust crusade. Conservatives masked their ambition to dismantle much of the New Deal behind the argument that such programs impeded war mobilization.

In the election of 1942 Roosevelt avoided Woodrow Wilson's error of making an off-year election a referendum on war policies; still the Republicans gained 44 seats in the House and 9 in the Senate. New York elected Thomas E. Dewey as governor, the first Republican since 1920. Republicans won 26 governorships in states that held 342 out of 531 electoral votes. More striking was the character of New Deal losses and conservative gains. Progressives like Senator George Norris of Nebraska lost, while diehard isolationists like Hamilton Fish (from Roosevelt's home county), won handily. The GOP began eyeing the White House.

Organized Labor

Wartime labor politics introduced a disruptive factor into Roosevelt's New Deal coalition. Though the president had never fully embraced organized labor, unions had become an important element in the Democratic party as well as a rich source of campaign funds. More conservative elements in the party wanted to curb union power. Wartime prosperity brought unprecedented gains for unions, though not without a continuation of the sometime violent struggles of the 1930s. Even as surging employment brought 1.5 million new members into the union fold, skilled workers of the American Federation of Labor and industrial workers of the Congress of Industrial Organizations vied for dominance. Just as divisive was the failure of labor leaders to agree to support Roosevelt's policies. And most workers had grievances with management. In 1941 alone more than 2 million workers walked off their jobs over wages and access to unions.

In 1942 Roosevelt moved to end labor strife. He established the War Labor Board (WLB), modeled on the old World War I agency, with the authority to impose arbitration in any labor dispute. To protect major interests, the WLB included equal representation for labor, management, and consumers. If the parties rejected the final decision, the president could seize the plants in question. In its most far-reaching decision the WLB adopted a "maintenance of membership" policy. Employers had always fought for the "open shop" where workers were free to be union members or not. Labor leaders demanded the "closed shop," which forced all workers in a plant to join a single union. The WLB formulated a compromise that gave workers 15 days to leave the union after a contract was signed. Any worker who remained a member had to pay union dues for the life of the contract. That policy led to an almost 40 percent growth in union membership between 1941 and 1945, when a record 14.75 million workers had union cards.

Labor's ability to redress its grievances was restricted by a "no-strike" pledge adopted shortly after Pearl Harbor. By 1943 workers saw the pledge as a burden. They pressed for repudiation even if it provoked a backlash in Congress and the press. A rash of new strikes threatened to disrupt war production. In 1943 some 3.1 million workers walked off their jobs. Railroad workers threatened to block the war effort when they tied up the rail lines just before Christmas. General George C. Marshall cursed it as the "damnedest crime ever committed against America." Finally the government seized the railroads and then granted wage increases. Between 1941 and 1945, almost 15,000 work stoppages took some 6.75 million workers off the job. All told, nearly 40 million work days were lost.

Such an account creates the impression that wartime labor policy was a failure. In reality the Roosevelt administration managed to limit the impact of quarrels between labor and management. Put another way, statistics reveal worker dedication to the war effort. Stoppages actually accounted for only about one-tenth of a percent of total work time during the war. Workers most often struck in defiance of their union leadership and left their jobs for just a few days.

One union, the United Mine Workers (UMW), and its leader, John L. Lewis, were responsible for a disproportionate share of disruptions. Wartime inflation affected coal miners more severely than most other workers. Wage scales were low. As Lewis angrily charged, "The coal miners of America are hungry. They are ill-fed and undernourished." Much of the animosity toward unions was provoked by Lewis' tactics in 1943, when he authorized a series of short strikes. Finally Roosevelt seized the mines and ran them for a time. Roosevelt had no love for Lewis, who had fought him in 1940 and whose militancy caused him nothing but political headaches. At times the president considered arresting UMW leaders and drafting striking miners, but as Secretary of the Interior Harold Ickes reminded him, a "jailed miner produces no more coal than a striking miner." The president, moreover, did not wish to antagonize more moderate labor leaders. With his blessings Ickes negotiated a settlement giving the miners generous benefits.

In helping the UMW, Lewis hurt the cause of labor. A huge coal shortage along the East Coast had left homes dark and cold. Most Americans thought of Lewis as public enemy number one. "John L. Lewis—Damn your coal black soul," wrote the military newspaper *Stars and Stripes.* In the fall of 1943 antiunion elements in Congress pushed through the Smith–Connolly Anti-Strike, or War Labor Disputes Act. It gave the president more authority to seize vital war plants shut by strikes and required union leaders to observe a 30-day "cooling-off" period before striking. Roosevelt wanted even more power, but he recognized the anti-

John L. Lewis.

union goals of Smith–Connolly supporters. He vetoed the bill, only to be overridden in both houses by large margins. In the end Roosevelt gained the authority he sought but maintained labor's support for the difficult 1944 presidential campaign.

1944: A Fourth Term

In the spring of 1944 no one knew whether Roosevelt would seek an unprecedented fourth term. The president's health had declined noticeably. Pallid skin, sagging shoulders, and shaking hands seemed open signs that he had aged too much to run. In July, one week before the Democratic convention, Roosevelt announced his decision: "All that is within me cries out to go back to my home on the Hudson River. . . . But as a good soldier . . . I will accept and serve."

Conservative Democrats wanted to rid the ticket of Vice President Henry A. Wallace, leader of the most progressive wing of the party and an outspoken internationalist. The CIO warmly endorsed him. Roosevelt left the public impression that he wanted Wallace on the ticket but before the convention tried to replace him with James Byrnes of South Carolina, the head of the Office of War Mobilization. The president had not reckoned on CIO leader Sidney Hillman, who supported Wallace and opposed Byrnes as an enemy of labor and of civil rights. At the convention the divided delegates settled on Harry S. Truman of Missouri, a loyal New Dealer who had distinguished himself during the war as head of the Senate committee monitoring defense expenditures.

The Republican ticket rejected the liberal internationalist Wendell Willkie in favor of the moderate governor of New York, Thomas E. Dewey. Dewey never had a chance. Countless reports of victory in Europe and the Pacific undermined his charges that Roosevelt had mismanaged the war. Both candidates warmly endorsed postwar American participation in international affairs. On domestic issues Dewey often sounded like a New Dealer. The GOP platform had so few criticisms of actual programs that one historian called it "the most significant endorsement of Roosevelt's policies yet written." Republicans fell back on old strategies of attack, condemning inefficiency and waste in government, excessive centralization of political power, and the destruction of free enterprise.

Roosevelt's campaign championed two reforms popular with liberals and soldiers. In his January State of the Union message the president outlined a bill aimed to ensure economic security and prosperity after the war. It was, he suggested, "a second Bill of Rights" that would guarantee jobs, decent living standards, greater opportunities for small businesses, better housing, and more protection against unemployment, old age, sickness, and injury. It was an agenda for a good society, not a plan to revive the New Deal, and once reelected Roosevelt did little to achieve it.

By contrast the "GI Bill of Rights" of 1944 was perhaps the most significant social legislation of the war years. Sociologists have identified occupation, place of residence, and level of education as three crucial determinants of social class. The GI Bill granted veterans the means to improve their status in these areas and more. It gave them occupational guidance, priority for jobs, loans to establish small businesses and farms, educational benefits and technical training, and mortgage assistance to buy homes. Later amendments added health care, particularly for those disabled by the war. Since the bill applied to soldiers only, it gained support even among those who normally opposed such social programs. Seeing the legislation as an opportunity to win the gratitude of veterans, the normally conservative American Legion gave its wholehearted endorsement.

By late summer Dewey's campaign had failed to excite many voters. Alice Roosevelt Longworth, the daughter of Theodore Roosevelt, compared Dewey to the little man on a wedding cake. Eventually Dewey and other frustrated GOP candidates resorted to "red baiting." Victory for Roosevelt would bring Communist labor leaders like Sidney Hillman into the White House, they charged. Latent anti-Semitism and nativism made Hillman and other ethnic labor leaders favorite targets. Voters turned away from such extremism. They gave Roosevelt and the Democrats 25.6 million popular votes to Dewey's 22 million. Roosevelt swamped his rival in the electoral college by a count of 432 to 99. The Democrats lost just one seat in the Senate, picked up 20 in the House, and captured 5 new governorships. In defeat, many frustrated GOP leaders decided to make "red baiting" their focus in future elections.

VICTORY

As he was sworn in on April 12, 1945, Harry Truman recognized the awesome task of replacing Franklin Roosevelt. In the brief period he had served as vice president, Truman had met with Roosevelt fewer than 10 times. He knew almost nothing about the president's postwar plans and promises. When a newspaperman addressed him as "Mr. President," he winced. "I wish you didn't have to call me that," he said. He asked the press corps to pray for him, but prayers would not prevent foreign leaders from taking advantage of his inexperience, so Truman adopted a tough pose and made his mind up quickly. People welcomed the new president's decisiveness as a relief from Roosevelt's evasions. Too often, though, he acted before the issues were clear.

As Truman assumed the presidency, the Allies had already launched the final blows against the Axis. The victory in the Pacific promised to be bloody. At Okinawa, just 370 miles south of Japan, American amphibious forces ran into fierce resistance. Over 3500 kamikaze pilots targeted the invasion fleet, inflicting serious damage. Japanese defenders threw nightly human wave assaults against Allied troops. The Americans suffered 50,000 casualties and the Japanese 100,000 deaths before the island fell in late June. Victory in Europe was much closer. By spring an army of 150 Russian divisions had reached the Oder River just to the east of Berlin. In March American troops commanded by General Omar Bradley had captured Cologne on the west bank of the Rhine and by a great stroke of luck captured an undamaged bridge at Remagen. By April Bradley's forces were sweeping into central Germany as British forces under General Bernard Montgomery moved to the north.

The Holocaust

The invading armies were not prepared for the horror of the concentration camps they discovered. As part of a plan to implement "the final solution" to Germany's problems, Hitler had ordered in areas under Nazi rule the systematic extermination of all European Jews as well as Gypsies, homosexuals, and others considered deviant. The SS, Hitler's security force, had established six extermination centers in Poland at Chełmno, Belzec, Majdanek, Sobibór, Treblinka, and Auschwitz. By rail from all over Europe they shipped Jews to die in the gas chambers.

In April 1945, at the concentration camp in Buchenwald, Germany, Senator Alben Barkley of Kentucky viewed a grisly reminder of the horrors of the Nazis' "final solution." As vice president under Harry Truman, Barkley urged the administration to support an independent homeland for Jews in Israel.

No issue of World War II more starkly raised questions of human good and evil than the Holocaust. And tragically, the United States could have done more to save at least some of the 6 million Jews the Nazis killed. Until the fall of 1941 the Nazis permitted Jews to leave Europe, but few countries, including the United States, would accept them. American restrictions, which had been lowered slightly in 1938, became progressively tighter. There are three factors explaining the exclusionary policy. First and foremost was the Depression. Many Americans feared that any rise in immigration would make joblessness worse. That concern coincided with a second impulse to tighten rather than loosen the restriction system established under the Immigration Act of 1924. Opinion polls showed that in 1938, as Nazi persecution of Jews increased, 71 to 85 percent of all Americans opposed easing quotas to help refugees. In 1939 some 66 percent objected to a one-time exception that would have admitted 10,000 children. The war in no way eased opposition to the admission of European refugees.

A third factor was an ugly strain of anti-Semitism that peaked in 1944 when pollster Elmo Roper warned that it "had spread all over the nation and is particularly virulent in urban centers." According to the polls Americans mistrusted Jews more than any European people except Italians. With the exception of a few bitter cranks, anti-Semites refrained from advocating outright persecution. More common was a kind of passive anti-Semitism that nurtured negative feelings but no overt hostilities. Jewish leaders feared, probably with cause, that pressure to ease immigration restrictions would make anti-Semitism worse. "I see in the papers that 200,000 Refugee Jews in Hungary will not live through the week," a typical letter to Congress began. "Thats too Damn Bad what in the Hell do we care about Jews in Hungary."

What was more tragic was the anti-Semitism of senior State Department officials who systematically frustrated Jewish efforts to emigrate to the United States. Immigration policy fell under the authority of Assistant Secretary of State Breckinridge Long, who embraced the upper-class American tradition of unmodulated anti-Semitism. President Roosevelt could have used an executive order to clear the obstacles Long and his officials created, but for several reasons he did not. For one, he was no stranger to gentlemanly anti-Semitism and thus discounted the virulence with which Long enforced his prejudices.

The president also received mixed signals from the American Jewish community. Jews wanted to help refugees, especially after 1942 as news of the death camps leaked from Europe, but they were not sure how to do so without aggravating anti-Semitism. Until the last year of the war polls showed that most Americans thought that only about 100,000 Jews had been killed. Jews were also split on the question of Zionism and the pressures to establish a Jewish homeland in Palestine. The British had blocked Jewish emigration to Palestine and opposed Zionism to avoid alienating the Arabs. Roosevelt and his advisers ultimately decided that the best way to save Jews was to win the war quickly. That still does not explain why the Allies did not do more: they could have bombed the rail lines to the camps, sent commando forces, or tried to destroy the death factories.

Treasury Secretary Henry Morgenthau, the one Jew in Roosevelt's cabinet, had at first gone along with the president and the British on the questions of Palestine and refugees. Then his staff informed him that the State Department at Breckenridge Long's insistence had since 1942 prevented information on the "final solution" from reaching the United States. In 1943 Long also blocked a plan Morgenthau and Roosevelt both approved to ransom Jews in Romania and 6000 Jewish children in France. By January 1944 Morganthau became so exasperated with the State Department that he sent Roosevelt a report entitled "The Acquiesence of this Government in the Murder of the Jews." Roosevelt stripped Long of his authority and appointed a War Refugee Board charged with saving as many Jews as possible. In the 1944 election both parties adopted pro-Zionist planks, and Roosevelt promised to seek the establishment of a Jewish commonwealth in Palestine. But some 18 precious "long and heartbreaking" months had been lost and with them an untold number of lives.

At Yalta, the Big Three did not discuss, much less resolve the issue of Palestine. Returning home in February 1945, Roosevelt stopped for talks with King Ibn Saud of Saudi Arabia. He impressed Roosevelt with Arab determination to end further Jewish immigration to Palestine. To many American Jews, the president now seemed to waver on his election promises, but it was Harry Truman who would face the survivors and their dreams of a Jewish homeland.

The United Nations

Truman also inherited responsibility for establishment of the United Nations Organization (UNO). The breakdown of the world economy during the 1930s followed by the horrors of World War II led the Allies to seek a new framework for the international system. That system, many Americans believed, required an end to economic nationalism, trade barriers, and currency problems that had led to depression and war. Most postwar planners defended the "open door" to trade. At the Chicago Aviation Conference in 1944 they had insisted on ready access for American airlines to routes and airports around the globe. At a 1944 meeting at Bretton Woods, a resort in New Hampshire, the Americans had created two new economic organizations: the International Monetary Fund (IMF) and the International Bank for Reconstruction and Development (the World Bank). The IMF would promote trade by stabilizing national currencies while the World Bank would invest in economic growth. Since the United States supplied most of the capital for both organizations, it would also dictate policy.

In late summer 1944 the Allies met at Dumbarton Oaks, a Washington estate, to lay out the structure for the UNO. An 11-member Security Council would oversee a General Assembly composed of all members. At Yalta, Roosevelt had won Stalin's support for the UNO but the price was high. Fearful that the Western powers would control the General Assembly, Stalin demanded three extra seats for the Soviet Union. He argued the fiction that the Ukrainian, Belorussian, and Lithuanian republics were independent states. Roosevelt at first resisted but gave in under pressure from Churchill to admit the Ukraine and Belorussia.

Although Truman had no intention of altering Roosevelt's course on the UNO or other wartime agreements, he almost immediately adopted a more hostile approach to Stalin and the Soviet Union. Truman had heard the same message from many sources: the Soviets could not be trusted. They had already begun to violate agreements on eastern Europe made at Yalta. Only if the United States stood firm, advisers counseled, could the Soviets be forced to keep their word. When Foreign Commissar V. M. Molotov stopped in Washington on his way to the organizational meeting of the UNO in San Francisco on April 25, Truman delivered a severe tongue-lashing to the startled Soviet leader. When Molotov objected, Truman retorted, "Keep your agreements and you won't be talked to that way."

Truman soon discovered that tough talk did not easily solve Allied differences. The April 1945 meeting in San Francisco to establish the new United Nations Organization revealed deep divisions between the Soviets and Americans. When United States delegates urged the admission of Argentina, the Soviets scoffed at permitting the entrance of a fascist regime. The United States prevailed, and it became clear that the UNO would favor the Western powers in most postwar disputes.

Ending the War

While the UNO convened, the Axis collapsed. As Mussolini attempted to escape to Germany antifascist mobs in Italy had captured and slaughtered him like a pig. Adolf Hitler committed suicide in his Berlin bunker on April 30. Two weeks later General Eisenhower accepted the German surrender. Allied leaders then planned to meet in July at Potsdam, just outside of Berlin, to consider the future of Europe and victory over Japan. With reports that Japan might fight for another five years, Truman wanted Stalin to enter the Pacific war. He was chagrined to learn that overzealous aides had abruptly canceled lend-lease shipments to Russia. Ships already at sea were ordered home. Truman countermanded the order, but not before he received a torrent of bitter complaints from the Soviet Union.

To repair the rifts, Truman asked Roosevelt's trusted adviser Harry Hopkins to see Stalin in Moscow. Though near death, Hopkins made the arduous trip and reached a series of important compromises. Stalin agreed to bring members of the Polish government-in-exile in London into the Communist regime running Poland. That left the Communists in charge but saved face for Churchill and Truman. Stalin also repeated his commitment to join the Pacific war, accepted an American formula for voting in the Security Council of the UNO, and promised to meet Truman in Germany.

Though Hopkins' trip improved the tone of Soviet–American relations, irreconcilable differences over postwar political settlements, especially in Germany and eastern Europe, split the Allies. At Potsdam Truman met Churchill (who lost office during the conference) and Stalin for the first time. Talks lasted for two and a half weeks without substantial agreement. Two issues dominated the meeting. Both sides agreed that Germany should be occupied and demilitarized. But whereas the British and Americans did not want to burden Germany with excessive reparations as they had after World War I, Stalin insisted that Russia receive a minimum of $10 billion regardless of the impact on the postwar German or European economy. A complicated compromise allowed Britain and the United States to restrict reparations from their zones but eliminated prospects for a centralized government in Germany.

Atomic Diplomacy

The most crucial issue never reached the bargaining table at Potsdam. On July 16, 1945, the first atomic fireball rose from the desert in Alamagordo, New Mexico. The next day news of the successful test was flashed to Truman at Potsdam from the Manhattan Project director, General Leslie Groves. Two questions loomed: Should the United States warn Japan before using the bomb? And even more to the point, should Truman tell Stalin? The possibility of not using the bomb or offering a demonstration, as a number of concerned Manhattan Project scientists urged, had been dismissed by a high-level committee of administrators, scientists, and political and military leaders.

Truman seemed a changed man—firmer, more confident—after he received the word from Alamagordo. He "told the Russians just where they got on and off and generally bossed the whole meeting," observed Churchill. The president chose not to tell Stalin about the bomb, only mentioning obliquely that the United States possessed a weapon of "awesome destructiveness." Instead of being cowed, Stalin smiled, remarking casually that he hoped the Americans would use their new weapon to good effect against Japan. (Most likely, spies had already informed Stalin about the atomic bomb, so Truman's reference came as no surprise.) Atomic diplomacy had failed its first test. If, as some historians believe, Stalin immediately stepped up the Russian program to build an atomic bomb, then the decision to keep the bomb secret helped launch the nuclear arms race.

Without consulting Stalin, Truman and Churchill decided to use the bomb with only an implied warning to the Japanese. Along with Chiang Kai-shek of China they issued an ominous ultimatum, threatening "prompt and utter destruction" if Japan did not surrender. On two points the Potsdam Declaration was silent. It never mentioned the atom bomb and it gave no indication that the vanquished could retain their emperor, a sacred institution to the Japanese. Tokyo made no formal reply.

Moderates in Japan had been pressing for peace since April 1945. They needed only assurances on keeping the emperor to overcome military diehards. Truman and Churchill knew Japan was on the verge of defeat and were aware that peace feelers had been sent to the Russians. Why then did the Allies offer no compromise on the emperor and instead cling to their policy of unconditional surrender? Some historians have charged that Secretary of State James Byrnes, a staunch anticommunist, wanted a combat demonstration of the bomb as a dramatic warning to the Soviet Union. Aware of the bomb's potential, Stalin would have reason to resolve issues on British and American terms.

Most evidence indicates that Truman decided to drop the bomb to end the war quickly. In doing so he followed the recommendations of the high-level Interim Committee appointed to review bomb policy. Military leaders believed Japan would not surrender without an invasion. The estimated cost in Allied lives ran as high as half a million to a million casualties. The terror of kamikaze attacks and the fierce resistance encountered at Okinawa served as grim reminders of Japanese fanaticism. Byrnes, among others, thought the American public would accept no formula that departed from unconditional surrender. And most American officials did not think the Japanese peace feelers were serious. Late in July 1945 Truman ordered crews on Tinian Island in the South Pacific to drop the bomb as soon as weather permitted.

When the president left Potsdam on August 2, nothing of importance had been settled. Germany's future as well as the question of reparations remained clouded. The agenda for a peace conference had still to be decided. Allied leaders had not even agreed when, if ever, they would meet again. Truman hoped that James Byrnes would be able to negotiate at future meetings of Allied foreign ministers, and both believed that "the bomb assured ultimate success in negotiations."

Before Truman's ship reached the United States the world learned what atomic warfare might mean. On August 6, 1945, the *Enola Gay*, a B-29 bomber, dropped a uranium bomb called "Little Boy" on Hiroshima, an industrial and military center. The blast leveled four square miles of the city, killing nearly 80,000 people (including 20 American prisoners of war). A German priest came upon dazed soldiers who had looked up as the bomb exploded. Their eyeballs had melted from their sockets. Another eyewitness spoke of survivors "so broken and confused that they moved and behaved like automatons." Two days later the Soviet Union declared war on Japan, and on August 9 a second atomic bomb (a plutonium weapon nicknamed "Fat Man") exploded over the port of Nagasaki. Another 60,000 were killed instantly. In both cities people who lived through the horror began to sicken and die. Radiation poisoning, unexpected by many of the scientists who built the bomb, claimed tens of thousands of additional lives.

Truman told his cabinet he could not bear the thought of killing more women and children and ordered a halt to the bombing. No more bombs were necessary. Breaking all precedents, the emperor intervened and declared openly for peace. On September 3 a humiliated Japanese delegation boarded the battleship *Missouri* in Tokyo Bay and signed the document of surrender. World War II had ended.

Frozen forever at 8:16 a.m., Japanese time: the moment when an atomic bomb exploded over Hiroshima.

"World War II changed everything," observed a retired admiral long after the war. Before the war Americans seldom exerted leadership in world affairs. In its wake the world looked to the United States to rebuild the economies of Europe and Asia and to maintain peace. World War II not only had shown the global interdependence of economic and political systems, but also increased that interdependence. Out of the war developed a truly international economy.

At home the trends toward bigness and centralization vastly accelerated. Supported by government, old industries grew and new industries like synthetic rubber sprang up. Advances in electronics, communications, and aviation brought the world closer to every home. Government grew, too. The size of the national debt alone guaranteed that Washington would continue to dominate the economy. The military services might shrink, but never again would they starve as they had between the wars. Americans would learn that a strong defense required a large federal bureaucracy and a generous military budget.

Three fears loomed, even as victory parades snaked down the nation's main streets. First, cutbacks in military spending might bring on another depression. The middle classes, greatly expanded by wartime prosperity, increasingly looked to government not to extend New Deal reforms but to help them preserve and continue their recent gains. Second, Stalin's efforts to control eastern Europe threatened the liberal peace plans of Franklin Roosevelt. Finally, there was the atomic bomb. The United States might control it for the present, but what if it fell into unfriendly hands? In the atomic age no one in the world, not even the United States, was safe any more.

SIGNIFICANT EVENTS

1941 — A. Philip Randolph plans march on Washington; Roosevelt creates Fair Employment Practices Commission

1942 — War Production Board and War Labor Board created; rubber shortage; Office of Price Administration provokes controversy; Revenue Act; Roosevelt lifts restrictions on enemy aliens; internment of Japanese-Americans

1943 — Office of War Mobilization replaces WPB; payroll deductions adopted; suspension of antitrust prosecutions; race riot in Detroit; zoot-suit riots; Smith–Connolly Act

1944 — Strikes in Philadelphia; *Smith v. Allwright*; Dumbarton Oaks and Bretton Woods meetings; Roosevelt wins fourth term; G.I. Bill of Rights; War Refugee Board created

1945 — Truman becomes president; Allied troops liberate extermination camps; first United Nations Organization meeting; Germany surrenders; Potsdam Conference; atom bombs dropped on Japan; World War II ends

PART 6

THE UNITED STATES IN A NUCLEAR AGE

At Los Alamos in July 1945, during the final feverish days of work on the first atomic bomb, a few scientists calculated the possible unexpected effects of an atomic blast. The strategic bombings at Dresden and Tokyo showed how a firestorm, once started, sucked oxygen from the surrounding atmosphere, feeding upon itself and enlarging the inferno. No one had ever set off an atomic explosion, and some scientists worried that an even greater chain reaction might follow, one that would not only ignite the atmosphere around it but would envelop the earth's atmosphere, leaving the planet in ashes. Members of the team checked and rechecked the calculations before deciding those fears were invalid.

In the half-century since Hiroshima, the atomic nightmare has returned repeatedly to haunt the world. The threat now appears to be not from the detonation of a single bomb but from an all-too-human chain reaction, in which escalating violence leads to atomic strike and counterstrike, followed by a decades-long radioactive "nuclear winter," from which intelligent life could never fully recover.

During the heady victory celebrations of 1945, the threat of nuclear annihilation seemed distant. Although President Truman and many other American leaders had become increasingly distrustful of Stalin, the United States preserved a clear atomic monopoly. The dangers from radioactive fallout had impressed only a handful of officials and even fewer of the public, who were treated to cheery fantasies of the peacetime use of atomics, including an article in the May 1947 *Collier's* magazine in which a recovered paraplegic emerged from the mushroom

cloud of his atomic treatment, his wheelchair almost miraculously left behind. By 1949, when fallout from Russian atomic tests indicated the U.S. monopoly had been broken, the grim global realignment was already well established. Two superpowers, the Soviet Union and the United States, had replaced the players in the old "balance of power" politics that had defined European politics for two centuries.

The polarization of the globe into two camps, each dominated by a superpower, would have seemed strange even 20 years earlier. But in the long view, the result was not surprising. Ever since the beginning of expansion in the sixteenth century, Europe's greatest growth came along its peripheries, both west and east. Along the continent's west-facing rim, the Portuguese, Spanish, Dutch, French, and English reached beyond themselves for commercial and colonial empires. By the late nineteenth century England's colonial offshoot, the United States, was coming into its own even farther west. Over these same centuries of expansion, Europe's eastern flank saw Russian settlers pushing across the steppes of Eurasia, turning more and more grasslands into cultivated fields. Farther north, Russian fur traders were bringing the forest and tundra of Siberia into the Russian orbit, just as French and English fur traders were encroaching on the forests of the Canadian shield.

In area and vastness of resources, the Soviet Union surpassed even the United States, its boundaries encompassing 12 time zones. Given the centuries-long tradition of authoritarian rule (*czar* is the Russian derivative of Caesar), the Russian Revolution of 1917 took a firmly centralized approach to modernization. At sometimes frightful cost (the attempt to collectivize its peasant farmers alone starved or killed 10 million) Stalin brought the Soviet Union to its position as superpower by the end of World War II. The peripheral powers of Europe—the United States and Russia—had become dominant. And by 1960 both were relying on large stockpiles of nuclear weapons as the ultimate guarantors of their security and power.

Able to annihilate each other many times over, the two superpowers hoped to guarantee the peace through a system of deterrence. The knowledge of "mutual assured destruction," nuclear strategists suggested, would prevent either side from being the first to launch a missile attack. Yet that strategy was a frightening one precisely because the globe could not be cut simply into two halves—communist and noncommunist—each with clearly unified political and economic interests. Just as the "federal union" of the United States had been often riven by ethnic, religious, or economic rivalries, conflicts worldwide were arising out of similar dynamics, threatening to widen into war where the prestige of either superpower became critically involved.

Both the Soviets and the Americans discovered the limits of projecting their power and prestige in regional conflicts. For more than a decade, the United States sought unsuccessfully to win a war against North Vietnam by conventional means, before withdrawing in defeat. For another decade, the Soviet Union waged a similarly unsuccessful war in Afghanistan. In both cases, though the rival superpowers justified their involvement in terms of a battle for democracy and liberty or for democratic socialism, regional rivalries clearly played a dominant role. In the Vietnam conflict, the Communist Ho Chi Minh was enough of a nationalist to prefer nearly any form of government, including French colonial rule, to domination by Vietnam's traditional enemy, China. It mattered not that China was ruled by a Communist "comrade," Mao Tse-tung. During their war in Afghanistan, the Soviets quickly discovered that their dogged rebel opposition was inspired by an Islamic faith. The 1979 revolution in Iran brought the Ayatollah Khomeini to power and further demonstrated that Islamic fundamentalism would play a crucial role in the Middle East and the Saharan subcontinent.

1079

Thus the world of the 1980s and 1990s was shaping up to be less a bipolar world, divided between two superpowers, than multipolar, with a great many regional rivalries and interests. These regional strains and conflicts could not be ignored, for the technology of industrialization had created a truly global theater of markets, cultures, and politics. Beginning in the 1970s, even the natural limits of the globe were becoming apparent.

In America, the boom and development mentality of the 1950s and 1960s was tempered in the 1970s as the environmental costs of air and water pollutants, strip mining, pesticides, and a host of other abuses became obvious. Similarly, by the mid-1970s most major rivers in the Soviet Union had been polluted by industrial wastes, significant fish kills being reported in the Ural, Volga, and Dnieper rivers. China, whose coal reserves are as great as those of the United States and the Soviet Union combined, was boosting its coal-fired electric generating plants from a 35,000-megawatt output in 1980 to a projected 92,000 megawatts in the year 2000. Already northern Chinese cities are heavily polluted by the burning of coal, and damage from acid rain can be charted in neighboring regions. China, the United States, and the Soviet Union combined account for nearly half of all humanly produced emissions of carbon dioxide, whose addition to the atmosphere threatens to raise the earth's temperature, creating a greenhouse effect that could change the world drastically. In the late 1980s recurring drought ravaged sub-Saharan Africa, leading to thousands of deaths from famine. As heat waves and drought severely damaged American crops in 1988, some scientists warned that the global warming trend had begun.

A nuclear winter or a greenhouse summer? Both grim alternatives make it clear that, half a millennium after the civilizations of two hemispheres achieved sustained contact, their ultimate fates are indivisibly intertwined.

CHRONOLOGY

AMERICAN EVENT	YEAR		GLOBAL EVENT
First atomic weapon detonated	1945	TRUMAN	United Nations founded
Truman Doctrine proclaimed	1947		
Marshall Plan aids postwar Europe	1948		Czechoslovakia falls to the Communists
			State of Israel created
	1949		U.S.S.R. explodes atomic bomb
			Communists seize power in China
McCarthy begins anticommunist campaign	1950		Korean War begins
	1953	EISENHOWER	Armistice in Korea
Brown v. Board of Education	1954		French defeated in Indochina
Postwar baby boom peaks	1957		Soviet Union launches *Sputnik*
	1959		Castro wins power in Cuba
	1961	KENNEDY	First Soviet manned space flight
			Soviets erect Berlin Wall
	1962		Cuban missile crisis
Civil rights march on Washington	1963	JOHNSON	U.S.-U.S.S.R. nuclear test-ban treaty
Kennedy assassinated			
Johnson launches war on poverty; escalates war in Vietnam	1964		Beatles become international rock stars
Voting Rights Act passed	1965		Mao Tse-tung launches radical "Cultural Revolution"
Chavez leads farm workers campaign			
	1967		Israeli-Arab Six-Day War
Martin Luther King assassinated	1968		Viet Cong launch Tet Offensive
Robert Kennedy assassinated			
First human flight to the moon	1969	NIXON	
Watergate burglars arrested	1972		SALT I signed
Indians protest at Wounded Knee	1973		Vietnam peace accord signed
			Yom Kippur War
			OPEC oil boycott
Nixon resigns	1974	FORD	
	1977	CARTER	Panama Canal treaty signed
	1978		Camp David accords signed
			Islamic revolution in Iran
U.S. recognizes Communist China	1979		Soviet Union invades Afghanistan
Nuclear accident at Three Mile Island			
"Reagan Revolution" tax and budget cuts	1981	REAGAN	Japan is graduating more engineers per year than the United States
Gramm–Rudman Act passed	1985		Mikhail Gorbachev becomes Soviet premier
Arms-for-hostage deal with Iran	1986		Fire at Chernobyl nuclear reactor
	1989	BUSH	
More than half of U.S. city landfills exhausted	1990		
	2000		Three out of five cities with population greater than 15 million are in third world

30

Cold War America

he war had been over for almost five months and still troop ships
steamed into New York and other ports, discharging soldiers eager to
meet their wives or perhaps a little anxious if they happened to spend
their last military hours in floating crap games where thousands of dollars changed hands. Timuel Black was packing his duffel below decks when he
heard some of the white soldiers calling, "There she is! The Statue of Liberty!"
Black felt a little bitter about the war. He'd been drafted in Chicago in 1943, just
after the race riots, and his father, a strong supporter of civil rights, was angry.
"What the hell are you goin' to fight in Europe for? The fight is here." He wanted
to go off with his boy to demonstrate in Detroit—and he would have, except the
roads were being blocked and the buses and trains screened to prevent Negroes'
coming in to make trouble.

In any case, Black was soon off to fight the Nazis, in a segregated army, with
separate mess halls, separate bunks, even separate towns in Britain to visit on
weekends off. He'd gone ashore during the D-Day invasion, survived the Battle of
the Bulge, and marched through one of the German concentration camps. "The
first thing you get is the stench," he recalled. "Everybody knows that's human
stench. You begin to realize something terrible had happened. There's quietness.
You get closer and you begin to see what's happened to these creatures. And you
get—I got more passionately angry than I guess I'd ever been." He thought: if it
could happen here, to the Germans, it could happen anywhere. It could happen to
black folk in America. So when the white soldiers called to come up and see the
Statue of Liberty, Black's reaction was, "Hell, I'm not goin' up there. Damn that."
But after all, he went up. "All of a sudden, I found myself with tears, cryin' and
saying the same thing [the white soldiers] were saying. Glad to be home, proud of
my country, as irregular as it is. Determined that it could be better. Just happy
that I had survived and buoyed up by the enthusiasm of the moment."

Across the other side of the continent, Betty Basye was working as a nurse in
a burn-and-blind center at Menlo Park, California. Soldiers from the Pacific were
shipped back there: "Blind young men. Eyes gone, legs gone. Parts of the face.
Burns—you'd land with a fire bomb and be up in flames." She'd joke with the
men, trying to keep their spirits up, talking about times to come. And when word
of V-J Day was broadcast, the hospital erupted in celebration. "Our superintendent of nurses led a conga line up and down the hospital, serpentine, up past

The mushroom-cloud image captured both the spectacle and potential horror of atomic warfare. With scant regard for the effects of radioactive fallout, the Defense Department conducted above-ground tests like this one near Las Vegas, Nevada, in 1953.

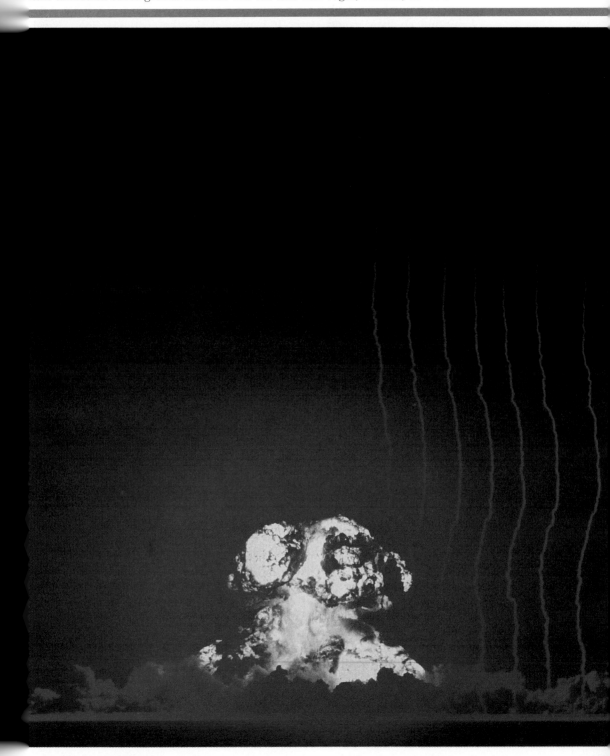

every bed. This took hours, because it was ward after ward. . . . Absolute bed-lam." And then Basye had to think about her own future. She kept her job for a while and was transferred to Pasadena, along with many of her patients. She would take one favorite of hers, Bill, for walks downtown. Half of Bill's face was gone, and civilians would stare. It happened to other patients, too. "Nicely dressed women, absolutely staring, just standing there staring." Some people wrote the local paper, wondering why disfigured vets couldn't be kept on their own grounds and off the streets. Basye sensed an indignation welling up. The war was over—"and we're still here." After a time, she started dating a soldier back from the South Pacific. "I got busy after the war," she recalled, "getting married and having my four children. That's what you were supposed to do. And getting your house in suburbia."

When Joe Hanley returned home he wasn't thinking about a house in subur-bia or even settling down. Getting off the streetcar in his old neighborhood, Chi-cago's North Side, the first thing he saw was a bar: "I'll have a shot and a beer," he said, and the bartender didn't take his money. "Welcome back, kid." Hanley didn't feel that welcome. He'd gone to war half convinced he'd be only "part of the cannon fodder. The sacrificial lamb. . . . It was a big surprise to everybody when you came home. What are you doing here? You know?" During the war, his foxhole buddy Kevin and he had been charging up a hill. "He went in one direc-tion and I went in another, hit the ground," and the next thing Hanley knew, Kevin was dead. It got to him. Kevin had a wife and young daughter; Hanley, nobody. The wrong man had been killed. After the Allies swept through Ger-many, his unit was sent to guard POWs. The Germans kept telling them, "Within 10 years you'll be fighting the Russians." Crazy! A lot of Germans felt that way. Back in Chicago, Hanley got a job in a local tavern and became the neighborhood bookie. He felt life was a joke. "Why worry about anything if within a moment or two you might die? Why get serious about it?" When gambling didn't provide enough action, he joined the police, hoping for more danger. But it seemed like child's play next to war. He did feel an obligation to Kevin and looked up his widow to tell her how it had been at the end and to befriend the young daughter. The acquaintance turned into friendship, and in 1949 Hanley married Kevin's wife. Life was slowly returning to normal.

Yet as Hanley, Basye, and Black were soon to discover, what was "normal" in these first years of peace was not entirely clear. The first truly global war had left a large part of Europe in ruins and the old balance of power shattered. Even if most Americans and their leaders wished to return to their isolationist attitudes of the 1930s—and, by and large, they did not—the dramatic events occurring month after month during 1945 and 1946 made it clear that the affairs of the wider world would not go away. For in the end, the United States converted not so much to peace as to a "cold war" against its former ally, the Soviet Union.

This undeclared war came to affect not only American foreign affairs, but almost every aspect of American life. Abroad, it justified a far wider military and economic role for the United States in areas like the Middle East and the Pacific rim from Korea to Southeast Asia. At home it sent major and minor politicians scurrying across the land in a search for Communist spies and "subversives" that took them from the State Department to Hollywood and into college classrooms. It influenced the curriculum teachers felt free to teach and even dictated the kinds of movies Americans watched. It dramatically increased the role of the military–industrial–university complex formed during World War II. "Reconversion" to peace, then, proved to be a process leading in unexpected directions.

CONVERSION: "THE AMERICAN PEOPLE WANT A REST"

At war's end, many business leaders feared that a sudden drop in government purchases would bring back the hard times of the 1930s. Munitions and aircraft factories would stand idle, while once-booming war communities like Willow Run became ghost towns. Instead, Americans went on a buying spree. High war wages had piled up in savings accounts and war bonds. Eager consumers set off to find the new cars, appliances, and foods unavailable during the war. Despite a sharp drop in government spending (from $83 billion in 1945 to only $31 billion in 1946), the gross national product fell less than 1 percent and employment actually increased. Consumers had taken up the slack.

In fact, demand was so high that shortages were widespread. Consumers found the lines in stores long, prices rising, and goods scarce. By the time the Office of Price Administration (OPA) lifted wage and price controls in June 1946, the inflation rate had jumped from an average of 2 percent during the war years to over 16 percent. And with demand so high, the scramble for goods became feverish. A customer determined to have fresh meat might be inspired to tip the butcher for the difficult task of lifting an order across the counter. Fresh hundred-dollar bills dropped at a salesman's feet circumvented the long wait for a new car. Builders held lotteries to see which lucky few out of thousands of applicants could have a new house.

Postwar Work

The transition from war to peace also meant significant dislocations in the job market. With millions of veterans looking for peacetime jobs, workers on the home front, especially women and minorities, found themselves out of work. By 1946 some 2.25 million women had left their jobs and another million were laid off. Yet heavy postwar consumer demand allowed 2.75 million women to find jobs, so that by 1950 women constituted 28 percent of the work force, up from 24 percent in 1940.

More to the point, the status of women's work declined. Their employment in the professions and managerial roles fell. Most women who returned to jobs after being laid off lost their seniority and had to move into lower positions that paid less. Most were concentrated in jobs that mirrored their traditional family responsibilities for nurturing: they were nurses, not doctors; teachers, not principals; tellers, not bankers. Far more worked in service (as maids, waitresses, or secretaries) than in manufacturing. The combined demands of work and family forced many women into low-paying part-time and unskilled jobs. Most places of employment were heavily segregated by gender. About 75 percent of women worked at female-only jobs. In fact, gender segregation in the workplace was worse in 1950 than in 1900 and more complete than segregation by race.

Equally important was the shift in attitudes in the prevailing culture. War employment had given many women their first taste of economic independence. As peace came, almost 75 percent of the working women in one survey indicated that they hoped to continue their jobs. But with peace came pressure for women to return to their more traditional roles. Male social scientists stressed how important it was for women to accept "more than the wife's usual responsibility for her marriage" and offer "lavish—and undemanding—affection" to returning GIs. One marriage counselor urged women to let their husbands know "you are tired of living alone, that you want him now to take charge."

For minorities, the end of the war brought a return of an old labor practice, "last hired, first fired." At the height of the war over 200,000 blacks and Hispanics had found jobs in shipbuilding. By 1946 that number had dwindled to less than 10,000. The influx of Mexican laborers under the bracero program temporarily halted. In the South, where the large majority of blacks lived, wartime labor shortages had become surpluses. Returning black and Hispanic veterans discovered that for them conditions at home had hardly improved.

Those workers who were not union members had no way to protest being laid off, but organized labor was determined to preserve the gains made during the war. As reconversion brought an abrupt decline in hours and overtime, unions demanded pay increases of up to 30 percent to make up for lost wages. When management balked, strikes spread across the nation. Autoworkers walked off the job in the fall of 1945; steelworkers in January 1946; miners in April. Strikes in such key industries seriously threatened to impede peacetime production. In 1946 some 5 million workers struck, a rate triple that of any previous year. Antiunion sentiment soared.

Most labor–management confrontations came eventually to the White House, where negotiators generally settled on wage increases ranging between 18 and 22 percent. But the crisis peaked in May 1946 with a threatened national rail strike, which would have paralyzed the nation's transportation network. An outraged President Truman asked, "What decent American would pull a rail strike at a time like this?" On May 23 he announced that the government would seize the railroads, while he requested power to draft striking workers into the military. The strike was settled before the threat could be carried out, but Truman's action startled liberals and conservatives alike. Few people approved the idea of using the draft as a punitive tool. Labor leaders, for their part, became convinced they had lost their friend at the White House.

The New Deal at Bay

Inflation, shortages, and labor unrest spelled political trouble for Harry Truman. In September 1945 he had boldly claimed his intention to extend the New Deal into the postwar era, with legislation to guarantee full employment, subsidized public housing, national health insurance, and a peacetime version of the Fair Employment Practices Commission to fight job discrimination. But by 1946 the spirit of reform had given way to a more conservative agenda. Truman's political stock had fallen in and out of Washington. Most of Franklin Roosevelt's old advisers had left the administration to lead more peaceful and private lives. In Congress, a coalition of conservative Republicans and southern Democrats stymied the president's attempts at further reform. All he achieved was a watered-down full-employment bill, which created the Council of Economic Advisors to guide the president's policies and at least established the principle that the government rather than the private sector was responsible for maintaining full employment.

As the elections of 1946 approached, Republicans harped on the production shortages, the procession of strikes, the mismanagement of the economy. "To err is Truman," proclaimed the campaign buttons—or, more simply, "Had Enough?" Evidently many voters had. The Republicans gained control of both houses of

Congress and 25 of 48 governorships. Not since 1928 had the Democrats fared so poorly.

Leading the rightward swing was Senator Robert A. Taft of Ohio, son of former president William Howard Taft. Bob Taft not only wanted to halt the spread of the New Deal—he wanted to dismantle it entirely, and especially limit the power of unions. "We have to get over the corrupting idea we can legislate prosperity, legislate equality, legislate opportunity," he said in dismissing the liberal agenda. In 1947 he led the fight to pass the Taft–Hartley Act, over Truman's veto. In the event of a strike, the bill allowed the president to order workers back on the job during a 90-day "cooling-off" period while collective bargaining continued. It also permitted states to adopt "right-to-work" laws, which banned the closed shop by eliminating union membership as a prerequisite for many jobs. Union leaders criticized the new law as a "slave-labor" act but discovered they could live with it, though it did hurt union efforts to organize, especially in the South.

Thus by 1947 the domestic conversion from war to peace was largely completed. In leaving behind the war and the Great Depression, most Americans did not repudiate the major accomplishments of the New Deal: Social Security, minimum wages, a more active role for government in reducing unemployment. But by and large they were not prepared to extend those reforms. As Truman himself conceded, "The American people have been through a lot of experiments and they want a rest."

Yet they were not to get one—at least not the sort they had been counting on. As the economy gradually shifted into a postwar boom, the rest of the world struggled to recover from years of devastation. Power had shifted from Europe to the periphery where in the new alignment the United States and the Soviet Union regarded each other as the world's two reigning superpowers—and as mortal enemies. Since this realignment had such serious and long-lasting consequences, it is worth looking in some detail at the pivotal events of 1945 and 1946. What happened that led the Western powers to split with their Soviet allies? How did the breach become irreparable?

THE RISE OF THE COLD WAR

In October 1944, with France recently liberated and the Allies on the offensive, Winston Churchill journeyed to Moscow to see Joseph Stalin. Getting down to work only at ten in the evening (Stalin loved to do business late at night), the two men discussed how the great powers might prevent conflicts from arising once the war was won. Churchill took out a sheet of paper and jotted down a number of smaller nations. Beside each he put a percentage indicating the amount of influence Britain or Russia might have. Romania—90 percent for the Russians. Greece—90 percent for the British, along with the Americans. Bulgaria—75 percent for the Russians. Hungary and Yugoslavia—50 percent each. Stalin read the list impassively, then handed it back to Churchill, who became a bit embarrassed at so baldly dividing the world into spheres of influence. He suggested burning the paper and also told Stalin that, as far as more public discussions went, it was "better to express these things in diplomatic terms and not to use the phrase 'dividing into spheres' because the Americans might be shocked. But as long as he and Marshal Stalin understood each other, he could explain matters to the President"—that is, of course, Roosevelt.

Roosevelt was not as naive about world affairs as this account might suggest. He too could speak matter-of-factly about the postwar world being managed by the "Four Policemen"—the United States, Russia, Britain, and China. And with Stalin as one of the policemen, Roosevelt was ready to concede that the Soviet Union could not be denied its own "sphere of influence." But he also knew that such big-power settlements went against long-cherished American ideals. Since the early Republic, Americans had championed, in principle at least, the right of small nations to determine their own fates, with their freedom guaranteed by treaties and international organizations. Such idealism inspired Woodrow Wilson's hopes for the League of Nations and Roosevelt's later support for the United Nations. In a sense, Roosevelt sought to balance two strands of thought: the traditional idealism of Wilson and the more practical recognition that the United States could not guarantee democracy in every nation and under every circumstance. Spheres of influence would inevitably continue to exist.

Truman was a different man. Lacking Roosevelt's experience or his easy confidence that he could manage "Uncle Joe," the new president approached the Sovi-

President Harry Truman and his Secretary of State James Byrnes relax on their return from the Potsdam Conference. At his first meeting with Stalin, Truman believed he needed to "stand up" to the Russians, and Byrnes consistently reinforced this approach as the cold war set in.

ets with a good deal more suspicion. "Stalin is an SOB, but of course he thinks I'm one, too," Truman commented after their meeting at Potsdam in July 1945. Behind all the diplomatic bowing and bluffing, what were the Soviets' real intentions? Stalin had spoken of adjusting Poland's borders, which could be chalked up as a matter of legitimate defensive security. But he had also asked that Russia assume joint control of the Dardanelles, Turkey's gateway to the Mediterranean. And he asked that the Soviet Union become trustee of Libya, Italy's former African colony. As one British diplomat at Potsdam aptly put it, the great debate was "whether Russia [is] peaceful and wants to join the Western Club but is suspicious of us, or whether she is out to dominate the world and is hoodwinking us." Truman and his advisers, like the diplomat, tended to opt for the same answer: "It always seems safer to go on the worse assumption."

With the war over, the Soviets resumed their claims to Libya and the Dardanelles. Furthermore, local Communists led the fighting to overturn the traditional monarchy in nearby Greece. And in November 1945 Soviet forces occupying part of Iran lent support to rebels seeking autonomy from the Iranian government. Asia, too, seemed a target for Soviet ambitions. Russian occupation forces in Manchuria were turning over captured Japanese arms to the Chinese Communist forces of Mao Tse-tung. Russian troops controlled the northern half of Korea. In other areas like Vietnam leftist nationalists were fighting against the return of colonial rule. To deal with this combination of menace and disorder Harry Truman and his advisers sought to frame a policy.

The View from West and East

Americans tended to suspect the worst of the Soviets, and for several reasons. To begin with, a deep ideological gulf had long separated the two nations. Since the October Revolution of 1917, most Americans viewed the Bolsheviks with a mixture of fear, suspicion, and loathing. Marxists, after all, had rejected both religion and the notion of private enterprise, two institutions central to the American dream. Further, Stalin's brutal purges during the late 1930s horrified the public and, even more important, left a lasting imprint on the American diplomatic corps. Finally, Soviet propagandists had made no secret of their intention to export revolution throughout the world, including the United States.

The most recent lesson of history—the war itself—seemed to dictate a stiff response to the Soviets. When Neville Chamberlain attempted a policy of appeasement with Hitler in 1938, it only emboldened German expansionism. After the war, Secretary of the Navy James Forrestal applied the Munich analogy when he argued that acceding to Russian demands would seem like an attempt "to buy their understanding and sympathy. We tried that once with Hitler. . . . There are no returns on appeasement." To many of Truman's advisers, the Soviet dictator seemed to be every bit as much bent on world conquest as Hitler had been.

Of course, Stalin's true intentions remain an open question, for historians have little information about the inner workings of the Soviet state. But the case can at least be made that after the war, Soviet attitudes did not center on a scheme for world domination. As they evaluated their situation, they saw the United States quite vigorously at work establishing its global influence. American occupation forces in Europe and Asia ringed the Soviet Union. American corporations owned or controlled vast oil fields in the Middle East and, along with the French and British, were a strong presence in Southeast Asia. In Latin America, the

United States had its own well-established sphere of influence. At the new United Nations, countries friendly to the United States far outnumbered those with links to the Soviet Union. And, of course, the United States alone possessed the atomic bomb. Stalin had reason to fear that the anticommunists in the American government would seek to exploit the weakness of his war-ravaged nation.

The Russians, too, had mastered their own lessons of history. Napoleon had invaded their nation in 1812; the "big powers" had forced Russia to give up territory after the Crimean War and at the Congress of Berlin. Germany had violated their land twice during the twentieth century. Given such precedents, Stalin might well have wished to protect the Soviet Union by controlling the nations surrounding him. Indeed, for a dictator accustomed to absolute power within his own territory, such an outlook was almost sheer habit. As one Yugoslav Communist leader remarked of Stalin, "Everything beyond the control of his police was a potential enemy."

The superiority of the American economy created another source of conflict. While Russia had been left devastated by Germany's invasion, the war had doubled the gross national product of the United States. The efficiency of American farms and factories, the quality of American consumer goods, along with technological innovation in the military and civilian sectors, gave Soviet leaders a feeling of inferiority. They realized that the Soviet Union could not compete successfully in the open world system the United States sought to establish after World War II. To make matters worse, the United States had quickly terminated its lend-lease program after V-J Day and refused a large loan that Stalin desperately needed to begin rebuilding his nation. As a final irritant, Americans were becoming increasingly reluctant to allow the Soviets to claim reparations from the Germans to help Russia back on its feet.

Toward Containment

The disagreements and mutual suspicion arising out of these conflicting points of view came to a head in the first months of 1946. For his part, Stalin announced in February that the Soviet Union would have to take unilateral steps to preserve its national security. In a world dominated by capitalism, he warned, future wars were inevitable. To assure against "any eventuality," the Russian people must be prepared to accept a new five-year plan for economic development.

Although some Americans thought Stalin was merely rallying Russian support for his domestic program, the speech confirmed the Truman administration's worst fears. "I'm tired of babying the Soviets," remarked the president, who in any case seldom wore kid gloves. Even Truman's mother passed along a message: "Tell Harry to be good, be honest, and behave himself, but I think it is now time for him to get tough with someone." *Time* magazine, an early voice for a "get tough" policy, called Stalin's speech "the most warlike pronouncement uttered by any top-rank statesman since V-J day" and was soon publishing maps showing the global threat of "Communist Contagion." In March Winston Churchill warned that the Soviets had dropped an "Iron Curtain" between their satellites and the free world.

Joseph Stalin.

As policymakers groped for an effective way to deal with these developments, the State Department received a diplomatic cable, extraordinary for both its 8000-word length and its impact on policy in Washington. The author, George Kennan, chargé d'affaires in Moscow and long a student of Soviet ways, argued that Russian leaders, including Stalin, were so paranoid that it was impossible to reach useful accommodations with them. "Nothing short of complete disarmament, delivery of our air and naval forces to Russia, and resigning of the powers of government to American Communists would even dent this problem," he wrote. Without the respectable cloak of Marxist ideology, Stalin "would stand before history, at best, as only the last in that succession of cruel and wasteful Russian rulers."

While Kennan's analysis was not particularly new, it did provide a clear framework for analyzing Soviet behavior and a strategic concept for responding to the Russians—"containment." By bringing to bear firm diplomatic, economic, and military counterpressure, the United States could block Soviet aggression wherever it occurred. Out of frustration the Soviets would be forced to drop their plans of conquest and alter their domestic institutions. Only then would an accommodation between East and West be possible. Hundreds of copies of Kennan's "long telegram" were made and sent to high officials in Washington as well as American diplomats abroad. Truman wholeheartedly adopted the doctrine of containment.

The Truman Doctrine

During the rest of 1946, the administration found few opportunities to apply the policy of containment. At first it seemed that Iran, with its strategic location and British-run oil fields, might serve the purpose. The Joint Chiefs of Staff, the combined American military command, had declared Iran's independence vital to the United States, for Iran held the key to secure oil fields in the Persian Gulf region. An oil mission sent to the area in 1943 had reported that vast Middle East oil fields would soon displace those in the United States as the center of world production. American oil companies had already established a major position in the region. During the war the U.S. government had taken a far more active role in the affairs

---

As American fears of Soviet intentions increased, journalists often described communism as though it were a disease, an inhuman force, or savage predator. In April 1946, *Time* magazine, a particularly outspoken source of anticommunist rhetoric, portrayed the spread of "infection" throughout Europe and Asia by the "Red Menace."

of Iran, Turkey, Saudi Arabia, and other Middle East states. Although Great Britain lost much of its regional influence to the United States, British diplomats welcomed the American presence as a safeguard against future Soviet expansion.

Iran seemed a likely Soviet target. British, American, and Russian troops occupied much of the country during the war. All three had negotiated unsuccessfully for oil concessions. By December 1945 the British and Americans had largely withdrawn, but the Soviet forces remained as part of a strategy to wrest economic and political concessions. In March 1946 Secretary of State James Byrnes went to the United Nations, determined to force a showdown over Soviet occupation of northern Iran. But before he could extract his pound of Russian flesh, the Soviets reached an agreement with Iran to withdraw their troops.

The critical cold war moment came in early 1947. As Europe reeled under severe winter storms and a depressed postwar economy, Great Britain announced it could no longer send aid to the beleaguered governments of Greece and Turkey. Truman decided to adopt a militant posture. Specifically, he wanted $400 million in military and economic aid for Greece and Turkey. The president went before Congress in March, determined to "scare hell out of the country." With the world divided into two hostile camps, he warned, the United States had to be prepared to step forward and help "free people" threatened by "totalitarian regimes." This position soon became known as the Truman Doctrine.

Critics were quick to point out that Truman had placed no limits on the American commitment. His was a proposal not simply to contain the communist threat to Greece and Turkey but also to resist Soviet expansion everywhere. Robert Taft thought it was a mistake to talk about a bipolar world divided into communist and anticommunist camps. Truman painted the alternatives in such strong colors, however, that Congress voted overwhelmingly to grant aid. In doing so, the nation took the critical step in entering the cold war. It linked Soviet communism with rebel movements all across the globe. It committed Americans to a relatively open-ended conflict. It expanded the president's powers to act in the face of a communist threat. All these actions would be debated in the decades to come, but by 1947 the die had been cast. Anticommunism had been established as a dominant theme in American policy, both foreign and domestic.

The Marshall Plan

For all its importance, the Truman Doctrine did not address the area of primary concern to Washington, Western Europe. Postwar economic collapse had left national treasuries empty, city streets dark, homes without heat, people starving, and factories closed. By 1947 American diplomats were warning that without American aid to revive the European economy, Communists would seize power in Germany, Italy, and France.

In June 1947 Secretary of State George C. Marshall stepped before a Harvard commencement audience to announce a New Deal–style recovery plan for Europe. He invited all European nations, East or West, to request assistance to rebuild their economies. Unlike the Truman Doctrine proposals, Marshall's speech made no mention of the communist menace, but his plan to provide Europe massive economic aid was designed to eliminate conditions that allowed Communists to take advantage of discontent. At the same time, generous credits would create far greater European demand for American goods, thus assuring markets and prosperity for the United States. And the secretary was gambling that fears of American economic penetration would lead the Soviets and their allies to reject his offer. At first neo-isolationists in Congress stymied aid under the guise of exercising fiscal conservatism. But when Communists expelled the non-Communists from Czechoslovakia's government, Congress approved the Marshall Plan, as it became known. And as the secretary anticipated, the Soviets blocked the efforts of Czechoslovakia and Poland to participate. The onus for dividing Europe fell, as Marshall guessed it would, on the Soviet Union, not the United States.

The Fall of Eastern Europe

Aggressive American efforts to stabilize Europe and the eastern Mediterranean placed Stalin on the defensive. At home he waged a battle against Western cultural influence. Even Russian soldiers and former prisoners of war were tainted, in his eyes, for allowing themselves to be captured or simply exposed to the West. Thousands were sent off to the Siberian labor camps, among them writer Alexander Solzhenitsyn, who later described the experience in *One Day in the Life of Ivan Denisovich.*

More shocking to the Western nations were Stalin's steps to consolidate Soviet political and military domination of Eastern Europe. In 1947 Stalin had moved even more forcefully against the moderate governments in Hungary and Czechoslovakia. Since 1945 Hungary had been ruled by a government chosen under relatively free elections. In June 1947 Soviet forces imposed a Communist regime subservient to Moscow. President Truman described that action as an "outrage." In February 1948 the duly elected government of Czechoslovakia was toppled and, shortly after, it was announced that the popular Czech foreign minister, Jan Masaryk, had fallen to his death from a small bathroom window. Suicide was the official explanation, but many suspected murder. In response to the Marshall Plan, Soviet foreign minister V. M. Molotov initiated a series of bilateral trade agreements tightly linking the Soviet and Eastern European economies in the COMECON (Council of Mutual Economic Assistance). In addition, he established the Cominform (Communist Information Bureau) to assert greater political control over foreign Communist parties.

Stalin's aggressive steps provoked further American efforts to win the cold war. By 1949 the United States and Canada had joined with Britain, France, Belgium, the Netherlands, and Luxembourg to establish the North Atlantic Treaty Organization (NATO) as a mutual defense pact. For the first time since Washington's Farewell Address in 1793 the United States during peacetime had entered into entangling alliances with European nations.

A crisis over Germany had precipitated that departure from tradition. In the process of forming NATO the Western powers had decided to transform their occupation zones into an independent West German state. The Western-controlled sectors of Berlin, however, lay over 100 miles to the east, well within the Soviet zone. On June 24 the Soviets reacted by blockading land access to Berlin. Truman's response was unequivocal: "We are going to stay, period." But he resisted the proposal of General Lucius Clay to shoot his way through the blockade. Instead, the United States began a massive airlift that lasted almost a year. In May 1949 Stalin lifted the blockade, conceding that he could not prevent the creation of West Germany.

Truman's firm handling of the Berlin crisis won him applause from both Dem-

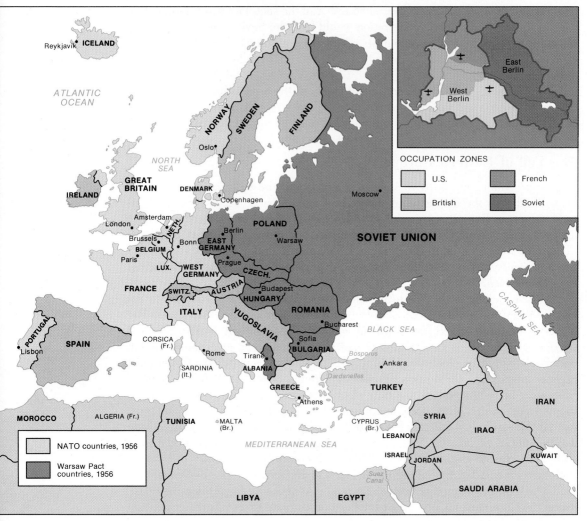

COLD WAR EUROPE
By 1956 the postwar occupation of Europe had hardened into rigid cold war boundaries. The United States reacted to the presence of Soviet conventional forces in Eastern Europe by rearming West Germany and creating the NATO alliance (1949) for the defense of nations from the North Atlantic through the Mediterranean basin. The U.S.S.R. formed a counteralliance under the Warsaw Pact (1955). While Bonn became the de facto capital of West Germany, Berlin remained the official capital and into the 1960s the focus of the most severe cold war tensions.

ocrats and Republicans. They were equally enthusiastic about another bold presidential action, the recognition of Israel in May 1948, minutes after the Israelis announced their independence. Truman had previously supported the immigration of Jews into Palestine, despite the opposition of oil-rich Arab states and diplomats in the State Department. Though the president was sympathetic to the idea of a Jewish homeland, he was also sensitive to the advice of political advisers preparing for the 1948 presidential campaign. As British Prime Minister Clement

Atlee observed, "There's no Arab vote in America, but there's a heavy Jewish vote and the Americans are always having elections."

The Atomic Shield versus the Iron Curtain

During the first months of the Berlin blockade, Truman and his advisers considered the possibility of war and its new ultimate question: would the atom bomb be used? Truman said he prayed not, but if the need arose, he would not flinch. The Department of Defense, planning for every eventuality, initiated a request for the transfer of bombing authority. But Truman drew the line: he was not going to have "some dashing lieutenant colonel decide when would be the proper time to drop one."

Increasingly the bomb loomed like a shadow falling across the developments of the postwar world. Truman's dilemma pointed up a major question: who would control the use of such monumental power, American civil or military authorities? In the international arena, should there be any controls over its development? What should happen if the Soviets developed their own bomb? In 1946 Americans were shocked to discover that Russian spies had been caught stealing Canadian atomic secrets. It was naive to think similar efforts were not being made in the United States. Truman asked how soon the Soviets might get the bomb, and he was assured by General Leslie Groves, head of the wartime Manhattan Project, that it would be at least 20 years, although American atomic scientists warned that the day might come within 5 years.

For the time being, however, Americans had their monopoly. In August 1946 President Truman signed the McMahon Bill, which established the Atomic Energy Commission (AEC) as a civilian agency with control over all fissionable materials for both peacetime and military applications. But General Groves had been working behind the scenes to give the military a decisive voice. It was Groves who had leaked information to the press about the spy ring delivering secrets to the Soviet Union. He wanted Congress as well as the public to doubt that scientists and civilians could be trusted with key secrets (though privately Groves admitted that no vital information had been lost). His campaign succeeded in amending the McMahon Act to give the military review over many civilian decisions. It also imposed such severe restrictions that sharing of information with Britain and Canada became virtually impossible. Under its terms, the AEC could not even permit the export of radioactive isotopes for medical research to neutral Sweden and Norway.

The idea of international control of atomic energy through the United Nations proved similarly vulnerable to cold war fears. Undersecretary of State Dean Acheson, TVA Director David Lilienthal, and physicist Robert Oppenheimer headed a committee that proposed to give a United Nations agency authority over the mining, refining, and use of the world's atomic raw materials. They believed that the Acheson–Lilienthal plan would afford the United States more security in the long run than a short-lived nuclear monopoly. But Truman put his adviser Bernard Baruch in charge of presenting the recommendations to the United Nations in June 1946. Baruch, a staunch cold warrior, was determined the United States would not give up its nuclear monopoly. His revised proposal ensured that the United States would be able to use the international agency not only to protect its own atomic resources but also to monitor the industrial and military uses of atomic energy within the Soviet Union.

The Soviets, naturally, rejected Baruch's proposal and instead introduced their own plan calling first for destruction of all nuclear bombs, then for an agreement never to use them, and, finally, for discussions about controls. Baruch had no intention of bargaining. It was either his plan or nothing, he announced. And so it was nothing, as the last serious attempt to achieve international cooperation collapsed. And while the United Nations debated, the United States conducted a nuclear bomb test on Bikini Atoll in the Pacific Ocean. The Truman administration had never seriously intended to sacrifice the American nuclear monopoly.

Atomic Deterrence

Ironically, because of the strict secrecy in developing the bomb, many of the military planners in charge of integrating it into American strategic planning knew little about it. Even Truman, in 1946, had no idea how many bombs the United States actually possessed. (For the two years after Hiroshima, it was never more than two.) The chiefs of the armed forces had at first tended to dismiss the weapon, in part from ignorance and in part from fears that too great a reliance on it might encourage the public to believe that conventional forces had become obsolete. But the situation soon changed.

By 1947 a tight-fisted Congress had cut the size of America's army down to a million soldiers. At the same time, the cold war was heating up in earnest. George Marshall, who had commanded some 8 million soldiers during the war as Army Chief of Staff, was now under pressure as secretary of state "to give the Russians hell." But as he ruefully observed, "My facilities for giving them hell—and I am a soldier and know something about the ability to give hell—was $1\frac{1}{3}$ divisions over the entire United States. That is quite a proposition when you deal with someone who has over 260 [divisions] and you have $1\frac{1}{3}$." Thus military planners were almost forced to adopt a nuclear strategy as the only deterrent to the overwhelming superiority of conventional Soviet forces in Europe.

At first what passed for nuclear strategies were little more than doomsday scenarios to incinerate vast areas of the Soviet Union. A 1946 war plan, "Pincher," modestly projected the obliteration of 20 Soviet cities in response to an attack on Western Europe. But the Joint Chiefs of Staff kept pressing the civilian AEC to permit stockpiling of more and more bombs. In 1948 "Fleetwood" raised the tally of cities to 77, with 8 bombs aimed for Moscow, 7 for Leningrad. Not until "Dropshot," the following year, did planners correct a major flaw in Fleetwood. If Moscow and Leningrad disappeared, who would be left to surrender? Dropshot recommended sparing those two cities until the second week. As military use of atomic materials continued to mount, David Lilienthal, the demoralized head of the Atomic Energy Commission, confessed that rather than promoting peaceful applications of nuclear energy, his agency had become "nothing more than a defense contractor for the Defense Department."

By 1948, then, not only was the cold war in full swing, but many Americans had hopes that the United States would win it. The Joint Chiefs of Staff had committed themselves to nuclear deterrence based on an American nuclear monopoly. Western Europe was on its way to economic recovery, thanks to the Marshall Plan. Soviet pressures on Greece, Turkey, and Iran had abated. Yet in one sense, success brought little comfort. The ideology of the cold war portrayed the Soviet Union as more than simply a major power seeking to protect its interests and expand where opportunity permitted. The Soviets were bent on dominating the world, even overthrowing the United States either from without or within. This was a war being fought not only across the globe but right in America, by unseen agents using underhanded means. In this way, the cold war mentality soon came to shape the lives of Americans at home much as it did American policy abroad.

THE COLD WAR AT HOME

With the worries of subversion and espionage increasing, President Truman acted to protect his own administration from the disloyalty of "Reds, phonies, and 'parlor pinks'" on the one hand and from the attacks of the Republican right on the other. On March 22, 1947, ten days after proposing the Truman Doctrine with its aid to Greece and Turkey, he signed an executive order establishing a Federal Employee Loyalty Program. Since there were over 2 million people employed by the government, plus another half million applying for jobs every year, it would be impossible for the Federal Bureau of Investigation (FBI) to examine them all; the order required supervisors to review and certify the loyalties of those who worked below them, reporting to a system of federal loyalty review boards. The FBI was to follow up any "derogatory information" that was unearthed.

The system quickly got out of hand. The conservative head of the Loyalty Review Board, Seth Richardson, made it clear that, in his opinion, the government could "discharge any employee for reasons which seem sufficient to the Government, and without extending to such employee any hearing whatsoever." Those accused would have no right to confront their accusers. After several years the difficulty of proving that employees were actually disloyal became clear, and Truman allowed the boards to fire those who were "potentially" disloyal or "bad security risks," such as alcoholics, homosexuals, and debtors. Suspected employees, in other words, were assumed guilty until proven innocent. After some 5 million investigations, the program identified a few hundred employees who, though not Communists, had at one time been associated with suspect groups. Rather than calm public fears, the loyalty program gave credibility to the growing "red scare."

HUAC, Hollywood, and Hiss

About the same time, the House Committee on Un-American Activities (HUAC) joined the hunt. Established in the 1930s, it gained the national limelight in 1947 with an investigation of communist influence in the film industry. Hollywood, with its wealth, glamour, and highly visible Jewish and foreign celebrities, had long aroused a mixture of attraction and suspicion among traditional Americans. "Large numbers of moving pictures that come out of Hollywood carry the communist line," charged committee member John Rankin of Mississippi. Indeed, during the Depression some Hollywood figures had developed ties to the Communist party or had become sympathetic to party causes. To generate support for the Allied cause during the war, with Roosevelt's blessing, Hollywood produced films with a positive view of the Soviet Union like *Mission to Moscow* and *Song of Russia*.

In 1947 HUAC interrogated a parade of movie stars, screen writers, and

Daily Lives

POLITICAL CULTURE

Film Noir in an Uncertain Cold War

For many years film had been recognized as a powerful medium of communication, for political purposes as much as for entertainment. During World War I, American audiences were rallied to support the Liberty Loan program with movies like *Stake Uncle Sam to Play Your Hand*, in which evil Germans in pointed helmets ravished innocent Belgian women. During World War II, Hollywood willingly promoted the war effort, whether highlighting Nazi atrocities in *Hitler's Children* or promoting the virtues of America's new-found Soviet ally in *Song of Russia*.

Such films were overt propaganda. But commercial and artistic films could also reflect the political temper of an era, conveying more subtle nuances within American culture. Outwardly, the public mood following World War II seemed one of celebration and joy. In the face of both the Great Depression and the horrors of World War II the United States had won its way to economic prosperity and triumph abroad. Yet beneath the surface of public optimism flowed a surprising current of pessimism and alienation. That darker mood produced a distinctive style, especially in the movies of the postwar era.

The gangster and hard-boiled detective films of the 1930s had already introduced audiences to an urban world of violence and disorder. But many films of the 1940s were more disturbing. Called *film noir* (literally, black film) by French critics, the new genre was visually darker and more abstract, dealing in pessimistic themes and brutal, even pathological characters. Sinister forces from without

menaced the heroes or heroines, who themselves had become psychologically more complex. Sexual and spiritual confusion replaced altruism and moral decency as motives. Gone were the prostitutes with hearts of gold, the stoic wives, and the sweet marriageable girls. The *femmes noires* tended to be sulky sirens, temptresses, or sinister black widows, who might double-cross their men or ensnare them in webs of suffocating domesticity.

What brought this dark mood into the traditionally upbeat Hollywood scene? Partially, it reflected a European influence on the home-grown film industry. Just as émigrés fleeing from Nazi regimes influenced the sciences and arts, European directors like Fritz Lang, Billy Wilder, and Otto Preminger brought their cosmopolitan tastes and a visually abstract style to the American cinema. They favored scenes with sharp contrasts of dark and light in which only a portion of the screen was lit and the rest left dark. When the war came, that style became a practical necessity. Shortages of lights, electricity, and technical crews forced directors to underlight their sets. Thematically, stark lighting was used to produce a bleaker image that emphasized the shadowy world of films dealing with urban crime, international intrigue, personal anxiety, and totalitarian evil. British director Alfred Hitchcock in *Suspicion* (1941) and *Shadow of a Doubt* (1943) introduced audiences to heroes—played by matinée idols like Cary Grant and Joseph Cotton—who seemed breezy and cheerful at first, but as the plot advanced, appeared more and more to be calculating murderers.

Even after wartime restrictions had ended, directors continued to use the same visual effects by choice, in part due

Daily Lives

Son John: A Communist so low, he lied with a hand on the family Bible.

to the change in the political climate. With the cold war in full swing and two atomic superpowers confronting each other, the attitudes of *film noir* had ample reason to flourish. Many Americans suspected that the masters of science and progress had unwittingly unleashed fundamentally destructive forces of nature. In friendly hands, such power promised safety; in alien hands, it threatened American survival. News that Soviet spies had stolen atomic secrets fed a national fear. How could America be safe from enemies it could neither see nor recognize, in a world where people of privilege betrayed society's trust? Such issues echoed *film noir*'s preoccupation with mistaken identity and misplaced loyalties.

Thus, the protagonist in the 1949 *film noir* classic *D.O.A.* (the abbreviation for "Dead on Arrival"), fleeing to the big city in search of liberation, discovers that he has been mysteriously poisoned by a fatal radioactive drug, prompting him to devote the remaining hours of his life to tracking down his murderer, killing him, and then giving himself up to the police. Similarly bleak films, focusing on corrupt police, fascistic authorities, or even invaders from outer space, allowed Americans to address new fears of dehumanizing communism and nuclear annihilation through stories that were old and familiar. Similar themes of distrust and betrayal were widespread in American culture, appearing in the writings of authors as varied in style, subject, and background as James Jones and Norman Mailer, who wrote about World War II (*From Here to Eternity* and *The Naked and the Dead*), the black novelist Ralph Ellison (*The Invisible Man*), and J. D. Salinger (*The Catcher in the Rye*).

The conviction that film had the power to shape as well as reflect public attitudes brought the House Un-American Activities Committee to Hollywood in order to drive "subversives" out of the film industry. Chastened producers soon jumped on the anticommunist bandwagon, producing a succession of staunchly patriotic films. In *My Son John* (1952), for example, two doting parents discover that their boy has become a Communist spy willing to lie even with his hand on the Holy Bible. Still, despite these pious pleas for conformity, congressional critics came to realize that the Hollywood "dream factory" could spin out *film noir* nightmares as easily as it manufactured patriotic fantasies.

producers about subversive influences in the film industry. Some witnesses were considered "friendly" because, like Gary Cooper, Robert Montgomery, and Ronald Reagan, they answered committee questions or supplied names of suspected leftists. But some refused to inform on others or to answer questions about prior ties to the Communist party. Eventually 10 uncooperative witnesses, known as the "Hollywood Ten," refused on First Amendment grounds to say whether they were or ever had been Communists. They served prison terms for contempt of Congress. Also serving time was Chairman J. Parnell Thomas, who was convicted of payroll fraud.

For all its probing, HUAC never offered any convincing evidence that film-makers were spreading subversive propaganda. About the most damning evidence presented was that one eager left-leaning extra, when asked to "whistle something" during his walk-on part, hummed a few bars of the Communist anthem, the "Internationale." The investigations did, however, inspire Hollywood to produce such films as *The Iron Curtain* (1948), in which a Russian spy ring in Canada is exposed, as well as *Red Menace* (1949), *I Was a Communist for the FBI* (1950), and *My Son John* (1952). The studios also purged actors suspected of disloyalty, adopting a "blacklist" that prevented admitted or accused Communists from finding work. Since no judicial proceedings were involved, victims of false charges, rumors, or spiteful accusations found it nearly impossible to clear their names.

In addition to congressional hearings, the government employed a variety of legal, political, and investigatory strategies to harass suspected subversives. The Taft–Hartley Act required union officials, but not management, to sign affidavits pledging no Communist affiliation. Under such pressures, the CIO expelled 11 left-wing unions because the members had democratically elected Communists or suspected Communists to union posts. CIO leader Philip Murray defended the action as necessary to remove "the dirty, filthy traitors." The Justice Department undertook a direct attack on the small and largely ineffective American Communist party. It charged the leadership under the wartime Smith Act (1940) with conspiring to advocate the violent overthrow of the government. Prosecutors built their case largely on the testimony of FBI informers who had infiltrated the party, though it was not an illegal organization.

Suspicion of aliens and immigrants led finally to the passage, over Truman's veto, of the McCarran International Security Act (1950). It required all Communists to register with the attorney general, forbade the entry of anyone who had belonged to a totalitarian organization, and allowed the Justice Department to detain suspect aliens indefinitely during deportation hearings. It was supported overwhelmingly in Congress (three future presidents voted for it—Kennedy, Johnson, and Nixon). Among the handful of representatives who dared to criticize it was Senator William Langer, an independent Republican of North Dakota, who called it "one of the most vicious, most dangerous pieces of legislation against the people that has ever been passed."

The notion that subversives were undermining the government seemed confirmed in 1950 when a jury convicted former State Department official Alger Hiss of perjury. Hiss, an adviser to Roosevelt at the Yalta Conference, had been accused by former Communist Whittaker Chambers of passing secrets to the Soviet Union during the 1930s. The hunt for evidence, first led by the young Congressman Richard M. Nixon of HUAC, took the press and public on a dramatic journey, including a trip to Chambers' farm where three microfilms were extracted from a hollow pumpkin, said to be a drop for spy secrets. Though the evidence in the case was far from conclusive, the jury convicted Hiss, not of espionage, but for lying about his association with Chambers. While the trial was in progress, the nation was further shocked by news from Britain that a high-ranking physicist, Klaus Fuchs, had spied for the Russians while working on the Manhattan Project. Evidence in the Fuchs trial led to the 1951 prosecution of Ethel and Julius Rosenberg as part of an atomic spy ring. The Rosenbergs were convicted of espionage and then executed in 1953 despite appeals for clemency.

The Ambitions of Senator McCarthy

Into this climate of fear, where legitimate concerns mixed with irrational hysteria, stepped Joseph R. McCarthy, the junior senator from Wisconsin. McCarthy, a corrupt Senate mediocrity in search of an issue to get him reelected, settled on anticommunism. To an audience in Wheeling, West Virginia, in February 1950 he waved a sheaf of papers in the air and announced that he had a list of 205—or perhaps 81, 57, or "a lot" of—Communists in the State Department. (No one, including the senator, could remember the number, which he continually changed.) In the following months McCarthy announced charge after charge. He had penetrated the "iron curtain" of the State Department to discover "card-carrying Communists," the "top Russian espionage agent" in the United States, "egg-sucking phony liberals," and "Communists and queers" who wrote "perfumed notes."

It seemed not to matter that McCarthy never substantiated his charges. When examined, his lists proved to be of people who had left the State Department long before or who had been cleared by the FBI. When forced into a corner, McCarthy simply lied and went on to another accusation. No one seemed beyond reach. In the summer of 1950 a Senate committee headed by Millard F. Tydings of Maryland concluded that McCarthy's charges were "a fraud and a hoax," but few in government were bold enough to attack "Jolting Joe" from Wisconsin, especially after 1950 when he helped defeat Tydings and several other Senate critics.

McCarthy was in one sense a maverick who over time wreaked havoc on the political system and both parties. He may even have sincerely opposed communism. Certainly, his imagination for communist demonology was almost without bounds. But in another sense, McCarthyism was the bitter fruit Truman and the Democrats reaped from their own attempts to exploit the anticommunist mood. McCarthy, more than Truman, had tapped the fears and hatreds of a broad coalition of Catholic leaders, conservatives, and neo-isolationists who harbored suspicion of things foreign, liberal, internationalist, cosmopolitan, or vaguely intellectual. They saw McCarthy and his fellow witch hunters as the protectors of a vaguely defined but deeply felt spirit of Americanism. For them the notion that all Americans, including Communists, were entitled to free speech smacked of heresy. Those who criticized America or defended its enemies were not entitled to its freedoms, the McCarthyites and many cold war liberals had concluded.

By the time Truman stepped down as president, 32 states had laws requiring teachers to take loyalty oaths, government loyalty boards were asking employees what newspapers they subscribed to or phonograph records they collected, and a library in Indiana had banned *Robin Hood* because the idea of stealing from the rich to give to the poor seemed rather too leftish. As one historian commented, "Opening the valve of anticommunist hysteria was a good deal simpler than closing it."

THE CULTURE OF PROSPERITY

No matter how strident it might be, anticommunist hysteria could not dampen the simple joys of getting and spending. The postwar years opened an era of unprecedented prosperity. Two forces drove this economic boom. One was unbridled consumer and business spending that followed 16 years of depression and war. The other was a rapid expansion in government expenditures at the local, state, and federal levels. The three major growth industries since World War II—health care, education, and government—were spurred by public spending. Equally important was the federal government's expenditure in the military–industrial sector. The defense budget, which fell to $9 billion in 1947, reached $50 billion by the time Truman left office.

What this growth made clear was that Americans, despite their wish to avoid any more "experiments," did not abandon the basic premises of the New Deal. The government maintained its commitment to setting a minimum wage, raising it again in 1950 from 45 to 75 cents. Social Security coverage was broadened to cover an additional 10 million workers. Furthermore, a growing list of welfare programs benefited not only the poor, but veterans, middle-income families, the elderly, and students. The most striking of these was the GI Bill of 1944.

Soldiers as Civilians

For returning veterans, the GI Bill of Rights created unparalleled opportunity. Between 1945 and 1952 the federal government spent some $13.5 billion on education and training. Veterans with more than two years service received all tuition and fees plus $50 a month ($75 for married GIs) for three years of college education at any school. States like New York and California rapidly expanded their university systems to meet the demand from veterans. By 1948 the government was paying the college costs of almost 50 percent of all male students as over 2 million veterans went to college on the GI Bill.

Increased educational levels encouraged a shift from blue- to white-collar work and self-employment. Although available jobs in areas like mining and manufacturing increased little if at all, work in areas like insurance, teaching, state and local governments, construction, and retailing expanded rapidly. Veterans also received low-interest loans to start businesses or farms of their own and to buy homes. By the 1950s the Veterans Administration (VA), which doled out this federal largesse, funded the purchase of some 20 percent of all new houses.

The GI Bill accelerated trends that would transform American society into a prosperous, better educated, heavily middle class suburban nation. Between 1945 and 1970 veterans, especially those with college educations, earned over 40 percent more than nonveterans. The GI Bill also contributed to the economic advantages white males held over minorities and females. Few women received benefits under the bill. Many lost their jobs or seniority to returning veterans. Blacks and Hispanics, even those eligible for veterans' benefits, were hampered by Jim Crow restrictions in segregated universities and jobs in both the public and private sectors. The Federal Housing Administration even helped draw up "model" restrictive housing covenants neighborhoods could adopt in order to "retain stability" by segregating according to "social and racial classes."

The Baby Boom

For many Americans the Depression followed by the war had interrupted plans for beginning a family. The postwar era changed that dramatically. In 1946 Americans married in record numbers, twice as many as in 1932. The United States had in fact one of the highest marriage rates in the world. (The divorce rate peaked, too, in 1946, but most of those divorced promptly remarried.) The brides were younger, which translated into unusual fertility. During the Depression birth rates had been at an all-time low, about 18 to 19 per thousand. They began to rise during the war and by 1952 had passed 25, one of the highest fertility rates in the world. Americans also chose to have larger families, as the number with three children tripled and those with four or more quadrupled. "Just imagine how much these extra people, these new markets, will absorb—in food, in clothing, in gadgets, in housing, in services," one newspaper columnist predicted. Not only did the baby boom contribute to the expanding economy; the prosperity and newer attitudes that came with it also reshaped childrearing practices.

The new preoccupation with courtship and marriage focused attention on issues of sexuality. One controversial foray into this territory was *Sexual Behavior in the Human Male* (1948, followed by *Sexual Behavior in American Women*, 1952), written by social researcher Alfred Kinsey. Commentators called the *Kinsey Report* "the most talked about book of the twentieth century." Polls indicated that 20 percent of the nation had read it or knew about it. Kinsey revealed among other things that about a third of all males had experienced some form of homosex-

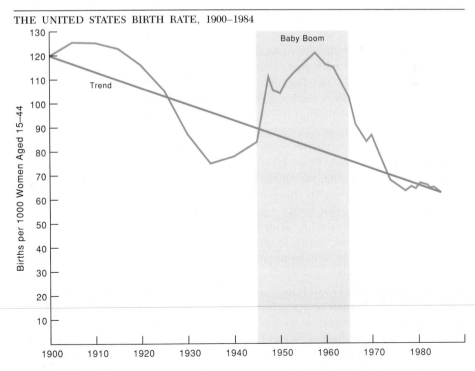

THE UNITED STATES BIRTH RATE, 1900–1984

Sources: U.S. Bureau of the Census, *Historical Statistics of the United States* and *Statistical Abstract of the United States*, various years.

ual activity, that extramarital sex was common for both men and women, and that women enjoyed sex in much the same way men did. Socioeconomic factors of race, class, ethnicity, and age often dictated sexual preferences. Middle-class whites avoided premarital intercourse more than lower class whites. At the same time, the middle class did more petting, kissing, and masturbating, while the lower classes were shy about kissing but less shy about intercourse.

It is difficult in more sexually liberated times to appreciate the impact of Kinsey's work. Perhaps most controversial was his claim that couples who had premarital sex tended to be better adjusted in marriage. Critics charged that Kinsey was a "menace to society" who would destroy the morals of the nation. Some accused him of abetting communism and called on Senator McCarthy's Permanent Investigating Subcommittee to investigate him. Other Americans found liberation in the discovery that behaviors once treated as sinful or perverse were widely accepted.

Hail, Suburbia

The boom in marriage and families created a need for housing; the growing prosperity, an intense desire for a home of one's own. At war's end, 5 million families were searching, eager to find anything, tired of living doubled up with other families, or in basements, or even in coal cellars. Housing was so scarce that one newspaper carried an advertisement offering a large icebox "which could be fixed up to live in." But with the help of the GI Bill and the rising prosperity, the chance to own, not merely rent, housing became a reality for over half of American families (up to 55 percent in 1950, from 43.6 in 1940).

In the postwar era a house was more often in a suburb than in a city. By the 1950s urban growth outside the South and West had virtually stopped, while the population in communities ringing central cities grew almost 50 percent. Urbanites wanting to escape the crowding and chaos of large cities were drawn to more pastoral communities with names like Park Forest, Briarcliff Manor, or Pacific Palisades. During the 1940s the increasing movement of the poor, Hispanics, and blacks into urban centers encouraged more affluent whites to move to the suburbs. Here families could find the detached single-family house with a lawn and garden idealized in American culture.

In the 1940s inexpensive suburban housing became synonymous with the name of William Levitt. From building houses for war workers, Levitt learned how to use mass production techniques. In 1947 he began construction of a 17,000-house community in the New York City suburb of Hempstead. All the materials for a Levittown house were precut and assembled at a factory, then moved to the site for assembly. If all went according to schedule, a new house was erected on a cement slab every 16 minutes. Buoyed by his success in Hempstead, Levitt later built other developments in Bucks County, Pennsylvania, and Willingboro, New Jersey.

The typical early Levitt house, a "Cape Codder," had a living room, kitchen, bath, and two bedrooms on the ground floor and an expansion attic, all for $7990. None had custom features, insulation, or any amenities that complicated construction. "The reason we have it so good in this country," Levitt said, "is that we can produce lots of things at low prices through mass production." Uniformity in house style extended to behavior as well. Levitt discouraged owners from changing colors or adding distinctive features to the house or yard. Buyers promised to cut the grass each week of the summer and not to hang out wash on weekends.

In the wake of the baby boom and a demand for new homes, mass-produced houses soon filled suburban developments all across the United States. By varying styles only slightly, developers were able to construct houses quickly at prices many young couples could afford.

Blacks were expressly excluded. Other suburban communities excluded Jews and ethnics in the restrictive covenants that dictated who could take up residence.

By 1950 some 5 million new housing units had been built, many in the new suburbs. But over 2.5 million families still lived doubled up. In California, a state with three cars registered for every four residents, suburbs bloomed across the landscape. By 1962 California had become the nation's most populous state. Growth was greatest around Los Angeles, once the center of the most extensive (1100 miles) urban electric railroad system in the world. In 1940 city planners launched construction of a freeway system to lure shoppers into downtown Los Angeles. Instead, white Angelinos saw the road network as an opportunity to migrate to the suburbs. Eventually one-third of the Los Angeles area was covered by highways, parking lots, and interchanges, increasing to two-thirds in the downtown areas. Los Angeles County developed a higher percentage of detached housing (about 67 percent) than other major cities like Chicago with 28 percent, New York with 20 percent, and Philadelphia with 15 percent.

Much of the white population that moved to the suburbs was replaced by blacks and Hispanics, who were part of larger migrations, especially of millions of southern black families leaving the South over the next two decades to search for work in urban centers. The majority headed for the Northeast and Upper Midwest. While central cities lost 3.6 million whites they gained 4.5 million blacks. Indeed, by 1960 half of all black Americans would live in central cities. Blacks and Hispanics were also drawn to California. In 1940 only 1.8 percent of California's population was black. By 1950 that percentage increased to 4.3 (and to 8 by 1970). As of 1945, only Mexico City had a larger Hispanic population than Los Angeles. And by the 1960s the 3 million Hispanic Californians made up 16 percent of the

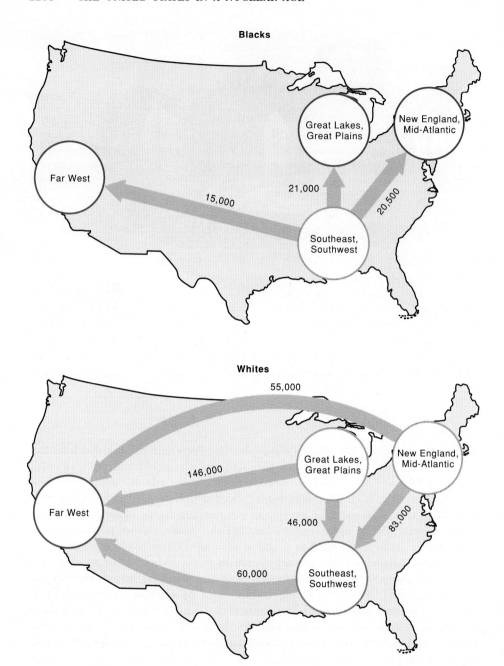

Source: Frank Levy, *Dollars and Dreams: The Changing American Income Distribution* (New York: Russell Sage Foundation, 1987), p. 106.

AVERAGE ANNUAL REGIONAL MIGRATION, 1947–1960

While African-Americans were moving in significant numbers to urban centers in the Northeast, Midwest, and Far West, whites were being drawn to the increasingly diversified economy of the South as well as the new industries stimulated by the war in the Far West. By the 1970s, the trend became known as the "Sunbelt" phenomenon.

population. Although most came from rural Mexico, 85 percent eventually settled in cities.

When poor black and Hispanic migrants poured into cities after the war, their prospects were particularly bleak. Earlier waves of European immigrants had been absorbed by the expanding urban economy, but during the 1950s the flight of jobs and middle-class population to the suburbs made it impossible for blacks and Hispanics to follow the same path. With fewer jobs and declining educational systems due to the loss of middle-class taxpayers, the cities were no longer well equipped to acculturate the newcomers and integrate them into the economy. Unemployment for the most recently arrived was over 40 percent in the worst areas.

Since few blacks or Hispanics could afford the cost of suburban living, they accounted for less than 5 percent of the population there. Black suburbanites were poorer, held lower status jobs, lived in more ramshackle housing, and had less education than blacks in the cities. The pattern for whites was just the opposite. The few black suburbs that existed dated from before the war and had little in common with the newer white "bedroom communities." Blacks who could afford to move could not find suitable housing at any price. Real estate agents refused to show them houses; bankers would not provide mortgages. And many communities adopted either restrictive covenants or zoning regulations that kept blacks and other "undesirables" out. William Myers finally managed in 1957 to buy a house from a white family in Levittown, Pennsylvania, but the developers did not sell directly to blacks until 1960.

The Flickering Gray Screen

The move to the suburbs, combined with generally shorter working hours in white-collar jobs, influenced the way Americans spent leisure time. Nowhere can this better be seen than in the popularity of television.

Television was not new in the 1940s. The technology had existed since 1927, and in 1939 the National Broadcasting Company (NBC) and Columbia Broadcasting System (CBS) had begun regular broadcasting. Programs included bits of musicals, vaudeville acts, and sports, transmitted by some 23 stations around the country. The war halted broadcasting as skilled personnel and equipment were shifted to military work, but with the coming of peace television quickly realized its potential as a mass medium. The Radio Corporation of America (RCA) rushed to produce modestly priced black-and-white sets and to improve the quality of picture tubes. By 1949 Americans owned a million television sets tuned into 108 licensed stations. Just three years later 15 million sets had been sold and by 1960 there were 46 million sets. Indeed, more Americans had televisions than had bathrooms.

The networks offered sports, news (with film produced by movie studios), dramatic series, and puppet shows like "Kukla, Fran, and Ollie" and "The Howdy Doody Show" for children. In 1948 the networks assumed an important role in politics as they covered both the Democratic and Republican conventions. Two years later, the medium showed its ability to combine entertainment, politics, and news by televising a series of hearings on organized crime chaired by Senator Estes Kefauver. Some 30 million viewers watched the New York City hearings broadcast live. The star attraction was mobster Frank Costello, who headed a large interstate criminal organization with close ties to city governments. Forbidden to show the witness himself, the television cameras focused on his hands as he nervously tore up bits of paper before finally walking out. Senator Kefauver gained such widespread fame that he emerged as a leading presidential candidate in the 1952 elections.

The spread of television soon transformed traditional habits of entertainment. At war's end, Americans had been a nation of moviegoers. About 75 percent of the potential audience went to the movies three times a month. Radio satisfied the need for news and information in over 90 percent of all homes, with listeners tuning in an average of five hours a day. By the early 1950s both media had experienced a dramatic decline in popularity. Movie attendance dropped to half of its 1946 peak and over 4000 neighborhood theaters closed in cities around the country. Many of them were replaced in the suburbs by popular drive-ins, which allowed whole families to enjoy movies in the comfort of their cars. But even that novelty failed to attract people in the same numbers. Radio suffered, too, as television lured away established comedians like Jack Benny, George Burns and Gracie Allen, and "Amos 'n' Andy."

The move to the suburbs reinforced this pattern. The big theaters and sports stadiums were still in the cities, where attendance was dropping; the fans were increasingly in the suburbs. In the more decentralized environment, baby boom parents spent much of their free time at home with their children. They could watch sports and movies on television. Even restaurant owners felt the squeeze. When Sid Caesar and Imogene Coca appeared on Saturday nights in "Your Show of Shows," diners rushed home to their television sets.

Television was no less immune to the red scare than Hollywood had been. In 1950 broadcasters and advertisers received an ominous booklet with a red hand closing over a microphone. "The Cominform and the Communist Party U.S.A. now rely more on radio and TV than the press and motion pictures as 'belts' to transmit pro-Sovietism to the American public," announced the authors of *Red Channels: The Report of Communist Influence in Radio and Television*. Then followed a list of some 151 of the most widely admired and talented names in broadcasting. Many people thought at first the list was a joke, but the authors were dead earnest. And though most of the named celebrities had been unjustly accused, many suddenly found themselves "controversial" and their shows canceled.

THE POLITICS OF FRUSTRATION

Going into the 1948 elections, Harry Truman had two strong suits. The first was the economy, which was back on track. The second was the bipartisan support won for his anti-Soviet foreign policy. But for all that, Truman found himself in deep trouble. The conservative mood that gave the Republicans control of the 80th Congress seemed to guarantee them victory in 1948. A coalition of Republicans and southern Democrats had eviscerated the president's legislative program. Inflation threatened to erode economic gains. And there was the problem of Truman himself. He seemed to lack, as one newspaper observed, "the stature, the vision, the social and economic grasp, or sense of history required to lead the nation in time of crisis." As much as people might admire Truman's spunk, his feisty spirit, and his honesty, many Democratic politicians would have preferred war hero Dwight Eisenhower as their candidate.

As if that were not enough, the New Deal coalition which Franklin Roosevelt had held together for so long seemed to be coming apart. On the left stood Henry Wallace, a capable secretary of agriculture and vice president under Roosevelt, then secretary of commerce under Truman. But Wallace wanted to pursue New Deal reforms even more vigorously than did Truman, and he continually voiced his sympathy for the Soviets at a time when the rest of the administration was moving rightward. Truman had fired him in 1946. Two years later, disaffected liberals bolted the Democratic party to support Henry Wallace at the head of a third-party Progressive ticket.

At the same time, the southern conservative wing of the party bitterly opposed Truman's moderate civil rights programs, which included proposals for a voting rights bill and an antilynching law. Truman sincerely opposed discrimination and knew, as well, that it was good politics to hold on to the black vote, which Roosevelt had wooed away from the Republican party for the first time since Reconstruction. But Truman also hailed from the border state of Missouri and knew how strong the sentiment for segregation was. At the 1948 Democratic National Convention he hoped to soft-pedal civil rights in the party platform, but he was outvoted by the liberal wing of the party. At that point delegates from several Deep South states stalked out of the convention. Soon they banded together to create the States' Rights or "Dixiecrat" party, with J. Strom Thurmond, the segregationist governor of South Carolina, as their candidate.

With the Democrats seemingly hopelessly divided, the Republicans had turned confidently once again to New York Governor Thomas Dewey and, as his running mate, the popular liberal governor of California, Earl Warren. The aloof Dewey inspired little enthusiasm, but he also had few enemies. "You have to know Dewey well to really dislike him," one disgruntled supporter of Robert Taft quipped. Two months before the election political pollster Elmo Roper stopped canvassing the voters. It seemed clear that Dewey would walk away with the election.

Truman, however, would not roll over and play dead. He launched an all-out attack against the "reactionaries" in Congress: that "bunch of old mossbacks . . . gluttons of privilege . . . all set to do a hatchet job on the New Deal." Hiring a

ELECTION OF 1948

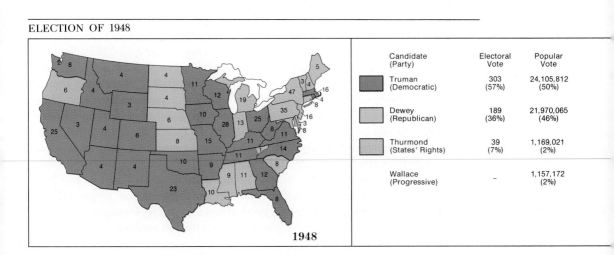

Candidate (Party)	Electoral Vote	Popular Vote
Truman (Democratic)	303 (57%)	24,105,812 (50%)
Dewey (Republican)	189 (36%)	21,970,065 (46%)
Thurmond (States' Rights)	39 (7%)	1,169,021 (2%)
Wallace (Progressive)	–	1,157,172 (2%)

1948

train, he whistle-stopped 30,000 miles across the country, making almost 400 speeches in eight weeks. Over and over he hammered away at the "do-nothing" 80th Congress, which, he told farmers, "had stuck a pitchfork" in their backs. As Truman pounded on the podium to emphasize his attack, someone would yell, "Give 'em hell, Harry!" "I'm a-doin' it," the president would shoot back. Still, on election day the odds makers were giving Dewey the edge by as much as 20 to 1. Hours before the polls closed the archconservative Chicago *Tribune* happily headlined "Dewey Defeats Truman." Once again, the experts were wrong. Not only did the voters return Truman by over 2 million popular votes, but they also gave the Democrats commanding majorities in the House and Senate.

The defection of the liberal and conservative extremes had allowed Truman to hold the New Deal coalition together. He had been the first major presidential candidate to campaign in Harlem. Jews grateful for his stand on Israel, Catholics loyal to the Democratic party, and ethnics all supported him. Farmers hurt by falling prices had deserted the Republicans. An easing of inflation had reminded middle-income Americans that they had benefited enormously under Democratic leadership. "I have a new car and am much better off than my parents were. Why change?" one suburban voter remarked.

The Fair Deal

As Harry Truman assumed the presidency in his own right, he expressed his conviction that all Americans were entitled to a "Fair Deal" from their government. His agenda called for a vigorous revival of New Deal programs and, echoing an old Populist idea, an effort to forge stronger links between farmers and labor.

In reality New Deal liberalism was in a period of decline. The coalition of Democratic and Republican conservatives in Congress rejected plans for a St. Lawrence Seaway in the Northeast, a TVA-style project in the Missouri River Valley, and other regional projects. The American Medical Association lobbied strongly to block a program of national health insurance. The Catholic church opposed federal aid to education, since it did not authorize subsidies to parochial schools. Furthermore, Truman could not forge a working coalition between farmers and labor. The farm block would not support labor in its attempts to repeal the Taft–Hartley Act, nor would labor vote to help pass farm price supports designed to encourage family farms at the expense of larger agribusinesses.

Civil rights legislation proved even more frustrating. Truman's Committee on Civil Rights had published its report, *To Secure These Rights*, in 1947. The committee exposed a racial caste system that denied blacks employment opportunities, equal education, voting rights, and decent housing. But every time Truman appealed to Congress to implement the committee's recommendations southern senators threatened to filibuster. Truman was forced to resort to executive authority to achieve even modest results. In his most direct attack on segregation, he issued an executive order in July 1948 banning discrimination in the armed forces. Segregationists predicted disaster, but experience would soon show that integrated units had little racial tension and fought well. Truman also appointed the first black federal judge and another black as governor of the Virgin Islands.

Several Supreme Court decisions gave added impetus to Truman's civil rights initiatives. In cases that indicated a growing willingness to reconsider the doctrine that black facilities could be "separate but equal" (*Plessy v. Ferguson*, 1896) the Court in *McLaurin v. Oklahoma State Regents* and *Sweatt v. Painter* (1950) struck down state education laws clearly designed to create separate but inferior facilities. But even if the courts moved in Truman's direction, Congress did not. On the domestic front Truman remained largely the conservator of Franklin Roosevelt's legacy.

Beyond Containment

Leadership in foreign affairs had been a strong point in Truman's first term. In his second term, success deserted him. American scientists reported in August 1949 that rains monitored in the Pacific contained undeniable traces of hot nuclear waste. Only one conclusion seemed possible. The Soviet Union had exploded a bomb more powerful than either of those used on Hiroshima and Nagasaki. When Truman announced the news, Congress was debating whether to spend $1.5 billion for military aid to the newly formed NATO alliance. The House stopped debating and voted the bill through, while Truman directed that research into a newer, more powerful fusion or hydrogen bomb continue. Senator Arthur Vandenberg, a leading Republican spokesman on foreign policy, summed up the reaction of many to the end of the American nuclear monopoly: "This is now a different world."

Then in December came more bad news. The long embattled Nationalist government of Chiang Kai-shek fled mainland China to the offshore island of Formosa. Chiang's defeat at the hands of Communist forces led by Mao Tse-tung came as no surprise to the State Department, which had long been monitoring the situation. The Nationalists' corruption and inefficiency had bedeviled American efforts to bring stability to China both during and after World War II. In 1947 full-scale civil war broke out. By February 1949 almost half of Chiang's demoralized troops had defected to the Communists. So the December defeat was hardly unexpected.

But Republicans, who had up until 1949 supported the president's foreign policy, now broke ranks. For some time, a group of wealthy conservatives and Republican senators had resented the administration's preoccupation with Europe. Time–Life publisher Henry Luce used his magazines to campaign for a greater concern for Asian affairs, and especially more aid to defeat Mao Tse-tung. Luce and his associates, known as the "China Lobby," were supported in part with funds from the Chinese Embassy, and when Chiang at last collapsed, his American backers charged the Democrats with letting the Communists win. Secretary of State Dean Acheson published State Department documents showing that nothing short of direct American intervention would have saved Chiang's corrupt and unpopular regime. But the China Lobby charged that Acheson's defense was nothing more than a "whitewash." And it was soon after that Joseph McCarthy began his hunt for "traitors" in the State Department.

Though irritated by such charges, the Truman administration itself was moving to a more assertive foreign policy—one that would militarize containment. The new policy was developed by the National Security Council (NSC), formed in 1947 when Congress attempted to make the military services more efficient by unifying them into a single Department of Defense. (The Central Intelligence Agency was also created at this time.) From the beginning, the NSC had lobbied for an active policy to win the cold war, "in which our national security is a stake and from which we cannot withdraw short of eventual national suicide." In April 1950 it sent Truman a document, NSC-68, which came to serve as the framework for American policy over the next 20 years.

NSC-68 argued that rather than hold the Soviets at bay, the United States should "strive for victory." To that end NSC-68 called for an immediate increase in defense spending from $13 billion to $50 billion a year, to be paid for with a large tax increase. Most of the funds would go to rebuild conventional forces, but the NSC saw the need to develop the hydrogen bomb to offset the Soviets' nuclear capacity. At the same time the American people had to be mobilized to make the necessary sacrifices, while the United States worked (NSC-68 never explained how) to make "the Russian people our Allies" in undermining their totalitarian government. Once again, national defense planners assumed that American policy could force the Soviets to liberalize their society while creating conditions under which "our free society can flourish."

Efforts to implement the policy provisions of NSC-68 at first aroused widespread opposition. Critics like George Kennan, the "father of containment," argued that the Soviets had no immediate plans for domination outside the Communist bloc and that NSC-68 recommendations were too simplistic and militaristic. Fiscal conservatives, both Democrat and Republican, resisted any proposal for higher taxes. Truman's own secretary of defense, Louis Johnson, claimed the new military budget would bankrupt the country. But all such reservations were swept away on June 25, 1950. "Korea came along and saved us," Acheson later remarked.

Korea

In 1950 Korea was about the last place Americans could have imagined themselves fighting a war. Since World War II the country had been divided along the 38th parallel, the north controlled by the Communist government of Kim Il Sung, the south by the dictatorship of Syngman Rhee. Preoccupied with China and the rebuilding of Japan, the Truman administration's interest had dwindled steadily after the war. When Secretary of State Dean Acheson discussed American policy in Asia for the National Press Club in January 1950, he did not even mention Korea.

On June 24 Harry Truman was enjoying a leisurely break from politics at the family home in Independence, Missouri. In Korea it was already Sunday morning when Acheson called the president to report that North Korean troops had crossed the 38th parallel, possibly to fulfill Kim Il Sung's proclaimed intention to "liberate" the South. Soon Acheson confirmed that a full-scale invasion had taken place. The United Nations, meeting in emergency session, had already ordered a ceasefire, which the North Koreans were ignoring. With that, Truman flew back to Washington, convinced that Stalin and his Chinese Communist allies had ordered the invasion. Kim, Truman reasoned, would hardly have acted on his own. Thus the threat of a third world war, this one atomic, seemed agonizingly real. Truman and his advisers wanted to respond to the crisis firmly enough to deter aggression, but without provoking a larger war with the Soviet Union or China.

Truman did not hesitate; American troops would fight the North Koreans, though the United States would not declare war. The fighting in Korea would be a "police action" supervised by the United Nations. On June 27 the United States' delegate to the Security Council succeeded in passing a resolution to send United Nations forces to Korea. That move succeeded only because the Soviet delegate, who had veto power, had walked out six months earlier in protest over the Council's refusal to seat mainland China. (Indeed, his absence from the Security Coun-

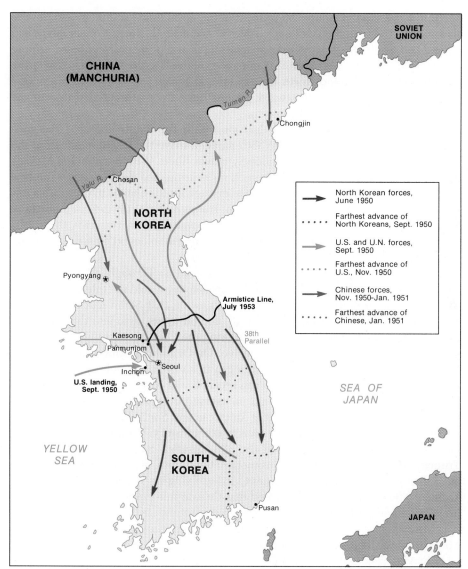

Legend:

→ North Korean forces, June 1950

···· Farthest advance of North Koreans, Sept. 1950

→ U.S. and U.N. forces, Sept. 1950

···· Farthest advance of U.S., Nov. 1950

→ Chinese forces, Nov. 1950-Jan. 1951

···· Farthest advance of Chinese, Jan. 1951

THE KOREAN WAR
In their opening offensive North Korean troops almost pushed South Korean and American forces into the sea at Pusan, but MacArthur rallied United Nations forces, made a successful landing at Inchon behind North Korean lines, and then crossed the 38th parallel into North Korea. Red Chinese troops counterattacked, inflicting on U.S. troops one of the most humiliating defeats in American military history. Fighting continued for another two years.

cil vote undermines the idea that Stalin, rather than Kim Il Sung, had masterminded the North Korean attack.)

Truman's forceful response won immediate approval across America, while Congress quickly voted the huge increase in defense funds needed to carry out the recommendations of NSC-68. American allies were less committed to the action. Though 16 nations contributed to the war effort, the United States provided 50 percent of the ground troops, 86 percent of the naval units, and 93 percent of the air force. By the time the UN forces could be marshalled, North Korean forces had pinned the South Koreans within a small defensive perimeter centered around Pusan. Then Douglas MacArthur, commander of the UN forces, launched a daring amphibious attack behind North Korean lines at Inchon, near the western end of the 38th parallel. Fighting eastward, MacArthur's troops threatened to trap the invaders, who fled back to the North.

Now Truman made a fateful decision. With the South liberated, he gave MacArthur permission to cross the 38th parallel, drive the Communists from the North, and reunite the country under Syngman Rhee. With Senator Joe McCarthy on the attack at home, the 1950 elections nearing, and the McCarran Internal Security Act just passed, Truman was glad enough for the chance to vanquish a few North Koreans. By Thanksgiving American troops had roundly defeated northern forces and were advancing on several fronts toward the frozen Yalu River, the boundary between Korea and China. MacArthur, emboldened by success, promised that the boys would be home by Christmas.

China, however, had grown increasingly restive. Throughout the fall offensive, Premier Zhou Enlai had warned that his country would not tolerate an American presence on its border. Washington, knowing that Stalin had declared the Korean conflict to be merely a "civil war" and off limits, assumed that Mao Tse-tung was essentially a Soviet puppet. Ignoring the Chinese warnings, MacArthur grandly launched his end-the-war offensive. On October 26 American troops captured a Chinese prisoner "so that you began to know at that point something was happening," Secretary of State Acheson recalled. On November 26 some 400,000 Chinese troops poured across the Yalu, smashing through the lightly defended UN lines. At Chosan they trapped 20,000 American and South Korean troops, inflicting one of the worst defeats in American military history. Within three weeks they had driven UN forces back behind the 38th parallel. So total was the rout that Truman wondered publicly about using the atom bomb. That remark sent a frightened British prime minister Clement Attlee flying to Washington to dissuade Truman. The president readily agreed that the war must remain limited and withdrew his nuclear threat.

Military stalemate in Korea brought into the open a simmering feud between MacArthur and Truman. The general had made no secret of his political ambitions or of his differences with Truman over American policy in Asia. He was eager to bomb Chinese and Russian supply bases across the Korean border, to blockade China's coast, and to unleash Chiang Kai-shek on mainland China. On March 23 he issued a personal ultimatum to Chinese military commanders demanding total surrender. To his Republican congressional supporters he sent a letter declaring, "We must win. There is no substitute for victory."

Truman saw MacArthur's public statements as a threat to the tradition of civilian leadership and his strategy as an open invitation to another world war. Outraged by such insubordination, he made plans to discipline the general. When Omar Bradley reported that the rumors of dismissal had reached the Far East and that MacArthur might try to resign, the irate Truman replied, "The son of a bitch isn't going to resign on me. I want him fired!" Military leaders agreed that MacArthur had to go. On April 11 a stunned nation learned that the celebrated military commander had been relieved of his duties. As cheering crowds greeted MacArthur in one of the largest ticker-tape parades in New York City's history, Truman's move seemed one of the great political mistakes of his career. MacArthur had the unprecedented opportunity to address a joint session of Congress before a national television audience. Rabid supporters tried to impeach Truman and Acheson.

Behind the personal feud raged an important debate over foreign policy. While MacArthur demanded an all-out effort in Asia, Acheson told Congress that Korea was but one link in a worldwide "collective security system." General war in Asia would threaten American interests in Europe. The Korean War had to be fought with Europe always foremost in American strategy. Or as General Omar Bradley argued, a showdown in Asia would lead to "the wrong war, at the wrong place, at the wrong time, and with the wrong enemy." Congressional leaders were thus persuaded of the need to accompany limited war in Korea with a military build-up in Europe. As for MacArthur, it was soon apparent that in his 14 years abroad he had lost touch with American political realities. His verbosity at congressional hearings bored even his own supporters. He soon retired to an expensive suite in a New York hotel to await the Republican presidential nomination, which, to his amazement, never came.

Korea took its toll on Truman's political fortunes as well. After July 1951, aimless peace talks dragged on along the border at Panmunjon. While the negotiators argued over the reunification of Korea and what to do with North Korean prisoners of war who refused to go home, the United States suffered another 32,000 casualties in an ugly war of attrition. There were no brilliant victories, only month after month of trench warfare, exhausted GIs, and sagging morale. Secretary of State Acheson spent much of his energy defending the Korean stalemate before hostile Republican senators like Richard Nixon of California, who inveighed against "Dean Acheson's cowardly college of Communist containment." In March 1952 Truman's popularity had sunk so low that he lost the New Hampshire presidential primary to Senator Estes Kefauver of Tennessee. With that defeat, he announced he would not run for reelection in 1952.

K1C2: The Election of 1952

The Republican formula for victory in 1952 was simple. Exploit the Truman administration's obvious weaknesses. Domestically, that did not include the economy, which remained remarkably healthy. Wage and price controls put in place by the administration prevented the sharp inflation that was expected to follow increased wartime spending. But the Republicans could capitalize on the protracted stalemate over Korea. And several of Truman's advisers had been forced to resign for accepting mink coats and deep freezes in return for political favors. The campaign strategy was summed up in the formula K1C2: Korea, corruption, and communism.

The bigger problem for Republicans lay in choosing a candidate. Once General Dwight D. Eisenhower formally joined the Republican party, he became the choice of moderates and the northeastern establishment. Party regulars and the conservative wing were heavily committed to Robert A. Taft, who ran surprisingly well in the party primaries. But Ike's popularity allowed his backers to maneuver their candidate to a first-ballot nomination. To heal the breach with the Taft delegates, the convention chose the staunch anticommunist Senator Richard M. Nixon as Eisenhower's running mate.

With no candidate as popular as Eisenhower, the Democrats drafted Illinois Governor Adlai E. Stevenson. Few candidates could match Stevenson's eloquence, but, like Dewey before him, Stevenson lacked the common touch. Re-

Two strange bedfellows of politics, the moderate Republican presidential candidate Dwight Eisenhower raises the hand of his ardent anticommunist running mate, Richard Nixon.

publican strategists turned his intelligence into a liability by dismissing him and his intellectual supporters as "eggheads." The GOP's campaign against communism and corruption, led by Nixon, left the Democratic candidate on the defensive. Eisenhower, meanwhile, took the high road above the mudslinging and promised voters that if elected, he would go to Korea to seek an end to the war.

Righteous indignation over corruption almost mired the Republicans in a scandal of their own when the New York *Post* revealed that a group of wealthy Californians had provided Richard Nixon with an $18,000 "slush fund" to help cover personal expenses. With his place on the ticket in peril, Nixon made an impassioned television appearance to defend himself as an honest, ordinary American, with car payments, a small life insurance policy, and a mortgage. He could afford to dress his wife only in a sensible "Republican cloth coat," not furs. And yes, his daughter Tricia had received a cocker spaniel puppy named "Checkers," but no matter what his enemies might say, his family was going to keep the dog. The speech was an immediate success, demonstrating clearly the newfound power of television to influence public opinion. More important, Nixon had successfully identified himself with the swelling middle-class center of American society: those who had escaped the Depression and were now determined to secure recent economic advances and savor the taste of prosperity.

The election outcome was never much in doubt. Eisenhower's broad smile and confident manner promised an era of effective leadership, and he received over 55 percent of the vote. The GOP also won a one-vote majority in the Senate and a slim edge in the House. "The great problem of America today," Ike had said during the campaign, "is to take that straight road down the middle." Most Americans who voted for him were comforted to think that was just where they were headed.

If Eisenhower's course pointed to a road down the middle, it is worth noting just how much that sense of "middle" had changed. In 1945, at the end of the war, there were large questions about what kind of peacetime society Americans would return to. The Great Depression had blended almost insensibly into world war. There had been no time to step back and assess the sizable changes that had been wrought. But in a broad sense, the political system was slowly adjusting to the idea that America's economy was inseparably tied to that of the emerging global order. The crash in 1929, with its worldwide effects, had demonstrated the closeness of the links. And the activist policies of the New Deal showed that Americans were willing to give the federal government power to influence American society in major new ways. If anything, the war gave the governments and private businesses greater power to move supplies and shape global policies. So when peace came in 1945, it gradually became clear that the "middle road" did not mean a return to the laissez-faire economics or politics of the 1920s.

Furthermore, the shift from war to peace demonstrated that it was no longer possible to make global war without making a global peace. Under the striking new balance of power in the postwar world, the United States and the Soviet Union stood alone as preeminent "superpowers," swiftly developing the military capability to annihilate each other and the rest of the world. In an environment of competing interests and atomic diplomacy, the suspicions on both sides led to a world where a "limited" war—over Korea, Berlin, Greece, or Iran—could not easily be isolated from larger conflicts. Perhaps the knowledge that there was no retreating from political as well as economic commitment was one reason that the rhetoric of anticommunism became so strident. Life in the shadow of a cold war, too, became part of the middle road Americans walked. And there was no simple way of turning back.

SIGNIFICANT EVENTS

1945	Iran crisis; civil war in Greece
1946	OPA lifts price controls; labor unrest; Kennan's "long telegram"; Stalin and Churchill "cold war" speeches; Republican congressional victories; McMahon Bill creates Atomic Energy Commission; Baruch plan fails at United Nations
1947	Truman Doctrine; Taft–Hartley Act; Marshall announces European recovery plan; Federal Loyalty Oath; HUAC investigates Hollywood; National Security Act creates Defense Department and CIA; Levittown construction begins
1948	Marshall Plan adopted; Berlin blockade; Truman upsets Dewey; Truman recognizes Israel
1949	Soviet A-bomb test; China falls to the Communists; NATO established; Truman orders work on H-bomb
1950	McCarthy's Wheeling, West Virginia, speech; Korean War begins; McCarran Act; NSC-68 adopted; Alger Hiss convicted; Kefauver crime hearings; *McLaurin* and *Sweatt* cases
1951	Rosenbergs accused; Truman fires MacArthur; peace talks in Korea
1952	Fertility rate in the United States reaches new high; Richard Nixon's "Checkers" speech; Eisenhower defeats Stevenson
1957	First black moves into Levittown, Pennsylvania

31

The Suburban Era

I f the 1950s had a symbol, it was the automobile: big, boxy, glittering with chrome, sprouting ever more outrageous fins, and careening down the road with the roar of an overpowered V-8 engine. A four-door Plymouth, Ford, or Chevy sedan served both for commuting and for driving the family to church. Rich kids and young-at-heart adults drove sporty convertibles. Harried suburban housewives preferred a station wagon to tote children and groceries. For the upwardly mobile executive or celebrity, a Cadillac, Lincoln, or Imperial was a must. Their huge wheelbases, Torque Flight transmissions, and feather-touch power steering gave them about as much feel for the road as a slab of ice slaloming down the road.

No longer were families scraping together to buy their first car or nursing the old one along until it died. Buyers were trading up, the bigger the better. With the suburbs and new shopping plazas spread so far apart, many families decided they needed two cars in the garage. Kids—mere *teenagers*—were saving enough spare change to buy cars, mostly used. The "hot-rodders" seemed to prefer older coupes, chopped, blocked, and channeled. Their radios would blare out songs like "Mabelline" and "Teen Angel," and guys with greased-back hair courtesy of Vitalis would head off to the drive-in with their girls to watch Steve McQueen in *The Blob*—or even worse, tool up to the overlook at Buena Vista bluff. But what could parents do to stop them? The kids all had jobs, cars, money of their own, and time to kill.

To draw customers to the auto showrooms, manufacturers advertised more than ever before. In an era when the advertising industry was experiencing the biggest boom in its history, 9 out of the top 10 ad campaigns were for cars. (The tenth was for the ubiquitous Coca-Cola.) Chrysler Corporation even hired a psychological consultant from Vienna to lay bare the buyers' automotive ids and egos. When buying a car, Dr. Ernest Dichter reported, a man subconsciously wanted to acquire a mistress. He set his eyes lovingly on a convertible—then, recalling his family responsibilities, settled for a four-door sedan. Chrysler eased the male dilemma by introducing the four-door hardtop, just as convenient, but with the slightly more rakish profile of the convertible.

The "Big Three" auto manufacturers—General Motors, Ford, and Chrysler— raced one another to redesign their annual models, each one boxier and more chrome-laden than the last. Harley Earl, head of the Art and Color Section at General Motors, was inspired by the swept-back silhouette of the Lockheed P-38

In *Easter Morning, Norman Rockwell gently satirized the gap between church membership and attendance. This sheepish suburban father's sanctuary is a "womb" chair designed by one of the most noted architects of the 1950s, Eero Saarinen.*

fighter plane to put the first modest tailfins on the 1948 Cadillac. Jet planes inspired other automakers after 1955 to try ever more outrageous fins. Chrysler's new "Forward Look," created by chief of styling Virgil Exner, embodied the mixture of the big brassy box with futuristic fascination. In the lingo of the Detroit stylists, these designs were "gasaroony," an adjective *Popular Mechanics* magazine translated as "terrific, overpowering, weird." By the time the 1959 Cadillac reached showrooms, pedestrians were learning to tread carefully behind the behemoth creations, lest they be impaled when the car backed up.

Fins, roadside motels, "gaseterias," drive-in burger huts, freeways, interstate highways, shopping centers, and, of course, suburbs were all part of a culture of mobility that was both physical and social in the 1950s. Americans continued their exodus from rural areas to cities and from the cities to the suburbs. As mechanization transformed cotton farming, blacks left the South in ever larger numbers, heading for industrial centers in the Northeast, Midwest, and West Coast. Mexican-Americans concentrated in southwestern cities; Puerto Ricans came largely to New York. And for Americans in the snow belt, the climate of the West and South (at least when civilized by air conditioning) made the Sunbelt irresistible to ever larger numbers.

Social mobility, too, burgeoned as affluence swelled the ranks of middle-class America. Having worried during the Depression era that divisions of class, ethnicity, and race might lead to social violence and political disorder, social scientists now spoke about consensus. In a positive light consensus reflected the triumph of the melting pot and an agreement among the wide majority of Americans about fundamental values. They rejected radical ideas at home and opposed the spread of communism abroad. But some social critics worried that too strong a consensus could breed a mindless conformity. In the things they owned, in the places they lived, in their churches and school, and in the values they held, Americans were becoming dangerously homogenized.

The baby boomers who reached adolescence in this era seldom worried about such issues. In the White House President Eisenhower radiated a comforting sense that the affairs of the nation and the world were in capable hands. That left teenagers free to worry about what really mattered: a first date, a first kiss, a first job, a first choice for college, and whether or not to "go all the way" before marriage.

TRANSFORMING WHEELS

The "mass automobility" of the 1950s defined a highly mobile and affluent consumer society. Almost every aspect of American life—work, family, and leisure, not to mention sex and personal self-expression—centered on the automobile. Of course, the American love affair with the automobile was hardly new. It had helped define the consumer culture of the 1920s: by the end of that decade nearly 27 million cars were on the road—one for every five Americans. The Depression and the war put a drag on new car sales, but Americans clung to the cars they had, even in hard times. "People give up everything in the world but their car," one observer noted. The postwar boom set autos again in motion. In 1946 Americans purchased 2 million cars; a decade later that figure had jumped to 8 million.

Like a freak of evolution run riot, automotive tailfins metamorphosed from the modest stubs of a 1948 Cadillac (top) into the sweeping wedges of Chrysler's "Forward Look," the batwing curves of a '59 Chevy, and the monstrous protrusions of the 1959 Cadillac (bottom), which also sported bomblike tail lights.

For many, and especially suburbanites, the automobile had become both a status symbol and a necessity. About two out of every three Americans drove a car to work. With about 6 percent of the world's population, Americans owned 50 percent of its automobiles. One out of every six jobs was involved in the manufacture or use of cars. When the automakers flourished, as in 1955, the American economy expanded. During the industry slump of 1958 the economy went into recession. But the automobile affected more than mere prosperity. The transforming power of its wheels changed the way Americans organized their personal lives and the space in which they lived. In the 1950s suburbs grew 40 times faster than cities. By 1960 half of the American people lived in suburbs. Such massive migration affected all aspects of class, religious, ethnic, and race relations. It also altered the economy, as manufacturing and trade followed the population to the suburbs. In the late 1940s almost 75 percent of the Levittowners on Long Island commuted into New York City to work. By the 1960s about 60 percent worked within their home county.

If railroads and mass transit were the vital arteries of urban America, highways carried the lifeblood of suburbia. Nine out of every ten suburban families owned a car and one in five had at least two. Almost all suburban activities depended on the availability of cars, cheap gasoline, and accessible roads. Shopping centers, the predecessors of more elaborate malls, were perhaps the best expression of the new auto-centered life. At the end of World War II the United States had just eight of these retail complexes, their cluster of stores set in a sea of asphalt parking space. By 1960 almost every community had at least one highway strip dotted with drive-in movies, stores, bowling alleys, gas stations, auto dealers, and fast-food joints. Even a few churches and funeral homes provided drive-in facilities to attract people committed to life behind the wheel. By 1960 the nation's approximately 3840 shopping centers covered as much land as all the central business districts.

To ease the burden on congested suburban roads, the Eisenhower administration proposed a 20-year plan for the construction of a massive interstate highway system of some 41,000 miles of freeway. Backed by a commission drawn from the trucking, oil, construction, and automobile industries, Eisenhower argued that not only would the new system ease congestion, but it would also provide easy evacuation of cities in case of nuclear attack. In 1956 Congress passed the Interstate Highway Act, which initiated the largest public works project in history. The federal government picked up 90 percent of the cost through a Highway Trust Fund, financed by special taxes on cars, gas, tires, lubricants, and auto parts.

The Interstate Highway Act had an enormous impact on American life. In all, the country spent some $250 billion on roads and highways in the 25 years after World War II. Average annual driving increased by 400 percent. Travelers had easier access to national parks, historic sites, and vacation areas. Whole new communities sprouted along the beltways around the nation's cities. Yet the new highway system was hardly a panacea. Congestion often worsened as motorists shifted routes to take advantage of the new roads. The massive transfer of dollars from the cities to the suburbs contributed to the eroding quality of urban life: 75 percent of all government transportation dollars (local, state, and federal) went to subsidize travel by car and truck; only 1 percent was earmarked for urban mass transit. Improved highways in turn benefited the largely more affluent suburbanites, who could afford to commute to their jobs. At the same time, many low-paying, unskilled jobs disappeared from the cities, forcing the urban poor into reverse commuting from city to suburb.

As intercity rail service and mass transit deteriorated, cities became less attractive places to live or do business. By the end of the 1950s most cities devoted at least a third of their downtown areas to parking lots and roads to accommodate automobile traffic. Once-thriving shopping districts became virtual ghost towns at night, as commuters returned to their bedroom communities. With fewer well-to-do taxpayers to draw upon, city governments lacked the tax base to finance public services. A vicious cycle ensued that proved most damaging to the urban poor, who had few means of escape.

THE SHAPE OF THE SUBURBS

For those who joined the mass migration to the suburbs, what did they hope to gain and how did they wish to live? First and foremost, the suburban ideal centered on a single-family dwelling owned by those who lived in it. The ideal itself could be traced back to the agrarian dream of being a self-sufficient farmer, carving a homestead from frontier lands. Over the years, the desire for an independent homestead survived the decline of family farming. Like the old agrarian model, suburban living consumed extensive amounts of land. Low-density housing spread over acre after acre of winding tracts, in sharp contrast to densely populated urban apartments. When the booming economy of the 1950s made homeownership possible for many Americans, they leapt at the chance.

Suburban homeownership was popularly associated with the broad middle classes: those workers who held white- or blue-collar jobs and made enough income to afford the housing. Indeed, class distinctions seemed to blur somewhat in the suburbs. "We see eye to eye on most things," commented one Levittown resident, "about raising kids, doing things together with your husband . . . we have practically the same identical background." Unlike many urban neighborhoods, where immigrant parents or grandparents might be living on the same block or even in the same apartment, single-family dwellers often left their relatives and in-laws behind. As a result, ethnic lifestyles were less pronounced in the suburbs. The restrictive immigration policies of the 1920s had also eroded ethnicity by reducing the number of newly arrived foreign-born Americans.

Class distinctions were reduced in other ways. As the GI Bill encouraged colleges and state university systems to expand, college diplomas and professional training became less a badge of the well-to-do. Furthermore, the developing bureaucratic and service economy created new jobs of indeterminate status. Television repair might be similar to blue-collar manufacturing, but what if the repairman also owned his own business? Was teaching or computer programming a higher status job? Class distinctions were more pronounced between suburban communities than within them. The rich tended to cluster in older developments, often centered around country clubs. Working-class suburbs sprouted on the outskirts of large manufacturing centers. Though middle class only on the basis of wages, the residents of blue-collar communities, like most suburbanites, had still escaped the city, owned their own homes, and depended on their cars.

American Civil Religion

If the move to the suburbs gradually stripped many ethnics of their native customs and languages, it seldom forced them to abandon their religious identity. Religion continued to be a distinctive and segregating factor during the 1950s. Catholics, Protestants, and Jews generally married within their own faiths, and in the suburbs they kept their social distance as well. Communities that showed no obvious class distinctions were sometimes deeply divided along religious lines. Catholics attended parochial rather than public schools, formed their own clubs, and gener-

Baptist Billy Graham led the revival of evangelistic denominations and sects. While his message emphasized the traditional fundamentalist themes of sin, redemption, and the Second Coming of Christ, his up-to-date methods took advantage of television, advertising, radio, and paperback books to reach the widest possible audience.

ally did not socialize with their Protestant neighbors. Protestant and Catholic members of the same country club usually did not play golf or tennis in the same foursomes. As for Jews, social historian Richard Polenberg has remarked that whereas a gulf divided many Catholics and Protestants, Jews and Gentiles "seem to have lived on the opposite sides of a religious Grand Canyon." Even superficial signs of friendliness masked underlying mistrust and the persistence of old stereotypes.

Although such religious boundaries remained distinct, the consensus increased that religion was central to American life. Church membership rose to over 50 percent for the first time in the twentieth century, and by 1957 the census bureau reported that 96 percent of the American people cited a specific affiliation when asked the question "What is your religion?" The religious upswing was supported in part by the prevailing cold war mood, since Communists were avowedly atheist. Patriotic and anticommunist themes were quite strong in the preaching of Billy Graham, a Baptist revival preacher who first attracted national attention at a tent meeting in Los Angeles in 1949. Following in the tradition of nineteenth-century revivalists like Charles Finney and Dwight Moody, Graham soon achieved even wider impact by televising his meetings. Though no revivalist, the Roman Catholic Bishop Fulton J. Sheen made the transition from a radio to a television ministry, where he spoke out strongly in favor of traditional values and against communism.

Religion also flourished because it was one crucial way suburbanites maintained a sense of identity and community, even as ethnic identity decreased. For gray-suited "organization men," swallowed up in the stress of corporate competition, religion offered a disciplined calm. So too it offered calm to the suburban homemaker, oppressed by seemingly endless diapers or floors in need of scrubbing. Rabbi Joshua Liebman's *Peace of Mind* became a best seller in 1946; the Reverend Norman Vincent Peale had even greater success with his *Power of Positive Thinking* in 1952. Throughout American culture, the benefits of religion—of *any* religion—were lauded. President Eisenhower made the point quite clear. "Our government makes no sense unless it is founded on a deeply religious faith," he proclaimed, "—and I don't care what it is." Congress, bowing to the popular mood, in 1954 added the phrase "under God" to the pledge of allegiance. And every Friday afternoon children watching "The Howdy Doody Show" were exhorted by "Buffalo Bob" to worship "at the church or synagogue of your choice."

"Homemaking" Women in the Workaday World

The growth of a suburban culture revealed a contradiction in the lives of middle-class women. Never before were their traditional roles as housewives and mothers so central to American society. Yet never before had more women joined the work force outside the home.

For housewives, the single-family dwelling of the suburbs required more labor to keep clean, while the baby boom left mothers with more children to tend with less help from relatives and grandparents, who no longer lived nearby. Increased dependence on automobiles made many a suburban housewife the chauffeur for her family. In the 1920s grocers, milkmen, or knife-sharpeners might deliver their goods or practice their trade from door to door. But by the 1950s delivery services were being replaced by housewives doing "errands."

Yet between 1940 and 1960 the percentage of wives working outside the home doubled from 15 to 30 percent. While the greatest increase occurred among women over 40, whose children were generally grown, by 1960 almost 40 percent of women with children between 6 and 16 held jobs. Some women took jobs simply to help make ends meet, but sheer financial necessity was not the only explanation. Middle-class married women went to work as often as lower class wives, and women with college degrees were the most likely to get a job. Two-income families were able to spend far more on gifts, education, recreation, and household appliances. In addition, women found status and self-fulfillment in their jobs. Wage work was clearly more rewarding to many than unpaid house-work. So was the opportunity for social contacts and personal growth.

More women were going to college, too: in 1950 men outnumbered them 2 to 1 on campus, but by 1960 the ratio was only 5 to 3. The increased education did not translate into economic equality, however; the percentage of women holding professional jobs actually dropped between 1950 and 1960. In fact the gap be-tween men's and women's wages was greater than in any other industrial nation. Women professionals earned only 64 percent of what males earned and those in sales earned just 41 percent. Over all, the median wage for women was less than half that for men.

Despite women's wider roles in society, the modern media continued to portray them either as sex objects or as housewives and mothers. A typical article appearing in *Redbook* in 1957 made a heroine of Junior, a "little freckle-faced brunette" who had given up work. As the story closed, Junior nursed her baby at two in the morning, crooning "I'm glad, glad, glad I'm just a housewife." In 1950 Lynn White, the president of Mills College for women, advocated a curriculum that displaced traditional academic subjects with those that were "distinctly femi-nine." Crafts were more suitable to women than the fine arts, he argued, and home economics had more relevance than a course in post-Kantian philosophy.

The media trivialized women in other ways. Advertisers constantly portrayed them as mindless consumers of household goods. Where the films of the 1930s and 1940s starred strong women like Mae West, Katharine Hepburn, and Barbara Stanwyck, confident in their intelligence, sexuality, and independence, the hero-ines of the 1950s appeared more vulnerable. Marilyn Monroe's voluptuous sensu-ality, combined with a little-girl innocence, clearly appealed to male tastes. Simi-larly, women's fashions portrayed a male vision of femininity. In 1947 Christian Dior introduced his "new look": narrow waistlines emphasizing shapely hips and a full bosom, rarely achieved without constricting foundation garments. The heels on shoes became ever higher and the toes pointier. As historian Lois Banner concluded, "Not since the Victorian era had women's fashions been so confining."

Women's sphere, then, remained limited during the 1950s. But the currents for change were present. Betty Friedan, a college graduate who had given up a career in psychology to raise a family, began to sense that other housewives were similarly frustrated at being merely "a server of food and putter-on of pants and a bedmaker." Her growing disillusionment with such a male-dominated culture led her to catalog its restrictive aspects in *The Feminine Mystique* (1963). By the end of the fifties other women were moving in the same direction.

The "Organization Man" in a Conglomerate World

If the new suburban culture affected middle-class women's lives both at home and at work, the postwar boom of the 1950s shaped the lives of suburban men in new

Daily Lives

PUBLIC SPACE/PRIVATE SPACE

The New Suburbia

Prosperity in the 1950s brought a greater demand for houses that, like automobiles, were larger and more ornamented. By the mid-1950s a builder like William Levitt no longer limited his offerings to the standard 900-square-foot Cape Cod saltbox efficiency house. New development designs, often created by builders rather than architects, haphazardly mixed styles and colors. California single-story ranch houses and one-and-a-half story New England Capes often stood side-by-side in the same developments. "Pink, orange, and turquoise may seem a weird combination," one newspaper commented, but reported that this exterior color scheme won its designer an award and a three-week vacation in Italy.

Despite an eclecticism that sometimes bordered on zaniness, suburban design did evolve from major architectural traditions. The most renowned of all suburban features, the picture window, traced its roots to architect Frank Lloyd Wright. Wright had come of age in the 1890s, at a time when "streetcar suburbs" were expanding around major urban areas. Wright's turn-of-the-century innovations combined open interior space, wide windows for natural lighting, and a horizontal, single-story layout. California architects translated Wright's ideas into the "ranch house," where rooms flowed into each other and indoor spaces opened to the outdoors to take advantage of the mild climate. Houses with fewer walls and defined spaces discouraged formality and even privacy.

Developers across the country seized upon the California "fantasy" style to conjure up for home buyers dreams of informal living along with a touch of glamour. While the reality was usually either a rectangular or L-shaped box, builders followed automobile designers in breaking the boxy profile with longer lines, decorator touches, or different planes defined by shapes, materials, colors, or textures. Developers added picture windows to make small houses seem more spacious, only to discover that they were popular in houses of all sizes and design.

Critics of suburban living suggested that the picture window was a means to ensure conformity. Why, after all, was the window most often placed looking onto the front yard, except to afford homeowners a means to keep an eye on neighbors who were watching them through their own picture windows? In truth, it made sense to have a picture window look onto the street in order to keep an eye on children. More important, it provided about the only vantage point from which people could enjoy their front yards. Few suburbanites sat out front or used the lawn for anything other than ornamental purposes. But since front yards made an important statement about houses and their owners, families decorated and tended them with special care.

By 1955, economics rather than aesthetics forced developers to forsake the basic suburban box. Surveys showed that three-quarters of all would-be buyers wanted a single-story house. But with land prices rising and new zoning codes being enforced, builders could not fit enough floor space onto typical lots. To build a two-story house without seeming to do so, they hit upon the split-level or "raised ranch": something, as one critic wryly noted, that "looked like a ranch-style house that had fallen out of the air and landed on something else." The front door

Daily Lives

This custom-built 1957 house reflected what so many suburban home buyers desired: plenty of glass and an open room structure that encouraged informality.

opened onto a landing halfway between the upper and lower floors, creating an illusion that it was only half the distance from one floor to the next. The basic construction, two simple boxes side-by-side, was cheap to build. By placing half the living space—either the kitchen, dining, and family rooms or the bedrooms—in what would otherwise be a basement, the split level created more habitable living space at little additional cost. Buyers approved, in part because the concept was novel, in larger part because they got more space at an affordable price.

Most of all, homeowners in the 1950s wanted family rooms and "live-in kitchens." One magazine described the family room as "the newest room in the house, but also the oldest," for the concept originated in the middle-class Victorian front parlor. Like it, the 1950s living room acquired more elegant furnishings for use during holidays or special entertaining. That led to the conversion of what often had been a basement "rumpus" room for the kids into a family room. Here, families sought a cozier feel with pine paneling and furniture designed for comfort and dura-

bility, with the television as the focus of the room. The "live-in" kitchen suited the growing families of the late 1950s who needed more space to prepare and eat meals. Earlier kitchens had normally been small and limited largely to food preparation. Meals were eaten in a combined living-dining area. The new larger kitchens were designed, one advertiser claimed, to make "mother a member of the family again," where everyone could gather while mother cooked. The same space would also hold appliances like dishwashers, dual ovens, and televisions, which became common kitchen features.

Clearly, suburban houses were more than

Little boxes on the hillside
Little boxes all the same.

as one folk-singing critic of the 1960s complained. To the people who flocked to suburbia, their homes represented a compromise between fantasy and practicality, fulfilling the American dream, "To own your own home."

ways as well. The 1950s witnessed the first sustained peacetime expansion of the economy since the 1920s. Buoyed by the new prosperity, large corporations moved increasingly toward product diversification and the conglomerate form of mergers. Each was a hedge against conditions that ravaged corporations in the 1930s, when a giant like General Electric, which had concentrated on equipment for generating electric power and light, suddenly found its markets evaporating. General Electric responded by entering markets for appliances, X-ray machines, and elevators, all products that involved application of the fruits of the company's research labs. In the postwar era General Electric diversified even further into nuclear power, jet engines, television, and industrial automation systems.

Diversification was practical for large industrial firms with the manufacturing base and profits to support extensive research and development (R&D). During the 1950s firms in the chemical, electronics, transportation, foods, and petroleum industries led the trend. Most large manufacturers produced in at least five industries, while the largest firms generally operated in twice as many. Large corporations also expanded their overseas operations. They took advantage of weak foreign economies to buy out potential competitors or to establish branches of their domestic operations. Most dynamic in the 1950s were the large integrated oil companies like Mobil and Standard Oil of New Jersey (Exxon), which developed huge oil fields in the Middle East and markets around the free world.

For some giants such as International Telephone and Telegraph (ITT) and for the small but aggressive firms such as Textron, Ling Temco Vought (LTV), and TRW the conglomerate merger served as a way to meet recessions and to seize opportunities for expansion. Unlike the earlier horizontal and vertical mergers, which had been limited to a core industry like automobiles and related manufacturing, conglomerate mergers brought together companies with seemingly unrelated products. Over a 20-year period ITT branched out from its basic communications business into baking, hotels and motels, car rental, home building, and insurance. In this way aggressive entrepreneurs like James Ling of LTV turned tiny local businesses into combinations of as many as 50 formerly independent companies. Between the late 1940s and early 1960s the 200 largest firms increased their share of the value added by manufacturing from around 30 percent to more than 40 percent. But bigger and more diversified did not always mean better or more profitable. Managers who knew how to market toasters did not necessarily know how to run hotels. New layers of managers added to paperwork, complicated decision making, and increased the size of the bureaucracy.

Despite fears that concentration would stifle competition and add to bureaucratic inefficiencies, economists judged concentration and diversification as stabilizing to the economy. In fact, in the critical science-based industries like electronics and chemicals responsible for much of the nation's technological innovation, competition increased. The top six firms in key industries never accounted for more than 45 percent of product value. Economists in banking and research centers like the Brookings Institution produced econometric models, which used statistics to enhance large firms' efficiency in managing inventory and investing revenues.

One key to managing these modern corporate giants was the advent of electronic data processing. In the early 1950s computers were virtually unknown in private industry. But banks and insurance companies saw computers as an answer to their need to manipulate huge quantities of records and statistical data. Manufacturers, especially in the petroleum, chemical, automotive, and electronics industries, began to use computers to monitor their production lines, quality control, and inventory. Americans began to have a sense of the automated workplace: more efficient, quieter, cleaner, and sometimes threateningly impersonal. Many skilled laborers became little more than caretakers of machines. This was a process, of course, that had been well under way since the Civil War. Now large corporations required that middle-level executives submerge their individual goals in the processes and work routines of a large bureaucracy. The corporate structure emphasized the need to work in teams and on committees rather than as individuals pursuing independent ideas.

David Riesman, a sociologist, attracted widespread attention when he outlined the consequences of the new corporate atmosphere in *The Lonely Crowd* (1950). In nineteenth-century America, Riesman argued, Americans had been "inner directed." It was their own consciences that formed their values and drove them to seek success. In contrast, modern workers had developed a personality shaped not so much by inner convictions as by the opinions of their peers. The new "other-directed" society of suburbia preferred security to success. "Go along to get along" was its motto. In a bureaucratized economy, it was important to please others, to conform to the group, and to cooperate. Other-directed people were, Riesman concluded, more superficial or shallow, having no deep convictions of their own.

William Whyte carried Riesman's critique from the workplace to the suburb in *The Organization Man* (1956). Here he found rootless families, shifted from town to town by the whims of impersonal corporations. (IBM, went one standard joke, stood for "I've Been Moved.") The typical "organization man" was sociable but not terribly ambitious. He sought primarily to "keep up with the Joneses" and the number of consumer goods they owned. He seemed all too ready to adopt the tastes and manners of the neighborhood. He lived in a suburban "split-level trap," as one critic put it, one among millions of "haggard" men, "tense and anxious" women, and "the gimme kids," who, like the cartoon character "Dennis the Menace," looked up from the litter under the Christmas tree to ask, "Is that all?"

No doubt such portraits were overdrawn and overly alarmist. (Where, after all, did Riesman's nineteenth-century inner-directed Americans get their values, if not from the society around them?) But they indicated the problems of adjustment faced by those working within large bureaucratic organizations and living in suburbs that were decentralized and self-contained.

THE POLITICS OF CALM

In presiding over these vast changes in American society, President Dwight David Eisenhower projected an aura of paternal calm. Eisenhower had been raised in a large Kansas farm family and his parents, though poor, offered him a warm, caring home steeped in religious faith. In an era of organization men, Eisenhower succeeded by organizing his way to the top of the military pyramid. A graduate of West Point, he was neither a scholar nor an aggressive general like George Patton. Rather, "Ike" had made his way upward by mastering bureaucratic politics. In the placid years between the two world wars, his skills at golf, poker, and bridge often proved as valuable as his military expertise. Yet such genial sociability could not hide his ambition or his ability to judge character shrewdly. It took a gifted organizer to coordinate the D-Day invasion and to hold together the conglomeration of egocentric generals who pushed west to Berlin. After the war Eisenhower presided for a time as president of Columbia University and then as commander of NATO forces in Europe. When the Republicans made the call in 1952, he was ready for a new challenge.

In shaping his administration, Eisenhower called upon his army ways. A good general, he believed, left the details to his staff while concentrating most attention on grand strategy. He also preferred private negotiation to public confrontation and kept such a low political profile that some critics thought he conceived the president to be almost a figurehead, like a constitutional monarch. In reality, he operated more of a "hidden hand" presidency, privately making decisions and setting directions but publicly letting others speak for him (and take the heat). At press conferences, his answers to questions were often garbled or rambling, giving the impression that he didn't always have a firm grasp of his policies. In truth, he was shrewder than his critics believed, sometimes even using his imprecision to bamboozle the press. "Don't worry," he once reassured his press secretary, "if that question comes [up], I'll just confuse them."

Yet for all his ability to organize and negotiate behind the scenes, Eisenhower still remained more aloof than most presidents. He often failed to use his prestige on major issues like civil rights. His chief of staff, Sherman Adams, a New Hampshire businessman and former governor, organized the flow of information so strictly that the president's briefing papers were boiled down to one-page summaries, which could be quickly and easily digested. Ever the organization man, Eisenhower surrounded himself with business executives who were dedicated to the status quo. The *New Republic* described the cabinet as "eight millionaires and a plumber"—the plumber being Secretary of Labor Martin P. Durkin, who soon became uncomfortable hobnobbing with so many thoroughbred Republicans and resigned.* Secretary of Defense Charles Wilson, former president of General Motors, best articulated the probusiness creed of the administration when he told a Senate committee that he had always believed, "What was good for our country was good for General Motors and vice versa."

Modern Republicanism

In office, Eisenhower pursued a course he described as "modern Republicanism." He resisted the demands of conservatives to dismantle New Deal programs and even agreed to increases in Social Security, unemployment insurance, and the minimum wage. He supported a small public housing program and a modest federally supported medical insurance plan for the needy. But he rejected more far-reaching liberal proposals on housing and universal health care through the Social Security system. And his secretary of the treasury, George M. Humphrey, soon became a forceful spokesman for a conservative domestic agenda. Humphrey, the former executive of a profitable conglomerate, cut back federal jobs whenever he could, eliminated construction projects, and resisted any pressure to raise defense spending. He preferred legislation favored by the business community, like the Submerged Lands Act of 1953, a bill that turned rich coastal oil deposits over to the states, which were far more easily influenced by the lobbies of the oil industry.

*When the Department of Health, Education and Welfare was established in 1953, Eisenhower did appoint a woman, Oveta Culp Hobby of Texas, making his cabinet eight millionaires and a millionairess.

To make modern Republicanism successful, Eisenhower had to woo away from the Democrats voters who were joining the newly affluent middle class. Success in that effort hinged on how well the administration could manage the economy. The Democrats of the New Deal had established a tradition of activism: when the economy faltered, deficit spending and tax cuts were used to stimulate it. Eisenhower, in contrast, wanted to reduce federal spending and the government's role in the economy. When a recession struck in 1953–54, the administration was concerned more with balancing the budget and holding inflation in line than with reducing unemployment through government spending. But these policies worked poorly enough (and the voters expressed their resentment in midterm elections) so that when recessions again hit in 1957–1958 and 1960–1961 there was less talk of balancing the budget. Indeed, Eisenhower achieved that goal in only three of eight fiscal years; and in 1959 he faced what was then the largest peacetime deficit in history. The result was that while the economy grew during the Eisenhower years, the pattern of that growth remained uneven, leaving the city and rural poor largely untouched.

Eisenhower followed a similar pragmatic approach in other areas. When major projects called for federal leadership, as with the Highway Act, he supported the policy. In 1954 he signed the St. Lawrence Seaway Act, which joined the United States and Canada in an ambitious engineering project to open the Great Lakes to ocean shipping. Like the highway program, the Seaway was fiscally acceptable because the funding came from user tolls and taxes rather than from general revenues.

In dealing with farmers, Eisenhower was not about to commit political suicide by trying to abolish price supports established during the New Deal. But as more and more government silos filled with farmers' surplus grain, Eisenhower's secretary of agriculture, Ezra Taft Benson, proposed a system of lower support payments designed to discourage farmers from overproducing basic commodities like corn, cotton, and wheat. Benson also established a soil bank program to pay farmers for taking land out of production. Still, agriculture continued to be transformed by the processes of modern technology. Automated harvesters, fertilizers, and new varieties of plants increased farm outputs as prices continued to drop. In an age of continuing centralization, more and more small farms were being replaced by larger agribusinesses.

The Fall of Joseph McCarthy

When Eisenhower hit on the notion of calling himself a modern Republican, he was looking for some way to distance himself from what he called the more "hidebound" members of the GOP. Their continuing anticommunist campaigns were causing him increasing embarrassment. Senator McCarthy's reckless antics, at first directed at Democrats, now had become less discriminating. In 1953 the Wisconsin senator tried to defeat the appointment of Soviet expert Charles E. Bohlen as ambassador to Moscow. Only the parliamentary skill of Senator Robert Taft saved the appointment and grave embarrassment to the administration. By the summer of 1953 the senator was on a rampage. He dispatched two of his staff members, Roy M. Cohn and G. David Schine, to investigate the Voice of America and the State Department's overseas information agency. Behaving more like college pranksters, the two conducted a whirlwind 18-day witch hunt through Western Europe. To the chagrin of the administration, they insisted on purging government library shelves of "subversive" books, including those by John Dewey and Foster Rhea Dulles, a conservative historian and cousin of the secretary of state. Some librarians, fearing for their careers, burned a number of books. That drove President Eisenhower to denounce "book burners," though he soon after reassured McCarthy's rabid supporters that he did not advocate free speech for communists.

Meanwhile, the administration's own behavior contributed to the red hysteria on which McCarthy thrived. The president launched a loyalty campaign, which he claimed resulted in 3000 firings and 5000 resignations of government employees. It was a godsend to McCarthyites: What further proof was needed that subversives were lurking in the federal bureaucracy? In addition, Eisenhower refused pleas to commute the death sentences of Julius and Ethel Rosenberg to life imprisonment. Such a severe sentence was unusual even in cases of espionage (and here the evidence was not conclusive), but the Rosenbergs were still executed on June 13, 1953. A year later the Atomic Energy Commission turned its investigative eyes on physicist J. Robert Oppenheimer. During World War II it was Oppenheimer's administrative and scientific genius that had led to the development of the atomic bomb. Widely respected by his colleagues, he had raised the hackles of many politicians in 1949 when he opposed the construction of a hydrogen bomb. Despite a few left-wing associations from the 1930s (which army officials had known about when Oppenheimer was working on the bomb), no one had ever accused him of passing on national security information. Nonetheless, the Atomic

With the ruthless Roy Cohn (left) and David Schine (right) providing legal counsel, Senator Joseph McCarthy made a minor Senate subcommittee into a major power center and his name synonymous with inquisitional politics.

Energy Commission in effect suggested Oppenheimer was a traitor by barring him from sensitive research.

In such a climate—where Democrats remained silent for fear of being called leftists and Eisenhower cautiously refused to "get in the gutter with *that* guy"—McCarthy eventually lost all sense of proportion. In that he was driven on by his overly ambitious and ruthless aide Roy Cohn. When the army denied David Schine a commission, Cohn persuaded McCarthy to investigate communism in the army. The new American Broadcasting Company network, eager to fill its afternoon program slots, decided to televise the hearings. The public had an opportunity to see McCarthy badger witnesses and make a mockery of Senate procedures. When Joseph L. Welch, the outraged lawyer for the army, asked, "Have you no sense of decency, sir?" he laid bare the senator's weak spot, to the applause of the gallery and the satisfaction of the wide television audience. As McCarthy's popularity dwindled and the 1954 elections safely passed, the Senate finally moved to censure him. McCarthy died three years later, destroyed by alcohol and the habit of throwing so many reckless punches.

The Politics of the Middle

Despite his aloof public posture, Eisenhower could not escape partisan politics. Just as Truman had been pricked occasionally by revelations of corrupt aides, key members of Eisenhower's administration were exposed for improperly accepting gifts and peddling influence. Most disturbing to Eisenhower was the resignation in 1958 of Sherman Adams, his most trusted adviser, who had accepted gifts in return for favors. None of these instances involved any hint of corruption on the president's part, and his political stock remained high. But poor economic performance took its toll on the GOP. In the wake of the 1954 recession the Democrats gained a 29-member majority in the House and a one-vote edge in the Senate. Never again would Eisenhower work with a Republican congressional majority. Even when he won a smashing victory over Adlai Stevenson (57 to 42 percent) in the 1956 presidential election, the Democrats' House majority increased to 33. In 1958 recession produced an even greater setback, giving the Democrats a 68-seat majority in the House and 30 seats in the Senate.

Eisenhower's triumph in 1956 had been the one electoral bright spot for the Republicans. A major heart attack in 1955 and abdominal surgery in 1956 had slowed the president, but rather than resulting in questions about his health, led to an outpouring of public sympathy. With the economy strong in 1955–1956 Stevenson never stood a chance. Eisenhower's political strategists also made effective use of television, hiring the advertising firm of Batten, Barton, Durstine, and Osborne to mount a campaign. BBDO pioneered the use of the five-minute trailer, which followed regular programs so that Ike's ads did not disturb the audience.

NATIONALISM IN AN AGE OF SUPERPOWERS

Prosperity at home depended on the maintenance of a stable international system of markets and resources. Before World War II European nations played a central role in that system, particularly in colonial areas of the Middle East, Africa, and Southeast Asia. With the collapse of the European global order, the United States and the Soviet Union had become the dominating superpowers in world affairs. But the war disrupted the old colonial relationships too. In Latin America and the Middle East nationalism often meant freeing states like Venezuela and Iran from burdensome debts and concessions to foreigners. In Asia Vietnamese nationalist forces led by Ho Chi Minh had driven Japanese occupation forces out of Indochina and were continuing their fight against French colonial forces. And within Soviet Eastern Europe, national feeling among nations like Poland and Hungary remained strong.

Given the atmosphere of the cold war, both superpowers tended to see the unrest, revolution, and nationalism in these smaller nations in terms of their bipolar struggle. By fits and starts, both the Soviet Union and the United States waxed hostile then conciliatory toward one another. And both competed for the allegiance of the smaller, newly independent nations across the globe.

To the Brink?

The conduct of foreign policy under Eisenhower was shared by the president with his secretary of state, John Foster Dulles. Eisenhower, of course, was no stranger to world politics, having done his stint of diplomatic maneuvering as a general fighting a global war and as commander of NATO. And Dulles approached his job with a somber enthusiasm; indeed, he had been on a virtual campaign for the position since advising presidential hopeful Thomas Dewey in 1944. Coming from a family of missionaries and diplomats, Dulles had within him a touch of both. He saw the Soviet–American struggle in almost religious terms: a fight of good against evil, in which the differences between the two superpowers were irreconcilable. Admirers praised his global vision of the world; detractors saw him as "the wooliest type of pontificating American." Certainly Dulles did not lack confidence. "With my understanding of the intricate relationship between the peoples of the world," he told Eisenhower, "and your sensitiveness to the political considerations, we will make the most successful team in history."

In the end, the two men's differing temperaments led to a policy that seesawed from confrontation to conciliation. Both men were cautious, but Eisenhower was less consistently aggressive in his attitudes toward the Soviets. Dulles, on the other hand, more often threw up cautionary roadblocks when the Russians suggested compromise. Despite that difference, the two men remained firmly committed to an anticommunist posture. "Freedom is pitted against slavery," Eisenhower declared, "lightness against dark."

The first priority for Eisenhower was to end the Korean War, which had settled into a drawn-out, bone-wearying stalemate. Even before taking office, the president-elect had fulfilled his campaign promise "to go to Korea" and appraise the situation firsthand. Once in office, he and Dulles made ominous noises about resorting to nuclear war against Communist China at the same time that they renewed negotiations with North Korea. On July 27, 1953, the Communists and the United Nations forces signed an armistice ending a "police action" in which 54,000 Americans had died. Korea itself remained divided, almost as it had been in 1950. Communism had been "contained" in Korea, but little more than that.

The administration, however, was determined to turn containment from what they charged had been a defensive strategy under Truman to a more offensive one.

Dulles wanted the United States to aid in liberating the "captive peoples" of Eastern Europe and other Communist nations. That seemed to require a larger military budget, however, at a time when Eisenhower was equally determined to cut back military spending and troop levels in order to keep the budget balanced. The president, who knew how the military services and their allies in defense industries vied for government money, was irked at the "fantastic programs" the Pentagon kept coming up with. "If we demand too much in taxes in order to build planes and ships," he argued, "we will tend to dry up the accumulations of capital that are necessary to provide jobs for the million or more new workers that we must absorb each year."

The solution Eisenhower and Dulles hit on for solving the problem was to rely less on ground forces and more on the threat of massive nuclear retaliation in order to intimidate the Soviets into political accommodations. Dulles proclaimed that Americans could not shrink from the threat of nuclear war. "If you are scared to go to the brink, you are lost," he argued. And as Secretary of Defense Charles Wilson put it, a nuclear strategy was much cheaper—"a bigger bang for the buck." Henceforth American foreign policy would have a "new look," though behind the rhetoric lay an ongoing commitment to containment.

Moving beyond the rhetoric of "brinksmanship" did not prove easy, however. When Dulles announced American intentions to "unleash" Chiang Kai-shek to attack mainland China from his outpost on Taiwan, China's foreign minister Zhou Enlai threatened to liberate Taiwan from the nationalists. At that, Eisenhower ordered the Seventh Fleet into the area to protect rather than unleash Chiang. By

ASIAN TROUBLE SPOTS

After the Geneva accords divided Indochina into North and South Vietnam, Secretary of State John Foster Dulles organized SEATO to resist Communist aggression in Southeast Asia. In addition to the conflict in Vietnam, tensions were fueled by the mutual hostility between mainland Communist China and Chiang Kai-shek's Taiwan, as well as the offshore islands of Quemoy and Matsu.

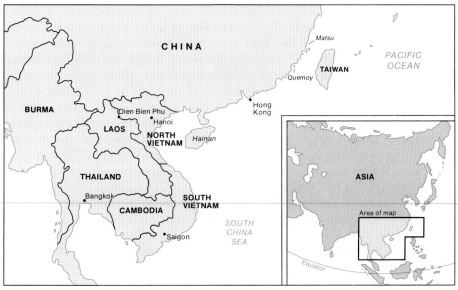

1955 Dulles had staked the defense of Taiwan on tiny coastal islands, especially Quemoy and Matsu. If the Communists attacked, he bluntly stated, "we'll have to use atomic weapons."

Nuclear weapons also figured in the American response to a crisis in Indo-china. Between 1950 and 1954, the United States had given France $1.2 billion in military aid (70 percent of the French military budget) to support the war against Ho Chi Minh. Viewing the countries of Southeast Asia like a row of dominoes, Eisenhower warned that any settlement with the Communists would lead to the loss of the entire region. "You have a row of dominoes set up, you knock over the first one. . . . You could have the beginning of a disintegration that would have the most profound influences."

Worn down by a war they seemed unable to win, the French in 1954 tried to force a final showdown with Ho's forces at Dien Bien Phu. With Vietnamese and Chinese troops holding the surrounding hilltops, the French garrison of 12,000 could not have picked a worse place to do battle. Desperate, the French government pleaded for more American aid, and Admiral Arthur Radford, head of the Joint Chiefs of Staff, volunteered a massive American air raid to relieve the besieged French forces. Radford did not rule out tactical nuclear weapons. But again Eisenhower pulled back. The idea of American involvement in another Asian war aroused opposition from both allies and domestic political leaders like Senate majority leader Lyndon B. Johnson. Without the capacity to win, the French surrendered at Dien Bien Phu in May and convened an international peace conference at Geneva, co-sponsored by the British and Soviet Union. Ho Chi Minh agreed to withdraw his forces north of the 17th parallel in anticipation of elections within two years, confident this would bring him to power in the South as well as the North. But Dulles, having limited the American role to observer at the Geneva peace conference, convinced Eisenhower to support a South Vietnamese government under Ngo Dinh Diem. Diem, Dulles argued, was not bound by the Geneva Accords. The United States then stepped further into the quagmire by sending a military mission to train Diem's army and keep him in power.

The Covert Side of the "New Look"

Dulles and Eisenhower pursued an activist foreign policy in less open ways with the help of John Foster Dulles' brother, Allen Dulles, director of the Central Intelligence Agency (CIA), which had been created in 1947 to coordinate foreign intelligence gathering and conduct covert operations against enemies. In Iran, a nationalist government under Mohammed Mossadeq had in 1951 seized British Petroleum, the British government's single most valuable overseas asset. American oil companies too had developed vast holdings in the region, and government policymakers viewed Iran as a key barrier against Soviet expansion into the Middle East. As relations worsened between Mossadeq and Iran's pro-Western monarch, Shah Mohammad Reza Pahlavi, Dulles feared that Mossadeq would turn to the Soviets. He and Eisenhower approved a covert CIA operation to topple Mossadeq's government. Led by Teddy Roosevelt's grandson, Kermit Roosevelt, "Operation Ajax" recruited a mob to help the Iranian armed forces drive Mossadeq out and return the Shah to his throne in August 1953. The following year a consortium of American oil companies assumed a major role in marketing Iranian oil, and disillusioned nationalists branded the Shah an American puppet.

Seeing how cheaply and quickly American influence had been restored in

Iran, Secretary Dulles looked for similar results in Guatemala. The decision to intervene, however, raised even more vexing ethical questions. Unlike Iran, Guatemala had a duly elected democratic government under Colonel Jacobo Arbenz Guzmán. Arbenz was determined to alleviate the severe poverty in his country by expropriating the idle farmland of rich landowners and giving it to the peasants. Guatemala's richest landowner was the Boston-based United Fruit Company, which had long supported conservative governments, paid few taxes, and shipped its profits back to the United States. Not coincidentally, United Fruit was an old client of Sullivan and Cromwell, a law firm in which both of the Dulles brothers had been partners.

When the Arbenz government seized 400,000 acres from United Fruit, its agents launched a publicity campaign to brand Arbenz a Communist. As the American ambassador to Guatemala later put it, "It seemed to me that the man thought like a communist and talked like a communist, and if not actually one, would do until one came along." When the Soviet Union permitted Czechoslovakia to send Guatemala 1900 tons of small arms, Dulles ordered a CIA-trained band of 1950 Guatemalan and Honduran mercenaries into Guatemala, aided by bombing raids carried out by American P-51 fighter planes. Within a week the army deserted Arbenz, who then fled the country. The leader of the Guatemalan rebels, Carlos Castillo Armas, established a military dictatorship which quickly returned the expropriated lands to United Fruit.

Success in Iran and Guatemala greatly enhanced the reputation of the CIA and created among American policymakers a misplaced faith in covert operations to achieve dramatic results at low cost. But in overthrowing popular governments, the United States gained a dubious reputation in many Third World countries as a foe of national liberation, popular democracy, and social reform. In 1958 the depth of anti-American feeling became obvious when angry crowds in several Latin American countries attacked Vice President Richard Nixon's car, spat at him, and pelted him with eggs and stones.

The Superpowers

Korea, Indochina, Iran, Guatemala—in the eyes of the administration, the crises in all these countries could be traced back to the Soviet dictatorship. Although nationalist movements around the globe were leading nations like India to declare themselves neutral or nonaligned, Dulles continually warned them that they could not sit on the fence: they must choose either the "free world" or the Communist bloc. Throughout the 1950s the secretary of state crisscrossed the globe, setting up mutual defense pacts patterned on NATO, to solidify American security. Yet in all this, it was becoming harder to decide what the motives of the Soviets themselves might be.

Joseph Stalin had died in March 1953, after becoming increasingly isolated, arbitrary, vengeful, and perhaps even paranoiac. For a time the Soviet Union was governed by "collective leadership," but power soon fell to Nikita Khrushchev, a party stalwart with a formidable intellect and peasant origins in the farm country of the Ukraine. In some ways Khrushchev resembled another farm-belt politician, Harry Truman. Both were unsophisticated yet shrewd, earthy in their sense of humor, energetic, irascible, and largely inexperienced in international affairs. Khrushchev kept American diplomats off balance: at times genial and conciliatory, he would suddenly become demanding and boastful.

At home Khrushchev established a relatively moderate regime, gradually shifting the economy toward production of consumer goods. Internationally, the Soviets called for an easing of tensions and reduced forces in Europe, in a bid to wean Western Europeans from dependence on the United States. In Washington the administration was unsure of how to receive the new overtures. The spirit of McCarthyism still reigned, so that compromise with the Soviets involved great political risk. And Secretary Dulles was temperamentally suspicious of all "Godless" Communists. It was actually Winston Churchill who suggested that the Russians might be serious about negotiating. In May 1953 he called on world leaders to hold a summit conference. Dulles and Eisenhower were distinctly cool to the proposition, but further Soviet overtures finally brought the Americans, British, French, and Soviets together in Geneva, Switzerland in 1955.

Little came of the summit other than a cordial "spirit of Geneva," which promised a cooling in the arms race. Neither side had been able to agree about how East and West Germany might be reunified, since both recognized that Germany held the key to Europe's balance of power. Eisenhower did manage a propaganda coup with a policy he called "Open Skies." In a dramatic, unexpected speech, the president announced that the United States would allow the Soviets to photograph American territory from the air and inspect military facilities if the Soviets would grant the same rights to Americans. As the president concluded his remarks to the thunderstruck audience, real lightning suddenly flashed, knocking out the power. The British and French heartily endorsed Open Skies, but Khrushchev condemned it as little more than a "transparent espionage device." Since the Soviets knew the location of American military sites, Open Skies would merely allow the United States to compile more accurate intelligence about the Soviet Union's facilities.

The spirit of Geneva was quickly disturbed by nationalist unrest in 1956. Within the Soviet Union, Khrushchev had undertaken a campaign condemning Stalin's crimes and excesses, and this more liberal attitude encouraged open dissent among Russia's Eastern European allies. Riots erupted in Poland in June, while in Hungary students took to the streets demanding that a coalition government under Imre Nagy replace the Stalinist puppet regime. When the rioting spread, Moscow accepted Nagy and began to remove Soviet tanks from Budapest. But when Nagy announced that Hungary would withdraw from the Warsaw Pact, that was too much. On October 31 tanks rolled into Budapest to crush the uprising. Nagy was imprisoned in Russia and executed in 1957. The American State Department issued formal protests but did nothing to help liberate the "captive nations." For all its tough talk, the "New Look" foreign policy recognized that the Soviets possessed a sphere of influence where the United States would not intervene.

Action would have been difficult because the United States faced a crisis in Egypt. Colonel Gamal Abdel Nasser, a nationalist, had come to power in 1952 and for several years had been attempting to modernize his country and rebuild his army. In 1955 Dulles sought to win Nasser's friendship by offering American aid to build the Aswan Dam, a massive power project on the Nile River. But when Nasser formed an Arab alliance against the young state of Israel and continued to pursue economic ties with the Warsaw bloc, Dulles decided to teach him a lesson. He withdrew the American pledge on Aswan. Nasser angrily upped the ante by seizing the British-owned Universal Suez Canal Company, which ran the waterway through which tankers carried most of Europe's oil.

By 1955 Nikita Khrushchev had emerged as the most powerful Soviet leader. At the Geneva summit (center, front), he was all smiles, claiming, "Things are different now." But like U.S. foreign policy, Khrushchev's waivered between "brinksmanship" and "peaceful coexistence."

Events then began to move quickly. Israel, alarmed at Nasser's Arab alliance, invaded Egypt's Sinai peninsula on October 29, the day Hungary announced it was leaving the Warsaw Pact. Three days later French and British forces seized the canal in an attempt to restore their own interests and prestige. Eisenhower, angered that his allies had not consulted him, for once joined the Soviet Union in supporting a United Nations resolution condemning Britain, France, and Israel and demanding an immediate cease-fire. By December American pressures forced Britain and France to remove their forces. Few events placed so much strain on the Western alliance as the Suez crisis. At the same time Nasser had demonstrated to the industrial powers the potential force of Third World nationalism.

Given the unstable situation, Eisenhower went before Congress in January 1957 and asked for a resolution empowering him to use force in the Middle East against any communist attack. What became known as the Eisenhower Doctrine in effect allowed the president to preempt the war-making authority of Congress in the event of a crisis. Even though the Democrats controlled Congress, fear of Soviet designs on the Middle East persuaded them to give Eisenhower the power he requested. The following year he used it, when Nasser's alliance, known as the United Arab Republic, aided nationalists in ousting a pro-Western government from Iraq. The Christian president of Lebanon, fearing that the unrest would spill into his strife-torn nation, appealed to Eisenhower for aid. Invoking his power under the Eisenhower Doctrine, the president ordered marines into Lebanon. Sunbathers on the beaches of Beirut, Lebanon's capital, were startled on July 15 as 5000 combat-clad marines stormed ashore.

Eventually the United States sent 15,000 troops to Lebanon. No fighting occurred and the American forces turned their peacekeeping role over to the United Nations. Startled by the aggressive American response, Iraq gave assurances that Western oil interests were safe. Nasser, for his part, discovered that Moscow's promise of help amounted to little more than rhetoric. Dulles claimed that the United States had once again turned back the communist drive into the emerging nations, but in reality, nationalism more than communism had been at the root of Middle Eastern turmoil.

Nationalist forces were also in ferment in Latin America, where rapid population growth and maldistribution of wealth and property (2 percent of the people controlled 75 percent of the land) increased social pressures. Repressive dictatorships exercised power and foreign interests—especially American—dominated

Latin American economies, making any conversion to democratic government highly unlikely. Cuba, only 90 miles south of American shores, was typical.

The United States owned many Cuban economic resources, including 80 percent of its utilities, and operated a major naval base at Guantánamo Bay. Cuban dictator Fulgencio Batista had close ties both to the American government and to major crime figures who operated gambling, prostitution, and drug rings in Havana. In 1956 a disgruntled middle-class lawyer, Fidel Castro, sought and quickly gained the support of impoverished peasants in Cuba's mountains to overthrow the corrupt regime. On January 1, 1959, Castro drove Batista from power.

At first many Americans applauded the Cuban revolution, welcoming Castro to the United States in April. But President Eisenhower was distinctly cool to the cigar-smoking Cuban. By summer Castro had filled key positions with Cuban Communists, launched an agricultural reform program, and confiscated American properties. Retaliating, Eisenhower embargoed Cuban sugar and mobilized opposition to Castro in other Latin American countries. Cut off from American markets and aid, Castro turned to the Soviet Union.

Thaws and Freezes

Throughout the series of continuing crises, each superpower found it difficult to interpret the other's motives. The Russians moved to exploit nationalist revolutions where the opportunity offered—more so in Cuba, less in Egypt—and at such times Nikita Khrushchev spoke belligerently of aiding national wars of liberation. "We will bury you," he once admonished the United States, though it was unclear whether this Russian colloquialism meant through peaceful competition or military confrontation. Khrushchev's most outrageous rhetoric came in a speech to the United Nations, where, to make his point, he took off his shoe and pounded it angrily on the table. More seriously, the Soviet premier issued an ultimatum to the Western powers in November 1958 to withdraw their troops from West Berlin within six months, declare it a free city, and negotiate access to it with the East Germans, a government the Western powers had refused to recognize. Eisenhower flatly rejected the ultimatum and Khrushchev backed away from his hardline stance.

By the time John Foster Dulles died of cancer in April 1959, Eisenhower had determined that the last 18 months of his presidency would be devoted to improving Soviet–American relations. In September, at the president's invitation, Khrushchev visited the United States. Though meetings at Camp David produced no significant results, the two leaders agreed to hold another summit meeting in Europe. And Khrushchev concluded his stay with a picturesque tour across America, swapping comments about manure with Iowa farmers, reacting puritanically to movie cancan dancers, and grumping when his visit to the new capitalist marvel, Disneyland, was canceled for security reasons.

Eisenhower's plans for a return visit to the Soviet Union were abruptly canceled on May 17, as the Paris summit conference collapsed. Two weeks earlier the Russians had announced they had shot down a high-altitude U-2 American spy plane. At first Eisenhower claimed that the plane had strayed off course while doing weather research, but Khrushchev sprang his trap: the CIA pilot, Gary Powers, had been captured alive. The president then admitted that he had personally authorized the U-2 overflights for reasons of national security. That epi-

The *Sputnik* launching in 1957 made Americans aware that vast distances no longer protected them from nuclear attack. But even before that discomforting event, Americans had begun devising "fallout shelters" for protection from the aftereffects of a nuclear attack. This one was exhibited in 1955.

sode ended Eisenhower's hopes that his personal diplomacy might create a new framework for Soviet–American relations.

Meanwhile, Congress and the American public had become increasingly worried about Soviet technical achievements. The Russians had developed a hydrogen bomb by 1954. In 1957 they stunned America by launching into outer space the first satellite, dubbed *Sputnik*. And by 1959, when Khrushchev arrived in Washington, the Soviets had crash-landed a much larger payload on the moon. If the Russians could target the moon, they surely could launch nuclear missiles against America, whereas the American space program had been so plagued with delays and mishaps that satellites were being nicknamed "flopniks" and "kaputniks." How had the Soviets managed to catch up with American nuclear technology so quickly? In 1958 Eisenhower joined Congress to pass a National Defense Education Act designed to strengthen graduate education and the teaching of science, mathematics, and foreign languages. At the same time, crash programs proliferated to build basement fallout shelters to protect Americans in case of a nuclear attack.

Democrats charged that the administration had ignored the nation's defense needs. The United States faced an unacceptable "missile gap," they claimed. Disgruntled army officers and defense experts called for a rebuilding of American conventional forces to correct a foreign policy that relied too heavily on nuclear retaliation. Eisenhower knew from American intelligence, but could not admit publicly, that the "missile gap" was not real. While willing to spend more on missile development, he refused to heed his critics' cry for a "crash" defense program at any cost. Eisenhower was not as readily impressed as later presidents by the promises of new weapon systems. He left office with a warning that too much military spending would lead to "an unwarranted influence, whether sought or unsought" by the "military–industrial complex" at the expense of democratic institutions. In looking back over his two terms he could take some comfort from his conduct of foreign policy. A less mature and sophisticated president might have led the United States into more severe conflict or even war. On the other hand, Eisenhower had not been able to place Soviet–American relations in a stable framework.

CIVIL RIGHTS AND THE NEW SOUTH

The history of black Americans and their struggle for equality from the 1940s on is filled with ironies. Just as barriers to legal segregation in the South were tumbling, millions of blacks were leaving for regions where suburbanization imposed new forms of residential discrimination not easily redressed by law. The South they left behind was in the early stages of an economic boom. The cities where they migrated had entered a period of decline that would make them the centers of the nation's worst poverty. Yet, as if to close a circle, the rise of large black voting blocs in major cities created political pressures that forced the nation to dismantle the most blatant legal and institutional barriers to racial equality. For blacks, it might be said that these were the best of times and the worst of times.

The New South's Effect on Blacks

After World War II the southern economy began to grow significantly faster than the national economy. And as it grew, what had for many years been a distinct regional economy was integrated into the larger national and international systems. Where cotton and other agricultural staples had once been king, new centers for manufacturing, the military, petroleum and natural gas, recreation, and finance flourished. None of these newer economic activities depended heavily on the low-wage, unskilled, and non-union labor that had previously been the most distinctive feature of the southern economy.

This remarkable about-face began during the war, with an influx of federal dollars to build and maintain military bases and defense plants. It continued in the postwar period. Congressman Mendel Rivers of South Carolina, for example, was so successful in steering defense projects into his district that critics complained that it might sink under the weight of military installations. As the improved business climate attracted outside capital and skilled labor into the region, wages began to match those elsewhere. And the South attracted new business because it offered a "clean slate." As opposed to more mature economies in the Northeast and Upper Midwest, the region had few unions, little regulation and bureaucracy, and low wages and taxes. Finally, there was the matter of climate, which later became known as the "Sunbelt phenomenon." Especially with improvements in air conditioning, the southern climate and amenities grew more attractive to affluent retirees, skilled professionals, and corporate managers.

Several additional factors more centrally affected the situation of blacks. Before World War II 80 percent of all blacks lived in the South. They constituted a large portion of the low-wage, unskilled labor pool that operated the South's major economic enterprises. The majority worked as sharecroppers and tenant farmers. During the war, about 3 million blacks and whites left farms for the army and urban industrial centers in search of higher wages. After the war that outflow continued.

The departure of so much labor created a crisis in cotton farming, where harvesting remained a labor-intensive task. For the first time cotton farmers had an incentive to mechanize the harvest and International Harvester cooperated by producing a workable machine. In 1950 just 5 percent of the cotton crop was mechanically picked; by 1960 it reached 50 percent. Farmers began to consolidate land into larger holdings. Tenant farmers, sharecroppers, and hired labor of both races, no longer in short supply, left the countryside for the city.

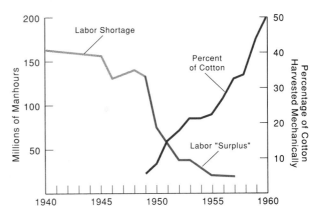

THE MECHANIZATION OF COTTON HARVESTING, 1940–1960

The percentage of cotton harvested by mechanical pickers jumped from only 5 percent in 1950 to 50 percent in 1960 (purple line). As a result, fewer man-hours were needed in the fields (red line), so that after 1949 there was an increasing surplus of labor, spurring black migration out of the cotton belt.

Note: Figure shows unskilled labor for all crops in the Mississippi Delta.

The federal minimum wage also had a profound impact on southern labor. The minimum wage law slowed the growth of low-wage employment everywhere in the country, but nowhere as much as in the South. Low-wage industries like textiles, lumber, paper, furniture, leather, and food processing, which for years had provided the bulk of jobs, became far less important. In addition, steel and other industries with strong national unions and manufacturers with plants around the country set wages by national standards. That brought southern wages close to the national average by the 1960s.

As wages rose and unskilled work disappeared, job opportunities for blacks declined. Outside of cotton farming, the single largest source of jobs for black teenagers was sawmills and lumber factories. As the minimum wage law drove up wages from 1950 to 1960, black teenage employment in lumber dropped 74 percent. New high-wage jobs were reserved for whites. Outside industries arriving in the South made no effort to disturb local employment patterns. So the ultimate irony arose. As per capita income rose and industrialization brought in new jobs, blacks poured out of the region in search of work. They arrived in cities that had little use for their labor or tolerance for racial differences.

The Movement for Civil Rights

In the post–World War II era the NAACP established itself as the great foe of racial segregation. Its chief weapon was the increased national political influence blacks achieved as they migrated in great numbers out of the South. No longer could northern politicians readily ignore the demands black leaders made for greater equality. The Swedish scholar Gunnar Myrdal had amply documented the black case in his landmark work *The American Dilemma* (1944), sponsored by the Carnegie Corporation. Presidents Roosevelt and Truman had taken small but significant steps to address the worst forms of legal and economic discrimination. And across the South black churches and colleges became centers for organized resistance to Jim Crow.

As blacks concentrated their attack on legal forms of discrimination, Thurgood Marshall emerged as the NAACP's leading attorney. Marshall had gone to law school in the 1930s at Howard University in Washington, where the dean, Charles Houston, was in the midst of revamping the school and turning out sharp, dedicated lawyers. Marshall was not only sharp, but he had the common touch. "Before he came along," one observer noted, "the principal black leaders—men like Du Bois and James Weldon Johnson and Charles Houston—didn't talk the language of the people. They were upper-class and upper-middle-class Negroes. Thurgood Marshall was *of* the people. . . . Out in Texas or Oklahoma or down the street here in Washington at the Baptist church, he would make these rousing speeches that would have 'em all jumping out of their seats. . . . 'We ain't gettin' what we should,' was what it came down to, and he made them see that."

During the late 1930s and early 1940s Marshall toured the South (in "a little old beat-up '29 Ford"), typing out legal briefs in the back seat, trying to get teachers to sue for equal pay, and defending blacks accused of murder in a Klan-infested county in Florida. He was friendly with whites, not shy, and blacks who had never even considered the possibility that a member of their race might win a legal battle "would come for miles, some of them on muleback or horseback, to see 'the nigger lawyer' who stood up in white men's courtrooms." For years NAACP lawyers worked hard to organize local chapters, to support members of the community willing to risk their jobs, property, and lives in order to challenge segregation. But they had waged a moderate, pragmatic campaign. They chose not to attack head-on the Supreme Court decision (*Plessy v. Ferguson*, 1896) that permitted "separate but equal" segregated facilities. They simply demonstrated that a black college or school might be separate, but it was hardly equal if it lacked a law school or even indoor plumbing.

But in 1950 the NAACP changed tactics: it would now try to convince the Supreme Court to overturn the separate but equal doctrine itself. Oliver Brown was one of the people who provided a way. Brown was dissatisfied that his daughter Linda had to walk past an all-white school on her way to catch the bus to her segregated black school in Topeka, Kansas. A three-judge federal panel rejected Brown's suit because the schools in Topeka, while segregated, did meet the test of equality. But after two years of arguments the Supreme Court in *Brown v. Board of Education* (1954) overturned the lower court ruling.

Marshall and his colleagues succeeded in part because of a change in the Court itself. The year before, President Eisenhower had appointed Earl Warren, a liberal Republican from California, as Chief Justice. Warren, a forceful advocate, managed to persuade the last of his reluctant judicial colleagues that segregation as defined in *Plessy* rested on an untenable theory of racial supremacy. The Court thus ruled unanimously that separate facilities were inherently unequal. To keep black children segregated solely on the basis of race, it ruled, "generates a feeling of inferiority as to their status in the community that may affect their hearts and minds in a way unlikely ever to be undone."

At the time of the *Brown* decision, 21 states and the District of Columbia operated segregated school systems. All of them had to decide, in some way, how to comply with the new ruling. The Court allowed a certain amount of leeway, handing down a second ruling in 1955 that required that desegregation be carried out "with all deliberate speed." Some border states reluctantly decided to comply, but in the Deep South, many called for diehard defiance. In 1956, a "Southern Manifesto" was issued by 19 United States senators and 81 representatives; it declared their intent to use "all lawful means" to reestablish legalized segregation.

The *Brown* decision did not end segregation, but it combined with political and economic forces to usher in a new era of southern race relations. In December 1955 Rosa Parks, a 43-year-old black civil rights activist, was riding the bus home in Montgomery, Alabama. She was no longer willing to relinquish her seat to a white man, as Alabama Jim Crow laws required. For refusing to do so, she was arrested and fined $10. That incident provoked long-simmering anger in the city's black community. Determined to overturn the law, the leaders organized a boycott of Montgomery buses, whose ridership was predominantly black. The white community, in an effort to halt this unprecedented black challenge, resorted to various forms of legal and physical intimidation. No local agent would insure cars used to carpool black workers. A bomb exploded in the house of the Reverend Martin Luther King, Jr., the key boycott leader. And when that failed to provoke the violence whites could use to justify harsh reprisals, 90 black leaders were arrested for organizing an illegal boycott. Still they held out until November 23, 1956, when the Supreme Court ruled bus segregation was illegal.

The triumph was especially sweet for Martin Luther King, Jr., whose leadership in Montgomery had brought him national fame. Prior to his arrival at the Dexter Street Baptist Church King had little personal contact with the worst forms of white racism. He had grown up in the relatively affluent middle-class black community of Atlanta, Georgia, the son of one of the city's most prominent black ministers. He attended Morehouse College, an academically respected black school in Atlanta, and the Crozer Theological Seminary in Philadelphia before entering the doctoral program in theology at Boston University. He heeded the call to Dexter Street in 1954 with the idea of becoming a theologian after he served his active ministry and finished his dissertation.

Graduate school provided King with the philosophy he would apply as leader of the bus boycott. He built his activism on the Social Gospel of Walter Rauschenbusch and other progressive theological reformers, his vision of modern man's fallen condition on the ideas of theologian Reinhold Niebuhr, and his concept of pacifism and nonviolence on the writings of Henry David Thoreau and Mohandas K. Gandhi, the architect of India's successful drive for independence from Great Britain. The southern black tradition of preaching taught King to speak in the moving "call and response" style, inspiring and energizing his listeners. His powerful sermons and personal magnetism made him the choice of other local black leaders to head the Montgomery Improvement Association (MIA), and to the MIA fell the task of leading the bus boycott.

As the boycott leader it was King's responsibility to rally black support without triggering violence. Since local officials were all too eager for any excuse to use force, King's nonviolent approach was the ideal strategy. King offered his audience two visions. First, he reminded them of the many injustices they had been forced to endure. The boycott, he asserted, was a good way to seek redress. Then he counseled his followers to avoid the actions of their oppressors: "In our protest there will be no cross burnings. No white person will be taken from his home by a hooded Negro mob and brutally murdered." And he evoked the Christian and republican ideals that would become the themes of his civil rights crusade. "If we protest courageously, and yet with dignity and Christian love," he said, "when the future history books are written, somebody will have to say, 'There lived a race of people, of black people, of people who had the moral courage to stand up for their rights. And thereby they injected a new meaning into the history of civilization.'"

Indeed, the blacks of Montgomery did set an example of moral courage that rewrote the pages of American race relations. That made the Supreme Court

Angry white students, opposed to integration, menace black students during a recess at Little Rock's Central High. This was the first civil rights crisis covered by television; for weeks NBC correspondent John Chancellor took a chartered plane daily to Oklahoma City to deliver film footage for the nightly news program.

decision against segregated buses all the more gratifying to King. On December 20, 1956, he took what he described as a "great ride" on the first integrated bus. One white attuned to the decline in municipal services remarked that the boycott had only won blacks "the same lousy service I've been getting every day," but in fact King had won the attention of the national news media as well. He appeared on the cover of conservative *Time* magazine. More important, the probing eye of national news media prevented local whites from greater acts of violence. In Montgomery blacks had developed tactics and leadership that would launch a more aggressive phase of the civil rights movement.

The spotlight moved the following year to Little Rock, Arkansas, a city ironically without a history of racial violence and with a plan for integrating its schools with the most deliberate lack of speed. Nine black students were scheduled to enroll in September 1957 at formerly segregated Central High School. Instead, the school board urged them to stay home when Governor Orval Faubus, generally a moderate on race relations, called out the Arkansas National Guard on the excuse of maintaining order. President Eisenhower tacitly supported Faubus in his defiance of court-ordered integration by remarking "that you cannot change people's hearts merely by laws." The Justice Department won an injunction against Faubus, but as the nine blacks returned on September 23 a mob of 1000 irate and abusive whites greeted them. So great was national attention to the crisis that President Eisenhower was forced to act. To uphold the authority of the federal courts, he sent in 1000 federal troops and took control of the National Guard.

For one year the Guardsmen preserved order until Faubus, in a last-ditch maneuver, closed all the schools. Only in 1959, under the pressure of another federal court ruling, did the Little Rock schools reopen and resume the plan for gradual integration.

Little Rock marked the advent of television news coverage in the civil rights struggle. For weeks, NBC news correspondent John Chancellor appeared on the new "Huntley–Brinkley Report" with film footage of ugly white mobs intimidating neatly dressed and dignified black students. This was only the first in a string of embarrassing racial episodes that television would serve up to national audiences. Moderate southern business leaders recognized they could not attract new industrial development under the shadow of such bad publicity. Often what they advocated to improve the South's image was mere tokenism and an appearance of racial harmony rather than substantive change. Governor James (Big Jim) Folsom of Alabama assured moderates that "we ain't going to force our fine colored folks to go to school with white people."

In the face of such attitudes, Martin Luther King and his followers recognized that the fight had only begun with the skirmishes of Montgomery and Little Rock. Cultural attitudes and customs were not about to give way overnight.

THE CULTURE WARS

The fifties, then, were not a time of consensus on civil rights. Nor, despite the placid surface of the suburban era, were they an era of orthodoxy for either the fine arts or mass entertainment. New York City became an international center for painting and architecture, while mass circulation paperback books revolutionized popular reading habits. American network television became the world's most powerful instrument of mass communication. And rock and roll became the musical idiom of a youth culture spawned by the postwar baby boom. Along with its economic and military power, the United States became a dominant force in world culture.

Cultural ferment provoked widespread commentary, much critical, some even apocalyptic, in warning against moral decadence and spiritual decline. On one level, "highbrow" intellectuals argued that mass culture was vulgarizing and even destroying the great traditions of Western arts. From quite another quarter, the middle class, came the accusation that television, advertising, comic books, movies, and rock music were creating a generation of juvenile delinquents. For both the "highbrow" and "middlebrow" critics, the culture of the 1950s threatened the future of American civilization.

During the 1920s and 1930s many intellectuals had welcomed the idea of mass society. Modern communications, they believed, would break down the barriers of race, class, religion, and nationality. A more homogeneous and harmonious order would emerge. But fascist and communist dictators, with their rabble-rousing mobs and media propaganda, turned these hopes to disillusionment. By the 1950s intellectuals more often argued that the mass media threatened to consume and destroy all valuable culture. In British novelist George Orwell's bleak reading of the future, *1984*, the government's "Ministry of Truth" controlled newspapers, television, film, and radio.

At Columbia University a group of refugees from Nazi Germany, known as the "Frankfurt school," argued that modern media had become the opiate of the masses. The constant repetition of television programs and commercials, Theodor Adorno claimed, tended "to make for automatized reactions and to weaken forces of individual resistance." Dwight Macdonald, another prominent critic, sarcastically attacked the culture of the suburban middle classes, which he called "midcult": books, films, and theater that pretended to be high art but in reality were little more than oversimplified treatments of serious issues. The democratization of American culture, he believed, led to banal conformity and mediocrity. Others, including Leslie Fiedler, stepped in to defend popular tastes. The criticism now leveled against television and popular music echoed criticism of the Elizabethan theater, Fiedler pointed out, as well as the novel, the opera, and film in their early years. Through it all, of course, the vast majority of suburban brows—high, middle, and low—tended to ignore the bombshells critics were lobbing at one another.

Juvenile Delinquency

Many parents and public figures believed that mass media were corrupting America's youth. Dance crazes, outlandish clothing styles, strange jargon, rebelliousness toward parents, and sexual precociousness—all these seemed to be symptoms of more threatening antisocial behavior. America had spawned a generation of rebellious juvenile delinquents. Psychologist Frederic Wertheim told a group of doctors, "You cannot understand present-day juvenile delinquency if you do not take into account the pathogenic and pathoplastic [infectious] influence of comic books." Others laid the blame on films and the lyrics of popular music.

The worry about youth resulted partly from the demographic changes in society. The baby boom children were becoming teenagers in the 1950s. And the general prosperity meant that more of them held after-school jobs, earned more of their own disposable income, and had more leisure time than parents growing up during the Depression and World War II. The center of the new teen culture was the high school. Whether in consolidated rural school districts, new suburban schools, or city systems, the large, comprehensive high schools of the 1950s were often miniature melting pots where middle-class students were exposed to, and often adopted, the style of the lower classes and blacks. Many districts, of course, sustained patterns of social class and racial isolation. All the same, high schools were more likely than neighborhood schools to encourage social integration.

Rock and Roll: Idiom of a Youth Culture

In many ways the argument about juvenile delinquency was an argument about social class and, to a lesser degree, race. When adults complained that "delinquent" teenagers dressed poorly, lacked ambition, were irresponsible and sexually promiscuous, these were the same arguments traditionally used to denigrate other outsiders—immigrants, the poor, and blacks. Nowhere were these racial and class undertones more evident than in the hue and cry which greeted the arrival of rock and roll.

Before 1954 popular music had been divided into three major categories: "pop," country and western, and rhythm and blues. A handful of major record companies with almost exclusively white singers dominated the pop charts. Off on one fringe of the popular field was country and western, often split into cowboy musicians like Roy Rogers and Gene Autry and the hillbilly style associated with

Nashville. The music industry generally treated rhythm and blues as "race music," whose performers and audience were largely black. Nationally, their radio and record market was relatively small. Each of these musical traditions, it is worth noting, grew out of regional cultures. Just as the West and the South saw the gradual breakdown of their colonial economies, so these musical subcultures were being gradually integrated into the national mainstream.

By the mid-1950s the distinctiveness of the three styles began to blur. Singers on the white pop charts recorded a few songs from country and rhythm and blues. The popularity of crossovers such as "Sh-boom," "Tutti-Frutti," and "Earth Angel" indicated that a major shift in taste and market was under way. Lyrics still reflected the pop fields's preoccupation with young love, marriage, and happiness, but the music reflected the rawer and earthier style of rhythm and blues. Country and western singer Bill Haley brought the new blend to the fore in 1954 with "Shake, Rattle, and Roll," the first rock song to reach the top of the pop charts.

And then—calamity! Millions of middle-class roofs nearly blew off with the appearance in 1955 of the rhythmic and raucous Elvis Presley. By background, Elvis was a country boy whose musical style combined elements of gospel, country, and blues. But it was his hip-swinging, pelvis-plunging performances that electrified teenage audiences. To more conservative adults, Presley's long hair, sideburns, and tight jeans seemed menacingly delinquent. His music and sensuous movement appeared to them an expression of hostile rebellion. What they often resented but rarely admitted was that Elvis looked lower class, sounded black, and really could sing.

Two phenomena helped assure the mass popularity of rock and roll. One was the introduction of the 45-rpm record at a price teenage consumers could afford. More important was the development of "top forty" rock radio. Having lost much of their traditional audience to television, radio stations discovered a new market among teenagers. Disc jockeys like Alan Freed developed a frenetic style that reflected the music's excited rhythms.

The Unblinking Eye

No medium played a more central role in the popular culture of the 1950s than television. It had a powerful political impact in the Kefauver hearings, in the 1952 and 1956 elections, and in the Army–McCarthy hearings. No candidate for office could ignore it; no manufacturer could capture the consumer market without it. As a rapidly emerging institution of power and influence, it experienced growing pains and found itself at the center of a debate over its influence in American life.

During the early 1950s advertisers rather than the networks produced most programs. Shows like the "Kraft Television Theater" and "U.S. Steel Hour" were named after the sponsor, not the performers or the content. Without any established history, television at first experimented with ideas drawn from other media such as theater and radio. Eighty percent of all shows were performed live. Original plays, for example, offered a showcase for young writers, directors, and performers such as Sidney Poitier, Paul Newman, and Joanne Woodward. Television news programs like Edward R. Murrow's "See It Now" occasionally probed subjects as sensitive as McCarthyism.

Elvis Presley.

In the mid-1950s television entered a new phase. Controversy surrounding Murrow's probe of McCarthy encouraged the networks to downgrade news and public affairs programs. At the same time they began working out a profitable arrangement with Hollywood film studios. The studios, seeking to regain revenue lost to television, produced telefilm series for the networks, which, in turn, sold time to advertisers. This gave the networks, rather than the sponsors, ultimate control over program content. By 1959 live television was virtually a thing of the past. Westerns, detective shows, and old movies led the ratings. Newscasts, dominated by filmed stories, became an important mechanism for building an audience for prime-time shows.

Critics of television charged that the new shows encouraged violence and juvenile delinquency. Impressionable children, they complained, were regularly exposed to manslaughter and mayhem, followed by appeals for soft drinks and cigarettes, rather than to programs of solid educational value. But those who had the power to regulate television—the president, Congress, the Federal Communications Commission (FCC)—chose not to extend a restraining hand. The only effort to promote "better" programs came in 1952, when the FCC allocated a number of channels, but no funding, to educational television.

Abstract Art and Architecture

Controversy over culture was hardly restricted to the popular arts. The modern paintings and buildings of the postwar era disturbed many Americans dedicated to traditional notions of art and architecture. The avant-garde styles of the 1950s were linked by an international flavor and self-conscious concern for abstraction. Their creators seemed determined to break with the past.

In 1951 the Museum of Modern Art in New York mounted a striking exhibit of American painters whose work baffled many viewers. Artists such as Jackson Pollock, Willem de Kooning, and Mark Rothko specifically rejected the representational style of those like Thomas Hart Benton, popular in the 1930s and 1940s, who celebrated American regional scenes and folkways. Pollock, himself a student of Benton, had become gradually more expressive and abstract, until finally, by dripping and spattering paints rather than brushing them on, he created patterns of action that revealed no controlling influence of the artist's hand. This was abstraction indeed.

For many architects, the decision to build geometric forms sheathed in glass and steel had more to do with economics than aesthetics. Simply put, modern buildings were cheaper to erect. Glass was the material of the decade because it was inexpensive and easy to use. Skilled masons and stonecutters were less available to do the ornate detailing common on public buildings of the prewar era. If modern buildings made any symbolic statement, it was about the faceless bureaucrats housed within the glass and steel boxes that looked like all the other boxes. The best of these, however, earned a well-deserved reputation for innovation and beauty, such as the United Nations complex erected along New York's East River in 1950. Its architects were an international team led by Walter Harrison of New York.

Moving from the East Coast to the West, and from the sublime to the flamboyantly ridiculous, a much more popular style of architecture, dubbed "California Crazy," delighted in producing restaurants in the shape of a hamburger, gas stations that looked like a flying wing, and neon palaces for gamblers in Las Vegas.

Perhaps the ultimate statement of car and home culture came as one architect incorporated the garage into the family room.

Americans in 1960 had reason to be satisfied with the accomplishments of the past decade. Despite periodic recession, income rose dramatically and unemployment remained low. The country had avoided war. The National Aeronautics and Space Administration (NASA) had sent satellites into orbit. A vast highway network linked the nation's urban centers and allowed motorists easier access to both city and countryside. Suburbs had provided millions of families an escape from the crowded center cities.

Yet as the 1950s ended, small cracks appeared in the national consensus. In run-down urban neighborhoods and college towns, motley collections of artists, intellectuals, musicians, and middle-class students had dropped out of mainstream society to form a "beat" subculture. Experimenting openly with drugs, mystical religions, Oriental philosophy, and sex, the "beatniks" self-consciously rejected what they viewed as the excessive materialism and spiritual bankruptcy of America's middle-class culture. A popular president left office warning that an overgrown defense establishment threatened to strangle democratic institutions. The currents of political reform, crushed temporarily by the purges of the McCarthyites, were again on the rise. Antinuclear groups like SANE (Committee for a Sane Nuclear Policy) protested the nuclear arms race. Blacks had shown they were less willing to accept inequality. In the midst of postwar peace and prosperity, the United States began to build a new social and political agenda.

SIGNIFICANT EVENTS

1950	David Riesman's *The Lonely Crowd* published
1951	First major exhibit of abstract expressionism at the Museum of Modern Art
1953	Submerged Lands Act; Rosenbergs executed; Korean armistice; Mossadeq overthrown in Iran
1954	*Brown v. Board of Education;* St. Lawrence Seaway Act; Robert Oppenheimer denied security clearance; Army–McCarthy hearings; McCarthy censured; CIA overthrows Arbenz in Guatemala; Geneva summit
1955	Montgomery bus boycott; Elvis Presley ignites rock and roll
1956	Interstate Highway Act; Eisenhower reelected; Suez crisis; "Southern Manifesto"
1957	*Sputnik* launched; Little Rock crisis; Civil Rights Act; Eisenhower Doctrine
1958	Sherman Adams resigns; Richard Nixon attacked in Latin America; marines sent into Lebanon; Berlin crisis; National Defense Education Act; NASA established
1959	Castro seizes power in Cuba; Khrushchev visits United States; Soviet probe hits moon
1960	Soviet Union captures CIA pilot; Paris summit canceled
1961	Eisenhower farewell address warns of military–industrial complex
1963	Betty Friedan's *The Feminine Mystique* published

32

Liberalism and
Beyond

Six-year-old Ruby knew the lessons. Her father and mother had drilled them into her. She was to look straight ahead—not to one side or the other—and especially not at *them*. She was to keep walking. And above all, she was not to look back once she'd passed, because that would encourage them. Ruby knew these things, but it was still hard to keep her eyes straight. The first day of school, and federal marshals were there along with her parents. And hundreds of white people, it seemed, had come from all over New Orleans. The marshals kept them from getting at her, but they came near enough to yell things like, "You little nigger, we'll get you and kill you." Worse things, too, she didn't want to think about. Then she was within the building's quiet halls and alone with her teacher. She was the only person in class: none of the white students had come. As the days went by during that autumn of 1960, the marshals stopped walking with her but the hecklers were still there. And once in a while Ruby couldn't help looking back, trying to see if she recognized the face of one woman in particular.

Ruby's parents were not social activists. They signed their daughter up for the white school because "we thought it was for all the colored to do, and we never thought Ruby would be alone." Her father's white employer fired him and the neighborhood store refused to do business with the family. Letters and phone calls threatened their lives and home. Through it all Ruby seemed remarkably resilient, playing with friends after school and taking things in stride. When she drew pictures, though, some of her feelings came out. White children appeared in large, bold outlines, their features carefully sketched. They had teeth, lips, 10 fingers, and 10 toes. But when she drew herself or other black children, an ear might be missing, or a thumb, or a nose. "When I draw a white girl, I know she'll be okay," she explained once, "but with the colored it's not so okay. So I try to give the colored as even a chance as I can, even if that's not the way it will end up being." Ruby's parents were more disturbed because she was not eating the way she used to. Often she left her school lunch untouched, or refused anything other than packaged food such as potato chips. It was only after a time that the problem was traced to the hecklers. "They tells me I'm going to die, and that it'll be soon. And that one lady tells me every morning I'm getting poisoned soon, when she can fix it." Ruby was convinced that the woman owned the variety store nearby and would carry out her threat by poisoning the family's food.

On August 28, 1963, more than 250,000 demonstrators joined the great civil rights March on Washington. The day belonged to the Reverend Martin Luther King, Jr., who movingly called on blacks and whites to join together in a color-blind society.

Ruby's drawings of a white girl (left) and herself.

Over the course of a year, white students gradually returned to class and life settled into a new routine. By the time Ruby was 10, she had developed a remarkably clear perception of herself. "Maybe because of all the trouble going to school in the beginning I learned more about my people. Maybe I would have anyway; because when you get older you see yourself and the white kids; and you find out the difference. You try to forget it, and say there is none; and if there is you won't say what it be. Then you say it's my own people, and so I can be proud of them instead of ashamed."

If the new ways were hard for Ruby, they were not easy for white southerners either—even those who saw the need for change. One woman, for years a dedicated teacher in Atlanta, vividly recalled a traumatic summer 10 years earlier, when she went north to New York City to take courses in education. There were black students living in the dormitory, an integrated situation she was not used to. One day as she stepped from her shower to dry off, so did a black student from the nearby stall. "When I saw her I didn't know what to do," the woman recalled. "I felt sick all over, and frightened. What I remember—I'll never forget it—is that horrible feeling of being caught in a terrible trap, and not knowing what to do about it. I thought of running out of the room and screaming, or screaming at the woman to get out, or running back into the shower. . . . My sense of propriety was with me, though—miraculously—and I didn't want to hurt the woman. It wasn't *her* that was upsetting me. I knew that, even in that moment of sickness and panic." So she ducked back into the shower until the other woman left.

It took her most of the summer before she felt comfortable eating with blacks at the same table. And when she returned home, she told no one about her experiences. "At that time people would have thought one of two things: I was crazy (for being so upset and ashamed) or a fool who in a summer had become a dangerous 'race mixer.'" She continued to love the South and to speak up for its traditions of dignity, neighborliness, and honor, but she saw the need for change. And so in 1961 she volunteered to teach one of the first integrated high school classes in Atlanta, even though she had her doubts. By the end of two years she concluded that she had never spent a more exciting time teaching. "I've never felt so useful, so constantly useful, not just to the children but to our whole society. American as well as Southern. Those children, all of them, have given me more than I've given them. They've helped me realize that some unpleasant times in my own life were not spent in vain. That's a privilege, to be able to have your life tested and found somewhat consistent, at least over the long haul. I guess I grew up there in New York, and used the strength from it down here later on."

A LIBERAL AGENDA FOR REFORM

The changes that swept America in the 1960s were wrenching to most people. From the schoolrooms and lunch counters of the South to the college campuses of the North, from eastern slums to western migrant labor camps, American society was in ferment. On the face of it, such agitation seemed to be a dramatic reversal of the placid fifties: turbulence and change overturning stability and order.

Yet the new decade grew naturally out of the social conditions that preceded it. Consensus had given society a sense of stability; prosperity bred confidence that nagging problems like poverty might finally be resolved. In the 1960s, wrote one of the era's optimistic liberals, "the world seemed more plastic, more subject to modification by human will"; we believed that "the energy and commitment of multitudes could be linked to compel the enrichment of human life." Such confidence always has the danger of becoming hubris; such hopes too often bring bitter disappointments despite striking successes. So it was with the liberal faith of the 1960s.

The Social Structures of Change

The 1950s sustained an economic expansion unlike any since the 1920s. A general prosperity had enlarged the middle class and given its members money to spend on suburban homes, time-saving appliances, televisions, automobiles. Furthermore, the baby boom created a generation of children who grew up under conditions of relative affluence. They had discretionary income to spend, a greater chance of going to college, and some freedom to think twice about what they might do or become as adults. These were luxuries not available to most young adults during the Depression or World War II.

At the same time, the economic tide of the 1950s did not raise all areas of the nation equally. While suburbs flourished, urban areas decayed. While more whites went to college, more blacks found themselves out of work on southern farms or desperate for jobs in northern ghettos. Mexican-Americans in cities lacked decent housing and jobs. Migrant workers, picking grapes in California or following the harvest north from Texas, felt their employers' sharp hostility with every attempt to unionize and improve their wages. Yet the general prosperity remained for all to see. And the success of the NAACP in wringing a policy of integration from the Supreme Court gave minorities new hopes.

The expansive years of the 1950s, in other words, made it possible for several major reform elements to emerge during the 1960s. The economic boom made minorities aware of the possibilities of economic opportunity. National liberation movements sweeping Africa and other Third World areas gave broader meaning to reforms at home. And the baby-boomers of the middle class came of age at a time when they had enough wealth and leisure to question the prosperity their parents had gained. These social forces, more than politicians or any of society's traditional leaders, were at the root of the decade's change. Time and again, the political system would be challenged to deal with what the 1950s had done—and what had been left undone.

The Election of 1960

The first president to face these currents of reform was John Fitzgerald Kennedy, at 43 the youngest man ever elected to the presidency. On the face of it, Kennedy's 1960 campaign promised to bring the breezes of change to Washington. While Eisenhower played golf, the Russians had launched *Sputnik*, Kennedy complained. While Ike talked about the budget gap, Kennedy pointed to the missile gap and charged that America was losing the cold war. The nation needed to find new challenges and "new frontiers," he proclaimed. The candidate's rhetoric was noble, but the direction in which Kennedy would take the nation was far from clear.

Aside from political issues, there was a social one to be met. Jack Kennedy was a Roman Catholic out of Irish Boston, and no Catholic other than Al Smith in 1928 had run for president as a major party candidate. Conservative Protestants, many concentrated in the heavily Democratic South, were convinced that a Catholic president would never be "free to exercise his own judgment" if the pope ordered otherwise. Despite warnings from his advisers, Kennedy chose to confront the issue head-on. In September he entered the lions' den, addressing an association of hostile ministers in Houston. The speech was the best of his campaign. "I believe in an America where the separation of church and state is absolute," he said, "—where no Catholic prelate would tell the President (should he be Catholic) how to act, and no Protestant minister would tell his parishioners how to vote." House Speaker Sam Rayburn, an old Texas pol, was astonished by Kennedy's bravura performance. "My God! . . . He's eating them blood raw."

Kennedy's opponent, Vice President Richard Nixon, agreed and thus did not make religion a campaign issue. Although Nixon ran on his record as an experienced leader and staunch anticommunist, by October the economy had tailed off into a recession and unemployment was up. Nixon had agreed to a series of debates with Kennedy—the first to be televised nationally. At the time of the first debate he was overtired and his "Lazy Shave" makeup failed to hide his five-o'clock shadow. By contrast, Kennedy seemed relaxed and was able to convince many voters that he had the experience needed to handle the job. Interest in the election ran so high that 64 percent of voters turned out, the largest number in 50 years. Out of 68.3 million ballots cast, Kennedy won by a margin of just 118,000.

In the end religion, ethnicity, and race played decisive roles. One voter was asked if he voted for Kennedy because he was a Catholic. "No, because *I* am," he answered; and in key states Catholic support made a difference. "Hyphenated"

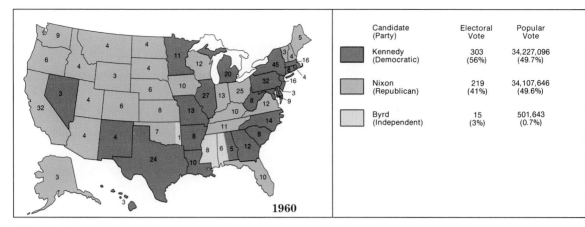

Candidate (Party)	Electoral Vote	Popular Vote
Kennedy (Democratic)	303 (56%)	34,227,096 (49.7%)
Nixon (Republican)	219 (41%)	34,107,646 (49.6%)
Byrd (Independent)	15 (3%)	501,643 (0.7%)

1960

THE ELECTION OF 1960

Americans—Hispanic, Jewish, Irish, Italian, Polish, and German—voted Democratic in record numbers, while much of the black vote which had gone to Eisenhower in 1956 returned to the Democratic fold. Indeed, when Martin Luther King was imprisoned during a civil rights protest in Georgia, Kennedy attracted the support of blacks by telephoning his sympathy to Dr. King's wife. Nixon ran strongest among white Protestant middle Americans. Kennedy became president by a whisker (there was solid evidence of voting fraud in Chicago and Texas), but he was victor nonetheless.

The Hard-Nosed Idealists of Camelot

To many observers, the Kennedy White House seemed to embody the best and brightest of the liberal Democratic promise. The administration was soon dubbed "Camelot," after King Arthur's magical court. In a popular Lerner and Lowe musical of 1960, Camelot had been pictured as a land where skies were fair, men brave, women pretty, and the days full of challenge and excitement. With similar panache, the president invited artists, musicians, and intellectuals to the White House, where his wife Jacqueline proved to be a host with infectious charm. During impromptu touch football games, a rough-and-tumble playfulness shone forth, akin to Arthur's jousting tournaments of old.

Yet Kennedy was by neither birth nor experience a liberal at all. His father, Joseph P. Kennedy, had made a fortune in stock market speculation and Hollywood real estate. Determined to build a family political dynasty, Joe Kennedy sent his boys to prestigious prep schools and then Harvard, to hobnob with the Protestant elite. Jack had followed the appointed regimen, was handsome and intelligent to boot, and possessed an ironic, self-deprecating humor. As a PT boat commander in World War II, he had been decorated for heroism, though he might as easily have been cashiered for carelessness. After the war he was elected to Congress, where he led an undistinguished career, supported Joe McCarthy, and earned a reputation as a lightweight and a playboy. But once Kennedy set his sights on the White House, he was a changed man. He revealed an astonishing capacity for political maneuver and organization. To woo the liberals, he adopted

John F. Kennedy's carefully cultivated image of a "Camelot" administration blended a concern for youth, verve, and life (his son John stands before him) with a determination to appear militarily "tough" against the communists.

their agenda and brought a distinguished group of intellectuals and academics to his campaign staff.

The grand designs of fascism had left many liberals disillusioned with all-encompassing ideologies for change. By the 1960s they had come to favor a pragmatic approach to reforming American society. Economists like John Kenneth Galbraith no longer attacked capitalism, since the strategies of John Maynard Keynes (page 1004) offered a means to make the system work. Rather than embrace a social welfare state, Kennedy liberals preferred to extend benefits piecemeal to solve the nation's lingering social ills. In foreign affairs Kennedy surrounded himself with cold war liberals who were no less dedicated than conservatives to fighting communism.

The Kennedy advisers were convinced that they, more than the likes of John Foster Dulles, had flexible and efficient ways to contain the Soviet Union. McGeorge Bundy, a former intelligence officer and Harvard dean, was both steely and brilliant; he headed the National Security Council. Walt Whitman Rostow, an MIT economist, was known for his theories of how developing nations could prosper and avoid the pitfalls of communism. And as secretary of defense, Robert Strange McNamara came determined to tame the sprawling bureaucracy of the Pentagon. McNamara, a former Harvard Business School professor and president of Ford Motors, specialized in using new quantitative tools like systems analysis to streamline business management. He had been one of the postwar breed of "whiz kids" who moved from the universities into the board rooms of once-staid corporations.

Kennedy liked all these men—witty, brilliant, intellectual—because they seemed not only to have high ideals, but to be at home with power. They were not afraid to use it. If Khrushchev spoke of waging guerrilla "wars of liberation,"

Americans could play that game too. A similar taste was reflected in Kennedy's spare-time reading: the popular James Bond spy novels. Agent 007, with his license to kill, was exactly to the president's taste: sophisticated, a cool womanizer (which Kennedy himself continued to be), and ready to use power and the latest technology to deal with communists or other bizarre enemies. Ironically, Bond demonstrated that there could be plenty of glamour and romance in being "hard-nosed" and pragmatic. That illicit pleasure was the underside, perhaps, of Camelot's high ideals.

NEW FRONTIERS

When Kennedy appointed Dean Rusk secretary of state, he indicated that foreign policy would be conducted from the White House. Rusk was an unassertive diplomat who would preside only over the Department of State, while the president and his national security advisers set broad policy. Kennedy wanted to bring to bear a more flexible range of military and economic options. Above all, he believed that Eisenhower had not realized how much the cold war had shifted from the traditional battlefronts of Europe to the developing nations in Asia, Africa, and Latin America.

Kennedy set the tone for his administration when he announced in the spring of 1961 a new "Alliance for Progress" with the nations of Latin America. The goal of the Alliance was the prevention of future Castro-style revolutions. Kennedy promised to provide $20 billion in foreign aid over 10 years—about four times the aid Latin America had been getting under Truman and Eisenhower. In return, Latin American nations would agree to reform unfair tax policies and begin agricultural land reforms. The administration also set up the Peace Corps, a program that sent idealistic young men and women to Third World nations to provide technical, educational, and public health services. Under the Alliance, a majority of Peace Corps volunteers were assigned to Latin America.

In what seemed the ultimate call to new frontiers, the president established a national commitment to send a man to the moon and bring him back by the end of the decade. But this "star trek" was another phase of the cold war. The Russians had launched their own successful manned space flight in 1959 and Kennedy was eager to beat them in a space race. In May Alan Shepard, Jr., completed a 20-minute suborbital flight. By February 1962 John Glenn had circled the earth three times. Longer flights followed, as Americans discovered in the astronauts heroes for a new age.

But in more down-to-earth ways, high ideals were not easily translated into practical results. Latin American governments were eager to accept aid but much less able or willing to carry out reforms. Few welcomed the intrusive Yankee diplomats who came from north of the border to inspect their programs. Instability remained a key problem, for in the first five years of the Alliance, nine Latin American governments were overthrown by military coups. The Peace Corps, for its part, proved a tremendous public relations success and helped thousands of Third World farmers on a people-to-people basis. But individual Peace Corps workers could do little to change corrupt policies on a national level, and many returned home convinced the Third World needed revolution, not reform.

Kennedy was determined to back economic policies with military measures. As the Alliance for Progress was getting under way, the Pentagon directed jungle warfare schools at Fort Bragg, North Carolina, and in the Canal Zone. These schools trained Latin American police and paramilitary groups to fight guerrilla wars; they also trained American "special forces" like the Green Berets. The administration wanted the capacity to send American forces or their allies into wars of liberation the way the Soviets had.

The prime target for "liberation" was Fidel Castro, whose Communist regime lay only 90 miles south of Florida. Since breaking diplomatic relations in 1960, the Eisenhower administration had authorized the CIA to organize an invasion of Cuba, and Kennedy approved an attack scheduled for April. The CIA assured the president that its 1400-member army of Cuban exiles could inspire their countrymen to overthrow Castro. But the invasion proved to be a mismanaged disaster. The poorly equipped rebel forces landed at the Bay of Pigs in a swamp, with no protective cover for miles. Within two days Castro's army had rounded them up. Taking responsibility for the entire fiasco, Kennedy suffered a bitter humiliation. That did not discourage further covert operations or cold war confrontation. Unrepentant for its first fiasco the CIA secretly hatched plans to embarrass or murder the Cuban leader.* It even tried to enlist the services of organized crime figures eager to renew their profitable operations in Havana.

Kennedy's advisers took a similar approach to the problem of South Vietnam, where a religious war within a civil war was under way. The autocratic government of Prime Minister Ngo Dinh Diem, a Catholic, remained in power, although it was growing more unpopular by the month. South Vietnamese Communists, known as the Vietcong, with support from North Vietnam waged a guerrilla war against Diem. Buddhist elements backed the rebellion. In May 1961, a month after the Bay of Pigs invasion, Kennedy secretly ordered 500 Green Berets and military advisers to Vietnam in hopes of helping Diem defeat the Vietcong. By 1963 the number of "military advisers" had risen to over 16,000 men, who were increasingly being drawn into combat situations. Kennedy publicly defended the aid, supporting Eisenhower's domino theory. "If South Vietnam went, it . . . would give the impression that the wave of the future in Southeast Asia was China and the Communists," he told the press.

By 1963 the situation had badly degenerated. Diem was ruthlessly suppressing Buddhist opposition groups. His corruption and police state tactics created a great deal of bad publicity, and he was not even winning the war. The administration tacitly encouraged a military coup that captured Diem and, to Washington's surprise, shot him in November 1963. Despite Kennedy's policy of pragmatic idealism, the United States found itself mired in a Vietnamese civil war, which it had no clear strategy for winning.

The Missiles of October

Vietnam and Cuba were only two areas in the Third World where the Kennedy administration sought to project its power against Communist forces. But the conflict between the United States and the Soviet Union soon overshadowed developments in Asia, Africa, and Latin America.

---

*The most notorious of these plans was a special CIA shoe polish, never successfully used, whose ingredients were designed to cause Castro's trademark beard to fall out, thus supposedly embarrassing the revolutionary leader.

June 1961 was the president's first chance to take the measure of Nikita Khrushchev, at a summit meeting held in Vienna. For two long days, Khrushchev was brash and belligerent. Germany must be reunited, he demanded. The Berlin problem must be settled within six months. Kennedy was shocked by the Soviet leader's vehemence and tried to respond in kind, but he left Vienna worried that Khrushchev perceived him as weak and inexperienced. In August his fears were confirmed when the Soviets threw up a heavily guarded wall dividing East from West Berlin, to prevent disillusioned East Germans from escaping to the western sector. But the Soviets did not seal off West Berlin's access to West Germany. Although the president strongly protested the move, the wall became a permanent fixture of Berlin life.

Continuing tensions with the Soviet Union also led the administration to rethink the American approach to nuclear warfare. Under the Dulles doctrine of massive retaliation, almost any incident might trigger a launch of the full arsenal of nuclear missiles. Kennedy and McNamara sought to establish a "flexible response doctrine" that would limit the level of a first nuclear strike and therefore leave room for negotiation. In that case, however, conventional forces in Europe would have to be built up, so that they could better deter aggression. McNamara proposed equipping them with smaller tactical nuclear weapons.

But what if the Soviets were tempted to launch a first-strike attack to knock out American missiles? McNamara's flexible response policy required that enough American missiles survive in order to retaliate. If the Soviets knew the United States could survive a first strike, they would then be less likely to launch a surprise attack. So McNamara began a program to bury missile sites underground and develop submarine-launched missiles. Ironically, American intelligence estimates showed that there was no "missile gap," despite Kennedy's campaign charges. The Soviets had far fewer missiles. Still, the new flexible response policies resulted in a 15 percent increase in the 1961 military budget, compared with only 2 percent increases during the last two Eisenhower years. In this sense, the effort to make American defenses more flexible served only to accelerate the arms race. And critics like George Kennan later concluded that nuclear "flexibility" was a dangerous idea, for there was "no way in which [some] nuclear weapons could be used that would not involve the possibility . . . of escalation into a general nuclear disaster."

The peril of nuclear confrontation became dramatically clear in the Cuban missile crisis of October 1962. In public statements President Kennedy had emphasized repeatedly that the United States would treat any attempt to place offensive weapons in Cuba as an unacceptable threat. Khrushchev had simultaneously promised that the Soviet Union had no such intention. Thus Kennedy was outraged when a CIA U-2 overflight on October 14 confirmed that offensive missile sites were being constructed. "He can't do that to me," the president snapped. For a week, top security advisers met in secret strategy sessions. Hawkish advisers urged Kennedy to order air strikes against the missile sites, but the president worried that such an attack might lead to nuclear war. In the end he decided to impose a naval blockade to intercept "all offensive military equipment under shipment to Cuba." Stunned Americans learned of the crisis on October 22, when the president announced the news on national television.

Tensions mounted as a Soviet submarine approached the line of American ships. On October 25 the navy stopped an oil tanker. Several Soviet ships reversed course. Kennedy was making strenuous efforts to resolve the crisis through diplomatic channels, and on October 26 he received a rambling message from Khrushchev agreeing to remove the missiles in return for an American promise not to invade Cuba. The next day came a more troubling message, insisting the United States must also dismantle its missile bases in Turkey, which bordered on the Soviet Union. Unwilling to strike that deal publicly, Kennedy decided to ignore the second letter and accept the offer in the first. When the Soviets agreed, the faceoff ended on terms that saved either side from overt humiliation.

The Cuban missile crisis was the closest the world had come to full-scale nuclear war, and the confrontation affected both superpowers profoundly. Khru-

THE WORLD OF THE SUPERPOWERS

This map shows the extent of the cold war Soviet and American military buildup. The United States established a worldwide network of bases and alliances surrounding Soviet bloc nations, from Japan and South Korea, South Vietnam, Pakistan, and Turkey in Asia to the nations of the NATO alliance in Europe. Soviet efforts to expand its influence in the Third World led to the creation of an outpost in Cuba. Around these strategic perimeters "hotspots" and centers of crisis continued to simmer.

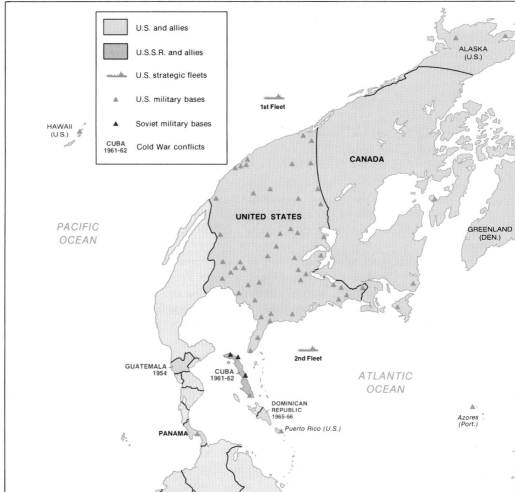

shchev found himself under heavy attack from China and from many of his rivals within the Communist party Politboro, who also chafed at the failure of his economic policies. He was finally removed from power in 1964, but not before the Soviets launched a program to close the real missile gap.

In some ways the crisis sobered Kennedy and his advisers and increased their determination to control the nuclear arms race. "If we cannot end now all our differences, at least we can help make the world safe for diversity," he proclaimed in June 1963. "For . . . we all inhabit this small planet. We all breathe the same air. We all cherish our children's future. And we are all mortal." Following through, the administration negotiated a nuclear test ban with the Soviets, prohibiting all above-ground nuclear tests. A telephone "hotline" was also installed, providing a direct communications link between the White House and the Kremlin for use in times of crisis. At the same time Kennedy's prestige soared for "standing up" to the Soviets. If cold war toughness paid political dividends, then the Kennedy team would look for new contests, confident of their mastery of the subtle uses of power.

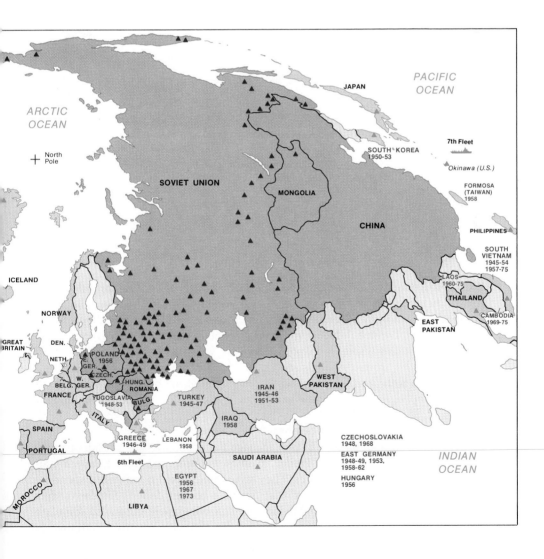

The discovery of Soviet offensive missile sites in Cuba, revealed by low-level American reconnaissance flights, led to the first nuclear showdown of the cold war. For several tense days in October 1962, President Kennedy met with his National Security Council to debate alternative responses.

The (Somewhat) New Frontier at Home

President Kennedy had campaigned on a liberal platform, calling for bold initiatives at home as well as abroad. Once in the White House, however, he found himself hemmed in by a Democratic Congress dominated by conservatives. As his vice president Lyndon Johnson quipped, Kennedy had the congressional minnows, but not the whales: the power brokers who controlled committees and determined the course of legislation. As a result, the president's legislative achievements were modest. The Area Redevelopment Act of 1961 provided financial aid to depressed industrial and rural areas while Congress raised the minimum wage to $1.25. But on key issues, including aid to education and medical health insurance, Kennedy made no headway.

He wavered, too, on how to best manage the economy. The president's economic advisers, led by Walter Heller, Paul Samuelson, and John Kenneth Galbraith, were all disciples of Keynes. They favored increased government spending to reduce unemployment, even if that meant a budget deficit. Similarly, they argued that tax cuts could be used to increase consumer spending and so stimulate the economy. Kennedy toyed with both remedies, but conservatives continued to push for a balanced budget—always Eisenhower's goal, and one even Harry Truman endorsed. So Kennedy moved cautiously, relieved at first to discover that the economy was growing quite nicely without a tax cut. Only in 1963 did he send such a proposal to Congress.

Despite his advisers' liberal bent, Kennedy hoped to work amicably with the leaders of big business. He firmly believed that prosperity for large firms spelled growth for the whole nation. Thus the president asked Congress to ease antitrust restrictions and grant investment credits and tax breaks—all actions that perfectly suited corporate interests. But he did believe that the government needed to limit the power of both large corporations and unions to set prices and wages. The alternative was an inflationary spiral, where wage increases would be followed by price increases followed by even higher wage demands.

To prevent that, the Council of Economic Advisors urged that wage increases be given to workers only if their increased productivity allowed prices to remain stable. In April 1962 the United Steel Workers, like most other major unions, agreed to a new contract within the administration's guidelines. The large steel corporations, however, broke their part of the informal bargain, announcing a 3.5 percent rise in steel prices. Feeling betrayed, Kennedy struck back. He called for investigations into price fixing, mounted antitrust proceedings, and shifted Pentagon purchases to smaller steel companies that had not raised prices. Eventually the big companies gave in, but the larger business community remained suspicious of Kennedy's intentions.

The Reforms of the Warren Court

For all of John Kennedy's talk of new frontiers and reform, he remained unwilling—or unable, given the opposition in Congress—to do much more than propose a liberal agenda. Ironically, it was the Supreme Court, traditionally the least activist branch of government, which—under Chief Justice Earl Warren—broke the reform logjam. Until Warren's retirement in 1969, the Court continued to hand down a series of landmark decisions in broad areas of civil liberties and civil rights.

In 1960 the rights of citizens accused of a crime but not yet convicted were often unclear. Those too poor to afford lawyers could be forced to go to trial without representation. The police and the courts often did not inform those accused of crime of their rights guaranteed under the Constitution. In a series of decisions, the Court ruled that the Fourteenth Amendment provided broad guarantees of due process under the law. *Gideon v. Wainwright* (1963), initiated by a Florida prisoner, made it clear that citizens—however poor they might be—were entitled to legal counsel in all cases involving a possible jail sentence. In *Escobedo v. Illinois* (1964) and *Miranda v. Arizona* (1966) the Court declared that individuals detained for a crime must be informed of the charges against them, of their right to remain silent, and of their right to have an attorney present during questioning. Any statement they made might be used against them. Though these decisions applied to all citizens, they were primarily intended to benefit the poor, who were most likely to be in trouble with the law and least likely to understand their rights. As a result, the decisions greatly angered law enforcement agencies and middle-class groups distressed by what they saw as a breakdown of "law and order."

Especially troubling to conservative religious groups was *Engel v. Vitale* (1962), in which the Court ruled that the separation of church and state had been violated in New York State, where the Board of Regents had written a nonsectarian prayer to be recited in school. Even if dissenting children could be excused, the Court ruled, they faced indirect pressure to recite the prayer. *Abington v. Schempp* (1963) extended the ban on school prayer to cover the reading of the Bible and the Lord's Prayer. Reaction against the Court's ruling was so strong that members of Congress introduced nearly 150 proreligious proposals, including one requesting that states require all applicants for a driver's license to state their belief in a supreme being. None were passed.

In a different vein, the Court in *Griswold v. Connecticut* (1964) overturned a nineteenth-century law banning the sale of contraceptives or providing medical advice about their use. And in another step liberalizing the social climate, the Court demonstrated its distaste for book censorship by greatly narrowing the legal definition of obscenity. A book had to be "utterly without redeeming social value" to permit censorship. The combination of decisions reforming criminal rights, prayer, and morality outraged conservatives of almost all social and political backgrounds. The right-wing John Birch Society dotted the landscape with billboards calling for the impeachment of Chief Justice Earl Warren.

The Court's most far-reaching decision was probably one of its least controversial, though politically most sensitive. The explosive growth of cities and suburbs had created enormous problems of legislative apportionment. Rural elements refused to redraw state legislative or congressional district lines to reflect new demographic patterns. In *Baker v. Carr* (1962) and a series of subsequent cases the Court ruled that the states must apportion seats not by "land or trees or pastures," but as closely as possible by the principle of "one person, one vote."

THE CIVIL RIGHTS CRUSADE

Nothing did more to propel the liberalism of the 1960s—and in the end, to push beyond it—than the campaign for civil rights. By the late 1950s a generation of southern blacks, many having moved from farms to cities, was no longer willing to accept second-class citizenship. But how could they overturn the legal bulwarks of segregation in the South as well as the racism evident in everyday life across the nation? As the decade progressed, it became clear that blacks were opting for not one but many strategies. Some tactics were rooted in the doctrines of integration and Christian nonviolence; some focused on winning gains through the courts. More militant blacks sought power over their own lives through direct action or even by separating from white reformers and white society. And from the heat and despair of the ghettos, some blacks spoke with the violence borne of pent-up frustration and rage.

Riding to Freedom

The movement for black civil rights gained momentum not through national movements but through a host of individual decisions by local groups and citizens. When new Orleans schools were desegregated in 1960, young Ruby's parents had not been urged to make a social statement. But once involved, they refused to back down. In Greensboro, North Carolina, that same year, four black students attending North Carolina Agricultural and Technical College happened to read a pamphlet describing the 1955 bus boycott in Montgomery, Alabama. Though all were members of the NAACP Youth Council, they decided to stage an independent sit-in at a segregated lunch counter. "The waitress looked at me as if I were from outer space," recalled one of the protesters. Word of the action spread and within two weeks, 15 sit-ins had taken place across the South. By the end of the year, 50,000 people had demonstrated, 3000 had gone to jail, and black civil rights organizations were actively working to keep the momentum going.

Prior to the 1960s two organizations, the NAACP and the Urban League, had led the civil rights struggle. These groups continued to take legal action to desegregate public facilities, but leadership within the movement had passed by the early 1960s to direct action groups. Since organizing the Montgomery boycott, Martin Luther King and his Southern Christian Leadership Conference (SCLC) had continued to advocate nonviolent protest: "To resist without bitterness; to be cursed and not reply; to be beaten and not hit back." A second key organization, the Congress of Racial Equality (CORE), was more willing than the SCLC to force confrontations with the segregationist system. Another group, the Student Non-Violent Coordinating Committee (SNCC, pronounced "Snick") grew out of the Greensboro sit-in. SNCC represented the more militant, younger generation of black reformers, who, as time went on, became impatient with the slow pace of integration.

In May 1961 CORE director James Farmer led a group of black and white "freedom riders" on a bus trip from Washington to New Orleans. Moving from city to city, they hoped to call attention to segregated facilities—and attention they received. In South Carolina, thugs beat divinity student John Lewis as he tried to enter an all-white waiting room. Freedom riders were also assaulted by mobs in Anniston, Alabama, where one of the buses was burned, and in Birmingham, Alabama.

Like President Roosevelt before him, Kennedy preferred words to action on civil rights. The national attention to freedom riders made his position on the fence uncomfortable. He needed black and liberal votes to win reelection. Yet he also needed the support of southern Democratic committee chairmen to get legislation through Congress. So he hedged on his promise to introduce major civil rights legislation, as he had promised during the campaign. He would, he told black leaders, use executive orders to eliminate discrimination in the government civil service and in businesses filling government contracts. He appointed several blacks to high administrative positions and five, including Thurgood Marshall, to the federal courts. The Justice Department, run by the president's brother Robert Kennedy, beefed up its civil rights enforcement procedures.

When the freedom riders launched their campaign, Kennedy hoped to avoid federal intervention by convincing Alabama officials to protect the demonstrators, so that federal forces would not have to be sent. His hopes were dashed when John Doar, a Justice Department official, relayed what was happening directly to Robert Kennedy from a phone booth outside the bus terminal in Montgomery. "Now the passengers are coming off," Doar reported, as the attorney general listened in shocked silence. "They're standing on a corner of the platform. Oh, there are fists, punching. A bunch of men led by a guy with a bleeding face are beating them. There are no cops. It's terrible. It's terrible. There's not a cop in sight. People are yelling, 'Get 'em, get 'em.' It's awful." Appalled, Robert Kennedy ordered in 400 federal marshals, who barely managed to hold off the mob. Martin Luther King,

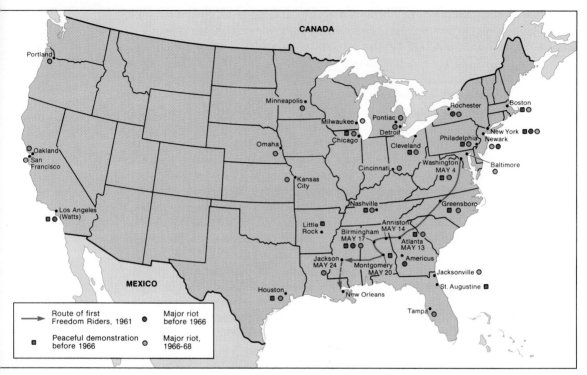

CIVIL RIGHTS: PATTERNS OF PROTEST AND UNREST
The first phase of the civil rights movement was confined largely to the South, where the
Freedom Ride of 1961 dramatized the issue of segregation. Urban unrest beginning in the
summer of 1964 turned the issue of race and politics into a national concern. Severe rioting
followed the murder of Martin Luther King, Jr., in 1968, after which the worst violence
subsided.

who was addressing a church meeting, phoned the attorney general to say that the
situation was becoming desperate. As Kennedy later recalled, "I said that we were
doing the best that we could and that he'd be as dead as Kelsey's nuts if it hadn't
been for the marshals and the efforts that we made."

Liberalism at High Tide

While CORE and the SCLC pulled back temporarily after the confrontation in
Montgomery, the more militant SNCC continued the bus rides from Montgomery
on to Jackson, Mississippi. By summer Robert Kennedy had persuaded SNCC to
shift its efforts from confrontation to voter registration, in hopes that the issue of
voting would prove less controversial. Voting booths, Kennedy noted, were not
like schools, where people would protest, "We don't want our little blond daughter going to school with a Negro." But as SNCC workers arrived in southern towns
the following fall and spring, they encountered legal harassment, jailings, beatings, bombings, and murders. Terrorized workers who called on the administration for protection found it woefully lacking. FBI agents often stood by taking
notes while SNCC workers were assaulted. "Every time I saw FBI men in Albany
[Georgia], they were with the local police force," Dr. King complained. At the
same time, SNCC workers made it clear they intended to stay. Fanning out across

the countryside, they spoke with farmers and poor blacks who had never before been involved in politics.

Confrontation increased, too, when a federal court ordered, over the protests of Governor Ross Barnett, the segregated University of Mississippi to admit James Meredith, a black applicant. In September 1962 Kennedy faced the same crisis that had confronted Eisenhower at Little Rock in 1957. After Governor Barnett personally blocked Meredith's registration, several hundred federal marshals quietly escorted Meredith into a university dormitory. The president announced on national television that the university had been integrated and asked students to follow the law of the land. Instead, a mob moved on campus, shooting out street lights, commandeering a bulldozer, and throwing rocks and bottles. To save the marshals, Kennedy finally sent in federal troops, but not before 2 people were killed and 375 wounded.

In Mississippi, President Kennedy had begun to lose control of the civil rights issue. Black militants urged bolder action than the president was willing to take. The House of Representatives, influenced by television coverage of the violence, introduced a number of civil rights measures. And Martin Luther King led a group to Birmingham, Alabama, to force a showdown against segregation. From a prison cell there, he produced one of the most eloquent documents of the civil rights movement, his "Letter from Birmingham Jail." Addressed to a local minister who had counseled an end to confrontation, King defended the use of civil disobedience. The choice, he warned, was not between obeying the law and nonviolently breaking it to bring about change; it was between his way and streets "flowing with blood," as restive black masses turned toward more militant ideologies.

By May King was again free and leading demonstrations. With arrests depleting his ranks, he organized thousands of children to march. Television cameras were on hand as Birmingham police chief "Bull" Connor, a man with a short fuse, unleashed attack dogs, club-wielding police, and fire hoses powerful enough to

---

Birmingham, Alabama, firefighters used high-pressure hoses to disperse civil rights demonstrators. The force of the hoses was great enough to tear bark off trees. Pictures like this one aroused widespread sympathy for the civil rights movement.

peel the bark off trees. The scenes enlisted as never before the support of northern liberals for the civil rights cause. But there was a grimmer push for reform in Birmingham. When segregationist bombs went off in black neighborhoods, black mobs retaliated with their own riot, burning a number of shops and businesses owned by whites. In the 10 weeks following the Birmingham demonstration there were over 750 riots in 186 cities and towns, both North and South. King's warning of streets "flowing with blood" seemed no longer far-fetched, and his own nonviolent protest appeared moderate by comparison.

Kennedy sensed that the time had come to take up the civil rights issue. In phrases which, like King's, drew heavily on Christian and republican rhetoric, he asked the nation, "If [an American with dark skin] cannot enjoy the full and free life all of us want, then who among us would be content to have the color of his skin changed and stand in his place? Who among us would then be content with counsels of patience and delay?" The president also threw his weight behind a strong civil rights bill to end segregation and protect black voters. When King announced a massive march on Washington for August 1963, Kennedy at first tried to persuade him that it would undermine support for his bill. "I have never engaged in any direct action movement which did not seem ill-timed," King replied. Faced with the inevitable, Kennedy made the march his own. He convinced the organizers to use the event to publicize and support the administration's bill, much to the disgust of militant CORE and SNCC factions.

On August 28 some 250,000 people gathered at the Lincoln Memorial to demonstrate their support for civil rights and racial harmony. Appropriately, the day belonged to King. In the powerful tones of a southern preacher, he reminded the crowd that the Declaration of Independence was a promise that applied to all people, black and white. "I have a dream," he told them, that one day "all of God's children, black men and white men, Jews and Gentiles, Protestants and Catholics, will be able to join hands and sing in the words of the old Negro spiritual, 'Free at last! Free at last! Thank God Almighty, we are free at last!'" Congress began deliberation of the civil rights bill, which was reported out of the Judiciary Committee on October 23.

The Fire Next Time

Support for civil rights paid Kennedy political dividends. Liberals embraced him as a hero. Though substantial numbers of southern whites and northern ethnics deserted him, appreciative blacks balanced those losses. All the same, the president decided he would make a trip to Texas in an effort to recoup some southern support for his reelection. On November 22, 1963, as his motorcade was making its way along the streets of Dallas, a sniper's rifle fired several times, fatally wounding him. His assassin, Lee Harvey Oswald, was caught hours later. He appeared to be an unstable man who, although having spent several years in the Soviet Union, acted independently and for his own reasons. But Oswald's story was never fully told, because only two days later—in full view of television cameras—he was gunned down by Jack Ruby, a disgruntled nightclub operator. Although an investigative commission headed by Chief Justice Warren concluded that the assassin acted alone, its hasty job prompted critics to suggest that Oswald was part of a larger conspiracy of undetermined origin.

The assassination struck at the heart of the political system. In the face of such violence, could the programs of political liberalism, gradual reform, or nonviolence hold the nation together? A few blacks believed that the Kennedy assassination was a case of a debt being repaid to a system that had tolerated its own racial violence—the "chickens coming home to roost," as black separatist Malcolm X put it. Many younger black leaders were aware that civil rights received the greatest national coverage when white, not black demonstrators were killed. They increasingly questioned how far liberal reform would take them. They wondered too how Kennedy's successor, Lyndon Johnson, a consummate southern politician, would approach the civil rights programs.

The new president, however, saw the need for action. Just as the Catholic issue had tested Kennedy's ability to lead, Johnson knew that without strong leadership on civil rights, "I'd be dead before I could ever begin." On November 23, his first day in office, he promised one civil rights leader after another that he would pass Kennedy's bill. By the following summer a southern filibuster in the Senate had been outmaneuvered and the Civil Rights Act of 1964 was law.

The bill marked one of the great moments in the history of American reform. Embodying all the provisions of the Kennedy bill, it barred discrimination in public accommodations such as lunch counters, bus stations, and hotels; it authorized the attorney general to bring suit to desegregate schools, museums, and other public facilities; it outlawed discrimination in employment by race, color, religion, sex, or national origin; and it gave additional protection to voting rights. Within months, the Supreme Court upheld the controversial public accommodations section, in what Justice Arthur Goldberg described as a "vindication of human dignity."

The Civil Rights Act did not deter some southern registrars from using literacy tests and other technicalities to prevent blacks from voting. Again in 1965 Martin Luther King led a series of demonstrations, culminating in a 54-mile walk

Martin Luther King (left) and his wife Coretta lead the march from Selma to Montgomery in March 1964. Already, however, activists from SNCC and CORE were insisting that tactics more radical than King's were needed.

from Selma to Montgomery, Alabama. President Johnson, who like Kennedy was not eager to offend southern voters, squirmed before federalizing the National Guard to protect the marchers. He then sent Congress even stronger legislation, which was passed in August 1965. The Voting Rights Act suspended literacy tests and other such devices. It also authorized federal officials to supervise elections in districts that had used the tests and in which less than half the population voted in 1964. Never shy about glorifying his own achievements, Johnson with some justice called the act "one of the most monumental laws in the entire history of American freedom." Within a five-year period black registration in the South jumped from 35 to 65 percent. In Mississippi, the scene of so much violence, the number went from 7 to 67 percent.

Black Power at the Ballot Box and on the Street

The civil rights laws, as comprehensive as they were, did not strike at what northern black leaders saw as the most invidious forms of discrimination. These were the de facto systems of segregation not codified in law, but practiced through unwritten custom and long force of habit. In large areas of America, de facto segregation locked blacks out of suburbs, kept them out of decent schools, barred them from exclusive clubs, and denied them all but the most menial jobs. Nor did the Voting Rights Act deal with the sources of urban black poverty, where the median income for blacks was approximately half of what whites earned and where black unemployment was double that of whites and five times as high for black men between the ages of 18 and 25.

In such an atmosphere, militants sharply questioned the liberal goal of integration. Since the 1940s the Black Muslim religious sect, dedicated to complete separation from white society, had attracted as many as 100,000 members, mostly young men. During the early 1960s the sect drew even wider attention through the energetic efforts of Malcolm X, a charismatic leader who spoke the language of the downtrodden from his own experience as a former hustler, gambler, and prison inmate. Malcolm broke with the Black Muslims and was moving toward a more moderate position in 1965, though one that still emphasized black community action, when he was gunned down by rivals. But by 1965–1966, even CORE and SNCC had begun to give up working with white liberals for nonviolent change. They began carrying guns to defend themselves and argued that for blacks to liberate themselves fully, they could not merely accept rights that were "given" to them by whites. They had to claim their rights. In 1966 Stokely Carmichael of SNCC gave the militants a slogan—"Black Power"—and the defiant symbol of a gloved fist raised in the air.

In its moderate form, the black power movement encouraged blacks to recover their cultural roots, their African heritage, and a new sense of identity. African clothes and natural hair styles became popular, while on college campuses black students pressed universities to hire black faculty, institute black studies programs, and provide segregated social and residential space. It was one of the great ironies of the 1960s that just as the civil rights movement broke down the legal barriers to integration, the black nationalist movement pressed for new forms of segregation, though now based on black pride rather than racial inferiority.

Black militants, on the other hand, perceived black power as an element of a broader Marxist ideology that treated violence as a useful revolutionary tool. The most militant among militants was the Black Panther party of Oakland, California. The Panthers, led by Huey P. Newton and Eldridge Cleaver, shocked white sensibilities by calling for the black community to arm themselves. Since California law forbade carrying concealed weapons, Newton and his followers openly brandished their weapons as they patrolled the streets to protect blacks from police harassment. In February 1967 Newton found the showdown he had been looking for, waving his loaded shotgun at one police officer and calling, "O.K., you big fat racist pig, draw your gun!" The police retreated, making Newton a hero in the ghetto.

When Newton was jailed after another gun battle, in which he was shot in the stomach, Eldridge Cleaver assumed leadership of the party and later attracted attention with his searing autobiography, *Soul on Ice*. But even at the height of their power, the Panthers never counted more than 2000 members nationwide. In the end, revolutionary black nationalism faded not because of white repression, but because radicals failed to define a political program that rallied large numbers from the black masses. Most remained committed to the goals defined by the civil rights movement, preferring nonviolence to armed confrontation, integration to segregation.

Beyond any consciously shaped ideology, however, a reservoir of frustration and despair existed in the ghettos. Riots broke out in Harlem and Rochester, New York, in 1964, the Watts area of Los Angeles in 1965, Chicago in 1966, and Newark and Detroit in 1967. Often disturbances were sparked by a seemingly minor incident like an arrest or an argument on the streets. A mob would gather and police cars and white-owned stores would be firebombed or looted. As police and the National Guard were ordered in, the violence escalated. In the riot at Watts, over $200 million in property lay in ruins and 34 people were dead, all of them black. It took nearly 5000 troops to end the bloodiest rioting in Detroit, where 40 died, 2000 were injured, and 5000 were left homeless.

To most whites the violence was unfathomable and inexcusable. Lyndon Johnson echoed the thoughts of many when he argued that "neither old wrongs nor new fears can justify arson and murder." Martin Luther King, still pursuing the tactics of nonviolence, was saddened by the destruction but discovered first-hand some of the anger behind it. Touring Watts only days after the riots, he was approached by a band of young blacks. "We won," they told him proudly. "How can you say you won," King countered, "when thirty-four Negroes are dead, your

A National Guardsman watches as flames consume large areas of the Watts section of Los Angeles during the 1965 riot. Often, a seemingly trivial event set off such scenes of violence, suggesting the depth of explosive rage harbored within the ghettos.

community is destroyed, and whites are using the riot as an excuse for inaction?" The youngsters were unmoved. "We won because we made them pay attention to us."

For Johnson, the explosion of ghetto violence and black militance seemed to mock his efforts to achieve national unity. The Civil Rights and Voting Rights acts were essential parts of the "Great Society" he hoped to build. In that effort he had achieved a legislative record virtually unequaled by any president in the nation's history. What Kennedy had promised, Johnson delivered. But the anger exploding in the nation's cities exposed serious flaws in the theory and practice of liberal reform.

LYNDON JOHNSON AND THE GREAT SOCIETY

Like the state he hailed from, Lyndon Baines Johnson was in all things bigger than life. His gifts were greater, his flaws more glaring. Insecurity was his Achilles heel and the engine that drove him. If Kennedy had been good as president, Johnson would be "the greatest of them all, the whole bunch of them." If FDR won in a landslide in 1936, Johnson would produce an even larger margin in 1964. And to anyone who displeased him, he could be ruthlessly cruel. He was vulgar, too—sometimes astonishingly so. He could summon a foreign dignitary to an audience as he sat, as if enthroned, on his toilet. His scatological language and preoccupation with barnyard sex amused few and offended many. After a 1965 operation, he shocked a national audience by lifting his shirt to expose a jagged scar and corpulent belly. That was not the "plain folks" Americans appreciated. The president was sometimes driven to ask why so few people genuinely liked him; once a courageous diplomat actually answered: "Because, Mr. President, you are not a very likeable man."

The irrepressible Lyndon Johnson had difficulty playing second fiddle to anyone, even when he was vice president. But his shrewd political instincts and folksy charm, which he knew how to deploy to good effect, often allowed him to outmaneuver his opponents.

Johnson was born in Stonewall, Texas, in the hill country outside Austin, where the dry climate and rough terrain only grudgingly yielded up a living. Schooled in manners by his overbearing mother and in politics by his father and his cronies, Johnson arrived in Washington in 1932 as an ardent New Dealer who loved the political game. When he became majority leader of the Senate in 1954, he cultivated an image as a moderate conservative who knew what strings to pull or levers to jog to get the job done. Johnson knew what made his colleagues run. On an important bill, he latched onto the undecided votes until they succumbed to the famous "Johnson treatment," a combination of arguments, threats, emotional or patriotic appeals, and enticing rewards.

Despite his overbearing nature and insecurity, Johnson possessed certain bedrock strengths. Though he could not help trying to control every person and situation, he was remarkably adept at hammering out compromises among competing interest groups. To those who served him well he could be loyal and generous. As president, he cared sincerely about society's underdogs. His support for civil rights, aid to the poor, education, and the welfare of the elderly came from genuine conviction. He made the betterment of such people the goal of his administration.

The Origins of the Great Society

In the first months after the assassination of John Kennedy, Johnson acted as the conservator of the Kennedy legacy. "Let us continue," he told a grief-stricken nation. Kennedy's assistants would stay on as his assistants; Kennedy's foreign policy would be his foreign policy; Kennedy's domestic agenda would shape his legislative program. Liberals who had dismissed Johnson as an unprincipled power broker begrudgingly came to respect the energy he showed in steering reform through Congress. The Civil Rights Act and tax cut legislation were only two of the most conspicuous pieces of Kennedy business Johnson quickly finished.

Kennedy had come to recognize that prosperity alone would not ease the plight of America's poor. In 1962 Michael Harrington's book *The Other America* brought widespread attention to the mass poverty that persisted in the face of general affluence. Attention focused particularly on the hills of Appalachia, stretching from western Pennsylvania south to Alabama, where in some counties a quarter of the population was trying to survive on a diet of flour and dried-milk paste supplied by federal surplus food programs. Under Kennedy Congress had passed a new food stamp program as well as laws designed to revive the economies of poor areas, replacing urban slums with newer housing and retraining the unemployed. Robert Kennedy also headed a presidential committee to fight juvenile delinquency in urban slums by involving the poor in "community action" programs. Direct participation, they hoped, would help overcome "a sense of resignation and fatalism" that sociologist Oscar Lewis had found while studying the Puerto Rican community of New York City.

It fell to Lyndon Johnson to shape a legislative package that could fight Kennedy's "war on poverty." By August 1964 he had driven through Congress the most sweeping social welfare bill since the New Deal. The Economic Opportunity Act addressed almost every major cause of poverty. It included training programs such as the Job Corps, which brought poor and unemployed recruits to rural or urban camps to receive six-month courses in new job skills. It granted loans to rural families and urban small businesses as well as aid to migrant workers, and it launched a domestic version of the Peace Corps, known as VISTA (Volunteers in Service to America). The price tag for these programs was high. Johnson committed almost $1 billion to Sargent Shriver, a Kennedy brother-in-law, who directed the new Office of Economic Opportunity (OEO). When Michael Harrington complained that even $1 billion could barely scratch the surface, Shriver tartly replied, "Maybe you've spent a billion dollars before, but this is my first time around."

Unfortunately, in his eagerness to move quickly Johnson sponsored a program that presented problems over the long haul. Shriver had to share jurisdiction over OEO programs with the departments of Labor and Health, Education and Welfare. Those bureaucracies had their own well-entrenched constituencies who were reluctant to share power with the politically unorganized poor. To take only one example, the Job Corps was forced to locate many of its retraining centers in remote rural conservation camps, due to the demands of the conservation lobby. Hapless recruits frequently found themselves bused a thousand miles from home. And when OEO workers tried to organize "community action" neighborhood groups, they often found themselves confronting the old-style bosses of city hall, setting up voter registration drives to oust corrupt officials or sponsoring rent strikes to improve conditions in public housing. In Syracuse, New York, the director of city housing reacted typically: "We are experiencing a class struggle in the traditional Karl Marx style in Syracuse, and I do not like it." In such battles for power and bureaucratic turf, federal poverty programs suffered.

The Election of 1964

In 1964, however, these long-term flaws were not yet evident. Johnson's political stock remained high. To an audience at the University of Michigan in May, he announced his ambition to forge a "Great Society," in which poverty and racial injustice no longer existed. The chance to fulfill his dreams seemed open to him, for the Republicans nominated Senator Barry Goldwater of Arizona as their presidential candidate. Few men in politics have been so genuinely well liked as Goldwater. Ruggedly handsome, he was a true son of the West who flew military jets in his spare time and spoke his mind with refreshing candor. But Goldwater's politics were so libertarian, he wished to rein in the federal government much more severely than most Americans believed necessary. Government should not dispense welfare, subsidize farmers, tax incomes on a progressive basis, or aid public education, he argued. At the same time, Goldwater's profound anticommunism led him into an unreserved support for a large defense establishment.

Such extreme views worried even moderate Republicans, and Johnson's election would have seemed a foregone conclusion except for Governor George Wallace of Alabama. Running in several Democratic primaries, Wallace's segregationist campaign won nearly a third or more of the votes in Wisconsin, Indiana, and Maryland—hardly the Deep South. In the end, however, he was persuaded to drop out of the race. In the one-sided contest that followed, Johnson portrayed himself as a responsible moderate, choosing Minnesota's liberal senator Hubert Humphrey to balance the ticket. Goldwater did not help himself by suggesting that the popular Social Security system be made voluntary or that military commanders be given the power to launch tactical nuclear weapons without presidential authority.

The election produced the landslide Johnson craved. Carrying every state except Arizona and four in the Deep South, he received 61 percent of the vote. Democrats gained better than two-to-one majorities in the Senate and House. All the same, the election was probably more a repudiation of Goldwater than a mandate for Johnson. The president was politically shrewd enough to realize that he had to move rapidly to exploit the momentum of his 1964 majority.

The Great Society

In January 1965 Johnson announced a vast legislative program to build the Great Society. In essence he proposed to extend state welfare programs on a scale beyond even Franklin Roosevelt's New Deal. For the poor it meant a doubling of the war on poverty; for the sick and disabled, a program of "Medicare"; for blacks, tougher civil rights enforcement; and for ethnic groups, a reform of restrictive immigration laws. The young would gain from aid to education, and for future generations, environmental legislation would preserve open space and clean up polluted air and water. By the end of 1965 fifty bills had been passed, many of them major pieces of legislation, with more on the agenda for the following year.

Education was a cornerstone of the Johnson program. To compensate the poor for their disadvantaged homes, Johnson as a former teacher wanted a strong educational system. Under the Elementary and Secondary School Act, students in low-income school districts were to receive educational equipment, money for books, and enrichment programs like "Project Headstart" for nursery-age children. But for all its benefits, the bill did not provide money for certain basics, such as badly needed new classrooms or increased teachers' salaries. And although eager schools scrambled to create programs that would tap federal money, they sometimes used the act to fund programs for middle-class as much as poor students. Administrative overhead often cost more than the actual programs. In the end, the Elementary and Secondary School Act gave as many benefits to middle-class educational professionals as to lower income students.

President Johnson also pushed through the Medicare Act, which provided the elderly with mandatory health insurance to cover their hospital costs. Since the days of Harry Truman, Congress had debated whether to provide some kind of health insurance for all Americans. Medicare targeted the elderly, because studies had shown that older people used hospitals three times more than other Ameri-

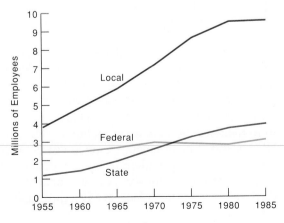

GROWTH OF GOVERNMENT, 1955–1985
Government has been a major growth industry since World War II. But even during the Great Society, government employment was most significant at the state and local levels. It grew more at the federal level during Ronald Reagan's presidency.

Source: U.S. Bureau of the Census.

cans and generally had incomes only half as large. Premiums would be paid into
the social security system and financed by it. Citizens could also make voluntary
payments that would cover doctors' and surgical fees. Since Medicare made no
provision for the poor who were not elderly, Congress also passed a program
called Medicaid. Participating states would receive matching grants from the federal government to pay the medical expenses of those on welfare or too poor to
afford medical care.

In one sense, Medicare and Medicaid worked. The poor and elderly did
receive significantly more help when facing catastrophic illnesses. But as increased numbers of patients used hospital services, Medicare budgets rose. In
addition, nothing in the act restricted hospitals or doctors from raising their fees.
The cost of the programs soared by over 500 percent in the first 10 years. In the
year after Congress approved Medicare, hospitals raised their fees by 14 percent,
double the increase of the year before. Doctors began to charge for care they once
gave free, raising their fees about 7 percent every year. Those increases wiped out
the benefits many of the elderly and poor received, so that actual medical expenses remained constant. What was saved in hospital bills went for more costly
drugs, dental work, and doctors' fees not covered under Medicare or Medicaid.

Ten days after signing the Medicare bill, Johnson signed the Omnibus Housing Act, designed to subsidize rents for poor families unable to find adequate
public housing. Four days later came the Voting Rights Act. Within two weeks
Congress approved creation of a new cabinet-level Department of Housing and
Urban Development (HUD) to be headed by Robert Weaver, a former president
of the NAACP. And in the tradition of the New Deal, which had patronized the
arts under the WPA, Johnson created the National Foundation of the Arts and
Humanities. Colleges and their students received support for scholarships and
loans, research equipment, and libraries. And on another front, Great Society
programs reformed American immigration policy. Although the United States still
admitted just 170,000 people each year, the Immigration Act of 1965 abolished the
national origins system, which favored northern Europeans over those from other
areas of Europe. Racial provisions restricting Asian immigration were eliminated,
although limits were still placed on immigration from other parts of the Western
Hemisphere.

Nor did Johnson, in his efforts to outdo the New Deal, slight the environment. By the mid-1960s many Americans had become increasingly concerned
about the acrid smog from factories and automobiles; lakes and rivers polluted by
detergents, pesticides, and industrial wastes; and the disappearance of wildlife. In
1964 Congress had already passed the National Wilderness Preservation System
Act to set aside 9.1 million acres of wilderness as "forever wild." Lady Bird Johnson, the president's wife, led a campaign to eliminate the garish billboards and
junkyards that marred the views along so many of the nation's roads. And Congress established pollution standards for interstate waterways and a year later
provided funds for sewage treatment and water purification. Similar standards
were tightened to diminish air pollution. The programs for the environment, like
other Great Society measures, often ran afoul of entrenched interests. Mining,
cattle-grazing, and lumbering businesses lobbied to continue using portions of
public wilderness lands for their own benefit. On the other hand, the new standards did result in a gradual, steady improvement in water and air quality in many
areas.

In 1966 Johnson pushed through bills to raise the minimum wage, improve
auto safety, aid mass transit, and develop "model cities." But by then he had

encountered mounting opposition from legislators worried that they were voting too much power and money to the executive branch. "Doesn't matter what kind of majority you come in with," Johnson had predicted early on. "You've got just one year when they treat you right, and before they start worrying about themselves." Yet as late as 1968 he was able to get major legislation through Congress to ban discrimination in housing (Fair Housing Act), to build public housing, to protect consumers from unfair credit practices (Truth-in-Lending Act), and to protect scenic rivers and expand the national park system.

The unparalleled successes of the Great Society carried a higher price tag than anyone had predicted, and the results were not all unmitigated successes. Statistics suggested that general prosperity, accelerated by the tax cut bill, did more to fight poverty than all the OEO programs. And the inevitable scandals began to surface: Job Corps retrainees burglarizing homes in their off-hours, school equipment purchased that no one knew how to use, and so on. Conservatives and radicals alike objected that the liberal welfare state was intruding into too many areas of people's lives. Ethnic groups like Italian- and Polish-Americans objected to what they considered favoritism accorded blacks and Hispanics under most poverty programs. And the mayors of large cities continued to oppose all community action programs that they did not control themselves.

Most of all, Johnson's consensus collapsed amid the growing controversy over the Vietnam War. By 1966 the war had expanded sharply, and it was no longer clear that the United States could afford to pay for troops and bombs as well as massive social programs. Inflation was one clear result of the president's determination to have both "guns and butter" without higher taxes. Thus the Great Society programs proved to be the high-water mark for the liberal approach to government begun under Franklin Roosevelt. By the mid-1960s civil rights organizations and the poor were not the only groups fighting to reach beyond liberal solutions; dissatisfied members of the middle class—and especially the young—had joined them.

THE COUNTERCULTURE

In the civil rights movement, a young generation of black leaders pushed for more extreme measures. College students had started the sit-in movement at Greensboro, and SNCC continued the freedom rides when CORE felt the situation had become too explosive. As the voting rights drive made headlines in the Deep South, white college students became involved too, getting their first taste of political action. In 1964 some 800 students from Berkeley, Oberlin, and other colleges met to receive training in preparation for the voter registration campaign in the South. Middle-class students who had grown up in peaceful white suburbs found themselves being trained by protest-hardened SNCC coordinators: when beaten by police, assume the fetal position—hands protecting the neck, elbows covering the temples to minimize injuries from nightsticks. It was a sober awakening, and students came back shocked that such things could happen in America.

Activists on the New Left

More than a few students returned home disillusioned with the slow pace of reform, seeing a need to overturn the "establishment"—regardless of whether it

Daily Lives

CLOTHING AND FASHION

The Politics of Dress

Three-piece suits, fur coats, berets, Grateful Dead T-shirts—clothing has always made a statement about the social class and values of the wearer. In the 1950s that statement was conformity. The khaki slacks and brush-cut hair popular with middle-class boys hinted at military regimentation. Rock-and-rollers, lower class kids, and farm boys often wore dungarees and T-shirts, perhaps with a cigarette pack tucked in the rolled-up sleeve. Beatniks advertised their nonconformity by adopting an exotic look: long hair, goatees, turtlenecks, and sandals.

During the 1960s clothing signaled the coming of a political upheavel as nonconformity became the norm. The pattern was closely tied to music, as middle-class teenagers rejected sentimental pop tunes for serious "folk" music or the raucous rhythms of rock and roll. The revolution began in earnest with the coming of the Beatles, four British rockers from working-class Liverpool. John, Paul, George, and Ringo inspired fan hysteria beyond anything seen before. Their "mod"-style British clothes and longish, page-boy hair caused as much commotion as their music. As young Americans embraced the Beatles and all things British, London supplanted Paris and New York as a fashion center.

Suddenly it was the young and working class, not the rich, who set trends in style. At first, women's hemlines rose well above the knees, as the "miniskirt" became the rage, but its popularity was eventually rivaled by the floor-length "maxi." Designer Rudi Gernreich, mostly with his tongue firmly in cheek, introduced the "topless" look with a swimsuit

In men's clothing, flowered prints, bold colors, and zany combinations of style replaced traditionally conservative fashions.

Daily Lives

bottom hung by a thin cord around the neck. Soon anarchy reigned in the world of fashion. Men especially broke with past tradition. Sideburns lengthened and moustaches and beards flourished as they had not since the nineteenth century. Men began to wear jewelry, furs, perfume, and shoulder-length hair. Subdued tweeds and narrow lapels gave way to bell-bottoms, broad floral ties, and wide-collared, sometimes psychedelic shirts.

All these fashions represented a desire to break social constraints in favor of greater sensuality and freedom of expression. Nowhere was that more evident than in the theatrical costuming of the counter-culture. Early in the decade, it was only beatniks and Hell's Angels-style motorcycle gangs who sported long hair and distinctive clothes. Then in the mid-1960s, middle-class students began to let their hair grow and replaced their khakis and pleated skirts with jeans and Army–Navy store military surplus. The original impulse was less rebellion than a distinct youthful identity that blurred social class lines, just as rock and roll did.

"Hippies" added a more colorful twist. They rejected commercial fashion, synthetic fabrics, and cosmetics in favor of a natural look. To express a return to nature, they adopted the Hispanic shawl and serape, the Indian fringed buckskin, beads, and moccasins, and the bright coloring of Oriental and Caribbean cotton fabrics. Much of their clothing and accessories were handcrafted and sold largely through street vendors, medieval-style craft fairs, and small shops. Often these same shops, located in college towns and artsy urban neighborhoods, did a lively business selling water pipes, "bongs," rolling papers, roach clips, strobe lights, posters, Indian print bedspreads, and

other paraphernalia of the drug culture. Military surplus and the varieties of neo-Indian garb became standard wear at folk and rock music festivals and "be-ins," as well as at political demonstrations.

Fashion had become a function of politics and rebellion. Traditional Americans saw beads, long hair, sandals, drugs, radical politics, and rock and roll as elements of a revolution. To them, hippies and radicals were equally threatening. They struck back by trying to censor and even outlaw the trappings of the counter-culture. Schools expelled boys when their hair was too long and girls when their skirts were too short. It became indecent to desecrate the flag by sewing patches of red, white, and blue on torn blue jeans. Short-haired blue-collar workers harassed long-haired hippies and antiwar protestors. The personal fashions of the youth rebellion came to symbolize a "generation gap" between the young and their elders.

Yet by the early 1970s, even some revolutionaries were having second thoughts. Feminists rejected the more extreme styles as an example of the male-dominated fashion world that treated women as sex objects. Hippie garb, which was impractical in the office, was replaced by knee-length skirts or pants suits. And as the once-shocking innovations became commonplace, even middle-aged men and women donned boots, let their hair grow a bit fuller, and slipped into modified bell-bottoms. Commercial success, not legal repression, had signaled an end to the revolution in fashion. Before long, three-piece suits, khakis, and short hair were back, although the democratic and eclectic spirit of the 1960s persisted. The new informality provided Americans of both sexes with a wider range of choice in fashions.

was liberal or conservative. Tom Hayden, from a working-class family in a suburb of Detroit, went to college at the University of Michigan, then traveled to Berkeley, and soon joined civil rights workers in Mississippi. "At first, you thought, well, the southern system is some kind of historical vestige," he recalled. "Instead, we found out that the structure of power was very tied into the structure of power in the whole U.S. You'd find that Harvard was investing in Mississippi Power and Light, which was a company that economically dominated Mississippi. You'd find that the southern wing of the Democratic Party held all the seniority positions in Congress."

Hayden, along with Al Haber, another student at the University of Michigan, was a driving force in forming the radical Students for a Democratic Society (SDS). Members of SDS had given up on change through the electoral system. They had little sympathy with an "old left" generation of radicals who grew up in the 1930s and were still debating the merits of Marxism. Action was the route that needed to be taken, Hayden argued: through sit-ins, protest marches, and direct confrontation. At a meeting in Port Huron, Michigan, in 1962 the group condemned the modern bureaucratic society exemplified by the "organization man" of the 1950s. The Port Huron Statement called for "participatory democracy," where large organizations run by bureaucrats would be broken down, decentralized, and reformed into face-to-face communities where individual participation mattered.

The bold theories of the Port Huron Statement did not exactly revolutionize America; only 60,000 copies of it were ever sold. The entire nation, however, heard in 1964 about Mario Savio and the Free Speech Movement at Berkeley. To most liberals, Berkeley was the gem of the California state university system. Like so many other universities, it had educated a generation of GIs following World War II. And when the Russians launched *Sputnik*, it had led American universities in setting higher standards. But to people like Tom Hayden and the SDS, Berkeley was a bureaucratic monster, enrolling more than 30,000 students. Like other large universities, it had impersonal lecture halls filled with classes taught by remote professors. Seminars seemed most often to be led by inexperienced graduate students. In the fall of 1964, Berkeley informed students that the one small area where political organizations had been allowed to advertise their causes was now off limits. When university police tried to remove a recruiter for CORE, thousands of angry students surrounded the police car for 32 hours.

Mario Savio, a graduate student in philosophy, soon became the leader of the Free Speech Movement. "In our free-speech fight, we have come up against what may emerge as the greatest problem of our nation—depersonalized, unresponsive bureaucracy," Savio proclaimed. When the university's president, Clark Kerr, threatened to expel him, 6000 students took control of the administration building, stopped classes with a strike, and convinced many faculty members to join them. Kerr backed down, placing no limits to free speech on campus except those that applied to society at large. But the lines between students and administrators had been drawn. Berkeley continued to be a hotbed of political demonstrations throughout the 1960s. And the rebellious spirit spread to other major universities like Michigan, Yale, and Columbia, and then to campuses across the nation.

The Rise of the Counterculture

Political action was only one way the younger generation responded to an impersonal, bureaucratic society. Disaffected rebels also condemned American society as being too preoccupied with abundance and economic materialism. More alienated students began to grope toward spiritual, nonmaterial goals. "Turn on to the scene, tune in to what is happening, and drop out of high school, college, grad school, junior executive," advised Timothy Leary, a Harvard psychology professor who dropped out himself. Those who heeded Leary's message embraced poverty as a superior way of life that afforded time to experiment with music, sex, and drugs. Observers labeled the new movement a "counterculture."

The counterculture of the 1960s had much in common with earlier religious revival and utopian movements. It admired the quirky individualism of Henry David Thoreau and, like Thoreau, it turned to Oriental philosophy such as Zen Buddhism. Like Brook Farm and other nineteenth-century utopian communities, the new "hippie" communes sought perfection along the fringes of society. Communards built geodesic domes based on the designs of architect Buckminster Fuller; they "learned how to scrounge materials, tear down abandoned buildings, use the unusable," as one member of the "Drop City" commune put it. Sexual freedom became a means to liberate them from the repressive inhibitions that distorted the lives of their "uptight" parents. Drugs appeared to open the inner mind to a higher state of consciousness. No longer would people be bound by conventional relationships and the goals of a liberal, bourgeois society.

The early threads of the sixties counterculture led back to the fifties and the subculture of the beat generation. The "beats" viewed themselves as being driven to the margins of society, like the black jazz musicians and underworld "hipsters" they so admired. "I saw the best minds of my generation destroyed by madness, starving hysterical naked," wrote Allen Ginsberg in his 1955 poem *Howl*. They had become "angelheaded hipsters . . . who in poverty and tatters and hollow-eyed and high sat up smoking in the supernatural darkness of cold-water flats floating across the tops of cities contemplating jazz." Jack Kerouac tapped the frenzied energy that lay beneath the beatniks' cool facade in *On the Road* (1957), a novel based on his travels across the country with his friend Neal Cassady. Kerouac finished the novel in one frenetic three-week binge, feeding a 120-foot roll of teletype paper through his typewriter and spilling out tales of pot, jazz, crazy sex, and all-night raps undertaken in a search for "IT"—the ultimate transcendental moment when mind and experience mesh. Indeed, Neal Cassady ended up driving the bus for a new generation of "hippies" as they sped off in 1964 on another wild chase across America. The antics of novelist Ken Kesey's "Merry Pranksters" were recorded in Tom Wolfe's *Electric Kool-Aid Acid Test*.

Unconventional drugs had long been a part of the beat scene of the 1950s, but their use expanded dramatically during the 1960s. Timothy Leary began experimenting with hallucinogenic mushrooms in Mexico and soon moved on to LSD, an even more potent drug. It "blew his mind," he announced, and he became so enthusiastic in making converts that Harvard blew him straight out of its hallowed doors. By 1966 Leary had joined the psychedelic lecture circuit, going from college to college describing the joys of drug use. Those students who were uncomfortable about taking LSD had the option of smoking marijuana, which by the late sixties was widely used on many campuses.

The Rock Revolution

While Kerouac, Ginsberg, and others preached sermons of liberation, the hymns of the movement surfaced in new forms of popular music. In 1958 a group called the Kingston Trio popularized folk music that appealed more to college than high school audiences. Compared to the spontaneous and irreverent style of rock and roll, folk music was self-consciously historical and serious. (The Kingston Trio's first hit, "Tom Dooley," was a revival of a nineteenth-century ballad.) As the audience for folk music grew, the lyrics increasingly focused on social or political issues. Joan Baez, with a voice one critic found as pure and clear "as air in autumn," dressed simply, wore no makeup, and rejected the commercialism of popular music. She joined folk singer Bob Dylan in the civil rights march on Washington in 1963, singing "We Shall Overcome" and "Blowin' in the Wind." Such folk singers reflected the activist side of the counterculture as they sought to provoke their audiences to political commitment and social action.

In 1964 a new sound, imported from England, exploded on the American scene. Within a year the Beatles, four musicians from Liverpool, had generated more excitement than any previous phenomenon in popular music. Their concerts and appearances on the Ed Sullivan television show attracted frenzied teen audiences who screamed and swooned as the "mod" crooners sang "I Want to Hold Your Hand." Part of the Beatles' appeal came from their distinctly English style. With hair considered long in the sixties, modish clothes, fresh faces, and irreverent wit, they looked and sounded like nothing young Americans had experienced. Their boyish enthusiasm for life captured the Dionysian spirit of the new counterculture. But the Beatles' enormous commercial success also reflected the creativity of their music. Along with other English groups, like the Rolling Stones, they reconnected American audiences with the rhythm-and-blues roots of rock and roll, which they had drawn upon when creating their own songs.

Until 1965 Bob Dylan was the essential folk artist, writing about nuclear weapons, pollution, and racism. He appeared at concerts with longish frizzy hair, working-class clothes, an unamplified guitar, and a harmonica suspended on a wire support. But then Dylan shocked his fans by donning a black leather jacket and shifting to a "folk-rock" style featuring an electric guitar. His new songs seemed to suggest that the old America was almost beyond redemption. Meanwhile, the Beatles completed a pilgrimage to India to study transcendental meditation and returned to produce *Sergeant Pepper's Lonely Hearts Club Band*, possibly the most influential album of the decade. It blended sound effects with music, alluded to trips taken with "Lucy in the Sky with Diamonds" (LSD), and concluded, "I'd love to turn you on." The new format was innovative, too. No longer were songs limited to the three-minute length of 45-rpm records and popular radio. Out in San Francisco, bands like the Grateful Dead pioneered "acid rock" with long pieces aimed to echo drug-induced states of mind.

The debt of white rock musicians to rhythm and blues led to increased integration in the music world. Prior to the 1960s black rhythm-and-blues bands played primarily to black audiences, in segregated clubs, or over black radio stations. Black artists like Little Richard, Chuck Berry, and Ray Charles wrote numerous hit songs made popular by white performers. With the success of the civil rights movement and a rising black social and political consciousness came "soul" music. Blacks became "soul brothers" and "soul sisters," and for the first time their music was played on major radio stations. One black disc jockey described

Folk singer Bob Dylan became a kind of unofficial spokesperson of the 1960s youth rebellion. His songs expressed the anger, alienation, and despair of both political activists and apolitical cultural dropouts.

soul as "the last to be hired, first to be fired, brown all year round, sit-in-the-back-of-the-bus feeling." Soul was the quality that expressed black pride and separatism: "You've got to live with us or you don't have it." Out of Detroit came the "Motown sound," which combined elements of gospel, blues, and big band jazz. Diana Ross and the Supremes, the Temptations, Stevie Wonder, and other groups under contract to Berry Gordy's Motown Record Company appealed to black and white audiences alike. Yet while soul music promoted black consciousness, it had little to offer by way of social commentary. It evoked the traditional blues themes of unrequited love, workday woes, unhappy marriages, and the troubles between men and women.

The West Coast Scene

For all of its themes of alienation, rebellion, and utopian quest, the counterculture also signaled the increasing importance of the West Coast in American popular culture. In the 1950s the shift of television production from the stages of New York to the film lots of Hollywood helped establish Los Angeles as a communications center. San Francisco became notorious as a center of the beat movement.

Then in 1958 the unthinkable happened. The Brooklyn Dodgers, followed soon after by the New York Giants, two baseball teams that had helped make New York City the national sports capital, fled the East Coast for Los Angeles and San Francisco. When Alaska and Hawaii became states in 1959, the national center of gravity shifted westward. Richard Nixon, a Californian, narrowly missed being elected president in 1960. By 1963 the "surfing sound" of West Coast rock groups like the Beach Boys and Jan and Dean had made Southern California's preoccupation with surfing and cars into a national fad. And Mario Savio and his Free Speech Movement soon attracted the attention of the nation.

Before 1967 Americans were only vaguely aware of another West Coast phenomenon, the "hippies." But in January a loose coalition of drug freaks, Zen cultists, and political activists banded together to hold the first well-publicized "Be-In." Allen Ginsberg was on hand to offer spiritual guidance. The Grateful Dead and Jefferson Airplane, acid rock groups based in San Francisco, provided entertainment. An unknown organization called the Diggers somehow managed to supply free food and drink, while the notorious Hell's Angels motorcycle gang policed the occasion. Drugs of all kinds were plentiful. And a crowd attired in a bizarre mix of Native American, circus, Oriental, army surplus, and other exotic costumes came to enjoy it all. The West Coast had long been a magnet for Americans seeking opportunity, escape, and alternative lifestyles; now the San Francisco Bay Area staked its claim as the spiritual center of the counterculture. The more politically conscious dropouts gravitated toward Berkeley; the apolitical "flower children" moved into Haight–Ashbury, a run-down San Francisco neighborhood of apartments, Victorian houses, and "head shops" selling drug paraphernalia, wall posters, Indian bedspreads, and other coveted accessories.

Haight–Ashbury became a model replicated across the nation. Communes sprang up in the Rocky Mountains; yoga classes appeared in Ohio; Chinese woks were used in Ketchum, Idaho; students enrolled in high schools of ecology in Kennebunk, Maine. Colleges became centers of hip culture, offering alternative courses, eliminating strict requirements, and tolerating the new sexual mores of their students. In the summer of 1969 all the positive forces of the counterculture converged on Bethel, New York, in the Catskill Mountain resort area, to celebrate the promise of peace, love, and freedom. The Woodstock Music Festival attracted 400,000 people to the largest rock concert ever organized. For one long weekend the audience and performers joined to form an ephemeral community based on sex, drugs, and rock and roll.

Even then, the counterculture was dying. Four months after Woodstock, the hippie world reconvened on the West Coast at Altamont, California, to celebrate again, in the last month of the sixties. Over this assemblage presided the Rolling Stones, who delighted in being called "their satanic majesties" and had always cultivated a somewhat hostile, sexually ambiguous image. This time peace and love turned into anger and violence. With Stones leader Mick Jagger singing "Street Fighting Man" and "Sympathy for the Devil," the Hell's Angels police force randomly assaulted members of the audience with chains and broken pool cues. Movie cameras whirred as a group of Angels ran down a black street hood and knifed him to death. Just as Woodstock had symbolized the vitality of the counterculture, Altamont suggested its self-destructive potential.

Violence also intruded on the laid-back urban communities hippies had formed. Organized crime and drug pushers muscled in on the lucrative trade in LSD, amphetamines, and marijuana. Bad drugs and addiction took their toll. Criminals and psychopaths often passed themselves off as hippies. Urban slum dwellers turned hostile to the strange middle-class dropouts who, in ways the poor could not fathom, found poverty ennobling. Free sex often became an excuse for rape, exploitation, and loveless gratification.

Commercial acceptance undermined the counterculture's innocence by integrating its irreverant and rebellious style into mainstream pop culture. Much that had once seemed outrageous in the hippie world was readily absorbed into the marketplace. By 1968, for example, ABC had introduced *The Mod Squad*, a television series featuring three hippie types as undercover police officers. Rock groups became big business enterprises commanding huge fees. Slick concerts with expensive tickets replaced communal dances with psychedelic light shows. Yogurt, granola, and herbal teas appeared on supermarket shelves. Ironically, the world that hippies forged was coopted by the society they had rejected.

By the late 1960s most dreams of human betterment seemed shattered—whether John Kennedy's New Frontier, Lyndon Johnson's Great Society, or the communal society of the hippie counterculture. Recession and inflation brought an end to the easy affluence that made liberal reform programs and alternative lifestyles seem so easily affordable. In 1965 presidential adviser Daniel Patrick Moynihan was still optimistically suggesting that Keynesian management of the economy had created permanent abundance. The challenge, as Moynihan saw it, was to find new problems for reformers to solve. "The immediate *supply* of resources available for social purposes might actually outrun the immediate *demand* of established programs," he speculated in a giddy moment. By the end of the decade that unbridled optimism had turned to gloom, despite the Great Society's successes in altering the political landscape. Poverty and unemployment menaced even middle-class youth who had found havens in communes, colleges, and graduate schools. Racial tensions had divided black militants and the white liberals of the civil rights movement into sometimes hostile camps.

But the Vietnam War more than any other single factor destroyed the promise of Camelot. After 1965 the nation was deeply divided over the American military role in Southeast Asia. Radicals on the left who opposed the war insisted on a new utopian political consciousness that would rid America of a capitalist system that promoted race and class conflict at home and imperialism and military adventurism abroad. Conservatives on the right who supported the war called for a return to more traditional values like law and order. Both the left and the right attacked the liberal center. Their combined opposition helped to undermine the consensus Lyndon Johnson had worked so hard to build.

SIGNIFICANT EVENTS

1958 — Kingston Trio popularizes folk music

1960 — Kennedy–Nixon debates; Greensboro sit-ins; Kennedy elected president

1961 — Alliance for Progress; Peace Corps begun; Alan Shepard, Jr., first American in space; Bay of Pigs invasion; Kennedy steps up U.S. role in Vietnam; Vienna summit; Berlin Wall built; Area Redevelopment Act; CORE freedom rides begin

1962 — John Glenn orbits earth; Michael Harrington's *The Other America* published; Cuban missile crisis; James Meredith desegregates University of Mississippi; *Engel v. Vitale; Baker v. Carr;* SDS Port Huron Statement

1963 — Diem assassinated in Vietnam; nuclear test ban treaty; University of Alabama desegregation crisis; Kennedy introduces Civil Rights Bill; March on Washington; *Gideon v. Wainwright;* Kennedy assassinated

1964 — *Escobedo v. Illinois; Griswold v. Connecticut;* Civil Rights Act passed; SNCC Freedom Summer; Harlem and Rochester race riots; Johnson enacts Kennedy tax cuts; Economic Opportunity Act; VISTA established; Wilderness Preservation System Act; Johnson defeats Goldwater; Berkeley "Free Speech" Movement; Beatles introduce British rock

1965 — Johnson launches the Great Society; King's Selma protest; Voting Rights Act; Watts riots; Malcolm X assassinated; Medicare and Medicaid acts; Elementary and Secondary School Act; Omnibus Housing Act; Immigration Act; escalation in Vietnam

1966 — *Miranda v. Arizona;* Stokely Carmichael of SNCC coins "Black Power" slogan; Model Cities Act; minimum wages raised

1967 — Black Panthers battle Oakland, California, police; first "Be-In"

1968 — Fair Housing Act

1969 — Woodstock Music Festival; Altamont concert

Generations of the Republic

The Baby Boomers (1940–   )

To Americans the end of World War II augured an era of peace, power, and, above all, abundance. The economy was booming, the war had done relatively little damage to the nation's people and natural resources, and U.S. global power was underscored by the monopoly on atomic weapons. For the generation being born at the start of this new era, the contours of abundance shaped their world too.

There was, to begin with, an abundance of postwar children. The baby boom of the mid-twentieth century was especially remarkable given that for two and a half centuries the fertility rate among American women had dropped, as American society changed from a rural-agricultural to an urban-industrial culture. In 1942, however, the rate began a 15-year rise to a high of 122.9 births per thousand in 1957. The baby boom cut across virtually all sectors of American society. Furthermore, the trends also affected other highly industrialized nations.

The sharp rise did not reflect a return to the large-family pattern of earlier centuries, when women married in their early twenties and gave birth, on average, to six or seven children. Baby-boom families were only slightly larger than those of the 1920s and 1930s, jumping from an average of about two children to three. What accounted for the difference was that greater numbers of women were marrying, and at a markedly younger age. Fully one-third of all mothers during the baby-boom years set up housekeeping by the age of 19. Moreover, most chose to stop having children by their early or mid-thirties, unlike most mothers of earlier centuries, who continued to bear children well into their forties.

As young couples moved away from older communities with extended families to single-family suburban tracts, they often found themselves without the advice needed to deal with the challenges of childrearing. They turned eagerly to Dr. Benjamin Spock's *Baby and Child Care* (1946), which eventually sold over 30 million copies, second only to the Bible. Dr. Spock urged parents to follow their instincts, "be flexible and adjust to the baby's needs and happiness." Spock's ideal mother stayed home with her children, while avoiding becoming either

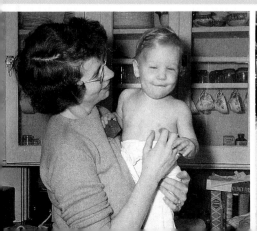

over-protective or indifferent to her child's welfare. "Don't be afraid to love him and enjoy him. Every baby needs to be smiled at, talked to, played with, fondled—gently and lovingly—just as much as he needs vitamins and calories."

When the baby boomers went to school, enrollments jumped by over 60 percent. Schools put up new wings and new buildings to accommodate the overflow and struggled to improve curricula to "keep up" with the Russians. During air-raid drills, lines of obedient children were led to basements, or sheltered themselves along interior walls. They were admonished, too, to "duck and cover" if caught at their desks when the first flash of an atomic blast came. Yet the cold war only occasionally intruded on the joys of getting and spending as this generation matured.

Continuing a trend of two centuries, the younger generation took increasingly longer to enter adulthood. The demand for technically skilled labor as well as parents' conviction that children were more likely to succeed with a higher education both served to lengthen the period of adolescence. The average boom child spent 12.9 years in school, with 84 percent finishing high school. Blacks were just as likely as whites to finish high school, but Hispanics lagged behind. As for college education, 44 percent of baby boomers were exposed to at least a year of it, and 25 percent graduated.

Given a prolonged period of adolescence, the 1950s economy of relative abundance was increasingly shaped by teenaged desires, styles and tastes. Adolescents had begun to accumulate money of their own to spend. In 1960 more than 25 percent of all teenaged boys and 14 percent of girls worked at least part time, and less of that money went, as it might have earlier in the century, to support the family. Teenagers controlled some $9.5 billion (out of GNP of $504 billion), which they spent on automobiles, clothes and records, not to mention candy bars, gum, soft drinks, and ice cream.

As a generation of youth came of age in the 1960s, the culture of abundance led many to look beyond the freedom of material well-being to "liberation" in other areas of life. Raised in child-centered, democratic, egalitarian families, college students became less willing to abide by university requirements for military training, chapel services, dress codes, or dormitory closing hours. Similarly, the currents of change touched more conservative courtship rituals. During the 1950s the practice of "going steady" had become common, with college fraternity brothers "pinning" women who would presumably become their wives. The sixties marked a return to more open dating patterns, and for the first time since the 1920s, the rate of premarital intercourse rose significantly. The wider availability of oral contraceptives, beginning in the late 1950s, increased the amount of control young

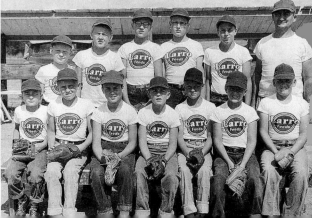

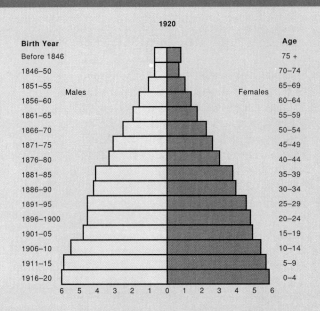

1920

Birth Year | | Age
Before 1846 | | 75 +
1846–50 | | 70–74
1851–55 | Males   Females | 65–69
1856–60 | | 60–64
1861–65 | | 55–59
1866–70 | | 50–54
1871–75 | | 45–49
1876–80 | | 40–44
1881–85 | | 35–39
1886–90 | | 30–34
1891–95 | | 25–29
1896–1900 | | 20–24
1901–05 | | 15–19
1906–10 | | 10–14
1911–15 | | 5–9
1916–20 | | 0–4

6 5 4 3 2 1 0 1 2 3 4 5 6

adults exerted over their sexual habits.

Liberation, abundance, control over one's future—these were the hallmarks of the new generation. Although only a fringe of the counterculture experimented with open marriage or communal living, liberation for many women meant being able to postpone or subordinate marriage to a full-time career. Often, this was a conscious decision arising out of a new appreciation for women's rights. But even the necessity of working in a blue-collar job fostered independence. One Puerto Rican woman in New York City reacted against the traditional pattern of male dominance in her marriage: "Whether I have a husband or not, I work. So I do what I want,

and if my husband dare to complain, I throw him out." As more women worked, they postponed marriage. In 1980, 20 percent of women between the ages of 25 and 29 were still unmarried—double the percentage a decade earlier and at its highest point since 1890. It was a sharp reversal of the pattern set by the baby boomers' own parents.

With that reversal came an increasing awareness of the limits of a culture of abundance. During the mid-1970s and 1980s, as baby boomers matured, they discovered economic, social, and even biological limits on their independence. As single and even married women increasingly worked full-time outside the home, they increased the competition for jobs. When these pressures were added to the economic problems of the mid-1970s to early 1980s, wages and income levels began to stagnate or even shrink. Families in which wives also worked could make up for much of this loss. But in single-parent families, especially those headed by women, the burden of poverty proved especially heavy. By 1980, one out of seven families was headed by a woman and those families accounted for 40 percent of people below the poverty level.

In addition, women who postponed marriage for the sake of career were, in their mid-thirties, realizing that they would have to begin having children soon or risk the medical complications of an older childbirth. Biological constraints

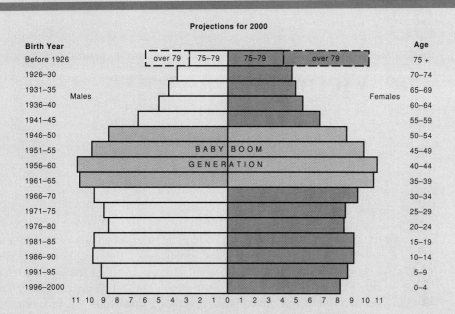

Projections for 2000

Birth Year		Age
Before 1926	over 79 / 75–79 / 75–79 / over 79	75 +
1926–30		70–74
1931–35		65–69
1936–40	Males / Females	60–64
1941–45		55–59
1946–50		50–54
1951–55	BABY BOOM	45–49
1956–60	GENERATION	40–44
1961–65		35–39
1966–70		30–34
1971–75		25–29
1976–80		20–24
1981–85		15–19
1986–90		10–14
1991–95		5–9
1996–2000		0–4

11 10 9 8 7 6 5 4 3 2 1 0 1 2 3 4 5 6 7 8 9 10 11

also served to limit social experimentation, as sexually transmitted diseases such as herpes in the 1970s and, more seriously, AIDS in the 1980s made casual sex a riskier proposition.

As baby boomers advanced toward old age, serious long-term issues about the nature of American society were becoming clearer. For most of American history, the shape of the population in any given year resembled a pyramid, as in 1920. The high birth rates provided a broad base at the bottom and mortality rates winnowed the population to a small tip of elderly. But as fertility rates continued their two-century decline and higher living standards made it possible for Americans to live longer,

the pyramid was being transformed more nearly into a cylinder. Only the temporary bulge of the baby boom distorted the shape.

With the period of adolescent education lengthening on the one hand and the number of retirees rising on the other hand, the proportion of the population working as productive adults will steadily decrease. At the same time, the burden of supporting both the education of their children and the care of elderly parents seems likely to increase. The generation raised to a sense of abundance, liberation, and control of its own destiny is finding itself experiencing limits that have always been a part of history.

33

The Vietnam Era

Vietnam from afar looked almost like an emerald paradise. "I remember getting up on the flight deck and seeing one of the most beautiful visions I've ever seen in my life," recalled Thomas Bird, an army rifleman sent there in 1965: "A beautiful white beach with thick jungle background. The only thing missing was naked women running down the beach, waving and shouting 'Hello, hello, hello.'" Upon landing, Bird and his buddies were each issued a "Nine-Rule" card outlining proper behavior toward the Vietnamese. "Treat the women with respect, we are guests in this country and here to help these people."

But who were they helping and who were they fighting? When American troops sought to engage Vietcong forces, the VC generally disappeared into the jungle beyond the villages and rice fields. John Muir, a Marine rifleman, walked into a typical hamlet with a Korean lieutenant. To Muir the place looked ordinary, but the Korean had been in Vietnam a while. "We have a little old lady and a little old man and two very small children," he pointed out. "According to them, the rest of the family has been spirited away . . . either been drafted into one army or the other. So there's only four of them and they have a pot of rice that's big enough to feed fifty people. And rice, once it's cooked, will not keep. They gotta be feeding the VC." Muir, whose only experience with rice till then had been Minute Rice or Uncle Ben's, watched as the lieutenant set the house on fire. The roof "started cooking off ammunition because all through the thatch they had ammunition stored."

GIs soon learned to walk down jungle trails with a cautious shuffle, looking for a wire or a piece of vine that seemed too straight. "We took more casualties from booby traps than we did from actual combat," recalled David Ross, a medic. "It was very frustrating because how do you fight back against a booby trap? You're just walking along and all of a sudden your buddy doesn't have a leg. Or you don't have a leg." Yet somehow the villagers would walk the same paths and never get hurt. Who was the enemy and who the friend? "It's very easy to slip into a primitive state of mind," noted Marine Douglas Anderson, "particularly if your life is in danger and you can't trust anyone. . . . In one case I saw a young [American soldier], probably eighteen years old, push an old man into his family bunker inside his hootch [hut] and throw a grenade in after him. We'd been hit a lot that week and pressure had been building up. It wasn't anything that happened that day. But I remember this guy distinctly because he had a tattoo of a little red devil

*In Vietnam helicopters gave infantry unusual mobility—a critical element in a war
with no real front line, since troops could be quickly carried from one battle to
another. These soldiers await a pickup amidst rice paddies south of Saigon.*

on his left arm and he had his shirt off when he threw the old man into the bunker and threw the grenade in after him."

Who was the friend and who the enemy? The same question was being asked half a globe away, on the campus of Kent State University in May 1970. By then the Vietnam War had dragged on for over five years, had driven President Lyndon Johnson from office and embroiled his successor, Richard Nixon, in a controversy over whether the fighting should be expanded into Cambodia. Kent State, just east of Akron, Ohio, was one of the many campuses that flourished in the 1950s and 1960s to accommodate the children of the baby boom. Normally it was an apolitical community, but opposition to the war had become so intense that 300 students had torn the Constitution from a history text and, in a formal ceremony, buried it, announcing that "President Nixon has murdered it." That evening demonstrators spilled over into the nearby town, smashed shop windows, and returned to campus to burn down an old Army ROTC building. The panicked mayor declared a state of emergency and Governor James Rhodes ordered in 750 of the National Guard. Student dissidents were the "worst type of people we harbor in America," he announced. "We are going to eradicate the problem."

By background and education, the National Guard troops were little different from the students they had come to police. Almost all were white, between 18 and 30, and from Ohio. Most had received only four months of active training before returning to their hometown units. Many treated the Guard much as they would a volunteer fire company. For some it was a second income; for others a weekend off every month with the guys; and for all, a sure way to avoid combat in Vietnam. Still, a political gulf separated most guardsmen from the student protesters. Many soldiers objected to the way antiwar forces criticized the president and the country. The officers, often veterans of World War II or Korea, particularly disap-

Crisis at Kent State: Who was the enemy, who the friend?

proved of students who evaded or openly rejected their military obligations. As his troops arrived at Kent, Guard Commander General Robert Canterbury remarked that "these students are going to have to find out what law and order is all about."

When the demonstrators assembled for a noon rally on the college commons, the Guard ordered them to disperse, although the troops' legal right to break up a peaceful demonstration was debatable. When the protesters did not disband the guardsmen advanced, wearing full battle gear and armed with M-1 rifles, whose high-velocity bullets had a horizontal range of almost two miles. Some students scattered; a few picked up rocks and threw them. The guardsmen then leveled their rifles and fired into the crowd, which included students passing back and forth from classes. Incredulous, a young woman knelt at the side of Jeffrey Miller, a student who lay dead. By the time calm was restored, three other students had been killed and nine more wounded, some caught innocently in the Guard's indiscriminate fire.

News of the killings swept the nation. At Jackson State, a black college in Mississippi, antiwar protesters seized a women's dormitory. On May 14 state police surrounded the building and without evident provocation opened fire, killing two more students and wounding a dozen. In both incidents the demonstrators had been unarmed. Before Kent and Jackson State there were sporadic strikes to protest the U.S. incursion of Cambodia. Afterward, hundreds of schools canceled classes for the week; nearly a third of all colleges had strikes of some sort. The ideals of the United States, it seemed to many, had been betrayed by those forces of law and order who were sworn to protect them.

Who was the friend and who the enemy? Time and again the war in Vietnam propelled conflicts in American society to the center of the political life of the nation. Vietnam did not create the counterculture and the radical student movement, but those elements would never have become so influential if the debate over Vietnam had not moved off college campuses and into the homes of middle Americans, where sons went off to fight and the war came home each night on the evening news. Vietnam did not create the civil rights issue, but it raised questions, as most wars do, of whether Vietnam was a "rich man's war and a poor man's fight," where sons of the upper and middle classes escaped battle by going to college while blacks and other poor draftees became sniper's targets along jungle trails. As no other war had, Vietnam seemed to stand the nation on its head. When American soldiers shot at Vietnamese "hostiles," who could not always be separated from "friendlies," or when National Guardsmen fired on their neighbors across a college green, who were the enemies and who were the friends?

THE ROAD TO VIETNAM

"The enemy must fight his battles far from his home base for a long time," one Vietnamese strategist wrote. "We must further weaken him by drawing him into protracted campaigns. Once his initial dash is broken, it will be easier to destroy him." The enemy in question was not American soldiers or even the French, but the Mongol invaders of A.D. 1284. For several thousand years Vietnam had struggled periodically to fight off foreign invasions. Influenced by Buddhist culture traveling eastward from India, it had also been invaded and ruled periodically by

The Geography of Vietnam

CHINA

NORTH VIETNAM

Lao Cai

Thai Nguyen

Dien Bien Phu

BURMA

Hanoi

Haiphong

Red R.

Black R.

GULF OF TONKIN

Luang Prabang

PLAIN OF JARS

Thanh Hoa

LAOS

Mekong R.

Vinh

Hainan

Vientiane

ANNAMESE

Con Thien
Quang Tri

Sepone

Khe Sanh

SOUTH CHINA SEA

THAILAND

Yom R.

Ping R.

Po Sak R.

Hue

Da Nang

CORDILLERA

My Lai
Quang Ngai

Mun R.

Dak To

Kon Tum

Kong R.

Pleiku

Qui Nhon

Bangkok

CAMBODIA

Tonle Sap

CENTRAL HIGHLANDS

Tuy Hoa

SOUTH VIETNAM

Pursat

Mekong R.

Nha Trang

GULF OF THAILAND

Phnom Penh

Da Lat

Song Be

Chau Doc

PLAIN OF REEDS

Saigon

Ben Tre

Can Tho

MEKONG RIVER DELTA

| 0 | 100 | 200 Miles |
| 0 | 100 | 200 Kilometers |

Ho Chi Minh Trail

★ Major battles of Tet offensive

Stretching along a thousand-mile curve along the South China Sea, Vietnam covers an area about 20 percent smaller than California but 20 percent longer. The spine of the peninsula, the Annamese Cordillera, proved a formidable battleground for war. "We were flying parallel to the mountains," Philip Caputo recalled; "the Cordillera spread out before us, and it was the most forbidding thing I had ever seen. An unbroken mass of green stretched westward, one ridgeline and mountain range after another, some more than a mile high and covered with forests that looked solid enough to walk on." Near the border between North and South Vietnam, the terrain was particularly steep. "The Rockpile" (top left) a 1200-foot pyramid near Khe Sanh, commanded a strategic view of five valleys. "Its top had enough flat space for about two medium-sized dinner tables," reported one journalist, "and when weather permitted, helicopters ferried soldiers on and off via a rickety platform inches from a 900-foot drop."

North Vietnam established the Ho Chi Minh Trail through "neutral" Laos (center) in order to supply the Vietcong. In the early stages of the war, supplies were brought in on foot by soldiers carrying knapsacks as well as rice in socks wrapped around their waists. By 1964 the North Vietnamese were building roads and bridges that could handle heavy trucks. Because of the dense rain forest, even low-flying U.S. helicopters found it difficult to locate and bomb the trail.

In the flatter terrain of the Mekong River delta to the south, rice paddies and jungle swamps proved equally hazardous (bottom). "On one patrol," recalled an artillery captain, "we had a man who had collected 80 leeches on his body. He died later from exhaustion and loss of blood. Another had a leech crawl through his penis into his bladder. Most of us are wearing prophylactics on patrol to prevent that, because it's painful as hell." In this war, geography, vegetation, and climate often proved as perilous foes as the Vietcong.

Nguyen Ai Quoc, who became Ho Chi Minh, once worked at London's posh Carlton Hotel in the pastry kitchen of the renowned French chef Escoffier. But he was soon swept up in socialist and nationalist politics, appearing at the Versailles Peace Conference (left) to plead for an independent Vietnam. By the time the United States was increasing its involvement in Vietnam, Ho had accumulated a lifetime of anticolonialist and revolutionary activity and become a revered leader of his people.

the Chinese from the north. After 1856 the French entered as a colonial power, bringing with them a strong Catholic tradition.

Ho Chi Minh was one Vietnamese who hoped his country would throw off the French influence as well as the Chinese. In 1912, at the age of 22, Ho gave up the poor life of a schoolteacher and hired out as a messboy on a French ocean liner. Traveling from Asia to Africa to Europe he lived quite literally on the underside of the colonial system: the rich and wealthy vacationing on the upper decks, the darker skinned laborers like Ho serving them below. On a brief visit to America he heard about the campaigns of the Ku Klux Klan. At the end of World War I, when President Wilson came to Versailles calling for self-determination for small nations, Ho bought a formal pin-striped suit at a second-hand store and attended the peace conference, petitioning on behalf of Vietnam. When his plea for independence was ignored, he became a communist, taking the recent Russian Revolution as his model. Visits to Moscow followed, with Ho returning to the Indochina region to organize revolutionary activity.

But it was only after the Japanese were driven out of Vietnam in 1945 that he was able to take advantage of the power vacuum and unite the country under a nationalist government. When France moved to recover control of its old colony, some of Ho's colleagues wanted to approach the Chinese Communists for help. But Ho was first and foremost a nationalist. He saw the age of colonialism dying and worried that Chinese aid might lead to permanent domination. "I prefer to smell French dung for five years rather than Chinese dung for the rest of my life," he concluded, and he allowed the French to return. Negotiations for independence soon broke down, however, so his forces fought eight years of guerrilla war before the French surrendered at Dien Bien Phu in 1954 (page 1136). At a peace conference held in Geneva, Ho agreed to withdraw his forces north of the 17th parallel, limiting his government to North Vietnam in return for the promise of free elections in both the North and the South. When the American-backed government of Ngo Dinh Diem refused to hold elections, South Vietnamese communists—the Vietcong—began their guerrilla war once again. "I think the Americans greatly underestimate the determination of the Vietnamese people," Ho remarked in 1962, as President Kennedy was committing more American advisers to South Vietnam.

Escalation at Tonkin Gulf

For Kennedy, Vietnam had been just one of many communist skirmishes which his activist advisers wanted to fight—in Cuba, in Africa, in Laos (Vietnam's western neighbor). But even 16,000 American "advisers" had been unable to help the unpopular Diem, who was overthrown by the military in November 1963. With renewed attention focused on Vietnam, Kennedy accepted President Eisenhower's "domino theory": if the pro-Western Catholic government fell to the Communists, the other nations of Southeast Asia would collapse like a row of dominos. The United States therefore had to support this government. When Kennedy was assassinated the same month as Diem, the problem of Vietnam was left to Lyndon Johnson.

Johnson's political instincts told him to keep the Vietnam War at arm's length. He felt like a catfish, he remarked, who had "just grabbed a big juicy worm with a right sharp hook in the middle of it." His primary concerns were with domestic issues: passing a tax cut, pushing his war on poverty, and drawing up the Great Society programs. Yet despite his caution, Johnson moved steadily toward deeper American involvement in Vietnam. He shared the cold war assumptions of Kennedy holdovers like National Security Adviser McGeorge Bundy and Defense Secretary Robert McNamara and succumbed to their pressure to apply containment to Vietnam's civil war. Johnson also was sensitive in 1964 to criticism from the Republican presidential candidate Barry Goldwater, who called for an end to appeasement and a "let's-win" policy of total military victory.

Until August 1964 American action had focused on combating the Vietcong within South Vietnam. North Vietnam, for its part, had been infiltrating a modest amount of men and supplies along the Ho Chi Minh Trail, a primitive network of jungle routes threading through Laos and Cambodia into the highlands of South Vietnam. In the summer of 1964 North Vietnam began to modernize the trail, allowing it to handle large trucks in addition to the peasants who carried supplies on their backs or used modified bicycles. At the time American officials were unaware of the change, but they realized all too well that the Vietcong already controlled some 40 percent of South Vietnamese territory. Pressure mounted in Washington to turn matters around. One option was to put more pressure on North Vietnam itself.

So President Johnson sent a number of American ships to the Gulf of Tonkin. Laden with electronic snooping gear, they patrolled the North Vietnamese coast while South Vietnamese ships conducted raids. On August 2, three North Vietnamese patrol boats exchanged fire with the American destroyer *Maddox*—neither side hurting the other—and then the Vietnamese boats fled. An outraged Johnson chided several shamefaced admirals. "You've got a whole fleet and all those airplanes, and you can't even sink three little ol' PT boats?" Two nights later, in inky blackness and a heavy thunderstorm, radar operators on the *C. Turner Joy* reported a torpedo attack. But a follow-up investigation could not be sure whether enemy ships had even been near the scene. "The Gulf is a very funny place," explained one communications officer. "You get inversion layers there that will give you very solid radar contacts . . . that just aren't there. That may have happened to us." The president was not pleased. "For all I know our navy might have been shooting at whales out there," he remarked privately.

Whatever his doubts, the president announced publicly that American ships had been attacked. Calling the incidents "open aggression on the high sea," he ordered retaliatory air raids on North Vietnam. He did not disclose that the Navy and South Vietnamese forces had been conducting secret military operations at the time. Such deception would become standard practice. It abetted Johnson's decision to ask Congress for authority to take "all necessary measures" to "repel any armed attack" on American forces and to "prevent future aggression." Congress jumped at the opportunity, passing what became known as the Gulf of Tonkin resolution by a lopsided vote of 414–0 in the House and 88–2 in the Senate. The action seemed to show Goldwater supporters that Johnson, too, could act firmly, and his popularity rose sharply.

Senator Ernest Gruening of Alaska, who with Wayne Morse of Oregon had been the only lawmakers to object, warned that the Tonkin Gulf Resolution gave the president "a blank check" to declare war, a power which the Constitution specifically reserved to Congress. Johnson insisted—no doubt sincerely at the time—that he had no such intention. But as pressure for an American victory increased, the president exploited the powers the resolution gave him.

Rolling Thunder

No sooner had Johnson taken the oath of office in January 1965 than he received a disturbing memorandum from McGeorge Bundy and Robert McNamara. "Both of us are now pretty well convinced that our present policy can lead only to disastrous defeat," they said. The United States should either increase its attack— "escalate" was the term coined in 1965—or simply withdraw. The idea behind escalation was to increase military pressure to the point at which further resistance cost more than the enemy was willing to risk, either militarily or politically. By taking gradual steps, the United States would demonstrate its resolve to win while leaving the door open to negotiations. But the theory that made so much sense in the planning rooms of the Pentagon did not work well in practice. Each stage of American escalation only hardened the resolve of the Vietcong and North Vietnamese. When a Vietcong mortar attack in February killed seven Marines stationed at Pleiku airbase, Johnson informed the nation that U.S. planes would begin bombing North Vietnam. Privately, McGeorge Bundy admitted that Pleiku was only an excuse to act. "Pleikus are like street cars," he remarked; "there's one every ten minutes."

Restricted air strikes did not satisfy more hawkish leaders like retired Air Force Chief of Staff General Curtis LeMay. "We are swatting flies when we should be going after the whole manure pile," he complained. In March Johnson ordered Operation Rolling Thunder, a systematic bombing campaign aimed at bolstering confidence in South Vietnam and cutting the flow of supplies from the North. At the same time, he declared his willingness to negotiate and consider a vast irrigation project, TVA-style, once North Vietnamese troops had left the South. But

LEVELS OF U.S. TROOPS IN
VIETNAM (AT YEAR-END)

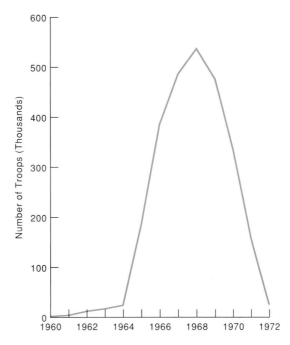

Source : U.S. Department of Defense.

Rolling Thunder achieved none of its goals. An impenetrable jungle canopy made the Ho Chi Minh Trail nearly impossible for American fighter pilots to spot from the air, so that supplies and troops flowed south without interruption. Even when bombs found their targets, North Vietnamese crews quickly filled in craters or spanned rivers with pontoon bridges made of bamboo stalks. Equally discouraging, the ever-changing military governments in South Vietnam carried on ineptly while Ho Chi Minh refused to negotiate unless the bombing stopped and American troops went home.

Once the Americans established bases from which to launch the new air strikes, these too became vulnerable to guerrilla attacks. When General William Westmoreland, the chief of American military operations in Vietnam, requested combat troops to defend the bases, Johnson sent in 3500 Marines, almost without considering the implication of his decision. Until then, only military "advisers" to the South Vietnamese had been sent. Once the crucial decision to commit combat troops had been taken, the urge to send more—to shore up and protect those already there—became strong. Another 40,000 soldiers arrived in May and 50,000 more by July. By then Johnson realized how serious his commitment was, but fearful of a political backlash, he deliberately downplayed the escalation. McNamara ordered the decision carried out in a "low-keyed manner," both to prevent Soviet or Chinese intervention and "to avoid undue concern and excitement in the Congress and in domestic public opinion." By the end of 1965 almost 185,000 American troops had landed—and still the call for more continued. In 1968, at the height of the war, 536,000 American troops were being supported with helicopters, jet aircraft, and other advanced military technologies. This was "escalation" with a vengeance.

SOCIAL CONSEQUENCES OF THE WAR

The greatest social impact of the war, naturally enough, fell first on the baby-boom generation of the 1950s. These young people came of age at a time when, on the one hand, draft calls for the armed services were rising and, on the other, the civil rights movement and the growing counterculture were encouraging students to question the goals of establishment America. The social experiences of both the Americans who fought and those who protested at home eventually forced Americans of all ages to come to grips with Vietnam.

The Soldiers' War

The social structure determining which Americans would be required to fight and which would remain civilian was the draft. The system in place generally favored the middle and upper classes, since college students and graduate students at first received deferments. Thus the Vietnam War increased male enrollment in colleges. As the war escalated the draft was changed, so that some students were called up through a lottery system. Still, those who knew the medical requirements might be able to produce a doctor's affidavit certifying a weak knee, flat feet, or bad eyes—all grounds for flunking the physical. About half of the potential draftees flunked—two to three times the rejection rate of those called up by the NATO allies. Of the 1200 men in Harvard's class of 1970, only 56 served in the military, and only 2 of them in Vietnam. The poorest and least educated were also likely to escape service, because the Armed Forces Qualification Test and the physical often screened them out. Thus the sons of blue-collar America were most likely to accept Uncle Sam's letter of induction, as were the sons of Hispanic and black Americans who, having fewer skills, were more often assigned to combat duty. The draft also made it a relatively young man's war. The average soldier serving in Vietnam was 19, compared with 26 years old for World War II.

Once in Vietnam, life for the ordinary "grunt"—infantry man—was a matter of trying to fight an uncertain enemy. Most soldiers came to Vietnam fairly well trained and with high morale, but the physical and psychological hardships took their toll. In a war of continual small skirmishes, booby traps, and search and destroy missions, it was hard to relax. What was especially frustrating was that success could not be measured in terms of territory gained. An American force would fight its way into a communist-controlled hamlet, clear and burn it, move on—and be ordered back to the same place days or weeks later, because the enemy had moved in again. The main measure of success in such a war soon became the "body count": the number of Vietcong who had been killed. And since most officers wanted to look as good as possible, body counts were inflated as the numbers were passed up the ranks. Furthermore, the strain of not being able to tell who was friendly and who was hostile made it all too easy for GIs to take out their frustrations on innocent civilians.

Other social factors affected morale and the way soldiers fought. Most new recruits were sent to Vietnam as individuals, not as part of units. This was a departure from usual military tradition, and it meant that there was little camaraderie between soldiers—a key requirement for good fighting. Combat veterans felt less sympathy for the raw replacements who joined them and often despised the rear-echelon or "REMF" soldiers who superintended supply depots or received combat pay for being lifeguards at beaches near Da Nang. Paradoxically, the miracles of modern technology also made the war hard to cope with. Because helicopters could whisk GIs from the front lines of a steaming jungle back to Saigon—where they could catch overnight flights to Hawaii or the mainland—the transition from the hell of war to civilian peace could be wrenching. John Kerry, later to become senator from Massachusetts, recalled his homecoming: "There I was, a week out of the jungle, flying from San Francisco to New York. I fell asleep and woke up yelling, probably a nightmare. The other passengers moved away from me—a reaction I noticed more and more in the months ahead. . . . The feeling toward [Vietnam vets] was, 'Stay away—don't contaminate us with whatever you've brought back from Vietnam.'"

Technology and Its Limits

Escalation of the war meant that American forces brought in the most technologically advanced equipment available. The transformation of South Vietnam was astonishing. By 1967 a million tons of supplies was being shipped to Vietnam each month—an average of a hundred pounds a day for every American in the country. Huge cranes, tractors, and barges built warehouses, barracks, and airfields. South Vietnam's airports soon handled more flight traffic than New York, Rome, Tokyo, or any other city in the world. The average soldier carried an automatic rifle that could discharge hundreds of rounds a minute, compared to French forces from the 1950s, whose rifles had clips of 8 or 10 rounds. Ground forces could also count on repeated air strikes to strafe or bomb enemy territory with thousands of shells before they marched in. Troops were provided with infrared sniper scopes and other instruments to help spot nighttime attackers. If technology could have won the war, Americans would have triumphed.

But technology alone could not make the difference, and it raised ethical issues as well. War is always hell, but where friendly and hostile civilian populations were mixed, the chances for deadly error increased. Bombs of napalm (jellied gasoline) and white phosphorus rained liquid fire from the skies, coating everything from village huts to the flesh of fleeing humans. Cluster bombs were designed to explode hundreds of pellets in midair, spraying the enemy with high-velocity shrapnel. To clear jungle canopies and expose Vietcong camps and roads, American planes sprayed more than 100 million pounds of defoliants such as Agent Orange. ("Only You Can Prevent Forests" was the sardonic motto of one unit assigned to the task.) The forests that were destroyed totaled over one-third of South Vietnam's timberlands—an area approximately the size of the state of Rhode Island. The long-term health and ecological effects were severe.

By 1967 the United States was spending more than $2 billion a month on the war. It dropped more bombs on Vietnam than it had during all of World War II. After one air attack on the communist-held provincial capital of Ben Tre, American troops walked into the remains, now mostly ruined buildings and rubble. "We had to destroy the town in order to save it," an officer explained. As the human and material costs of the war increased, that statement stuck in the minds of many observers. How far could the technology of war be taken before it ran headlong into limits? Such questions provoked anguished debate among Americans as the effects of the war came home.

Daily Lives

TIME AND TRAVEL

The Race to the Moon

In campaigning for the presidency in 1960 John F. Kennedy chided the Republicans for a losing effort in the space race with the Soviet Union. While the American program limped along, the Soviets leapt ahead. Only a few months after Kennedy's inauguration, Russian cosmonaut Yuri Gagarin orbited the world in a five-ton spacecraft lifted aloft by rocket engines far more powerful than any the United States possessed. On May 6, 1961, an Atlas rocket did carry Commander Alan Shepard into space, but that was merely a 15-minute suborbital flight of 300 miles. Kennedy feared that in losing the space race, the United States might lose the cold war as well. Nations around the world whose hearts and minds the superpowers struggled to win might conclude that the Soviet Union possessed superior technology and leadership.

Thus Kennedy ordered his science advisers "to shift our efforts in space from low to high gear." To Congress and a national television audience he announced that the United States would do something truly dramatic: land a man on the moon and bring him back alive "before the decade is out." The cost in money and scientific talent would be considerable, but to Kennedy, the investment was sound. "This is not merely a race," he remarked in an allusion to the Soviets' success. "Space is open to us now; and our eagerness to share its meaning is not governed by the efforts of others. We must go into space because whatever mankind must undertake, free men must fully share."

The president's enthusiasm for this enormous undertaking did not win universal acclaim. Former President Eisenhower thought anyone was "nuts" to spend billions for a space spectacular that promised little in the way of scientific discoveries. Nor was it clear that NASA could achieve such a feat in so short a time. Yet Congress, perhaps seeing the space program as a huge pork barrel, voted to fund Kennedy's "great new American enterprise." From then on the space program achieved a string of triumphs. In February 1962 Colonel John Glenn successfully circled the earth three times in "a fireball of a ride"; an unmanned satellite passed Venus later that year; and a Telstar communications satellite began relaying television broadcasts, launching an era of truly global mass communications.

One after another, the space spectaculars continued, much to the public's delight. In March 1965 American astronauts first maneuvered their capsule; in May Edward White took America's first space walk; the following year two vehicles met and docked for the first time. The Gemini program was followed by the Apollo missions, whose Saturn rockets provided the power necessary to launch payloads into lunar orbit. From there, two astronauts planned to pilot a separate module to the moon's surface, while a third remained in the orbiting command module waiting for them and the return trip. Although a fire during ground tests killed three astronauts in 1967, by Christmas eve 1968 a successful Apollo 8 mission was circling the moon. It seemed a "vast, lonely and forbidding sight," one astronaut remarked to hundreds of millions in a live telecast.

On July 20, 1969, the lunar module of Apollo 11 at last touched down on the earth's closest neighbor. Commander Neil Armstrong, moving awkwardly in his bulky spacesuit, worked his way down a ladder to the white, chalky surface. He

Daily Lives

Landing on the moon may have been one small step for a man, but NASA spent $25 billion on the project, over $2 billion for each of the 12 astronauts who took lunar walks.

was not alone. Besides Edwin Aldrin, who followed him, and Michael Collins, orbiting in the command module, Armstrong brought along a quarter of the world's population, who monitored the moment live on television. "That's one small step for a man, one giant leap for mankind," he proclaimed. By the time the Apollo series concluded its missions in 1972, American astronauts had roamed the lunar surface in roving vehicles, taken geologic samples, and left behind devices to measure seismic tremors and solar winds.

Exploration had come a long way in the centuries since the first European mariners pressed westward across the Atlantic. In both cases, exploring parties ventured outward with only the most tenuous links to their home bases. But twentieth-century astronauts were backed by an immense array of instruments, detailed photographic mapping of their proposed landing sites, and hundreds of mission controllers monitoring everything from blood pressure to fuel-tank valves. The economic commitment and the necessary second-by-second coordination could have been provided only by a technologically complex industrial society.

Still, the politics of both eras shaped the course of exploration, whether to the Americas or to the moon. Machines, after all, could have performed most of the moon mission's tasks, at far less risk and expense. Just as Portugal, England, and Spain used explorers to vie for national advantage, so Kennedy seized on the moon missions as a demonstration of American enterprise in the cold war. And NASA bureaucrats cannily recognized that the glamour of a manned space program established the necessary popular support for billion-dollar outlays.

While critics argued that those billions might better have been funneled into research on more earthly problems, Presidents Kennedy, Johnson, and Nixon all responded to the need for symbolic conquests along New Frontiers—and so, apparently, did the public. The creators of television's "Star Trek," a science fiction program originally popular in the 1960s, put its Kennedyesque hero, Captain James T. Kirk, in command of the starship *Enterprise,* "to boldly go where no man has gone before."

The War Comes Home

College campuses became the center of growing opposition to American involvement in Vietnam. Faculty members held "teach-ins" to explain the issues to concerned students. Scholars familiar with Southeast Asia, like George Kahin at Cornell University and foreign affairs specialist Hans Morgenthau, questioned every major assumption the president used to justify escalation. The United States and South Vietnam had instigated the war, Kahin charged, by violating the Geneva accords of 1954. Moreover, the Vietcong were an indigenous rebel force with legitimate grievances against Saigon's corrupt government. That made the war a civil war among the Vietnamese, not an effort by Soviet or Chinese Communists to conquer Southeast Asia, as Eisenhower, Kennedy, and Johnson had claimed. Finally, dissidents argued that profound differences in Asian and Western culture made it impossible to impose an American solution with troops or diplomacy.

By 1966 national leaders had similarly divided into opposing camps of "hawks" and "doves." The hawks argued that America must win in Vietnam to save Southeast Asia from Communism, to preserve the nation's prestige, and to protect the lives of American soldiers fighting the war. A large majority of the American people supported those views. The doves were nonetheless a prominent minority. They included New Left radicals like Tom Hayden, actress Jane Fonda, and folk singer Joan Baez as well as respected editorialist Walter Lippmann, Senator J. William Fulbright, head of the Foreign Relations Committee, and Dr. Benjamin Spock, the physician whose child-care manuals had raised the generation of baby-boomers sent to fight in Vietnam. Blacks as a group were far less likely than whites to support the war. Some resented the diversion of resources from the cities to the war effort. Even more important, many blacks' heightened sense of racial consciousness led them to identify with the Vietnamese people. Martin Luther King, SNCC, and CORE all opposed the war. Black heavyweight champion Muhammad Ali joined the Black Muslims and the international Islamic movement, refusing to be inducted into the army on religious grounds. And black poet Nikki Giovanni set into vivid phrases her own sense of alienation:

> We kill in Vietnam
> for them
> We kill for UN&NATO&SEATO&US
> And everywhere for all alphabet but BLACK.

By 1967 the antiwar crusade had swept college campuses. Students and faculty turned out in crowds of thousands to express their outrage: "Hey, hey, LBJ, how many kids have you killed today?" Over 300,000 people attended the demonstration organized in April 1967 in New York City. Sixty college protesters organized by SDS leaders from Cornell University burned their draft cards in defiance of federal law. In the fall more violent protests erupted as antiwar radicals stormed a draft induction center in Oakland, California. The next day 55,000 protesters including the novelist Norman Mailer and poet Robert Lowell ringed the Pentagon in Washington. Again, mass arrests followed.

Student protests and demonstrations forced policymakers and citizens to take a sobering look at the justice of the war. But the guerrilla tactics of more radical elements alienated many. It would be hard to exaggerate the shock university communities felt when radicals shut down Columbia University and clashed with

Lyndon Johnson shocked reporters in October 1965 when he publicly exposed his surgical scar from a gallbladder operation. Political caricaturist David Levine caught the underlying tragedy of the Johnson presidency by drawing the scar in the shape of Vietnam.

police for a week in 1968 or the following year when black militant students—bandoleers draped across their shoulders, shotguns at their sides—seized the student union at Cornell. Even more shocking, a graduate student at the University of Wisconsin was killed in his lab when a bomb exploded there. The device had been planted by radicals protesting government-sponsored defense research.

On the other hand, key moderates both within and outside the government became convinced that victory was beyond the resources of the United States. Senator Fulbright, who helped President Johnson push the Tonkin Gulf Resolution through the Senate, held televised hearings that were highly critical of American policy. *Time* and *Life* magazines, run by the hawkish publisher Henry Luce, made a dramatic editorial turnabout in 1967. Even the strongest supporters of the war felt the pressure. Secretary of State Dean Rusk, a hard-liner throughout, was dismayed to hear his relatives back home in Cherokee County, Georgia: "Dean, if you can't tell us when this war is going to end, well then, maybe we just ought to chuck it."

Defense Secretary Robert McNamara became the most dramatic defector from the establishment position. For years the statistically minded secretary had struggled to quantify the success of the war effort. General William Westmoreland duly provided body counts, number of bombs dropped, and pacification reports, all sufficient to convince McNamara that there was indeed a "light at the end of the tunnel." But by 1967 the secretary had become skeptical. If Americans actually were killing 300,000 Vietnamese, enemy forces should be shrinking. Instead, intelligence estimates indicated that North Vietnamese infiltration had risen from 35,000 a year in 1965 to 150,000 by the end of 1967. McNamara had also come to have doubts about the morality of the situation. "The picture of the world's greatest superpower killing or seriously injuring 1,000 non-combatants a week, while trying to pound a tiny, backward nation into submission on an issue whose merits are hotly disputed, is not a pretty one," he advised. Johnson, however, was determined not to be labeled the first American president who lost a war, especially when hawks like Senator John Stennis of Mississippi and General Westmoreland were pressing to escalate further. And so McNamara resigned.

As the war dragged on, it had one other social consequence: inflation. With the president unwilling to negotiate a retreat, the cost of the war soared to over $50 billion a year. Medicare, education, housing, and other Great Society programs raised the domestic budget sharply too. Through it all Johnson refused to raise taxes, and the result was a rise in wages and prices. From 1950 to 1960 the average rate of inflation hovered at about 2 percent a year. From 1965 to 1970, as the war escalated, it jumped to around 4 percent. The rise was not perceived as serious at first, but the seeds were sown for future trouble.

THE UNRAVELING

Almost all the forces dividing America seemed to converge in 1968, when some of the harsh costs of the war became clear. Until January of that year, most Americans had reason to believe that the United States was gaining ground, whatever private doubts had arisen among Lyndon Johnson's advisers and whatever campus protesters might say. Military leaders sent back optimistic figures about mounting enemy casualties. Television relayed home footage of American soldiers on helicopter raids, search and destroy patrols, bombing missions. With the exception of a few correspondents like David Halberstam of the New York *Times* and independent journalists like Bernard Fall, almost no one provided insight into the Vietnamese side of the war. As one network journalist commented, "It's an American war in Asia and that's the only story the American audience is interested in."

Tet Offensive

The Vietcong's Tet offensive in January 1968 changed the American perspective. Tet, the most festive of Vietnamese celebrations, marks the coming of the lunar new year. In previous years it had been observed by an informal cease-fire. But on the night of January 30, 1968, Vietcong guerrillas launched a concerted attack on 36 of the 44 provincial capitals of South Vietnam. Assault targets included Saigon's major airport, the South Vietnamese presidential palace, and Hue, the ancient Vietnamese imperial capital. Perhaps most unnerving to Americans, 19 crack Vietcong commandos blasted a hole in the wall of the American embassy compound in Saigon and stormed in. When they were unable to breach the embassy's heavy main door, they fought in the courtyard until all 19 lay dead. One reporter, stunned by the carnage, compared the courtyard to a "butcher shop."

The Tet offensive had been in the planning for nearly half a year. Deliberately, the North Vietnamese had lured American troops to the hinterlands of South Vietnam to engage in pitched battles at remote outposts like Khe Sanh, Con Thien, Song Be, and Dak To. As American forces were deployed in response, the Vietcong infiltrated major population areas of Saigon and the delta region. Weapons were smuggled in on vegetable carts and a few audacious VC, disguised as South Vietnamese soldiers, even hitched rides on American jeeps and trucks. The attack caught American troops off guard, but they quickly counterattacked, repulsing most of the assaults. Hue, the communists' biggest conquest, took three weeks to retake. Appearing before the American press, General Westmoreland announced that the Vietcong had "very deceitfully" taken advantage of the Vietnamese holiday "to create maximum consternation" and that their "well-laid plans went afoul."

In a narrow military sense, Westmoreland was right. The enemy had been driven back, sustaining perhaps 40,000 deaths compared to 1100 American and 2300 South Vietnamese soldiers' lives lost—a ratio of over 10 to 1 (though 12,500 civilians died). But such military considerations paled beside the message that Americans at home received from Tet. Westmoreland, Johnson, and other officials had repeatedly asserted that the Vietcong were on their last legs. Yet as Ho Chi Minh had cooly informed the French after World War II, "You can kill ten of my men for every one I kill of yours . . . even at those odds, you will lose and I will win." Now the Vietcong had launched a nationwide offense and even penetrated the defenses of the American embassy. Tet created a "credibility gap" between the administration's promises and the harsh reality of the situation. Highly respected CBS news anchor Walter Cronkite drew a gloomy lesson of Tet for his national audience: "To say that we are mired in stalemate seems the only realistic, yet unsatisfactory, conclusion."

The sheer brutality of the war came home, too. Americans were used to combat footage on the nightly news, but few were prepared for an NBC report from Saigon at the height of Tet. It showed South Vietnamese police chief Nguyen Ngoc Loan approaching a recently captured Vietcong suspect, brusquely pulling out his pistol, and shooting him through the head. Two months later, with American troops increasingly edgy about Vietcong attacks, Lieutenant William Calley moved American troops into the hamlet of My Lai, rounded up the villagers, and executed over 200 men, women, and children. The dead of My Lai would have been just more figures in the "body count," except that an army photographer had taken pictures and a helicopter pilot intervened. If returning veterans were to be believed, there had been hundreds of similar incidents, though perhaps few as bloody. On the communist side, vengeance was at times even more severe. Before Hue could be retaken, the Vietcong had shot, clubbed to death, or buried alive perhaps 3000 residents, many of them innocent civilians.

The Tet offensive left Lyndon Johnson sobered and unsure how to react. On the one hand, General Westmoreland was requesting an additional 206,000 troops on top of the half million already in Vietnam. The Joint Chiefs of Staff backed him. But the new secretary of defense, Clark Clifford, became a surprise convert for deescalation. Clifford was a Johnson loyalist through and through, and a stalwart believer in the war. But in sizing up the situation in his new position as defense secretary, he could get no satisfactory answers from his generals. "How long would it take to succeed in Vietnam?" Clifford recalled asking them.

> They didn't know. How many more troops would it take? They couldn't say. Were two hundred thousand the answer? They weren't sure. Might they need more? Yes, they might need more. Could the enemy build up [their own troop strength] in exchange? Probably. So what was the plan to win the war? Well, the only plan was that attrition would wear out the Communists, and they would have had enough. Was there any indication that we've reached that point? No, there wasn't.

Clifford backed up his own judgment by bringing together a panel of "wise men," including such respected pillars of the cold war establishment as Dean Acheson,

Harry Truman's secretary of state; Henry Cabot Lodge, a Republican and former ambassador to South Vietnam; and several distinguished retired generals. The panel told the president that his advisers had led him "down the garden path" on Vietnam. The war could not be won, and he should seek a negotiated settlement.

Meanwhile, the antiwar forces had found a political champion in Senator Eugene McCarthy from Wisconsin. McCarthy was something of a maverick in the Senate—he wrote poetry in his spare time—but he announced that no matter what the odds, he would challenge Johnson by running for the presidency. Idealistic college students, instructed to get haircuts and shaves in order to look "clean for Gene," canvassed New Hampshire voters, lining up support for the first presidential primary. Johnson had not formally entered the 1968 presidential race, but his supporters sponsored a write-in campaign, confident of a decisive win. When the votes were counted, McCarthy had lost by only 300 out of 50,000 votes cast (crossover voting allowed Republicans to vote for him). For the president, so slim a victory was a stunning defeat. It encouraged Robert Kennedy, John Kennedy's younger brother, to announce his own candidacy in opposition to the war.

"I've got to get me a peace proposal," the president told Clifford, and the White House speechwriters went to work. They finally put together an announcement that bombing raids against North Vietnam would be halted, at least partially, in hopes that peace talks could begin. They were still trying to write an ending when Johnson told them, "Don't worry; I may have a little ending of my own." On March 31 he supplied it, announcing: "I have concluded that I should not permit the presidency to become involved in the partisan divisions that are developing in this political year. . . . Accordingly I shall not seek, and I will not accept, the nomination of my party for another term as your president."

The announcement shocked Johnson's advisers and, perhaps even more, those who had opposed him for so long. The Vietnam War had pulled down one of the savviest, most effective politicians of the era. North Vietnam, for its part, responded to the speech by sending delegates to a peace conference in Paris, where negotiations quickly bogged down. And American attention soon focused on the chaotic situation at home, where all the turbulence, discontent, and violence of the 1960s seemed to be coming together.

The Shocks of 1968

On April 4 Martin Luther King, Jr., traveled to Memphis to lead a demonstration in support of striking sanitation workers. He had checked into his motel room and was relaxing on the balcony when James Earl Ray, an escaped convict, fatally shot him with a sniper's rifle. Over the years King had maintained his commitment to nonviolence, despite more militant calls for black power. But the frustration and anger that greeted news of his death could not be contained. Riots broke out that evening in ghetto areas of the nation's capital; by the end of the week, 125 more neighborhoods across the country had seen similar disturbances. Almost before Americans could recover, a disgruntled Arab nationalist, Sirhan Sirhan, assassinated Robert Kennedy on the evening of June 5. Running in opposition to the war, Kennedy had just won a crucial primary victory in California.

The deaths of King and Kennedy raised painful questions about lost possibilities in American politics. In their own ways, both men exemplified the liberal tradition, which reached its high-water mark in the 1960s. King espoused a Christian theology of nonviolence to bring about change without resorting to the lan-

Enthusiastic crowds followed Robert Kennedy on his Democratic primary campaign during the 1968 presidential election. The evening of his victory in California he was assassinated by a Palestinian refugee, Sirhan Sirhan, who later claimed he admired Kennedy.

guage of the gun. He had broadened his campaign in his final years to include the poor of all races. Robert Kennedy had begun his career as a pragmatic politician who, like his brother John, had not hesitated to use power ruthlessly. But Kennedy, like King, had a capacity to change and grow. He had come to reject the war which his brother had supported, and despite his upper-class background he seemed genuinely to sympathize with the poor and minorities. At the same time, he had a good deal of popularity among traditional white ethnics and blue-collar workers. Would the liberal political tradition have had a longer life if these two charismatic figures had survived the turbulence of the sixties?

Violence denied them the chance to answer. And with Eugene McCarthy failing to gain the support of blacks, traditional workers, or party professionals, it became clear that Lyndon Johnson's faithful vice president, Hubert Humphrey, would be the choice of the Democrats when their convention met at Chicago in August. It meant, too, that no major candidate would speak for the growing numbers of Americans disillusioned with the war and searching for ways to bring the currents of reform into the mainstream of politics. The Republicans had already chosen Richard Nixon, a traditional anticommunist (now reborn as the "new," more moderate Nixon), along with little-known conservative governor from Maryland, Spiro Agnew, for vice president. As much as radicals disliked Johnson, they had an even greater distaste for Nixon, "new" or old. And although Hubert Humphrey had begun his career as a progressive and a strong supporter of civil rights, he was now intimately associated with the war and the old-style liberal reforms that could never satisfy radicals.

Chicago, where the Democratic National Convention met, was the fiefdom of

Mayor Richard Daley, long the symbol of machine politics and backroom deals. Daley was determined that the radicals who poured into Chicago would not disrupt "his" convention, just as the radicals were equally determined that they would. For a week the police skirmished with demonstrators: police clubs, riot gear, and tear gas versus the demonstrators' eggs, rocks, and balloons filled with paint and urine. When Daley refused to allow a peaceful march past the convention site, the radicals marched anyway and, with the mayor's blessing, the police turned on the crowd in what a federal commission later labeled a police riot. In one pitched battle, many officers took off their badges and waded into the crowd, nightsticks swinging, chanting, "Kill, kill, kill." Reporters, medics, and other innocent bystanders were injured; at 3:00 a.m. police invaded candidate Eugene McCarthy's hotel headquarters and pulled some of his assistants from their beds. With feelings running so high, President Johnson did not dare to make an appearance at his own party's convention. Theodore White, a veteran journalist covering the assemblage, scribbled his verdict in a notebook as police chased hippies down Michigan Avenue. "The Democrats are finished," he wrote.

Whose Silent Majority?

Radicals were not the only Americans alienated from the political system in 1968. Governor George Wallace of Alabama sensed that the times were ripe for an appeal to disgruntled voters among the "average man on the street, this man in the textile mill, this man in the steel mill, this barber, this beautician, the policeman on the beat." In short, he sought the support of blue-collar workers and the lower middle classes. Wallace had first come to national attention as he stood at the door barring integration of the University of Alabama, and then as a feisty presidential candidate in 1964. For the race in 1968 he formed his own American Independent party and chose as his running mate the hawkish General Curtis LeMay, who spoke belligerently of the United States' ability to bomb North Vietnam "back to the stone age."

Wallace made no effort to mask his appeal to divisiveness. His enemies were the "liberals, intellectuals, and long hairs [who] have run this country for too long." He gleefully taunted the bearded protesters who came to heckle him. "You can come up here and I'll autograph your sandals," he would call, and the pro-Wallace crowd roared its support. Indeed, when security became too tight at a New York City rally, Wallace's managers secretly dispensed a number of tickets to radicals in order to provoke the desired confrontation. On the other hand, Wallace's campaign was not merely an appeal to law and order, militarism, and white backlash; he was too sharp for that. Coming out of a tradition of southern populism, he called for federal job-training programs, stronger unemployment benefits, national health insurance, a higher minimum wage, and a further extension of union rights. Polls in September revealed that many supporters of Robert Kennedy had shifted their allegiance to Wallace. A quarter of all union members backed him, compared with 32 percent for Nixon and 34 percent for Humphrey. Without the tug of party loyalties, many more workers would have defected.

In fact, Wallace had tapped true discontent among the working class. Many blue-collar workers who despised hippies and peace marchers nonetheless wanted the United States out of Vietnam. And they were suspicious, as Wallace was, of the upper-class "establishment" which held power. "We can't understand how all those rich kids—the kids with beards from the suburbs—how they got off when my son had to go over there and maybe get his head shot off," one blue-collar parent complained. Old-style radicals of the 1930s might have tried to channel and organize such discontent, but the leaders of the New Left by and large gave up on traditional workers, preferring to aim their appeal at the newer minorities: students, Hispanics, blacks, and the unorganized poor.

Who, then, would earn the votes of this shifting group of workers, white ethnic groups, and "ordinary" Americans fed up with the war? Martin Luther King and Robert Kennedy had tried to include them in a newer definition of liberal reform. George Wallace appealed to traditional populist themes and underlying racial resentment. And Richard Nixon, too, sought to bring these traditionally Democratic voters, especially disaffected southern Democrats, into the Republican party.

The Republicans, of course, had been reviled by the populists of old as representatives of the Money Power, Monopoly, and the old-line establishment. (Eisenhower's cabinet, after all, had been characterized as "eight millionaires and a plumber.") But Richard Nixon himself had modest roots. His parents owned a general store in Whittier, California, where he had worked to help the family out. His high school grades were good enough to earn him a scholarship to Harvard, but he turned it down in favor of nearby Whittier College, fearing he could not afford the cost of transportation. At Duke Law School he was so pinched for funds he lived in an abandoned toolshed, and his dogged hard work earned him the somewhat dubious nickname of "iron pants." If ever there had been a candidate who had pulled himself up by his bootstraps, Horatio Alger–style, it was Nixon. And he well understood the disdain ordinary laborers felt for "kids with the beards from the suburbs"—hippies who wore flags sewn to the seat of their pants—who seemed always to be insisting, protesting, *demanding*. Nixon believed himself a representative of the "silent majority," as he later described it, not a vocal minority.

He thus set two fundamental requirements for his campaign: to distance himself from President Johnson on Vietnam and to turn Wallace's "average Americans" into a Republican "silent majority." The Vietnam issue was delicate, because Nixon had generally supported the president's desire to end the war and his efforts to work through Soviet leaders to find a solution. He told his aide Richard

THE ELECTION OF 1968

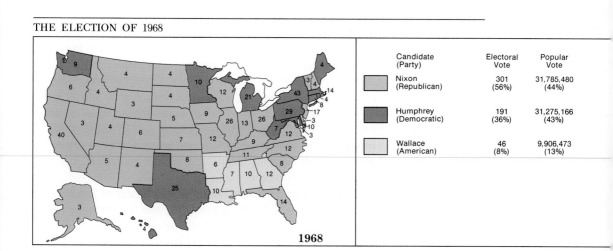

Candidate (Party)	Electoral Vote	Popular Vote
Nixon (Republican)	301 (56%)	31,785,480 (44%)
Humphrey (Democratic)	191 (36%)	31,275,166 (43%)
Wallace (American)	46 (8%)	9,906,473 (13%)

1968

Whalen, "I've come to the conclusion that there's no way to win the war. But we can't say that, of course. In fact, we have to seem to say the opposite." For most of his campaign he hinted that he had a secret plan to end the war but steadfastly refused to disclose it. He pledged only to find an honorable solution.

As for wooing his silent majority, Nixon tried to evoke "the traditional values of middle-class America," as one of his advisers explained: "hard work, individual enterprise, orderly behavior, love of country, moral piety, material progress." He also touched on their fears by promising more police to promote "law and order" while cracking down on "pot," pornography, protest, and permissiveness. He reassured Wallace's populist following that the Republicans would not dismantle the welfare state. At the same time, conservatives took heart in his pledge to unshackle "the greatest engine of progress ever developed in the history of man— American private enterprise."

While Nixon's managers worked to expose their candidate mostly through controlled television appearances, Hubert Humphrey sought to put together a campaign out of the ruins of the Chicago convention. All through September antiwar protesters dogged his trail with "Dump the Hump" posters. Finally the vice president gave a speech distancing his position on Vietnam, however slightly, from that of his unpopular boss. The protests then faded, Humphrey picked up energy, morale, and momentum, and he began appealing to traditional blue-collar Democrats to return to the fold. By November his rallies were enthusiastic and well attended. But the late surge was not enough to turn the tide. Nixon captured 43.4 percent of the popular vote to 42.7 percent for Humphrey and 13.5 percent for Wallace. More important, Nixon's "southern strategy" paid off. He and Wallace carried the entire southern tier of states except Texas. The "Solid South," which had remained in the Democratic camp since the days of Republican carpetbaggers, was solid no longer. And the majority of the American electorate seemed to have turned their back on liberal reform.

THE NIXON ERA

In Richard Nixon, Americans had elected two men to the presidency. On the public side, he appeared as the traditional small-town conservative who cherished individual initiative, Chamber-of-Commerce capitalism, Fourth-of-July patriotism, county-fair culture, and middle-class Victorian mores. At the same time, the private Nixon had worked so hard to make his Horatio Alger story come true that he often became cynical about the symbols of America in which he wrapped himself. His language among intimates was caustic and profane, and he waxed bitter toward those who crossed him. He had never taken naturally to public speaking and was physically rather awkward—a White House aide once found toothmarks on a "child-proof" aspirin cap which the president had been unable to pry open. But Nixon never shirked difficult tasks—indeed, he seemed to search them out as challenges—"crises" to face and conquer.

The new president prided himself on mastering the grand strategies and global consequences of foreign policy. A settlement of the war thus became one of his first priorities upon taking office. He had a congenial ally to work with, National Security Adviser Henry Kissinger. Kissinger at first seemed an unlikely

Nixon protégé. After fleeing Nazi Germany as a young man, he attended Harvard and became a professor there as well as an adviser to Governor Nelson Rockefeller of New York, one of the "eastern liberal" types distrusted by many main-line Republicans. But Kissinger was an intensely ambitious man. He worked for a time for Lyndon Johnson, trying to open negotiations with the North Vietnamese; and when Nixon was running for president, Kissinger secretly supplied the Republicans with information about Johnson's maneuvering. After the election he joined the new administration. Like Nixon, Kissinger strove for a global vision of foreign affairs and the use of grand strategy. Like Nixon, he had a tendency to pursue his ends secretly, circumventing the traditional bureaucracies of government such as the Department of State.

Vietnamization—and Cambodia

Nixon and Kissinger worked closely to devise a new policy for Vietnam. The president wanted to negotiate a settlement that would bring American troops home, but he wanted only "peace with honor," which meant preserving a pro-American South Vietnamese government. The strategy he adopted was "Vietnam-ization," which involved a carrot and a stick. On its own initiative, the United States began gradually withdrawing troops as a way to advance the peace talks in Paris. The burden of fighting would shift to the South Vietnamese army, equipped now with massive amounts of American supplies. Although to critics this strategy meant little more than "changing the color of the corpses," it helped reduce anti-war protests at home. At the same time the media shifted their focus from the war to the peace talks, thus creating the impression the war was winding down.

Using the stick, President Nixon hoped to drive the North Vietnamese into negotiating peace on American terms. Quite consciously, he traded on his reputation as a cold warrior who would stop at nothing to win. As he explained to his chief of staff Robert Haldeman,

> I call it the Madman Theory, Bob. I want the North Vietnamese to believe that I've reached the point where I might do anything to stop the war. We'll just slip the word to them that, "for God's sake, you know Nixon is obsessed about Communists. We can't restrain him when he's angry—and he has his hand on the nuclear button"—and Ho Chi Minh himself will be in Paris in two days begging for peace.

To underline his point, Nixon launched a series of bombing attacks in the spring of 1969 against North Vietnamese supply depots inside neighboring Cambodia. Johnson had refused to widen the war in this manner, fearing domestic reaction, but Nixon simply kept the raids secret. Over the next 15 months some 100,000 pounds of bombs were dropped in Operation MENU, whose various sorties, in the strange lingo of the Pentagon, were code-named BREAKFAST, LUNCH, SNACK, and DESSERT.

But the North Vietnamese were willing to risk the additional bombing and the threats of the "Madman." Even after Ho Chi Minh died in 1969, his successors continued to reject any offer that did not end with complete American withdrawal and an abandonment of the South Vietnamese military government. And as American bombing raids forced the VC to push deeper into Cambodia, that country became less stable under its neutral government of Prince Sihanouk. Right-wing forces under General Lon Nol overthrew Sihanouk, and a civil war between the communists and the generals ensued.

Once again Nixon decided to turn up the heat. Although his secretaries of defense and state were opposed, he ordered a ground invasion of Cambodia by American troops in order to wipe out North Vietnamese bases there. This, to be sure, was Johnson's old policy of escalation—just the opposite of the withdrawal Nixon had promised. But the Joint Chiefs argued that such an attack would buy time to strengthen the South Vietnamese army, and Nixon decided there would be no point in taking half-measures. He recognized the storm of protest that would arise (the administration was "going to get unshirted hell for doing this," he noted) but decided to "go for all the marbles." On April 30 he announced the "incursion" of American troops into Cambodia, proclaiming that he would not allow "the world's most powerful nation" to act "like a pitiful helpless giant." The wave of protests that followed included the Kent State tragedy as well as another march on Washington by 100,000 protesters. Even Congress was upset enough to repeal the Tonkin Gulf Resolution, a symbolic rejection of Nixon's invasion. After two months American troops left Cambodia, having achieved little.

Morale in a No-Win War

For a time, Vietnamization seemed to be making some headway. More American troops were sent home while the South Vietnamese forces' ability to fight improved modestly. But morale became a serious problem for American GIs. Until the Tet offensive American troops had fought well, however frustrating the conditions of battle. But Tet made it all too clear that the United States was not simply engaged in a "mopping up" operation. The American troops who remained during Vietnamization tended to become more cynical. Obviously the United States was getting out, so why were they still being asked to put their lives on the line? When overly eager officers led their men into battle too often, frustrated GIs became hostile. Fred Hickey, a helicopter pilot, recalled that the men under one arrogant and incompetent lieutenant

> booby-trapped his hooch with a smoke grenade, yellow smoke, which was a warning. But he didn't take any heed. Then they tried another, red smoke, which said the next one was going to be a hand grenade or a white phosphorus grenade. He obviously didn't believe it. The last one was a hand grenade, and he was eliminated and replaced. Grenades leave no fingerprints. Nobody's going to go to jail.

Reports of such "fraggings"—incidents involving fragmentation grenades—rose to over 2000 during the Vietnamization process.

In addition, the same forces that troubled American society were eroding the army's fighting effectiveness. At a time when Timothy Leary was inviting young Americans to "turn on" to marijuana and hallucinogens, the drug culture affected Americans in Vietnam as well. The Pentagon estimated that by 1971 nearly a third of American troops there had experimented with either opium or heroin, easily obtained in Southeast Asia. And just as the civil rights movement sparked increased black consciousness at home, so too abroad. Robert Rawls, a black GI, recalled that his friends "used to make a shoestring that they braided up and tied around their wrist, and everywhere a whole lot of blacks used to go, they'd give a power sign." One white medic noticed that Muhammad Ali's refusal to be drafted had a noticeable effect on the blacks in his unit. They began "to question why they were fighting the Honky's war against other Third World people. I saw very interesting relationships happening between your quick-talking, sharp-witted Northern blacks and your kind of easygoing, laid-back Southern blacks. . . . Many Southern blacks changed their entire point of view by the end of their tour and went home extremely angry."

The problem with morale only underlined the dilemma facing President Nixon. If the troops had become restive, domestic opposition to the war was even greater. By repealing the Gulf of Tonkin Resolution, Congress itself had put the president on notice that he would have to negotiate a settlement soon. Yet the North Vietnamese refused to yield, even after the American assaults in Cambodia.

The Move Toward Détente

As the daily situation reports came in from Vietnam, Nixon attempted to keep the war within a larger global perspective. The United States had a vast—but not limitless—defense arsenal to support the fighting. Committing half a million troops and billions of dollars to Vietnam meant that other resources were stretched. Both Kissinger and Nixon recognized that the United States no longer had the strength to exercise unchallenged dominance across the globe. The Soviets, for one, had undertaken a steady build-up of arms and missiles ever since Khrushchev had backed down at the Cuban missile crisis in 1962. Furthermore, the expanding economies of Japan and Western Europe challenged the dominance in world trade that had benefited the United States following World War II. Continued instability in Southeast Asia, the Middle East, and other Third World areas threatened the strength of the non-Communist bloc. Thus Vietnam had become a bottomless pit consuming valuable military and economic resources.

In what the White House labeled the new "Nixon Doctrine," the United States announced it would no longer expect to fight every battle, win every war, or draw every line to keep the global peace. Instead, Americans would shift some of the military burden for containment to such allies as Japan in the Pacific, the Shah of Iran in the Middle East, Zaire in central Africa, and the apartheid government in South Africa. Over the next six years American foreign military sales jumped from $1.8 billion to $15.2 billion. At the same time, Nixon and Kissinger looked for new ways to contain Soviet power not simply by the traditional threat of arms but through a negotiated easing of tensions. The United States would agree to ease the burdens the cold war placed on the Soviet economy if the Soviets would limit the arms race and put pressure on their Vietnamese allies to negotiate an end to the war. The name of the policy, borrowed from the French, was détente. Kissinger and Nixon also hoped to check Soviet power by playing what they called a "China card." Rather than view Mao Tse-tung as an archenemy, they would open diplomatic relations with the Chinese. By playing on deep-seated Soviet fears of their neighbor, they would force the Soviets to be more conciliatory toward the United States.

The strategy of détente was a remarkable departure from traditional cold war policy, which had long maintained that the Soviets understood force alone and that they were united with China in a monolithic Communist conspiracy. Indeed, although the Soviets had attended a brief summit meeting with Lyndon Johnson in 1967, the new regime of Leonid Brezhnev seemed hardly eager for reform. Nikita Khrushchev had attacked Stalin's excesses, but Brezhnev seemed very

Richard Nixon and Soviet Premier Leonid Brezhnev relax at Brezhnev's dacha on the Black Sea, during a June 1974 summit. For all their differences, the staunch anticommunist and the Soviet bureaucrat were both shrewd, even cynical judges of political power and human nature. Both regarded détente as in their mutual interest.

much in the mold of an old-style Stalinist bureaucrat. In 1968 he had sent Soviet troops into Czechoslovakia to crack down on the more liberal Communist government there. As for the Chinese, beginning in 1966 Mao had led his followers on a "cultural revolution," systematically eradicating all Western influence from China. The Cultural Revolution unleashed a virtual reign of terror at the hands of millions of youthful "Red Guards." Their victims were largely cultural and political figures stigmatized as "capitalist roaders," those who would use capitalist means to promote economic growth. Republicans in particular had regularly denounced the idea of even recognizing Mao's government, although it had been in power for 20 years. Now Richard Nixon, the man who had built a career fighting Communism, was embarked on a policy that broke dramatically with his past.

Characteristically, he and Kissinger moved secretly at first. Quiet talks in Poland between the Chinese and American ambassadors established a bridge, and in 1971 the Chinese indicated they would welcome a vist from an American Ping-Pong team. Since the Chinese were among the world's best Ping-Pong players and the Americans among the worst, bracing athletic competition was clearly not the point. Then in July Henry Kissinger disappeared from public view while visiting Pakistan—nursing a stomachache, according to his aides. A day later he surfaced in Beijing, the Chinese capital, to announce that the president would visit China in early 1972. Nixon's visit lasted nearly a week. He pledged to normalize relations; this included recognizing China's claims on Taiwan as an internal matter, which outraged Chiang Kai-shek, who still controlled the so-called nationalist regime there. Conservative Republicans were irritated, but the president's popularity with the public was high. Only a politician with Nixon's impeccable anticommunist credentials could have managed such an about-face in American foreign policy.

The trip to China was followed by another diplomatic coup, a summit visit to Moscow in May 1972. Brezhnev, troubled by food shortages and a weak consumer economy, was eager to strike a deal for United States grain and technology; for Nixon the Soviet market promised to ease American trade deficits and crop surpluses. The two leaders struck a major wheat deal, but the most important benefit of the meeting was the signing of the first Strategic Arms Limitation Treaty (SALT I). In the agreement, both sides pledged not to develop a new system of antiballistic missiles (ABMs), which would have sparked a costly arms race for both countries. And they agreed to limit the number of intercontinental ballistic missiles (ICBMs) each side would deploy.

Both the China and Moscow visits strengthened Nixon's reputation as a global strategist. But it remained to be seen whether the prestige he gained at lofty summits would help him extricate the United States from Vietnam as well as surmount the domestic divisions the war had raised at home. On those fronts, the president proved less successful.

The New Federalist

As a Republican, Nixon was skeptical of the liberal reliance on federal planning and he looked for ways to decentralize government social policy. "After a third of a century of power flowing from the people and the states to Washington," he argued, "it is time for a New Federalism in which power, funds, and responsibility will flow from Washington to the states and to the people." To accomplish this, he proposed a system of revenue-sharing, where federal money was turned over in block grants to state and local governments. Instead of earmarking the funds for specific purposes, localities could decide which problems needed attention and how best to attack them. Congress passed a revenue-sharing act in 1972, which distributed $30 billion over the following five years.

A similar approach influenced aid to individuals. Liberal programs from Franklin Roosevelt to Lyndon Johnson often provided specific services to individuals: job retraining programs, head-start programs for preschoolers, food supplement programs for nursing mothers. Republicans argued that such a "service strategy" too often assumed that federal bureaucrats best understood what services the poor needed. Nixon favored an "income strategy" instead, which simply gave recipients money and allowed them to spend it as they saw fit. Such grants would encourage individual initiatives, increase personal freedom, and reduce government bureaucracy.

In this spirit Nixon encouraged a renegade liberal academic, Daniel Patrick Moynihan, to develop a program favored by conservatives to reduce the welfare bureaucracy while increasing the incentive for those receiving welfare to find jobs. Moynihan had earlier completed a study which argued that harsh urban conditions and welfare programs had contributed to a serious erosion of the black family. Since the current welfare system favored poor families headed by single females over those with two parents, it sometimes drove fathers away. Moreover, Moynihan was convinced that existing federal programs and civil rights efforts had raised the black standard of living high enough so that further welfare legislation was unnecessary.

He proposed instead a government policy of "benign neglect" and the replacement of the welfare system with a new "Family Assistance Plan." Rather than go through the demeaning welfare process of demonstrating need to unsympathetic bureaucrats, poor families would be guaranteed a minimum annual income of $1600. The emphasis on family would encourage fathers to stay at home. The plan also required recipients to register for employment to satisfy conservative critics who usually envisioned all welfare recipients as able-bodied workers addicted to handouts and too lazy to work. Though Moynihan's proposals died in Congress, they defined the general terms in which poverty and assistance to the poor would be debated in the future.

In the polarized atmosphere of the Vietnam era, Nixon's "new federalism" provoked sharp dissent. Critics feared that if local governments did not have to raise money from local voters, they would have little incentive to spend tax money wisely. In addition, "block grants" would be parceled out to rich and poor districts alike. Why subsidize wealthy suburbs at the expense of underprivileged slums? Furthermore, grants to individuals did not address structural problems in society. A "no-strings-attached" check given to a family whose children needed a good education was of little help if the schools in the area were run-down and inadequate.

In any case, the administration's new federalism was a matter of emphasis, for the new Nixon supported many New Deal–style social programs. In 1970 he signed a bill establishing an Occupational Safety and Health Agency (OSHA) to enforce health and safety standards in the workplace. And although the president was no crusader for the environment, he did support a Clean Air Act to reduce car exhaust emissions as well as a Clean Water Act to make polluters liable for their negligence and to deal with disastrous oil spills. Just as Nixon's pragmatic style allowed him to change course in foreign policy, so too he made accommodations in domestic affairs.

Indeed, the worsening economy stretched his pragmatism even further, for by 1970 the nation had entered its first recession in a decade. Traditionally a recession brought a decrease in demand for goods and a rise in unemployment as workers were laid off. Manufacturers then cut wages and prices in order to preserve profit margins and encourage demand for their goods. But in the recession of 1970, while unemployment rose as expected, wages and prices were also rising in an inflationary spiral. Foreign trade surpluses turned into deficits. Americans were getting the worst of two worlds: a stagnant economy combined with rising prices—or "stagflation." Unfriendly Democrats labeled the phenomenon "Nixonomics," in which "all things that should go up—the stock market, corporate profits, real spendable income, productivity—go down, and all things that should go down—unemployment, prices, interest rates—go up."

But to charge the president with the failings of the economy was hardly fair. Lyndon Johnson had brought on inflation by refusing to raise taxes to pay for the war and Great Society social programs. In addition, wages continued their inflationary rise partly because powerful unions had negotiated automatic cost-of-living increases into their contracts. Similarly, in industries dominated by a few large corporations, like steel and oil, prices did not follow the market forces of a recession. So prices and wages continued to rise as demand and employment fell.

At first Nixon responded by cutting federal spending, hoping that inflation would slow even if unemployment continued to rise. But by December unemployment had risen to 6 percent and so had inflation—the worst level since the Korean War. Interest rates were at their highest point in a century. Mindful that his own "silent majority" were the people most pinched by the slower economy, Nixon decided that unemployment posed a greater threat than inflation. Announcing "I am now a Keynesian," he adopted a deficit budget designed to stimulate the growth of jobs. He announced an even more surprising piece of news in August 1971: to provide short-term relief, wages and prices would be frozen for 90 days. For a Republican to advocate federal wage and price controls was almost as heretical as seeking to establish diplomatic relations with China. Yet Nixon did not hesitate. For another year federal wage and price boards enforced the ground rules for any increases; most controls were lifted in January 1973. Nixon also devalued the dollar in order to reverse the foreign trade deficit. Cheaper dollars raised the price of imports like the popular Volkswagen Beetle and made American exports more competitive in foreign markets.

By the fall of 1972 the economy was again booming. As in foreign policy, Nixon had reversed long-cherished economic policies to achieve practical results.

"SILENT" MAJORITIES AND VOCAL MINORITIES

During the 1968 campaign Richard Nixon had noticed a placard carried by a hopeful voter—"Bring Us Together"—and adopted it as his campaign theme. Yet of necessity political coalitions cannot bring everyone together. Their goal is simply to assemble a majority on election day. Nixon recognized quite well that in the three-way race of 1968, his 43 percent did not add up to a majority. But when Wallace's vote was added, the total came to an impressive 60 percent. Nixon set out to add discontented southerners and blue-collar workers to the traditional GOP base. In doing so, he tried to identify them with the "silent majority," at the same time excluding other vocal minorities who had been actively campaigning for increased civil rights. The black movement had received the most national attention during the mid-1960s, but other minorities also adopted more radical tactics to achieve their ends. Their new, more assertive visibility was crucial to Nixon's attempt to form his own counter-majority.

Hispanic Activism

Outside the southwestern states, southeastern Florida, and New York City few Americans prior to the 1960s and 1970s had much contact with the nation's Hispanic population. The major immigration from Mexico and Puerto Rico began only after World War II and, in the case of Cubans, after the 1959 revolution that brought Castro to power. While historical, cultural, ethnic, and geographic differences among the three major Hispanic groups made it difficult to develop a common political agenda, activist leaders did seek greater Hispanic unity.

The acquisition of Puerto Rico in 1898 gave the United States control over an island population of one million people, whose diverse mixture of classes and races resulted from the intermarriage of African, Indian, and Spanish peoples. Their political status remained uncertain until 1947, when the island acquired a new constitution. Puerto Rico became neither a state nor an independent nation, but a commonwealth. Island people were defined as U.S. citizens subject to the draft, free from federal income taxes, and ineligible for benefits under federal social service programs.

After World War II a weak island economy and the lure of prosperity on the mainland brought over a million Puerto Ricans into New York City. As citizens of the United States, they could move freely to the mainland and back home again. That dual consciousness discouraged many from establishing deep roots stateside. Equally important, the newcomers were startled to discover that, whatever their

Cesar Chavez mobilized the largely Hispanic migrant workers into the United Farm Workers Union. His demands for recognition of the union by California growers led to a bitter
strike in 1966. A call for boycotts in 1969 against grapes and lettuce gained Chavez and the
union national attention. In July 1970, after five years of conflict, the growers agreed to
recognize the union.

status at home, on the mainland they were subject to racial discrimination and
most often segregated into rundown urban slums. Approximately half of the recent
immigrants lived below the poverty level in 1964, according to the Puerto Rican
Forum, and their unemployment was three times greater than for whites and 50
percent higher than for blacks. When light-skinned migrants escaped those conditions by blending into the middle class as "Latin Americans," the Puerto Rican
community lost some of the leadership it needed to assert its political rights. Still,
a shared island orientation preserved a strong group identity. By the 1960s, the
urban *barrios* gained greater political consciousness as groups like "Aspira"
adopted the strategies of civil rights activists and organizations like the Black and
Puerto Rican Caucus created links with other minority groups.

The Cubans who arrived in the United States after 1959—some 350,000 over
the course of the decade—forged fewer ties with other Hispanics. Most settled
around Miami. An unusually large number came from Cuba's professional, business, and government class, were racially white and politically conservative. Mexican-Americans, on the other hand, constituted the largest segment of the Hispanic population. Until the 1940s most were farmers and farm laborers in Texas,

New Mexico, and California. But during the 1950s, the process of mechanization had affected them, just as it had southern blacks. By 1969 about 85 percent of Mexican-Americans had settled in cities. With urbanization came a slow improvement of the range and quality of jobs they held. A body of skilled workers, middle class professionals, and entrepreneurs emerged.

In 1960, frustrated by years of neglect by major parties, Hispanic political leaders from the region formed the Mexican-American Political Association. MAPA declared its intent to be "proudly Mexican American, *openly* political, and *necessarily* bipartisan." By 1964 four Mexican-Americans had been elected to Congress, but the growing activism across the nation altered traditional Hispanic approaches to politics. Younger Mexican-Americans began to call themselves Chicanos. In 1965 Cesar Chavez gained national attention by his efforts to organize migrant laborers into the United Farm Workers and lead them in *La Huelga*—The Strike—as they struck farm growers and set in motion a national boycott of California lettuce and grapes. Corky Gonzales, a Denver social worker, established *La Crusada Para Justicia* (Crusade for Justice) to support strikes by Chicano high school students, protest police brutality, and oppose the Vietnam War. The more militant Reies Tijerina and his supporters in New Mexico occupied the Kit Carson National Forest to dramatize disputes over old Spanish land titles.

By the late 1960s Mexican-Americans had clearly established an ethnic consciousness and a movement. Like blacks, Chicanos saw themselves as a deculturated people: their heritage rejected, their labor exploited, their opportunity for advancement denied. The new ethnic militancy led to the formation of *La Raza Unida* (The Race United), a third-party movement which sought to gain power in communities where Chicanos were a majority and to extract concessions from the Democrats and Republicans. The more militant "Brown Berets" adopted the paramilitary tactics and radical rhetoric of the Black Panthers.

The Choices of Native Americans

Like blacks and Hispanics, Indians resorted to the strategies of protest and demonstration; yet the unique situation of Native Americans (as many now called themselves) set them apart from other minorities. Despite a largely hostile white culture that had most often worked either to exterminate or assimilate, the traditions and identities of American Indians survived through their tribes, bands, villages, and other kin associations. From a low in population of only 250,000 in 1920, Native Americans grew steadily to around 800,000 by 1970. Leaders of Indian tribal councils, many of them World War II veterans, pressed for expanded civil rights; and in 1948 the Supreme Court required states to grant Indians the right to vote (*Trujillo v. Garley*).

But the growing pressures for civil rights that inspired that decision created another threat to Indian tribal identities. Liberals came to see the reservations not as oases of Indian culture, but as rural ghettos. During the 1950s they joined conservatives eager to repeal the New Deal and western state politicians eyeing tribal resources to adopt a policy of "termination." Under this approach, the Bureau of Indian Affairs would reduce federal services, gradually sell off tribal lands, and push Indians into the "mainstream" of American life. Although most full-blood Indians objected to the policy, some mixed bloods and Indians already assimilated into white society supported the move. The resulting relocation of approximately 35,000 Native Americans accelerated a shift of Indian population from rural areas to cities. The urban population, which had been barely 30,000 in 1940, reached over 300,000 by the 1970s. But the tribal cultures that emphasized communal sharing had not prepared most Indians to deal with regular wage employment, budgeting, the need for personal savings, or an adversary legal system. Less than 10 percent of those relocated in the 1950s found permanent jobs. Unemployment translated into poverty, which in turn led to unusually high levels of disease, alcoholism, and other signs of social disintegration.

The social activism of the 1960s inspired Indian leaders to shape a new political agenda. Tribes in the state of Washington held "fish-ins" to protest restrictions on their fishing rights. In 1968 urban activists in Minneapolis created AIM, the American Indian Movement, and a year later similarly minded Indians living in the San Francisco Bay area formed Indians of All Tribes. Because the Bureau of Indian Affairs refused to address the problems of urban Indians, more militant members of the organization dramatized their dissatisfaction by seizing the abandoned federal prison on Alcatraz Island in San Francisco Bay.

The Alcatraz action inspired a national push for Indian rights, and a determination to join in a pan-Indian movement. Richard Oakes, a Mohawk Indian from New York, declared that the Alcatraz protest was not "a movement to liberate the island, but to liberate ourselves." Then in 1973, AIM organizers Russell Means and Dennis Banks led a dramatic takeover of a trading post at Wounded Knee, on a Sioux reservation in South Dakota. Ever since white cavalry had gunned down more than 200 Sioux in 1890 (page 743), Wounded Knee had symbolized for Indians the betrayal of white promises and the bankruptcy of reservation policy.

At the same time, the Wounded Knee incident demonstrated the problems that Indian activists faced. When federal officers surrounded the trading post, militants discovered that other Indians did not support their tactics, and they were forced to leave. A pan-Indian movement was difficult to achieve when so many tribes were determined to go their own ways, as distinct, self-regulating communities. Less activist tribes often already commanded substantial resources, gained from exploiting oil, timber or mineral rights that went with their lands. Other tribes, like the Penobscot and Passamaquoddy Indians of Maine, turned to the courts to recover land that had been given them in long-ignored treaties. Thus even activists who supported the pan-Indian movement found themselves splintering. During the 1970s over 100 different organizations were formed to unite various tribes pursuing political and legal agendas at the local, state, and federal level.

Social Policies and the Court

The militance of Indian, Hispanic, and black protesters alarmed many of the "silent majority" Nixon hoped to attract to an expanded Republican coalition. The blue-collar and southern Democratic voters he sought to detach distrusted the entire activist counterculture: long-haired demonstrators, drug-users, sexually permissive radicals. In addition, Wallace supporters had been particularly vocal in opposing school desegregation. Nixon capitalized on the themes of law and order in his 1968 campaign and, increasingly, turned his attention to finding an ally in the Supreme Court.

Fifteen years after *Brown v. Board of Education* had ruled that racially separate school systems must be desegregated, many localities still had not complied. Busing was one method of achieving racial balance, but it aroused determined opposition from white neighborhoods, where parents resented their children being bused away from their neighborhood to more distant, formerly all-black schools. For their part, blacks worried about their reception in hostile white neighborhoods, but by and large they supported busing as a means to better education. President Nixon, however, became an outspoken critic of busing and in 1969, when lawyers for Mississippi asked the Supreme Court to delay an integration plan, the Justice Department filed a brief supporting the state. Federal policy had taken a 180-degree turn. The Court rejected that proposal, holding in *United States v. Jefferson County Board of Education* that all state systems, including Mississippi's, had an obligation "to terminate dual systems at once and to operate now and hereafter only unitary schools." Two years later, in *Swann v. Charlotte–Mecklenburg Board of Education* (1971), the Court further ruled that busing, balancing ratios, and redrawing of school district lines were all acceptable ways to achieve integration.

Such decisions indicated that even though Earl Warren had retired as Chief Justice in 1969, the Court was still a force for liberal social policy. Nixon resolved to change that by filling vacancies in the court with more conservative justices. As Earl Warren's replacement as Chief Justice, he nominated Warren Burger, a somewhat lackluster jurist who accepted most of the Court's precedents but had no wish to break new ground. When another vacancy occurred in 1969, Nixon tried twice to appoint conservative southern judges. But both nominees, Clement Haynsworth of South Carolina and G. Harrold Carswell of Florida, had reputations on the federal bench for opposing civil rights and labor unions. Although Haynsworth was an able jurist, he had heard cases in which he had a financial stake. By contrast, Carswell was so undistinguished that one of his defenders, Senator Roman Hruska of Nebraska, was reduced to arguing that the quality of mediocrity deserved "a little representation" on the Court. Congress rejected both.

In the end, Nixon succeeded with Minnesotan Harry Blackmun, a moderate judge of unimpeachable integrity. In 1971 he made two additional appointments: Lewis Powell, a highly regarded Virginia lawyer, and William Rehnquist of Arizona, an extremely conservative attorney who had supported the efforts of the Nixon Justice Department to restrict civil rights and civil liberties. With the successive appointments of Burger, Blackmun, Powell, and Rehnquist, the Court would no longer lead the fight for minority rights. But neither would it reverse the achievements of the Warren Court.

Us versus Them

Shaping the Supreme Court was only one element of Nixon's strategy to fashion a silent majority out of the turmoil of the sixties. He also worked to portray those who opposed him—opponents of the incursion into Cambodia, civil rights activists, liberal Democrats—as standing beyond the bounds of traditional American values. Just as Nixon had tended to equate liberal reformers with communist "pinkos" during the 1950s, now his administration blurred the lines between honest dissent and radical criminals. And in doing so, it reflected a side of the president that tended to see issues in terms of "'us' against 'them,'" as loyal aide

Charles Colson later recalled. Nixon's reaction to Congress when it repealed the Tonkin Gulf Resolution reflected that attitude. There would be no more "screwing around" with Congress, he told his staff. "Don't worry about divisiveness. Having drawn the sword, don't take it out—stick it in hard."

Under Attorney General John Mitchell, the Justice Department launched a systematic campaign against radicals and civil rights activists. The strategy went beyond public denunciations to harassment through legal prosecution. Targets included Vietnam Veterans Against the War, the leaders of demonstrations during the 1968 Democratic convention, socially-conscious members of the Catholic clergy, the Black Panthers, SDS activists, and leaders of the peace movement like Yale chaplain William Sloane Coffin and Dr. Benjamin Spock. Even when Mitchell's department lacked a strong case, it prosecuted anyway, hoping to force dissenters to commit their limited resources to staying out of jail rather than furthering their causes. Meanwhile, in its war against drug users, the administration proposed a bill that would allow police to stage "no-knock" raids and use "preventive detention" to keep suspected criminals in jail without bail. It also lobbied for permission to make greater use of phone taps and other means of electronic surveillance.

In the political arena, Nixon gave Vice President Spiro Agnew the task of traveling the low road, just as Nixon himself had been appointed "point man" during the Eisenhower administration. Aided by speechwriter William Safire, Agnew launched such alliterative assaults as his description of the press and television news commentators as "nattering nabobs of negativism" and "troubadours of trouble" who contributed to the "creeping permissiveness that afflicted America." He reduced antiwar demonstrators to "an effete corps of impudent snobs." Even opponents in the Senate were accused of being "radical liberals." As Agnew's attacks continued, it became clear that his speeches were part of an administration campaign to control or discredit the news media. In the campaign between "us" and "them," the national press corps was clearly seen as "them," a hostile establishment slanting the news. Agnew pointedly reminded the networks that broadcast licenses were subject to public review; to drive the point home, the administration challenged the renewals of two Florida stations owned by the Washington *Post*, a paper critical of the administration.

Triumph

As the election of 1972 approached, Nixon's majority seemed to be falling into place. George Wallace had returned to the Democratic party to run for president, his tone this time a bit more moderate. But at a shopping mall in Maryland a would-be assassin with no evident political motives seriously wounded Wallace and ended his campaign. Some of his support might have gone to Senator Edmund Muskie of Maine, a Democratic moderate who had been a dignified vice-presidential nominee in 1968. But then New Hampshire's largest newspaper, the Manchester *Union-Leader*, printed a letter charging Muskie with disparaging the large French-Canadian population there. When the newspaper's right-wing publisher, William Loeb, added his own slurs about Muskie's wife, the candidate made an impassioned defense, in which tears filled his eyes. And political etiquette damned any man who broke down and cried before the television cameras. Only later was it discovered that the offending letter had been planted by a staff member of the Nixon administration in charge of campaign "dirty tricks."

With Muskie and Wallace effectively out of the race, the antiwar candidacy of Senator George McGovern of South Dakota became unstoppable. Under new party rules, which McGovern had helped write, the delegate selection process was opened to all party members, providing proportional representation for minorities, women, and young people. No longer would party bosses hand-pick the delegates. But with McGovern receiving the nomination, Nixon had his split between "us" and "them" arranged just the way he had hoped. The Democratic platform called for immediate withdrawal from Vietnam, abolition of the draft, amnesty for war resisters, and a minimun guaranteed income for the poor. None of those issues appealed to the traditional New Deal coalition of urban bosses, southerners, labor leaders, and ethnics.

By November the only question was how large Nixon's majority would be. An unsolved burglary at the Watergate complex in Washington, D.C., while vaguely linked to the White House, had not touched the president. He even captured some antiwar sentiment by announcing on election eve that peace in Vietnam was at hand. When the smoke cleared, only liberal Massachusetts and the heavily black District of Columbia gave McGovern a majority. Nixon received almost 61 percent of the popular vote and an impressive 520 out of 538 electoral votes. His biggest gains came among disaffected Democrats in the South and among blue-collar workers. Yet on closer analysis, the smashing victory seemed more a rejection of McGovern than approval of administration policies. In the races for the Senate and governorships the Democrats actually made gains, while losing only 13 House seats. As one pollster concluded, "Richard Nixon's 'new American majority' was the creation of George McGovern."

Victory by a wide margin did not leave the president satisfied. The day after the election, he shocked his White House staff by briefly thanking them for their efforts and then making way for chief of staff H. R. Haldeman, who announced that all cabinet members and senior staff would be required to submit formal letters of resignation so that the president would have the option of "cleaning house." His intentions toward his political opponents were even more ominous. "We have not used the power in the first four years, as you know," he remarked to Haldeman during the campaign. "We haven't used the Bureau [FBI] and we haven't used the Justice Department, but things are going to change now. And they *are* going to change and they're going to get it, right?" Haldeman could only agree.

The End of an Era

The president was particularly frustrated because victory still eluded him in Vietnam. Campus protests had subsided after the furor over Cambodia, partly because only 39,000 American troops remained in Vietnam. But the North Vietnamese refused to negotiate any settlement that left the South Vietnamese government of General Nguyen Van Thieu in power. Nixon wanted to subdue his opponents through force, but sending new American reinforcements was out of the question. To step up the pressure he ordered Haiphong harbor mined and blockaded in May 1972, along with a sustained bombing campaign. "The bastards have never been bombed like they're going to be bombed this time," he told one aide. Despite his preelection peace claims, Nixon on December 18 launched an even greater wave of attacks, as American planes dropped more bombs on the North in 12 days than they had during the entire campaign from 1969 to 1971.

Once again, Kissinger returned to Paris, hoping that the combination of threats and conciliation would bring a settlement. Ironically the Americans' ally, General Thieu, threw up the most stumbling blocks, for he was rightly convinced that his regime would not last long once the United States departed. But in January 1973 a treaty was finally arranged, smoothed by Kissinger's promise of aid to the North Vietnamese to help in postwar reconstruction, as well as a secret pledge to Thieu to send troops again if they were needed. By March the last American units were home.

"The enemy must fight his battles . . . [in] protracted campaigns," wrote the Vietnamese strategist in 1284. Ho Chi Minh had taken 8 years to outlast the French and had seen another 15 elapse before he died in 1969 on the way to outlasting the Americans. For all concerned it had been a bloody, wearying conflict. Between 1961 and 1973 the war claimed some 58,000 American lives and left over 300,000 wounded. The cost to Southeast Asia in lives and destruction was almost impossible to calculate. Over a million Vietnamese soldiers and perhaps half a million civilians died. Some 6.5 million South Vietnamese became refugees along with 3 million Cambodians and Laotians.

When the Americans pulled out, they left behind the shell of a mighty military complex. On paper, South Vietnam had the world's fourth largest air force, but probably no more than 10 percent of its planes and helicopters could actually fly. On paper, Nixon achieved the "peace with honor" he had insisted on, but experienced observers predicted that South Vietnam's days were numbered. By any real measure of military success the Vietcong peasant guerrillas and their lightly armed North Vietnamese allies had held off—and in that sense defeated— the world's greatest military power.

For most Americans the lessons of Vietnam were painful. In fundamental ways, the era of optimism rising out of World War II had ended. In those first heady postwar days, the United States had emerged as one of the two preeminent superpowers of the world, embarked on a policy of containment wherever it was needed. Truman had set the policy by becoming a feisty anticommunist; Richard Nixon had begun his political career by attacking Truman for not being tough enough. Yet it was Nixon, in the end, who was pragmatic enough to see that the United States did not have inexhaustible military resources to contain communism everywhere. Sometimes the United States would have to tolerate neutralism and the forces of nationalism. Nixon's policy of détente, based on the rivalry between the Soviet Union and the People's Republic of China, clearly recognized that communism was not monolithic. The enemy too had its divisions and limits.

The scars of Vietnam affected more than just the nation's ability to fight a far-flung guerrilla war. It shattered the liberal optimism of the early sixties: the belief that with enough brilliant intellectuals or enough federal programs, poverty and discontent could be eliminated and the world made safe for democracy. Vietnam was John Kennedy's war as well as Richard Nixon's; and Vietnam brought the reforms of Lyndon Johnson to a halt. Johnson had seen himself as the rightful heir to the liberal Roosevelt, his Great Society a capstone of the New Deal. Like Roosevelt, he had gone to war determined not only to win it, but to triumph over his critics at home, who seemed not to understand his liberal hopes. He died on January 22, 1973, not far from his Texas ranch, one day before the American war in Vietnam ended.

SIGNIFICANT EVENTS

1945 — Ho Chi Minh unifies Vietnam

1947 — Puerto Rico given commonwealth status

1948 — *Trujillo v. Garley*

1954 — French defeat at Dien Bien Phu; Geneva accords

1963 — Diem assassinated; United States has 16,000 "advisers" in Vietnam

1964 — Tonkin Gulf incident; Tonkin Gulf Resolution

1965 — Rolling Thunder begins bombing of North Vietnam; antiwar "teach-ins" on college campuses; Cesar Chavez leads national campaign on behalf of farm workers

1967 — March on the Pentagon; Johnson's advisers oppose war

1968 — U.S. troop levels in Vietnam peak at 536,000; Tet offensive; My Lai massacre; peace talks begin in Paris; Eugene McCarthy challenges Johnson in New Hampshire primary; Johnson withdraws from race; Martin Luther King, Jr., assassinated; Robert Kennedy enters race and is assassinated; riots at Democratic Convention in Chicago; George Wallace candidacy; Nixon wins election

1969 — Secret bombing of Cambodia; Vietnamization leads to reduction of American forces; Nixon Doctrine; Senate defeats Haynsworth and Carswell nominations

1970 — U.S. troops invade Cambodia; killings at Kent State and Jackson State; march on Washington; Clean Air and Water acts; creation of OSHA; recession creates stagflation; repeal of Tonkin Gulf Resolution

1971 — Nixon adopts wage and price controls; *Swann v. Charlotte–Mecklenburg Board of Education;* Pentagon Papers published

1972 — Nixon trip to China; détente with Soviet Union; SALT I; Revenue Sharing Act; Watergate break-in; Nixon reelected; mining of Haiphong Harbor; Christmas bombings of North Vietnam

1973 — Vietnam peace treaty; AIM supporters occupy Wounded Knee

34

The Age of Limits

n July 1969 newsmen, diplomats, and celebrities from around the world converged on Cape Kennedy to witness the launching of *Apollo 11*, the first
manned space flight to the moon. With them came tens of thousands of the
curious and a handful of protestors, including a mule-cart procession led by
the Reverend Ralph Abernathy, whose Poor People's March hoped to dramatize
the problem of poverty. Abernathy, however, was so overwhelmed by the *Saturn
5's* thunderous ignition and fiery rocket blast that he prayed instead for the safety
of the crew. The emotion of the drama caught him up just as it did the millions of
Americans who, days later, celebrated when Armstrong and Aldrin walked across
a lunar landscape.

President Nixon called the flight of *Apollo 11* the best week's work since the
Creation. And undoubtedly the triumph had been epochal. Had not humankind
set new outer limits for what it might accomplish? And yet a certain skepticism
lingered over what it all meant. One scientist took comfort that after *Apollo* humankind could always go elsewhere, no matter how much a mess was made of the
planet earth. That was no small consideration given the increasing problems of
smog, water pollution, and toxic wastes. There had been some dramatic warnings.
In 1967 an oil tanker, the *Torrey Canyon*, spilled 100,000 tons of oil into the
English Channel. Detergents used to clean up the spill left the area clean but
without plant and animal life for years after.

Such dangers were of grave concern to city officials in Santa Barbara, California, an outpost of paradise along the Pacific Coast. In the channel stretching
between there and Los Angeles, 90 miles to the south, oil companies had drilled
some 925 wells in the coastal tidelands. State efforts to impose stringent regulations on federal oil leases offshore had failed, but the Department of Interior
repeatedly assured local officials they had "nothing to fear." That changed on
January 28, 1969, when Union Oil Company's well A-21 blew a billow of thick
crude oil into the channel. Crews quickly capped the hole only to discover that
pressure from the well had opened a fissure in the ocean floor, through which
natural gas and oil seeped to the surface. "It looked like a massive, inflamed
abscess bursting with reddish-brown pus," one dismayed observer commented.

By February 1, an oil slick had covered five miles of Santa Barbara's once-
pristine white beaches. Only after 11 days of struggle were oil workers able to seal
the leak, which spouted more than 200,000 barrels and left a slick that extended
for some 800 miles. Beaches, boats, and wildlife as far south as San Diego were

At the end of a decade in which Americans landed on the moon, a series of down-to-earth crises, like the oil spill that fouled these waters off Santa Barbara, California, underscored the limits of American power and technology both at home and abroad.

coated with the black, gooey tar. "Cormorants and grebes dived into the the oily swells for fish, most never to surface alive. All along the mucky shoreline, birds lay dead or dying, unable to raise their oil-soaked feathers," one reporter wrote. Despite the heroic efforts of environmentalists, thousands of shore birds died, and detergents claimed the entire population of limpets, abalones, lobsters, sea urchins, mussels, clams, and some fish. One environmentalist warned that "a drastic ecological imbalance" was inevitable.

Few people in Santa Barbara were surprised to learn that Union Oil was operating well below federal and state standards when the well blew. The company was widely known as a polluter and twice in 1967 had been charged with polluting Los Angeles harbor. Two weeks before the Santa Barbara disaster it was accused of dumping 1500 barrels of oil into the Santa Anna River. Outspoken Union Oil President Fred Hartley dismissed the leak as "Mother Earth letting some oil come out." "I'm amazed at the publicity for the loss of a few birds," he told a group of dismayed U.S. Senate conservationists. The Senate responded by passing the Water Quality Improvement Act, which established fines for oil spills.

It was Santa Barbara, not *Apollo 11*, that served as a portent of the coming decade. There would be more Apollo missions, and Vice President Agnew would try briefly to initiate a new race to Mars. But Americans discovered more pressing concerns closer to home: war in the Middle East, the dramatic announcement of the Arab members of the Organization of Petroleum Exporting Countries (OPEC) that they would embargo oil shipments to the West, growing concern over environmental deterioration, the shocking revelations of the Watergate scandals, and the continuing rise of inflation signaled an end to an optimistic faith that American technological know-how could solve any problem or that economic growth was both inevitable and beneficial. No longer could Americans pursue their dreams, whether of conquering space or frontiers closer to home, without calculating the costs. Elliot Richardson, the Nixon administration's secretary of health, education and welfare (HEW), drew the appropriate lesson when he remarked, "We must recognize, as we have with both foreign affairs and natural resources, that resources we thought were boundless . . . are indeed severely limited." The United States had entered an era of limits.

THE LIMITS OF REFORM

Like the space program, the reform movements of the early 1960s had begun with a sense of possibility, of remaking society in a way that preserved both past values and future prospects. But as the decade wore on those movements—for civil rights, against the atomic bomb and the Vietnam War, for a more democratic society, for more meaningful lifestyles—had fragmented into rival, even warring, factions. The nonviolent civil rights movement continued, but so too did radical black nationalism, urban guerrilla violence, and rioting. Out of the radical SDS had come the Weathermen and terrorist Weather Underground. America still seemed a nation in need of reforming, much as it had before, but President Kennedy's call to national sacrifice gave way to narrow preoccupations with self-awareness and personal improvement. According to social observer Tom Wolfe, the self-obsessed "Me Generation" had displaced the crusading New Left.

Amid frustrated hopes, some elements of the reform movement kept alive the idea of restructuring society in substantial ways. Environmentalists, feminists, and consumer advocates utilized many of the same strategies of nonviolent protest and legal maneuver that worked so effectively in the civil rights crusade. But unlike the radicalism of the 1960s, these movements each had long been associated with the American reform tradition. And though they often had radical goals, their leadership most frequently came from the political mainstream and won some major victories, even if they failed ultimately to transform American society.

Environmentalism

The Santa Barbara oil spill was hardly the first warning that Americans were reaching limits to the abuse the environment could take. Searing clouds of acrid smog over Los Angeles had for years hinted at the danger posed by auto emissions in a region where freeways dominated the landscape. Or possibly the first warning came from the recognition that radioactive fallout from nuclear bomb tests in Nevada might well threaten schoolchildren in Troy, New York. Rachel Carson in *Silent Spring* (1962) had so convincingly enumerated the environmental hazards of the pesticide DDT that 40 state legislatures had passed restrictive laws. Certainly, no one with a sense of irony could help but marvel that the Cuyahoga River running through Cleveland, Ohio, had become a major fire hazard. Smog, fallout, dangerous pesticides, hazardous consumer goods, and polluted rivers were all by-products of industrial technology. By the late 1960s Americans started to recognize that a deteriorating environment was the not-so-hidden cost of unbridled economic growth.

The environmental movement that emerged marked a departure from both traditional conservation associated with Teddy Roosevelt, Gifford Pinchot, and Harold Ickes and preservationists like John Muir and the Sierra Club. Conservationists had always stressed the idea of proper *use* of both renewable and nonrenewable resources as a way to ensure the nation's future prosperity. Engineers, lawyers, and economists shaped the conservation agenda. Preservationists shared the Romantics' vision of humankind's spiritual links to nature. They sought largely to save unique wilderness areas like Yellowstone, Yosemite, and the Grand Canyon from development and commercial exploitation.

The new environmental movement incorporated elements of both conservation and preservation into the field of ecology, the biological science that since the early twentieth century has been demonstrating the linkages and dependencies of life processes. Barry Commoner in his book *The Closing Circle* (1971) argued that modern society lived under the illusion it could "improve on nature." In doing so it imposed a terrible price on the environment. American farmers, for example, had shifted from animal manures to artificial fertilizers to increase farm productivity. But the change also raised costs, left soil sterile, and poisoned nearby water sources. After laundry detergents artificially "whitened" clothes, they created foamy scum in lakes and rivers while nourishing deadly algae blooms. Industry profited in the short run, Commoner argued, but in the long run the environment might be bankrupt. Nothing short of a "new social ethic" or transformation of cultural values could produce an ecologically responsible society, warned microbiologist René Dubos.

Increased concern with environmental issues led to greater appreciation of wilderness areas like Yosemite National Park, above. Paradoxically, the influx of new visitors turned once peaceful trails into five-lane thoroughfares, threatening the wilderness with being "loved to death."

By the end of the decade, environmentalists were organizing to implement such an ethic in concrete ways. They brought a lawsuit to block the plan of a consortium of oil companies to build an 800-mile pipeline across Alaska's fragile wilderness. In addition, they successfully lobbied in Congress to defeat a bill authorizing support for the supersonic transport plane, the SST, a plane whose high-altitude flights threatened to deplete the vital ozone layer around the earth. Similarly, a coalition of environmental groups fought a proposed jet airport that threatened south Florida's water supply and the ecology of Florida's Everglades National Park.

The airport battle drew clear lines between the new ethic of environmental restraint and traditional champions of economic growth. Few states have been as receptive to such projects or suffered so much environmental dislocation from development as Florida. Walt Disney, among others, wanted the airport to bring tourists to his huge Disney World project near Orlando; and no one more deeply believed in technology's ability to improve on nature than the king of synthetic culture, Disney himself. At Disneyland in California he had constructed a world that eliminated the accidental or natural in favor of plastic animals, fake forests, and even artificial rocks. Although Disney had a reputation for representing all that was clean and innocent in popular culture, environmentalists defeated the airport project.

"There is a new kind of revolutionary movement under way in this country," declared Senator Henry Jackson of Washington. Even President Nixon, normally a friend of business and real estate interests, responded to the call for more stringent environmental regulation. His administration banned the use of DDT (though not its sale abroad) and supported the National Environmental Policy Act of 1969, which required environmental impact statements for most public projects and made the government responsible for representing the public interest. Nixon also established the Environmental Protection Agency to enforce the law. Echoing Barry Commoner, he announced, "We must learn not how to master nature but how to master ourselves, our institutions, and our technology."

By the spring of 1970 a healthy environment had become such a popular cause that Senator Gaylord Nelson of Wisconsin suggested a national "Earth Day" to celebrate this new consciousness. On April 22, 1970, for at least a few hours pedestrians reclaimed downtown city streets, millions of schoolchildren planted trees and picked up litter, college students demonstrated, and Congress adjourned. The enthusiasm reflected the movement's dual appeal: it combined the rationalism of science with a religious vision of life's organic unity. One California congressman recognized that Americans did not fully appreciate what this celebration could mean: "The Establishment sees this as a great big anti-litter campaign. Wait until they find out what it really means . . . to clean up our earth."

Earth Day was more an end than a beginning. President Nixon, for one, was unwilling to see environmental causes restrict economic development. In his own Earth Day speech he threw the administration's support behind the oil industry's Alaskan pipeline project, which survived a long series of court challenges before construction began in 1973. The president also personally lobbied for the SST. Having helped kill the environmentally destructive Cross-Florida Barge Canal project in 1969, he went to Alabama in 1971 to launch the equally ill-conceived Tombigbee–Tennessee Waterway. "We are not going to allow the environmental issue . . . to destroy the system," he announced in 1972.

Beyond the matter of high principles or pragmatic choices, Nixon's political instincts were shrewd. Conflict between social classes underlay the environmental debate. Many middle-class veterans of the counterculture, civil rights, and anti-war movements had found a new outlet in environmental activism. To workers and the silent majority, facing rising inflation and unemployment, the issue came down to jobs versus the environment. "Out of work? Hungry? Eat an environmentalist," declared one popular bumper sticker. To workers and upwardly mobile middle Americans, environmentalism too often seemed suspiciously like a scenario in which those who already possessed access to the good life wanted to close the door, leaving the less privileged standing on the outside.

Consumerism

In 1965 a thin young man with jet black hair and intense dark eyes shocked the automotive world by publishing *Unsafe at Any Speed*, an exposé that relentlessly criticized the "Big Three" automakers in Detroit for emphasizing style, horsepower, comfort, and sales over any concern with safety, fuel economy, or reliability. The author, Ralph Nader, argued that too many automobiles unnecessarily imperiled their occupants even during minor collisions. Rather than add safety features, the industry lobbied with Washington to block regulation. Nader's particular target was the Chevrolet Corvair, a rear-engined small car which General Motors had produced to compete with the popular German Volkswagen Beetle. Crash reports, as well as internal GM engineering studies, indicated that the

Daily Lives

FOOD AND DRINK
Fast-Food America

If people are what they eat (as well as where and how), American society reveals a good deal about itself through its national eating habits. Three long-term trends in particular became evident during the 1970s: Americans increasingly were eating outside the home; the frequency with which families sat together for the three basic meals of the day declined steadily; and diet itself was altered significantly.

Eating foods prepared by a non–family member was once largely the exclusive privilege of the rich, who had access to servants, restaurants, and clubs; or it was the misfortune of the very poor, who took their meals in prisons, soup kitchens, or other institutional settings. By the 1970s the consumption of prepared foods and meals had become common for most Americans. Fast-food chains, school and office cafeterias, vending machines, and other public facilities served up over 40 percent of the meals Americans ate. Many home meals consisted of packaged foods like TV dinners or frozen entrées that required nothing but temperature change prior to consumption. Whether at home or away, the emphasis at mealtime was increasingly on the speed, convenience, or economy with which food was prepared.

Before the 1960s most American restaurants offered a limited range of foods, featuring meats and potatoes baked, broiled, or fried, vegetables steamed or boiled, eggs over easy, and cakes, pies, and ice cream for dessert. An adventurous eater could discover fine French cooking or ethnic foods in urban areas, but even pizza or sweet-and-sour pork were novelties in suburbia. Affluence in the 1950s and 1960s encouraged Americans to become more cosmopolitan in their eating habits. As people traveled, they experienced the world's cuisine. *Picadinho a Brasileira* and *carbonnades à la Flamande* began to replace beef stew. Immigrants to the United States, especially large numbers of Hispanics and Asians, greatly expanded American tastes. Instead of chop suey and chow mein, diners could choose a variety of regional Chinese styles—Mandarin, Cantonese, or spicy Hunan and Szechwan. Lunch might mean a Kosher delicatessen. Texas and California developed variants of Mexican cooking, as Americans graduated from tacos and Fritos to enchiladas and burritos. California steak houses introduced Americans to salad bars. And many people discovered the differences between northern and southern Italian cooking, as well as the vast array of Asian cuisines from India to Thailand to Korea.

As prepared foods became more popular, meals as social occasions for families became rarer. Common meals required the participants to foresake personal preferences and time schedules to share the same foods, served in the same order, at the same time. But in an age of convenience, fast-food chains, and ethnic takeouts, it became practical for individual family members to eat different foods at the same time or to break the "one-cook-to-one-family" pattern. In the process, eating became desocialized. The two most communal meals, breakfast and dinner, no longer brought families together as they once did. By the end of the 1970s some 75 percent of American families did not have breakfast together, and the average family sat down to dinner less than three times a week for a meal that lasted no more than 20 minutes. As formal meals lost their

Daily Lives

Once limited largely to hamburgers, ice cream, and pancakes, fast food chains now allow Americans to bolt down indifferently synthesized varieties of ethnic and regional foods as well.

importance, snacking became common. Individual family members ingested food in some fashion as often as 20 times a day. More and more often, people combined the consumption of foods with activities other than meals: popcorn and movies, beer and TV sports, coffee and commuting.

As important as where and how people ate were nutritional changes in diet. In earlier societies meals had consisted largely of a core complex carbohydrate (rice, bread, potatoes, or noodles), served up with a fringe complement of meats, vegetables, fruits, and seasoned perhaps with a sauce. The core carbohydrate pro-

vided most nutrition, calories, and satisfaction; the fringe abetted the eating of the core. In modern Western society, including the United States, that pattern reversed over time. By the 1970s the bulk of most Americans' calories had long come from protein foods like meat and eggs, and even more from foods rich in sugars and fats.

As preoccupation with slimness grew, consumption of sugar as a sweetener added to food or eaten in candy declined. But since most Americans ate more and more prepared and precooked foods, the indirect consumption of sugar and sweeteners increased, through desserts, baked goods, soft drinks, and ice cream. Food manufacturers discovered that sugars and dense fats like palm and coconut oil improved flavor, texture, taste, and shelf life. Thus they included sweeteners or fats in places where most people did not expect them: table salt, coatings for fried foods, peanut butter, and "health" foods like granola. By the late 1970s the average American consumed some 130 pounds of sugar and sweeteners per year and about 40 percent of all calories in the form of animal and vegetable fats. The consequence was a steady increase in obesity and diet-related heart diseases and cancers.

An increasing awareness of the relation between diet and disease made the American public, especially the middle and upper classes, more willing to alter eating habits in order to prolong life and health. But with sugars and fats continuing to sell, marketers catered to these preferences. Whether Americans' increasing control over the variety and timing of their meals will eventually lead to long-term increases in longevity remains to be seen.

Corvair sometimes tended to roll over in routine turns and quickly lost control when it skidded.

Almost from its beginnings the auto industry had employed carefully orchestrated public relations to shield itself from such criticism. General Motors thus did not take kindly to Nader's revelations. As a defense against this counterculture David, the corporate Goliath decided on a policy of harassment and sent out a private investigator to dig up dirt from Nader's personal life. What they discovered was no hippie disguised in a suit, but an ascetic, penny-pinching example of the American dream. As the son of immigrant parents, he had graduated from Princeton and Harvard Law School. He worked hard, wore his hair short, and never used drugs. And when he discovered GM's intentions, he sued.

GM's embarrassed president James Roche publicly apologized, but by then Nader was a hero and *Unsafe at Any Speed* a best seller. In 1966 Congress passed the National Traffic and Motor Vehicle Safety Act and the Highway Safety Act, which for the first time required safety standards for cars, tires, and roads. Nader used $425,000 from his successful lawsuit against GM to launch his Washington-based Center for the Study of Responsive Law (1969) with a staff of five lawyers and a hundred college volunteers. "Nader's Raiders" as the group soon became known, investigated a wide range of consumer and political issues, including consumer-oriented government agencies, water pollution, Congress, old-age homes, and auto safety.

After 1970 the consumer movement adopted a broad agenda to make business more responsible. It identified unsafe toys, dangerous food additives, and pollutants. It insisted that businesses hire more women and minorities. It brought suit against unethical marketing strategies like "bait-and-switch advertising," against hidden credit costs that plagued the poor, and against defective products, dubbed "lemons." Nader and a host of similar advocates formed powerful lobbying groups and investigating teams; they used legal tools like the "class-action suit," which allowed individuals with common damages from hazardous products or negligence to sue as a group rather than bringing a series of individual suits.

As the consumer movement cast its net more widely, it lost focus. Many of its concerns overlapped with the environmental, civil rights, and women's movements. Like so many leaders from those causes, upper middle-class consumer advocates provoked the skepticism of middle Americans, who worried more about the availability of credit than its fairness. Despite some dramatic victories, consumerism did not shift the location of power in the system. In taking on General Motors once again in the 1970s in Campaign GM, Nader's Raiders had placed their faith in the pressure of public opinion as a way to force corporations to serve the public interest. In response auto executives proved they could appeal to the public as well as Nader's public interest lawyers did. More important, Campaign GM never tapped into the discontent of General Motors workers or forged an alliance with the powerful United Auto Workers Union, which represented them. When public interest lawyers defended the rights of women or minorities or when they attacked specific marketing abuses, they often were more successful. But Nader was never able to establish consumerism as the basis for a mass political reform movement.

Feminism

Undoubtedly the most historically rooted and controversial of the three major "isms" of the 1960s and 1970s was feminism. Organized struggle for women's rights and equality in the United States began before the Civil War. Sustained political efforts had won women the vote in 1920 and shifting economic forces had brought more women into the job market throughout the twentieth century. Yet increasing affluence could not hide the reality that during the post–World War II era, the role of women as housewives and homemakers had been glorified at the expense of two-job families and the aspirations of many women to have careers of their own. In *The Feminine Mystique* (1963) Betty Friedan wrote poignantly about the "problem that has no name," a dispiriting boredom or emptiness in the midst of affluent lives. "Our culture does not permit women to accept or gratify their basic need to grow and fulfill their potentialities as human beings."

The Feminine Mystique acted as an important catalyst to the women's rights movement. The Commission on the Status of Women appointed by President Kennedy proposed the 1963 Equal Pay Act and helped add gender to the forms of discrimination proscribed by the 1964 Civil Rights Act. Women had also assumed an important role in both the civil rights and antiwar movements. But those politically conscious women discovered that like those for whom they struggled, they too were victims of discrimination. During the voter registration drives women were often restricted to behind-the-scenes services such as cooking, doing laundry, and fulfilling others' sexual impulses. Antiwar activists occasionally exploited women's vulnerability as a way to expose the brutality of police and National Guardsmen. As marchers approached hostile forces, up went the cry "Broads on line!" Women who were denied a role in formulating strategy and making decisions were asked to bear much of the violence aimed against protesters.

By 1966 activist women were less willing to see their grievances eclipsed by other political constituencies. Friedan joined a group of 24 women and 2 men who formed the National Organization for Women (NOW). The new feminists sought to force the Johnson administration to take bolder action to eliminate discrimination in such areas as jobs and pay. When feminists argued "sexism" was not qualitatively different from racism, Johnson accepted the argument and in 1967 he included women as well as blacks, Hispanics, and other minorities covered by federal affirmative action programs.

Changes in work, family, education, and sexual mores established a receptive climate for the feminist appeal. After 1957 the birth rate began a rapid decline; affluence and improved methods of contraception, such as the birth control pill, encouraged smaller family size. Women who in the 1950s had children at a young age were free by the 1960s to enter the labor force. By 1970 over 40 percent of all women, an unprecedented number, were employed outside the home. Education also spurred the shift from home to the job market and increased consciousness of women's issues. Higher educational levels allowed women to enter an economy oriented increasingly to white-collar service industries rather than blue-collar manufacturing. Women, especially black women, were more likely than men to be high school graduates.

Between 1960 and 1970 the number of female college students doubled. Former bastions of sexual exclusivity like Yale and Vassar became coeducational. In a social atmosphere that stressed greater freedom for all individuals, college women discovered both the opportunity and pressure for greater experimentation: they contemplated courses in the sciences or careers in law, dated without rules that specified when they had to return to dormitories, and no longer faced a rigid double standard that encouraged men to seek premarital sex that "sweet, marriageable girls" had long been warned to refuse. After college, women could more readily live as singles or in open relationships.

As much as women sought liberation from old restrictions, their new circumstances raised new problems. Men did not readily share traditional family responsibilities with working women; obligations of a job were added to domestic routines. Because they often took part-time jobs or jobs treated as "female" work, women earned far less than men. Many college women continued to view the future "through a wedding band," shunning personal ambition, achievement, and competitiveness as bars to marriage. As a result, they were less likely to choose careers that brought high pay, status, and power. And though greater sexual freedom implied more gender equality, the media continued to promote the image of women as sex objects. To some feminists, the revolution in easy sex and "free" love favored men, since they could more readily escape domestic obligations without loss of sexual companionship.

Such confusing social cross-currents made it difficult for the growing feminist movement to translate its grievances into a coherent political agenda. NOW members could agree in 1967 to a "Bill of Rights" that called for maternity leave for working mothers, federally supported day-care facilities, child-care tax deductions, and equal education and job training. But they divided on two other issues: the passage of an Equal Rights Amendment and a repeal of all state antiabortion laws. Women labor leaders feared that absolute equality would deprive women of necessary protections in the workplace. Socially conservative feminists were offended at the idea that women should have "reproductive freedom." The more radical feminists pushed NOW to adopt both positions.

By the early 1970s the feminists had captured the media's attention. Fifty thousand women participated in NOW's Strike for Equality Parade down New York's Fifth Avenue. Television cameras zeroed in on signs with such slogans as "Don't Cook Dinner—Starve a Rat Today." Some newscasters reported that marchers had burned their bras to protest sexual stereotyping. "Bra burners" became the media's condescending phrase used to deny credibility to militant feminists like Kate Millett, whose *Sexual Politics* (1970) condemned a male-dominated "patriarchal" society.

Political action brought all the major women's organizations together in support of an Equal Rights Amendment (ERA) to the Constitution. A similar effort had gone down to defeat in 1946, but its advocates were more unified by the 1970s. Even the majority of American men were sympathetic to both the ERA and abortion reform. Yet many women feared that the ERA would deprive them of certain protections under the law, while still others saw the amendment as part of a liberation movement they opposed. In 1972 both the House and Senate passed the amendment virtually without opposition. It outlawed all forms of gender discrimination. Within a year 28 of the necessary 38 states had approved the ERA.

Initial success of the ERA drive reflected the growing influence of women in politics. At the 1972 Democratic National Convention the outspoken members of the National Women's Political Caucus captured the party's endorsement for the ERA and helped nominate George McGovern, although the convention would not adopt their platform resolutions supporting gay rights and reproductive freedom. And in 1973 the Supreme Court, even with its conservative Nixon appointees, voted 7–2 in *Roe v. Wade* to strike down 46 state laws restricting a woman's access to abortion. In his opinion for the majority, Justice Harry Blackmun observed that a woman in the nineteenth century had "enjoyed a substantially broader right to terminate a pregnancy than she does in most states today." As legal abortion in the

Feminists recognized the need to strengthen bonds among women in order to provide a new sense of identity not linked to traditional female roles and stereotypes. In this 1970 demonstration they marched to assert their rights, following not only in the footsteps of the New Left but also in the traditions of the women's rights movements of the previous hundred years.

first three months of pregnancy became more readily available, the rate of maternal deaths from illegal operations, especially among minorities, declined.

The early success of the ERA and the feminist triumph with *Roe v. Wade* masked underlying divisions among women's groups in the country. The Supreme Court decision triggered a sharp backlash from many Catholics, Protestant fundamentalists, and socially conservative women. Catholics and fundamentalists alike believed that since human life began with conception, abortion was nothing less than murder under any circumstances. Their outrage inspired a crusade for a "right-to-life" amendment to the Constitution. A similar conservative backlash breathed new life into the "STOP-ERA" crusade of Phyllis Schlafly, an Illinois political organizer who, although a professional herself, believed that women should embrace their traditional role as homemakers subordinate to their husbands. "Every change [that the ERA] requires will deprive women of a right, benefit, or exemption that they now enjoy," Schlafly argued. Many women and men outside the urban professional circle that dominated NOW shared Schlafly's reservations.

In the middle ground stood many women (and a considerable number of men) who wanted the political system to correct the worst inequalities. The forces for moderate reform won several victories, including a ruling forbidding discrimination in colleges receiving federal aid, a court decision ordering the American Telephone and Telegraph Company to open all jobs to women, and the integration of the aggressively masculine military service academies. More far-reaching goals would take longer to achieve. Within a year after Congress passed the ERA, the National Women's Political Caucus conceded that the momentum to pass the amendment had declined. With support waning, Congress in 1979 extended the deadline for ratification from March 22, 1979, to June 30, 1982. Of a necessary 38 state legislatures, 35 had ratified the ERA by 1980, although 5 had rescinded their approval and it was clear that the amendment would fail. Even though determined feminists vowed to continue the fight, they too had discovered the limits of the era.

The Activist Legacy

To say that the organized environmental, consumer, and feminist movements lost ground after the early 1970s is not to say that they failed. Rather, each crusade fell short in its effort to forge a national consensus. There would be no new ecological consciousness, no consumer-directed economy, and no absolute gender equality. Indeed, none of the movements could ever agree just what those ideas would mean in practice.

Instead, the United States was left after the early 1970s with more awareness of ecology, consumer rights, and the blatant and subtle forms of sexism. Advocates of reform had learned to use the media, to lobby politicians, to fight in the courts, and to organize. Old organizations like the National Audobon Society and League of Women Voters had been revitalized. New organizations like NOW and Friends of the Earth had become part of the political infrastructure. Within government the EPA, FTC, and other agencies had a mandate to enforce the court decisions and laws that reformers had won. In that way the advocates of reform achieved a political and social legacy in the tradition of progressivism and the New Deal.

POLITICAL LIMITS: WATERGATE

To Richard Nixon, the triumph of his 1972 reelection must have seemed sweet revenge. In 49 of the 50 states he had defeated George McGovern, the patron saint of liberal environmentalists, consumer advocates, feminists, and the youthful counterculture. Yet while Nixon sought to stem the liberal tide, in the matter of executive power, he continued a trend of concentration and expansion of an "imperial presidency" that had been under way since the early twentieth century. More than any other factor, the cold war with its sense of ongoing crisis had encouraged a steady accumulation of power in the presidency. That expansion involved not only proliferating agencies, both public and secret like the National

Security Agency, but also ever-greater symbolic trappings of political power. Where Franklin Roosevelt had a White House staff of 100, Nixon had over 6000. Emboldened by his victory over McGovern, Nixon determined to use the power of the presidency even more broadly.

The Perils of Power

Part of the president's penchant for wielding power was undoubtedly personal. His lists of enemies and resentments grew ever longer. The impoverished law student who had lived in an abandoned toolshed now reveled in the pomp, the splendor of the presidency, the success and respect it accorded. Where other presidents had seemed content with one or perhaps two vacation retreats, Nixon opted for three. A fleet of 36 planes and helicopters stood ready to ferry members of the White House entourage wherever they might go, while the official yacht *Sequoia* came in for presidential complaint because it was not elegantly enough appointed. Nixon even tried dressing the White House guards in fancy new uniforms, but he was forced to abandon the practice after having them heartily ridiculed as something out of comic opera.

But the matter of power was more than a personal issue. The president and his advisers were particularly eager to act forcefully because they were convinced that the radical reformers of the counterculture menaced American society. As the atmosphere of confrontation during the late sixties encouraged the president to see political debate as a matter of "them" versus "us," members of his staff began compiling an "enemies list"—including everyone from CBS correspondent Daniel Schorr to actress and antiwar activist Jane Fonda. Twenty in particular were targeted for audits by the Internal Revenue Service or similar harassment. In the national debate over Vietnam, Nixon had been particularly irate when in June 1971 the New York *Times* published a secret, often highly critical military study of the war, soon dubbed the Pentagon Papers. Counterattacking, the president authorized his aide John Ehrlichman to organize a team known as "the plumbers," to find and plug security leaks. The government not only prosecuted Daniel Ellsberg, the disillusioned official who had leaked the Pentagon Papers, but the plumbers burglarized the files of Ellsberg's psychiatrist in hopes of finding personally damaging material.

Democrats in Congress had become increasingly concerned about the open assertion of presidential power known as impoundment. When Congress passed a number of social programs Nixon opposed, he simply refused to spend the appropriated money. By 1973 Nixon had used impoundment to make cuts in over a hundred federal programs amounting to some $15 billion. The courts eventually ruled that impoundment was illegal, but meanwhile the president continued his campaign to consolidate power and reshape the more liberal social policies of Congress to his own liking. To that end, he appointed a conservative ideologue to head up Lyndon Johnson's antipoverty agency, the Office of Economic Opportunity, with orders to incapacitate it as much as possible. And Nixon vetoed a host of welfare and environmental bills.

Convinced of the need for firm action in a crisis, suspicious not only of the radical left but also of the liberals in Congress, delighting in personal trappings of power—all these elements made it easier for Richard Nixon to break or bend the rules of power in the service of what he believed was a good cause. In the end, his refusal to acknowledge the limits of power or the ethics of using it brought him down.

Break-In

Nixon's fall began with an apparently minor item that hit the newspapers in June 1972: a petty burglary of Democratic National Committee headquarters, located in Washington's plush Watergate apartment complex. The matter seemed so routine at first that the Washington *Post* assigned the story to a couple of cub reporters, Bob Woodward and Carl Bernstein. But the five burglars proved an unusual lot. They wore business suits, carried walkie-talkies as well as bugging devices and tear-gas guns, and had over $2000 in the form of hundred-dollar bills with sequential serial numbers.

The laconic ivy-league Woodward and the manic, city-smart Bernstein made a true "odd couple." Yet despite their relative inexperience, they sensed the large dimensions of the Watergate affair. One of the burglars, James McCord, had worked for the CIA; another had been captured with an address book whose phone numbers included one belonging to a Howard Hunt at the "W. House." Woodward called the number and discovered that Hunt was indeed a White House consultant. When asked to comment on the story, Nixon's press secretary Ron Ziegler called the break-in "a third rate burglary attempt" and warned that "certain elements may try to stretch this beyond what it is." In August Nixon himself announced that White House Counsel John Dean had conducted a thorough investigation and concluded that "no one on the White House staff . . . was involved in this very bizarre incident. What really hurts in matters of this sort is not the fact that they occur," the president continued. "What really hurts is if you try to cover up."

Matters were not easily settled, however. Woodward and Bernstein traced some of the burglars' money back to the Nixon campaign's Committee to Re-elect the President (popularly known as CREEP). CREEP had "laundered" the money and also established a secret "slush fund" of some $350,000 to be used for projects against the Democrats. The dirty tricks undertaken included forged letters distributed on the letterheads of Democratic candidates, false news leaks, and spying on Democratic campaign workers. But by election time, Woodward and Bernstein had run out of fresh leads. So frustrated was the editor at the Washington *Post*, Benjamin C. Bradlee, that he later confessed that he was "ready to hold both Woodward's and Bernstein's heads in a pail of water until they came up with another story."

In January 1973 the five burglars plus White House aides E. Howard Hunt, Jr., and G. Gordon Liddy went on trial before Judge John J. Sirica. A stern man, "Maximum John" Sirica was not satisfied with the defendants' guilty plea; he wanted to know whether anyone else had directed the burglars and why "these hundred dollar bills were floating around like coupons." Threatened with a stiff jail sentence, James McCord finally cracked. In a letter that Sirica read to the court, McCord admitted that other officials had been involved, that the defendants had been pressured and bribed to plead guilty, and that they had perjured themselves during the trial. In a flight of Orwellian "newspeak," presidential press secretary Ron Ziegler announced on April 17 that all previous administration statements on the Watergate scandal had become "inoperative." With regret, the president announced on April 30 that he had accepted the resignations of his two closest aides,

H.R. Haldeman and John Erlichman. He also fired John W. Dean III, his White House counsel, who had agreed to cooperate with prosecutors.

Over the summer of 1973 televised Senate hearings chaired by Senator Sam Ervin of North Carolina heard testimony from a string of administration officials, each witness taking the trail of the burglary and its cover-up higher and higher into White House circles. It became clear that Attorney General John Mitchell, then the highest ranking law officer of the land, had attended meetings in 1972 where Gordon Liddy outlined preliminary plans for a campaign of dirty tricks, illegal wiretaps, call girl schemes, and burglary of the Democratic National Committee's Watergate office. McCord, Liddy, Hunt, and others had also worked directly for John Erlichman as members of the plumber's unit. When these illegal actions became known, the judge presiding over the Ellsberg Pentagon Papers trial declared a mistrial.

To the Oval Office

Despite these damning revelations most Americans were not quite prepared for the testimony offered by White House counsel John Dean. Young, with a boy scout's face, Dean testified in a quiet monotone that the president had personally been involved in the cover up as recently as April. When McCord threatened to tell all, Dean had met with the president, Haldeman, and Erlichman to discuss raising up to a million dollars in hush money to buy the burglars' silence. Still, Dean was the only witness whose testimony had involved the president. It was his word against Nixon's—until the Senate committee's staff discovered, almost by chance, that the president had been secretly recording all his conversations and phone calls in the Oval Office since 1970. The reliability of Dean's testimony was no longer central, for the tapes could tell all.

Obtaining that evidence proved no easy task. In an effort to restore confidence in the White House, Nixon had appointed Elliot Richardson as attorney general to succeed Richard Kleindienst, who like John Mitchell had fallen under suspicion. Richardson in turn appointed Harvard law professor Archibald Cox as a special prosecutor to investigate the new Watergate disclosures. When Cox subpoenaed the tapes, the president refused to turn them over, citing executive privilege and matters of national security. The courts, however, overruled this position.

As that battle raged and the astonished public wondered if matters could possibly get worse, they did. An investigation unrelated to Watergate found evidence that Vice President Spiro Agnew had systematically solicited graft, not just as governor of Maryland, but while serving in Washington. Agnew loudly denounced the charges while quietly negotiating with prosecutors for permission to plead *nolo contendere* (no contest) to a single charge of federal income tax evasion. In return, he agreed to resign the vice presidency in October. The rambunctious rhetorician of law and order suddenly appeared no better than a petty crook. Under provisions of the Twenty-Fifth Amendment, Nixon appointed popular Michigan congressman Gerald R. Ford to replace Agnew.

Meanwhile, Special Prosecutor Archibald Cox remained unrelenting in his demands to examine the tapes. The president had countered by offering to submit written summaries of conversations rather than the tapes themselves. But trust in the president had by now been so greatly undermined that Cox rejected the offer, especially since the president also demanded that Cox agree to ask for no further

Under the leadership of North Carolina Senator Sam Ervin (left), the Senate Committee investigating the Watergate scandal attracted a large television audience. John Dean (right), the former White House legal counsel, provided the most damning testimony linking President Nixon to the cover-up. But only when the existence of secretly recorded White House tapes became known was there a chance to corroborate his account.

documents. On Saturday night, October 20, Nixon ordered Cox fired. Elliot Richardson and his assistant, William Ruckelshaus, refused and resigned instead; Solicitor General Robert Bork finally fired him. Reaction to the "Saturday Night Massacre" was overwhelming: 150,000 telegrams poured into Washington and by the following Tuesday 84 House members sponsored 16 different bills of impeachment. The beleaguered president agreed to comply with Judge Sirica's order to hand over the tapes. And he appointed Texas lawyer Leon Jaworski as a new special prosecutor.

No sooner had the smoke cleared from the Saturday Night Massacre, however, than White House counsel J. Fred Buzhardt admitted that sections of the subpoenaed tapes were missing, including a crucial 18-minute gap in the conversation in which the president first discussed the Watergate burglary, three days after it occurred. Nixon's loyal secretary Rose Mary Woods tried to take the blame and White House chief of staff Alexander Haig suggested an unaccountable "sinister force" might have caused the blank space, but experts later verified that the gap was the result of intentional erasure.

By April 24, 1974, Jaworski's investigations led him to request additional tapes. Again the president refused; then he grudgingly agreed to supply some 1200 pages of typed transcripts, though not the tapes themselves. Even the transcripts damaged the president's case. The conversations were littered with profanity ("[expletive deleted]," the transcripts read), revealing a vulgar, mean-spirited White House staff. And they suggested a president very much a part of the cover-up process. On March 21, 1973, he had talked with Dean about how to "take care of the jackasses who are in jail." When Dean estimated it might take a million dollars to shut them up, Nixon replied, "We could get that. . . . You could get a million dollars. And you could get it in cash. I know where it could be gotten. I mean it's not easy, but it could be done." And when the matter of perjury came up Nixon suggested a way out: "You can say, 'I don't remember.' You can say, 'I can't recall.'"

Even those devastating revelations did not produce the "smoking gun" the president's defenders demanded as a basis for impeachment. They wanted clear proof that the president had actively participated in the cover-up from its earliest moments. When Jaworski petitioned the Supreme Court to order release of additional tapes to use in the trial of six former Nixon aides, the Court in *United States v. Nixon* on July 24 ruled unanimously in the prosecutor's favor.

The end came quickly. The House Judiciary Committee adopted three articles of impeachment, charging that Nixon had illegally obstructed justice, had abused his constitutional authority in improperly using federal agencies to harass citizens, and had impeded the committee's effort to investigate the cover-up. The tapes produced the smoking gun. Conversations with Haldeman on June 23, 1972, only a few days after the break-in, showed that Nixon knew the burglars were tied to the White House staff, knew that his attorney general had been involved, and knew that Mitchell had acted to limit FBI investigation. Even the president's staunchest supporters deserted him. Knowing that the Senate had the votes to make him the first president convicted in an impeachment trial, Nixon resigned on August 8, 1974. The following day Gerald Ford became president. "The Constitution works," Ford told a relieved nation. "Our long national nightmare is over."

Had the system worked? In one sense, yes. The wheels of justice had turned, even if slowly. For the first time a president had been forced to leave office. Four cabinet officers, John Mitchell, Commerce Secretary Maurice Stans, Agriculture Secretary Earl Butz, and Mitchell's successor Richard Kleindienst were all convicted of crimes. Twenty-five Nixon aides eventually served prison terms ranging from 25 days to over 4 years.

Yet what would have happened if Ben Bradlee had found his pail of water? With the exception of the Washington *Post* and one or two other newspapers, the media had accepted the administration's cover-up at face value. And despite the revelations of widespread political abuses, federal agencies still have it within their power to harass innocent citizens arbitrarily. Later abuses within the executive branch such as the "Irangate" scandals under Ronald Reagan have demonstrated that the imperial powers of the presidency are still largely unchecked. Secret agencies and covert operations remain standard procedure. The Fair Campaign Practices Act adopted in 1974 to eliminate "fat-cat" contributions and to enforce greater financial accountability on campaigns succeeded largely in complicating the efforts of third parties to initiate campaigns. Political action committees (PACs) representing special interest groups became major sources of campaign funding. The system works, as the Founding Fathers understood, only when citizens and public servants respect the limits of government power.

A FORD, NOT A LINCOLN

Gerald Ford inherited a presidential office almost crippled by the Watergate scandals. As the first unelected president, he had no popular mandate. He was little known outside Washington and his home district around Grand Rapids, Michigan. Ford's success as the House minority leader came from personal popularity, political reliability, and plodding determination, qualities that suited a congressman but not an unelected president. Lyndon Johnson once quipped that "Gerry Ford is so dumb he can't walk and chew gum at the same time." Yet Ford had a kind of respect for tradition and inner solidity that came as a relief after the mercurial styles of Johnson and Nixon. He had been a star football player at the University of Michigan and later earned a law degree from Yale. By all instincts a conservative, Ford was determined to continue Nixon's aggressive foreign policy and a domestic program of social and fiscal conservatism.

Kissinger Regnant

As Nixon's star fell, that of his Secretary of State and National Security Advisor Henry Kissinger rapidly rose. Kissinger cultivated reporters who relished his witty quips, intellectual breadth, and willingness to leak stories to the press. He was a ruthless political infighter who rid the White House of his chief rivals. With Nixon desperate for a foreign policy success to offset Watergate in the summer of 1974, he took Kissinger on a trip to Moscow and the Middle East. As the end neared, it was Kissinger who warned military commanders to ignore presidential orders.

Kissinger had struggled to prevent Vietnam and Watergate from eroding the president's power to conduct an independent foreign policy. Congress was too sensitive to public opinion and special interest pressure groups to pursue consistent long-term policies, he warned. But after Vietnam congressional leaders were eager to curtail presidential powers. In 1971 they had repealed the Gulf of Tonkin Resolution (p. 1200), and by 1975 they had passed bills barring American troops from returning to Vietnam or from new involvements in strifetorn Angola without congressional approval. More important, the War Powers Act of 1973 required the president to consult Congress whenever possible before committing troops, to send an explanation for his actions within 2 days, and to withdraw any troops after 60 days unless Congress voted to retain them.

In all his political machinations, Kissinger viewed himself as a realist, a man for whom order and stability were more important than principle. In that way he offended idealists on the political left and right. Quoting the German writer Goethe, Kissinger acknowledged, "If I had to choose between justice and disorder, on the one hand, and injustice and order on the other, I would always choose the latter." He most ruthlessly applied that approach to quell political ferment in Chile.

In 1970 Chile ranked as one of South America's few viable democracies. When a coalition of Socialists, Communists, and radicals succeeeded in electing Salvador Allende Gossens as president, the CIA determined that his victory created a danger to the United States. Kissinger pressed the CIA to bribe the Chilean Congress and to promote a military coup against Allende. When those attempts failed, Kissinger resorted to economic warfare between the United States and the

Allende government. By 1973 a Chilean coalition of disgruntled conservatives, high-paid union workers, and foreign business leaders with CIA backing had joined to drive the Socialists from power. On September 17 the Chilean military attacked the presidential palace and killed Allende. The United States immediately recognized the new government, which over the next decade deteriorated into a brutally repressive dictatorship. Kissinger argued that the United States had the right to destroy this democracy because communists were antidemocratic.

The Decline of American Hegemony

As a political realist, Kissinger understood that the United States no longer had the economic strength to dominate the affairs of the noncommunist bloc of nations. The country faced a process of decolonization that meant loosening its grip in areas like Central America and the Middle East, though it was politically impossible to admit that to the public. Kissinger was particularly vulnerable to hostile Republican conservatives suspicious of his old Rockefeller ties and eager to restore prestige lost during Vietnam.

At home inflation had begun to soar. A short-term economic boom in 1972–1973 following the devaluation of the dollar led to increased prices. American industries with inefficient production, products of poor quality, and high wages struggled against mounting competition from manufacturers in Europe and the Pacific rim (Japan, South Korea, Taiwan, Hong Kong, Singapore, and the Philippines). American-based multinational corporations began to establish their manu-

After having won a Nobel Peace Prize in 1973 for his role in ending the Vietnam War, Henry Kissinger entered the Ford administration as something of a hero. But his efforts to improve relations with the Soviet Union by strengthening détente aroused the ire of the Republican right wing, while liberals accused Kissinger of being too secretive and friendly to dictators.

facturing centers overseas to take advantage of lower costs and cheap labor. The bellwether industry of the American economy, automobiles, steadily lost sales to Japan and Germany. Speaking on behalf of its blue-collar constituency, the AFL–CIO complained that the loss of high-wage manufacturing jobs would create "a nation of hamburger stands, a country stripped of industrial capacity . . . , a nation of citizens busily buying and selling cheeseburgers and root beer floats."

And when it seemed matters could hardly become worse, along came the Yom Kippur War and the OPEC oil boycott. Here was decolonization with a vengeance. On October 6, 1973, Syria and Egypt launched a devastating surprise attack against Israel. The Soviet Union airlifted supplies to the Arabs; the United States countered on October 15 by resupplying its Israeli allies while pressing the two sides to accept a cease-fire. The seven Arab members of OPEC backed Egypt and Syria. They imposed a boycott of oil sales to countries seen as friendly to Israel. Since the 1920s the major multinational oil companies, known after World War II as the Seven Sisters (Exxon, Shell, Gulf, Mobil, British Petroleum, Socal, and Texaco), had dominated world marketing. Never before had the OPEC nations controlled the distribution of their oil, but the boycott from October 1973 until March 1974 devastated the countries of Western Europe and Japan, which imported 80 to 90 percent of their oil from the Middle East. The rise of oil prices from $2 to $8 a barrel set off recessionary pressures that staggered the industrial economies of the world.

Since the United States relied on the Middle East for just 12 percent of its oil consumption (other imports came from Venezuela, Mexico, and Canada), American oil experts were confident that the boycott would end before the United States suffered appreciably. That confidence soon collapsed when it became obvious that Americans were far more dependent on foreign oil than most people had ever appreciated. With just 7 percent of the world's population, the United States consumed about 30 percent of its energy. The nation's postwar prosperity came in large part from the use of cheap energy. Among the technologies that spurred postwar economic growth were high-compression automobile engines, commercial airliners, detergents, artificial fertilizers, synthetic fabrics, plastics, and disposable containers.

In November 1973 President Nixon had announced to the nation, "We are heading toward the most acute shortage of energy since World War II." Americans felt the crunch in every aspect of their lives. As the price of petroleum-based plastics soared, everything from records to raincoats cost more. In some places motorists hoping to buy a few gallons of gas waited for hours in lines miles long. Nixon pledged to "make the United States energy-independent by 1980," but his Watergate woes interfered with efforts to frame a coherent energy policy.

To Kissinger fell the role of shoring up the West's energy fortunes by using American influence to stabilize the politics of the Middle East. If the Arab states saw the United States as a neutral in their conflict with Israel, they would be less likely to resort to future oil blackmail. And in linking the oil boycott to the cold war, Kissinger thought the revival of American prestige would allow him to reduce Soviet influence in the region. Egypt's President Anwar Sadat had recently exposed Soviet vulnerability by expelling 10,000 Russian advisers from his country. From January to April 1974 Kissinger intermittently engaged in "shuttle diplomacy" between Sadat's government in Cairo and the Israeli government of Golda Meir in Jerusalem. By the end of January Kissinger had persuaded Israel to withdraw its troops from the west bank of the Suez Canal; in May he arranged disengagement between Israel and Syria in the Golan Heights.

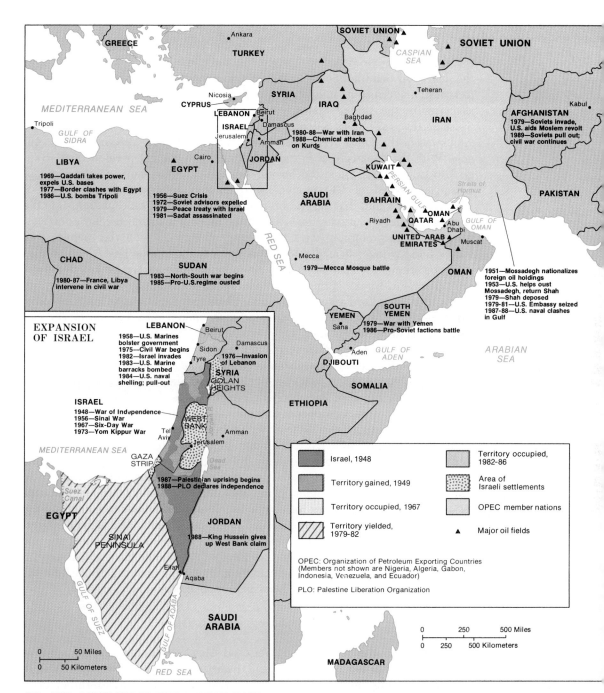

Map labels (main map):

GREECE · Ankara · SOVIET UNION · SOVIET UNION · CASPIAN SEA · TURKEY · Teheran · Kabul

MEDITERRANEAN SEA · Nicosia · SYRIA · IRAQ · AFGHANISTAN
1979—Soviets invade, U.S. aids Moslem revolt
1989—Soviets pull out; civil war continues

CYPRUS · LEBANON · Beirut · Baghdad · IRAN
Tripoli · ISRAEL · Damascus · 1980-88—War with Iran
1988—Chemical attacks on Kurds

GULF OF SIDRA · Jerusalem · Amman · PAKISTAN

LIBYA · Cairo · JORDAN · KUWAIT · PERSIAN GULF · Straits of Hormuz
1969—Qaddafi takes power, expels U.S. bases
1977—Border clashes with Egypt
1986—U.S. bombs Tripoli

EGYPT · SAUDI ARABIA · BAHRAIN · OMAN
1956—Suez Crisis
1972—Soviet advisors expelled
1979—Peace treaty with Israel
1981—Sadat assassinated

Riyadh · QATAR · Abu Dhabi · GULF OF OMAN
UNITED ARAB EMIRATES · Muscat

CHAD · SUDAN · RED SEA · Mecca · OMAN
1980-87—France, Libya intervene in civil war
1983—North-South war begins
1985—Pro-U.S. regime ousted
1979—Mecca Mosque battle

1951—Mossadegh nationalizes foreign oil holdings
1953—U.S. helps oust Mossadegh, return Shah
1979—Shah deposed
1979-81—U.S. Embassy seized
1987-88—U.S. naval clashes in Gulf

YEMEN · Sana · SOUTH YEMEN
1979—War with Yemen
1986—Pro-Soviet factions battle

DJIBOUTI · Aden · GULF OF ADEN · ARABIAN SEA

SOMALIA · ETHIOPIA · MADAGASCAR

Inset map — EXPANSION OF ISRAEL:

LEBANON · Beirut
1958—U.S. Marines bolster government
1975—Civil War begins
1982—Israel invades
1983—U.S. Marine barracks bombed
1984—U.S. naval shelling; pull-out

Sidon · Damascus
Tyre · 1976—Invasion of Lebanon
SYRIA · GOLAN HEIGHTS

ISRAEL
1948—War of Independence
1956—Sinai War
1967—Six-Day War
1973—Yom Kippur War

WEST BANK · Amman
Tel Aviv · Jerusalem · Dead Sea

MEDITERRANEAN SEA · GAZA STRIP
1987—Palestinian uprising begins
1988—PLO declares independence

EGYPT · Suez Canal · JORDAN
1988—King Hussein gives up West Bank claim

SINAI PENINSULA · Elat · Aqaba

GULF OF SUEZ · GULF OF AQABA

SAUDI ARABIA · RED SEA

0   50 Miles
0   50 Kilometers

Legend:

Israel, 1948
Territory gained, 1949
Territory occupied, 1967
Territory yielded, 1979-82
Territory occupied, 1982-86
Area of Israeli settlements
OPEC member nations
▲ Major oil fields

OPEC: Organization of Petroleum Exporting Countries (Members not shown are Nigeria, Algeria, Gabon, Indonesia, Venezuela, and Ecuador)

PLO: Palestine Liberation Organization

0   250   500 Miles
0   250   500 Kilometers

OIL AND CONFLICT IN THE MIDDLE EAST

What the Balkans had been before World War I the Middle East became after World War II: a vital geopolitical region beset by big-power rivalry and complicated by tribal, ethnic, and religious divisions and political instability. Much of the world's known oil reserves lie along the Persian Gulf. Proximity to the Soviet Union and vital trade routes like the Suez Canal define the region's geographic importance. Revolutions in Iran and Afghanistan, intermittent warfare between Arabs and Jews, the unresolved questions of Israel's borders and a Palestinian homeland, the disintegration of Lebanon, and a long, bloody war between Iran and Iraq have been among the conflicts that have unsettled the region.

That was just one strand in the web Kissinger sought to weave. He also saw the possibility of indirectly asserting American power through a client state. To that end he and Nixon had authorized the sale of the most advanced weapons to the shah of oil-rich Iran. Some 40,000 American military and civilian advisers went to Iran to modernize its military and civilian economies. In regional conflicts the shah, unlike the United States, could threaten pro-Soviet states like Iraq and Syria. In that same spirit Kissinger asserted American power in less strategically vital areas of the Third World, especially in the southwest African nation of Angola. With the departure of Portugal's colonial government, rival factions struggled to gain power. Since the Soviet Union backed the more powerful group, Kissinger ordered the CIA to give covert aid to pro-Western elements.

Kissinger found that despite his almost heroic efforts, he could not stem the erosion of American power. As involvement in Angola stirred memories of Vietnam, Congress prohibited the CIA from spending money for the Angolan civil war. While Kissinger struggled to restore order to the Middle East, the American client government in Vietnam fell. In 1973 President Thieu had broken the cease-fire agreement. By the spring of 1975 the South Vietnamese forces faced certain defeat. President Ford asked Congress for $1 billion in aid to Vietnam, Cambodia, and Laos, but Congress refused to spend more money on a lost cause. The end came almost immediately after. Desperate South Vietnamese civilian and military leaders rushed to escape Communist retribution.

Even in the Western Hemisphere American hegemony eroded. The OPEC boycott heightened the dependence of the United States on Mexico, Venezuela, and Canada for much of its imported energy. While those countries benefited from higher oil prices, oil-dependent economies like Brazil's suffered. As a result, Brazil and other exporters tried to do with coffee and other raw materials what the Arabs had done with oil. Even the normally cooperative Canadians showed an inclination to establish more economic distance. Americans owned or controlled large economic interests in Canada, and much of Canada's popular culture came from the United States. Under Prime Minister Pierre Elliot Trudeau, Canada pursued a more independent foreign policy. It established ties to China and the Soviet Union while limiting the level of foreign investments. And as OPEC tightened its noose, Canada cut back exports to the United States to meet its own energy needs. As much as Kissinger saw Europe, the Middle East, and Asia as the arena for big power initiatives, he could not ignore the growing disaffection between the United States and its hemispheric neighbors.

Détente

Vietnam, Chile, the Yom Kippur War, and Angola indicated that the spirit of détente had not ended Soviet–American rivalry over the Third World. Seeking to ease tensions, Ford met with Soviet leader Leonid Brezhnev in November 1974. Since economic stagnation had dogged the Soviet Union, Brezhnev came to Vladivostok eager for more American trade; Ford and Kissinger wanted a limit on nuclear weapons that preserved the current American advantage. Though many issues could not be resolved, the two sides agreed in principle to a framework for a second SALT treaty.

A similar hope to extend détente brought Ford and Brezhnev together with European leaders at Helsinki, Finland, in August 1975. There they agreed to recognize the political boundaries that had divided Eastern and Western Europe since 1945. For the first time the United States sent an ambassador to East Germany. In return Brezhnev eased restrictions on the rights of Soviet Jews to emigrate. That issue had led numerous senators and congressmen to oppose trade agreements with the Soviet Union.

The erosion of American power, symbolized by Kissinger's overtures to the Soviet Union, led outraged Republican conservatives like 1976 presidential hopeful Ronald Reagan to criticize Ford and Kissinger for trafficking with the Communists. When the administration proposed to return operating control of the Panama Canal to Panama in order to ease tensions in Latin America, the conservatives charged Ford with selling out American interests and weakening the nation's power. In an effort to subdue the critics, Ford in 1976 stripped Kissinger of his post as National Security Advisor.

An Embattled Presidency

Every president has a "honeymoon" during which the press and opposing politicians restrain criticism. Ford's presidential honeymoon was much shorter than most. His first setback came when he appointed former New York governor Nelson A. Rockefeller as vice-president. Liberals had never forgiven Rockefeller for violent police actions in 1971 at Attica Prison which left 33 prisoners and 10 hostages dead. Populist conservatives resented Rockefeller's inherited wealth and viewed him, along with his protégé Henry Kissinger, as the embodiment of the eastern establishment's liberal internationalism.

If the conservatives were angry about Rockefeller, almost everyone was outraged when Ford pardoned Richard Nixon on September 8, 1974. Pardon meant no prosecution, leaving charges unanswered and crimes unpunished. In trying to put Watergate in the past, Ford reopened the wounds. He did the same in refusing charity to the draft resisters from the Vietnam War. He offered them conditional amnesty after review by a government panel. Most of the 350,000 resisters refused the terms, which still held them guilty for an act of conscience. Conservatives and veterans' groups objected to leniency for those they saw as disloyal citizens.

Then Ford inadvertently exposed widespread abuses by the CIA and FBI. Upon taking office, he had incautiously admitted the CIA was involved in the overthrow of Salvador Allende. Soon after, Seymour Hersh of the New York *Times* uncovered illegal CIA domestic espionage operations. A commission headed by Vice President Rockefeller reported that the abuses were more widespread than at first expected. The CIA routinely kept citizens under surveillance, had conducted drug experiments on unwitting subjects, had used Operation CHAOS to infiltrate protest organizations, and had done political dirty work for the White House.

A Senate committee headed by Frank Church of Idaho produced equally disturbing information. The CIA had been involved in numerous assassinations or attempted murders of foreign leaders, including Fidel Castro of Cuba, Patrice Lumumba of the Congo, Rafael Trujillo of the Dominican Republic, and Ngo Dinh Diem of South Vietnam, as well as Allende. The FBI had similarly used illegal means to infiltrate and disrupt domestic dissidents, including an attempt by J. Edgar Hoover to smear Martin Luther King. A chastened President Ford ordered the creation of an Intelligence Oversight Board to monitor the CIA, while the Senate created its own watchdog committee.

Most presidents' fortunes rise and fall with the economy. Ford faced the twin scourges of inflation and recession. As a conservative, he rejected the pressures to impose wage and price controls. Nor did he heed warnings from Democrats to avoid policies that used increased unemployment and lower earnings to fight rising prices. Donning a button with the inscription "WIN" (Whip Inflation Now), he declared inflation the nation's number one problem and opted for a mixture of lower government spending and voluntary restraints. With the economy reeling, the Democrats made major gains during the 1974 election, adding 49 seats in the House and 5 in the Senate as well as 4 governorships.

Election successes masked the deep divisions within the Democratic party in the wake of the 1972 McGovern campaign disaster. No more than the Republicans did the Democrats have a coherent program to restore the economy to health. When Ford went before Congress to give his first State of the Union message in January 1975, the country faced its worst slump since the Great Depression. During the previous quarter the gross national product had fallen over 9 percent, inflation had climbed to almost 14 percent, and unemployment exceeded 7 percent.

At the heart of the economic crisis lay the problem of rising energy costs. By 1976 consumption had returned to 1973 levels, even though domestic oil production had fallen by over 1 million barrels. Imports of Middle Eastern oil priced at almost $14 a barrel were needed to supply the nation's profligate thirst for energy. In 1975 Congress adopted the Energy Policy and Conservation Act, which increased the authority of the Federal Energy Administration to order utilities to burn abundant coal rather than expensive oil. In addition, the act created a strategic petroleum reserve as a hedge against future boycotts and ordered the auto industry to improve energy efficiency (mileage per gallon of fuel). And as a final—but environmentally dangerous—stopgap measure, the government encouraged the rapid development of nuclear power plants.

Rising energy costs struck hardest at the older industrial centers of the Northeast and Upper Midwest, which imported most of their energy. Housing and plants built in the days of cheap energy proved wasteful and inefficient. Nixon's

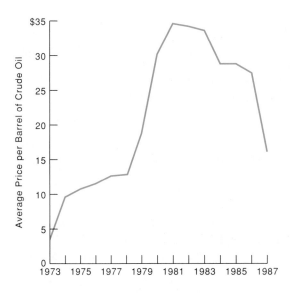

OPEC OIL PRICES, 1973–1987
Prices fell even further than the chart shows after 1980 because the dollar was worth much less than in 1973.

and Ford's fiscal conservatism hurt too. Cutbacks in federal spending fell hardest on major cities with shrinking tax bases, outmoded industries, and heavy social service costs. The crisis for "rust belt" cities came to a head in October 1975 when New York announced it stood on the brink of bankruptcy.

New York's problems stemmed in part from its extensive welfare services, its careless budgetary practices, and its bloated municipal employee unions and in part from the loss of jobs in the private sector. With few ways left to raise taxes or borrow money, Mayor Abraham D. Beame appealed to the federal government for help. When Ford refused, the New York *Daily News'* headline stated, "FORD TO CITY: DROP DEAD." Only after New York had overhauled its finances and won concessions from city workers did Ford authorize loans. His grudging response, which forced much-needed reforms, seemed highly insensitive to the beleaguered people of New York and other strapped municipalities.

The Election of 1976

In the 1976 presidential campaign the greatest debates occurred within rather than between the major parties. Ford's greatest challenge came from former California governor, movie actor, and television pitchman Ronald Reagan. Once a supporter of Franklin Roosevelt, Reagan discovered true conservatism after his marriage to actress Nancy Davis. Although Ford's appearances lost him votes, the polished Reagan won crowds with an aggressive style that radiated amiability. "Under Messrs. Nixon and Ford this nation has become Number Two in military power," he would tell enthusiastic audiences. Reagan had the race deadlocked until the convention, where Ford eked out the nomination while the Reagan forces controlled the party platform, which attacked détente, opposed busing, called for constitutional amendments on balanced budgets, school prayer, and prohibition of abortions, and generally favored reduction of government in Washington wherever possible.

Among Democratic hopefuls James Earl (Jimmy) Carter's anonymity before 1976 proved a strength. His southern accent marked him as a Washington outsider. His image as a "born-again" Christian reassured those Americans searching for renewed faith. And one pledge—"I would not tell a lie"—seemed a welcome antidote to cover-ups and deceptions. Somehow Carter managed to address controversial issues such as abortion or busing without offending large groups on either side. He was "personally opposed to abortion" as a Christian but against a constitutional amendment overturning *Roe v. Wade.* In their platform, rather than their candidate, the Democrats established some distance from the rival GOP. They supported federal health insurance, job programs, and the ERA while opposing an antiabortion amendment and reluctantly accepting busing as a last-ditch tool to achieve integration.

Seldom has an election generated so little interest. "Don't Vote. It Only Encourages Them," one popular bumper sticker proclaimed. No matter who won, American politics in the age of limits would have a conservative flavor. Partisanship proved stronger than ever as most voters (80 percent of Democrats and 90 percent of Republicans) backed their party's candidate. It added up to 50.1 percent for Carter, a popular edge of almost 1.7 million, and a 57-vote lead (297–240) in the Electoral College. Carter's overwhelming margin among blacks (90 percent) carried the South and offset Ford's margin among whites, especially in the western states, which all went Republican. Resounding Democratic majorities in the

Senate (62–38), House (292–143), and governorships (37–12–1) indicated more accurately than the presidential race how much the weak economy had hurt the Republicans.

JIMMY CARTER, RESTORING THE FAITH

"If after the inauguration you find a Cy Vance as secretary of state and Zbigniew Brzezinski as head of national security, then I would say we have failed," Carter's chief aide Hamilton Jordan told reporters during the campaign. The new administration promised to bring fresh faces to Washington. But once elected Carter turned to hiring familiar figures. He appointed establishment lawyer Cyrus Vance as secretary of state and Columbia professor Zbigniew Brzezinski as national security adviser. The New York *Times* warned Carter against such a contradiction because he "lacks the eloquence to hide it." But more than any political shortcoming, the weak economy and small electoral margin denied Carter an opportunity for bold leadership.

The Carter Style

Carter tried to remove some of the trappings from the imperial presidency and infuse a simpler style into the White House. Rather than the usual Inauguration Day ride down Pennsylvania Avenue in the presidential limousine, the president and his wife Rosalynn walked. He shunned the formal morning coat and tails for a business suit. And he cut perquisites and brought into his cabinet many Washington newcomers, whose lack of familiarity with federal administration probably made them unsuitable for high office. Consumer advocate Ralph Nader warned that Carter's "conservatives with high integrity would follow the wrong policies straight instead of crooked."

If Carter had any overriding sense of direction, it remained obscure throughout his administration. He had a tremendous grasp of information but often focused so narrowly on details that he failed to clarify his larger goals. On the one hand, he appointed as ambassador to the United Nations former Georgia congressman and black activist Andrew Young, who hoped to improve American relations with the nonwhite peoples of the Southern Hemisphere. On the other hand, Carter chose as attorney general a Georgian, Griffin Bell, who had belonged to racially and religiously segregated clubs and held generally conservative views on political and social issues. Would the conservative outsider Bell or the liberal Washington veteran Young indicate the course of the new administration?

In foreign policy Carter accepted the realities of decolonization. The United States, he suggested, should exert "leadership without hegemony." Inordinate fear of Communism had led the United States in the past to support any right-wing dictator who happened to oppose Communism. Under Carter, the United States would reassert its moral purpose by giving a higher priority to the preservation of human rights. And in his Inaugural Address, the former nuclear submarine officer established as his ultimate goal "the elimination of all nuclear weapons from this earth." His direction of foreign policy was confused, however, by the rivalry between Zbigniew Brzezinski and Secretary of State Cyrus Vance. Brzezinski profoundly mistrusted the Soviet Union. He had the staunch cold warrior's concern with containing the Communist menace. Vance believed negotiations were both possible and potentially profitable. Stronger economic ties would reduce the risk of superpower conflict. Carter gravitated in both directions.

The president found it most difficult to sustain his good intentions on the domestic front. He set out to make government more efficient, responsive to the people, and ethical. Yet when he first tried to impose these standards by eliminating 19 expensive pork barrel water projects, the leaders of his own party threatened to bury his legislative program. And his efforts to restore faith in government ran afoul of revelations of widespread congressional corruption. Perhaps as many as a hundred congressmen had received bribes from the South Korean government. Others were involved in various kickback schemes and accepted bribes from federal agents posing as Arabs in the "Abscam" investigation. When the dubious financial dealings of his brother Billy and his Georgia friend and budget director Burt Lance came to light, Carter remained loyal to family and friend. But the failure to discipline the two made the president seem hypocritical.

With congressional leaders unwilling and unable to discipline Senate and House members, Carter found it almost impossible to push through a legislative program. And like Gerald Ford, he learned that the wounds of Vietnam were slow to heal. In response to a campaign pledge, he granted amnesty to Vietnam War draft resisters but not to veterans with dishonorable discharges. Conservatives like Barry Goldwater were outraged and many veterans were bitter. As the American Civil Liberties Union pointed out, the veterans with tainted discharges were more likely to be the undereducated poor from minority groups.

The Moral Equivalent of War

In 1977 even the weather seemed to conspire against the Carter administration. One of the most severe winters in modern history created temporary shortages of heating fuels and drove prices up. Heavy snows and fierce cold forced many schools and factories to close. Like Ford, Carter preferred to ask for voluntary restraint rather than enforce mandatory government policies to conserve energy and control fuel costs. To meet the energy crisis the nation had to adopt conservation measures as the "moral equivalent of war," he announced in April 1977.

Carter correctly sensed that conservation was the cheapest and most environmentally desirable way to discourage dependence on foreign oil. But homilies about "helping our neighbors" did not sell the president's program of new taxes aimed to discourage wasteful energy consumption. The American way, as domestic oil producers were quick to argue, was to produce more, not live with less. The oil industry insisted that deregulation of energy prices would stimulate sufficient production to meet the nation's needs. Americans in general were too wedded to large gas-guzzling cars, air conditioners, inefficient electrical appliances, and warm houses to accept limits as long as fuel was available. Although Congress did agree to establish a cabinet-level Department of Energy, it rejected most of Carter's energy taxes and proposals to encourage solar alternatives.

By 1978 the "moral equivalent of war" looked more like its acronym: MEOW. Renewed administration efforts resulted in a weak National Energy Act, which provided tax credits for installation of energy-saving equipment, encouraged utility conversion to coal, and allowed prices to rise for newly discovered natural gas. As a result, the nation was ill-prepared for the dislocation in international oil markets that followed the 1978 revolution against the shah of Iran. Brief shortages allowed OPEC to raise prices 14.5 percent. Carter could only complain that such hikes were unfair while asking Americans to lower thermostats to 65 degrees and, if car trips were essential, observe the new 55 mile per hour speed limit.

As a diversion from the worries of energy shortages, many Americans flocked to see antinuclear activist Jane Fonda in the movie *China Syndrome*, a tale of faulty construction resulting in a meltdown of the core of a nuclear power plant. Then on March 28, 1979, a stuck valve at the Three Mile Island nuclear power plant in Pennsylvania released a cloud of radioactive gas into the atmosphere. It took two weeks before the reactor was shut down. A hundred thousand nearby residents fled their homes. Since the early 1950s public utilities had promoted nuclear power as the answer to future energy needs. Construction of plants raced ahead of technological safeguards and solutions to the problem of nuclear waste disposal. By the time of Three Mile Island, huge construction cost overruns and concerns about safety had inspired a growing antinuclear backlash. Experts now admitted that nuclear plants were no more than a temporary response to the nation's long-term needs.

In the wake of Three Mile Island, President Carter appealed anew for a strong energy program, most of which Congress rejected. By May motorists once

The danger of depending on nuclear power as an alternate source of energy became evident in 1979 when an accident closed this plant at Three Mile Island near Harrisburg, Pennsylvania. The large towers are part of the cooling system in which the accident occurred. Huge construction costs, the unsolved problem of nuclear waste disposal, and safety issues soon soured the public on nuclear energy.

INCOME PROJECTIONS OF
TWO-INCOME FAMILIES,
1967–1984
In the age of limits family income stayed relatively even only because more wives entered the work force. Wages for individual workers fell, when calculated in real dollars.

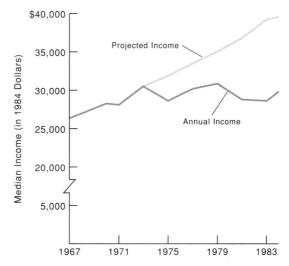

Source: Frank Levy, *Dollars and Dreams: The Changing American Income Distribution* (New York: Norton, 1988), p. 204.

again faced long lines at the gas pumps. OPEC announced plans for a 50 percent price hike. Not until spring 1980 did Congress pass a bill taxing windfall profits (although not significantly), regulating nuclear power more stringently, establishing a Synthetic Fuels Corporation and a solar-energy program, and reviving the Strategic Petroleum Reserve. Carter had promoted sacrifice as a way to "seize control of our common destiny"; Congress preferred halfhearted measures that left America's energy future in OPEC's hands.

A Sick Economy

An economy dependent on inexpensive fuel could hardly absorb rapid OPEC price hikes without serious dislocations. Colleges that had allocated 10 percent of their budgets to energy soon had to pay as much as 50 percent. All costs began a dramatic rise as inflation shot from just below 6 percent in 1976 to almost 14 percent by 1979. Workers' wages could not keep pace. People took home more dollars, but real earnings steadily eroded. Federal policies made matters worse. Government payments to farmers, higher minimum wages, import protection for key industries like steel, and new Social Security taxes added to inflationary pressures. So too did declines in the productivity of American labor, where output for each workhour kept dropping. Outmoded industrial plants, ineffective management practices, burdensome union rules, and inflexible wage contracts with built-in cost-of-living adjustments lowered the competitive standing of American industry in world markets.

As has been true since the early twentieth century, the automobile industry played a determining and symbolic economic role. In 1978 the industry was sick, with the Chrysler Corporation at death's door. The company had for years made serious mistakes in styling and had been unable to design and build small cars in time to respond to shifting consumer demand. Unless the government provided a billion-dollar tax credit, warned Chrysler president Lee Iacocca, the nation's tenth largest business enterprise faced bankruptcy.

"Are we going to guarantee businessmen against their own incompetence?" asked an angry Senator William Proxmire. "No one should hold half a million workers responsible for the decisions of a few officials long since gone," replied Michigan congressman James Blanchard in defense of the Chrysler bailout. In the end the reality of unemployed autoworkers weighed more heavily than the abstractions of free market rhetoric. After wringing wage concessions from Chrysler employees, Congress agreed to guarantee a $1.5 billion loan that did bring Chrysler off the critical list. Still, disgruntled liberals and conservatives appreciated the lyrics of folk singer Tom Paxton as he announced,

> I'm changing my name to Chrysler.
> I'll be waiting in that great receiving line.
> So when they hand a billion grand out,
> I'll be standing with my hand out;
> Mister I'll get by.

The Chrysler loan was little more than a bandage on a badly wounded economy. "Hard choices" were needed to stem inflation, reverse mounting trade deficits, ease rising interest rates, and reduce the federal deficit, the *Wall Street Journal* argued. But Carter called only for voluntary restraints on prices and wages, while seeking to restore the strength of the dollar in international trade. The high interest rates favored by conservatives struck hardest at American consumers addicted to installment and credit-card buying. Before Carter's economic remedies could work, OPEC began another round of oil price hikes that increased energy costs almost 60 percent. Interest rates shot up to almost 20 percent. Mortgage money disappeared. New "housing starts" (the number of homes under construction), second in economic importance only to automobiles, dwindled, while older homes went unsold. With Federal Reserve rates at 15 percent, an anti-inflationary recession in 1980 doomed Carter's political future.

Leadership, Not Hegemony

Presidents battered on the domestic front often see a strong foreign policy as one way to restore power and prestige. Carter achieved a stunning breakthrough in mediating the longstanding hostility between Israel and Egypt, only to fall hostage to OPEC and to Islamic revolutionaries in Iran.

For all the carping from hardboiled liberals and conservatives, Carter's human rights policy did make a difference. At least one Argentinian Nobel Peace Prize winner, Adolfo Pérez Esquivel, claimed he owed his life to it. So did hundreds of others in countries like the Philippines, South Korea, Argentina, and Chile, where dissidents were routinely murdered and tortured. The Carter administration exerted economic pressures to promote more humane policies. Yet when rich minerals, oil, or other national security interests were involved, the administration managed to ignore flagrant abuses. The shah of Iran was so good a customer for American arms and such a major oil exporter that Carter ignored the terror of the shah's secret police, SAVAK, against Iranian political prisoners. Joseph Mobutu, dictator of Zaire in Central Africa, had one of the world's most indefensible records on human rights. His nation also controlled vast mineral resources exploited by European companies, so when rebels from nearby Angola threatened Mobutu, the United States flew in Moroccan and French troops and provided financial aid.

Declining American influence in the Third World underlay a growing debate over Panama. To many Americans the Panama Canal symbolized the American role as a great power. Most Americans believed the United States owned the canal, but in reality it held sovereignty in a ten-mile-wide strip called the Canal Zone and ran the canal under a perpetual lease. Since the 1960s Panamanians had resented and sometimes rioted against American dominance. Pushed by Secretary of State Vance to ease anti-American sentiment in the region, Carter won Senate approval in 1977 of several treaties that returned sovereignty over the canal to Panama by 1999 but maintained the American right to defend and use the waterway. Senator S. I. Hayakawa of California spoke for the defenders of the American imperial tradition when he argued, "It's ours. We stole it fair and square."

Cyrus Vance had pushed the canal treaties as part of a policy of negotiation and conciliation that greatly enhanced American prestige in Central America. From 1979 on, however, it was not Vance but Zbigniew Brzezinski who dominated the administration's foreign policy. Brzezinski was determined to reimpose a cold war framework, even in Latin America. Unrest troubled all the region's struggling nations, especially Nicaragua. The corrupt government of Anastasio Somoza had proven so venal and predatory that it alienated the normally conservative propertied classes. When leading Nicaraguan business figures threw their support behind the rebel Sandinista movement, Carter tried to rally the Organization of American States (OAS) to prevent a rebel victory.

No other nation proved willing to support Somoza and after the rebels assumed power they rejected American aid in favor of a nonaligned status and friendliness toward Cuba. As revolution spread in neighboring El Salvador, the Sandinistas sent supplies. The Carter administration could not make a case for the Salvadoran government, which had systematically murdered its own people as well as four American Catholic churchwomen. Still Carter and his successor Ronald Reagan would assist El Salvador while encouraging the overthrow of the leftist government in Nicaragua.

The United States under Carter was not the only superpower with a flagging economy and problems in the Third World. The Soviet Union struggled with an aging leadership and an economy that produced guns but little butter. Even rising oil prices did not help, although the Russians led the world in oil production. Gains from oil were drained off by inefficient industries, support for impoverished allies in Eastern Europe, Cuba, and Vietnam, and attempts to extend Soviet influence in the Middle East and Africa. Economic weakness made the Soviets receptive to greater cooperation with the United States. In that spirit Carter and Soviet premier Leonid Brezhnev in 1977 issued a joint statement on a Middle East Peace.

Opposition to a Soviet Middle Eastern role was immediate and powerful. Carter quickly learned, as had every politician since Harry Truman, that Soviet bashing made far better domestic politics than did easing of cold war tensions. He quickly rendered his understanding with Brezhnev inoperative. The Soviets then renewed arms shipments to Israel's archenemy, Syria. And in that troubled environment, Zbigniew Brzezinski flew off to Beijing to revive the China card. The United States extended formal recognition to China in 1979. Trade doubled within a single year. The Chinese in return exploited the new relationship to launch a punitive invasion of Vietnam.

For the Russians the China card created a potential Japanese–Chinese–American alliance on their Asian border. In a last attempt to save détente Brezhnev met Carter at a Vienna summit conference in 1979. Their main subject was arms control under SALT II. The treaty did limit nuclear launchers to 2400 and MIRVs (missiles with multiple warheads) to 1320 on each side. But neither side would agree to scrap key weapons systems—the Soviets' 300 huge land-based ICBMs and the new American radar-evading cruise missiles. The cold war lobby led by Paul Nitze, author of NSC-68 (page 1111), killed the treaty even though Brezhnev allowed the emigration of 50,000 Soviet Jews in support of improved Soviet–American relations. Opponents objected to the idea of nuclear weapons' parity as symbolic of declining American power. They never acknowledged that part of the Soviet arsenal was aimed at China, not Western Europe or the United States. Nor did they include in the American arsenal the added potential of British and French nuclear forces.

Stung by hostility to the Vance policy of negotiations and accommodations, Carter turned increasingly to Brzezinski, confrontation, and a military buildup. The president expanded the defense budget, built American bases in the Persian Gulf region, sent aid to anticommunist dictators whatever their record on human rights, and created a Rapid Deployment Force to defend exposed American interests in the Middle East. The Soviet Union responded with similar truculence.

The Middle East: Hope and Hostages

What the unstable Balkans were to Europe in the pre–World War I era the Middle East promised to be for the superpowers in the 1970s and 1980s. Oil and proximity to the Soviet's southern border gave the area its geopolitical importance. Religious, tribal, national, and ethnic rivalries created chronic instability dramatized by the endless bloodletting in Beirut, Lebanon, and the outbreak of war between Israel and its Arab neighbors in 1948, 1956, 1967, and 1973. The United States had strong ties to oil-rich Saudi Arabia, a commitment to the survival of Israel, and a determination to prevent the Soviet Union from extending its influence into the area.

Preservation of the peace was one key to American policy. As a result, Americans were greatly encouraged when President Anwar Sadat of Egypt made an unprecedented trip to Israel to meet with Prime Minister Menachem Begin. To encourage the peace process, Carter invited Begin and Sadat to Camp David in Maryland in September 1978. For 13 days the three men argued, threatened, and cajoled. When it was over, Carter had helped the two reach an agreement ending the 30-year state of war between Israel and Egypt. Israel accommodated Egypt by agreeing to withdraw from the Sinai Peninsula, which it had occupied since 1967; Carter compensated Israel by offering $3 billion in military aid. Begin and Sadat shared a Nobel Peace Prize that might just as fairly have gone to Carter for his critical role in forcing the two to compromise their profound differences.

Camp David established only a momentary hope for Middle Eastern stability. Throughout the 1970s, policymakers had seen the shah of Iran, with his huge American-equipped military forces, as a possible regional policeman. Equally important, a stable Iran blocked Soviet access to the Persian Gulf and its oil. While American intelligence agents scoured the world for signs of potential leftist revolutions, they virtually ignored the possibility of a religious revolution from the

It was at Camp David, in private talks sponsored by President Jimmy Carter (center), that Egyptian President Anwar el-Sadat (left) and Israeli Prime Minister Menachem Begin (right) hammered out a "Framework for Peace in the Middle East" as a first step toward ending decades of war and mistrust. For their efforts Begin and Sadat shared the Nobel Peace Prize of 1978, but the prize justifiably might have gone to Carter.

right in a country as important to the United States as Iran. Thus in the fall of 1978 the dramatic collapse of the Pahlevi dynasty and the rise of Islamic fundamentalists led by the Ayatollah Ruholla Khomeini took the United States almost completely by surprise.

Brzezinski urged Carter to support the shah with troops if necessary; Vance recommended meetings with the revolutionary leaders, distance from the shah, and military restraint. Carter waffled between the two by encouraging the shah to resist with force but holding back any American participation. Indecision created the worst of two worlds. The shah fell in February 1979 and the revolutionaries declared a holy war against the modernizing Western influence the United States had so liberally sowed in Iran. By the fall of 1979 Kissinger, Brzezinski, and other friends of the shah persuaded Carter to admit the dying monarch into the United States for medical treatment. That enraged the Islamic fundamentalists, who saw the shah as a traitor and criminal. They stormed the American embassy in Iran and held 53 Americans hostage.

The hostage crisis seemed to symbolize the inability of the Carter administration to maintain American power and prestige abroad. Concern arose that the Shiite fundamentalists would spread revolutionary instability throughout the region or, worse yet, the Soviets might prey upon a weakened Iran. But the Soviets also worried that religious zeal might spread to restless minorities, especially those within their own borders. With China hostile and Iran in turmoil, Brezhnev on December 27, 1979, ordered Soviet troops into neighboring Afghanistan to subdue anticommunist Muslim guerrillas.

An outraged President Carter condemned the invasion. He withdrew SALT II from the Senate (where it stood no chance of passage), renewed registration for the draft, accelerated the military buildup, embargoed sales of American wheat and technology to the Soviet Union, and forced the United States to withdraw from the 1980 Olympic games in Moscow. And in the tradition of presidents since World War II, he announced the Carter Doctrine, a commitment to intervene unilaterally if the Soviet Union threatened American interests in the Persian Gulf.

The spectacle of "America Held Hostage" shown on nightly newscasts killed Carter's hopes for another term. It did not help that Iran's turmoil led to another round of OPEC price hikes and new inflationary pressures. Nor did it help that Americans eager to confront the Soviet Union were reluctant to sacrifice personally to do so. Agricultural interests, Olympic athletes, the new generation of draft resisters, and feminists all had complaints: Why should the American farmer shoulder the burden of a grain embargo? What do sports have to do with politics? Why should military buildup require draft registration? And shouldn't the draft include women?

Once again Carter faced a test of his leadership. Even more than the 53 Americans in Tehran, Jimmy Carter had been taken hostage by events in the Middle East. His ratings in national polls sank to record lows (77 percent negative). He responded by reviving the cold war rhetoric of the 1950s and accelerating the development of nuclear weapons. But whereas the CIA in 1953 had successfully overthrown an Iranian government, the American military in 1980 proved incapable of organizing a mission to free the hostages (or perhaps to kidnap Khomeini). Eight Marines died in the collision of two helicopters and a plane in Iran's central desert. Cyrus Vance, a lonely voice of moderation, finally resigned.

By 1980 the United States was mired in what Carter himself described as "a crisis of confidence." Visions of Vietnam, Central America, and the Middle East produced a nightmare of waning American power and prestige. Economic dislocations at home revived fears of a depression. And an accompanying spiritual malaise left the American people looking for some way to restore their lost faith. None of these problems had begun with Jimmy Carter. The inflationary cycle and declining American productivity had their roots in the Vietnam era. And ironically, America's lost hegemony reflected long-term success in bringing economic growth to Europe, the Pacific rim, and to a lesser degree Brazil, Mexico, India, and Saudi Arabia.

Thus Carter's failure was more symbolic. He lost the leadership issue to prophets on the political right who campaigned to restore American hegemony by expanding the military and revitalizing the cold war crusade. And in the "me generation" Carter's appeals to sacrifice could not overcome the hawkers of self-help therapy, fundamentalist defenders of the faith, and more traditional commercial vendors of the American dream who promised spiritual renewal in the 1980s.

SIGNIFICANT EVENTS

1962 — Rachel Carson's *Silent Spring* published

1965 — Ralph Nader's *Unsafe at Any Speed* published

1966 — National Traffic and Motor Vehicle Safety Act; NOW established

1969 — Apollo 11 moon mission; Santa Barbara oil spill; National Environmental Policy Act

1970 — First Earth Day; Environmental Protection Agency created; NOW organizes Strike for Equality; CIA assists overthrow of Allende in Chile

1971 — Barry Commoner's *The Closing Circle* published

1972 — Congress passes Equal Rights Amendment; Woodward and Bernstein investigate Watergate burglary

1973 — Watergate burglars convicted; *Roe v. Wade*; Haldeman and Erlichman resign; Ervin Committee hearings; Archibald Cox appointed special prosecutor; Spiro Agnew resigns; Saturday Night Massacre; War Powers Act; OPEC oil boycott triggers U.S. recession

1974 — *United States v. Nixon*; House adopts articles of impeachment; Nixon resigns; Ford becomes president; Fair Campaign Practices Act; Kissinger Arab–Israeli "shuttle" diplomacy; Ford–Brezhnev meeting at Vladivostok; Ford pardons Nixon; Church Committee exposes CIA and FBI abuses

1975 — Thieu government falls in South Vietnam; Helsinki Summit; Energy Policy and Conservation Act; New York City faces bankruptcy

1976 — Carter defeats Ford

1977 — Hyde Amendment limiting abortions; congressional scandals; Department of Energy established; Panama Canal treaties

1978 — Revolution in Iran; Chrysler bailout; Camp David meetings

1979 — Three Mile Island crisis; energy crisis; United States recognizes Peoples' Republic of China; SALT II agreement; Iran hostage crisis; Soviet Union invades Afghanistan

1980 — Inflation and recession hurt economy; Carter adopts sanctions against the Soviet Union; U.S. hostage mission fails

1982 — Ratification of ERA fails

35

A Nation
Still Divisible

n the early 1970s San Diego city officials looked out at a downtown that was growing seedier each year, as stores and shoppers continued their flight to the suburbs. As once-thriving downtown retail centers disintegrated, becoming virtual ghost towns at the close of the business day, the task of revitalizing cities confronted urban planners across the nation. San Diego, with 13 separate malls in suburbs ringing the city's perimeter, was typical. So the city came up with a $3 billion redevelopment plan, calling for a convention center, marina, hotels, and apartment complexes.

The city also intended to beat the suburbs at their own game by erecting Horton Plaza, a mall on a grand scale. By 1985 construction crews had transformed the city center into a shopping complex with the look of an Italian hill town. Stores with stucco facades fronted twisting pedestrian thoroughfares, where Renaissance arches and contrasting-striped stonework lured customers to upscale stores like Banana Republic (which sold safari-style travel clothes), to jewelers, and to sporting goods shops. Jugglers and clowns wandered the streets, while paid guitarists serenaded passersby. Horton Plaza's imitation of Old World architecture in trendy southern California soon followed the zoo and Sea World as San Diego's third-ranked tourist attraction, drawing over 12 million shoppers and tourists in 1986 alone.

Although Horton Plaza was more extravagant than most of its competitors, it was hardly an innovation. The first enclosed mall, Southdale Center, had been completed nearly 20 years earlier in Edina, Minnesota, near Minneapolis. Edina had good reason for enclosure: with chilling winters and 100 days a year of rain, shopping conditions were hardly ideal for outdoor strollers. The mall's planners approached Victor Gruen, an architect who had been seeking ways to reclaim urban downtowns from what he saw as the tyranny of the automobile. Gruen contrasted the pedestrian-dominated streets and fountain-filled squares of European villages with the acres of sterile parking lots surrounding suburban shopping centers. As he noted in his manifesto, *The Tired Heart of Our Cities*, automobiles added pollution and congestion to the urban environment. They decentralized and dehumanized cities with their space-consuming superhighways, inner loops, cloverleafs and exitways, parking lots, gas stations, and auto repair shops. Southdale provided an alternative model: a climate-controlled (68 degrees year-round)

Bringing a touch of Disney World–style magic to urban redevelopment, San Diego succeeded in luring shoppers back to its downtown retail center with Horton Plaza, a replica of an Italian hill town.

marketplace where shoppers could browse or get a bite to eat at a café without dodging cars or inhaling exhaust fumes.

Retailers elsewhere in the nation were at first reluctant to join the move to malls, fearing that if customers couldn't drive by their stores or park in front, they wouldn't stop and shop. There was no arguing, however, with success: virtually all the new malls turned handsome profits. By 1985, when Horton Plaza opened, Southdale had expanded to a three-level, 144-store complex, spreading over 1.1 million square feet. Nationwide, there were more shopping centers (25,000) than either school districts or hospitals. Some 2800 were enclosed, like Southdale. Furthermore, shopping malls accounted for over 50 percent of all retail sales, excluding the sale of automobile supplies.

Indeed, malls had become money-making machines, crafted to provide the right blend of stores for maximizing a consumer's buying opportunities. The mall manager at Southdale in 1986, Greg Bergan, could call upon sales figures that precisely defined his prime customers as women averaging 40.3 years in age with a household income of $33,750. Their purchases ran most often to clothes; thus 26 separate women's apparel stores took up a fifth of Southdale's floor space. The bottom line in profits was measured in sales per square foot. Jewelry stores led the way, with over $600 per square foot; shoe stores, a popular attraction, averaged over $300. Bergan was continually fine-tuning his retail mix. A Woolworth's store had long occupied a central spot in the mall, but its lease was not renewed. "This was crazy," he explained. "Who was shopping in it? The guy was paying me $3 a square foot." On the other hand a Lens Crafter store, which offered one-hour service on optical prescriptions, seemed a perfect addition. Customers had an hour to kill waiting for their glasses and spent it shopping in other stores. Malls like Southdale had become so profitable that investors with large amounts of capital, like pension funds and insurance companies, sought them out. Southdale was only one of a hundred malls owned by the Equitable Life Assurance Company.

If malls had become rewarding generators of income for investors, to consumers they were the cathedrals of American material culture. Shopping on Sunday seemed to rival churchgoing as the weekly family ritual. Whereas American youth culture had centered on the high school in the 1950s and on college campuses in the 1960s, in the 1970s and 1980s it gravitated toward mall fast-food stores and video amusement arcades. For single men and women malls became a place to find a date. Older people in search of a regimen of moderate exercise discovered that the controlled climate was ideal for "mall walking." For consumers of all stripes, malls were fantasy cities where no one lived but anyone could find a slice of the American dream.

The new cathedrals of consumption serve as an appropriate symbol of a society that in the late 1970s and 1980s turned away from protests and crusades back to the traditions of a consumer culture. Self-improvement replaced social reform as the road to a more perfect society. In the face of declining economic expectations and an age of limits, Americans found it difficult to sustain the commitment to systemic reform or to the liberal philosophies of government intervention. In seeking spiritual fulfillment, they turned in increasing numbers to evangelical religion, with its emphasis on the conversion of "born-again" individuals, private charities, and the virtues of the traditional family. Along less orthodox paths, the "human potential movement" focused on such techniques as yoga, transcendental meditation, and "bioenergetics" to bring inward personal fulfillment.

American politics too had a charismatic leader who celebrated conservative virtues. Against Jimmy Carter's recognition of the inevitability of limits at home and abroad, Ronald Reagan declared it was time for "America to stand tall again." Reagan evoked Puritan John Winthrop's seventeenth-century vision of an American "city on a hill," inspiring the rest of the world. He called for an America liberated from the shackles of the federal government's regulatory jungle, a nation that would resume its position as the number one military power in the world and encourage its citizens to promote the public good through the pursuit of private wealth.

At the same time, Reagan's ideal of limited government failed to address many of the unresolved issues of the 1970s. Indeed, the policies of deregulation, the shift of budget priorities to military spending, and a retreat from social intervention served to increase the gap between the rich and the poor. Environmental decay—whether in the form of acid rain, toxic waste dumps, or nuclear accidents—continued to threaten public health. On many levels the Reagan agenda called for a flight from public responsibility into a fantasy world no more authentic than the Italian hill town nestled in downtown San Diego. At times John Winthrop's austere vision seemed to have become a city on a hill with climate control, where the proprietors of Muzak-filled walkways banished all problems beyond the perimeters of the parking lots. Yet Ronald Reagan tapped the public's deep and abiding feelings of both resentment and hope. He confounded his critics with a capacity to sustain broad support for his image of a born-again America.

THE CONSERVATIVE REBELLION

In 1964 conservative Barry Goldwater had proclaimed his campaign slogan on billboards across America: "In Your Heart You Know He's Right." Beneath one of the billboards an unknown Democratic wag unfurled his own banner: "Yes—Extreme Right." In 1964 most citizens voted with the wag, perceiving Goldwater's platform as too conservative, too extreme, too dangerous for the times.

Two decades later, in the wake of social change at home and a wrenching war abroad, the public mood had changed. During the 1970s economic uncertainties caused by falling real incomes, energy shortages, and rising prices fed a growing resistance to a liberal political or social agenda. Hard-pressed workers resented increased competition from minorities, especially those supported by quotas and government programs. Taxpayers resisted the demands of government, especially at the local and state levels, for increased revenues to support social welfare spending. Rising divorce rates, single-parent households, and declining marriage rates made many Americans fear for the survival of the family. The media, whether television, movies, or popular music, purveyed a culture dominated by explicit sexuality and violence. Sexual permissiveness and the freedom to choose an abortion seemed to many traditional Catholics, orthodox Jews, and evangelical Protestants part of a wholesale assault on decency. Increasingly the political agenda was determined by those who wanted to restore a strong family, traditional religious values, reinvigorated patriotism, and limited government.

During the late 1970s and the 1980s conservatives increasingly spoke out against abortion and in favor of the right to life for unborn children. Adopting the tactics of protest and civil disobedience once common to radicals in the 1960s, they clash here with pro-choice demonstrators outside Faneuil Hall in Boston.

Born Again

One of the central threads in the conservative rebellion was a call for a renewed revival of religion, and that call came most vocally from white Protestant evangelicals. Fundamentalist Protestants had increasingly separated themselves from the older, more liberal denominations since the 1920s (page 928). In the decades after World War II their membership grew dramatically—between 400 and 700 percent, compared with under 90 percent for the older main-line denominations. By the 1980s they had become a significant third force in Christian America, after Roman Catholics and traditional Protestants. The election of Jimmy Carter, himself a professed born-again Christian, was one reflection of their newfound visibility.

Like most mass movements, evangelical Protestantism was more complex and divided than it appeared to outsiders. Fundamentalists, believing that the Holy Spirit had not spoken to individuals directly since the time of Christ, focused their attention on the literal words and message of the Bible as the key to divine guidance. Pentacostalists, on the other hand, insisted that the Holy Spirit still moved the faithful directly; some believers spoke "in tongues," their bodies and voices contorted by the spirit in them. Thus a fundamentalist like the Reverend Jerry Falwell had strong theological disagreements with a Pentacostalist like the Reverend Pat Robertson. Still, evangelicals found a good deal of common ground in what they saw as the corruptions of American society. They rejected feminism in favor of the patriarchal family, in which men were the breadwinners and spiritual heads and women raised children in the home. They attacked the Supreme Court for decisions which they believed helped open the floodgates of pornography. The demands of homosexuals for "gay rights" particularly offended their belief that the Bible condemned homosexuality as an unqualified sin.

Just as fundamentalists of the 1920s had sought to overturn the trend toward a more secular system of education, the evangelicals of the 1980s sought to refashion it. They pressed states and the federal government to adopt a "school prayer" amendment allowing officially sanctioned prayer in classrooms. They urged the teaching of "Creationism" as an acceptable alternative to Darwinian evolution. When frustrated with public school curricula, they created thousands of "Christian Academies" to insulate their children from the pervasive influence of "secular humanism." Few people charged with being secular humanists knew what the term meant, but to the Christian right it referred generally to the modernist notions that all truths were relative, not absolute, and that ethics were defined by circumstances, not moral verities.

Although evangelicals condemned the modern media as agents of liberalism and secular humanism, they eagerly used the new technology for their own purposes. Cable and satellite broadcasting allowed "televangelists" to reach national audiences. The Reverend Pat Robertson, the son of a Virginia politician, introduced his "700 Club" over the Christian Broadcast Network from Virginia Beach, Virginia. His success inspired a "700 Club" regular, Jim Bakker, to launch a spin-off program called the "Praise the Lord Club"—PTL for short. Within a few years PTL had the largest audience of any daily show in the world. The content was Pentacostal in background: gospel singing, fervent sermons, faith-healing, and speaking in tongues. The format, however, imitated that of sophisticated network "talk shows," including Bakker's Christian monologue, testimonials from celebrity guests, and musical entertainment.

Spiritual leadership easily translated into commercial and political success. Televangelists were determined fund-raisers. By the end of the 1970s, Robertson and Bakker had each received between $25 million and $30 million in contributions. But their coffers were not so full as those of the Reverend Jerry Falwell, spiritual leader of the Thomas Road Baptist Church in Lynchburg, Virginia, and television host of "The Old Time Gospel Hour." It was Falwell who first made the step from religious to political activism. In 1979 he formed the Moral Majority, Inc., an organization to attract campaign contributions and to examine candidates around the country and their views on key issues like school prayer, the Equal Rights Amendment, secular humanism, and abortion. America, Falwell proclaimed, possessed "more God-fearing citizens per capita than any other nation on earth," and they needed to make their voices heard politically. Moral Majority soon developed extensive computerized mailing lists to identify donors and target audiences for mass mailings. In the 1980 election it sent out over a billion pieces of mail in an attempt to unseat liberal senators and members of Congress.

American Catholics faced their own decisions about the degree to which religion and politics should mix. In the 1960s conservative Catholics organized opposition to school aid that did not include parochial schools. At the same time liberal

The Reverend Jerry Falwell's Moral Majority attempted to apply religious convictions in the political arena. Falwell actively supported Ronald Reagan's military buildup and political candidates who shared the Moral Majority's social agenda, including opposition to abortion.

Catholics, long commited to social causes, found a vocal leader in Father Robert Drinan, an activist member of Congress from Massachusetts, as well as in the radical priests Philip and Daniel Berrigan, who protested American involvement in the arms race and in Vietnam. Their social activism reflected a more general movement in the church that had arisen out of the church council known as Vatican II (1962–1965). Convened by Pope John XXIII and continued by his successor, Pope Paul VI, the council sought to revitalize the church and to reappraise its role in the modern world. The reforms of Vatican II reduced the amount of Latin in the mass, invited greater lay participation, and encouraged the ecumenical movement for closer ties to other Christians and to Jews.

Catholic conservatives, disturbed by these currents, found support for their views when the charismatic John Paul II assumed the papacy in 1979. The Polish-born John Paul reined in the liberal trends inspired by Vatican II and energetically promoted his views by traveling internationally. His ruling that clergy could not hold political office forced priests like Father Drinan out of politics. He resisted a wider role for women but offered no solution to the crisis American Catholics faced from the sharp decline in young men and women willing to adopt celibate lives as priests and nuns.

Though sometimes wary of one another, conservative Catholics found common cause with Protestant evangelicals. Both groups lobbied for the government to provide federal aid to parochial schools and fundamentalist academies. But it was the issue of abortion that attracted the greatest mutual support. Pope John Paul reaffirmed the church's teaching that all life begins at conception and that abortion amounts to murder of the "unborn." Evangelicals, long suspicious of the power of secular technology and science, attacked abortion as another instance where science had upset the natural moral order of life. Those who believed that women's primary role is motherhood rejected the feminist argument that abortion was "pro-choice" because it allowed women to control their lives.

The Liberal Media

If evangelists like Jerry Falwell and Pat Robertson launched their own shows, and even their own broadcast networks, to champion conservative causes, it was partly because they were convinced that the mass media were staffed and run by an establishment that was liberal in its political orientation and overly permissive in its personal outlook.

The issue was hardly new. In 1928 songwriter Cole Porter teased his audiences with the sly innuendo that "Birds do it, bees do it, even educated fleas do it. . . . Let's fall in love." Indirection was dictated by strict moral standards such as the film industry's Production Code, which forbade graphic violence, offensive language, or any hint of explicit sex or nudity. Even married couples slept in separate beds and had children without ever mentioning the word "pregnant." But by the 1950s a new permissiveness had begun to creep into much of American popular culture. In the case of movies, it reflected in part an effort to recapture some of the mass audience lost to television. Traditional genres like westerns and musicals had lost their appeal, but sex and violence still sold, especially since television was bound by code restrictions. The Supreme Court eased pressures further with a series of landmark decisions on obscenity that limited censorship.

Hollywood did rejuvenate some of its traditional genre subjects without injecting sex or violence. The success of *Planet of the Apes* (1968) launched a series of science fiction film cycles such as *Superman*, *Star Wars*, and *Star Trek*, which recalled much of the innocence of 1930s films. Furthermore, to placate critics, the industry had adopted in 1968 a rating system (G, PG, R, and X) meant to protect moviegoers. This concession could not hide the fact that by the 1970s film had lost any evident moral boundaries or direction. Soft-core pornography with simulated sex and partial nudity gave way to explicit hard-core films like *Deep Throat* and *The Devil in Miss Jones*. *The Texas Chain Saw Massacre* inspired a round of horror and violence films that strove mainly to titillate audiences with mindless murder, dripping gore, and comic mutilation. Even the boundary between horror and patriotism blurred in Sylvester Stallone's *Rambo* series, in which a muscular superpatriot, equipped with enough ammunition to stock several battalions, took on whole nations singlehandedly. Thus the movie industry found itself under attack from two directions. Intellectuals and critics deplored Hollywood's tendency to appeal to the lowest common denominator to attract a mass audience while religious, educational, and community groups were offended by movies that assaulted traditional values.

Television provoked similar condemnation. Parents' organizations charged that young viewers were especially vulnerable to discussions of controversial subject matter, suggestive sexuality and violence, and programs with themes critical of established institutions such as big business, authority, and the family. Women and minorities complained that television portrayed them as stereotypes, when it bothered to portray them at all. Intellectuals despaired that the large majority of Americans spent over five hours a day watching a range of soap operas, quiz shows, rerun movies, series, sports, and news that seldom dealt with any serious issues in a substantial way. Even television's popular "Sixty Minutes," which purported to be the best sort of hard-hitting journalism, combined uneven dashes of muckraking, human interest, and editorializing. The producers routinely reduced hours of interviews to a few selected comments and often gave equal weight to issues of great and minor importance.

Television also attracted criticism because its old standby, the situation comedy (or "sitcom"), became more topical during the 1970s. Traditionally sitcoms had taken lighthearted looks at middle-class family life and avoided controversy. But in 1971 producer Norman Lear introduced the first episode of his new comedy, "All in the Family," with a warning: "The program you are about to see . . . seeks to throw a humorous spotlight on our frailties, prejudices, and concerns." With that advisory, Archie Bunker exploded into prime time. Seething with fears and prejudices, Archie treated his addlepated wife like a doormat, struggled to understand his modestly rebellious daughter, and shouted endless insults at his Polish-American son-in-law. Minority groups, nonconformists, bosses, and liberals all offended his uninformed, blue-collar sensibilities. Out of his mouth came phrases like "Hebes," "Spics," "pansies," "fags," and "Commie crapola" that never before had survived the censors' "bleep." Americans were supposed to laugh at Archie's dumb and outrageous sentiments. "If your Spics and Spades want their rightful share of the American dream, let 'em go out and hustle for it just like I done," Archie shouts at his son-in-law from the shabby security of his living room chair. But large parts of the audience were not laughing. Some minority leaders charged that by making Archie lovable, the show legitimized the very prejudices it seemed to attack.

Benjamin Franklin "Hawkeye" Pierce was every bit as irreverent as Archie Bunker was irascible. Inspired by Robert Altman's movie hit *M*A*S*H* (1970), the television series, launched in 1972, portrayed the lives of army surgeons and nurses during the Korean War. The show's liberal, egalitarian comedy twitted bureaucracy, authority, pretense, bigotry, and snobbery for over 10 years, running 7 years longer than the war itself. During that time the central characters evolved in ways that reflected significant social change in American society. The one major African-American character disappeared during the first season. Hawkeye and his companions began as hard-drinking, womanizing foes of war and army life. Ten years later they still hated the army and war, but Hawkeye had become more vulnerable, respectful to women, and less of a wiseguy. The intensely faithful husband B. J. Hunicutt had replaced the randy "Trapper" John MacIntyre. "Hotlips" Hoolihan was transformed from a military martinet and raving patriot into Margaret Hoolihan, a career woman struggling for respect. Having treated heavy drinking as a mix of college partying and an escape from the horrors of war, the show began to deal with alcoholism.

Critics of television entertainment were most likely to focus their ire on violent cop shows, sexually frank dramatic series, or Saturday morning cartoon mayhem. For children, who were among the heaviest consumers of network programming, television was a virtual wasteland. Even the success of such Public Broadcasting System (PBS) series as "Sesame Street" and "Mister Rogers' Neigh-

Archie Bunker, from "All in the Family", played by Carroll O'Connor.

borhood" could not reduce childhood addiction to commercial television. Advertisements beckoned the undiscriminating young viewer to feast on sugar-laden cereals and candies before dragging their parents off to buy the latest in military toys, space weapons, or leggy Barbie's ever-expanding wardrobe.

Thus television, like the movies, became a battleground over which conservatives and liberals clashed. Norman Lear, Archie Bunker's creator, went on to form a lobbying group, People for the American Way, to push for more diversity in American life and counteract pressure groups like the Moral Majority. The conservatives, looking to take their cause to the political arena, found an amiable actor who had already made a successful transition from movies to politics.

The Election of 1980

Jimmy Carter might be born again, but Ronald Reagan spoke the language of true conservatism. "I think there is a hunger in this land for a spiritual revival, a return to a belief in moral absolutes," he told his followers. Such a commitment to fundamentalist articles of faith was more important than the fact that Reagan actually had no church affiliation and seldom attended services. By contrast, the more religiously active Carter seemed too liberal for the politically conservative Christian right.

The defection of traditionally Democratic evangelical Protestants was just one liability Carter faced. His rapid military buildup and cutbacks in social programs offended liberals, while rampant inflation and a weak economy alienated blue-collar voters. As the Iran hostage crisis dragged on, the president remained preoccupied with it and refrained from vigorous campaigning. By July 1980 only 32 percent of the nation approved of Carter's performance. In Republican primaries, Ronald Reagan easily outdistanced a host of other conservative hopefuls and survived George Bush's charge that his conception of finance amounted to "voodoo economics." As Reagan captured the right and center, Representative John Anderson of Illinois led the frustrated liberal wing into a third party.

THE ELECTION OF 1980

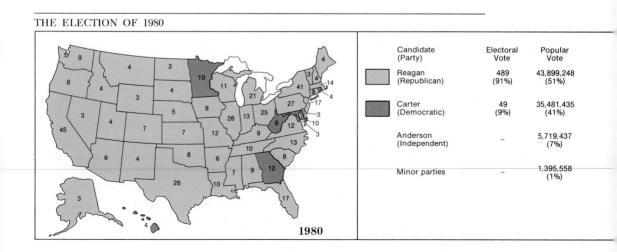

Candidate (Party)	Electoral Vote	Popular Vote
Reagan (Republican)	489 (91%)	43,899,248 (51%)
Carter (Democratic)	49 (9%)	35,481,435 (41%)
Anderson (Independent)	–	5,719,437 (7%)
Minor parties	–	1,395,558 (1%)

1980

Against Reagan's promise to restore America to greatness, Carter tried to sell the less popular notion that the United States needed to sacrifice in order to survive in a world of scarcity. It was an approach Reagan gleefully challenged. In a nationally televised debate he asked the American people, "Are you better off than you were four years ago?" Undecided voters saw in Reagan a candidate with the power to lead. Frustrated by Carter's inability to restore the economy or resolve the hostage crisis, they turned the race into a landslide: 51 percent for Reagan, 41 percent for Carter, 7 percent for Anderson. Equally impressive, the Republicans won their first majority in the Senate since 1954, claiming that the margin of victory was a popular mandate for a conservative agenda.

On that count, however, the verdict was not clear. Certainly the landslide was not of historic proportions: Eisenhower, Lyndon Johnson, and Richard Nixon (in 1972) had all won by larger margins. Only 52 percent of the eligible electorate went to the polls, the lowest total in 32 years. "It's a fed-up vote," argued Carter's political analyst Patrick Caddell. Two-thirds of the voters complained about high taxes, inflation, and unemployment. The more liberal elements, especially the young, blacks, and the poor, stayed away in record numbers, whereas Reagan's majority was greatest among those over 45, white, and earning more than $50,000 per year. Still, Reagan had significantly splintered the New Deal Democratic coalition. He made striking gains among union workers, southern white Protestants, Catholics, and Jews. Whether or not these voters became part of a permanent conservative coalition depended on the new administration's capacity to reduce popular dissatisfaction with government.

PRIME TIME WITH RONALD REAGAN

Jimmy Carter thought simplicity would appeal to Americans fed up with an imperial presidency. Ronald Reagan brought the bright lights of Hollywood to Washington, staging one of the most extravagant inaugurations in the nation's history. White House events took on the air of Hollywood premieres, with celebrities decked out in expensive designer originals. Nancy Reagan became the most fashion-conscious first lady since Jackie Kennedy. The Reagan presidency made the conspicuous display of wealth once again a sign of success and power. During Reagan's first term sales of stretch limousines doubled every year. Poverty rates rose too, as the gulf between rich and poor widened.

The Great Communicator

The message Ronald Reagan brought to Washington was simple and attractive. "It is time to reawaken the industrial giant, to get government back within its means, and to lighten our punitive tax burden," he announced on inauguration day. A strong national defense and a determined effort to revive the cold war crusade against the Soviet Union would reestablish the United States as the number one power in the world. So enthusiastically received was his message that commentators began referring to the president as "the great communicator," whose uncanny ability to use television and radio unsettled his liberal adversaries.

Reagan's skill as a veteran trouper often managed to obscure the contradictions between rhetoric and reality. With his jaunty wave and jutting jaw, he projected physical vitality and the charismatic good looks of John Kennedy. Yet at age 69, he was the oldest president to take office, and none since Calvin Coolidge had slept as soundly or as much. Reagan had begun his political life in the 1930s as an avid New Deal Democrat, but the rise of Stalinism had left him disillusioned, as it had many liberals. By the 1950s Reagan had become an ardent anticommunist who gained a reputation among conservatives as an engaging after-dinner speaker and corporate spokesperson for General Electric. In 1966 he was elected governor of California and served for eight years. As governor he spoke of paring down government programs and balancing budgets, although spending jumped sharply during his term in office. Similarly, he continued to champion family values, although he was divorced and estranged from some of his children.

Similar inconsistencies marked his leadership as president. Outsiders applauded Reagan's "hands-off" management as exactly what the nation needed after Jimmy Carter, the knowledgeable technocrat who immersed himself in details but was unable to inspire or lead. Reagan seemed to set a clear tone and direction, letting his advisers take care of the details. On the other hand, cabinet officials like Secretary of the Treasury Donald Regan were shocked to find the new president remarkably ignorant about important matters of policy and seemingly uninterested in learning more. "The Presidential mind was not cluttered with facts," Regan lamented. Then, too, Reagan appeared uncomfortable with confrontation and disliked reining in members of his administration. To outsiders, that quality appeared to be loyalty; some insiders saw an inability to control his advisers and staff. Nancy Reagan often dictated his schedule (aided by an astrologer), helped select his advisers, and even sometimes determined the major issues the president addressed. Yet the public believed he was firmly in charge and, until the Iran arms scandal in 1986, consistently expressed approval of his handling of the office. His capacity for deflecting responsibility for mistakes from himself to others earned him a reputation as the "Teflon president," since no criticism seemed to stick.

In addition, Reagan was blessed by remarkably good fortune: a number of events beyond his control broke in his favor. The deaths of three aging Soviet leaders, Leonid Brezhnev in 1982, Yuri Andropov in 1984, and Konstantin Chernenko in 1985, compounded that country's persistent economic weakness and reduced Russian influence abroad. Members of the OPEC oil cartel quarreled among themselves, exceeded production quotas, and thus forced oil prices lower, removing one major inflationary pressure. The day Reagan took office, the Iranians released the American hostages, relieving the president of his first major foreign policy crisis. And when a would-be assassin shot the president in the chest on March 30, 1981, the wound was not life threatening. Plans for a conservative Reagan revolution moved ahead.

The Reagan Agenda

Reagan's first task was to restore prestige to a presidential office that Gerald Ford once described as more imperiled than imperial. Here Reagan achieved perhaps his single greatest success. He summoned respect for an executive branch battered by debate over Vietnam, the scandals of Watergate, and the lackluster Ford and Carter administrations. Congress once again looked to the White House to set the legislative agenda. Ironically, Reagan wanted to strengthen the presidency as a way to weaken big government. His budget would become an instrument to reduce bureaucracy and to undermine agencies responsible for what seemed to him excessive meddling in the areas of civil rights, environmental and consumer protection, economic regulation, poverty programs, urban renewal, transportation, the arts, and education. In essence, Reagan wanted to return government to the size and responsibility it had had in the 1950s before the reforms of Kennedy and Johnson. He soon recognized that most programs were so deeply entrenched and their constituencies so attached to them that he could at first only scale back, not destroy them, as his more radical supporters demanded.

At the heart of the Reagan revolution was a commitment to "supply-side" economics, a program with a striking resemblance to the trickle-down economic theories of the Harding–Coolidge era. Supply-side theorists argued that high taxes and government regulation stifled entrepreneurship and economic expansion. If the government wanted employment and the economy to grow, it needed to assure higher profits, reduce the risk of innovation, and guarantee fatter paychecks. More money in private hands would mean more demand for goods. Not coincidentally, the key to this economic revival lay in a politically popular and economically controversial solution, a large tax cut. Such a cut threatened to reduce revenues and increase the deficit, of course—except that supply-side economist Arthur Laffer claimed that the economy would be so stimulated that tax revenues would actually rise, even though the rate was cut.

The second target of Reagan's agenda was the "silent thief," inflation, which had systematically robbed Americans during the Ford–Carter years. Reagan resisted certain traditional cures for inflation: tight money, high interest rates, and wage-and-price controls. He frequently sparred with Federal Reserve Chairman Paul Volker for keeping interest rates high and a tight rein on the money supply. Reagan preferred two approaches unpopular with Democrats, higher unemployment and breaking the power of major unions, which would reduce labor costs.

Lower public spending, a favorite Republican remedy, might have seemed one likely method of reducing inflation. But the third element of Reagan's agenda was a sharp rise in military outlays: a total of $1.5 trillion to be spent over five years. His strategic goal was to provide the United States with the strength to act unilaterally anywhere in the world to beat back any communist threat. This was a remarkably ambitious goal: John Kennedy had wanted the United States prepared to fight two and a half potential wars—one, for example, in Europe, one in Southeast Asia, and a smaller scale skirmish in Central America. Richard Nixon had recognized the rising importance of regional power blocs like Western Europe, with whom the United States might cooperate to guarantee security without bankrupting the economy. Reagan recognized no such limits. The United States would act unilaterally to guarantee its security. And rather than emphasize either nuclear defense or conventional warmaking powers, Defense Secretary Caspar Weinberger lobbied Congress for both.

In opting for such an inclusive approach, the administration seemed undecided about where America's most crucial interests lay if hard choices had to be made. Did the oil-rich Middle East deserve the most attention, or did America's economically and politically unstable neighbor, Latin America? The economically vibrant Pacific rim, or the traditional allies of Europe? All these areas presented important issues to be faced: energy dependence on the Middle East, a mounting Third World debt owed American lenders, the flight of high-wage jobs to low-wage countries, the instability of Eastern Europe. The president tended to view these issues, when he heeded them, through the traditional lenses of the cold warrior. "The Soviet Union underlies all the unrest that is going on. If they weren't engaged in a game of dominoes, there wouldn't be any hot spots in the world," he asserted in 1980. Thus his foreign policy agenda remained staunchly anticommunist.

The Reagan Revolution in Practice

Soon after taking office, the administration found itself with a chance to "hang tough" when PATCO, the union representing air traffic controllers, went on strike. Strikes by civil service employees were technically illegal, but the controllers maintained that a strike was the only way to win better working conditions and ensure greater air safety. Reagan responded in the spirit of Governor Calvin Coolidge breaking the 1919 Boston police strike. Setting aside the merits of the controllers' complaints, he refused to compromise and fired them for violating their contract. The public generally approved what it saw as a blow against big labor's continual appetite for less work at higher wages. Then, too, the air controllers were already receiving solidly middle-class wages for skilled labor, so they hardly appeared to be in the ranks of the downtrodden and impoverished. The administration's hard-line stance, combined with a recession that soon enveloped the nation, allowed major corporations to wrest substantial concessions from unions on wages and work rules. Organized labor witnessed a steady decline in membership and political power.

At the same time, the president's war against government regulation took special aim at rules protecting the environment. Western conservatives had long looked askance at government intervention to preserve wild lands, especially when the policy seemed directed at halting economic development in their areas for the benefit of "nature lovers." Reagan appointed westerner James Watt, an outspoken champion of this "sagebrush rebellion," to head the Interior Department. Watt, in turn, devoted himself to opening federal lands for private development, including lumbering and offshore oil drilling. Similarly, Anne Burford Gorsuch set out to cut back the Environmental Protection Agency's efforts to enforce antipollution regulations. Watt's outrageous statements forced his resignation in 1983 and scandal over mismanagement at the EPA drove Gorsuch out, but the administration continued to oppose most efforts to regulate or protect the environment. Reagan, who once claimed trees were a source of air pollution, refused to accept the conclusion of scientists that the smoke from coal-fired power plants in the Ohio valley was sending destructive acid rain over the lakes and forests of eastern Canada and the United States.

Most important, by the summer of 1981 Reagan had also pushed through Congress his supply-side tax legislation. The Economic Recovery Tax Act (ERTA) provided a 25 percent across-the-board reduction for all taxpayers. The president hailed it, along with recently passed budget cuts, as an antidote to "big government's" addiction to spending and a stimulus to the economy. Opponents called it a bonanza for the rich, pointing out that an "equal" cut of 25 percent for all taxpayers meant a much larger windfall for the wealthy, who paid larger taxes to begin with. Even Budget Director David Stockman admitted that parts of the legislation had been particularly beneficial to special interests. "Do you realize the greed that came to the forefront? The hogs were really feeding," he recalled. "The greed level, the level of opportunism, just got out of control."

The administration's impact on the economy was mixed. By 1982 a recession had pushed unemployment above 10 percent. The Federal Reserve Board's tight money policies and high interest rates deepened the recession. Key industries like automobiles staggered under the pressure of foreign competition and their own inefficiency. But the combination of falling energy costs, the stimulus of federal spending, improved industrial productivity, and easier monetary policy in 1983 brought on an economic expansion that lasted through Reagan's presidency. While many workers earned less per hour, the flow of women into the labor market kept family incomes from falling too much. Recovery also spurred higher corporate profits, but not the increased savings and investment rates that supply-side theorists had predicted. Much of the expansion was financed by borrowing and investment from foreigners, especially the Japanese and British.

Whatever the performance of the economy as a whole, the Reagan tax cut was one of a series of policy changes that brought about a substantial transfer of wealth from the poor and lower middle-class workers to the upper middle classes and the rich. Dedicated to a free market philosophy, the administration barely responded as jobs that paid blue-collar workers relatively high wages flowed to Mexico and Asia, where laborers worked for less. It had no solution either as cheap imported foods cut into the American farmers' share of the domestic market and huge international surpluses created a depression in the agricultural sector. Many once-prosperous farmers found themselves dangerously in debt or their mortgaged farms foreclosed. And Reagan aimed the sharpest edge of his budget axe at programs for the poor. The administration cut most from programs that gave direct benefits to the poor: food stamps, Aid to Families with Dependent Children, Medicaid, school lunches, and housing assistance. The programs least affected were middle-class entitlements like Social Security and Medicare, which affected those over 65 who, as social activist Michael Harrington observed, "are not now, and for a long time have not been, poor."

The shift in wealth distribution caused by the tax cut, rising unemployment, and lost federal benefits hit home for tens of millions of Americans. "For every 25-year-old I read about making $300,000 a year on Wall Street," one economist noted, "there are hundreds of 25-year-olds working as fast-food people or hospital orderlies earning $3.50 an hour." During the 1950s and 1960s family earnings increased some 30 percent each decade. But the 1970s brought a period of decline, which continued into the 1980s.

With a combination of income transfers, agricultural depression, and job flight, the percentage of Americans living below the poverty level rose from 11.7 percent in 1980 to 15 percent by 1982, where it stayed for the rest of the Reagan administration. Reagan's successful war on inflation, which dropped to less than 2 percent by 1986, contributed to a rise in unemployment. Joblessness peaked at over 10 percent (12 million) in 1982 and hovered around 7 percent during the recovery and stock market boom, finally dropping below 6 percent before the 1988 election. (By contrast, the highest rate under Jimmy Carter was 5.9 percent.) Somewhere around 1.5 million people simply gave up trying to find work. Millions of others fled to the booming economies of Texas and the Southwest only to

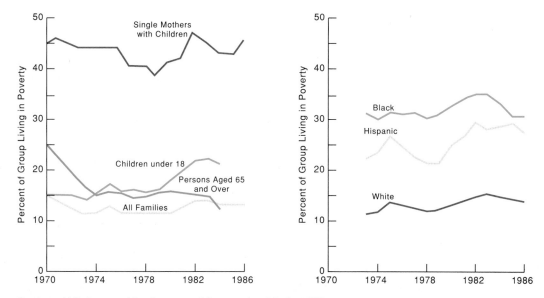

Sources: U.S. Bureau of the Census and Congressional Budget Office.
POVERTY IN AMERICA, 1970–1986
While Social Security and other income supplements to older Americans reduced their rate of poverty, the circumstances of single mothers with children significantly worsened.

see the bottom fall out as oil prices plunged from over $40 to $13 a barrel and domestic production slumped. Thus the Reagan recovery was an uneven one, despite its continued expansion.

The Surge in Military Spending

An equally significant part of the Reagan revolution was the sharp rise in military spending. Known as "Cap the Knife" for his budget cutting under Richard Nixon, Defense Secretary Caspar Weinberger surprised many by being more aggressive than the most hawkish generals in seeking a bigger budget. Outlays rose from under $200 billion (an average of 4.9 percent of the GNP) under Presidents Ford and Carter to almost $300 billion (6.2 percent of the GNP) in 1985, when growing opposition led to some restraint. The largest increases were for strategic nuclear weapons, especially the B-1 bomber (rejected by Carter as outmoded), aircraft carrier task forces and Trident missile subs for the navy, the huge land-based MX intercontinental ballistic missiles, and subsonic cruise missiles. The administration argued that a nuclear buildup would strengthen the position of American negotiators during arms reductions talks.

This vast buildup inspired three major lines of criticism. First, the rise in spending accompanied by increasingly tough talk by Reagan defense planners about the possibility of "winning" a nuclear exchange sparked a revival of antinuclear peace groups across Europe and America. The bishops of the American Catholic church felt moved to announce their opposition to nuclear war. In *The Fate of the Earth* (1982), Jonathan Schell speculated on the grisly destruction even a limited nuclear exchange might cause. Scientists warned that debris in the atmosphere might cause a "nuclear winter" fatal to all life on earth.

Equally vocal were those outraged by the cost and complexity of the Pentagon's armament list. Stories of $600 toilet seats and $7000 coffee pots made headlines, but more serious were the failures of entire multibillion-dollar weapons systems, like the army's Bradley troop carriers and Sergeant York antiaircraft guns. Many weapons were so complicated that they seldom worked and could not be repaired by military personnel. Repeated scandals revealed widespread fraud in defense industry billing and Defense Department procurement.

The public heard little, however, from critics concerned that the military buildup had scant connection to strategic needs. Their primary target was the president's Strategic Defense Initiative (SDI, nicknamed "Star Wars" after the popular futuristic movie series of the era). The goal of SDI was to establish a space-based missile system that would be merely "defensive," knocking enemy missiles out of the sky well before they reached their targets. Almost all reputable scientists argued that the system was technically flawed, yet, beginning in 1983, the administration won billions of dollars each year to pursue development of the idea, hoping as well to wring concessions from the Soviets during arms talks. Critics countered that Reagan's defense buildup amounted to very little bang for trillions of bucks.

The combination of massive defense spending and substantial tax cuts left the federal government awash in red ink. Annual deficits soared to over $200 billion. The vast borrowing required to pay this debt kept interest rates high until recovery set in during 1983–1984. In turn, the high interest rates attracted investors from Europe and Asia, who poured capital into the United States, aggravating the debt crisis in the Third World. But Reagan steadfastly refused any tax increases,

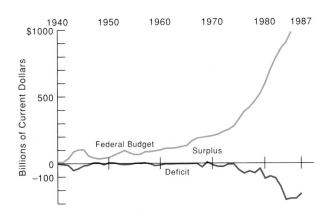

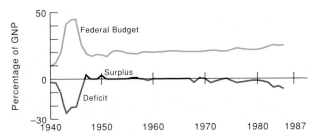

THE FEDERAL BUDGET AND SURPLUS/DEFICIT, 1940–1987

Despite Reagan's campaign pledge to reduce federal spending, the federal deficit soared higher during his presidency than at any other time in the nation's history.

took no steps to curb the rapid growth in foreign oil imports, and ignored mounting foreign trade deficits, as the United States, a creditor nation since World War
I, became by 1986 the world's largest debtor.

Whether the large budget deficits were truly a threat to the American economy remained a hotly debated topic. Some economists argued that, just as corporations routinely went into debt and borrowed money to build new factories, it
was healthy for the federal government to go into debt to build roads, bridges,
schools—the necessary infrastructure of American society. But Reagan largely
ignored those expenditures and the general public was convinced cutbacks were
needed. Neither the administration nor Congress could agree on where to begin.
As a stopgap measure, Congress in 1985 passed the Gramm–Rudman Act, which
established a set of steadily declining limits on the federal budget each year, to
achieve a balanced budget in 1993. These limits were meant to force Congress and
the president to make hard choices; if they did not, automatic across-the-board
cuts would go into effect. Not only was the constitutionality of this approach in
doubt, but in addition, successive Congresses, as well as presidents Reagan and
Bush, accepted unrealistic budget projections that defeated the purpose of the
Gramm–Rudman Act.

The Election of 1984

No matter how loudly Reagan's critics complained, the president remained popular with the American people. Even among African-Americans and other minorities he received generally favorable ratings, despite his hostility to affirmative
action and social welfare programs. Massive foreign borrowing and deficit spending fueled an economic expansion that assured the president, though not the
Republican party, electoral success. The only real questions in 1984 were which

In the 1984 presidential campaign,
Jesse Jackson called for a "Rainbow coalition" of citizens of all colors who had been hurt by the Reagan revolution. But his positions
seemed too liberal for most Americans at the time.

Democrat would lose to Reagan and by how much. A challenge by Jesse Jackson and his "Rainbow Coalition" raised the prospect of an African-American candidate. But the honor went to the former Carter vice president, Walter Mondale of Minnesota, a moderate who embraced traditional New Deal liberalism.

The Democrats perceived one small ray of hope in what pollsters had identified as a gender gap. Reagan's standing among women was lower than with men, even though he had appointed Sandra Day O'Connor the first female justice of the Supreme Court and Elizabeth Hanford Dole secretary of transportation. Most of his appointments went, however, to white Protestant males who met the conservative test of ideological purity on issues like abortion, tax cuts, military spending, and anticommunist crusades in the Third World. To exploit the gender gap, Mondale chose Representative Geraldine Ferraro of New York as his running mate. In doing so, he paid his debt to the National Organization for Women for its support and fulfilled his campaign pledge to work for greater opportunity for all Americans.

But the continuing economic recovery, along with the president's affable charm, brought to Reagan even greater numbers of traditional New Deal Democrats, especially southern evangelicals and blue-collar workers. Baby-boom voters also favored Reagan by wide margins. He even won a majority of the women's vote (57 percent) as well as a crushing majority (59 percent) of the popular vote and victory in 49 states. Women suffered an additional political setback as 9 women candidates for the Senate and all but 2 women out of the 41 running for Congress went down to defeat. At least in 1984, the gender gap did not translate into an identifiable women's vote.

SECOND-TERM BLUES

Second terms have been hard on many popular presidents, especially those re-elected by wide margins. For George Washington it was factionalism that marred his second term; for Thomas Jefferson, the embargo; for Franklin Roosevelt, the Court-packing plan; for Lyndon Johnson, the Vietnam War; and for Richard Nixon, Watergate. So too Ronald Reagan suffered a precipitous drop in his political fortunes as scandals racked his administration.

A good deal of the problem could be traced to the president's hands-off approach to governing. In March 1987, at the administration's low point, former senator Howard Baker of Tennessee was brought in as chief-of-staff to reorganize the White House. One of Baker's aides was shocked to discover how far matters had slipped:

> There was no pattern of analysis, no coming together. Individual cabinet members were just doing what they wanted to do—the ones that were smart had realized that the White House really didn't matter. . . . [Aides] felt free to sign [the president's] initials on documents without noting that they were acting for him. When I asked a group of them, who among them thought they had authority to sign in the president's name, there was a long, uncomfortable silence. Then one answered, "Well—everybody, and nobody."

Yet Reagan again confounded his critics with his political resilience. The Iran–Contra scandal, the worst of his problems, passed without precipitating an impeachment, as Watergate had. The president presided over an economic expansion that became the longest in peacetime history without a recession, and he concluded with the Soviet Union an Intermediate Nuclear Force Treaty (INF) that promised to eliminate a whole class of missiles from Europe. He left office with his personal popularity still high.

Triumph Before the Storm

Indeed, the second term began well enough, with inflation under control, the economy continuing to expand, and the stock market reaching new highs. The president could claim partial credit for a major reform in the tax system, though its passage owed just as much to the persistence of Senator Bill Bradley of New Jersey and Representative Richard Gephardt of Missouri. The bill, passed in August 1986, was designed to be "revenue neutral"—that is, the changes would not raise or lower the total amount of taxes collected. But it removed many of the old inequities and loopholes that had often allowed the people with the highest incomes to pay the lowest taxes. Tax avoidance had become something of a national obsession, influencing when and what people bought in order to gain tax deductions. Under the new law individuals were far less likely to base a spending decision on tax consequences rather than on whether it made economic sense on its own merits.

Furthermore, vacancies in the Supreme Court allowed the president to shift its ideological balance further to the right. When Chief Justice Warren Burger resigned in 1986, Reagan elevated Justice William Rehnquist to that position, filling Rehnquist's vacancy with distinguished conservative jurist Antonin Scalia. But the limits of the president's influence became clear when the Senate rejected Robert Bork, a more combative conservative. Bork's long history of polemical articles and speeches challenging long-established Court policies on privacy and civil rights made many Republicans hesitate. Even so, a moderately conservative judge from California, Anthony Kennedy, won easy approval in 1988.

As of July 1986, the president's popularity seemed unassailable as he stood in the glare of Fourth-of-July patriotic fireworks, lighting the torch of a newly refurbished Statue of Liberty. "The 75-year-old man is hitting home runs," rhapsodized *Time* magazine. In reality, he was about to enter the most wrenching years of his presidency. The crisis was sparked by two longstanding traits of the administration: Reagan's indifference to the details of his office and his determination to pursue a more aggressive anticommunist foreign policy abroad.

Standing Tall

In his public life Ronald Reagan had stood firm in defense of the principles of liberty and freedom. Most often, his administration focused attention on human rights abuses in communist nations, turning a blind eye toward the excesses of right-wing dictatorships. This ideological approach, as one analyst pointed out, tended to give Reagan policymakers an "absolute certainty of their own rightness." Since they were operating with "pure hearts," they found it all too easy to justify working with "dirty hands." In some cases, noble ends were used to justify dubious tactics.

Three areas of the world commanded the administration's attention. First, Reagan was determined to counter a Soviet arms buildup and adventurism with American arms and interventionism. In Central America, the shadow of Fidel Castro's communist regime loomed, the Sandinistas of Nicaragua had established a leftist government, and instability threatened to spread revolution. Finally, the Reaganites sought to stabilize the Middle East, where Soviet troops were bogged down in Afghanistan, a bloody war dragged on between Iran and Iraq, the governments of Syria and Libya supported international terrorists, chaos engulfed Lebanon, and tensions between Israel and its neighbors simmered.

The administration's first test came in 1982, after Israel invaded war-torn Lebanon to drive out the guerrilla forces of the Palestine Liberation Organization (PLO). Once Israeli troops reached Beirut, Syrian-armed Muslim groups struck back. A bloody stalemate resulted. Secretary of State George Shultz proposed that the Israelis be replaced by a European–American peacekeeping force. Although Defense Secretary Weinberger objected that troops might be drawn into an indefensible situation with an uncertain mission, Reagan agreed with Shultz and sent American marines to support the embattled Christian minority government. Soon the peacekeeping forces became the target of rival Muslim factions. Terrorists backed by the Khomeini regime in Iran succeeded in bombing the American Embassy and, six months later in October 1983, blew up a U.S. Marine barracks, killing 239. At Weinberger's urging, the president reconsidered his position and ordered American troops withdrawn. In Lebanon, Reagan found it difficult to project American force.

Grenada, a Caribbean island with a medical school attended by a number of American students, proved more susceptible to forceful intervention. With civil war threatening to bring a Marxist government to power there, the president sent in an invasion force that not only airlifted the American students to safety, but crushed the forces of the unpopular leftist rebels. Although troop actions were not particularly well coordinated (one desperate officer was forced to open a communications link with his air cover by making a collect call to Washington over a local pay phone), the American public generally approved the show of force. The military, the president seemed to be saying, would no longer be shackled by the agony of Vietnam.

Still, a constructive response to the Middle East with its wars, political upheavals, and terrorists eluded the Reagan administration. In 1985 Iranian-backed terrorists took additional hostages in Lebanon, a number of them American. Terrorists also struck airlines. In the most dramatic incident they hijacked a TWA flight between Athens and Rome in June 1985. In such situations, Reagan's public response was always uncompromising: "Let terrorists beware: when the rules of international behavior are violated, our policy will be one of swift and effective retribution." But against whom should the United States seek revenge? There was little intelligence about the many political and terrorist factions. Only in the case of the hijacked cruise ship *Achille Lauro* did the United States strike back effectively. When Egyptian authorities allowed the captured terrorists to quietly board a plane for Tunisia, American F-14 Tomcat fighters forced the plane to land in Italy.

In its war on terrorists, the Reagan government increasingly focused on Libya and its eccentric, vocally anti-American leader Colonel Muammar Qadhafi. Intelligence sources indicated that Qadhafi's supporters were behind at least some of the terrorist attacks on American tourists and servicemen. In the Gulf of Sidra, Libyan gunboats periodically played cat-and-mouse with an American naval task force, while American jets retaliated with attacks on radar installations. Then a terrorist bombing killed a U.S. serviceman in West Berlin. Reagan ordered 30 air force and navy bombers to attack selected targets, including Qadhafi's headquarters. The show of force impressed the American public, although European leaders, with the exception of Prime Minister Margaret Thatcher of Great Britain, opposed the raids. Later intelligence reports indicated that the majority of terrorist attacks were supported not by Libya, but by Syria—a nation much less isolated from the international community, and one the administration seemed more wary of challenging openly.

Clean Hearts and Dirty Hands in Central America

In South and Central America the gap between American ideals and American power proved even larger. The greatest long-term crisis involved the mounting debts that undermined the economic and political stability of the region. So large were the sums involved that paying the interest alone strained the debtor nations' economies. American banks, which had loaned billions of dollars, were themselves threatened if the nations decided to default. By 1988 the debt crisis across the entire Third World had expanded to $1.2 trillion. As interest rates rose, hard-pressed debtor nations were forced to spend valuable resources servicing interest on their debt rather than promoting industry, building needed roads and hospitals, or offering public services. Since the problem seemed intractable, the administration did little to look for ways to ease the crisis.

Communism, not economics, preoccupied Reagan. In El Salvador, leftist rebels increasingly gained ground in their attempt to overthrow the reigning dictatorship. In response, private right-wing "death squads" exacted their own retribution, murdering anyone suspected of opposition, including a few Americans in the area. Thus moderate forces were caught in the crossfire, with approximately 40,000 civilians killed in the period between 1979 and 1984. The combination of American pressure and foreign aid finally led to the election of a moderate conservative government for El Salvador under José Napoleón Duarte. A slowdown in the guerrilla war and civilian murders followed, but there was little improvement in conditions for El Salvador's impoverished peasants.

In neighboring Nicaragua the circumstances were reversed. Since 1979 the left-wing Sandinista government had gravitated steadily toward Cuba and had repressed the country's internal political opposition. For all that, most neutral observers conceded that a majority of Nicaraguans supported Sandinista efforts to introduce land, educational, and health reforms. Reagan had campaigned in 1980 for a harder line against Nicaragua, however, and cut off American aid during his first year in office. At the same time, he extended help to the rebel "Contra" forces trying to overthrow the Sandinistas. When critics accused Reagan of fomenting another Vietnam in Central America, he called the Contras "freedom fighters," comparing them to the Founding Fathers. While the Contras did include disaffected Sandinistas and moderate democrats, a good many of their leaders were refugees from the Somoza dictatorship, whose repressive policies had helped make the Sandinistas so welcome to Nicaraguans.

Congress at first refused to support the Contras with anything more than limited supplies for "humanitarian" purposes. Most Central American govern-ments were similarly loathe to intervene; indeed, four of Nicaragua's regional neighbors, known as the Contadora group—Venezuela, Mexico, Panama, and Colombia—sought to negotiate a solution and avoid an expanded war. But Reagan was determined to overthrow the Sandinistas. The CIA helped the Contras to mine Nicaraguan harbors, damaging seven foreign ships and violating interna-tional law in the process. Even conservative senators like Barry Goldwater were outraged, and Congress adopted (and the president signed) an amendment spon-sored by Representative Edward Boland of Massachusetts explicitly forbidding the CIA or "any other agency or entity involved in intelligence activities" from spending money to support the Contras "directly or indirectly." Despite adminis-tration pressures, Congress remained leery of providing more military aid.

The Iran–Contra Connection

Thus by mid-1985 Reagan policymakers felt two major frustrations. For one, Con-gress had limited their support of the Contras in Central America; and second, Iranian-backed terrorists continued to hold hostages in Lebanon. In the summer of 1985, soon after the anguishing TWA hijacking, a course of events was set in motion that eventually linked these two issues.

The president made it increasingly clear he wanted to find a way to free the remaining hostages in Lebanon. Robert McFarlane, his stoic national security adviser, suggested the administration try to open a channel to moderate factions in the Iranian government. A former Israeli intelligence officer had hinted that such moderates did exist and hoped to improve relations with Western nations, espe-cially since Iran was embroiled in a protracted war with Iraq. If the United States sold Iran a few weapons, the grateful Iranians might use their influence in Leba-non to free the hostages.

There were major problems with this scenario. No one knew whether any influential moderates existed in Iran. The only available contact was a glib-tongued, arms-dealing Iranian named Manucher Ghorbanifar. Even if an agree-ment exchanging arms for hostages could be made, it violated the president's often-repeated vow never to negotiate or pay ransom to terrorists. "This is almost too absurd to comment on," Secretary Weinberger replied, upon hearing of the idea to supply Iran with arms. "It's like asking Qadhafi to Washington for a cozy chat." Still, the president apparently approved the initiative—or at least McFar-lane believed he had. In August 500 missiles were shipped to Iran from Israel, while the United States replaced the missiles in Israel's arsenal.

Over the following year, three more secret arms shipments were made to Iran, once using Israel as a go-between and twice more directly. The man who seemed to pull so much of the negotiations together was a junior officer under McFarlane in the National Security Council, Lieutenant Colonel Oliver North. North, a decorated Vietnam veteran with a flair for the dramatic, had already orchestrated the bold midair interception of the *Achille Lauro* terrorists. He was a "can-do" sort, impatient with bureaucrats and bureaucratic procedures. In the most astonishing initiative to Iran he and McFarlane flew to the capital, Teheran, in May 1986, using false Irish passports, carrying gift-wrapped .357-caliber pistols, a chocolate layer cake, and poison pills, in case the mission went awry. Despite four separate arms shipments, only one hostage was released.

Secretaries Weinberger and Shultz had strongly opposed the idea of exchang-

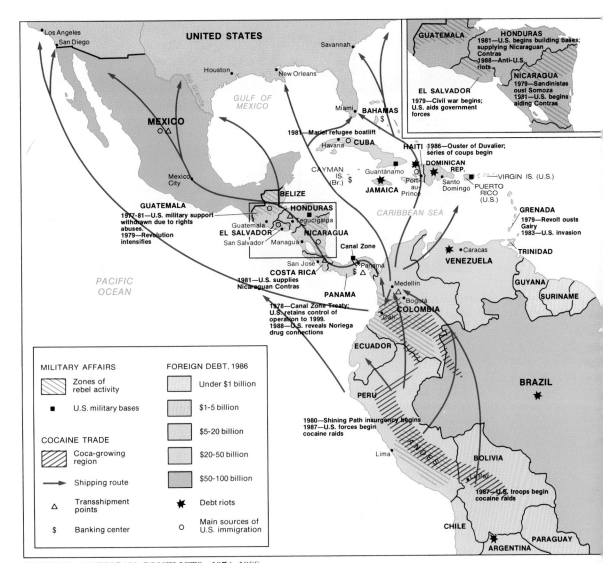

CENTRAL AMERICAN CONFLICTS, 1974–1988

President Reagan's attempts to overthrow the Sandinista government in Nicaragua and to contain communism focused American attention on Latin America. So too did the staggering debts Latin countries owed to banks in America and elsewhere. Equally distorting to the hemisphere's social and economic fabric was the sharp rise in the drug trade organized by criminal syndicates. Most notorious was the Medellin cartel, which operated from a remote region in Colombia, shipping drugs through havens in Panama and the Bahamas into the United States while depositing its enormous profits in banks in Miami and offshore banking centers like the Cayman Islands.

ing arms for hostages. What was perhaps most astonishing is that they were largely uninformed of the initiatives, precisely because their opposition was well known. McFarlane's successor as national security adviser, Admiral John Poindexter, had the president sign a secret intelligence "finding" that allowed him, North, and others to pursue their mission without informing anyone in Congress or even four

Oliver North successfully took the offensive in his testimony before the congressional committee investigating the Iran–Contra scandals. Here he delivers a pro-Contra lecture to his interrogators.

of the eight members of Poindexter's own National Security Council, including the secretaries of defense and state. With the president so inattentive to the details of foreign policy, McFarlane, Poindexter, and North derived an immense amount of power to act on their own.

North and McFarlane had already been acting without the knowledge of Congress to supply the Contras with arms in Central America. To do so, they devised ways to circumvent the Boland Amendment and its prohibitions against military aid. McFarlane made clear to Saudi Arabia and several other friendly allies that the Contras were desperately in need of funds. Between the summers of 1984 and 1985, the Saudis deposited at least $30 million in Swiss bank accounts set up to launder the money. North then recruited to the cause Richard Secord, a former major general who had been forced to retire from the air force under suspicion of having sold arms at a profit to Libya. Secord set up a delivery system, buying weapons with the laundered money, making a tidy profit, and delivering them to Central America. In addition, North illegally helped private conservative fund-raisers within the United States raise money for what he nobly referred to as Project Democracy. Secord, his sights set a trifle lower, merely referred to it as "the Enterprise."

The two strands of North's secret missions came together in January 1986, in a meeting with Ghorbanifar to work out the third arms sale to Iran. It occurred to North that the excess profits from the sale of U.S. missiles could be deposited in a Swiss account and then siphoned off to benefit the Contras. Ghorbanifar thought the idea a capital one: "I think this is now, Ollie, the best chance, because . . . we never get such good money out of this," he laughed, as he was recorded on a tape North himself made. "We do everything. We do hostages free of charge; we do all terrorists free of charge; Central America free of charge." By secretly selling government property at a profit, funds were made available for a rogue covert operation, without having the funds appropriated by Congress through the usual constitutional process.

Cover Blown

Through the fall of 1986, both operations had remained hidden from view, but that changed abruptly as the congressional elections drew near. A hostage, David Jacobsen, was released in return for a fifth shipment of TOW missiles. But the news that McFarlane and North had visited Teheran in May was leaked to a Lebanese newspaper, *Al Shiraa*, which gleefully published it. As corroborating evidence appeared, the administration was swamped by incredulous reporters, trying to determine how its policy of secret arms sales could be squared with its vocal antiterrorist campaign. Within the administration, both Weinberger and Shultz were outraged that the negotiations had been kept from them (although critics claimed they had too easily turned a blind eye, once they had seen that their advice was being rejected). Then, during the investigation of the Iranian affair, the link between the arms sales and the Contras was discovered. Attorney General Edwin Meese undertook an investigation to piece together the complete story, but he was so leisurely in pursuing the matter that North and his secretary were able to spend the bulk of one weekend shredding crucial documents. Enough of a paper trail remained, however—along with crucial computer files that had not been erased—that the dimensions of Project Democracy became clear.

As the controversy unfolded, the president defended the arms sales to Iran as negotiations unrelated to the release of hostages. He accepted Poindexter's resignation and dismissed Oliver North, though referring to him as a national hero. He seemed singularly uninterested in discovering what his subordinates had been doing, ostensibly in his name, but because of the public outcry agreed to appoint an investigative commission of three, led by former senator John Tower of Texas. The following week, on December 4, the House and Senate launched their own nine-month joint investigation into the Iran–Contra affair. And Attorney General Meese reluctantly appointed Lawrence Walsh as an independent prosecutor to investigate possible illegalities.

The press immediately began referring to the scandal as "Irangate," making the obvious comparison to Richard Nixon's Watergate scandal. But the two episodes had different dynamics and different outcomes. Watergate led eventually to the Oval Office, implicating the president in a cover-up from the very beginning. But the Iran–Contra congressional hearings, held during the summer of 1987, left the role of the president unexplained. "I assumed that the president was aware of what I was doing and had, through my superiors, approved it," North told Congress. But his superior, Admiral Poindexter, claimed he had deliberately kept Reagan in ignorance, "so that I could insulate him from the decision. . . . On this whole issue, you know, the buck stops here, with me." Since the committee had no desire to proceed with impeachment, the hearings came to a sputtering end, although the independent prosecutor did win convictions against North in 1989 and Poindexter in 1990.

So Irangate was not Watergate; perhaps it was worse. Harry Truman coined the phrase "The buck stops here," meaning that the president bore final responsibility for the actions of his subordinates. Iran–Contra revealed a presidency in which an unelected segment within the government took upon itself the power to intercept the buck's upward movement and launch a series of illegal diversions of government money to finance an unapproved war. "Dirty hands" worked diligently for the ideals of "clean hearts."

From Cold War to *Glasnost*

Still, the president's Teflon coating held. By the end of his term, Reagan's popularity returned, in part because of substantial progress achieved in Soviet–American relations. The 1980s had been difficult for the Soviet Union, with its stagnant economy, unstable leadership, and the loss of influence in Africa and the Middle East. The war in Afghanistan had become a Russian Vietnam. When Soviet jets in 1983 shot down a South Korean airliner that had penetrated its air space, killing all 269 passengers (including a member of Congress from Georgia), the world community condemned the brutality. Reagan, aware of the strains in the Soviet economy, at first accelerated the arms race to place additional pressure on the Russians to negotiate. In 1983 the United States deployed both intermediate-range Pershing II and cruise missiles in Europe, placing Moscow within a 10-minute missile flight from the launch site. Despite the pressure, the beleaguered Soviets walked out of the negotiations.

By 1985 the choice of Mikhail Gorbachev as premier created new possibilities in Soviet–American relations. Unlike his aged predecessors, Gorbachev was young, saw the need for reform within the Soviet Union, and rivaled Reagan as a shaper of world opinion. The fundamental restructuring, or *perestroika*, conceived by Gorbachev entailed improving relations with the United States, reduc-

Soviet Premier Gorbachev (right) used his summits with Ronald Reagan to reduce Soviet–American tensions, although the spirit of *glasnost* did not ease the skirmishes between his wife Raisa and Nancy Reagan, who waged a quiet war over fashion and ideology. Gorbachev came to rival Reagan as a "great communicator," with many Americans applauding his efforts to reform Soviet society and to slow the arms race.

ing military commitments, and adopting a policy of openness (*glasnost*) about problems in the Soviet Union. The Reagan administration soon found itself on the defensive over arms limitations. Gorbachev unilaterally ended all nuclear tests; Reagan refused to make a similar move, since American tests were needed to develop his controversial Strategic Defense Initiative. To many foreign observers it seemed Reagan was determined to extend the arms race into space. In June 1986, he announced that the United States would unilaterally exceed the limits of SALT II, an agreement which, though never ratified, had been since 1979 the only fragile restraint on the arms race.

In October, when the two leaders held their second summit in Reykjavík, Iceland, Gorbachev dangled the possibility of abolishing all nuclear weapons. Reagan seemed receptive to the idea, apparently unaware that if both sides eliminated all nuclear weapons, Soviet conventional forces would far outnumber NATO troops in Europe. In the end, the president refused to sacrifice his Star Wars for an all-or-nothing Soviet proposal. Many of his advisers were stunned that he had been so ill-prepared to negotiate. Although the Reykjavík summit proved a giddy exercise in hasty diplomacy, negotiations continued. In December 1987 Reagan traveled to Moscow, where he signed an agreement to eliminate an entire class of missiles. These intermediate-range nuclear forces (INFs) were land-based missiles, with ranges of 600 to 3400 miles. Both sides agreed to allow on-site inspections of missile bases and facilities where missiles were destroyed. Only two significant groups objected. Western European leaders feared a weakening of their defenses, and the right wing of Reagan's own party refused to believe that the Soviets could be trusted. They were not convinced, as Reagan was, that Gorbachev needed to shift resources from military buildup to domestic economic reforms. On May 27, 1988, the Senate approved the treaty by a 93–5 margin, marking a major step back from the brink of nuclear confrontation.

THE REAGAN LEGACY AND AN UNFINISHED SOCIAL AGENDA

As the election of 1988 approached, Ronald Reagan, against all odds, appeared to have made a comeback. What remained less clear was the long-term consequences of his years in office. The aura of prosperity, like the president's own aura of amiability, seemed at times to mask deeper problems requiring serious attention if the republic was to prosper and grow.

The Uncertain Legacy

The Reagan era most certainly proved that conservatives remained alive and well in America. For many years, the intellectual high ground of political thought had been held by liberal think tanks like the Brookings Institution. By the 1980s, conservative centers like the Hoover Institute and the American Enterprise Institute were energetically providing the Reagan administration with personnel and advice. Few Democrats seemed willing to call themselves liberals, and such traditional constituencies as labor unions were increasingly condemned as unhealthy interest groups.

Daily Lives

POLITICAL CULTURE
Life in the Underclass

During the 1880s Jacob Riis "discovered" a class of people largely invisible to the "better half" of society. Drawing on his investigative reporting for the New York *Tribune*, he described them as "individuals who have lost connection with home life, or never had any, or whose homes had ceased to be sufficiently separated, decent, and desireable to afford what are regarded as ordinary wholesome influences of home and family." A century later investigators for the Chicago *Tribune* discovered that there still existed in American cities "a lost society dwelling in enclaves of despair and chaos that infect and threaten the communities at large." This world, comprising as many as 5 million Americans, was also invisible, except when its behavior became so violent or criminal that newspapers and television news could not ignore it.

The trials of this underclass, numbing when seen as aggregate statistics, were searing when the *Tribune* reporters described individual lives, like that of Dorothy Sands. In 1957 Dorothy, her mother, Ora Streeter, and the rest of her family lived in a one-room shack in rural Mississippi. The family made a bare living picking cotton. But Dorothy's stepfather drank heavily and beat her mother in his intoxication, until finally Ora decided to escape the South, her job, and her abusive husband to take six small children to Chicago, where her mother lived. For young Dorothy, "It was something like going to a new world."

Life in Chicago imposed disappointments and cruelties of its own. Streeter's husband tracked the family down. After a brief reconciliation, the drinking and the

Early teen pregnancies trapped many poverty-stricken families in a recurring cycle of poverty.

beatings began anew. The couple separated and Streeter moved her children to a poorer neighborhood, where rents were lower. When arthritis prevented her from working she signed up for public assistance. Dorothy, the oldest child, assumed responsibility for the household, caring for the other children. With what little time she had for herself, she reached the ninth grade at school. But when she was 15 her dream of a nursing career ended when she discovered she was pregnant. In 1965, after her mother died, Dorothy began a relationship with Carra Little, a man who promised he could not get her pregnant.

Daily Lives

Within a year, Dorothy had her second child. She asked the doctors to sterilize her, but they refused. And the children kept arriving—four more of them. "When you are young, you don't really think about the future," Dorothy recalled. "You say, 'if I have another baby, then I have another child.'"

Though Little and Dorothy never married, he shared some of the household burdens and had regular work. But he also drank heavily, had affairs with other women, and beat her. And in 1976 he died of a heart attack. The household soon disintegrated. Dorothy did not even notice until seven months had passed that her oldest daughter, Barbara, like her mother and grandmother before her, was pregnant at age 15. By 1985 Dorothy was suffering from chronic depression and had considered suicide. At age 37 she was a grandmother living in a three-room apartment with five of her six children, her daughter LaWanda's new boyfriend, two grandchildren ages 7 and 2, and two teenaged girls who had run away from home. In 20 years the family had never been off welfare and no one in the household had held a regular job. Only one of her children attended school for more than brief periods.

With public assistance money Dorothy could afford only to house her family in a dilapidated three-story building on Chicago's West Side, where they were the sole tenants in eight apartments. Each evening people from the neighborhood pried open the front door to do "crack" or drink 100 percent grain alcohol. Sometime in 1985 the family stopped bathing because every time they turned on the water, plaster fell into the tub. The building manager reneged on his promise to make repairs. So the children just stood over the sink and washed their clothes by hand. An electrical wire attached to a bare bulb doubled as a clothesline.

This apartment, without heat or gas for cooking, rented for $275, which Dorothy paid out of her welfare allotment of $868 a month, comprising support payments and food stamps. Only she had a room of her own, which she kept neat and cleaned. To protect her few personal items from her family or intruders, she kept them padlocked in a closet. The girls slept on canvas cots in one room, while the boys took turns between cots and a mattress on the living room floor. Meals were irregular affairs, since money was scarce and no one liked to cook. For two weeks each month the family splurged on eggs for breakfast and Spam for dinner. More often they got by on hot dogs, rice, and beans.

Of this neighborhood's 61,500 people, over half received some form of welfare. People lucky enough to find work quickly moved away. The social agencies that existed to help people in trouble had largely stopped trying, leaving what one government official described as "a caste of people almost totally dependent on the state, with little hope of breaking free." The combination of Reagan administration cuts in welfare, inept and overburdened public agencies, depressed urban economies, as well as crime, drug addiction, and other social pathologies had left a permanent urban underclass. As citizens too depressed, apathetic, distracted, or ignorant of electoral procedures to vote, these people remained a largely voiceless part of the body politic.

For the rest of the American people, more fortunate in their circumstances, a question persisted: How could the problems of the largely invisible underclass be solved before the violence and desperation of the streets threatened the identity of American democracy itself?

There seemed limits, however, to the conservative rebellion. Although Ronald Reagan championed the agenda of conservative religious leaders, he did little to act on the issues they raised, including school prayer, amendments to the Constitution requiring a balanced budget and outlawing abortion, and forceful antidrug legislation. Moreover, the taint of self-interest and scandal hampered the administration's effectiveness. Key Reagan advisers Lyn Nofziger and Michael Deaver were both indicted and later convicted for profiting illegally from their connections with the president and his administration. Attorney General Edwin Meese was never indicted but was so often criticized for misusing his office to help friends in private business that the Justice Department's own committee on ethics issued a critical report after his resignation. In all, over 100 members of the Reagan administration had either resigned or been forced out of office by criticism of their ethical or legal conduct.

The Democratic Congress might have provided the counterweight of visible, effective leadership, but for the most part, Congress seemed unwilling to grapple with serious issues. The tax reform legislation of 1986 was an exception; so, in 1988, was a compromise between conservatives and liberals for overhauling the welfare system. That bill incorporated liberal demands for increases in child-care payments, Medicaid, and welfare with conservative requirements for recipients either to work or to enroll in job training and educational programs. In other areas, however, Congress remained skittish. Virtually all members condemned the record-high deficits of the Reagan years, but with the president so adamantly opposed to new taxes, they appointed a bipartisan commission to issue recommendations, which turned out to be useless. As the rising tide of drug traffic placed increasing pressure on the urban social fabric, Congress passed a hastily drawn bill to strengthen law enforcement and treatment programs during the election year—but failed to fund the programs adequately.

Unsolved Problems

The seeming inability of both the executive and legislative branches to act vigorously was even more alarming because of deeper structural problems in the economy and society. Ironically, one crisis stemmed from the Reagan administration's inability to put into practice its "free enterprise" philosophy of reining in government bureaucracy. The bureaucracy most in need of reining in was the military's. Investigations of Pentagon procurement procedures showed that millions of dollars were being misspent when contracts were not let out for competitive bidding, as they would have under free-market conditions. On the other hand, the lack of oversight at the military's nuclear power plants showed that the bureaucracy suffered equally from too little regulation. By the end of the Reagan years, 17 sites had been closed down due to safety hazards involved in processing nuclear wastes. Because these sites were military installations, they were exempt from—and had often ignored—some of the most elementary regulations in place for civilian nuclear power plants. The prolonged inattention meant that the cost of repair might reach $200 billion. Similar problems plagued the space program, as the explosion of the space shuttle *Challenger* demonstrated in January 1986. Flaws in other military rocket designs left the American space program temporarily crippled.

In the area of public health, the spread of AIDS (acquired immune deficiency syndrome) posed a challenge that caught the administration particularly unprepared. The disease at first struck especially hard at the male homosexual community, at a time when both lesbians and gays were becoming more vocal in asserting their rights as citizens. Since the 1970s increasing numbers of people had begun to "come out of the closet" by making their sexual orientation known publicly and fighting for "gay rights" and an end to legal discrimination. Although a number of outspoken conservatives were themselves gay, most evangelical Christians, conservative Catholics, and other traditional groups continued to condemn homosexual acts as immoral. Intravenous drug users also were hard-hit by AIDS. Public health officials warned that the enormous expense of treating AIDS patients threatened the health care system, but the Reagan administration moved with extreme caution in providing research funds or care for those afflicted. Much of the burden fell on states like New York and California, where a high percentage of the gay and drug-addicted population lived.

The health of the nation's financial system seemed equally shaky, despite the continuing prosperity. After a surging bull market broke repreated records, on October 19, 1987, the Dow Jones industrial averages dropped over 500 points. On paper, that meant a loss of almost 20 percent in the value of stocks in a single day, forcing investors to recall the catastrophic crash of 1929. A presidential commission found evidence that the severe loss came from unregulated market practices like buying and selling on the basis of computer programs, not from weakness in the economy. Yet neither Congress nor the administration acted on the commission's recommendations. At the same time, savings and loans banks around the country were failing at the highest rate since the Great Depression. The Reagan administration had significantly cut back its regulation of savings and loan industry investments. Under the new, more liberal rules, many savings banks jumped into highly speculative deals or even engaged in outright fraud. Since depositors' money was backed by the Federal Savings and Loan Insurance Corporation (FSLIC), the government was faced with paying back depositors if these thrift institutions failed. The administration ignored the problem, as experts warned that a bailout might cost as much as $250 billion.

While the administration's economic policy had helped create 14.5 million jobs through 1988, the jobs were spread unevenly through the economic sector. Over 2 million of them were in finance, insurance, real estate, and law, all services used by the wealthy, not the poor. In the highly paid "Wall Street" jobs—those involving financial services—over 70 percent went to white males, only 2 percent to African-Americans. New employment for women was concentrated in the areas of health, education, social services, and government, where approximately 3 million jobs opened, most dependent on government support. New jobs for the poor (over 3 million) were largely restricted to minimum wage or poverty-level employment in hotels, fast-food restaurants, and retail stores. Here, in unskilled, often part-time, and usually dead-end jobs, almost 2 million blacks and Hispanics found work. Finally, there were almost 2.5 million new jobs for people (mostly male) who handled or moved things. Jobs for "light truck drivers," for example, increased five times as fast as any other employment.

For the wealthiest 20 percent of Americans, the 1980s had been the best of times. Demand for doctors, lawyers, engineers, and MBAs soared. What counterculture hippies were to the 1960s, high-salaried yuppies (young, upwardly mobile professionals) were to the 1980s. While the middle 60 percent of the population saw their earnings fall slightly, earnings dropped 8 percent for the poorest 20 percent and rose 9 percent for the top 20 percent. Over one-third of all tax savings ($3.6 billion) went to those 162,000 American families earning over $200,000, compared to $2.9 billion to the 31.7 million families with incomes under $15,000 a year.

A Question of Civil Rights

By the 1980s the African-American community had seemingly split in two. A significant minority had successfully lived the American dream. Almost three times more African-Americans were elected to public office in the 1970s and 1980s than in the 1960s. Tom Bradley in Los Angeles, Andrew Young in Atlanta, Harold Washington in Chicago, and Wilson Goode in Philadelphia had become mayors of some of the nation's largest cities. Blacks made substantial strides in the professions, management, sports, and entertainment. The earnings of households headed by blacks rose faster than those for whites in the 1970s, although they remained 20 percent lower.

But the surge of African-Americans into middle-class occupations tended to disguise the persistence of poverty tied to race, along with age and sex. In the 1970s and 1980s, while many of the elderly escaped poverty with the aid of Social Security payments, more young families were counted among the nation's poor. Those families were increasingly headed by single women. Over 40 percent of all black families (versus 12 percent for whites) were headed by women, and the number was growing. Here was the hard core of poverty. And for blacks as well as whites the divorce rate continued to rise. To make matters worse, the largest numbers of black families were concentrated in urban areas hard hit by the recessionary economy. Black unemployment, particularly severe among teenagers and young adults, was twice the national average.

The issue of racial prejudice, one of the oldest problems in American history, provided new cause for concern in the 1980s. During the 1970s, judicially active courts had forced officials in many large cities to take affirmative action to counter the long-term effects of segregation. That trend was challenged when the Supreme Court decided *Bakke v. Regents of the University of California* (1978). Allan Bakke, a white man, had been rejected by the medical school at the University of California at Davis, even though he had higher grades than most of the minority applicants admitted under a quota system. In a divided, ambiguous ruling, the Court ruled 5–4 that fixed quotas were illegal and that Bakke was to be admitted. On the other hand, Justice Powell's concurring opinion acknowledged that race could be a factor in admissions programs in order to secure a more diversified student body. Similar cases (decided in closely split decisions) left many observers unsure of the Court's direction, except that in general it was taking a more stringent attitude toward quota systems and affirmative action.

In the realm of everyday life, African-Americans received all too many signs that prejudice continued to operate in American society. Howard Beach, a white area of New York City, attracted national attention in 1987 when a gang of white youths beat several blacks who had strayed into the neighborhood, chasing one onto a highway where he was run over and killed. Racial incidents increased on college campuses, including the universities of Michigan and Massachusetts and the ivy league campus of Dartmouth. Equally disturbing, a black agent working for the Federal Bureau of Investigation, the nation's highest law enforcement agency, accused white co-workers of harassing him with death threats. The combination of persisting race discrimination and an economy that perpetuated a despairing underclass posed problems that could not be ignored.

The New Immigration

During the 1980s, according to provisional figures, about 6 million immigrants entered the country legally—more than in any decade in American history except

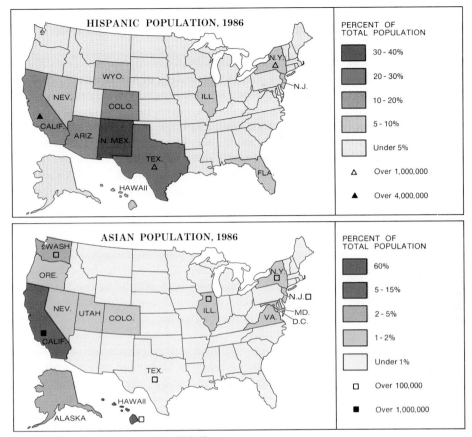

HISPANIC POPULATION, 1986

PERCENT OF
TOTAL POPULATION

30 - 40%

20 - 30%

10 - 20%

5 - 10%

Under 5%

△   Over 1,000,000

▲   Over 4,000,000

ASIAN POPULATION, 1986

PERCENT OF
TOTAL POPULATION

60%

5 - 15%

2 - 5%

1 - 2%

Under 1%

☐   Over 100,000

■   Over 1,000,000

HISPANIC AND ASIAN POPULATIONS
Hispanics and Asians have been the two fastest-growing population groups in the United States over the past several decades. Demographers predict that Hispanics will soon displace African-Americans as the nation's single largest minority group. Both Asians and Hispanics have been especially drawn to the climate and job opportunities in California.

1901–1910. Adding another 300,000 to 500,000 illegal immigrants each year, the total was even greater than the 8.8 million arriving in the first decade of the century.

Latin American immigrants accounted for approximately 35 to 40 percent of the influx each year, as they had since the 1960s. The greatest number settled in sunbelt states of Florida, Texas, and California, as well as Illinois and New York. However, the increased visibility of Hispanics did not readily translate into economic gains. In an economy increasingly divided between highly skilled jobs in the service sectors and low-paying unskilled jobs, Hispanics lagged behind anglos and blacks in education. Often, the lack of adequate English-language skills discouraged academic success. As housing costs soared during the late 1970s, only 43 percent of Hispanics owned their homes, compared to 63 percent of all Americans.

Larger families with less money translated into crowded conditions. Like immigrant families at the turn of the century, the more established Hispanic families provided housing for newer immigrants, who were often single. The new-comers hoped to save enough money from their weekly paycheck to send it to relatives in Mexico or Central America.

At the same time, some of the new immigration patterns reversed established ones. Traditionally, the majority of immigrants arriving in America have taken the lowest paying jobs, gradually assimilating into society and working their way up. Census figures from the mid-1980s indicated, however, that newcomers often did better than natives. Thus foreign-born black and Hispanic people appeared more likely to have jobs than native-born ones. Riots in Miami during 1989 revealed growing tension between newly arrived Haitians and African-Americans. Heavy immigration also disturbed relations between Hispanics and Central Americans.

By the 1980s Asians had surpassed Hispanics in numbers of legal immigrants. By eliminating the national origins quota system, the Immigration Act of 1965 opened the door on a first-come, first-qualified basis, making possible the influx of people from China and Taiwan, Korea, Japan, the Philippines, Vietnam, Cambodia, Laos, Thailand, and India. As of 1990 about 6.5 million Asian-Americans lived in the United States. Like earlier immigrants from Europe, those from the Pacific rim came in waves. Some, like the Vietnamese "boat people" of the late 1970s, were driven from their homes by economic or political turmoil; others were drawn to reunite families or realize greater opportunities in the Western Hemisphere. Professional and educated Asian Indians emigrated in search of better jobs in the United States. Doctors and nurses constituted a large percentage of the early Korean immigrants. But letters home to relatives and other nationals soon attracted a more diverse population, which concentrated in small businesses. By the mid-1980s Indians owned over 50 percent of the non–chain motels in the United States, and Koreans often replaced Jews and Italians as owners of small inner-city delicatessens and produce stores.

A wave of Asian immigrants has changed the style of America's cities much as European immigrants did a century before. This shopping plaza in Westminster, California, includes both a Chinese supermarket and "B.B.Q. Deli" as well as various Vietnamese enterprises. The overseas package and mail service indicates continued links to Asia.

The presence of other Asian-Americans and an international atmosphere drew many Asian-Americans to New York City, but climate made Hawaii and California particularly popular destinations. In 1977 alone some 40,000 Filipinos, many eager to escape from the corrupt regime of dictator Ferdinand Marcos, migrated to Honolulu. Of the 400,000 Korean-Americans in 1980 some 100,000 lived around Los Angeles. So, too, the half million Japanese-Americans settled primarily in California and Hawaii. By contrast, the federal government attempted to disperse the large influx of Vietnamese (as well as Cambodians and Laotians) who fled after the American withdrawal from Southeast Asia.

Many of the new immigrants achieved success while facing subtle forms of discrimination. With the exception of the Vietnamese, whose average income had been lowered by the presence of newly arrived boat people, the census bureau's 1980 figures of average yearly income showed many Asians leading not only other immigrant groups, but full-time American wage earners:

Asian Indian	$18,707
Japanese	16,829
Chinese	15,753
White	15,572
Korean	14,224
Filipino	13,690
Hispanic	11,650
Vietnamese	11,641
African-American	11,327

The high rate of success resulted partly from previous business and educational experience, as well as a powerful work ethic. One survey indicated that while the average American student spent 19.6 hours a week on academic work, the average Japanese-American spent 32.6 hours and Chinese-Americans, 40.4.

Racial tensions, made worse by job losses and the U.S. trade deficit with Asian countries, soon gave way to scattered acts of violence. In the ports of Texas and Louisiana the Ku Klux Klan joined with angry shrimp fishermen to mount a campaign of harassment and terror against newly arrived Vietnamese shrimpers. During a 1982 recession, some Detroit blue-collar workers vented their fear of Japanese auto imports by beating a Chinese-American to death. Many inner-city Korean merchants faced vandalism from local street gangs. The increasing numbers of both Asians and Hispanics also raised fears that they would not assimilate into American society. To spur acculturation conservatives called for the elimination of bilingual education. In 1981 the outspoken Max Rafferty, a nativist California educator, told Hispanics, "Immigrating was *your* idea. So the burden of learning the new language falls upon you—or should." In 1986 California voters reinforced the message. They passed a state referendum ending bilingual education. Other states such as Florida followed suit.

Congress also attacked the problem of increasing illegal immigration along the nation's southern border. After debating the issue for several years, in 1987 it passed a compromise version of the Simpson–Mazzoli Bill, which for the first time punished employers for hiring illegal aliens. To ease the plight of those aliens illegally in the country, the new law allowed those resident since January 1982 to become citizens. The Immigration and Naturalization Service used stricter guidelines for determining which immigrants would be granted political asylum, although critics complained that the anticommunist Reagan administration was much more generous in admitting Nicaraguans fleeing the Sandinistas than it was El Salvadoreans fleeing the American-backed government.

The new wave of immigration created serious local stresses. In the long view, though, it did not constitute a pressing crisis. Despite the "flood" of new arrivals, incoming immigrants made up only 0.3 percent of the population every year—about half the percentage that had entered, on average, over the past two centuries. In 1985, the total foreign-born population in the United States was 7 percent, compared with 11 percent for France, 16 percent for Canada, and 20 percent for Australia. In general, the traditional forces favoring assimilation seemed still at work.

The Election of 1988

All of these underlying problems—the role of the military bureaucracy, the savings and loan crisis, the need for racial tolerance, and the place of new immigrants—were fit topics for discussion in the election of 1988. Yet both candidates avoided them. The race to succeed Ronald Reagan in the White House proved a drawn-out affair that failed, above all, to define a new political agenda. Among seven major Democratic candidates only Jesse Jackson showed a real ability to excite the voters, both positively and negatively. He called for a national crusade to ease the plight of the poor. But as an African-American with a record of distinctly liberal ideas, Jackson could not capture the center of the Democratic party. That was the target of Massachusetts governor Michael Dukakis. Little-known outside New England, Dukakis ran a cautious but effective primary campaign

George Bush accepts the 1988 Republican nomination for president. Despite his controversial selection of Senator J. Danforth Quayle (looking on) as his vice-presidential running mate, Bush defeated the Democratic nominee, Michael Dukakis.

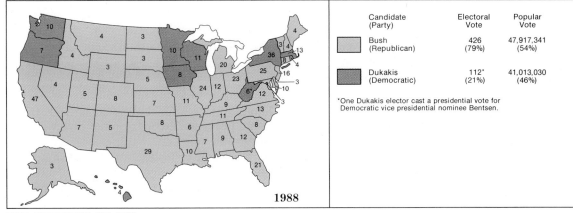

Candidate (Party)	Electoral Vote	Popular Vote
Bush (Republican)	426 (79%)	47,917,341 (54%)
Dukakis (Democratic)	112* (21%)	41,013,030 (46%)

*One Dukakis elector cast a presidential vote for Democratic vice presidential nominee Bentsen.

1988

THE ELECTION OF 1988

based on a record of administrative competence and a call to revive the economic fortunes of the poor and middle classes.

As the heir apparent to Ronald Reagan, George Bush appealed most to Republican party professionals and the affluent middle class that had benefited from Reagonomics. Bush had some evident weaknesses. He had been involved in the disastrous decision to trade arms for hostages. Women voters showed a preference for Dukakis and his support for free choice on the abortion issue. Many blue-collar workers hurt by the loss of high-wage jobs seemed ready to return to the Democratic fold. To emphasize his own stature, Bush selected one of the least qualified candidates in American political history, conservative Senator J. Danforth Quayle of Indiana, as his running mate.

More than Dukakis, Bush evaded major campaign issues and draped himself in the flag. Like Reagan, he emphasized the Republican themes of strong national defense and anti-Soviet policies. In addition, Americans seemed reluctant to change the political course so long as the economy kept growing. In a campaign that ultimately focused on media images rather than issues, Bush won by a comfortable margin (54 to 46 percent) while achieving an Electoral College advantage of 426 to 112. The people had spoken, though not very loudly.

George Washington had begun his first term in office exactly 200 years earlier, presiding over a fragile republic whose future seemed uncertain at best. Yet that republic survived, flourished, and developed a remarkably democratic system for adjudicating the rival needs and claims of its diverse citizenry. To George Bush fell the responsibility of articulating an agenda for a nation of nations that remained divided, as always, along lines of class, gender, race, religion, section, generation, and ideology.

SIGNIFICANT EVENTS

1978 — *Bakke v. Regents of the University of California*

1979 — Moral Majority established; Sandinistas overthrow Somoza in Nicaragua

1980 — Reagan defeats Carter

1980s — Asians pass Hispanics in numbers of legal immigrants

1981 — Reagan shot; military buildup; Reagan breaks PATCO strike; recession sets in; Economic Recovery Tax Act; United States begins aiding Nicaraguan Contras

1982 — Jonathan Schell's *Fate of the Earth* published; attack on U.S. Marine barracks in Lebanon

1983 — Reagan proposes SDI; invasion of Grenada; Soviets shoot down South Korean airliner; Pershing missiles deployed in Europe

1984 — Boland Amendment passed; Geraldine Ferraro nominated for vice president; Reagan defeats Mondale

1985 — Gramm–Rudman Act; U.S. bombing raid on Libya; increase in hostages taken by terrorists; United States begins secret arms-for-hostages negotiations with Iran

1986 — *Challenger* shuttle disaster; Oliver North begins diverting Iran arms sales profits to Contras; California restricts bilingual education; Tax Reform Act; American jets attack Libya; Reykjavík summit; Immigration Reform Act; Iran–Contra scandal breaks

1987 — Iran–Contra hearings; United States and Soviet Union agree on INF treaty; stock market plunge

1988 — Congress passes drug and welfare reform bills; Bush defeats Dukakis

1989 — Miami riots; Oliver North convicted

APPENDIX

THE DECLARATION OF INDEPENDENCE

In Congress, July 4, 1776,

THE UNANIMOUS DECLARATION OF THE
THIRTEEN UNITED STATES OF AMERICA

When, in the course of human events, it becomes necessary for one people to dissolve the political bands which have connected them with another, and to assume, among the powers of the earth, the separate and equal station to which the laws of nature and of nature's God entitle them, a decent respect to the opinions of mankind requires that they should declare the causes which impel them to the separation.

We hold these truths to be self-evident, that all men are created equal; that they are endowed by their Creator with certain unalienable rights; that among these, are life, liberty, and the pursuit of happiness. That, to secure these rights, governments are instituted among men, deriving their just powers from the consent of the governed; that, whenever any form of government becomes destructive of these ends, it is the right of the people to alter or to abolish it, and to institute a new government, laying its foundation on such principles, and organizing its powers in such form, as to them shall seem most likely to effect their safety and happiness. Prudence, indeed, will dictate that governments long established, should not be changed for light and transient causes; and, accordingly, all experience hath shown, that mankind are more disposed to suffer, while evils are sufferable, than to right themselves by abolishing the forms to which they are accustomed. But, when a long train of abuses and usurpations, pursuing invariably the same object, evinces a design to reduce them under absolute despotism, it is their right, it is their duty, to throw off such government and to provide new guards for their future security. Such has been the patient sufferance of these colonies, and such is now the necessity which constrains them to alter their former systems of government. The history of the present King of Great Britain is a history of repeated injuries and usurpations, all having, in direct object, the establishment of an absolute tyranny over these States. To prove this, let facts be submitted to a candid world:

He has refused his assent to laws the most wholesome and necessary for the public good.

He has forbidden his governors to pass laws of immediate and pressing importance, unless suspended in their operation till his assent should be obtained; and, when so suspended, he has utterly neglected to attend to them.

He has refused to pass other laws for the accommodation of large districts of people, unless those people would relinquish the right of representation in the legislature; a right inestimable to them, and formidable to tyrants only.

He has called together legislative bodies at places unusual, uncomfortable, and distant from the depository of their public records, for the sole purpose of fatiguing them into compliance with his measures.

He has dissolved representative houses repeatedly for opposing, with manly firmness, his invasions on the rights of the people.

He has refused, for a long time after such dissolutions, to cause others to be elected; whereby the legislative powers, incapable of annihilation, have returned to the people at large for their exercise; the state remaining, in the meantime, exposed to all the danger of invasion from without, and convulsions within.

He has endeavored to prevent the population of these States; for that purpose, obstructing the laws for naturalization of foreigners, refusing to pass others to encourage their migration hither, and raising the conditions of new appropriations of lands.

He had obstructed the administration of justice, by refusing his assent to laws for establishing judiciary powers.

He has made judges dependent on his will alone, for the tenure of their offices, and the amount and payment of their salaries.

He has erected a multitude of new offices, and sent hither swarms of officers to harass our people, and eat out their substance.

He has kept among us, in time of peace, standing armies, without the consent of our legislatures.

He has affected to render the military independent of, and superior to, the civil power.

He has combined, with others, to subject us to a jurisdiction foreign to our Constitution, and unacknowledged by our laws; giving his assent to their acts of pretended legislation:

For quartering large bodies of armed troops among us:

For protecting them by a mock trial, from punishment, for any murders which they should commit on the inhabitants of these States:

For cutting off our trade with all parts of the world:

For imposing taxes on us without our consent:

For depriving us, in many cases, of the benefit of trial by jury:

For transporting us beyond seas to be tried for pretended offences:

For abolishing the free system of English laws in a neighboring province, establishing therein an arbitrary government, and enlarging its boundaries, so as to render it at once an example and fit instrument for introducing the same absolute rule into these colonies:

For taking away our charters, abolishing our most valuable laws, and altering, fundamentally, the powers of our governments:

For suspending our own legislatures, and declaring themselves invested with power to legislate for us in all cases whatsoever.

He had abdicated government here, by declaring us out of his protection, and waging war against us.

He has plundered our seas, ravaged our coasts, burnt our towns, and destroyed the lives of our people.

He is, at this time, transporting large armies of foreign mercenaries to complete the works of death, desolation, and tyranny, already begun, with circumstances of cruelty and perfidy scarcely paralleled in the most barbarous ages, and totally unworthy the head of a civilized nation.

He has constrained our fellow citizens, taken captive on the high seas, to bear arms against their country, to become the executioners of their friends, and brethren, or to fall themselves by their hands.

He has excited domestic insurrections amongst us, and has endeavored to bring on the inhabitants of our frontiers, the merciless Indian savages, whose known rule of warfare is an undistinguished destruction of all ages, sexes, and conditions.

In every stage of these oppressions, we have petitioned for redress, in the most humble terms; our repeated petitions have been answered only by repeated injury. A prince, whose character is thus marked by every act which may define a tyrant, is unfit to be the ruler of a free people.

Nor have we been wanting in attention to our British brethren. We have warned them, from time to time, of attempts made by their legislature to extend an unwarrantable jurisdiction over us. We have reminded them of the circumstances of our emigration and settlement here. We have appealed to their native justice and magnanimity, and we have conjured them, by the ties of our common kindred, to disavow these usurpations, which would inevitably interrupt our connections and correspondence. They, too, have been deaf to the voice of justice and consanguinity. We must, therefore, acquiesce in the necessity which denounces our separation, and hold them as we hold the rest of mankind, enemies in war, in peace, friends.

We, therefore, the representatives of the United States of America, in general Congress assembled, appealing to the Supreme Judge of the world for the rectitude of our intentions, do, in the name, and by the authority of the good people of these colonies, solemnly publish and declare, that these united colonies are, and of right ought to be, free and independent states: that they are absolved from all allegiance to the British Crown, and that all political connection between them and the state of Great Britain is, and ought to be, totally dissolved; and that, as free and independent states, they have full power to levy war, conclude peace, contract alliances, establish commerce, and to do all other acts and things which independent states may of right do. And, for the support of this declaration, with a firm reliance on the protection of Divine Providence, we mutually pledge to each other our lives, our fortunes, and our sacred honor.

The foregoing Declaration was, by order of Congress, engrossed, and signed by the following members:

JOHN HANCOCK

New Hampshire
Josiah Bartlett
William Whipple
Matthew Thornton

New York
William Floyd
Philip Livingston
Francis Lewis
Lewis Morris

Delaware
Caesar Rodney
George Reed
Thomas M'Kean

North Carolina
William Hooper
Joseph Hewes
John Penn

Massachusetts Bay
Samuel Adams
John Adams
Robert Treat Paine
Elbridge Gerry

New Jersey
Richard Stockton
John Witherspoon
Francis Hopkinson
John Hart
Abraham Clark

Maryland
Samuel Chase
William Paca
Thomas Stone
Charles Carroll,
    of Carrollton

South Carolina
Edward Rutledge
Thomas Heyward, Jr.
Thomas Lynch, Jr.
Arthur Middleton

Rhode Island
Stephen Hopkins
William Ellery

Connecticut
Roger Sherman
Samuel Huntington
William Williams
Oliver Wolcott

Pennsylvania
Robert Morris
Benjamin Rush
Benjamin Franklin
John Morton
George Clymer
James Smith
George Taylor
James Wilson
George Ross

Virginia
George Wythe
Richard Henry Lee
Thomas Jefferson
Benjamin Harrison
Thomas Nelson, Jr.
Francis Lightfoot Lee
Carter Braxton

Georgia
Button Gwinnett
Lyman Hall
George Walton

Resolved, That copies of the Declaration be sent to the several assemblies, conventions, and committees, or councils of safety, and to the several commanding officers of the continental troops; that it be proclaimed in each of the United States, at the head of the army.

THE CONSTITUTION OF THE UNITED STATES OF AMERICA[1]

We the People of the United States, in Order to form a more perfect Union, establish Justice, insure domestic Tranquility, provide for the common defence, promote the general Welfare, and secure the Blessings of Liberty to ourselves and our Posterity, do ordain and establish this CONSTITUTION for the United States of America.

ARTICLE 1

Section 1. All legislative Powers herein granted shall be vested in a Congress of the United States, which shall consist of a Senate and House of Representatives.

Section 2. The House of Representatives shall be composed of Members chosen every second Year by the People of the several States, and the Electors in each State shall have the Qualifications requisite for Electors of the most numerous Branch of the State Legislature.

No Person shall be a Representative who shall not have attained to the Age of twenty-five Years, and been seven Years a Citizen of the United States, and who shall not, when elected, be an Inhabitant of that State in which he shall be chosen.

[Representatives and direct Taxes[2] shall be apportioned among the several States which may be included within this Union, according to their respective Numbers, which shall be determined by adding to the whole Number of free Persons, including those bound to Service for a Term of Years, and excluding Indians not taxed, three fifths of all other Persons.][3] The actual Enumeration shall be made within three Years after the first Meeting of the Congress of the United States, and within every subsequent Term of ten Years, in such Manner as they shall by Law direct. The Number of Representatives shall not exceed one for every thirty Thousand, but each State shall have at Least one Representative; and until such enumeration shall be made, the State of New Hampshire shall be entitled to chuse three, Massachusetts eight, Rhode-Island and Providence Plantations one, Connecticut five, New York six, New Jersey four, Pennsylvania eight, Delaware one, Maryland six, Virginia ten, North Carolina five, South Carolina five, and Georgia three.

When vacancies happen in the Representation from any State, the Executive Authority thereof shall issue Writs of Election to fill such Vacancies.

The House of Representatives shall chuse their Speaker and other Officers; and shall have the sole Power of Impeachment.

Section 3. The Senate of the United States shall be composed of two Senators from each State, chosen by the Legislature thereof, for six Years; and each Senator shall have one Vote.

Immediately after they shall be assembled in Consequence of the first Election, they shall be divided as equally as may be into three Classes. The Seats of the Senators of the first Class shall be vacated at the Expiration of the second Year, of the second Class at the Expiration of the fourth Year, and of the third Class at the Expiration of the sixth Year, so that one-third may be chosen every second Year; and if Vacancies happen by Resignation, or otherwise, during the Recess of the Legislature of any State, the Executive thereof may make temporary Appointments until the next Meeting of the Legislature, which shall then fill such Vacancies.

No Person shall be a Senator who shall not have attained to the Age of thirty Years, and been nine Years a Citizen of the United States, and who shall not, when elected, be an Inhabitant of that State for which he shall be chosen.

The Vice President of the United States shall be President of the Senate, but shall have no vote, unless they be equally divided.

The Senate shall chuse their other Officers, and also a President pro tempore, in the absence of the Vice President, or when he shall exercise the Office of President of the United States.

The Senate shall have the sole Power to try all Impeachments. When sitting for that pur-

---

[1]This version follows the original Constitution in capitalization and spelling. It is adapted from the text published by the United States Department of the Interior, Office of Education.

[2]Altered by the Sixteenth Amendment.

[3]Negated by the Fourteenth Amendment.

pose they shall be on Oath or Affirmation. When the President of the United States is tried, the Chief Justice shall preside: And no person shall be convicted without the Concurrence of two thirds of the Members present.

Judgment in Cases of Impeachment shall not extend further than to removal from Office, and disqualification to hold and enjoy any Office of honor, Trust, or Profit under the United States: but the Party convicted shall nevertheless be liable and subject to Indictment, Trial, Judgment, and Punishment, according to Law.

Section 4. The Times, Places and Manner of holding Elections for Senators and Representatives, shall be prescribed in each State by the Legislature thereof; but the Congress may at any time by Law make or alter such Regulations, except as to the Places of Chusing Senators.

The Congress shall assemble at least once in every Year, and such Meeting shall be on the first Monday in December, unless they shall by Law appoint a different Day.

Section 5. Each House shall be the Judge of the Elections, Returns and Qualifications of its own Members, and a Majority of each shall constitute a Quorum to do Business; but a smaller number may adjourn from day to day, and may be authorized to compel the Attendance of absent Members, in such Manner, and under such Penalties, as each House may provide.

Each House may determine the Rules of its Proceedings, punish its Members for disorderly Behaviour, and, with the Concurrence of two thirds, expel a Member.

Each House shall keep a Journal of its Proceedings, and from time to time publish the same, excepting such Parts as may in their Judgment require Secrecy; and the Yeas and Nays of the Members of either House on any question shall, at the Desire of one fifth of those Present, be entered on the Journal.

Neither House, during the Session of Congress, shall, without the Consent of the other, adjourn for more than three days, nor to any other Place than that in which the two Houses shall be sitting.

Section 6. The Senators and Representatives shall receive a Compensation for their Services, to be ascertained by Law, and paid out of the Treasury of the United States. They shall in all Cases, except Treason, Felony, and Breach of the Peace, be privileged from Arrest during their Attendance at the Session of their respective Houses, and in going to and returning from the same; and for any Speech or Debate in either House, they shall not be questioned in any other Place.

No Senator or Representative shall, during the Time for which he was elected, be appointed to any civil Office under the Authority of the United States, which shall have been created, or the Emoluments whereof shall have been increased, during such time; and no Person holding any Office under the United States shall be a Member of either House during his continuance in Office.

Section 7. All Bills for raising Revenue shall originate in the House of Representatives; but the Senate may propose or concur with Amendments as on other bills.

Every Bill which shall have passed the House of Representatives and the Senate, shall, before it become a Law, be presented to the President of the United States; If he approve he shall sign it, but if not he shall return it, with his Objections, to that House in which it shall have originated, who shall enter the Objections at large on their Journal, and proceed to reconsider it. If after such Reconsideration two thirds of that House shall agree to pass the bill, it shall be sent, together with the objections, to the other House, by which it shall likewise be reconsidered, and if approved by two thirds of that House, it shall become a Law. But in all such Cases the Votes of both Houses shall be determined by Yeas and Nays, and the Names of the Persons voting for and against the Bill shall be entered on the Journal of each House respectively. If any Bill shall not be returned by the President within ten Days (Sundays excepted) after it shall have been presented to him, the Same shall be a Law, in like Manner as if he had signed it, unless the Congress by their Adjournment prevent its Return, in which Case it shall not be a Law.

Every Order, Resolution, or Vote to which the Concurrence of the Senate and House of Representatives may be necessary (except on a question of Adjournment) shall be presented to the President of the United States; and before the Same shall take Effect, shall be approved by him, or being disapproved by him, shall be repassed by two thirds of the Senate and House of Representatives, according to the Rules and Limitations prescribed in the Case of a Bill.

Section 8. The Congress shall have Power To lay and collect Taxes, Duties, Imposts and Excises, to pay the Debts and provide for the common Defence and general Welfare of the United States; but all Duties, Imposts and Excises shall be uniform throughout the United States;

To borrow money on the credit of the United States;

To regulate Commerce with foreign Nations, and among the several States, and with the Indian Tribes;

To establish an uniform rule of Naturalization, and uniform Laws on the subject of Bankruptcies throughout the United States;

To coin Money, regulate the Value thereof, and of foreign Coin, and fix the Standard of Weights and Measures;

To provide for the Punishment of counterfeiting the Securities and current Coin of the United States;

To establish Post Offices and post Roads;

To promote the Progress of Science and useful Arts, by securing for limited Times to Authors and Inventors the exclusive Right to their respective Writings and Discoveries;

To constitute Tribunals inferior to the Supreme Court;

To define and punish Piracies and Felonies committed on the high Seas, and Offenses against the Law of Nations;

To declare War, grant Letters of Marque and Reprisal, and make Rules concerning Captures on Land and Water;

To raise and support Armies, but no Appropriation of Money to that Use shall be for a longer Term than two Years;

To provide and maintain a Navy;

To make Rules for the Government and Regulation of the land and naval forces;

To provide for calling forth the Militia to execute the Laws of the Union, suppress Insurrections and repel Invasions;

To provide for organizing, arming, and disciplining the Militia, and for governing such Part of them as may be employed in the Service of the United States, reserving to the States respectively, the Appointment of the Officers, and the Authority of training the Militia according to the discipline prescribed by Congress;

To exercise exclusive Legislation in all Cases whatsoever, over such District (not exceeding ten Miles square) as may, by Cession of particular States, and the acceptance of Congress, become the Seat of the Government of the United States, and to exercise like Authority over all Places purchased by the Consent of the Legislature of the State in which the Same shall be, for the Erection of Forts, Magazines, Arsenals, Dock-yards, and other needful Buildings;—And

To make all Laws which shall be necessary and proper for carrying into Execution the foregoing Powers, and all other Powers vested by this Constitution in the Government of the United States, or in any Department or Officer thereof.

Section 9. The Migration or Importation of such Persons as any of the States now existing shall think proper to admit, shall not be prohibited by the Congress prior to the Year one thousand eight hundred and eight, but a tax or duty may be imposed on such Importation, not exceeding ten dollars for each Person.

The privilege of the Writ of Habeas Corpus shall not be suspended, unless when in Cases of Rebellion or Invasion the public Safety may require it.

No bill of Attainder or ex post facto Law shall be passed.

No capitation, or other direct, Tax shall be laid unless in Proportion to the Census or Enumeration herein before directed to be taken.

No Tax or Duty shall be laid on Articles exported from any State.

No Preference shall be given by any Regulation of Commerce or Revenue to the Ports of one State over those of another: nor shall Vessels bound to, or from, one State, be obliged to enter, clear, or pay Duties in another.

No Money shall be drawn from the Treasury, but in Consequence of Appropriations made by Law; and a regular Statement and Account of the Receipts and Expenditures of all public Money shall be published from time to time.

No Title of Nobility shall be granted by the United States: And no Person holding any Office of Profit or Trust under them, shall, without the Consent of the Congress, accept of any present, Emolument, Office, or Title, of any kind whatever, from any King, Prince, or foreign State.

Section 10. No State shall enter into any Treaty, Alliance, or Confederation; grant Letters of Marque and Reprisal; coin Money; emit Bills of Credit; make any Thing but gold and silver Coin a Tender in Payment of Debts; pass any Bill of Attainder, ex post facto Law, or Law impairing the Obligation of Contracts, or grant any Title of Nobility.

No State shall, without the Consent of the Congress, lay any Imposts or Duties on Imports or Exports, except what may be absolutely necessary for executing its inspection Laws; and the net Produce of all Duties and Imposts, laid by any State on Imports or Exports, shall be for the use of the Treasury of the United States; and all such Laws shall be subject to the Revision and Control of the Congress.

No state shall, without the Consent of Congress, lay any duty of Tonnage, keep Troops, or Ships of War in time of Peace, enter into any Agreement or Compact with another State, or with a foreign Power, or engage in War, unless actually invaded, or in such imminent Danger as will not admit of delay.

ARTICLE II

Section 1. The executive Power shall be vested in a President of the United States of America. He shall hold his Office during the Term of four years, and, together with the Vice President, chosen for the same Term, be elected, as follows:

Each State shall appoint, in such Manner as the Legislature thereof may direct, a Number of Electors, equal to the whole Number of Senators and Representatives to which the State may be entitled in the Congress: but no Senator or Representative, or Person holding an Office of Trust or Profit under the United States, shall be appointed an Elector.

[The Electors shall meet in their respective States, and vote by Ballot for two persons, of whom one at least shall not be an Inhabitant of the same State with themselves. And they shall make a List of all the Persons voted for, and of the Number of Votes for each; which List they shall sign and certify, and transmit sealed to the Seat of the Government of the United States, directed to the President of the Senate. The President of the Senate shall, in the Presence of the Senate and House of Representatives, open all the Certificates, and the Votes shall then be counted. The Person having the greatest Number of Votes shall be the President, if such Number be a Majority of the whole Number of Electors appointed; and if there be more than one who have such Majority, and have an equal Number of Votes, then the House of Representatives shall immediately chuse by Ballot one of them for President; and if no Person have a Majority, then from the five highest on the List the said House shall in like Manner chuse the President. But in chusing the President, the Votes shall be taken by States, the Representation from each State having one Vote; a quorum for this Purpose shall consist of a Member or Members from two-thirds of the States, and a Majority of all the States shall be necessary to a Choice. In every Case, after the Choice of the President, the Person having the greatest Number of Votes of the Electors shall be the Vice President. But if there should remain two or more who have equal votes, the Senate shall chuse from them by Ballot the Vice President.][4]

The Congress may determine the Time of chusing the Electors, and the Day on which they shall give their Votes; which Day shall be the same throughout the United States.

No person except a natural-born Citizen, or a Citizen of the United States, at the time of the Adoption of this Constitution, shall be eligible to the Office of President; neither shall any Person be eligible to that Office who shall not have attained to the Age of thirty-five years, and been fourteen Years a Resident within the United States.

In Case of the Removal of the President from Office, or of his Death, Resignation, or Inability to discharge the Powers and Duties of the said Office, the same shall devolve on the Vice President, and the Congress may by Law provide for the Case of Removal, Death, Resignation, or Inability, both of the President and Vice President, declaring what Officer shall then act as President, and such Officer shall act accordingly, until the disability be removed, or a President shall be elected.

The President shall, at stated Times, receive for his Services a Compensation, which shall neither be increased nor diminished during the Period for which he shall have been elected, and he shall not receive within that Period any other Emolument from the United States, or any of them.

Before he enter on the execution of his Office, he shall take the following Oath or Affirma-

---

[4] Revised by the Twelfth Amendment.

tion:—"I do solemnly swear (or affirm) that I will faithfully execute the Office of President of the United States, and will, to the best of my Ability, preserve, protect, and defend the Constitution of the United States."

Section 2. The President shall be Commander in Chief of the Army and Navy of the United States, and of the Militia of the several States, when called into the actual Service of the United States; he may require the Opinion, in writing, of the principal Officer in each of the executive Departments, upon any subject relating to the Duties of their respective Offices, and he shall have Power to Grant Reprieves and Pardons for Offenses against the United States, except in Cases of Impeachment.

He shall have Power, by and with the Advice and Consent of the Senate, to make Treaties, provided two-thirds of the Senators present concur; and he shall nominate, and by and with the Advice and Consent of the Senate, shall appoint Ambassadors, other public Ministers and Consuls, Judges of the supreme Court, and all other Officers of the United States, whose Appointments are not herein otherwise provided for, and which shall be established by Law: but the Congress may by Law vest the Appointment of such inferior Officers, as they think proper, in the President alone, in the Courts of Law, or in the Heads of Departments.

The President shall have Power to fill up all Vacancies that may happen during the Recess of the Senate, by granting Commissions which shall expire at the End of their next Session.

Section 3. He shall from time to time give to the Congress Information of the State of the Union, and recommend to their Consideration such Measures as he shall judge necessary and expedient; he may, on extraordinary occasions, convene both Houses, or either of them, and in Case of Disagreement between them, with respect to the Time of Adjournment, he may adjourn them to such Time as he shall think proper; he shall receive Ambassadors and other public Ministers; he shall take care that the Laws be faithfully executed, and shall Commission all the Officers of the United States.

Section 4. The President, Vice President and all civil Officers of the United States, shall be removed from Office on Impeachment for, and Conviction of, Treason, Bribery, or other high Crimes and Misdemeanors.

ARTICLE III

Section 1. The judicial Power of the United States, shall be vested in one supreme Court, and in such inferior Courts as the Congress may from time to time ordain and establish. The Judges, both of the supreme and inferior Courts, shall hold their Offices during good Behaviour, and shall, at stated Times, receive for their Services, a Compensation, which shall not be diminished during their Continuance in Office.

Section 2. The judicial Power shall extend to all Cases, in Law and Equity, arising under this Constitution, the Laws of the United States, and Treaties made, or which shall be made, under their Authority;—to all Cases affecting ambassadors, other public ministers and consuls;—to all cases of admiralty and maritime Jurisdiction;—to Controversies to which the United States shall be a Party;—to Controversies between two or more States;—between a State and Citizens of another State;[5]—between Citizens of different States—between Citizens of the same State claiming Lands under Grants of different States, and between a State, or the Citizens thereof, and foreign States, Citizens, or Subjects.

In all Cases affecting Ambassadors, other public Ministers and Consuls, and those in which a State shall be Party, the supreme Court shall have original Jurisdiction. In all the other Cases before mentioned, the supreme Court shall have appellate Jurisdiction, both as to Law and Fact, with such Exceptions, and under such Regulations as the Congress shall make.

The trial of all Crimes, except in Cases of Impeachment, shall be by Jury; and such Trial shall be held in the State where the said Crimes shall have been committed; but when not committed within any State, the Trial shall be at such Place or Places as the Congress may by Law have directed.

Section 3. Treason against the United States, shall consist only in levying War against them,

[5]Qualified by the Eleventh Amendment.

or in adhering to their Enemies, giving them Aid and Comfort. No Person shall be convicted of Treason unless on the Testimony of two Witnesses to the same overt Act, or on Confession in open Court.

The Congress shall have power to declare the Punishment of Treason, but no Attainder of Treason shall work Corruption of Blood, or Forfeiture except during the Life of the Person attainted.

ARTICLE IV

Section 1. Full Faith and Credit shall be given in each State to the public Acts, Records, and judicial Proceedings of every other State. And the Congress may by general Laws prescribe the Manner in which such Acts, Records and Proceedings shall be proved, and the Effect thereof.

Section 2. The Citizens of each State shall be entitled to all Privileges and Immunities of Citizens in the several States.

A Person charged in any State with Treason, Felony, or other Crime, who shall flee from Justice, and be found in another State, shall on demand of the executive Authority of the State from which he fled, be delivered up, to be removed to the State having Jurisdiction of the crime.

No Person held to Service or Labour in one State, under the Laws thereof, escaping into another, shall, in Consequence of any Law or Regulation therein, be discharged from such Service or Labour, but shall be delivered up on Claim of the Party to whom such Service or Labour may be due.

Section 3. New States may be admitted by the Congress into this Union; but no new State shall be formed or erected within the Jurisdiction of any other State; nor any State be formed by the Junction of two or more States, or parts of States, without the Consent of the Legislatures of the States concerned as well as of the Congress.

The Congress shall have Power to dispose of and make all needful Rules and Regulations respecting the Territory or other Property belonging to the United States; and nothing in this Constitution shall be so construed as to Prejudice any Claims of the United States, or of any particular State.

Section 4. The United States shall guarantee to every State in this Union a Republican Form of Government, and shall protect each of them against Invasion; and on Application of the Legislature, or of the Executive (when the Legislature cannot be convened) against domestic Violence.

ARTICLE V

The Congress, whenever two-thirds of both Houses shall deem it necessary, shall propose Amendments to this Constitution, or, on the Application of the Legislatures of two-thirds of the several States, shall call a Convention for proposing Amendments, which, in either Case, shall be valid to all Intents and Purposes, as part of this Constitution, when ratified by the Legislatures of three-fourths of the several States, or by Conventions in three-fourths thereof, as the one or the other Mode of Ratification may be proposed by the Congress; Provided that no Amendment which may be made prior to the Year One thousand eight hundred and eight shall in any Manner affect the first and fourth Clauses in the Ninth Section of the first Article; and that no State, without its Consent, shall be deprived of its equal Suffrage in the Senate.

ARTICLE VI

All Debts contracted and Engagements entered into, before the Adoption of this Constitution, shall be as valid against the United States under this Constitution, as under the Confederation.

This Constitution, and the Laws of the United States which shall be made in Pursuance thereof; and all Treaties made, or which shall be made, under the Authority of the United States, shall be the supreme Law of the Land; and the Judges in every State shall be bound thereby, any Thing in the Constitution or Laws of any State to the Contrary notwithstanding.

The Senators and Representatives before mentioned, and the Members of the several State Legislatures, and all executive and judicial Officers, both of the United States and of the several States, shall be bound by Oath or Affirmation to support this Constitution; but no religious Tests shall ever be required as a qualification to any Office or public Trust under the United States.

ARTICLE VII

The Ratification of the Conventions of nine States shall be sufficient for the Establishment of this Constitution between the States so ratifying the same.

Done in Convention by the Unanimous Consent of the States present the Seventeenth Day of September in the Year of our Lord one thousand seven hundred and Eighty seven, and of the Independence of the United States of America the Twelfth. In Witness whereof We have hereunto subscribed our Names.[6]

GEORGE WASHINGTON

PRESIDENT AND DEPUTY FROM VIRGINIA

New Hampshire
John Langdon
Nicholas Gilman

Massachusetts
Nathaniel Gorham
Rufus King

Connecticut
William Samuel
  Johnson
Roger Sherman

New York
Alexander Hamilton

New Jersey
William Livingston
David Brearley
William Paterson
Jonathan Dayton

Pennsylvania
Benjamin Franklin
Thomas Mifflin
Robert Morris
George Clymer
Thomas FitzSimons
Jared Ingersoll
James Wilson
Gouverneur Morris

Delaware
George Read
Gunning Bedford, Jr.
John Dickinson
Richard Bassett
Jacob Broom

Maryland
James McHenry
Daniel of
  St. Thomas Jenifer
Daniel Carroll

Virginia
John Blair
James Madison, Jr.

North Carolina
William Blount
Richard Dobbs
  Spaight
Hugh Williamson

South Carolina
John Rutledge
Charles Cotesworth
  Pinckney
Charles Pinckney
Pierce Butler

Georgia
William Few
Abraham Baldwin

Articles in Addition to, and Amendment of, the Constitution of the United States of America, Proposed by Congress, and Ratified by the Legislatures of the Several States, Pursuant to the Fifth Article of the Original Constitution[7]

[AMENDMENT I]

Congress shall make no law respecting an establishment of religion, or prohibiting the free exercise thereof; or abridging the freedom of speech, or of the press; or the right of the people peaceably to assemble, and to petition the Government for a redress of grievances.

[AMENDMENT II]

A well regulated Militia, being necessary to the security of a free State, the right of the people to keep and bear Arms shall not be infringed.

[AMENDMENT III]

No Soldier shall, in time of peace, be quartered in any house, without the consent of the Owner, nor in time of war, but in a manner to be prescribed by law.

[AMENDMENT IV]

The right of the people to be secure in their persons, houses, papers, and effects, against unreasonable searches and seizures, shall not be violated, and no Warrants shall issue, but

[6]These are the full names of the signers, which in some cases are not the signatures on the document.

[7]This heading appears only in the joint resolution submitting the first ten amendments, known as the Bill of Rights.

upon probable cause, supported by Oath or affirmation, and particularly describing the place to be searched, and the persons or things to be seized.

[AMENDMENT V]

No person shall be held to answer for a capital or otherwise infamous crime, unless on a presentment or indictment of a Grand Jury, except in cases arising in the land or naval forces, or in the Militia, when in actual service in time of War or public danger; nor shall any person be subject for the same offence to be twice put in jeopardy of life or limb; nor shall be compelled in any criminal case to be a witness against himself, nor be deprived of life, liberty, or property, without due process of law; nor shall private property be taken for public use, without just compensation.

[AMENDMENT VI]

In all criminal prosecutions, the accused shall enjoy the right to a speedy and public trial, by an impartial jury of the State and district wherein the crime shall have been committed, which district shall have been previously ascertained by law, and to be informed of the nature and cause of the accusation; to be confronted with the witnesses against him; to have compulsory process for obtaining witnesses in his favour, and to have the Assistance of Counsel for his defence.

[AMENDMENT VII]

In suits at common law, where the value in controversy shall exceed twenty dollars, the right of trial by jury shall be preserved, and no fact tried by a jury, shall be otherwise reexamined in any Court of the United States, than according to the rules of the common law.

[AMENDMENT VIII]

Excessive bail shall not be required, nor excessive fines imposed, nor cruel and unusual punishments inflicted.

[AMENDMENT IX]

The enumeration of the Constitution, of certain rights, shall not be construed to deny or disparage others retained by the people.

[AMENDMENT X]

The powers not delegated to the United States by the Constitution, nor prohibited by it to the States, are reserved to the States respectively, or to the people.

[Amendments I–X, in force 1791.]

[AMENDMENT XI][8]

The Judicial power of the United States shall not be construed to extend to any suit in law or equity, commenced or prosecuted against one of the United States by Citizens of another State, or by Citizens or Subjects of any Foreign State.

[AMENDMENT XII][9]

The Electors shall meet in their respective States and vote by ballot for President and Vice-President, one of whom, at least, shall not be an inhabitant of the same State with themselves; they shall name in their ballots the person voted for as President, and in distinct ballots the person voted for as Vice-President, and they shall make distinct lists of all persons voted for as President, and of all persons voted for as Vice-President, and of the number of votes for each, which lists they shall sign and certify, and transmit sealed to the seal of the government of the United States, directed to the President of the Senate;—The President of the Senate shall, in the presence of the Senate and House of Representatives, open all the certificates and the votes shall then be counted;—The person having the greatest number of votes for President, shall be the President, if such number be a majority of the whole number of Electors appointed; and if no person have such majority, then from the persons having the highest numbers not exceeding three on the list of those

[8]Adopted in 1798.
[9]Adopted in 1804.

voted for as President, the House of Representatives shall choose immediately, by ballot, the President. But in choosing the President, the votes shall be taken by states, the representation from each state having one vote; a quorum for this purpose shall consist of a member or members from two-thirds of the states, and a majority of all the states shall be necessary to a choice. And if the House of Representatives shall not choose a President whenever the right of choice shall devolve upon them, before the fourth day of March next following, then the Vice-President shall act as President, as in the case of the death or other constitutional disability of the President.—The person having the greatest number of votes as Vice-President, shall be the Vice-President, if such number be a majority of the whole number of Electors appointed, and if no person have a majority, then from the two highest numbers on the list, the Senate shall choose the Vice-President; a quorum for the purpose shall consist of two-thirds of the whole number of Senators, and a majority of the whole number shall be necessary to a choice. But no person constitutionally ineligible to the office of President shall be eligible to that of Vice-President of the United States.

[AMENDMENT XIII][10]

Section 1. Neither slavery nor involuntary servitude, except as a punishment for crime whereof the party shall have been duly convicted, shall exist within the United States, or any place subject to their jurisdiction.

Section 2. Congress shall have power to enforce this article by appropriate legislation.

[AMENDMENT XIV][11]

Section 1. All persons born or naturalized in the United States, and subject to the jurisdiction thereof, are citizens of the United States and of the State wherein they reside. No State shall abridge the privileges or immunities of citizens of the United States; nor shall any State deprive any person of life, liberty, or property, without due process of law; nor deny to any person within its jurisdiction the equal protection of the laws.

Section 2. Representatives shall be apportioned among the several States according to their respective numbers, counting the whole number of persons in each State, excluding Indians not taxed. But when the right to vote at any election for the choice of electors for President and Vice-President of the United States, Representatives in Congress, the Executive and Judicial officers of a State, or the members of the Legislature thereof, is denied to any of the male inhabitants of such State, being twenty-one years of age, and citizens of the United States, or in any way abridged, except for participation in rebellion, or other crime, the basis of representation therein shall be reduced in the proportion which the number of such male citizens shall bear to the whole number of male citizens twenty-one years of age in such State.

Section 3. No person shall be a Senator or Representative in Congress, or elector of President and Vice-President, or hold any office, civil or military, under the United States, or under and State, who, having previously taken an oath, as a member of Congress, or as an officer of the United States, or as a member of any State legislature, or as an executive or judicial officer of any State, to support the Constitution of the United States, shall have engaged in insurrection or rebellion against the same, or given aid or comfort to the enemies thereof. But Congress may by a vote of two-thirds of each House, remove such disability.

Section 4. The validity of the public debt of the United States, authorized by law, including debts incurred for payment of pensions and bounties for services in suppressing insurrection or rebellion, shall not be questioned. But neither the United States nor any State shall assume or pay any debts or obligation incurred in aid of insurrection or rebellion against the United States, or any claim for the loss or emancipation of any slave; but all such debts, obligations, and claims shall be held illegal and void.

Section 5. The Congress shall have the power to enforce, by appropriate legislation, the provisions of this article.

[10]Adopted in 1865.
[11]Adopted in 1868.

[AMENDMENT XV][12]

Section 1. The right of citizens of the United States to vote shall not be denied or abridged by the United States or by any State on account of race, color, or previous condition of servitude—

Section 2. The Congress shall have power to enforce this article by appropriate legislation.

[AMENDMENT XVI][13]

The Congress shall have power to lay and collect taxes on incomes, from whatever source derived, without apportionment among the several States, and without regard to any census or enumeration.

[AMENDMENT XVII][14]

The Senate of the United States shall be composed of two Senators from each State, elected by the people thereof, for six years; and each Senator shall have one vote. The electors in each State shall have the qualifications requisite for electors of the most numerous branch of the State legislatures.

When vacancies happen in the representation of any State in the Senate, the executive authority of such State shall issue writs of election to fill such vacancies: *Provided,* That the legislature of any State may empower the executive thereof to make temporary appointments until the people fill the vacancies by election as the legislature may direct.

This amendment shall not be so construed as to affect the election or term of any Senator chosen before it becomes valid as part of the Constitution.

[AMENDMENT XVIII][15]

Section 1. After one year from the ratification of this article the manufacture, sale, or transportation of intoxicating liquors within, the importation thereof into, or the exportation

thereof from the United States and all territory subject to the jurisdiction thereof for beverage purposes is hereby prohibited.

Section 2. The Congress and the several States shall have concurrent power to enforce this article by appropriate legislation.

Section 3. This article shall be inoperative unless it shall have been ratified as an amendment to the Constitution by the legislatures of the several States, as provided in the Constitution, within seven years from the date of the submission hereof to the States by the Congress.

[AMENDMENT XIX][16]

The right of citizens of the United States to vote shall not be denied or abridged by the United States or by any State on account of sex.

Congress shall have power to enforce this article by appropriate legislation.

[AMENDMENT XX][17]

Section 1. The terms of the President and Vice-President shall end at noon on the 20th day of January, and the terms of Senators and Representatives at noon on the 3d day of January, of the years in which such terms would have ended if this article had not been ratified; and the terms of their successors shall then begin.

Section 2. The Congress shall assemble at least once in every year, and such meeting shall begin at noon on the 3d day of January, unless they shall by law appoint a different day.

Section 3. If, at the time fixed for the beginning of the term of the President, the President elect shall have died, the Vice-President elect shall become President. If a President shall not have been chosen before the time fixed for the beginning of his term or if the President elect shall have failed to qualify, then the Vice-President elect shall act as President until a President shall have qualified; and the Congress may by law provide for the case wherein neither a President elect nor a Vice-President elect shall

[12]Adopted in 1870.
[13]Adopted in 1913.
[14]Adopted in 1913.
[15]Adopted in 1918.

[16]Adopted in 1920.
[17]Adopted in 1933.

have qualified, declaring who shall then act as President, or the manner in which one who is to act shall be selected, and such person shall act accordingly until a President or Vice-President shall have qualified.

Section 4. The Congress may by law provide for the case of the death of any of the persons from whom the House of Representatives may choose a President whenever the right of choice shall have devolved upon them, and for the case of the death of any of the persons from whom the Senate may choose a Vice-President whenever the right of choice shall have devolved upon them.

Section 5. Sections 1 and 2 shall take effect on the 15th day of October following the ratification of this article.

Section 6. This article shall be inoperative unless it shall have been ratified as an amendment to the Constitution by the legislatures of three-fourths of the several States within seven years from the date of its submission.

[AMENDMENT XXI][18]

Section 1. The eighteenth article of amendment to the Constitution of the United States is hereby repealed.

Section 2. The transportation or importation into any State, Territory, or possession of the United States for delivery or use therein of intoxicating liquors, in violation of the laws thereof, is hereby prohibited.

Section 3. This article shall be inoperative unless it shall have been ratified as an amendment to the Constitution by conventions in the several States, as provided in the Constitution, within seven years from the date of the submission hereof to the States by the Congress.

[AMENDMENT XXII][19]

No person shall be elected to the office of the President more than twice, and no person who has held the office of President, or acted as President, for more than two years of a term to

[18]Adopted in 1933.
[19]Adopted in 1961.

which some other person was elected President shall be elected to the office of the President more than once.

But this Article shall not apply to any person holding the office of President when this Article was proposed by the Congress, and shall not prevent any person who may be holding the office of President, or acting as President, during the term within which this Article becomes operative from holding the office of President or acting as President during the remainder of such term.

This article shall be inoperative unless it shall have been ratified as an amendment to the Constitution by the legislatures of three-fourths of the several states within seven years from the date of its submission to the states by the Congress.

[AMENDMENT XXIII][20]

Section 1. The District constituting the seat of Government of the United States shall appoint in such manner as the Congress may direct:

A number of electors of President and Vice-President equal to the whole number of Senators and Representatives in Congress to which the District would be entitled if it were a State, but in no event more than the least populous State; they shall be in addition to those appointed by the States, but they shall be considered, for the purpose of the election of President and Vice-President, to be electors appointed by a State; and they shall meet in the District and perform such duties as provided by the twelfth article of amendment.

Section 2. The Congress shall have power to enforce this article by appropriate legislation.

[AMENDMENT XXIV][21]

Section 1. The right of citizens of the United States to vote in any primary or other election for President or Vice-President, for electors for President or Vice-President, or for Senator or Representative in Congress, shall not be denied or abridged by the United States or any state by reason of failure to pay any poll tax or other tax.

[20]Adopted in 1961.
[21]Adopted in 1964.

Section 2. The Congress shall have the power to enforce this article by appropriate legislation.

[AMENDMENT XXV][22]

Section 1. In case of the removal of the President from office or of his death or resignation, the Vice-President shall become President.

Section 2. Whenever there is a vacancy in the office of the Vice President, the President shall nominate a Vice President who shall take office upon confirmation by a majority vote of both Houses of Congress.

Section 3. Whenever the President transmits to the President Pro Tempore of the Senate and the Speaker of the House of Representatives his written declaration that he is unable to discharge the powers and duties of his office, and until he transmits to them a written declaration to the contrary, such powers and duties shall be discharged by the Vice-President as Acting President.

Section 4. Whenever the Vice-President and a majority of either the principal officers of the executive departments or of such other body as Congress may by law provide, transmit to the President Pro Tempore of the Senate and the Speaker of the House of Representatives their written declaration that the President is unable to discharge the powers and duties of his office, the Vice President shall immediately assume the powers and duties of the office as Acting President.

Thereafter, when the President transmits to the President Pro Tempore of the Senate and the Speaker of the House of Representatives his written declaration that no inability exists, he shall resume the powers and duties of his office unless the Vice President and a majority of either the principal officers of the executive departments or of such other body as Congress may by law provide, transmit within four days to the President Pro Tempore of the Senate and the Speaker of the House of Representatives their written declaration that the President is unable to discharge the powers and duties of his office. Thereupon Congress shall decide the issue, assembling within forty-eight hours for that purpose if not in session. If the Congress, within twenty-one days after receipt of the latter written declaration, or, if Congress is not in session, within twenty-one days after Congress is required to assemble, determines by two-thirds vote of both Houses that the President is unable to discharge the powers and duties of his office, the Vice President shall continue to discharge the same as Acting President; otherwise, the President shall resume the powers and duties of his office.

[AMENDMENT XXVI][23]

Section 1. The right of citizens of the United States, who are eighteen years of age or older, to vote shall not be denied or abridged by the United States or by any State on account of age.

Section 2. The Congress shall have power to enforce this article by appropriate legislation.

---

[22]Adopted in 1967.

[23]Adopted in 1971.

PRESIDENTIAL ELECTIONS

Year	Candidates	Parties	Popular Vote	% of Popular Vote	Electoral Vote	% Voter Partici- pation
1789	George Washington				69	
	John Adams				34	
	Other candidates				35	
1792	George Washington				132	
	John Adams				77	
	George Clinton				50	
	Other candidates				5	
1796	John Adams	Federalist			71	
	Thomas Jefferson	Dem.-Rep.			68	
	Thomas Pinckney	Federalist			59	
	Aaron Burr	Dem.-Rep.			30	
	Other candidates				48	
1800	Thomas Jefferson	Dem.-Rep.			73	
	Aaron Burr	Dem.-Rep.			73	
	John Adams	Federalist			65	
	Charles C. Pinckney	Federalist			64	
	John Jay	Federalist			1	
1804	Thomas Jefferson	Dem.-Rep.			162	
	Charles C. Pinckney	Federalist			14	
1808	James Madison	Dem.-Rep.			122	
	Charles C. Pinckney	Federalist			47	
	George Clinton	Dem.-Rep.			6	
1812	James Madison	Dem.-Rep.			128	
	DeWitt Clinton	Federalist			89	
1816	James Monroe	Dem.-Rep.			183	
	Rufus King	Federalist			34	
1820	James Monroe	Dem.-Rep.			231	
	John Quincy Adams	Indep.-Rep.			1	
1824	John Quincy Adams	Dem.-Rep.	108,740	31	84	26.9
	Andrew Jackson	Dem.-Rep.	153,544	43	99	
	Henry Clay	Dem.-Rep.	47,136	13	37	
	William H. Crawford	Dem.-Rep.	46,618	13	41	
1828	Andrew Jackson	Democratic	647,286	56.0	178	57.6
	John Quincy Adams	National Republican	508,064	44.0	83	
1832	Andrew Jackson	Democratic	688,242	54.5	219	55.4
	Henry Clay	National Republican	473,462	37.5	49	
	William Wirt	Anti-Masonic	101,051	8.0	7	
	John Floyd	Democratic			11	
1836	Martin Van Buren	Democratic	765,483	50.9	170	57.8
	William H. Harrison	Whig			73	
	Hugh L. White	Whig	739,795	49.1	26	
	Daniel Webster	Whig			14	
	W. P. Mangum	Whig			11	

Year	Candidates	Parties	Popular Vote	% of Popular Vote	Electoral Vote	% Voter Partici- pation
1840	**William H. Harrison**	Whig	1,275,016	53	234	80.2
	Martin Van Buren	Democratic	1,129,102	47	60	
1844	**James K. Polk**	Democratic	1,338,464	49.6	170	78.9
	Henry Clay	Whig	1,300,097	48.1	105	
	James G. Birney	Liberty	62,300	2.3		
1848	**Zachary Taylor**	Whig	1,360,967	47.4	163	72.7
	Lewis Cass	Democratic	1,222,342	42.5	127	
	Martin Van Buren	Free Soil	291,263	10.1		
1852	**Franklin Pierce**	Democratic	1,601,117	50.9	254	69.6
	Winfield Scott	Whig	1,385,453	44.1	42	
	John P. Hale	Free Soil	155,825	5.0		
1856	**James Buchanan**	Democratic	1,832,955	45.3	174	78.9
	John C. Fremont	Republican	1,339,932	33.1	114	
	Millard Fillmore	American	871,731	21.6	8	
1860	**Abraham Lincoln**	Republican	1,866,452	39.8	180	81.2
	Stephen A. Douglas	Democratic	1,375,157	29.5	12	
	John C. Breckinridge	Democratic	847,953	18.1	72	
	John Bell	Constitutional Union	590,631	12.6	39	
1864	**Abraham Lincoln**	Republican	2,206,938	55.0	212	73.8
	George B. McClellan	Democratic	1,803,787	45.0	21	
1868	**Ulysses S. Grant**	Republican	3,013,421	52.7	214	78.1
	Horatio Seymour	Democratic	2,706,829	47.3	80	
1872	**Ulysses S. Grant**	Republican	3,596,745	55.6	286	71.3
	Horace Greeley	Democratic	2,843,446	43.9	66	
1876	**Rutherford B. Hayes**	Republican	4,036,298	48.0	185	81.8
	Samuel J. Tilden	Democratic	4,300,590	51.0	184	
1880	**James A. Garfield**	Republican	4,453,295	48.5	214	79.4
	Winfield S. Hancock	Democratic	4,414,082	48.1	155	
	James B. Weaver	Greenback-Labor	308,578	3.4		
1884	**Grover Cleveland**	Democratic	4,879,507	48.5	219	77.5
	James G. Blaine	Republican	4,850,293	48.2	182	
	Benjamin F. Butler	Greenback-Labor	175,370	1.8		
	John P. St. John	Prohibition	150,369	1.5		
1888	**Benjamin Harrison**	Republican	5,477,129	47.9	233	79.3
	Grover Cleveland	Democratic	5,537,857	48.6	168	
	Clinton B. Fisk	Prohibition	249,506	2.2		
	Anson J. Streeter	Union Labor	146,935	1.3		
1892	**Grover Cleveland**	Democratic	5,555,426	46.1	277	74.7
	Benjamin Harrison	Republican	5,182,690	43.0	145	
	James B. Weaver	People's	1,029,846	8.5	22	
	John Bidwell	Prohibition	264,133	2.2		
1896	**William McKinley**	Republican	7,104,779	52.0	271	79.3
	William J. Bryan	Democratic	6,502,925	48.0	176	
1900	**William McKinley**	Republican	7,218,491	51.7	292	73.2
	William J. Bryan	Democratic; Populist	6,356,734	45.5	155	
	John C. Wooley	Prohibition	208,914	1.5		
1904	**Theodore Roosevelt**	Republican	7,628,461	57.4	336	65.2
	Alton B. Parker	Democratic	5,084,223	37.6	140	
	Eugene V. Debs	Socialist	402,283	3.0		
	Silas C. Swallow	Prohibition	258,536	1.9		

Year	Candidates	Parties	Popular Vote	% of Popular Vote	Electoral Vote	% Voter Partici- pation
1908	**William H. Taft**	Republican	7,675,320	51.6	321	65.4
	William J. Bryan	Democratic	6,412,294	43.1	162	
	Eugene V. Debs	Socialist	420,793	2.8		
	Eugene W. Chafin	Prohibition	253,840	1.7		
1912	**Woodrow Wilson**	Democratic	6,293,454	42.0	435	58.8
	Theodore Roosevelt	Progressive	4,119,538	28.0	88	
	William H. Taft	Republican	3,484,980	24.0	8	
	Eugene V. Debs	Socialist	900,672	6.0		
	Eugene W. Chafin	Prohibition	206,275	1.4		
1916	**Woodrow Wilson**	Democratic	9,129,606	49.4	277	61.6
	Charles E. Hughes	Republican	8,538,221	46.2	254	
	A. L. Benson	Socialist	585,113	3.2		
	J. Frank Hanly	Prohibition	220,506	1.2		
1920	**Warren G. Harding**	Republican	16,143,407	60.4	404	49.2
	James M. Cox	Democratic	9,130,328	34.2	127	
	Eugene V. Debs	Socialist	919,799	3.4		
	P. P. Christensen	Farmer-Labor	265,411	1.0		
1924	**Calvin Coolidge**	Republican	15,718,211	54.0	382	48.9
	John W. Davis	Democratic	8,385,283	28.8	136	
	Robert M. La Follette	Progressive	4,831,289	16.6	13	
1928	**Herbert C. Hoover**	Republican	21,391,381	58.2	444	56.9
	Alfred E. Smith	Democratic	15,016,443	40.9	87	
1932	**Franklin D. Roosevelt**	Democratic	22,821,857	57.4	472	56.9
	Herbert C. Hoover	Republican	15,761,841	39.7	59	
	Norman Thomas	Socialist	881,951	2.2		
1936	**Franklin D. Roosevelt**	Democratic	27,751,597	60.8	523	61.0
	Alfred M. Landon	Republican	16,679,583	36.5	8	
	William Lemke	Union	882,479	1.9		
1940	**Franklin D. Roosevelt**	Democratic	27,307,819	54.8	449	62.5
	Wendell L. Wilkie	Republican	22,321,018	44.8	82	
1944	**Franklin D. Roosevelt**	Democratic	25,606,585	53.5	432	55.9
	Thomas E. Dewey	Republican	22,014,745	46.0	99	
1948	**Harry S Truman**	Democratic	24,105,812	50.0	303	53.0
	Thomas E. Dewey	Republican	21,970,065	46.0	189	
	J. Strom Thurmond	States' Rights	1,169,021	2	39	
	Henry A. Wallace	Progressive	1,157,172	2		
1952	**Dwight D. Eisenhower**	Republican	33,936,234	55.1	442	63.3
	Adlai E. Stevenson	Democratic	27,314,992	44.4	89	
1956	**Dwight D. Eisenhower**	Republican	35,590,472	57.6	457	60.6
	Adlai E. Stevenson	Democratic	26,022,752	42.1	73	
1960	**John F. Kennedy**	Democratic	34,227,096	49.7	303	62.8
	Richard M. Nixon	Republican	34,107,646	49.6	219	
	Harry F. Byrd	Independent	501,643		15	
1964	**Lyndon B. Johnson**	Democratic	43,129,566	61.1	486	61.7
	Barry M. Goldwater	Republican	27,178,188	38.5	52	
1968	**Richard M. Nixon**	Republican	31,785,480	44.0	301	60.6
	Hubert H. Humphrey	Democratic	31,275,166	42.7	191	
	George C. Wallace	American Independent	9,906,473	13.5	46	
1972	**Richard M. Nixon**	Republican	47,169,911	60.7	520	55.2
	George S. McGovern	Democratic	29,170,383	37.5	17	
	John G. Schmitz	American	1,099,482	1.4		

Year	Candidates	Parties	Popular Vote	% of Popular Vote	Electoral Vote	% Voter Partici-pation
1976	**Jimmy Carter**	Democratic	40,830,763	50.1	297	53.5
	Gerald R. Ford	Republican	39,147,793	48.0	240	
1980	**Ronald Reagan**	Republican	43,899,248	51.0	489	52.6
	Jimmy Carter	Democratic	35,481,432	41.0	49	
	John B. Anderson	Independent	5,719,437	7.0	0	
	Ed Clark	Libertarian	920,859	1.0	0	
1984	**Ronald Reagan**	Republican	54,451,521	58.8	525	53.3
	Walter Mondale	Democratic	37,565,334	40.5	13	
1988	**George H. Bush**	Republican	47,917,341	54.0	426	48.6*
	Michael Dukakis	Democratic	41,013,030	46.0	112	

*Estimate

PRESIDENTIAL ADMINISTRATIONS

The Washington Administration (1789–1797)

Vice President	John Adams	1789–1797
Secretary of State	Thomas Jefferson	1789–1793
	Edmund Randolph	1794–1795
	Timothy Pickering	1795–1797
Secretary of Treasury	Alexander Hamilton	1789–1795
	Oliver Wolcott	1795–1797
Secretary of War	Henry Knox	1789–1794
	Timothy Pickering	1795–1796
	James McHenry	1796–1797
Attorney General	Edmund Randolph	1789–1793
	William Bradford	1794–1795
	Charles Lee	1795–1797
Postmaster General	Samuel Osgood	1789–1791
	Timothy Pickering	1791–1794
	Joseph Habersham	1795–1797

The John Adams Administration (1797–1801)

Vice President	Thomas Jefferson	1797–1801
Secretary of State	Timothy Pickering	1797–1800
	John Marshall	1800–1801
Secretary of Treasury	Oliver Wolcott	1797–1800
	Samuel Dexter	1800–1801
Secretary of War	James McHenry	1797–1800
	Samuel Dexter	1800–1801
Attorney General	Charles Lee	1797–1801
Postmaster General	Joseph Habersham	1797–1801
Secretary of Navy	Benjamin Stoddert	1798–1801

The Jefferson Administration (1801–1809)

Vice President	Aaron Burr	1801–1805
	George Clinton	1805–1809
Secretary of State	James Madison	1801–1809
Secretary of Treasury	Samuel Dexter	1801
	Albert Gallatin	1801–1809
Secretary of War	Henry Dearborn	1801–1809
Attorney General	Levi Lincoln	1801–1805
	Robert Smith	1805
	John Breckinridge	1805–1806
	Caesar Rodney	1807–1809
Postmaster General	Joseph Habersham	1801
	Gideon Granger	1801–1809
Secretary of Navy	Robert Smith	1801–1809

The Madison Administration (1809–1817)

Vice President	George Clinton	1809–1813
	Elbridge Gerry	1813–1817
Secretary of State	Robert Smith	1809–1811
	James Monroe	1811–1817
Secretary of Treasury	Albert Gallatin	1809–1813
	George Campbell	1814
	Alexander Dallas	1814–1816
	William Crawford	1816–1817
Secretary of War	William Eustis	1809–1812
	John Armstrong	1813–1814
	James Monroe	1814–1815
	William Crawford	1815–1817
Attorney General	Caesar Rodney	1809–1811
	William Pinkney	1811–1814
	Richard Rush	1814–1817
Postmaster General	Gideon Granger	1809–1814
	Return Meigs	1814–1817
Secretary of Navy	Paul Hamilton	1809–1813
	William Jones	1813–1814
	Benjamin Crowninshield	1814–1817

The Monroe Administration (1817–1825)

Vice President	Daniel Tompkins	1817–1825
Secretary of State	John Quincy Adams	1817–1825
Secretary of Treasury	William Crawford	1817–1825
Secretary of War	George Graham	1817
	John C. Calhoun	1817–1825
Attorney General	Richard Rush	1817
	William Wirt	1817–1825
Postmaster General	Return Meigs	1817–1823
	John McLean	1823–1825
Secretary of Navy	Benjamin Crowninshield	1817–1818
	Smith Thompson	1818–1823
	Samuel Southard	1823–1825

The John Quincy Adams Administration (1825–1829)

Vice President	John C. Calhoun	1825–1829
Secretary of State	Henry Clay	1825–1829
Secretary of Treasury	Richard Rush	1825–1829
Secretary of War	James Barbour	1825–1828
	Peter Porter	1828–1829

Attorney General	William Wirt	1825–1829
Postmaster General	John McLean	1825–1829
Secretary of Navy	Samuel Southard	1825–1829

The Jackson Administration (1829–1837)

Vice President	John C. Calhoun	1829–1833
	Martin Van Buren	1833–1837
Secretary of State	Martin Van Buren	1829–1831
	Edward Livingston	1831–1833
	Louis McLane	1833–1834
	John Forsyth	1834–1837
Secretary of Treasury	Samuel Ingham	1829–1831
	Louis McLane	1831–1833
	William Duane	1833
	Roger B. Taney	1833–1834
	Levi Woodbury	1834–1837
Secretary of War	John H. Eaton	1829–1831
	Lewis Cass	1831–1837
	Benjamin Butler	1837
Attorney General	John M. Berrien	1829–1831
	Roger B. Taney	1831–1833
	Benjamin Butler	1833–1837
Postmaster General	William Barry	1829–1835
	Amos Kendall	1835–1837
Secretary of Navy	John Branch	1829–1831
	Levi Woodbury	1831–1834
	Mahlon Dickerson	1834–1837

The Van Buren Administration (1837–1841)

Vice President	Richard M. Johnson	1837–1841
Secretary of State	John Forsyth	1837–1841
Secretary of Treasury	Levi Woodbury	1837–1841
Secretary of War	Joel Poinsett	1837–1841
Attorney General	Benjamin Butler	1837–1838
	Felix Grundy	1838–1840
	Henry D. Gilpin	1840–1841
Postmaster General	Amos Kendall	1837–1840
	John M. Niles	1840–1841
Secretary of Navy	Mahlon Dickerson	1837–1838
	James Paulding	1838–1841

The William Harrison Administration (1841)

Vice President	John Tyler	1841
Secretary of State	Daniel Webster	1841
Secretary of Treasury	Thomas Ewing	1841

Secretary of War	John Bell	1841
Attorney General	John J. Crittenden	1841
Postmaster General	Francis Granger	1841
Secretary of Navy	George Badger	1841

The Tyler Administration (1841–1845)

Vice President	None	
Secretary of State	Daniel Webster	1841–1843
	Hugh S. Legaré	1843
Secretary of State	Abel P. Upshur	1843–1844
	John C. Calhoun	1844–1845
Secretary of Treasury	Thomas Ewing	1841
	Walter Forward	1841–1843
	John C. Spencer	1843–1844
	George Bibb	1844–1845
Secretary of War	John Bell	1841
	John C. Spencer	1841–1843
	James M. Porter	1843–1844
	William Wilkins	1844–1845
Attorney General	John J. Crittenden	1841
	Hugh S. Legaré	1841–1843
	John Nelson	1843–1845
Postmaster General	Francis Granger	1841
	Charles Wickliffe	1841
Secretary of Navy	George Badger	1841
	Abel P. Upshur	1841
	David Henshaw	1843–1844
	Thomas Gilmer	1844
	John Y. Mason	1844–1845

The Polk Administration (1845–1849)

Vice President	George M. Dallas	1845–1849
Secretary of State	James Buchanan	1845–1849
Secretary of Treasury	Robert J. Walker	1845–1849
Secretary of War	William L. Marcy	1845–1849
Attorney General	John Y. Mason	1845–1846
	Nathan Clifford	1846–1848
	Isaac Toucey	1848–1849
Postmaster General	Cave Johnson	1845–1849
Secretary of Navy	George Bancroft	1845–1846
	John Y. Mason	1846–1849

The Taylor Administration (1849–1850)

Vice President	Millard Fillmore	1849–1850
Secretary of State	John M. Clayton	1849–1850

The Taylor Administration (1849–1850) (continued)

Secretary of Treasury	William Meredith	1849–1850
Secretary of War	George Crawford	1849–1850
Attorney General	Reverdy Johnson	1849–1850
Postmaster General	Jacob Collamer	1849–1850
Secretary of Navy	William Preston	1849–1850
Secretary of Interior	Thomas Ewing	1849–1850

The Fillmore Administration (1850–1853)

Vice President	None	
Secretary of State	Daniel Webster	1850–1852
	Edward Everett	1852–1853
Secretary of Treasury	Thomas Corwin	1850–1853
Secretary of War	Charles Conrad	1850–1853
Attorney General	John J. Crittenden	1850–1853
Postmaster General	Nathan Hall	1850–1852
	Sam D. Hubbard	1852–1853
Secretary of Navy	William A. Graham	1850–1852
	John P. Kennedy	1852–1853
Secretary of Interior	Thomas McKennan	1850
	Alexander Stuart	1850–1853

The Pierce Administration (1853–1857)

Vice President	William R. King	1853–1857
Secretary of State	William L. Marcy	1853–1857
Secretary of Treasury	James Guthrie	1853–1857
Secretary of War	Jefferson Davis	1853–1857
Attorney General	Caleb Cushing	1853–1857
Postmaster General	James Campbell	1853–1857
Secretary of Navy	James C. Dobbin	1853–1857
Secretary of Interior	Robert McClelland	1853–1857

The Buchanan Administration (1857–1861)

Vice President	John C. Breckinridge	1857–1861
Secretary of State	Lewis Cass	1857–1860
	Jeremiah S. Black	1860–1861
Secretary of Treasury	Howell Cobb	1857–1860
	Philip Thomas	1860–1861
	John A. Dix	1861
Secretary of War	John B. Floyd	1857–1861
	Joseph Holt	1861
Attorney General	Jeremiah S. Black	1857–1860
	Edwin M. Stanton	1860–1861
Postmaster General	Aaron V. Brown	1857–1859
	Joseph Holt	1859–1861
	Horatio King	1861
Secretary of Navy	Isaac Toucey	1857–1861
Secretary of Interior	Jacob Thompson	1857–1861

The Lincoln Administration (1861–1865)

Vice President	Hannibal Hamlin	1861–1865
	Andrew Johnson	1865
Secretary of State	William H. Seward	1861–1865
Secretary of Treasury	Samuel P. Chase	1861–1864
	William P. Fessenden	1864–1865
	Hugh McCulloch	1865
Secretary of War	Simon Cameron	1861–1862
	Edwin M. Stanton	1862–1865
Attorney General	Edward Bates	1861–1864
	James Speed	1864–1865
Postmaster General	Horatio King	1861
	Montgomery Blair	1861–1864
	William Dennison	1864–1865
Secretary of Navy	Gideon Welles	1861–1865
Secretary of Interior	Caleb B. Smith	1861–1863
	John P. Usher	1863–1865

The Andrew Johnson Administration (1865–1869)

Vice President	None	
Secretary of State	William H. Seward	1865–1869
Secretary of Treasury	Hugh McCulloch	1865–1869
Secretary of War	Edwin M. Stanton	1865–1867
	Ulysses S. Grant	1867–1868
	Lorenzo Thomas	1868
	John M. Schofield	1868–1869

Attorney General	James Speed	1865–1866
	Henry Stanbery	1866–1868
	William M. Evarts	1868–1869
Postmaster General	William Dennison	1865–1866
	Alexander Randall	1866–1869
Secretary of Navy	Gideon Welles	1865–1869
Secretary of Interior	John P. Usher	1865
	James Harlan	1865–1866
	Orville H. Browning	1866–1869

The Grant Administration (1869–1877)

Vice President	Schuyler Colfax	1869–1873
	Henry Wilson	1873–1877
Secretary of State	Elihu B. Washburne	1869
	Hamilton Fish	1869–1877
Secretary of Treasury	George S. Boutwell	1869–1873
	William Richardson	1873–1874
	Benjamin Bristow	1874–1876
	Lot M. Morrill	1876–1877
Secretary of War	John A. Rawlins	1869
	William T. Sherman	1869
	William W. Belknap	1869–1876
	Alphonso Taft	1876
	James D. Cameron	1876–1877
Attorney General	Ebenezer Hoar	1869–1870
	Amos T. Ackerman	1870–1871
	G. H. Williams	1871–1875
	Edwards Pierrepont	1875–1876
	Alphonso Taft	1876–1877
Postmaster General	John A. J. Creswell	1869–1874
	James W. Marshall	1874
	Marshall Jewell	1874–1876
	James N. Tyner	1876–1877
Secretary of Navy	Adolph E. Borie	1869
	George M. Robeson	1869–1877
Secretary of Interior	Jacob D. Cox	1869–1870
	Columbus Delano	1870–1875
	Zachariah Chandler	1875–1877

The Hayes Administration (1877–1881)

| Vice President | William A. Wheeler | 1877–1881 |
| Secretary of State | William M. Evarts | 1877–1881 |

Secretary of Treasury	John Sherman	1877–1881
Secretary of War	George W. McCrary	1877–1879
	Alex Ramsey	1879–1881
Attorney General	Charles Devens	1877–1881
Postmaster General	David M. Key	1877–1880
	Horace Maynard	1880–1881
Secretary of Navy	Richard W. Thompson	1877–1880
	Nathan Goff, Jr.	1881
Secretary of Interior	Carl Schurz	1877–1881

The Garfield Administration (1881)

Vice President	Chester A. Arthur	1881
Secretary of State	James G. Blaine	1881
Secretary of Treasury	William Windom	1881
Secretary of War	Robert T. Lincoln	1881
Attorney General	Wayne MacVeagh	1881
Postmaster General	Thomas L. James	1881
Secretary of Navy	William H. Hunt	1881
Secretary of Interior	Samuel J. Kirkwood	1881

The Arthur Administration (1881–1885)

Vice President	None	
Secretary of State	F. T. Frelinghuysen	1881–1885
Secretary of Treasury	Charles J. Folger	1881–1884
	Walter Q. Gresham	1884
	Hugh McCulloch	1884–1885
Secretary of War	Robert T. Lincoln	1881–1885
Attorney General	Benjamin H. Brewster	1881–1885
Postmaster General	Timothy O. Howe	1881–1883
	Walter Q. Gresham	1883–1884
	Frank Hatton	1884–1885
Secretary of Navy	William H. Hunt	1881–1882
	William E. Chandler	1882–1885
Secretary of Interior	Samuel J. Kirkwood	1881–1882
	Henry M. Teller	1882–1885

The Cleveland Administration (1885–1889)

Vice President	Thomas A. Hendricks	1885–1889
Secretary of State	Thomas F. Bayard	1885–1889
Secretary of Treasury	Daniel Manning	1885–1887
	Charles S. Fairchild	1887–1889
Secretary of War	William C. Endicott	1885–1889
Attorney General	Augustus H. Garland	1885–1889
Postmaster General	William F. Vilas	1885–1888
	Don M. Dickinson	1888–1889
Secretary of Navy	William C. Whitney	1885–1889
Secretary of Interior	Lucius Q. C. Lamar	1885–1888
	William F. Vilas	1888–1889
Secretary of Agriculture	Norman J. Colman	1889

The Benjamin Harrison Administration (1889–1893)

Vice President	Levi P. Morton	1889–1893
Secretary of State	James G. Blaine	1889–1892
	John W. Foster	1892–1893
Secretary of Treasury	William Windom	1889–1891
	Charles Foster	1891–1893
Secretary of War	Redfield Proctor	1889–1891
	Stephen B. Elkins	1891–1893
Attorney General	William H. H. Miller	1889–1891
Postmaster General	John Wanamaker	1889–1893
Secretary of Navy	Benjamin F. Tracy	1889–1893
Secretary of Interior	John W. Noble	1889–1893
Secretary of Agriculture	Jeremiah M. Rusk	1889–1893

The Cleveland Administration (1893–1897)

Vice President	Adlai E. Stevenson	1893–1897
Secretary of State	Walter Q. Gresham	1893–1895
	Richard Olney	1895–1897
Secretary of Treasury	John G. Carlisle	1893–1897
Secretary of War	Daniel S. Lamont	1893–1897
Attorney General	Richard Olney	1893–1895
	James Harmon	1895–1897
Postmaster General	Wilson S. Bissell	1893–1895
	William L. Wilson	1895–1897
Secretary of Navy	Hilary A. Herbert	1893–1897
Secretary of Interior	Hoke Smith	1893–1896
	David R. Francis	1896–1897
Secretary of Agriculture	Julius S. Morton	1893–1897

The McKinley Administration (1897–1901)

Vice President	Garret A. Hobart	1897–1901
Secretary of State	Theodore Roosevelt	1901
	John Sherman	1897–1898
	William R. Day	1898
	John Hay	1898–1901
Secretary of Treasury	Lyman J. Gage	1897–1901
Secretary of War	Russell A. Alger	1897–1899
	Elihu Root	1899–1901
Attorney General	Joseph McKenna	1897–1898
	John W. Griggs	1898–1901
	Philander C. Knox	1901
Postmaster General	James A. Gary	1897–1898
	Charles E. Smith	1898–1901
Secretary of Navy	John D. Long	1897–1901
Secretary of Interior	Cornelius N. Bliss	1897–1899
	Ethan A. Hitchcock	1899–1901
Secretary of Agriculture	James Wilson	1897–1901

The Theodore Roosevelt Administration (1901–1909)

Vice President	Charles Fairbanks	1905–1909
Secretary of State	John Hay	1901–1905
	Elihu Root	1905–1909
	Robert Bacon	1909
Secretary of Treasury	Lyman J. Gage	1901–1902
	Leslie M. Shaw	1902–1907
	George B. Cortelyou	1907–1909
Secretary of War	Elihu Root	1901–1904
	William H. Taft	1904–1908
	Luke E. Wright	1908–1909
Attorney General	Philander C. Knox	1901–1904
	William H. Moody	1904–1906
	Charles J. Bonaparte	1906–1909
Postmaster General	Charles E. Smith	1901–1902
	Henry C. Payne	1902–1904
	Robert J. Wynne	1904–1905

	George B. Cortelyou	1905–1907
	George von L. Meyer	1907–1909
Secretary of Navy	John D. Long	1901–1902
	William H. Moody	1902–1904
	Paul Morton	1904–1905
	Charles J. Bonaparte	1905–1906
	Victor H. Metcalf	1906–1908
	Truman H. Newberry	1908–1909
Secretary of Interior	Ethan A. Hitchcock	1901–1907
	James R. Garfield	1907–1909
Secretary of Agriculture	James Wilson	1901–1909
Secretary of Labor and Commerce	George B. Cortelyou	1903–1904
	Victor H. Metcalf	1904–1906
	Oscar S. Straus	1906–1909
	Charles Nagel	1909

The Taft Administration (1909–1913)

Vice President	James S. Sherman	1909–1913
Secretary of State	Philander C. Knox	1909–1913
Secretary of Treasury	Franklin MacVeagh	1909–1913
Secretary of War	Jacob M. Dickinson	1909–1911
	Henry L. Stimson	1911–1913
Attorney General	George W. Wickersham	1909–1913
Postmaster General	Frank H. Hitchcock	1909–1913
Secretary of Navy	George von L. Meyer	1909–1913
Secretary of Interior	Richard A. Ballinger	1909–1911
	Walter L. Fisher	1911–1913
Secretary of Agriculture	James Wilson	1909–1913
Secretary of Labor and Commerce	Charles Nagel	1909–1913

The Wilson Administration (1913–1921)

Vice President	Thomas R. Marshall	1913–1921
Secretary of State	William J. Bryan	1913–1915
	Robert Lansing	1915–1920
	Bainbridge Colby	1920–1921
Secretary of Treasury	William G. McAdoo	1913–1918
	Carter Glass	1918–1920
	David F. Houston	1920–1921
Secretary of War	Lindley M. Garrison	1913–1916
	Newton D. Baker	1916–1921
Attorney General	James C. McReyolds	1913–1914
	Thomas W. Gregory	1914–1919
	A. Mitchell Palmer	1919–1921
Postmaster General	Albert S. Burleson	1913–1921
Secretary of Navy	Josephus Daniels	1913–1921
Secretary of Interior	Franklin K. Lane	1913–1920
	John B. Payne	1920–1921
Secretary of Agriculture	David F. Houston	1913–1920
	Edwin T. Meredith	1920–1921
Secretary of Commerce	William C. Redfield	1913–1919
	Joshua W. Alexander	1919–1921
Secretary of Labor	William B. Wilson	1913–1921

The Harding Administration (1921–1923)

Vice President	Calvin Coolidge	1921–1923
Secretary of State	Charles E. Hughes	1921–1923
Secretary of Treasury	Andrew Mellon	1921–1923
Secretary of War	John W. Weeks	1921–1923
Attorney General	Harry M. Daugherty	1921–1923
Postmaster General	Will H. Hays	1921–1922
	Hubert Work	1922–1923
	Harry S. New	1923
Secretary of Navy	Edwin Denby	1921–1923
Secretary of Interior	Albert B. Fall	1921–1923
	Hubert Work	1923
Secretary of Agriculture	Henry C. Wallace	1921–1923
Secretary of Commerce	Herbert C. Hoover	1921–1923
Secretary of Labor	James J. Davis	1921–1923

The Coolidge Administration (1923–1929)

Vice President	Charles G. Dawes	1925–1929
Secretary of State	Charles E. Hughes	1923–1925
	Frank B. Kellogg	1925–1929
Secretary of Treasury	Andrew Mellon	1923–1929
Secretary of War	John W. Weeks	1923–1925
	Dwight F. Davis	1925–1929
Attorney General	Henry M. Daugherty	1923–1924
	Harlan F. Stone	1924–1925
	John G. Sargent	1925–1929
Postmaster General	Harry S. New	1923–1929
Secretary of Navy	Edwin Derby	1923–1924
	Curtis D. Wilbur	1924–1929
Secretary of Interior	Hubert Work	1923–1928
	Roy O. West	1928–1929
Secretary of Agriculture	Henry C. Wallace	1923–1924
	Howard M. Gore	1924–1925
	William M. Jardine	1925–1929
Secretary of Commerce	Herbert C. Hoover	1923–1928
	William F. Whiting	1928–1929
Secretary of Labor	James J. Davis	1923–1929

The Hoover Administration (1929–1933)

Vice President	Charles Curtis	1929–1933
Secretary of State	Henry L. Stimson	1929–1933
Secretary of Treasury	Andrew Mellon	1929–1932
	Ogden L. Mills	1932–1933
Secretary of War	James W. Good	1929
	Patrick J. Hurley	1929–1933
Attorney General	William D. Mitchell	1929–1933
Postmaster General	Walter F. Brown	1929–1933
Secretary of Navy	Charles F. Adams	1929–1933
Secretary of Interior	Ray L. Wilbur	1929–1933
Secretary of Agriculture	Arthur M. Hyde	1929–1933
Secretary of Commerce	Robert P. Lamont	1929–1932
	Roy D. Chapin	1932–1933
Secretary of Labor	James J. Davis	1929–1930
	William N. Doak	1930–1933

The Franklin D. Roosevelt Administration (1933–1945)

Vice President	John Nance Garner	1933–1941
	Henry A. Wallace	1941–1945
	Harry S. Truman	1945
Secretary of State	Cordell Hull	1933–1944
	Edward R. Stettinius, Jr.	1944–1945
Secretary of Treasury	William H. Woodin	1933–1934
	Henry Morgenthau, Jr.	1934–1945
Secretary of War	George H. Dern	1933–1936
	Henry A. Woodring	1936–1940
	Henry L. Stimson	1940–1945
Attorney General	Homer S. Cummings	1933–1939
	Frank Murphy	1939–1940
	Robert H. Jackson	1940–1941
Attorney General	Francis Biddle	1941–1945
Postmaster General	James A. Farley	1933–1940
	Frank C. Walker	1940–1945
Secretary of Navy	Claude A. Swanson	1933–1940
	Charles Edison	1940
	Frank Knox	1940–1944
	James V. Forrestal	1944–1945
Secretary of Interior	Harold L. Ickes	1933–1945
Secretary of Agriculture	Henry A. Wallace	1933–1940
	Claude R. Wickard	1940–1945
Secretary of Commerce	Daniel C. Roper	1933–1939
	Harry L. Hopkins	1939–1940
	Jesse Jones	1940–1945
	Henry A. Wallace	1945
Secretary of Labor	Frances Perkins	1933–1945

The Truman Administration (1945–1953)

Vice President	Alben W. Barkley	1949–1953
Secretary of State	Edward R. Stettinius, Jr.	1945
	James F. Byrnes	1945–1947
	George C. Marshall	1947–1949
	Dean G. Acheson	1949–1953
Secretary of Treasury	Fred M. Vinson	1945–1946
	John W. Snyder	1946–1953
Secretary of War	Robert P. Patterson	1945–1947
	Kenneth C. Royall	1947

Attorney General	Tom C. Clark	1945–1949
	J. Howard McGrath	1949–1952
	James P. McGranery	1952–1953
Postmaster General	Frank C. Walker	1945
	Robert E. Hannegan	1945–1947
	Jesse M. Donaldson	1947–1953
Secretary of Navy	James V. Forrestal	1945–1947
Secretary of Interior	Harold L. Ickes	1945–1946
	Julius A. Krug	1946–1949
	Oscar L. Chapman	1949–1953
Secretary of Agriculture	Clinton P. Anderson	1945–1948
	Charles F. Brannan	1948–1953
Secretary of Commerce	Henry A. Wallace	1945–1946
	W. Averell Harriman	1946–1948
	Charles W. Sawyer	1948–1953
Secretary of Labor	Lewis B. Schwellenbach	1945–1948
	Maurice J. Tobin	1948–1953
Secretary of Defense	James V. Forrestal	1947–1949
	Louis A. Johnson	1949–1950
	George C. Marshall	1950–1951
	Robert A. Lovett	1951–1953

The Eisenhower Administration (1953–1961)

Vice President	Richard M. Nixon	1953–1961
Secretary of State	John Foster Dulles	1953–1959
	Christian A. Herter	1959–1961
Secretary of Treasury	George M. Humphrey	1953–1957
	Robert B. Anderson	1957–1961
Attorney General	Herbert Brownell, Jr.	1953–1958
	William P. Rogers	1958–1961
Postmaster General	Arthur E. Summerfield	1953–1961
Secretary of Interior	Douglas McKay	1953–1956
	Fred A. Seaton	1956–1961
Secretary of Agriculture	Ezra T. Benson	1953–1961
Secretary of Commerce	Sinclair Weeks	1953–1958
	Lewis L. Strauss	1958–1959
	Frederick H. Mueller	1959–1961

Secretary of Labor	Martin P. Durkin	1953
	James P. Mitchell	1953–1961
Secretary of Defense	Charles E. Wilson	1953–1957
	Neil H. McElroy	1957–1959
	Thomas S. Gates Jr.	1959–1961
Secretary of Health, Education, and Welfare	Oveta Culp Hobby	1953–1955
	Marion B. Folsom	1955–1958
	Arthur S. Flemming	1958–1961

The Kennedy Administration (1961–1963)

Vice President	Lyndon B. Johnson	1961–1963
Secretary of State	Dean Rusk	1961–1963
Secretary of Treasury	C. Douglas Dillon	1961–1963
Attorney General	Robert F. Kennedy	1961–1963
Postmaster General	J. Edward Day	1961–1963
	John A. Gronouski	1963
Secretary of Interior	Stewart L. Udall	1961–1963
Secretary of Agriculture	Orville L. Freeman	1961–1963
Secretary of Commerce	Luther H. Hodges	1961–1963
Secretary of Labor	Arthur J. Goldberg	1961–1962
	W. Willard Wirtz	1962–1963
Secretary of Defense	Robert S. McNamara	1961–1963
Secretary of Health, Education, and Welfare	Abraham A. Ribicoff	1961–1962
	Anthony J. Celebrezze	1962–1963

The Lyndon Johnson Administration (1963–1969)

Vice President	Hubert H. Humphrey	1965–1969
Secretary of State	Dean Rusk	1963–1969
Secretary of Treasury	C. Douglas Dillon	1963–1965
	Henry H. Fowler	1965–1969
Attorney General	Robert F. Kennedy	1963–1964
	Nicholas Katzenbach	1965–1966
	Ramsey Clark	1967–1969
Postmaster General	John A. Gronouski	1963–1965
	Lawrence F. O'Brien	1965–1968
	Marvin Watson	1968–1969

The Lyndon Johnson Administration (1963–1969)

Secretary of Interior	Stewart L. Udall	1963–1969
Secretary of Agriculture	Orville L. Freeman	1963–1969
Secretary of Commerce	Luther H. Hodges	1963–1064
	John T. Connor	1964–1967
	Alexander B. Trowbridge	1967–1968
	Cyrus R. Smith	1968–1969
Secretary of Labor	W. Willard Wirtz	1963–1969
Secretary of Defense	Robert F. McNamara	1963–1968
	Clark Clifford	1968–1969
Secretary of Health, Education, and Welfare	Anthony J. Celebrezze	1963–1965
	John W. Gardner	1965–1968
	Wilbur J. Cohen	1968–1969
Secretary of Housing and Urban Development	Robert C. Weaver	1966–1969
	Robert C. Wood	1969
Secretary of Transportation	Alan S. Boyd	1967–1969

The Nixon Administration (1969–1974)

Vice President	Spiro T. Agnew	1969–1973
	Gerald R. Ford	1973–1974
Secretary of State	William P. Rogers	1969–1973
	Henry A. Kissinger	1973–1974
Secretary of Treasury	David M. Kennedy	1969–1970
	John B. Connally	1971–1972
	George P. Shultz	1972–1974
	William E. Simon	1974
Attorney General	John N. Mitchell	1969–1972
	Richard G. Kleindienst	1972–1973
	Elliot L. Richardson	1973
	William B. Saxbe	1973–1974
Postmaster General	Winton M. Blount	1969–1971
Secretary of Interior	Walter J. Hickel	1969–1970
	Rogers Morton	1971–1974
Secretary of Agriculture	Clifford M. Hardin	1969–1971
	Earl L. Butz	1971–1974
Secretary of Commerce	Maurice H. Stans	1969–1972
	Peter G. Peterson	1972–1973
	Frederick B. Dent	1973–1974

Secretary of Labor	George P. Shultz	1969–1970
	James D. Hodgson	1970–1973
	Peter J. Brennan	1973–1974
Secretary of Defense	Melvin R. Laird	1969–1973
	Elliot L. Richardson	1973
	James R. Schlesinger	1973–1974
Secretary of Health, Education, and Welfare	Robert H. Finch	1969–1970
	Elliot L. Richardson	1970–1973
	Caspar W. Weinberger	1973–1974
Secretary of Housing and Urban Development	George Romney	1969–1973
	James T. Lynn	1973–1974
Secretary of Transportation	John A. Volpe	1969–1973
	Claude S. Brinegar	1973–1974

The Ford Administration (1974–1977)

Vice President	Nelson A. Rockefeller	1974–1977
Secretary of State	Henry A. Kissinger	1974–1977
Secretary of Treasury	William E. Simon	1974–1977
Attorney General	William Saxbe	1974–1975
	Edward Levi	1975–1977
Secretary of Interior	Rogers Morton	1974–1975
	Stanley K. Hathaway	1975
	Thomas Kleppe	1975–1977
Secretary of Agriculture	Earl L. Butz	194–1976
	John A. Knebel	1976–1977
Secretary of Commerce	Frederick B. Dent	1974–1975
	Rogers Morton	1975–1976
	Elliot L. Richardson	1976–1977
Secretary of Labor	Peter J. Brennan	1974–1975
	John T. Dunlop	1975–1976
	W. J. Usery	1976–1977
Secretary of Defense	James R. Schlesinger	1974–1975
	Donald Rumsfeld	1975–1977
Secretary of Health, Education, and Welfare	Caspar Weinberger	1974–1975
	Forrest D. Mathews	1975–1977
Secretary of Housing and Urban Development	James T. Lynn	1974–1975
	Carla A. Hills	1975–1977
Secretary of Transportation	Claude Brinegar	1974–1975
	William T. Coleman	1975–1977

The Carter Administration (1977–1981)

Vice President	Walter F. Mondale	1977–1981
Secretary of State	Cyrus R. Vance	1977–1980
	Edmund Muskie	1980–1981
Secretary of Treasury	W. Michael Blumenthal	1977–1979
	G. William Miller	1979–1981
Attorney General	Griffin Bell	1977–1979
	Benjamin R. Civiletti	1979–1981
Secretary of Interior	Cecil D. Andrus	1977–1981
Secretary of Agriculture	Robert Bergland	1977–1981
Secretary of Commerce	Juanita M. Kreps	1977–1979
	Philip M. Klutznick	1979–1981
Secretary of Labor	F. Ray Marshall	1977–1981
Secretary of Defense	Harold Brown	1977–1981
Secretary of Health, Education, and Welfare	Joseph A. Califano	1977–1979
	Patricia R. Harris	1979
Secretary of Health and Human Services	Patricia R. Harris	1979–1981
Secretary of Education	Shirley M. Hufstedler	1979–1981
Secretary of Housing and Urban Development	Patricia R. Harris	1977–1979
	Moon Landrieu	1979–1981
Secretary of Transportation	Brock Adams	1977–1979
	Neil E. Goldschmidt	1979–1981
Secretary of Energy	James R. Schlesinger	1977–1979
	Charles W. Duncan	1979–1981

The Reagan Administration (1981–1989)

Vice President	George Bush	1981–1989
Secretary of State	Alexander M. Haig	1981–1982
	George P. Shultz	1982–1989
Secretary of Treasury	Donald Regan	1981–1985
	James A. Baker, III	1985–1988
	Nicholas Brady	1988–1989
Attorney General	William F. Smith	1981–1985
	Edwin A. Meese, III	1985–1988
	Richard Thornburgh	1988–1989
Secretary of Interior	James Watt	1981–1983
	William P. Clark, Jr.	1983–1985
	Donald P. Hodel	1985–1989
Secretary of Agriculture	John Block	1981–1986
	Richard E. Lyng	1986–1989
Secretary of Commerce	Malcolm Baldridge	1981–1987
	C. William Verity, Jr.	1987–1989
Secretary of Labor	Raymond Donovan	1981–1985
	William E. Brock	1985–1987
	Ann D. McLaughlin	1987–1989
Secretary of Defense	Caspar Weinberger	1981–1987
	Frank Carlucci	1987–1989
Secretary of Health and Human Services	Richard Schweiker	1981–1983
	Margaret Heckler	1983–1985
	Otis R. Bowen	1985–1989
Secretary of Education	Terrel H. Bell	1981–1985
	William J. Bennett	1985–1988
	Laura F. Cavazos	1988–1989
Secretary of Housing and Urban Development	Samuel Pierce	1981–1989
Secretary of Transportation	Drew Lewis	1981–1983
	Elizabeth Dole	1983–1987
	James H. Burnley	1987–1989
Secretary of Energy	James Edwards	1981–1982
	Donald P. Hodel	1982–1985
	John S. Herrington	1985–

The Bush Administration (1989–   )

Vice President	J. Danforth Quayle	1989–
Secretary of State	James A. Baker III	1989–
Secretary of Treasury	Nicholas Brady	1989–
Attorney General	Richard Thornburgh	1989–
Secretary of Interior	Manuel Lujan	1989–
Secretary of Agriculture	Clayton Yeutter	1989–
Secretary of Commerce	Robert Mosbacher	1989–
Secretary of Labor	Elizabeth Dole	1989–
Secretary of Defense	Richard Cheney	1989–

The Bush Administration (1989–) (continued)			Secretary of Transportation	Samuel K. Skinner	1989–
Secretary of Health and Human Services	Louis W. Sullivan	1989–	Secretary of Energy	James Watkins	1989–
Secretary of Housing and Urban Development	Jack Kemp	1989–	Secretary of Veterans Affairs	Edwin Derwinski	1989–

JUSTICES OF THE SUPREME COURT

	Term of Service	Years of Service	Life Span		Term of Service	Years of Service	Life Span
John Jay	1789–1795	5	1745–1829	John M. Harlan	1877–1911	34	1833–1911
John Rutledge	1789–1791	1	1739–1800	William B. Woods	1880–1887	7	1824–1887
William Cushing	1789–1810	20	1732–1810	Stanley Matthews	1881–1889	7	1824–1889
James Wilson	1789–1798	8	1742–1798	Horace Gray	1882–1902	20	1828–1902
John Blair	1789–1796	6	1732–1800	Samuel Blatchford	1882–1893	11	1820–1893
Robert H. Harrison	1789–1790	—	1745–1790	Lucius Q. C. Lamar	1888–1893	5	1825–1893
James Iredell	1790–1799	9	1751–1799	*Melville W. Fuller*	1888–1910	21	1833–1910
Thomas Johnson	1791–1793	1	1732–1819	David J. Brewer	1890–1910	20	1837–1910
William Paterson	1793–1806	13	1745–1806	Henry B. Brown	1890–1906	16	1836–1913
*John Rutledge**	1795	—	1739–1800	George Shiras, Jr.	1892–1903	10	1832–1924
Samuel Chase	1796–1811	15	1741–1811	Howell E. Jackson	1893–1895	2	1832–1895
Oliver Ellsworth	1796–1800	4	1745–1807	Edward D. White	1894–1910	16	1845–1921
Bushrod Washington	1798–1829	31	1762–1829	Rufus W. Peckham	1895–1909	14	1838–1909
Alfred Moore	1799–1804	4	1755–1810	Joseph McKenna	1898–1925	26	1843–1926
John Marshall	1801–1835	34	1755–1835	Oliver W. Holmes	1902–1932	30	1841–1935
William Johnson	1804–1834	30	1771–1834	William R. Day	1903–1922	19	1849–1923
H. Brockholst Livingston	1806–1823	16	1757–1823	William H. Moody	1906–1910	3	1853–1917
Thomas Todd	1807–1826	18	1765–1826	Horace H. Lurton	1910–1914	4	1844–1914
Joseph Story	1811–1845	33	1779–1845	Charles E. Hughes	1910–1916	5	1862–1948
Gabriel Duval	1811–1835	24	1752–1844	Willis Van Devanter	1911–1937	26	1859–1941
Smith Thompson	1823–1843	20	1768–1843	Joseph R. Lamar	1911–1916	5	1857–1916
Robert Trimble	1826–1828	2	1777–1828	*Edward D. White*	1910–1921	11	1845–1921
John McLean	1829–1861	32	1785–1861	Mahlon Pitney	1912–1922	10	1858–1924
Henry Baldwin	1830–1844	14	1780–1844	James C. McReynolds	1914–1941	26	1862–1946
James M. Wayne	1835–1867	32	1790–1867	Louis D. Brandeis	1916–1939	22	1856–1941
Roger B. Taney	1836–1864	28	1777–1864	John H. Clarke	1916–1922	6	1857–1945
Philip P. Barbour	1836–1841	4	1783–1841	William H. Taft	1921–1930	8	1857–1930
John Catron	1837–1865	28	1786–1865	George Sutherland	1922–1938	15	1862–1942
John McKinley	1837–1852	15	1780–1852	Pierce Butler	1922–1939	16	1866–1939
Peter V. Daniel	1841–1860	19	1784–1860	Edward T. Sanford	1923–1930	7	1865–1930
Samuel Nelson	1845–1872	27	1792–1873	Harlan F. Stone	1925–1941	16	1872–1946
Levi Woodbury	1845–1851	5	1789–1851	*Charles E. Hughes*	1930–1941	11	1862–1948
Robert C. Grier	1846–1870	23	1794–1870	Owen J. Roberts	1930–1945	15	1875–1955
Benjamin R. Curtis	1851–1857	6	1809–1874	Benjamin N. Cardozo	1932–1938	6	1870–1938
John A. Campbell	1853–1861	8	1811–1889	Hugo L. Black	1937–1971	34	1886–1971
Nathan Clifford	1858–1881	23	1803–1881	Stanley F. Reed	1938–1957	19	1884–1980
Noah H. Swayne	1862–1881	18	1804–1884	Felix Frankfurter	1939–1962	23	1882–1965
Samuel F. Miller	1862–1890	28	1816–1890	William O. Douglas	1939–1975	36	1898–1980
David Davis	1862–1877	14	1815–1886	Frank Murphy	1940–1949	9	1890–1949
Stephen J. Field	1863–1897	34	1816–1899	*Harlan F. Stone*	1941–1946	5	1872–1946
Salmon P. Chase	1864–1873	8	1808–1873	James F. Byrnes	1941–1942	1	1879–1972
William Strong	1870–1880	10	1808–1895	Robert H. Jackson	1941–1954	13	1892–1954
Joseph P. Bradley	1870–1892	22	1813–1892	Wiley B. Rutledge	1943–1949	6	1894–1949
Ward Hunt	1873–1882	9	1810–1886	Harold H. Burton	1945–1958	13	1888–1964
Morrison R. Waite	1874–1888	14	1816–1888	*Fred M. Vinson*	1946–1953	7	1890–1953
				Tom C. Clark	1949–1967	18	1899–1977

	Term of Service	Years of Service	Life Span		Term of Service	Years of Service	Life Span
Sherman Minton	1949–1956	7	1890–1965	Abe Fortas	1965–1969	4	1910–
Earl Warren	1953–1969	16	1891–1974	Thurgood Marshall	1967–	—	1908–
John Marshall Harlan	1955–1971	16	1899–1971	Warren C. Burger	1969–	—	1907–
William J. Brennan, Jr.	1956–	—	1906–	Harry A. Blackmun	1970–	—	1908–
Charles E. Whittaker	1957–1962	5	1901–1973	Lewis F. Powell, Jr.	1971–	—	1907–
Potter Stewart	1958–1981	23	1915–	William H. Rehnquist	1971–	—	1924–
Byron R. White	1962–	—	1917–	John P. Stevens, III	1975–	—	1920–
Arthur J. Goldberg	1962–1965	3	1908–	Sandra Day O'Connor	1981–	—	1930–
				William H. Rehnquist	1986–	—	1924–
				Antonin Scalia	1986–	—	1936–
				Anthony M. Kennedy	1987–	—	1936–

*Appointed and served one term, but not confirmed by the Senate.

Note: Chief justices are in italics.

A SOCIAL PROFILE OF THE AMERICAN REPUBLIC

POPULATION

Year	Population	Percent Increase	Population Per Square Mile	Percent Urban/ Rural	Percent Male/ Female	Percent White/ Nonwhite	Persons Per Household	Median Age
1790	3,929,214		4.5	5.1/94.9	NA/NA	80.7/19.3	5.79	NA
1800	5,308,483	35.1	6.1	6.1/93.9	NA/NA	81.1/18.9	NA	NA
1810	7,239,881	36.4	4.3	7.3/92.7	NA/NA	81.0/19.0	NA	NA
1820	9,638,453	33.1	5.5	7.2/92.8	50.8/49.2	81.6/18.4	NA	16.7
1830	12,866,020	33.5	7.4	8.8/91.2	50.8/18.1	81.9/18.1	NA	17.2
1840	17,069,453	32.7	9.8	10.8/89.2	50.9/49.1	83.2/16.8	NA	17.8
1850	23,191,876	35.9	7.9	15.3/84.7	51.0/49.0	84.3/15.7	5.55	18.9
1860	31,443,321	35.6	10.6	19.8/80.2	51.2/48.8	85.6/14.4	5.28	19.4
1870	39,818,449	26.6	13.4	25.7/74.3	50.6/49.4	86.2/13.8	5.09	20.2
1880	50,155,783	26.0	16.9	28.2/71.8	50.9/49.1	86.5/13.5	5.04	20.9
1890	62,947,714	25.5	21.2	35.1/64.9	51.2/48.8	87.5/12.5	4.93	22.0
1900	75,994,575	20.7	25.6	39.6/60.4	51.1/48.9	87.9/12.1	4.76	22.9
1910	91,972,266	21.0	31.0	45.6/54.4	51.5/48.5	88.9/11.1	4.54	24.1
1920	105,710,620	14.9	35.6	51.2/48.8	51.0/49.0	89.7/10.3	4.34	25.3
1930	122,775,046	16.1	41.2	56.1/43.9	50.6/49.4	89.8/10.2	4.11	26.4
1940	131,669,275	7.2	44.2	56.5/43.5	50.2/49.8	89.8/10.2	3.67	29.0
1950	150,697,361	14.5	50.7	64.0/36.0	49.7/50.3	89.5/10.5	3.37	30.2
1960	179,323,175	18.5	50.6	69.9/30.1	49.3/50.7	88.6/11.4	3.33	29.5
1970	203,302,031	13.4	57.4	73.5/26.5	48.7/51.3	87.6/12.4	3.14	28.0
1980	226,545,805	11.4	64.0	73.7/26.3	48.6/51.4	86.0/14.0	2.76	30.0
1990*	250,410,000	9.9	70.8	NA	48.8/51.2	84.1/15.9	NA	32.1**
2000*	268,266,000	7.1	75.8	NA	48.9/51.1	82.6/17.4	NA	NA

NA = Not available.
* Projections.
**1987 figure.

VITAL STATISTICS (rates per thousand)

Year	Births	Year	Births	Deaths*	Marriage*	Divorces*
1800	55.0	1900	32.3	17.2	NA	NA
1810	54.3	1910	30.1	14.7	NA	NA
1820	55.2	1920	27.7	13.0	12.0	1.6
1830	51.4	1930	21.3	11.3	9.2	1.6
1840	51.8	1940	19.4	10.8	12.1	2.0
1850	43.3	1950	24.1	9.6	11.1	2.6
1860	44.3	1960	23.7	9.5	8.5	2.2
1870	38.3	1970	18.4	9.5	10.6	3.5
1880	39.8	1980	15.9	8.8	10.6	5.2
1890	31.5	1987	15.7	8.7	9.9	4.8

NA = Not available.
*Data not available before 1900.

LIFE EXPECTANCY (in years)

Year	Total Population	White Females	Nonwhite Females	White Males	Nonwhite Males
1900	47.3	48.7	33.5	46.6	32.5
1910	50.1	52.0	37.5	48.6	33.8
1920	54.1	55.6	45.2	54.4	45.5
1930	59.7	63.5	49.2	59.7	47.3
1940	62.9	66.6	54.9	62.1	51.5
1950	68.2	72.2	62.9	66.5	59.1
1960	69.7	74.1	66.3	67.4	61.1
1970	70.9	75.6	69.4	68.0	61.3
1980	73.7	78.1	73.6	70.7	65.3
1987	74.9	78.3	75.4	71.5	67.6

THE CHANGING AGE STRUCTURE

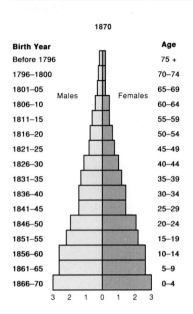

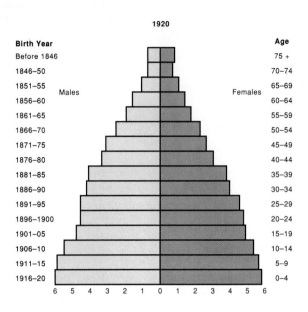

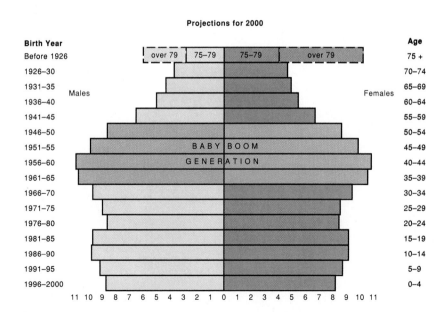

For more explanation of these population pyramids, see pages 714–15 and 1190–91.

REGIONAL ORIGIN OF IMMIGRANTS (percent)

Years	Total Number of Immigrants	Total Europe	North and West	East and Central	South and Other	Western Hemisphere	Asia
1821–1830	143,389	69.2	67.1	—	2.1	8.4	—
1831–1840	599,125	82.8	81.8	—	1.0	5.5	—
1841–1850	1,713,251	93.8	92.9	0.1	0.3	3.6	—
1851–1860	2,598,214	94.4	93.6	0.1	0.8	2.9	1.6
1861–1870	2,314,824	89.2	87.8	0.5	0.9	7.2	2.8
1871–1880	2,812,191	80.8	73.6	4.5	2.7	14.4	4.4
1881–1890	5,246,613	90.3	72.0	11.9	6.3	8.1	1.3
1891–1900	3,687,546	96.5	44.5	32.8	19.1	1.1	1.9
1901–1910	8,795,386	92.5	21.7	44.5	6.3	4.1	2.8
1911–1920	5,735,811	76.3	17.4	33.4	25.5	19.9	3.4
1921–1930	4,107,209	60.3	31.7	14.4	14.3	36.9	2.4
1931–1940	528,431	65.9	38.8	11.0	16.1	30.3	2.8
1941–1950	1,035,039	60.1	47.5	4.6	7.9	34.3	3.1
1951–1960	2,515,479	52.8	17.7	24.3	10,8	39.6	6.0
1961–1970	3,321,677	33.8	11.7	9.4	12.9	51.7	12.9
1971–1980	4,384,000	18.3	4.3	5.6	8.4	44.0	37.3

Dash indicates less than 0.1 percent.

RECENT TRENDS IN IMMIGRATION (in thousands)

	1961–1970	1971–1980	Percent 1961–1970	Percent 1971–1980	1985	1987
All countries	3,321.7	4,493.3	100.0	100.0	570.0	601.5
Europe	1,123.5	800.4	33.8	17.8	69.5	68.0
Austria	20.6	9.5	0.6	0.2	1.9	2.4
Hungary	5.4	6.6	0.2	0.1	0.6	—
Belgium	9.2	5.3	0.3	0.1	0.8	0.9
Czechoslovakia	3.3	6.0	0.1	0.1	0.7	0.7
Denmark	9.2	4.4	0.3	0.1	0.5	0.5
Finland	4.2	2.9	0.1	0.1	0.2	0.3
France	45.2	25.1	1.4	0.6	3.5	3.8
Germany	190.8	74.4	5.7	1.7	10.2	9.9
Great Britain	214.5	137.4	6.5	3.1	15.6	15.9
Greece	86.0	92.4	2.6	2.1	3.5	4.1
Ireland	33.0	11.5	1.0	0.3	1.3	3.0
Italy	214.1	129.4	6.4	7.9	6.4	4.7
Netherlands	30.6	10.5	.9	0.2	1.2	1.3
Norway	15.5	3.9	.5	0.1	0.4	0.4
Poland	53.5	37.2	1.6	0.8	7.4	5.8
Portugal	76.1	101.7	2.3	2.3	3.8	4.0
Spain	44.7	39.1	1.3	0.9	2.3	2.1
Sweden	17.1	6.5	.5	0.1	1.2	1.2
Switzerland	18.5	8.2	.6	0.2	1.0	0.1
U.S.S.R.	2.5	39.0	.1	0.9	1.5	1.1
Yugoslavia	20.4	30.5	.6	0.7	1.5	1.8
Other Europe	9.1	18.9	.2	0.2	4.0	4.0
Asia	427.6	1,588.2	12.9	35.2	255.2	248.3
China	34.8	124.3	1.0	2.8	33.1	18.6
Hong Kong	75.0	113.5	2.3	2.5	10.8	8.8
India	27.2	164.1	0.8	3.7	24.5	26.4

RECENT TRENDS IN IMMIGRATION (continued)

	1961–1970	1971–1980	Percent 1961–1970	Percent 1971–1980	1985	1987
Iran	10.3	45.1	0.3	1.0	12.3	10.3
Israel	29.6	37.7	0.9	0.8	4.3	4.8
Japan	40.0	49.8	1.2	1.1	4.6	4.7
Jordan	11.7	27.5	0.4	0.6	2.7	2.8
Korea	34.5	267.6	1.0	6.0	34.8	35.4
Lebanon	15.2	41.3	0.5	0.9	2.5	3.0
Philippines	98.4	355.0	3.0	7.9	53.1	58.3
Turkey	10.1	13.4	0.3	0.3	1.7	2.1
Vietnam	4.3	172.8	1.1	3.8	20.4	13.1
Other Asia	36.5	176.1	1.1	3.8	50.4	60.0
America	1,716.4	1,982.5	51.7	44.3	225.5	265.0
Argentina	49.7	29.9	1.5	0.7	1.9	2.2
Brazil	29.3	17.8	0.9	0.4	2.6	2.7
Canada	413.3	169.9	12.4	3.8	16.4	16.7
Colombia	72.0	77.3	2.2	1.7	11.8	11.5
Cuba	208.5	264.9	6.3	5.9	17.1	27.4
Dominican Rep.	93.3	148.1	2.8	3.3	23.9	24.9
Ecuador	36.8	50.1	1.1	1.1	4.6	4.7
El Salvador	15.0	34.4	0.5	0.8	10.1	10.6
Guatemala	15.9	25.9	0.5	0.6	4.4	5.8
Haiti	34.5	56.3	1.0	1.3	9.9	14.8
Honduras	15.7	17.4	0.5	0.4	3.7	72.5
Mexico	453.9	640.3	13.7	14.3	61.3	2.8
Panamá	19.4	23.5	0.6	0.5	3.2	5.8
Peru	19.1	29.2	0.6	0.6	4.1	5.8
West Indies	133.9	271.8	4.0	6.1	28.5	48.3
Other America	106.1	125.7	3.1	2.8	22.0	9.7

Figures may not add to total due to rounding.

AMERICAN WORKERS AND FARMERS

Year	Total Number of Workers (thousands)	Percent of Workers Male/Female	Percent of Female Workers Married	Percent of Workers in Female Population	Percent of Workers in Labor Unions	Farm Population (thousands)	Farm Population as Percent of Total Population
1870	12,506	85/15	NA	NA	NA	NA	NA
1880	17,392	85/15	NA	NA	NA	21,973	43.8
1890	23,318	83/17	13.9	18.9	NA	24,771	42.3
1900	29,073	82/18	15.4	20.6	3	29,875	41.9
1910	38,167	79/21	24.7	25.4	6	32,077	34.9
1920	41,614	79/21	23.0	23.7	12	31,974	30.1
1930	48,830	78/22	28.9	24.8	7	30,529	24.9
1940	53,011	76/24	36.4	27.4	27	30,547	23.2
1950	59,643	72/28	52.1	31.4	25	23,048	15.3
1960	69,877	68/32	59.9	37.7	26	15,635	8.7
1970	82,049	63/37	63.4	43.4	25	9,712	4.8
1980	108,544	58/42	59.7	51.5	23	6,051	2.7
1987	119,865	55/45	59.1	55.4	19	4,986	2.0

THE ECONOMY AND FEDERAL SPENDING

| Year | Gross National Product (GNP) (in billions) | Foreign Trade (in millions) | | | Federal Budget (in billions) | Federal Surplus/Deficit (in billions) | Federal Debt (in billions) |
		Exports	Imports	Balance of Trade			
1790	NA	$ 20	$ 23	$ −3	$ 0.004	$ +0.00015	$ 0.076
1800	NA	71	91	−20	0.011	+0.0006	0.083
1810	NA	67	85	−18	0.008	+0.0012	0.053
1820	NA	70	74	−4	0.018	−0.0004	0.091
1830	NA	74	71	+3	0.015	+0.100	0.049
1840	NA	132	107	+25	0.024	−0.005	0.004
1850	NA	152	178	−26	0.040	+0.004	0.064
1860	NA	400	362	−38	0.063	−0.01	0.065
1870	$ 7.4	451	462	−11	0.310	+0.10	2.4
1880	11.2	853	761	+92	0.268	+0.07	2.1
1890	13.1	910	823	+87	0.318	+0.09	1.2
1900	18.7	1,499	930	+569	0.521	+0.05	1.2
1910	35.3	1,919	1,646	+273	0.694	−0.02	1.1
1920	91.5	8,664	5,784	+2,880	6.357	+0.3	24.3
1930	90.7	4,013	3,500	+513	3.320	+0.7	16.3
1940	100.0	4,030	7,433	−3,403	9.6	−2.7	43.0
1950	286.5	10,816	9,125	+1,691	43.1	−2.2	257.4
1960	506.5	19,600	15,046	+4,556	92.2	+0.3	286.3
1970	992.7	42,700	40,189	+2,511	195.6	−2.8	371.0
1980	2,631.7	220,783	244,871	+24,088	590.9	−73.8	907.7
1987	4,526.7	252,866	424,082	−171,216	1,015.6	−173.2	2,350.3

GREENLAND
(KALALLIT-NUNAAT)
(Den.)

80°N

ALASKA
(U.S.)

60°N

CANADA

NORTH
AMERICA

40°N

UNITED STATES

ATLANTIC
OCEAN

BERMUDA
(Br.)

MEXICO

BAHAMAS

CUBA

CAPE
VERDE

20°N

DOMINICAN
REP. 18

HAITI
BELIZE

PUERTO 27
RICO (U.S.) 26
25

HAWAII
(U.S.)

GUATEMALA
EL SALVADOR
NICARAGUA
COSTA RICA
PANAMA

HONDURAS 20
29
24 23
21 22 19
28

PACIFIC
OCEAN

VENEZUELA
GUYANA
SURINAME
FR. GUIANA

COLOMBIA

ECUADOR

0° Equator

SOUTH
AMERICA

WESTERN
SAMOA

AMERICAN
SAMOA

FRENCH
POLYNESIA

PERU

BRAZIL

BOLIVIA

PARAGUAY

20°S

TONGA

CHILE

ARGENTINA

URUGUAY

40°S

FALKLAND
IS. (Br.)

60°S

80°S

160°W   140°W   120°W   100°W   80°W   60°W

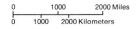

0   1000   2000 Miles

0   1000   2000 Kilometers

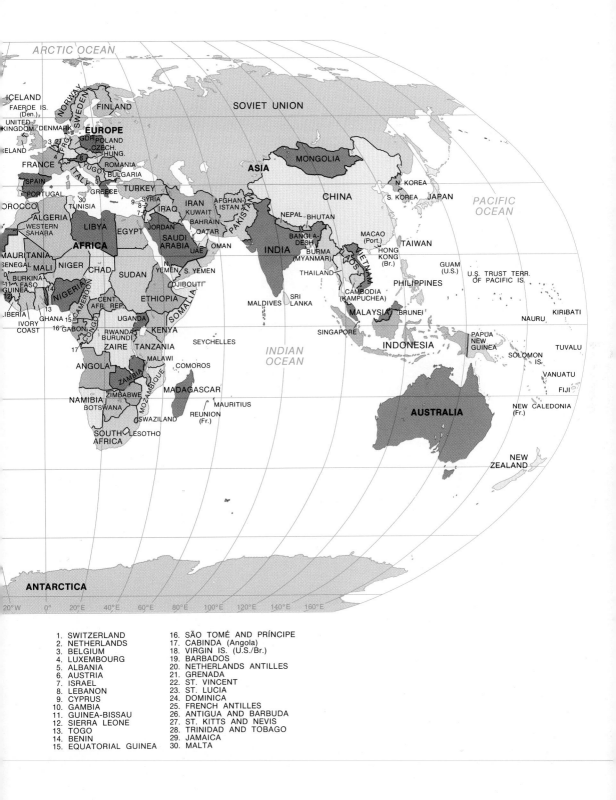

ARCTIC OCEAN

ICELAND
FAEROE IS.
(Den.)
UNITED
KINGDOM DENMARK
IRELAND

NORWAY
SWEDEN
FINLAND

SOVIET UNION

EUROPE
GDR
FRG POLAND
CZECH.
HUNG.

FRANCE
ITALY
ROMANIA
BULGARIA

ASIA

MONGOLIA

N. KOREA

SPAIN
PORTUGAL
GREECE
TURKEY

S. KOREA JAPAN

PACIFIC
OCEAN

MOROCCO
TUNISIA
SYRIA
IRAQ
IRAN
AFGHAN-
ISTAN

CHINA

ALGERIA
LIBYA
EGYPT

KUWAIT
JORDAN
BAHRAIN
QATAR

PAKISTAN

NEPAL BHUTAN

MACAO
(Port.)
TAIWAN

WESTERN
SAHARA

SAUDI
ARABIA

UAE OMAN

INDIA

BANGLA-
DESH

BURMA
(MYANMAR)

HONG
KONG
(Br.)

AFRICA

MAURITANIA

MALI NIGER CHAD

N.
YEMEN S. YEMEN

SUDAN

LAOS
VIETNAM

GUAM
(U.S.)

U.S. TRUST TERR.
OF PACIFIC IS.

SENEGAL
BURKINA
FASO
GUINEA
NIGERIA
CAMEROON
CENT.
AFR. REP.

DJIBOUTI

THAILAND

PHILIPPINES

ETHIOPIA

CAMBODIA
(KAMPUCHEA)

KIRIBATI

NAURU

IVORY
COAST
LIBERIA
GHANA
GABON
CONGO

UGANDA
KENYA

SOMALIA

MALDIVES

SRI
LANKA

MALAYSIA
BRUNEI

RWANDA
BURUNDI

ZAIRE TANZANIA

SINGAPORE

SEYCHELLES

INDONESIA

PAPUA
NEW
GUINEA

SOLOMON
IS.

TUVALU

INDIAN
OCEAN

ANGOLA

MALAWI
COMOROS

VANUATU

ZAMBIA
MOZAMBIQUE

FIJI

NAMIBIA
BOTSWANA

ZIMBABWE

MADAGASCAR

MAURITIUS

AUSTRALIA

NEW CALEDONIA
(Fr.)

SWAZILAND
REUNION
(Fr.)

SOUTH
AFRICA
LESOTHO

NEW
ZEALAND

ANTARCTICA

20°W   0°   20°E   40°E   60°E   80°E   100°E   120°E   140°E   160°E

1. SWITZERLAND
2. NETHERLANDS
3. BELGIUM
4. LUXEMBOURG
5. ALBANIA
6. AUSTRIA
7. ISRAEL
8. LEBANON
9. CYPRUS
10. GAMBIA
11. GUINEA-BISSAU
12. SIERRA LEONE
13. TOGO
14. BENIN
15. EQUATORIAL GUINEA

16. SÃO TOMÉ AND PRÍNCIPE
17. CABINDA (Angola)
18. VIRGIN IS. (U.S./Br.)
19. BARBADOS
20. NETHERLANDS ANTILLES
21. GRENADA
22. ST. VINCENT
23. ST. LUCIA
24. DOMINICA
25. FRENCH ANTILLES
26. ANTIGUA AND BARBUDA
27. ST. KITTS AND NEVIS
28. TRINIDAD AND TOBAGO
29. JAMAICA
30. MALTA

BIBLIOGRAPHY

CHAPTER 1

Discovery and Exploration in the Sixteenth Century
Kenneth R. Andrews, *Trade, Plunder, and Settlement: Maritime Enterprise and the Genesis of the British Empire, 1480–1630* (1985); K. R. Andrews, N. P. Canny, and P. E. H. Hair, eds., *The Westward Enterprise: English Activities in Ireland, the Atlantic, and America, 1480–1650* (1979); Ralph Davis, *The Rise of Atlantic Economies* (1973); J. H. Elliott, *The Old World and the New, 1492–1650* (1970); James Lang, *Conquest and Commerce: Spain and England in the Americas* (1975); W. H. McNeil, *The Rise of the West* (1963); Samuel Eliot Morison, *The European Discovery of America: The Northern Voyage, 500–1600* (1971), and *The European Discovery of America: The Southern Voyages, 1492–1616* (1974); J. H. Parry, *The Age of Reconnaissance* (1963); David Beers Quinn, *England and the Discovery of America, 1481–1620* (1974), *North America from Earliest Discovery to First Settlements* (1977), and *Set Fair for Roanoke* (1985).

Native American Civilizations
Alfred W. Crosby, Jr., *The Columbian Exchange: Biological and Cultural Consequences of 1492* (1972); Nigel Davies, *The Aztecs* (1973); Harold Driver, *Indians of North America* (2d ed., 1970); Peter Farb, *Man's Rise to Civilization* (1968); R. C. Padden, *The Hummingbird and the Hawk* (1962); M. Leon Portilla, *The Broken Spears: The Aztec Account of the Conquest of Mexico* (1962); Wilcomb E. Washburn, *The Indian in America* (1975).

The Spanish Empire in the Sixteenth Century
Fernand Braudel, *The Mediterranean and the Mediterranean World in the Age of Philip the Second*, Vols. 1 and 2 (1976); J. H. Elliott, *Imperial Spain, 1469–1716* (1963); Charles Gibson, *The Aztecs Under Spanish Rule* (1964); James Lockhart, *Spanish Peru, 1532–1560* (1968); James Lockhart and Stuart B. Schwartz, *Early Latin America: A History of Colonial Spanish America and Brazil* (1983).

The Protestant Reformation
Owen Chadwick, *The Reformation* (1964); Patrick Collinson, *The Elizabethan Puritan Movement* (1967); A. G. Dickens, *The English Reformation* (1974); Richard Dunn, *The Age of Religious Wars, 1159–1689* (1979); Erik Erikson, *Young Man Luther* (1962); Charles George and Katherine George, *The Protestant Mind of the English Reformation* (1961); De Lamar Jensen, *Reformation Europe, Age of Reform and Revolution* (1981); Steven Ozment, *The Reformation in the Cities* (1975); Keith Thomas, *Religion and the Decline of Magic* (1971); Michael Walzer, *The Revolution of the Saints* (1965).

Elizabethan and Stuart England
Trevor Ashton, ed., *Crisis in Europe, 1560–1660* (1965); Carl Bridenbaugh, *Vexed and Troubled Englishmen, 1590–1642* (1968); Mildred Campbell, *The English Yeoman Under Elizabeth and the Early Stuarts* (1942); Peter Laslett, *The World We Have Lost* (1965); Wallace Notestein, *The English People on the Eve of Colonization, 1603–1630* (1954); Laurence Stone, *The Crisis of the Aristocracy, 1558–1641* (1965); Keith Wrightson, *English Society, 1580–1680* (1982).

Ireland in the Sixteenth Century
Nicholas Canny, *The Elizabethan Conquest of Ireland* (1976), and *Kingdom and Colony: Ireland in the Atlantic World, 1560–1800* (1988); David Beers Quinn, *The Elizabethans and the Irish* (1976).

CHAPTER 2

General Histories
Charles M. Andrews, *The Colonial Period in American History, (1934–1938)*; Wesley Frank Craven, *The Southern Colonies in the Seventeenth Century, 1607–1689* (1949); David Galenson, *White Servitude in Colonial America* (1981); Sidney Mintz, *Sweetness and Power: The Place of Sugar in Modern History* (1985); Gary Nash, *Red, White and Black: The Peoples of Early America* (1974); John E. Pomfret, *Founding the American Colonies, 1583–1660* (1970); R. C. Simmons, *The American Colonies* (1976).

Native Americans in the Early South
Karen Kupperman, *Settling with the Indians: The Meeting of English and Indian Cultures in America, 1580–1640* (1980); J. Leitch Wright, Jr., *The Only Land They Knew: The Tragic Story of American Indians in the Old South* (1981); Nancy Lurie, "Indian Cultural Adjustment to European Civilization," in *Seventeenth-Century*

America, ed. James M. Smith (1959); James H. Merrell, *The Indians' New World: Catawbas and Their Neighbors* (1989).

Race and Slavery
Wesley Frank Craven, *White, Red, and Black: The Seventeenth-Century Virginian* (1971); Philip Curtin, *The Atlantic Slave Trade* (1969); Basil Davidson, *The African Genius* (1970); David B. Davis, *The Problem of Slavery in Western Culture* (1966); Carl N. Degler, *Neither White Nor Black: Slavery and Race Relations in Brazil and the United States* (1971); Winthrop Jordan, *White over Black* (1968); Herbert Klein, *The Middle Passage* (1978), and *Slavery in the Americas: A Comparative Study of Virginia and Cuba* (1967); Peter Kolchin, *Unfree Labor: American Slavery and Russian Serfdom* (1987); Richard Olaniyan, *African History and Culture* (1982); Roland Oliver, ed., *The Cambridge History of Africa*, Vol. 3: *c. 1050–c. 1600* (1977); Orlando Patterson, *Slavery and Social Death: A Comparative Study* (1982); James A. Rawley, *The Transatlantic Slave Trade* (1981); Walter Rodney, *West Africa and the Atlantic Slave Trade* (1969); Peter Wood, *Black Majority: Negroes in Colonial South Carolina from 1670 Through the Stono Rebellion* (1974), and "'I Did the Best I Could for My Day': The Study of Early Black History During the Second Reconstruction, 1960 to 1976," *William and Mary Quarterly*, (1978).

The Early Chesapeake Colonies
Philip L. Barbour, *The Three Worlds of Captain John Smith* (1964); Warren M. Billings, John E. Selby, and Thad W. Tate, *Colonial Virginia* (1986); Lois Green Carr, Philip D. Morgan, and Jean B. Russo, *Colonial Chesapeake Society* (1989); Lois Green Carr and Lorena Walsh, "The Planter's Wife: The Experience of White Women in Seventeenth-Century Maryland," *William and Mary Quarterly* (1977); Carville Earle, *The Evolution of a Tidewater Settlement Pattern: All Hallows Parish, Maryland 1650–1783* (1975); Ivor Noel Hume, *Martin's Hundred: The Discovery of a Lost Virginia Settlement* (1979); Allan Kulikoff, *Tobacco and Slaves* (1987); Aubrey C. Land, *Colonial Maryland* (1981); Gloria Main, *Tobacco Colony: Life in Early Maryland, 1650–1720* (1982); Edmund S. Morgan, *American Slavery, American Freedom* (1975); Darrett Rutman and Anita Rutman, *A Place in Time: Middlesex County, Virginia, 1650–1750* (1984); Thad Tate and David Ammerman, eds., *The Chesapeake in the Seventeenth Century* (1979); Alden Vaughan, *American Genesis: Captain John Smith and the Founding of Virginia* (1975).

The English Revolution
Christopher Hill, *The Century of Revolution, 1603–1714* (1961), and *The World Turned Upside Down* (1972); Lawrence Stone, *The Causes of the English Revolution, 1529–1642* (1972).

The Carolinas
Verner Crane, *The Southern Frontier, 1670–1732* (1929); Daniel C. Littlefield, *Rice and Slaves: Ethnicity and the Slave Trade in Colonial South Carolina* (1981); H. T. Merrens, *Colonial North Carolina* (1964); M. Eugene Sirmans, *Colonial South Carolina* (1966); Clarence

L. Ver Steeg, *Origins of a Southern Mosaic* (1975); Robert Weir, *Colonial South Carolina* (1982).

Georgia
Harold E. Davis, *The Fledgling Province: Social and Cultural Life in Colonial Georgia, 1733–1776* (1976); Hardy Jackson and Phinizy Spalding, eds., *Forty Years of Diversity: Essays on Colonial Georgia* (1984); Phinizy Spalding, *Oglethorpe in America* (1977).

The British Caribbean
Richard Dunn, *Sugar and Slaves: The Rise of the Planter Class in the English West Indies, 1624–1713* (1972); Gary Puckrein, *Little England: Plantation Society and Anglo-Barbadian Politics, 1627–1700* (1984).

The Spanish Empire in the Southwest
Sherbune F. Cook, *The Conflict Between the California Indian and White Civilization* (1943); Charles Gibson, *Spain in America* (1966); Edward H. Spicer, *Cycles of Conquest: The Impact of Spain, Mexico, and the United States on the Indians of the Southwest, 1533–1960* (1962).

CHAPTER 3

Native Americans and Northern Colonials
James Axtell, *The European and the Indian* (1981), and *The Invasion Within: The Contest of Cultures in Colonial North America* (1985); Charles E. Clark, *The Eastern Frontier: The Settlement of Northern New England, 1610–1763* (1970); William Cronon, *Changes in the Land: Indians, Colonists and the Ecology of New England* (1983); Francis Jennings, *The Ambiguous Iroquois Empire* (1984), and *The Invasion of America* (1975); Douglas Leach, *Flintlock and Tomahawk: New England in King Philip's War* (1958); Calvin Martin, *Keepers of the Game: Indian–Animal Relationships and the Fur Trade* (1978); Daniel K. Richter and James H. Merrell, *Beyond the Covenant Chain: The Iroquois and Their Neighbors in Indian North America, 1600–1800* (1987); Neal Salisbury, *Manitou and Providence: Indians, Europeans and the Making of New England* (1982); Allen W. Trelease, *Indian Affairs in Colonial New York* (1960); Bruce G. Trigger, *The Children of Aataentsic: A History of the Huron People to 1660* (1976); Alden Vaughan, *The New England Frontier* (1965); Anthony F. C. Wallace, *The Death and Rebirth of the Seneca* (1972).

The French in North America
W. J. Eccles, *The Canadian Frontier, 1534–1760* (1969), and *France in America* (1972); Allan Greer, *Peasant, Lord and Merchant: Rural Society in Three Quebec Parishes, 1740–1840* (1985); Richard Colebrook Harris, *The Seigneurial System in Early Canada* (1966); C. E. O'Neill, *Church and State in French Colonial Louisiana* (1966).

New England Puritanism
Francis Bremer, *The Puritan Experiment* (1976); Stephen Foster, *Their Solitary Way: The Puritan Social Ethic in the First Century of Settlement in New England* (1971); Charles Hambrick-Stowe, *The Practice of Piety:*

Puritan Devotional Literature in Seventeenth-Century New England (1982); Robert Middlekauff, *The Mathers* (1971); Perry Miller, *The New England Mind: From Colony to Province* (1953); Edmund S. Morgan, *Visible Saints* (1963); Harry Stout, *The New England Soul* (1986).

The New England Colonies
Paul Boyer and Stephen Nissenbaum, *Salem Possessed: The Social Origins of Witchcraft* (1974); Richard Bushman, *From Puritan to Yankee: Character and the Social Order in Connecticut, 1690–1765* (1967); David Cressy, *Coming Over: Migration and Communication Between England and New England in the Seventeenth Century* (1987); John P. Demos, *Entertaining Satan: Witchcraft and the Culture of Early New England* (1982), and *A Little Commonwealth: Family Life in Plymouth Colony* (1970); Philip Greven, *Four Generations: Land, Population, and Family in Colonial Andover, Massachusetts* (1970); Stephen Innes, *To Labor in a New Land: Economy and Society in Seventeenth-Century Springfield* (1983); Sydney V. James, *Colonial Rhode Island* (1975); Carol Karlsen, *The Devil in the Shape of a Woman: Witchcraft in Colonial New England* (1987); George Langdon, *Pilgrim Colony* (1960); Kenneth Lockridge, *A New England Town: Dedham, Massachusetts, 1636–1737* (1970); Edmund S. Morgan, *The Puritan Dilemma: The Story of John Winthrop* (1958), and *The Puritan Family*, rev. ed. (1966); Darrett Rutman, *Winthrop's Boston* (1965); David E. Stannard, *The Puritan Way of Death* (1977); Laurel Ulrich, *Good Wives: Image and Reality in the Lives of Women in Northern New England, 1650–1750* (1982).

The Middle Colonies
Patricia Bonomi, *A Factious People: Politics and Society in Colonial New York* (1971); Edwin Bronner, *William Penn's "Holy Experiment"* (1962); Thomas J. Condon, *New York Beginnings* (1968); Wesley Frank Craven, *New Jersey and the English Colonization of North America* (1964); Mary Maples Dunn, *William Penn* (1967); Melvin B. Endy, *William Penn and Early Quakerism* (1973); Joseph Illick, *Colonial Pennsylvania* (1976); Michael Kammen, *Colonial New York* (1975); Gary B. Nash, *Quakers and Politics: Pennsylvania, 1681–1726* (1968); J. E. Pomfret, *Colonial New Jersey* (1973); Oliver A. Rink, *Holland on the Hudson: An Economic and Social History of Dutch New York* (1986); Robert C. Ritchie, *The Duke's Province: A Study of Politics and Society in Colonial New York, 1660–1691*; Alan Tully, *William Penn's Legacy* (1977).

The Imperial Connection
Michael Hall, *Edward Randolph and the American Colonies, 1676–1703* (1960); Richard R. Johnson, *Adjustment to Empire* (1981); Michael Kammen, *Empire and Interest: The American Colonies and the Politics of Mercantilism* (1970); David Lovejoy, *The Glorious Revolution in America* (1972); J. M. Sosin, *English America and the Revolution of 1688* (1982); Ian K. Steele, *Politics of Colonial Policy: The Board of Trade in Colonial Administration* (1968); Stephen Saunders Webb, *The Governors–General: The English Army and the Definition of Empire, 1569–1681* (1979).

CHAPTER 4

General Histories
Patricia Bonomi, *Under the Cope of Heaven: Religion, Society, and Politics in Colonial America* (1986); Philip Greven, *The Protestant Temperament: Patterns of Childrearing, Religious Experience, and Self in Early America* (1977); James Henretta, *The Evolution of American Society, 1700–1815* (1973); Stephen Innes, ed., *Work and Labor in Early America* (1988); Alice Hanson Jones, *Wealth of a Nation to Be: The American Colonies on the Eve of the Revolution* (1980); John McCusker and Russell Menard, *The Economy of British America, 1607–1787* (1985); Jackson Turner Main, *The Social Structure of Revolutionary America* (1965); D. W. Meinig, *The Shaping of America: A Geographical Perspective on 500 Years of History*, Vol. 1: *Atlantic America, 1492–1800* (1986); Mary Beth Norton, *Liberty's Daughters: The Revolutionary Experience of American Women, 1750–1800* (1980); Gary M. Walton and James F. Shepherd, *The Economic Rise of Early America* (1979); Robert V. Wells, *The Population of the British Colonies in America Before 1776* (1975).

Immigration
Bernard Bailyn, *Voyagers to the West: A Passage in the Peopling of America on the Eve of the American Revolution* (1986); J. M. Bumsted, *The People's Clearance: Highland Emigration to British North America, 1770–1815* (1982); Jon Butler, *The Huguenots in America* (1983); R. J. Dickson, *Ulster Immigration to Colonial America, 1718–1775* (1966); Ned Landsman, *Scotland and Its First American Colony, 1683–1765* (1985).

Rural Society in Eighteenth-Century America
Charles Grant, *Democracy in the Frontier Town of Kent* (1961); James Henretta, "Farms and Families: Mentalite in Pre-Industrial America," *William and Mary Quarterly* (1978); Christopher M. Jedrey, *The World of John Cleaveland* (1979); Sung Bok Kim, *Landlord and Tenant in Colonial New York* (1978); James T. Lemon, *The Best Poor Man's Country: A Geographical Study of Early Southeastern Pennsylvania* (1972); Gregory Stiverson, *Poverty in the Land of Plenty: Tenancy in Eighteenth-Century Maryland* (1978); Michael Zuckerman, *Peaceable Kingdoms: New England Towns in the Eighteenth Century* (1970).

The Frontier
Richard Aquila, *The Iroquois Restoration: Iroquois Diplomacy on the Colonial Frontier, 1701–1754* (1983); Richard Beeman, *The Evolution of the Southern Backcountry* (1984); Richard M. Brown, *The South Carolina Regulators* (1963); David H. Corkran, *The Cherokee Frontier: Conflict and Survival, 1740–1762* (1962), and *The Creek Frontier, 1540–1783* (1967); Robert D. Mitchell, *Commercialism and Frontier: Perspectives on the Early Shenandoah Valley* (1977); Malcolm J. Rohrbough, *The Trans-Appalachian Frontier* (1978).

Provincial Seaports
Carl Bridenbaugh, *Cities in the Wilderness* (1938), and *Cities in Revolt* (1955); Elaine Forman Crane, *A Dependent People: Newport, Rhode Island in the Revolutionary Era* (1985); Thomas Doerflinger, *A Vigorous Spirit*

of Enterprise: Merchants and Economic Development in Revolutionary Philadelphia (1986); Christine Leigh Heyrman, Commerce and Culture: The Maritime Communities of Colonial Massachusetts, 1690–1750 (1984); Gary B. Nash, The Urban Crucible: Social Change, Political Consciousness, and the Origins of the American Revolution (1979); Jacob M. Price, "Economic Function and the Growth of American Port Towns in the Eighteenth Century," Perspectives in American History (1974); Marcus Rediker, Between the Devil and the Deep Blue Sea: Merchant Seamen, Pirates, and the Anglo-American Maritime Works, 1700–1750 (1987); Frederick B. Tolles, Meetinghouse and Countinghouse: The Quaker Merchants of Colonial Philadelphia (1948); Gerald B. Warden, Boston, 1687–1776 (1970); Stephanie Grauman Wolf, Urban Village: Population, Community, and Family Structure in Germantown, Pennsylvania, 1683–1800 (1976).

Blacks in Eighteenth-Century America
Ira Berlin, "Time, Space, and the Evolution of Afro-American Society in British Mainland America," American Historical Review (1980); Thomas J. Davis, A Rumor of Revolt: The "Great Negro Plot" in Colonial New York (1985); Herbert Gutman, The Black Family in Slavery and Freedom, 1750–1925 (1976); Alan Kulikoff, "The Origins of Afro-American Society in Tidewater Maryland and Virginia, 1700–1790," William and Mary Quarterly (1978); Jean Butenhoff Lee, "The Problem of the Slave Community in the Eighteenth-Century Chesapeake," William and Mary Quarterly (1986); Gerald W. Mullin, Flight and Rebellion: Slave Resistance in Eighteenth-Century Virginia (1972); Jean R. Soderlund, Quakers and Slavery (1985); Betty Wood, Slavery in Colonial Georgia, 1730–1775 (1984).

The Eighteenth-Century South
Carl Bridenbaugh, Myths and Realities: Societies of the Colonial South (1952); Paul G. E. Clemens, The Atlantic Economy and Colonial Maryland's Eastern Shore: From Tobacco to Grain (1980); A. Roger Ekirch, "Poor Carolina": Politics and Society in Colonial North Carolina, 1729–1776 (1981); Rhys Isaac, The Transformation of Virginia, 1740–1790 (1982); Jan Lewis, The Pursuit of Happiness: Family and Values in Jefferson's Virginia (1983); Daniel Blake Smith, Inside the Great House: Planter Family Life in Eighteenth-Century Chesapeake Society (1980); Julia Cherry Spruill, Women's Life and Work in the Southern Colonies (1938); Charles Sydnor, Gentlemen Freeholders: Political Practices in Washington's Virginia (1956).

The Enlightenment
Henry May, The Enlightenment in America (1976); Esmond Wright, Franklin of Philadelphia (1986); Louis B. Wright, The Cultural Life of the American Colonies (1957).

The Great Awakening
Edwin Scott Gaustad, The Great Awakening in New England (1957); Alan Heimert, Religion and the American Mind: From the Great Awakening to the American Revolution (1966); Patricia Tracy, Jonathan Edwards, Pastor (1979).

Colonial Political Development in the Eighteenth Century
Bernard Bailyn, The Origins of American Politics (1968); Edward M. Cook, The Fathers of the Towns: Leadership and Community Structure in Eighteenth-Century New England (1976); Jack P. Greene, The Quest for Power: The Lower Houses of Assembly in the Southern Royal Colonies, 1689–1776 (1963); Robert C. Newbold, The Albany Congress and the Plan of Union of 1754 (1955); Robert Zemsky, Merchants, Farmers, and River Gods: An Essay on Eighteenth Century American Politics (1971).

CHAPTER 5

General Histories
Charles M. Andrews, The Colonial Background of the American Revolution, rev. ed. (1931); Ian Christie and Benjamin Labaree, Empire or Independence, 1760–1776 (1976); Edward Countryman, The American Revolution (1985); Lawrence Henry Gipson, The Coming of the Revolution, 1763–1775 (1954); Edmond S. Morgan, The Birth of the Republic, 1763–1789 (1956); Alfred Young, ed., The American Revolution: Explorations in the History of American Radicalism (1976).

The Seven Years' War
Fred Anderson, A People's Army: Massachusetts Soldiers and Society in the Seven Years War (1984); France Jennings, Empire of Fortune: Crown, Colonies, and Tribes in the Seven Years War in America (1989); Howard H. Peckham, The Colonial Wars, 1689–1762 (1963); Alan Rogers, Empire and Liberty (1974).

British Society and Politics
John Brewer, Party Ideology and Popular Politics at the Accession of George III (1976); John Brooke, King George III (1972); J. C. D. Clark, English Society, 1688–1832 (1985); Bernard Donoughue, British Politics and the American Revolution (1965); M. Dorothy George, London Life in the Eighteenth Century (1965); Lawrence Henry Gipson, The British Empire Before the American Revolution (1936–1970); Michael Kammen, A Rope of Sand: The Colonial Agents, British Politics, and the American Revolution (1968); Lewis B. Namier, England in the Age of the American Revolution, 2d ed. (1961); Richard Pares, King George III and the Politicians (1953); J. H. Plumb, The First Four Georges (1956); W. A. Speck, Stability and Strife: England, 1714–1760 (1979).

The Intellectual Sources of Resistance and Revolution
Bernard Bailyn, The Ideological Origins of the American Revolution (1967); Trevor Colburn, The Lamp of Experience: Whig History and the Intellectual Origins of the American Revolution (1965); Nathan O. Hatch, The Sacred Cause of Liberty: Republican Thought and the Millennium in Revolutionary New England (1977); Isaac Kramnick, Bolingbroke and His Circle: The Politics of Nostalgia in the Age of Walpole (1968); Edmund S. Morgan, The Challenge of the American Revolution (1976), and Inventing the People: The Rise of Popular Sovereignty in England and America (1988); J. G. A. Pocock, The Machiavellian Moment: Florentine Political Thought

and the Atlantic Republican Tradition (1975); Caroline Robbins, *The Eighteenth-Century Commonwealthman: Studies in the Transmission, Development, and Circumstances of English Liberal Thought from the Restoration of Charles II Until the War with the Thirteen Colonies* (1959).

A Decade of Resistance
David Ammerman, *In the Common Cause: The American Response to the Coercive Acts of 1774* (1974); Timothy Breen, *Tobacco Culture: The Mentality of the Great Tidewater Planters on the Eve of the Revolution* (1985); Richard D. Brown, *Revolutionary Politics in Massachusetts: The Boston Committee of Correspondence and the Towns, 1772–1774* (1970); Joseph Ernst, *Money and Politics in America, 1755–1775* (1973); Paul A. Gilje, *The Road to Mobocracy: Popular Disorder in New York City, 1763–1834* (1987); Dirk Hoerder, *Crowd Action in Revolutionary Massachusetts, 1765–1780* (1977); Benjamin Labaree, *The Boston Tea Party* (1964); Pauline Maier, *From Resistance to Revolution* (1972); Edmund S. Morgan and Helen M. Morgan, *The Stamp Act Crisis* (1953); Gregory H. Nobles, *Divisions Throughout the Whole: Politics and Society in Hampshire County, Massachusetts, 1740–1775* (1983); William Penack, *War, Politics, and Revolution in Provincial Massachusetts* (1981); Peter Shaw, *American Patriots and the Rituals of Revolution* (1981); John Shy, *Toward Lexington: The Role of the British Army in the Coming of the American Revolution* (1965); Richard Walsh, *Charleston's Sons of Liberty: A Study of the Artisans, 1763–1789* (1959); Hiller B. Zobel, *The Boston Massacre* (1970).

Leaders of the American Resistance
Richard Beeman, *Patrick Henry* (1982); Eric Foner, *Tom Paine and Revolutionary America* (1976); David Hawke *Paine* (1974); Pauline Maier, *The Old Revolutionaries: Political Lives in the Age of Samuel Adams* (1980); Peter Shaw, *The Character of John Adams* (1976); John J. Waters, *The Otis Family in Provincial and Revolutionary Massachusetts* (1968).

CHAPTER 6

General
John R. Alden, *The American Revolution* (1964); Ira Gruber, *The Howe Brothers and the American Revolution* (1972); Don Higginbotham, *The American War for Independence* (1971); Piers Makesy, *The War for America* (1964); Robert Middlekauff, *The Glorious Cause: The American Revolution, 1763–1789* (1982); John Shy, *A People Numerous and Armed* (1976).

Thomas Jefferson and the Declaration of Independence
Carl Becker, *The Declaration of Independence* (1922); Dumas Malone, *Jefferson the Virginian* (1948); Garry Willis, *Inventing America* (1978).

The Loyalists
Bernard Bailyn, *The Ordeal of Thomas Hutchinson* (1974); Wallace Brown, *The King's Friends* (1966); Robert M. Calhoon, *The Loyalists in Revolutionary America* (1973); Neil MacKinnon, *This Unfriendly Soil: The Loy-*

alist Experience in Nova Scotia, 1783–1791 (1986); Mary Beth Norton, *The British-Americans* (1972).

George Washington and the Continental Army
E. Wayne Carp, *To Starve the Army at Pleasure: Continental Army Administration and American Political Culture, 1775–1783* (1984); James T. Flexner, *George Washington in the American Revolution* (1968); Douglas Southall Freeman, *George Washington* (1948–1957); James Kirby Martin and Mark Lender, *A Respectable Army: The Military Origins of the Republic, 1763–1789* (1982); Charles Royster, *A Revolutionary People at War* (1979).

Diplomacy
Samuel F. Bemis, *The Diplomacy of the American Revolution* (1935); Jonathan R. Dull, *A Diplomatic History of the American Revolution* (1985); Ronald Hoffman and Peter J. Albert, eds., *Peace and the Peacemakers: The Treaty of 1783* (1986); Richard B. Morris, *The Peacemakers: The Great Powers and American Independence* (1965); Gerald Stourzh, *Benjamin Franklin and American Foreign Policy* (rev. ed., 1969).

The North and the American Revolution
Edward Countryman, *A People in Revolution: The American Revolution and Political Society in New York, 1760–1790* (1981); Robert A. Gross, *The Minutemen and Their World* (1976); Robert J. Taylor, *Western Massachusetts in the Revolution* (1954); Donald Wallace White, *A Village at War: Chatham, New Jersey and the American Revolution* (1979); Alfred F. Young, "George Robert Twelves Hewes (1742–1840): A Boston Shoemaker and the Memory of the American Revolution," *William and Mary Quarterly* (1981).

Native Americans and the Revolutionary Frontier
Barbara Graymont, *The Iroquois in the American Revolution* (1972); Isabel Thomson Kelsey, *Joseph Brant, 1743–1807: Man of Two Worlds* (1984); James H. O'Donnell III, *Southern Indians in the American Revolution* (1973); J. M. Sosin, *The Revolutionary Frontier, 1763–1783* (1967).

The South and the American Revolution
John R. Alden, *The South in the Revolution, 1763–1789* (1957); Jeffrey J. Crow and Larry E. Tise, eds., *The Southern Experience in the American Revolution* (1978); Ronald Hoffman, Thad W. Tate, and Peter J. Albert, eds., *An Uncivil War: The Southern Backcountry During the American Revolution* (1985); Jerome J. Nadelhaft, *The Disorders of War: The Revolution in South Carolina* (1981).

The Black Experience and the American Revolution
Ira Berlin and Ronald Hoffman, eds., *Slavery and Freedom in the Age of the American Revolution* (1983); Jeffrey Crow, "Slave Rebelliousness and Social Conflict in North Carolina, 1775–1802," *William and Mary Quarterly* (1980); David Brion Davis, *The Problem of Slavery in the Age of Revolution* (1975); Duncan MacLeod, *Slavery, Race, and the American Revolution* (1974); Benjamin Quarles, *The Negro in the American Revolution* (1961).

Women and the American Revolution
Joy Day Buel and Richard Buel, Jr., *The Way of Duty: A Woman and Her Family in Revolutionary America* (1984); Linda Grant DePauw, *Founding Mothers* (1975); Linda Kerber, *Women of the Republic: Intellect and Ideology in Revolutionary America* (1980).

CHAPTER 7

General
Forrest McDonald, *E Pluribus Unum: The Formation of the American Republic, 1776–1790* (1965); Curtis P. Nettels, *The Emergence of a National Economy, 1775–1815* (1962); Robert R. Palmer, *The Age of Democratic Revolution: A Political History of Europe and America, 1760–1800* (1959, 1964); Gordon Wood, *The Creation of the American Republic* (1969).

State Politics and State Constitutions
Willi Paul Adams, *The First American Constitutions* (1980); Ronald Hoffman and Peter Albert, eds., *Sovereign States in an Age of Uncertainty* (1981); Jackson Turner Main, *The Sovereign States, 1775–1783* (1973), and *Political Parties Before the Constitution* (1973); Stephen E. Patterson, *Political Parties in Revolutionary Massachusetts* (1973); David Szatmary, *Shays' Rebellion: The Making of an Agrarian Insurrection* (1980).

The Articles of Confederation
Joseph L. Davis, *Sectionalism in American Politics, 1774–1787* (1977); E. James Ferguson, *The Power of the Purse: A History of American Public Finance, 1776–1790* (1961); H. James Henderson, *Party Politics in the Continental Congress* (1974); Merrill D. Jensen, *The Articles of Confederation*, rev. ed. (1959), and *The New Nation* (1950); Peter S. Onuf, *The Origins of the Federal Republic: Jurisdictional Controversies in the United States, 1775–1787* (1983); Jack N. Rakove, *The Beginnings of National Politics* (1979).

Society in the New Republic
Nancy Cott, "Divorce and the Changing Status of Women in Massachusetts," *William and Mary Quarterly* (1976); Joseph J. Ellis, *After the Revolution: Profiles of Early American Culture* (1979); Jay Fliegelman, *Prodigals and Pilgrims: The American Revolution Against Patriarchal Authority, 1750–1800* (1982); J. Franklin Jameson, *The American Revolution Considered as a Social Movement* (1962); Benjamin W. Labaree, *The Merchants of Newburyport, 1764–1815* (1962); Jan Lewis, "The Republican Wife: Virtue and Seduction in the Early Republic," *William and Mary Quarterly* (1987); Forrest McDonald and Ellen Shapiro McDonald, "The Ethnic Origins of the American People, 1790," *William and Mary Quarterly* (1980); Donald L. Robinson, *Slavery in the Structure of American Politics, 1765–1820* (1971); Howard Rock, *Artisans of the New Republic: Tradesmen of New York City in the Age of Jefferson* (1979); Charles G. Steffen, *The Mechanics of Baltimore: Workers and Politics in the Age of Revolution, 1763–1812* (1984); Lynne Withey, *Dearest Friend: A Life of Abigail Adams* (1981); Arthur Zilversmit, *The First Emancipation: The Abolition of Slavery in the North* (1967).

The Federal Constitution
Douglass Adair, *Fame and the Founding Fathers* (1974);

Lance Banning, "James Madison and the Nationalists, 1780–1783," *William and Mary Quarterly* (1983); Charles Beard, *An Economic Interpretation of the Constitution of the United States* (1913); Richard Beeman, Stephen Botein, and Edward C. Carter II, eds., *Beyond Confederation: Origins of the Constitution and American National Identity* (1987); Irving Brant, *James Madison: The Nationalist, 1780–1787* (1948); Robert E. Brown, *Charles Beard and the Constitution* (1956); Linda Grant DePauw, *The Eleventh Pillar: New York State and the Federal Constitution* (1966); John P. Diggins, *The Lost Soul of American Politics: Virtue, Self-Interest, and the Foundations of Liberalism* (1984); Max Farrand, *The Framing of the Constitution* (1913); Ralph Ketcham, *James Madison* (1971); Leonard Levy, ed., *Essays on the Making of the Constitution* (1969); Staughton Lynd, *Class Conflict, Slavery, and the United States Constitution* (1967); Forrest McDonald, *We the People: The Economic Origins of the Constitution* (1958), and *Novus Ordo Seclorum: The Intellectual Origins of the Constitution* (1985); Clinton Rossiter, *1787: The Grand Convention* (1973); Gerald Stourzh, *Alexander Hamilton and the Idea of Republican Government* (1970); Garry Wills, *Explaining America: The Federalist* (1981).

The Anti-Federalists
Cecilia Kenyon, "Men of Little Faith: The Anti-Federalists and the Nature of Representative Government," *William and Mary Quarterly* (1955); Jackson Turner Main, *The Anti-Federalists* (1981); Robert A. Rutland, *The Ordeal of the Constitution: The Anti-Federalists and the Ratification Struggle of 1787–88* (1966).

CHAPTER 8

Society
Nancy F. Cott, *The Bonds of Womanhood: "Woman's Sphere" in New England, 1780–1835* (1977); J. Hector St. John de Crèvecoeur, *Letters from an American Farmer* (1782, paper 1981); Joseph J. Ellis, *After the Revolution: Profiles of Early American Culture* (1979); Benjamin Franklin, *The Autobiography and Other Writings* (1986); Reginald Horsman, *The Frontier in the Formative Years, 1783–1815* (1970); Malcolm J. Rohrbough, *The Trans-Appalachian Frontier: Peoples, Societies, and Institutions, 1775–1850* (1978); Charles G. Steffen, *The Mechanics of Baltimore: Workers and Politics in the Age of Revolution, 1763–1812* (1984).

National Government
Ralph Adams Brown, *The Presidency of John Adams* (1975); Manning J. Dauer, *The Adams Federalists* (1953); Richard Hofstadter, *The Idea of a Party System: The Rise of Legitimate Opposition in the United States, 1780–1840* (1969); Richard H. Kohn, *Eagle and Sword: The Federalists and the Creation of a Military Establishment in America, 1783–1802* (1975); Stephan G. Kurtz, *The Presidency of John Adams: The Collapse of Federalism 1795–1800* (1957); Forrest McDonald, *The Presidency of George Washington* (1974); John C. Miller, *The Foundation Era, 1789–1801* (1960).

Party Politics
Richard Beeman, *The Old Dominion and the New Nation, 1788–1801* (1972); William Nisbet Chambers, *Political Parties in the New Nation: The American Experi-*

ence (1963); Joseph Charles, *The Origins of the American Party System* (1956); Noble Cunningham, *The Jeffersonian Republicans: The Formation of Party Organization, 1789–1801* (1957); Paul Goodman, *The Democratic Republicans of Massachusetts* (1964); John F. Hoadley, *Origins of American Political Parties, 1789–1803* (1986); Norman Risjord, *Chesapeake Politics, 1781–1800* (1978); Thomas P. Slaughter, *The Whiskey Rebellion: Frontier Epilogue to the American Revolution* (1986); Alfred Young, *The Democratic Republicans of New York: The Origins, 1763–1797* (1967).

Party Ideology
Joyce Appleby, *Capitalism and a New Social Order: The Republican Vision of the 1790s* (1984); Lance Banning, *The Jeffersonian Persuasion: The Evolution of a Party Ideology* (1978); Richard W. Buel, Jr., *Securing the Republic: Ideology in American Politics, 1789–1815* (1972); Drew R. McCoy, *The Elusive Republic: Political Economy in Jeffersonian America* (1980); John R. Nelson, Jr., *Liberty and Property: Political Economy and Policymaking in the New Nation, 1789–1812* (1987); Gerald Stourzh, *Alexander Hamilton and the Idea of Republican Government* (1970); John Zvesper, *Political Philosophy and Rhetoric: A Study of the Origins of Party Politics* (1977).

Constitutional Developments
Leonard Levy, *Legacy of Suppression: Freedom of Speech and Press in Early American History* (1960); Robert A. Rutland, *The Birth of the Bill of Rights, 1776–1791* (1955); Bernard Schwartz, *The Great Rights of Mankind: A History of the American Bill of Rights* (1977); James M. Smith, *Freedom's Fetters: The Alien and Sedition Laws and American Civil Liberties* (1956).

Foreign Policy
Harry Ammon, *The Genet Mission* (1973); Jerald Combs, *The Jay Treaty: Political Battleground of the Founding Fathers* (1970); Alexander DeConde, *Entangling Alliance: Politics and Diplomacy Under George Washington* (1958), and *The Quasi-War: The Politics and Diplomacy of the Undeclared War with France, 1797–1801* (1966); Felix Gilbert, *To the Farewell Address: Ideas of Early American Foreign Policy* (1961); Bradford Perkins, *The First Rapprochement: England and the United States, 1795–1805* (1955); William Stinchcombe, *The XYZ Affair* (1980); Paul A. Varg, *Foreign Policies of the Founding Fathers* (1963).

Biographies
Gay Wilson Allen and Roger Asselineau, *St. John de Crèvecoeur: The Life of an American Farmer* (1987); Irving Brant, *James Madison: Father of the Constitution, 1787–1800* (1950); Jacob E. Cooke, *Alexander Hamilton* (1982); Marcus Cunliffe, *George Washington: Man and Monument* (1958); John C. Miller, *Alexander Hamilton: Portrait in Paradox* (1959); Merrill Peterson, *Thomas Jefferson and the New Nation* (1970); Page Smith, *John Adams* (1962); Garry Wills, *Cincinnatus: George Washington and the Enlightenment* (1984).

CHAPTER 9

General Histories
Richard Hofstadter, *The Idea of a Party System: The Rise of Legitimate Opposition in the United States, 1780–1840* (1969); George Dangerfield, *The Era of Good Feelings* (1952), and *The Awakening of American Nationalism, 1815–1828* (1965); Marshall Smelser, *The Democratic Republic, 1801–1815* (1968); James Sterling Young, *The Washington Community, 1800–1828* (1966).

Biographies
Harry Ammon, *James Monroe: The Quest for National Identity* (1979); Leonard Baker, *John Marshall: A Life in Law* (1974); Samuel F. Bemis, *John Quincy Adams and the Foundations of American Foreign Policy* (1949); Noble E. Cunningham, Jr., *In Pursuit of Reason: The Life of Thomas Jefferson* (1987); Ralph Ketcham, *James Madison: A Biography* (1971); Dumas Malone, *Jefferson the President: First Term, 1801–1805* (1970), and *Jefferson the President: Second Term, 1805–1809* (1974); Drew R. McCoy, *The Last of the Fathers: James Madison and the Republican Legacy* (1989); Merrill Peterson, *Thomas Jefferson and the New Nation: A Biography* (1970); Robert Remini, *Andrew Jackson and the Course of American Empire, 1767–1821* (1977).

Jeffersonians in Power
Alexander Balinky, *Albert Gallatin: Fiscal Theories and Policy* (1958); James Banner, *To the Hartford Convention: The Federalists and the Origins of Party Politics in the Early Republic, 1789–1815* (1970); Noble E. Cunningham, Jr., *The Jeffersonian Republicans in Power: Party Operations, 1801–1809* (1963), and *The Process of Government Under Jefferson* (1978); David Hackett Fischer, *The Revolution of American Conservatism: The Federalist Party in the Era of Jeffersonian Democracy* (1965); Paul Goodman, *The Democratic Republicans of Massachusetts* (1964); Linda K. Kerber, *Federalists in Dissent: Imagery and Ideology in Jeffersonian America* (1970); Drew R. McCoy, *The Elusive Republic: Political Economy in Jeffersonian America* (1980); Norman K. Risjord, *The Old Republicans: Southern Conservatism in the Age of Jefferson* (1965); Howard Rock, *Artisans of the New Republic: The Tradesman of New York City in the Age of Thomas Jefferson* (1979).

Indian Affairs and Western Expansion
John Boles, *The Great Revival in the South, 1787–1805* (1972); R. David Edmunds, *The Shawnee Prophet* (1983), and *Tecumseh and the Quest for Indian Leadership* (1984); Reginald Horsman, *Expansion and American Indian Policy, 1783–1812* (1967), and *The Frontier in the Formative Years, 1783–1815* (1970); Donald Jackson, *Thomas Jefferson and the Stony Mountains: Exploring the West from Monticello* (1979); Malcolm J. Rohrbough, *The Trans-Appalachian Frontier: Peoples, Societies, and Institutions, 1775–1850* (1978); Henry Savage, Jr., *Discovering America, 1700–1875* (1979); Bernard W. Sheehan, *Seeds of Extinction: Jeffersonian Philanthropy and the American Indians* (1973).

The Judiciary
Richard E. Ellis, *The Jeffersonian Crisis: Courts and Politics in the Early Republic* (1971); Robert K. Faulkner, *The Jurisprudence of John Marshall* (1968); Morton J. Horowitz, *The Transformation of American Law, 1780–1860* (1977); R. K. Newmyer, *The Supreme Court Under Marshall and Taney* (1968).

Foreign Affairs and the War of 1812
Roger H. Brown, *The Republic in Peril: 1812* (1964); Harry L. Coles, *The War of 1812* (1965); Alexander DeConde, *This Affair of Louisiana* (1976); Reginald Horsman, *The War of 1812* (1969); Ernest R. May, *The Making of the Monroe Doctrine* (1976); Bradford Perkins, *First Rapprochement: England and the United States, 1795–1805* (1955), and *Prologue to War: England and the United States, 1805–1812* (1961); Robert A. Rutland, *Madison's Alternatives: The Jeffersonian Republicans and the Coming of War, 1805–1812* (1975); J. C. A. Stagg, *Mr. Madison's War: Politics, Diplomacy, and Warfare in the Early Republic, 1783–1830* (1983).

CHAPTER 10

General Histories
W. Elliot Brownlee, *Dynamics of Ascent: A History of the American Economy* (1974); Stuart Bruchey, *The Roots of American Economic Growth, 1607–1861* (1965); Douglass C. North, *The Economic Growth of the United States, 1790–1860* (1961).

Transportation
Carter Goodrich, *Government Promotion of American Canals and Railroads* (1960); Erik F. Haites et al., *Western River Transportation: The Era of Early Internal Development, 1810–1860* (1975); Louis C. Hunter, *Steamboats on the Western Rivers: An Economic and Technological History* (1949); Philip D. Jordan, *The National Road* (1948); Harry N. Scheiber, *Ohio Canal Era: A Case Study of Government and the Economy, 1820–1861* (1969); Ronald E. Shaw, *Erie Water West: A History of the Erie Canal* (1966); George R. Taylor, *The Transportation Revolution, 1815–1860* (1951).

Industrialization
Alfred D. Chandler, Jr., *The Visible Hand: Managerial Revolution in American Business* (1977); Thomas C. Cochran, *Frontiers of Change: Early Industrialism in America* (1981); Robert F. Dalzell, Jr., *Enterprising Elite: The Boston Associates and the World They Made* (1987); Constance M. Green, *Eli Whitney and the Birth of American Technology* (1956); David J. Jeremy, *Transatlantic Industrial Revolution: The Diffusion of Textile Technology Between Britain and America, 1790–1830* (1981); Nathan Rosenberg, *Technology and American Economic Growth* (1972); Peter Temin, *Iron and Steel in Nineteenth Century America* (1964); Caroline F. Ware, *The Early New England Cotton Manufacture* (1931).

Agriculture
Percy W. Bidwell and John Falconer, *History of Agriculture in the Northern United States* (1925); Clarence Danhof, *Changes in Agriculture: The Northern United States, 1820–1870* (1969); Paul W. Gates, *The Farmer's Age: Agriculture, 1815–1860* (1960); Lewis C. Gray, *History of Agriculture in the Southern United States* (1933).

Workers and Community Studies
Stuart M. Blumin, *The Urban Threshold: Growth and Change in a Nineteenth-Century American Community* (1976); Thomas Dublin, *Women at Work: The Transformation of Work and Community in Lowell, Massachusetts, 1826–1860* (1979); Paul G. Faler, *Mechanics and Manufacturers in the Early Industrial Revolution: Lynn, Massachusetts, 1780–1860* (1981); Bruce Laurie, *Working People of Philadelphia, 1800–1850* (1980), and *Artisans into Workers: Labor in Nineteenth-Century America* (1989); Brian C. Mitchell, *The Paddy Camps: The Irish of Lowell, 1821–61* (1988); Jonathan Prude, *The Coming of Industrial Order: Town and Factory Life in Rural Massachusetts, 1810–1860* (1983); W. J. Rorabaugh, *The Craft Apprentice: From Franklin to the Machine Age in America* (1986); Steven J. Ross, *Workers on the Edge: Work, Leisure, and Politics in Industrializing Cincinnati, 1788–1890* (1985); Christine Stansell, *City of Women: Sex and Class in New York, 1789–1860* (1986); Sean Wilentz, *Chants Democratic: New York City and the Rise of the American Working Class, 1788–1850* (1984).

Society and Values
Daniel J. Boorstin, *The Americans: The National Experience* (1965); Michel Chevalier, *Society, Manners and Politics in the United States* (1839, reprinted 1961), Russel B. Nye, *Society and Culture in America, 1830–1860* (1974); Edward Pessen, *Jacksonian America: Society, Personality, and Politics*, rev. ed. (1978), and *Riches, Class, and Power Before the Civil War* (1973); Alexis de Tocqueville, *Democracy in America* (1945 ed.).

Land and the West
John Mack Faragher, *Sugar Creek: Life on the Illinois Prairie* (1986); Roy M. Robbins, *Our Landed Heritage: The Public Domain* (1942); Malcolm J. Rohrbough, *The Land Office Business: The Settlement and Administration of American Public Lands, 1789–1837* (1968); Dale Van Every, *The Final Challenge: The American Frontier, 1804–1845* (1964); Richard C. Wade, *The Urban Frontier: The Rise of Western Cities, 1790–1840* (1973); David J. Wishart, *The Fur Trade of the American West, 1817–1840* (1979).

Politics and Law
George Dangerfield, *The Awakening of American Nationalism, 1815–1828* (1965); Robert K. Faulkner, *The Jurisprudence of John Marshall* (1968); Morton J. Horwitz, *The Transformation of American Law, 1780–1860* (1977); Glover Moore, *The Missouri Controversy, 1819–1821* (1953); R. Kent Newmyer, *The Supreme Court Under Marshall and Taney* (1968); M. N. Rothbard, *The Panic of 1819: Reactions and Policies* (1962); Charles Sydnor, *The Development of Southern Sectionalism, 1819–1848* (1948).

CHAPTER 11

General Histories
George Dangerfield, *The Awakening of American Nationalism, 1815–1828* (1965); Edward Pessen, *Jacksonian America: Society, Personality, and Politics*, rev. ed. (1978); Arthur Schlesinger, Jr., *The Age of Jackson* (1945); Glyndon G. Van Deusen, *The Jacksonian Era, 1828–1845* (1959).

Biographies
Samuel F. Bemis, *John Quincy Adams and the Union* (1956); Gerald M. Capers, *John C. Calhoun, Opportunist* (1960); Donald Cole, *Martin Van Buren and the American Political System* (1984); Richard N. Current,

Daniel Webster and the Rise of National Conservativism (1955); Thomas P. Govan, *Nicholas Biddle: Nationalist and Public Banker* (1959); John Niven, *John C. Calhoun and the Price of Union: A Biography* (1988), and *Martin Van Buren: The Romantic Age of American Politics* (1983); Merrill D. Peterson, *The Great Triumvirate: Webster, Clay, and Calhoun* (1987); Robert V. Remini, *Andrew Jackson and the Course of American Freedom, 1822–1832* (1981), and *Andrew Jackson and the Course of American Democracy, 1833–1845* (1984); Glyndon G. Van Deusen, *The Life of Henry Clay* (1937); Charles W. Wiltse, *John C. Calhoun, Nullifier, 1829–1839* (1949).

Society and Values
Michel Chevalier, *Society, Manners, and Politics in the United States* (1961); Charles Dickens, *American Notes for General Circulation* (1842, reprinted 1972); Francis J. Grund, *Aristocracy in America* (1839, reprinted 1959); Harriet Martineau, *Society in America* (1837); Douglas T. Miller, *Jacksonian Aristocracy: Class and Democracy in New York, 1830–1860* (1967); Russel B. Nye, *Society and Culture in America, 1830–1860* (1960); Edward Pessen, *Riches, Class, and Power Before the Civil War* (1973); Alexis de Tocqueville, *Democracy in America* (1945); Frances Trollope, *Domestic Manners of the Americans* (1832, reprinted 1984); John William Ward, *Andrew Jackson: Symbol for an Age* (1955).

The Emergence of Democracy
James S. Chase, *Emergence of the Presidential Nominating Convention, 1789–1832* (1973); Richard Hofstadter, *The Idea of a Party System: The Rise of Legitimate Opposition in the United States, 1780–1840* (1969); Richard P. McCormick, *The Presidential Game: The Origins of American Presidential Politics* (1982); Chilton Williamson, *American Suffrage from Property to Democracy, 1760–1860* (1960).

The Jacksonian Party System
Lee Benson, *The Concept of Jacksonian Democracy: New York as a Test Case* (1961); James C. Curtis, *The Fox at Bay: Martin Van Buren and the Presidency, 1837–1841* (1970); Paul Goodman, *Towards a Christian Republic: Antimasonry and the Great Transition in New England, 1826–1836* (1988); Robert G. Gunderson, *The Log Cabin Campaign* (1957); Mary W. M. Hargreaves, *The Presidency of John Quincy Adams* (1985); Daniel Walker Howe, *The Political Culture of the American Whigs* (1979); Lawrence Frederick Kohl, *The Politics of Individualism: Parties and the American Character in the Jacksonian Era* (1988); Richard B. Latner, *the Presidency of Andrew Jackson: White House Politics, 1829–1837* (1979); Richard P. McCormick, *The Second American Party System: Party Formation in the Jacksonian Era* (1966); Marvin Meyers, *The Jacksonian Persuasion: Politics and Belief* (1957); Robert Remini, *The Election of Andrew Jackson* (1963).

Banking and the Economy
Bray Hammond, *Banks and Politics in America from the Revolution to the Civil War* (1957); John M. McFaul, *The Politics of Jacksonian Finance* (1972); Robert Remini, *Andrew Jackson and the Bank War* (1967); William G. Shade, *Banks or No Banks: The Money Issue in Western Politics, 1832–1865* (1972); James Roger Sharp, *The Jacksonians Versus the Banks: Politics in the States*

After the Panic of 1837 (1970); Peter Temin, *The Jacksonian Economy* (1969).

Nullification
Richard Ellis, *The Union at Risk: Jacksonian Democracy, States' Rights and the Nullification Crisis* (1987); William W. Freehling, *Prelude to Civil War: The Nullification Controversy in South Carolina* (1966); Merrill D. Peterson, *Olive Branch and Sword: The Compromise of 1833* (1982); Charles S. Sydnor, *The Development of Southern Sectionalism, 1819–1848* (1948).

Indian Removal
Arthur H. DeRosier, Jr., *The Removal of the Choctaw Indians* (1970); Michael D. Green, *The Politics of Indian Removal: Creek Government and Society in Crisis* (1982); John K. Mahon, *History of the Second Seminole War, 1835–1842* (1967); William G. McLoughlin, *Cherokee Renascence in the New Republic* (1986); Francis P. Prucha, *American Indian Policy in the Formative Years* (1962); Ronald N. Satz, *American Indian Policy in the Jacksonian Era* (1975).

CHAPTER 12

General Histories
Perry Miller, *The Life of the Mind in America: From the Revolution to the Civil War* (1966); Russel B. Nye, *Society and Culture in America, 1830–1860* (1974); Alice Tyler, *Freedom's Ferment: Phases of American Social History from the Colonial Period to the Outbreak of Civil War* (1944); Ronald G. Walters, *American Reformers, 1815–1860* (1978).

Revivalism
Whitney R. Cross, *The Burned-Over District: The Social and Intellectual History of Enthusiastic Religion in Western New York, 1800–1850* (1950); Paul Johnson, *A Shopkeeper's Millennium: Society and Revivals in Rochester, New York, 1815–1837* (1978); William G. McLoughlin, *Modern Revivalism: Charles Grandison Finney to Billy Graham* (1959).

Women's Sphere and Feminism
Nancy F. Cott, *The Bonds of Womanhood: "Woman's Sphere" in New England, 1780–1835* (1977); Carl Degler, *At Odds: Women and the Family in America from the Revolution to the Present* (1980); Ann Douglas, *The Feminization of American Culture* (1977); Ellen C. DuBois, *Feminism and Suffrage: The Emergence of an Independent Women's Movement in America, 1848–1869* (1978); Keith E. Melder, *Beginnings of Sisterhood: The American Women's Rights Movement, 1800–1850* (1977); James Reed, *From Private Vice to Public Virtue: The Birth Control Movement in America* (1978); Mary P. Ryan, *Cradle of the Middle Class: The Family in Oneida County, New York, 1790–1865* (1981); Nancy Woloch, *Women and the American Experience* (1984).

American Romanticism
Paul F. Boller, Jr., *American Transcendentalism, 1830–1860: An Intellectual Inquiry* (1974); F. O. Matthiessen, *American Renaissance: Art and Expression in the Age of Emerson and Whitman* (1941); Anne C. Rose, *Transcendentalism as a Social Movement, 1830–1850* (1981).

Utopian Communities
Arthur Bestor, *Backwoods Utopias: The Sectarian and Owenite Phases of Communitarian Socialism in America, 1663–1829* (1950); Maren L. Carden, *Oneida: Utopian Community to Modern Corporation* (1971); Henri Destroche, *The American Shakers from Neo-Christianity to Pre-Socialism* (1971); Lawrence Foster, *Religion and Sexuality: Three American Communal Experiments of the Nineteenth Century* (1981); J. F. C. Harrison, *Quest for the New Moral World: Robert Owen and the Owenites in Britain and America* (1969); Louis Kern, *An Ordered Love: Sex Roles and Sexuality in Victorian Utopias* (1981).

Reform Movements
Lawrence A. Cremin, *American Education: The National Experience* (1980); Ellen Dwyer, *Homes for the Mad: Life Inside Two Nineteenth-Century Asylums* (1987); Barbara Leslie Epstein, *The Politics of Domesticity: Women, Evangelism, and Temperance in Nineteenth-Century America* (1981); Carl F. Kaestle, *Pillars of the Republic: Common Schools and American Society, 1780–1860* (1983); Stephen Nissenbaum, *Sex, Diet, and Debility in Jacksonian America: Sylvester Graham and Health Reform* (1980); W. J. Rorabaugh, *The Alcoholic Republic: An American Tradition* (1979); David Rothman, *The Discovery of the Asylum: Social Order and Disorder in the New Republic* (1971); Ian R. Tyrrell, *Sobering Up: From Temperance to Prohibition in Antebellum America, 1800–1860* (1979); Rush Welter, *Popular Education and Democratic Thought in America* (1962).

Abolitionism
R. J. M. Blackett, *Building an Antislavery Wall: Black Americans in the Abolitionist Movement, 1830–1860* (1983); Aileen Kraditor, *Means and Ends in American Abolitionism: Garrison and His Critics on Strategy and Tactics, 1834–1850* (1967); Donald G. Mathews, *Slavery and Methodism* (1965); John R. McKivigan, *The War Against Proslavery Religion: Abolitionism and the Northern Churches* (1984); Russel B. Nye, *Fettered Freedom: Civil Liberties and the Slavery Controversy, 1830–1860*, rev. ed. (1963); Benjamin Quarles, *Black Abolitionists* (1969); Leonard Richards, *"Gentlemen of Property and Standing": Anti-Abolition Mobs in Jacksonian America* (1970); James B. Stewart, *Holy Warriors: The Abolitionists and American Slavery* (1976).

Biographies
Robert Abzug, *Passionate Liberator: Theodore Dwight Weld and the Dilemma of Reform* (1980); Lois Banner, *Elizabeth Cady Stanton: A Radical for Woman's Rights* (1980); Betty Fladeland, *James Gillespie Birney: Slaveholder to Abolitionist* (1955); Keith J. Hardman, *Charles Grandison Finney, 1792–1875: Revivalist and Reformer* (1987); Nathan Huggins, *Slave and Citizen: The Life of Frederick Douglass* (1980); Gerda Lerner, *The Grimké Sisters of South Carolina: Rebels Against Slavery* (1967); Katherine Kish Sklar, *Catharine Beecher: A Study in American Domesticity* (1973); James Brewer Stewart, *Wendell Phillips: Liberty's Hero* (1986); John L. Thomas, *The Liberator: William Lloyd Garrison* (1963); Robert D. Thomas, *The Man Who Would Be Perfect: John Humphrey Noyes and the Utopian Impulse* (1977); Bertram Wyatt-Brown, *Lewis Tappan and the Evangelical War Against Slavery* (1969).

CHAPTER 13

General Histories
Monroe Billington, *The American South* (1971); Clement Eaton, *A History of the Old South*, 3d ed. (1975); Charles S. Sydnor, *The Development of Southern Sectionalism, 1819–1848* (1948).

Southern Society
Ira Berlin, *Slaves Without Masters: The Free Negro in the Antebellum South* (1976); Dickson D. Bruce, Jr., *Violence and Culture in the Antebellum South* (1979); Everett Dick, *The Dixie Frontier: A Social History of the Southern Frontier from the First Transmontane Beginnings to the Civil War* (1948); Clement Eaton, *The Growth of the Southern Civilization, 1790–1860* (1961); Drew Gilpin Faust, *James Henry Hammond and the South: A Design for Mastery* (1967); John Hope Franklin, *The Militant South, 1800–1861* (1956); Lewis C. Gray, *History of Agriculture in the Southern United States to 1860* (1933); J. William Harris, *Plain Folk and Gentry in a Slave Society: White Liberty and Black Slavery in Augusta's Hinterlands* (1985); Michael P. Johnson and James L. Roark, *Black Masters: A Free Family of Color in the Old South* (1984); Donald G. Mathews, *Religion in the Old South* (1977); John Hebron Moore, *The Emergence of the Cotton Kingdom in the Old Southwest: Mississippi, 1770–1860* (1988); James Oakes, *The Ruling Race: A History of American Slaveholders* (1982); Frederick Law Olmsted, *The Cotton Kingdom* (1861, reprinted 1984); Frank L. Owsley, *Plain Folk of the Old South* (1949); Theodore Rosengarten, *Tombee: Portrait of a Cotton Planter* (1986); Steven M. Stowe, *Intimacy and Power in the Old South: Ritual in the Lives of the Planters* (1987); Gavin Wright, *The Political Economy of the Cotton South: Households, Markets, and Wealth in the Nineteenth Century* (1978); Bertram Wyatt-Brown, *Honor and Violence in the Old South* (1986).

Southern Women
Jane Turner Censer, *North Carolina Planters and Their Children, 1800–1860* (1984); Catherine Clinton, *The Plantation Mistress: Woman's World in the Old South* (1983); Elizabeth Fox-Genovese, *Within the Plantation Household: Black and White Women of the Old South* (1988); Frances Anne Kemble, *Journal of the Residence on a Georgian Plantation in 1838–1839* (1863, reprinted 1961); Suzanne Lebsock, *Free Women of Petersburg: Status and Culture in a Southern Town, 1784–1860* (1984); Anne Firor Scott, *The Southern Lady: From Pedestal to Politics, 1830–1930* (1970); Deborah G. White, *Ar'n't I a Woman? Female Slaves in the Plantation South* (1985); C. Vann Woodward, ed., *Mary Chesnut's Civil War* (1981).

Slavery
Carl N. Degler, *Neither Black Nor White: Slavery and Race Relations in Brazil and the United States* (1971); Ulrich B. Phillips, *American Negro Slavery* (1918), and *Life and Labor in the Old South* (1929); Kenneth M. Stampp, *The Peculiar Institution: Slavery in the Antebellum South* (1956); Robert S. Starobin, *Industrial Slavery in the Old South* (1970); William L. Van Deburg, *The Slave Drivers: Black Agricultural Labor Supervisors in the Antebellum South* (New York, 1988); Richard C. Wade, *Slavery in the Cities* (1964).

Slave Culture

John W. Blassingame, *The Slave Community: Plantation Life in the Ante-Bellum South*, rev. ed. (1979); Frederick Douglass, *My Bondage and My Freedom* (1855, reprint 1969); Eugene D. Genovese, *Roll, Jordan, Roll: The World the Slaves Made* (1974); Herbert G. Gutman, *The Black Family in Slavery and Freedom, 1750–1925* (1976); Charles Joyner, *Down by the Riverside: A South Carolina Slave Community* (1984); Lawrence Levine, *Black Culture and Black Consciousness: Afro-American Folk Thought from Slavery to Freedom* (1977); Albert J. Raboteau, *Slave Religion: The "Invisible Institution" in the Antebellum South* (1978); Sterling Stuckey, *Slave Culture: Nationalist Theory and the Foundations of Black America* (1987).

The Defense of Slavery

William J. Cooper, Jr., *The South and the Politics of Slavery, 1828–1856* (1978); Clement Eaton, *Freedom of Thought in the Old South* (1940); Drew Gilpin Faust, *A Sacred Circle: The Dilemma of the Intellectual in the Old South* (1977); George M. Fredrickson, *The Black Image in the White Mind: The Debate on Afro-American Character and Destiny, 1817–1914* (1971); Alison Goodyear Freehling, *Drift Toward Dissolution: The Virginia Slavery Debate of 1831–1832* (1982); Kenneth S. Greenberg, *Masters and Statesmen: The Political Culture of American Slavery* (1985).

CHAPTER 14

General Histories

Ray A. Billington, *The Far Western Frontier, 1830–1860* (1956); Ray A Billington and Martin Ridge, *Westward Expansion*, 5th ed. (1982); Frederick Merk, *History of the Westward Movement* (1978).

American Expansionism

Bernard De Voto, *The Year of Decision: 1846* (1943); John Mack Faragher, *Women and Men on the Overland Trail* (1979); Norman A. Graebner, *Empire on the Pacific: A Study of American Continental Expansionism* (1955); Thomas R. Hietala, *Manifest Design: Anxious Aggrandizement in Late Jacksonian America* (1985); Reginald Horsman, *Race and Manifest Destiny: The Origins of American Racial Anglo-Saxonism* (1981); Frederick Merk, *Manifest Destiny and Mission in American History* (1963), *The Monroe Doctrine and American Expansionism, 1843–1849* (1966), and *The Oregon Question: Essays in Anglo-American Diplomacy and Politics* (1967); John D. Unruh, Jr., *The Plains Across: The Overland Emigrants and the Trans-Mississippi West, 1840–60* (1979).

Societies in the West

Leonard J. Arrington, *Great Basin Kingdom: An Economic History of the Latter-Day Saints* (1958); Leonard J. Arrington and Davis Bitton, *The Mormon Experience: A History of the Latter-Day Saints* (1979); Gunther Barth, *Instant Cities: Urbanization and the Rise of San Francisco and Denver* (1975); William C. Binkley, *The Texas Revolution* (1952); John W. Caughey, *Gold is the Cornerstone* (1948); Malcolm Clark, Jr., *Eden Seekers: The Settlement of Oregon, 1812–1862* (1981); Robert F. Heizer and Alan J. Almquist, *The Other Californians: Prejudice and Discrimination under Spain, Mexico, and* *the United States to 1920* (1971); Donald D. Jackson, *Gold Dust* (1980); Julie Roy Jeffrey, *Frontier Women: The Trans-Mississippi West, 1840–1860* (1979); Dorothy O. Johansen and Charles M. Gates, *Empire on the Columbia: A History of the Pacific Northwest*, 2d ed. (1967); Sandra L. Myres, *Westering Women and the Frontier Experience, 1800–1915* (1982); Rodman Paul, *California Gold: The Beginning of Mining in the Far West* (1947); Leonard Pitt, *The Decline of the Californios: A Social History of the Spanish-Speaking Californians, 1846–1890* (1966); David J. Weber, *The Mexican Frontier, 1821–1846: The American Southwest Under Mexico* (1982).

Expansion and the Party System

Paul B. Bergeron, *The Presidency of James K. Polk* (1987); William R. Brock, *Parties and Political Conscience: American Dilemmas, 1840–1850* (1979); Frederick Merk, *Slavery and the Annexation of Texas* (1972); Robert J. Morgan, *A Whig Embattled: The Presidency Under John Tyler* (1954); James C. N. Paul, *Rift in the Democracy* (1961); George R. Poage, *Henry Clay and the Whig Party* (1936).

The War with Mexico

K. Jack Bauer, *The Mexican War, 1846–1848* (1974); Seymour V. Connor and Odie B. Faulk, *North America Divided: The Mexican War, 1846–1848* (1971); Neal Harlow, *California Conquered: The Annexation of a Mexican Province, 1846–1850* (1982); Robert W. Johannsen, *To the Halls of the Montezumas: The Mexican War in the American Imagination* (1985); David M. Pletcher, *The Diplomacy of Annexation: Texas, Oregon, and the Mexican War* (1973); John H. Schroeder, *Mr. Polk's War: American Opposition and Dissent, 1846–1848* (1973).

The Sectional Crisis and the Expansion of Slavery

John Barnwell, *Love of Order: South Carolina's First Secession Crisis* (1982); Eugene H. Berwanger, *The Frontier Against Slavery: Western Anti-Negro Prejudice and the Slavery Extension Controversy* (1967); Frederick J. Blue, *The Free Soilers: Third Party Politics, 1848–1854* (1973); William J. Cooper, Jr., *The South and the Politics of Slavery, 1828–1856* (1978); Holman Hamilton, *Prologue to Conflict: The Crisis and Compromise of 1850* (1964); Michael F. Holt, *The Political Crisis of the 1850s* (1978); Chaplain W. Morrison, *Democratic Politics and Sectionalism: The Wilmot Proviso Controversy* (1967); Allan Nevins, *Ordeal of the Union* (1947); David M. Potter, *The Impending Crisis, 1848–1861* (1976); Joseph G. Rayback, *Free Soil: The Election of 1848* (1970); Richard H. Sewell, *Ballots for Freedom: Antislavery Politics in the United States, 1837–1860* (1976).

Biographies

Leonard J. Arrington, *Brigham Young: American Moses* (1985); K. Jack Bauer, *Zachary Taylor: Soldier, Planter, Statesman of the Old Southwest* (1985); Robert F. Dalzell, *Daniel Webster and the Trial of American Nationalism, 1843–1852* (1972); Holman Hamilton, *Zachary Taylor: Soldier in the White House* (1951); Robert W. Johannsen, *Stephen A. Douglas* (1973); Charles G. Sellers, Jr., *James K. Polk: Continentalist, 1843–1846* (1966); Glyndon G. Van Deusen, *The Life of Henry Clay* (1937).

CHAPTER 15

General Histories
Avery Craven, *The Coming of the Civil War*, 2d ed. rev. (1957), and *The Growth of Southern Nationalism, 1848–1861* (1953); Allan Nevins, *Ordeal of the Union* (1947), and *The Emergence of Lincoln* (1950); David M. Potter, *The Impending Crisis, 1848–1861* (1976).

Biographies
David Donald, *Charles Sumner and the Coming of the Civil War* (1960); Don E. Fehrenbacher, *Prelude to Greatness: Lincoln in the 1850s* (1962); Robert W. Johannsen, *Stephen A. Douglas* (1973); Philip Shriver Klein, *President James Buchanan* (1962); Roy F. Nichols, *Franklin Pierce: Young Hickory of the Granite Hills*, 2d ed. rev. (1958); Stephen B. Oates, *To Purge This Land With Blood: A Biography of John Brown* (1970), and *With Malice Toward None: A Life of Abraham Lincoln* (1977); Benjamin P. Thomas, *Abraham Lincoln* (1952).

Economic Development
Alfred D. Chandler, ed., *The Railroads: The Nation's First Big Business* (1965); Albert Fishlow, *American Railroads and the Transformation of the Antebellum Economy* (1965); Paul W. Gates, *The Farmer's Age: Agriculture, 1815–1860* (1960); James Huston, *The Panic of 1857 and the Coming of the Civil War* (1987); Douglass C. North, *The Economic Growth of the United States, 1790–1860* (1961); John F. Stover, *Iron Road to the West: American Railroads in the 1850s* (1978).

Immigration and Nativism
Ray A. Billington, *The Protestant Crusade, 1800–1860* (1938); John P. Dolan, *The Immigrant Church: New York's Irish and German Catholics, 1815–1865* (1975); Robert Ernst, *Immigrant Life in New York City, 1825–1863* (1949); Oscar Handlin, *Boston's Immigrants: A Study of Acculturation*, rev. ed. (1959); Michael F. Holt, "The Antimasonic and Know Nothing Parties," in Arthur M. Schlesinger, Jr., ed., *History of U.S. Political Parties* (1973), vol. 1, 575-737; W. Darrell Overdyke, *The Know-Nothing Party in the South* (1950); Philip D. Taylor, *The Distant Magnet: European Emigration to the U.S.A.* (1971).

Southern Sectionalism and Nationalism
Fred Bateman and Thomas Weiss, *A Deplorable Scarcity: The Failure of Industrialization in the Slave Economy* (1981); Charles H. Brown, *Agents for Manifest Destiny: The Lives and Times of the Filibusterers* (1979); William J. Cooper, Jr., *The South and the Politics of Slavery, 1828–1856* (1978); Robert E. May, *The Southern Dream of a Caribbean Empire, 1854–1861* (1973); John McCardell, *The Idea of a Southern Nation: Southern Nationalists and Southern Nationalism, 1830–1860* (1979); William R. Taylor, *Cavalier and Yankee: The Old South and American National Character* (1961).

Sectionalism and National Politics
Eugene H. Berwanger, *The Frontier Against Slavery: Western Anti-Negro Prejudice and the Slavery Extension Controversy* (1967); Don E. Fehrenbacher, *Slavery, Law, and Politics: The Dred Scott Case in Historical Perspective* (1981); Eric Foner, *Free Soil, Free Labor, Free Men: The Ideology of the Republican Party before the Civil War* (1970); Paul W. Gates, *Fifty Million Acres: Conflict Over Kansas Land Policy, 1854–1890* (1954); William E. Gienapp, *The Origins of the Republican Party, 1852–1856* (1987); Michael F. Holt, *The Political Crisis of the 1850s* (1978); Robert W. Johannsen, ed., *The Lincoln-Douglas Debates* (1965); Roy F. Nichols, *The Disruption of American Democracy* (1848); James A. Rawley, *Race and Politics: "Bleeding Kansas" and the Coming of the Civil War* (1969); Richard H. Sewell, *Ballots for Freedom: Antislavery Politics in the United States, 1837–1860* (1976); Mark W. Summers, *The Plundering Generation: Corruption and the Crisis of the Union, 1849–1861* (1987).

Secession and the Outbreak of War
William L. Barney, *The Secessionist Impulse: Alabama and Mississippi in 1860* (1974); Steven A. Channing, *Crisis of Fear: Secession in South Carolina* (1974); Daniel W. Crofts, *Reluctant Confederates: Upper South Unionists in the Secession Crisis* (1989); Richard N. Current, *Lincoln and the First Shot* (1963); George N. Knoles, ed., *The Crisis of the Union, 1860–1861* (1965); David M. Potter, *Lincoln and His Party in the Secession Crisis* (1942); Kenneth M. Stampp, *And the War Came: The North and the Secession Crisis, 1860–1861* (1950); Ralph Wooster, *The Secession Conventions of the South* (1862).

The Causes of the Civil War
David M. Potter, *The South and the Sectional Conflict* (1969); Thomas J. Pressly, *Americans Interpret Their Civil War* (1954); Kenneth M. Stampp, ed., *The Causes of the Civil War*, rev. ed. (1974).

CHAPTER 16

General Histories
Richard E. Beringer et al., *The Elements of Confederate Defeat: Nationalism, War Aims, and Religion* (1989); David Donald, *Why the North Won the Civil War* (1960); Allan Nevins, *The War for the Union*, 4 vols. (1959–1971); James M. McPherson, *Battle Cry of Freedom* (1988); James G. Randall and David Donald, *The Civil War and Reconstruction*, 2d ed. (1961); Edmund Wilson, *Patriotic Gore: Studies in the Literature of the American Civil War* (1962).

Biographies
Bruce Catton, *Grant Moves South* (1960), and *Grant Takes Command* (1969); Douglas Southall Freeman, *R. E. Lee* (1934–1935); Lloyd Lewis, *Sherman: Fighting Prophet* (1932); William S. McFeely, *Grant: A Biography* (1981); Stephen B. Oates, *With Malice Toward None: The Life of Abraham Lincoln* (1977); James G. Randall and Richard N. Current, *Lincoln the President* (1945–1955); Hudson Strode, *Jefferson Davis*, 3 vols. (1955–1964); Benjamin P. Thomas, *Abraham Lincoln* (1952); Benjamin P. Thomas and Harold Hyman, *Stanton: The Life and Times of Lincoln's Secretary of War* (1962); Glyndon G. Van Deusen, *Willian Henry Seward* (1967).

Military History
Bern Anderson, *By Sea and by River: The Naval History of the Civil War* (1962); Bruce Catton, *The Centennial History of the Civil War* (1961–1965); Thomas L. Con-

nelly, *Army of the Heartland: The Army of Tennessee, 1861–1862* (1967), and *Autumn of Glory: The Army of Tennessee, 1862–1865* (1971); Thomas L. Connelly and Archer Jones, *The Politics of Command: Factions and Ideas in Confederate Strategy* (1973); Burke Davis, *Sherman's March* (1980); Herman Hattaway and Archer Jones, *How the North Won: A Military History of the Civil War* (1983); Gerald F. Linderman, *Embattled Courage: The Experience of Combat in the American Civil War* (1987); Reid Mitchell, *Civil War Soldiers: Their Expectations and Their Experiences* (1988); Bell I. Wiley, *The Life of Johnny Reb* (1943), and *The Life of Billy Yank* (1952); T. Harry Williams, *Lincoln and His Generals* (1952).

The Confederacy
Thomas B. Alexander and Richard E. Beringer, *The Anatomy of the Confederate Congress* (1972); Curtis A. Amlund, *Federalism in the Southern Confederacy* (1966); Paul D. Escott, *After Secession: Jefferson Davis and the Failure of Confederate Nationalism* (1978); Drew Gilpin Faust, *The Creation of Confederate Nationalism: Ideology and Identity in the Civil War South* (1988); Mary Elizabeth Massey, *Refugee Life in the Confederacy* (1964); Robert M. Myers, ed., *Children of Pride: A True Story of Georgia and the Civil War* (1972); Frank L. Owsley, *State Rights in the Confederacy* (1925); Charles W. Ramsdell, *Behind the Lines in the Southern Confederacy* (1944); James L. Roark, *Masters Without Slaves: Southern Planters in the Civil War and Reconstruction* (1977); Emory M. Thomas, *The Confederate Nation, 1861–1865* (1979); Richard C. Todd, *Confederate Finance* (1954); Bell I. Wiley, *The Plain People of the Confederacy* (1943), and *The Road to Appomattox* (1956); Wilfred B. Yearns, *The Confederate Congress* (1960).

The Union
Ralph Andreano, ed., *The Economic Impact of the American Civil War* (1962); Adrian Cook, *The Armies of the Streets: The New York City Draft Riots of 1863* (1974); Leonard P. Curry, *Blueprint for Modern America: Non-Military Legislation of the First Civil War Congress* (1968); George Fredrickson, *The Inner Civil War: Northern Intellectuals and the Crisis of the Union* (1965); Paul W. Gates, *Agriculture and the Civil War* (1965); William B. Hesseltine, *Lincoln and the War Governors* (1948); Harold M. Hyman, *A More Perfect Union: The Impact of the Civil War and Reconstruction on the Constitution* (1973); Frank L. Klement, *The Copperheads in the Middle West* (1960); James H. Moorhead, *American Apocalypse: Yankee Protestants and the Civil War, 1860–1869* (1978); Philip S. Paludan, *A Covenant with Death: The Constitution, the Law, and Equality in the Civil War Era* (1975), and *"A People's Contest": The Union and Civil War, 1861–1865* (1988); James A. Rawley, *The Politics of Union: Northern Politics During the Civil War* (1974); Joel H. Silbey, *A Respectable Minority: The Democratic Party in the Civil War Era* (1977); George Winston Smith and Charles Burnet Judah, *Life in the North During the Civil War* (1966); Hans L. Trefousse, *The Radical Republicans: Lincoln's Vanguard for Racial Justice* (1969).

Women and the Civil War
Mary Elizabeth Massey, *Bonnet Brigades: American Women and the Civil War* (1966); George C. Rable, *Civil Wars: Women and the Crisis of Southern Nationalism* (1989); C. Vann Woodward, ed., *Mary Chesnut's Civil War* (1981); Agatha Young, *Women and the Crisis: Women of the North in the Civil War* (1959).

Emancipation and the Black Experience
Dudley Cornish, *The Sable Arm: Negro Troops in the Union Army, 1861–1865* (1956); LaWanda Cox, *Lincoln and Black Freedom: A Study in Presidential Leadership* (1981); Barbara Jeanne Fields, *Slavery and Freedom on the Middle Ground: Maryland During the Nineteenth Century* (1985); John Hope Franklin, *The Emancipation Proclamation* (1963); Louis Gerteis, *From Contraband to Freedman: Federal Policy Toward Southern Blacks, 1861–1865* (1973); Leon Litwack, *Been in the Storm So Long: The Aftermath of Slavery* (1979); James M. McPherson, *The Struggle for Equality: Abolitionists and the Negro in the Civil War and Reconstruction* (1964); Clarence L. Mohr, *On the Threshold of Freedom: Masters and Slaves in Civil War Georgia* (1986); Willie Lee Rose, *Rehearsal for Reconstruction: The Port Royal Experiment* (1964); V. Jacque Voegli, *Free but Not Equal: The Midwest and the Negro During the Civil War* (1967).

Diplomacy
David P. Crook, *Diplomacy During the American Civil War* (1975); Norman Ferris, *The Trent Affair: A Diplomatic Crisis* (1977); Brian Jenkins, *Britain and the War for the Union* (1974); Frank L. Owsley, *King Cotton Diplomacy*, rev. ed. (1959).

CHAPTER 17
General Histories
Eric Foner, *Reconstruction: America's Unfinished Revolution, 1863–1877* (1988); James McPherson, *Ordeal by Fire: The Civil War and Reconstruction* (1982); James G. Randall and David Donald, *The Civil War and Reconstruction*, 2d ed. (1961); Kenneth M. Stampp, *The Era of Reconstruction, 1865–1877* (1965).

Biographies
Fawn M. Brodie, *Thaddeus Stevens: Scourge of the South* (1959); David Donald, *Charles Sumner and the Rights of Man* (1970); William S. McFeely, *Yankee Stepfather: General O. O. Howard and the Freedmen* (1968), and *Grant: A Biography* (1981).

National Politics
Richard H. Abbott, *The Republican Party and the South, 1855–1877: The First Southern Strategy* (1986); Herman Belz, *Emancipation and Equal Rights: Politics and Constitutionalism in the Civil War Era* (1978); Michael Les Benedict, *A Compromise of Principle: Congressional Republicans and Reconstruction* (1974), and *The Impeachment and Trial of Andrew Johnson* (1973); W. R. Brock, *An American Crisis: Congress and Reconstruction, 1865–1867* (1963); John Cox and LaWanda Cox, *Politics, Principles, and Prejudice, 1865–1866* (1963); Eric L. McKitrick, *Andrew Johnson and Reconstruction* (1966); James M. McPherson, *The Struggle for Equality: Abolitionists and the Negro in the Civil War and Reconstruction* (1964); John G. Sproat, *"The Best Men": Liberal Reformers in the Gilded Age* (1968); Hans

L. Trefousse, *The Radical Republicans: Lincoln's Vanguard for Racial Justice* (1969).

Reconstruction and the Constitution
William Gillette, *The Right to Vote: Politics and the Passage of the Fifteenth Amendment* (1965); Harold M. Hyman, *A More Perfect Union: The Impact of the Civil War and Reconstruction on the Constitution* (1973); Joseph James, *The Framing of the Fourteenth Amendment* (1956); Stanley I. Kutler, *Judicial Power and Reconstruction Politics* (1968).

The Black Experience in Reconstruction
Herbert G. Gutman, *The Black Family in Slavery and Freedom, 1750–1925* (1976); Janet Sharp Hermann, *The Pursuit of a Dream* (1981); Thomas Holt, *Black Over White: Negro Political Leadership in South Carolina* (1977); Leon Litwack, *Been in the Storm So Long: The Aftermath of Slavery* (1979); Howard Rabinowitz, ed., *Southern Black Leaders in Reconstruction* (1982); Willie Lee Rose, *Rehearsal for Reconstruction: The Port Royal Experiment* (1964); Vernon L. Wharton, *The Negro in Mississippi, 1865–1890* (1947); Joel Williamson, *After Slavery: The Negro in South Carolina During Reconstruction* (1966).

Reconstruction in the South
Dan T. Carter, *When the War Was Over: The Failure of Self-Reconstruction in the South, 1865–1867* (1985); Richard N. Current, *Those Terrible Carpetbaggers: A Reinterpretation* (1988); William C. Harris, *Day of the Carpetbagger: Republican Reconstruction in Mississippi* (1979); Elizabeth Studley Nathans, *Losing the Peace: Georgia Republicans and Reconstruction, 1865–1871* (1968); Michael Perman, *Reunion Without Compromise: The South and Reconstruction, 1865–1868* (1973), and *The Road to Redemption: Southern Politics, 1869–1880* (1984); George C. Rable, *But There Was No Peace: The Role of Violence in the Politics of Reconstruction* (1984); James Sefton, *The United States Army and Reconstruction, 1865–1877* (1967); Allen Trelease, *White Terror: The Ku Klux Klan Conspiracy and Southern Reconstruction* (1967); Ted Tunnell, *Crucible of Reconstruction: War, Radicalism, and Race in Louisiana, 1862–1877* (1974); Sarah Woolfolk Wiggins, *The Scalawag in Alabama Politics, 1865–1881* (1977).

Social and Economic Reconstruction
George R. Bentley, *A History of the Freedmen's Bureau* (1955); Eric Foner, *Nothing But Freedom: Emancipation and Its Legacy* (1983); Steven Hahn, *The Roots of Southern Populism: Yeoman Farmers and the Transformation of the Georgia Upcountry, 1850–1890* (1983); Jacqueline Jones, *Soldiers of Light and Love: Northern Teachers and Georgia Blacks, 1865–1873* (1980); Donald Nieman, *To Set the Law in Motion: The Freedmen's Bureau and the Legal Rights of Blacks, 1865–1868* (1979); Lawrence N. Powell, *New Masters: Northern Planters During the Civil War and Reconstruction* (1984); Roger L. Ransom and Richard Sutch, *One Kind of Freedom: The Economic Consequences of Emancipation* (1977); James Roark, *Masters Without Slaves: Southern Planters in the Civil War and Reconstruction* (1977); Mark W. Summers, *Railroads, Reconstruction, and the Gospel of Prosperity* (1984).

The End of Reconstruction
Paul Buck, *The Road to Reunion, 1865–1900* (1937); William Gillette, *Retreat from Reconstruction, 1869–1879* (1980); Keith Ian Polakoff, *The Politics of Inertia: The Election of 1876 and the End of Reconstruction* (1973); C. Vann Woodward, *Reunion and Reaction: The Compromise of 1877 and the End of Reconstruction* (1951).

CHAPTER 18

General Studies
Daniel Boorstin, *The Americans: The Democratic Experience* (1973); John A. Garraty, *The New Commonwealth* (1968); Ray Ginger, *The Age of Excess* (1963); Samuel P. Hays, *The Response to Industrialism, 1885–1914* (1957); Edward C. Kirkland, *Industry Comes of Age: Business, Labor and Public Policy, 1860–1897* (1961); Robert Wiebe, *The Search for Order, 1877–1920* (1968).

The Economy
Frederick Lewis Allen, *The Great Pierpont Morgan* (1949); W. Elliott Brownlee, *Dynamics of Ascent: A History of the American Economy*, rev. ed. (1979); Stuart Brunchey, *Growth of the Modern American Economy* (1975); Milton Friedman and Anna Schwartz, *Monetary History of the United States, 1867–1960* (1963); Robert L. Heilbroner, *The Economic Transformation of America* (1977); Robert Higgs, *The Transformation of the American Economy, 1865–1914* (1971); Susan Previant Lee and Peter Passell, *A New Economic View of American History* (1979).

The Railroads
Alfred D. Chandler, Jr., *The Railroads: The Nation's First Big Business* (1965); Robert Fogel, *Railroads and American Economic Growth* (1964); Julius Grodinsky, *Jay Gould* (1957); Gabriel Kolko, *Railroads and Regulation, 1877–1916* (1965); Albro Martin, *James J. Hill and the Opening of the Northwest* (1976); George H. Miller, *Railroads and the Granger Laws* (1971); John F. Stover, *American Railroads* (1970).

The Rise of Big Business
Alfred Chandler, *Pierre S. DuPont and the Making of the Modern Corporation* (1971); Alfred Chandler, *Strategy and Structure: Chapters in the History of American Industrial Enterprise* (1962), and *The Visible Hand: The Managerial Revolution in American Business* (1977); Thomas Cochrane, *Business in American Life* (1972); Harold C. Livesay, *Andrew Carnegie and the Rise of Big Business* (1975); Alan Nevins, *Study in Power: John D. Rockefeller*, 2 vols. (1953); Glenn Porter, *The Rise of Big Business* (1973); Alan Trachtenberg, *The Incorporation of America* (1982); Joseph Wall, *Andrew Carnegie* (1970).

Invention and Industry
Robert Bruce, *Alexander Graham Bell and the Conquest of Solitude* (1973); Robert Conot, *A Streak of Luck* (1979); John F. Kasson, *Civilizing the Machine* (1976); Harold Passer, *The Electrical Manufacturers, 1875–1900* (1953); Nathan Rosenberg, *Technology and American Economic Growth* (1972); Peter Temin, *Iron and Steel in Nineteenth Century America* (1964); Frederick

A. White, *American Industrial Research Laboratories* (1961).

Capitalism and Its Critics
Robert Bannister, *Social Darwinism: Science and Myth in Anglo-American Social Thought* (1979); Sidney Fine, *Laissez Faire and the General Welfare State: A Study of Conflict in American Thought, 1865–1900* (1956); Louis Galambos, *The Public Image of Big Business in America, 1880–1940: A Quantitative Study of Social Change* (1975); Richard Hofstader, *Social Darwinism in American Thought* (rev. ed., 1955); Edward C. Kirkland, *Dream and Thought in the Business Community, 1860–1900* (1956); T. Jackson Lears, *No Place of Grace: Antimodernism and the Transformation of American Culture, 1880–1920* (1981); John Thomas, *Alternative America: Henry George, Edward Bellamy, and the Adversary Tradition* (1983).

The Culture of Work
John Bodnar, *Immigration and Industrialization: Ethnicity in an American Mill Town* (1977); Michael Frisch and Daniel Walkowitz, eds., *Working-Class America: Essays on Labor, Community, and American Society* (1983); James R. Green, *World of the Worker: Labor in Twentieth Century America* (1980); Herbert Gutman, *Work, Culture, and Society in Industrializing America* (1976); Tamara Hareven, *Family, Time, and Industrial Time: The Relationship Between the Family and Work in a New England Industrial Community* (1982); Susan Kennedy, *If All We Did Was To Weep At Home: A History of White Working Class Women in America* (1979); Alice Kessler-Harris, *Out of Work: A History of Wage-Earning Women in the United States* (1982); Walter Licht, *Working for the Railroad: The Organization of Work in the Nineteenth Century* (1983); David Montgomery, *Workers' Control in America: Studies in the History of Work, Technology, and Labor Struggles* (1979); Daniel Nelson, *Managers and Workers: Origins of the New Factory System* (1975); Daniel T. Rodgers, *The Work Ethic in Industrial America, 1850–1920* (1978); Stephan Thernstrom, *The Other Bostonians: Poverty and Progress in the American Metropolis, 1880–1970* (1973).

The Labor Movement
Mari Jo Buhle, *Women and American Socialism, 1870–1920* (1981); Melvyn Dubofsky, *Industrialism and the American Worker, 1865–1920* (1975); Melvyn Dubofsky, *We Shall Be All: A History of the Industrial Workers of the World* (1969); Leon Fink, *Workingmen's Discovery: The Knights of Labor and American Politics* (1983); Philip Foner, *Women and the American Labor Movement*, 2 vols. (1979); William H. Harris, *The Harder We Run: Black Workers Since the Civil War* (1982); Stuart Kaufman, *Samuel Gompers and the Origins of the American Federation of Labor* (1973); Gwendolyn Mink, *Old Labor and New Immigrants in American Political Development: Union, Party, and State, 1875–1920* (1986); Nick Salvatore, *Eugene V. Debs: Citizen and Socialist* (1982); David Shannon, *The Socialist Party* (1955); Lloyd Ulman, *The Rise of the National Trade Union: The Development and Significance of Its Structure, Governing Institutions, and Economic Policies* (1955).

CHAPTER 19

General Studies
Howard P. Chudacoff, *The Evolution of American Urban Society* (rev. ed., 1981); Charles Glabb and A. Theodore Brown, *A History of Urban America* (rev. ed., 1976); Blake McKelvey, *The Urbanization of America, 1860–1915* (1963); Allan Pred, *Spatial Dynamics of U.S. Urban Growth, 1800–1914* (1971); John Stilgoe, *Borderland: Origins of the American Suburb, 1820–1939* (1988); Stephan Thernstrom and Richard Sennett, eds., *19th Century Cities: Essays in the New Urban History* (1969); Sam Bass Warner, Jr., *Streetcar Suburbs* (1962), and *The Urban Wilderness* (1972).

Immigration and Immigrants
Josef Barton, *Peasants and Strangers: Italians, Rumanians, and Slovaks in an American City* (1975); Jack Chen, *The Chinese of America* (1980); Leonard Dinnerstein, Roger Nichols, and David Reimers, *Natives and Strangers* (1979); John Duff, *The Irish in the United States* (1971); Mario Garcia, *Desert Immigrants: The Mexicans of El Paso, 1880–1920* (1981); Yuji Ichioka, *The Issei: The World of the First Generation Japanese Americans, 1885–1924* (1988); Edward Kantowicz, *Polish-American Politics in Chicago* (1975); Thomas Kessner, *The Golden Door: Italian and Jewish Immigrant Mobility in New York City, 1880–1915* (1977); Alan M. Kraut, *The Huddled Masses: The Immigrant in American Society, 1880–1921* (1982); Joseph Lopreato, *Italian Americans* (1970); James Stuart Olsen, *The Ethnic Dimension in American History*, vol. II (1979); Moses Richin, *The Promised City: New York's Jews* (1962); Jacob Riis, *How the Other Half Lives* (1890); Philip Taylor, *The Distant Magnet: European Emigration to the U.S.A.* (1971); Virginia Yans-McLaughlin, *Family and Community: Italian Immigrants in Buffalo, 1880–1930* (1977); Olivier Zunz, *The Changing Face of Inequality: Urbanization, Industrial Development, and Immigrants in Detroit, 1880–1920* (1982).

Nativism and Race
Louis Harlan, *Booker T. Washington: The Making of a Black Leader, 1856–1901* (1972), and *Booker T. Washington: The Wizard of Tuskegee, 1901–1915* (1953); John Higham, *Strangers in the Land: Patterns of American Nativism, 1880–1925* (1955), and *Send These to Me* (1975); Kenneth Kusmer, *A Ghetto Takes Shape* (1976); Gilbert Osofsky, *Harlem: The Making of a Ghetto* (1966); Allan H. Spear, *Black Chicago* (1967); Donald Spivey, *Schooling for the New Slavery: Black Industrial Education, 1868–1915* (1978).

Politics and Poverty
John Allswang, *Bosses, Machines, and Urban Voters* (1977); Robert H. Bremner, *From the Depths: The Discovery of Poverty in the United States* (1956); Lyle Dorsett, *The Pendergast Machine* (1968); Steven Erie, *Rainbow's End: Irish-Americans and the Dilemmas of Urban Machine Politics, 1840–1985* (1988); Leo Hershkowitz, *Tweed's New York: Another Look* (1977); Zane Miller, *Boss Cox's Cincinnati* (1968); James T. Patterson, *America's Struggle Against Poverty* (1981); Thomas Philpott, *The Slum and the Ghetto* (1978); William L. Riordon, *Plunkitt of Tammany Hall* (1963); Lloyd Wendt and Herman Kogan, *Bosses in Lusty Chicago* (2d. ed., 1971).

Reform
Jane Addams, *Twenty Years at Hull-House* (1910); Ruth Bordin, *Woman and Temperance: The Quest for Power and Liberty, 1860–1900* (1981); Allen Davis, *Spearheads for Reform: The Social Settlements and the Progressive Movement, 1890–1914* (1967), and *American Heroine: The Life and Legend of Jane Addams* (1973); Marvin Lazerson, *Origins of the Urban School* (1971); Eric Monkonnen, *Police in Urban America, 1860–1920* (1981); David Pivar, *Purity Crusade: Sexual Morality and Social Control, 1868–1900* (1973); Barbara Rosencrantz, *Public Health and the State* (1972); Martin Schiesl, *The Politics of Efficiency: Municipal Administration and Reform in America* (1977); David Tyack, *The One Best System: A History of American Urban Education* (1974); Morris Vogel, *The Invention of the Modern Hospital: Boston, 1870–1930* (1980); James C. Whorton, *Crusaders for Fitness: The History of American Health Reformers* (1982).

Urban Life, Work, and Culture
Cindy Aron, *Ladies and Gentlemen of the Civil Service: Middle Class Workers in Victorian America* (1987); Gunther Barth, *City People: The Rise of Modern City Culture in 19th Century America* (1980); Allan Brandt, *No Magic Bullet: A Social History of Venereal Disease in the United States Since 1880* (rev. ed., 1985); Robert Cross, *The Church and the City* (1967); Ronald Davies, *A History of Music in American Life, Volume II: The Gilded Years, 1865–1920* (1980); Tamara K. Hareven and Randolph Langenbach, *Amoskeag: Life and Work in an American Factory* (1978); Neil Harris, *Humbug: The Art of P. T. Barnum* (1973); Lawrence Kasson, *Amusing the Million: Coney Island at the Turn of the Century* (1978); Richard Lingeman, *Theodore Dreiser: At the Gates of the City, 1871–1907* (1986); John Lucas and Ronald Smith, *Saga of American Sport* (1978); Henry F. May, *Protestant Churches and Urban America* (1949); Katherine Morello, *The Invisible Bar: The Woman Lawyer in America, 1638 to the Present* (1986); Joseph Musselman, *Music in the Cultured Generation: A Social History of Music in America, 1870–1900* (1971); Russel Nye, *The Unembarrassed Muse: The Popular Arts in America* (1970); Roy Rosenzweig, *Eight Hours for What We Will: Workers & Leisure in An Industrial City, 1870–1920* (1983); Robert H. Walker, *Life in the Age of Enterprise, 1865–1900* (1967).

Women and Family
Harvey Green, *The Light of the Home: An Intimate View of the Lives of Women in Victorian America* (1983); John S. Haller and Robin M. Haller, *The Physician and Sexuality in Victorian America* (1986); N. Ray Hiner and Joseph Hawes, eds., *Growing Up in America: Children in Historical Perspective* (1985); David Katzman, *Seven Days a Week: Women and Domestic Service in Industrializing America* (1978); Judith Leavitt, *Brought to Bed: Childbearing in America, 1750–1950* (1988); Elaine May, *Great Expectations: Marriage and Divorce in Post-Victorian America* (1980); Steven Mintz, *A Prison of Expectations: The Family in Victorian Culture* (1983); Steven Mintz and Susan Kellogg, *Domestic Revolutions: A Social History of American Family Life* (1988); Ellen Rothman, *Hands and Hearts: A History of Courtship in America* (1984); Carroll Smith-Rosenberg, *Disorderly Conduct: Visions of Gender in Victorian America* (1986);

Susan Strasser, *Never Done: A History of American Housework* (1983).

CHAPTER 20

The New South: History, Politics, and Culture
Orville Vernon Burton, *In My Father's House* (1985); W. J. Cash, *The Mind of the South* (1941); Thomas D. Clark and Albert Kirwan, *The South Since Appomattox* (1967); Thomas L. Connelly, *God and General Longstreet: The Lost Cause and the Southern Mind* (1982); John M. Cooper, *Walter Hines Page: The Southerner as American, 1855–1918* (1977); Carl N. Degler, *The Other South: Southern Dissenters in the Nineteenth Century* (1974); Vincent P. DeSantis, *Republicans Face the Southern Question: The New Departure Years, 1877–1897* (1959); Robert Durden, *The Self-Inflicted Wound: Southern Politics in the Nineteenth Century* (1985); John S. Ezell, *The South Since 1865* (1975); Paul Gaston, *The New South Creed* (1970); Richard Gray, *Writing the South: The Idea of an American Region* (1986); J. Morgan Kousser, *The Shaping of Southern Politics: Suffrage Restriction and Establishment of the One Party South* (1974); J. Morgan Kousser and James McPherson, eds., *Region, Race, and Reconstruction* (1982); Lawrence Larsen, *The Rise of the Urban South* (1985); Raymond B. Nixon, *Henry W. Grady: Spokesman of the New South* (1969); David M. Potter, *The South and the Concurrent Majority* (1972); Charles R. Wilson, *Baptized in Blood: The Religion of the Lost Cause, 1865–1920* (1980); C. Vann Woodward, *The Origins of the New South* (1951); C. Vann Woodward, *Tom Watson: Agrarian Rebel* (1938).

The Southern Economy and Race
David Carlton, *Mill and Town in South Carolina, 1880–1920* (1982); Pete Daniels, *Breaking the Land: The Transformation of Cotton, Tobacco, and Rice Cultures Since 1880* (1985); Steven Hahn, *The Roots of Southern Populism: Yeoman Farmers and the Transformation of the Georgia Upcountry, 1850–1890* (1983); Louis T. Harlan, *Booker T. Washington* (1972), and *Booker T. Washington: The Wizard of Tuskegee* (1983); Robert Higgs, *Competition and Coercion: Blacks in the American Economy, 1865–1890* (1977); J. M. McPherson, *The Abolitionist Legacy: From Reconstruction to the NAACP* (1975); August Meier, *Negro Thought in America, 1880–1915: Racial Ideologies in the Age of Booker T. Washington* (1963); Howard Rabinowitz, *Race Relations in the Urban South, 1865–1890* (1978); Roger Ransom and Richard Sutch, *One Kind of Freedom: The Economic Consequences of Emancipation* (1977); Donald Spivey, *Schooling for the New Slavery: Black Industrial Education* (1978); J. F. Stover, *The Railroads of the South* (1955); Edward Wheeler, *Uplifting the Race: The Black Minister in the New South, 1865–1902* (1986); Joel Williamson, *The Crucible of Race: Black-White Relations in the American South Since Emancipation* (1984), and *After Slavery* (1965); C. Vann Woodward, *The Strange Career of Jim Crow* (3rd rev. ed., 1974); Gavin Wright, *Old South, New South* (1986).

Opening of the West
Walton Bean, *California* (1978); Ray A. Billington, *Westward Expansion* (1967); Thomas D. Clark, *Frontier America* (rev. ed., 1969); Robert Hine, *The American*

West (2d, rev. ed., 1984); Paul Hutton, ed., *Soldiers West: Biographies from the Military Frontier* (1987); Howard Lamar, *The Reader's Encyclopedia of the American West* (1977), and *The Far Southwest, 1846–1912* (1966); Gerald McFarland, *A Scattered People: An American Family Moves West* (1985); Leo Marx, *The Machine in the Garden* (1964); Donald W. Meinig, *The Southwest: Three People in Geographical Change, 1600–1970* (1971); Frederick Merk, *History of the Westward Movement* (1978); Roderick Nash, *Wilderness and the American Mind* (3rd ed., 1982); Earl Pomery, *The Pacific Slope* (1968); Wallace Stegner, *Beyond the Hundredth Meridian: John Welsey Powell and the Second Opening of the West* (1954); Henry Nash Smith, *Virgin Land* (1950); Donald Worster, *Rivers of Empire: Water, Aridity and the Growth of the American West* (1985).

The Peoples of the West
Rudolfo Acuna, *Occupied America: A History of Chicanos* (1981); Ralph Andrist, *The Long Death: The Last Days of the Sioux Nation* (1964); Robert Athearn, *In Search of Canaan: Black Migration in Kansas, 1879–1880* (1978); Gunther Barth, *Bitter Strength: A History of the Chinese in the United States, 1850–1870* (1964); Gretchen Bataille and Charles Silet, *The Pretend Indians: Images of Native Americans in the Movies* (1980); Beverly Beeton, *Women Vote in the West: The Woman Suffrage Movement, 1869–1896* (1986); Thomas Berger, *Little Big Man* (1964); Robert Berkhofer, Jr., *The White Man's Indian* (1978); Dee Brown, *Bury My Heart at Wounded Knee: An Indian History of the American West* (1970); Dee Brown, *The Gentle Tamers: Women of the Old West* (1958); Edward Curtis, *The North American Indian* (1972); David Dary, *Cowboy Culture* (1981); Everett Dick, *Sod House Frontier* (1954); Carol Fairbanks, *Prairie Women: Images in American and Canadian Fiction* (1986); John Mack Faragher, *Women and Men on the Overland Trail* (1979); Christine Fisher, ed., *Let Them Speak for Themselves: Women in the American West, 1849–1900* (1977); Joe B. Frantz and Julian Choate, *The American Cowboy: The Myth and Reality* (1955); Julie Roy Jeffrey, *Frontier Women: The Trans-Mississippi West, 1840–1880* (1979); Alvin Josephy, *The Indian Heritage in America* (1969); William Katz, *The Black West* (1971); Polly W. Kaufman, *Women Teachers on the Frontier* (1984); William Leckie, *The Buffalo Soldiers: A Narrative History of the Negro Cavalry* (1967); Frederick Luebke, *Ethnicity on the Great Plains* (1980); Robert Mardock, *Reformers and the American Indian* (1971); M. S. Meier and Feliciano Rivera, *The Chicanos: A History of the Mexican Americans* (1972); Sandra Myres, *Western Women and the Frontier Experience, 1880–1915* (1982); James S. Olsen and Raymond Wilson, *Native Americans in the Twentieth Century* (1984); Nell Painter, *The Exodusters: Black Migration to Kansas after Reconstruction* (1976); Paul Prucha, *American Indian Policy in Crisis* (1976); Harriet and Fred Rochlin, *Pioneer Jews: A New Life in the Far West* (1984); Mari Sandoz, *Cheyenne Autumn* (1954); William Savage, *The Cowboy Hero: His Image in American History and Culture* (1979), and as ed., *Cowboy Life* (1975); Kent Steckmesser, *The Western Hero in History and Legend* (1965); Elinor Pruitt Stewart, *Letters of a Woman Homesteader* (1913, 14); Joanna Stratton, *Pioneer Women: Voices of the Kansas Frontier* (1981); John Tebbel and Keith Jennison, *The American Indian Wars* (1960); Robert Utley,

High Noon in Lincoln: Violence on the Western Frontier (1987); Robert Utley, *The Indian Frontier of the American West, 1846–1890* (1984), and *Frontier Regulars: The United States Army and the Indian, 1866–1891* (1974); Sylvia Van Kirk, *Many Tender Ties: Women in Fur Trade Society* (1983); Wilcomb Washburn, *The Indian in America* (1975).

The Western Economy
Lewis Atherton, *Cattle Kings* (1961); Gunther Barth, *Instant Cities* (1975); Edward Dale, *The Range Cattle Industry* (rev. ed., 1969); David Dary, *Entrepreneurs of the Old West* (1986); Robert Dykstra, *The Cattle Towns* (1968); Gilbert Fite, *The Farmer's Frontier* (1966); Paul Gates, *History of Public Land Development* (1968); William Greever, *The Bonanza West: The Story of the Western Mining Rushes* (1963); Gene M. Gressley, *Bankers and Cattlemen* (1966); Robert West Howard, *The Great Iron Trail: The Story of the First Transcontinental Railroad* (1963); Donald Jackson, *Gold Dust* (1980); Richard Lingenfelter, *The Hardrock Miners: A History of the Mining Labor Movement in the American West, 1863–1893* (1974); Rodman Paul, *Mining Frontiers of the Far West, 1848–1880* (1963); Mari Sandoz, *Old Jules* (1962); Mari Sandoz, *The Buffalo Hunters: The Story of the Hide Men* (1978); Fred A. Shannon, *The Farmer's Last Frontier, 1860–1897* (1945); J. M. Skaggs, *The Cattle Trailing Industry* (1973); George R. Taylor and Irene Neu, *The American Railroad Network, 1861–1890* (1956); Mark Twain, *Roughing It* (1872); James Ward, *Railroads and the Character of America, 1820–1887* (1986); Walter Prescott Webb, *The Great Plains* (1931); Mark Wyman, *Hard Rock Epic: Western Miners and the Industrial Revolution, 1860–1910* (1979).

CHAPTER 21

General Studies
James Bryce, *The American Commonwealth*, 2 vols. (1888); Sean Cashman, *America and the Gilded Age* (1984); John Dobson, *Politics in the Gilded Age* (1978); Harold Faulkner, *Politics, Reform, and Expansion, 1890–1900* (1959); Richard Hoftstader, *The Age of Reform: From Bryan to FDR* (1955); Nancy Eleanor Flexner, *Century of Struggle: The Women's Rights Movement in the United States* (1959); Morton Keller, *Affairs of State: Public Life in Late 19th Century America* (1977); H. Wayne Morgan, *From Hayes to McKinley* (1969); H. Wayne Morgan, ed., *The Gilded Age* (1970); Stephen Skowronek, *Building a New American State: The Expansion of National Administrative Capacities* (1982).

Ideology and Politics
Kenneth Davison, *The Presidency of Rutherford B. Hayes* (1972); Margaret Forster, *Significant Sisters: The Grassroots of Active Feminism, 1839–1939* (1986); Lewis Gould, *The Presidency of William McKinley* (1981); David C. Hammack, *Power and Society: Greater New York at the Turn of the Century* (1982); S. P. Hirshson, *Farewell to the Bloody Shirt: Northern Republicans and the Southern Negro, 1877–1893* (1962); Richard Jensen, *The Winning of the Midwest: Social and Political Conflict, 1888–1896* (1971); David Jordan, *Roscoe Conkling of New York* (1971); Paul Kleppner, *The Cross of Culture: A Social Analysis of Midwestern Politics* (1970), and

The Third Electoral System, 1853–1892: Voters, Parties, and Political Cultures (1979); Robert Marcus, Grand Old Party: Political Structure in the Gilded Age (1971); Robert McCloskey, American Conservatism in the Age of Enterprise (1951); Michael McGerr, The Decline of Politics: The American North, 1865–1928 (1988); Allan Nevins, Grover Cleveland: A Study in Courage (New York, 1932); Arnold Paul, Conservative Crisis and the Rule of Law: Attitudes of Bar and Bench, 1887–1895 (1969); Allan Peskin, Garfield (1978); Thomas Reeves, Gentlemen Boss: The Life of Chester Alan Arthur (1975); David Rothman, Politics and Power: The United States Senate, 1869–1901 (1966); R. Hal Williams, Years of Decision: American Politics in the 1890s (1978).

Protest and Reform
Geoffrey Blodgett, The Gentle Reformers (1966); William Dick, Labor and Socialism in America (1972); John Diggins, The American Left in the Twentieth Century (1973); Ari Hoogenboom, Outlawing the Spoils: A History of the Civil Service Movement, 1865–1883 (1961); John Laslett, Labor and the Left (1970); Charles Lofgren, The Plessy Case: A Legal-Historical Interpretation (1987); Walter Nugent, Money and American Society (1968); John Sproat, The Best Men: Liberal Reformers in the Gilded Age (1968); Irwin Unger, The Greenback Era: A Social and Political History of American Finance, 1865–1879 (1964).

Populism
Peter Argersinger, Populism and Politics: William Alfred Peffer and the People's Party (1974); Lawrence Goodwyn, Democratic Promise: The Populist Movement in America (1976); Steven Hahn, The Roots of Southern Populism: Yeoman Farmers and the Transformation of the Georgia Upcountry (1983); Sheldon Hackney, Populism to Progressivism in Alabama (1969); John Hicks, The Populist Revolt (1931); Robert McMath, Populist Vanguard (1975); Bruce Palmer, Man Over Money (1980); Norman Pollack, The Populist Response to Industrial America (1962); Theodore Saloutos, Farmer Movements in the South, 1865–1933 (1960); Barton Shaw, The Wool-Hat Boys: Georgia's Populist Party (1984); C. Vann Woodward, Tom Watson, Agrarian Rebel (1938), and The Origins of the New South (1972); Allan Weinstein, Prelude to Populism: Origins of the Silver Issue (1970).

The Depression of 1893 and the Election of 1896
Paolo Coletta, William Jennings Bryan: Political Evangelist (1964); Robert F. Durden, The Climax of Populism: The Election of 1896 (1965); Ray Ginger, Altgeld's America (1958); Paul W. Glad, McKinley, Bryan, and the People (1964), and The Trumpet Soundeth (1960); Charles Hoffman, The Depression of the Nineties: An Economic History (1970); J. Rogers Hollingsworth, The Whirligig of Politics: The Democracy of Cleveland and Bryan (1963); Stanley Jones, The Presidential Election of 1896 (1964); Louis Koenig, Bryan (1971); Samuel McSeveney, The Politics of Depression (1972).

CHAPTER 22

General
Richard Bannister, Social Darwinism (1979); Robert Beisner, From the Old Diplomacy to the New, 1865–1900 (1975); Charles Campbell, The Transformation of Amer-

ican Foreign Relations, 1865–1900 (1976), and From Revolution to Rapprochement: The United States and Great Britain, 1783–1903 (1974); Richard Challener, Admirals, Generals and American Foreign Policy, 1889–1914 (1973); John Dobson, America's Ascent: The United States Becomes a Great Power, 1880–1914 (1978); John Lewis Gaddis, Russia, the Soviet Union, and the United States (1978); John A. S. Grenville and George Young, Politics, Strategy, and American Diplomacy (1967); Richard Hofstadter, Social Darwinism in American Thought (rev. ed., 1959); Ronald Jensen, The Alaska Purchase and Russian-American Relations (1970); David Pletcher, The Awkward Years (1962); Emily Rosenberg, Spreading the American Dream (1982); Tom Terrill, The Tariff, Politics, and American Foreign Policy, 1874–1901 (1973); Mira Wilkins, The Emergence of the Multinational Enterprise (1970); William A. Williams, The Tragedy of American Diplomacy (rev. ed., 1962).

The Question of Imperialism
David Anderson, Imperialism and Idealism: American Diplomats in China, 1861–1898 (1986); William Becker, The Dynamics of Business-Government Relations (1982); Robert L. Beisner, Twelve Against Empire (1968); Phillip Darby, Three Faces of Imperialism: British and American Approaches to Asia and Africa, 1870–1970 (1987); Philip S. Foner, The Spanish-Cuban-American War and the Birth of American Imperialism, 2 vols., (1972); Frank Friedel, The Splendid Little War (1958); Willard Gatewood, Jr., Black Americans and the White Man's Burden, 1898–1903 (1975); Kenneth Hagan, American Gun-Boat Diplomacy, 1877–1889 (1973); David Healy, U.S. Expansionism (1970); Michael Hunt, Ideology and U.S. Foreign Policy (1987); Walter LaFeber, The New Empire (1963); Frederick Merk, Manifest Destiny and Mission in American History (1963); Wolfgang Mommsen and Jurgen Osterhammel, eds., Imperialism and After (1986); H. Wayne Morgan, America's Road to Empire: The War With Spain and Overseas Expansion (1965); Thomas J. Osborne, Empire Can Wait: American Opposition to Hawaiian Annexation, 1893–1898 (1981); Ernest Paolino, The Foundations of American Empire (1973); Thomas Paterson, ed., Imperialism and Anti-Imperialism (1973); Bradford Perkins, The Great Rapprochement (1968); Julius Pratt, The Expansionists of 1898 (1936); Tony Smith, The Pattern of Imperialism: The United States, Great Britain and the Late Industrializing World Since 1815 (1982); Richard Turk, The Ambiguous Relationship: Theodore Roosevelt and Alfred Thayer Mahan (1987).

The United States and Asia
David Anderson, Imperialism and Idealism: American Diplomacy in China, 1861–1898 (1985); Warren Cohen, America's Response to China (rev. ed., 1980); Michael Hunt, The Making of a Special Relationship: The United States and China to 1914 (1983); Jane Hunter, The Gospel of Gentility: American Women Missionaries in Turn-of-the-Century China (1984); Akira Iriye, Across the Pacific (1967) and Pacific Estrangement: Japanese and American Expansion, 1897–1911 (1972); Yur-Bok Lee and Wayne Patterson, eds., One Hundred Years of Korean-American Relations, 1882–1982 (1986); Ernest May and John Fairbanks, eds., America's China Trade in Historical Perspective (1986); Glenn May, Social Engineering in the Philippines (1980); Thomas McCormick, China

Market: America's Quest for Informal Empire, 1893–1901 (1968); Charles Neu, *The Troubled Encounter* (1975); Peter Stanley, *A Nation in the Making: The Philippines and the United States* (1974); Randall Stross, *The Hard Earth: American Agriculturalists on Chinese Soil, 1898–1937* (1986); James Thomson, Peter Stanley, and John Perry, *Sentimental Imperialists: The American Experience in East Asia* (1981); Robert Welch, Jr., *Response to Imperialism: The United States and the Philippine-American War, 1899–1902* (1979); Marilyn B. Young, *Rhetoric of Empire: American China Policy, 1895–1901* (1968).

The United States and the Americas
Robert Brown, *Canada's National Policy, 1883–1900* (1964); Kenneth Bourne, *Britain and the Balance of Power in North America, 1815–1908* (1967); Walter LaFeber, *Inevitable Revolutions: The United States in Central America* (rev. ed., 1984); Lester Langley, *The Banana Wars* (1983), and *The United States and the Caribbean, 1900–1970* (1980); Louis Perez, Jr., *Cuba under the Platt Amendment, 1902–1934* (1986), and *Cuba Between Empires, 1878–1902* (1983); Dexter Perkins, *The Monroe Doctrine, 1867–1907* (1937); Ramon Ruiz, *Cuba* (1968); Karl Schmitt, *Mexico and the United States, 1821–1973* (1974); Josefina Vazquez and Lorenzo Meyer, *The United States and Mexico* (1985).

CHAPTER 23

General Studies
John Chambers II, *The Tyranny of Change: America in the Progressive Era, 1900–1917* (1980); Arthur Ekrich, *Progressivism in America* (1974); Lewis Gould, ed., *The Progressive Era* (1974); Richard Hofstader, *The Age of Reform: From Bryan to FDR* (1955); Gabriel Kolko, *The Triumph of Conservatism* (1963); Arthur Link and Richard L. McCormick, *Progressivism* (1983); William O'Neill, *The Progressive Years* (1975); James Weinstein, *The Corporate Ideal in the Liberal States, 1900–1918* (1969); Robert Wiebe, *Businessmen and Reform: A Study of the Progressive Movement* (1962).

The Progressive Impulse
Daniel Aaron, *Men of Good Hope: A Story of American Progressives* (1951); Richard Abrams, *The Burdens of Progress* (1978); Robert H. Bremner, *From the Depths: The Discovery of Poverty in the United States* (1956); David Chalmers, *The Social and Political Ideas of the Muckrakers* (1964); Clarke Chambers, *Paul U. Kellog and the Survey* (1971); Robert Crunden, *Ministers of Reform: The Progressives' Achievements in American Civilization, 1889–1920* (1982); Charles Forcey, *The Crossroads of Liberalism: Croly, Weyl, Lippmann and the Progressive Era, 1900–1925* (1961); William Hutchinson, *The Modernist Impulse in American Protestantism* (1976); Roy Lubove, *The Professional Altruist: The Emergence of Social Work as a Career, 1880–1930* (1965); D. W. Marcell, *Progress and Pragmatism: James, Dewey, Beard and the American Idea of Progress* (1974); Daniel Nelson, *Frederick W. Taylor and the Rise of Scientific Management* (1980); David Noble, *The Progressive Mind, 1890–1917* (rev. ed., 1981); Morton White, *Social Thought in America: The Revolt Against Formalism,* (1949); Harold Wilson, *McClure's Magazine and the Muckrakers* (1970).

Social Reform and Minority Rights
Allen F. Davis, *American Heroine: The Life and Legend of Jane Addams* (1973), and *Spearheads of Reform: The Social Settlements and the Progressive Movement, 1890–1919* (1967); Louis Harlan, *Separate and Unequal: Public School Campaigns and Racism in the Southern Seaboard States, 1900–1915* (1968); Charles F. Kellogg, *NAACP: A History of the National Association for the Advancement of Colored People, 1909–1920* (1967); Roy Lubove, *The Progressives and the Slums: Tenement House Reform in New York City* (1962); James McPherson, *The Abolitionist Legacy: From Reconstruction to the NAACP* (1975); David Musto, *The American Disease: Origins of Narcotics Control* (1973); Elliot M. Rudwick, *W.E.B. DuBois* (1968); James Timberlake, *Prohibition and the Progressive Campaign* (1963).

Women
Paula Baker, *Gender and the Transformation of Politics: Public and Private Life in New York, 1870–1930* (1989); Nancy F. Cott, *The Grounding of Modern Feminism* (1987); Nancy Dye, *As Equals and Sisters: Feminism, the Labor Movement, and the Women's Trade Union League of New York* (1980); Linda Gordon, *Woman's Body, Woman's Right: A Social History of Birth Control* (1976); David Kennedy, *Birth Control in America: The Career of Margaret Sanger* (1970); Aileen Kraditor, *Ideas of the Woman Suffrage Movement* (1965); Ellen Lagemann, *A Generation of Women: Education in the Lives of Progressive Reformers* (1979); David Morgan, *Suffragists and Democrats: The Politics of Woman Suffrage in America* (1972); William O'Neil, *Divorce in the Progressive Era* (1967); Ruth Rosen, *The Lost Sisterhood: Prostitutes in America, 1900–1918* (1982); Rosalind Rosenberg, *Beyond Separate Spheres: Intellectual Roots of Modern Feminism* (1982).

Education, the New Professionalism, and Entertainment
Burton Bledstein, *The Culture of Professionalism* (1976); Lawrence Cremin, *The Transformation of the School: Progressivism in American Education* (1961); John DiMeglio, *Vaudeville U.S.A.* (1973); Lewis Erenberg, *Steppin' Out: New York Nightlife and the Transformation of American Culture, 1890–1930* (1981); James Farrell, *Inventing the American Way of Death, 1830–1920* (1980); Thomas Haskell, *The Emergence of Professional Social Science* (1977); Bruce Kuklick, *The Rise of American Philosophy* (1977); Martin Laforse and James Drake, *Popular Culture and American Life: Selected Topics in the Study of American Popular Culture* (1981); Robert Sklar, *Movie-Made America: A Social History of the American Movies* (1975); Paul Starr, *The Social Transformation of American Medicine* (1982); David Tyack and Elizabeth Hansot, *Managers of Virtue: Public School Leadership in America, 1820–1980* (1982); Lawrence Vesey, *The Emergence of the American University* (1970).

Local and State Reform
Richard Abrams, *Conservatism in a Progressive Era: Massachusetts Politics, 1900–1912* (1964); John Buenker, *Urban Liberalism and Progressive Reform* (1973); James Crooks, *Politics and Progress: The Rise of Urban Progressivism in Baltimore, 1895–1911* (1968); Dewey Grantham, *Southern Progressivism: The Recon-*

ciliation of Progress and Tradition (1983); Melvin Holli, *Reform in Detroit: Hazen S. Pingree and Urban Politics* (1969); Jack Kirby, *Darkness at Dawning: Race and Reform in the Progressive South* (1972); Richard L. McCormick, *From Realignment to Reform: Political Change in New York State, 1893–1910* (1981); George Mowry, *The California Progressives* (1951); Bradley Rice, *Progressive Cities: The Commission Government Movement in America, 1901–1920* (1977); Jack Tager, *The Intellectual as Urban Reformer: Brand Whitlock and The Progressive Movement* (1968); David P. Thelen, *The New Citizenship: Origins of Progressivism in Wisconsin* (1972), and *Robert LaFollette and the Insurgent Spirit* (1976).

National Politics and Public Policy
Donald Anderson, *William Howard Taft* (1973); John Blum, *The Republican Roosevelt* (1954); John Blum, *Woodrow Wilson and the Politics of Morality* (1954); John Milton Cooper, Jr., *The Warrior and the Priest: Woodrow Wilson and Theodore Roosevelt* (1983); John Gable, *The Bull Moose Years* (1978); Alexander George and Juliette George, *Woodrow Wilson and Colonel House: A Personality Study* (1956); Lewis Gould, *Reform and Regulation: American Politics, 1900–1916* (1978); Samuel Hays, *Conservation and the Gospel of Efficiency: The Progressive Conservation Movement, 1890–1920* (1959); James Holt, *Congressional Insurgents and the Party System* (1969); Arthur Link, *Woodrow Wilson,* 5 vols. (1947–1965), and *Woodrow Wilson and the Progressive Era, 1910–1917* (1954); Albro Martin, *Enterprise Denied: Origins of the Decline of American Railroads, 1897–1917*; David McCullough, *Mornings on Horseback* (1981); Michael McGerr, *The Decline of Popular Politics: The American North, 1865–1928* (1986); Edmund Morris, *The Rise of Theodore Roosevelt* (1979); George Mowry, *The Era of Theodore Roosevelt* (1958); James Penick, *Progressive Politics and Conservation: The Ballinger-Pinchot Affair* (1968); Harold Pinkett, *Gifford Pinchot: Private and Public Forester* (1970); Edwin Weinstein, *Woodrow Wilson: A Medical and Psychological Biography* (1981); Craig West, *Banking Reform and the Federal Reserve, 1863–1923* (1977); Clifton Yearley, *The Money Machines* (1970).

CHAPTER 24

General
Paul Abrahams, *The Foreign Expansion of American Finance and Its Relationship to Foreign Economic Policies of the United States, 1907–1921* (1976); Robert Beisner, *From the Old Diplomacy to the New, 1865–1900* (1975); John Dobson, *America's Ascent: The United States Becomes a Great Power, 1880–1914* (1978); Morrell Heald and Lawrence Kaplan, *Culture and Diplomacy* (1977); Peter Karsten, *The Naval Aristocracy* (1972); Robert Osgood, *Ideals and Self-Interest in America's Foreign Relations* (1953); Emily Rosenberg, *Spreading the American Dream: American Economic and Cultural Expansion, 1890–1945* (1982); Robert Schulzinger, *American Diplomacy in the Twentieth Century* (1984); Tom Terrill, *The Tariff, Politics, and American Foreign Policy, 1874–1901* (1973); Rubin Weston, *Racism and U.S. Imperialism, 1865–1946* (1971); Mira Wilkins, *The Emergence of the Multinational Enterprise* (1970).

Roosevelt, Taft, and Wilson
Howard K. Beale, *Theodore Roosevelt and the Rise of America to World Power* (1956); David Burton, *Theodore Roosevelt: Confident Imperialist* (1968); Robert W. Cherney, *A Righteous Cause: The Life of William Jennings Bryan* (1985); Richard H. Collin, *Theodore Roosevelt, Culture, Diplomacy, and Expansion* (1985); John Cooper, Jr., *Walter Hines Page* (1977); Lloyd Gardner, *Wilson and Revolutions, 1913–1921* (1976); *William Jennings Bryan: Missionary Isolationist* (1983); Arthur Link, *Wilson: The Diplomatist* (1957) and *Woodrow Wilson: Revolution, War, and Peace* (1979); Frederick Marks III, *Velvet on Iron: The Diplomacy of Theodore Roosevelt* (1979); Ralph E. Minger, *William Howard Taft and United States Foreign Policy* (1975).

Asia, the Pacific, and Latin America
Warren Cohen, *America's Response to China* (rev. ed., 1980); Akira Iriye, *Pacific Estrangement: Japanese and American Expansion, 1897–1911* (1972); Jerry Israel, *Progressivism and the Open Door* (1971); David Healy, *Gunboat Diplomacy in the Wilson Era: The U.S. Navy in Haiti, 1915–1916* (1976); Walter LaFeber, *The Panama Canal* (1978); Lester Langley, *Struggle for the American Mediterranean* and *The United States and the Caribbean, 1900–1970* (1980); Glenn May, *Social Engineering in the Philippines* (1980); Robert McClellan, *The Heathen Chinese: A Study of American Attitudes Toward China* (1971); David McCullough, *The Path Between the Seas: The Creation of the Panama Canal, 1870–1914* (1977); Dana Munro, *Intervention and Dollar Diplomacy in the Caribbean, 1900–1920* (1964); Charles Neu, *The Troubled Encounter* (1975); Robert Smith, *The United States and Revolutionary Nationalism in Mexico, 1916–1932* (1972); Peter Stanley, *A Nation in the Making: The Philippines and the United States, 1899–1921* (1974).

From Neutrality to War
Thomas Baily and Paul Ryan, *The Lusitania Disaster* (1975); John Coogan, *The End of Neutrality: The United States, Britain, and Maritime Rights, 1899–1915* (1981); John Cooper, *The Vanity of Power: American Isolationism and the First World War* (1969); Patrick Devlin, *Too Proud to Fight: Woodrow Wilson's Neutrality* (1974); Ross Gregory, *The Origins of American Intervention in the First World War* (1977); Burton Kaufman, *Efficiency and Expansion: Foreign Trade Organization in the Wilson Administration* (1974); Roland Marchand, *The American Peace Movement and Social Reform* (1973); Ernest May, *The World War and American Isolationism, 1914–1917* (1959); Jeffrey Safford, *Wilsonian Maritime Diplomacy* (1977).

The First World War Abroad
Arthur Barbeau and Henri Florette, *The Unknown Soldiers: Black American Troops in World War I* (1974); Edward Coffman, *The War to End All Wars: The American Military Experience in World War I* (1968); Paul Fussell, *The Great War and Modern Memory* (1975); John Gifford, *The Citizen Soldiers* (1972); Otis Graham, *The Great Campaigns* (1971); Maurine Greenwald, *Women, War, and Work* (1980); N. Gordon Levin, Jr., *Woodrow Wilson and World Politics: America's Response to War and Revolution* (1968); Laurence Stallings, *The Doughboys: The Story of the AEF, 1917–1918*

(1963); Frank Vandiver, *The Life and Times of John J. Pershing*, 2 vols. (1977).

The Homefront

Valerie Conner, *The National War Labor Board: Stability, Social Justice, and the Voluntary State in World War I* (1983); Robert Cuff, *The War Industries Board: Business Government-Relations During World War I* (1973); Carol Gruber, *Mars and Minerva: World War I and the Uses of Higher Learning in America* (1975); Ellis Hawley, *The Great War and the Search for Modern Order* (1979); Robert Haynes, *A Night of Violence: The Houston Riot of 1917* (1976); David Kennedy, *Over Here: The First World War and American Society* (1980); Seward Livermore, *Politics Is Adjourned: Woodrow Wilson and the War Congress, 1917–1918* (1966); Frederick Luebke, *Bonds of Loyalty: German Americans and World War I* (1974); Paul Murphy, *World War I and the Origins of Civil Liberties* (1979); Jordan Schwarz, *The Speculator: Bernard M. Baruch in Washington, 1917–1965* (1981); Barbara Steinson, *American Women's Activism in World War I* (1982); Stephen Vaughn, *Holding Fast the Inner Lines: Democracy, Nationalism, and the Committee on Public Information* (1979); James Weinstein, *The Decline of Socialism in America, 1912–1923* (1967).

Versailles

Thomas Bailey, *Woodrow Wilson and the Great Betrayal* (1945), and *Woodrow Wilson and the Lost Peace* (1944); Robert Ferrell, *Woodrow Wilson and World War I* (1985); Inga Floto, *Colonel House at Paris* (1980); John Gaddis, *Russia, the Soviet Union, and the United States* (1978); Lloyd Gardner, *Safe for Democracy: The Anglo-American Response to Revolution, 1913–1923* (1984); Arno Mayer, *Politics and Diplomacy of Peacemaking* (1965); Charles Mee, Jr., *The End of Order, Versailles, 1919* (1980); Ralph Stone, *The Irreconcilables: The Fight Against the League of Nations* (1970); Ralph Stone, *The Irreconcilables* (1970).

Aftermath

David Brody, *Labor in Crisis* (1965); Stanley Coben, *A. Mitchell Palmer* (1963); Stanley Cooperman, *World War I and the American Mind* (1970); Roberta Feuerlicht, *Justice Crucified* (1977); Robert Murray, *The Red Scare* (1955); Burl Noggle, *Into the Twenties* (1977); Stuart Rochester, *American Liberal Disillusionment in the Wake of World War I* (1977); Francis Russell, *A City in Terror* (1975); William Tuttle, Jr., *Race Riot: Chicago in the Red Summer of 1919* (1970); Stephen Ward, ed., *The War Generation: Veterans of the First World War* (1975).

CHAPTER 25

General Studies

Frederick Lewis Allen, *Only Yesterday: An Informal History of the 1920s* (1931); John Braeman et al., ed., *Change and Continuity in Twentieth Century America: The 1920s* (1968); John Hicks, *The Republican Ascendancy, 1921–1933* (1960); Isabel Leighton, ed., *The Aspirin Age* (1949); William Leuchtenburg, *The Perils of Prosperity, 1914–1932* (1958); Donald McCoy, *Coming of Age* (1973); Geoffrey Perrett, *America in the Twenties* (1982); Arthur Schlesinger, Jr., *The Crisis of the Old Order* (1957); David Shannon, *Between the Wars: America, 1919–1940* (1979).

Economics, Business, and Labor

Irving Bernstein, *The Lean Years: A History of the American Worker, 1920–1933* (1960); David Brody, *Steelworkers in America* (1960), and *Workers in Industrial America* (1980); Alfred Chandler, *Strategy and Structure: Chapters in the History of American Inustrial Enterprise* (1962); Ed Cray, *Chrome Colossus: General Motors and Its Times* (1980); Gilbert Fite, *George Peek and the Fight for Farm Parity* (1954); James Flink, *The Car Culture* (1975); Louis Galambos, *Competition and Cooperation* (1966); James Gilbert, *Designing the Industrial State* (1972); Allan Nevins and Frank Hill, *Ford*, 3 vols. (1954–1963); Jim Potter, *The American Economy Between the Wars* (1974); John Rae, *American Automobile* (1965), and *The Road and the Car in American Life* (1971); George Soule, *Prosperity Decade* (1947); Keith Sward, *The Legend of Henry Ford* (1948); Leslie Woodcock Tentler, *Wage Earning Women: Industrial Work and Family Life in the United States, 1900–1930* (1979); Bernard Weisberger, *The Dream Maker* (1979) [about Will Durant, President of General Motors]; Robert Zieger, *Republicans and Labor, 1919–1929* (1969).

Mass Society and Mass Culture

Erick Barnouw, *A Tower of Babel: A History of American Broadcasting in the United States to 1933* (1966); Daniel Boorstin, *The Americans: The Democratic Experience* (1973); Paul Carter, *Another Part of the Twenties* (1977); Robert Creamer, *Babe* (1974); Kenneth Davis, *The Hero: Charles A. Lindbergh* (1954); Stuart Ewing, *Captains of Consciousness* (1976); Robert Lynd and Helen Lynd, *Middletown: A Study in Modern Culture* (1929); Roland Marchand, *Advertising the American Dream: Making Way for Modernity, 1920–1940* (1985); Lary May, *Screening Out the Past* (1980); Leonard Mosley, *Lindbergh: A Biography* (1976); Otis Pease, *The Responsibilities of American Advertising* (1959); Daniel Pope, *The Making of Modern Advertising* (1983); Randy Roberts, *Jack Dempsey, The Manassa Mauler* (1979); Philip Rosen, *The Modern Stentors: Radio Broadcasting and the Federal Government, 1920–1933* (1980); Robert Sklar, *Movie-Made America: A Cultural History of American Movies* (1975).

High Culture

Carlos Baker, *Hemingway* (1956); Malcolm Cowley, *Exile's Return* (1934); Robert Crunden, *From Self to Society: Transition in Modern Thought, 1919–1941* (1972); Frederick Hoffman, *The Twenties* (1949); Arthur Mizner, *The Far Side of Paradise* (1951); Roderick Nash, *The Nervous Generation: American Thought, 1917–1930* (1969); Mark Shorer, *Sinclair Lewis* (1961); Marvin Singleton, *H.L. Mencken and the "American Mercury" Adventure* (1962); Edmund Wilson, *The Twenties* (1975).

Women, Youth, and Minorities

Lois Banner, *American Beauty* (1983); William Chafe, *The American Women: Her Changing Social, Economic, and Political Roles, 1920–1970* (1972); David Cronon, *Black Moses: The Story of Marcus Garvey* (1955); Paula Fass, *The Damned and Beautiful: American Youth in the 1920s* (1977); Linda Gordon, *Woman's Body, Woman's Right: A Social History of Birth Control in America*

(1976); Nathan Huggins, *Harlem Renaissance* (1971); J. Stanley Lemons, *The Woman Citizen: Social Feminism in the 1920s* (1973); David Lewis, *When Harlem Was in Vogue* (1981); Glenna Matthews, *"Just a Housewife!" The Rise and Fall of Domesticity in America* (1987); Wilson Moses, *The Golden Age of Black Nationalism, 1850–1925* (1988); Arnold Rampersad, *The Life of Langston Hughes,* 2 vols. (1986–1988); Ricardo Romo, *East Los Angeles: History of a Barrio* (1983); Lois Scharf, *To Work and to Wed* (1980); Alan Spear, *Black Chicago* (1967); Joe Trotter, *Black Milwaukee: The Making of an Industrial Proletariat* (1985); Theodore Vincent, *Black Power and the Garvey Movement* (1971); Winifred Wandersee, *Women's Work and Family Values, 1920–1940* (1981).

Political Fundamentalism

David Burner, *The Politics of Provincialism* (1968); David Chalmers, *Hooden Americanism: The History of the Ku Klux Klan* (1965); Norman Clark, *Deliver Us from Evil* (1976); Robert Divine, *American Immigration Policy* (1957); Norman Furniss, *The Fundamentalist Controversy, 1918–1933* (1954); Ray Ginger, *Six Days or Forever? Tennessee v. John Scopes* (1958); Joseph Gusfeld, *Symbolic Crusade* (1963); John Higham, *Strangers in the Land: Patterns of American Nativism, 1860–1925* (1955); Kenneth Jackson, *The Ku Klux Klan in the City, 1915–1930* (1967); Don Kirschner, *City and Country: Rural Responses to Urbanization in the 1920s* (1970); George Marsden, *Fundamentalism and American Culture* (1980); Andrew Sinclair, *Prohibition: The Era of Excess* (1962); William Wilson, *Coming of Age: Urban America, 1915–1945* (1974).

Politics, Public Policy, and the Election of 1928

Kristi Andersen, *The Creation of a Democratic Majority* (1979); Paula Edler, *Governor Alfred E. Smith: The Politician as Reformer* (1983); James Giglio, *H. M. Daugherty and the Politics of Expediency* (1978); Oscar Handlin, *Al Smith and His America* (1958); Ellis Hawley, *Herbert Hoover as Secretary of Commerce: Studies in New Era Thought and Practice* (1974); Robert Himmelberg, *The Origins of the National Recovery Administration: Business, Government, and the Trade Association Issue, 1921–1933* (1976); J. Joseph Huthmacher, *Massachusetts People and Politics, 1919–1933* (1959); Alan Lichtman, *Prejudice and the Old Politics* (1979); Richard Lowitt, *George Norris,* 2 vols. (1971); Donald McCoy, *Calvin Coolidge* (1967); Robert Murray, *The Harding Era* (1969), and *The Politics of Normalcy* (1973); Burl Noggle, *Teapot Dome* (1962); Elisabeth Perry, *Belle Moskowitz: Feminine Politics and the Exercise of Power in the Age of Alfred E. Smith* (1987); George Tindall, *The Emergence of the New South* (1967); Eugene Trani and David Wilson, *The Presidency of Warren G. Harding* (1977).

CHAPTER 26

General Studies

Frederick Lewis Allen, *Since Yesterday* (1939); Lester Chandler, *America's Greatest Depression, 1929–1941* (1970); John Garraty, *The Great Depression: An Inquiry into the Causes, Course, and Consequences of the Worldwide Depression of the Nineteen Thirties as Seen by Contemporaries and in the Light of History* (1987); Charles Kindler, *The World in Depression* (1973); Robert McElvaine, *The Great Depression: America, 1929–1941* (1984); Broadus Mitchell, *Depression Decade* (1947); Arthur Schlesinger, Jr., *The Crisis of the Old Order* (1957).

The Great Crash and the Origins of the Great Depression

Milton Friedman and Ana Schwartz, *The Great Contraction* (1965); John Galbraith, *The Great Crash* (1988); Susan Kennedy, *The Banking Crisis of 1933* (1973); Robert Sobel, *The Great Bull Market: Wall Street in the 1920s* (1968); Peter Temin, *Did Monetary Forces Cause the Great Depression?* (1976); Gordon Thomas and Max Morgan-Witts, *The Day the Bubble Burst: The Social History of the Wall Street Crash of 1929* (1979).

Depression Life

Edward Anderson, *Hungry Men* (1935); Robert Angell, *The Family Encounters the Depression* (1936); Ann Banks, *First Person America* (1980); Caroline Bird, *The Invisible Scar* (1966); The Federal Writers' Project, *These Are Our Lives* (1939); John Garraty, *Unemployment in History: Economic Thought and Public Policy* (1978); Mirra Komarovsky, *The Unemployed Man and His Family* (1940); Robert Lynd and Helen Lynd, *Middletown in Transition* (1937); Robert McElvaine, ed., *Down & Out in the Great Depression* (1983); H. Wayne Morgan, *Drugs in America: A Social History, 1800–1980* (1981); David Musto, *The American Disease, Origins of Narcotics Control* (rev. ed., 1988); Lois Scharf, *To Work and to Wed: Female Employment, Feminism, and the Great Depression* (1980); Studs Terkel, *Hard Times: An Oral History of the Great Depression* (1970); Tom Terrill and Jerrold Hirsch, eds., *Such as Us: Southern Voices of the Thirties* (1978); Winifred Wandersee, *Women's Work and Family Values, 1920–1940* (1981); Susan Ware, *Holding Their Own: American Women in the 1930s* (1982); Jeane Westin, *Making Do: How Women Survived the '30s* (1976).

Ethnicity and Race

Rodolfo Acuna, *Occupied America* (rev. ed., 1981); Ralph Bunche, *The Political Status of the Negro in the Age of FDR* (1973); Dan Carter, *Scottsboro: A Tragedy of the American South* (1969); Sarah Deutsch, *No Separate Refuge: Culture, Class, and Gender on an Anglo-Hispanic Frontier in the American Southwest, 1880–1940* (1987); Abraham Hoffman, *Unwanted Mexican-Americans in the Great Depression* (1974); Richard Polenberg, *One Nation Divisible: Class, Race, and Ethnicity in the United States Since 1938* (1980); Bernard Sternsher, ed., *The Negro in Depression and War* (1969); Robert Weisbrot, *Father Divine and the Struggle for Racial Equality* (1983); Nancy Weiss, *The National Urban League* (1974); Raymond Wolters, *Negroes and the Great Depression* (1970).

Depression Culture

Daniel Aaron, *Writers on the Left* (1961); James Agee, *Let Us Now Praise Famous Men* (1941); Andrew Bergman, *We're in the Money: Depression America and Its Films* (1971); Eileen Eagan, *Class, Culture and the Classroom* (1981); Neal Gabler, *An Empire of Their Own: How the Jews Invented Hollywood* (1988); Richard Pells, *Radical Visions and American Dreams* (1973);

John Steinbeck, *The Grapes of Wrath* (1939); William Stott, *Documentary Expressionism and Thirties America* (1973); Warren Susman, *Culture as History: The Transformation of American Society in the Twentieth Century* (1984); Twelve Southerners, *I'll Take My Stand: The South and the Agrarian Tradition* (1937).

Radicalism and Protest
Irving Bernstein, *The Lean Years: A History of the American Worker, 1920–1933* (1960); Roger Daniels, *The Bonus March* (1971); John Hevener, *Which Side You On? The Harlan County Coal Miners, 1931–1939* (1978); Harvey Klehr, *The Heyday of American Communism: The Depression Decade* (1983); Donald Lisio, *The President and Protest: Hoover, Conspiracy, and the Bonus Riot* (1974); Mark Naison, *Communists in Harlem During the Depression* (1983); Theodore Saloutos and John Hicks, *Twentieth Century Populism: Agrarian Protest in the Middle West, 1900–1939* (1951); John Shover, *Cornbelt Rebellion: The Farmers' Holiday Association* (1965).

The Hoover Years
David Burner, *Herbert Hoover: A Public Life* (1979); Martin Fausold, *The Presidency of Herbert C. Hoover* (1985); Martin Fausold and George Mazuzun, eds, *The Hoover Presidency* (1974); George Nash, *The Life of Herbert Hoover* (1983); James Olson, *Herbert Hoover and the Reconstruction Finance Corporation* (1977); Albert Romasco, *The Poverty of Abundance: Hoover, The Nation, The Depression* (1965); Elliot A. Rosen, *Hoover, Roosevelt, and the Brains Trust: From Depression to New Deal* (1977); Jordan Schwarz, *The Interregnum of Despair* (1970); Joan Hoff Wilson, *Herbert Hoover: Forgotten Progressive* (1975).

CHAPTER 27

General Studies
John Braeman et al., *The New Deal*, 2 vols. (1975); Paul Conkin, *The New Deal* (1967); Otis Graham, Jr., *Encore for Reform: The Old Progressives and the New Deal* (1967); Barry Karl, *The Uneasy State* (1983); William Leuchtenburg, *Franklin D. Roosevelt and the New Deal* (1963); Robert McElvaine, *The Great Depression: America, 1929–1941* (1984); Gerald Nash, *The Great Depression and World War II* (1979); Harvard Sitkoff, ed., *Fifty Years Later: The New Deal Evaluated* (1985).

Franklin and Eleanor
James Burns, *Roosevelt: The Lion and the Fox* (1956); Kenneth Davis, *FDR*, 2 vols. (1972–1986); Frank Freidel, *Franklin D. Roosevelt*, 4 vols. (1952–1973); Joseph Lash, *Eleanor and Franklin* (1971); Ted Morgan, *FDR: A Biography* (1985); Eleanor Roosevelt, *This Is My Story* (1937), and *This I Remember* (1949); Lois Scharf, *Eleanor Roosevelt: First Lady of American Liberalism* (1987); Arthur Schlesinger, Jr., *The Age of Roosevelt*, 3 vols. (1957–1960); Rexford Tugwell, *The Democratic Roosevelt: A Biography of Franklin D. Roosevelt* (1957); Geoffrey Ward, *Before the Trumpet: Young Franklin Roosevelt* (1985), and *A First Class Temperament: The Emergence of Franklin Roosevelt* (1989).

The New Dealers
Michael Beschloss, *Kennedy and Roosevelt: The Uneasy Alliance* (1980); John Blum, *From the Morgenthau Diaries*, 3 vols. (1959–1965); Harold Ickes, *The Secret Diaries of Harold L. Ickes*, 3 vols. (1953–1954); Peter Irons, *The New Deal Lawyers* (1982); Joseph Lash, *Dealers and Dreamers: A New Look at the New Deal* (1988); Katie Lochheim, ed., *The Making of the New Deal: The Insiders Speak* (1983); George Martin, *Madame Secretary: Frances Perkins* (1976); George McJimsey, *Harry Hopkins: Ally of the Poor and Defender of Democracy* (1987); Raymond Moley, *After Seven Years* (1939); Frances Perkins, *The Roosevelt I Knew* (1946); Samuel Rosenman, *Working for Roosevelt* (1952); Jordan Schwarz, *Liberal: Adolf A. Berle and the Vision of an American Era* (1987); Robert Sherwood, *Roosevelt and Hopkins: An Intimate History* (1948); Bernard Sternsher, *Rexford Tugwell and the New Deal* (1964); Susan Ware, *Partner and I: Molly Dewson, Feminism, and New Deal Politics* (1987).

Recovery and Reform
Bernard Belush, *The Failure of the NRA* (1975); Ellis Hawley, *The New Deal and the Problems of Monopoly* (1966); Barry Karl, *Executive Reorganization and Reform in the New Deal* (1963); Mark Leff, *The Limits of Symbolic Reform: The New Deal and Taxation, 1933–1939* (1984); Thomas McCraw, *TVA and the Public Power Fight* (1970); James Olson, *Saving Capitalism: The RFC and the New Deal, 1933–1940* (1988); Michael Parrish, *Securities Regulation and the New Deal* (1970); Richard Polenberg, *Reorganizing Roosevelt's Government* (1966); Albert Romasco, *The Politics of Recovery: Roosevelt's New Deal* (1983).

Agriculture
Sidney Baldwin, *Poverty and Politics: The Rise and Decline of the Farm Security Administration* (1967); David Conrad, *The Forgotten Farmers: The Story of Sharecroppers in the New Deal* (1965); Richard Kirkendall, *Social Scientists and Farm Politics in the Age of Roosevelt* (1966); Paul Mertz, *The New Deal and Southern Rural Poverty* (1978); W. D. Rowley, *M. L. Wilson and the Campaign for Domestic Allotment* (1970); Walter Stein, *California and the Dust Bowl Migration* (1973); Van Perkins, *Crisis in Agriculture* (1969); Donald Worster, *Dust Bowl: The Southern Plains in the 1930s* (1979).

Relief and the Rise of the Semi-Welfare State
Searle Charles, *Minister of Relief* (1963) [about Harry Hopkins]; Paul Conkin, *FDR and the Origins of the Welfare State* (1967) and *Tomorrow a New World* (1971); Phoebe Cutler, *The Public Landscape of the New Deal* (1986); Richard Lowitt and Maurine Beasley, eds., *One Third of a Nation: Lorena Hickok Reports on the Great Depression* (1981); Roy Lubove, *The Struggle for Social Security* (1968); Jerre Mangione, *The Dream and the Deal: The Federal Writers' Project, 1935–1943* (1972); Jane deHart Matthews, *The Federal Theater, 1935–1939* (1967); Richard McKinzie, *The New Deal for Artists* (1973); Francis O'Connor, ed., *Art for the Millions: Essays from the 1930s by Artists and Administrators of the WPA Federal Art Project* (1973); Karen Becker Orhn, *Dorothea Lange and the Documentary Tradition* (1980); Marlene Park and Gerald Markowitz, *Democratic Vistas: Post Offices and Public Art in the New Deal* (1984); John Salmond, *The Civilian Conservation Corps* (1967); Bonnie Schwartz, *The Civil Works Administration, 1933–1934* (1984).

Dissent and Protest
Alan Brinkley, *Voices of Protest: Huey Long, Father Coughlin, and the Great Depression* (1982); Donald Grubbs, *Cry from Cotton: The Southern Tenant Farmers Union and the New Deal* (1971); Abraham Holzman, *The Townsend Movement* (1963); Glen Jeansonne, *Gerald L. K. Smith: Minister of Hate* (1988); R. Alan Lawson, *The Failure of Independent Liberalism, 1930–1941* (1971); Leo Ribuffo, *The Old Christian Right: The Protestant Far Right from the Great Depression to the Cold War* (1983); Charles Tull, *Father Coughlin and the New Deal* (1965); T. Harry Williams, *Huey Long* (1969); Frank Warren, *Liberals and Communism: The "Red Decade" Revisited* (1966), and *An Alternative Vision: The Socialist Party in the 1930s* (1976); George Wolfskill, *Revolt of the Conservatives: A History of the American Liberty League, 1934–1940* (1962).

Labor
Jerold Auerbach, *Labor and Liberty: The La Follette Committee and the New Deal* (1966); John Barnard, *Walter Reuther and the Rise of the Auto Workers* (1983); Irving Bernstein, *Turbulent Years: A History of the American Worker, 1933–1941* (1969); Melvyn Dubofsky and Warren Van Tine, *John L. Lewis: A Biography* (1977); Sidney Fine, *Sit-Down: The General Motors Strike of 1936-1937* (1969); Peter Friedlander, *The Emergence of a UAW Local* (1975); August Meier and Elliott Rudwick, *Black Detroit and the Rise of the UAW* (1979); David Milton, *The Politics of U.S. Labor: From the Great Depression to the New Deal* (1980); Ronald Schatz, *The Electrical Workers* (1983).

New Deal Politics
John Allswang, *The New Deal in American Politics* (1978); Frank Freidel, *FDR and the South* (1965); J. Joseph Huthmacher, *Senator Robert Wagner and the Rise of Urban Liberalism* (1968); James Patterson, *Congressional Conservatism and the New Deal* (1967), and *The New Deal and the States* (1969); William Leuchtenburg, "The Origins of Franklin D. Roosevelt's 'Court Packing' Plan," in Philip Kurland, ed., *The Supreme Court Review* (1966).

Minorities
Laurence Kelly, *The Assault on Assimilation: John Collier and the Origins of Indian Policy Reform, 1920–1954* (1983); John Kirby, *Black Americans in the Roosevelt Era: Liberalism and Race* (1980); Carey McWilliams, *North from Mexico* (1949); Donald Parman, *The New Deal and the Navajoes* (1976); Kenneth Philp, *John Collier's Crusade for Indian Reform, 1920–1934* (1977); Francis Prucha, *The Indians in American Society: From the Revolutionary War to the Present* (1985); Mark Reisler, *By the Sweat of Their Brow: Mexican Immigrant Labor in the United States, 1900–1940* (1976); Harvard Sitkoff, *A New Deal for Blacks* (1978); Raymond Walters, *Negroes and the Great Depression: The Problem of Economic Recovery* (1970); Nancy Weiss, *Farewell to the Party of Lincoln: Black Politics in the Age of FDR* (1983); Robert Zangrando, *The NAACP Crusade Against Lynching* (1980).

CHAPTER 28

Diplomacy Before the War
Selig Adler, *The Uncertain Giant* (1965); Thomas Buckley, *The United States and the Washington Naval Conference, 1921–1922* (1970); Charles Chatfield, *For Peace and Justice: Pacifism in America, 1914–1941* (1971); Warren Cohen, *Empire Without Tears: American Foreign Relations, 1921–1933* (1988); Frank Costigliola, *Awkward Dominion: American Political, Economic, and Cultural Relations with Europe, 1919–1933* (1985); Charles DeBenedetti, *The Peace Reform Movement in American History* (1980), and *Origins of the Modern American Peace Movement, 1915–1929* (1978); Roger Dingman, *Power in the Pacific: The Origins of Naval Arms Limitation, 1914–1922* (1976); Robert Ferrell, *Peace in Their Time* (1952), and *American Diplomacy in the Great Depression* (1970); Peter Filene, *Americans and the Soviet Experiment, 1917–1933* (1967); John Lewis Gaddis, *Russia, the Soviet Union, and the United States* (1978); Akira Iriye, *After Imperialism: The Search for a New Order in the Far East, 1921–1931* (1965); Harold Josephson, *James T. Shotwell and the Rise of Internationalism in America* (1976); Melvyn Leffler, *The Elusive Quest* (1979); Elting E. Morison, *Turmoil and Tradition* (1964) [on Henry Stimson]; Arnold Offner, *The Origins of the Second World War* (1975); Stephen Rabe, *The Road to OPEC: U.S. Relations with Venezuela, 1919–1976* (1982); Raymond Sontag, *A Broken World, 1919–1939* (1971); Robert Schulzinger, *The Wise Men of Foreign Affairs: A History of the Council on Foreign Relations* (1984); Adam Ulam, *Expansion and Coexistence: Soviet Foreign Policy from 1917 to 1973* (rev. ed., 1974); Joan Hoff Wilson, *American Business and Foreign Policy, 1920–1933* (1968), and *Herbert Hoover* (1975).

The Roosevelt Era and the Coming of World War II
Dorothy Borg, *The United States and the Far Eastern Crisis of 1933–1938* (1964); James MacGregor Burns, *Roosevelt: The Lion and the Fox* (1956); Robert Dallek, *Franklin D. Roosevelt and American Foreign Policy, 1932–1945* (1979); Robert Divine, *The Reluctant Belligerent* (2d ed., 1979); Herbert Feis, *The Road to Pearl Harbor* (1950); John Findling, *Close Neighbors, Distant Friends: United States-Central American Relations* (1987); Lloyd Gardner, *Economic Aspects of New Deal Diplomacy* (1964); Irwin Gellman, *Good Neighbor Diplomacy* (1979); Betty Glad, *Key Pittman: The Tragedy of a Senate Insider* (1986); Patrick Headen, *Roosevelt Confronts Hitler: America's Entry into World War II* (1987); Warren Kimball, *The Most Unsordid Act: Lend Lease, 1939–1941* (1969); Walter LaFeber, *Inevitable Revolutions: The United States in Central America* (1983); Douglas Little, *Malevolent Neutrality: The United States, Great Britain, and the Origins of the Spanish Civil War* (1985); Lorenzo Meyer, *Mexico and the United States in the Oil Controversy, 1917–1942* (1977); Arthur Morse, *While Six Million Died* (1968); Gordon Prange, *At Dawn We Slept* (1981); David Reynolds, *The Creation of the Anglo-American Alliance, 1937–1941* (1982); John Toland, *Infamy* (1982); Jonathan Utley, *Going to War with Japan, 1937–1941* (1985); Roberta Wohlstetter, *Pearl Harbor: Warning and Decision* (1962); Bryce Wood, *The Making of the Good Neighbor Policy* (1961); David Wyman, *The Abandonment of the Jews* (1984).

War and Strategy
John Dower, *War Without Mercy: Race and Power in the Pacific War* (1986); David Eisenhower, *Eisenhower at War, 1943–1945* (1986); B. H. Liddell Hart, *History*

of the Second World War (1970); Max Hastings, OVER-
LORD: D-Day and the Battle of Normandy (1984); Akira
Iriye, Power and Culture: The Japanese-American War,
1941–1945 (1981); D. Clayton James, The Years of Mac-
Arthur, 1941–1945 (1975) and (with Anne Sharp Wells),
A Time for Giants: Politics of the American High Com-
mand During World War II (1987); Eric Larabee, Com-
mander in Chief: Franklin Delano Roosevelt, His Lieu-
tenants, and Their War (1987); William Manchester,
American Caesar (1979); Samuel Eliot Morison, The
Two Ocean War (1963); Bernard C. Nalty, Strength for
the Fight: A History of Black Americans in the Military
(1986); Forrest Pogue, George C. Marshall, 3 vols.
(1963–1975); Ronald Schaffer, Wings of Judgment:
American Bombing in World War II (1985); Michael
Sherry, The Rise of American Air Power (1987); Bradley
Smith, The Shadow Warriors: O.S.S. and the Origins of
the C.I.A. (1983); Ronald Spector, The Eagle Against the
Sun: The American War With Japan (1985); James
Stokesbury, A Short History of World War II (1980).

War and Diplomacy
Henry Blumenthal, Illusion and Reality in Franco-
American Diplomacy, 1914–1945 (1982); Russell Buhite,
Decision at Yalta (1986); James MacGregor Burns, Roo-
sevelt: The Soldier of Freedom (1970); Winston Church-
ill, The Second World War, 6 vols. (1948–1953); Diane
Shaver Clemens, Yalta (1970); Robert Divine, Roosevelt
and World War II (1969); Herbert Feis, Roosevelt,
Churchill, Stalin: The War They Waged and the Peace
They Sought (1957); Fraser J. Harbutt, The Iron Cur-
tain: Churchill, America, and the Origins of the Cold
War (1986); George Herring, Aid to Russia, 1941–1946
(1977); Warren Kimball, ed., Churchill and Roosevelt:
The Complete Correspondence, 1939–1945 (1984); Ga-
briel Kolko, The Politics of War (1968); William Roger
Louis, Imperialism at Bay: The United States and the
Decolonization of the British Empire, 1941–1945 (1978);
Mark H. Lytle, The Origins of the Iranian-American
Alliance, 1941–1953 (1987); William Hardy McNeill,
America, Britain, and Russia (1953); David Painter, Oil
and the American Century: The Political Economy of
U.S. Foreign Oil Policy, 1941–1954 (1986); Keith
Sainsbury, Roosevelt, Stalin, Churchill, and Chaing Kai
Shek, 1943: The Moscow, Cairo, and Tehran Confer-
ences (1985); Martin Sherwin, A World Destroyed: The
Atomic Bomb and the Grand Alliance (1975); Gaddis
Smith, American Diplomacy During the Second World
War, 1941–1945 (2d ed., 1985); Michael B. Stoff, Oil,
War, and American Security: The Search for a National
Policy on Foreign Oil, 1941–1947 (1980); Christopher
Thorne, Allies of a Kind: The United States, Great Brit-
ain, and the War Against Japan, 1941–1945 (1978);
David Wyman, The Abandonment of the Jews: America
and the Holocaust, 1941–1945 (1984).

CHAPTER 29

Organizing for War

John M. Blum, "V" Was for Victory: Politics and Ameri-
can Culture During World War II (1976); David Brink-
ley, Washington Goes to War (1988); Bruce Catton, The
War Lords of Washington (1948); George Flynn, The
Mess in Washington: Manpower Mobilization in World
War II (1979); Philip Funginiello, The Challenge to
Urban Liberalism: Federal-City Relations During World
War II (1978); Mark Harris et al., The Homefront (1984);
Philip Knightly, The First Casualty (1975); Clayton
Koppes and Gregory Black, Hollywood Goes to War
(1987); Richard Lingeman, Don't You Know There's a
War On? The American Home Front, 1941–1945 (1970);
Gerald Nash, The American West Transformed: The
Impact of the Second World War (1985); Geoffrey Per-
rett, Days of Sadness, Years of Triumph: The American
People, 1939–1945 (1973); Richard Polenberg, War and
Society: The United States, 1941–1945 (1972); Studs
Terkel, "The Good War:" An Oral History of World
War II (1984); Harold Vatter, The American Economy in
World War II (1985); Allan Winkler, The Politics of
Propaganda: The Office of War Information, 1942–1945
(1978).

Workers and Women at War
Karen T. Anderson, Wartime Women: Sex Roles, Family
Relations, and the Status of American Women During
World War II (1981); Matthew Baigall and Julia Wil-
liams, eds., Artists Against War and Fascism (1986);
M. Joyce Baker, Images of Women on Film: The War
Years, 1941–1945 (1981); James Foster, The Union Poli-
tic: The C.I.O. Political Action Committee (1975);
Sherna Berger Gluck, Rosie the Riveter Revisited:
Women, the War, and Social Change (1987); John Har-
ris, The Right to Manage (1982); Susan Hartmann, The
Home Front and Beyond: American Women in the 1940s
(1982); Maurice Isserman, Which Side Were You On?
The American Communist Party During the Second
World War (1982); Paul Koistinen, The Hammer and the
Sword: Labor, the Military, and Industrial Mobiliza-
tion, 1920–1945 (1979); Nelson Lichtenstein, Labor's
War at Home (1982); Ruth Milkman, Gender at Work:
The Dynamics of Job Segregation by Sex During World
War II (1987).

Minorities and the War
A. Russell Buchanan, Black-Americans in World War II
(1977); Dominic Capeci, Jr., Race Relations in Wartime
Detroit (1984), and The Harlem Race Riot of 1943 (1977);
Richard Dalfiume, Desegregation of the U.S. Armed
Forces (1969); Lee Finkel, Forum for Protest: The Black
Press During World War II (1975); Mauricio Mazon, The
Zoot Suit Riots (1984); Phillip McGuire, ed., Taps for a
Jim Crow Army: Letters from Black Soldiers in World
War II (1982); Patrick Washburn, A Question of Sedi-
tion: The Federal Government and the Investigation of
the Black Press During World War II (1986); Neil Wynn,
The Afro-American and the Second World War (1976).

Internees and Refugees
Robert Abzug, Inside the Vicious Heart: Americans and
the Liberation of the Nazi Concentration Camps (1985);
Richard Breitman and Alan Kraut, American Refugee
Policy and European Jewry, 1933–1945 (1987); Commis-
sion on Wartime Relocation and Internment of Civilians,
Personal Justice Denied (1982); P. Scott Corbett, Quiet
Passages: The Exchange of Civilians Between the United
States and Japan during World War II (1987); Roger
Daniels, Concentration Camps U.S.A. (1971); Leonard
Dinnerstein, America and the Survivors of the Holo-
caust (1982); Richard Drinnon, Keeper of Concentration
Camps: Dillon S. Myer and American Racism (1987);
Masayo Umezawa Duus, Unlikely Liberators: The Men
of the 100th and 442nd (1987); Bill Hosokawa, Nisei
(1969); Peter Irons, Justice at War: The Story of the Jap-
anese American Internment Cases (1983); Deborah

Lipstadt, *Beyond Belief: The American Press and the Coming of the Holocaust, 1933–1945* (1986); Michi Weglyn, *Years of Infamy: The Untold Story of America's Concentration Camps* (1976); David Wyman, *The Abandonment of the Jews* (1984); Norman Zucker and Naomi Flink Zucker, *The Guarded Gate: The Reality of American Refugee Policy* (1987).

Atoms and the End of WW II
Gar Alperovitz, *Atomic Diplomacy* (rev. ed., 1985); Nuel Davis, *Lawrence and Oppenheimer* (1969); Robert Donovan, *Conflict and Crisis* (1977); Herbert Feis, *Between War and Peace: The Potsdam Conference* (1960); Herbert Feis, *The Atomic Bomb and the End of World War II* (2d ed., 1966); John L. Gaddis, *The United States and the Origins of the Cold War* (1971); John Gilkenson, Jr., *Gathering Rare Ores: The Diplomacy of Uranium Acquisition, 1943–1954* (1987); John Hersey, *Hiroshima* (1946); Richard Hewlett and Oscar Anderson, *The New World* (1962); Dan Kurzman, *Day of the Bomb: Countdown to Hiroshima* (1986); Vojtech Mastny, *Russia's Road to the Cold War* (1979); Thomas Paterson, *On Every Front: The Making of the Cold War* (1979); Richard Rhodes, *The Making of the Atomic Bomb* (1986); Lisle Rose, *After Yalta* (1973); Martin Sherwin, *A World Destroyed* (1975).

CHAPTER 30

The Postwar Era
Erik Barnouw, *Tube of Plenty: The Evolution of American Television* (1975); Paul Boyer, *By the Bomb's Early Light* (1986); Serge Gilbaut, *How New York Stole the Idea of Modern Art* (1983); James Gilbert, *Another Chance* (1981); James Gilbert, *A Cycle of Outrage* (1986); Eric Goldman, *The Crucial Decade and After* (rev. ed., 1960); Alonzo Hamby, *The Imperial Years* (1976); Kenneth Jackson, *Crabgrass Frontier: The Suburbanization of the United States* (1985); Landon Jones, *Great Expectations: America and the Babyboom Generation* (1980); Richard Kluger, *Simple Justice: The History of the Brown v. Board of Education and Black America's Struggle for Equality* (1975); George Lipsitz, *Class and Culture in Postwar America* (1981); David Marc, *Demographic Vistas* (1984); James O'Connor, ed., *American History/American Television* (1983); William O'Neill, *American High* (1986); Richard Pells, *The Liberal Mind in a Conservative Age* (1985); Dana Polan, *Power and Paranoia: History, Narrative, and the American Cinema, 1940–1950* (1986); Richard Polenberg, *One Nation Divisible* (1980); Leila Rupp and Verta Taylor, *Survival in the Doldrums: The American Women's Rights Movement, 1945 to the 1960s* (1987); Mark Silk, *Spiritual Politics: Religion and America Since World War II* (1988); Jules Tygiel, *Baseball's Great Experiment: Jackie Robinson and His Legacy* (1983).

The Cold War in the West
Dean Acheson, *Present at the Creation* (1969); Stephen Ambrose, *The Rise to Globalism* (3rd ed., 1983); Robin Edmonds, *Setting the Mold: The United States and Great Britain, 1945–1950* (1986); Richard Wightman Fox, *Reinhold Niebuhr: A Biography* (1985); Lawrence Freedman, *The Evolution of Nuclear Strategy* (1983); Richard Freeland, *The Truman Doctrine and the Origins of McCarthyism* (1970); John L. Gaddis, *The United States and the Origins of the Cold War* (1972), *Strategies of Containment* (1982), and *The Long Peace: Inquiries into the History of the Cold War* (1987); Lloyd Gardner, *Architects of Illusion* (1970); David Green, *The Containment of Latin America* (1971); Gregg Herken, *The Winning Weapon* (1980); Michael Hogan, *The Marshall Plan: America, Britain, and the Reconstruction of Western Europe, 1947–1952* (1987); Fred Kaplan, *The Wizards of Armageddon* (1983); Laurence Kaplan, *The United States and NATO* (1984); George Kennan, *Memoirs*, 2 vols. (1967, 1972); Bruce Kuniholm, *The Origins of the Cold War in the Near East* (1980); Walter LaFeber, *America, Russia, and the Cold War* (5th ed., 1985); Mark H. Lytle, *The Origins of the Iranian-American Alliance, 1941–1953* (1987); Robert Messer, *The End of an Alliance* (1982); Aaron D. Miller, *Search for Security* (1980); James Miller, *The United States and Italy, 1940–1950* (1986); Thomas Paterson, *On Every Front* (1979); Robert Pollard, *Economic Security and the Origins of the Cold War* (1985); Ronald Pruessen, *John Foster Dulles* (1982); Cheryl Rubenberg, *Israel and the American National Interest* (1986); Gaddis Smith, *Dean Acheson* (1972); Hugh Thomas, *Armed Truce: The Beginnings of the Cold War, 1945–1946* (1987); Dan Tschirgi, *The Politics of Indecision* (1983); Adam Ulam, *The Rivals* (1971); Immanuel Wexler, *The Marshall Plan Revisited* (1983); Lawrence Wittner, *American Intervention in Greece, 1943–1949* (1982); Daniel Yergin, *Shattered Peace* (1977).

The Cold War in Asia
Robert Blum, *Drawing the Line: The Origin of the American Containment Policy in East Asia* (1982); Warren I. Cohen, *America's Response to China* (2d ed., 1980); Ronald Caridi, *The Korean War and American Politics* (1969); Bruce Cummings, *The Origins of the Korean War* (1980), and as ed., *Child of Conflict: The Korean-American Relationship, 1943–1953* (1983); William Head, *America's China Sojourn* (1983); Gary Hess, *The United States' Emergence as a Southeast Asian Power, 1940–1950* (1987); Akira Iriye, *The Cold War in Asia* (1974); Burton Kaufman, *The Korean War* (1986); Charles Neu, *The Troubled Encounter: The United States and Japan* (1975); Michael Schaller, *The United States and China in the Twentieth Century* (1979); Michael Schaller, *The American Occupation of Japan: The Coming of the Cold War to Asia* (1985); John W. Spanier, *The Truman-MacArthur Controversy and the Korean War* (1959); William Stueck, Jr., *The Road to Confrontation* (1981); Christopher Thorne, *Allies of a Kind* (1978); Nancy Tucker, *Patterns in the Dust: Chinese-American Relations and the Recognition Controversy, 1949–1950* (1983).

The Domestic Cold War
Michael Belknap, *Cold War Political Justice: The Smith Act, the Communist Party, and American Civil Liberties* (1977); David Caute, *The Great Fear* (1978); Larry Ceplair and Steven Englund, *The Inquisition in Hollywood* (1983); Robert Griffin, *The Politics of Fear* (1970); Stanley I. Kutler, *The American Inquisition: Justice and Injustice in the Cold War* (1982); Robert Lamphere and Tom Shachtman, *The FBI-KGB War* (1986); Victor Navasky, *Naming Names* (1980); William O'Neill, *A Better World: Stalinism and the American Intellectuals* (1983); Michael Oshinsky, *A Conspiracy So Immense:*

The World of Joe McCarthy (1983); Ronald Radosh and Joyce Radosh, *The Rosenberg File* (1983); Thomas Reeves, *The Life and Times of Joe McCarthy* (1982); Paul Rogin, *The Intellectuals and McCarthy* (1969); Richard Rovere, *Senator Joe McCarthy* (1959); Nora Sayre, *Running Time: Films on the Cold War* (1982); Nancy Lynn Schwartz, *The Hollywood Writers' War* (1982); Ellen Shrecker, *No Ivory Tower: McCarthyism and the Universities* (1984); Peter Steinberg, *The Great "Red Menace:" United States Prosecution of American Communists, 1947–1952* (1984); Athan Theoharis, *Seeds of Repression: Harry S Truman and the Origins of McCarthyism* (1971); Allen Weinstein, *Perjury: The Hiss-Chambers Case* (1978); Robert Williams, *Klaus Fuchs: Atom Spy* (1987).

The Truman Administration
Jack Ballard, *The Shock of Peace: Military and Economic Demobilization after World War II* (1983); William Berman, *The Politics of Civil Rights in the Truman Administration* (1970); Barton Bernstein, ed., *Politics and Policies of the Truman Administration* (1970); Richard Dalfiume, *Desegregation of the U.S. Armed Forces* (1969); Robert Donovan, *Conflict and Crisis* (1977) and *Years of Tumult* (1982); Andrew Dunar, *The Truman Scandals and the Politics of Morality* (1984); Robert Ferrell, *Harry S Truman and the Modern American Presidency* (1983); Donald Fixico, *Termination and Relocation: Federal Indian Policy, 1945–1960* (1986); Alonzo Hamby, *Beyond the New Deal* (1973); Alton Lee, *Truman and Taft-Hartley* (1966); Maeva Marcus, *Truman and the Steel Seizure* (1977); Norman Markowitz, *The Rise and Fall of the People's Century: Henry A. Wallace and American Liberalism, 1941–1948* (1973); Allen Matusow, *Farm Politics and Policies in the Truman Years* (1967); Donald McCoy, *The Presidency of Harry S Truman* (1984); Donald McCoy and Richard Ruetten, *Quest and Response: Minority Rights and the Truman Administration* (1973); Merle Miller, *Plain Speaking* (1973); Richard Miller, *Truman: The Rise to Power* (1986); Allen Yarnell, *Democrats and Progressives: The 1948 Presidential Election as a Test of Postwar Liberalism* (1974).

CHAPTER 31

General
James Gilbert, *Another Chance* (1981); Eric Goldman, *The Critical Decade and After, 1945–1960* (1960); Godfrey Hodgson, *America in Our Time* (1976); Martin Jezer, *The Dark Ages: Life in the United States, 1945–1960* (1982); William Leuchtenberg, *A Troubled Feast* (1979); Peter Lewis, *The Fifties* (1977); Douglas Miller and Marion Nowak, *The Fifties: The Way We Really Were* (1977); Ronald Oakley, *God's Country: America in the 1950s* (1986); William O'Neill, *American High* (1986).

American Life and Culture
Erik Barnouw, *Tube of Plenty* (1975); Daniel Bell, *The End of Ideology* (1960); Carl Belz, *The Story of Rock* (2d ed., 1972); Victoria Byerly, *Hard Times Cotton Mill Girls* (1986); Paul Carter, *Another Part of the Fifties* (1983); William Chafe, *The American Woman, 1920–1970* (1972); Bruce Cook, *The Beat Generation* (1970);

Richard Davies, *The Age of Asphalt* (1975); Carl Degler, *At Odds* (1980); John D'Emillio and Estelle Freedman, *Intimate Matters: A History of Sexuality in America* (1988); James Flink, *The Car Culture in America* (1973); Betty Friedan, *The Feminine Mystique* (1963); John Kenneth Galbraith, *The Affluent Society* (1958); Herbert Gans, *The Levittowners* (1967); James Gilbert, *A Cycle of Outrage* (1986); Charlie Gillett, *The Sound of the City: The Rise of Rock and Roll* (1970); Will Herberg, *Protestant-Catholic-Jew* (1956); Thomas Hine, *Populux* (1986); Kenneth Jackson, *Crabgrass Frontier* (1985); David Marc, *Demographic Vistas* (1984); Mary McAuliffe, *Crisis on the Left* (1978); C. Wright Mills, *The Power Elite* (1956) and *White Collar* (1951); George Nash, *The Conservative Intellectual Movement in America* (1976); Richard Pells, *The Liberal Mind in a Conservative Age* (1985); David Potter, *People of Plenty* (1956); David Riesman, *The Lonely Crowd* (1950); Gaye Tuchman et al., eds., *Hearth and Home: Images of Women in the Mass Media* (1978); Ed Ward et al., *Rock of Ages: The Rolling Stone History of Rock and Roll* (1986); Carol Warren, *Madwives: Schizophrenic Women in the 1950s* (1987); William Whyte, *The Organization Man* (1956).

Foreign Policy in the Eisenhower Era
Stephen Ambrose, *Ike's Spies: Eisenhower and the Espionage Establishment* (1981); Richard Barnet, *Intervention and Revolution* (rev. ed., 1972); Blanche W. Cook, *The Declassified Eisenhower* (1981); Chester Cooper, *The Lion's Last Roar: Suez, 1956* (1978); Robert Divine, *Eisenhower and the Cold War* (1981), and *Blowin' in the Wind: The Nuclear Test Ban Debate, 1954–1960* (1978); Townsend Hoopes, *The Devil and John Foster Dulles* (1973); Richard Immerman, *The CIA in Guatemala* (1982); Madeline Kalb, *The Congo Cables: The Cold War in Africa from Eisenhower to Kennedy* (1982); Burton Kaufman, *Trade and Aid: Eisenhower's Economic Policy* (1982); Richard Melanson and David Mayers, eds., *Reevaluating Eisenhower: American Foreign Policy in the 1950s* (1987); Kermit Roosevelt, *Counter-Coup* (1979,80); Stephen Schlesinger and Steven Kinzer, *Bitter Fruit* (1981); Richard Welch, Jr., *Response to Revolution: The United States and the Cuban Revolution, 1954–1961* (1985); Mira Wilkins, *The Maturing of Multinational Enterprise* (1974).

Civil Rights
Numan Bartley, *The Rise of Massive Resistance: Race and Politics in the South during the 1950s* (1969); Jack Bloom, *Class, Race, and the Civil Rights Movement* (1987); James Duram, *Moderate Among Extremists: Dwight D. Eisenhower and the School Desegregation Crisis* (1981); David Garrow, *Bearing the Cross* (1986); Vincent Harding, *There is a River: The Black Struggle for Freedom in America* (1981); Elizabeth Huckaby, *The Crisis at Central High: Little Rock 1957–1958* (1980); Richard Kluger, *Simple Justice* (1975); Anthony Lewis et al., *Portrait of a Decade* (1964); August Meier and Elliott Rudwick, *Core: A Study in the Civil Rights Movement, 1942–1968* (1975); Stephen Oates, *Let the Trumpet Sound: The Life and Times of Martin Luther King, Jr.* (1982); Bernard Schwartz, *Inside the Warren Court* (1983); C. Vann Woodward, *The Strange Career of Jim Crow* (3rd ed., 1974); Juan Williams, *Eyes on the Prize: America's Civil Rights Years, 1954–1965* (1987).

Domestic Politics
Stephen Ambrose, *Eisenhower the President* (1984); Alexander Bickel, *Politics and the Warren Court* (1965); Piers Brendon, *Ike* (1986); Larry Burt, *Tribalism in Crisis: Federal Indian Policy, 1953–1961* (1982); Barbara Clowse, *Brainpower for the Cold War: The Sputnik Crisis and the National Defense Education Act of 1958* (1981); Donald Fixico, *Termination and Relocation: Federal Indian Policy, 1945–1960* (1986); Fred Greenstein, *The Hidden Hand Presidency: Eisenhower as Leader* (1982); Robert Heilbroner, *The Limits of American Capitalism* (1965); Joann Krieg, ed., *Dwight D. Eisenhower: Soldier, President, and Statesman* (1987); David W. Reinhard, *The Republican Right Since 1945* (1983); Elmo Richardson, *The Presidency of Dwight D. Eisenhower* (1979); Mark Rose, *Interstate: Express Highway Politics, 1941–1956* (1979); Michael Straight, *Trial by Television* (1954); Herbert Vatter, *The U.S. Economy in the 1950s* (1963); Gary Wills, *Nixon Agonistes* (1970).

CHAPTER 32

General
Todd Gitlin, *The Sixties* (1987); Richard Goodwin, *Remembering America: A Voice from the Sixties* (1988); Godfrey Hodgson, *America in Our Time* (1976); Landon Y. Jones, *Great Expectations: America and the Baby Boom Generation* (1981); Allen Matusow, *The Unraveling of America: A History of Liberalism in the 1960s* (1984); Lawrence Wright, *The New World: Growing Up in America, 1960–1984* (1988).

The Counterculture and New Left
Serge Denisoff, *Great Day Coming: Folk Music and the American Left* (1971); Morris Dickstein, *The Gates of Eden;* Joan Didion, *Slouching Towards Bethlehem* (1968), and *White Album* (1979); Todd Gitlin, *The Whole World Is Watching: The Mass Media in the Making and Unmaking of the New Left* (1981); Paul Goodman, *Growing Up Absurd* (1960); Maurice Isserman, *If I Had a Hammer . . . : The Death of the Old Left and the Birth of the New Left* (1987); Judy Kaplan and Linn Shapiro, *Red Diaper Babies: Children on the Left* (1985); Kenneth Keniston, *The Uncommitted* (1965); Lawrence Lader, *Power on the Left* (1979); Martin Lee and Bruce Shlain, *Acid Dreams: The CIA, LSD, and the Sixties Rebellion* (1985); Dennis McNally, *Desolate Angel: Jack Kerouac, the Beat Generation, and America* (1979); William O'Neill, *Coming Apart* (1971); Theodore Roszak, *The Making of a Counter Culture* (1969); Stanley Rothman and S. Robert Lichter, *Roots of Rebellion* (1982); Kirkpatrick Sale, *SDS* (1973); Anthony Scaduto, *Bob Dylan* (1971); Philip Slater, *The Pursuit of Loneliness* (1970); Students for a Democratic Society, *The Port Huron Statement* (1962); Hunter Thompson, *Hell's Angels* (1967) and *Fear and Loathing in Las Vegas* (1971); Ed Ward et al., *Rock of Ages: The Rolling Stone History of Rock and Roll* (1986); Tom Wolfe, *Electric Kool-Aid Acid Test* (1968).

Civil Rights and Black Power
Michael Belknap, *Federal Law and Southern Order: Racial Violence and Constitutional Conflict in the Post-Brown South* (1987); Derrick Bell, *And We Are Not Saved: The Elusive Quest for Racial Justice* (1987); Jack Bloom, *Class, Race, and the Civil Rights Movement* (1987); Taylor Branch, *Parting the Waters* (1988); Carl Brauer, *John F. Kennedy and the Second Reconstruction* (1980); Stokely Carmichael and Charles Hamilton, *Black Power* (1967); Clayborne Carson, *In Struggle: SNCC and the Black Awakening of the 1960s* (1981); William Chafe, *Civilities and Civil Rights* (1980) and *The Unfinished Journey* (1986); Joe Feagin and Harlan Hahn, *Ghetto Revolts* (1973); David Garrow, *Bearing the Cross* (1986) and *The FBI and Martin Luther King* (1981); Vincent Harding, *There is a River: The Black Struggle for Freedom in America* (1981); Otto Kerner et al., *The Report of the National Advisory Commission on Civil Disorders* (1968); Steven Lawson, *Black Ballots* (1976) and *In Pursuit of Power* (1985); Malcolm X (with Alex Haley), *The Autobiography of Malcolm X* (1966); August Meier and Elliott Rudwick, *Core: A Study in the Civil Rights Movement, 1942–1968* (1975); Stephen Oates, *Let the Trumpet Sound: The Life and Times of Martin Luther King, Jr.* (1982); Bernard Schwartz, *Inside the Warren Court* (1983); Harvard Sitkoff, *The Struggle for Black Equality, 1954–1980* (1981); Juan Williams, *Eyes on the Prize: America's Civil Rights Years, 1954–1965* (1987); Harris Wofford, *Of Kennedy and Kings* (1980); Eugene Wolfenstein, *The Victims of Democracy: Malcolm X and the Black Revolutionaries* (1981).

The Kennedys and Lyndon Johnson
Robert Caro, *The Years of Lyndon Johnson: The Path to Power* (1982); Paul Conkin, *Big Daddy from the Pedernales: Lyndon Baines Johnson* (1986); Ronnie Dugger, *The Politician* (1982); Jim Heath, *Decade of Disillusionment* (1975); Henry Hurt, *Reasonable Doubt: An Investigation into the Assassination John F. Kennedy* (1985); Lyndon Johnson, *Vantage Point* (1971); Doris Kearns, *Lyndon Johnson and the American Dream* (1976); Bruce Miroff, *Pragmatic Illusions* (1976); Herbert Parmet, *Jack* (1980), and *JFK—The Presidency of John F. Kennedy* (1983); Arthur Schlesinger, Jr., *The Thousand Days* (1965), and *Robert Kennedy and His Times* (1978); Earl Warren et al., *The Report of the Warren Commission* (1964); Theodore White, *The Making of the President, 1960* (1961).

**Politics and Foreign Policy in the
Kennedy-Johnson Era**
Henry Aaron, *Politics and the Professors* (1978); Graham Allison, *Essence of Decision: Explaining the Cuban Missile Crisis* (1971); James Anderson and Jared Hazelton, *Managing Macroeconomic Policy: The Johnson Presidency* (1986); Desmond Ball, *Politics and Force Levels: The Strategic Missile Program of the Kennedy Administration* (1980); Warren Cohen, *Dean Rusk* (1980); Hugh Graham Davis, *Uncertain Trumpet* (1984); Greg Duncan, *Years of Poverty, Years of Plenty* (1984); Robert Haveman, ed., *A Decade of Federal Antipoverty Programs* (1977); Walter LaFeber, *America, Russia, and the Cold War, 1945–1984* (5th ed., 1985); Sar Levitan and Robert Taggart, *The Promise of Greatness* (1976); Richard Mahoney, *JFK: Ordeal in Africa* (1983); Walter McDougall, *...The Heavens and the Earth: A Political History of the Space Age* (1985); Charles Murray, *Losing Ground: American Social Policy, 1950–1980* (1984); Thomas Noer, *Cold War and Black Liberation: The United States and White Rule in Africa, 1948–1968* (1985); Francis Fox Piven and Richard Cloward, *Regulating the Poor* (1971); Emmette Redford and Richard

McCulley, *White House Operations: The Johnson Presidency* (1986); Gerald Rice, *The Bold Experiment: JFK's Peace Corps* (1985); Glenn Seaborg, *Kennedy, Khrushchev, and the Test Ban* (1981); R. B. Smith, *An International History of the Vietnam War: The Kennedy Strategy* (1985); Tom Wicker, *JFK and LBJ* (1968); Bryce Wood, *The Dismantling of the Good Neighbor Policy* (1985); Peter Wyden, *The Bay of Pigs* (1979).

CHAPTER 33

The United States and the Vietnam War

Loren Baritz, *Backfire: A History of How American Culture Led Us into Vietnam and Made Us Fight the Way We Did* (1985); Larry Berman, *Planning a Tragedy* (1982); William Broyles, *Brothers in Arms: A Journey From War to Peace* (1986); Richard Dean Burns and Milton Leitenberg, eds., *The Wars in Vietnam, Cambodia, and Laos, 1945–1982* (1984); Larry Cable, *Conflict of Myths: The Development of American Counterinsurgency Doctrine and the Vietnam War* (1986); Francis Fitzgerald, *Fire in the Lake* (1972); Leslie Gelb and Richard Betts, *The Irony of Vietnam: The System Worked* (1979); Mike Gravel et al., *The Pentagon Papers*, (1975); David Halberstam, *The Best and the Brightest* (1972) and *The Making of a Quagmire* (rev. ed., 1987); George Herring, *America's Longest War* (2d ed., 1986); George Kahin, *Intervention: How America Became Involved in Vietnam* (1986); Stanley Karnow, *Vietnam* (1983); Gabriel Kolko, *Anatomy of a War* (1985); Andrew Krepinevich, Jr., *The Army and Vietnam* (1986); Guenter Lewy, *America in Vietnam* (1978); Kathryn Marshall, *In the Combat Zone: An Oral History of Women in the Vietnam War, 1966–1975* (1987); Tim Page, *Nam* (1983); Bruce Palmer, Jr., *The 25-Year War* (1984); Archimedes Patti, *Why Viet Nam?* (1983); Norman Podhoretz, *Why We Were in Vietnam* (1982); Al Santoli, *Everything We Had: An Oral History of the Vietnam War by Thirty Three American Soldiers Who Fought It* (1981); Neil Sheehan, *A Bright Shining Lie: John Paul Vann and America in Vietnam* (1988); Ronald Spector, *The United States Army in Vietnam* (1983); Shelby Stanton, *Rises and Fall of an American Army: U.S. Ground Forces, Vietnam, 1965–1973* (1985) and *Green Berets at War* (1985); Harry Summers, Jr., *On Strategy: A Critical Analysis of the Vietnam War* (1981); Wallace Terry, *Bloods: An Oral History of the Vietnam War by Black Veterans* (1984); William Turley, *The Second Indochina War: A Short Political and Military History* (1986).

Dissent Against the War

William Berman, *William Fulbright and the Vietnam War* (1988); Eugene Brown, *William Fulbright: Advise and Dissent* (1984); David Caute, *The Year of the Barricades, 1968* (1988); Gloria Emerson, *Winners and Losers* (1976); David Farber, *Chicago '68* (1988); Todd Gitlin, *The Sixties* (1987); Myra MacPherson, *Long Time Passing: Vietnam and the Haunted Generation* (1984); Norman Mailer, *Armies of the Night* (1968) and *Miami and the Siege of Chicago* (1969); James Miller, *Democracy Is in the Streets* (1987); Thomas Powers, *Vietnam: The War at Home* (1973); Herbert Schandler, *The Unmaking of a President: Lyndon Johnson and Vietnam* (1977); Melvin Small, *Johnson, Nixon, and the Doves* (1988); William Strauss, *Chance and Circumstance* (1978); Irwin Unger,

The Movement (1974); Lawrence Wittner, *Rebels Against War: The American Peace Movement, 1933–1983* (1984); Nancy Zaroulis and Gerald Sullivan, *Who Spoke Up? American Protest Against the War in Vietnam* (1984).

The Nixon Presidency Before Watergate

Richard Barnet, *The Giants: Russia and America* (1977); Fawn Brodie, *Richard Nixon* (1981); John Erlichman, *Witness to Power* (1982); Raymond Garthoff, *Détente and Confrontation: American-Soviet Relations from Nixon to Reagan* (1985); Seymour Hersh, *The Price of Power: Kissinger in the Nixon White House* (1983); Henry Kissinger, *The White House Years* (1979) and *Years of Upheaval* (1982); Robert Litwack, *Détente and the Nixon Doctrine* (1984); Morris Morley, *The United States and Chile* (1975); Roger Morris, *Uncertain Greatness: Henry Kissinger and American Foreign Policy* (1977); Daniel Patrick Moynihan, *The Politics of a Guaranteed Income* (1973); Richard Nixon, *RN* (1978); Leon Panetta and Peter Gall, *Bring Us Together: The Nixon Team and the Civil Rights Retreat* (1971); William Safire, *Before the Fall* (1975); William Shawcross, *Sideshow: Nixon, Kissinger, and the Destruction of Cambodia* (1978); Robert Sutter, *The China Quandary* (1983); Theodore White, *The Making of the President, 1968* (1969); Gary Wills, *Nixon Agonistes* (1970).

Minorities: Background and Politics

Rodolfo Acuna, *Occupied America* (2d ed., 1981); Mario Barerra, *Race and Class in the Southwest* (1979); John Burma, ed., *Mexican-Americans in the United States* (1970); Albert Camarillo, *Hispanics in a Changing Society* (1979); Tony Castro, *Chicano Power* (1974); Vine Deloria, *Behind the Veil of Broken Treaties* (1974); Patrick Gallagher, *The Cuban Exile* (1980); Hazel W. Hertzberg, *The Search for an American Indian Identity: Modern Pan-Indian Movements* (1971); Peter Iverson, *The Navajo Nation* (1981); Virginia Sanchez Korrol, *From Colonia to Community* (1983); Darcy McNickle, *Native American Tribalism* (1973); Joan Moore and Harry Pachon, *Hispanics in the United States* (1985); Joan Moore et al., *Homeboys* (1978); Roger Nichols, *The American Indian: Past and Present* (3rd ed. 1986); James Olsen and Raymond Wilson, *Native Americans in the Twentieth Century* (1984); A. Petit, *Images of Mexican-American in Fiction and Film* (1980); Thomas Sanders and Walter Peek, *Literature of the American Indian* (1976); Ronald Taylor, *Chavez and the Farm Workers* (1975); Dennis Tedlock and Barbara Tedlock, eds., *Teachings from the American Earth: Indian Religion and Philosophy* (1975); Arnulfo Trejo, ed., *The Chicanos: As We See Ourselves* (1979); Karl Wagenheim, *Puerto Rico: A Profile* (1975).

CHAPTER 34

American Society and the Economy in the 1970s

Richard Barnet, *The Lean Years* (1980); John Blair, *The Control of Oil* (1976); Barry Bluestone and Bennett Harrison, *The Deindustrialization of America* (1982); Peter Calleo, *The Imperious Economy* (1982); Peter Carroll, *It Seemed Like Nothing Happened: The Tragedy and Promise of America in the 1970s* (1982); Peter Clecak, *America's Quest for an Ideal Self* (1983); Barry Commoner, *The Politics of Energy* (1979); Jim Hougan, *Dec-*

adence: Radical Nostalgia, Narcissism, and Decline in the 1970s (1975); Christopher Lasch, The Culture of Narcissism (1978); J. Anthony Lukas, Common Ground: A Turbulent Decade in the Lives of Three American Families (1986); Martin Melosi, Coping with Abundance: Energy and Environment in Industrial America (1985); John Schwarz, America's Hidden Success (rev. ed., 1988); Robert Sherrill, The Oil Follies of 1970–1980 (1983); Lester Thurow, The Zero-Sum Society (1980).

Environmentalism
Rachel Carson, Silent Spring (1962); Barry Caspar and Paul Wellstone, Powerline (1981); Barry Commoner, The Closing Circle (1971); Albert Cowdry, This Land, This South: An Environmental History (1983); Thomas Dunlap, DDT: Scientists, Citizens, and Public Policy (1981); Edith Efron, The Apocalyptics (1984); Sam Hays, Beauty, Health, and Permanence: Environmental Politics in the United States, 1955–1985 (1987); Ronald Inglehart, The Silent Revolution (1977); Ian McHarg, Design with Nature (1969); Daniel Martin, Three Mile Island (1980); Lester Milbrath, Environmentalists: Vanguard for a New Society (1984); Ralph Nader and John Abbotts, The Menace of Atomic Energy (1977); Roderick Nash, Wilderness and the American Mind (3rd ed., 1982); Marc Reisner, Cadillac Desert: The American West and Its Disappearing Water (1986); Robert Stobaugh and Daniel Yergin, eds., Energy Future (1979); James Trefethen, An American Crusade for Wildlife (1975); Thomas Whiteside, The Pendulum and the Toxic Cloud (1979); Donald Worster, Rivers of Empire: Water Aridity, and the Growth of the American West (1985).

Feminism, Sexual Politics, and the Family
Rae Andre, Homemakers: The Forgotten Workers (1981); Judith Barwick, In Transition: How Feminism, Sexual Liberation, and the Search for Self-Fulfillment Have Altered America (1979); Peter Berger and Bridgett Berger, The War Over the Family: Capturing the Middle Ground (1983); Mary Frances Berry, Why ERA Failed: Politics, Women's Rights, and the Amending Process of the Constitution (1986); Caroline Bird, Born Female: The High Cost of Keeping Women Down (1969); Susan Brownmiller, Against Our Will: Men, Women, and Rape (1975); William Chafe, Women and Equality: Changing Patterns in American Culture (1977); Robert Coles and Geoffrey Stokes, Sex and the American Teenager (1985); Angela Davis, Women, Race, and Class (1981); Barbara Deckard, The Women's Movement (1975); Carl Degler, At Odds (1980); John D'Emilio, Sexual Politics, Sexual Communities: The Making of a Homosexual Minority in the United States, 1940–1970 (1983); John D'Emilio and Estelle Freedman, Intimate Matters: A History of Sexuality in America (1988); Andrea Dworkin, Right-Wing Women (1983); Barbara Ehrenreich, The Hearts of Men: American Dreams and the Flight From Commitment (1983); Susan Estebrook, If All We Did Was to Weep at Home: A History of White Working-Class Women in America (1979); Sara Evans, Personal Politics: The Roots of Women's Liberation in the Civil Rights Movement and the New Left (1979); Lillian Faderman, Surpassing the Love of Men (1979); Shulamith Firestone, The Dialectic of Sex: The Case for the Feminist Revolution (1970); Jo Freeman, The Politics of Women's Liberation (1975); Victor Fuchs, How We Live: An Economic Perspective

on Americans from Birth to Death (1983); Carol Gilligan, In Another Voice: Psychological Theory and Women's Development (1982); Germaine Greer, The Female Eunuch (1972); Alice Kessler Harris, Out to Work (1982); Judith Hole and Ellen Levine, The Rebirth of Feminism (1971); Louis Kapp Howe, Pink Collar Workers: Inside the World of Women's Work (1977); Gloria Hull et al., But Some of Us Are Brave: Black Women Studies (1982); Morton Hunt, Sexual Behavior in the 1970s (1974); Elizabeth Janeway, Cross Sections from a Decade of Change (1983); Jonathan Katz, ed., Gay American History (1976); Linda Kerber and Jane Matthews, eds., America: Refocusing the Past (1981); Christopher Lasch, Haven in a Hostile World (1979); Kate Millett, Sexual Politics (1970); Steven Mintz and Susan Kellogg, Domestic Revolutions: A Social History of American Family Life (1988); Robin Morgan, ed., Sisterhood Is Powerful: An Anthology (1970); Helen Rogan, Mixed Company: Women in the Modern Army (1981); La Frances Rodgers-Rose, ed., The Black Woman (1980); Sheila Rothman, Woman's Proper Place (1978); Nancy Seifer, Nobody Speaks for Me: Self-Portraits of American Working-Class Women (1976); Gloria Steinem, Outrageous Acts and Everyday Rebellions (1983); Nancy Wolloch, Women and the American Experience (1984).

Watergate
Richard Ben-Veniste and George Frampton, Stonewall (1978); John Dean, Blind Ambition (1976); J. Anthony Lukas, Nightmare: The Underside of the Nixon Years (rev. ed., 1988); Richard Nixon, RN: The Memoirs of Richard Nixon (1978); Arthur Schlesinger, Jr., The Imperial Presidency (1973); Jonathan Schell, The Time of Illusion (1975); John Sirica, To Set the Record Straight (1979); Theodore White, Breach of Faith (1975); Bob Woodward and Carl Bernstein, All the President's Men (1974), and The Final Days (1976).

Politics and Diplomacy in the Ford-Carter Years
Zbigniew Brzezinski, Power and Principle (1983); Jimmy Carter, Keeping the Faith (1982); Rosalynn Carter, First Lady from Plains (1984); Terry Deibel, Presidents, Public Opinion, and Power: The Nixon, Carter, and Reagan Years (1987); Gerald Ford, A Time to Heal (1979); Millicent Gates and Bruce Geelhoed, The Dragon and the Snake: An American Account of the Turmoil in China, 1976–1977 (1986); Robert Hartman, Palace Politics (1980); Michael Hogan, The Panama Canal in American Politics (1986); Henry Jackson, From the Congo to Soweto: U.S. Foreign Policy Toward Africa Since 1960 (1982); Hamilton Jordan, Crisis (1982); Walter LaFeber, The Panama Canal (rev. ed., 1989); Clark Mollenhoff, The President Who Failed (1980); Richard Pipes, U.S.-Soviet Relations in the Era of Détente (1981); William Quandt, Camp David (1986); Stephen Rabe, The Road to OPEC: U.S. Relations with Venezuela, 1919–1976 (1982); R. K. Ramazani, The U.S. and Iran (1982); A. James Reichley, Conservatives in an Age of Change: The Nixon and Ford Administrations (1981); Kirkpatrick Sale, Power Shift (1975); Gary Sick, All Fall Down (1985); Gaddis Smith, Morality, Reason, and Power (1986); Robert Sutter, The China Quandary (1983); Strobe Talbot, Endgame (1979); Seth Tillman, The U.S. in the Middle East (1982); Cyrus Vance, Hard Choices (1983).

CHAPTER 35

Contemporary American Society

Robert Bellah et al., *Habits of the Heart: Individualism and Commitment in American Life* (1985); Thomas Edsall, *The New Politics of Inequality* (1984); Michael Goldfield, *The Decline of Organized Labor in the United States* (1987); Michael Harrington, *The New American Poverty* (1984); Jonathan Kwitny, *The Crimes of Patriots: A True Tale of Dope, Dirty Money, and the CIA* (1987); Frank Levy *Dollars and Dreams: The Changing American Income Distribution* (1987); Jane Mansbridge, *Why We Lost the ERA* (1986); David Marc, *Demographic Vistas: Television in American Culture* (1984); Robert McElvaine, *The End of the Conservative Era: Liberalism After Reagan* (1987); Michael Piore and Charles Sabal, *The Second Industrial Divide: Possibilities for Prosperity* (1987); Frances Fox Piven and Richard Cloward, *The New Class War* (1982); Robert Sklar, *Prime Time* (1980); Robert Spitzer, *The Right to Life Movement and Third Party Politics* (1987); Peter Steinfels, *The Neo-Conservatives* (1979); Studs Terkel, *The Great Divide* (1988); John Woodridge, *The Evangelicals* (1975).

The Reagan Presidency

Frank Ackerman, *Reaganomics* (1982); Stephen Cimbala, *The Reagan Defense Program* (1986); Joan Claybrook, *Retreat from Safety: Reagan's Attack on American Health* (1984); Robert Dallek, *Ronald Reagan: The Politics of Symbolism* (1984); Michael Deaver, *Behind the Scenes* (1987); Ronnie Duggar, *On Reagan* (1983); Rowland Evans and Robert Novak, *The Reagan Revolution* (1981); Jonathan Lash, *A Season of Spoils: The Story of the Reagan Administration's Attack on the Environment* (1984); Robert Lekachman, *Greed Is Not Enough* (1983); Jane Mayer and Doyle McManus, *Landslide: The Unmaking of the President, 1984–1988* (1988); Austin Ranney, ed., *The American Elections of 1984* (1985); Richard Reeves, *The Reagan Detour* (1985); Donald Regan, *For the Record* (1988); Larry Speakes, *Speaking Out* (1988); Paul Stares, *Space and National Security* (1987); David Stockman, *The Triumph of Politics: The Inside Story of the Reagan Revolution* (1986); Gary Wills, *Reagan's America* (1987).

Foreign Policy in the 1980s

Lawrence Barrett, *Gambling with History* (1984); Tom Barry et al., *The Other Side of Paradise: Foreign Control in the Caribbean* (1984); Karl Bermann, *Under the Big Stick* (1985); Raymond Bonner, *Weakness and Deceit: U.S. Policy and El Salvador* (1984); Tom Buckley, *Violent Neighbors* (1984); Bradford Burns, *At War with Nicaragua* (1987); Leslie Cockburn, *Out of Control* (1987); Christopher Coker, *The United States and South Africa, 1968–1985* (1986); Stephen Emerson, *Secret Warriors* (1988); Carl Feldbaum and Ronald Bee, *Looking the Tiger in the Eye: Confronting the Nuclear Threat* (1988); Roy Gutman, *Banana Diplomacy* (1988); Alexander Haig, Jr., *Caveat: Realism, Reagan, and Foreign Policy* (1984); Jerry Hough, *The Struggle for the Third World* (1986); Bruce Jentleson, *Pipeline Politics: The Complex Political Economy of East-West Trade* (1986); Walter LaFeber, *Inevitable Revolutions* (2d ed., 1984); David Martin and John Wolcott, *Best Laid Plans* (1988); Morris Morley, *The Imperial State and Revolution* (1987); Robert Pastor, *Condemned to Repetition: The United States and Nicaragua* (1987); Stephen Randall, *U.S. Foreign Oil Policy, 1919–1984* (1985); Jonathan Schell, *The Fate of the Earth* (1982); Lars Schoultz, *National Security and U.S. Policy Toward Latin America* (1987); Strobe Talbott, *Deadly Gambits: The Reagan Administration and the Stalemate in Nuclear Arms Control* (1984), and *The Russians and Reagan* (1984); Sanford Ungar, *Africa* (1985); Thomas Walker, ed., *Reagan Versus the Sandinistas* (1987); Bob Woodward, *Veil: The Secret Wars of the CIA* (1987).

Minority Relations and the New Immigration

Ken Auletta, *The Underclass* (1982); John Crewden, *The Tarnished Door: The New Immigrants and the Transformation of America* (1983); Roger Daniels et al., eds., *Japanese-Americans: From Relocation to Redress* (1986); Leonard Dinnerstein and David Reimers, *Ethnic Americans* (2d ed., 1982); Reynolds Farley and Walter Allen, *The Color Line and the Quality of Life in America* (1987); Douglas Glasgow, *The Black Underclass* (1980); Stanford Lyman, *Chinese Americans* (1974); Joan Moore and Harry Pachon, *Hispanics in the United States* (1985); Adolph Reed, *The Jesse Jackson Phenomenon: The Crisis of Purpose in Afro-American Politics* (1986); David Reimers, *Still the Golden Door: The Third World Comes to America* (1985); The Staff of the *Chicago Tribune*, *The American Millstone: An Examination of the Nation's Permanent Underclass* (1986); Shih-Shan Henry Tsai, *The Chinese Experience in America* (1986); William J. Wilson, *The Declining Significance of Race: Blacks and Changing American Institutions* (2d ed., 1980).

PHOTO CREDITS

Historical Society, New York City; **247** Culver Pictures; **252** Independence National Historical Park; **254** Independence National Historical Park; **256** Colonial Williamsburg Foundation.

GENERATIONS OF THE REPUBLIC

258-L The Library Company of Philadelphia; **258-R** Thomas Coram, "View of Mulberry Plantation." Oil on paper, 10 × 17.6 cm. The Gibbes Museum of Art/Carolina Art Association; **259-L** The Detroit Institute of Arts, Founders Society Purchase, Gibbs-Williams Fund; **259-C** Maryland Historical Society, Baltimore, Md. Bequest of Miss Ellen C. Gaingerfield; **259-R** Maryland Historical Society, Baltimore, Md.; **260-L** Colonial Williamsburg Foundation; **260-C** Collection of Dr. Alexander A. McBurney; **260-R** The Valentine Museum, Richmond, Va.; **261-L** Abby Aldrich Rockefeller Folk Art Center; **261-R** "Renty, Congo. Plantation of B. F. Taylor, Esq." Original daguerrotype by J. T. Zealy, Columbia, S.C., 1850. Courtesy of the Peabody Museum, Harvard University.

CHAPTER 8

263 Courtesy of the New York Historical Society, New York City; **264** American Antiquarian Society; **269** Addison Gallery of American Art, Phillips Academy, Andover, Mass.; **277-L** Independence National Historical Park; **277-R** National Gallery of Art, Washington, D.C.; **281** Culver Pictures; **284** Courtesy of the New York Historical Society, New York City; **289** U.S. Department of the Interior, National Park Service. Adams National Historic Site, Quincy, Mass.; **294** Courtesy of The Henry Francis Du Pont Winterthur Museum (detail).

CHAPTER 9

299 New York State Historical Association (detail); **300** Courtesy of the New York Public Library; **301** Library of Congress; **306** Boston Athenaeum (detail); **313** Library of Congress; **319** George Catlin, "The Open Door, known as The Prophet, brother of Tecumseh," 1830. Oil on canvas, 29 × 24 in. National Museum of American Art, Smithsonian Institution. Gift of Mrs. Joseph Harrison, Jr.; **324** The Historical Society of Pennsylvania; **328-L** New Orleans Museum of Art. Gift of Edgar William and Bernice Chrysler Garbish; **328-R** Yale University Art Gallery, Mabe;l Brady Garvan Collection; **331** New York State Office of Parks, Recreation and Historic Preservation. Philips Manor Hall State Historic Site; **334** Bibliothèque Nationale (detail); **335** Bildarchiv Preussischer Kulturbesitz.

CHAPTER 10

339 The Bettmann Archive; **342** Smithsonian Institution, Textile Division; **343** Courtesy of the New York Historical Society, New York City; **349** Anglo-American Art Museum, Louisiana State University, Baton Rouge. Gift of Mrs. Mamie Persac Lusk; **353** Beinecke Rare Book and Manuscript Library, Yale University; **357** Missouri Historical Society; **361** Baker Library Manuscripts & Archives, Harvard Business School. Harvard University; **369** Alfred Jacob Miller, "Caravan en Route." Courtesy Boatmens BancShares, Inc. St. Louis, Mo.

CHAPTER 11

375 Roosevelt Library; **377** Courtesy of the Historical Society of York County, Penna.; **377** Courtesy of the New York Historical Society, New York City; **384** The St. Louis Art Museum; **390** New Orleans Museum of Art. Gift of William E. Groves; **391** Historical Picture Service, Inc.; **395-L** Fogg Art Museum, Harvard University (detail); **395-R** Collection of Jay P. Altmayer; **398** Boston Art Commission, Office of the Arts and Humanities; **404** Museum of the City of New York, The Clarence Davies Collection; **407** Courtesy of The Cincinnati Historical Society.

CHAPTER 12

413 Print Collection, Miriam and Ira D. Wallach Division of Arts, Prints and Photographs. New York Public Library, Astor, Lenox, and Tilden Foundations; **414** The Stowe-Day Foundation, Hartford, Conn.; **416** Allen Memorial Art Museum. Gift of Lewis Tappan; **421** Historical Picture Service, Inc.; **423** Bettmann ArchiveBBC Hulton; **425** Library of Congress; **427** Rare Book Division, New York Public Library, Astor, Lenox, and Tilden Foundations; **428** Culver Pictures; **436-L** Rare Books and Manuscripts, Boston Public Library. Photo courtesy Geoffrey Stein Studios; **436-R** The Bettmann Archive; **438** The Bettmann Archive; **441** Courtesy of Rhoda Barney Jenkins.

GENERATIONS OF THE REPUBLIC

446-L Colonial Williamsburg Foundation; **446-C** Fraktur. Andrew Mayberry-Margaret Trott Family Record, Heart & Hand artist, Windam, Me. Watercolor and ink on woven paper, 13⅜″ × 9⅜″. Collection of the Museum of American Folk Art, New York City. Gift of Mr. and Mrs. Philip M. Isaacson; **446-R** The Nelson-Atkins Museum of Art, Kansas City Missouri. Gift of Mrs. Edith Gregor Halpert; **447-L** Colonial Williamsburg Foundation; **447-C** Gift of Belle Greene and Henry Copley Greene, in memory of their mother, Mary Abbey Greene. Courtesy of the Museum of Fine Arts, Boston; **447-R** "The Emerson School" by Southworth and Hawes, American Daguerreotype (1840–1862). The Metropolitan Museum of Art. Gift of I. N. Phelps Stokes, Edward S. Hawes, Alice Mary Hawes, Marion Augusta Hawes, 1937; **448-L** The Bettmann Archive; **448-R** Library of Congress; **449-L** Library of Congress; **449-C** National Archives; **449-R** Division of Photographic History, National Museum of American History. Smithsonian Institution, Washington, D.C.

CHAPTER 13

451 Historic New Orleans Collection; **454–455** Museum of the City of New York, Harry T. Peters Collection; **465** Historic New Orleans Collection; **467** San Antonio Museum Association, San Antonio, Tex.; **475** Kennedy Galleries, New York City; **477** Courtesy of The Charleston Museum, Charleston, S.C.; **483** Courtesy of the New York Historical Society, New York City.

CHAPTER 14

487 Library of Congress; **491** Alfred Sully, "Monterey, California Rancho Scene," n.d. Watercolor, 8″ × 10″. Kahn Collection. The Oakland Museum, Oakland, Calif.; **494** Courtesy, Archives Division, Texas State Library; **497** J. Goldsborough Bruff. Courtesy of the Yale University Library; **503** George Peter Alexander Healy, "James K. Polk." In the collection of The Corcoran Gallery of Art, Museum Purchase, Gallery Fund;

506 Courtesy of the New York Historical Society, New York City; **519** Library of Congress.

CHAPTER 15

523 Culver Pictures; **525** Kansas State Historical Society, Topeka, Kans.; **531** Museum of the City of New York; **541** Print Collection, Miriam and Ira D. Wallach Division of Arts, Prints and Photographs. New York Public Library, Astor, Lenox, and Tilden Foundations; **545** Missouri Historical Society; **545** Library of Congress; **547-L** The Bettmann Archive; **547-R** Illinois State Historical Library; **552** Boston Athenaeum; **556** *Harper's Weekly;* **549** Library of Congress.

CHAPTER 16

561 Winslow Homer, "A Rainy Day in Camp." The Metropolitan Museum of Art. Gift of Mrs. William F. Milton, 1932; **562** *Harper's Weekly;* **563** Chicago Historical Society; **571** Library of Congress; **574** Library of Congress; **578** Frank W. and Marie T. Wood Print Collection, Alexandria, Va.; **582** U.S. Army Military History Institute, Carlisle Barracks, Penna.; **583** M. and M. Karolik Collection. Courtesy, Museum of Fine Arts, Boston; **586** Dale S. Snair Collection, Richmond, Va.; **585** Larry B. Wilford Collection, Civil War Photohistorian; **597-L** Library of Congress; **597-R** The Valentine Museum of the Life and History of Richmond, Cook Collection.

CHAPTER 17

603 Winslow Homer, "A Visit from the Old Mistress," 1876. Oil on canvas, 18″ × 24⅛″. National Museum of American Art, Smithsonian Institution. Gift of William T. Evans; **607-L** Library of Congress; **607-R** U.S. Army Military History Institute, Carlisle Barracks, Penna.; **609** Library of Congress; **610** The Library Company of Philadelphia; **616** Library of Congress; **618** Library of Congress; **623** Courtesy of the New York Historical Society, New York City; **625** Richard Norris Brooke, "A Pastoral Visit, Virginia." In the collection of The Corcoran Gallery of Art, Museum Purchase, Gallery Fund; **629** The Valentine Museum of the Life and History of Richmond, Cook Collection; **631-L** Courtesy of the American Antiquarian Society; **631-R** Sophie Smith Collection, Smith College; **633** The Granger Collection; **636** Rutherford B. Hayes Presidential Center; **638** United States Senate, Committee on Rules and Administration; **639** Library of Congress, Division of Rare Books and Manuscripts; **642** The Bettmann Archive; **643** Courtesy of The British Library, London.

CHAPTER 18

647 The Granger Collection; **649** Library of Congress; **651** The Bettmann Archive; **652** The Margaret Woodbury Strong Museum, Rochester, N.Y.; **654** Culver Pictures; **657** Library of Congress; **666** Courtesy of Exxon; **669** Lee Boltin Picture Library; **674** Courtesy of the Metropolitan Life Insurance Company, N.Y.; **678** Collection of Lee Baxandall.

CHAPTER 19

683 Theodore Groll, German, 1857–1913: "Washington Street, Indianapolis at Dusk," 1892–95. Oil on canvas, 76″ × 98½″. Copyright 1989 Indianapolis Museum of Art. Gift of a Couple of Old Hoosiers; **684** Library of Congress; **685** "Cliff Dwellers," 1913. George Wesley Bellows, United States, 1882–1925. Oil on canvas, 39½″ × 41½″. Los Angeles County Museum of Art, Los Angeles County Funds; **692** National Archives. Photo courtesy Rudolph Vetter/Interpretive Photography; **694** Courtesy of the New York Public Library, Astor, Lenox, and Tilden Foundations; **698** Milwaukee Art Museum, Layton Art Collection; **700** *Good Housekeeping,* March 1, 1889; **702** The Margaret Woodbury Strong Museum, Rochester, N.Y.; **707** Staten Island Historical Society; **711** Museum of Art, Rhode Island School of Design, Joseph Metcalf and Walter H. Kimball Funds.

GENERATIONS OF THE REPUBLIC

714-L The Fine Arts Museum of San Francisco. Gift of Mr. and Mrs. John D. Rockefeller, 3rd; **714-C** Milwaukee County Historical Society; **714-R** Courtesy of the Museum of Modern Art, N.Y. Museum Purchase; **715-C** Library of Congress; **715-C** University of Oregon Library; **715-R** Library of Congress; **716-L** The Bettmann Archive; **716-C** Museum of the City of New York; **716-R** Minneapolis Institute of Arts; **717-L** Tuskegee University Archives, Chester Higgins Collection; **717-C** Ashfield Historical Society, Howes Brothers Photograph; **717-R** Ashfield Historical Society, Howes Brothers Photograph.

CHAPTER 20

719 Idaho State Historical Society; **721** Courtesy of the New York Public Library; **723** Robert P. Coggins Collection of Southern American Art; **727** Brown Brothers; **735** Library of Congress; **742** National Anthropological Archives, Smithsonian Institution; **746** Henry E. Huntington Library and Art Gallery; **748** Courtesy, Wichita Art Museum, the Roland P. Murdock Collection; **753** Nebraska State Historical Society, Solomon D. Butcher Collection; **754** Greeley Municipal Museum.

CHAPTER 21

759 Courtesy of the New York Historical Society, New York City; **760** Culver Pictures; **761** Library of Congress; **763** Chicago Historical Society; **765** Bancroft Library; **769** Library of Congress; **770** California State Library; **775** The Kansas State Historical Society, Topeka, Kans. **779** Courtesy, Dover Publications, N.Y.; **782** Museum of American Political Life, University of Hartford, Conn.; **783** Library of Congress; **787** Library of Congress.

CHAPTER 22

791 Tsuneo Tambu Collection, Yokohama, Japan. Photo courtesy Laurie Platt Winfrey, Inc.; **792** "Bugler," from *Colliers,* September 10, 1898, p. 13. Courtesy of the New York Public Library; **797** Fred Pansing. "Naval Parade," August 20, 1898. Oil on canvas. Courtesy of the Museum of the City of New York; **803** Library of Congress (both); **806** Hawaii State Archives; **813** Library of Congress; **816** Library of Congress (both); **819** New York Public Library, Lewis Hine Collection.

CHAPTER 23

823 Library of Congress (detail); **824** Brown Brothers; **825** "The Four Suffragettes." *Colliers,* 1912. Courtesy of the New York Public Library; **829** Culver Pictures; **833** San Diego Historical Society, Ticor Collection; **837** The Henry E. Huntington Library, San Marino, Calif.; **840** Drawing by Charles Dana Gibson. Dover Publications; **844-L** Brown Brothers; **844-R** Library of Congress; **845** Library of Congress; **850** Culver Pictures;

856 Edmund Charles Tarbell, 1862–1938. "Thomas Woodrow Wilson," 1921. Oil on canvas, 46″ × 36 1/4″. NPG.65.42. National Portrait Gallery, Smithsonian Institution. Transfer from the NMAA; gift of the City of New York through the National Art Committee.

CHAPTER 24

861 George Luks. "Armistice Night." 1918. Oil on canvas, 37″ × 68 3/4″. Collection of Whitney Museum of American Art. Anonymous gift. 54.58; 864 Theodore Roosevelt Collection, Harvard College Library; 871 Brown Brothers; 876 Trustees of the Imperial War Museum, London (both); 881 National Archives; 883 U.S. Military Academy, West Point Museum Collection; 885 National Archives, U.S. War Department; 891 Earl Lonsbury. "Battle Engagement," WPA Photo Collection. Archives of American Art, Smithsonian Institution; 892 Trustees of the Imperial War Museum, London; 896 Brown Brothers; 898 Collection of Albert Craig; 899 Bildarchiv Preussischer Kulturbesitz.

CHAPTER 25

903 Western Illinois University Art Gallery/Museum; 904 The Bettmann Archives; 908 From the Collections of Henry Ford Museum & Greenfield Village; 911 Gerrit Beneker (American 1882–1934). "Portrait of Homer White." Collection of the Canton Art Institute, Canton, O.; 913 American Quarterly, Vol. 10, 1958, p. 419; 914 Library of Congress; 916 The Bettmann Archives; 919 Lief Neandross. "The Roxy Theater." Watercolor. Courtesy of the Rambusch Co., N.Y.; 922 The Bettmann Archives; 927 Paul Cadmus. "To the Lynching!" 1935. Pencil and watercolor on paper, 20 1/2″ × 15 3/4″. Collection of Whitney Museum of American Art. Purchase 36.32; 931 UPI/Bettmann Newsphotos.

GENERATIONS OF THE REPUBLIC 5

936-L Idaho State Historical Society, Photo #60-139.13; 936-C Library of Congress, Arnold Genthe Collection; 936-R Ashfield Historical Society Museum, Howes Brothers Photograph; 937-L Alice Lloyd College Photo Archives, Astor Dobson Collection; 937-C Richard Samuel Roberts Collection; 937-R Culver Pictures; 938-L Laura Gilpin. "Fransworth-Hazelhurst Wedding," 1926, 79.130/97. Courtesy Amon Carter Museum, Ft. Worth, Tex. Copyright 1981; 938-C Library of Congress; 938-R Library of Congress; 939-L Library of Congress; 939-C Library of Congress; 939-R Wayne Miller/Magnum.

CHAPTER 26

941 Library of Congress (both); 946 Vanity Fair, October 1933. Courtesy of the New York Public Library; 950 Brown Brothers; 953 Library of Congress; 957 UPI/Bettmann Newsphotos; 958 Photofest; 960 Library of Congress; 961 Library of Congress; 962 Library of Congress; 966 United States Air Force.

CHAPTER 27

975 Franklin D. Roosevelt Library; 976-T Franklin D. Roosevelt Library; 976-B Elizabeth Olds. "Miner Joe," 1937. National Museum of American Art, Smithsonian Institution; 978 UPI/Bettmann Newsphotos; 982 Library of Congress; 986 UPI/Bettmann Newsphotos; 987 Peter Hopkins. "Riot at Union Square, March 6, 1930," 1947. Courtesy of the Museum of the City of New York;

993 The Bettmann Archives; 1001 Tom Lea. "Back Home: Pleasant Hill, Mo., 1865." National Archives; 1003 Library of Congress.

CHAPTER 28

1009 National Archives; 1010T AP/Wide World; 1010B United States Marine Corps Historical Center; 1015 UPI/Bettmann Newsphotos; 1021 UPI/Bettmann Newsphotos; 1029 United States Marine Corps, Defense Department; 1031 AP/Wide World; 1032 Jacob Lawrence. "War Series: Shipping Out," 1947. Egg tempera on composition board, 20″ × 16″. Collection of Whitney Museum of American Art. Gift of Mr. And Mrs. Roy R. Neuberger. 51.7; 1037 United States Coast Guard; 1039 B. Anthony Stewart, 1951. National Geographic Society.

CHAPTER 29

1047 Franklin D. Roosevelt Library; 1051 William Strout, LIFE MAGAZINE, copyright TIME Inc.; 1055 Courtesy Du Pont, Inc.; 1056 Library of Congress; 1058 Library of Congress; 1061 Library of Congress; 1065 UPI/Bettmann Newsphotos; 1069 UPI/Bettmann Newsphotos; 1072 National Archives, United States Army Signal Corps; 1076 Brian Brake/Photo Researchers; 1078 Colliers, May 3, 1947. Courtesy Library of Congress; 1079 Andy Hernandez/Picture Group.

CHAPTER 30

1083 J.R. Eyerman, LIFE MAGAZINE, copyright TIME Inc.; 1088 United States Navy, Courtesy Harry S Truman Library; 1089 Copyright 1946, TIME Inc. Reprinted by permission; 1090 AP/Wide World; 1099 Museum of Modern Art, Film Stills Archive, N.Y.; 1105 The Bettmann Archives; 1116 AP/Wide World.

CHAPTER 31

1119 Copyright 1959 by Norman Rockwell. Reproduced by permission of the Norman Rockwell Estate. Photo courtesy of Mike Cluff; 1121 Courtesy Cadillac Motor Cars (both); 1123 Elliott Erwitt/Magnum; 1127 Russell R. Klein House. Kentfield, Calif. From Architectural Record, Vol. 121, No. 6, May 1957; 1132 Eve Arnold/Magnum; 1139 United Press Associations; 1141 AP/Wide World; 1146 Burt Glinn/Magnum; 1149 The Bettmann Archives.

CHAPTER 32

1153 Fred Ward/Black Star; 1154 Drawing by Ruby. Reprinted with permission from Robert Coles, Children in Crisis: A Study of Courage and Fear (1964–1967). Little, Brown and Company; 1158 The Bettmann Archives; 1164 AP/Wide World; 1169 Charles Moore/Black Star; 1171 UPI/Bettmann Newsphotos; 1172 UPI/Bettmann Newsphotos; 1173 Michael Alexander/Black Star; 1174 ; 1180 Friedel/Black Star; 1184 UPI/Bettmann Newsphotos.

GENERATIONS OF THE REPUBLIC 6

1188L Courtesy of James West Davidson; 1188C Spencer Museum of Art, University of Kansas, Gift of Marion Palfi (1917–1978); 1188R David S. Strickler/Picture Cube; 1189L Courtesy of Christine Leigh Heyrman; 1189C Courtesy of Michael B. Stoff; 1189R Courtesy of William E. Gienapp; 1190L Bruce Davidson/Magnum; 1190C Courtesy of Mark H. Lytle; 1190R Leonard

Index

Page numbers in *italic* refer to illustrations, tables, and charts. Page numbers followed by *n.* (e.g., 1160*n.*) refer to footnotes. Book titles and the names of magazines and journals are listed under "Books" and "Magazines and journals," respectively, and not as main headings. Legislative acts and U.S. Supreme Court cases are listed both as main headings and under "Legislation" and "Supreme Court, U.S.," respectively.

A & P stores, 708, 909
ABC powers, 870
Abenaki Indians, 99–100
Abercromby, James, 164
Abernathy, Ralph, 1230
Abington v. Schempp (1963), 1166
Abolitionism, 336, 435–441, 444–445, 484
Abortion, 424, 1240–1241, 1255, *1270*, 1272–1273
Abraham Lincoln Brigade, 1016–1017
Abrams v. United States (1919), 887
Abscam investigation (1970s), 1257
Abstract art, 1150, 1151
Acadia (*see* Nova Scotia)
Acadia Conference (1941), 1026
Acheson, Dean, 1095, 1111, 1112, 1114, 1115, 1209
Achille Lauro (ship), 1286, 1288
ACLU (American Civil Liberties Union), 1257
Adams, Abigail, 248
Adams, Brooks, 798–799
Adams, Charles Francis, Jr., 778
Adams, Henry, 718, 779, 798–799, 802, *844*
Adams, John, 224, 252, *289*, 379
  on "citizen-soldiers," 212
  at Continental Congress (First), 185
  at Continental Congress (Second), 195
  death of, 332–333
  and election of 1796, 287
  and election of 1800, 292
  on fighting, in 1775, 202, 203
  on French Revolution, 283
  legacy of, 296
  local loyalty of, 226
  on presidency, 289
  presidency of, 289–297
    and France:
      mission to, 292
      war with, 290
    and Alexander Hamilton, rivalry with, 289
    and "midnight appointments," 305
  as vice president, 272–273
  and women's rights, 248
Adams, John Quincy, *331*, 341
  on campaign techniques, 407
  in election of 1824, 380, *381*
  in election of 1828, 386

Adams, John Quincy (*Cont.*):
  on impressment, 321
  as president, 385–386
  as Secretary of State, 330–331
  on War of 1812, 325, 329
Adams, Samuel, 179–182, *181*, 185–188, 232, 252
Adams, Samuel Hopkins, 848
Adams, Sherman, 1130, 1133, 1151
Adams-Onís Treaty (1819), 330
Adamson Act (1917), 857
Addams, Jane, 699, 826, 831, 835–836, 840, 874, 951
Adjusted Compensation Certificates, 970
Adolescents (teen-agers), 1189
Adorno, Theodore, 1148
Advertising, 708, 912–913, 1067, 1118, 1275
AEC (Atomic Energy Commission), 1095, 1117, 1132
Afghanistan, Soviet invasion of, 1079, 1081, 1264
AFL (*see* American Federation of Labor)
Africa, 5, 14–16, 61, *793*, *1018*, 1028–1029
African-Americans:
  and abolitionism, 438
  in armed forces, 221–222, 813, *813*, 846, 880–881, *881*, 884–885, *1032*, 1216–1217
  and civil rights movement, 1143–1147, 1166–1168, 1166–1174, 1172–1174
  and cocaine, 957
  in colonial times:
    in American Revolution, 220–222
    in Caribbean Basin, 66–67
    in Chesapeake region, 59–62, 79, 126, 136–139
    family life of, 137–138
    in Georgia, 75–76
    in New Netherlands, 102
    population of, *137*, *137*, *239*
    and religion, 240
    in seaports, 133–134
    in 1740–1800, 258–261
    in South Carolina, 73–74, 126, 136–139
    in Spanish colonies, 27
  education of, 393, 611, 625–626, 628, 705, 707, 731, *731*, *953*, 1189

African-Americans: education of (*Cont.*):
    and school integration, 1145–1146, 1151, 1152–1154
  in elections, 758, 760, 1157
  family life of, 137–138, 447, 449, 474–475, 624, 717, 938
  and Fourteenth Amendment, 611–612
  and Marcus Garvey, 922, 923, 935
  and GI Bill, 1102
  in gold rush, 509–510
  during Great Depression, *953*, 963–964, 993–994, 998, 999
  and Harlem Renaissance, *903*
  in late 19th century:
    and Alliance movement, 774
    and disfranchisement, 732–733
    education of, 707, 731, *731*
    in elections, 758, 760
    family life of, 717
    and Jim Crow system, 730–733, 785–787
    in Kansas, 718–720
    in lumber industry, 728–729
    and Booker T. Washington, 786–787
    as workers, 674, 722
  migration of, 659, 1105–1107, 1142
  in 1920s, 922–923
  in North, 392–394, *905*
  population of:
    in 1775, 137, *137*, 239
    in 1790, 264
    in 1820–1860, in South, *458*, 458–459, 460–461
    in 1860, in North, 392
  during Reagan's administration, 1298
  and religion, 240, 313, 314–315, 393, 478–479, 625, 625–626
  and rock and roll, 1184–1185
  and Theodore Roosevelt, 845–846
  in 1740–1800, 258–261
  in South:
    in American Revolution, 220–222
    and disfranchisement, 732–733
    during Great Depression, *953*
    and Jim Crow system, 730–733, 785–787
    in lumber industry, 728–729
    population of, in 1820–1860, *458*, 458–459, 460–461
    and racism and segregation, 730–732, 784–785

African-Americans: in South (*Cont.*):
    during Reconstruction, 602–605,
        639
    aspirations of, 604, 614, 617,
        618, 621–628, 629
    education of, 611, 625–626, 628
    family life of, 624
    and freedom, response to, 621–
        624
    housing of, 622–623, *623*
    income of, per capita, 627
    and officeholding, 617–618
    and religion, *625*, 625–626
    and sharecropping, 622–623,
        623, 626–627, *627*, 723
    and suffrage, 610–611, 617,
        630–631, 732–733
    and school integration, 1152–
        1155
    and wages, 626, 722
    after World War II, 1141–1143
    in suburbs, 1105, 1107
and suffrage, 385, 392, *393*, 610–
    611, 617, 630–631, 732–733
during Truman's administration,
    1110
and Vietnam War, 1206, 1216–1217
as workers:
    discrimination against, 674
    for Henry Ford, 908
    on Panama Canal construction,
        863
    during Reconstruction, 626–627
    and strikes, 674, 774
    in unions, 901
    wages of, 626, 722, 993–994, 1301
    during World War I, 883, 884
    after World War II, 1086
    during World War II, 1058, 1063,
        1064
during World War II, 1058, 1063–
    1066
as writers, and FWP, 998
(*See also* Lynchings; Race and rac-
    ism; Segregation; Slaves and
    slavery)
Agee, James, 999
Agelino, Joseph T., 971
Agnew, Spiro, 1211, 1226, 1232, 1245,
    1265
Agricultural Adjustment Act (1933),
    984, *1006*
Agricultural Adjustment Act (1938),
    985
Agricultural Adjustment Administra-
    tion (AAA), 984–985
Agricultural Marketing Act (1929), 973
Agriculture:
    among American Indians, 18–21, 84,
        268–269
    and capital, scarcity of, in 1790, 271
    after Civil War, 581
    in colonial times:
        in backcountry, 126–128, 268–269,
            270
        in England, 146
        in Middle Colonies, 126
        in New England, 93, 123
        in Pennsylvania, 107
        in Spanish America, 27
    commercialization of, 1850–1860,
        527–530
    during Eisenhower's administration,
        1131
    during Great Depression, 960–962,
        984–985

Agriculture (*Cont.*):
    in late 19th century, 721–730, 750,
        751–752, 772, 798
    in Ohio Territory, 312
    and railroads, 526
    during Reagan's administration, 1280
    in South:
        in 1830s–1860, 453–456, 551
        during Reconstruction, 626–630
    and transportation revolution of
        1830–1850, 347, 526
    during World War II, 1053
    (*See also* Farmers; Land; Planters
        and plantations; Sharecropping;
        Tenancy; *specific crops, e.g.,*
        Cotton and cotton growing;
        Sugar; Tobacco growing and
        tobacco industry)
Aguinaldo, Emilio, 814, 817
AIDS (acquired immune deficiency
    syndrome), 1296–1297
Aiken, Conrad, 998
AIM (American Indian Movement),
    1224
Air-raid drills, 1189
Air traffic controllers' strike (1981),
    1279
Air travel, 1039, *1039*
Aircraft industry, 1052
Airplanes, 1034, 1035–1036, 1038–1039
Aix-la-Chappelle, Treaty of (1748), 120
Alabama, 453–454, 457, 462, 551, 594,
    613–614, 619, 1167–1168, *1169*,
    1169–1170
Alabama, University of, 1187
Alamance, Battle of (1771), 130, 155
Alaska, 17–18, 157, 804, 821, 1235
Albany, New York (Fort Orange), 101,
    118, 208
Albany Congress (1754), 120–121, 154–
    155, 158, 184–185
Albemarle Sound (North Carolina), 67
Alcatraz Island (California), 1224
Alcohol (*see* Drinking; Prohibition;
    Temperance movement)
Alcott, Bronson, 425
Aldrich, Nelson W., 846, 850
Aldrin, Edwin, 1205
Alexander II (Russian czar), 687, 819,
    821
Algonquin (ship), 878
Algonquin Indians, 82
Ali, Muhammad, 1206, 1216–1217
Alien and Sedition Acts (1798), 291–
    292, 303
"All in the Family" (TV program), 1274
Allegheny Mountains, 2
Allen, Ethan, 130, 234
Allen, Florence, 995
Allen, Fred, 918
Allen, Frederick Lewis, 904, 913
Allen, Horace, 803–804
Allende Gossens, Salvador, 1248–1249,
    1253, 1265
Alliance movement, 773–775, 776, 789
Alliance for Progress, 1159, 1187
Allison, William B., 846
Alsberg, Henry, 998
Altamont, California, 1186
Altgeld, John P., 679
Altman, Robert, 1274
AMA (American Medical Association),
    1110
Amadas, Philip, 38
Amalgamated Iron and Steel Workers,
    679

Amazon River, 101
Amendments, Constitutional (*see* Con-
    stitution, U.S.)
America First Committee, 901, 1019
American Birth Control League, 916,
    935
American Board of Customs Commis-
    sioners, 179
American Broadcasting Company
    (ABC), 1133
American Chemical Society, 653
American Civil Liberties Union
    (ACLU), 1257
American Enterprise Institute, 1293
American Federation of Labor (AFL),
    645, 676–677, 681, 884, 924, 996–
    997
American Independent party, 1212
American Indian Movement (AIM),
    1224
American Indians (*see* Indians,
    American)
American Legion, 1070
American Liberty League, 986
American Medical Association (AMA),
    1110
American Museum, 914
American party (Know-Nothings), 538–
    539
American Philosophical Society, 141,
    155
American Plan, 910
American Protective Association, 697
American Railway Union, 679
American Revolution (*see* Revolution,
    American)
American Sugar Refining Company,
    847
American System, 403
American Telegraph and Telephone
    Company, 654
American Tobacco Company, 728
American Union Against Militarism,
    874
Ames, Fisher, 283, 294
Amherst, Jeffrey, 164, 169, 192
"Amos 'n' Andy" (radio program), 919
Amusement parks, 836–837
Anarchism, 780, 895–897, 924
Anderson, Douglas, 1192
Anderson, John, 1275
Anderson, Marian, 1007
Anderson, Sherwood, 811, 922
Andros, Edmund, 110, 113
Angelus Temple, The, 902
Angley, Edward, 967
Anglicans, 107–108, 110, 111, 142,
    144, 201, 249
    (*See also* Church of England)
Anglo-American Treaty (1871), 801
Angola, 61, 1248, 1252, 1260
Annamese Cordillera, 1197
Annapolis, Maryland, 232
Annapolis Convention, 251, 257
Anne I (English queen), 155
Anniston, Alabama, 1167
Anthony, Susan B., 423, 440, 631–632,
    701, 704
Anti-Comintern Pact (1937), 1017
Anti-Imperialist League, 821
Anti-Masonry, 381, 383
Anti-Saloon League, 766, 838, 859
Anti-Semitism, 645, 777, 819, 901,
    988, 1071–1073, *1072–1073*
Antietam, Battle of (1862), 569–570,
    572, 591

Antinomianism, 97–98
Antislavery movement (*see* Abolitionism)
Antitrust suits, 847, 851, 1051
  (*See also* Sherman Antitrust Act)
Antrobus, John, 451
Apache Indians, 77, 742
Apollo 11 (spacecraft), 1230, 1265
Apollo program, 1204–1205, 1230
Appalachian Mountains, 169, *171*, 233–234
Apprenticeship system, 340, 357, 362, 447
Arabic (British ship), 875, 897
Arabs, 1073
  (*See also specific Arab countries, e.g.,* Egypt; Saudi Arabia)
Arapaho Indians, 486
Arawak Indians, 17
Arbenz Guzmán, Jacobo, 1137
Architecture, 1126, 1150–1151
Area Redevelopment Act (1961), 1164, 1187
Argentia Bay (Newfoundland), 1020
Argentina, 26
Arikara Indians, 486, 488
Aristocracy, 265, 277, 279, 293, 376, 381, 401, 405, 408–409, 543
Arizona, 18–19, 25, 76, 518
Arizona (battleship), 1008
Arkansas, 354, 372, 457, 462, 553, 565, 593, 605–606, 619
Armas, Carlos Castillo, 1137
Armed forces (*see* Army; Continental Army; Military; Militia; Navy)
Armory Show (1913), 645
Armour, Philip, 681
Arms control, 1293
Arms race, 1011–1012
Arms sales, 1016, 1252, 1288–1292
Armstrong, Louis, 921
Armstrong, Neil, 1204–1205
Army, U.S., 290, 305, 810–811, 813, *813*, 846, 887, 889, 890–891
  (*See also* Continental Army)
Arnautoff, Victor, 999
Arnold, Benedict, 209, 223
Arnold, Thurman, 1004, 1050–1051
Art, *685*, 830, 921, 998–1002, 1150–1151, 1178
  (*See also* Architecture)
Arthur, Chester A., 692, 769, 769–770, 789
Arthurdale, West Virginia, 994
Articles of Confederation, 231–232, 236, 239, 243, 250–251, 254, 257, 273
Artisans, 132–133, 174, 177, 180–181, 235, 242–244, 246–247, 269–270, 357
Asch Building (New York City), 822
Ashcan School (art), *685*, 830, 921
Asia, 14–16, 802–804, *1135*
  (*See also specific countries, e.g.,* China; Japan)
Asian-Americans, *1299, 1300,* 1300–1301
Assembly lines, 907, 908, 935, 997
Associationalism, 932
Assumption (fiscal policy), 276, 305
Astaire, Fred, 958
Astor, John Jacob, 366, 368, 379
Aswan Dam (Egypt), 1138
Asylum movement, 434
Atatürk, Kemal, 898, 901
Atchison, David Rice, 524, 539

Atchison, Topeka, and Santa Fe Railroad, 662, 747
Atlanta, Georgia, 593–594, 846
Atlantic Charter, 1020, 1040, 1045
Atlantic City, New Jersey, 914–915
Atlantis, 21
Atomic energy (*see* Nuclear power plants; Nuclear weapons)
Atomic Energy Commission (AEC), 1095, 1117, 1132
Atomic weapons (*see* Nuclear weapons)
Attica Prison (New York), 1253
Attlee, Clement, 1094–1095, 1114
Augsburg, League of, 119, 155
Austin, Ann, 98
Austin, Stephen, 492–493
Australia, 156
Australian-Americans, 509, 511
Austria, 74, 162, 901, 1017
Austria-Hungary, 872
Automation, 1128–1129
Automobile industry, 907–909, 912–913, 944, 997, 1050, 1118–1120, 1235–1238, 1259–1260
Automobiles, 650, 907–909, 1118, 1120–1122, 1266
  (*See also* Automobile industry)
Azores, 15, 37
Aztecs, 7, 20–21, 24–27, 42

B-1 (aircraft), 1281
B-29 (aircraft), 1038
Baby boom, 1103, 1188–1191
Back Home: April 1865 (mural), 1000, *1001*
Back to Africa movement, *922*
Backcountry (*see* Frontier)
Bacon, Nathaniel, 57–58
Baer, George, 846
Baez, Joan, 1184, 1206
Bahamas, 17, 65
Baja peninsula, 18, 29, 76
Baker, George, 964
Baker, Howard, 1284
Baker, Newton, 882, 890
Baker, Ray Stannard, 828, 886
Baker v. Carr (1962), 1166, 1187
Bakke, Allan, 1298
Bakker, Jim, 1271
Balance of trade, 1870–1910, *798*
Balboa, Vasco Nuñez de, 13, 25
Baldwin, William, 693
Ballinger, Richard, 850–851
Balloon frame house, 352
Baltimore, Maryland, 344, 346, 356, 406, 435, 457
Baltimore and Ohio Railroad, 660, 677
"Banana republics," 791
Bancroft, George, 369
Bank of the United States, First, 276, 278, 305, 341
Bank of the United States, Second, 341, 350, 399–402, 408
Banking Act (1935), 990
Bankruptcy, 350
Banks, Dennis, 1224
Banks and banking:
  and Banking Act (1935), 990
  during Civil War, 580
  during Great Depression, 947, 967, 968, 980–981
  in Jacksonian era, 400–403, 408, 410
  in 1920s, 945
  and railroads, 663–664
  and savings and loan industry crisis, 1297

Banks and banking (*Cont.*):
  during Woodrow Wilson's administration, 855–856
  and World War I, 1015
  (*See also* Bank of the United States, First; Bank of the United States, Second)
Banner, Lois, 1125
Baptists:
  and Anti-Masonry, 381
  and blacks, 313, 626
  in colonial America, 70, 72, 107
    and First Great Awakening, 144
    and Salem witchcraft trials, 111
  and Jeffersonian Republican party, 287
  and party system, 442
  during Reconstruction, 626
  and Second Great Awakening, 312–313, 419
  and slavery, 437, 485
Bara, Theda, 918
Barbados, 66–67, 70, 73
Barbed wire, 751, 757
Barkley, Alben, 1068, *1072*
Barlowe, Arthur, 38, 41
Barnard, Thomas, 167
Barnett, Ross, 1169
Barnum, Phineas T., 914
Barton, Bruce, 903, 935
Barton, Clara, 581–582
Baruch, Bernard, 882–883, 942, 1016–1017, 1095–1096
Baseball, 673, 710, *711*, 713, 920, 1185
Basketball, 710, 713
Basye, Betty, 1082–1084
Bathing suits, 1054
Batista, Fulgencio, 1140
Baton Rouge, Louisiana, 463
Battle Annie, 696
Bay of Pigs invasion (1961), 1160, 1187
Bayard, Margaret (*see* Smith, Margaret)
Be-ins, 1185
Beach Boys (music group), 1185
Beacon Hill (Boston), 192
Beame, Abraham D., 1255
Bear Flag Revolt (1846), 505
Beatles (music group), 1081, 1180, 1184, 1187
Beatniks, 1151, 1180, 1183
Beauregard, Pierre, 557, 560
Beauty contests, 914–915
Beauty parlors, 917
Beaver Indians, 18
Beckley, John, 286
Becky Sharp (film), 955
Bede (the Venerable Bede), 68, 69
Beecher, Catharine, *414*, 420–421, 422–423, 425, 434
Beecher, Henry Ward, 779
Beecher, Lyman, 412–417, *414*, 420, 422, 425, 435, 437, 439, 443
Begin, Menachem, 1262, *1263*
Behavioral psychology, 827
Belgians, in colonial America, 102
Belgium, 872
Belize, 790
Bell, Alexander Graham, 645, 653, 654, 681, 792
Bell, Griffin, 1256
Bell, John, 554
Bell Telephone Company, 653–656
Bellamy, Edward, 671, 713
Bellow, Saul, 998

Bellows, George, *685*, *698*, 830, 921
Bemis Heights (New York), 208, 209
Ben Tre, South Vietnam, 1203
Benezet, Anthony, 245
Bennett, James Gordon, 699
Bennington, Battle of (1777), 209
Benson, Ezra Taft, 1131
Benton, Thomas Hart (artist), 1150
Benton, Thomas Hart (U.S. senator), 400, 403, 490
Beothuk Indians, 11
Bergan, Greg, 1268
Bering Strait, 17–18
Berkeley, Busby, 958
Berkeley, William, 57–58, 66
Berkeley, University of California at, 1182
Berkman, Alexander, 896
Berle, Adolf, 980, 1005
Berlin, Germany, 1081, 1093, *1094*, 1140, 1161
Berlin Conference (1885), 645
Berlin Decree (1806), 321
Bernstein, Carl, 1244, 1265
Berrigan, Daniel and Philip, 1272
Bessemer, Henry, 650
Bessemer process, *647*, 650, 666
Bethel, New York, 1185
Bethlehem Steel, 910
Bethune, Mary McLeod, 993, *993*, 994
Beveridge, Albert, 863
Beverly Hills, California, 906
Bicycling, 709
Biddle, Nicholas, 400–402
Bikini Atoll, 1096
Bilingual education, 1301
Bill of Rights, 256–257, 274
Bimetallism, 768
Birch (John) Society, 1166
Bird, Thomas, 1192
Birmingham, Alabama, 686, 729, 757, *1169*, 1169–1170
Birney, James G., 436, 444–445, 483, 502
Birth control, 424, 832, 916, 936, 951, 1166
Birth rate, 264, 353, 424, 446–447, 714, 722, 936, 951, 1103, *1103*, 1188, 1239
Bison (buffalo), 739, *745*, 757
Black, Timuel, 1082
"Black blizzards," 959, *960*
Black codes, 608–609, *610*
Black Death, 5, 7, 22–23, *23*, 42, 68
"Black" graft, 684
Black Hawk (Indian chief), 391
Black Hills (South Dakota), 740
Black Hoof (Indian chief), 318
Black Kettle (Indian chief), 739
Black market during World War II, 1056
Black Muslims, 1172
Black Panther party, 1172–1173, 1187
Black power movement, 1172–1174
Black Thursday (October 24, 1929), 945–946
Black Tuesday (October 29, 1929), *946*
Blackmun, Harry, 1225, 1240
Blacks:
   and abolitionism, 438
   in armed forces, 221–222, 813, *813*, 846, 880–881, *881*, 884–885, *1032*, 1216–1217
   and civil rights movement, 1143–1147, 1166–1174

Blacks (*Cont.*):
   and cocaine, 957
   in colonial times:
      in American Revolution, 220–222
      in Caribbean Basin, 66–67
      in Chesapeake region, 59–62, 79, 126, 136–139
      family life of, 137–138
      in Georgia, 75–76
      in New Netherlands, 102
      population of, 137, *137*, 239
      and religion, *240*
      in seaports, 133–134
      in 1740–1800, 258–261
      in South Carolina, 73–74, 126, 136–139
      in Spanish colonies, 27
   education of, *393*, 611, 625–626, 628, 705, 707, 731, *731*, *953*, 1189
      and school integration, 1145–1146, 1151, 1152–1154
   in elections, 758, 760, 1157
   family life of, 137–138, 447, 449, 474–475, 624, 717, 938
   and Fourteenth Amendment, 611–612
   and Marcus Garvey, 922, 923, 935
   and GI Bill, 1102
   in gold rush, 509–510
   during Great Depression, *953*, 963–964, 993–994, 998, 999
   and Harlem Renaissance, *903*
   in late 19th century:
      and Alliance movement, 774
      and disfranchisement, 732–733
      education of, 707, 731, *731*
      in elections, 758, 760
      family life of, 717
      and Jim Crow system, 730–733, 785–787
      in Kansas, 718–720
      in lumber industry, 728–729
      and Booker T. Washington, 786–787
      as workers, 674, 722
   migration of, 659, 1105–1107, 1142
   in 1920s, 922–923
   in North, 392–394, *905*
   population of:
      in 1775, 137, *137*, 239
      in 1790, 264
      in 1820–1860, in South, *458*, 458–459, 460–461
      in 1860, in North, 392
   during Reagan's administration, 1298
   and religion, *240*, 313, 314–315, *393*, 478–479, 625, 625–626
   and rock and roll, 1184–1185
   and Theodore Roosevelt, 845–846
   in 1740–1800, 258–261
   in South:
      in American Revolution, 220–222
      and disfranchisement, 732–733
      during Great Depression, *953*
      and Jim Crow system, 730–733, 785–787
      in lumber industry, 728–729
      population of, in 1820–1860, *458*, 458–459, 460–461
      and racism and segregation, 730–732, 784–785
      during Reconstruction, 602–605, 639
      aspirations of, 604, 614, 617, *618*, 621–628, 629

Blacks: in South: during Reconstruction (*Cont.*):
      education of, 611, 625–626, 628
      family life of, 624
      and freedom, response to, 621–624
      housing of, 622–623, *623*
      income of, per capita, 627
      and officeholding, 617–618
      and religion, 625, 625–626
      and sharecropping, 622–623, *623*, 626–627, *627*, 723
      and suffrage, 610–611, 617, 630–631, 732–733
   and school integration, 1152–1155
   and wages, 626, 722
   after World War II, 1141–1143
   in suburbs, 1105, 1107
   and suffrage, 385, 392, *393*, 610–611, 617, 630–631, 732–733
   during Truman's administration, 1110
   and Vietnam War, 1206, 1216–1217
   as workers:
      discrimination against, 674
      for Henry Ford, 908
      on Panama Canal construction, 863
      during Reconstruction, 626–627
      and strikes, 674, 774
      in unions, 901
      wages of, 626, 722, 993–994, 1301
      during World War I, 883, 884
      after World War II, 1086
      during World War II, 1058, 1063, 1064
   during World War II, 1058, 1063–1066
   as writers, and FWP, 998
   (*See also* Lynchings; Race and racism; Segregation; Slaves and slavery)
Blackwell, Elizabeth, 704
Blaine, James G., 766, 770, 801–802, 804–805
Blanchard, James, 1260
Bland-Allison Act (1878), 768–769, 789
Bleecker, Ann Eliza, 214
Blizzards, 750, 753, 756
Block grants, 1219, 1220
Blockade (Civil War), 566
Bloomer, Amelia, 422
Bloomers, 422–423, *423*, 701
Blue Eagle symbol, *982*, 984
Board of Trade and Plantations, 112–113, 151, 169
Boeing 707 (aircraft), 1039
Boeing Stratocruiser (aircraft), 1039, *1039*
Bohlen, Charles E., 1131
Bohr, Niels, 1035
Boland, Edward, 1288, 1304
Boleyn, Anne, 33–34
Bolingbroke, Henry St. John, 150
Bolivia, 7, 26, 1013–1014
Bonanza farms, 752
Bond, James, 1159
Bonds (*see* Stocks and bonds)
Bonsack, James, 727–728
Bontemps, Arna, 998
Bonus Bill (1816), 342
Bonus march (1932), 901, 970–971, 979
"Boodle," 684
Books:
   American Dilemma, The (Gunnar Myrdal), 1143
   Applied Christianity (Washington Gladden), 698

Books (*Cont.*):
  Babbitt (Sinclair Lewis), 901, 909,
    922, 935
  Baby and Child Care (Benjamin
    Spock), 1188–1189
  Being and Nothingness (Jean-Paul
    Sartre), 901
  Book of Mormon, 512
  Caesar's Column (Ignatius
    Donnelly), 777
  Cato's Letters (John Trenchard and
    Thomas Gordon), 151, 183
  censorship of, 1132
  Closing Circle, The (Barry Com-
    moner), 1233, 1265
  Coin's Financial School (William
    Harvey), 782
  Common Law, The (Oliver Wendell
    Holmes, Jr.), 827
  Common Sense (Thomas Paine), 190,
    194, 196–197, 225
  Electric Kool-Aid Acid Test (Tom
    Wolfe), 1183
  *Engineers and the Price System,
    The* (Thorstein Veblen), 827
  Fate of the Earth, The (Jonathan
    Schell), 1281, 1304
  Feminine Mystique, The (Betty
    Friedan), 1125, 1151, 1239
  Fundamentals, The, 928
  Gilded Age, The (Mark Twain and
    Charles Dudley Warner), 765
  Gone with the Wind (Margaret
    Mitchell), 955
  Good Earth, The (Pearl Buck), 955
  Grapes of Wrath, The (John
    Steinbeck), 901, 961
  Great Gatsby, The (F. Scott
    Fitzgerald), 901
  How the Other Half Lives
    (Jacob Riis), 693, 713
  Huckleberry Finn (Mark Twain),
    645, 765
  In His Steps (Charles L. Sheldon), 698
  Index of American Design, 999
  Infant Care, 937
  *Influence of Sea Power Upon His-
    tory* (Alfred Mahan), 821
  Jungle, The (Upton Sinclair), 645,
    848, 859
  Kinsey Report (Alfred Kinsey),
    1103–1104
  Let Us Now Praise Famous Men
    (James Agee and Walker
    Evans), 999
  *Letters on the Condition of Women
    and the Equality of the Sexes*
    (Sarah Grimké), 440
  Lonely Crowd, The (David
    Riesman), 1129, 1151
  Looking Backward (Edward
    Bellamy), 671, 713
  Main Street (Sinclair Lewis), 922
  Man Nobody Knows, The (Bruce
    Barton), 903, 935
  Middletown (Helen and Robert
    Lynd), 912, 935
  Native Son (Richard Wright), 998
  1984 (George Orwell), 1147
  Oh Yeah! (Edward Angley), 967
  On the Road (Jack Kerouac), 1183
  *One Day in the Life of Ivan
    Denisovich* (Alexander
    Solzhenitsyn), 1093
  100,000,000 Guinea Pigs (Fred
    Schlink), 955

Books (*Cont.*):
  Only Yesterday (Frederick Lewis
    Allen), 904
  Organization Man, The (William
    Whyte), 1129
  Other America, The (Michael
    Harrington), 1175, 1187
  Passing of the Great Race, The
    (Madison Grant), 835
  Peace of Mind (Joshua Liebman),
    1124
  Pilgrim's Progress (John Bunyan),
    828
  Poverty (Robert Hunter), 830, 859
  Power of Positive Thinking, The
    (Norman Vincent Peale), 1124
  Pragmatism (William James), 859
  Progress and Poverty (Henry
    George), 670–671
  *Red Channels: The Report of Com-
    munist Influence in Radio and
    Television*, 1108
  Rise of David Levinsky, The, 688
  Robin Hood, 1101
  Sex in Education (Edward Clarke),
    706–707
  Sexual Politics (Kate Millett), 1240
  Shame of the Cities, The (Lincoln
    Steffens), 859
  Silent Spring (Rachel Carson), 1233,
    1265
  Social Control (Edward A. Ross),
    827
  Soul on Ice (Eldridge Cleaver), 1173
  Souls of Black Folk, The (W. E. B.
    Du Bois), 787, 789
  Theory of the Leisure Class, The
    (Thorstein Veblen), 827
  Tired Heart of Our Cities, The
    (Victor Gruen), 1266
  To Secure These Rights (report),
    1110
  Tom Sawyer (Mark Twain), 655
  Ulysses (James Joyce), 901
  Uncle Tom's Cabin (Harriet Beecher
    Stowe), 439, 520, 542, 548–549,
    549
  Unsafe at Any Speed (Ralph Nader),
    1235–1238, 1265
  and urbanization, 687
  War of the Worlds, The (H. G.
    Wells), 955
  White Shadows (Claude McKay),
    923
  Winesburg, Ohio (Sherwood
    Anderson), 922
  Women and Economics (Charlotte
    Perkins Gilman), 704, 831
  Yellow Wall Paper, The (Charlotte
    Perkins Gilman), 704
  Your Money's Worth (Fred Schlink),
    955
  (*See also* Literature; Magazines and
    journals)
Boom-and-bust business cycle, 370,
  379, 418, 426, 670, *670*
Boom towns, 744
Boomers, 751
Boone, Daniel, *171*, 250
Boonesborough, Kentucky, *171*
Booth, George, 63
Bork, Robert, 1246, 1285
Boston, Massachusetts, 160–161, 176–
  177, 179–180, 182, 184, 186–189,
  192–194, 202–205, 262–263, 356,
  365, 412–416, 645, 713, 930

Boston Massacre (1770), 176, 180, 191
Boston Port Bill (1774), 183, 186
Boston Tea Party (1773), 157, 159,
  182, 191, 197
Boucher, Jonathan, 201
Bouquet, Henry, *171*
Bow, Clara, 918
Box mill, *754*
Boxer Rebellion (China), 645, 817–818,
  821
Braddock, Edward, 163, 191
Bradford, William, 87
Bradlee, Benjamin C., 1244
Bradley, Bill, 1285
Bradley, Omar N., 1037, 1071, 1114
Bradley, Tom, 1009, 1298
Bradstreet, John, 164
Brains Trust, 979–980
Brandeis, Louis D., 827–828, 857, 887
Brandywine, Battle of (1777), 206, 225
Brant, Joseph (Thayendangea), 214
Brazil, 16, 66, 68, 102, 139, 645, 1252
Bread lines, 779
Breckinridge, John C., 553–554
Breed's Hill (Boston), 192–194
Brendan (saint), 21
Bretton Woods Conference (1944),
  1074
Brezhnev, Leonid, 1217–1219, *1218*,
  1252–1253, 1261, 1265
Briand, Aristide, 1012
Brinksmanship, 1135
Britain, Battle of (1940–1941), 1038
British Honduras, 790
British North America Act (1867), 801
British Petroleum, 1136
Bronson House (Los Angeles), 699
Brook Farm, 422, 428
Brookings Institution, 1293
Brooklyn, New York, 356, 365
Brooklyn Bridge, 666, 692, 713
Brooklyn Heights, Battle of (1776), 205
Brooks, Preston S., 540
Brotherhood of Locomotive Firemen
  and Engineers, 1064
Brotherhood of Sleeping Car Porters,
  1063
Brouwer, Adriaen, *51*
Brown, John, 524, 552, *552*, 718
Brown, Linda, 1144
Brown, Mrs. James, *719*
Brown, Oliver, 1144
Brown v. Board of Education (1954),
  1081, 1144, 1151, 1224–1225
Brownsville, Texas, 846
Bruff, Joseph Goldsborough, *497*
Bryan, Charles W., 934
Bryan, William Jennings, 782–784,
  783, 816, 849, 869, 874–875, 875,
  897, 929, 934
Bryce, James, 761
Bryn Mawr College, 706
Brzezinski, Zbigniew, 1256–1257,
  1261–1263
Buchanan, James, 490, 541, 543, 545,
  545–546, 558
Buchenwald (concentration camp), *1072*
Buck, Pearl, 955
Budget and Accounting Act (1921), 935
Buena Vista, Battle of (1847), 506, 590
Buffalo (bison), 739, *745*, 757
Buford (ship), 896
Bulge, Battle of the (1945), 1037
"Bull Moose" party (*see* Progressive
  party)
Bull Run, First Battle of (1861), 560–561

Bull Run, Second Battle of (1862), 569
Bunau-Varilla, Philippe, 861
Bundy, McGeorge, 1158, 1199, 1200
Bunker, Archie, 1274, *1274*
Bunker Hill, Battle of (1775), 192–194, *193*, 225
Bureau of Indian Affairs, 1223–1224
Burger, Warren, 1225, 1285
Burgoyne, John, 208–209, 214
Burke, Edmund, 112, 188
Burleson, Albert, 895
Burlingame Treaty (1868), 802
"Burned-Over District" (New York State), 423, 512
Burnham, Daniel, 693
Burns, Euchre Kate, 696
Burnside, Ambrose, 571
Burr, Aaron, 292, 295
Bush, George, 1275, *1302*, 1302–1303
Bush, Vannevar, 1034
Bushy Run, Pennsylvania, *171*
Business and commerce:
    and advertising, 708, 912–913, 1067, 1118, 1275
    and codes of fair practices, 983–984
    and consumerism, 1235–1238
    in 18th century, 132–133
        and American Revolution, 241–242
        of cities, 135
        and merchants' wealth, 136
        and Navigation Acts, 55–56, 109, 153
        and nonimportation, 180, 186
        of northern colonies, 95, 103, 107
        in 1790, 269–271
        and smuggling, 168, 170
    in England, 16th–18th centuries, 36, 48, 62, 146, 175
    and government regulation, 842–843, 847–849, 855–857
    and John F. Kennedy, 1165
    and management, 660–661, 910
    and John Marshall's Supreme Court, 350–351
    and mergers and acquisitions, 668, 909, 1128
    in 1920s, 909–913
    and Theodore Roosevelt, 846–848
    and shopping malls, 1266–1268, *1267*
    during World War I, 1015
    (*See also* Banks and banking; Consumer goods; Corporations; Depressions and panics; Economy and economic conditions; Foreign trade; Industrialization; Prices; Wages and salaries)
Busing, 1225
Butler, George Washington, 928
Butler v. United States (1936), 985, 1007
Butz, Earl, 1247
Buzhardt, J. Fred, 1246
Byrd, William, 138, 146
Byrnes, James, 1050, 1070, 1076, *1088*, 1092

C. Turner Joy (warship), 1200
Cabinet (president's), origin of, 273
Cable lines (urban transport), 690
Cabot, John, 10, 37, 42
Cabral, Pedro Alvares, 16
Caddell, Patrick, 1276
Cadillac (automobile), *1121*
Caesar, Sid, 1108
Cahill, Holger, 998

Cahuilla Indians, 18
Calhoun, John C., 341, *398*, *519*, 525, 599
    and Bonus Bill, 342
    and Compromise of 1850, 518–519
    and Andrew Jackson, 386, 387
    and nullification theory, 397
    as presidential candidate, 379–380, 383
    and slavery, 484, 515
    and tariff of 1833, 399
    and War Hawks, 325
California, 309
    acquisition of, 508
    admission of, 354, 517–520
    Asian-Americans in, 1301
    bilingual education in, 1301
    and Black Panther party, 1172–1173
    blacks in, 1105–1107
    Chinese-Americans in, 488, 802
    in 1845, 491–492
    in 1860 election, 553
    and gold rush, 509–511
    Mexican-Americans in, 514–515, 1063, 1105–1107
    in Mexican War, 505–506
    under Mexico, 492
    migrants to, during Great Depression, 961–962
    and 1960s counterculture, 1185–1186
    and Ronald Reagan, 1277
    Upton Sinclair and Democratic party in, 986
    and slavery, 551
    Spanish settlers in, 76
    suburbs in, 1105
    Watts riot in, *1173*, 1173–1174
    (*See also* Los Angeles; San Francisco)
Calley, William, 1209
Calvert family, 54, 58, 67, 78–79
Calvin, John, 32–33, 84–85, 96, 416
Calvinism, 34, 83, 88, 97, 141–144, 150
    (*See also* Puritanism)
Cambodia, 1081, 1215–1216, 1229
Cambridge, Massachusetts, 192, 202
Cambridge University, 147
Camden, Battle of (1780), 218–219
Camp David accords (1978), 1081, 1262, *1263*, 1265
Camp meetings, *313*, 314–315, *315*, 467
Canada, 80–83, 119, 154, 160, 164–165, 195, 233–234, 800–801, 1061, 1252
Canals, 343–346, *345*
Canary Islands, 13, 15–16, 65, 68
Cane Ridge revival (1801), 312–313, 314, 316, 416, 430
Canned food, 907
Cannon, Joseph G., 846, 850
Cannonball Express (railroad), 660
Canterbury, Robert, 1195
Cape Ann (Massachusetts), 87
Cape Hatteras (North Carolina), 42
Cape Verde Islands, 16
"Capital deepening," 656
Capone, Al, 926
Capper-Volstead Act (1922), 932, 935
Caputo, Philip, 1197
Caravel (ship), 15
Caribbean region:
    and American Revolution, 195, 211, 224
    Anglo-French rivalry in, 119
    English settlement in, 65–67, 79

Caribbean region (*Cont.*):
    and Molasses Act and Sugar Act, 170
    and Theodore Roosevelt, 864–865
    and slavery, 27, 66–67, 139
    and South Carolina, 65, 67, 70, *71*, 73–74
    in Spanish empire, 16–17, 25, 27, 29
    sugar economy in, 66, 68–69, 79
    and trade with northern colonies, 95, 100, 107, 132
    U.S. interventions in, 867
    and Woodrow Wilson, 869
    (*See also specific countries, e.g.,* Cuba; Dominican Republic)
Carleton, Guy, 204, 208
Carlisle Commission, 210, 225
Carmel, California, 77
Carmichael, Stokely, 1172, 1187
Carnegie, Andrew, *647*, 665–666, 786, 814, 874
Carnegie Steel Company, 645, 681
Carpentier, Georges, 920
Carranza, Venustiano, 870
Carson, Price, and Scott department store (Chicago), 693
Carson, Rachel, 1233, 1265
Carswell, G. Harrold, 1225
Carter, Billy, 1257
Carter, James Earl (Jimmy), 1256–1265, *1263*, 1265, 1277, 1304
    and Camp David accords, 1262
    in election of 1976, 1255
    in election of 1980, 1275–1276
    and energy crisis, 1257–1259
    foreign policy of, 1256, 1260–1262
    and human rights, 1260
    and inflation, 1260
    and Iranian revolution and hostage crisis, 1262–1264
    and Nicaragua, 1261
    problems and failures of, 1264
    and Soviet invasion of Afghanistan, 1264
Carteret, George, 105
Cartier, Jacques, 82, 113
Carver, George Washington, 722–723
Case, Theodore S., 695
Cass, Lewis, 515–516
Cassady, Neal, 1183
Cassidy, Butch, 747
Cast Iron Palace (New York City), 708
Castro, Fidel, 1081, 1140, 1151, 1160, 1253
Catalogue sales, 708–709
Catherine of Aragon, 33
Catherine the Great (Russian empress), 157, 159
Catholics (*see* Roman Catholic Church)
Catt, Carrie Chapman, 833–834, 917
Cattle ranching, *748*, 748–750, 757
Caughnawaga Indians, *104*
Cayuga Indians, 104
CCC (Civilian Conservation Corps), 981, 996, *1006*
Cellophane, 907
Censorship, 1131–1132, 1166
Census, U.S.:
    of 1790, 264
    of 1820, 353
    of 1850, 353, 356
    of 1870, 686
    of 1890, 669, 673, 721
    of 1920, 904
Census Bureau, 859
Center for the Study of Responsive Law, 1238

Central America, 790, 790–792, 1287, 1289
  (*See also* Latin America; *specific countries, e.g.,* Guatemala; Nicaragua; Panama)
Central Intelligence Agency (CIA), 1136, 1137, 1160, 1160*n.*, 1248–1249, 1252, 1253, 1265, 1288
Central Pacific Railroad, 745–746
Central Park (New York City), 713, 836
Centralia, Washington, 896
Cerro Gordo, Battle of (1847), 506
Chadwick, Edwin, 643
Chain stores, 708
Challenger (space shuttle), 1304
Chamber of Commerce, U.S., 910
Chamberlain, Neville, 1017, 1089
Chambers, Whittaker, 1100–1101
Champlain, Samuel de, 82, 113
Chancellor, John, 1146, 1147
Chancellorsville, Battle of (1863), 591
Chandler, Samuel, 228
Chanute, Octave, 692
Chapultepec, Mexico, 506
Charity (philanthropy), 706, 965
Charles I (English king), 55, 67, 79, 87, 96, 110, 113
Charles II (English king), 55–56, 67, 92, 102, 106, 113
Charles River Bridge v. Warren Bridge (1837), 409
Charleston, South Carolina, 67, 72, 131–132, 135, 179, 215–217, 219, 221, 225, 346, 396–397, 462, 472, 481
Charlestown, Massachusetts, 184, 189, 192–194
Chase, Salmon, 516
Chase, Samuel, 307
Chavez, Cesar, 962, 1081, 1222, 1223, 1229
Chavez, Dennis, 994
Cheever, John, 998
Chernobyl nuclear accident, 1081
Cherokee Indians, 74, 139, 163, 169, 264, 327, 388–392
Chesapeake affair (1807), 322
Chesapeake Bay, 39, 42, 44, 48, 54, 206, 219, 222–224
Chesapeake region, 44–65, 53
  and Bacon's Rebellion and Coode's Rebellion, 57–58
  blacks in, 59–62, 136–139
  English policy changes in, 55–56
  family life in, 52, 62, 114–117
  gentry of, 62–65
  and Maryland and Indian wars, 54–55
  versus northern colonies, 84, 86, 92–93, 95, 99–100, 103
  and tobacco growing, 49–52
  unrest in, 56–57
  and Virginia Company, 48–49
  (*See also* Maryland; Virginia)
Chesnut, Mary, 465–466, 594
Chevrolet Corvair (automobile), 1235–1238
Cheyenne Indians, 486, 488, 735, 739, 740, 741, 799, 1001
Chiang Kai-shek, 1043, 1075, 1111, 1135, 1218
Chicago, Illinois:
  antiblack riots in, in 1919, 885
  Columbian Exposition in, in 1893, 700, 713, 836–837

Chicago, Illinois (*Cont.*):
  Democratic party convention in, in 1968, 1211–1212
  fire in, in 1871, 713
  First Ward Ball in, in 1908, 762–763
  garbage collection in, in 1890s, 840–841
  during Great Depression, 950
  growth of, 356, 686
  Haymarket Massacre in, in 1886, 678–679
  immigrants in, in 1860, 532
  Midway Plaisance in, 837
  municipal governments of, 695
  prostitution in, in 1910, 839
  and railroads, 346, 527–529
  Republic Steel Company strike in, in 1937, 997
  skyscrapers in, 693
Chicago, University of, 706, 826
Chicago Aviation Conference (1944), 1074
Chicago Vice Commission, 839
Chicago (warship), 796
Chicanos, 1223
  (*See also* Mexican-Americans)
Chickasaw Indians, 264, 320, 327, 388, 391
Child labor, 673, 779, 832–833, 857, 911, 1053
Child raising, 446–448
Childbirth, 1900–1945, 937
Children, 694, 714–715, 937–938, 949–950, 953, 954, 1274–1275
  (*See also* Birth rate; Child labor; Childbirth; Family and family life; Infant mortality; Juvenile delinquency; Teen-agers)
Children's Bureau, 937
Chile, 26, 1248–1249
China, 7, 14, 16, 228
  Communist revolution in, 1081, 1111
  environmental problems in, 1080
  and Four Policemen, 1041
  and imperialism, 793
  and Japan, 901, 1017
  and Korea, 804
  and Korean War, 1114
  "open door" policy in, 817–818
  and Taiwan, 1135, 1135–1136
  and U.S.:
    during Carter's administration, 1261–1262
    and Richard Nixon, 1217–1219
    recognition of, 1081
    and Theodore Roosevelt, 865
    and William Henry Seward, 802
    Singer sewing machines in, 792
    and Taft's dollar diplomacy, 867–868
    and Woodrow Wilson, 869
    after World War I, 900, 1012–1013
    and Yalta Conference, 1043
"China Lobby," 1111
Chinese-Americans, 488, 509–512, 689, 746, 770, 802, 1301
Chinese Exclusion Act (1882), 713, 821
Chippewa Indians, 169, 238, 320
Chisholm Trail, 749
Chivington, John, 739
Chloral hydrate, 956
Chloroform, 956
Choctaw Indians, 163, 264, 320, 327–328, 388, 390, 390–391
Christian missionaries, in late 19th century, 795

Christianity (*see specific groups and institutions, e.g.,* Baptists; Protestantism; Roman Catholic Church)
Christie, Howard Chandler, 915
Chrysler Corporation, 1118–1120, 1259–1260, 1265
Church, Frank, 1253, 1265
Church of England, 33–34, 52, 63–64, 70, 85, 88, 94, 96
  (*See also* Anglicans)
Church of Jesus Christ of Latter Day Saints (*see* Mormons)
Churchill, Winston, 945, 978, 1020, 1021, 1025–1028, 1040–1044, 1075, 1087–1088, 1138
CIA (Central Intelligence Agency), 1136, 1137, 1160, 1160*n.*, 1248–1249, 1252, 1253, 1265
Cigar Makers' Union, 676
Cigarettes, 727–728
Cincinnati, Ohio, 238, 356, 365, 392, 435, 437, 532
Cinema (*see* Films and filmmaking)
CIO (Congress of Industrial Organizations), 997, 1070, 1100
Citadel, 216
Cities:
  American Indians in, 1223–1224
  18th-century seaports, 131–135
  electric lighting in, 652
  during energy crisis, 1255
  and family life, 936
  during Great Depression, 948, 965
  and immigration, 532–533
  during industrial revolution, 643
  in late 19th century, 686, 772
  and mass transit, 643, 691, 1122
  migration to:
    of blacks and Hispanics, 1105–1107
    of rural workers, 1865–1920, 659
    in 1950s, 1122
  and progressivism, 824–825, 829–831, 832, 835, 838–842
  and Prohibition, 926
  and shopping malls, 1266
  in South, 457, 467–468, 576
  in Third World, 1081
  wealth in, distribution of, in 1825 and 1860, 365
  in West, 511–514
  (*See also specific cities, e.g.,* Chicago; London; Los Angeles; New York City)
Citizens' League for Fair Play, 994
Civil liberties and civil rights:
  and American Indians, 1223–1224
  and Civil Rights Act (1964), 1171
  and civil rights movement, 1179–1182
  before Civil War, 393–394, 483
  in Civil War, 547–548, 583–584
  in election of 1948, 1109
  in 1950s, 1143–1147
  in 1960s, 1166–1174, 1179–1182
  during Reagan's administration, 1298
  during Reconstruction, 610–611
  during Red Scare of 1919, 895–896
  in 1790s, 290–292
  during Truman's administration, 1110
  and Warren court, 1165–1166
  during World War I, 886–887
  during World War II, 1059–1066
  (*See also* Abolitionism; Slaves and slavery)

Civil rights (*see* Civil liberties and civil rights)
Civil Rights Act (1875), 731
Civil Rights Act (1957), 1151
Civil Rights Act (1964), 1171, 1187, 1239
Civil Rights Cases (1883), 731, 757
Civil Service Act (1883), 767
Civil service system, 767
Civil War:
   beginning of, 556–557, 560–562, 565–566
   and blockade, 566–567
   and border states, 564–565
   combat in, 568, 570, 589–591, 590, 592, 595
   and Confederate home front, 575–579
      economy of, 575–576
      finance and government of, 577–578
      hardships of, 578–579
      and women, 576
   and diplomacy, 566–567
   in East, stalemate in, 569–571
   and election of 1860, 553–554
   and emancipation, 571–575
   and Harper's Ferry, 552
   impact of, 598–599
      on family, 449
   naval war in, 566
   political leadership in, 563–564
   and resources of Union and Confederacy in 1861, 562
   roots of, 556–558
      and economic differences of North and South, 643
      and political realignment of 1850s, 534–543
         and election of 1856, 541–543
         in Kansas, 522–525, 539–540
         and Kansas-Nebraska Act, 536–537
         and Know-Nothings, 538
         and party system, collapse of, 537–539
         and Charles Sumner, whipping of, 540–541
      and sectional changes in U.S. society, 525–534
         and agriculture, commercialization of, 527–530
         and immigration, 530–533
         and industrialization, 530
         and railroad economy, growth of, 526–527
         and South, problems of, 533–534
      and worsening crisis, 543–552
         and *Dred Scott* decision, 543–544
         and Lecompton Constitution, 545–546
         and Lincoln-Douglas debates, 546–550
         and Panic of 1857, 544–545
         and South, problems of, 551
      (*See also* Books, *Uncle Tom's Cabin*)
   and secession, 554–555
   soldier's life in, 584–589
      in battle, 589–591
      camp life, 561, 584–588, 586
      of Confederate soldiers, 588–589
      and disease and medical care, 585, 588
      and food, 586–587

Civil War: soldier's life in (*Cont.*):
      and morals, 588
   as total war, 561–563
   and Union home front, 579–584
      and civil liberties and dissent, 583–584
      government finance and economy of, 575–576
      and women and work force, 581–582
   Union victory in, 591–598
   veterans of, support for, 766
   in West, Grant in, 567–569
   (*See also specific battles, e.g.,* Antietam; Bull Run; Gettysburg)
Civil Works Administration (CWA), 981
Civilian Conservation Corps (CCC), 981, 996, 1006
Clark, "Champ," 880
Clark, George Rogers, 213–214, 224
Clark, William, 2–3, 309–311
Clarke, Charity, 199
Clarke, Edward, 706
Clay, Cassius (Muhammed Ali), 1206, 1216–1217
Clay, Henry, 324, 341, 342, 519
   and John Quincy Adams, 380
   and Nicholas Biddle, 401
   and Compromise of 1850, 518–519
   and Andrew Jackson, 387
   and Missouri Compromise, 372
   and National Republicans, 386
   and nullification, 399
   as presidential candidate, 379–380, 402, 502
   and War Hawks, 325
   and Whig party, 403
Clay, Lucius, 1093
Clayton Antitrust Act (1914), 856, 859
Clayton-Bulwer Treaty (1850), 790, 804, 821
Clean Air Act (1970), 1229
Clean Water Act (1970), 1229
Cleaver, Eldridge, 1172, 1173
Clemenceau, Georges, 882, 888, 889
Clemens, Samuel (Mark Twain), 645, 655, 690, 765, 814
Clement VII (pope), 33
Cleveland, Grover, 697, 770–771, 789
   and Cuba, 809
   and depression of 1893–1897, 780–781
   in election of 1892, 776–777
   and Great Britain and Venezuela, 807
   and Hawaii, 807
   and Philippines, 814
   and protective tariff, 768
   and Pullman strike, 679
Cleveland, Ohio, 666–667, 694, 841
Clifford, Clark, 1209
Clinton, De Witt, 343
Clinton, Henry, 211, 213, 215–216, 221, 224
Clive, John, 164
Clothing (*see* Fashion and dress)
Cloudscrapers, 692
Coal industry, 780, 846, 1069, 1080
Coca, Imogene, 1108
Coca-Cola, 956, 1056
Cocaine, 956, 957
Cochise (Indian chief), 742
Cocoanuts, The (film), 940
Codes of fair practices, 983–984

Coercive Acts (1774), 182–188, 191
Coeur d'Alene, Idaho, 679, 744, 757
Coffee, 754
Coffin, William Sloane, 1226
Cohan, George M., 886
Cohens v. Virginia (1821), 306
Cohn, Roy M., 1131, 1132, 1133
Cold war, 1082–1117, 1087–1097, 1094, 1097–1101, 1162
Colden, Cadwallader, 176
Cole, Nathan, 142
Colleges (*see* Higher education)
Colleton, John, 67
Collier, John, 995
Collins, Michael, 1205
Colombia, 860–861, 1289
Colonialism, 893
   (*See also* Imperialism)
Colonies:
   English:
      and American Indians, 72–73, 75, 120, 168
      in Anglo-French Wars, 119–120, 162–164, 167
      in Caribbean region, 66–67
      in Carolinas, 67, 70–74
      in Chesapeake region, 48–65
      disunity of, 118–121, 123, 130–131, 140–142, 144, 168, 181 187
      and England, attitudes toward, 144–153, 160–161, 173
      and England, resistance to, 173–177, 179–186
      English policies toward, 47–48, 55–56, 109–110, 112–113, 151–152, 153, 168–179, 172, 178–179, 180, 182–183
      and Enlightenment, 140–141
      and First Great Awakening, 141–144
      immigration to, in 18th-century, 121–122
      Middle Colonies, 100–108
      in New England, 85–89, 92–100
      plantation economies in, 72–74, 76, 136–139, 145
      political culture in, 147–148, 150–151
      population of, in 18th century, 119, 123
      rural communities in, 123, 126
      social structure and mobility in, 146–147
      urbanization in, 131–136
      and westward expansion, 120, 126–129, 141
      (*See also specific colonies, e.g.,* New York; Pennsylvania)
   French:
      in Caribbean region, 209, 211
      in mainland North America, 80, 82–83, 113, 119–120, 164–165
      (*See also* New France)
   Spanish, 27–29, 76–77
   (*See also* Chesapeake region; Revolution, American; subheadings "in 17th century," "in 18th century," and "in colonial times" under relevant headings, e.g., Agriculture; Blacks; Business and commerce; Economy and economic conditions; Equality and inequality; Family and family life; Frontier; Health and sanitation; Immigrants and im-

Colonies: Spanish: see also (*Cont.*): migration; Indians, American; Land; New England; Politics; Population; Religion and religious life; Slaves and slavery; South; Women)
Colonization movement (1820s), 435
Colorado, 518
Colored Farmers' National Alliance and Cooperative Union, 774
Colson, Charles, 1226
Columbia University, 141, 1147, 1206–1207
Columbian Exposition (Chicago, 1893), 700, 713, 836–837
Columbus, Christopher, 7, 11, 16–17, 25, *41*, 42
Columbus, New Mexico, 870
COMECOM (Council of Mutual Economic Assistance), 1093
Cominform, 1093
Commerce Department, U.S., 931–932
Commission on the Status of Women, 1239
Commission on Training Camp Activities, 882
Committee for Industrial Organization (*see* Congress of Industrial Organizations)
Committee on Public Information (CPI), 886
Committee to Defend America by Aiding the Allies, 1019
Committees of correspondence, 181–182
Committees of inspection, 180, 188
Commoner, Barry, 1233, 1235, 1265
Commonwealth v. Hunt (1842), 364
Communications, in late 19th century, 653–656
  (*See also* Films and filmmaking; Mass media; Newspapers; Post Office, U.S.; Radio broadcasting; Telegraph; Telephones; Television; Transportation)
Communist Labor party, 895
Communist party (U.S.), 895, 969, 1100
Communists and communism:
  in Cuba, 1140
  in Guatemala, 1137
  and Marshall Plan, 1092–1093
  and Truman Doctrine, 1091–1092
  in U.S., 895–896, 987, 999, 1071, 1097–1101, 1108, 1131–1132
  in Vietnam, 1198–1199
Compact theory of the Union, 291, 397–398
Company of Hundred Associates, 82
Composers Forum Laboratory, 998
Compromise of 1850, *517*, 517–520, 525–526
Compromise of 1877, 637, 730, 757
Computers, 1128–1129
Comstock, Anthony, 704
Comstock Law, 704
Concord and Lexington, Battle of (1775), 189–192, 214
Coney Island (New York), 836
Confederacy (*see* Civil War)
Confiscation Act, First (1861), 572
Confiscation Act, Second (1862), 572, 614
Conglomerates, 1128
Congregationalists, 430
  and Anti-Masonry, 381

Congregationalists (*Cont.*):
  in early New England, 87–88, 93–94, 96–98, 110, 249–250
  in England, 87–88
  and Federalist party, 287
  and First Great Awakening, 142–144, 154
  in Middle Colonies, 102, 105
  and party system, 442
  and Second Great Awakening, 312, 419
  (*See also* Pilgrims; Puritanism)
Congress, U.S. (*see* Legislation)
Congress of Industrial Organizations (CIO), 997, 1070, 1100
Congress of Racial Equality (CORE), 1066, 1167, 1172
Congressional Union, 834
Conkling, Roscoe, 765, 769
Connecticut, 92, 96, 109–110, 112, 214, 329, 365, 392
Connecticut River Valley, 95, 101, 123, 143
Connor, "Bull," 1169, *1169*
Conquistadors, 14, 25–27, 37, 42
Conrad, Frank, 918
Conroy, Jack, 998
Conscientious objectors, 880
Conscription, 577–578, 584, 880, 890, 1030–1031, 1202
Conservation (*see* Environment, human effects on)
Constitution, U.S.:
  amendments to:
    First, 291
    Tenth, 274
    Twelfth, 292
    Thirteenth, 596, 608
    Fourteenth, 611–612, 631, 731
    Fifteenth, 630–632
    Sixteenth, 851
    Seventeenth, 842
    Eighteenth, 925, 935
    Nineteenth, 645, 834, 917, 935
    and Hartford Convention (1814), 329
    (*See also* Bill of Rights; Equal Rights Amendment)
  broad versus strict construction of, 278–279, 288, 309, 350–351
  contract clause in, 350
  framing of, 252–255
  and nullification, 397–399
  ratification struggle of, 271–72
  and Reconstruction, 611–612, 615–617, 616–617, 630–631, 639
  and secession, 555–556, 617
  (*See also* Supreme Court, U.S.)
Constitutional Convention (1787), 253–255, 257
Construction industry, 906–907, 944
Consumer goods, 664–665, 707–709, 1056, 1085, 1235–1238
Consumer price index, 882
Consumerism, 1235–1238
Contadora group, 1288
Continental Army, 226, 231, 233
  blacks in, 221
  and Boston, siege of, 202, 204
  character of, 202–204, 212, 224–225
  creation of, 195, 225
  and middle states, campaigns in, 205–209, 213, 225
  and southern campaigns, 218–219, 223–224
  unrest in, *212*, 213

Continental Army (*Cont.*):
  at Valley Forge, 211–213
  (*See also* specific battles, e.g., Saratoga; Yorktown)
Continental Association, 186, 188, 216
Continental Congress:
  First, 184–187, 191
  Second:
    and Articles of Confederation, 231–232
    and Continental Army, 202–203, 211–213, 223, 225
    and Declaration of Independence, 194–197, *196*
    and fiscal problems, 242
    and French alliance, 210
    and western lands, 234–239
Continental system, 321, 324
Contraception (*see* Birth control)
Contras (Nicaragua), 1287–1288, 1290–1292
Coode, John, 58
Coolidge, Calvin, 909, 922, 930–933, *931*, 935, 947, 966, 1011, 1013
Coolidge, Grace, *931*
Cooper, Anthony Ashley, 67, 78
Cooper, Frankie, 1054
Cooper, Gary, 1100
Cooper, James Fenimore, 426–427
Copland, Aaron, 998
Copperheads, 583–584
Copse Hill (Boston), 192
Coral Sea, Battle of (1942), 1028
CORE (Congress of Racial Equality), 1067, 1167, 1172
Corn, 355, *355*, 456
Cornell University, 730, 1207
Cornwallis, Lord Charles, 206, 216, 218–219, 223–225, 232
Coronado, Francisco Vásquez de, 25
Corporations, 351–352, 656–657, 668, 669–671, 882, 909–910, 945, 1128–1129
Corruption in government, 746, 930, 1133, 1257, 1296
Corsets, 700
Cortés, Hernando, 7, 13–14, 25–26, 156
Cortina, Juan, 515
Costa Rica, 17, 790–791, 821
Costello, Frank, 1107–1108
Cotton, John, 97
Cotton, Joseph, 1099
Cotton and cotton growing:
  and Cherokee Indians, 388–389
  and cotton gin, 335, 342, *342*, 454, 726–727
  and depression of 1837–1843, 403–405
  in 1808 and 1811, 341
  in 1820s–1840s, 342, 453–456, *456*
  in Kansas, 720
  in late 19th century, 722–723, *724*, 725, 726–727
  in 1950s, 1142, *1143*
  and panic of 1819, 370
  prices of:
    1810–1860, 533
    1860–1890, 772
    during Reconstruction, and black farmers, 603–604
  and slave labor system, 643
Coughlin, "Bathhouse" John, 762–763
Coughlin, Charles, 987–988, 992, 1007
Council of Economic Advisors, 1086
Counterculture (1960s), 1179–1187
Counterreformation, 82–84

Country Party (see Opposition, The)
Courts, federal, 274, 305–307, 1002–1004
    (See also Law; Supreme Court, U.S.)
Cousins, Norman, 952
Cowboys, 748, 749
Cowpens, Battle of (1781), 219, 225
Cox, Archibald, 1245–1246, 1265
Cox, James, 929, 970
Coxey, Jacob, 780
Coxey's Army, 789
Craftsworkers (see Artisans)
Crandall, Prudence, 439
Crawford, George Gordon, 729
Crawford, William, 943
Crawford, William H., 379–380
Crazy Horse (Indian chief), 740, 757
Creationism, 1271
Credit (finance), 726, 912–913, 932, 944, 985, 1102
Crédit Mobilier, 681
Creek Indians, 72–73, 162, 169, 262, 265, 327, 388–389, 391
Creel, George, 886, 889
Crèvecoeur, Hector St. John de, 265, 268, 270, 271–272, 332, 335–336, 340–341, 347, 367, 378, 410
Crime (see Corruption in government)
Crittenden, John C., 555, 572
Croatoan, 42
Crocker, Charles, 745, 746
Crockett, David, 385, 494
Croker, Richard, 695
Croly, Herbert, 852
Cromwell, Oliver, 55, 102
Cronkite, Walter, 1209
Crook, George, 739
Crop-lien system, 726, 773
Croquet, 709
Cross-Florida Barge Canal, 1235
Crow Indians, 486
Crown Point (New York), 163, 165
Cruise missiles, 1292
Cuba, 13, 17, 36, 65, 160, 165, 331, 460, 535–536, 808–810, 812–814, 864, 1013, 1140, 1160
    (See also Cuban missile crisis)
Cuban-Americans, 1222
Cuban missile crisis (1962), 1081, 1160–1163, 1164
Cudahy, Eddie, 669
Cultural Revolution (China), 1081, 1218
Culture (see Art; Films and filmmaking; Leisure and entertainment; Literature; Mass culture; Music; Radio broadcasting; Television; Theater)
Cumberland Gap, 171, 234
Curley, James, 984
Currency, 276–279, 399–405, 577, 579–580, 634, 768–769, 782–784, 982
    (See also Banks and banking; Gold standard; Money supply; Silver standard)
Currency Act (1764), 170, 191
Curtis, Edward, 735
Custer, George Armstrong, 740
Customs collectors, 170, 179–180
Cuyahoga River, 694, 1233
CWA (Civil Works Administration), 981
Czechoslovakia, 1017, 1081, 1093, 1137
Czolgosz, Leon, 843, 859

D-Day (1945), 1036, 1037
Daladier, Edouard, 1017
Dalay, Augustin, 710
Daley, Richard, 1212
Dallas, Texas, 1170
Darrow, Clarence, 929
Dartmouth College, 883
Dartmouth College v. Woodward (1819), 351
Darwin, Charles, 645, 670, 799
Daugherty, Harry, 930
Daughters of Liberty, 181, 198, 214
Davies, Jeff, 1053
Davies, "Little Bob," 696
Davis, Jefferson, 462, 563, 579, 596, 602, 603, 639
    character of, 563
    criticism of, 577
    election of, as Confederate president, 554
    leadership of, 563–564
    and outbreak of war, 556–557
    power centralized by, 577
    on slavery, 482
Davis, John W., 934
Davis, Nancy (see Reagan, Nancy)
Davis Bend, black community at, 602–604, 639
Dawes, Charles G., 1011
Dawes, William, 189
Dawes Plan (1924), 1045
Dawes Severalty Act (1887), 743, 757, 995
Daylight savings time, 883
Dayton, Tennessee, 928–929
DDT (pesticide), 1035, 1233, 1235
De Havilland Comet (aircraft), 1039
de Kooning, Willem, 999, 1150
De Leon, Daniel, 671
de Lesseps, Ferdinand, 860
de Lôme, Enrique Dupuy, 809–810
de Soto, Hernando, 25
De Witt, John, 1061
Dean, John W., III, 1244, 1245, 1246, 1247
Deane, Silas, 210
Deaver, Michael, 1296
Debs, Eugene V., 679, 680, 847, 854, 887, 895, 897, 929
Debt, 726, 773, 906, 944, 945
Debt crisis in Third World, 1287
Declaration of Independence (1776), 177, 179, 195–196, 225–226, 229, 239, 485
Declaration of Rights and Grievances (1774), 185
Declaratory Act, 175, 191
Deere, John, 527, 530
Deficit, federal, 1282, 1282–1283
DeLancey, James, 118, 120
Delaware, 4, 100, 107–108, 187, 221, 234, 249, 460, 564
Delaware River, 101, 105, 107, 146, 152, 205, 207
Democracy, 334–336
    and Federalists versus Republicans, 288
    and Manifest Destiny, 490
    in old South, 485
    perils of, 898–900
    and race, 388–396
        and American Indians, 388–392
        and free blacks in North, 392–396
    and Reconstruction, 604
    rise of, 1820s–1840s, 374–410
        and bank war, 399–403

Democracy: rise of, 1820s–1840s (Cont.):
    and equality and opportunity, 377–379
    and Andrew Jackson, 385–388
    and nullification crisis, 396–399
    political culture of, 379–385
        and Anti-Masonry, 380–382
        and election of 1824, 380
        and log cabin campaign, 406–407
        and parties, acceptance of, 383–384
        and parties, in Jacksonian era, 408–410
        and politics of common man, 384–385
        social sources of, 382–383
    and temperance, 432–433
    and Martin Van Buren and depression of 1837–1843, 403–405
    and western expansion, 236
Democratic party, 383
    and blacks, 392, 732, 993
    in Civil War, 583
    and Eisenhower Doctrine, 1139
    and elections:
        of 1840, 405–407
        of 1848, 516–517
        of 1852, 520
        of 1860, 553–554
        of 1884, 770
        of 1892, 758–761, 777
        of 1896, 782–784
        of 1910, 851
        of 1916, 877–878
        of 1918, 893
        of 1928, 933, 933–934
        of 1932, 971–972
        of 1934, 985
        of 1936, 992
        of 1938, 1005
        of 1944, 1070–1071
        of 1946, 1086–1087
        of 1948, 1108–1109
        of 1952, 1115–1116
        of 1954, 1133
        of 1956 and 1958, 1133
        of 1960, 1156–1157
        of 1964, 1176–1177
        of 1968, 1211
        of 1972, 1226–1227
        of 1974, 1254
        of 1976, 1255–1256
        of 1980, 1275–1276
        of 1988, 1302–1303
    and feminism, 1240
    ideology of, 408–409, 484
    in Jacksonian era, 410, 442, 484
    and Ku Klux Klan, 927
    in late 19th century, 761–765
        and Alliance movement, 774, 775
        and depression of 1893–1897, 781
        and Jim Crow system, 730
        and Panic of 1873, 634
        as "party of treason," 766
        and protective tariffs, 768
    and Nixon's "dirty tricks," 1244
    origins of, 380, 382, 386
    popular vote for, 1860–1912, 853
    realignment of, in 1850s, 536–537
    and reformers, 442
    and Upton Sinclair, 986
    and Smith v. Allwright (1944), 1066

Democratic party (*Cont.*):
  in South, 484, 635–636
  and temperance, 443
  and Texas, annexation of, 501–502
  and women, during New Deal, 996
Dempsey, Jack, 920, 946
Denmark, 184
Denver, Colorado, 986
Department stores, 708
Depression (1930s), 900, 947–973
  ecological disaster during, 959–962
  and family life, 939, 951–954
  and Great Crash, 946–947
  Lorena Hickok reports on, 974–976
  and Herbert Hoover, 964–973
  and mass culture, 954–959
  minorities during, 962–964
  (*See also* New Deal)
Depressions and panics (economic):
  of 1819, 370–372, 382, 396, 399–400, 405
  of 1833 (Biddle's Panic), 402
  of 1837–1843, 338, 364, 403–405
  of 1857, 544–545
  of 1873, 634
  of 1893–1897, 668, 777–789
  [*See also* Depression (1930s)]
Derleth, August, 904
Desert Land Act (1877), 751, 757
Détente, 1217–1219, *1249*, 1252–1253
Deterrence policy, 1079, 1096
Detroit, Michigan, 213, 841, 901, 965, 1065, 1173
Devastation (British warship), 796
Devery, William, 696
Dewey, Alice, 826
Dewey, George, 810, 811, 821
Dewey, John, 826, 1132
Dewey, Thomas E., 1068, 1070, 1071, 1109, 1134
Dewson, Mary W. "Molly," 996
Dias, Bartolomeu, 15, 42
Díaz, Adolfo, 867
Díaz, Porfirio, 801, 870
Dichter, Ernest, 1118
Dickens, Charles, 830
Dickinson, John, 149, 179, *179*, 195, 252
Diderot, Denis, 159
Diegueño Indians, 18
Diem, Ngo Dinh, 1136, 1160, 1187, 1199, 1229, 1253
Dien Bien Phu, Indochina, 1136, 1229
Dies, Martin, 999
Diet and nutrition:
  of Civil War soldiers, 586–587
  and fast eating, in 1830s, 352, *353*
  of free blacks, 394
  during Great Depression, 949
  in late 19th century, 702
  and New England Kitchen, 829–830
  in 1920s, 907
  in 1970s, 1236–1237
  of slaves, 476–477, *477*
  on steamboats, 349
  and sugar, 68–69
  (*See also* Food)
Diggers (1960s social group), 1185
Dillingham Commission, 838
Dingley Tariff (1897), 788
Diomede Islands, 18
Dior, Christian, 1125
Diplomacy, 566–567, 863–871, 874–876, 1014–1025, 1040–1044
Disarmament, 1012, 1293
  (*See also* SALT I; SALT II)

Disease (*see* Health and sanitation)
Disestablishment, 144, 249–250
Disfranchisement, 732–733, 785–786, 966
Disney, Walt, 958, 1140, 1234
District of Columbia (*see* Washington, D.C.)
Divine, M. J. (Father Divine), 964
Divorces, 831, 1103
Dix, Dorothea, 434, 581
Dixiecrat party (States' Rights party), 1109
D.O.A. (film), 1098
Doar, John, 1167
Dodd, Samuel C. T., 667, 668
Dole, Elizabeth Hanford, 1284
Dollar diplomacy, 866–868
Dolphin (warship), 870
Domesticity, ideal of, 420–421, *421*
Dominican Republic, 865, 1229
Domino theory, 1199
Donnelly, Ignatius, 775, 776, 777
Doolittle, James, 1028
Dorchester Heights (Massachusetts), 204
Dos Passos, John, 790, 922
Doughboys, 890–891
Douglas, Stephen A., 515, 519–520, 522, 536, 539, 541, 544–547, *547*, 550, 553–554
Douglass, Frederick, 394, 438, 474–475, 479, 574
Doyle, H. S., 760
Draft, military (*see* Conscription)
Drake, Edwin M., 650
Drake, Francis, 38–39
Drayton, William Henry, 241
Dreadnought (British warship), 797
Dred Scott decision (1857), 543–544, 572
Dreiser, Theodore, 826, 830
Dresden, Germany, 1036
Dress (*see* Fashion and dress)
Drew, Daniel, 662
Drinan, Robert, 1272
Drinker, Elizabeth, 208
Drinking, 244–245, *433*
  (*See also* Immigrants and immigration, and drinking; Prohibition; Saloons; Temperance movement)
Drug, Incorporated, 909
Drugs and drug taking, 1181, 1183, 1216, *1289*, 1296, 1297
  (*See also* Pharmaceuticals)
Du Bois, W. E. B., 787, 789, 884, 1144
Du Pont (E. I.) de Nemours & Company, 653
Duarte, José Napoleón, 1287
Dubos, René, 1233
Dukakis, Michael, 1302–1303
Duke, James Buchanan, 728
Duke's Laws, 103
Dulany, Daniel, 197
Dulles, Allen, 1136
Dulles, Foster Rhea, 1132
Dulles, John Foster, 1134–1138, *1135*, 1140
Dumbarton Oaks Conference (1944), 1074
"Dumbbell" tenements, 694, *694*
Dunkards, 142
Dunmore, Lord, 195–196, 221
Dunne, Peter Finley, 799, 841
Durant, William, 943

Durkin, Martin P., 1130
Durr, Virginia, 948
Dust Bowl, 959–960
Dutch-Americans, 102, 105, 107, 108, 111, 131, 135, 532
Dutch Reformed Church, 102–103, 142
Dutch West India Company, 101–102
Dyer, L. C., 927
Dyer, Mary, 98
Dylan, Bob, 1184, *1184*

Eads, James B., 649, 692
Eakins, Thomas, *711*
Earl, Harley, 1118
Earth Day (1970), 1235, 1265
East Germany, 1253
East Indian Company, 182–183, 186
Easter Morning (painting), *1119*
Eastman, George, 652
Eccles, Marriner, 1004
Ecology, 1233
Economic Opportunity Act (1964), 1175–1176, 1187
Economic Recovery Tax Act (1981), 1279–1280, 1304
Economy Act (1933), 980
Economy and economic conditions:
  and boom-and-bust business cycle, 370, 379, 418, 426
  in colonial times:
    during American Revolution, 241–243
    in Carolinas, 70–73
    in Georgia, 74–76
    in New England, 92–93
  and Dwight D. Eisenhower, 1131
  and Alexander Hamilton's financial program, 275–279
  in Jacksonian era, 408–409
  and market revolution of 1820s–1850s, 340–352
    agriculture in, 347–350
    and corporations, 351–352
    and cotton trade, 342
    and federal government, 341–342
    and John Marshall's Supreme Court, 350–351
    and transportation revolution, 342–347, *345*, *346*
    and canals, 343–344
    and railroads, 346–347
    and steamboats, 344–346, 348–349
  and mercantilism, 47–48
  in 1920s, 906–913, 931–933, 940–945
  in 1950s, 1118–1120, 1128–1129
  in 1970s, recession in, 1249–1250, 1254–1255, 1259–1260
  during Nixon's administration, 1220
  during Reagan's administration, 1280, *1280*–1283, 1297
  and wealth, distribution of, 1815–1860, 365–366
  after World War I, 1011
  during World War I, 882–883
  after World War II, 1085, 1102
  during World War II, 1048–1059, 1066–1068
  (*See also* Agriculture; Business and commerce; Credit; Currency; Debt; Depressions and panics; Income, personal; Industrialization; Inflation; Money supply; Planters and plantations; Prices; Slaves and slavery; South,

Economy and economic conditions: see also (*Cont.*): economy of; Taxes and taxation; Wages and salaries; Work and workers)
Ecuador, 26
Edenton, North Carolina, *183*
Edina, Minnesota, 1266
Edinburgh, Scotland, 147
Edison, Thomas Alva, *651*, 651–652, 681, 792
Edison Electric Light Company, 652
Education:
  and baby boomers, 1189
  bilingual education, 1301
  and busing, 1225
  and John and Alice Dewey, 826–827
  in early 20th century, 938
  in 1830s–1850s, 433–434
  and Elementary and Secondary School Act (1965), 1177
  and *Engel v. Vitale* (1962), 1165–1166
  during Great Depression, 953, *953*
  and high schools, 1148
  for immigrants, 706
  integration in, 1110–1111, 1144–1147, 1151, 1152–1154
  and intelligence tests, 881
  in late 19th century, 704–706
  and *McLaurin v. Oklahoma State Regents* (1950), 1110–1111
  and religious revival of 1980s, 1271
  and Scopes trial, 928–929
  in South, 730, *731*
  store catalogues used in, 709
  and *Sweatt v. Painter* (1950), 1110–1111
  (*See also* Blacks, education of; Higher education; Women, education of)
Edward VI (English king), 33
Edwards, Jonathan, 143, 412, 416
Edwards, Malenda, *339*
Egypt, 1138–1139, 1250, 1262
Ehrlichman, John, 1243, 1245, 1265
Einstein, Albert, 645, 1035
Einstein, Izzy, 925
Eisenhower, Dwight D., *1116*, 1129–1130, 1151
  and Bonus marchers, 970
  and Eisenhower Doctrine, 1139
  in election of 1948, 1108
  in election of 1952, 1115–1116
  and foreign policy, 1134–1141
  and Indochina, 1136
  and interstate highway system, 1122
  and Lebanon, 1139
  and Little Rock civil rights crisis, 1146
  and Joseph McCarthy, 1132
  and military budget, 1135, 1141
  and National Defense Education Act, 1141
  and politics, 1133
  on religion, 1124
  and Rosenbergs, 1132
  and space exploration, 1204
  and Suez Crisis, 1139
  and Taiwan, 1135–1136
  in World War II, 1029, 1036
Eisenhower, Milton, 1062
El Dorado, 42, 78
El Salvador, 1261, 1287
Elderly, 717, 939, 988, 1177–1178, 1191

Elections:
  congressional:
    of 1854, 537
    of 1860, 554
    of 1862, 573
    of 1866, 612–613
    of 1874, 634
    of 1876, 768
    of 1890, 775
    of 1892, 777
    of 1894, 781
    of 1910, 851
    of 1914, 857
    of 1918, 893
    of 1930, 969
    of 1934, 985
    of 1938, 1004–1005
    of 1942, 1068
    of 1946, 1086–1087
    of 1954, 1133
    of 1974, 1254
    in late 19th century, 764
  presidential:
    of 1796, 286–287
    of 1800, 292, *292*
    of 1804, 320
    of 1808, 323
    of 1812, 330
    of 1816, 330
    of 1820, 330
    of 1824, 380, *381*
    of 1828, 386
    of 1832, 402
    of 1836, 403, 484, 495
    of 1840, 405–408, *409*
    of 1844, 502–503
    of 1848, 516–517
    of 1852, 520
    of 1856, 541–543
    of 1860, 553, 553–554
    of 1864, 594–595
    of 1868, 630
    of 1872, 633
    of 1876, 636–638, *637*, *638*, 769
    of 1880, 769
    of 1884, 770
    of 1888, 771
    of 1892, 776–777
    of 1896, 781–784, *785*
    of 1904, 847–848
    of 1912, *855*
    of 1916, 877, 877–878
    of 1920, 929
    of 1924, 930, 934
    of 1928, *933*, 933–934
    of 1932, *971*, 971–973
    of 1936, 991–992, *993*
    of 1940, 1020
    of 1944, 1070–1071
    of 1948, 1108–1109, *1109*
    of 1952, 1115–1116
    of 1956, 1133
    of 1960, 1156–1157, *1157*
    of 1964, 1176–1177
    of 1968, 1211–1214, *1213*
    of 1972, 1226–1227
    of 1976, 1255
    of 1980, *1275*, 1275–1276
    of 1984, 1283–1284
    of 1988, 1302–1303
    voting shifts in, 781n
  and progressivism, 842
Electoral College, 254
Electricity and electrical technology, 651–652, 690–691, 992–993

Elementary and Secondary School Act (1965), 1177, 1187
Elevated railways, 690
Elevators, 693
Eliot, T. S., 922, 935
Elizabeth I (English queen), 33–34, 36, 38–39, 42, 84–85
Elk Hill, California, 930
Elkins Act (1903), 847, 859
Ellis, Powhatan, 374, 376, 463
Ellis Island (New York City), 713
Ellison, Ralph, 998, 1098
Ellsberg, Daniel, 1243, 1245
Ellsworth, Oliver, 252
Emancipation Proclamation (1862), 573–574, 596
Embargo Act (1807), 323–324, 330, 332, 341, 348
Emergency Banking Act (1933), 980
Emergency Relief and Construction Act (1932), 969
Emergency Relief Appropriation Act (1935), 989, *1006*
Emerson, Ralph Waldo, 257, *425*, 425–429, 507, 552
Emigration during Great Depression, 948
Empire State Building (New York City), 906
Employees (*see* Work and workers)
Employment and unemployment:
  of blacks, 963, 1107
  during depression of 1837–1843, 404–405
  during depression of 1893–1897, 778–779
  during Great Depression, 948, 952, 968–969, 981, 988–989, 1004
  in 1920s, 911, 945
  in 1925–1945, *949*
  during Nixon's administration, 1220
  during Reagan's administration, 1280, 1297
  during World War II, 1053
  after World War II, of blacks and Hispanics, 1107
  (*See also* Work and workers)
Endo, Mitsue, 1062
Energy Policy and Conservation Act (1975), 1254, 1265
Energy resources, 1250, 1252, 1254, 1257–1258
Engel v. Vitale (1962), 1165–1166, 1187
England (*see* Great Britain)
English-Americans, 44, 48–50, 54, 66, 67, 84–89, 442, 509, 532
Enlightenment, 140–141, 157, 303, 334, 380, 425
Enola Gay (aircraft), 1076
Enterprise (aircraft carrier), 1028
Entertainment (*see* Leisure and entertainment)
Enumerated powers, 278–279
Environment, human effects on:
  and American Indians, 734
  and environmentalist movement, 1233–1235
  and gold mining, *719*
  during Great Depression, 959–962, 981–982
  and Great Society program, 1178
  and industrialization, 650
  and lumber industry, 728
  and mining, 744
  in 1970s–1980s, 1080

Environment, human effects on (*Cont.*):
  and Richard Nixon, 1220
  and oil spills, 1230, 1230–1232, *1231*
  regulation of, 848–849, 850–851
  and James Watt, 1279
Environmental Protection Agency
    (EPA), 1235
Episcopal Church, 462
Equal Pay Act (1963), 1239
Equal Rights Amendment (ERA), 917,
    1240–1242, 1265
Equality and inequality:
  after American Revolution, 228,
      239–241, 243, 246–251, 278
  and Anti-Masonry, 381
  belief in, 265, 279, 288, 377–378
  and clothing, 377
  in colonial times, 123–124, 127, 135–
      136, 146, 179
  and Declaration of Independence,
      197
  in England, 145–148
  in New England, 92–93
  and republicanism, 243, 246–248
  in South, 52, 56–58, 62, 64, 66,
      74–75
  definition of, 379, 485
  European visitors on, 377–378
  and evangelicalism, 419
  and manners, 378
  and opportunity, 377–379, 485
  and second party system, 378–379,
      405, 410
  and Transcendentalism, 426
  (*See also* Democracy; Indentured
      servants; Race and racism;
      Slaves and slavery)
Equitable Life Assurance Company,
    1268
ERA (Equal Rights Amendment), 917,
    1240–1242, 1265
Era of Good Feelings, 330, 379
Erdman Act (1898), 788
Ericsson, Leif, 4, 7, 24
Erie Canal, 343, *343*, 345
Erie Railroad, 660, 662
Erie Wars, 662
Ervin, Sam, 1245, *1246*, 1265
Escobedo v. Illinois (1964), 1165, 1187
Eskimo Indians, 18, 36–37
Espionage Act (1917), 886, 897
Ether, 956
Ethiopia, 901, 1016
Ethnic groups (*see* Immigrants and
    immigration; *specific groups, e.g.,*
    Asian-Americans; Hispanics;
    Italian-Americans; Jews; Mexican-
    Americans)
Eugenics, 835
Europe:
  American workers from, 1870–1920,
      658–659
  and cold war, *1094*
  eastern, in 16th–18th centuries, 157
  in 14th–15th centuries, 5, 14, 21–24
  Great Depression in, 947
  and Marshall Plan, 1092–1093
  population of, 1750–1850, 686
  after World War I, and German war
      debt, 1011
  during World War II, 1018–1021,
      1036–1037
  after World War II, Communist gov-
      ernments in, 1093
Eutaw Springs, Battle of (1781), 219
Evangelicalism, 416*n.*

Evangelicalism (*Cont.*):
  and Anti-Masonry, 381
  of Billy Graham, *1123*
  and Aimee Semple McPherson,
      902–903
  and market, 418
  in 1980s, 1270–1271
  and J. Frank Norris, 903
  and party system, 442
  and Second Great Awakening, 416,
      419
  and temperance, 443
  and urban poor, 697
  (*See also* Millennialism)
Evans, Walker, 999
Everest, Wesley, 896
Everglades National Park, 1234
Evironmental Protection Agency
    (EPA), 1265
Evolution (biology), 928–929
Ex parte Endo (1944), 1062
Ex parte McCardle (1868), 617
Ex parte Milligan (1866), 583, 616
Excise taxes, 276, 280–281, 305
Executive Reorganization Act (1938),
    1007
Exner, Virgil, 1120
Exodusters, 720, 757
Expansionism:
  after American Revolution, 279–282
  in Jeffersonian era, 307–311
  in late 19th century, 736–738
  and Manifest Destiny, 489–491
  and Mexican borderlands, 491–492
  and Overland Trail, 496–501
  political origins of, 501–508
  and population growth, 353–354
  William H. Seward on, 357
  and slavery, 507–508, 515–520
  and Texas, 492–495, 501–502
  (*See also* Frontier; Imperialism;
      West)
Exports, 284–285, 321–322, *322*, 324,
    341, 348, 454

Facsimile (fax) machines, 655
Factory system (*see* Industrialization)
Fair Campaign Practices Act (1974),
    1247, 1265
Fair Employment Practices Commis-
    sion (FEPC), 1063–1064, 1077
Fair Housing Act (1968), 1179, 1187
Fair Labor Standards Act (1938), *1006*,
    1007
Fall, Albert, 930
Fall, Bernard, 1208
Fallen Timbers, Battle of (1794), 280
Fallout shelters, *1141*
Falwell, Jerry, 1271, *1272*
Family and family life:
  and baby boom, 1188–1189
  of blacks, 137–138, 447, 449,
      474–475, 624, 717, 938
  in colonial times:
    in New England, 91–93, 98,
        116–117
    of slaves, 137–138
    in South, 52, 62, 72, 114–117
  in 1815–1875, 446–449
  on frontier, in Jeffersonian era, 312
  during Great Depression, 951–954
  of immigrants, 689–690
  and industrialization, 365, 420, 424,
      449
  and meals, in 1970s, 1236–1237
  of middle class, in 1800–1850, 424

Family and family life (*Cont.*):
  in 1900–1960, 936–939
  on Overland Trail, 496–499
  and urbanization, 702–703, 714–717
  and utopian communities, 430–431
  (*See also* Birth control; Children;
      Infant mortality; Marriage;
      Women)
Family rooms, 1127
Farben, I. G., 1051
Farewell Address (Washington's), 287,
    331
Farm Credit Administration, 985
Farm Holiday Association, 969
Farm Security Administration, *1006*
Farmer, James, 1167
Farmer-Labor party, 986
Farmers:
  in colonial times:
    in backcountry, 127, 268
    in Chesapeake region, 52–53
    in New England, 123
  during Great Depression, 960–961
  in late 19th century:
    and currency controversy, 768
    politics of, 772–777
    in West, 718–721, 750–756
  in 1920s, 900, 931, 932
  and Rural Electrification Administra-
      tion, 992–993
  and Shay's Rebellion, 251
  during Truman's administration,
      1110
  and Woodrow Wilson, 857
  during World War I, 883
  yeoman farmers, in old South,
      451–452, 466–468, *467*
  (*See also* Agriculture; Sharecropping)
Farragut, David, 566, 594–595
Fascism, 899–900, 1014, 1016–1017
Fashion and dress:
  in 18th century, 198–199, *199*
  in 1820s, 377
  and garment industry, 701, 707, 822
  and 1960s counterculture, 1180–1181
  of 17th-century Indians and
      Europeans, 40–41
  of slaves, 471
  for women:
    in 1850s–1860s, 422–423
    in late 19th century, 700–701
    in 1920s, 904
    in 1950s, 1125
    during World War II, 1054–1055
Fass, Paula, 939
Fast-food chains, 1237, *1237*
Father Divine, 964
Faubus, Orval, 1146–1147
Fawkes, Guy, 177
Fax machines, 655
FBI (Federal Bureau of Investigation),
    1097, 1168, 1253, 1298
FDIC (Federal Deposit Insurance Cor-
    poration), 980–981, *1006*
Federal Art Project (FAP), 998–999, 1000
Federal Bureau of Investigation (FBI),
    1097, 1168, 1253, 1298
Federal Bureau of Narcotics, *957*
Federal Communications Commission
    (FCC), 1150
Federal Deposit Insurance Corporation
    (FDIC), 980–981, *1006*
Federal Emergency Relief Act (1933),
    1006
Federal Emergency Relief Administra-
    tion (FERA), 981, 996

Federal Energy Administration, 1254
Federal Farm Board, 967
Federal Farm Loan Act (1916), 857
Federal government:
  budget of, 1920–1940, 968
  employees of:
    blacks as, during World War II, 1063
    and Federal Employee Loyalty Program, 1097
    during Great Depression, 953
    number of, 931, 1005, 1048, 1177
    women as, 995
    during World War I, 883
  and federal deficit, 1282, 1282–1283
  in management-labor disputes, 679, 680
  in people's lives, 975–976, 1000
  (See also Presidency; Legislation; Regulation, governmental)
Federal Highway Act (1916), 857
Federal Housing Administration (FHA), 1102
Federal Land Banks, 967
Federal Music Project (FMP), 998
Federal Reserve Act (1913), 856, 859
Federal Reserve Board, 856, 944, 990
Federal Theater Project (FTP), 999
Federal Trade Commission (FTC), 856, 859
Federal Trade Commission Act (1914), 856
Federal Writers Project (FWP), 998
Federalist Papers, The (essays, James Madison, Alexander Hamilton, and John Jay), 255–257
Federalist party, 286–296, 334, 351
  achievements of, 296
  campaign techniques of, 323
  death of, 330, 332, 380, 505
  in election of 1796, 287
  in election of 1804, 320
  and electioneering, 294–295
  founding of, 277, 286
  and France, quasi-war with, 290
  and French Revolution, 283
  and Great Britain, 283
  and Hartford Convention, 329–330
  ideology of, 288
  and War of 1812, 324
  and West, 280–282, 307
Federalists (supporters of Constitution), 255–257, 262, 272, 279, 287
Feminism (see Women)
Fenian Brotherhood, 801
FEPC (Fair Employment Practices Commission), 1063–1064, 1077
FERA (Federal Emergency Relief Administration), 981, 996
Ferber, Edna, 701
Ferdinand (Spanish king), 16, 24
Ferdinando, Simon, 39, 42
Ferguson, Miriam "Ma," 917
Ferguson, Robert, 646
Fermi, Enrico, 1035
Ferraro, Geraldine, 1284, 1304
Ferris, George, 837
Ferris wheel, 837
Fessenden, William Pitt, 609–610
Fetterman, William, 740
FHA (Federal Housing Administration), 1102
Fiedler, Leslie, 1148
Filipino-Americans, 1301

Fillmore, Millard, 519, 541, 543
Film noir (film genre), 1098–1099
Films and filmmaking, 900, 918, 955–959, 1097–1100, 1108, 1150, 1273
Finance (see Banks and banking; Money supply)
Fine Arts Section (FAS), 1000
Finland, 901, 1019
Finney, Charles Grandison, 415–418, 416, 421, 426, 430, 437, 439, 490
Finnish-Americans, 102, 107–108
Fireside chats (Franklin D. Roosevelt), 979
First Great Awakening, 7, 141–144, 154
Fish, Hamilton, Jr., 1015, 1068
Fisher, Carl G., 940
Fisher, Mary, 98
Fishing industry, 8, 10–11, 95
Fisk, James, Jr., 662
Fitzgerald, F. Scott, 901, 917, 922
Fitzhugh, George, 482
Flagg, James, 886
Flanagan, Hallie, 999
Flappers (women, 1920s), 917
Flatiron Building (New York City), 692
Fletcher v. Peck (1810), 306, 350–351
Florida, 165, 309, 325, 328, 330, 391, 618, 620, 636–637, 940, 1234
Flu (influenza), 937
Flynn, "Honest" Ed, 697
Folk music, 1184
Folsom, James "Big Jim," 1147
Fonda, Jane, 1206, 1243
Food, 848, 883
  (See also Diet and nutrition)
Food Administration, 883
Football, 710, 920
Foraker Act (1900), 817, 821
Force Act (1870), 635
Force Bill (1833), 399, 501
Ford, Gerald, 1248, 1265
  in election of 1976, 1255
  and Henry Kissinger, 1249, 1253
  and New York City fiscal crisis, 1255
  and Nixon pardon, 1253
  and Nixon resignation, 1247
  on presidency, 1277
  and Nelson Rockefeller, 1253
  as vice president, 1245
  and Vietnam War, 1252
    and amnesty for draft resisters, 1253
Ford, Henry, 859, 899, 907–908, 908, 935, 997, 1057
Ford Motor Company, 907–908, 969, 1118–1120
Fordney-McCumber Tariff (1922), 931, 935, 1011, 1045
Foreign policy (U.S.):
  during John Adams's administration, 290, 292
  and containment policy, 1091
  during Eisenhower's administration, 1134–1141
  during Jefferson's administration, 308–309
  in late 19th century, 794–800
  and League of Nations, 893
  during Monroe's administration, 329–332
  during Truman's administration, 1111–1112
  during Washington's administration, 284–285
  after World War I, 1010–1011

Foreign policy (U.S.) (Cont.):
  (See also Diplomacy; Imperialism; specific wars, e.g., Spanish-American War; War of 1812; World War I)
Foreign trade, 795, 798, 798, 864, 874, 1011
  (See also Exports; Imports; Tariffs)
Foreman, Clark, 993
Forrestal, James, 1089
Fort Carillon, 163–164
Fort Detroit, 164, 169
Fort Duquesne, 120, 153, 163–164
Fort Frontenac, 164–165
Fort Harmar, Treaties of (1789), 280
Fort Laramie, Treaty of (1851), 500–501
Fort Necessity, 153–155, 162, 202
Fort Niagara, 164, 214
Fort Oswego, 163
Fort Sumter, 556, 556
Fort Ticonderoga, 164, 302
Fort Wayne, Treaty of (1809), 320
Fort William Henry, 163
Forten, Charlotte, 394
Foster, William Z., 969
Fountain of Youth, 25
Four Policemen policy, 1041
Fourierism, 431
Fourteen Points speech, 887–888
Fourtune, Henry, 677
Fourtune, Malvina, 677
Frémont, John C., 505–506, 541, 543
France:
  and American Indians, 80, 82–83, 99, 104, 120
  and American Revolution, 209–211, 223–225, 292
  and Canada, 80, 82–83, 113, 119–120, 169
  and Caribbean region, 66, 209, 211
  and England, 34, 55, 118–121, 153–154, 159
    and Seven Years' War, 162–165
    and trade with colonies, 168, 170
  in 15th century, 5
  and Indochina, 1136, 1198–1199
  and Louisiana Purchase, 308–309
  and neutral rights, 284–285
  in Newfoundland, 10, 13
  North American explorations of, 44, 72, 76, 80, 82
  quasi-war with, 290
  and slavery, 336
  and Suez crisis, 1139
  in World War I, 872
    U.S. image of, 873
    U.S. soldiers in, 890–891
  after World War I, and German rearmament, 1012
  in World War II, 1019, 1036
Francis I (French king), 24, 80
Franco, Francisco, 1016–1017
Franco-Prussian War, 645
Franklin, Benjamin, 332
  and Albany Congress, 118–121, 144
  and commercial economy, 270–271
  at Constitutional Convention, 253, 254
  at Continental Congress, 196
  on drinking, 244
  in France, 210, 211
  and frontier society, 129
  and Masonry, 380
  on population growth, 156, 159
  and slavery, 139–140

Franklin, proposed state of, 234
Franz Ferdinand (Austro-Hungarian
    archduke), 872
Fredricksburg, Battle of (1862), 571
Free Soil party, 516–517, 520
Free Speech Movement, 1182, 1187
Free State Hotel (Lawrence, Kansas),
    525
Freedman's Bureau, 610–611, 625,
    627–629
Freedom riders, 1167, 1187
Freeman's Farm, 209
Freemasonry (see Masonry)
Freeport Doctrine, 550
French-Americans, 509, 511
French and Indian War (see Seven
    Years' War)
French Revolution, 283, 332, 334–335
Freud, Sigmund, 645, 916, 935, 956
Frick, Henry Clay, 666, 679, 777
Friedan, Betty, 1125, 1151, 1239
Frobisher, Martin, 36–37, 37, 39, 42
Frontier:
    in 18th century, 126–131
        after American Revolution, 233–
            239
        Appalachian frontier, 171
        boundary disputes and tenant
            wars on, 130–131
        economy of, 268–269
        First Great Awakening on, 144
        Indian and white conflicts on, 169
        and Jay-Gardoqui Treaty, 250–251
        marriage age on, 264, 267
        settlement of, 126–129
        social conflicts on, 129–130, 142
    in 1800–1850s:
        and transportation revolution,
            342–347
        whites and Indians on, 311–320,
            486–489
            and Black Hoof and assimila-
                tion, 316–318
            and camp meetings, 314–315
            and Overland Trail, 499–501
            and Second Great Awakening,
                312–316
            and Tecumseh and pan-Indian
                movement, 318–320
            and Trail of Tears, 390–392
        women on, 268, 311, 508–510,
            513
    (See also Expansionism; Indians,
        American, on frontier; West)
Fuchs, Klaus, 1101
Fuel Administration, 883
Fugitive slave law of 1850, 518–520,
    556
Fulbright, J. William, 1206, 1207
Fuller, Albert, 951
Fuller, Buckminster, 1183
Fulton, Robert, 346
Fundamental Constitutions of South
    Carolina, 70
Fundamentalism (religion), 928, 1123,
    1270–1271
Funerals, 939
Fur trade, 72–73, 82–83, 103–104,
    119–120, 157, 159, 368–369, 369,
    734

Gadsden, Christopher, 187
Gadsden Purchase (1853), 535
Gag law, 444, 484
Gagarin, Yuri, 1204
Gage, Thomas, 187–189, 192, 194, 204

Galbraith, John Kenneth, 1158, 1164
Gallatin, Albert, 304–305
Galloway, Joseph, 186–187, 197
Galveston, Texas, 841, 859
Gama, Vasco da, 7, 15, 42
Gandhi, Mohandas K., 898, 1145
Gangsters, and Prohibition, 925–926
Garcia, John, 1008
Gardoqui, Diego de, 250
Garfield, James, 767, 769, 789
Garland, Hamlin, 672
Garment industry, 701, 822
Garner, John Nance, 1017
Garrison, William Lloyd, 435–437,
    436, 439–440, 441, 444, 481, 516
Garvey, Marcus, 922, 923, 935
Gasoline, 1051
Gaspee Commission, 181, 185, 191
Gast, John, 487
Gastonia, North Carolina, 911
Gates, Horatio, 208–209, 218, 224
Gay rights (see Homosexuals and ho-
    mosexuality)
General Electric Company, 653, 910,
    1128
General Federation of Women's Clubs,
    832, 859
General Managers Association, 679
General Motors Acceptance Corpora-
    tion, 913
General Motors Corporation, 908, 997,
    1118–1120, 1235–1238
Genêt, Edmond, 285
Geneva, 33–34
Geneva Accords (1954), 1136
George I (English king), 155
George II (English king), 74, 154–155
George III (English king), 160, 165,
    175, 177–178, 182, 185, 190–191,
    195, 197, 208, 211, 224
George, David Lloyd, 889
George, Henry, 670–671, 681, 712
Georgia, 74–76, 79, 112, 185, 201,
    215, 229, 230, 389, 391, 457, 596,
    608, 614, 786, 926
Gephardt, Richard, 1285
Germain, George, 195, 204, 208, 224
German-Americans, 108, 122, 130,
    442, 443, 532, 538, 886, 1060
Germantown, Battle of (1777), 207,
    225
Germany:
    and Austria, 901
    and Berlin blockade, 1093
    fascism in, 900, 1014
    and Great Britain, 808
    Hessians from, in American Revolu-
        tion, 202
    inflation in, in 1920s, 901
    and Martin Luther, 32
    navy of, 645
    and Rapallo Treaty (1922), 1012
    social security system of, 645
    in World War I, 872–878, 1011
    in World War II, 901, 1020, 1027,
        1038–1039, 1042–1043, 1075
Gernreich, Rudi, 1180
Geronimo (Indian chief), 742, 742–743
Gerry, Elbridge, 252, 290
Gershwin, George, 921
Getty, J. Paul, 951
Gettysburg, Battle of (1863), 584, 589,
    591
Ghent, Treaty of (1814), 329
Ghorbanifar, Manucher, 1288, 1290
Ghost Dance, 743, 757

GI Bill (1944), 1070, 1102
Gibbons v. Ogden (1824), 350
Gibraltar, Strait of, 21, 224
Gibson, Charles Dana, 779, 840
Gibson, Katherine, 752
Gideon v. Wainwright (1963), 1187
Gifford, Walter, 967
Gilbert, Humphrey, 14, 30, 34–38, 39,
    42, 48, 67, 78
Gilbert Islands, 1029
Gilman, Charlotte Perkins, 704, 831,
    874
Gilmore, Patrick, 711
Gilpin, William, 736, 744
Ginsberg, Allen, 1183, 1185
Ginsburg, David, 1048
Giovanni, Nikki, 1206
Gitlow, Benjamin, 895
Gladden, Washington, 698
Glasnost (Soviet policy), 1292, 1293
Glass, Carter, 855
Glass-Steagall Banking Act (1932), 968
Glass-Steagall Banking Act (1933), 980
Glenn, John, 1187, 1204
Glidden, Joseph, 751
Glorious Revolution, 7, 110, 112–113,
    119, 150–151
Glyn, Elinor, 918
Glynn, Martin, 877
Goering, Herman, 1038
Goethe, Johann Wolfgang von, 1248
Gold, 719, 744, 757, 807
"Gold Bug" pin, 782
Gold Coast, 61
Gold reserves, 1893–1897, 778
Gold rush (California), 509–511
Gold standard, 768, 782–784, 947,
    982
Goldberg, Arthur, 1171
Goldman, Emma, 896
Goldmark, Josephine, 828
Goldwater, Barry, 1176–1177, 1199,
    1257, 1269, 1288
Gompers, Samuel, 676, 680, 884, 915
Gonzalez, Corky, 1223
Good Neighbor policy, 901
Goode, Wilson, 1298
Goodman, Benny, 955
Goodyear Tire & Rubber Company,
    997
Gorbachev, Mikhail, 1081, 1292,
    1292–1293
Gorbachev, Raisa, 1292
Gordon, Thomas, 151, 184
Gordy, Berry, 1185
Gorgas, William, 862
Gorman, Margaret, 914, 915
Gorsuch, Anne Burford, 1279
"Gospel Car," 902
Gotham Court (New York City), 694
Gould, Jay, 662, 676, 680, 743
Government (see Civil liberties and
    civil rights; Constitution, U.S.;
    Elections; Federal government;
    Foreign policy; Legislation; Mili-
    tary; Politics; Popular sovereignty;
    Regulation, governmental; Repre-
    sentative government; Republican-
    ism; State governments; Supreme
    Court, U.S.; Taxes and taxation)
Grady, Henry, 721
Graham, Billy, 1123, 1124
Graham, Sylvester, 422, 429
Gramm-Rudman Act (1985), 1081,
    1283, 1304
Gramophone, 652

Granada, 16
Grand Army of the Republic, 766
Grandfather clauses, 785
Grange, Harold "Red," 920
Granges, 773–774
Grant, Cary, 1099
Grant, Madison, 835
Grant, Ulysses S., 597, 632–634, 633
　and "Mother" Bickerdyke, 582
　character of, 567–568
　as commanding general, 593
　and Comstock Law, 704
　in Congress's battle with Johnson, 615
　corruption under, 632–633
　in election of 1868, 630
　in election of 1872, 633
　first victories of, 567
　and Indians in Black Hills, 740
　and Lee's surrender, 598
　and Reconstruction, 632–633
　at Shiloh, 567–569
　at Vicksburg, 593
　and Virgin Islands, 804
　and Virginia campaign, 593–594, 597
Grasse, Comte de, 224
Grateful Dead (music group), 1184, 1185
"Graveyard vote," 696
Great Atlantic and Pacific Tea Company, 708, 909
Great Awakening (see First Great Awakening; Second Great Awakening)
Great Britain:
　and American colonies, 144–153
　administration of, 47–48, 55–56, 109–112, 151–153
　before American Revolution, 160–191
　and Coercive Acts, 182–184
　and Common Sense, 190
　and First Continental Congress, 185–187
　and frontier troubles, 169
　and Grenville's measures, 169–172
　and resistance, beginning of, 172–173, 181–182
　after Seven Years' War, 167–168
　and Seven Years' War, 162–166
　and Townshend Acts, 178–181
　and early colonization efforts, 36–39, 42–43
　and economic development and inequality, 145–148
　and imperial system before 1760, 151–153
　and politics, 148–151
　settlement of:
　　Chesapeake and Carolinas, 47–52, 56, 64–65, 69–70, 73
　　Middle Colonies, 102–103, 105–106
　　New England, 84–85, 87–88
　　in 17th century, 108–113
　　and urban life, 145
　　(See also Colonies, English)
　and American Indians, 120, 169, 280, 325, 327, 331
　and Bank of England, 278
　and Canada, 800–801

Great Britain (Cont.):
　and Caribbean region, settlement of, 65–66
　and Central America, 790, 804
　and China, 817
　Civil War and Restoration in, 7, 55, 84, 89, 113, 150
　and Confederacy, 566–567
　Corn Laws of, 347
　in 18th-century, 145–151
　factories in, 358
　and France, 118–121, 153–154, 159, 160–165, 162, 165, 166
　and Greece and Turkey, 1092
　industrial revolution in, 335, 643
　and Ireland, 34–35
　in late 19th century, rivals of, 808
　and Netherlands, 35–36
　and neutral rights, 284–285, 290, 321–322, 324
　Orders in Council of, 321–322, 324
　in Pacific region, 805
　and Panama Canal, 860
　political parties in, 282
　religion in, 32–34, 84–85
　and Russia, 820
　in 17th-century, 84–85
　in 16th-century, 5–6, 35–36
　and Spain, 29–30, 33, 35–36, 38, 42, 55, 65–66, 72
　and Suez Crisis, 1139
　suffrage in, 834, 898
　and U.S.:
　　during John Adams's administration, 290
　　early relations with, 233–234, 242, 283
　　during Jefferson's administration, 308, 321–322, 324
　　during Madison's administration, 324
　　and Monroe Doctrine, 331–332
　　and Oregon, 503
　　after War of 1812, 330–331
　　and War of 1812, 324–329
　　during Washington's administration, 284–285
　　(See also Revolution, American)
　and Venezuela, 807–808
　in World War I, 872–874
　in World War II, 1019–1020, 1038–1039
　and Zionism, 1073
　(See also Churchill, Winston)
Great Depression (see Depression)
Great Lakes, 119, 164, 169
Great Northern Railroad, 747
Great Plains, 733, 752–756
Great Pueblo Revolt (1680), 77
Great Society program (1960s), 1175–1179
Great Train Robbery, The (film), 935
Greater East-Asia Co-Prosperity Sphere, 1021
Greece, 184, 1092
Greek-Americans, 688
Greeley, Horace, 407, 431, 544, 560, 572, 633, 685
Green, William, 996
Green Corn Rebellion, 880
Green Mountain Boys, 130, 234
Greenback party, 766, 768, 789
Greenbacks (currency), 580, 634, 768
Greene, Nathanael, 218, 218–219, 224–225
Greenhouse effect, 1080

Greenland, 4
Greensboro, North Carolina, 1166–1167
Greenville, Treaty of (1795), 280, 311, 318
Grenada, 1286, 1304
Grenville, George, 170, 172–173, 178
Grenville, Richard, 39
Gresham, Walter, 807
Grimké, Angelina, 436, 440, 483
Grimké, Sarah, 394, 436, 440, 444, 483
Griswold v. Connecticut (1964), 1166, 1187
Groll, Theodore, 683
Grosse Point, Michigan, 906
Groves, Leslie, 1075, 1095
Gruen, Victor, 1266
Gruening, Ernest, 1200
Guadalupe Hidalgo, Treaty of (1848), 508, 514
Guatemala, 791, 1137
Guilford Courthouse, Battle of (1781), 219, 225
Guiteau, Charles, 767, 769
Guy Fawkes Day, 177
Gwinnet, Ann, 247

Habeas corpus, writ of, 577, 583, 635
Haber, Al, 1182
Hadden, Briton, 920
Haig, Alexander, 1246
Haight-Ashbury (San Francisco), 1185
Haiti, 867
Hakluyt, Richard (the elder), 38
Hakluyt, Richard (the younger), 38–39, 48
Halberstam, David, 1208
Haldeman, H. R., 1215, 1227, 1245, 1247, 1265
Hale, Edward Everett, 788
Haley, Bill, 1149
"Half-Breeds," 766
Halifax, Nova Scotia, 204–205
Hall, Newman, 648
Hallucinogens (drugs), 1183
Hamilton, Alexander, 252, 277, 302, 852
　and John Adams, 289
　attacks on, 293
　and Bill of Rights, 274
　character of, 275
　on Constitution, broad construction of, 279, 350
　on Constitution, ratification of, 256
　and election of 1796, 287
　and election of 1800, 292, 295
　and Federalist Papers, 255
　and Federalist party, 286
　financial program of, 275, 275–279, 305
　and Great Britain, 283, 285
　on import duty, 242
　and Jay's Treaty, 285
　on manufacturing, 268
　as secretary of Treasury, 273
　and Whiskey Rebellion, 280–281
Hamilton, Henry, 213
Hammond, James Henry, 454, 471, 482, 545
Hammond, William, 956
Hampton, Wade, 731, 732
Hampton Institute, 786
Hancock, John, 179, 196
Hanley, Joe, 1084
Hanna, Marcus Alonzo, 782, 784
Hanson, Ole, 895

Harding, Warren G., 896, 898, 929–930, 935, 1010
Hariot, Thomas, 39
Harlem Heights, Battle of (1776), 205
Harlem Renaissance, *903*, 923
Harmar, Josiah, 280
Harper, William, 397, 399
Harriman, E. H., 847
Harriman, Florence Jaffrey, 995
Harrington, James, 150
Harrington, Michael, 1175, 1176, 1187, 1280
Harrison, Benjamin, 767, 769, 771, 776–777, 806
Harrison, Walter, 1150
Harrison, William Henry, 316, 320, 327, 403, 405–407, *409*, 495, 501
Harrison Anti-Narcotic Act (1914), 957
Harte, Bret, 747
Hartford Convention (1814), 329–330
Hartley, Fred, 1232
Harvard University, 141, 155, 909
Harvey, William, 782
Haugen, Gilbert, 932
Haussmann, Georges, 643
Havana Conference (1940), 1014
Hawaii, 805–807, 814, 821, 1301
Hawkins, John, 29
Hawley-Smoot Tariff (1930), 967, 973, 1045
Hawthorne, Nathaniel, 428
Hay, John, 799, 808, 809, 810, 817–818, 819, 820, 860
Hay-Herran Convention (1903), 860
Hay-Pauncefote Treaty (1901), 808, 821, 897
Hayakawa, S. I., 1261
Hayden, Tom, 1182, 1206
Hayes, Rutherford B., 636–637, 653, 718, 767, 769
Haymarket Massacre (1886), 678–679
Hayne, Robert, 397, *398*, 444
Haynsworth, Clement, 1225
Headright system, 50
Health, Education and Welfare, Department of, 1130*n*.
Health and sanitation:
  and advertising, in 1920s, 912
  and AIDS epidemic, 1296–1297
  among American Indians, 7, 26, 29, 65, 77, 156, 487–488, 739
  and Chicago garbage collection, 840–841
  in cities, 643, 694, 717
  among Civil War soldiers, 585
  in colonial times:
    during American Revolution, 214
    in New England, 91–92
    in seaports, 135
    in South Carolina, 72
    on transatlantic voyages, 124–125
    in Virginia, 48, 51–52
  and diet, in 1970s, 1237
  in Dust Bowl, 959–960
  in early 20th century, 936–938
  during Great Depression, 949–950, 994
  and Medicare and Medicaid, 1177–1178
  of pioneer families, 755
  among slaves, 471–472
  and women's dress, 701
  during World War I, of soldiers, 890
  during World War II, 1033, 1035
  (*See also* Birth control; Diet and nutrition)

Hearst, William Randolph, 809
Helicopters, *1193*
Hell-Cat Maggie, 696
Heller, Walter, 1164
Hell's Angels (motorcycle gang), 1185, 1186
Hemingway, Ernest, 922
Hemp, 456, 484
Hempstead, New York, 1104
Henderson, Leon, 1046–1048, 1056
Hendrik, 120–121, 154
Henri, Robert, 921
Henry VII (English king), 10, 24
Henry VIII (English king), 33, 35
Henry (Portuguese prince), 14–15
Henry, Patrick, 173, 186, 226, 245, *256*, 257, 481
Hepburn, Katharine, 1125
Hepburn Act (1906), 848, 859
Heroin, 956
Herran, Tomas, 860
Hersh, Seymour, 1253
Hessians, 202, 205–206, 209, 212, 214
Hetch-Hetchy valley, 849
Hiawatha, 104
Hickey, Fred, 1216
Hickok, Lorena, 974–976, *976*
High schools, in 1950s, 1148
Higher education:
  and baby boom, 1189
  in early 20th century, 938
  in 18th century, 64, 141, 147
  and GI Bill, 1102
  during Great Depression, 953
  in late 19th century, 706–707
  and New Left, 1182
  of women:
    in 1870–1910, 831
    in 1920s, 917
    in 1950s, 1125
    in 1960s, 1239
  (*See also* Students)
Highway Safety Act (1966), 1238
Hill, James J., 847
Hillman, Sidney, 1070, 1071
Hillsboro, North Carolina, 218
Hillsborough, Lord, 180
Hippies, 1181, 1183, 1185, 1186
Hirabayashi v. United States (1943), 1062
Hiroshima, Japan, 1076, *1076*
Hispanics:
  in California, 1063–1066, 1105–1107
  education of, 1189
  and GI Bill, 1102
  migration of, after World War II, 1105–1107
  and New Deal, 994
  in 1980s, 1299–1300
  1986 population of, *1299*
  during Nixon's administration, 1221–1222
  as workers:
    wages of, 1301
    after World War II, 1086
  (*See also specific groups, e.g.,* Cuban-Americans; Mexican-Americans; Puerto Ricans)
Hispaniola (Haiti), 6, 13, 17, 25, 65
Hiss, Alger, 1100–1101, 1117
Hitchcock, Alfred, 1099
Hitler, Adolf, 900, 901, 969, 1014, *1015*, 1016–1020, 1024, 1036–1041, 1071, 1074
Ho Chi Minh, 898, 1079, 1136, *1198*, 1198–1199, 1215, 1228, 1229

Ho Chi Minh Trail, 1196, *1197*, 1199
Hoadley, Benjamin, 150
Hoar, George, 810
Hobby, Oveta Culp, 1130*n*.
Hoboken, New Jersey, *891*
Hoe printing press, 358–359
Hogarth, William, *147*
Holding companies, 668
Hole-in-the-Wall Gang, 747
Hollywood, California, 1097–1100
  (*See also* Films and filmmaking)
"Hollywood Ten," 1100
Holmes, Oliver Wendell, Jr., 827, 887, 895
Holocaust (Nazi exterminations), 1071–1073
Home economics education, 707
Home Life Insurance Building (Chicago), 692–693, 713
Home Owners' Loan Act (1934), 981, *1006*
Homelessness, during Great Depression, 950
Homer, Winslow, *603*
Homespun, 198–199
Homestead, Pennsylvania, 672, 679
Homestead Act (1862), 580, 725, 751, 765
Homestead Steel strike, 777
Homosexuals and homosexuality, 1271, 1296–1297
Honduras, 17, 790, 792, 867
Honeymoons, 716
Hooker, Isabella Beecher, 440
Hooker, Joseph, 571, 591
Hooker, Thomas, 96
Hoover, Herbert, 883, 930–934, 964–973, *966*, 973, 1013
Hoover, J. Edgar, 1253
Hoover Institute, 1293
Hoovervilles, *950*
Hopi Indians, 19, 77
Hopkins, Harry, 981, 988, 989, 998, 1075
Hopkins, Johns, 706
Hopkins, Mark, 745
Hornet (aircraft carrier), 1028
Horse-drawn railways, 690
Horseshoe Bend, Battle of (1814), 327
Horton Plaza (San Diego), 1266, *1267*
Hostage crisis (Iran-U.S.), 1263–1264
House, Edward M., 869, 878
House of Burgesses, 50, 173, 199, 226, 236
House Un-American Activities Committee (HUAC), 1097–1100
Household manufacturing, 268, 288, 357, 365, 420
Houseman, John, 999
Housing:
  in 18th century backcountry, 127
  and Fair Housing Act (1968), 1179
  and GI Bill, 1102
  during Great Depression, 950, 981
  in late 19th century, 702
  and Omnibus Housing Act (1965), 1178
  in suburbs, 1104–1107, 1122–1123, 1126–1127
  Vanderbilt's summer home, *669*
  after World War II, 1104–1107
  during World War II, 1048, 1057, 1065
Housing and Urban Development, Department of (HUD), 1178
Houston, Charles, 1144

Houston, Sam, *494*, 494–495
Houston, Texas, 881
Howard, O. O., 739
Howard Beach, New York, 1298
Howard University, 1144
Howe, Richard, 204–205, 208
Howe, William, 192–193, 204–208, 211
Howl (poem, Allen Ginsberg), 1183
Hruska, Roman, 1225
HUAC (House Un-American Activities
     Committee), 1097–1100
HUD (Housing and Urban Develop-
     ment, Department of), 1178
Hudson, T. S., 648
Hudson River, 101, 103–105, 131, 146,
     204, 206, 208
Hudson's Bay Company, 159
Hue, South Vietnam, 1208–1209
Huerta, Victoriano, 870
Hughes, Charles Evans, 877–878, 896,
     930, 1012
Huguenots, 34, 70, 83, 105
Hull, Cordell, 1013, 1014, 1016, 1024
Hull House (Chicago), 699, 713, 965
Hume, David, 255
Humphrey, George M., 1130
Humphrey, Hubert, 1176, 1211, 1214
Hungary, 1093, 1138
Hunt, E. Howard, Jr., 1244
Hunt, Richard Morris, *669*, 699
Hunter, Robert, 830, 859
Huntington, Collis P., 743, 745, 747,
     786
Huron Indians, 82, 103, 169
Hurricanes, 942
Hurston, Zora Neale, 998
Hutcheson, "Big Bill," 996
Hutchinson, Anne, 97–98
Hutchinson, Thomas, 174, 182, 187
Hy-Brasil, 21
Hyde Amendment (1977), 1265
Hyden, Kentucky, 904–905
Hydrogen bomb, 1117, 1132

Iacocca, Lee, 1259
Ibn Saud (Saudi king), 1073
Iceland, 8, 16
Ickes, Harold, 982, 993, 994, *1003*,
     1004, 1069
Idaho, 3, 18, 679, *719*
Idaho City, Idaho, *719*
Illegal aliens, 1301
Illinois, 237, 347, 371, 392, 457, 526,
     550, 772, 833, 859
     (*See also* Chicago)
Illinois Vice Commission, 839
Illiteracy (*see* Literacy and illiteracy)
IMF (International Monetary Fund),
     1074
Immigrants and immigration:
     and diet, 1236
     and drinking, 415, 443, 538
     in 18th century, 121–123, *122*, 130,
          135–136
          to Spanish colonies, 27
     in 1815–1830s, 353
     in 1840s–1850s, 530–533, *531*
     in election of 1796, 287
     European:
          1820–1920, 642
          1870–1920, 658–659
          and factory system, 361–362,
               530–532
          and family size, 447
          and gold rush, 509–512
          and Immigration Act (1965), 1178

Immigrants and immigration (*Cont.*):
     Jews:
          Russian, *819*
          during World War II, 1072–1073
     and Know-Nothings, 538
     literacy tests for, 859
     in municipal politics, 684
     in 1980s, 1298–1302, 1304
     and party system, 442, 538
     and population, 1860–1920, *687*
     and progressivism, 835–838
     public education for, 705–706
     restriction of, in 1920s, 924–925
     in 17th century:
          to Caribbean region, 66
          to Chesapeake and Carolinas, 44,
               48–50, 54, 67, 72
          to New England, 84–89
          to New Jersey, 105
          to New Netherlands, 101–102
          of Quakers, 105–107
          to Spanish colonies, 27
     in 1790–1820, 264, 353
     and transcontinental railroad con-
          struction, 746
     and urbanization, 686–690, 697–699,
          716
     as workers, 658–659, 673
     during World War I, 880
     (*See also specific groups, e.g.*, Asian-
          Americans; English-Americans;
          German-Americans; Hispanics;
          Irish-Americans; Italian-
          Americans; Jews; Mexican-
          Americans)
Immigration Act (1924), 1060
Immigration Act (1965), 1178, 1187,
     1300
Immigration Reform Act (1986), 1304
Immigration Restriction League, 697,
     713, 838
Impeachment of judges, 307
Imperial Valley, California, 962
Imperialism:
     1878–1900, *793*
     origins and spread of, 644
     of U.S., 790–820
          and Canada, 800–801
          and China, 817–818
          versus European imperialism, 794
          ideology of, 799–800
          and Latin America, 804–805
               and Central America, 790–792
               and Mexico, 801–802
               and Venezuela, 807–808
          in Pacific region, 805–807
          and Philippines, 814–817
          and Russian-American conflict,
               818–820
          and William Henry Seward, 802–
               804
          and Spanish-American War, 808–
               814
          and U.S. foreign-policy shapers,
               794–799
Implied powers, 279, 350, 397–398
Imports, 284, *322*, 323, 396, 566
Impoundment policy of Richard Nixon,
     1243
Impressment, 136, 284–285, 290, 321–
     322, 329
In re Debs (1895), 680
Incas, 26–27
Income, personal:
     and Great Depression, 948
     in Jacksonian era, 366

Income, personal (*Cont.*):
     in 1920s, 940
     in 1967–1984, *1259*
     during Reagan's administration,
          1280, 1297
     in South, 455, 599, 627, 630
     during World War II, 1053
     (*See also* Wages and salaries)
Income tax, 781, 851, 855, 931, 1068
Indentured servants, 50–52, 57, 59,
     61–62, 66, 95, 106, 123–125, 133,
     212
India, 7, 14–15, 68, 83, 162, 164, 224,
     898
Indian-Americans, 1300
Indian National Congress, 645
Indian Removal Act (1830), 734
Indian Reorganization Act (1934), 995
Indiana, 237, 344, 371, 392, 457
Indianapolis, Indiana, *683*
Indians, American:
     acculturation of, *742*
     and civil rights, 1223–1224
     and Dawes Severalty Act, 743, 757,
          795
     in 18th century:
          in American Revolution, 213–214
          economy of, 268–269
          on frontier, 169, 233–235,
               237–238, 268–269, 280
          and Iroquois League, 118–120
          in Pennsylvania, 107–108
          in Seven Years' War, 163–164,
               191
     before 1500, 6, 17–21, *19*
     on frontier:
          in 18th century, 169, 233–235,
               237–238, 268–269, 280
          in 19th century, 3, 311, 316–320,
               388–392, 396, 453, 499–501,
               721, 734–736, 738–743
     and New Deal, 994–995
     and racism, 721
     removal of, 280, 311, 316, 318, 320,
          388–392, 396, 453
     reservations for, *741, 743*
     in 16th and 17th centuries, 80, 82,
          83, 113
          in Caribbean region, 17, 65
          and disease, 7, 26, 29, 65, 77, 156
          dress among, 40–41
          in New England, 84, 99–100
          on Roanoke Island, 38–41, 42
          in South, 44–49, 57–58, 70–73,
               75–76, 79
          and Spanish conquest, 17, 25–27,
               76–77
     treaties with, 280, 311, 318, 320,
          388–392, 500–501
     (*See also specific tribes and peoples,
          e.g.*, Aztecs; Cheyenne Indians;
          Sioux Indians)
Indians of All Tribes, 1224
Indigo, 126, 132, 241
Individualism, 288–289, 415, 419,
     426–429, 490
Indochina, 1136
     (*See also* Vietnam; Vietnam War)
Industrial accidents, 672
Industrial design of automobiles,
     1118–1120, *1121*
Industrial revolution, 334–336,
     642–643
     (*See also* Industrialization)
Industrial Workers of the World
     (IWW), 886

Industrialization, 335, 341
  and cities, 684–685
  and Civil War, 575–576, 580, 599
  in 1850s, 530
  in 1860s–1880s, 648–680
    and big business, 664–671
      Carnegie's steel industry inte-
        gration, 665–666
      and consumer goods, 664–665
      critics of, 669–671
      Morgan's mergers, 668–669
      Rockefeller and Standard Oil,
        666–667
    industrial systems developed,
      649–659
      corporations, 656–657
      finance capital, 656
      labor pool, 657–659
      natural resources and industrial
        technology, 650
      systematic invention, 651–653
      transportation and communica-
        tion, 653–656
    railroads in, 659–664
      competition and consolidation
        of, 661–662
      and finance, 662–664
      and managerial revolution, 660–
        661
    in South, 457, 534, 551, 575–576,
      727–728, 728–730
    workers' response to, 362–364,
      671–680
      American Federation of Labor,
        676–677
      early unions, 675
      Knights of Labor, 675–676
      and limits of industrial systems,
        677–680
      workers' world, 671–675
  and factories, rise of, 357–364, 530
    and shoe industry, 362–363
    and technology, 358–359
    and textile factories, 359–362
    and workers, 362
      versus slaves, 482
      and unions, 363–364
  and family, 365, 420, 424, 447, 449
  Hamilton's program and, 278, 288
  and immigrants, 532
  and interchangeable parts, 338, 358
  and social conditions, 824
  (See also Industry)
Industry, 771–772, 906–907, 1049–
  1053
  (See also Industrialization; specific
    industries, e.g., Automobile
    industry; Steel industry)
Inequality (see Equality and inequality)
INF treaty (1988), 1293, 1304
Infant mortality, 446, 472, 936–937
Inflation, 882, 1220–1221, 1249, 1254,
  1259, 1278
Influenza, 937
Information systems, 654–655
Injunctions against strikers, 680
Inoculation, 140, 176
Installment buying, 913
Insull, Samuel, 652
Intelligence Oversight Board, 1253
Intelligence tests, 881
Interior, Department of the, 1279
Intermediate Credit Act (1923), 932
Intermediate-range nuclear forces
  (INF) agreement, 1293
Internal combustion engine, 650

International Bank for Reconstruction
  and Development (World Bank),
  1074
International Monetary Fund (IMF),
  1074
International Telephone and Telegraph
  (ITT), 1128
Interstate Commerce Act (1887), 771
Interstate Commerce Commission
  (ICC), 774, 789, 847, 848, 859
Interstate Highway Act (1956), 1122,
  1151
Interstate highway system, 1122
Invention (see Science and invention)
Investment trusts, 943–944
Iran, 1079, 1081, 1091–1092, 1136,
  1252, 1260, 1262–1264, 1265,
  1288–1292, 1304
Iran-Contra affair (1980s), 1288–1292,
  1304
Iraq, 1139
Ireland, 16, 34, 36, 39–40, 42, 122
Irish-Americans, 130, 245, 361–362,
  395, 442, 443, 509, 531, 531–532,
  538, 770, 801
  (See also Scots-Irish–Americans)
Irish Sweepstakes, 955
Iron and iron industry, 650, 729
Iroquois, League of the, 7, 19, 100,
  103–105, 113, 118, 120–121, 163–
  164, 169, 214
Iroquois Indians, 280
  (See also Iroquois, League of the)
Isabella (Spanish queen), 16, 24
Islam, 1079, 1081, 1172, 1263
Islands of the Blessed, 4, 8, 80
Isle of Jersey, 95
Isolationism, 1014–1025
Israel, 1081, 1094–1095, 1117, 1139,
  1250, 1262, 1286, 1288
Issei (see Japanese-Americans)
Italian-Americans, 74, 642, 688–689,
  1060
Italy, 5, 10–11, 16–17, 32, 34, 80, 899,
  901, 1014, 1036
ITT (International Telephone and Tele-
  graph), 1128
IWW (Industrial Workers of the
  World), 886

Jackson, Andrew, 599, 738
  and Bank of the U.S., 401–402
  and censorship of mails, 444
  character of, 387
  and democracy, 384–385, 387
  and Democratic party, 380, 382
  and election of 1824, 379–380
  and election of 1828, 386
  on equality, 379
  and Florida, 328, 330
  and Indians, 326–327, 388–392, 389,
    390
  at New Orleans, 326, 330
  and nullification, 397–399
  and perpetual union, 399
  and presidency, 402–403
  and Specie Circular, 403
  and Texas, 495
Jackson, Henry, 1234
Jackson, Jesse, 1283, 1284, 1302
Jackson, Robert, 1062
Jackson, Thomas "Stonewall," 560,
  569, 591
Jackson State University, 1195, 1229
Jacobsen, David, 1291
Jagger, Mick, 1186

Jamaica, 13, 65
James I (English king), 42, 44, 47–50,
  55, 79, 84–85, 177
James II (English king), 56, 102–103,
  105, 113
James, Frank and Jesse, 747
James, Ward, 952
James, William, 826, 859
James Island, South Carolina, 215
Jamestown, 7, 42, 44, 48–49, 49, 58,
  74, 76, 78–79
Jan and Dean (music group), 1185
Japan, 14, 17, 83
  and China, 868, 901, 1012–1013,
    1017
  and Korea, 804
  and Meiji Constitution, 645
  in 1920s, 899
  in 1930s, 1014
  and U.S., 791, 803, 865–866, 1021–
    1025
  in World War II, 901, 1027, 1039,
    1043, 1075–1076
Japanese-Americans, 806, 901, 1060–
  1062, 1301
Jaworski, Leon, 1246, 1247
Jay, John, 224, 242–243, 250, 255,
  274, 285
Jay-Gardoqui Treaty (1785), 250–251,
  257
Jay's Treaty (1795), 285–286, 290
Jazz, 904, 921
Jazz Singer, The (film), 935
Jeffers, William M., 1052
Jefferson, Thomas, 277, 324, 800
  character and beliefs of, 277, 288,
    302–305, 309
  on Constitutional Convention, 252
  at Continental Congress, 196
  death of, 332–333
  and drinking, 245
  economic policies of, 276, 278, 279,
    304–305
  and election of 1796, 287
  and election of 1800, 292, 293, 300
  and election of 1804, 320
  and Erie Canal, 343
  and Federalists, 295, 296
  and France, 283, 285
  on Hamilton-Adams conflict, 289
  and Hamilton's program, 276, 278,
    279, 304–395
  on impeachment of judges, 307
  inauguration of, 298, 300, 304
  and Indians, 316, 318, 388
  and Kentucky, 291, 397
  and Lewis and Clark expedition, 2,
    3, 309–311
  and Louisiana Purchase, 308–309
  and Marbury v. Madison, 306
  and Missouri crisis, 372
  and neutral rights, 322
  and Northwest Territory, 237–238
  and political conflicts, 293
  and political parties, 282, 320, 383
  and Republican party, 286
  as secretary of state, 273
  and slave trade, 372
  and Virginia, 173, 226, 229
  and Washington, D.C., 301, 301
  on Whiskey Rebellion, 281–282
Jefferson Airplane (music group), 1185
Jenney, William LeBaron, 692
Jerome, Chauncy, 338, 340, 358, 365,
  367, 370, 485
Jesuits (Society of Jesus), 83, 104, 113

Jesus Christ, 903
Jet airplanes, 1038–1039, *1039*
Jews, 16, 72, 75, 102, 123, 136, 687, 688, *819*, 1124, 1253, 1262
  (*See also* Anti-Semitism)
Jim Crow system, 730–733, 731*n.*, 785–787
  (*See also* Disfranchisement; Segregation)
Jitterbug (dance), *1065*
Job Corps, 1175, 1176
Jobs (*see* Employment and unemployment; Work and workers)
John XXIII (pope), 1272
John Birch Society, 1166
John Deere Plow Company, 658
John Paul II (pope), 1272
Johns Hopkins University, 706, 713
Johnson, Andrew, *607*
  and Congress, conflict with, 609–611
  and Joseph Davis, 602
  and election of 1864, 594
  and election of 1866, 612–613
  and Fourteenth Amendment, 612
  and Ulysses S. Grant, 630
  impeachment of, 615–616
  and land confiscation, 615
  Reconstruction program of, 607–609
Johnson, Hiram W., 924, 1015
Johnson, Hugh, 983
Johnson, James Weldon, 1144
Johnson, John H., 994
Johnson, Lady Bird, 1178
Johnson, Louis, 1112
Johnson, Lyndon B., 1081, *1174*, 1174–1175, 1187, *1207*, 1228, 1229
  and civil rights, 1171, 1172
  and election of 1964, 1176–1177
  and election of 1968, 1210
  and feminism, 1239
  and Great Society program, 979, 1175–1176, 1177–1179
  and John F. Kennedy, 1164
  and Henry Kissinger, 1215
  and race riots, 1173
  and Vietnam War, 1136, 1199–1201, 1207–1208
  and Voting Rights Act, 1171–1172
Johnson, Tom, 841
Johnston, Albert Sydney, 567
Johnston, Joseph, 569
Joint stock companies, 36–37, 48
Jones, Bobby, 920
Jones, James, 1098
Jones, John Luther "Casey," 660
Jones, Samuel, 841
Joplin, Scott, 711
Jordan, David Starr, 864
Jordan, Hamilton, 1256
Joseph (Indian chief), 742
Journals (*see* Magazines and journals)
Joyce, James, 901
Judicial review, 306, 398
Judiciary Act (1789), 274, 306
Judiciary Act (1801), 305
Juvenile delinquency, 1148, 1175

Kahin, George, 1206
Kahn, Otto, 943
Kaiser, Henry J., 1052
Kansas, 25, 522–525, 536–537, 539–540, 545–546, 551, 718–720
Kansas-Nebraska Act (1854), 535, 536–537

Keating-Owen Act (1916), 833, 857, 859
Keegan, Dennis, 1008
Kefauver, Estes, 1107–1108, 1115
Keith, Minor, 790–792, 794, 821
Keith-Albee Circuit (vaudeville), 840, 859
Kelley, Florence, 833
Kelley, Oliver Hudson, 773
Kellogg, Frank, 1012
Kellogg-Briand Pact (1928), 901, 1012, 1045
Kelly, William, 650
Kemble, Frances (Fanny), 378, 472, 476, 480
Kendall, Amos, 385–386
Kenna, Michael "Hinky Dink," 696, 762–763
Kennan, George, 820
Kennan, George F., 1091, 1112, 1161
Kennedy, Anthony, 1285
Kennedy, John, Jr., *1158*
Kennedy, John F., 1157–1159, *1158*, 1164–1165, 1175, 1187
  and Alliance for Progress, 1159
  assassination of, 1081, 1170–1171
  and Bay of Pigs invasion, 1160
  and civil rights, 1167, 1170
  and Cuban missile crisis, 1160–1163
  in election of 1960, 1156–1157
  and feminism, 1239
  and march on Washington, 1170
  and space exploration, 1204
  and University of Mississippi integration, 1169
  at Vienna summit, 1161
  and Vietnam, 1199
Kennedy, Joseph P., 1157
Kennedy, Robert F., 1081, 1167, 1168, 1175, 1210–1211, *1211*, 1229
Kent State University, *1194*, 1194–1195, 1229
Kentucky, 234, 264, 267, 280, 291, 309, 312, 371, 382, 388, 397, 468, 481, 484, 565
Kerouac, Jack, 1183
Kerr, Clark, 1182
Kerry, John, 1203
Kesey, Ken, 1183
Keynes, John Maynard, 948, 1004, 1007, 1067, 1158
Khomeini, Ruholla, 1079, 1263
Khrushchev, Nikita, 1137–1138, *1139*, 1140, 1161–1163
Kim Il Sung, 1112
Kindergartens, 706
King, Coretta, *1171*
King, Martin Luther, Jr., 1210–1211
  assassination of, 1081, 1210, 1229
  in Birmingham, Alabama, 1169
  and FBI, 1168, 1253
  and freedom riders, 1167–1168
  and march on Washington, *1153*, 1170
  and Montgomery bus boycott, 1145
  and race riots, 1173–1174
  and SCLC, 1167
  on Selma–Montgomery march, *1171*, 1171–1172
  and Vietnam War, 1206
King, Richard, 749
King, Rufus, 252
"King Caucus," 379
King George's War, 7, 120, 154–155
King Ranch (Texas), 749

King William's War, 7, 119, 155
King's College, 141
  (*See also* Columbia University)
King's Mountain, Battle of (1780), 217, 225
Kingston (New York), 367–369
Kingston Trio (music group), 1183–1184, 1187
Kino, Eusebio Francisco, 76
Kinsey, Alfred, 1103–1104
Kipling, Rudyard, 644
Kip's Bay (New York), 205
"Kiss-Me Clubs," 910
Kissinger, Henry, 1214–1215, 1217, 1218, 1228, 1248–1253, *1249*, 1263, 1265
Kit Carson National Forest, 1223
"Kitchen Cabinet," 387
Kitchens, 754–755, 1127
KKK (Ku Klux Klan), 635, *636*
Kleindienst, Richard, 1245, 1247
Knights of Labor, 675–676, 681
Know-Nothings (American party), 538–539
Knox, Frank, 991
Knox, Philander, 847, 866–868
Kodak cameras, 652
Konoye, Fumimaro, 1024
Korea, 803–804
Korean airliner disaster, 1292, 1304
Korean-Americans, 1300, 1301
Korean War, 1081, 1112–1115, *1113*, 1134, 1274
Korematsu v. United States (1944), 1062
Kosciuszko, Thaddeus, 218
Krimmel, Rudolf, *294*
Ku Klux Klan (KKK), 635, *636*, 926–928, 935, 1301
Ku Klux Klan Act (1871), 635

La Follette, Robert, 782, 842, 848, 859, 878
Labor (*see* Employment and unemployment; Unions; Work and workers)
Labor and Commerce, Department of, 859
Labor Contract Law, 658
Labor unions (*see* Unions)
Labrador, 36–37
Ladies Association of Philadelphia, 215
Lafayette, Marquis de, 332, 334
Laffer, Arthur, 1278
Lake Champlain, 163, 165, 208, 327
Lake Champlain, Battle of (1814), 327
Lake Erie, Battle of (1813), 325–327
Lake George, 163
Lake Ontario, 163
Lalawethika (Indian leader) (*see* Tenskwatawa)
Lamar, L. Q. C., 731
Lamb, William, 775
Lance, Burt, 1257
Land:
  and American Indians, 738–739, 743, 995
  (*See also* Indians, American, removal of)
  in colonial times:
    in backcountry, 127, 130–131
    in Chesapeake region, 49–50, 56
    in Georgia, 75
    in New England, 92, 93
    in South Carolina, 72
    in Virginia, 50

Land (*Cont.*):
  federal, sales of:
    in 1815–1850s, 354, *355*
    in 1830s, 403
    and 1889 land rush, 751
    under Jefferson, 307–308
  during gold rush, 514–515
  and panic of 1819, 370
  for railroads, 526, 746
  in South:
    in late 19th century, 721–722,
      723, 725, 726, 759–760
    and Reconstruction, 602–604,
      614–615, 639
  (*See also* Agriculture; Farmers;
    Frontier; Planters and planta-
    tions; Sharecropping; Tenancy;
    West)
Land Grant College Act, 580
Land-grant colleges, 580, 706
Landis, Kenesaw Mountain, 920
Landon, Alfred M. "Alf," 991–992
Lane, Ralph, 39
Lane Seminary, 417, 435–437
Lang, Fritz, 1099
Lange, Dorothea, *941*
Langer, William, 1100
Lansing, Robert, 875
Las Casas, Bartolomé, 29
Lasker, Albert, 912
Lathrop, Julia, 832–833
Latin America, 335
  conflicts in, 1974–1988, *1289*
  dictatorships in, 900
  during Great Depression, 950
  nationalism in, in 1950s, 1137, 1139–
    1140
  slaves in, 472
  and U.S.:
    and Alliance for Progress, 1159
    during Carter's administration,
      1261
    in late 19th century, 804–805
    and Monroe Doctrine, 332
    Nixon in, 1137
    and Taft's dollar diplomacy,
      866–867
    and Woodrow Wilson, 869
    after World War I, 1013–1014
  (*See also* Central America; *specific
    countries*):
Laud, William, 88
Laudanum, 956
Laurens, Henry, 221
Law, 657, 658, 667, 827
  (*See also* Legislation; Supreme
    Court, U.S.)
Law schools, 707
Lawrence, Jacob, *1032*
Lawrence, Kansas, 522, 524–525, *525*,
  539
Lawson, Thomas A., 828
League for the Protection of the Fam-
  ily, 779, 789
League of Nations, 893–894, 1013,
  1041
League of Women Voters, 917, 1015
Lear, Norman, 1274, 1275
Leary, Timothy, 1183, 1216
Lease, Mary Elizabeth, 775, *775*,
  776–777
Lebanon, 1139, 1286, 1288, 1304
Lecompton constitution, 545–546
Lee, Arthur, 210
Lee, "Mother" Ann, 429–430
Lee, Richard Henry, 187, 195–196

Lee, Robert E., 552, 569–571, 576,
  591–594, *597*, 597–598, 618
Leeds, England, 147
Legion of Decency, 959
Legislation:
  Adamson Act (1917), 857
  Agricultural Adjustment Act (1933),
    984
  Agricultural Adjustment Act (1938),
    985
  Agricultural Marketing Act (1929),
    973
  antilynching bills, 927
  Area Redevelopment Act (1961),
    1164
  Banking Act (1935), 990
  Bland-Allison Act (1878), 768–769
  Bonus Bill (1816), 342
  Budget and Accounting Act (1921),
    935
  Capper-Volstead Act (1922), 932
  Chinese Exclusion Act (1882), 713
  Civil Rights Act (1875), 731
  Civil Rights Act (1964), 1171, 1239
  Civil Service Act (1883), 767
  Clayton Antitrust Act (1914), 856
  Clean Air Act (1970), 1229
  Clean Water Act (1970), 1229
  Comstock Law (1873), 704
  Confiscation Act, First (1861), 572
  Confiscation Act, Second (1862),
    572, 614
  Dawes Severalty Act (1887), 743,
    995
  Desert Land Act (1877), 751
  Economic Opportunity Act (1964),
    1175–1176
  Economic Recovery Tax Act (1981),
    1279–1280
  Economy Act (1933), 980
  Elementary and Secondary School
    Act (1965), 1177
  Elkins Act (1903), 847
  Embargo Act (1807), 323–324, 330,
    332, 341, 348
  Emergency Banking Act (1933), 980
  Emergency Relief and Construction
    Act (1932), 969
  Emergency Relief Appropriation Act
    (1935), 989
  Energy Policy and Conservation Act
    (1975), 1254
  Equal Pay Act (1963), 1239
  Erdman Act (1898), 788
  Espionage Act (1917), 886, 897
  Executive Reorganization Act (1938),
    1007
  Fair Campaign Practices Act (1974),
    1247
  Fair Housing Act (1968), 1179
  Fair Labor Standards Act (1938),
    1006
  Federal Farm Loan Act (1916), 857
  Federal Highway Act (1916), 857
  Federal Reserve Act (1913), 856
  Federal Trade Commission Act
    (1914), 856
  Foraker Act (1907), 817
  Force Bill (1833), 399, 501
  Fordney-McCumber Tariff (1922),
    931
  GI Bill (1944), 1070, 1102
  Glass-Steagall Banking Act (1932),
    968
  Glass-Steagall Banking Act (1933),
    980

Legislation (*Cont.*):
  Gramm-Rudman Act (1985), 1283
  Harrison Anti-Narcotic Act (1914),
    957
  Hawley-Smoot Tariff (1930), 967
  Hepburn Railway Act (1906), 848
  Highway Safety Act (1966), 1238
  Home Owners' Loan Act (1933), 981
  Homestead Act (1862), 580, 725, 765
  Hyde Amendment (1977), 1265
  Immigration Act (1924), 1060
  Immigration Act (1965), 1178, 1300
  Immigration Reform Act (1986),
    1304
  Indian Removal Act (1830), 734
  Indian Reorganization Act (1934),
    995
  Intermediate Credit Act (1923), 932
  Interstate Commerce Act (1887), 771
  Interstate Highway Act (1956), 1122
  Judiciary Act (1789), 274, 306
  Judiciary Act (1801), 305
  Kansas-Nebraska Act (1854), 535,
    536–537
  Keating-Owen Act (1916), 833, 857
  Labor Contract Law, 658
  Lend-Lease Act (1941), 1020
  Lever Act (1917), 883
  Macon's Bill Number 2 (1810), 324
  Mann Act (1910), 839
  Marijuana Tax Act (1937), 957
  McCarran International Security Act
    (1950), 1100
  McKinley Tariff (1890), 768, 771
  McMahon Act (1946), 1095
  Meat Inspection Act (1906), 848
  Medicare Act (1965), 1177–1178
  Model Cities Act (1966), 1187
  Morrill Act (1862), 706
  National Defense Education Act
    (1958), 1141
  National Energy Act (1978), 1257
  National Environmental Policy Act
    (1969), 1235
  National Industrial Recovery Act
    (1933), 982
  National Labor Relations Act (1935),
    990
  National Origins Act (1924), 924
  National Public Housing Act (1937),
    1006
  National Traffic and Motor Vehicle
    Safety Act (1966), 1238
  Naval Appropriations Bill (1890), 821
  Neutrality Act (1935), 901, 1016
  Neutrality Act (1937), 1017
  during New Deal, *1006*
  Non-Intercourse Act (1809), 324
  Northwest Ordinance (1787),
    237–239, *238*
  Omnibus Bill (1850), 518–519
  Omnibus Housing Act (1965), 1178
  Overman Act (1918), 882
  Payne-Aldrich Tariff (1909), 859
  Public Utilities Holding Company
    Act (1935), 990
  Pure Food and Drug Act (1906),
    848, 956
  Reclamation Act (1902), 849
  Revenue Act (1932), 967
  Revenue Act (1935), 990
  Revenue Act (1942), 1068
  Seaman's Act (1916), 857
  Second Confiscation Act (1862), 614
  Second War Powers Act (1942), 1050
  Securities Act (1933), 981

Legislation (*Cont.*):
Securities Exchange Act (1934), 981
Sedition Act (1798), 291–292, 303
Sedition Act (1918), 886
Selective Service Act (1917), 880
Sheppard-Towner Federal Maternity and Infancy Act (1921), 917
Sherman Antitrust Act (1890), 645, 668, 680, 771
Sherman Silver Purchase Act (1890), 769, 771, 780–781
Simpson-Mazzoli Bill (1987), 1301
Smith Act (1940), 1100
Smith-Connally Anti-Strike Act (1943), 1069–1070
Social Security Act (1935), 717, 989
Soil Conservation and Domestic Allotment Act (1936), 985
St. Lawrence Seaway Act (1954), 1131
Submerged Lands Act (1953), 1130
Taft-Hartley Act (1947), 1087
Tax Reform Act (1986), 1285
Teller Amendment (1898), 810, 814, 821
Tenure of Office Act, 616
Trade Agreements Act (1934), 1013
Underwood-Simmons Tariff (1913), 855
Volstead Act (1919), 925
Voting Rights Act (1965), 1172
Wade-Davis Bill (1864), 605–606
War Powers Act (1973), 1248
Warehouse Act (1916), 857
Water Quality Improvement Act (1969), 1232
for welfare reform, 1296
Wilson-Gorman Tariff Act (1894), 781
Leisler, Jacob, 111
Leisure and entertainment, 709–712, 920–921, 954–959, 1056
(*See also* Films and filmmaking; Radio broadcasting; Television; Theater)
LeMay, Curtis, 1200, 1212
Lemke, William "Liberty Bill," 992
Lend-Lease Act (1941), 1020, 1045
Lend-lease program, 1020
Lenin, Vladimir, 879–880
Lenni Lenape Indians, 107–108, 169, 280, 320
Lenoir, Etienne, 650
Leonard, Daniel, 197
Leuchtenburg, William, 985
Lever Act (1917), 883
Levine, David, *1207*
Levitt, William, 1104, 1126
Levittown, 1104, 1117
Lewis, John, 1167
Lewis, John L., 996, 998, 1069, *1069*
Lewis, John Solomon, 723
Lewis, Meriwether, 2–3, 309–311
Lewis, Oscar, 1175
Lewis, Sinclair, 901, 909, 922, 935
Lewis and Clark expedition, 2–3, 309–311, *310*, 488
Lexington (aircraft carrier), 1028
Lexington and Concord, Battle of (1775), 189–192, 214
Leyte Gulf, Battle of (1945), 1040
Liberal Republican party, 632–633
Liberty party, 444, 502, 516
Liberty ships, 1052
Libya, 1286–1287, 1304
Liddy, G. Gordon, 1244, 1245

Liebman, Joshua, 1124
Life expectancy, 353, 394, 449, 472, 994
Life insurance companies, 663–664
Lighting systems, 652
Lilienthal, David, 1095, 1096
Liliuokalani (Hawaiian queen), 806
Lincoln, Abraham, *547*
assassination of, 598
and blacks, rights of, 550, 605–606
and border states, 564–565
character of, 546–547, 550, 598
and Civil War, as leader, 563–564
and Civil War, outbreak of, 556–557
and *Dred Scott* decision, 544, 550
in election of 1858, 546–547, 550
in election of 1860, 553, 553–554
in election of 1864, 594–595
and Lincoln-Douglas debates, 546–547, 550
on Mexican War, 505
and Reconstruction, 604–606, 608
and Santee Sioux Indians, 739
and slavery, 542, 546, 550, 556, 571–573, 596
and Thirteenth Amendment, 596
and writ of habeas corpus, 583
Lincoln, Benjamin, 216, 224
Lincoln, Mary Todd, 406
Lincoln-Douglas debates, 546–547, 550
Lindbergh, Charles, 935, 1019
Lindsey, Ben, 827
Ling, James, 1128
Lippmann, Walter, 913, 972, 1206
Literacy and illiteracy, 705, 994
(*See also* Literacy tests)
Literacy tests, 697, 732, 838, 859, 1172
Literature, 921–922, 998, 1098
(*See also* Books; Magazines and journals)
Little, Carra, 1294–1295
Little Big Horn, Battle of (1876), 645
Little Big Horn River, 740
Little Mothers' Leagues, 937
Little Rock, Arkansas, *1146*, 1146–1147, 1151
Little Rock and Fort Smith Railroad, 770
Livermore, Jesse, 943
Livingston, Margaret, 246
Livingston, Robert, 196, 308–309
Lloyd, Harold, 918
Local governments, employees of, *1177*
Locke, Alain, 923, 935
Locke, John, 70, 141, 172, 302, 482
Locusts, 753
Lodge, Henry Cabot, 799, 809, 870, 893, 894, 924, 1210
Loeb, William, 1226
Lomasney, Martin, 696
Lon Nol, 1216
London, England, 5, 20, 145, 149, 643
London Economic Conference (1933), 1014, 1045
"Lone Ranger, The" (radio program), 955
Long, Breckenridge, 1073
Long, Huey P., *986*, 986–987, 1007
Long, John, 810
Long Island, 98, 102, 105, 205, 206
Longworth, Alice Roosevelt, 925, 1071
Lorentz, Pare, 999
Los Angeles, California, 686, 747, 901, 902, 1009, 1065–1066, 1105, *1173*, 1173–1174

Loudoun, Lord (Joseph Campbell), 163–164, 167
Louis XIII (French king), 82
Louis XIV (French king), 113, 119
Louisbourg, 164, 165, 192
Louisiana, 371
in Civil War, 566, 575, 593
disfranchisement in, 785
and Huey Long, 986–987
and Reconstruction, 605–606, 609, 618, 620–621, 636–637
slavery in, 451
Spanish control of, in 1790, 234
suffrage in, 382
Louisiana (battleship), 861
Louisiana Purchase, 308–309, *310*, 330–331, 371–372, 508, 536–537
Lovejoy, Elijah, 439
Lowell, Massachusetts, 359–362, 405
Lowell, Robert, 1206
Loyalism, in American Revolution, 197, *200*, 201, 206, 208, 214–220, 246
Loyalty Review Board, 1097
LSD (drug), 1183
LTV Corporation, 1128
Luce, Henry R., 920, 1111, 1207
Lucky Strike cigarettes, 912
Luiseño Indians, 18
Luks, George, 830
Lumber industry, 728–729
Lumumba, Patrice, 1253
Luna Park (New York), 836, 837
Lundy, Benjamin, 435
Lusitania (British ship), 875, 897
Lusk, R. D., 959
Luther, Martin, 7, 31–32, 42
Lutherans, 32, 72, 83, 102, 142
Lynchings, 732, 774, 786, 885, 886, 927, 963–964, 993
Lynd, Helen and Robert, 912, 935, 952
Lynn, Massachusetts, 362–363, 405
Lyon, Matthew, 291, 293
McAdoo, William Gibbs, 882, 883, 934
MacArthur, Douglas, 970, 1022, 1026, 1037–1040, 1114–1115
Macaulay, Catherine, 150, 247
MacAuliffe, Tony, 1037
McCallum, Daniel, 661
McCarran International Security Act (1950), 1100
McCarthy, Eugene, 1210, 1211, 1229
McCarthy, Joseph, 1081, 1101, 1131–1133, *1132*, 1149–1150, 1151
McClellan, George, 563, 566, 569–571, 594–595
McClure, Samuel, 828
McCombs, William, 854
McCord, James, 1244, 1245
McCormick, Anne, 964
McCormick, Cyrus, 527, 530, 792
McCormick Harvester Company, 678
McCulloch v. Maryland (1819), 350, 401
Macdonald, Dwight, 1148
McFarlane, Robert, 1288
McGovern, George, 1227, 1240, 1242
MacIntyre, John, 792
McKay, Claude, 923
McKellar, Kenneth, 895
McKim, Mead & White, 699
McKinley, William, 782, 784, 788, 789, 809–810, 811, 812, 814, 843, 859
McKinley Tariff (1890), 768, 771, 805, 806

McLaurin v. Oklahoma State Regents (1950), 1110–1111
McMahon Act (1946), 1095, 1117
McNamara, Robert S., 1158, 1161, 1199, 1200, 1201, 1207
McNary, Charles, 932
Macon's Bill Number 2 (1810), 324
McPherson, Aimee Semple, 902–903, *904*
Macune, Charles W., 774, 775
Maddox (destroyer), 1199
Madeira Islands, 13, 15, 65, 68
Madero, Francisco, 870
Madison, Dolley, 323, 328
Madison, James, 252, 271, 481
  and Bill of Rights, 274
  character and beliefs of, 288, 323
  at Constitutional Convention, 252–256
  in election of 1808, 323
  in election of 1812, 330
  and Hamilton's financial program, 276–279
  on impeachment, 616
  and *Marbury v. Madison*, 306
  and Monroe Doctrine, 331
  and neutral rights, 324
  and new nationalism, 341–342
  and Republican party, 286
  and Virginia resolutions, 291, 397
  and War of 1812, 324, 328
  on George Washington, 273
Magazines and journals:
  Birth Control Review, 916
  Everybody's, 828
  Ladies Home Journal, The, 828
  Life, 883, 1207
  Lowell Offering, 359
  McCall's, 1055
  McClure's, 828
  Nation, The, 730
  New Republic, The, 898, 1130
  in 1920s, 920
  Reader's Digest, 920
  Redbook, 1125
  Time, 920, 935, 974, 1091, *1091*, 1207
Magellan, Ferdinand, 25, 38, 42
Mahan, Alfred Thayer, 795, 799, 821
Mahican Indians, 103
Mail (*see* Post Office, U.S.)
Mail order business, 708–709
Mailer, Norman, 1098, 1206
Maine, 92, 102, 110, 126, 371–372, 443
Maine (battleship), 809, 810, 821
Maine Law (1851), 443
  (*See also* Prohibition; Temperance movement)
Malcolm X, 1171, 1172, 1187
Malls (shopping malls), 1266–1268, *1267*
Manahoac Indians, 44, 47
Manchester, England, 147
Manchuria, 819–820, 901
Mandan Indians, 310, 486, 488
Manhattan Island, 102, 131, 205
Manhattan Project, 1035
Manifest Destiny, 487, 489–491
Mann, Horace, 433
Mann Act (1910), 839, 859
Manufacturing (*see* Household manufacturing; Industrialization)
Mao Tse-tung, 898, 1081, 1111, 1217, 1218
Marbury v. Madison (1803), 306

Marijuana, 957, 1183
Marijuana Tax Act (1937), 957
Marion, Francis, 217–218, *220*, 224–225
Market (*see* Business and commerce; Economy and economic conditions)
Marriage:
  age at, in 1790, 264
  and baby boom, 1188, 1190
  of blacks:
    in 1850, 394
    among slaves, 475
  in early 19th century, 419, 420–424, 447–449
  in early 20th century, 939
  in 1880–1916, 831
  during Great Depression, 951
  in late 19th century, 715–716
    among immigrants, 689–690
  and Oneida community, 430–431
  polygamous, of Mormons, 513
  after World War II, 1103
  (*See also* Divorces; Family and family life)
Marshall, George C., 1069, 1092–1093, 1096
Marshall, John, 290, 300, 306, *306*, 350–351, 391, 409
Marshall, Thurgood, 1143–1144, 1167
Marshall Plan, 1081, 1092–1093
Martha's Vineyard, 102
Martí, José, 808, 821
Martin v. Hunter's Lessee (1816), 306
Marx Brothers, 940, 958, *958*
Mary (English queen), 34
Mary II (English queen), 7, 110
Maryland:
  and Civil War, 565, 569–570
  Coode's Rebellion in, 58
  in election of 1856, 543
  free blacks in, 480
  and national bank, 350
  planters in, 462
  settlement of, 54, 79
  and slavery, 239, 241
  and western frontier, 234–236
  and workers' compensation, 843, 859
Masaryk, Jan, 1093
"MASH" (TV program), 1274
Mason jars, 951
Mason, George, 290
Masonry, 380–381
Mass culture, 900, 913–923, 954–959, 1147–1148
Mass media, 899, 918–920, 1226, 1273–1274
  (*See also* Films and filmmaking; Radio broadcasting; Television)
Mass production (*see* Assembly lines; Industrialization)
Mass transit, 691, 1122
Massachusetts:
  in American Revolution, 192–194, 204
  and Calvin Coolidge, 930
  educational reform in, 433–434
  free blacks in, 392
  and Hartford Convention, 329
  Know-Nothings in, 538
  land claims of, 234
  and Maine, 371
  and Mexican War, 505
  population of, in 1790, 264
  Shay's Rebellion in, 251
  and state regulatory commission, 789
  and ten-hour workday, 681

Massachusetts (*Cont.*):
  (*See also* Boston; Massachusetts Bay Colony)
Massachusetts Bay Colony:
  before American Revolution, 179–180, 184, 186–188
  and Dominion of New England, 109
  and Massachusetts Bay Company, 88–89
  religious divisions in, 96–98
  and Salem witchcraft trials, 110–111
  Scots-Irish in, 130
Massachusetts Bay Company, 88–89
Massachusetts Government Act (1774), 183–184
Massachusetts Institute of Technology, 730, 831
Materialism, 270, 366–367, 428–429, 577–581
Mather, Increase, 110
Matsu (island, China), *1135*
Matsuoka, Yosuke, 1014
Maximilian (Mexican emperor), 801, 821
Mayans, 20
Mayflower Compact, 87
Mayhew, Thomas, 158
Me Generation (1970s), 1233
Meade, George Gordon, 591, 593
Means, Russell, 1224
Meat Inspection Act (1906), 848, 859
Meat-packing, 665
Medellín cartel, *1289*
Medicaid, 1178
Medical schools, 707
Medicare Act (1965), 1177–1178
Medicine, 707, 831, 917, 937, 956–957, 1034, 1177–1178
  (*See also* Health and sanitation)
Medicines (pharmaceuticals), 848, 909
Mediterranean Sea, 5, 14–15, 36, 224
Meese, Edwin, 1291, 1296
Meiji Constitution (Japan), 645
Meiji restoration (Japan), 803
Meir, Golda, 1250
Mellon, Andrew, 930–931, *931*, 966
Melting Pot, The (play, Israel Zangwill), 712
Melville, Herman, *428*, 428–429, 803
Memphis, Tennessee, 566, 612, 694
Mencken, H. L., 933, 972
Mennonites, 142
Mercantilism, 47–48
Merchants (*see* Business and commerce)
Meredith, James, 1169, 1187
Mergers and acquisitions, 668, 909, 1128
Merrimack (ship), 566
Metacomet, 100
Methodist Church, 7, 142
Methodists, 626
  and Anti-Masonry, 381
  and blacks, 313, 626
  and Jeffersonian Republican party, 287
  and party system, 442
  and Second Great Awakening, 312–313, 419
  and slavery, 436, 485
Mexican-Americans, 488, 509–510, 514–515, 884, 957, 962–963, 994, 1063–1064, 1222–1223
  (*See also* Chicanos; Hispanics)
Mexican Revolution, 645

Mexican War, 427, 503–508, *504*, 506, 561
Mexico, 7, 18, 25–29, 491–495, 513, 535, 801–802, 870–871, 878, 1013, 1013–1014
(*See also* Mexican War)
Miami, Florida, 940, 942, 973
Miami Confederacy, 264, 280
Miami Indians, 169, 280, 320
Michigan, 237, 664–665, 965
(*See also* Detroit)
Micmac Indians, 11, 18, 80
Middle class:
  and domesticity, 420–421
  and education, 433
  and family, 365, 424, 446–449
  and fashion, 423
  during Great Depression, 948–949, 952, 981
  in late 19th century:
    birth rate among, 714
    in cities, 699–703
    housing for, 702
    and revivals, 418
  of rural-urban migrants, 1865–1920, 659
  on stock market, in 1920s, 942
  in West, 509
Middle Colonies, 101–108, 128, 131, 142–144, 201, 204–209, 211–213
(*See also* Delaware; New Jersey; New York; Pennsylvania)
Middle East, 1138–1139, 1250, *1251*, 1261, 1262–1264, 1286–1287
(*See also specific countries, e.g.*, Egypt; Israel)
Middle Passage, 61, 125
Midway, Battle of (1942), 901, 1028
Midway Island, 804, 901, 1028
Midway Plaisance (Chicago), 837
Migrant workers, 961–962
Milan Decree (1807), 322
Milburne, Jacob, 111
Military:
  and Dwight D. Eisenhower, 1141
  and Thomas Jefferson, 305
  during Reagan's administration, 1278, 1281–1282, 1296
  and Franklin D. Roosevelt, 1019
  and Theodore Roosevelt, 863
  segregation in, 813, *813*, 846, 1110
  during World War I, 877
  after World War II, 1096
  during World War II, 1030–1034
  (*See also* Army; Conscription; Continental Army; Militia; Navy; Veterans; *names of specific wars and battles*)
Militia (U.S., 17th–18th centuries), 52, 57, 73, 110–111, 169, 187, 189, 192, 194, 202–203, 206, 208, 216–218, 220–221, 224–225
Millennialism, *413*, 415, 417–418, 425, 429, 490, 599
Miller, Jeffrey, 1195
Millett, Kate, 1240
Milton, John, 150
Mining industry, 744
Miniskirts, 1180
Minneapolis, Minnesota, 986
Minnesota, 739, 776, 777, 986
Minor v. Happersett (1875), 764
Minorca, 224
Minorities (*see specific groups, e.g.*, Blacks; Hispanics; Italian-Americans; Jews; Mexican-Americans)

Minstrel show, *395*, 395–396
Miranda v. Arizona (1966), 1165, 1187
Miscegenation, 465–466
Miss America contest, 914–915, 935
Missiles (weapons), 1038, 1141, 1292
Missionaries, Christian, in late 19th century, 795
  (*See also* Missions)
Missions (Christian), 76–78, 77, 83, 283, 490
Mississippi:
  and busing, 1225
  civil rights movement in, 1169
    and black voters, 1172
  in Civil War, 593
  disfranchisement in, 732–733
  free blacks in, 480
  land concentration in, 551
  population of, in 1860, *460*
  and Reconstruction, 608–609, 614, 617, 621, 635–636
  schools in, in 1860, 457
  and Thirteenth Amendment, 608
Mississippi, University of, 1169, 1187
Mississippi Plan, 635–636
Mississippi River, 2–3, 7, 25, 119, 165, 195, 224, 233–234, 250, 282, 308–309, 593, 648, 649
Missouri, 354, 371–372, 384, 481, 512, 522, 539–540, 565
Missouri (battleship), 1076
Missouri Compromise (1820), *371*, 371–372, 515–517, 536–537, 543–544, 550, 555
Missouri Indians, 488
Missouri River, 2–3
Mitchell, Charles, 945
Mitchell, John, 1226, 1245, 1247
Mitchell, John A., 846
Mitchell, Margaret, 955
Mobile, Alabama, 328, 699
Mobile Bay, Battle of (1864), 594
Mobutu, Joseph, 1260
Moctezuma II (Aztec king), 25–26
Mod Squad, The (TV program), 1186
Model A (automobile), 908
Model Cities Act (1966), 1187
Model T (automobile), 859, 907
Mohawk Indians, 104, 120, 214
Mohegan Indians, 100
Molasses Act (1733), 170
Moley, Raymond, 979–980, 1014
Molotov, V. M., 1074, 1093
Monacan Indians, 44, 47
Mondale, Walter, 1284, 1304
Money (*see* Banks and banking; Currency; Money supply)
Money supply, 855–856, 882, 944, 947, 980, 987–988
Mongols, 7
Monitor (ship), 566
Monkey Business (film), *958*
Monmouth Courthouse, Battle of (1778), 213
Monongahela River, 650
Monopolies, 408, 667
Monroe, James, 308–309, 330–332, 342, 379, 383, 388
Monroe, Marilyn, 1125
Monroe Doctrine, 330–332, 897
Montagnais Indians, 18, 82
Montaigne, Michel de, 40
Montana, 2
Montcalm, Marquis de (Louis Joseph), 163–164
Montesquieu, 229

Montgomery, Benjamin, 602–604, 639, *639*
Montgomery, Bernard, 1029, 1071
Montgomery, Robert, 1100
Montgomery, Alabama, 1145, 1151, 1167–1168
Montgomery Improvement Association (MIA), 1145
Montgomery Ward, 708–709
Montreal, Canada, 82, 164
Montserrat, 66
Moody, Dwight, 697, 713
Moorehead v. Tipaldo (1936), 1002
Moral Majority, 1271, *1272*, 1304
More, Thomas, 37
Morehouse College, 1145
Morgan, Daniel, 218
Morgan, J. C., 995
Morgan, J. Pierpont, 645, 668, 847, 851, 943
Morgan, William, 380–381
Morgenthau, Hans, 1206
Morgenthau, Henry, 1004, 1043, 1067, 1073
Mormons, 512–514, 688n.
Morocco, 866
Morphine, 956
Morrill Act (1862), 706
Morris, Gouverneur, 252, 255
Morris, Robert, 242–243, 252
Morristown, New Jersey, 206
Morrow, Dwight, 1013
Morse, Samuel F. B., 358, 655
Morse, Wayne, 1200
Mortality rates, in late 19th century, 717
Moselle, Gertrude, 716
Mossadeq, Mohammed, 1136
Motion pictures (*see* Films and filmmaking)
Motley, Archibald, *903*
Motown music, 1185
Mott, Lucretia, 440
Mountain men, 368–369
Movies (*see* Films and filmmaking)
Moynihan, Daniel Patrick, 1186, 1219–1220
Muckrakers, 828
Mugwumps, 766
Muir, John, 849, 1192
Mulattoes, 394, 479–481
Muller, Curt, 827
Muller v. Oregon (1908), 828, 859
Mumford, Lewis, 693, 899
Muncie, Indiana, 839, 912, 918
Munich Conference (1938), 901, 1017, 1045
Munn v. Illinois (1877), 774, 789
Murals, during New Deal, 999–1001
Murieta, Joaquín, 515
Murphy, Frank, 997, 1062
Murphy, Shirley, 702
Murray, Judith Sargent, 247
Murray, Philip, 998, 1100
Murrow, Edward R., 1149
Museum of Modern Art (New York City), 1150, 1151
Music, 710–711, 955, 998, 1180
  (*See also* Rock and roll)
Muskie, Edmund, 1226
Muslims, 5, 7, 14, 16, 68
Mussolini, Benito, 899, 901, 1014, 1016, 1074
Mutual assured destruction, 1079
My Lai, South Vietnam, 1209, 1229
My Son John (film), 1098, 1100

Myers, William, 1107
Myrdal, Gunnar, 1143

NAACP (National Association for the Advancement of Colored People), 787, 789, 927, 993, 1143–1144, 1167
Nader, Ralph, 1235–1238, 1256, 1265
Nagasaki, Japan, 1076
Nagy, Imre, 1138
Naismith, James, 710
Nantucket Island, 102
Napoleon (French emperor), 308, 320–322, 324–325, 327, 334
Napoleon III (French emperor), 801
Narcotics, 956–957
Narragansett Bay, 181
Narragansett Indians, 87, 99–100
Narváez, Panfilo de, 25
NASA (National Aeronautics and Space Administration), 1151, 1204, 1205
Nashville (cruiser), 861
Nasser, Gamal Abdel, 1138–1139
Nast, Thomas, *610*
Natchez, Mississippi, 463
Natchez Indians, 20
National Aeronautics and Space Administration (NASA), 1151, 1204, 1205
National Association for the Advancement of Colored People (NAACP), 787, 789, 927, 993, 1143–1144, 1167
National Association of Manufacturers, 800, 910
National Birth Control League, 916
National Broadcasting Company, 919
National Civil Service Reform League, 767
National Consumers' League, 827–828, 833, 859
National debt, during World War I, 882
National Defense Council, 884
National Defense Education Act (1958), 1141, 1151
National Education Association, 831
National Energy Act (1978), 1257
National Environmental Policy Act (1969), 1235, 1265
National Farmers' Alliance, 774–775
National Farmers' Alliance and Industrial Union, 775
National Foundation of the Arts and Humanities, 1178
National Guard, at Kent State University, 1194–1195
National Industrial Recovery Act (1933), 982, *1006*
National Labor Relations Act (1935), 990, *1006*
National Labor Relations Board, 990
National Labor Union (NLU), 675, 681
National Municipal League, 772, 789
National Negro Business League, 787
National Organization for Women (NOW), 1239, 1265
National Origins Act (1924), 924
National Public Housing Act (1937), *1006*
National Recovery Administration (NRA), 982–984, 993–994, 995–996
National Republican party, 380, 386
National Security Act (1947), 1117
National Security Council (NSC), 1111

National Trades' Union, 363
National Traffic and Motor Vehicle Safety Act (1966), 1238, 1265
National Union for Social Justice, 987–988
National Union party, 612
National War Labor Board (NWLB), 884
National Wilderness Preservation System, 1178
National Woman Suffrage Association, 704, 764, 766, 789, 833–834, 917
National Woman's party, 834, 917
National Women's Political Caucus (NWPC), 1240
National Youth Administration (NYA), 989
Nationalism, 329–330, 333–334, 341–342, 371, 398–399, 555, 558, 564, 1133–1134, 1137, 1137–1140
Native Americans (*see* Indians, American)
Nativism, 510, 514–515, 533, 538–539, 924–925
NATO (North Atlantic Treaty Organization), 1093
Natural rights, 302
Naturalization Act, 290, 292
Naturalization (citizenship), 696
Nature, 426–427
Navajo Indians, 995
Naval Appropriations Bill (1890), 821
Navigation, 8, 13–15, 79, 168
Navigation Acts, 48, 55–56, 109, 153
Navy, British, and American Revolution, 202, 204, 224
Navy, U.S.:
   in Civil War, 566–567
   and France, war with, 290
   and "Great White Fleet," 866, 897
   Jefferson and, 305
   in late 19th century, 795–798
   in Mexican War, 505–506
   and Pearl Harbor, 1008, *1009*, 1024
   in Spanish-American War, 811–812, *812*
   and War of 1812, 325–327
   after World War I, 1011–1012
   in World War II, 1028, 1030
Nazi party (Germany), 969–970, 1014, 1071–1072
Nebraska, 536, 720
Negro Union Co-operative Aid Association, 718
Negroes (*see* Blacks)
Nelson, Donald M., 1050
Nelson, Gaylord, 1235
Netherlands, 34–36, 55, 57, 66, 85–86, 101–103, 119, 168, 170, 182, 242
Neutral rights, 284–285, 290, 321–325, 329, 566–567
Neutrality Act (1935), 901, 1016, 1045
Neutrality Act (1936), 1045
Neutrality Act (1937), 1017, 1045
Nevada, 18
Nevis, 66
New Amsterdam (New York City), 101, *101*, 103
New Brunswick, New Jersey, 206, 926
New Deal (1930s), 900, 901, 974–1007
   1933–1935, 976–985
   first hundred days of, 979–982
   and riddle of recovery, 982–985
   and Roosevelts, 977–979
   1935–1936, 985–992
   and election of 1936, 991–992

New Deal (1930s): 1935–1936 (*Cont.*):
   protests against, 985–988
   second hundred days of, 988–990
   1937–1940, 1002–1007, 1046
   and courts, 1002–1004
   problems of, 1004–1005
   legacy of, 1005–1007
   and U.S. society, 992–1002
   and art and culture, 998–1002
   and minorities, 993–995
   and organized labor, 996–998
   and women, 995–996
   after World War II, 1086–1087
   in election of 1948, 1109
   during World War II, 1068
New England, *86*
   and abolitionism, 437
   in 18th century:
      in American Revolution, 208
      backcountry of, 126–127
      farming in, 123, 126
      First Great Awakening in, 143
      and Green Mountain Boys, 130
      population of, in 1790, 267
      rural life in, 123
      and Seven Years' War, 163
   free blacks in, 392
   literacy in, in 1850, 457
   in 17th century, 83–100
      deviance and dissent in, 94–98
      and Dominion of New England, 109–110, 113
      families and local life in, 89–94, 116–117
      and Indians, 99–100
      and Long Island, 102–103
      and Puritans, 84–89
      and Salem witchcraft trials, 110–111
      women in, 98–99
   before 1620, 84
   and War of 1812, 323, 329
   (*See also* Connecticut; Maine; Massachusetts; Massachusetts Bay Colony; New Hampshire; Plymouth Colony; Rhode Island)
New England Emigrant Aid Company, 522, 539
New England Kitchen, 829–830, 859
New France, 80, 82–83, 113, 119–120, 164–165
New Hampshire, 88, 92, 109, 112, 127, 130, 262, 329
New Harmony community, 422, 431–432
New Haven, Connecticut, 653
New Haven Colony, 96, 105
New Jersey, 105, 109, 113, 201, 205–206, 213, 392, 553, 668
New Jersey Plan, 253
New Left, 1179–1182
New Mexico, 19, 25, 76–77, 488, 491–492, 503–504, 508, 514, 518, 519
New Nationalism, 341–342, 371–372, 851–852
New Netherlands, 101, 102, 102–104, 109, 113
New Orleans, Battle of (1815), 326, 328, 328–329
New Orleans, Louisiana, 7, 165, 271, 282, 308, 326, 328–329, 356, 457, 481, 527, 529, 612, 620, *691*, 1152
New York:
   asylum movement in, 434
   and black suffrage, 392
   in 18th century:

New York: in 18th century (*Cont.*):
  and American Revolution, 201,
    204–206, 207, 208–209,
    213–214
  and Constitution, *256*
  and Green Mountain Boys, 130
  population of, in 1790, 264
  and Seven Years' War, *162*
  and Townshend Acts, 178, 191
  and election of 1844, 502
  and Erie Canal, 343–344
  Know-Nothings in, 538
  and Franklin Roosevelt, 978
  in 17th century, 101–105, 109
    Leisler's Rebellion in, 111
  tenement code in, in 1912, 832
  (*See also* New York City)
New York Birth Control League, 859
New York Central Railroad, 660
New York City:
  Asian-Americans in, 1301
  Central Park in, 836
  Democratic party in, *759*
  in 18th century, 131, *132*
    and American Revolution, 204–206
    in elections of 1799 and 1800, 295
    and Stamp Act, 176
    George Washington's reception in,
      272
  fiscal crisis in, 1255, 1265
  Gotham Court of, 694
  during Great Depression, 965
    and Union Square protest, 987
  and Howard Beach attack, 1298
  Irish immigrants in, in 1847, *531*
  municipal governments of, 695
  and George Washington Plunkitt,
    682–684
  and progressivism, 843
  in 17th century, *101*
  skyline of, 906
  slums and tenements in, 693
  and Triangle Shirtwaist Company
    fire, 822, 824
  unemployment in, in 1840, 405
New York Stock Exchange, 656, 663,
  778, 943, 945–946
Newfoundland, 7, 10–11, 16, 18
Newlands, Frederick, 849
Newport, Rhode Island, 131, 198, 211
Newspapers, 265, 359, 689, 699, 708,
  710, 920
  Chicago *Tribune*, 1294
  Liberator, 435, 438, 481
  Manchester *Union-Leader*, 1226
  New York *Times*, 1243
  Washington Post, 1244
Newton, Huey P., 1172–1173
Newton, Isaac, 7, 141
Nez Percé Indians, 742
Niagara movement, 787
Nicaragua, 17, 645, 790, 867, 869,
  1013, 1081, 1261, 1287–1288,
  1290–1292, 1304
Nicholas II (Russian czar), 878
Nicholson, Francis, 111
Nickelodeons, 918
Nicolls, Richard, 105
Niebuhr, Reinhold, 1145
Nimitz, Chester W., 1040
Nipmuc Indians, 100
Nisei (*see* Japanese-Americans)
Nitze, Paul, 1262
Nixon, Richard M., 1081, 1100, *1116,*
  1214–1215, *1218,* 1229, 1242–
  1244, 1265

Nixon, Richard M. (*Cont.*):
  and Dean Acheson, 1115
  and *Apollo 11,* 1230
  and détente, 1217–1219
  and elections:
    of 1952, 1115
    of 1960, 1156–1157
    of 1968, 1211
    of 1969, 1213
    of 1972, 1227
  and energy crisis, 1250
  and environmentalism, 1234–1235,
    1235
  Gerald Ford's pardon of, 1253
  and impoundment policy, 1243
  and Henry Kissinger, 1248
  in Latin America, 1137
  "new federalism" of, 1219–1221
  and "slush fund" scandal, 1116
  and Supreme Court, 1225
  "us versus them" mentality of,
    1225–1226
  and Vietnam War, 1213–1214, 1215–
    1216, 1227–1228
  and Watergate affair, 1244–1247
N.L.R.B. v. Jones and Laughlin Steel
  Corporation (1937), 1003
NLU (National Labor Union), 675, 681
Nofziger, Lyn, 1296
Nominating conventions, 383
Nomura, Kichisaburo, 1024
Non-Intercourse Act (1809), 324
Nootka Indians, 735
Norfolk, Virginia, 196, 221
Norris, Frank, 830
Norris, George, 981, *983,* 1015, 1068
Norris, J. Frank, 903
Norris, Tennessee, 994
North, Lord, 181–182, 188–189
North, Oliver, 1288–1291, *1290,* 1304
North Atlantic Treaty Organization
  (NATO), 1093
North Bridge, 189–190
North Carolina, 256, 457, *460*
  American Revolution in, 201, 217–
    219, 222, 224–225
  and Constitution, 274
  population of, 264
  Regulation in, 129–130, 181
  settlement of, 67
  suffrage in, 382
Northern Alliance, 775
Northern Pacific Railroad, 747, 778
Northern Securities Company, 847, 859
Northwest Coast Indians, 734–735
Northwest Ordinance (1787), 237–239,
  238
Northwest Passage, 10, 36, 80–81
Northwest Territory, 237–238, *238*
Northwestern Alliance (National Farm-
  ers' Alliance), 774–775
Nova Scotia (Acadia), 37, 80, 82, 84,
  163, 169
NOW (National Organization for
  Women), 1239, 1265
Noyes, Alexander, 943
Noyes, John Humphrey, 430–431
NRA (National Recovery Administra-
  tion), 982–984, 993–994, 995–996
NSC-68 (document), 1111–1112, 1117,
  1262
NSC (National Security Council), 1111
Nuclear power plants, 1081, 1254,
  1258, *1258*
Nuclear test ban treaty (1963), 1081,
  1187

Nuclear weapons, 901, 1035,
  1075–1076, 1078–1079, *1083,*
  1095–1097, 1111, 1135–1136,
  1161, 1281
  (*See also* Arms control; Disarma-
    ment; Nuclear test ban treaty;
    SALT I; SALT II)
Nueces River, 503–505
Nullification, 397, 397–399, 484, 501
Nye, Gerald P., 1015
Nye Committee, 1045
Nylon stockings, *1055*

Oakes, Richard, 1224
Oakland, California, 1172–1173
Obscenity, definition of, 1166
Ocala Demands, 775, 789
Occupational Safety and Health
  Agency (OSHA), 1220
O'Connor, John J., 1005
O'Connor, Sandra Day, 1284
October War (Yom Kippur War)
  (1973), 1081, 1250
OEO (Office of Economic Opportu-
  nity), 1176, 1243
Office equipment, technology of, 655
Office of Economic Opportunity
  (OEO), 1176, 1243
Office of Minority Affairs, 994
Office of Price Administration (OPA),
  1056, 1077, 1085
Office of Scientific Research and De-
  velopment (OSRD), 1034
Office of War Mobilization (OWM),
  1049–1053, 1077
Office work, women in, *674*
Oglethorpe, James, 74
Ohio, 311, 344, 392, 406, 437, 512,
  526, 538, 769
Ohio Company, 153
Ohio River, 2–3, 238, 453
Ohio Valley, 120–121, 159, 162–164
Oil industry:
  early technology of, 650
  and expropriations by Bolivia and
    Mexico, 1013–1014
  and Iran, 1136
  and J. Paul Getty, 951
  in 1950s, 1128
  and oil spills, 1230, 1230–1232, *1231*
  and OPEC boycott, 1250, 1252
  and Rockefeller, 666–667
  and Submerged Lands Act (1953),
    1130
  (*See also* Oil resources)
Oil resources, 1091–1092, *1251,* 1254,
  1261
O'Keefe, Georgia, 921
Okhotsk, Russia, 157
Okinawa, 1071
Oklahoma, 25, 751, 757, *950*
Oklahoma City, Oklahoma, *950*
Old Age Revolving Pensions, Limited,
  988
"Old Time Gospel Hour, The" (TV
  program), 1271
Older, Fremont, 826
Olds, Sarah, 755
Oligopolies, 667, 909
Olive Branch Petition (1775), 195
Oliver, Joe "King," 921
Olmsted, Frederick Law, 454, 463,
  468–471, 473, 476, 836
Olney, Richard, 807, 809
Olson, Floyd B., 986

Olympic games of 1980, 1264
Omaha Indians, 487
Omnibus Bill (1850), 518–519
Omnibus Housing Act (1965), 1178, 1187
Oñate, Juan de, 76
Oneida community, 422–423, 430–431
Oneida Indians, 104
OPEC (Organization of Petroleum Exporting Countries), 1081, 1250, 1252, 1254, 1258, 1260, 1264, 1265
Opechancanough, 47, 54, 57
"Open door" policy in China, 817–818, 821
"Open Skies" policy, 1138
Opium, 956–957
Oppenheimer, J. Robert, 1078, 1095, 1132–1133, 1151
Opposition, The, 150–151, 172, 174, 183–184, 247
Orchestras, 710
Orders in Council, 321–322, 324
Oregon, 18, 310, 331, 354, 489–491, 495, 502, 503, 508, 516, 553, 827–828
Oregon (battleship), 860
Oregon Trail, 497, 498
Organization of Petroleum Exporting Countries (OPEC), 1081, 1250, 1252, 1254, 1258, 1260, 1264, 1265
Organization on Unemployment Relief, 967
Orlando, Vittorio, 889
Orozco, José Clemente, 999
Orwell, George, 1147
Osborn, Lollie, 703
Osceola (Indian chief), 391
OSHA (Occupational Safety and Health Agency), 1220
Ostend Manifesto (1854), 535–536
Ostrogorski, Moisei, 761
O'Sullivan, John L. 490
Oswald, Lee Harvey, 1170
Otis, Elisha Graves, 693
Oto Indians, 487
Ottawa Indians, 169, 238
Ottoman Empire, 5
Overland Trail, 496–501, 498, 500, 508, 512, 520
Overlanders, 733
Overman Act (1918), 882
Owen, Robert, 431
Owen, Ruth Bryan, 995
Oxford University, 147

Pachucos, 1065
Pacific Northwest, Indian tribes of, 20
Pacific Ocean, 13, 25, 38, 82, 157
Pacific region, 815, 1021–1025, 1022–1023, 1028, 1033, 1037–1040
Pacifism, 874
Padrones, 658
Pago Pago, Samoa, 805
Pahlavi, Mohammed Reza (Iranian shah), 1136, 1252, 1260, 1262–1263
Paine, Thomas, 190, 190–191, 194, 196–197
Palestine, 1073
(See also Israel)
Palm Beach, Florida, 940
Palmer, A. Mitchell, 895, 896
Pamunkey Indians, 44, 47
Pan-American Congress (1889), 805, 821

Panama, 13, 17, 25, 861, 1261
Panama Canal, 645, 808, 860–863, 862, 864, 897, 1081, 1253, 1261, 1265
Panay (gunboat), 1017, 1045
Panics, economic (see Depressions and panics)
Paris, France, 5, 643
Paris, Treaty of (1763), 160, 165, 191
Paris, Treaty of (1783), 224, 225, 233
Paris, Treaty of (1898), 821
Parker, Alton B., 847
Parker, Peter, 215
Parks, Rosa, 1145
Parties, political (see Political parties)
Passaic, New Jersey, 911
Pasteur, Louis, 686
Pastor, Tony, 839
PATCO (air traffic controllers union), 1279
Patents, number of, in 19th century, 318n., 651
Paterson, William, 253
Patman, Wright, 970
Patronage, 384, 387
Patronage, political, 305, 307, 767
Patrons of Husbandry, 773–774, 789
Patterson, Ben, 774
Patton, George S., Jr., 970, 1029, 1037
Paul VI (pope), 1272
Paul, Alice, 834, 917
Pauncefote, Julian, 808
Pawtucket Indians, 99–100
Paxton, Tom, 1260
Paxton Boys, 129, 155
Payne-Aldrich Tariff (1909), 859
Peace Corps, 1159, 1187
Peale, Norman Vincent, 1124
Pearl Harbor, Hawaii, 806, 901, 1008, 1009, 1024
PECE (President's Emergency Committee on Employment), 967
Peirce, Charles, 826
Pendleton Act (Civil Service Act) (1883), 767
Penn, William, 105–108, 106
Pennsylvania:
    asylum movement in, 434
    and black suffrage, 392
    in Civil War, 591–592
    in 18th century:
        in American Revolution, 206–208, 211–214
        and election of 1796, 286
        and French-English conflict, 120
        and Seven Years' War, 162–163
        population of, in 1790, 264, 267
    suffrage in, 230
    and Whiskey Rebellion, 280–281
    in election of 1856, 543
    Know-Nothings in, 538
    oil finds in, 650
    and William Penn and Quakers, 105–108
    and Three Mile Island, 1258, 1258
    (See also Philadelphia)
Pennsylvania Railroad, 660, 665–666
Pennsylvania (battleship), 1008
Pennsylvania, University of (Academy and College of Philadelphia), 141
Penobscot Indians, 18
Pensacola, Florida, 328
Pensions, 988, 989
Pentacostalists, 1270–1271
Pentagon Papers (documents), 1229, 1243, 1245

People for the American Way, 1275
People's party (see Populist party)
Pérez Esquivel, Adolfo, 1260
Perfectionism, 417, 422, 425, 429–430, 599
Perkins, Frances, 953, 990, 995
Perry, Matthew, 645, 803, 803, 821
Perry, Oliver Hazard, 327
Pershing, John "Black Jack," 871, 871, 887, 897
Pershing II missiles, 1292, 1304
Peru, 26, 28, 42, 76, 156, 945
Pet banks, 402
Peter the Great (Russian czar), 157
Petroleum industry (see Oil industry; Oil resources)
Pharmaceuticals, 848, 909
Philadelphia, Pennsylvania:
    blacks in, and 1944 transit strike, 1064
    in 18th century, 119
        in American Revolution, 206–208, 213
        Constitutional Convention in, 252–255
        First Continental Congress in, 184–187
        as national capital, 276
        population of, 107, 132
        Second Continental Congress in, 194–197
    free blacks in, 394
    railroads in, 527–529
    social mobility in, 1820–1860, 366
    Whig parade in, in 1840, 375
Philadelphia and Reading Railroad, 778
Philanthropy, 706, 965
Philip II (Spanish king), 34, 42
Philippines, 25, 162, 165, 810, 811, 814–817, 821, 869, 901, 1026, 1040
Phillips, Wendell, 436
Phonograph records, 711
Photocopying, 655
Photography, 652, 716, 941
Phrenology, 429
Pickford, Mary, 915
Picture windows, 1126
Pierce, Franklin, 520, 534–536, 541, 558, 563
Pike, Zebulon, 310
Pilgrims, 7, 85–86, 113
Pinchot, Gifford, 848, 850–851
Pinckney, Charles Cotesworth, 252, 290, 320, 323
Pinckney, Thomas, 282, 287
Pinckney's Treaty (1796), 282, 308
Pingree, Hazen, 841
Pinkerton detectives, 776
Pinzer, Maimie, 839
Pirates, 29, 72
Pitcairn, John, 189
Pitt, William, 154, 163–167, 178, 178, 188
Pittsburgh, Pennsylvania, 164, 169, 262, 281
Pittsburgh Bessemer Steel Company, 672
Pizarro brothers, 14, 26, 27
Plains Indians, 486–488, 499–501
    (See also specific tribes, e.g., Cheyenne Indians; Crow Indians)
Plains of Abraham, 164
Planet of the Apes (film), 1273
Planters and plantations:
    in colonial times:
        in Caribbean region, 66–67

Planters and plantations: in colonial
    times (*Cont.*):
  in Carolinas, 74
  in Chesapeake region, 62–65
  in old South, *461*, 461–462
    in 1850s, 551
    and plantation masters, 463–464
    and slavery, 458–460, 469–472
      and slave culture, 474–480
      and slave resistance, 472–474
    in Tidewater and on frontier,
      462–463
    and women, 464–466, *465*
    and yeoman farmers, 468
  during Reconstruction, 628–630, 635
Platt, Orville H., 846
Platt, Thomas, 788
Platt Amendment (1901), 821, 897,
  1013
Pleasant Hill, Missouri, 1000
Pleiku, South Vietnam, 1200
Plessy v. Ferguson (1896), 645, 705,
  732, 757, 1110, 1144
Plummer, Franklin E., 374, 376–378,
  383, 407, 462
Plunkitt, George Washington, 682–684
Plymouth Colony, 7, 87–88, 96, 100,
  108–110, 113
Pocahontas, 47
Poindexter, John, 1289–1291
Poland, 901, 1019, 1042, 1075
Polenberg, Richard, 1124
Police, 930, 1212
Polio, 978, *978*
Political parties:
  in Civil War, 564
  in 1840s, 442–445
    and abolitionism, 444–445
    and temperance movement, 443
    and woman suffrage, 442–443
  in 1850s, 534–543
    and election of 1856, 541–543
    and Kansas, 539–540
    and Kansas-Nebraska Act, 536–537
    and Know-Nothings, 538–539
    and second American party sys-
      tem, collapse of, 537
    and Charles Sumner, 540–541
  in Jacksonian era, 380–385, 408–410
    acceptance of, 383–384
    and Anti-Masonry, 380–382
    and election of 1824, 380
  in Jeffersonian era, 304
  in late 19th century, 761–766
  in 1790s, 282–289, 294–295
    and election of 1796, 287
    and Federalists and Republicans,
      285–289
    ideologies of, 288–289
    organization of, 285–286
    and French Revolution, 283
    and George Washington, 284–285
    [*See also* Federalist party; Repub-
      lican party (Jeffersonian)]
  and *Smith v. Allwright* (1944), 1066
  —by name:
  American Independent party, 1212
  American party (Know-Nothings),
    538–539
  Black Panther party, 1172–1173,
    1187
  Communist Labor party, 895
  Communist party (U.S.), 895, 969,
    1100
  Farmer-Labor party, 986
  Free Soil party, 516–517, 520

Political parties (*Cont.*):
  Greenback party, 766, 768, 789
  Liberty party, 444, 502, 516
  National Republican party, 380, 386
  National Union party, 612
  National Woman's party, 834, 917
  Progressive party, 853–854, 859,
    1109
  Prohibition party, 766, 789
  Raza Unida, La, 1223
  Socialist Labor party, 671
  States' Rights party, 1109
  Union party, 992
  (*See also* Democratic party; Federal-
    ist party; Republican party
    (Jeffersonian); Republican party
    (modern); Politics; Populist
    party; Whig party)
Politics:
  of American Indians, 18–20
    of Aztecs, 21, 24
    of Iroquois League, 104–105
    and Powhatan, 44, 47
    and Tecumseh and pan-Indian
      movement, 318–320
  and Civil War:
    and border states, 564–565
    and civil liberties and dissent,
      583–584
    and election of 1864, 594–596
    and emancipation of slaves, 571–
      573
    impact of, 599
    in South, 577–578
  in 1819–1820, 371–372
  in 1840s, and expansionism, 501–508
    and Oregon, 503
    and slavery, 507–508, 515–520
    and Texas and Mexican War, 501–
      507
  in Jacksonian era, 376–377, 379–387
    and John Quincy Adams' presi-
      dency, 385–386
    and Anti-Masonry, 380–382
    of common man, 384–385
    and election of 1824, 380
    and Jackson as president of the
      people, 386–387
    and "log cabin" campaign of 1840,
      405–407
    and market economy, 387
    and nullification crisis, 396–399
    and parties, acceptance of, 383–
      384
    social sources of, 382–383
  and Ku Klux Klan, 927
  in late 19th century:
    blacks in, 730–731
    in cities, 695–699
      and George Washington
        Plunkitt, 682–684
    traditional politics, failure of,
      758–789
      and Alliance movement,
        773–775
      and battle of standards,
        782–784
      blacks' response to, 786–788
      congressional politics, 766–769
      and depression of 1893,
        777–781
      and election of 1896, 784
      and farmers' revolt, 772–777
      and Jim Crow politics, 784–786
      and McKinley, 788–789
      and new realignment, 781–789

Politics: in late 19th century: tradi-
    tional politics, failure of (*Cont.*):
      and party politics, 761–766
      and Populist party, 776–777
      and presidential politics, 769–
        771
      and state and local politics, 771–
        772
  before 1789:
    and Articles of Confederation,
      231–232
    and Declaration of Independence,
      196–197
    in England versus America, 148–
      149
    and English imperial system be-
      fore 1600, 151–153
    and English Opposition and
      American political thought,
      149–151
    in 17th century:
      in Carolinas, 70, 73
      in Dominion of New England,
        109–110
      in Georgia, 75–76
      in Maryland, 54, 58
      in Massachusetts Bay Colony,
        88–89
      in New Hampshire, 92
      in New Jersey, 105
      in New York, 102–103
      in Pennsylvania, 106–108
      in Plymouth Colony, 87
      in Rhode Island and
        Connecticut, 92–94
      in Virginia, 50, 52, 63
    in 1700, 112–113
    and state constitutions, 229–231
  in 1790s, 294–295
    (*See also* Political parties, in
      1790s)
  in South:
    blacks in, 617–618, 730–731
    during Civil War, 577–578
    during Reconstruction, 605–621
      and blacks in office, 617–618
      and economic issues and cor-
        ruption, 620–621
      and Fourteenth Amendment,
        611–612
      and impeachment of Johnson,
        615–616
      and Johnson's program, 606–
        611
      and land for blacks, 614–615
      and Lincoln's plan, 605
      and northern disillusionment
        and white supremacy, 633–
        636
      and Republican party, 618–619
      and state governments, 619–
        620
    and slavery, 481–484, 515–520,
      551
    and *Dred Scott* decision, 543–
      544
    and election of 1860, 553–554
    and Kansas-Nebraska Act, 536–
      537
    and proslavery argument, 482–
      483
    and secession, 554–556
    and Virginia debate of 1832,
      481–482
    and Wilmot Proviso, 507
  during World War II, 1066–1071

Politics (*Cont.*):
(*See also* Constitution, U.S.; Elections; Equality and inequality; Political parties; Voting)
Polk, James K., 502–508, *503*, 516, 543
Polk, Leonidas, 776
Poll tax, 732–733
Pollock, Jackson, 999, 1150
Pollution (*see* Environment, human effects on)
Polo, Marco, 7, 14, 42
Polygamy, 513
Ponce de Leon, Juan, 25
Pontiac (Indian chief), 169, 191
Poor People's March (1969), 1230
Pope, John, 569, 739
Popé (Indian chief), 77
Pope's Day, 177, *177*
Popular music, 711
Popular sovereignty, 515, 518, 522, 524–525, 536, 539–540, 544, 546–549, 550
Population:
  age distribution of, *1190, 1191*
  of American Indians:
    in 1790, 264
    in 1920–1970, 1223
    and European diseases, 6–7, 26, 29, 65, 77, 99–100
    of Iroquois League, 104
    of Sioux, 488
  of blacks, 137, *137*, 239, 264, 267, 392, *458*, 458–459, 472
  in 18th century:
    of blacks, 137, *137*, 239, 264
    of British North America, 119, 123, 145, 156
    on frontier, 127, 233, 238, 264
    of New France, 119–120
    of seaports, 131, *132*
    in 1790, 264–265, *266*, 267, *267*
    worldwide growth of, 157, 159
  of Europe, 1750–1850, 686
  of immigrants, 1860–1920, *687*
  in 17th century:
    of New England, 91–92, 98
    of New York, 101–102
    of Pennsylvania, 106
    of South Carolina, 72
    of Virginia, 48, 51–52, 60
  of South, pre–Civil War, *460*, 460–461
  and urbanization, 685–686, 714, 1105–1107
  (*See also* Birth rate; Census, U.S.; Elderly; Immigrants and immigration)
Populist party, 758–761, 766, 775, 776–777, 781, 783–784, 789
Port Huron Statement (1962), 1182, 1187
Porter, Cole, 1273
Portsmouth, Treaty of (1905), 865, 897
Portugal, 5, 10, 13–16, 38, 42, 95
Portuguese-Americans, 102
Post, Louis, 896
Post Office, U.S., 265, 709, 713, 1000–1001, 1053
Potawatomi Indians, 169, 238, 320
Potosí, 27
Potsdam Conference (1945), 1074–1075, *1088*
Pound, Ezra, 922
Poverty:
  among baby boomers, 1190

Poverty (*Cont.*):
  and crime, 693
  and depression of 1893–1897, 779
  in 1890, 669
  among elderly, in late 19th century, 717
  and Great Society program, 1177–1178
  and Kennedy's and Johnson's programs, 1175–1176
  and life in the underclass, 1294–1295
  in 1920s, 911
  in 1970–1986, *1281*
  and Nixon's "new federalism," 1219–1220
  and *The Other America,* 1175
  and progressivism, 830
  during Reagan's administration, 1280, 1298
Powder Alarm (1774), 185
Powderly, Terence V., 675
Powell, John Wesley, 736–738
Powell, Lewis, 1225, 1298
Powers, Gary, 1140
Powers, Johnny, 841
Powhatan, 44–47, *49*, 78–79, 99, 103
Praeger, Robert, 886
Pragmatism (philosophy), 826
"Praise the Lord Club" (PTL), 1271
Preemption, 354
Preminger, Otto, 1099
Presbyterians, 70, 72, 87, 108, 142–144, 154, 312, 381, 419, 442
Prescott, William, 192–193
Preservationism, 849
Presidency, *289*, 402–403, *823*, 844, 979, 1005, 1139, 1242–1243
  (*See also* individual presidents)
President's Emergency Committee on Employment (PECE), 967
Presley, Elvis, 1149, *1149*, 1151
Prester John, 14–15, 82
Prices, 726, 906, 947, 1056, 1220–1221, 1254, *1254*
Priestley, Joseph, 150
Primaries (elections), 1066
Princeton, Battle of (1777), 206
Princeton, New Jersey, 206, 232
Princeton University, 141, 155, 854
Prison reform, 434
Private education, 706
Proclamation of 1763, 191, 233
Proclamation on Nullification (1832), 398
Progressive party, 853–854, 859, 1109
Progressivism, 822–858, 863–871, 1005
  and immigration, 835–838
  legacy of, 857–858
  and municipal reform, 840–842
  and poverty, 830–831
  and prostitution, 839
  and Theodore Roosevelt, 844–848
    and 1912 election, 851–854
    and government regulation of food, drugs, and environment, 848–849
  roots of, 825–829
  and social welfare and social justice, 832–833
  in states, 842–843
  and William Howard Taft, 849–851
  and temperance movement, 838
  and vaudeville, 839–840
  and Woodrow Wilson, 854–857
  and women, 831–832
    suffrage for, 833–834

Prohibition, 443, 537–538, 901, 925–926, 972
  (*See also* Temperance movement)
Prohibition party, 766, 789
Promontory Point, Utah, 746
Propaganda, 886, *1061*, 1098
Prophetstown, 319
Proprietary government, 54, 70, 73, 102–103, 105, 106
Prosser, Gabriel, 472
Prostitution, 135, 176, 839, 882, 952
Protest marches, 170, 780, 970, *987*, 1081, *1153*, 1206
Protestant Association, 58
Protestant Reformation, 7, 31–34, 84, 96, 98–99
Protestantism, 1124, 1270–1271
  (*See also* Evangelicalism; Fundamentalism; *names of specific branches, e.g.,* Baptists; Congregationalists; Methodists)
Providence, Rhode Island, 97
Proximity fuse, 1034–1035
Proxmire, William, 1260
Prudential Building (Buffalo, New York), 693
Prussia, 162–164
Psychedelic drugs, 1183
PTL ("Praise the Lord Club"), 1271
Public Utilities Holding Company Act (1935), 990, *1006*
Public Works Administration (PWA), 982, *1006*
Public works programs, 967–968, 969
  (*See also* Public Works Administration)
Pueblo Indians, 19, 77, 105
Puerto Ricans, 1039, 1221–1222
Puerto Rico, 13, 65, 817, 821, 1221, 1229
Pugachev, Emelian, 157, 159
Pujo Committee, 855
Pulitzer, Joseph, 708
Pullen, Frank, 813
Pullman, George, 679
Pullman, Illinois, 679
Pure Food and Drug Act (1906), 848, 859, 956
Puritanism, 34, 84–89, 90–91, 93–94, 96–98, 107
Put-in-Bay, Battle of (1813), 325
PWA (Public Works Administration), 982, *1006*
Pyle, Ernie, 1034

Qadhafi, Muammar, 1286–1287
Quadrant, 15
Quakers (Society of Friends), 97, 98, 105–108, 110, 111, 142–144, 240, 245
Quartering Act (1765), 170, 173, 178
Quartering Act (1774), 183
Quasi-War with France, 290, 305
Quay, Matthew, 788
Quayle, J. Danforth, *1302*
Quebec, Canada, 82, 113, 154, 163–165, *165*, 191, 208
Quebec Act (1774), 195
Queen Anne's War, 7, 119
Quemoy (island, China), *1135*

Race and racism:
  in 1820s, 388–396
    and free blacks in North, 392–394
    and Indians on frontier, 388–391
    and minstrel shows, 395, 395–396

Race and racism (*Cont.*):
  during Great Depression, 963–964,
      993–994
  and Japanese-Americans during
      World War II, 1060–1062
  in late 19th and early 20th centuries,
      784–786
    and Asians in San Francisco in
        1906, 865–866
    in 1870s–1880s, 721
    and immigrants, 835
    and imperialism and expansion-
        ism, 644, 799–800
    and intelligence tests, 881
    and Philippines after Spanish-
        American War, 814–815
    and poor, 760
    during Spanish-American War,
        813
    during World War I, 881, 885
  and Manifest Destiny, 490
  in 1980s, 1301
  during Reagan's administration, 1298
  and Reconstruction, 604, 610, 611–
      612, 617, 620–621, 629, 633–
      636, 638–639
  during World War II, 901, 1032,
      1063–1064, 1065–1066
  (*See also* Abolitionism; Lynchings;
      Segregation; Slaves and slavery;
      *specific racial and ethnic
      groups, e.g.,* Blacks; Hispanics;
      Indians, American; Jews)
Radford, Arthur, 1136
Radical Republicans, 605–616, 630
Radio broadcasting, 901, 918–920, 929,
    955, 979, 987–988, 1108, 1149
Radio Corporation of America (RCA),
    942, 943, 1107
Rafferty, Max, 1301
Railroad Administration, 883
Railroads:
  and buffalo, 739, *745*
  development of:
    in 1830–1850, 346–347
    in 1850s, 526–529, *528, 529*
    in 1850–1900, 659–664
  finance capital for, 656
  improvements in, in 1880s, 648
  inadequacies of, in 1866, 646–648
  industrial accidents on, 672
  and Knights of Labor, 676
  land grants to, 526, 751
  miles of track of, 1870–1890, *663*
  need for, 653
  and pace of life, 352
  regulation of, 771–772, 774, 842,
      847, 848
  in South, 620, *724, 725*
  strikes against, 677–680, 1069, 1086
  transcontinental railroad, 645,
      746–747
  and western development, 744–748
  during World War I, 883
  (*See also* Streetcars)
Rainford, William, 698
Raleigh, Walter, Jr., 14, 30, 34–35, 38,
    38–39, 42, 48, 67, 78
Raleigh, Walter, Sr., 29
Ranch houses, 1126
Rancheros, 491, 492, 514
Randolph, A. Philip, 1063, 1077
Randolph, Edmund, 252, 273, 278
Randolph, John, 305
Rankin, John, 1097
Raskob, John J., 940, 942

Rational Christianity, 141, 142
Rationing, during World War II, 1056
Raulston, John, 929
Rauschenbusch, Walter, 1145
Ray, James Earl, 1210
Rayburn, Sam, 1156
Raza Unida, La (Chicano party), 1223
RCA (Radio Corporation of America),
    942, 943, 1107
Reagan, Nancy, 1255, 1276, 1277, *1292*
Reagan, Ronald, 1253, 1269, 1276–
    1277, *1292,* 1304
  agenda of, 1277–1279
  and air traffic controllers' strike,
      1279
  and arms race and arms control,
      1292–1293
  and elections:
    of 1976, 1255
    of 1980, 1275–1276
    of 1984, 1283–1284
  and environmental issues, 1279
  and Grenada, 1286
  in Hollywood HUAC investigation,
      1100
  and Iran-Contra affair, 1291
  and Lebanon, 1286
    hostages in, 1288
  legacy of, 1293–1302
  second term of, 1284–1293
  and taxation, 1279–1280
Reclamation Act (1902), 849
Reconquista, 7, 16
Reconstruction, 602–640
  abandonment of, 630–639
    and election of 1876, 636–637, *638*
    and Ulysses S. Grant, 630, 632–633
    and northern disillusionment,
        633–634
    and racism, 638–639
    and white supremacy, 634–636,
        636
  and black aspirations, 602–604, *603,*
      621–630
    and family life, 622–623, *623,* 624
    and Freedmen's Bureau, 627–628
    and freedom, experience of, 621,
        624
    and plantations, *627,* 628–630
    and religion and education, *625,*
        625–626, *629*
    and working conditions, 626–627
  congressional Reconstruction, 613–
      617, 632–633
    and constitutional issues, 616–617
    and impeachment of Johnson,
        615–616
    and land for blacks, 614–615
  and Fifteenth Amendment, 630–631
  presidential Reconstruction, 604–613
    and election of 1866, 612–613
    and Fourteenth Amendment,
        611–612
    and Johnson's program, 606–611
      failure of, 608–609
      and Johnson's break with
          Congress, 609–611
      and Lincoln's plan, 605–606
      and mood of South, 606
  in South, 602–604, *614,* 617–621
    and black officeholding, 617–618,
        618
    and economic issues and corrup-
        tion, 620–621
    and state governments, 619–620
    and white Republicans, 618–619

Reconstruction Finance Corporation
    (RFC), 968
Red Bird (Cheyenne chief), 1001
Red Scare (1919), 895–897
Redeemers, 637, 730–731, 758
Reed, John, 895
Reed, Thomas, 771
Reform movements, 412–445
  and asylum movement, 434
  and Civil War, 599
  and James Fenimore Cooper and
      Henry David Thoreau, 426–427
  and educational reform, 433–434
  and Robert Owen and New Har-
      mony, 431–432
  and party system, 442–445
  and revivalism, 412–424
    and Lyman Beecher, 412–415
    and Charles Finney, 416
    and market economy, 417–418
    philosophy of, 416–417
  and Transcendentalism, 425–426
  and utopian communities, 429–431
  and Walt Whitman, Nathaniel
      Hawthorne, and Herman
      Melville, 427–429
  (*See also* Abolitionism; Blacks, and
      suffrage; Civil liberties and civil
      rights; Evangelicalism; Temper-
      ance movement; Women, suf-
      frage of)
Refregier, Anton, 999
Regan, Donald, 1277
*Regents of the University of California
    v. Bakke* (1978), 1298, 1304
Regulation, governmental, 774,
    842–843, 847–849, 855–857
  (*See also* Antitrust suits)
Regulators (South Carolina, 18th cen-
    tury), 129–130, 155, 201, 216
Rehnquist, William, 1225, 1285
Reliance Building (Chicago), 693
Relief (during Great Depression),
    965–966, 974, 981
Religion and religious life:
  among American Indians, 18–20, 46,
      99
  and blacks, *240,* 313, 314–315, 393,
      478–479, *625,* 625–626
  and Civil War soliders, 588
  in 18th century:
    in backcountry, 128
    and disestablishment, 144, 249–250
    and Enlightenment, 140–141
    and First Great Awakening,
        141–144
    in Middle Colonies, 102, 103,
        104, 105–108
    in New England colonies, 93–99,
        110, 123
    in seaports, 135–136
    in southern colonies, 54, 58, 64,
        70, 72, 74–75
  in first half of 19th century:
    and Anti-Masonry, 381
    among blacks, 313, 478–479
    and market economy, 417–418
    and party system, 442
    and Second Great Awakening,
        312–316, 418–419
  in late 19th century:
    and immigrants, 689
    and missionaries abroad, 795
    and party politics, 764–765
    and urban problems, 697–699
    in West, 756

Religion and religious life (*Cont.*):
and Reformation, 30–34
in 20th century:
in election of 1928, 934
and Father Divine, 964
and feminism, 1241
fundamentalism, 928, *1123*, 1270–1271
in 1980s, 1269–1273
in suburbs, 1123–1124
and Warren court, 1165–1166
(*See also* Evangelicalism; *specific religions, denominations, and religious groups, e.g.,* Anglicans; Islam; Jews; Presbyterians; Protestantism; Roman Catholic Church)
Remington Arms Company, 655
Remington (E.) and Sons, 681
Renaissance, 21
Reno, Milo, 969
Representative government:
in 18th century, 148–149
American views of, 172–175, 178–179, 183–185
and Declaration of Independence, 197
and English Opposition, 150–151
and frontier, 234, 236–239
and state constitutions, 230–231
and U.S. Constitution, 253, 255–256
in 17th century:
and Glorious Revolution, 112
in Middle Colonies, 103, 107–108
in New England, 89, 94
in Virginia, 50, 52, 57
Republic Steel Company, 997
Republican motherhood, 420
Republican party (Jeffersonian), 277, 286, 288, 292–293, 296
and Alien and Sedition Acts, 291–292
and election of 1796, 287
and election of 1800, 292, 303–304
and election of 1808, 323
and electioneering, 294
end of, 379–380
and New Nationalism, 341–342
and War of 1812, 324–325
Republican party (modern):
and blacks:
during New Deal, 993
suffrage of, 610, 630–631
as voters, 617
before Civil War, 537
and *Dred Scott* decision, 543–544
ideology of, 541–543, 558
and John Brown's raid, 552
and Kansas, 539–540
and slavery, 539–543
and Charles Sumner, 540–541, *542*
and Dwight D. Eisenhower, 1130–1131
and elections:
of 1856, 541–543, *542*
of 1860, 553–554
of 1866, 612–613
of 1888, 771
of 1894, 781
of 1896, 782, 788, 809
of 1910, 851
of 1912, 852–853
of 1916, 877–878
of 1918, 893
of 1928, *933*, 933–934
of 1932, 971–972

Republican party (modern): and elections (*Cont.*):
of 1936, 991–992
of 1938, 1005
of 1942, 1068
of 1944, 1070–1071
of 1946, 1086–1087
of 1948, 1108–1109
of 1952, 1115–1116
of 1954, 1133
of 1964, 1176–1177
of 1968, 1211, 1213
of 1976, 1255
of 1980, 1275–1276
in late 19th century, 761–766
and Alliance movement, 775
and Panic of 1873, 634
and protective tariffs, 767–768
in 1920s, 929–935
popular vote for, 1860–1912, 853
and Reconstruction:
abandonment of, 630–639
and election of 1876, 636–638
and Fifteenth Amendment, 630–632
and Ulysses S. Grant, 630, 632–633
and northern disillusionment, 633–634
and white supremacy, 634–636
and blacks, 610, 617–618, 630–631
and congressional Reconstruction, 613–616
and impeachment of Johnson, 615–616
and land for blacks, 614–615
and election of 1866, 612–613
and Fourteenth Amendment, 611
and Johnson's break with Congress, 609–611
and Johnson's program, 606–608
and Lincoln's plan, 605–606
in South:
and black officeholding, 617–618
and economic issues and corruption, 620–621
and state governments, 619–620
and white Republicans, 618–619
and Theodore Roosevelt, 846
and Upton Sinclair in California, 986
and William Howard Taft, 850
(*See also* Liberal Republican party; Radical Republicans)
Republicanism:
before American Revolution, 229–231, 249
and *Common Sense*, 190
and First Continental Congress, 185, 187
and slavery, 239–240, 397
and women, 247–248
and Civil War, 558
and equality, 379
and Republican party, 542–543
and U.S. Constitution, 254–257
Resettlement Administration, 985
Reuben James (destroyer), 1020
Reuther, Walter, 998
Revenue Act (1932), 967
Revenue Act (1935), 990, *1006*
Revenue Act (1942), 1068, 1077
Revenue Sharing Act (1972), 1229

Revere, Paul, 186–187, 189
Revivalism, 141–144, 312–316, 415–421
Revolt of the Beavers, The (play), 999
Revolution, American, 192–225
and Bunker Hill, Battle of, 192–194
and France, 209–211
and loyalists, 197, *200*, 201
in South, 215–220
in North, 202–209, *207*, 211–215
and American and British armies in 1775, 202–204
and American and British strategy in 1775, 204–205
on home front, 214–215
and New York and New Jersey campaigns, 205–206
and Philadelphia, British capture of, 206–208
and Saratoga, American victory at, 208–209
and Second Continental Congress, 194–197
in South, 215–222, *217*
and blacks, 220–222
and Charleston, siege of, 215–216
and Nathaniel Greene, 218–220
partisan struggle in, 216–218
in West, 213–214
(*See also* Continental Army; Militia)
Reynolds, Joshua, 145
Rhee, Syngman, 1112
Rhode Island, 94, 96–97, 109–110, 112, 181, 274, 382
Rhodes, James, 1194
Rhythm and blues (music), 1148–1149, 1184
Rice, 7, 72–74, 76, 126, 132, 186, 241, 453, 456
Richards, Ellen, 829–830, 831
Richardson, Ebenezer, *174*
Richardson, Elliot, 1232, 1245, 1246
Richardson, Seth, 1097
Richelieu, Cardinal, 82–83
Richmond, Virginia, 223, *578*, 690, 713
Rickets, 938
Riefensthal, Leni, 900
Riesman, David, 1129, 1151
Riis, Jacob, 693, 695, 712, 713, 830, 1294
Rio Grande, 503–505
Rivera, Diego, 999
Roads and roadbuilding, 906–907, 1121–1122
Roanoke Indians, 38
Roanoke Island, 38–39, 41–42
Roberts, Kenneth, 924
Roberts, Owen, 1062
Roberts, Peter, 838
Robertson, Pat, 1271
Rochambeau, Comte de, 223–224
Roche, James, 1238
Rochester, New York, 344, 418, 421
Rock and roll, 1148–1149, 1180, 1183–1185, *1185*
Rockefeller, John D., 645, *666*, 666–667, 681, 706, 829, 847, 895
Rockefeller, Nelson A., 1253
Rockets, 1038
(*See also* Missiles; Space exploration)
Rockingham, Marquis of, 175, 177
Rockwell, Norman, 915, *1119*
Rodney, Caesar, 187
Roe, Elizabeth, 753
Roe v. Wade (1973), 1240, 1265
Roebling, John, 692
Roebling, Washington, 692

Roebuck, Alvah C., 709
Rogers, Ginger, 958
Rogers, Will, 979
Rolfe, John, 47
Rolling Stones (music group), 1186
Roman Catholic Church:
  antinuclear movement in, 1281
  and Lyman Beecher, 415
  in Canada, 195
  in colonial America, 54, 58, 102,
    104, 107, 176–177
  and Counterreformation, 82–83
  and education, federal aid to, 1110
  and election of 1884, 770
  and feminism, 1241
  and immigrants, in 1840s–1860s, 532
  and John F. Kennedy, 1156
  and Know-Nothings, 538
  and Ku Klux Klan, 927
  in 1980s, 1271–1273
  and Reformation, 30–34
  and Alfred E. Smith, 934
  and suburbs, 1123–1124
Romanians, 157
Romanticism, 425–427
Rommel, Erwin, 1026, 1028, 1029
Roosevelt, Eleanor, 974, 976, 976–977,
  977, 979, 993, 995, 1007, 1044
Roosevelt, Franklin Delano, 901, 976,
  977–979, 978, 1003, 1021
  and atomic bomb, 1035
  and blacks, during World War II,
    1063
  and Bonus marchers, 971
  and civil liberties, 1059
  death of, 1044
  and elections:
    of 1932, 972–973
    of 1936, 991–992
    of 1944, 1070–1071
  and first hundred days, 979–982
  and foreign affairs, 1014–1017
  Four Policemen plan of, 1041
  Good Neighbor policy of, 1013–1014
  health of, 1042
  and Leon Henderson, 1048
  inauguration of, 975, 976–977
  and Japanese invasion of China,
    1017
  and Jews, during World War II,
    1073
  and Douglas MacArthur, 1040
  and narcotics, 956
  in 1936–1938, 1004–1005
  and Pearl Harbor, 1025
  people's hopes for, 975–976
  and postwar spheres of influence,
    1088
  and second hundred days, 988–990
  and Stalin, 1042
  and unions, during World War II,
    1068–1070
  as vice-presidential candidate in
    1920, 929
  and war costs, 1066–1068
  White House staff of, 1243
  and World War II, 1027, 1040–1044
  at Yalta Conference, 1074
Roosevelt, Kermit, 1136
Roosevelt, Theodore, 750, 789, 844–
  849
  and Henry and Brooks Adams, 799
  and antitrust suits, 846–847
  and Asia, 865
  and blacks, 845–846
  and Caribbean region, 864–865

Roosevelt, Theodore (Cont.):
  and conservation, 848–849
  and Cuba, 809, 810
  and elections:
    of 1904, 847–848
    of 1912, 851–854
    of 1916, 878
  "gospels" of, 828
  and Hepburn Railway Act, 848
  and Japan, 865–866
  on Robert La Follette, 842
  and Lusitania sinking, 875
  and muckrakers, 828
  and Navy, 797
  and Panama Canal, 860–863, 864
  personal qualities of, 844
  and presidency, 823
  and Franklin D. Roosevelt, 977
  and Russian Jews, 819
  and Spanish-American War, 810,
    811, 813
  "Square Deal" of, 846–847
  and strikes, 780, 846
  and Lawrence Veiller, 832
Root, Elihu, 864
Root-Takahira Agreement (1908), 866
Roper, Elmo, 1072, 1109
Rosenberg, Julius and Ethel, 1101,
  1132
Rosenman, Sam, 1043
Ross, David, 1192
Ross, Diana, 1185
Ross, Edward A., 827, 835
Ross, John, 388, 391, 391
Ross, Nellie, 917
Rostow, Walt Whitman, 1158
Rothko, Mark, 1150
Roxy theater (New York City), 919
Royal African Company, 61
Rubber industry, 997, 1050–1052
Ruby, Jack, 1170
Ruckelshaus, William, 1246
Rum, 132, 170, 244–245
Rural Electrification Administration
  (REA), 992–993, 1006
Rush, Benjamin, 147, 245, 247–248,
  278
Rush-Bagot Agreement (1817), 331
Rusk, Dean, 1159, 1207
Russell, Charles Edward, 828
Russell Sage Foundation, 830
Russia, 3, 36, 76, 157, 159, 804,
  818–820, 865, 872, 879–880, 892
  (See also Soviet Union)
Russian-Americans, 819
Russian Revolution (1917), 645
Russo-Japanese War, 645, 865, 897
Ruth, George Herman "Babe," 920
Rutherford, Lucy Mercer, 979
Rutledge, Edward, 232
Rutledge, John, 252
Ryswick, Treaty of (1697), 119

Saarinen, Eero, 1119
Sac Prairie, Wisconsin, 904
Sacagawea (Indian), 3
Sacco, Nicola, 924
Sachs, Sadie, 832
Sadat, Anwar, 1250, 1262, 1263
Safire, William, 1226
Salaries (see Wages and salaries)
Sales taxes, 1067–1068
Salina, Kansas, 1032–1033
Salinger, J. D., 1098
Saloons, 838, 926
SALT I (treaty), 1081, 1219, 1229

SALT II (treaty), 1262, 1264, 1265, 1293
Salt industry, 664–665
Salt Lake City, Utah, 513–514, 648
Salvation Army, 697
Samoa, 805
Samoan Treaty (1878), 821
Samoset, 87
Samuelson, Paul, 1164
San Bernardino, California, 747
San Diego, California, 1266, 1267
San Francisco, California, 511–512,
  532, 849, 865–866, 986, 1009,
  1010, 1185, 1186
San Jacinto, Battle of (1836), 494–495
San Juan Hill, Battle of (1898), 813,
  813–814
San Salvador, 17
Sand Creek, Colorado, 739
Sandinistas (Nicaragua), 1261, 1287–
  1288, 1304
Sandino, César Augusto, 1013
Sands, Barbara, 1295
Sands, Dorothy, 1294–1295
Sandwich Islands (see Hawaii)
Sandys, Edwin, 49
SANE (Committee for a Sane Nuclear
  Policy), 1151
Sanger, Margaret, 832, 859, 916, 916
Sanguenay, 82
Sankey, Ira David, 697
Santa Anna, Antonio Lopez de, 494–
  495, 506
Santa Barbara, California, 1230–1232,
  1231
Santa Fe, New Mexico, 7, 77, 79, 503
Santa Fe Railroad, 778
Santa Fe Trail, 492
Santee Sioux Indians, 739
Santo Domingo, 36
São Tomé, 16
Saratoga, Battle of (1777), 208–210, 225
Sartre, Jean-Paul, 901
Saudi Arabia, 1290
Sauk and Fox Indians, 320, 391
Savannah, Georgia, 75, 215, 219, 225
Savings and loan industry crisis
  (1980s), 1297
Savio, Mario, 1182
Sawdust Trail, The (painting, George
  Bellows), 698
Scalia, Antonin, 1285
Scandinavia, 4, 24, 34
Scandinavian-Americans, 532
Schaw, Janet, 124–125, 221
Schecter Poultry Corp. v. United
  States (1935), 984, 1007
Schell, Francis, 375
Schell, Jonathan, 1281, 1304
Schenck v. United States (1919), 887,
  897
Schiff, Jacob, 819
Schine, G. David, 1131, 1132, 1133
Schlafly, Phyllis, 1241
Schlink, Fred, 955
Schneiderman, Rose, 824
Schongauer, Martin, 31
Schools (see Education)
Schorr, Daniel, 1243
Schuman, William, 998
Schurz, Carl, 609, 633
Schuylkill River, 206
Schwab, Charles M., 666
Science and invention, 318n., 651–653,
  904, 906, 1034–1035
  (See also Technology)
Science fiction, 1273

SCLC (Southern Christian Leadership Conference), 1167
Scopes, John T., 928–929, 935
Scopes trial (1925), 901, 935
Scotland, 34, 55
Scots-Americans, 105, 123, 201, 245, 442
Scots-Irish–Americans, 72, 74, 95, 108, 121, 126–127, 129–130, 135
Scott, Dred, 543–544, *545*
Scott, Thomas, 665–666
Scott, Winfield, 506, 520, 564, 566
Scottsboro boys, 963–964
SDI (Strategic Defense Initiative), 1282, 1293
SDS (Students for a Democratic Society), 1182
Seaman's Act (1916), 857
Sears, Ricard W., 709
Sears, Roebuck, 709, 755, 916, 956
Seattle, Washington, *950*
SEC (Securities and Exchange Commission), 981
Secession, 397, 399, 520, 552, 554–557, *555*, 617
Second American party system, 382, 385, 537
Second Confiscation Act, 614
Second Great Awakening, 312–315, 412–419, 430, 437
Second War Powers Act (1942), 1050
Secord, Richard, 1290
Secret ballot, 696
Secrettown, California, *746*
Secular humanism, 1271
Securities Act (1933), 981
Securities and Exchange Commission (SEC), 981
Securities Exchange Act (1934), 981, *1006*
Sedition Act (1798), 291–292, 303
Sedition Act (1918), 886
Seeger, Charles, 998
Segregation, 393, 629, 633
    in armed forces, in World War II, 1032
    and black power movement, 1172
    and *Brown v. Board of Education,* 1081, 1144, 1151, 1224–1225
    and busing, 1225
    and Civil Rights Act (1964), 1171
    and civil rights movement, 1166–1167, 1169–1170
    and *Plessy v. Ferguson,* 645, 705, 732, 757, 1110, 1144
    during Franklin Roosevelt's administration, 993
    in South in late 19th century, 730–732
    during Truman's administration, 1110
    and Woodrow Wilson, 854
Selden, George, 650
Selective Service Act (1917), 880, 897
Seminole Indians, 264, 388, 391–392
Seneca Falls convention (1840), 440
Seneca Indians, 104, 169
Senegambia, 61
Separate-but-equal doctrine (in *Plessy v. Ferguson*), 732, 757, 1110, 1144
"Separate" Congregationalists, 144
Separatists (*see* Congregationalists; Pilgrims)
Sequoia (yacht), 1243
Serbia, 872
Serfdom, 157

Sergeant Pepper's Lonely Hearts Club Band (record album, Beatles), 1184
Serra, Junipero, 76
Serrano Indians, 18
Servants, in late 19th century, 702
    (*See also* Indentured servants)
Settlement houses, 698–699, 832
700 Club, 1271
Seven Years' War, 158–166, *162, 165, 166,* 169–170, 178, 190–192, 201–202, 209
Sewall, Arthur, 784
Sewall, Hannah, 90
Sewall, Jonathan, 160
Sewall, Samuel, 90–91
Seward, William H., 357, 519, 566, 594–595, 802–804
Sewing machines, 792
Sex and sexual morality:
    of baby boomers, 1189–1190, 1190–1191
    and counterculture of 1960s, 1183, 1186
    in early 20th century, 938–939
    and feminism, 1239–1240
    in late 19th century, 704, 715–716
    and mass media, 1273
    and miscegenation with slaves, 465–466
    in movies, during Great Depression, 959
    in 1920s, 916
    in Oneida Community, 430–431
    among Shakers, 430
    during World War I, 882
    after World War II, 1103–1104
    (*See also* Abortion; Homosexuals and homosexuality; Victorian morality; Women)
Seymour, Jane, 33
Shah of Iran (Mohammed Reza Pahlavi), 1136, 1252, 1260, 1262–1263
"Shake, Rattle, and Roll" (song), 1149
Shaker Heights, Ohio, 906
Shakers, 429–430
Shaman, 18, 80
Shantytowns, *950*
Share Our Wealth, 986
Sharecropping, 622–623, *623,* 626–627, *627,* 723–727
Shaw, Anna Howard, 834
Shaw, Pauline, 830
Shaw (warship), 1008
Shawnee Indians, 169, 238, 280, 318–319
Shays, Daniel, 251
Sheeler, Charles, 921
Sheen, Fulton J., 1124
Sheep raising, 750
Shelby, Gertrude, 940
Sheldon, Charles L., 698
Shepard, Alan, Jr., 1187, 1204
Sheppard-Towner Federal Maternity and Infancy Act (1921), 917, 935
Sheridan, Philip, 596
Sherman, Roger, 252
Sherman, William Tecumseh, 567, 593–597, 614
Sherman Antitrust Act (1890), 645, 668, 680, 771, 789, 847
Sherman Silver Purchase Act (1890), 769, 771, 780–781, 789
Shiloh, Battle of (1862), 567–569, 590–591, 593
Shipbuilding, 1052

Shipping Out (painting, Jacob Lawrence), *1032*
Shirley, William, 121
Shoe industry, 362–363
Sholes, C. Latham, 655
Shopping centers, 1121–1122
Shopping malls, 1266–1268, *1267*
Shoshone Indians, 18, 736
Shriver, Sargent, 1176
Shufeldt, Robert, 803, 821
Shultz, George, 1286, 1288
Siberia, 17–18, 157
Sibley, Henry, 739
Sidra, Gulf of, 1287
Sierra Club, 849, 859
Sierra Leone, 240
Sihanouk, Norodom, 1215–1216
Silk Road, 14
Silliman, Mary, 214
Silver mining, 744
Silver standard, 768–769, 780–781, 782–784
Simmons, William, 926
Simpson, "Sockless" Jerry, 775
Simpson-Mazzoli Bill (1987), 1301
Sims, Bill, 720
Sinclair, Upton, 645, 848, 859, 986
Singer, Isaac Merritt, 794
Singer Company, 792
"Single-tax" clubs, 671
Sino-Japanese War, 821
Sioux Indians, 486–488, *489,* 499, 501, 734, 739, 740, *741,* 743
Sirhan Sirhan, 1210, *1211*
Sirica, John J., 1244
Sitcoms (TV), 1274
Sitting Bull (Indian chief), 740, 743
Situation comedies (TV), 1274
Six-Day War (1967), 1081
"Sixty Minutes" (TV program), 1274
Skyscrapers, 692–693
Slater, Samuel, 335, 358–359
Slaves and slavery, 469–470
    and African slave trade, 16, *59,* 59–61, *60,* 121, 133, 253
    and American Indians, 70–71, 389
    and American Revolution, 195, 220–222, 239–241
    and antislavery societies, 240, 241
    in Brazil, abolished, 645
    and John Brown's raid on Harper's Ferry, 552
    in Civil War, 573–575, *574*
    in colonial times:
        in backcountry, 127
        in Caribbean region, 27, 66–67
        in Chesapeake region, 7, 59–62, 136–139
        dance and music of, *134*
        in Georgia, 75–76
        in Portuguese colonies, 16, 157
        in seaports, 133–134, 155
        in South Carolina, 73–74, 136–139
        in Spanish colonies, 27
    and culture of slaves, 474–481
        and community, 479–480
        and diet and health, 476–477
        and family life, 474–475
        and free blacks, 480–481
        and religion, 478–479
        and songs and stories, 475, 478–479
    distribution of, *458,* 458–459
    and *Dred Scott* decision, 543–544, 550, 553
    and economy of South, 456, 463, 551, 721

Slaves and slavery: and economy of
    South (*Cont.*):
  and slave prices, 456, *475,533,*
    534
  and emancipation, 571–573
  expansion of, to new states and terri-
    tories, 488, 515–516
    and Compromise of 1850, 517–520
    and election of 1848, 516–517
    and Kansas, 522–524, 539–540
      and Kansas-Nebraska Act, *535,*
      536–537
    after Mexican War, 507–508
    and Mexican War, 505, 507
    and Missouri Compromise,
      371–372
    and Texas, 502–503
    and Wilmot Proviso, 507
  and Know-Nothings, 539
  as labor system, 459–460
    and work and discipline, 470–471
  and Lincoln-Douglas debates, 546–
    547, 550
  and maintenance of slaves, 471
  and nullification, 397, 399
  number of, brought to Americas,
    642
  and Republican party, 539–543
  and resistance of slaves, 396–397,
    472–474
  and secession, *555,* 555–558
  and sectionalism, 484–485
  and slaveowners, 460–466
    and miscegenation, 465–466
  and southern society, 481–485
    and politics, 483–484
    and proslavery argument, 482–483
    and Virginia debate of 1832,
      481–482
  and *Uncle Tom's Cabin,* 439, 520,
    542, 548–549, *549*
  (*See also* Abolitionism; Blacks)
Slavic-Americans, 689
Slavs, 157
Slidell, John, 504–505
Sloan, Alfred, 908, 913
Sloan, John, 830
Sloughter, Henry, 111
Slums and tenements, 693–695, 832
Smallpox, 140
Smith, Adam, 47
Smith, Alfred E., 843, 934
Smith, Captain John, 40, *46,*46–47, 51
Smith, Joseph, 512
Smith, Margaret, 298, 300
Smith, Moe, 925
Smith Act (1940), 1100
Smith College, 706
Smith-Connolly Anti-Strike Act (1943),
  1069–1070
Smith v. Allwright (1944), 1066
Smokers, The (painting, Adriaen
  Brouwer), *51*
SNCC (Student Non-Violent Coordi-
  nating Committee), 1168–1169,
  1172
Sneider, Christopher, *174*
Social Darwinism, 670, 799–800
Social Security, 939
Social Security Act (1935), 717, 989,
  1006
Social work, 830–831
Socialism, 780
Socialist Labor party, 671
Socialist party, 854, 859, 887, 895
Society of Cincinnati, 249

Society of Friends (*see* Quakers)
Society of Jesus (*see* Jesuits)
Sociological jurisprudence, 827
Sod houses, 752, 753
Soil Conservation and Domestic Allot-
  ment Act (1936), 985
Sokoloff, Nicolai, 998
Solomon Islands, 1028
Solzhenitsyn, Alexander, 1093
Somohalla (Indian chief), 735
Somoza, Anastasio, 1261, 1304
Sonar, 1029
Sons of Liberty, 174, 176, 179–180, 182
Sooners, 751
Soul music, 1184–1185
South:
  cities in, 457, 467–468, 576
  civil rights movement in, 1166–1172
  before Civil War:
    and John Brown's raid, 552
    civil liberties and civil rights in,
      483
    democracy in, 485
    in early republic, 239–241, 249
    economy of, 453–455, 467, 534, 551
    education in, 434, 457, 468
    and immigrants, 534
    industrialization in, 457, 534, 551,
      575–576
    party system in, 484
    poor whites in, 460, 468–469
    population of, *460,*460–461
    and republicanism, 551, 558
    and urbanization, 356, 457,
      467–468
    and War of 1812, 325
    women in, 464–467
    yeoman farmers in, 451–452, 466–
      468
  in colonial times, 48–65, 70–76, 114–
    117, 126, 136–139
    American Indians in, 44–49, 57–
      58, 70–73, 75–76, 79
    backcountry of, 268
    equality and inequality in, 52,
      56–58, 62, 64, 66, 74–75
    family life in, 52, 62, 72, 114–117
    religion in, 54, 58, 64, 70, 72,
      74–75
  economy of:
    after American Revolution,
      239–241
    before Civil War, 453–455, 467,
      534, 551
    and industrialization, 457, 534,
      551, 575–576, 727–728,
      728–730
    in late 19th century, 721–730
      cotton in, 722–723
      in 1870s–1880s, 720–721
      farmers' debt in, 773
      and industrialization,
        727–728, 728–730
      reasons for nature of, 728–730
      sharecropping in, 723–727
      steel industry in, 729
      wages in, 722, 728
    manufacturing in, 457, 534, 551,
      575–576
    per capita income in, 455, *599,*
      627, 630
    and tariffs, 341, 396–399, 484,
      507, 534, 545
    wages in, 722–728, 756, 1143
    and wealth, concentration of, 365,
      463, 551, 599

South: economy of (*Cont.*):
  after World War II, 1142–1143
  (*See also* Agriculture, in South;
    Cotton and cotton growing;
    Planters and plantations;
    Slaves and slavery; Tobacco
    growing and tobacco industry)
  education in, 434, 457, 468, 705,
    730, *731*
  geography of, in late 19th century,
    724–725
  railroads in, 526, 528–529, 620,
    646–648, *724,* 725
  and states' rights, 429, 518–520, 551,
    554, 577–578
  and urbanization, 453, 457, 467–468,
    721
  (*See also* Blacks, in South; Civil
    War; Land, in South; Planters
    and plantations; Politics, in
    South; Reconstruction; Revolu-
    tion, American, in South; Slaves
    and slavery; *specific southern
    states, e.g.,* Alabama; South
    Carolina)
South America (*see* Latin America)
South Carolina, 65
  in American Revolution, 201,
    215–222, 224–225, 241
  black population in, 460, 617
  in Civil War, 597
  in colonial times, 7, 67, 70–74, *71,*
    79, 129, 136–139, 169, 181
  and election of 1796, 287
  and nullification, 396–399
  plantations in, 462
  and Reconstruction, 608, 609,
    614–615, 617–621, 636–637
  secession of, 554
  suffrage in, 382
South Carolina Exposition and Protest,
  397
Southdale Center (Edina, Minnesota),
  1266
Southern Alliance, 774–775
Southern Christian Leadership Conference (SCLC), 1167
Southern Tenant Farmers Union, 964
Southworth, E. D. N., 703
Soviet Union:
  and Afghanistan, 1081, 1264
  and Baltic nations, 901
  and Cuban missile crisis, 1160–1163
  and democracy, 899
  environmental problems in, 1080
  and Finland, 1019
  and Iran, 1091–1092
  and Korean War, 1112–1113
  and Nazis, 969–970, 1018–1019
  in 1950s, 1137–1138
  in 1980s, 1292–1293
  and nuclear weapons, 1081, 1096,
    1111
  and Poland and Finland, 1019
  and postwar spheres of influence,
    1087–1089
  and Rapallo Treaty, 1012
  and space exploration, 1204
  as superpower, 1078–1080
  and Third World, 1261
  and UN, 1074
  and U.S.:
    and détente, 1217–1219,
      1252–1253
    during Eisenhower's administra-
      tion, 1134

Soviet Union: and U.S. (*Cont.*):
and John F. Kennedy, 1161–1163
and lend-lease program, 1020
in 1959, 1140
perception of, 1089–1090
during Reagan's administration, 1276, 1277
and Franklin D. Roosevelt, 1014
after World War II, 1089–1090, 1093
in World War II, 901, 1020, 1029, 1044
and Yom Kippur War, 1250
(*See also* Brezhnev, Leonid; Gorbachev, Mikhail; Khrushchev, Nikita; Russia; Stalin, Joseph)
Space exploration, 1081, 1141, 1187, 1204–1205, 1296
Spain, 5, 7, 119, *267*, 290
and colonial America, 13, 16–17, 25–30, *28*, 33, 35–36, 42, 65–66, 76–78, *77*
and England, 29–30, 33, 35–36, 42, 65–66, 72
and Mexico, 491–492
and Seven Years' War, 160, 162, 165
and Treaty of Paris (1783), 224
and U.S.:
after American Revolution, 257
in 1895, 808–810
and Jay-Gardoqui Treaty (1785), 250–251
and Louisiana Purchase, 308
and Pinckney's Treaty (1796), 282
and Transcontinental Treaty (1819), 330
(*See also* Spanish-American War; Spanish Civil War)
Spanish-American War, 645, 797, 810–814, 821
Spanish Civil War, 901, 1016–1017
Spanish Main, 17, 36
Sparta, Georgia, 758
Specie Circular, 403
Spencer, Herbert, 670, 799
Split-level houses, 1126–1127
Spock, Benjamin, 1188, 1206, 1226
Spoils system, 387
Spooner, John, 846
Sports, in late 19th century, 709–710
(*See also specific sports, e.g.*, Baseball; Football)
Sprague, Frank Julian, 690–691
Sputnik (Soviet satellites), 1081, 1141, *1141*
Squanto (Indian), 87
SST (supersonic transport plane), 1234
St. Clair, Arthur, 280
St. John, Newfoundland, 11, 37
St. Kitts, 66
St. Lawrence River, 82, 113, 164–165
St. Lawrence Seaway, 1110, 1131
St. Lawrence Seaway Act (1954), 1131, 1151
St. Louis, Missouri, 356, *357*, 365, 457, 532, 648, 649, 718–719, 885
St. Louis Exposition (1905), 914
Stalin, Joseph, 901, 1018–1019, 1027, 1028, 1041–1044, 1074–1075, 1087–1091, *1090*, 1093, 1137
Stallone, Sylvester, 1273
"Stalwarts," 765
Stamp Act (1765), 170–175, 178, 184, 197
Stamp Act Congress, 174, 184
Standard Oil Company, 645, 653, 667, 668, 681, 792, 848, 1050–1051

Stanford, Leland, 706, 745, 746
Stanford University, 706
Stans, Maurice, 1247
Stanton, Edwin, 606, 614, 616, 630
Stanton, Elizabeth Cady, 422–423, 440, *441*, 631–632, 701
Stanwyck, Barbara, 1125
Star Trek (TV program), 1205
Star Wars program (Strategic Defense Initiative), 1282, 1293
Stark, John, 214
State Department, U.S., 1073, 1101
State governments, 229–230, 771–774, 777, 842–843, 965, *1177*
States' rights, 291, 305, 397, 429, 518–520, 551, 554, 577–578, 599
States' Rights party, 1109
Statue of Liberty, 713
Steam-powered ships, 653
Steamboats, 344–346, 348–349, *349*, 352
Steel industry:
and Bessemer process, *647*, 650
in 1880 and 1914, *649*
finance capital for, 656
integration of, by Carnegie, 665–666
and John F. Kennedy, 1165
mergers in, by Morgan, 668
and skyscrapers, 692
in South, in late 19th century, 729
unions and strikes in, 679, 997
working conditions in, in late 19th century, 672–673
Steel Workers' Organizing Committee (SWOC), 996–998
Steffens, Lincoln, 695, 828, 859
Steinbeck, John, 901, 961
Stephens, Alexander H., 577, 609, 731
Stephens, Uriah, 675
Stephenson, David, 928
Steuben, Friedrich Wilhelm von, 213, *213*, 218, 225
Stevens, Isaac, 738
Stevens, John, 806
Stevens, Thaddeus, 609, *609*, 615, 632
Stevenson, Adlai E., 1115–1116, 1133
Stewart, A. T., 708
Stewart, Helen Wiser, 749
Stewart, Lyman, 928
Stewart, Milton, 928
Stieglitz, Alfred, 830
Stimson, Henry, 1013, 1015, 1024
Stinkards, 20
Stockman, David, 1280
Stocks and bonds:
and depression of 1893–1897, 778
during Great Depression, 981
in 1920s, 910, 940, 942
and Great Bull Market, 943–945
and Great Crash, 901, 945–947
and 1987 crash, 1297
and railroads, 663–664
and trusts, 667
during World War I, 882
during World War II, 1067
(*See also* New York Stock Exchange)
Stone, Fred, 839
Stone, Harlan, 1001
Stone, Lucy, 440, 631, *631*
Stono Rebellion, 139, 155
Stowe, Harriet Beecher, 413, *414*, 439, 520, 542, 710
Straight, Willard, 868
Strategic Arms Limitation Treaties (*see* SALT I; SALT II)

Strategic Defense Initiative (SDI), 1282, 1293
Strategic Petroleum Reserve, 1259
Streetcar suburbs, *691*
Streetcars, 690–691, *691*
Streeter, Ora, 1294
Strikes:
by air traffic controllers, 1279
and blacks, 674, 774
in coal industry, in 1902, 846
in garment industry, in 1909–1910, 822
during Great Depression, 986, 997–998
in late 19th century, 677–680
in 1870s–1890s, 779–780
of miners, in Coeur d'Alene, Idaho, 744
in 1920s, 911
and Theodore Roosevelt, 846
and Taft-Hartley Act, 1087
in textile industry, in 1927, 911
after World War I, 895
during World War I, 884
after World War II, 1086
during World War II, 1069
Strong, Josiah, 697, 712
Stryker, Roy, 1002
Student Non-Violent Coordinating Committee (SNCC), 1167, 1168–1169, 1172
Students (college and university), 1179–1182, 1194–1195, 1202, 1206–1207
(*See also* Higher education)
Students for a Democratic Society (SDS), 1182
Sturges v. Crowninshield (1819), 351
Submarines, 875, 878, 1026, 1034
Submerged Lands Act (1953), 1130, 1151
Suburbs, 691, 1104–1107, 1121–1129
Subways, 645, 691
Suez Canal, 645, 862, 1138
Suez Crisis (1956), 1138–1139
Suffolk Resolves, 186
Suffrage (*see* Blacks, suffrage of; Constitution, U.S., amendments to, Fourteenth, Fifteenth, Nineteenth; Voting; Women, suffrage of)
Sugar, 66, 68–69, 453, 456, 484, 805, *806*, 808, 847
Sugar Act (1764), 159, 170, 172–174, 181, 184
Sugar Creek, Illinois, 368–369
Sullivan, Louis H., 693
Sullivan's Island, 215
Sully, Thomas, *331*
Summit conferences (U.S.-Soviet), 1138, *1139*, 1140, 1161, 1218–1219, 1252–1253, 1262, 1293
Sumner, Charles, 540–541, *541*, 572, 605, 609, 632–633, 804
Sumner, William Graham, 670, 799–800
Sumter, Thomas, 217–218, 224–225
Sunbelt phenomenon, *1106*, 1142
Sundance Kid, 747
Sunday, William Ashton "Billy," *698*
Supersonic transport plane (SST), 1234
Supply-side economics, 1278
Supreme Court, U.S.:
Abington v. Schempp (1963), 1166
Abrams v. United States (1919), 887
Baker v. Carr (1962), 1166

Supreme Court, U.S. (*Cont.*):
Louis D. Brandeis appointed to, 857
Brown v. Board of Education
    (1954), 1081, 1144, 1151,
    1224–1225
Butler v. United States (1936), 985,
    1007
*Charles River Bridge v. Warren
    Bridge* (1837), 409
and Civil Rights Act (1964), 1171
Civil Rights Cases (1883), 731, 757
and civil rights cases during
    Truman's administration,
    1110–1111
Cohen v. Virginia (1821), 306
Commonwealth v. Hunt (1842), 364
creation of, 274
Dartmouth College v. Woodward
    (1819), 351
Dred Scott decision (1857), 543–544
Engel v. Vitale (1962), 1165–1166,
    1187
Escobedo v. Illinois (1964), 1165, 1187
Ex parte Endo (1944), 1062
Ex parte McCardle (1868), 617
Ex parte Milligan (1866), 583, 616
Fletcher v, Peck (1810), 350–351
Gibbons v. Ogden (1824), 350
Gideon v. Wainwright (1963), 1187
and "Granger cases," 774
Griswold v. Connecticut (1964),
    1166, 1187
Hirabayashi v. United States (1943),
    1062
and Thomas Jefferson, 307
and judicial review, 398
and Keating-Owen Act (1916), 833n.
Korematsu v. United States (1944),
    1062
McCulloch v. Maryland (1819), 350,
    401
*McLaurin v. Oklahoma State Re-
    gents* (1950), 1110–1111
Marbury v. Madison (1803), 306
and John Marshall, 350–351
Martin v. Hunter's Lessee (1816),
    306
Minor v. Happersett (1875), 764
Miranda v. Arizona (1966), 1165,
    1187
Moorehead v. Tipaldo (1936), 1002
Muller v. Oregon (1908), 828, 859
Munn v. Illinois (1877), 774, 789
and New Deal, 1002–1003
during Nixon's administration,
    1224–1225
*N.L.R.B. v. Jones and Laughlin
    Steel Corporation* (1937), 1003
and Northern Securities Company
    antitrust suit, 847
and obscenity, 1273
Plessy v. Ferguson (1896), 645, 705,
    732, 757, 1110, 1144
In re Debs (1895), 680
and Ronald Reagan, 1285
and Reconstruction, 616–617
*Regents of the University of
    California v. Bakke* (1978),
    1298, 1304
Roe v. Wade (1973), 1240, 1265
and Franklin D. Roosevelt, 901,
    1003
*Schecter Poultry Corp. v. United
    States* (1935), 984, 1007
Schenck v. United States (1919),
    887, 897

Supreme Court, U.S. (*Cont.*):
and Scottsboro nine (1933), 963–964
and separate-but-equal doctrine,
    645, 705, 732, 757, 1110, 1144
and sit-down strikes, 997
Smith v. Allwright (1944), 1066
Sturges v. Crowninshield (1819), 351
*Swann v. Charlotte-Mecklenburg
    Board of Education* (1971),
    1225, 1229
Sweatt v. Painter (1950), 1110–1111
Texas v. White (1869), 617
Trujillo v. Garley (1948), 1223, 1229
United States v. E. C. Knight (1895),
    847, 859
*United States v. Hudson and
    Goodwin* (1812), 291
*United States v. Jefferson County
    Board of Education* (1969), 1225
United States v. Nixon (1974), 1247,
    1265
and Earl Warren, 1144, 1165–1166
and Wilson-Gorman Tariff Act
    (1894), 781
Worcester v. Georgia (1832), 391
Supremes (music group), 1185
Suspension bridges, 692
Susquehannock Indians, 57
Sussex (French ship), 875, 897
Svinin, Pavel Petrovich, 240
*Swann v. Charlotte-Mecklenburg
    Board of Education* (1971), 1225,
    1229
Sweatt v. Painter (1950), 1110–1111
Sweden, 184
Swedish-Americans, 4, 102, 107–108,
    123
Swift, Gustavus, 665
Swiss-Americans, 72, 74, 123
Switzerland, 34, 226
Sydney, Algernon, 150
Synthetic Fuels Corporation, 1259
Syracuse, New York, 1176
Syria, 1250, 1287
Szilard, Leo, 1035

Taft, Robert A., 1015, 1019, 1020,
    1087, 1115, 1131
Taft, William Howard, 817, 838,
    849–851, 850, 866–868
Taft-Hartley Act (1947), 1087, 1100,
    1117
Taiwan, 1135, 1135–1136, 1218
Tallmadge, James, 372
Tallmadge amendment (1819), 372
Tammany Hall, 682, 843
Tammany Society, 759
Tampa, Florida, 812–813, 821
Tampico, Mexico, 870
Taney, Roger, 402, 409, 544, 544
Taos Indians, 735
Tappan, Lewis, 436–437, 441
Tarahumara Indians, 77
Tarawa, 1029
Tarbell, Ida M., 828, 886
Tariffs:
during Civil War, 580
and depression of 1893–1897, 781
Dingley Tariff (1897), 788
of 1816, 341
of 1824, 396, 397
of 1832, 398
of 1833, 399
of 1846, 507
Fordney-McCumber Tariff (1922),
    931, 1011

Tariffs (*Cont.*):
and Alexander Hamilton's financial
    program, 276, 305
Hawley-Smoot Tariff (1930), 967
Payne-Aldrich Tariff (1909), 859
protective, in late 19th century,
    767–768, 771
South and, 341, 396–399, 484, 507,
    534, 545
and William Howard Taft, 850
and Trade Agreements Act (1934),
    1013
Wilson-Gorman Tariff Act (1894),
    781
and Woodrow Wilson, 855
Tarleton, Banastre, 219
Tasmanian dodge, 696
Tax Reform Act (1986), 1285, 1304
Taxes and taxation:
British, on Americans, 170, 172–175,
    178, 182
during Civil War, 579–580
in Confederacy, 577
on gasoline, 906–907
during Great Depression, 967, 989
and Alexander Hamilton's financial
    program, 275–281
and Thomas Jefferson's economic
    policies, 304–305
and John F. Kennedy, 1164–1165
and Andrew Mellon, 931
and Ronald Reagan, 1278,
    1279–1280, 1285
and Revenue Act (1942), 1068
during World War II, 1067–1068
(*See also* Income tax)
Taylor, Frederick W., 672–673
Taylor, Nathaniel, 416–417
Taylor, Zachary, 503–506, 516–519
Taylorism, 673
Tea Act (1773), 176, 182, 184, 201
Teach-ins, 1229
Teachers, 705, 706, 831
Teapot Dome scandal, 901, 930
Technology:
and agriculture, 527, 530, 581
and cotton gin, 335, 342, 342, 454
in first half of 19th century, 335,
    358–359
in late 19th century, 650, 729–730
and transportation, 342–347,
    526–529
and Vietnam War, 1203
(*See also* Industrialization; Science
    and invention)
Tecumseh (Indian leader), 316, 320,
    327
Teen-agers, of baby boom, 1189
Teheran Conference (1944), 1042
Telegraph, 358, 653, 655
Telephones, 648, 653–656
Televangelists, 1271
Television:
controversies over, 1273–1275
in election of 1956, 1133
in election of 1960, 1156
and Litle Rock civil rights crisis,
    1146, 1147
and Joseph McCarthy, 1133
in 1950s, 1149–1150
and 1960s counterculture, 1186
Nixon's "Checkers" speech on, 1116
and televangelists, 1271
Vietnam War on, 1209
after World War II, 1107–1108
Teller, Henry M., 782

Teller Amendment (1898), 810, 814, 821

Telstar (satellite), 1204

Temperance movement, 245, 318, 432–433, *433*, 838–839, 882
(*See also* Prohibition)

Temporary Emergency Relief Administration, 978

Temptations (music group), 1185

Tenancy, 130–131, 146, 155, 201, 725

Tenements (*see* Slums and tenements)

Tennent family, 143, 155

Tennessee, 233–234, 264, 267, 280, 481, 566–568, 593, 596–597, 605, 607, 612, 928–929

Tennessee Coal, Iron, and Railway Company (TCI), 729, 757, 851

Tennessee Valley Authority (TVA), 981–982, *983*

Tennis, 709

Tenochtitlán (Mexico City), 20, 25–26, 42

Tenskwatawa (Indian leader), *319*, 319–320, 515

Tenure of Office Act, 616

Tepehuane Indians, 77

Terrorism, 1286–1287

Tesla, Nikola, 652

Tet offensive (Vietnam War, 1968), 1208–1209

Texas, 76
annexation of, 502–503
cotton production in, 1850–1860, 454
and Miriam "Ma" Ferguson, 917
Hispanics in, 514–515, 1063–1064
and Mexican War, 503–504
and Mexico, 491, 492–495, 801
during Monroe's presidency, 330
population of, in 1860, *460*
revolution and republic in, 492–495
slavery in, 493, 502–503
Southern Alliance in, 774
and Thirteenth Amendment, 608

Texas and Pacific Railroad, 676

Texas v. White (1869), 617

Textile industry, 341, 359–362, *361*, 727, 911

Thailand, 14

Thames, Battle of the (1814), 326–327, 405

Thatcher, Margaret, 1287

Thayendanegea (Indian chief), 214

Thayer, Webster, 924

Theater, 710, 999
(*See also* Vaudeville)

Thieu, Nguyen Van, 1227, 1228

Third World, 1081, 1159, 1261, 1287
(*See also* Africa; Asia; Latin America; *specific countries*)

Thomas, J. Parnell, 1100

Thomas, Norman, 972, 992, 1019

Thompson, Dorothy, 992

Thoreau, Henry David, 427–428, 444, 1145, 1183

Three Little Pigs (film), 973

Three Mile Island nuclear power plant, 1081, *1258*, *1258*, 1265

Thurman, Allen B., *770*

Thurmond, J. Strom, 1109

Tijerina, Reies, 1223

Tilden, Bill, 920

Tilden, Samuel, 636–637, 769

Tillman, "Pitchfork" Ben, 774

Time, 338, 361–362, 367, 648, 883

Time-and-motion studies, 673

Tin Can Tourists Association, 909

Tippecanoe, Battle of (1811), 320, 405

Tire industry, *1051*

Titusville, Pennsylvania, 650, 681

Tobacco growing and tobacco industry, 47, 50–52, *51*, 79, 186, 239, 241, 453, 456, 727–728

Tocqueville, Alexis de, 352, 356, 366–367, 390, 396, 418, 420, 434, 818

Todd, Mary, 406

Tojo, Hideki, 1024

Tokyo, Japan, 1028

Toledo, Ohio, 841

Toltecs, 20

"Tom Dooley" (song), 1184

Tombigbee-Tennessee Waterway, 1235

Tonkin, Gulf of, 1199–1200, 1229

Topeka, Kansas, 1144

Torrey Canyon (oil tanker), 1230

Tower, John, 1291

Townsend, Francis, 988

Townshend, Charles, 178

Townshend Acts (1760s), 176, 178–181, 184, 191

Trade Agreements Act (1934), 1013

Trade associations, 932

Trade (*see* Foreign trade)

Trail of Tears, 390–391

Tramps' March on Washington (1894), 780

Trans-Siberian railroad, 645, 820

Transcendentalism, 425–426, 428

Transcontinental railroad, 645, 746–747

Transcontinental Treaty (1819), 330

Transportation:
in 1790, 265, 267, 270
in cities, in late 19th century, 643, 653, 690–691
revolution in, in first half of 19th century, 341–347
and canals, 343–346, *345*
and equality, 377–378
and railroads, 346–347
and speed, 352
and steamboats, 344, 346, 348–349, *349*, 352
transatlantic, in 18th century, 124–125
(*See also* Air travel; Airplanes; Automobiles; Mass transit; Railroads; Roads and roadbuilding)

Treasury Department, U.S., 957, *957*, 1000, 1067

Treasury notes, 769

Treaties:
Adams-Onís Treaty (1819), 320
Aix-la-Chapelle Treaty (1748), 120
Anglo-American Treaty (1871), 801
Anti-Comintern Pact (1937), 1017
Burlingame Treaty (1868), 802
Clayton-Bulwer Treaty (1850), 790
"cooling off" agreements under Woodrow Wilson, 869
Fort Harmar Treaty (1789), 280
Fort Laramie Treaty (1851), 500–501
Fort Wayne Treaty (1809), 320
Gadsden Purchase (1853), 535
Ghent Treaty (1814), 329
Greenville Treaty (1795), 280, 311, 318
Guadalupe Hidalgo Treaty (1848), 508, 514
Hay-Herran Convention (1903), 860
Hay-Pauncefote Treaty (1901), 808, 897
INF treaty (1988), 1293

Treaties (*Cont.*):
with Japan, in 1858, *791*
Jay-Gardoqui Treaty (1785), 250–251, 257
Jay's Treaty (1795), 285–286, 290
Kellogg-Briand Pact (1928), 901, 1012
Munich Pact (1938), 1017
and Panama Canal, 1261
Paris Treaty (1763), 160, 165, 191
Paris Treaty (1783), 224, 225, 233
Paris Treaty (1898), 821
Pinckney's Treaty (1796), 282, 308
Portsmouth Treaty (1905), 865, 897
Root-Takahira Agreement (1908), 866
Rush-Bagot Agreement (1817), 331
Ryswick Treaty (1697), 119
SALT I, 1081, 1219, 1229
SALT II, 1262, 1264, 1293
Samoan Treaty (1878), 805, 821
Transcontinental Treaty (1819), 330
Utrecht Treaty (1713), 119
Versailles Treaty (1919), 889–894
at Washington Naval Conference (1921), 1012

Trench warfare, 876

Trenchard, John, 151, 172, 183

Trent affair (1861), 566–567

Trenton, Battle of (1776), 205, 213, 225

Triangle Shirtwaist Company fire (1911), 822–824, *824*, 859

Triple-A Plowed Under (play), 999

Trist, Nicholas, 508

Trois-Rivières, 82

Trolley cars, 690–691

Tropical Fruit Company, 791

Trotsky, Leon, 880

Trudeau, Pierre Elliot, 1252

Trujillo, Rafael, 1253

Trujillo v. Garley (1948), 1223, 1229

Truman, Harry S., 1044, 1051, 1070, *1088*
and atomic bomb, 1075–1076
and Berlin crisis, 1093
and civil rights, 1110
and election of 1946, 1086–1087
and election of 1948, 1108–1109
and Federal Employee Loyalty Program, 1097
foreign policy of, 1111–1112
and Israel, 1094–1095
and Korean War, 1112–1115
and New Deal, 1110
and nuclear weapons, 1095
and Potsdam Conference, 1074–1075
and railroad strike, 1086
after Roosevelt's death, 1071
and Soviet Union, 1088–1089, 1091–1092
and UN, 1074

Truman Doctrine, 1081, 1091–1092

Trumbull, Lyman, 610

Trunk lines (railroads), 660

Trusts, 667, 847

Truth, Sojourner, 437, 1065

Tuberculosis, 694

Tubman, Harriet, 438, *438*

Tucker, Josiah, 168

Tugwell, Rexford G., 980, 999–1002

Tule Lake, California, 1062

Turkey, 898, 1092, 1162

Turner, Frederick Jackson, 733, 744, 757

Turner, Nat, 473, 480–481

Tuscarora Indians, 72, 104
Tushepaw Indians, 3
Tuskegee Institute, 786, 787, 789
TVA (Tennessee Valley Authority), 981–982, *983*
Twain, Mark, 645, 655, 690, 765, 814
Tweed, William, 696, 697, 713
Tydings, Millard F., 1101
Tyler, John, 501–503, 508
Tymkevich, Paul, 706
Typewriters, 655, 767

U-2 spy plane crisis (1959), 1140
UAW (United Auto Workers), 997
UMW (United Mine Workers), 846, 996, 1069
Underground Railroad, 438, *438*
Underwood-Simmons Tariff (1913), 855, 859
Unemployment (*see* Employment and unemployment)
UNIA (Universal Negro Improvement Association), 923, 935
Union, in Civil War (*see* Civil War)
Union Oil Company, 1230, 1232
Union Pacific Railroad, 746, 778
Union party, 992
Unions, 363–364
  and blacks, 394, 901, 1063, 1064
  early, 675
  and garment industry, 822
  during Great Depression, 984, 996–998
  and John F. Kennedy, 1165
  Knights of Labor, 675–676
  in late 19th century, 680
  and National Labor Relations Act, 990
  in 1920s, 908, 910, 911
  during Reagan's administration, 1279
  and right to strike, 364
  Southern Tenant Farmers Union, 964
  and Taft-Hartley Act (1947), 1087
  during World War I, 883
  after World War II, 1086
  during World War II, 1063, 1064, 1068–1070
  (*See also* Strikes; *specific unions,* e.g., American Federation of Labor; Congress of Industrial Organizations; United Farm Workers Union; United Mine Workers)
Unitarianism, 414, 417, 425, 442
United Arab Republic, 1139
United Auto Workers (UAW), 997
United Farm Workers of America, 962
United Farm Workers Union, *1222,* 1223
United Fruit Company, 791, 1137
United Kingdom (*see* Great Britain)
United Mine Workers (UMW), 846, 996, 1069
United Nations, 1073–1074, 1092, 1095, 1112–1113, 1139, 1256
United Nations Organization (UNO), 1073–1074
United Rubber Workers Union, 997
United States v. E. C. Knight (1895), 847, 859
United States v. Hudson and Goodwin (1812), 291
United States v. Jefferson County Board of Education (1969), 1225

United States v. Nixon (1974), 1247, 1265
United Steel Workers, 1165
Universal Negro Improvement Association (UNIA), 923, 935
Universal Suez Canal Company, 1138
Universities (*see* Higher education)
Union of Soviet Socialist Republics (*see* Soviet Union)
UNO (United Nations Organization), 1073–1074
Upper South, 455–456, 460, 470, 480
Ural Mountains, 157
Urban League, 993, 1167
Urbanization, 682–713
  in 18th century, 131–135, 145
  and city life and culture, 699–712
    and arts and entertainment, 709–712
    and college years, 706–707
    and family, 447–449, 714–717
    and middle class at home, 699–703
    and palaces of consumption, 707–709
    and school days, 704–706
    and Victorian mores, 703–704
  in first half of 19th century, 356
  in 1920s, 904, *905*
  and rise of cities, 684–695
    and bridges and skyscrapers, 692–693
    and global migration to cities, 686–688
    and immigrants, 688–690
    and shape of cities, 690
    and slums and tenements, 693–695
    and urban explosion, 685–686
    and urban transport, 690–692
  and running and reforming cities, 695–699
    and boss rule, 695–697
    and social conscience of cities, 697–699
  in South, 457, 467–468, 721
  (*See also* Cities)
U.S. Geological Survey, 738
U.S. Rubber Company, 653
U.S. Steel Corporation, 645, 668, 681, 729, 851, 910, 947–948, 997
USSR (*see* Soviet Union)
Utah, 518, 519, 688*n.*
Utah (battleship), 1008
Utopian communities, 415, 429–432, 603
Utrecht, Treaty of (1713), 119

V-1 (missile), 1038
V-2 (missile), 1038
VA (Veterans Administration), 1102
Valentino, Rudolph, 918
Vallandigham, Clement, 583, 594
Valley Forge, Pennsylvania, 211–212, 225
Van Buren, Martin, 383–386, 391, 401, 403–405, 408, 484, 495, 501–502, 516–517, 520
Van Devanter, Willis, 1003
Vance, Cyrus, 1256, 1256–1257, 1261, 1262, 1263, 1264
Vandenberg, Arthur, 1039, 1111
Vanderbilt, Cornelius, 657, 662
Vanderbilt, Cornelius, II, *669*
Vanderbilt, William H., 699
Vanderbilt family, 669
Vann, Robert, 993
Vanzetti, Bartolomeo, 924

Vatican II (1962–1965), 1272
Vaudeville, 839–840, 919
Veblen, Thorstein, 827
Veiller, Lawrence, 832
Venezuela, 17, 807–808, 865
Venice, Italy, 184
Venice Amusement Park (California), 837
Veracruz, Mexico, 870
Vergennes, Charles Gravier de, 209–210
Vermont, 127, 130, 228, 234, 329, 371
Verrazzano, Giovanni de, 80
Versailles, Treaty of (1919), 645, 889–895
Vesey, Denmark, 396–397, 472
Vespucci, Amerigo, 17
Veterans, 970–971, 1070, 1102, 1257
Veterans Administration (VA), 1102
Vice-admiralty courts, 170, 172, 177, 181
Vice presidency, 273
Vick, Sarah Pierce, *465*
Vicksburg, Mississippi, 463, 593
Victorian morality, 700–701, 703–704, 715–716
Vietcong, 1160, 1199, 1206
Vietnam, 1196–1197
  (*See also* Vietnam War)
Vietnam War, 1079, 1081, 1186–1187, 1192–1194, 1195–1201, 1229
  and amnesty for draft resisters, 1253, 1257
  domestic consequences of, 1194–1195, 1206–1208
  end of, 1227–1228, 1252
  and Great Society program, 1179
  and John F. Kennedy, 1160
  lessons of, 1228
  and Richard Nixon, 1213–1214
  Tet offensive in, 1208–1209
  and U.S. Congress, 1248
  U.S. troops in:
    conditions of, 1202–1203
    morale of, 1216–1217
    number of, 1201, *1201*
    and Vietnamization and Cambodia, 1215–1216
Vietnamese-Americans, 1301
Villa, Francisco "Pancho," 870–871, *871,* 897
Vincennes, 213
Vinland, 4, 7
Virgin Islands, 804, 1110
Virginia:
  agricultural reform in, 551
  in Civil War, 569, 571, 591, 593–594, 596–598
  in colonial times, 79
    American Revolution in, 223–224
    and Powhatan's confederacy, 44–47
    and Roanoke colony, 39, 42
    and Stamp Act, 173
    and Townshend Acts, 179
    western land claims of, 234, *235,* 236
  and Constitution, ratification of, 262
  and John Brown's raid, 552
  plantations in, 462
  in Reconstruction, 614
  and resolutions of 1798, 291–292
  and slavery, 59–62, 126, 136, 138–139, 239, 241, 459, 473, 481
  (*See also* Chesapeake region)
Virginia dynasty, 330

Virginia Plan, 253
VISTA (Volunteers in Service to America), 1176
Vocational education, 706
Volcker, Paul, 1278
Volstead Act (1919), 925
Voltaire, 141
Voting:
    after American Revolution, 294–295
    and *Baker v. Carr*, 1166
    of blacks, 392, 732–733, 758
    and civil rights movement, 1168–1170, 1171–1172
    and democratic reforms, 382–383
    in 1860–1912, 852, 853
    of immigrants, 835
    and municipal politics, 684, 696
    in presidential elections, 1876–1900, 764
    and *Smith v. Allwright*, 1066
    and *Trujillo v. Garley*, 1223
    and Voting Rights Act, 1172
    and women, 295, 385, 631–632
    (*See also* Blacks, and suffrage; Disfranchisement; Elections; Women, suffrage of)
Voting Rights Act (1965), 1081, 1172, 1187

WACs (Women's Army Corps), 1033
Wade, Benjamin F., 605, 609, 616, 632
Wade-Davis Bill (1864), 605–606
Wages and salaries:
    of blacks, 626, 722, 993–994, 1301
    in cattle ranching, 749
    by ethnic group, in 1980, 1301
    and Henry Ford, 908
    during Great Depression, 953, 989
    of industrial workers, in late 19th century, 673
    and John F. Kennedy, 1165
    in 1920s, 906, 944–945
    during Nixon's administration, 1220–1221
    and prostitution, 839
    in South, 722, 728, 756, 1143
    of women, 953, 1059, 1125
    after World War II, 1086
    (*See also* Income, personal)
Wagner, Robert F., 843, 990
Wagner Act (National Labor Relations Act) (1935), 990, *1006*
Wainwright Building (St. Louis), 693
Wald, Lillian, 874
Waldseemüller, Martin, 17
Wales, 95
Walker, Robert, 502
Walker, Thomas, *171*
Wall Street (New York City), 652, *654*, 896, 896–897
Wallace, DeWitt, 920
Wallace, George, 1176, 1212, 1214, 1226, 1229
Wallace, Henry A., 984, 1070, 1109
Wallace, Henry C., 930
Walsh, Christy, 920
Walsh, Lawrence, 1291
Wampanoag Indians, 87, 99–100
Wanapaun Indians, 735
War Advertising Council, 1067
War Hawks, 324–325
War Industries Board (WIB), 882–883, 897

War Labor Board (WLB), 1068–1069, 1077
War Labor Disputes Act (Smith-Connolly Anti-Strike Act) (1943), 1069–1070
War of 1812, 320–329, *326*, 341, 505
War Powers Act (1973), 1248, 1265
War Production Board (WPB), 1050, 1054, 1077
War Refugee Board, 1073, 1077
War Relocation Authority (WRA), 1062
Warburg, Paul, 943
Ward, Aaron Montgomery, 708–709
Ware, James E., 694
Warehouse Act (1916), 857
Warfare, 561, 738–743, 866, *876*, 1035–1036
    (*See also specific wars and battles*)
Warm Springs, Georgia, 978
Warner, Charles Dudley, 765
Warren, Charles, 1016
Warren, Earl, 1060, 1066, 1109, 1144, 1165–1166, 1170
Warren, James, 194, 212
Warsaw Pact (1955), *1094*
Washington, Booker T., 786–787, 789, 845
Washington, George, 272–274
    in American Revolution, 202–208, 211–213, 215, 223–224
    and Constitution, 271
    Farewell Address of, 287, 331
    and Federalist party, 286
    at First Continental Congress, 186
    at Fort Necessity, 153–155, 162
    in French crisis, 290
    and Alexander Hamilton, 275
    and Miami Confederacy, 280
    and national bank, 278–279
    and neutrality proclamation, 284
    on parties, 383
    and Pinckney's Treaty, 282
    on Republican party, 293
    at Second Continental Congress, 252–253
    in Seven Years' War, 163–164
    and Washington, D.C., 300
    and Whiskey Rebellion, 281
Washington, Harold, 1153
Washington, D.C., 298, 300–302, *301*, 452, 518, 519, 674, 1046, 1048–1049, *1153*
Washington Naval Disarmament Conference (1921–1922), 901, 1012, 1045
Waste Land, The (poem, T. S. Eliot), 935
Water Quality Improvement Act (1969), 1232
Water resources, 737, 738, 751, 754, 848–849
Watergate scandal (1970s), 1081, 1229, 1244–1247, 1265
Waters, Walter, 970
Watonga, Oklahoma, 1001
Watson, John B., 827, 912
Watson, Thomas E., 653, 758–761, 774, 775, 776, 777, 784, 786
Watt, James, 1279
Watts riot (Los Angeles, 1965), *1173*, 1173–1174
WAVEs, 1033
Wayne, Anthony, 280
WCTU (Women's Christian Temperance Union), 704, 717, 766, 789

Weapons (*see* Arms control; Arms race; Arms sales; Missiles; Nuclear weapons)
Weaver, James B., 776
Weaver, Robert, 1178
Weaver, Robert C., 993
Webster, Daniel, 386, *398*, 398–399, 401, 403, 408, 518, *519*
Webster, Noah, 292
Weimar Republic, 898
Weinberger, Caspar, 1278, 1281, 1286, 1288
Welch, Joseph L., 1133
Weld, Theodore Dwight, 435–439, *436*
Welfare, 1219–1220, 1296
    (*See also* Relief)
Welfare capitalism, 910, 932, 932–933
Welles, Orson, 955, 999
Welles, Sumner, 1063
Wellesley College, 706
Wellington bomber (aircraft), 1038
Wells, David A., 712
Wells, H. G., 955
Welsh-Americans, 106, 442
Wertheim, Frederic, 1148
Wesley, Charles, 7
Wesley, John, 7
West, H. T., *723*
West, Mae, 958, 1125
West:
    agriculture in, 347, 508–509, 527–530
    and gold rush, 509–511
    Japanese-Americans in, 1060–1062
    land rush in, in first half of 19th century, 354–355
    in late 19th century, 733–756
        and American Indians, 734–736, 738–743
        cattle ranching in, 748–750
        economy of, 720–721
        as final frontier, 750–756
        racism in, 721
        railroads in, 744–748
        whites in, 736–738
    and Mormons, 512–514
    natural environment of, 737
    and 1960s counterculture, 1185–1186
    water resources in, 751, 754, 848–849
    woman suffrage in, *834*
    during World War II, 1052, 1060–1062
    (*See also* Expansionism; Frontier; Indians, American, on frontier; *specific western states, e.g.,* California; Texas)
West Country of England, 8, 10–11, 16, 29, 38–39, 95
West Florida, 309, 328, 330
West Germany, 1093
West Indies (*see* Caribbean region)
West Virginia, 213, 565
West Virginia (battleship), 1008, *1009*
Western Electric Company, 910
Western Federation of Miners, 744
Westinghouse, George, 652, 681
Westinghouse Company, 652–653, 918
Westminster, California, *1300*
Westmoreland, William, 1201, 1207, 1209
Weyler, Valeriano, 809
Whalen, Richard, 1213–1214
Wheat, 107, 132, 239, 347, 355, *355*, 456, 751, 772
Whig party:
    death of, 538, 543
    and depression of 1837–1843, 404, *404*

Whig party (*Cont.*):
  and elections:
    of 1836, 403
    of 1840, *375*, 405–408
    of 1848, 516–517
    of 1852, 520
  ideology of, 408–410, 484
  and Lincoln's plan for Reconstruction, 604
  and Mexican War, 505
  origins of, 382, 403
  and reform movements, 442–443
  in South, 484
  and John Tyler, 501
Whiskey, 245, 318, 347, 432
Whiskey Rebellion, 280–282, *282*, 286
Whiskey tax, 276, 280–281, 286, 305
White, Edward, 1204
White, John, 39, 42
White, Lynn, 1125
White, Theodore, 1212
White, William Allen, 978, 1019
White-collar workers, 948
White Oaks Mill, 727
Whitefield, George, *142*, 142–144, 155, 416
Whiteman, Paul, 921
Whitman, Walt, *427*, 427–428, 660, 712
Whitney, Eli, 335, 342, 358
Whyte, William, 1129
WIB (War Industries Board), 882–883, 897
Wichita, Kansas, 748
Wilde, Oscar, 795
Wilder, Billy, 1099
Wilderness Preservation System Act (1964), 1187
Wiley, Harvey, 848
Wilhelm II (German kaiser), 872
Wilkes, John, 165–166
Wilkinson, Eliza, 246
Wilkinson, James, 250
Willard, Abijah, 192, 194
Willard, Emma Hunt, 434
Willard, Frances, 704
William and Mary College, 141
William of Orange, 7, 110
Williams, Roger, 96–97, 100
Williamson, Clara, *748*
Willkie, Wendell, 1020
Willow Run, Michigan, 1057
Wilmot Proviso (1846), 507–508, 515, 516, 520
Wilson, Charles, 1130, 1135
Wilson, Edith Bolling, 894
Wilson, Edmund, 965
Wilson, Ellen, 872
Wilson, James, 252
Wilson, Woodrow, 854–857, *856*, 929
  in election of 1912, 853–854
  in election of 1916, 877–878
  and Hetch-Hetchy valley controversy, 849
  and literacy tests for immigrants, 838
  moral diplomacy of, 868–871
  and National War Labor Board, 884
  and vaudeville, 840
  and World War I:
    Fourteen Points speech of, 887–888
    and U.S. economy, 882
    and U.S. entry into war, 878–879
    and U.S. neutrality, 872–877
    and Versailles Treaty, 889–895, 892
Wilson-Gorman Tariff Act (1894), 781
Windward Coast, 61

Wingina (Indian), 38–39
Winnebago Indians, 320
Winslow, John, 160
Winthrop, John, *88*, 88–89, 490, 1269
Wirt, William, 381
Wisconsin, 234, 237, 347, 842, 859
Wisconsin, University of, 842, 1207
Witchcraft, 110–111, 113
WLB (War Labor Board), 1068–1069, 1077
Wobblies (Industrial Workers of the World), 886
Wolfe, James, 164, 167
Wolfe, Tom, 1183, 1233
Women:
  and abolitionism, 440–441
  and American Revolution, 203, 204, 214, 246–247
  baby boomers, 1190–1191
  and beauty contests, 914–915
  and childbirth, 1900–1945, 937
  in colonial times, 52, 62, 89, 92, 95, 97–99, 114–117, 127–129, 133–135, 268, 312
    among American Indians, 19, 45, 104–105
    and American resistance, 181, *183*, 198–199
  education of:
    after American Revolution, 248
    in 1870–1910, 831
    in late 19th century, 706–707
    in medical schools, 707, 831
    in 1920s, 917
    in 1950s, 1125
    in 1960s, 1239
  and election of 1984, 1284
  and feminist movement, 440, 1238–1242
  on frontier, 268, 311, 508–510, 513
  and GI Bill, 1102
  during Great Depression, 939, 951–954, 995–996
  in Jacksonian era, 419–424
  in late 19th century:
    in Alliance movement, 775
    on cattle ranches, 749
    courtship age of, 715
    and depression of 1893–1897, 779
    dress of, 700–701
    education of, 706–707, 831
    and Fifteenth Amendment, 631–632
    on Great Plains farms, 752
    and marriage, 715
    suffrage of, 704, 764, 789
    as workers, 673–674
  in 1920s, 904, 913–917
  on Overland Trail, 495, 497–499
  and poverty, 1294–1295, 1298
  and progressivism, 831–834
  and Prohibition, 925
  and Ronald Reagan, 1284
  and religion, 143, 313–315, 419–421, 513
  and slavery, 465–466, 474–475
  in South:
    before Civil War, 464–467
    in Civil War, 576, 581–582, *582*
  in suburbs, 1124–1125
  suffrage of, 764, *834*, 898
    and Susan B. Anthony, 704
    after Civil War, 631–632
    in 1820s–1840s, 442–443
    in election of 1800, 295

Women: suffrage of (*Cont.*):
    and Fifteenth Amendment, 631–632
    in 1920s, 917
    and progressivism, 833–834
    and Woodrow Wilson, 857
    in Wyoming, 789
    (*See also* Constitution, U.S., amendments to, Nineteenth)
  and temperance, 432–433, 925
  and utopian communities, 430–431
  as workers:
    baby boomers, 1190
    during Civil War, 576, 582
    as clerks, *674*
    and depression of 1893–1897, 779
    eight-hour workday for, 859
    during Great Depression, 952–953
    and household manufacturing, 268, 357, 365, 420
    in late 19th century, 673–674
    and *Muller v. Oregon*, 827–828
    in 1920s, 917
    in 1940–1960, 1124–1125
    in 1970, 1239
    on Overland Trail, 498–499
    and progressivism, *833*
    in textile mills, 359–363
    wages of, 953, 1059, 1125
    during World War I, 883, 885, *885*
    after World War II, 1085
    during World War II, *1047*, 1057–1059, *1058*
  after World War II, 1085–1086
  during World War II, in armed forces, 1033
  (*See also* Abortion; Birth control; Family and family life; Fashion and dress; Marriage)
Women Ordnance Workers (WOW), *1047*
Women's Army Corps (WACs), 1033
Women's Christian Temperance Union (WCTU), 704, 713, 766, 789
Women's clubs, 832
Women's International League for Peace and Freedom, 874, 1016
Wonder, Stevie, 1185
Woodhull, Victoria, 704
Woodmason, Charles, 130
Woodruff, Robert, 1056
Woods, Arthur, 967
Woods, Rose Mary, 1246
Woodside, John A., *299*
Woodstock Music Festival (1969), 1185–1186, 1187
Woodward, Bob, 1244, 1265
Woodward, Mary, 756
Woolworth, F. W., 708, 713
Worcester v. Georgia (1832), 391
Work and workers:
  and apprenticeship system, 340, 357, 362, 447
  in Civil War, 576, 580, 582
  in 18th century:
    among American Indians, 268
    in seaports, 132–133
  in Europe in 18th and 19th centuries, 686
  and labor legislation during Great Depression, 990
  in late 19th century:
    on bonanza farms, 752
    and family life, 716
    and industrialization, 671–680

Work and workers: in late 19th century (*Cont.*):
and American Federation of
Labor, 676–677
conditions of, 672
and Knights of Labor, 675–676
and limits of industrial systems,
677–680
and unions, early, 675
and workers' world, 671–675
occupational distribution of,
657–660, *658*, 671–672,
677–680
in 1920s, 906, 908
and Prohibition, 926
and revivalism in 1840s, 418
during World War I, 883–885
after World War II, 1085–1086
during World War II, 1057, 1063–
1065
(*See also* Artisans; Blacks, as workers; Farmers; Household manufacturing; Indentured servants;
Industrialization; Slaves and
slavery; Strikes; Unions; Wages
and salaries; Women, as workers)
Workers' compensation, 672, 843, 857,
859
Works Progress Administration (WPA),
989, 994, 996, 998
World Bank (International Bank for
Reconstruction and
Development), 1074
World War I, 645, 871–897
armistice of, *861*
business profits during, 1015
final battles of, *888*
and U.S., 872–897
and election of 1916, 877–878
entry of, 878–879
neutrality of, 872–874
and diplomacy, 874–876
preparedness for, 876–877
and Red Scare, 895–897
and Versailles Treaty, 889–895
war and society, 879–889
and economic mobilization,
882–883
and propaganda and civil liberties, 886–887
and soldiers, 880–882, 890–891
and workers, 883–885
World War II, 901, 1008–1010, 1025–
1044

World War II (*Cont.*):
air power in, 1035–1036, 1038–1039
Allied strategies for, 1025–1026
Allied strengths in, 1027–1028
and diplomacy, 1040–1044
atomic diplomacy, 1075–1077
early course of, 1026–1027
end of, 1071–1077
in Europe, 1036–1037, 1071
in Japan, 1037–1040
in Europe, *1018*, 1018–1021, 1028–
1030, 1036–1037
geography of, 1022–1023
in Pacific, naval war, 1028
science and technology in, 1034–
1035
on U.S. home front, 1046–1071
and consumption, 1053–1056
and dress, 1054–1055
and minority rights, 1059–1066
of blacks, 1065–1066
of Italian-Americans, 1060
of Japanese-Americans,
1060–1062
and minority workers,
1063–1065
and politics, 1066–1071
and election of 1944,
1070–1071
and organized labor,
1068–1070
and reform, 1068
and war costs, 1066–1068
and war production, 1049–1050,
1052–1053
and rubber, 1050–1052
and war work, 1053–1059
and minority workers,
1063–1065
in Willow Run, Michigan, 1057
and women, *1047*, 1057–1059
and U.S. military branches,
1030–1033
and women, 1033, *1047*, 1057–1059
World's Columbian Exposition
(Chicago, 1893), 700, 713,
836–837
Wounded Knee, South Dakota, 743,
757, 1081, 1224, 1229
Wovoka (Paiute Indian), 743
WOW (Women Ordnance Workers),
1047
WPA (Works Progress Administration),
989, 994, 996, 998

WPB (War Production Board), 1050,
1054, 1077
WRA (War Relocation Authority),
1062
Wright, Frank Lloyd, 1126
Wright, Richard, 998
Wrigley, Philip, 1056
Writers and writing (*see* Books; Litera-
ture; Magazines and journals;
Newspapers)
Wyandot Indians, 320
Wyoming, 789, 917
Wyoming (warship), 803

XYZ Affair (1797), 290

Yale University, 141, 155
Yalta Conference (1945), 1042–1043,
1074
Yamamoto Isoruku, 1025, 1028
Yamasee Indians, 72–73, 79
Yaqui Indians, 77
Yellow dog contracts, 910
Yellowknife Indians, 18
Yeoman farmers, 451–452, 466–468,
467
Yom Kippur War (1973), 1081, 1250
Yorktown, Battle of (1781), 222, 223,
224–225
Yorktown (aircraft carrier), 1028
Yosemite National Park, *1234*
Young, Andrew, 1256, 1298
Young, Brigham, 513
Young, Owen D., 1011
Young America movement, 535
Your Show of Shows (TV program),
1108
Youth (*see* Children; Students; Teen-
agers)
Yuchi Indians, 75
Yuppies, 1297

Zaire, 1260–1261
Zangwill, Israel, 712
Zapata, Emiliano, 870
Zelaya, José, 867
Zhou Enlai, 1114, 1135
Ziegler, Ron, 1244
Zimmermann, Arthur, 878
Zionism, 1073
Zola, Emile, 708
Zoot suiters, *1065*, 1065–1066
Zuñi Indians, 19

ABOUT THE AUTHORS

JAMES WEST DAVIDSON received his Ph.D. from Yale University. A historian who has pursued a full-time writing career, he is the author of numerous books, among them *After the Fact: The Art of Historical Detection* (with Mark H. Lytle), *The Logic of Millennial Thought: Eighteenth-Century New England*, and *Great Heart: The History of a Labrador Adventure* (with John Rugge).

WILLIAM E. GIENAPP has a Ph.D. from the University of California, Berkeley. He is Professor of History at the University of Wyoming, where he was the 1988–1989 Seibold Professor. In 1988 he was given the Avery O. Craven Award for his work, *The Origins of the Republican Party, 1852–1856*. Currently he is at work on *Abraham Lincoln and Civil War America*.

CHRISTINE LEIGH HEYRMAN is Associate Professor of History at Brandeis University. She received a Ph.D. in American Studies from Yale University and is the author of *Commerce and Culture: The Maritime Communities of Colonial Massachusetts, 1690–1750*. Her professional activities include serving on the Editorial Board of the *Journal of American History* and as Council Secretary for the Institute of Early American History and Culture.

MARK H. LYTLE, who was awarded a Ph.D. from Yale University, is Professor of History and Environmental Studies and Chair of the American Studies Program at Bard College. He is also Director of the Master of Arts in Teaching Program at Bard. His publications include *The Origins of the Iranian–American Alliance, 1941–1953* and *After the Fact: The Art of Historical Detection* (with James West Davidson). In 1989 he received the Horace Kidger Award of the New England History Teachers Association. He is now at work on *The Uncivil War: America in the Vietnam Era*.

MICHAEL B. STOFF is Associate Professor of History at the University of Texas at Austin, where he directs the honors program in history. The recipient of a Ph.D. from Yale University, he wrote *Oil, War, and American Security: The Search for a National Policy on Foreign Oil, 1941–1947* and the forthcoming *Manhattan Project: A Documentary Introduction to the Development and Use of the Atomic Bomb*.

GREENLAND
(KALALLIT-NUNAAT)
(Den.)

ALASKA
(U.S.)

80°N

60°N

CANADA

NORTH
AMERICA

40°N

UNITED STATES

ATLANTIC
OCEAN

BERMUDA
(Br.)

HAWAII
(U.S.)

MEXICO

BAHAMAS

20°N

CUBA

DOMINICAN

CAPE
VERDE

HAITI

REP. 18

PACIFIC
OCEAN

GUATEMALA
EL SALVADOR
NICARAGUA
COSTA RICA
PANAMA

BELIZE
HONDURAS 20

PUERTO 27
RICO (U.S.) 29

26
25
24 23
22 19
28

0° Equator

COLOMBIA

VENEZUELA

GUYANA
SURINAME
FR. GUIANA

ECUADOR

SOUTH
AMERICA

WESTERN
SAMOA

PERU

BRAZIL

AMERICAN
SAMOA

FRENCH
POLYNESIA

BOLIVIA

20°S

TONGA

PARAGUAY

CHILE
ARGENTINA

URUGUAY

40°S

FALKLAND
IS. (Br.)

60°S

80°S

160°W 140°W 120°W 100°W 80°W 60°W

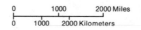

0   1000   2000 Miles
0   1000   2000 Kilometers